Webster's
Spanish-
English
Dictionary

Created in Cooperation with the Editors of
MERRIAM-WEBSTER

Webster's *Spanish-English* Dictionary

Spanish-English
English-Spanish

BARNES & NOBLE

NEW YORK

Contents

Preface

The volume you are holding is a new edition of a dictionary designed to meet the needs of English and Spanish speakers in a time of ever-expanding communication among the countries of the Western Hemisphere. It is intended for language learners, teachers, office workers, tourists, business travelers—anyone who needs to communicate effectively in the Spanish and English languages as they are spoken and written in the Americas. This new dictionary provides accurate and up-to-date coverage of current vocabulary in both languages, as well as abundant examples of words used in context to illustrate idiomatic usage. The selection of Spanish words and idioms was based on evidence drawn from a wide variety of modern Latin-American sources and interpreted by trained Merriam-Webster bilingual lexicographers. The English entries were chosen by Merriam-Webster editors from the most recent Merriam-Webster dictionaries, and they represent the current basic vocabulary of American English.

All of this material is presented in a format which is based firmly upon and, in many important ways, is similar to the traditional styling found in the Merriam-Webster monolingual dictionaries. The reader who is familiar with Merriam-Webster dictionaries will immediately recognize this style, with its emphasis on convenience and ease of use, clarity and conciseness of the information presented, precise discrimination of senses, and frequent inclusion of example phrases showing words in actual use. Other features include pronunciations (in the International Phonetic Alphabet) for all English words, full coverage of irregular verbs in both languages, a section on basic Spanish grammar, tables of the most common Spanish and English abbreviations, and a detailed Explanatory Notes section which answers any questions the reader might have concerning the use of this book.

This dictionary represents the combined efforts of many members of the Merriam-Webster Editorial Department, along with advice and assistance from consultants outside the company. The primary defining work was done by Charlene M. Chateauneuf, Seán O'Mannion-Espejo, James L. Rader, Donna L. Rickerby, Adrienne M. Scholz, Amy West, Karen L. Wilkinson, and Linda Picard Wood. Brian M. Sietsema, Ph.D., provided the pronunciations. Cross-reference services were provided by Donna L. Rickerby. Karen L. Levister assisted in inputting revisions. Carol Fugiel contributed many hours of clerical assistance and other valuable support. The editorial work relating to typesetting and production was begun by

Jennifer S. Goss and continued by Susan L. Brady, who also offered helpful suggestions regarding format. Madeline L. Novak provided guidance on typographic matters. John M. Morse was responsible for the conception of this book as well as for numerous ideas and continued support along the way.

Eileen M. Haraty
Editor

Explanatory Notes

Entries

1. Main Entries

A boldface letter, word, or phrase appearing flush with the left-hand margin of each column of type is a main entry or entry word. The main entry may consist of letters set solid, of letters joined by a hyphen, or of letters separated by a space:

> **cafetalero¹, -ra** *adj* ...
>
> **eye–opener** ... *n* ...
>
> **walk out** *vi* ...

The main entry, together with the material that follows it on the same line and succeeding indented lines, constitutes a dictionary entry.

2. Order of Main Entries

Alphabetical order throughout the book follows the order of the English alphabet, with one exception: words beginning with the Spanish letter *ñ* follow all entries for the letter *n*. The main entries follow one another alphabetically letter by letter without regard to intervening spaces or hyphens; for example, *shake-up* follows *shaker*.

Homographs (words with the same spelling) having different parts of speech are usually given separate dictionary entries. These entries are distinguished by superscript numerals following the entry word:

> **hail¹** ... *vt* ...
>
> **hail²** *n* ...
>
> **hail³** *interj* ...
>
> **madrileño¹, -ña** *adj* ...
>
> **madrileño², -ña** *n* ...

Numbered homograph entries are listed in the following order: verb, adverb, adjective, noun, conjunction, preposition, pronoun, interjection, article.

Homographs having the same part of speech are normally included at the same dictionary entry, without regard to their different semantic origins. On the English-to-Spanish side, however, separate entries are made if the homographs have distinct inflected forms or if they have distinct pronunciations.

3. Guide Words

A pair of guide words is printed at the top of each page, indicating the first and last main entries that appear on that page:

factura · faringe

4. Variants

When a main entry is followed by the word *or* and another spelling, the two spellings are variants. Both are standard, and either one may be used according to personal inclination:

jailer *or* **jailor** . . . *n* . . .

quizá *or* **quizás** *adv* . . .

Occasionally, a variant spelling is used only for a particular sense of a word. In these cases, the variant spelling is listed after the sense number of the sense to which it pertains:

electric . . . *adj* **1** *or* **electrical** . . .

Sometimes the entry word is used interchangeably with a longer phrase containing the entry word. For the purposes of this dictionary, such phrases are considered variants of the headword:

bunk² *n* **1** *or* **bunk bed** . . .

angina *nf* **1** *or* **angina de pecho** : angina . . .

Variant wordings of boldface phrases may also be shown:

madera *nf* . . . **3 madera dura** *or* **madera noble** . . .

atención[1] *nf* . . . **2 poner atención** *or* **prestar atención** . . .

5. Run-On Entries

A main entry may be followed by one or more derivatives or by a homograph with a different functional label. These are run-on entries. Each is introduced by a boldface dash and each has a functional label. They are not defined, however, since their equivalents can be readily derived by adding the corresponding foreign-language suffix to the terms used to define the entry word or, in the case of homographs, simply substituting the appropriate part of speech:

illegal . . . *adj* : ilegal — **illegally** *adv* (the Spanish adverb is *ilegalmente*)

transferir . . . *vt* trasladar : to transfer — **transferible** *adj* (the English adjective is **transferable**)

Bosnian *n* : bosnio *m*, -nia *f* — **Bosnian** *adj* (the Spanish adjective is *bosnio, -nia*)

On the Spanish side of the book, reflexive verbs are sometimes run on undefined:

enrollar *vt* : to roll up, to coil — **enrollarse** *vr*

The absence of a definition means that *enrollarse* has the simple reflexive meaning "to become rolled up or coiled," "to roll itself up."

6. Bold Notes

A main entry may be followed by one or more phrases containing the entry word or an inflected form of the entry word. These are bold notes. Each bold note is defined at its own numbered sense:

> **álamo** *nm* **1** : poplar **2 álamo temblón**
> : aspen

> **hold**[1] ... *vi* ... **4 to hold to** : ... **5 to
> hold with** : ...

If the bold note consists only of the entry word and a single preposition, the entry word is represented by a boldface swung dash ∼.

> **pegar** ... *vi* ... **3 ∼ con** : to match, to
> go with ...

The same bold note phrase may appear at two or more senses if it has more than one distinct meaning:

> **wear**[1] ... *vt* ... **3 to wear out** : gastar
> ⟨he wore out his shoes ... ⟩ **4 to wear
> out** EXHAUST : agotar, fatigar ⟨to wear
> oneself out ... ⟩ ...

> **estar** ... *vi* ... **15 ∼ por** : to be in favor
> of **16 ∼ por** : to be about to ⟨está por
> cerrar ... ⟩ ...

If the use of the entry word is commonly restricted to one particular phrase, then a bold note may be given as the entry word's only sense:

> **ward**[1] ... *vt* **to ward off** : ...

Pronunciation

1. Pronunciation of English Entry Words

The matter between a pair of brackets [ ] following the entry word of an English-to-Spanish entry indicates the pronunciation. The symbols used are explained in the International Phonetic Alphabet chart on page 58a.

The presence of variant pronunciations indicates that not all educated speakers pronounce words the same way. A second-place variant is not to be regarded as less acceptable than the pronunciation that is given first. It may, in fact, be used by as many educated speakers as the first variant, but the requirements of the printed page are such that one must precede the other:

tomato [təˈmeɪt̬o, -ˈmɑ-] ...

When a compound word has less than a full pronunciation, the missing part is to be supplied from the pronunciation at the entry for the unpronounced element of the compound:

gamma ray [ˈgæmə] ...

ray [ˈreɪ] ...

smoke[1] [ˈsmoːk] ...

smoke detector [dɪˈtɛktər] ...

In general, no pronunciation is given for open compounds consisting of two or more English words that are main entries at their own alphabetical place:

water lily *n* : nenúfar *m*

Only the first entry in a series of numbered homographs is given a pronunciation if their pronunciations are the same:

dab[1] [ˈdæb] *vt* ...

dab[2] *n* ...

No pronunciation is shown for principal parts of verbs that are formed by regular suffixation, nor for other derivative words formed by common suffixes.

2. Pronunciation of Spanish Entry Words

Spanish pronunciation is highly regular, so no pronunciations are given for most Spanish-to-English entries. Exceptions have been made for certain words (such as foreign borrowings) whose Spanish pronunciations are not evident from their spellings:

pizza [ˈpitsa, ˈpisa] ...

footing [ˈfuˌtɪŋ] ...

Functional Labels

An italic label indicating a part of speech or some other functional classification follows the pronunciation or, if no pronunciation is given, the main entry. The eight traditional parts of speech, adjective, adverb, conjunction, interjection, noun, preposition, pronoun, and verb, are indicated as follows:

> **daily²** *adj* . . .
>
> **vagamente** *adv* . . .
>
> **and** . . . *conj* . . .
>
> **huy** *interj* . . .
>
> **jackal** . . . *n* . . .
>
> **para** *prep* . . .
>
> **neither³** *pron* . . .
>
> **leer** . . . *v* . . .

Verbs that are intransitive are labeled *vi,* and verbs that are transitive are labeled *vt.* Entries for verbs that are both transitive and intransitive are labeled *v;* if such an entry includes irregular verb inflections, it is labeled *v* immediately after the main entry, with the labels *vi* and *vt* serving to introduce transitive and intransitive subdivisions when both are present:

> **deliberar** *vi* : to deliberate
>
> **necessitate** . . . *vt* **-tated; -tating** : necesitar, requerir
>
> **satisfy** . . . *v* **-fied; -fying** *vt* . . . — *vi* . . .

Two other labels are used to indicate functional classifications of verbs: *v aux* (auxiliary verb) and *v impers* (impersonal verb).

> **may** . . . *v aux, past* **might** . . .
>
> **haber¹** . . . *v aux* **1** : have . . . — *v impers*
> **1 hay** : there is, there are . . .

Gender Labels

In Spanish-to-English noun entries, the gender of the entry word is indicated by an italic *m* (masculine), *f* (feminine), or *mf* (masculine or feminine), immediately following the functional label:

> **magnesio** *nm* . . .
>
> **galaxia** *nf* . . .
>
> **turista** *nmf* . . .

If both the masculine and feminine forms are shown for a noun referring to a person, the label is simply *n:*

> **director, -tora** *n* . . .

Spanish noun equivalents of English entry words are also labeled for gender:

> **amnesia** . . . *n* : amnesia *f*
>
> **earache** . . . *n* : dolor *m* de oído
>
> **gamekeeper** . . . *n* : guardabosque *mf*

Inflected Forms

1. Nouns

The plurals of nouns are shown in this dictionary when they are irregular, when plural suffixation brings about a change in accentuation or in the spelling of the root word, when an English noun ends in a consonant plus *-o* or in *-ey,* when an English noun ends in *-oo,* when an English noun is a compound that pluralizes any element but the last, when a noun has variant plurals, or whenever the dictionary user might have reasonable doubts regarding the spelling of a plural:

> **tooth** . . . *n, pl* **teeth** . . .
>
> **garrafón** *nm, pl* **-fones** . . .
>
> **potato** . . . *n, pl* **-toes** . . .

> **abbey** ... *n, pl* **-beys** ...
>
> **cuckoo**[2] *n, pl* **-oos** ...
>
> **brother–in–law** ... *n, pl*
>   **brothers–in–law** ...
>
> **quail**[2] *n, pl* **quail** *or* **quails** ...
>
> **hábitat** *nm, pl* **-tats** ...
>
> **tahúr** *nm, pl* **tahúres** ...

Cutback inflected forms are used for most nouns on the English-to-Spanish side, regardless of the number of syllables. On the Spanish-to-English side, cutback inflections are given for nouns that have three or more syllables; plurals for shorter words are written out in full:

> **shampoo**[2] *n, pl* **-poos** ...
>
> **calamity** ... *n, pl* **-ties** ...
>
> **mouse** ... *n, pl* **mice** ...
>
> **sartén** *nmf, pl* **sartenes** ...
>
> **hámster** *nm, pl* **hámsters** ...
>
> **federación** *nf, pl* **-ciones** ...

If only one gender form has a plural which is irregular, that plural form will be given with the appropriate label:

> **campeón, -ona** *n, mpl* **-ones** : champi-
>   on

The plurals of nouns are usually not shown when the base word is unchanged by the addition of the regular plural suffix or when the noun is unlikely to occur in the plural:

> **apple** ... *n* : manzana *f*
>
> **inglés**[3] *nm* : English (language)

Nouns that are plural in form and that regularly occur in plural constructions are labeled as *npl* (for English nouns), *nmpl* (for Spanish masculine nouns), or *nfpl* (for Spanish feminine nouns):

> **knickers** ... *npl* ...
>
> **enseres** *nmpl* ...
>
> **mancuernas** *nfpl* ...

Entry words that are unchanged in the plural are labeled *ns &
pl* (for English nouns), *nms & pl* (for Spanish masculine nouns),
nfs & pl (for Spanish feminine nouns), and *nmfs & pl* (for Spanish
gender-variable nouns):

> **deer** . . . *ns & pl* . . .
>
> **lavaplatos** *nms & pl* . . .
>
> **tesis** *nfs & pl* . . .
>
> **rompehuelgas** *nmfs & pl* . . .

2. Verbs

ENGLISH VERBS

The principal parts of verbs are shown in English-to-Spanish
entries when they are irregular, when suffixation brings about a
change in spelling of the root word, when the verb ends in *-ey,*
when there are variant inflected forms, or whenever it is believed
that the dictionary user might have reasonable doubts about the
spelling of an inflected form:

> **break**[1] . . . *v* **broke** . . . ; **broken** . . . ;
>   **breaking** . . .
>
> **drag**[1] . . . *v* **dragged; dragging** . . .
>
> **monkey**[1] . . . *vi* **-keyed; -keying** . . .
>
> **label**[1] . . . *vt* **-beled** *or* **-belled; -beling**
>   *or* **-belling** . . .
>
> **imagine** . . . *vt* **-ined; -ining** . . .

Cutback inflected forms are usually used when the verb has
two or more syllables:

> **multiply** . . . *v* **-plied; -plying** . . .
>
> **bevel**[1] . . . *v* **-eled** *or* **-elled; -eling** *or*
>   **-elling** . . .
>
> **forgo** *or* **forego** . . . *vt* **-went; -gone;**
>   **-going** . . .
>
> **commit** . . . *vt* **-mitted; -mitting** . . .

The principal parts of an English verb are not shown when the
base word is unchanged by suffixation:

> **delay**[1] ... *vt*
>
> **pitch**[1] ... *vt*

SPANISH VERBS

Entries for irregular Spanish verbs are cross-referenced by number to the model conjugations appearing in the Conjugation of Spanish Verbs section:

> **abnegarse** {49} *vr* ...
>
> **volver** {89} *vi* ...

Entries for Spanish verbs with regular conjugations are not cross-referenced; however, model conjugations for regular Spanish verbs are included in the Conjugation of Spanish Verbs section beginning on page 38a.

Adverbs and Adjectives

The comparative and superlative forms of English adjective and adverb main entries are shown when suffixation brings about a change in spelling of the root word, when the inflection is irregular, and when there are variant inflected forms:

> **wet**[2] *adj* **wetter; wettest** ...
>
> **good**[2] *adj* **better** ... ; **best** ...
>
> **evil**[1] ... *adj* **eviler** *or* **eviller; evilest** *or* **evillest** ...

The superlative forms of adjectives and adverbs of two or more syllables are usually cut back; the superlative is shown in full, however, when it is desirable to indicate the pronunciation of the inflected form:

> **early**[1] ... *adv* **earlier; -est** ...
>
> **gaudy** ... *adj* **gaudier; -est** ...
>
> **secure**[2] *adj* **-curer; -est** ...
>
> *but*
>
> **young**[1] ... *adj* **younger** ['jʌŋgər]; **youngest** [-gəst] ...

At a few entries only the superlative form is shown:

mere *adj, superlative* **merest** . . .

The absence of the comparative form indicates that there is no evidence of its use.

The comparative and superlative forms of adjectives and adverbs are usually not shown when the base word is unchanged by suffixation:

quiet³ *adj* **1** . . .

Usage

1. Usage Labels

Two types of usage labels are used in this dictionary—regional and stylistic. Spanish words that are limited in use to a specific area or areas of Latin America, or to Spain, are given labels indicating the countries in which they are most commonly used:

guarachear *vi Cuba, PRi fam* . . .

bucket . . . *n* : . . . cubeta *f Mex*

The following regional labels are used in this book: *Arg* (Argentina), *Bol* (Bolivia), *CA* (Central America), *Car* (Caribbean), *Chile* (Chile), *Col* (Colombia), *CoRi* (Costa Rica), *Cuba* (Cuba), *DomRep* (Dominican Republic), *Ecua* (Ecuador), *Sal* (El Salvador), *Guat* (Guatemala), *Hond* (Honduras), *Mex* (Mexico), *Nic* (Nicaragua), *Pan* (Panama), *Par* (Paraguay), *Peru* (Peru), *PRi* (Puerto Rico), *Spain* (Spain), *Uru* (Uruguay), *Ven* (Venezuela).

Since this book focuses on the Spanish spoken in Latin America, only the most common regionalisms from Spain have been included in order to allow for more thorough coverage of Latin-American forms.

A number of Spanish words are given a *fam* (familiar) label as well, indicating that these words are suitable for informal contexts but would not normally be used in formal writing or speaking. The stylistic label *usu considered vulgar* is added for a word which is usually considered vulgar or offensive but whose widespread use justifies its inclusion in this book. The label is intended to warn the reader that the word in question may be inappropriate in polite conversation.

2. Usage Notes

Definitions are sometimes preceded by parenthetical usage notes that give supplementary semantic information:

> **not** ... *adv* **1** (*used to form a negative*) : no ...
>
> **within**[2] *prep* ... **2** (*in expressions of distance*) : ... **3** (*in expressions of time*) : ...
>
> **e**[2] *conj* (*used instead of* **y** *before words beginning with i or hi*) : ...
>
> **poder**[1] ... *v aux* ... **2** (*expressing possibility*) : ... **3** (*expressing permission*) : ...

Additional semantic orientation is also sometimes given in the form of parenthetical notes appearing within the definition:

> **calibrate** ... *vt* ... : calibrar (armas), graduar (termómetros)
>
> **palco** *nm* : box (in a theater or stadium)

Occasionally a usage note is used in place of a definition. This is usually done when the entry word has no single foreign-language equivalent. This type of usage note will be accompanied by examples of common use:

> **shall** ... *v aux* ... **1** (*used to express a command*) ⟨you shall do as I say : harás lo que te digo⟩ ...

3. Illustrations of Usage

Definitions are sometimes followed by verbal illustrations that show a typical use of the word in context or a common idiomatic usage. These verbal illustrations include a translation and are enclosed in angle brackets:

> **lejos** *adv* **1** : far away, distant ⟨a lo lejos
> : in the distance, far off⟩ . . .

> **make¹** . . . **9** . . . : ganar ⟨to make a liv-
> ing : ganarse la vida⟩ . . .

Sense Division

A boldface colon is used to introduce a definition:

> **fable** . . . *n* : fábula *f*

Boldface Arabic numerals separate the senses of a word that has more than one sense:

> **laguna** *nf* **1** : lagoon **2** : lacuna, gap

Whenever some information (such as a synonym, a boldface word or phrase, a usage note, a cross-reference, or a label) follows a sense number, it applies only to that specific numbered sense and not to any other boldface numbered senses:

> **abanico** *nm* . . . **2** GAMA : . . .
>
> **tonic²** *n* . . . **2** *or* **tonic water** : . . .
>
> **grillo** *nm* . . . **2 grillos** *nmpl* : . . .
>
> **fairy** . . . *n, pl* **fairies** . . . **2 fairy tale** : . . .
>
> **myself** . . . *pron* **1** (*used reflexively*) : . . .
>
> **pike** . . . *n* . . . **3** → **turnpike**
>
> **atado²** *nm* . . . **2** *Arg* : . . .

Cross-References

Three different kinds of cross-references are used in this dictionary: synonymous, cognate, and inflectional. In each instance the cross-reference is readily recognized by the boldface arrow following the entry word.

Synonymous and cognate cross-references indicate that a definition at the entry cross-referred to can be substituted for the entry word:

> **scapula** . . . → **shoulder blade**
>
> **amuck** . . . → **amok**

An inflectional cross-reference is used to identify the entry word as an inflected form of another word (as a noun or verb):

> **fue, etc.** → **ir, ser**
>
> **mice** → **mouse**

Synonyms

At many entries or senses in this book, a synonym in small capital letters is provided before the boldface colon and the following defining text. These synonyms are all main entries or bold notes elsewhere in the book. They serve as a helpful guide to the meaning of the entry or sense and also give the reader an additional term that might be substituted in a similar context. On the English-to-Spanish side synonyms are particularly abundant, since special care has been taken to guide the English speaker—by means of synonyms, verbal illustrations, or usage notes—to the meaning of the Spanish terms at each sense of a multisense entry.

Spanish Grammar

Accentuation

Spanish word stress is generally determined according to the following rules:

- Words ending in a vowel, or in -*n* or -*s,* are stressed on the penultimate syllable (*zapato*, *llaman*).

- Words ending in a consonant other than -*n* or -*s* are stressed on the last syllable (*perdiz, curiosidad*).

Exceptions to these rules have a written accent mark over the stressed vowel (*fácil*, *hablará*, *último*). There are also a few words which take accent marks in order to distinguish them from homonyms (*si*, *sí*; *que*, *qué*; *el*, *él*; etc.).

Adverbs ending in -*mente* have two stressed syllables since they retain both the stress of the root word and of the -*mente* suffix (*lentamente*, *difícilmente*). Many compounds also have two stressed syllables (*limpiaparabrisas*).

Punctuation and Capitalization

Questions and exclamations in Spanish are preceded by an inverted question mark ¿ and an inverted exclamation mark ¡, respectively:

> ¿Cuándo llamó Ana?
> Y tú, ¿qué piensas?
>
> ¡No hagas eso!
> Pero, ¡qué lástima!

In Spanish, unlike English, the following words are not capitalized:

- Names of days, months, and languages (*jueves, octubre, español*).

- Spanish adjectives or nouns derived from proper nouns (*los nicaragüenses, una teoría marxista*).

Articles

1. Definite Article

Spanish has five forms of the definite article: *el* (masculine singular), *la* (feminine singular), *los* (masculine plural), *las* (feminine plural), and *lo* (neuter). The first four agree in gender and number with the nouns they limit (*el carro,* the car; *las tijeras,* the scissors), although the form *el* is used with feminine singular nouns beginning with a stressed *a-* or *ha-* (*el águila, el hambre*).

The neuter article *lo* is used with the masculine singular form of an adjective to express an abstract concept (*lo mejor de este método,* the best thing about this method; *lo meticuloso de su trabajo,* the meticulousness of her work; *lo mismo para mí,* the same for me).

Whenever the masculine article *el* immediately follows the words *de* or *a,* it combines with them to form the contractions *del* and *al,* respectively (*viene **del** campo,* vi **al** hermano de Roberto*).

The use of *el, la, los,* and *las* in Spanish corresponds largely to the use of *the* in English; some exceptions are noted below.

The definite article is used:

- When referring to something as a class (*los gatos son ágiles,* cats are agile; *me gusta el café,* I like coffee).

- In references to meals and in most expressions of time (*¿comiste el almuerzo?,* did you eat lunch?; *vino el año pasado,* he came last year; *son las dos,* it's two o'clock; *prefiero el verano,* I prefer summer; *la reunión es el lunes,* the meeting is on Monday; but: *hoy es lunes,* today is Monday).

- Before titles (except *don, doña, san, santo, santa, fray,* and *sor*) in third-person references to people (*la señora Rivera llamó,* Mrs. Rivera called; but: *hola, señora Rivera,* hello, Mrs. Rivera).

- In references to body parts and personal possessions (*me duele la cabeza,* my head hurts; *dejó el sombrero,* he left his hat).

- To mean "the one" or "the ones" when the subject is already understood (*la de madera,* the wooden one; *los que vi ayer,* the ones I saw yesterday).

The definite article is omitted:

- Before a noun in apposition, if the noun is not modified (*Caracas, capital de Venezuela;* but: *Pico Bolívar, la montaña más alta de Venezuela*).

- Before a number in a royal title (*Carlos Quinto,* Charles the Fifth).

2. Indefinite Article

The forms of the indefinite article in Spanish are *un* (masculine singular), *una* (feminine singular), *unos* (masculine plural), and *unas* (feminine plural). They agree in number and gender with the nouns they limit (*una mesa,* a table; *unos platos,* some plates), although the form *un* is used with feminine singular nouns beginning with a stressed *a-* or *ha-* (*un ala, un hacha*).

The use of *un, una, unos,* and *unas* in Spanish corresponds largely to the use of *a, an,* and *some* in English, with some exceptions:

- Indefinite articles are generally omitted before nouns identifying someone or something as a member of a class or category (*Paco es profesor/católico,* Paco is a professor/Catholic; *se llama páncreas,* it's called a pancreas).

- They are also often omitted in instances where quantity is understood from context (*vine sin chaqueta,* I came without a jacket; *no tengo carro,* I don't have a car).

Nouns

1. Gender

Nouns in Spanish are either masculine or feminine. A noun's gender can often be determined according to the following guidelines:

- Nouns ending in *-aje, -o,* or *-or* are usually masculine (*el traje, el libro, el sabor*), with some exceptions (*la mano, la foto, la labor,* etc.).

- Nouns ending in *-a, -dad, -ión, -tud,* or *-umbre* are usually feminine (*la alfombra, la capacidad, la excepción, la juventud, la certidumbre*). Exceptions include: *el día, el mapa,* and many learned borrowings ending in *-ma* (*el idioma, el tema*).

Most nouns referring to people or animals agree in gender with the subject (*el hombre, la mujer; el hermano, la hermana; el perro, la perra*). However, some nouns referring to people, including those ending in *-ista,* use the same form for both sexes (*el artista, la artista; el modelo, la modelo;* etc.).

A few names of animals exist in only one gender form (*la jirafa, el sapo,* etc.). In these instances, the adjectives *macho* and *hembra* are sometimes used to distinguish males and females (*una jirafa macho,* a male giraffe).

2. Pluralization

Plurals of Spanish nouns are formed as follows:

- Nouns ending in an unstressed vowel or an accented *-é* are pluralized by adding *-s* (*la vaca, las vacas; el café, los cafés*).

- Nouns ending in a consonant other than *-s,* or in a stressed vowel other than *-é,* are generally pluralized by adding *-es* (*el papel, los papeles; el rubí, los rubíes*). Exceptions include *papá* (*papás*) and *mamá* (*mamás*).

- Nouns with an unstressed final syllable ending in *-s* usually have a zero plural (*la crisis, las crisis; el jueves, los jueves*). Other nouns ending in *-s* add *-es* to form the plural (*el mes, los meses; el país, los países*).

- Nouns ending in *-z* are pluralized by changing the *-z* to *-c* and adding *-es* (*el lápiz, los lápices; la vez, las veces*).

- Many compound nouns have a zero plural (*el paraguas, los paraguas; el aguafiestas, los aguafiestas*).

- The plurals of *cualquiera* and *quienquiera* are *cualesquiera* and *quienesquiera,* respectively.

Adjectives

1. Gender and Number

Most adjectives agree in gender and number with the nouns they modify (un chico *alto,* una chica *alta,* unos chicos *altos,* unas chicas *altas*). Some adjectives, including those ending in *-e* and *-ista* (*fuerte, altruista*) and comparative adjectives ending in *-or* (*mayor, mejor*), vary only for number.

Adjectives whose masculine singular forms end in *-o* generally change the *-o* to *-a* to form the feminine (*pequeño* → *pequeña*). Masculine adjectives ending in *-án, -ón,* or *-dor,* and masculine adjectives of nationality which end in a consonant, usually add *-a* to form the feminine (*holgazán* → *holgazana*; *llorón* → *llorona*; *trabajador* → *trabajadora*; *irlandés* → *irlandesa*).

Adjectives are pluralized in much the same manner as nouns:

- The plurals of adjectives ending in an unstressed vowel or an accented *-é* are formed by adding an *-s* (un postre *rico,* unos postres *ricos;* una camisa *café,* unas camisas *cafés*).

- Adjectives ending in a consonant, or in a stressed vowel other than *-é,* are generally pluralized by adding *-es* (un niño *cortés,* unos niños *corteses;* una persona *iraní,* unas personas *iraníes*).

- Adjectives ending in *-z* are pluralized by changing the *-z* to *-c* and adding *-es* (una respuesta *sagaz,* unas respuestas *sagaces*).

2. Shortening

- The following masculine singular adjectives drop their final *-o* when they occur before a masculine singular noun: *bueno* (*buen*), *malo* (*mal*), *uno* (*un*), *alguno* (*algún*), *ninguno* (*ningún*), *primero* (*primer*), *tercero* (*tercer*).

- *Grande* shortens to *gran* before any singular noun.

- *Ciento* shortens to *cien* before any noun.

- The title *Santo* shortens to *San* before all masculine names except those beginning with *To-* or *Do-* (*San Juan, Santo Tomás*).

3. Position

Descriptive adjectives generally follow the nouns they modify (*una cosa útil, un actor famoso*). However, adjectives that express an inherent quality often precede the noun (*la blanca nieve*).

Some adjectives change meaning depending on whether they occur before or after the noun: *un pobre niño,* a poor (pitiable) child; *un niño pobre,* a poor (not rich) child; *un gran hombre,* a great man; *un hombre grande,* a big man; *el único libro,* the only book; *el libro único,* the unique book, etc.

4. Comparative and Superlative Forms

The comparative of Spanish adjectives is generally rendered as *más . . . que* (more . . . than) or *menos . . . que* (less . . . than): *soy más alta que él,* I'm taller than he; *son menos inteligentes que tú,* they're less intelligent than you.

The superlative of Spanish adjectives usually follows the formula *definite article + (noun +) más/menos + adjective: ella es la estudiante más trabajadora,* she is the hardest-working student; *él es el menos conocido,* he's the least known.

A few Spanish adjectives have irregular comparative and superlative forms:

Adjective	Comparative/Superlative
bueno (good)	**mejor** (better, best)
malo (bad)	**peor** (worse, worst)
grande[1] (big, great), **viejo** (old)	**mayor** (greater, older; greatest, oldest)
pequeño[1] (little), **joven** (young)	**menor** (lesser, younger; least, youngest)
mucho (much), **muchos** (many)	**más** (more, most)
poco (little), **pocos** (few)	**menos** (less, least)

[1] These words have regular comparative and superlative forms when used in reference to physical size: *él es más grande que yo; nuestra casa es la más pequeña.*

ABSOLUTE SUPERLATIVE

The absolute superlative is formed by placing *muy* before the adjective, or by adding the suffix *-ísimo* (*ella es muy simpática* or *ella es simpatiquísima,* she is very nice). The absolute superlative using *-ísimo* is formed according to the following rules:

- Adjectives ending in a consonant other than *-z* simply add the *-ísimo* ending (*fácil → facilísimo*).

- Adjectives ending in *-z* change this consonant to *-c* and add *-ísimo* (*feliz → felicísimo*).

- Adjectives ending in a vowel or diphthong drop the vowel or diphthong and add *-ísimo* (*claro → clarísimo; amplio → amplísimo*).

- Adjectives ending in *-co* or *-go* change these endings to *qu* and *gu*, respectively, and add *-ísimo* (*rico → riquísimo; largo → larguísimo*).

- Adjectives ending in *-ble* change this ending to *-bil* and add *-ísimo* (*notable → notabilísimo*).

- Adjectives containing the stressed diphthong *ie* or *ue* will sometimes change these to *e* and *o*, respectively (*ferviente → fervientísimo* or *ferventísimo; bueno → buenísimo* or *bonísimo*).

Adverbs

Adverbs can be formed by adding the adverbial suffix *-mente* to virtually any adjective (*fácil → fácilmente*). If the adjective varies for gender, the feminine form is used as the basis for forming the adverb (*rápido → rápidamente*).

Pronouns

1. Personal Pronouns

The personal pronouns in Spanish are:

Person		Singular	Plural	
FIRST	**yo**	I	**nosotros, nosotras**	we
SECOND	**tú**	you (familiar)	**vosotros[2], vosotras[2]**	you, all of you
	vos[1]	you		
	usted	you (formal)	**ustedes[3]**	you, all of you
THIRD	**él**	he	**ellos, ellas**	they
	ella	she		
	ello	it (neuter)		

[1] Familiar form used in addition to *tú* in South and Central America.

[2] Familiar form used in Spain.

[3] Formal form used in Spain; familiar and formal form used in Latin America.

FAMILIAR VS. FORMAL

The second person personal pronouns exist in both familiar and formal forms. The familiar forms are generally used when addressing relatives, friends, and children, although usage varies considerably from region to region; the formal forms are used in other contexts to show courtesy, respect, or emotional distance.

In Spain and in the Caribbean, *tú* is used exclusively as the familiar singular "you." In South and Central America, however, *vos* either competes with *tú* to varying degrees or replaces it entirely. (For a more detailed explanation of *vos* and its corresponding verb forms, refer to the Conjugation of Spanish Verbs section.)

The plural familiar form *vosotros, -as* is used only in Spain, where *ustedes* is reserved for formal contexts. In Latin America, *vosotros, -as* is not used, and *ustedes* serves as the all-purpose plural "you."

It should be noted that while *usted* and *ustedes* are regarded as second person pronouns, they take the third person form of the verb.

USAGE

In Spanish, personal pronouns are generally omitted (*voy al cine,* I'm going to the movies; *¿llamaron?,* did they call?), although they are sometimes used for purposes of emphasis or clarity (*se* *lo diré yo,* I will tell them; *vino ella, pero él se quedó,* she came, but he stayed behind). The forms *usted* and *ustedes* are usually included out of courtesy (*¿cómo está usted?,* how are you?).

Personal pronouns are not generally used in reference to inanimate objects or living creatures other than humans; in these instances, the pronoun is most often omitted (*¿es nuevo? no, es viejo,* is it new? no, it's old).

The neuter third person pronoun *ello* is reserved for indefinite subjects (as abstract concepts): *todo ello implica* . . . , all of this implies . . . ; *por si ello fuera poco* . . . , as if that weren't enough . . . . It most commonly appears in formal writing and speech. In less formal contexts, *ello* is often either omitted or replaced with *esto, eso,* or *aquello.*

2. Prepositional Pronouns

Prepositional pronouns are used as the objects of prepositions (*¿es para mí?,* is it for me?; *se lo dio a ellos,* he gave it to them).

The prepositional pronouns in Spanish are:

Singular		Plural	
mí	me	**nosotros, nosotras**	us
ti	you	**vosotros[1], vosotras[1]**	you
usted	you (formal)	**ustedes**	you
él	him	**ellos, ellas**	them
ella	her		
ello	it (neuter)		
sí	yourself, himself, herself, itself, oneself	**sí**	yourselves, themselves

[1] Used primarily in Spain.

When the preposition *con* is followed by *mí, ti,* or *sí,* both words are replaced by *conmigo, contigo,* and *consigo,* respectively (*¿vienes conmigo?,* are you coming with me?; *habló contigo,* he spoke with you; *no lo trajo consigo,* she didn't bring it with her).

3. Object Pronouns

DIRECT OBJECT PRONOUNS

Direct object pronouns represent the primary goal or result of the action of a verb. The direct object pronouns in Spanish are:

Singular		Plural	
me	me	nos	us
te	you	os[1]	you
le[2]	you, him	les[2]	you, them
lo	you, him, it	los	you, them
la	you, her, it	las	you, them

[1] Used only in Spain.
[2] Used mainly in Spain.

Agreement

The third person forms agree in both gender and number with the nouns they replace or the people they refer to (*pintó las paredes,* she painted the walls → *las pintó,* she painted them; *visitaron al señor Juárez,* they visited Mr. Juárez → *lo visitaron,* they visited him). The remaining forms vary only for number.

Position

Direct object pronouns are normally affixed to the end of an affirmative command, a simple infinitive, or a present participle (¡*hazlo!,* do it!; *es difícil hacerlo,* it's difficult to do it; *haciéndolo, aprenderás,* you'll learn by doing it). With constructions involving an auxiliary verb and an infinitive or present participle, the pronoun may occur either immediately before the construction or suffixed to it (*lo voy a hacer* or *voy a hacerlo,* I'm going to do it; *estoy haciéndolo* or *lo estoy haciendo,* I'm doing it). In all other cases, the pronoun immediately precedes the conjugated verb (*no lo haré,* I won't do it).

Regional Variation

In Spain and in a few areas of Latin America, *le* and *les* are used in place of *lo* and *los* when referring to or addressing people (*le vieron,* they saw him; *les vistió,* she dressed them). In most parts of Latin America, however, *los* and *las* are used for the second person plural in both formal and familiar contexts.

The second person plural familiar form *os* is restricted to Spain.

INDIRECT OBJECT PRONOUNS

Indirect object pronouns represent the secondary goal of the action of a verb (*me dio el regalo,* he gave me the gift; *les dije que no,* I told them no). The indirect object pronouns in Spanish are:

Singular		**Plural**	
me	(to, for, from) me	**nos**	(to, for, from) us
te	(to, for, from) you	**os**[1]	(to, for, from) you
le	(to, for, from) you, him, her, it	**les**	(to, for, from) you, them
se[2]		**se**[2]	

[1]Used only in Spain.
[2]See explanation below.

Position

Indirect object pronouns follow the same rules as direct object pronouns with regard to their position in relation to verbs. When they occur with direct object pronouns, the indirect object pronoun always precedes (*nos lo dio,* she gave it to us; *estoy trayéndotela,* I'm bringing it to you).

Use of *Se*

When the indirect object pronouns *le* or *les* occur before any direct object pronoun beginning with an *l-,* the indirect object pronouns *le* and *les* convert to *se* (*les mandé la carta,* I sent them the letter → *se la mandé,* I sent it to them; *vamos a comprarle los aretes,* let's buy her the earrings → *vamos a comprárselos,* let's buy them for her).

4. Reflexive Pronouns

Reflexive pronouns are used to refer back to the subject of the verb (*me hice daño,* I hurt myself; *se vistieron,* they got dressed, they dressed themselves; *nos lo compramos,* we bought it for ourselves).

The reflexive pronouns in Spanish are:

	Singular		**Plural**
me	myself	**nos**	ourselves
te	yourself	**os**[1]	yourselves
se	yourself, himself, herself, itself	**se**	yourselves, themselves

[1]Used only in Spain.

Reflexive pronouns are also used:

- When the verb describes an action performed to one's own body, clothing, etc. (*me quité los zapatos,* I took off my shoes; *se arregló el pelo,* he fixed his hair).

- In the plural, to indicate reciprocal action (*se hablan con frecuencia,* they speak with each other frequently).

- In the third person singular and plural, as an indefinite subject reference (*se dice que es verdad,* they say it's true; *nunca se sabe,* one never knows; *se escribieron miles de páginas,* thousands of pages were written).

It should be noted that many verbs which take reflexive pronouns in Spanish have intransitive equivalents in English (*ducharse,* to shower; *quejarse,* to complain; etc.).

5. Relative Pronouns

Relative pronouns introduce subordinate clauses acting as nouns or modifiers (*el libro que escribió* . . . , the book that he wrote . . . ; *las chicas a quienes conociste* . . . , the girls whom you met . . .). In Spanish, the relative pronouns are:

que (that, which, who, whom)

quien, quienes (who, whom, that, whoever, whomever)

el cual, la cual, los cuales, las cuales (which, who)

el que, la que, los que, las que (which, who, whoever)

lo cual (which)

lo que (what, which, whatever)

cuanto, cuanta, cuantos, cuantas (all those that, all that, whatever, whoever, as much as, as many as)

Relative pronouns are not omitted in Spanish as they often are in English: *el carro que vi ayer,* the car (that) I saw yesterday. When relative pronouns are used with prepositions, the preposition precedes the clause (*la película sobre la cual le hablé,* the film I spoke to you about).

The relative pronoun *que* can be used in reference to both people and things. Unlike other relative pronouns, *que* does not take the personal *a* when used as a direct object referring to a person (*el hombre que llamé,* the man that I called; but: *el hombre a quien llamé,* the man whom I called).

Quien is used only in reference to people. It varies in number with the explicit or implied antecedent (*las mujeres con quienes charlamos . . . ,* the women we chatted with; *quien lo hizo pagará,* whoever did it will pay).

El cual and *el que* vary for both number and gender, and are therefore often used in situations where *que* or *quien(es)* might create ambiguity: *nos contó algunas cosas sobre los libros, las cuales eran interesantes,* he told us some things about the books which (the things) were interesting.

Lo cual and *lo que* are used to refer back to a whole clause, or to something indefinite (*dijo que iría, lo cual me alegró,* he said he would go, which made me happy; *pide lo que quieras,* ask for whatever you want).

Cuanto varies for both number and gender with the implied antecedent: *conté a cuantas (personas) pude,* I counted as many (people) as I could. If an indefinite mass quantity is referred to, the masculine singular form is used (*anoté cuanto decía,* I jotted down whatever he said).

Possessives

1. Possessive Adjectives

UNSTRESSED FORMS

Singular		Plural	
mi(s)	my	**nuestro(s), nuestra(s)**	our
tu(s)	your	**vuestro(s)[1], vuestra(s)[1]**	your
su(s)	your, his, her, its	**su(s)**	your, their

[1] Used only in Spain.

STRESSED FORMS

Singular		Plural	
mío(s), **mía(s)**	my, mine, of mine	**nuestro(s),** **nuestra(s)**	our, ours, of ours
tuyo(s), **tuya(s)**	your, yours, of yours	**vuestro(s)¹,** **vuestra(s)¹**	your, yours, of yours
suyo(s), **suya(s)**	your, yours, of yours; his, of his; her, hers, of hers; its, of its	**suyo(s),** **suya(s)**	your, yours, of yours; their, theirs, of theirs

[1]Used only in Spain.

The unstressed forms of possessive adjectives precede the nouns they modify (*mis zapatos,* my shoes; *nuestra escuela,* our school).

The stressed forms occur after the noun and are often used for purposes of emphasis (*el carro tuyo,* your car; *la pluma es mía,* the pen is mine; *unos amigos nuestros,* some friends of ours).

All possessive adjectives agree with the noun in number. The stressed forms, as well as the unstressed forms *nuestro* and *vuestro,* also vary for gender.

2. Possessive Pronouns

The possessive pronouns have the same forms as the stressed possessive adjectives (see table above). They are always preceded by the definite article, and they agree in number and gender with the nouns they replace (*las llaves mías,* my keys → *las mías,* mine; *los guantes nuestros,* our gloves → *los nuestros,* ours).

Demonstratives

1. Demonstrative Adjectives

The demonstrative adjectives in Spanish are:

Singular		Plural	
este, esta	this	**estos, estas**	these
ese, esa	that	**esos, esas**	those
aquel, aquella	that	**aquellos, aquellas**	those

Demonstrative adjectives agree with the nouns they modify in gender and number (*esta chica, aquellos árboles*). They normally precede the noun, but may occasionally occur after for purposes of emphasis or to express contempt: *en la época aquella de cambio,* in that era of change; *el perro ese ha ladrado toda la noche,* that (awful, annoying, etc.) dog barked all night long.

The forms *aquel, aquella, aquellos,* and *aquellas* are generally used in reference to people and things that are relatively distant from the speaker in space or time: *ese libro,* that book (a few feet away); *aquel libro,* that book (way over there).

2. Demonstrative Pronouns

The demonstrative pronouns in Spanish are orthographically identical to the demonstrative adjectives except that they take an accent mark over the stressed vowel (*éste, ése, aquél,* etc.). In addition, there are three neuter forms—*esto, eso,* and *aquello*—which are used when referring to abstract ideas or unidentified things (*¿te dijo eso?,* he said that to you?; *¿qué es esto?,* what is this?; *tráeme todo aquello,* bring me all that stuff).

Except for the neuter forms, demonstrative pronouns agree in gender and number with the nouns they replace (*esta silla,* this chair → *ésta,* this one; *aquellos vasos,* those glasses → *aquéllos,* those ones).

Abbreviations in This Work

adj	adjective	*nm*	masculine noun
adv	adverb	*nmf*	masculine or feminine noun
Arg	Argentina		
Bol	Bolivia	*nmfpl*	plural noun invariable for gender
Brit	British		
CA	Central America	*nmfs & pl*	noun invariable for both gender and number
Car	Caribbean region		
Col	Colombia		
conj	conjunction	*nmpl*	masculine plural noun
CoRi	Costa Rica		
DomRep	Dominican Republic	*nms & pl*	invariable singular or plural masculine noun
Ecua	Ecuador		
esp	especially	*npl*	plural noun
f	feminine	*ns & pl*	noun invariable for plural
fam	familiar or colloquial		
fpl	feminine plural	*Pan*	Panama
Guat	Guatemala	*Par*	Paraguay
Hond	Honduras	*pl*	plural
interj	interjection	*pp*	past participle
m	masculine	*prep*	preposition
Mex	Mexico	*PRi*	Puerto Rico
mf	masculine or feminine	*pron*	pronoun
		s	singular
mfpl	masculine or feminine plural	*Sal*	El Salvador
		Uru	Uruguay
mpl	masculine plural	*usu*	usually
n	noun	*v*	verb (transitive and intransitive)
nf	feminine noun		
nfpl	feminine plural noun	*v aux*	auxiliary verb
		Ven	Venezuela
nfs & pl	invariable singular or plural feminine noun	*vi*	intransitive verb
		v impers	impersonal verb
		vr	reflexive verb
Nic	Nicaragua	*vt*	transitive verb

Conjugation of Spanish Verbs

Simple Tenses

Tense	Regular Verbs Ending in -AR	
	hablar	
PRESENT INDICATIVE	hablo	hablamos
	hablas	habláis
	habla	hablan
PRESENT SUBJUNCTIVE	hable	hablemos
	hables	habléis
	hable	hablen
PRETERIT INDICATIVE	hablé	hablamos
	hablaste	hablasteis
	habló	hablaron
IMPERFECT INDICATIVE	hablaba	hablábamos
	hablabas	hablabais
	hablaba	hablaban
IMPERFECT SUBJUNCTIVE	hablara	habláramos
	hablaras	hablarais
	hablara	hablaran
	or	
	hablase	hablásemos
	hablases	hablaseis
	hablase	hablasen
FUTURE INDICATIVE	hablaré	hablaremos
	hablarás	hablaréis
	hablará	hablarán
FUTURE SUBJUNCTIVE	hablare	habláremos
	hablares	hablareis
	hablare	hablaren
CONDITIONAL	hablaría	hablaríamos
	hablarías	hablaríais
	hablaría	hablarían
IMPERATIVE		hablemos
	habla	hablad
	hable	hablen
PRESENT PARTICIPLE (GERUND)	hablando	
PAST PARTICIPLE	hablado	

Regular Verbs Ending in -ER comer		Regular Verbs Ending in -IR vivir	
como	comemos	vivo	vivimos
comes	coméis	vives	vivís
come	comen	vive	viven
coma	comamos	viva	vivamos
comas	comáis	vivas	viváis
coma	coman	viva	vivan
comí	comimos	viví	vivimos
comiste	comisteis	viviste	vivisteis
comió	comieron	vivió	vivieron
comía	comíamos	vivía	vivíamos
comías	comíais	vivías	vivíais
comía	comían	vivía	vivían
comiera	comiéramos	viviera	viviéramos
comieras	comierais	vivieras	vivierais
comiera	comieran	viviera	vivieran
or		*or*	
comiese	comiésemos	viviese	viviésemos
comieses	comieseis	vivieses	vivieseis
comiese	comiesen	viviese	viviesen
comeré	comeremos	viviré	viviremos
comerás	comeréis	vivirás	viviréis
comerá	comerán	vivirá	vivirán
comiere	comiéremos	viviere	viviéremos
comieres	comiereis	vivieres	viviereis
comiere	comieren	viviere	vivieren
comería	comeríamos	viviría	viviríamos
comerías	comeríais	vivirías	viviríais
comería	comerían	viviría	vivirían
	comamos		vivamos
come	comed	vive	vivid
coma	coman	viva	vivan
comiendo		viviendo	
comido		vivido	

Compound Tenses

1. Perfect Tenses

The perfect tenses are formed with *haber* and the past participle:

PRESENT PERFECT
> he hablado, etc. (*indicative*);
> haya hablado, etc. (*subjunctive*)

PAST PERFECT
> había hablado, etc. (*indicative*);
> hubiera hablado, etc. (*subjunctive*)
> *or*
> hubiese hablado, etc. (*subjunctive*)

PRETERIT PERFECT
> hube hablado, etc. (*indicative*)

FUTURE PERFECT
> habré hablado, etc. (*indicative*)

CONDITIONAL PERFECT
> habría hablado, etc. (*indicative*)

2. Progressive Tenses

The progressive tenses are formed with *estar* and the present participle:

PRESENT PROGRESSIVE
> estoy llamando, etc. (*indicative*);
> esté llamando, etc. (*subjunctive*)

IMPERFECT PROGRESSIVE
> estaba llamando, etc. (*indicative*);
> estuviera llamando, etc. (*subjunctive*)
> *or*
> estuviese llamando, etc. (*subjunctive*)

PRETERIT PROGRESSIVE

estuve llamando, etc. (*indicative*)

FUTURE PROGRESSIVE

estaré llamando, etc. (*indicative*)

CONDITIONAL PROGRESSIVE

estaría llamando, etc. (*indicative*)

PRESENT PERFECT PROGRESSIVE

he estado llamando, etc. (*indicative*);
haya estado llamando, etc. (*subjunctive*)

PAST PERFECT PROGRESSIVE

había estado llamando, etc. (*indicative*);
hubiera estado llamando, etc. (*subjunctive*)
or
hubiese estado llamando, etc. (*subjunctive*)

Use of *Vos*

In parts of South and Central America, *vos* often replaces or competes with *tú* as the second person familiar personal pronoun. It is particularly well established in the Río de la Plata region and much of Central America.

The pronoun *vos* often takes a distinct set of verb forms, usually in the present tense and the imperative. These vary widely from region to region; examples of the most common forms are shown below.

INFINITIVE FORM	hablar	comer	vivir
PRESENT INDICATIVE	vos hablás	vos comés	vos vivís
PRESENT SUBJUNCTIVE	vos hablés	vos comás	vos vivás
IMPERATIVE	hablá	comé	viví

In some areas, *vos* may take the *tú* or *vosotros* forms of the verb, while in others (as Uruguay), *tú* is combined with the *vos* verb forms.

Irregular Verbs

The *imperfect subjunctive*, the *future subjunctive*, the *conditional*, and most forms of the *imperative* are not included in the model conjugations list, but can be derived as follows:

The *imperfect subjunctive* and the *future subjunctive* are formed from the third person plural form of the preterit tense by removing the last syllable (*-ron*) and adding the appropriate suffix:

PRETERIT INDICATIVE, THIRD PERSON PLURAL (querer)	quisieron
IMPERFECT SUBJUNCTIVE (querer)	quisiera, quisieras, etc. *or* quisiese, quisieses, etc.
FUTURE SUBJUNCTIVE (querer)	quisiere, quisieres, etc.

The conditional uses the same stem as the future indicative:

FUTURE INDICATIVE (poner)	pondré, pondrás, etc.
CONDITIONAL (poner)	pondría, pondrías, etc.

The third person singular, first person plural, and third person plural forms of the *imperative* are the same as the corresponding forms of the present subjunctive.

The second person plural *(vosotros)* form of the *imperative* is formed by removing the final *-r* of the infinitive form and adding a *-d* (ex.: *oír → oíd*).

Model Conjugations of Irregular Verbs

The model conjugations below include the following simple tenses: the *present indicative* (IND), the *present subjunctive* (SUBJ), the *preterit indicative* (PRET), the *imperfect indicative* (IMPF), the *future indicative* (FUT), the second person singular form of the *imperative* (IMPER), the *present participle* or *gerund* (PRP), and the *past participle* (PP). Each set of conjugations is preceded by the corresponding infinitive form of the verb, shown in bold type. Only tenses containing irregularities are listed, and the irregular verb forms within each tense are displayed in bold type.

Each irregular verb entry in the Spanish-English section of this dictionary is cross-referred by number to one of the following model conjugations. These cross-reference numbers are shown in curly braces { } immediately following the entry's functional label.

1 **abolir** *(defective verb)* : IND abolimos, abolís *(other forms not used)*; SUBJ *(not used)*; IMPER *(only second person plural is used)*

2 **abrir** : PP abierto

3 **actuar** : IND **actúo, actúas, actúa,** actuamos, actuáis, **actúan;** SUBJ **actúe, actúes, actúe,** actuemos, actuéis, **actúen;** IMPER **actúa**

4 **adquirir** : IND **adquiero, adquieres, adquiere,** adquirimos, adquirís, **adquieren;** SUBJ **adquiera, adquieras, adquiera,** adquiramos, adquiráis, **adquieran;** IMPER **adquiere**

5 **airar** : IND **aíro, aíras, aíra,** airamos, airáis, **aíran;** SUBJ **aíre, aíres, aíre,** airemos, airéis, **aíren;** IMPER **aíra**

6 **andar** : PRET **anduve, anduviste, anduvo, anduvimos, anduvisteis, anduvieron**

7 **asir** : IND **asgo,** ases, ase, asimos, asís, asen; SUBJ **asga, asgas, asga, asgamos, asgáis, asgan**

8 **aunar** : IND **aúno, aúnas, aúna,** aunamos, aunáis, **aúnan;** SUBJ **aúne, aúnes, aúne,** aunemos, aunéis, **aúnen;** IMPER **aúna**

9 **avergonzar** : IND **avergüenzo, avergüenzas, avergüenza,** avergonzamos, avergonzáis, **avergüenzan;** SUBJ **avergüence, avergüences, avergüence, avergoncemos, avergoncéis, avergüencen;** PRET **avergoncé;** IMPER **avergüenza**

10 **averiguar** : SUBJ **averigüe, averigües, averigüe, averigüemos, averigüéis, averigüen;** PRET **averigüé,** averiguaste, averiguó, averiguamos, averiguasteis, averiguaron

11 **bendecir** : *IND* **bendigo, bendices, bendice,** bendecimos, bendecís, **bendicen;** *SUBJ* **bendiga, bendigas, bendiga, bendigamos, bendigáis, bendigan;** *PRET* **bendije, bendijiste, bendijo, bendijimos, bendijisteis, bendijeron;** *IMPER* **bendice**

12 **caber** : *IND* **quepo,** cabes, cabe, cabemos, cabéis, caben; *SUBJ* **quepa, quepas, quepa, quepamos, quepáis, quepan;** *PRET* **cupe, cupiste, cupo, cupimos, cupisteis, cupieron;** *FUT* **cabré, cabrás, cabrá, cabremos, cabréis, cabrán**

13 **caer** : *IND* **caigo,** caes, cae, caemos, caéis, caen; *SUBJ* **caiga, caigas, caiga, caigamos, caigáis, caigan;** *PRET* **caí, caíste, cayó, caímos, caísteis, cayeron;** *PRP* **cayendo;** *PP* **caído**

14 **cocer** : *IND* **cuezo, cueces, cuece,** cocemos, cocéis, **cuecen;** *SUBJ* **cueza, cuezas, cueza, cozamos, cozáis, cuezan;** *IMPER* **cuece**

15 **coger** : *IND* **cojo,** coges, coge, cogemos, cogéis, cogen; *SUBJ* **coja, cojas, coja, cojamos, cojáis, cojan**

16 **colgar** : *IND* **cuelgo, cuelgas, cuelga,** colgamos, colgáis, **cuelgan;** *SUBJ* **cuelgue, cuelgues, cuelgue, colguemos, colguéis, cuelguen;** *PRET* **colgué,** colgaste, colgó, colgamos, colgasteis, colgaron; *IMPER* **cuelga**

17 **concernir** *(defective verb; used only in the third person singular and plural of the present indicative, present subjunctive, and imperfect subjunctive) see* 25 **discernir**

18 **conocer** : *IND* **conozco,** conoces, conoce, conocemos, conocéis, conocen; *SUBJ* **conozca, conozcas, conozca, conozcamos, conozcáis, conozcan**

19 **contar** : *IND* **cuento, cuentas, cuenta,** contamos, contáis, **cuentan;** *SUBJ* **cuente, cuentes, cuente,** contemos, contéis, **cuenten;** *IMPER* **cuenta**

20 **creer** : *PRET* creí, **creíste, creyó, creímos, creísteis, creyeron;** *PRP* **creyendo;** *PP* **creído**

21 **cruzar** : *SUBJ* **cruce, cruces, cruce, crucemos, crucéis, crucen;** *PRET* **crucé,** cruzaste, cruzó, cruzamos, cruzasteis, cruzaron

22 **dar** : *IND* **doy,** das, da, damos, **dais,** dan; *SUBJ* **dé,** des, **dé,** demos, **deis,** den; *PRET* **di, diste, dio, dimos, disteis, dieron**

23 **decir** : *IND* **digo, dices, dice,** decimos, decís, **dicen;** *SUBJ* **diga, digas, diga, digamos, digáis, digan;** *PRET* **dije, dijiste, dijo, dijimos, dijisteis, dijeron;** *FUT* **diré, dirás, dirá, diremos, diréis, dirán;** *IMPER* **di;** *PRP* **diciendo;** *PP* **dicho**

24 **delinquir** : *IND* **delinco,** delinques, delinque, delinquimos, delinquís, delinquen; *SUBJ* **delinca, delincas, delinca, delincamos, delincáis, delincan**

25 **discernir** : *IND* **discierno, disciernes, discierne,** discernimos, discernís, **disciernen;** *SUBJ* **discierna, disciernas, discierna,** discernamos, discernáis, **disciernan;** *IMPER* **discierne**

26 **distinguir** : *IND* **distingo,** distingues, distingue, distinguimos, distinguís, distinguen; *SUBJ* **distinga, distingas, distinga, distingamos, distingáis, distingan**

27 **dormir** : *IND* **duermo, duermes, duerme,** dormimos, dormís, **duermen;** *SUBJ* **duerma, duermas, duerma, durmamos, durmáis, duerman;** *PRET* dormí, dormiste, **durmió,** dormimos, dormisteis, **durmieron;** *IMPER* **duerme;** *PRP* **durmiendo**

28 **elegir** : *IND* **elijo, eliges, elige,** elegimos, elegís, **eligen;** *SUBJ* **elija, elijas, elija, elijamos, elijáis, elijan;** *PRET* elegí, elegiste, **eligió,** elegimos, elegisteis, **eligieron;** *IMPER* **elige;** *PRP* **eligiendo**

29 **empezar** : *IND* **empiezo, empiezas, empieza,** empezamos, empezáis, **empiezan;** *SUBJ* **empiece, empieces, empiece, empecemos, empecéis, empiecen;** *PRET* **empecé,** empezaste, empezó, empezamos, empezasteis, empezaron; *IMPER* **empieza**

30 **enraizar** : *IND* **enraízo, enraízas, enraíza,** enraizamos, enraizáis, **enraízan;** *SUBJ* **enraíce, enraíces, enraíce, enraicemos, enraicéis, enraícen;** *PRET* **enraicé,** enraizaste, enraizó, enraizamos, enraizasteis, enraizaron; *IMPER* **enraíza**

31 **erguir** : *IND* **irgo** *or* **yergo, irgues** *or* **yergues, irgue** *or* **yergue,** erguimos, erguís, **irguen** *or* **yerguen;** *SUBJ* **irga** *or* **yerga, irgas** *or* **yergas, irga** *or* **yerga, irgamos, irgáis, irgan** *or* **yergan;** *PRET* erguí, erguiste, **irguió,** erguimos, erguisteis, **irguieron;** *IMPER* **irgue** *or* **yergue;** *PRP* **irguiendo**

32 **errar** : *IND* **yerro, yerras, yerra,** erramos, erráis, **yerran;** *SUBJ* **yerre, yerres, yerre,** erremos, erréis, **yerren;** *IMPER* **yerra**

33 **escribir** : *PP* **escrito**

34 **estar** : *IND* **estoy, estás, está,** estamos, estáis, **están;** *SUBJ* **esté, estés, esté,** estemos, estéis, **estén;** *PRET* **estuve, estuviste, estuvo, estuvimos, estuvisteis, estuvieron;** *IMPER* **está**

35 **exigir** : *IND* **exijo,** exiges, exige, exigimos, exigís, exigen; *SUBJ* **exija, exijas, exija, exijamos, exijáis, exijan**

36 **forzar** : *IND* **fuerzo, fuerzas, fuerza,** forzamos, forzáis, **fuerzan;** *SUBJ* **fuerce, fuerces, fuerce, forcemos, forcéis, fuercen;** *PRET* **forcé,** forzaste, forzó, forzamos, forzasteis, forzaron; *IMPER* **fuerza**

37 **freír** : *IND* **frío, fríes, fríe,** freímos, freís, **fríen;** *SUBJ* **fría, frías, fría, friamos, friáis, fríen;** *PRET* freí, **freíste, frió, freímos, freísteis, frieron;** *IMPER* **fríe;** *PRP* **friendo;** *PP* **frito**

38 **gruñir** : *PRET* **gruñí,** gruñiste, **gruñó,** gruñimos, gruñisteis, **gruñeron;** *PRP* **gruñendo**

39 **haber** : *IND* **he, has, ha, hemos,** habéis, **han;** *SUBJ* **haya, hayas, haya, hayamos, hayáis, hayan;** *PRET* **hube, hubiste, hubo, hubimos, hubisteis, hubieron;** *FUT* **habré, habrás, habrá, habremos, habréis, habrán;** *IMPER* **he**

40 **hacer** : *IND* **hago,** haces, hace, hacemos, hacéis, hacen; *SUBJ* **haga, hagas, haga, hagamos, hagáis, hagan;** *PRET* **hice, hiciste, hizo, hicimos, hicisteis, hicieron;** *FUT* **haré, harás, hará, haremos, haréis, harán;** *IMPER* **haz;** *PP* **hecho**

41 **huir** : *IND* **huyo, huyes, huye,** huimos, huís, **huyen;** *SUBJ* **huya, huyas, huya, huyamos, huyáis, huyan;** *PRET* **huí,** huiste, **huyó,** huimos, huisteis, **huyeron;** *IMPER* **huye;** *PRP* **huyendo**

42 **imprimir** : *PP* **impreso**

43 **ir** : *IND* **voy, vas, va, vamos, vais, van;** *SUBJ* **vaya, vayas, vaya, vayamos, vayáis, vayan;** *PRET* **fui, fuiste, fue, fuimos, fuisteis, fueron;** *IMPF* **iba, ibas, iba, íbamos, ibais, iban;** *IMPER* **ve;** *PRP* **yendo;** *PP* **ido**

44 **jugar** : *IND* **juego, juegas, juega,** jugamos, jugáis, **juegan;** *SUBJ* **juegue, juegues, juegue, juguemos, juguéis, jueguen;** *PRET*

jugué, jugaste, jugó, jugamos, jugasteis, jugaron; *IMPER* **juega**

45 **lucir** : *IND* **luzco,** luces, luce, lucimos, lucís, lucen; *SUBJ* **luzca, luzcas, luzca, luzcamos, luzcáis, luzcan**

46 **morir** : *IND* **muero, mueres, muere,** morimos, morís, **mueren;** *SUBJ* **muera, mueras, muera, muramos, muráis, mueran;** *PRET* morí, moriste, **murió,** morimos, moristeis, **murieron;** *IMPER* **muere;** *PRP* **muriendo;** *PP* **muerto**

47 **mover** : *IND* **muevo, mueves, mueve,** movemos, movéis, **mueven;** *SUBJ* **mueva, muevas, mueva,** movamos, mováis, **muevan;** *IMPER* **mueve**

48 **nacer** : *IND* **nazco,** naces, nace, nacemos, nacéis, nacen; *SUBJ* **nazca, nazcas, nazca, nazcamos, nazcáis, nazcan**

49 **negar** : *IND* **niego, niegas, niega,** negamos, negáis, **niegan;** *SUBJ* **niegue, niegues, niegue, neguemos, neguéis, nieguen;** *PRET* **negué,** negaste, negó, negamos, negasteis, negaron; *IMPER* **niega**

50 **oír** : *IND* **oigo, oyes, oye, oímos,** oís, **oyen;** *SUBJ* **oiga, oigas, oiga, oigamos, oigáis, oigan;** *PRET* **oí, oíste, oyó, oímos, oísteis, oyeron;** *IMPER* **oye;** *PRP* **oyendo;** *PP* **oído**

51 **oler** : *IND* **huelo, hueles, huele,** olemos, oléis, **huelen;** *SUBJ* **huela, huelas, huela,** olamos, oláis, **huelan;** *IMPER* **huele**

52 **pagar** : *SUBJ* **pague, pagues, pague, paguemos, paguéis, paguen;** *PRET* **pagué,** pagaste, pagó, pagamos, pagasteis, pagaron

53 **parecer** : *IND* **parezco,** pareces, parece, parecemos, parecéis, parecen; *SUBJ* **parezca, parezcas, parezca, parezcamos, parezcáis, parezcan**

54 **pedir** : *IND* **pido, pides, pide,** pedimos, pedís, **piden;** *SUBJ* **pida, pidas, pida, pidamos, pidáis, pidan;** *PRET* pedí, pediste, **pidió,** pedimos, pedisteis, **pidieron;** *IMPER* **pide;** *PRP* **pidiendo**

55 **pensar** : *IND* **pienso, piensas, piensa,** pensamos, pensáis, **piensan;** *SUBJ* **piense, pienses, piense,** pensemos, penséis, **piensen;** *IMPER* **piensa**

56 **perder** : *IND* **pierdo, pierdes, pierde,** perdemos, perdéis, **pierden;** *SUBJ* **pierda, pierdas, pierda,** perdamos, perdáis, **pierdan;** *IMPER* **pierde**

57 **placer** : *IND* **plazco,** places, place, placemos, placéis, placen; *SUBJ* **plazca, plazcas, plazca, plazcamos, plazcáis, plazcan;** *PRET* plací, placiste, plació *or* **plugo,** placimos, placisteis, placieron *or* **pluguieron**

58 **poder** : *IND* **puedo, puedes, puede,** podemos, podéis, **pueden;** *SUBJ* **pueda, puedas, pueda,** podamos, podáis, **puedan;** *PRET* **pude, pudiste, pudo, pudimos, pudisteis, pudieron;** *FUT* **podré, podrás, podrá, podremos, podréis, podrán;** *IMPER* **puede;** *PRP* **pudiendo**

59 **podrir** *or* **pudrir** : *PP* **podrido** *(all other forms based on* pudrir*)*

60 **poner** : *IND* **pongo,** pones, pone, ponemos, ponéis, ponen; *SUBJ* **ponga, pongas, ponga, pongamos, pongáis, pongan;** *PRET* **puse, pusiste, puso, pusimos, pusisteis, pusieron;** *FUT* **pondré, pondrás, pondrá, pondremos, pondréis, pondrán;** *IMPER* **pon;** *PP* **puesto**

61 **producir** : *IND* **produzco,** produces, produce, producimos, producís, producen; *SUBJ* **produzca, produzcas, produzca, produzcamos, produzcáis, produzcan;** *PRET* **produje, produjiste, produjo, produjimos, produjisteis, produjeron**

62 **prohibir** : *IND* **prohíbo, prohíbes, prohíbe,** prohibimos, prohibís, **prohíben;** *SUBJ* **prohíba, prohíbas, prohíba,** prohibamos, prohibáis, **prohíban;** *IMPER* **prohíbe**

63 **proveer** : *PRET* **proveí, proveíste, proveyó, proveímos, proveísteis, proveyeron;** *PRP* **proveyendo;** *PP* **provisto**

64 **querer** : *IND* **quiero, quieres, quiere,** queremos, queréis, **quieren;** *SUBJ* **quiera, quieras, quiera,** queramos, queráis, **quieran;** *PRET* **quise, quisiste, quiso, quisimos, quisisteis, quisieron;** *FUT* **querré, querrás, querrá, querremos, querréis, querrán;** *IMPER* **quiere**

65 **raer** : *IND* **rao** *or* **raigo** *or* **rayo,** raes, rae, raemos, raéis, raen; *SUBJ* **raiga** *or* **raya, raigas** *or* **rayas, raiga** *or* **raya, raigamos** *or* **rayamos, raigáis** *or* **rayáis, raigan** *or* **rayan;** *PRET* **raí, raíste, rayó, raímos, raísteis, rayeron;** *PRP* **rayendo;** *PP* **raído**

66 **reír** : *IND* **río, ríes, ríe, reímos,** reís, **ríen;** *SUBJ* **ría, rías, ría, riamos, riáis, rían;** *PRET* **reí, reíste, rió, reímos, reísteis, rieron;** *IMPER* **ríe;** *PRP* **riendo;** *PP* **reído**

67 **reñir** : *IND* **riño, riñes, riñe,** reñimos, reñís, **riñen;** *SUBJ* **riña, riñas, riña, riñamos, riñáis, riñan;** *PRET* reñí, reñiste, **riñó,** reñimos, reñisteis, **riñeron;** *IMPER* riñe; *PRP* riñendo

68 **reunir** : *IND* **reúno, reúnes, reúne,** reunimos, reunís, **reúnen;** *SUBJ* **reúna, reúnas, reúna,** reunamos, reunáis, **reúnan;** *IMPER* **reúne**

69 **roer** : *IND* roo *or* **roigo** *or* **royo,** roes, roe, roemos, roéis, roen; *SUBJ* roa *or* **roiga** *or* **roya,** roas *or* **roigas** *or* **royas,** roa *or* **roiga** *or* **roya,** roamos *or* **roigamos** *or* **royamos,** roáis *or* **roigáis** *or* **royáis,** roan *or* **roigan** *or* **royan;** *PRET* roí, **roíste, royó, roímos, roísteis, royeron;** *PRP* **royendo;** *PP* **roído**

70 **romper** : *PP* **roto**

71 **saber** : *IND* **sé,** sabes, sabe, sabemos, sabéis, saben; *SUBJ* **sepa, sepas, sepa, sepamos, sepáis, sepan;** *PRET* **supe, supiste, supo, supimos, supisteis, supieron;** *FUT* **sabré, sabrás, sabrá, sabremos, sabréis, sabrán**

72 **sacar** : *SUBJ* **saque, saques, saque, saquemos, saquéis, saquen;** *PRET* **saqué,** sacaste, sacó, sacamos, sacasteis, sacaron

73 **salir** : *IND* **salgo,** sales, sale, salimos, salís, salen; *SUBJ* **salga, salgas, salga, salgamos, salgáis, salgan;** *FUT* **saldré, saldrás, saldrá, saldremos, saldréis, saldrán;** *IMPER* **sal**

74 **satisfacer** : *IND* **satisfago,** satisfaces, satisface, satisfacemos, satisfacéis, satisfacen; *SUBJ* **satisfaga, satisfagas, satisfaga, satisfagamos, satisfagáis, satisfagan;** *PRET* **satisfice, satisficiste, satisfizo, satisficimos, satisficisteis, satisficieron;** *FUT* **satisfaré, satisfarás, satisfará, satisfaremos, satisfaréis, satisfarán;** *IMPER* **satisfaz** *or* satisface; *PP* **satisfecho**

75 **seguir** : *IND* **sigo, sigues, sigue,** seguimos, seguís, **siguen;** *SUBJ* **siga, sigas, siga, sigamos, sigáis, sigan;** *PRET* seguí, seguiste, **siguió,** seguimos, seguisteis, **siguieron;** *IMPER* **sigue;** *PRP* **siguiendo**

76 **sentir** : *IND* **siento, sientes, siente,** sentimos, sentís, **sienten;** *SUBJ* **sienta, sientas, sienta, sintamos, sintáis, sientan;** *PRET*

sentí, sentiste, **sintió**, sentimos, sentisteis, **sintieron**; *IMPER* **siente**; *PRP* **sintiendo**

77 **ser** : *IND* **soy, eres, es, somos, sois, son**; *SUBJ* **sea, seas, sea, seamos, seáis, sean**; *PRET* **fui, fuiste, fue, fuimos, fuisteis, fueron**; *IMPF* **era, eras, era, éramos, erais, eran**; *IMPER* **sé**; *PRP* **siendo**; *PP* **sido**

78 **soler** *(defective verb; used only in the present, preterit, and imperfect indicative, and the present and imperfect subjunctive) see* 47 **mover**

79 **tañer** : *PRET* **tañí**, tañiste, **tañó**, tañimos, tañisteis, **tañeron**; *PRP* **tañendo**

80 **tener** : *IND* **tengo, tienes, tiene,** tenemos, tenéis, **tienen**; *SUBJ* **tenga, tengas, tenga, tengamos, tengáis, tengan**; *PRET* **tuve, tuviste, tuvo, tuvimos, tuvisteis, tuvieron**; *FUT* **tendré, tendrás, tendrá, tendremos, tendréis, tendrán**; *IMPER* **ten**

81 **traer** : *IND* **traigo**, traes, trae, traemos, traéis, traen; *SUBJ* **traiga, traigas, traiga, traigamos, traigáis, traigan**; *PRET* **traje, trajiste, trajo, trajimos, trajisteis, trajeron**; *PRP* **trayendo**; *PP* **traído**

82 **trocar** : *IND* **trueco, truecas, trueca**, trocamos, trocáis, **truecan**; *SUBJ* **trueque, trueques, trueque, troquemos, troquéis, truequen**; *PRET* **troqué**, trocaste, trocó, trocamos, trocasteis, trocaron; *IMPER* **trueca**

83 **uncir** : *IND* **unzo**, unces, unce, uncimos, uncís, uncen; *SUBJ* **unza, unzas, unza, unzamos, unzáis, unzan**

84 **valer** : *IND* **valgo**, vales, vale, valemos, valéis, valen; *SUBJ* **valga, valgas, valga, valgamos, valgáis, valgan**; *FUT* **valdré, valdrás, valdrá, valdremos, valdréis, valdrán**

85 **variar** : *IND* **varío, varías, varía**, variamos, variáis, **varían**; *SUBJ* **varíe, varíes, varíe**, variemos, variéis, **varíen**; *IMPER* **varía**

86 **vencer** : *IND* **venzo**, vences, vence, vencemos, vencéis, vencen; *SUBJ* **venza, venzas, venza, venzamos, venzáis, venzan**

87 **venir** : *IND* **vengo, vienes, viene**, venimos, venís, **vienen**; *SUBJ* **venga, vengas, venga, vengamos, vengáis, vengan**; *PRET* **vine, viniste, vino, vinimos, vinisteis, vinieron**; *FUT* **vendré**,

vendrás, vendrá, vendremos, vendréis, vendrán; *IMPER* **ven;**
PRP **viniendo**

88 **ver** : *IND* **veo, ves, ve, vemos, veis, ven;** *PRET* **vi, viste, vio,
vimos, visteis, vieron;** *IMPER* **ve;** *PRP* **viendo;** *PP* **visto**

89 **volver** : *IND* **vuelvo, vuelves, vuelve,** volvemos, volvéis, **vuel-
ven;** *SUBJ* **vuelva, vuelvas, vuelva,** volvamos, volváis, **vuel-
van;** *IMPER* **vuelve;** *PP* **vuelto**

90 **yacer** : *IND* **yazco** *or* **yazgo** *or* **yago,** yaces, yace, yacemos,
yacéis, yacen; *SUBJ* **yazca** *or* **yazga** *or* **yaga, yazcas** *or* **yaz-
gas** *or* **yagas, yazca** *or* **yazga** *or* **yaga, yazcamos** *or* **yazg-
amos** *or* **yagamos, yazcáis** *or* **yazgáis** *or* **yagáis, yazcan** *or*
yazgan *or* **yagan;** *IMPER* yace *or* **yaz**

Irregular English Verbs

INFINITIVE	PAST	PAST PARTICIPLE
arise	arose	arisen
awake	awoke	awoken *or* awaked
be	was, were	been
bear	bore	borne
beat	beat	beaten *or* beat
become	became	become
befall	befell	befallen
begin	began	begun
behold	beheld	beheld
bend	bent	bent
beseech	beseeched *or* besought	beseeched *or* besought
beset	beset	beset
bet	bet	bet
bid	bade *or* bid	bidden *or* bid
bind	bound	bound
bite	bit	bitten
bleed	bled	bled
blow	blew	blown
break	broke	broken
breed	bred	bred
bring	brought	brought
build	built	built
burn	burned *or* burnt	burned *or* burnt
burst	burst	burst
buy	bought	bought
can	could	—
cast	cast	cast
catch	caught	caught
choose	chose	chosen
cling	clung	clung
come	came	come
cost	cost	cost
creep	crept	crept
cut	cut	cut
deal	dealt	dealt
dig	dug	dug
do	did	done
draw	drew	drawn
dream	dreamed *or* dreamt	dreamed *or* dreamt
drink	drank	drunk *or* drank
drive	drove	driven
dwell	dwelled *or* dwelt	dwelled *or* dwelt

INFINITIVE	PAST	PAST PARTICIPLE
eat	ate	eaten
fall	fell	fallen
feed	fed	fed
feel	felt	felt
fight	fought	fought
find	found	found
flee	fled	fled
fling	flung	flung
fly	flew	flown
forbid	forbade	forbidden
forecast	forecast	forecast
forego	forewent	foregone
foresee	foresaw	foreseen
foretell	foretold	foretold
forget	forgot	forgotten *or* forgot
forgive	forgave	forgiven
forsake	forsook	forsaken
freeze	froze	frozen
get	got	got *or* gotten
give	gave	given
go	went	gone
grind	ground	ground
grow	grew	grown
hang	hung	hung
have	had	had
hear	heard	heard
hide	hid	hidden *or* hid
hit	hit	hit
hold	held	held
hurt	hurt	hurt
keep	kept	kept
kneel	knelt *or* kneeled	knelt *or* kneeled
know	knew	known
lay	laid	laid
lead	led	led
lean	leaned	leaned
leap	leaped *or* leapt	leaped *or* leapt
learn	learned	learned
leave	left	left
lend	lent	lent
let	let	let
lie	lay	lain
light	lit *or* lighted	lit *or* lighted
lose	lost	lost
make	made	made
may	might	—

INFINITIVE	PAST	PAST PARTICIPLE
mean	meant	meant
meet	met	met
mow	mowed	mowed *or* mown
pay	paid	paid
put	put	put
quit	quit	quit
read	read	read
rend	rent	rent
rid	rid	rid
ride	rode	ridden
ring	rang	rung
rise	rose	risen
run	ran	run
saw	sawed	sawed *or* sawn
say	said	said
see	saw	seen
seek	sought	sought
sell	sold	sold
send	sent	sent
set	set	set
shake	shook	shaken
shall	should	—
shear	sheared	sheared *or* shorn
shed	shed	shed
shine	shone *or* shined	shone *or* shined
shoot	shot	shot
show	showed	shown *or* showed
shrink	shrank *or* shrunk	shrunk *or* shrunken
shut	shut	shut
sing	sang *or* sung	sung
sink	sank *or* sunk	sunk
sit	sat	sat
slay	slew	slain
sleep	slept	slept
slide	slid	slid
sling	slung	slung
smell	smelled *or* smelt	smelled *or* smelt
sow	sowed	sown *or* sowed
speak	spoke	spoken
speed	sped *or* speeded	sped *or* speeded
spell	spelled	spelled
spend	spent	spent
spill	spilled	spilled
spin	spun	spun
spit	spit *or* spat	spit *or* spat
split	split	split

INFINITIVE	PAST	PAST PARTICIPLE
spoil	spoiled	spoiled
spread	spread	spread
spring	sprang *or* sprung	sprung
stand	stood	stood
steal	stole	stolen
stick	stuck	stuck
sting	stung	stung
stink	stank *or* stunk	stunk
stride	strode	stridden
strike	struck	struck
swear	swore	sworn
sweep	swept	swept
swell	swelled	swelled *or* swollen
swim	swam	swum
swing	swung	swung
take	took	taken
teach	taught	taught
tear	tore	torn
tell	told	told
think	thought	thought
throw	threw	thrown
thrust	thrust	thrust
tread	trod	trodden *or* trod
wake	woke	woken *or* waked
waylay	waylaid	waylaid
wear	wore	worn
weave	wove *or* weaved	woven *or* weaved
wed	wedded	wedded
weep	wept	wept
will	would	—
win	won	won
wind	wound	wound
withdraw	withdrew	withdrawn
withhold	withheld	withheld
withstand	withstood	withstood
wring	wrung	wrung
write	wrote	written

Spelling-to-Sound Correspondences in Spanish

For example words for the phonetic symbols below, see
  Pronunciation Symbols on page 58a.

VOWELS

a [a]

e [e] in open syllables
   (syllables ending with
   a vowel); [ɛ] in closed
   syllables (syllables
   ending with a conso-
   nant)

i [i]; before another vowel
   in the same syllable
   pronounced as [j] ([ʒ] or
   [ʃ] in Argentina and
   Uruguay; [dʒ] when at
   the beginning of a word
   in the Caribbean)

o [o] in open syllables
   (syllables ending with
   a vowel); [ɔ] in closed
   syllables (syllables
   ending with a conso-
   nant)

u [u]; before another vowel
   in the same syllable
   pronounced as [w]

y [i]; before another vowel
   in the same syllable
   pronounced as [j] ([ʒ] or
   [ʃ] in Argentina and
   Uruguay; [dʒ] when at
   the beginning of a word
   in the Caribbean)

CONSONANTS

b [b] at the beginning of a
   word or after m or n; [β]
   elsewhere

c [s] before i or e in Latin
   America and parts of
   southern Spain, [θ] in
   northern Spain; [k]
   elsewhere

ch [tʃ]; frequently [ʃ] in Chile
   and Panama; sometimes
   [ts] in Chile

d [d] at the beginning of a
   word or after n or l; [ð]
   elsewhere, frequently
   silent between vowels

f [f]; [Φ] in Honduras (no
   English equivalent for
   this sound; like [f] but
   made with both lips)

g [x] before i or e ([h] in the
   Caribbean and Central
   America); [g] at the
   beginning of a word or
   after n and not before i
   or e; [ɣ] elsewhere,
   frequently silent
   between vowels

gu [gw] at the beginning of a
   word before a, o; [ɣw]
   elsewhere before a, o;
   frequently just [w]
   between vowels; [g] at
   the beginning of a word
   before i, e; [ɣ] elsewhere
   before i, e; frequently
   silent between vowels

gü [gw] at the beginning of a
   word, [ɣw] elsewhere;
   frequently just [w]
   between vowels

h silent

j [x] ([h] in the Caribbean
   and Central America)

k [k]

l [l]

ll [j]; [ʒ] or [ʃ] in Argentina
   and Uruguay; [dʒ] when
   at the beginning of a
   word in the Caribbean;

[lʲ] in Bolivia, Paraguay, Peru, and parts of northern Spain (no English equivalent; like "lli" in *million*)

m   [m]

n   [n]; frequently [ŋ] at the end of a word when next word begins with a vowel

ñ   [ɲ]

p   [p]

qu   [k]

r   [r] (no English equivalent; a trilled sound) at the beginning of words; [t̪]/[ɾ] elsewhere

rr   [r] (no English equivalent; a trilled sound)

s   [s]; frequently [z] before *b, d, g, m, n, l, r*; at the end of a word [h] or silent in many parts of Latin America and some parts of Spain

t   [t]

v   [b] at the beginning of a word or after *m* or *n*; [β] elsewhere

x   [ks] or [gz] between vowels; [s] before consonants

z   [s] in Latin America and parts of southern Spain, [θ] in northern Spain; at the end of a word [h] or silent in many parts of Latin America and some parts of Spain

Pronunciation Symbols

VOWELS

æ	**a**sk, b**a**t, gl**a**d
ɑ	c**o**t, b**o**mb
a	*New England* **au**nt, *British* **a**sk, gl**a**ss, *Spanish* c**a**sa
e	*Spanish* p**e**so, j**e**fe
ɛ	**e**gg, b**e**t, f**e**d
ə	**a**bout, jav**e**lin, Al**a**bama
ə̣	when italicized as in əl, əm, ən, indicates a syllabic pronunciation of the consonant as in bott**le**, pris**m**, butt**on**
i	v**e**ry, an**y**, thirt**y**, *Spanish* pi**ñ**a
i:	**ea**t, b**ea**d, b**ee**
ɪ	**i**d, b**i**d, p**i**t
o	**O**hio, yell**o**wer, potat**o**, *Spanish* **ó**valo
o:	**oa**ts, **ow**n, z**o**ne, bl**ow**
ɔ	**aw**l, m**au**l, c**au**ght, p**aw**
ʊ	s**u**re, sh**ou**ld, c**ou**ld
u	*Spanish* **u**va, c**u**lpa
u:	b**oo**t, f**ew**, c**oo**
ʌ	**u**nder, p**u**tt, b**u**d
eɪ	**ei**ght, w**a**de, b**ay**
aɪ	**i**ce, b**i**te, t**ie**
aʊ	**ou**t, g**ow**n, pl**ow**
ɔɪ	**oy**ster, c**oi**l, b**oy**
ər	f**ur**ther, st**ir**
ɒ	*British* b**o**nd, g**o**d
:	indicates that the preceding vowel is long. Long vowels are almost always diphthongs in English, but not in Spanish.

CONSONANTS

b	**b**a**b**y, la**b**or, ca**b**
β	*Spanish* ca**b**o, ó**v**alo
d	**d**ay, rea**d**y, ki**d**
ʤ	**j**ust, ba**dg**er, fu**dg**e
ð	**th**en, ei**th**er, ba**th**e
f	**f**oe, tou**gh**, bu**ff**
g	**g**o, bi**gg**er, ba**g**
ɣ	*Spanish* tra**g**ar, da**g**a
h	**h**ot, a**h**a
j	**y**es, vine**y**ard
k	**c**at, **k**eep, la**c**quer, flo**ck**
l	**l**aw, ho**ll**ow, boi**l**
m	**m**at, he**m**p, ha**mm**er, ri**m**
n	**n**ew, te**n**t, te**n**or, ru**n**
ŋ	ru**ng**, ha**ng**, swi**ng**er
ɲ	*Spanish* caba**ñ**a, pi**ñ**a
p	**p**ay, la**p**se, to**p**
r	**r**ope, bu**rn**, ta**r**
s	**s**ad, mi**s**t, ki**ss**
ʃ	**sh**oe, mi**ss**ion, slu**sh**
t	**t**oe, bu**tt**on, ma**t**
ţ	indicates that some speakers of English pronounce this as a voiced alveolar flap [ɾ], as in la**t**er, ca**tt**y, ba**tt**le
ʧ	**ch**oose, ba**tch**
θ	**th**in, e**th**er, ba**th**
v	**v**at, ne**v**er, ca**v**e
w	**w**et, soft**w**are
x	*German* Ba**ch**, *Scots* lo**ch**, *Spanish* **g**ente, **j**efe
z	**z**oo, ea**s**y, bu**zz**
ʒ	**j**aborandi, a**z**ure, bei**ge**
h, k,	when italicized indicate
p, t	sounds which are present in the pronunciation of some speakers of English but absent in that of others, so that *whence* ['*h*wɛns] can be pronounced as ['wɛns], ['hwɛns], ['wɛnts], or ['hwɛnts]

STRESS MARKS

ˈ high stress	**pen**manship
ˌ low stress	penman**ship**

Spanish–English
Dictionary

A

a¹ *nf* : first letter of the Spanish alphabet

a² *prep* **1** : to ⟨nos vamos a México : we're going to Mexico⟩ **2** (*used before direct or indirect objects referring to persons*) ⟨¿llamaste a tu papá? : did you call your dad?⟩ ⟨como a usted le guste : as you wish⟩ **3** : in the manner of ⟨papas a la francesa : french fries⟩ **4** : on, by means of ⟨a pie : on foot⟩ **5** : per, each ⟨tres pastillas al día : three pills per day⟩ **6** : at ⟨a las dos : at two o'clock⟩ ⟨al principio : at first⟩ **7** (*with infinitive*) ⟨enséñales a leer : teach them to read⟩ ⟨problemas a resolver : problems to be solved⟩

ábaco *nm* : abacus

abad *nm* : abbot

abadesa *nf* : abbess

abadía *nf* : abbey

abajo *adv* **1** : down ⟨póngalo más abajo : put it further down⟩ ⟨arriba y abajo : up and down⟩ **2** : downstairs **3** : under, beneath ⟨el abajo firmante : the undersigned⟩ **4** : down with ⟨¡abajo la inflación! : down with inflation!⟩ **5** ~ **de** : under, beneath **6 de** ~ : bottom ⟨el cajón de abajo : the bottom drawer⟩ **7 hacia** ~ *or* **para** ~ : downwards **8 cuesta abajo** : downhill **9 río abajo** : downstream

abalanzarse {21} *vr* : to hurl oneself, to rush

abanderado, -da *n* : standard-bearer

abandonado, -da *adj* **1** : abandoned, deserted **2** : neglected **3** : slovenly, unkempt

abandonar *vt* **1** DEJAR : to abandon, to leave **2** : to give up, to quit ⟨abandonaron la búsqueda : they gave up the search⟩ — **abandonarse** *vr* **1** : to neglect oneself **2** ~ **a** : to succumb to, to give oneself over to

abandono *nm* **1** : abandonment **2** : neglect **3** : withdrawal ⟨ganar por abandono : to win by default⟩

abanicar {72} *vt* : to fan — **abanicarse** *vr*

abanico *nm* **1** : fan **2** GAMA : range, gamut

abaratamiento *nm* : price reduction

abaratar *vt* : to lower the price of — **abaratarse** *vr* : to go down in price

abarcar {72} *vt* **1** : to cover, to include, to embrace **2** : to undertake **3** : to monopolize

abaritonado, -da *adj* : baritone

abarrotado, -da *adj* : packed, crammed

abarrotar *vt* : to fill up, to pack

abarrotería *nf CA, Mex* : grocery store

abarrotero, -ra *n Col, Mex* : grocer

abarrotes *nmpl* **1** : groceries, supplies **2 tienda de abarrotes** : general store, grocery store

abastecedor, -dora *n* : supplier

abastecer {53} *vt* : to supply, to stock — **abastecerse** *vr* : to stock up

abastecimiento → **abasto**

abasto *nm* : supply, supplying ⟨no da abasto : there isn't enough for all⟩

abatido, -da *adj* : dejected, depressed

abatimiento *nm* **1** : drop, reduction **2** : dejection, depression

abatir *vt* **1** DERRIBAR : to demolish, to knock down **2** : to shoot down **3** DEPRIMIR : to depress, to bring low — **abatirse** *vr* **1** DEPRIMIRSE : to get depressed **2** ~ **sobre** : to swoop down on

abdicación *nf, pl* **-ciones** : abdication

abdicar {72} *vt* : to relinquish, to abdicate

abdomen *nm, pl* **-dómenes** : abdomen

abdominal *adj* : abdominal

abecé *nm* : ABC's *pl*

abecedario *nm* ALFABETO : alphabet

abedul *nm* : birch (tree)

abeja *nf* : bee

abejorro *nm* : bumblebee

aberración *nf, pl* **-ciones** : aberration

aberrante *adj* : aberrant, perverse

abertura *nf* **1** : aperture, opening **2** AGUJERO : hole **3** : slit (in a skirt, etc.) **4** GRIETA : crack

abeto *nm* : fir (tree)

abierto¹ *pp* → **abrir**

abierto², -ta *adj* **1** : open **2** : candid, frank **3** : generous — **abiertamente** *adv*

abigarrado, -da *adj* : multicolored, variegated

abigeato *nm* : rustling (of livestock)

abismal *adj* : abysmal, vast

abismo *nm* : abyss, chasm ⟨al borde del abismo : on the brink of ruin⟩

abjurar *vi* ~ **de** : to abjure — **abjuración** *nf*

ablandamiento *nm* : softening, moderation

ablandar *vt* **1** SUAVIZAR : to soften **2** CALMAR : to soothe, to appease — *vi* : to moderate, to get milder — **ablandarse** *vr* **1** : to become soft, to soften **2** CEDER : to yield, to relent

ablución *nf, pl* **-ciones** : ablution

abnegación *nf, pl* **-ciones** : abnegation, self-denial

abnegado, -da *adj* : self-sacrificing, selfless

abnegarse {49} *vr* : to deny oneself

abobado, -da *adj* **1** : silly, stupid **2** : bewildered

abocarse {72} *vr* **1** DIRIGIRSE : to head, to direct oneself **2** DEDICARSE : to dedicate oneself

abochornar *vt* AVERGONZAR : to embarrass, to shame — **abochornarse** *vr*

abofetear *vt* : to slap

abogacía *nf* : law, legal profession

abogado, -da *n* : lawyer, attorney

abogar {52} *vi* ~ **por** : to plead for, to defend, to advocate

abolengo *nm* LINAJE : lineage, ancestry
abolición *nf, pl* **-ciones** : abolition
abolir {1} *vt* DEROGAR : to abolish, to repeal
abolladura *nf* : dent
abollar *vt* : to dent
abombar *vt* : to warp, to cause to bulge — **abombarse** *vr* : to decompose, to go bad
abominable *adj* ABORRECIBLE : abominable
abominación *nf, pl* **-ciones** : abomination
abominar *vt* ABORRECER : to abominate, to abhor
abonado, -da *n* : subscriber
abonar *vt* **1** : to pay **2** FERTILIZAR : to fertilize — **abonarse** *vr* : to subscribe
abono *nm* **1** : payment, installment **2** FERTILIZANTE : fertilizer **3** : season ticket
abordaje *nm* : boarding
abordar *vt* **1** : to address, to broach **2** : to accost, to waylay **3** : to come on board
aborigen[1] *adj, pl* **-rígenes** : aboriginal, native
aborigen[2] *nmf, pl* **-rígenes** : aborigine, indigenous inhabitant
aborrecer {53} *vt* ABOMINAR, ODIAR : to abhor, to detest, to hate
aborrecible *adj* ABOMINABLE, ODIOSO : abominable, detestable
aborrecimiento *nm* : abhorrence, loathing
abortar *vi* : to have an abortion — *vt* **1** : to abort **2** : to quash, to suppress
abortista *nmf* : abortionist
abortivo, -va *adj* : abortive
aborto *nm* **1** : abortion **2** : miscarriage
abotonar *vt* : to button — **abotonarse** *vr* : to button up
abovedado, -da *adj* : vaulted
abrasador, -dora *adj* : burning, scorching
abrasar *vt* QUEMAR : to burn, to sear, to scorch
abrasivo[1]**, -va** *adj* : abrasive
abrasivo[2] *nm* : abrasive
abrazadera *nf* : clamp, brace
abrazar {21} *vt* : to hug, to embrace — **abrazarse** *vr*
abrazo *nm* : hug, embrace
abrebotellas *nms & pl* : bottle opener
abrelatas *nms & pl* : can opener
abrevadero *nm* BEBEDERO : watering trough
abreviación *nf, pl* **-ciones** : abbreviation
abreviar *vt* **1** : to abbreviate **2** : to shorten, to cut short
abreviatura → **abreviación**
abridor *nm* : bottle opener, can opener
abrigadero *nm* : shelter, windbreak
abrigado, -da *adj* **1** : sheltered **2** : warm, wrapped up (with clothing)
abrigar {52} *vt* **1** : to shelter, to protect **2** : to keep warm, to dress warmly **3** : to cherish, to harbor ⟨abrigar esperanzas : to cherish hopes⟩ — **abrigarse** *vr* : to dress warmly
abrigo *nm* **1** : coat, overcoat **2** : shelter, refuge
abril *nm* : April
abrillantador *nm* : polish
abrillantar *vt* : to polish, to shine
abrir {2} *vt* **1** : to open **2** : to unlock, to undo **3** : to turn on (a tap or faucet) — *vi* : to open, to open up — **abrirse** *vr* **1** : to open up **2** : to clear (of the skies)
abrochar *vt* : to button, to fasten — **abrocharse** *vr* : to fasten, to hook up
abrogación *nf, pl* **-ciones** : abrogation, annulment, repeal
abrogar {52} *vt* : to abrogate, to annul, to repeal
abrojo *nm* : bur (of a plant)
abrumador, -dora *adj* : crushing, overwhelming
abrumar *vt* **1** AGOBIAR : to overwhelm **2** OPRIMIR : to oppress, to burden
abrupto, -ta *adj* **1** : abrupt **2** ESCARPADO : steep — **abruptamente** *adv*
absceso *nm* : abscess
absolución *nf, pl* **-ciones** **1** : absolution **2** : acquittal
absolutismo *nm* : absolutism
absoluto, -ta *adj* **1** : absolute, unconditional **2 en ～** : not at all ⟨no me gustó en absoluto : I did not like it at all⟩ — **absolutamente** *adv*
absolver {89} *vt* **1** : to absolve **2** : to acquit
absorbente *adj* **1** : absorbent **2** : absorbing, engrossing
absorber *vt* **1** : to absorb, to soak up **2** : to occupy, to take up, to engross
absorción *nf, pl* **-ciones** : absorption
absorto, -ta *adj* : absorbed, engrossed
abstemio[1]**, -mia** *adj* : abstemious, teetotal
abstemio[2]**, -mia** *n* : teetotaler
abstención *nf, pl* **-ciones** : abstention
abstenerse {80} *vr* : to abstain, to refrain
abstinencia *nf* : abstinence
abstracción *nf, pl* **-ciones** : abstraction
abstracto, -ta *adj* : abstract
abstraer {81} *vt* : to abstract — **abstraerse** *vr* : to lose oneself in thought
abstraído, -da *adj* : preoccupied, withdrawn
abstruso, -sa *adj* : abstruse
abstuvo, etc. → **abstenerse**
absuelto *pp* → **absolver**
absurdo[1]**, -da** *adj* DISPARATADO, RIDÍCULO : absurd, ridiculous — **absurdamente** *adv*
absurdo[2] *nm* : absurdity
abuchear *vt* : to boo, to jeer
abucheo *nm* : booing, jeering
abuela *nf* **1** : grandmother **2** : old woman **3 ¡tu abuela!** *fam* : no way!, forget about it!
abuelo *nm* **1** : grandfather **2** : old man **3 abuelos** *nmpl* : grandparents, ancestors

abulia *nf* : apathy, lethargy
abúlico, -ca *adj* : lethargic, apathetic
abultado, -da *adj* : bulging, bulky
abultar *vi* : to bulge — *vt* : to enlarge, to expand
abundancia *nf* : abundance
abundante *adj* : abundant, plentiful — **abundantemente** *adv*
abundar *vi* **1** : to abound, to be plentiful **2** ~ **en** : to be in agreement with
aburrido, -da *adj* **1** : bored, tired, fed up **2** TEDIOSO : boring, tedious
aburrimiento *nm* : boredom, weariness
aburrir *vt* : to bore, to tire — **aburrirse** *vr* : to get bored
abusado, -da *adj Mex fam* : sharp, on the ball
abusador, -dora *n* : abuser
abusar *vi* **1** : to go too far, to do something to excess **2** ~ **de** : to abuse (as drugs) **3** ~ **de** : to take unfair advantage of
abusivo, -va *adj* **1** : abusive **2** : outrageous, excessive
abuso *nm* **1** : abuse **2** : injustice, outrage
abyecto, -ta *adj* : despicable, contemptible
acá *adv* AQUÍ : here, over here ⟨¡ven acá! : come here!⟩
acabado¹, -da *adj* **1** : finished, done, completed **2** : old, worn-out
acabado² *nm* : finish ⟨un acabado brillante : a glossy finish⟩
acabar *vi* **1** TERMINAR : to finish, to end **2** ~ **de** : to have just (done something) ⟨acabo de ver a tu hermano : I just saw your brother⟩ **3** ~ **con** : to put an end to, to stamp out — *vt* TERMINAR : to finish — **acabarse** *vr* TERMINARSE : to come to an end, to run out ⟨se me acabó el dinero : I ran out of money⟩
acacia *nf* : acacia
academia *nf* : academy
académico¹, -ca *adj* : academic, scholastic — **académicamente** *adv*
académico², -ca *n* : academic, academician
acaecer {53} *vt (3rd person only)* : to happen, to take place
acalambrarse *vr* : to cramp up, to get a cramp
acallar *vt* : to quiet, to silence
acalorado, -da *adj* : emotional, heated
acaloramiento *nm* **1** : heat **2** : ardor, passion
acalorar *vt* : to heat up, to inflame — **acalorarse** *vr* : to get upset, to get worked up
acampada *nf* : camp, camping ⟨ir de acampada : to go camping⟩
acampar *vi* : to camp
acanalar *vt* **1** : to groove, to furrow **2** : to corrugate
acantilado *nm* : cliff
acanto *nm* : acanthus
acantonar *vt* : to station, to quarter
acaparador, -dora *adj* : greedy, selfish

acaparar *vt* **1** : to stockpile, to hoard **2** : to monopolize
acápite *nm* : paragraph
acariciar *vt* : to caress, to stroke, to pet
ácaro *nm* : mite
acarrear *vt* **1** : to haul, to carry **2** : to bring, to give rise to ⟨los problemas que acarrea : the problems that come along with it⟩
acarreo *nm* : transport, haulage
acartonarse *vr* **1** : to stiffen **2** : to become wizened
acaso *adv* **1** : perhaps, by any chance **2 por si acaso** : just in case
acatamiento *nm* : compliance, observance
acatar *vt* : to comply with, to respect
acaudalado, -da *adj* RICO : wealthy, rich
acaudillar *vt* : to lead, to command
acceder *vi* ~ **a** **1** : to accede to, to agree to **2** : to assume (a position) **3** : to gain access to
accesar *vt* : to access (on a computer)
accesibilidad *nf* : accessibility
accesible *adj* ASEQUIBLE : accessible, attainable
acceso *nm* **1** : access **2** : admittance, entrance
accesorio¹, -ria *adj* **1** : accessory **2** : incidental
accesorio² *nm* **1** : accessory **2** : prop (in the theater)
accidentado¹, -da *adj* **1** : eventful, turbulent **2** : rough, uneven **3** : injured
accidentado², -da *n* : accident victim
accidental *adj* : accidental, unintentional — **accidentalmente** *adv*
accidentarse *vr* : to have an accident
accidente *nm* **1** : accident **2** : unevenness **3 accidente geográfico** : geographical feature
acción *nf, pl* **acciones** **1** : action **2** ACTO : act, deed **3** : share, stock
accionamiento *nm* : activation
accionar *vt* : to put into motion, to activate — *vi* : to gesticulate
accionario, -ria *adj* : stock ⟨mercado accionario : stock market⟩
accionista *nmf* : stockholder, shareholder
acebo *nm* : holly
acechar *vt* **1** : to watch, to spy on **2** : to stalk, to lie in wait for
acecho *nm* **al acecho** : lying in wait
acedera *nf* : sorrel (herb)
acéfalo, -la *adj* : leaderless
aceitar *vt* : to oil
aceite *nm* **1** : oil **2 aceite de ricino** : castor oil **3 aceite de oliva** : olive oil
aceitera *nf* **1** : cruet (for oil) **2** : oilcan **3** *Mex* : oil refinery
aceitoso, -sa *adj* : oily
aceituna *nf* OLIVA : olive
aceituno *nm* OLIVO : olive tree
aceleración *nf, pl* **-ciones** : acceleration, speeding up
acelerado, -da *adj* : accelerated, speedy
acelerador *nm* : accelerator

aceleramiento *nm* → **aceleración**

acelerar *vt* **1** : to accelerate, to speed up **2** AGILIZAR : to expedite — *vi* : to accelerate (of an automobile) — **acelerarse** *vr* : to hasten, to hurry up

acelga *nf* : chard, Swiss chard

acendrado, -da *adj* : pure, unblemished

acendrar *vt* : to purify, to refine

acento *nm* **1** : accent **2** : stress, emphasis

acentuación *nf, pl* **-ciones** : accentuation

acentuado, -da *adj* : marked, pronounced

acentuar {3} *vt* **1** : to accent **2** : to emphasize, to stress — **acentuarse** *vr* : to become more pronounced

acepción *nf, pl* **-ciones** SIGNIFICADO : sense, meaning

aceptabilidad *nf* : acceptability

aceptable *adj* : acceptable

aceptación *nf, pl* **-ciones 1** : acceptance **2** APROBACIÓN : approval

aceptar *vt* **1** : to accept **2** : to approve

acequia *nf* **1** : irrigation ditch **2** *Mex* : sewer

acera *nf* : sidewalk

acerado, -da *adj* **1** : made of steel **2** : steely, tough

acerbo, -ba *adj* **1** : harsh, cutting ⟨comentarios acerbos : cutting remarks⟩ **2** : bitter — **acerbamente** *adv*

acerca *prep* ~ **de** : about, concerning

acercamiento *nm* : rapprochement, reconciliation

acercar {72} *vt* APROXIMAR, ARRIMAR : to bring near, to bring closer — **acercarse** *vr* APROXIMARSE, ARRIMARSE : to approach, to draw near

acería *nf* : steel mill

acerico *nm* : pincushion

acero *nm* : steel ⟨acero inoxidable : stainless steel⟩

acérrimo, -ma *adj* **1** : staunch, steadfast **2** : bitter ⟨un acérrimo enemigo : a bitter enemy⟩

acertado, -da *adj* CORRECTO : accurate, correct, on target — **acertadamente** *adv*

acertante[1] *adj* : winning

acertante[2] *nmf* : winner

acertar {55} *vt* : to guess correctly — *vi* **1** ATINAR : to be correct, to be on target **2** ~ **a** : to manage to

acertijo *nm* ADIVINANZA : riddle

acervo *nm* **1** : pile, heap **2** : wealth, heritage ⟨el acervo artístico del instituto : the artistic treasures of the institute⟩

acetato *nm* : acetate

acético, -ca *adj* : acetic ⟨ácido acético : acetic acid⟩

acetileno *nm* : acetylene

acetona *nf* **1** : acetone **2** : nail-polish remover

achacar {72} *vt* : to attribute, to impute ⟨te achaca todos sus problemas : he blames all his problems on you⟩

achacoso, -sa *adj* : frail, sickly

achaparrado, -da *adj* : stunted, scrubby ⟨árboles achaparrados : scrubby trees⟩

achaques *nmpl* : aches and pains

achatar *vt* : to flatten

achicar {72} *vt* **1** REDUCIR : to make smaller, to reduce **2** : to intimidate **3** : to bail out (water) — **achicarse** *vr* : to become intimidated

achicharrar *vt* : to scorch, to burn to a crisp

achicoria *nf* : chicory

achispado, -da *adj fam* : tipsy

achote *or* **achiote** *nm* : annatto seed

achuchón *nm, pl* **-chones 1** : push, shove **2** *fam* : squeeze, hug **3** *fam* : mild illness

aciago, -ga *adj* : fateful, unlucky

acicalar *vt* **1** PULIR : to polish **2** : to dress up, to adorn — **acicalarse** *vr* : to get dressed up

acicate *nm* **1** : spur **2** INCENTIVO : incentive, stimulus

acidez *nf, pl* **-deces 1** : acidity **2** : sourness **3 acidez estomacal** : heartburn

acidificar {72} *vt* : to acidify

ácido[1]**, -da** *adj* AGRIO : acid, sour

ácido[2] *nm* : acid

acierto *nm* **1** : correct answer, right choice **2** : accuracy, skill, deftness

acimut *nm* : azimuth

acitronar *vt Mex* : to fry until crisp

aclamación *nf, pl* **-ciones** : acclaim, acclamation

aclamar *vt* : to acclaim, to cheer, to applaud

aclaración *nf, pl* **-ciones** CLARIFICACIÓN : clarification, explanation

aclarar *vt* **1** CLARIFICAR : to clarify, to explain, to resolve **2** : to lighten **3 aclarar la voz** : to clear one's throat — *vi* **1** : to get light, to dawn **2** : to clear up — **aclararse** *vr* : to become clear

aclaratorio, -ria *adj* : explanatory

aclimatar *vt* : to acclimatize — **aclimatarse** *vr* ~ **a** : to get used to — **aclimatación** *nf*

acné *nm* : acne

acobardar *vt* INTIMIDAR : to frighten, to intimidate — **acobardarse** *vr* : to be frightened, to cower

acodarse *vr* ~ **en** : to lean (one's elbows) on

acogedor, -dora *adj* : cozy, warm, friendly

acoger {15} *vt* **1** REFUGIAR : to take in, to shelter **2** : to receive, to welcome — **acogerse** *vr* **1** REFUGIARSE : to take refuge **2** ~ **a** : to resort to, to avail oneself of

acogida *nf* **1** AMPARO, REFUGIO : refuge, protection **2** RECIBIMIENTO : reception, welcome

acolchar *vt* **1** : to pad (a wall, etc.) **2** : to quilt

acólito *nm* **1** MONAGUILLO : altar boy **2** : follower, helper, acolyte

acomedido, -da *adj* : helpful, obliging

acometer *vt* **1** ATACAR : to attack, to assail **2** EMPRENDER : to undertake, to begin — *vi* ~ **contra** : to rush against
acometida *nf* ATAQUE : attack, assault
acomodado, -da *adj* **1** : suitable, appropriate **2** : well-to-do, prosperous
acomodador, -dora *n* : usher, usherette *f*
acomodar *vt* **1** : to accommodate, to make room for **2** : to adjust, to adapt — **acomodarse** *vr* **1** : to settle in **2** ~ **a** : to adapt to
acomodaticio, -cia *adj* : accommodating, obliging
acomodo *nm* **1** : job, position **2** : arrangement, placement **3** : accommodation, lodging
acompañamiento *nm* : accompaniment
acompañante *nmf* **1** COMPAÑERO : companion **2** : accompanist
acompañar *vt* : to accompany, to go with
acompasado, -da *adj* : rhythmic, regular, measured
acomplejado, -da *adj* : full of complexes, neurotic
acondicionado, -da *adj* **1** : equipped, fitted-out **2 bien acondicionado** : in good shape, in a fit state
acondicionador *nm* **1** : conditioner **2 acondicionador de aire** : air conditioner
acondicionar *vt* **1** : to condition **2** : to fit out, to furnish
acongojado, -da *adj* : distressed, upset
acongojarse *vr* : to grieve, to become distressed
aconsejable *adj* : advisable
aconsejar *vt* : to advise, to counsel
acontecer {53} *vt* (*3rd person only*) : to occur, to happen
acontecimiento *nm* SUCESO : event
acopiar *vt* : to gather, to collect, to stockpile
acopio *nm* : collection, stock
acoplamiento *nm* : connection, coupling
acoplar *vt* : to couple, to connect — **acoplarse** *vr* : to fit together
acoquinar *vt* : to intimidate
acorazado¹, -da *adj* BLINDADO : armored
acorazado² *nm* : battleship
acordado, -da *adj* : agreed upon
acordar {19} *vt* **1** : to agree on **2** OTORGAR : to award, to bestow — **acordarse** *vr* RECORDAR : to remember, to recall
acorde¹ *adj* **1** : in agreement, in accordance **2** ~ **con** : in keeping with
acorde² *nm* : chord
acordeón *nm, pl* **-deones** : accordion — **acordeonista** *nmf*
acordonar *vt* **1** : to cordon off **2** : to lace up **3** : to mill (coins)
acorralar *vt* ARRINCONAR : to corner, to hem in, to corral
acortar *vt* : to shorten, to cut short — **acortarse** *vr* **1** : to become shorter **2** : to end early

acosar *vt* PERSEGUIR : to pursue, to hound, to harass
acoso *nm* ASEDIO : harassment ⟨acoso sexual : sexual harassment⟩
acostar {19} *vt* **1** : to lay (something) down **2** : to put to bed — **acostarse** *vr* **1** : to lie down **2** : to go to bed
acostumbrado, -da *adj* **1** HABITUADO : accustomed **2** HABITUAL : usual, customary
acostumbrar *vt* : to accustom — *vi* : to be accustomed, to be in the habit — **acostumbrarse** *vr*
acotación *nf, pl* **-ciones** **1** : marginal note **2** : stage direction
acotado, -da *adj* : enclosed
acotamiento *nm Mex* : shoulder (of a road)
acotar *vt* **1** ANOTAR : to note, to annotate **2** DELIMITAR : to mark off (land), to demarcate
acre¹ *adj* **1** : acrid, pungent **2** MORDAZ : caustic, biting
acre² *nm* : acre
acrecentamiento *nm* : growth, increase
acrecentar {55} *vt* AUMENTAR : to increase, to augment
acreditación *nf, pl* **-ciones** : accreditation
acreditado, -da *adj* **1** : accredited, authorized **2** : reputable
acreditar *vt* **1** : to accredit, to authorize **2** : to credit **3** : to prove, to verify — **acreditarse** *vr* : to gain a reputation
acreedor¹, -dora *adj* : deserving, worthy
acreedor², -dora *n* : creditor
acribillar *vt* **1** : to riddle, to pepper (with bullets, etc.) **2** : to hound, to harass
acrílico *nm* : acrylic
acrimonia *nf* **1** : pungency **2** : acrimony
acrimonioso, -sa *adj* : acrimonious
acriollarse *vr* : to adopt local customs, to go native
acritud *nf* **1** : pungency, bitterness **2** : intensity, sharpness **3** : harshness, asperity
acrobacia *nf* : acrobatics
acróbata *nmf* : acrobat
acrobático, -ca *adj* : acrobatic
acrónimo *nm* : acronym
acta *nf* **1** : document, certificate ⟨acta de nacimiento : birth certificate⟩ **2 actas** *nfpl* : minutes (of a meeting)
actitud *nf* **1** : attitude **2** : posture, position
activación *nf, pl* **-ciones** **1** : activation, stimulation **2** ACELERACIÓN : acceleration, speeding up
activar *vt* **1** : to activate **2** : to stimulate, to energize **3** : to speed up
actividad *nf* : activity
activista *nmf* : activist
activo¹, -va *adj* : active — **activamente** *adv*
activo² *nm* : assets *pl* ⟨activo y pasivo : assets and liabilities⟩

acto *nm* **1** ACCIÓN : act, deed **2** : act (in a play) **3 el acto sexual** : sexual intercourse **4 en el acto** : right away, on the spot **5 acto seguido** : immediately after

actor *nm* ARTISTA : actor

actriz *nf, pl* **actrices** ARTISTA : actress

actuación *nf, pl* **-ciones 1** : performance **2 actuaciones** *nfpl* DILIGENCIAS : proceedings

actual *adj* PRESENTE : present, current

actualidad *nf* **1** : present time ⟨en la actualidad : at present⟩ **2 actualidades** *nfpl* : current affairs

actualización *nf, pl* **-ciones** : updating, modernization

actualizar {21} *vt* : to modernize, to bring up to date

actualmente *adv* : at present, nowadays

actuar {3} *vi* : to act, to perform

actuarial *adj* : actuarial

actuario, -ria *n* : actuary

acuarela *nf* : watercolor

acuario *nm* : aquarium

Acuario *nmf* : Aquarius, Aquarian

acuartelar *vt* : to quarter (troops)

acuático, -ca *adj* : aquatic, water

acuchillar *vt* APUÑALAR : to knife, to stab

acuciante *adj* : pressing, urgent

acucioso, -sa → **acuciante**

acudir *vi* **1** : to go, to come (someplace for a specific purpose) ⟨acudió a la puerta : he went to the door⟩ ⟨acudimos en su ayuda : we came to her aid⟩ **2** : to be present, to show up ⟨acudí a la cita : I showed up for the appointment⟩ **3** ~ **a** : to turn to, to have recourse to ⟨hay que acudir al médico : you must consult the doctor⟩

acueducto *nm* : aqueduct

acuerdo *nm* **1** : agreement **2 estar de acuerdo** : to agree **3 de acuerdo con** : in accordance with **4 de** ~ : OK, all right

acuicultura *nf* : aquaculture

acullá *adv* : yonder, over there

acumulación *nf, pl* **-ciones** : accumulation

acumulador *nm* : storage battery

acumular *vt* : to accumulate, to amass — **acumularse** *vr* : to build up, to pile up

acumulativo, -va *adj* : cumulative — **acumulativamente** *adv*

acunar *vt* : to rock, to cradle

acuñar *vt* : to coin, to mint

acuoso, -sa *adj* : aqueous, watery

acupuntura *nf* : acupuncture

acurrucarse {72} *vr* : to cuddle, to nestle, to curl up

acusación *nf, pl* **-ciones 1** : accusation, charge **2 la acusación** : the prosecution

acusado[1], -da *adj* : prominent, marked

acusado[2], -da *n* : defendant

acusador, -dora *n* **1** : accuser **2** FISCAL : prosecutor

acusar *vt* **1** : to accuse, to charge **2** : to reveal, to betray ⟨sus ojos acusaban la desconfianza : his eyes revealed distrust⟩ — **acusarse** *vr* : to confess

acusativo *nm* : objective (in grammar)

acusatorio, -ria *adj* : accusatory

acuse *nm* **acuse de recibo** : acknowledgment of receipt

acústica *nf* : acoustics

acústico, -ca *adj* : acoustic

adagio *nm* **1** REFRÁN : adage, proverb **2** : adagio

adalid *nm* : leader, champion

adaptable *adj* : adaptable — **adaptabilidad** *nf*

adaptación *nf, pl* **-ciones** : adaptation, adjustment

adaptado, -da *adj* : suited, adapted

adaptador *nm* : adapter (in electricity)

adaptar *vt* **1** MODIFICAR : to adapt **2** : to adjust, to fit — **adaptarse** *vr* : to adapt oneself, to conform

adecentar *vt* : to tidy up

adecuación *nf, pl* **-ciones** ADAPTACIÓN : adaptation

adecuadamente *adv* : adequately

adecuado, -da *adj* **1** IDÓNEO : suitable, appropriate **2** : adequate

adecuar {8} *vt* : to adapt, to make suitable — **adecuarse** *vr* ~ **a** : to be appropriate for, to fit in with

adefesio *nm* : eyesore, monstrosity

adelantado, -da *adj* **1** : advanced, ahead **2** : fast (of a clock or watch) **3 por** ~ : in advance

adelantamiento *nm* **1** : advancement **2** : speeding up

adelantar *vt* **1** : to advance, to move forward **2** : to overtake, to pass **3** : to reveal (information) in advance **4** : to advance, to lend (money) — **adelantarse** *vr* **1** : to advance, to get in front **2** ~ **a** : to forestall, to preempt

adelante *adv* **1** : ahead, in front, forward **2 más adelante** : further on, later on **3 ¡adelante!** : come in!

adelanto *nm* **1** : advance, progress **2** : advance payment **3** : earliness ⟨llevamos una hora de adelanto : we're running an hour ahead of time⟩

adelfa *nf* : oleander

adelgazar {21} *vt* : to thin, to reduce — *vi* : to lose weight

ademán *nm, pl* **-manes 1** GESTO : gesture **2 ademanes** *nmpl* : manners

además *adv* **1** : besides, furthermore **2** ~ **de** : in addition to, as well as

adenoides *nfpl* : adenoids

adentrarse *vr* ~ **en** : to go into, to penetrate

adentro *adv* : inside, within

adentros *nmpl* **decirse para sus adentros** : to say to oneself ⟨me dije para mis adentros que nunca regresaría : I told myself that I'd never go back⟩

adepto[1], -ta *adj* : supportive ⟨ser adepto a : to be a follower of⟩

adepto[2], -ta *n* PARTIDARIO : follower, supporter

aderezar {21} *vt* **1** SAZONAR : to season, to dress (salad) **2** : to embellish, to adorn

aderezo *nm* **1** : dressing, seasoning **2** : adornment, embellishment

adeudar *vt* **1** : to debit **2** DEBER : to owe

adeudo *nm* **1** DÉBITO : debit **2** *Mex* : debt, indebtedness

adherencia *nf* **1** : adherence, adhesiveness **2** : appendage, accretion

adherente *adj* : adhesive, sticky

adherirse {76} *vr* : to adhere, to stick

adhesión *nf, pl* **-siones** **1** : adhesion **2** : attachment, commitment (to a cause, etc.)

adhesivo¹, **-va** *adj* : adhesive

adhesivo² *nm* : adhesive

adicción *nf, pl* **-ciones** : addiction

adición *nf, pl* **-ciones** : addition

adicional *adj* : additional — **adicionalmente** *adv*

adicionar *vt* : to add

adictivo, -va *adj* : addictive

adicto¹, **-ta** *adj* **1** : addicted **2** : devoted, dedicated

adicto², **-ta** *n* **1** : addict **2** PARTIDARIO : supporter, advocate

adiestrador, -dora *n* : trainer

adiestramiento *nm* : training

adiestrar *vt* : to train

adinerado, -da *adj* : moneyed, wealthy

adiós *nm, pl* **adioses** **1** DESPEDIDA : farewell, good-bye **2** ¡adiós! : good-bye!

aditamento *nm* : attachment, accessory

aditivo *nm* : additive

adivinación *nf, pl* **-ciones** **1** : guess **2** : divination, prediction

adivinanza *nf* ACERTIJO : riddle

adivinar *vt* **1** : to guess **2** : to foretell, to predict

adivino, -na *n* : fortune-teller

adjetivo¹, **-va** *adj* : adjectival

adjetivo² *nm* : adjective

adjudicación *nf, pl* **-ciones** **1** : adjudication **2** : allocation, awarding, granting

adjudicar {72} *vt* **1** : to adjudge, to adjudicate **2** : to assign, to allocate ⟨adjudicar la culpa : to assign the blame⟩ **3** : to award, to grant

adjuntar *vt* : to enclose, to attach

adjunto¹, **-ta** *adj* : enclosed, attached

adjunto², **-ta** *n* : deputy, assistant

adjunto³ *nm* : adjunct

administración *nf, pl* **-ciones** **1** : administration, management **2** administración de empresas : business administration

administrador, -dora *n* : administrator, manager

administrar *vt* : to administer, to manage, to run

administrativo, -va *adj* : administrative

admirable *adj* : admirable, impressive — **admirablemente** *adv*

admiración *nf, pl* **-ciones** : admiration

admirador, -dora *n* : admirer

admirar *vt* **1** : to admire **2** : to amaze, to astonish — **admirarse** *vr* : to be amazed

admirativo, -va *adj* : admiring

admisibilidad *nf* : admissibility

admisible *adj* : admissible, allowable

admisión *nf, pl* **-siones** : admission, admittance

admitir *vt* **1** : to admit, to let in **2** : to acknowledge, to concede **3** : to allow, to make room for ⟨la ley no admite cambios : the law doesn't allow for changes⟩

admonición *nf, pl* **-ciones** : admonition, warning

admonitorio, -ria *adj* : admonitory

ADN *nm* (*ácido desoxirribonucleico*) : DNA

adobar *vt* : to marinate

adobe *nm* : adobe

adobo *nm* **1** : marinade, seasoning **2** *Mex* : spicy marinade used for cooking pork

adoctrinamiento *nm* : indoctrination

adoctrinar *vt* : to indoctrinate

adolecer {53} *vi* PADECER : to suffer ⟨adolece de timidez : he suffers from shyness⟩

adolescencia *nf* : adolescence

adolescente¹ *adj* : adolescent, teenage

adolescente² *nmf* : adolescent, teenager

adonde *conj* : where ⟨el lugar adonde vamos es bello : the place where we're going is beautiful⟩

adónde *adv* : where ⟨¿adónde vamos? : where are we going?⟩

adondequiera *adv* : wherever, anywhere ⟨adondequiera que vayas : anywhere you go⟩

adopción *nf, pl* **-ciones** : adoption

adoptar *vt* **1** : to adopt (a measure), to take (a decision) **2** : to adopt (children)

adoptivo, -va *adj* **1** : adopted (children, country) **2** : adoptive (parents)

adoquín *nm, pl* **-quines** : paving stone, cobblestone

adorable *adj* : adorable, lovable

adoración *nf, pl* **-ciones** : adoration, worship

adorador¹, **-dora** *adj* : adoring, worshipping

adorador², **-dora** *n* : worshipper

adorar *vt* : to adore, to worship

adormecer {53} *vt* **1** : to make sleepy, to lull to sleep **2** : to numb — **adormecerse** *vr* **1** : to doze off **2** : to go numb

adormecimiento *nm* **1** SUEÑO : drowsiness, sleepiness **2** INSENSIBILIDAD : numbness

adormilarse *vr* : to doze, to drowse

adornar *vt* DECORAR : to decorate, to adorn

adorno *nm* : ornament, decoration

adquirido, -da *adj* **1** : acquired **2** mal adquirido : ill-gotten

adquirir {4} *vt* **1** : to acquire, to gain **2** COMPRAR : to purchase

adquisición *nf, pl* **-ciones 1** : acquisition **2** COMPRA : purchase
adquisitivo, -va *adj* **poder adquisitivo** : purchasing power
adrede *adv* : intentionally, on purpose
adrenalina *nf* : adrenaline
adscribir {33} *vt* : to assign, to appoint — **adscribirse** *vr* ~ **a** : to become a member of
adscripción *nf, pl* **-ciones** : assignment, appointment
adscrito *pp* → **adscribir**
aduana *nf* : customs, customs office
aduanero¹, -ra *adj* : customs
aduanero², -ra *n* : customs officer
aducir {61} *vt* : to adduce, to offer as proof
adueñarse *vr* ~ **de** : to take possession of, to take over
adulación *nf, pl* **-ciones** : adulation, flattery
adulador¹, -dora *adj* : flattering
adulador², -dora *n* : flatterer, toady
adular *vt* LISONJEAR : to flatter
adulteración *nf, pl* **-ciones** : adulteration
adulterar *vt* : to adulterate
adulterio *nm* : adultery
adúltero¹, -ra *adj* : adulterous
adúltero², -ra *n* : adulterer
adultez *nf* : adulthood
adulto, -ta *adj & n* : adult
adusto, -ta *adj* : harsh, severe
advenedizo, -za *n* **1** : upstart, parvenu **2** : newcomer
advenimiento *nm* : advent
adverbio *nm* : adverb — **adverbial** *adj*
adversario¹, -ria *adj* : opposing, contrary
adversario², -ria *n* OPOSITOR : adversary, opponent
adversidad *nf* : adversity
adverso, -sa *adj* DESFAVORABLE : adverse, unfavorable — **adversamente** *adv*
advertencia *nf* AVISO : warning
advertir {76} *vt* **1** AVISAR : to warn **2** : to notice, to tell ⟨no advertí que estuviera enojada : I couldn't tell she was angry⟩
Adviento *nm* : Advent
adyacente *adj* : adjacent
aéreo, -rea *adj* **1** : aerial, air **2 correo aéreo** : airmail
aeróbic *nm* : aerobics
aeróbico, -ca *adj* : aerobic
aerobio, -bia *adj* : aerobic
aerodinámica *nf* : aerodynamics
aerodinámico, -ca *adj* : aerodynamic, streamlined
aeródromo *nm* : airfield
aeroespacial *adj* : aerospace
aerolínea *nf* : airline
aeromozo, -za *n* : flight attendant, steward *m*, stewardess *f*
aeronáutica *nf* : aeronautics
aeronáutico, -ca *adj* : aeronautical
aeronave *nf* : aircraft

aeropostal *adj* : airmail
aeropuerto *nm* : airport
aerosol *nm* : aerosol, aerosol spray
aeróstata *nmf* : balloonist
aerotransportado, -da *adj* : airborne
aerotransportar *vt* : to airlift
afabilidad *nf* : affability
afable *adj* : affable — **afablemente** *adv*
afamado, -da *adj* : well-known, famous
afán *nm, pl* **afanes 1** ANHELO : eagerness, desire **2** EMPEÑO : effort, determination
afanador, -dora *n Mex* : cleaning person, cleaner
afanarse *vr* : to toil, to strive
afanosamente *adv* : zealously, industriously, busily
afanoso, -sa *adj* **1** : eager, industrious **2** : arduous, hard
afear *vt* : to make ugly, to disfigure
afección *nf, pl* **-ciones 1** : fondness, affection **2** : illness, complaint
afectación *nf, pl* **-ciones** : affectation
afectado, -da *adj* **1** : affected, mannered **2** : influenced **3** : afflicted **4** : feigned
afectar *vt* **1** : to affect **2** : to upset **3** : to feign, to pretend
afectísimo, -ma *adj* **suyo afectísimo** : yours truly
afectivo, -va *adj* : emotional
afecto¹, -ta *adj* **1** : affected, afflicted **2** : fond, affectionate
afecto² *nm* CARIÑO : affection
afectuoso, -sa *adj* CARIÑOSO : affectionate, caring
afeitadora *nf* : shaver, electric razor
afeitar *vt* RASURAR : to shave — **afeitarse** *vr*
afelpado, -da *adj* : plush
afeminado, -da *adj* : effeminate
aferrado, -da *adj* : obstinate, stubborn
aferrarse {55} *vr* : to cling, to hold on
affidávit *nm, pl* **-dávits** : affidavit
afgano, -na *adj & n* : Afghan
AFI *nm* (Alfabeto Fonético Internacional) : IPA
afianzar {21} *vt* **1** : to secure, to strengthen **2** : to guarantee, to vouch for — **afianzarse** *vr* ESTABLECERSE : to establish oneself
afiche *nm* : poster
afición *nf, pl* **-ciones 1** : enthusiasm, penchant, fondness ⟨afición al deporte : love of sports⟩ **2** PASATIEMPO : hobby
aficionado¹, -da *adj* ENTUSIASTA : enthusiastic, keen
aficionado², -da *n* **1** ENTUSIASTA : enthusiast, fan **2** : amateur
áfido *nm* : aphid
afiebrado, -da *adj* : feverish
afilado, -da *adj* **1** : sharp **2** : long, pointed ⟨una nariz afilada : a sharp nose⟩
afilador *nm* : sharpener
afilalápices *nms & pl* : pencil sharpener
afilar *vt* : to sharpen
afiliación *nf, pl* **-ciones** : affiliation

afiliado[1], **-da** *adj* : affiliated
afiliado[2], **-da** *n* : member
afiliarse *vr* : to become a member, to join, to affiliate
afín *adj, pl* **afines** 1 PARECIDO : related, similar ⟨la biología y disciplinas afines : biology and related disciplines⟩ 2 PRÓXIMO : adjacent, nearby
afinación *nf, pl* **-ciones** 1 : tune-up 2 : tuning (of an instrument)
afinador, -dora *n* : tuner (of musical instruments)
afinar *vt* 1 : to perfect, to refine 2 : to tune (an instrument) — *vi* : to sing or play in tune
afincarse {72} *vr* : to establish oneself, to settle in
afinidad *nf* : affinity, similarity
afirmación *nf, pl* **-ciones** 1 : statement 2 : affirmation
afirmar *vt* 1 : to state, to affirm 2 REFORZAR : to make firm, to strengthen
afirmativo, -va *adj* : affirmative — **afirmativamente** *adv*
aflicción *nf, pl* **-ciones** DESCONSUELO, PESAR : grief, sorrow
afligido, -da *adj* : grief-stricken, sorrowful
afligir {35} *vt* 1 : to distress, to upset 2 : to afflict — **afligirse** *vr* : to grieve
aflojar *vt* 1 : to loosen, to slacken 2 *fam* : to pay up, to fork over — *vi* : to slacken, to ease up — **aflojarse** *vr* : to become loose, to slacken
afloramiento *nm* : outcropping, emergence
aflorar *vi* : to come to the surface, to emerge
afluencia *nf* 1 : flow, influx 2 : abundance, plenty
afluente *nm* : tributary
afluir {41} *vi* : to flock ⟨la gente afluía a la frontera : people were flocking to the border⟩ 2 : to flow
aforismo *nm* : aphorism
aforo *nm* 1 : appraisal, assessment 2 : maximum capacity (of a theater, highway, etc.)
afortunado, -da *adj* : fortunate, lucky — **afortunadamente** *adv*
afrecho *nm* : bran, mash
afrenta *nf* : affront, insult
afrentar *vt* : to affront, to dishonor, to insult
africano, -na *adj & n* : African
afroamericano, -na *adj & n* : Afro-American
afrodisiaco *or* **afrodisíaco** *nm* : aphrodisiac
afrontamiento *nm* : confrontation
afrontar *vt* : to confront, to face up to
afrutado, -da *adj* : fruity
afuera *adv* 1 : out ⟨¡afuera! : get out!⟩ 2 : outside, outdoors
afueras *nfpl* ALEDAÑOS : outskirts
agachadiza *nf* : snipe (bird)
agachar *vt* : to lower (a part of the body) ⟨agachar la cabeza : to bow one's head⟩

— agacharse *vr* : to crouch, to stoop, to bend down
agalla *nf* 1 BRANQUIA : gill 2 **tener agallas** *fam* : to have guts, to have courage
agarradera *nf* ASA, ASIDERO : handle, grip
agarrado, -da *adj fam* : cheap, stingy
agarrar *vt* 1 : to grab, to grasp 2 : to catch, to take — *vi* **agarrar y** *fam* : to do (something) abruptly ⟨el día siguiente agarró y se fue : the next day he up and left⟩ — **agarrarse** *vr* 1 : to hold on, to cling 2 *fam* : to get into a fight ⟨se agarraron a golpes : they came to blows⟩
agarre *nm* : grip, grasp
agarrotarse *vr* 1 : to stiffen up 2 : to seize up
agasajar *vt* : to fête, to wine and dine
agasajo *nm* : lavish attention
ágata *nf* : agate
agave *nm* : agave
agazaparse *vr* 1 AGACHARSE : to crouch 2 : to hide
agencia *nf* : agency, office
agenciar *vt* : to obtain, to procure — **agenciarse** *vr* : to manage, to get by
agenda *nf* 1 : agenda 2 : appointment book
agente *nmf* 1 : agent 2 **agente de viajes** : travel agent 3 **agente de bolsa** : stockbroker 4 **agente de tráfico** : traffic officer
agigantado, -da *adj* GIGANTESCO : gigantic
agigantar *vt* 1 : to increase greatly, to enlarge 2 : to exaggerate
ágil *adj* 1 : agile, nimble 2 : sharp, lively (of a response, etc.) — **ágilmente** *adv*
agilidad *nf* : agility, nimbleness
agilizar {21} *vt* ACELERAR : to expedite, to speed up
agitación *nf, pl* **-ciones** 1 : agitation 2 NERVIOSISMO : nervousness
agitado, -da *adj* 1 : agitated, excited 2 : choppy, rough, turbulent
agitador, -dora *n* PROVOCADOR : agitator
agitar *vt* 1 : to agitate, to shake 2 : to wave, to flap 3 : to stir up — **agitarse** *vr* 1 : to toss about, to flap around 2 : to get upset
aglomeración *nf, pl* **-ciones** 1 : conglomeration, mass 2 GENTÍO : crowd
aglomerar *vt* : to cluster, to amass — **aglomerarse** *vr* : to crowd together
aglutinar *vt* : to bring together, to bind
agnóstico, -ca *adj & n* : agnostic
agobiado, -da *adj* : weary, worn-out, weighted-down
agobiante *adj* 1 : exhausting, overwhelming 2 : stifling, oppressive
agobiar *vt* 1 OPRIMIR : to oppress, to burden 2 ABRUMAR : to overwhelm 3 : to wear out, to exhaust
agonía *nf* : agony, death throes
agonizante *adj* : dying

agonizar {21} *vi* **1** : to be dying **2** : to be in agony **3** : to dim, to fade

agorero, -ra *adj* : ominous

agostar *vt* **1** : to parch **2** : to wither — **agostarse** *vr*

agosto *nm* **1** : August **2 hacer uno su agosto** : to make a fortune, to make a killing

agotado, -da *adj* **1** : exhausted, used up **2** : sold out **3** FATIGADO : worn-out, tired

agotador, -dora *adj* : exhausting

agotamiento *nm* FATIGA : exhaustion

agotar *vt* **1** : to exhaust, to use up **2** : to weary, to wear out — **agotarse** *vr*

agraciado¹, -da *adj* **1** : attractive **2** : fortunate

agraciado², -da *n* : winner

agradable *adj* GRATO, PLACENTERO : pleasant, agreeable — **agradablemente** *adv*

agradar *vi* : to be pleasing ⟨nos agradó mucho el resultado : we were very pleased with the result⟩

agradecer {53} *vt* **1** : to be grateful for **2** : to thank

agradecido, -da *adj* : grateful, thankful

agradecimiento *nm* : gratitude, thankfulness

agrado *nm* **1** GUSTO : taste, liking ⟨no es de su agrado : it's not to his liking⟩ **2** : graciousness, agreeableness **3 con ~** : with pleasure, willingly ⟨lo haré con agrado : I will be happy to do it⟩

agrandar *vt* **1** : to exaggerate **2** : to enlarge — **agrandarse** *vr*

agrario, -ria *adj* : agrarian, agricultural

agravación *nf, pl* **-ciones** : aggravation, worsening

agravante *adj* : aggravating

agravar *vt* **1** : to increase (weight), to make heavier **2** EMPEORAR : to aggravate, to worsen — **agravarse** *vr*

agraviar *vt* INJURIAR, OFENDER : to offend, to insult

agravio *nm* INJURIA : affront, offense, insult

agredir {1} *vt* : to assail, to attack

agregado¹, -da *n* **1** : attaché **2** : assistant professor

agregado² *nm* **1** : aggregate **2** AÑADIDURA : addition, something added

agregar {52} *vt* **1** AÑADIR : to add, to attach **2** : to appoint — **agregarse** *vr* : to join

agresión *nf, pl* **-siones** **1** : aggression **2** ATAQUE : attack

agresividad *nf* : aggressiveness, aggression

agresivo, -va *adj* : aggressive — **agresivamente** *adv*

agresor¹, -sora *adj* : hostile, attacking

agresor², -sora *n* **1** : aggressor **2** : assailant, attacker

agreste *adj* **1** CAMPESTRE : rural **2** : wild, untamed

agriar *vt* **1** : to sour, to make sour **2** : to embitter — **agriarse** *vr* : to turn sour

agrícola *adj* : agricultural

agricultor, -tora *n* : farmer, grower

agricultura *nf* : agriculture, farming

agridulce *adj* **1** : bittersweet **2** : sweet-and-sour

agrietar *vt* : to crack — **agrietarse** *vr* **1** : to crack **2** : to chap

agrimensor, -sora *n* : surveyor

agrimensura *nf* : surveying

agrio, agria *adj* **1** ÁCIDO : sour **2** : caustic, acrimonious

agriparse *vr* : to catch the flu

agroindustria *nf* : agribusiness

agronomía *nf* : agronomy

agropecuario, -ria *adj* : pertaining to livestock and agriculture

agrupación *nf, pl* **-ciones** GRUPO : group, association

agrupamiento *nm* : grouping, concentration

agrupar *vt* : to group together

agua *nf* **1** : water **2 agua oxigenada** : hydrogen peroxide **3 aguas negras** *or* **aguas residuales** : sewage **4 como agua para chocolate** *Mex fam* : furious **5 echar aguas** *Mex fam* : to keep an eye out, to be on the lookout

aguacate *nm* : avocado

aguacero *nm* : shower, downpour

aguado, -da *adj* **1** DILUIDO : watered-down, diluted **2** *CA, Col, Mex fam* : soft, flabby **3** *Mex, Peru fam* : dull, boring

aguafiestas *nmfs & pl* : killjoy, stick-in-the-mud, spoilsport

aguafuerte *nm* : etching

aguamanil *nm* : ewer, pitcher

aguanieve *nf* : sleet ⟨caer aguanieve : to be sleeting⟩

aguantar *vt* **1** SOPORTAR : to bear, to tolerate, to withstand **2** : to hold **3 aguantar las ganas** : to resist an urge ⟨no pude aguantar las ganas de reír : I couldn't keep myself from laughing⟩ — *vi* : to hold out, to last — **aguantarse** *vr* **1** : to resign oneself **2** : to restrain oneself

aguante *nm* **1** TOLERANCIA : tolerance, patience **2** RESISTENCIA : endurance, strength

aguar {10} *vt* **1** : to water down, to dilute **2 aguar la fiesta** *fam* : to spoil the party

aguardar *vt* ESPERAR : to wait for, to await — *vi* : to be in store

aguardiente *nm* : clear brandy

aguarrás *nm* : turpentine

agudeza *nf* **1** : keenness, sharpness **2** : shrillness **3** : witticism

agudizar {21} *vt* : to intensify, to heighten

agudo, -da *adj* **1** : acute, sharp **2** : shrill, high-pitched **3** PERSPICAZ : clever, shrewd

agüero *nm* AUGURIO, PRESAGIO : augury, omen

aguijón *nm, pl* **-jones** **1** : stinger (of a bee, etc.) **2** : goad

aguijonear *vt* : to goad
águila *nf* **1** : eagle **2 águila o sol** *Mex* : heads or tails
aguileño, -ña *adj* : aquiline
aguilera *nf* : aerie, eagle's nest
aguilón *nm, pl* **-lones** : gable
aguinaldo *nm* **1** : Christmas bonus, year-end bonus **2** *PRi, Ven* : Christmas carol
agüitarse *vr Mex fam* : to have the blues, to feel discouraged
aguja *nf* **1** : needle **2** : steeple, spire
agujerear *vt* : to make a hole in, to pierce
agujero *nm* **1** : hole **2 agujero negro** : black hole (in astronomy)
agujeta *nf* **1** *Mex* : shoelace **2 agujetas** *nfpl* : muscular soreness or stiffness
agusanado, -da *adj* : worm-eaten
aguzar {21} *vt* **1** : to sharpen ⟨aguzar el ingenio : to sharpen one's wits⟩ **2 aguzar el oído** : to prick up one's ears
ah *interj* : oh!
ahí *adv* **1** : there ⟨ahí está : there it is⟩ **2 por ~** : somewhere, thereabouts **3 de ahí que** : with the result that, so that **~** : for the time being
ahijado, -da *n* : godchild, godson *m,* goddaughter *f*
ahijar {5} *vt* : to adopt (a child)
ahínco *nm* : eagerness, zeal
ahogar {52} *vt* **1** : to drown **2** : to smother **3** : to choke back, to stifle — **ahogarse** *vr*
ahogo *nm* : breathlessness, suffocation
ahondar *vt* : to deepen — *vi* : to elaborate, to go into detail
ahora *adv* **1** : now **2 ahora mismo** : right now **3 hasta ~** : so far **4 por ~** : for the time being
ahorcar {72} *vt* : to hang, to kill by hanging — **ahorcarse** *vr*
ahorita *adv fam* : right now, right away
ahorquillado, -da *adj* : forked
ahorrador, -dora *adj* : thrifty
ahorrar *vt* **1** : to save (money) **2** : to spare, to conserve — *vi* : to save up — **ahorrarse** *vr* : to spare oneself
ahorrativo, -va *adj* : thrifty, frugal
ahorro *nm* : saving ⟨cuenta de ahorros : savings account⟩
ahuecar {72} *vt* **1** : to hollow out **2** : to cup (one's hands) **3** : to plump up, to fluff up
ahuizote *nm Mex fam* : annoying person, pain in the neck
ahumar {8} *vt* : to smoke, to cure
ahuyentar *vt* **1** : to scare away, to chase away **2** : to banish, to dispel ⟨ahuyentar las dudas : to dispel doubts⟩
airado, -da *adj* FURIOSO : angry, irate
airar {5} *vt* : to make angry, to anger
aire *nm* **1** : air **2 aire acondicionado** : air-conditioning **3 darse aires** : to give oneself airs
airear *vt* : to air, to air out — **airearse** *vr* : to get some fresh air
airoso, -sa *adj* **1** : elegant, graceful **2 salir airoso** : to come out winning
aislacionismo *nm* : isolationism

aislacionista *adj & nmf* : isolationist
aislado, -da *adj* : isolated, alone
aislador *nm* : insulator (part)
aislamiento *nm* **1** : isolation **2** : insulation
aislante *nm* : insulator, nonconductor
aislar {5} *vt* **1** : to isolate **2** : to insulate
ajado, -da *adj* **1** : worn, shabby **2** : wrinkled, crumpled
ajar *vt* : to wear out, to spoil
ajardinado, -da *adj* : landscaped
ajedrecista *nmf* : chess player
ajedrez *nm, pl* **-dreces 1** : chess **2** : chess set
ajeno, -na *adj* **1** : alien **2** : of another, of others ⟨propiedad ajena : somebody else's property⟩ **3 ~ a** : foreign to **4 ~ de** : devoid of, free from
ajetreado, -da *adj* : hectic, busy
ajetrearse *vr* : to bustle about, to rush around
ajetreo *nm* : hustle and bustle, fuss
ají *nm, pl* **ajíes** : chili pepper
ajo *nm* : garlic
ajonjolí *nm, pl* **-líes** : sesame
ajuar *nm* : trousseau
ajustable *adj* : adjustable
ajustado, -da *adj* **1** CEÑIDO : tight, tight-fitting **2** : close, tight ⟨una ajustada victoria : a close victory⟩
ajustar *vt* **1** : to adjust, to adapt **2** : to take in (clothing) **3** : to settle, to resolve — **ajustarse** *vr* : to fit, to conform
ajuste *nm* **1** : adjustment **2** : tightening
ajusticiar *vt* EJECUTAR : to execute, to put to death
al *prep* (contraction of a and el) → **a²**
ala *nf* **1** : wing **2** : brim (of a hat)
Alá *nm* : Allah
alabanza *nf* ELOGIO : praise
alabar *vt* : to praise — **alabarse** *vr* : to boast
alabastro *nm* : alabaster
alabear *vt* : to warp — **alabearse** *vr*
alabeo *nm* : warp, warping
alacena *nf* : cupboard, larder
alacrán *nm, pl* **-cranes** ESCORPIÓN : scorpion
alado, -da *adj* : winged
alambique *nm* : still (to distill alcohol)
alambre *nm* **1** : wire **2 alambre de púas** : barbed wire
alameda *nf* **1** : poplar grove **2** : tree-lined avenue
álamo *nm* **1** : poplar **2 álamo temblón** : aspen
alar *nm* : eaves *pl*
alarde *nm* **1** : show, display **2 hacer alarde de** : to make show of, to boast about
alardear *vi* PRESUMIR : to boast, to brag
alargado, -da *adj* : elongated, slender
alargamiento *nm* : lengthening, extension, elongation
alargar {52} *vt* **1** : to extend, to lengthen **2** PROLONGAR : to prolong — **alargarse** *vr*

alarido *nm* : howl, shriek

alarma *nf* : alarm

alarmante *adj* : alarming — **alarmante-mente** *adv*

alarmar *vt* : to alarm

alazán *nm, pl* **-zanes** : sorrel (color or animal)

alba *nf* AMANECER : dawn, daybreak

albacea *nmf* TESTAMENTARIO : executor, executrix *f*

albahaca *nf* : basil

albanés, **-nesa** *adj & n, mpl* **-neses** : Albanian

albañil *nmf* : bricklayer, mason

albañilería *nf* : bricklaying, masonry

albaricoque *nm* : apricot

albatros *nm* : albatross

albedrío *nm* : will ⟨libre albedrío : free will⟩

alberca *nf* **1** : reservoir, tank **2** *Mex* : swimming pool

albergar {52} *vt* ALOJAR : to house, to lodge, to shelter

albergue *nm* **1** : shelter, refuge **2** : hostel

albino, **-na** *adj & n* : albino — **albinismo** *nm*

albóndiga *nf* : meatball

albor *nm* **1** : dawning, beginning **2** BLANCURA : whiteness

alborada *nf* : dawn

alborear *v impers* : to dawn

alborotado, **-da** *adj* **1** : excited, agitated **2** : rowdy, unruly

alborotador[1], **-dora** *adj* **1** : noisy, boisterous **2** : rowdy, unruly

alborotador[2], **-dora** *n* : agitator, troublemaker, rioter

alborotar *vt* **1** : to excite, to agitate **2** : to incite, to stir up — **alborotarse** *vr* **1** : to get excited **2** : to riot

alboroto *nm* **1** : disturbance, ruckus **2** MOTÍN : riot

alborozado, **-da** *adj* : jubilant

alborozar {21} *vt* : to gladden, to cheer

alborozo *nm* : joy, elation

álbum *nm* : album ⟨álbum de recortes : scrapbook⟩

albúmina *nf* : albumin

albur *nm* **1** : chance, risk **2** *Mex* : pun

alca *nf* : auk

alcachofa *nf* : artichoke

alcahuete, **-ta** *n* CHISMOSO : gossip

alcaide *nm* : warden (in a prison)

alcalde, **-desa** *n* : mayor

alcaldía *nf* **1** : mayoralty **2** AYUNTAMIENTO : city hall

álcali *nm* : alkali

alcalino, **-na** *adj* : alkaline — **alcalinidad** *nf*

alcance *nm* **1** : reach **2** : range, scope

alcancía *nf* **1** : piggy bank, money box **2** : collection box (for alms, etc.)

alcanfor *nm* : camphor

alcantarilla *nf* CLOACA : sewer, drain

alcanzar {21} *vt* **1** : to reach **2** : to catch up with **3** LOGRAR : to achieve, to attain — *vi* **1** DAR : to suffice, to be enough **2** ∼ **a** : to manage to

alcaparra *nf* : caper

alcapurria *nf* PRi : stuffed fritter made with taro and green banana

alcaravea *nf* : caraway

alcatraz *nm, pl* **-traces** : gannet

alcázar *nm* : fortress, castle

alce[1], etc. → **alzar**

alce[2] *nm* : moose, European elk

alcoba *nf* : bedroom

alcohol *nm* : alcohol

alcohólico, **-ca** *adj & n* : alcoholic

alcoholismo *nm* : alcoholism

alcoholizarse {21} *vr* : to become an alcoholic

alcornoque *nm* **1** : cork oak **2** *fam* : idiot, fool

alcurnia *nf* : ancestry, lineage

aldaba *nf* : door knocker

aldea *nf* : village

aldeano[1], **-na** *adj* : village, rustic

aldeano[2], **-na** *n* : villager

aleación *nf, pl* **-ciones** : alloy

alear *vt* : to alloy

aleatorio, **-ria** *adj* : random, fortuitous — **aleatoriamente** *adv*

alebrestar *vt* : to excite, to make nervous — **alebrestarse** *vr*

aledaño, **-ña** *adj* : bordering, neighboring

aledaños *nmpl* AFUERAS : outskirts, surrounding area

alegar {52} *vt* **1** : to assert, to allege — *vi* DISCUTIR : to argue

alegato *nm* **1** : allegation, claim **2** *Mex* : argument, summation (in law) **3** : argument, dispute

alegoría *nf* : allegory

alegórico, **-ca** *adj* : allegorical

alegrar *vt* : to make happy, to cheer up — **alegrarse** *vr* : to be glad, to rejoice

alegre *adj* **1** : glad, cheerful **2** : colorful, bright **3** *fam* : tipsy

alegremente *adv* : happily, cheerfully

alegría *nf* : joy, cheer, happiness

alejado, **-da** *adj* : remote

alejamiento *nm* **1** : removal, separation **2** : estrangement

alejar *vt* **1** : to remove, to move away **2** : to estrange, to alienate — **alejarse** *vr* **1** : to move away, to stray **2** : to drift apart

alelado, **-da** *adj* **1** : bewildered, stupefied **2** : foolish, stupid

aleluya *interj* : hallelujah!, alleluia!

alemán[1], **-mana** *adj & n, mpl* **-manes** : German

alemán[2] *nm* : German (language)

alentador, **-dora** *adj* : encouraging

alentar {55} *vt* : to encourage, to inspire — *vi* : to breathe

alerce *nm* : larch

alérgeno *nm* : allergen

alergia *nf* : allergy

alérgico, **-ca** *adj* : allergic

alero *nm* **1** : eaves *pl* **2** : forward (in basketball)

alerón *nm, pl* **-rones** : aileron
alerta[1] *adv* : on the alert
alerta[2] *adj & nf* : alert
alertar *vt* : to alert
aleta *nf* **1** : fin **2** : flipper **3** : small wing
aletargado, -da *adj* : lethargic, sluggish, torpid
aletargarse {52} *vr* : to feel drowsy, to become lethargic
aletear *vi* : to flutter, to flap one's wings
aleteo *nm* : flapping, flutter
alevín *nm, pl* **-vines 1** : fry, young fish **2** PRINCIPIANTE : beginner
alevosía *nf* **1** : treachery **2** : premeditation
alevoso, -sa *adj* : treacherous
alfabético, -ca *adj* : alphabetical — **alfabéticamente** *adv*
alfabetismo *nm* : literacy
alfabetizado, -da *adj* : literate
alfabetizar {21} *vt* : to alphabetize
alfabeto *nm* : alphabet
alfalfa *nf* : alfalfa
alfanje *nm* : cutlass, scimitar
alfarería *nf* : pottery
alfarero, -ra *n* : potter
alféizar *nm* : sill, windowsill
alfeñique *nm fam* : wimp, weakling
alférez *nmf, pl* **-reces 1** : second lieutenant **2** : ensign
alfil *nm* : bishop (in chess)
alfiler *nm* **1** : pin **2** BROCHE : brooch
alfiletero *nm* : pincushion
alfombra *nf* : carpet, rug
alfombrado *nm* : carpeting
alfombrar *vt* : to carpet
alfombrilla *nf* : small rug, mat
alforfón *nm, pl* **-fones** : buckwheat
alforja *nf* : saddlebag
alforza *nf* : pleat, tuck
alga *nf* **1** : aquatic plant, alga **2** : seaweed
algarabía *nf* **1** : gibberish, babble **2** : hubbub, uproar
álgebra *nf* : algebra
algebraico, -ca *adj* : algebraic
álgido, -da *adj* **1** : critical, decisive **2** : icy cold
algo[1] *adv* : somewhat, rather ⟨es simpático, pero algo tacaño : he's nice but rather stingy⟩
algo[2] *pron* **1** : something **2** ~ **de** : some, a little ⟨tengo algo de dinero : I've got some money⟩
algodón *nm, pl* **-dones** : cotton
algoritmo *nm* : algorithm
alguacil *nm* : constable
alguien *pron* : somebody, someone
alguno[1], **-na** *adj* (**algún** *before masculine singular nouns*) **1** : some, any ⟨algún día : someday, one day⟩ **2** (*in negative constructions*) : not any, not at all ⟨no tengo noticia alguna : I have no news at all⟩ **3 algunas veces** : sometimes
alguno[2], **-na** *pron* **1** : one, someone, somebody ⟨alguno de ellos : one of them⟩ **2 algunos, -nas** *pron pl* : some,

a few ⟨algunos quieren trabajar : some want to work⟩
alhaja *nf* : jewel, gem
alhajar *vt* : to adorn with jewels
alharaca *nf* : fuss
alhelí *nm* : wallflower
aliado[1], **-da** *adj* : allied
aliado[2], **-da** *n* : ally
alianza *nf* : alliance
aliarse {85} *vr* : to form an alliance, to ally oneself
alias *adv & nm* : alias
alicaído, -da *adj* : depressed, discouraged
alicates *nmpl* PINZAS : pliers
aliciente *nm* **1** INCENTIVO : incentive **2** ATRACCIÓN : attraction
alienación *nf, pl* **-ciones** : alienation, derangement
alienar *vt* ENAJENAR : to alienate
aliento *nm* **1** : breath **2** : courage, strength **3 dar aliento a** : to encourage
aligerar *vt* **1** : to lighten **2** ACELERAR : to hasten, to quicken
alijo *nm* : cache, consignment (of contraband)
alimaña *nf* : pest, vermin
alimentación *nf, pl* **-ciones** NUTRICIÓN : nutrition, nourishment
alimentar *vt* **1** NUTRIR : to feed, to nourish **2** MANTENER : to support (a family) **3** FOMENTAR : to nurture, to foster — **alimentarse** *vr* ~ **con** : to live on
alimentario, -ria → **alimenticio**
alimenticio, -cia *adj* **1** : nutritional, food, dietary **2** : nutritious, nourishing
alimento *nm* : food, nourishment
aliñar *vt* **1** : to dress (salad) **2** CONDIMENTAR : to season
alineación *nf, pl* **-ciones 1** : alignment **2** : lineup (in sports)
alineamiento *nm* : alignment
alinear *vt* **1** : to align **2** : to line up — **alinearse** *vr* **1** : to fall in, to line up **2** ~ **con** : to align oneself with
aliño *nm* : seasoning, dressing
alipús *nm, pl* **-puses** *Mex fam* : booze, drink
alisar *vt* : to smooth
aliso *nm* : alder
alistamiento *nm* : enlistment, recruitment
alistar *vt* **1** : to recruit **2** : to make ready — **alistarse** *vr* : to join up, to enlist
aliteración *nf, pl* **-ciones** : alliteration
aliviar *vt* MITIGAR : to relieve, to alleviate, to soothe — **aliviarse** *vr* : to recover, to get better
alivio *nm* : relief
aljaba *nf* : quiver (for arrows)
aljibe *nm* : cistern, well
allá *adv* **1** : there, over there **2 más allá** : farther away **3 más allá de** : beyond **4 allá tú** : that's up to you

allanamiento *nm* **1** : (police) raid **2 allanamiento de morada** : breaking and
entering
allanar *vt* **1** : to raid, to search **2** : to resolve, to solve **3** : to smooth, to level
out
allegado[1], **-da** *adj* : close, intimate
allegado[2], **-da** *n* : close friend, relation
⟨parientes y allegados : friends and re-
lations⟩
allegar {52} *vt* : to gather, to collect
allende[1] *adv* : beyond, on the other side
allende[2] *prep* : beyond ⟨allende las montañas : beyond the mountains⟩
allí *adv* : there, over there ⟨allí mismo
: right there⟩ ⟨hasta allí : up to that
point⟩
alma *nf* **1** : soul **2** : person, human being **3 no tener alma** : to be pitiless **4
tener el alma en un hilo** : to have one's
heart in one's mouth
almacén *nm, pl* **-cenes 1** BODEGA
: warehouse, storehouse **2** TIENDA
: shop, store **3 gran almacén** *Spain*
: department store
almacenaje → **almacenamiento**
almacenamiento *nm* : storage ⟨almace-
namiento de datos : data storage⟩
almacenar *vt* : to store, to put in storage
almacenero, -ra *n* : shopkeeper
almacenista *nm* MAYORISTA : wholesaler
almádena *nf* : sledgehammer
almanaque *nm* : almanac
almeja *nf* : clam
almendra *nf* **1** : almond **2** : kernel
almendro *nm* : almond tree
almiar *nm* : haystack
almíbar *nm* : syrup
almidón *nm, pl* **-dones** : starch
almidonar *vt* : to starch
alminar *nm* MINARETE : minaret
almirante *nm* : admiral
almizcle *nm* : musk
almohada *nf* : pillow
almohadilla *nf* **1** : small pillow, cushion
2 : bag, base (in baseball)
almohadón *nm, pl* **-dones** : bolster,
cushion
almohazar {21} *vt* : to curry (a horse)
almoneda *nf* SUBASTA : auction
almorranas *nfpl* HEMORROIDES : hemorrhoids, piles
almorzar {36} *vi* : to have lunch — *vt* : to
have for lunch
almuerzo *nm* : lunch
alocado, -da *adj* **1** : crazy **2** : wild, reckless **3** : silly, scatterbrained
alocución *nf, pl* **-ciones** : speech, address
áloe *or* **aloe** *nm* : aloe
alojamiento *nm* : lodging, accommodations *pl*
alojar *vt* ALBERGAR : to house, to lodge
— **alojarse** *vr* : to lodge, to room
alondra *nf* : lark, skylark
alpaca *nf* : alpaca

alpinismo *nm* : mountain climbing,
mountaineering
alpinista *nmf* : mountain climber
alpino, -na *adj* : Alpine, alpine
alpiste *nm* : birdseed
alquilar *vt* ARRENDAR : to rent, to lease
alquiler *nm* ARRENDAMIENTO : rent,
rental
alquimia *nf* : alchemy
alquimista *nmf* : alchemist
alquitrán *nm, pl* **-tranes** BREA : tar
alquitranar *vt* : to tar, to cover with tar
alrededor[1] *adv* **1** : around ⟨todo
temblaba alrededor : all around things
were shaking⟩ **2 ~ de** : around, approximately ⟨alrededor de quince personas : around fifteen people⟩
alrededor[2] *prep* **~ de** : around, about
⟨corrió alrededor de la casa : she ran
around the house⟩ ⟨llegaré alrededor
de diciembre : I will get there around
December⟩
alrededores *nmpl* ALEDAÑOS : surroundings, outskirts
alta *nf* **1** : admission, entry, enrollment
2 dar de alta : to release, to discharge
(a patient)
altanería *nf* ALTIVEZ, ARROGANCIA : arrogance, haughtiness
altanero, -ra *adj* ALTIVO, ARROGANTE
: arrogant, haughty — **altaneramente**
adv
altar *nm* : altar
altavoz *nm, pl* **-voces** ALTOPARLANTE
: loudspeaker
alteración *nf, pl* **-ciones 1** MODIFI-
CACIÓN : alteration, modification **2**
PERTURBACIÓN : disturbance, disruption
alterado, -da *adj* : upset
alterar *vt* **1** MODIFICAR : to alter, to
modify **2** PERTURBAR : to disturb, to
disrupt — **alterarse** *vr* : to get upset,
to get worked up
altercado *nm* DISCUSIÓN, DISPUTA : altercation, argument, dispute
alternador *nm* : alternator
alternancia *nf* : alternation, rotation
alternar *vi* **1** : to alternate **2** : to mix,
to socialize — *vt* : to alternate — **al-
ternarse** *vr* : to take turns
alternativa *nf* OPCIÓN : alternative, option
alternativo, -va *adj* **1** : alternating **2** : alternative — **alternativamente** *adv*
alterno, -na *adj* : alternate ⟨corriente alterna : alternating current⟩
alteza *nf* **1** : loftiness, lofty height **2 Alteza** : Highness
altibajos *nmpl* **1** : unevenness (of terrain) **2** : ups and downs
altímetro *nm* : altimeter
altiplanicie *nf* → **altiplano**
altiplano *nm* : high plateau, upland
altisonante *adj* **1** : pompous, affected
(of language) **2** *Mex* : rude, obscene
(of language)
altitud *nf* : altitude

altivez *nf, pl* **-veces** ALTANERÍA, ARRO-
GANCIA : arrogance, haughtiness
altivo, -va *adj* ALTANERO, ARROGANTE
: arrogant, haughty
alto[1] *adv* **1** : high **2** : loud, loudly
alto[2], **-ta** *adj* **1** : tall, high **2** : loud ⟨en
voz alta : aloud, out loud⟩
alto[3] *nm* **1** ALTURA : height, elevation
2 : stop, halt **3 altos** *nmpl* : upper floors
alto[4] *interj* : halt!, stop!
altoparlante *nm* ALTAVOZ : loudspeaker
altozano *nm* : hillock
altruismo *nm* : altruism
altruista[1] *adj* : altruistic
altruista[2] *nmf* : altruist
altura *nf* **1** : height **2** : altitude **3** : loftiness, nobleness **4 a la altura de** : near,
up by ⟨en la avenida San Antonio a la
altura de la Calle Tres : on San Antonio Avenue up near Third Street⟩ **5 a
estas alturas** : at this point, at this
stage of the game
alubia *nf* : kidney bean
alucinación *nf, pl* **-ciones** : hallucination
alucinante *adj* : hallucinatory
alucinar *vi* : to hallucinate
alucinógeno[1], **-na** *adj* : hallucinogenic
alucinógeno[2] *nm* : hallucinogen
alud *nm* AVALANCHA : avalanche, landslide
aludido, -da *n* **1** : person in question ⟨el
aludido : the aforesaid⟩ **2 darse por
aludido** : to take it personally
aludir *vi* : to allude, to refer
alumbrado *nm* ILUMINACIÓN : lighting
alumbramiento *nm* **1** : lighting **2**
: childbirth
alumbrar *vt* **1** ILUMINAR : to light, to illuminate **2** : to give birth to
alumbre *nm* : alum
aluminio *nm* : aluminum
alumnado *nm* : student body
alumno, -na *n* **1** : pupil, student **2**
ex–alumno, -na : alumnus, alumna *f* **3**
ex–alumnos, -nas *npl* : alumni, alum-
nae *f*
alusión *nf, pl* **-siones** : allusion, reference
alusivo, -va *adj* **1** : allusive **2** ∼ **a** : in
reference to, regarding
aluvión *nm, pl* **-viones** : flood, barrage
alza *nf* SUBIDA : rise ⟨precios en alza
: rising prices⟩
alzamiento *nm* LEVANTAMIENTO : uprising, insurrection
alzar {21} *vt* **1** ELEVAR, LEVANTAR : to
lift, to raise **2** : to erect — **alzarse** *vr*
LEVANTARSE : to rise up
ama *nf* → **amo**
amabilidad *nf* : kindness
amable *adj* : kind, nice — **amablemente**
adv
amado[1], **-da** *adj* : beloved, darling
amado[2], **-da** *n* : sweetheart, loved one
amaestrar *vt* : to train (animals)
amafiarse *vr Mex fam* : to conspire, to
be in cahoots

amagar {52} *vt* **1** : to show signs of (an
illness, etc.) **2** : to threaten — *vi* **1** : to
be imminent, to threaten **2** : to feint,
to dissemble
amago *nm* **1** AMENAZA : threat **2** : sign,
hint
amainar *vi* : to abate, to ease up, to die
down
amalgama *nf* : amalgam
amalgamar *vt* : to amalgamate, to unite
amamantar *v* : to breast-feed, to nurse,
to suckle
amanecer[1] {53} *v impers* **1** : to dawn **2**
: to begin to show, to appear **3** : to
wake up (in the morning)
amanecer[2] *nm* ALBA : dawn, daybreak
amanerado, -da *adj* : affected, mannered
amansar *vt* **1** : to tame **2** : to soothe, to
calm down — **amansarse** *vr*
amante[1] *adj* : loving, fond
amante[2] *nmf* : lover
amañar *vt* : to rig, to fix, to tamper with
— **amañarse** *vr* **amañárselas** : to manage
amaño *nm* **1** : skill, dexterity **2** : trick,
ruse
amapola *nf* : poppy
amar *vt* : to love — **amarse** *vr*
amargado, -da *adj* : embittered, bitter
amargar {52} *vt* : to make bitter, to embitter — *vi* : to taste bitter
amargo[1], **-ga** *adj* : bitter — **amargamente** *adv*
amargo[2] *nm* : bitterness, tartness
amargura *nf* **1** : bitterness **2** : grief, sorrow
amarilis *nf* : amaryllis
amarillear *vi* : to yellow, to turn yellow
amarillento, -ta *adj* : yellowish
amarillismo *nm* : yellow journalism,
sensationalism
amarillo[1], **-lla** *adj* : yellow
amarillo[2] *nm* : yellow
amarra *nf* **1** : mooring, mooring line **2
soltar las amarras de** : to loosen one's
grip on
amarrar *vt* **1** : to moor (a boat) **2** ATAR
: to fasten, to tie up, to tie down
amartillar *vt* : to cock (a gun)
amasar *vt* **1** : to amass **2** : to knead **3**
: to mix, to prepare
amasijo *nm* : jumble, hodgepodge
amasio, -sia *n* : lover, paramour
amateur *adj & nmf* : amateur — **ama-
teurismo** *nm*
amatista *nf* : amethyst
amatorio, -ria *adj* : amatory, sexual
⟨poesía amatoria : love poems⟩
amazona *nf* **1** : Amazon (in mythology)
2 : horsewoman
amazónico, -ca *adj* : amazonian
ambages *nmpl sin* ∼ : without hesitation, straight to the point
ámbar *nm* **1** : amber **2 ámbar gris** : ambergris
ambición *nf, pl* **-ciones** : ambition
ambicionar *vt* : to aspire to, to seek

ambicioso, -sa *adj* : ambitious — **ambiciosamente** *adv*
ambidextro, -tra *adj* : ambidextrous
ambientación *nf, pl* -**ciones** : setting, atmosphere
ambiental *adj* : environmental — **ambientalmente** *adv*
ambientalista *nmf* : environmentalist
ambientar *vt* : to give atmosphere to, to set (in literature and drama) — **ambientarse** *vr* : to adjust, to get one's bearings
ambiente *nm* 1 : atmosphere 2 : environment 3 : surroundings *pl*
ambigüedad *nf* : ambiguity
ambiguo, -gua *adj* : ambiguous
ámbito *nm* : domain, field, area
ambivalencia *nf* : ambivalence
ambivalente *adj* : ambivalent
ambos, -bas *adj & pron* : both
ambulancia *nf* : ambulance
ambulante *adj* 1 : traveling, itinerant 2 **vendedor ambulante** : street vendor
ameba *nf* : amoeba
amedrentar *vt* : to frighten, to intimidate — **amedrentarse** *vr*
amén *nm* 1 : amen 2 ~ **de** : in addition to, besides 3 **en un decir amén** : in an instant
amenaza *nf* : threat, menace
amenazador, -dora *adj* : threatening, menacing
amenazante → **amenazador**
amenazar {21} *v* : to threaten
amenguar {10} *vt* 1 : to diminish 2 : to belittle, to dishonor
amenidad *nf* : pleasantness, amenity
amenizar {21} *vt* 1 : to make pleasant 2 : to brighten up, to add life to
ameno, -na *adj* : agreeable, pleasant
amento *nm* : catkin
americano, -na *adj & n* : American
amerindio, -dia *adj & n* : Amerindian
ameritar *vt* MERECER : to deserve
ametralladora *nf* : machine gun
amianto *nm* : asbestos
amiba → **ameba**
amigable *adj* : friendly, amicable — **amigablemente** *adv*
amígdala *nf* : tonsil
amigdalitis *nf* : tonsilitis
amigo¹, -ga *adj* : friendly, close
amigo², -ga *n* : friend
amigote *nm* : crony, pal
amilanar *vt* 1 : to frighten 2 : to daunt, to discourage — **amilanarse** *vr* : to lose heart
aminoácido *nm* : amino acid
aminorar *vt* : to reduce, to lessen — *vi* : to diminish
amistad *nf* : friendship
amistoso, -sa *adj* : friendly — **amistosamente** *adv*
amnesia *nf* : amnesia
amnésico, -ca *adj & n* : amnesiac, amnesic
amnistía *nf* : amnesty
amnistiar {85} *vt* : to grant amnesty to

amo, ama *n* 1 : master *m*, mistress *f* 2 : owner, keeper (of an animal) 3 **ama de casa** : housewife 4 **ama de llaves** : housekeeper
amodorrado, -da *adj* : drowsy
amolar {19} *vt* 1 : to grind, to sharpen 2 : to pester, to annoy
amoldable *adj* : adaptable
amoldar *vt* 1 : to mold 2 : to adapt, to adjust — **amoldarse** *vr*
amonestación *nf, pl* -**ciones** 1 APERCIBIMIENTO : admonition, warning 2 **amonestaciones** *nfpl* : banns
amonestar *vt* APERCIBIR : to admonish, to warn
amoníaco *or* amoniaco *nm* : ammonia
amontonamiento *nm* : accumulation, piling up
amontonar *vt* 1 APILAR : to pile up, to heap up 2 : to collect, to gather 3 : to hoard — **amontonarse** *vr*
amor *nm* 1 : love 2 : loved one, beloved 3 **amor propio** : self-esteem 4 **hacer el amor** : to make love
amoral *adj* : amoral
amoratado, -da *adj* : black-and-blue, bruised, livid
amordazar {21} *vt* 1 : to gag, to muzzle 2 : to silence
amorfo, -fa *adj* : shapeless, amorphous
amorío *nm* : love affair, fling
amoroso, -sa *adj* 1 : loving, affectionate 2 : amorous ⟨una mirada amorosa : an amorous glance⟩ 3 : charming, cute — **amorosamente** *adv*
amortiguación *nf* : cushioning, absorption
amortiguador *nm* : shock absorber
amortiguar {10} *vt* : to soften (an impact)
amortizar {21} *vt* : to amortize, to pay off — **amortización** *nf*
amotinado¹, -da *adj* : rebellious, insurgent, mutinous
amotinado², -da *n* : rebel, insurgent, mutineer
amotinamiento *nm* : uprising, rebellion
amotinar *vt* : to incite (to riot), to agitate — **amotinarse** *vr* 1 : to riot, to rebel 2 : to mutiny
amparar *vt* : to safeguard, to protect — **ampararse** *vr* 1 ~ **de** : to take shelter from 2 ~ **en** : to have recourse to
amparo *nm* ACOGIDA, REFUGIO : protection, refuge
amperímetro *nm* : ammeter
amperio *nm* : ampere
ampliable *adj* : expandable, enlargeable, extendible
ampliación *nf, pl* -**ciones** : expansion, extension
ampliar {85} *vt* 1 : to expand, to extend 2 : to widen 3 : to enlarge (photographs) 4 : to elaborate on, to develop (ideas)
amplificador *nm* : amplifier
amplificar {72} *vt* : to amplify — **amplificación** *nf*

amplio, -plia *adj* : broad, wide, ample —
ampliamente *adj*
amplitud *nf* **1** : breadth, extent **2** : spaciousness
ampolla *nf* **1** : blister **2** : vial, ampoule
ampollar *vt* : to blister — **ampollarse** *vr*
ampolleta *nf* **1** : small vial **2** : hourglass
3 *Chile* : light bulb
ampulosidad *nf* : pompousness, bombast
ampuloso, -sa *adj* GRANDILOCUENTE
: pompous, bombastic — **ampulosamente** *adv*
amputar *vt* : to amputate — **amputación** *nf*
amueblar *vt* : to furnish
amuleto *nm* TALISMÁN : amulet, charm
amurallar *vt* : to wall in, to fortify
anacardo *nm* : cashew nut
anaconda *nf* : anaconda
anacrónico, -ca *adj* : anachronistic
anacronismo *nm* : anachronism
ánade *nmf* **1** : duck **2 ánade real** : mallard
anagrama *nm* : anagram
anal *adj* : anal
anales *nmpl* : annals
analfabetismo *nm* : illiteracy
analfabeto, -ta *adj & n* : illiterate
analgésico¹, -ca *adj* : analgesic, painkilling
analgésico² *nm* : painkiller, analgesic
análisis *nm* : analysis
analista *nmf* **1** : analyst **2** : annalist
analítico, -ca *adj* : analytical, analytic
— **analíticamente** *adv*
analizar {21} *vt* : to analyze
analogía *nf* : analogy
analógico, -ca *adj* **1** : analogical **2** : analog ⟨computadora analógica : analog computer⟩
análogo, -ga *adj* : analogous, similar
ananá *or* **ananás** *nm, pl* **-nás** : pineapple
anaquel *nm* REPISA : shelf
anaranjado¹, -da *adj* NARANJA : orange-colored
anaranjado² *nm* NARANJA : orange (color)
anarquía *nf* : anarchy
anárquico, -ca *adj* : anarchic
anarquismo *nm* : anarchism
anarquista *adj & nmf* : anarchist
anatema *nm* : anathema
anatomía *nf* : anatomy — **anatomista** *nmf*
anatómico, -ca *adj* : anatomical — **anatómicamente** *adv*
anca *nf* **1** : haunch, hindquarter **2 ancas de rana** : frogs' legs
ancestral *adj* **1** : ancient, traditional **2** : ancestral
ancestro *nm* ASCENDIENTE : ancestor, forefather *m*
ancho¹, -cha *adj* **1** : wide, broad **2** : ample, loose-fitting
ancho² *nm* : width, breadth
anchoa *nf* : anchovy

anchura *nf* : width, breadth
ancianidad *nf* SENECTUD : old age
anciano¹, -na *adj* : aged, old, elderly
anciano², -na *n* : elderly person
ancla *nf* : anchor
ancladero → **anclaje**
anclaje *nm* : anchorage
anclar *v* FONDEAR : to anchor
andadas *nfpl* **1** : tracks **2 volver a las andadas** : to go back to one's old ways, to backslide
andador¹ *nm* **1** : walker, baby walker **2** *Mex* : walkway
andador², -dora *n* : walker, one who walks
andadura *nf* : course, journey ⟨su agotadora andadura al campeonato : his exhausting journey to the championship⟩
andaluz, -luza *adj & n, mpl* **-luces** : Andalusian
andamiaje *nm* **1** : scaffolding **2** ESTRUCTURA : structure, framework
andamio *nm* : scaffold
andanada *nf* **1** : volley, broadside **2 soltar una andanada a** : to reprimand
andanzas *nfpl* : adventures
andar¹ {6} *vi* **1** CAMINAR : to walk **2** IR
: to go, to travel **3** FUNCIONAR : to run, to function ⟨el auto anda bien : the car runs well⟩ **4** : to ride ⟨andar a caballo : to ride on horseback⟩ **5** : to be ⟨anda sin dinero : he's broke⟩ — *vt* : to walk, to travel
andar² *nm* : walk, gait
andas *nfpl* : stand (for a coffin), bier
andén *nm, pl* **andenes** **1** : (train) platform **2** *CA, Col* : sidewalk
andino, -na *adj* : Andean
andorrano, -na *adj & n* : Andorran
andrajos *nmpl* : rags, tatters
andrajoso, -sa *adj* : ragged, tattered
andrógino, -na *adj* : androgynous
andurriales *nmpl* : remote place
anea *nf* : cattail
anécdota *nf* : anecdote
anecdótico, -ca *adj* : anecdotal
anegar {52} *vt* **1** INUNDAR : to flood **2** AHOGAR : to drown **3** : to overwhelm
— **anegarse** *vr* : to be flooded
anejo *nm* → **anexo²**
anemia *nf* : anemia
anémico, -ca *adj* : anemic
anémona *nf* : anemone
anestesia *nf* : anesthesia
anestesiar *vt* : to anesthetize
anestésico¹, -ca *adj* : anesthetic
anestésico² *nm* : anesthetic
anestesista *nmf* : anesthetist
aneurisma *nmf* : aneurysm
anexar *vt* : to annex, to attach
anexión *nf, pl* **-xiones** : annexation
anexo¹, -xa *adj* : attached, joined, annexed
anexo² *nm* **1** : annex **2** : supplement (to a book), appendix
anfetamina *nf* : amphetamine

anfibio¹, -bia *adj* : amphibious
anfibio² *nm* : amphibian
anfiteatro *nm* **1** : amphitheater **2** : lecture hall
anfitrión, -triona *n, mpl* **-triones** : host, hostess *f*
ánfora *nf* **1** : amphora **2** *Mex, Peru* : ballot box
ángel *nm* : angel
angelical *adj* : angelic, angelical
angélico, -ca *adj* → **angelical**
angina *nf* **1** *or* **angina de pecho** : angina **2** *Mex* : tonsil
anglicano, -na *adj & n* : Anglican
angloparlante¹ *adj* : English-speaking
angloparlante² *nmf* : English speaker
anglosajón, -jona *adj & n, mpl* **-jones** : Anglo-Saxon
angoleño, -ña *adj & n* : Angolan
angora *nf* : angora
angostar *vt* : to narrow — **angostarse** *vr*
angosto, -ta *adj* : narrow
angostura *nf* : narrowness
anguila *nf* : eel
angular *adj* : angular — **angularidad** *nf*
ángulo *nm* **1** : angle **2** : corner **3** **ángulo muerto** : blind spot
anguloso, -sa *adj* : angular, sharp ⟨una cara angulosa : an angular face⟩ — **angulosidad** *nf*
angustia *nf* **1** CONGOJA : anguish, distress **2** : anxiety, worry
angustiar *vt* **1** : to anguish, to distress **2** : to worry — **angustiarse** *vr*
angustioso, -sa *adj* **1** : anguished, distressed **2** : distressing, worrisome
anhelante *adj* : yearning, longing
anhelar *vt* : to yearn for, to crave
anhelo *nm* : longing, yearning
anidar *vi* **1** : to nest **2** : to make one's home, to dwell — *vt* : to shelter
anillo *nm* SORTIJA : ring
ánima *n* ALMA : soul
animación *nf, pl* **-ciones** **1** : animation **2** VIVEZA : liveliness
animado, -da *adj* **1** : animated, lively **2** : cheerful — **animadamente** *adv*
animador, -dora *n* **1** : (television) host **2** : cheerleader
animadversión *nf, pl* **-siones** ANIMOSIDAD : animosity, antagonism
animal¹ *adj* **1** : animal **2** ESTÚPIDO : stupid, idiotic **3** : rough, brutish
animal² *nm* : animal
animal³ *nmf* **1** IDIOTA : idiot, fool **2** : brute, beastly person
animar *vt* **1** ALENTAR : to encourage, to inspire **2** : to animate, to enliven **3** : to brighten up, to cheer up — **animarse** *vr*
anímico, -ca *adj* : mental ⟨estado anímico : state of mind⟩
ánimo *nm* **1** ALMA : spirit, soul **2** : mood, spirits *pl* **3** : encouragement **4** PROPÓSITO : intention, purpose ⟨sociedad sin ánimo de lucro : nonprofit organization⟩ **5** : energy, vitality

animosidad *nf* ANIMADVERSIÓN : animosity, ill will
animoso, -sa *adj* : brave, spirited
aniñado, -da *adj* : childlike
aniquilación *nf* → **aniquilamiento**
aniquilamiento *nm* : annihilation, extermination
aniquilar *vt* **1** : to annihilate, to wipe out **2** : to overwhelm, to bring to one's knees — **aniquilarse** *vr*
anís *nm* **1** : anise **2 semilla de anís** : aniseed
aniversario *nm* : anniversary
ano *nm* : anus
anoche *adv* : last night
anochecer¹ {53} *v impers* : to get dark
anochecer² *nm* : dusk, nightfall
anodino, -na *adj* : insipid, dull
ánodo *nm* : anode
anomalía *nf* : anomaly
anómalo, -la *adj* : anomalous
anonadado, -da *adj* : dumbfounded, speechless
anonadar *vt* : to dumbfound, to stun
anonimato *nm* : anonymity
anónimo, -ma *adj* : anonymous — **anónimamente** *adv*
anorexia *nf* : anorexia
anoréxico, -ca *adj* : anorexic
anormal *adj* : abnormal — **anormalmente** *adv*
anormalidad *nf* : abnormality
anotación *nf, pl* **-ciones** **1** : annotation, note **2** : scoring (in sports) ⟨lograron una anotación : they managed to score a goal⟩
anotar *vt* **1** : to annotate **2** APUNTAR, ESCRIBIR : to write down, to jot down **3** : to score (in sports) — *vi* : to score
anquilosado, -da *adj* **1** : stiff-jointed **2** : stagnated, stale
anquilosamiento *nm* **1** : stiffness (of joints) **2** : stagnation, paralysis
anquilosarse *vr* **1** : to stagnate **2** : to become stiff or paralyzed
anquilostoma *nm* : hookworm
ánsar *nm* : goose
ansarino *nm* : gosling
ansia *nf* **1** INQUIETUD : apprehensiveness, uneasiness **2** ANGUSTIA : anguish, distress **3** ANHELO : longing, yearning
ansiar {85} *vt* : to long for, to yearn for
ansiedad *nf* : anxiety
ansioso, -sa *adj* **1** : anxious, worried **2** : eager — **ansiosamente** *adv*
antagónico, -ca *adj* : conflicting, opposing
antagonismo *nm* : antagonism
antagonista¹ *adj* : antagonistic
antagonista² *nmf* : antagonist, opponent
antagonizar {21} *vt* : to antagonize
antaño *adv* : yesteryear, long ago
antártico, -ca *adj* **1** : antarctic **2 círculo antártico** : antarctic circle
ante¹ *nm* **1** : elk, moose **2** : suede
ante² *prep* **1** : before, in front of **2** : considering, in view of **3 ante todo** : first and foremost, above all

anteanoche *adv* : the night before last
anteayer *adv* : the day before yesterday
antebrazo *nm* : forearm
antecedente[1] *adj* : previous, prior
antecedente[2] *nm* **1** : precedent **2 antecedentes** *nmpl* : record, background
anteceder *v* : to precede
antecesor, -sora *n* **1** ANTEPASADO : ancestor **2** PREDECESOR : predecessor
antedicho, -cha *adj* : aforesaid, above
antelación *nf, pl* **-ciones 1** : advance notice **2 con ~** : in advance, beforehand
antemano *adv* **de ~** : in advance ⟨se lo agradezco de antemano : I thank you in advance⟩
antena *nf* : antenna
antenoche → **anteanoche**
anteojera *nf* **1** : eyeglass case **2 anteojeras** *nfpl* : blinders
anteojos *nmpl* GAFAS : glasses, eyeglasses
antepasado[1], -da *adj* : before last ⟨el domingo antepasado : the Sunday before last⟩
antepasado[2], -da *n* ANTECESOR : ancestor
antepecho *nm* **1** : guardrail **2** : ledge, sill
antepenúltimo, -ma *adj* : third from last
anteponer {60} *vt* **1** : to place before ⟨anteponer al interés de la nación el interés de la comunidad : to place the interests of the community before national interest⟩ **2** : to prefer
anteproyecto *nm* **1** : draft, proposal **2 anteproyecto de ley** : bill
antera *nf* : anther
anterior *adj* **1** : previous **2** : earlier ⟨tiempos anteriores : earlier times⟩ **3** : anterior, forward, front
anterioridad *nf* **1** : priority **2 con ~** : beforehand, in advance
anteriormente *adv* : previously, beforehand
antes *adv* **1** : before, earlier **2** : formerly, previously **3** : rather, sooner ⟨antes prefiero morir : I'd rather die⟩ **4 ~ de** : before, previous to ⟨antes de hoy : before today⟩ **5 antes que** : before ⟨antes que llegue Luis : before Luis arrives⟩ **6 cuanto antes** : as soon as possible **7 antes bien** : on the contrary
antesala *nf* **1** : anteroom, waiting room, lobby **2** : prelude, prologue
antiaborto, -ta *adj* : antiabortion
antiácido *nm* : antacid
antiadherente *adj* : nonstick
antiaéreo, -rea *adj* : antiaircraft
antiamericano, -na *adj* : anti-American
antibalas *adj* : bulletproof
antibiótico[1], -ca *adj* : antibiotic
antibiótico[2] *nm* : antibiotic
antichoque *adj* : shockproof
anticipación *nf, pl* **-ciones 1** : expectation, anticipation **2 con ~** : in advance

anticipado, -da *adj* **1** : advance, early **2 por ~** : in advance
anticipar *vt* **1** : to anticipate, to forestall, to deal with in advance **2** : to pay in advance — **anticiparse** *vr* **1** : to be early **2** ADELANTARSE : to get ahead
anticipo *nm* **1** : advance (payment) **2** : foretaste, preview
anticlerical *adj* : anticlerical
anticlimático, -ca : anticlimactic
anticlímax *nm* : anticlimax
anticomunismo *nm* : anticommunism
anticomunista *adj & nmf* : anticommunist
anticoncepción *nf, pl* **-ciones** : birth control, contraception
anticonceptivo *nm* : contraceptive
anticongelante *nm* : antifreeze
anticuado, -da *adj* : antiquated, outdated
anticuario[1], -ria *adj* : antique, antiquarian
anticuario[2], -ria *n* : antiquarian, antiquary
anticuario[3] *nm* : antique shop
anticuerpo *nm* : antibody
antidemocrático, -ca *adj* : antidemocratic
antideportivo, -va *adj* : unsportsmanlike
antidepresivo *nm* : antidepressant
antídoto *nm* : antidote
antidrogas *adj* : antidrug
antier → **anteayer**
antiestético, -ca *adj* : unsightly, unattractive
antifascista *adj & nmf* : antifascist
antifaz *nm, pl* **-faces** : mask
antifeminista *adj & nmf* : antifeminist
antífona *nf* : anthem
antígeno *nm* : antigen
antigualla *nf* **1** : antique **2** : relic, old thing
antiguamente *adv* **1** : formerly, once **2** : long ago
antigüedad *nf* **1** : antiquity **2** : seniority **3** : age ⟨con siglos de antigüedad : centuries-old⟩ **4 antigüedades** *nfpl* : antiques
antiguo, -gua *adj* **1** : ancient, old **2** : former **3** : old-fashioned ⟨a la antigua : in the old-fashioned way⟩ **4 Antiguo Testamento** : Old Testament
antihigiénico, -ca *adj* INSALUBRE : unhygienic, unsanitary
antihistamínico *nm* : antihistamine
antiimperialismo *nm* : anti-imperialism
antiimperialista *adj & nmf* : anti-imperialist
antiinflacionario, -ria *adj* : anti-inflationary
antiinflamatorio, -ria *adj* : anti-inflammatory
antillano[1], -na *adj* CARIBEÑO : Caribbean, West Indian
antillano[2], -na *n* : West Indian
antílope *nm* : antelope
antimilitarismo *nm* : antimilitarism

antimilitarista *adj & nmf* : antimilitarist
antimonio *nm* : antimony
antimonopolista *adj* : antimonopoly, antitrust
antinatural *adj* : unnatural, perverse
antipatía *nf* : aversion, dislike
antipático, -ca *adj* : obnoxious, unpleasant
antipatriótico, -ca *adj* : unpatriotic
antirrábico, -ca *adj* : antirabies ⟨vacuna antirrábica : rabies vaccine⟩
antirreglamentario, -ria *adj* 1 : unlawful, illegal 2 : foul (in sports)
antirrevolucionario, -ria *adj & n* : antirevolutionary
antirrobo, -ba *adj* : antitheft
antisemita *adj* : anti-Semitic
antisemitismo *nm* : anti-Semitism
antiséptico¹, -ca *adj* : antiseptic
antiséptico² *nm* : antiseptic
antisocial *adj* : antisocial
antitabaco *adj* : antismoking
antiterrorista *adj* : antiterrorist
antítesis *nf* : antithesis
antitoxina *nf* : antitoxin
antitranspirante *nm* : antiperspirant
antojadizo, -za *adj* CAPRICHOSO : capricious
antojarse *vr* 1 APETECER : to be appealing, to be desirable ⟨se me antoja un helado : I feel like having ice cream⟩ 2 : to seem, to appear ⟨los árboles se antojaban fantasmas : the trees seemed like ghosts⟩
antojitos *nmpl Mex* : traditional Mexican snack foods
antojo *nm* 1 CAPRICHO : whim 2 : craving
antología *nf* 1 : anthology 2 **de ~** *fam* : fantastic, incredible
antónimo *nm* : antonym
antonomasia *nf* **por ~** : par excellence
antorcha *nf* : torch
antracita *nf* : anthracite
antro *nm* 1 : cave, den 2 : dive, seedy nightclub
antropofagia *nf* CANIBALISMO : cannibalism
antropófago¹, -ga *adj* : cannibalistic
antropófago², -ga *n* CANÍBAL : cannibal
antropoide *adj & nmf* : anthropoid
antropología *nf* : anthropology
antropológico, -ca *adj* : anthropological
antropólogo, -ga *n* : anthropologist
anual *adj* : annual, yearly — **anualmente** *adv*
anualidad *nf* : annuity
anuario *nm* : yearbook, annual
anudar *vt* : to knot, to tie in a knot — **anudarse** *vr*
anuencia *nf* : consent
anulación *nf*, *pl* **-ciones** : annulment, nullification
anular *vt* : to annul, to cancel
anunciador, -dora *n* → **anunciante**
anunciante *nmf* : advertiser
anunciar *vt* 1 : to announce 2 : to advertise

anuncio *nm* 1 : announcement 2 : advertisement, commercial
anzuelo *nm* 1 : fishhook 2 **morder el anzuelo** : to take the bait
añadido *nm* : addition
añadidura *nf* 1 : additive, addition 2 **por ~** : in addition, furthermore
añadir *vt* 1 AGREGAR : to add 2 AUMENTAR : to increase
añejar *vt* : to age, to ripen
añejo, -ja *adj* 1 : aged, vintage 2 : age-old, musty, stale
añicos *nmpl* : smithereens, bits ⟨hacer(se) añicos : to shatter⟩
añil *nm* 1 : indigo 2 : bluing
año *nm* 1 : year ⟨en el año 1990 : in (the year) 1990⟩ ⟨tiene diez años : she is ten years old⟩ 2 : grade ⟨cuarto año : fourth grade⟩ 3 **año bisiesto** : leap year 4 **año luz** : light-year 5 **Año Nuevo** : New Year
añoranza *nf* : longing, yearning
añorar *vt* 1 DESEAR : to long for 2 : to grieve for, to miss — *vi* : to mourn, to grieve
añoso, -sa *adj* : aged, old
aorta *nf* : aorta
apabullante *adj* : overwhelming, crushing
apabullar *vt* : to overwhelm
apacentar {55} *vt* : to pasture, to put to pasture
apache *adj & nmf* : Apache
apachurrado, -da *adj fam* : depressed, down
apachurrar *vt* : to crush, to squash
apacible *adj* : gentle, mild, calm — **apaciblemente** *adv*
apaciguador, -dora *adj* : calming
apaciguamiento *nm* : appeasement
apaciguar {10} *vt* APLACAR : to appease, to pacify — **apaciguarse** *vr* : to calm down
apadrinar *vt* 1 : to be a godparent to 2 : to sponsor, to support
apagado, -da *adj* 1 : off, out ⟨la luz está apagada : the light is off⟩ 2 : dull, subdued
apagador *nm Mex* : switch
apagar {52} *vt* 1 : to turn off, to shut off 2 : to extinguish, to put out — **apagarse** *vr* 1 : to go out, to fade 2 : to wane, to die down
apagón *nm, pl* **-gones** : blackout (of power)
apalancamiento *nm* : leverage
apalancar {72} *vt* 1 : to jack up 2 : to pry open
apalear *vt* : to beat up, to thrash
apantallar *vt Mex* : to dazzle, to impress
apañar *vt* 1 : to seize, to grasp 2 : to repair, to mend — **apañarse** *vr* : to manage, to get along
apaño *nm fam* 1 : patch 2 HABILIDAD : skill, knack
apapachar *vt Mex fam* : to cuddle, to caress — **apapacharse** *vr*

aparador *nm* **1** : sideboard, cupboard
2 ESCAPARATE, VITRINA : shop window
aparato *nm* **1** : machine, appliance, apparatus ⟨aparato auditivo : hearing
aid⟩ ⟨aparato de televisión : television
set⟩ **2** : system ⟨aparato digestivo : digestive system⟩ **3** : display, ostentation
⟨sin aparato : without ceremony⟩ **4**
aparatos *nmpl* : braces (for the teeth)
aparatoso, -sa *adj* **1** : ostentatious **2**
: spectacular
aparcamiento *nm Spain* **1** : parking **2**
: parking lot
aparcar {72} *v Spain* : to park
aparcero, -ra *n* : sharecropper
aparear *vt* **1** : to mate (animals) **2** : to
match up — **aparearse** *vr* : to mate
aparecer {53} *vi* **1** : to appear **2** PRE-
SENTARSE : to show up **3** : to turn up,
to be found — **aparecerse** *vr* : to appear
aparejado, -da *adj* **1** ir aparejado con
: to go hand in hand with **2** llevar
aparejado : to entail
aparejar *vt* **1** PREPARAR : to prepare, to
make ready **2** : to harness (a horse) **3**
: to fit out (a ship)
aparejo *nm* **1** : equipment, gear **2** : harness, saddle **3** : rig, rigging (of a ship)
aparentar *vt* **1** : to seem, to appear ⟨no
aparentas tu edad : you don't look your
age⟩ **2** FINGIR : to feign, to pretend
aparente *adj* **1** : apparent **2** : showy,
striking — **aparentemente** *adv*
aparición *nf, pl* **-ciones** **1** : appearance
2 PUBLICACIÓN : publication, release
3 FANTASMA : apparition, vision
apariencia *nf* **1** ASPECTO : appearance,
look **2** en ~ : seemingly, apparently
apartado *nm* **1** : section, paragraph **2**
apartado postal : post office box
apartamento *nm* DEPARTAMENTO
: apartment
apartar *vt* **1** ALEJAR : to move away, to
put at a distance **2** : to put aside, to set
aside, to separate — **apartarse** *vr* **1** : to
step aside, to move away **2** DESVIARSE
: to stray
aparte[1] *adv* **1** : apart, aside ⟨modestia
aparte : if I say so myself⟩ **2** : separately **3** ~ **de** : apart from, besides
aparte[2] *adj* : separate, special
aparte[3] *nm* : aside (in theater)
apartheid *nm* : apartheid
apasionado, -da *adj* : passionate, enthusiastic — **apasionadamente** *adv*
apasionante *adj* : fascinating, exciting
apasionar *vt* : to enthuse, to excite —
apasionarse *vr*
apatía *nf* : apathy
apático, -ca *adj* : apathetic
apearse *vr* **1** DESMONTAR : to dismount
2 : to get out of or off (a vehicle)
apedrear *vt* : to stone, to throw stones
at
apegado, -da *adj* : attached, close, devoted ⟨es muy apegado a su familia : he
is very devoted to his family⟩

apegarse {52} *vr* ~ **a** : to become attached to, to grow fond of
apego *nm* AFICIÓN : attachment, fondness, inclination
apelación *nf, pl* **-ciones** : appeal (in
court)
apelar *vi* **1** : to appeal **2** ~ **a** : to resort
to
apelativo *nm* APELLIDO : last name,
surname
apellidarse *vr* : to have for a last name
⟨¿cómo se apellida? : what is your last
name?⟩
apellido *nm* : last name, surname
apelotonar *vt* : to roll into a ball, to bundle up
apenar *vt* : to aggrieve, to sadden —
apenarse *vr* **1** : to be saddened **2** : to
become embarrassed
apenas[1] *adv* : hardly, scarcely
apenas[2] *conj* : as soon as
apéndice *nm* **1** : appendix **2** : appendage
apendicectomía *nf* : appendectomy
apendicitis *nf* : appendicitis
apercibimiento *nm* **1** : preparation **2**
AMONESTACIÓN : warning
apercibir *vt* **1** DISPONER : to prepare, to
make ready **2** AMONESTAR : to warn
3 OBSERVAR : to observe, to perceive
— **apercibirse** *vr* **1** : to get ready **2** ~
de : to notice
aperitivo *nm* **1** : appetizer **2** : aperitif
apero *nm* : tool, implement
apertura *nf* **1** : opening, aperture **2**
: commencement, beginning **3** : openness
apesadumbrar *vt* : to distress, to sadden
— **apesadumbrarse** *vr* : to be weighed
down
apestar *vt* **1** : to infect with the plague
2 : to corrupt — *vi* **1** : to stink
apestoso, -sa *adj* : stinking, foul
apetecer {53} *vt* **1** : to crave, to long for
⟨apeteció la fama : he longed for fame⟩
2 : to appeal to ⟨me apetece un bistec
: I feel like having a steak⟩ ⟨¿cuándo
te apetece ir? : when do you want to
go?⟩ — *vi* **1** : to be appealing
apetecible *adj* : appetizing, appealing
apetito *nm* : appetite
apetitoso, -sa *adj* : appetizing
apiario *nm* : apiary
ápice *nm* **1** : apex, summit **2** PIZCA : bit,
smidgen
apicultor, -tora *n* : beekeeper
apicultura *nf* : beekeeping
apilar *vt* AMONTONAR : to heap up, to
pile up — **apilarse** *vr*
apiñado, -da *adj* : jammed, crowded
apiñar *vt* : to pack, to cram — **apiñarse**
vr : to crowd together, to huddle
apio *nm* : celery
apisonadora *nf* : steamroller
apisonar *vt* : to pack down, to tamp
aplacamiento *nm* : appeasement
aplacar {72} *vt* APACIGUAR : to appease,
to placate — **aplacarse** *vr* : to calm
down

aplanadora *nf* : steamroller
aplanar *vt* : to flatten, to level
aplastante *adj* : crushing, overwhelming
aplastar *vt* : to crush, to squash
aplaudir *v* : to applaud
aplauso *nm* 1 : applause, clapping 2 : praise, acclaim
aplazamiento *nm* : postponement
aplazar {21} *vt* : to postpone, to defer
aplicable *adj* : applicable — **aplicabilidad** *nf*
aplicación *nf, pl* -**ciones** 1 : application 2 : diligence, dedication
aplicado, -da *adj* : diligent, industrious
aplicador *nm* : applicator
aplicar {72} *vt* : to apply — **aplicarse** *vr* : to apply oneself
aplique *or* **apliqué** *nm* : appliqué
aplomar *vt* : to plumb, to make vertical
aplomo *nm* : aplomb, composure
apocado, -da *adj* : timid
apocalipsis *nms & pl* : apocalypse ⟨el Libro del Apocalipsis : the Book of Revelation⟩
apocalíptico, -ca *adj* : apocalyptic
apocamiento *nm* : timidity
apocarse {72} *vr* 1 : to shy away, to be intimidated 2 : to humble oneself, to sell oneself short
apócrifo, -fa *adj* : apocryphal
apodar *vt* : to nickname, to call — **apodarse** *vr*
apoderado, -da *n* : proxy, agent
apoderar *vt* : to authorize, to empower — **apoderarse** *vr* ~ **de** : to seize, to take over
apodo *nm* SOBRENOMBRE : nickname
apogeo *nm* : acme, peak, zenith
apología *nf* : defense, apology
apoplejía *nf* : apoplexy, stroke
apoplético, -ca *adj* : apoplectic
aporrear *vt* : to bang on, to beat, to bludgeon
aportación *nf, pl* -**ciones** : contribution
aportar *vt* CONTRIBUIR : to contribute, to provide
aporte *nm* → **aportación**
apostador, -dora *n* : bettor, better
apostar {19} *v* : to bet, to wager ⟨apuesto que no viene : I bet he's not coming⟩
apostasía *nf* : apostasy
apóstata *nmf* : apostate
apostilla *nf* : note
apostillar *vt* : to annotate
apóstol *nm* : apostle
apostólico, -ca *adj* : apostolic
apóstrofe *nmf* : apostrophe
apostura *nf* : elegance, gracefulness
apoyacabezas *nms & pl* : headrest
apoyapiés *nms & pl* : footrest
apoyar *vt* 1 : to support, to back 2 : to lean, to rest — **apoyarse** *vr* 1 ~ **en** : to lean on 2 ~ **en** : to be based on, to rest on
apoyo *nm* : support, backing
apreciable *adj* : appreciable, substantial, considerable

apreciación *nf, pl* -**ciones** 1 : appreciation 2 : appraisal, evaluation
apreciar *vt* 1 ESTIMAR : to appreciate, to value 2 EVALUAR : to appraise, to assess — **apreciarse** *vr* : to appreciate, to increase in value
aprecio *nm* 1 ESTIMO : esteem, appreciation 2 EVALUACIÓN : appraisal, assessment
aprehender *vt* 1 : to apprehend, to capture 2 : to conceive of, to grasp
aprehensión *nf, pl* -**siones** : apprehension, capture, arrest
apremiante *adj* : pressing, urgent
apremiar *vt* INSTAR : to pressure, to urge — *vi* URGIR : to be urgent ⟨el tiempo apremia : time is of the essence⟩
apremio *nm* : pressure, urgency
aprender *v* : to learn — **aprenderse** *vr*
aprendiz, -diza *n, mpl* -**dices** : apprentice, trainee
aprendizaje *nm* : apprenticeship
aprensión *nf, pl* -**siones** : apprehension, dread
aprensivo, -va *adj* : apprehensive, worried
apresamiento *nm* : seizure, capture
apresar *vt* : to capture, to seize
aprestar *vt* : to make ready, to prepare — **aprestarse** *vr* : to get ready
apresuradamente *adv* 1 : hurriedly 2 : hastily, too fast
apresurado, -da *adj* : hurried, in a rush
apresuramiento *nm* : hurry, haste
apresurar *vt* : to quicken, to speed up — **apresurarse** *vr* : to hurry up, to make haste
apretado, -da *adj* 1 : tight 2 *fam* : cheap, tightfisted — **apretadamente** *adv*
apretar {55} *vt* 1 : to press, to push (a button) 2 : to tighten 3 : to squeeze — *vi* 1 : to press, to push 2 : to fit tightly, to be too tight ⟨los zapatos me aprietan : my shoes are tight⟩
apretón *nm, pl* -**tones** 1 : squeeze 2 **apretón de manos** : handshake
apretujar *vt* : to squash, to squeeze — **apretujarse** *vr*
aprieto *nm* APURO : predicament, difficulty ⟨estar en un aprieto : to be in a fix⟩
aprisa *adv* : quickly, hurriedly
aprisionar *vt* 1 : to imprison 2 : to trap, to box in
aprobación *nf, pl* -**ciones** : approval, endorsement
aprobar {19} *vt* 1 : to approve of 2 : to pass (a law, an exam) — *vi* : to pass (in school)
aprobatorio, -ria *adj* : approving
apropiación *nf, pl* -**ciones** : appropriation
apropiado, -da *adj* : appropriate, proper, suitable — **apropiadamente** *adv*
apropiarse *vr* ~ **de** : to take possession of, to appropriate
aprovechable *adj* : usable

aprovechado[1], **-da** *adj* **1** : diligent, hardworking **2** : pushy, opportunistic

aprovechado[2], **-da** *n* : pushy person, opportunist

aprovechamiento *nm* : use, exploitation

aprovechar *vt* : to take advantage of, to make good use of — *vi* **1** : to be of use **2** : to progress, to improve — **aprovecharse** *vr* ~ **de** : to take advantage of, to exploit

aprovisionamiento *nm* : provisions *pl*, supplies *pl*

aprovisionar *vt* : to provide, to supply (with provisions)

aproximación *nf*, *pl* **-ciones 1** : approximation, estimate **2** : rapprochement

aproximado, -da *adj* : approximate, estimated — **aproximadamente** *adv*

aproximar *vt* ACERCAR, ARRIMAR : to approximate, to bring closer — **aproximarse** *vr* ACERCARSE, ARRIMARSE : to approach, to move closer

aptitud *nf* : aptitude, capability

apto, -ta *adj* **1** : suitable, suited, fit **2** HÁBIL : capable, competent

apuesta *nf* : bet, wager

apuesto, -ta *adj* : elegant, good-looking

apuntador, -dora *n* : prompter

apuntalar *vt* : to prop up, to shore up

apuntar *vt* **1** : to aim, to point **2** ANOTAR : to write down, to jot down **3** INDICAR, SEÑALAR : to point to, to point out **4** : to prompt (in the theater) — *vi* **1** : to take aim **2** : to become evident — **apuntarse** *vr* **1** : to sign up, to enroll **2** : to score

apunte *nm* : note

apuñalar *vt* : to stab

apuradamente *adv* **1** : with difficulty **2** : hurriedly, hastily

apurado, -da *adj* **1** APRESURADO : rushed, pressured **2** : poor, needy **3** : difficult, awkward **4** : embarrassed

apurar *vt* **1** APRESURAR : to hurry, to rush **2** : to use up, to exhaust **3** : to trouble — **apurarse** *vr* **1** APRESURARSE : to hurry up **2** PREOCUPARSE : to worry

apuro *nm* **1** APRIETO : predicament, jam **2** : rush, hurry **3** : embarrassment

aquejar *vt* : to afflict

aquel, aquella *adj*, *mpl* **aquellos** : that, those

aquél, aquélla *pron*, *mpl* **aquéllos 1** : that (one), those (ones) **2** : the former

aquello *pron* (*neuter*) : that, that matter, that business ⟨aquello fue algo serio : that was something serious⟩

aquí *adv* **1** : here **2** : now ⟨de aquí en adelante : from now on⟩ **3 por** ~ : around here, hereabouts

aquiescencia *nf* : acquiescence, approval

aquietar *vt* : to allay, to calm — **aquietarse** *vr* : to calm down

aquilatar *vt* **1** : to assay **2** : to assess, to size up

ara *nf* **1** : altar **2 en aras de** : in the interests of, for the sake of

árabe[1] *adj & nmf* : Arab, Arabian

árabe[2] *nm* : Arabic (language)

arabesco *nm* : arabesque — **arabesco, -ca** *adj*

arábigo, -ga *adj* **1** : Arabic, Arabian **2 número arábigo** : Arabic numeral

arable *adj* : arable

arado *nm* : plow

aragonés, -nesa *adj & n*, *mpl* **-neses** : Aragonese

arancel *nm* : tariff, duty

arándano *nm* : blueberry

arandela *nf* : washer (for a faucet, etc.)

araña *nf* **1** : spider **2** : chandelier

arañar *v* : to scratch, to claw

arañazo *nm* : scratch

arar *v* : to plow

arbitraje *nm* **1** : arbitration **2** : refereeing (in sports)

arbitrar *v* **1** : to arbitrate **2** : to referee, to umpire

arbitrariedad *nf* **1** : arbitrariness **2** INJUSTICIA : injustice, wrong

arbitrario, -ria *adj* **1** : arbitrary **2** : unfair, unjust — **arbitrariamente** *adv*

arbitrio *nm* **1** ALBEDRÍO : will **2** JUICIO : judgment

árbitro, -tra *n* **1** : arbitrator, arbiter **2** : referee, umpire

árbol *nm* **1** : tree **2 árbol genealógico** : family tree

arbolado[1], **-da** *adj* : wooded

arbolado[2] *nm* : woodland

arboleda *nf* : grove, wood

arbóreo, -rea *adj* : arboreal

arbusto *nm* : shrub, bush, hedge

arca *nf* **1** : ark **2** : coffer, chest

arcada *nf* **1** : arcade, series of arches **2 arcadas** *nfpl* : retching ⟨hacer arcadas : to retch⟩

arcaico, -ca *adj* : archaic

arcángel *nm* : archangel

arcano, -na *adj* : arcane

arce *nm* : maple tree

arcén *nm*, *pl* **arcenes** : hard shoulder, berm

archidiócesis *nfs & pl* : archdiocese

archipiélago *nm* : archipelago

archivador *nm* : filing cabinet

archivar *vt* **1** : to file **2** : to archive

archivero, -ra *n* : archivist

archivista *nmf* : archivist

archivo *nm* **1** : file **2** : archive, archives *pl*

arcilla *nf* : clay

arco *nm* **1** : arch, archway **2** : bow (in archery) **3** : arc **4** : wicket (in croquet) **5** PORTERÍA : goal, goalposts *pl* **6 arco iris** : rainbow

arder *vi* **1** : to burn ⟨el bosque está ardiendo : the forest is in flames⟩ ⟨arder de ira : to burn with anger, to be seething⟩ **2** : to smart, to sting, to burn ⟨le ardía el estómago : he had heartburn⟩

ardid *nm* : scheme, ruse

ardiente *adj* **1** : burning **2** : ardent, passionate — **ardientemente** *adv*
ardilla *nf* **1** : squirrel **2** *or* **ardilla listada** : chipmunk
ardor *nm* **1** : heat **2** : passion, ardor
ardoroso, -sa *adj* : heated, impassioned
arduo, -dua *adj* : arduous, grueling — **arduamente** *adv*
área *nf* : area
arena *nf* **1** : sand ⟨arena movediza : quicksand⟩ **2** : arena
arenga *nf* : harangue, lecture
arengar {52} *vt* : to harangue, to lecture
arenilla *nf* **1** : fine sand **2 arenillas** *nfpl* : kidney stones
arenisca *nf* : sandstone
arenoso, -sa *adj* : sandy, gritty
arenque *nm* : herring
arepa *nf* : cornmeal bread
arete *nm* : earring
argamasa *nf* : mortar (cement)
argelino, -na *adj & n* : Algerian
argentino, -na *adj & n* : Argentinian, Argentine
argolla *nf* : hoop, ring
argón *nm* : argon
argot *nm* : slang
argucia *nf* : sophistry, subtlety
argüir {41} *vi* : to argue — *vt* **1** ARGUMENTAR : to contend, to argue **2** INFERIR : to deduce **3** PROBAR : to prove
argumentación *nf, pl* **-ciones** : line of reasoning, argument
argumentar *vt* : to argue, to contend
argumento *nm* **1** : argument, reasoning **2** : plot, story line
aria *nf* : aria
aridez *nf, pl* **-deces** : aridity, dryness
árido, -da *adj* : arid, dry
Aries *nmf* : Aries
ariete *nm* : battering ram
arisco, -ca *adj* : surly, sullen, unsociable
arista *nf* **1** : ridge, edge **2** : beard (of a plant) **3 aristas** *nfpl* : rough edges, complications, problems
aristocracia *nf* : aristocracy
aristócrata *nmf* : aristocrat
aristocrático, -ca *adj* : aristocratic
aritmética *nf* : arithmetic
aritmético, -ca *adj* : arithmetic, arithmetical — **aritméticamente** *adv*
arlequín *nm, pl* **-quines** : harlequin
arma *nf* **1** : weapon **2 armas** *nfpl* : armed forces **3 arma de fuego** : firearm
armada *nf* : navy, fleet
armadillo *nm* : armadillo
armado, -da *adj* **1** : armed **2** : assembled, put together **3** *PRi* : obstinate, stubborn
armador, -dora *n* : shipowner
armadura *nf* **1** : armor **2** ARMAZÓN : skeleton, framework
armamento *nm* : armament, arms *pl*, weaponry
armar *vt* **1** : to assemble, to put together **2** : to create, to cause ⟨armar un es-

cándalo : to cause a scene⟩ **3** : to arm — **armarse** *vr* **armarse de valor** : to steel oneself
armario *nm* **1** CLÓSET, ROPERO : closet **2** ALACENA : cupboard
armatoste *nm fam* : monstrosity, contraption
armazón *nmf, pl* **-zones 1** ESQUELETO : framework, skeleton ⟨armazón de acero : steel framework⟩ **2** : frames *pl* (of eyeglasses)
armenio, -nia *adj & n* : Armenian
armería *nf* **1** : armory **2** : arms museum **3** : gunsmith's shop **4** : gunsmith's craft
armiño *nm* : ermine
armisticio *nm* : armistice
armonía *nf* : harmony
armónica *nf* : harmonica
armónico, -ca *adj* **1** : harmonic **2** : harmonious — **armónicamente** *adv*
armonioso, -sa *adj* : harmonious — **armoniosamente** *adv*
armonizar {21} *vt* **1** : to harmonize **2** : to reconcile — *vi* : to harmonize, to blend together
arnés *nm, pl* **arneses** : harness
aro *nm* **1** : hoop **2** : napkin ring **3** *Arg, Chile, Uru* : earring
aroma *nm* : aroma, scent
aromático, -ca *adj* : aromatic
arpa *nf* : harp
arpegio *nm* : arpeggio
arpía *nf* : shrew, harpy
arpillera *nf* : burlap
arpista *nmf* : harpist
arpón *nm, pl* **arpones** : harpoon — **arponear** *vt*
arquear *vt* : to arch, to bend — **arquearse** *vr* : to bend, to bow
arqueología *nf* : archaeology
arqueológico, -ca *adj* : archaeological
arqueólogo, -ga *n* : archaeologist
arquero, -ra *n* **1** : archer **2** PORTERO : goalkeeper, goalie
arquetípico, -ca *adj* : archetypal
arquetipo *nm* : archetype
arquitecto, -ta *n* : architect
arquitectónico, -ca *adj* : architectural — **aquitectónicamente** *adv*
arquitectura *nf* : architecture
arrabal *nm* **1** : slum **2 arrabales** *nmpl* : outskirts, outlying area
arracada *nf* : hoop earring
arracimarse *vr* : to cluster together
arraigado, -da *adj* : deep-seated, ingrained
arraigar {52} *vi* : to take root, to become established — **arraigarse** *vr*
arraigo *nm* : roots *pl* ⟨con mucho arraigo : deep-rooted⟩
arrancar {72} *vt* **1** : to pull out, to tear out **2** : to pick, to pluck (a flower) **3** : to start (an engine) **4** : to boot (a computer) — *vi* **1** : to start an engine **2** : to get going — **arrancarse** *vr* : to pull out, to pull off

arrancón *nm, pl* **-cones** *Mex* **1** : sudden loud start (of a car) **2 carrera de arrancones** : drag race

arranque *nm* **1** : starter (of a car) **2** ARREBATO : outburst, fit **3 punto de arranque** : beginning, starting point

arrasar *vt* **1** : to level, to smooth **2** : to devastate, to destroy **3** : to fill to the brim

arrastrar *vt* **1** : to drag, to tow **2** : to draw, to attract — *vi* : to hang down, to trail — **arrastrarse** *vr* **1** : to crawl **2** : to grovel

arrastre *nm* **1** : dragging **2** : pull, attraction **3 red de arrastre** : dragnet, trawling net

arrayán *nm, pl* **-yanes 1** MIRTO : myrtle **2 arrayán brabántico** : bayberry, wax myrtle

arrear *vt* : to urge on, to drive — *vi* : to hurry along

arrebatado, -da *adj* **1** PRECIPITADO : impetuous, hotheaded, rash **2** : flushed, blushing

arrebatar *vt* **1** : to snatch, to seize **2** CAUTIVAR : to captivate — **arrebatarse** *vr* : to get carried away (with anger, etc.)

arrebato *nm* ARRANQUE : fit, outburst

arreciar *vi* : to intensify, to worsen

arrecife *nm* : reef

arreglado, -da *adj* **1** : fixed, repaired **2** : settled, sorted out **3** : neat, tidy **4** : smart, dressed-up

arreglar *vt* **1** COMPONER : to repair, to fix **2** : to tidy up ⟨arregla tu cuarto : pick up your room⟩ **3** : to solve, to work out ⟨quiero arreglar este asunto : I want to settle this matter⟩ — **arreglarse** *vr* **1** : to get dressed (up) ⟨arreglarse el pelo : to get one's hair done⟩ **2 arreglárselas** *fam* : to get by, to manage

arreglo *nm* **1** : repair **2** : arrangement **3** : agreement, understanding

arrellanarse *vr* : to settle (in a chair)

arremangarse {52} *vr* : to roll up one's sleeves

arremeter *vi* EMBESTIR : to attack, to charge

arremetida *nf* EMBESTIDA : attack, onslaught

arremolinarse *vr* **1** : to crowd around, to mill about **2** : to swirl (about)

arrendador, -dora *n* **1** : landlord, landlady *f* **2** : tenant, lessee

arrendajo *nm* : jay

arrendamiento *nm* **1** ALQUILER : rental, leasing **2 contrato de arrendamiento** : lease

arrendar {55} *vt* ALQUILAR : to rent, to lease

arrendatario, -ria *n* : tenant, lessee, renter

arreos *nmpl* GUARNICIONES : tack, harness, trappings

arrepentido, -da *adj* : repentant, remorseful

arrepentimiento *nm* : regret, remorse, repentance

arrepentirse {76} *vr* **1** : to regret, to be sorry **2** : to repent

arrestar *vt* DETENER : to arrest, to detain

arresto *nm* **1** DETENCIÓN : arrest **2 arrestos** *nmpl* : boldness, daring

arriar {85} *vt* **1** : to lower (a flag, etc.) **2** : to slacken (a rope, etc.)

arriate *nm Mex, Spain* : bed (for plants), border

arriba *adv* **1** : up, upwards **2** : above, overhead **3** : upstairs **4** ∼ **de** : more than **5 de arriba abajo** : from top to bottom, from head to foot

arribar *vi* **1** : to arrive **2** : to dock, to put into port

arribista *nmf* : parvenu, upstart

arribo *nm* : arrival

arriendo *nm* ARRENDAMIENTO : rent, rental

arriero, -ra *n* : mule driver, muleteer

arriesgado, -da *adj* **1** : risky **2** : bold, daring

arriesgar {52} *vt* : to risk, to venture — **arriesgarse** *vr* : to take a chance

arrimado, -da *n Mex fam* : sponger, freeloader

arrimar *vt* ACERCAR, APROXIMAR : to bring closer, to draw near — **arrimarse** *vr* ACERCARSE, APROXIMARSE : to approach, to get close

arrinconar *vt* **1** ACORRALAR : to corner, to box in **2** : to push aside, to abandon

arroba *nf* : arroba (Spanish unit of measurement)

arrobamiento *nm* : rapture, ecstasy

arrobar *vt* : to enrapture, to enchant — **arrobarse** *vr*

arrocero¹, -ra *adj* : rice

arrocero², -ra *n* : rice grower

arrodillarse *vr* : to kneel (down)

arrogancia *nf* ALTANERÍA, ALTIVEZ : arrogance, haughtiness

arrogante *adj* ALTANERO, ALTIVO : arrogant, haughty

arrogarse {52} *vr* : to usurp, to arrogate

arrojado, -da *adj* : daring, fearless

arrojar *vt* **1** : to hurl, to cast, to throw **2** : to give off, to spew out **3** : to yield, to produce **4** *fam* : to vomit — **arrojarse** *vr* PRECIPITARSE : to throw oneself, to leap

arrojo *nm* : boldness, fearlessness

arrollador, -dora *adj* : sweeping, overwhelming

arrollar *vt* **1** : to sweep away, to carry away **2** : to crush, to overwhelm **3** : to run over (with a vehicle)

arropar *vt* : to clothe, to cover (up) — **arroparse** *vr*

arrostrar *vt* : to confront, to face (up to)

arroyo *nm* **1** RIACHUELO : brook, creek, stream **2** : gutter

arroz *nm, pl* **arroces** : rice

arrozal *nm* : rice field, rice paddy

arruga *nf* : wrinkle, fold, crease

arrugado, -da *adj* : wrinkled, creased, lined

arrugar {52} *vt* : to wrinkle, to crease, to pucker — **arrugarse** *vr*

arruinar *vt* : to ruin, to wreck — **arruinarse** *vr* **1** : to be ruined **2** : to fall into ruin, to go bankrupt

arrullar *vt* : to lull to sleep — *vi* : to coo

arrullo *nm* **1** : lullaby **2** : coo (of a dove)

arrumaco *nm fam* : kissing, cuddling

arrumbar *vt* **1** : to lay aside, to put away **2** : to floor, to leave speechless

arsenal *nm* : arsenal

arsénico *nm* : arsenic

arte *nmf* (*usually m in singular, f in plural*) **1** : art ⟨artes y oficios : arts and crafts⟩ ⟨bellas artes : fine arts⟩ **2** HABILIDAD : skill **3** : cunning, cleverness

artefacto *nm* **1** : artifact **2** DISPOSITIVO : device

artemisa *nf* : sagebrush

arteria *nf* : artery — **arterial** *adj*

arteriosclerosis *nf* : arteriosclerosis, hardening of the arteries

artero, -ra *adj* : wily, crafty

artesanal *adj* : pertaining to crafts or craftsmanship, handmade

artesanía *nf* **1** : craftsmanship **2** : handicrafts *pl*

artesano, -na *n* : artisan, craftsman *m*, craftsperson

artesiano, -na *adj* : artesian ⟨pozo artesiano : artesian well⟩

ártico, -ca *adj* : arctic

articulación *nf, pl* **-ciones** **1** : articulation, pronunciation **2** COYUNTURA : joint

articular *vt* **1** : to articulate, to utter **2** : to connect with a joint **3** : to coordinate, to orchestrate

articulista *nmf* : columnist

artículo *nm* **1** : article, thing **2** : item, feature, report **3 artículo de comercio** : commodity **4 artículos de primera necesidad** : essentials **5 artículos de tocador** : toiletries

artífice *nmf* **1** ARTESANO : artisan **2** : mastermind, architect

artificial *adj* **1** : artificial, man-made **2** : feigned, false — **artificialmente** *adv*

artificio *nm* **1** HABILIDAD : skill **2** APARATO : device, appliance **3** ARDID : artifice, ruse

artificioso, -sa *adj* **1** : skillful **2** : cunning, deceptive

artillería *nf* : artillery

artillero, -ra *n* : artilleryman *m*, gunner

artilugio *nm* : gadget, contraption

artimaña *nf* : ruse, trick

artista *nmf* **1** : artist **2** ACTOR, ACTRIZ : actor, actress *f*

artístico, -ca *adj* : artistic — **artísticamente** *adv*

artrítico, -ca *adj* : arthritic

artritis *nfs & pl* : arthritis

artrópodo *nm* : arthropod

arveja *nf* GUISANTE : pea

arzobispado *nm* : archbishopric

arzobispo *nm* : archbishop

as *nm* : ace

asa *nf* AGARRADERA, ASIDERO : handle, grip

asado¹, -da *adj* : roasted, grilled, broiled

asado² *nm* **1** : roast **2** : barbecued meat **3** : barbecue, cookout

asador *nm* : spit, rotisserie

asaduras *nfpl* : entrails, offal

asalariado¹, -da *adj* : wage-earning, salaried

asalariado², -da *n* : wage earner

asaltante *nmf* **1** : mugger, robber **2** : assailant

asaltar *vt* **1** : to assault **2** : to mug, to rob **3 asaltar al poder** : to seize power

asalto *nm* **1** : assault **2** : mugging, robbery **3** : round (in boxing) **4 asalto al poder** : coup d'etat

asamblea *nf* : assembly, meeting

asambleísta *nmf* : assemblyman *m*, assemblywoman *f*

asar *vt* : to roast, to grill — **asarse** *vr fam* : to roast, to be dying from heat

asbesto *nm* : asbestos

ascendencia *nf* **1** : ancestry, descent **2** ~ **sobre** : influence over

ascendente *adj* : ascending, upward ⟨un curso ascendente : an upward trend⟩

ascender {56} *vt* **1** : to ascend, to rise up **2** : to be promoted ⟨ascendió a gerente : she was promoted to manager⟩ **3** ~ **a** : to amount to, to reach ⟨las deudas ascienden a 20 millones de pesos : the debt amounts to 20 million pesos⟩ — *vt* : to promote

ascendiente¹ *nmf* ANCESTRO : ancestor

ascendiente² *nm* INFLUENCIA : influence, ascendancy

ascensión *nf, pl* **-siones** **1** : ascent, rise **2 Fiesta de la Ascensión** : Ascension Day

ascenso *nm* **1** : ascent, rise **2** : promotion

ascensor *nm* ELEVADOR : elevator

asceta *nmf* : ascetic

ascético, -ca *adj* : ascetic

ascetismo *nm* : asceticism

asco *nm* **1** : disgust ⟨¡qué asco! : that's disgusting!, how revolting!⟩ **2 darle asco (a alguien)** : to sicken, to revolt **3 estar hecho un asco** : to be filthy **4 hacerle ascos a** : to turn up one's nose at

ascua *nf* **1** BRASA : ember **2 estar en ascuas** *fam* : to be on edge

asear *vt* **1** : to wash, to clean **2** : to tidy up — **asearse** *vr*

asechanza *nf* : snare, trap

asechar *vt* : to set a trap for

asediar *vt* **1** SITIAR : to besiege **2** ACOSAR : to harass

asedio *nm* **1** : siege **2** ACOSO : harassment

asegurador¹, -dora *adj* **1** : insuring, assuring **2** : pertaining to insurance

asegurador², **-dora** *n* : insurer, underwriter
aseguradora *nf* : insurance company
asegurar *vt* **1** : to assure **2** : to secure **3** : to insure — **asegurarse** *vr* **1** CERCIORARSE : to make sure **2** : to take out insurance, to insure oneself
asemejar *vt* **1** : to make similar ⟨ese bigote te asemeja a tu abuelo : that mustache makes you look like your grandfather⟩ **2** *Mex* : to be similar to, to resemble — **asemejarse** *vr* ~ **a** : to look like, to resemble
asentaderas *nfpl fam* : bottom, buttocks *pl*
asentado, **-da** *adj* : settled, established
asentamiento *nm* : settlement
asentar {55} *vt* **1** : to lay down, to set down, to place **2** : to settle, to establish **3** *Mex* : to state, to affirm — **asentarse** *vr* **1** : to settle **2** ESTABLECERSE : to settle down, to establish oneself
asentimiento *nm* : assent, consent
asentir {76} *vi* : to consent, to agree
aseo *nm* : cleanliness
aséptico, **-ca** *adj* : aseptic, germ-free
asequible *adj* ACCESIBLE : accessible, attainable
aserción *nf* → **aserto**
aserradero *nm* : sawmill
aserrar {55} *vt* : to saw
aserrín *nm, pl* **-rrines** : sawdust
aserto *nm* : assertion, affirmation
asesinar *vt* **1** : to murder **2** : to assassinate
asesinato *nm* **1** : murder **2** : assassination
asesino¹, **-na** *adj* : murderous, homicidal
asesino², **-na** *n* **1** : murderer, killer **2** : assassin
asesor, **-sora** *n* : advisor, consultant
asesoramiento *nm* : advice, counsel
asesorar *vt* : to advise, to counsel — **asesorarse** *vr* ~ **de** : to consult
asesoría *nf* **1** : consulting, advising **2** : consultant's office
asestar {55} *vt* **1** : to aim, to point (a weapon) **2** : to deliver, to deal (a blow)
aseveración *nf, pl* **-ciones** : assertion, statement
aseverar *vt* : to assert, to state
asexual *adj* : asexual — **asexualmente** *adv*
asfaltado¹, **-da** *adj* : asphalted, paved
asfaltado² *nm* PAVIMENTO : pavement, asphalt
asfaltar *vt* : to pave, to blacktop
asfalto *nm* : asphalt
asfixia *nf* : asphyxia, asphyxiation, suffocation
asfixiar *vt* : to asphyxiate, to suffocate, to smother — **asfixiarse** *vr*
asga, etc. → **asir**
así¹ *adv* **1** : like this, like that **2** : so, thus ⟨así sea : so be it⟩ **3** ~ **de** : so, about so ⟨una caja así de grande : a box about so big⟩ **4 así que** : so, therefore

5 ~ **como** : as well as **6 así así** : so-so, fair
así² *adj* : such, such a ⟨un talento así es inestimable : a talent like that is priceless⟩
así³ *conj* AUNQUE : even if, even though ⟨no irá, así le paguen : he won't go, even if they pay him⟩
asiático¹, **-ca** *adj* : Asian, Asiatic
asiático², **-ca** *n* : Asian
asidero *nm* **1** AGARRADERA, ASA : grip, handle **2** AGARRE : grip, hold
asiduamente *adv* : regularly, frequently
asiduidad *nf* **1** : assiduousness **2** : regularity, frequency
asiduo, **-dua** *adj* **1** : assiduous **2** : frequent, regular
asiento *nm* **1** : seat, chair ⟨asiento trasero : back seat⟩ **2** : location, site
asignación *nf, pl* **-ciones** **1** : allocation **2** : appointment, designation **3** : allowance, pay **4** *PRi* : homework, assignment
asignar *vt* **1** : to assign, to allocate **2** : to appoint
asignatura *nf* MATERIA : subject, course
asilado, **-da** *n* : exile, refugee
asilo *nm* : asylum, refuge, shelter
asimetría *nf* : asymmetry
asimétrico, **-ca** *adj* : asymmetrical, asymmetric
asimilación *nf, pl* **-ciones** : assimilation
asimilar *vt* : to assimilate — **asimilarse** *vr* ~ **a** : to be similar to, to resemble
asimismo *adv* **1** IGUALMENTE : similarly, likewise **2** TAMBIÉN : as well, also
asir {7} *vt* : to seize, to grasp — **asirse** *vr* ~ **a** : to cling to
asistencia *nf* **1** : attendance **2** : assistance **3** : assist (in sports)
asistente¹ *adj* : attending, in attendance
asistente² *nmf* **1** : assistant **2 los asistentes** : those present, those in attendance
asistir *vi* : to attend, to be present ⟨asistir a clase : to attend class⟩ — *vt* : to aid, to assist
asma *nf* : asthma
asmático, **-ca** *adj* : asthmatic
asno *nm* BURRO : ass, donkey
asociación *nf, pl* **-ciones** **1** : association, relationship **2** : society, group, association
asociado¹, **-da** *adj* : associate, associated
asociado², **-da** *n* : associate, partner
asociar *vt* **1** : to associate, to connect **2** : to pool (resources) **3** : to take into partnership — **asociarse** *vr* **1** : to become partners **2** ~ **a** : to join, to become a member of
asolar {19} *vt* : to devastate, to destroy
asoleado, **-da** *adj* : sunny
asolear *vt* : to put in the sun — **asolearse** *vr* : to sunbathe
asomar *vt* : to show, to stick out — *vi* : to appear, to become visible — **aso-**

marse *vr* **1** : to show, to appear **2** : to lean out, to look out ⟨se asomó por la ventana : he leaned out the window⟩
asombrar *vt* MARAVILLAR : to amaze, to astonish — **asombrarse** *vr* : to marvel, to be amazed
asombro *nm* : amazement, astonishment
asombroso, -sa *adj* : amazing, astonishing — **asombrosamente** *adv*
asomo *nm* **1** : hint, trace **2 ni por asomo** : by no means
aspa *nf* : blade (of a fan or propeller)
aspaviento *nm* : exaggerated movement, fuss, flounce
aspecto *nm* **1** : aspect **2** APARIENCIA : appearance, look
aspereza *nf* RUDEZA : roughness, coarseness
áspero, -ra *adj* : rough, coarse, abrasive — **ásperamente** *adv*
aspersión *nf, pl* **-siones** : sprinkling
aspersor *nm* : sprinkler
aspiración *nf, pl* **-ciones 1** : inhalation, breathing in **2** ANHELO : aspiration, desire
aspiradora *nf* : vacuum cleaner
aspirante *nmf* : applicant, candidate
aspirar *vi* ∼ **a** : to aspire to — *vt* : to inhale, to breathe in
aspirina *nf* : aspirin
asquear *vt* : to sicken, to disgust
asquerosidad *nf* : filth, foulness
asqueroso, -sa *adj* : disgusting, sickening, repulsive — **asquerosamente** *adv*
asta *nf* **1** : flagpole ⟨a media asta : at half-mast⟩ **2** : horn, antler **3** : shaft (of a weapon)
ástaco *nm* : crayfish
astado, -da *adj* : horned
aster *nm* : aster
asterisco *nm* : asterisk
asteroide *nm* : asteroid
astigmatismo *nm* : astigmatism
astil *nm* : shaft (of an arrow or feather)
astilla *nf* **1** : splinter, chip **2 de tal palo, tal astilla** : like father, like son
astillar *vt* : to splinter — **astillarse** *vr*
astillero *nm* : dry dock, shipyard
astral *adj* : astral
astringente *adj & nm* : astringent — **astringencia** *nf*
astro *nm* **1** : heavenly body **2** : star
astrología *nf* : astrology
astrológico, -ca *adj* : astrological
astrólogo, -ga *n* : astrologer
astronauta *nmf* : astronaut
astronáutica *nf* : astronautics
astronáutico, -ca *adj* : astronautic, astronautical
astronave *nf* : spaceship
astronomía *nf* : astronomy
astronómico, -ca *adj* : astronomical — **astronómicamente** *adv*
astrónomo, -ma *n* : astronomer
astroso, -sa *adj* DESALIÑADO : slovenly, untidy
astucia *nf* **1** : astuteness, shrewdness **2** : cunning, guile

astuto, -ta *adj* **1** : astute, shrewd **2** : crafty, tricky — **astutamente** *adv*
asueto *nm* : time off, break
asumir *vt* **1** : to assume, to take on ⟨asumir el cargo : to take office⟩ **2** SUPONER : to assume, to suppose
asunción *nf, pl* **-ciones** : assumption
asunto *nm* **1** CUESTIÓN, TEMA : affair, matter, subject **2 asuntos** *nmpl* : affairs, business
asustadizo, -za *adj* : nervous, jumpy, skittish
asustado, -da *adj* : frightened, afraid
asustar *vt* ESPANTAR : to scare, to frighten — **asustarse** *vr*
atacante *nmf* : assailant, attacker
atacar {72} *v* : to attack
atado¹, -da *adj* : shy, inhibited
atado² *nm* **1** : bundle, bunch **2** *Arg* : pack (of cigarettes)
atadura *nf* LIGADURA : tie, bond
atajar *vt* **1** IMPEDIR : to block, to stop **2** INTERRUMPIR : to interrupt, to cut off **3** CONTENER : to hold back, to restrain — *vi* ∼ **por** : to take a shortcut through
atajo *nm* : shortcut
atalaya *nf* **1** : watchtower **2** : vantage point
atañer {79} *vt* ∼ **a** (*3rd person only*) : to concern, to have to do with ⟨eso no me atañe : that does not concern me⟩
ataque *nm* **1** : attack, assault **2** : fit ⟨ataque de risa : fit of laughter⟩ **3 ataque de nervios** : nervous breakdown **4 ataque cardíaco** *or* **ataque al corazón** : heart attack
atar *vt* AMARRAR : to tie, to tie up, to tie down — **atarse** *vr*
atarantado, -da *adj fam* **1** : restless **2** : dazed, stunned
atarantar *vt fam* : to daze, to stun
atarazana *nf* : shipyard
atardecer¹ {53} *v impers* : to get dark
atardecer² *nm* : late afternoon, dusk
atareado, -da *adj* : busy, overworked
atascar {72} *vt* **1** ATORAR : to block, to clog, to stop up **2** : to hinder — **atascarse** *vr* **1** : to become obstructed **2** : to get bogged down **3** PARARSE : to stall
atasco *nm* **1** : blockage **2** EMBOTELLAMIENTO : traffic jam
ataúd *nm* : coffin, casket
ataviar {85} *vt* : to dress, to clothe — **ataviarse** *vr* : to dress up
atavío *nm* ATUENDO : dress, attire
ateísmo *nm* : atheism
atemorizar {21} *vt* : to frighten, to intimidate — **atemorizarse** *vr*
atemperar *vt* : to temper, to moderate
atención¹ *nf, pl* **-ciones 1** : attention **2 poner atención** *or* **prestar atención** : to pay attention **3 llamar la atención** : to attract attention **4 en atención a** : in view of
atención² *interj* **1** : attention! **2** : watch out!

atender {56} *vt* **1** : to help, to wait on **2** : to look after, to take care of **3** : to heed, to listen to — *vi* : to pay attention

atenerse {80} *vr* : to abide ⟨tendrás que atenerte a las reglas : you will have to abide by the rules⟩

atentado *nm* : attack, assault

atentamente *adv* **1** : attentively, carefully **2** (*used in correspondence*) : sincerely, sincerely yours

atentar {55} *vi* ~ **contra** : to make an attempt on, to threaten ⟨atentaron contra su vida : they made an attempt on his life⟩

atento, -ta *adj* **1** : attentive, mindful **2** CORTÉS : courteous

atenuación *nf, pl* **-ciones 1** : lessening **2** : understatement

atenuante[1] *adj* : extenuating, mitigating

atenuante[2] *nmf* : extenuating circumstance, excuse

atenuar {3} *vt* **1** MITIGAR : to extenuate, to mitigate **2** : to dim (light), to tone down (colors) **3** : to minimize, to lessen

ateo[1]**, atea** *adj* : atheistic

ateo[2]**, atea** *n* : atheist

aterciopelado, -da *adj* : velvety, downy

aterido, -da *adj* : freezing, frozen

aterrador, -dora *adj* : terrifying

aterrar {55} *vt* : to terrify, to frighten

aterrizaje *nm* : landing (of a plane)

aterrizar {21} *vt* : to land, to touch down

aterrorizar {21} *vt* **1** : to terrify **2** : to terrorize — **aterrorizarse** *vr* : to be terrified

atesorar *vt* : to hoard, to amass

atestado, -da *adj* : crowded, packed

atestar {55} *vt* **1** ATIBORRAR : to crowd, to pack **2** : to witness, to testify to — *vi* : to testify

atestiguar {10} *vt* : to testify to, to bear witness to — *vi* DECLARAR : to testify

atiborrar *vt* : to pack, to crowd — **atiborrarse** *vr* : to stuff oneself

ático *nm* **1** : penthouse **2** BUHARDILLA, DESVÁN : attic

atigrado, -da *adj* : tabby (of cats), striped (of fur)

atildado, -da *adj* : smart, neat, dapper

atildar *vt* **1** : to put a tilde over **2** : to clean up, to smarten up — **atildarse** *vr* : to get spruced up

atinar *vi* ACERTAR : to be accurate, to be on target

atingencia *nf* : bearing, relevance

atípico, -ca *adj* : atypical

atiplado, -da *adj* : shrill, high-pitched

atirantar *vt* : to make taut, to tighten

atisbar *vt* **1** : to spy on, to watch **2** : to catch a glimpse of, to make out

atisbo *nm* : glimpse, sign, hint

atizador *nm* : poker (for a fire)

atizar {21} *vt* **1** : to poke, to stir, to stoke (a fire) **2** : to stir up, to rouse **3** *fam* : to give, to land (a blow)

atlántico, -ca *adj* : Atlantic

atlas *nm* : atlas

atleta *nmf* : athlete

atlético, -ca *adj* : athletic

atletismo *nm* : athletics

atmósfera *nf* : atmosphere

atmosférico, -ca *adj* : atmospheric

atole *nm Mex* **1** : thick hot beverage prepared with corn flour **2 darle atole con el dedo (a alguien)** : to string (someone) along

atollarse *vr* : to get stuck, to get bogged down

atolón *nm, pl* **-lones** : atoll

atolondrado, -da *adj* **1** ATURDIDO : bewildered, dazed **2** DESPISTADO : scatterbrained, absentminded

atómico, -ca *adj* : atomic

atomizador *nm* : atomizer

atomizar {21} *vt* FRAGMENTAR : to fragment, to break into bits

átomo *nm* : atom

atónito, -ta *adj* : astonished, amazed

atontar *vt* **1** : to stupefy **2** : to bewilder, to confuse

atorar *vt* ATASCAR : to block, to clog — **atorarse** *vr* **1** ATASCARSE : to get stuck **2** ATRAGANTARSE : to choke

atormentador, -dora *n* : tormenter

atormentar *vt* : to torment, to torture — **atormentarse** *vr* : to torment oneself, to agonize

atornillar *vt* : to screw (in, on, down)

atorrante *nmf Arg* : bum, loafer

atosigar {52} *vt* : to harass, to annoy

atracadero *nm* : dock, pier

atracador, -dora *n* : robber, mugger

atracar {72} *vt* : to dock, to land — *vt* : to hold up, to rob, to mug — **atracarse** *vr fam* ~ **de** : to gorge oneself with

atracción *nf, pl* **-ciones** : attraction

atraco *nm* : holdup, robbery

atractivo[1]**, -va** *adj* : attractive

atractivo[2] *nm* : attraction, appeal, charm

atraer {81} *vt* : to attract — **atraerse** *vr* **1** : to attract (each other) **2** GANARSE : to gain, to win

atragantarse *vr* : to choke (on food)

atrancar {72} *vt* : to block, to bar — **atrancarse** *vr*

atrapada *nf* : catch

atrapar *vt* : to trap, to capture

atrás *adv* **1** DETRÁS : back, behind ⟨se quedó atrás : he stayed behind⟩ **2** ANTES : ago ⟨mucho tiempo atrás : long ago⟩ **3 para** ~ *or* **hacia** ~ : backwards, toward the rear **4** ~ **de** : in back of, behind

atrasado, -da *adj* **1** : late, overdue **2** : backward **3** : old-fashioned **4** : slow (of a clock or watch)

atrasar *vt* : to delay, to put off — *vi* : to lose time — **atrasarse** *vr* : to fall behind

atraso *nm* **1** RETRASO : lateness, delay ⟨llegó con 20 minutos de atraso : he was 20 minutes late⟩ **2** : backwardness **3 atrasos** *nmpl* : arrears

atravesar {55} *vt* **1** CRUZAR : to cross, to go across **2** : to pierce **3** : to lay across **4** : to go through (a situation or crisis) — **atravesarse** *vr* **1** : to be in the way ⟨se me atravesó : it blocked my path⟩ **2** : to interfere, to meddle

atrayente *adj* : attractive

atreverse *vr* **1** : to dare **2** : to be insolent

atrevido, -da *adj* **1** : bold, daring **2** : insolent

atrevimiento *nm* **1** : daring, boldness **2** : insolence

atribución *nf, pl* **-ciones** : attribution

atribuible *adj* IMPUTABLE : attributable, ascribable

atribuir {41} *vt* **1** : to attribute, to ascribe **2** : to grant, to confer — **atribuirse** *vr* : to take credit for

atribular *vt* : to afflict, to trouble — **atribularse** *vr*

atributo *nm* : attribute

atril *nm* : lectern, stand

atrincherar *vt* : to entrench — **atrincherarse** *vr* **1** : to dig in, to entrench oneself **2** ~ **en** : to hide behind

atrio *nm* **1** : atrium **2** : portico

atrocidad *nf* : atrocity

atrofia *nf* : atrophy

atrofiar *v* : to atrophy

atronador, -dora *adj* : thunderous, deafening

atropellado, -da *adj* **1** : rash, hasty **2** : brusque, abrupt

atropellamiento → **atropello**

atropellar *vt* **1** : to knock down, to run over **2** : to violate, to abuse — **atropellarse** *vr* : to rush through (a task), to trip over one's words

atropello *nm* : abuse, violation, outrage

atroz *adj, pl* **atroces** : atrocious, appalling — **atrozmente** *adv*

atuendo *nm* ATAVÍO : attire, costume

atufar *vt* : to vex, to irritate — **atufarse** *vr* **1** : to get angry **2** : to smell bad, to stink

atún *nm, pl* **atunes** : tuna fish, tuna

aturdimiento *nm* : bewilderment, confusion

aturdir *vt* **1** : to stun, to shock **2** : to bewilder, to confuse, to stupefy

atuvo, etc. → **atenerse**

audacia *nf* OSADÍA : boldness, audacity

audaz *adj, pl* **audaces** : bold, audacious, daring — **audazmente** *adv*

audible *adj* : audible

audición *nf, pl* **-ciones** **1** : hearing **2** : audition

audiencia *nf* : audience

audífono *nm* **1** : hearing aid **2** **audífonos** *nmpl* : headphones, earphones

audio *nm* : audio

audiovisual *adj* : audiovisual

auditar *vt* : to audit

auditivo, -va *adj* : auditory, hearing, aural ⟨aparato auditivo : hearing aid⟩

auditor, -tora *n* : auditor

auditoría *nf* : audit

auditorio *nm* **1** : auditorium **2** : audience

auge *nm* **1** : peak, height **2** : boom, upturn

augur *nm* : augur

augurar *vt* : to predict, to foretell

augurio *nm* AGÜERO, PRESAGIO : augury, omen

augusto, -ta *adj* : august

aula *nf* : classroom

aullar {8} *vt* : to howl, to wail

aullido *nm* : howl, wail

aumentar *vt* ACRECENTAR : to increase, to raise — *vi* : to rise, to increase, to grow

aumento *nm* INCREMENTO : increase, rise

aun *adv* **1** : even ⟨ni aun en coche llegaría a tiempo : I wouldn't arrive on time even if I drove⟩ **2 aun así** : even so **3 aun más** : even more

aún *adv* **1** TODAVÍA : still, yet ⟨¿aún no ha llegado el correo? : the mail still hasn't come?⟩ **2 más aún** : furthermore

aunar {8} *vt* : to join, to combine — **aunarse** *vr* : to unite

aunque *conj* **1** : though, although, even if, even though **2 aunque sea** : at least

aura *nf* **1** : aura **2** : turkey buzzard

áureo, -rea *adj* : golden

aureola *nf* **1** : halo **2** : aura (of power, fame, etc.)

aurícula *nf* : auricle

auricular *nm* : telephone receiver

aurora *nf* **1** : dawn **2 aurora boreal** : aurora borealis

ausencia *nf* : absence

ausentarse *vr* **1** : to leave, to go away **2** ~ **de** : to stay away from

ausente¹ *adj* : absent, missing

ausente² *nmf* **1** : absentee **2** : missing person

auspiciar *vt* **1** PATROCINAR : to sponsor **2** FOMENTAR : to foster, to promote

auspicios *nmpl* : sponsorship, auspices

austeridad *nf* : austerity

austero, -ra *adj* : austere

austral¹ *adj* : southern

austral² *nm* : former monetary unit of Argentina

australiano, -na *adj & n* : Australian

austriaco *or* **austríaco, -ca** *adj & n* : Austrian

autenticar {72} *vt* : to authenticate — **autenticación** *nf*

autenticidad *nf* : authenticity

auténtico, -ca *adj* : authentic — **auténticamente** *adv*

autentificar {72} *vt* : to authenticate — **autentificación** *nf*

autismo *nm* : autism

autista *adj* : autistic

auto *nm* : auto, car

autoayuda *nf* : self-help

autobiografía *nf* : autobiography

autobiográfico, -ca *adj* : autobiographical

autobús *nm, pl* **-buses** : bus

autocompasión *nf* : self-pity
autocontrol *nm* : self-control
autocracia *nf* : autocracy
autócrata *nmf* : autocrat
autocrático, -ca *adj* : autocratic
autóctono, -na *adj* : indigenous, native
⟨arte autóctono : indigenous art⟩
autodefensa *nf* : self-defense
autodestrucción *nf* : self-destruction —
autodestructivo, -va *adj*
autodeterminación *nf* : self-determination
autodidacta[1] *adj* : self-taught
autodidacta[2] *nmf* : self-taught person, autodidact
autodidacto[1], **-ta** *adj* → **autodidacta**[1]
autodidacto[2], **-ta** *n* → **autodidacta**[2]
autodisciplina *nf* : self-discipline
autoestima *nf* : self-esteem
autogobierno *nm* : self-government
autografiar *vt* : to autograph
autógrafo *nm* : autograph
autoinfligido, -da *adj* : self-inflicted
automación → **automatización**
autómata *nm* : automaton
automático, -ca *adj* : automatic — **automáticamente** *adv*
automatización *nf* : automation
automatizar {21} *vt* : to automate
automotor, -tora *adj* **1** : self-propelled **2** : automotive, car
automotriz[1] *adj, pl* **-trices** : automotive, car
automotriz[2] *nf, pl* **-trices** : automaker
automóvil *nm* : automobile
automovilista *nmf* : motorist
automovilístico, -ca *adj* : automobile, car ⟨accidente automovilístico : automobile accident⟩
autonombrado, -da *adj* : self-appointed
autonomía *nf* : autonomy
autónomo, -ma *adj* : autonomous — **autónomamente** *adv*
autopista *nf* : expressway, highway
autoproclamado, -da *adj* : self-proclaimed, self-appointed
autopropulsado, -da *adj* : self-propelled
autopsia *nf* : autopsy
autor, -tora *n* **1** : author **2** : perpetrator
autoría *nf* : authorship
autoridad *nf* : authority
autoritario, -ria *adj* : authoritarian
autorización *nf, pl* **-ciones** : authorization
autorizado, -da *adj* **1** : authorized **2** : authoritative
autorizar {21} *vt* : to authorize, to approve
autorretrato *nm* : self-portrait
autoservicio *nm* **1** : self-service restaurant **2** SUPERMERCADO : supermarket
autostop *nm* **1** : hitchhiking **2 hacer autostop** : to hitchhike
autostopista *nmf* : hitchhiker
autosuficiencia *nf* : self-sufficiency — **autosuficiente** *adj*
auxiliar[1] *vt* : to aid, to assist

auxiliar[2] *adj* : assistant, auxiliary
auxiliar[3] *nmf* **1** : assistant, helper **2 auxiliar de vuelo** : flight attendant
auxilio *nm* **1** : aid, assistance **2 primeros auxilios** : first aid
aval *nm* : guarantee, endorsement
avalancha *nf* ALUD : avalanche
avalar *vt* : to guarantee, to endorse
avaluar {3} *vt* : to evaluate, to appraise
avalúo *nm* : appraisal, evaluation
avance *nm* ADELANTO : advance
avanzado, -da *adj* **1** : advanced **2** : progressive
avanzar {21} *v* : to advance, to move forward
avaricia *nf* CODICIA : greed, avarice
avaricioso, -sa *adj* : avaricious, greedy
avaro[1], **-ra** *adj* : miserly, greedy
avaro[2], **-ra** *n* : miser
avasallador, -dora *adj* : overwhelming
avasallamiento *nm* : subjugation, domination
avasallar *vt* : to overpower, to subjugate
ave *nf* **1** : bird **2 aves de corral** : poultry **3 ave rapaz** *or* **ave de presa** : bird of prey
avecinarse *vr* : to approach, to come near
avecindarse *vr* : to settle, to take up residence
avellana *nf* : hazelnut, filbert
avellano *nm* : hazel
avena *nf* **1** : oat, oats *pl* **2** : oatmeal
avenencia *nf* : agreement, pact
avenida *nf* : avenue
avenir {87} *vt* : to reconcile, to harmonize — **avenirse** *vr* **1** : to agree, to come to terms **2** : to get along
aventajado, -da *adj* : outstanding
aventajar *vt* **1** : to be ahead of, to lead **2** : to surpass, to outdo
aventar {55} *vt* **1** : to fan **2** : to winnow **3** *Col, Mex* : to throw, to toss — **aventarse** *vr* **1** *Col, Mex* : to hurl oneself **2** *Mex fam* : to dare, to take a chance
aventón *nm, pl* **-tones** *Col, Mex fam* : ride, lift
aventura *nf* **1** : adventure **2** RIESGO : venture, risk **3** : love affair
aventurado, -da *adj* : hazardous, risky
aventurar *vt* : to venture, to risk — **aventurarse** *vr* : to take a risk
aventurero[1], **-ra** *adj* : adventurous
aventurero[2], **-ra** *n* : adventurer
avergonzado, -da *adj* **1** : ashamed **2** : embarrassed
avergonzar {9} *vt* APENAR : to shame, to embarrass — **avergonzarse** *vr* APENARSE : to be ashamed, to be embarrassed
avería *nf* **1** : damage **2** : breakdown, malfunction
averiado, -da *adj* **1** : damaged, faulty **2** : broken down
averiar {85} *vt* : to damage — **averiarse** *vr* : to break down
averiguación *nf, pl* **-ciones** : investigation, inquiry

averiguar {10} *vt* **1** : to find out, to ascertain **2** : to investigate
aversión *nf, pl* **-siones** : aversion, dislike
avestruz *nm, pl* **-truces** : ostrich
avezado, -da *adj* : seasoned, experienced
aviación *nf, pl* **-ciones** : aviation
aviador, -dora *n* : aviator, flyer
aviar {85} *vt* **1** : to prepare, to make ready **2** : to tidy up **3** : to equip, to supply
avicultor, -tora *n* : poultry farmer
avicultura *nf* : poultry farming
avidez *nf, pl* **-deces** : eagerness
ávido, -da *adj* : eager, avid — **ávidamente** *adv*
avieso, -sa *adj* **1** : twisted, distorted **2** : wicked, depraved
avinagrado, -da *adj* : vinegary, sour
avío *nm* **1** : preparation, provision **2** : loan (for agriculture or mining) **3** **avíos** *nmpl* : gear, equipment
avión *nm, pl* **aviones** : airplane
avioneta *nf* : light airplane
avisar *vt* **1** : to notify, to inform **2** : to advise, to warn
aviso *nm* **1** : notice **2** : advertisement, ad **3** ADVERTENCIA : warning **4 estar sobre aviso** : to be on the alert
avispa *nf* : wasp
avispado, -da *adj fam* : clever, sharp
avispero *nm* : wasps' nest
avispón *nm, pl* **-pones** : hornet
avistar *vt* : to sight, to catch sight of
avituallar *vt* : to suppy with food, to provision
avivar *vt* **1** : to enliven, to brighten **2** : to strengthen, to intensify
avizorar *vt* **1** ACECHAR : to spy on, to watch **2** : to observe, to perceive ⟨se avizoran dificultades : difficulties are expected⟩
axila *nf* : underarm, armpit
axioma *nm* : axiom
axiomático, -ca *adj* : axiomatic
ay *interj* **1** : oh! **2** : ouch!, ow!
ayer[1] *adv* : yesterday
ayer[2] *nm* ANTAÑO : yesteryear, days gone by
ayote *nm CA, Mex* : squash, pumpkin
ayuda *nf* **1** : help, assistance **2 ayuda de cámara** : valet
ayudante *nmf* : helper, assistant

ayudar *vt* : to help, to assist — **ayudarse** *vr* ～ **de** : to make use of
ayunar *vi* : to fast
ayunas *nfpl* **en** ～ : fasting ⟨este medicamento ha de tomarse en ayunas : this medication should be taken on an empty stomach⟩
ayuno *nm* : fast
ayuntamiento *nm* **1** : town hall, city hall **2** : town or city council
azabache *nm* : jet ⟨negro azabache : jet black⟩
azada *nf* : hoe
azafata *nf* **1** : stewardess *f* **2** : hostess *f* (on a TV show)
azafrán *nm, pl* **-franes 1** : saffron **2** : crocus
azahar *nm* : orange blossom
azalea *nf* : azalea
azar *nm* **1** : chance ⟨juegos de azar : games of chance⟩ **2** : accident, misfortune **3 al azar** : at random, randomly
azaroso, -sa *adj* **1** : perilous, hazardous **2** : turbulent, eventful
azimut *nm* : azimuth
azogue *nm* : mercury, quicksilver
azorar *vt* **1** : to alarm, to startle **2** : to fluster, to embarrass — **azorarse** *vr* : to get embarrassed
azotar *vt* **1** : to whip, to flog **2** : to lash, to batter **3** : to devastate, to afflict
azote *nm* **1** LÁTIGO : whip, lash **2** *fam* : spanking, licking **3** : calamity, scourge
azotea *nf* : flat roof, terraced roof
azteca *adj & nmf* : Aztec
azúcar *nmf* : sugar — **azucarar** *vt*
azucarado, -da *adj* : sweetened, sugary
azucarera *nf* : sugar bowl
azucarero, -ra *adj* : sugar ⟨industria azucarera : sugar industry⟩
azucena *nf* : white lily
azuela *nf* : adze
azufre *nm* : sulphur — **azufroso, -sa** *adj*
azul *adj & nm* : blue
azulado, -da *adj* : bluish
azulejo *nm* : ceramic tile, floor tile
azuloso, -sa *adj* : bluish
azulete *nm* : bluing
azur[1] *adj* CELESTE : azure
azur[2] *n* CELESTE : azure, sky blue
azuzar {21} *vt* : to incite, to egg on

B

b *nf* : second letter of the Spanish alphabet
baba *nf* **1** : spittle, saliva **2** : dribble, drool (of a baby) **3** : slime, ooze
babear *vi* **1** : to drool, to slobber **2** : to ooze
babel *nmf* : babel, chaos, bedlam
babero *nm* : bib
babor *nm* : port, port side

babosa *nf* : slug (mollusk)
babosada *nf CA, Mex* : silly act or remark
baboso, -sa *adj* **1** : drooling, slobbering **2** : slimy **3** *CA, Mex fam* : silly, dumb
babucha *nf* : slipper
babuino *nm* : baboon
bacalao *nm* : cod (fish)

bache *nm* **1** : pothole **2** *PRi* : deep puddle **3** : bad period, rough time ⟨bache
económico : economic slump⟩
bachiller *nmf* : high school graduate
bachillerato *nm* : high school diploma
bacilo *nm* : bacillus
bacon *nm Spain* : bacon
bacteria *nf* : bacterium
bacteriano, -na *adj* : bacterial
bacteriología *nf* : bacteriology
bacteriológico, -ca *adj* : bacteriologic,
bacteriological
bacteriólogo, -ga *n* : bacteriologist
báculo *nm* **1** : staff, stick **2** : comfort,
support
badajo *nm* : clapper (of a bell)
badén *nm, pl* **badenes 1** : (paved) ford,
channel **2** : dip, ditch (in a road) **3**
: speed bump
bádminton *nm* : badminton
bafle *or* **baffle** *nm* **1** : baffle **2** : speaker, loudspeaker
bagaje *nm* **1** EQUIPAJE : baggage, luggage **2** : background ⟨bagaje cultural
: cultural baggage⟩
bagatela *nf* : trifle, trinket
bagre *nm* : catfish
bahía *nf* : bay
bailar *vt* : to dance — *vi* **1** : to dance **2**
: to spin **3** : to be loose, to be too big
bailarín[1], **-rina** *adj, mpl* **-rines 1** : dancing **2** : fond of dancing
bailarín[2], **-rina** *n, mpl* **-rines 1** : dancer
2 : ballet dancer, ballerina *f*
baile *nm* **1** : dance **2** : dance party, ball
3 llevarse al baile a *Mex fam* : to take
for a ride, to take advantage of
baja *nf* **1** DESCENSO : fall, drop **2**
: slump, recession **3** : loss, casualty **4**
dar de baja : to discharge, to dismiss
5 darse de baja : to withdraw, to drop
out
bajada *nf* **1** : descent **2** : dip, slope **3**
: decrease, drop
bajar *vt* **1** DESCENDER : to lower, to let
down, to take down **2** REDUCIR : to reduce (prices) **3** INCLINAR : to lower,
to bow (the head) **4** : to go down, to
descend **5 bajar de categoría** : to
downgrade — *vi* **1** : to drop, to fall **2**
: to come down, to go down **3** : to ebb
(of tides) — **bajarse** *vr* ∼ **de** : to get
off, to get out of (a vehicle)
bajeza *nf* **1** : low or despicable act **2**
: baseness
bajío *nm* **1** : lowland **2** : shoal, sandbank, shallows
bajista *nmf* : bass player, bassist
bajo[1] *adv* **1** : down, low **2** : softly, quietly ⟨habla más bajo : speak more soft-
ly⟩
bajo[2], **-ja** *adj* **1** : low **2** : short (of stature)
3 : soft, faint, deep (of sounds) **4** : low-
er ⟨el bajo Amazonas : the lower Ama-
zon⟩ **5** : lowered ⟨con la mirada baja
: with lowered eyes⟩ **6** : base, vile **7
los bajos fondos** : the underworld

bajo[3] *nm* **1** : bass (musical instrument)
2 : first floor, ground floor **3** : hemline
bajo[4] *prep* : under, beneath, below
bajón *nm, pl* **bajones** : sharp drop,
slump
bajorrelieve *nm* : bas-relief
bala *nf* **1** : bullet **2** : bale
balacera *nf* TIROTEO : shoot-out, gunfight
balada *nf* : ballad
balance *nm* **1** : balance **2** : balance
sheet
balancear *vt* **1** : to balance **2** : to swing
(one's arms, etc.) **3** : to rock (a boat)
— **balancearse** *vr* **1** OSCILAR : to
swing, to sway, to rock **2** VACILAR : to
hesitate, to vacillate
balanceo *nm* **1** : swaying, rocking **2**
: vacillation
balancín *nm, pl* **-cines 1** : rocking chair
2 SUBIBAJA : seesaw
balandra *nf* : sloop
balanza *nf* BÁSCULA : scales *pl,* balance
balar *vi* : to bleat
balaustrada *nf* : balustrade
balaustre *nm* : baluster
balazo *nm* **1** TIRO : shot, gunshot **2**
: bullet wound
balboa *nf* : balboa (monetary unit of
Panama)
balbucear *vi* **1** : to mutter, to stammer
2 : to prattle, to babble ⟨los niños están balbuceando : the children are
prattling away⟩
balbuceo *nm* : mumbling, stammering
balbucir → **balbucear**
balcánico, -ca *adj* : Balkan
balcón *nm, pl* **balcones** : balcony
balde *nm* **1** CUBO : bucket, pail **2 en**
∼ : in vain, to no avail
baldío[1], **-día** *adj* **1** : fallow, uncultivated **2** : useless, vain
baldío[2] *nm* **1** : wasteland **2** *Mex* : vacant lot
baldosa *nf* LOSETA : floor tile
balear *vt* : to shoot, to shoot at
balero *nm* **1** *Mex* : ball bearing **2** *Mex,
PRi* : cup-and-ball toy
balido *nm* : bleat
balín *nm, pl* **balines** : pellet
balística *nf* : ballistics
balístico, -ca *adj* : ballistic
baliza *nf* **1** : buoy **2** : beacon (for aircraft)
ballena *nf* : whale
ballenero[1], **-ra** *adj* : whaling
ballenero[2], **-ra** *n* : whaler
ballenero[3] *nm* : whaleboat, whaler
ballesta *nf* **1** : crossbow **2** : spring (of
an automobile)
ballet *nm* : ballet
balneario *nm* : spa, bathing resort
balompié *nm* FUTBOL : soccer
balón *nm, pl* **balones** : ball
baloncesto *nm* BASQUETBOL : basketball
balsa *nf* **1** : raft **2** : balsa **3** : pond, pool
balsámico, -ca *adj* : soothing

bálsamo *nm* : balsam, balm
báltico, -ca *adj* : Baltic
baluarte *nm* BASTIÓN : bulwark, bastion
bambolear *vi* 1 : to sway, to swing 2 : to wobble — **bambolearse** *vr*
bamboleo *nm* 1 : swaying, swinging 2 : wobbling
bambú *nm, pl* **bambúes** *or* **bambús** : bamboo
banal *adj* : banal, trivial
banalidad *nf* : banality
banana *nf* : banana
bananero[1], -ra *adj* : banana
bananero[2] *nm* : banana tree
banano *nm* 1 : banana tree 2 *CA, Col* : banana
banca *nf* 1 : banking 2 BANCO : bench
bancada *nf* 1 : group, faction 2 : workbench
bancal *nm* 1 : terrace (in agriculture) 2 : plot (of land)
bancario, -ria *adj* : bank, banking
bancarrota *nf* QUIEBRA : bankruptcy
banco *nm* 1 : bank ⟨banco central : central bank⟩ ⟨banco de datos : data bank⟩ ⟨banco de arena : sandbank⟩ ⟨banco de sangre : blood bank⟩ 2 BANCA : stool, bench 3 : pew 4 : school (of fish)
banda *nf* 1 : band, strip 2 *Mex* : belt ⟨banda transportadora : conveyor belt⟩ 3 : band (of musicians) 4 : gang (of persons), flock (of birds) 5 **banda de rodadura** : tread (of a tire, etc.) 6 **banda sonora** *or* **banda de sonido** : sound track
bandada *nf* : flock (of birds), school (of fish)
bandazo *nm* : swerving, lurch
bandearse *vr* : to look after oneself, to cope
bandeja *nf* : tray, platter
bandera *nf* : flag, banner
banderazo *nm* : starting signal (in sports)
banderilla *nf* : banderilla, dart (in bullfighting)
banderín *nm, pl* **-rines** : pennant, small flag
bandidaje *nm* : banditry
bandido, -da *n* BANDOLERO : bandit, outlaw
bando *nm* 1 FACCIÓN : faction, side 2 EDICTO : proclamation
bandolerismo *nm* : banditry
bandolero, -ra *n* BANDIDO : bandit, outlaw
bangladesí *adj & nmf* : Bangladeshi
banjo *nm* : banjo
banquero, -ra *n* : banker
banqueta *nf* 1 : footstool, stool, bench 2 *Mex* : sidewalk
banquete *nm* : banquet
banquetear *v* : to feast
banquillo *nm* 1 : bench (in sports) 2 : dock, defendant's seat
bañadera *nf* → **bañera**

bañar *vt* 1 : to bathe, to wash 2 : to immerse, to dip 3 : to coat, to cover ⟨bañado en lágrimas : bathed in tears⟩ — **bañarse** *vr* 1 : to take a bath, to bathe 2 : to go for a swim
bañera *nf* TINA : bathtub
bañista *nmf* : bather
baño *nm* 1 : bath 2 : swim, dip 3 : bathroom 4 **baño María** : double boiler
baqueta *nf* 1 : ramrod 2 **baquetas** *nfpl* : drumsticks
bar *nm* : bar, tavern
baraja *nf* : deck of cards
barajar *vt* 1 : to shuffle (cards) 2 : to consider, to toy with
baranda *nf* : rail, railing
barandal *nm* 1 : rail, railing 2 : bannister, handrail
barandilla *nf Spain* : bannister, handrail, railing
barata *nf* 1 *Mex* : sale, bargain 2 *Chile* : cockroach
baratija *nf* : bauble, trinket
baratillo *nm* : rummage sale, flea market
barato[1] *adv* : cheap, cheaply ⟨te lo vendo barato : I'll sell it to you cheap⟩
barato[2], -ta *adj* : cheap, inexpensive
baratura *nf* 1 : cheapness 2 : cheap thing
barba *nf* 1 : beard, stubble 2 : chin
barbacoa *nf* : barbecue
bárbaramente *adv* : barbarously
barbaridad *nf* 1 : barbarity, atrocity 2 **¡qué barbaridad!** : that's outrageous!
barbarie *nf* : barbarism, savagery
bárbaro[1] *adv fam* : wildly ⟨anoche lo pasamos bárbaro : we had a wild time last night⟩
bárbaro[2], -ra *adj* 1 : barbarous, wild, uncivilized 2 *fam* : great, fantastic
bárbaro[3], -ra *n* : barbarian
barbecho *nm* : fallow land ⟨dejar en barbecho : to leave fallow⟩
barbero, -ra *n* : barber
barbilla *nf* MENTÓN : chin
barbitúrico *nm* : barbiturate
barbudo[1], -da *adj* : bearded
barbudo[2] *nm* : bearded man
barca *nf* 1 : boat 2 **barca de pasaje** : ferryboat
barcaza *nf* : barge
barcia *nf* : chaff
barco *nm* 1 BARCA : boat 2 BUQUE, NAVE : ship
bardo *nm* : bard
bario *nm* : barium
barítono *nm* : baritone
barlovento *nm* : windward
barman *nm* : bartender
barniz *nm, pl* **barnices** 1 LACA : varnish, lacquer 2 : glaze (on ceramics, etc.)
barnizar {21} *vt* 1 : to varnish 2 : to glaze
barométrico, -ca *adj* : barometric
barómetro *nm* : barometer
barón *nm, pl* **barones** : baron

baronesa *nf* : baroness
baronet *nm* : baronet
barquero, -ra : boatman *m*, boatwoman *f*
barquillo *nm* : wafer, thin cookie or cracker
barra *nf* : bar
barraca *nf* **1** CABAÑA, CHOZA : hut, cabin **2** : booth, stall
barracuda *nf* : barracuda
barranca *nf* **1** : hillside, slope **2** → **barranco**
barranco *nm* : ravine, gorge
barredora *nf* : street sweeper (machine)
barrena *nf* **1** TALADRO : drill, auger, gimlet **2** : tailspin
barrenar *vt* **1** : to drill **2** : to undermine
barrendero, -ra *n* : sweeper, street cleaner
barrer *v* : to sweep — **barrerse** *vr* : to slide (in sports)
barrera *nf* OBSTÁCULO : barrier, obstacle ⟨barrera de sonido : sound barrier⟩
barreta *nf* : crowbar
barriada *nf* **1** : district, quarter **2** : slums *pl*
barrica *nf* BARRIL, TONEL : barrel, cask, keg
barricada *nf* : barricade
barrida *nf* **1** : sweep **2** : slide (in sports)
barrido *nm* : sweeping
barriga *nf* PANZA : belly, paunch
barrigón, -gona *adj, mpl* **-gones** *fam* : potbellied, paunchy
barril *nm* **1** BARRICA : barrel, keg **2 cerveza de barril** : draft beer
barrio *nm* **1** : neighborhood, district **2 barrios bajos** : slums *pl*
barro *nm* **1** LODO : mud **2** ARCILLA : clay **3** ESPINILLA, GRANO : pimple, blackhead
barroco, -ca *adj* : baroque
barroso, -sa *adj* ENLODADO : muddy
barrote *nm* : bar (on a window)
barrunto *nm* **1** SOSPECHA : suspicion **2** INDICIO : sign, indication, hint
bártulos *nmpl* : things, belongings ⟨liar los bártulos : to pack one's things⟩
barullo *nm* BULLA : racket, ruckus
basa *nf* : base, pedestal
basalto *nm* : basalt
basar *vt* FUNDAR : to base — **basarse** *vr* FUNDARSE ~ **en** : to be based on
báscula *nf* BALANZA : balance, scales *pl*
base *nf* **1** : base, bottom **2** : base (in baseball) **3** FUNDAMENTO : basis, foundation **4 base de datos** : database **5 a base de** : based on, by means of **6 en base a** : based on, on the basis of
básico, -ca *adj* FUNDAMENTAL : basic — **básicamente** *adv*
basílica *nf* : basilica
basquetbol *or* **básquetbol** *nm* BALONCESTO : basketball
basset *nm* : basset hound
bastante[1] *adv* **1** : enough, sufficiently ⟨he trabajado bastante : I have worked enough⟩ **2** : fairly, rather, quite ⟨llegaron bastante temprano : they arrived quite early⟩
bastante[2] *adj* : enough, sufficient
bastante[3] *pron* : enough ⟨hemos visto bastante : we have seen enough⟩
bastar *vi* : to be enough, to suffice
bastardilla *nf* CURSIVA : italic type, italics *pl*
bastardo, -da *adj & n* : bastard
bastidor *nm* **1** : framework, frame **2** : wing (in theater) ⟨entre bastidores : backstage, behind the scenes⟩
bastilla *nf* : hem
bastión *nf, pl* **bastiones** BALUARTE : bastion, bulwark
basto, -ta *adj* : coarse, rough
bastón *nm, pl* **bastones 1** : cane, walking stick **2** : baton **3 bastón de mando** : staff (of authority)
basura *nf* DESECHOS : garbage, waste, refuse
basurero[1]**, -ra** *n* : garbage collector
basurero[2] *nm Mex* : garbage can
bata *nf* **1** : bathrobe, housecoat **2** : smock, coverall, lab coat
batalla *nf* **1** : battle **2** : fight, struggle **3 de** ~ : ordinary, everyday ⟨mis zapatos de batalla : my everyday shoes⟩
batallar *vi* LIDIAR, LUCHAR : to battle, to fight
batallón *nm, pl* **-llones** : battalion
batata *nf* : yam, sweet potato
batazo *nm* HIT : hit (in baseball)
bate *nm* : baseball bat
batea *nf* **1** : tray, pan **2** : flat-bottomed boat, punt
bateador, -dora *n* : batter, hitter
batear *vi* : to bat — *vt* : to hit
bateo *nm* : batting (in baseball)
batería *nf* **1** PILA : battery **2** : drum kit, drums *pl* **3 batería de cocina** : kitchen utensils *pl*
baterista *nmf* : drummer
batido *nm* LICUADO : milk shake
batidor *nm* : eggbeater, whisk, mixer
batidora *nf* : (electric) mixer
batir *vt* **1** GOLPEAR : to beat, to hit **2** VENCER : to defeat **3** REVOLVER : to mix, to beat **4** : to break (a record) — **batirse** *vr* : to fight
batista *nf* : batiste, cambric
batuta *nf* **1** : baton **2 llevar la batuta** : to be the leader, to call the tune
baúl *nm* : trunk, chest
bautismal *adj* : baptismal
bautismo *nm* : baptism, christening
bautista *adj & nmf* : Baptist
bautizar {21} *vt* : to baptize, to christen
bautizo → **bautismo**
bávaro, -ra *adj & n* : Bavarian
baya *nf* **1** : berry **2 baya de saúco** : elderberry
bayeta *nf* : cleaning cloth
bayoneta *nf* : bayonet
baza *nf* **1** : trick (in card games) **2 meter baza en** : to butt in on
bazar *nm* : bazaar
bazo *nm* : spleen

bazofia *nf* 1 : table scraps *pl* 2 : slop, swill 3 : hogwash, rubbish
bazuca *nf* : bazooka
beagle *nm* : beagle
beatificar {72} *vt* : to beatify — **beatificación** *nf*
beatífico, -ca *adj* : beatific
beatitud *nf* : beatitude
beato, -ta *adj* 1 : blessed 2 : pious, devout 3 : sanctimonious, overly devout
bebé *nm* : baby
bebedero *nm* 1 ABREVADERO : watering trough 2 *Mex* : drinking fountain
bebedor, -dora *n* : drinker
beber *v* TOMAR : to drink
bebida *nf* : drink, beverage
beca *nf* : grant, scholarship
becado, -da *n* : scholar, scholarship holder
becerro, -rra *n* : calf
begonia *nf* : begonia
beige *adj* & *nm* : beige
beisbol *or* **béisbol** *nm* : baseball
beisbolista *nmf* : baseball player
beldad *nf* BELLEZA, HERMOSURA : beauty
belén *nf, pl* **belenes** NACIMIENTO : Nativity scene
belga *adj* & *nmf* : Belgian
beliceño, -ña *adj* & *n* : Belizean
belicista[1] *adj* : militaristic
belicista[2] *nmf* : warmonger
bélico, -ca *adj* GUERRERO : war, fighting ⟨esfuerzos bélicos : war efforts⟩
belicosidad *nf* : bellicosity
belicoso, -sa *adj* 1 : warlike, martial 2 : aggressive, belligerent
beligerancia *nf* : belligerence
beligerante *adj* & *nmf* : belligerent
bellaco[1]**, -ca** *adj* : sly, cunning
bellaco[2]**, -ca** *n* : rogue, scoundrel
belleza *nf* BELDAD, HERMOSURA : beauty
bello, -lla *adj* 1 HERMOSO : beautiful 2 **bellas artes** : fine arts
bellota *nf* : acorn
bemol *nm* : flat (in music) — **bemol** *adj*
benceno *nm* : benzene
bendecir {11} *vt* 1 CONSAGRAR : to bless, to consecrate 2 ALABAR : to praise, to extol 3 **bendecir la mesa** : to say grace
bendición *nf, pl* **-ciones** : benediction, blessing
bendiga, bendijo etc. → **bendecir**
bendito, -ta *adj* 1 : blessed, holy 2 : fortunate 3 : silly, simple-minded
benedictino, -na *adj* & *n* : Benedictine
benefactor[1]**, -tora** *adj* : beneficent
benefactor[2]**, -tora** *n* : benefactor, benefactress *f*
beneficencia *nf* : beneficence, charity
beneficiar *vt* : to benefit, to be of assistance to — **beneficiarse** *vr* : to benefit, to profit
beneficiario, -ria *n* : beneficiary
beneficio *nm* 1 GANANCIA, PROVECHO : gain, profit 2 : benefit

beneficioso, -sa *adj* PROVECHOSO : beneficial
benéfico, -ca *adj* : charitable, beneficent
benemérito, -ta *adj* : meritorious, worthy
beneplácito *nm* : approval, consent
benevolencia *nf* BONDAD : benevolence, kindness
benévolo, -la *adj* BONDADOSO : benevolent, kind, good
bengala *nf* **luz de bengala** 1 : flare (signal) 2 : sparkler
bengalí[1] *adj* & *nmf* : Bengali
bengalí[2] *nm* : Bengali (language)
benignidad *nf* : mildness, kindness
benigno, -na *adj* : benign, mild
beninés, -nesa *adj* & *n* : Beninese
benjamín, -mina *n, mpl* **-mines** : youngest child
beodo[1]**, -da** *adj* : drunk, inebriated
beodo[2]**, -da** *n* : drunkard
berberecho *nm* : cockle
berbiquí *nm* : brace (in carpentry)
berenjena *nf* : eggplant
bergantín *nm, pl* **-tines** : brig (ship)
berilo *nm* : beryl
bermudas *nfpl* : Bermuda shorts
berrear *vi* 1 : to bellow, to low 2 : to bawl, to howl
berrido *nm* 1 : bellowing 2 : howl, scream
berrinche *nm fam* : tantrum, conniption
berro *nm* : watercress
berza *nf* : cabbage
besar *vt* : to kiss
beso *nm* : kiss
bestia[1] *adj* 1 : ignorant, stupid 2 : boorish, rude
bestia[2] *nf* : beast, animal
bestia[3] *nmf* 1 IGNORANTE : ignoramus 2 : brute
bestial *adj* 1 : bestial, beastly 2 *fam* : huge, enormous ⟨hace un frío bestial : it's terribly cold⟩ 3 *fam* : great, fantastic
besuquear *vt fam* : to cover with kisses — **besuquearse** *vr fam* : to neck, to smooch
betabel *nm Mex* : beet
betún *nm, pl* **betunes** 1 : shoe polish 2 *Mex* : icing
bianual *adj* : biannual
biatlón *nm, pl* **-lones** : biathlon
biberón *nm, pl* **-rones** : baby's bottle
biblia *nf* 1 : bible 2 **la Biblia** : the Bible
bíblico, -ca *adj* : biblical
bibliografía *nf* : bibliography
bibliográfico, -ca *adj* : bibliographic, bibliographical
bibliógrafo, -fa *n* : bibliographer
biblioteca *nf* : library
bibliotecario, -ria *n* : librarian
bicameral *adj* : bicameral
bicarbonato *nm* 1 : bicarbonate 2 **bicarbonato de soda** : sodium bicarbonate, baking soda
bicentenario *nm* : bicentennial

bíceps *nms & pl* : biceps
bicho *nm* : small animal, bug, insect
bici *nf fam* : bike
bicicleta *nf* : bicycle
bicolor *adj* : two-tone
bicúspide *adj* : bicuspid
bidón *nm, pl* **bidones** : large can, (oil) drum
bien[1] *adv* **1** : well ⟨¿dormiste bien? : did you sleep well?⟩ **2** CORRECTAMENTE : correctly, properly, right ⟨hay que hacerlo bien : it must be done correctly⟩ **3** : very, quite ⟨el libro era bien divertido : the book was very amusing⟩ **4** : easily ⟨bien puede acabarlo en un día : he can easily finish it in a day⟩ **5** : willingly, readily ⟨bien lo aceptaré : I'll gladly accept it⟩ **6 bien que** : although **7 más bien** : rather
bien[2] *adj* **1** : well, OK, all right ⟨¿te sientes bien? : are you feeling all right?⟩ **2** : pleasant, agreeable ⟨las flores huelen bien : the flowers smell very nice⟩ **3** : satisfactory **4** : correct, right
bien[3] *nm* **1** : good ⟨el bien y el mal : good and evil⟩ **2 bienes** *nmpl* : property, goods, possessions
bienal *adj & nf* : biennial — **bienalmente** *adv*
bienaventurado, -da *adj* **1** : blessed **2** : fortunate, happy
bienaventuranzas *nfpl* : Beatitudes
bienestar *nm* **1** : welfare, well-being **2** CONFORT : comfort
bienhechor[1], **-chora** *adj* : beneficent, benevolent
bienhechor[2], **-chora** *n* : benefactor, benefactress *f*
bienintencionado, -da *adj* : well-meaning
bienvenida *nf* **1** : welcome **2 dar la bienvenida a** : to welcome
bienvenido, -da *adj* : welcome
bies *nm* : bias (in sewing)
bife *nm Arg, Chile, Uru* : steak
bífido, -da *adj* : forked
bifocal *adj* : bifocal
bifocales *nmpl* : bifocals
bifurcación *nf, pl* **-ciones** : fork (in a river or road)
bifurcarse {72} *vr* : to fork
bigamia *nf* : bigamy
bígamo, -ma *n* : bigamist
bigote *nm* **1** : mustache **2** : whisker (of an animal)
bigotudo, -da *adj* : mustached, having a big mustache
bikini *nm* : bikini
bilateral *adj* : bilateral — **bilateralmente** *adv*
bilingüe *adj* : bilingual
bilioso, -sa *adj* **1** : bilious **2** : irritable
bilis *nf* : bile
billar *nm* : pool, billiards
billete *nm* **1** : bill ⟨un billete de cinco dólares : a five-dollar bill⟩ **2** BOLETO : ticket ⟨billete de ida y vuelta : round-trip ticket⟩

billetera *nf* : billfold, wallet
billón *nm, pl* **billones** **1** : billion (Great Britain) **2** : trillion (U.S.A.)
bimestral *adj* : bimonthly — **bimestralmente** *adv*
bimotor *adj* : twin-engined
binacional *adj* : binational
binario, -ria *adj* : binary
bingo *nm* : bingo
binocular *adj* : binocular
binoculares *nmpl* : binoculars
binomio *nm* **1** : binomial **2** PAREJA : pair, duo
biodegradable *adj* : biodegradable
biodegradarse *vr* : to biodegrade
biodiversidad *nf* : biodiversity
biofísica *nf* : biophysics
biofísico[1], **-ca** *adj* : biophysical
biofísico[2], **-ca** *n* : biophysicist
biografía *nf* : biography
biográfico, -ca *adj* : biographical
biógrafo, -fa *n* : biographer
biología *nf* : biology
biológico, -ca *adj* : biological, biologic — **biológicamente** *adv*
biólogo, -ga *n* : biologist
biombo *nm* MAMPARA : folding screen, room divider
biomecánica *nf* : biomechanics
biopsia *nf* : biopsy
bioquímica *nf* : biochemistry
bioquímico[1], **-ca** *adj* : biochemical
bioquímico[2], **-ca** *n* : biochemist
biosfera *or* **biósfera** *nf* : biosphere
biotecnología *nf* : biotechnology
biótico, -ca *adj* : biotic
bipartidismo *nm* : two-party system
bipartidista *adj* : bipartisan
bípedo *nm* : biped
birlar *vt fam* : to swipe, to pinch
birmano, -na *adj & n* : Burmese
bis[1] *adv* **1** : twice, again (in music) **2** : a, A ⟨artículo 47 bis : Article 47A⟩ ⟨calle Bolívar, número 70 bis : Bolívar Street, number 70A⟩
bis[2] *nm* : encore
bisabuelo, -la *n* : great-grandfather *m*, great-grandmother *f*, great-grandparent
bisagra *nf* : hinge
bisecar {72} *vt* : bisect — **bisección** *nf*
bisel *nm* : bevel
biselar *vt* : to bevel
bisexual *adj* : bisexual
bisiesto *adj* **año bisiesto** : leap year
bismuto *nm* : bismuth
bisnieto, -ta *n* : great-grandson *m*, great-granddaughter *f*, great-grandchild
bisonte *nm* : bison, buffalo
bisoñé *nm* : hairpiece, toupee
bisoño[1], **-ña** *adj* : inexperienced, green
bisoño[2], **-ña** *n* : rookie, greenhorn
bistec *nm* : steak, beefsteak
bisturí *nm* ESCALPELO : scalpel
bisutería *nf* : costume jewelry
bit *nm* : bit (unit of information)
bivalvo *nm* : bivalve
bizarría *nf* **1** : courage, gallantry **2** : generosity

bizarro, -rra *adj* **1** VALIENTE : courageous, valiant **2** GENEROSO : generous
bizco, -ca *adj* : cross-eyed
bizcocho *nm* **1** : sponge cake **2** : biscuit **3** *Mex* : breadstick
bizquera *nf* : crossed eyes, squint
blanco¹, -ca *adj* : white
blanco², -ca *n* : white person
blanco³ *nm* **1** : white **2** : target, bull's-eye ⟨dar en el blanco : to hit the target, to hit the nail on the head⟩ **3** : blank space, blank ⟨un cheque en blanco : a blank check⟩
blancura *nf* : whiteness
blancuzco, -ca *adj* **1** : whitish, off-white **2** PÁLIDO : pale
blandir {1} *vt* : to wave, to brandish
blando, -da *adj* **1** SUAVE : soft, tender **2** : weak (in character) **3** : lenient
blandura *nf* **1** : softness, tenderness **2** : leniency
blanqueador *nm* : bleach, whitener
blanquear *vt* **1** : to whiten, to bleach **2** : to shut out (in sports) **3** : to launder (money) — *vi* : to turn white
blanquillo *nm* *CA, Mex* : egg
blasfemar *vi* : to blaspheme
blasfemia *nf* : blasphemy
blasfemo, -ma *adj* : blasphemous
blazer *nm* : blazer
bledo *nm* **no me importa un bledo** *fam* : I couldn't care less, I don't give a damn
blindado, -da *adj* ACORAZADO : armored
blindaje *nm* **1** : armor, armor plating **2** : shield (for cables, machinery, etc.)
bloc *nm, pl* **blocs** : writing pad, pad of paper
blof *nm* *Col, Mex* : bluff
blofear *vi* *Col, Mex* : to bluff
blondo, -da *adj* : blond, flaxen
bloque *nm* **1** : block **2** GRUPO : bloc ⟨el bloque comunista : the Communist bloc⟩
bloquear *vt* **1** OBSTRUIR : to block, to obstruct **2** : to blockade
bloqueo *nm* **1** OBSTRUCCIÓN : blockage, obstruction **2** : blockade
blusa *nf* : blouse
blusón *nm, pl* **blusones** : loose shirt, smock
boa *nf* : boa
boato *nm* : ostentation, show
bobada *nf* **1** : stupid remark or action **2 decir bobadas** : to talk nonsense
bobalicón, -cona *adj, mpl* **-cones** *fam* : silly, stupid
bobina *nf* CARRETE : bobbin, reel
bobo¹, -ba *adj* : silly, stupid
bobo², -ba *n* : fool, simpleton
boca *nf* **1** : mouth **2 boca arriba** : face up, on one's back **3 boca abajo** : face down, prone **4 boca de riego** : hydrant **5 en boca de** : according to
bocacalle *nf* : entrance to a street ⟨gire a la última bocacalle : take the last turning⟩
bocadillo *nm* *Spain* : sandwich

bocado *nm* **1** : bite, mouthful **2** FRENO : bit (of a bridle)
bocajarro *nm* **a** ~ : point-blank, directly
bocallave *nf* : keyhole
bocanada *nf* **1** : swig, swallow **2** : puff, mouthful (of smoke) **3** : gust (of air) **4** : stream (of people)
boceto *nm* : sketch, outline
bochinche *nm fam* : ruckus, uproar
bochorno *nm* **1** VERGÜENZA : embarrassment **2** : hot and humid weather **3** : hot flash
bochornoso, -sa *adj* **1** EMBARAZOSO : embarrassing **2** : hot and muggy
bocina *nf* **1** : horn, trumpet **2** : automobile horn **3** : mouthpiece (of a telephone) **4** *Mex* : loudspeaker
bocinazo *nm* : honk (of a horn)
bocio *nm* : goiter
bocón, -cona *n, mpl* **bocones** *fam* : blabbermouth, loudmouth
boda *nf* : wedding
bodega *nf* **1** : wine cellar **2** *Chile, Col, Mex* : storeroom, warehouse **3** (*in various countries*) : grocery store
bofetada *nf* CACHETADA : slap on the face
bofetear *vt* CACHETEAR : to slap
bofetón *nm* → **bofetada**
bofo, -fa *adj* : flabby
boga *nf* : fashion, vogue ⟨estar en boga : to be in style⟩
bogotano¹, -na *adj* : of or from Bogotá
bogotano², -na *n* : person from Bogotá
bohemio, -mia *adj & n* : bohemian, Bohemian
boicot *nm, pl* **boicots** : boycott
boicotear *vt* : to boycott
boina *nf* : beret
boiserie *nf* : wood paneling, wainscoting
boj *nm, pl* **bojes** : box (plant), boxwood
bola *nf* **1** : ball ⟨bola de nieve : snowball⟩ **2** *fam* : lie, fib **3** *Mex fam* : bunch, group ⟨una bola de rateros : a bunch of thieves⟩ **4** *Mex* : uproar, tumult
bolear *vt* *Mex* : to polish (shoes)
bolera *nf* : bowling alley
bolero *nm* : bolero
boleta *nf* **1** : ballot **2** : ticket **3** : receipt
boletería *nf* TAQUILLA : box office, ticket office
boletín *nm, pl* **-tines** **1** : bulletin **2** : journal, review **3 boletín de prensa** : press release
boleto *nm* BILLETE : ticket
boliche *nm* **1** BOLOS : bowling **2** *Arg* : bar, tavern
bólido *nm* **1** : race car **2** METEORO : meteor
bolígrafo *nm* : ballpoint pen
bolillo *nm* **1** : bobbin **2** *Mex* : roll, bun
bolívar *nm* : bolivar (monetary unit of Venezuela)
boliviano¹, -na *adj & n* : Bolivian
boliviano² *nm* : boliviano (monetary unit of Bolivia)

bollo *nm* : bun, sweet roll
bolo *nm* : bowling pin, tenpin
bolos *nmpl* BOLICHE : bowling
bolsa *nf* 1 : bag, sack 2 *Mex* : pocketbook, purse 3 *Mex* : pocket 4 **la Bolsa** : the stock market, the stock exchange 5 **bolsa de trabajo** : employment agency
bolsear *vi Mex* : to pick pockets
bolsillo *nm* 1 : pocket 2 **dinero de bolsillo** : pocket change, loose change
bolso *nm* : pocketbook, handbag
bomba *nf* 1 : bomb 2 : bubble 3 : pump ⟨bomba de gasolina : gas pump⟩
bombachos *nmpl* : baggy pants, bloomers
bombardear *vt* 1 : to bomb 2 : to bombard
bombardeo *nm* 1 : bombing, shelling 2 : bombardment
bombardero *nm* : bomber (airplane)
bombástico, -ca *adj* : bombastic
bombear *vt* : to pump
bombero, -ra *n* : firefighter, fireman *m*
bombilla *nf* : lightbulb
bombillo *nm CA, Col, Ven* : lightbulb
bombo *nm* 1 : bass drum 2 *fam* : exaggerated praise, hype ⟨con bombos y platillos : with great fanfare⟩
bombón *nm, pl* **bombones** 1 : bonbon, chocolate 2 *Mex* : marshmallow
bonachón¹, -chona *adj, mpl* **-chones** *fam* : good-natured, kindhearted
bonachón², -chona *n, mpl* **-chones** *fam* BUENAZO : kindhearted person
bonaerense¹ *adj* : of or from Buenos Aires
bonaerense² *nmf* : person from Buenos Aires
bonanza *nf* 1 PROSPERIDAD : prosperity ⟨bonanza económica : economic boom⟩ 2 : calm weather 3 : rich ore deposit, bonanza
bondad *nf* BENEVOLENCIA : goodness, kindness ⟨tener la bondad de hacer algo : to be kind enough to do something⟩
bondadoso, -sa *adj* BENÉVOLO : kind, kindly, good — **bondadosamente** *adv*
bonete *nm* : cap, mortarboard
boniato *nm* : sweet potato
bonificación *nf, pl* **-ciones** 1 : discount 2 : bonus, extra
bonito¹ *adv* : nicely, well ⟨¡qué bonito canta tu hermana! : your sister sings wonderfully!⟩
bonito², -ta *adj* LINDO : pretty, lovely ⟨tiene un apartamento bonito : she has a nice apartment⟩
bonito³ *nm* : bonito (tuna)
bono *nm* 1 : bond ⟨bono bancario : bank bond⟩ 2 : voucher
boqueada *nf* : gasp ⟨dar la última boqueada : to give one's last gasp⟩
boquear *vi* 1 : to gasp 2 : to be dying
boquete *nm* : gap, opening, breach
boquiabierto, -ta *adj* : open-mouthed, speechless, agape

boquilla *nf* : mouthpiece (of a musical instrument)
borbollar *vi* : to bubble
borbotar *or* **borbotear** *vi* : to boil, to bubble, to gurgle
borboteo *nm* : bubbling, gurgling
borda *nf* : gunwale
bordado *nm* : embroidery, needlework
bordar *v* : to embroider
borde *nm* 1 : border, edge 2 **al borde de** : on the verge of ⟨estoy al borde de la locura : I'm about to go crazy⟩
bordear *vt* 1 : to border, to skirt ⟨el Río Este bordea Manhattan : the East River borders Manhattan⟩ 2 : to border on ⟨bordea la irrealidad : it borders on unreality⟩ 3 : to line ⟨una calle bordeada de árboles : a street lined with trees⟩
bordillo *nm* : curb
bordo *nm* **a ∼** : aboard, on board
boreal *adj* : northern
borgoña *nf* : burgundy
bórico, -ca *adj* : boric ⟨ácido bórico : boric acid⟩
boricua *adj & nmf fam* : Puerto Rican
borinqueño, -ña → **boricua**
borla *nf* 1 : pom-pom, tassel 2 : powder puff
boro *nm* : boron
borrachera *nf* : drunkenness ⟨agarró una borrachera : he got drunk⟩
borrachín, -china *n, mpl* **-chines** *fam* : lush, drunk
borracho¹, -cha *adj* EBRIO : drunk, intoxicated
borracho², -cha *n* : drunk, drunkard
borrador *nm* 1 : rough copy, first draft ⟨en borrador : in the rough⟩ 2 : eraser
borrar *vt* : to erase, to blot out — **borrarse** *vr* 1 : to fade, to fade away 2 : to resign, to drop out 3 *Mex fam* : to split, to leave ⟨me borro : I'm out of here⟩
borrascoso, -sa *adj* : gusty, blustery
borrego, -ga *n* 1 : lamb, sheep 2 : simpleton, fool
borrico → **burro**
borrón *nm, pl* **borrones** : smudge, blot ⟨borrón y cuenta nueva : let's start on a clean slate, let's start over again⟩
borronear *vt* : to smudge, to blot
borroso, -sa *adj* 1 : blurry, smudgy 2 CONFUSO : unclear, confused
boscoso, -sa *adj* : wooded
bosnio, -nia *adj & n* : Bosnian
bosque *nm* : woods, forest
bosquecillo *nm* : grove, copse, thicket
bosquejar *vt* ESBOZAR : to outline, to sketch
bosquejo *nm* 1 TRAZADO : outline, sketch 2 : draft
bostezar {21} *vi* : to yawn
bostezo *nm* : yawn
bota *nf* 1 : boot 2 : wineskin
botana *nf Mex* : snack, appetizer
botanear *vi Mex* : to have a snack
botánica *nf* : botany

botánico[1], **-ca** *adj* : botanical
botánico[2], **-ca** *n* : botanist
botar *vt* **1** ARROJAR : to throw, to fling, to hurl **2** TIRAR : to throw out, to throw away **3** : to launch (a ship)
bote *nm* **1** : small boat ⟨bote de remos : rowboat⟩ **2** : can, jar **3** : jump, bounce **4** *Mex fam* : jail
botella *nf* : bottle
botica *nf* FARMACIA : drugstore, pharmacy
boticario, -ria *n* FARMACÉUTICO : pharmacist, druggist
botín *nm, pl* **botines 1** : baby's bootee **2** : ankle boot **3** : booty, plunder
botiquín *nm, pl* **-quines 1** : medicine cabinet **2** : first-aid kit
botón *nm, pl* **botones 1** : button **2** : bud **3** INSIGNIA : badge
botones *nmfs & pl* : bellhop
botulismo *nm* : botulism
boulevard [ˌbuleˈvar] → **bulevar**
bouquet *nm* **1** : fragrance, bouquet (of wine) **2** RAMILLETE : bouquet (of flowers)
boutique *nf* : boutique
bóveda *nf* **1** : vault, dome **2** CRIPTA : crypt
bovino, -na *adj* : bovine
box *nm, pl* **boxes 1** : pit (in auto racing) **2** *Mex* : boxing
boxeador, -dora *n* : boxer
boxear *vi* : to box
boxeo *nm* : boxing
boya *nf* : buoy
boyante *adj* **1** : buoyant **2** : prosperous, thriving
bozal *nm* **1** : muzzle **2** : halter (for a horse)
bracear *vi* **1** : to wave one's arms **2** : to make strokes (in swimming)
bracero, -ra *n* : migrant worker, day laborer
braguero *nm* : truss (in medicine)
bragueta *nf* : fly, pants zipper
braille *adj & nm* : braille
bramante *nm* : twine, string
bramar *vi* **1** RUGIR : to roar, to bellow **2** : to howl (of the wind)
bramido *nm* : bellowing, roar
brandy *nm* : brandy
branquia *nf* AGALLA : gill
brasa *nf* ASCUA : ember, live coal
brasero *nm* : brazier
brasier *nm* *Col, Mex* : brassiere, bra
brasileño, -ña *adj & n* : Brazilian
bravata *nf* **1** JACTANCIA : boast, bravado **2** AMENAZA : threat
bravo, -va *adj* **1** FEROZ : ferocious, fierce ⟨un perro bravo : a ferocious dog⟩ **2** EXCELENTE : excellent, great ⟨¡bravo! : bravo!, well done!⟩ **3** : rough, rugged, wild **4** : annoyed, angry
bravucón, -cona *n, mpl* **-cones** : bully
bravuconadas *nfpl* : bravado
bravura *nf* **1** FEROCIDAD : fierceness, ferocity **2** VALENTÍA : bravery

braza *nf* **1** : breaststroke **2** : fathom (unit of length)
brazada *nf* : stroke (in swimming)
brazalete *nm* PULSERA : bracelet, bangle
brazo *nm* **1** : arm **2 brazo derecho** : right-hand man **3 brazos** *nmpl* : hands, laborers
brea *nf* ALQUITRÁN : tar, pitch
brebaje *nm* : potion, brew
brecha *nf* **1** : gap, breach ⟨estar siempre en la brecha : to be always there when needed, to stay in the thick of things⟩ **2** : gash
brécol *nm* : broccoli
brega *nf* **1** LUCHA : struggle, fight **2** : hard work
bregar {52} *vi* **1** LUCHAR : to struggle **2** : to toil, to work hard **3** ~ **con** : to deal with
brete *nm* : jam, tight spot
breve *adj* **1** CORTO : brief, short **2 en** ~ : shortly, in short — **brevemente** *adv*
brevedad *nf* : brevity, shortness
breviario *nm* : breviary
brezal *nm* : heath, moor
brezo *nm* : heather
bribón, -bona *n, mpl* **bribones** : rascal, scamp
bricolaje *or* **bricolage** *nm* : do-it-yourself
brida *nf* : bridle
brigada *nf* **1** : brigade **2** : gang, team, squad
brigadier *nm* : brigadier
brillante[1] *adj* : brilliant, bright — **brillantemente** *adv*
brillante[2] *nm* DIAMANTE : diamond
brillantez *nf* : brilliance, brightness
brillar *vi* : to shine, to sparkle
brillo *nm* **1** LUSTRE : luster, shine **2** : brilliance
brilloso, -sa *adj* LUSTROSO : lustrous, shiny
brincar {72} *vi* **1** SALTAR : to jump around, to leap about **2** : to frolic, to gambol
brinco *nm* **1** SALTO : jump, leap, skip **2 pegar un brinco** : to give a start, to jump
brindar *vi* : to drink a toast ⟨brindó por los vencedores : he toasted the victors⟩ — *vt* OFRECER, PROPORCIONAR : to offer, to provide — **brindarse** *vr* : to offer one's assistance, to volunteer
brindis *nm* : toast, drink ⟨hacer un brindis : to drink a toast⟩
brinque, etc. → **brincar**
brío *nm* **1** : force, determination **2** : spirit, verve
brioso, -sa *adj* : spirited, lively
briqueta *nf* : briquette
brisa *nf* : breeze
británico[1], **-ca** *adj* : British
británico[2], **-ca** *n* **1** : British person **2 los británicos** : the British
brizna *nf* **1** : strand, thread **2** : blade (of grass)

broca *nf* : drill bit
brocado *nm* : brocade
brocha *nf* : paintbrush
broche *nm* **1** ALFILER : brooch **2** : fastener, clasp **3 broche de oro** : finishing touch
brocheta *nf* : skewer
brócoli *nm* : broccoli
broma *nf* **1** CHISTE : joke, prank **2** : fun, merriment **3 en ~** : in jest, jokingly
bromear *vi* : to joke, to fool around ⟨sólo estaba bromeando : I was only kidding⟩
bromista[1] *adj* : fun-loving, joking
bromista[2] *nmf* : joker, prankster
bromo *nm* : bromine
bronca *nf fam* : fight, quarrel, fuss
bronce *nm* : bronze
bronceado[1], **-da** *adj* **1** : tanned, suntanned **2** : bronze
bronceado[2] *nm* **1** : suntan, tan **2** : bronzing
broncearse *vr* : to get a suntan
bronco, -ca *adj* **1** : harsh, rough **2** : untamed, wild
bronquial *adj* : bronchial
bronquio *nm* : bronchial tube, bronchus
bronquitis *nf* : bronchitis
broqueta *nf* : skewer
brotar *vi* **1** : to bud, to sprout **2** : to spring up, to stream, to gush forth **3** : to break out, to appear
brote *nm* **1** : outbreak **2** : sprout, bud, shoot
broza *nf* **1** : brushwood **2** MALEZA : scrub, undergrowth
brujería *nf* HECHICERÍA : witchcraft, sorcery
brujo[1], **-ja** *adj* : bewitching
brujo[2], **-ja** *n* : warlock *m*, witch *f*, sorcerer
brújula *nf* : compass
bruma *nf* : haze, mist
brumoso, -sa *adj* : hazy, misty
bruñir {38} *vt* : to burnish, to polish (metals)
brusco, -ca *adj* **1** SÚBITO : sudden, abrupt **2** : curt, brusque — **bruscamente** *adv*
brusquedad *nf* **1** : abruptness, suddenness **2** : brusqueness
brutal *adj* **1** : brutal **2** *fam* : incredible, terrific — **brutalmente** *adv*
brutalidad *nf* CRUELDAD : brutality
brutalizar {21} *vt* : to brutalize, to maltreat
bruto[1], **-ta** *adj* **1** : gross ⟨peso bruto : gross weight⟩ ⟨ingresos brutos : gross income⟩ **2** : unrefined ⟨petróleo bruto : crude oil⟩ **3** : brutish, stupid
bruto[2], **-ta** *n* **1** : brute **2** : dunce, blockhead
bubónico, -ca *adj* : bubonic
bucal *adj* : oral
bucanero *nm* : buccaneer, pirate
buccino *nm* : whelk
buceador, -dora *n* : diver, scuba diver

bucear *vi* **1** : to dive, to swim underwater **2** : to explore, to delve
buceo *nm* **1** : diving, scuba diving **2** : exploration, searching
buche *nm* **1** : crop (of a bird) **2** *fam* : belly, gut **3** : mouthful ⟨hacer buches : to rinse one's mouth⟩
bucle *nm* **1** : curl, ringlet **2** : loop
bucólico, -ca *adj* : bucolic
budín *nm, pl* **budines** : pudding
budismo *nm* : Buddhism
budista *adj & nmf* : Buddhist
buen *adj* → **bueno**[1]
buenamente *adv* **1** : easily **2** : willingly
buenaventura *nf* **1** : good luck **2** : fortune, future ⟨le dijo la buenaventura : she told his fortune⟩
buenazo, -za *n fam* BONACHÓN : kindhearted person
bueno[1], **-na** *adj* (**buen** *before masculine singular nouns*) **1** : good ⟨una buena idea : a good idea⟩ **2** BONDADOSO : nice, kind **3** APROPIADO : proper, appropriate **4** SANO : well, healthy **5** : considerable, goodly ⟨una buena cantidad : a lot⟩ **6 buenos días** : hello, good day **7 buenas tardes** : good afternoon **8 buenas noches** : good evening, good night
bueno[2] *interj* **1** : OK!, all right! **2** *Mex* : hello! (on the telephone)
buey *nm* : ox, steer
búfalo *nm* **1** : buffalo **2 búfalo de agua** : water buffalo
bufanda *nf* : scarf, muffler
bufar *vi* : to snort
bufet *or* **bufé** *nm* : buffet-style meal
bufete *nm* **1** : law firm, law office **2** : writing desk
bufido *nm* : snort
bufo, -fa *adj* : comic
bufón, -fona *n, mpl* **bufones** : clown, buffoon, jester
bufonada *nf* **1** : jest, buffoonery **2** : sarcasm
buhardilla *nf* **1** ÁTICO, DESVÁN : attic **2** : dormer window
búho *nm* **1** : owl **2** *fam* : hermit, recluse
buhonero, -ra *n* MERCACHIFLE : peddler
buitre *nm* : vulture
bujía *nf* : spark plug
bula *nf* : papal bull
bulbo *nm* : bulb
bulboso, -sa *adj* : bulbous
bulevar *nm* : boulevard
búlgaro, -ra *adj & n* : Bulgarian
bulla *nf* BARULLO : racket, rowdiness
bullicio *nm* **1** : ruckus, uproar **2** : hustle and bustle
bullicioso, -sa *adj* : noisy, busy, turbulent
bullir {38} *vi* **1** HERVIR : to boil **2** MOVERSE : to stir, to bustle about
bulto *nm* **1** : package, bundle **2** : piece of luggage, bag **3** : size, bulk, volume **4** : form, shape **5** : lump (on the body), swelling, bulge

bumerán nm, pl **-ranes** : boomerang
búnker nm, pl **búnkers** : bunker
búnquer → **búnker**
buñuelo nm : fried pastry
buque nm BARCO : ship, vessel
burbuja nf : bubble, blister (on a surface)
burbujear vi 1 : to bubble 2 : to fizz
burbujeo nm : bubbling
burdel nm : brothel, whorehouse
burdo, -da adj 1 : coarse, rough 2 : crude, clumsy ⟨una burda mentira : a clumsy lie⟩ — **burdamente** adj
burgués, -guesa adj & n, mpl **burgueses** : bourgeois
burguesía nf : bourgeoisie, middle class
burla nf 1 : mockery, ridicule 2 : joke, trick 3 **hacer burla de** : to make fun of, to mock
burlar vt ENGAÑAR : to trick, to deceive — **burlarse** vr ~ **de** : to make fun of, to ridicule
burlesco, -ca adj : burlesque, comic
burlón[1], -lona adj, mpl **burlones** : joking, mocking
burlón[2], -lona n, mpl **burlones** : joker
burocracia nf : bureaucracy
burócrata nmf : bureaucrat
burocrático, -ca adj : bureaucratic
burrada nf fam : stupid act, nonsense
burrito nm : burrito
burro[1], -rra adj fam : dumb, stupid

burro[2], -rra n 1 ASNO : donkey, ass 2 fam : dunce, poor student
burro[3] nm 1 : sawhorse 2 Mex : ironing board 3 Mex : stepladder
bursátil adj : stock-market
bursitis nf : bursitis
burundés, -desa adj & n : Burundian
bus nm : bus
busca nf : search
buscador, -dora n : hunter (for treasure, etc.), prospector
buscapersonas nms & pl : beeper, pager
buscapleitos nmfs & pl : troublemaker
buscar {72} vt 1 : to look for, to seek 2 : to pick up, to collect 3 : to provoke — vi : to look, to search ⟨buscó en los bolsillos : he searched through his pockets⟩
buscavidas nmf & pl 1 : busybody 2 : go-getter
busque, etc. → **buscar**
búsqueda nf : search
busto nm : bust
butaca nf 1 SILLÓN : armchair 2 : seat (in a theatre) 3 Mex : pupil's desk
butano nm : butane
buzo[1], -za adj Mex fam : smart, astute ⟨¡ponte buzo! : get with it!, get on the ball!⟩
buzo[2] nm : diver, scuba diver
buzón nm, pl **buzones** : mailbox
byte nm : byte

C

c nf : third letter of the Spanish alphabet
cabal adj 1 : exact, correct 2 : complete 3 : upright, honest
cabales nmpl **no estar en sus cabales** : not to be in one's right mind
cabalgar {52} vi : to ride (on horseback)
cabalgata nf : cavalcade, procession
cabalidad nf a ~ : thoroughly, conscientiously
caballa nf : mackerel
caballada nf 1 : herd of horses 2 fam : nonsense, stupidity, outrageousness
caballar adj EQUINO : horse, equine
caballeresco, -ca adj : gallant, chivalrous
caballería nf 1 : cavalry 2 : horse, mount 3 : knighthood, chivalry
caballeriza nf : stable
caballero[1] → **caballeroso**
caballero[2] nm 1 : gentleman 2 : knight
caballerosidad nf : chivalry, gallantry
caballeroso, -sa adj : gentlemanly, chivalrous
caballete nm 1 : ridge 2 : easel 3 : trestle (for a table, etc.) 4 : bridge (of the nose) 5 : sawhorse
caballista nmf : horseman m, horsewoman f
caballito nm 1 : rocking horse 2 **caballito de mar** : seahorse 3 **caballitos** nmpl : merry-go-round

caballo nm 1 : horse 2 : knight (in chess) 3 **caballo de fuerza** or **caballo de vapor** : horsepower
cabalmente adv : fully, exactly
cabaña nf CHOZA : cabin, hut
cabaret nm, pl **-rets** : nightclub, cabaret
cabecear vt : to head (in soccer) — vi 1 : to nod one's head 2 : to lurch, to pitch
cabecera nf 1 : headboard 2 : head ⟨cabecera de la mesa : head of the table⟩ 3 : heading, headline 4 : headwaters pl 5 **médico de cabecera** : family doctor 6 **cabecera municipal** CA, Mex : downtown area
cabecilla nmf : ringleader, kingpin
cabellera nf : head of hair, mane
cabello nm : hair
cabelludo, -da adj 1 : hairy 2 **cuero cabelludo** : scalp
caber {12} vi 1 : to fit, to go ⟨no sé si cabremos todos en el coche : I don't know if we'll all fit in the car⟩ 2 : to be possible ⟨no cabe duda alguna : there's no doubt about it⟩ ⟨cabe que llegue mañana : he may come tomorrow⟩
cabestrillo nm : sling ⟨llevo el brazo en cabestrillo : my arm is in a sling⟩
cabestro nm : halter (for an animal)
cabeza nf 1 : head 2 **cabeza hueca** : scatterbrain 3 **de** ~ : head first 4 **dolor de cabeza** : headache

cabezada *nf* **1** : butt, blow with the head **2** : nod ⟨echar una cabezada : to take a nap, to doze off⟩
cabezal *nm* : bolster
cabezazo *nm* : butt, blow with the head
cabezón, -zona *adj, mpl* **-zones** *fam* **1** : having a big head **2** : pigheaded, stubborn
cabida *nf* **1** : room, space, capacity **2 dar cabida a** : to accommodate, to hold
cabildear *vi* : to lobby
cabildeo *nm* : lobbying
cabildero, -ra *n* : lobbyist
cabildo *nm* AYUNTAMIENTO **1** : town or city hall **2** : town or city council
cabina *nf* **1** : cabin **2** : booth **3** : cab (of a truck), cockpit (of an airplane)
cabizbajo, -ja *adj* : dejected, downcast
cable *nm* : cable
cableado *nm* : wiring
cabo *nm* **1** : end ⟨al cabo de dos semanas : at the end of two weeks⟩ **2** : stub, end piece **3** : corporal **4** : cape, headland ⟨el Cabo Cañaveral : Cape Canaveral⟩ **5 al fin y al cabo** : after all, in the end **6 llevar a cabo** : to carry out, to do
caboverdiano, -na *adj & n* : Cape Verdean
cabrá, etc. → caber
cabra *nf* : goat
cabrestante *nm* : windlass
cabrío, -ría *adj* : goat, caprine
cabriola *nf* **1** : skip, jump **2 hacer cabriolas** : to prance
cabriolar *vi* : to prance
cabrito *nm* : kid, baby goat
cabús *nm, pl* **cabuses** *Mex* : caboose
cacahuate *or* **cacahuete** *nm* : peanut
cacalote *nm Mex* : crow
cacao *nm* : cacao, cocoa bean
cacarear *vi* : to crow, to cackle, to cluck — *vt fam* : to boast about, to crow about ⟨cacarear un huevo : to brag about an accomplishment⟩
cacareo *nm* **1** : clucking (of a hen), crowing (of a rooster) **2** : boasting
cacatúa *nf* : cockatoo
cace, etc. → cazar
cacería *nf* **1** CAZA : hunt, hunting **2** : hunting party
cacerola *nf* : pan, saucepan
cacha *nf* : butt (of a gun)
cachar *vt fam* : to catch
cacharro *nm* **1** *fam* : thing, piece of junk **2** *fam* : jalopy **3 cacharros** *nmpl* : pots and pans
cache *nm* : cache, cache memory
caché *nm* : cachet
cachear *vt* : to search, to frisk
cachemir *nm* : cashmere
cachetada *nf* BOFETADA : slap on the face
cachete *nm* : cheek
cachetear *vt* BOFETEAR : to slap
cachiporra *nf* : bludgeon, club, blackjack
cachirul *nm Mex fam* : cheating ⟨hacer cachirul : to cheat⟩

cachivache *nm fam* : thing ⟨mete tus cachivaches en el maletero : put your stuff in the trunk⟩
cacho *nm fam* : piece, bit
cachorro, -rra *n* **1** : cub **2** PERRITO : puppy
cachucha *nf Mex* : cap, baseball cap
cacique *nm* **1** : chief (of a tribe) **2** : boss (in politics)
cacofonía *nf* : cacophony
cacofónico, -ca *adj* : cacophonous
cacto *nm* : cactus
cactus → cacto
cada *adj* **1** : each ⟨cuestan diez pesos cada una : they cost ten pesos each⟩ **2** : every ⟨cada vez : every time⟩ **3** : such, some ⟨sales con cada historia : you come up with such crazy stories⟩ **4 cada vez más** : more and more, increasingly **5 cada vez menos** : less and less
cadalso *nm* : scaffold, gallows
cadáver *nm* : corpse, cadaver
cadavérico, -ca *adj* **1** : cadaverous **2** PÁLIDO : deathly pale
caddie *or* **caddy** *nmf, pl* **caddies** : caddy
cadena *nf* **1** : chain **2** : network, channel **3 cadena de montaje** : assembly line **4 cadena perpetua** : life sentence
cadencia *nf* : cadence, rhythm
cadencioso, -sa *adj* : rhythmic, rhythmical
cadera *nf* : hip
cadete *nmf* : cadet
cadmio *nm* : cadmium
caducar {72} *vi* : to expire
caducidad *nf* : expiration
caduco, -ca *adj* **1** : outdated, obsolete **2** : deciduous
caer {13} *vi* **1** : to fall, to drop **2** : collapse **3** : to hang (down) **4 caer bien** *fam* : to be pleasant, to be likeable ⟨me caes bien : I like you⟩ **5 caer mal** *or* **caer gordo** *fam* : to be unpleasant, to be unlikeable — **caerse** *vr* : to fall down
café¹ *adj* : brown ⟨ojos cafés : brown eyes⟩
café² *nm* **1** : coffee **2** : café
cafeína *nf* : caffeine
cafetal *nm* : coffee plantation
cafetalero¹, -ra *adj* : coffee ⟨cosecha cafetalera : coffee harvest⟩
cafetalero², -ra *n* : coffee grower
cafetera *nf* : coffeepot, coffeemaker
cafetería *nf* **1** : coffee shop, café **2** : lunchroom, cafeteria
cafetero¹, -ra *adj* : coffee-producing
cafetero², -ra *n* : coffee grower
cafeticultura *nf Mex* : coffee industry
caguama *nf* **1** : large Caribbean turtle **2** *Mex* : large bottle of beer
caída *nf* **1** BAJA, DESCENSO : fall, drop **2** : collapse, downfall
caiga, etc. → caer
caimán *nm, pl* **caimanes** : alligator, caiman

caimito *nm* : star apple
caja *nf* **1** : box, case **2** : cash register, checkout counter **3** : bed (of a truck) **4** *fam* : coffin **5 caja fuerte** *or* **caja de caudales** : safe **6 caja de seguridad** : safe-deposit box **7 caja torácica** : rib cage
cajero, -ra *n* **1** : cashier **2** : teller **3 cajero automático** : automated teller machine, ATM
cajeta *nf Mex* : a sweet caramel-flavored spread
cajetilla *nf* : pack (of cigarettes)
cajón *nm, pl* **cajones 1** : drawer, till **2** : crate, case **3 cajón de estacionamiento** *Mex* : parking space
cajuela *nf Mex* : trunk (of a car)
cal *nf* : lime, quicklime
cala *nf* : cove, inlet
calabacín *nm, pl* **-cines** : zucchini
calabacita *nf Mex* : zucchini
calabaza *nf* **1** : pumpkin, squash **2** : gourd **3 dar calabazas a** : to give the brush-off to, to jilt
calabozo *nm* **1** : prison **2** : jail cell
calado¹, -da *adj* **1** : drenched **2** : openworked
calado² ** *nm* **1 : draft (of a ship) **2** : openwork
calafatear *vt* : to caulk
calamar *nm* **1** : squid **2 calamares** *nmpl* : calamari
calambre *nm* **1** ESPASMO : cramp **2** : electric shock, jolt
calamidad *nf* DESASTRE : calamity, disaster
calamina *nf* : calamine
calamitoso, -sa *adj* : calamitous, disastrous
calaña *nf* : ilk, kind, sort ⟨una persona de mala calaña : a bad sort⟩
calar *vt* **1** : to soak through **2** : to pierce, to penetrate — *vi* : to catch on — **calarse** *vr* : to get drenched
calavera¹ *nf* **1** : skull **2** *Mex* : taillight
calavera² *nm* : rake, rogue
calcar {72} *vt* **1** : to trace **2** : to copy, to imitate
calce, etc. → **calzar**
calceta *nf* : knee-high stocking
calcetería *nf* : hosiery
calcetín *nm, pl* **-tines** : sock
calcificar {72} *v* : to calcify — **calcificarse** *vr*
calcinar *vt* : to char, to burn
calcio *nm* : calcium
calco *nm* **1** : transfer, tracing **2** : copy, image
calcomanía *nf* : decal, transfer
calculador, -dora *adj* : calculating
calculadora *nf* : calculator
calcular *vt* **1** : to calculate, to estimate **2** : to plan, to scheme
cálculo *nm* **1** : calculation, estimation **2** : calculus **3** : plan, scheme **4 cálculo biliar** : gallstone **5 hoja de cálculo** : spreadsheet
caldas *nfpl* : hot springs

caldear *vt* : to heat, to warm — **caldearse** *vr* **1** : to heat up **2** : to become heated, to get tense
caldera *nf* **1** : cauldron **2** : boiler
caldo *nm* **1** CONSOMÉ : broth, stock **2 caldo de cultivo** : culture medium, breeding ground
caldoso, -sa *adj* : watery
calefacción *nf, pl* **-ciones** : heating, heat
calefactor *nm* : heater
caleidoscopio → **calidoscopio**
calendario *nm* **1** : calendar **2** : timetable, schedule
caléndula *nf* : marigold
calentador *nm* : heater
calentamiento *nm* **1** : heating, warming **2** : warm-up (in sports)
calentar {55} *vt* **1** : to heat, to warm **2** *fam* : to annoy, to anger **3** *fam* : to excite, to turn on — **calentarse** *vr* **1** : to get warm, to heat up **2** : to warm up (in sports) **3** *fam* : to become sexually aroused **4** *fam* : to get mad
calentura *nf* **1** FIEBRE : temperature, fever **2** : cold sore
calibrador *nm* : gauge, calipers *pl*
calibrar *vt* : to calibrate — **calibración** *nf*
calibre *nm* **1** : caliber, gauge **2** : importance, excellence **3** : kind, sort ⟨un problema de grueso calibre : a serious problem⟩
calidad *nf* **1** : quality, grade **2** : position, status **3 en calidad de** : as, in the capacity of
cálido, -da *adj* **1** : hot ⟨un clima cálido : a hot climate⟩ **2** : warm ⟨una cálida bienvenida : a warm welcome⟩
calidoscopio *nm* : kaleidoscope
caliente *adj* **1** : hot, warm ⟨mantenerse caliente : to stay warm⟩ **2** : heated, fiery ⟨una disputa caliente : a heated argument⟩ **3** *fam* : sexually excited, horny
califa *nm* : caliph
calificación *nf, pl* **-ciones 1** NOTA : grade (for a course) **2** : rating, score **3** CLASIFICACIÓN : qualification, qualifying ⟨ronda de calificación : qualifying round⟩
calificar {72} *vt* **1** : to grade **2** : to describe, to rate ⟨la calificaron de buena alumna : they described her as a good student⟩ **3** : to qualify, to modify (in grammar)
calificativo¹, -va *adj* : qualifying
calificativo² *nm* : qualifier, epithet
caligrafía *nf* **1** ESCRITURA : handwriting **2** : calligraphy
calipso *nm* : calypso
calistenia *nf* : calisthenics
cáliz *nm, pl* **cálices 1** : chalice, goblet **2** : calyx
caliza *nf* : limestone
callado, -da *adj* : quiet, silent — **calladamente** *adv*
callar *vi* : to keep quiet, to be silent — *vt* **1** : to silence, to hush ⟨¡calla a los

niños! : keep the children quiet!⟩ **2** : to keep secret — **callarse** *vr* : to remain silent ⟨¡cállate! : be quiet!, shut up!⟩

calle *nf* : street, road

callejear *vi* : to wander about the streets, to hang out

callejero, -ra *adj* : street ⟨perro callejero : stray dog⟩

callejón *nm, pl* **-jones** **1** : alley **2 callejón sin salida** : dead-end street

callo *nm* **1** : callus, corn **2 callos** *nmpl* : tripe

calloso, -sa *adj* : callous

calma *nf* : calm, quiet

calmante¹ *adj* : calming, soothing

calmante² *nm* : tranquilizer, sedative

calmar *vt* TRANQUILIZAR : to calm, to soothe — **calmarse** *vr* : to calm down

calmo, -ma *adj* TRANQUILO : calm, tranquil

calmoso, -sa *adj* **1** TRANQUILO : calm, quiet **2** LENTO : slow, sluggish

calor *nm* **1** : heat ⟨hace calor : it's hot outside⟩ ⟨tener calor : to feel hot⟩ **2** : warmth, affection **3** : ardor, passion

caloría *nf* : calorie

calórico, -ca *adj* : caloric

calorífico, -ca *adj* : caloric

calque, etc. → calcar

calumnia *nf* : slander, libel — **calumnioso, -sa** *adj*

calumniar *vt* : to slander, to libel

caluroso, -sa *adj* **1** : hot **2** : warm, enthusiastic

calva *nf* : bald spot, bald head

calvario *nm* **1** : Calvary **2** : Stations of the Cross *pl* **3 vivir un calvario** : to suffer great adversity

calvicie *nf* : baldness

calvo¹, -va *adj* : bald

calvo², -va *n* : bald person

calza *nf* : block, wedge

calzada *nf* : roadway, avenue

calzado *nm* : footwear

calzador *nm* : shoehorn

calzar {21} *vt* **1** : to wear (shoes) ⟨¿de cuál calza? : what is your shoe size?⟩ ⟨siempre calzaban tenis : they always wore sneakers⟩ **2** : to provide with shoes

calzo *nm* : chock, wedge

calzoncillos *nmpl* : underpants, briefs

calzones *nmpl* : underpants, panties

cama *nf* **1** : bed **2 cama elástica** : trampoline

camada *nf* : litter, brood

camafeo *nm* : cameo

camaleón *nm, pl* **-leones** : chameleon

cámara *nf* **1** : camera **2** : chamber, room **3** : house (in government) **4** : inner tube

camarada *nmf* **1** : comrade, companion **2** : colleague

camaradería *nf* : camaraderie

camarero, -ra *n* **1** MESERO : waiter, waitress *f* **2** : bellhop *m*, chambermaid *f* (in a hotel) **3** : steward *m*, stewardess *f* (on a ship, etc.)

camarilla *nf* : political clique

camarógrafo, -fa *n* : cameraman *m*, camerawoman *f*

camarón *nm, pl* **-rones** **1** : shrimp **2** : prawn

camarote *nm* : cabin, stateroom

camastro *nm* : small hard bed, pallet

cambalache *nm fam* : swap

cambiante *adj* **1** : changing **2** VARIABLE : changeable, variable

cambiar *vt* **1** ALTERAR, MODIFICAR : to change **2** : to exchange, to trade — *vi* **1** : to change **2 cambiar de velocidad** : to shift gears — **cambiarse** *vr* **1** : to change (clothing) **2** MUDARSE : to move (to a new address)

cambio *nm* **1** : change, alteration **2** : exchange **3** : change (money) **4 en cambio** : instead **5 en cambio** : however, on the other hand

cambista *nmf* : exchange broker

camboyano, -na *adj & n* : Cambodian

cambur *nm Ven* : banana

camelia *nf* : camellia

camello *nm* : camel

camellón *nm, pl* **-llones** *Mex* : traffic island

camerino *nm* : dressing room

camerunés, -nesa *adj, mpl* **-neses** : Cameroonian

camilla *nf* : stretcher

camillero, -ra *n* : orderly (in a hospital)

caminante *nmf* : wayfarer, walker

caminar *vi* ANDAR : to walk, to move — *vt* : to walk, to cover (a distance)

caminata *nf* : hike, long walk

camino *nm* **1** : path, road **2** : journey ⟨ponerse en camino : to set off⟩ **3** : way ⟨a medio camino : halfway there⟩

camión *nm, pl* **camiones** **1** : truck **2** *Mex* : bus

camionero, -ra *n* **1** : truck driver **2** *Mex* : bus driver

camioneta *nf* : light truck, van

camisa *nf* **1** : shirt **2 camisa de fuerza** : straitjacket

camiseta *nf* **1** : T-shirt **2** : undershirt

camisón *nm, pl* **-sones** : nightshirt, nightgown

camorra *nf fam* : fight, trouble ⟨buscar camorra : to pick a fight⟩

camote *nm* **1** : root vegetable similar to the sweet potato **2 hacerse camote** *Mex fam* : to get mixed up

campal *adj* : pitched, fierce ⟨batalla campal : pitched battle⟩

campamento *nm* : camp

campana *nf* : bell

campanada *nf* TAÑIDO : stroke (of a bell), peal

campanario *nm* : bell tower, belfry

campanilla *nf* **1** : small bell, handbell **2** : uvula

campante *adj* : nonchalant, smug ⟨seguir tan campante : to go on as if nothing had happened⟩

campaña *nf* **1** CAMPO : countryside, country **2** : campaign **3 tienda de campaña** : tent
campañol *nm* : vole
campechana *nf Mex* : puff pastry
campechanía *nf* : geniality
campechano, -na *adj* : open, cordial, friendly
campeón, -peona *n, mpl* **-peones** : champion
campeonato *nm* : championship
cámper *nm* : camper (vehicle)
campero, -ra *adj* : country, rural
campesino, -na *n* : peasant, farm laborer
campestre *adj* : rural, rustic
camping *nm* **1** : camping **2** : campsite
campiña *nf* CAMPO : countryside, country
campista *nmf* : camper
campo *nm* **1** CAMPAÑA : countryside, country **2** : field ⟨campo de aviación : airfield⟩ ⟨su campo de responsabilidad : her field of responsibility⟩
camposanto *nm* : graveyard, cemetery
campus *nms & pl* : campus
camuflaje *nm* : camouflage
camuflajear *vt* : to camouflage
camuflar → **camuflajear**
can *nm* : hound, dog
cana *nf* **1** : gray hair **2 salirle canas** : to go gray, to get gray hair **3 echar una cana al aire** : to let one's hair down
canadiense *adj & nmf* : Canadian
canal[1] *nm* **1** : canal **2** : channel
canal[2] *nmf* : gutter, groove
canalé *nm* : rib, ribbing (in fabric)
canaleta *nf* : gutter
canalete *nm* : paddle
canalizar {21} *vt* : to channel
canalla[1] *adj fam* : low, rotten
canalla[2] *nmf fam* : bastard, swine
canapé *nm* **1** : hors d'oeuvre, canapé **2** SOFÁ : couch, sofa
canario[1], **-ria** *adj* : of or from the Canary Islands
canario[2], **-ria** *n* : Canarian, Canary Islander
canario[3] *nm* : canary
canasta *nf* **1** : basket **2** : canasta (card game)
cancel *nm* **1** : sliding door **2** : partition
cancelación *nf, pl* **-ciones** **1** : cancellation **2** : payment in full
cancelar *vt* **1** : to cancel **2** : to pay off, to settle
cáncer *nm* : cancer
Cáncer *nmf* : Cancer
cancerígeno[1], **-na** *adj* : carcinogenic
cancerígeno[2] *nm* : carcinogen
canceroso, -sa *adj* : cancerous
cancha *nf* : court, field (for sports)
canciller *nm* : chancellor
cancillería *nf* : chancellery, ministry
canción *nf, pl* **canciones** **1** : song **2 canción de cuna** : lullaby
cancionero[1] *nm* : songbook
cancionero[2], **-ra** *n Mex* : songster, songstress *f*

candado *nm* : padlock
candela *nf* **1** : flame, fire **2** : candle
candelabro *nm* : candelabra
candelero *nm* **1** : candlestick **2 estar en el candelero** : to be the center of attention
candente *adj* : red-hot
candidato, -ta *n* : candidate, applicant
candidatura *nf* : candidacy
candidez *nf* **1** : simplicity **2** INGENUIDAD : naïveté, ingenuousness
cándido, -da *adj* **1** : simple, unassuming **2** INGENUO : naive, ingenuous
candil *nm* : oil lamp
candilejas *nfpl* : footlights
candor *nm* : naïveté, innocence
candoroso, -sa *adj* : naive, innocent
canela *nf* : cinnamon
canesú *nm* : yoke (of clothing)
cangrejo *nm* JAIBA : crab
canguro *nm* **1** : kangaroo **2 hacer de canguro** *Spain* : to baby-sit
caníbal[1] *adj* : cannibalistic
caníbal[2] *nmf* ANTROPÓFAGO : cannibal
canibalismo *nm* ANTROPOFAGIA : cannibalism
canibalizar {21} *vt* : to cannibalize
canica *nf* : marble ⟨jugar a las canicas : to play marbles⟩
caniche *nm* : poodle
canijo, -ja *adj* **1** *fam* : puny, weak **2** *Mex fam* : tough, hard ⟨un examen muy canijo : a very tough exam⟩
canilla *nf* **1** : shin, shinbone **2** *Arg, Uru* : faucet
canino[1], **-na** *adj* : canine
canino[2] *nm* **1** COLMILLO : canine (tooth) **2** : dog, canine
canje *nm* INTERCAMBIO : exchange, trade
canjear *vt* INTERCAMBIAR : to exchange, to trade
cannabis *nm* : cannabis
cano, -na *adj* : gray ⟨un hombre de pelo cano : a gray-haired man⟩
canoa *nf* : canoe
canon *nm, pl* **cánones** : canon
canónico, -ca *adj* **1** : canonical **2 derecho canónico** : canon law
canónigo *nm* : canon (of a church)
canonizar {21} *vt* : to canonize — **canonización** *nf*
canoso, -sa → **cano**
cansado, -da *adj* **1** : tired ⟨estar cansado : to be tired⟩ **2** : tiresome, wearying ⟨ser cansado : to be tiring⟩
cansancio *nm* FATIGA : fatigue, weariness
cansar *vt* FATIGAR : to wear out, to tire — *vi* : to be tiresome — **cansarse** *vr* **1** : to wear oneself out **2** : to get bored
cansino, -na *adj* : slow, weary, lethargic
cantaleta *nf fam* : nagging ⟨la misma cantaleta : the same old story⟩
cantalupo *nm* : cantaloupe
cantante *nmf* : singer
cantar[1] *v* : to sing

cantar[2] *nm* : song, ballad
cántaro *nm* **1** : pitcher, jug **2 llover a cántaros** *fam* : to rain cats and dogs
cantata *nf* : cantata
cantera *nf* : quarry ⟨cantera de piedra : stone quarry⟩
cántico *nm* : canticle, chant
cantidad[1] *adv fam* : really ⟨ese carro me costó cantidad : that car cost me plenty⟩
cantidad[2] *nf* **1** : quantity **2** : sum, amount (of money) **3** *fam* : a lot, a great many ⟨había cantidad de niños en el parque : there were tons of kids in the park⟩
cantimplora *nf* : canteen, water bottle
cantina *nf* **1** : tavern, bar **2** : canteen, mess, dining quarters *pl*
cantinero, -ra *n* : bartender
canto *nm* **1** : singing **2** : chant ⟨canto gregoriano : Gregorian chant⟩ **3** : song (of a bird) **4** : edge, end ⟨de canto : on end, sideways⟩ **5 canto rodado** : boulder
cantón *nm, pl* **cantones 1** : canton **2** *Mex fam* : place, home
cantonés[1], **-nesa** *adj & n, mpl* **-neses** : Cantonese
cantonés[2] *nm, pl* **-neses** : Cantonese (language)
cantor[1], **-tora** *adj* **1** : singing **2 pájaro cantor** : songbird
cantor[2], **-tora** *n* **1** : singer **2** : cantor
caña *nf* **1** : cane ⟨caña de azúcar : sugarcane⟩ **2** : reed **3 caña de pescar** : fishing rod **4 caña del timón** : tiller (of a boat)
cañada *nf* : ravine, gully
cáñamo *nm* : hemp
cañaveral *nm* : sugarcane field
cañería *nf* TUBERÍA : pipes *pl*, piping
caño *nm* **1** : pipe **2** : spout **3** : channel (for navigation)
cañón *nm, pl* **cañones 1** : cannon **2** : barrel (of a gun) **3** : canyon
cañonear *vt* : to shell, to bombard
cañoneo *nm* : shelling, bombardment
cañonero *nm* : gunboat
caoba *nf* : mahogany
caolín *nm* : kaolin
caos *nm* : chaos
caótico, -ca *adj* : chaotic
capa *nf* **1** : cape, cloak **2** : coating **3** : layer, stratum **4** : (social) class, stratum
capacidad *nf* **1** : capacity **2** : capability, ability
capacitación *nf, pl* **-ciones** : training
capacitar *vt* : to train, to qualify
caparazón *nm, pl* **-zones** : shell, carapace
capataz *nmf, pl* **-taces** : foreman *m*, forewoman *f*
capaz *adj, pl* **capaces 1** APTO : capable, able **2** COMPETENTE : competent **3** : spacious ⟨capaz para : with room for⟩
capcioso, -sa *adj* : cunning, deceptive ⟨pregunta capciosa : trick question⟩

capea *nf* : amateur bullfight
capear *vt* **1** : to make a pass with the cape (in bullfighting) **2** : to dodge, to weather ⟨capear el temporal : to ride out the storm⟩
capellán *nm, pl* **-llanes** : chaplain
capilar *nm* : capillary — **capilar** *adj*
capilla *nf* : chapel
capirotada *nf Mex* : traditional bread pudding
capirotazo *nm* : flip, flick
capital[1] *adj* **1** : capital **2** : chief, principal
capital[2] *nm* : capital ⟨capital de riesgo : venture capital⟩
capital[3] *nf* : capital, capital city
capitalino[1], **-na** *adj* : of or from a capital city
capitalino[2], **-na** *n* : inhabitant of a capital city
capitalismo *nm* : capitalism
capitalista *adj & nmf* : capitalist
capitalizar {21} *vt* : to capitalize — **capitalización** *nf*
capitán, -tana *n, mpl* **-tanes** : captain
capitanear *vt* : to captain, to command
capitanía *nf* : captaincy
capitel *nm* : capital (of a column)
capitolio *nm* : capitol
capitulación *nf, pl* **-ciones** : capitulation
capitular *vi* : to capitulate, to surrender
capítulo *nm* **1** : chapter, section **2** : matter, subject
capó *nm* : hood (of a car)
capón *nm, pl* **capones** : capon
caporal *nm* **1** : chief, leader **2** : foreman (on a ranch)
capota *nf* : top (of a convertible)
capote *nm* **1** : cloak, overcoat **2** : bullfighter's cape **3** *Mex* COFRE : hood (of a car)
capricho *nm* ANTOJO : whim, caprice
caprichoso, -sa *adj* ANTOJADIZO : capricious, fickle
Capricornio *nmf* : Capricorn
cápsula *nf* : capsule
captar *vt* **1** : to catch, to grasp **2** : to gain, to attract **3** : to harness, to collect (waters)
captor, -tora *n* : captor
captura *nf* : capture, seizure
capturar *vt* : to capture, to seize
capucha *nf* : hood, cowl
capuchina *nf* : nasturtium
capuchino *nm* **1** : Capuchin (monk) **2** : capuchin (monkey) **3** : cappuccino
capullo *nm* **1** : cocoon **2** : bud (of a flower)
caqui *adj & nm* : khaki
cara *nf* **1** : face **2** ASPECTO : look, appearance ⟨¡qué buena cara tiene ese pastel! : that cake looks delicious!⟩ **3** *fam* : nerve, gall **4** ~ **a** *or* **de cara a** : facing **5 de cara a** : in view of, in the light of
carabina *nf* : carbine
caracol *nm* **1** : snail **2** CONCHA : conch, seashell **3** : cochlea **4** : ringlet

caracola *nf* : conch
carácter *nm, pl* caracteres 1 ÍNDOLE : character, kind, nature 2 TEMPERAMENTO : disposition, temperament 3 : letter, symbol ⟨caracteres chinos : Chinese characters⟩
característica *nf* RASGO : trait, feature, characteristic
característico, -ca *adj* : characteristic — característicamente *adv*
caracterizar {21} *vt* : to characterize — caracterización *nf*
caramba *interj* 1 (*expressing annoyance*) : darn!, heck! 2 (*expressing disgust or surprise*) : jeez!
carámbano *nm* : icicle
carambola *nf* 1 : carom 2 : ruse, trick ⟨por carambola : by a lucky chance⟩
caramelo *nm* 1 : caramel 2 DULCE : candy
caramillo *nm* 1 : pipe, small flute 2 : heap, pile
caraqueño[1], -ña *adj* : of or from Caracas
caraqueño[2], -ña *n* : person from Caracas
carátula *nf* 1 : title page 2 : cover, dust jacket 3 CARETA : mask 4 *Mex* : face, dial (of a clock or watch)
caravana *nf* 1 : caravan 2 : convoy, motorcade 3 REMOLQUE : trailer
caray → caramba
carbohidrato *nm* : carbohydrate
carbón *nm, pl* carbones 1 : coal 2 : charcoal
carbonatado, -da *adj* : carbonated
carbonato *nm* : carbonate
carboncillo *nm* : charcoal
carbonera *nf* : coal cellar, coal bunker (on a ship)
carbonero, -ra *adj* : coal
carbonizar {21} *vt* : to carbonize, to char
carbono *nm* : carbon
carbunco *or* carbunclo *nm* : carbuncle
carburador *nm* : carburetor
carburante *nm* : fuel
carca *nmf fam* : old fogy
carcacha *nf fam* : jalopy, wreck
carcaj *nm* : quiver (for arrows)
carcajada *nf* : loud laugh, guffaw ⟨reírse a carcajadas : to roar with laughter⟩
carcajearse *vr* : to roar with laughter, to be in stitches
cárcel *nf* PRISIÓN : jail, prison
carcelero, -ra *n* : jailer
carcinogénico, -ca *adj* : carcinogenic
carcinógeno *nm* CANCERÍGENO : carcinogen
carcinoma *nm* : carcinoma
carcomer *vt* : to eat away at, to consume
carcomido, -da *adj* 1 : worm-eaten 2 : decayed, rotten
cardán *nm, pl* cardanes : universal joint
cardar *vt* : to card, to comb
cardenal *nm* 1 : cardinal (in religion) 2 : bruise
cardíaco *or* cardiaco, -ca *adj* : cardiac, heart

cárdigan *nm, pl* -gans : cardigan
cardinal *adj* : cardinal
cardiología *nf* : cardiology
cardiólogo, -ga *n* : cardiologist
cardiovascular *adj* : cardiovascular
cardo *nm* : thistle
cardumen *nm* : school of fish
carear *vt* : to bring face-to-face
carecer {53} *vi* ~ de : to lack ⟨el cheque carecía de fondos : the check lacked funds⟩
carencia *nf* 1 FALTA : lack 2 ESCASEZ : shortage 3 DEFICIENCIA : deficiency
carente *adj* ~ de : lacking (in)
carero, -ra *adj fam* : pricey
carestía *nf* 1 : rise in cost ⟨la carestía de la vida : the high cost of living⟩ 2 : dearth, scarcity
careta *nf* MÁSCARA : mask
carey *nm* 1 : hawksbill turtle, sea turtle 2 : tortoiseshell
carga *nf* 1 : loading 2 : freight, load, cargo 3 : burden, responsibility 4 : charge ⟨carga eléctrica : electrical charge⟩ 5 : attack, charge
cargado, -da *adj* 1 : loaded 2 : bogged down, weighted down 3 : close, stuffy 4 : charged ⟨cargado de tensión : charged with tension⟩ 5 FUERTE : strong ⟨café cargado : strong coffee⟩ 6 cargado de hombros : stoop-shouldered
cargador[1], -dora *n* : longshoreman *m*, longshorewoman *f*
cargador[2] *nm* 1 : magazine (for a firearm) 2 : charger (for batteries)
cargamento *nm* : cargo, load
cargar {52} *vt* 1 : to carry 2 : to load, to fill 3 : to charge — *vi* 1 : to load 2 : to rest (in architecture) 3 ~ sobre : to fall upon
cargo *nm* 1 : burden, load 2 : charge ⟨a cargo de : in charge of⟩ 3 : position, office
cargue, etc. → cargar
carguero[1], -ra *adj* : freight, cargo ⟨tren carguero : freight train⟩
carguero[2] *nm* : freighter, cargo ship
cariarse *vr* : to decay (of teeth)
caribe *adj* : Caribbean ⟨el mar Caribe : the Caribbean Sea⟩
caribeño, -ña *adj* : Caribbean
caribú *nm* : caribou
caricatura *nf* 1 : caricature 2 : cartoon
caricaturista *nmf* : caricaturist, cartoonist
caricaturizar {21} *vt* : to caricature
caricia *nf* 1 : caress 2 hacer caricias : to pet, to stroke
caridad *nf* 1 : charity 2 LIMOSNA : alms *pl*
caries *nfs & pl* : cavity (in a tooth)
carillón *nm, pl* -llones 1 : carillon 2 : glockenspiel
cariño *nm* AFECTO : affection, love
cariñoso, -sa *adj* AFECTUOSO : affectionate, loving — cariñosamente *adv*
carioca[1] *adj* : of or from Rio de Janeiro

carioca[2] *nmf* : person from Rio de Janeiro

carisma *nf* : charisma

carismático, -ca *adj* : charismatic

carita *adj Mex fam* : cute (said of a man) ⟨tu primo se cree muy carita : your cousin thinks he's gorgeous⟩

caritativo, -va *adj* : charitable

cariz *nm, pl* **carices** : appearance, aspect

carmesí *adj & nm* : crimson

carmín *nm, pl* **carmines** 1 : carmine 2 **carmín de labios** : lipstick

carnada *nf* CEBO : bait

carnal *adj* 1 : carnal 2 **primo carnal** : first cousin

carnaval *nm* : carnival

carnaza *nf* : bait

carne *nf* 1 : meat ⟨carne molida : ground beef⟩ 2 : flesh ⟨carne de gallina : goose bumps⟩

carné → **carnet**

carnero *nm* 1 : ram, sheep 2 : mutton

carnet *nm* 1 : identification card, ID 2 : membership card 3 **carnet de conducir** *Spain* : driver's license

carnicería *nf* 1 : butcher shop 2 MATANZA : slaughter, carnage

carnicero, -ra *n* : butcher

carnívoro[1], **-ra** *adj* : carnivorous

carnívoro[2] *nm* : carnivore

carnoso, -sa *adj* : fleshy, meaty

caro[1] *adv* : dearly, a lot ⟨pagué caro : I paid a high price⟩

caro[2], **-ra** *adj* 1 : expensive, dear 2 QUERIDO : dear, beloved

carpa *nf* 1 : carp 2 : big top (of a circus) 3 : tent

carpelo *nm* : carpel

carpeta *nf* : folder, binder, portfolio (of drawings, etc.)

carpetazo *nm* **dar carpetazo a** : to shelve, to defer

carpintería *nf* 1 : carpentry 2 : carpenter's workshop

carpintero, -ra *n* : carpenter

carraspear *vi* : to clear one's throat

carraspera *nf* : hoarseness ⟨tener carraspera : to have a frog in one's throat⟩

carrera *nf* 1 : run, running ⟨a la carrera : at full speed⟩ ⟨de carrera : hastily⟩ 2 : race 3 : course of study 4 : career, profession 5 : run (in baseball)

carreta *nf* : cart, wagon

carrete *nm* 1 BOBINA : reel, spool 2 : roll of film

carretel → **carrete**

carretera *nf* : highway, road ⟨carretera de peaje : turnpike⟩

carretero, -ra *adj* : highway ⟨el sistema carretero nacional : the national highway system⟩

carretilla *nf* 1 : wheelbarrow 2 **carretilla elevadora** : forklift

carril *nm* 1 : lane ⟨carretera de doble carril : two-lane highway⟩ 2 : rail (on a railroad track)

carrillo *nm* : cheek, jowl

carrito *nm* : cart ⟨carrito de compras : shopping cart⟩

carrizo *nm* JUNCO : reed

carro *nm* 1 COCHE : car 2 : cart 3 *Chile, Mex* : coach (of a train) 4 **carro alegórico** : float (in a parade)

carrocería *nf* : bodywork, body (of a vehicle)

carroña *nf* : carrion

carroñero, -ra *n* : scavenger (animal)

carroza *nf* 1 : carriage 2 : float (in a parade)

carruaje *nm* : carriage

carrusel *nm* 1 : merry-go-round 2 : carousel ⟨carrusel de equipaje : luggage carousel⟩

carta *nf* 1 : letter 2 NAIPE : playing card 3 : charter, constitution 4 MENÚ : menu 5 : map, chart 6 **tomar cartas en** : to intervene in

cártamo *nm* : safflower

cartearse *vr* ESCRIBIRSE : to write to one another, to correspond

cartel *nm* 1 : sign, poster

cártel *or* **cartel** *nm* : cartel

cartelera *nf* 1 : billboard 2 : marquee

cartera *nf* 1 BILLETERA : wallet, billfold 2 BOLSO : pocketbook, purse 3 : portfolio ⟨cartera de acciones : stock portfolio⟩

carterista *nmf* : pickpocket

cartero, -ra *n* : letter carrier, mailman *m*

cartilaginoso, -sa *adj* : cartilaginous, gristly

cartílago *nm* : cartilage

cartilla *nf* 1 : primer, reader 2 : booklet ⟨cartilla de ahorros : bankbook⟩

cartografía *nf* : cartography

cartógrafo, -fa *n* : cartographer

cartón *nm, pl* **cartones** 1 : cardboard ⟨cartón madera : fiberboard⟩ 2 : carton

cartucho *nm* : cartridge

cartulina *nf* : poster board, cardboard

carúncula *nf* : wattle (of a bird)

casa *nf* 1 : house, building 2 HOGAR : home 3 : household, family 4 : company, firm 5 **echar la casa por la ventana** : to spare no expense

casaca *nf* : jacket

casado[1], **-da** *adj* : married

casado[2], **-da** *n* : married person

casamentero, -ra *n* : matchmaker

casamiento *nm* 1 : marriage 2 BODA : wedding

casar *vt* : to marry — *vi* : to go together, to match up — **casarse** *vr* 1 : to get married 2 **~ con** : to marry

casateniente *nmf Mex* : landlord, landlady *f*

cascabel[1] *nm* : small bell

cascabel[2] *nf* : rattlesnake

cascada *nf* CATARATA, SALTO : waterfall, cascade

cascajo *nm* 1 : pebble, rock fragment 2 *fam* : piece of junk

cascanueces *nms & pl* : nutcracker

cascar {72} *vt* : to crack (a shell) — **cascarse** *vr* : to crack, to chip

cáscara *nf* 1 : skin, peel, rind, husk 2 : shell (of a nut or egg)

cascarón *nm, pl* **-rones** 1 : eggshell 2 *Mex* : shell filled with confetti

cascarrabias *nmfs & pl fam* : grouch, crab

casco *nm* 1 : helmet 2 : hull 3 : hoof 4 : fragment, shard 5 : center (of a town) 6 *Mex* : empty bottle 7 **cascos** *nmpl* : headphones

caserío *nm* 1 : country house 2 : hamlet

casero¹, -ra *adj* 1 : domestic, household 2 : homemade

casero², -ra *n* DUEÑO : landlord *m*, landlady *f*

caseta *nf* : booth, stand, stall ⟨caseta telefónica : telephone booth⟩

casete → **cassette**

casi *adv* 1 : almost, nearly, virtually 2 (*in negative phrases*) : hardly ⟨casi nunca : hardly ever⟩

casilla *nf* 1 : booth 2 : pigeonhole 3 : box (on a form)

casino *nm* 1 : casino 2 : (social) club

caso *nm* 1 : case 2 **en caso de** : in case of, in the event of 3 **hacer caso de** : to pay attention to, to notice 4 **hacer caso omiso de** : to ignore, to take no notice of 5 **no venir al caso** : to be beside the point

caspa *nf* : dandruff

casque, etc. → **cascar**

casquete *nm* 1 : skullcap 2 **casquete glaciar** : ice cap 3 **casquete corto** *Mex* : crew cut

casquillo *nm* : case, casing (of a bullet)

cassette *nmf* : cassette

casta *nf* 1 : caste 2 : lineage, stock ⟨de casta : thoroughbred, purebred⟩ 3 **sacar la casta** *Mex* : to come out ahead

castaña *nf* : chestnut

castañetear *vi* : to chatter (of teeth)

castaño¹, -ña *adj* : chestnut, brown

castaño² *nm* 1 : chestnut tree 2 : chestnut, brown

castañuela *nf* : castanet

castellano¹, -na *adj & n* : Castilian

castellano² *nm* ESPAÑOL : Spanish, Castilian (language)

castidad *nf* : chastity

castigar {52} *vt* : to punish

castigo *nm* : punishment

castillo *nm* 1 : castle 2 **castillo de proa** : forecastle

casto, -ta *adj* : chaste, pure — **castamente** *adv*

castor *nm* : beaver

castración *nf, pl* **-ciones** : castration

castrar *vt* 1 : to castrate, to spay, to neuter, to geld 2 DEBILITAR : to weaken, to debilitate

castrense *adj* : military

casual *adj* 1 FORTUITO : fortuitous, accidental 2 *Mex* : casual (of clothing)

casualidad *nf* 1 : chance 2 **por** ~ *or* **de** ~ : by chance, by any chance

casualmente *adv* : accidentally, by chance

casucha *or* **casuca** *nf* : shanty, hovel

cataclismo *nm* : cataclysm

catacumbas *nfpl* : catacombs

catador, -dora *n* : wine taster

catalán¹, -lana *adj & n, mpl* **-lanes** : Catalan

catalán² *nm* : Catalan (language)

catálisis *nf* : catalysis

catalítico, -ca *adj* : catalytic

catalizador *nm* 1 : catalyst 2 : catalytic converter

catalogar {52} *vt* : to catalog, to classify

catálogo *nm* : catalog

catamarán *nm, pl* **-ranes** : catamaran

cataplasma *nf* : poultice

catapulta *nf* : catapult

catapultar *vt* : to catapult

catar *vt* 1 : to taste, to sample 2 : to look at, to examine

catarata *nf* CASCADA, SALTO : waterfall 2 : cataract

catarro *nm* RESFRIADO : cold, catarrh

catarsis *nf* : catharsis

catártico, -ca *adj* : cathartic

catástrofe *nf* DESASTRE : catastrophe, disaster

catastrófico, -ca *adj* DESASTROSO : catastrophic, disastrous

catcher *nmf* : catcher (in baseball)

catecismo *nm* : catechism

cátedra *nf* 1 : chair, professorship 2 : subject, class 3 **libertad de cátedra** : academic freedom

catedral *nf* : cathedral

catedrático, -ca *n* PROFESOR : professor

categoría *nf* 1 CLASE : category 2 RANGO : rank, standing 3 **categoría gramatical** : part of speech 4 **de** ~ : first-rate, outstanding

categórico, -ca *adj* : categorical, unequivocal — **categóricamente** *adv*

catéter *nm* : catheter

cátodo *nm* : cathode

catolicismo *nm* : Catholicism

católico, -ca *adj & n* : Catholic

catorce *adj & nm* : fourteen

catorceavo *nm* : fourteenth

catre *nm* : cot

catsup *nm* : ketchup

caucásico, -ca *adj & n* : Caucasian

cauce *nm* 1 LECHO : riverbed 2 : means *pl*, channel

caucho *nm* 1 GOMA : rubber 2 : rubber tree 3 *Ven* : tire

caución *nf, pl* **cauciones** FIANZA : bail, security

caudal *nm* 1 : volume of water 2 RIQUEZA : capital, wealth 3 ABUNDANCIA : abundance

caudillaje *nm* : leadership

caudillo *nm* : leader, commander

causa *nf* **1** MOTIVO : cause, reason, motive ⟨a causa de : because of⟩ **2** IDEAL : cause ⟨morir por una causa : to die for a cause⟩ **3** : lawsuit
causal[1] *adj* : causal
causal[2] *nm* : cause, grounds *pl*
causalidad *nf* : causality
causante[1] *adj* ~ **de** : causing, responsible for
causante[2] *nmf Mex* : taxpayer
causar *vt* **1** : to cause **2** : to provoke, to arouse ⟨eso me causa gracia : that strikes me as being funny⟩
cáustico, -ca *adj* : caustic
cautela *nf* : caution, prudence
cautelar *adj* : precautionary, preventive
cauteloso, -sa *adj* : cautious, prudent — **cautelosamente** *adv*
cauterizar {21} *vt* : to cauterize
cautivador, -dora *adj* : captivating
cautivar *vt* HECHIZAR : to captivate, to charm
cautiverio *nm* : captivity
cautivo, -va *adj & n* : captive
cauto, -ta *adj* : cautious, careful
cavar *vt* : to dig — *vi* ~ **en** : to delve into, to probe
caverna *nf* : cavern, cave
cavernoso, -sa *adj* **1** : cavernous **2** : deep, resounding
caviar *nm* : caviar
cavidad *nf* : cavity
cavilar *vi* : to ponder, to deliberate
cayado *nm* : crook, staff, crosier
cayena *nf* : cayenne pepper
cayó, etc. → **caer**
caza[1] *nf* **1** CACERÍA : hunt, hunting **2** : game
caza[2] *nm* : fighter plane
cazador, -dora *n* **1** : hunter **2 cazador furtivo** : poacher
cazar {21} *vt* **1** : to hunt **2** : to catch, to bag **3** *fam* : to land (a job, a spouse) — *vi* : to go hunting
cazatalentos *nmfs & pl* : talent scout
cazo *nm* **1** : saucepan, pot **2** CUCHARÓN : ladle
cazuela *nf* **1** : pan, saucepan **2** : casserole
cazurro, -ra *adj* : sullen, surly
CD *nm* : CD, compact disk
cebada *nf* : barley
cebar *vt* **1** : to bait **2** : to feed, to fatten **3** : to prime (a pump, etc.) — **cebarse** *vr* ~ **en** : to take it out on
cebo *nm* **1** CARNADA : bait **2** : feed **3** : primer (for firearms)
cebolla *nf* : onion
cebolleta *nf* : scallion, green onion
cebollino *nm* **1** : chive **2** : scallion
cebra *nf* : zebra
cebú *nm, pl* **cebús** *or* **cebúes** : zebu (cattle)
cecear *vi* : to lisp
ceceo *nm* : lisp
cecina *nf* : dried beef, beef jerky
cedazo *nm* : sieve

ceder *vi* **1** : to yield, to give way **2** : to diminish, to abate **3** : to give in, to relent — *vt* : to cede, to hand over
cedro *nm* : cedar
cédula *nf* : document, certificate
céfiro *nm* : zephyr
cegador, -dora *adj* : blinding
cegar {49} *vt* **1** : to blind **2** : to block, to stop up — *vi* : to be blinded, to go blind
cegatón, -tona *adj, mpl* **-tones** *fam* : blind as a bat
ceguera *nf* : blindness
ceiba *nf* : ceiba, silk-cotton tree
ceja *nf* **1** : eyebrow ⟨fruncir las cejas : to knit one's brows⟩ **2** : flange, rim
cejar *vi* : to give in, to back down
celada *nf* : trap, ambush
celador, -dora *n* GUARDIA : guard, warden
celda *nf* : cell (of a jail)
celebración *nf, pl* **-ciones** : celebration
celebrado, -da *adj* CÉLEBRE, FAMOSO : famous, celebrated
celebrante *nmf* OFICIANTE : celebrant
celebrar *vt* **1** FESTEJAR : to celebrate **2** : to hold (a meeting) **3** : to say (Mass) **4** : to welcome, to be happy about — *vi* : to be glad — **celebrarse** *vr* **1** : to be celebrated, to fall **2** : to be held, to take place
célebre *adj* CELEBRADO, FAMOSO : celebrated, famous
celebridad *nf* **1** : celebrity **2** FAMA : fame, renown
celeridad *nf* : celerity, swiftness
celeste[1] *adj* **1** : celestial **2** : sky blue, azure
celeste[2] *nm* : sky blue
celestial *adj* : heavenly, celestial
celibato *nm* : celibacy
célibe *adj & nmf* : celibate
cello *nm* : cello
celo *nm* **1** : zeal, fervor **2** : heat (of females), rut (of males) **3 celos** *nmpl* : jealousy ⟨tenerle celos a alguien : to be jealous of someone⟩
celofán *nm, pl* **-fanes** : cellophane
celosía *nf* **1** : lattice window **2** : latticework, trellis
celoso, -sa *adj* **1** : jealous **2** : zealous — **celosamente** *adv*
celta[1] *adj* : Celtic
celta[2] *nmf* : Celt
célula *nf* : cell
celular *adj* : cellular
celuloide *nm* **1** : celluloid **2** : film, cinema
celulosa *nf* : cellulose
cementar *vt* : to cement
cementerio *nm* : cemetery
cemento *nm* : cement
cena *nf* : supper, dinner
cenador *nm* : arbor
cenagal *nm* : bog, quagmire
cenagoso, -sa *adj* : swampy
cenar *vi* : to have dinner, to have supper — *vt* : to have for dinner or supper

⟨anoche cenamos tamales : we had tamales for supper last night⟩
cencerro *nm* : cowbell
cenicero *nm* : ashtray
ceniciento, -ta *adj* : ashen
cenit *nm* : zenith, peak
ceniza *nf* 1 : ash 2 **cenizas** *nfpl* : ashes (of a deceased person)
cenizo, -za *n* : jinx
cenote *nm Mex* : natural deposit of spring water
censar *vt* : to take a census of
censo *nm* : census
censor, -sora *n* : censor, critic
censura *nf* 1 : censorship 2 : censure, criticism
censurable *adj* : reprehensible, blameworthy
censurar *vt* 1 : to censor 2 : to censure, to criticize
centauro *nm* : centaur
centavo *nm* 1 : cent (in English-speaking countries) 2 : unit of currency in various Latin-American countries
centella *nf* 1 : lightning flash 2 : spark
centellear *vi* 1 : to twinkle 2 : to gleam, to sparkle
centelleo *nm* : twinkling, sparkle
centenar *nm* 1 : hundred 2 **a centenares** : by the hundreds
centenario¹, -ria *adj & n* : centenarian
centenario² *nm* : centennial
centeno *nm* : rye
centésimo¹, -ma *adj* : hundredth
centésimo² *nm* : hundredth
centígrado *adj* : centigrade, Celsius
centigramo *nm* : centigram
centímetro *nm* : centimeter
centinela *nmf* : sentinel, sentry
central¹ *adj* 1 : central 2 PRINCIPAL : main, principal
central² *nf* 1 : main office, headquarters 2 **central camionera** *Mex* : bus terminal
centralita *nf* : switchboard
centralizar {21} *vt* : to centralize — **centralización** *nf*
centrar *vt* 1 : to center 2 : to focus — **centrarse** *vr* ~ **en** : to focus on, to concentrate on
céntrico, -ca *adj* : central
centrífugo, -ga *adj* : centrifugal
centrípeto, -ta *adj* : centripetal
centro¹ *nmf* : center (in sports)
centro² *nm* 1 MEDIO : center ⟨centro de atención : center of attention⟩ ⟨centro de gravedad : center of gravity⟩ 2 : downtown 3 **centro de mesa** : centerpiece
centroamericano, -na *adj & n* : Central American
ceñido, -da *adj* AJUSTADO : tight, tight-fitting
ceñir {67} *vt* 1 : to encircle, to surround 2 : to hug, to cling to ⟨me ciñe demasiado : it's too tight on me⟩ — **ceñirse** *vr* ~ **a** : to restrict oneself to, to stick to

ceño *nm* 1 : frown, scowl 2 **fruncir el ceño** : to frown, to knit one's brows
cepa *nf* 1 : stump (of a tree) 2 : stock (of a vine) 3 LINAJE : ancestry, stock
cepillar *vt* 1 : to brush 2 : to plane (wood) — **cepillarse** *vr*
cepillo *nm* 1 : brush ⟨cepillo de dientes : toothbrush⟩ 2 : plane (for woodworking)
cepo *nm* : trap (for animals)
cera *nf* 1 : wax ⟨cera de abejas : beeswax⟩ 2 : polish
cerámica *nf* 1 : ceramics *pl* 2 : pottery
cerámico, -ca *adj* : ceramic
ceramista *nmf* ALFARERO : potter
cerca¹ *adv* 1 : close, near, nearby 2 ~ **de** : nearly, almost
cerca² *nf* 1 : fence 2 : (stone) wall
cercado *nm* : enclosure
cercanía *nf* 1 PROXIMIDAD : proximity, closeness 2 **cercanías** *nfpl* : outskirts, suburbs
cercano, -na *adj* : near, close
cercar {72} *vt* 1 : to fence in, to enclose 2 : to surround
cercenar *vt* 1 : to cut off, to amputate 2 : to diminish, to curtail
cerceta *nf* : teal (duck)
cerciorarse *vr* ASEGURARSE ~ **de** : to make sure of, to verify
cerco *nm* 1 : siege 2 : cordon, circle 3 : fence
cerda *nf* 1 : bristle 2 : sow
cerdo *nm* 1 : pig, hog 2 **carne de cerdo** : pork
cereal *nm* : cereal — **cereal** *adj*
cerebelo *nm* : cerebellum
cerebral *adj* : cerebral
cerebro *nm* : brain
ceremonia *nf* : ceremony — **ceremonial** *adj*
ceremonioso, -sa *adj* : ceremonious
cereza *nf* : cherry
cerezo *nm* : cherry tree
cerilla *nf* 1 : match 2 : earwax
cerillo *nm* (*in various countries*) : match
cerner {56} *vt* : to sift — **cernerse** *vr* 1 : to hover 2 ~ **sobre** : to loom over, to threaten
cernidor *nm* : sieve
cernir → **cerner**
cero *nm* : zero
ceroso, -sa *adj* : waxy
cerque, etc. → **cercar**
cerquita *adv fam* : very close, very near
cerrado, -da *adj* 1 : closed, shut 2 : thick, broad ⟨tiene un acento cerrado : she has a thick accent⟩ 3 : cloudy, overcast 4 : quiet, reserved 5 : dense, stupid
cerradura *nf* : lock
cerrajería *nf* : locksmith's shop
cerrajero, -ra *n* : locksmith
cerrar {55} *vt* 1 : to close, to shut 2 : to turn off 3 : to bring to an end — *vi* 1 : to close up, to lock up 2 : to close down — **cerrarse** *vr* 1 : to close 2 : to fasten, to button up 3 : to conclude, to end

cerrazón *nf, pl* **-zones** : obstinacy, stubbornness
cerro *nm* COLINA, LOMA : hill
cerrojo *nm* PESTILLO : bolt, latch
certamen *nm, pl* **-támenes** : competition, contest
certero, -ra *adj* : accurate, precise — **certeramente** *adv*
certeza *nf* : certainty
certidumbre *nf* : certainty
certificable *adj* : certifiable
certificación *nf, pl* **-ciones** : certification
certificado[1]**, -da** *adj* 1 : certified 2 : registered (of mail)
certificado[2] *nm* 1 : certificate 2 : registered letter
certificar {72} *vt* 1 : to certify 2 : to register (mail)
cervato *nm* : fawn
cervecera *nf* : brewery
cervecería *nf* 1 : brewery 2 : beer hall, bar
cerveza *nf* : beer ⟨cerveza de barril : draft beer⟩
cervical *adj* : cervical
cerviz *nf, pl* **cervices** : nape of the neck, cervix
cesación *nf, pl* **-ciones** : cessation, suspension
cesante *adj* : laid off, unemployed
cesantía *nf* : unemployment
cesar *vi* : to cease, to stop — *vt* : to dismiss, to lay off
cesárea *nf* : cesarean, C-section
cese *nm* 1 : cessation, stop ⟨cese del fuego : cease-fire⟩ 2 : dismissal
cesio *nm* : cesium
cesión *nf, pl* **cesiones** : transfer, assignment ⟨cesión de bienes : transfer of property⟩
césped *nm* : lawn, grass
cesta *nf* 1 : basket 2 : jai alai racket
cesto *nm* 1 : hamper 2 : basket (in basketball) **3 cesto de (la) basura** : wastebasket
cetrería *nf* : falconry
cetrino, -na *adj* : sallow
cetro *nm* : scepter
chabacano[1]**, -na** *adj* : tacky, tasteless
chabacano[2] *nm Mex* : apricot
chacal *nm* : jackal
cháchara *nf fam* 1 : small talk, chatter 2 **chácharas** *nfpl* : trinkets, junk
chacharear *vi fam* : to chatter, to gab
chacra *nf Arg, Chile, Peru* : small farm
chadiano, -na *adj & n* : Chadian
chal *nm* MANTÓN : shawl
chalado[1]**, -da** *adj fam* : crazy, nuts
chalado[2]**, -da** *n* : nut, crazy person
chalán *nm, pl* **chalanes** *Mex* : barge
chalé → **chalet**
chaleco *nm* : vest
chalet *nm Spain* : house
chalupa *nf* 1 : small boat 2 *Mex* : small stuffed tortilla
chamaco, -ca *n Mex fam* : kid, boy *m*, girl *f*

chamarra *nf* 1 : sheepskin jacket 2 : poncho, blanket
chamba *nf Mex, Peru fam* : job, work
chambear *vi Mex, Peru fam* : to work
chamo, -ma *n Ven fam* 1 : kid, boy *m*, girl *f* 2 : buddy, pal
champaña *or* **champán** *nm* : champagne
champiñón *nm, pl* **-ñones** : mushroom
champú *nm, pl* **-pus** *or* **-púes** : shampoo
champurrado *nm Mex* : hot chocolate thickened with cornstarch
chamuco *nm Mex fam* : devil
chamuscar {72} *vt* : to singe, to scorch — **chamuscarse** *vr*
chamusquina *nf* : scorch
chance *nm* OPORTUNIDAD : chance, opportunity
chancho[1]**, -cha** *adj fam* : dirty, filthy, gross
chancho[2]**, -cha** *n* 1 : pig, hog 2 *fam* : slob
chanchullero, -ra *adj fam* : shady, crooked
chanchullo *nm fam* : shady deal, scam
chancla *nf* 1 : thong sandal, slipper 2 : old shoe
chancleta → **chancla**
chanclo *nm* 1 : clog 2 **chanclos** *nmpl* : overshoes, galoshes, rubbers
chancro *nm* : chancre
changarro *nm Mex* : small shop, stall
chango, -ga *n Mex* : monkey
chantaje *nm* : blackmail
chantajear *vt* : to blackmail
chantajista *nmf* : blackmailer
chanza *nf* 1 : joke, jest 2 *Mex fam* : chance, opportunity
chapa *nf* 1 : sheet, panel, veneer 2 : lock 3 : badge
chapado, -da *adj* 1 : plated 2 **chapado a la antigua** : old-fashioned
chapar *vt* 1 : to veneer 2 : to plate (metals)
chaparrón *nm, pl* **-rrones** 1 : downpour 2 : great quantity, torrent
chapeado, -da *adj Col, Mex* : flushed
chapopote *nm Mex* : tar, blacktop
chapotear *vi* : to splash about
chapucero[1]**, -ra** *adj* 1 : crude, shoddy 2 *Mex fam* : dishonest
chapucero[2]**, -ra** *n* 1 : sloppy worker, bungler 2 *Mex fam* : cheat, swindler
chapulín *nm, pl* **-lines** *CA, Mex* : grasshopper, locust
chapuza *nf* 1 : botched job 2 *Mex fam* : fraud, trick ⟨hacer chapuzas : to cheat⟩
chapuzón *nm, pl* **-zones** : dip, swim ⟨darse un chapuzón : to go for a quick dip⟩
chaqueta *nf* : jacket
charada *nf* : charades (game)
charango *nm* : traditional Andean stringed instrument
charca *nf* : pond, pool
charco *nm* : puddle, pool

charcutería *nf* : delicatessen
charla *nf* : chat, talk
charlar *vi* : to chat, to talk
charlatán[1], **-tana** *adj* : talkative, chatty
charlatán[2], **-tana** *n, mpl* **-tanes** 1 : chatterbox 2 FARSANTE : charlatan, phony
charlatanear *vi* : to chatter away
charol *nm* 1 : lacquer, varnish 2 : patent leather 3 : tray
charola *nf Bol, Mex, Peru* : tray
charreada *nf Mex* : charro show, rodeo
charretera *nf* : epaulet
charro[1], **-rra** *adj* 1 : gaudy, tacky 2 *Mex* : pertaining to charros
charro[2], **-rra** *n Mex* : charro (Mexican cowboy or cowgirl)
chascarrillo *nm fam* : joke, funny story
chasco *nm* 1 BROMA : trick, joke 2 DECEPCIÓN, DESILUSIÓN : disillusionment, disappointment
chasis *or* **chasís** *nm* : chassis
chasquear *vt* 1 : to click (the tongue, fingers, etc.) 2 : to snap (a whip)
chasquido *nm* 1 : click (of the tongue or fingers) 2 : snap, crack
chatarra *nf* : scrap metal
chato, -ta *adj* 1 : pug-nosed 2 : flat
chauvinismo *nm* : chauvinism
chauvinista[1] *adj* : chauvinistic
chauvinista[2] *nmf* : chauvinist
chaval, -vala *n fam* : kid, boy *m,* girl *f*
chavo[1], **-va** *adj Mex fam* : young
chavo[2], **-va** *n Mex fam* : kid, boy *m,* girl *f*
chavo[3] *nm fam* : cent, buck ⟨no tengo un chavo : I'm broke⟩
chayote *nm* : chayote (plant, fruit)
checar {72} *vt Mex* : to check, to verify
checo[1], **-ca** *adj & n* : Czech
checo[2] *nm* : Czech (language)
checoslovaco, -ca *adj & n* : Czechoslovakian
chef *nm* : chef
chelín *nm, pl* **chelines** : shilling
cheque[1], etc. → **checar**
cheque[2] *nm* 1 : check 2 **cheque de viajero** : traveler's check
chequear *vt* 1 : to check, to verify 2 : to check in (baggage)
chequeo *nm* 1 INSPECCIÓN : check, inspection 2 : checkup, examination
chequera *nf* : checkbook
chévere *adj fam* : great, fantastic
chic *adj & nm* : chic
chica → **chico**
chicano, -na *adj & n* : Chicano *m,* Chicana *f*
chicha *nf* : fermented alcoholic beverage made from corn
chícharo *nm* : pea
chicharra *nf* 1 CIGARRA : cicada 2 : buzzer
chicharrón *nm, pl* **-rrones** 1 : pork rind 2 **darle chicharrón a** *Mex fam* : to get rid of
chichón *nm, pl* **chichones** : bump, swelling

chicle *nm* : chewing gum
chicloso *nm Mex* : taffy
chico[1], **-ca** *adj* 1 : little, small 2 : young
chico[2], **-ca** *n* 1 : child, boy *m,* girl *f* 2 : young man *m,* young woman *f*
chicote *nm* LÁTIGO : whip, lash
chiffon → **chifón**
chiflado[1], **-da** *adj fam* : nuts, crazy
chiflado[2], **-da** *n fam* : crazy person, lunatic
chiflar *vi* : to whistle — *vt* : to whistle at, to boo — **chiflarse** *vr fam* ~ **por** : to be crazy about
chiflido *nm* : whistle, whistling
chiflón *nm, pl* **chiflones** : draft (of air)
chifón *nm, pl* **chifones** : chiffon
chilango[1], **-ga** *adj Mex fam* : of or from Mexico City
chilango[2], **-ga** *n Mex fam* : person from Mexico City
chilaquiles *nmpl Mex* : shredded tortillas in sauce
chile *nm* : chili pepper
chileno, -na *adj & n* : Chilean
chillar *vi* 1 : to squeal, to screech 2 : to scream, to yell 3 : to be gaudy, to clash
chillido *nm* 1 : scream, shout 2 : squeal, screech, cry (of an animal)
chillo *nm PRi* : red snapper
chillón, -llona *adj, mpl* **chillones** 1 : piercing, shrill 2 : loud, gaudy
chilpayate *nmf Mex fam* : child, little kid
chimenea *nf* 1 : chimney 2 : fireplace
chimichurri *nm Arg* : traditional hot sauce
chimpancé *nm* : chimpanzee
china *nf* 1 : pebble, small stone 2 *PRi* : orange
chinchar *vt fam* : to annoy, to pester — **chincharse** *vr fam* : to put up with something, to grin and bear it
chinchayote *nm Mex* : chayote root
chinche[1] *nf* 1 : bedbug 2 *Ven* : ladybug 3 : thumbtack
chinche[2] *nmf fam* : nuisance, pain in the neck
chinchilla *nf* : chinchilla
chino[1], **-na** *adj* 1 : Chinese 2 *Mex* : curly, kinky
chino[2], **-na** *n* : Chinese person
chino[3] *nm* : Chinese (language)
chip *nm, pl* **chips** : chip ⟨chip de memoria : memory chip⟩
chipote *nm Mex fam* : bump (on the head)
chipotle *nm Mex* : type of chili pepper
chipriota *adj & nmf* : Cypriot
chiquear *vt Mex* : to spoil, to indulge
chiquero *nm* POCILGA : pigpen, pigsty
chiquillada *nf* : childish prank
chiquillo[1], **-lla** *adj* : very young, little
chiquillo[2], **-lla** *n* : kid, youngster
chiquito[1], **-ta** *adj* : tiny
chiquito[2], **-ta** *n* : little one, baby
chiribita *nf* 1 : spark 2 **chiribitas** *nfpl* : spots before the eyes
chiribitil *nm* 1 DESVÁN : attic, garret 2 : cubbyhole

chirigota *nf fam* : joke
chirimía *nf* : traditional reed pipe
chirimoya *nf* : cherimoya, custard apple
chiripa *nf* **1** : fluke **2 de ~** : by sheer luck
chirivía *nf* : parsnip
chirona *nf fam* : slammer, jail
chirriar {85} *vi* **1** : to squeak, to creak **2** : to screech — **chirriante** *adj*
chirrido *nm* **1** : squeak, squeaking **2** : screech, screeching
chirrión *nm, pl* **chirriones** *Mex* : whip, lash
chisme *nm* **1** : gossip, tale **2** *Spain fam* : gadget, thingamajig
chismear *vi* : to gossip
chismoso¹, -sa *adj* : gossipy, gossiping
chismoso², -sa *n* **1** : gossiper, gossip **2** *Mex fam* : tattletale
chispa¹ *adj* **1** *Mex fam* : lively, vivacious ⟨un perrito chispa : a frisky puppy⟩ **2** *Spain fam* : tipsy
chispa² *nf* **1** : spark **2 echar chispas** : to be furious
chispeante *adj* : sparkling, scintillating
chispear *vi* **1** : to give off sparks **2** : to sparkle
chisporrotear *vi* : to crackle, to sizzle
chiste *nm* **1** : joke, funny story **2 tener chiste** : to be funny **3 tener su chiste** *Mex* : to be tricky
chistoso¹, -sa *adj* **1** : funny, humorous **2** : witty
chistoso², -sa *n* : wit, joker
chivas *nfpl Mex fam* : stuff, odds and ends
chivo¹, -va *n* **1** : kid, young goat **2 chivo expiatorio** : scapegoat
chivo² *nm* **1** : billy goat **2** : fit of anger
chocante *adj* **1** : shocking **2** : unpleasant, rude
chocar {72} *vi* **1** : to crash, to collide **2** : to clash, to conflict **3** : to be shocking ⟨le chocó : he was shocked⟩ **4** *Mex, Ven fam* : to be unpleasant or obnoxious ⟨me choca tu jefe : I can't stand your boss⟩ — *vt* **1** : to shake (hands) **2** : to clink glasses
chochear *vi* **1** : to be senile **2 ~ por** : to dote on, to be soft on
chochín *nm, pl* **-chines** : wren
chocho, -cha *adj* **1** : senile **2** : doting
choclo *nm* **1** : ear of corn, corncob **2** : corn **3 meter el choclo** *Mex fam* : to make a mistake
chocolate *nm* **1** : chocolate **2** : hot chocolate, cocoa
chofer *or* **chófer** *nm* **1** : chauffeur **2** : driver
choke *nm* : choke (of an automobile)
chole *interj Mex fam* ¡ya chole! : enough!, cut it out!
cholo, -la *adj & n* : mestizo
cholla *nf fam* : head
chollo *nm Spain fam* : bargain
chongo *nm* **1** *Mex* : bun (chignon) **2 chongos** *nmpl Mex* : dessert made with fried bread

choque¹, etc. → chocar
choque² *nm* **1** : crash, collision **2** : clash, conflict **3** : shock
chorizo *nm* : chorizo, sausage
chorrear *vi* **1** : to drip **2** : to pour out, to gush out
chorrito *nm* : squirt, splash
chorro *nm* **1** : flow, stream, jet **2** *Mex fam* : heap, ton
choteado, -da *adj Mex fam* : worn-out, stale ⟨esa canción está bien choteada : that song's been played to death⟩
chotear *vt* : to make fun of
choteo *nm* : joking around, kidding
chovinismo, chovinista → chauvinismo, chauvinista
choza *nf* BARRACA, CABAÑA : hut, shack
chubasco *nm* : downpour, storm
chuchería *nf* : knickknack, trinket
chueco, -ca *adj* **1** : crooked, bent **2** *Chile, Mex fam* : dishonest, shady
chulada *nf Mex, Spain fam* : cute or pretty thing ⟨¡qué chulada de vestido! : what a lovely dress!⟩
chulear *vt Mex fam* : to compliment
chuleta *nf* : cutlet, chop
chulo¹, -la *adj* **1** *fam* : cute, pretty **2** *Spain fam* : cocky, arrogant
chulo² *nm Spain* : pimp
chupada *nf* **1** : suck, sucking **2** : puff, drag (on a cigarette)
chupado, -da *adj fam* **1** : gaunt, skinny **2** : plastered, drunk
chupaflor *nm* COLIBRÍ : hummingbird
chupamirto *nm Mex* : hummingbird
chupar *vt* **1** : to suck **2** : to absorb **3** : to puff on **4** *fam* : to drink, to guzzle — *vi* : to suckle — **chuparse** *vr* **1** : to waste away **2** *fam* : to put up with **3** ¡chúpate esa! *fam* : take that!
chupete *nm* **1** : pacifier **2** *Chile, Peru* : lollipop
chupetear *vt* : to suck (at)
chupón *nm, pl* **chupones** **1** : sucker (of a plant) **2** : baby bottle, pacifier
churrasco *nm* **1** : steak **2** : barbecued meat
churro *nm* **1** : fried dough **2** *fam* : botch, mess **3** *fam* : attractive person, looker
chusco, -ca *adj* : funny, amusing
chusma *nf* GENTUZA : riffraff, rabble
chutar *vi* : to shoot (in soccer)
chute *nm* : shot (in soccer)
cianuro *nm* : cyanide
cibernética *nf* : cybernetics
cicatriz *nf, pl* **-trices** : scar
cicatrizarse {21} *vr* : to form a scar, to heal
cíclico, -ca *adj* : cyclical
ciclismo *nm* : bicycling
ciclista *nmf* : bicyclist
ciclo *nm* : cycle
ciclomotor *nm* : moped
ciclón *nm, pl* **ciclones** : cyclone
cicuta *nf* : hemlock
cidra *nf* : citron (fruit)
ciega, ciegue etc. → cegar

ciego¹, -ga *adj* **1** INVIDENTE : blind **2** a ciegas : blindly **3** quedarse ciego : to go blind — ciegamente *adv*

ciego², -ga *n* INVIDENTE : blind person

cielo *nm* **1** : sky **2** : heaven **3** : ceiling

ciempiés *nms & pl* : centipede

cien¹ *adj* **1** : a hundred, hundred ⟨las primeras cien páginas : the first hundred pages⟩ **2** cien por cien *or* cien por ciento : a hundred percent, through and through, wholeheartedly

cien² *nm* : one hundred

ciénaga *nf* : swamp, bog

ciencia *nf* **1** : science **2** : learning, knowledge **3** a ciencia cierta : for a fact, for certain

cieno *nm* : mire, mud, silt

científico¹, -ca *adj* : scientific — científicamente *adv*

científico², -ca *n* : scientist

ciento¹ *adj* (*used in compound numbers*) : one hundred ⟨ciento uno : one hundred and one⟩

ciento² *nm* **1** : hundred, group of a hundred **2** por ~ : percent

cierne, etc. → cerner

cierra, etc. → cerrar

cierre *nm* **1** : closing, closure **2** : fastener, clasp, zipper

cierto, -ta *adj* **1** : true, certain, definite ⟨lo cierto es que . . . : the fact is that . . . ⟩ **2** : certain, one ⟨cierto día de verano : one summer day⟩ ⟨bajo ciertas circunstancias : under certain circumstances⟩ **3** por ~ : in fact, as a matter of fact — ciertamente *adv*

ciervo, -va *n* : deer, stag *m*, hind *f*

cifra *nf* **1** : figure, number **2** : quantity, amount **3** CLAVE : code, cipher

cifrar *vt* **1** : to write in code **2** : to place, to pin ⟨cifró su esperanza en la lotería : he pinned his hopes on the lottery⟩ — cifrarse *vr* : to amount ⟨la multa se cifra en millares : the fine amounts to thousands⟩

cigarra *nf* CHICHARRA : cicada

cigarrera *nf* : cigarette case

cigarrillo *nm* : cigarette

cigarro *nm* **1** : cigarette **2** PURO : cigar

cigoto *nm* : zygote

cigüeña *nf* : stork

cilantro *nm* : cilantro, coriander

cilíndrico, -ca *adj* : cylindrical

cilindro *nm* : cylinder

cima *nf* CUMBRE : peak, summit, top

cimarrón, -rrona *adj, mpl* -rrones : untamed, wild

címbalo *nm* : cymbal

cimbel *nm* : decoy

cimbrar *vt* : to shake, to rock — cimbrarse *vr* : to sway, to swing

cimentar {55} *vt* **1** : to lay the foundation of, to establish **2** : to strengthen, to cement

cimientos *nmpl* : base, foundation(s)

cinc *nm* : zinc

cincel *nm* : chisel

cincelar *vt* **1** : to chisel **2** : to engrave

cincha *nf* : cinch, girth

cinchar *vt* : to cinch (a horse)

cinco *adj & nm* : five

cincuenta *adj & nm* : fifty

cincuentavo¹, -va *adj* : fiftieth

cincuentavo² *nm* : fiftieth (fraction)

cine *nm* **1** : cinema, movies *pl* **2** : movie theater

cineasta *nmf* : filmmaker

cinematográfico, -ca *adj* : movie, film, cinematic ⟨la industria cinematográfica : the film industry⟩

cingalés¹, -lesa *adj & n* : Sinhalese

cingalés² *nm* : Sinhalese (language)

cínico¹, -ca *adj* **1** : cynical **2** : shameless, brazen — cínicamente *adv*

cínico², -ca *n* : cynic

cinismo *nm* : cynicism

cinta *nf* **1** : ribbon **2** : tape ⟨cinta métrica : tape measure⟩ **3** : strap, belt ⟨cinta transportadora : conveyor belt⟩

cinto *nm* : strap, belt

cintura *nf* **1** : waist, waistline **2** meter en cintura *fam* : to bring into line, to discipline

cinturón *nm, pl* -rones **1** : belt **2** cinturón de seguridad : seat belt

ciñe, etc. → ceñir

ciprés *nm, pl* cipreses : cypress

circo *nm* : circus

circón *nm, pl* circones : zircon

circonio *nm* : zirconium

circuitería *nf* : circuitry

circuito *nm* : circuit

circulación *nf, pl* -ciones **1** : circulation **2** : movement **3** : traffic

circular¹ *vi* **1** : to circulate **2** : to move along **3** : to drive

circular² *adj* : circular

circular³ *nf* : circular, flier

circulatorio, -ria *adj* : circulatory

círculo *nm* **1** : circle **2** : club, group

circuncidar *vt* : to circumcise

circuncisión *nf, pl* -siones : circumcision

circundar *vt* : to surround — circundante *adj*

circunferencia *nf* : circumference

circunflejo, -ja *adj* acento circunflejo : circumflex

circunlocución *nf, pl* -ciones : circumlocution

circunloquio *nm* → circunlocución

circunnavegar {52} *vt* : to circumnavigate — circunnavegación *nf*

circunscribir {33} *vt* : to circumscribe, to constrict, to limit — circunscribirse *vr*

circunscripción *nf, pl* -ciones **1** : limitation, restriction **2** : constituency

circunscrito *pp* → circunscribir

circunspección *nf, pl* -ciones : circumspection, prudence

circunspecto, -ta *adj* : circumspect, prudent

circunstancia *nf* : circumstance

circunstancial *adj* : circumstantial, incidental

circunstante *nmf* **1** : onlooker, bystander **2 los circunstantes** : those present

circunvalación *nf, pl* **-ciones** : surrounding, encircling ⟨carretera de circunvalación : bypass, beltway⟩

circunvecino, -na *adj* : surrounding, neighboring

cirio *nm* : large candle

cirro *nm* : cirrus (cloud)

cirrosis *nf* : cirrhosis

ciruela *nf* **1** : plum **2 ciruela pasa** : prune

cirugía *nf* : surgery

cirujano, -na *n* : surgeon

cisma *nm* : schism, rift

cisne *nm* : swan

cisterna *nf* : cistern, tank

cita *nf* **1** : quote, quotation **2** : appointment, date

citable *adj* : quotable

citación *nf, pl* **-ciones** EMPLAZAMIENTO : summons, subpoena

citadino¹, -na *adj* : of the city, urban

citadino², -na *n* : city dweller

citado, -da *adj* : said, aforementioned

citar *vt* **1** : to quote, to cite **2** : to make an appointment with **3** : to summon (to court), to subpoena — **citarse** *vr* ∼ **con** : to arrange to meet (someone)

cítara *nf* : zither

citatorio *nm* : subpoena

citoplasma *nm* : cytoplasm

cítrico¹, -ca *adj* : citric

cítrico² *nm* : citrus fruit

ciudad *nf* **1** : city, town **2 ciudad universitaria** : college or university campus **3 ciudad perdida** *Mex* : shantytown

ciudadanía *nf* **1** : citizenship **2** : citizenry, citizens *pl*

ciudadano¹, -na *adj* : civic, city

ciudadano², -na *n* **1** NACIONAL : citizen **2** HABITANTE : resident, city dweller

ciudadela *nf* : citadel, fortress

cívico, -ca *adj* **1** : civic **2** : public-spirited

civil¹ *adj* **1** : civil **2** : civilian

civil² *nmf* : civilian

civilidad *nf* : civility, courtesy

civilización *nf, pl* **-ciones** : civilization

civilizar {21} *vt* : to civilize

civismo *nm* : community spirit, civic-mindedness, civics

cizaña *nf* : discord, rift

clamar *vi* : to clamor, to raise a protest — *vt* : to cry out for

clamor *nm* : clamor, outcry

clamoroso, -sa *adj* : clamorous, resounding, thunderous

clan *nm* : clan

clandestinidad *nf* : secrecy ⟨en la clandestinidad : underground⟩

clandestino, -na *adj* : clandestine, secret

clara *nf* : egg white

claraboya *nf* : skylight

claramente *adv* : clearly

clarear *v impers* **1** : to clear, to clear up **2** : to get light, to dawn — *vi* : to go gray, to turn white

claridad *nf* **1** NITIDEZ : clarity, clearness **2** : brightness, light

clarificación *nf, pl* **-ciones** ACLARACIÓN : clarification, explanation

clarificar {72} *vt* ACLARAR : to clarify, to explain

clarín *nm, pl* **clarines** : bugle

clarinete *nm* : clarinet

clarividencia *nf* **1** : clairvoyance **2** : perspicacity, discernment

clarividente¹ *adj* **1** : clairvoyant **2** : perspicacious, discerning

clarividente² *nmf* : clairvoyant

claro¹ *adv* **1** : clearly ⟨habla más claro : speak more clearly⟩ **2** : of course, surely ⟨¡claro!, ¡claro que sí! : absolutely!, of course!⟩ ⟨claro que entendió : of course she understood⟩

claro², -ra *adj* **1** : bright, clear **2** : pale, fair, light **3** : clear, evident

claro³ *nm* **1** : clearing **2 claro de luna** : moonlight

clase *nf* **1** : class **2** ÍNDOLE, TIPO : sort, kind, type

clasicismo *nm* : classicism

clásico¹, -ca *adj* **1** : classic **2** : classical

clásico² *nm* : classic

clasificación *nf, pl* **-ciones** **1** : classification, sorting out **2** : rating **3** CALIFICACIÓN : qualification (in competitions)

clasificado, -da *adj* : classified ⟨aviso clasificado : classified ad⟩

clasificar {72} *vt* **1** : to classify, to sort out **2** : to rate, to rank — *vi* CALIFICAR : to qualify (in competitions) — **clasificarse** *vr*

claudicación *nf, pl* **-ciones** : surrender, abandonment of one's principles

claudicar {72} *vi* : to back down, to abandon one's principles

claustro *nm* : cloister

claustrofobia *nf* : claustrophobia

claustrofóbico, -ca *adj* : claustrophobic

cláusula *nf* : clause

clausura *nf* **1** : closure, closing **2** : closing ceremony **3** : cloister

clausurar *vt* **1** : to close, to bring to a close **2** : to close down

clavadista *nmf* : diver

clavado¹, -da *adj* **1** : nailed, fixed, stuck **2** *fam* : punctual, on the dot **3** *fam* : identical ⟨es clavado a su padre : he's the image of his father⟩

clavado² *nm* : dive

clavar *vt* **1** : to nail, to hammer **2** HINCAR : to plunge, to stick **3** : to fix (one's eyes) on — **clavarse** *vr* : to stick oneself (with a sharp object)

clave¹ *adj* : key, essential

clave² *nf* **1** CIFRA : code **2** : key ⟨la clave del misterio : the key to the mystery⟩ **3** : clef **4** : keystone

clavel *nm* : carnation

clavelito *nm* : pink (flower)

clavicémbalo *nm* : harpsichord
clavícula *nf* : collarbone
clavija *nf* **1** : plug **2** : peg, pin
clavo *nm* **1** : nail ⟨clavo grande : spike⟩ **2** : clove **3 dar en el clavo** : to hit the nail on the head
claxon *nm, pl* **cláxones** : horn (of an automobile)
clemencia *nf* : clemency, mercy
clemente *adj* : merciful
cleptomanía *nf* : kleptomania
cleptómano, -na *n* : kleptomaniac
clerecía *nf* : ministry, ministers *pl*
clerical *adj* : clerical
clérigo, -ga *n* : cleric, member of the clergy
clero *nm* : clergy
cliché *nm* **1** : cliché **2** : stencil **3** : negative (of a photograph)
cliente, -ta *n* : customer, client
clientela *nf* : clientele, customers *pl*
clima *nm* **1** : climate **2** AMBIENTE : atmosphere, ambience
climático, -ca *adj* : climatic
climatización *nf, pl* **-ciones** : air-conditioning
climatizar {21} *vt* : to air-condition — **climatizado, -da** *adj*
clímax *nm* : climax
clínica *nf* : clinic
clínico, -ca *adj* : clinical — **clínicamente** *adv*
clip *nm, pl* **clips 1** : clip **2** : paper clip
clítoris *nms & pl* : clitoris
cloaca *nf* ALCANTARILLA : sewer
clocar {82} *vi* : to cluck
cloche *nm CA, Car, Col, Ven* : clutch (of an automobile)
clon *nm* : clone
cloqué, etc. → **clocar**
cloquear *vi* : to cluck
clorar *vt* : to chlorinate — **cloración** *nf*
cloro *nm* : chlorine
clorofila *nf* : chlorophyll
cloroformo *nm* : chloroform
cloruro *nm* : chloride
clóset *nm, pl* **clósets 1** : closet **2** : cupboard
club *nm* : club
clueca, clueque etc. → **clocar**
coa *nf Mex* : hoe
coacción *nf, pl* **-ciones** : coercion, duress
coaccionar *vt* : to coerce
coactivo, -va *adj* : coercive
coagular *y* : to clot, to coagulate — **coagulación** *nf*
coágulo *nm* : clot
coalición *nf, pl* **-ciones** : coalition
coartada *nf* : alibi
coartar *vt* : to restrict, to limit
cobalto *nm* : cobalt
cobarde[1] *adj* : cowardly
cobarde[2] *nmf* : coward
cobardía *nf* : cowardice
cobaya *nf* : guinea pig
cobertizo *nm* : shed, shelter
cobertor *nm* COLCHA : bedspread, quilt

cobertura *nf* **1** : coverage **2** : cover, collateral
cobija *nf* FRAZADA, MANTA : blanket
cobijar *vt* : to shelter — **cobijarse** *vr* : to take shelter
cobra *nf* : cobra
cobrador, -dora *n* **1** : collector **2** : conductor (of a bus or train)
cobrar *vt* **1** : to charge **2** : to collect, to draw, to earn **3** : to acquire, to gain **4** : to recover, to retrieve **5** : to cash (a check) **6** : to claim, to take (a life) **7** : to shoot (game), to bag — *vi* **1** : to be paid **2 llamar por cobrar** *Mex* : to call collect
cobre *nm* : copper
cobrizo, -za *adj* : coppery
cobro *nm* : collection (of money), cashing (of a check)
coca *nf* **1** : coca **2** *fam* : coke, cocaine
cocaína *nf* : cocaine
cocal *nm* : coca plantation
cocción *nf, pl* **cocciones** : cooking
cocear *vi* : to kick (of an animal)
cocer {14} *vt* **1** COCINAR : to cook **2** HERVIR : to boil
cochambre *nmf fam* : filth, grime
cochambroso, -sa *adj* : filthy, grimy
coche *nm* **1** : car, automobile **2** : coach, carriage **3 coche cama** : sleeping car **4 coche fúnebre** : hearse
cochecito *nm* : baby carriage, stroller
cochera *nf* : garage, carport
cochinada *nf fam* **1** : filthy language **2** : disgusting behavior **3** : dirty trick
cochinillo *nm* : suckling pig, piglet
cochino[1]**, -na** *adj* **1** : dirty, filthy, disgusting **2** *fam* : rotten, lousy
cochino[2]**, -na** *n* : pig, hog
cocido[1]**, -da** *adj* **1** : boiled, cooked **2 bien cocido** : well-done
cocido[2] *nm* ESTOFADO, GUISADO : stew
cociente *nm* : quotient
cocimiento *nm* : cooking, baking
cocina *nf* **1** : kitchen **2** : stove **3** : cuisine, cooking
cocinar *v* : to cook
cocinero, -ra *n* : cook, chef
cocineta *nf Mex* : kitchenette
coco *nm* **1** : coconut **2** *fam* : head **3** *fam* : bogeyman
cocoa *nf* : cocoa, hot chocolate
cocodrilo *nm* : crocodile
cocotero *nm* : coconut palm
coctel *or* **cóctel** *nm* **1** : cocktail **2** : cocktail party
coctelera *nf* : cocktail shaker
codazo *nm* **1 darle un codazo a** : to elbow, to nudge **2 abrirse paso a codazos** : to elbow one's way through
codearse *vr* : to rub elbows, to hobnob
códice *nm* : codex, manuscript
codicia *nf* AVARICIA : avarice, covetousness
codiciar *vt* : to covet
codicilo *nm* : codicil
codicioso, -sa *adj* : avaricious, covetous

codificación *nf, pl* **-ciones 1** : codification **2** : coding, encoding

codificar {72} *vt* **1** : to codify **2** : to code, to encode

código *nm* **1** : code **2 código postal** : zip code **3 código morse** : Morse code

codo[1], **-da** *adj Mex* : cheap, stingy

codo[2], **-da** *n Mex* : tightwad, cheapskate

codo[3] *nm* : elbow

codorniz *nf, pl* **-nices** : quail

coeficiente *nm* **1** : coefficient **2 coeficiente intelectual** : IQ, intelligence quotient

coexistir *vi* : to coexist — **coexistencia** *nf*

cofa *nf* : crow's nest

cofre *nm* **1** BAÚL : trunk, chest **2** *Mex* CAPOTE : hood (of a car)

coger {15} *vt* **1** : to seize, to take hold of **2** : to catch **3** : to pick up **4** : to gather, to pick **5** : to gore — **cogerse** *vr* AGARRARSE : to hold on

cogida *nf* **1** : gathering, harvest **2** : goring

cognición *nf, pl* **-ciones** : cognition

cognitivo, -va *adj* : cognitive

cogollo *nm* **1** : heart (of a vegetable) **2** : bud, bulb **3** : core, crux ⟨el cogollo de la cuestión : the heart of the matter⟩

cogote *nm* : scruff, nape

cohabitar *vi* : to cohabit — **cohabitación** *nf*

cohechar *vt* SOBORNAR : to bribe

cohecho *nm* SOBORNO : bribe, bribery

coherencia *nf* : coherence — **coherente** *adj*

cohesión *nf, pl* **-siones** : cohesion

cohesivo, -va *adj* : cohesive

cohete *nm* : rocket

cohibición *nf, pl* **-ciones 1** : (legal) restraint **2** INHIBICIÓN : inhibition

cohibido, -da *adj* : inhibited, shy

cohibir {62} *vt* : to inhibit, to make self-conscious — **cohibirse** *vr* : to feel shy or embarrassed

cohorte *nf* : cohort

coima *nf Arg, Chile, Peru* : bribe

coimear *vt Arg, Chile, Peru* : to bribe

coincidencia *nf* : coincidence

coincidente *adj* **1** : coincident **2** ACORDE : coinciding

coincidir *vi* **1** : to coincide **2** : to agree

coito *nm* : sexual intercourse, coitus

coja, etc. → **coger**

cojear *vi* **1** : to limp **2** : to wobble, to rock **3 cojear del mismo pie** : to be two of a kind

cojera *nf* : limp

cojín *nm, pl* **cojines** : cushion, throw pillow

cojinete *nm* **1** : bearing, bushing **2 cojinete de bola** : ball bearing

cojo[1], **-ja** *adj* **1** : limping, lame **2** : wobbly **3** : weak, ineffectual

cojo[2], **-ja** *n* : lame person

cojones *nmpl usu considered vulgar* **1** : testicles *pl* **2** : guts *pl*, courage

col *nf* **1** REPOLLO : cabbage **2 col de Bruselas** : Brussels sprout **3 col rizada** : kale

cola *nf* **1** RABO : tail ⟨cola de caballo : ponytail⟩ **2** FILA : line (of people) ⟨hacer cola : to wait in line⟩ **3** : cola, drink **4** : train (of a dress) **5** : tails *pl* (of a tuxedo) **6** PEGAMENTO : glue **7** *fam* : buttocks *pl*, rear end

colaboracionista *nmf* : collaborator, traitor

colaborador, -dora *n* **1** : contributor (to a periodical) **2** : collaborator

colaborar *vi* : to collaborate — **colaboración** *nf*

colación *nf, pl* **-ciones 1** : light meal **2** : comparison, collation ⟨sacar a colación : to bring up, to broach⟩ **3** : conferral (of a degree)

colador *nm* **1** : colander, strainer **2** *PRi* : small coffeepot

colapso *nm* **1** : collapse **2** : standstill

colar {19} *vt* : to strain, to filter — **colarse** *vr* **1** : to sneak in, to cut in line, to gate-crash **2** : to slip up, to make a mistake

colateral[1] *adj* : collateral — **colateralmente** *adv*

colateral[2] *nm* : collateral

colcha *nf* COBERTOR : bedspread, quilt

colchón *nm, pl* **colchones 1** : mattress **2** : cushion, padding, buffer

colchoneta *nf* : mat (for gymnastic sports)

colear *vi* **1** : to wag its tail **2 vivito y coleando** *fam* : alive and kicking

colección *nf, pl* **-ciones** : collection

coleccionar *vt* : to collect, to keep a collection of

coleccionista *nmf* : collector

colecta *nf* : collection (of donations)

colectar *vt* : to collect

colectividad *nf* : community, group

colectivo[1], **-va** *adj* : collective — **colectivamente** *adv*

colectivo[2] *nm* **1** : collective **2** *Arg, Bol, Peru* : city bus

colector[1], **-tora** *n* : collector ⟨colector de impuestos : tax collector⟩

colector[2] *nm* **1** : sewer **2** : manifold (of an engine)

colega *nmf* **1** : colleague **2** HOMÓLOGO : counterpart **3** *fam* : buddy

colegiado[1], **-da** *adj* : collegiate

colegiado[2], **-da** *n* **1** ÁRBITRO : referee **2** : member (of a professional association)

colegial[1], **-giala** *adj* **1** : school, collegiate **2** *Mex fam* : green, inexperienced

colegial[2], **-giala** *n* : schoolboy *m*, schoolgirl *f*

colegiatura *nf Mex* : tuition

colegio *nm* **1** : school **2** : college ⟨colegio electoral : electoral college⟩ **3** : professional association

colegir {28} *vt* 1 JUNTAR : to collect, to gather 2 INFERIR : to infer, to deduce
cólera[1] *nm* : cholera
cólera[2] *nf* FURIA, IRA : anger, rage
colérico, -ca *adj* 1 FURIOSO : angry 2 IRRITABLE : irritable
colesterol *nm* : cholesterol
coleta *nf* 1 : ponytail 2 : pigtail
coletazo *nm* : lash, flick (of a tail)
colgado, -da *adj* 1 : hanging, hanged 2 : pending 3 **dejar colgado a** : to disappoint, to let down
colgante[1] *adj* : hanging, dangling
colgante[2] *nm* : pendant, charm (on a bracelet)
colgar {16} *vt* 1 : to hang (up), to put up 2 AHORCAR : to hang (someone) 3 : to hang up (a telephone) 4 *fam* : to fail (an exam) — **colgarse** *vr* 1 : to hang, to be suspended 2 AHORCARSE : to hang oneself 3 : to hang up a telephone
colibrí *nm* CHUPAFLOR : hummingbird
cólico *nm* : colic
coliflor *nf* : cauliflower
colilla *nf* : butt (of a cigarette)
colina *nf* CERRO, LOMA : hill
colindante *adj* CONTIGUO : adjacent, neighboring
colindar *vi* : to adjoin, to be adjacent
coliseo *nm* : coliseum
colisión *nf, pl* -siones : collision
colisionar *vi* : to collide
collage *nm* : collage
collar *nm* 1 : collar (for an animal) 2 : necklace ⟨collar de perlas : string of pearls⟩
colmado, -da *adj* : heaping
colmar *vt* 1 : to fill to the brim 2 : to fulfill, to satisfy 3 : to heap, to shower ⟨me colmaron de regalos : they showered me with gifts⟩
colmena *nf* : beehive
colmenar *nm* APIARIO : apiary
colmillo *nm* 1 CANINO : canine (tooth), fang 2 : tusk
colmilludo, -da *adj Mex, PRi* : astute, shrewd, crafty
colmo *nm* : height, extreme, limit ⟨el colmo de la locura : the height of folly⟩ ⟨¡eso es el colmo! : that's the last straw!⟩
colocación *nf, pl* -ciones 1 : placement, placing 2 : position, job 3 : investment
colocar {72} *vt* 1 PONER : to place, to put 2 : to find a job for 3 : to invest — **colocarse** *vr* 1 SITUARSE : to position oneself 2 : to get a job
colofón *nm, pl* -fones 1 : ending, finale 2 : colophon
colofonia *nf* : rosin
colombiano, -na *adj & n* : Colombian
colon *nm* : (intestinal) colon
colón *nm, pl* **colones** : Costa Rican and Salvadoran unit of currency
colonia *nf* 1 : colony 2 : cologne 3 *Mex* : residential area, neighborhood
colonial *adj* : colonial

colonización *nf, pl* -ciones : colonization
colonizador[1], **-dora** *adj* : colonizing
colonizador[2], **-dora** *n* : colonizer, colonist
colonizar {21} *vt* : to colonize, to settle
colono, -na *n* 1 : settler, colonist 2 : tenant farmer
coloquial *adj* : colloquial
coloquio *nm* 1 : discussion, talk 2 : conference, symposium
color *nm* 1 : color 2 : paint, dye 3 **colores** *nmpl* : colored pencils
coloración *nf, pl* -ciones : coloring, coloration
colorado[1], **-da** *adj* 1 ROJO : red 2 **ponerse colorado** : to blush 3 **chiste colorado** *Mex* : off-color joke
colorado[2] *nm* ROJO : red
colorante *nm* : coloring ⟨colorante de alimentos : food coloring⟩
colorear *vt* : to color — *vi* 1 : to redden 2 : to ripen
colorete *nm* : rouge, blusher
colorido *nm* : color, coloring
colorín *nm, pl* -rines 1 : bright color 2 : goldfinch
colosal *adj* : colossal
coloso *nm* : colossus
coludir *vi* : to be in collusion, to conspire
columna *nf* 1 : column 2 **columna vertebral** : spine, backbone
columnata *nf* : colonnade
columnista *nmf* : columnist
columpiar *vt* : to push (on a swing) — **columpiarse** *vr* : to swing
columpio *nm* : swing
colusión *nf, pl* -siones : collusion
colza *nf* : rape (plant)
coma[1] *nm* : coma
coma[2] *nf* : comma
comadre *nf* 1 : godmother of one's child 2 : mother of one's godchild 3 *fam* : neighbor, female friend 4 *fam* : gossip
comadrear *vi fam* : to gossip
comadreja *nf* : weasel
comadrona *nf* : midwife
comanche *nmf* : Comanche
comandancia *nf* 1 : command headquarters 2 : command
comandante *nmf* 1 : commander, commanding officer 2 : major
comandar *vt* : to command, to lead
comando *nm* 1 : commando 2 : command (for computers)
comarca *nf* REGIÓN : region
comarcal *adj* REGIONAL : regional, local
comatoso, -sa *adj* : comatose
combar *vt* : to bend, to curve — **combarse** *vr* 1 : to bend, to buckle 2 : to warp, to bulge, to sag
combate *nm* 1 : combat 2 : fight, boxing match
combatiente *nmf* : combatant, fighter
combatir *vt* : to combat, to fight against — *vi* : to fight

combatividad *nf* : fighting spirit
combativo, -va *adj* : combative, spirited
combinación *nf, pl* **-ciones** 1 : combination 2 : connection (in travel)
combinar *vt* 1 UNIR : to combine, to mix together 2 : to match, to put together — **combinarse** *vr* : to get together, to conspire
combo *nm* 1 : (musical) band 2 *Chile, Peru* : sledgehammer 3 *Chile, Peru* : punch
combustible[1] *adj* : combustible
combustible[2] *nm* : fuel
combustión *nf, pl* **-tiones** : combustion
comedero *nm* : trough, feeder
comedia *nf* : comedy
comediante *nmf* : actor, actress *f*
comedido, -da *adj* MESURADO : moderate, restrained
comediógrafo, -fa *n* : playwright
comedor *nm* : dining room
comején *nm, pl* **-jenes** : termite
comelón[1], **-lona** *adj, mpl* **-lones** *fam* : gluttonous
comelón[2], **-lona** *n, pl* **-lones** *fam* : big eater, glutton
comensal *nmf* : dinner guest
comentador, -dora *n* → **comentarista**
comentar *vt* 1 : to comment on, to discuss 2 : to mention, to remark
comentario *nm* 1 : comment, remark ⟨sin comentarios : no comment⟩ 2 : commentary
comentarista *nmf* : commentator
comenzar {29} *v* EMPEZAR : to begin, to start
comer[1] *vt* 1 : to eat 2 : to consume, to eat up, to eat into — *vi* 1 : to eat 2 CENAR : to have a meal 3 **dar de comer** : to feed — **comerse** *vr* : to eat up
comer[2] *nm* : eating, dining
comercial *adj & nm* : commercial — **comercialmente** *adv*
comercializar {21} *vt* 1 : to commercialize 2 : to market
comerciante *nmf* : merchant, dealer
comerciar *vi* : to do business, to trade
comercio *nm* 1 : commerce, trade 2 NEGOCIO : business, place of business
comestible *adj* : edible
comestibles *nmpl* VÍVERES : groceries, food
cometa[1] *nm* : comet
cometa[2] *nf* : kite
cometer *vt* 1 : to commit 2 **cometer un error** : to make a mistake
cometido *nm* : assignment, task
comezón *nf, pl* **-zones** PICAZÓN : itchiness, itching
comible *adj fam* : eatable, edible
comic *or* **cómic** *nm* : comic strip, comic book
comicastro, -tra *n* : second-rate actor, ham
comicidad *nf* HUMOR : humor, wit
comicios *nmpl* : elections, voting
cómico[1], **-ca** *adj* : comic, comical

cómico[2], **-ca** *n* HUMORISTA : comic, comedian, comedienne *f*
comida *nf* 1 : food 2 : meal 3 : dinner 4 **comida basura** : junk food 5 **comida rápida** : fast food
comidilla *nf* : talk, gossip
comienzo *nm* 1 : start, beginning 2 **al comienzo** : at first 3 **dar comienzo** : to begin
comillas *nfpl* : quotation marks ⟨entre comillas : in quotes⟩
comilón, -lona → **comelón, -lona**
comilona *nf fam* : feast
comino *nm* 1 : cumin 2 **me vale un comino** *fam* : not to matter to someone ⟨no me importa un comino : I couldn't care less⟩
comisaría *nf* : police station
comisario, -ria *n* : commissioner
comisión *nf, pl* **-siones** 1 : commission, committing 2 : committee 3 : percentage, commission ⟨comisión sobre las ventas : sales commission⟩
comisionado[1], **-da** *adj* : commissioned, entrusted
comisionado[2], **-da** *n* → **comisario**
comisionar *vt* : to commission
comité *nm* : committee
comitiva *nf* : retinue, entourage
como[1] *adv* 1 : around, about ⟨cuesta como 500 pesos : it costs around 500 pesos⟩ 2 : kind of, like ⟨tengo como mareos : I'm kind of dizzy⟩
como[2] *conj* 1 : how, as ⟨hazlo como dijiste que lo harías : do it the way you said you would⟩ 2 : since, given that ⟨como estaba lloviendo, no salí : since it was raining, I didn't go out⟩ 3 : if ⟨como lo vuelva a hacer lo arrestarán : if he does that again he'll be arrested⟩ 4 **como quiera** : in any way
como[3] *prep* 1 : like, as ⟨ligero como una pluma : light as a feather⟩ 2 **así como** : as well as
cómo *adv* : how ⟨¿cómo estás? : how are you?⟩ ⟨¿a cómo están las manzanas? : how much are the apples?⟩ ⟨¿cómo? : excuse me?, what was that?⟩ ⟨¿se puede? ¡cómo no! : may I? please do!⟩
cómoda *nf* : bureau, chest of drawers
comodidad *nf* 1 : comfort 2 : convenience
comodín *nm, pl* **-dines** 1 : joker, wild card 2 : all-purpose word or thing 3 : pretext, excuse
cómodo, -da *adj* 1 CONFORTABLE : comfortable 2 : convenient — **cómodamente** *adv*
comodoro *nm* : commodore
comoquiera *adv* 1 : in any way 2 **comoquiera que** : in whatever way, however ⟨comoquiera que sea eso : however that may be⟩
compa *nm fam* : buddy, pal
compactar *vt* : to compact, to compress
compacto, -ta *adj* : compact

compadecer · compra

64

compadecer {53} *vt* : to sympathize with, to feel sorry for — **compadecerse** *vr* **1** ~ **de** : to take pity on, to commiserate with **2** ~ **con** : to fit, to accord (with)

compadre *nm* **1** : godfather of one's child **2** : father of one's godchild **3** *fam* : buddy, pal

compaginar *vt* **1** COORDINAR : to combine, to coordinate **2** : to collate

compañerismo *nm* : comradeship, camaraderie

compañero, -ra *n* : companion, mate, partner

compañía *nf* **1** : company ⟨llegó en compañía de su madre : he arrived with his mother⟩ **2** EMPRESA, FIRMA : firm, company

comparable *adj* : comparable

comparación *nf, pl* **-ciones** : comparison

comparado, -da *adj* : comparative ⟨literatura comparada : comparative literature⟩

comparar *vt* : to compare

comparativo[1], -va *adj* : comparative, relative — **comparativamente** *adv*

comparativo[2] *nm* : comparative degree or form

comparecencia *nf* **1** : appearance (in court) **2 orden de comparecencia** : subpoena, summons

comparecer {53} *vi* : to appear (in court)

compartimiento *or* **compartimento** *nm* : compartment

compartir *vt* : to share

compás *nm, pl* **-pases 1** : beat, rhythm, time **2** : compass

compasión *nf, pl* **-siones** : compassion, pity

compasivo, -va *adj* : compassionate, sympathetic

compatibilidad *nf* : compatibility

compatible *adj* : compatible

compatriota *nmf* PAISANO : compatriot, fellow countryman

compeler *vt* : to compel

compendiar *vt* : to summarize, to condense

compendio *nm* : summary

compenetración *nf, pl* **-ciones** : rapport, mutual understanding

compenetrarse *vr* **1** : to understand each other **2** ~ **con** : to identify oneself with

compensación *nf, pl* **-ciones** : compensation

compensar *vt* : to compensate for, to make up for — *vi* : to be worth one's while

compensatorio, -ria *adj* : compensatory

competencia *nf* **1** : competition, rivalry **2** : competence

competente *adj* : competent, able — **competentemente** *adv*

competición *nf, pl* **-ciones** : competition

competidor[1], -dora *adj* RIVAL : competing, rival

competidor[2], -dora *n* RIVAL : competitor, rival

competir {54} *vi* : to compete

competitividad *nf* : competitiveness

competitivo, -va *adj* : competitive — **competitivamente** *adv*

compilar *vt* : to compile — **compilación** *nf*

compinche *nmf fam* **1** : buddy, pal **2** : partner in crime, accomplice

complacencia *nf* : pleasure, satisfaction

complacer {57} *vt* : to please — **complacerse** *vr* ~ **en** : to take pleasure in

complaciente *adj* : obliging, eager to please

complejidad *nf* : complexity

complejo[1], -ja *adj* : complex

complejo[2] *nm* : complex

complementar *vt* : to complement, to supplement — **complementarse** *vr*

complementario, -ria *adj* : complementary

complemento *nm* **1** : complement, supplement **2** : supplementary pay, allowance

completamente *adv* : completely, totally

completar *vt* TERMINAR : to complete, to finish

completo, -ta *adj* **1** : complete **2** : perfect, absolute **3** : full, detailed

complexión *nf, pl* **-xiones** : (physical) constitution

complicación *nf, pl* **-ciones** : complication

complicado, -da *adj* : complicated

complicar {72} *vt* **1** : to complicate **2** : to involve — **complicarse** *vr*

cómplice *nmf* : accomplice

complicidad *nf* : complicity

complot *nm, pl* **complots** CONFABULACIÓN, CONSPIRACIÓN : conspiracy, plot

componenda *nf* : shady deal, scam

componente *adj & nm* : component, constituent

componer {60} *vt* **1** ARREGLAR : to fix, to repair **2** CONSTITUIR : to make up, to compose **3** : to compose, to write **4** : to set (a bone) — **componerse** *vr* **1** : to improve, to get better **2** ~ **de** : to consist of

comportamiento *nm* CONDUCTA : behavior, conduct

comportarse *vr* : to behave, to conduct oneself

composición *nf, pl* **-ciones 1** OBRA : composition, work **2** : makeup, arrangement

compositor, -tora *n* : composer, songwriter

compostura *nf* **1** : composure **2** : mending, repair

compra *nf* **1** : purchase **2 ir de compras** : to go shopping **3 orden de compra** : purchase order

comprador, -dora *n* : buyer, shopper
comprar *vt* : to buy, to purchase
compraventa *nf* : buying and selling
comprender *vt* **1** ENTENDER : to comprehend, to understand **2** ABARCAR : to cover, to include — *vi* : to understand ⟨¡ya comprendo! : now I understand!⟩
comprensible *adj* : understandable — **comprensiblemente** *adv*
comprensión *nf, pl* **-siones 1** : comprehension, understanding, grasp **2** : understanding, sympathy
comprensivo, -va *adj* : understanding
compresa *nf* **1** : compress **2** *or* **compresa higiénica** : sanitary napkin
compresión *nf, pl* **-siones** : compression
compresor *nm* : compressor
comprimido *nm* PÍLDORA, TABLETA : pill, tablet
comprimir *vt* : to compress
comprobable *adj* : verifiable, provable
comprobación *nf, pl* **-ciones** : verification, confirmation
comprobante *nm* **1** : proof ⟨comprobante de identidad : proof of identity⟩ **2** : voucher, receipt ⟨comprobante de ventas : sales slip⟩
comprobar {19} *vt* **1** : to verify, to check **2** : to prove
comprometedor, -dora *adj* : compromising
comprometer *vt* **1** : to compromise **2** : to jeopardize **3** : to commit, to put under obligation — **comprometerse** *vr* **1** : to commit oneself **2** ∼ **con** : to get engaged to
comprometido, -da *adj* **1** : compromising, awkward **2** : committed, obliged **3** : engaged (to be married)
compromiso *nm* **1** : obligation, commitment **2** : engagement ⟨anillo de compromiso : engagement ring⟩ **3** : agreement **4** : awkward situation, fix
compuerta *nf* : floodgate
compuesto¹ *pp* → **componer**
compuesto², -ta *adj* **1** : fixed, repaired **2** : compound, composite **3** : decked out, spruced up **4** ∼ **de** : made up of, consisting of
compuesto³ *nm* : compound
compulsión *nf, pl* **-siones** : compulsion
compulsivo, -va *adj* **1** : compelling, urgent **2** : compulsive — **compulsivamente** *adv*
compungido, -da *adj* : contrite, remorseful
compungirse {35} *vr* : to feel remorse
compuso, etc. → **componer**
computable *adj* : countable ⟨años computables : years accrued⟩ ⟨ingresos computables : qualifying income⟩
computación *nf, pl* **-ciones** : computing, computers *pl*
computador *nm* → **computadora**
computadora *nf* **1** : computer **2 computadora portátil** : laptop computer

computar *vt* : to compute, to calculate
computarizar {21} *vt* : to computerize
cómputo *nm* : computation, calculation
comulgar {52} *vi* : to receive Communion
común *adj, pl* **comunes 1** : common **2 común y corriente** : ordinary, regular **3 por lo común** : generally, as a rule
comuna *nf* : commune
comunal *adj* : communal
comunicación *nf, pl* **-ciones 1** : communication **2** : access, link **3** : message, report
comunicado *nm* **1** : communiqué **2 comunicado de prensa** : press release
comunicar {72} *vt* **1** : to communicate, to convey **2** : to notify — **comunicarse** *vr* ∼ **con 1** : to contact, to get in touch with **2** : to be connected to
comunicativo, -va *adj* : communicative, talkative
comunidad *nf* : community
comunión *nf, pl* **-niones 1** : communion, sharing **2** : Communion
comunismo *nm* : communism, Communism
comunista *adj & nmf* : communist
comúnmente *adv* : commonly
con *prep* **1** : with ⟨vengo con mi padre : I'm going with my father⟩ ⟨¡con quién hablas? : who are you speaking to?⟩ **2** : in spite of ⟨con todo : in spite of it all⟩ **3** : to, towards ⟨ella es amable con los niños : she is kind to the children⟩ **4** : by ⟨con llegar temprano : by arriving early⟩ **5 con (tal) que** : as long as, so long as
conato *nm* : attempt, effort ⟨conato de robo : attempted robbery⟩
cóncavo, -va *adj* : concave
concebible *adj* : conceivable
concebir {54} *vt* **1** : to conceive **2** : to conceive of, to imagine — *vi* : to conceive, to become pregnant
conceder *vt* **1** : to grant, to bestow **2** : to concede, to admit
concejal, -jala *n* : councilman *m*, councilwoman *f*, alderman *m*, alderwoman *f*
concejo *nm* : council ⟨concejo municipal : town council⟩
concentración *nf, pl* **-ciones** : concentration
concentrado *nm* : concentrate
concentrar *vt* : to concentrate — **concentrarse** *vr*
concéntrico, -ca *adj* : concentric
concepción *nf, pl* **-ciones** : conception
concepto *nm* NOCIÓN : concept, idea, opinion
conceptuar {3} *vt* : to regard, to judge
concernir {17} *vi* : to be of concern
concertar {55} *vt* **1** : to arrange, to set up **2** : to agree on, to settle **3** : to harmonize — *vi* : to be in harmony
concesión *nf, pl* **-siones 1** : concession **2** : awarding, granting
concha *nf* : conch, seashell

conciencia *nf* **1** : conscience **2** : consciousness, awareness

concientizar {21} *vt* : to make aware — **concientizarse** *vr* ~ **de** : to realize, to become aware of

concienzudo, -da *adj* : conscientious

concierto *nm* **1** : concert **2** : agreement **3** : concerto

conciliador¹, -dora *adj* : conciliatory

conciliador², -dora *n* : arbitrator, peacemaker

conciliar *vt* : to conciliate, to reconcile — **conciliación** *nf*

conciliatorio, -ria *adj* → **conciliador¹**

concilio *nm* : (church) council

conciso, -sa *adj* : concise — **concisión** *nf*

conciudadano, -na *n* : fellow citizen

cónclave *nm* : conclave, private meeting

concluir {41} *vt* **1** TERMINAR : to conclude, to finish **2** DEDUCIR : to deduce, to infer — *vi* : to end, to conclude

conclusión *nf, pl* **-siones** : conclusion

concluyente *adj* : conclusive

concomitante *adj* : concomitant

concordancia *nf* : agreement, accordance

concordar {19} *vi* : to agree, to coincide — *vt* : to reconcile

concordia *nf* : concord, harmony

concretar *vt* **1** : to pinpoint, to specify **2** : to fulfill, to realize — **concretarse** *vr* : to become real, to take shape

concretizar → **concretar**

concreto¹, -ta *adj* **1** : concrete, actual **2** : definite, specific ⟨en concreto : specifically⟩ — **concretamente** *adv*

concreto² *nm* HORMIGÓN : concrete

concubina *nf* : concubine

concurrencia *nf* **1** : audience, turnout **2** : concurrence

concurrente *adj* : concurrent — **concurrentemente** *adv*

concurrido, -da *adj* : busy, crowded

concurrir *vi* **1** : to converge, to come together **2** : to concur, to agree **3** : to take part, to participate **4** : to attend, to be present ⟨concurrir a una reunión : to attend a meeting⟩ **5** ~ **a** : to contribute to

concursante *nmf* : contestant, competitor

concursar *vt* : to compete in — *vi* : to compete, to participate

concurso *nm* **1** : contest, competition **2** : concurrence, coincidence **3** : crowd, gathering **4** : cooperation, assistance

condado *nm* **1** : county **2** : earldom

conde, -desa *n* : count *m*, earl *m*, countess *f*

condecoración *nf, pl* **-ciones** : decoration, medal

condecorar *vt* : to decorate, to award (a medal)

condena *nf* **1** REPROBACIÓN : disapproval, condemnation **2** SENTENCIA : sentence, conviction

condenable *adj* : reprehensible

condenación *nf, pl* **-ciones** **1** : condemnation **2** : damnation

condenado¹, -da *adj* **1** : fated, doomed **2** : convicted, sentenced **3** *fam* : darn, damned

condenado², -da *n* : convict

condenar *vt* **1** : to condemn **2** : to sentence **3** : to board up, to wall up — **condenarse** *vr* : to be damned

condensación *nf, pl* **-ciones** : condensation

condensar *vt* : to condense

condesa *nf* → **conde**

condescendencia *nf* : condescension

condescender {56} *vi* **1** : to condescend **2** : to agree, to acquiesce

condición *nf, pl* **-ciones** **1** : condition, state **2** : capacity, position **3** **condiciones** *nfpl* : conditions, circumstances ⟨condiciones de vida : living conditions⟩

condicional *adj* : conditional — **condicionalmente** *adv*

condicionamiento *nm* : conditioning

condicionar *vt* **1** : to condition, to determine **2** ~ **a** : to be contingent on, to depend on

condimentar *vt* SAZONAR : to season, to spice

condimento *nm* : condiment, seasoning, spice

condiscípulo, -la *n* : classmate

condolencia *nf* : condolence, sympathy

condolerse {47} *vr* : to sympathize

condominio *nm* : condominium, condo

condón *nm, pl* **condones** : condom

cóndor *nm* : condor

conducción *nf, pl* **-ciones** **1** : conduction (of electricity, etc.) **2** DIRECCIÓN : management, direction

conducir {61} *vt* **1** DIRIGIR, GUIAR : to direct, to lead **2** MANEJAR : to drive (a vehicle) — *vi* **1** : to drive a vehicle **2** ~ **a** : to lead to — **conducirse** *vr* PORTARSE : to behave, to conduct oneself

conducta *nf* COMPORTAMIENTO : conduct, behavior

conducto *nm* : conduit, channel, duct

conductor¹, -tora *adj* : conducting, leading

conductor², -tora *n* : driver

conductor³ *nm* : conductor (of electricity, etc.)

conectar *vt* : to connect — *vi* ~ **con** : to link up with, to communicate with

conector *nm* : connector

conejera *nf* : rabbit hutch

conejillo *nm* **conejillo de Indias** : guinea pig

conejo, -ja *n* : rabbit

conexión *nf, pl* **-xiones** : connection

confabulación *nf, pl* **-ciones** COMPLOT, CONSPIRACIÓN : plot, conspiracy

confabularse *vr* : to plot, to conspire

confección *nf, pl* **-ciones** **1** : preparation **2** : tailoring, dressmaking

confeccionar *vt* : to make, to produce, to prepare

confederación *nf, pl* **-ciones** : confederation

confederarse *vr* : to confederate, to form a confederation

conferencia *nf* **1** REUNIÓN : conference, meeting **2** : lecture

conferenciante *nmf* : lecturer

conferencista → **conferenciante**

conferir {76} *vt* : to confer, to bestow

confesar {55} *v* : to confess — **confesarse** *vr* : to go to confession

confesión *nf, pl* **-siones 1** : confession **2** : creed, denomination

confesionario *nm* : confessional

confesor *nm* : confessor

confeti *nm* : confetti

confiable *adj* : trustworthy, reliable

confiado, -da *adj* **1** : confident, self-confident **2** : trusting — **confiadamente** *adv*

confianza *nf* **1** : trust ⟨de poca confianza : untrustworthy⟩ **2** : confidence, self-confidence

confianzudo, -da *adj* : forward, presumptuous

confiar {85} *vi* : to have trust, to be trusting — *vt* **1** : to confide **2** : to entrust — **confiarse** *vr* **1** : to be overconfident **2** ~ **a** : to confide in

confidencia *nf* : confidence, secret

confidencial *adj* : confidential — **confidencialmente** *adv*

confidencialidad *nf* : confidentiality

confidente *nmf* **1** : confidant, confidante *f* **2** : informer

configuración *nf, pl* **-ciones** : configuration, shape

configurar *vt* : to shape, to form

confín *nm, pl* **confines** : boundary, limit

confinamiento *nm* : confinement

confinar *vt* **1** : to confine, to limit **2** : to exile — *vi* ~ **con** : to border on

confirmación *nf, pl* **-ciones** : confirmation

confirmar *vt* : to confirm, to substantiate

confiscación *nf, pl* **-ciones** : confiscation

confiscar {72} *vt* DECOMISAR : to confiscate, to seize

confitado, -da *adj* : candied

confite *nm* : comfit, candy

confitería *nf* **1** DULCERÍA : candy store, confectionery **2** : tearoom, café

confitero, -ra *n* : confectioner

confitura *nf* : preserves, jam

conflagración *nf, pl* **-ciones 1** : conflagration, fire **2** : war

conflictivo, -va *adj* **1** : troubled **2** : controversial

conflicto *nm* : conflict

confluencia *nf* : junction, confluence

confluir {41} *vi* **1** : to converge, to join **2** : to gather, to assemble

conformar *vt* **1** : to form, to create **2** : to constitute, to make up — **conformarse** *vr* **1** RESIGNARSE : to resign

oneself **2** : to comply, to conform **3** ~ **con** : to content oneself with, to be satisfied with

conforme[1] *adj* **1** : content, satisfied **2** ~ **a** : in accordance with

conforme[2] *conj* : as ⟨entreguen sus tareas conforme vayan saliendo : hand in your homework as you leave⟩

conformidad *nf* **1** : agreement, consent **2** : resignation

confort *nm* : comfort

confortable *adj* CÓMODO : comfortable

confortar *vt* CONSOLAR : to comfort, to console

confraternidad *nf* : brotherhood, fraternity

confraternización *nf, pl* **-ciones** : fraternization

confraternizar *vi* : to fraternize

confrontación *nf, pl* **-ciones** : confrontation

confrontar *vt* **1** ENCARAR : to confront **2** : to compare **3** : to bring face-to-face — *vi* : to border — **confrontarse** *vr* ~ **con** : to face up to

confundir *vt* : to confuse, to mix up — **confundirse** *vr* : to make a mistake, to be confused ⟨confundirse de número : to get the wrong number⟩

confusión *nf, pl* **-siones** : confusion

confuso, -sa *adj* **1** : confused, mixed-up **2** : obscure, indistinct

congelación *nf, pl* **-ciones 1** : freezing **2** : frostbite

congelado, -da *adj* HELADO : frozen

congelador *nm* HELADORA : freezer

congelamiento *nm* → **congelación**

congelar *vt* : to freeze — **congelarse** *vr*

congeniar *vi* : to get along (with someone)

congénito, -ta *adj* : congenital

congestión *nf, pl* **-tiones** : congestion

congestionado, -da *adj* : congested

congestionamiento *nm* → **congestión**

congestionarse *vr* **1** : to become flushed **2** : to become congested

conglomerado[1]**, -da** *adj* : conglomerate, mixed

conglomerado[2] *nm* : conglomerate, conglomeration

congoja *nf* ANGUSTIA : anguish, grief

congoleño, -ña *adj & n* : Congolese

congraciarse *vr* : to ingratiate oneself

congratular *vt* FELICITAR : to congratulate

congregación *nf, pl* **-ciones** : congregation, gathering

congregar {52} *vt* : to bring together — **congregarse** *vr* : to congregate, to assemble

congresista *nmf* : congressman *m*, congresswoman *f*

congreso *nm* : congress, conference

congruencia *nf* **1** : congruence **2** COHERENCIA : coherence — **congruente** *adj*

cónico, -ca *adj* : conical, conic

conífera *nf* : conifer

conífero, -ra *adj* : coniferous
conjetura *nf* : conjecture, guess
conjeturar *vt* : to guess, to conjecture
conjugación *nf, pl* **-ciones** : conjugation
conjugar {52} *vt* **1** : to conjugate **2** : to combine
conjunción *nf, pl* **-ciones** : conjunction
conjuntivo, -va *adj* : connective ⟨tejido conjuntivo : connective tissue⟩
conjunto¹, -ta *adj* : joint
conjunto² *nm* **1** : collection, group **2** : ensemble, outfit ⟨conjunto musical : musical ensemble⟩ **3** : whole, entirety ⟨en conjunto : as a whole, altogether⟩
conjurar *vt* **1** : to exorcise **2** : to avert, to ward off — *vi* CONSPIRAR : to conspire, to plot
conjuro *nm* **1** : exorcism **2** : spell
conllevar *vt* **1** : to bear, to suffer **2** IMPLICAR : to entail, to involve
conmemorar *vt* : to commemorate — **conmemoración** *nf*
conmemorativo, -va *adj* : commemorative, memorial
conmigo *pron* : with me ⟨habló conmigo : he talked with me⟩
conminar *vt* AMENAZAR : to threaten, to warn
conmiseración *nf, pl* **-ciones** : pity, commiseration
conmoción *nf, pl* **-ciones** **1** : shock, upheaval **2** *or* **conmoción cerebral** : concussion
conmocionar *vt* : to shake, to shock
conmovedor, -dora *adj* EMOCIONANTE : moving, touching
conmover {47} *vt* **1** EMOCIONAR : to move, to touch **2** : to shake up — **conmoverse** *vr*
conmutador *nm* **1** : switch **2** : switchboard
conmutar *vt* **1** : to commute (a sentence) **2** : to switch, to exchange
connivencia *nf* : connivance
connotación *nf, pl* **-ciones** : connotation
connotar *vt* : to connote, to imply
cono *nm* : cone
conocedor¹, -dora *adj* : knowledgeable
conocedor², -dora *n* : connoisseur, expert
conocer {18} *vt* **1** : to know, to be acquainted with ⟨ya lo conocí : I've already met him⟩ **2** : to meet **3** RECONOCER : to recognize — **conocerse** *vr* **1** : to know each other **2** : to meet **3** : to know oneself
conocido¹, -da *adj* **1** : familiar **2** : well-known, famous
conocido², -da *n* : acquaintance
conocimiento *nm* **1** : knowledge **2** SENTIDO : consciousness
conque *conj* : so, so then, and so ⟨¡ah, conque esas tenemos! : oh, so that's what's going on!⟩
conquista *nf* : conquest
conquistador¹, -dora *adj* : conquering

conquistador², -dora *n* : conqueror
conquistar *vt* : to conquer
consabido, -da *adj* : usual, typical
consagración *nf, pl* **-ciones** : consecration
consagrar *vt* **1** : to consecrate **2** DEDICAR : to dedicate, to devote
consciencia → **conciencia**
consciente *adj* : conscious, aware — **conscientemente** *adv*
conscripción *nf, pl* **-ciones** : conscription, draft
conscripto, -ta *n* : conscript, inductee
consecución *nf, pl* **-ciones** : attainment
consecuencia *nf* **1** : consequence, result ⟨a consecuencia de : as a result of⟩ **2 en ～** : accordingly
consecuente *adj* : consistent — **consecuentemente** *adv*
consecutivo, -va *adj* : consecutive, successive — **consecutivamente** *adv*
conseguir {75} *vt* **1** : to get, to obtain **2** : to achieve, to attain **3** : to manage to ⟨consiguió acabar el trabajo : she managed to finish the job⟩
consejero, -ra *n* : adviser, counselor
consejo *nm* **1** : advice, counsel **2** : council ⟨consejo de guerra : court-martial⟩
consenso *nm* : consensus
consentido, -da *adj* : spoiled, pampered
consentimiento *nm* : consent, permission
consentir {76} *vt* **1** PERMITIR : to consent to, to allow **2** MIMAR : to pamper, to spoil — *vi* **～ en** : to agree to, to approve of
conserje *nmf* : custodian, janitor, caretaker
conserva *nf* **1** : preserve(s), jam **2 conservas** *nfpl* : canned goods
conservación *nf, pl* **-ciones** : conservation, preservation
conservacionista *nmf* : conservationist
conservador¹, -dora *adj & n* : conservative
conservador² *nm* : preservative
conservadurismo *nf* : conservatism
conservante *nm* : preservative
conservar *vt* **1** : to preserve **2** GUARDAR : to keep, to conserve
conservatorio *nm* : conservatory
considerable *adj* : considerable — **considerablemente** *adv*
consideración *nf, pl* **-ciones** **1** : consideration **2** : respect **3 de ～** : considerable, important
considerado, -da *adj* **1** : considerate, thoughtful **2** : respected
considerar *vt* **1** : to consider, to think over **2** : to judge, to deem **3** : to treat with respect
consigna *nf* **1** ESLOGAN : slogan **2** : assignment, orders *pl* **3** : checkroom
consignación *nf, pl* **-ciones** **1** : consignment **2** ASIGNACIÓN : allocation
consignar *vt* **1** : to consign **2** : to record, to write down **3** : to assign, to allocate

consigo *pron* : with her, with him, with you, with oneself ⟨se llevó las llaves consigo : she took the keys with her⟩
consiguiente *adj* **1** : resulting, consequent **2 por ~** : consequently, as a result
consistencia *nf* : consistency
consistente *adj* **1** : firm, strong, sound **2** : consistent — **consistentemente** *adv*
consistir *vi* **1 ~ en** : to consist of **2 ~ en** : to lie in, to consist in
consola *nf* : console
consolación *nf, pl* **-ciones** : consolation ⟨premio de consolación : consolation prize⟩
consolar {19} *vt* CONFORTAR : to console, to comfort
consolidar *vt* : to consolidate — **consolidación** *nf*
consomé *nm* CALDO : consommé, clear soup
consonancia *nf* **1** : consonance, harmony **2 en consonancia con** : in accordance with
consonante[1] *adj* : consonant, harmonious
consonante[2] *nf* : consonant
consorcio *nm* : consortium
consorte *nmf* : consort, spouse
conspicuo, -cua *adj* : eminent, famous
conspiración *nf, pl* **-ciones** COMPLOT, CONFABULACIÓN : conspiracy, plot
conspirador, -dora *n* : conspirator
conspirar *vi* CONJURAR : to conspire, to plot
constancia *nf* **1** PRUEBA : proof, certainty **2** : record, evidence ⟨que quede constancia : for the record⟩ **3** : perseverance, constancy
constante[1] *adj* : constant — **constantemente** *adv*
constante[2] *nf* : constant
constar *vi* **1** : to be evident, to be on record ⟨que conste : believe me, have no doubt⟩ **2 ~ de** : to consist of
constatación *nf, pl* **-ciones** : confirmation, proof
constatar *vt* **1** : to verify **2** : to state
constelación *nf, pl* **-ciones** : constellation
consternación *nf, pl* **-ciones** : consternation, dismay
consternar *vt* : to dismay, to appall
constipación *nf, pl* **-ciones** : constipation
constipado[1], **-da** *adj* **estar constipado** : to have a cold
constipado[2] *nm* RESFRIADO : cold
constiparse *vr* : to catch a cold
constitución *nf, pl* **-ciones** : constitution — **constitucional** *adj* — **constitucionalmente** *adv*
constitucionalidad *nf* : constitutionality
constituir {41} *vt* **1** FORMAR : to constitute, to make up, to form **2** FUNDAR : to establish, to set up — **constituirse**

vr ~ en : to set oneself up as, to become
constitutivo, -va *adj* : constituent, component
constituyente *adj* & *nmf* : constituent
constreñir {67} *vt* **1** FORZAR, OBLIGAR : to constrain, to oblige **2** LIMITAR : to restrict, to limit
construcción *nf, pl* **-ciones** : construction, building
constructivo, -va *adj* : constructive — **constructivamente** *adv*
constructor, -tora *n* : builder
constructora *nf* : construction company
construir {41} *vt* : to build, to construct
consuelo *nm* : consolation, comfort
consuetudinario, -ria *adj* **1** : customary, habitual **2 derecho consuetudinario** : common law
cónsul *nmf* : consul — **consular** *adj*
consulado *nm* : consulate
consulta *nf* **1** : consultation **2** : inquiry
consultar *vt* : to consult
consultor[1], **-tora** *adj* : consulting ⟨firma consultora : consulting firm⟩
consultor[2], **-tora** *n* : consultant
consultorio *nm* : office (of a doctor or dentist)
consumación *nf, pl* **-ciones** : consummation
consumado, -da *adj* : consummate, perfect
consumar *vt* **1** : to consummate, to complete **2** : to commit, to carry out
consumible *adj* : consumable
consumición *nf, pl* **-ciones** **1** : consumption **2** : drink (in a restaurant)
consumido, -da *adj* : thin, emaciated
consumidor, -dora *n* : consumer
consumir *vt* : to consume — **consumirse** *vr* : to waste away
consumo *nm* : consumption
contabilidad *nf* **1** : accounting, bookkeeping **2** : accountancy
contabilizar {21} *vt* : to enter, to record (in accounting)
contable[1] *adj* : countable
contable[2] *nmf* *Spain* : accountant, bookkeeper
contactar *vt* : to contact — *vi* **~ con** : to get in touch with, to contact
contacto *nm* : contact
contado[1], **-da** *adj* **1** : counted ⟨tenía los días contados : his days were numbered⟩ **2** : rare, scarce ⟨en contadas ocasiones : on rare occasions⟩
contado[2] *nm* **al contado** : cash ⟨pagar al contado : to pay in cash⟩
contador[1], **-dora** *n* : accountant
contador[2] *nm* : meter ⟨contador de agua : water meter⟩
contaduría *nf* **1** : accounting office **2** CONTABILIDAD : accountancy
contagiar *vt* **1** : to infect **2** : to transmit (a disease) — **contagiarse** *vr* **1** : to be contagious **2** : to become infected
contagio *nm* : contagion, infection

contagioso, -sa *adj* : contagious, catching

contaminación *nf, pl* **-ciones** : contamination, pollution

contaminante *nm* : pollutant, contaminant

contaminar *vt* : to contaminate, to pollute

contar {19} *vt* **1** : to count **2** : to tell **3** : to include — *vi* **1** : to count (up) **2** : to matter, to be of concern ⟨eso no cuenta : that doesn't matter⟩ **3** ~ **con** : to rely on, to count on — **contarse** *vr* ~ **entre** : to be numbered among

contemplación *nf, pl* **-ciones** : contemplation — **contemplativo, -va** *adj*

contemplar *vt* **1** : to contemplate, to ponder **2** : to gaze at, to look at

contemporáneo, -nea *adj & n* : contemporary

contención *nf, pl* **-ciones** : containment, holding

contencioso, -sa *adj* : contentious

contender {56} *vi* **1** : to contend, to compete **2** : to fight

contendiente *nmf* : contender

contenedor *nm* **1** : container, receptacle **2** : Dumpster™

contener {80} *vt* **1** : to contain, to hold **2** ATAJAR : to restrain, to hold back — **contenerse** *vr* : to restrain oneself

contenido¹, -da *adj* : restrained, reserved

contenido² *nm* : contents *pl*, content

contentar *vt* : to please, to make happy — **contentarse** *vr* : to be satisfied, to be pleased

contento¹, -ta *adj* : contented, glad, happy

contento² *nm* : joy, happiness

contestación *nf, pl* **-ciones 1** : answer, reply **2** : protest

contestar *vt* RESPONDER : to answer — *vi* **1** RESPONDER : to answer, to reply **2** REPLICAR : to answer back

contexto *nm* : context

contienda *nf* **1** : dispute, conflict **2** : contest, competition

contigo *pron* : with you ⟨voy contigo : I'm going with you⟩

contiguo, -gua *adj* COLINDANTE : contiguous, adjacent

continencia *nf* : continence

continente *nm* : continent — **continental** *adj*

contingencia *nf* : contingency, eventuality

contingente *adj & nm* : contingent

continuación *nf, pl* **-ciones 1** : continuation **2 a** ~ : next ⟨lo demás sigue a continuación : the rest follows⟩ **3 a continuación de** : after, following

continuar {3} *v* : to continue

continuidad *nf* : continuity

continuo, -nua *adj* : continuous, steady, constant — **continuamente** *adv*

contonearse *vr* : to sway one's hips

contoneo *nm* : swaying, wiggling (of the hips)

contorno *nm* **1** : outline **2 contornos** *nmpl* : outskirts

contorsión *nf, pl* **-siones** : contortion

contra¹ *nf* **1** *fam* : difficulty, snag **2 llevar la contra a** : to oppose, to contradict

contra² *nm* : con ⟨los pros y los contras : the pros and cons⟩

contra³ *prep* : against

contraalmirante *nm* : rear admiral

contraatacar {72} *v* : to counterattack — **contraataque** *nm*

contrabajo *nm* : double bass

contrabalancear *vt* : to counterbalance — **contrabalanza** *nf*

contrabandear *v* : to smuggle

contrabandista *nmf* : smuggler, black marketeer

contrabando *nm* **1** : smuggling **2** : contraband

contracción *nf, pl* **-ciones** : contraction

contracepción *nf, pl* **-ciones** : contraception

contraceptivo *nm* ANTICONCEPTIVO : contraceptive

contrachapado *nm* : plywood

contracorriente *nf* **1** : crosscurrent **2 ir a contracorriente** : to go against the tide

contractual *adj* : contractual

contradecir {11} *vt* DESMENTIR : to contradict — **contradecirse** *vr* DESDECIRSE : to contradict oneself

contradicción *nf, pl* **-ciones** : contradiction

contradictorio, -ria *adj* : contradictory

contraer {81} *vt* **1** : to contract (a disease) **2** : to establish by contract ⟨contraer matrimonio : to get married⟩ **3** : to tighten, to contract — **contraerse** *vr* : to contract, to tighten up

contrafuerte *nm* : buttress

contragolpe *nm* **1** : counterblow **2** : backlash

contrahecho, -cha *adj* : deformed, hunchbacked

contraindicado, -da *adj* : contraindicated — **contraindicación** *nf*

contralor, -lora *n* : comptroller

contralto *nmf* : contralto

contramaestre *nm* **1** : boatswain **2** : foreman

contramandar *vt* : to countermand

contramano *nm* **a** ~ : the wrong way (on a street)

contramedida *nf* : countermeasure

contraorden *nf* : countermand

contraparte *nf* **1** : counterpart **2 en** ~ : on the other hand

contrapartida *nf* : compensation

contrapelo *nm* **a** ~ : in the wrong direction, against the grain

contrapeso *nm* : counterbalance

contraponer {60} *vt* **1** : to counter, to oppose **2** : to contrast, to compare

contraposición *nf, pl* **-ciones** : comparison

contraproducente *adj* : counterproductive

contrapunto *nm* : counterpoint
contrariar {85} *vt* **1** : to contradict, to oppose **2** : to vex, to annoy
contrariedad *nf* **1** : setback, obstacle **2** : vexation, annoyance
contrario, -ria *adj* **1** : contrary, opposite ⟨al contrario : on the contrary⟩ **2** : conflicting, opposed
contrarrestar *vt* : to counteract
contrarrevolución *nf, pl* **-ciones** : counterrevolution — **contrarrevolucionario, -ria** *adj & n*
contrasentido *nm* : contradiction
contraseña *nf* : password
contrastante *adj* : contrasting
contrastar *vt* **1** : to resist **2** : to check, to confirm — *vi* : to contrast
contraste *nm* : contrast
contratar *vt* **1** : to contract for **2** : to hire, to engage
contratiempo *nm* **1** PERCANCE : mishap, accident **2** DIFICULTAD : setback, difficulty
contratista *nmf* : contractor
contrato *nm* : contract
contravenir {87} *vt* : to contravene, to infringe
contraventana *nf* : shutter
contribución *nf, pl* **-ciones** : contribution
contribuidor, -dora *n* : contributor
contribuir {41} *vt* **1** APORTAR : to contribute **2** : to pay (in taxes) — *vi* **1** : contribute, to help out **2** : to pay taxes
contribuyente[1] *adj* : contributing
contribuyente[2] *nmf* : taxpayer
contrición *nf, pl* **-ciones** : contrition
contrincante *nmf* : rival, opponent
contrito, -ta *adj* : contrite, repentant
control *nm* **1** : control **2** : inspection, check **3** : checkpoint, roadblock
controlador, -dora *n* : controller ⟨controlador aéreo : air traffic controller⟩
controlar *vt* **1** : to control **2** : to monitor, to check
controversia *nf* : controversy
controversial → **controvertido**
controvertido, -da *adj* : controversial
controvertir {76} *vt* : to dispute, to argue about — *vi* : to argue, to debate
contubernio *nm* : conspiracy
contumacia *nf* : obstinacy, stubbornness
contumaz *adj, pl* **-maces** : obstinate, stubbornly disobedient
contundencia *nf* **1** : forcefulness, weight **2** : severity
contundente *adj* **1** : blunt ⟨un objeto contundente : a blunt instrument⟩ **2** : forceful, convincing — **contundentemente** *adv*
contusión *nf, pl* **-siones** : bruise, contusion
contuvo, etc. → **contener**
convalecencia *nf* : convalescence
convalecer {53} *vi* : to convalesce, to recover

convaleciente *adj & nmf* : convalescent
convección *nf, pl* **-ciones** : convection
convencer {86} *vt* : to convince, to persuade — **convencerse** *vr*
convencimiento *nm* : belief, conviction
convención *nf, pl* **-ciones** **1** : convention, conference **2** : pact, agreement **3** : convention, custom
convencional *adj* : conventional — **convencionalmente** *adv*
convencionalismo *nm* : conventionality
conveniencia *nf* **1** : convenience **2** : fitness, suitability, advisability
conveniente *adj* **1** : convenient **2** : suitable, advisable
convenio *nm* PACTO : agreement, pact
convenir {87} *vi* **1** : to be suitable, to be advisable **2** : to agree
convento *nm* **1** : convent **2** : monastery
convergencia *nf* : convergence
convergente *adj* : convergent, converging
converger {15} *vi* **1** : to converge **2** ~ **en** : to concur on
conversación *nf, pl* **-ciones** : conversation
conversador, -dora *n* : conversationalist, talker
conversar *vi* : to converse, to talk
conversión *nf, pl* **-siones** : conversion
converso, -sa *n* : convert
convertible *adj & nm* : convertible
convertidor *nm* : converter
convertir {76} *vt* **1** : to convert **2** : to transform, to change **3** : to exchange (money) — **convertirse** *vr* ~ **en** : to turn into
convexo, -xa *adj* : convex
convicción *nf, pl* **-ciones** : conviction
convicto[1]**, -ta** *adj* : convicted
convicto[2]**, -ta** *n* : convict, prisoner
convidado, -da *n* : guest
convidar *vt* **1** INVITAR : to invite **2** : to offer
convincente *adj* : convincing — **convincentemente** *adv*
convivencia *nf* **1** : coexistence **2** : cohabitation
convivir *vi* **1** : to coexist **2** : to live together
convocación *nf, pl* **-ciones** : convocation
convocar {72} *vt* : to convoke, to call together
convocatoria *nf* : summons, call
convoy *nm* : convoy
convulsión *nf, pl* **-siones** **1** : convulsion **2** : agitation, upheaval
convulsionar *vt* : to shake, to convulse — **convulsionarse** *vr*
convulsivo, -va *adj* : convulsive
conyugal *adj* : conjugal
cónyuge *nmf* : spouse, partner
coñac *nm* : cognac, brandy
cooperación *nf, pl* **-ciones** : cooperation
cooperador, -dora *adj* : cooperative

cooperar *vi* : to cooperate
cooperativa *nf* : cooperative, co-op
cooperativo, -va *adj* : cooperative
cooptar *vt* : to co-opt
coordenada *nf* : coordinate
coordinación *nf, pl* **-ciones** : coordination
coordinador, -dora *n* : coordinator
coordinar *vt* COMPAGINAR : to coordinate, to combine
copa *nf* **1** : wineglass, goblet **2** : drink ⟨irse de copas : to go out drinking⟩ **3** : cup, trophy
copar *vt* **1** : to take ⟨ya está copado el puesto : the job is already taken⟩ **2** : to fill, to crowd
copartícipe *nmf* : joint partner
copete *nm* **1** : tuft (of hair) **2 estar hasta el copete** : to be completely fed up
copia *nf* **1** : copy **2** : imitation, replica
copiadora *nf* : photocopier
copiar *vt* : to copy
copiloto *nmf* : copilot
copioso, -sa *adj* : copious, abundant
copla *nf* **1** : popular song or ballad **2** : couplet, stanza
copo *nm* **1** : snowflake **2 copos de avena** : rolled oats **3 copos de maíz** : cornflakes
copra *nf* : copra
cópula *nf* : copulation
copular *vi* : to copulate
coque *nm* : coke (fuel)
coqueta *nf* : dressing table
coquetear *vi* : to flirt
coqueteo *nm* : flirting, coquetry
coqueto[1], -ta *adj* : flirtatious, coquettish
coqueto[2], -ta *n* : flirt
coraje *nm* **1** VALOR : valor, courage **2** IRA : anger ⟨darle coraje a alguien : to make someone angry⟩
corajudo, -da *adj* : brave
coral[1] *nm* **1** : coral **2** : chorale
coral[2] *nf* : choir
Corán *nm* **el Corán** : the Koran
coraza *nf* **1** : armor, armor plating **2** : shell (of an animal)
corazón *nm, pl* **-zones 1** : heart ⟨de todo corazón : wholeheartedly⟩ ⟨de buen corazón : kindhearted⟩ **2** : core **3** : darling, sweetheart
corazonada *nf* : hunch, impulse
corbata *nf* : tie, necktie
corcel *nm* : steed, charger
corchete *nm* **1** : hook and eye, clasp **2** : square bracket
corcho *nm* : cork
corcholata *nf Mex* : cap, bottle top
corcovear *vi* : to buck
cordel *nm* : cord, string
cordero *nm* : lamb
cordial[1] *adj* : cordial, affable — **cordialmente** *adv*
cordial[2] *nm* : cordial (liqueur)
cordialidad *nf* : cordiality, warmth
cordillera *nf* : mountain range
córdoba *nf* : Nicaraguan unit of currency

cordón *nm, pl* **cordones 1** : cord ⟨cordón umbilical : umbilical cord⟩ **2** : cordon
cordura *nf* **1** : sanity **2** : prudence, good judgment
coreano[1], -na *adj & n* : Korean
coreano[2] *nm* : Korean (language)
corear *vt* : to chant, to chorus
coreografía *nf* : choreography
coreografiar {85} *vt* : to choreograph
coreográfico, -ca *adj* : choreographic
coreógrafo, -fa *n* : choreographer
corista *nmf* **1** : chorister **2** : chorus girl *f*
cormorán *nm, pl* **-ranes** : cormorant
cornada *nf* : goring, butt (with the horns)
córnea *nf* : cornea
cornear *vt* : to gore
cornejo *nm* : dogwood (tree)
corneta *nf* : bugle, horn, cornet
cornisa *nf* : cornice
cornudo, -da *adj* : horned
coro *nm* **1** : choir **2** : chorus
corola *nf* : corolla
corolario *nm* : corollary
corona *nf* **1** : crown **2** : wreath, garland **3** : corona (in astronomy)
coronación *nf, pl* **-ciones** : coronation
coronar *vt* **1** : to crown **2** : to reach the top of, to culminate
coronario, -ria *adj* : coronary
coronel, -nela *n* : colonel
coronilla *nf* **1** : crown (of the head) **2 estar hasta la coronilla** : to be completely fed up
corpiño *nm* **1** : bodice **2** *Arg* : brassiere, bra
corporación *nf, pl* **-ciones** : corporation
corporal *adj* : corporal, bodily
corporativo, -va *adj* : corporate
corpóreo, -rea *adj* : corporeal, physical
corpulencia *nf* : corpulence, stoutness, sturdiness
corpulento, -ta *adj* ROBUSTO : robust, stout, sturdy
corpúsculo *nm* : corpuscle
corral *nm* **1** : farmyard **2** : corral, pen, stockyard **3** *or* **corralito** : playpen
correa *nf* : strap, belt
correcaminos *nms & pl* : roadrunner
corrección *nf, pl* **-ciones 1** : correction **2** : correctness, propriety **3** : rebuke, reprimand **4 corrección de pruebas** : proofreading
correccional *nm* REFORMATORIO : reformatory
correctivo, -va *adj* : corrective ⟨lentes correctivos : corrective lenses⟩
correcto, -ta *adj* **1** : correct, right **2** : courteous, polite — **correctamente** *adv*
corrector, -tora *n* : proofreader
corredizo, -za *adj* : sliding ⟨puerta corrediza : sliding door⟩
corredor[1], -dora *n* **1** : runner, racer **2** : agent, broker ⟨corredor de bolsa : stockbroker⟩
corredor[2] *nm* PASILLO : corridor, hallway

correduría *nf* → **corretaje**
corregir {28} *vt* 1 ENMENDAR : to correct, to emend 2 : to reprimand 3 **corregir pruebas** : to proofread — **corregirse** *vr* : to reform, to mend one's ways
correlación *nf, pl* **-ciones** : correlation
correo *nm* 1 : mail ⟨correo aéreo : airmail⟩ 2 : post office
correoso, -sa *adj* : leathery, rough
correr *vi* 1 : to run, to race 2 : to rush 3 : to flow — *vt* 1 : to travel over, to cover 2 : to move, to slide, to roll, to draw (curtains) 3 **correr un riesgo** : to run a risk — **correrse** *vr* 1 : to move along 2 : to run, to spill over
correspondencia *nf* 1 : correspondence, mail 2 : equivalence 3 : connection, interchange
corresponder *vi* 1 : to correspond 2 : to pertain, to belong 3 : to be appropriate, to fit 4 : to reciprocate — **corresponderse** *vr* : to write to each other
correspondiente *adj* : corresponding, respective
corresponsal *nmf* : correspondent
corretaje *nm* : brokerage
corretear *vi* 1 VAGAR : to loiter, to wander about 2 : to run around, to scamper about — *vt* : to pursue, to chase
corrida *nf* 1 : run, dash 2 : bullfight
corrido¹, -da *adj* 1 : straight, continuous 2 : worldly, experienced
corrido² *nm* : Mexican narrative folk song
corriente¹ *adj* 1 : common, everyday 2 : current, present 3 *Mex* : cheap, trashy 4 **perro corriente** *Mex* : mutt
corriente² *nf* 1 : current ⟨corriente alterna : alternating current⟩ ⟨direct current : corriente continua⟩ 2 : draft 3 TENDENCIA : tendency, trend
corrillo *nm* : small group, clique
corro *nm* : ring, circle (of people)
corroboración *nf, pl* **-ciones** : corroboration
corroborar *vt* : to corroborate
corroer {69} *vt* 1 : to corrode 2 : to erode, to wear away
corromper *vt* 1 : to corrupt 2 : to rot — **corromperse** *vr*
corrompido, -da *adj* CORRUPTO : corrupt, rotten
corrosión *nf, pl* **-siones** : corrosion
corrosivo, -va *adj* : corrosive
corrugar {52} *vt* : to corrugate — **corrugación** *nf*
corrupción *nf, pl* **-ciones** 1 : decay 2 : corruption
corruptela *nf* : corruption, abuse of power
corrupto, -ta *adj* CORROMPIDO : corrupt
corsario *nm* : privateer
corsé *nm* : corset
cortada *nf* : cut, gash
cortador, -dora *n* : cutter
cortadora *nf* : cutter, slicer
cortadura *nf* : cut, slash
cortafuegos *nms & pl* 1 : firebreak 2 : firewall (program)

cortante *adj* : cutting, sharp
cortar *vt* 1 : to cut, to slice, to trim 2 : to cut out, to omit 3 : to cut off, to interrupt 4 : to block, to close off 5 : to curdle (milk) — *vi* 1 : to cut 2 : to break up 3 : to hang up (the telephone) — **cortarse** *vr* 1 : to cut oneself ⟨cortarse el pelo : to cut one's hair⟩ 2 : to be cut off 3 : to sour (of milk)
cortauñas *nms & pl* : nail clippers
corte¹ *nm* 1 : cut, cutting ⟨corte de pelo : haircut⟩ 2 : style, fit
corte² *nf* 1 : court ⟨corte suprema : supreme court⟩ 2 **hacer la corte a** : to court, to woo
cortejar *vt* GALANTEAR : to court, to woo
cortejo *nm* 1 GALANTEO : courtship 2 : retinue, entourage
cortés *adj* : courteous, polite — **cortésmente** *adv*
cortesano¹, -na *adj* : courtly
cortesano², -na *n* : courtier
cortesía *nf* 1 : courtesy, politeness 2 **de ~** : complimentary, free
corteza *nf* 1 : bark 2 : crust 3 : peel, rind 4 : cortex ⟨corteza cerebral : cerebral cortex⟩
cortijo *nm* : farmhouse
cortina *nf* : curtain
cortisona *nf* : cortisone
corto, -ta *adj* 1 : short (in length or duration) 2 : scarce 3 : timid, shy 4 **corto de vista** : nearsighted
cortocircuito *nm* : short circuit
corvejón *nm, pl* **-jones** JARRETTE : hock
corvo, -va *adj* : curved, bent
cosa *nf* 1 : thing, object 2 : matter, affair 3 **otra cosa** : anything else, something else
cosecha *nf* : harvest, crop
cosechador, -dora *n* : harvester, reaper
cosechadora *nf* : harvester (machine)
cosechar *vt* 1 : to harvest, to reap 2 : to win, to earn, to garner — *vi* : to harvest
coser *vt* 1 : to sew 2 : to stitch up — *vi* : to sew
cosmético¹, -ca *adj* : cosmetic
cosmético² *nm* : cosmetic
cósmico, -ca *adj* : cosmic
cosmonauta *nmf* : cosmonaut
cosmopolita *adj & nmf* : cosmopolitan
cosmos *nm* : cosmos
cosquillas *nfpl* 1 : tickling 2 **hacer cosquillas** : to tickle
cosquilleo *nm* : tickling sensation, tingle
cosquilloso, -sa *adj* : ticklish
costa *nf* 1 : coast, shore 2 : cost ⟨a toda costa : at all costs⟩
costado *nm* 1 : side 2 **al costado** : alongside
costar {19} *v* : to cost ⟨¿cuánto cuesta? : how much does it cost?⟩
costarricense *adj & nmf* : Costa Rican
costarriqueño, -ña → **costarricense**
coste → **costo**
costear *vt* : to pay for, to finance

costero, -ra *adj* : coastal, coast
costilla *nf* **1** : rib **2** : chop, cutlet **3** *fam* : better half, wife
costo *nm* **1** : cost, price **2 costo de vida** : cost of living
costoso, -sa *adj* : costly, expensive
costra *nf* **1** : crust **2** POSTILLA : scab
costumbre *nf* **1** : custom **2** HÁBITO : habit
costura *nf* **1** : seam **2** : sewing, dressmaking **3 alta costura** : haute couture
costurera *nf* : seamstress *f*
cotejar *vt* : to compare, to collate
cotejo *nm* : comparison, collation
cotidiano, -na *adj* : daily, everyday ⟨la vida cotidiana : daily life⟩
cotización *nf, pl* **-ciones** **1** : market price **2** : quote, estimate
cotizado, -da *adj* : in demand, sought after
cotizar {21} *vt* : to quote, to value — **cotizarse** *vr* : to be worth
coto *nm* **1** : enclosure, reserve **2 poner coto a** : to put a stop to
cotorra *nf* **1** : small parrot **2** *fam* : chatterbox, windbag
cotorrear *vi fam* : to chatter, to gab, to blab
cotorreo *nm fam* : chatter, prattle
coyote *nm* **1** : coyote **2** *Mex fam* : smuggler (of illegal immigrants)
coyuntura *nf* **1** ARTICULACIÓN : joint **2** : occasion, moment
coz *nf, pl* **coces** : kick (of an animal)
crac *nm, pl* **cracs** : crash (of the stock market)
cozamos, etc. → **cocer**
craneal *adj* : cranial
cráneo *nf* : cranium, skull — **craneano, -na** *adj*
cráter *nm* : crater
crayón *nm, pl* **-yones** : crayon
creación *nf, pl* **-ciones** : creation
creador[1]**, -dora** *adj* : creative, creating
creador[2]**, -dora** *n* : creator
crear *vt* **1** : to create, to cause **2** : to originate
creatividad *nf* : creativity
creativo, -va *adj* : creative
crecer {53} *vi* **1** : to grow **2** : to increase
crecida *nf* : flooding, floodwater
crecido, -da *adj* **1** : grown, grown-up **2** : large (of numbers)
creciente *adj* **1** : growing, increasing **2 luna creciente** : waxing moon
crecientemente *adv* : increasingly
crecimiento *nm* **1** : growth **2** : increase
credencial *adj* **cartas credenciales** : credentials
credenciales *nfpl* : documents, documentation, credentials
credibilidad *nf* : credibility
crédito *nm* : credit
credo *nm* : creed, credo
credulidad *nf* : credulity
crédulo, -la *adj* : credulous, gullible
creencia *nf* : belief
creer {20} *v* **1** : to believe **2** : to suppose, to think ⟨creo que sí : I think so⟩

— **creerse** *vr* **1** : to believe, to think **2** : to regard oneself as ⟨se cree guapísimo : he thinks he's so handsome⟩
creíble *adj* : believable, credible
creído, -da *adj* **1** *fam* : conceited **2** : confident, sure
crema *nf* **1** : cream **2 la crema y nata** : the pick of the crop
cremación *nf, pl* **-ciones** : cremation
cremallera *nf* : zipper
cremar *vt* : to cremate
cremoso, -sa *adj* : creamy
crepa *nf Mex* : crepe (pancake)
crepe *or* **crep** *nmf* : crepe (pancake)
crepé *nm* **1** → **crespón** **2 papel crepé** : crepe paper
crepitar *vi* : to crackle
crepúsculo *nm* : twilight
crescendo *nm* : crescendo
crespo, -pa *adj* : curly, frizzy
crespón *nm, pl* **crespones** : crepe (fabric)
cresta *nf* **1** : crest **2** : comb (of a rooster)
creta *nf* : chalk (mineral)
cretino, -na *n* : cretin
creyente *nmf* : believer
creyó, etc. → **creer**
crezca, etc. → **crecer**
cría *nf* **1** : breeding, rearing **2** : young **3** : litter
criadero *nm* : hatchery
criado[1]**, -da** *adj* **1** : raised, brought up **2 bien criado** : well-bred
criado[2]**, -da** *n* : servant, maid *f*
criador, -dora *n* : breeder
crianza *nf* : upbringing, rearing
criar {85} *vt* **1** : to breed **2** : to bring up, to raise
criatura *nf* **1** : baby, child **2** : creature
criba *nf* : sieve, screen
cribar *vt* : to sift
cric *nm, pl* **crics** : jack
crimen *nm, pl* **crímenes** : crime
criminal *adj & nmf* : criminal
crin *nf* **1** : mane **2** : horsehair
criollo[1]**, -lla** *adj* **1** : Creole **2** : native, national ⟨comida criolla : native cuisine⟩
criollo[2]**, -lla** *n* : Creole
criollo[3] *nm* : Creole (language)
cripta *nf* : crypt
críptico, -ca *adj* **1** : cryptic, coded **2** : enigmatic, cryptic
criptón *nm* : krypton
críquet *nm* : cricket (game)
crisálida *nf* : chrysalis, pupa
crisantemo *nm* : chrysanthemum
crisis *nf* **1** : crisis **2 crisis nerviosa** : nervous breakdown
crisma *nf fam* : head ⟨romperle la crisma a alguien : to knock someone's block off⟩
crisol *nm* **1** : crucible **2** : melting pot
crispar *vt* **1** : to cause to contract **2** : to irritate, to set on edge ⟨eso me crispa : that gets on my nerves⟩ — **crisparse** *vr* : to tense up

cristal *nm* **1** VIDRIO : glass, piece of glass **2** : crystal

cristalería *nf* **1** : glassware shop ⟨como chivo en cristalería : like a bull in a china shop⟩ **2** : glassware, crystal

cristalino[1], **-na** *adj* : crystalline, clear

cristalino[2] *nm* : lens (of the eye)

cristalizar {21} *vi* : to crystallize — **cristalización** *nf*

cristiandad *nf* : Christendom

cristianismo *nm* : Christianity

cristiano, -na *adj & n* : Christian

Cristo *nm* : Christ

criterio *nm* **1** : criterion **2** : judgment, sense

crítica *nf* **1** : criticism **2** : review, critique

criticar {72} *vt* : to criticize

crítico[1], **-ca** *adj* : critical — **críticamente** *adv*

crítico[2], **-ca** *n* : critic

criticón[1], **-cona** *adj, mpl* **-cones** *fam* : hypercritical, captious

criticón[2], **-cona** *n, mpl* **-cones** *fam* : faultfinder, critic

croar *vi* : to croak

croata *adj & nmf* : Croatian

crocante *adj* : crunchy

croché *or* **crochet** *nm* : crochet

cromático, -ca *adj* : chromatic

cromo *nm* **1** : chromium, chrome **2** : picture card, sports card

cromosoma *nm* : chromosome

crónica *nf* **1** : news report **2** : chronicle, history

crónico, -ca *adj* : chronic

cronista *nmf* **1** : reporter, newscaster **2** HISTORIADOR : chronicler, historian

cronología *nf* : chronology

cronológico, -ca *adj* : chronological — **cronológicamente** *adv*

cronometrador, -dora *n* : timekeeper

cronometrar *vt* : to time, to clock

cronómetro *nm* : chronometer

croquet *nm* : croquet

croqueta *nf* : croquette

croquis *nm* : rough sketch

cruce[1], etc. → **cruzar**

cruce[2] *nm* **1** : crossing, cross **2** : crossroads, intersection ⟨cruce peatonal : crosswalk⟩

crucero *nm* **1** : cruise **2** : cruiser, warship **3** *Mex* : intersection

crucial *adj* : crucial — **crucialmente** *adv*

crucificar {72} *vt* : to crucify

crucifijo *nm* : crucifix

crucifixión *nf, pl* **-fixiones** : crucifixion

crucigrama *nm* : crossword puzzle

crudo[1], **-da** *adj* **1** : raw **2** : crude, harsh

crudo[2] *nm* : crude oil

cruel *adj* : cruel — **cruelmente** *adv*

crueldad *nf* : cruelty

cruento, -ta *adj* : bloody

crujido *nm* **1** : rustling **2** : creaking **3** : crackling (of a fire) **4** : crunching

crujiente *adj* : crunchy, crisp

crujir *vi* **1** : to rustle **2** : to creak, to crack **3** : to crunch

crup *nm* : croup

crustáceo *nm* : crustacean

crutón *nm, pl* **crutones** : crouton

cruz *nf, pl* **cruces** : cross

cruza *nf* : cross (hybrid)

cruzada *nf* : crusade

cruzado[1], **-da** *adj* : crossed ⟨espadas cruzadas : crossed swords⟩

cruzado[2] *nm* **1** : crusader **2** : Brazilian unit of currency

cruzar {21} *vt* **1** : to cross **2** : to exchange (words, greetings) **3** : to cross, to interbreed — **cruzarse** *vr* **1** : to intersect **2** : to meet, to pass each other

cuaderno *nm* LIBRETA : notebook

cuadra *nf* **1** : city block **2** : stable

cuadrado[1], **-da** *adj* : square

cuadrado[2] *nm* : square ⟨elevar al cuadrado : to square (a number)⟩

cuadragésimo[1] *adj* : fortieth, forty-

cuadragésimo[2], **-ma** *n* : fortieth, forty- (in a series)

cuadrante *nm* **1** : quadrant **2** : dial

cuadrar *vi* : to conform, to agree — *vt* : to square — **cuadrarse** *vr* : to stand at attention

cuadriculado *nm* : grid (on a map, etc.)

cuadrilátero *nm* **1** : quadrilateral **2** : ring (in sports)

cuadrilla *nf* : gang, team, group

cuadro *nm* **1** : square ⟨una blusa a cuadros : a checkered blouse⟩ **2** : painting, picture **3** : baseball diamond, infield **4** : panel, board, cadre

cuadrúpedo *nm* : quadruped

cuádruple *adj* : quadruple

cuadruplicar {72} *vt* : to quadruple — **cuadruplicarse** *vr*

cuajada *nf* : curd

cuajar *vi* **1** : to curdle **2** COAGULAR : to clot, to coagulate **3** : to set, to jell **4** : to be accepted ⟨su idea no cuajó : his idea didn't catch on⟩ — *vt* **1** : to curdle **2** ~ **de** : to fill with

cual[1] *prep* : like, as

cual[2] *pron* **1 el cual, la cual, los cuales, las cuales** : who, whom, which ⟨la razón por la cual lo dije : the reason I said it⟩ **2 lo cual** : which ⟨se rió, lo cual me dio rabia : he laughed, which made me mad⟩ **3 cada cual** : everyone, everybody

cuál[1] *adj* : which, what ⟨¿cuáles libros? : which books?⟩

cuál[2] *pron* **1** (*in questions*) : which (one), what (one) ⟨¿cuál es el mejor? : which one is the best?⟩ ⟨¿cuál es tu apellido? : what is your last name?⟩ **2 cuál más, cuál menos** : some more, some less

cualidad *nf* : quality, trait

cualitativo, -va *adj* : qualitative — **cualitativamente** *adv*

cualquier *adj* → **cualquiera**[1]

cualquiera[1] (**cualquier** *before nouns*) *adj, pl* **cualesquiera 1** : any, whichever ⟨cualquier persona : any person⟩ **2** : everyday, ordinary ⟨un hombre cualquiera : an ordinary man⟩

cualquiera² *pron, pl* **cualesquiera 1** : anyone, anybody, whoever **2** : whatever, whichever

cuán *adv* : how ⟨¡cuán risible fue todo eso! : how funny it all was!⟩

cuando¹ *conj* **1** : when ⟨cuando llegó : when he arrived⟩ **2** : since, if ⟨cuando lo dices : if you say so⟩ **3 cuando más** : at the most **4 de vez en cuando** : from time to time

cuando² *prep* : during, at the time of ⟨cuando la guerra : during the war⟩

cuándo *adv & conj* **1** : when ⟨¿cuándo llegará? : when will she arrive?⟩ ⟨no sabemos cuándo será : we don't know when it will be⟩ **2 ¿de cuándo acá?** : since when?, how come?

cuantía *nf* **1** : quantity, extent **2** : significance, import

cuántico, -ca *adj* : quantum ⟨teoría cuántica : quantum theory⟩

cuantioso, -sa *adj* **1** : abundant, considerable **2** : heavy, grave ⟨cuantiosos daños : heavy damage⟩

cuantitativo, -va *adj* : quantitative — **cuantitativamente** *adv*

cuanto¹ *adv* **1** : as much as ⟨come cuanto puedas : eat as much as you can⟩ **2 cuanto antes** : as soon as possible **3 en ~** : as soon as **4 en cuanto a** : as for, as regards

cuanto², -ta *adj* : as many, whatever ⟨llévate cuantas flores quieras : take as many flowers as you wish⟩

cuanto³, -ta *pron* **1** : as much as, all that, everything ⟨tengo cuanto deseo : I have all that I want⟩ **2 unos cuantos, unas cuantas** : a few

cuánto¹ *adv* : how much, how many ⟨¿a cuánto están las manzanas? : how much are the apples?⟩ ⟨no sé cuánto desean : I don't know how much they want⟩

cuánto², -ta *adj* : how much, how many ⟨¿cuántos niños tiene? : how many children do you have?⟩

cuánto³ *pron* : how much, how many ⟨¿cuántos quieren participar? : how many want to take part?⟩ ⟨¿cuánto cuesta? : how much does it cost?⟩

cuarenta *adj & nm* : forty

cuarentavo¹, -va *adj* : fortieth

cuarentavo² *nm* : fortieth (fraction)

cuarentena *nf* **1** : group of forty **2** : quarantine

Cuaresma *nf* : Lent

cuartear *vt* **1** : to quarter **2** : to divide up — **cuartearse** *vr* AGRIETARSE : to crack, to split

cuartel *nm* **1** : barracks, headquarters **2** : mercy ⟨una guerra sin cuartel : a merciless war⟩

cuartelazo *nm* : coup d'état

cuarteto *nm* : quartet

cuartilla *nf* : sheet (of paper)

cuarto¹, -ta *adj* : fourth

cuarto², -ta *n* : fourth (in a series)

cuarto³ *nm* **1** : quarter, fourth ⟨cuarto de galón : quart⟩ **2** HABITACIÓN : room

cuarzo *nm* : quartz

cuate, -ta *n Mex* **1** : twin **2** *fam* : buddy, pal

cuatrero, -ra *n* : rustler

cuatrillizo, -za *n* : quadruplet

cuatro *adj & nm* : four

cuatrocientos¹, -tas *adj* : four hundred

cuatrocientos² *nms & pl* : four hundred

cuba *nf* BARRIL : cask, barrel

cubano, -na *adj & n* : Cuban

cubertería *nf* : flatware, silverware

cubeta *nf* **1** : keg, cask **2** : bulb (of a thermometer) **3** *Mex* : bucket, pail

cúbico, -ca *adj* : cubic, cubed

cubículo *nm* : cubicle

cubierta *nf* **1** : covering **2** FORRO : cover, jacket (of a book) **3** : deck

cubierto¹ *pp* → **cubrir**

cubierto² *nm* **1** : cover, shelter ⟨bajo cubierto : under cover⟩ **2** : table setting **3** : utensil, piece of silverware

cubil *nm* : den, lair

cúbito *nm* : ulna

cubo *nm* **1** : cube **2** BALDE : pail, bucket, can ⟨cubo de basura : garbage can⟩ **3** : hub (of a wheel)

cubrecama *nm* COLCHA : bedspread

cubrir {2} *vt* : to cover — **cubrirse** *vr*

cucaracha *nf* : cockroach, roach

cuchara *nf* : spoon

cucharada *nf* : spoonful

cucharilla *or* **cucharita** *nf* : teaspoon

cucharón *nm, pl* **-rones** : ladle

cuchichear *vi* : to whisper

cuchicheo *nm* : whisper

cuchilla *nf* **1** : kitchen knife, cleaver **2** : blade ⟨cuchilla de afeitar : razor blade⟩ **3** : crest, ridge

cuchillada *nf* : stab, knife wound

cuchillo *nm* : knife

cuclillas *nfpl* **en ~** : squatting, crouching

cuco¹, -ca *adj fam* : pretty, cute

cuco² *nm* : cuckoo

cucurucho *nm* : ice-cream cone

cuece, cueza etc. → **cocer**

cuela, etc. → **colar**

cuelga, cuelgue etc. → **colgar**

cuello *nm* **1** : neck **2** : collar (of a shirt) **3 cuello del útero** : cervix

cuenca *nf* **1** : river basin **2** : eye socket

cuenco *nm* : bowl, basin

cuenta¹, etc. → **contar**

cuenta² *nf* **1** : calculation, count **2** : account **3** : check, bill **4 darse cuenta** : to realize **5 tener en cuenta** : to bear in mind

cuentagotas *nfs & pl* **1** : dropper **2 con ~** : little by little

cuentista *nmf* **1** : short story writer **2** *fam* : liar, fibber

cuento *nm* **1** : story, tale **2 cuento de hadas** : fairy tale **3 sin ~** : countless

cuerda *nf* **1** : cord, rope, string **2 cuerdas vocales** : vocal cords **3 darle cuerda a** : to wind up (a clock, a toy, etc.)

cuerdo, -da *adj* : sane, sensible
cuerno *nm* **1** : horn, antler **2** : cusp (of the moon) **3** : horn (musical instrument)
cuero *nm* **1** : leather, hide **2 cuero cabelludo** : scalp
cuerpo *nm* **1** : body **2** : corps
cuervo *nm* : crow, raven
cuesta[1], etc. → **costar**
cuesta[2] *nf* **1** : slope ⟨cuesta arriba : uphill⟩ **2 a cuestas** : on one's back
cuestión *nf, pl* **-tiones** ASUNTO, TEMA : matter, affair
cuestionable *adj* : questionable, dubious
cuestionar *vt* : to question
cuestionario *nm* **1** : questionnaire **2** : quiz
cueva *nf* : cave
cuidado *nm* **1** : care **2** : worry, concern **3 tener cuidado** : to be careful **4 ¡cuidado!** : watch out!, be careful!
cuidador, -dora *n* : caretaker
cuidadoso, -sa *adj* : careful, attentive — **cuidadosamente** *adv*
cuidar *vt* **1** : to take care of, to look after **2** : to pay attention to — *vi* **1** ∼ **de** : to look after **2 cuidar de que** : to make sure that — **cuidarse** *vr* : to take care of oneself
culata *nf* : butt (of a gun)
culatazo *nf* : kick, recoil
culebra *nf* SERPIENTE : snake
culi *nmf* : coolie
culinario, -ria *adj* : culinary
culminante *adj* **punto culminante** : peak, high point, climax
culminar *vi* : to culminate — **culminación** *nf*
culo *nm* **1** *fam* : backside, behind **2** : bottom (of a glass)
culpa *nf* **1** : fault, blame ⟨echarle la culpa a alguien : to blame someone⟩ **2** : sin
culpabilidad *nf* : guilt
culpable[1] *adj* : guilty
culpable[2] *nmf* : culprit, guilty party
culpar *vt* : to blame
cultivado, -da *adj* **1** : cultivated, farmed **2** : cultured
cultivador, -dora *n* : cultivator
cultivar *vt* **1** : to cultivate **2** : to foster
cultivo *nm* **1** : cultivation, farming **2** : crop
culto[1], **-ta** *adj* : cultured, educated
culto[2] *nm* **1** : worship **2** : cult
cultura *nf* : culture
cultural *adj* : cultural — **culturalmente** *adv*
cumbre *nf* CIMA : top, peak, summit
cumpleaños *nms & pl* : birthday
cumplido[1], **-da** *adj* **1** : complete, full **2** : courteous, correct
cumplido[2] *nm* : compliment, courtesy ⟨por cumplido : out of courtesy⟩ ⟨andarse con cumplidos : to stand on ceremony, to be formal⟩
cumplimentar *vt* **1** : to congratulate **2** : to carry out, to perform

cumplimiento *nm* **1** : completion, fulfillment **2** : performance
cumplir *vt* **1** : to accomplish, to carry out **2** : to comply with, to fulfill **3** : to attain, to reach ⟨su hermana cumple los 21 el viernes : her sister will be 21 on Friday⟩ — *vi* **1** : to expire, to fall due **2** : to fulfill one's obligations ⟨cumplir con el deber : to do one's duty⟩ ⟨cumplir con la palabra : to keep one's word⟩ — **cumplirse** *vr* **1** : to come true, to be fulfilled ⟨se cumplieron sus sueños : her dreams came true⟩ **2** : to run out, to expire
cúmulo *nm* **1** MONTÓN : heap, pile **2** : cumulus
cuna *nf* **1** : cradle **2** : birthplace ⟨Puerto Rico es la cuna de la música salsa : Puerto Rico is the birthplace of salsa music⟩
cundir *vi* **1** : to propagate, to spread ⟨cundió el pánico en el vecindario : panic spread throughout the neighborhood⟩ **2** : to progress, to make headway
cuneta *nf* : ditch (in a road), gutter
cuña *nf* : wedge
cuñado, -da *n* : brother-in-law *m*, sister-in-law *f*
cuño *nm* : die (for stamping)
cuota *nf* **1** : fee, dues **2** : quota, share **3** : installment, payment
cupé *nm* : coupe
cupo[1], etc. → **caber**
cupo[2] *nm* **1** : quota, share **2** : capacity, room
cupón *nm, pl* **cupones 1** : coupon, voucher **2 cupón federal** : food stamp
cúpula *nf* : dome, cupola
cura[1] *nm* : priest
cura[2] *nf* **1** CURACIÓN, TRATAMIENTO : cure, treatment **2** : dressing, bandage
curación *nf, pl* **-ciones** CURA, TRATAMIENTO : cure, treatment
curandero, -ra *nm* **1** : witch doctor **2** : quack, charlatan
curar *vt* **1** : to cure, to heal **2** : to treat, to dress **3** CURTIR : to tan **4** : to cure (meat) — *vi* : to get well, to recover — **curarse** *vr*
curativo, -va *adj* : curative, healing
curiosear *vi* **1** : to snoop, to pry **2** : to browse — *vt* : to look over, to check
curiosidad *nf* **1** : curiosity **2** : curio
curioso, -sa *adj* **1** : curious, inquisitive **2** : strange, unusual, odd — **curiosamente** *adv*
currículo → **currículum**
currículum *nm, pl* **-lums 1** : résumé, curriculum vitae **2** : curriculum, course of study
curry ['kurri] *nm, pl* **-rries 1** : curry powder **2** : curry (dish)
cursar *vt* **1** : to attend (school), to take (a course) **2** : to dispatch, to pass on
cursi *adj fam* : affected, pretentious
cursilería *nf* **1** : vulgarity, poor taste **2** : pretentiousness

cursiva *nf* BASTARDILLA : italic type, italics *pl*
curso *nm* **1** : course, direction **2** : school year **3** : course, subject (in school)
cursor *nm* : cursor
curtido, -da *adj* : weather-beaten, leathery (of skin)
curtidor, -dora *n* : tanner
curtiduría *nf* : tannery
curtir *vt* **1** : to tan **2** : to harden, to weather — **curtirse** *vr*
curva *nf* : curve, bend
curvar *vt* : to bend

curvatura *nf* : curvature
curvilíneo, -nea *adj* : curvaceous, shapely
curvo, -va *adj* : curved, bent
cúspide *nf* : zenith, apex, peak
custodia *nf* : custody
custodiar *vt* : to guard, to look after
custodio, -dia *n* : keeper, guardian
cúter *nm* : cutter (boat)
cutícula *nf* : cuticle
cutis *nms & pl* : skin, complexion
cuyo, -ya *adj* **1** : whose, of whom, of which **2 en cuyo caso** : in which case

D

d *nf* : fourth letter of the Spanish alphabet
dable *adj* : feasible, possible
dactilar *adj* **huellas dactilares** : fingerprints
dádiva *nf* : gift, handout
dadivoso, -sa *adj* : generous
dado, -da *adj* **1** : given **2 dado que** : given that, since
dador, -dora *n* : giver, donor
dados *nmpl* : dice
daga *nf* : dagger
dalia *nf* : dahlia
dálmata *nm* : dalmatian
daltónico, -ca *adj* : color-blind
daltonismo *nm* : color blindness
dama *nf* **1** : lady **2 damas** *nfpl* : checkers
damasco *nm* : damask
damisela *nf* : damsel
damnificado, -da *n* : victim (of a disaster)
damnificar {72} *vt* : to damage, to injure
dance, etc. → **danzar**
dandi *nm* : dandy, fop
danés¹, -nesa *adj* : Danish
danés², -nesa *n, mpl* **daneses** : Dane, Danish person
danza *nf* : dance, dancing ⟨danza folklórica : folk dance⟩
danzante, -ta *n* BAILARÍN : dancer
danzar {21} *v* BAILAR : to dance
dañar *vt* **1** : to damage, to spoil **2** : to harm, to hurt — **dañarse** *vr*
dañino, -na *adj* : harmful
daño *nm* **1** : damage **2** : harm, injury **3 hacer daño a** : to harm, to damage **4 daños y perjuicios** : damages
dar {22} *vt* **1** : to give **2** ENTREGAR : to deliver, to hand over **3** : to hit, to strike **4** : to yield, to produce **5** : to perform **6** : to give off, to emit **7 ～ como** or **～ por** : to regard as, to consider — *vi* **1** ALCANZAR : to suffice, to be enough ⟨no me da para dos pasajes : I don't have enough for two fares⟩ **2 ～ a** or **～ sobre** : to overlook, to look out on **3 ～ con** : to run into **4 ～ con** : to hit upon (an idea) **5 dar de sí** : to give, to stretch — **darse** *vr* **1** : to give in, to

surrender **2** : to occur, to arise **3** : to grow, to come up **4 ～ con** or **～ contra** : to hit oneself against **5 dárselas de** : to boast about ⟨se las da de muy listo : he thinks he's very smart⟩
dardo *nm* : dart
datar *vt* : to date — *vi* **～ de** : to date from, to date back to
dátil *nm* : date (fruit)
dato *nm* **1** : fact, piece of information **2 datos** *nmpl* : data, information
dé → **dar**
de *prep* **1** : of ⟨la casa de Pepe : Pepe's house⟩ ⟨un niño de tres años : a three-year-old boy⟩ **2** : from ⟨es de Managua : she's from Managua⟩ ⟨salió del edificio : he left the building⟩ **3** : in, at ⟨a las tres de la mañana : at three in the morning⟩ ⟨salen de noche : they go out at night⟩ **4** : than ⟨más de tres : more than three⟩
deambular *vi* : to wander, to roam
debacle *nf* : debacle
debajo *adv* **1** : underneath, below, on the bottom **2 ～ de** : under, underneath **3 por ～** : below, beneath
debate *nm* : debate
debatir *vt* : to debate, to discuss — **debatirse** *vr* : to struggle
debe *nm* : debit column, debit
deber¹ *vt* : to owe — *v aux* **1** : must, have to ⟨debo ir a la oficina : I must go to the office⟩ **2** : should, ought to ⟨deberías buscar trabajo : you ought to look for work⟩ **3** (*expressing probability*) : must ⟨debe ser mexicano : he must be Mexican⟩ — **deberse** *vr* **～ a** : to be due to
deber² *nm* **1** OBLIGACIÓN : duty, obligation **2 deberes** *nmpl, Spain* : homework
debidamente *adv* : properly, duly
debido, -da *adj* **1** : right, proper, due **2 ～ a** : due to, owing to
débil *adj* : weak, feeble — **débilmente** *adv*
debilidad *nf* : weakness, debility, feebleness
debilitamiento *nm* : debilitation, weakening

debilitar *vt* : to debilitate, to weaken — **debilitarse** *vr*
debilucho[1], **-cha** *adj* : weak, frail
debilucho[2], **-cha** *n* : weakling
debitar *vt* : to debit
débito *nm* **1** DEUDA : debt **2** : debit
debut [de'but] *nm, pl* **debuts** : debut
debutante[1] *nmf* : beginner, newcomer
debutante[2] *nf* : debutante *f*
debutar *vi* : to debut, to make a debut
década *nf* DECENIO : decade
decadencia *nf* **1** : decadence **2** : decline
decadente *adj* **1** : decadent **2** : declining
decaer {13} *vi* **1** : to decline, to decay, to deteriorate **2** FLAQUEAR : to weaken, to flag
decaiga, etc. → **decaer**
decano, -na *n* **1** : dean **2** : senior member
decantar *vt* : to decant
decapitar *vt* : to decapitate, to behead
decayó, etc. → **decaer**
decena *nf* : group of ten
decencia *nf* : decency
decenio *nm* DÉCADA : decade
decente *adj* : decent — **decentemente** *adv*
decepción *nf, pl* **-ciones** : disappointment, letdown
decepcionante *adj* : disappointing
decepcionar *vt* : to disappoint, to let down — **decepcionarse** *vr*
deceso *nm* DEFUNCIÓN : death, passing
dechado *nm* **1** : sampler (of embroidery) **2** : model, paragon
decibelio *or* **decibel** *nm* : decibel
decidido, -da *adj* : decisive, determined, resolute — **decididamente** *adv*
decidir *vt* **1** : to decide, to determine ⟨no he decidido nada : I haven't made a decision⟩ **2** : to persuade, to decide ⟨su padre lo decidió a estudiar : his father persuaded him to study⟩ — *vi* : to decide — **decidirse** *vr* : to make up one's mind
decimal *adj* : decimal
décimo, -ma *adj* : tenth — **décimo, -ma** *n*
decimoctavo[1], **-va** *adj* : eighteenth
decimoctavo[2], **-va** *n* : eighteenth (in a series)
decimocuarto[1], **-ta** *adj* : fourteenth
decimocuarto[2], **-ta** *n* : fourteenth (in a series)
decimonoveno[1], **-na** *or* **decimonono**, **-na** *adj* : nineteenth
decimonoveno[2], **-na** *or* **decimonono**, **-na** *n* : nineteenth (in a series)
decimoquinto[1], **-ta** *adj* : fifteenth
decimoquinto[2], **-ta** *n* : fifteenth (in a series)
decimoséptimo[1], **-ma** *adj* : seventeenth
decimoséptimo[2], **-ma** *n* : seventeenth (in a series)
decimosexto[1], **-ta** *adj* : sixteenth
decimosexto[2], **-ta** *n* : sixteenth (in a series)

decimotercero[1], **-ra** *adj* : thirteenth
decimotercero[2], **-ra** *n* : thirteenth (in a series)
decir[1] {23} *vt* **1** : to say ⟨dice que no quiere ir : she says she doesn't want to go⟩ **2** : to tell ⟨dime lo que estás pensando : tell me what you're thinking⟩ **3** : to speak, to talk ⟨no digas tonterías : don't talk nonsense⟩ **4** : to call ⟨me dicen Rosy : they call me Rosy⟩ **5 es decir** : that is to say **6 querer decir** : to mean — **decirse** *vr* **1** : to say to oneself **2** : to be said ⟨¿cómo se dice "lápiz" en francés? : how do you say "pencil" in French?⟩
decir[2] *nm* DICHO : saying, expression
decisión *nf, pl* **-siones** : decision, choice
decisivo, -va *adj* : decisive, conclusive — **decisivamente** *adv*
declamar *vi* : to declaim — *vt* : to recite
declaración *nf, pl* **-ciones** **1** : declaration, statement **2** TESTIMONIO : deposition, testimony **3 declaración de derechos** : bill of rights **4 declaración jurada** : affidavit
declarado, -da *adj* : professed, open — **declaradamente** *adv*
declarar *vt* : to declare, to state — *vi* ATESTIGUAR : to testify — **declararse** *vr* **1** : to declare oneself, to make a statement **2** : to confess one's love **3** : to plead (in court) ⟨declararse inocente : to plead not guilty⟩
declinación *nf, pl* **-ciones** **1** : drop, downward trend **2** : declination **3** : declension (in grammar)
declinar *vt* : to decline, to turn down — *vi* **1** : to draw to a close **2** : to diminish, to decline
declive *nm* **1** DECADENCIA : decline **2** : slope, incline
decodificador *nm* : decoder
decolar *vi Chile, Col, Ecua* : to take off (of an airplane)
decolorar *vt* : to bleach — **decolorarse** *vr* : to fade
decomisar *vt* CONFISCAR : to seize, to confiscate
decomiso *nm* : seizure, confiscation
decoración *nf, pl* **-ciones** **1** : decoration **2** : decor **3** : stage set, scenery
decorado *nm* : stage set, scenery
decorador, -dora *n* : decorator
decorar *vt* ADORNAR : to decorate, to adorn
decorativo, -va *adj* : decorative, ornamental
decoro *nm* : decorum, propriety
decoroso, -sa *adj* : decent, proper, respectable
decrecer {53} *vi* : to decrease, to wane, to diminish — **decreciente** *adj*
decrecimiento *nm* : decrease, decline
decrépito, -ta *adj* : decrepit
decretar *vt* : to decree, to order
decreto *nm* : decree
decúbito *nm* : horizontal position ⟨en decúbito prono : prone⟩ ⟨en decúbito supino : supine⟩

dedal *nm* : thimble
dedalera *nf* DIGITAL : foxglove
dedicación *nf, pl* **-ciones** : dedication, devotion
dedicar {72} *vt* CONSAGRAR : to dedicate, to devote — **dedicarse** *vr* ~ **a** : to devote oneself to, to engage in
dedicatoria *nf* : dedication (of a book, song, etc.)
dedo *nm* **1** : finger ⟨dedo meñique : little finger⟩ **2 dedo del pie** : toe
deducción *nf, pl* **-ciones** : deduction
deducible *adj* **1** : deducible, inferable **2** : deductible
deducir {61} *vt* **1** INFERIR : to deduce **2** DESCONTAR : to deduct
defecar {72} *vi* : to defecate — **defecación** *nf*
defecto *nm* **1** : defect, flaw, shortcoming **2 en su defecto** : lacking that, in the absence of that
defectuoso, -sa *adj* : defective, faulty
defender {56} *vt* : to defend, to protect — **defenderse** *vr* **1** : to defend oneself **2** : to get by, to know the basics ⟨su inglés no es perfecto pero se defiende : his English isn't perfect but he gets by⟩
defendible *adj* : defensible, tenable
defensa[1] *nf* : defense
defensa[2] *nmf* : defender, back (in sports)
defensiva *nf* : defensive, defense
defensivo, -va *adj* : defensive — **defensivamente** *adv*
defensor[1], **-sora** *adj* : defending, defense
defensor[2], **-sora** *n* **1** : defender, advocate **2** : defense counsel
defeño, -ña *n* : person from the Federal District (Mexico City)
deferencia *nf* : deference
deficiencia *nf* : deficiency, flaw
deficiente *adj* : deficient
déficit *nm, pl* **-cits 1** : deficit **2** : shortage, lack
definición *nf, pl* **-ciones** : definition
definido, -da *adj* : definite, well-defined
definir *vt* **1** : to define **2** : to determine
definitivamente *adv* **1** : finally **2** : permanently, for good **3** : definitely, absolutely
definitivo, -va *adj* **1** : definitive, conclusive **2 en definitiva** : all in all, on the whole **3 en definitiva** *Mex* : permanently, for good
deflación *nf, pl* **-ciones** : deflation
deforestación *nf, pl* **-ciones** : deforestation
deformación *nf, pl* **-ciones** **1** : deformation **2** : distortion
deformar *vt* **1** : to deform, to disfigure **2** : to distort — **deformarse** *vr*
deforme *adj* : deformed, misshapen
deformidad *nf* : deformity
defraudación *nf, pl* **-ciones** : fraud
defraudar *vt* **1** ESTAFAR : to defraud, to cheat **2** : to disappoint
defunción *nf, pl* **-ciones** DECESO : death, passing

degeneración *nf, pl* **-ciones 1** : degeneration **2** : degeneracy, depravity
degenerado, -da *adj* DEPRAVADO : degenerate
degenerar *vi* : to degenerate
degenerativo, -va *adj* : degenerative
degollar {19} *vt* **1** : to slit the throat of, to slaughter **2** DECAPITAR : to behead **3** : to ruin, to destroy
degradación *nf, pl* **-ciones 1** : degradation **2** : demotion
degradar *vt* **1** : to degrade, to debase **2** : to demote
degustación *nf, pl* **-ciones** : tasting, sampling
degustar *vt* : to taste
deidad *nf* : deity
deificar {72} *vt* : to idolize, to deify
dejado, -da *adj* **1** : slovenly **2** : careless, lazy
dejar *vt* **1** : to leave **2** ABANDONAR : to abandon, to forsake **3** : to let be, to let go **4** PERMITIR : to allow, to permit — *vi* ~ **de** : to stop, to quit ⟨dejar de fumar : to quit smoking⟩ — **dejarse** *vr* **1** : to let oneself be ⟨se deja insultar : he lets himself be insulted⟩ **2** : to forget, to leave ⟨me dejé las llaves en el carro : I left the keys in the car⟩ **3** : to neglect oneself, to let oneself go **4** : to grow ⟨nos estamos dejando el pelo largo : we're growing our hair long⟩
dejo *nm* **1** : aftertaste **2** : touch, hint **3** : (regional) accent
del (*contraction of* **de** *and* **el**) → **de**
delación *nf, pl* **-ciones** : denunciation, betrayal
delantal *nm* **1** : apron **2** : pinafore
delante *adv* **1** ENFRENTE : ahead, in front **2** ~ **de** : before, in front of
delantera *nf* **1** : front, front part, front row ⟨tomar la delantera : to take the lead⟩ **2** : forward line (in sports)
delantero[1], **-ra** *adj* **1** : front, forward **2 tracción delantera** : front-wheel drive
delantero[2], **-ra** *n* : forward (in sports)
delatar *vt* **1** : to betray, to reveal **2** : to denounce, to inform against
delegación *nf, pl* **-ciones** : delegation
delegado, -da *n* : delegate, representative
delegar {52} *vt* : to delegate
deleitar *vt* : to delight, to please — **deleitarse** *vr*
deleite *nm* : delight, pleasure
deletrear *vi* : to spell ⟨¿como se deletrea? : how do you spell it?⟩
deleznable *adj* **1** : brittle, crumbly **2** : slippery **3** : weak, fragile ⟨una excusa deleznable : a weak excuse⟩
delfín *nm, pl* **delfines 1** : dolphin **2** : dauphin, heir apparent
delgadez *nf* : thinness, skinniness
delgado, -da *adj* **1** FLACO : thin, skinny **2** ESBELTO : slender, slim **3** DELICADO : delicate, fine **4** AGUDO : sharp, clever
deliberación *nf, pl* **-ciones** : deliberation

deliberado, -da *adj* : deliberate, intentional — **deliberadamente** *adv*
deliberar *vi* : to deliberate
deliberativo, -va *adj* : deliberative
delicadeza *nf* **1** : delicacy, fineness **2** : gentleness, softness **3** : tact, discretion, consideration
delicado, -da *adj* **1** : delicate, fine **2** : sensitive, frail **3** : difficult, tricky **4** : fussy, hard to please **5** : tactful, considerate
delicia *nf* : delight
delicioso, -sa *adj* **1** RICO : delicious **2** : delightful
delictivo, -va *adj* : criminal
delictuoso, -sa → **delictivo**
delimitación *nf, pl* **-ciones 1** : demarcation **2** : defining, specifying
delimitar *vt* **1** : to demarcate **2** : to define, to specify
delincuencia *nf* : delinquency, crime
delincuente[1] *adj* : delinquent
delincuente[2] *nmf* CRIMINAL : delinquent, criminal
delinear *vt* **1** : to delineate, to outline **2** : to draft, to draw up
delinquir {24} *vi* : to break the law
delirante *adj* : delirious
delirar *vi* **1** DESVARIAR : to be delirious **2** : to rave, to talk nonsense
delirio *nm* **1** DESVARÍO : delirium **2** DISPARATE : nonsense, ravings *pl* ⟨delirios de grandeza : delusions of grandeur⟩ **3** FRENESÍ : mania, frenzy ⟨¡fue el delirio! : it was wild!⟩
delito *nm* : crime, offense
delta *nm* : delta
demacrado, -da *adj* : emaciated, gaunt
demagogia *nf* : demagogy
demagógico, -ca *adj* : demagogic, demagogical
demagogo, -ga *n* : demagogue
demanda *nf* **1** : demand ⟨la oferta y la demanda : supply and demand⟩ **2** : petition, request **3** : lawsuit
demandado, -da *n* : defendant
demandante *nmf* : plaintiff
demandar *vt* **1** : to demand **2** REQUERIR : to call for, to require **3** : to sue, to file a lawsuit against
demarcar {72} *vt* : to demarcate — **demarcación** *nf*
demás[1] *adj* : remaining ⟨acabó las demás tareas : she finished the rest of the chores⟩
demás[2] *pron* **1** lo (la, los, las) **demás** : the rest, everyone else, everything else ⟨Pepe, Rosa, y los demás : Pepe, Rosa, and everybody else⟩ **2** estar por **demás** : to be of no use, to be pointless ⟨no estaría por demás : it couldn't hurt, it's worth a try⟩ **3** por demás : extremely **4** por lo demás : otherwise **5** y demás : and so on, et cetera
demasía *nf* en ∼ : excessively, in excess
demasiado[1] *adv* **1** : too ⟨vas demasiado aprisa : you're going too fast⟩ **2** : too

much ⟨estoy comiendo demasiado : I'm eating too much⟩
demasiado[2], **-da** *adj* : too much, too many, excessive
demencia *nf* **1** : dementia **2** LOCURA : madness, insanity
demente[1] *adj* : insane, mad
demente[2] *nmf* : insane person
demeritar *vt* **1** : to detract from **2** : to discredit
demérito *nm* **1** : fault **2** : discredit, disrepute
democracia *nf* : democracy
demócrata[1] *adj* : democratic
demócrata[2] *nmf* : democrat
democrático, -ca *adj* : democratic — **democráticamente** *adv*
democratizar {21} *vt* : to democratize, to make democratic
demografía *nf* : demography
demográfico, -ca *adj* : demographic
demoledor, -dora *adj* : devastating
demoler {47} *vt* DERRIBAR, DERRUMBAR : to demolish, to destroy
demolición *nf, pl* **-ciones** : demolition
demonio *nm* DIABLO : devil, demon
demora *nf* : delay
demorar *vt* **1** RETRASAR : to delay **2** TARDAR : to take, to last ⟨la reparación demorará varios días : the repair will take several days⟩ — *vi* : to delay, to linger — **demorarse** *vr* **1** : to be slow, to take a long time **2** : to take too long
demostración *nf, pl* **-ciones** : demonstration
demostrar {19} *vt* : to demonstrate, to show
demostrativo, -va *adj* : demonstrative
demudar *vt* : to change, to alter — **demudarse** *vr* : to change one's expression
denegación *nf, pl* **-ciones** : denial, refusal
denegar {49} *vt* : to deny, to turn down
denigrante *adj* : degrading, humiliating
denigrar *vt* **1** DIFAMAR : to denigrate, to disparage **2** : to degrade, to humiliate
denodado, -da *adj* : bold, dauntless
denominación *nf, pl* **-ciones 1** : name, designation **2** : denomination (of money)
denominador *nm* : denominator
denominar *vt* : to designate, to name
denostar {19} *vt* : to revile
denotar *vt* : to denote, to show
densidad *nf* : density, thickness
denso, -sa *adj* : dense, thick — **densamente** *adv*
dentado, -da *adj* SERRADO : serrated, jagged
dentadura *nf* **1** : teeth *pl* **2** dentadura postiza : dentures *pl*
dental *adj* : dental
dentellada *nf* **1** : bite **2** : tooth mark
dentera *nf* **1** : envy, jealousy **2** dar dentera : to set one's teeth on edge
dentición *nf, pl* **-ciones 1** : teething **2** : dentition, set of teeth

dentífrico *nm* : toothpaste
dentista *nmf* : dentist
dentro *adv* 1 : in, inside 2 : indoors 3 ~ **de** : within, inside, in 4 **dentro de poco** : soon, shortly 5 **dentro de todo** : all in all, all things considered 6 **por** ~ : inwardly, inside
denuedo *nm* : valor, courage
denuesto *nm* : insult
denuncia *nf* 1 : denunciation, condemnation 2 : police report
denunciante *nmf* : accuser (of a crime)
denunciar *vt* 1 : to denounce, to condemn 2 : to report (to the authorities)
deparar *vt* : to have in store for, to provide with ⟨no sabemos lo que nos depara el destino : we don't know what fate has in store for us⟩
departamental *adj* 1 : departmental 2 **tienda departamental** *Mex* : department store
departamento *nm* 1 : department 2 APARTAMENTO : apartment
departir *vi* : to converse
dependencia *nf* 1 : dependence, dependency ⟨dependencia emocional : emotional dependence⟩ ⟨dependencia del alcohol : dependence on alcohol⟩ 2 : agency, branch office
depender *vi* 1 : to depend 2 ~ **de** : to depend on 3 ~ **de** : to be subordinate to
dependiente[1] *adj* : dependent
dependiente[2], **-ta** *n* : clerk, salesperson
deplorable *adj* : deplorable
deplorar *vt* 1 : to deplore 2 LAMENTAR : to regret
deponer {60} *vt* 1 : to depose, to overthrow 2 : to abandon (an attitude or stance) 3 **deponer las armas** : to lay down one's arms — *vi* 1 TESTIFICAR : to testify, to make a statement 2 EVACUAR : to defecate
deportación *nf, pl* **-ciones** : deportation
deportar *vt* : to deport
deporte *nm* : sport, sports *pl* ⟨hacer deporte : to engage in sports⟩
deportista[1] *adj* 1 : fond of sports 2 : sporty
deportista[2] *nmf* 1 : sports fan 2 : athlete, sportsman *m*, sportswoman *f*
deportividad *nf Spain* : sportsmanship
deportivo, -va *adj* 1 : sports, sporting ⟨artículos deportivos : sporting goods⟩ 2 : sporty
deposición *nf, pl* **-ciones** 1 : statement, testimony 2 : removal from office
depositante *nmf* : depositor
depositar *vt* 1 : to deposit, to place 2 : to store — **depositarse** *vr* : to settle
depósito *nm* 1 : deposit 2 : warehouse, storehouse
depravación *nf, pl* **-ciones** : depravity
depravado, -da *adj* DEGENERADO : depraved, degenerate
depravar *vt* : to deprave, to corrupt
depreciación *nf, pl* **-ciones** : depreciation

depreciar *vt* : to depreciate, to reduce the value of — **depreciarse** *vr* : to lose value
depredación *nf* SAQUEO : depredation, plunder
depredador[1], **-dora** *adj* : predatory
depredador[2] *nm* 1 : predator 2 SAQUEADOR : plunderer
depresión *nf, pl* **-siones** 1 : depression 2 : hollow, recess 3 : drop, fall 4 : slump, recession
depresivo[1], **-va** *adj* 1 : depressive 2 : depressant
depresivo[2] *nm* : depressant
deprimente *adj* : depressing
deprimir *vt* 1 : to depress 2 : to lower — **deprimirse** *vr* ABATIRSE : to get depressed
depuesto *pp* → **deponer**
depuración *nf, pl* **-ciones** 1 PURIFICACIÓN : purification 2 PURGA : purge 3 : refinement, polish
depurar *vt* 1 PURIFICAR : to purify 2 PURGAR : to purge
depuso, etc. → **deponer**
derecha *nf* 1 : right 2 : right hand, right side 3 : right wing, right (in politics)
derechazo *nm* 1 : pass with the cape on the right hand (in bullfighting) 2 : right (in boxing) 3 : forehand (in tennis)
derechista[1] *adj* : rightist, right-wing
derechista[2] *nmf* : right-winger
derecho[1] *adv* 1 : straight 2 : upright 3 : directly
derecho[2], **-cha** *adj* 1 : right 2 : right-hand 3 RECTO : straight, upright, erect
derecho[3] *nm* 1 : right ⟨derechos humanos : human rights⟩ 2 : law ⟨derecho civil : civil law⟩ 3 : right side (of cloth or clothing)
deriva *nf* 1 : drift 2 **a la deriva** : adrift
derivación *nf, pl* **-ciones** 1 : derivation 2 RAMIFICACIÓN : ramification, consequence
derivar *vi* 1 : to drift 2 ~ **de** : to come from, to derive from 3 ~ **en** : to result in — *vt* : to steer, to direct ⟨derivó la discusión hacia la política : he steered the discussion over to politics⟩ — **derivarse** *vr* : to be derived from, to arise from
dermatología *nf* : dermatology
dermatológico, -ca *adj* : dermatological
dermatólogo, -ga *n* : dermatologist
derogación *nf, pl* **-ciones** : abolition, repeal
derogar {52} *vt* ABOLIR : to abolish, to repeal
derramamiento *nm* 1 : spilling, overflowing 2 **derramamiento de sangre** : bloodshed
derramar *vt* 1 : to spill 2 : to shed (tears, blood) — **derramarse** *vr* 1 : to spill over 2 : to scatter
derrame *nm* 1 : spilling, shedding 2 : leakage, overflow 3 : discharge, hemorrhage
derrapar *vi* : to skid

derrape *nm* : skid
derredor *nm* **al derredor** *or* **en derredor** : around, round about
derrengado, -da *adj* **1** : bent, twisted **2** : exhausted
derretir {54} *vt* : to melt, to thaw — **derretirse** *vr* **1** : to melt, to thaw **2** ~ **por** *fam* : to be crazy about
derribar *vt* **1** DEMOLER, DERRUMBAR : to demolish, to knock down **2** : to shoot down, to bring down (an airplane) **3** DERROCAR : to overthrow
derribo *nm* **1** : demolition, razing **2** : shooting down **3** : overthrow
derrocamiento *nm* : overthrow
derrocar {72} *vt* DERRIBAR : to overthrow, to topple
derrochador[1], -dora *adj* : extravagant, wasteful
derrochador[2], -dora *n* : spendthrift
derrochar *vt* : to waste, to squander
derroche *nm* : extravagance, waste
derrota *nf* **1** : defeat, rout **2** : course (at sea)
derrotar *vt* : to defeat
derrotero *nm* RUTA : course
derrotista *adj* & *nmf* : defeatist
derruir {41} *vt* : to demolish, to tear down
derrumbamiento *nm* : collapse
derrumbar *vt* **1** DEMOLER, DERRIBAR : to demolish, to knock down **2** DESPEÑAR : to cast down, to topple — **derrumbarse** *vr* DESPLOMARSE : to collapse, to break down
derrumbe *nm* **1** DESPLOME : collapse, fall ⟨el derrumbe del comunismo : the fall of Communism⟩ **2** : landslide
desabastecimiento *nm* : shortage, scarcity
desabasto *nm Mex* : shortage, scarcity
desabrido, -da *adj* : tasteless, bland
desabrigar {52} *vt* **1** : to undress **2** : to uncover **3** : to deprive of shelter
desabrochar *vt* : to unbutton, to undo — **desabrocharse** *vr* : to come undone
desacatar *vt* **1** DESAFIAR : to defy **2** DESOBEDECER : to disobey
desacato *nm* **1** : disrespect **2** : contempt (of court)
desacelerar *vi* : to decelerate, to slow down
desacertado, -da *adj* **1** : mistaken **2** : unwise
desacertar {55} *vi* ERRAR : to err, to be mistaken
desacierto *nm* ERROR : error, mistake
desaconsejable *adj* : inadvisable
desaconsejado, -da *adj* : ill-advised, unwise
desacorde *adj* **1** : conflicting **2** : discordant
desacostumbrado, -da *adj* : unaccustomed, unusual
desacreditar *vt* DESPRESTIGIAR : to discredit, to disgrace
desactivar *vt* : to deactivate, to defuse
desacuerdo *nm* : disagreement
desafiante *adj* : defiant

desafiar {85} *vt* RETAR : to defy, to challenge
desafilado, -da *adj* : blunt
desafinado, -da *adj* : out-of-tune, off-key
desafinarse *vr* : to go out of tune
desafío *nm* **1** RETO : challenge **2** RESISTENCIA : defiance
desafortunado, -da *adj* : unfortunate, unlucky — **desafortunadamente** *adv*
desafuero *nm* ABUSO : injustice, outrage
desagradable *adj* : unpleasant, disagreeable — **desagradablemente** *adv*
desagradar *vi* : to be unpleasant, to be disagreeable
desagradecido, -da *adj* : ungrateful
desagrado *nm* **1** : displeasure **2 con** ~ : reluctantly
desagravio *nm* **1** : apology **2** : amends, reparation
desagregarse {52} *vr* : to break up, to disintegrate
desaguar {10} *vi* : to drain, to empty
desagüe *nm* **1** : drain **2** : drainage
desahogado, -da *adj* **1** : well-off, comfortable **2** : spacious, roomy
desahogar {52} *vt* **1** : to relieve, to ease **2** : to give vent to — **desahogarse** *vr* **1** : to recover, to feel better **2** : to unburden oneself, to let off steam
desahogo *nm* **1** : relief, outlet **2 con** ~ : comfortably
desahuciar *vt* **1** : to deprive of hope **2** : to evict — **desahuciarse** *vr* : to lose all hope
desahucio *nm* : eviction
desairar {5} *vt* : to snub, to rebuff
desaire *nm* : rebuff, snub, slight
desajustar *vt* **1** : to disarrange, to put out of order **2** : to upset (plans)
desajuste *nm* **1** : maladjustment **2** : imbalance **3** : upset, disruption
desalentador, -dora *adj* : discouraging, disheartening
desalentar {55} *vt* DESANIMAR : to discourage, to dishearten — **desalentarse** *vr*
desaliento *nm* : discouragement
desaliñado, -da *adj* : slovenly, untidy
desalmado, -da *adj* : heartless, callous
desalojar *vt* **1** : to remove, to clear **2** EVACUAR : to evacuate, to vacate **3** : to evict
desalojo *nm* **1** : removal, expulsion **2** : evacuation **3** : eviction
desamor *nm* **1** FRIALDAD : indifference **2** ENEMISTAD : dislike, enmity
desamparado, -da *adj* DESVALIDO : helpless, destitute
desamparar *vt* : to abandon, to forsake
desamparo *nm* **1** : abandonment, neglect **2** : helplessness
desamueblado, -da *adj* : unfurnished
desandar {6} *vt* : to go back, to return to the starting point
desangelado, -da *adj* : dull, lifeless
desangrar *vt* : to bleed, to bleed dry — **desangrarse** *vr* **1** : to be bleeding **2** : to bleed to death

desanimar *vt* DESALENTAR : to discourage, to dishearten — **desanimarse** *vr*

desánimo *nm* DESALIENTO : discouragement, dejection

desanudar *vt* : to untie, to disentangle

desapacible *adj* : unpleasant, disagreeable

desaparecer {53} *vt* : to cause to disappear — *vi* : to disappear, to vanish

desaparecido[1], **-da** *adj* **1** : late, deceased **2** : missing

desaparecido[2], **-da** *n* : missing person

desaparición *nf, pl* **-ciones** : disappearance

desapasionado, -da *adj* : dispassionate, impartial — **desapasionadamente** *adv*

desapego *nm* : coolness, indifference

desapercibido, -da *adj* **1** : unnoticed **2** DESPREVENIDO : unprepared, off guard

desaprobación *nf, pl* **-ciones** : disapproval

desaprobar {19} *vt* REPROBAR : to disapprove of

desaprovechar *vt* MALGASTAR : to waste, to misuse — *vi* : to lose ground, to slip back

desarmador *nm Mex* : screwdriver

desarmar *vt* **1** : to disarm **2** DESMONTAR : to disassemble, to take apart

desarme *nm* : disarmament

desarraigado, -da *adj* : rootless

desarraigar {52} *vt* : to uproot, to root out

desarreglado, -da *adj* : untidy, disorganized

desarreglar *vt* **1** : to mess up **2** : to upset, to disrupt

desarreglo *nm* **1** : untidiness **2** : disorder, confusion

desarrollar *vt* : to develop — **desarrollarse** *vr* : to take place

desarrollo *nm* : development

desarticulación *nf, pl* **-ciones** **1** : dislocation **2** : breaking up, dismantling

desarticular *vt* **1** DISLOCAR : to dislocate **2** : to break up, to dismantle

desaseado, -da *adj* **1** : dirty **2** : messy, untidy

desastre *nm* CATÁSTROFE : disaster

desastroso, -sa *adj* : disastrous, catastrophic

desatar *vt* **1** : to undo, to untie **2** : to unleash **3** : to trigger, to precipitate — **desatarse** *vr* : to break out, to erupt

desatascar {72} *vt* : to unblock, to clear

desatención *nf, pl* **-ciones** **1** : absentmindedness, distraction **2** : discourtesy

desatender {56} *vt* **1** : to disregard **2** : to neglect

desatento, -ta *adj* **1** DISTRAÍDO : absentminded **2** GROSERO : discourteous, rude

desatinado, -da *adj* : foolish, silly

desatino *nm* : folly, mistake

desautorizar {21} *vt* : to deprive of authority, to discredit

desavenencia *nf* DISCORDANCIA : disagreement, dispute

desayunar *vi* : to have breakfast — *vt* : to have for breakfast

desayuno *nm* : breakfast

desazón *nf, pl* **-zones** INQUIETUD : uneasiness, anxiety

desbalance *nm* : imbalance

desbancar {72} *vt* : to displace, to oust

desbandada *nf* : scattering, dispersal

desbarajuste *nm* DESORDEN : disarray, disorder, mess

desbaratar *vt* **1** ARRUINAR : to destroy, to ruin **2** DESCOMPONER : to break, to break down — **desbaratarse** *vr* : to fall apart

desbloquear *vt* **1** : to open up, to clear, to break through **2** : to free, to release

desbocado, -da *adj* : unbridled, rampant

desbocarse {72} *vr* : to run away, to bolt

desbordamiento *nm* : overflowing

desbordante *adj* : overflowing, bursting ⟨desbordante de energía : bursting with energy⟩

desbordar *vt* **1** : to overflow, to spill over **2** : to surpass, to exceed — **desbordarse** *vr*

descabellado, -da *adj* : outlandish, ridiculous

descafeinado, -da *adj* : decaffeinated

descalabrar *vt* : to hit on the head — **descalabrarse** *vr*

descalabro *nm* : setback, misfortune, loss

descalificación *nf, pl* **-ciones** **1** : disqualification **2** : disparaging remark

descalificar {72} *vt* **1** : to disqualify **2** DESACREDITAR : to discredit — **descalificarse** *vr*

descalzarse {21} *vr* : take off one's shoes

descalzo, -za *adj* : barefoot

descansado, -da *adj* **1** : rested, refreshed **2** : restful, peaceful

descansar *vi* : to rest, to relax — *vt* : to rest ⟨descansar la vista : to rest one's eyes⟩

descansillo *nm* : landing (of a staircase)

descanso *nm* **1** : rest, relaxation **2** : break **3** : landing (of a staircase) **4** : intermission

descapotable *adj & nm* : convertible

descarado, -da *adj* : brazen, impudent — **descaradamente** *adv*

descarga *nf* **1** : discharge **2** : unloading

descargar {52} *vt* **1** : to discharge **2** : to unload **3** : to release, to free **4** : to take out, to vent (anger, etc.) — **descargarse** *vr* **1** : to unburden oneself **2** : to quit **3** : to lose power

descargo *nm* **1** : unloading **2** : defense ⟨testigo de descargo : witness for the defense⟩

descarnado, -da *adj* : scrawny, gaunt

descaro *nm* : audacity, nerve

descarriado, -da *adj* : lost, gone astray
descarrilar *vi* : to derail — **descarrilarse** *vr*
descartar *vt* : to rule out, to reject — **descartarse** *vr* : to discard
descascarar *vt* : to peel, to shell, to husk — **descascararse** *vr* : to peel off, to chip
descendencia *nf* **1** : descendants *pl* **2** LINAJE : descent, lineage
descendente *adj* : downward, descending
descender {56} *vt* **1** : to descend, to go down **2** BAJAR : to lower, to take down, to let down — *vi* **1** : to descend, to come down **2** : to drop, to fall **3** ~ **de** : to be a descendant of
descendiente *adj* & *nm* : descendant
descenso *nm* **1** : descent **2** BAJA, CAÍDA : drop, fall
descentralizar {21} *vt* : to decentralize — **descentralizarse** *vr* — **descentralización** *nf*
descifrable *adj* : decipherable
descifrar *vt* : to decipher, to decode
descodificar {72} *vt* : to decode
descolgar {16} *vt* **1** : to take down, to let down **2** : to pick up, to answer (the telephone)
descollar {19} *vi* SOBRESALIR : to stand out, to be outstanding, to excel
descolorarse *vr* : to fade
descolorido, -da *adj* : discolored, faded
descomponer {60} *vt* **1** : to rot, to decompose **2** DESBARATAR : to break, to break down — **descomponerse** *vr* **1** : to break down **2** : to decompose
descomposición *nf, pl* **-ciones 1** : breakdown, decomposition **2** : decay
descompresión *nf* : decompression
descompuesto[1] *pp* → **descomponer**
descompuesto[2]**, -ta** *adj* **1** : broken down, out of order **2** : rotten, decomposed
descomunal *adj* **1** ENORME : enormous, huge **2** EXTRAORDINARIO : extraordinary
desconcertante *adj* : disconcerting
desconcertar {55} *vt* : to disconcert — **desconcertarse** *vr*
desconchar *vt* : to chip — **desconcharse** *vr* : to chip off, to peel
desconcierto *nm* : uncertainty, confusion
desconectar *vt* **1** : to disconnect, to switch off **2** : to unplug
desconfiado, -da *adj* : distrustful, suspicious
desconfianza *nf* RECELO : distrust, suspicion
desconfiar {85} *vi* ~ **de** : to distrust, to be suspicious of
descongelar *vt* **1** : to thaw **2** : to defrost **3** : to unfreeze (assets — **descongelarse** *vr*
descongestionante *adj* & *nm* : decongestant

desconocer {18} *vt* **1** IGNORAR : to be unaware of **2** : to fail to recognize
desconocido[1]**, -da** *adj* : unknown, unfamiliar
desconocido[2]**, -da** *n* EXTRAÑO : stranger
desconocimiento *nm* : ignorance
desconsiderado, -da *adj* : inconsiderate, thoughtless — **desconsideradamente** *adj*
desconsolado, -da *adj* : disconsolate, heartbroken
desconsuelo *nm* AFLICCIÓN : grief, distress, despair
descontaminar *vt* : to decontaminate — **descontaminación** *nf*
descontar {19} *vt* **1** : to discount, to deduct **2** EXCEPTUAR : to except, to exclude
descontento[1]**, -ta** *adj* : discontented, dissatisfied
descontento[2] *nm* : discontent, dissatisfaction
descontrol *nm* : lack of control, disorder, chaos
descontrolarse *vr* : to get out of control, to be out of hand
descorazonado, -da *adj* : disheartened, discouraged
descorazonador, -dora *adj* : disheartening, discouraging
descorrer *vt* : to draw back
descortés *adj, pl* **-teses** : discourteous, rude
descortesía *nf* : discourtesy, rudeness
descrédito *nm* DESPRESTIGIO : discredit
descremado, -da *adj* : nonfat, skim
describir {33} *vt* : to describe
descripción *nf, pl* **-ciones** : description
descriptivo, -va *adj* : descriptive
descrito *pp* → **describir**
descuartizar {21} *vt* **1** : to cut up, to quarter **2** : to tear to pieces
descubierto[1] *pp* → **descubrir**
descubierto[2]**, -ta** *adj* **1** : exposed, revealed **2 al descubierto** : out in the open
descubridor, -dora *n* : discoverer, explorer
descubrimiento *nm* : discovery
descubrir {2} *vt* **1** HALLAR : to discover, to find out **2** REVELAR : to uncover, to reveal — **descubrirse** *vr*
descuento *nm* REBAJA : discount
descuidado, -da *adj* **1** : neglectful, careless **2** : neglected, unkempt
descuidar *vt* : to neglect, to overlook — *vi* : to be careless — **descuidarse** *vr* **1** : to be careless, to drop one's guard **2** : to let oneself go
descuido *nm* **1** : carelessness, negligence **2** : slip, oversight
desde *prep* **1** : from **2** : since **3 desde ahora** : from now on **4 desde entonces** : since then **5 desde hace** : for, since (a time) ⟨ha estado nevando desde hace dos días : it's been snowing for

two days⟩ 6 **desde luego** : of course
7 **desde que** : since, ever since 8 **desde ya** : right now, immediately
desdecir {11} vi 1 ~ **de** : to be unworthy of 2 ~ **de** : to clash with — **desdecirse** vr 1 CONTRADECIRSE : to contradict oneself 2 RETRACTARSE : to go back on one's word
desdén nm, pl **desdenes** DESPRECIO : disdain, scorn
desdentado, -da adj : toothless
desdeñar vt DESPRECIAR : to disdain, to scorn, to despise
desdeñoso, -sa adj : disdainful, scornful — **desdeñosamente** adv
desdibujar vt : to blur — **desdibujarse** vr
desdicha nf 1 : misery 2 : misfortune
desdichado[1], -da adj 1 : unfortunate 2 : miserable, unhappy
desdichado[2], -da n : wretch
desdicho pp → **desdecir**
desdiga, desdijo etc. → **desdecir**
desdoblar vt DESPLEGAR : to unfold
deseable adj : desirable
desear vt 1 : to wish ⟨te deseo buena suerte : I wish you good luck⟩ 2 QUERER : to want, to desire
desecar {72} vt : to dry (flowers, etc.)
desechable adj : disposable
desechar vt 1 : to discard, to throw away 2 RECHAZAR : to reject
desecho nm 1 : reject 2 **desechos** nmpl RESIDUOS : rubbish, waste
desembarazarse {21} vr ~ **de** : to get rid of
desembarcadero nm : jetty, landing pier
desembarcar {72} vi : to disembark — vt : to unload
desembarco nm 1 : landing, arrival 2 : unloading
desembarque → **desembarco**
desembocadura nf 1 : mouth (of a river) 2 : opening, end (of a street)
desembocar {72} vi ~ **en** or ~ **a** 1 : to flow into, to join 2 : to lead to, to result in
desembolsar vt PAGAR : to disburse, to pay out
desembolso nm PAGO : disbursement, payment
desempacar {72} v : to unpack
desempate nm : tiebreaker, play-off
desempeñar vt 1 : to play (a role) 2 : to fulfill, to carry out 3 : to redeem (from a pawnshop) — **desempeñarse** vr : to function, to act
desempeño nm 1 : fulfillment, carrying out 2 : performance
desempleado[1], -da adj : unemployed
desempleado[2], -da n : unemployed person
desempleo nm : unemployment
desempolvar vt 1 : to dust off 2 : to resurrect, to revive
desencadenar vt 1 : to unchain 2 : to trigger, to unleash — **desencadenarse** vr

desencajar vt 1 : to dislocate 2 : to disconnect, to disengage
desencantar vt : to disenchant, to disillusion — **desencantarse** vr
desencanto nm : disenchantment, disillusionment
desenchufar vt : to disconnect, to unplug
desenfadado, -da adj 1 : uninhibited, carefree 2 : confident, self-assured
desenfado nm 1 DESENVOLTURA : self-assurance, confidence 2 : naturalness, ease
desenfrenadamente adv : wildly, with abandon
desenfrenado, -da adj : unbridled, unrestrained
desenfreno nm : abandon, unrestraint
desenganchar vt : to unhitch, to uncouple
desengañar vt : to disillusion, to disenchant — **desengañarse** vr
desengaño nm : disenchantment, disillusionment
desenlace nm : ending, outcome
desenlazar {21} vt 1 : to untie 2 : to clear up, to resolve
desenmarañar vt : to disentangle, to unravel
desenmascarar vt : to unmask, to expose
desenredar vt : to untangle, to disentangle
desenrollar vt : to unroll, to unwind
desentenderse {56} vr 1 ~ **de** : to want nothing to do with, to be uninterested in 2 ~ **de** : to pretend ignorance of
desenterrar {55} vt 1 EXHUMAR : to exhume 2 : to unearth, to dig up
desentonar vi 1 : to clash, to conflict 2 : to be out of tune, to sing off-key
desentrañar vt : to get to the bottom of, to unravel
desenvainar vt : to draw, to unsheathe (a sword)
desenvoltura nf 1 DESENFADO : confidence, self-assurance 2 ELOCUENCIA : eloquence, fluency
desenvolver {89} vt : to unwrap, to open — **desenvolverse** vr 1 : to unfold, to develop 2 : to manage, to cope
desenvuelto[1] pp → **desenvolver**
desenvuelto[2], -ta adj : confident, relaxed, self-assured
deseo nm : wish, desire
deseoso, -sa adj : eager, anxious
desequilibrar vt : to unbalance, to throw off balance — **desequilibrarse** vr
desequilibrio nm : imbalance
deserción nf, pl **-ciones** : desertion, defection
desertar vi 1 : to desert, to defect 2 ~ **de** : to abandon, to neglect
desertor, -tora n : deserter, defector
desesperación nf, pl **-ciones** : desperation, despair

desesperado, -da *adj* : desperate, despairing, hopeless — **desesperadamente** *adv*

desesperanza *nf* : despair, hopelessness

desesperar *vt* : to exasperate — *vi* : to despair, to lose hope — **desesperarse** *vr* : to become exasperated

desestimar *vt* **1** : to reject, to disallow **2** : to have a low opinion of

desfachatez *nf, pl* **-teces** : audacity, nerve, cheek

desfalcador, -dora *n* : embezzler

desfalcar {72} *vt* : to embezzle

desfalco *nm* : embezzlement

desfallecer {53} *vi* **1** : to weaken **2** : to faint

desfallecimiento *nm* **1** : weakness **2** : fainting

desfasado, -da *adj* **1** : out of sync **2** : out of step, behind the times

desfase *nm* : gap, lag ⟨desfase horario : jet lag⟩

desfavorable *adj* : unfavorable, adverse — **desfavorablemente** *adv*

desfavorecido, -da *adj* : underprivileged

desfigurar *vt* **1** : to disfigure, to mar **2** : to distort, to misrepresent

desfiladero *nm* : narrow gorge, defile

desfilar *vi* : to parade, to march

desfile *nm* : parade, procession

desfogar {52} *vt* **1** : to vent **2** *Mex* : to unclog, to unblock — **desfogarse** *vr* : to vent one's feelings, to let off steam

desforestación *nf, pl* **-ciones** : deforestation

desgajar *vt* **1** : to tear off **2** : to break apart — **desgajarse** *vr* : to come apart

desgana *nf* **1** INAPETENCIA : lack of appetite **2** APATÍA : apathy, unwillingness, reluctance

desgano *nm* → **desgana**

desgarbado, -da *adj* : ungainly

desgarrador, -dora *adj* : heartrending, heartbreaking

desgarradura *nf* : tear, rip

desgarrar *vt* **1** : to tear, to rip **2** : to break (one's heart) — **desgarrarse** *vr*

desgarre *nm* → **desgarro**

desgarro *nm* : tear

desgarrón *nm, pl* **-rrones** : rip, tear

desgastar *vt* **1** : to use up **2** : to wear away, to wear down

desgaste *nm* : deterioration, wear and tear

desglosar *vt* : to break down, to itemize

desglose *nm* : breakdown, itemization

desgobierno *nm* : anarchy, disorder

desgracia *nf* **1** : misfortune **2** : disgrace **3 por** ~ : unfortunately

desgraciadamente *adv* : unfortunately

desgraciado[1], -da *adj* **1** : unfortunate, unlucky **2** : vile, wretched

desgraciado[2], -da *n* : unfortunate person, wretch

desgranar *vt* : to shuck, to shell

deshabitado, -da *adj* : unoccupied, uninhabited

deshacer {40} *vt* **1** : to destroy, to ruin **2** DESATAR : to undo, to untie **3** : to break apart, to crumble **4** : to dissolve, to melt **5** : to break, to cancel — **deshacerse** *vr* **1** : to fall apart, to come undone **2** ~ **de** : to get rid of

deshecho[1] *pp* → **deshacer**

deshecho[2], -cha *adj* **1** : destroyed, ruined **2** : devastated, shattered **3** : undone, untied

desheredado, -da *adj* MARGINADO : dispossessed, destitute

desheredar *vt* : to disinherit

deshicieron, etc. → **deshacer**

deshidratar *vt* : to dehydrate — **deshidratación** *nf*

deshielo *nm* : thaw, thawing

deshilachar *vt* : to fray — **deshilacharse** *vr*

deshizo → **deshacer**

deshonestidad *nf* : dishonesty

deshonesto, -ta *adj* : dishonest

deshonra *nf* : dishonor, disgrace

deshonrar *vt* : to dishonor, to disgrace

deshonroso, -sa *adj* : dishonorable, disgraceful

deshuesar *vt* **1** : to pit (a fruit, etc.) **2** : to bone, to debone

deshumanizar {21} *vt* : to dehumanize — **deshumanización** *nf*

desidia *nf* **1** APATÍA : apathy, indolence **2** NEGLIGENCIA : negligence, sloppiness

desierto[1], -ta *adj* : deserted, uninhabited

desierto[2] *nm* : desert

designación *nf, pl* **-ciones** NOMBRAMIENTO : appointment, naming (to an office, etc.)

designar *vt* NOMBRAR : to designate, to appoint, to name

designio *nm* : plan

desigual *adj* **1** : unequal **2** DISPAREJO : uneven

desigualdad *nf* **1** : inequality **2** : unevenness

desilusión *nf, pl* **-siones** DESENCANTO, DESENGAÑO : disillusionment, disenchantment

desilusionar *vt* DESENCANTAR, DESENGAÑAR : to disillusion, to disenchant — **desilusionarse** *vr*

desinfectante *adj & nm* : disinfectant

desinfectar *vt* : to disinfect — **desinfección** *nf*

desinflar *vt* : to deflate — **desinflarse** *vr*

desinhibido, -da *adj* : uninhibited, unrestrained

desintegración *nf, pl* **-ciones** : disintegration

desintegrar *vt* : to disintegrate, to break up — **desintegrarse** *vr*

desinterés *nm* **1** : lack of interest, indifference **2** : unselfishness

desinteresado, -da *adj* GENEROSO : unselfish

desintoxicar {72} *vt* : to detoxify, to detox

desistir *vi* **1** : to desist, to stop **2** ~ **de** : to give up, to relinquish
deslave *nm Mex* : landslide
desleal *adj* INFIEL : disloyal — **deslealmente** *adv*
deslealtad *nf* : disloyalty
desleír {66} *vt* : to dilute, to dissolve
desligar {52} *vt* **1** : to separate, to undo **2** : to free (from an obligation) — **desligarse** *vr* ~ **de** : to extricate oneself from
deslindar *vt* **1** : to mark the limits of, to demarcate **2** : to define, to clarify
deslinde *nm* : demarcation
desliz *nm, pl* **deslices** : error, mistake, slip ⟨desliz de la lengua : slip of the tongue⟩
deslizar {21} *vt* **1** : to slide, to slip **2** : to slip in — **deslizarse** *vr* **1** : to slide, to glide **2** : to slip away
deslucido, -da *adj* **1** : unimpressive, dull **2** : faded, dingy, tarnished
deslucir {45} *vt* **1** : to spoil **2** : to fade, to dull, to tarnish **3** : to discredit
deslumbrar *vt* : to dazzle — **deslumbrante** *adj*
deslustrado, -da *adj* : dull, lusterless
deslustrar *vt* : to tarnish, to dull
deslustre *nm* : tarnish
desmán *nm, pl* **desmanes 1** : outrage, abuse **2** : misfortune
desmandarse *vr* : to behave badly, to get out of hand
desmantelar *vt* DESMONTAR : to dismantle
desmañado, -da *adj* : clumsy, awkward
desmayado, -da *adj* **1** : fainting, weak **2** : dull, pale
desmayar *vi* : to lose heart, to falter — **desmayarse** *vr* DESVANECERSE : to faint, to swoon
desmayo *nm* **1** : faint, fainting **2 sufrir un desmayo** : to faint
desmedido, -da *adj* DESMESURADO : excessive, undue
desmejorar *vt* : to weaken, to make worse — *vi* : to decline (in health), to get worse
desmembramiento *nm* : dismemberment
desmembrar {55} *vt* **1** : to dismember **2** : to break up
desmemoriado, -da *adj* : absentminded, forgetful
desmentido *nm* : denial
desmentir {76} *vt* **1** NEGAR : to deny, to refute **2** CONTRADECIR : to contradict
desmenuzar {21} *vt* **1** : to break down, to scrutinize **2** : to crumble, to shred — **desmenuzarse** *vr*
desmerecer {53} *vt* : to be unworthy of — *vi* **1** : to decline in value **2** ~ **de** : to compare unfavorably with
desmesurado, -da *adj* DESMEDIDO : excessive, inordinate — **desmesuradamente** *adv*
desmigajar *vt* : to crumble — **desmigajarse** *vr*

desmilitarizado, -da *adj* : demilitarized
desmontar *vt* **1** : to clear, to level off **2** DESMANTELAR : to dismantle, to take apart — *vi* : to dismount
desmonte *nm* : clearing, leveling
desmoralizador, -dora *adj* : demoralizing
desmoralizar {21} *vt* DESALENTAR : to demoralize, to discourage
desmoronamiento *nm* : crumbling, falling apart
desmoronar *vt* : to wear away, to erode — **desmoronarse** *vr* : to crumble, to deteriorate, to fall apart
desmotadora *nf* : gin, cotton gin
desmovilizar {21} *vt* : to demobilize — **desmovilización** *nf*
desnaturalizar {21} *vt* **1** : to denature **2** : to distort, to alter
desnivel *nm* **1** : disparity, difference **2** : unevenness (of a surface)
desnivelado, -da *adj* **1** : uneven **2** : unbalanced
desnudar *vt* **1** : to undress **2** : to strip, to lay bare — **desnudarse** *vr* : to undress, to strip off one's clothing
desnudez *nf, pl* **-deces** : nudity, nakedness
desnudismo → **nudismo**
desnudista → **nudista**
desnudo[1], -da *adj* : nude, naked, bare
desnudo[2] *nm* : nude
desnutrición *nf, pl* **-ciones** MALNUTRICIÓN : malnutrition, undernourishment
desnutrido, -da *adj* MALNUTRIDO : malnourished, undernourished
desobedecer {53} *v* : to disobey
desobediencia *nf* : disobedience — **desobediente** *adj*
desocupación *nf, pl* **-ciones** : unemployment
desocupado, -da *adj* **1** : vacant, empty **2** : free, unoccupied **3** : unemployed
desocupar *vt* **1** : to empty **2** : to vacate, to move out of — **desocuparse** *vr* : to leave, to quit (a job)
desodorante *adj* & *nm* : deodorant
desolación *nf, pl* **-ciones** : desolation
desolado, -da *adj* **1** : desolate **2** : devastated, distressed
desolador, -dora *adj* **1** : devastating **2** : bleak, desolate
desollar *vt* : to skin, to flay
desorbitado, -da *adj* **1** : excessive, exorbitant **2 con los ojos desorbitados** : with eyes popping out of one's head
desorden *nm, pl* **desórdenes 1** DESBARAJUSTE : disorder, mess **2** : disorder, disturbance, upset
desordenado, -da *adj* **1** : untidy, messy **2** : disorderly, unruly
desordenar *vt* : to mess up — **desordenarse** *vr* : to get messed up
desorganización *nf, pl* **-ciones** : disorganization
desorganizar {21} *vt* : to disrupt, to disorganize

desorientación *nf, pl* **-ciones** : disorientation, confusion

desorientar *vt* : to disorient, to mislead, to confuse — **desorientarse** *vr* : to become disoriented, to lose one's way

desovar *vi* : to spawn

despachar *vt* **1** : to complete, to conclude **2** : to deal with, to take care of, to handle **3** : to dispatch, to send off **4** *fam* : to finish off, to kill — **despacharse** *vr fam* : to gulp down, to polish off

despacho *nm* **1** : dispatch, shipment **2** OFICINA : office, study

despacio *adv* LENTAMENTE, LENTO : slowly, slow ⟨¡despacio! : take it easy!, easy does it!⟩

desparasitar *vt* : to worm (an animal), to delouse

desparpajo *nm fam* **1** : self-confidence, nerve **2** *CA* : confusion, muddle

desparramar *vt* **1** : to spill, to splatter **2** : to spread, to scatter

despatarrarse *vr* : to sprawl (out)

despavorido, -da *adj* : terrified, horrified

despecho *nm* **1** : spite **2 a despecho de** : despite, in spite of

despectivo, -va *adj* **1** : contemptuous, disparaging **2** : derogatory, pejorative

despedazar {21} *vt* : to cut to pieces, to tear apart

despedida *nf* **1** : farewell, good-bye **2 despedida de soltera** : bridal shower

despedir {54} *vt* **1** : to see off, to show out **2** : to dismiss, to fire **3** EMITIR : to give off, to emit ⟨despedir un olor : to give off an odor⟩ — **despedirse** *vr* : to take one's leave, to say good-bye

despegado, -da *adj* **1** : separated, detached **2** : cold, distant

despegar {52} *vt* : to remove, to detach — *vi* : to take off, to lift off, to blast off

despegue *nm* : takeoff, liftoff

despeinado, -da *adj* : disheveled, tousled ⟨estoy despeinada : my hair's a mess⟩

despeinarse *vr* **1** : to mess up one's hair **2** : to become disheveled ⟨me despeiné : my hair got messed up⟩

despejado, -da *adj* **1** : clear, fair **2** : alert, clear-headed **3** : uncluttered, unobstructed

despejar *vt* **1** : to clear, to free **2** : to clarify — *vi* **1** : to clear up **2** : to punt (in sports)

despeje *nm* **1** : clearing **2** : punt (in sports)

despellejar *vt* : to skin (an animal)

despenalizar {21} *vt* : to legalize — **despenalización** *nf*

despensa *nf* **1** : pantry, larder **2** PROVISIONES : provisions *pl*, supplies *pl*

despeñar *vt* : to hurl down

despepitar *vt* : to seed, to remove the seeds from

desperdiciar *vt* **1** DESAPROVECHAR, MALGASTAR : to waste **2** : to miss, to miss out on

desperdicio *nm* **1** : waste **2 desperdicios** *nmpl* RESIDUOS : refuse, scraps, rubbish

desperdigar {52} *vt* DISPERSAR : to disperse, to scatter

desperfecto *nm* **1** DEFECTO : flaw, defect **2** : damage

despertador *nm* : alarm clock

despertar {55} *vi* : to awaken, to wake up — *vt* **1** : to arouse, to wake **2** EVOCAR : to elicit, to evoke — **despertarse** *vr* : to wake (oneself) up

despiadado, -da *adj* CRUEL : cruel, merciless, pitiless — **despiadadamente** *adv*

despido *nm* : dismissal, layoff

despierto, -ta *adj* **1** : awake, alert **2** LISTO : clever, sharp ⟨con la mente despierta : with a sharp mind⟩

despilfarrador¹, -dora *adj* : extravagant, wasteful

despilfarrador², -dora *n* : spendthrift, prodigal

despilfarrar *vt* MALGASTAR : to squander, to waste

despilfarro *nm* : extravagance, wastefulness

despintar *vt* : to strip the paint from — **despintarse** *vr* : to fade, to wash off, to peel off

despistado¹, -da *adj* **1** DISTRAÍDO : absentminded, forgetful **2** CONFUSO : confused, bewildered

despistado², -da *n* : scatterbrain, absentminded person

despistar *vt* : to throw off the track, to confuse — **despistarse** *vr*

despiste *nm* **1** : absentmindedness **2** : mistake, slip

desplantador *nm* : garden trowel

desplante *nm* : insolence, rudeness

desplazamiento *nm* **1** : movement, displacement **2** : journey

desplazar {21} *vt* **1** : to replace, to displace **2** TRASLADAR : to move, to shift

desplegar {49} *vt* **1** : to display, to show, to manifest **2** DESDOBLAR : to unfold, to unfurl **3** : to spread (out) **4** : to deploy

despliegue *nm* **1** : display **2** : deployment

desplomarse *vr* **1** : to plummet, to fall **2** DERRUMBARSE : to collapse, to break down

desplome *nm* **1** : fall, drop **2** : collapse

desplumar *vt* : to pluck (a chicken, etc.)

despoblado¹, -da *adj* : uninhabited, deserted

**despoblado² *nm* : open country, deserted area

despoblar {19} *vt* : to depopulate

despojar *vt* **1** : to strip, to clear **2** : to divest, to deprive — **despojarse** *vr* **1** ~ **de** : to remove (clothing) **2** ~ **de** : to relinquish, to renounce

despojos *nmpl* **1** : remains, scraps **2** : plunder, spoils

desportilladura *nf* : chip, nick

desportillar *vt* : to chip — **desportillarse** *vr*

desposeer {20} *vt* : to dispossess

déspota *nmf* : despot, tyrant

despotismo *nm* : despotism — **despótico, -ca** *adj*

despotricar {72} *vi* : to rant and rave, to complain excessively

despreciable *adj* **1** : despicable, contemptible **2** : negligible ⟨nada despreciable : not inconsiderable, significant⟩

despreciar *vt* DESDEÑAR, MENOSPRECIAR : to despise, to scorn, to disdain

despreciativo, -va *adj* : scornful, disdainful

desprecio *nm* DESDÉN, MENOSPRECIO : disdain, contempt, scorn

desprender *vt* **1** SOLTAR : to detach, to loosen, to unfasten **2** EMITIR : to emit, to give off — **desprenderse** *vr* **1** : to come off, to come undone **2** : to be inferred, to follow **3** ~ **de** : to part with, to get rid of

desprendido, -da *adj* : generous, unselfish, disinterested

desprendimiento *nm* **1** : detachment **2** GENEROSIDAD : generosity **3** **desprendimiento de tierras** : landslide

despreocupación *nf, pl* **-ciones** : indifference, lack of concern

despreocupado, -da *adj* : carefree, easygoing, unconcerned

desprestigiar *vt* DESACREDITAR : to discredit, to disgrace — **desprestigiarse** *vr* : to lose prestige

desprestigio *nm* DESCRÉDITO : discredit, disrepute

desprevenido, -da *adj* DESAPERCIBIDO : unprepared, off guard, unsuspecting

desproporción *nf, pl* **-ciones** : disproportion, disparity

desproporcionado, -da : out of proportion

despropósito *nm* : piece of nonsense, absurdity

desprotegido, -da *adj* : unprotected, vulnerable

desprovisto, -ta *adj* ~ **de** : devoid of, lacking in

después *adv* **1** : afterward, later **2** : then, next **3** ~ **de** : after, next after ⟨después de comer : after eating⟩ **4** **después (de) que** : after ⟨después que lo acabé : after I finished it⟩ **5** **después de todo** : after all **6** **poco después** : shortly after, soon thereafter

despuntado, -da *adj* : blunt, dull

despuntar *vt* : to blunt — *vi* **1** : to dawn **2** : to sprout **3** : to excel, to stand out

desquiciar *vt* **1** : to unhinge (a door) **2** : to drive crazy — **desquiciarse** *vr* : to go crazy

desquitarse *vr* **1** : to get even, to retaliate **2** ~ **con** : to take it out on

desquite *nm* : revenge

desregulación *nf, pl* **-ciones** : deregulation

desregular *vt* : to deregulate

desregularización *nf* → **desregulación**

destacadamente *adv* : outstandingly, prominently

destacado, -da *adj* **1** : outstanding, prominent **2** : stationed, posted

destacamento *nm* : detachment (of troops)

destacar {72} *vt* **1** ENFATIZAR, SUBRAYAR : to emphasize, to highlight, to stress **2** : to station, to post — *vi* : to stand out

destajo *nm* **1** : piecework **2 a** ~ : by the item, by the job

destapador *nm* : bottle opener

destapar *vt* **1** : to open, to take the top off **2** DESCUBRIR : to reveal, to uncover **3** : to unblock, to unclog

destape *nm* : uncovering, revealing

destartalado, -da *adj* : dilapidated, tumbledown

destellar *vi* **1** : to sparkle, to flash, to glint **2** : to twinkle

destello *nm* **1** : flash, sparkle, twinkle **2** : glimmer, hint

destemplado, -da *adj* **1** : out of tune **2** : irritable, out of sorts **3** : unpleasant (of weather)

desteñir {67} *vi* : to run, to fade — **desteñirse** *vr* DESCOLORARSE : to fade

desterrado[1], -da *adj* : banished, exiled

desterrado[2], -da *n* : exile

desterrar {55} *vt* **1** EXILIAR : to banish, to exile **2** ERRADICAR : to eradicate, to do away with

destetar *vt* : to wean

destiempo *adv* **a** ~ : at the wrong time

destierro *nm* EXILIO : exile

destilación *nf, pl* **-ciones** : distillation

destilador, -dora *n* : distiller

destilar *vt* **1** : to exude **2** : to distill

destilería *nf* : distillery

destinación *nf, pl* **-ciones** DESTINO : destination

destinado, -da *adj* : destined, bound

destinar *vt* **1** : to appoint, to assign **2** ASIGNAR : to earmark, to allot

destinatario, -ria *n* **1** : addressee **2** : payee

destino *nm* **1** : destiny, fate **2** DESTINACIÓN : destination **3** : use **4** : assignment, post

destitución *nf, pl* **-ciones** : dismissal, removal from office

destituir {41} *vt* : to dismiss, to remove from office

destorcer {14} *vt* : to untwist

destornillador *nm* : screwdriver

destornillar *vt* : to unscrew

destrabar *vt* **1** : to untie, to undo, to ease up **2** : to separate

destreza *nf* HABILIDAD : dexterity, skill

destronar *vt* : to depose, to dethrone

destrozado, -da *adj* **1** : ruined, destroyed **2** : devastated, brokenhearted

destrozar {21} *vt* **1** : to smash, to shatter **2** : to destroy, to wreck — **destrozarse** *vr*
destrozo *nm* **1** DAÑO : damage **2** : havoc, destruction
destrucción *nf, pl* **-ciones** : destruction
destructivo, -va *adj* : destructive
destructor[1], -tora *adj* : destructive
destructor[2] *nm* : destroyer (ship)
destruir {41} *vt* : to destroy — **destruirse** *vr*
desubicado, -da *adj* **1** : out of place **2** : confused, disoriented
desunión *nf, pl* **-niones** : disunity
desunir *vt* : to split, to divide
desusado, -da *adj* **1** INSÓLITO : unusual **2** OBSOLETO : obsolete, disused, antiquated
desuso *nm* : disuse, obsolescence ⟨caer en desuso : to fall into disuse⟩
desvaído, -da *adj* **1** : pale, washed-out **2** : vague, blurred
desvainar *vt* : to shell
desvalido, -da *adj* DESAMPARADO : destitute, helpless
desvalijar *vt* **1** : to ransack **2** : to rob
desvalorización *nf, pl* **-ciones** **1** DEVALUACIÓN : devaluation **2** : depreciation
desvalorizar {21} *vt* : to devalue
desván *nm, pl* **desvanes** ÁTICO, BUHARDILLA : attic
desvanecer {53} *vt* **1** DISIPAR : to make disappear, to dispel **2** : to fade, to blur — **desvanecerse** *vr* **1** : to vanish, to disappear **2** : to fade **3** DESMAYARSE : to faint, to swoon
desvanecimiento *nm* **1** : disappearance **2** DESMAYO : faint **3** : fading
desvariar {85} *vi* **1** DELIRAR : to be delirious **2** : to rave, to talk nonsense
desvarío *nm* DELIRIO : delirium
desvelado, -da *adj* : sleepless
desvelar *vt* **1** : to keep awake **2** REVELAR : to reveal, to disclose — **desvelarse** *vr* **1** : to stay awake **2** : to do one's utmost
desvelo *nm* **1** : sleeplessness **2** **desvelos** *nmpl* : efforts, pains
desvencijado, -da *adj* : dilapidated, rickety
desventaja *nf* : disadvantage, drawback
desventajoso, -sa *adj* : disadvantageous, unfavorable
desventura *nf* INFORTUNIO : misfortune
desventurado, -da *adj* : unfortunate, ill-fated
desvergonzado, -da *adj* : shameless, impudent
desvergüenza *nf* : shamelessness, impudence
desvestir {54} *vt* : to undress — **desvestirse** *vr* : to get undressed
desviación *nf, pl* **-ciones** **1** : deviation, departure **2** : detour, diversion
desviar {85} *vt* **1** : to change the course of, to divert **2** : to turn away, to deflect — **desviarse** *vr* **1** : to branch off **2** APARTARSE : to stray
desvinculación *nf, pl* **-ciones** : dissociation
desvincular *vt* ~ **de** : to separate from, to dissociate from — **desvincularse** *vr*
desvío *nm* **1** : diversion, detour **2** : deviation
desvirtuar {3} *vt* **1** : to impair, to spoil **2** : to detract from **3** : to distort, to misrepresent
detalladamente *adv* : in detail, at great length
detallar *vt* : to detail
detalle *nm* **1** : detail **2 al detalle** : retail
detallista[1] *adj* **1** : meticulous **2** : retail
detallista[2] *nmf* **1** : perfectionist **2** : retailer
detección *nf, pl* **-ciones** : detection
detectar *vt* : to detect — **detectable** *adj*
detective *nmf* : detective
detector *nm* : detector ⟨detector de mentiras : lie detector⟩
detención *nf, pl* **-ciones** **1** ARRESTO : detention, arrest **2** : stop, halt **3** : delay, holdup
detener {80} *vt* **1** ARRESTAR : to arrest, to detain **2** PARAR : to stop, to halt **3** : to keep, to hold back — **detenerse** *vr* **1** : to stop **2** : to delay, to linger
detenidamente *adv* : thoroughly, at length
detenimiento *nm* **con** ~ : carefully, in detail
detentar *vt* : to hold, to retain
detergente *nm* : detergent
deteriorado, -da *adj* : damaged, worn
deteriorar *vt* ESTROPEAR : to damage, to spoil — **deteriorarse** *vr* **1** : to get damaged, to wear out **2** : to deteriorate, to worsen
deterioro *nm* **1** : deterioration, wear **2** : worsening, decline
determinación *nf, pl* **-ciones** **1** : determination, resolve **2 tomar una determinación** : to make a decision
determinado, -da *adj* **1** : certain, particular **2** : determined, resolute
determinante[1] *adj* : determining, deciding
determinante[2] *nm* : determinant
determinar *vt* **1** : to determine **2** : to cause, to bring about — **determinarse** *vr* : to make up one's mind, to decide
detestar *vt* : to detest — **detestable** *adj*
detonación *nf, pl* **-ciones** : detonation
detonador *nm* : detonator
detonante[1] *adj* : detonating, explosive
detonante[2] *nm* **1** → **detonador 2** : catalyst, cause
detonar *vi* : to detonate, to explode
detractor, -tora *n* : detractor, critic
detrás *adv* **1** : behind **2** ~ **de** : in back of **3 por** ~ : from behind
detrimento *nm* : detriment ⟨en detrimento de : to the detriment of⟩
detuvo, etc. → **detener**

deuda *nf* **1** DÉBITO : debt **2 en deuda con** : indebted to
deudo, -da *n* : relative
deudor¹, -dora *adj* : indebted
deudor², -dora *n* : debtor
devaluación *nf, pl* **-ciones** DESVAL-ORIZACIÓN : devaluation
devaluar {3} *vt* : to devalue — **devaluarse** *vr* : to depreciate
devanarse *vr* **devanarse los sesos** : to rack one's brains
devaneo *nm* **1** : flirtation, fling **2** : idle pursuit
devastador, -dora *adj* : devastating
devastar *vt* : to devastate — **devastación** *nf*
devenir {87} *vi* **1** : to come about **2 ~ en** : to become, to turn into
devoción *nf, pl* **-ciones** : devotion
devolución *nf, pl* **-ciones** REEMBOLSO : return, refund
devolver {89} *vt* **1** : to return, to give back **2** REEMBOLSAR : to refund, to pay back **3** : to vomit, to bring up — *vi* : to vomit, to throw up — **devolverse** *vr* : to return, to come back, to go back
devorar *vt* **1** : to devour **2** : to consume
devoto¹, -ta *adj* : devout — **devotamente** *adv*
devoto², -ta *n* : devotee, admirer
di → **dar, decir**
día *nm* **1** : day ⟨todos los días : every day⟩ **2** : daytime, daylight ⟨de día : by day, in the daytime⟩ ⟨en pleno día : in broad daylight⟩ **3 al día** : up-to-date **4 en su día** : in due time
diabetes *nf* : diabetes
diabético, -ca *adj & n* : diabetic
diablillo *nm* : little devil, imp
diablo *nm* DEMONIO : devil
diablura *nf* **1** : prank **2 diabluras** *nfpl* : mischief
diabólico, -ca *adj* : diabolical, diabolic, devilish
diaconisa *nf* : deaconess
diácono *nm* : deacon
diacrítico, -ca *adj* : diacritic, diacritical
diadema *nf* : diadem, crown
diáfano, -na *adj* : diaphanous
diafragma *nm* : diaphragm
diagnosticar {72} *vt* : to diagnose
diagnóstico¹, -ca *adj* : diagnostic
diagnóstico² *nm* : diagnosis
diagonal *adj & nf* : diagonal — **diagonalmente** *adv*
diagrama *nm* **1** : diagram **2 diagrama de flujo** ORGANIGRAMA : flowchart
dial *nm* : dial (on a radio, etc.)
dialecto *nm* : dialect
dialogar {52} *vi* : to have a talk, to converse
diálogo *nm* : dialogue
diamante *nm* : diamond
diametral *adj* : diametric, diametrical — **diametralmente** *adv*
diámetro *nm* : diameter
diana *nf* **1** : target, bull's-eye **2** *or* **toque de diana** : reveille

diapositiva *nf* : slide, transparency
diario¹ *adv Mex* : every day, daily
diario², -ria *adj* : daily, everyday — **diariamente** *adv*
diario³ *nm* **1** : diary **2** PERIÓDICO : newspaper
diarrea *nf* : diarrhea
diatriba *nf* : diatribe, tirade
dibujante *nmf* **1** : draftsman *m*, draftswoman *f* **2** CARICATURISTA : cartoonist
dibujar *vt* **1** : to draw, to sketch **2** : to portray, to depict
dibujo *nm* **1** : drawing **2** : design, pattern **3 dibujos animados** : (animated) cartoons
dicción *nf, pl* **-ciones** : diction
diccionario *nm* : dictionary
dícese → **decir**
dicha *nf* **1** SUERTE : good luck **2** FELICIDAD : happiness, joy
dicho¹ *pp* → **decir**
dicho², -cha *adj* : said, aforementioned
dicho³ *nm* DECIR : saying, proverb
dichoso, -sa *adj* **1** : blessed **2** FELIZ : happy **3** AFORTUNADO : fortunate, lucky
diciembre *nm* : December
diciendo → **decir**
dictado *nm* : dictation
dictador, -dora *n* : dictator
dictadura *nf* : dictatorship
dictamen *nm, pl* **dictámenes** **1** : report **2** : judgment, opinion
dictaminar *vt* : to report — *vi* : to give an opinion, to pass judgment
dictar *vt* **1** : to dictate **2** : to pronounce (a judgment) **3** : to give, to deliver ⟨dictar una conferencia : to give a lecture⟩
dictatorial *adj* : dictatorial
didáctico, -ca *adj* : didactic
diecinueve *adj & nm* : nineteen
diecinueveavo¹, -va *adj* : nineteenth
diecinueveavo² *nm* : nineteenth (fraction)
dieciocho *adj & nm* : eighteen
dieciochoavo¹, -va *or* **dieciochavo, -va** *adj* : eighteenth
dieciochoavo² *or* **dieciochavo** *nm* : eighteenth (fraction)
dieciséis *adj & nm* : sixteen
dieciseisavo¹, -va *adj* : sixteenth
dieciseisavo² *nm* : sixteenth (fraction)
diecisiete *adj & nm* : seventeen
diecisieteavo¹, -va *adj* : seventeenth
diecisieteavo² *nm* : seventeenth
diente *nm* **1** : tooth ⟨diente canino : eyetooth, canine tooth⟩ **2** : tusk, fang **3** : prong, tine **4 diente de león** : dandelion
dieron, etc. → **dar**
diesel [ˈdisɛl] *nm* : diesel
diestra *nf* : right hand
diestramente *adv* : skillfully, adroitly
diestro¹, -tra *adj* **1** : right **2** : skillful, accomplished
diestro² *nm* : bullfighter, matador
dieta *nf* : diet

dietética *nf* : dietetics
dietético, -ca *adj* : dietetic
dietista *nmf* : dietitian
diez *adj & nm, pl* **dieces** : ten
difamación *nf, pl* **-ciones** : defamation, slander
difamar *vt* : to defame, to slander
difamatorio, -ria *adj* : slanderous, defamatory, libelous
diferencia *nf* **1** : difference **2 a diferencia de** : unlike, in contrast to
diferenciación *nf, pl* **-ciones** : differentiation
diferenciar *vt* : to differentiate between, to distinguish — **diferenciarse** *vr* : to differ
diferendo *nm* : dispute, conflict
diferente *adj* DISTINTO : different — **diferentemente** *adv*
diferir {76} *vt* DILATAR, POSPONER : to postpone, to put off — *vi* : to differ
difícil *adj* : difficult, hard
difícilmente *adv* **1** : with difficulty **2** : hardly
dificultad *nf* : difficulty
dificultar *vt* : to make difficult, to obstruct
dificultoso, -sa *adj* : difficult, hard
difteria *nf* : diphtheria
difundir *vt* **1** : to diffuse, to spread out **2** : to broadcast, to spread
difunto, -ta *adj & n* FALLECIDO : deceased
difusión *nf, pl* **-siones** **1** : spreading **2** : diffusion (of heat, etc.) **3** : broadcast, broadcasting ⟨los medios de difusión : the media⟩
difuso, -sa *adj* : diffuse, widespread
diga, etc. → **decir**
digerir {76} *vt* : to digest — **digerible** *adj*
digestión *nf, pl* **-tiones** : digestion
digestivo, -va *adj* : digestive
digital[1] *adj* : digital — **digitalmente** *adv*
digital[2] *nf* **1** DEDALERA : foxglove **2** : digitalis
dígito *nm* : digit
dignarse *vr* : to deign, to condescend ⟨no se dignó contestar : he didn't deign to answer⟩
dignatario, -ria *n* : dignitary
dignidad *nf* **1** : dignity **2** : dignitary
dignificar {72} *vt* : to dignify
digno, -na *adj* **1** HONORABLE : honorable **2** : worthy — **dignamente** *adv*
digresión *nf, pl* **-ciones** : digression
dije *nm* : charm (on a bracelet)
dijo, etc. → **decir**
dilación *nf, pl* **-ciones** : delay
dilapidar *vt* : to waste, to squander
dilatar *vt* **1** : to dilate, to widen, to expand **2** DIFERIR, POSPONER : to put off, to postpone — **dilatarse** *vr* **1** : to expand (of gases, metals, etc.) **2** *Mex* : to take long, to be long
dilatorio, -ria *adj* : dilatory, delaying
dilema *nm* : dilemma
diletante *nmf* : dilettante

diligencia *nf* **1** : diligence, care **2** : promptness, speed **3** : action, step **4** : task, errand **5** : stagecoach **6 diligencias** *nfpl* : judicial procedures, formalities
diligente *adj* : diligent — **diligentemente** *adv*
dilucidar *vt* : to elucidate, to clarify
dilución *nf, pl* **-ciones** : dilution
diluir {41} *vt* : to dilute
diluviar *v impers* : to pour (with rain), to pour down
diluvio *nm* **1** : flood **2** : downpour
dimensión *nf, pl* **-siones** : dimension — **dimensional** *adj*
dimensionar *vt* : to measure, to gauge
diminutivo[1]**, -va** *adj* : diminutive
diminutivo[2] *nm* : diminutive
diminuto, -ta *adj* : minute, tiny
dimisión *nf, pl* **-siones** : resignation
dimitir *vi* : to resign, to step down
dimos → **dar**
dinámica *nf* : dynamics
dinámico, -ca *adj* : dynamic — **dinámicamente** *adv*
dinamismo *nm* : energy, vigor
dinamita *nf* : dynamite
dinamitar *vt* : to dynamite
dínamo *or* **dinamo** *nm* : dynamo
dinastía *nf* : dynasty
dineral *nm* : fortune, large sum of money
dinero *nm* : money
dinosaurio *nm* : dinosaur
dintel *nm* : lintel
dio, etc. → **dar**
diocesano, -na *adj* : diocesan
diócesis *nfs & pl* : diocese
dios, diosa *n* : god, goddess *f*
Dios *nm* : God
diploma *nm* : diploma
diplomacia *nf* : diplomacy
diplomado[1]**, -da** *adj* : qualified, trained
diplomado[2] *nm Mex* : seminar
diplomático[1]**, -ca** *adj* : diplomatic — **diplomáticamente** *adv*
diplomático[2]**, -ca** *n* : diplomat
diptongo *nm* : diphthong
diputación *nf, pl* **-ciones** : deputation, delegation
diputado, -da *n* : delegate, representative
dique *nm* : dike
dirá, etc. → **decir**
dirección *nf, pl* **-ciones** **1** : address **2** : direction **3** : management, leadership **4** : steering (of an automobile)
direccional[1] *adj* : directional
direccional[2] *nf* : directional, turn signal
directa *nf* : high gear
directamente *adv* : straight, directly
directiva *nf* **1** ORDEN : directive **2** DIRECTORIO, JUNTA : board of directors
directivo[1]**, -va** *adj* : executive, managerial
directivo[2]**, -va** *n* : executive, director
directo, -ta *adj* **1** : direct, straight, immediate **2 en** ~ : live (in broadcasting)

director, -tora *n* **1** : director, manager, head **2** : conductor (of an orchestra)
directorial *adj* : managing, executive
directorio *nm* **1** : directory **2** DIRECTI-VA, JUNTA : board of directors
directriz *nf, pl* **-trices** : guideline
dirigencia *nf* : leaders *pl*, leadership
dirigente[1] *adj* : directing, leading
dirigente[2] *nmf* : director, leader
dirigible *nm* : dirigible, blimp
dirigir {35} *vt* **1** : to direct, to lead **2** : to address **3** : to aim, to point **4** : to conduct (music) — **dirigirse** *vr* ~ **a 1** : to go towards **2** : to speak to, to address
dirimir *vt* **1** : to resolve, to settle **2** : to annul, to dissolve (a marriage)
discapacidad *nf* MINUSVALÍA : disability, handicap
discapacitado[1], **-da** *adj* : disabled, handicapped
discapacitado[2], **-da** *n* : disabled person, handicapped person
discar {72} *v* : to dial
discernimiento *nm* : discernment
discernir {25} *v* : to discern, to distinguish
disciplina *nf* : discipline
disciplinar *vt* : to discipline — **disciplinario, -ria** *adj*
discípulo, -la *n* : disciple, follower
disc jockey [ˌdiskˈʤoke, -ˈʤo-] *nmf* : disc jockey
disco *nm* **1** : phonograph record **2** : disc, disk ⟨disco compacto : compact disc⟩ **3** : discus
díscolo, -la *adj* : unruly, disobedient
disconforme *adj* : in disagreement
discontinuidad *nf* : discontinuity
discontinuo, -nua *adj* : discontinuous
discordancia *nf* DESAVENENCIA : conflict, disagreement
discordante *adj* **1** : discordant **2** : conflicting
discordia *nf* : discord
discoteca *nf* **1** : disco, discotheque **2** *CA, Mex* : record store
discreción *nf, pl* **-ciones** : discretion
discrecional *adj* : discretionary
discrepancia *nf* : discrepancy
discrepar *vi* **1** : to disagree **2** : to differ
discreto, -ta *adj* : discreet — **discretamente** *adv*
discriminación *nf, pl* **-ciones** : discrimination
discriminar *vt* **1** : to discriminate against **2** : to distinguish, to differentiate
discriminatorio, -ria *adj* : discriminatory
disculpa *nf* **1** : apology **2** : excuse
disculpable *adj* : excusable
disculpar *vt* : to excuse, to pardon — **disculparse** *vr* : to apologize
discurrir *vi* **1** : to flow **2** : to pass, to go by **3** : to ponder, to reflect
discurso *nm* **1** ORACIÓN : speech, address **2** : discourse, treatise

discusión *nf, pl* **-siones 1** : discussion **2** ALTERCADO, DISPUTA : argument
discutible *adj* : arguable, debatable
discutidor, -dora *adj* : argumentative
discutir *vt* **1** : to discuss **2** : to dispute — *vi* ALTERCAR : to argue, to quarrel
disecar {72} *vt* **1** : to dissect **2** : to stuff (for preservation)
disección *nf, pl* **-ciones** : dissection
diseminación *nf, pl* **-ciones** : dissemination, spreading
diseminar *vt* : to disseminate, to spread
disensión *nf, pl* **-siones** : dissension, disagreement
disentería *nf* : dysentery
disentir {76} *vi* : to dissent, to disagree
diseñador, -dora *n* : designer
diseñar *vt* **1** : to design, to plan **2** : to lay out, to outline
diseño *nm* : design
disentimiento *nm* : dissent
disertación *nf, pl* **-ciones 1** : lecture, talk **2** : dissertation
disertar *vi* : to lecture, to give a talk
disfraz *nm, pl* **disfraces 1** : disguise **2** : costume **3** : front, pretense
disfrazar {21} *vt* **1** : to disguise **2** : to mask, to conceal — **disfrazarse** *vr* : to wear a costume, to be in disguise
disfrutar *vt* : to enjoy — *vi* : to enjoy oneself, to have a good time
disfrute *nm* : enjoyment
disfunción *nf, pl* **-ciones** : dysfunction — **disfuncional** *adj*
disgresión → **digresión**
disgustar *vt* : to upset, to displease, to make angry — **disgustarse** *vr*
disgusto *nm* **1** : annoyance, displeasure **2** : argument, quarrel **3** : trouble, misfortune
disidencia *nf* : dissidence, dissent
disidente *adj & nmf* : dissident
disímbolo, -la *adj Mex* : dissimilar
disímil *adj* : dissimilar
disimulado, -da *adj* **1** : concealed, disguised **2** : furtive, sly
disimular *vi* : to dissemble, to pretend — *vt* : to conceal, to hide
disimulo *nm* **1** : dissembling, pretense **2** : slyness, furtiveness **3** : tolerance
disipar *vt* **1** : to dissipate, to dispel **2** : to squander — **disiparse** *vr*
diskette [diˈsket] *nm* : floppy disk, diskette
dislocar {72} *vt* : to dislocate — **dislocación** *nf*
disminución *nf, pl* **-ciones** : decrease, drop, fall
disminuir {41} *vt* REDUCIR : to reduce, to decrease, to lower — *vi* **1** : to lower **2** : to drop, to fall
disociación *nf, pl* **-ciones** : dissociation
disociar *vt* : to dissociate, to separate
disolución *nf, pl* **-ciones 1** : dissolution, dissolving **2** : breaking up **3** : dissipation
disoluto, -ta *adj* : dissolute, dissipated

disolver {89} *vt* **1** : to dissolve **2** : to break up — **disolverse** *vr*
disonancia *nf* : dissonance — **disonante** *adj*
dispar *adj* **1** : different, disparate **2** DIVERSO : diverse **3** DESIGUAL : inconsistent
disparado, -da *adj* salir disparado *fam* : to take off in a hurry, to rush away
disparar *vi* **1** : to shoot, to fire **2** *Mex fam* : to pay — *vt* **1** : to shoot **2** *Mex fam* : to treat to, to buy — **dispararse** *vr* : to shoot up, to skyrocket
disparatado, -da *adj* ABSURDO, RIDÍCULO : absurd, ridiculous, crazy
disparate *nm* : silliness, stupidity ⟨decir disparates : to talk nonsense⟩
disparejo, -ja *adj* DESIGUAL : uneven
disparidad *nf* : disparity
disparo *nm* TIRO : shot
dispendio *nm* : wastefulness, extravagance
dispendioso, -sa *adj* : wasteful, extravagant
dispensa *nf* : dispensation
dispensable *adj* **1** : dispensable **2** : excusable
dispensar *vt* **1** : to dispense, to give, to grant **2** EXCUSAR : to excuse, to forgive **3** EXIMIR : to exempt
dispensario *nm* **1** : dispensary, clinic **2** *Mex* : dispenser
dispersar *vt* DESPERDIGAR : to disperse, to scatter
dispersión *nf, pl* -siones : dispersion
disperso, -sa *adj* : dispersed, scattered
displicencia *nf* : indifference, coldness, disdain
displicente *adj* : indifferent, cold, disdainful
disponer {60} *vt* **1** : to arrange, to lay out **2** : to stipulate, to order **3** : to prepare — *vi* ~ **de** : to have at one's disposal — **disponerse** *vr* ~ **a** : to prepare to, to be about to
disponibilidad *nf* : availability
disponible *adj* : available
disposición *nf, pl* -ciones **1** : disposition **2** : aptitude, talent **3** : order, arrangement **4** : willingness, readiness **5** última disposición : last will and testament
dispositivo *nm* **1** APARATO, MECANISMO : device, mechanism **2** : force, detachment
dispuesto[1] *pp* → **disponer**
dispuesto[2], **-ta** *adj* PREPARADO : ready, prepared, disposed
dispuso, etc. → **disponer**
disputa *nf* ALTERCADO, DISCUSIÓN : dispute, argument
disputar *vi* : to argue, to contend, to vie — *vt* : to dispute, to question — **disputarse** *vr* : to be in competition for ⟨se disputan la corona : they're fighting for the crown⟩
disquera *nf* : record label, recording company

disquete → **diskette**
disquisición *nf, pl* -ciones **1** : formal discourse **2** disquisiciones *nfpl* : digressions
distancia *nf* : distance
distanciamiento *nm* **1** : distancing **2** : rift, estrangement
distanciar *vt* **1** : to space out **2** : to draw apart — **distanciarse** *vr* : to grow apart, to become estranged
distante *adj* **1** : distant, far-off **2** : aloof
distar *vi* ~ **de** : to be far from ⟨dista de ser perfecto : he is far from perfect⟩
diste → **dar**
distender {56} *vt* : to distend, to stretch
distensión *nf, pl* -siones : distension
distinción *nf, pl* -ciones : distinction
distinguible *adj* : distinguishable
distinguido, -da *adj* : distinguished, refined
distinguir {26} *vt* **1** : to distinguish **2** : to honor — **distinguirse** *vr*
distintivo, -va *adj* : distinctive, distinguishing
distinto, -ta *adj* **1** DIFERENTE : different **2** CLARO : distinct, clear, evident
distorsión *nf, pl* -siones : distortion
distorsionar *vt* : to distort
distracción *nf, pl* -ciones **1** : distraction, amusement **2** : forgetfulness **3** : oversight
distraer {81} *vt* **1** : to distract **2** ENTRETENER : to entertain, to amuse — **distraerse** *vr* **1** : to get distracted **2** : to amuse oneself
distraídamente *adv* : absentmindedly
distraído[1] *pp* → **distraer**
distraído[2], **-da** *adj* **1** : distracted, preoccupied **2** DESPISTADO : absentminded
distribución *nf, pl* -ciones : distribution
distribuidor, -dora *n* : distributor
distribuir {41} *vt* : to distribute
distributivo, -va *adj* : distributive
distrital *adj* : district, of the district
distrito *nm* : district
distrofia *nf* : dystrophy ⟨distrofia muscular : muscular dystrophy⟩
disturbio *nm* : disturbance
disuadir *vt* : to dissuade, to discourage
disuasión *nf, pl* -siones : dissuasion
disuasivo, -va *adj* : deterrent, discouraging
disuasorio, -ria *adj* : discouraging
disuelto *pp* → **disolver**
disyuntiva *nf* : dilemma
DIU ['diu] *nm* (*d*ispositivo *i*ntra*u*terino) : IUD, intrauterine device
diurético[1], **-ca** *adj* : diuretic
diurético[2] *nm* : diuretic
diurno, -na *adj* : day, daytime
diva *nf* → **divo**
divagar {52} *vi* : to digress
diván *nm, pl* divanes : divan
divergencia *nf* : divergence, difference
divergente *adj* : divergent, differing
divergir {35} *vi* **1** : to diverge **2** : to differ, to disagree

diversidad *nf* : diversity, variety
diversificación *nf, pl* **-ciones** : diversification
diversificar {72} *vt* : to diversify
diversión *nf, pl* **-siones** ENTRETENIMIENTO : fun, amusement, diversion
diverso, -sa *adj* : diverse, various
divertido, -da *adj* 1 : amusing, funny 2 : entertaining, enjoyable
divertir {76} *vt* ENTRETENER : to amuse, to entertain — **divertirse** *vr* : to have fun, to have a good time
dividendo *nm* : dividend
dividir *vt* 1 : to divide, to split 2 : to distribute, to share out — **dividirse** *vr*
divieso *nm* : boil
divinidad *nf* : divinity
divino, -na *adj* : divine
divisa *nf* 1 : currency 2 LEMA : motto 3 : emblem, insignia
divisar *vt* : to discern, to make out
divisible *adj* : divisible
división *nf, pl* **-siones** : division
divisionismo *nm* : factionalism
divisivo, -va *adj* : divisive
divisor *nm* : denominator
divisorio, -ria *adj* : dividing
divo, -va *n* 1 : prima donna 2 : celebrity, star
divorciado¹, -da *adj* 1 : divorced 2 : split, divided
divorciado², -da *n* : divorcé *m*, divorcée *f*
divorciar *vt* : to divorce — **divorciarse** *vr* : to get a divorce
divorcio *nm* : divorce
divulgación *nf, pl* **-ciones** 1 : spreading, dissemination 2 : popularization
divulgar {52} *vt* 1 : to spread, to circulate 2 REVELAR : to divulge, to reveal 3 : to popularize — **divulgarse** *vr*
dizque *adv* : supposedly, apparently
dobladillar *vt* : to hem
dobladillo *nm* : hem
doblar *vt* 1 : to double 2 PLEGAR : to fold, to bend 3 : to turn ⟨doblar la esquina : to turn the corner⟩ 4 : to dub — *vi* 1 : to turn 2 : to toll, to ring — **doblarse** *vr* 1 : to fold up, to double over 2 : to give in, to yield
doble¹ *adj* : double — **doblemente** *adv*
doble² *nm* 1 : double 2 : toll (of a bell), knell
doble³ *nmf* : stand-in, double
doblegar {52} *vt* 1 : to fold, to crease 2 : to force to yield — **doblegarse** *vr* : to yield, to bow
doblez¹ *nm, pl* **dobleces** : fold, crease
doblez² *nmf* : duplicity, deceitfulness
doce *adj & nm* : twelve
doceavo¹, -va *adj* : twelfth
doceavo² *nm* : twelfth (fraction)
docena *nf* 1 : dozen 2 **docena de fraile** : baker's dozen
docencia *nf* : teaching
docente¹ *adj* : educational, teaching
docente² *n* : teacher, lecturer
dócil *adj* : docile — **dócilmente** *adv*

docilidad *nf* : docility
docto, -ta *adj* : learned, erudite
doctor, -tora *n* : doctor
doctorado *nm* : doctorate
doctrina *nf* : doctrine — **doctrinal** *adj*
documentación *nf, pl* **-ciones** : documentation
documental *adj & nm* : documentary
documentar *vt* : to document
documento *nm* : document
dogma *nm* : dogma
dogmático, -ca *adj* : dogmatic
dogmatismo *nm* : dogmatism
dólar *nm* : dollar
dolencia *nf* : ailment, malaise
doler {47} *vi* 1 : to hurt, to ache 2 : to grieve — **dolerse** *vr* 1 : to be distressed 2 : to complain
doliente *nmf* : mourner, bereaved
dolor *nm* 1 : pain, ache ⟨dolor de cabeza : headache⟩ 2 PENA, TRISTEZA : grief, sorrow
dolorido, -da *adj* 1 : sore, aching 2 : hurt, upset
doloroso, -sa *adj* 1 : painful 2 : distressing — **dolorosamente** *adv*
doloso, -sa *adj* : fraudulent — **dolosamente** *adv*
domador, -dora *n* : tamer
domar *vt* : to tame, to break in
domesticado, -da *adj* : domesticated, tame
domesticar {72} *vt* : to domesticate, to tame
doméstico, -ca *adj* : domestic, household
domiciliado, -da *adj* : residing
domiciliario, -ria *adj* 1 : home 2 **arresto domiciliario** : house arrest
domiciliarse *vr* RESIDIR : to reside
domicilio *nm* : home, residence ⟨cambio de domicilio : change of address⟩
dominación *nf, pl* **-ciones** : domination
dominancia *nf* : dominance
dominante *adj* 1 : dominant 2 : domineering
dominar *vt* 1 : to dominate 2 : to master, to be proficient at — *vi* : to predominate, to prevail — **dominarse** *vr* : to control oneself
domingo *nm* : Sunday
dominical *adj* : Sunday ⟨periódico dominical : Sunday newspaper⟩
dominicano, -na *adj & n* : Dominican
dominio *nm* 1 : dominion, power 2 : mastery 3 : domain, field
dominó *nm, pl* **-nós** 1 : domino (tile) 2 : dominoes *pl* (game)
domo *nm* : dome
don¹ *nm* 1 : gift, present 2 : talent
don² *nm* 1 : title of courtesy preceding a man's first name 2 **don nadie** : nobody, insignificant person
dona *nf Mex* : doughnut, donut
donación *nf, pl* **-ciones** : donation
donador, -dora *n* : donor
donaire *nm* 1 GARBO : grace, poise 2 : witticism

donante *nf* → donador
donar *vt* : to donate
donativo *nm* : donation
doncella *nf* : maiden, damsel
doncellez *nf* : maidenhood
donde[1] *conj* : where, in which ⟨el pueblo donde vivo : the town where I live⟩
donde[2] *prep* : over by ⟨lo encontré donde la silla : I found it over by the chair⟩
dónde *adv* : where ⟨¿dónde está su casa? : where is your house?⟩
dondequiera *adv* 1 : anywhere, no matter where 2 dondequiera que : wherever, everywhere
doña *nf* : title of courtesy preceding a woman's first name
doquier *adv* por ～ : everywhere, all over
dorado[1], -da *adj* : gold, golden
dorado[2], -da *nm* : gilt
dorar *vt* 1 : to gild 2 : to brown (food)
dormido, -da *adj* 1 : asleep 2 : numb ⟨tiene el pie dormido : her foot's numb, her foot's gone to sleep⟩
dormilón, -lona *n* : sleepyhead, late riser
dormir {27} *vt* : to put to sleep — *vi* : to sleep — dormirse *vr* : to fall asleep
dormitar *vi* : to snooze, to doze
dormitorio *nm* 1 : bedroom 2 : dormitory
dorsal[1] *adj* : dorsal
dorsal[2] *nm* : number (worn in sports)
dorso *nm* 1 : back ⟨el dorso de la mano : the back of the hand⟩ 2 *Mex* : backstroke
dos *adj & nm* : two
doscientos[1], -tas *adj* : two hundred
doscientos[2] *nms & pl* : two hundred
dosel *nm* : canopy
dosificación *nf, pl* -ciones : dosage
dosis *nfs & pl* 1 : dose 2 : amount, quantity
dossier *nm* : dossier
dotación *nf, pl* -ciones 1 : endowment, funding 2 : staff, personnel
dotado, -da *adj* 1 : gifted 2 ～ de : endowed with, equipped with
dotar *vt* 1 : to provide, to equip 2 : to endow
dote *nf* 1 : dowry 2 dotes *nfpl* : talent, gift
doy → dar
draga *nf* : dredge
dragado *nm* : dredging
dragar {52} *vt* : to dredge
dragón *nm, pl* dragones 1 : dragon 2 : snapdragon
drague, etc. → dragar
drama *nm* : drama
dramático, -ca *adj* : dramatic — dramáticamente *adv*
dramatizar {21} *vt* : to dramatize — dramatización *nf*
dramaturgo, -ga *n* : dramatist, playwright

drástico, -ca *adj* : drastic — drásticamente *adv*
drenaje *nm* : drainage
drenar *vt* : to drain
drene *nm Mex* : drain
driblar *vi* : to dribble (in basketball)
drible *nm* : dribble (in basketball)
droga *nf* : drug
drogadicción *nf, pl* -ciones : drug addiction
drogadicto, -ta *n* : drug addict
drogar {52} *vt* : to drug — drogarse *vr* : to take drugs
drogue, etc. → drogar
droguería *nf* FARMACIA : drugstore
dromedario *nm* : dromedary
dual *adj* : dual
dualidad *nf* : duality
dualismo *nm* : dualism
ducha *nf* : shower ⟨darse una ducha : to take a shower⟩
ducharse *vr* : to take a shower
ducho, -cha *adj* : experienced, skilled, expert
dúctil *adj* : ductile
ducto *nm* 1 : duct, shaft 2 : pipeline
duda *nf* : doubt ⟨no cabe duda : there's no doubt about it⟩
dudar *vt* : to doubt — *vi* ～ en : to hesitate to ⟨no dudes en pedirme ayuda : don't hesitate to ask me for help⟩
dudoso, -sa *adj* 1 : doubtful 2 : dubious, questionable — dudosamente *adv*
duele, etc. → doler
duelo *nm* 1 : duel 2 LUTO : mourning
duende *nm* 1 : elf, goblin 2 ENCANTO : magic, charm ⟨una bailarina que tiene duende : a dancer with a certain magic⟩
dueño, -ña *n* 1 : owner, proprietor, proprietress *f* 2 : landlord, landlady *f*
duerme, etc. → dormir
dueto *nm* : duet
dulce[1] *adv* : sweetly, softly
dulce[2] *adj* 1 : sweet 2 : mild, gentle, mellow — dulcemente *adv*
dulce[3] *nm* : candy, sweet
dulcería *nf* : candy store
dulcificante *nm* : sweetener
dulzura *nf* 1 : sweetness 2 : gentleness, mellowness
duna *nf* : dune
dúo *nm* : duo, duet
duodécimo[1], -ma *adj* : twelfth
duodécimo[2], -ma *nm* : twelfth (in a series)
dúplex *nms & pl* : duplex apartment
duplicación *nf, pl* -ciones : duplication, copying
duplicado *nm* : duplicate, copy
duplicar {72} *vt* 1 : to double 2 : to duplicate, to copy
duplicidad *nf* : duplicity
duque *nm* : duke
duquesa *nf* : duchess
durabilidad *nf* : durability
durable → duradero

duración *nf, pl* **-ciones** : duration, length
duradero, -ra *adj* : durable, lasting
duramente *adv* **1** : harshly, severely **2** : hard
durante *prep* : during ⟨durante todo el día : all day long⟩ ⟨trabajó durante tres horas : he worked for three hours⟩
durar *vi* : to last, to endure
durazno *nm* **1** : peach **2** : peach tree

dureza *nf* **1** : hardness, toughness **2** : severity, harshness
durmiente[1] *adj* : sleeping
durmiente[2] *nmf* : sleeper
durmió, etc. → **dormir**
duro[1] *adv* : hard ⟨trabajé tan duro : I worked so hard⟩
duro[2], **-ra** *adj* **1** : hard, tough **2** : harsh, severe

E

e[1] *nf* : fifth letter of the Spanish alphabet
e[2] *conj* (*used instead of* y *before words beginning with* i- *or* hi-) : and
ebanista *nmf* : cabinetmaker
ebanistería *nf* : cabinetmaking
ébano *nm* : ebony
ebriedad *nf* EMBRIAGUEZ : inebriation, drunkenness
ebrio, -bria *adj* EMBRIAGADO : inebriated, drunk
ebullición *nf, pl* **-ciones** : boiling
eccéntrico → **excéntrico**
echar *vt* **1** LANZAR : to throw, to cast, to hurl **2** EXPULSAR : to throw out, to expel **3** EMITIR : to emit, give off **4** BROTAR : to sprout, to put forth **5** DESPEDIR : to fire, to dismiss **6** : to put in, to add **7 echar a perder** : to spoil, to ruin **8 echar de menos** : to miss ⟨echan de menos a su madre : they miss their mother⟩ — *vi* **1** : to start off **2** ~ **a** : to begin to — **echarse** *vr* **1** : to throw oneself **2** : to lie down **3** : to put on **4** ~ **a** : to start to **5 echarse a perder** : to go bad, to spoil **6 echárselas de** : to pose as
ecléctico, -ca *adj* : eclectic
eclesiástico[1], **-ca** *adj* : ecclesiastical, ecclesiastic
eclesiástico[2] *nm* CLÉRIGO : cleric, clergyman
eclipsar *vt* **1** : to eclipse **2** : to outshine, to surpass
eclipse *nm* : eclipse
eco *nm* : echo
ecografía *nf* : ultrasound scanning
ecología *nf* : ecology
ecológico, -ca *adj* : ecological — **ecológicamente** *adv*
ecologista *nmf* : ecologist, environmentalist
ecólogo, -ga *n* : ecologist
economía *nf* **1** : economy **2** : economics
económicamente *adv* : financially
económico, -ca *adj* : economic, economical
economista *nmf* : economist
economizar {21} *vt* : to save, to economize on — *vi* : to save up, to be frugal
ecosistema *nm* : ecosystem
ecuación *nf, pl* **-ciones** : equation
ecuador *nm* : equator

ecuánime *adj* **1** : even-tempered **2** : impartial
ecuanimidad *nf* **1** : equanimity **2** : impartiality
ecuatorial *adj* : equatorial
ecuatoriano, -na *adj & n* : Ecuadorian
ecuestre *adj* : equestrian
ecuménico, -ca *adj* : ecumenical
eczema *nm* : eczema
edad *nf* **1** : age ⟨¿qué edad tiene? : how old is she?⟩ **2** ÉPOCA, ERA : epoch, era
edema *nm* : edema
Edén *nm, pl* **Edenes** : Eden, paradise
edición *nf, pl* **-ciones** **1** : edition **2** : publication, publishing
edicto *nm* : edict, proclamation
edificación *nf, pl* **-ciones** **1** : edification **2** : construction, building
edificante *adj* : edifying
edificar {72} *vt* **1** : to edify **2** CONSTRUIR : to build, to construct
edificio *nm* : building, edifice
editar *vt* **1** : to edit **2** PUBLICAR : to publish
editor[1], **-tora** *adj* : publishing ⟨casa editora : publishing house⟩
editor[2], **-tora** *n* **1** : editor **2** : publisher
editora *nf* : publisher, publishing company
editorial[1] *adj* **1** : publishing **2** : editorial
editorial[2] *nm* : editorial
editorial[3] *nf* : publishing house
editorializar {21} *vi* : to editorialize
edredón *nm, pl* **-dones** COBERTOR, COLCHA : comforter, eiderdown, quilt
educable *adj* : educable, teachable
educación *nf, pl* **-ciones** **1** ENSEÑANZA : education **2** : manners *pl* — **educacional** *adj*
educado, -da *adj* : polite, well-mannered
educador, -dora *n* : educator
educando, -da *n* ALUMNO, PUPILO : pupil, student
educar {72} *vt* **1** : to educate **2** CRIAR : to bring up, to raise **3** : to train — **educarse** *vr* : to be educated
educativo, -va *adj* : educational
efectista *adj* : dramatic, sensational
efectivamente *adv* : really, actually
efectividad *nf* : effectiveness

efectivo¹, -va *adj* **1** : effective **2** : real, actual **3** : permanent, regular (of employment)

efectivo² *nm* : cash

efecto *nm* **1** : effect **2 en ~** : actually, in fact **3 efectos** *nmpl* : goods, property ⟨efectos personales : personal effects⟩

efectuar {3} *vt* : to carry out, to bring about

efervescencia *nf* **1** : effervescence **2** : vivacity, high spirits *pl*

efervescente *adj* **1** : effervescent **2** : vivacious

eficacia *nf* **1** : effectiveness, efficacy **2** : efficiency

eficaz *adj, pl* **-caces 1** : effective **2** EFICIENTE : efficient — **eficazmente** *adv*

eficiencia *nf* : efficiency

eficiente *adj* EFICAZ : efficient — **eficientemente** *adv*

eficientizar {21} *vt Mex* : to streamline, to make more efficient

efigie *nf* : effigy

efímera *nf* : mayfly

efímero, -ra *adj* : ephemeral

efusión *nf, pl* **-siones 1** : effusion **2** : warmth, effusiveness **3 con ~** : effusively

efusivo, -va *adj* : effusive — **efusivamente** *adv*

egipcio, -cia *adj & n* : Egyptian

eglefino *nm* : haddock

ego *nm* : ego

egocéntrico, -ca *adj* : egocentric, self-centered

egoísmo *nm* : selfishness, egoism

egoísta¹ *adj* : selfish, egoistic

egoísta² *nmf* : egoist, selfish person

egotismo *nm* : egotism, conceit

egotista¹ *adj* : egotistic, egotistical, conceited

egotista² *nmf* : egotist, conceited person

egresado, -da *n* : graduate

egresar *vi* : to graduate

egreso *nm* **1** : graduation **2 ingresos y egresos** : income and expenditure

eh *interj* **1** : hey! **2** : eh?, huh?

eje *nm* **1** : axle **2** : axis

ejecución *nf, pl* **-ciones** : execution

ejecutante *nmf* : performer

ejecutar *vt* **1** : to execute, to put to death **2** : to carry out, to perform

ejecutivo, -va *adj & n* : executive

ejecutor, -tora *n* : executor

ejemplar¹ *adj* : exemplary, model

ejemplar² *nm* **1** : copy (of a book, magazine, etc.) **2** : specimen, example

ejemplificar {72} *vt* : to exemplify, to illustrate

ejemplo *nm* **1** : example **2 por ~** : for example **3 dar ejemplo** : to set an example

ejercer {86} *vi* **~ de** : to practice as, to work as — *vt* **1** : to practice **2** : exercise (a right) **3** : to exert

ejercicio *nm* **1** : exercise **2** : practice

ejercitar *vt* **1** : to exercise **2** ADIESTRAR : to drill, to train

ejército *nm* : army

ejidal *adj Mex* : cooperative

ejido *nm* **1** : common land **2** *Mex* : cooperative

ejote *nm Mex* : green bean

el¹ *pron (referring to masculine nouns)* **1** : the one ⟨tengo mi libro y el tuyo : I have my book and yours⟩ ⟨de los cantantes me gusta el de México : I prefer the singer from México⟩ **2 el que** : he who, whoever, the one that ⟨el que vino ayer : the one who came yesterday⟩ ⟨el que trabaja duro estará contento : he who works hard will be happy⟩

el², la *art, pl* **los, las** : the ⟨los niños están en la casa : the boys are in the house⟩ ⟨me duele el pie : my foot hurts⟩

él *pron* : he, him ⟨él es mi amigo : he's my friend⟩ ⟨hablaremos con él : we will speak with him⟩

elaboración *nf, pl* **-ciones 1** PRODUCCIÓN : production, making **2** : preparation, devising

elaborado, -da *adj* : elaborate

elaborar *vt* **1** : to make, to produce **2** : to devise, to draw up

elasticidad *nf* : elasticity

elástico¹, -ca *adj* **1** FLEXIBLE : flexible **2** : elastic

elástico² *nm* **1** : elastic (material) **2** : rubber band

elección *nf, pl* **-ciones 1** SELECCIÓN : choice, selection **2** : election

electivo, -va *adj* : elective

electo, -ta *adj* : elect ⟨el presidente electo : the president-elect⟩

elector, -tora *n* : elector, voter

electorado *nm* : electorate

electoral *adj* : electoral, election

electricidad *nf* : electricity

electricista *nmf* : electrician

eléctrico, -ca *adj* : electric, electrical

electrificar {72} *vt* : to electrify — **electrificación** *nf*

electrizar {21} *vt* : to electrify, to thrill — **electrizante** *adj*

electrocardiógrafo *nm* : electrocardiograph

electrocardiograma *nm* : electrocardiogram

electrocutar *vt* : to electrocute — **electrocución** *nf*

electrodo *nm* : electrode

electrodoméstico *nm* : electric appliance

electroimán *nm, pl* **-manes** : electromagnet

electrólisis *nfs & pl* : electrolysis

electrolito *nm* : electrolyte

electromagnético, -ca *adj* : electromagnetic

electromagnetismo *nm* : electromagnetism

electrón *nm, pl* **-trones** : electron

electrónica *nf* : electronics

electrónico, -ca *adj* : electronic — **electrónicamente** *adv*

elefante, -ta *n* : elephant

elegancia *nf* : elegance

elegante *adj* : elegant, smart — **elegantemente** *adv*

elegía *nf* : elegy

elegíaco, -ca *adj* : elegiac

elegibilidad *nf* : eligibility

elegible *adj* : eligible

elegido, -da *adj* **1** : chosen, selected **2** : elected

elegir {28} *vt* **1** ESCOGER, SELECCIONAR : to choose, to select **2** : to elect

elemental *adj* **1** : elementary, basic **2** : fundamental, essential

elemento *nm* : element

elenco *nm* : cast (of actors)

elepé *nm* : long-playing record

elevación *nf, pl* **-ciones** : elevation, height

elevado, -da *adj* **1** : elevated, lofty **2** : high

elevador *nm* ASCENSOR : elevator

elevar *vt* ALZAR : to raise, to lift **2** AUMENTAR : to raise, to increase **3** : to elevate (in a hierarchy), to promote **4** : to present, to submit — **elevarse** *vr* : to rise

elfo *nm* : elf

eliminación *nf, pl* **-ciones** : elimination, removal

eliminar *vt* **1** : to eliminate, to remove **2** : to do in, to kill

elipse *nf* : ellipse

elipsis *nf* : ellipsis

elíptico, -ca *adj* : elliptical, elliptic

elite *or* **élite** *nf* : elite

elixir *or* **elíxir** *nm* : elixir

ella *pron* : she, her ⟨ella es mi amiga : she is my friend⟩ ⟨nos fuimos con ella : we left with her⟩

ello *pron* : it ⟨es por ello que me voy : that's why I'm going⟩

ellos, ellas *pron pl* **1** : they, them **2 de ellos, de ellas** : theirs

elocución *nf, pl* **-ciones** : elocution

elocuencia *nf* : eloquence

elocuente *adj* : eloquent — **elocuentemente** *adv*

elogiar *vt* ENCOMIAR : to praise

elogio *nm* : praise

elote *nm* **1** *Mex* : corn, maize **2** *CA, Mex* : corncob

elucidación *nf, pl* **-ciones** ESCLARECIMIENTO : elucidation

elucidar *vt* ESCLARECER : to elucidate

eludir *vt* EVADIR : to evade, to avoid, to elude

emanación *nf, pl* **-ciones** : emanation

emanar *vi* ~ **de** : to emanate from — *vt* : to exude

emancipar *vt* : to emancipate — **emancipación** *nf*

embadurnar *vt* EMBARRAR : to smear, to daub

embajada *nf* : embassy

embajador, -dora *n* : ambassador

embalaje *nm* : packing, packaging

embalar *vt* EMPAQUETAR : to pack

embaldosar *vt* : to tile, to pave with tiles

embalsamar *vt* : to embalm

embalsar *vt* : to dam, to dam up

embalse *nm* : dam, reservoir

embarazada *adj* ENCINTA, PREÑADA : pregnant, expecting

embarazar {21} *vt* **1** : to obstruct, to hamper **2** PREÑAR : to make pregnant

embarazo *nm* : pregnancy

embarazoso, -sa *adj* : embarrassing, awkward

embarcación *nf, pl* **-ciones** : boat, craft

embarcadero *nm* : wharf, pier, jetty

embarcar {72} *vi* : to embark, to board — *vt* : to load

embarco *nm* : embarkation

embargar {52} *vt* **1** : to seize, to impound **2** : to overwhelm

embargo *nm* **1** : seizure **2** : embargo **3 sin** ~ : however, nevertheless

embarque *nm* **1** : embarkation **2** : shipment

embarrancar {72} *vi* **1** : to run aground **2** : to get bogged down

embarrar *vt* **1** : to cover with mud **2** EMBADURNAR : to smear

embarullar *vt fam* : to muddle, to confuse — **embarullarse** *vr fam* : to get mixed up

embate *nm* **1** : onslaught **2** : battering (of waves or wind)

embaucador, -dora *n* : swindler, deceiver

embaucar {72} *vt* : to trick, to swindle

embeber *vt* : to absorb, to soak up — *vi* : to shrink

embelesado, -da *adj* : spellbound

embelesar *vt* : to enchant, to captivate

embellecer {53} *vt* : to embellish, to beautify

embellecimiento *nm* : beautification, embellishment

embestida *nf* **1** : charge (of a bull) **2** ARREMETIDA : attack, onslaught

embestir {54} *vt* : to hit, to run into, to charge at — *vi* ARREMETER : to charge, to attack

emblanquecer {53} *vt* BLANQUEAR : to bleach, to whiten — **emblanquecerse** *vr* : to turn white

emblema *nm* : emblem

emblemático, -ca *adj* : emblematic

embolia *nf* : embolism

émbolo *nm* : piston

embolsarse *vr* **1** : to pocket (money) **2** : to collect (payment)

emborracharse *vr* EMBRIAGARSE : to get drunk

emborronar *vt* **1** : to blot, to smudge **2** GARABATEAR : to scribble

emboscada *nf* : ambush

emboscar {72} *vt* : to ambush — **emboscarse** *vr* : to lie in ambush

embotadura *nf* : bluntness, dullness

embotar *vt* **1** : to dull, to blunt **2** : to weaken, to enervate

embotellamiento *nm* ATASCO : traffic jam

embotellar *vt* ENVASAR : to bottle
embragar {52} *vi* : to engage the clutch
embrague *nm* : clutch
embravecerse {53} *vr* **1** : to get furious **2** : to get rough ⟨el mar se embraveció : the sea became tempestuous⟩
embriagado, -da *adj* : inebriated, drunk
embriagador, -dora *adj* : intoxicating
embriagarse {52} *vr* EMBORRACHARSE : to get drunk
embriaguez *nf* EBRIEDAD : drunkenness, inebriation
embrión *nm, pl* **embriones** : embryo
embrionario, -ria *adj* : embryonic
embrollo *nm* ENREDO : imbroglio, confusion
embrujar *vt* HECHIZAR : to bewitch
embrujo *nm* : spell, curse
embudo *nm* : funnel
embuste *nm* **1** MENTIRA : lie, fib **2** ENGAÑO : trick, hoax
embustero¹, -ra *adj* : lying, deceitful
embustero², -ra *n* : liar, cheat
embutido *nm* **1** : sausage **2** : inlaid work
embutir *vt* **1** : to cram, to stuff, to jam **2** : to inlay
emergencia *nf* **1** : emergency **2** : emergence
emergente *adj* **1** : emergent **2** : consequent, resultant
emerger {15} *vi* : to emerge, to surface
emético¹, -ca *adj* : emetic
emético² *nm* : emetic
emigración *nf, pl* **-ciones 1** : emigration **2** : migration
emigrante *adj & nmf* : emigrant
emigrar *vi* **1** : to emigrate **2** : to migrate
eminencia *nf* : eminence
eminente *adj* : eminent, distinguished
eminentemente *adv* : basically, essentially
emisario¹, -ria *n* : emissary
emisario² *nm* : outlet (of a body of water)
emisión *nf, pl* **-siones 1** : emission **2** : broadcast **3** : issue ⟨emisión de acciones : stock issue⟩
emisor *nm* TRANSMISOR : television or radio transmitter
emisora *nf* : radio station
emitir *vt* **1** : to emit, to give off **2** : to broadcast **3** : to issue **4** : to cast (a vote)
emoción *nf, pl* **-ciones** : emotion — **emocional** *adj* — **emocionalmente** *adv*
emocionado, -da *adj* **1** : moved, affected by emotion **2** ENTUSIASMADO : excited
emocionante *adj* **1** CONMOVEDOR : moving, touching **2** EXCITANTE : exciting, thrilling
emocionar *vt* **1** CONMOVER : to move, to touch **2** : to excite, to thrill — **emocionarse** *vr*
emotivo, -va *adj* : emotional, moving
empacador, -dora *n* : packer

empacar {72} *vt* **1** EMPAQUETAR : to pack **2** : to bale — *vi* **1** : to pack — **empacarse** *vr* **1** : to balk, to refuse to budge **2** *Col, Mex fam* : to eat ravenously, to devour
empachar *vt* **1** ESTORBAR : to obstruct **2** : to give indigestion to **3** DISFRAZAR : to disguise, to mask — **empacharse** *vr* **1** INDIGESTARSE : to get indigestion **2** AVERGONZARSE : to be embarrassed
empacho *nm* **1** INDIGESTIÓN : indigestion **2** VERGÜENZA : embarrassment **3** **no tener empacho en** : to have no qualms about
empadronarse *vr* : to register to vote
empalagar {52} *vt* **1** : to cloy, to surfeit **2** FASTIDIAR : to annoy, to bother
empalagoso, -sa *adj* MELOSO : cloying, excessively sweet
empalar *vt* : to impale
empalizada *nf* : palisade (fence)
empalmar *vt* **1** : to splice, to link **2** : to combine — *vi* **1** : to meet, to converge
empalme *nm* **1** CONEXIÓN : connection, link **2** : junction
empanada *nf* : pie, turnover
empanadilla *nf* : meat or seafood pie
empanar *vt* : to bread
empantanado, -da *adj* : bogged down, delayed
empañar *vt* **1** : to steam up **2** : to tarnish, to sully
empapado, -da *adj* : soggy, sodden
empapar *vt* MOJAR : to soak, to drench — **empaparse** *vr* **1** : to get soaking wet **2** ~ **de** : to absorb, to be imbued with
empapelar *vt* : to wallpaper
empaque *nm fam* **1** : presence, bearing **2** : pomposity **3** DESCARO : impudence, nerve
empaquetar *vt* EMBALAR : to pack, to package — **empaquetarse** *vr fam* : to dress up
emparedado *nm* : sandwich
emparedar *vt* : to wall in, to confine
emparejar *vt* **1** : to pair, to match up **2** : to make even — *vi* : to catch up — **emparejarse** *vr* : to pair up
emparentado, -da *adj* : related
emparentar {55} *vi* : to become related by marriage
emparrillado *nm Mex* : gridiron (in football)
empastar *vt* **1** : to fill (a tooth) **2** : to bind (a book)
empaste *nm* : filling (of a tooth)
empatar *vt* : to tie, to connect — *vi* : to result in a draw, to be tied — **empatarse** *vr Ven* : to hook up, to link together
empate *nm* : draw, tie
empatía *nf* : empathy
empecinado, -da *adj* TERCO : stubborn
empecinarse *vr* OBSTINARSE : to be stubborn, to persist
empedernido, -da *adj* INCORREGIBLE : hardened, inveterate
empedrado *nm* : paving, pavement

empedrar {55} *vt* : to pave (with stones)
empeine *nm* : instep
empellón *nm, pl* **-llones** : shove, push
empelotado, -da *adj* **1** *Mex fam* : madly in love **2** *fam* : stark naked
empeñado, -da *adj* : determined, committed
empeñar *vt* **1** : to pawn **2** : to pledge, to give (one's word) — **empeñarse** *vr* **1** : to insist stubbornly **2** : to make an effort
empeño *nm* **1** : pledge, commitment **2** : insistence **3** ESFUERZO : effort, determination **4** : pawning ⟨casa de empeños : pawnshop⟩
empeoramiento *nm* : worsening, deterioration
empeorar *vi* : to deteriorate, to get worse — *vt* : to make worse
empequeñecer {53} *vi* : to diminish, to become smaller — *vt* : to minimize, to make smaller
emperador *nm* : emperor
emperatriz *nf, pl* **-trices** : empress
empero *conj* : however, nevertheless
empezar {29} *v* COMENZAR : to start, to begin
empinado, -da *adj* : steep
empinar *vt* ELEVAR : to lift, to raise — **empinarse** *vr* : to stand on tiptoe
empírico, -ca *adj* : empirical — **empíricamente** *adv*
emplasto *nm* : poultice, dressing
emplazamiento *nm* **1** : location, site **2** CITACIÓN : summons, subpoena
emplazar {21} *vt* **1** CONVOCAR : to convene, to summon **2** : to subpoena **3** UBICAR : to place, to position
empleado, -da *n* : employee
empleador, -dora *n* PATRÓN : employer
emplear *vt* **1** : to employ **2** USAR : to use — **emplearse** *vr* **1** : to get a job **2** : to occupy oneself
empleo *nm* **1** OCUPACIÓN : employment, occupation, job **2** : use, usage
empobrecer {53} *vt* : to impoverish — *vi* : to become poor — **empobrecerse** *vr*
empobrecimiento *nm* : impoverishment
empollar *vi* : to brood eggs — *vt* : to incubate
empolvado, -da *adj* **1** : dusty **2** : powdered, powdery
empolvar *vt* **1** : to cover with dust **2** : to powder — **empolvarse** *vr* **1** : to gather dust **2** : to powder one's face
emporio *nm* **1** : center, capital, empire ⟨un emporio cultural : a cultural center⟩ ⟨un emporio financiero : a financial empire⟩ **2** : department store
empotrado, -da *adj* : built-in ⟨armarios empotrados : built-in cabinets⟩
empotrar *vt* : to build into, to embed
emprendedor, -dora *adj* : enterprising
emprender *vt* : to undertake, to begin

empresa *nf* **1** COMPAÑÍA, FIRMA : company, corporation, firm **2** : undertaking, venture
empresariado *nm* **1** : business world **2** : management, managers *pl*
empresarial *adj* : business, managerial, corporate
empresario, -ria *n* **1** : manager **2** : businessman *m*, businesswoman *f* **3** : impresario
empréstito *nm* : loan
empujar *vi* : to push, to shove — *vt* **1** : to push **2** PRESIONAR : to spur on, to press
empuje *nm* : impetus, drive
empujón *nm, pl* **-jones** : push, shove
empuñadura *nf* MANGO : hilt, handle
empuñar *vt* **1** ASIR : to grasp **2** empuñar las armas : to take up arms
emú *nm* : emu
emular *vt* IMITAR : to emulate — **emulación** *nf*
emulsión *nf, pl* **-siones** : emulsion
emulsionante *nm* : emulsifier
emulsionar *vt* : to emulsify
en *prep* **1** : in ⟨en el bolsillo : in one's pocket⟩ ⟨en una semana : in a week⟩ **2** : on ⟨en la mesa : on the table⟩ **3** : at ⟨en casa : at home⟩ ⟨en el trabajo : at work⟩ ⟨en ese momento : at that moment⟩
enagua *nf* : petticoat, slip
enajenación *nf, pl* **-ciones** **1** : transfer (of property) **2** : alienation **3** : absentmindedness
enajenado, -da *adj* : out of one's mind
enajenar *vt* **1** : to transfer (property) **2** : to alienate **3** : to enrapture — **enajenarse** *vr* **1** : to become estranged **2** : to go mad
enaltecer {53} *vt* : to praise, to extol
enamorado[1], -da *adj* : in love
enamorado[2], -da *n* : lover, sweetheart
enamoramiento *nm* : infatuation, crush
enamorar *vt* : to enamor, to win the love of — **enamorarse** *vr* : to fall in love
enamoriscarse {72} *vr fam* : to have a crush, to be infatuated
enamorizado, -da *adj* : amorous, passionate
enano[1], -na *adj* : tiny, minute
enano[2], -na *n* : dwarf, midget
enarbolar *vt* **1** : to hoist, to raise **2** : to brandish
enarcar {72} *vt* : to arch, to raise
enardecer {53} *vt* **1** : to arouse (anger, passions) **2** : to stir up, to excite — **enardecerse** *vr*
encabezado *nm Mex* : headline
encabezamiento *nm* **1** : heading **2** : salutation, opening
encabezar {21} *vt* **1** : to head, to lead **2** : to put a heading on
encabritarse *vr* **1** : to rear up **2** *fam* : to get angry
encadenar *vt* **1** : to chain **2** : to connect, to link **3** INMOVILIZAR : to immobilize

encajar *vi* : to fit, to fit together, to fit in — *vt* **1** : to insert, to stick **2** : to take, to cope with ⟨encajó el golpe : he withstood the blow⟩
encaje *nm* **1** : lace **2** : financial reserve
encajonar *vt* **1** : to box, to crate **2** : to cram in
encalar *vt* : to whitewash
encallar *vi* **1** : to run aground **2** : to get stuck
encallecido, -da *adj* : callused
encamar *vt* : to confine to a bed
encaminado, -da *adj* **1** : on the right track **2** ~ **a** : aimed at, designed to
encaminar *vt* **1** : to direct, to channel **2** : to head in the right direction — **encaminarse** *vr* ~ **a** : to head for, to aim at
encandilar *vt* : to dazzle
encanecer {53} *vi* : to gray, to go gray
encantado, -da *adj* **1** : charmed, bewitched **2** : delighted
encantador¹, -dora *adj* : charming, delightful
encantador², -dora *n* : magician
encantamiento *nm* : enchantment, spell
encantar *vt* **1** : to enchant, to bewitch **2** : to charm, to delight ⟨me encanta esta canción : I love this song⟩
encanto *nm* **1** : charm, fascination **2** HECHIZO : spell **3** : delightful person or thing
encañonar *vt* : to point (a gun) at, to hold up
encapotado, -da *adj* : cloudy, overcast
encapotarse *vr* : to cloud over, to become overcast
encaprichado, -da *adj* : infatuated
encaprichamiento *nm* : infatuation
encapuchado, -da *adj* : hooded
encarado, -da *adj* **estar mal encarado** *fam* : to be ugly-looking, to look mean
encaramar *vt* : to raise, to lift up — **encaramarse** *vr* : to perch
encarar *vt* CONFRONTAR : to face, to confront
encarcelación *nf* → **encarcelamiento**
encarcelamiento *nm* : incarceration, imprisonment
encarcelar *vt* : to incarcerate, to imprison
encarecer {53} *vt* **1** : to increase, to raise (price, value) **2** : to beseech, to entreat — **encarecerse** *vr* : to become more expensive
encarecidamente *adv* : insistently, urgently
encarecimiento *nm* : increase, rise (in price)
encargado¹, -da *adj* : in charge
encargado², -da *n* : manager, person in charge
encargar {52} *vt* **1** : to put in charge of **2** : to recommend, to advise **3** : to order, to request — **encargarse** *vr* ~ **de** : to take charge of
encargo *nm* **1** : errand **2** : job assignment **3** : order ⟨hecho de encargo : custom-made, made to order⟩

encariñarse *vr* ~ **con** : to become fond of, to grow attached to
encarnación *nf*, *pl* **-ciones** : incarnation, embodiment
encarnado¹, -da *adj* **1** : incarnate **2** : flesh-colored **3** : red **4** : ingrown
encarnado² *nm* : red
encarnar *vt* : to incarnate, to embody — **encarnarse** *vr* **encarnarse una uña** : to have an ingrown nail
encarnizado, -da *adj* **1** : bloodshot, inflamed **2** : fierce, bloody
encarnizar {21} *vt* : to enrage, to infuriate — **encarnizarse** *vr* : to be brutal, to attack viciously
encarrilar *vt* : to guide, to put on the right track
encasillar *vt* CLASIFICAR : to classify, to pigeonhole, to categorize
encausar *vt* : to prosecute, to charge
encauzar {21} *vt* : to channel, to guide — **encauzarse** *vr*
encebollado, -da *adj* : cooked with onions
encefalitis *nms & pl* : encephalitis
enceguecedor, -dora *n* : blinding
encendedor *nm* : lighter
encender {56} *vi* : to light — *vt* **1** : to light, to set fire to **2** PRENDER : to switch on **3** : to start (a motor) **4** : to arouse, to kindle — **encenderse** *vr* **1** : to get excited **2** : to blush
encendido¹, -da *adj* **1** : burning **2** : flushed **3** : fiery, passionate
encendido² *nm* : ignition
encerado *nm* **1** : waxing, polishing **2** : blackboard
encerar *vt* : to wax, to polish
encerrar {55} *vt* **1** : to lock up, to shut away **2** : to contain, to include **3** : to involve, to entail
encerrona *nf* **1** TRAMPA : trap, setup **2 prepararle una encerrona a alguien** : to set a trap for someone, to set someone up
encestar *vi* : to make a basket (in basketball)
enchapado *nm* : plating, coating (of metal)
encharcamiento *nm* : flood, flooding
encharcar {72} *vt* : to flood, to swamp — **encharcarse** *vr*
enchilada *nf* : enchilada
enchilar *vt Mex* : to season with chili
enchuecar {72} *vt Chile, Mex fam* : to make crooked, to twist
enchufar *vt* **1** : to plug in **2** : to connect, to fit together
enchufe *nm* **1** : connection **2** : plug, socket
encía *nf* : gum (tissue)
encíclica *nf* : encyclical
enciclopedia *nf* : encyclopedia
enciclopédico, -ca *adj* : encyclopedic
encierro *nm* **1** : confinement **2** : enclosure
encima *adv* **1** : on top, above **2** ADEMÁS : as well, besides **3** ~ **de** : on, on top

of, over **4 por encima de** : above, beyond ⟨por encima de la ley : above the law⟩ **5 echarse encima** : to take upon oneself **6 estar encima de** *fam* : to nag, to criticize **7 quitarse de encima** : to get rid of

encina *nf* : evergreen oak

encinta *adj* EMBARAZADA, PREÑADA : pregnant, expecting

enclaustrado, -da *adj* : cloistered, shut away

enclavado, -da *adj* : buried

enclenque *adj* : weak, sickly

encoger {15} *vt* **1** : to shrink, to make smaller **2** : to intimidate — *vi* : to shrink, to contract — **encogerse** *vr* **1** : to shrink **2** : to be intimidated, to cower, to cringe **3 encogerse de hombros** : to shrug (one's shoulders)

encogido, -da *adj* **1** : shriveled, shrunken **2** TÍMIDO : shy, inhibited

encogimiento *nm* **1** : shrinking, shrinkage **2** : shrug **3** TIMIDEZ : shyness

encolar *vt* : to paste, to glue

encolerizar {21} *vt* ENFURECER : to enrage, to infuriate — **encolerizarse** *vr*

encomendar {55} *vt* CONFIAR : to entrust, to commend — **encomendarse** *vr*

encomiable *adj* : commendable, praiseworthy

encomiar *vt* ELOGIAR : to praise, to pay tribute to

encomienda *nf* **1** : charge, mission **2** : royal land grant **3** : parcel

encomio *nm* : praise, eulogy

encomioso, -sa *adj* : eulogistic, laudatory

enconar *vt* **1** : to irritate, to anger **2** : to inflame — **enconarse** *vr* **1** : to become heated **2** : to fester

encono *nm* **1** RENCOR : animosity, rancor **2** : inflammation, infection

encontrado, -da *adj* : contrary, opposing

encontrar {19} *vt* **1** HALLAR : to find **2** : to encounter, to meet — **encontrarse** *vr* **1** REUNIRSE : to meet **2** : to clash, to conflict **3** : to be ⟨su abuelo se encuentra mejor : her grandfather is doing better⟩

encorvar *vt* : to bend, to curve — **encorvarse** *vr* : to hunch over, to stoop

encrespar *vt* **1** : to curl, to ruffle, to ripple **2** : to annoy, to irritate — **encresparse** *vr* **1** : to curl one's hair **2** : to become choppy **3** : to get annoyed

encrucijada *nf* : crossroads

encuadernación *nf, pl* **-ciones** : bookbinding

encuadernar *vt* EMPASTAR : to bind (a book)

encuadrar *vt* **1** ENMARCAR : to frame **2** ENCAJAR : to fit, to insert **3** COMPRENDER : to contain, to include

encubierto *pp* → **encubrir**

encubrimiento *nm* : cover-up

encubrir {2} *vt* : to cover up, to conceal

encuentro *nm* **1** : meeting, encounter **2** : conference, congress

encuerado, -da *adj fam* : naked

encuerar *vt fam* : to undress

encuesta *nf* **1** INVESTIGACIÓN, PESQUISA : inquiry, investigation **2** SONDEO : survey

encuestador, -dora *n* : pollster

encuestar *vt* : to poll, to take a survey of

encumbrado, -da *adj* **1** : lofty, high **2** : eminent, distinguished

encumbrar *vt* **1** : to exalt, to elevate **2** : to extol — **encumbrarse** *vr* : to reach the top

encurtir *vt* ESCABECHAR : to pickle

ende *adv* **por ~** : therefore, consequently

endeble *adj* : feeble, weak

endeblez *nf* : weakness, frailty

endémico, -ca *adj* : endemic

endemoniado, -da *adj* : fiendish, diabolical

endentecer {53} *vi* : to teethe

enderezar {21} *vt* **1** : to straighten (out) **2** : to stand on end, to put upright

endeudado, -da *adj* : in debt, indebted

endeudamiento *nm* : indebtedness

endeudarse *vr* **1** : to go into debt **2** : to feel obliged

endiabladamente *adv* : extremely, diabolically

endiablado, -da *adj* **1** : devilish, diabolical **2** : complicated, difficult

endibia *or* **endivia** *nf* : endive

endilgar {52} *vt fam* : to spring, to foist ⟨me endilgó la responsabilidad : he saddled me with the responsibility⟩

endocrino, -na *adj* : endocrine

endogamia *nf* : inbreeding

endosar *vt* : to endorse

endoso *nm* : endorsement

endulzante *nm* : sweetener

endulzar {21} *vt* **1** : to sweeten **2** : to soften, to mellow — **endulzarse** *vr*

endurecer {53} *vt* : to harden, to toughen — **endurecerse** *vr*

enebro *nm* : juniper

eneldo *nm* : dill

enema *nm* : enema

enemigo, -ga *adj & n* : enemy

enemistad *nf* : enmity, hostility

enemistar *vt* : to make enemies of — **enemistarse** *vr* **~ con** : to fall out with

energía *nf* : energy

enérgico, -ca *adj* **1** : energetic, vigorous **2** : forceful, emphatic — **enérgicamente** *adv*

energúmeno, -na *n fam* : lunatic, crazy person

enero *nm* : January

enervar *vt* **1** : to enervate **2** *fam* : to annoy, to get on one's nerves — **enervante** *adj*

enésimo, -ma *adj* : umpteenth, nth

enfadar *vt* **1** : to annoy, to make angry **2** *Mex fam* : to bore — **enfadarse** *vr* : to get angry, to get annoyed

enfado *nm* : anger, annoyance
enfadoso, -sa *adj* : irritating, annoying
enfardar *vt* : to bale
énfasis *nms & pl* : emphasis
enfático, -ca *adj* : emphatic — **enfáticamente** *adv*
enfatizar {21} *vt* DESTACAR, SUBRAYAR : to emphasize
enfermar *vt* : to make sick — *vi* : to fall ill, to get sick — **enfermarse** *vr*
enfermedad *nf* 1 INDISPOSICIÓN : sickness, illness 2 : disease
enfermería *nf* : infirmary
enfermero, -ra *n* : nurse
enfermizo, -za *adj* : sickly
enfermo[1], -ma *adj* : sick, ill
enfermo[2], -ma *n* 1 : sick person, invalid 2 PACIENTE : patient
enfilar *vt* 1 : to take, to go along ⟨enfiló la carretera de Montevideo : she went up the road to Montevideo⟩ 2 : to line up, to put in a row 3 : to string, to thread 4 : to aim, to direct — *vi* : to make one's way
enflaquecer {53} *vi* : to lose weight, to become thin — *vt* : to emaciate
enfocar {72} *vt* 1 : to focus (on) 2 : to consider, to look at
enfoque *nm* : focus
enfrascamiento *nm* : immersion, absorption
enfrascarse {72} *vr* ~ **en** : to immerse oneself in, to get caught up in
enfrentamiento *nm* : clash, confrontation
enfrentar *vt* : to confront, to face — **enfrentarse** *vr* 1 ~ **con** : to clash with 2 ~ **a** : to face up to
enfrente *adv* 1 DELANTE : in front 2 : opposite
enfriamiento *nm* 1 CATARRO : chill, cold 2 : cooling off, damper
enfriar {85} *vt* 1 : to chill, to cool 2 : to cool down, to dampen — *vi* : to get cold — **enfriarse** *vr* : to get chilled, to catch a cold
enfundar *vt* : to sheathe, to encase
enfurecer {53} *vt* ENCOLERIZAR : to infuriate — **enfurecerse** *vr* : to fly into a rage
enfurecido, -da *adj* : furious, raging
enfurruñarse *vr fam* : to sulk
engalanar *vt* : to decorate, to deck out — **engalanarse** *vr* : to dress up
enganchar *vt* : to hook, to snag 2 : to attach, to hitch up — **engancharse** *vr* 1 : to get snagged, to get hooked 2 : to enlist
enganche *nm* 1 : hook 2 : coupling, hitch 3 *Mex* : down payment
engañar *vt* 1 EMBAUCAR : to trick, to deceive, to mislead 2 : to cheat on, to be unfaithful to — **engañarse** *vr* 1 : to be mistaken 2 : to deceive oneself
engaño *nm* 1 : deception, trick 2 : fake, feint (in sports)
engañoso, -sa *adj* 1 : deceitful 2 : misleading, deceptive

engarrotarse *vr* : to stiffen up, to go numb
engatusamiento *nm* : cajolery
engatusar *vt* : to coax, to cajole
engendrar *vt* 1 : to beget, to father 2 : to give rise to, to engender
engentarse *vr Mex* : to be in a daze
englobar *vt* : to include, to embrace
engomar *vt* : to glue
engordar *vt* : to fatten, to fatten up — *vi* : to gain weight
engorro *nm* : nuisance, bother
engorroso, -sa *adj* : bothersome
engranaje *nm* : gears *pl*, cogs *pl*
engranar *vt* : to mesh, to engage — *vi* : to mesh gears
engrandecer {53} *vt* 1 : to enlarge 2 : to exaggerate 3 : to exalt
engrandecimiento *nm* 1 : enlargement 2 : exaggeration 3 : exaltation
engrane *nm Mex* : cogwheel
engrapadora *nf* : stapler
engrapar *vt* : to staple
engrasar *vt* : to grease, to lubricate
engrase *nm* : greasing, lubrication
engreído, -da *adj* PRESUMIDO, VANIDOSO : vain, conceited, stuck-up
engreimiento *nm* ARROGANCIA : arrogance, conceit
engreír {66} *vt* ENVANECER : to make vain — **engreírse** *vr* : to become conceited
engrosar {19} *vt* : to enlarge, to increase, to swell — *vi* ENGORDAR : to gain weight
engrudo *nm* : paste
engullir {38} *vt* : to gulp down, to gobble up — **engullirse** *vr*
enharinar *vt* : to flour
enhebrar *vt* ENSARTAR : to string, to thread
enhiesto, -ta *adj* 1 : erect, upright 2 : lofty, towering
enhilar *vt* : to thread (a needle, etc.)
enhorabuena *nf* FELICIDADES : congratulations *pl*
enigma *nm* : enigma, mystery
enigmático, -ca *adj* : enigmatic — **enigmáticamente** *adv*
enjabonar *vt* : to soap up, to lather — **enjabonarse** *vr*
enjaezar {21} *vt* : to harness
enjalbegar {52} *vt* : to whitewash
enjambrar *vi* : to swarm
enjambre *nm* 1 : swarm 2 MUCHEDUMBRE : crowd, mob
enjaular *vt* 1 : to cage 2 *fam* : to jail, to lock up
enjuagar {52} *vt* : to rinse — **enjuagarse** *vr* : to rinse out
enjuague *nm* 1 : rinse 2 **enjuague bucal** : mouthwash
enjugar {52} *vt* : to wipe away (tears)
enjuiciar *vt* 1 : to indict, to prosecute 2 JUZGAR : to try
enjundioso, -sa *adj* : substantial, weighty
enjuto, -ta *adj* : lean, gaunt

enlace *nm* **1** : bond, link, connection **2** : liaison

enladrillado *nm* : brick paving

enladrillar *vt* : to pave with bricks

enlatar *vt* ENVASAR : to can

enlazar {21} *v* : to join, to link, to fit together

enlistar *vt* : to list — **enlistarse** *vr* : to enlist

enlodado, -da *adj* BARROSO : muddy

enlodar *vt* **1** : to cover with mud **2** : to stain, to sully — **enlodarse** *vr*

enlodazar → enlodar

enloquecedor, -dora *adj* : maddening

enloquecer {53} *vt* ALOCAR : to drive crazy — **enloquecerse** *vr* : to go crazy

enlosado *nm* : flagstone pavement

enlosar *vt* : to pave with flagstone

enlutarse *vr* : to go into mourning

enmaderado *nm* **1** : wood paneling **2** : hardwood floor

enmarañar *vt* **1** : to tangle **2** : to complicate **3** : to confuse, to mix up — **enmarañarse** *vr*

enmarcar {72} *vt* **1** ENCUADRAR : to frame **2** : to provide the setting for

enmascarar *vt* : to mask, to disguise

enmasillar *vt* : to putty, to caulk

enmendar {55} *vt* **1** : to amend **2** CORREGIR : to emend, to correct **3** COMPENSAR : to compensate for — **enmendarse** *vr* : to mend one's ways

enmienda *nf* **1** : amendment **2** : correction, emendation

enmohecerse {53} *vr* **1** : to become moldy **2** OXIDARSE : to rust, to become rusty

enmudecer {53} *vt* : to mute, to silence — *vi* : to fall silent

enmugrar *vt* : to soil, to make dirty — **enmugrarse** *vr* : to get dirty

ennegrecer {53} *vt* : to blacken, to darken — **ennegrecerse** *vr*

ennoblecer {53} *vt* **1** : to ennoble **2** : to embellish

enojadizo, -za *adj* IRRITABLE : irritable, cranky

enojado, -da *adj* **1** : annoyed **2** : angry, mad

enojar *vt* **1** : to anger **2** : to annoy, to upset — **enojarse** *vr*

enojo *nm* **1** CÓLERA : anger **2** : annoyance

enojón, -jona *adj, pl* **-jones** *Chile, Mex fam* : irritable, cranky

enojoso, -sa *adj* FASTIDIOSO, MOLESTOSO : annoying, irritating

enorgullecer {53} *vt* : to make proud — **enorgullecerse** *vr* : to pride oneself

enorme *adj* INMENSO : enormous, huge — **enormemente** *adv*

enormidad *nf* **1** : enormity, seriousness **2** : immensity, hugeness

enraizado, -da *adj* : deep-seated, deeply rooted

enraizar {30} *vi* : to take root

enramada *nf* : arbor, bower

enramar *vt* : to cover with branches

enrarecer {53} *vt* : to rarefy — **enrarecerse** *vr*

enredadera *nf* : climbing plant, vine

enredar *vt* **1** : to tangle up, to entangle **2** : to confuse, to complicate **3** : to involve, to implicate — **enredarse** *vr*

enredo *nm* **1** EMBROLLO : muddle, confusion **2** MARAÑA : tangle

enredoso, -sa *adj* : complicated, tricky

enrejado *nm* **1** : railing **2** : grating, grille **3** : trellis, lattice

enrevesado, -da *adj* : complicated, involved

enriquecer {53} *vt* : to enrich — **enriquecerse** *vr* : to get rich

enriquecido, -da *adj* : enriched

enriquecimiento *nm* : enrichment

enrojecer {53} *vt* : to make red, to redden — **enrojecerse** *vr* : to blush

enrolar *vt* RECLUTAR : to recruit — **enrolarse** *vr* INSCRIBIRSE : to enlist, to sign up

enrollar *vt* : to roll up, to coil — **enrollarse** *vr*

enronquecerse {53} *vr* : to become hoarse

enroscar {72} *vt* TORCER : to twist — **enroscarse** *vr* : to coil, to twine

ensacar {72} *vt* : to bag (up)

ensalada *nf* : salad

ensaladera *nf* : salad bowl

ensalmo *nm* : incantation, spell

ensalzar {21} *vt* **1** : to praise, to extol **2** EXALTAR : to exalt

ensamblaje *nm* : assembly

ensamblar *vt* **1** : to assemble **2** : to join, to fit together

ensanchar *vt* **1** : to widen **2** : to expand, to extend — **ensancharse** *vr*

ensanche *nm* **1** : widening **2** : expansion, development

ensangrentado, -da *adj* : bloody, bloodstained

ensañarse *vr* : to act cruelly, to be merciless

ensartar *vt* **1** ENHEBRAR : to string, to thread **2** : to skewer, to pierce

ensayar *vi* : to rehearse — *vt* **1** : to try out, to test **2** : to assay

ensayista *nmf* : essayist

ensayo *nm* **1** : essay **2** : trial, test **3** : rehearsal **4** : assay (of metals)

enseguida *adv* INMEDIATAMENTE : right away, immediately, at once

ensenada *nf* : cove, inlet

enseña *nf* **1** INSIGNIA : emblem, insignia **2** : standard, banner

enseñanza *nf* **1** EDUCACIÓN : education **2** : teaching

enseñar *vt* **1** : to teach **2** MOSTRAR : to show, to display — **enseñarse** *vr* ~ **a** : to learn to, to get used to

enseres *nmpl* : equipment, furnishings *pl* ⟨enseres domésticos : household goods⟩

ensillar *vt* : to saddle (up)

ensimismado, -da *adj* : absorbed, engrossed

ensimismarse *vr* : to lose oneself in thought

ensoberbecerse {53} *vr* : to become haughty

ensombrecer {53} *vt* : to cast a shadow over, to darken — **ensombrecerse** *vr*

ensoñación *nf, pl* **-ciones** : fantasy

ensopar *vt* **1** : to drench **2** : to dunk, to dip

ensordecedor, -dora *adj* : deafening, thunderous

ensordecer {53} *vt* : to deafen — *vi* : to go deaf

ensuciar *vt* : to soil, to dirty — **ensuciarse** *vr*

ensueño *nm* **1** : daydream, revery **2** FANTASÍA : illusion, fantasy

entablar *vt* **1** : to cover with boards **2** : to initiate, to enter into, to start

entallar *vt* AJUSTAR : to tailor, to fit, to take in — *vi* QUEDAR : to fit

ente *nm* **1** : being, entity **2** : body, organization ⟨ente rector : ruling body⟩ **3** *fam* : eccentric, crackpot

enteco, -ca *adj* : gaunt, frail

entenado, -da *n Mex* : stepchild, stepson *m*, stepdaughter *f*

entender[1] {56} *vt* **1** COMPRENDER : to understand **2** OPINAR : to think, to believe **3** : to mean, to intend **4** DEDUCIR : to infer, to deduce — *vi* **1** : to understand ⟨¡ya entiendo! : now I understand!⟩ **2** ~ **de** : to know about, to be good at **3** ~ **en** : to be in charge of — **entenderse** *vr* **1** : to be understood **2** : to get along well, to understand each other **3** ~ **con** : to deal with

entender[2] *nm* **a mi entender** : in my opinion

entendible *adj* : understandable

entendido[1], **-da** *adj* **1** : skilled, expert **2 tener entendido** : to understand, to be under the impression ⟨teníamos entendido que vendrías : we were under the impression you would come⟩ **3 darse por entendido** : to go without saying

entendido[2] *nm* : expert, authority, connoisseur

entendimiento *nm* **1** : intellect, mind **2** : understanding, agreement

enterado, -da *adj* : aware, well-informed ⟨estar enterado de : to be privy to⟩

enteramente *adv* : entirely, completely

enterar *vt* INFORMAR : to inform — **enterarse** *vr* INFORMARSE : to find out, to learn

entereza *nf* **1** INTEGRIDAD : integrity **2** FORTALEZA : fortitude **3** FIRMEZA : resolve

enternecedor, -dora *adj* CONMOVEDOR : touching, moving

enternecer {53} *vt* CONMOVER : to move, to touch

entero[1], **-ra** *adj* **1** : entire, whole **2** : complete, absolute **3** : intact — **enteramente** *adv*

entero[2] *nm* **1** : integer, whole number **2** : point (in finance)

enterramiento *nm* : burial

enterrar {55} *vt* : to bury

entibiar *vt* : to cool (down) — **entibiarse** *vr* : to become lukewarm

entidad *nf* **1** ENTE : entity **2** : body, organization **3** : firm, company **4** : importance, significance

entierro *nm* **1** : burial **2** : funeral

entintar *vt* : to ink

entoldado *nm* : awning

entomología *nf* : entomology

entomólogo, -ga *n* : entomologist

entonación *nf, pl* **-ciones** : intonation

entonar *vi* : to be in tune — *vt* **1** : to intone **2** : to tone up

entonces *adv* **1** : then **2 desde** ~ : since then **3 en aquel entonces** : in those days

entornado, -da *adj* ENTREABIERTO : half-closed, ajar

entornar *vt* ENTREABRIR : to leave ajar

entorno *nm* : surroundings *pl*, environment

entorpecer {53} *vt* **1** : to hinder, to obstruct **2** : to dull — **entorpecerse** *vr* : to dull the senses

entrada *nf* **1** : entrance, entry **2** : ticket, admission **3** : beginning, onset **4** : entrée **5** : cue (in music) **6 entradas** *nfpl* : income ⟨entradas y salidas : income and expenditures⟩ **7 tener entradas** : to have a receding hairline

entrado, -da *adj* **entrado en años** : elderly

entramado *nm* : framework

entrampar *vt* **1** ATRAPAR : to entrap, to ensnare **2** ENGAÑAR : to deceive, to trick

entrante *adj* **1** : next, upcoming ⟨el año entrante : next year⟩ **2** : incoming, new ⟨el presidente entrante : the president elect⟩

entraña *nf* **1** MEOLLO : core, heart, crux **2 entrañas** *nfpl* VÍSCERAS : entrails

entrañable *adj* : close, intimate

entrañar *vt* : to entail, to involve

entrar *vi* **1** : to enter, to go in, to come in **2** : to begin — *vt* **1** : to bring in, to introduce **2** : to access

entre *prep* **1** : between **2** : among

entreabierto[1] *pp* → entreabrir

entreabierto[2], **-ta** *adj* ENTORNADO : half-open, ajar

entreabrir {2} *vt* ENTORNAR : to leave ajar

entreacto *nm* : intermission, interval

entrecano, -na *adj* : grayish, graying

entrecejo *nm* **fruncir el entrecejo** : to knit one's brows

entrecomillar *vt* : to place in quotation marks

entrecortado, -da *adj* **1** : labored, difficult ⟨respiración entrecortada : shortness of breath⟩ **2** : faltering, hesitant ⟨con la voz entrecortada : with a catch in his voice⟩

entrecruzar {21} *vt* ENTRELAZAR : to interweave, to intertwine — **entrecruzarse** *vr*
entredicho *nm* **1** DUDA : doubt, question **2** : prohibition
entrega *nf* **1** : delivery **2** : handing over, surrender **3** : installment ⟨entrega inicial : down payment⟩
entregar {52} *vt* **1** : to deliver **2** DAR : to give, to present **3** : to hand in, to hand over — **entregarse** *vr* **1** : to surrender, to give in **2** : to devote oneself
entrelazar {21} *vt* ENTRECRUZAR : to interweave, to intertwine
entremedias *adv* **1** : in between, halfway **2** : in the meantime
entremés *nm, pl* **-meses** **1** APERITIVO : appetizer, hors d'oeuvre **2** : interlude, short play
entremeterse → **entrometerse**
entremetido *nm* → **entrometido**
entremezclar *vt* : to intermingle
entrenador, -dora *n* : trainer, coach
entrenamiento *nm* : training, drill, practice
entrenar *vt* : to train, to drill, to practice — **entrenarse** *vr* : to train, to spar (in boxing)
entreoír {50} *vt* : to hear indistinctly
entrepierna *nf* **1** : inner thigh **2** : crotch **3** : inseam
entrepiso *nm* ENTRESUELO : mezzanine
entresacar {72} *vt* **1** SELECCIONAR : to pick out, to select **2** : to thin out
entresuelo *nm* ENTREPISO : mezzanine
entretanto[1] *adv* : meanwhile
entretanto[2] *nm* **en el entretanto** : in the meantime
entretejer *vt* : to interweave
entretela *nf* : facing (of a garment)
entretener {80} *vt* **1** DIVERTIR : to entertain, to amuse **2** DISTRAER : to distract **3** DEMORAR : to delay, to hold up — **entretenerse** *vr* **1** : to amuse oneself **2** : to dally
entretenido, -da *adj* DIVERTIDO : entertaining, amusing
entretenimiento *nm* **1** : entertainment, pastime **2** DIVERSIÓN : fun, amusement
entrever {88} *vt* **1** : to catch a glimpse of **2** : to make out, to see indistinctly
entreverar *vt* : to mix, to intermingle
entrevero *nm* : confusion, disorder
entrevista *nf* : interview
entrevistador, -dora *n* : interviewer
entrevistar *vt* : to interview — **entrevistarse** *vr* REUNIRSE ~ **con** : to meet with
entristecer {53} *vt* : to sadden
entrometerse *vr* : to interfere, to meddle
entrometido, -da *n* : meddler, busybody
entroncar {72} *vt* RELACIONAR : to establish a relationship between, to connect — *vi* **1** : to be related **2** : to link up, to be connected
entronque *nm* **1** : kinship **2** VÍNCULO : link, connection

entuerto *nm* : wrong, injustice
entumecer {53} *vt* : to make numb, to be numb — **entumecerse** *vr* : to go numb, to fall asleep
entumecido, -da *adj* **1** : numb **2** : stiff (of muscles, joints, etc.)
entumecimiento *nm* : numbness
enturbiar *vt* **1** : to cloud **2** : to confuse — **enturbiarse** *vr*
entusiasmar *vt* : to excite, to fill with enthusiasm — **entusiasmarse** *vr* : to get excited
entusiasmo *nm* : enthusiasm
entusiasta[1] *adj* : enthusiastic
entusiasta[2] *nmf* AFICIONADO : enthusiast
enumerar *vt* : to enumerate — **enumeración** *nf*
enunciación *nf, pl* **-ciones** : enunciation, statement
enunciar *vt* : to enunciate, to state
envainar *vt* : to sheathe
envalentonar *vt* : to make bold, to encourage — **envalentonarse** *vr*
envanecer {53} *vt* ENGREÍR : to make vain — **envanecerse** *vr*
envasar *vt* **1** EMBOTELLAR : to bottle **2** ENLATAR : to can **3** : to pack in a container
envase *nm* **1** : packaging, packing **2** : container **3** LATA : can **4** : empty bottle
envejecer {53} *vt* : to age, to make look old — *vi* : to age, to grow old
envejecido, -da *adj* : aged, old-looking
envejecimiento *nm* : aging
envenenamiento *nm* : poisoning
envenenar *vt* **1** : to poison **2** : to embitter
envergadura *nf* **1** : span, breadth, spread **2** : importance, scope
envés *nm, pl* **enveses** : reverse, opposite side
enviado, -da *n* : envoy, correspondent
enviar {85} *vt* **1** : to send **2** : to ship
envidia *nf* : envy, jealousy
envidiar *vt* : to envy — **envidiable** *adj*
envidioso, -sa *adj* : envious, jealous
envilecer {53} *vt* : to degrade, to debase
envilecimiento *nm* : degradation, debasement
envío *nm* **1** : shipment **2** : remittance
enviudar *vi* : to be widowed, to become a widower
envoltorio *nm* **1** : bundle, package **2** : wrapping, wrapper
envoltura *nf* : wrapper, wrapping
envolver {89} *vt* **1** : to wrap **2** : to envelop, to surround **3** : to entangle, to involve — **envolverse** *vr* **1** : to become involved **2** : to wrap oneself (up)
envuelto *pp* → **envolver**
enyerbar *vt Mex* : to bewitch
enyesar *vt* **1** : to plaster **2** ESCAYOLAR : to put in a plaster cast
enzima *nf* : enzyme
éon *nm, pl* **eones** : aeon
eperlano *nm* : smelt (fish)

épico, -ca *adj* : epic
epicúreo¹, -rea *adj* : epicurean
epicúreo², -rea *n* : epicure
epidemia *nf* : epidemic
epidémico, -ca *adj* : epidemic
epidermis *nf* : epidermis
epifanía *nf* : feast of the Epiphany (January 6th)
epigrama *nm* : epigram
epilepsia *nf* : epilepsy
epiléptico, -ca *adj & n* : epileptic
epílogo *nm* : epilogue
episcopal *adj* : episcopal
episcopaliano, -na *adj & n* : Episcopalian
episódico, -ca *adj* : episodic
episodio *nm* : episode
epístola *nf* : epistle
epitafio *nm* : epitaph
epíteto *nm* : epithet, name
epítome *nm* : summary, abstract
época *nf* **1** EDAD, ERA, PERÍODO : epoch, age, period **2** : time of year, season **3 de ~** : vintage, antique
epopeya *nf* : epic poem
equidad *nf* JUSTICIA : equity, justice, fairness
equilátero, -ra *adj* : equilateral
equilibrado, -da *adj* : well-balanced
equilibrar *vt* : to balance — **equilibrarse** *vr*
equilibrio *nm* **1** : balance, equilibrium ⟨perder el equilibrio : to lose one's balance⟩ ⟨equilibrio político : balance of power⟩ **2** : poise, aplomb
equilibrista *nmf* ACRÓBATA, FUNÁMBULO : acrobat, tightrope walker
equino, -na *adj* : equine
equinoccio *nm* : equinox
equipaje *nm* BAGAJE : baggage, luggage
equipamiento *nm* : equipping, equipment
equipar *vt* : to equip — **equiparse** *vr*
equiparable *adj* : comparable
equiparar *vt* **1** IGUALAR : to put on a same level, to make equal **2** COMPARAR : to compare
equipo *nm* **1** : team, crew **2** : gear, equipment
equitación *nf, pl* **-ciones** : horseback riding, horsemanship
equitativo, -va *adj* JUSTO : equitable, fair, just — **equitativamente** *adv*
equivalencia *nf* : equivalence
equivalente *adj & nm* : equivalent
equivaler {84} *vi* : to be equivalent
equivocación *nf, pl* **-ciones** ERROR : error, mistake
equivocado, -da *adj* : mistaken, wrong — **equivocadamente** *adv*
equivocar {72} *vt* : to mistake, to confuse — **equivocarse** *vr* : to make a mistake, to be wrong
equívoco¹, -ca *adj* AMBIGUO : ambiguous, equivocal
equívoco² *nm* : misunderstanding
era¹, etc. → **ser**
era² *nf* EDAD, ÉPOCA : era, age

erario *nm* : public treasury
erección *nf, pl* **-ciones** : erection, raising
eremita *nmf* ERMITAÑO : hermit
ergonomía *nf* : ergonomics
erguido, -da *adj* : erect, upright
erguir {31} *vt* : to raise, to lift up — **erguirse** *vr* : to straighten up
erial *nm* : uncultivated land
erigir {35} *vt* : to build, to erect — **erigirse** *vr* **~ en** : to set oneself up as
erizado, -da *adj* : bristly
erizarse {21} *vr* : to bristle, to stand on end
erizo *nm* **1** : hedgehog **2 erizo de mar** : sea urchin
ermitaño¹, -ña *n* EREMITA : hermit, recluse
ermitaño² *nm* : hermit crab
erogación *nf, pl* **-ciones** : expenditure
erogar {52} *vt* **1** : to pay out **2** : to distribute
erosión *nf, pl* **-siones** : erosion
erosionar *vt* : to erode
erótico, -ca *adj* : erotic
erotismo *nm* : eroticism
errabundo, -da *adj* ERRANTE, VAGABUNDO : wandering
erradicar {72} *vt* : to eradicate — **erradicación** *nf*
errado, -da *adj* : wrong, mistaken
errante *adj* ERRABUNDO, VAGABUNDO : errant, wandering
errar {32} *vt* FALLAR : to miss — *vi* **1** DESACERTAR : to be wrong, to be mistaken **2** VAGAR : to wander
errata *nf* : misprint, error
errático, -ca *adj* : erratic — **erráticamente** *adv*
erróneo, -nea *adj* EQUIVOCADO : erroneous, wrong — **erróneamente** *adv*
error *nm* EQUIVOCACIÓN : error, mistake
eructar *vi* : to belch, to burp
eructo *nm* : belch, burp
erudición *nf, pl* **-ciones** : erudition, learning
erudito¹, -ta *adj* LETRADO : erudite, learned
erudito², -ta *n* : scholar
erupción *nf, pl* **-ciones** **1** : eruption **2** SARPULLIDO : rash
eruptivo, -va *adj* : eruptive
es → **ser**
esbelto, -ta *adj* DELGADO : slender, slim
esbirro *nm* : henchman
esbozar {21} *vt* BOSQUEJAR : to sketch, to outline
esbozo *nm* **1** : sketch **2** : rough draft
escabechar *vt* **1** ENCURTIR : to pickle **2** *fam* : to kill, to rub out
escabeche *nm* : brine (for pickling)
escabechina *nf* MASACRE : massacre, bloodbath
escabel *nm* : footstool
escabroso, -sa *adj* **1** : rugged, rough **2** : difficult, tough **3** : risqué
escabullirse {38} *vr* : to slip away, to escape

escala *nf* **1** : scale **2** ESCALERA : ladder **3** : stopover
escalada *nf* : ascent, climb
escalador, -dora *n* ALPINISTA : mountain climber
escalafón *nm, pl* **-fones 1** : list of personnel **2** : salary scale, rank
escalar *vt* : to climb, to scale — *vi* **1** : to go climbing **2** : to escalate
escaldar *vt* : to scald
escalera *nf* **1** : ladder ⟨escalera de tijera : stepladder⟩ **2** : stairs *pl*, staircase **3 escalera mecánica** : escalator
escalfador *nm* : chafing dish
escalfar *vt* : to poach (eggs)
escalinata *nf* : flight of stairs
escalofriante *adj* : horrifying, blood-curdling
escalofrío *nm* : shiver, chill, shudder
escalón *nm, pl* **-lones 1** : echelon **2** : step, rung
escalonado, -da *adj* GRADUAL : gradual, staggered
escalonar *vt* **1** : to terrace **2** : to stagger, to alternate
escalpelo *nm* BISTURÍ : scalpel
escama *nf* **1** : scale (of fish or reptiles) **2** : flake (of skin)
escamar *vt* **1** : to scale (fish) **2** : to make suspicious
escamocha *nf Mex* : fruit salad
escamoso, -sa *adj* : scaly
escamotear *vt* **1** : to palm, to conceal **2** *fam* : to lift, to swipe **3** : to hide, to cover up
escandalizar {21} *vt* : to shock, to scandalize — *vi* : to make a fuss — **escandalizarse** *vr* : to be shocked
escándalo *nm* **1** : scandal **2** : scene, commotion
escandaloso, -sa *adj* **1** : shocking, scandalous **2** RUIDOSO : noisy, rowdy **3** : flagrant, outrageous — **escandalosamente** *adv*
escandinavo, -va *adj & n* : Scandinavian
escandir *vt* : to scan (poetry)
escanear *vt* : to scan
escáner *nm* : scanner, scan
escaño *nm* **1** : seat (in a legislative body) **2** BANCO : bench
escapada *nf* HUIDA : flight, escape
escapar *vi* HUIR : to escape, to flee, to run away — **escaparse** *vr* : to escape notice, to leak out
escaparate *nm* **1** : shop window **2** : showcase
escapatoria *nf* **1** : loophole, excuse, pretext ⟨no tener escapatoria : to have no way out⟩ **2** ESCAPADA : escape, flight
escape *nm* **1** FUGA : escape **2** : exhaust (from a vehicle)
escapismo *nm* : escapism
escápula *nf* OMÓPLATO : scapula, shoulder blade
escapulario *nm* : scapular
escarabajo *nm* : beetle
escaramuza *nf* **1** : skirmish **2** : scrimmage

escaramuzar {21} *vi* : to skirmish
escarapela *nf* : rosette (ornament)
escarbar *vt* **1** : to dig, to scratch up **2** : to poke, to pick **3** ~ **en** : to investigate, to pry into
escarcha *nf* **1** : frost **2** *Mex, PRi* : glitter
escarchar *vt* **1** : to frost (a cake) **2** : to candy (fruit)
escardar *vt* **1** : to weed, to hoe **2** : to weed out
escariar *vt* : to ream
escarlata *adj & nf* : scarlet
escarlatina *nf* : scarlet fever
escarmentar {55} *vt* : to punish, to teach a lesson to — *vi* : to learn one's lesson
escarmiento *nm* **1** : lesson, warning **2** CASTIGO : punishment
escarnecer {53} *vt* RIDICULIZAR : to ridicule, to mock
escarnio *nm* : ridicule, mockery
escarola *nf* : escarole
escarpa *nf* : escarpment, steep slope
escarpado, -da *adj* : steep, sheer
escarpia *nf* : hook, spike
escasamente *adv* : scarcely, barely
escasear *vi* : to be scarce, to run short
escasez *nf, pl* **-seces** : shortage, scarcity
escaso, -sa *adj* **1** : scarce, scant **2** ~ **de** : short of
escatimar *vt* : to skimp on, to be sparing with ⟨no escatimar esfuerzos : to spare no effort⟩
escayola *nf* **1** : plaster (for casts) **2** : plaster cast
escayolar *vt* : to put in a plaster cast
escena *nf* **1** : scene **2** : stage
escenario *nm* **1** ESCENA : stage **2** : setting, scene ⟨el escenario del crimen : the scene of the crime⟩
escénico, -ca *adj* **1** : scenic **2** : stage
escenificar {72} *vt* : to stage, to dramatize
escepticismo *nm* : skepticism
escéptico[1], -ca *adj* : skeptical
escéptico[2], -ca *n* : skeptic
escindirse *vr* **1** : to split **2** : to break away
escisión *nf, pl* **-siones 1** : split, division **2** : excision
esclarecer {53} *vt* **1** ELUCIDAR : to elucidate, to clarify **2** ILUMINAR : to illuminate, to light up
esclarecimiento *nm* ELUCIDACIÓN : elucidation, clarification
esclavitud *nf* : slavery
esclavización *nf, pl* **-ciones** : enslavement
esclavizar {21} *vt* : to enslave
esclavo, -va *n* : slave
esclerosis *nf* **esclerosis múltiple** : multiple sclerosis
esclusa *nf* : floodgate, lock (of a canal)
escoba *nf* : broom
escobilla *nf* : small broom, brush, whisk broom
escobillón *nm, pl* **-llones** : swab

escocer {14} *vi* ARDER : to smart, to sting — **escocerse** *vr* : to be sore

escocés[1], -cesa *adj, mpl* -ceses 1 : Scottish 2 : tartan, plaid

escocés[2], -cesa *n, mpl* -ceses : Scottish person, Scot

escocés[3] *nm* 1 : Scots (language) 2 *pl* -ceses : Scotch (whiskey)

escofina *nf* : file, rasp

escoger {15} *vt* ELEGIR, SELECCIONAR : to choose, to select

escogido, -da *adj* : choice, select

escolar[1] *adj* : school

escolar[2] *nmf* : student, pupil

escolaridad *nf* : schooling ⟨escolaridad obligatoria : compulsory education⟩

escolarización *nf, pl* -ciones : education, schooling

escollo *nm* 1 : reef 2 OBSTÁCULO : obstacle

escolta *nmf* : escort

escoltar *vt* : to escort, to accompany

escombro *nm* 1 : debris, rubbish 2 escombros *nmpl* : ruins, rubble

esconder *vt* OCULTAR : to hide, to conceal

escondidas *nfpl* 1 : hide-and-seek 2 a ~ : secretly, in secret

escondimiento *nm* : concealment

escondite *nm* 1 ENCONDRIJO : hiding place 2 ESCONDIDAS : hide-and-seek

escondrijo *nm* ESCONDITE : hiding place

escopeta *nf* : shotgun

escoplear *vt* : to chisel (out)

escoplo *nm* : chisel

escora *nf* : list, heeling

escorar *vi* : to list, to heel (of a boat)

escorbuto *nm* : scurvy

escoria *nf* 1 : slag, dross 2 HEZ : dregs *pl*, scum ⟨la escoria de la sociedad : the dregs of society⟩

Escorpio *or* Escorpión *nmf* : Scorpio

escorpión *nm, pl* -piones ALACRÁN : scorpion

escote *nm* 1 : low neckline 2 pagar a escote : to go dutch

escotilla *nf* : hatch, hatchway

escotillón *nf, pl* -llones : trapdoor

escozor *nm* : smarting, stinging

escriba *nm* : scribe

escribano, -na *n* 1 : court clerk 2 NOTARIO : notary public

escribir {33} *v* 1 : to write 2 : to spell — escribirse *vr* CARTEARSE : to write to one another, to correspond

escrito[1] *pp* → escribir

escrito[2], -ta *adj* : written

escrito[3] *nm* 1 : written document 2 escritos *nmpl* : writings, works

escritor, -tora *n* : writer

escritorio *nm* : desk

escritorzuelo, -la *n* : hack (writer)

escritura *nf* 1 : writing, handwriting 2 : deed 3 las Escrituras : the Scriptures

escroto *nm* : scrotum

escrúpulo *nm* : scruple

escrupuloso, -sa *adj* 1 : scrupulous 2 METICULOSO : exact, meticulous — escrupulosamente *adv*

escrutador, -dora *adj* : penetrating, searching

escrutar *vt* ESCUDRIÑAR : to scrutinize, to examine closely

escrutinio *nm* : scrutiny

escuadra *nf* 1 : square (instrument) 2 : fleet, squadron

escuadrilla *nf* : squadron, formation, flight

escuadrón *nm, pl* -drones : squadron

escuálido, -da *adj* 1 : skinny, scrawny 2 INMUNDO : filthy, squalid

escuchar *vt* 1 : to listen to 2 : to hear — *vi* : to listen — escucharse *vr*

escudar *vt* : to shield — escudarse *vr* ~ en : to hide behind

escudero *nm* : squire

escudo *nm* 1 : shield 2 escudo de armas : coat of arms

escudriñar *vt* 1 ESCRUTAR : to scrutinize 2 : to inquire into, to investigate

escuela *nf* : school

escueto, -ta *adj* 1 : plain, simple 2 : succinct, concise — escuetamente *adv*

escuincle, -cla *n Mex fam* : child, kid

esculcar {72} *vt* : to search

esculpir *vt* 1 : to sculpt 2 : to carve, to engrave — *vi* : to sculpt

escultor, -tora *n* : sculptor

escultórico, -ca *adj* : sculptural

escultura *nf* : sculpture

escultural *adj* : statuesque

escupidera *nf* : spittoon, cuspidor

escupir *v* : to spit

escupitajo *nm* : spit

escurridizo, -za *adj* : slippery, elusive

escurridor *nm* 1 : dish rack 2 : colander

escurrir *vt* 1 : to wring out 2 : to drain — *vi* 1 : to drain 2 : to drip, to drip-dry — escurrirse *vr* : to slip away

ese, esa *adj, mpl* esos : that, those

ése, ésa *pron, mpl* ésos : that one, those ones *pl*

esencia *nf* : essence

esencial *adj* : essential — esencialmente *adv*

esfera *nf* 1 : sphere 2 : face, dial (of a watch)

esférico[1], -ca *adj* : spherical

esférico[2] *nm* : ball (in sports)

esfinge *nf* : sphinx

esforzado, -da *adj* 1 : energetic, vigorous 2 VALIENTE : courageous, brave

esforzar {36} *vt* : to strain — esforzarse *vr* : to make an effort

esfuerzo *nm* 1 : effort 2 ÁNIMO, VIGOR : spirit, vigor 3 sin ~ : effortlessly

esfumar *vt* : to tone down, to soften — esfumarse *vr* 1 : to fade away, to vanish 2 *fam* : to take off, to leave

esgrima *nf* : fencing (sport)

esgrimidor, -dora *n* : fencer

esgrimir *vt* 1 : to brandish, to wield 2 : to use, to resort to — *vi* : to fence

esguince *nm* : sprain, strain (of a muscle)

eslabón *nm, pl* **-bones** : link

eslabonar *vt* : to link, to connect, to join

eslavo[1], **-va** *adj* : Slavic

eslavo[2], **-va** *n* : Slav

eslogan *nm, pl* **-lóganes** : slogan

eslovaco, -ca *adj & n* : Slovakian, Slovak

esloveno, -na *adj & nm* : Slovene, Slovenian

esmaltar *vt* : to enamel

esmalte *nm* **1** : enamel **2 esmalte de uñas** : nail polish

esmerado, -da *adj* : careful, painstaking

esmeralda *nf* : emerald

esmerarse *vr* : to take great pains, to do one's utmost

esmeril *nm* : emery

esmero *nm* : meticulousness, great care

esmoquin *nm, pl* **-quins** : tuxedo

esnob[1] *adj, pl* **esnobs** : snobbish

esnob[2] *nmf, pl* **esnobs** : snob

esnobismo *nm* : snobbery, snobbishness

eso *pron (neuter)* **1** : that ⟨eso no me gusta : I don't like that⟩ **2 ¡eso es!** : that's it!, that's right! **3 a eso de** : around ⟨a eso de las tres : around three o'clock⟩ **4 en ～** : at that point, just then

esófago *nm* : esophagus

esos → **ese**

ésos → **ése**

esotérico, -ca *adj* : esoteric — **esotéricamente** *adv*

espabilado, -da *adj* : bright, smart

espabilarse *vr* **1** : to awaken **2** : to get a move on **3** : to get smart, to wise up

espacial *adj* **1** : space **2** : spatial

espaciar *vt* DISTANCIAR : to space out, to spread out

espacio *nm* **1** : space, room **2** : period, length (of time) **3 espacio exterior** : outer space

espacioso, -sa *adj* : spacious, roomy

espada[1] *nf* **1** : sword **2 espadas** *nfpl* : spades (in playing cards)

espada[2] *nm* MATADOR, TORERO : bullfighter, matador

espadaña *nf* **1** : belfry **2** : cattail

espadilla *nf* : scull, oar

espagueti *nm or* **espaguetis** *nmpl* : spaghetti

espalda *nf* **1** : back **2 espaldas** *nfpl* : shoulders, back **3 por la espalda** : from behind

espaldarazo *nm* **1** : recognition, support **2** : slap on the back

espaldera *nf* : trellis

espantajo *nm* : scarecrow

espantapájaros *nms & pl* : scarecrow

espantar *vt* ASUSTAR : to scare, to frighten — **espantarse** *vr*

espanto *nm* : fright, fear, horror

espantoso, -sa *adj* **1** : frightening, terrifying **2** : frightful, dreadful

español[1], **-ñola** *adj* : Spanish

español[2], **-ñola** *n* : Spaniard

español[3] *nm* CASTELLANO : Spanish (language)

esparadrapo *nm* : adhesive bandage, Band-Aid™

esparcimiento *nm* **1** DIVERSIÓN, RECREO : entertainment, recreation **2** DESCANSO : relaxation **3** DISEMINACIÓN : dissemination, spreading

esparcir {83} *vt* DISPERSAR : to scatter, to spread — **esparcirse** *vr* **1** : to spread out **2** DESCANSARSE : to take it easy **3** DIVERTIRSE : to amuse oneself

espárrago *nm* : asparagus

espartano, -na *adj* : severe, austere

espasmo *nm* : spasm

espasmódico, -ca *adj* : spasmodic

espástico, -ca *adj* : spastic

espátula *nf* : spatula

especia *nf* : spice

especial *adj & nm* : special

especialidad *nf* : specialty

especialista *nmf* : specialist, expert

especialización *nf, pl* **-ciones** : specialization

especializarse {21} *vr* : to specialize

especialmente *adv* : especially, particularly

especie *nf* **1** : species **2** CLASE, TIPO : type, kind, sort

especificación *nf, pl* **-ciones** : specification

especificar {72} *vt* : to specify

específico, -ca *adj* : specific — **específicamente** *adv*

espécimen *nm, pl* **especímenes** : specimen

especioso, -sa *adj* : specious

espectacular *adj* : spectacular — **espectacularmente** *adv*

espectáculo *nm* **1** : spectacle, sight **2** : show, performance

espectador, -dora *n* : spectator, onlooker

espectro *nm* **1** : ghost, specter **2** : spectrum

especulación *nf, pl* **-ciones** : speculation

especulador, -dora *n* : speculator

especular *vi* : to speculate

especulativo, -va *adj* : speculative

espejismo *nm* **1** : mirage **2** : illusion

espejo *nm* : mirror

espejuelos *nmpl* ANTEOJOS : spectacles, glasses

espeluznante *adj* : hair-raising, terrifying

espera *nf* : wait

esperado, -da *adj* : anticipated

esperanza *nf* : hope, expectation

esperanzado, -da *adj* : hopeful

esperanzador, -dora *adj* : encouraging, promising

esperanzar {21} *vt* : to give hope to

esperar *vt* **1** AGUARDAR : to wait for, to await **2** : to expect **3** : to hope ⟨espero poder trabajar : I hope to be able to work⟩ ⟨espero que sí : I hope so⟩ — *vi*

: to wait — **esperarse** *vr* **1** : to expect, to be hoped ⟨como podría esperarse : as would be expected⟩ **2** : to hold on, to hang on ⟨espérate un momento : hold on a minute⟩
esperma *nmf* : sperm
esperpéntico, -ca *adj* GROTESCO : grotesque
esperpento *nm fam* MAMARRACHO : sight, fright ⟨voy hecha un esperpento : I really look a sight⟩
espesante *nm* : thickener
espesar *vt* : to thicken — **espesarse** *vr*
espeso, -sa *adj* : thick, heavy, dense
espesor *nm* : thickness, density
espesura *nf* **1** : thickness **2** : thicket
espetar *vt* **1** : to blurt out **2** : to skewer
espía *nmf* : spy
espiar {85} *vt* : to spy on, to observe — *vi* : to spy
espiga *nf* **1** : ear (of wheat) **2** : spike (of flowers)
espigado, -da *adj* : willowy, slender
espigar {52} *vt* : to glean, to gather — **espigarse** *vr* : to grow quickly, to shoot up
espigón *nm, pl* **-gones** : breakwater
espina *nf* **1** : thorn **2** : spine ⟨espina dorsal : spinal column⟩ **3** : fish bone
espinaca *nf* **1** : spinach (plant) **2 espinacas** *nfpl* : spinach (food)
espinal *adj* : spinal
espinazo *nm* : backbone
espineta *nf* : spinet
espinilla *nf* **1** BARRO, GRANO : pimple **2** : shin
espino *nm* : hawthorn
espinoso, -sa *adj* **1** : thorny, prickly **2** : bony (of fish) **3** : knotty, difficult
espionaje *nm* : espionage
espiración *nf, pl* **-ciones** : exhalation
espiral *adj & nf* : spiral
espirar *vt* EXHALAR : to breathe out, to give off — *vi* : to exhale
espiritismo *nm* : spiritualism
espiritista *nmf* : spiritualist
espíritu *nm* **1** : spirit **2** ÁNIMO : state of mind, spirits *pl* **3 el Espíritu Santo** : the Holy Ghost
espiritual *adj* : spiritual — **espiritualmente** *adv*
espiritualidad *nf* : spirituality
espita *nf* : spigot, tap
esplendidez *nf, pl* **-deces** ESPLENDOR : magnificence, splendor
espléndido, -da *adj* **1** : splendid, magnificent **2** : generous, lavish — **espléndidamente** *adv*
esplendor *nm* ESPLENDIDEZ : splendor
esplendoroso, -sa *adj* MAGNÍFICO : magnificent, grand
espliego *nm* LAVANDA : lavender
espolear *vt* : to spur on
espoleta *nf* **1** DETONADOR : detonator, fuse **2** : wishbone
espolón *nm, pl* **-lones** : spur (of poultry), fetlock (of a horse)

espolvorear *vt* : to sprinkle, to dust
esponja *nf* **1** : sponge **2 tirar la esponja** : to throw in the towel
esponjado, -da *adj* : spongy
esponjoso, -sa *adj* **1** : spongy **2** : soft, fluffy
esponsales *nmpl* : betrothal, engagement
espontaneidad *nf* : spontaneity
espontáneo, -nea *adj* : spontaneous — **espontáneamente** *adv*
espora *nf* : spore
esporádico, -ca *adj* : sporadic — **esporádicamente** *adv*
esposar *vt* : to handcuff
esposas *nfpl* : handcuffs
esposo, -sa *n* : spouse, wife *f*, husband *m*
esprint *nm* : sprint
esprintar *vi* : to sprint
esprínter *nmf* : sprinter
espuela *nf* : spur
espuerta *nf* : two-handled basket
espulgar {52} *vt* **1** : to delouse **2** : to scrutinize
espuma *nf* **1** : foam **2** : lather **3** : froth, head (on beer)
espumar *vi* : to foam, to froth — *vt* : to skim off
espumoso, -sa *adj* : foamy, frothy
espurio, -ria *adj* : spurious
esputar *v* : to expectorate, to spit
esputo *nm* : spit, sputum
esqueje *nm* : cutting (from a plant)
esquela *nf* **1** : note **2** : notice, announcement
esquelético, -ca *adj* : emaciated, skeletal
esqueleto *nm* **1** : skeleton **2** ARMAZÓN : framework
esquema *nf* BOSQUEJO : outline, sketch, plan
esquemático, -ca *adj* : schematic
esquí *nm* **1** : ski **2 esquí acuático** : water ski, waterskiing
esquiador, -dora *n* : skier
esquiar {85} *vi* : to ski
esquife *nm* : skiff
esquila *nf* **1** CENCERRO : cowbell **2** : shearing
esquilar *vt* TRASQUILAR : to shear
esquimal *adj & nmf* : Eskimo
esquina *nf* : corner
esquinazo *nm* **1** : corner **2 dar esquinazo a** *fam* : to stand up, to give the slip to
esquirla *nf* : splinter (of bone, glass, etc.)
esquirol *nm* ROMPEHUELGAS : strikebreaker, scab
esquisto *nm* : shale
esquivar *vt* **1** EVADIR : to dodge, to evade **2** EVITAR : to avoid
esquivez *nf, pl* **-veces** **1** : aloofness **2** TIMIDEZ : shyness
esquivo, -va *adj* **1** HURAÑO : aloof, unsociable **2** : shy **3** : elusive, evasive
esquizofrenia *nf* : schizophrenia
esquizofrénico, -ca *adj & n* : schizophrenic

esta *adj* → **este**[1]
ésta → **éste**
estabilidad *nf* : stability
estabilización *nf, pl* **-ciones** : stabilization
estabilizador *nm* : stabilizer
estabilizar {21} *vt* : to stabilize — **estabilizarse** *vr*
estable *adj* : stable, steady
establecer {53} *vt* FUNDAR, INSTITUIR : to establish, to found, to set up — **establecerse** *vr* INSTALARSE : to settle, to establish oneself
establecimiento *nm* **1** : establishing **2** : establishment, institution, office
establo *nm* : stable
estaca *nf* : stake, picket, post
estacada *nf* **1** : picket fence **2** : stockade
estacar {72} *vt* **1** : to stake out **2** : to fasten down with stakes — **estacarse** *vr* : to remain rigid
estación *nf, pl* **-ciones** **1** : station ⟨estación de servicio : service station, gas station⟩ **2** : season
estacional *adj* : seasonal
estacionamiento *nm* **1** : parking **2** : parking lot
estacionar *vt* **1** : to place, to station **2** : to park — **estacionarse** *vr* **1** : to park **2** : to remain stationary
estacionario, -ria *adj* **1** : stationary **2** : stable
estada *nf* : stay
estadía *nf* ESTANCIA : stay, sojourn
estadio *nm* **1** : stadium **2** : phase, stage
estadista *nmf* : statesman
estadística *nf* **1** : statistic, figure **2** : statistics
estadístico[1], **-ca** *adj* : statistical — **estadísticamente** *adv*
estadístico[2], **-ca** *n* : statistician
estado *nm* **1** : state **2** : status ⟨estado civil : marital status⟩ **3** CONDICIÓN : condition
estadounidense *adj & nmf* AMERICANO, NORTEAMERICANO : American
estafa *nf* : swindle, fraud
estafador, -dora *n* : cheat, swindler
estafar *vt* DEFRAUDAR : to swindle, to defraud
estalactita *nf* : stalactite
estalagmita *nf* : stalagmite
estallar *vi* **1** REVENTAR : to burst, to explode, to erupt **2** : to break out
estallido *nm* **1** EXPLOSIÓN : explosion **2** : report (of a gun) **3** : outbreak, outburst
estambre *nm* **1** : worsted (fabric) **2** : stamen
estampa *nf* **1** ILUSTRACIÓN, IMAGEN : printed image, illustration **2** ASPECTO : appearance, demeanor
estampado[1], **-da** *adj* : patterned, printed
estampado[2] *nm* : print, pattern
estampar *vt* : to stamp, to print, to engrave

estampida *nf* : stampede
estampilla *nf* **1** : rubber stamp **2** SELLO, TIMBRE : postage stamp
estancado, -da *adj* : stagnant
estancamiento *nm* : stagnation
estancar {72} *vt* **1** : to dam up, to hold back **2** : to bring to a halt, to deadlock — **estancarse** *vr* **1** : to stagnate **2** : to be brought to a standstill, to be deadlocked
estancia *nf* **1** ESTADÍA : stay, sojourn **2** : ranch, farm
estanciero, -ra *n* : rancher, farmer
estanco, -ca *adj* : watertight
estándar *adj & nm* : standard
estandarización *nf, pl* **-ciones** : standardization
estandarizar {21} *vt* : to standardize
estandarte *nm* : standard, banner
estanque *nm* **1** : pool, pond **2** : tank, reservoir
estante *nm* REPISA : shelf
estantería *nf* : shelves *pl*, bookcase
estaño *nm* : tin
estaquilla *nf* **1** : peg **2** ESPIGA : spike
estar {34} *v aux* : to be ⟨estoy aprendiendo inglés : I'm learning English⟩ ⟨está terminado : it's finished⟩ — *vi* **1** (*indicating a state or condition*) : to be ⟨está muy alto : he's so tall, he's gotten very tall⟩ ⟨¿ya estás mejor? : are you feeling better now?⟩ ⟨estoy casado : I'm married⟩ **2** (*indicating location*) : to be ⟨están en la mesa : they're on the table⟩ ⟨estamos en la página 2 : we're on page 2⟩ **3** : to be at home ⟨¿está Maria? : is Maria in?⟩ **4** : to remain ⟨estaré aquí 5 días : I'll be here for 5 days⟩ **5** : to be ready, to be done ⟨estará para las diez : it will be ready by ten o'clock⟩ **6** : to agree ⟨¿estamos? : are we in agreement?⟩ ⟨estoy contigo : I'm with you⟩ **7** ¿**cómo estás?** : how are you? **8** ¡**está bien!** : all right!, that's fine! **9** ~ **a** : to cost **10** ~ **a** : to be ⟨¿a qué día estamos? : what's today's date?⟩ **11** ~ **con** : to have ⟨está con fiebre : she has a fever⟩ **12** ~ **de** : to be ⟨estoy de vacaciones : I'm on vacation⟩ ⟨está de director hoy : he's acting as director today⟩ **13 estar bien (mal)** : to be well (sick) **14** ~ **para** : to be in the mood for **15** ~ **por** : to be in favor of **16** ~ **por** : to be about to ⟨está por cerrar : it's on the verge of closing⟩ **17 estar de más** : to be unnecessary **18 estar que** : to be (in a state or condition) ⟨está que echa chispas : he's hopping mad⟩ — **estarse** *vr* QUEDARSE : to stay, to remain ⟨estáte quieto! : be still!⟩
estarcir {83} *vt* : to stencil
estatal *adj* : state, national
estática *nf* : static
estático, -ca *adj* : static
estatizar {21} *vt* : to nationalize — **estatización** *nf*
estatua *nf* : statue

estatuilla *nf* : statuette, figurine
estatura *nf* : height, stature ⟨de mediana estatura : of medium height⟩
estatus *nm* : status, prestige
estatutario, -ria *adj* : statutory
estatuto *nm* : statute
este[1], **esta** *adj, mpl* **estos** : this, these
este[2] *adj* : eastern, east
este[3] *nm* **1** ORIENTE : east **2** : east wind **3 el Este** : the East, the Orient
éste, ésta *pron, mpl* **éstos 1** : this one, these ones *pl* **2** : the latter
estela *nf* **1** : wake (of a ship) **2** RASTRO : trail (of dust, smoke, etc.)
estelar *adj* : stellar
estelarizar {21} *vt Mex* : to star in, to be the star of
esténcil *nm* : stencil
estentóreo, -rea *adj* : loud, thundering
estepa *nf* : steppe
éster *nf* : ester
estera *nf* : mat
estercolero *nm* : dunghill
estéreo *adj & nm* : stereo
estereofónico, -ca *adj* : stereophonic
estereotipado, -da *adj* : stereotyped
estereotipar *vt* : to stereotype
estereotipo *nm* : stereotype
estéril *adj* **1** : sterile, germ-free **2** : infertile, barren **3** : futile, vain
esterilidad *nf* **1** : sterility **2** : infertility
esterilizar {21} *vt* **1** : to sterilize, to disinfect **2** : to sterilize (a person), to spay (an animal) — **esterilización** *nf*
esterlina *adj* : sterling
esternón *nm, pl* **-nones** : sternum
estero *nm* : estuary
estertor *nm* : death rattle
estética *nf* : aesthetics
estético, -ca *adj* : aesthetic — **estéticamente** *adv*
estetoscopio *nm* : stethoscope
estibador, -dora *n* : longshoreman, stevedore
estibar *vt* : to load (freight)
estiércol *nm* : dung, manure
estigma *nm* : stigma
estigmatizar {21} *vt* : to stigmatize, to brand
estilarse *vr* : to be in fashion
estilete *nm* : stiletto
estilista *nmf* : stylist
estilizar {21} *vt* : to stylize
estilo *nm* **1** : style **2** : fashion, manner **3** : stylus
estima *nf* ESTIMACIÓN : esteem, regard
estimable *adj* **1** : considerable **2** : estimable, esteemed
estimación *nf, pl* **-ciones 1** ESTIMA : esteem, regard **2** : estimate
estimado, -da *adj* : esteemed, dear ⟨Estimado señor Ortiz : Dear Mr. Ortiz⟩
estimar *vt* **1** APRECIAR : to esteem, to respect **2** EVALUAR : to estimate, to appraise **3** OPINAR : to consider, to deem
estimulación *nf, pl* **-ciones** : stimulation
estimulante[1] *adj* : stimulating
estimulante[2] *nm* : stimulant

estimular *vt* **1** : to stimulate **2** : to encourage
estímulo *nm* **1** : stimulus **2** INCENTIVO : incentive, encouragement
estío *nm* : summertime
estipendio *nm* **1** : salary **2** : stipend, remuneration
estipular *vt* : to stipulate — **estipulación** *nf*
estirado, -da *adj* **1** : stretched, extended **2** PRESUMIDO : stuck-up, conceited
estiramiento *nm* **1** : stretching **2 estiramiento facial** : face-lift
estirar *vt* : to stretch (out), to extend — **estirarse** *vr*
estirón *nm, pl* **-rones 1** : pull, tug **2 dar un estirón** : to grow quickly, to shoot up
estirpe *nf* LINAJE : lineage, stock
estival *adj* VERANIEGO : summer
esto *pron (neuter)* **1** : this ⟨¿qué es esto? : what is this?⟩ **2 en ~** : at this point **3 por ~** : for this reason
estocada *nf* **1** : final thrust (in bullfighting) **2** : thrust, lunge (in fencing)
estofa *nf* CLASE : class, quality ⟨de baja estofa : low-class, poor-quality⟩
estofado *nm* COCIDO, GUISADO : stew
estofar *vt* GUISAR : to stew
estoicismo *nm* : stoicism
estoico[1], **-ca** *adj* : stoic, stoical
estoico[2], **-ca** *n* : stoic
estola *nf* : stole
estomacal *adj* GÁSTRICO : stomach, gastric
estómago *nm* : stomach
estoniano, -na *adj & n* : Estonian
estonio, -nia *adj & n* : Estonian
estopa *nf* **1** : tow (yarn or cloth) **2** : burlap
estopilla *nf* : cheesecloth
estoque *nm* : rapier, sword
estorbar *vt* OBSTRUIR : to obstruct, to hinder — *vi* : to get in the way
estorbo *nm* **1** : obstacle, hindrance **2** : nuisance
estornino *nm* : starling
estornudar *vi* : to sneeze
estornudo *nm* : sneeze
estos *adj* → **este**[1]
éstos → **éste**
estoy → **estar**
estrabismo *nm* : squint
estrado *nm* **1** : dais, platform, bench (of a judge) **2 estrados** *nmpl* : courts of law
estrafalario, -ria *adj* ESTRAMBÓTICO, EXCÉNTRICO : eccentric, bizarre
estragar {52} *vt* DEVASTAR : to ruin, to devastate
estragón *nm* : tarragon
estragos *nmpl* **1** : ravages, destruction, devastation ⟨los estragos de la guerra : the ravages of war⟩ **2 hacer estragos en** or **causar estragos entre** : to play havoc with
estrambótico, -ca *adj* ESTRAFALARIO, EXCÉNTRICO : eccentric, bizarre

estrangulamiento *nm* : strangling, strangulation

estrangular *vt* AHOGAR : to strangle — **estrangulación** *nf*

estratagema *nf* ARTIMAÑA : stratagem, ruse

estratega *nmf* : strategist

estrategia *nf* : strategy

estratégico, -ca *adj* : strategic, tactical — **estratégicamente** *adv*

estratificación *nf, pl* **-ciones** : stratification

estratificado, -da *adj* : stratified

estrato *nm* : stratum, layer

estratosfera *nf* : stratosphere

estratosférico, -ca *adj* **1** : stratospheric **2** : astronomical, exorbitant

estrechamiento *nm* **1** : narrowing **2** : narrow point **3** : tightening, strengthening (of relations)

estrechar *vt* **1** : to narrow **2** : to tighten, to strengthen (a bond) **3** : to hug, to embrace **4 estrechar la mano de** : to shake hands with — **estrecharse** *vr*

estrechez *nf, pl* **-checes 1** : tightness, narrowness **2 estrecheces** *nfpl* : financial problems

estrecho[1], -cha *adj* **1** : tight, narrow **2** ÍNTIMO : close — **estrechamente** *adv*

estrecho[2] *nm* : strait, narrows

estrella *nf* **1** ASTRO : star ⟨estrella fugaz : shooting star⟩ **2** : destiny ⟨tener buena estrella : to be born lucky⟩ **3** : movie star **4 estrella de mar** : starfish

estrellado, -da *adj* **1** : starry **2** : star-shaped **3 huevos estrellados** : fried eggs

estrellamiento *nm* : crash, collision

estrellar *vt* : to smash, to crash — **estrellarse** *vr* : to crash, to collide

estrellato *nm* : stardom

estremecedor, -dora *adj* : horrifying

estremecer {53} *vt* : to cause to shake — *vi* : to tremble, to shake — **estremecerse** *vr* : to shudder, to shiver (with emotion)

estremecimiento *nm* : trembling, shaking, shivering

estrenar *vt* **1** : to use for the first time **2** : to premiere, to open — **estrenarse** *vr* : to make one's debut

estreno *nm* DEBUT : debut, premiere

estreñimiento *nm* : constipation

estreñirse {67} *vr* : to be constipated

estrépito *nm* ESTRUENDO : clamor, din

estrepitoso, -sa *adj* : clamorous, noisy — **estrepitosamente** *adv*

estrés *nm, pl* **estreses** : stress

estresante *adj* : stressful

estresar *vt* : to stress, to stress out

estría *nf* : fluting, groove

estribación *nf, pl* **-ciones 1** : spur, ridge **2 estribaciones** *nfpl* : foothills

estribar *vi* FUNDARSE ~ **en** : to be due to, to stem from

estribillo *nm* : refrain, chorus

estribo *nm* **1** : stirrup **2** : abutment, buttress **3 perder los estribos** : to lose one's temper

estribor *nm* : starboard

estricnina *nf* : strychnine

estricto, -ta *adj* SEVERO : strict, severe — **estrictamente** *adv*

estridente *adj* : strident, shrill, loud — **estridentemente** *adv*

estrofa *nf* : stanza, verse

estrógeno *nm* : estrogen

estropajo *nm* : scouring pad

estropear *vt* **1** ARRUINAR : to ruin, to spoil **2** : to break, to damage — **estropearse** *vr* **1** : to spoil, to go bad **2** : to break down

estropicio *nm* DAÑO : damage, breakage

estructura *nf* : structure, framework

estructuración *nf, pl* **-ciones** : structuring, structure

estructural *adj* : structural — **estructuralmente** *adv*

estructurar *vt* : to structure, to organize

estruendo *nm* ESTRÉPITO : racket, din, roar

estruendoso, -sa *adj* : resounding, thunderous

estrujar *vt* APRETAR : to press, to squeeze

estuario *nm* : estuary

estuche *nm* : kit, case

estuco *nm* : stucco

estudiado, -da *adj* : affected, mannered

estudiantado *nm* : student body, students *pl*

estudiante *nmf* : student

estudiantil *adj* : student ⟨la vida estudiantil : student life⟩

estudiar *v* : to study

estudio *nm* **1** : study **2** : studio **3 estudios** *nmpl* : studies, education

estudioso, -sa *adj* : studious

estufa *nf* **1** : stove, heater **2** *Col, Mex* : cooking stove, range

estupefacción *nf, pl* **-ciones** : stupefaction, astonishment

estupefaciente[1] *adj* : narcotic

estupefaciente[2] *nm* DROGA, NARCÓTICO : drug, narcotic

estupefacto, -ta *adj* : astonished, stunned

estupendo, -da *adj* MARAVILLOSO : stupendous, marvelous — **estupendamente** *adv*

estupidez *nf, pl* **-deces 1** : stupidity **2** : nonsense

estúpido[1], -da *adj* : stupid — **estúpidamente** *adj*

estúpido[2], -da *n* IDIOTA : idiot, fool

estupor *nm* **1** : stupor **2** : amazement

esturión *nm, pl* **-riones** : sturgeon

estuvo, etc. → **estar**

etano *nm* : ethane

etanol *nm* : ethanol

etapa *nf* FASE : stage, phase

etcétera[1] : et cetera, and so on

etcétera[2] *nmf* : et cetera

éter *nm* : ether

etéreo, -rea *adj* : ethereal, heavenly
eternidad *nf* : eternity
eternizar {21} *vt* PERPETUAR : to make eternal, to perpetuate — **eternizarse** *vr fam* : to take forever
eterno, -na *adj* : eternal, endless — **eternamente** *adv*
ética *nf* : ethics
ético, -ca *adj* : ethical — **éticamente** *adv*
etimología *nf* : etymology
etimológico, -ca *adj* : etymological
etimólogo, -ga *n* : etymologist
etíope *adj & nmf* : Ethiopian
etiqueta *nf* **1** : etiquette **2** : tag, label **3 de ~** : formal, dressy
etiquetar *vt* : to label
étnico, -ca *adj* : ethnic
etnología *nf* : ethnology
etnólogo, -ga *n* : ethnologist
eucalipto *nm* : eucalyptus
Eucaristía *nf* : Eucharist, communion
eucarístico, -ca *adj* : eucharistic
eufemismo *nm* : euphemism
eufemístico, -ca *adj* : euphemistic
eufonía *nf* : euphony
eufónico, -ca *adj* : euphonious
euforia *nf* : euphoria, joyousness
eufórico, -ca *adj* : euphoric, exuberant, joyous — **eufóricamente** *adv*
eunuco *nm* : eunuch
europeo, -pea *adj & n* : European
euskera *nm* : Basque (language)
eutanasia *nf* : euthanasia
evacuación *nf, pl* **-ciones** : evacuation
evacuar *vt* **1** : to evacuate, to vacate **2** : to carry out — *vi* : to have a bowel movement
evadir *vt* ELUDIR : to evade, to avoid — **evadirse** *vr* : to escape, to slip away
evaluación *nf, pl* **-ciones** : assessment, evaluation
evaluador, -dora *n* : assessor
evaluar {3} *vt* : to evaluate, to assess, to appraise
evangélico, -ca *adj* : evangelical — **evangélicamente** *adv*
evangelio *nm* : gospel
evangelismo *nm* : evangelism
evangelista *nm* : evangelist
evangelizador, -dora *n* : evangelist, missionary
evaporación *nf, pl* **-ciones** : evaporation
evaporar *vt* : to evaporate — **evaporarse** *vr* ESFUMARSE : to disappear, to vanish
evasión *nf, pl* **-siones** **1** : escape, flight **2** : evasion, dodge
evasiva *nf* : excuse, pretext
evasivo, -va *adj* : evasive
evento *nm* : event
eventual *adj* **1** : possible **2** : temporary ⟨trabajadores eventuales : temporary workers⟩ — **eventualmente** *adv*
eventualidad *nf* : possibility, eventuality
evidencia *nf* **1** : evidence, proof **2 poner en evidencia** : to demonstrate, to make clear

evidenciar *vt* : to demonstrate, to show — **evidenciarse** *vr* : to be evident
evidente *adj* : evident, obvious, clear — **evidentemente** *adv*
eviscerar *vt* : to eviscerate
evitable *adj* : avoidable, preventable
evitar *vt* **1** : to avoid **2** PREVENIR : to prevent **3** ELUDIR : to escape, to elude
evocación *nf, pl* **-ciones** : evocation
evocador, -dora *adj* : evocative
evocar {72} *vt* **1** : to evoke **2** RECORDAR : to recall
evolución *nf, pl* **-ciones** **1** : evolution **2** : development, progress
evolucionar *vi* **1** : to evolve **2** : to change, to develop
evolutivo, -va *adj* : evolutionary
exabrupto *nm* : pointed remark
exacción *nf, pl* **-ciones** : levying, exaction
exacerbar *vt* **1** : to exacerbate, to aggravate **2** : to irritate, to exasperate
exactamente *adv* : exactly
exactitud *nf* PRECISIÓN : accuracy, precision, exactitude
exacto, -ta *adj* PRECISO : accurate, precise, exact
exageración *nf, pl* **-ciones** : exaggeration
exagerado, -da *adj* **1** : exaggerated **2** : excessive — **exageradamente** *adv*
exagerar *v* : to exaggerate
exaltación *nf, pl* **-ciones** **1** : exaltation **2** : excitement, agitation
exaltado[1]**, -da** *adj* : excitable, hotheaded
exaltado[2]**, -da** *n* : hothead
exaltar *vt* **1** ENSALZAR : to exalt, to extol **2** : to excite, to agitate — **exaltarse** *vr* ACALORARSE : to get overexcited
ex–alumno → alumno
examen *nm, pl* **exámenes** **1** : examination, test **2** : consideration, investigation
examinar *vt* **1** : to examine **2** INSPECCIONAR : to inspect — **examinarse** *vr* : to take an exam
exánime *adj* **1** : lifeless **2** : exhausted
exasperante *adj* : exasperating
exasperar *vt* IRRITAR : to exasperate, to irritate — **exasperación** *nf*
excavación *nf, pl* **-ciones** : excavation
excavadora *nf* : excavator
excavar *v* : to excavate, to dig
excedente[1] *adj* **1** : excessive **2** : excess, surplus
excedente[2] *nm* : surplus, excess
exceder *vt* : to exceed, to surpass — **excederse** *vr* : to go too far
excelencia *nf* **1** : excellence **2** : excellency ⟨Su Excelencia : His Excellency⟩
excelente *adj* : excellent — **excelentemente** *adv*
excelso, -sa *adj* : lofty, sublime
excentricidad *nf* : eccentricity
excéntrico, -ca *adj & n* : eccentric
excepción *nf, pl* **-ciones** : exception
excepcional *adj* EXTRAORDINARIO : exceptional, extraordinary, rare

excepto *prep* SALVO : except
exceptuar {3} *vt* EXCLUIR : to except, to exclude
excesivo, -va *adj* : excessive — **excesivamente** *adv*
exceso *nm* 1 : excess 2 excesos *nmpl* : excesses, abuses 3 exceso de velocidad : speeding
excitabilidad *nf* : excitability
excitación *nf, pl* -ciones : excitement
excitante *adj* : exciting
excitar *vt* : to excite, to arouse — **excitarse** *vr*
exclamación *nf, pl* -ciones : exclamation
exclamar *v* : to exclaim
excluir {41} *vt* EXCEPTUAR : to exclude, to leave out
exclusión *nf, pl* -siones : exclusion
exclusividad *nf* 1 : exclusiveness 2 : exclusive rights *pl*
exclusivista *adj & nmf* : exclusivist
exclusivo, -va *adj* : exclusive — **exclusivamente** *adv*
excomulgar {52} *vt* : to excommunicate
excomunión *nf, pl* -niones : excommunication
excreción *nf, pl* -ciones : excretion
excremento *nm* : excrement
excretar *vt* : to excrete
exculpar *vt* : to exonerate, to exculpate — **exculpación** *nf*
excursión *nf, pl* -siones : excursion, outing
excursionista *nmf* 1 : sightseer, tourist 2 : hiker
excusa *nf* 1 PRETEXTO : excuse 2 DISCULPA : apology
excusado *nm Mex* : toilet
excusar *vt* 1 : to excuse 2 : to exempt — **excusarse** *vr* : to apologize, to send one's regrets
execrable *adj* : detestable, abominable
exención *nf, pl* -ciones : exemption
exento, -ta *adj* 1 : exempt, free 2 exento de impuestos : tax-exempt
exequias *nfpl* FUNERALES : funeral rites
exhalación *nf, pl* -ciones 1 : exhalation 2 : shooting star ⟨salió como una exhalación⟩ : he took off like a shot⟩
exhalar *vt* ESPIRAR : to exhale, to give off
exhaustivo, -va *adj* : exhaustive — **exhaustivamente** *adv*
exhausto, -ta *adj* AGOTADO : exhausted, worn-out
exhibición *nf, pl* -ciones 1 : exhibition, show 2 : showing
exhibir *vt* : to exhibit, to show, to display — **exhibirse** *vr*
exhortación *nf, pl* -ciones : exhortation
exhortar *vt* : to exhort
exhumar *vt* DESENTERRAR : to exhume — **exhumación** *nf*
exigencia *nf* : demand, requirement
exigente *adj* : demanding, exacting
exigir {35} *vt* 1 : to demand, to require 2 : to exact, to levy

exiguo, -gua *adj* : meager
exiliado[1], -da *adj* : exiled, in exile
exiliado[2], -da *n* : exile
exiliar *vt* DESTERRAR : to exile, to banish — **exiliarse** *vr* : to go into exile
exilio *nm* DESTIERRO : exile
eximio, -mia *adj* : distinguished, eminent
eximir *vt* EXONERAR : to exempt
existencia *nf* 1 : existence 2 existencias *nfpl* MERCANCÍA : goods, stock
existente *adj* 1 : existing, in existence 2 : in stock
existir *vi* : to exist
éxito *nm* 1 TRIUNFO : success, hit 2 tener éxito : to be successful
exitoso, -sa *adj* : successful — **exitosamente** *adv*
éxodo *nm* : exodus
exoneración *nf, pl* -ciones EXENCIÓN : exoneration, exemption
exonerar *vt* 1 EXIMIR : to exempt, to exonerate 2 DESPEDIR : to dismiss
exorbitante *adj* : exorbitant
exorcismo *nm* : exorcism — **exorcista** *nmf*
exorcizar {21} *vt* : to exorcise
exótico, -ca *adj* : exotic
expandir *vt* EXPANSIONAR : to expand — **expandirse** *vr* : to spread
expansión *nf, pl* -siones 1 : expansion, spread 2 DIVERSIÓN : recreation, relaxation
expansionar *vt* EXPANDIR : to expand — **expansionarse** *vr* 1 : to expand 2 DIVERTIRSE : to amuse oneself, to relax
expansivo, -va *adj* : expansive
expatriado, -da *adj & n* : expatriate
expatriarse {85} *vr* 1 EMIGRAR : to emigrate 2 : to go into exile
expectación *nf, pl* -ciones : expectation, anticipation
expectante *adj* : expectant
expectativa *nf* 1 : expectation, hope 2 expectativas *nfpl* : prospects
expedición *nf, pl* -ciones : expedition
expediente *nm* 1 : expedient, means 2 ARCHIVO : file, dossier, record
expedir {54} *vt* 1 EMITIR : to issue 2 DESPACHAR : to dispatch, to send
expedito, -ta *adj* 1 : free, clear 2 : quick, easy
expeler *vt* : to expel, to eject
expendedor, -dora *n* : dealer, seller
expendio *nm* TIENDA : store, shop
expensas *nfpl* 1 : expenses, costs 2 a expensas de : at the expense of
experiencia *nf* 1 : experience 2 EXPERIMENTO : experiment
experimentación *nf, pl* -ciones : experimentation
experimental *adj* : experimental
experimentar *vi* : to experiment — *vt* 1 : to experiment with, to test out 2 : to experience
experimento *nm* EXPERIENCIA : experiment

experto, -ta *adj & n* : expert
expiación *nf, pl* **-ciones** : expiation, atonement
expiar {85} *vt* : to expiate, to atone for
expiración *nf, pl* **-ciones** VENCIMIENTO : expiration
expirar *vi* **1** FALLECER, MORIR : to pass away, to die **2** : to expire
explanada *nf* : esplanade, promenade
explayar *vt* : to extend — **explayarse** *vr* : to expound, to speak at length
explicable *adj* : explicable, explainable
explicación *nf, pl* **-ciones** : explanation
explicar {72} *vt* : to explain — **explicarse** *vr* : to understand
explicativo, -va *adj* : explanatory
explicitar *vt* : to state explicitly, to specify
explícito, -ta *adj* : explicit — **explícitamente** *adv*
exploración *nf, pl* **-ciones** : exploration
explorador, -dora *n* : explorer, scout
explorar *vt* : to explore — **exploratorio, -ria** *adj*
explosión *nf, pl* **-siones** **1** ESTALLIDO : explosion **2** : outburst ⟨una explosión de ira : an outburst of anger⟩
explosionar *vi* : to explode
explosivo, -va *adj* : explosive
explotación *nf, pl* **-ciones** **1** : exploitation **2** : operation, running
explotar *vt* **1** : to exploit **2** : to operate, to run — *vi* ESTALLAR, REVENTAR : to explode — **explotable** *adj*
exponencial *adj* : exponential — **exponencialmente** *adv*
exponente *nm* : exponent
exponer {60} *vt* **1** : to exhibit, to show, to display **2** : to explain, to present, to set forth **3** : to expose, to risk — *vi* : to exhibit
exportación *nf, pl* **-ciones** **1** : exportation **2 exportaciones** *nfpl* : exports
exportador, -dora *n* : exporter
exportar *vt* : to export — **exportable** *adj*
exposición *nf, pl* **-ciones** **1** EXHIBICIÓN : exposition, exhibition **2** : exposure **3** : presentation, statement
expositor, -tora *n* **1** : exhibitor **2** : exponent
exprés *nms & pl* **1** : express, express train **2** : espresso
expresamente *adv* : expressly, on purpose
expresar *vt* : to express — **expresarse** *vr*
expresión *nf, pl* **-siones** : expression
expresivo, -va *adj* **1** : expressive **2** CARIÑOSO : affectionate — **expresivamente** *adv*
expreso[1], -sa *adj* : express, specific
expreso[2] *nm* : express train, express
exprimidor *nm* : squeezer, juicer
exprimir *vt* **1** : to squeeze **2** : to exploit
expropiar *vt* : to expropriate, to commandeer — **expropiación** *nf*
expuesto[1] *pp* → **exponer**
expuesto[2], -ta *adj* **1** : exposed **2** : hazardous, risky

expulsar *vt* : to expel, to eject
expulsión *nf, pl* **-siones** : expulsion
expurgar {52} *vt* : to expurgate
expuso, etc. → **exponer**
exquisitez *nf, pl* **-teces** **1** : exquisiteness, refinement **2** : delicacy, special dish
exquisito, -ta *adj* **1** : exquisite **2** : delicious
extasiarse {85} *vr* : to be in ecstasy, to be enraptured
éxtasis *nms & pl* : ecstasy, rapture
extático, -ca *adj* : ecstatic
extemporáneo, -nea *adj* **1** : unseasonable **2** : untimely
extender {56} *vt* **1** : to spread out, to stretch out **2** : to broaden, to expand ⟨extender la influencia : to broaden one's influence⟩ **3** : to draw up (a document), to write out (a check) — **extenderse** *vr* **1** : to spread **2** : to last
extendido, -da *adj* **1** : outstretched **2** : widespread
extensamente *adv* : extensively, at length
extensible *adj* : extensible, extendable
extensión *nf, pl* **-siones** **1** : extension, stretching **2** : expanse, spread **3** : extent, range **4** : length, duration
extensivo, -va *adj* **1** : extensive **2 hacer extensivo** : to extend
extenso, -sa *adj* **1** : extensive, detailed **2** : spacious, vast
extenuar {3} *vt* : to exhaust, to tire out — **extenuarse** *vr* — **extenuante** *adj*
exterior[1] *adj* **1** : exterior, external **2** : foreign ⟨asuntos exteriores : foreign affairs⟩
exterior[2] *nm* **1** : outside **2** : abroad
exteriorizar {21} *vt* : to express, to reveal
exteriormente *adv* : outwardly
exterminar *vt* : to exterminate — **exterminación** *nf*
exterminio *nm* : extermination
externar *vt Mex* : to express, to display
externo, -na *adj* : external, outward
extinción *nf, pl* **-ciones** : extinction
extinguidor *nm* : fire extinguisher
extinguir {26} *vt* **1** APAGAR : to extinguish, to put out **2** : to wipe out — **extinguirse** *vr* **1** APAGARSE : to go out, to fade out **2** : to die out, to become extinct
extinto, -ta *adj* : extinct
extintor *nm* : extinguisher
extirpación *n, pl* **-ciones** : removal, excision
extirpar *vt* : to eradicate, to remove, to excise — **extirparse** *vr*
extorsión *nf, pl* **-siones** **1** : extortion **2** : harm, trouble
extorsionar *vt* : to extort
extra[1] *adv* : extra
extra[2] *adj* **1** : additional, extra **2** : superior, top-quality
extra[3] *nmf* : extra (in movies)

extra[4] *nm* : extra expense ⟨paga extra : bonus⟩
extracción *nf, pl* **-ciones** : extraction
extracto *nm* **1** : extract ⟨extracto de vainilla : vanilla extract⟩ **2** : abstract, summary
extractor *nm* : extractor
extracurricular *adj* : extracurricular
extradición *nf, pl* **-ciones** : extradition
extraditar *vt* : to extradite
extraer {81} *vt* : to extract
extraído *pp* → **extraer**
extrajudicial *adj* : out-of-court
extramatrimonial *adj* : extramarital
extranjerizante *adj* : foreign-sounding, foreign-looking
extranjero[1], **-ra** *adj* : foreign
extranjero[2], **-ra** *n* : foreigner
extranjero[3] *nm* : foreign countries *pl* ⟨viajó al extranjero : he traveled abroad⟩ ⟨trabajan en el extranjero : they work overseas⟩
extrañamente *adv* : strangely, oddly
extrañamiento *nm* ASOMBRO : amazement, surprise, wonder
extrañar *vt* : to miss (someone) — **extrañarse** *vr* : to be surprised
extrañeza *nf* **1** : strangeness, oddness **2** : surprise
extraño[1], **-ña** *adj* **1** RARO : strange, odd **2** EXTRANJERO : foreign
extraño[2], **-ña** *n* DESCONOCIDO : stranger
extraoficial *adj* OFICIOSO : unofficial — **extraoficialmente** *adv*
extraordinario, -ria *adj* EXCEPCIONAL : extraordinary — **extraordinariamente** *adv*
extrasensorial *adj* : extrasensory ⟨percepción extrasensorial : extrasensory perception⟩
extraterrestre *adj & nmf* : extraterrestrial, alien

extravagancia *nf* : extravagance, outlandishness, flamboyance
extravagante *adj* : extravagant, outrageous, flamboyant
extraviar {85} *vt* **1** : to mislead, to lead astray **2** : to misplace, to lose — **extraviarse** *vr* : to get lost, to go astray
extravío *nm* **1** PÉRDIDA : loss, misplacement **2** : misconduct
extremado, -da *adj* : extreme — **extremadamente** *adv*
extremar *vt* : to carry to extremes — **extremarse** *vr* : to do one's utmost
extremidad *nf* **1** : extremity, tip, edge **2 extremidades** *nfpl* : extremities
extremista *adj & nmf* : extremist
extremo[1], **-ma** *adj* **1** : extreme, utmost **2** EXCESIVO : excessive **3 en caso extremo** : as a last resort
extremo[2] *nm* **1** : extreme, end **2 al extremo de** : to the point of **3 en ~** : in the extreme
extrovertido[1], **-da** *adj* : extroverted, outgoing
extrovertido[2], **-da** *n* : extrovert
extrudir *vt* : to extrude
exuberancia *nf* **1** : exuberance **2** : luxuriance, lushness
exuberante *adj* : exuberant, luxuriant — **exuberantemente** *adv*
exudar *vt* : to exude
exultación *nf, pl* **-ciones** : exultation, elation
exultante *adj* : exultant, elated — **exultantemente** *adv*
exultar *vi* : to exult, to rejoice
eyacular *vi* : to ejaculate — **eyaculación** *nf*
eyección *nf, pl* **-ciones** : ejection, expulsion
eyectar *vt* : to eject, to expel — **eyectarse** *vr*

F

f *nf* : sixth letter of the Spanish alphabet
fábrica *nf* FACTORÍA : factory
fabricación *nf, pl* **-ciones** : manufacture
fabricante *nmf* : manufacturer
fabricar {72} *vt* MANUFACTURAR : to manufacture, to make
fabril *adj* INDUSTRIAL : industrial, manufacturing
fábula *nf* **1** : fable **2** : fabrication, fib
fabuloso, -sa *adj* **1** : fabulous, fantastic **2** : mythical, fabled
facción *nf, pl* **facciones 1** : faction **2 facciones** *nfpl* RASGOS : features
faccioso, -sa *adj* : factious
faceta *nf* : facet
facha *nf* : appearance, look ⟨estar hecho una facha : to look a sight⟩
fachada *nf* : facade
facial *adj* : facial

fácil *adj* **1** : easy **2** : likely, probable ⟨es fácil que no pase : it probably won't happen⟩
facilidad *nf* **1** : facility, ease **2 facilidades** *nfpl* : facilities, services **3 facilidades** *nfpl* : opportunities
facilitar *vt* **1** : to facilitate **2** : to provide, to supply
fácilmente *adv* : easily, readily
facsímil *or* **facsímile** *nm* **1** : facsimile, copy **2** : fax
facsimilar *adj* : facsimile
factibilidad *nf* : feasibility
factible *adj* : feasible, practicable
facticio, -cia *adj* : artificial, factitious
factor[1], **-tora** *n* **1** : agent, factor **2** : baggage clerk
factor[2] *nm* ELEMENTO : factor, element
factoría *nf* FÁBRICA : factory
factótum *nm* : factotum

factura *nf* **1** : making, manufacturing **2** : bill, invoice

facturación *nf, pl* **-ciones 1** : invoicing, billing **2** : check-in

facturar *vt* **1** : to bill, to invoice **2** : to register, to check in

facultad *nf* **1** : faculty, ability ⟨facultades mentales : mental faculties⟩ **2** : authority, power **3** : school (of a university) ⟨facultad de derecho : law school⟩

facultar *vt* : to authorize, to empower

facultativo, -va *adj* **1** OPTATIVO : voluntary, optional **2** : medical ⟨informe facultativo : medical report⟩

faena *nf* : task, job, work ⟨faenas domésticas : housework⟩

faenar *vi* **1** : to work, to labor **2** PESCAR : to fish

fagot *nm* : bassoon

faisán *nm, pl* **faisanes** : pheasant

faja *nf* **1** : sash, belt **2** : girdle **3** : strip (of land)

fajar *vt* **1** : to wrap (a sash or girdle) around **2** : to hit, to thrash — **fajarse** *vr* **1** : to put on a sash or girdle **2** : to come to blows

fajín *nm, pl* **-jines** : sash, belt

fajo *nm* : bundle, sheaf ⟨un fajo de billetes : a wad of cash⟩

falacia *nf* : fallacy

falaz, -laza *adj, mpl* **falaces** FALSO : fallacious, false

falda *nf* **1** : skirt ⟨falda escocesa : kilt⟩ **2** REGAZO : lap (of the body) **3** VERTIENTE : side, slope

faldón *nm, pl* **-dones 1** : tail (of a shirt, etc.) **2** : full skirt **3 faldón bautismal** : christening gown

falible *adj* : fallible

fálico, -ca *adj* : phallic

falla *nf* **1** : flaw, defect **2** : (geological) fault **3** : fault, failing

fallar *vi* **1** FRACASAR : to fail, to go wrong **2** : to rule (in a court of law) — *vt* **1** ERRAR : to miss (a target) **2** : to pronounce judgment on

fallecer {53} *vi* MORIR : to pass away, to die

fallecido, -da *adj & n* DIFUNTO : deceased

fallecimiento *nm* : demise, death

fallido, -da *adj* : failed, unsuccessful

fallo *nm* **1** SENTENCIA : sentence, judgment, verdict **2** : error, fault

falo *nm* : phallus, penis

falsamente *adv* : falsely

falsear *vt* **1** : to falsify, to fake **2** : to distort — *vi* **1** CEDER : to give way **2** : to be out of tune

falsedad *nf* **1** : falseness, hypocrisy **2** MENTIRA : falsehood, lie

falsete *nm* : falsetto

falsificación *nf, pl* **-ciones 1** : counterfeit, forgery **2** : falsification

falsificador, -dora *n* : counterfeiter, forger

falsificar {72} *vt* **1** : to counterfeit, to forge **2** : to falsify

falso, -sa *adj* **1** FALAZ : false, untrue **2** : counterfeit, forged

falta *nf* **1** CARENCIA : lack ⟨hacer falta : to be lacking, to be needed⟩ **2** DEFECTO : defect, fault, error **3** : offense, misdemeanor **4** : foul (in basketball), fault (in tennis)

faltar *vi* **1** : to be lacking, to be needed ⟨me falta tiempo : I don't have enough time⟩ **2** : to be absent, to be missing **3** QUEDAR : to remain, to be left ⟨faltan pocos días para la fiesta : the party is just a few days away⟩ **4** ¡no faltaba más! : don't mention it!, you're welcome!

falto, -ta *adj* ~ **de** : lacking (in), short of

fama *nf* **1** : fame **2** REPUTACIÓN : reputation **3 de mala fama** : disreputable

famélico, -ca *adj* HAMBRIENTO : starving, famished

familia *nf* **1** : family **2 familia política** : in-laws

familiar[1] *adj* **1** CONOCIDO : familiar **2** : familial, family **3** INFORMAL : informal

familiar[2] *nmf* PARIENTE : relation, relative

familiaridad *nf* **1** : familiarity **2** : informality

familiarizarse {21} *vr* ~ **con** : to familiarize oneself with

famoso[1], **-sa** *adj* CÉLEBRE : famous

famoso[2], **-sa** *n* : celebrity

fanal *nm* **1** : beacon, signal light **2** *Mex* : headlight

fanático, -ca *adj & n* : fanatic

fanatismo *nm* : fanaticism

fandango *nm* : fandango

fanfarria *nf* **1** : (musical) fanfare **2** : pomp, ceremony

fanfarrón[1], **-rrona** *adj, mpl* **-rrones** *fam* : bragging, boastful

fanfarrón[2], **-rrona** *n, mpl* **-rrones** *fam* : braggart

fanfarronada *nf* : boast, bluster

fanfarronear *vi* : to brag, to boast

fango *nm* LODO : mud, mire

fangosidad *nf* : muddiness

fangoso, -sa *adj* LODOSO : muddy

fantasear *vi* : to fantasize, to daydream

fantasía *nf* **1** : fantasy **2** : imagination

fantasioso, -sa *adj* : fanciful

fantasma *nm* : ghost, phantom

fantasmagórico, -ca *adj* : phantasmagoric

fantasmal *adj* : ghostly

fantástico, -ca *adj* **1** : fantastic, imaginary, unreal **2** *fam* : great, fantastic

faquir *nm* : fakir

farándula *nf* : show business, theater

faraón *nm, pl* **faraones** : pharaoh

fardo *nm* **1** : bale **2** : bundle

farfulla *nf* : jabbering

farfullar *v* : to jabber, to gabble

faringe *nf* : pharynx

faríngeo, -gea *adj* : pharyngeal
fariña *nf* : coarse manioc flour
farmacéutico[1]**, -ca** *adj* : pharmaceutical
farmacéutico[2]**, -ca** *n* : pharmacist
farmacia *nf* : drugstore, pharmacy
fármaco *nm* : medicine, drug
farmacodependencia *nf* : drug addiction
farmacología *nf* : pharmacology
faro *nm* **1** : lighthouse **2** : headlight
farol *nm* **1** : streetlight **2** : lantern, lamp **3** *fam* : bluff **4** *Mex* : headlight
farola *nf* **1** : lamppost **2** : streetlight
farolero, -ra *n fam* : bluffer
farra *nf* : spree, revelry
fárrago *nm* REVOLTIJO : hodgepodge, jumble
farsa *nf* **1** : farce **2** : fake, sham
farsante *nmf* CHARLATÁN : charlatan, fraud, phony
fascículo *nm* : fascicle, part (of a publication)
fascinación *nf, pl* **-ciones** : fascination
fascinante *adj* : fascinating
fascinar *vt* **1** : to fascinate **2** : to charm, to captivate
fascismo *nm* : fascism
fascista *adj & nmf* : fascist
fase *nf* : phase, stage
fastidiar *vt* **1** MOLESTAR : to annoy, to bother, to hassle **2** ABURRIR : to bore — *vi* : to be annoying or bothersome
fastidio *nm* **1** MOLESTIA : annoyance, nuisance, hassle **2** ABURRIMIENTO : boredom
fastidioso, -sa *adj* **1** MOLESTO : annoying, bothersome **2** ABURRIDO : boring
fatal *adj* **1** MORTAL : fatal **2** *fam* : awful, terrible **3** : fateful, unavoidable
fatalidad *nf* **1** : fatality **2** DESGRACIA : misfortune, bad luck
fatalismo *nm* : fatalism
fatalista[1] *adj* : fatalistic
fatalista[2] *nmf* : fatalist
fatalmente *adv* **1** : unavoidably **2** : unfortunately
fatídico, -ca *adj* : fateful, momentous
fatiga *nf* CANSANCIO : fatigue
fatigado, -da *adj* AGOTADO : weary, tired
fatigar {52} *vt* CANSAR : to fatigue, to tire — **fatigarse** *vr* : to wear oneself out
fatigoso, -sa *adj* : fatiguing, tiring
fatuidad *nf* **1** : fatuousness **2** VANIDAD : vanity, conceit
fatuo, -tua *adj* **1** : fatuous **2** PRESUMIDO : vain
fauces *nfpl* : jaws *pl*, maw
faul *nm, pl* **fauls** : foul, foul ball
fauna *nf* : fauna
fausto *nm* : splendor, magnificence
favor *nm* **1** : favor **2 a favor de** : in favor of **3 por ~** : please
favorable *adj* : favorable — **favorablemente** *adv*
favorecedor, -dora *adj* : becoming, flattering
favorecer {53} *vt* **1** : to favor **2** : to look well on, to suit

favorecido, -da *adj* **1** : flattering **2** : fortunate
favoritismo *nm* : favoritism
favorito, -ta *adj & n* : favorite
fax *nm* : fax, facsimile
fayuca *nf Mex* **1** : contraband **2** : black market
fayuquero *nm Mex* : smuggler, black marketeer
faz *nf* **1** : face, countenance ⟨la faz de la tierra : the face of the earth⟩ **2** : side (of coins, fabric, etc.)
fe *nf* **1** : faith **2** : assurance, testimony ⟨dar fe de : to bear witness to⟩ **3** : intention, will ⟨de buena fe : bona fide, in good faith⟩
fealdad *nf* : ugliness
febrero *nm* : February
febril *adj* : feverish — **febrilmente** *adv*
fecal *adj* : fecal
fecha *nf* **1** : date **2 fecha de caducidad** *or* **fecha de vencimiento** : expiration date **3 fecha límite** : deadline
fechar *vt* : to date, to put a date on
fechoría *nf* : misdeed
fécula *nf* : starch
fecundar *vt* : to fertilize (an egg) — **fecundación** *nf*
fecundidad *nf* **1** : fecundity, fertility **2** : productiveness
fecundo, -da *adj* FÉRTIL : fertile, fecund
federación *nf, pl* **-ciones** : federation
federal *adj* : federal
federalismo *nm* : federalism
federalista *adj & nmf* : federalist
federar *vt* : to federate
fehaciente *adj* : reliable, irrefutable — **fehacientemente** *adv*
feldespato *nm* : feldspar
felicidad *nf* **1** : happiness **2 ¡felicidades!** : best wishes!, congratulations!, happy birthday!
felicitación *nf, pl* **-ciones** **1** : congratulation ⟨¡felicitaciones! : congratulations!⟩ **2** : greeting card
felicitar *vt* CONGRATULAR : to congratulate — **felicitarse** *vr* ~ **de** : to be glad about
feligrés, -gresa *n, mpl* **-greses** : parishioner
feligresía *nf* : parish
felino, -na *adj & n* : feline
feliz *adj, pl* **felices** **1** : happy **2 Feliz Navidad** : Merry Christmas
felizmente *adv* **1** : happily **2** : fortunately, luckily
felonía *nf* : felony
felpa *nf* **1** : terry cloth **2** : plush
felpudo *nm* : doormat
femenil *adj* : women's, girls' ⟨futbol femenil : women's soccer⟩
femenino, -na *adj* **1** : feminine **2** : women's ⟨derechos femeninos : women's rights⟩ **3** : female
femineidad *nf* : femininity
feminidad *nf* : femininity
feminismo *nm* : feminism
feminista *adj & nmf* : feminist

femoral *adj* : femoral
fémur *nm* : femur, thighbone
fenecer {53} *vi* **1** : to die, to pass away **2** : to come to an end, to cease
fénix *nm* : phoenix
fenomenal *adj* **1** : phenomenal **2** *fam* : fantastic, terrific — **fenomenalmente** *adv*
fenómeno *nm* **1** : phenomenon **2** : prodigy, genius
feo[1] *adv* : badly, bad
feo[2], **fea** *adj* **1** : ugly **2** : unpleasant, nasty
féretro *nm* ATAÚD : coffin, casket
feria *nf* **1** : fair, market **2** : festival, holiday **3** *Mex* : change (money)
feriado, -da *adj* día feriado : public holiday
ferial *nm* : fairground
fermentar *v* : to ferment — **fermentación** *nf*
fermento *nm* : ferment
ferocidad *nf* : ferocity, fierceness
feroz *adj, pl* **feroces** FIERO : ferocious, fierce — **ferozmente** *adv*
férreo, -rrea *adj* **1** : iron **2** : strong, steely ⟨una voluntad férrea : an iron will⟩ **3** : strict, severe **4 vía férrea** : railroad track
ferretería *nf* **1** : hardware store **2** : hardware **3** : foundry, ironworks
férrico, -ca *adj* : ferric
ferrocarril *nm* : railroad, railway
ferrocarrilero → **ferroviario**
ferroso, -sa *adj* : ferrous
ferroviario, -ria *adj* : rail, railroad
ferry *nm, pl* **ferrys** : ferry
fértil *adj* FECUNDO : fertile, fruitful
fertilidad *nf* : fertility
fertilizante[1] *adj* : fertilizing ⟨droga fertilizante : fertility drug⟩
fertilizante[2] *nm* ABONO : fertilizer
fertilizar *vt* ABONAR : to fertilize — **fertilización** *nf*
ferviente *adj* FERVOROSO : fervent
fervor *nm* : fervor, zeal
fervoroso, -sa *adj* FERVIENTE : fervent, zealous
festejar *vt* **1** CELEBRAR : to celebrate **2** AGASAJAR : to entertain, to wine and dine **3** *Mex fam* : to thrash, to beat
festejo *nm* : celebration, festivity
festín *nm, pl* **festines** : banquet, feast
festinar *vt* : to hasten, to hurry up
festival *nm* : festival
festividad *nf* **1** : festivity **2** : (religious) feast, holiday
festivo, -va *adj* **1** : festive **2 día festivo** : holiday — **festivamente** *adv*
fetal *adj* : fetal
fetiche *nm* : fetish
fétido, -da *adj* : fetid, foul
feto *nm* : fetus
feudal *adj* : feudal — **feudalismo** *nm*
feudo *nm* **1** : fief **2** : domain, territory
fiabilidad *nf* : reliability, trustworthiness
fiable *adj* : trustworthy, reliable
fiado, -da *adj* : on credit

fiador, -dora *n* : bondsman, guarantor
fiambrería *nf* : delicatessen
fiambres *nfpl* : cold cuts
fianza *nf* **1** CAUCIÓN : bail, bond **2** : surety, deposit
fiar {85} *vt* **1** : to sell on credit **2** : to guarantee — **fiarse** *vr* ~ **de** : to place trust in
fiasco *nm* FRACASO : fiasco, failure
fibra *nf* **1** : fiber **2 fibra de vidrio** : fiberglass
fibrilar *vi* : to fibrillate — **fibrilación** *nf*
fibroso, -sa *adj* : fibrous
ficción *nf, pl* **ficciones** **1** : fiction **2** : fabrication, lie
ficha *nf* **1** : index card **2** : file, record **3** : token **4** : domino, checker, counter, poker chip
fichar *vt* **1** : to open a file on **2** : to sign up — *vi* : to punch in, to punch out
fichero *nm* **1** : card file **2** : filing cabinet
ficticio, -cia *adj* : fictitious
fidedigno, -na *adj* FIABLE : reliable, trustworthy
fideicomisario, -ria *n* : trustee
fideicomiso *nm* : trusteeship, trust ⟨guardar en fideicomiso : to hold in trust⟩
fidelidad *nf* : fidelity, faithfulness
fideo *nm* : noodle
fiduciario[1], **-ria** *adj* : fiduciary
fiduciario[2], **-ria** *n* : trustee
fiebre *nf* **1** CALENTURA : fever, temperature ⟨fiebre amarilla : yellow fever⟩ ⟨fiebre palúdica : malaria⟩ **2** : fever, excitement
fiel[1] *adj* **1** : faithful, loyal **2** : accurate — **fielmente** *adv*
fiel[2] *nm* **1** : pointer (of a scale) **2 los fieles** : the faithful
fieltro *nm* : felt
fiera *nf* **1** : wild animal, beast **2** : fiend, demon ⟨una fiera para el trabajo : a demon for work⟩
fiereza *nf* : fierceness, ferocity
fiero, -ra *adj* FEROZ : fierce, ferocious
fierro *nm* HIERRO : iron
fiesta *nf* **1** : party, fiesta **2** : holiday, feast day
figura *nf* **1** : figure **2** : shape, form **3 figura retórica** : figure of speech
figurado, -da *adj* : figurative — **figuradamente** *adv*
figurar *vi* **1** : to figure, to be included ⟨Rivera figura entre los más grandes pintores de México : Rivera is among Mexico's greatest painters⟩ **2** : to be prominent, to stand out — *vt* : to represent ⟨esta línea figura el horizonte : this line represents the horizon⟩ — **figurarse** *vr* : to imagine, to think ⟨¡figúrate el lío en que se metió! : imagine the mess she got into!⟩
fijación *nf, pl* **-ciones** **1** : fixation, obsession **2** : fixing, establishing **3** : fastening, securing
fijador *nm* **1** : fixative **2** : hair spray

fijamente *adv* : fixedly
fijar *vt* **1** : to fasten, to affix **2** ES-TABLECER : to establish, to set up **3** CONCRETAR : to set, to fix ⟨fijar la fecha : to set the date⟩ — **fijarse** *vr* **1** : to settle, to become fixed **2** ~ **en** : to notice, to pay attention to
fijeza *nf* **1** : firmness (of convictions) **2** : persistence, constancy ⟨mirar con fijeza a : to stare at⟩
fijiano, -na *adj & n* : Fijian
fijo, -ja *adj* **1** : fixed, firm, steady **2** PERMANENTE : permanent
fila *nf* **1** HILERA : line, file ⟨ponerse en fila : to get in line⟩ **2** : rank, row **3** **filas** *nfpl* : ranks ⟨cerrar filas : to close ranks⟩
filamento *nm* : filament
filantropía *nf* : philanthropy
filantrópico, -ca *adj* : philanthropic
filántropo, -pa *n* : philanthropist
filatelia *nf* : philately, stamp collecting
filatelista *nmf* : stamp collector, philatelist
fildeador, -dora *n* : fielder
filete *nm* **1** : fillet **2** SOLOMILLO : sirloin **3** : thread (of a screw)
filiación *nf, pl* **-ciones** **1** : affiliation, connection **2** : particulars *pl,* (police) description
filial[1] *adj* : filial
filial[2] *nf* : affiliate, subsidiary
filibustero *nm* : freebooter, pirate
filigrana *nf* **1** : filigree **2** : watermark (on paper)
filipino, -na *adj & n* : Filipino
filmación *nf, pl* **-ciones** : filming, shooting
filmar *vt* : to film, to shoot
filme *or* **film** *nm* PELÍCULA : film, movie
filmina *nf* : slide, transparency
filo *nm* **1** : cutting edge, blade **2** : edge ⟨al filo del escritorio : at the edge of the desk⟩ ⟨al filo de la medianoche : at the stroke of midnight⟩
filología *nf* : philology
filólogo, -ga *n* : philologist
filón *nm, pl* **filones** **1** : seam, vein (of minerals) **2** *fam* : successful business, gold mine
filoso, -sa *adj* : sharp
filosofar *vi* : to philosophize
filosofía *nf* : philosophy
filosófico, -ca *adj* : philosophic, philosophical — **filosóficamente** *adv*
filósofo, -fa *n* : philosopher
filtración *nf* : seepage, leaking
filtrar *v* : to filter — **filtrarse** *vr* : to seep through, to leak
filtro *nm* : filter
filudo, -da *adj* : sharp
fin *nm* **1** : end **2** : purpose, aim, objective **3** **en** ~ : in short **4** **fin de semana** : weekend **5** **por** ~ : finally, at last
finado, -da *adj & n* DIFUNTO : deceased
final[1] *adj* : final, ultimate — **finalmente** *adv*

final[2] *nm* : end, conclusion, finale
final[3] *nf* : final, play-off
finalidad *nf* **1** : purpose, aim **2** : finality
finalista *nmf* : finalist
finalización *nf* : completion, end
finalizar {21} *v* : to finish, to end
financiación *nf, pl* **-ciones** : financing, funding
financiamiento *nm* → **financiación**
financiar *vt* : to finance, to fund
financiero[1], **-ra** *adj* : financial
financiero[2], **-ra** *n* : financier
financista *nmf* : financier
finanzas *nfpl* : finances, finance ⟨altas finanzas : high finance⟩
finca *nf* **1** : farm, ranch **2** : country house
fineza *nf* FINURA, REFINAMIENTO : refinement
fingido, -da *adj* : false, feigned
fingimiento *nm* : pretense
fingir {35} *v* : to feign, to pretend
finiquitar *vt* **1** : to settle (an account) **2** : to conclude, to bring to an end
finiquito *nm* : settlement (of an account)
finito, -ta *adj* : finite
finja, etc. → **fingir**
finlandés, -desa *adj & n* : Finnish
fino, -na *adj* **1** : fine, excellent **2** : delicate, slender **3** REFINADO : refined **4** : sharp, acute ⟨olfato fino : keen sense of smell⟩ **5** : subtle
finta *nf* : feint
fintar *or* **fintear** *vi* : to feint
finura *nf* **1** : fineness, high quality **2** FINEZA, REFINAMIENTO : refinement
fiordo *nm* : fjord
fique *nm* : sisal
firma *nf* **1** : signature **2** : signing **3** EMPRESA : firm, company
firmamento *nm* : firmament, sky
firmante *nmf* : signer, signatory
firmar *v* : to sign
firme *adj* **1** : firm, resolute **2** : steady, stable
firmemente *adv* : firmly
firmeza *nf* **1** : firmness, stability **2** : strength, resolve
firuletes *nmpl* : frills, adornments
fiscal[1] *adj* : fiscal — **fiscalmente** *adv*
fiscal[2] *nmf* : district attorney, prosecutor
fiscalizar {21} *vt* **1** : to audit, to inspect **2** : to oversee **3** : to criticize
fisco *nm* : national treasury, exchequer
fisgar {52} *vt* HUSMEAR : to pry into, to snoop on
fisgón, -gona *n, mpl* **fisgones** : snoop, busybody
fisgonear *vi* : to snoop, to pry
fisgue, etc. → **fisgar**
física *nf* : physics
físico[1], **-ca** *adj* : physical — **físicamente** *adv*
físico[2], **-ca** *n* : physicist
físico[3] *nm* : physique, figure
fisiología *nf* : physiology

fisiológico, -ca *adj* : physiological, physiologic
fisiólogo, -ga *n* : physiologist
fisión *nf, pl* **fisiones** : fission — **fisionable** *adj*
fisionomía → **fisonomía**
fisioterapeuta *nmf* : physical therapist
fisioterapia *nf* : physical therapy
fisonomía *nf* : physiognomy, features *pl*
fistol *nm Mex* : tie clip
fisura *nf* : fissure, crevasse
fláccido, -da *or* **flácido, -da** *adj* : flaccid, flabby
flaco, -ca *adj* 1 DELGADO : thin, skinny 2 : feeble, weak ⟨una flaca excusa : a feeble excuse⟩
flagelar *vt* : to flagellate — **flagelación** *nf*
flagelo *nm* 1 : scourge, whip 2 : calamity
flagrante *adj* : flagrant, glaring, blatant — **flagrantemente** *adv*
flama *nf* LLAMA : flame
flamante *adj* 1 : bright, brilliant 2 : brand-new
flamear *vi* 1 LLAMEAR : to flame, to blaze 2 ONDEAR : to flap, to flutter
flamenco¹, -ca *adj* 1 : flamenco 2 : Flemish
flamenco², -ca *n* : Fleming, Flemish person
flamenco³ *nm* 1 : Flemish (language) 2 : flamingo 3 : flamenco (music or dance)
flanco *nm* : flank, side
flanquear *vt* : to flank
flaquear *vi* DECAER : to flag, to weaken
flaqueza *nf* 1 DEBILIDAD : frailty, feebleness 2 : thinness 3 : weakness, failing
flato *nm* : gloom, melancholy
flatulento, -ta *adj* : flatulent — **flatulencia** *nf*
flauta *nf* 1 : flute 2 **flauta dulce** : recorder
flautín *nm, pl* **flautines** : piccolo
flautista *nmf* : flute player, flutist
flebitis *nf* : phlebitis
flecha *nf* : arrow
fleco *nm* 1 : bangs *pl* 2 : fringe
flema *nf* : phlegm
flemático, -ca *adj* : phlegmatic, stolid, impassive
flequillo *nm* : bangs *pl*
fletar *vt* 1 : to charter, to hire 2 : to load (freight)
flete *nm* 1 : charter fee 2 : shipping cost 3 : freight, cargo
fletero *nm* : shipper, carrier
flexibilidad *nf* : flexibility
flexibilizar {21} *vt* : to make more flexible
flexible¹ *adj* : flexible
flexible² *nm* 1 : flexible electrical cord 2 : soft hat
flirtear *vi* : to flirt
flojear *vi* 1 DEBILITARSE : to weaken, to flag 2 : to idle, to loaf around

flojedad *nf* : weakness
flojera *nf fam* 1 : lethargy, feeling of weakness 2 : laziness
flojo, -ja *adj* 1 SUELTO : loose, slack 2 : weak, poor ⟨está flojo en las ciencias : he's weak in science⟩ 3 PEREZOSO : lazy
flor *nf* 1 : flower 2 **flor de Pascua** : poinsettia
flora *nf* : flora
floración *nf* : flowering ⟨en plena floración : in full bloom⟩
floral *adj* : floral
floreado, -da *adj* : flowered, flowery
florear *vi* FLORECER : to flower, to bloom — *vt* 1 : to adorn with flowers 2 *Mex* : to flatter, to compliment
florecer {53} *vi* 1 : to bloom, to blossom 2 : to flourish, to thrive
floreciente *adj* 1 : flowering 2 PRÓSPERO : flourishing, thriving
florecimiento *nm* : flowering
floreo *nm* : flourish
florería *nf* : flower shop, florist's
florero¹, -ra *n* : florist
florero² *nm* JARRÓN : vase
floresta *nf* 1 : glade, grove 2 BOSQUE : woods
florido, -da *adj* 1 : full of flowers 2 : florid, flowery ⟨escritos floridos : flowery prose⟩
florista *nmf* : florist
floritura *nf* : frill, embellishment
flota *nf* : fleet
flotabilidad *nf* : buoyancy
flotación *nf, pl* **-ciones** : flotation
flotador *nm* 1 : float 2 : life preserver
flotante *adj* : floating, buoyant
flotar *vi* : to float
flote *nm* a ~ : afloat
flotilla *nf* : flotilla, fleet
fluctuar {3} *vi* 1 : to fluctuate 2 VACILAR : to vacillate — **fluctuación** *nf* — **fluctuante** *adj*
fluidez *nf* 1 : fluency 2 : fluidity
fluido¹, -da *adj* 1 : flowing 2 : fluent 3 : fluid
fluido² *nm* : fluid
fluir {41} *vi* : to flow
flujo *nm* 1 : flow 2 : discharge
flúor *nm* : fluorine
fluoración *nf, pl* **-ciones** : fluoridation
fluorescencia *nf* : fluorescence — **fluorescente** *adj*
fluorizar {21} *vt* : to fluoridate
fluoruro *nm* : fluoride
fluvial *adj* : fluvial, river
fluye, etc. → **fluir**
fobia *nf* : phobia
foca *nf* : seal (animal)
focal *adj* : focal
focha *nf* : coot
foco *nm* 1 : focus 2 : center, pocket 3 : lightbulb 4 : spotlight 5 : headlight
fofo, -fa *adj* 1 ESPONJOSO : soft, spongy 2 : flabby
fogaje *nm* 1 FUEGO : skin eruption, cold sore 2 BOCHORNO : hot and humid weather

fogata *nf* : bonfire
fogón *nm, pl* **fogones** : bonfire
fogonazo *nm* : flash, explosion
fogonero, -ra *n* : stoker (of a furnace), fireman
fogoso, -sa *adj* ARDIENTE : ardent
foguear *vt* : to inure, to accustom
foja *nf* : sheet (of paper)
folículo *nm* : follicle
folio *nm* : folio, leaf
folklore *nm* : folklore
folklórico, -ca *adj* : folk, traditional
follaje *nm* : foliage
folleto *nm* : pamphlet, leaflet, circular
fomentar *vt* **1** : to foment, to stir up **2** PROMOVER : to promote, to foster
fomento *nm* : promotion, encouragement
fonda *nf* **1** POSADA : inn **2** : small restaurant
fondeado, -da *adj fam* : rich, in the money
fondear *vt* **1** : to sound **2** : to sound out, to examine **3** *Mex* : to fund, to finance — *vi* ANCLAR : to anchor — **fondearse** *vr fam* : to get rich
fondeo *nm* **1** : anchoring **2** *Mex* : funding, financing
fondillos *mpl* : seat, bottom (of clothing)
fondo *nm* **1** : bottom **2** : rear, back, end **3** : depth **4** : background **5** : sea bed **6** : fund ⟨fondo de inversiones : investment fund⟩ **7** *Mex* : slip, petticoat **8** **fondos** *nmpl* : funds, resources ⟨cheque sin fondos : bounced check⟩ **9 a ~** : thoroughly, in depth **10 en ~** : abreast
fonema *nm* : phoneme
fonética *nf* : phonetics
fonético, -ca *adj* : phonetic
fontanería *nf* PLOMERÍA : plumbing
fontanero, -ra *n* PLOMERO : plumber
footing ['fu,tɪŋ] *nm* : jogging ⟨hacer footing : to jog⟩
foque *nm* : jib
forajido, -da *n* : bandit, fugitive, outlaw
foráneo, -nea *adj* : foreign, strange
forastero, -ra *n* : stranger, outsider
forcejear *vi* : to struggle
forcejeo *nm* : struggle
fórceps *nms & pl* : forceps *pl*
forense *adj* : forensic, legal
forestal *adj* : forest
forja *nf* FRAGUA : forge
forjar *vt* **1** : to forge **2** : to shape, to create ⟨forjar un compromiso : to hammer out a compromise⟩ **3** : to invent, to concoct
forma *nf* **1** : form, shape **2** MANERA, MODO : manner, way **3** : fitness ⟨estar en forma : to be fit, to be in shape⟩ **4** **formas** *nfpl* : appearances, conventions
formación *nf, pl* **-ciones 1** : formation **2** : training ⟨formación profesional : vocational training⟩

formal *adj* **1** : formal **2** : serious, dignified **3** : dependable, reliable
formaldehído *nm* : formaldehyde
formalidad *nf* **1** : formality **2** : seriousness, dignity **3** : dependability, reliability
formalizar {21} *vt* : to formalize, to make official
formalmente *adv* : formally
formar *vt* **1** : to form, to make **2** CONSTITUIR : to constitute, to make up **3** : to train, to educate — **formarse** *vr* **1** DESARROLLARSE : to develop, to take shape **2** EDUCARSE : to be educated
formatear *vt* : to format
formativo, -va *adj* : formative
formato *nm* : format
formidable *adj* **1** : formidable, tremendous **2** *fam* : fantastic, terrific
formón *nm, pl* **formones** : chisel
fórmula *nf* : formula
formulación *nf, pl* **-ciones** : formulation
formular *vt* **1** : to formulate, to draw up **2** : to make, to lodge (a protest or complaint)
formulario *nm* : form ⟨rellenar un formulario : to fill out a form⟩
fornicar {72} *vi* : to fornicate — **fornicación** *nf*
fornido, -da *adj* : well-built, burly, hefty
foro *nm* **1** : forum **2** : public assembly, open discussion
forraje *nm* **1** : forage, fodder **2** : foraging **3** *fam* : hodgepodge
forrajear *vi* : to forage
forrar *vt* **1** : to line (a garment) **2** : to cover (a book)
forro *nm* **1** : lining **2** CUBIERTA : book cover
forsitia *nf* : forsythia
fortachón, -chona *adj, pl* **-chones** *fam* : brawny, strong, tough
fortalecer {53} *vt* : to strengthen, to fortify — **fortalecerse** *vr*
fortalecimiento *nm* **1** : strengthening, fortifying **2** : fortifications
fortaleza *nf* **1** : fortress **2** FUERZA : strength **3** : resolution, fortitude
fortificación *nf, pl* **-ciones** : fortification
fortificar {72} *vt* **1** : to fortify **2** : to strengthen
fortín *nm, pl* **fortines** : small fort
fortuito, -ta *adj* : fortuitous
fortuna *nf* **1** SUERTE : fortune, luck **2** RIQUEZA : wealth, fortune
forzar {36} *vt* **1** OBLIGAR : to force, to compel **2** : to force open **3** : to strain ⟨forzar los ojos : to strain one's eyes⟩
forzosamente *adv* **1** : forcibly, by force **2** : necessarily, inevitably ⟨forzosamente tendrán que pagar : they'll have no choice but to pay⟩
forzoso, -sa *adj* **1** : forced, compulsory **2** : necessary, inevitable
fosa *nf* **1** : ditch, pit ⟨fosa séptica : septic tank⟩ **2** TUMBA : grave **3** : cavity ⟨fosas nasales : nasal cavities, nostrils⟩
fosfato *nm* : phosphate

fosforescencia *nf* : phosphorescence — **fosforescente** *adj*

fósforo *nm* **1** CERILLA : match **2** : phosphorus

fósil[1] *adj* : fossilized, fossil

fósil[2] *nm* : fossil

fosilizarse {21} *vr* : to fossilize, to become fossilized

foso *nm* **1** FOSA, ZANJA : ditch **2** : pit (of a theater) **3** : moat

foto *nf* : photo, picture

fotocopia *nf* : photocopy — **fotocopiar** *vt*

fotocopiadora *nf* COPIADORA : photocopier

fotoeléctrico, -ca *adj* : photoelectric

fotogénico, -ca *adj* : photogenic

fotografía *nf* **1** : photograph **2** : photography

fotografiar {85} *vt* : to photograph

fotográfico, -ca *adj* : photographic — **fotográficamente** *adv*

fotógrafo, -fa *n* : photographer

fotosíntesis *nf* : photosynthesis

fotosintético, -ca *adj* : photosynthetic

fracasado[1], **-da** *adj* : unsuccessful, failed

fracasado[2], **-da** *n* : failure

fracasar *vi* **1** FALLAR : to fail **2** : to fall through

fracaso *nm* FIASCO : failure

fracción *nf, pl* **fracciones 1** : fraction **2** : part, fragment **3** : faction, splinter group

fraccionamiento *nm* **1** : division, breaking up **2** *Mex* : residential area, housing development

fraccionar *vt* : to divide, to break up

fraccionario, -ria *adj* : fractional

fractura *nf* **1** : fracture **2 fractura complicada** : compound fracture

fracturarse *vr* QUEBRARSE, ROMPERSE : to fracture, to break ⟨fracturarse el brazo : to break one's arm⟩

fragancia *nf* : fragrance, scent

fragante *adj* : fragrant

fragata *nf* : frigate

frágil *adj* **1** : fragile **2** : frail, delicate

fragilidad *nf* **1** : fragility **2** : frailty, delicacy

fragmentar *vt* : to fragment — **fragmentación** *nf*

fragmentario, -ria *adj* : fragmentary, sketchy

fragmento *nm* **1** : fragment, shard **2** : bit, snippet **3** : excerpt, passage

fragor *nm* : clamor, din, roar

fragoroso, -sa *adj* : thunderous, deafening

fragoso, -sa *adj* **1** : rough, uneven **2** : thick, dense

fragua *nf* FORJA : forge

fraguar {10} *vt* **1** : to forge **2** : to conceive, to concoct, to hatch — *vi* : to set, to solidify

fraile *nm* : friar, monk

frambuesa *nf* : raspberry

francamente *adv* **1** : frankly, candidly **2** REALMENTE : really ⟨es francamente admirable : it's really impressive⟩

francés[1], **-cesa** *adj, mpl* **franceses** : French

francés[2], **-cesa** *n, mpl* **franceses** : French person, Frenchman *m*, Frenchwoman *f*

francés[3] *nm* : French (language)

franciscano, -na *adj & n* : Franciscan

francmasón, -sona *n, mpl* **-sones** : Freemason — **francmasonería** *nf*

franco[1], **-ca** *adj* **1** CÁNDIDO : frank, candid **2** PATENTE : clear, obvious **3** : free ⟨franco a bordo : free on board⟩

franco[2] *nm* : franc

francotirador, -dora *n* : sniper

franela *nf* : flannel

franja *nf* **1** : stripe, band **2** : border, fringe

franquear *vt* **1** : to clear **2** ATRAVESAR : to cross, to go through **3** : to pay the postage on

franqueo *nm* : postage

franqueza *nf* : frankness

franquicia *nf* **1** EXENCIÓN : exemption **2** : franchise

frasco *nm* : small bottle, flask, vial

frase *nf* **1** : phrase **2** ORACIÓN : sentence

frasear *vt* : to phrase

fraternal *adj* : fraternal, brotherly

fraternidad *nf* **1** : brotherhood **2** : fraternity

fraternizar {21} *vi* : to fraternize — **fraternización** *nf*

fraterno, -na *adj* : fraternal, brotherly

fratricida *adj* : fratricidal

fratricidio *nm* : fratricide

fraude *nm* : fraud

fraudulento, -ta *adj* : fraudulent — **fraudulentamente** *adv*

fray *nm* : brother (title of a friar) ⟨Fray Bartolomé : Brother Bartholomew⟩

frazada *nf* COBIJA, MANTA : blanket

frecuencia *nf* : frequency

frecuentar *vt* : to frequent, to haunt

frecuente *adj* : frequent — **frecuentemente** *adv*

fregadera *nf fam* : hassle, pain in the neck

fregadero *nm* : kitchen sink

fregado[1], **-da** *adj fam* : annoying, bothersome

fregado[2] *nm* **1** : scrubbing, scouring **2** *fam* : mess, muddle

fregar {49} *vt* **1** : to scrub, to scour, to wash ⟨fregar los trastes : to do the dishes⟩ ⟨fregar el suelo : to scrub the floor⟩ **2** *fam* : to annoy — *vi* **1** : to wash the dishes **2** : to clean, to scrub **3** *fam* : to be annoying

freidera *nf Mex* : frying pan

freír {37} *vt* : to fry — **freírse** *vr*

frenar *vt* **1** : to brake **2** DETENER : to curb, to check — *vi* : to apply the brakes — **frenarse** *vr* : to restrain oneself

frenesí *nm* : frenzy

frenético, -ca *adj* : frantic, frenzied — **frenéticamente** *adv*

freno *nm* **1** : brake **2** : bit (of a bridle) **3** : check, restraint **4 frenos** *nmpl Mex* : braces (for teeth)

frente[1] *nm* **1** : front ⟨al frente de : at the head of⟩ ⟨en frente : in front, opposite⟩ **2** : facade **3** : front line, sphere of activity **4** : front (in meteorology) ⟨frente frío : cold front⟩ **5 hacer frente a** : to face up to, to brave

frente[2] *nf* **1** : forehead, brow **2 frente a frente** : face to face

fresa *nf* **1** : strawberry **2** : drill (in dentistry)

fresco[1], **-ca** *adj* **1** : fresh **2** : cool **3** *fam* : insolent, nervy

fresco[2] *nm* **1** : coolness **2** : fresh air ⟨al fresco : in the open air, outdoors⟩ **3** : fresco

frescor *nm* : cool air ⟨el frescor de la noche : the cool of the evening⟩

frescura *nf* **1** : freshness **2** : coolness **3** : calmness **4** DESCARO : nerve, audacity

fresno *nm* : ash (tree)

freza *nf* : spawn, roe

frezar {21} *vi* DESOVAR : to spawn

friable *adj* : friable

frialdad *nf* **1** : coldness **2** INDIFERENCIA : indifference, unconcern

fríamente *adv* : coldly, indifferently

fricasé *nm* : fricassee

fricción *nf, pl* **-cciones 1** : friction **2** : rubbing, massage **3** : discord, disagreement ⟨fricción entre los hermanos : friction between the brothers⟩

friccionar *vt* **1** FROTAR : to rub **2** : to massage

friega[1], **friegue, etc.** → **fregar**

friega[2] *nf* **1** FRICCIÓN : rubdown, massage **2** : annoyance, bother

frigidez *nf* : (sexual) frigidity

frigorífico *nm Spain* : refrigerator

frijol *nm* : bean ⟨frijoles refritos : refried beans⟩

frío[1], **fría** *adj* **1** : cold **2** INDIFERENTE : cool, indifferent

frío[2] *nm* **1** : cold ⟨hace mucho frío esta noche : it's very cold tonight⟩ **2** INDIFERENCIA : coldness, indifference **3 tener frío** : to feel cold ⟨tengo frío : I'm cold⟩ **4 tomar frío** RESFRIARSE : to catch a cold

friolento, -ta *adj* : sensitive to cold

friolera *nf* (*used ironically or humorously*) : trifling amount ⟨una friolera de mil dólares : a mere thousand dollars⟩

friso *nm* : frieze

fritar *vt* : to fry

frito[1] *pp* → **freír**

frito[2], **-ta** *adj* **1** : fried **2** *fam* : worn-out, fed up ⟨tener frito a alguien : to get on someone's nerves⟩ **3** *fam* : fast asleep ⟨se quedó frito en el sofá : she fell asleep on the couch⟩

fritura *nf* **1** : frying **2** : fried food

frivolidad *nf* : frivolity

frívolo, -la *adj* : frivolous — **frívolamente** *adv*

fronda *nf* **1** : frond **2 frondas** *nfpl* : foliage

frondoso, -sa *adj* : leafy, luxuriant

frontal *adj* : frontal, head-on ⟨un choque frontal : a head-on collision⟩

frontalmente *adv* : head-on

frontera *nf* : border, frontier

fronterizo, -za *adj* : border, on the border ⟨estados fronterizos : neighboring states⟩

frontispicio *nm* : frontispiece

frotar *vt* **1** : to rub **2** : to strike (a match) — **frotarse** *vr* : to rub (together)

frote *nm* : rubbing, rub

fructífero, -ra *adj* : fruitful, productive

fructificar {72} *vi* **1** : to bear or produce fruit **2** : to be productive

fructuoso, -sa *adj* : fruitful

frugal *adj* : frugal, thrifty — **frugalmente** *adv*

frugalidad *adj* : frugality

frunce *nm* : gather (in cloth), pucker

fruncido *nm* : gathering, shirring

fruncir {83} *vt* **1** : to gather, to shirr **2 fruncir el ceño** : to knit one's brow, to frown **3 fruncir la boca** : to pucker up, to purse one's lips

frunza, etc. → **fruncir**

frustración *nf, pl* **-ciones** : frustration

frustrado, -da *adj* **1** : frustrated **2** : failed, unsuccessful

frustrante *adj* : frustrating

frustrar *vt* : to frustrate, to thwart — **frustrarse** *vr* FRACASAR : to fail, to come to nothing ⟨se frustraron sus esperanzas : his hopes were dashed⟩

fruta *nf* : fruit

frutal[1] *adj* : fruit, fruit-bearing

frutal[2] *nm* : fruit tree

frutilla *nf* : South American strawberry

fruto *nm* **1** : fruit, agricultural product ⟨los frutos de la tierra : the fruits of the earth⟩ **2** : result, consequence ⟨los frutos de su trabajo : the fruits of his labor⟩

fucsia *adj & nm* : fuchsia

fue, etc. → **ir, ser**

fuego *nm* **1** : fire **2** : light ⟨¿tienes fuego? : have you got a light?⟩ **3** : flame, burner (on a stove) **4** : ardor, passion **5** FOGAJE : skin eruption, cold sore **6 fuegos artificiales** *nmpl* : fireworks

fuelle *nm* : bellows

fuente *nf* **1** MANANTIAL : spring **2** : fountain **3** ORIGEN : source ⟨fuentes informativas : sources of information⟩ **4** : platter, serving dish

fuera *adv* **1** : outside, out **2** : abroad, away **3** ~ **de** : outside of, out of, beyond **4** ~ **de** : besides, in addition to ⟨fuera de eso : aside from that⟩ **5 fuera de lugar** : out of place, amiss

fuerce, fuerza etc. → **forzar**

fuero *nm* **1** JURISDICCIÓN : jurisdiction **2** : privilege, exemption **3 fuero interno** : conscience, heart of hearts

fuerte[1] *adv* **1** : strongly, tightly, hard **2** : loudly **3** : abundantly

fuerte[2] *adj* **1** : strong **2** : intense ⟨un fuerte dolor : an intense pain⟩ **3** : loud **4** : extreme, excessive

fuerte[3] *nm* **1** : fort, stronghold **2** : forte, strong point

fuerza *nf* **1** : strength, vigor ⟨fuerza de voluntad : willpower⟩ **2** : force ⟨fuerza bruta : brute force⟩ **3** : power, might ⟨fuerza de brazos : manpower⟩ **4 fuerzas** *nfpl* : forces ⟨fuerzas armadas : armed forces⟩ **5 a fuerza de** : by, by dint of

fuetazo *nm* : lash

fuga *nf* **1** HUIDA : flight, escape **2** : fugue **3** : leak ⟨fuga de gas : gas leak⟩

fugarse {52} *vr* **1** : to escape **2** HUIR : to flee, to run away **3** : to elope

fugaz *adj, pl* **fugaces** : brief, fleeting

fugitivo, -va *adj & n* : fugitive

fulana *nf* : hooker, slut

fulano, -na *n* : so-and-so, what's-his-name, what's-her-name ⟨fulano, mengano, y zutano : Tom, Dick, and Harry⟩ ⟨señora fulana de tal : Mrs. so-and-so⟩

fulcro *nm* : fulcrum

fulgor *nm* : brilliance, splendor

fulgurar *vi* : to shine brightly, to gleam, to glow

fulminante *adj* **1** : fulminating, explosive **2** : devastating, terrible ⟨una mirada fulminante : a withering look⟩

fulminar *vt* **1** : to strike with lightning **2** : to strike down ⟨fulminar a alguien con la mirada : to look daggers at someone⟩

fumador, -dora *n* : smoker

fumar *v* : to smoke

fumble *nm* : fumble (in football)

fumblear *vt* : to fumble (in football)

fumigante *nm* : fumigant

fumigar {52} *vt* : to fumigate — **fumigación** *nf*

funámbulo, -la *n* EQUILIBRISTA : tightrope walker

función *nf, pl* **funciones 1** : function **2** : duty **3** : performance, show

funcional *adj* : functional — **funcionalmente** *adv*

funcionamiento *nm* **1** : functioning **2 en ~** : in operation

funcionar *vi* **1** : to function **2** : to run, to work

funcionario, -ria *n* : civil servant, official

funda *nf* **1** : case, cover, sheath **2** : pillowcase

fundación *nf, pl* **-ciones** : foundation, establishment

fundado, -da *adj* : well-founded, justified

fundador, -dora *n* : founder

fundamental *adj* BÁSICO : fundamental, basic — **fundamentalmente** *adv*

fundamentalismo *nm* : fundamentalism

fundamentalista *nmf* : fundamentalist

fundamentar *vt* **1** : to lay the foundations for **2** : to support, to back up **3** : to base, to found

fundamento *nm* : basis, foundation, groundwork

fundar *vt* **1** ESTABLECER, INSTITUIR : to found, to establish **2** BASAR : to base — **fundarse** *vr* ~ **en** : to be based on, to stem from

fundición *nf, pl* **-ciones 1** : founding, smelting **2** : foundry

fundir *vt* **1** : to melt down, to smelt **2** : to fuse, to merge **3** : to burn out (a lightbulb) — **fundirse** *vr* **1** : to fuse together, to blend, to merge **2** : to melt, to thaw **3** : to fade (in television or movies)

fúnebre *adj* **1** : funeral, funereal **2** LÚGUBRE : gloomy, mournful

funeral[1] *adj* : funeral, funerary

funeral[2] *nm* **1** : funeral **2 funerales** *nmpl* EXEQUIAS : funeral rites

funeraria *nf* **1** : funeral home, funeral parlor **2 director de funeraria** : funeral director, undertaker

funerario, -ria *adj* : funeral

funesto, -ta *adj* : terrible, disastrous ⟨consecuencias funestas : disastrous consequences⟩

fungicida[1] *adj* : fungicidal

fungicida[2] *nm* : fungicide

fungir {35} *vi* : to act, to function ⟨fungir de asesor : to act as a consultant⟩

fungoso, -sa *adj* : fungous

funja, etc. → **fungir**

furgón *nm, pl* **furgones 1** : van, truck **2** : freight car, boxcar **3 furgón de cola** : caboose

furgoneta *nf* : van

furia *nf* **1** CÓLERA, IRA : fury, rage **2** : violence, fury ⟨la furia de la tormenta : the fury of the storm⟩

furibundo, -da *adj* : furious

furiosamente *adv* : furiously, frantically

furioso, -sa *adj* **1** AIRADO : furious, irate **2** : intense, violent

furor *nm* **1** : fury, rage **2** : violence (of the elements) **3** : passion, frenzy **4** : enthusiasm ⟨hacer furor : to be all the rage⟩

furtivo, -va *adj* : furtive — **furtivamente** *adv*

furúnculo *nm* DIVIESO : boil

fuselaje *nm* : fuselage

fusible *nm* : (electrical) fuse

fusil *nm* : rifle

fusilar *vt* **1** : to shoot, to execute (by firing squad) **2** *fam* : to plagiarize, to pirate

fusilería *nf* **1** : rifles *pl*, rifle fire **2 descarga de fusilería** : fusillade

fusión *nf, pl* **fusiones 1** : fusion **2** : union, merger

fusionar *vt* **1** : to fuse **2** : to merge, to amalgamate — **fusionarse** *vr*
fusta *nf* : riding crop
fustigar {52} *vt* **1** AZOTAR : to whip, to lash **2** : to upbraid, to berate
futbol *or* **fútbol** *nm* **1** : soccer **2 futbol americano** : football

futbolista *nmf* : soccer player
futesa *nf* **1** : small thing, trifle **2 futesas** *nfpl* : small talk
fútil *adj* : trifling, trivial
futurista *adj* : futuristic
futuro[1], **-ra** *adj* : future
futuro[2] *nm* PORVENIR : future

G

g *nf* : seventh letter of the Spanish alphabet
gabán *nm, pl* **gabanes** : topcoat, overcoat
gabardina *nf* **1** : gabardine **2** : trench coat, raincoat
gabarra *nf* : barge
gabinete *nm* **1** : cabinet (in government) **2** : study, office (in the home) **3** : (professional) office
gablete *nm* : gable
gabonés, -nesa *adj & n, mpl* **-neses** : Gabonese
gacela *nf* : gazelle
gaceta *nf* : gazette, newspaper
gachas *nfpl* : porridge
gacho, -cha *adj* **1** : drooping, turned downward **2** *Mex fam* : nasty, awful **3 ir a gachas** *fam* : to go on all fours
gaélico[1], **-ca** *adj* : Gaelic
gaélico[2] *nm* : Gaelic (language)
gafas *nfpl* ANTEOJOS : eyeglasses, glasses
gaita *nf* : bagpipes *pl*
gajes *nmpl* **gajes del oficio** : occupational hazards
gajo *nm* **1** : broken branch (of a tree) **2** : cluster, bunch (of fruit) **3** : segment (of citrus fruit)
gala *nf* **1** : gala ⟨vestido de gala : formal dress⟩ ⟨tener algo a gala : to be proud of something⟩ **2 galas** *nfpl* : finery, attire
galáctico, -ca *adj* : galactic
galán *nm, pl* **galanes** **1** : ladies' man, gallant **2** : leading man, hero **3** : boyfriend, suitor
galano, -na *adj* **1** : elegant **2** *Mex* : mottled
galante *adj* : gallant, attentive — **galantemente** *adv*
galantear *vt* **1** CORTEJAR : to court, to woo **2** : to flirt with
galanteo *nm* **1** CORTEJO : courtship **2** : flirtation, flirting
galantería *nf* **1** : gallantry, attentiveness **2** : compliment
galápago *nm* : aquatic turtle
galardón *nm, pl* **-dones** : award, prize
galardonado, -da *adj* : prize-winning
galardonar *vt* : to give an award to
galaxia *nf* : galaxy
galeno *nm fam* : physician, doctor
galeón *nm, pl* **galeones** : galleon
galera *nf* : galley

galería *nf* **1** : gallery, balcony (in a theater) ⟨galería comercial : shopping mall⟩ **2** : corridor, passage
galerón *n, mpl* **-rones** *Mex* : large hall
galés[1], **-lesa** *adj* : Welsh
galés[2], **-lesa** *n, mpl* **galeses** **1** : Welshman *m*, Welshwoman *f* **2 los galeses** : the Welsh
galés[3] *nm* : Welsh (language)
galgo *nm* : greyhound
galimatías *nms & pl* : gibberish, nonsense
galio *nm* : gallium
gallardete *nm* : pennant, streamer
gallardía *nf* **1** VALENTÍA : bravery **2** APOSTURA : elegance, gracefulness
gallardo, -da *adj* **1** VALIENTE : brave **2** APUESTO : elegant, graceful
gallear *vi* : to show off, to strut around
gallego[1], **-ga** *adj* **1** : Galician **2** *fam* : Spanish
gallego[2], **-ga** *n* **1** : Galician **2** *fam* : Spaniard
galleta *nf* **1** : cookie **2** : cracker
gallina *nf* **1** : hen **2 gallina de Guinea** : guinea fowl
gallinazo *nm* : vulture, buzzard
gallinero *nm* : chicken coop, henhouse
gallito, -ta *adj fam* : cocky, belligerent
gallo *nm* **1** : rooster, cock **2** *fam* : squeak or crack in the voice **3** *Mex* : serenade **4 gallo de pelea** : gamecock
galo[1], **-la** *adj* **1** : Gaulish **2** : French
galo[2], **-la** *n* **1** : Frenchman *m*, Frenchwoman *f*
galocha *nf* : galosh
galón *nm, pl* **galones** **1** : gallon **2** : stripe (military insignia)
galopada *nf* : gallop
galopante *adj* : galloping ⟨inflación galopante : galloping inflation⟩
galopar *vi* : to gallop
galope *nm* : gallop
galpón *nm, pl* **galpones** : shed, storehouse
galvanizar {21} *vt* : to galvanize — **galvanización** *nf*
gama *nf* **1** : range, spectrum, gamut **2** → **gamo**
gamba *nf* : large shrimp, prawn
gamberro, -rra *n Spain* : hooligan, troublemaker
gambiano, -na *adj & n* : Gambian
gambito *nm* : gambit (in chess)
gameto *nm* : gamete

gamo, -ma *n* : fallow deer
gamuza *nf* **1** : suede **2** : chamois
gana *nf* **1** : desire, inclination **2 de bue-**
na gana : willingly, readily, gladly **3**
de mala gana : reluctantly, halfheartedly **4 tener ganas de** : to feel like, to
be in the mood for ⟨tengo ganas de
bailar : I feel like dancing⟩ **5 ponerle**
ganas a algo : to put effort into something
ganadería *nf* **1** : cattle raising, stock-
breeding **2** : cattle ranch **3** GANADO
: cattle *pl*, livestock
ganadero¹, -ra *adj* : cattle, ranching
ganadero², -ra *n* : rancher, stockbreed-
er
ganado *nm* **1** : cattle *pl*, livestock **2**
ganado ovino : sheep *pl* **3 ganado por-**
cino : swine *pl*
ganador¹, -dora *adj* : winning
ganador², -dora *n* : winner
ganancia *nf* **1** : profit **2 ganancias** *nfpl*
: winnings, gains
ganancioso, -sa *adj* : profitable
ganar *vt* **1** : to win **2** : to gain ⟨ganar
tiempo : to buy time⟩ **3** : to earn ⟨ga-
nar dinero : to make money⟩ **4** : to acquire, to obtain — *vi* **1** : to win **2** : to
profit ⟨salir ganando : to come out
ahead⟩ — **ganarse** *vr* **1** : to gain, to
win ⟨ganarse a alguien : to win someone over⟩ **2** : to earn ⟨ganarse la vida
: to make a living⟩ **3** : to deserve
gancho *nm* **1** : hook **2** : clothes hanger **3** : hairpin, bobby pin **4** *Col* : safety pin
gandul¹ *nm* *CA, Car, Col* : pigeon pea
gandul², -dula *n fam* : idler, lazybones
gandulear *vi* : to idle, to loaf, to lounge
about
ganga *nf* : bargain
ganglio *nm* **1** : ganglion **2** : gland
gangrena *nf* : gangrene — **gangrenoso,**
-sa *adj*
gángster *nmf, pl* **gángsters** : gangster
gansada *nf* : silly thing, nonsense
ganso, -sa *n* **1** : goose, gander *m* **2** : idiot, fool
gañido *nm* : yelp (of a dog)
gañir {38} *vi* : to yelp
garabatear *v* : to scribble, to scrawl, to
doodle
garabato *nm* **1** : doodle **2 garabatos**
nmpl : scribble, scrawl
garaje *nm* : garage
garante *nmf* : guarantor
garantía *nf* **1** : guarantee, warranty **2**
: security ⟨garantía de trabajo : job se-
curity⟩
garantizar {21} *vt* : to guarantee
garapiña *nf* : pineapple drink
garapiñar *vt* : to candy
garbanzo *nm* : chickpea, garbanzo
garbo *nm* **1** DONAIRE : grace, poise **2**
: jauntiness
garboso, -sa *adj* **1** : graceful **2** : elegant, stylish
garceta *nf* : egret

gardenia *nf* : gardenia
garfio *nm* : hook, gaff, grapnel
gargajo *nm fam* : phlegm
garganta *nf* **1** : throat **2** : neck (of a
person or a bottle) **3** : ravine, narrow
pass
gargantilla *nf* : choker, necklace
gárgara *nf* **1** : gargle, gargling **2 hacer**
gárgaras : to gargle
gargarizar *vi* : to gargle
gárgola *nf* : gargoyle
garita *nf* **1** : cabin, hut **2** : sentry box,
lookout post
garoso, -sa *adj Col, Ven* : gluttonous,
greedy
garra *nf* **1** : claw **2** : hand, paw **3 garr-**
as *nfpl* : claws, clutches ⟨caer en las
garras de alguien : to fall into someone's clutches⟩
garrafa *nf* : decanter, carafe
garrafal *adj* : terrible, monstrous
garrafón *nm, pl* **-fones** : large decanter,
large bottle
garrapata *nf* : tick
garrobo *nm CA* : large lizard, iguana
garrocha *nf* **1** PICA : lance, pike **2** : pole
⟨salto con garrocha : pole vault⟩
garrotazo *nm* : blow (with a club)
garrote *nm* **1** : club, stick **2** *Mex* : brake
garúa *nf* : drizzle
garuar {3} *v impers* LLOVIZNAR : to drizzle
garza *nf* : heron
gas *nm* : gas, vapor, fumes *pl* ⟨gas la-
grimógeno : tear gas⟩
gasa *nf* : gauze
gasear *vt* **1** : to gas **2** : to aerate (a liquid)
gaseosa *nf* REFRESCO : soda, soft drink
gaseoso, -sa *adj* **1** : gaseous **2** : carbonated, fizzy
gasoducto *nm* : gas pipeline
gasolina *nf* : gasoline, gas
gasolinera *nf* : gas station, service station
gastado, -da *adj* **1** : spent **2** : worn,
worn-out
gastador¹, -dora *adj* : extravagant,
spendthrift
gastador², -dora *n* : spendthrift
gastar *vt* **1** : to spend **2** CONSUMIR : to
consume, to use up **3** : to squander, to
waste **4** : to wear ⟨gasta un bigote : he
sports a mustache⟩ — **gastarse** *vr* **1**
: to spend, to expend **2** : to run down,
to wear out
gasto *nm* **1** : expense, expenditure **2**
DETERIORO : wear **3 gastos gen-**
erales *or* **gastos indirectos** : overhead
gástrico, -ca *adj* : gastric
gastritis *nf* : gastritis
gastronomía *nf* : gastronomy
gastronómico, -ca *adj* : gastronomic
gastrónomo, -ma *n* : gourmet
gatas *adv* **andar a gatas** : to crawl, to
go on all fours
gatear *vi* **1** : to crawl **2** : to climb, to
clamber (up)

gatillero *nm Mex* : gunman
gatillo *nm* : trigger
gatito, -ta *n* : kitten
gato¹, -ta *n* : cat
gato² *nm* : jack (for an automobile)
gauchada *nf Arg, Uru* : favor, kindness
gaucho *nm* : gaucho
gaveta *nf* CAJÓN : drawer 2 : till
gavilla *nf* 1 : gang, band 2 : sheaf
gaviota *nf* : gull, seagull
gay ['ge, 'gai] *adj* : gay (homosexual)
gaza *nf* : loop
gazapo *nm* 1 : young rabbit 2 : misprint, error
gazmoñería *nf* MOJIGATERÍA : prudery, primness
gazmoño¹, -ña *adj* : prudish, prim
gazmoño², -ña *n* MOJIGATO : prude, prig
gaznate *nm* : throat, gullet
gazpacho *nm* : gazpacho
géiser *or* **géyser** *nm* : geyser
gel *nm* : gel
gelatina *nf* : gelatin
gélido, -da *adj* : icy, freezing cold
gelificarse *vr* : to jell
gema *nf* : gem
gemelo¹, -la *adj & n* MELLIZO : twin
gemelo² *nm* 1 : cuff link 2 **gemelos** *nmpl* BINOCULARES : binoculars
gemido *nm* : moan, groan, wail
Géminis *nmf* : Gemini
gemir {54} *vi* : to moan, to groan, to wail
gen *or* **gene** *nm* : gene
gendarme *nmf* POLICÍA : police officer, policeman *m*, policewoman *f*
gendarmería *nf* : police
genealogía *nf* : genealogy
genealógico, -ca *adj* : genealogical
generación *nf, pl* **-ciones** 1 : generation ⟨tercera generación : third generation⟩ 2 : generating, creating 3 : class ⟨la generación del '97 : the class of '97⟩
generacional *adj* : generation, generational
generador *nm* : generator
general¹ *adj* 1 : general 2 **en ~** *or* **por lo general** : in general, generally
general² *nmf* 1 : general 2 **general de división** : major general
generalidad *nf* 1 : generality, generalization 2 : majority
generalización *nf, pl* **-ciones** 1 : generalization 2 : escalation, spread
generalizado, -da *adj* : generalized, widespread
generalizar {21} *vi* : to generalize — *vt* : to spread, to spread out — **generalizarse** *vr* : to become widespread
generalmente *adv* : usually, generally
generar *vt* : to generate — **generarse** *vr*
genérico, -ca *adj* : generic
género *nm* 1 : genre, class, kind ⟨el género humano : the human race, mankind⟩ 2 : gender (in grammar) 3 **géneros** *nmpl* : goods, commodities
generosidad *nf* : generosity
generoso, -sa *adj* 1 : generous, unselfish 2 : ample — **generosamente** *adv*

genética *nf* : genetics
genético, -ca *adj* : genetic — **genéticamente** *adv*
genetista *nmf* : geneticist
genial *adj* 1 AGRADABLE : genial, pleasant 2 : brilliant ⟨una obra genial : a work of genius⟩ 3 *fam* FORMIDABLE : fantastic, terrific
genialidad *nf* 1 : genius 2 : stroke of genius 3 : eccentricity
genio *nm* 1 : genius 2 : temper, disposition ⟨de mal genio : bad-tempered⟩ 3 : genie
genital *adj* : genital
genitales *nmpl* : genitals, genitalia
genocidio *nm* : genocide
genotipo *nm* : genotype
gente *nf* 1 : people 2 : relatives *pl*, folks *pl* 3 **gente menuda** *fam* : children, kids *pl* 4 **ser buena gente** : to be nice, to be kind
gentil¹ *adj* 1 AMABLE : kind 2 : gentile
gentil² *nmf* : gentile
gentileza *nf* 1 AMABILIDAD : kindness 2 CORTESÍA : courtesy
gentilicio, -cia *adj* 1 : national, tribal 2 : family
gentío *nm* MUCHEDUMBRE, MULTITUD : crowd, mob
gentuza *nf* CHUSMA : riffraff, rabble
genuflexión *nf, pl* **-xiones** 1 : genuflection 2 **hacer una genuflexión** : to genuflect
genuino, -na *adj* : genuine — **genuinamente** *adv*
geofísica *nf* : geophysics
geofísico, -ca *adj* : geophysical
geografía *nf* : geography
geográfico, -ca *adj* : geographic, geographical — **geográficamente** *adv*
geógrafo, -fa *n* : geographer
geología *nf* : geology
geológico, -ca *adj* : geologic, geological — **geológicamente** *adv*
geólogo, -ga *n* : geologist
geometría *nf* : geometry
geométrico, -ca *adj* : geometric, geometrical — **geométricamente** *adv*
geopolítica *nf* : geopolitics
geopolítico, -ca *adj* : geopolitical
georgiano, -na *adj & n* : Georgian
geranio *nm* : geranium
gerbo *nm* : gerbil
gerencia *nf* : management, administration
gerencial *adj* : managerial
gerente *nmf* : manager, director
geriatría *nf* : geriatrics
geriátrico, -ca *adj* : geriatric
germanio *nm* : germanium
germano, -na *adj* : Germanic, German
germen *nm, pl* **gérmenes** : germ
germicida *nf* : germicide
germinación *nf, pl* **-ciones** : germination
germinar *vi* : to germinate, to sprout
gerontología *nf* : gerontology
gerundio *nm* : gerund

gesta *nf* : deed, exploit
gestación *nf*, *pl* **-ciones** : gestation
gesticulación *nf*, *pl* **-ciones** : gesturing, gesticulation
gesticular *vi* : to gesticulate, to gesture
gestión *nf*, *pl* **gestiones** **1** TRÁMITE : procedure, step **2** ADMINISTRACIÓN : management **3 gestiones** *nfpl* : negotiations
gestionar *vt* **1** : to negotiate, to work towards **2** ADMINISTRAR : to manage, to handle
gesto *nm* **1** ADEMÁN : gesture **2** : facial expression **3** MUECA : grimace
gestor¹, -tora *adj* : facilitating, negotiating, managing
gestor², -tora *n* : facilitator, manager
géyser → **géiser**
ghanés, -nesa *adj & n*, *mpl* **ghaneses** : Ghanaian
ghetto → **gueto**
giba *nf* **1** : hump (of an animal) **2** : hunchback (of a person)
gibón *nm*, *pl* **gibones** : gibbon
giboso¹, -sa *adj* : hunchbacked, humpbacked
giboso², -sa *n* : hunchback, humpback
gigabyte *nm* : gigabyte
gigante¹ *adj* : giant, gigantic
gigante², -ta *n* : giant
gigantesco, -ca *adj* : gigantic, huge
gime, etc. → **gemir**
gimnasia *nf* : gymnastics
gimnasio *nm* : gymnasium, gym
gimnasta *nmf* : gymnast
gimnástico, -ca *adj* : gymnastic
gimotear *vi* LLORIQUEAR : to whine, to whimper
gimoteo *nm* : whimpering
ginebra *nf* : gin
ginecología *nf* : gynecology
ginecológico, -ca *adj* : gynecologic, gynecological
ginecólogo, -ga *n* : gynecologist
ginseng *nm* : ginseng
gira *nf* : tour
giralda *nf* : weather vane
girar *vi* **1** : to turn around, to revolve **2** : to swing around, to swivel — *vt* **1** : to turn, to twist, to rotate **2** : to draft (checks) **3** : to transfer (funds)
girasol *nm* MIRASOL : sunflower
giratorio, -ria *adj* : revolving
giro *nm* **1** VUELTA : turn, rotation **2** : change of direction ⟨giro de 180 grados : U-turn, about-face⟩ **3 giro bancario** : bank draft **4 giro postal** : money order
giroscopio *or* **giróscopo** *nm* : gyroscope
gis *nm Mex* : chalk
gitano, -na *adj & n* : Gypsy
glacial *adj* : glacial, icy — **glacialmente** *adv*
glaciar *nm* : glacier
gladiador *nm* : gladiator
gladiolo *or* **gladíolo** *nm* : gladiolus
glándula *nf* : gland — **glandular** *adj*

glaseado *nm* : glaze, icing
glasear *vt* : to glaze
glaucoma *nm* : glaucoma
glicerina *nf* : glycerin, glycerol
glicinia *nf* : wisteria
global *adj* **1** : global, worldwide **2** : full, comprehensive **3** : total, overall
globalizar {21} *vt* **1** ABARCAR : to include, to encompass **2** : to extend worldwide
globalmente *adv* : globally, as a whole
globo *nm* **1** : globe, sphere **2** : balloon **3 globo ocular** : eyeball
glóbulo *nm* **1** : globule **2** : blood cell, corpuscle
gloria *nf* **1** : glory **2** : fame, renown **3** : delight, enjoyment **4** : star, legend ⟨las glorias del cine : the great names in motion pictures⟩
glorieta *nf* **1** : rotary, traffic circle **2** : bower, arbor
glorificar {72} *vt* ALABAR : to glorify — **glorificación** *nf*
glorioso, -sa *adj* : glorious — **gloriosamente** *adv*
glosa *nf* **1** : gloss **2** : annotation, commentary
glosar *vt* **1** : to gloss **2** : to annotate, to comment on (a text)
glosario *nm* : glossary
glotis *nf* : glottis
glotón¹, -tona *adj*, *mpl* **glotones** : gluttonous
glotón², -tona *n*, *mpl* **glotones** : glutton
glotón³ *nm*, *pl* **glotones** : wolverine
glotonería *nf* GULA : gluttony
glucosa *nf* : glucose
glutinoso, -sa *adj* : glutinous
gnomo ['nomo] *nm* : gnome
gobernación *nf*, *pl* **-ciones** : governing, government
gobernador, -dora *n* : governor
gobernante¹ *adj* : ruling, governing
gobernante² *nmf* : ruler, leader, governor
gobernar {55} *vt* **1** : to govern, to rule **2** : to steer, to sail (a ship) — *vi* **1** : to govern **2** : to steer
gobierno *nm* : government
goce¹, etc. → **gozar**
goce² *nm* **1** PLACER : enjoyment, pleasure **2** : use, possession
gol *nm* : goal (in soccer)
golear *vt* : to rout, to score many goals against (in soccer)
goleta *nf* : schooner
golf *nm* : golf
golfista *nmf* : golfer
golfo *nm* : gulf, bay
golondrina *nf* **1** : swallow (bird) **2 golondrina de mar** : tern
golosina *nf* : sweet, snack
goloso, -sa *adj* : fond of sweets ⟨ser goloso : to have a sweet tooth⟩
golpazo *nm* : heavy blow, bang, thump
golpe *nm* **1** : blow ⟨caerle a golpes a alguien : to give someone a beating⟩ **2** : knock **3 de ~** : suddenly **4 de un**

golpe : all at once, in one fell swoop **5**
golpe de estado : coup, coup d'etat **6**
golpe de suerte : stroke of luck
golpeado, -da *adj* **1** : beaten, hit **2**
: bruised (of fruit) **3** : dented
golpear *vt* **1** : to beat (up), to hit **2** : to
slam, to bang, to strike — *vi* **1** : to
knock (at a door) **2** : to beat ⟨la lluvia
golpeaba contra el tejado : the rain beat
against the roof⟩ — **golpearse** *vr*
golpetear *v* **1** : to knock, to rattle, to tap
golpeteo *nm* : banging, knocking, tapping
goma *nf* **1** : gum ⟨goma de mascar
: chewing gum⟩ **2** CAUCHO : rubber
⟨goma espuma : foam rubber⟩ **3** PEGA-
MENTO : glue **4** : rubber band **5** *Arg*
: tire **6** *or* **goma de borrar** : eraser
gomita *nf* : rubber band
gomoso, -sa *adj* : gummy, sticky
góndola *nf* : gondola
gong *nm* : gong
gonorrea *nf* : gonorrhea
gorda *nf Mex* : thick corn tortilla
gordinflón[1], **-flona** *adj, mpl* **-flones** *fam*
: chubby, pudgy
gordinflón[2], **-flona** *n, mpl* **-flones** *fam*
: chubby person
gordo[1], **-da** *adj* **1** : fat **2** : thick **3** : fatty, greasy, oily **4** : unpleasant ⟨me cae
gorda tu tía : I can't stand your aunt⟩
gordo[2], **-da** *n* : fat person
gordo[3] *nm* **1** GRASA : fat **2** : jackpot
gordura *nf* : fatness, flab
gorgojo *nm* : weevil
gorgotear *vi* : to gurgle, to bubble
gorgoteo *nm* : gurgle
gorila *nm* : gorilla
gorjear *vi* **1** : to chirp, to tweet, to warble **2** : to gurgle
gorjeo *nm* **1** : chirping, warbling **2**
: gurgling
gorra *nf* **1** : bonnet **2** : cap **3 de ~** *fam*
: for free, at someone else's expense
⟨vivir de gorra : to sponge, to freeload⟩
gorrear *vt fam* : to bum, to scrounge —
vi fam : to freeload
gorrero, -ra *n fam* : freeloader, sponger
gorrión *nm, pl* **gorriones** : sparrow
gorro *nm* **1** : cap **2 estar hasta el gorro** : to be fed up
gorrón, -rrona *n, mpl* **gorrones** *fam*
: freeloader, scrounger
gorronear *vt fam* : to bum, to scrounge
— *vi fam* : to freeload
gota *nf* **1** : drop ⟨una gota de sudor : a
bead of sweat⟩ ⟨como dos gotas de
agua : like two peas in a pod⟩ ⟨sudar
la gota gorda : to sweat buckets, to
work very hard⟩ **2** : gout
gotear *v* **1** : to drip **2** : to leak — *v
impers* LLOVIZNAR : to drizzle
goteo *nm* : drip, dripping
gotera *nf* **1** : leak **2** : stain (from dripping water)
gotero *nm* : (medicine) dropper
gótico, -ca *adj* : Gothic
gourmet *nmf* : gourmet

gozar {21} *vi* **1** : to enjoy oneself, to have
a good time **2 ~ de** : to enjoy, to have,
to possess ⟨gozar de buena salud : to
enjoy good health⟩ **3 ~ con** : to take
delight in
gozne *nm* BISAGRA : hinge
gozo *nm* **1** : joy **2** PLACER : enjoyment,
pleasure
gozoso, -sa *adj* : joyful
grabación *nf, pl* **-ciones** : recording
grabado *nm* **1** : engraving **2 grabado
al aguafuerte** : etching
grabador, -dora *n* : engraver
grabadora *nf* : tape recorder
grabar *vt* **1** : to engrave **2** : to record,
to tape — *vi* **grabar al aguafuerte** : to
etch — **grabarse** *vr* **grabársele a alguien en la memoria** : to become en-
graved on someone's mind
gracia *nf* **1** : grace **2** : favor, kindness
3 : humor, wit ⟨su comentario no me
hizo gracia : I wasn't amused by his re-
mark⟩ **4 gracias** *nfpl* : thanks ⟨¡gracias! : thank you!⟩ ⟨dar gracias : to give
thanks⟩
grácil *adj* **1** : graceful **2** : delicate, slender, fine
gracilidad *nm* : gracefulness
gracioso, -sa *adj* **1** CHISTOSO : funny,
amusing **2** : cute, attractive
grada *nf* **1** : harrow **2** PELDAÑO : step,
stair **3 gradas** *nfpl* : bleachers, grandstand
gradación *nf, pl* **-ciones** : gradation,
scale
gradar *vt* : to harrow, to hoe
gradería *nf* : tiers *pl*, stands *pl*, rows *pl*
(in a theater)
gradiente *nf* : gradient, slope
grado *nm* **1** : degree (in meteorology
and mathematics) ⟨grado centígrado
: degree centigrade⟩ **2** : extent, level,
degree ⟨en grado sumo : greatly, to the
highest degree⟩ **3** RANGO : rank **4**
: year, class (in education) **5 de buen
grado** : willingly, readily
graduable *adj* : adjustable
graduación *nf, pl* **-ciones** **1** : graduation (from a school) **2** GRADO : rank
3 : alcohol content, proof
graduado[1], **-da** *adj* **1** : graduated **2
lentes graduados** : prescription lens-
es
graduado[2], **-da** *n* : graduate
gradual *adj* : gradual — **gradualmente**
adv
graduar {3} *v* **1** : to regulate, to adjust
2 CALIBRAR : to calibrate, to gauge —
graduarse *vr* : to graduate (from a
school)
graffiti *or* **grafiti** *nmpl* : graffiti *pl*
gráfica *nf → **gráfico**[2]
gráfico[1], **-ca** *adj* : graphic — **gráficamente** *adv*
gráfico[2] *nm* **1** : graph, chart **2** : graphic (for a computer, etc.) **3 gráfico de
barras** : bar graph
grafismo *nm* : graphics *pl*

grafito *nm* : graphite
gragea *nf* **1** : coated pill or tablet **2**
  grageas *nfpl* : sprinkles, jimmies
grajo *nm* : rook (bird)
grama *nf* : grass
gramática *nf* : grammar
gramatical *adj* : grammatical — **gra-**
  maticalmente *adv*
gramo *nm* : gram
gran → **grande**
grana *nf* : scarlet, deep red
granada *nf* **1** : pomegranate **2** : grenade
  ⟨granada de mano : hand grenade⟩
granadero *nm* **1** : grenadier **2**
  granaderos *nmpl Mex* : riot squad
granadino, -na *adj & n* : Grenadian
granado, -da *adj* **1** DISTINGUIDO : distinguished **2** : choice, select
granate *nm* **1** : garnet **2** : deep red, maroon
grande *adj* (**gran** *before singular nouns*)
  1 : large, big ⟨un libro grande : a big
  book⟩ **2** ALTO : tall **3** NOTABLE : great
  ⟨un gran autor : a great writer⟩ **4** (*in-*
  dicating intensity) : great ⟨con gran
  placer : with great pleasure⟩ **5** : old,
  grown-up ⟨hijos grandes : grown chil-
  dren⟩
grandeza *nf* **1** MAGNITUD : greatness,
  size **2** : nobility **3** : generosity, graciousness **4** : grandeur, magnificence
grandilocuencia *nf* : grandiloquence —
  grandilocuente *adj*
grandiosidad *nf* : grandeur
grandioso, -sa *adj* **1** MAGNÍFICO
  : grand, magnificent **2** : grandiose
granel *adv* **1 a ~** : galore, in great quan-
  tities **2 a ~** : in bulk ⟨vender a granel
  : to sell in bulk⟩
granero *nm* : barn, granary
granito *nm* : granite
granizada *nf* : hailstorm
granizar {21} *v impers* : to hail
granizo *nm* : hail
granja *nf* : farm
granjear *vt* : to earn, to win —
  granjearse *vr* : to gain, to earn
granjero, -ra *n* : farmer
grano *nm* **1** PARTÍCULA : grain, particle
  ⟨un grano de arena : a grain of sand⟩
  2 : grain (of rice, etc.), bean (of coffee),
  seed **3** : grain (of wood or rock) **4** BAR-
  RO, ESPINILLA : pimple **5 ir al grano**
  : to get to the point
granuja *nmf* PILLUELO : rascal, urchin
granular[1] *vt* : to granulate — **granularse**
  vr : to break out in spots
granular[2] *adj* : granular, grainy
granza *nf* : chaff
grapa *nf* **1** : staple **2** : clamp
grapadora *nf* ENGRAPADORA : stapler
grapar *vt* ENGRAPAR : to staple
grasa *nf* **1** : grease **2** : fat **3** *Mex* : shoe
  polish
grasiento, -ta *adj* : greasy, oily
graso, -sa *adj* **1** : fatty **2** : greasy, oily
grasoso, -sa *adj* GRASIENTO : greasy,
  oily

gratificación *nf, pl* **-ciones 1** SATISFAC-
  CIÓN : gratification **2** : bonus **3** REC-
  OMPENSA : recompense, reward
gratificar {72} *vt* **1** SATISFACER : to satisfy, to gratify **2** RECOMPENSAR : to reward **3** : to give a bonus to
gratinado, -da *adj* : au gratin
gratis[1] *adv* GRATUITAMENTE : free, for
  free, gratis
gratis[2] *adj* GRATUITO : free, gratis
gratitud *nf* : gratitude
grato, -ta *adj* AGRADABLE, PLACEN-
  TERO : pleasant, agreeable — **grata-**
  mente *adv*
gratuitamente *adv* **1** : gratuitously **2**
  GRATIS : free, for free, gratis
gratuito, -ta *adj* **1** : gratuitous, unwarranted **2** GRATIS : free, gratis
grava *nf* : gravel
gravamen *nm, pl* **-vámenes 1** : burden,
  obligation **2** : (property) tax
gravar *vt* **1** : to burden, to encumber **2**
  : to levy (a tax)
grave *adj* **1** : grave, important **2** : serious, somber **3** : serious (of an illness)
gravedad *nf* **1** : gravity ⟨centro de
  gravedad : center of gravity⟩ **2** : seriousness, severity
gravemente *adv* : gravely, seriously
gravilla *nf* : (fine) gravel
gravitación *nf, pl* **-ciones** : gravitation
gravitacional *adj* : gravitational
gravitar *vi* **1** : to gravitate **2 ~ sobre**
  : to rest on **3 ~ sobre** : to loom over
gravoso, -sa *adj* **1** ONEROSO : burdensome, onerous **2** : costly
graznar *vi* : to caw, to honk, to quack,
  to squawk
graznido *nm* : cawing, honking, quack-
  ing, squawking
gregario, -ria *adj* : gregarious
gregoriano, -na *adj* : Gregorian
gremial *adj* SINDICAL : union, labor
gremio *nm* SINDICATO : union, guild
greña *nf* **1** : mat, tangle **2 greñas** *nfpl*
  MELENAS : shaggy hair, mop
greñudo, -da *n* HIPPIE, MELENUDO
  : longhair, hippie
grey *nf* : congregation, flock
griego[1], **-ga** *adj & n* : Greek
griego[2] *nm* : Greek (language)
grieta *nf* : crack, crevice
grifo *nm* **1** : faucet ⟨agua del grifo : tap
  water⟩ **2** : griffin
grillete *nm* : shackle
grillo *nm* **1** : cricket **2 grillos** *nmpl* : fetters, shackles
grima *nf* **1** : disgust, uneasiness **2 dar-**
  le grima a alguien : to get on someone's nerves
gringo, -ga *adj & n* YANQUI : Yankee,
  gringo
gripa *nf Col, Mex* : flu
gripe *nf* : flu
gris *adj* **1** : gray **2** : overcast, cloudy
grisáceo, -cea *adj* : grayish
gritar *v* : to shout, to scream, to cry
gritería *nf* : shouting, clamor

grito *nm* : shout, scream, cry ⟨a grito pelado : at the top of one's voice⟩
groenlandés, -desa *adj & n* : Greenlander
grogui *adj fam* : dazed, groggy
grosella *nf* 1 : currant 2 **grosella espinosa** : gooseberry
grosería *nf* 1 : insult, coarse language 2 : rudeness, discourtesy
grosero¹, -ra *adj* 1 : rude, fresh 2 : coarse, vulgar
grosero², -ra *n* : rude person
grosor *nm* : thickness
grosso *adj* **a grosso modo** : roughly, broadly, approximately
grotesco, -ca *adj* : grotesque, hideous
grúa *nf* 1 : crane (machine) 2 : tow truck
gruesa *nf* : gross
grueso¹, -sa *adj* 1 : thick, bulky 2 : heavy, big 3 : heavyset, stout
grueso² *nm* 1 : thickness 2 : main body, mass 3 **en ∼** : in bulk
grulla *nf* : crane (bird)
grumo *nm* : lump, glob
gruñido *nm* : growl, grunt
gruñir {38} *vi* 1 : to growl, to grunt 2 : to grumble
gruñón¹, -ñona *adj, mpl* **gruñones** *fam* : grumpy, crabby
gruñón², -ñona *n, mpl* **gruñones** *fam* : grumpy person, nag
grupa *nf* : rump, hindquarters *pl*
grupo *nm* : group
gruta *nf* : grotto, cave
guacal *nm Col, Mex, Ven* : crate
guacamayo *nm* : macaw
guacamole *or* **guacamol** *nm* : guacamole
guacamote *nm Mex* : yuca, cassava
guachinango → **huachinango**
guacho, -cha *adj* 1 *Arg, Col, Chile, Peru* : orphaned 2 *Chile, Peru* : odd, unmatched
guadaña *nf* : scythe
guagua *nf* 1 *Arg, Col, Chile, Peru* : baby 2 *Cuba, PRi* : bus
guaira *nf* 1 *CA* : traditional flute 2 *Peru* : smelting furnace
guajiro, -ra *n Cuba* : peasant
guajolote *nm Mex* : turkey
guanábana *nf* : guanabana, soursop (fruit)
guanaco *nm* : guanaco
guandú *nm CA, Car, Col* : pigeon pea
guango, -ga *adj Mex* 1 : loose-fitting, baggy 2 : slack, loose
guano *nm* : guano
guante *nm* 1 : glove ⟨guante de boxeo : boxing glove⟩ 2 **arrojarle el guante (a alguien)** : to throw down the gauntlet (to someone)
guantelete *nm* : gauntlet
guapo, -pa *adj* 1 : handsome, good-looking, attractive 2 : elegant, smart 3 *fam* : bold, dashing
guapura *nf fam* : handsomeness, attractiveness, good looks *pl* ⟨¡qué guapura! : what a vision!⟩

guarache → **huarache**
guarachear *vi Cuba, PRi fam* : to go on a spree, to go out on the town
guaraní¹ *adj & nmf* : Guarani
guaraní² *nm* : Guarani (language of Paraguay)
guarda *nmf* 1 GUARDIÁN : security guard 2 : keeper, custodian
guardabarros *nms & pl* : fender, mudguard
guardabosque *nmf* : forest ranger, gamekeeper
guardacostas¹ *nmfs & pl* : coastguardsman
guardacostas² *nms & pl* : coast guard vessel
guardaespaldas *nmfs & pl* : bodyguard
guardafangos *nms & pl* : fender, mudguard
guardameta *nmf* ARQUERO, PORTERO : goalkeeper, goalie
guardapelo *nm* : locket
guardapolvo *nm* 1 : dustcover 2 : duster, housecoat
guardar *vt* 1 : to guard 2 : to maintain, to preserve 3 CONSERVAR : to put away 4 RESERVAR : to save 5 : to keep (a secret or promise) — **guardarse** *vr* 1 **∼ de** : to refrain from 2 **∼ de** : to guard against, to be careful not to
guardarropa *nm* 1 : cloakroom, checkroom 2 ARMARIO : closet, wardrobe
guardería *nf* : nursery, day-care center
guardia¹ *nf* 1 : guard, defense 2 : guard duty, watch 3 **en ∼** : on guard
guardia² *nmf* 1 : sentry, guardsman, guard 2 : police officer, policeman *m*, policewoman *f*
guardiamarina *nmf* : midshipman
guardián, -diana *n, mpl* **guardianes** 1 GUARDA : security guard, watchman 2 : guardian, keeper 3 **perro guardián** : watchdog
guarecer {53} *vt* : to shelter, to protect — **guarecerse** *vr* : to take shelter
guarida *nf* 1 : den, lair 2 : hideout
guarismo *nm* : figure, numeral
guarnecer {53} *vt* 1 : to adorn 2 : to garnish 3 : to garrison
guarnición *nf, pl* **-ciones** 1 : garnish 2 : garrison 3 : decoration, trimming, setting (of a jewel)
guaro *nm CA* : liquor distilled from sugarcane
guasa *nf fam* 1 : joking, fooling around 2 **de ∼** : in jest, as a joke
guasón¹, -sona *adj, mpl* **guasones** *fam* : funny, witty
guasón², -sona *n, mpl* **guasones** *fam* : joker, clown
guatemalteco, -ca *adj & n* : Guatemalan
guau *interj* : wow!
guayaba *nf* : guava (fruit)
gubernamental *adj* : governmental
gubernativo, -va → **gubernamental**
gubernatura *nf Mex* : governing body
guepardo *nm* : cheetah
güero, -ra *adj Mex* : blond, fair

guerra *nf* **1** : war ⟨declarar la guerra : to declare war⟩ ⟨guerra sin cuartel : all-out war⟩ **2** : warfare **3** LUCHA : conflict, struggle
guerrear *vi* : to wage war
guerrero[1], **-ra** *adj* **1** : war, fighting **2** : warlike
guerrero[2], **-ra** *n* : warrior
guerrilla *nf* : guerrilla warfare
guerrillero, -ra *adj & n* : guerrilla
gueto *nm* : ghetto
guía[1] *nf* **1** : directory, guidebook **2** ORIENTACIÓN : guidance, direction ⟨la conciencia me sirve como guía : conscience is my guide⟩
guía[2] *nmf* : guide, leader ⟨guía de turismo : tour guide⟩
guiar {85} *vt* **1** : to guide, to lead **2** CONDUCIR : to manage — **guiarse** *vr* : to be guided by, to go by
guija *nf* : pebble
guijarro *nm* : pebble
guillotina *nf* : guillotine — **guillotinar** *vt*
guinda[1] *adj & nm Mex* : burgundy (color)
guinda[2] *nf* : morello (cherry)
guineo *nm Car* : banana
guinga *nf* : gingham
guiñada → **guiño**
guiñar *vi* : to wink
guiño *nm* : wink
guión *nm, pl* **guiones 1** : script, screenplay **2** : hyphen, dash **3** ESTANDARTE : standard, banner
guirnalda *nf* : garland
guisa *nf* **1** : manner, fashion **2 a guisa de** : like, by way of **3 de tal guisa** : in such a way

guisado ESTOFADO *nm* : stew
guisante *nm* : pea
guisar *vt* **1** ESTOFAR : to stew **2** *Spain* : to cook
guiso *nm* **1** : stew **2** : casserole
güisqui → **whisky**
guita *nf* : string, twine
guitarra *nf* : guitar
guitarrista *nmf* : guitarist
gula *nf* GLOTONERÍA : gluttony, greed
gusano *nm* **1** LOMBRIZ : worm, earthworm ⟨gusano de seda : silkworm⟩ **2** : caterpillar, maggot, grub
gustar *vt* **1** : to taste **2** : to like ⟨¿gustan pasar? : would you like to come in?⟩ — *vi* **1** : to be pleasing ⟨me gustan los dulces : I like sweets⟩ ⟨a María le gusta Carlos : Maria is attracted to Carlos⟩ ⟨no me gusta que me griten : I don't like to be yelled at⟩ **2 ~ de** : to like, to enjoy ⟨no gusta de chismes : she doesn't like gossip⟩ **3 como guste** : as you wish, as you like
gustativo, -va *adj* : taste ⟨papilas gustativas : taste buds⟩
gusto *nm* **1** : flavor, taste **2** : taste, style **3** : pleasure, liking **4** : whim, fancy ⟨a gusto : at will⟩ **5 a ~** : comfortable, at ease **6 al gusto** : to taste, as one likes **7 mucho gusto** : pleased to meet you
gustosamente *adv* : gladly
gustoso, -sa *adj* **1** : willing, glad ⟨nuestra empresa participará gustosa : our company will be pleased to participate⟩ **2** : zesty, tasty
gutural *adj* : guttural

H

h *nf* : eighth letter of the Spanish alphabet
ha → **haber**
haba *nf* : broad bean
habanero[1], **-ra** *adj* : of or from Havana
habanero[2], **-ra** *n* : native or resident of Havana
haber[1] {39} *v aux* **1** : have, has ⟨no ha llegado el envío : the shipment hasn't arrived⟩ **2 ~ de** : must ⟨ha de ser tarde : it must be late⟩ — *v impers* **1 hay** : there is, there are ⟨hay dos mensajes : there are two messages⟩ ⟨¿qué hay de nuevo? : what's new?⟩ **2 hay que** : it is necessary ⟨hay que trabajar más rápido : you have to work faster⟩
haber[2] *nm* **1** : assets *pl* **2** : credit, credit side **3 haberes** *nmpl* : salary, income, remuneration
habichuela *nf* **1** : bean, kidney bean **2** : green bean
hábil *adj* **1** : able, skillful **2** : working ⟨días hábiles : working days⟩
habilidad *nf* CAPACIDAD : ability, skill
habilidoso, -sa *adj* : skillful, clever

habilitación *nf, pl* **-ciones 1** : authorization **2** : furnishing, equipping
habilitar *vt* **1** : to enable, to authorize, to empower **2** : to equip, to furnish
hábilmente *adv* : skillfully, expertly
habitable *adj* : habitable, inhabitable
habitación *nf, pl* **-ciones 1** CUARTO : room **2** DORMITORIO : bedroom **3** : habitation, occupancy
habitante *nmf* : inhabitant, resident
habitar *vt* : to inhabit — *vi* : to reside, to dwell
hábitat *nm, pl* **-tats** : habitat
hábito *nm* **1** : habit, custom **2** : habit (of a monk or nun)
habitual *adj* : habitual, customary — **habitualmente** *adv*
habituar {3} *vt* : to accustom, to habituate — **habituarse** *vr* **~ a** : to get used to, to grow accustomed to
habla *nf* **1** : speech **2** : language, dialect **3 de ~** : speaking ⟨de habla inglesa : English-speaking⟩
hablado, -da *adj* **1** : spoken **2 mal hablado** : foulmouthed

hablador¹, -dora *adj* : talkative
hablador², -dora *n* : chatterbox
habladuría *nf* **1** : rumor **2 habladurías**
nfpl : gossip, scandal
hablante *nmf* : speaker
hablar *vi* **1** : to speak, to talk ⟨hablar en
broma : to be joking⟩ **2 ~ de** : to mention, to talk about **3 dar que hablar**
: to make people talk — *vt* **1** : to speak
(a language) **2** : to talk about, to discuss ⟨háblalo con tu jefe : discuss it
with your boss⟩ — **hablarse** *vr* **1** : to
speak to each other, to be on speaking
terms **2 se habla inglés (etc.)** : English (etc.) spoken
habrá, etc. → **haber**
hacedor, -dora *n* : creator, maker, doer
hacendado, -da *n* : landowner
hacer {40} *vt* **1** : to make **2** : to do, to
perform **3** : to force, to oblige ⟨los hice
esperar : I made them wait⟩ — *vi* : to
act ⟨haces bien : you're doing the right
thing⟩ — *v impers* **1** (*referring to weather*) ⟨hacer frío : to be cold⟩ ⟨hace viento : it's windy⟩ **2 hace** : ago ⟨hace mucho tiempo : a long time ago, for a long
time⟩ **3 no le hace** : it doesn't matter,
it makes no difference **4 hacer falta**
: to be necessary, to be needed — **hacerse** *vr* **1** : to become **2** : to pretend,
to act, to play ⟨hacerse el tonto : to
play dumb⟩ **3** : to seem ⟨el examen se
me hizo difícil : the exam seemed difficult to me⟩ **4** : to get, to grow ⟨se
hace tarde : it's growing late⟩
hacha *nf* : hatchet, ax
hachazo *nm* : blow, chop (with an ax)
hachís *nm* : hashish
hacia *prep* **1** : toward, towards ⟨hacia
abajo : downward⟩ ⟨hacia adelante
: forward⟩ **2** : near, around, about
⟨hacia las seis : about six o'clock⟩
hacienda *nf* **1** : estate, ranch, farm **2**
: property **3** : livestock **4 la Hacienda**
: department of revenue, tax office
hacinar *vt* **1** : to pile up, to stack **2** : to
overcrowd — **hacinarse** *vr* : to crowd
together
hada *nf* : fairy
hado *nm* : destiny, fate
haga, etc. → **hacer**
haitiano, -na *adj & n* : Haitian
hala *interj Spain* **1** (*expressing encouragement or disbelief*) : come on! **2** (*expressing surprise*) : wow! **3** (*expressing
protest*) : hey!
halagador¹, -dora *adj* : flattering
halagador², -dora *n* : flatterer
halagar {52} *vt* : to flatter, to compliment
halago *nm* : flattery, praise
halagüeño, -ña *adj* **1** : flattering **2** : encouraging, promising
halar *vt CA, Car →* **jalar**
halcón *nm, pl* **halcones** : hawk, falcon
halibut *nm, pl* **-buts** : halibut
hálito *nm* **1** : breath **2** : gentle breeze

hallar *vt* **1** ENCONTRAR : to find **2** DE-
SCUBRIR : to discover, to find out —
hallarse *vr* **1** : to be situated, to find
oneself **2** : to feel ⟨no se halla bien : he
doesn't feel comfortable, he feels out
of place⟩
hallazgo *nm* **1** : discovery **2** : find ⟨¡es
un verdadero hallazgo! : it's a real
find!⟩
halo *nm* **1** : halo **2** : aura
halógeno *nm* : halogen
hamaca *nf* : hammock
hambre *nf* **1** : hunger **2** : starvation **3
tener hambre** : to be hungry **4 dar
hambre** : to make hungry
hambriento, -ta *adj* : hungry, starving
hambruna *nf* : famine
hamburguesa *nf* : hamburger
hampa *nf* : criminal underworld
hampón, -pona *n, mpl* **hampones**
: criminal, thug
hámster ['xamster] *nm, pl* **hámsters**
: hamster
han → **haber**
handicap *or* **hándicap** ['handi‚kap] *nm,
pl* **-caps** : handicap (in sports)
hangar *nm* : hangar
hará, etc. → **hacer**
haragán¹, -gana *adj, mpl* **-ganes** : lazy,
idle
haragán², -gana *n, mpl* **-ganes** HOL-
GAZÁN : slacker, good-for-nothing
haraganear *vi* : to be lazy, to waste one's
time
haraganería *nf* : laziness
harapiento, -ta *adj* : ragged, tattered
harapos *nmpl* ANDRAJOS : rags, tatters
hardware ['hard‚wer] *nm* : computer
hardware
harén *nm, pl* **harenes** : harem
harina *nf* **1** : flour **2 harina de maíz**
: cornmeal
hartar *vt* **1** : to glut, to satiate **2** FAS-
TIDIAR : to tire, to irritate, to annoy —
hartarse *vr* : to be weary, to get fed up
harto¹ *adv* : most, extremely, very
harto², -ta *adj* **1** : full, satiated **2** : fed
up
hartura *nf* **1** : surfeit **2** : abundance,
plenty
has → **haber**
hasta¹ *adv* : even
hasta² prep 1 : until, up until ⟨hasta entonces : until then⟩ ⟨¡hasta luego! : see
you later!⟩ **2** : as far as ⟨nos fuimos
hasta Managua : we went all the way
to Managua⟩ **3** : up to ⟨hasta cierto
punto : up to a certain point⟩ **4 hasta
que** : until
hastiar {85} *vt* **1** : to make weary, to
bore **2** : to disgust, to sicken — **has-
tiarse** *vr* **~ de** : to get tired of
hastío *nm* **1** TEDIO : tedium **2** REPUG-
NANCIA : disgust
hato *nm* **1** : flock, herd **2** : bundle (of
possessions)
hawaiano, -na *adj & n* : Hawaiian
hay → **haber¹**

haya[1], etc. → **haber**
haya[2] *nf* : beech (tree and wood)
hayuco *nm* : beechnut
haz[1] → **hacer**
haz[2] *nm, pl* **haces** **1** FARDO : bundle **2** : beam (of light)
haz[3] *nf, pl* **haces** **1** : face **2 haz de la tierra** : surface of the earth
hazaña *nf* PROEZA : feat, exploit
hazmerreír *nm fam* : laughingstock
he[1] {39} → **haber**
he[2] *v impers* **he aquí** : here is, here are, behold
hebilla *nf* : buckle, clasp
hebra *nf* : strand, thread
hebreo[1], **-brea** *adj & n* : Hebrew
hebreo[2] *nm* : Hebrew (language)
hecatombe *nf* **1** MATANZA : massacre **2** : disaster
heces → **hez**
hechicería *nf* **1** BRUJERÍA : sorcery, witchcraft **2** : curse, spell
hechicero[1], **-ra** *adj* : bewitching, enchanting
hechicero[2], **-ra** *n* : sorcerer, sorceress *f*
hechizar {21} *vt* **1** EMBRUJAR : to bewitch **2** CAUTIVAR : to charm
hechizo *nm* **1** SORTILEGIO : spell, enchantment **2** ENCANTO : charm, fascination
hecho[1] *pp* → **hacer**
hecho[2], **-cha** *adj* **1** : made, done **2** : ready-to-wear **3** : complete, finished ⟨hecho y derecho : full-fledged⟩
hecho[3] *nm* **1** : fact **2** : event ⟨hechos históricos : historic events⟩ **3** : act, action **4 de ∼** : in fact, in reality
hechura *nf* **1** : style **2** : craftsmanship, workmanship **3** : product, creation
hectárea *nf* : hectare
heder {56} *vi* : to stink, to reek
hediondez *nf, pl* **-deces** : stink, stench
hediondo, **-da** *adj* MALOLIENTE : foul-smelling, stinking
hedor *nm* : stench, stink
hegemonía *nf* **1** : dominance **2** : hegemony (in politics)
helada *nf* : frost (in meteorology)
heladería *nf* : ice-cream parlor, ice-cream stand
helado[1], **-da** *adj* **1** GÉLIDO : icy, freezing cold **2** CONGELADO : frozen
helado[2] *nm* : ice cream
heladora *nf* CONGELADOR : freezer
helar {55} *v* CONGELAR : to freeze — *impers* : to produce frost ⟨anoche heló : there was frost last night⟩ — **helarse** *vr*
helecho *nm* : fern, bracken
hélice *nf* **1** : spiral, helix **2** : propeller
helicóptero *nm* : helicopter
helio *nm* : helium
helipuerto *nm* : heliport
hembra *adj & nf* : female
hemisférico, **-ca** *adj* : hemispheric, hemispherical
hemisferio *nm* : hemisphere
hemofilia *nf* : hemophilia

hemofílico, **-ca** *adj & n* : hemophiliac
hemoglobina *nf* : hemoglobin
hemorragia *nf* **1** : hemorrhage **2 hemorragia nasal** : nosebleed
hemorroides *nfpl* ALMORRANAS : hemorrhoids, piles
hemos → **haber**
henchido, **-da** *adj* : swollen, bloated
henchir {54} *vt* **1** : to stuff, to fill **2** : to swell, to swell up — **henchirse** *vr* **1** : to stuff oneself **2** LLENARSE : to fill up, to be full
hender {56} *vt* : to cleave, to split
hendidura *nf* : crack, crevice, fissure
henequén *nm, pl* **-quenes** : sisal hemp
heno *nm* : hay
hepatitis *nf* : hepatitis
heráldica *nf* : heraldry
heráldico, **-ca** *adj* : heraldic
heraldo *nm* : herald
herbario, **-ria** *adj* : herbal
herbicida *nm* : herbicide, weed killer
herbívoro[1], **-ra** *adj* : herbivorous
herbívoro[2] *nm* : herbivore
herbolario, **-ria** *n* : herbalist
hercio *nm* : hertz
hercúleo, **-lea** *adj* : herculean
heredar *vt* : to inherit
heredero, **-ra** *n* : heir, heiress *f*
hereditario, **-ria** *adj* : hereditary
hereje *nmf* : heretic
herejía *nf* : heresy
herencia *nf* **1** : inheritance **2** : heritage **3** : heredity
herético, **-ca** *adj* : heretical
herida *nf* : injury, wound
herido[1], **-da** *adj* **1** : injured, wounded **2** : hurt, offended
herido[2], **-da** *n* : injured person, casualty
herir {76} *vt* **1** : to injure, to wound **2** : to hurt, to offend
hermafrodita *nmf* : hermaphrodite
hermanar *vt* **1** : to unite, to bring together **2** : to match up, to twin (cities)
hermanastro, **-tra** *n* : half brother *m*, half sister *f*
hermandad *nf* **1** FRATERNIDAD : brotherhood ⟨hermandad de mujeres : sisterhood, sorority⟩ **2** : association
hermano, **-na** *n* : sibling, brother *m*, sister *f*
hermético, **-ca** *adj* : hermetic, watertight — **herméticamente** *adv*
hermoso, **-sa** *adj* BELLO : beautiful, lovely — **hermosamente** *adv*
hermosura *nf* BELLEZA : beauty, loveliness
hernia *nf* : hernia
héroe *nm* : hero
heroicidad *nf* : heroism, heroic deed
heroico, **-ca** *adj* : heroic — **heroicamente** *adv*
heroína *nf* **1** : heroine **2** : heroin
heroísmo *nm* : heroism
herpes *nms & pl* **1** : herpes **2** : shingles
herradura *nf* : horseshoe
herraje *nm* : ironwork

herramienta *nf* : tool
herrar {55} *vt* : to shoe (a horse)
herrería *nf* : blacksmith's shop
herrero, -ra *n* : blacksmith
herrumbre *nf* ORÍN : rust
herrumbroso, -sa *adj* OXIDADO : rusty
hertzio *nm* : hertz
hervidero *nm* **1** : mass, swarm **2** : hotbed (of crime, etc.)
hervidor *nm* : kettle
hervir {76} *vi* **1** BULLIR : to boil, to bubble **2 ~ de** : to teem with, to be swarming with — *vt* : to boil
hervor *nm* **1** : boiling **2** : fervor, ardor
heterogeneidad *nf* : heterogeneity
heterogéneo, -nea *adj* : heterogeneous
heterosexual *adj & nmf* : heterosexual
heterosexualidad *nf* : heterosexuality
hexágono *nm* : hexagon — **hexagonal** *adj*
hez *nf, pl* **heces 1** ESCORIA : scum, dregs *pl* **2** : sediment, lees *pl* **3 heces** *nfpl* : feces, excrement
hiato *nm* : hiatus
hibernar *vi* : to hibernate — **hibernación** *nf*
híbrido¹, -da *adj* : hybrid
híbrido² *nm* : hybrid
hicieron, etc. → hacer
hidalgo, -ga *n* : nobleman *m*, noblewoman *f*
hidrante *nm CA, Col* : hydrant
hidratar *vt* : to moisturize — **hidratante** *adj*
hidrato *nm* **1** : hydrate **2 hidrato de carbono** : carbohydrate
hidráulico, -ca *adj* : hydraulic
hidroavión *nm, pl* **-viones** : seaplane
hidrocarburo *nm* : hydrocarbon
hidroeléctrico, -ca *adj* : hydroelectric
hidrofobia *nf* RABIA : hydrophobia, rabies
hidrófugo, -ga *adj* : water-repellent
hidrógeno *nm* : hydrogen
hidroplano *nm* : hydroplane
hiede, etc. → heder
hiedra *nf* **1** : ivy **2 hiedra venenosa** : poison ivy
hiel *nf* **1** BILIS : bile **2** : bitterness
hiela, etc. → helar
hielo *nm* **1** : ice **2** : coldness, reserve ⟨romper el hielo : to break the ice⟩
hiena *nf* : hyena
hiende, etc. → hender
hierba *nf* **1** : herb **2** : grass **3 mala hierba** : weed
hierbabuena *nf* : mint, spearmint
hiere, etc. → herir
hierra, etc. → herrar
hierro *nm* **1** : iron ⟨hierro fundido : cast iron⟩ **2** : branding iron
hierve, etc. → hervir
hígado *nm* : liver
higiene *nf* : hygiene
higiénico, -ca *adj* : hygienic — **higiénicamente** *adv*
higienista *nmf* : hygienist
higo *nm* **1** : fig **2 higo chumbo** : prickly pear (fruit)

higrómetro *nm* : hygrometer
higuera *nf* : fig tree
hijastro, -tra *n* : stepson *m*, stepdaughter *f*
hijo, -ja *n* **1** : son *m*, daughter *f* **2 hijos** *nmpl* : children, offspring
híjole *interj Mex* : wow!, good grief!
hilacha *nf* **1** : ravel, loose thread **2 mostrar la hilacha** : to show one's true colors
hilado *nm* **1** : spinning **2** HILO : yarn, thread
hilar *vt* **1** : to spin (thread) **2** : to consider, to string together (ideas) — *vi* **1** : to spin **2 hilar delgado** : to split hairs
hilarante *adj* **1** : humorous, hilarious **2 gas hilarante** : laughing gas
hilaridad *nf* : hilarity
hilera *nf* FILA : file, row, line
hilo *nm* **1** : thread ⟨colgar de un hilo : to hang by a thread⟩ ⟨hilo dental : dental floss⟩ **2** LINO : linen **3** : (electric) wire **4** : theme, thread (of a discourse) **5** : trickle (of water, etc.)
hilvanar *vt* **1** : to baste, to tack **2** : to piece together
himnario *nm* : hymnal
himno *nm* **1** : hymn **2 himno nacional** : national anthem
hincapié *nm* **hacer hincapié en** : to emphasize, to stress
hincar {72} *vt* CLAVAR : to stick, to plunge — **hincarse** *vr* **hincarse de rodillas** : to kneel down, to fall to one's knees
hinchado, -da *adj* **1** : swollen, inflated **2** : pompous, overblown
hinchar *vt* **1** INFLAR : to inflate **2** : to exaggerate — **hincharse** *vr* **1** : to swell up **2** : to become conceited, to swell with pride
hinchazón *nf, pl* **-zones** : swelling
hinche, etc. → henchir
hindi *nm* : Hindi
hindú *adj & nmf* : Hindu
hinduismo *nm* : Hinduism
hiniesta *nf* : broom (plant)
hinojo *nm* **1** : fennel **2 de hinojos** : on bended knee
hinque, etc. → hincar
hipar *vi* : to hiccup
hiperactividad *nf* : hyperactivity
hiperactivo, -va *adj* : hyperactive, overactive
hipérbole *nf* : hyperbole
hiperbólico, -ca *adj* : hyperbolic, exaggerated
hipercrítico, -ca *adj* : hypercritical
hipermetropía *nf* : farsightedness
hipersensibilidad *nf* : hypersensitivity
hipersensible *adj* : hypersensitive
hipertensión *nf, pl* **-siones** : hypertension, high blood pressure
hip-hop [ˌxipˈxop] *nm* : hip-hop (music)
hípico, -ca *adj* : equestrian ⟨concurso hípico : horse show⟩
hipil → huipil
hipnosis *nfs & pl* : hypnosis

hipnótico, -ca *adj* : hypnotic
hipnotismo *nm* : hypnotism
hipnotizador[1], -dora *adj* **1** : hypnotic **2** : spellbinding, mesmerizing
hipnotizador[2], -dora *n* : hypnotist
hipnotizar {21} *vt* : to hypnotize
hipo *nm* : hiccup, hiccups *pl*
hipocampo *nm* : sea horse
hipocondría *nf* : hypochondria
hipocondríaco, -ca *adj & n* : hypochondriac
hipocresía *nf* : hypocrisy
hipócrita[1] *adj* : hypocritical — **hipócritamente** *adv*
hipócrita[2] *nmf* : hypocrite
hipodérmico, -ca *adj* **aguja hipodérmica** : hypodermic needle
hipódromo *nm* : racetrack
hipopótamo *nm* : hippopotamus
hipoteca *nf* : mortgage
hipotecar {72} *vt* **1** : to mortgage **2** : to compromise, to jeopardize
hipotecario, -ria *adj* : mortgage
hipotensión *nf* : low blood pressure
hipotenusa *nf* : hypotenuse
hipótesis *nfs & pl* : hypothesis
hipotético, -ca *adj* : hypothetical — **hipotéticamente** *adv*
hippie *or* **hippy** ['hipi] *nmf, pl* **hippies** [-pis] : hippie
hiriente *adj* : hurtful, offensive
hirió, etc. → **herir**
hirsuto, -ta *adj* **1** : hirsute, hairy **2** : bristly, wiry
hirviente *adj* : boiling
hirvió, etc. → **hervir**
hisopo *nm* **1** : hyssop **2** : cotton swab
hispánico, -ca *adj & n* : Hispanic
hispano[1], -na *adj* : Hispanic ⟨de habla hispana : Spanish-speaking⟩
hispano[2], -na *n* : Hispanic (person)
hispanoamericano[1], -na *adj* LATINOAMERICANO : Latin-American
hispanoamericano[2], -na *n* LATINOAMERICANO : Latin American
hispanohablante[1] *adj* : Spanish-speaking
hispanohablante[2] *nmf* : Spanish speaker
histerectomía *nf* : hysterectomy
histeria *nf* **1** : hysteria **2** : hysterics
histérico, -ca *adj* : hysterical — **histéricamente** *adv*
histerismo *nm* **1** : hysteria **2** : hysterics
historia *nf* **1** : history **2** NARRACIÓN, RELATO : story
historiador, -dora *n* : historian
historial *nm* **1** : record, document **2** CURRÍCULUM : résumé, curriculum vitae
histórico, -ca *adj* **1** : historical **2** : historic, important — **históricamente** *adv*
historieta *nf* : comic strip
histrionismo *nm* : histrionics, acting
hit ['hit] *nm, pl* **hits** **1** ÉXITO : hit, popular song **2** : hit (in baseball)
hito *nm* : milestone, landmark

hizo → **hacer**
hobby ['hɔbi] *nm, pl* **hobbies** [-bis] : hobby
hocico *nm* : snout, muzzle
hockey ['hɔke, -ki] *nm* : hockey
hogar *nm* **1** : home **2** : hearth, fireplace
hogareño, -ña *adj* **1** : home-loving **2** : domestic, homelike
hogaza *nf* : large loaf (of bread)
hoguera *nf* **1** FOGATA : bonfire **2 morir en la hoguera** : to burn at the stake
hoja *nf* **1** : leaf, petal, blade (of grass) **2** : sheet (of paper), page (of a book) ⟨hoja de cálculo : spreadsheet⟩ **3** FORMULARIO : form ⟨hoja de pedido : order form⟩ **4** : blade (of a knife) ⟨hoja de afeitar : razor blade⟩
hojalata *nf* : tinplate
hojaldre *nm* : puff pastry
hojarasca *nf* : fallen leaves *pl*
hojear *vt* : to leaf through (a book or magazine)
hojuela *nf* **1** : leaflet, young leaf **2** : flake
hola *interj* : hello!, hi!
holandés[1], -desa *adj, mpl* **-deses** : Dutch
holandés[2], -desa *n, mpl* **-deses** : Dutch person, Dutchman *m*, Dutchwoman *f* ⟨los holandeses : the Dutch⟩
holandés[3] *nm* : Dutch (language)
holgadamente *adv* : comfortably, easily ⟨vivir holgadamente : to be well-off⟩
holgado, -da *adj* **1** : loose, baggy **2** : at ease, comfortable
holganza *nf* : leisure, idleness
holgazán[1], -zana *adj, mpl* **-zanes** : lazy
holgazán[2], -zana *n, mpl* **-zanes** HARAGÁN : slacker, idler
holgazanear *vi* HARAGANEAR : to laze around, to loaf
holgazanería *nf* PEREZA : idleness, laziness
holgura *nf* **1** : looseness **2** COMODIDAD : comfort, ease
holístico, -ca *adj* : holistic
hollar {19} *vt* : to tread on, to trample
hollín *nm, pl* **hollines** TIZNE : soot
holocausto *nm* : holocaust
holograma *nm* : hologram
hombre *nm* **1** : man ⟨el hombre : man, mankind⟩ **2 hombre de estado** : statesman **3 hombre de negocios** : businessman **4 hombre lobo** : werewolf
hombrera *nf* **1** : shoulder pad **2** : epaulet
hombría *nf* : manliness
hombro *nm* : shoulder ⟨encogerse de hombros : to shrug one's shoulders⟩
hombruno, -na *adj* : mannish
homenaje *nm* : homage, tribute ⟨rendir homenaje a : to pay tribute to⟩
homenajear *vt* : to pay homage to, to honor
homeopatía *nf* : homeopathy
homicida[1] *adj* : homicidal, murderous
homicida[2] *nmf* ASESINO : murderer
homicidio *nm* ASESINATO : homicide, murder

homilía *nf* : homily, sermon
homófono *nm* : homophone
homogeneidad *nf* : homogeneity
homogeneización *nf* : homogenization
homogeneizar {21} *vt* : to homogenize
homogéneo, -nea *adj* : homogeneous
homógrafo *nm* : homograph
homologación *nf, pl* **-ciones** **1** : sanctioning, approval **2** : parity
homologar {52} *vt* **1** : to sanction **2** : to bring into line
homólogo¹, -ga *adj* : homologous, equivalent
homólogo², -ga *n* : counterpart
homónimo¹, -ma *n* TOCAYO : namesake
homónimo² *nm* : homonym
homosexual *adj & nmf* : homosexual
homosexualidad *nf* : homosexuality
honda *nf* : sling
hondo¹ *adv* : deeply
hondo², -da *adj* PROFUNDO : deep ⟨en lo más hondo de : in the depths of⟩ — **hondamente** *adv*
hondonada *nf* **1** : hollow, depression **2** : ravine, gorge
hondura *nf* : depth
hondureño, -ña *adj & n* : Honduran
honestidad *nf* **1** : decency, modesty **2** : honesty, uprightness
honesto, -ta *adj* **1** : decent, virtuous **2** : honest, honorable — **honestamente** *adv*
hongo *nm* **1** : fungus **2** : mushroom
honor *nm* **1** : honor ⟨en honor a la verdad : to be quite honest⟩ **2 honores** *nmpl* : honors ⟨hacer los honores : to do the honors⟩
honorable *adj* HONROSO : honorable — **honorablemente** *adv*
honorario, -ria *adj* : honorary
honorarios *nmpl* : payment, fees (for professional services)
honorífico, -ca *adj* : honorary ⟨mención honorífica : honorable mention⟩
honra *nf* **1** : dignity, self-respect ⟨tener a mucha honra : to take great pride in⟩ **2** : good name, reputation
honradamente *adv* : honestly, decently
honradez *nf, pl* **-deces** : honesty, integrity, probity
honrado, -da *adj* **1** HONESTO : honest, upright **2** : honored
honrar *vt* **1** : to honor **2** : to be a credit to ⟨su generosidad lo honra : his generosity does him credit⟩
honroso, -sa *adj* HONORABLE : honorable — **honrosamente** *adv*
hora *nf* **1** : hour ⟨media hora : half an hour⟩ ⟨a la última hora : at the last minute⟩ ⟨a la hora en punto : on the dot⟩ ⟨horas de oficina : office hours⟩ **2** : time ⟨¿qué hora es? : what time is it?⟩ **3** CITA : appointment
horario *nm* : schedule, timetable, hours *pl* ⟨horario de visita : visiting hours⟩
horca *nf* **1** : gallows *pl* **2** : pitchfork
horcajadas *nfpl* a ~ : astride, astraddle
horcón *nm, pl* **horcones** : wooden post, prop

horda *nf* : horde
horizontal *adj* : horizontal — **horizontalmente** *adv*
horizonte *nm* : horizon, skyline
horma *nf* **1** : shoe tree **2** : shoemaker's last
hormiga *nf* : ant
hormigón *nm, pl* **-gones** CONCRETO : concrete
hormigonera *nf* : cement mixer
hormigueo *nm* **1** : tingling, pins and needles *pl* **2** : uneasiness
hormiguero *nm* **1** : anthill **2** : swarm (of people)
hormona *nf* : hormone — **hormonal** *adj*
hornacina *nf* : niche, recess
hornada *nf* : batch
hornear *vt* : to bake
hornilla *nf* : burner (of a stove)
horno *nm* **1** : oven ⟨horno crematorio : crematorium⟩ ⟨horno de microondas : microwave oven⟩ **2** : kiln
horóscopo *nm* : horoscope
horqueta *nf* **1** : fork (in a river or road) **2** : crotch (in a tree) **3** : small pitchfork
horquilla *nf* **1** : hairpin, bobby pin **2** : pitchfork
horrendo, -da *adj* : horrendous, horrible
horrible *adj* : horrible, dreadful — **horriblemente** *adv*
horripilante *adj* : horrifying, hair-raising
horripilar *vt* : to horrify, to terrify
horror *nm* : horror, dread
horrorizado, -da *adj* : terrified
horrorizar {21} *vt* : to horrify, to terrify — **horrorizarse** *vr*
horroroso, -sa *adj* **1** : horrifying, terrifying **2** : dreadful, bad
hortaliza *nf* **1** : vegetable **2 hortalizas** *nfpl* : garden produce
hortera *adj Spain fam* : tacky, gaudy
hortícola *adj* : horticultural
horticultor, -ra *n* : horticulturist
horticultura *nf* : horticulture
hosco, -ca *adj* : sullen, gloomy
hospedaje *nm* : lodging, accommodations *pl*
hospedar *vt* : to provide with lodging, to put up — **hospedarse** *vr* : to stay, to lodge
hospicio *nm* : orphanage
hospital *nm* : hospital
hospitalario, -ria *adj* : hospitable
hospitalidad *nf* : hospitality
hospitalización *nf, pl* **-ciones** : hospitalization
hospitalizar {21} *vt* : to hospitalize — **hospitalizarse** *vr*
hostería *nf* POSADA : inn
hostia *nf* : host, Eucharist
hostigamiento *nm* : harassment
hostigar {52} *vt* ACOSAR, ASEDIAR : to harass, to pester
hostil *adj* : hostile

hostilidad *nf* **1** : hostility, antagonism **2 hostilidades** *nfpl* : (military) hostilities
hostilizar {21} *vt* : to harass
hotel *nm* : hotel
hotelero[1], **-ra** *adj* : hotel ⟨la industria hotelera : the hotel business⟩
hotelero[2], **-ra** *n* : hotel manager, hotelier
hoy *adv* **1** : today ⟨hoy mismo : right now, this very day⟩ **2** : now, nowadays ⟨de hoy en adelante : from now on⟩
hoyo *nm* AGUJERO : hole
hoyuelo *nm* : dimple
hoz *nf, pl* **hoces** : sickle
hozar {21} *vi* : to root (of a pig)
huachinango *nm Mex* : red snapper
huarache *nm* : huarache sandal
hubo, etc. → **haber**
hueco[1], **-ca** *adj* **1** : hollow, empty **2** : soft, spongy **3** : hollow-sounding, resonant **4** : proud, conceited **5** : superficial
hueco[2] *nm* **1** : hole, hollow, cavity **2** : gap, space **3** : recess, alcove
huele, etc. → **oler**
huelga *nf* **1** PARO : strike **2 hacer huelga** : to strike, to go on strike
huelguista *nmf* : striker
huella[1], **etc.** → **hollar**
huella[2] *nf* **1** : footprint ⟨seguir las huellas de alguien : to follow in someone's footsteps⟩ **2** : mark, impact ⟨dejar huella : to leave one's mark⟩ ⟨sin dejar huella : without a trace⟩ **3 huella digital** *or* **huella dactilar** : fingerprint
huérfano[1], **-na** *adj* **1** : orphan, orphaned **2** : defenseless **3** ~ **de** : lacking, devoid of
huérfano[2], **-na** *n* : orphan
huerta *nf* **1** : large vegetable garden, truck farm **2** : orchard **3** : irrigated land
huerto *nm* **1** : vegetable garden **2** : orchard
hueso *nm* **1** : bone **2** : pit, stone (of a fruit)
huésped[1], **-peda** *n* INVITADO : guest
huésped[2] *nm* : host ⟨organismo huésped : host organism⟩
huestes *nfpl* **1** : followers **2** : troops, army
huesudo, -da *adj* : bony
hueva *nf* : roe, spawn
huevo *nm* : egg ⟨huevos revueltos : scrambled eggs⟩
huida *nf* : flight, escape
huidizo, -za *adj* **1** ESCURRIDIZO : elusive, slippery **2** : shy, evasive
huipil *nm CA, Mex* : traditional sleeveless blouse or dress
huir {41} *vi* **1** ESCAPAR : to escape, to flee **2** ~ **de** : to avoid
huiro *nm Chile, Peru* : seaweed
huizache *nm* : huisache, acacia
hule *nm* **1** : oilcloth, oilskin **2** *Mex* : rubber **3 hule espuma** *Mex* : foam rubber
humanidad *nf* **1** : humanity, mankind

2 : humaneness **3 humanidades** *nfpl* : humanities *pl*
humanismo *nm* : humanism
humanista *nmf* : humanist
humanístico, -ca *adj* : humanistic
humanitario, -ria *adj & n* : humanitarian
humano[1], **-na** *adj* **1** : human **2** BENÉVOLO : humane, benevolent — **humanamente** *adv*
humano[2] *nm* : human being, human
humareda *nf* : cloud of smoke
humeante *adj* **1** : smoky **2** : smoking, steaming
humear *vi* **1** : to smoke **2** : to steam
humectante[1] *adj* : moisturizing
humectante[2] *nm* : moisturizer
humedad *nf* **1** : humidity **2** : dampness, moistness
humedecer {53} *vt* **1** : to humidify **2** : to moisten, to dampen
húmedo, -da *adj* **1** : humid **2** : moist, damp
humidificador *nm* : humidifier
humidificar {72} *vt* : to humidify
humildad *nf* **1** : humility **2** : lowliness
humilde *adj* **1** : humble **2** : lowly ⟨gente humilde : poor people⟩
humildemente *adv* : meekly, humbly
humillación *nf, pl* **-ciones** : humiliation
humillante *adj* : humiliating
humillar *vt* : to humiliate — **humillarse** *vr* : to humble oneself ⟨humillarse a hacer algo : to stoop to doing something⟩
humo *nm* **1** : smoke, steam, fumes **2 humos** *nmpl* : airs *pl*, conceit
humor *nm* **1** : humor **2** : mood, temper ⟨está de buen humor : she's in a good mood⟩
humorada *nf* **1** BROMA : joke, witticism **2** : whim, caprice
humorismo *nm* : humor, wit
humorista *nmf* : humorist, comedian, comedienne *f*
humorístico, -ca *adj* : humorous — **humorísticamente** *adv*
humoso, -sa *adj* : smoky, steamy
humus *nm* : humus
hundido, -da *adj* **1** : sunken **2** : depressed
hundimiento *nm* **1** : sinking **2** : collapse, ruin
hundir *vt* **1** : to sink **2** : to destroy, to ruin — **hundirse** *vr* **1** : to sink down **2** : to cave in **3** : to break down, to go to pieces
húngaro[1], **-ra** *adj & n* : Hungarian
húngaro[2] *nm* : Hungarian (language)
huracán *nm, pl* **-canes** : hurricane
huraño, -ña *adj* **1** : unsociable, aloof **2** : timid, skittish (of an animal)
hurgar {52} *vt* : to poke, to jab, to rake (a fire) — *vi* ~ **en** : to rummage in, to poke through
hurgue, etc. → **hurgar**
hurón *nm, pl* **hurones** : ferret
huronear *vi* : to pry, to snoop

hurra *interj* : hurrah!, hooray!
hurtadillas *nfpl* **a ~** : stealthily, on the sly
hurtar *vt* ROBAR : to steal
hurto *nm* **1** : theft, robbery **2** : stolen property, loot
husmear *vt* **1** : to follow the scent of, to track **2** : to sniff out, to pry into — *vi* **1** : to pry, to snoop **2** : to sniff around (of an animal)
huso *nm* **1** : spindle **2 huso horario** : time zone
huy *interj* : ow!, ouch!
huye, etc. → **huir**

I

i *nf* : ninth letter of the Spanish alphabet
iba, etc. → **ir**
ibérico, -ca *adj* : Iberian
ibero, -ra *or* **íbero, -ra** *adj & n* : Iberian
iberoamericano, -na *adj* HISPANO-AMERICANO, LATINOAMERICANO : Latin-American
ibis *nfs & pl* : ibis
ice, etc. → **izar**
iceberg *nm, pl* **icebergs** : iceberg
icono *nm* : icon
iconoclasia *nf* : iconoclasm
iconoclasta *nmf* : iconoclast
ictericia *nf* : jaundice
ida *nf* **1** : going, departure **2 ida y vuelta** : round-trip **3 idas y venidas** : comings and goings
idea *nf* **1** : idea, notion **2** : opinion, belief **3** PROPÓSITO : intention
ideal *adj & nm* : ideal — **idealmente** *adv*
idealismo *nm* : idealism
idealista[1] *adj* : idealistic
idealista[2] *nmf* : idealist
idealizar {21} *vt* : to idealize — **idealización** *nf*
idear *vt* : to devise, to think up
ideario *nm* : ideology
ídem *nm* : idem, the same, ditto
idéntico, -ca *adj* : identical, alike — **idénticamente** *adv*
identidad *nf* : identity
identificable *adj* : identifiable
identificación *nf, pl* **-ciones** **1** : identification, identifying **2** : identification document, ID
identificar {72} *vt* : to identify — **identificarse** *vr* **1** : to identify oneself **2 ~ con** : to identify with
ideología *nf* : ideology — **ideológicamente** *adv*
ideológico, -ca *adj* : ideological
idílico, -ca *adj* : idyllic
idilio *nm* : idyll
idioma *nm* : language ⟨el idioma inglés : the English language⟩
idiomático, -ca *adj* : idiomatic — **idiomáticamente** *adv*
idiosincrasia *nf* : idiosyncrasy
idiosincrásico, -ca *adj* : idiosyncratic
idiota[1] *adj* : idiotic, stupid, foolish
idiota[2] *nmf* : idiot, foolish person
idiotez *nf, pl* **-teces** **1** : idiocy **2** : idiotic act or remark ⟨¡no digas idioteces! : don't talk nonsense!⟩
ido *pp* → **ir**

idólatra[1] *adj* : idolatrous
idólatra[2] *nmf* : idolater
idolatrar *vt* : to idolize
idolatría *nf* : idolatry
ídolo *nm* : idol
idoneidad *nf* : suitability
idóneo, -nea *adj* ADECUADO : suitable, fitting
iglesia *nf* : church
iglú *nm* : igloo
ignición *nf, pl* **-ciones** : ignition
ignífugo, -ga *adj* : fire-resistant, fireproof
ignominia *nf* : ignominy, disgrace
ignominioso, -sa *adj* : ignominious, shameful
ignorancia *nf* : ignorance
ignorante[1] *adj* : ignorant
ignorante[2] *nmf* : ignorant person, ignoramus
ignorar *vt* **1** : to ignore **2** DESCONOCER : to be unaware of ⟨lo ignoramos por absoluto : we have no idea⟩
ignoto, -ta *adj* : unknown
igual[1] *adv* **1** : in the same way **2 por ~** : equally
igual[2] *adj* **1** : equal **2** IDÉNTICO : the same, alike **3** : even, smooth **4** SEMEJANTE : similar **5** CONSTANTE : constant
igual[3] *nmf* : equal, peer
igualación *nf* **1** : equalization **2** : leveling, smoothing **3** : equating (in mathematics)
igualado, -da *adj* **1** : even (of a score) **2** : level **3** *Mex* : disrespectful
igualar *vt* **1** : to equalize **2** : to tie ⟨igualar el marcador : to even the score⟩
igualdad *nf* **1** : equality **2** UNIFORMIDAD : evenness, uniformity
igualmente *adv* **1** : equally **2** ASIMISMO : likewise
iguana *nf* : iguana
ijada *nf* : flank, loin, side
ijar *nm* → **ijada**
ilegal[1] *adj* : illegal, unlawful — **ilegalmente** *adv*
ilegal[2] *nmf CA, Mex* : illegal alien
ilegalidad *nf* : illegality, unlawfulness
ilegibilidad *nf* : illegibility
ilegible *adj* : illegible — **ilegiblemente** *adv*
ilegitimidad *nf* : illegitimacy
ilegítimo, -ma *adj* : illegitimate, unlawful

ileso, -sa *adj* : uninjured, unharmed
ilícito, -ta *adj* : illicit — **ilícitamente** *adv*
ilimitado, -da *adj* : unlimited
ilógico, -ca *adj* : illogical — **ilógicamente** *adv*
iluminación *nf, pl* **-ciones 1** : illumination **2** ALUMBRADO : lighting
iluminado, -da *adj* : illuminated, lighted
iluminar *vt* **1** : to illuminate, to light (up) **2** : to enlighten
ilusión *nf, pl* **-siones 1** : illusion, delusion **2** ESPERANZA : hope ⟨hacerse ilusiones : to get one's hopes up⟩
ilusionado, -da *adj* ESPERANZADO : hopeful, eager
ilusionar *vt* : to build up hope, to excite — **ilusionarse** *vr* : to get one's hopes up
iluso¹, -sa *adj* : naive, gullible
iluso², -sa *n* SOÑADOR : dreamer, visionary
ilusorio, -ria *adj* ENGAÑOSO : illusory, misleading
ilustración *nf, pl* **-ciones 1** : illustration **2** : erudition, learning ⟨la Ilustración : the Enlightenment⟩
ilustrado, -da *adj* **1** : illustrated **2** DOCTO : learned, erudite
ilustrador, -dora *n* : illustrator
ilustrar *vt* **1** : to illustrate **2** ACLARAR, CLARIFICAR : to explain
ilustrativo, -va *adj* : illustrative
ilustre *adj* : illustrious, eminent
imagen *nf, pl* **imágenes** : image, picture
imaginable *adj* : imaginable, conceivable
imaginación *nf, pl* **-ciones** : imagination
imaginar *vt* : to imagine — **imaginarse** *vr* **1** : to suppose, to imagine **2** : to picture
imaginario, -ria *adj* : imaginary
imaginativo, -va *adj* : imaginative — **imaginativamente** *adv*
imaginería *nf* **1** : imagery **2** : image making (in religion)
imán *nm, pl* **imanes** : magnet
imantar *vt* : to magnetize
imbatible *adj* : unbeatable
imbécil¹ *adj* : stupid, idiotic
imbécil² *nmf* **1** : imbecile **2** *fam* : idiot, dope
imborrable *adj* : indelible
imbuir {41} *vt* : to imbue — **imbuirse** *vr*
imitación *nf, pl* **-ciones 1** : imitation **2** : mimicry, impersonation
imitador¹, -dora *adj* : imitative
imitador², -dora *n* **1** : imitator **2** : mimic
imitar *vt* **1** : to imitate, to copy **2** : to mimic, to impersonate
imitativo, -va *adj* → **imitador¹**
impaciencia *nf* : impatience
impacientar *vt* : to make impatient, to exasperate — **impacientarse** *vr*
impaciente *adj* : impatient — **impacientemente** *adv*
impactado, -da *adj* : shocked, stunned
impactante *adj* **1** : shocking **2** : impressive, powerful

impactar *vt* **1** GOLPEAR : to hit **2** IMPRESIONAR : to impact, to affect — **impactarse** *vr*
impacto *nm* **1** : impact, effect **2** : shock, collision
impagable *adj* **1** : unpayable **2** : priceless
impago *nm* : nonpayment
impalpable *adj* INTANGIBLE : impalpable, intangible
impar¹ *adj* : odd ⟨números impares : odd numbers⟩
impar² *nm* : odd number
imparable *adj* : unstoppable
imparcial *adj* : impartial — **imparcialmente** *adv*
imparcialidad *nf* : impartiality
impartir *vt* : to impart, to give
impasible *adj* : impassive, unmoved — **impasiblemente** *adv*
impasse *nm* : impasse
impávido, -da *adj* : undaunted, unperturbed
impecable *adj* INTACHABLE : impeccable, faultless — **impecablemente** *adv*
impedido, -da *adj* : disabled, crippled
impedimento *nm* **1** : impediment, obstacle **2** : disability
impedir {54} *vt* **1** : to prevent, to block **2** : to impede, to hinder
impeler *vt* **1** : to drive, to propel **2** : to impel
impenetrable *adj* : impenetrable — **impenetrabilidad** *nf*
impenitente *adj* : unrepentant, impenitent
impensable *adj* : unthinkable
impensado, -da *adj* : unforeseen, unexpected
imperante *adj* : prevailing
imperar *vi* **1** : to reign, to rule **2** PREDOMINAR : to prevail
imperativo¹, -va *adj* : imperative
imperativo² *nm* : imperative
imperceptible *adj* : imperceptible — **imperceptiblemente** *adv*
imperdible *nm* *Spain* : safety pin
imperdonable *adj* : unpardonable, unforgivable
imperecedero, -ra *adj* **1** : imperishable **2** INMORTAL : immortal, everlasting
imperfección *nf, pl* **-ciones 1** : imperfection **2** DEFECTO : defect, flaw
imperfecto¹, -ta *adj* : imperfect, flawed
imperfecto² *nm* : imperfect tense
imperial *adj* : imperial
imperialismo *nm* : imperialism
imperialista *adj & nmf* : imperialist
impericia *nf* : lack of skill, incompetence
imperio *nm* : empire
imperioso, -sa *adj* **1** : imperious **2** : pressing, urgent — **imperiosamente** *adv*
impermeabilizante *adj* : water-repellent
impermeabilizar {21} *vt* : to waterproof
impermeable¹ *adj* **1** : impervious **2** : impermeable, waterproof
impermeable² *nm* : raincoat

impersonal *adj* : impersonal — **impersonalmente** *adv*

impertinencia *nf* INSOLENCIA : impertinence, insolence

impertinente *adj* **1** INSOLENTE : impertinent, insolent **2** INOPORTUNO : inappropriate, uncalled-for **3** IRRELEVANTE : irrelevant

imperturbable *adj* : imperturbable, impassive, stolid

ímpetu *nm* **1** : impetus, momentum **2** : vigor, energy **3** : force, violence

impetuoso, -sa *adj* : impetuous, impulsive — **impetuosamente** *adv*

impiedad *nf* : impiety

impío, -pía *adj* : impious, ungodly

implacable *adj* : implacable, relentless — **implacablemente** *adv*

implantación *nf, pl* **-ciones** **1** : implantation **2** ESTABLECIMIENTO : establishment, introduction

implantado, -da *adj* : well-established

implantar *vt* **1** : to implant **2** ESTABLECER : to establish, to introduce — **implantarse** *vr*

implante *nm* : implant

implementar *vt* : to implement — **implementarse** *vr* — **implementación** *nf*

implemento *nm* : implement, tool

implicación *nf, pl* **-ciones** : implication

implicar {72} *vt* **1** ENREDAR, ENVOLVER : to involve, to implicate **2** : to imply

implícito, -ta *adj* : implied, implicit — **implícitamente** *adv*

implorar *vt* : to implore

implosión *nf, pl* **-siones** : implosion — **implosivo, -va** *adj*

implosionar *vi* : to implode

imponderable *adj & nm* : imponderable

imponente *adj* : imposing, impressive

imponer {60} *vt* **1** : to impose **2** : to confer — *vi* : to be impressive, to command respect — **imponerse** *vr* **1** : to take on (a duty) **2** : to assert oneself **3** : to prevail

imponible *adj* : taxable

impopular *adj* : unpopular — **impopularidad** *nf*

importación *nf, pl* **-ciones** **1** : importation **2** **importaciones** *nfpl* : imports

importado, -da *adj* : imported

importador[1], **-dora** *adj* : importing

importador[2], **-dora** *n* : importer

importancia *nf* : importance

importante *adj* : important — **importantemente** *adv*

importar *vi* : to matter, to be important ⟨no le importa lo que piensen : she doesn't care what they think⟩ — *vt* : to import

importe *nm* **1** : price, cost **2** : sum, amount

importunar *vt* : to bother, to inconvenience — *vi* : to be inconvenient

importuno, -na *adj* **1** : inopportune, inconvenient **2** : bothersome, annoying

imposibilidad *nf* : impossibility

imposibilitado, -da *adj* **1** : disabled, crippled **2 verse imposibilitado** : to be unable (to do something)

imposibilitar *vt* **1** : to make impossible **2** : to disable, to incapacitate — **imposibilitarse** *vr* : to become disabled

imposible *adj* : impossible

imposición *nf, pl* **-ciones** **1** : imposition **2** EXIGENCIA : demand, requirement **3** : tax **4** : deposit

impositivo, -va *adj* : tax ⟨tasa impositiva : tax rate⟩

impostor, -tora *n* : impostor

impostura *nf* **1** : fraud, imposture **2** CALUMNIA : slander

impotencia *nf* **1** : impotence, powerlessness **2** : impotence (in medicine)

impotente *adj* **1** : powerless **2** : impotent

impracticable *adj* : impracticable

imprecisión *nf, pl* **-siones** **1** : imprecision, vagueness **2** : inaccuracy

impreciso, -sa *adj* **1** : imprecise, vague **2** : inaccurate

impredecible *adj* : unpredictable

impregnar *vt* : to impregnate

imprenta *nf* **1** : printing **2** : printing shop, press

imprescindible *adj* : essential, indispensable

impresentable *adj* : unpresentable, unfit

impresión *nf, pl* **-siones** **1** : print, printing **2** : impression, feeling

impresionable *adj* : impressionable

impresionante *adj* : impressive, incredible, amazing — **impresionantemente** *adv*

impresionar *vt* **1** : to impress, to strike **2** : to affect, to move — *vi* : to make an impression — **impresionarse** *vr* : to be affected, to be removed

impresionismo *nm* : impressionism

impresionista[1] *adj* : impressionist, impressionistic

impresionista[2] *nmf* : impressionist

impreso[1] *pp* → **imprimir**

impreso[2], **-sa** *adj* : printed

impreso[3] *nm* PUBLICACIÓN : printed matter, publication

impresor, -sora *n* : printer

impresora *nf* : (computer) printer

imprevisible *adj* : unforeseeable

imprevisión *nf, pl* **-siones** : lack of foresight, thoughtlessness

imprevisto[1], **-ta** *adj* : unexpected, unforeseen

imprevisto[2] *nm* : unexpected occurrence, contingency

imprimir {42} *vt* **1** : to print **2** : to imprint, to stamp, to impress

improbabilidad *nf* : improbability

improbable *adj* : improbable, unlikely

improcedente *adj* **1** : inadmissible **2** : inappropriate, improper

improductivo, -va *adj* : unproductive

improperio *nm* : affront, insult

impropiedad *nf* : impropriety

impropio, -pia *adj* **1** : improper, incorrect **2** INADECUADO : unsuitable, inappropriate

improvisación *nf, pl* **-ciones** : improvisation, ad-lib

improvisado, -da *adj* : improvised, ad-lib

improvisar *v* : to improvise, to ad-lib

improviso *adj* **de ~** : all of a sudden, unexpectedly

imprudencia *nf* INDISCRECIÓN : imprudence, indiscretion

imprudente *adj* INDISCRETO : imprudent, indiscreet — **imprudentemente** *adv*

impúdico, -ca *adj* : shameless, indecent

impuesto[1] *pp* → **imponer**

impuesto[2] *nm* : tax

impugnar *vt* : to challenge, to contest

impulsar *vt* : to propel, to drive

impulsividad *nf* : impulsiveness

impulsivo, -va *adj* : impulsive — **impulsivamente** *adv*

impulso *nm* **1** : drive, thrust **2** : impulse, urge

impune *adj* : unpunished

impunemente *adv* : with impunity

impunidad *nf* : impunity

impureza *nf* : impurity

impuro, -ra *adj* : impure

impuso, etc. → **imponer**

imputable *adj* ATRIBUIBLE : attributable

imputación *nf, pl* **-ciones 1** : attribution, imputation **2** : accusation

imputar *vt* ATRIBUIR : to impute, to attribute

inacabable *adj* : endless

inacabado, -da *adj* INCONCLUSO : unfinished

inaccesibilidad *nf* : inaccessibility

inaccesible *adj* **1** : inaccessible **2** : unattainable

inacción *nf, pl* **-ciones** : inactivity, inaction

inaceptable *adj* : unacceptable

inactividad *nf* : inactivity, idleness

inactivo, -va *adj* : inactive, idle

inadaptado[1], **-da** *adj* : maladjusted

inadaptado[2], **-da** *n* : misfit

inadecuación *nf, pl* **-ciones** : inadequacy

inadecuado, -da *adj* **1** : inadequate **2** IMPROPIO : inappropriate — **inadecuadamente** *adv*

inadmisible *adj* **1** : inadmissible **2** : unacceptable

inadvertencia *nf* : oversight

inadvertidamente *adv* : inadvertently

inadvertido, -da *adj* **1** : unnoticed ⟨pasar inadvertido : to go unnoticed⟩ **2** DESPISTADO, DISTRAÍDO : inattentive, distracted

inagotable *adj* : inexhaustible

inaguantable *adj* INSOPORTABLE : insufferable, unbearable

inalámbrico, -ca *adj* : wireless, cordless

inalcanzable *adj* : unreachable, unattainable

inalienable *adj* : inalienable

inalterable *adj* **1** : unalterable, unchangeable **2** : impassive **3** : colorfast

inamovible *adj* : immovable, fixed

inanición *nf, pl* **-ciones** : starvation

inanimado, -da *adj* : inanimate

inapelable *adj* : indisputable

inapetencia *nf* : lack of appetite

inaplicable *adj* : inapplicable

inapreciable *adj* **1** : imperceptible, negligible **2** : invaluable

inapropiado, -da *adj* : inappropriate, unsuitable

inarticulado, -da *adj* : inarticulate, unintelligible — **inarticuladamente** *adv*

inasequible *adj* : unattainable, inaccessible

inasistencia *nf* AUSENCIA : absence

inatacable *adj* : unassailable, indisputable

inaudible *adj* : inaudible

inaudito, -ta *adj* : unheard-of, unprecedented

inauguración *nf, pl* **-ciones** : inauguration

inaugural *adj* : inaugural, opening

inaugurar *vt* **1** : to inaugurate **2** : to open

inca *adj & nmf* : Inca

incalculable *adj* : incalculable

incalificable *adj* : indescribable

incandescencia *nf* : incandescence — **incandescente** *adj*

incansable *adj* INFATIGABLE : tireless — **incansablemente** *adv*

incapacidad *nf* **1** : inability, incapacity **2** : disability, handicap

incapacitado, -da *adj* **1** : disqualified **2** : disabled, handicapped

incapacitar *vt* **1** : to incapacitate, to disable **2** : to disqualify

incapaz *adj, pl* **-paces 1** : incapable, unable **2** : incompetent, inept

incautación *nf, pl* **-ciones** : seizure, confiscation

incautar *vt* CONFISCAR : to confiscate, to seize, **-incautarse** *vr*

incauto, -ta *adj* : unwary, unsuspecting

incendiar *vt* : to set fire to, to burn (down) — **incendiarse** *vr* : to catch fire

incendiario[1], **-ria** *adj* : incendiary, inflammatory

incendiario[2], **-ria** *n* : arsonist

incendio *nm* **1** : fire **2 incendio premeditado** : arson

incensario *nm* : censer

incentivar *vt* : to encourage, to stimulate

incentivo *nm* : incentive

incertidumbre *nf* : uncertainty, suspense

incesante *adj* : incessant — **incesantemente** *adv*

incesto *nm* : incest

incestuoso, -sa *adj* : incestuous

incidencia *nf* **1** : incident **2** : effect, impact **3 por ~** : by chance, accidentally

incidental *adj* : incidental
incidentalmente *adv* : by chance
incidente *nm* : incident, occurrence
incidir *vi* 1 ~ **en** : to fall into, to enter into ⟨incidimos en el mismo error : we fell into the same mistake⟩ 2 ~ **en** : to affect, to influence, to have a bearing on
incienso *nm* : incense
incierto, -ta *adj* 1 : uncertain 2 : untrue 3 : unsteady, insecure
incineración *nf, pl* **-ciones** 1 : incineration 2 : cremation
incinerador *nm* : incinerator
incinerar *vt* 1 : to incinerate 2 : to cremate
incipiente *adj* : incipient
incisión *nf, pl* **-siones** : incision
incisivo¹, -va *adj* : incisive
incisivo² *nm* : incisor
inciso *nm* : digression, aside
incitación *nf, pl* **-ciones** : incitement
incitador¹, -dora *n* : instigator, agitator
incitador², -dora *adj* : provocative
incitante *adj* : provocative
incitar *vt* : to incite, to rouse
incivilizado, -da *adj* : uncivilized
inclemencia *nf* : inclemency, severity
inclemente *adj* : inclement
inclinación *nf, pl* **-ciones** 1 PROPENSIÓN : inclination, tendency 2 : incline, slope
inclinado, -da *adj* 1 : sloping 2 : inclined, apt
inclinar *vt* : to tilt, to lean, to incline ⟨inclinar la cabeza : to bow one's head⟩ — **inclinarse** *vr* 1 : to lean, to lean over 2 ~ **a** : to be inclined to
incluir {41} *vt* : to include
inclusión *nf, pl* **-siones** : inclusion
inclusive *adv* : inclusively, up to and including
inclusivo, -va *adj* : inclusive
incluso *adv* 1 AUN : even, in fact ⟨es importante e incluso crucial : it is important and even crucial⟩ 2 : inclusively
incógnita *nf* 1 : unknown quantity (in mathematics) 2 : mystery
incógnito, -ta *adj* 1 : unknown 2 **de incógnito** : incognito
incoherencia *nf* : incoherence
incoherente *adj* : incoherent — **incoherentemente** *adv*
incoloro, -ra *adj* : colorless
incombustible *adj* : fireproof
incomible *adj* : inedible
incomodar *vt* 1 : to make uncomfortable 2 : to inconvenience — **incomodarse** *vr* : to put oneself out, to take the trouble
incomodidad *nf* 1 : discomfort, awkwardness 2 MOLESTIA : inconvenience, bother
incómodo, -da *adj* 1 : uncomfortable, awkward 2 INCONVENIENTE : inconvenient
incomparable *adj* : incomparable

incompatibilidad *nf* : incompatibility
incompatible *adj* : incompatible, uncongenial
incompetencia *nf* : incompetence
incompetente *adj & nmf* : incompetent
incompleto, -ta *adj* : incomplete
incomprendido, -da *adj* : misunderstood
incomprensible *adj* : incomprehensible
incomprensión *nf, pl* **-siones** : lack of understanding, incomprehension
incomunicación *nf, pl* **-ciones** : lack of communication
incomunicado, -da *adj* 1 : cut off, isolated 2 : in solitary confinement
inconcebible *adj* : inconceivable, unthinkable — **inconcebiblemente** *adv*
inconcluso, -sa *adj* INACABADO : unfinished
incondicional *adj* : unconditional — **incondicionalmente** *adv*
inconexo, -xa *adj* : unconnected, disconnected
inconfesable *adj* : unspeakable, shameful
inconforme *adj & nmf* : nonconformist
inconformidad *nf* : nonconformity
inconformista *adj & nmf* : nonconformist
inconfundible *adj* : unmistakable, obvious — **inconfundiblemente** *adv*
incongruencia *nf* : incongruity
incongruente *adj* : incongruous
inconmensurable *adj* : vast, immeasurable
inconquistable *adj* : unyielding
inconsciencia *nf* 1 : unconsciousness, unawareness 2 : irresponsibility
inconsciente¹ *adj* 1 : unconscious, unaware 2 : reckless, needless — **inconscientemente** *adv*
inconsciente² *nm* **el inconsciente** : the unconscious
inconsecuente *adj* : inconsistent — **inconsecuencia** *nf*
inconsiderado, -da *adj* : inconsiderate, thoughtless
inconsistencia *nf* : inconsistency
inconsistente *adj* 1 : weak, flimsy 2 : inconsistent, weak (of an argument)
inconsolable *adj* : inconsolable — **inconsolablemente** *adv*
inconstancia *nf* : inconstancy
inconstante *adj* : inconstant, fickle, changeable
inconstitucional *adj* : unconstitutional
inconstitucionalidad *nf* : unconstitutionality
incontable *adj* INNUMERABLE : countless, innumerable
incontenible *adj* : uncontrollable, unstoppable
incontestable *adj* INCUESTIONABLE, INDISCUTIBLE : irrefutable, indisputable
incontinencia *nf* : incontinence — **incontinente** *adj*
incontrolable *adj* : uncontrollable
incontrolado, -da *adj* : uncontrolled, out of control

incontrovertible *adj* : indisputable
inconveniencia *nf* **1** : inconvenience, trouble **2** : unsuitability, inappropriateness **3** : tactless remark
inconveniente[1] *adj* **1** INCÓMODO : inconvenient **2** INAPROPIADO : improper, unsuitable
inconveniente[2] *nm* : obstacle, problem, snag ⟨no tengo inconveniente en hacerlo : I don't mind doing it⟩
incorporación *nf, pl* **-ciones** : incorporation
incorporar *vt* **1** : to incorporate **2** : to add, to include — **incorporarse** *vr* **1** : to sit up **2** ~ **a** : to join
incorpóreo, -rea *adj* : incorporeal, bodiless
incorrección *n, pl* **-ciones** : impropriety, improper word or action
incorrecto, -ta *adj* : incorrect — **incorrectamente** *adv*
incorregible *adj* : incorrigible — **incorregibilidad** *nf*
incorruptible *adj* : incorruptible
incredulidad *nf* : incredulity, skepticism
incrédulo[1]**, -la** *adj* : incredulous, skeptical
incrédulo[2]**, -la** *n* : skeptic
increíble *adj* : incredible, unbelievable — **increíblemente** *adv*
incrementar *vt* : to increase — **incrementarse** *vr*
incremento *nm* AUMENTO : increase
incriminar *vt* : to incriminate — **incriminación** *nf*
incriminatorio, -ria *adj* : incriminating, incriminatory
incruento, -ta *adj* : bloodless
incrustación *nf, pl* **-ciones** : inlay
incrustar *vt* **1** : to embed **2** : to inlay — **incrustarse** *vr* : to become embedded
incubación *nf, pl* **-ciones** : incubation
incubadora *nf* : incubator
incubar *v* : to incubate
incuestionable *adj* INCONTESTABLE, INDISCUTIBLE : unquestionable, indisputable — **incuestionablemente** *adv*
inculcar {72} *vt* : to inculcate, to instill
inculpar *vt* ACUSAR : to accuse, to charge
inculto, -ta *adj* **1** : uncultured, ignorant **2** : uncultivated, fallow
incumbencia *nf* : obligation, responsibility
incumbir *vi* (*3rd person only*) ~ **a** : to be incumbent upon, to be of concern to ⟨a mí no me incumbe : it's not my concern⟩
incumplido, -da *adj* : irresponsible, unreliable
incumplimiento *nm* **1** : nonfulfillment, neglect **2 incumplimiento de contrato** : breach of contract
incumplir *vt* : to fail to carry out, to break (a promise, a contract)
incurable *adj* : incurable
incurrir *vi* **1** ~ **en** : to incur ⟨incurrir en gastos : to incur expenses⟩ **2** ~ **en** : to fall into, to commit ⟨incurrió en un error : he made a mistake⟩

incursión *nf, pl* **-siones** : incursion, raid
incursionar *vi* **1** : to raid **2** ~ **en** : to go into, to enter ⟨el actor incursionó en el baile : the actor worked in dance for awhile⟩
indagación *nf, pl* **-ciones** : investigation, inquiry
indagar {52} *vt* : to inquire into, to investigate
indebido, -da *adj* : improper, undue — **indebidamente** *adv*
indecencia *nf* : indecency, obscenity
indecente *adj* : indecent, obscene
indecible *adj* : indescribable, inexpressible
indecisión *nf, pl* **-siones** : indecision
indeciso, -sa *adj* **1** IRRESOLUTO : indecisive **2** : undecided
indeclinable *adj* : unavoidable
indecoro *nm* : impropriety, indecorousness
indecoroso, -sa *adj* : indecorous, unseemly
indefectible *adj* : unfailing, sure
indefendible *adj* : indefensible
indefenso, -sa *adj* : defenseless, helpless
indefinible *adj* : indefinable
indefinido, -da *adj* **1** : undefined, vague **2** INDETERMINADO : indefinite — **indefinidamente** *adv*
indeleble *adj* : indelible — **indeleblemente** *adv*
indelicado, -da *adj* : indelicate, tactless
indemnización *nf, pl* **-ciones** **1** : indemnity **2 indemnización por despido** : severance pay
indemnizar {21} *vt* : to indemnify, to compensate
independencia *nf* : independence
independiente *adj* : independent — **independientemente** *adv*
independizarse {21} *vr* : to become independent, to gain independence
indescifrable *adj* : indecipherable
indescriptible *adj* : indescribable — **indescriptiblemente** *adv*
indeseable *adj & nmf* : undesirable
indestructible *adj* : indestructible
indeterminación *nf, pl* **-ciones** : indeterminacy
indeterminado, -da *adj* **1** INDEFINIDO : indefinite **2** : indeterminate
indexar *vt* INDICIAR : to index (wages, prices, etc.)
indicación *nf, pl* **-ciones** **1** : sign, signal **2** : direction, instruction **3** : suggestion, hint
indicado, -da *adj* **1** APROPIADO : appropriate, suitable **2** : specified, indicated ⟨al día indicado : on the specified day⟩
indicador *nm* **1** : gauge, dial, meter **2** : indicator ⟨indicadores económicos : economic indicators⟩
indicar {72} *vt* **1** SEÑALAR : to indicate **2** ENSEÑAR, MOSTRAR : to show
indicativo[1]**, -va** *adj* : indicative
indicativo[2] *nm* : indicative (mood)

índice *nm* **1** : index **2** : index finger, forefinger **3** INDICIO : indication
indiciar *vt* : to index (prices, wages, etc.)
indicio *nm* : indication, sign
indiferencia *nf* : indifference
indiferente *adj* **1** : indifferent, unconcerned **2 ser indiferente** : to be of no concern ⟨me es indiferente : it doesn't matter to me⟩
indígena[1] *adj* : indigenous, native
indígena[2] *nmf* : native
indigencia *nf* MISERIA : poverty, destitution
indigente *adj & nmf* : indigent
indigestarse *vr* **1** EMPACHARSE : to have indigestion **2** *fam* : to nauseate, to disgust ⟨ese tipo se me indigesta : that guy makes me sick⟩
indigestión *nf, pl* **-tiones** EMPACHO : indigestion
indigesto, -ta *adj* : indigestible, difficult to digest
indignación *nf, pl* **-ciones** : indignation
indignado, -da *adj* : indignant
indignante *adj* : outrageous, infuriating
indignar *vt* : to outrage, to infuriate — **indignarse** *vr*
indignidad *nf* : indignity
indigno, -na *adj* : unworthy
índigo *nm* : indigo
indio[1]**, -dia** *adj* **1** : American Indian, Indian, Amerindian **2** : Indian (from India)
indio[2]**, -dia** *n* **1** : American Indian **2** : Indian (from India)
indirecta *nf* **1** : hint, innuendo **2 echar indirectas** *or* **lanzar indirectas** : to drop a hint, to insinuate
indirecto, -ta *adj* : indirect — **indirectamente** *adv*
indisciplina *nf* : indiscipline, unruliness
indisciplinado, -da *adj* : undisciplined, unruly
indiscreción *nf, pl* **-ciones 1** IMPRUDENCIA : indiscretion **2** : tactless remark
indiscreto, -ta *adj* IMPRUDENTE : indiscreet, imprudent — **indiscretamente** *adv*
indiscriminado, -da *adj* : indiscriminate — **indiscriminadamente** *adv*
indiscutible *adj* INCONTESTABLE, INCUESTIONABLE : indisputable, unquestionable — **indiscutiblemente** *adv*
indispensable *adj* : indispensable — **indispensablemente** *adv*
indisponer {60} *vt* **1** : to spoil, to upset **2** : to make ill — **indisponerse** *vr* **1** : to become ill **2 ~ con** : to fall out with
indisposición *nf, pl* **-ciones** : indisposition, illness
indispuesto, -ta *adj* : unwell, indisposed
indistinguible *adj* : indistinguishable
indistintamente *adv* **1** : indistinctly **2** : indiscriminately
indistinto, -ta *adj* : indistinct, vague, faint

individual *adj* : individual — **individualmente** *adv*
individualidad *nf* : individuality
individualismo *nm* : individualism
individualista[1] *adj* : individualistic
individualista[2] *nmf* : individualist
individualizar {21} *vt* : to individualize
individuo *nm* : individual, person
indivisible *adj* : indivisible — **indivisibilidad** *nf*
indocumentado, -da *n* : illegal immigrant
índole *nf* **1** : nature, character **2** CLASE, TIPO : sort, kind
indolencia *nf* : indolence, laziness
indolente *adj* : indolent, lazy
indoloro, -ra *adj* : painless
indomable *adj* **1** : indomitable **2** : unruly, unmanageable
indómito, -ta *adj* : indomitable
indonesio, -sia *adj & n* : Indonesian
inducción *nf, pl* **-ciones** : induction
inducir {61} *vt* **1** : to induce, to cause **2** : to infer, to deduce
inductivo, -va *adj* : inductive
indudable *adj* : unquestionable, beyond doubt
indudablemente *adv* : undoubtedly, unquestionably
indulgencia *nf* **1** : indulgence, leniency **2** : indulgence (in religion)
indulgente *adj* : indulgent, lenient
indultar *vt* : to pardon, to reprieve
indulto *nm* : pardon, reprieve
indumentaria *nf* : clothing, attire
industria *nf* : industry
industrial[1] *adj* : industrial
industrial[2] *nmf* : industrialist, manufacturer
industrialización *nf, pl* **-ciones** : industrialization
industrializar {21} *vt* : to industrialize
industrioso, -sa *adj* : industrious
inédito, -ta *adj* **1** : unpublished **2** : unprecedented
inefable *adj* : ineffable
ineficacia *nf* **1** : inefficiency **2** : ineffectiveness
ineficaz *adj, pl* **-caces 1** : inefficient **2** : ineffective — **ineficazmente** *adv*
ineficiencia *nf* : inefficiency
ineficiente *adj* : inefficient — **ineficientemente** *adv*
inelegancia *nf* : inelegance — **inelegante** *adj*
inelegible *adj* : ineligible — **inelegibilidad** *nf*
ineludible *adj* : inescapable, unavoidable — **ineludiblemente** *adv*
ineptitud *nf* : ineptitude, incompetence
inepto, -ta *adj* : inept, incompetent
inequidad *nf* : inequity
inequitativo, -va *adj* : inequitable
inequívoco, -ca *adj* : unequivocal, unmistakable — **inequívocamente** *adv*
inercia *nf* **1** : inertia **2** : apathy, passivity **3 por ~** : out of habit
inerme *adj* : unarmed, defenseless

inerte *adj* : inert
inescrupuloso, -sa *adj* : unscrupulous
inescrutable *adj* : inscrutable
inesperado, -da *adj* : unexpected — **inesperadamente** *adv*
inestabilidad *nf* : instability, unsteadiness
inestable *adj* : unstable, unsteady
inestimable *adj* : inestimable, invaluable
inevitabilidad *nf* : inevitability
inevitable *adj* : inevitable, unavoidable — **inevitablemente** *adv*
inexactitud *nf* : inaccuracy
inexacto, -ta *adj* : inexact, inaccurate
inexcusable *adj* : inexcusable, unforgivable
inexistencia *nf* : lack, nonexistence
inexistente *adj* : nonexistent
inexorable *adj* : inexorable — **inexorablemente** *adv*
inexperiencia *nf* : inexperience
inexperto, -ta *adj* : inexperienced, unskilled
inexplicable *adj* : inexplicable — **inexplicablemente** *adv*
inexplorado, -da *adj* : unexplored
inexpresable *adj* : inexpressible
inexpresivo, -va *adj* : inexpressive, expressionless
inexpugnable *adj* : impregnable
inextinguible *adj* 1 : inextinguishable 2 : unquenchable
inextricable *adj* : inextricable — **inextricablemente** *adv*
infalibilidad *nf* : infallibility
infalible *adj* : infallible — **infaliblemente** *adv*
infame *adj* 1 : infamous 2 : loathsome, vile ⟨tiempo infame : terrible weather⟩
infamia *nf* : infamy, disgrace
infancia *nf* 1 NIÑEZ : infancy, childhood 2 : children *pl* 3 : beginnings *pl*
infante *nm* 1 : infante, prince 2 : infantryman
infantería *nf* : infantry
infantil *adj* 1 : childish, infantile 2 : child's, children's
infantilismo *nm* 1 : infantilism 2 INMADUREZ : childishness
infarto *nm* : heart attack
infatigable *adj* : indefatigable, tireless — **infatigablemente** *adv*
infección *nf, pl* **-ciones** : infection
infeccioso, -sa *adj* : infectious
infectar *vt* : to infect — **infectarse** *vr*
infecto, -ta *adj* 1 : infected 2 : repulsive, sickening
infecundidad *nf* : infertility
infecundo, -da *adj* : infertile, barren
infelicidad *nf* : unhappiness
infeliz[1] *adj, pl* **-lices** 1 : unhappy 2 : hapless, unfortunate, wretched
infeliz[2] *nmf, pl* **-lices** : wretch
inferencia *nf* : inference
inferior[1] *adj* : inferior, lower
inferior[2] *nmf* : inferior, underling
inferioridad *nf* : inferiority

inferir {76} *vt* 1 DEDUCIR : to infer, to deduce 2 : to cause (harm or injury), to inflict
infernal *adj* : infernal, hellish
infestación *n, pl* **-ciones** : infestation
infestar *vt* 1 : to infest 2 : to overrun, to invade
infición *nf, pl* **-ciones** *Mex* : pollution
infidelidad *nf* : unfaithfulness, infidelity
infiel[1] *adj* : unfaithful, disloyal
infiel[2] *nmf* : infidel, heathen
infierno *nm* 1 : hell 2 el quinto infierno : the middle of nowhere
infiltrar *vt* : to infiltrate — **infiltrarse** *vr* — **infiltración** *nf*
infinidad *nf* 1 : infinity 2 SINFÍN : great number, huge quantity ⟨una infinidad de veces : countless times⟩
infinitesimal *adj* : infinitesimal
infinitivo *nm* : infinitive
infinito[1] *adv* : infinitely, vastly
infinito[2], -ta *adj* 1 : infinite 2 : limitless, endless 3 hasta lo infinito : ad infinitum — **infinitamente** *adv*
infinito[3] *nm* : infinity
inflable *adj* : inflatable
inflación *nf, pl* **-ciones** : inflation
inflacionario, -ria *adj* : inflationary
inflacionista → **inflacionario**
inflamable *adj* : flammable
inflamación *nf, pl* **-ciones** : inflammation
inflamar *vt* : to inflame
inflamatorio, -ria *adj* : inflammatory
inflar *vt* HINCHAR : to inflate — **inflarse** *vr* 1 : to swell 2 : to become conceited
inflexibilidad *nf* : inflexibility
inflexible *adj* : inflexible, unyielding
inflexión *nf, pl* **-xiones** : inflection
infligir {35} *vt* : to inflict
influencia *nf* INFLUJO : influence
influenciable *adj* : easily influenced, suggestible
influenciar *vt* : to influence
influenza *nf* : influenza
influir {41} *vt* : to influence — *vi* ~ **en** *or* ~ **sobre** : to have an influence on, to affect
influjo *nm* INFLUENCIA : influence
influyente *adj* : influential
información *nf, pl* **-ciones** 1 : information 2 INFORME : report, inquiry 3 NOTICIAS : news
informado, -da *adj* : informed ⟨bien informado : well-informed⟩
informador, -dora *n* : informer, informant
informal *adj* 1 : unreliable (of persons) 2 : informal, casual — **informalmente** *adv*
informalidad *nf* : informality
informante *nmf* : informant
informar *vt* ENTERAR : to inform — *vi* : to report — **informarse** *vr* ENTERARSE : to get information, to find out
informática *nf* : computer science, computing

informativo[1], **-va** *adj* : informative
informativo[2] *nm* : news program, news
informatización *nf, pl* **-ciones** : computerization
informatizar {21} *vt* : to computerize
informe[1] *adj* AMORFO : shapeless, formless
informe[2] *nm* **1** : report **2** : reference (for employment) **3 informes** *nmpl* : information, data
infortunado, -da *adj* : unfortunate, unlucky
infortunio *nm* **1** DESGRACIA : misfortune **2** CONTRATIEMPO : mishap
infracción *nf, pl* **-ciones** : violation, offense, infraction
infractor, -tora *n* : offender
infraestructura *nf* : infrastructure
infrahumano, -na *adj* : subhuman
infranqueable *adj* **1** : impassable **2** : insurmountable
infrarrojo, -ja *adj* : infrared
infrecuente *adj* : infrequent
infringir {35} *vt* : to infringe, to breach
infructuoso, -sa *adj* : fruitless — **infructuosamente** *adv*
ínfulas *nfpl* **1** : conceit **2 darse ínfulas** : to put on airs
infundado, -da *adj* : unfounded, baseless
infundio *nm* : false story, lie, tall tale ⟨todo eso son infundios : that's a pack of lies⟩
infundir *vt* **1** : to instill **2 infundir ánimo a** : to encourage **3 infundir miedo a** : to intimidate
infusión *nf, pl* **-siones** : infusion
ingeniar *vt* : to devise, to think up — **ingeniarse** *vr* : to manage, to find a way
ingeniería *nf* : engineering
ingeniero, -ra *n* : engineer
ingenio *nm* **1** : ingenuity **2** CHISPA : wit, wits **3** : device, apparatus **4 ingenio azucarero** : sugar refinery
ingenioso, -sa *adj* **1** : ingenious **2** : clever, witty — **ingeniosamente** *adv*
ingente *adj* : huge, enormous
ingenuidad *nf* : naïveté, ingenuousness
ingenuo[1], **-nua** *adj* CÁNDIDO : naive — **ingenuamente** *adv*
ingenuo[2], **-nua** *n* : naive person
ingerencia → injerencia
ingerir {76} *vt* : to ingest, to consume
ingestión *nf, pl* **-tiones** : ingestion
ingle *nf* : groin
inglés[1], **-glesa** *adj, mpl* **ingleses** : English
inglés[2], **-glesa** *n, mpl* **ingleses** : Englishman *m*, Englishwoman *f*
inglés[3] *nm* : English (language)
inglete *nm* : miter joint
ingobernable *adj* : ungovernable, lawless
ingratitud *nf* : ingratitude
ingrato[1], **-ta** *adj* **1** : ungrateful **2** : thankless
ingrato[2], **-ta** *n* : ingrate
ingrediente *nm* : ingredient

ingresar *vt* **1** : to admit ⟨ingresaron a Luis al hospital : Luis was admitted into the hospital⟩ **2** : to deposit — *vi* **1** : to enter, to go in **2 ~ en** : to join, to enroll in
ingreso *nm* **1** : entrance, entry **2** : admission **3 ingresos** *nmpl* : income, earnings *pl*
íngrimo, -ma *adj* : all alone, all by oneself
inhábil *adj* : unskillful, clumsy
inhabilidad *nf* **1** : unskillfulness **2** : unfitness
inhabilitar *vt* **1** : to disqualify, to bar **2** : to disable
inhabitable *adj* : uninhabitable
inhabituado, -da *adj* **~ a** : unaccustomed to
inhalador *nm* : inhaler
inhalante *nm* : inhalant
inhalar *vt* : to inhale — **inhalación** *nf*
inherente *adj* : inherent
inhibición *nf, pl* **-ciones** COHIBICIÓN : inhibition
inhibir *vt* : to inhibit — **inhibirse** *vr*
inhóspito, -ta *adj* : inhospitable
inhumación *nf, pl* **-ciones** : interment, burial
inhumanidad *nf* : inhumanity
inhumano, -na *adj* : inhuman, cruel, inhumane
inhumar *vt* : to inter, to bury
iniciación *nf, pl* **-ciones** **1** : initiation **2** : introduction
iniciado, -da *n* : initiate
iniciador[1], **-dora** *adj* : initiatory
iniciador[2], **-dora** *n* : initiator, originator
inicial[1] *adj* : initial, original — **inicialmente** *adv*
inicial[2] *nf* : initial (letter)
iniciar *vt* COMENZAR : to initiate, to begin — **iniciarse** *vr*
iniciativa *nf* : initiative
inicio *nm* COMIENZO : beginning
inicuo, -cua *adj* : iniquitous, wicked
inigualado, -da *adj* : unequaled
inimaginable *adj* : unimaginable
inimitable *adj* : inimitable
ininteligible *adj* : unintelligible
ininterrumpido, -da *adj* : uninterrupted, continuous — **ininterrumpidamente** *adv*
iniquidad *nf* : iniquity, wickedness
injerencia *nf* : interference
injerirse {76} *vr* ENTROMETERSE, INMISCUIRSE : to meddle, to interfere
injertar *vt* : to graft
injerto *nm* : graft ⟨injerto de piel : skin graft⟩
injuria *nf* AGRAVIO : affront, insult
injuriar *vt* INSULTAR : to insult, to revile
injurioso, -sa *adj* : insulting, abusive
injusticia *nf* : injustice, unfairness
injustificable *adj* : unjustifiable
injustificadamente *adv* : unjustifiably, unfairly
injustificado, -da *adj* : unjustified, unwarranted

injusto, -ta *adj* : unfair, unjust — **injustamente** *adv*

inmaculado, -da *adj* : immaculate, spotless

inmadurez *nf, pl* **-reces** : immaturity

inmaduro, -ra *adj* **1** : immature **2** : unripe

inmediaciones *nfpl* : environs, surrounding area

inmediatamente *adv* ENSEGUIDA : immediately

inmediatez *nf, pl* **-teces** : immediacy

inmediato, -ta *adj* **1** : immediate **2** CONTIGUO : adjoining **3 de ~** : immediately, right away **4 ~ a** : next to, close to

inmejorable *adj* : excellent, unbeatable

inmemorial *adj* : immemorial ⟨tiempos inmemoriales : time immemorial⟩

inmensidad *nf* : immensity, vastness

inmenso, -sa *adj* ENORME : immense, huge, vast — **inmensamente** *adv*

inmensurable *adj* : boundless, immeasurable

inmerecido, -da *adj* : undeserved — **inmerecidamente** *adv*

inmersión *nf, pl* **-siones** : immersion

inmerso, -sa *adj* **1** : immersed **2** : involved, absorbed

inmigración *nf, pl* **-ciones** : immigration

inmigrado, -da *adj & n* : immigrant

inmigrante *adj & nmf* : immigrant

inmigrar *vi* : to immigrate

inminencia *nf* : imminence

inminente *adj* : imminent — **inminentemente** *adv*

inmiscuirse {41} *vr* ENTROMETERSE, INJERIRSE : to meddle, to interfere

inmobiliario, -ria *adj* : real estate, property

inmoderación *n, pl* **-ciones** : immoderation, intemperance

inmoderado, -da *adj* : immoderate, excessive — **inmoderamente** *adv*

inmodestia *nf* : immodesty — **inmodesto, -ta** *adj*

inmolar *vt* : to immolate — **inmolación** *nf*

inmoral *adj* : immoral

inmoralidad *nf* : immorality

inmortal *adj & nmf* : immortal

inmortalidad *nf* : immortality

inmortalizar {21} *vt* : to immortalize

inmotivado, -da *adj* **1** : unmotivated **2** : groundless

inmovible *adj* : immovable, fixed

inmóvil *adj* **1** : still, motionless **2** : steadfast

inmovilidad *nf* : immobility

inmovilizar {21} *vt* : to immobilize

inmueble *nm* : building, property

inmundicia *nf* : dirt, filth, trash

inmundo, -da *adj* : dirty, filthy, nasty

inmune *adj* : immune

inmunidad *nf* : immunity

inmunizar {21} *vt* : to immunize — **inmunización** *nf*

inmunología *nf* : immunology

inmunológico, -ca *adj* : immune ⟨sistema inmunológico : immune system⟩

inmutabilidad *nf* : immutability

inmutable *adj* : immutable, unchangeable

innato, -ta *adj* : innate, inborn

innecesario, -ria *adj* : unnecessary — **innecesariamente** *adv*

innegable *adj* : undeniable

innoble *adj* : ignoble — **innoblemente** *adv*

innovación *nf, pl* **-ciones** : innovation

innovador, -dora *adj* : innovative

innovar *vt* : to introduce — *vi* : to innovate

innumerable *adj* INCONTABLE : innumerable, countless

inobjetable *adj* : indisputable, unobjectionable

inocencia *nf* : innocence

inocente¹ *adj* **1** : innocent **2** INGENUO : naive — **inocentemente** *adv*

inocente² *nmf* : innocent person

inocentón¹, -tona *adj, mpl* **-tones** : naive, gullible

inocentón², -tona *n, mpl* **-tones** : simpleton, dupe

inocuidad *nf* : harmlessness

inocular *vt* : to inoculate, to vaccinate — **inoculación** *nf*

inocuo, -cua *adj* : innocuous, harmless

inodoro¹, -ra *adj* : odorless

inodoro² *nm* : toilet

inofensivo, -va *adj* : inoffensive, harmless

inolvidable *adj* : unforgettable

inoperable *adj* : inoperable

inoperante *adj* : ineffective, inoperative

inopinado, -da *adj* : unexpected — **inopinadamente** *adv*

inoportuno, -na *adj* : untimely, inopportune, inappropriate

inorgánico, -ca *adj* : inorganic

inoxidable *adj* **1** : rustproof **2 acero inoxidable** : stainless steel

inquebrantable *adj* : unshakable, unwavering

inquietante *adj* : disturbing, worrisome

inquietar *vt* PREOCUPAR : to disturb, to upset, to worry — **inquietarse** *vr*

inquieto, -ta *adj* **1** : anxious, uneasy, worried **2** : restless

inquietud *nf* **1** : anxiety, uneasiness, worry **2** AGITACIÓN : restlessness

inquilinato *nm* : tenancy

inquilino, -na *n* : tenant, occupant

inquina *nf* **1** : aversion, dislike **2** : ill will ⟨tener inquina a alguien : to have a grudge against someone⟩

inquirir {4} *vi* : to make inquiries — *vt* : to investigate

inquisición *nf, pl* **-ciones** : investigation, inquiry

inquisidor, -dora *adj* : inquisitive

inquisitivo, -va *adj* : inquisitive, curious — **inquisitivamente** *adv*

insaciable *adj* : insatiable

insalubre *adj* **1** : unhealthy **2** ANTIHIGIÉNICO : unsanitary

insalubridad *nf* : unhealthiness
insalvable *adj* : insuperable, insurmountable
insano, -na *adj* **1** LOCO : insane, mad **2** INSALUBRE : unhealthy
insatisfacción *nf, pl* **-ciones** : dissatisfaction
insatisfactorio *nm* : unsatisfactory
insatisfecho, -cha *adj* **1** : dissatisfied **2** : unsatisfied
inscribir {33} *vt* **1** MATRICULAR : to enroll, to register **2** GRABAR : to engrave — **inscribirse** *vr* : to register, to sign up
inscripción *nf, pl* **-ciones 1** MATRÍCULA : enrollment, registration **2** : inscription
inscrito *pp* → **inscribir**
insecticida¹ *adj* : insecticidal
insecticida² *nm* : insecticide
insecto *nm* : insect
inseguridad *nf* **1** : insecurity **2** : lack of safety **3** : uncertainty
inseguro, -ra *adj* **1** : insecure **2** : unsafe **3** : uncertain
inseminar *vt* : to inseminate — **inseminación** *nf*
insensatez *nf, pl* **-teces** : foolishness, stupidity
insensato¹, -ta *adj* : foolish, senseless
insensato², -ta *n* : fool
insensibilidad *nf* : insensitivity
insensible *adj* : insensitive, unfeeling
inseparable *adj* : inseparable — **inseparablemente** *adv*
inserción *nf, pl* **-ciones** : insertion
insertar *vt* : to insert
inservible *adj* INÚTIL : useless, unusable
insidia *nf* **1** : snare, trap **2** : malice
insidioso, -sa *adj* : insidious
insigne *adj* : noted, famous
insignia *nf* ENSEÑA : insignia, emblem, badge
insignificancia *nf* **1** : insignificance **2** NIMIEDAD : trifle, triviality
insignificante *adj* : insignificant
insincero, -ra *adj* : insincere — **insinceridad** *nf*
insinuación *nf, pl* **-ciones** : insinuation, hint
insinuante *adj* : suggestive
insinuar {3} *vt* : to insinuate, to hint at — **insinuarse** *vr* **1** ~ **a** : to make advances to **2** ~ **en** : to worm one's way into
insipidez *nf, pl* **-deces** : insipidness, blandness
insípido, -da *adj* : insipid, bland
insistencia *nf* : insistence
insistente *adj* : insistent — **insistentemente** *adv*
insistir *v* : to insist
insociable *adj* : unsociable
insolación *nf, pl* **-ciones** : sunstroke
insolencia *nf* IMPERTINENCIA : insolence
insolente *adj* IMPERTINENTE : insolent
insólito, -ta *adj* : rare, unusual

insoluble *adj* : insoluble — **insolubilidad** *nf*
insolvencia *nf* : insolvency, bankruptcy
insolvente *adj* : insolvent, bankrupt
insomne *adj* & *nmf* : insomniac
insomnio *nm* : insomnia
insondable *adj* : fathomless, deep
insonorizado, -da *adj* : soundproof
insoportable *adj* INAGUANTABLE : unbearable, intolerable
insoslayable *adj* : unavoidable, inescapable
insospechado, -da *adj* : unexpected, unforeseen
insostenible *adj* : untenable
inspección *nf, pl* **-ciones** : inspection
inspeccionar *vt* : to inspect
inspector, -tora *n* : inspector
inspiración *nf, pl* **-ciones 1** : inspiration **2** INHALACIÓN : inhalation
inspirador, -dora *adj* : inspiring
inspirar *vt* : to inspire — *vi* INHALAR : to inhale
instalación *nf, pl* **-ciones** : installation
instalar *vt* **1** : to install **2** : to instate — **instalarse** *vr* ESTABLECERSE : to settle, to establish oneself
instancia *nf* **1** : petition, request **2 en última instancia** : as a last resort
instantánea *nf* : snapshot
instantáneo, -nea *adj* : instantaneous — **instantáneamente** *adv*
instante *nm* **1** : instant, moment **2 al instante** : immediately **3 a cada instante** : frequently, all the time **4 por instantes** : constantly, incessantly
instar *vt* APREMIAR : to urge, to press — *vi* URGIR : to be urgent or pressing ⟨insta que vayamos pronto : it is imperative that we leave soon⟩
instauración *nf, pl* **-ciones** : establishment
instaurar *vt* : to establish
instigador, -dora *n* : instigator
instigar {52} *vt* : to instigate, to incite
instintivo, -va *adj* : instinctive — **instintivamente** *adv*
instinto *nm* : instinct
institución *nf, pl* **-ciones** : institution
institucional *adj* : institutional — **institucionalmente** *adv*
institucionalización *nf, pl* **-ciones** : institutionalization
institucionalizar {21} *vt* : to institutionalize
instituir {41} *vt* ESTABLECER, FUNDAR : to institute, to establish, to found
instituto *nm* : institute
institutriz *nf, pl* **-trices** : governess *f*
instrucción *nf, pl* **-ciones 1** EDUCACIÓN : education **2 instrucciones** *nfpl* : instructions, directions
instructivo, -va *adj* : instructive, educational
instructor, -tora *n* : instructor
instruir {41} *vt* **1** ADIESTRAR : to instruct, to train **2** ENSEÑAR : to educate, to teach

instrumentación *nf, pl* **-ciones** : orchestration
instrumental *adj* : instrumental
instrumentar *vt* : to orchestrate
instrumentista *nmf* : instrumentalist
instrumento *nm* : instrument
insubordinado, -da *adj* : insubordinate — **insubordinación** *nf*
insubordinarse *vr* : to rebel
insuficiencia *nf* **1** : insufficiency, inadequacy **2 insuficiencia cardíaca** : heart failure
insuficiente *adj* : insufficient, inadequate — **insuficientemente** *adv*
insufrible *adj* : insufferable
insular *adj* : insular
insularidad *nf* : insularity
insulina *nf* : insulin
insulso, -sa *adj* **1** INSÍPIDO : insipid, bland **2** : dull
insultante *adj* : insulting
insultar *vt* : to insult
insulto *nm* : insult
insumos *nmpl* : supplies ⟨insumos agrícolas : agricultural supplies⟩
insuperable *adj* : insuperable, insurmountable
insurgente *adj & nmf* : insurgent — **insurgencia** *nf*
insurrección *nf, pl* **-ciones** : insurrection, uprising
insustancial *adj* : insubstantial, flimsy
insustituible *adj* : irreplaceable
intachable *adj* : irreproachable, faultless
intacto, -ta *adj* : intact
intangible *adj* IMPALPABLE : intangible, impalpable
integración *nf, pl* **-ciones** : integration
integral *adj* **1** : integral, essential **2 pan integral** : whole grain bread
integrante[1] *adj* : integrating, integral
integrante[2] *nmf* : member
integrar *vt* : to make up, to compose — **integrarse** *vr* : to integrate, to fit in
integridad *nf* **1** RECTITUD : integrity, honesty **2** : wholeness, completeness
integrismo *nm* : fundamentalism
integrista *adj & nmf* : fundamentalist
íntegro, -gra *adj* **1** : honest, upright **2** ENTERO : whole, complete **3** : unabridged
intelecto *nm* : intellect
intelectual *adj & nmf* : intellectual — **intelectualmente** *adv*
intelectualidad *nf* : intelligentsia
inteligencia *nf* : intelligence
inteligente *adj* : intelligent — **inteligentemente** *adv*
inteligible *adj* : intelligible — **inteligibilidad** *nf*
intemperancia *adj* : intemperance, excess
intemperie *nf* **1** : bad weather, elements *pl* **2 a la intemperie** : in the open air, outside
intempestivo, -va *adj* : inopportune, untimely — **intempestivamente** *adv*

intención *nf, pl* **-ciones** : intention, plan
intencionado, -da → **intencional**
intencional *adj* : intentional — **intencionalmente** *adv*
intendencia *nf* : management, administration
intendente *nmf* : quartermaster
intensidad *nf* : intensity
intensificación *nf, pl* **-ciones** : intensification
intensificar {72} *vt* : to intensify — **intensificarse** *vr*
intensivo, -va *adj* : intensive — **intensivamente** *adv*
intenso, -sa *adj* : intense — **intensamente** *adv*
intentar *vt* : to attempt, to try
intento *nm* **1** PROPÓSITO : intent, intention **2** TENTATIVA : attempt, try
interacción *nf, pl* **-ciones** : interaction
interactivo, -va *adj* : interactive
interactuar {3} *vi* : to interact
intercalar *vt* : to intersperse, to insert
intercambiable *adj* : interchangeable
intercambiar *vt* CANJEAR : to exchange, to trade
intercambio *nm* CANJE : exchange, trade
interceder *vi* : to intercede
intercepción *nf, pl* **-ciones** : interception
interceptar *vt* **1** : to intercept, to block **2 interceptar las líneas** : to wiretap
intercesión *nf, pl* **-siones** : intercession
intercomunicación *nf, pl* **-ciones** : intercommunication
interconexión *nf, pl* **-xiones** : interconnection
interconfesional *adj* : interdenominational
interdepartamental *adj* : interdepartmental
interdependencia *nf* : interdependence — **interdependiente** *adj*
interdicción *nf, pl* **-ciones** : interdiction, prohibition
interés *nm, pl* **-reses** : interest
interesado, -da *adj* **1** : interested **2** : selfish, self-seeking
interesante *adj* : interesting
interesar *vt* : to interest — *vi* : to be of interest, to be interesting — **interesarse** *vr*
interestatal *adj* : interstate ⟨autopista interestatal : interstate highway⟩
interestelar *adj* : interstellar
interfase → **interfaz**
interfaz *nf, pl* **-faces** : interface
interferencia *nf* : interference, static
interferir {76} *vi* : to interfere, to meddle — *vt* : to interfere with, to obstruct
intergaláctico, -ca *adj* : intergalactic
intergubernamental *adj* : intergovernmental
interín[1] *or* **ínterin** *adv* : meanwhile
interín[2] *or* **ínterin** *nm, pl* **-rines** : meantime, interim ⟨en el interín : in the meantime⟩

interinamente *adv* : temporarily
interino, -na *adj* : acting, temporary, interim
interior[1] *adj* : interior, inner
interior[2] *nm* **1** : interior, inside **2** : inland region
interiormente *adv* : inwardly
interjección *nf, pl* **-ciones** : interjection
interlocutor, -tora *n* : interlocutor, speaker
interludio *nm* : interlude
intermediario, -ria *adj & n* : intermediary, go-between
intermedio[1]**, -dia** *adj* : intermediate
intermedio[2] *nm* **1** : intermission **2 por intermedio de** : by means of
interminable *adj* : interminable, endless — **interminablemente** *adv*
intermisión *nf, pl* **-siones** : intermission, pause
intermitente[1] *adj* **1** : intermittent **2** : flashing, blinking (of a light) — **intermitentemente** *adv*
intermitente[2] *nm* : blinker, turn signal
internacional *adj* : international — **internacionalmente** *adv*
internacionalismo *nm* : internationalism
internacionalizar {21} *vt* : to internationalize
internado *nm* : boarding school
internar *vt* : to commit, to confine — **internarse** *vr* **1** : to penetrate, to advance into **2 ~ en** : to go into, to enter
internista *nmf* : internist
interno[1]**, -na** *adj* : internal — **internamente** *adv*
interno[2]**, -na** *n* **1** : intern **2** : inmate, internee
interpelación *nf, pl* **-ciones** : appeal, plea
interpelar *vt* : to question (formally)
interpersonal *adj* : interpersonal
interpolar *vt* : to insert, to interpolate
interponer {60} *vt* : to interpose — **interponerse** *vr* : to intervene
interpretación *nf, pl* **-ciones** : interpretation
interpretar *vt* **1** : to interpret **2** : to play, to perform
interpretativo, -va *adj* : interpretive
intérprete *nmf* **1** TRADUCTOR : interpreter **2** : performer
interpuesto *pp* → **interponer**
interracial *adj* : interracial
interrelación *nf, pl* **-ciones** : interrelationship
interrelacionar *vi* : to interrelate
interrogación *nf, pl* **-ciones** **1** : interrogation, questioning **2 signo de interrogación** : question mark
interrogador, -dora *n* : interrogator, questioner
interrogante[1] *adj* : questioning
interrogante[2] *nm* **1** : question mark **2** : query
interrogar {52} *vt* : to interrogate, to question

interrogativo, -va *adj* : interrogative
interrogatorio *nm* : interrogation, questioning
interrumpir *v* : to interrupt
interrupción *nf, pl* **-ciones** : interruption
interruptor *nm* **1** : (electrical) switch **2** : circuit breaker
intersección *nf, pl* **-ciones** : intersection
intersticio *nm* : interstice — **intersticial** *adj*
interuniversitario, -ria *adj* : intercollegiate
interurbano, -na *adj* **1** : intercity **2** : long-distance ⟨llamadas interurbanas : long-distance calls⟩
intervalo *nm* : interval
intervención *nf, pl* **-ciones** **1** : intervention **2** : audit **3 intervención quirúrgica** : operation
intervencionista *adj & nmf* : interventionist
intervenir {87} *vi* **1** : to take part **2** INTERCEDER : to intervene, to intercede — *vt* **1** : to control, to supervise **2** : to audit **3** : to operate on **4** : to tap (a telephone)
interventor, -tora *n* **1** : inspector **2** : auditor, comptroller
intestado, -da *adj* : intestate
intestinal *adj* : intestinal
intestino *nm* : intestine
intimar *vi* **~ con** : to become friendly with — *vt* : to require, to call on
intimidación *nf, pl* **-ciones** : intimidation
intimidad *nf* **1** : intimacy **2** : privacy, private life
intimidar *vt* ACOBARDAR : to intimidate
íntimo, -ma *adj* **1** : intimate, close **2** PRIVADO : private — **íntimamente** *adv*
intitular *vt* : to entitle, to title
intocable *adj* : untouchable
intolerable *adj* : intolerable, unbearable
intolerancia *nf* : intolerance
intolerante[1] *adj* : intolerant
intolerante[2] *nmf* : intolerant person, bigot
intoxicación *nf, pl* **-ciones** : poisoning
intoxicante *nm* : poison
intoxicar {72} *vt* : to poison
intranquilidad *nf* PREOCUPACIÓN : worry, anxiety
intranquilizar {21} *vt* : to upset, to make uneasy — **intranquilizarse** *vr* : to get worried, to be anxious
intranquilo, -la *adj* PREOCUPADO : uneasy, worried
intransigencia *nf* : intransigence
intransigente *adj* : intransigent, unyielding
intransitable *adj* : impassable
intransitivo, -va *adj* : intransitive
intrascendente *adj* : unimportant, insignificant
intratable *adj* **1** : intractable **2** : awkward **3** : unsociable
intravenoso, -sa *adj* : intravenous

intrepidez *nf* : fearlessness
intrépido, -da *adj* : intrepid, fearless
intriga *nf* : intrigue
intrigante *nmf* : schemer
intrigar {52} *v* : to intrigue — **intrigante** *adj*
intrincado, -da *adj* : intricate, involved
intrínseco, -ca *adj* : intrinsic — **intrínsecamente** *adv*
introducción *nf, pl* **-ciones** : introduction
introducir {61} *vt* **1** : to introduce **2** : to bring in **3** : to insert **4** : to input, to enter — **introducirse** *vr* : to penetrate, to get into
introductorio, -ria *adj* : introductory
intromisión *nf, pl* **-siones** : interference, meddling
introspección *nf, pl* **-ciones** : introspection
introspectivo, -va *adj* : introspective
introvertido¹, -da *adj* : introverted
introvertido², -da *n* : introvert
intrusión *nf, pl* **-siones** : intrusion
intruso¹, -sa *adj* : intrusive
intruso², -sa *n* : intruder
intuición *nf, pl* **-ciones** : intuition
intuir {41} *vt* : to intuit, to sense
intuitivo, -va *adj* : intuitive — **intuitivamente** *adv*
inundación *nf, pl* **-ciones** : flood, inundation
inundar *vt* : to flood, to inundate
inusitado, -da *adj* : unusual, uncommon — **inusitadamente** *adv*
inusual *adj* : unusual, uncommon — **inusualmente** *adv*
inútil¹ *adj* INSERVIBLE : useless — **inútilmente** *adv*
inútil² *nmf* : good-for-nothing
inutilidad *nf* : uselessness
inutilizar {21} *vt* **1** : to make useless **2** INCAPACITAR : to disable, to put out of commission
invadir *vt* : to invade
invalidar *vt* : to nullify, to invalidate
invalidez *nf, pl* **-deces 1** : invalidity **2** : disablement
inválido, -da *adj & n* : invalid
invalorable *adj* : invaluable
invariable *adj* : invariable — **invariablemente** *adv*
invasión *nf, pl* **-siones** : invasion
invasivo, -va *adj* : invasive
invasor¹, -sora *adj* : invading
invasor², -sora *n* : invader
invectiva *nf* : invective, abuse
invencibilidad *nf* : invincibility
invencible *adj* **1** : invincible **2** : insurmountable
invención *nf, pl* **-ciones 1** INVENTO : invention **2** MENTIRA : fabrication, lie
inventar *vt* **1** : to invent **2** : to fabricate, to make up
inventariar {85} *vt* : to inventory
inventario *nm* : inventory
inventiva *nf* : ingenuity, inventiveness
inventivo, -va *adj* : inventive

invento *nm* INVENCIÓN : invention
inventor, -tora *n* : inventor
invernadero *nm* : greenhouse, hothouse
invernal *adj* : winter, wintry
invernar {55} *vi* **1** : to spend the winter **2** HIBERNAR : to hibernate
inverosímil *adj* : unlikely, far-fetched
inversión *nf, pl* **-siones 1** : inversion **2** : investment
inversionista *nmf* : investor
inverso¹, -sa *adj* **1** : inverse, inverted **2** CONTRARIO : opposite **3 a la inversa** : on the contrary, vice versa **4 en orden inverso** : in reverse order — **inversamente** *adv*
inverso² *n* : inverse
inversor, -sora *n* : investor
invertebrado¹, -da *adj* : invertebrate
invertebrado² *nm* : invertebrate
invertir {76} *vt* **1** : to invert, to reverse **2** : to invest — *vi* : to make an investment — **invertirse** *vr* : to be reversed
investidura *nf* : investiture, inauguration
investigación *nf, pl* **-ciones 1** ENCUESTA, INDAGACIÓN : investigation, inquiry **2** : research
investigador¹, -dora *adj* : investigative
investigador², -dora *n* **1** : investigator **2** : researcher
investigar {52} *vt* **1** INDAGAR : to investigate **2** : to research — *vi* ~ **sobre** : to do research into
investir {54} *vt* **1** : to empower **2** : to swear in, to inaugurate
inveterado, -da *adj* : inveterate, deep-seated
invicto, -ta *adj* : undefeated
invidente¹ *adj* CIEGO : blind, sightless
invidente² *nmf* CIEGO : blind person
invierno *nm* : winter, wintertime
inviolable *adj* : inviolable — **inviolabilidad** *nf*
inviolado, -da *adj* : inviolate, pure
invisibilidad *nf* : invisibility
invisible *adj* : invisible — **invisiblemente** *adv*
invitación *nf, pl* **-ciones** : invitation
invitado, -da *n* : guest
invitar *vt* : to invite
invocación *nf, pl* **-ciones** : invocation
invocar {72} *vt* : to invoke, to call on
involucramiento *nm* : involvement
involucrar *vt* : to implicate, to involve — **involucrarse** *vr* : to get involved
involuntario, -ria *adj* : involuntary — **involuntariamente** *adv*
invulnerable *adj* : invulnerable
inyección *nf, pl* **-ciones** : injection, shot
inyectado, -da *adj* **ojos inyectados** : bloodshot eyes
inyectar *vt* : to inject
ion *nm* : ion
iónico, -ca *adj* : ionic
ionizar {21} *vt* : to ionize — **ionización** *nf*
ionosfera *nf* : ionosphere
ir {43} *vi* **1** : to go ⟨ir a pie : to go on foot, to walk⟩ ⟨ir a caballo : to ride

horseback⟩ ⟨ir a casa : to go home⟩ **2**
: to lead, to extend, to stretch ⟨el
camino va de Cali a Bogotá : the road
goes from Cali to Bogotá⟩ **3** FUN-
CIONAR : to work, to function ⟨esta
computadora ya no va : this computer
doesn't work anymore⟩ **4** : to get on,
to get along ⟨¿cómo te va? : how are
you?, how's it going?⟩ ⟨el negocio no
va bien : the business isn't doing well⟩
5 : to suit ⟨ese vestido te va bien : that
dress really suits you⟩ **6** ~ **con** : to be
⟨ir con prisa : to be in a hurry⟩ **7** ~
por : to follow, to go along ⟨fueron por
la costa : they followed the shoreline⟩
8 dejarse ir : to let oneself go **9 ir a**
parar : to end up **10 vamos a ver** : let's
see — *v aux* **1** (*with present participle*)
⟨ir caminando : to walk⟩ ⟨¡voy corriendo! : I'll be right there!⟩ **2** ~ **a** : to
be going to ⟨voy a hacerlo : I'm going
to do it⟩ ⟨el avión va a despegar : the
plane is about to take off⟩ — **irse** *vr* **1**
: to leave, to go ⟨¡vámonos! : let's go!⟩
⟨todo el mundo se fue : everyone left⟩
2 ESCAPARSE : to leak **3** GASTARSE : to
be used up, to be gone
ira *nf* CÓLERA, FURIA : wrath, anger
iracundo, -da *adj* : irate, angry
iraní *adj & nmf* : Iranian
iraquí *adj & nmf* : Iraqi
irascible *adj* : irascible, irritable — **iras-**
cibilidad *nf*
irga, irgue etc. → **erguir**
iridio *nm* : iridium
iridiscencia *nf* : iridescence — **iridis-**
cente *adj*
iris *nms & pl* **1** : iris **2 arco iris** : rainbow
irlandés[1], **-desa** *adj, mpl* **-deses** : Irish
irlandés[2], **-desa** *n, pl* **-deses** : Irish person, Irishman *m*, Irishwoman *f*
irlandés[3] *nm* : Irish (language)
ironía *nf* : irony
irónico, -ca *adj* : ironic, ironical —
irónicamente *adv*
irracional *adj* : irrational — **irracional-**
mente *adv*
irracionalidad *nf* : irrationality
irradiación *nf, pl* **-ciones** : irradiation
irradiar *vt* : to radiate, to irradiate
irrazonable *adj* : unreasonable
irreal *adj* : unreal
irrebatible *adj* : unanswerable, irrefutable
irreconciliable *adj* : irreconcilable
irreconocible *adj* : unrecognizable
irrecuperable *adj* : irrecoverable, irretrievable
irredimible *adj* : irredeemable
irreductible *adj* : unyielding
irreemplazable *adj* : irreplaceable
irreflexión *nf, pl* **-xiones** : thoughtlessness, impetuosity
irreflexivo, -va *adj* : rash, unthinking —
irreflexivamente *adv*
irrefrenable *adj* : uncontrollable, unstoppable ⟨un impulso irrefrenable : an
irresistible urge⟩

irrefutable *adj* : irrefutable
irregular *adj* : irregular — **irregular-**
mente *adv*
irregularidad *nf* : irregularity
irrelevante *adj* : irrelevant — **irrele-**
vancia *nf*
irreligioso, -sa *adj* : irreligious
irremediable *adj* : incurable — **irreme-**
diablemente *adv*
irreparable *adj* : irreparable
irreprimible *adj* : irrepressible
irreprochable *adj* : irreproachable
irresistible *adj* : irresistible — **irre-**
sistiblemente *adv*
irresolución *nf, pl* **-ciones** : indecision,
hesitation
irresoluto, -ta *adj* INDECISO : undecided
irrespeto *nm* : disrespect
irrespetuoso, -sa *adj* : disrespectful —
irrespetuosamente *adv*
irresponsabilidad *nf* : irresponsibility
irresponsable *adj* : irresponsible — **irr-**
esponsablemente *adv*
irrestricto, -ta *adj* : unrestricted, unconditional
irreverencia *nf* : disrespect
irreverente *adj* : disrespectful
irreversible *adj* : irreversible
irrevocable *adj* : irrevocable — **irrevo-**
cablemente *adv*
irrigar {52} *vt* : to irrigate — **irrigación**
nf
irrisible *adj* : laughable
irrisión *nf, pl* **-siones** : derision, ridicule
irrisorio, -ria *adj* RISIBLE : ridiculous,
ludicrous
irritabilidad *nf* : irritability
irritable *adj* : irritable
irritación *nf, pl* **-ciones** : irritation
irritante *adj* : irritating
irritar *vt* : to irritate — **irritación** *nf*
irrompible *adj* : unbreakable
irrumpir *vi* ~ **en** : to burst into
irrupción *nf, pl* **-ciones** **1** : irruption **2**
: invasion
isla *nf* : island
islámico, -ca *adj* : Islamic, Muslim
islandés[1], **-desa** *adj, mpl* **-deses** : Icelandic
islandés[2], **-desa** *n, mpl* **-deses** : Icelander
islandés[3] *nm* : Icelandic (language)
isleño, -ña *n* : islander
islote *nm* : islet
isometría *nfs & pl* : isometrics
isométrico, -ca *adj* : isometric
isósceles *adj* : isosceles ⟨triángulo
isósceles : isosceles triangle⟩
isótopo *nm* : isotope
israelí *adj & nmf* : Israeli
istmo *nm* : isthmus
itacate *nm Mex* : pack, provisions *pl*
italiano[1], **-na** *adj & n* : Italian
italiano[2] *nm* : Italian (language)
iterbio *nm* : ytterbium
itinerante *adj* AMBULANTE : traveling,
itinerant
itinerario *nm* : itinerary, route

itrio *nm* : yttrium
izar {21} *vt* : to hoist, to raise ⟨izar la bandera : to raise the flag⟩
izquierda *nf* : left
izquierdista *adj & nmf* : leftist
izquierdo, -da *adj* : left

J

j *nf* : tenth letter of the Spanish alphabet
ja *interj* **1** : ha! **2 ja, ja** : ha-ha!
abalí *nm* : wild boar
abalina *nf* : javelin
abón *nm, pl* **jabones** : soap
abonar *vt* ENJABONAR : to soap up, to lather — **jabonarse** *vr*
abonera *nf* : soap dish
abonoso, -sa *adj* : soapy
aca *nf* **1** : pony **2** YEGUA : mare
acal *nm Mex* : shack, hut
acinto *nm* : hyacinth
actancia *nf* **1** : boastfulness **2** : boasting, bragging
actancioso[1], -sa *adj* : boastful
actancioso[2], -sa *n* : boaster, braggart
actarse *vr* : to boast, to brag
ade *nm* : jade
adear *vi* : to pant, to gasp, to puff — **jadeante** *adj*
adeo *nm* : panting, gasping, puffing
aez *nm, pl* **jaeces 1** : harness **2** : kind, sort, ilk **3 jaeces** *nmpl* : trappings
aguar *nm* : jaguar
ai alai *nm* : jai alai
aiba *nf* CANGREJO : crab
alapeño *nm Mex* : jalapeño pepper
alar *vt* **1** : to pull, to tug **2** *fam* : to attract, to draw in ⟨las ideas nuevas lo jalan : new ideas appeal to him⟩ — *vi* **1** : to pull, to pull together **2** *fam* : to hurry up, to get going **3** *Mex fam* : to be in working order ⟨esta máquina no jala : this machine doesn't work⟩
albegue *nm* : whitewash
alea *nf* : jelly
alear *vt* : to encourage, to urge on
aleo *nm* **1** *fam* : uproar, ruckus, racket **2** *fam* : confusion, hassle **3** : cheering and clapping (for a dance)
alón *nm, pl* **jalones 1** : milestone, landmark **2** TIRÓN : pull, tug
alonar *vt* : to mark, to stake out
alonear *vt Mex, Peru fam* : to tug at — *vi* **1** *fam* : to pull, to tug **2** *CA fam* : to haggle
amaica *nf* : hibiscus
amaicano, -na → **jamaiquino**
amaiquino, -na *adj & n* : Jamaican
amás *adv* **1** NUNCA : never **2 nunca jamás** *or* **jamás de los jamases** : never ever **3 para siempre jamás** : for ever and ever
amba *nf* : jamb
amelgo *nm* : nag (horse)
amón *nm, pl* **jamones** : ham
Januká *nmf* : Hanukkah
japonés[1], -nesa *adj & n, mpl* **-neses** : Japanese

japonés[2] *nm, pl* **-neses** : Japanese (language)
jaque *nm* **1** : check (in chess) ⟨jaque mate : checkmate⟩ **2 tener en jaque** : to intimidate, to bully
jaqueca *nf* : headache, migraine
jarabe *nm* **1** : syrup **2** : Mexican folk dance
jarana *nf* **1** *fam* : revelry, partying, spree **2** *fam* : joking, fooling around **3** : small guitar
jaranear *vi fam* : to go on a spree, to party
jarcia *nf* **1** : rigging **2** : fishing tackle
jardín *nm, pl* **jardines 1** : garden **2 jardín de niños** : kindergarten **3 los jardines** *nmpl* : the outfield
jardinería *nf* : gardening
jardinero, -ra *n* **1** : gardener **2** : outfielder (in baseball)
jarra *nf* **1** : pitcher, jug **2** : stein, mug **3 de jarras** *or* **en jarras** : akimbo
jarrete *nm* **1** : back of the knee **2** CORVEJÓN : hock
jarro *nm* **1** : pitcher, jug **2** : mug
jarrón *nm, pl* **jarrones** FLORERO : vase
jaspe *nm* : jasper
jaspeado, -da *adj* **1** VETEADO : streaked, veined **2** : speckled, mottled
jaula *nf* : cage
jauría *nf* : pack of hounds
javanés, -nesa *adj & n* : Javanese
azmín *nm, pl* **jazmines** : jasmine
azz [ˈjas, ˈʤas] *nm* : jazz
eans [ˈjins, ˈʤins] *nmpl* : jeans
eep [ˈjip, ˈʤip] *nm, pl* **jeeps** : jeep
efatura *nf* **1** : leadership **2** : headquarters ⟨jefatura de policía : police headquarters⟩
efe, -fa *n* **1** : chief, head, leader ⟨jefe de bomberos : fire chief⟩ **2** : boss
Jehová *nm* : Jehovah
ején *nm, pl* **jejenes** : gnat, small mosquito
engibre *nm* : ginger
eque *nm* : sheikh, sheik
erarca *nmf* : leader, chief
erarquía *nf* **1** : hierarchy **2** RANGO : rank
erárquico, -ca *adj* : hierarchical
erbo *nm* : gerbil
erez *nm, pl* **jereces** : sherry
erga *nf* **1** : jargon, slang **2** : coarse cloth
erigonza *nf* GALIMATÍAS : mumbo jumbo, gibberish
eringa *nf* : syringe
eringar {52} *vt* **1** : to inject **2** *fam* JOROBAR : to annoy, to pester — *vi fam*

JOROBAR : to be annoying, to be a nuisance

jeringuear → **jeringar**
jeringuilla → **jeringa**
jeroglífico *nm* : hieroglyphic
jersey *nm, pl* **jerseys 1** : jersey (fabric) **2** *Spain* : sweater
Jesucristo *nm* : Jesus Christ
jesuita *adj & nm* : Jesuit
Jesús *nm* **1** : Jesus **2 ¡Jesús!** : goodness!, good heavens!
jeta *nf* **1** : snout **2** *fam* : face, mug
jíbaro, -ra *adj* **1** : Jivaro **2** : rustic, rural
jibia *nf* : cuttlefish
jícama *nf* : jicama
jícara *nf Mex* : calabash
jilguero *nm* : European goldfinch
jinete *nmf* : horseman, horsewoman *f*, rider
jinetear *vt* **1** : to ride, to perform (on horseback) **2** DOMAR : to break in (a horse) — *vi* CABALGAR : to ride horseback
jingoísmo [ˌʤɪŋgoˈizmo, ˌʤɪŋ-] *nm* : jingoism
jingoísta *adj* : jingoist, jingoistic
jiote *nm Mex* : rash
jira *nf* : outing, picnic
jirafa *nf* **1** : giraffe **2** : boom microphone
jirón *nm, pl* **jirones** : shred, rag ⟨hecho jirones : in tatters⟩
jitomate *nm Mex* : tomato
jockey [ˈʤɔki, ˈʤo-] *nmf, pl* **jockeys** [-kis] : jockey
jocosidad *nf* : humor, jocularity
jocoso, -sa *adj* : playful, jocular — **jocosamente** *adv*
jofaina *nf* : washbowl
jogging [ˈʤɔgɪŋ, ˈʤo-] *nm* : jogging
jolgorio *nm* : merrymaking, fun
jonrón *nm, pl* **jonrones** : home run
jordano, -na *adj & n* : Jordanian
jornada *nf* **1** : expedition, day's journey **2 jornada de trabajo** : working day **3 jornadas** *nfpl* : conference, congress
jornal *nm* **1** : day's pay **2 a ∼** : by the day
jornalero, -ra *n* : day laborer
joroba *nf* **1** GIBA : hump **2** *fam* : nuisance, pain in the neck
jorobado¹, -da *adj* GIBOSO : hunchbacked, humpbacked
jorobado², -da *n* GIBOSO : hunchback, humpback
jorobar *vt fam* JERINGAR : to bother, to annoy — *vi fam* JERINGAR : to be annoying, to be a nuisance
jorongo *nm Mex* : full-length poncho
jota *nf* **1** : jot, bit ⟨no entiendo ni jota : I don't understand a word of it⟩ ⟨no se ve ni jota : you can't see a thing⟩ **2** : jack (in playing cards)
joven¹ *adj, pl* **jóvenes 1** : young **2** : youthful
joven² *nmf, pl* **jóvenes** : young man *m*, young woman *f*, young person

jovial *adj* : jovial, cheerful — **jovialmente** *adv*
jovialidad *nf* : joviality, cheerfulness
joya *nf* **1** : jewel, piece of jewelry **2** : treasure, gem ⟨la nueva empleada es una joya : the new employee is a real gem⟩
joyería *nf* **1** : jewelry store **2** : jewelry **3 joyería de fantasía** : costume jewelry
joyero, -ra *n* : jeweler
juanete *nm* : bunion
jubilación *nf, pl* **-ciones 1** : retirement **2** PENSIÓN : pension
jubilado¹, -da *adj* : retired, in retirement
jubilado², -da *nmf* : retired person, retiree
jubilar *vt* **1** : to retire, to pension off **2** *fam* : to get rid of, to discard — **jubilarse** *vr* : to retire
jubileo *nm* : jubilee
júbilo *nm* : jubilation, joy
jubiloso, -sa *adj* : jubilant, joyous
judaico, -ca *adj* : Judaic, Jewish
judaísmo *nm* : Judaism
judía *nf* **1** : bean **2** *or* **judía verde** : green bean, string bean
judicatura *nf* **1** : judiciary, judges *pl* **2** : office of judge
judicial *adj* : judicial — **judicialmente** *adv*
judío¹, -día *adj* : Jewish
judío², -día *n* : Jewish person, Jew
judo [ˈjuðo, ˈʤu-] *nm* : judo
juega, juegue, etc. → **jugar**
juego *nm* **1** : play, playing ⟨poner en juego : to bring into play⟩ **2** : game, sport ⟨juego de cartas : card game⟩ ⟨Juegos Olímpicos : Olympic Games⟩ **3** : gaming, gambling ⟨estar en juego : to be at stake⟩ **4** : set ⟨un juego de llaves : a set of keys⟩ **5 hacer juego** : to go together, to match **6 juego de manos** : conjuring trick, sleight of hand
juerga *nf* : partying, binge ⟨irse de juerga : to go on a spree⟩
juerguista *nmf* : reveler, carouser
jueves *nms & pl* : Thursday
juez¹ *nmf, pl* **jueces 1** : judge **2** ÁRBITRO : umpire, referee
juez², jueza *n* → **juez¹**
jugada *nf* **1** : play, move **2** : trick ⟨hacer una mala jugada : to play a dirty trick⟩
jugador, -dora *n* **1** : player **2** : gambler
jugar ⟨44⟩ *vi* **1** : to play ⟨jugar a la pelota : to play ball⟩ **2** APOSTAR : to gamble, to bet **3** : to joke, to kid — *vt* **1** : to play ⟨jugar un papel : to play a role⟩ ⟨jugar una carta : to play a card⟩ **2** : to bet — **jugarse** *vr* **1** : to risk, to gamble away ⟨jugarse la vida : to risk one's life⟩ **2 jugarse el todo por el todo** : to risk everything
jugarreta *nf fam* : prank, dirty trick
juglar *nm* : minstrel

jugo *nm* **1** : juice **2** : substance, essence ⟨sacarle el jugo a algo : to get the most out of something⟩
jugosidad *nf* : juiciness, succulence
jugoso, -sa *adj* : juicy
juguete *nm* : toy
juguetear *vi* **1** : to play, to cavort, to frolic **2** : to toy, to fiddle
juguetería *nf* : toy store
juguetón, -tona *adj, mpl* **-tones** : playful — **juguetonamente** *adv*
juicio *nm* **1** : good judgment, reason, sense **2** : opinion ⟨a mi juicio : in my opinion⟩ **3** : trial ⟨llevar a juicio : to take to court⟩
juicioso, -sa *adj* : judicious, wise — **juiciosamente** *adv*
julio *nm* : July
juncia *nf* : sedge
junco *nm* **1** : reed, rush **2** : junk (boat)
jungla *nf* : jungle
junio *nm* : June
junquillo *nm* : jonquil
junta *nf* **1** : board, committee ⟨junta directiva : board of directors⟩ **2** REUNIÓN : meeting, session **3** : junta **4** : joint, gasket
juntamente *adv* **1** : jointly, together ⟨juntamente con : together with⟩ **2** : at the same time
juntar *vt* **1** UNIR : to unite, to combine, to put together **2** REUNIR : to collect, to gather together, to assemble **3** : to close partway ⟨juntar la puerta : to leave the door ajar⟩ — **juntarse** *vr* **1** : to join together **2** : to socialize, to get together
junto, -ta *adj* **1** UNIDO : joined, united **2** : close, adjacent ⟨colgaron los dos retratos juntos : they hung the two paintings side by side⟩ **3** (*used adverbially*) : together ⟨llegamos juntos : we arrived together⟩ **4** ~ **a** : next to, alongside of **5** ~ **con** : together with, along with
juntura *nf* : joint, coupling
Júpiter *nm* : Jupiter
jura *nf* : oath, pledge ⟨jura de bandera : pledge of allegiance⟩

jurado[1] *nm* : jury
jurado[2]**, -da** *n* : juror
juramento *nm* **1** : oath ⟨juramento hipocrático : Hippocratic oath⟩ **2** : swearword, oath
jurar *vt* **1** : to swear ⟨jurar lealtad : to swear loyalty⟩ **2** : to take an oath ⟨el alcalde juró su cargo : the mayor took the oath of office⟩ — *vi* : to curse, to swear
jurídico, -ca *adj* : legal
jurisdicción *nf, pl* **-ciones** : jurisdiction
jurisdiccional *adj* : jurisdictional, territorial
jurisprudencia *nf* : jurisprudence, law
jurista *nmf* : jurist
justa *nf* **1** : joust **2** TORNEO : tournament, competition
justamente *adv* **1** PRECISAMENTE : precisely, exactly **2** : justly, fairly
justar *vi* : to joust
justicia *nf* **1** : justice, fairness ⟨hacerle justicia a : to do justice to⟩ ⟨ser de justicia : to be only fair⟩ **2 la justicia** : the law ⟨tomarse la justicia por su mano : to take the law into one's own hands⟩
justiciero, -ra *adj* : righteous, avenging
justificable *adj* : justifiable
justificación *nf, pl* **-ciones** : justification
justificante *nm* **1** : justification **2** : proof, voucher
justificar {72} *vt* **1** : to justify **2** : to excuse, to vindicate
justo[1] *adv* **1** : justly **2** : right, exactly ⟨justo a tiempo : just in time⟩ **3** : tightly
justo[2]**, -ta** *adj* **1** : just, fair **2** : right, exact **3** : tight ⟨estos zapatos me quedan muy justos : these shoes are too tight⟩
justo[3]**, -ta** *n* : just person ⟨los justos : the just⟩
juvenil *adj* **1** : juvenile, young, youthful **2** ADOLESCENTE : teenage
juventud *nf* **1** : youth **2** : young people
juzgado *nm* TRIBUNAL : court, tribunal
juzgar {52} *vt* **1** : to try, to judge (a case in court) **2** : to pass judgment on **3** CONSIDERAR : to consider, to deem
juzgue, etc. → **juzgar**

K

k *nf* : eleventh letter of the Spanish alphabet
káiser *nm* : kaiser
kaki → **caqui**
kaleidoscopio → **caleidoscopio**
kamikaze *adj & nm* : kamikaze
kampucheano, -na *adj & n* : Kampuchean
kan *nm* : khan
karaoke *nm* : karaoke
karate *or* **kárate** *nm* : karate
kayac *or* **kayak** *nm, pl* **kayacs** *or* **kayaks** : kayak

keniano, -na *adj & n* : Kenyan
kepí *nm* : kepi
kermesse *or* **kermés** [kɛr'mɛs] *nf, pl* **kermesses** *or* **kermeses** [-'mɛsɛs] : charity fair, bazaar
kerosene *or* **kerosén** *or* **keroseno** *nm* : kerosene, paraffin
kibutz *or* **kibbutz** *nms & pl* : kibbutz
kilo *nm* **1** : kilo, kilogram **2** *fam* : large amount
kilobyte [ˌkilo'bait] *nm* : kilobyte
kilocíclo *nm* : kilocycle
kilogramo *nm* : kilogram

kilohertzio *nm* : kilohertz
kilometraje *nm* : distance in kilometers, mileage
kilométrico, -ca *adj fam* : endless, very long
kilómetro *nm* : kilometer
kilovatio *nm* : kilowatt
kimono *nm* : kimono
kinder [ˈkɪndɛr] → **kindergarten**
kindergarten [ˌkɪndɛrˈgartɛn] *nm, pl* **kindergartens** [-tɛns] : kindergarten, nursery school
kinesiología *nf* : physical therapy

kinesiólogo, -ga *n* : physical therapist
kiosco → **quiosco**
kit *nm, pl* **kits** : kit
kiwi [ˈkiwi] *nm* **1** : kiwi (bird) **2** : kiwifruit
klaxon → **claxon**
knockout [nɔˈkaut] → **nocaut**
koala *nm* : koala bear
kriptón *nm* : krypton
kurdo¹, -da *adj* : Kurdish
kurdo², -da *n* : Kurd
kuwaití [kuˌwaiˈti] *adj & nmf* : Kuwaiti

L

l *nf* : twelfth letter of the Spanish alphabet
la¹ *pron* **1** : her, it ⟨llámala hoy : call her today⟩ ⟨sacó la botella y la abrió : he took out the bottle and opened it⟩ **2** (*formal*) : you ⟨no la vi a usted, Señora Díaz : I didn't see you, Mrs. Díaz⟩ **3** : the one ⟨mi casa y la de la puerta roja : my house and the one with the red door⟩ **4 la que** : the one who
la² *art* → **el²**
laberíntico, -ca *adj* : labyrinthine
laberinto *nm* : labyrinth, maze
labia *nf fam* : gift of gab ⟨tu amigo tiene labia : your friend has a way with words⟩
labial *adj* : labial, lip ⟨lápiz labial : lipstick⟩
labio *nm* **1** : lip **2 labio leporino** : harelip
labor *nf* : work, labor
laborable *adj* **1** : arable **2 día laborable** : workday, business day
laboral *adj* : work, labor ⟨costos laborales : labor costs⟩
laborar *vi* : to work
laboratorio *nm* : laboratory, lab
laboriosidad *nf* : industriousness, diligence
laborioso, -sa *adj* **1** : laborious, hard **2** : industrious, hardworking
labrado¹, -da *adj* **1** : cultivated, tilled **2** : carved, wrought
labrado² *nm* : cultivated field
labrador, -dora *n* : farmer
labranza *nf* : farming
labrar *vt* **1** : to carve, to work (metal) **2** : to cultivate, to till **3** : to cause, to bring about
laca *nf* **1** : lacquer, shellac **2** : hair spray **3 laca de uñas** : nail polish
lacayo *nm* : lackey
lace, etc. → **lazar**
lacear *vt* : to lasso
laceración *nf, pl* **-ciones** : laceration
lacerante *adj* : hurtful, wounding
lacerar *vt* **1** : to lacerate, to cut **2** : to hurt, to wound (one's feelings)
lacio, -cia *adj* **1** : limp, lank **2 pelo lacio** : straight hair

lacónico, -ca *adj* : laconic — **lacónicamente** *adv*
lacra *nf* **1** : scar, mark (on the skin) **2** : stigma, blemish
lacrar *vt* : to seal (with wax)
lacrimógeno, -na *adj* **gas lacrimógeno** : tear gas
lacrimoso, -sa *adj* : tearful, moving
lactancia *nf* **1** : lactation **2** : breast-feeding
lactante *nmf* : nursing infant, suckling
lactar *v* : to breast-feed
lácteo, -tea *adj* **1** : dairy **2 Vía Láctea** : Milky Way
láctico, -ca *adj* : lactic
lactosa *nf* : lactose
ladeado, -da *adj* : crooked, tilted, lopsided
ladear *vt* : to tilt, to tip — **ladearse** *vr* : to bend (over)
ladera *nf* : slope, hillside
ladino¹, -na *adj* **1** : cunning, shrewd **2** *CA, Mex* : mestizo
ladino², -na *n* **1** : trickster **2** *CA, Mex* : Spanish-speaking Indian **3** *CA, Mex* : mestizo
lado *nm* **1** : side **2** PARTE : place ⟨miró por todos lados : he looked everywhere⟩ **3 al lado de** : next to, beside **4 de ~** : tilted, sideways ⟨está de lado : it's lying on its side⟩ **5 hacerse a un lado** : to step aside **6 lado a lado** : side by side **7 por otro lado** : on the other hand
ladrar *vi* : to bark
ladrido *nm* : bark (of a dog), barking
ladrillo *nm* **1** : brick **2** AZULEJO : tile
ladrón, -drona *n, mpl* **ladrones** : robber, thief, burglar
lagartija *nf* : small lizard
lagarto *nm* **1** : lizard **2 lagarto de Indias** : alligator
lago *nm* : lake
lágrima *nf* : tear, teardrop
lagrimear *vi* **1** : to water (of eyes) **2** : to weep easily
laguna *nf* **1** : lagoon **2** : lacuna, gap
laicado *nm* : laity
laico¹, -ca *adj* : lay, secular
laico², -ca *n* : layman *m*, laywoman *f*

laja *nf* : slab
lama[1] *nf* : slime, ooze
lama[2] *nm* : lama
lamber *vt* : to lick
lamé *nm* : lamé
lamentable *adj* **1** : unfortunate, lamentable **2** : pitiful, sad
lamentablemente *adv* : unfortunately, regrettably
lamentación *nf, pl* **-ciones** : lamentation, groaning, moaning
lamentar *vt* **1** : to lament **2** : to regret ⟨lo lamento : I'm sorry⟩ — **lamentarse** *vr* : to grumble, to complain
lamento *nm* : lament, groan, cry
lamer *vt* **1** : to lick **2** : to lap against
lamida *nf* : lick
lámina *nf* **1** PLANCHA : sheet, plate **2** : plate, illustration
laminado[1], **-da** *adj* : laminated
laminado[2] *nm* : laminate
laminar *vt* : to laminate — **laminación** *nf*
lámpara *nf* : lamp
lampiño, -ña *adj* : hairless
lamprea *nf* : lamprey
lana *nf* **1** : wool ⟨lana de acero : steel wool⟩ **2** *Mex fam* : money, dough
lance[1], etc. → **lanzar**
lance[2] *nm* **1** INCIDENTE : event, incident **2** RIÑA : quarrel **3** : throw, cast (of a net, etc.) **4** : move, play (in a game), throw (of dice)
lancear *vt* : to spear
lanceta *nf* : lancet
lancha *nf* **1** : small boat, launch **2** **lancha motora** : motorboat, speedboat
langosta *nf* **1** : lobster **2** : locust
langostino *nm* : prawn, crayfish
languidecer {53} *vi* : to languish
languidez *nf, pl* **-deces** : languor, listlessness
lánguido, -da *adj* : languid, listless — **lánguidamente** *adv*
lanolina *nf* : lanolin
lanudo, -da *adj* : woolly
lanza *nf* : spear, lance
lanzadera *nf* **1** : shuttle (for weaving) **2** **lanzadera espacial** : space shuttle
lanzado, -da *adj* **1** : impulsive, brazen **2** : forward, determined ⟨ir lanzado : to hurtle along⟩
lanzador, -dora *n* : thrower, pitcher
lanzallamas *nms & pl* : flamethrower
lanzamiento *nm* **1** : throw **2** : pitch (in baseball) **3** : launching, launch
lanzar {21} *vt* **1** : to throw, to hurl **2** : to pitch **3** : to launch — **lanzarse** *vr* **1** : to throw oneself (at, into) **2** ~ **a** : to embark upon, to undertake
laosiano, -na *adj & n* : Laotian
lapicero *nm* **1** : mechanical pencil **2** *CA, Peru* : ballpoint pen
lápida *nf* : marker, tombstone
lapidar *vt* APEDREAR : to stone
lapidario, -ria *adj & n* : lapidary
lápiz *nm, pl* **lápices 1** : pencil **2 lápiz de labios** *or* **lápiz labial** : lipstick

lapón, -pona *adj & n, mpl* **lapones** : Lapp
lapso *nm* : lapse, space (of time)
lapsus *nms & pl* : error, slip
laptop *nm, pl* **laptops** : laptop
laquear *vt* : to lacquer, to varnish, to shellac
largamente *adv* **1** : at length, extensively **2** : easily, comfortably **3** : generously
largar {52} *vt* **1** SOLTAR : to let loose, to release **2** AFLOJAR : to loosen, to slacken **3** *fam* : to give, to hand over **4** *fam* : to hurl, to let fly (insults, etc.) — **largarse** *vr fam* : to scram, to beat it
largo[1], **-ga** *adj* **1** : long **2 a lo largo** : lengthwise **3 a lo largo de** : along **4 a la larga** : in the long run
largo[2] *nm* : length ⟨tres metros de largo : three meters long⟩
largometraje *nm* : feature film
largue, etc. → **largar**
larguero *nm* : crossbeam
largueza *nf* : generosity, largesse
larguirucho, -cha *adj fam* : lanky
largura *nf* : length
laringe *nf* : larynx
laringitis *nfs & pl* : laryngitis
larva *nf* : larva — **larval** *adj*
las → **el**[2], **los**[1]
lasaña *nf* : lasagna
lasca *nf* : chip, chipping
lascivia *nf* : lasciviousness, lewdness
lascivo, -va *adj* : lascivious, lewd — **lascivamente** *adv*
láser *nm* : laser
lasitud *nf* : lassitude, weariness
laso, -sa *adj* : languid, weary
lástima *nf* **1** : compassion, pity **2** PENA : shame, pity ⟨¡qué lástima! : what a shame!⟩
lastimadura *nf* : injury, wound
lastimar *vt* **1** DAÑAR, HERIR : to hurt, to injure **2** AGRAVIAR : to offend — **lastimarse** *vr* : to hurt oneself
lastimero, -ra *adj* : pitiful, wretched
lastimoso, -sa *adj* **1** : shameful **2** : pitiful, terrible
lastrar *vt* **1** : to ballast **2** : to burden, to encumber
lastre *nm* **1** : burden **2** : ballast
lata *nf* **1** : tinplate **2** : tin can **3** *fam* : pest, bother, nuisance **4 dar lata** *fam* : to bother, to annoy
latencia *nf* : latency
latente *adj* : latent
lateral[1] *adj* **1** : lateral, side **2** : indirect — **lateralmente** *adv*
lateral[2] *nm* : end piece, side
látex *nms & pl* : latex
latido *nm* : beat, throb ⟨latido del corazón : heartbeat⟩
latifundio *nm* : large estate
latigazo *nm* : lash (with a whip)
látigo *nm* AZOTE : whip
latín *nm* : Latin (language)
latino[1], **-na** *adj* **1** : Latin **2** *fam* : Latin-American

latino², -na *n fam* : Latin American
latinoamericano¹, -na *adj* HISPANO-AMERICANO : Latin American
latinoamericano, -na *n* : Latin American
latir *vi* **1** : to beat, to throb **2 latirle a uno** *Mex fam* : to have a hunch ⟨me late que no va a venir : I have a feeling he's not going to come⟩
latitud *nf* **1** : latitude **2** : breadth
lato, -ta *adj* **1** : extended, lengthy **2** : broad (in meaning)
latón *nm, pl* **latones** : brass
latoso¹, -sa *adj fam* : annoying, bothersome
latoso², -sa *n fam* : pest, nuisance
latrocinio *nm* : larceny
laúd *nm* : lute
laudable *adj* : laudable, praiseworthy
laudo *nm* : findings, decision
laureado, -da *adj & n* : laureate
laurear *vt* : to award, to honor
laurel *nm* **1** : laurel **2** : bay leaf **3 dormirse en sus laureles** : to rest on one's laurels
lava *nf* : lava
lavable *adj* : washable
lavabo *nm* **1** LAVAMANOS : sink, washbowl **2** : lavatory, toilet
lavadero *nm* : laundry room
lavado *nm* **1** : laundry, wash **2** : laundering ⟨lavado de dinero : money laundering⟩
lavadora *nf* : washing machine
lavamanos *nms & pl* LAVABO : sink, washbowl
lavanda *nf* ESPLIEGO : lavender
lavandería *nf* : laundry (service)
lavandero, -ra *n* : launderer, laundress *f*
lavaplatos *nms & pl* **1** : dishwasher **2** *Chile, Col, Mex* : kitchen sink
lavar *vt* **1** : to wash, to clean **2** : to launder (money) **3 lavar en seco** : to dry-clean — **lavarse** *vr* **1** : to wash oneself **2 lavarse las manos de** : to wash one's hands of
lavativa *nf* : enema
lavatorio *nm* : lavatory, washroom
lavavajillas *nms & pl* : dishwasher
laxante *adj & nm* : laxative
laxitud *nf* : laxity, slackness
laxo, -xa *adj* : lax, slack
lazada *nf* : bow, loop
lazar {21} *vt* : to rope, to lasso
lazo *nm* **1** VÍNCULO : link, bond **2** : bow, ribbon **3** : lasso, lariat
le *pron* **1** : to her, to him, to it ⟨¿qué le dijiste? : what did you tell him?⟩ **2** : from her, from him, from it ⟨el ladrón le robó la cartera : the thief stole his wallet⟩ **3** : for her, for him, for it ⟨cómprale flores a tu mamá : buy your mom some flowers⟩ **4** (*formal*) : to you, for you ⟨le traje un regalo : I brought you a gift⟩
leal *adj* : loyal, faithful — **lealmente** *adv*
lealtad *nf* : loyalty, allegiance

lebrel *nm* : hound
lección *nf, pl* **lecciones** : lesson
lechada *nf* **1** : whitewash **2** : grout
lechal *adj* : suckling, unweaned ⟨cordero lechal : suckling lamb⟩
leche *nf* **1** : milk ⟨leche en polvo : powdered milk⟩ ⟨leche de magnesia : milk of magnesia⟩ **2** : milky sap
lechera *nf* **1** : milk jug **2** : dairymaid *f*
lechería *nf* : dairy store
lechero¹, -ra *adj* : dairy
lechero², -ra *n* : milkman *m*, milk dealer
lecho *nm* **1** : bed ⟨un lecho de rosas : a bed of roses⟩ ⟨lecho de muerte : deathbed⟩ **2** : riverbed **3** : layer, stratum (in geology)
lechón, -chona *n, mpl* **lechones** : suckling pig
lechoso, -sa *adj* : milky
lechuga *nf* : lettuce
lechuza *nf* BÚHO : owl, barn owl
lectivo, -va *adj* : school ⟨año lectivo : school year⟩
lector¹, -tora *adj* : reading ⟨nivel lector : reading level⟩
lector², -tora *n* : reader
lector³ *nm* : scanner, reader ⟨lector óptico : optical scanner⟩
lectura *nf* **1** : reading **2** : reading matter
leer {20} *v* : to read
legación *nf, pl* **-ciones** : legation
legado *nm* **1** : legacy, bequest **2** : legate, emissary
legajo *nm* : dossier, file
legal *adj* : legal, lawful — **legalmente** *adv*
legalidad *nf* : legality, lawfulness
legalista *adj* : legalistic
legalizar {21} *vt* : to legalize — **legalización** *nf*
legar {52} *vt* **1** : to bequeath, to hand down **2** DELEGAR : to delegate
legendario, -ria *adj* : legendary
legible *adj* : legible
legión *nf, pl* **legiones** : legion
legionario, -ria *n* : legionnaire
legislación *nf* **1** : legislation, lawmaking **2** : laws *pl*, legislation
legislador¹, -dora *adj* : legislative
legislador², -dora *n* : legislator
legislar *vi* : to legislate
legislativo, -va *adj* : legislative
legislatura *nf* **1** : legislature **2** : term of office
legitimar *vt* **1** : to legitimize **2** : to authenticate — **legitimación** *nf*
legitimidad *nf* : legitimacy
legítimo, -ma *adj* **1** : legitimate **2** : genuine, authentic — **legítimamente** *adv*
lego¹, -ga *adj* **1** : secular, lay **2** : uninformed, ignorant
lego², -ga *n* : layperson, layman *m*, laywoman *f*
legua *nf* **1** : league **2 notarse a leguas** : to be very obvious ⟨se notaba a leguas : you could tell from a mile away⟩

legue, etc. → **legar**
legumbre *nf* **1** HORTALIZA : vegetable
2 : legume
leíble *adj* : readable
leída *nf* : reading, read ⟨de una leída : in
one reading, at one go⟩
leído[1] *pp* → **leer**
leído[2], **-da** *adj* : well-read
lejanía *nf* : remoteness, distance
lejano, -na *adj* : remote, distant, far
away
lejía *nf* **1** : lye **2** : bleach
lejos *adv* **1** : far away, distant ⟨a lo lejos
: in the distance, far off⟩ ⟨desde lejos
: from a distance⟩ **2** : long ago, a long
way off ⟨está lejos de los 50 años : he's
a long way from 50 years old⟩ **3 de ∼**
: by far ⟨esta decisión fue de lejos la
más fácil : this decision was by far the
easiest⟩ **4 ∼ de** : far from ⟨lejos de ser
reprobado, recibió una nota de B : far
from failing, he got a B⟩
lelo, -la *adj* : silly, stupid
lema *nm* : motto, slogan
lencería *nf* : lingerie
lengua *nf* **1** : tongue ⟨morderse la
lengua : to bite one's tongue⟩ **2** IDIOMA
: language ⟨lengua materna : mother
tongue, native language⟩ ⟨lengua
muerta : dead language⟩
lenguado *nm* : sole, flounder
lenguaje *nm* **1** : language, speech **2**
lenguaje gestual *or* **lenguaje de
gestos** : sign language **3 lenguaje de
programación** : programming language
lengüeta *nf* **1** : tongue (of a shoe), tab,
flap **2** : reed (of a musical instrument)
3 : barb, point
lengüetada *nf* **beber a lengüetadas** : to
lap (up)
lenidad *nf* : leniency
lenitivo, -va *adj* : soothing
lente *nmf* **1** : lens ⟨lentes de contacto
: contact lenses⟩ **2 lentes** *nmpl* AN-
TEOJOS : eyeglasses ⟨lentes de sol : sun-
glasses⟩
lenteja *nf* : lentil
lentejuela *nf* : sequin, spangle
lentitud *nf* : slowness
lento[1] *adv* DESPACIO : slowly
lento[2], **-ta** *adj* **1** : slow **2** : slow-witted,
dull — **lentamente** *adv*
leña *nf* : wood, firewood
leñador, -dora *n* : lumberjack, woodcutter
leñera *nf* : woodshed
leño *nm* : log
leñoso, -sa *adj* : woody
Leo *nmf* : Leo
león, -ona *n, mpl* **leones 1** : lion, lioness
f **2** (*in various countries*) : puma, cougar
leonado, -da *adj* : tawny
leonino, -na *adj* **1** : leonine **2** : one-
sided, unfair
leopardo *nm* : leopard
leotardo *nm* MALLA : leotard, tights *pl*
leperada *nf Mex* : obscenity

lépero, -ra *adj Mex* : vulgar, coarse
lepra *nf* : leprosy
leproso[1], **-sa** *adj* : leprous
leproso[2], **-sa** *n* : leper
lerdo, -da *adj* **1** : clumsy **2** : dull, oafish,
slow-witted
les *pron* **1** : to them ⟨dales una propina
: give them a tip⟩ **2** : from them ⟨se
les privó de su herencia : they were de-
prived of their inheritance⟩ **3** : for
them ⟨les hice sus tareas : I did their
homework for them⟩ **4** : to you *pl*, for
you *pl* ⟨les compré un regalo : I bought
you all a present⟩
lesbiana *nf* : lesbian — **lesbiano, -na** *adj*
lesbianismo *nm* : lesbianism
lesión *nf, pl* **lesiones** HERIDA : lesion,
wound, injury ⟨una lesión grave : a serious injury⟩
lesionado, -da *adj* HERIDO : injured,
wounded
lesionar *vt* : to injure, to wound — **le-
sionarse** *vr* : to hurt oneself
lesivo, -va *adj* : harmful, damaging
letal *adj* MORTÍFERO : deadly, lethal —
letalmente *adv*
letanía *nf* **1** : litany **2** *fam* : spiel, song
and dance
letárgico, -ca *adj* : lethargic
letargo *nm* : lethargy, torpor
letón[1], **-tona** *adj & n, mpl* **letones** : Latvian
letón[2] *nm* : Latvian (language)
letra *nf* **1** : letter **2** CALIGRAFÍA : handwriting, lettering **3** : lyrics *pl* **4 al pie
de la letra** : word for word, by the book
5 letras *nfpl* : arts (in education)
letrado[1], **-da** *adj* ERUDITO : learned, erudite
letrado[2], **-da** *n* : attorney-at-law, lawyer
letrero *nm* RÓTULO : sign, notice
letrina *nf* : latrine
letrista *nmf* : lyricist, songwriter
leucemia *nf* : leukemia
leva *nf* : cam
levadizo, -za *adj* **1** : liftable **2 puente
levadizo** : drawbridge
levadura *nf* **1** : yeast, leavening **2
levadura en polvo** : baking powder
levantamiento *nm* **1** ALZAMIENTO : uprising **2** : raising, lifting ⟨levantamien-
to de pesas : weight lifting⟩
levantar *vt* **1** ALZAR : to lift, to raise **2**
: to put up, to erect **3** : to call off, to
adjourn **4** : to give rise to, to arouse
⟨levantar sospechas : to arouse suspi-
cion⟩ — **levantarse** *vr* **1** : to rise, to
stand up **2** : to get out of bed
levar *vt* **levar anclas** : to weigh anchor
leve *adj* **1** : light, slight **2** : trivial, unimportant — **levemente** *adv*
levedad *nf* : lightness
levemente *adv* LIGERAMENTE : lightly,
softly
leviatán *nm, pl* **-tanes** : leviathan
léxico[1], **-ca** *adj* : lexical
léxico[2] *nm* : lexicon, glossary
lexicografía *nf* : lexicography

lexicográfico, -ca *adj* : lexicographical, lexicographic
lexicógrafo, -fa *n* : lexicographer
ley *nf* **1** : law ⟨fuera de la ley : outside the law⟩ ⟨la ley de gravedad : the law of gravity⟩ **2** : purity (of metals) ⟨oro de ley : pure gold⟩
leyenda *nf* **1** : legend **2** : caption, inscription
leyó, etc. → **leer**
liar {85} *vt* **1** ATAR : to bind, to tie (up) **2** : to roll (a cigarette) **3** : to confuse — **liarse** *vr* : to get mixed up
libanés, -nesa *adj & n, mpl* **-neses** : Lebanese
libar *vt* **1** : to suck (nectar) **2** : to sip, to swig (liquor, etc.)
libelo *nm* **1** : libel, lampoon **2** : petition (in court)
libélula *nf* : dragonfly
liberación *nf, pl* **-ciones** : liberation, deliverance ⟨liberación de la mujer : women's liberation⟩
liberado, -da *adj* **1** : liberated ⟨una mujer liberada : a liberated woman⟩ **2** : freed, delivered
liberal *adj & nmf* : liberal
liberalidad *nf* : generosity, liberality
liberalismo *nm* : liberalism
liberalizar {21} *vt* : to liberalize — **liberalización** *nf*
liberar *vt* : to liberate, to free — **liberarse** *vr* : to get free of
liberiano, -na *adj & n* : Liberian
libertad *nf* **1** : freedom, liberty ⟨tomarse la libertad de : to take the liberty of⟩ **2 libertad bajo fianza** : bail **3 libertad condicional** : parole
libertador[1], -dora *adj* : liberating
libertador[2], -dora *n* : liberator
libertar *vt* LIBRAR : to set free
libertario, -ria *adj & n* : libertarian
libertinaje *nm* : licentiousness, dissipation
libertino[1], -na *adj* : licentious, dissolute
libertino[2], -na *n* : libertine
libidinoso, -sa *adj* : lustful, lewd
libido *nf* : libido
libio, -bia *adj & n* : Libyan
libra *nf* **1** : pound **2 libra esterlina** : pound sterling
Libra *nmf* : Libra
libramiento *nm* **1** : liberating, freeing **2** LIBRANZA : order of payment **3** *Mex* : beltway
libranza *nf* : order of payment
librar *vt* **1** LIBERTAR : to deliver, to set free **2** : to wage ⟨librar batalla : to do battle⟩ **3** : to issue ⟨librar una orden : to issue an order⟩ — **librarse** *vr* ∼ **de** : to free oneself from, to get out of
libre[1] *adj* **1** : free ⟨un país libre : a free country⟩ ⟨libre de : free from, exempt from⟩ ⟨libre albedrío : free will⟩ **2** DESOCUPADO : vacant **3 día libre** : day off
libre[2] *nm Mex* : taxi
librea *nf* : livery

librecambio *nm* : free trade
libremente *adv* : freely
librería *nf* : bookstore
librero[1], -ra *n* : bookseller
librero[2] *nm Mex* : bookcase
libresco, -ca *adj* : bookish
libreta *nf* CUADERNO : notebook
libretista *nmf* **1** : librettist **2** : scriptwriter
libreto *nm* : libretto, script
libro *nm* **1** : book ⟨libro de texto : textbook⟩ **2 libros** *nmpl* : books (in bookkeeping), accounts ⟨llevar los libros : to keep the books⟩
licencia *nf* **1** : permission **2** : leave, leave of absence **3** : permit, license ⟨licencia de conducir : driver's license⟩
licenciado, -da *n* **1** : university graduate **2** ABOGADO : lawyer
licenciar *vt* **1** : to license, to permit, to allow **2** : to discharge **3** : to grant a university degree to — **licenciarse** *vr* : to graduate
licenciatura *nf* **1** : college degree **2** : course of study (at a college or university)
licencioso, -sa *adj* : licentious, lewd
liceo *nm* : secondary school, high school
licitación *nf, pl* **-ciones** : bid, bidding
licitar *vt* : to bid on
lícito, -ta *adj* **1** : lawful, licit **2** JUSTO : just, fair
licor *nm* **1** : liquor **2** : liqueur
licorera *nf* : decanter
licuado *nm* BATIDO : milk shake
licuadora *nf* : blender
licuar {3} *vt* : to liquefy — **licuarse** *vr*
lid *nf* **1** : fight, combat **2** : argument, dispute **3 lides** *nfpl* : matters, affairs **4 en buena lid** : fair and square
líder[1] *adj* : leading, foremost
líder[2] *nmf* : leader
liderar *vt* DIRIGIR : to lead, to head
liderato *nm* : leadership, leading
liderazgo → **liderato**
lidiar *vt* : to fight — *vi* BATALLAR, LUCHAR : to struggle, to battle, to wrestle
liebre *nf* : hare
liendre *nf* : nit
lienzo *nm* **1** : linen **2** : canvas, painting **3** : stretch of wall or fencing
liga *nf* **1** ASOCIACIÓN : league **2** GOMITA : rubber band **3** : garter
ligado, -da *adj* : linked, connected
ligadura *nf* **1** ATADURA : tie, bond **2** : ligature
ligamento *nm* : ligament
ligar {52} *vt* : to bind, to tie (up)
ligeramente *adv* **1** : slightly **2** LEVEMENTE : lightly, gently **3** : casually, flippantly
ligereza *nf* **1** : lightness **2** : flippancy **3** : agility
ligero, -ra *adj* **1** : light, lightweight **2** : slight, minor **3** : agile, quick **4** : lighthearted, superficial
lignito *nm* : lignite

ligue, etc. → **ligar**
lija *nf or* **papel de lija** : sandpaper
lijar *vt* : to sand
lila[1] *adj* : lilac, light purple
lila[2] *nf* : lilac
lima *nf* **1** : lime (fruit) **2** : file ⟨lima de uñas : nail file⟩
limadora *nf* : polisher
limar *vt* **1** : to file **2** : to polish, to put the final touch on **3** : to smooth over ⟨limar las diferencias : to iron out differences⟩
limbo *nm* **1** : limbo **2** : limb (in botany and astronomy)
limeño[1], **-ña** *adj* : of or from Lima, Peru
limeño[2], **-ña** *n* : person from Lima, Peru
limero *nm* : lime tree
limitación *nf, pl* **-ciones 1** : limitation **2** : limit, restriction ⟨sin limitación : unlimited⟩
limitado, -da *adj* **1** RESTRINGIDO : limited **2** : dull, slow-witted
limitar *vt* RESTRINGIR : to limit, to restrict — *vi* ~ **con** : to border on — **limitarse** *vr* ~ **a** : to limit oneself to
límite *nm* **1** : boundary, border **2** : limit ⟨el límite de mi paciencia : the limit of my patience⟩ ⟨límite de velocidad : speed limit⟩ **3 fecha límite** : deadline
limítrofe *adj* LINDANTE, LINDERO : bordering, adjoining
limo *nm* : slime, mud
limón *nm, pl* **limones 1** : lemon **2** : lemon tree **2 limón verde** *Mex* : lime
limonada *nf* : lemonade
limosna *nf* : alms, charity
limosnear *vi* : to beg (for alms)
limosnero, -ra *n* MENDIGO : beggar
limoso, -sa *adj* : slimy
limpiabotas *nmfs & pl* : bootblack
limpiador[1], **-dora** *adj* : cleaning
limpiador[2], **-dora** *n* : cleaning person, cleaner
limpiamente *adv* : cleanly, honestly, fairly
limpiaparabrisas *nms & pl* : windshield wiper
limpiar *vt* **1** : to clean, to cleanse **2** : to clean up, to remove defects **3** *fam* : to clean out (in a game) **4** *fam* : to swipe, to pinch — *vi* : to clean — **limpiarse** *vr*
limpiavidrios *nmfs & pl Mex* : windshield wiper
límpido, -da *adj* : limpid
limpieza *nf* **1** : cleanliness, tidiness **2** : cleaning **3** HONRADEZ : integrity, honesty **4** DESTREZA : skill, dexterity
limpio[1] *adv* : fairly
limpio[2], **-pia** *adj* **1** : clean, neat **2** : honest ⟨un juego limpio : a fair game⟩ **3** : free ⟨limpio de impurezas : pure, free from impurities⟩ **4** : clear, net ⟨ganancia limpia : clear profit⟩
limusina *nf* : limousine
linaje *nm* ABOLENGO : lineage, ancestry
linaza *nf* : linseed
lince *nm* : lynx

linchamiento *nm* : lynching
linchar *vt* : to lynch
lindante *adj* LIMÍTROFE, LINDERO : bordering, adjoining
lindar *vi* **1** ~ **con** : to border, to skirt **2** ~ **con** BORDEAR : to border on, to verge on
linde *nmf* : boundary, limit
lindero[1], **-ra** *adj* LIMÍTROFE, LINDANTE : bordering, adjoining
lindero[2] *nm* : boundary, limit
lindeza *nf* **1** : prettiness **2** : clever remark **3 lindezas** *nfpl,* (*used ironically*) : insults
lindo[1] *adv* **1** : beautifully, wonderfully ⟨canta lindo tu mujer : your wife sings beautifully⟩ **2 de lo lindo** : a lot, a great deal ⟨los zancudos nos picaban de lo lindo : the mosquitoes were biting away at us⟩
lindo[2], **-da** *adj* **1** BONITO : pretty, lovely **2** MONO : cute
línea *nf* **1** : line ⟨línea divisoria : dividing line⟩ ⟨línea de banda : sideline⟩ **2** : line, course, position ⟨línea de conducta : course of action⟩ ⟨en líneas generales : in general terms, along general lines⟩ **3** : line, service ⟨línea aérea : airline⟩ ⟨línea telefónica : telephone line⟩
lineal *adj* : linear
linfa *nf* : lymph
linfático, -ca *adj* : lymphatic
lingote *nm* : ingot
lingüista *nmf* : linguist
lingüística *nf* : linguistics
lingüístico, -ca *adj* : linguistic
linimento *nm* : liniment
lino *nm* **1** : linen **2** : flax
linóleo *nm* : linoleum
linterna *nf* **1** : lantern **2** : flashlight
lío *nm fam* **1** : confusion, mess **2** : hassle, trouble, jam ⟨meterse en un lío : to get into a jam⟩ **3** : affair, liaison
liofilizar {21} *vt* : to freeze-dry
lioso, -sa *adj fam* **1** : confusing, muddled **2** : troublemaking
liquen *nm* : lichen
liquidación *nf, pl* **-ciones 1** : liquidation **2** : clearance sale **3** : settlement, payment
liquidar *vt* **1** : to liquefy **2** : to liquidate **3** : to settle, to pay off **4** *fam* : to rub out, to kill
liquidez *nf, pl* **-deces** : liquidity
líquido[1], **-da** *adj* **1** : liquid, fluid **2** : net ⟨ingresos líquidos : net income⟩
líquido[2] *nm* **1** : liquid, fluid ⟨líquido de frenos : brake fluid⟩ **2** : ready cash, liquid assets
lira *nf* : lyre
lírica *nf* : lyric poetry
lírico, -ca *adj* : lyric, lyrical
lirio *nm* **1** : iris **2 lirio de los valles** MUGUETE : lily of the valley
lirismo *nm* : lyricism
lirón *nm, pl* **lirones** : dormouse
lisiado[1], **-da** *adj* : disabled, crippled

lisiado[2], **-da** *n* : disabled person, cripple
lisiar *vt* : to cripple, to disable — **lisiarse** *vr*
liso, -sa *adj* **1** : smooth **2** : flat **3** : straight ⟨pelo liso : straight hair⟩ **4** : plain, unadorned ⟨liso y llano : plain and simple⟩
lisonja *nf* : flattery
lisonjear *vt* ADULAR : to flatter
lista *nf* **1** : list **2** : roster, roll ⟨pasar lista : to take attendance⟩ **3** : stripe, strip **4** : menu
listado[1], **-da** *adj* : striped
listado[2] *nm* : listing
listar *vt* : to list
listeza *nf* : smartness, alertness
listo, -ta *adj* **1** DISPUESTO, PREPARADO : ready ⟨¿estás listo? : are you ready?⟩ **2** : clever, smart
listón *nm, pl* **listones 1** : ribbon **2** : strip (of wood), lath **3** : high bar (in sports)
lisura *nf* : smoothness
litera *nf* : bunk bed, berth
literal *adj* : literal — **literalmente** *adv*
literario, -ria *adj* : literary
literato, -ta *n* : writer, author
literatura *nf* : literature
litigante *adj & nmf* : litigant
litigar {52} *vi* : to litigate, to be in litigation
litigio *nm* **1** : litigation, lawsuit **2 en ~** : in dispute
litigioso, -sa *adj* : litigious
litio *nm* : lithium
litografía *nf* **1** : lithography **2** : lithograph
litógrafo, -fa *n* : lithographer
litoral[1] *adj* : coastal
litoral[2] *nm* : shore, seaboard
litosfera *nf* : lithosphere
litro *nm* : liter
lituano[1], **-na** *adj & n* : Lithuanian
lituano[2] *nm* : Lithuanian (language)
liturgia *nf* : liturgy
litúrgico, -ca *adj* : liturgical — **litúrgicamente** *adv*
liviandad *nf* LIGEREZA : lightness
liviano, -na *adj* **1** : light, slight **2** INCONSTANTE : fickle
lividez *nf* PALIDEZ : pallor
lívido, -da *adj* **1** AMORATADO : livid **2** PÁLIDO : pallid, extremely pale
living *nm* : living room
llaga *nf* : sore, wound
llama *nf* **1** : flame **2** : llama
llamada *nf* : call ⟨llamada a larga distancia : long-distance call⟩ ⟨llamada al orden : call to order⟩
llamado[1], **-da** *adj* : named, called ⟨una mujer llamada Rosa : a woman called Rosa⟩
llamado[2] → **llamamiento**
llamador *nm* : door knocker
llamamiento *nm* : call, appeal
llamar *vt* **1** : to name, to call **2** : to call, to summon **3** : to phone, to call up — **llamarse** *vr* : to be called, to be named ⟨¿cómo te llamas? : what's your name?⟩

llamarada *nf* **1** : flare-up, sudden blaze **2** : flushing (of the face)
llamativo, -va *adj* : flashy, showy, striking
llameante *adj* : flaming, blazing
llamear *vi* : to flame, to blaze
llana *nf* **1** : trowel **2** → **llano**[2]
llanamente *adv* : simply, plainly, straightforwardly
llaneza *nf* : simplicity, naturalness
llano[1], **-na** *adj* **1** : even, flat **2** : frank, open **3** LISO : plain, simple
llano[2] *nm* : plain
llanta *nf* **1** NEUMÁTICO : tire **2** : rim
llantén *nm, pl* **llantenes** : plantain (weed)
llanto *nm* : crying, weeping
llanura *nf* : plain, prairie
llave *nf* **1** : key **2** : faucet **3** INTERRUPTOR : switch **4** : brace (punctuation mark) **5 llave inglesa** : monkey wrench
llavero *nm* : key chain, key ring
llegada *nf* : arrival
llegar {52} *vi* **1** : to arrive, to come **2 ~ a** : to arrive at, to reach, to amount to **3 ~ a** : to manage to ⟨llegó a terminar la novela : she managed to finish the novel⟩ **4 llegar a ser** : to become ⟨llegó a ser un miembro permanente : he became a permanent member⟩
llegue, etc. → **llegar**
llenar *vt* **1** : to fill, to fill up, to fill in **2** : to meet, to fulfill ⟨los regalos no llenaron sus expectativas : the gifts did not meet her expectations⟩ — **llenarse** *vr* : to fill up, to become full
llenito, -ta *adj fam* REGORDETE : chubby, plump
lleno[1], **-na** *adj* **1** : full, filled **2 de ~** : completely, fully **3 estar lleno de sí mismo** : to be full of oneself
lleno[2] *nm* **1** *fam* : plenty, abundance **2** : full house, sellout
llevadero, -ra *adj* : bearable
llevar *vt* **1** : to take away, to carry ⟨me gusta, me lo llevo : I like it, I'll take it⟩ **2** : to wear **3** : to take, to lead ⟨llevamos a Pedro al cine : we took Pedro to the movies⟩ **4 llevar a cabo** : to carry out **5 llevar adelante** : to carry on, to keep going — *vi* : to lead ⟨un problema lleva al otro : one problem leads to another⟩ — *v aux* : to have ⟨llevo mucho tiempo buscándolo : I've been looking for it for a long time⟩ ⟨lleva leído medio libro : he's halfway through the book⟩ — **llevarse** *vr* **1** : to take away, to carry off **2** : to get along ⟨siempre nos llevábamos bien : we always got along well⟩
llorar *vi* : to cry, to weep — *vt* : to mourn, to bewail
lloriquear *vi* : to whimper, to whine
lloriqueo *nm* : whimpering, whining
llorón, -rona *n, mpl* **llorones** : crybaby, whiner
lloroso, -sa *adj* : tearful, sad

llovedizo, -za *adj* : rain ⟨agua llovediza : rainwater⟩
llover {47} *v impers* : to rain ⟨está lloviendo : it's raining⟩ ⟨llover a cántaros : to rain cats and dogs⟩ — *vi* : to rain down, to shower ⟨le llovieron regalos : he was showered with gifts⟩
llovizna *nf* : drizzle, sprinkle
lloviznar *v impers* : to drizzle, to sprinkle
llueve, etc. → **llover**
lluvia *nf* **1** : rain, rainfall **2** : barrage, shower
lluvioso, -sa *adj* : rainy
lo[1] *pron* **1** : him, it ⟨lo vi ayer : I saw him yesterday⟩ ⟨lo entiendo : I understand it⟩ ⟨no lo creo : I don't believe so⟩ **2** (*formal, masculine*) : you ⟨disculpe, señor, no lo oí : excuse me sir, I didn't hear you⟩ **3 lo que** : what, that which ⟨eso es lo que más le gusta : that's what he likes the most⟩
lo[2] *art* **1** : the ⟨lo mejor : the best, the best thing⟩ **2** : how ⟨sé lo bueno que eres : I know how good you are⟩
loa *nf* : praise
loable *adj* : laudable, praiseworthy — **loablemente** *adv*
loar *vt* : to praise, to laud
lobato, -ta *n* : wolf cub
lobby *nm* : lobby, pressure group
lobo, -ba *n* : wolf
lóbrego, -ga *adj* SOMBRÍO : gloomy, dark
lobulado, -da *adj* : lobed
lóbulo *nm* : lobe ⟨lóbulo de la oreja : earlobe⟩
locación *nf, pl* **-ciones 1** : location (in moviemaking) **2** *Mex* : place
local[1] *adj* : local — **localmente** *adv*
local[2] *nm* : premises *pl*
localidad *nf* : town, locality
localización *nf, pl* **-ciones 1** : locating, localization **2** : location
localizar {21} *vt* **1** UBICAR : to locate, to find **2** : to localize — **localizarse** *vr* UBICARSE : to be located ⟨se localiza en el séptimo piso : it is located on the seventh floor⟩
locatario, -ria *n* : tenant
loción *nf, pl* **lociones** : lotion
lócker *nm, pl* **lóckers** : locker
loco[1], **-ca** *adj* **1** DEMENTE : crazy, insane, mad **2 a lo loco** : wildly, recklessly **3 volverse loco** : to go mad
loco[2], **-ca** *n* **1** : crazy person, lunatic **2 hacerse el loco** : to act the fool
locomoción *nf, pl* **-ciones** : locomotion
locomotor, -tora *adj* : locomotive
locomotora *nf* **1** : locomotive **2** : driving force
locuacidad *nf* : loquacity, talkativeness
locuaz *adj, pl* **locuaces** : loquacious, talkative
locución *nf, pl* **-ciones** : locution, phrase ⟨locución adverbial : adverbial phrase⟩
locura *nf* **1** : insanity, madness **2** : crazy thing, folly

locutor, -tora *n* : announcer
lodazal *nm* : bog, quagmire
lodo *nm* BARRO : mud, mire
lodoso, -sa *adj* : muddy
logaritmo *nm* : logarithm
logia *nf* : lodge ⟨logia masónica : Masonic lodge⟩
lógica *nf* : logic
lógico, -ca *adj* : logical — **lógicamente** *adv*
logística *nf* : logistics *pl*
logístico, -ca *adj* : logistic, logistical
logo → **logotipo**
logotipo *nm* : logo
logrado, -da *adj* : successful, well done
lograr *vt* **1** : to get, to obtain **2** : to achieve, to attain — **lograrse** *vr* : to be successful
logro *nm* : achievement, attainment
loma *nf* : hill, hillock
lombriz *nf, pl* **lombrices** : worm ⟨lombriz de tierra : earthworm, night crawler⟩ ⟨lombriz solitaria : tapeworm⟩ ⟨tener lombrices : to have worms⟩
lomo *nm* **1** : back (of an animal) **2** : loin ⟨lomo de cerdo : pork loin⟩ **3** : spine (of a book) **4** : blunt edge (of a knife)
lona *nf* : canvas
loncha *nf* LONJA, REBANADA : slice
lonche *nm* **1** ALMUERZO : lunch **2** *Mex* : submarine sandwich
lonchería *nf Mex* : luncheonette
londinense[1] *adj* : of or from London
londinense[2] *nmf* : Londoner
longaniza *nf* : spicy pork sausage
longevidad *nf* : longevity
longevo, -va *adj* : long-lived
longitud *nf* **1** LARGO : length ⟨longitud de onda : wavelength⟩ **2** : longitude
longitudinal *adj* : longitudinal
lonja *nf* LONCHA, REBANADA : slice
lontananza *nf* : background ⟨en lontananza : in the distance, far away⟩
lord *nm, pl* **lores** (*title in England*) : lord
loro *nm* : parrot
los[1], **las** *pron* **1** : them ⟨hice galletas y se las di a los nuevos vecinos : I made cookies and gave them to the new neighbors⟩ **2** : you ⟨voy a llevarlos a los dos : I am going to take both of you⟩ **3 los que, las que** : those, who, the ones ⟨los que van a cantar deben venir temprano : those who are singing must come early⟩ **4** (*used with* **haber**) ⟨los hay en varios colores : they come in various colors⟩
los[2] *art* → **el**[2]
losa *nf* : flagstone, paving stone
loseta *nf* BALDOSA : floor tile
lote *nm* **1** : part, share **2** : batch, lot **3** : plot of land, lot
lotería *nf* : lottery
loto *nm* : lotus
loza *nf* **1** : crockery, earthenware **2** : china
lozanía *nf* **1** : healthiness, robustness **2** : luxuriance, lushness

lozano, -na *adj* **1** : robust, healthy-looking ⟨un rostro lozano : a smooth, fresh face⟩ **2** : lush, luxuriant
LSD *nm* : LSD
lubricante[1] *adj* : lubricating
lubricante[2] *nm* : lubricant
lubricar {72} *vt* : to lubricate, to oil — **lubricación** *nf*
lucero *nm* : bright star ⟨lucero del alba : morning star⟩
lucha *nf* **1** : struggle, fight **2** : wrestling
luchador, -dora *n* **1** : fighter **2** : wrestler
luchar *vi* **1** : to fight, to struggle **2** : to wrestle
luchón, -chona *adj, mpl* **luchones** *Mex* : industrious, hardworking
lucidez *nf, pl* **-deces** : lucidity, clarity
lucido, -da *adj* MAGNÍFICO : magnificent, splendid
lúcido, -da *adj* : lucid
luciérnaga *nf* : firefly, glowworm
lucimiento *nm* **1** : brilliance, splendor, sparkle **2** : triumph, success ⟨salir con lucimiento : to succeed with flying colors⟩
lucio *nm* : pike (fish)
lucir {45} *vi* **1** : to shine **2** : to look good, to stand out **3** : to seem, to appear ⟨ahora luce contento : he looks happy now⟩ — *vt* **1** : to wear, to sport **2** : to flaunt, to show off — **lucirse** *vr* **1** : to distinguish oneself, to excel **2** : to show off
lucrarse *vr* : to make a profit
lucrativo, -va *adj* : lucrative, profitable — **lucrativamente** *adv*
lucro *nm* GANANCIA : profit, gain
luctuoso, -sa *adj* : mournful, tragic
luego[1] *adv* **1** DESPUÉS : then, afterwards **2** : later (on) **3** desde ~ : of course **4** ¡hasta luego! : see you later! **5** **luego que** : as soon as **6** **luego luego** *Mex fam* : right away, immediately
luego[2] *conj* : therefore ⟨pienso, luego existo : I think, therefore I am⟩
lugar *nm* **1** : place, position ⟨se llevó el primer lugar en su división : she took first place in her division⟩ **2** ESPACIO : space, room **3** **dar lugar a** : to give rise to, to lead to **4** **en lugar de** : in-

stead of **5** **lugar común** : cliché, platitude **6** **tener lugar** : to take place
lugareño[1], **-ña** *adj* : village, rural
lugareño[2], **-ña** *n* : villager
lugarteniente *nmf* : lieutenant, deputy
lúgubre *adj* : gloomy, lugubrious
lujo *nm* **1** : luxury **2** **de ~** : deluxe
lujoso, -sa *adj* : luxurious
lujuria *nf* : lust, lechery
lujurioso, -sa *adj* : lustful, lecherous
lumbago *nm* : lumbago
lumbar *adj* : lumbar
lumbre *nf* **1** FUEGO : fire **2** : brilliance, splendor **3** **poner en la lumbre** : to put on the stove, to warm up
lumbrera *nf* **1** : skylight **2** : vent, port **3** : brilliant person, luminary
luminaria *nf* **1** : altar lamp **2** LUMBRERA : luminary, celebrity
luminiscencia *nf* : luminescence — **luminiscente** *adj*
luminosidad *nf* : luminosity, brightness
luminoso, -sa *adj* : shining, luminous
luna *nf* **1** : moon **2** **luna de miel** : honeymoon
lunar[1] *adj* : lunar
lunar[2] *nm* **1** : mole, beauty spot **2** : defect, blemish **3** : polka dot
lunático, -ca *adj & n* : lunatic
lunes *nms & pl* : Monday
luneta *nf* **1** : lens (of eyeglasses) **2** : windshield (of an automobile) **3** : crescent
lupa *nf* : magnifying glass
lúpulo *nm* : hops (plant)
lustrar *vt* : to shine, to polish
lustre *nm* **1** BRILLO : luster, shine **2** : glory, distinction
lustroso, -sa *adj* BRILLOSO : lustrous, shiny
luto *nm* : mourning ⟨estar de luto : to be in mourning⟩
luz *nf, pl* **luces** **1** : light **2** : lighting **3** *fam* : electricity **4** : window, opening **5** : light, lamp **6** : span, spread (between supports) **7** **a la luz de** : in light of **8** **dar a luz** : to give birth **9** **traje de luces** : matador's costume
luzca, etc. → **lucir**

M

m *nf* : thirteenth letter of the Spanish alphabet
macabro, -bra *adj* : macabre
macaco[1], **-ca** *adj* : ugly, misshapen
macaco[2], **-ca** *n* : macaque
macadán *nm, pl* **-danes** : macadam
macana *nf* **1** : club, cudgel **2** *fam* : nonsense, silliness **3** *fam* : lie, fib
macanudo, -da *adj fam* : great, fantastic
macarrón *nm, pl* **-rrones** **1** : macaroon **2** **macarrones** *nmpl* : macaroni
maceta *nf* **1** : flowerpot **2** : mallet **3** *Mex fam* : head

macetero *nm* **1** : plant stand **2** TIESTO : flowerpot, planter
machacar {72} *vt* **1** : to crush, to grind **2** : to beat, to pound — *vi* : to insist, to go on (about)
machacón, -cona *adj, mpl* **-cones** : insistent, tiresome
machete *nm* : machete
machetear *vt* : to hack with a machete — *vi Mex fam* : to plod, to work tirelessly
machismo *nm* **1** : machismo **2** : male chauvinism
machista *nm* : male chauvinist

macho¹ *adj* **1** : male **2** : macho, virile, tough
macho² *nm* **1** : male **2** : he-man
machote *nm* **1** *fam* : tough guy, he-man **2** *CA, Mex* : rough draft, model **3** *Mex* : blank form
machucar {72} *vt* **1** : to pound, to beat, to crush **2** : to bruise
machucón *nm, pl* **-cones 1** MORETÓN : bruise **2** : smashing, pounding
macilento, -ta *adj* : gaunt, wan
macis *nm* : mace (spice)
macizo, -za *adj* **1** : solid ⟨oro macizo : solid gold⟩ **2** : strong, strapping **3** : massive
macrocosmo *nm* : macrocosm
mácula *nf* : blemish, stain
madeja *nf* **1** : skein, hank **2** : tangle (of hair)
madera *nf* **1** : wood **2** : lumber, timber **3 madera dura** *or* **madera noble** : hardwood
maderero, -ra *adj* : timber, lumber
madero *nm* : piece of lumber, plank
madrastra *nf* : stepmother
madrazo *nm Mex fam* : punch, blow ⟨se agarraron a madrazos : they beat each other up⟩
madre *nf* **1** : mother **2 madre política** : mother-in-law **3 la Madre Patria** : the mother country (said of Spain)
madrear *vt Mex fam* : to beat up
madreperla *nf* NÁCAR : mother-of-pearl
madreselva *nf* : honeysuckle
madriguera *nf* : burrow, den, lair
madrileño¹, **-ña** *adj* : of or from Madrid
madrileño², **-ña** *n* : person from Madrid
madrina *nf* **1** : godmother **2** : bridesmaid **3** : sponsor
madrugada *nf* **1** : early morning, wee hours **2** ALBA : dawn, daybreak
madrugador, -dora *n* : early riser
madrugar {52} *vi* **1** : to get up early **2** : to get a head start
madurar *v* **1** : to ripen **2** : to mature
madurez *nf, pl* **-reces 1** : maturity **2** : ripeness
maduro, -ra *adj* **1** : mature **2** : ripe
maestría *nf* **1** : mastery, skill **2** : master's degree
maestro¹, **-tra** *adj* **1** : masterly, skilled **2** : chief, main **3** : trained ⟨un elefante maestro : a trained elephant⟩
maestro², **-tra** *n* **1** : teacher (in grammar school) **2** : expert, master **3** : maestro
Mafia *nf* : Mafia
mafioso, -sa *n* : mafioso, gangster
magdalena *nf* : bun, muffin
magenta *adj & n* : magenta
magia *nf* : magic
mágico, -ca *adj* : magic, magical — **mágicamente** *adv*
magisterio *nm* **1** : teaching **2** : teachers *pl*, teaching profession
magistrado, -da *n* : magistrate, judge
magistral *adj* **1** : masterful, skillful **2** : magisterial

magistralmente *adv* : masterfully, brilliantly
magistratura *nf* : judgeship, magistracy
magma *nm* : magma
magnanimidad *nf* : magnanimity
magnánimo, -ma *adj* GENEROSO : magnanimous — **magnánimamente** *adv*
magnate *nmf* : magnate, tycoon
magnesia *nf* : magnesia
magnesio *nm* : magnesium
magnético, -ca *adj* : magnetic
magnetismo *nm* : magnetism
magnetizar {21} *vt* : to magnetize
magnetófono *nm* : tape recorder
magnetofónico, -ca *adj* **cinta magnetofónica** : magnetic tape
magnificar {72} *vt* **1** : to magnify **2** EXAGERAR : to exaggerate **3** ENSALZAR : to exalt, to extol, to praise highly
magnificencia *nf* : magnificence, splendor
magnífico, -ca *adj* ESPLENDOROSO : magnificent, splendid — **magníficamente** *adv*
magnitud *nf* : magnitude
magnolia *nf* : magnolia (flower)
magnolio *nm* : magnolia (tree)
mago, -ga *n* **1** : magician **2** : wizard (in folk tales, etc.) **3 los Reyes Magos** : the Magi
magro, -gra *adj* **1** : lean (of meat) **2** : meager
maguey *nm* : maguey
magulladura *nf* MORETÓN : bruise
magullar *vt* : to bruise — **magullarse** *vr*
mahometano¹, **-na** *adj* ISLÁMICO : Islamic, Muslim
mahometano², **-na** *n* : Muslim
mahonesa → **mayonesa**
maicena *nf* : cornstarch
mainframe ['meın,freım] *nm* : mainframe
maíz *nm* : corn, maize
maizal *nm* : cornfield
maja *nf* : pestle
majadería *nf* **1** TONTERÍA : stupidity, foolishness **2** *Mex* LEPERADA : insult, obscenity
majadero¹, **-ra** *adj* **1** : foolish, silly **2** *Mex* LÉPERO : crude, vulgar
majadero², **-ra** *n* **1** TONTO : fool **2** *Mex* : rude person, boor
majar *vt* : to crush, to mash
majestad *nf* : majesty ⟨Su Majestad : Your Majesty⟩
majestuosamente *adv* : majestically
majestuosidad *nf* : majesty, grandeur
majestuoso, -sa *adj* : majestic, stately
majo, -ja *adj Spain* **1** : nice, likeable **2** GUAPO : attractive, good-looking
mal¹ *adv* **1** : badly, poorly ⟨baila muy mal : he dances very badly⟩ **2** : wrong, incorrectly ⟨me entendió mal : she misunderstood me⟩ **3** : with difficulty, hardly ⟨mal puedo oírte : I can hardly hear you⟩ **4 de mal en peor** : from bad to worse **5 menos mal** : it could have been worse

mal² *adj* → **malo**
mal³ *nm* **1** : evil, wrong **2** DAÑO : harm, damage **3** DESGRACIA : misfortune **4** ENFERMEDAD : illness, sickness
malabar *adj* **juegos malabares** : juggling
malabarista *nmf* : juggler
malaconsejado, -da *adj* : ill-advised
malacostumbrado, -da *adj* CONSENTIDO : spoiled, pampered
malacostumbrar *vt* : to spoil
malagradecido, -da *adj* INGRATO : ungrateful
malaisio → **malasio**
malaquita *nf* : malachite
malaria *nf* PALUDISMO : malaria
malasio, -sia *adj & n* : Malaysian
malauiano, -na *adj & n* : Malawian
malaventura *nf* : misadventure, misfortune
malaventurado, -da *adj* MALHADADO : ill-fated, unfortunate
malayo, -ya *adj & n* : Malay, Malayan
malbaratar *vt* **1** MALGASTAR : to squander **2** : to undersell
malcriado¹, -da *adj* **1** : ill-bred, ill-mannered **2** : spoiled, pampered
malcriado², -da *n* : spoiled brat
maldad *nf* **1** : evil, wickedness **2** : evil deed
maldecir {11} *vt* : to curse, to damn — *vi* **1** : to curse, to swear **2** ∼ **de** : to speak ill of, to slander, to defame
maldición *nf, pl* **-ciones** : curse
maldiga, maldijo etc. → **maldecir**
maldito, -ta *adj* **1** : cursed, damned ⟨¡maldita sea! : damn it all!⟩ **2** : wicked
maldoso, -sa *adj Mex* : mischievous
maleable *adj* : malleable
maleante *nmf* : crook, thug
malecón *nm, pl* **-cones** : jetty, breakwater
maleducado, -da *adj* : ill-mannered, rude
maleficio *nm* : curse, hex
maléfico, -ca *adj* : evil, harmful
malentender {56} *vt* : to misunderstand
malentendido *nm* : misunderstanding
malestar *nm* **1** : discomfort **2** IRRITACIÓN : annoyance **3** INQUIETUD : uneasiness, unrest
maleta *nf* : suitcase, bag ⟨haz tus maletas : pack your bags⟩
maletero¹, -ra *n* : porter
maletero² *nm* : trunk (of an automobile)
maletín *nm, pl* **-tines 1** PORTAFOLIO : briefcase **2** : overnight bag, satchel
malevolencia *nf* : malevolence, wickedness
malévolo, -la *adj* : malevolent, wicked
maleza *nf* **1** : thicket, underbrush **2** : weeds *pl*
malformación *nf, pl* **-ciones** : malformation
malgache *adj & nmf* : Madagascan
malgastar *vt* : to squander (resources), to waste (time, effort)
malhablado, -da *adj* : foul-mouthed

malhadado, -da *adj* MALAVENTURADO : ill-fated
malhechor, -chora *n* : criminal, delinquent, wrongdoer
malherir {76} *vt* : to injure seriously
malhumor *nm* : bad mood, sullenness
malhumorado, -da *adj* : bad-tempered, cross
malicia *nf* **1** : wickedness, malice **2** : mischief, naughtiness **3** : cunning, craftiness
malicioso, -sa *adj* **1** : malicious **2** PÍCARO : mischievous
malignidad *nf* **1** : malignancy **2** MALDAD : evil
maligno, -na *adj* **1** : malignant ⟨un tumor maligno : a malignant tumor⟩ **2** : evil, harmful, malign
malinchismo *nm Mex* : preference for foreign goods or people — **malinchista** *adj*
malintencionado, -da *adj* : malicious, spiteful
malinterpretar *vt* : to misinterpret
malla *nf* **1** : mesh **2** LEOTARDO : leotard, tights *pl* **3** **malla de baño** : bathing suit
mallorquín, -quina *adj & n* : Majorcan
malnutrición *nf, pl* **-ciones** DESNUTRICIÓN : malnutrition
malnutrido, -da *adj* DESNUTRIDO : malnourished, undernourished
malo¹, -la *adj* (**mal** *before masculine singular nouns*) **1** : bad ⟨mala suerte : bad luck⟩ **2** : wicked, naughty **3** : cheap, poor (quality) **4** : harmful ⟨malo para la salud : bad for one's health⟩ **5** (*using the form* **mal**) : unwell ⟨estar mal del corazón : to have heart trouble⟩ **6** **estar de malas** : to be in a bad mood
malo², -la *n* : villain, bad guy (in novels, movies, etc.)
malogrado, -da *adj* : failed, unsuccessful
malograr *vt* **1** : to spoil, to ruin **2** : to waste (an opportunity, time) — **malograrse** *vr* **1** FRACASAR : to fail **2** : to die young
malogro *nm* **1** : untimely death **2** FRACASO : failure
maloliente *adj* HEDIONDO : foul-smelling, smelly
malparado, -da *adj* **salir malparado** *or* **quedar malparado** : to come out of (something) badly, to end up in a bad state
malpensado, -da *adj* : distrustful, suspicious, nasty-minded
malquerencia *nf* AVERSIÓN : ill will, dislike
malquerer {64} *vt* : to dislike
malquiso, etc. → **malquerer**
malsano, -na *adj* : unhealthy
malsonante *adj* : rude, offensive ⟨palabras malsonantes : foul language⟩
malta *nf* : malt
malteada *nf* : malted milk ⟨malteada de chocolate : chocolate malt⟩

maltés, -tesa *adj & n, mpl* **malteses** : Maltese
maltratar *vt* **1** : to mistreat, to abuse **2** : to damage, to spoil
maltrato *nm* : mistreatment, abuse
maltrecho, -cha *adj* : battered, damaged
malucho, -cha *adj fam* : sick, under the weather
malva *adj & nm* : mauve
malvado¹, -da *adj* : evil, wicked
malvado², -da *n* : evildoer, wicked person
malvavisco *nm* : marshmallow
malvender *vt* : to sell at a loss
malversación *nf, pl* **-ciones** : misappropriation (of funds), embezzlement
malversador, -dora *n* : embezzler
malversar *vt* : to embezzle
malvivir *vi* : to live badly, to just scrape by
mamá *nf fam* : mom, mama
mamar *vi* **1** : to suckle **2 darle de mamar a** : to breast-feed — *vt* **1** : to suckle, to nurse **2** : to learn from childhood, to grow up with — **mamarse** *vr fam* : to get drunk
mamario, -ria *adj* : mammary
mamarracho *nm fam* **1** ESPERPENTO : mess, sight **2** : laughingstock, fool **3** : rubbish, junk
mambo *nm* : mambo
mami *nf fam* : mommy
mamífero¹, -ra *adj* : mammalian
mamífero² *nm* : mammal
mamila *nf* **1** : nipple **2** *Mex* : baby bottle, pacifier
mamografía *nf* : mammogram
mamola *nf* : pat, chuck under the chin
mamotreto *nm fam* **1** : huge book, tome **2** ARMATOSTE : hulk, monstrosity
mampara *nf* BIOMBO : screen, room divider
mamparo *nm* : bulkhead
mampostería *nf* : masonry, stonemasonry
mampostero *nm* : mason, stonemason
mamut *nm, pl* **mamuts** : mammoth
maná *nm* : manna
manada *nf* **1** : flock, herd, pack **2** *fam* : horde, mob ⟨llegaron en manada : they came in droves⟩
manantial *nm* **1** FUENTE : spring **2** : source
manar *vi* **1** : to flow **2** : to abound
manatí *nm* : manatee
mancha *nf* **1** : stain, spot, mark ⟨mancha de sangre : bloodstain⟩ **2** : blemish, blot ⟨una mancha en su reputación : a blemish on his reputation⟩ **3** : patch
manchado, -da *adj* : stained
manchar *vt* **1** ENSUCIAR : to stain, to soil **2** DESHONRAR : to sully, to tarnish — **mancharse** *vr* : to get dirty
mancillar *vt* : to sully, to besmirch
manco, -ca *adj* : one-armed, one-handed
mancomunar *vt* : to combine, to pool — **mancomunarse** *vr* : to unite, to join together

mancomunidad *nf* **1** : commonwealth **2** : association, confederation
mancuernas *nfpl* : cuff links
mancuernillas *nf Mex* : cuff links
mandadero, -ra *n* : errand boy *m*, errand girl *f*, messenger
mandado *nm* **1** : order, command **2** : errand ⟨hacer los mandados : to run errands, to go shopping⟩
mandamás *nmf, pl* **-mases** *fam* : boss, bigwig, honcho
mandamiento *nm* **1** : commandment **2** : command, order, warrant ⟨mandamiento judicial : warrant, court order⟩
mandar *vt* **1** ORDENAR : to command, to order **2** ENVIAR : to send ⟨te manda saludos : he sends you his regards⟩ **3** ECHAR : to hurl, to throw **4 ¿mande?** *Mex* : yes?, pardon? — *vi* : to be the boss, to be in charge — **mandarse** *vr Mex* : to take liberties, to take advantage
mandarín *nm* : Mandarin
mandarina *nf* : mandarin orange, tangerine
mandatario, -ria *n* **1** : leader (in politics) ⟨primer mandatario : head of state⟩ **2** : agent (in law)
mandato *nm* **1** : term of office **2** : mandate
mandíbula *nf* **1** : jaw **2** : mandible
mandil *nm* **1** DELANTAL : apron **2** : horse blanket
mandilón *nm, pl* **-lones** *fam* : wimp, coward
mandioca *nf* **1** : manioc, cassava **2** : tapioca
mando *nm* **1** : command, leadership **2** : control (for a device) ⟨mando a distancia : remote control⟩ **3 al mando de** : in charge of **4 al mando de** : under the command of
mandolina *nf* : mandolin
mandón, -dona *adj, mpl* **mandones** : bossy, domineering
mandonear *vt fam* MANGONEAR : to boss around
mandrágora *nf* : mandrake
manecilla *nf* : hand (of a clock), pointer
manejable *adj* **1** : manageable **2** : docile, easily led
manejar *vt* **1** CONDUCIR : to drive (a car) **2** OPERAR : to handle, to operate **3** : to manage **4** : to manipulate (a person) — *vi* : to drive — **manejarse** *vr* **1** COMPORTARSE : to behave **2** : to get along, to manage
manejo *nm* **1** : handling, operation **2** : management
manera *nf* **1** MODO : way, manner, fashion **2 de cualquier manera** *or* **de todas maneras** : anyway, anyhow **3 de manera que** : so, in order that **4 de ninguna manera** : by no means, absolutely not **5 manera de ser** : personality, demeanor

manga *nf* **1** : sleeve **2** MANGUERA : hose
manganeso *nm* : manganese
mangle *nm* : mangrove
mango *nm* **1** : hilt, handle **2** : mango
mangonear *vt fam* : to boss around, to bully — *vi* **1** : to be bossy **2** : to loaf, to fool around
mangosta *nf* : mongoose
manguera *nf* : hose
manguito *nm* **1** : muff **2** : sleeve (of a pipe, etc.), hose (of a car)
maní *nm, pl* **maníes** : peanut
manía *nf* **1** OBSESIÓN : mania, obsession **2** : craze, fad **3** : odd habit, peculiarity **4** : dislike, aversion
maníaco¹, -ca *adj* : maniacal
maníaco², -ca *n* : maniac
maniatar *vt* : to tie the hands of, to manacle
maniático¹, -ca *adj* **1** MANÍACO : maniacal **2** : obsessive **3** : fussy, finicky
maniático², -ca *n* **1** MANÍACO : maniac, lunatic **2** : obsessive person, fanatic **3** : eccentric, crank
manicomio *nm* : insane asylum, madhouse
manicura *nf* : manicure
manicuro, -ra *n* : manicurist
manido, -da *adj* : hackneyed, stale, trite
manifestación *nf, pl* **-ciones 1** : manifestation, sign **2** : demonstration, rally
manifestante *nmf* : demonstrator
manifestar {55} *vt* **1** : to demonstrate, to show **2** : to declare — **manifestarse** *vr* **1** : to be or become evident **2** : to state one's position ⟨se han manifestado a favor del acuerdo : they have declared their support for the agreement⟩ **3** : to demonstrate, to rally
manifiesto¹, -ta *adj* : manifest, evident, clear — **manifiestamente** *adv*
manifiesto² *nm* : manifesto
manija *nf* MANGO : handle
manilla → **manecilla**
manillar *nm* : handlebars *pl*
maniobra *nf* : maneuver, stratagem
maniobrar *v* : to maneuver
manipulación *nf, pl* **-ciones** : manipulation
manipulador¹, -dora *adj* : manipulating, manipulative
manipulador², -dora *n* : manipulator
manipular *vt* **1** : to manipulate **2** MANEJAR : to handle
maniquí¹ *nmf, pl* **-quíes** : mannequin, model
maniquí² *nm, pl* **-quíes** : mannequin, dummy
manirroto¹, -ta *adj* : extravagant
manirroto², -ta *n* : spendthrift
manivela *nf* : crank
manjar *nm* : delicacy, special dish
mano¹ *nf* **1** : hand **2** : coat (of paint or varnish) **3 a ~** : by hand **4 a ~** *or* **a la mano** : handy, at hand, nearby **5 darse la mano** : to shake hands **6 de la mano** : hand in hand ⟨la política y la economía van de la mano : politics

and economics go hand in hand⟩ **7 de primera mano** : firsthand, at firsthand **8 de segunda mano** : secondhand ⟨ropa de segunda mano : secondhand clothing⟩ **9 mano a mano** : one-on-one **10 mano de obra** : labor, manpower **11 mano de mortero** : pestle **12 echar una mano** : to lend a hand **13 mano negra** *Mex fam* : shady dealings *pl*
mano², -na *n Mex fam* : buddy, pal ⟨¡oye, mano! : hey man!⟩
manojo *nm* PUÑADO : handful, bunch
manopla *nf* **1** : mitten, mitt **2** : brass knuckles *pl*
manosear *vt* **1** : to handle or touch excessively **2** ACARICIAR : to fondle, to caress
manotazo *nm* : slap, smack, swipe
manotear *vi* : to wave one's hands, to gesticulate
mansalva *adv* **a ~** : at close range
mansarda *nf* BUHARDILLA : attic
mansedumbre *nf* **1** : gentleness, meekness **2** : tameness
mansión *nf, pl* **-siones** : mansion
manso, -sa *adj* **1** : gentle, meek **2** : tame — **mansamente** *adv*
manta *nf* **1** COBIJA, FRAZADA : blanket **2** : poncho **3** *Mex* : coarse cotton fabric
manteca *nf* **1** GRASA : lard, fat **2** : butter
mantecoso, -sa *adj* : buttery
mantel *nm* **1** : tablecloth **2** : altar cloth
mantelería *nf* : table linen
mantener {80} *vt* **1** SUSTENTAR : to support, to feed ⟨mantener uno su familia : to support one's family⟩ **2** CONSERVAR : to keep, to preserve **3** CONTINUAR : to keep up, to sustain ⟨mantener una correspondencia : to keep up a correspondence⟩ **4** AFIRMAR : to maintain, to affirm — **mantenerse** *vr* **1** : to support oneself, to subsist **2 mantenerse firme** : to hold one's ground
mantenimiento *nm* **1** : maintenance, upkeep **2** : sustenance, food **3** : preservation
mantequera *nf* **1** : churn **2** : butter dish
mantequería *nf* **1** : creamery, dairy **2** : grocery store
mantequilla *nf* : butter
mantilla *nf* : mantilla
mantis *nf* **mantis religiosa** : praying mantis
manto *nm* **1** : cloak **2** : mantle (in geology)
mantón *nm, pl* **-tones** CHAL : shawl
mantuvo, etc. → **mantener**
manual¹ *adj* **1** : manual ⟨trabajo manual : manual labor⟩ **2** : handy, manageable — **manualmente** *adv*
manual² *nm* : manual, handbook
manualidades *nfpl* : handicrafts (in schools)
manubrio *nm* **1** : handle, crank **2** : handlebars *pl*

manufactura *nf* **1** FABRICACIÓN : manufacture **2** : manufactured item, product **3** FÁBRICA : factory
manufacturar *vt* FABRICAR : to manufacture
manufacturero¹, -ra *adj* : manufacturing
manufacturero², -ra *n* FABRICANTE : manufacturer
manuscrito¹, -ta *adj* : handwritten
manuscrito² *nm* : manuscript
manutención *nf, pl* **-ciones** : maintenance, support
manzana *nf* **1** : apple **2** CUADRA : block (enclosed by streets or buildings) **3** *or* **manzana de Adán** : Adam's apple
manzanal *nm* **1** : apple orchard **2** MANZANO : apple tree
manzanar *nm* : apple orchard
manzanilla *nf* **1** : chamomile **2** : chamomile tea
manzano *nm* : apple tree
maña *nf* **1** : dexterity, skill **2** : cunning, guile **3 mañas** *or* **malas mañas** *nfpl* : bad habits, vices
mañana *nf* **1** : morning **2** : tomorrow
mañanero, -ra *adj* MATUTINO : morning ⟨rocío mañanero : morning dew⟩
mañanitas *nfpl Mex* : birthday serenade
mañoso, -sa *adj* **1** HÁBIL : skillful **2** ASTUTO : cunning, crafty **3** : fussy, finicky
mapa *nm* CARTA : map
mapache *nm* : raccoon
mapamundi *nm* : map of the world
maqueta *nf* : model, mock-up
maquillador, -dora *n* : makeup artist
maquillaje *nm* : makeup
maquillarse *vr* : to put on makeup, to make oneself up
máquina *nf* **1** : machine ⟨máquina de coser : sewing machine⟩ ⟨máquina de escribir : typewriter⟩ **2** LOCOMOTORA : engine, locomotive **3** : machine (in politics) **4 a toda máquina** : at full speed
maquinación *nf, pl* **-ciones** : machination, scheme, plot
maquinal *adj* : mechanical, automatic — **maquinalmente** *adv*
maquinar *vt* : to plot, to scheme
maquinaria *nf* **1** : machinery **2** : mechanism, works *pl*
maquinilla *nf* **1** : small machine or device **2** *CA, Car* : typewriter
maquinista *nmf* **1** : machinist **2** : railroad engineer
mar *nmf* **1** : sea ⟨un mar agitado : a rough sea⟩ ⟨hacerse a la mar : to set sail⟩ **2 alta mar** : high seas
maraca *nf* : maraca
maraña *nf* **1** : thicket **2** ENREDO : tangle, mess
marasmo *nm* : paralysis, stagnation
maratón *nm, pl* **-tones** : marathon
maravilla *nf* **1** : wonder, marvel ⟨a las mil maravillas : wonderfully, mar-

velously⟩ ⟨hacer maravillas : to work wonders⟩ **2** : marigold
maravillar *vt* ASOMBRAR : to astonish, to amaze — **maravillarse** *vr* : to be amazed, to marvel
maravilloso, -sa *adj* ESTUPENDO : wonderful, marvelous — **maravillosamente** *adv*
marbete *nm* **1** ETIQUETA : label, tag **2** *PRi* : registration sticker (of a car)
marca *nf* **1** : mark **2** : brand, make **3** : trademark ⟨marca registrada : registered trademark⟩ **4** : record (in sports) ⟨batir la marca : to beat the record⟩
marcado, -da *adj* : marked ⟨un marcado contraste : a marked contrast⟩
marcador *nm* **1** TANTEADOR : scoreboard **2** : marker, felt-tipped pen **3 marcador de libros** : bookmark
marcaje *nm* **1** : scoring (in sports) **2** : guarding (in sports)
marcapasos *nms & pl* : pacemaker
marcar {72} *vt* **1** : to mark **2** : to brand (livestock) **3** : to indicate, to show **4** RESALTAR : to emphasize **5** : to dial (a telephone) **6** : to guard (an opponent) **7** ANOTAR : to score (a goal, a point) — *vi* **1** ANOTAR : to score **2** : to dial
marcha *nf* **1** : march **2** : hike, walk ⟨ir de marcha : to go hiking⟩ **3** : pace, speed ⟨a toda marcha : at top speed⟩ **4** : gear (of an automobile) ⟨marcha atrás : reverse, reverse gear⟩ **5 en ～** : in motion, in gear, under way
marchar *vi* **1** IR : to go, to travel **2** ANDAR : to walk **3** FUNCIONAR : to work, to go **4** : to march — **marcharse** *vr* : to leave
marchitar *vi* : to make wither, to wilt — **marchitarse** *vr* **1** : to wither, to shrivel up, to wilt **2** : to languish, to fade away
marchito, -ta *adj* : withered, faded
marcial *adj* : martial, military
marco *nm* **1** : frame, framework **2** : goalposts *pl* **3** AMBIENTE : setting, atmosphere **4** : mark (unit of currency)
marea *nf* : tide
mareado, -da *adj* **1** : dizzy, lightheaded **2** : queasy, nauseous **3** : seasick
marear *vt* **1** : to make sick ⟨los gases me marearon : the fumes made me sick⟩ **2** : to bother, to annoy — **marearse** *vr* **1** : to get sick, to become nauseated **2** : to feel dizzy **3** : to get tipsy
marejada *nf* **1** : surge, swell (of the sea) **2** : undercurrent, ferment, unrest
maremoto *nm* : tidal wave
mareo *nm* **1** : dizzy spell **2** : nausea **3** : seasickness, motion sickness **4** : annoyance, vexation
marfil *nm* : ivory
margarina *nf* : margarine
margarita *nf* **1** : daisy **2** : margarita (cocktail)
margen¹ *nf, pl* **márgenes** : bank (of a river), side (of a street)

margen[2] *nm, pl* **márgenes 1** : edge, border **2** : margin ⟨margen de ganancia : profit margin⟩
marginación *nf, pl* **-ciones** : marginalization, exclusion
marginado[1], **-da** *adj* **1** DESHEREDADO : outcast, alienated, dispossessed **2 clases marginadas** : underclass
marginado[2], **-da** *n* : outcast, misfit
marginal *adj* : marginal, fringe
marginalidad *nf* : marginality
marginar *vt* : to ostracize, to exclude
mariachi *nm* : mariachi musician or band
maridaje *nm* : marriage, union
maridar *vt* UNIR : to marry, to unite
marido *nm* ESPOSO : husband
marihuana *or* **mariguana** *or* **marijuana** *nf* : marihuana
marimacho *nmf fam* **1** : mannish woman **2** : tomboy
marimba *nf* : marimba
marina *nf* **1** : coast, coastal area **2** : navy, fleet ⟨marina mercante : merchant marine⟩
marinada *nf* : marinade
marinar *vt* : to marinate
marinero[1], **-ra** *adj* **1** : seaworthy **2** : sea, marine
marinero[2] *nm* : sailor
marino[1], **-na** *adj* : marine, sea
marino[2] *nm* : sailor, seaman
marioneta *nf* TÍTERE : puppet, marionette
mariposa *nf* **1** : butterfly **2 mariposa nocturna** : moth
mariquita[1] *nf* : ladybug
mariquita[2] *nm fam* : sissy, wimp
mariscal *nm* **1** : marshal **2 mariscal de campo** : field marshal (in the military), quarterback (in football)
marisco *nm* **1** : shellfish **2 mariscos** *nmpl* : seafood
marisma *nf* : marsh, salt marsh
marital *adj* : marital, married ⟨la vida marital : married life⟩
marítimo, -ma *adj* : maritime, shipping ⟨la industria marítima : the shipping industry⟩
marmita *nf* : (cooking) pot
mármol *nm* : marble
marmóreo, -rea *adj* : marble, marmoreal
marmota *nf* **1** : marmot **2 marmota de América** : woodchuck, groundhog
maroma *nf* **1** : rope **2** : acrobatic stunt **3** *Mex* : somersault
marque, etc. → **marcar**
marqués, -quesa *n, mpl* **marqueses** : marquis *m*, marquess *m*, marquise *f*, marchioness *f*
marquesina *nf* : marquee, canopy
marqueta *nf Mex* : block (of chocolate), lump (of sugar or salt)
marranada *nf* **1** : disgusting thing **2** : dirty trick
marrano[1], **-na** *adj* : filthy, disgusting
marrano[2], **-na** *n* **1** CERDO : pig, hog **2** : dirty pig, slob

marrar *vt* : to miss (a target) — *vi* : to fail, to go wrong
marras *adv* **1** : long ago **2 de ~** : said, aforementioned ⟨el individuo de marras : the individual in question⟩
marrasquino *nm* : maraschino
marrón *adj & nm, pl* **marrones** CASTAÑO : brown
marroquí *adj & nmf, pl* **-quíes** : Moroccan
marsopa *nf* : porpoise
marsupial *nm* : marsupial
marta *nf* **1** : marten **2 marta cebellina** : sable (animal)
Marte *nm* : Mars
martes *nms & pl* : Tuesday
martillar *v* : to hammer
martillazo *nm* : blow with a hammer
martillo *nm* **1** : hammer **2 martillo neumático** : jackhammer
martinete *nm* **1** : heron **2** : pile driver
mártir *nmf* : martyr
martirio *nm* **1** : martyrdom **2** : ordeal, torment
martirizar {21} *vt* **1** : to martyr **2** ATORMENTAR : to torment
marxismo *nm* : Marxism
marxista *adj & nmf* : Marxist
marzo *nm* : March
mas *conj* PERO : but
más[1] *adv* **1** : more ⟨¿hay algo más grande? : is there anything bigger?⟩ **2** : most ⟨Luis es el más alto : Luis is the tallest⟩ **3** : longer ⟨el sabor dura más : the flavor lasts longer⟩ **4** : rather ⟨más querría andar : I would rather walk⟩ **5 a ~** : besides, in addition **6 más allá** : further **7 qué ... más ...** : what ..., what a ... ⟨¡qué día más bonito! : what a beautiful day!⟩
más[2] *adj* **1** : more ⟨dáme dos kilos más : give me two more kilos⟩ **2** : most ⟨la que ganó más dinero : the one who earned the most money⟩ **3** : else ⟨¿quién más quiere vino? : who else wants wine?⟩
más[3] *n* : plus sign
más[4] *prep* : plus ⟨tres más dos es igual a cinco : three plus two equals five⟩
más[5] *pron* **1** : more ⟨¿tienes más? : do you have more?⟩ **2 a lo más** : at most **3 de ~** : extra, excess **4 más o menos** : more or less, approximately **5 por más que** : no matter how much ⟨por más que corras no llegarás a tiempo : no matter how fast you run you won't arrive on time⟩
masa *nf* **1** : mass, volume ⟨masa atómica : atomic mass⟩ ⟨producción en masa : mass production⟩ **2** : dough, batter **3 masas** *nfpl* : people, masses ⟨las masas populares : the common people⟩ **4 masa harina** *Mex* : corn flour (for tortillas, etc.)
masacrar *vt* : to massacre
masacre *nf* : massacre
masaje *nm* : massage
masajear *vt* : to massage

masajista *nmf* : masseur *m*, masseuse *f*
mascar {72} *v* MASTICAR : to chew
máscara *nf* **1** CARETA : mask **2** : appearance, pretense **3 máscara antigás** : gas mask
mascarada *nf* : masquerade
mascarilla *nf* **1** : mask (in medicine) ⟨mascarilla de oxígeno : oxygen mask⟩ **2** : facial mask (in cosmetology)
mascota *nf* : mascot
masculinidad *nf* : masculinity
masculino, -na *adj* **1** : masculine, male **2** : manly **3** : masculine (in grammar)
mascullar *v* : to mumble, to mutter
masificado, -da *adj* : overcrowded
masilla *nf* : putty
masivamente *adv* : en masse
masivo, -va *adj* : mass ⟨comunicación masiva : mass communication⟩
masón *nm, pl* **masones** FRANCMASÓN : Mason, Freemason
masonería *nf* FRANCMASONERÍA : Masonry, Freemasonry
masónico, -ca *adj* : Masonic
masoquismo *nm* : masochism
masoquista[1] *adj* : masochistic
masoquista[2] *nmf* : masochist
masque, etc. → **mascar**
masticar {72} *v* MASCAR : to chew, to masticate
mástil *nm* **1** : mast **2** ASTA : flagpole **3** : neck (of a stringed instrument)
mastín *nm, pl* **mastines** : mastiff
mástique *nm* : putty, filler
mastodonte *nm* : mastodon
masturbación *nf, pl* **-ciones** : masturbation
masturbarse *vr* : to masturbate
mata *nf* **1** ARBUSTO : bush, shrub **2** : plant ⟨mata de tomate : tomato plant⟩ **3** : sprig, tuft **4 mata de pelo** : mop of hair
matadero *nm* : slaughterhouse, abattoir
matado, -da *adj Mex* : strenuous, exhausting
matador *nm* TORERO : matador, bullfighter
matamoscas *nms & pl* : flyswatter
matanza *nf* MASACRE : slaughter, butchering
matar *vt* **1** : to kill **2** : to slaughter, to butcher **3** APAGAR : to extinguish, to put out (fire, light) **4** : to tone down (colors) **5** : to pass, to waste (time) **6** : to trump (in card games) — *vi* : to kill — **matarse** *vr* **1** : to be killed **2** SUICIDARSE : to commit suicide **3** *fam* : to exhaust oneself ⟨se mató tratando de terminarlo : he knocked himself out trying to finish it⟩
matasanos *nms & pl fam* : quack
matasellar *vt* : to cancel (a stamp), to postmark
matasellos *nms & pl* : postmark
matatena *nf Mex* : jacks
mate[1] *adj* : matte, dull
mate[2] *nm* **1** : maté **2 jaque mate** : checkmate ⟨darle mate a *or* darle jaque mate a : to checkmate⟩

matemática → **matemáticas**
matemáticas *nfpl* : mathematics, math
matemático[1], **-ca** *adj* : mathematical — **matemáticamente** *adv*
matemático[2], **-ca** *n* : mathematician
materia *nf* **1** : matter ⟨materia gris : gray matter⟩ **2** : material ⟨materia prima : raw material⟩ **3** : (academic) subject **4 en materia de** : on the subject of, concerning
material[1] *adj* **1** : material, physical, real **2 daños materiales** : property damage
material[2] *nm* **1** : material ⟨material de construcción : building material⟩ **2** EQUIPO : equipment, gear
materialismo *nm* : materialism
materialista[1] *adj* : materialistic
materialista[2] *nmf* **1** : materialist **2** *Mex* : truck driver
materializar {21} *vt* : to bring to fruition, to realize — **materializarse** *vr* : to materialize, to come into being
materialmente *adv* **1** : materially, physically ⟨materialmente imposible : physically impossible⟩ **2** : really, absolutely
maternal *adj* : maternal, motherly
maternidad *nf* **1** : maternity, motherhood **2** : maternity hospital, maternity ward
materno, -na *adj* : maternal
matinal *adj* MATUTINO : morning ⟨la pálida luz matinal : the pale morning light⟩
matinée *or* **matiné** *nf* : matinee
matiz *nm, pl* **matices** **1** : hue, shade **2** : nuance
matización *nf, pl* **-ciones** **1** : tinting, toning, shading **2** : clarification (of a statement)
matizar {21} *vt* **1** : to tinge, to tint (colors) **2** : to vary, to modulate (sounds) **3** : to qualify (statements)
matón *nm, pl* **matones** : thug, bully
matorral *nm* **1** : thicket **2** : scrub, scrubland
matraca *nf* **1** : rattle, noisemaker **2 dar la matraca a** : to pester, to nag
matriarca *nf* : matriarch
matriarcado *nm* : matriarchy
matrícula *nf* **1** : list, roll, register **2** INSCRIPCIÓN : registration, enrollment **3** : license plate, registration number
matriculación *nf, pl* **-ciones** : matriculation, registration
matricular *vt* **1** INSCRIBIR : to enroll, to register (a person) **2** : to register (a vehicle) — **matricularse** *vr* : to matriculate
matrimonial *adj* : marital, matrimonial ⟨la vida matrimonial : married life⟩
matrimonio *nm* **1** : marriage, matrimony **2** : married couple
matriz *nf, pl* **matrices** **1** : uterus, womb **2** : original, master copy **3** : main office, headquarters **4** : stub (of a check) **5** : matrix ⟨matriz de puntos : dot matrix⟩

matrona *nf* : matron
matronal *adj* : matronly
matutino¹, -na *adj* : morning ⟨la edición matutina : the morning edition⟩
matutino² *nm* : morning paper
maullar {8} *vi* : to meow
maullido *nm* : meow
mauritano, -na *adj & n* : Mauritanian
mausoleo *nm* : mausoleum
maxilar *nm* : jaw, jawbone
máxima *nf* : maxim
máxime *adv* ESPECIALMENTE : especially, principally
maximizar {21} *vt* : to maximize
máximo¹, -ma *adj* : maximum, greatest, highest
máximo² *nm* **1** : maximum **2 al máximo** : to the utmost **3 como ∼** : at the most, at the latest
maya¹ *adj & nmf* : Mayan
maya² *nmf* : Maya, Mayan
mayo *nm* : May
mayonesa *nf* : mayonnaise
mayor¹ *adj* **1** (*comparative of* **grande**) : bigger, larger, greater, elder, older **2** (*superlative of* **grande**) : biggest, largest, greatest, eldest, oldest **3** : grown-up, mature **4** : main, major **5 mayor de edad** : of (legal) age **6 al por mayor** *or* **por ∼** : wholesale
mayor² *nmf* **1** : major (in the military) **2** : adult
mayoral *nm* CAPATAZ : foreman, overseer
mayordomo *nm* : butler, majordomo
mayoreo *nm* : wholesale
mayores *nmpl* : grown-ups, elders
mayoría *nf* **1** : majority **2 en su mayoría** : on the whole
mayorista¹ *adj* ALMACENISTA : wholesale
mayorista² *nmf* : wholesaler
mayoritariamente *adv* : primarily, chiefly
mayoritario, -ria *adj & n* : majority ⟨un consenso mayoritario : a majority consensus⟩
mayormente *adv* : primarily, chiefly
mayúscula *nf* : capital letter
mayúsculo, -la *adj* **1** : capital, uppercase **2** : huge, terrible ⟨un problema mayúsculo : a huge problem⟩
maza *nf* **1** : mace (weapon) **2** : drumstick **3** *fam* : bore, pest
mazacote *nm* **1** : concrete **2** : lumpy mess (of food) **3** : eyesore, crude work of art
mazapán *nm, pl* **-panes** : marzipan
mazmorra *nf* CALABOZO : dungeon
mazo *nm* **1** : mallet **2** : pestle **3** MANOJO : handful, bunch
mazorca *nf* **1** CHOCLO : cob, ear of corn **2 pelar la mazorca** *Mex fam* : to smile from ear to ear
me *pron* **1** : me ⟨me vieron : they saw me⟩ **2** : to me, for me, from me ⟨dame el libro : give me the book⟩ ⟨me lo compró : he bought it for me⟩ ⟨me robaron la cartera : they stole my pocketbook⟩
3 : myself, to myself, for myself, from myself ⟨me preparé una buena comida : I cooked myself a good dinner⟩ ⟨me equivoqué : I made a mistake⟩
mecánica *nf* : mechanics
mecánico¹, -ca *adj* : mechanical — **mecánicamente** *adv*
mecánico², -ca *n* **1** : mechanic **2** : technician ⟨mecánico dental : dental technician⟩
mecanismo *nm* : mechanism
mecanización *nf, pl* **-ciones** : mechanization
mecanizar {21} *vt* : to mechanize
mecanografía *nf* : typing
mecanografiar {85} *vt* : to type
mecanógrafo, -fa *n* : typist
mecate *nm* *CA, Mex, Ven* : rope, twine, cord
mecedor *nm* : glider (seat)
mecedora *nf* : rocking chair
mecenas *nmfs & pl* : patron (of the arts), sponsor
mecenazgo *nm* PATROCINIO : sponsorship, patronage
mecer {86} *vt* **1** : to rock **2** COLUMPIAR : to push (on a swing) — **mecerse** *vr* : to rock, to swing, to sway
mecha *nf* **1** : fuse **2** : wick **3 mechas** *nfpl* : highlights (in hair)
mechero *nm* **1** : burner **2** *Spain* : lighter
mechón *nm, pl* **mechones** : lock (of hair)
medalla *nf* : medal, medallion
medallista *nmf* : medalist
medallón *nm, pl* **-llones 1** : medallion **2** : locket
media *nf* **1** CALCETÍN : sock **2** : average, mean **3 medias** *nfpl* : stockings, hose, tights **4 a medias** : by halves, half and half, halfway ⟨ir a medias : to go halves⟩ ⟨verdad a medias : half-truth⟩
mediación *nf, pl* **-ciones** : mediation
mediado, -da *adj* **1** : half full, half empty, half over **2** : halfway through ⟨mediada la tarea : halfway through the job⟩
mediador, -dora *n* : mediator
mediados *nmpl* **a mediados de** : halfway through, in the middle of ⟨a mediados del mes : towards the middle of the month, mid-month⟩
medialuna *nf* **1** : crescent **2** : croissant, crescent roll
medianamente *adv* : fairly, moderately
medianero, -ra *adj* **1** : dividing **2** : mediating
medianía *nf* **1** : middle position **2** : mediocre person, mediocrity
mediano, -na *adj* **1** : medium, average ⟨la mediana edad : middle age⟩ **2** : mediocre
medianoche *nf* : midnight
mediante *prep* : through, by means of ⟨Dios mediante : God willing⟩
mediar *vi* **1** : to mediate **2** : to be in the middle, to be halfway through **3** : to elapse, to pass ⟨mediaron cinco años entre el inicio de la guerra y el armisti-

cio : five years passed between the start
of the war and the armistice⟩ **4** : to be
a consideration ⟨media el hecho de que
cuesta mucho : one must take into account that it is costly⟩ **5** : to come up,
to happen ⟨medió algo urgente : something pressing came up⟩
mediatizar {21} *vt* : to influence, to interfere with
medicación *nf, pl* **-ciones** : medication,
treatment
medicamento *nm* : medication, medicine, drug
medicar {72} *vt* : to medicate —
medicarse *vr* : to take medicine
medicina *nf* : medicine
medicinal *adj* **1** : medicinal **2** : med-
icated
medicinar *vt* : to give medication to, to
dose
medición *nf, pl* **-ciones** : measuring,
measurement
médico¹, -ca *adj* : medical ⟨una receta
médica : a doctor's prescription⟩
médico², -ca *n* DOCTOR : doctor, physician
medida *nf* **1** : measurement, measure
⟨hecho a medida : custom-made⟩ **2**
: measure, step ⟨tomar medidas : to
take steps⟩ **3** : moderation, prudence
⟨sin medida : immoderately⟩ **4** : extent, degree ⟨en gran medida : to a
great extent⟩
medidor *nm* : meter, gauge
medieval *adj* : medieval — **medieval-
ista** *nmf*
medievo → **medioevo**
medio¹ *adv* **1** : half ⟨está medio dormi-
da : she's half asleep⟩ **2** : rather, kind
of ⟨está medio aburrida esta fiesta : this
party is rather boring⟩
medio², -dia *adj* **1** : half ⟨una media
hora : half an hour⟩ ⟨medio hermano
: half brother⟩ ⟨a media luz : in the
half-light⟩ ⟨son las tres y media : it's
half past three, it's three-thirty⟩ **2**
: midway, halfway ⟨a medio camino
: halfway there⟩ **3** : middle ⟨la clase
media : the middle class⟩ **4** : average
⟨la temperatura media : the average
temperature⟩
medio³ *nm* **1** CENTRO : middle, center
⟨en medio de : in the middle of, amid⟩
2 AMBIENTE : milieu, environment **3**
: medium, spiritualist **4** : means *pl*, way
⟨por medio de : by means of⟩ ⟨los
medios de comunicación : the media⟩
5 medios *nmpl* : means, resources
mediocampista *nmf* : midfielder
mediocre *adj* : mediocre, average
mediocridad *nf* : mediocrity
mediodía *nm* : noon, midday
medioevo *nm* : Middle Ages
medir {54} *vt* **1** : to measure **2** : to weigh,
to consider ⟨medir los riesgos : to
weigh the risks⟩ — *vi* : to measure —
medirse *vr* : to be moderate, to exercise restraint

meditabundo, -da *adj* PENSATIVO : pensive, thoughtful
meditación *nf, pl* **-ciones** : meditation,
thought
meditar *vi* : to meditate, to think ⟨med-
itar sobre la vida : to contemplate life⟩
— *vt* **1** : to think over, to consider **2**
: to plan, to work out
meditativo, -va *adj* : pensive
mediterráneo, -nea *adj* : Mediterranean
medrar *vi* **1** PROSPERAR : to prosper, to
thrive **2** AUMENTAR : to increase, to
grow
medro *nm* PROSPERIDAD : prosperity,
growth
medroso, -sa *adj* : fainthearted, fearful
médula *nf* **1** : marrow, pith **2 médula
espinal** : spinal cord
medular *adj* : fundamental, core ⟨el
punto medular : the crux of the mat-
ter⟩
medusa *nf* : jellyfish, medusa
megabyte *nm* : megabyte
megáfono *nm* : megaphone
megahercio *nm* : megahertz
megahertzio *nm* : megahertz
megatón *nm, pl* **-tones** : megaton
megavatio *nm* : megawatt
mejicano → **mexicano**
mejilla *nf* : cheek
mejillón *nm, pl* **-llones** : mussel
mejor¹ *adv* **1** : better ⟨Carla cocina
mejor que Ana : Carla cooks better
than Ann⟩ **2** : best ⟨ella es la que lo
hace mejor : she's the one who does it
best⟩ **3** : rather ⟨mejor morir que
rendirme : I'd rather die than give up⟩
4 : it's better that ... ⟨mejor te vas
: you'd better go⟩ **5 a lo mejor** : maybe,
perhaps
mejor² *adj* **1** (*comparative of* **bueno**)
: better ⟨a falta de algo mejor : for lack
of something better⟩ **2** (*comparative of*
bien) : better ⟨está mucho mejor : he's
much better⟩ **3** (*superlative of* **bueno**)
: best, the better ⟨mi mejor amigo : my
best friend⟩ **4** (*superlative of* **bien**)
: best, the better ⟨duermo mejor en un
clima seco : I sleep best in a dry cli-
mate⟩ **5** PREFERIBLE : preferable, better **6 lo mejor** : the best thing, the best
part
mejor³ *nmf* (*with definite article*) : the
better (one), the best (one)
mejora *nf* : improvement
mejoramiento *nm* : improvement
mejorana *nf* : marjoram
mejorar *vt* : to improve, to make better
— *vi* : to improve, to get better — **mejorarse** *vr*
mejoría *nf* : improvement, betterment
mejunje *nm* : concoction, brew
melancolía *nf* : melancholy, sadness
melancólico, -ca *adj* : melancholy, sad
melanoma *nm* : melanoma
melaza *nf* : molasses
melena *nf* **1** : mane **2** : long hair **3 melenas** *nfpl* GREÑAS : shaggy hair, mop

melenudo¹, -da *adj fam* : longhaired
melenudo², -da *n* GREÑUDO : longhair, hippie
melindres *nmpl* **1** : affectation, airs *pl* **2** : finickiness
melindroso¹, -sa *adj* **1** : affected **2** : fussy, finicky
melindroso², -sa *n* : finicky person, fuss-budget
melisa *nf* : lemon balm
mella *nf* **1** : dent, nick **2 hacer mella en** : to have an effect on, to make an impression on
mellado, -da *adj* **1** : chipped, dented **2** : gap-toothed
mellar *vt* : to dent, to nick
mellizo, -za *adj* & *n* GEMELO : twin
melocotón *nm, pl* **-tones** : peach
melodía *nf* : melody, tune
melódico, -ca *adj* : melodic
melodioso, -sa *adj* : melodious
melodrama *nm* : melodrama
melodramático, -ca *adj* : melodramatic
melón *nm, pl* **melones** : melon, cantaloupe
meloso, -sa *adj* **1** : honeyed, sweet **2** EMPALAGOSO : cloying, saccharine
membrana *nf* **1** : membrane **2 membrana interdigital** : web, webbing (of a bird's foot) — **membranoso, -sa** *adj*
membresía *nf* : membership, members *pl*
membrete *nm* : letterhead, heading
membrillo *nm* : quince
membrudo, -da *adj* FORNIDO : muscular, well-built
memez *nf, pl* **memeces** : stupid thing
memo, -ma *adj* : silly, stupid
memorabilia *nf* : memorabilia
memorable *adj* : memorable
memorándum *or* **memorando** *nm, pl* **-dums** *or* **-dos** **1** : memorandum, memo **2** : memo book, appointment book
memoria *nf* **1** : memory ⟨de memoria : by heart⟩ ⟨hacer memoria : to try to remember⟩ ⟨traer a la memoria : to call to mind⟩ **2** RECUERDO : remembrance, memory ⟨su memoria perdurará para siempre : his memory will live forever⟩ **3** : report ⟨memoria annual : annual report⟩ **4 memorias** *nfpl* : memoirs
memorizar {21} *vt* : to memorize — **memorización** *nf*
mena *nf* : ore
menaje *nm* : household goods *pl*, furnishings *pl*
mención *nf, pl* **-ciones** : mention
mencionar *vt* : to mention, to refer to
mendaz *adj, pl* **mendaces** : mendacious, lying
mendicidad *nf* : begging
mendigar {52} *vi* : to beg — *vt* : to beg for
mendigo, -ga *n* LIMOSNERO : beggar
mendrugo *nm* : crust (of bread)

menear *vt* **1** : to shake (one's head) **2** : to sway, to wiggle (one's hips) **3** : to wag (a tail) **4** : to stir (a liquid) — **menearse** *vr* **1** : to wiggle one's hips **2** : to fidget
meneo *nm* **1** : movement **2** : shake, toss **3** : swaying, wagging, wiggling **4** : stir, stirring
menester *nm* **1** : activity, occupation, duties *pl* **2 ser menester** : to be necessary ⟨es menester que vengas : you must come⟩
mengano, -na → **fulano**
mengua *nf* **1** : decrease, decline **2** : lack, want **3** : discredit, dishonor
menguar *vt* : to diminish, to lessen — *vi* **1** : to decline, to decrease **2** : to wane — **menguante** *adj*
meningitis *nf* : meningitis
menisco *nm* : meniscus, cartilage
menjurje → **mejunje**
menopausia *nf* : menopause
menor¹ *adj* **1** (*comparative of* **pequeño**) : smaller, lesser, younger **2** (*superlative of* **pequeño**) : smallest, least, youngest **3** : minor **4 al por menor** : retail **5 ser menor de edad** : to be a minor, to be underage
menor² *nmf* : minor, juvenile
menos¹ *adv* **1** : less ⟨llueve menos en agosto : it rains less in August⟩ **2** : least ⟨el coche menos caro : the least expensive car⟩ **3 ∼ de** : less than, fewer than
menos² *adj* **1** : less, fewer ⟨tengo más trabajo y menos tiempo : I have more work and less time⟩ **2** : least, fewest ⟨la clase que tiene menos estudiantes : the class that has the fewest students⟩
menos³ *prep* **1** SALVO, EXCEPTO : except **2** : minus ⟨quince menos cuatro son once : fifteen minus four is eleven⟩
menos⁴ *pron* **1** : less, fewer ⟨no deberías aceptar menos : you shouldn't accept less⟩ **2 al menos** *or* **por lo menos** : at least **3 a menos que** : unless
menoscabar *vt* **1** : to lessen, to diminish **2** : to disgrace, to discredit **3** PERJUDICAR : to harm, to damage
menoscabo *nm* **1** : lessening, diminishing **2** : disgrace, discredit **3** : harm, damage
menospreciar *vt* **1** DESPRECIAR : to scorn, to look down on **2** : to underestimate, to undervalue
menosprecio *nm* DESPRECIO : contempt, scorn
mensaje *nm* : message
mensajero, -ra *n* : messenger
menso, -sa *adj Mex fam* : foolish, stupid
menstrual *adj* : menstrual
menstruar {3} *vi* : to menstruate — **menstruación** *nf*
mensual *adj* : monthly
mensualidad *nf* **1** : monthly payment, installment **2** : monthly salary
mensualmente *adv* : every month, monthly

mensurable *adj* : measurable
menta *nf* **1** : mint, peppermint **2 menta verde** : spearmint
mentado, -da *adj* **1** : aforementioned **2** FAMOSO : renowned, famous
mental *adj* : mental, intellectual — **mentalmente** *adv*
mentalidad *nf* : mentality
mentar {55} *vt* **1** : to mention, to name **2 mentar la madre a** *fam* : to insult, to swear at
mente *nf* : mind ⟨tener en mente : to have in mind⟩
mentecato¹, -ta *adj* : foolish, simple
mentecato², -ta *n* : fool, idiot
mentir {76} *vi* : to lie
mentira *nf* : lie
mentiroso¹, -sa *adj* EMBUSTERO : lying, untruthful
mentiroso², -sa *n* EMBUSTERO : liar
mentís *nm, pl* **mentises** : denial, repudiation ⟨dar el mentís a : to deny, to refute⟩
mentol *nm* : menthol
mentón *nm, pl* **mentones** BARBILLA : chin
mentor *nm* : mentor, counselor
menú *nm, pl* **menús** : menu
menudear *vi* : to occur frequently — *vt* : to do repeatedly
menudencia *nf* **1** : trifle **2 menudencias** *nfpl* : giblets
menudeo *nm* : retail, retailing
menudillos *nmpl* : giblets
menudo¹, -da *adj* **1** : minute, small **2 a ~** FRECUENTEMENTE : often, frequently
menudo² *nm* **1** *Mex* : tripe stew **2 menudos** *nmpl* : giblets
meñique *nm or* **dedo meñique** : little finger, pinkie
meollo *nm* **1** MÉDULA : marrow **2** SESO : brains *pl* **3** ENTRAÑA : essence, core ⟨el meollo del asunto : the heart of the matter⟩
mequetrefe *nm fam* : good-for-nothing
mercachifle *nm* : peddler, hawker
mercadeo *nm* : marketing
mercadería *nf* : merchandise, goods *pl*
mercado *nm* : market ⟨mercado de trabajo *or* mercado laboral : labor market⟩ ⟨mercado de valores *or* mercado bursátil : stock market⟩
mercadotecnia *nf* : marketing
mercancía *nf* : merchandise, goods *pl*
mercante *nmf* : merchant, dealer
mercantil *adj* COMERCIAL : commercial, mercantile
merced *nf* **1** : favor **2 ~ a** : thanks to, due to **3 a merced de** : at the mercy of
mercenario, -ria *adj & n* : mercenary
mercería *nf* : notions store
Mercosur *nm* : economic community consisting of Argentina, Brazil, Paraguay, and Uruguay
mercurio *nm* : mercury
Mercurio *nm* : Mercury (planet)

merecedor, -dora *adj* : deserving, worthy
merecer {53} *vt* : to deserve, to merit — *vi* : to be worthy
merecidamente *adv* : rightfully, deservedly
merecido *nm* : something merited, due ⟨recibieron su merecido : they got their just deserts⟩
merecimiento *nm* : merit, worth
merendar {55} *vi* : to have an afternoon snack — *vt* : to have as an afternoon snack
merendero *nm* **1** : lunchroom, snack bar **2** : picnic area
merengue *nm* **1** : meringue **2** : merengue (dance)
meridiano¹, -na *adj* **1** : midday **2** : crystal clear
meridiano² *nm* : meridian
meridional *adj* SUREÑO : southern
merienda *nf* : afternoon snack, tea
mérito *nm* : merit
meritorio¹, -ria *adj* : deserving, meritorious
meritorio², -ria *n* : intern, trainee
merluza *nf* : hake
merma *nf* **1** : decrease, cut **2** : waste, loss
mermar *vi* : to decrease, to diminish — *vt* : to reduce, to cut down
mermelada *nf* : marmalade, jam
mero¹, -ra *adv Mex fam* **1** : nearly, almost ⟨ya mero me caí : I almost fell⟩ **2** : just, exactly ⟨aquí mero : right here⟩
mero², -ra *adj* **1** : mere, simple **2** *Mex fam (used as an intensifier)* : very ⟨en el mero centro : in the very center of town⟩
mero³ *nm* : grouper
merodeador, -dora *n* **1** : marauder **2** : prowler
merodear *vi* **1** : to maraud, to pillage **2** : to prowl around, to skulk
mes *nm* : month
mesa *nf* **1** : table **2** : committee, board
mesada *nf* : allowance, pocket money
mesarse *vr* : to pull at ⟨mesarse los cabellos : to tear one's hair⟩
mesero, -ra *n* CAMARERO : waiter, waitress *f*
meseta *nf* : plateau, tableland
Mesías *nm* : Messiah
mesón *nm, pl* **mesones** : inn
mesonero, -ra *nm* : innkeeper
mestizo¹, -za *adj* **1** : of mixed ancestry **2** HÍBRIDO : hybrid
mestizo², -za *n* : person of mixed ancestry
mesura *nf* **1** MODERACIÓN : moderation, discretion **2** CORTESÍA : courtesy **3** GRAVEDAD : seriousness, dignity
mesurado, -da *adj* COMEDIDO : moderate, restrained
mesurar *vt* : to moderate, to restrain, to temper — **mesurarse** *vr* : to restrain oneself
meta *nf* : goal, objective

metabólico, -ca *adj* : metabolic
metabolismo *nm* : metabolism
metabolizar {21} *vt* : to metabolize
metafísica *nf* : metaphysics
metafísico, -ca *adj* : metaphysical
metáfora *nf* : metaphor
metafórico, -ca *adj* : metaphoric,
metaphorical
metal *nm* 1 : metal 2 : brass section (in
an orchestra)
metálico, -ca *adj* : metallic, metal
metalistería *nf* : metalworking
metalurgia *nf* : metallurgy
metalúrgico¹, -ca *adj* : metallurgical
metalúrgico², -ca *n* : metallurgist
metamorfosis *nfs & pl* : metamorphosis
metano *nm* : methane
metedura *nf* **metedura de pata** : blunder, faux pas
meteórico, -ca *adj* : meteoric
meteorito *nm* : meteorite
meteoro *nm* : meteor
meteorología *nf* : meteorology
meteorológico, -ca *adj* : meteorologic,
meteorological
meteorólogo, -ga *n* : meteorologist
meter *vt* 1 : to put (in) ⟨metieron su
dinero en el banco : they put their money in the bank⟩ 2 : to fit, to squeeze
⟨puedes meter dos líneas más en esa
página : you can fit two more lines on
that page⟩ 3 : to place (in a job) ⟨lo
metieron de barrendero : they got him
a job as a street sweeper⟩ 4 : to involve
⟨lo metió en un buen lío : she got him
in an awful mess⟩ 5 : to make, to cause
⟨meten demasiado ruido : they make
too much noise⟩ 6 : to spread (a rumor) 7 : to strike (a blow) 8 : to take
up, to take in (clothing) 9 **a todo meter** : at top speed — **meterse** *vr* 1 : to
get into, to enter 2 *fam* : to meddle ⟨no
te metas en lo que no te importa : mind
your own business⟩ 3 ~ **con** *fam* : to
pick a fight with, to provoke ⟨no te
metas conmigo : don't mess with me⟩
metiche¹ *adj Mex fam* : nosy
metiche² *nmf Mex fam* : busybody
meticulosidad *nf* : thoroughness, meticulousness
meticuloso, -sa *adj* : meticulous, thorough — **meticulosamente** *adv*
metida *nf* **metida de pata** *fam* : blunder,
gaffe, blooper
metódico, -ca *adj* : methodical —
metódicamente *adv*
metodista *adj & nmf* : Methodist
método *nm* : method
metodología *nf* : methodology
metomentodo *nmf fam* : busybody
metraje *nm* : length (of a film) ⟨de largo
metraje : feature-length⟩
metralla *nf* : shrapnel
metralleta *nf* : submachine gun
métrico, -ca *adj* 1 : metric 2 **cinta
métrica** : tape measure
metro *nm* 1 : meter 2 : subway
metrónomo *nm* : metronome

metrópoli *nf or* **metrópolis** *nfs & pl* : metropolis
metropolitano, -na *adj* : metropolitan
mexicanismo *nm* : Mexican word or expression
mexicano, -na *adj & n* : Mexican
mexicoamericano, -na *adj & n* : Mexi-
can-American
meza, etc. → **mecer**
mezcla *nf* 1 : mixing 2 : mixture, blend
3 : mortar (masonry material)
mezclar *vt* 1 : to mix, to blend 2 : to
mix up, to muddle 3 INVOLUCRAR : to
involve — **mezclarse** *vr* 1 : to get
mixed up (in) 2 : to mix, to mingle (socially)
mezclilla *nf Chile, Mex* : denim ⟨pan-
talones de mezclilla : jeans⟩
mezcolanza *nf* : jumble, hodgepodge
mezquindad *nf* 1 : meanness, stinginess
2 : petty deed, mean action
mezquino¹, -na *adj* 1 : mean, petty 2
: stingy 3 : paltry
mezquino² *nm Mex* : wart
mezquita *nf* : mosque
mezquite *nm* : mesquite
mi *adj* : my
mí *pron* 1 : me ⟨es para mí : it's for me⟩
⟨a mí no me importa : it doesn't matter to me⟩ 2 **mí mismo, mí misma** : myself
miasma *nm* : miasma
miau *nm* : meow
mica *nf* : mica
mico *nm* : monkey, long-tailed monkey
micra *nf* : micron
microbio *nm* : microbe, germ
microbiología *nf* : microbiology
microbiológico, -ca *adj* : microbiologi-
cal
microbús *nm, pl* **-buses** : minibus
microcomputadora *nf* : microcomputer
microcosmos *nms & pl* : microcosm
microficha *nf* : microfiche
microfilm *nm, pl* **-films** : microfilm
micrófono *nm* : microphone
micrómetro *nm* : micrometer
microonda *nf* : microwave
microondas *nms & pl* : microwave, microwave oven
microordenador *nm Spain* : microcomputer
microorganismo *nm* : microorganism
microprocesador *nm* : microprocessor
microscópico, -ca *adj* : microscopic
microscopio *nm* : microscope
mide, etc. → **medir**
miedo *nm* 1 TEMOR : fear ⟨le tiene
miedo al perro : he's scared of the dog⟩
⟨tenían miedo de hablar : they were
afraid to speak⟩ 2 **dar miedo** : to
frighten
miedoso, -sa *adj* TEMEROSO : fearful
miel *nf* : honey
miembro *nm* 1 : member 2 EXTREMI-
DAD : limb, extremity
mienta, etc. → **mentar**
miente, etc. → **mentir**

mientras[1] *adv* **1** *or* **mientras tanto** : meanwhile, in the meantime **2 mientras más** : the more ⟨mientras más como, más quiero : the more I eat, the more I want⟩

mientras[2] *conj* **1** : while, as ⟨roncaba mientras dormía : he snored while he was sleeping⟩ **2** : as long as ⟨luchará mientras pueda : he will fight as long as he is able⟩ **3 mientras que** : while, whereas ⟨él es alto mientras que ella es muy baja : he is tall, whereas she is very short⟩

miércoles *nms & pl* : Wednesday

miga *nf* **1** : crumb **2 hacer buenas (malas) migas con** : to get along well (poorly) with

migaja *nf* **1** : crumb **2 migajas** *nfpl* SO-BRAS : leftovers, scraps

migración *nf, pl* **-ciones** : migration

migrante *nmf* : migrant

migraña *nf* : migraine

migratorio, -ria *adj* : migratory

mijo *nm* : millet

mil[1] *adj* : thousand

mil[2] *nm* : one thousand, a thousand

milagro *nm* : miracle ⟨de milagro : miraculously⟩

milagroso, -sa *adj* : miraculous, marvelous — **milagrosamente** *adv*

milenio *nm* : millennium

milésimo, -ma *adj* : thousandth — **milésimo** *nm*

milicia *nf* **1** : militia **2** : military service

miligramo *nm* : milligram

mililitro *nm* : milliliter

milímetro *nm* : millimeter

militancia *nf* : militancy

militante[1] *adj* : militant

militante[2] *nmf* : militant, activist

militar[1] *vi* **1** : to serve (in the military) **2** : to be active (in politics)

militar[2] *adj* : military

militar[3] *nmf* SOLDADO : soldier

militarismo *nm* : militarism

militarista *adj & nmf* : militarist

militarizar {21} *vt* : to militarize

milla *nf* : mile

millar *nm* : thousand

millón *nm, pl* **millones** : million

millonario, -ria *n* : millionaire

millonésimo[1], **-ma** *adj* : millionth

millonésimo[2] *nm* : millionth

mil millones *nms & pl* : billion

milpa *nf CA, Mex* : cornfield

milpiés *nms & pl* : millipede

mimar *vt* CONSENTIR : to pamper, to spoil

mimbre *nm* : wicker

mimeógrafo *nm* : mimeograph

mímica *nf* **1** : mime, sign language **2** IMITACIÓN : mimicry

mimo *nm* **1** : pampering, indulgence ⟨hacerle mimos a alguien : to pamper someone⟩ **2** : mime

mimoso, -sa *adj* **1** : fussy, finicky **2** : affectionate, clinging

mina *nf* **1** : mine **2** : lead (for pencils)

minar *vt* **1** : to mine **2** DEBILITAR : to undermine

minarete *nm* ALMINAR : minaret

mineral *adj & nm* : mineral

minería *nf* : mining

minero[1], **-ra** *adj* : mining

minero[2], **-ra** *n* : miner, mine worker

miniatura *nf* : miniature

minicomputadora *nf* : minicomputer

minifalda *nf* : miniskirt

minifundio *nm* : small farm

minimizar {21} *vt* : to minimize

mínimo[1], **-ma** *adj* **1** : minimum ⟨salario mínimo : minimum wage⟩ **2** : least, smallest **3** : very small, minute

mínimo[2] *nm* **1** : minimum, least amount **2** : modicum, small amount **3 como ~** : at least

minino, -na *n fam* : pussy, pussycat

miniserie *nf* : miniseries

ministerial *adj* : ministerial

ministerio *nm* : ministry, department

ministro, -tra *n* : minister, secretary ⟨primer ministro : prime minister⟩ ⟨Ministro de Defensa : Secretary of Defense⟩

minivan [ˌminiˈban, -ˈvan] *nf, pl* **-vanes** : minivan

minoría *nf* : minority

minorista[1] *adj* : retail

minorista[2] *nmf* : retailer

minoritario, -ria *adj* : minority

mintió, etc. → **mentir**

minuciosamente *adv* **1** : minutely **2** : in great detail **3** : thoroughly, meticulously

minucioso, -sa *adj* **1** : minute **2** DE-TALLADO : detailed **3** : thorough, meticulous

minué *nm* : minuet

minúsculo, -la *adj* DIMINUTO : tiny, miniscule

minusvalía *nf* : disability, handicap

minusválido[1], **-da** *adj* : handicapped, disabled

minusválido[2], **-da** *n* : handicapped person

minuta *nf* **1** BORRADOR : rough draft **2** : bill, fee

minutero *nm* : minute hand

minuto *nm* : minute

mío[1], **mía** *adj* **1** : my, of mine ⟨¡Dios mío! : my God!, good heavens!⟩ ⟨una amiga mía : a friend of mine⟩ **2** : mine ⟨es mío : it's mine⟩

mío[2], **mía** *pron* (*with definite article*) : mine, my own ⟨tus zapatos son iguales a los míos : your shoes are just like mine⟩

miope *adj* : nearsighted, myopic

miopía *nf* : myopia, nearsightedness

mira *nf* **1** : sight (of a firearm or instrument) **2** : aim, objective ⟨con miras a : with the intention of, with a view to⟩ ⟨de amplias miras : broad-minded⟩ ⟨poner la mira en : to aim at, to aspire to⟩

mirada *nf* **1** : look, glance, gaze **2** EXPRESIÓN : look, expression ⟨una mirada de sorpresa : a look of surprise⟩

mirado, -da *adj* **1** : cautious, careful **2** : considerate **3 bien mirado** : well thought of **4 mal mirado** : disliked, disapproved of

mirador *nm* : balcony, lookout, vantage point

miramiento *nm* **1** CONSIDERACIÓN : consideration, respect **2 sin miramientos** : without due consideration, carelessly

mirar *vt* **1** : to look at **2** OBSERVAR : to watch **3** REFLEXIONAR : to consider, to think over — *vi* **1** : to look **2** : to face, to overlook **3** ∼ **por** : to look after, to look out for — **mirarse** *vr* **1** : to look at oneself **2** : to look at each other

mirasol *nm* GIRASOL : sunflower

miríada *nf* : myriad

mirlo *nm* : blackbird

mirra *nf* : myrrh

mirto *nm* ARRAYÁN : myrtle

misa *nf* : Mass

misantropía *nf* : misanthropy

misantrópico, -ca *adj* : misanthropic

misántropo, -pa *n* : misanthrope

miscelánea *nf* : miscellany

misceláneo, -nea *adj* : miscellaneous

miserable *adj* **1** LASTIMOSO : miserable, wretched **2** : paltry, meager **3** MEZQUINO : stingy, miserly **4** : despicable, vile

miseria *nf* **1** POBREZA : poverty **2** : misery, suffering **3** : pittance, meager amount

misericordia *nf* COMPASIÓN : mercy, compassion

misericordioso, -sa *adj* : merciful

mísero, -ra *adj* **1** : wretched, miserable **2** : stingy **3** : paltry, meager

misil *nm* : missile

misión *nf, pl* **misiones** : mission

misionero, -ra *adj & n* : missionary

misiva *nf* : missive, letter

mismísimo, -ma *adj* (used as an intensifier) : very, selfsame ⟨el mismísimo día : that very same day⟩

mismo[1] *adv* (used as an intensifier) : right, exactly ⟨hazlo ahora mismo : do it right now⟩ ⟨te llamará hoy mismo : he'll definitely call you today⟩

mismo[2], -ma *adj* **1** : same **2** (used as an intensifier) : very ⟨en ese mismo momento : at that very moment⟩ **3** : oneself ⟨lo hizo ella misma : she made it herself⟩ **4 por lo mismo** : for that reason

misoginia *nf* : misogyny

misógino *nm* : misogynist

misterio *nm* : mystery

misterioso, -sa *adj* : mysterious — **misteriosamente** *adv*

misticismo *nm* : mysticism

místico[1], -ca *adj* : mystic, mystical

místico[2], -ca *n* : mystic

mitad *nf* **1** : half ⟨mitad y mitad : half and half⟩ **2** MEDIO : middle ⟨a mitad de : halfway through⟩ ⟨por la mitad : in half⟩

mítico, -ca *adj* : mythical, mythic

mitigar {52} *vt* ALIVIAR : to mitigate, to alleviate — **mitigación** *nf*

mitin *nm, pl* **mítines** : (political) meeting, rally

mito *nm* LEYENDA : myth, legend

mitología *nf* : mythology

mitológico, -ca *adj* : mythological

mitosis *nfs & pl* : mitosis

mitra *nf* : miter (bishop's hat)

mixto, -ta *adj* **1** : mixed, joint **2** : coeducational

mixtura *nf* : mixture, blend

mnemónico, -ca *adj* : mnemonic

mobiliario *nm* : furniture

mocasín *nm, pl* **-sines** : moccasin

mocedad *nf* **1** JUVENTUD : youth **2** : youthful prank

mochila *nf* MORRAL : backpack, knapsack

moción *nf, pl* **-ciones** **1** MOVIMIENTO : motion, movement **2** : motion (to a court or assembly)

moco *nm* **1** : mucus **2** *fam* : snot ⟨limpiarse los mocos : to wipe one's (runny) nose⟩

mocoso, -sa *n* : kid, brat

moda *nf* **1** : fashion, style **2 a la moda** *or* **de** ∼ : in style, fashionable **3 moda pasajera** : fad

modales *nmpl* : manners

modalidad *nf* **1** CLASE : kind, type **2** MANERA : way, manner

modelar *vt* : to model, to mold — **modelarse** *vr* : to model oneself after, to emulate

modelo[1] *adj* : model ⟨una casa modelo : a model home⟩

modelo[2] *nm* : model, example, pattern

modelo[3] *nmf* : model, mannequin

módem *or* **modem** [ˈmoðɛm] *nm* : modem

moderación *nf, pl* **-ciones** MESURA : moderation

moderado, -da *adj & n* : moderate — **moderadamente** *adv*

moderador, -dora *n* : moderator, chair

moderar *vt* **1** TEMPERAR : to temper, to moderate **2** : to curb, to reduce ⟨moderar gastos : to curb spending⟩ **3** PRESIDIR : to chair (a meeting) — **moderarse** *vr* **1** : to restrain oneself **2** : to diminish, to calm down

modernidad *nf* **1** : modernity, modernness **2** : modern age

modernismo *nm* : modernism

modernista[1] *adj* : modernist, modernistic

modernista[2] *nmf* : modernist

modernizar {21} *vt* : to modernize — **modernización** *nf*

moderno, -na *adj* : modern, up-to-date

modestia *nf* : modesty

modesto, -ta *adj* : modest — **modestamente** *adv*

modificación *nf, pl* **-ciones** : alteration

modificador¹, -dora *adj* : modifying, moderating

modificador² → **modificante**

modificante *nm* : modifier

modificar {72} *vt* ALTERAR : to modify, to alter, to adapt

modismo *nm* : idiom

modista *nmf* 1 : dressmaker 2 : fashion designer

modo *nm* 1 MANERA : way, manner, mode ⟨de un modo u otro : one way or another⟩ ⟨a mi modo de ver : to my way of thinking⟩ 2 : mood (in grammar) 3 : mode (in music) 4 **a modo de** : by way of, in the manner of, like ⟨a modo de ejemplo : by way of example⟩ 5 **de cualquier modo** : in any case, anyway 6 **de modo que** : so, in such a way that 7 **de todos modos** : in any case, anyway 8 **en cierto modo** : in a way, to a certain extent

modorra *nf* : drowsiness, lethargy

modular¹ *v* : to modulate — **modulación** *nf*

modular² *adj* : modular

módulo *nm* : module, unit

mofa *nf* 1 : mockery, ridicule 2 **hacer mofa de** : to make fun of, to ridicule

mofarse *vr* ~ **de** : to scoff at, to make fun of

mofeta *nf* ZORRILLO : skunk

mofle *nm* CA, Mex : muffler (of a car)

moflete *nm fam* : fat cheek

mofletudo, -da *adj fam* : fat-cheeked, chubby

mohín *nm, pl* **mohines** : grimace, face

mohino, -na *adj* : gloomy, melancholy

moho *nm* 1 : mold, mildew 2 : rust

mohoso, -sa *adj* 1 : moldy 2 : rusty

moisés *nm, pl* **moiseses** : bassinet, cradle

mojado¹, -da *adj* : wet

mojado², -da *n Mex fam* : illegal immigrant

mojar *vt* 1 : to wet, to moisten 2 : to dunk — **mojarse** *vr* : to get wet

mojigatería *nf* 1 : hypocrisy 2 GAZMOÑERÍA : primness, prudery

mojigato¹, -ta *adj* : prudish, prim — **mojigatamente** *adv*

mojigato², -ta *n* : prude, prig

mojón *nm, pl* **mojones** : boundary stone, marker

molar *nm* MUELA : molar

molcajete *nm Mex* : mortar

molde *nm* 1 : mold, form 2 **letras de molde** : printing, block lettering

moldear *vt* 1 FORMAR : to mold, to shape 2 : to cast

moldura *nf* : molding

mole¹ *nm Mex* 1 : spicy sauce made with chilies and usually chocolate 2 : meat served with mole sauce

mole² *nf* : mass, bulk

molécula *nf* : molecule — **molecular** *adj*

moler {47} *vt* 1 : to grind, to crush 2 CANSAR : to exhaust, to wear out

molestar *vt* 1 FASTIDIAR : to annoy, to bother 2 : to disturb, to disrupt — *vi* : to be a nuisance — **molestarse** *vr* ~ **en** : to take the trouble to

molestia *nf* 1 FASTIDIO : annoyance, bother, nuisance 2 : trouble ⟨se tomó la molestia de investigar : she took the trouble to investigate⟩ 3 MALESTAR : discomfort

molesto, -ta *adj* 1 ENOJADO : bothered, annoyed 2 FASTIDIOSO : bothersome, annoying

molestoso, -sa *adj* : bothersome, annoying

molido, -da *adj* 1 MACHACADO : ground, crushed 2 **estar molido** : to be exhausted

molienda *nf* : milling, grinding

molinero, -ra *n* : miller

molinillo *nm* : grinder, mill ⟨molinillo de café : coffee grinder⟩

molino *nm* 1 : mill 2 **molino de viento** : windmill

molla *nf* : soft fleshy part, flesh (of fruit), lean part (of meat)

molleja *nf* : gizzard

molusco *nm* : mollusk

momentáneamente *adv* : momentarily

momentáneo, -nea *adj* 1 : momentary 2 TEMPORARIO : temporary

momento *nm* 1 : moment, instant ⟨espera un momentito : wait just a moment⟩ 2 : time, period of time ⟨momentos difíciles : hard times⟩ 3 : present, moment ⟨los atletas del momento : the athletes of the moment, today's popular athletes⟩ 4 : momentum 5 **al momento** : right away, at once 6 **de** ~ : at the moment, for the moment 7 **de un momento a otro** : any time now 8 **por momentos** : at times

momia *nf* : mummy

monaguillo *nm* ACÓLITO : altar boy

monarca *nmf* : monarch

monarquía *nf* : monarchy

monárquico, -ca *n* : monarchist

monasterio *nm* : monastery

monástico, -ca *adj* : monastic

mondadientes *nms* & *pl* PALILLO : toothpick

mondar *vt* : to peel

mondongo *nm* ENTRAÑAS : innards *pl*, insides *pl*, guts *pl*

moneda *nf* 1 : coin 2 : money, currency

monedero *nm* : change purse

monetario, -ria *adj* : monetary, financial

mongol, -gola *adj* & *n* : Mongol, Mongolian

monitor¹, -tora *n* : instructor (in sports)

monitor² *nm* : monitor ⟨monitor de televisión : television monitor⟩

monitorear *vt* : to monitor

monja *nf* : nun

monje *nm* : monk

mono¹, -na *adj fam* : lovely, pretty, cute, darling

mono², **-na** *n* : monkey
monóculo *nm* : monocle
monogamia *nf* : monogamy
monógamo, **-ma** *adj* : monogamous
monografía *nf* : monograph
monograma *nm* : monogram
monolingüe *adj* : monolingual
monolítico, **-ca** *adj* : monolithic
monolito *nm* : monolith
monólogo *nm* : monologue
monomanía *nf* : obsession
monopatín *nm*, *pl* **-tines 1** : scooter **2** : skateboard
monopolio *nm* : monopoly
monopolizar {21} *vt* : to monopolize — **monopolización** *nf*
monosilábico, **-ca** *adj* : monosyllabic
monosílabo *nm* : monosyllable
monoteísmo *nm* : monotheism
monoteísta¹ *adj* : monotheistic
monoteísta² *nmf* : monotheist
monotonía *nf* **1** : monotony **2** : monotone
monótono, **-na** *adj* : monotonous — **monótonamente** *adv*
monóxido *nm* : monoxide ⟨monóxido de carbono : carbon monoxide⟩
monserga *nf* : gibberish, drivel
monstruo *nm* : monster
monstruosidad *nf* : monstrosity
monstruoso, **-sa** *adj* : monstrous — **monstruosamente** *adv*
monta *nf* **1** : sum, total **2** : importance, value ⟨de poca monta : unimportant, insignificant⟩
montaje *nm* **1** : assembling, assembly **2** : montage
montante *nm* : transom, fanlight
montaña *nf* **1** MONTE : mountain **2** montaña rusa : roller coaster
montañero, **-ra** *n* : mountaineer, mountain climber
montañoso, **-sa** *adj* : mountainous
montar *vt* **1** : to mount **2** ESTABLECER : to set up, to establish **3** ARMAR : to assemble, to put together **4** : to edit (a film) **5** : to stage, to put on (a show) **6** : to cock (a gun) **7** montar en bicicleta : to get on a bicycle **8** montar a caballo CABALGAR : to ride horseback
monte *nm* **1** MONTAÑA : mountain, mount **2** : woodland, scrubland ⟨monte bajo : underbrush⟩ **3** : outskirts (of a town), surrounding country **4** monte de piedad : pawnshop
montés *adj*, *pl* **monteses** : wild (of animals or plants)
montículo *nm* **1** : mound, heap **2** : hillock, knoll
monto *nm* : amount, total
montón *nm*, *pl* **-tones 1** : heap, pile **2** *fam* : ton, load ⟨un montón de preguntas : a ton of questions⟩ ⟨montones de gente : loads of people⟩
montura *nf* **1** : mount (horse) **2** : saddle, tack **3** : setting, mounting (of jewelry) **4** : frame (of glasses)

monumental *adj fam* **1** : tremendous, terrific **2** : massive, huge
monumento *nm* : monument
monzón *nm*, *pl* **monzones** : monsoon
moño *nm* **1** : bun (chignon) **2** LAZO : bow, knot ⟨corbata de moño : bow tie⟩
moquear *vi* : to snivel
moquillo *nm* : distemper
mora *nf* **1** : blackberry **2** : mulberry
morada *nf* RESIDENCIA : dwelling, abode
morado¹, **-da** *adj* : purple
morado² *nm* : purple
morador, **-dora** *n* : dweller, inhabitant
moral¹ *adj* : moral — **moralmente** *adv*
moral² *nf* **1** MORALIDAD : ethics, morality, morals *pl* **2** ÁNIMO : morale, spirits *pl*
moraleja *nf* : moral (of a story)
moralidad *nf* : morality
moralista¹ *adj* : moralistic
moralista² *nmf* : moralist
morar *vi* : to dwell, to reside
moratoria *nf* : moratorium
mórbido, **-da** *adj* : morbid
morboso, **-sa** *adj* : morbid — **morbosidad** *nf*
morcilla *nf* : blood sausage, blood pudding
mordacidad *nf* : bite, sharpness
mordaz *adj* : caustic, scathing
mordaza *nf* **1** : gag **2** : clamp
mordedura *nf* : bite (of an animal)
morder {47} *v* : to bite
mordida *nf* **1** : bite **2** *CA, Mex* : bribe, payoff
mordisco *nm* : bite, nibble
mordisquear *vt* : to nibble (on), to bite
morena *nf* **1** : moraine **2** : moray (eel)
moreno¹, **-na** *adj* **1** : brunette **2** : dark, dark-skinned
moreno², **-na** *n* **1** : brunette **2** : dark-skinned person
moretón *nm*, *pl* **-tones** : bruise
morfina *nf* : morphine
morfología *nf* : morphology
morgue *nf* : morgue
moribundo¹, **-da** *adj* : dying, moribund
moribundo², **-da** *n* : dying person
morillo *nm* : andiron
morir {46} *vi* **1** FALLECER : to die **2** APAGARSE : to die out, to go out
mormón, **-mona** *adj & n*, *pl* **mormones** : Mormon
moro¹, **-ra** *adj* : Moorish
moro², **-ra** *n* **1** : Moor **2** : Muslim
morosidad *nf* **1** : delinquency (in payment) **2** : slowness
moroso, **-sa** *adj* **1** : delinquent, in arrears ⟨cuentas morosas : delinquent accounts⟩ **2** : slow, sluggish
morral *nm* MOCHILA : backpack, knapsack
morralla *nf* **1** : small fish **2** : trash, riffraff **3** *Mex* : small change
morriña *nf* : homesickness
morro *nm* HOCICO : snout

morsa *nf* : walrus
morse *nm* : Morse code
mortaja *nf* SUDARIO : shroud
mortal[1] *adj* **1** : mortal **2** FATAL : fatal,
 deadly — **mortalmente** *adv*
mortal[2] *nmf* : mortal
mortalidad *nf* : mortality
mortandad *nf* **1** : loss of life, death toll
 2 : carnage, slaughter
mortero *nm* : mortar (bowl, cannon, or
 building material)
mortífero, -ra *adj* LETAL : deadly, fatal
mortificación *nf, pl* **-ciones 1** : mortification **2** TORMENTO : anguish, torment
mortificar {72} *vt* **1** : to mortify **2** TOR-
 TURAR : to trouble, to torment — **mor-
 tificarse** *vr* : to be mortified, to feel embarrassed
mosaico *nm* : mosaic
mosca *nf* **1** : fly **2 mosca común**
 : housefly
moscada *adj* **nuez moscada** : nutmeg
moscovita *adj & nmf* : Muscovite
mosquearse *vr* **1** : to become suspicious
 2 : to take offense
mosquete *nm* : musket
mosquetero *nm* : musketeer
mosquitero *nm* : mosquito net
mosquito *nm* ZANCUDO : mosquito
mostachón *nm, pl* **-chones** : macaroon
mostaza *nf* : mustard
mostrador *nm* : counter (in a store)
mostrar {19} *vt* **1** : to show **2** EXHIBIR
 : to exhibit, to display — **mostrarse** *vr*
 : to show oneself, to appear
mota *nf* **1** : fleck, speck **2** : defect, blemish
mote *nm* SOBRENOMBRE : nickname
moteado, -da *adj* : dotted, spotted, dappled
motel *nm* : motel
motín *nm, pl* **motines 1** : riot **2** : rebellion, mutiny
motivación *nf, pl* **-ciones** : motivation
 — **motivacional** *adj*
motivar *vt* **1** CAUSAR : to cause **2** IM-
 PULSAR : to motivate
motivo *nm* **1** MÓVIL : motive **2** CAUSA
 : cause, reason **3** TEMA : theme, motif
moto *nf* : motorcycle, motorbike
motocicleta *nf* : motorcycle
motociclismo *nm* : motorcycling
motociclista *nmf* : motorcyclist
motor[1], **-ra** *adj* MOTRIZ : motor
motor[2] *nm* **1** : motor, engine **2** : driving
 force, cause
motorista *nmf* : motorist
motriz *adj, pl* **motrices** : driving
motu proprio *adv* **de motu proprio** [de
 'motu'proprio] : voluntarily, of one's
 own accord
mousse ['mus] *nmf* : mousse
mover {47} *vt* **1** TRASLADAR : to move,
 to shift **2** AGITAR : to shake, to nod
 (the head) **3** ACCIONAR : to power, to
 drive **4** INDUCIR : to provoke, to cause
 5 : to excite, to stir — **moverse** *vr* **1**

: to move, to move over **2** : to hurry,
 to get a move on **3** : to get moving, to
 make an effort
movible *adj* : movable
movida *nf* : move (in a game)
móvil[1] *adj* : mobile
móvil[2] *nm* **1** MOTIVO : motive **2** : mobile
movilidad *nf* : mobility
movilizar {21} *vt* : to mobilize — **movi-
 lización** *nf*
movimiento *nm* : movement, motion
 ⟨movimiento del cuerpo : bodily move-
 ment⟩ ⟨movimiento sindicalista : labor
 movement⟩
mozo[1], **-za** *adj* : young, youthful
mozo[2], **-za** *n* **1** JOVEN : young man *m*,
 young woman *f*, youth **2** : helper, servant **3** *Arg, Chile, Col, Peru* : waiter *m*,
 waitress *f*
mucamo, -ma *n* : servant, maid *f*
muchacha *nf* : maid
muchacho, -cha *n* **1** : kid, boy *m*, girl *f*
 2 JOVEN : young man *m*, young woman
 f
muchedumbre *nf* MULTITUD : crowd,
 multitude
mucho[1] *adv* **1** : much, a lot ⟨mucho más
 : much more⟩ ⟨le gusta mucho : he
 likes it a lot⟩ **2** : long, a long time
 ⟨tardó mucho en venir : he was a long
 time getting here⟩ **3 por mucho que**
 : no matter how much
mucho[2], **-cha** *adj* **1** : a lot of, many,
 much ⟨mucha gente : a lot of people⟩
 ⟨hace mucho tiempo que no lo veo : I
 haven't seen him in ages⟩ **2 muchas
 veces** : often
mucho[3], **-cha** *pron* **1** : a lot, many, much
 ⟨hay mucho que hacer : there is a lot
 to do⟩ ⟨muchas no vinieron : many did-
 n't come⟩ **2 cuando ~** *or* **como ~**
 : at most **3 con ~** : by far **4 ni mucho menos** : not at all, far from it
mucílago *nm* : mucilage
mucosidad *nf* : mucus
mucoso, -sa *adj* : mucous, slimy
muda *nf* **1** : change ⟨muda de ropa
 : change of clothes⟩ **2** : molt, molting
mudanza *nf* **1** CAMBIO : change **2**
 TRASLADO : move, moving
mudar *v* **1** CAMBIAR : to change **2** : to
 molt, to shed — **mudarse** *vr* **1**
 TRASLADARSE : to move (one's residence) **2** : to change (clothes)
mudo[1], **-da** *adj* SILENCIOSO : silent ⟨el
 cine mudo : silent films⟩ **2** : mute,
 dumb
mudo[2], **-da** *n* : mute
mueble *nm* **1** : piece of furniture **2
 muebles** *nmpl* : furniture, furnishings
mueblería *nf* : furniture store
mueca *nf* : grimace, face
muela *nf* **1** : tooth, molar ⟨dolor de
 muelas : toothache⟩ ⟨muela de juicio
 : wisdom tooth⟩ **2** : millstone **3** : whetstone
muele, *etc.* → **moler**

muelle[1] *adj* : soft, comfortable, easy
muelle[2] *nm* **1** : wharf, dock **2** RESORTE : spring
muérdago *nm* : mistletoe
muerde, etc. → **morder**
muere, etc. → **morir**
muerte *nf* : death
muerto[1] *pp* → **morir**
muerto[2], **-ta** *adj* **1** : dead **2** : lifeless, flat, dull **3** ~ **de** : dying of ⟨estoy muerto de hambre : I'm dying of hunger⟩
muerto[3], **-ta** *nm* DIFUNTO : dead person, deceased
muesca *nf* : nick, notch
muestra[1], **etc.** → **mostrar**
muestra[2] *nf* **1** : sample **2** SEÑAL : sign, show ⟨una muestra de respeto : a show of respect⟩ **3** EXPOSICIÓN : exhibition, exposition **4** : pattern, model
mueve, etc. → **mover**
mugido *nm* : moo, lowing, bellow
mugir {35} *vi* : to moo, to low, to bellow
mugre *nf* SUCIEDAD : grime, filth
mugriento, -ta *adj* : filthy
muguete *nm* : lily of the valley
muja, etc. → **mugir**
mujer *nf* **1** : woman **2** ESPOSA : wife
mulato, -ta *adj & n* : mulatto
muleta *nf* : crutch
mullido, -da *adj* **1** : soft, fluffy **2** : spongy, springy
mulo, -la *n* : mule
multa *nf* : fine
multar *vt* : to fine
multicolor *adj* : multicolored
multicultural *adj* : multicultural
multidisciplinario, -ria *adj* : multidisciplinary
multifacético, -ca *adj* : multifaceted
multifamiliar *adj* : multifamily
multilateral *adj* : multilateral
multimedia *nf* : multimedia
multimillonario, -ria *n* : multimillionaire
multinacional *adj* : multinational
múltiple *adj* : multiple
multiplicación *nf, pl* **-ciones** : multiplication
multiplicar {72} *v* **1** : to multiply **2** : to increase — **multiplicarse** *vr* : to multiply, to reproduce
multiplicidad *nf* : multiplicity
múltiplo *nm* : multiple
multitud *nf* MUCHEDUMBRE : crowd, multitude
multiuso, -sa *adj* : multipurpose
multivitamínico, -ca *adj* : multivitamin
mundano, -na *adj* : worldly, earthly
mundial *adj* : world, worldwide
mundialmente *adv* : worldwide, all over the world

mundo *nm* **1** : world **2 todo el mundo** : everyone, everybody
municiones *nfpl* : ammunition, munitions
municipal *adj* : municipal
municipio *nm* **1** : municipality **2** AYUNTAMIENTO : town council
muñeca *nf* **1** : doll **2** MANIQUÍ : mannequin **3** : wrist
muñeco *nm* **1** : doll, boy doll **2** MARIONETA : puppet
muñón *nm, pl* **muñones** : stump (of an arm or leg)
mural *adj & nm* : mural
muralista *nmf* : muralist
muralla *nf* : rampart, wall
murciélago *nm* : bat (animal)
murga *nf* : band of street musicians
murió, etc. → **morir**
murmullo *nm* **1** : murmur, murmuring **2** : rustling, rustle ⟨el murmullo de las hojas : the rustling of the leaves⟩
murmurar *vt* **1** : to murmur, to mutter **2** : to whisper (gossip) — *vi* **1** : to murmur **2** CHISMEAR : to gossip
muro *nm* : wall
musa *nf* : muse
musaraña *nf* : shrew
muscular *adj* : muscular
musculatura *nf* : muscles *pl,* musculature
músculo *nm* : muscle
musculoso, -sa *adj* : muscular, brawny
muselina *nf* : muslin
museo *nm* : museum
musgo *nm* : moss
musgoso, -sa *adj* : mossy
música *nf* : music
musical *adj* : musical — **musicalmente** *adv*
músico[1], **-ca** *adj* : musical
músico[2], **-ca** *n* : musician
musitar *vt* : to mumble, to murmur
muslo *nm* : thigh
musulmán, -mana *adj & n, mpl* **-manes** : Muslim
mutación *nf, pl* **-ciones** : mutation
mutante *adj & nm* : mutant
mutar *v* : to mutate
mutilar *vt* : to mutilate — **mutilación** *nf*
mutis *nm* **1** : exit (in theater) **2** : silence
mutual *adj* : mutual
mutuo, -tua *adj* : mutual, reciprocal — **mutuamente** *adv*
muy *adv* **1** : very, quite ⟨es muy inteligente : she's very intelligent⟩ ⟨muy bien : very well, fine⟩ ⟨eso es muy americano : that's typically American⟩ **2** : too ⟨es muy grande para él : it's too big for him⟩

N

n *nf* : fourteenth letter of the Spanish alphabet

nabo *nm* : turnip

nácar *nm* MADREPERLA : nacre, mother-of-pearl

nacarado, -da *adj* : pearly

nacer {48} *vi* **1** : to be born ⟨nací en Guatemala : I was born in Guatemala⟩ ⟨no nació ayer : he wasn't born yesterday⟩ **2** : to hatch **3** : to bud, to sprout **4** : to rise, to originate **5 nacer para algo** : to be born to be something **6 volver a nacer** : to have a lucky escape

nacido¹, -da *adj* **1** : born **2 recién nacido** : newborn

nacido², -da *n* **1 los nacidos** : those born (at a particular time) **2 recién nacido** : newborn baby

naciente *adj* **1** : newfound, growing **2** : rising ⟨el sol naciente : the rising sun⟩

nacimiento *nm* **1** : birth **2** : source (of a river) **3** : beginning, origin **4** BELÉN : Nativity scene, crèche

nación *nf, pl* **naciones** : nation, country, people (of a country)

nacional¹ *adj* : national

nacional² *nmf* CIUDADANO : national, citizen

nacionalidad *nf* : nationality

nacionalismo *nm* : nationalism

nacionalista¹ *adj* : nationalist, nationalistic

nacionalista² *nmf* : nationalist

nacionalización *nf, pl* **-ciones 1** : nationalization **2** : naturalization

nacionalizar {21} *vt* **1** : to nationalize **2** : to naturalize (as a citizen) — **nacionalizarse** *vr*

naco, -ca *adj Mex* : trashy, vulgar, common

nada¹ *adv* : not at all, not in the least ⟨no estamos nada cansados : we are not at all tired⟩

nada² *nf* **1** : nothingness **2** : smidgen, bit ⟨una nada le disgusta : the slightest thing upsets him⟩

nada³ *pron* **1** : nothing ⟨no estoy haciendo nada : I'm not doing anything⟩ **2 casi nada** : next to nothing **3 de ~** : you're welcome **4 dentro de nada** : very soon, in no time **5 nada más** : nothing else, nothing more

nadador, -dora *n* : swimmer

nadar *vi* **1** : to swim **2 ~ en** : to be swimming in, to be rolling in — *vt* : to swim

nadería *nf* : small thing, trifle

nadie *pron* : nobody, no one ⟨no vi a nadie : I didn't see anyone⟩

nadir *nm* : nadir

nado *nm* **1** *Mex* : swimming **2 a ~** : swimming ⟨cruzó el río a nado : he swam across the river⟩

nafta *nf* **1** : naphtha **2** (*in various countries*) : gasoline

naftalina *nf* : naphthalene, mothballs *pl*

náhuatl¹ *adj & nmf, pl* **nahuas** : Nahuatl

náhuatl² *nm* : Nahuatl (language)

nailon → **nilón**

naipe *nm* : playing card

nalga *nf* **1** : buttock **2 nalgas** *nfpl* : buttocks, bottom

nalgada *nf* : smack on the bottom, spanking

namibio, -bia *adj & n* : Namibian

nana *nf* **1** : lullaby **2** *fam* : grandma **3** *CA, Col, Mex, Ven* : nanny

nanay *interj fam* : no way!, not likely!

naranja¹ *adj & nm* : orange (color)

naranja² *nf* : orange (fruit)

naranjal *nm* : orange grove

naranjo *nm* : orange tree

narcisismo *nm* : narcissism

narcisista¹ *adj* : narcissistic

narcisista² *nmf* : narcissist

narciso *nm* : narcissus, daffodil

narcótico¹, -ca *adj* : narcotic

narcótico² *nm* : narcotic

narcotizar {21} *vt* : to drug, to dope

narcotraficante *nmf* : drug trafficker

narcotráfico *nm* : drug trafficking

narigón, -gona *adj, mpl* **-gones** : big-nosed

narigudo → **narigón**

nariz *nf, pl* **narices 1** : nose ⟨sonar(se) la nariz : to blow one's nose⟩ **2** : sense of smell

narración *nf, pl* **-ciones** : narration, account

narrador, -dora *n* : narrator

narrar *vt* : to narrate, to tell

narrativa *nf* : narrative, story

narrativo, -va *adj* : narrative

narval *nm* : narwhal

nasa *nf* : creel

nasal *adj* : nasal

nata *nf* **1** : cream ⟨nata batida : whipped cream⟩ **2** : skin (on boiled milk)

natación *nf, pl* **-ciones** : swimming

natal *adj* : native, natal

natalicio *nm* : birthday ⟨el natalicio de George Washington : George Washington's birthday⟩

natalidad *nf* : birthrate

natillas *nfpl* : custard

natividad *nf* : birth, nativity

nativo, -va *adj & n* : native

nato, -ta *adj* : born, natural

natural¹ *adj* **1** : natural **2** : normal ⟨como es natural : naturally, as expected⟩ **3 ~ de** : native of, from **4 de tamaño natural** : life-size

natural² *nm* **1** CARÁCTER : disposition, temperament **2** : native ⟨un natural de Venezuela : a native of Venezuela⟩

naturaleza *nf* **1** : nature ⟨la madre naturaleza : mother nature⟩ **2** ÍNDOLE : nature, disposition, constitution ⟨la naturaleza humana : human nature⟩ **3 naturaleza muerta** : still life

naturalidad *nf* : simplicity, naturalness
naturalismo *nm* : naturalism
naturalista[1] *adj* : naturalistic
naturalista[2] *nmf* : naturalist
naturalización *nf, pl* **-ciones** : naturalization
naturalizar {21} *vt* : to naturalize — **naturalizarse** *vr* NACIONALIZARSE : to become naturalized
naturalmente *adv* **1** : naturally, inherently **2** : of course
naufragar {52} *vi* **1** : to be shipwrecked **2** FRACASAR : to fail, to collapse
naufragio *nm* **1** : shipwreck **2** FRACASO : failure, collapse
náufrago[1], **-ga** *adj* : shipwrecked, castaway
náufrago[2], **-ga** *n* : shipwrecked person, castaway
náusea *nf* **1** : nausea **2 dar náuseas** : to nauseate, to disgust **3 náuseas matutinas** : morning sickness
nauseabundo, -da *adj* : nauseating, sickening
náutica *nf* : navigation
náutico, -ca *adj* : nautical
nautilo *nm* : nautilus
navaja *nf* **1** : pocketknife, penknife ⟨navaja de muelle : switchblade⟩ **2 navaja de afeitar** : straight razor, razor blade
navajo, -ja *adj & n* : Navajo
naval *adj* : naval
nave *nf* **1** : ship ⟨nave capitana : flagship⟩ ⟨nave espacial : spaceship⟩ **2** : nave ⟨nave lateral : aisle⟩ **3 quemar uno sus naves** : to burn one's bridges
navegabilidad *nf* : navigability
navegable *adj* : navigable
navegación *nf, pl* **-ciones** : navigation
navegante[1] *adj* : sailing, seafaring
navegante[2] *nmf* : navigator
navegar {52} *v* : to navigate, to sail
Navidad *nf* : Christmas, Christmastime ⟨Feliz Navidad : Merry Christmas⟩
navideño, -ña *adj* : Christmas
naviero, -ra *adj* : shipping
náyade *nf* : naiad
nazca, etc. → **nacer**
nazi *adj & nmf* : Nazi
nazismo *nm* : Nazism
nébeda *nf* : catnip
neblina *nf* : light fog, mist
neblinoso, -sa *adj* : misty, foggy
nebulosa *nf* : nebula
nebulosidad *nf* : mistiness, haziness
nebuloso, -sa *adj* **1** : hazy, misty **2** : nebulous, vague
necedad *nf* : stupidity, foolishness ⟨decir necedades : to talk nonsense⟩
necesariamente *adv* : necessarily
necesario, -ria *adj* **1** : necessary **2 si es necesario** : if need be **3 hacerse necesario** : to be required
neceser *nm* : toilet kit, vanity case
necesidad *nf* **1** : need, necessity **2** : poverty, want **3 necesidades** *nfpl* : hardships **4 hacer sus necesidades** : to relieve oneself

necesitado, -da *adj* : needy
necesitar *vt* **1** : to need **2** : to necessitate, to require — *vi* ∼ **de** : to have need of
necio[1], **-cia** *adj* **1** : foolish, silly, dumb **2** *fam* : naughty
necio[2], **-cia** *n* ESTÚPIDO : fool, idiot
necrología *nf* : obituary
necrópolis *nfs & pl* : cemetery
néctar *nm* : nectar
nectarina *nf* : nectarine
neerlandés[1], **-desa** *adj, mpl* **-deses** HOLANDÉS : Dutch
neerlandés[2], **-desa** *n, mpl* **-deses** HOLANDÉS : Dutch person, Dutchman *m*
nefando, -da *adj* : unspeakable, heinous
nefario, -ria *adj* : nefarious
nefasto, -ta *adj* **1** : ill-fated, unlucky **2** : disastrous, terrible
negación *nf, pl* **-ciones** **1** : negation, denial **2** : negative (in grammar)
negar {49} *vt* **1** : to deny **2** REHUSAR : to refuse **3** : to disown — **negarse** *vr* **1** : to refuse **2** : to deny oneself
negativa *nf* **1** : denial **2** : refusal
negativo[1], **-va** *adj* : negative
negativo[2] *nm* : negative (of a photograph)
negligé *nm* : negligee
negligencia *nf* : negligence
negligente *adj* : neglectful, negligent — **negligentemente** *adv*
negociable *adj* : negotiable
negociación *nf, pl* **-ciones** **1** : negotiation **2 negociación colectiva** : collective bargaining
negociador, -dora *n* : negotiator
negociante *nmf* : businessman *m*, businesswoman *f*
negociar *vt* : to negotiate — *vi* : to deal, to do business
negocio *nm* **1** : business, place of business **2** : deal, transaction **3 negocios** *nmpl* : commerce, trade, business
negrero, -ra *n* **1** : slave trader **2** *fam* : slave driver, brutal boss
negrita *nf* : boldface (type)
negro[1], **-gra** *adj* **1** : black, dark **2** BRONCEADO : suntanned **3** : gloomy, awful, desperate ⟨la cosa se está poniendo negra : things are looking bad⟩ **4 mercado negro** : black market
negro[2], **-gra** *n* **1** : dark-skinned person, black person **2** *fam* : darling, dear
negro[3] *nm* : black (color)
negrura *nf* : blackness
negruzco, -ca *adj* : blackish
nene, -na *n* : baby, small child
nenúfar *nm* : water lily
neocelandés → **neozelandés**
neoclasicismo *nm* : neoclassicism
neoclásico, -ca *adj* : neoclassical
neófito, -ta *n* : neophyte, novice
neologismo *nm* : neologism
neón *nm, pl* **neones** : neon
neoyorquino[1], **-na** *adj* : of or from New York

neoyorquino[2], **-na** *n* : New Yorker
neozelandés[1], **-desa** *adj, mpl* **-deses**
 : of or from New Zealand
neozelandés[2], **-desa** *n, mpl* **-deses**
 : New Zealander
nepalés, -lesa *adj & n, mpl* **-leses**
 : Nepali
nepotismo *nm* : nepotism
neptunio *nm* : neptunium
Neptuno *nm* : Neptune
nervio *nm* **1** : nerve **2** : tendon, sinew,
 gristle (in meat) **3** : energy, drive **4**
 : rib (of a vault) **5 nervios** *nmpl*
 : nerves ⟨estar mal de los nervios : to
 be a bundle of nerves⟩ ⟨ataque de
 nervios : nervous breakdown⟩
nerviosamente *adv* : nervously
nerviosidad → **nerviosismo**
nerviosismo *nf* : nervousness, anxiety
nervioso, -sa *adj* **1** : nervous, nerve ⟨sis-
 tema nervioso : nervous system⟩ **2**
 : high-strung, restless, anxious ⟨pon-
 erse nervioso : to get nervous⟩ **3** : vigorous, energetic
nervudo, -da *adj* : sinewy, wiry
neta *nf Mex fam* : truth ⟨la neta es que
 me cae mal : the truth is, I don't like
 her⟩
netamente *adv* : clearly, obviously
neto, -ta *adj* **1** : net ⟨peso neto : net
 weight⟩ **2** : clear, distinct
neumático[1], **-ca** *adj* : pneumatic
neumático[2] *nm* LLANTA : tire
neumonía *nf* PULMONÍA : pneumonia
neural *adj* : neural
neuralgia *nf* : neuralgia
neuritis *nf* : neuritis
neurología *nf* : neurology
neurológico, -ca *adj* : neurological,
 neurologic
neurólogo, -ga *n* : neurologist
neurosis *nfs & pl* : neurosis
neurótico, -ca *adj & n* : neurotic
neutral *adj* : neutral
neutralidad *nf* : neutrality
neutralizar {21} *vt* : to neutralize — **neutralización** *nf*
neutro, -tra *adj* **1** : neutral **2** : neuter
neutrón *nm, pl* **neutrones** : neutron
nevada *nf* : snowfall
nevado, -da *adj* **1** : snowcapped **2**
 : snow-white
nevar {55} *v impers* : to snow
nevasca *nf* : snowstorm, blizzard
nevera *nf* REFRIGERADOR : refrigerator
nevería *nf Mex* : ice cream parlor
nevisca *nf* : light snowfall, flurry
nevoso, -sa *adj* : snowy
nexo *nm* VÍNCULO : link, connection,
 nexus
ni *conj* **1** : neither, nor ⟨afuera no hace
 ni frío ni calor : it's neither cold nor
 hot outside⟩ **2 ni que** : not even if, not
 as if ⟨ni que me pagaran : not even if
 they paid me⟩ ⟨ni que fuera (yo) su
 madre : it's not as if I were his moth-
 er⟩ **3 ni siquiera** : not even ⟨ni siquiera
 nos llamaron : they didn't even call us⟩

nicaragüense *adj & nmf* : Nicaraguan
nicho *nm* : niche
nicotina *nf* : nicotine
nido *nm* **1** : nest **2** : hiding place, den
niebla *nf* : fog, mist
niega, niegue etc. → **negar**
nieto, -ta *n* **1** : grandson *m*, granddaughter *f* **2 nietos** *nmpl* : grandchil-
 dren
nieva, etc. → **nevar**
nieve *nf* **1** : snow **2** *Cuba, Mex, PRi*
 : sherbet
nigeriano, -na *adj & n* : Nigerian
nigua *nf* : sand flea, chigger
nihilismo *nm* : nihilism
nilón *or* **nilon** *nm, pl* **nilones** : nylon
nimbo *nm* **1** : halo **2** : nimbus
nimiedad *nf* INSIGNIFICANCIA : trifle,
 triviality
nimio, -mia *adj* INSIGNIFICANTE : insignificant, trivial
ninfa *nf* : nymph
ningunear *vt Mex fam* : to disrespect
ninguno[1], **-na** (**ningún** *before masculine
 singular nouns*) *adj, mpl* **ningunos** : no,
 none ⟨no es ninguna tonta : she's no
 fool⟩ ⟨no debe hacerse en ningún momento : that should never be done⟩
ninguno[2], **-na** *pron* **1** : neither, none
 ⟨ninguno de los dos ha vuelto aún : neither one has returned yet⟩ **2** : no one,
 no other ⟨te quiero más que a ninguna : I love you more than any other⟩
niña *nf* **1** PUPILA : pupil (of the eye) **2**
 la niña de los ojos : the apple of one's
 eye
niñada *nf* **1** : childishness **2** : trifle, silly thing
niñería → **niñada**
niñero, -ra *n* : baby-sitter, nanny
niñez *nf, pl* **niñeces** INFANCIA : childhood
niño, -ña *n* : child, boy *m*, girl *f*
niobio *nm* : niobium
nipón, -pona *adj & n, mpl* **nipones**
 JAPONÉS : Japanese
níquel *nm* : nickel
nitidez *nf, pl* **-deces** CLARIDAD : clarity, vividness, sharpness
nítido, -da *adj* CLARO : clear, vivid, sharp
nitrato *nm* : nitrate
nítrico, -ca *adj* **ácido nítrico** : nitric acid
nitrito *nm* : nitrite
nitrógeno *nm* : nitrogen
nitroglicerina *nf* : nitroglycerin
nivel *nm* **1** : level, height ⟨nivel del mar
 : sea level⟩ **2** : level, standard ⟨nivel
 de vida : standard of living⟩
nivelar *vt* : to level (out)
nixtamal *nm Mex* : limed corn used for
 tortillas
no *adv* **1** : no ⟨¿quieres ir al mercado?
 no, voy más tarde : do you want to go
 shopping? no, I'm going later⟩ **2** : not
 ⟨¡no hagas eso! : don't do that!⟩ ⟨creo
 que no : I don't think so⟩ **3** : non- ⟨no
 fumador : non-smoker⟩ **4 ¡como no!**
 : of course! **5 no bien** : as soon as, no
 sooner

nobelio *nm* : nobelium
noble[1] *adj* : noble — **noblemente** *adv*
noble[2] *nmf* : nobleman *m*, noblewoman *f*
nobleza *nf* **1** : nobility **2** HONRADEZ : honesty, integrity
nocaut *nm* : knockout, KO
noche *nf* **1** : night, nighttime, evening **2 buenas noches** : good evening, good night **3 de noche** *or* **por la noche** : at night **4 hacerse de noche** : to get dark
Nochebuena *nf* : Christmas Eve
nochecita *nf* : dusk
Nochevieja *nf* : New Year's Eve
noción *nf, pl* **nociones 1** CONCEPTO : notion, concept **2 nociones** *nfpl* : smattering, rudiments *pl*
nocivo, -va *adj* DAÑINO : harmful, noxious
noctámbulo, -la *n* **1** : sleepwalker **2** : night owl
nocturno[1]**, -na** *adj* : night, nocturnal
nocturno[2] *nm* : nocturne
nodriza *nf* : wet nurse
nódulo *nm* : nodule
nogal *nm* **1** : walnut tree **2** *Mex* : pecan tree **3 nogal americano** : hickory
nómada[1] *adj* : nomadic
nómada[2] *nmf* : nomad
nomás *adv* : only, just ⟨lo hice nomás porque sí : I did it just because⟩ ⟨nomás de recordarlo me enojo : I get angry just remembering it⟩ ⟨nomás faltan dos semanas para Navidad : there are only two weeks left till Christmas⟩
nombradía *nf* RENOMBRE : fame, renown
nombrado, -da *adj* : famous, well-known
nombramiento *nm* : appointment, nomination
nombrar *vt* **1** : to appoint **2** : to mention, to name
nombre *nm* **1** : name ⟨nombre de pluma : pseudonym, pen name⟩ ⟨en nombre de : on behalf of⟩ ⟨sin nombre : nameless⟩ **2** : noun ⟨nombre propio : proper noun⟩ **3** : fame, renown
nomenclatura *nf* : nomenclature
nomeolvides *nmfs & pl* : forget-me-not
nómina *nf* : payroll
nominación *nf, pl* **-ciones** : nomination
nominal *adj* : nominal — **nominalmente** *adv*
nominar *vt* : to nominate
nominativo[1]**, -va** *adj* : nominative
nominativo[2] *nm* : nominative (case)
nomo *nm* : gnome
non[1] *adj* IMPAR : odd, not even
non[2] *nm* : odd number
nonagésimo[1]**, -ma** *adj* : ninetieth, ninety-
nonagésimo[2]**, -ma** *n* : ninetieth, ninety- (in a series)
nono, -na *adj* : ninth — **nono** *nm*
nopal *nm* : nopal, cactus
nopalitos *nmpl Mex* : pickled cactus leaves
noquear *vt* : to knock out, to KO

norcoreano, -na *adj & n* : North Korean
nordeste[1] *or* **noreste** *adj* **1** : northeastern **2** : northeasterly
nordeste[2] *or* **noreste** *nm* : northeast
nórdico, -ca *adj & n* **1** ESCANDINAVO : Scandinavian **2** : Norse
noreste → **nordeste**
noria *nf* **1** : waterwheel **2** : Ferris wheel
norirlandés[1]**, -desa** *adj, mpl* **-deses** : Northern Irish
norirlandés[2]**, -desa** *n, mpl* **-deses** : person from Northern Ireland
norma *nf* **1** : rule, regulation **2** : norm, standard
normal *adj* **1** : normal, usual **2** : standard **3 escuela normal** : teacher-training college
normalidad *nf* : normality, normalcy
normalización *nf, pl* **-ciones** *nf* **1** REGULARIZACIÓN : normalization **2** ESTANDARIZACIÓN : standardization
normalizar {21} *vt* **1** REGULARIZAR : to normalize **2** ESTANDARIZAR : to standardize — **normalizarse** *vr* : to return to normal
normalmente *adv* GENERALMENTE : ordinarily, generally
noroeste[1] *adj* **1** : northwestern **2** : northwesterly
noroeste[2] *nm* : northwest
norte[1] *adj* : north, northern
norte[2] *nm* **1** : north **2** : north wind **3** META : aim, objective
norteamericano, -na *adj & n* **1** : North American **2** AMERICANO, ESTADOUNIDENSE : American, native or inhabitant of the United States
norteño[1]**, -ña** *adj* : northern
norteño[2]**, -ña** *n* : Northerner
noruego[1]**, -ga** *adj & n* : Norwegian
noruego[2] *nm* : Norwegian (language)
nos *pron* **1** : us ⟨nos enviaron a la frontera : they sent us to the border⟩ **2** : ourselves ⟨nos divertimos muchísimo : we enjoyed ourselves a great deal⟩ **3** : each other, one another ⟨nos vimos desde lejos : we saw each other from far away⟩ **4** : to us, for us, from us ⟨nos lo dio : he gave it to us⟩ ⟨nos lo compraron : they bought it from us⟩
nosotros, -tras *pron* **1** : we ⟨nosotros llegamos ayer : we arrived yesterday⟩ **2** : us ⟨ven con nosotros : come with us⟩ **3 nosotros mismos** : ourselves ⟨lo arreglamos nosotros mismos : we fixed it ourselves⟩
nostalgia *nf* **1** : nostalgia, longing **2** : homesickness
nostálgico, -ca *adj* **1** : nostalgic **2** : homesick
nota *nf* **1** : note, message **2** : announcement ⟨nota de prensa : press release⟩ **3** : grade, mark (in school) **4** : characteristic, feature, touch **5** : note (in music) **6** : bill, check (in a restaurant)

notable *adj* **1** : notable, noteworthy **2** : outstanding

notación *nf, pl* **-ciones** : notation

notar *vt* **1** : to notice ⟨hacer notar algo : to point out something⟩ **2** : to tell ⟨la diferencia se nota inmediatamente : you can tell the difference right away⟩ — **notarse** *vr* **1** : to be evident, to show **2** : to feel, to seem

notario, -ria *n* : notary, notary public

noticia *nf* **1** : news item, piece of news **2 noticias** *nfpl* : news

noticiero *nm* : news program, newscast

noticioso, -sa *adj* : news ⟨agencia noticiosa : news agency⟩

notificación *nf, pl* **-ciones** : notification

notificar {72} *vt* : to notify, to inform

notoriedad *nf* **1** : knowledge, obviousness **2** : fame, notoriety

notorio, -ria *adj* **1** OBVIO : obvious, evident **2** CONOCIDO : well-known

novato¹, -ta *adj* : inexperienced, new

novato², -ta *n* : beginner, novice

novecientos¹, -tas *adj* : nine hundred

novecientos² *nms & pl* : nine hundred

novedad *nf* **1** : newness, novelty **2** : innovation

novedoso, -sa *adj* : original, novel

novel *adj* NOVATO : inexperienced, new

novela *nf* **1** : novel **2** : soap opera

novelar *vt* : to fictionalize, to make a novel out of

novelesco, -ca *adj* **1** : fictional **2** : fantastic, fabulous

novelista *nmf* : novelist

novena *nf* : novena

noveno, -na *adj* : ninth — **noveno, -na** *n*

noventa *adj & nm* : ninety

noventavo¹, -va *adj* : ninetieth

noventavo² *nm* : ninetieth (fraction)

noviazgo *nm* **1** : courtship, relationship **2** : engagement, betrothal

novicio, -cia *n* **1** : novice (in religion) **2** PRINCIPIANTE : novice, beginner

noviembre *nm* : November

novilla *nf* : heifer

novillada *nf* : bullfight featuring young bulls

novillero, -ra *n* : apprentice bullfighter

novillo *nm* : young bull

novio, -via *n* **1** : boyfriend *m*, girlfriend *f* **2** PROMETIDO : fiancé *m*, fiancée *f* **3** : bridegroom *m*, bride *f*

novocaína *nf* : novocaine

nubarrón *nm, pl* **-rrones** : storm cloud

nube *nf* **1** : cloud ⟨andar en las nubes : to have one's head in the clouds⟩ ⟨por las nubes : sky-high⟩ **2** : cloud (of dust), swarm (of insects, etc.)

nublado¹, -da *adj* **1** NUBOSO : cloudy, overcast **2** : clouded, dim

nublado² *nm* **1** : storm cloud **2** AMENAZA : menace, threat

nublar *vt* **1** : to cloud **2** OSCURECER : to obscure — **nublarse** *vr* : to get cloudy

nubosidad *nf* : cloudiness

nuboso, -sa *adj* NUBLADO : cloudy

nuca *nf* : nape, back of the neck

nuclear *adj* : nuclear

núcleo *nm* **1** : nucleus **2** : center, heart, core

nudillo *nm* : knuckle

nudismo *nm* : nudism

nudista *adj & nmf* : nudist

nudo *nm* **1** : knot ⟨nudo de rizo : square knot⟩ ⟨un nudo en la garganta : a lump in one's throat⟩ **2** : node **3** : junction, hub ⟨nudo de comunicaciones : communication center⟩ **4** : crux, heart (of a problem, etc.)

nudoso, -sa *adj* : knotty, gnarled

nuera *nf* : daughter-in-law

nuestro¹, -tra *adj* : our

nuestro², -tra *pron* (*with definite article*) : ours, our own ⟨el nuestro es más grande : ours is bigger⟩ ⟨es de los nuestros : it's one of ours⟩

nuevamente *adv* : again, anew

nuevas *nfpl* : tidings *pl*

nueve *adj & nm* : nine

nuevecito, -ta *adj* : brand-new

nuevo, -va *adj* **1** : new ⟨una casa nueva : a new house⟩ ⟨¿qué hay de nuevo? : what's new?⟩ **2 de ~** : again, once more **3 Nuevo Testamento** : New Testament

nuez *nf, pl* **nueces** **1** : nut **2** : walnut **3** *Mex* : pecan **4 nuez de Adán** : Adam's apple **5 nuez moscada** : nutmeg

nulidad *nf* **1** : nullity **2** : incompetent person ⟨¡es una nulidad! : he's hopeless!⟩

nulo, -la *adj* **1** : null, null and void **2** INEPTO : useless, inept ⟨es nula para la cocina : she's hopeless at cooking⟩

numen *nm* : poetic muse, inspiration

numerable *adj* : countable

numeración *nf, pl* **-ciones** **1** : numbering **2** : numbers *pl*, numerals *pl* ⟨numeración romana : Roman numerals⟩

numerador *nm* : numerator

numeral *adj* : numeral

numerar *vt* : to number

numerario, -ria *adj* : long-standing, permanent ⟨profesor numerario : tenured professor⟩

numérico, -ca *adj* : numerical — **numéricamente** *adv*

número *nm* **1** : number ⟨número impar : odd number⟩ ⟨número ordinal : ordinal number⟩ ⟨número arábico : Arabic numeral⟩ ⟨número quebrado : fraction⟩ **2** : issue (of a publication) **3 sin ~** : countless

numeroso, -sa *adj* : numerous

numismática *nf* : numismatics

nunca *adv* **1** : never, ever ⟨nunca es tarde : it's never too late⟩ ⟨no trabaja casi nunca : he hardly ever works⟩ **2 nunca más** : never again **3 nunca jamás** : never ever

nuncio *nm* : harbinger, herald

nupcial *adj* : nuptial, wedding

nupcias *nfpl* : nuptials *pl*, wedding

nutria *nf* **1** : otter **2** : nutria
nutrición *nf, pl* **-ciones** : nutrition, nourishment
nutrido, -da *adj* **1** : nourished ⟨mal nutrido : undernourished, malnourished⟩ **2** : considerable, abundant ⟨de nutrido : full of, abounding in⟩
nutriente *nm* : nutrient
nutrimento *nm* : nutriment
nutrir *vt* **1** ALIMENTAR : to feed, to nourish **2** : to foster, to provide
nutritivo, -va *adj* : nourishing, nutritious

nylon → **nilón**
ñ *nf* : fifteenth letter of the Spanish alphabet
ñame *nm* : yam
ñandú *nm* : rhea
ñapa *nf* : extra amount ⟨de ñapa : for good measure⟩
ñoñear *vi fam* : to whine
ñoño, -ña *adj fam* : whiny, fussy ⟨no seas tan ñoño : don't be such a wimp⟩
ñoquis *nmpl* : gnocchi *pl*
ñu *nm* : gnu, wildebeest

O

o[1] *nf* : sixteenth letter of the Spanish alphabet
o[2] *conj* (**u** *before words beginning with o- or ho-*) **1** : or ⟨¿vienes con nosotros o te quedas? : are you coming with us or staying?⟩ **2** : either ⟨o vienes con nosotros o te quedas : either you come with us or you stay⟩ **3 o sea** : that is to say, in other words
oasis *nms & pl* : oasis
obcecado, -da *adj* **1** : blinded ⟨obcecado por la ira : blinded by rage⟩ **2** : stubborn, obstinate
obcecar {72} *vt* : to blind (by emotions) — **obcecarse** *vr* : to become stubborn
obedecer {53} *vt* : to obey ⟨obedecer órdenes : to obey orders⟩ ⟨obedece a tus padres : obey your parents⟩ — *vi* **1** : to obey **2** ~ **a** : to respond to **3** ~ **a** : to be due to, to result from
obediencia *nf* : obedience
obediente *adj* : obedient — **obedientemente** *adv*
obelisco *nm* : obelisk
obertura *nf* : overture
obesidad *nf* : obesity
obeso, -sa *adj* : obese
óbice *nm* : obstacle, impediment
obispado *nm* DIÓCESIS : bishopric, diocese
obispo *nm* : bishop
obituario *nm* : obituary
objeción *nf, pl* **-ciones** : objection ⟨ponerle objeciones a algo : to object to something⟩
objetar *v* : to object ⟨no tengo nada que objetar : I have no objections⟩
objetividad *nf* : objectivity
objetivo[1]**, -va** *adj* : objective — **objetivamente** *adv*
objetivo[2] *nm* **1** META : objective, goal, target **2** : lens
objeto *nm* **1** COSA : object, thing **2** OBJETIVO : objective, purpose ⟨con objeto de : in order to, with the aim of⟩ **3 objeto volador no identificado** : unidentified flying object
objetor, -tora *n* : objector ⟨objetor de conciencia : conscientious objector⟩
oblea *nf* **1** : wafer **2 hecho una oblea** *fam* : skinny as a rail

oblicuo, -cua *adj* : oblique — **oblicuamente** *adv*
obligación *nf, pl* **-ciones 1** DEBER : obligation, duty **2** : bond, debenture
obligado, -da *adj* **1** : obliged **2** : obligatory, compulsory **3** : customary
obligar {52} *vt* : to force, to require, to oblige — **obligarse** *vr* : to commit oneself, to undertake (to do something)
obligatorio, -ria *adj* : mandatory, required, compulsory
obliterar *vt* : to obliterate, to destroy — **obliteración** *nf*
oblongo, -ga *adj* : oblong
obnubilación *nf, pl* **-ciones** : bewilderment, confusion
obnubilar *vt* : to daze, to bewilder
oboe[1] *nm* : oboe
oboe[2] *nmf* : oboist
obra *nf* **1** : work ⟨obra de arte : work of art⟩ ⟨obra de teatro : play⟩ ⟨obra de consulta : reference work⟩ **2** : deed ⟨una buena obra : a good deed⟩ **3** : construction work **4 obra maestra** : masterpiece **5 obras públicas** : public works **6 por obra de** : thanks to, because of
obrar *vt* : to work, to produce ⟨obrar milagros : to work miracles⟩ — *vi* **1** : to act, to behave ⟨obrar con cautela : to act with caution⟩ **2 obrar en poder de** : to be in possession of
obrero[1]**, -ra** *adj* : working ⟨la clase obrera : the working class⟩
obrero[2]**, -ra** *n* : worker, laborer
obscenidad *nf* : obscenity
obsceno, -na *adj* : obscene
obscurecer, obscuridad, obscuro → **oscurecer, oscuridad, oscuro**
obsequiar *vt* REGALAR : to give, to present ⟨lo obsequiaron con una placa : they presented him with a plaque⟩
obsequio *nm* REGALO : gift, present
obsequiosidad *nf* : attentiveness, deference
obsequioso, -sa *adj* : obliging, attentive
observable *adj* : observable
observación *nf, pl* **-ciones 1** : observation, watching **2** : remark, comment
observador[1]**, -dora** *adj* : observant

observador[2], **-dora** *n* : observer, watcher

observancia *nf* : observance

observante *adj* : observant ⟨los judíos observantes : observant Jews⟩

observar *vt* **1** : to observe, to watch ⟨estábamos observando a los niños : we were watching the children⟩ **2** NOTAR : to notice **3** ACATAR : to obey, to abide by **4** COMENTAR : to remark, to comment

observatorio *nm* : observatory

obsesión *nf, pl* **-siones** : obsession

obsesionar *vt* : to obsess, to preoccupy excessively — **obsesionarse** *vr*

obsesivo, -va *adj* : obsessive

obseso, -sa *adj* : obsessed

obsolescencia *nf* DESUSO : obsolescence — **obsolescente** *adj*

obsoleto, -ta *adj* DESUSADO : obsolete

obstaculizar {21} *vt* IMPEDIR : to obstruct, to hinder

obstáculo *nm* IMPEDIMENTO : obstacle

obstante[1] *conj* **no obstante** : nevertheless, however

obstante[2] *prep* **no obstante** : in spite of, despite ⟨mantuvo su inocencia no obstante la evidencia : he maintained his innocence in spite of the evidence⟩

obstar *v impers* ∼ **a** *or* ∼ **para** : to hinder, to prevent ⟨eso no obsta para que me vaya : that doesn't prevent me from leaving⟩

obstetra *nmf* TOCÓLOGO : obstetrician

obstetricia *nf* : obstetrics

obstétrico, -ca *adj* : obstetric, obstetrical

obstinación *nf, pl* **-ciones 1** TERQUEDAD : obstinacy, stubbornness **2** : perseverance, tenacity

obstinado, -da *adj* **1** TERCO : obstinate, stubborn **2** : persistent — **obstinadamente** *adv*

obstinarse *vr* EMPECINARSE : to be obstinate, to be stubborn

obstrucción *nf, pl* **-ciones** : obstruction, blockage

obstruccionismo *nm* : obstructionism, filibustering

obstruccionista *adj* : obstructionist, filibustering

obstructor, -tora *adj* : obstructive

obstruir {41} *vt* BLOQUEAR : to obstruct, to block, to clog — **obstruirse** *vr*

obtención *nf* : obtaining, procurement

obtener {80} *vt* : to obtain, to secure, to get — **obtenible** *adj*

obturador *nm* : shutter (of a camera)

obtuso, -sa *adj* : obtuse

obtuvo, etc. → **obtener**

obús *nm, pl* **obuses 1** : mortar (weapon) **2** : mortar shell

obviar *vt* : to get around (a difficulty), to avoid

obvio, -via *adj* : obvious — **obviamente** *adv*

oca *nf* : goose

ocasión *nf, pl* **-siones 1** : occasion, time **2** : opportunity, chance **3** : bargain **4 de** ∼ : secondhand **5 aviso de ocasión** *Mex* : classified ad

ocasional *adj* **1** : occasional **2** : chance, fortuitous

ocasionalmente *adv* **1** : occasionally **2** : by chance

ocasionar *vt* CAUSAR : to cause, to occasion

ocaso *nm* **1** ANOCHECER : sunset, sundown **2** DECADENCIA : decline, fall

occidental *adj* : western, occidental

occidente *nm* **1** OESTE, PONIENTE : west **2 el Occidente** : the West

oceánico, -ca *adj* : oceanic

océano *nm* : ocean

oceanografía *nf* : oceanography

oceanográfico, -ca *adj* : oceanographic

ocelote *nm* : ocelot

ochenta *adj & nm* : eighty

ochentavo[1], **-va** *adj* : eightieth

ochentavo[2] *nm* : eightieth (fraction)

ocho *adj & nm* : eight

ochocientos[1], **-tas** *adj* : eight hundred

ochocientos[2] *ms & pl* : eight hundred

ocio *nm* **1** : free time, leisure **2** : idleness

ociosidad *nf* : idleness, inactivity

ocioso, -sa *adj* **1** INACTIVO : idle, inactive **2** INÚTIL : pointless, useless

ocre *nm* : ocher

octágono *nm* : octagon — **octagonal** *adj*

octava *nf* : octave

octavo, -va *adj* : eighth — **octavo, -va** *n*

octeto *nm* **1** : octet **2** : byte

octogésimo[1], **-ma** *adj* : eightieth, eighty-

octogésimo[2], **-ma** *n* : eightieth, eighty- (in a series)

octubre *nm* : October

ocular *adj* **1** : ocular, eye ⟨músculos oculares : eye muscles⟩ **2 testigo ocular** : eyewitness

oculista *nmf* : oculist, ophthalmologist

ocultación *nf, pl* **-ciones** : concealment

ocultar *vt* ESCONDER : to conceal, to hide — **ocultarse** *vr*

oculto, -ta *adj* **1** ESCONDIDO : hidden, concealed **2** : occult

ocupación *nf, pl* **-ciones 1** : occupation, activity **2** : occupancy **3** EMPLEO : employment, job

ocupacional *adj* : occupational, job-related

ocupado, -da *adj* **1** : busy **2** : taken ⟨este asiento está ocupado : this seat is taken⟩ **3** : occupied ⟨territorios ocupados : occupied territories⟩ **4 señal de ocupado** : busy signal

ocupante *nmf* : occupant

ocupar *vt* **1** : to occupy, to take possession of **2** : to hold (a position) **3** : to employ, to keep busy **4** : to fill (space, time) **5** : to inhabit (a dwelling) **6** : to bother, to concern — **ocuparse** *vr* ∼ **de 1** : to be concerned with **2** : to take care of

ocurrencia *nf* **1** : occurrence, event **2** : witticism **3** : bright idea
ocurrente *adj* **1** : witty **2** : clever, sharp
ocurrir *vi* : to occur, to happen — **ocurrirse** *vr* ~ **a** : to occur to, to strike ⟨se me ocurrió una mejor idea : a better idea occurred to me⟩
oda *nf* : ode
odiar *vt* ABOMINAR, ABORRECER : to hate
odio *nm* : hate, hatred
odioso, -sa *adj* ABOMINABLE, ABORRECIBLE : hateful, detestable
odisea *nf* : odyssey
odontología *nf* : dentistry, dental surgery
odontólogo, -ga *n* : dentist, dental surgeon
oeste¹ *adj* **1** : west, western ⟨la región oeste : the western region⟩ **2** : westerly
oeste² *nm* **1** : west, West **2** : west wind
ofender *vt* AGRAVIAR : to offend, to insult — *vi* : to offend, to be insulting — **ofenderse** *vr* : to take offense
ofensa *nf* : offense, insult
ofensiva *nf* : offensive ⟨pasar a la ofensiva : to go on the offensive⟩
ofensivo, -va *adj* : offensive, insulting
ofensor, -sora *n* : offender
oferente *nmf* **1** : supplier **2** FUENTE : source ⟨un oferente no identificado : an unidentified source⟩
oferta *nf* **1** : offer **2** : sale, bargain ⟨las camisas están en oferta : the shirts are on sale⟩ **3 oferta y demanda** : supply and demand
ofertar *vt* OFRECER : to offer
oficial¹ *adj* : official — **oficialmente** *adv*
oficial² *nmf* **1** : officer, police officer, commissioned officer (in the military) **2** : skilled worker
oficializar {21} *vt* : to make official
oficiante *nmf* : celebrant
oficiar *vt* **1** : to inform officially **2** : to officiate at, to celebrate (Mass) — *vi* ~ **de** : to act as
oficina *nf* : office
oficinista *nmf* : office worker
oficio *nm* **1** : trade, profession ⟨es electricista de oficio : he's an electrician by trade⟩ **2** : function, role **3** : official communication **4** : experience ⟨tener oficio : to be experienced⟩ **5** : religious ceremony
oficioso, -sa *adj* **1** EXTRAOFICIAL : unofficial **2** : officious — **oficiosamente** *adv*
ofrecer {53} *vt* **1** : to offer **2** : to provide, to give **3** : to present (an appearance, etc.) — **ofrecerse** *vr* **1** : to offer oneself, to volunteer **2** : to open up, to present itself
ofrecimiento *nm* : offer, offering
ofrenda *nf* : offering
oftalmología *nf* : ophthalmology
oftalmólogo, -ga *n* : ophthalmologist
ofuscación *nf, pl* **-ciones** : blindness, confusion

ofuscar {72} *vt* **1** : to blind, to dazzle **2** CONFUNDIR : to bewilder, to confuse — **ofuscarse** *vr* ~ **con** : to be blinded by
ogro *nm* : ogre
ohm *nm, pl* **ohms** : ohm
ohmio → **ohm**
oídas *nfpl* **de** ~ : by hearsay
oído *nm* **1** : ear ⟨oído interno : inner ear⟩ **2** : hearing ⟨duro de oído : hard of hearing⟩ **3 tocar de oído** : to play by ear
oiga, etc. → **oír**
oír {50} *vi* : to hear — *vt* **1** : to hear **2** ESCUCHAR : to listen to **3** : to pay attention to, to heed **4 ¡oye!** *or* **¡oiga!** : listen!, excuse me!, look here!
ojal *nm* : buttonhole
ojalá *interj* **1** : I hope so!, if only!, God willing! **2** : I hope, I wish, hopefully ⟨¡ojalá que le vaya bien! : I hope things go well for her!⟩ ⟨¡ojalá no llueva! : hopefully it won't rain!⟩
ojeada *nf* : glimpse, glance ⟨echar una ojeada : to have a quick look⟩
ojear *vt* : to eye, to have a look at
ojete *nm* : eyelet
ojiva *nf* : warhead
ojo *nm* **1** : eye **2** : judgment, sharpness ⟨tener buen ojo para : to be a good judge of, to have a good eye for⟩ **3** : hole (in cheese), eye (in a needle), center (of a storm) **4** : span (of a bridge) **5 a ojos vistas** : openly, publicly **6 andar con ojo** : to be careful **7 ojo de agua** *Mex* : spring, source **8 ¡ojo!** : look out!, pay attention!
ola *nf* **1** : wave **2 ola de calor** : heat wave
oleada *nf* : swell, wave ⟨una oleada de protestas : a wave of protests⟩
oleaje *nm* : waves *pl*, surf
óleo *nm* **1** : oil **2** : oil painting
oleoducto *nm* : oil pipeline
oleoso, -sa *adj* : oily
oler {51} *vt* **1** : to smell **2** INQUIRIR : to pry into, to investigate **3** AVERIGUAR : to smell out, to uncover — *vi* **1** : to smell ⟨huele mal : it smells bad⟩ **2** ~ **a** : to smell like, to smell of ⟨huele a pino : it smells like pine⟩ — **olerse** *vr* : to have a hunch, to suspect
olfatear *vt* **1** : to sniff **2** : to sense, to sniff out
olfativo, -va *adj* : olfactory
olfato *nm* **1** : sense of smell **2** : nose, instinct
oligarquía *nf* : oligarchy
olimpiada *or* **olimpíada** *nf* **1** : Olympiad **2** *or* **olimpiadas** *nfpl* : Olympics *pl*
olímpico, -ca *adj* : Olympic
olisquear *vt* : to sniff at
oliva *nf* ACEITUNA : olive ⟨aceite de oliva : olive oil⟩
olivo *nm* : olive tree
olla *nf* **1** : pot ⟨olla de presión : pressure cooker⟩ **2 olla podrida** : Spanish stew

olmeca *adj & nmf* : Olmec
olmo *nm* : elm
olor *nm* : smell, odor
oloroso, -sa *adj* : scented, fragrant
olote *nm Mex* : cob, corncob
olvidadizo, -za *adj* : forgetful, absent-minded
olvidar *vt* **1** : to forget, to forget about ⟨olvida lo que pasó : forget about what happened⟩ **2** : to leave behind ⟨olvidé mi chequera en la casa : I left my checkbook at home⟩ — **olvidarse** *vr* : to forget ⟨se me olvidó mi cuaderno : I forgot my notebook⟩ ⟨se le olvidó llamarme : he forgot to call me⟩
olvido *nm* **1** : forgetfulness **2** : oblivion **3** DESCUIDO : oversight
omaní *adj & nmf* : Omani
ombligo *nm* : navel, belly button
ombudsman *nmfs & pl* : ombudsman
omelette *nmf* : omelet
ominoso, -sa *adj* : ominous — **ominosamente** *adv*
omisión *nf, pl* **-siones** : omission, neglect
omiso, -sa *adj* **1** NEGLIGENTE : neglectful **2 hacer caso omiso de** : to ignore
omitir *vt* **1** : to omit, to leave out **2** : to fail to ⟨omitió dar su nombre : he failed to give his name⟩
ómnibus *n, pl* **-bus** *or* **-buses** : bus, coach
omnipotencia *nf* : omnipotence
omnipotente *adj* TODOPODEROSO : omnipotent, almighty
omnipresencia *nf* : ubiquity, omnipresence
omnipresente *adj* : ubiquitous, omnipresent
omnisciente *adj* : omniscient — **omnisciencia** *nf*
omnívoro, -ra *adj* : omnivorous
omóplato *or* **omoplato** *nm* : shoulder blade
once *adj & nm* : eleven
onceavo¹, -va *adj* : eleventh
**onceavo² ** *nm* : eleventh (fraction)
onda *nf* **1** : wave, ripple, undulation ⟨onda sonora : sound wave⟩ **2** : wave (in hair) **3** : scallop (on clothing) **4** *fam* : wavelength, understanding ⟨agarrar la onda : to get the point⟩ ⟨en la onda : on the ball, with it⟩ **5 ¿qué onda?** *fam* : what's happening?, what's up?
ondear *vi* : to ripple, to undulate, to flutter
ondulación *nf, pl* **-ciones** : undulation
ondulado, -da *adj* **1** : wavy ⟨pelo ondulado : wavy hair⟩ **2** : undulating
ondulante *adj* : undulating
ondular *vt* : to wave (hair) — *vi* : to undulate, to ripple
oneroso, -sa *adj* GRAVOSO : onerous, burdensome
ónix *nm* : onyx
onza *nf* : ounce

opacar {72} *vt* **1** : to make opaque or dull **2** : to outshine, to overshadow
opacidad *nf* **1** : opacity **2** : dullness
opaco, -ca *adj* **1** : opaque **2** : dull
ópalo *nm* : opal
opción *nf, pl* **opciones** **1** ALTERNATIVA : option, choice **2** : right, chance ⟨tener opción a : to be eligible for⟩
opcional *adj* : optional — **opcionalmente** *adv*
ópera *nf* : opera
operación *nf, pl* **-ciones** **1** : operation **2** : transaction, deal
operacional *adj* : operational
operador, -dora *n* **1** : operator **2** : cameraman, projectionist
operante *adj* : operating, working
operar *vt* **1** : to produce, to bring about **2** INTERVENIR : to operate on **3** *Mex* : to operate, to run (a machine) — *vi* **1** : to operate, to function **2** : to deal, to do business — **operarse** *vr* **1** : to come about, to take place **2** : to have an operation
operario, -ria *n* : laborer, worker
operático, -ca → **operístico**
operativo¹, -va *adj* **1** : operating ⟨capacidad operativa : operating capacity⟩ **2** : operative
**operativo² ** *nm* : operation ⟨operativo militar : military operation⟩
opereta *nf* : operetta
operístico, -ca *adj* : operatic
opiato *nm* : opiate
opinable *adj* : arguable
opinar *vi* **1** : to think, to have an opinion **2** : to express an opinion **3 opinar bien de** : to think highly of — *vt* : to think ⟨opinamos lo mismo : we're of the same opinion, we're in agreement⟩
opinión *nf, pl* **-niones** : opinion, belief
opio *nm* : opium
oponente *nmf* : opponent
oponer {60} *vt* **1** CONTRAPONER : to oppose, to place against **2 oponer resistencia** : to resist, to put up a fight — **oponerse** *vr* ~ **a** : to object to, to be against
oporto *nm* : port (wine)
oportunamente *adv* **1** : at the right time, opportunely **2** : appropriately
oportunidad *nf* : opportunity, chance
oportunismo *nm* : opportunism
oportunista¹ *adj* : opportunistic
**oportunista² ** *nmf* : opportunist
oportuno, -na *adj* **1** : opportune, timely **2** : suitable, appropriate
oposición *nf, pl* **-ciones** : opposition
opositor, -tora *n* ADVERSARIO : opponent
oposum *nm* ZARIGÜEYA : opossum
opresión *nf, pl* **-siones** **1** : oppression **2 opresión de pecho** : tightness in the chest
opresivo, -va *adj* : oppressive
opresor¹, -sora *adj* : oppressive
opresor², -sora *n* : oppressor

oprimir *vt* **1** : to oppress **2** : to press, to squeeze ⟨oprima el botón : push the button⟩

oprobio *nm* : opprobrium, shame

optar *vi* **1** ~ **por** : to opt for, to choose **2** ~ **a** : to aspire to, to apply for ⟨dos candidatos optan a la presidencia : two candidates are running for president⟩

optativo, -va *adj* FACULTATIVO : optional

óptica *nf* **1** : optics **2** : optician's shop **3** : viewpoint

óptico¹, -ca *adj* : optical, optic

óptico², -ca *n* : optician

optimismo *nm* : optimism

optimista¹ *adj* : optimistic

optimista² *nmf* : optimist

óptimo, -ma *adj* : optimum, optimal

optometría *nf* : optometry — **optometrista** *nmf*

opuesto¹ *pp* → **oponer**

opuesto² *adj* **1** : opposite, contrary **2** : opposed

opulencia *nf* : opulence — **opulento, -ta** *adj*

opus *nm* : opus

opuso, etc. → **oponer**

ora *conj* : now ⟨los matices eran variados, ora verdes, ora ocres : the hues were varied, now green, now ocher⟩

oración *nf, pl* **-ciones 1** DISCURSO : oration, speech **2** PLEGARIA : prayer **3** FRASE : sentence, clause

oráculo *nm* : oracle

orador, -dora *n* : speaker, orator

oral *adj* : oral — **oralmente** *adv*

órale *interj Mex fam* **1** : sure!, OK! ⟨¿los dos por cinco pesos? ¡órale! : both for five pesos? you've got a deal!⟩ **2** : come on! ⟨¡órale, vámonos! : come on, let's go!⟩

orangután *nm, pl* **-tanes** : orangutan

orar *vi* REZAR : to pray

oratoria *nf* : oratory

oratorio *nm* **1** CAPILLA : oratory, chapel **2** : oratorio

orbe *nm* **1** : orb, sphere **2** GLOBO : globe, world

órbita *nf* **1** : orbit **2** : eye socket **3** ÁMBITO : sphere, field

orbitador *nm* : space shuttle, orbiter

orbital *adj* : orbital

orbitar *v* : to orbit

orden¹ *nm, pl* **órdenes 1** : order ⟨todo está en orden : everything's in order⟩ ⟨por orden cronológico : in chronological order⟩ **2 orden del día** : agenda (at a meeting) **3 orden público** : law and order

orden² *nf, pl* **órdenes 1** : order ⟨una orden religiosa : a religious order⟩ ⟨una orden de tacos : an order of tacos⟩ **2 orden de compra** : purchase order **3 estar a la orden del día** : to be the order of the day, to be prevalent

ordenación *nf, pl* **-ciones 1** : ordination **2** : ordering, organizing

ordenadamente *adv* : in an orderly fashion, neatly

ordenado, -da *adj* : orderly, neat

ordenador *nm Spain* : computer

ordenamiento *nm* **1** : ordering, organizing **2** : code (of laws)

ordenanza¹ *nf* REGLAMENTO : ordinance, regulation

ordenanza² *nm* : orderly (in the armed forces)

ordenar *vt* **1** MANDAR : to order, to command **2** ARREGLAR : to put in order, to arrange **3** : to ordain (a priest)

ordeñar *vt* : to milk

ordeño *nm* : milking

ordinal *nm* : ordinal (number)

ordinariamente *adv* **1** : usually **2** : coarsely

ordinariez *nf* : coarseness, vulgarity

ordinario, -ria *adj* **1** : ordinary **2** : coarse, common, vulgar **3 de** ~ : usually

orear *vt* : to air

orégano *nm* : oregano

oreja *nf* : ear

orfanato *nm* : orphanage

orfanatorio *nm Mex* : orphanage

orfebre *nmf* : goldsmith, silversmith

orfebrería *nf* : articles of gold or silver

orfelinato *nm* : orphanage

orgánico, -ca *adj* : organic — **orgánicamente** *adv*

organigrama *nm* : organization chart, flowchart

organismo *nm* **1** : organism **2** : agency, organization

organista *nmf* : organist

organización *nf, pl* **-ciones** : organization

organizador¹, -dora *adj* : organizing

organizador², -dora *n* : organizer

organizar {21} *vt* : to organize, to arrange — **organizarse** *vr* : to get organized

organizativo, -va *adj* : organizational

órgano *nm* : organ

orgasmo *nm* : orgasm

orgía *nf* : orgy

orgullo *nm* : pride

orgulloso, -sa *adj* : proud — **orgullosamente** *adv*

orientación *nf, pl* **-ciones 1** : orientation **2** DIRECCIÓN : direction, course **3** GUÍA : guidance, direction

oriental¹ *adj* **1** : eastern **2** : oriental **3** *Arg, Uru* : Uruguayan

oriental² *nmf* **1** : Easterner **2** : Oriental **3** *Arg, Uru* : Uruguayan

orientar *vt* **1** : to orient, to position **2** : to guide, to direct — **orientarse** *vr* **1** : to orient oneself, to get one's bearings **2** ~ **hacia** : to turn towards, to lean towards

oriente *nm* **1** : east, East **2 el Oriente** : the Orient

orífice *nmf* : goldsmith

orificio *nm* : orifice, opening

origen *nm, pl* **orígenes 1** : origin **2** : lineage, birth **3 dar origen a** : to give rise to **4 en su origen** : originally

original *adj & nm* : original — **origi-nalmente** *adv*
originalidad *nf* : originality
originar *vt* : to originate, to give rise to — **originarse** *vr* : to originate, to begin
originario, -ria *adj* ~ **de** : native of
originariamente *adv* : originally
orilla *nf* 1 BORDE : border, edge 2 : bank (of a river) 3 : shore
orillar *vt* 1 : to skirt, to go around 2 : to trim, to edge (cloth) 3 : to settle, to wind up 4 *Mex* : to pull over (a vehicle)
orín *nm* 1 HERRUMBRE : rust 2 **orines** *nmpl* : urine
orina *nf* : urine
orinación *nf* : urination
orinal *nm* : urinal (vessel)
orinar *vi* : to urinate — **orinarse** *vr* : to wet oneself
oriol *nm* OROPÉNDOLA : oriole
oriundo, -da *adj* ~ **de** : native of
orla *nf* : border, edging
orlar *vt* : to edge, to trim
ornamentación *nf, pl* -ciones : ornamentation
ornamental *adj* : ornamental
ornamentar *vt* ADORNAR : to ornament, to adorn
ornamento *nm* : ornament, adornment
ornar *vt* : to adorn, to decorate
ornitología *nf* : ornithology
ornitólogo, -ga *n* : ornithologist
ornitorrinco *nm* : platypus
oro *nm* : gold
orondo, -da *adj* 1 : rounded, potbellied (of a container) 2 *fam* : smug, self-satisfied
oropel *nm* : glitz, glitter, tinsel
oropéndola *nf* : oriole
orquesta *nf* : orchestra — **orquestal** *adj*
orquestar *vt* : to orchestrate — **orquestación** *nf*
orquídea *nf* : orchid
ortiga *nf* : nettle
ortodoncia *nf* : orthodontics
ortodoncista *nmf* : orthodontist
ortodoxia *nf* : orthodoxy
ortodoxo, -xa *adj* : orthodox
ortografía *nf* : orthography, spelling
ortográfico, -ca *adj* : orthographic, spelling
ortopedia *nf* : orthopedics
ortopédico, -ca *adj* : orthopedic
ortopedista *nmf* : orthopedist
oruga *nf* 1 : caterpillar 2 : track (of a tank, etc.)
orzuelo *nm* : sty, stye (in the eye)
os *pron pl* (*objective form of* **vosotros**) *Spain* 1 : you, to you 2 : yourselves, to yourselves 3 : each other, to each other
osa *nf* → **oso**
osadía *nf* 1 VALOR : boldness, daring 2 AUDACIA : audacity, nerve
osado, -da *adj* 1 : bold, daring 2 : audacious, impudent — **osadamente** *adv*

osamenta *nf* : skeletal remains *pl*, bones *pl*
osar *vi* : to dare
oscilación *nf, pl* -ciones 1 : oscillation 2 : fluctuation 3 : vacillation, wavering
oscilar *vi* 1 BALANCEARSE : to swing, to sway, to oscillate 2 FLUCTUAR : to fluctuate 3 : to vacillate, to waver
oscuramente *adv* : obscurely
oscurecer {53} *vt* 1 : to darken 2 : to obscure, to confuse, to cloud 3 **al oscurecer** : at dusk, at nightfall — *v impers* : to grow dark, to get dark — **oscurecerse** *vr* : to darken, to dim
oscuridad *nf* 1 : darkness 2 : obscurity
oscuro, -ra *adj* 1 : dark 2 : obscure 3 **a oscuras** : in the dark, in darkness
óseo, ósea *adj* : skeletal, bony
ósmosis *or* **osmosis** *nf* : osmosis
oso, osa *n* 1 : bear 2 **Osa Mayor** : Big Dipper 3 **Osa Menor** : Little Dipper 4 **oso blanco** : polar bear 5 **oso hormiguero** : anteater 6 **oso de peluche** : teddy bear
ostensible *adj* : ostensible, apparent — **ostensiblemente** *adv*
ostentación *nf, pl* -ciones : ostentation, display
ostentar *vt* 1 : to display, to flaunt 2 POSEER : to have, to hold ⟨ostenta el récord mundial : he holds the world record⟩
ostentoso, -sa *adj* : ostentatious, showy — **ostentosamente** *adv*
osteópata *nmf* : osteopath
osteopatía *n* : osteopathy
osteoporosis *nf* : osteoporosis
ostión *nm, pl* **ostiones** 1 *Mex* : oyster 2 *Chile* : scallop
ostra *nf* : oyster
ostracismo *nm* : ostracism
otear *vt* : to scan, to survey, to look over
otero *nm* : knoll, hillock
otomana *nf* : ottoman (mueble)
otomano, -na *adj & n* : Ottoman
otoñal *adj* : autumn, autumnal
otoño *nm* : autumn, fall
otorgamiento *nm* : granting, awarding
otorgar {52} *vt* 1 : to grant, to award 2 : to draw up, to frame (a legal document)
otro¹, otra *adj* 1 : other 2 : another ⟨en otro juego, ellos ganaron : in another game, they won⟩ 3 **otra vez** : again 4 **de otra manera** : otherwise 5 **otra parte** : elsewhere 6 **en otro tiempo** : once, formerly
otro², otra *pron* 1 : another one ⟨dame otro : give me another⟩ 2 : other one ⟨el uno o el otro : one or the other⟩ 3 **los otros, las otras** : the others, the rest ⟨me dio una y se quedó con las otras : he gave me one and kept the rest⟩
ovación *nf, pl* -ciones : ovation
ovacionar *vt* : to cheer, to applaud

oval → **ovalado**
ovalado, -da *adj* : oval
óvalo *nm* : oval
ovárico, -ca *adj* : ovarian
ovario *nm* : ovary
oveja *nf* **1** : sheep, ewe **2 oveja negra** : black sheep
overol *nm* : overalls *pl*
ovillar *vt* : to roll into a ball
ovillo *nm* **1** : ball (of yarn) **2** : tangle
ovni *or* **OVNI** *nm* (*o*bjeto *v*olador *no i*dentificado) : UFO
ovoide *adj* : ovoid, ovoidal
ovulación *nf, pl* **-ciones** : ovulation
ovular *vi* : to ovulate
óvulo *nm* : ovum

oxidación *nf, pl* **-ciones 1** : oxidation **2** : rusting
oxidado, -da *adj* : rusty
oxidar *vt* **1** : to cause to rust **2** : to oxidize — **oxidarse** *vr* : to rust, to become rusty
óxido *nm* **1** HERRUMBRE, ORÍN : rust **2** : oxide
oxigenar *vt* **1** : to oxygenate **2** : to bleach (hair)
oxígeno *nm* : oxygen
oxiuro *nm* : pinworm
oye, etc. → **oír**
oyente *nmf* **1** : listener **2** : auditor, auditing student
ozono *nm* : ozone

P

p *nf* : seventeenth letter of the Spanish alphabet
pabellón *nm, pl* **-llones 1** : pavilion **2** : summerhouse, lodge **3** : flag (of a vessel)
pabilo *nm* MECHA : wick
paca *nf* FARDO : bale
pacana *nf* : pecan
pacer {48} *v* : to graze, to pasture
paces → **paz**
pachanga *nf fam* : party, bash
paciencia *nf* : patience
paciente *adj & nmf* : patient — **pacientemente** *adv*
pacificación *nf, pl* **-ciones** : pacification
pacíficamente *adv* : peacefully, peaceably
pacificar {72} *vt* : to pacify, to calm — **pacificarse** *vr* : to calm down, to abate
pacífico, -ca *adj* : peaceful, pacific
pacifismo *nm* : pacifism
pacifista *adj & nmf* : pacifist
pacotilla *nf de* ∼ : shoddy, trashy
pactar *vt* : to agree on — *vi* : to come to an agreement
pacto *nm* CONVENIO : pact, agreement
padecer {53} *vt* : to suffer, to endure — *vi* ADOLECER ∼ **de** : to suffer from
padecimiento *nm* **1** : suffering **2** : ailment, condition
padrastro *nm* **1** : stepfather **2** : hangnail
padre¹ *adj Mex fam* : fantastic, great
padre² *nm* **1** : father **2 padres** *nmpl* : parents
padrenuestro *nm* : Lord's Prayer, paternoster
padrino *nm* **1** : godfather **2** : best man **3** : sponsor, patron
padrón *nm, pl* **padrones** : register, roll ⟨padrón municipal : city register⟩
paella *nf* : paella
paga *nf* **1** : payment **2** : pay, wages *pl*
pagadero, -ra *adj* : payable
pagado, -da *adj* **1** : paid **2 pagado de sí mismo** : self-satisfied, smug
pagador, -dora *n* : payer

paganismo *nm* : paganism
pagano, -na *adj & n* : pagan
pagar {52} *vt* : to pay, to pay for, to repay — *vi* : to pay
pagaré *nm* VALE : promissory note, IOU
página *nf* : page
pago *nm* **1** : payment **2 en pago de** : in return for
pagoda *nf* : pagoda
pague, etc. → **pagar**
país *nm* **1** NACIÓN : country, nation **2** REGIÓN : region, territory
paisaje *nm* : scenery, landscape
paisano, -na *n* COMPATRIOTA : compatriot, fellow countryman
paja *nf* **1** : straw **2** *fam* : trash, tripe
pajar *nm* : hayloft, haystack
pajarera *nf* : aviary
pájaro *nm* : bird ⟨pájaro cantor : songbird⟩ ⟨pájaro bobo : penguin⟩ ⟨pájaro carpintero : woodpecker⟩
pajita *nf* : (drinking) straw
pajote *nm* : straw, mulch
pala *nf* **1** : shovel, spade **2** : blade (of an oar or a rotor) **3** : paddle, racket
palabra *nf* **1** VOCABLO : word **2** PROMESA : word, promise ⟨un hombre de palabra : a man of his word⟩ **3** HABLA : speech **4** : right to speak ⟨tener la palabra : to have the floor⟩
palabrería *nf* : empty talk
palabrota *nf* : swearword
palacio *nm* **1** : palace, mansion **2 palacio de justicia** : courthouse
paladar *nm* **1** : palate **2** GUSTO : taste
paladear *vt* SABOREAR : to savor
paladín *nm, pl* **-dines** : champion, defender
palanca *nf* **1** : lever, crowbar **2** *fam* : leverage, influence **3 palanca de cambio** *or* **palanca de velocidad** : gearshift
palangana *nf* : washbowl
palanqueta *nf* : jimmy, small crowbar
palco *nm* : box (in a theater or stadium)
palear *vt* **1** : to shovel **2** : to paddle
palenque *nm* **1** ESTACADA : stockade, palisade **2** : arena, ring

paleontología *nf* : paleontology
paleontólogo, -ga *n* : paleontologist
palestino, -na *adj & n* : Palestinian
palestra *nf* : arena ⟨salir a la palestra : to join the fray⟩
paleta *nf* **1** : palette **2** : trowel **3** : spatula **4** : blade, vane **5** : paddle **6** *CA, Mex* : lollipop, Popsicle
paletilla *nf* : shoulder blade
paliar *vt* MITIGAR : to alleviate, to palliate
paliativo¹, -va *adj* : palliative
paliativo² *nm* : palliative
palidecer {53} *vi* : to turn pale
palidez *nf, pl* **-deces** : paleness, pallor
pálido, -da *adj* : pale
palillo *nm* **1** MONDADIENTES : toothpick **2 palillos** *nmpl* : chopsticks **3 palillo de tambor** : drumstick
paliza *nf* : beating, pummeling ⟨darle una paliza a : to beat, to thrash⟩
palma *nf* **1** : palm (of the hand) **2** : palm (tree or leaf) **3 batir palmas** : to clap, to applaud **4 llevarse la palma** *fam* : to take the cake
palmada *nf* **1** : pat **2** : slap **3** : clap
palmarés *nm* : record (of achievements)
palmario, -ria *adj* MANIFIESTO : clear, manifest
palmeado, -da *adj* : webbed
palmear *vt* : to slap on the back — *vi* : to clap, to applaud
palmera *nf* : palm tree
palmo *nm* **1** : span, small amount **2 palmo a palmo** : bit by bit, inch by inch **3 dejar con un palmo de narices** : to disappoint
palmotear *vi* : to applaud
palmoteo *nm* : clapping, applause
palo *nm* **1** : stick, pole, post **2** : shaft, handle ⟨palo de escoba : broomstick⟩ **3** : mast, spar **4** : wood **5** : blow (with a stick) **6** : suit (of cards)
paloma *nf* **1** : pigeon, dove **2 paloma mensajera** : carrier pigeon
palomilla *nf* : moth
palomitas *nfpl* : popcorn
palpable *adj* : palpable, tangible
palpar *vt* : to feel, to touch
palpitación *nf, pl* **-ciones** : palpitation
palpitar *vi* : to palpitate, to throb — **palpitante** *adj*
palta *nf* : avocado
paludismo *nm* MALARIA : malaria
palurdo, -da *n* : boor, yokel, bumpkin
pampa *nf* : pampa
pampeano, -na *adj* : pampean, pampas
pampero → **pampeano**
pan *nm* **1** : bread **2** : loaf of bread **3** : cake, bar ⟨pan de jabón : bar of soap⟩ **4 pan dulce** *CA, Mex* : traditional pastry **5 pan tostado** : toast **6 ser pan comido** *fam* : to be a piece of cake, to be a cinch
pana *nf* : corduroy
panacea *nf* : panacea
panadería *nf* : bakery, bread shop
panadero, -ra *n* : baker

panal *nm* : honeycomb
panameño, -ña *adj & n* : Panamanian
pancarta *nf* : placard, sign
pancita *nf Mex* : tripe
páncreas *nms & pl* : pancreas
panda *nmf* : panda
pandeado, -da *adj* : warped
pandearse *vr* **1** : to warp **2** : to bulge, to sag
pandemonio *or* **pandemónium** *nm* : pandemonium
pandereta *nf* : tambourine
pandero *nm* : tambourine
pandilla *nf* **1** : group, clique **2** : gang
panecito *nm* : roll, bread roll
panegírico¹, -ca *adj* : eulogistic, panegyrical
panegírico² *nm* : eulogy, panegyric
panel *nm* : panel — **panelista** *nmf*
panera *nf* : bread box
panfleto *nm* : pamphlet
pánico *nm* : panic
panorama *nm* **1** VISTA : panorama, view **2** : scene, situation ⟨el panorama nacional : the national scene⟩ **3** PERSPECTIVA : outlook
panorámico, -ca *adj* : panoramic
panqueque *nm* : pancake
pantaletas *nfpl* : panties
pantalla *nf* **1** : screen, monitor **2** : lampshade **3** : fan
pantalón *nm, pl* **-lones 1** : pants *pl*, trousers *pl* **2 pantalones vaqueros** : jeans **3 pantalones de mezclilla** *Chile, Mex* : jeans **4 pantalones de montar** : jodhpurs
pantano *nm* **1** : swamp, marsh, bayou **2** : reservoir **3** : obstacle, difficulty
pantanoso, -sa *adj* **1** : marshy, swampy **2** : difficult, thorny
panteón *nm, pl* **-teones 1** CEMENTERIO : cemetery **2** : pantheon, mausoleum
pantera *nf* : panther
pantimedias *nfpl Mex* : panty hose
pantomima *nf* : pantomime
pantorrilla *nf* : calf (of the leg)
pantufla *nf* ZAPATILLA : slipper
panza *nf* BARRIGA : belly, paunch
panzón, -zona *adj, mpl* **panzones** : potbellied, paunchy
pañal *nm* : diaper
pañería *nf* **1** : cloth, material **2** : fabric store
pañito *nm* : doily
paño *nm* **1** : cloth **2** : rag, dust cloth **3 paño de cocina** : dishcloth **4 paño higiénico** : sanitary napkin
pañuelo *nm* **1** : handkerchief **2** : scarf
papa¹ *nm* : pope
papa² *nf* **1** : potato **2 papa dulce** : sweet potato **3 papas fritas** : potato chips, french fries **4 papas a la francesa** *Mex* : french fries
papá *nm fam* **1** : dad, pop **2 papás** *nmpl* : parents, folks
papada *nf* **1** : double chin, jowl **2** : dewlap
papagayo *nm* LORO : parrot

papal *adj* : papal
papalote *nm Mex* : kite
papaya *nf* : papaya
papel *nm* **1** : paper, piece of paper **2** : role, part **3 papel de estaño** : tinfoil **4 papel de empapelar** *or* **papel pintado** : wallpaper **5 papel higiénico** : toilet paper **6 papel de lija** : sandpaper
papeleo *nm* : paperwork, red tape
papelera *nf* : wastebasket
papelería *nf* : stationery store
papelero, -ra *adj* : paper
papeleta *nf* **1** : ballot **2** : ticket, slip
paperas *nfpl* : mumps
papi *nm fam* : daddy, papa
papilla *nf* **1** : pap, mash **2 hacer papilla** : to beat to a pulp
papiro *nm* : papyrus
paquete *nm* BULTO : package, parcel
paquistaní *adj & nmf* : Pakistani
par¹ *adj* : even (in number)
par² *nm* 1 : pair, couple **2** : equal, peer ⟨sin par : matchless, peerless⟩ **3** : par (in golf) **4** : rafter **5 de par en par** : wide open
par³ *nf* **1** : par ⟨por encima de la par : above par⟩ **2 a la par que** : at the same time as, as well as ⟨interesante a la par que instructivo : both interesting and informative⟩
para *prep* **1** : for ⟨para ti : for you⟩ ⟨alta para su edad : tall for her age⟩ ⟨una cita para el lunes : an appointment for Monday⟩ **2** : to, towards ⟨para la derecha : to the right⟩ ⟨van para el río : they're heading towards the river⟩ **3** : to, in order to ⟨lo hace para molestarte : he does it to annoy you⟩ **4** : around, by (a time) ⟨para mañana estarán listos : they'll be ready by tomorrow⟩ **5 para adelante** : forwards **6 para atrás** : backwards **7 para que** : so, so that, in order that ⟨te lo digo para que sepas : I'm telling you so you'll know⟩
parabién *nm, pl* **-bienes** : congratulations *pl*
parábola *nf* **1** : parable **2** : parabola
parabrisas *nms & pl* : windshield
paracaídas *nms & pl* : parachute
paracaidista *nmf* **1** : parachutist **2** : paratrooper
parachoques *nms & pl* : bumper
parada *nf* **1** : stop ⟨parada de autobús : bus stop⟩ **2** : catch, save, parry (in sports) **3** DESFILE : parade
paradero *nm* : whereabouts
paradigma *nm* : paradigm
paradisíaco, -ca *or* **paradisiaco, -ca** *adj* : heavenly
parado, -da *adj* **1** : motionless, idle, stopped **2** : standing (up) **3** : confused, bewildered **4 bien (mal) parado** : in good (bad) shape ⟨salió bien parado : it turned out well for him⟩
paradoja *nf* : paradox
paradójico, -ca *adj* : paradoxical
parafernalia *nf* : paraphernalia

parafina *nf* : paraffin
parafrasear *vt* : to paraphrase
paráfrasis *nfs & pl* : paraphrase
paraguas *nms & pl* : umbrella
paraguayo, -ya *adj & n* : Paraguayan
paraíso *nm* **1** : paradise, heaven **2 paraíso fiscal** : tax shelter
paraje *nm* : spot, place
paralelismo *nm* : parallelism, similarity
paralelo¹, -la *adj* : parallel
paralelo² *nm* : parallel
paralelogramo *nm* : parallelogram
parálisis *nfs & pl* **1** : paralysis **2** : standstill **3 parálisis cerebral** : cerebral palsy
paralítico, -ca *adj & n* : paralytic
paralizar {21} *vt* **1** : to paralyze **2** : to bring to a standstill — **paralizarse** *vr*
parámetro *nm* : parameter
páramo *nm* : barren plateau, moor
parangón *nm, pl* **-gones 1** : comparison **2 sin ~** : incomparable
paraninfo *nm* : auditorium, assembly hall
paranoia *nf* : paranoia
paranoico, -ca *adj & n* : paranoid
parapeto *nm* : parapet, rampart
parapléjico, -ca *adj & n* : paraplegic
parar *vt* **1** DETENER : to stop **2** : to stand, to prop — *vi* **1** CESAR : to stop **2** : to stay, to put up **3 ir a parar** : to end up, to wind up — **pararse** *vr* **1** : to stop **2** ATASCARSE : to stall (out) **3** : to stand up, to get up
pararrayos *nms & pl* : lightning rod
parasitario, -ria *adj* : parasitic
parasitismo *nm* : parasitism
parásito *nm* : parasite
parasol *nm* SOMBRILLA : parasol
parcela *nf* : parcel, tract of land
parcelar *vt* : to parcel (land)
parchar *vt* : to patch, to patch up
parche *nm* : patch
parcial *adj* : partial — **parcialmente** *adv*
parcialidad *nf* : partiality, bias
parco, -ca *adj* **1** : sparing, frugal **2** : moderate, temperate
pardo, -da *adj* : brownish grey
pardusco → **pardo**
parecer¹ {53} *vi* **1** : to seem, to look, to appear to be ⟨parece bien fácil : it looks very easy⟩ ⟨así parece : so it seems⟩ ⟨pareces una princesa : you look like a princess⟩ **2** : to think, to have an opinion ⟨me parece que sí : I think so⟩ **3** : to like, to be in agreement ⟨si te parece : if you like, if it's all right with you⟩ — **parecerse** *vr* **~ a** : to resemble
parecer² *nm* **1** OPINIÓN : opinion **2** ASPECTO : appearance ⟨al parecer : apparently⟩
parecido¹, -da *adj* **1** : similar, alike **2 bien parecido** : good-looking
parecido² *nm* : resemblance, similarity
pared *nf* : wall
pareja *nf* **1** : couple, pair **2** : partner, mate

parejo, -ja *adj* **1** : even, smooth, level **2** : equal, similar

parentela *nf* : relations *pl*, kinfolk

parentesco *nm* : relationship, kinship

paréntesis *nms & pl* **1** : parenthesis **2** : digression

parentético, -ca *adj* : parenthetic, parenthetical

paria *nmf* : pariah, outcast

paridad *nf* : parity, equality

pariente *nmf* : relative, relation

parir *vi* : to give birth — *vt* : to give birth to, to bear

parking *nm* : parking lot

parlamentar *vi* : to talk, to parley

parlamentario[1], **-ria** *adj* : parliamentary

parlamentario[2], **-ria** *n* : member of parliament

parlamento *nm* **1** : parliament **2** : negotiations *pl*, talks *pl*

parlanchín[1], **-china** *adj, mpl* **-chines** : chatty, talkative

parlanchín[2], **-china** *n, mpl* **-chines** : chatterbox

parlante *nm* ALTOPARLANTE : loudspeaker

parlotear *vi fam* : to gab, to chat, to prattle

parloteo *nm fam* : prattle, chatter

paro *nm* **1** HUELGA : strike **2** : stoppage, stopping **3 paro forzoso** : layoff

parodia *nf* : parody

parodiar *vt* : to parody

paroxismo *nm* **1** : fit, paroxysm **2** : peak, height ⟨llevar al paroxismo : to carry to the extreme⟩

parpadear *vi* **1** : to blink **2** : to flicker

parpadeo *nm* **1** : blink, blinking **2** : flickering

párpado *nm* : eyelid

parque *nm* **1** : park **2 parque de atracciones** : amusement park

parquear *vt* : to park — **parquearse** *vr*

parqueo *nm* : parking

parquet *or* **parqué** *nm* : parquet

parquímetro *nm* : parking meter

parra *nf* : vine, grapevine

párrafo *nm* : paragraph

parranda *nf fam* : party, spree

parrilla *nf* **1** : broiler, grill **2** : grate

parrillada *nf* BARBACOA : barbecue

párroco *nm* : parish priest

parroquia *nf* **1** : parish **2** : parish church **3** : customers *pl*, clientele

parroquial *adj* : parochial

parroquiano, -na *n* **1** : parishioner **2** : customer, patron

parsimonia *nf* **1** : calm **2** : parsimony, thrift

parsimonioso, -sa *adj* **1** : calm, unhurried **2** : parsimonious, thrifty

parte[1] *nm* : report, dispatch

parte[2] *nf* **1** : part, share **2** : part, place ⟨en alguna parte : somewhere⟩ ⟨por todas partes : everywhere⟩ **3** : party (in negotiations, etc.) **4 de parte de** : on behalf of **5 ¿de parte de quién?** : may I ask who's calling? **6 tomar parte** : to take part

partero, -ra *n* : midwife

partición *nf, pl* **-ciones** : division, sharing

participación *nf, pl* **-ciones** **1** : participation **2** : share, interest **3** : announcement, notice

participante *nmf* **1** : participant **2** : competitor, entrant

participar *vi* **1** : to participate, to take part **2 ~ en** : to have a share in — *vt* : to announce, to notify

partícipe *nmf* : participant

participio *nm* : participle

partícula *nf* : particle

particular[1] *adj* **1** : particular, specific **2** : private, personal **3** : special, unique

particular[2] *nm* **1** : matter, detail **2** : individual

particularidad *nf* : characteristic, peculiarity

particularizar {21} *vt* **1** : to distinguish, to characterize **2** : to specify

partida *nf* **1** : departure **2** : item, entry **3** : certificate ⟨partida de nacimiento : birth certificate⟩ **4** : game, match, hand **5** : party, group

partidario, -ria *n* : follower, supporter

partido *nm* **1** : (political) party **2** : game, match ⟨partido de futbol : soccer game⟩ **3** APOYO : support, following **4** PROVECHO : profit, advantage ⟨sacar partido de : to profit from⟩

partir *vt* **1** : to cut, to split **2** : to break, to crack **3** : to share (out), to divide — *vi* **1** : to leave, to depart **2 ~ de** : to start from **3 a partir de** : as of, from ⟨a partir de hoy : as of today⟩ — **partirse** *vr* **1** : to smash, to split open **2** : to chap

partisano, -na *adj & n* : partisan

partitura *nf* : (musical) score

parto *nm* **1** : childbirth, delivery, labor ⟨estar de parto : to be in labor⟩ **2** : product, creation, brainchild

parvulario *nm* : nursery school

párvulo, -la *n* : toddler, preschooler

pasa *nf* **1** : raisin **2 pasa de Corinto** : currant

pasable *adj* : passable, tolerable — **pasablemente** *adv*

pasada *nf* **1** : passage, passing **2** : pass, wipe, coat (of paint) **3 de ~** : in passing **4 mala pasada** : dirty trick

pasadizo *nm* : passageway, corridor

pasado[1], **-da** *adj* **1** : past ⟨el año pasado : last year⟩ ⟨pasado mañana : the day after tomorrow⟩ ⟨pasadas las siete : after seven o'clock⟩ **2** : stale, bad, overripe **3** : old-fashioned, out-of-date **4** : overripe, slightly spoiled

pasado[2] *nm* : past

pasador *nm* **1** : bolt, latch **2** : barrette **3** *Mex* : bobby pin

pasaje *nm* **1** : ticket (for travel) **2** TARIFA : fare **3** : passageway **4** : passengers *pl*

pasajero[1], **-ra** *adj* : passing, fleeting

pasajero[2], **-ra** *n* : passenger

pasamanos *nms & pl* **1** : handrail **2**
: bannister
pasante *nmf* : assistant
pasaporte *nm* : passport
pasar *vi* **1** : to pass, to go by, to come
by **2** : to come in, to enter ⟨¿se puede
pasar? : may we come in?⟩ **3** : to happen ⟨¿qué pasa? : what's happening?,
what's going on?⟩ **4** : to manage, to get
by **5** : to be over, to end **6** ~ **de** : to
exceed, to go beyond **7** ~ **por** : to pretend to be — *vt* **1** : to pass, to give ⟨¿me
pasas la sal? : would you pass me the
salt?⟩ **2** : to pass (a test) **3** : to go over,
to cross **4** : to spend (time) **5** : to tolerate **6** : to go through, to suffer **7** : to
show (a movie, etc.) **8** : to overtake, to
pass, to surpass **9** : to pass over, to wipe
up **10 pasarlo bien** *or* **pasarla bien** : to
have a good time **11 pasarlo mal** *or*
pasarla mal : to have a bad time, to
have a hard time **12 pasar por alto** : to
overlook, to omit — **pasarse** *vr* **1** : to
move, to pass, to go away **2** : to slip
one's mind, to forget **3** : to go too far
pasarela *nf* **1** : gangplank **2** : footbridge
3 : runway, catwalk
pasatiempo *nm* : pastime, hobby
Pascua *nf* **1** : Easter **2** : Passover **3**
: Christmas **4 Pascuas** *nfpl* : Christmas season
pase *nm* **1** PERMISO : pass, permit **2**
pase de abordar *Mex* : boarding pass
pasear *vi* : to take a walk, to go for a
ride — *vt* **1** : to take for a walk **2** : to
parade around, to show off —
pasearse *vr* : to walk around
paseo *nm* **1** : walk, stroll **2** : ride **3** EX-
CURSIÓN : outing, trip **4** : avenue, walk
5 *or* **paseo marítimo** : boardwalk
pasiflora *nf* : passionflower
pasillo *nm* CORREDOR : hallway, corridor, aisle
pasión *nf, pl* **pasiones** : passion
pasional *adj* : passionate ⟨crimen pasional : crime of passion⟩
pasionaria → **pasiflora**
pasivo¹, -va *adj* : passive — **pasiva-
mente** *adv*
pasivo² *nm* **1** : liability ⟨activos y pa-
sivos : assets and liabilities⟩ **2** : debit
side (of an account)
pasmado, -da *adj* : stunned, flabber-
gasted
pasmar *vt* : to amaze, to stun — **pas-
marse** *vr*
pasmo *nm* **1** : shock, astonishment **2**
: wonder, marvel
pasmoso, -sa *adj* : incredible, amazing
— **pasmosamente** *adv*
paso¹, -sa *adj* : dried ⟨ciruela pasa
: prune⟩
paso² *nm* **1** : passage, passing ⟨de paso
: in passing, on the way⟩ **2** : way, path
⟨abrirse paso : to make one's way⟩ **3**
: crossing ⟨paso de peatones : cross-
walk⟩ ⟨paso a desnivel : underpass⟩
⟨paso elevado : overpass⟩ **4** : step

⟨paso a paso : step by step⟩ **5** : pace,
gait ⟨a buen paso : quickly, at a good
rate⟩
pasta *nf* **1** : paste ⟨pasta de dientes *or*
pasta dental : toothpaste⟩ **2** : pasta **3**
: pastry dough **4 libro en pasta dura**
: hardcover book **5 tener pasta de** : to
have the makings of
pastar *vi* : to graze — *vt* : to put to pasture
pastel¹ *adj* : pastel
pastel² *nm* **1** : cake ⟨pastel de cumpleaños : birthday cake⟩ **2** : pie, turnover
3 : pastel
pastelería *nf* : pastry shop
pasteurización *nf, pl* **-ciones** : pasteurization
pasteurizar {21} *vt* : to pasteurize
pastilla *nf* **1** COMPRIMIDO, PÍLDORA
: pill, tablet **2** : lozenge ⟨pastilla para
la tos : cough drop⟩ **3** : cake (of soap),
bar (of chocolate)
pastizal *nm* : pasture, grazing land
pasto *nm* **1** : pasture **2** HIERBA : grass,
lawn
pastor, -tora *n* **1** : shepherd, shepherdess *f* **2** : minister, pastor
pastoral *adj & nf* : pastoral
pastorear *vt* : to shepherd, to tend
pastorela *nf* **1** : pastoral, pastourelle **2**
Mex : a traditional Christmas play
pastoso, -sa *adj* **1** : pasty, doughy **2**
: smooth, mellow (of sounds)
pata *nf* **1** : paw, leg (of an animal) **2**
: foot, leg (of furniture) **3 patas de gallo** : crow's-feet **4 meter la pata** *fam* : to
put one's foot in it, to make a blunder
patada *nf* **1** PUNTAPIÉ : kick **2** : stamp
(of the foot)
patalear *vi* **1** : to kick **2** : to stamp one's
feet
pataleta *nf fam* : tantrum
patán¹ *adj, pl* **patanes** : boorish, crude
patán² *nm, pl* **patanes** : boor, lout
patata *nf Spain* : potato
pateador, -dora *n* : kicker (in sports)
patear *vt* : to kick — *vi* : to stamp one's
foot
patentar *vt* : to patent
patente¹ *adj* EVIDENTE : obvious, patent
— **patentemente** *adv*
patente² *nf* : patent
paternal *adj* : fatherly, paternal
paternidad *nf* **1** : fatherhood, paternity
2 : parenthood **3** : authorship
paterno, -na *adj* : paternal ⟨abuela pa-
terna : paternal grandmother⟩
patético, -ca *adj* : pathetic, moving
patetismo *nm* : pathos
patíbulo *nm* : gallows, scaffold
patillas *nfpl* : sideburns
patín *nm, pl* **patines** : skate ⟨patín de
ruedas : roller skate⟩
patinador, -dora *n* : skater
patinaje *nm* : skating
patinar *vi* **1** : to skate **2** : to skid, to slip
3 *fam* : to slip up, to blunder
patinazo *nm* **1** : skid **2** *fam* : blunder,
slipup

patineta *nf* **1** : scooter **2** : skateboard
patinete *nm* : scooter
patio *nm* **1** : courtyard, patio **2 patio de recreo** : playground
patito, -ta *n* : duckling
pato, -ta *n* **1** : duck **2 pato real** : mallard **3 pagar el pato** *fam* : to take the blame
patología *nf* : pathology
patológico, -ca *adj* : pathological
patólogo, -ga *n* : pathologist
patraña *nf* : tall tale, humbug, nonsense
patria *nf* : native land
patriarca *nm* : patriarch — **patriarcal** *adj*
patriarcado *nm* : patriarchy
patrimonio *nm* : patrimony, legacy
patrio, -tria *adj* **1** : native, home ⟨suelo patrio : native soil⟩ **2** : paternal
patriota[1] *adj* : patriotic
patriota[2] *nmf* : patriot
patriotería *nf* : jingoism, chauvinism
patriotero[1], **-ra** *adj* : jingoistic, chauvinistic
patriotero[2], **-ra** *n* : jingoist, chauvinist
patriótico, -ca *adj* : patriotic
patriotismo *nm* : patriotism
patrocinador, -dora *n* : sponsor, patron
patrocinar *vt* : to sponsor
patrocinio *nm* : sponsorship, patronage
patrón[1], **-trona** *n, mpl* **patrones 1** JEFE : boss **2** : patron saint
patrón[2] *nm, pl* **patrones 1** : standard **2** : pattern (in sewing)
patronal *adj* **1** : management, employers' ⟨sindicato patronal : employers' association⟩ **2** : pertaining to a patron saint ⟨fiesta patronal : patron saint's day⟩
patronato *nm* **1** : board, council **2** : foundation, trust
patrono, -na *n* **1** : employer **2** : patron saint
patrulla *nf* **1** : patrol **2** : police car, cruiser
patrullar *v* : to patrol
patrullero *nm* **1** : police car **2** : patrol boat
paulatino, -na *adj* : gradual
paupérrimo, -ma *adj* : destitute, poverty-stricken
pausa *nf* : pause, break
pausado[1] *adv* : slowly, deliberately ⟨habla más pausado : speak more slowly⟩
pausado[2], **-da** *adj* : slow, deliberate — **pausadamente** *adv*
pauta *nf* **1** : rule, guideline **2** : lines *pl* (on paper)
pava *nf Arg, Bol, Chile* : kettle
pavimentar *vt* : to pave
pavimento *nm* : pavement
pavo, -va *n* **1** : turkey **2 pavo real** : peacock **3 comer pavo** : to be a wallflower
pavón *nm, pl* **pavones** : peacock
pavonearse *vr* : to strut, to swagger
pavoneo *nm* : strut, swagger
pavor *nm* TERROR : dread, terror

pavoroso, -sa *adj* ATERRADOR : dreadful, terrifying
payasada *nf* BUFONADA : antic, buffoonery
payasear *vi* : to clown around
payaso, -sa *n* : clown
paz *nf, pl* **paces 1** : peace **2 dejar en paz** : to leave alone **3 hacer las paces** : to make up, to reconcile
pazca, etc. → **pacer**
PC *nmf* : PC, personal computer
peaje *nm* : toll
peatón *nm, pl* **-tones** : pedestrian
peatonal *adj* : pedestrian
peca *nf* : freckle
pecado *nm* : sin
pecador[1], **-dora** *adj* : sinful, sinning
pecador[2], **-dora** *n* : sinner
pecaminoso, -sa *adj* : sinful
pecar {72} *vi* **1** : to sin **2 ~ de** : to be too much (something) ⟨no pecan de amabilidad : they're not overly friendly⟩
pécari *or* **pecarí** *nm* : peccary
pececillo *nm* : small fish
pecera *nf* : fishbowl, fish tank
pecho *nm* **1** : chest **2** SENO : breast, bosom **3** : heart, courage **4 dar el pecho** : to breast-feed **5 tomar a pecho** : to take to heart
pechuga *nf* : breast (of fowl)
pecoso, -sa *adj* : freckled
pectoral *adj* : pectoral
peculado *nm* : embezzlement
peculiar *adj* **1** CARACTERÍSTICO : particular, characteristic **2** RARO : peculiar, uncommon
peculiaridad *nf* : peculiarity
pecuniario, -ria *adj* : pecuniary
pedagogía *nf* : pedagogy
pedagógico, -ca *adj* : pedagogic, pedagogical
pedagogo, -ga *n* : educator, pedagogue
pedal *nm* : pedal
pedalear *vi* : to pedal
pedante[1] *adj* : pedantic
pedante[2] *nmf* : pedant
pedantería *nf* : pedantry
pedazo *nm* TROZO : piece, bit, chunk ⟨caerse a pedazos : to fall to pieces⟩ ⟨hacer pedazos : to tear into shreds, to smash to pieces⟩
pedernal *nm* : flint
pedestal *nm* : pedestal
pedestre *adj* : commonplace, pedestrian
pediatra *nmf* : pediatrician
pediatría *nf* : pediatrics
pediátrico, -ca *adj* : pediatric
pedido *nm* **1** : order (of merchandise) **2** : request
pedigrí *nm* : pedigree
pedir {54} *vt* **1** : to ask for, to request ⟨le pedí un préstamo a Claudia : I asked Claudia for a loan⟩ **2** : to order (food, merchandise) **3 pedir disculpas** *or* **pedir perdón** : to apologize — *vi* **1** : to order **2** : to beg

pedrada *nf* **1** : blow (with a rock or stone) ⟨la ventana se quebró de una pedrada : the window was broken by a rock⟩ **2** *fam* : cutting remark, dig
pedregal *nm* : rocky ground
pedregoso, -sa *adj* : rocky, stony
pedrera *nf* CANTERA : quarry
pedrería *nf* : precious stones *pl*, gems *pl*
pegado, -da *adj* **1** : glued, stuck, stuck together **2** ~ **a** : right next to
pegajoso, -sa *adj* **1** : sticky, gluey **2** : catchy ⟨una tonada pegajosa : a catchy tune⟩
pegamento *nm* : adhesive, glue
pegar {52} *vt* **1** : to glue, to stick, to paste **2** : to attach, to sew on **3** : to infect with, to give ⟨me pegó el resfriado : he gave me his cold⟩ **4** GOLPEAR : to hit, to deal, to strike ⟨me pegaron un puntapié : they gave me a kick⟩ **5** : to give (out with) ⟨pegó un grito : she let out a yell⟩ — *vi* **1** : to adhere, to stick **2** ~ **en** : to hit, to strike (against) **3** ~ **con** : to match, to go with — **pegarse** *vr* **1** GOLPEARSE : to hit oneself, to hit each other **2** : to stick, to take hold **3** : to be contagious **4** *fam* : to tag along, to stick around
pegote *nm* **1** : sticky mess **2** *Mex* : sticker, adhesive label
pegue, etc. → pegar
peinado *nm* : hairstyle, hairdo
peinador, -dora *n* : hairdresser
peinar *vt* : to comb — **peinarse** *vr*
peine *nm* : comb
peineta *nf* : ornamental comb
peladez *nf, pl* **-deces** *Mex fam* : obscenity, bad language
pelado, -da *adj* **1** : bald, hairless **2** : peeled **3** : bare, barren **4** : broke, penniless **5** *Mex fam* : coarse, crude
pelador *nm* : peeler
pelagra *nf* : pellagra
pelaje *nm* : coat (of an animal), fur
pelar *vt* **1** : to peel, to shell **2** : to skin **3** : to pluck **4** : to remove hair from **5** *fam* : to clean out (of money) — **pelarse** *vr* **1** : to peel **2** *fam* : to get a haircut **3** *Mex fam* : to split, to leave
peldaño *nm* **1** : step, stair **2** : rung
pelea *nf* **1** LUCHA : fight **2** : quarrel
pelear *vi* **1** LUCHAR : to fight **2** DISPUTAR : to quarrel — **pelearse** *vr*
peleón, -ona *adj, mpl* **-ones** *Spain* : quarrelsome, argumentative
peleonero, -ra *adj Mex* : quarrelsome
peletería *nf* **1** : fur shop **2** : fur trade
peletero, -ra *n* : furrier
peliagudo, -da *adj* : tricky, difficult, ticklish
pelícano *nm* : pelican
película *nf* **1** : movie, film **2** : (photographic) film **3** : thin covering, layer
peligrar *vi* : to be in danger
peligro *nm* **1** : danger, peril **2** : risk ⟨correr peligro de : to run the risk of⟩
peligroso, -sa *adj* : dangerous, hazardous

pelirrojo[1], -ja *adj* : red-haired, redheaded
pelirrojo[2], -ja *n* : redhead
pellejo *nm* **1** : hide, skin **2 salvar el pellejo** : to save one's neck
pellizcar {72} *vt* **1** : to pinch **2** : to nibble on
pellizco *nm* : pinch
pelo *nm* **1** : hair **2** : fur **3** : pile, nap **4 a pelo** : bareback **5 con pelos y señales** : in great detail **6 no tener pelos en la lengua** : to not mince words, to be blunt **7 tomarle el pelo a alguien** : to tease someone, to pull someone's leg
pelón, -lona *adj, mpl* **pelones 1** : bald **2** *fam* : broke **3** *Mex fam* : tough, difficult
pelota *nf* **1** : ball **2** *fam* : head **3 en pelotas** *fam* : naked **4 pelota vasca** : jai alai **5 pasar la pelota** *fam* : to pass the buck
pelotón *nm, pl* **-tones** : squad, detachment
peltre *nm* : pewter
peluca *nf* : wig
peluche *nm* : plush (fabric)
peludo, -da *adj* : hairy, shaggy, bushy
peluquería *nf* **1** : hairdresser's, barber shop **2** : hairdressing
peluquero, -ra *n* : barber, hairdresser
peluquín *nm, pl* **-quines** TUPÉ : hairpiece, toupee
pelusa *nf* : lint, fuzz
pélvico, -ca *adj* : pelvic
pelvis *nfs & pl* : pelvis
pena *nf* **1** CASTIGO : punishment, penalty ⟨pena de muerte : death penalty⟩ **2** AFLICCIÓN : sorrow, grief ⟨morir de pena : to die of a broken heart⟩ ⟨¡qué pena! : what a shame!, how sad!⟩ **3** DOLOR : pain, suffering **4** DIFICULTAD : difficulty, trouble ⟨a duras penas : with great difficulty⟩ **5** VERGÜENZA : shame, embarrassment **6 valer la pena** : to be worthwhile
penacho *nm* **1** : crest, tuft **2** : plume (of feathers)
penal[1] *adj* : penal
penal[2] *nm* CÁRCEL : prison, penitentiary
penalidad *nf* **1** : hardship **2** : penalty, punishment
penalizar {21} *vt* : to penalize
penalty *nm* : penalty (in sports)
penar *vt* : to punish, to penalize — *vi* : to suffer, to grieve
pendenciero, -ra *adj* : argumentative, quarrelsome
pender *vi* **1** : to hang **2** : to be pending
pendiente[1] *adj* **1** : pending **2 estar pendiente de** : to be watchful of, to be on the lookout for
pendiente[2] *nm Spain* : earring
pendiente[3] *nf* : slope, incline
pendón *nm, pl* **pendones** : banner
péndulo *nm* : pendulum
pene *nm* : penis

penetración *nf, pl* **-ciones 1** : penetration **2** : insight
penetrante *adj* **1** : penetrating, piercing **2** : sharp, acute **3** : deep (of a wound)
penetrar *vi* **1** : to penetrate, to sink in **2 — por** *or* **~ en** : to pierce, to go in, to enter into ⟨el frío penetra por la ventana : the cold comes right in through the window⟩ — *vt* **1** : to penetrate, to permeate **2** : to pierce ⟨el dolor penetró su corazón : sorrow pierced her heart⟩ **3** : to fathom, to understand
penicilina *nf* : penicillin
península *nf* : peninsula — **peninsular** *adj*
penitencia *nf* : penance, penitence
penitenciaría *nf* : penitentiary
penitente *adj* & *nmf* : penitent
penol *nm* : yardarm
penoso, -sa *adj* **1** : painful, distressing **2** : difficult, arduous **3** : shy, bashful
pensado, -da *adj* **1 bien pensado** : well thought-out **2 en el momento menos pensado** : when least expected **3 poco pensado** : badly thought-out **4 mal pensado** : evil-minded
pensador, -dora *n* : thinker
pensamiento *nm* **1** : thought **2** : thinking **3** : pansy
pensar {55} *vi* **1** : to think **2 ~ en** : to think about — *vt* **1** : to think **2** : to think about **3** : to intend, to plan on — **pensarse** *vr* : to think over
pensativo, -va *adj* : pensive, thoughtful
pensión *nf, pl* **pensiones 1** JUBILACIÓN : pension **2** : boarding house **3 pensión alimenticia** : alimony
pensionado, -da *n* → **pensionista**
pensionista *nmf* **1** JUBILADO : pensioner, retiree **2** : boarder, lodger
pentágono *nm* : pentagon — **pentagonal** *adj*
pentagrama *nm* : staff (in music)
penúltimo, -ma *adj* : next to last, penultimate
penumbra *nf* : semidarkness
penuria *nf* **1** ESCASEZ : shortage, scarcity **2** : poverty
peña *nf* : rock, crag
peñasco *nm* : crag, large rock
peñón → **peñasco**
peón *nm, pl* **peones 1** : laborer, peon **2** : pawn (in chess)
peonía *nf* : peony
peor[1] *adv* **1** (*comparative of* **mal**) : worse ⟨se llevan peor que antes : they get along worse than before⟩ **2** (*superlative of* **mal**) : worst ⟨me fue peor que a nadie : I did the worst of all⟩
peor[2] *adj* **1** (*comparative of* **malo**) : worse ⟨es peor que el original : it's worse than the original⟩ **2** (*superlative of* **malo**) : worst ⟨el peor de todos : the worst of all⟩
pepa *nf* : seed, pit (of a fruit)
pepenador, -dora *n* CA, Mex : scavenger
pepenar *vt* CA, Mex : to scavenge, to scrounge

pepinillo *nm* : pickle, gherkin
pepino *nm* : cucumber
pepita *nf* **1** : seed, pip **2** : nugget **3** Mex : dried pumpkin seed
peque, etc. → **pecar**
pequeñez *nf, pl* **-ñeces 1** : smallness **2** : trifle, triviality **3 pequeñez de espíritu** : pettiness
pequeño[1], **-ña** *adj* **1** : small, little ⟨un libro pequeño : a small book⟩ **2** : young **3** BAJO : short
pequeño[2], **-ña** *n* : child, little one
pera *nf* : pear
peraltar *vt* : to bank (a road)
perca *nf* : perch (fish)
percal *nm* : percale
percance *nm* : mishap, misfortune
percatarse *vr* **~ de** : to notice, to become aware of
percebe *nm* : barnacle
percepción *nf, pl* **-ciones 1** : perception **2** : idea, notion **3** COBRO : receipt (of payment), collection
perceptible *adj* : perceptible, noticeable — **perceptiblemente** *adv*
percha *nf* **1** : perch **2** : coat hanger **3** : coatrack, coat hook
perchero *nm* : coatrack
percibir *vt* **1** : to perceive, to notice, to sense **2** : to earn, to draw (a salary)
percudido, -da *adj* : grimy
percudir *vt* : to make grimy — **percudirse** *vr*
percusión *nf, pl* **-siones** : percussion
percusor *or* **percutor** *nm* : hammer (of a firearm)
perdedor[1], **-dora** *adj* : losing
perdedor[2], **-dora** *n* : loser
perder {56} *vt* **1** : to lose **2** : to miss ⟨perdimos la oportunidad : we missed the opportunity⟩ **3** : to waste (time) — *vi* : to lose — **perderse** *vr* EXTRAVIARSE : to get lost, to stray
perdición *nf, pl* **-ciones** : perdition, damnation
pérdida *nf* **1** : loss **2 pérdida de tiempo** : waste of time
perdidamente *adv* : hopelessly
perdido, -da *adj* **1** : lost **2** : inveterate, incorrigible ⟨es un caso perdido : he's a hopeless case⟩ **3** : in trouble, done for **4 de ~** Mex fam : at least
perdigón *nm, pl* **-gones** : shot, pellet
perdiz *nf, pl* **perdices** : partridge
perdón[1] *nm, pl* **perdones** : forgiveness, pardon
perdón[2] *interj* : excuse me!, sorry!
perdonable *adj* : forgivable
perdonar *vt* **1** DISCULPAR : to forgive, to pardon **2** : to exempt, to excuse
perdurable *adj* : lasting
perdurar *vi* : to last, to endure, to survive
perecedero, -ra *adj* : perishable
perecer {53} *vi* : to perish, to die
peregrinación *nf, pl* **-ciones** : pilgrimage
peregrinaje *nm* → **peregrinación**

peregrino[1], **-na** *adj* **1** : unusual, odd **2** MIGRATORIO : migratory
peregrino[2], **-na** *n* : pilgrim
perejil *nm* : parsley
perenne *adj* : perennial
perentorio, -ria *adj* **1** : peremptory **2** URGENTE : urgent **3** FIJO : fixed, set
pereza *nf* FLOJERA, HOLGAZANERÍA : laziness, idleness
perezoso[1], **-sa** *adj* FLOJO, HOLGAZÁN : lazy
perezoso[2] *nm* : sloth (animal)
perfección *nf, pl* **-ciones** : perfection
perfeccionamiento *nm* : perfecting, refinement
perfeccionar *vt* : to perfect, to refine
perfeccionismo *nm* : perfectionism
perfeccionista *nmf* : perfectionist
perfecto, -ta *adj* : perfect — **perfectamente** *adv*
perfidia *nf* : perfidy, treachery
pérfido, -da *adj* : perfidious
perfil *nm* **1** : profile **2 de ∼** : sideways, from the side **3 perfiles** *nmpl* RASGOS : features, characteristics
perfilar *vt* : to outline, to define — **perfilarse** *vr* **1** : to be outlined, to be silhouetted **2** : to take shape
perforación *nf, pl* **-ciones 1** : perforation **2** : drilling
perforadora *nf* **1** : hole punch (for paper) **2** : drill (in mining, etc.)
perforar *vt* **1** : to perforate, to pierce **2** : to drill, to bore
perfumar *vt* : to perfume, to scent — **perfumarse** *vr*
perfume *nm* : perfume, scent
pergamino *nm* : parchment
pérgola *nf* : pergola, arbor
pericia *nf* : skill, expertise
pericial *adj* : expert ⟨testigo pericial : expert witness⟩
perico *nm* COTORRA : small parrot
periferia *nf* : periphery
periférico[1], **-ca** *adj* : peripheral
periférico[2] *nm* **1** *CA, Mex* : beltway **2** : peripheral
perilla *nf* **1** : goatee **2** : pommel (on a saddle) **3** *Col, Mex* : knob, handle **4 perilla de la oreja** : earlobe **5 de perillas** *fam* : handy, just right
perímetro *nm* : perimeter
periódico[1], **-ca** *adj* : periodic — **periódicamente** *adv*
periódico[2] *nm* DIARIO : newspaper
periodismo *nm* : journalism
periodista *nmf* : journalist
periodístico, -ca *adj* : journalistic, news
período *or* **periodo** *nm* : period
peripecia *nf* VICISITUD : vicissitude, reversal ⟨las peripecias de su carrera : the ups and downs of her career⟩
periquito *nm* **1** : parakeet **2 periquito australiano** : budgerigar
periscopio *nm* : periscope
perito, -ta *adj & n* : expert
perjudicar {72} *vt* : to harm, to be detrimental to

perjudicial *adj* : harmful, detrimental
perjuicio *nm* **1** : harm, damage **2 en perjuicio de** : to the detriment of
perjurar *vi* : to perjure oneself
perjurio *nm* : perjury
perjuro, -ra *n* : perjurer
perla *nf* **1** : pearl **2 de perlas** *fam* : wonderfully ⟨me viene de perlas : it suits me just fine⟩
permanecer {53} *vi* **1** QUEDARSE : to remain, to stay **2** SEGUIR : to remain, to continue to be
permanencia *nf* **1** : permanence, continuance **2** ESTANCIA : stay
permanente[1] *adj* **1** : permanent **2** : constant — **permanentemente** *adv*
permanente[2] *nf* : permanent (wave)
permeabilidad *nf* : permeability
permeable *adj* : permeable
permisible *adj* : permissible, allowable
permisividad *nf* : permissiveness
permisivo, -va *adv* : permissive
permiso *nm* **1** : permission **2** : permit, license **3** : leave, furlough **4 con ∼** : excuse me, pardon me
permitir *vt* : to permit, to allow — **permitirse** *vr*
permuta *nf* : exchange
permutar *vt* INTERCAMBIAR : to exchange
pernicioso, -sa *adj* : pernicious, destructive
pernil *nm* **1** : haunch (of an animal) **2** : leg (of meat), ham **3** : trouser leg
perno *nm* : bolt, pin
pernoctar *vi* : to stay overnight, to spend the night
pero[1] *nm* **1** : fault, defect ⟨ponerle peros a : to find fault with⟩ **2** : objection
pero[2] *conj* : but
perogrullada *nf* : truism, platitude, cliché
peroné *nm* : fibula
perorar *vi* : to deliver a speech
perorata *nf* : oration, long-winded speech
peróxido *nm* : peroxide
perpendicular *adj & nf* : perpendicular
perpetrar *vt* : to perpetrate
perpetuar {3} *vt* ETERNIZAR : to perpetuate
perpetuidad *nf* : perpetuity
perpetuo, -tua *adj* : perpetual — **perpetuamente** *adv*
perplejidad *nf* : perplexity
perplejo, -ja *adj* : perplexed, puzzled
perrada *nf fam* : dirty trick
perrera *nf* : kennel, dog pound
perrero, -ra *n* : dogcatcher
perrito, -ta *n* CACHORRO : puppy, small dog
perro, -rra *n* **1** : dog, bitch *f* **2 perro caliente** : hot dog **3 perro salchicha** : dachshund **4 perro faldero** : lapdog **5 perro cobrador** : retriever
persa[1] *adj & nmf* : Persian
persa[2] *nm* : Persian (language)

persecución *nf, pl* **-ciones 1** : pursuit, chase **2** : persecution
perseguidor, -dora *n* **1** : pursuer **2** : persecutor
perseguir {75} *vt* **1** : to pursue, to chase **2** : to persecute **3** : to pester, to annoy
perseverancia *nf* : perseverance
perseverar *vi* : to persevere
persiana *nf* : blind, venetian blind
persignarse *vr* SANTIGUARSE : to cross oneself, to make the sign of the cross
persistir *vi* : to persist — **persistencia** *nf* — **persistente** *adj*
persona *nf* : person
personaje *nm* **1** : character (in drama or literature) **2** : personage, celebrity
personal[1] *adj* : personal — **personalmente** *adv*
personal[2] *nm* : personnel, staff
personalidad *nf* : personality
personalizar {21} *vt* : to personalize
personificar {72} *vi* : to personify — **personificación** *nf*
perspectiva *nf* **1** : perspective, view **2** : prospect, outlook
perspicacia *nf* : shrewdness, perspicacity, insight
perspicaz *adj, pl* **-caces** : shrewd, perspicacious
persuadir *vt* : to persuade — **persuadirse** *vr* : to become convinced
persuasión *nf, pl* **-siones** : persuasion
persuasivo, -va *adj* : persuasive
pertenecer {53} *vi* : to belong
perteneciente *adj* ～ **a** : belonging to
pertenencia *nf* **1** : membership **2** : ownership **3 pertenencias** *nfpl* : belongings, possessions
pértiga *nf* GARROCHA : pole ⟨salto de pértiga : pole vault⟩
pertinaz *adj, pl* **-naces 1** OBSTINADO : obstinate **2** PERSISTENTE : persistent
pertinencia *nf* : pertinence, relevance — **pertinente** *adj*
pertrechos *nmpl* : equipment, gear
perturbación *nf, pl* **-ciones** : disturbance, disruption
perturbador, -dora *adj* **1** INQUIETANTE : disturbing, troubling **2** : disruptive
perturbar *vt* **1** : to disturb, to trouble **2** : to disrupt
peruano, -na *adj & n* : Peruvian
perversidad *nf* : perversity, depravity
perversión *nf, pl* **-siones** : perversion
perverso, -sa *adj* : wicked, depraved
pervertido[1], **-da** *adj* DEPRAVADO : perverted, depraved
pervertido[2], **-da** *n* : pervert
pervertir {76} *vt* : to pervert, to corrupt
pesa *nf* **1** : weight **2 levantamiento de pesas** : weightlifting
pesadamente *adv* **1** : heavily **2** : slowly, clumsily
pesadez *nf, pl* **-deces 1** : heaviness **2** : slowness **3** : tediousness
pesadilla *nf* : nightmare

pesado[1], **-da** *adj* **1** : heavy **2** : slow **3** : irritating, annoying **4** : tedious, boring **5** : tough, difficult
pesado[2], **-da** *n fam* : bore, pest
pesadumbre *nf* AFLICCIÓN : grief, sorrow, sadness
pésame *nm* : condolences *pl* ⟨mi más sentido pésame : my heartfelt condolences⟩
pesar[1] *vt* **1** : to weigh **2** EXAMINAR : to consider, to think over — *vi* **1** : to weigh ⟨¿cuánto pesa? : how much does it weigh?⟩ **2** : to be heavy **3** : to weigh heavily, to be a burden ⟨no le pesa : it's not a burden on him⟩ ⟨pesa sobre mi corazón : it weighs upon my heart⟩ **4** INFLUIR : to carry weight, to have bearing **5** (*with personal pronouns*) : to grieve, to sadden ⟨me pesa mucho : I'm very sorry⟩ **6 pese a** : in spite of, despite
pesar[2] *nm* **1** AFLICCIÓN, PENA : sorrow, grief **2** REMORDIMIENTO : remorse **3 a pesar de** : in spite of, despite
pesaroso, -sa *adj* **1** : sad, mournful **2** ARREPENTIDO : sorry, regretful
pesca *nf* : fishing
pescadería *nf* : fish market
pescado *nm* : fish (as food)
pescador, -dora *n* : fisherman *m*, fisherwoman *f*
pescar {72} *vt* **1** : to fish for **2** : to catch **3** *fam* : to get a hold of, to land — *vi* : to fish, to go fishing
pescuezo *nm* : neck
pesebre *nm* : manger
pesero *nm Mex* : minibus
peseta *nf* : peseta (Spanish unit of currency)
pesimismo *nm* : pessimism
pesimista[1] *adj* : pessimistic
pesimista[2] *nmf* : pessimist
pésimo, -ma *adj* : dreadful, abominable
peso *nm* **1** : weight, heaviness **2** : burden, responsibility **3** : weight (in sports) **4** BÁSCULA : scales *pl* **5** : peso
pesque, etc. → **pescar**
pesquería *nf* : fishery
pesquero[1], **-ra** *adj* : fishing ⟨pueblo pesquero : fishing village⟩
pesquero[2] *nm* : fishing boat
pesquisa *nf* INVESTIGACIÓN : inquiry, investigation
pestaña *nf* **1** : eyelash **2** : flange, rim
pestañear *vi* : to blink
pestañeo *nm* : blink
peste *nf* **1** : plague, pestilence **2** : stench, stink **3** : nuisance, pest
pesticida *nm* : pesticide
pestilencia *nf* **1** : stench, foul odor **2** : pestilence
pestilente *adj* **1** : foul, smelly **2** : pestilent
pestillo *nm* CERROJO : bolt, latch
petaca *nf* **1** *Mex* : suitcase **2 petacas** *nfpl Mex fam* : bottom, behind
pétalo *nm* : petal
petardear *vi* : to backfire

petardeo *nm* : backfiring
petardo *nm* : firecracker
petate *nm Mex* : mat
petición *nf, pl* -**ciones** : petition, request
peticionar *vt* : to petition
peticionario, -ria *n* : petitioner
petirrojo *nm* : robin
peto *nm* : bib (of clothing)
pétreo, -trea *adj* : stone, stony
petrificar {72} *vt* : to petrify
petróleo *nm* : oil, petroleum
petrolero¹, -ra *adj* : oil ⟨industria petrolera : oil industry⟩
petrolero² *nm* : oil tanker
petrolífero, -ra *adj* → **petrolero¹**
petulancia *nf* INSOLENCIA : insolence, petulance
petulante *adj* INSOLENTE : insolent, petulant — **petulantemente** *adv*
petunia *nf* : petunia
peyorativo, -va *adj* : pejorative
pez¹ *nm, pl* **peces** 1 : fish 2 **pez de colores** : goldfish 3 **pez espada** : swordfish 4 **pez gordo** : big shot
pez² *nf, pl* **peces** : pitch, tar
pezón *nm, pl* **pezones** : nipple
pezuña *nf* : hoof ⟨pezuña hendida : cloven hoof⟩
pi *nf* : pi
piadoso, -sa *adj* 1 : compassionate, merciful 2 DEVOTO : pious, devout
pianista *nmf* : pianist, piano player
piano *nm* : piano
piar {85} *vi* : to chirp, to cheep, to tweet
pibe, -ba *n Arg, Uru fam* : kid, child
pica *nf* 1 : pike, lance 2 : goad (in bullfighting) 3 : spade (in playing cards)
picada *nf* 1 : bite, sting (of an insect) 2 : sharp descent
picadillo *nm* 1 : minced meat, hash 2 **hacer picadillo a** : to beat to a pulp
picado, -da *adj* 1 : perforated 2 : minced, chopped 3 : decayed (of teeth) 4 : choppy, rough 5 *fam* : annoyed, miffed
picador *nm* : picador
picadura *nf* 1 : sting, bite 2 : prick, puncture 3 : decay, cavity
picaflor *nm* COLIBRÍ : hummingbird
picana *nf* : goad, prod
picante¹ *adj* 1 : hot, spicy 2 : sharp, cutting 3 : racy, risqué
picante² *nm* 1 : spiciness 2 : hot spices *pl*, hot sauce
picaporte *nm* 1 : latch 2 : door handle 3 ALDABA : door knocker
picar {72} *vt* 1 : to sting, to bite 2 : to peck at 3 : to nibble on 4 : to prick, to puncture, to punch (a ticket) 5 : to grind, to chop 6 : to goad, to incite 7 : to pique, to provoke — *vi* 1 : to itch 2 : to sting 3 : to be spicy 4 : to nibble 5 : to take the bait 6 ~ **en** : to dabble in 7 **picar muy alto** : to aim too high — **picarse** *vr* 1 : to get a cavity, to decay 2 : to get annoyed, to take offense
picardía *nf* 1 : cunning, craftiness 2 : prank, dirty trick

picaresco, -ca *adj* 1 : picaresque 2 : rascally, roguish
pícaro¹, -ra *adj* 1 : mischievous 2 : cunning, sly 3 : off-color, risqué
pícaro², -ra *n* 1 : rogue, scoundrel 2 : rascal
picazón *nf, pl* -**zones** COMEZÓN : itch
picea *nf* : spruce (tree)
pichel *nm* : pitcher, jug
pichón, -chona *n, mpl* **pichones** 1 : young pigeon, squab 2 *Mex fam* : novice, greenhorn
picnic *nm* : picnic
pico *nm* 1 : peak 2 : point, spike 3 : beak, bill 4 : pick, pickax 5 **y pico** : and a little, and a bit ⟨las siete y pico : a little after seven⟩ ⟨dos metros y pico : a bit over two meters⟩
picor *nm* : itch, irritation
picoso, -sa *adj Mex* : very hot, spicy
picota *nf* 1 : pillory, stock 2 **poner a alguien en la picota** : to put someone on the spot
picotada *nf* → **picotazo**
picotazo *nm* : peck (of a bird)
picotear *vt* : to peck — *vi* : to nibble, to pick
pictórico, -ca *adj* : pictorial
picudo, -da *adj* 1 : pointy, sharp 2 ~ **para** *Mex fam* : clever at, good at
pide, etc. → **pedir**
pie *nm* 1 : foot ⟨a pie : on foot⟩ ⟨de pie : on one's feet, standing⟩ 2 : base, bottom, stem, foot ⟨pie de la cama : foot of the bed⟩ ⟨pie de una lámpara : base of a lamp⟩ ⟨pie de la escalera : bottom of the stairs⟩ ⟨pie de una copa : stem of a glass⟩ 3 : foot (in measurement) ⟨pie cuadrado : square foot⟩ 4 : cue (in theater) 5 **dar pie a** : to give cause for, to give rise to 6 **en pie de igualdad** : on equal footing
piedad *nf* 1 COMPASIÓN : mercy, pity 2 DEVOCIÓN : piety, devotion
piedra *nf* 1 : stone 2 : flint (of a lighter) 3 : hailstone 4 **piedra de afilar** : whetstone, grindstone 5 **piedra angular** : cornerstone 6 **piedra arenisca** : sandstone 7 **piedra caliza** : limestone 8 **piedra imán** : lodestone 9 **piedra de molino** : millstone 10 **piedra de toque** : touchstone
piel *nf* 1 : skin 2 CUERO : leather, hide ⟨piel de venado : deerskin⟩ 3 : fur, pelt 4 CÁSCARA : peel, skin 5 **piel de gallina** : goose bumps *pl* ⟨me pone la piel de gallina : it gives me goose bumps⟩
piélago *nm* **el piélago** : the deep, the ocean
piensa, etc. → **pensar**
pienso *nm* : feed, fodder
pierde, etc. → **perder**
pierna *nf* : leg
pieza *nf* 1 ELEMENTO : piece, part, component ⟨vestido de dos piezas : two-piece dress⟩ ⟨pieza de recambio : spare part⟩ ⟨pieza clave : key element⟩ 2 : piece (in chess) 3 OBRA : piece, work

⟨pieza de teatro : play⟩ **4** : room, bedroom
pifia *nf fam* : goof, blunder
pigargo *nm* : osprey
pigmentación *nf, pl* **-ciones** : pigmentation
pigmento *nm* : pigment
pigmeo, -mea *adj & n* : pygmy, Pygmy
pijama *nm* : pajamas *pl*
pila *nf* **1** BATERÍA : battery ⟨pila de linterna : flashlight battery⟩ **2** MONTÓN : pile, heap **3** : sink, basin, font ⟨pila bautismal : baptismal font⟩ ⟨pila para pájaros : birdbath⟩
pilar *nm* **1** : pillar, column **2** : support, mainstay
píldora *nf* PASTILLA : pill
pillaje *nm* : pillage, plunder
pillar *vt* **1** *fam* : to catch ⟨¡cuidado! ¡nos pillarán! : watch out! they'll catch us!⟩ **2** *fam* : to grasp, to catch on ⟨¿no lo pillas? : don't you get it?⟩
pillo[1], -lla *adj* : cunning, crafty
pillo[2], -lla *n* **1** : rascal, brat **2** : rogue, scoundrel
pilluelo, -la *n* : urchin
pilón *nm, pl* **pilones 1** PILA : basin **2** : pillar, tower (for cables), pylon (of a bridge) **3** *Mex* : extra, lagniappe
pilotar *vt* : to pilot, to drive
pilote *nm* : pile (stake)
pilotear → **pilotar**
piloto *nm* **1** : pilot, driver **2** : pilot light
piltrafa *nf* **1** : poor quality meat **2** : wretch **3 piltrafas** *nfpl* : food scraps
pimentero *nm* : pepper shaker
pimentón *nm, pl* **-tones 1** : paprika **2** : cayenne pepper
pimienta *nf* **1** : pepper (condiment) **2 pimienta de Jamaica** : allspice
pimiento *nm* : pepper (fruit) ⟨pimiento verde : green pepper⟩
pináculo *nm* **1** : pinnacle (of a building) **2** : peak, acme
pincel *nm* : paintbrush
pincelada *nf* **1** : brushstroke **2 últimas pinceladas** : final touches
pinchar *vt* **1** PICAR : to puncture (a tire) **2** : to prick, to stick **3** : to goad, to tease, to needle — *vi* **1** : to be prickly **2** : to get a flat tire **3** *fam* : to get beaten, to lose out — **pincharse** *vr* : to give oneself an injection
pinchazo *nm* **1** : prick, jab **2** : puncture, flat tire
pingüe *adj* **1** : rich, huge (of profits) **2** : lucrative
pingüino *nm* : penguin
pininos *or* **pinitos** *nmpl* : first steps ⟨hacer pininos : to take one's first steps, to toddle⟩
pino *nm* : pine, pine tree
pinta *nf* **1** : dot, spot **2** : pint **3** *fam* : aspect, appearance ⟨las peras tienen buena pinta : the pears look good⟩ **4 pintas** *nfpl Mex* : graffiti
pintadas *nfpl* : graffiti

pintar *vt* **1** : to paint **2** : to draw, to mark **3** : to describe, to depict — *vi* **1** : to paint, to draw **2** : to look ⟨no pinta bien : it doesn't look good⟩ **3** *fam* : to count ⟨aquí no pinta nada : he has no say here⟩ — **pintarse** *vr* **1** MAQUILLARSE : to put on makeup **2 pintárselas solo** *fam* : to manage by oneself, to know it all
pintarrajear *vt* : to daub (with paint)
pinto, -ta *adj* : speckled, spotted
pintor, -tora *n* **1** : painter **2 pintor de brocha gorda** : housepainter, dauber
pintoresco, -ca *adj* : picturesque, quaint
pintura *nf* **1** : paint **2** : painting (art, work of art)
pinza *nf* **1** : clothespin **2** : claw, pincer **3** : pleat, dart **4 pinzas** *nfpl* : tweezers **5 pinzas** *nfpl* ALICATES : pliers, pincers
pinzón *nm, pl* **pinzones** : finch
piña *nf* **1** : pineapple **2** : pine cone
piñata *nf* : piñata
piñón *nm, pl* **piñones 1** : pine nut **2** : pinion
pío[1], pía *adj* **1** DEVOTO : pious, devout **2** : piebald, pied, dappled
pío[2] *nm* : peep, tweet, cheep
piocha *nf* **1** : pickax **2** *Mex* : goatee
piojo *nm* : louse
piojoso, -sa *adj* **1** : lousy **2** : filthy
pionero[1], -ra *adj* : pioneering
pionero[2], -ra *n* : pioneer
pipa *nf* : pipe (for smoking)
pipián *nm, pl* **pipianes** *Mex* : a spicy sauce or stew
pipiolo, -la *n fam* **1** : greenhorn, novice **2** : kid, youngster
pique[1], etc. → **picar**
pique[2] *nm* **1** : pique, resentment **2** : rivalry, competition **3 a pique de** : about to, on the verge of **4 irse a pique** : to sink, to founder
piqueta *nf* : pickax
piquete *nm* **1** : picketers *pl*, picket line **2** : squad, detachment **3** *Mex* : prick, jab
piquetear *vt* **1** : to picket **2** *Mex* : to prick, to jab
pira *nf* : pyre
piragua *nf* : canoe — **piragüista** *nmf*
pirámide *nf* : pyramid
piraña *nf* : piranha
pirata[1] *adj* : bootleg, pirated
pirata[2] *nmf* **1** : pirate **2** : bootlegger **3 pirata aéreo** : hijacker
piratear *vt* **1** : to hijack, to commandeer **2** : to bootleg, to pirate
piratería *nf* : piracy, bootlegging
piromanía *nf* : pyromania
pirómano, -na *n* : pyromaniac
piropo *nm* : flirtatious compliment
pirotecnia *nf* : fireworks *pl*, pyrotechnics *pl*
pirotécnico, -ca *adj* : fireworks, pyrotechnic
pírrico, -ca *adj* : Pyrrhic
pirueta *nf* : pirouette
pirulí *nm* : cone-shaped lollipop

pisada *nf* **1** : footstep **2** HUELLA : footprint

pisapapeles *nms & pl* : paperweight

pisar *vt* **1** : to step on, to set foot in **2** : to walk all over, to mistreat — *vi* : to step, to walk, to tread

piscina *nf* **1** : swimming pool **2** : fish pond

Piscis *nmf* : Pisces

piso *nm* **1** PLANTA : floor, story **2** SUELO : floor **3** *Spain* : apartment

pisotear *vt* **1** : to stamp on, to trample **2** PISAR : to walk all over **3** : to flout, to disregard

pisotón *nm, pl* **-tones** : stamp, step ⟨sufrieron empujones y pisotones : they were pushed and stepped on⟩

pista *nf* **1** RASTRO : trail, track ⟨siguen la pista de los sospechosos : they're on the trail of the suspects⟩ **2** : clue **3** CAMINO : road, trail **4** : track, racetrack **5** : ring, arena, rink **6 pista de aterrizaje** : runway, airstrip **7 pista de baile** : dance floor

pistacho *nm* : pistachio

pistilo *nm* : pistil

pistola *nf* **1** : pistol, handgun **2** : spray gun

pistolera *nf* : holster

pistolero *nm* : gunman

pistón *nm, pl* **pistones** : piston

pita *nf* **1** : agave **2** : pita fiber **3** : twine

pitar *vi* **1** : to blow a whistle **2** : to whistle, to boo **3** : to beep, to honk, to toot — *vt* : to whistle at, to boo

pitido *nm* **1** : whistle, whistling **2** : beep, honk, toot

pito *nm* **1** SILBATO : whistle **2 no me importa un pito** *fam* : I don't give a damn

pitón *nm, pl* **pitones** **1** : python **2** : point of a bull's horn

pituitario, -ria *adj* : pituitary

pívot *nmf, pl* **pívots** : center (in basketball)

pivote *nm* : pivot

piyama *nmf* : pajamas *pl*

pizarra *nf* **1** : slate **2** : blackboard **3** : scoreboard

pizarrón *nm, pl* **-rrones** : blackboard, chalkboard

pizca *nf* **1** : pinch ⟨una pizca de canela : a pinch of cinnamon⟩ **2** : speck, trace ⟨ni pizca : not a bit⟩ **3** *Mex* : harvest

pizcar {72} *vt Mex* : to harvest

pizque, etc. → **pizcar**

pizza ['pitsa, 'pisa] *nf* : pizza

pizzería *nf* : pizzeria, pizza parlor

placa *nf* **1** : sheet, plate **2** : plaque, nameplate **3** : plate (in photography) **4** : badge, insignia **5 placa de matrícula** : license plate, tag **6 placa dental** : plaque, tartar

placebo *nm* : placebo

placenta *nf* : placenta, afterbirth

placentero, -ra *adj* AGRADABLE, GRATO : pleasant, agreeable

placer[1] {57} *vi* GUSTAR : to be pleasing ⟨hazlo como te plazca : do it however you please⟩

placer[2] *nm* **1** : pleasure, enjoyment **2 a ~** : as much as one wants

plácido, -da *adj* TRANQUILO : placid, calm

plaga *nf* **1** : plague, infestation, blight **2** CALAMIDAD : disaster, scourge

plagado, -da *adj* **~ de** : filled with, covered with

plagar {52} *vt* : to plague

plagiar *vt* **1** : to plagiarize **2** SECUESTRAR : to kidnap, to abduct

plagiario, -ria *n* **1** : plagiarist **2** SECUESTRADOR : kidnapper, abductor

plagio *nm* **1** : plagiarism **2** SECUESTRO : kidnapping, abduction

plague, etc. → **plagar**

plan *nm* **1** : plan, strategy, program ⟨plan de inversiones : investment plan⟩ ⟨plan de estudios : curriculum⟩ **2** PLANO : plan, diagram **3** : attitude, intent, purpose ⟨ponte en plan serio : be serious⟩ ⟨estamos en plan de divertirnos : we're looking to have some fun⟩

plana *nf* **1** : page ⟨noticias en primera plana : front-page news⟩ **2 plana mayor** : staff (in the military)

plancha *nf* **1** : iron, ironing **2** : grill, griddle ⟨a la plancha : grilled⟩ **3** : sheet, plate ⟨plancha para hornear : baking sheet⟩ **4** *fam* : blunder, blooper

planchada *nf* : ironing, pressing

planchado *nm* → **planchada**

planchar *v* : to iron

planchazo *nm fam* : goof, blunder

plancton *nm* : plankton

planeación *nf* → **planeamiento**

planeador *nm* : glider (aircraft)

planeamiento *nm* : plan, planning

planear *vt* : to plan — *vi* : to glide (in the air)

planeo *nm* : gliding, soaring

planeta *nm* : planet

planetario[1], **-ria** *adj* **1** : planetary **2** : global, worldwide

planetario[2] *nm* : planetarium

planicie *nf* : plain

planificación *nf* : planning ⟨planificación familiar : family planning⟩

planificar {72} *vt* : to plan

planilla *nf* **1** LISTA : list **2** NÓMINA : payroll **3** TABLA : chart, table **4** *Mex* : slate, ticket (of candidates) **5 planilla de cálculo** *Arg, Chile* : spreadsheet

plano[1], **-na** *adj* : flat, level, plane

plano[2] *nm* **1** PLAN : map, plan **2** : plane (surface) **3** NIVEL : level ⟨en un plano personal : on a personal level⟩ **4** : shot (in photography) **5 de ~** : flatly, outright, directly ⟨se negó de plano : he flatly refused⟩

planta *nf* **1** : plant ⟨planta de interior : houseplant⟩ **2** FÁBRICA : plant, factory **3** PISO : floor, story **4** : staff, employees *pl* **5** : sole (of the foot)

plantación *nf, pl* **-ciones** 1 : plantation 2 : planting
plantado, -da *adj* 1 : planted 2 **dejar plantado** : to stand up (a date), to dump (a lover)
plantar *vt* 1 : to plant, to sow ⟨plantar de flores : to plant with flowers⟩ 2 : to put in, to place 3 *fam* : to plant, to land ⟨plantar un beso : to plant a kiss⟩ 4 *fam* : to leave, to jilt — **plantarse** *vr* 1 : to stand firm 2 *fam* : to arrive, to show up 3 *fam* : to balk
planteamiento *nm* 1 : approach, position ⟨el planteamiento feminista : the feminist viewpoint⟩ 2 : explanation, exposition 3 : proposal, suggestion, plan
plantear *vt* 1 : to set forth, to bring up, to suggest 2 : to establish, to set up 3 : to create, to pose (a problem) — **plantearse** *vr* 1 : to think about 2 : to arise
plantel *nm* 1 : educational institution 2 : staff, team
planteo → **planteamiento**
plantilla *nf* 1 : insole 2 : pattern, template, stencil 3 *Mex, Spain* : staff, roster of employees
plantío *nm* : field (planted with a crop)
plantón *nm, pl* **plantones** 1 : seedling 2 : long wait ⟨darle a alguien un plantón : to stand someone up⟩
plañidero¹, -ra *adj* : mournful
plañidero², -ra *nf* : hired mourner
plañir {38} *v* : to mourn, to lament
plasma *nm* : plasma
plasmar *vt* : to express, to give form to — **plasmarse** *vr*
plasta *nf* : soft mass, lump
plástica *nf* : modeling, sculpture
plasticidad *nf* : plasticity
plástico¹, -ca *adj* : plastic
plástico² *nm* : plastic
plastificar {72} *vt* : to laminate
plata *nf* 1 : silver 2 : money
plataforma *nf* ESTRADO, TARIMA : platform, dais 2 : platform (in politics) 3 : springboard, stepping stone 4 **plataforma continental** : continental shelf 5 **plataforma de lanzamiento** : launchpad 6 **plataforma petrolífera** : oil rig (at sea)
platal *nm* : large sum of money, fortune
platanal *nm* : banana plantation
platanero¹, -ra *adj* : banana, banana-producing
platanero², -ra *n* : banana grower
plátano *nm* 1 : banana 2 : plantain 3 **plátano macho** *Mex* : plantain
platea *nf* : orchestra, pit (in a theater)
plateado, -da *adj* 1 : silver, silvery 2 : silver-plated
plática *nf* 1 : talk, lecture 2 : chat, conversation
platicar {72} *vi* : to talk, to chat — *vt Mex* : to tell, to say
platija *nf* : flatfish, flounder

platillo *nm* 1 : saucer ⟨platillo volador : flying saucer⟩ 2 : cymbal 3 *Mex* : dish ⟨platillos típicos : local dishes⟩
platino *nm* : platinum
plato *nm* 1 : plate, dish ⟨lavar los platos : to do the dishes⟩ 2 : serving, helping 3 : course (of a meal) 4 : dish ⟨plato típico : typical dish⟩ 5 : home plate (in baseball) 6 **plato hondo** : soup bowl
plató *nm* : set (in the movies)
platónico, -ca *adj* : platonic
playa *nf* : beach, seashore
playera *nf* 1 : canvas sneaker 2 *CA, Mex* : T-shirt
plaza *nf* 1 : square, plaza 2 : marketplace 3 : room, space, seat (in a vehicle) 4 : post, position 5 **plaza fuerte** : stronghold, fortified city 6 **plaza de toros** : bullring
plazca, etc. → **placer**
plazo *nm* 1 : period, term ⟨un plazo de cinco días : a period of five days⟩ ⟨a largo plazo : long-term⟩ 2 ABONO : installment ⟨pagar a plazos : to pay in installments⟩
pleamar *nf* : high tide
plebe *nf* : common people, masses *pl*
plebeyo¹, -ya *adj* : plebeian
plebeyo², -ya *n* : plebeian, commoner
plegable *adj* : folding, collapsible
plegadizo → **plegable**
plegar {49} *vt* DOBLAR : to fold, to bend — **plegarse** *vr* : to give in, to yield
plegaria *nf* ORACIÓN : prayer
pleito *nm* 1 : lawsuit 2 : fight, argument, dispute
plenamente *adv* COMPLETAMENTE : fully, completely
plenario, -ria *adj* : plenary, full
plenilunio *nm* : full moon
plenipotenciario, -ria *n* : plenipotentiary
plenitud *nf* : fullness, abundance
pleno, -na *adj* COMPLETO ((*often used as an intensifier*)) : full, complete ⟨en pleno uso de sus facultades : in full command of his faculties⟩ ⟨en plena noche : in the middle of the night⟩ ⟨en pleno corazón de la ciudad : right in the heart of the city⟩
plétora *nf* : plethora
pleuresía *nf* : pleurisy
pliega, pliegue etc. → **plegar**
pliego *nm* 1 HOJA : sheet of paper 2 : sealed document
pliegue *nm* 1 DOBLEZ : crease, fold 2 : pleat
plisar *vt* : to pleat
plomada *nf* 1 : plumb line 2 : sinker
plomería *nf* FONTANERÍA : plumbing
plomero, -ra *n* FONTANERO : plumber
plomizo, -za *adj* : leaden
plomo *nm* 1 : lead 2 : plumb line 3 : fuse 4 *fam* : bore, drag 5 **a** ~ : plumb, straight
plugo, etc. → **placer**
pluma *nf* 1 : feather 2 : pen 3 **pluma fuente** : fountain pen

plumaje *nm* : plumage
plumero *nm* : feather duster
plumilla *nf* : nib
plumón *nm, pl* **plumones** : down
plumoso, -sa *adj* : feathery, downy
plural *adj & nm* : plural
pluralidad *nf* : plurality
pluralizar {21} *vt* : to pluralize
pluriempleado, -da *adj* : holding more than one job
pluriempleo *nm* : moonlighting
plus *nm* : bonus
plusvalía *nf* : appreciation, capital gain
Plutón *nm* : Pluto
plutocracia *nf* : plutocracy
plutonio *nm* : plutonium
población *nf, pl* **-ciones** 1 : population 2 : city, town, village
poblado¹, -da *adj* 1 : inhabited, populated 2 : full, thick ⟨cejas pobladas : bushy eyebrows⟩
poblado² *nm* : village, settlement
poblador, -dora *n* : settler
poblar {19} *vt* 1 : to populate, to inhabit 2 : to settle, to colonize 3 ~ **de** : to stock with, to plant with — **poblarse** *vr* : to fill up, to become crowded
pobre¹ *adj* 1 : poor, impoverished 2 : unfortunate ⟨¡pobre de mí! : poor me!⟩ 3 : weak, deficient ⟨una dieta pobre : a poor diet⟩
pobre² *nmf* : poor person ⟨los pobres : the poor⟩ ⟨¡pobre! : poor thing!⟩
pobremente *adv* : poorly
pobreza *nf* : poverty
pocilga *nf* CHIQUERO : pigsty, pigpen
pocillo *nm* : small coffee cup, demitasse
poción *nf, pl* **pociones** : potion
poco¹ *adv* 1 : little, not much ⟨poco probable : not very likely⟩ ⟨come poco : he doesn't eat much⟩ 2 : a short time, a while ⟨tardaremos poco : we won't be very long⟩ 3 **poco antes** : shortly before 4 **poco después** : shortly after
poco², -ca *adj* 1 : little, not much, (a) few ⟨tengo poco dinero : I don't have much money⟩ ⟨en no pocas ocasiones : on more than a few occasions⟩ ⟨poca gente : few people⟩ 2 **pocas veces** : rarely
poco³, -ca *pron* 1 : little, few ⟨le falta poco para terminar : he's almost finished⟩ ⟨uno de los pocos que quedan : one of the remaining few⟩ 2 **un poco** : a little, a bit ⟨un poco de vino : a little wine⟩ ⟨un poco extraño : a bit strange⟩ 3 **a ~** *Mex* (*used to express disbelief*) ⟨¿a poco no se te hizo difícil? : you mean you didn't find it difficult?⟩ 4 **de a poco** : little by little 5 **hace poco** : not long ago 6 **poco a poco** : little by little 7 **dentro de poco** : shortly, in a little while 8 **por ~** : nearly, almost
podar *vt* : to prune, to trim
poder¹ {58} *v aux* 1 : to be able to, can ⟨no puede hablar : he can't speak⟩ 2 (*expressing possibility*) : might, may ⟨puede llover : it may rain at any mo-

ment⟩ ⟨¿cómo puede ser? : how can that be?⟩ 3 (*expressing permission*) : can, may ⟨¿puedo ir a la fiesta? : can I go to the party?⟩ ⟨¿se puede? : may I come in?⟩ — *vi* 1 : to beat, to defeat ⟨cree que le puede a cualquiera : he thinks he can beat anyone⟩ 2 : to be possible ⟨¿crees que vendrán? — puede (que sí) : do you think they'll come? — maybe⟩ 3 ~ **con** : to cope with, to manage ⟨¡no puedo con estos niños! : I can't handle these children!⟩ 4 **no poder más** : to have had enough ⟨no puede más : she can't take anymore⟩ 5 **no poder menos que** : to not be able to help ⟨no pudo menos que asombrarse : she couldn't help but be amazed⟩
poder² *nm* 1 : control, power ⟨poder adquisitivo : purchasing power⟩ 2 : authority ⟨el poder legislativo : the legislature⟩ 3 : possession ⟨está en mi poder : it's in my hands⟩ 4 : strength, force ⟨poder militar : military might⟩
poderío *nm* 1 : power 2 : wealth, influence
poderoso, -sa *adj* 1 : powerful 2 : wealthy, influential 3 : effective
podiatría *nf* : podiatry
podio *nm* : podium
pódium → **podio**
podología *nf* : podiatry, chiropody
podólogo, -ga *n* : podiatrist, chiropodist
podrá, etc. → **poder**
podredumbre *nf* 1 : decay, rottenness 2 : corruption
podrido, -da *adj* 1 : rotten, decayed 2 : corrupt
podrir → **pudrir**
poema *nm* : poem
poesía *nf* 1 : poetry 2 POEMA : poem
poeta *nmf* : poet
poético, -ca *adj* : poetic, poetical
pogrom *nm* : pogrom
póker *or* **poker** *nm* : poker (card game)
polaco¹, -ca *adj* : Polish
polaco², -ca *n* : Pole, Polish person
polaco³ *nm* : Polish (language)
polar *adj* : polar
polarizar {21} *vt* : to polarize — **polarizarse** *vr* — **polarización** *nf*
polea *nf* : pulley
polémica *nf* CONTROVERSIA : controversy, polemics
polémico, -ca *adj* CONTROVERTIDO : controversial, polemical
polen *nm, pl* **pólenes** : pollen
policía¹ *nf* : police
policía² *nmf* : police officer, policeman *m*, policewoman *f*
policíaco, -ca *or* **policiaco, -ca** *adj* : police ⟨novela policíaca : detective story⟩
policial *adj* : police
poliéster *nm* : polyester
poligamia *nf* : polygamy
polígamo¹, -ma *adj* : polygamous
polígamo², -ma *n* : polygamist
polígono *nm* : polygon — **polígonal** *adj*

poliinsaturado, -da *adj* : polyunsaturated

polilla *nf* : moth

polimerizar {21} *vt* : to polymerize

polímero *nm* : polymer

polinesio, -sia *adj & n* : Polynesian

polinizar {21} *vt* : to pollinate — **polinización** *nf*

polio *nf* : polio

poliomielitis *nf* : poliomyelitis, polio

polisón *nm, pl* **-sones** : bustle (on clothing)

politécnico, -ca *adj* : polytechnic

politeísmo *nm* : polytheism — **politeísta** *adj & nmf*

política *nf* 1 : politics 2 : policy

políticamente *adv* : politically

político¹, -ca *adj* 1 : political 2 : tactful, politic 3 : by marriage ⟨padre político : father-in-law⟩

político², -ca *n* : politician

póliza *nf* : policy ⟨póliza de seguros : insurance policy⟩

polizón *nm, pl* **-zones** : stowaway ⟨viajar de polizón : to stow away⟩

polka *nf* : polka

polla *nf* APUESTA : bet

pollera *nf* 1 : chicken coop 2 : skirt

pollero, -ra *n* 1 : poulterer 2 : poultry farm 3 *Mex fam* COYOTE : smuggler of illegal immigrants

pollito, -ta *n* : chick, young bird, fledgling

pollo, -lla *n* 1 : chicken 2 POLLITO : chick 3 JOVEN : young man *m*, young lady *f*

polluelo *nm* → **pollito**

polo *nm* 1 : pole ⟨el Polo Norte : the North Pole⟩ ⟨polo negativo : negative pole⟩ 2 : polo (sport) 3 : polo shirt 4 : focal point, center 5 **polo opuesto** : exact opposite

polución *nf, pl* **-ciones** CONTAMINACIÓN : pollution

polvareda *nf* 1 : cloud of dust 2 : uproar, fuss

polvera *nf* : compact (for face powder)

polvo *nm* 1 : dust 2 : powder 3 **polvos** *nmpl* : face powder 4 **polvos de hornear** : baking powder 5 **hacer polvo** *fam* : to crush, to shatter ⟨vas a hacer polvo el reloj : you're going to destroy your watch⟩

pólvora *nf* 1 : gunpowder 2 : fireworks *pl*

polvoriento, -ta *adj* : dusty, powdery

polvorín *nm, pl* **-rines** : magazine, storehouse (for explosives)

pomada *nf* : ointment, cream

pomelo *nm* : grapefruit

pómez *nf or* **piedra pómez** : pumice

pomo *nm* 1 : pommel (on a sword) 2 : knob, handle 3 : perfume bottle

pompa *nf* 1 : bubble 2 : pomp, splendor 3 **pompas fúnebres** : funeral

pompón *nm, pl* **pompones** BORLA : pom-pom

pomposidad *nf* 1 : pomp, splendor 2 : pomposity, ostentation

pomposo, -sa *adj* : pompous — **pomposamente** *adv*

pómulo *nm* : cheekbone

pon → **poner**

ponchadura *nf Mex* : puncture, flat (tire)

ponchar *vt* 1 : to strike out (in baseball) 2 *Mex* : to puncture — **poncharse** *vr* 1 *Col, Ven* : to strike out (in baseball) 2 *Mex* : to blow out (of a tire)

ponche *nm* 1 : punch (drink) 2 **ponche de huevo** : eggnog

poncho *nm* : poncho

ponderación *nf, pl* **-ciones** 1 : consideration, deliberation 2 : high praise

ponderar *vt* 1 : to weigh, to consider 2 : to speak highly of

pondrá, etc. → **poner**

ponencia *nf* 1 DISCURSO : paper, presentation, address 2 INFORME : report

ponente *nmf* : speaker, presenter

poner {60} *vt* 1 COLOCAR : to put, to place ⟨pon el libro en la mesa : put the book on the table⟩ 2 AGREGAR, AÑADIR : to put in, to add 3 : to put on (clothes) 4 CONTRIBUIR : to contribute 5 ESCRIBIR : to put in writing ⟨no le puso su nombre : he didn't put his name on it⟩ 6 IMPONER : to set, to impose 7 EXPONER : to put, to expose ⟨lo puso en peligro : she put him in danger⟩ 8 : to prepare, to arrange ⟨poner la mesa : to set the table⟩ 9 : to name ⟨le pusimos Ana : we called her Ana⟩ 10 ESTABLECER : to set up, to establish ⟨puso un restaurante : he opened up a restaurant⟩ 11 INSTALAR : to install, to put in 12 (*with an adjective or adverb*) : to make ⟨siempre lo pones de mal humor : you always put him in a bad mood⟩ 13 : to turn on, to switch on 14 SUPONER : to suppose ⟨pongamos que no viene : supposing he doesn't come⟩ 15 : to lay (eggs) 16 **~ a** : to start (someone doing something) ⟨lo puse a trabajar : I put him to work⟩ 17 **~ de** : to place as ⟨la pusieron de directora : they made her director⟩ 18 **~ en** : to put in (a state or condition) ⟨poner en duda : to call into question⟩ — *vi* 1 : to contribute 2 : to lay eggs — **ponerse** *vr* 1 : to move (into a position) ⟨ponerse de pie : to stand up⟩ 2 : to put on, to wear 3 : to become, to turn ⟨se puso colorado : he turned red⟩ 4 : to set (of the sun or moon)

poni *or* **poney** *nm* : pony

ponga, etc. → **poner**

poniente *nm* 1 OCCIDENTE : west 2 : west wind

ponqué *nm Col, Ven* : cake

pontifical *adj* : pontifical

pontificar {72} *vi* : to pontificate

pontífice *nm* : pontiff, pope

pontón *nm, pl* **pontones** : pontoon

ponzoña *nf* VENENO : poison — **ponzoñoso, -sa** *adj*

popa *nf* **1** : stern **2 a** ~ : astern, abaft, aft

popelín *nm, pl* **-lines** : poplin

popelina *nf* : poplin

popote *nm Mex* : (drinking) straw

populachero, -ra *adj* : common, popular, vulgar

populacho *nm* : rabble, masses *pl*

popular *adj* **1** : popular **2** : traditional **3** : colloquial

popularidad *nf* : popularity

popularizar {21} *vt* : to popularize — **popularizarse** *vr*

populista *adj & nmf* : populist — **populismo** *nm*

populoso, -sa *adj* : populous

popurrí *nm* : potpourri

por *prep* **1** : for, during ⟨se quedaron allí por la semana : they stayed there during the week⟩ ⟨por el momento : for now, at the moment⟩ **2** : around, during ⟨por noviembre empieza a nevar : around November it starts to snow⟩ ⟨por la mañana : in the morning⟩ **3** : around (a place) ⟨debe estar por allí : it must be over there⟩ ⟨por todas partes : everywhere⟩ **4** : by, through, along ⟨por la puerta : through the door⟩ ⟨pasé por tu casa : I stopped by your house⟩ ⟨por la costa : along the coast⟩ **5** : for, for the sake of ⟨lo hizo por su madre : he did it for his mother⟩ ⟨¡por Dios! : for heaven's sake!⟩ **6** : because of, on account of ⟨llegué tarde por el tráfico : I arrived late because of the traffic⟩ ⟨dejar por imposible : to give up as impossible⟩ **7** : per ⟨60 millas por hora : 60 miles per hour⟩ ⟨por docena : by the dozen⟩ **8** : for, in exchange for, instead of ⟨su hermana habló por él : his sister spoke on his behalf⟩ **9** : by means of ⟨hablar por teléfono : to talk on the phone⟩ ⟨por escrito : in writing⟩ **10** : as for ⟨por mí : as far as I'm concerned⟩ **11** : times ⟨tres por dos son seis : three times two is six⟩ **12** SEGÚN : from, according to ⟨por lo que dices : judging from what you're telling me⟩ **13** : as, for ⟨por ejemplo : for example⟩ **14** : by ⟨hecho por mi abuela : made by my grandmother⟩ ⟨por correo : by mail⟩ **15** : for, in order to ⟨lucha por ganar su respeto : he struggles to win her respect⟩ **16 estar por** : to be about to **17 por ciento** : percent **18 por favor** : please **19 por lo tanto** : therefore, consequently **20 ¿por qué?** : why? **21 por que → porque 22 por . . . que** : no matter how ⟨por mucho que intente : no matter how hard I try⟩ **23 por si** *or* **por si acaso** : just in case

porcelana *nf* : china, porcelain

porcentaje *nm* : percentage

porche *nm* : porch

porción *nf, pl* **porciones 1** : portion **2** PARTE : part, share **3** RACIÓN : serving, helping

pordiosear *vi* MENDIGAR : beg

pordiosero, -ra *n* MENDIGO : beggar

porfiado, -da *adj* OBSTINADO, TERCO : obstinate, stubborn — **porfiadamente** *adv*

porfiar {85} *vi* : to insist, to persist

pormenor *nm* DETALLE : detail

pormenorizar {21} *vi* : to go into detail — *vt* : to tell in detail

pornografía *nf* : pornography

pornográfico, -ca *adj* : pornographic

poro *nm* : pore

poroso, -sa *adj* : porous — **porosidad** *nf*

poroto *nm Arg, Chile, Uru* : bean

porque *conj* **1** : because **2** *or* **por que** : in order that

porqué *nm* : reason, cause

porquería *nf* **1** SUCIEDAD : dirt, filth **2** : nastiness, vulgarity **3** : worthless thing, trifle **4** : junk food

porra *nf* **1** : nightstick, club **2** *Mex* : cheer, yell ⟨los aficionados le echaban porras : the fans cheered him on⟩

porrazo *nm* **1** : blow, whack **2 de golpe y porrazo** : suddenly

porrista *nmf* **1** : cheerleader **2** : fan, supporter

portaaviones *nms & pl* : aircraft carrier

portada *nf* **1** : title page **2** : cover **3** : facade, front

portador, -dora *n* : carrier, bearer

portafolio *or* **portafolios** *nm, pl* **-lios 1** MALETÍN : briefcase **2** : portfolio (of investments)

portal *nm* **1** : portal, doorway **2** VESTÍBULO : vestibule, hall

portar *vt* **1** : to carry, to bear **2** : to wear — **portarse** *vr* CONDUCIRSE : to behave ⟨pórtate bien : behave yourself⟩

portátil *adj* : portable

portaviandas *nms & pl* : lunch box

portaviones *nm → **portaaviones**

portavoz *nmf, pl* **-voces** : spokesperson, spokesman *m*, spokeswoman *f*

portazo *nm* : slam (of a door)

porte *nm* **1** ASPECTO : bearing, demeanor **2** TRANSPORTE : transport, carrying ⟨porte pagado : postage paid⟩

portento *nm* MARAVILLA : marvel, wonder

portentoso, -sa *adj* MARAVILLOSO : marvelous, wonderful

porteño, -ña *adj* : of or from Buenos Aires

portería *nf* **1** ARCO : goal, goalposts *pl* **2** : superintendent's office

portero, -ra *n* **1** ARQUERO : goalkeeper, goalie **2** : doorman *m* **3** : janitor, superintendent

pórtico *nm* : portico

portilla *nf* : porthole

portón *nm, pl* **portones 1** : main door **2** : gate

portugués[1], **-guesa** *adj & n, mpl* **-gueses** : Portuguese

portugués[2] *nm* : Portuguese (language)

porvenir *nm* FUTURO : future
pos *adv* **en pos de** : in pursuit of
posada *nf* **1** : inn **2** *Mex* : Advent celebration
posadero, -ra *n* : innkeeper
posar *vi* : to pose — *vt* : to place, to lay — **posarse** *vr* **1** : to land, to light, to perch **2** : to settle, to rest
posavasos *nms & pl* : coaster (for drinks)
posdata → **postdata**
pose *nf* : pose
poseedor, -dora *n* : possessor, holder
poseer {20} *vt* : to possess, to hold, to have
poseído, -da *adj* : possessed
posesión *nf, pl* **-siones** : possession
posesionarse *vr* ~ **de** : to take possession of, to take over
posesivo[1]**, -va** *adj* : possessive
posesivo[2] *nm* : possessive case
posguerra *nf* : postwar period
posibilidad *nf* **1** : possibility **2 posibilidades** *nfpl* : means, income
posibilitar *vt* : to make possible, to permit
posible *adj* : possible — **posiblemente** *adv*
posición *nf, pl* **-ciones** **1** : position, place **2** : status, standing **3** : attitude, stance
posicionar *vt* **1** : to position, to place **2** : to establish — **posicionarse** *vr*
positivo[1]**, -va** *adj* : positive
positivo[2] *nm* : print (in photography)
poso *nm* **1** : sediment, dregs *pl* **2** : grounds *pl* (of coffee)
posoperatorio, -ria *adj* : postoperative
posponer {60} *vt* **1** : to postpone **2** : to put behind, to subordinate
pospuso, etc. → **posponer**
posta *nf* : relay race
postal[1] *adj* : postal
postal[2] *nf* : postcard
postdata *nf* : postscript
poste *nm* : post, pole ⟨poste de teléfonos : telephone pole⟩
póster *or* **poster** *nm, pl* **pósters** *or* **posters** : poster, placard
postergación *nf, pl* **-ciones** : postponement, deferring
postergar {52} *vt* **1** : to delay, to postpone **2** : to pass over (an employee)
posteridad *nf* : posterity
posterior *adj* **1** ULTERIOR : later, subsequent **2** TRASERO : back, rear
postgrado *nm* : graduate course
postgraduado, -da *n* : graduate student, postgraduate
postigo *nm* **1** CONTRAVENTANA : shutter **2** : small door, wicket gate
postilla *nf* : scab
postizo, -za *adj* : artificial, false ⟨dentadura postiza : dentures⟩
postnatal *adj* : postnatal
postor, -tora *n* : bidder ⟨mejor postor : highest bidder⟩

postración *nf, pl* **-ciones** **1** : prostration **2** ABATIMIENTO : depression
postrado, -da *adj* **1** : prostrate **2 postrado en cama** : bedridden
potranco, -ca *n* → **potro**[1]
postrar *vt* DEBILITAR : to debilitate, to weaken — **postrarse** *vr* : to prostrate oneself
postre *nm* : dessert
postrero, -ra *adj* (**postrer** *before masculine singular nouns*) ÚLTIMO : last
postulación *nf, pl* **-ciones** **1** : collection **2** : nomination (of a candidate)
postulado *nm* : postulate, assumption
postulante, -ta *n* **1** : postulant **2** : candidate, applicant
postular *vt* **1** : to postulate **2** : to nominate **3** : to propose — **postularse** *vr* : to run, to be a candidate
póstumo, -ma *adj* : posthumous — **póstumamente** *adv*
postura *nf* **1** : posture, position (of the body) **2** ACTITUD, POSICIÓN : position, stance
potable *adj* : drinkable, potable
potaje *nm* : thick vegetable soup, pottage
potasa *nf* : potash
potasio *nm* : potassium
pote *nm* **1** OLLA : pot **2** : jar, container
potencia *nf* **1** : power ⟨potencias extranjeras : foreign powers⟩ ⟨elevado a la tercera potencia : raised to the third power⟩ **2** : capacity, potency
potencial *adj & nm* : potential
potenciar *vt* : to promote, to foster
potenciómetro *nm* : dimmer, dimmer switch
potentado, -da *n* **1** SOBERANO : potentate, sovereign **2** MAGNATE : tycoon, magnate
potente *adj* **1** : powerful, strong **2** : potent, virile
potestad *nf* **1** AUTORIDAD : authority, jurisdiction **2 patria potestad** : custody, guardianship
potrero *nm* **1** : field, pasture **2** : cattle ranch
potro[1]**, -tra** *n* : colt *m*, filly *f*
potro[2] *nm* **1** : rack (for torture) **2** : horse (in gymnastics)
pozo *nm* **1** : well ⟨pozo de petróleo : oil well⟩ **2** : deep pool (in a river) **3** : mine shaft **4** *Arg, Par, Uru* : pothole **5 pozo séptico** : cesspool
pozole *nm* *Mex* : spicy stew made with pork and hominy
práctica *nf* **1** : practice, experience **2** EJERCICIO : exercising ⟨la práctica de la medicina : the practice of medicine⟩ **3** APLICACIÓN : application, practice ⟨poner en práctica : to put into practice⟩ **4 prácticas** *nfpl* : training
practicable *adj* : practicable, feasible
prácticamente *adv* : practically
practicante[1] *adj* : practicing ⟨católicos practicantes : practicing Catholics⟩

practicante[2] *nmf* : practicer, practitioner

practicar {72} *vt* **1** : to practice **2** : to perform, to carry out **3** : to exercise (a profession) — *vi* : to practice

práctico, -ca *adj* : practical, useful

pradera *nf* : grassland, prairie

prado *nm* **1** CAMPO : field, meadow **2** : park

pragmático, -ca *adj* : pragmatic — **pragmáticamente** *adv*

pragmatismo *nm* : pragmatism

preámbulo *nm* **1** INTRODUCCIÓN : preamble, introduction **2** RODEO : evasion ⟨gastar preámbulos : to beat around the bush⟩

prebélico, -ca *adj* : antebellum

prebenda *nf* : privilege, perquisite

precalentar {55} *vt* : to preheat

precariedad *nf* : precariousness

precario, -ria *adj* : precarious — **precariamente** *adv*

precaución *nf, pl* **-ciones** **1** : precaution ⟨medidas de precaución : precautionary measures⟩ **2** PRUDENCIA : caution, care ⟨con precaución : cautiously⟩

precautorio, -ria *adj* : precautionary

precaver *vt* PREVENIR : to prevent, to guard against — **precaverse** *vr* PREVENIRSE : to take precautions, to be on guard

precavido, -da *adj* CAUTELOSO : cautious, prudent

precedencia *nf* : precedence, priority

precedente[1] *adj* : preceding, previous

precedente[2] *nm* : precedent

preceder *v* : to precede

precepto *nm* : rule, precept

preciado, -da *adj* : esteemed, prized, valuable

preciarse *vr* **1** JACTARSE : to boast, to brag **2** ~ **de** : to pride oneself on

precinto *nm* : seal

precio *nm* **1** : price **2** : cost, sacrifice ⟨a cualquier precio : whatever the cost⟩

preciosidad *nf* : beautiful thing ⟨este vestido es una preciosidad : this dress is lovely⟩

precioso, -sa *adj* **1** HERMOSO : beautiful, exquisite **2** VALIOSO : precious, valuable

precipicio *nm* **1** : precipice **2** RUINA : ruin

precipitación *nf, pl* **-ciones** **1** PRISA : haste, hurry, rush **2** : precipitation, rain, snow

precipitado, -da *adj* **1** : hasty, sudden **2** : rash — **precipitadamente** *adv*

precipitar *vt* **1** APRESURAR : to hasten, to speed up **2** ARROJAR : to hurl, to throw — **precipitarse** *vr* **1** APRESURARSE : to rush **2** : to act rashly **3** ARROJARSE : to throw oneself

precisamente *adv* JUSTAMENTE : precisely, exactly

precisar *vt* **1** : to specify, to determine exactly **2** NECESITAR : to need, to require — *vi* : to be necessary

precisión *nf, pl* **-siones** **1** EXACTITUD : precision, accuracy **2** CLARIDAD : clarity (of style, etc.) **3** NECESIDAD : necessity ⟨tener precisión de : to have need of⟩

preciso, -sa *adj* **1** EXACTO : precise **2** : very, exact ⟨en ese preciso instante : at that very instant⟩ **3** NECESARIO : necessary

precocidad *nf* : precocity

precocinar *vt* : to precook

preconcebir {54} *vt* : to preconceive

precondición *nf, pl* **-ciones** : precondition

preconizar {21} *vt* **1** : to recommend, to advocate **2** : to extol

precoz *adj, pl* **precoces** **1** : precocious **2** : early, premature — **precozmente** *adv*

precursor, -sora *n* : forerunner, precursor

predecesor, -sora *n* ANTECESOR : predecessor

predecir {11} *vt* : to foretell, to predict

predestinado, -da *adj* : predestined, fated

predestinar *vt* : to predestine — **predestinación** *nf*

predeterminar *vt* : to predetermine

prédica *nf* SERMÓN : sermon

predicado *nm* : predicate

predicador, -dora *n* : preacher

predicar {72} *v* : to preach

predicción *nf, pl* **-ciones** **1** : prediction **2** PRONÓSTICO : forecast ⟨predicción del tiempo : weather forecast⟩

prediga, predijo etc. → **predecir**

predilección *nf, pl* **-ciones** : predilection, preference

predilecto, -ta *adj* : favorite

predio *nm* : property, piece of land

predisponer {60} *vt* **1** : to predispose, to incline **2** : to prejudice, to bias

predisposición *nf, pl* **-ciones** **1** : predisposition, tendency **2** : prejudice, bias

predominante *adj* : predominant — **predominantemente** *adv*

predominar *vi* PREVALECER : to predominate, to prevail

predominio *nm* : predominance, prevalence

preeminente *adj* : preeminent — **preeminencia** *nf*

preescolar *adj & nm* : preschool

preestreno *nm* : preview

prefabricado, -da *adj* : prefabricated

prefacio *nm* : preface

prefecto *nm* : prefect

preferencia *nf* **1** : preference **2** PRIORIDAD : priority **3 de** ~ : preferably

preferencial *adj* : preferential

preferente *adj* : preferential, special ⟨trato preferente : special treatment⟩

preferentemente *adv* : preferably

preferible *adj* : preferable
preferido, -da *adj & n* : favorite
preferir {76} *vt* : to prefer
prefigurar *vt* : foreshadow, prefigure
prefijo *nm* : prefix
pregonar *vt* 1 : to proclaim, to announce 2 : to hawk (merchandise) 3 : to extol 4 : to reveal, to disclose
pregunta *nf* 1 : question 2 hacer una pregunta : to ask a question
preguntar *vt* : to ask, to question — *vi* : to ask, to inquire — preguntarse *vr* : to wonder
preguntón, -tona *adj, mpl* -tones : inquisitive
prehistórico, -ca *adj* : prehistoric
prejuiciado, -da *adj* : prejudiced
prejuicio *nm* : prejudice
prejuzgar {52} *vt* : to prejudge
prelado *nm* : prelate
preliminar *adj & nm* : preliminary
preludio *nm* : prelude
prematrimonial *adj* : premarital
prematuro, -ra *adj* : premature
premeditación *nf, pl* -ciones : premeditation
premeditar *vt* : to premeditate, to plan
premenstrual *adj* : premenstrual
premiado, -da *adj* : winning, prizewinning
premiar *vt* 1 : to award a prize to 2 : to reward
premier *nmf* : premier, prime minister
premio *nm* 1 : prize ⟨premio gordo : grand prize, jackpot⟩ 2 : reward 3 : premium
premisa *nf* : premise, basis
premolar *nm* : bicuspid (tooth)
premonición *nf, pl* -ciones : premonition
premura *nf* : haste, urgency
prenatal *adj* : prenatal
prenda *nf* 1 : piece of clothing 2 : security, pledge
prendar *vt* 1 : to charm, to captivate 2 : to pawn, to pledge — prendarse *vr* ~ de : to fall in love with
prendedor *nm* : brooch, pin
prender *vt* 1 SUJETAR : to pin, to fasten 2 APRESAR : to catch, to apprehend 3 : to light (a cigarette, a match) 4 : to turn on ⟨prende la luz : turn on the light⟩ 5 prender fuego a : to set fire to — *vi* 1 : to take root 2 : to catch fire 3 : to catch on
prensa *nf* 1 : printing press 2 : press ⟨conferencia de prensa : press conference⟩
prensar *vt* : to press
prensil *adj* : prehensile
preñado, -da *adj* 1 : pregnant 2 ~ de : filled with
preñar *vt* EMBARAZAR : to make pregnant
preñez *nf, pl* preñeces : pregnancy
preocupación *nf, pl* -ciones INQUIETUD : worry, concern
preocupante *adj* : worrisome

preocupar *vt* INQUIETAR : to worry, to concern — preocuparse *vr* APURARSE : to worry, to be concerned
preparación *nf, pl* -ciones 1 : preparation, readiness 2 : education, training 3 : (medicinal) preparation
preparado[1], -da *adj* 1 : ready, prepared 2 : trained
preparado[2] *nm* : preparation, mixture
preparar *vt* 1 : to prepare, to make ready 2 : to teach, to train, to coach — prepararse *vr*
preparativos *nmpl* : preparations
preparatoria *nf Mex* : high school
preparatorio, -ria *adj* : preparatory
preponderante *adj* : preponderant, predominant — preponderancia *nf* — preponderantemente *adv*
preposición *nf, pl* -ciones : preposition — preposicional *adj*
prepotente *adj* : arrogant, domineering, overbearing — prepotencia *nf*
prerrogativa *nf* : prerogative, privilege
presa *nf* 1 : capture, seizure ⟨hacer presa de : to seize⟩ 2 : catch, prey ⟨presa de : prey to, seized with⟩ 3 : claw, fang 4 DIQUE : dam 5 : morsel, piece (of food)
presagiar *vt* : to presage, to portend
presagio *nm* : omen, portent
presbiterio *nm* : presbytery, sanctuary (of a church)
presbítero *nm* : presbyter
presciencia *nf* : prescience
prescindible *adj* : expendable, dispensable
prescindir *vi* 1 ~ de : to do without, to dispense with 2 DESATENDER : to ignore, to disregard 3 OMITIR : to omit, to skip
prescribir {33} *vt* : to prescribe
prescripción *nf, pl* -ciones : prescription
prescrito *pp* → prescribir
presencia *nf* 1 : presence 2 ASPECTO : appearance
presenciar *vt* : to be present at, to witness
presentable *adj* : presentable
presentación *nf, pl* -ciones 1 : presentation 2 : introduction 3 : appearance
presentador, -dora *n* : newscaster, anchorman *m*, anchorwoman *f*
presentar *vt* 1 : to present, to show 2 : to offer, to give 3 : to submit (a document), to launch (a product) 4 : to introduce (a person) — presentarse *vr* 1 : to show up, to appear 2 : to arise, to come up 3 : to introduce oneself
presente[1] *adj* 1 : present, in attendance 2 : present, current 3 tener presente : to keep in mind
presente[2] *nm* 1 : present (time, tense) 2 : one present ⟨entre los presentes se encontraban ... : those present included ... ⟩
presentimiento *nm* : premonition, hunch, feeling

presentir {76} *vt* : to sense, to intuit ⟨presentía lo que iba a pasar : he sensed what was going to happen⟩

preservación *nf, pl* **-ciones** : preservation

preservar *vt* **1** : to preserve **2** : to protect

preservativo *nm* CONDÓN : condom

presidencia *nf* **1** : presidency **2** : chairmanship

presidencial *adj* : presidential

presidente, -ta *n* **1** : president **2** : chair, chairperson **3** : presiding judge

presidiario, -ria *n* : convict, prisoner

presidio *nm* : prison, penitentiary

presidir *vt* **1** MODERAR : to preside over, to chair **2** : to dominate, to rule over

presilla *nf* : eye, loop, fastener

presión *nf, pl* **presiones 1** : pressure **2 presión arterial** : blood pressure

presionar *vt* **1** : to pressure **2** : to press, to push — *vi* : to put on the pressure

preso[1]**, -sa** *adj* : imprisoned

preso[2]**, -sa** *n* : prisoner

prestado, -da *adj* **1** : borrowed, on loan **2 pedir prestado** : to borrow

prestamista *nmf* : moneylender, pawnbroker

préstamo *nm* : loan

prestar *vt* **1** : to lend, to loan **2** : to render (a service), to give (aid) **3 prestar atención** : to pay attention **4 prestar juramento** : to take an oath — **prestarse** *vr* : to lend oneself ⟨se presta a confusiones : it lends itself to confusion⟩

prestatario, -ria *n* : borrower

presteza *nf* : promptness, speed

prestidigitación *nf, pl* **-ciones** : sleight of hand, prestidigitation

prestidigitador, -dora *n* : conjurer, magician

prestigio *nm* : prestige — **prestigioso, -sa** *adj*

presto[1] *adv* : promptly, at once

presto[2]**, -ta** *adj* **1** : quick, prompt **2** DISPUESTO, PREPARADO : ready

presumido, -da *adj* VANIDOSO : conceited, vain

presumir *vt* SUPONER : to presume, to suppose — *vi* **1** ALARDEAR : to boast, to show off **2 ~ de** : to consider oneself ⟨presume de inteligente : he thinks he's intelligent⟩

presunción *nf, pl* **-ciones 1** SUPOSICIÓN : presumption, supposition **2** VANIDAD : conceit, vanity

presunto, -ta *adj* : presumed, supposed, alleged — **presuntamente** *adv*

presuntuoso, -sa *adj* : conceited

presuponer {60} *vt* : to presuppose

presupuestal *adj* : budget, budgetary

presupuestar *vi* : to budget — *vt* : to budget for

presupuestario, -ria *adj* : budget, budgetary

presupuesto *nm* **1** : budget, estimate **2** : assumption, supposition

presurizar {21} *vt* : to pressurize

presuroso, -sa *adj* : hasty, quick

pretencioso, -sa *adj* : pretentious

pretender *vt* **1** INTENTAR : to attempt, to try ⟨pretendo estudiar : I'm trying to study⟩ **2** AFIRMAR : to claim ⟨pretende ser pobre : he claims he's poor⟩ **3** : to seek, to aspire to ⟨¿qué pretendes tú? : what are you after?⟩ **4** CORTEJAR : to court **5 pretender que** : to expect ⟨¿pretendes que lo crea? : do you expect me to believe you?⟩

pretendiente[1] *nmf* **1** : candidate, applicant **2** : pretender, claimant (to a throne, etc.)

pretendiente[2] *nm* : suitor

pretensión *nf, pl* **-siones 1** : intention, hope, plan **2** : pretension ⟨sin pretensiones : unpretentious⟩

pretexto *nm* EXCUSA : pretext, excuse

pretil *nm* : parapet, railing

prevalecer {53} *vi* : to prevail, to triumph

prevaleciente *adj* : prevailing, prevalent

prevalerse {84} *vr* **~ de** : to avail oneself of, to take advantage of

prevención *nf, pl* **-ciones 1** : prevention **2** : preparation, readiness **3** : precautionary measure **4** : prejudice, bias

prevenido, -da *adj* **1** PREPARADO : prepared, ready **2** ADVERTIDO : forewarned **3** CAUTELOSO : cautious

prevenir {87} *vt* **1** : to prevent **2** : to warn — **prevenirse** *vr* **~ contra** *or* **~ de** : to take precautions against

preventivo, -va *adj* : preventive, precautionary

prever {88} *vt* ANTICIPAR : to foresee, to anticipate

previo, -via *adj* **1** : previous, prior **2** : after, upon ⟨previo pago : after paying, upon payment⟩

previsible *adj* : foreseeable

previsión *nf, pl* **-siones 1** : foresight **2** : prediction, forecast **3** : precaution

previsor, -sora *adj* : farsighted, prudent

prieto, -ta *adj* **1** : blackish, dark **2** : dark-skinned, swarthy **3** : tight, compressed

prima *nf* **1** : premium **2** : bonus **3** → **primo**

primacía *nf* **1** : precedence, priority **2** : superiority, supremacy

primado *nm* : primate (bishop)

primario, -ria *adj* : primary

primate *nm* : primate

primavera *nf* **1** : spring (season) **2** PRÍMULA : primrose

primaveral *adj* : spring, springlike

primero[1] *adv* **1** : first **2** : rather, sooner

primero[2]**, -ra** *adj* (**primer** *before masculine singular nouns*) **1** : first **2** : top, leading **3** : fundamental, basic **4 de primera** : first-rate

primero[3]**, -ra** *n* : first

primicia *nf* **1** : first fruits **2** : scoop, exclusive

primigenio, -nia *adj* : original, primary
primitivo, -va *adj* **1** : primitive **2** ORIG-INAL : original
primo, -ma *n* : cousin
primogénito, -ta *adj & n* : firstborn
primor *nm* **1** : skill, care **2** : beauty, elegance
primordial *adj* **1** : primordial **2** : basic, fundamental
primoroso, -sa *adj* **1** : exquisite, fine, delicate **2** : skillful
prímula *nf* : primrose
princesa *nf* : princess
principado *nm* : principality
principal¹ *adj* **1** : main, principal **2** : foremost, leading
principal² *nm* : capital, principal
príncipe *nm* : prince
principesco, -ca *adj* : princely
principiante¹ *adj* : beginning
principiante² *nmf* : beginner, novice
principiar *vt* EMPEZAR : to begin
principio *nm* **1** COMIENZO : beginning **2** : principle **3 al principio** : at first **4 a principios de** : at the beginning of ⟨a principios de agosto : at the beginning of August⟩ **5 en ∼** : in principle
pringar {52} *vt* **1** : to dip (in grease) **2** : to soil, to spatter (with grease) — **pringarse** *vr*
pringoso, -sa *adj* : greasy
pringue¹, etc. → **pringar**
pringue² *nm* : grease, drippings *pl*
prior, priora *n* : prior *m*, prioress *f*
priorato *nm* : priory
prioridad *nf* : priority, precedence
prisa *nf* **1** : hurry, rush **2 a ∼** *or* **de ∼** : quickly, fast **3 a toda prisa** : as fast as possible **4 darse prisa** : to hurry **5 tener prisa** : to be in a hurry
prisión *nf*, *pl* **prisiones 1** CÁRCEL : prison, jail **2** ENCARCELAMIENTO : imprisonment
prisionero, -ra *n* : prisoner
prisma *nm* : prism
prismáticos *nmpl* : binoculars
prístino, -na *adj* : pristine
privacidad *nf* : privacy
privación *nf*, *pl* **-ciones 1** : deprivation **2** : privation, want
privado, -da *adj* : private — **privadamente** *adv*
privar *vt* **1** DESPOJAR : to deprive **2** : to stun, to knock out — **privarse** *vr* : to deprive oneself
privativo, -va *adj* : exclusive, particular
privilegiado, -da *adj* : privileged
privilegiar *vt* : to grant a privilege to, to favor
privilegio *nm* : privilege
pro¹ *nm* **1** : pro, advantage ⟨los pros y contras : the pros and cons⟩ **2 en pro de** : for, in favor of
pro² *prep* : for, in favor of ⟨grupos pro derechos humanos : groups supporting human rights⟩
proa *nf* : bow, prow
probabilidad *nf* : probability

probable *adj* : probable, likely
probablemente *adv* : probably
probar {19} *vt* **1** : to demonstrate, to prove **2** : to test, to try out **3** : to try on (clothing) **4** : to taste, to sample — *vi* : to try — **probarse** *vr* : to try on (clothing)
probeta *nf* : test tube
probidad *nf* : probity
problema *nm* : problem
problemática *nf* : set of problems ⟨la problemática que debemos enfrentar : the problems we must face⟩
probóscide *nf* : proboscis
problemático, -ca *adj* : problematic
procaz *adj*, *pl* **procaces 1** : insolent, impudent **2** : indecent
procedencia *nf* : origin, source
procedente *adj* **1** : proper, fitting **2 ∼ de** : coming from
proceder *vi* **1** AVANZAR : to proceed **2** : to act, to behave **3** : to be appropriate, to be fitting **4 ∼ de** : to originate from, to come from
procedimiento *nm* : procedure, process
prócer *nmf* : eminent person, leader
procesado, -da *n* : accused, defendant
procesador *nm* : processor ⟨procesador de textos : word processor⟩
procesamiento *nm* : processing ⟨procesamiento de datos : data processing⟩
procesar *vt* **1** : to prosecute, to try **2** : to process
procesión *nf*, *pl* **-siones** : procession
proceso *nm* **1** : process **2** : trial, proceedings *pl*
proclama *nf* : proclamation
proclamación *nf*, *pl* **-ciones** : proclamation
proclamar *vt* : to proclaim — **proclamarse** *vr*
proclive *adj* **∼ a** : inclined to, prone to
proclividad *nf* : proclivity, inclination
procrear *vi* : to procreate — **procreación** *nf*
procurador, -dora *n* ABOGADO : attorney
procurar *vt* **1** INTENTAR : to try, to endeavor **2** CONSEGUIR : to obtain, to procure **3 procurar hacer** : to manage to do
prodigar {52} *vt* : to lavish, to be generous with
prodigio *nm* : wonder, marvel
prodigioso, -sa *adj* : prodigious, marvelous
pródigo¹, -ga *adj* **1** : generous, lavish **2** : wasteful, prodigal
pródigo², -ga *n* : spendthrift, prodigal
producción *nf*, *pl* **-ciones 1** : production **2 producción en serie** : mass production
producir {61} *vt* **1** : to produce, to make, to manufacture **2** : to cause, to bring about **3** : to bear (interest) — **producirse** *vr* : to take place, to occur
productividad *nf* : productivity
productivo, -va *adj* **1** : productive **2** LUCRATIVO : profitable

producto *nm* **1** : product **2** : proceeds *pl*, yield
productor, -tora *n* : producer
proeza *nf* HAZAÑA : feat, exploit
profanar *vt* : to profane, to desecrate — **profanación** *nf*
profano¹, -na *adj* **1** : profane **2** : worldly, secular
profano², -na *n* : nonspecialist
profecía *nf* : prophecy
proferir {76} *vt* **1** : to utter **2** : to hurl (insults)
profesar *vt* **1** : to profess, to declare **2** : to practice, to exercise
profesión *nf, pl* **-siones** : profession
profesional *adj & nmf* : professional — **profesionalmente** *adv*
profesionalismo *nm* : professionalism
profesionalizar {21} *vt* : to professionalize
profesionista *nmf Mex* : professional
profesor, -sora *n* **1** MAESTRO : teacher **2** : professor
profesorado *nm* **1** : faculty **2** : teaching profession
profeta *nm* : prophet
profético, -ca *adj* : prophetic
profetisa *nf* : prophetess, prophet
profetizar {21} *vt* : to prophesy
prófugo, -ga *adj & n* : fugitive
profundidad *nf* : depth, profundity
profundizar {21} *vt* **1** : to deepen **2** : to study in depth — *vi* ~ **en** : to go deeply into, to study in depth
profundo, -da *adj* **1** HONDO : deep **2** : profound — **profundamente** *adv*
profusión *nf, pl* **-siones** : abundance, profusion
profuso, -sa *adj* : profuse, abundant, extensive
progenie *nf* : progeny, offspring
progenitor, -tora *n* ANTEPASADO : ancestor, progenitor
progesterona *nf* : progesterone
prognóstico *nm* : prognosis
programa *nm* **1** : program **2** : plan **3 programa de estudios** : curriculum
programable *adj* : programmable
programación *nf, pl* **-ciones** **1** : programming **2** : planning
programador, -dora *n* : programmer
programar *vt* **1** : to schedule, to plan **2** : to program (a computer, etc.)
progresar *vi* : to progress, to make progress
progresista *adj & nmf* : progressive
progresivo, -va *adj* : progressive, gradual
progreso *nm* : progress
prohibición *nf, pl* **-ciones** : ban, prohibition
prohibir {62} *vt* : to prohibit, to ban, to forbid
prohibitivo, -va *adj* : prohibitive
prohijar {5} *vt* ADOPTAR : to adopt
prójimo *nm* : neighbor, fellow man
prole *nf* : offspring, progeny
proletariado *nm* : proletariat, working class

proletario, -ria *adj & n* : proletarian
proliferar *vi* : to proliferate — **proliferación** *nf*
prolífico, -ca *adj* : prolific
prolijo, -ja *adj* : wordy, long-winded
prólogo *nm* : prologue, preface, foreword
prolongación *nf, pl* **-ciones** : extension, lengthening
prolongar {52} *vt* **1** : to prolong **2** : to extend, to lengthen — **prolongarse** *vr* CONTINUAR : to last, to continue
promediar *vt* **1** : to average **2** : to divide in half — *vi* : to be half over
promedio *nm* **1** : average **2** : middle, midpoint
promesa *nf* : promise
prometedor, -dora *adj* : promising, hopeful
prometer *vt* : to promise — *vi* : to show promise — **prometerse** *vr* COMPROMETERSE : to get engaged
prometido¹, -da *adj* : engaged
prometido², -da *n* NOVIO : fiancé *m*, fiancée *f*
prominente *adj* : prominent — **prominencia** *nf*
promiscuo, -cua *adj* : promiscuous — **promiscuidad** *nf*
promisorio, -ria *adj* **1** : promising **2** : promissory
promoción *nf, pl* **-ciones** **1** : promotion **2** : class, year **3** : play-off (in soccer)
promocionar *vt* : to promote — **promocional** *adj*
promontorio *nm* : promontory, headland
promotor, -tora *n* : promoter
promover {47} *vt* **1** : to promote, to advance **2** FOMENTAR : to foster, to encourage **3** PROVOCAR : to provoke, to cause
promulgación *nf, pl* **-ciones** **1** : enactment **2** : proclamation, enactment
promulgar {52} *vt* **1** : to promulgate, to proclaim **2** : to enact (a law or decree)
prono, -na *adj* : prone
pronombre *nm* : pronoun
pronosticar {72} *vt* : to predict, to forecast
pronóstico *nm* **1** PREDICCIÓN : forecast, prediction **2** : prognosis
prontitud *nf* **1** PRESTEZA : promptness, speed **2 con** ~ : promptly, quickly
pronto¹ *adv* **1** : quickly, promptly **2** : soon **3 de** ~ : suddenly **4 lo más pronto posible** : as soon as possible **5 tan pronto como** : as soon as
pronto², -ta *adj* **1** RÁPIDO : quick, speedy, prompt **2** PREPARADO : ready
pronunciación *nf, pl* **-ciones** : pronunciation
pronunciado, -da *adj* **1** : pronounced, sharp, steep **2** : marked, noticeable
pronunciamiento *nm* **1** : pronouncement **2** : military uprising
pronunciar *vt* **1** : to pronounce, to say **2** : to give, to deliver (a speech) **3 pro-**

nunciar un fallo : to pronounce sentence — **pronunciarse** *vr* : to declare oneself

propagación *nf, pl* **-ciones** : propagation, spreading

propaganda *nf* 1 : propaganda 2 PUBLICIDAD : advertising

propagar {52} *vt* 1 : to propagate 2 : to spread, to disseminate — **propagarse** *vr*

propalar *vt* 1 : to divulge 2 : to spread

propano *nm* : propane

propasarse *vr* : to go too far, to overstep one's bounds

propensión *nf, pl* **-siones** INCLINACIÓN : inclination, propensity

propenso, -sa *adj* : prone, susceptible

propiamente *adv* 1 : properly, correctly 2 : exactly, precisely ⟨propiamente dicho : strictly speaking⟩

propiciar *vt* 1 : to propitiate 2 : to favor, to foster

propicio, -cia *adj* : favorable, propitious

propiedad *nf* 1 : property ⟨propiedad privada : private property⟩ 2 : ownership 3 CUALIDAD : property, quality 4 : suitability, appropriateness

propietario¹, -ria *adj* : proprietary

propietario², -ria *n* DUEÑO : owner, proprietor

propina *nf* : tip, gratuity

propinar *vt* : to give, to strike ⟨propinar una paliza : to give a beating⟩

propio, -pia *adj* 1 : own ⟨su propia casa : his own house⟩ ⟨sus recursos propios : their own resources⟩ 2 APROPIADO : appropriate, suitable 3 CARACTERÍSTICO : characteristic, typical 4 MISMO : oneself ⟨el propio director : the director himself⟩

proponer {60} *vt* 1 : to propose, to suggest 2 : to nominate — **proponerse** *vr* : to intend, to plan, to set out ⟨lo que se propone lo cumple : he does what he sets out to do⟩

proporción *nf, pl* **-ciones** 1 : proportion 2 : ratio (in mathematics) 3 **proporciones** *nfpl* : proportions, size ⟨de grandes proporciones : very large⟩

proporcionado, -da *adj* 1 : proportionate 2 : proportioned ⟨bien proporcionado : well-proportioned⟩ — **proporcionadamente** *adv*

proporcional *adj* : proportional — **proporcionalmente** *adv*

proporcionar *vt* 1 : to provide, to give 2 : to proportion, to adapt

proposición *nf, pl* **-ciones** : proposal, proposition

propósito *nm* 1 INTENCIÓN : purpose, intention 2 a ∼ : by the way 3 a ∼ : on purpose, intentionally

propuesta *nf* PROPOSICIÓN : proposal

propulsar *vt* 1 IMPULSAR : to propel, to drive 2 PROMOVER : to promote, to encourage

propulsión *nf, pl* **-siones** : propulsion

propulsor *nm* : propellant

propuso, etc. → **proponer**

prorrata *nf* 1 : share, quota 2 a ∼ : pro rata, proportionately

prórroga *nf* 1 : extension, deferment 2 : overtime (in sports)

prorrogar {52} *vt* 1 : to extend (a deadline) 2 : to postpone

prorrumpir *vi* : to burst forth, to break out ⟨prorrumpí en lágrimas : I burst into tears⟩

prosa *nf* : prose

prosaico, -ca *adj* : prosaic, mundane

proscribir {33} *v* 1 PROHIBIR : to prohibit, to ban, to proscribe 2 DESTERRAR : to banish, to exile

proscripción *nf, pl* **-ciones** 1 PROHIBICIÓN : ban, proscription 2 DESTIERRO : banishment

proscrito¹ *pp* → **proscribir**

proscrito², -ta *n* 1 DESTERRADO : exile 2 : outlaw

prosecución *nf, pl* **-ciones** 1 : continuation 2 : pursuit

proseguir {75} *vt* 1 CONTINUAR : to continue 2 : to pursue (studies, goals) — *vi* : to continue, to go on

prosélito, -ta *n* : proselyte

prospección *nf, pl* **-ciones** : prospecting, exploration

prospectar *vi* : to prospect

prospecto *nm* : prospectus, leaflet, brochure

prosperar *vi* : to prosper, to thrive

prosperidad *nf* : prosperity

próspero, -ra *adj* : prosperous, flourishing

próstata *nf* : prostate

prostitución *nf, pl* **-ciones** : prostitution

prostituir {41} *vt* : to prostitute — **prostituirse** *vr* : to prostitute oneself

prostituto, -ta *n* : prostitute

protagonista *nmf* 1 : protagonist, main character 2 : leader

protagonizar {21} *vt* : to star in

protección *nf, pl* **-ciones** : protection

protector¹, -tora *adj* : protective

protector², -tora *n* 1 : protector, guardian 2 : patron

protector³ *nm* : protector, guard ⟨chaleco protector : chest protector⟩

protectorado *nm* : protectorate

proteger {15} *vt* : to protect, to defend — **protegerse** *vr*

protegido, -da *n* : protégé

proteína *nf* : protein

prótesis *nfs & pl* : prosthesis

protesta *nf* 1 : protest 2 *Mex* : promise, oath

protestante *adj & nmf* : Protestant

protestantismo *nm* : Protestantism

protestar *vi* : to protest, to object — *vt* 1 : to protest, to object to 2 : to declare, to profess

protocolo *nm* : protocol

protón *nm, pl* **protones** : proton

protoplasma *nm* : protoplasm

prototipo *nm* : prototype

protozoario *or* **protozoo** *nm* : protozoan

protuberancia *nf* : protuberance — **pro-tuberante** *adj*
provecho *nm* : benefit, advantage
provechoso, -sa *adj* BENEFICIOSO : beneficial, profitable, useful — **provechosamente** *adv*
proveedor, -dora *n* : provider, supplier
proveer {63} *vt* : to provide, to supply — **proveerse** *vr* ~ **de** : to obtain, to supply oneself with
provenir {87} *vi* ~ **de** : to come from
provenzal[1] *adj* : Provençal
provenzal[2] *nmf* : Provençal
provenzal[3] *nm* : Provençal (language)
proverbio *nm* REFRÁN : proverb — **proverbial** *adj*
providencia *nf* 1 : providence, foresight 2 : Providence, God 3 **providencias** *nfpl* : steps, measures
providencial *adj* : providential
provincia *nf* : province — **provincial** *adj*
provinciano, -na *adj* : provincial, unsophisticated
provisión *nf, pl* **-siones** : provision
provisional *adj* : provisional, temporary
provisionalmente *adv* : provisionally, tentatively
provisorio, -ria *adj* : provisional, temporary
provisto *pp* → **proveer**
provocación *nf, pl* **-ciones** : provocation
provocador[1], **-dora** *adj* : provocative, provoking
provocador[2], **-dora** *n* AGITADOR : agitator
provocar {72} *vt* 1 CAUSAR : to provoke, to cause 2 IRRITAR : to provoke, to pique
provocativo, -va *adj* : provocative
proxeneta *nmf* : pimp *m*
próximamente *adv* : shortly, soon
proximidad *nf* 1 : nearness, proximity 2 **proximidades** *nfpl* : vicinity
próximo, -ma *adj* 1 : near, close ⟨la Navidad está próxima : Christmas is almost here⟩ 2 SIGUIENTE : next, following ⟨la próxima semana : the following week⟩
proyección *nf, pl* **-ciones** 1 : projection 2 : showing, screening (of a film) 3 : range, influence, diffusion
proyectar *vt* 1 : to plan 2 LANZAR : to throw, to hurl 3 : to project, to cast (light or shadow) 4 : to show, to screen (a film)
proyectil *nm* : projectile, missile
proyecto *nm* 1 : plan, project 2 **proyecto de ley** : bill
proyector *nm* 1 : projector 2 : spotlight
prudencia *nf* : prudence, care, discretion
prudente *adj* : prudent, sensible, reasonable
prueba[1], etc. → **probar**
prueba[2] *nf* 1 : proof, evidence 2 : trial, test 3 : proof (in printing or photography) 4 : event, qualifying round (in sports) 5 **a prueba de agua** : waterproof 6 **prueba de fuego** : acid test 7 **poner a prueba** : to put to the test
prurito *nm* 1 : itching 2 : desire, urge
psicoanálisis *nm* : psychoanalysis — **psicoanalista** *nmf*
psicoanalítico, -ca *adj* : psychoanalytic
psicoanalizar {21} *vt* : to psychoanalyze
psicología *nf* : psychology
psicológico, -ca *adj* : psychological — **psicológicamente** *adv*
psicólogo, -ga *n* : psychologist
psicópata *nmf* : psychopath
psicopático, -ca *adj* : psycopathic
psicosis *nfs & pl* : psychosis
psicosomático, -ca *adj* : psychosomatic
psicoterapeuta *nmf* : psychotherapist
psicoterapia *nf* : psychotherapy
psicótico, -ca *adj & n* : psychotic
psique *nf* : psyche
psiquiatra *nmf* : psychiatrist
psiquiatría *nf* : psychiatry
psiquiátrico[1], **-ca** *adj* : psychiatric
psiquiátrico[2] *nm* : mental hospital
psíquico, -ca *adj* : psychic
psiquis *nfs & pl* : psyche
psoriasis *nf* : psoriasis
ptomaína *nf* : ptomaine
púa *nf* 1 : barb ⟨alambre de púas : barbed wire⟩ 2 : tooth (of a comb) 3 : quill, spine
pubertad *nf* : puberty
pubiano → **púbico**
púbico, -ca *adj* : pubic
publicación *nf, pl* **-ciones** : publication
publicar {72} *vt* 1 : to publish 2 DIVULGAR : to divulge, to disclose
publicidad *nf* 1 : publicity 2 : advertising
publicista *nmf* : publicist
publicitar *vt* 1 : to publicize 2 : to advertise
publicitario, -ria *adj* : advertising, publicity ⟨agencia publicitaria : advertising agency⟩
público[1], **-ca** *adj* : public — **públicamente** *adv*
público[2] *nm* 1 : public 2 : audience, spectators *pl*
puchero *nm* 1 : pot 2 : stew 3 : pout ⟨hacer pucheros : to pout⟩
pucho *nm* 1 : waste, residue 2 : cigarette butt 3 **a puchos** : little by little, bit by bit
púdico, -ca *adj* : chaste, modest
pudiente *adj* 1 : powerful 2 : rich, wealthy
pudín *nm, pl* **pudines** BUDÍN : pudding
pudo, etc. → **poder**
pudor *nm* : modesty, reserve
pudoroso, -sa *adj* : modest, reserved, shy
pudrir {59} *vt* 1 : to rot 2 *fam* : to annoy, to upset — **pudrirse** *vr* 1 : to rot 2 : to languish
pueblerino, -na *adj* : provincial, countrified

puebla, etc. → **poblar**
pueblo *nm* **1** NACIÓN : people **2** : common people **3** ALDEA, POBLADO : town, village
puede, etc. → **poder**
puente *nm* **1** : bridge ⟨puente levadizo : drawbridge⟩ **2** : denture, bridge **3 puente aéreo** : airlift
puerco[1], **-ca** *adj* : dirty, filthy
puerco[2], **-ca** *n* **1** CERDO, MARRANO : pig, hog **2** : pig, dirty or greedy person **3 puerco espín** : porcupine
pueril *adj* : childish, puerile
puerro *nm* : leek
puerta *nf* **1** : door, entrance, gate **2 a puerta cerrada** : behind closed doors
puerto *nm* **1** : port, harbor **2** : mountain pass **3 puerto marítimo** : seaport
puertorriqueño, -ña *adj & n* : Puerto Rican
pues *conj* **1** : since, because, for ⟨no puedo ir, pues no tengo plata : I can't go, since I don't have any money⟩ ⟨lo hace, pues a él le gusta : he does it because he likes to⟩ **2** (*used interjectionally*) : well, then ⟨¡pues claro que sí! : well, of course!⟩ ⟨¡pues no voy! : well then, I'm not going!⟩
puesta *nf* **1** : setting ⟨puesta del sol : sunset⟩ **2** : laying (of eggs) **3 puesta a punto** : tune-up **4 puesta en marcha** : start, starting up
puestero, -ra *n* : seller, vendor
puesto[1] *pp* → **poner**
puesto[2], **-ta** *adj* : dressed ⟨bien puesto : well-dressed⟩
puesto[3] *nm* **1** LUGAR, SITIO : place, position **2** : position, job **3** : kiosk, stand, stall **4 puesto que** : since, given that
pugilato *nm* BOXEO : boxing, pugilism
pugilista *nm* BOXEADOR : boxer, pugilist
pugna *nf* **1** CONFLICTO, LUCHA : conflict, struggle **2 en** ~ : at odds, in conflict
pugnar *vi* LUCHAR : to fight, to strive, to struggle
pugnaz *adj* : pugnacious
pujante *adj* : mighty, powerful
pujanza *nf* : strength, vigor ⟨pujanza económica : economic strength⟩
pulcritud *nf* **1** : neatness, tidiness **2** ESMERO : meticulousness
pulcro, -cra *adj* **1** : clean, neat **2** : exquisite, delicate, refined
pulga *nf* **1** : flea **2 tener malas pulgas** : to be bad-tempered
pulgada *nf* : inch
pulgar *nm* **1** : thumb **2** : big toe
pulir *vt* **1** : to polish, to shine **2** REFINAR : to refine, to perfect
pulla *nf* **1** : cutting remark, dig, gibe **2** : obscenity
pulmón *nm, pl* **pulmones** : lung
pulmonar *adj* : pulmonary
pulmonía *nf* NEUMONÍA : pneumonia
pulpa *nf* : pulp, flesh
pulpería *nf* : small grocery store

púlpito *nm* : pulpit
pulpo *nm* : octopus
pulsación *nf, pl* **-ciones 1** : beat, pulsation, throb **2** : keystroke
pulsar *vt* **1** APRETAR : to press, to push **2** : to strike (a key) **3** : to assess — *vi* : to beat, to throb
pulsera *nf* : bracelet
pulso *nm* **1** : pulse ⟨tomarle el pulso a alguien : to take someone's pulse⟩ ⟨tomarle el pulso a la opinión : to sound out opinion⟩ **2** : steadiness (of hand) ⟨dibujo a pulso : freehand sketch⟩
pulular *vi* ABUNDAR : to abound, to swarm ⟨en el río pululan los peces : the river is teeming with fish⟩
pulverizador *nm* **1** : atomizer, spray **2** : spray gun
pulverizar {21} *vt* **1** : to pulverize, to crush **2** : to spray
puma *nf* : cougar, puma
puna *nf* : bleak Andean tableland
punción *nf, pl* **punciones** : puncture
punible *adj* : punishable
punitivo, -va *adj* : punitive
punce, etc. → **punzar**
punta *nf* **1** : tip, end ⟨punta del dedo : fingertip⟩ ⟨en la punta de la lengua : at the tip of one's tongue⟩ **2** : point (of a weapon or pencil) ⟨punta de lanza : spearhead⟩ **3** : point, headland **4** : bunch, lot ⟨una punta de ladrones : a bunch of thieves⟩ **5 a punta de** : by, by dint of
puntada *nf* **1** : stitch (in sewing) **2** PUNZADA : sharp pain, stitch, twinge **3** *Mex* : witticism, quip
puntal *nm* **1** : prop, support **2** : stanchion
puntapié *nm* PATADA : kick
puntazo *nm* CORNADA : wound (from a goring)
puntear *vt* **1** : to pluck (a guitar) **2** : to lead (in sports)
puntería *nf* : aim, marksmanship
puntero *nm* **1** : pointer **2** : leader
puntiagudo, -da *adj* : sharp, pointed
puntilla *nf* **1** : lace edging **2** : dagger (in bullfighting) **3 de puntillas** : on tiptoe
puntilloso, -sa *adj* : punctilious
punto *nm* **1** : dot, point **2** : period (in punctuation) **3** : item, question **4** : spot, place **5** : moment, stage, degree **6** : point (in a score) **7** : stitch **8 en** ~ : on the dot, sharp ⟨a las dos en punto : at two o'clock sharp⟩ **9 al punto** : at once **10 a punto fijo** : exactly, certainly **11 dos puntos** : colon **12 hasta cierto punto** : up to a point **13 punto decimal** : decimal point **14 punto de vista** : point of view **15 punto y coma** : semicolon **16 y punto** : period ⟨es el mejor que hay y punto : it's the best there is, period⟩ **17 puntos cardinales** : points of the compass

puntuación *nf, pl* **-ciones 1** : punctuation **2** : scoring, score, grade

puntual *adj* **1** : prompt, punctual **2** : exact, accurate — **puntualmente** *adv*

puntualidad *nf* **1** : promptness, punctuality **2** : exactness, accuracy

puntualizar {21} *vt* **1** : to specify, to state **2** : to point out

puntuar {3} *vt* : to punctuate — *vi* : to score points

punzada *nf* : sharp pain, twinge, stitch

punzante *adj* **1** : sharp **2** CÁUSTICO : biting, caustic

punzar {21} *vt* : to pierce, to puncture

punzón *nm, pl* **punzones 1** : awl **2** : hole punch

puñado *nm* **1** : handful **2 a puñados** : lots of, by the handful

puñal *nm* DAGA : dagger

puñalada *nf* : stab, stab wound

puñetazo *nm* : punch (with the fist)

puño *nm* **1** : fist **2** : handful, fistful **3** : cuff (of a shirt) **4** : handle, hilt

pupila *nf* : pupil (of the eye)

pupilo, -la *n* **1** : pupil, student **2** : ward, charge

pupitre *nm* : writing desk

puré *nm* : purée ⟨puré de papas : mashed potatoes⟩

pureza *nf* : purity

purga *nf* **1** : laxative **2** : purge

purgante *adj & nm* : laxative, purgative

purgar {52} *vt* **1** : to purge, to cleanse **2** : to liquidate (in politics) **3** : to give a

laxative to — **purgarse** *vr* **1** : to take a laxative **2** ~ **de** : to purge oneself of

purgatorio *nm* : purgatory

purgue, etc. → **purgar**

purificador *nm* : purifier

purificar {72} *vt* : to purify — **purificación** *nf*

puritano¹, -na *adj* : puritanical, puritan

puritano², -na *n* **1** : Puritan **2** : puritan

puro¹ *adv* : sheer, much ⟨de puro terco : out of sheer stubbornness⟩

puro², -ra *adj* **1** : pure ⟨aire puro : fresh air⟩ **2** : plain, simple, sheer ⟨por pura curiosidad : from sheer curiosity⟩ **3** : only, just ⟨emplean puras mujeres : they only employ women⟩ **4 pura sangre** : Thoroughbred horse

puro³ *nm* : cigar

púrpura *nf* : purple

purpúreo, -rea *adj* : purple

purpurina *nf* : glitter (for decoration)

pus *nm* : pus

pusilánime *adj* COBARDE : pusillanimous, cowardly

puso, etc. → **poner**

pústula *nf* : pustule, pimple

puta *nf* : whore, slut

putrefacción *nf, pl* **-ciones** : putrefaction

putrefacto, -ta *adj* **1** PODRIDO : putrid, rotten **2** : decayed

pútrido, -da *adj* : putrid, rotten

puya *nf* **1** : point (of a lance) **2 lanzar una puya** : to gibe, to taunt

Q

q *nf* : eighteenth letter of the Spanish alphabet

que¹ *conj* **1** : that ⟨dice que está listo : he says that he's ready⟩ ⟨espero que lo haga : I hope that he does it⟩ **2** : than ⟨más que nada : more than anything⟩ **3** (*implying permission or desire*) ⟨¡que entre! : send him in!⟩ ⟨¡que te vaya bien! : I wish you well!⟩ **4** (*indicating a reason or cause*) ⟨¡cuidado, que te caes! : be careful, you're about to fall!⟩ ⟨no provoques al perro, que te va a morder : don't provoke the dog or (else) he'll bite⟩ **5 es que** : the thing is that, I'm afraid that **6 yo que tú** : if I were you

que² *pron* **1** : who, that ⟨la niña que viene : the girl who is coming⟩ **2** : whom, that ⟨los alumnos que enseñé : the students that I taught⟩ **3** : that, which ⟨el carro que me gusta : the car that I like⟩ **4 el (la, lo, las, los) que** → **el¹, la¹, lo¹, los¹**

qué¹ *adv* : how, what ⟨¡qué bonito! : how pretty!⟩

qué² *adj* : what, which ⟨¿qué hora es? : what time is it?⟩

qué³ *pron* : what ⟨¿qué quieres? : what do you want?⟩

quebracho *nm* : quebracho (tree)

quebrada *nf* DESFILADERO : ravine, gorge

quebradizo, -za *adj* FRÁGIL : breakable, delicate, fragile

quebrado¹, -da *adj* **1** : bankrupt **2** : rough, uneven **3** ROTO : broken

quebrado² *nm* : fraction

quebrantamiento *nm* **1** : breaking **2** : deterioration, weakening

quebrantar *vt* **1** : to break, to split, to crack **2** : to weaken **3** : to violate (a law or contract)

quebranto *nm* **1** : break, breaking **2** AFLICCIÓN : affliction, grief **3** PÉRDIDA : loss

quebrar {55} *vt* **1** ROMPER : to break **2** DOBLAR : to bend, to twist — *vi* **1** : to go bankrupt **2** : to fall out, to break up — **quebrarse** *vr*

queda *nf* : curfew

quedar *vi* **1** PERMANECER : to remain, to stay **2** : to be ⟨quedamos contentos con las mejoras : we were pleased with the improvements⟩ **3** : to be situated ⟨queda muy lejos : it's very far, it's too far away⟩ **4** : to be left ⟨quedan sólo dos alternativas : there are only two options left⟩ **5** : to fit, to suit ⟨estos zapatos no me quedan : these shoes don't fit⟩ **6 quedar bien (mal)** : to turn out well (badly) **7** ~ **en** : to agree, to arrange ⟨¿en qué quedamos? : what's the arrangement, then?⟩ — **quedarse** *vr* **1** : to stay ⟨se quedó en casa : she stayed at home⟩ **2** : to keep on ⟨se quedó esperando : he kept on waiting⟩ **3 quedarse atrás** : to stay behind ⟨no quedarse atrás : to be no slouch⟩ **4** ~ **con** : to remain ⟨me quedé con hambre después de comer : I was still hungry after I ate⟩

quedo¹ *adv* : softly, quietly

quedo², -da *adj* : quiet, still

quehacer *nm* **1** : work **2 quehaceres** *nmpl* : chores

queja *nf* : complaint

quejarse *vr* **1** : to complain **2** : to groan, to moan

quejido *nm* **1** : groan, moan **2** : whine, whimper

quejoso, -sa *adj* : complaining, whining

quejumbroso, -sa *adj* : querulous, whining

quema *nf* **1** FUEGO : fire **2** : burning

quemado, -da *adj* **1** : burned, burnt **2** : annoyed **3** : burned-out

quemador *nm* : burner

quemadura *nf* : burn

quemar *vt* : to burn, to set fire to — *vi* : to be burning hot — **quemarse** *vr*

quemarropa *nf a* ~ : point-blank

quemazón *nf, pl* **-zones 1** : burning **2** : intense heat **3** : itch **4** : cutting remark

quena *nf* : Peruvian reed flute

quepa, etc. → **caber**

querella *nf* **1** : complaint **2** : lawsuit

querellante *nmf* : plaintiff

querellarse *vr* ~ **contra** : to bring suit against, to sue

querer¹ {64} *vt* **1** DESEAR : to want, to desire ⟨quiere ser profesor : he wants to be a teacher⟩ ⟨¿cuánto quieres por esta computadora? : how much do you want for this computer?⟩ **2** : to love, to like, to be fond of ⟨te quiero : I love you⟩ **3** (*indicating a request*) ⟨¿quieres pasarme la leche? : please pass the milk⟩ **4 querer decir** : to mean **5 sin** ~ : unintentionally — *vi* : like, want ⟨si quieras : if you like⟩

querer² *nm* : love, affection

querido¹, -da *adj* : dear, beloved

querido², -da *n* : dear, sweetheart

queroseno *nm* : kerosene

querrá, etc. → **querer**

querúbico, -ca *adj* : cherubic

querubín *nm, pl* **-bines** : cherub

quesadilla *nf* : quesadilla

quesería *nf* : cheese shop

queso *nm* : cheese

quetzal *nm* **1** : quetzal (bird) **2** : monetary unit of Guatemala

quicio *nm* **1 estar fuera de quicio** : to be beside oneself **2 sacar de quicio** : to exasperate, to drive crazy

quid *nm* : crux, gist ⟨el quid de la cuestión : the crux of the matter⟩

quiebra¹, etc. → **quebrar**

quiebra² *nf* **1** : break, crack **2** BANCARROTA : failure, bankruptcy

quien *pron, pl* **quienes 1** : who, whom ⟨no sé quien ganará : I don't know who will win⟩ ⟨las personas con quienes trabajo : the people with whom I work⟩ **2** : whoever, whomever ⟨quien quiere salir que salga : whoever wants to can leave⟩ **3** : anyone, some people ⟨hay quienes no están de acuerdo : some people don't agree⟩

quién *pron, pl* **quiénes 1** : who, whom ⟨¿quién sabe? : who knows?⟩ ⟨¿con quién hablo? : with whom am I speaking?⟩ **2 de** ~ : whose ⟨¿de quién es este libro? : whose book is this?⟩

quienquiera *pron, pl* **quienesquiera** : whoever, whomever

quiere, etc. → **querer**

quieto, -ta *adj* **1** : calm, quiet **2** INMÓVIL : still

quietud *nf* **1** : calm, tranquility **2** INMOVILIDAD : stillness

quijada *nf* : jaw, jawbone

quijotesco, -ca *adj* : quixotic

quilate *nm* : karat

quilla *nf* : keel

quimera *nf* : chimera, illusion

quimérico, -ca *adj* : chimeric, fanciful

química *nf* : chemistry

químico¹, -ca *adj* : chemical

químico², -ca *n* : chemist

quimioterapia *nf* : chemotherapy

quimono *nm* : kimono

quince *adj & nm* : fifteen

quinceañero, -ra *n* : fifteen-year-old, teenager

quinceavo¹, -va *adj* : fifteenth

quinceavo² *nm* : fifteenth (fraction)

quincena *nf* : two week period, fortnight

quincenal *adj* : bimonthly, twice a month

quincuagésimo¹, -ma *adj* : fiftieth, fifty-

quincuagésimo², -ma *n* : fiftieth, fifty- (in a series)

quingombó *nm* : okra

quiniela *nf* : sports lottery

quinientos¹, -tas *adj* : five hundred

quinientos² *nms & pl* : five hundred

quinina *nf* : quinine

quino *nm* : cinchona

quinqué *nm* : oil lamp

quinquenal *adj* : five-year ⟨un plan quinquenal : a five-year plan⟩

quinta *nf* : country house, villa

quintaesencia *nf* : quintessence — **quintaesencial** *adj*

quintal *nm* : hundredweight

quinteto *nm* : quintet

quintillizo, -za *n* : quintuplet

quinto, -ta *adj* : fifth — **quinto, -ta** *n*

quíntuplo, -la *adj* : quintuple, five-fold

quiosco *nm* **1** : kiosk **2** : newsstand **3 quiosco de música** : bandstand

quirófano *nm* : operating room

quiromancia *nf* : palmistry
quiropráctica *nf* : chiropractic
quiropráctico, -ca *n* : chiropractor
quirúrgico, -ca *adj* : surgical — **quirúrgicamente** *adv*
quiso, etc. → **querer**
quisquilloso¹, -sa *adj* : fastidious, fussy
quisquilloso², -sa *n* : fussy person, fussbudget
quiste *nm* : cyst
quitaesmalte *nm* : nail polish remover
quitamanchas *nms & pl* : stain remover

quitanieves *nms & pl* : snowplow
quitar *vt* **1** : to remove, to take away **2** : to take off (clothes) **3** : to get rid of, to relieve — **quitarse** *vr* **1** : to withdraw, to leave **2** : to take off (one's clothes) **3** ~ **de** : to give up (a habit) **4 quitar de encima** : to get rid of
quitasol *nm* : parasol
quiteño¹, -ña *adj* : of or from Quito
quiteño², -ña *n* : person from Quito
quizá *or* **quizás** *adv* : maybe, perhaps
quórum *nm, pl* **quórums** : quorum

R

r *nf* : nineteenth letter of the Spanish alphabet
rábano *nm* **1** : radish **2 rábano picante** : horseradish
rabí *nmf, pl* **rabíes** : rabbi
rabia *nf* **1** HIDROFOBIA : rabies, hydrophobia **2** : rage, anger
rabiar *vi* **1** : to rage, to be furious **2** : to be in great pain **3 a** ~ *fam* : like crazy, like mad
rabieta *nf* BERRINCHE : tantrum
rabino, -na *n* : rabbi
rabioso, -sa *adj* **1** : enraged, furious **2** : rabid
rabo *nm* **1** COLA : tail **2 el rabo del ojo** : the corner of one's eye
racha *nf* **1** : gust of wind **2** : run, series, string ⟨racha perdedora : losing streak⟩
racheado, -da *adj* : gusty, windy
racial *adj* : racial
racimo *nm* : bunch, cluster ⟨un racimo de uvas : a bunch of grapes⟩
raciocinio *nm* : reason, reasoning
ración *nf, pl* **raciones 1** : share, ration **2** PORCIÓN : portion, helping
racional *adj* : rational, reasonable — **racionalmente** *adv*
racionalidad *nf* : rationality
racionalización *nf, pl* **-ciones** : rationalization
racionalizar {21} *vt* **1** : to rationalize **2** : to streamline
racionamiento *nm* : rationing
racionar *vt* : to ration
racismo *nm* : racism
racista *adj & nmf* : racist
radar *nm* : radar
radiación *nf, pl* **-ciones** : radiation, irradiation
radiactividad *nf* : radioactivity
radiactivo, -va *adj* : radioactive
radiador *nm* : radiator
radial *adj* **1** : radial **2** : radio, broadcasting ⟨emisora radial : radio transmitter⟩
radiante *adj* : radiant
radiar *vt* **1** : to radiate **2** : to irradiate **3** : to broadcast (on the radio)
radical¹ *adj* : radical, extreme — **radicalmente** *adv*

radical² *nmf* : radical
radicalismo *nm* : radicalism
radicar {72} *vi* **1** : to be found, to lie **2** ARRAIGAR : to take root — **radicarse** *vr* : to settle, to establish oneself
radio¹ *nm* **1** : radius **2** : radium
radio² *nmf* : radio
radioactividad *nf* : radioactivity
radioactivo, -va *adj* : radioactive
radioaficionado, -da *n* : ham radio operator
radiodifusión *nf, pl* **-siones** : radio broadcasting
radiodifusora *nf* : radio station
radioemisora *nf* : radio station
radiofaro *nm* : radio beacon
radiofónico, -ca *adj* : radio ⟨estación radiofónica pública : public radio station⟩
radiofrecuencia *nf* : radio frequency
radiografía *nf* : X ray (photograph)
radiografiar {85} *vt* : to x-ray
radiología *nf* : radiology
radiólogo, -ga *n* : radiologist
radón *nm* : radon
raer {65} *vt* RASPAR : to scrape, to scrape off
ráfaga *nf* **1** : gust (of wind) **2** : flash, burst ⟨una ráfaga de luz : a flash of light⟩
raid *nm* CA, Mex fam : lift, ride
raído, -da *adj* : worn, shabby
raiga, etc. → **raer**
raíz *nf, pl* **raíces 1** : root **2** : origin, source **3 a raíz de** : following, as a result of **4 echar raíces** : to take root
raja *nf* **1** : crack, slit **2** : slice, wedge
rajá *nm* : raja
rajadura *nf* : crack, split
rajar *vt* HENDER : to crack, to split — *vi* **1** *fam* : to chatter **2** *fam* : to boast, to brag — **rajarse** *vr* **1** : to crack, to split open **2** *fam* : to back out
rajatabla *adv* **a** ~ : strictly, to the letter
ralea *nf* : kind, sort, ilk ⟨son de la misma valea : they're two of a kind⟩
ralentí *nm* **dejar al ralentí** : to leave (a motor) idling
rallado, -da *adj* **1** : grated **2 pan rallado** : bread crumbs *pl*
rallador *nm* : grater

rallar *vt* : to grate
ralo, -la *adj* : sparse, thin
RAM *nf* : RAM, random-access memory
rama *nf* : branch
ramaje *nm* : branches *pl*
ramal *nm* 1 : branchline 2 : halter, strap
ramera *nf* : harlot, prostitute
ramificación *nf, pl* **-ciones** : ramification
ramificarse {72} *vr* : to branch out, to divide into branches
ramillete *nm* 1 RAMO : bouquet 2 : select group, cluster
ramo *nm* 1 : branch 2 RAMILLETE : bouquet 3 : division (of science or industry) 4 **Domingo de Ramos** : Palm Sunday
rampa *nf* : ramp, incline
rana *nf* 1 : frog 2 **rana toro** : bullfrog
ranchera *nf Mex* : traditional folk song
ranchería *nf* : settlement
ranchero, -ra *n* : rancher, farmer
rancho *nm* 1 : ranch, farm 2 : hut 3 : settlement, camp 4 : food, mess (for soldiers, etc.)
rancio, -cia *adj* 1 : aged, mellow (of wine) 2 : ancient, old 3 : rancid
rango *nm* 1 : rank, status 2 : high social standing 3 : pomp, splendor
ranúnculo *nm* : buttercup
ranura *nf* : groove, slot
rap *nm* : rap (music)
rapacidad *nf* : rapacity
rapar *vt* 1 : to crop 2 : to shave
rapaz¹ *adj, pl* **rapaces** : rapacious, predatory
rapaz², -paza *n, mpl* **rapaces** : youngster, child
rape *nm* : close haircut
rapé *nm* : snuff
rapero, -ra *n* : rapper, rap artist
rapidez *nf* : rapidity, speed
rápido¹ *adv* : quickly, fast ⟨¡manejas tan rápido! : you drive so fast!⟩
rápido², -da *adj* : rapid, quick — **rápidamente** *adv*
rápido³ *nm* 1 : express train 2 **rápidos** *nmpl* : rapids
rapiña *nf* 1 : plunder, pillage 2 **ave de rapiña** : bird of prey
raposa *nf* : vixen (fox)
rapsodia *nf* : rhapsody
raptar *vt* SECUESTRAR : to abduct, to kidnap
rapto *nm* 1 SECUESTRO : kidnapping, abduction 2 ARREBATO : fit, outburst
raptor, -tora *n* SECUESTRADOR : kidnapper
raque *nm* : beachcombing
raquero, -ra *n* : beachcomber
raqueta *nf* 1 : racket (in sports) 2 : snowshoe
raquítico, -ca *adj* 1 : scrawny, weak 2 : measly, skimpy
raquitismo *nm* : rickets
raramente *adv* : seldom, rarely
rareza *nf* 1 : rarity 2 : peculiarity, oddity

raro, -ra *adj* 1 EXTRAÑO : odd, strange, peculiar 2 : unusual, rare 3 : exceptional 4 **rara vez** : seldom, rarely
ras *nm* **a ras de** : level with
rasar *vt* 1 : to skim, to graze 2 : to level
rascacielos *nms & pl* : skyscraper
rascar {72} *vt* 1 : to scratch 2 : to scrape — **rascarse** *vr* : to scratch an itch
rasgadura *nf* : tear, rip
rasgar {52} *vt* : to rip, to tear — **rasgarse** *vr*
rasgo *nm* 1 : stroke (of a pen) ⟨a grandes rasgos : in broad outlines⟩ 2 CARACTERÍSTICA : trait, characteristic 3 : gesture, deed 4 **rasgos** *nmpl* FACCIONES : features
rasgón *nm, pl* **rasgones** : rip, tear
rasgue, etc. → rasgar
rasguear *vt* : to strum
rasguñar *vt* 1 : to scratch 2 : to sketch, to outline
rasguño *nm* 1 : scratch 2 : sketch
raso¹, -sa *adj* 1 : level, flat 2 **soldado raso** : private (in the army) ⟨los soldados rasos : the ranks⟩
raso² *nm* : satin
raspadura *nf* 1 : scratching, scraping 2 **raspaduras** *nfpl* : scrapings
raspar *vt* 1 : to scrape 2 : to file down, to smooth — *vi* : to be rough
rasque, etc. → rascar
rastra *nf* 1 : harrow 2 **a rastras** : by dragging, unwillingly
rastrear *vt* 1 : to track, to trace 2 : to comb, to search 3 : to trawl
rastrero, -ra *adj* 1 : creeping, crawling 2 : vile, despicable
rastrillar *vt* : to rake, to harrow
rastrillo *nm* 1 : rake 2 *Mex* : razor
rastro *nm* 1 PISTA : trail, track 2 VESTIGIO : trace, sign
rastrojo *nm* : stubble (of plants)
rasuradora *nf Mex, CA* : electric razor, shaver
rasurar *vt* AFEITAR : to shave — **rasurarse** *vr*
rata¹ *nm fam* : pickpocket, thief
rata² *nf* 1 : rat 2 *Col, Pan, Peru* : rate, percentage
ratear *vt* : to pilfer, to steal
ratero, -ra *n* : petty thief
ratificación *nf, pl* **-ciones** : ratification
ratificar {72} *vt* 1 : to ratify 2 : to confirm
rato *nm* 1 : while 2 **pasar el rato** : to pass the time 3 **a cada rato** : all the time, constantly ⟨les sacaba dinero a cada rato : he was always taking money from them⟩ 4 **al poco rato** : later, shortly after
ratón¹, -tona *n, mpl* **ratones** 1 : mouse 2 **ratón de biblioteca** *fam* : bookworm
ratón² *nm, pl* **ratones** 1 : (computer) mouse 2 *CoRi* : biceps
ratonera *nf* : mousetrap
raudal *nm* 1 : torrent 2 **a raudales** : in abundance

raya¹, etc. → **raer**
raya² *nf* **1** : line **2** : stripe **3** : skate, ray **4** : part (in the hair) **5** : crease (in clothing)
rayar *vt* **1** ARAÑAR : to scratch **2** : to scrawl on, to mark up ⟨rayaron las paredes : they covered the walls with graffiti⟩ — *vi* **1** : to scratch **2** AMANECER : to dawn, to break ⟨al rayar el alba : at break of day⟩ **3** ~ **con** : to be adjacent to, to be next to **4** ~ **en** : to border on, to verge on ⟨su respuesta raya en lo ridículo : his answer borders on the ridiculous⟩ — **rayarse** *vr*
rayo *nm* **1** : ray, beam ⟨rayo láser : laser beam⟩ ⟨rayo de gamma : gamma ray⟩ ⟨rayo de sol : sunbeam⟩ **2** RELÁMPAGO : lightning bolt **3 rayo X** : X-ray
rayón *nm, pl* **rayones** : rayon
raza *nf* **1** : race ⟨raza humana : human race⟩ **2** : breed, strain **3 de ~** : thoroughbred, pedigreed
razón *nf, pl* **razones** **1** MOTIVO : reason, motive ⟨en razón de : by reason of, because of⟩ **2** JUSTICIA : rightness, justice ⟨tener razón : to be right⟩ **3** : reasoning, sense ⟨perder la razón : to lose one's mind⟩ **4** : ratio, proportion
razonable *adj* : reasonable — **razonablemente** *adv*
razonado, -da *adj* : itemized, detailed
razonamiento *nm* : reasoning
razonar *v* : to reason, to think
reabastecimiento *nm* : replenishment
reabierto {2} *pp* → **reabrir**
reabrir {2} *vt* : to reopen — **reabrirse** *vr*
reacción *nf, pl* **-ciones** **1** : reaction **2 motor a reacción** : jet engine
reaccionar *vi* : to react, to respond
reaccionario, -ria *adj & n* : reactionary
reacio, -cia *adj* : resistant, opposed
reacondicionar *vt* : to recondition
reactivación *nf, pl* **-ciones** : reactivation, revival
reactivar *vt* : to reactivate, revive
reactor *nm* **1** : reactor ⟨reactor nuclear : nuclear reactor⟩ **2** : jet engine **3** : jet airplane, jet
reafirmar *vt* : to reaffirm, to assert, to strengthen
reajustar *vt* : to readjust, to adjust
reajuste *nm* : readjustment ⟨reajuste de precios : price increase⟩
real *adj* **1** : real, true **2** : royal
realce *nm* **1** : embossing, relief **2 dar realce** : to highlight, to bring out
realeza *nf* : royalty
realidad *nf* **1** : reality **2 en ~** : in truth, actually
realinear *vt* : to realign
realismo *nm* **1** : realism **2** : royalism
realista¹ *adj* **1** : realistic **2** : realist : royalist
realista² *nmf* **1** : realist **2** : royalist
realización *nf, pl* **-ciones** : execution, realization

realizar {21} *vt* **1** : to carry out, to execute **2** : to produce, to direct (a film or play) **3** : to fulfill, to achieve **4** : to realize (a profit) — **realizarse** *vr* **1** : to come true **2** : to fulfill oneself
realmente *adv* : really, in reality
realzar {21} *vt* **1** : to heighten, to raise **2** : to highlight, to enhance
reanimación *nf, pl* **-ciones** : revival, resuscitation
reanimar *vt* **1** : to revive, to restore **2** : to resuscitate — **reanimarse** *vr* : to come around, to recover
reanudación *nf, pl* **-ciones** : resumption, renewal
reanudar *vt* : to resume, to renew — **reanudarse** *vr* : to resume, to continue
reaparecer {53} *vi* **1** : to reappear **2** : to make a comeback
reaparición *nf, pl* **-ciones** : reappearance
reapertura *nf* : reopening
reata *nf* **1** : rope **2** *Mex* : lasso, lariat **3 de ~** : single file
reavivar *vt* : to revive, to reawaken
rebaja *nf* **1** : reduction **2** DESCUENTO : discount **3 rebajas** *nfpl* : sale
rebajar *vt* **1** : to reduce, to lower ⟨a precios rebajados : at reduced prices, on sale⟩ **2** : to lessen, to diminish **3** : to humiliate — **rebajarse** *vr* **1** : to humble oneself **2 rebajarse a** : to stoop to
rebanada *nf* : slice
rebañar *vt* : to mop up, to sop up
rebaño *nm* **1** : flock **2** : herd
rebasar *vt* **1** : to surpass, to exceed **2** *Mex* : to pass, to overtake
rebatiña *nf* : scramble, fight (over something)
rebatir *vt* REFUTAR : to refute
rebato *nm* **1** : surprise attack **2 tocar a rebato** : to sound the alarm
rebelarse *vr* : to rebel
rebelde¹ *adj* : rebellious, unruly
rebelde² *nmf* **1** : rebel **2** : defaulter
rebeldía *nf* **1** : rebelliousness **2 en ~** : in default
rebelión *nf, pl* **-liones** : rebellion
rebobinar *vt* : to rewind
reborde *nm* : border, flange, rim
rebosante *adj* : brimming, overflowing ⟨rebosante de salud : brimming with health⟩
rebosar *vi* **1** : to overflow **2** ~ **de** : to abound in, to be bursting with — *vt* : to radiate
rebotar *vi* **1** : to bounce **2** : to ricochet, to rebound
rebote *nm* **1** : bounce **2** : rebound, ricochet
rebozar {21} *vt* : to coat in batter
rebozo *nm* **1** : shawl, wrap **2 sin ~** : frankly, openly
rebullir {38} *v* : to move, to stir — **rebullirse** *vr*
rebuscado, -da *adj* : affected, pretentious
rebuscar {72} *vi* : to search thoroughly

rebuznar *vi* : to bray
rebuzno *nm* : bray, braying
recabar *vt* **1** : to gather, to obtain, to collect **2 recabar fondos** : to raise money
recado *nm* **1** : message ⟨mandar recado : to send word⟩ **2** *Spain* : errand
recaer {13} *vi* **1** : to relapse **2** ~ **en** *or* ~ **sobre** : to fall on, to fall to
recaída *nf* : relapse
recaiga, etc. → **recaer**
recalar *vi* : to arrive
recalcar {72} *vt* : to emphasize, to stress
recalcitrante *adj* : recalcitrant
recalentar {55} *vt* **1** : to reheat, to warm up **2** : to overheat
recámara *nf* **1** *Col, Mex, Pan* : bedroom **2** : chamber (of a firearm)
recamarera *nf Mex* : chambermaid
recambio *nm* **1** : spare part **2** : refill (for a pen, etc.)
recapacitar *vi* **1** : to reconsider **2** ~ **en** : to reflect on, to weigh
recapitular *v* : to recapitulate — **recapitulación** *nf*
recargable *adj* : rechargeable
recargado, -da *adj* : overly elaborate or ornate
recargar {52} *vt* **1** : to recharge **2** : to overload
recargo *nm* : surcharge
recatado, -da *adj* MODESTO : modest, demure
recato *nm* PUDOR : modesty
recaudación *nf, pl* **-ciones 1** : collection **2** : earnings *pl*, takings *pl*
recaudador, -dora *n* **recaudador de impuestos** : tax collector
recaudar *vt* : to collect
recaudo *nm* : safe place ⟨a (buen) recaudo : in safe keeping⟩
recayó, etc. → **recaer**
rece, etc. → **rezar**
recelo *nm* : distrust, suspicion
receloso, -sa *adj* : distrustful, suspicious
recepción *nf, pl* **-ciones** : reception
recepcionista *nmf* : receptionist
receptáculo *nm* : receptacle
receptividad *nf* : receptivity, receptiveness
receptivo, -va *adj* : receptive
receptor¹, -tora *adj* : receiving
receptor², -tora *n* **1** : recipient **2** : catcher (in baseball), receiver (in football)
receptor³ *nm* : receiver ⟨receptor de televisión : television set⟩
recesión *nf, pl* **-siones** : recession
recesivo, -va *adj* : recessive
receso *nm* : recess, adjournment
receta *nf* **1** : recipe **2** : prescription
recetar *vt* : to prescribe (medications)
rechazar {21} *vt* **1** : to reject **2** : to turn down, to refuse
rechazo *nm* : rejection, refusal
rechifla *nf* : booing, jeering
rechinar *vi* **1** : to squeak **2** : to grind, to gnash ⟨hacer rechinar los dientes : to grind one's teeth⟩

rechoncho, -cha *adj fam* : chubby, squat
recibidor *nm* : vestibule, entrance hall
recibimiento *nm* : reception, welcome
recibir *vt* **1** : to receive, to get **2** : to welcome — *vi* : to receive visitors — **recibirse** *vr* ~ **de** : to qualify as
recibo *nm* : receipt
reciclable *adj* : recyclable
reciclado → **reciclaje**
reciclaje *nm* **1** : recycling **2** : retraining
reciclar *vt* **1** : to recycle **2** : to retrain
recién *adv* **1** : newly, recently ⟨recién nacido : newborn⟩ ⟨recién casados : newlyweds⟩ ⟨recién llegado : newcomer⟩ **2** : just, only just ⟨recién ahora me acordé : I just now remembered⟩
reciente *adj* : recent — **recientemente** *adv*
recinto *nm* **1** : enclosure **2** : site, premises *pl*
recio¹ *adv* **1** : strongly, hard **2** : loudly, loud
recio², -cia *adj* **1** : severe, harsh **2** : tough, strong
recipiente¹ *nm* : container, receptacle
recipiente² *nmf* : recipient
reciprocar {72} *vi* : to reciprocate
reciprocidad *nf* : reciprocity
recíproco, -ca *adj* : reciprocal, mutual
recitación *nf, pl* **-ciones** : recitation, recital
recital *nm* : recital
recitar *vt* : to recite
reclamación *nf, pl* **-ciones 1** : claim, demand **2** QUEJA : complaint
reclamar *vt* **1** EXIGIR : to demand, to require **2** : to claim — *vi* : to complain
reclamo *nm* **1** : bird call, lure **2** : lure, decoy **3** : inducement, attraction **4** : advertisement **5** : complaint
reclinar *vt* : to rest, to lean — **reclinarse** *vr* : to recline, to lean back
recluir {41} *vt* : to confine, to lock up — **recluirse** *vr* : to shut oneself up, to withdraw
reclusión *nf, pl* **-siones** : imprisonment
recluso, -sa *n* **1** : inmate, prisoner **2** SOLITARIO : recluse
recluta *nmf* : recruit, draftee
reclutamiento *nm* : recruitment, recruiting
reclutar *vt* ENROLAR : to recruit, to enlist
recobrar *vt* : to recover, to regain — **recobrarse** *vr* : to recover, to recuperate
recocer {14} *vt* : to overcook, to cook again
recodo *nm* : bend
recogedor *nm* : dustpan
recoger {15} *vt* **1** : to collect, to gather **2** : to get, to retrieve, to pick up **3** : to clean up, to tidy (up)
recogido, -da *adj* : quiet, secluded
recogimiento *nm* **1** : collecting, gathering **2** : withdrawal **3** : absorption, concentration

recolección *nf, pl* **-ciones 1** : collection ⟨recolección de basura : trash pickup⟩ **2** : harvest

recolectar *vt* **1** : to gather, to collect **2** : to harvest, to pick

recomendable *adj* : advisable, recommended

recomendación *nf, pl* **-ciones** : recommendation

recomendar {55} *vt* **1** : to recommend **2** ACONSEJAR : to advise

recompensa *nf* : reward, recompense

recompensar *vt* **1** PREMIAR : to reward **2** : to compensate

reconciliación *nf, pl* **-ciones** : reconciliation

reconciliar *vt* : to reconcile — **reconciliarse** *vr*

recóndito, -ta *adj* **1** : remote, isolated **2** : hidden, recondite **3 en lo más recóndito de** : in the depths of

reconfortar *vt* : to comfort — **reconfortante** *adj*

reconocer {18} *vt* **1** : to recognize **2** : to admit **3** : to examine

reconocible *adj* : recognizable

reconocido, -da *adj* **1** : recognized, accepted **2** : grateful

reconocimiento *nm* **1** : acknowledgment, recognition, avowal **2** : (medical) examination **3** : reconnaissance

reconquista *nf* : reconquest

reconquistar *vt* **1** : to reconquer, to recapture **2** RECUPERAR : to regain, to recover

reconsiderar *vt* : to reconsider — **reconsideración** *nf*

reconstrucción *nf, pl* **-ciones** : reconstruction

reconstruir {41} *vt* **1** : to rebuild, to reconstruct

reconversión *nf, pl* **-siones** : restructuring

reconvertir {76} *vt* **1** : to restructure **2** : to retrain

recopilación *nf, pl* **-ciones 1** : summary **2** : collection, compilation

recopilar *vt* : to compile, to collect

récord *or* **record** ['rekɔr] *nm, pl* **récords** *or* **records** [-kɔrs] : record ⟨record mundial : world record⟩ — **récord** *or* **record** *adj*

recordar {19} *vt* **1** : to recall, to remember **2** : to remind — *vi* **1** ACORDARSE : to remember **2** DESPERTAR : to wake up

recordatorio¹, -ria *adj* : commemorative

recordatorio² *nm* : reminder

recorrer *vt* **1** : to travel through, to tour **2** : to cover (a distance) **3** : to go over, to look over

recorrido *nm* **1** : journey, trip **2** : path, route, course **3** : round (in golf)

recortar *vt* **1** : to cut, to reduce **2** : cut out **3** : to trim, to cut off **4** : to outline — **recortarse** *vr* : to stand out ⟨los árboles se recortaban en el horizonte : the trees were silhouetted against the horizon⟩

recorte *nm* **1** : cut, reduction **2** : clipping ⟨recortes de periódicos : newspaper clippings⟩

recostar {19} *vt* : to lean, to rest — **recostarse** *vr* : to lie down, recline

recoveco *nm* **1** VUELTA : bend, turn **2** : nook, corner **3 recovecos** *nmpl* : intricacies, ins and outs

recreación *nf, pl* **-ciones 1** : re-creation **2** DIVERSIÓN : recreation, entertainment

recrear *vt* **1** : to re-create **2** : to entertain, to amuse — **recrearse** *vr* : to enjoy oneself

recreativo, -va *adj* : recreational

recreo *nm* **1** DIVERSIÓN : entertainment, amusement **2** : recess, break

recriminación *nf, pl* **-ciones** : reproach, recrimination

recriminar *vt* : to reproach — *vi* : to recriminate — **recriminarse** *vr*

recrudecer {53} *v* : to intensify, to worsen — **recrudecerse** *vr*

rectal *adj* : rectal

rectangular *adj* : rectangular

rectángulo *nm* : rectangle

rectificación *nf, pl* **-ciones** : rectification, correction

rectificar {72} *vt* **1** : to rectify, to correct **2** : to straighten (out)

rectitud *nf* **1** : straightness **2** : honesty, rectitude

recto¹ *adv* : straight

recto², -ta *adj* **1** : straight **2** : upright, honorable **3** : sound

recto³ *nm* : rectum

rector¹, -tora *adj* : governing, managing

rector², -tora *n* : rector

rectoría *nf* : rectory

recubierto *pp* → **recubrir**

recubrir {2} *vt* : to cover, to coat

recuento *nm* : recount, count ⟨un recuento de los votos : a recount of the votes⟩

recuerdo *nm* **1** : memory **2** : souvenir, memento **3 recuerdos** *nmpl* : regards

recular *vi* **1** : to back up **2** REPLEGARSE : to retreat, to fall back **3** RETRACTARSE : to back down

recuperación *nf, pl* **-ciones 1** : recovery, recuperation **2 recuperación de datos** : data retrieval

recuperar *vt* **1** : to recover, to get back, to retrieve **2** : to recuperate **3** : to make up for ⟨recuperar el tiempo perdido : to make up for lost time⟩ — **recuperarse** *vr* ~ **de** : to recover from, to get over

recurrente *adj* : recurrent, recurring

recurrir *vi* **1** ~ **a** : to turn to, to appeal to **2** ~ **a** : to resort to **3** : to appeal (in law)

recurso *nm* **1** : recourse ⟨el último recurso : the last resort⟩ **2** : appeal (in law) **3 recursos** *nmpl* : resources, means ⟨recursos naturales : natural resources⟩

red *nf* **1** : net, mesh **2** : network, system, chain **3** : trap, snare
redacción *nf, pl* **-ciones 1** : writing, composition **2** : editing
redactar *vt* **1** : to write, to draft **2** : to edit
redactor, -tora *n* : editor
redada *nf* **1** : raid **2** : catch, haul
redefinir *vt* : to redefine — **redefinición** *nf*
redención *nf, pl* **-ciones** : redemption
redentor¹, -tora *adj* : redeeming
redentor², -tora *n* : redeemer
redescubierto *pp* → **redescubrir**
redescubrir {2} *vt* : to rediscover
redicho, -cha *adj fam* : affected, pretentious
redil *nm* **1** : sheepfold **2 volver al redil** : to return to the fold
redimir *vt* : to redeem, to deliver (from sin)
rediseñar *vt* : to redesign
redistribuir {41} *vt* : to redistribute — **redistribución** *nf*
rédito *nm* : return, yield
redituar {3} *vt* : to produce, to yield
redoblar *vt* : to redouble, to strengthen — **redoblado, -da** *adj*
redoble *nm* : drum roll
redomado, -da *adj* **1** : sly, crafty **2** : utter, out-and-out
redonda *nf* **1** : region, surrounding area **2 a la redonda** ALREDEDOR : around ⟨de diez millas a la redonda : for ten miles around⟩
redondear *vt* : to round off, to round out
redondel *nm* **1** : ring, circle **2** : bullring, arena
redondez *nf* : roundness
redondo, -da *adj* **1** : round ⟨mesa redonda : round table⟩ **2** : great, perfect ⟨un negocio redondo : an excellent deal⟩ **3** : straightforward, flat ⟨un rechazo redondo : a flat refusal⟩ **4** *Mex* : round-trip **5 en ∼** : around
reducción *nf, pl* **-ciones** : reduction, decrease
reducido, -da *adj* **1** : reduced, limited **2** : small
reducir {61} *vt* **1** DISMINUIR : to reduce, to decrease, to cut **2** : to subdue **3** : to boil down — **reducirse** *vr* ∼ **a** : to come down to, to be nothing more than
redundancia *nf* : redundancy
redundante *adj* : redundant
reedición *nf, pl* **-ciones** : reprint
reelegir {28} *vt* : to reelect — **reelección** *nf*
reembolsable *adj* : refundable
reembolsar *vt* **1** : to refund, to reimburse **2** : to repay
reembolso *nm* : refund, reimbursement
reemplazable *adj* : replaceable
reemplazar {21} *vt* : to replace, to substitute
reemplazo *nm* : replacement, substitution
reencarnación *nf, pl* **-ciones** : reincarnation

reencuentro *nm* : reunion
reestablecer {53} *vt* : to reestablish
reestructurar *vt* : to restructure
reexaminar *vt* : to reexamine
refaccionar *vt* : to repair, to renovate
refacciones *nfpl* : repairs, renovations
referencia *nf* **1** : reference **2 hacer referencia a** : to refer to
referendo → **referéndum**
referéndum *nm, pl* **-dums** : referendum
referente *adj* ∼ **a** : concerning
réferi *or* **referi** ['referi] *nmf* : referee
referir {76} *vt* **1** : to relate, to tell **2** : to refer ⟨nos refirió al diccionario : she referred us to the dictionary⟩ — **referirse** *vr* ∼ **a 1** : to refer to **2** ∼ **a** : to be concerned, to be in reference to ⟨en lo que se refiere a la educación : as far as education is concerned⟩
refinado¹, -da *adj* : refined
refinado² *nm* : refining
refinamiento *nm* **1** : refining **2** FINURA : refinement
refinanciar *vt* : to refinance
refinar *vt* : to refine
refinería *nf* : refinery
reflectante *adj* : reflective, reflecting
reflector¹, -tora *adj* : reflecting
reflector² *nm* **1** : spotlight, searchlight **2** : reflector
reflejar *vt* : to reflect — **reflejarse** *vr* : to be reflected ⟨la decepción se refleja en su rostro : the disappointment shows on her face⟩
reflejo *nm* **1** : reflection **2** : reflex **3 reflejos** *nmpl* : highlights, streaks (in hair)
reflexión *nf, pl* **-xiones** : reflection, thought
reflexionar *vi* : to reflect, to think
reflexivo, -va *adj* **1** : reflective, thoughtful **2** : reflexive
reflujo *nm* : ebb, ebb tide
reforma *nf* **1** : reform **2** : alteration, renovation
reformador, -dora *n* : reformer
reformar *vt* **1** : to reform **2** : to change, to alter **3** : to renovate, to repair — **reformarse** *vr* : to mend one's ways
reformatorio *nm* : reformatory
reformular *vt* : to reformulate — **reformulación** *nf*
reforzar {36} *vt* **1** : to reinforce, to strengthen **2** : to encourage, to support
refracción *nf, pl* **-ciones** : refraction
refractar *vt* : to refract — **refractarse** *vr*
refractario, -ria *adj* : refractory, obstinate
refrán *nm, pl* **refranes** ADAGIO : proverb, saying
refregar {49} *vt* : to scrub
refrenar *vt* **1** : to rein in (a horse) **2** : to restrain, to check — **refrenarse** *vr* : to restrain oneself
refrendar *vt* **1** : to countersign, to endorse **2** : to stamp (a passport)
refrescante *adj* : refreshing

refrescar {72} *vt* **1** : to refresh, to cool **2** : to brush up (on) **3 refrescar la memoria** : to refresh one's memory — *vi* : to turn cooler

refresco *nm* : refreshment, soft drink

refriega *nf* : skirmish, scuffle

refrigeración *nf, pl* **-ciones 1** : refrigeration **2** : air-conditioning

refrigerador *nmf* NEVERA : refrigerator

refrigeradora *nf Col, Peru* : refrigerator

refrigerante *nm* : coolant

refrigerar *vt* **1** : to refrigerate **2** : to air-condition

refrigerio *nm* : snack, refreshments *pl*

refrito¹, -ta *adj* : refried

refrito² *nm* : rehash

refuerzo *nm* : reinforcement, support

refugiado, -da *n* : refugee

refugiar *vt* : to shelter — **refugiarse** *vr* ACOGERSE : to take refuge

refugio *nm* : refuge, shelter

refulgencia *nf* : brilliance, splendor

refulgir {35} *vi* : to shine brightly

refundir *vt* **1** : to recast (metals) **2** : to revise, to rewrite

refunfuñar *vi* : to grumble, to groan

refutar *vt* : to refute — **refutación** *nf*

regadera *nf* **1** : watering can **2** : shower head, shower **3** : sprinkler

regaderazo *nm Mex* : shower

regalar *vt* **1** OBSEQUIAR : to present (as a gift), to give away **2** : to regale, to entertain **3** : to flatter, to make a fuss over — **regalarse** *vr* : to pamper oneself

regalía *nf* : royalty, payment

regaliz *nm, pl* **-lices** : licorice

regalo *nm* **1** OBSEQUIO : gift, present **2** : pleasure, comfort **3** : treat

regañadientes *mpl* **a ~** : reluctantly, unwillingly

regañar *vt* : to scold, to give a talking to — *vi* **1** QUEJARSE : to grumble, to complain **2** REÑIR : to quarrel, to argue

regaño *nm fam* : scolding

regañon, -ñona *adj, mpl* **-ñones** *fam* : grumpy, irritable

regar {49} *vt* **1** : to irrigate **2** : to water **3** : to wash, to hose down **4** : to spill, to scatter

regata *nf* : regatta, yacht race

regate *nm* : dodge, feint

regatear *vt* **1** : to haggle over **2** ESCATIMAR : to skimp on, to be sparing with — *vi* : to bargain, to haggle

regateo *nm* : bargaining, haggling

regatón *nm, pl* **-tones** : ferrule, tip

regazo *nm* : lap (of a person)

regencia *nf* : regency

regenerar *vt* : to regenerate — **regenerarse** *vr* — **regeneración** *nf*

regentar *vt* : to run, to manage

regente *nmf* : regent

regidor, -dora *n* : town councillor

régimen *nm, pl* **regímenes 1** : regime **2** : diet **3** : regimen, rules *pl* ⟨régimen de vida : lifestyle⟩

regimiento *nm* : regiment

regio, -gia *adj* **1** : great, magnificent **2** : regal, royal

región *nf, pl* **regiones** : region, area

regional *adj* : regional — **regionalmente** *adv*

regir {28} *vt* **1** : to rule **2** : to manage, to run **3** : to control, to govern ⟨las costumbres que rigen la conducta : the customs which govern behavior⟩ — *vi* : to apply, to be in force ⟨las leyes rigen en los tres países : the laws apply in all three countries⟩ — **regirse** *vr* **~ por** : to go by, to be guided by

registrador¹, -dora *adj* **caja registradora** : cash register

registrador², -dora *n* : registrar, recorder

registrar *vt* **1** : to register, to record **2** GRABAR : to record, to tape **3** : to search, to examine — **registrarse** *vr* **1** INSCRIBIRSE : to register **2** OCURRIR : to happen, to occur

registro *nm* **1** : register **2** : registration **3** : registry, record office **4** : range (of a voice or musical instrument) **5** : search

regla *nf* **1** NORMA : rule, regulation **2** : ruler ⟨regla de cálculo : slide rule⟩ **3** MENSTRUACIÓN : period, menstruation

reglamentación *nf, pl* **-ciones 1** : regulation **2** : rules *pl*

reglamentar *vt* : to regulate, to set rules for

reglamentario, -ria *adj* : regulation, official ⟨equipo reglamentario : standard equipment⟩

reglamento *nm* : regulations *pl*, rules *pl* ⟨reglamento de tráfico : traffic regulations⟩

regocijar *vt* : to gladden, to delight — **regocijarse** *vr* : to rejoice

regocijo *nm* : delight, rejoicing

regordete, -ta *adj fam* LLENITO : chubby

regresar *vt* DEVOLVER : to give back — *vi* : to return, to come back, to go back

regresión *nf, pl* **-siones** : regression, return

regresivo, -va *adj* : regressive

regreso *nm* **1** : return **2 estar de regreso** : to be back, to be home

reguero *nm* **1** : irrigation ditch **2** : trail, trace **3 propagarse como reguero de pólvora** : to spread like wildfire

regulable *adj* : adjustable

regulación *nf, pl* **-ciones** : regulation, control

regulador¹, -dora *adj* : regulating, regulatory

regulador² *nm* **1** : regulator, governor **2 regulador de tiro** : damper (in a chimney)

regular¹ *vt* : to regulate, to control

regular² *adj* **1** : regular **2** : fair, OK, so-so **3** : medium, average **4 por lo regular** : in general, generally

regularidad *nf* : regularity

regularización *nf, pl* **-ciones** NORMAL-IZACIÓN : normalization

regularizar {21} *vt* NORMALIZAR : to normalize, to make regular

regularmente *adv* : regularly

regusto *nm* : aftertaste

rehabilitar *vt* **1** : to rehabilitate **2** : to reinstate **3** : renovate, to restore — **rehabilitación** *nf*

rehacer {40} *vt* **1** : to redo **2** : to remake, to repair, to renew — **rehacerse** *vr* **1** : to recover **2** ~ **de** : to get over

rehecho *pp* → **rehacer**

rehén *nm, pl* **rehenes** : hostage

rehicieron, etc. → **rehacer**

rehizo → **rehacer**

rehuir {41} *vt* : to avoid, to shun

rehusar {8} *v* : to refuse

reimprimir *vt* : to reprint

reina *nf* : queen

reinado *nm* : reign

reinante *adj* **1** : reigning **2** : prevailing, current

reinar *vi* **1** : to reign **2** : to prevail

reincidencia *nf* : recidivism, relapse

reincidente *nmf* : backslider, recidivist

reincidir *vi* : to backslide, to retrogress

reincorporar *vt* : to reinstate — **reincorporarse** *vr* ~ **a** : to return to, to rejoin

reiniciar *vt* **1** : to resume, to restart **2** : to reboot (a computer)

reino *nm* : kingdom, realm ⟨reino animal : animal kingdom⟩

reinstalar *vt* **1** : to reinstall **2** : to reinstate

reintegración *nf, pl* **-ciones** **1** : reinstatement, reintegration **2** : refund, reimbursement

reintegrar *vt* **1** : to reintegrate, reinstate **2** : to refund, to reimburse — **reintegrarse** *vr* ~ **a** : to return to, to rejoin

reír {66} *vi* : to laugh — *vt* : to laugh at — **reírse** *vr*

reiteración *nf, pl* **-ciones** : reiteration, repetition

reiterado, -da *adj* : repeated ⟨lo explicó en reiteradas ocasiones : he explained it repeatedly⟩ — **reiteradamente** *adv*

reiterar *vt* : to reiterate, to repeat

reiterativo, -va *adj* : repetitive, repetitious

reivindicación *nf, pl* **-ciones** **1** : demand, claim **2** : vindication

reivindicar {72} *vt* **1** : to vindicate **2** : to demand, to claim **3** : to restore

reja *nf* **1** : grille, grating ⟨entre rejas : behind bars⟩ **2** : plowshare

rejilla *nf* : grille, grate, screen

rejuvenecer {53} *vt* : to rejuvenate — *vi* : to be rejuvenated — **rejuvenecerse** *vr*

rejuvenecimiento *nm* : rejuvenation

relación *nf, pl* **-ciones** **1** : relation, connection, relevance **2** : relationship **3** RELATO : account **4** LISTA : list **5 con relación a** *or* **en relación con** : in relation to, concerning **6 relaciones-públicas** : public relations

relacionar *vt* : to relate, to connect — **relacionarse** *vr* ~ **con** : to be connected to, to be linked with

relajación *nf, pl* **-ciones** : relaxation

relajado, -da *adj* **1** : relaxed, loose **2** : dissolute, depraved

relajante *adj* : relaxing

relajar *vt* : to relax, to slacken — *vi* : to be relaxing — **relajarse** *vr*

relajo *nm* **1** : commotion, ruckus **2** : joke, laugh ⟨lo hizo de relajo : he did it for a laugh⟩

relamerse *vr* : to smack one's lips, to lick one's chops

relámpago *nm* : flash of lightning

relampaguear *vi* : to flash

relanzar {21} *vt* : to relaunch

relatar *vt* : to relate, to tell

relatividad *nf* : relativity

relativo, -va *adj* **1** : relative **2 en lo relativo a** : with regard to, concerning — **relativamente** *adv*

relato *nm* **1** : story, tale **2** : account

releer {20} *vt* : to reread

relegar {52} *vt* **1** : to relegate **2 relegar al olvido** : to consign to oblivion

relevante *adj* : outstanding, important

relevar *vt* **1** : to relieve, to take over from **2** ~ **de** : to exempt from — **relevarse** *vr* : to take turns

relevo *nm* **1** : relief, replacement **2** : relay ⟨carrera de relevos : relay race⟩

relicario *nm* **1** : reliquary **2** : locket

relieve *nm* **1** : relief, projection ⟨mapa en relieve : relief map⟩ ⟨letras en relieve : embossed letters⟩ **2** : prominence, importance **3 poner en relieve** : to highlight, to emphasize

religión *nf, pl* **-giones** : religion

religiosamente *adv* : religiously, faithfully

religioso[1], **-sa** *adj* : religious

religioso[2], **-sa** *n* : monk *m*, nun *f*

relinchar *vi* : to neigh, to whinny

relincho *nm* : neigh, whinny

reliquia *nf* **1** : relic **2 reliquia de familia** : family heirloom

rellenar *vt* **1** : to refill **2** : to stuff, to fill **3** : to fill out

relleno[1], **-na** *adj* : stuffed, filled

relleno[2] *nm* : stuffing, filling

reloj *nm* **1** : clock **2** : watch **3 reloj de arena** : hourglass **4 reloj de pulsera** : wristwatch **5 como un reloj** : like clockwork

relojería *nf* **1** : watchmaker's shop **2** : watchmaking, clockmaking

reluciente *adj* : brilliant, shining

relucir {45} *vi* **1** : to glitter, to shine **2 salir a relucir** : to come to the surface **3 sacar a relucir** : to bring up, to mention

relumbrante *adj* : dazzling

relumbrar *vi* : to shine brightly

relumbrón *nm, pl* **-brones** **1** : flash, glare **2 de** ~ : flashy, showy

remachar *vt* **1** : to rivet **2** : to clinch (a nail) **3** : to stress, to drive home — *vi* : to smash, to spike (a ball)

remache *nm* **1** : rivet **2** : smash, spike (in sports)

remanente *nm* **1** : remainder, balance **2** : surplus

remanso *nm* : pool

remar *vi* **1** : to row, to paddle **2** : to struggle, to toil

remarcar {72} *vt* : to emphasize, to stress

rematado, -da *adj* : utter, complete

rematador, -dora *n* : auctioneer

rematar *vt* **1** : to finish off **2** : to auction — *vi* **1** : to shoot **2** : to end

remate *nm* **1** : shot (in sports) **2** : auction **3** : end, conclusion **4 como ~** : to top it off **5 de ~** : completely, utterly

remecer {86} *vt* : to sway, to swing

remedar *vt* **1** IMITAR : to imitate, to copy **2** : to mimic, to ape

remediar *vt* **1** : to remedy, to repair **2** : to help out, to assist **3** EVITAR : to prevent, to avoid

remedio *nm* **1** : remedy, cure **2** : solution **3** : option ⟨no me quedó más remedio : I had no other choice⟩ ⟨no hay remedio : it can't be helped⟩ **4 poner remedio a** : to put a stop to **5 sin ~** : unavoidable, inevitable

remedo *nm* : imitation

rememorar *vi* : to recall ⟨rememorar los viejos tiempos : to reminisce⟩

remendar {55} *vt* **1** : to mend, to patch, to darn **2** : to correct

remero, -ra *n* : rower

remesa *nf* **1** : remittance **2** : shipment

remezón *nm, pl* **-zones** : mild earthquake, tremor

remiendo *nm* **1** : patch **2** : correction

remilgado, -da *adj* **1** : prim, prudish **2** : affected

remilgo *nm* : primness, affectation

reminiscencia *nf* : reminiscence

remisión *nf, pl* **-siones 1** ENVÍO : sending, delivery **2** : remission **3** : reference, cross-reference

remiso, -sa *adj* **1** : lax, remiss **2** : reluctant

remitente[1] *nm* : return address

remitente[2] *nmf* : sender (of a letter, etc.)

remitir *vt* **1** : to send, to remit **2 ~ a** : to refer to, to direct to ⟨nos remitió al diccionario : he referred us to the dictionary⟩ — *vi* : to subside, to let up

remo *nm* **1** : paddle, oar **2** : rowing (sport)

remoción *nf, pl* **-ciones 1** : removal **2** : dismissal

remodelación *nf, pl* **-ciones 1** : remodeling **2** : reorganization, restructuring

remodelar *vt* **1** : to remodel **2** : to restructure

remojar *vt* **1** : to soak, to steep **2** : to dip, to dunk **3** : to celebrate with a drink

remojo *nm* **1** : soaking, steeping **2 poner en remojo** : to soak, to leave soaking

remolacha *nf* : beet

remolcador *nm* : tugboat

remolcar {72} *vt* : to tow, to haul

remolino *nm* **1** : whirlwind **2** : eddy, whirlpool **3** : crowd, throng **4** : cowlick

remolque *nm* **1** : towing, tow **2** : trailer **3 a ~** : in tow

remontar *vt* **1** : to overcome **2** SUBIR : to go up — **remontarse** *vr* **1** : to soar **2 ~ a** : to date from, to go back to

rémora *nf* : obstacle, hindrance

remorder {47} *vt* INQUIETAR : to trouble, to distress

remordimiento *nm* : remorse

remotamente *adv* : remotely, vaguely

remoto, -ta *adj* **1** : remote, unlikely ⟨hay una posibilidad remota : there is a slim possibility⟩ **2** : distant, far-off

remover {47} *vt* **1** : to stir **2** : to move around, to turn over **3** : to stir up **4** : to remove **5** : to dismiss

remozamiento *nm* : renovation

remozar {21} *vt* **1** : to renew, to brighten up **2** : to redo, to renovate

remuneración *nf, pl* **-ciones** : remuneration, pay

remunerar *vt* : to pay, to remunerate

remunerativo, -va *adj* : remunerative

renacer {48} *vi* : to be reborn, to revive

renacimiento *nm* **1** : rebirth, revival **2 el Renacimiento** : the Renaissance

renacuajo *nm* : tadpole, pollywog

renal *adj* : renal, kidney

rencilla *nf* : quarrel

renco, -ca *adj* : lame

rencor *nm* **1** : rancor, enmity, hostility **2 guardar rencor** : to hold a grudge

rencoroso, -sa *adj* : resentful, rancorous

rendición *nf, pl* **-ciones 1** : surrender, submission **2** : yield, return

rendido, -da *adj* **1** : submissive **2** : worn-out, exhausted **3** : devoted

rendija *nf* GRIETA : crack, split

rendimiento *nm* **1** : performance **2** : yield

rendir {54} *vt* **1** : to render, to give ⟨rendir las gracias : to give thanks⟩ ⟨rendir homenaje a : to pay homage to⟩ **2** : to yield **3** CANSAR : to exhaust — *vi* **1** CUNDIR : to progress, to make headway **2** : to last, to go a long way — **rendirse** *vr* : to surrender, to give up

renegado, -da *n* : renegade

renegar {49} *vi* **1 ~ de** : to renounce, to disown, to give up **2 ~ de** : to complain about — *vt* **1** : to deny vigorously **2** : to abhor, to hate

renegociar *vt* : to renegotiate — **renegociación** *nf*

renglón *nm, pl* **renglones 1** : line (of writing) **2** : merchandise, line (of products)

rengo, -ga *adj* : lame
renguear *vi* : to limp
reno *nm* : reindeer
renombrado, -da *adj* : renowned, famous
renombre *nm* NOMBRADÍA : renown, fame
renovable *adj* : renewable
renovación *nf, pl* **-ciones 1** : renewal ⟨renovación de un contrato : renewal of a contract⟩ **2** : change, renovation
renovar {19} *vt* **1** : to renew, to restore **2** : to renovate
renquear *vi* : to limp, to hobble
renquera *nf* COJERA : limp, lameness
renta *nf* **1** : income **2** : rent **3 impuesto sobre la renta** : income tax
rentable *adj* : profitable
rentar *vt* **1** : to produce, to yield **2** ALQUILAR : to rent
renuencia *nf* : reluctance, unwillingness
renuente *adj* : reluctant, unwilling
renuncia *nf* **1** : resignation **2** : renunciation **3** : waiver
renunciar *vi* **1** : to resign **2 ~ a** : to renounce, to relinquish ⟨renunció al título : he relinquished the title⟩
reñido, -da *adj* **1** : tough, hard-fought **2** : at odds, on bad terms
reñir {67} *vi* **1** : to argue **2 ~ con** : to fall out with, to go up against — *vt* : to scold, to reprimand
reo, rea *n* **1** : accused, defendant **2** : offender, culprit
reojo *nm* **de ~** : out of the corner of one's eye ⟨una mirada de reojo : a sidelong glance⟩
reorganizar {21} *vt* : to reorganize — **reorganización** *nf*
repantigarse {52} *vr* : to slouch, to loll about
reparación *nf, pl* **-ciones 1** : reparation, amends **2** : repair
reparar *vt* **1** : to repair, to fix, to mend **2** : to make amends for **3** : to correct **4** : to restore, to refresh — *vi* **1 ~ en** : to observe, to take notice of **2 ~ en** : to consider, to think about
reparo *nm* **1** : repair, restoration **2** : reservation, qualm ⟨no tuvieron reparos en decírmelo : they didn't hesitate to tell me⟩ **3 poner reparos a** : to find fault with, to object to
repartición *nf, pl* **-ciones 1** : distribution **2** : department, division
repartidor¹, -dora *adj* : delivery ⟨camión repartidor : delivery truck⟩
repartidor², -dora *n* : delivery person, distributor
repartimiento *nm* → **repartición**
repartir *vt* **1** : to allocate **2** DISTRIBUIR : to distribute, to hand out **3** : to spread
reparto *nm* **1** : allocation **2** : distribution **3** : cast (of characters)
repasar *vt* **1** : to pass by again **2** : to review, to go over **3** : to mend
repaso *nm* **1** : review **2** : mending **3** : checkup, overhaul

repatriar {85} *vt* : to repatriate — **repatriación** *nf*
repavimentar *vt* : to resurface
repelente¹ *adj* : repellent, repulsive
repelente² *nm* : repellent ⟨repelente de insectos : insect repellent⟩
repeler *vt* **1** : to repel, to resist, to repulse **2** : to reject **3** : to disgust ⟨el sabor me repele : I find the taste repulsive⟩
repensar {55} *v* : to rethink, to reconsider
repente *nm* **1** : sudden movement, start ⟨de repente : suddenly⟩ **2** : fit, outburst ⟨un repente de ira : a fit of anger⟩
repentino, -na *adj* : sudden — **repentinamente** *adv*
repercusión *nf, pl* **-siones** : repercussion
repercutir *vi* **1** : to reverberate, to echo **2 ~ en** : to have effects on, to have repercussions on
repertorio *nm* : repertoire
repetición *nf, pl* **-ciones 1** : repetition **2** : rerun, repeat
repetidamente *adv* : repeatedly
repetido, -da *adj* **1** : repeated, numerous **2 repetidas veces** : repeatedly, time and again
repetir {54} *vt* **1** : to repeat **2** : to have a second helping of — **repetirse** *vr* **1** : to repeat oneself **2** : to recur
repetitivo, -va *adj* : repetitive, repetitious
repicar {72} *vt* : to ring — *vi* : to ring out, to peal
repique *nm* : ringing, pealing
repisa *nf* : shelf, ledge ⟨repisa de chimenea : mantelpiece⟩ ⟨repisa de ventana : windowsill⟩
replantear *vt* : to redefine, to restate — **replantearse** *vr* : to reconsider
replegar {49} *vt* : to fold — **replegarse** *vr* RETIRARSE : to retreat, to withdraw
repleto, -ta *adj* **1** : replete, full **2 ~ de** : packed with, crammed with
réplica *nf* **1** : reply **2** : replica, reproduction **3** *Chile, Mex* : aftershock
replicación *nf, pl* **-ciones** : replication
replicar {72} *vi* **1** : to reply, to retort **2** : to argue, to answer back
repliegue *nm* **1** : fold **2** : retreat, withdrawal
repollo *nm* COL : cabbage
reponer {60} *vt* **1** : to replace, to put back **2** : to reinstate **3** : to reply — **reponerse** *vr* : to recover
reportaje *nm* : article, story, report
reportar *vt* **1** : to check, to restrain **2** : to bring, to carry, to yield ⟨me reportó numerosos beneficios : it brought me many benefits⟩ **3** : to report — **reportarse** *vr* **1** CONTENERSE : to control oneself **2** PRESENTARSE : to report, to show up
reporte *nm* : report
reportear *vt* : to report on, to cover

reportero, -ra n **1** : reporter **2 reportero gráfico** : photojournalist
reposado, -da adj : calm
reposar vi **1** : to rest, to repose **2** : to stand, to settle ⟨deje reposar la masa media hora : let the dough stand for half an hour⟩ **3** : to lie, to be buried — **reposarse** vr : to settle
reposición nf, pl **-ciones 1** : replacement **2** : reinstatement **3** : revival
repositorio nm : repository
reposo nm : repose, rest
repostar vi **1** : to stock up **2** : to refuel
repostería nf **1** : confectioner's shop **2** : pastry-making
repostero, -ra n : confectioner
repreguntar vt : to cross-examine
represguntas nfpl : cross-examination
reprender vt : to reprimand, to scold
reprensible adj : reprehensible
represa nf : dam
represalia nf **1** : reprisal, retaliation **2 tomar represalias** : to retaliate
represar vt : to dam
representación nf, pl **-ciones 1** : representation **2** : performance **3 en representación de** : on behalf of
representante nmf **1** : representative **2** : performer
representar vt **1** : to represent, to act for **2** : to perform **3** : to look, to appear as **4** : to symbolize, to stand for **5** : to signify, to mean — **representarse** vr : to imagine, to picture
representativo, -va adj : representative
represión nf, pl **-siones** : repression
represivo, -va adj : repressive
reprimenda nf : reprimand
reprimir vt **1** : to repress **2** : to suppress, to stifle
reprobable adj : reprehensible, culpable
reprobación nf : disapproval
reprobar {19} vt **1** DESAPROBAR : to condemn, to disapprove of **2** : to fail (a course)
reprobatorio, -ria adj : disapproving, admonitory
reprochable adj : reprehensible, reproachable
reprochar vt : to reproach — **reprocharse** vr
reproche nm : reproach
reproducción nf, pl **-ciones** : reproduction
reproducir {61} vt : to reproduce — **reproducirse** vr **1** : to breed, to reproduce **2** : to recur
reproductor, -tora adj : reproductive
reptar vi : to crawl, to slither
reptil[1] adj : reptilian
reptil[2] nm : reptile
república nf : republic
republicanismo nm : republicanism
republicano, -na adj & n : republican
repudiar vt : to repudiate — **repudiación** nf
repudio nm : repudiation
repuesto[1] pp → **reponer**

repuesto[2] nm **1** : spare part **2 de ~** : spare ⟨rueda de repuesto : spare wheel⟩
repugnancia nf : repugnance
repugnante adj : repulsive, repugnant, revolting
repugnar vt : to cause repugnance, to disgust — **repugnarse** vr
repujar vt : to emboss
repulsivo, -va adj : repulsive
repuntar vt Arg, Chile : to round up (cattle) — vi : to begin to appear — **repuntarse** vr : to fall out, to quarrel
repuso, etc. → **reponer**
reputación nf, pl **-ciones** : reputation
reputar vt : to consider, to deem
requerir {76} vt **1** : to require, to call for **2** : to summon, to send for
requesón nm, pl **-sones** : curd cheese, cottage cheese
réquiem nm : requiem
requisa nf **1** : requisition **2** : seizure **3** : inspection
requisar vt **1** : to requisition **2** : to seize **3** INSPECCIONAR : to inspect
requisito nm **1** : requirement **2 requisito previo** : prerequisite
res nf **1** : beast, animal **2** CA, Mex : beef **3 reses** nfpl : cattle ⟨60 reses : 60 head of cattle⟩
resabio nm **1** VICIO : bad habit, vice **2** DEJO : aftertaste
resaca nf **1** : undertow **2** : hangover
resaltar vi **1** SOBRESALIR : to stand out **2 hacer resaltar** : to bring out, to highlight — vt : to stress, to emphasize
resarcimiento nm **1** : compensation **2** : reimbursement
resarcir {83} vt : to compensate, to indemnify — **resarcirse** vr ~ **de** : to make up for
resbaladizo, -za adj **1** RESBALOSO : slippery **2** : tricky, ticklish, delicate
resbalar vi **1** : to slip, to slide **2** : to slip up, to make a mistake **3** : to skid — **resbalarse** vr
resbalón nm, pl **-lones** : slip
resbaloso, -sa adj : slippery
rescatar vt **1** : to rescue, to save **2** : to recover, to get back
rescate nm **1** : rescue **2** : recovery **3** : ransom
rescindir vt : to rescind, to annul, to cancel
rescisión nf, pl **-siones** : annulment, cancellation
rescoldo nm : embers pl
resecar {72} vt : to make dry, to dry up — **resecarse** vr : to dry up
reseco, -ca adj : dry, dried-up
resentido, -da adj : resentful
resentimiento nm : resentment
resentirse {76} vr **1** : to suffer, to be weakened **2** OFENDERSE : to be upset ⟨se resintió porque la insultaron : she got upset when they insulted her, she resented being insulted⟩ **3** ~ **de** : to feel the effects of

reseña *nf* **1** : report, summary, review **2** : description

reseñar *vt* **1** : to review **2** DESCRIBIR : to describe

reserva *nf* **1** : reservation **2** : reserve **3** : confidence, privacy ⟨con la mayor reserva : in strictest confidence⟩ **4 de ~** : spare, in reserve **5 reservas** *nfpl* : reservations, doubts

reservación *nf, pl* **-ciones** : reservation

reservado, -da *adj* **1** : reserved, reticent **2** : confidential

reservar *vt* : to reserve — **reservarse** *vr* **1** : to save oneself **2** : to conceal, to keep to oneself

reservorio *nm* : reservoir, reserve

resfriado *nm* CATARRO : cold

resfriar {85} *vt* : to cool — **resfriarse** *vr* **1** : to cool off **2** : to catch a cold

resfrío *nm* : cold

resguardar *vt* : to safeguard, to protect — **resguardarse** *vr*

resguardo *nm* **1** : safeguard, protection **2** : receipt, voucher **3** : border guard, coast guard

residencia *nf* **1** : residence **2** : boarding house

residencial *adj* : residential

residente *adj & nmf* : resident

residir *vi* **1** VIVIR : to reside, to dwell **2** **~ en** : to lie in, to consist of

residual *adj* : residual

residuo *nm* **1** : residue **2** : remainder **3 residuos** *nmpl* : waste ⟨residuos nucleares : nuclear waste⟩

resignación *nf, pl* **-ciones** : resignation

resignar *vt* : to resign — **resignarse** *vr* **~ a** : to resign oneself to

resina *nf* **1** : resin **2 resina epoxídica** : epoxy

resistencia *nf* **1** : resistance **2** AGUANTE : endurance, strength, stamina

resistente *adj* **1** : resistant **2** : strong, tough

resistir *vt* **1** : to stand, to bear, to tolerate **2** : to withstand — *vi* : to resist ⟨resistió hasta el último minuto : he held out until the last minute⟩ — **resistirse** *vr* **~ a** : to be resistant to, to be reluctant

resollar {19} *vi* : to breathe heavily, to wheeze

resolución *nf, pl* **-ciones** **1** : resolution, settlement **2** : decision **3** : determination, resolve

resolver {89} *vt* **1** : to resolve, to settle **2** : to decide — **resolverse** *vr* : to make up one's mind

resonancia *nf* **1** : resonance **2** : impact, repercussions *pl*

resonante *adj* **1** : resonant **2** : tremendous, resounding ⟨un éxito resonante : a resounding success⟩

resonar {19} *vi* : to resound, to ring

resoplar *vi* **1** : to puff, to pant **2** : to snort

resoplo *nm* **1** : puffing, panting **2** : snort

resorte *nm* **1** MUELLE : spring **2** : elasticity **3** : influence, means *pl* ⟨tocar resortes : to pull strings⟩

resortera *nf Mex* : slingshot

respaldar *vt* : to back, to support, to endorse — **respaldarse** *vr* : to lean back

respaldo *nm* **1** : back (of an object) **2** : support, backing

respectar *vt* : to concern, to relate to ⟨por lo que a mí respecta : as far as I'm concerned⟩

respectivo, -va *adj* : respective — **respectivamente** *adv*

respecto *nm* **1 ~ a** : in regard to, concerning **2 al respecto** : on this matter, in this respect

respetable *adj* : respectable — **respetabilidad** *nf*

respetar *vt* : to respect

respeto *nm* **1** : respect, consideration **2 respetos** *nmpl* : respects ⟨presentar sus respetos : to pay one's respects⟩

respetuosidad *nf* : respectfulness

respetuoso, -sa *adj* : respectful — **respetuosamente** *adv*

respingo *nm* : start, jump

respiración *nf, pl* **-ciones** : respiration, breathing

respiradero *nm* : vent, ventilation shaft

respirador *nm* : respirator

respirar *v* : to breathe

respiratorio, -ria *adj* : respiratory

respiro *nm* **1** : breath **2** : respite, break

resplandecer {53} *vi* **1** : to shine **2** : to stand out

resplandeciente *adj* **1** : resplendent, shining **2** : radiant

resplandor *nm* **1** : brightness, brilliance, radiance **2** : flash

responder *vt* : to answer — *vi* **1** : to answer, to reply, to respond **2 ~ a** : to respond to ⟨responder al tratamiento : to respond to treatment⟩ **3 ~ de** : to answer for, to vouch for (something) **4 ~ por** : to vouch for (someone)

responsabilidad *nf* : responsibility

responsable *adj* : responsible — **responsablemente** *adv*

respuesta *nf* : answer, response

resquebrajar *vt* : to split, to crack — **resquebrajarse** *vr*

resquemor *nm* : resentment, bitterness

resquicio *nm* **1** : crack **2** : opportunity, chance **3** : trace ⟨sin un resquicio de remordimiento : without a trace of remorse⟩ **4 resquicio legal** : loophole

resta *nf* SUSTRACCIÓN : subtraction

restablecer {53} *vt* : to reestablish, to restore — **restablecerse** *vr* : to recover

restablecimiento *nm* **1** : reestablishment, restoration **2** : recovery

restallar *vi* : to crack, to crackle, to click

restallido *nm* : crack, crackle

restante *adj* **1** : remaining **2 lo restante, los restantes** : the rest

restañar *vt* : to stanch

restar *vt* **1** : to deduct, to subtract ⟨restar un punto : to deduct a point⟩

2 : to minimize, to play down — *vi* : to remain, to be left

restauración *nf, pl* **-ciones** 1 : restoration 2 : catering, food service

restaurante *nm* : restaurant

restaurar *vt* : to restore

restitución *nf, pl* **-ciones** : restitution, return

restituir {41} *vt* : to return, to restore, to reinstate

resto *nm* 1 : rest, remainder 2 **restos** *nmpl* : remains ⟨restos de comida : leftovers⟩ ⟨restos arqueológicos : archeological ruins⟩ 3 **restos mortales** : mortal remains

restorán *nm, pl* **-ranes** : restaurant

restregadura *nf* : scrub, scrubbing

restregar {49} *vt* 1 : to rub 2 : to scrub — **restregarse** *vr*

restricción *nf, pl* **-ciones** : restriction, limitation

restrictivo, -va *adj* : restrictive

restringido, -da *adj* LIMITADO : limited, restricted

restringir {35} *vt* LIMITAR : to restrict, to limit

restructuración *nf* : restructuring

restructurar *vt* : to restructure

resucitación *nf* : resuscitation ⟨resucitación cardiopulmonar : CPR, cardiopulmonary resuscitation⟩

resucitar *vt* 1 : to resuscitate, to revive, to resurrect 2 : to revitalize

resuello *nm* 1 : puffing, heavy breathing, wheezing 2 : break, breather

resuelto[1] *pp* → **resolver**

resuelto[2], **-ta** *adj* : determined, resolved, resolute

resulta *nf* 1 : consequence, result 2 **a resultas de** *or* **de resultas de** : as a result of

resultado *nm* : result, outcome

resultante *adj & nf* : resultant

resultar *vi* 1 : to work, to work out ⟨mi idea no resultó : my idea didn't work out⟩ 2 : to prove, to turn out to be ⟨resultó bien simpático : he turned out to be very nice⟩ 3 ~ **en** : to lead to, to result in 4 ~ **de** : to be the result of

resumen *nm, pl* **-súmenes** 1 : summary, summation 2 **en** ~ : in summary, in short

resumidero *nm* : drain

resumir *v* : to summarize, to sum up

resurgimiento *nm* : resurgence

resurgir {35} *vi* : to reappear, to revive

resurrección *nf, pl* **-ciones** : resurrection

retablo *nm* 1 : tableau 2 : altarpiece

retador, -dora *n* : challenger (in sports)

retaguardia *nf* : rear guard

retahíla *nf* : string, series ⟨una retahíla de insultos : a volley of insults⟩

retaliación *nf, pl* **-ciones** : retaliation

retama *nf* : broom (plant)

retar *vt* DESAFIAR : to challenge, to defy

retardante *adj* : retardant

retardar *vt* 1 RETRASAR : to delay, to retard 2 : to postpone

retazo *nm* 1 : remnant, scrap 2 : fragment, piece ⟨retazos de su obra : bits and pieces from his writings⟩

retención *nf, pl* **-ciones** 1 : retention 2 : deduction, withholding

retener {80} *vt* 1 : to retain, to keep 2 : to withhold 3 : to detain

retentivo, -va *adj* : retentive

reticencia *nf* 1 : reluctance, reticence 2 : insinuation

reticente *adj* 1 : reluctant, reticent 2 : insinuating, misleading

retina *nf* : retina

retintín *nm, pl* **-tines** 1 : jingle, jangle 2 **con** ~ : sarcastically

retirada *nf* 1 : retreat ⟨batirse en retirada : to withdraw, to beat a retreat⟩ 2 : withdrawal (of funds) 3 : retirement 4 : refuge, haven

retirado, -da *adj* 1 : remote, distant, far off 2 : secluded, quiet

retirar *vt* 1 : to remove, to take away, to recall 2 : to withdraw, to take out — **retirarse** *vr* 1 REPLEGARSE : to retreat, to withdraw 2 JUBILARSE : to retire

retiro *nm* 1 JUBILACIÓN : retirement 2 : withdrawal, retreat 3 : seclusion

reto *nm* DESAFÍO : challenge, dare

retocar {72} *vt* : to touch up

retoñar *vi* : to sprout

retoño *nm* : sprout, shoot

retoque *nm* : retouching

retorcer {14} *vt* 1 : to twist 2 : to wring — **retorcerse** *vr* 1 : to get twisted, to get tangled up 2 : to squirm, to writhe, to wiggle about

retorcijón *nm, pl* **-jones** : cramp, sharp pain

retorcimiento *nm* 1 : twisting, wringing 2 : deviousness

retórica *nf* : rhetoric

retórico, -ca *adj* : rhetorical — **retóricamente** *adv*

retornar *v* : to return

retorno *nm* : return

retozar {21} *vi* : to frolic, to romp

retozo *nm* : frolicking

retozón, -zona *adj, mpl* **-zones** : playful

retracción *nf, pl* **-ciones** : retraction, withdrawal

retractable *adj* : retractable

retractación *nf, pl* **-ciones** : retraction (of a statement, etc.)

retractarse *vr* 1 : to withdraw, to back down 2 ~ **de** : to take back, to retract

retraer {81} *vt* 1 : to bring back 2 : to dissuade — **retraerse** *vr* 1 RETIRARSE : to withdraw, to retire 2 REFUGIARSE : to take refuge

retraído, -da *adj* : withdrawn, retiring, shy

retraimiento *nm* 1 : shyness, timidity 2 : withdrawal

retrasado, -da *adj* 1 : retarded, mentally slow 2 : behind, in arrears 3

: backward (of a country) **4** : slow (of a watch)

retrasar *vt* **1** DEMORAR, RETARDAR : to delay, to hold up **2** : to put off, to postpone — **retrasarse** *vr* **1** : to be late **2** : to fall behind

retraso *nm* **1** ATRASO : delay, lateness **2 retraso mental** : mental retardation

retratar *vt* **1** : to portray, to depict **2** : to photograph **3** : to paint a portrait of

retrato *nm* **1** : depiction, portrayal **2** : portrait, photograph

retrete *nm* : restroom, toilet

retribución *nf, pl* **-ciones 1** : pay, payment **2** : reward

retribuir {41} *vt* **1** : to pay **2** : to reward

retroactivo, -va *adj* : retroactive — **retroactivamente** *adv*

retroalimentación *nf, pl* **-ciones** : feedback

retroceder *vi* **1** : to move back, to turn back **2** : to back off, to back down **3** : to recoil (of a firearm)

retroceso *nm* **1** : backward movement **2** : backing down **3** : setback, relapse **4** : recoil

retrógrado, -da *adj* **1** : reactionary **2** : retrograde

retropropulsión *nf* : jet propulsion

retrospectiva *nf* : retrospective, hindsight

retrospectivo, -va *adj* **1** : retrospective **2 mirada retrospectiva** : backward glance

retrovisor *nm* : rearview mirror

retruécano *nm* : pun, play on words

retumbar *vi* **1** : to boom, to thunder **2** : to resound, to reverberate

retumbo *nm* : booming, thundering, roll

retuvo, etc. → **retener**

reubicar {72} *vt* : to relocate — **reubicación** *nf*

reuma *or* **reúma** *nmf* → **reumatismo**

reumático, -ca *adj* : rheumatic

reumatismo *nm* : rheumatism

reunión *nf, pl* **-niones 1** : meeting **2** : gathering, reunion

reunir {68} *vt* **1** : to unite, to join, to bring together **2** : to have, to possess ⟨reunieron los requisitos necesarios : they fulfilled the necessary requirements⟩ **3** : to gather, to collect, to raise (funds) — **reunirse** *vr* : to meet

reutilizable *adj* : reusable

reutilizar {21} *vt* **1** : to recycle, to reuse

revalidar *vt* **1** : to confirm, to ratify **2** : to defend (a title)

revaluar {3} *vt* : to reevaluate — **revaluación** *n*

revancha *nf* **1** DESQUITE : revenge, requital **2** : rematch

revelación *nf, pl* **-ciones** : revelation

revelado *nm* : developing (of film)

revelador¹, -dora *adj* : revealing

revelador² *nm* : developer

revelar *vt* **1** : to reveal, to disclose **2** : to develop (film)

revendedor, -dora *n* **1** : scalper **2** DETALLISTA : retailer

revender *vt* **1** : to resell **2** : to scalp

reventa *nf* **1** : resale **2** : scalping

reventar {55} *vi* **1** ESTALLAR, EXPLOTAR : to burst, to blow up **2 ~ de** : to be bursting with — *vt* **1** : to burst **2** *fam* : to annoy, to rile

reventón *nm, pl* **-tones 1** : burst, bursting **2** : blowout, flat tire **3** *Mex fam* : bash, party

reverberar *vi* : to reverberate — **reverberación** *nf*

reverdecer {53} *vi* **1** : to grow green again **2** : to revive

reverencia *nf* **1** : reverence **2** : bow, curtsy

reverenciar *vt* : to revere, to venerate

reverendo¹, -da *adj* **1** : reverend **2** *fam* : total, absolute ⟨es un reverendo imbécil : he is a complete idiot⟩

reverendo², -da *n* : reverend

reverente *adj* : reverent

reversa *nf Col, Mex* : reverse (gear)

reversible *adj* : reversible

reversión *nf, pl* **-siones** : reversion

reverso *nm* **1** : back, other side **2 el reverso de la medalla** : the complete opposite

revertir {76} *vi* **1** : to revert, to go back **2 ~ en** : to result in, to end up as

revés *nm, pl* **reveses 1** : back, wrong side **2** : setback, reversal **3** : backhand (in sports) **4 al revés** : the other way around, upside down, inside out **5 al revés de** : contrary to

revestimiento *nm* : covering, facing (of a building)

revestir {54} *vt* **1** : to coat, to cover, to surface **2** : to conceal, to disguise **3** : to take on, to assume ⟨la reunión revistió gravedad : the meeting took on a serious note⟩

revisar *vt* **1** : to examine, to inspect, to check **2** : to check over, to overhaul (machinery) **3** : to revise

revisión *nf, pl* **-siones 1** : revision **2** : inspection, check

revisor, -sora *n* **1** : inspector **2** : conductor (on a train)

revista *nf* **1** : magazine, journal **2** : revue **3 pasar revista** : to review, to inspect

revistar *vt* : to review, to inspect

revitalizar {21} *vt* : to revitalize — **revitalización** *nf*

revivir *vi* : to revive, to come alive again — *vt* : to relive

revocación *nf, pl* **-ciones** : revocation, repeal

revocar {72} *vt* **1** : to revoke, to repeal **2** : to plaster (a wall)

revolcar {82} *vt* : to knock over, to knock down — **revolcarse** *vr* : to roll around, to wallow

revolcón *nm, pl* **-cones** *fam* : tumble, fall

revolotear *vi* : to flutter around, to flit

revoloteo *nm* : fluttering, flitting

revoltijo *nm* **1** FÁRRAGO : mess, jumble **2** *Mex* : traditional seafood dish
revoltoso, -sa *adj* : unruly, rebellious
revolución *nf, pl* **-ciones** : revolution
revolucionar *vt* : to revolutionize
revolucionario, -ria *adj & n* : revolutionary
revolver {89} *vt* **1** : to move about, to mix, to shake, to stir **2** : to upset (one's stomach) **3** : to mess up, to rummage through ⟨revolver la casa : to turn the house upside down⟩ — **revolverse** *vr* **1** : to toss and turn **2** VOLVERSE : to turn around
revólver *nm* : revolver
revoque *nm* : plaster
revuelo *nm* **1** : fluttering **2** : commotion, stir
revuelta *nf* : uprising, revolt
revuelto[1] *pp* → **revolver**
revuelto[2], **-ta** *adj* **1** : choppy, rough ⟨mar revuelto : rough sea⟩ **2** : untidy **3 huevos revueltos** : scrambled eggs
rey *nm* : king
reyerta *nf* : brawl, fight
rezagado, -da *n* : straggler, latecomer
rezagar {52} *vt* **1** : to leave behind **2** : to postpone — **rezagarse** *vr* : to fall behind, to lag
rezar {21} *vi* **1** : to pray **2** : to say ⟨como reza el refrán : as the saying goes⟩ **3** **~ con** : to concern, to have to do with — *vt* : to say, to recite ⟨rezar un Ave María : to say a Hail Mary⟩
rezo *nm* : prayer, praying
rezongar {52} *vi* : to gripe, to grumble
rezumar *v* : to ooze, to leak
ría[1], **etc.** → **reír**
ría[2] *nf* : estuary
riachuelo *nm* ARROYO : brook, stream
riada *nf* : flood
ribera *nf* : bank, shore
ribete *nm* **1** : border, trim **2** : frill, adornment **3 ribetes** *nmpl* : hint, touch ⟨tiene sus ribetes de genio : there's a touch of genius in him⟩
ribetear *vt* : to border, to edge, to trim
ricamente *adv* : richly, splendidly
rice, etc. → **rizar**
rico[1], **-ca** *adj* **1** : rich, wealthy **2** : fertile **3** : luxurious, valuable **4** : delicious **5** : adorable, lovely **6** : great, wonderful
rico[2], **-ca** *n* : rich person
ridiculez *nf, pl* **-leces** : ridiculousness, absurdity
ridiculizar {21} *vt* : to ridicule
ridículo[1], **-la** *adj* ABSURDO, DISPARATADO : ridiculous, ludicrous — **ridículamente** *adv*
ridículo[2], **-la** *n* **1 hacer el ridículo** : to make a fool of oneself **2 poner en ridículo** : to ridicule
ríe, etc. → **reír**
riega, riegue etc. → **regar**
riego *nm* : irrigation
riel *nm* : rail, track

rienda *nf* **1** : rein **2 dar rienda suelta a** : to give free rein to **3 llevar las riendas** : to be in charge **4 tomar las riendas** : to take control
riesgo *nm* : risk
riesgoso, -sa *adj* : risky
rifa *nf* : raffle
rifar *vt* : to raffle — *vi* : to quarrel, to fight
rifle *nm* : rifle
rige, rija etc. → **regir**
rigidez *nf, pl* **-deces** **1** : rigidity, stiffness ⟨rigidez cadavérica : rigor mortis⟩ **2** : inflexibility
rígido, -da *adj* **1** : rigid, stiff **2** : strict — **rígidamente** *adv*
rigor *nm* **1** : rigor, harshness **2** : precision, meticulousness **3 de ~** : usual ⟨la respuesta de rigor : the standard reply⟩ **4 de ~** : essential, obligatory **5 en ~** : strictly speaking, in reality
riguroso, -sa *adj* : rigorous — **rigurosamente** *adv*
rima *nf* **1** : rhyme **2 rimas** *nfpl* : verse, poetry
rimar *vi* : to rhyme
rimbombante *adj* **1** : grandiose, showy **2** : bombastic, pompous
rímel *or* **rimel** *nm* : mascara
rin *nm Col, Mex* : wheel, rim (of a tire)
rincón *nm, pl* **rincones** : corner, nook
rinde, etc. → **rendir**
rinoceronte *nm* : rhinoceros
riña *nf* **1** : fight, brawl **2** : dispute, quarrel
riñe, etc. → **reñir**
riñón *nm, pl* **riñones** : kidney
río[1] → **reír**
río[2] *nm* **1** : river **2** : torrent, stream ⟨un río de lágrimas : a flood of tears⟩
ripio *nm* **1** : debris, rubble **2** : gravel
riqueza *nf* **1** : wealth, riches *pl* **2** : richness **3 riquezas naturales** : natural resources
risa *nf* **1** : laughter, laugh **2 dar risa** : to make laugh ⟨me dio mucha risa : I found it very funny⟩ **3** *fam* **morirse de la risa** : to die laughing, to crack up
risco *nm* : crag, cliff
risible *adj* IRRISORIO : ludicrous, laughable
risita *nf* : giggle, titter, snicker
risotada *nf* : guffaw
ristra *nf* : string, series *pl*
risueño, -ña *adj* **1** : cheerful, pleasant **2** : promising
rítmico, -ca *adj* : rhythmical, rhythmic — **rítmicamente** *adv*
ritmo *nm* **1** : rhythm **2** : pace, tempo ⟨trabajó a ritmo lento : she worked at a slow pace⟩
rito *nm* : rite, ritual
ritual *adj & nm* : ritual — **ritualmente** *adv*
rival *adj & nmf* COMPETIDOR : rival
rivalidad *nf* : rivalry, competition
rivalizar {21} *vi* **~ con** : to rival, to compete with

rizado, -da *adj* **1** : curly **2** : ridged **3** : ripply, undulating
rizar {21} *vt* **1** : to curl **2** : to ripple, to ruffle (a surface) **3** : to crumple, to fold — **rizarse** *vr* **1** : to frizz **2** : to ripple
rizo *nm* **1** : curl **2** : loop (in aviation)
robalo *or* **róbalo** *nm* : sea bass
robar *vt* **1** : to steal **2** : to rob, to burglarize **3** SECUESTRAR : to abduct, to kidnap **4** : to captivate — *vi* ～ **en** : to break into
roble *nm* : oak
robo *nm* : robbery, theft
robot *nm, pl* **robots** : robot
robótica *nf* : robotics
robustecer {53} *vt* : to grow stronger, to strengthen
robustez *nf* : sturdiness, robustness
robusto, -ta *adj* : robust, sturdy
roca *nf* : rock, boulder
roce[1], etc. → **rozar**
roce[2] *nm* **1** : rubbing, chafing **2** : brush, graze, touch **3** : close contact, familiarity **4** : friction, disagreement
rociador *nm* : sprinkler
rociar {85} *vt* : to spray, to sprinkle
rocío *nm* **1** : dew **2** : shower, light rain
rock *or* **rock and roll** *nm* : rock, rock and roll
rocola *nf* : jukebox
rocoso, -sa *adj* : rocky
rodada *nf* : track (of a tire), rut
rodado, -da *adj* **1** : wheeled **2** : dappled (of a horse)
rodadura *nf* : rolling, taxiing
rodaja *nf* : round, slice
rodaje *nm* **1** : filming, shooting **2** : breaking in (of a vehicle)
rodamiento *nm* **1** : bearing ⟨rodamiento de bolas : ball bearings⟩ **2** : rolling
rodante *adj* : rolling
rodar {19} *vi* **1** : to roll, to roll down, to roll along ⟨rodé por la escalera : I tumbled down the stairs⟩ ⟨todo rodaba bien : everthing was going along well⟩ **2** GIRAR : to turn, to go around **3** : to move about, to travel ⟨andábamos rodando por todas partes : we drifted along from place to place⟩ — *vt* **1** : to film, to shoot **2** : to break in (a new vehicle)
rodear *vt* **1** : to surround **2** : to round up (cattle) — *vi* **1** : to go around **2** : to beat around the bush — **rodearse** *vr* ～ **de** : to surround oneself with
rodeo *nm* **1** : rodeo, roundup **2** DESVÍO : detour **3** : evasion ⟨andar con rodeos : to beat around the bush⟩ ⟨sin rodeos : without reservations⟩
rodilla *nf* : knee
rodillo *nm* **1** : roller **2** : rolling pin
rododendro *nm* : rhododendron
roedor[1], **-dora** *adj* : gnawing
roedor[2] *nm* : rodent
roer {69} *vt* **1** : to gnaw **2** : to eat away at, to torment
rogar {16} *vt* **1** : to beg, to request — *vi* **1** : to beg, to plead **2** : to pray

roiga, etc. → **roer**
rojez *nf* : redness
rojizo, -za *adj* : reddish
rojo[1], **-ja** *adj* **1** : red **2 ponerse rojo** : to blush
rojo[2] *nm* : red
rol *nm* **1** : role **2** : list, roll
rollo *nm* **1** : roll, coil ⟨un rollo de cinta : a roll of tape⟩ ⟨en rollo : rolled up⟩ **2** *fam* : roll of fat **3** *fam* : boring speech, lecture
romance *nm* **1** : Romance language **2** : ballad **3** : romance **4 en buen romance** : simply stated, simply put
romano, -na *adj & n* : Roman
romanticismo *nm* : romanticism
romántico, -ca *adj* : romantic — **románticamente** *adv*
rombo *nm* : rhombus
romería *nf* **1** : pilgrimage, procession **2** : crowd, gathering
romero[1], **-ra** *n* PEREGRINO : pilgrim
romero[2] *nm* : rosemary
romo, -ma *adj* : blunt, dull
rompecabezas *nms & pl* : puzzle, riddle
rompehielos *nms & pl* : icebreaker (ship)
rompehuelgas *nmfs & pl* ESQUIROL : strikebreaker, scab
rompenueces *nms & pl* : nutcracker
rompeolas *ns & pl* : breakwater, jetty
romper {70} *vt* **1** : to break, to smash **2** : to rip, to tear **3** : to break off (relations), to break (a contract) **4** : to break through, to break down **5** GASTAR : to wear out — *vi* **1** : to break ⟨al romper del día : at the break of day⟩ **2** ～ **a** : to begin to, to burst out with ⟨romper a llorar : to burst into tears⟩ **3** ～ **con** : to break off with
rompope *nm CA, Mex* : drink similar to eggnog
ron *nm* : rum
roncar {72} *vi* **1** : to snore **2** : to roar
ronco, -ca *adj* **1** : hoarse **2** : husky (of the voice) — **roncamente** *adv*
ronda *nf* **1** : beat, patrol **2** : round (of drinks, of negotiations, of a game)
rondar *vt* **1** : to patrol **2** : to hang around ⟨siempre está rondando la calle : he's always hanging around the street⟩ **3** : to be approximately ⟨debe rondar los cincuenta : he must be about 50⟩ — *vi* **1** : to be on patrol **2** : to prowl around, to roam about
ronque, etc. → **roncar**
ronquera *nf* : hoarseness
ronquido *nm* **1** : snore **2** : roar
ronronear *vi* : to purr
ronroneo *nm* : purr, purring
ronzal *nm* : halter (for an animal)
ronzar {21} *v* : to munch, to crunch
roña *nf* **1** : mange **2** : dirt, filth **3** *fam* : stinginess
roñoso, -sa *adj* **1** : mangy **2** : dirty **3** *fam* : stingy
ropa *nf* **1** : clothes *pl*, clothing **2 ropa interior** : underwear

ropaje *nm* : apparel, garments *pl*, regalia

ropero *nm* ARMARIO, CLÓSET : wardrobe, closet

rosa[1] *adj* : rose-colored, pink

rosa[2] *nm* : rose, pink (color)

rosa[3] *nf* → rose (flower)

rosáceo, -cea *adj* : pinkish

rosado[1], **-da** *adj* **1** : pink **2 vino rosado** : rosé

rosado[2] *nm* : pink (color)

rosal *nm* : rosebush

rosario *nm* **1** : rosary **2** : series ⟨un rosario de islas : a string of islands⟩

rosbif *nm* : roast beef

rosca *nf* **1** : thread (of a screw) ⟨una tapa a rosca : a screw top⟩ **2** : ring, coil

roseta *nf* : rosette

rosquilla *nf* : ring-shaped pastry, doughnut

rostro *nm* : face, countenance

rotación *nf, pl* **-ciones** : rotation

rotar *vt* : to rotate, to turn — *vi* : to turn, to spin

rotativo[1], **-va** *adj* : rotary

rotativo[2] *nm* : newspaper

rotatorio, -ria *adj* → rotativo[1]

roto[1] *pp* → romper

roto[2], **-ta** *adj* **1** : broken **2** : ripped, torn

rotonda *nf* **1** : traffic circle, rotary **2** : rotunda

rotor *nm* : rotor

rótula *nf* : kneecap

rotular *vt* **1** : to head, to entitle **2** : to label

rótulo *nm* **1** : heading, title **2** : label, sign

rotundo, -da *adj* **1** REDONDO : round **2** : categorical, absolute ⟨un éxito rotundo : a resounding success⟩ — **rotundamente** *adv*

rotura *nf* : break, tear, fracture

roya *nf* : plant rust

roya, etc. → roer

rozado, -da *adj* GASTADO : worn

rozadura *nf* **1** : scratch, abrasion **2** : rubbed spot, sore

rozar {21} *vt* **1** : to chafe, to rub against **2** : to border on, to touch on **3** : to graze, to touch lightly — **rozarse** *vr* ∼ **con** *fam* : to rub shoulders with

ruandés, -desa *adj & n* : Rwandan

ruano, -na *adj* : roan

rubí *nm, pl* **rubíes** : ruby

rubio, -bia *adj & n* : blond

rublo *nm* : ruble

rubor *nm* **1** : flush, blush **2** : rouge, blusher

ruborizarse {21} *vr* : to blush

rubrica *nf* : title, heading

rubricar {72} *vt* **1** : to sign with a flourish ⟨firmado y rubricado : signed and sealed⟩ **2** : to endorse, to sanction

rubro *nm* **1** : heading, title **2** : line, area (in business)

rudeza *nf* ASPEREZA : roughness, coarseness

rudimentario, -ria *adj* : rudimentary — **rudimentariamente** *adv*

rudimento *nm* : rudiment, basics *pl*

rudo, -da *adj* **1** : rough, harsh **2** : coarse, unpolished — **rudamente** *adv*

rueda[1], **etc.** → rodar

rueda[2] *nf* **1** : wheel **2** RODAJA : round slice **3** : circle, ring **4 rueda de andar** : treadmill **5 rueda de prensa** : press conference **6 ir sobre ruedas** : to go smoothly

ruedita *nf* : caster (on furniture)

ruedo *nm* **1** : bullring, arena **2** : rotation, turn **3** : hem

ruega, ruegue etc. → rogar

ruego *nm* : request, appeal, plea

rugido *nm* : roar

rugir {35} *vi* : to roar

ruibarbo *nm* : rhubarb

ruido *nm* : noise, sound

ruidoso, -sa *adj* : loud, noisy — **ruidosamente** *adv*

ruin *adj* **1** : base, despicable **2** : mean, stingy

ruina *nf* **1** : ruin, destruction **2** : downfall, collapse **3 ruinas** *nfpl* : ruins, remains

ruinoso, -sa *adj* **1** : run-down, dilapidated **2** : ruinous, disastrous

ruiseñor *nm* : nightingale

ruja, etc. → rugir

ruleta *nf* : roulette

rulo *nm* : curler, roller

rumano, -na *n* : Romanian, Rumanian

rumbo *nm* **1** : direction, course ⟨con rumbo a : bound for, heading for⟩ ⟨perder el rumbo : to go off course, to lose one's bearings⟩ ⟨sin rumbo : aimless, aimlessly⟩ **2** : ostentation, pomp **3** : lavishness, generosity

rumiante *adj & nm* : ruminant

rumiar *vt* : to ponder, to mull over — *vi* **1** : to chew the cud **2** : to ruminate, to ponder

rumor *nm* **1** : rumor **2** : murmur

rumorearse *or* **rumorarse** *vr* : to be rumored ⟨se rumorea que se va : rumor has it that she's leaving⟩

rumoroso, -sa *adj* : murmuring, babbling ⟨un arroyo rumoroso : a babbling brook⟩

rupia *nf* : rupee

ruptura *nf* **1** : break **2** : breaking, breach (of a contract) **3** : breaking off, breakup

rural *adj* : rural

ruso[1], **-sa** *adj & n* : Russian

ruso[2] *nm* : Russian (language)

rústico[1], **-ca** *adj* : rural, rustic

rústico[2], **-ca** *n* : rustic, country dweller

ruta *nf* : route

rutina *nf* : routine, habit

rutinario, -ria *adj* : routine, ordinary ⟨visita rutinaria : routine visit⟩ — **rutinariamente** *adv*

S

s *nf* : twentieth letter of the Spanish alphabet

sábado *nm* **1** : Saturday **2** : Sabbath

sábalo *nm* : shad

sabana *nf* : savanna

sábana *nf* : sheet, bedsheet

sabandija *nf* BICHO : bug, small reptile, pesky creature

sabático, -ca *adj* : sabbatical

sabedor, -dora *adj* : aware, informed

sabelotodo *nmf fam* : know-it-all

saber[1] {71} *vt* **1** : to know **2** : to know how to, to be able to ⟨sabe tocar el violín : she can play the violin⟩ **3** : to learn, to find out **4** ~ : to wit, namely — *vi* **1** : to know, to suppose **2** : to be informed ⟨supimos del desastre : we heard about the disaster⟩ **3** : to taste ⟨esto no sabe bien : this doesn't taste right⟩ **4** ~ **a** : to taste like ⟨sabe a naranja : it tastes like orange⟩ — **saberse** *vr* : to know ⟨ese chiste no me lo sé : I don't know that joke⟩

saber[2] *nm* : knowledge, learning

sabiamente *adv* : wisely

sabido, -da *adj* : well-known

sabiduría *nf* **1** : wisdom **2** : learning, knowledge

sabiendas *adv* **1 a** ~ : knowingly **2 a sabiendas de que** : knowing full well that

sabio[1], **-bia** *adj* **1** PRUDENTE : wise, sensible **2** DOCTO : learned

sabio[2], **-bia** *n* **1** : wise person **2** : savant, learned person

sable *nm* : saber, cutlass

sabor *nm* **1** : flavor, taste **2 sin** ~ : flavorless

saborear *vt* **1** : to taste, to savor **2** : to enjoy, to relish

sabotaje *nm* : sabotage

saboteador, -dora *n* : saboteur

sabotear *vt* : to sabotage

sabrá, etc. → saber

sabroso, -sa *adj* **1** RICO : delicious, tasty **2** AGRADABLE : pleasant, nice, lovely

sabueso *nm* **1** : bloodhound **2** *fam* : detective, sleuth

sacacorchos *nms & pl* : corkscrew

sacapuntas *nms & pl* : pencil sharpener

sacar {72} *vt* **1** : to pull out, to take out ⟨saca el pollo del congelador : take the chicken out of the freezer⟩ **2** : to get, to obtain ⟨saqué un 100 en el examen : I got 100 on the exam⟩ **3** : to get out, to extract ⟨le saqué la información : I got the information from him⟩ **4** : to stick out ⟨sacar la lengua : to stick out one's tongue⟩ **5** : to bring out, to introduce ⟨sacar un libro : to publish a book⟩ ⟨sacaron una moda nueva : they introduced a new style⟩ **6** : to take (photos) **7** : to make (copies) — *vi* **1**

: to kick off (in soccer or football) **2** : to serve (in sports)

sacarina *nf* : saccharin

sacarosa *nf* : sucrose

sacerdocio *nm* : priesthood

sacerdotal *adj* : priestly

sacerdote, -tisa *n* : priest *m*, priestess *f*

saciar *vt* **1** HARTAR : to sate, to satiate **2** SATISFACER : to satisfy

saciedad *nf* : satiety

saco *nm* **1** : bag, sack **2** : sac **3** : jacket, sport coat

sacramento *nm* : sacrament — **sacramental** *adj*

sacrificar {72} *vt* : to sacrifice — **sacrificarse** *vr* : to sacrifice oneself, to make sacrifices

sacrificio *nm* : sacrifice

sacrilegio *nm* : sacrilege

sacrílego, -ga *adj* : sacrilegious

sacristán *nm, pl* **-tanes** : sexton, sacristan

sacristía *nf* : sacristy, vestry

sacro, -cra *adj* SAGRADO : sacred ⟨arte sacro : sacred art⟩

sacrosanto, -ta *adj* : sacrosanct

sacudida *nf* **1** : shaking **2** : jerk, jolt, shock **3** : shake-up, upheaval

sacudir *vt* **1** : to shake, to beat **2** : to jerk, to jolt **3** : to dust off **4** CONMOVER : to shake up, to shock — **sacudirse** *vr* : to shake off

sacudón *nm, pl* **-dones** : intense jolt or shake-up

sádico[1], **-ca** *adj* : sadistic

sádico[2], **-ca** *n* : sadist

sadismo *nm* : sadism

safari *nm* : safari

saga *nf* : saga

sagacidad *nf* : sagacity, shrewdness

sagaz *adj, pl* **sagaces** PERSPICAZ : shrewd, discerning, sagacious

Sagitario *nmf* : Sagittarius, Sagittarian

sagrado, -da *adj* : sacred, holy

sainete *nm* : comedy sketch, one-act farce ⟨este proceso es un sainete : these proceedings are a farce⟩

sajar *vt* : to lance, to cut open

sal[1] → salir

sal[2] *nf* **1** : salt **2** *CA, Mex* : misfortune, bad luck

sala *nf* **1** : living room **2** : room, hall ⟨sala de conferencias : lecture hall⟩ ⟨sala de urgencias : emergency room⟩ ⟨sala de baile : ballroom⟩

salado, -da *adj* **1** : salty **2 agua salada** : salt water

salamandra *nf* : salamander

salami *nm* : salami

salar *vt* **1** : to salt **2** : to spoil, to ruin **3** *CoRi, Mex* : to jinx, to bring bad luck

salarial *adj* : salary, salary-related

salario *nm* **1** : salary **2 salario mínimo** : minimum wage

salaz *adj, pl* **salaces** : salacious, lecherous

salchicha *nf* **1** : sausage **2** : frankfurter, wiener

salchichón *nf, pl* **-chones** : a type of deli meat

salchichonería *nf Mex* **1** : delicatessen **2** : cold cuts *pl*

saldar *vt* : to settle, to pay off ⟨saldar una cuenta : to settle an account⟩

saldo *nm* **1** : settlement, payment **2** : balance ⟨saldo de cuenta : account balance⟩ **3** : remainder, leftover merchandise

saldrá, etc. → **salir**

salero *nm* **1** : saltshaker **2** : wit, charm

salga, etc. → **salir**

salida *nf* **1** : exit ⟨salida de emergencia : emergency exit⟩ **2** : leaving, departure **3** SOLUCIÓN : way out, solution **4** : start (of a race) **5** OCURRENCIA : wisecrack, joke **6 salida del sol** : sunrise

saliente¹ *adj* **1** : departing, outgoing **2** : projecting **3** DESTACADO : salient, prominent

saliente² *nm* **1** : projection, protrusion **2 ventana en saliente** : bay window

salinidad *nf* : salinity, saltiness

salino, -na *adj* : saline ⟨solución salina : saline solution⟩

salir {73} *vi* **1** : to go out, to come out, to get out ⟨salimos todas las noches : we go out every night⟩ ⟨su libro acaba de salir : her book just came out⟩ **2** PARTIR : to leave, to depart **3** APARECER : to appear ⟨salió en todos los diarios : it came out in all the papers⟩ **4** : to project, to stick out **5** : to cost, to come to **6** RESULTAR : to turn out, to prove **7** : to come up, to occur ⟨salga lo que salga : whatever happens⟩ ⟨salió una oportunidad : an opportunity came up⟩ **8** ~ **a** : to take after, to look like, to resemble **9** ~ **con** : to go out with, to date — **salirse** *vr* **1** : to escape, to get out, to leak out **2** : to come loose, to come off **3 salirse con la suya** : to get one's own way

saliva *nf* : saliva

salivar *vi* : to salivate

salmo *nm* : psalm

salmón¹ *adj* : salmon-colored

salmón² *nm, pl* **salmones** : salmon

salmuera *nf* : brine

salobre *adj* : brackish, briny

salón *nm, pl* **salones 1** : hall, large room ⟨salón de clase : classroom⟩ ⟨salón de baile : ballroom⟩ **2** : salon ⟨salón de belleza : beauty salon⟩ **3** : parlor, sitting room

salpicadera *nf Mex* : fender

salpicadura *nf* : spatter, splash

salpicar {72} *vt* **1** : to spatter, to splash **2** : to sprinkle, to scatter about

salpimentar {55} *vt* **1** : to season (with salt and pepper) **2** : to spice up

salsa *nf* **1** : sauce ⟨salsa picante : hot sauce⟩ ⟨salsa inglesa : Worcestershire sauce⟩ ⟨salsa tártara : tartar sauce⟩ **2** : gravy **3** : salsa (music) **4 salsa mexicana** : salsa (sauce)

salsero, -ra *n* : salsa musician

saltador, -dora *n* : jumper

saltamontes *nms & pl* : grasshopper

saltar *vi* **1** BRINCAR : to jump, to leap **2** : to bounce **3** : to come off, to pop out **4** : to shatter, to break **5** : to explode, to blow up — *vt* **1** : to jump, to jump over **2** : to skip, to miss — **saltarse** *vr* OMITIR : to skip, to omit ⟨me salté ese capítulo : I skipped that chapter⟩

saltarín, -rina *adj, mpl* **-rines** : leaping, hopping ⟨frijol saltarín : jumping bean⟩

salteado, -da *adj* **1** : sautéed **2** : jumbled up ⟨los episodios se transmitieron salteados : the episodes were broadcast in random order⟩

salteador *nm* : highwayman

saltear *vt* **1** SOFREÍR : to sauté **2** : to skip around, to skip over

saltimbanqui *nmf* : acrobat

salto *nm* **1** BRINCO : jump, leap, skip **2** : jump, dive (in sports) **3** : gap, omission **4 dar saltos** : to jump up and down **5** *or* **salto de agua** CATARATA : waterfall

saltón, -tona *adj, mpl* **saltones** : bulging, protruding

salubre *adj* : healthful, salubrious

salubridad *nf* : healthfulness, health

salud *nf* **1** : health ⟨buena salud : good health⟩ **2 ¡salud!** : bless you! (when someone sneezes) **3 ¡salud!** : cheers!, to your health!

saludable *adj* **1** SALUBRE : healthful **2** SANO : healthy, well

saludar *vt* **1** : to greet, to say hello to **2** : to salute — **saludarse** *vr*

saludo *nm* **1** : greeting, regards *pl* **2** : salute

salutación *nf, pl* **-ciones** : salutation

salva *nf* **1** : salvo, volley **2 salva de aplausos** : round of applause

salvación *nf, pl* **-ciones 1** : salvation **2** RESCATE : rescue

salvado *nm* : bran

salvador, -dora *n* **1** : savior, rescuer **2 el Salvador** : the Savior

salvadoreño, -ña *adj & n* : Salvadoran, El Salvadoran

salvaguardar *vt* : to safeguard

salvaguardia *or* **salvaguarda** *nf* : safeguard, defense

salvajada *nf* ATROCIDAD : atrocity, act of savagery

salvaje¹ *adj* **1** : wild ⟨animales salvajes : wild animals⟩ **2** : savage, cruel **3** : primitive, uncivilized

salvaje² *nmf* : savage

salvajismo *nm* : savagery

salvamento *nm* **1** : rescuing, lifesaving **2** : salvation **3** : refuge

salvar *vt* **1** : to save, to rescue **2** : to cover (a distance) **3** : to get around (an obstacle), to overcome (a difficulty) **4**

: to cross, to jump across **5 salvando**
: except for, excluding — **salvarse** *vr*
1 : to survive, to escape **2** : to save one's
soul
salvavidas[1] *nms & pl* **1** : life preserver
2 bote salvavidas : lifeboat
salvavidas[2] *nmf* : lifeguard
salvedad *nf* **1** EXCEPCIÓN : exception
2 : proviso, stipulation
salvia *nf* : sage (plant)
salvo[1], **-va** *adj* **1** : unharmed, sound
⟨sano y salvo : safe and sound⟩ **2 a ~**
: safe from danger
salvo[2] *prep* **1** EXCEPTO : except (for),
save ⟨todos asistirán salvo Jaime : all
will attend except for Jaime⟩ **2 salvo
que** : unless ⟨salvo que llueva : unless
it rains⟩
salvoconducto *nm* : safe-conduct
samba *nf* : samba
San *adj* → **santo**[1]
sanar *vt* : to heal, to cure — *vi* : to get
well, to recover
sanatorio *nm* **1** : sanatorium **2** : clinic, private hospital
sanción *nf, pl* **sanciones** : sanction
sancionar *vt* **1** : to penalize, to impose
a sanction on **2** : to sanction, to approve
sancochar *vt* : to parboil
sandalia *nf* : sandal
sándalo *nm* : sandalwood
sandez *nf, pl* **sandeces** ESTUPIDEZ
: nonsense, silly thing to say
sandía *nf* : watermelon
sandwich ['sandwiʧ, 'saŋgwiʧ] *nm, pl*
sandwiches [-dwiʧɛs, -gwi-] EMPARE-
DADO : sandwich
saneamiento *nm* **1** : cleaning up, sanitation **2** : reorganizing, streamlining
sanear *vt* **1** : to clean up, to sanitize **2**
: to reorganize, to streamline
sangrante *adj* **1** : bleeding **2** : flagrant,
blatant
sangrar *vi* : to bleed — *vt* : to indent (a
paragraph, etc.)
sangre *nf* **1** : blood **2 a sangre fría** : in
cold blood **3 a sangre y fuego** : by violent force **4 pura sangre** : thoroughbred
sangría *nf* **1** : bloodletting **2** : sangria
(wine punch) **3** : drain, draining ⟨una
sangría fiscal : a financial drain⟩ **4** : indentation, indenting
sangriento, -ta *adj* **1** : bloody **2** : cruel
sanguijuela *nf* **1** : leech, bloodsucker **2**
: sponger, leech
sanguinario, -ria *adj* : bloodthirsty
sanguíneo, -nea *adj* **1** : blood ⟨vaso
sanguíneo : blood vessel⟩ **2** : sanguine,
ruddy
sanidad *nf* **1** : health **2** : public health,
sanitation
sanitario[1], **-ria** *adj* **1** : sanitary **2** : health
⟨centro sanitario : health center⟩
sanitario[2], **-ria** *n* : sanitation worker
sanitario[3] *nm Col, Mex, Ven* : toilet ⟨los
sanitarios : the toilets, the restroom⟩

sano, -na *adj* **1** SALUDABLE : healthy **2**
: wholesome **3** : whole, intact
santiaguino, -na *adj* : of or from Santi-
ago, Chile
santiamén *nm* **en un santiamén** : in no
time at all
santidad *nf* : holiness, sanctity
santificar {72} *vt* : to sanctify, to consecrate, to hallow
santiguarse {10} *vr* PERSIGNARSE : to
cross oneself
santo[1], **-ta** *adj* **1** : holy, saintly ⟨el Santo Padre : the Holy Father⟩ ⟨una vida
santa : a saintly life⟩ **2 Santo, Santa**
(San *before names of masculine saints
except those beginning with D or T*)
: Saint ⟨Santa Clara : Saint Claire⟩
⟨Santo Tomás : Saint Thomas⟩ ⟨San
Francisco : Saint Francis⟩
santo[2], **-ta** *n* : saint
santo[3] *nm* **1** : saint's day **2** CUMPLE-
AÑOS : birthday
santuario *nm* : sanctuary
santurrón, -rrona *adj, mpl* **-rrones**
: overly pious, sanctimonious — **santurronamente** *adv*
saña *nf* **1** : fury, rage **2** : viciousness
⟨con saña : viciously⟩
sapo *nm* : toad
saque[1], etc. → **sacar**
saque[2] *nm* **1** : kickoff (in soccer or football) **2** : serve, service (in sports)
saqueador, -dora *n* DEPREDADOR
: plunderer, looter
saquear *vt* : to sack, to plunder, to loot
saqueo *nm* DEPREDACIÓN : sacking,
plunder, looting
sarampión *nm* : measles *pl*
sarape *nm CA, Mex* : serape, blanket
sarcasmo *nm* : sarcasm
sarcástico, -ca *adj* : sarcastic
sarcófago *nm* : sarcophagus
sardina *nf* : sardine
sardónico, -ca *adj* : sardonic
sarga *nf* : serge
sargento *nmf* : sergeant
sarna *nf* : mange
sarnoso, -sa *adj* : mangy
sarpullido *nm* ERUPCIÓN : rash
sarro *nm* **1** : deposit, coating **2** : tartar,
plaque
sarta *nf* **1** : string, series (of insults, etc.)
2 : string (of pearls, etc.)
sartén *nmf, pl* **sartenes** **1** : frying pan
2 tener la sartén por el mango : to call
the shots, to be in control
sasafrás *nm* : sassafras
sastre, -tra *n* : tailor
sastrería *nf* **1** : tailoring **2** : tailor's shop
Satanás *or* **Satán** *nm* : Satan, the devil
satánico, -ca *adj* : satanic
satélite *nm* : satellite
satín *or* **satén** *nm, pl* **satines** *or* **satenes**
: satin
satinado, -da *adj* : satiny, glossy
sátira *nf* : satire
satírico, -ca *adj* : satirical, satiric
satirizar {21} *vt* : to satirize

sátiro *nm* : satyr

satisfacción *nf, pl* **-ciones** : satisfaction

satisfacer {74} *vt* **1** : to satisfy **2** : to fulfill, to meet **3** : to pay, to settle — **satisfacerse** *vr* **1** : to be satisfied **2** : to take revenge

satisfactorio, -ria *adj* : satisfactory — **satisfactoriamente** *adv*

satisfecho, -cha *adj* : satisfied, content, pleased

saturación *nf, pl* **-ciones** : saturation

saturar *vt* **1** : to saturate, to fill up **2** : to satiate, to surfeit

saturnismo *nm* : lead poisoning

Saturno *nm* : Saturn

sauce *nm* : willow

saúco *nm* : elder (tree)

saudí *or* **saudita** *adj & nmf* : Saudi, Saudi Arabian

sauna *nmf* : sauna

savia *nf* : sap

saxofón *nm, pl* **-fones** : saxophone

sazón¹ *nf, pl* **sazones** **1** : flavor, seasoning **2** : ripeness, maturity ⟨en sazón : in season, ripe⟩ **3 a la sazón** : at that time, then

sazón² *nmf, pl* **sazones** *Mex* : flavor, seasoning

sazonar *vt* CONDIMENTAR : to season, to spice

scanner *nm* → **escáner**

sé → **saber, ser**

se *pron* **1** : to him, to her, to you, to them ⟨se los daré a ella : I'll give them to her⟩ **2** : each other, one another ⟨se abrazaron : they hugged each other⟩ **3** : himself, herself, itself, yourself, yourselves, themselves ⟨se afeitó antes de salir : he shaved before leaving⟩ **4** (*used in passive constructions*) ⟨se dice que es hermosa : they say she's beautiful⟩ ⟨se habla inglés : English spoken⟩

sea, etc. → **ser**

sebo *nm* **1** : grease, fat **2** : tallow **3** : suet

secado *nm* : drying

secador *nm* : hair dryer

secadora *nf* **1** : dryer, clothes dryer **2** *Mex* : hair dryer

secante *nm* : blotting paper, blotter

secar {72} *v* : to dry — **secarse** *vr* **1** : to get dry **2** : to dry up

sección *nf, pl* **secciones** **1** : section ⟨sección transversal : cross section⟩ **2** : department, division

seco, -ca *adj* **1** : dry **2** DISECADO : dried ⟨fruta seca : dried fruit⟩ **3** : thin, lean **4** : curt, brusque **5** : sharp ⟨un golpe seco : a sharp blow⟩ **6 a secas** : simply, just ⟨se llama Chico, a secas : he's just called Chico⟩ **7 en ~** : abruptly, suddenly ⟨frenar en seco : to make a sudden stop⟩

secoya *nf* : sequoia, redwood

secreción *nf, pl* **-ciones** : secretion

secretar *vt* : to secrete

secretaría *nf* **1** : secretariat, administrative department **2** *Mex* : ministry, cabinet office

secretariado *nm* **1** : secretariat **2** : secretarial profession

secretario, -ria *n* : secretary — **secretarial** *adj*

secreto¹, -ta *adj* **1** : secret **2** : secretive — **secretamente** *adv*

secreto² *nm* **1** : secret **2** : secrecy

secta *nf* : sect

sectario, -ria *adj & n* : sectarian

sector *nm* : sector

secuaz *nmf, pl* **secuaces** : follower, henchman, underling

secuela *nf* : consequence, sequel ⟨las secuelas de la guerra : the aftermath of the war⟩

secuencia *nf* : sequence

secuestrador, -dora *n* **1** : kidnapper, abductor **2** : hijacker

secuestrar *vt* **1** RAPTAR : to kidnap, to abduct **2** : to hijack, to commandeer **3** CONFISCAR : to confiscate, to seize

secuestro *nm* **1** RAPTO : kidnapping, abduction **2** : hijacking **3** : seizure, confiscation

secular *adj* : secular — **secularismo** *nm* — **secularización** *nf*

secundar *vt* : to support, to second

secundaria *nf* **1** : secondary education, high school **2** *Mex* : junior high school, middle school

secundario, -ria *adj* : secondary

secuoya *nf* : sequoia

sed *nf* **1** : thirst ⟨tener sed : to be thirsty⟩ **2 tener sed de** : to hunger for, to thirst for

seda *nf* : silk

sedación *nf, pl* **-ciones** : sedation

sedal *nm* : fishing line

sedán *nm, pl* **sedanes** : sedan

sedante *adj & nm* CALMANTE : sedative

sedar *vt* : to sedate

sede *nf* **1** : seat, headquarters **2** : venue, site **3 la Santa Sede** : the Holy See

sedentario, -ria *adj* : sedentary

sedición *nf, pl* **-ciones** : sedition — **sedicioso, -sa** *adj*

sediento, -ta *adj* : thirsty, thirsting

sedimentación *nf, pl* **-ciones** : sedimentation

sedimentario, -ria *adj* : sedimentary

sedimento *nm* : sediment

sedoso, -sa *adj* : silky, silken

seducción *nf, pl* **-ciones** : seduction

seducir {61} *vt* **1** : to seduce **2** : to captivate, to charm

seductivo, -va *adj* : seductive

seductor¹, -tora *adj* **1** SEDUCTIVO : seductive **2** ENCANTADOR : charming, alluring

seductor², -tora *n* : seducer

segador, -dora *n* : harvester

segar {49} *vt* **1** : to reap, to harvest, to cut **2** : to sever abruptly ⟨una vida segada por la enfermedad : a life cut short by illness⟩

seglar¹ *adj* LAICO : lay, secular

seglar² *nm* LAICO : layperson, layman *m*, laywoman *f*

segmentación *nf, pl* **-ciones** : segmentation

segmentado, -da *adj* : segmented

segmento *nm* : segment

segregar {52} *vt* **1** : to segregate **2** SECRETAR : to secrete

seguida *nf* **en** ~ : right away, immediately ⟨vuelvo en seguida : I'll be right back⟩

seguidamente *adv* **1** : next, immediately after **2** : without a break, continuously

seguido[1] *adv* **1** RECTO : straight, straight ahead **2** : often, frequently

seguido[2]**, -da** *adj* **1** CONSECUTIVO : consecutive, successive ⟨tres días seguidos : three days in a row⟩ **2** : straight, unbroken **3** ~ **por** *or* ~ **de** : followed by

seguidor, -dora *n* : follower, supporter

seguimiento *nm* **1** : following, pursuit **2** : continuation **3** : tracking, monitoring

seguir {75} *vt* **1** : to follow ⟨el sol sigue la lluvia : sunshine follows the rain⟩ ⟨seguiré tu consejo : I'll follow your advice⟩ ⟨me siguieron con la mirada : they followed me with their eyes⟩ **2** : to go along, to keep on ⟨seguimos toda la carretera panamericana : we continued along the PanAmerican Highway⟩ ⟨siguió hablando : he kept on talking⟩ ⟨seguir el curso : to stay on course⟩ **3** : to take (a course, a treatment) — *vi* **1** : to go on, to keep going ⟨sigue adelante : keep going, carry on⟩ **2** : to remain, to continue to be ⟨¿todavía sigues aquí? : you're still here?⟩ ⟨sigue con vida : she's still alive⟩ **3** : to follow, to come after ⟨la frase que sigue : the following sentence⟩

según[1] *adv* : it depends ⟨según y como : it all depends on⟩

según[2] *conj* **1** COMO, CONFORME : as, just as ⟨según lo dejé : just as I left it⟩ **2** : depending on how ⟨según se vea : depending on how one sees it⟩

según[3] *prep* **1** : according to ⟨según los rumores : according to the rumors⟩ **2** : depending on ⟨según los resultados : depending on the results⟩

segundo[1]**, -da** *adj* : second ⟨el segundo lugar : second place⟩

segundo[2]**, -da** *n* **1** : second (in a series) **2** : second (person), second-in-command

segundo[3] *nm* : second ⟨sesenta segundos : sixty seconds⟩

seguramente *adv* **1** : for sure, surely **2** : probably

seguridad *nf* **1** : safety, security **2** : (financial) security ⟨seguridad social : Social Security⟩ **3** CERTEZA : certainty, assurance ⟨con toda seguridad : with complete certainty⟩ **4** : confidence, self-confidence

seguro[1] *adv* : certainly, definitely ⟨va a llover, seguro : it's going to rain for sure⟩ ⟨¡seguro que sí! : of course!⟩

seguro[2]**, -ra** *adj* **1** : safe, secure **2** : sure, certain ⟨estoy segura que es él : I'm sure that's him⟩ **3** : reliable, trustworthy **4** : self-assured

seguro[3] *nm* **1** : insurance ⟨seguro de vida : life insurance⟩ **2** : fastener, clasp **3** *Mex* : safety pin

seis *adj & nm* : six

seiscientos[1]**, -tas** *adj* : six hundred

seiscientos[2] *nms & pl* : six hundred

selección *nf, pl* **-ciones** **1** ELECCIÓN : selection, choice **2** **selección natural** : natural selection

seleccionar *vt* ELEGIR : to select, to choose

selectivo, -va *adj* : selective — **selectivamente** *adv*

selecto, -ta *adj* **1** : choice, select **2** EXCLUSIVO : exclusive

selenio *nm* : selenium

sellar *vt* **1** : to seal **2** : to stamp

sello *nm* **1** : seal **2** ESTAMPILLA, TIMBRE : postage stamp **3** : hallmark, characteristic

selva *nf* **1** BOSQUE : woods *pl*, forest ⟨selva húmeda : rain forest⟩ **2** JUNGLA : jungle

selvático, -ca *adj* **1** : forest, jungle ⟨sendero selvático : jungle path⟩ **2** : wild

semáforo *nm* **1** : traffic light **2** : stop signal

semana *nf* : week

semanal *adj* : weekly — **semanalmente** *adv*

semanario *nm* : weekly (publication)

semántica *nf* : semantics

semántico, -ca *adj* : semantic

semblante *nm* **1** : countenance, face **2** : appearance, look

semblanza *nf* : biographical sketch, profile

sembrado *nm* : cultivated field

sembrador, -dora *n* : planter, sower

sembradora *nf* : seeder (machine)

sembrar {55} *vt* **1** : to plant, to sow **2** : to scatter, to strew ⟨sembrar el pánico : to spread panic⟩

semejante[1] *adj* **1** PARECIDO : similar, alike **2** TAL : such ⟨nunca he visto cosa semejante : I have never seen such a thing⟩

semejante[2] *nm* PRÓJIMO : fellowman

semejanza *nf* PARECIDO : similarity, resemblance

semejar *vi* : to resemble, to look like — **semejarse** *vr* : to be similar, to look alike

semen *nm* : semen

semental *nm* : stud (animal) ⟨caballo semental : stallion⟩

semestre *nm* : semester

semicírculo *nm* : semicircle, half circle

semiconductor *nm* : semiconductor

semidiós *nm, pl* **-dioses** : demigod *m*

semifinal *nf* : semifinal

semifinalista[1] *adj* : semifinal

semifinalista[2] *nmf* : semifinalist

semiformal *adj* : semiformal
semilla *nf* : seed
semillero *nm* **1** : seedbed **2** : hotbed, breeding ground
seminario *nm* **1** : seminary **2** : seminar, graduate course
seminarista *nm* : seminarian
semiprecioso, -sa *adj* : semiprecious
semita[1] *adj* : Semitic
semita[2] *nmf* : Semite
sémola *nf* : semolina
sempiterno, -na *adj* ETERNO : eternal, everlasting
senado *nm* : senate
senador, -dora *n* : senator
sencillamente *adv* : simply, plainly
sencillez *nf* : simplicity
sencillo[1], **-lla** *adj* **1** : simple, easy **2** : plain, unaffected **3** : single
sencillo[2] *nm* **1** : single (recording) **2** : small change (coins) **3** : one-way ticket
senda *nf* CAMINO, SENDERO : path, way
sendero *nm* CAMINO, SENDA : path, way
sendos, -das *adj pl* : each, both ⟨llevaban sendos vestidos nuevos : they were each wearing a new dress⟩
senectud *nf* ANCIANIDAD : old age
senegalés, -lesa *adj & n, mpl* **-leses** : Senegalese
senil *adj* : senile — **senilidad** *nf*
seno *nm* **1** : breast, bosom ⟨los senos : the breasts⟩ ⟨el seno de la familia : the bosom of the family⟩ **2** : sinus **3 seno materno** : womb
sensación *nf, pl* **-ciones 1** IMPRESIÓN : feeling ⟨tener la sensación : to have a feeling⟩ **2** : sensation ⟨causar sensación : to cause a sensation⟩
sensacional *adj* : sensational
sensacionalista *adj* : sensationalistic, lurid
sensatez *nf* **1** : good sense **2 con ~** : sensibly
sensato, -ta *adj* : sensible, sound — **sensatamente** *adv*
sensibilidad *nf* **1** : sensitivity, sensibility **2** SENSACIÓN : feeling
sensibilizar {21} *vt* : to sensitize
sensible *adj* **1** : sensitive **2** APRECIABLE : considerable, significant
sensiblemente *adv* : considerably, significantly
sensiblería *nf* : sentimentality, mush
sensiblero, -ra *adj* : mawkish, sentimental, mushy
sensitivo, -va *adj* **1** : sense ⟨órganos sensitivos : sense organs⟩ **2** : sentient, capable of feeling
sensor *nm* : sensor
sensorial *adj* : sensory
sensual *adj* : sensual, sensuous — **sensualmente** *adv*
sensualidad *nf* : sensuality
sentado, -da *adj* **1** : sitting, seated **2** : established, settled ⟨dar por sentado : to take for granted⟩ ⟨dejar sentado : to make clear⟩ **3** : sensible, steady, judicious

sentar {55} *vt* **1** : to seat, to sit **2** : to establish, to set — *vi* **1** : to suit ⟨ese color te sienta : that color suits you⟩ **2** : to agree with (of food or drink) ⟨las cebollas no me sientan : onions don't agree with me⟩ **3** : to please ⟨le sentó mal el paseo : she didn't enjoy the trip⟩ — **sentarse** *vr* : to sit, to sit down ⟨siéntese, por favor : please have a seat⟩
sentencia *nf* **1** : sentence, judgment **2** : maxim, saying
sentenciar *vt* : to sentence
sentido[1], **-da** *adj* **1** : heartfelt, sincere ⟨mi más sentido pésame : my sincerest condolences⟩ **2** : touchy, sensitive **3** : offended, hurt
sentido[2] *nm* **1** : sense ⟨sentido común : common sense⟩ ⟨los cinco sentidos : the five senses⟩ ⟨sin sentido : senseless⟩ **2** CONOCIMIENTO : consciousness **3** SIGNIFICADO : meaning, sense ⟨doble sentido : double entendre⟩ **4** : direction ⟨calle de sentido único : one-way street⟩
sentimental[1] *adj* **1** : sentimental **2** : love, romantic ⟨vida sentimental : love life⟩
sentimental[2] *nmf* : sentimentalist
sentimentalismo *nm* : sentimentality, sentimentalism
sentimiento *nm* **1** : feeling, emotion **2** PESAR : regret, sorrow
sentir {76} *vt* **1** : to feel, to experience ⟨no siento nada de dolor : I don't feel any pain⟩ ⟨sentía sed : he was feeling thirsty⟩ ⟨sentir amor : to feel love⟩ **2** PERCIBIR : to perceive, to sense ⟨sentir un ruido : to hear a noise⟩ **3** LAMENTAR : to regret, to feel sorry for ⟨lo siento mucho : I'm very sorry⟩ — *vi* **1** : to have feeling, to feel **2 sin ~** : without noticing, inadvertently — **sentirse** *vr* **1** : to feel ⟨¿te sientes mejor? : are you feeling better?⟩ **2** *Chile, Mex* : to take offense
seña *nf* **1** : sign, signal **2 dar señas de** : to show signs of
señal *nf* **1** : signal **2** : sign ⟨señal de tráfico : traffic sign⟩ **3** INDICIO : indication ⟨en señal de : as a token of⟩ **4** VESTIGIO : trace, vestige **5** : scar, mark **6** : deposit, down payment
señalado, -da *adj* : distinguished, notable
señalador *nm* : marker ⟨señalador de libros : bookmark⟩
señalar *vt* **1** INDICAR : to indicate, to show **2** : to mark **3** : to point out, to stress **4** : to fix, to set — **señalarse** *vr* : to distinguish oneself
señor, -ñora *n* **1** : gentleman *m*, man *m*, lady *f*, woman *f*, wife *f* **2** : Sir *m*, Madam *f* ⟨estimados señores : Dear Sirs⟩ **3** : Mr. *m*, Mrs. *f* **4** : lord *m*, lady *f* ⟨el Señor : the Lord⟩
señoría *nf* **1** : lordship **2 Su Señoría** : Your Honor
señorial *adj* : stately, regal

señorío *nm* **1** : manor, estate **2** : dominion, power **3** : elegance, class
señorita *nf* **1** : young lady, young woman **2** : Miss
señuelo *nm* **1** : decoy **2** : bait
sépalo *nm* : sepal
sepa, etc. → **saber**
separación *nf, pl* **-ciones 1** : separation, division **2** : gap, space
separadamente *adv* : separately, apart
separado, -da *adj* **1** : separated **2** : separate ⟨vidas separadas : separate lives⟩ **3 por ~** : separately
separar *vt* **1** : to separate, to divide **2** : to split up, to pull apart — **separarse** *vr*
sepelio *nm* : interment, burial
sepia¹ *adj & nm* : sepia
sepia² *nf* : cuttlefish
septentrional *adj* : northern
séptico, -ca *adj* : septic
septiembre *nm* : September
séptimo¹, -ma *adj* : seventh
séptimo² *nm* : seventh
septuagésimo¹, -ma *adj* : seventieth
septuagésimo² *nm* : seventieth
sepulcral *adj* **1** : sepulchral **2** : dismal, gloomy
sepulcro *nm* TUMBA : tomb, sepulchre
sepultar *vt* ENTERRAR : to bury
sepultura *nf* **1** : burial **2** TUMBA : grave, tomb
seque, etc. → **secar**
sequedad *nf* **1** : dryness **2** : brusqueness, curtness
sequía *nf* : drought
séquito *nm* : retinue, entourage
ser¹ {77} *vi* **1** : to be ⟨él es mi hermano : he is my brother⟩ ⟨Camila es linda : Camila is pretty⟩ **2** : to exist, to live ⟨ser, o no ser : to be or not to be⟩ **3** : to take place, to occur ⟨el concierto es el domingo : the concert is on Sunday⟩ **4** (*used with expressions of time, date, season*) ⟨son las diez : it's ten o'clock⟩ ⟨hoy es el 9 : today's the 9th⟩ **5** : to cost, to come to ⟨¿cuánto es? : how much is it?⟩ **6** (*with the future tense*) : to be able to be ⟨¿será posible? : can it be possible?⟩ **7 ~ de** : to come from ⟨somos de Managua : we're from Managua⟩ **8 ~ de** : to belong to ⟨ese lápiz es de Juan : that's Juan's pencil⟩ **9 es que** : the thing is that ⟨es que no lo conozco : it's just that I don't know him⟩ **10 ¡sea!** : agreed!, all right! **11 sea...sea** : either...or — *v aux* (*used in passive constructions*) : to be ⟨la cuenta ha sido pagada : the bill has been paid⟩ ⟨él fue asesinado : he was murdered⟩
ser² *nm* : being ⟨ser humano : human being⟩
seráfico, -ca *adj* : angelic, seraphic
serbio¹, -bia *adj & n* : Serb, Serbian
serbio² *nm* : Serbian (language)
serbocroata¹ *adj* : Serbo-Croatian
serbocroata² *nm* : Serbo-Croatian (language)

serenar *vt* : to calm, to soothe — **serenarse** *vr* CALMARSE : to calm down
serenata *nf* : serenade
serendipia *nf* : serendipity
serenidad *nf* : serenity, calmness
sereno¹, -na *adj* **1** SOSEGADO : serene, calm, composed **2** : fair, clear (of weather) **3** : calm, still (of the sea) — **serenamente** *adv*
sereno² *nm* : night watchman
seriado, -da *adj* : serial
serial *nm* : serial (on radio or television)
seriamente *adv* : seriously
serie *nf* **1** : series **2** SERIAL : serial **3 fabricación en serie** : mass production **4 fuera de serie** : extraordinary, amazing
seriedad *nf* **1** : seriousness, earnestness **2** : gravity, importance
serio, -ria *adj* **1** : serious, earnest **2** : reliable, responsible **3** : important **4 en ~** : seriously, in earnest — **seriamente** *adv*
sermón *nm, pl* **sermones 1** : sermon **2** *fam* : harangue, lecture
sermonear *vt fam* : to harangue, to lecture
serpentear *vi* : to twist, to wind — **serpenteante** *adj*
serpentina *nf* : paper streamer
serpiente *nf* : serpent, snake
serrado, -da *adj* DENTADO : serrated
serranía *nf* : mountainous area
serrano, -na *adj* : from the mountains
serrar {55} *vt* : to saw
serrín *nm, pl* **serrines** : sawdust
serruchar *vt* : to saw up
serrucho *nm* : saw, handsaw
servicentro *nm Peru* : gas station
servicial *adj* : obliging, helpful
servicio *nm* **1** : service **2** SAQUE : serve (in sports) **3 servicios** *nmpl* : restroom
servidor, -dora *n* **1** : servant **2 su seguro servidor** : yours truly (in correspondence)
servidumbre *nf* **1** : servitude **2** : help, servants *pl*
servil *adj* **1** : servile, subservient **2** : menial
servilismo *nm* : servility, subservience
servilleta *nf* : napkin
servir {54} *vt* **1** : to serve, to be of use to **2** : to serve, to wait **3** SURTIR : to fill (an order) — *vi* **1** : to work ⟨mi radio no sirve : my radio isn't working⟩ **2** : to be of use, to be helpful ⟨esa computadora no sirve para nada : that computer's perfectly useless⟩ — **servirse** *vr* **1** : to help oneself to **2** : to be kind enough ⟨sírvase enviarnos un catálogo : please send us a catalog⟩
sésamo *nm* AJONJOLÍ : sesame, sesame seeds *pl*
sesenta *adj & nm* : sixty
sesentavo¹, -va *adj* : sixtieth
sesentavo² *n* : sixtieth (fraction)
sesgado, -da *adj* **1** : inclined, tilted **2** : slanted, biased

sesgar {52} *vt* **1** : to cut on the bias **2** : to tilt **3** : to bias, to slant
sesgo *nm* : bias
sesgue, etc. → **sesgar**
sesión *nf, pl* **sesiones 1** : session **2** : showing, performance
sesionar *vi* REUNIRSE : to meet, to be in session
seso *nm* **1** : brains, intelligence **2 sesos** *nmpl* : brains (as food)
sesudo, -da *adj* **1** : prudent, sensible **2** : brainy
set *nm, pl* **sets** : set (in tennis)
seta *nf* : mushroom
setecientos[1], **-tas** *adj* : seven hundred
setecientos[2] *nms & pl* : seven hundred
setenta *adj & nm* : seventy
setentavo[1], **-va** *adj* : seventieth
setentavo[2] *nm* : seventieth
setiembre → **septiembre**
seto *nm* **1** : fence, enclosure **2 seto vivo** : hedge
seudónimo *nm* : pseudonym
severidad *nf* **1** : harshness, severity **2** : strictness
severo, -ra *adj* **1** : harsh, severe **2** ES-TRICTO : strict — **severamente** *adv*
sexagésimo[1], **-ma** *adj* : sixtieth, sixty-
sexagésimo[2], **-ma** *n* : sixtieth, sixty- (in a series)
sexismo *nm* : sexism — **sexista** *adj & nmf*
sexo *nm* : sex
sextante *nm* : sextant
sexteto *nm* : sextet
sexto, -ta *adj* : sixth — **sexto, -ta** *n*
sexual *adj* : sexual, sex ⟨educación sexual : sex education⟩ — **sexualmente** *adv*
sexualidad *nf* : sexuality
sexy *adj, pl* **sexy** *or* **sexys** : sexy
shock ['ʃɔk, 'tʃɔk] *nm* : shock ⟨estado de shock : state of shock⟩
short *nm, pl* **shorts** : shorts *pl*
show *nm, pl* **shows** : show
si *conj* **1** : if ⟨lo haré si me pagan : I'll do it if they pay me⟩ ⟨si lo supiera te lo diría : if I knew it I would tell you⟩ **2** : whether, if ⟨no importa si funciona o no : it doesn't matter whether it works (or not)⟩ **3** (*expressing desire, protest, or surprise*) ⟨si supiera la verdad : if only I knew the truth⟩ ⟨¡si no quiero! : but I don't want to!⟩ **4 si bien** : although ⟨si bien se ha progresado : although progress has been made⟩ **5 si no** : otherwise, or else ⟨si no, no voy : otherwise I won't go⟩
sí[1] *adv* **1** : yes ⟨sí, gracias : yes, please⟩ ⟨creo que sí : I think so⟩ **2** : indeed, absolutely ⟨esta vez sí que ganaré : this time I'm sure to win⟩ **3 porque sí** *fam* : because, just because ⟨lo hizo porque sí : she did it just because⟩
sí[2] *nm* : yes ⟨dar el sí : to say yes, to express consent⟩
sí[3] *pron* **1 de por sí** *or* **en sí** : by itself, in itself, per se **2 fuera de sí** : beside

oneself **3 para sí (mismo)** : to himself, to herself, for himself, for herself **4 entre** ∼ : among themselves
siamés, -mesa *adj & n, mpl* **siameses** : Siamese
sibilante *adj & nf* : sibilant
siciliano, -na *adj & n* : Sicilian
sico- → **psico-**
sicomoro *or* **sicómoro** *nm* : sycamore
SIDA *or* **sida** *nm* (síndrome de inmunodeficiencia adquirida) : AIDS
siderurgia *nf* : iron and steel industry
siderúrgico, -ca *adj* : steel, iron ⟨la industria siderúrgica : the steel industry⟩
sidra *nf* : hard cider
siega[1], **siegue,** etc. → **segar**
siega[2] *nf* **1** : harvesting **2** : harvest time **3** : harvested crop
siembra[1], etc. → **sembrar**
siembra[2] *nf* **1** : sowing **2** : sowing season **3** SEMBRADO : cultivated field
siempre *adv* **1** : always ⟨siempre tienes hambre : you're always hungry⟩ **2** : still ⟨¿siempre te vas? : are you still going?⟩ **3** *Mex* : after all ⟨siempre no fui : I didn't go after all⟩ **4 siempre que** : whenever, every time ⟨siempre que pasa : every time he walks by⟩ **5 para** ∼ : forever, for good **6 siempre y cuando** : provided that
sien *nf* : temple (on the forehead)
sienta, etc. → **sentar**
siente, etc. → **sentir**
sierpe *nf* : serpent, snake
sierra[1], etc. → **serrar**
sierra[2] *nf* **1** : saw ⟨sierra de vaivén : jigsaw⟩ **2** CORDILLERA : mountain range **3** : mountains *pl* ⟨viven en la sierra : they live in the mountains⟩
siervo, -va *n* **1** : slave **2** : serf
siesta *nf* : nap, siesta
siete *adj & nm* : seven
sífilis *nf* : syphilis
sifón *nm, pl* **sifones** : siphon
siga, sigue etc. → **seguir**
sigilo *nm* : secrecy, stealth
sigiloso, -sa *adj* FURTIVO : furtive, stealthy — **sigilosamente** *adv*
sigla *nf* : acronym, abbreviation
siglo *nm* **1** : century **2** : age ⟨el Siglo de Oro : the Golden Age⟩ ⟨hace siglos que no te veo : I haven't seen you in ages⟩ **3** : world, secular life
signar *vt* : to sign (a treaty or agreement)
signatario, -ria *n* : signatory
significación *nf, pl* **-ciones 1** : significance, importance **2** : signification, meaning
significado *nm* **1** : sense, meaning **2** : significance
significante *adj* : significant
significar {72} *vt* **1** : to mean, to signify **2** : to express, to make known — **significarse** *vr* **1** : to draw attention, to become known **2** : to take a stance
significativo, -va *adj* **1** : significant, important **2** : meaningful — **significativamente** *adv*

signo *nm* **1** : sign ⟨signo de igual : equal sign⟩ ⟨un signo de alegría : a sign of happiness⟩ **2** : (punctuation) mark ⟨signo de interrogación : question mark⟩ ⟨signo de admiración : exclamation point⟩ ⟨signo de intercalación : caret⟩
siguiente *adj* : next, following
sílaba *nf* : syllable
silábico, -ca *adj* : syllabic
silbar *v* : to whistle
silbato *nm* PITO : whistle
silbido *nm* : whistle, whistling
silenciador *nm* **1** : muffler (of an automobile) **2** : silencer
silenciar *vt* **1** : to silence **2** : to muffle
silencio *nm* **1** : silence, quiet ⟨¡silencio! : be quiet!⟩ **2** : rest (in music)
silencioso, -sa *adj* : silent, quiet — **silenciosamente** *adv*
sílice *nf* : silica
silicio *nm* : silicon
silla *nf* **1** : chair **2 silla de ruedas** : wheelchair
sillón *nm, pl* **sillones** : armchair, easy chair
silo *nm* : silo
silueta *nf* **1** : silhouette **2** : figure, shape
silvestre *adj* : wild ⟨flor silvestre : wildflower⟩
silvicultor, -tora *n* : forester
silvicultura *nf* : forestry
sima *nf* ABISMO : chasm, abyss
simbólico, -ca *adj* : symbolic — **simbólicamente** *adj*
simbolismo *nm* : symbolism
simbolizar {21} *vt* : to symbolize
símbolo *nm* : symbol
simetría *nf* : symmetry
simétrico, -ca *adj* : symmetrical, symmetric
simiente *nf* : seed
símil *nm* **1** : simile **2** : analogy, comparison
similar *adj* SEMEJANTE : similar, alike
similitud *nf* : similarity, resemblance
simio *nm* : ape
simpatía *nf* **1** : liking, affection ⟨tomarle simpatía a : to take a liking to⟩ **2** : warmth, friendliness **3** : support, solidarity
simpático, -ca *adj* : nice, friendly, likeable
simpatizante *nf* : sympathizer, supporter
simpatizar {21} *vi* **1** : to get along, to hit it off ⟨simpaticé mucho con él : I really liked him⟩ **2** ~ **con** : to sympathize with, to support
simple[1] *adj* **1** SENCILLO : plain, simple, easy **2** : pure, mere ⟨por simple vanidad : out of pure vanity⟩ **3** : simpleminded, foolish
simple[2] *n* : fool, simpleton
simplemente *adv* : simply, merely, just
simpleza *nf* **1** : foolishness, simpleness **2** NECEDAD : nonsense
simplicidad *nf* : simplicity

simplificar {72} *vt* : to simplify — **simplificación** *nf*
simplista *adj* : simplistic
simposio *or* **simposium** *nm* : symposium
simulación *nf, pl* **-ciones** : simulation
simulacro *nm* : imitation, sham ⟨simulacro de juicio : mock trial⟩
simular *vt* **1** : to simulate **2** : to feign, to pretend
simultáneo, -nea *adj* : simultaneous — **simultáneamente** *adv*
sin *prep* **1** : without ⟨sin querer : unintentionally⟩ ⟨sin refinar : unrefined⟩ **2 sin que** : without ⟨lo hicimos sin que él se diera cuenta : we did it without him noticing⟩
sinagoga *nf* : synagogue
sinceridad *nf* : sincerity
sincero, -ra *adj* : sincere, honest, true — **sinceramente** *adv*
síncopa *nf* : syncopation
sincopar *vt* : to syncopate
sincronizar {21} *vt* : to synchronize — **sincronización** *nf*
sindical *adj* GREMIAL : union, labor ⟨representante sindical : union representative⟩
sindicalización *nf, pl* **-ciones** : unionizing, unionization
sindicalizar {21} *vt* : to unionize — **sindicalizarse** *vr* **1** : to form a union **2** : to join a union
sindicar → **sindicalizar**
sindicato *nm* GREMIO : union, guild
síndrome *nm* : syndrome
sinecura *nf* : sinecure
sinfín *nm* : endless number ⟨un sinfín de problemas : no end of problems⟩
sinfonía *nf* : symphony
sinfónica *nf* : symphony orchestra
sinfónico, -ca *adj* : symphonic, symphony
singular[1] *adj* **1** : singular, unique **2** PARTICULAR : peculiar, odd **3** : singular (in grammar) — **singularmente** *adv*
singular[2] *nm* : singular
singularidad *nf* : uniqueness, singularity
singularizar {21} *vt* : to make unique or distinct — **singularizarse** *vr* : to stand out, to distinguish oneself
siniestrado, -da *adj* : damaged, wrecked ⟨zona siniestrada : disaster zone⟩
siniestro[1], **-tra** *adj* **1** IZQUIERDO : left, left-hand **2** MALVADO : sinister, evil
siniestro[2] *nm* : accident, disaster
sinnúmero → **sinfín**
sino *conj* **1** : but, rather ⟨no será hoy, sino mañana : it won't be today, but tomorrow⟩ **2** EXCEPTO : but, except ⟨no hace sino despertar suspicacias : it does nothing but arouse suspicion⟩
sinónimo[1], **-ma** *adj* : synonymous
sinónimo[2] *nm* : synonym
sinopsis *nfs & pl* RESUMEN : synopsis, summary
sinrazón *nf, pl* **-zones** : wrong, injustice

sinsabores *nmpl* : woes, troubles
sinsonte *nm* : mockingbird
sintáctico, -ca *adj* : syntactic, syntactical
sintaxis *nfs & pl* : syntax
síntesis *nfs & pl* **1** : synthesis, fusion **2** SINOPSIS : synopsis, summary
sintético, -ca *adj* : synthetic — **sintéticamente** *adv*
sintetizar {21} *vt* **1** : to synthesize **2** RESUMIR : to summarize
sintió, etc. → **sentir**
síntoma *nm* : symptom
sintomático, -ca *adj* : symptomatic
sintonía *nf* **1** : tuning in (of a radio) **2** **en sintonía con** : in tune with, attuned to
sintonizador *nm* : tuner, knob for tuning (of a radio, etc.)
sintonizar {21} *vt* : to tune (in) to — *vi* **1** : to tune in **2** ~ **con** : to be in tune with, to empathize with
sinuosidad *nf* : sinuosity
sinuoso, -sa *adj* **1** : winding, sinuous **2** : devious
sinvergüenza¹ *adj* **1** DESCARADO : shameless, brazen, impudent **2** TRAVIESO : naughty
sinvergüenza² *nmf* **1** : rogue, scoundrel **2** : brat, rascal
sionista *adj & nmf* : Zionist — **sionismo** *nm*
siqui- → **psiqui-**
siquiera *adv* **1** : at least ⟨dame siquiera un poquito : at least give me a little bit⟩ **2** (*in negative constructions*) : not even ⟨ni siquiera nos saludaron : they didn't even say hello to us⟩
sirena *nf* **1** : mermaid **2** : siren ⟨sirena de niebla : foghorn⟩
sirio, -ria *adj & n* : Syrian
sirope *nm* : syrup
sirve, etc. → **servir**
sirviente, -ta *n* : servant, maid *f*
sisal *nm* : sisal
sisear *vi* : to hiss
siseo *nm* : hiss
sísmico, -ca *adj* : seismic
sismo *nm* **1** TERREMOTO : earthquake **2** TEMBLOR : tremor
sismógrafo *nm* : seismograph
sistema *nm* : system
sistemático, -ca *adj* : systematic — **sistemáticamente** *adv*
sistematizar {21} *vt* : to systematize
sistémico, -ca *adj* : systemic
sitiar *vt* ASEDIAR : to besiege
sitio *nm* **1** LUGAR : place, site ⟨vámonos a otro sitio : let's go somewhere else⟩ **2** ESPACIO : room, space ⟨hacer sitio a : to make room for⟩ **3** : siege ⟨estado de sitio : state of siege⟩ **4** *Mex* : taxi stand
situación *nf, pl* **-ciones** : situation
situado, -da *adj* : situated, placed
situar {3} *vt* UBICAR : to situate, to place, to locate — **situarse** *vr* **1** : to be placed, to be located **2** : to make a place for oneself, to do well

sketch *nm* : sketch, skit
slip *nm* : briefs *pl*, underpants *pl*
smog *nm* : smog
smoking *nm* ESMOQUIN : tuxedo
snob → **esnob**
so *prep* : under ⟨so pena de : under penalty of⟩
sobaco *nm* : armpit
sobado, -da *adj* **1** : worn, shabby **2** : well-worn, hackneyed
sobar *vt* **1** : to finger, to handle **2** : to knead **3** : to rub, to massage **4** *fam* : to beat, to pummel
soberanía *nf* : sovereignty
soberano, -na *adj & n* : sovereign
soberbia *nf* **1** ORGULLO : pride, arrogance **2** MAGNIFICENCIA : magnificence
soberbio, -bia *adj* **1** : proud, arrogant **2** : grand, magnificent
sobornable *adv* : venal, bribable
sobornar *vt* : to bribe
soborno *nm* **1** : bribery **2** : bribe
sobra *nf* **1** : excess, surplus **2 de** ~ : extra, to spare **3 sobras** *nfpl* : leftovers, scraps
sobrado, -da *adj* : abundant, excessive, more than enough
sobrante¹ *adj* : remaining, superfluous
sobrante² *nm* : remainder, surplus
sobrar *vi* : to be in excess, to be superfluous ⟨más vale que sobre a que falte : it's better to have too much than not enough⟩
sobre¹ *nm* **1** : envelope **2** : packet ⟨un sobre de sazón : a packet of seasoning⟩
sobre² *prep* **1** : on, on top of ⟨sobre la mesa : on the table⟩ **2** : over, above **3** : about ⟨¿tiene libros sobre Bolivia? : do you have books on Bolivia?⟩ **4 sobre todo** : especially, above all
sobrealimentar *vt* : to overfeed
sobrecalentar {55} *vt* : to overheat — **sobrecalentarse** *vr*
sobrecama *nmf* : bedspread
sobrecargar {52} *vt* : to overload, to overburden, to weigh down
sobrecoger {15} *vt* **1** : to surprise, to startle **2** : to scare — **sobrecogerse** *vr*
sobrecubierta *nf* : dust jacket
sobredosis *nfs & pl* : overdose
sobreentender {56} *vt* : to infer, to understand
sobreestimar *vt* : to overestimate, to overrate
sobreexcitado, -da *adj* : overexcited
sobreexponer {60} *vt* : to overexpose
sobregirar *vt* : to overdraw
sobregiro *nm* : overdraft
sobrehumano, -na *adj* : superhuman
sobrellevar *vt* : to endure, to bear
sobremanera *adv* : exceedingly
sobremesa *nf* : after-dinner conversation
sobrenatural *adj* : supernatural
sobrenombre *nm* APODO : nickname
sobrentender → **sobreentender**

sobrepasar *vt* : to exceed, to surpass —
 sobrepasarse *vr* PASARSE : to go too
 far
sobrepelliz *nf, pl* **-pellices** : surplice
sobrepeso *nm* **1** : excess weight **2**
 : overweight, obesity
sobrepoblación, sobrepoblado → **superpoblación, superpoblado**
sobreponer {60} *vt* **1** SUPERPONER : to
 superimpose **2** ANTEPONER : to put
 first, to give priority to — **sobrepon-
 erse** *vr* **1** : to pull oneself together **2**
 ~ **a** : to overcome
sobreprecio *nm* : surcharge
sobreproducción *nf, pl* **-ciones** : over-
 production
sobreproducir {61} *vt* : to overproduce
sobreprotector, -tora *adj* : overprotec-
 tive
sobreproteger {15} *vt* : to overprotect
sobresaliente[1] *adj* **1** : protruding, projecting **2** : outstanding, noteworthy **3**
 : significant, salient
sobresaliente[2] *nmf* : understudy
sobresalir {73} *vi* **1** : to protrude, to jut
 out, to project **2** : to stand out, to excel
sobresaltar *vt* : to startle, to frighten —
 sobresaltarse *vr*
sobresalto *nm* : start, fright
sobresueldo *nm* : bonus, additional pay
sobretasa *nf* : surcharge ⟨sobretasa a la
 gasolina : gas tax⟩
sobretodo *nm* : overcoat
sobrevalorar *or* **sobrevaluar** {3} *vt* : to
 overvalue, to overrate
sobrevender *vt* : to oversell
sobrevenir {87} *vi* ACAECER : to take
 place, to come about ⟨podrían sobrevenir complicaciones : complications could occur⟩
sobrevivencia → **supervivencia**
sobreviviente → **superviviente**
sobrevivir *vi* : to survive — *vt* : to outlive, to outlast
sobrevolar {19} *vt* : to fly over, to overfly
sobriedad *nf* : sobriety, moderation
sobrino, -na *n* : nephew *m*, niece *f*
sobrio, -bria *adj* : sober — **sobriamente**
 adv
socarrón, -rrona *adj, mpl* **-rrones 1**
 : sly, cunning **2** : sarcastic
socavar *vt* : to undermine
sociabilidad *nf* : sociability
sociable *adj* : sociable
social *adj* : social — **socialmente** *adv*
socialista *adj & nmf* : socialist — **socialismo** *nm*
sociedad *nf* **1** : society **2** : company,
 enterprise **3 sociedad anónima** : in-
 corporated company
socio, -cia *n* **1** : member **2** : partner
socioeconómico, -ca *adj* : socioeconomic
sociología *nf* : sociology
sociológico, -ca *adj* : sociological —
 sociológicamente *adv*

sociólogo, -ga *n* : sociologist
socorrer *vt* : to assist, to come to the aid
 of
socorrido, -da *adj* ÚTIL : handy, practical
socorrista *nmf* **1** : rescue worker **2**
 : lifeguard
socorro *nm* AUXILIO **1** : aid, help
 ⟨equipo de socorro : rescue team⟩ **2**
 ¡**socorro!** : help!
soda *nf* : soda, soda water
sodio *nf* : sodium
soez *adj, pl* **soeces** GROSERO : rude,
 vulgar — **soezmente** *adv*
sofá *nm* : couch, sofa
sofistería *nf* : sophistry — **sofista** *nmf*
sofisticación *nf, pl* **-ciones** : sophistication
sofisticado, -da *adj* : sophisticated
sofocante *adj* : suffocating, stifling
sofocar {72} *vt* **1** AHOGAR : to suffocate,
 to smother **2** EXTINGUIR : to extinguish, to put out (a fire) **3** APLASTAR
 : to crush, to put down ⟨sofocar una
 rebelión : to crush a rebellion⟩ — **sofocarse** *vr* **1** : to suffocate **2** *fam* : to
 get upset, to get mad
sofreír {66} *vt* : to sauté
sofrito[1], **-ta** *adj* : sautéed
sofrito[2] *nm* : seasoning sauce
softbol *nm* : softball
software *nm* : software
soga *nf* : rope
soja → **soya**
sojuzgar *vt* : to subdue, to conquer, to
 subjugate
sol *nm* **1** : sun **2** : Peruvian unit of currency
solamente *adv* SÓLO : only, just
solapa *nf* **1** : lapel (of a jacket) **2** : flap
 (of an envelope)
solapado, -da *adj* : secret, underhanded
solapar *vt* : to cover up, to keep secret
 — **solaparse** *vr* : to overlap
solar[1] {19} *vt* : to floor, to tile
solar[2] *adj* : solar, sun
solar[3] *nm* **1** TERRENO : lot, piece of
 land, site **2** *Cuba, Peru* : tenement
 building
solariego, -ga *adj* : ancestral
solaz *nm, pl* **solaces 1** CONSUELO : solace, comfort **2** DESCANSO : relaxation, recreation
solazarse {21} *vr* : to relax, to enjoy oneself
soldado *nm* **1** : soldier **2 soldado raso**
 : private, enlisted man
soldador[1], **-dora** *n* : welder
soldador[2] *nm* : soldering iron
soldadura *nf* **1** : welding **2** : soldering,
 solder
soldar {19} *vt* **1** : to weld **2** : to solder
soleado, -da *adj* : sunny
soledad *nf* : loneliness, solitude
solemne *adj* : solemn — **solemne-
 mente** *adv*
solemnidad *nf* : solemnity

soler {78} *vi* : to be in the habit of, to tend to ⟨solía tomar café por la tarde : she usually drank coffee in the afternoon⟩ ⟨eso suele ocurrir : that frequently happens⟩

solera *nf* 1 : prop, support 2 : tradition

solicitante *nmf* : applicant

solicitar *vt* 1 : to request, to solicit 2 : to apply for ⟨solicitar empleo : to apply for employment⟩

solícito, -ta *adj* : solicitous, attentive, obliging

solicitud *nf* 1 : solicitude, concern 2 : request 3 : application

solidaridad *nf* : solidarity

solidario, -ria *adj* : supportive, united in support ⟨se declararon solidarios con la nueva ley : they declared their support for the new law⟩ ⟨espíritu solidario : spirit of solidarity⟩

solidarizar {21} *vi* : to be in solidarity ⟨solidarizamos con la huelga : we support the strike⟩

solidez *nf* 1 : solidity, firmness 2 : soundness (of an argument, etc.)

solidificar {72} *vt* : to solidify, to make solid — **solidificarse** *vr* — **solidificación** *nf*

sólido¹, -da *adj* 1 : solid, firm 2 : sturdy, well-made 3 : sound, well-founded — **sólidamente** *adv*

sólido² *nm* : solid

soliloquio *nm* : soliloquy

solista *nmf* : soloist

solitaria *nf* TENIA : tapeworm

solitario¹, -ria *adj* 1 : lonely 2 : lone, solitary 3 DESIERTO : deserted, lonely ⟨una calle solitaria : a deserted street⟩

solitario², -ria *n* : recluse, loner

solitario³ *nm* : solitaire

sollozar {21} *vi* : to sob

sollozo *nm* : sob

solo¹, -la *adj* 1 : alone, by oneself 2 : lonely 3 ÚNICO : only, sole, unique ⟨hay un solo problema : there's only one problem⟩ 4 **a solas** : alone

solo² *nm* : solo

sólo *adv* SOLAMENTE : just, only ⟨sólo quieren comer : they just want to eat⟩

solomillo *nm* : sirloin, loin

solsticio *nm* : solstice

soltar {19} *vt* 1 : to let go of, to drop 2 : to release, to set free 3 AFLOJAR : to loosen, to slacken

soltería *nf* : bachelorhood, spinsterhood

soltero¹, -ra *adj* : single, unmarried

soltero², -ra *n* 1 : bachelor *m*, single man *m*, single woman *f* 2 **apellido de soltera** : maiden name

soltura *nf* 1 : looseness, slackness 2 : fluency (of language) 3 : agility, ease of movement

soluble *adj* : soluble — **solubilidad** *nf*

solución *nf*, *pl* **-ciones** 1 : solution (in a liquid) 2 : answer, solution

solucionar *vt* RESOLVER : to solve, to resolve — **solucionarse** *vr*

solvencia *nf* 1 : solvency 2 : settling, payment (of debts) 3 : reliability ⟨solvencia moral : trustworthiness⟩

solvente¹ *adj* 1 : solvent 2 : reliable, trustworthy

solvente² *nm* : solvent

somalí *adj* & *nmf* : Somalian

sombra *nf* 1 : shadow 2 : shade 3 **sombras** *nfpl* : darkness, shadows *pl* 4 **sin sombra de duda** : without a shadow of a doubt

sombreado, -da *adj* 1 : shady 2 : shaded, darkened

sombrear *vt* : to shade

sombrerero, -ra *n* : milliner, hatter

sombrero *nm* 1 : hat 2 **sin ~** : bareheaded 3 **sombrero hongo** : derby

sombrilla *nf* : parasol, umbrella

sombrío, -bría *adj* LÓBREGO : dark, somber, gloomy — **sombríamente** *adv*

someramente *adv* : cursorily, summarily

somero, -ra *adj* : superficial, cursory, shallow

someter *vt* 1 : to subjugate, to conquer 2 : to subordinate 3 : to subject (to treatment or testing) 4 : to submit, to present — **someterse** *vr* 1 : to submit, to yield 2 : to undergo

sometimiento *nm* 1 : submission, subjection 2 : presentation

somnífero¹, -ra *adj* : soporific

somnífero² *nm* : sleeping pill

somnolencia *nf* : drowsiness, sleepiness

somnoliento, -ta *adj* : drowsy, sleepy

somorgujo *or* **somormujo** *nm* : loon, grebe

somos → ser¹

son¹ → ser

son² *nm* 1 : sound ⟨al son de la trompeta : at the sound of the trumpet⟩ 2 : news, rumor 3 **en son de** : as, in the manner of, by way of ⟨en son de broma : as a joke⟩ ⟨en son de paz : in peace⟩

sonado, -da *adj* : celebrated, famous, much-discussed

sonaja *nf* : rattle

sonajero *nm* : rattle (toy)

sonámbulo, -la *n* : sleepwalker

sonar¹ {19} *vi* 1 : to sound ⟨suena bien : it sounds good⟩ 2 : to ring (bells) 3 : to look or sound familiar ⟨me suena ese nombre : that name rings a bell⟩ 4 **~ a** : to sound like — *vt* 1 : to ring 2 : to blow (a trumpet, a nose) — **sonarse** *vr* : to blow one's nose

sonar² *nm* : sonar

sonata *nf* : sonata

sonda *nf* 1 : sounding line 2 : probe 3 CATÉTER : catheter

sondar *vt* 1 : to sound, to probe (in medicine, drilling, etc.) 2 : to probe, to explore (outer space)

sondear *vt* 1 : to sound 2 : to probe 3 : to sound out, to test (opinions, markets)

sondeo *nm* **1** : sounding, probing **2** : drilling **3** ENCUESTA : survey, poll
soneto *nm* : sonnet
sónico, -ca *adj* : sonic
sonido *nm* : sound
sonoridad *nf* : sonority, resonance
sonoro, -ra *adj* **1** : resonant, sonorous, voiced (in linguistics) **2** : resounding, loud **3 banda sonora** : soundtrack
sonreír {66} *vi* : to smile
sonriente *adj* : smiling
sonrisa *nf* : smile
sonrojar *vt* : to cause to blush — **sonrojarse** *vr* : to blush
sonrojo *nm* RUBOR : blush
sonrosado, -da *adj* : rosy, pink
sonsacar {72} *vt* : to wheedle, to extract
sonsonete *nm* **1** : tapping **2** : drone **3** : mocking tone
soñador¹, -dora *adj* : dreamy
soñador², -dora *n* : dreamer
soñar {19} *v* **1** : to dream **2 ~ con** : to dream about **3 soñar despierto** : to daydream
soñoliento, -ta *adj* : sleepy, drowsy
sopa *nf* **1** : soup **2 estar hecho una sopa** : to be soaked to the bone
sopera *nf* : soup tureen
sopesar *vt* : to weigh, to evaluate
soplar *vi* : to blow — *vt* : to blow on, to blow out, to blow off
soplete *nm* : blowtorch
soplido *nm* : puff
soplo *nm* : puff, gust
soplón, -plona *n, mpl* **soplones** *fam* : tattletale, sneak
sopor *nm* SOMNOLENCIA : drowsiness, sleepiness
soporífero, -ra *adj* : soporific
soportable *adj* : bearable, tolerable
soportar *vt* **1** SOSTENER : to support, to hold up **2** RESISTIR : to withstand, to resist **3** AGUANTAR : to bear, to tolerate
soporte *nm* : base, stand, support
soprano *nmf* : soprano
sor *nf* : Sister (religious title)
sorber *vt* **1** : to sip, to suck in **2** : to absorb, to soak up
sorbete *nm* : sherbet
sorbo *nm* **1** : sip, gulp, swallow **2 beber a sorbos** : to sip
sordera *nf* : deafness
sordidez *nf, pl* **-deces** : sordidness, squalor
sórdido, -da *adj* : sordid, dirty, squalid
sordina *nf* : mute (for a musical instrument)
sordo, -da *adj* **1** : deaf **2** : muted, muffled
sordomudo, -da *n* : deaf-mute
sorgo *nm* : sorghum
soriasis *nfs & pl* : psoriasis
sorna *nf* : sarcasm, mocking tone
sorprendente *adj* : surprising — **sorprendentemente** *adv*
sorprender *vt* : to surprise — **sorprenderse** *vr*

sorpresa *nf* : surprise
sorpresivo, -va *adj* **1** : surprising, surprise **2** IMPREVISTO : sudden, unexpected
sortear *vt* **1** RIFAR : to raffle, to draw lots for **2** : to dodge, to avoid
sorteo *nm* : drawing, raffle
sortija *nf* **1** ANILLO : ring **2** : curl, ringlet
sortilegio *nm* **1** HECHIZO : spell, charm **2** HECHICERÍA : sorcery
SOS *nm* : SOS
sosegado, -da *adj* SERENO : calm, tranquil, serene
sosegar {49} *vt* : to calm, to pacify — **sosegarse** *vr*
sosiego *nm* : tranquillity, serenity, calm
soslayar *vt* ESQUIVAR : to dodge, to evade
soslayo *nm* **de ~** : obliquely, sideways ⟨mirar de soslayo : to look askance⟩
soso, -sa *adj* **1** INSÍPIDO : bland, flavorless **2** ABURRIDO : dull, boring
sospecha *nf* : suspicion
sospechar *vt* : to suspect — *vi* : to be suspicious
sospechosamente *adv* : suspiciously
sospechoso¹, -sa *adj* : suspicious, suspect
sospechoso², -sa *n* : suspect
sostén *nm, pl* **sostenes 1** APOYO : support **2** : sustenance **3** : brassiere, bra
sostener {80} *vt* **1** : to support, to hold up **2** : to hold ⟨sostenme la puerta : hold the door for me⟩ ⟨sostener una conversación : to hold a conversation⟩ **3** : to sustain, to maintain — **sostenerse** *vr* **1** : to stand, to hold oneself up **2** : to continue, to remain
sostenible *adj* : sustainable, tenable
sostenido¹, -da *adj* **1** : sustained, prolonged **2** : sharp (in music)
sostenido² *nm* : sharp (in music)
sostuvo, etc. → **sostener**
sotana *nf* : cassock
sótano *nm* : basement
sotavento *nm* : lee ⟨a sotavento : leeward⟩
soterrar {55} *vt* **1** : to bury **2** : to conceal, to hide away
soto *nm* : grove, copse
souvenir *nm, pl* **-nirs** RECUERDO : souvenir, memento
soviético, -ca *adj* : Soviet
soy → **ser**
soya *nf* : soy, soybean
spaghetti → **espagueti**
sport [ɛˈspor] *adj* : sport, casual
sprint [ɛˈsprin, -ˈsprint] *nm* : sprint — **sprinter** *nmf*
squash [ɛˈskwaʃ, -ˈskwatʃ] *nm* : squash (sport)
Sr. *nm* : Mr.
Sra. *nf* : Mrs., Ms.
Srta. *or* **Srita.** *nf* : Miss, Ms.
standard → **estándar**
stress → **estrés**
su *adj* **1** : his, her, its, their, one's ⟨su libro : her book⟩ ⟨sus consecuencias

: its consequences⟩ 2 (*formal*) : your ⟨tómese su medicina, señor : take your medicine, sir⟩

suave *adj* 1 BLANDO : soft 2 LISO : smooth 3 : gentle, mild 4 *Mex fam* : great, fantastic

suavemente *adv* : smoothly, gently, softly

suavidad *nf* : softness, smoothness, mellowness

suavizante *nm* : softener, fabric softener

suavizar {21} *vt* 1 : to soften, to smooth out 2 : to tone down — **suavizarse** *vr*

subacuático, -ca *adj* : underwater

subalterno¹, -na *adj* 1 SUBORDINADO : subordinate 2 SECUNDARIO : secondary

subalterno², -na *n* SUBORDINADO : subordinate

subarrendar {55} *vt* : to sublet

subasta *nf* : auction

subastador, -dora *n* : auctioneer

subastar *vt* : to auction, to auction off

subcampeón, -peona *n, mpl* **-peones** : runner-up

subcomité *nm* : subcommittee

subconsciente *adj & nm* : subconscious — **subconscientemente** *adv*

subcontratar *vt* : to subcontract

subcontratista *nmf* : subcontractor

subcultura *nf* : subculture

subdesarrollado, -da *adj* : underdeveloped

subdirector, -tora *n* : assistant manager

súbdito, -ta *n* : subject (of a monarch)

subdividir *vt* : to subdivide

subdivisión *nf, pl* **-siones** : subdivision

subestimar *vt* : to underestimate, to undervalue

subexponer {60} *vt* : to underexpose

subexposición *nf, pl* **-ciones** : underexposure

subgrupo *nm* : subgroup

subibaja *nm* : seesaw

subida *nf* 1 : ascent, climb 2 : rise, increase 3 : slope, hill ⟨ir de subida : to go uphill⟩

subido, -da *adj* 1 : intense, strong ⟨amarillo subido : bright yellow⟩ 2 **subido de tono** : risqué

subir *vt* 1 : to bring up, to take up 2 : to climb, to go up 3 : to raise — *vi* 1 : to go up, to come up 2 : to rise, to increase 3 : to be promoted 4 **~ a** : to get on, to mount ⟨subir a un tren : to get on a train⟩ — **subirse** *vr* 1 : to climb (up) 2 : to pull up (clothing) 3 **subirse a la cabeza** : to go to one's head

súbito, -ta *adj* 1 REPENTINO : sudden 2 **de ~** : all of a sudden, suddenly — **súbitamente** *adv*

subjetivo, -va *adj* : subjective — **subjetivamente** *adv* — **subjetividad** *nf*

subjuntivo¹, -va *adj* : subjunctive

subjuntivo² *nm* : subjunctive

sublevación *nf, pl* **-ciones** ALZAMIENTO : uprising, rebellion

sublevar *vt* : to incite to rebellion — **sublevarse** *vr* : to rebel, to rise up

sublimar *vt* : to sublimate — **sublimación** *nf*

sublime *adj* : sublime

submarinismo *nm* : scuba diving

submarinista *nmf* : scuba diver

submarino¹, -na *adj* : submarine, undersea

submarino² *nm* : submarine

suboficial *nmf* : noncommissioned officer, petty officer

subordinado, -da *adj & n* : subordinate

subordinar *vt* : to subordinate — **subordinarse** *vr* — **subordinación** *nf*

subproducto *nm* : by-product

subrayar *vt* 1 : to underline, to underscore 2 ENFATIZAR : to highlight, to emphasize

subrepticio, -cia *adj* : surreptitious — **subrepticiamente** *adv*

subsahariano, -na *adj* : sub-Saharan

subsanar *vt* 1 RECTIFICAR : to rectify, to correct 2 : to overlook, to excuse 3 : to make up for

subscribir → suscribir

subsecretario, -ria *n* : undersecretary

subsecuente *adj* : subsequent — **subsecuentemente** *adv*

subsidiar *vt* : to subsidize

subsidiaria *nf* : subsidiary

subsidio *nm* : subsidy

subsiguiente *adj* : subsequent

subsistencia *nf* 1 : subsistence 2 : sustenance

subsistir *vi* 1 : to subsist, to live 2 : to endure, to survive

substancia → sustancia

subteniente *nmf* : second lieutenant

subterfugio *nm* : subterfuge

subterráneo¹, -nea *adj* : underground, subterranean

subterráneo² *nm* 1 : underground passage, tunnel 2 *Arg, Uru* : subway

subtítulo *nm* : subtitle, subheading

subtotal *nm* : subtotal

suburbano, -na *adj* : suburban

suburbio *nm* 1 : suburb 2 : slum (outside a city)

subvención *nf, pl* **-ciones** : subsidy, grant

subvencionar *vt* : to subsidize

subversivo, -va *adj & n* : subversive — **subversión** *nf*

subvertir {76} *vt* : to subvert

subyacente *adj* : underlying

subyugar {52} *vt* : to subjugate — **subyugación** *nf*

succión *nf, pl* **succiones** : suction

succionar *vt* : to suck up, to draw in

sucedáneo *nm* : substitute ⟨sucedáneo de azucar : sugar substitute⟩

suceder *vi* 1 OCURRIR : to happen, to occur ⟨¿qué sucede? : what's going on?⟩ ⟨suceda lo que suceda : come what may⟩ 2 **~ a** : to follow, to succeed ⟨suceder al trono : to succeed to the throne⟩ ⟨a la primavera sucede el verano : summer follows spring⟩

sucesión *nf, pl* **-siones** **1** : succession **2** : sequence, series **3** : issue, heirs *pl*
sucesivamente *adv* : successively, consecutively ⟨y así sucesivamente : and so on⟩
sucesivo, -va *adj* : successive ⟨en los días sucesivos : in the days that followed⟩
suceso *nm* **1** : event, happening, occurrence **2** : incident, crime
sucesor, -sora *n* : successor
suciedad *nf* **1** : dirtiness, filthiness **2** MUGRE : dirt, filth
sucinto, -ta *adj* CONCISO : succinct, concise — **sucintamente** *adv*
sucio, -cia *adj* : dirty, filthy
sucre *nm* : Ecuadoran unit of currency
suculento, -ta *adj* : succulent
sucumbir *vi* : to succumb
sucursal *nf* : branch (of a business)
sudadera *nf* : sweatshirt
sudado, -da → **sudoroso**
sudafricano, -na *adj & n* : South African
sudamericano, -na *adj & n* : South American
sudanés, -nesa *adj & n, mpl* **-neses** : Sudanese
sudar *vi* TRANSPIRAR : to sweat, to perspire
sudario *nm* : shroud
sudeste → **sureste**
sudoeste → **suroeste**
sudor *nm* TRANSPIRACIÓN : sweat, perspiration
sudoroso, -sa *adj* : sweaty
sueco¹, -ca *adj* : Swedish
sueco², -ca *n* : Swede
sueco³ *nm* : Swedish (language)
suegro, -gra *n* **1** : father-in-law *m*, mother-in-law *f* **2 suegros** *nmpl* : in-laws
suela *nf* : sole (of a shoe)
suelda, etc. → **soldar**
sueldo *nm* : salary, wage
suele, etc. → **soler**
suelo *nm* **1** : ground ⟨caerse al suelo : to fall down, to hit the ground⟩ **2** : floor, flooring **3** TIERRA : soil, land
suelta, etc. → **soltar**
suelto¹, -ta *adj* : loose, free, unattached
suelto² *nm* : loose change
suena, etc. → **sonar**
sueña, etc. → **soñar**
sueño *nm* **1** : dream **2** : sleep ⟨perder el sueño : to lose sleep⟩ **3** : sleepiness ⟨tener sueño : to be sleepy⟩
suero *nm* **1** : serum **2** : whey
suerte *nf* **1** FORTUNA : luck, fortune ⟨tener suerte : to be lucky⟩ ⟨por suerte : luckily⟩ **2** DESTINO : fate, destiny, lot **3** CLASE, GÉNERO : sort, kind ⟨toda suerte de cosas : all kinds of things⟩
suertudo, -da *adj fam* : lucky
suéter *nm* : sweater
suficiencia *nf* **1** : adequacy, sufficiency **2** : competence, fitness **3** : smugness, self-satisfaction
suficiente *adj* **1** BASTANTE : enough, sufficient ⟨tener suficiente : to have

enough⟩ **2** : suitable, fit **3** : smug, complacent
suficientemente *adv* : sufficiently, enough
sufijo *nm* : suffix
suflé *nm* : soufflé
sufragar {52} *vt* **1** AYUDAR : to help out, to support **2** : to defray (costs) — *vi* : to vote
sufragio *nm* : suffrage, vote
sufrido, -da *adj* **1** : long-suffering, patient **2** : sturdy, serviceable (of clothing)
sufrimiento *nm* : suffering
sufrir *vt* **1** : to suffer ⟨sufrir una pérdida : to suffer a loss⟩ **2** : to tolerate, to put up with ⟨ella no lo puede sufrir : she can't stand him⟩ — *vi* : to suffer
sugerencia *nf* : suggestion
sugerir {76} *vt* **1** PROPONER, RECOMENDAR : to suggest, to recommend, to propose **2** : to suggest, to bring to mind
sugestión *nf, pl* **-tiones** : suggestion, prompting ⟨poder de sugestión : power of suggestion⟩
sugestionable *adj* : suggestible, impressionable
sugestionar *vt* : to influence, to sway — **sugestionarse** *vr* ~ **con** : to talk oneself into, to become convinced of
sugestivo, -va *adj* **1** : suggestive **2** : interesting, stimulating
suicida¹ *adj* : suicidal
suicida² *nmf* : suicide victim, suicide
suicidarse *vr* : to commit suicide
suicidio *nm* : suicide
suite *nf* : suite
suizo, -za *adj & n* : Swiss
sujeción *nf, pl* **-ciones** **1** : holding, fastening **2** : subjection
sujetador *nm* **1** : fastener **2** : holder ⟨sujetador de tazas : cup holder⟩
sujetalibros *nms & pl* : bookend
sujetapapeles *nms & pl* CLIP : paper clip
sujetar *vt* **1** : to hold on to, to steady, to hold down **2** FIJAR : to fasten, to attach **3** DOMINAR : to subdue, to conquer — **sujetarse** *vr* **1** : to hold on, to hang on **2** ~ **a** : to abide by
sujeto¹, -ta *adj* **1** : secure, fastened **2** ~ **a** : subject to
sujeto² *nm* **1** INDIVIDUO : individual, character **2** : subject (in grammar)
sulfúrico, -ca *adj* : sulfuric
sulfuro *nm* : sulfur
sultán *nm, pl* **sultanes** : sultan
suma *nf* **1** CANTIDAD : sum, quantity **2** : addition
sumamente *adv* : extremely, exceedingly
sumar *vt* **1** : to add, to add up **2** : to add up to, to total — *vi* : to add up — **sumarse** *vr* ~ **a** : to join
sumario¹, -ria *adj* SUCINTO : succinct, summary — **sumariamente** *adv*
sumario² *nm* : summary

sumergir {35} *vt* : to submerge, to immerse, to plunge — **sumergirse** *vr*

sumersión *nf, pl* **-siones** : submersion, immersion

sumidero *nm* : drain, sewer

suministrar *vt* : to supply, to provide

suministro *nm* : supply, provision

sumir *vt* SUMERGIR : to plunge, to immerse, to sink — **sumirse** *vr*

sumisión *nf, pl* **-siones 1** : submission **2** : submissiveness

sumiso, -sa *adj* : submissive, acquiescent, docile

sumo, -ma *adj* **1** : extreme, great, high ⟨la suma autoridad : the highest authority⟩ **2 a lo sumo** : at the most — **sumamente** *adv*

suntuoso, -sa *adj* : sumptuous, lavish — **suntuosamente** *adv*

supeditar *vt* SUBORDINAR : to subordinate — **supeditación** *nf*

super[1] *or* **súper** *adj fam* : super, great

super[2] *nm* SUPERMERCADO : market, supermarket

superable *adj* : surmountable

superabundancia *nf* : overabundance, superabundance — **superabundante** *adj*

superar *vt* **1** : to surpass, to exceed **2** : to overcome, to surmount — **superarse** *vr* : to improve oneself

superávit *nm, pl* **-vit** *or* **-vits** : surplus

superchería *nf* : trickery, fraud

supercomputadora *nf* : supercomputer

superestructura *nf* : superstructure

superficial *adj* : superficial — **superficialmente** *adv*

superficialidad *nf* : superficiality

superficie *nf* **1** : surface **2** : area ⟨la superficie de un triángulo : the area of a triangle⟩

superfluidad *nf* : superfluity

superfluo, -flua *adj* : superfluous

superintendente *nmf* : supervisor, superintendent

superior[1] *adj* **1** : superior **2** : upper ⟨nivel superior : upper level⟩ **3** : higher ⟨educación superior : higher education⟩ **4 ~ a** : above, higher than, in excess of

superior[2] *nm* : superior

superioridad *nf* : superiority

superlativo[1], **-va** *adj* : superlative

superlativo[2] *nm* : superlative

supermercado *nm* : supermarket

superpoblación *nf, pl* **-ciones** : overpopulation

superpoblado, -da *adj* : overpopulated

superponer {60} *vt* : to superimpose

superpotencia *nf* : superpower

superproducción → **sobreproducción**

supersónico, -ca *adj* : supersonic

superstición *nf, pl* **-ciones** : superstition

supersticioso, -sa *adj* : superstitious

supervisar *vt* : to supervise, to oversee

supervisión *nf, pl* **-siones** : supervision

supervisor, -sora *n* : supervisor, overseer

supervivencia *nf* : survival

superviviente *nmf* : survivor

supino, -na *adj* : supine

suplantar *vt* : to supplant, to replace

suplemental → **suplementario**

suplementario, -ria *adj* : supplementary, additional, extra

suplemento *nm* : supplement

suplencia *nf* : substitution, replacement

suplente *adj & nmf* : substitute ⟨equipo suplente : replacement team⟩

supletorio, -ria *adj* : extra, additional ⟨teléfono supletorio : extension phone⟩ ⟨cama supletoria : spare bed⟩

súplica *nf* : plea, entreaty

suplicar {72} *vt* IMPLORAR, ROGAR : to entreat, to implore, to supplicate

suplicio *nm* TORMENTO : ordeal, torture

suplir *vt* **1** COMPENSAR : to make up for, to compensate for **2** REEMPLAZAR : to replace, to substitute

supo, etc. → **saber**

suponer {60} *vt* **1** PRESUMIR : to suppose, to assume ⟨supongo que sí : I guess so, I suppose so⟩ ⟨se supone que van a llegar mañana : they're supposed to arrive tomorrow⟩ **2** : to imply, to suggest **3** : to involve, to entail ⟨el éxito supone mucho trabajo : success involves a lot of work⟩

suposición *nf, pl* **-ciones** PRESUNCIÓN : supposition, assumption

supositorio *nm* : suppository

supremacía *nf* : supremacy

supremo, -ma *adj* : supreme

supresión *nf, pl* **-siones 1** : suppression, elimination **2** : deletion

suprimir *vt* **1** : to suppress, to eliminate **2** : to delete

supuestamente *adv* : supposedly, allegedly

supuesto, -ta *adj* **1** : supposed, alleged **2 por ~** : of course, absolutely

supurar *vi* : to ooze, to discharge

supuso, etc. → **suponer**

sur[1] *adj* : southern, southerly, south

sur[2] *nm* **1** : south, South **2** : south wind

surafricano, -na → **sudafricano**

suramericano, -na → **sudamericano**

surcar {72} *vt* **1** : to plow (through) **2** : to groove, to score, to furrow

surco *nm* : groove, furrow, rut

sureño[1], **-ña** *adj* : southern, Southern

sureño[2], **-ña** *n* : Southerner

sureste[1] *adj* **1** : southeast, southeastern **2** : southeasterly

sureste[2] *nm* : southeast, Southeast

surf *nm* : surfing

surfear *vi* : to surf

surfing → **surf**

surfista *nmf* : surfer

surgimiento *nm* : rise, emergence

surgir {35} *vi* **1** : to rise, to arise, to emerge

suroeste[1] *adj* **1** : southwest, southwestern **2** : southwesterly

suroeste[2] *nm* : southwest, Southwest

surtido[1], **-da** *adj* **1** : assorted, varied **2** : stocked, provisioned

surtido² *nm* : assortment, selection
surtidor *nm* **1** : jet, spout **2** *Arg, Chile, Spain* : gas pump
surtir *vt* **1** : to supply, to provide ⟨surtir un pedido : to fill an order⟩ **2 surtir efecto** : to have an effect — *vi* : to spout, to spurt up — **surtirse** *vr* : to stock up
susceptible *adj* : susceptible, sensitive — **susceptibilidad** *nf*
suscitar *vt* : to provoke, to give rise to
suscribir {33} *vt* **1** : to sign (a formal document) **2** : to endorse, to sanction — **suscribirse** *vr* ~ **a** : to subscribe to
suscripción *nf, pl* **-ciones 1** : subscription **2** : endorsement, sanction **3** : signing
suscriptor, -tora *n* : subscriber
susodicho, -cha *adj* : aforementioned, aforesaid
suspender *vt* **1** COLGAR : to suspend, to hang **2** : to suspend, to discontinue **3** : to suspend, to dismiss
suspensión *nf, pl* **-siones** : suspension
suspenso *nm* : suspense
suspicacia *nf* : suspicion, mistrust
suspicaz *adj, pl* **-caces** DESCONFIADO : suspicious, wary
suspirar *vi* : to sigh
suspiro *nm* : sigh
surque, etc. → **surcar**
suscrito *pp* → **suscribir**
sustancia *nf* **1** : substance **2 sin** ~ : shallow, lacking substance
sustancial *adj* **1** : substantial **2** ESENCIAL, FUNDAMENTAL : essential, fundamental — **sustancialmente** *adv*
sustancioso, -sa *adj* **1** NUTRITIVO : hearty, nutritious **2** : substantial, solid
sustantivo *nm* : noun

sustentación *nf, pl* **-ciones** SOSTÉN : support
sustentar *vt* **1** : to support, to hold up **2** : to sustain, to nourish **3** : to maintain, to hold (an opinion) — **sustentarse** *vr* : to support oneself
sustento *nm* **1** : means of support, livelihood **2** : sustenance, food
sustitución *nf, pl* **-ciones** : replacement, substitution
sustituir {41} *vt* **1** : to replace, to substitute for **2** : to stand in for
sustituto, -ta *n* : substitute, stand-in
susto *nm* : fright, scare
sustracción *nf, pl* **-ciones 1** RESTA : subtraction **2** : theft
sustraer {81} *vt* **1** : to remove, to take away **2** RESTAR : to subtract **3** : to steal — **sustraerse** *vr* ~ **a** : to avoid, to evade
susurrar *vi* **1** : to whisper **2** : to murmur **3** : to rustle (leaves, etc.) — *vt* : to whisper
susurro *nm* **1** : whisper **2** : murmur **3** : rustle, rustling
sutil *adj* **1** : delicate, thin, fine **2** : subtle
sutileza *nf* **1** : delicacy **2** : subtlety
sutura *nf* : suture
suturar *vt* : to suture
suyo¹, -ya *adj* **1** : his, her, its, theirs ⟨los libros suyos : his books⟩ ⟨un amigo suyo : a friend of hers⟩ ⟨esta casa es suya : this house is theirs⟩ **2** (*formal*) : yours ⟨¿este abrigo es suyo, señor? : is this your coat, sir?⟩
suyo², -ya *pron* **1** : his, hers, theirs ⟨mi guitarra y la suya : my guitar and hers⟩ ⟨ellos trajeron las suyas : they brought theirs, they brought their own⟩ **2** (*formal*) : yours ⟨usted olvidó la suya : you forgot yours⟩
switch *nm* : switch

T

t *nf* : twenty-first letter of the Spanish alphabet
taba *nf* : anklebone
tabacalero¹, -ra *adj* : tobacco ⟨industria tabacalera : tobacco industry⟩
tabacalero², -ra *n* : tobacco grower
tabaco *nm* : tobacco
tábano *nm* : horsefly
taberna *nf* : tavern, bar
tabernáculo *nm* : tabernacle
tabicar {72} *vt* : to wall up
tabique *nm* : thin wall, partition
tabla *nf* **1** : table, list ⟨tabla de multiplicar : multiplication table⟩ **2** : board, plank, slab ⟨tabla de planchar : ironing board⟩ **3** : plot, strip (of land) **4 tablas** *nfpl* : stage, boards *pl*
tablado *nm* **1** : floor **2** : platform, scaffold **3** : stage
tablero *nm* **1** : bulletin board **2** : board (in games) ⟨tablero de ajedrez : chess-

board⟩ ⟨tablero de damas : checkerboard⟩ **3** PIZARRA : blackboard **4** : switchboard **5 tablero de instrumentos** : dashboard, instrument panel
tableta *nf* **1** COMPRIMIDO, PÍLDORA : tablet, pill **2** : bar (of chocolate)
tabletear *vi* : to rattle, to clack
tableteo *nm* : clack, rattling
tablilla *nf* **1** : small board or tablet **2** : bulletin board **3** : splint
tabloide *nm* : tabloid
tablón *nm, pl* **tablones 1** : plank, beam **2 tablón de anuncios** : bulletin board
tabú¹ *adj* : taboo
tabú² *nm, pl* **tabúes** *or* **tabús** : taboo
tabulador *nm* : tabulator
tabular¹ *vt* : to tabulate
tabular² *adj* : tabular
taburete *nm* : footstool, stool
tacañería *nf* : miserliness, stinginess

tacaño¹, -ña *adj* MEZQUINO : stingy, miserly

tacaño², -ña *n* : miser, tightwad

tacha *nf* 1 : flaw, blemish, defect 2 **poner tacha a** : to find fault with 3 **sin ~** : flawless

tachadura *nf* : erasure, correction

tachar *vt* 1 : to cross out, to delete 2 **~ de** : to accuse of, to label as ⟨lo tacharon de mentiroso : they accused him of being a liar⟩

tachón *nm, pl* **tachones** : stud, hobnail

tachonar *vt* : to stud

tachuela *nf* : tack, hobnail, stud

tácito, -ta *adj* : tacit, implicit — **tácitamente** *adv*

taciturno, -na *adj* 1 : taciturn 2 : sullen, gloomy

tacle *nm* : tackle

taclear *vt* : to tackle (in football)

taco *nm* 1 : wad, stopper, plug 2 : pad (of paper) 3 : cleat 4 : heel (of a shoe) 5 : cue (in billiards) 6 : light snack, bite 7 : taco

tacón *nm, pl* **tacones** : heel (of a shoe) ⟨de tacón alto : high-heeled⟩

táctica *nf* : tactic, tactics *pl*

táctico¹, -ca *adj* : tactical

táctico², -ca *n* : tactician

táctil *adj* : tactile

tacto *nm* 1 : touch, touching, feel 2 DELICADEZA : tact

tafetán *nm, pl* **-tanes** : taffeta

tahúr *nm, pl* **tahúres** : gambler

tailandés¹, -desa *adj & n, pl* **-deses** : Thai

tailandés² *nm* : Thai (language)

taimado, -da *adj* 1 : crafty, sly 2 *Chile* : sullen, sulky

tajada *nf* 1 : slice 2 **sacar tajada** *fam* : to get one's share

tajante *adj* 1 : cutting, sharp 2 : decisive, categorical

tajantemente *adj* : emphatically, categorically

tajar *vt* : to cut, to slice

tajo *nm* 1 : cut, slash, gash 2 ESCARPA : steep cliff

tal¹ *adv* 1 : so, in such a way 2 **tal como** : just as ⟨tal como lo hice : just the way I did it⟩ 3 **con tal que** : provided that, as long as 4 **¿qué tal?** : how are you?, how's it going?

tal² *adj* 1 : such, such a 2 **tal vez** : maybe, perhaps

tal³ *pron* 1 : such a one, someone 2 : such a thing, something 3 **tal para cual** : two of a kind

tala *nf* : felling (of trees)

taladrar *vt* : to drill

taladro *nm* : drill, auger ⟨taladro eléctrico : power drill⟩

talante *nm* 1 HUMOR : mood, disposition 2 VOLUNTAD : will, willingness

talar *vt* 1 : to cut down, to fell 2 DEVASTAR : to devastate, to destroy

talco *nm* 1 : talc 2 : talcum powder

talego *nm* : sack

talento *nm* : talent, ability

talentoso, -sa *adj* : talented, gifted

talismán *nm, pl* **-manes** AMULETO : talisman, charm

talla *nf* 1 ESTATURA : height 2 : size (in clothing) 3 : stature, status 4 : sculpture, carving

tallar *vt* 1 : to sculpt, to carve 2 : to measure (someone's height) 3 : to deal (cards)

tallarín *nf, pl* **-rines** : noodle

talle *nm* 1 : size 2 : waist, waistline 3 : figure, shape

taller *nm* 1 : shop, workshop 2 : studio (of an artist)

tallo *nm* : stalk, stem ⟨tallo de maíz : cornstalk⟩

talón *nm, pl* **talones** 1 : heel (of the foot) 2 : stub (of a check) 3 **talón de Aquiles** : Achilles' heel

talud *nm* : slope, incline

tamal *nm* : tamale

tamaño¹, -ña *adj* : such a big ⟨¿crees tamaña mentira? : do you believe such a lie?⟩

tamaño² *nm* 1 : size 2 **de tamaño natural** : life-size

tamarindo *nm* : tamarind

tambalearse *vr* 1 : to teeter 2 : to totter, to stagger, to sway — **tambaleante** *adj*

tambaleo *nm* : staggering, lurching, swaying

también *adv* : too, as well, also

tambor *nm* : drum

tamborilear *vi* : to drum, to tap

tamborileo *nm* : tapping, drumming

tamiz *nm* : sieve

tamizar {21} *vt* : to sift

tampoco *adv* : neither, not either ⟨ni yo tampoco : me neither⟩

tampón *nm, pl* **tampones** 1 : ink pad 2 : tampon

tam–tam *nm* : tom-tom

tan *adv* 1 : so, so very ⟨no es tan difícil : it is not that difficult⟩ 2 : as ⟨tan pronto como : as soon as⟩ 3 **tan siquiera** : at least, at the least 4 **tan sólo** : only, merely

tanda *nf* 1 : turn, shift 2 : batch, lot, series

tándem *nm* 1 : tandem (bicycle) 2 : duo, pair

tangente *adj & nf* : tangent — **tangencial** *adj*

tangible *adj* : tangible

tango *nm* : tango

tanino *nm* : tannin

tanque *nm* 1 : tank, reservoir 2 : tanker, tank (vehicle)

tanteador *nm* MARCADOR : scoreboard

tantear *vt* 1 : to feel, to grope 2 : to size up, to weigh — *vi* 1 : to keep score 2 : to feel one's way

tanteo *nm* 1 : estimate, rough calculation 2 : testing, sizing up 3 : scoring

tanto¹ *adv* 1 : so much ⟨tanto mejor : so much the better⟩ 2 : so long ⟨¿por qué te tardaste tanto? : why did you take so long?⟩

tanto², -ta *adj* **1** : so much, so many, such ⟨no hagas tantas preguntas : don't ask so many questions⟩ ⟨tiene tanto encanto : he has such charm, he's so charming⟩ **2** : as much, as many ⟨come tantos dulces como yo : she eats as many sweets as I do⟩ **3** : odd, however many ⟨cuarenta y tantos años : forty-odd years⟩

tanto³ *nm* **1** : certain amount **2** : goal, point (in sports) **3 al tanto** : abreast, in the picture **4 un tanto** : somewhat, rather ⟨un tanto cansado : rather tired⟩

tanto⁴, -ta *pron* **1** : so much, so many ⟨tiene tanto que hacer : she has so much to do⟩ ⟨¡no me des tantos! : don't give me so many!⟩ **2 entre ~** : meanwhile **3 por lo tanto** : therefore

tañer {79} *vt* **1** : to ring (a bell) **2** : to play (a musical instrument)

tañido *nm* **1** CAMPANADA : ring, peal, toll **2** : sound (of an instrument)

tapa *nf* **1** : cover, top, lid **2** *Spain* : bar snack

tapacubos *nms & pl* : hubcap

tapadera *nf* **1** : cover, lid **2** : front, cover (for an organization or person)

tapar *vt* **1** CUBRIR : to cover, to cover up **2** OBSTRUIR : to block, to obstruct — **taparse** *vr*

tapete *nm* **1** : small rug, mat **2** : table cover **3 poner sobre el tapete** : to bring up for discussion

tapia *nf* : (adobe) wall, garden wall

tapiar *vt* **1** : to wall in **2** : to enclose, to block off

tapicería *nf* **1** : upholstery **2** TAPIZ : tapestry

tapicero, -ra *n* : upholsterer

tapioca *nf* : tapioca

tapir *nm* : tapir

tapiz *nm, pl* **tapices** : tapestry

tapizar {21} *vt* **1** : to upholster **2** : to cover, to carpet

tapón *nm, pl* **tapones** **1** : cork **2** : bottle cap **3** : plug, stopper

tapujo *nm* **1** : deceit, pretension **2 sin tapujos** : openly, frankly

taquigrafía *nf* : stenography, shorthand

taquigráfico, -ca *adj* : stenographic

taquígrafo, -fa *n* : stenographer

taquilla *nf* **1** : box office, ticket office **2** : earnings *pl*, take

taquillero, -ra *adj* : box-office, popular ⟨un éxito taquillero : a box-office success⟩

tarántula *nf* : tarantula

tararear *vt* : to hum

tardanza *nf* : lateness, delay

tardar *vi* **1** : to delay, to take a long time **2** : to be late **3 a más tardar** : at the latest — *vt* DEMORAR : to take (time) ⟨tarda una hora : it takes an hour⟩

tarde¹ *adv* **1** : late **2 tarde o temprano** : sooner or later

tarde² *nf* **1** : afternoon, evening **2 ¡buenas tardes!** : good afternoon!, good evening! **3 en la tarde** *or* **por la tarde** : in the afternoon, in the evening

tardío, -día *adj* : late, tardy

tardo, -da *adj* : slow

tarea *nf* **1** : task, job **2** : homework

tarifa *nf* **1** : rate ⟨tarifas postales : postal rates⟩ **2** : fare (for transportation) **3** : price list **4** ARANCEL : duty

tarima *nf* PLATAFORMA : dais, platform, stage

tarjeta *nf* : card ⟨tarjeta de crédito : credit card⟩ ⟨tarjeta postal : postcard⟩

tarro *nm* **1** : jar, pot **2** *Arg, Chile* : can, tin

tarta *nf* **1** : tart **2** : cake

tartaleta *nf* : tart

tartamudear *vi* : to stammer, to stutter

tartamudeo *nm* : stutter, stammer

tartán *nm, pl* **tartanes** : tartan, plaid

tártaro *nm* : tartar

tasa *nf* **1** : rate ⟨tasa de desempleo : unemployment rate⟩ **2** : tax, fee **3** : appraisal, valuation

tasación *nf, pl* **-ciones** : appraisal, assessment

tasador, -dora *n* : assessor, appraiser

tasar *vt* **1** VALORAR : to appraise, to value **2** : to set the price of **3** : to ration, to limit

tasca *nf* : cheap bar, dive

tatuaje *nm* : tattoo, tattooing

tatuar {3} *vt* : to tattoo

taurino, -na *adj* : bull, bullfighting

Tauro *nm* : Taurus

tauromaquia *nf* : (art of) bullfighting

taxi *nm, pl* **taxis** : taxi, taxicab

taxidermia *nf* : taxidermy

taxidermista *nmf* : taxidermist

taxímetro *nm* : taximeter

taxista *nmf* : taxi driver

taza *nf* **1** : cup **2** : cupful **3** : (toilet) bowl **4** : basin (of a fountain)

tazón *nm, pl* **tazones** **1** : bowl **2** : large cup, mug

te *pron* **1** : you ⟨te quiero : I love you⟩ **2** : for you, to you, from you ⟨me gustaría dártelo : I would like to give it to you⟩ **3** : yourself, for yourself, to yourself, from yourself ⟨¡cálmate! : calm yourself!⟩ ⟨¿te guardaste uno? : did you keep one for yourself?⟩ **4** : thee

té *nm* **1** : tea **2** : tea party

tea *nf* : torch

teatral *adj* : theatrical — **teatralmente** *adv*

teatro *nm* **1** : theater **2 hacer teatro** : to put on an act, to exaggerate

teca *nf* : teak

techado *nm* **1** : roof **2 bajo techado** : under cover, indoors

techar *vt* : to roof, to shingle

techo *nm* **1** TEJADO : roof **2** : ceiling **3** : upper limit, ceiling

techumbre *nf* : roofing

tecla *nf* **1** : key (of a musical instrument or a machine) **2 dar en la tecla** : to hit the nail on the head

teclado *nm* : keyboard
teclear *vt* : to type in, to enter
técnica *nf* **1** : technique, skill **2** : technology
técnico¹, -ca *adj* : technical — **técnicamente** *adv*
técnico², -ca *n* : technician, expert, engineer
tecnología *nf* : technology
tecnológico, -ca *adj* : technological — **tecnológicamente** *adv*
tecolote *nm Mex* : owl
tedio *nm* : tedium, boredom
tedioso, -sa *adj* : tedious, boring — **tediosamente** *adv*
teja *nf* : tile
tejado *nm* TECHO : roof
tejedor, -dora *n* : weaver
tejer *vt* **1** : to knit, to crochet **2** : to weave **3** FABRICAR : to concoct, to make up, to fabricate
tejido *nm* **1** TELA : fabric, cloth **2** : weave, texture **3** : tissue ⟨tejido muscular : muscle tissue⟩
tejo *nm* **1** : yew **2** : hopscotch (children's game)
tejón *nm, pl* **tejones** : badger
tela *nf* **1** : fabric, cloth, material **2 tela de araña** : spiderweb **3 poner en tela de juicio** : to call into question, to doubt
telar *nm* : loom
telaraña *nf* : spiderweb, cobweb
tele *nf fam* : TV, television
telecomunicación *nf, pl* **-ciones** : telecommunication
teleconferencia *nf* : teleconference
teledifusión *nf, pl* **-siones** : television broadcasting
teledirigido, -da *adj* : remote-controlled
telefonear *v* : to telephone, to call
telefónico, -ca *adj* : phone, telephone ⟨llamada telefónica : phone call⟩
telefonista *nmf* : telephone operator
teléfono *nm* **1** : telephone **2 llamar por teléfono** : to telephone, to make a phone call
telegrafiar {85} *v* : to telegraph
telegráfico, -ca *adj* : telegraphic
telégrafo *nm* : telegraph
telegrama *nm* : telegram
telenovela *nf* : soap opera
telepatía *nf* : telepathy
telepático, -ca *adj* : telepathic — **telepáticamente** *adv*
telescópico, -ca *adj* : telescopic
telescopio *nm* : telescope
telespectador, -dora *n* : television viewer
telesquí *nm, pl* **-squís** : ski lift
televidente *nmf* : television viewer
televisar *vt* : to televise
televisión *nf, pl* **-siones** : television, TV
televisivo, -va *adj* : television ⟨serie televisiva : television series⟩
televisor *nm* : television set
telón *nm, pl* **telones** **1** : curtain (in theater) **2 telón de fondo** : backdrop, background

tema *nm* **1** ASUNTO : theme, topic, subject **2** MOTIVO : motif, central theme
temario *nm* **1** : set of topics (for study) **2** : agenda
temática *nf* : subject matter
temático, -ca *adj* : thematic
temblar {55} *vi* **1** : to tremble, to shake, to shiver ⟨le temblaban las rodillas : his knees were shaking⟩ **2** : to shudder, to be afraid ⟨tiemblo con sólo pensarlo : I shudder to think of it⟩
temblor *nm* **1** : shaking, trembling **2** : tremor, earthquake
tembloroso, -sa *adj* : tremulous, trembling, shaking ⟨con la voz temblorosa : with a shaky voice⟩
temer *vt* : to fear, to dread — *vi* : to be afraid
temerario, -ria *adj* : reckless, rash — **temerariamente** *adv*
temeridad *nf* **1** : temerity, recklessness, rashness **2** : rash act
temeroso, -sa *adj* MIEDOSO : fearful, frightened
temible *adj* : fearsome, dreadful
temor *nm* MIEDO : fear, dread
témpano *nm* : ice floe
temperamento *nm* : temperament — **temperamental** *adj*
temperancia *nf* : temperance
temperar *vt* MODERAR : to temper, to moderate — *vi* : to have a change of air
temperatura *nf* : temperature
tempestad *nf* **1** : storm, tempest **2 tempestad de arena** : sandstorm
tempestuoso, -sa *adj* : tempestuous, stormy
templado, -da *adj* **1** : temperate, mild **2** : moderate, restrained **3** : warm, lukewarm **4** VALIENTE : courageous, bold
templanza *nf* **1** : temperance, moderation **2** : mildness (of weather)
templar *vt* **1** : to temper (steel) **2** : to restrain, to moderate **3** : to tune (a musical instrument) **4** : to warm up, to cool down — **templarse** *vr* **1** : to be moderate **2** : to warm up, to cool down
temple *nm* **1** : temper (of steel, etc.) **2** HUMOR : mood ⟨de buen temple : in a good mood⟩ **3** : tuning **4** VALOR : courage
templo *nm* **1** : temple **2** : church, chapel
tempo *nm* : tempo (in music)
temporada *nf* **1** : season, time ⟨temporada de béisbol : baseball season⟩ **2** : period, spell ⟨por temporadas : on and off⟩
temporal¹ *adj* **1** : temporal **2** : temporary
temporal² *nm* **1** : storm **2 capear el temporal** : to weather the storm
temporalmente *adv* : temporarily
temporario, -ria *adj* : temporary — **temporariamente** *adv*
temporero¹, -ra *adj* : temporary, seasonal

temporero², -ra *n* : temporary or seasonal worker
temporizador *nm* : timer
tempranero, -ra *adj* **1** : early **2** : early-rising
temprano¹ *adv* : early ⟨lo más temprano posible : as soon as possible⟩
temprano², -na *adj* : early ⟨la parte temprana del siglo : the early part of the century⟩
ten → **tener**
tenacidad *nf* : tenacity, perseverance
tenaz *adj, pl* **tenaces 1** : tenacious, persistent **2** : strong, tough
tenaza *nf, or* **tenazas** *nfpl* **1** : pliers, pincers **2** : tongs **3** : claw (of a crustacean)
tenazmente *adv* : tenaciously
tendedero *nm* : clothesline
tendencia *nf* **1** PROPENSIÓN : tendency, inclination **2** : trend
tendencioso, -sa *adj* : tendentious, biased
tendente → **tendiente**
tender {56} *vt* **1** EXTENDER : to spread out, to lay out **2** : to hang out (clothes) **3** : to lay (cables, etc.) **4** : to set (a trap) — *vi* ∼ **a** : to tend to, to have a tendency towards — **tenderse** *vr* : to stretch out, to lie down
tendero, -ra *n* : shopkeeper, storekeeper
tendido *nm* **1** : laying (of cables, etc.) **2** : seats *pl*, section (at a bullfight)
tendiente *adj* ∼ **a** : aimed at, designed to
tendón *nm, pl* **tendones** : tendon
tenebrosidad *nf* : darkness, gloom
tendrá, etc. → **tener**
tenebroso, -sa *adj* **1** OSCURO : gloomy, dark **2** SINIESTRO : sinister
tenedor¹, -dora *n* **1** : holder **2 tenedor de libros, tenedora de libros** : bookkeeper
tenedor² *nm* : table fork
tenencia *nf* **1** : possession, holding **2** : tenancy **3** : tenure
tener {80} *vt* **1** : to have ⟨tiene ojos verdes : she has green eyes⟩ ⟨tengo mucho que hacer : I have a lot to do⟩ ⟨tiene veinte años : he's twenty years old⟩ ⟨tiene un metro de largo : it's one meter long⟩ **2** : to hold ⟨ten esto un momento : hold this for a moment⟩ **3** : to feel, to make ⟨tengo frío : I'm cold⟩ ⟨eso nos tiene contentos : that makes us happy⟩ **4** ∼ **por** : to think, to consider ⟨me tienes por loco : you think I'm crazy⟩ — *v aux* **1 tener que** : to have to ⟨tengo que salir : I have to leave⟩ ⟨tiene que estar aquí : it has to be here, it must be here⟩ **2** (*with past participle*) ⟨tenía pensado escribirte : I've been thinking of writing to you⟩ — **tenerse** *vr* **1** : to stand up **2** ∼ **por** : to consider oneself ⟨me tengo por afortunado : I consider myself lucky⟩
tenería *nf* CURTIDURÍA : tannery
tenga, etc. → **tener**
tenia *nf* SOLITARIA : tapeworm

teniente *nmf* **1** : lieutenant **2 teniente coronel** : lieutenant colonel
tenis *nms & pl* **1** : tennis **2 tenis** *nmpl* : sneakers *pl*
tenista *nmf* : tennis player
tenor *nm* **1** : tenor **2** : tone, sense
tensar *vt* **1** : to tense, to make taut **2** : to draw (a bow) — **tensarse** *vr* : to become tense
tensión *nf, pl* **tensiones 1** : tension, tautness **2** : stress, strain **3 tensión arterial** : blood pressure
tenso, -sa *adj* : tense
tentación *nf, pl* **-ciones** : temptation
tentáculo *nm* : tentacle, feeler
tentador¹, -dora *adj* : tempting
tentador², -dora *n* : tempter, temptress *f*
tentar {55} *vt* **1** TOCAR : to feel, to touch **2** PROBAR : to test, to try **3** ATRAER : to tempt, to entice
tentativa *nf* : attempt, try
tentempié *nm fam* : snack, bite
tenue *adj* **1** : tenuous **2** : faint, weak, dim **3** : light, fine **4** : thin, slender
teñir {67} *vt* **1** : to dye **2** : to stain
teodolito *nm* : theodolite, transit (for surveying)
teología *nf* : theology
teológico, -ca *adj* : theological
teólogo, -ga *n* : theologian
teorema *nm* : theorem
teoría *nf* : theory
teórico¹, -ca *adj* : theoretical — **teóricamente** *adv*
teórico², -ca *n* : theorist
teorizar {21} *vi* : to theorize
tepe *nm* : sod, turf
teponaztle *nm Mex* : traditional drum
tequila *nm* : tequila
terapeuta *nmf* : therapist
terapéutica *nf* : therapeutics
terapéutico, -ca *adj* : therapeutic
terapia *nf* **1** : therapy **2 terapia intensiva** : intensive care
tercer → **tercero**
tercermundista *adj* : third-world
tercero¹, -ra *adj* (**tercer** *before masculine singular nouns*) **1** : third **2 el Tercer Mundo** : the Third World
tercero², -ra *n* : third (in a series)
terceto *nm* **1** : tercet, triplet (in literature) **2** : trio (in music)
terciar *vt* **1** : to place diagonally **2** : to divide into three parts — *vi* **1** : to mediate **2** ∼ **en** : to take part in
terciario, -ria *adj* : tertiary
tercio¹, -cia → **tercero**
tercio² *nm* : third ⟨dos tercios : two thirds⟩
terciopelo *nm* : velvet
terco, -ca *adj* OBSTINADO : obstinate, stubborn
tergiversación *nf, pl* **-ciones** : distortion
tergiversar *vt* : to distort, to twist
termal *adj* : thermal, hot
termas *nfpl* : hot springs
térmico, -ca *adj* : thermal, heat ⟨energía térmica : thermal energy⟩

terminación *nf, pl* **-ciones** : termination, conclusion

terminal[1] *adj* : terminal — **terminalmente** *adv*

terminal[2] *nm* (*in some regions f*) : (electric or electronic) terminal

terminal[3] *nf* (*in some regions m*) : terminal, station

terminante *adj* : final, definitive, categorical — **terminantemente** *adv*

terminar *vt* **1** CONCLUIR : to end, to conclude **2** ACABAR : to complete, to finish off — *vi* **1** : to finish **2** : to stop, to end — **terminarse** *vr* **1** : to run out **2** : to come to an end

término *nm* **1** CONCLUSIÓN : end, conclusion **2** : term, expression **3** : period, term of office **4 término medio** : happy medium **5 términos** *nmpl* : terms, specifications ⟨los términos del acuerdo : the terms of the agreement⟩

terminología *nf* : terminology

termita *nf* : termite

termo *nm* : thermos

termodinámica *nf* : thermodynamics

termómetro *nm* : thermometer

termostato *nm* : thermostat

ternera *nf* : veal

ternero, -ra *n* : calf

terno *nm* **1** : set of three **2** : three-piece suit

ternura *nf* : tenderness

terquedad *nf* OBSTINACIÓN : obstinacy, stubbornness

terracota *nf* : terra-cotta

terraplén *nm, pl* **-plenes** : terrace, embankment

terráqueo, -quea *adj* **1** : earth **2 globo terráqueo** : the earth, globe (of the earth)

terrateniente *nmf* : landowner

terraza *nf* **1** : terrace, veranda **2** : balcony (in a theater) **3** : terrace (in agriculture)

terremoto *nm* : earthquake

terrenal *adj* : worldly, earthly

terreno *nm* **1** : terrain **2** SUELO : earth, ground **3** : plot, tract of land **4 perder terreno** : to lose ground **5 preparar el terreno** : to pave the way

terrestre *adj* : terrestrial

terrible *adj* : terrible, horrible — **terriblemente** *adv*

terrier *nmf* : terrier

territorial *adj* : territorial

territorio *nm* : territory

terrón *nm, pl* **terrones 1** : clod (of earth) **2 terrón de azúcar** : lump of sugar

terror *nm* : terror

terrorífico, -ca *adj* : horrific, terrifying

terrorismo *nm* : terrorism

terrorista *adj & nmf* : terrorist

terroso, -sa *adj* : earthy ⟨colores terrosos : earthy colors⟩

terruño *nm* : native land, homeland

terso, -sa *adj* **1** : smooth **2** : glossy, shiny **3** : polished, flowing (of a style)

tersura *nf* **1** : smoothness **2** : shine

tertulia *nf* : gathering, group ⟨tertulia literaria : literary circle⟩

tesauro *nm* : thesaurus

tesis *nfs & pl* : thesis

tesón *nm* : persistence, tenacity

tesonero, -ra *adj* : persistent, tenacious

tesorería *nf* : treasurer's office

tesorero, -ra *n* : treasurer

tesoro *nm* **1** : treasure **2** : thesaurus

test *nm* : test

testaferro *nm* : figurehead

testamentario[1], **-ria** *adj* : testamentary

testamentario[2], **-ria** *n* ALBACEA : executor, executrix *f*

testamento *nm* : testament, will

testar *vi* : to draw up a will

testarudo, -da *adj* : stubborn, pigheaded

testículo *nm* : testicle

testificar {72} *v* : to testify

testigo *nmf* : witness

testimonial *adj* **1** : testimonial **2** : token

testimoniar *vi* : to testify

testimonio *nm* : testimony, statement

teta *nf* : teat

tétano *or* **tétanos** *nm* : tetanus, lockjaw

tetera *nf* **1** : teapot **2** : teakettle

tetilla *nf* **1** : teat **2** : nipple

tetina *nf* : nipple (on a bottle)

tétrico, -ca *adj* : somber, gloomy

textil *adj & nm* : textile

texto *nm* : text

textual *adj* : literal, exact — **textualmente** *adv*

textura *nf* : texture

tez *nf, pl* **teces** : complexion, coloring

ti *pron* **1** : you ⟨es para ti : it's for you⟩ **2 ti mismo, ti misma** : yourself **3** : thee

tía → **tío**

tiamina *nf* : thiamine

tianguis *nm Mex* : open-air market

tibetano[1], **-na** *adj & n* : Tibetan

tibetano[2] *nm* : Tibetan (language)

tibia *nf* : tibia

tibieza *nf* **1** : tepidness **2** : halfheartedness

tibio, -bia *adj* **1** : lukewarm, tepid **2** : cool, unenthusiastic

tiburón *nm, pl* **-rones 1** : shark **2** : raider (in finance)

tic *nm* **1** : click, tick **2 tic nervioso** : tic

tico, -ca *adj & n fam* : Costa Rican

tictac *nm* **1** : ticking, tick-tock **2 hacer tictac** : to tick

tiembla, etc. → **temblar**

tiempo *nm* **1** : time ⟨justo a tiempo : just in time⟩ ⟨perder tiempo : to waste time⟩ ⟨tiempo libre : spare time⟩ **2** : period, age ⟨en los tiempos que corren : nowadays⟩ **3** : season, moment ⟨antes de tiempo : prematurely⟩ **4** : weather ⟨hace buen tiempo : the weather is fine, it's nice outside⟩ **5** : tempo (in music) **6** : half (in sports) **7** : tense (in grammar)

tienda *nf* **1** : store, shop **2** *or* **tienda de campaña** : tent

tiende, etc. → **tender**

tiene, etc. → **tener**
tienta¹, etc. → **tentar**
tienta² *nf* **andar a tientas** : to feel one's way, to grope around
tiernamente *adv* : tenderly
tierno, -na *adj* **1** : affectionate, tender **2** : tender, young
tierra *nf* **1** : land **2** SUELO : ground, earth **3** : country, homeland, soil **4** **tierra natal** : native land **5 tierras altas** : highlands **6 la Tierra** : the Earth
tieso, -sa *adj* **1** : stiff, rigid **2** : upright, erect
tiesto *nm* **1** : potsherd **2** MACETA : flowerpot
tiesura *nf* : stiffness, rigidity
tifoidea *nf* : typhoid
tifoideo, -dea *adj* : typhoid ⟨fiebre tifoidea : typhoid fever⟩
tifón *nm, pl* **tifones** : typhoon
tifus *nm* : typhus
tigre, -gresa *n* **1** : tiger, tigress *f* **2** : jaguar
tijera *nf* **1** *or* **tijeras** *nfpl* : scissors **2 de** ∼ : folding ⟨escalera de tijera : stepladder⟩
tijereta *nf* : earwig
tijeretada *nf or* **tijeretazo** *nm* : cut, snip
tildar *vt* ∼ **de** : to brand as, to call ⟨lo tildaron de traidor : they branded him as a traitor⟩
tilde *nf* **1** : accent mark **2** : tilde (accent over *ñ*)
tilo *nm* : linden (tree)
timador, -dora *n* : swindler
timar *vt* : to swindle, to cheat
timbal *nm* **1** : kettledrum **2 timbales** *nmpl* : timpani
timbre *nm* **1** : bell ⟨tocar el timbre : to ring the doorbell⟩ **2** : tone, timbre **3** SELLO : seal, stamp **4** *CA, Mex* : postage stamp
timidez *nf* : timidity, shyness
tímido, -da *adj* : timid, shy — **tímidamente** *adv*
timo *nm fam* : swindle, trick, hoax
timón *nm, pl* **timones** : rudder ⟨estar al timón : to beat the helm⟩
timonel *nm* : helmsman, coxswain
timorato, -ta *adj* **1** : timorous **2** : sanctimonious
tímpano *nm* **1** : eardrum **2 tímpanos** *nmpl* : timpani, kettledrums
tina *nf* **1** BAÑERA : tub, bathtub **2** : vat
tinaco *nm Mex* : water tank
tinieblas *nfpl* **1** OSCURIDAD : darkness **2** : ignorance
tino *nm* **1** : good judgment, sense **2** : tact, sensitivity, insight
tinta *nf* : ink
tinte *nm* **1** : dye, coloring **2** : overtone ⟨tintes raciales : racial overtones⟩
tintero *nm* **1** : inkwell **2 quedarse en el tintero** : to remain unsaid
tintinear *vt* : to jingle, to clink, to tinkle
tintineo *nm* : clink, jingle, tinkle
tinto, -ta *adj* **1** : dyed, stained ⟨tinto en sangre : bloodstained⟩ **2** : red (of wine)

tintorería *nf* : dry cleaner (service)
tintura *nf* **1** : dye, tint **2** : tincture ⟨tintura de yodo : tincture of iodine⟩
tiña *nf* : ringworm
tiñe, etc. → **teñir**
tío, tía *n* **1** : uncle *m*, aunt *f*
tiovivo *nm* : merry-go-round
tipi *nm* : tepee
típico, -ca *adj* : typical — **típicamente** *adv*
tipificar {72} *vt* **1** : to classify, to categorize **2** : to typify
tiple *nm* : soprano
tipo¹ *nm* **1** CLASE : type, kind, sort **2** : figure, build, appearance **3** : rate ⟨tipo de interés : interest rate⟩ **4** : (printing) type, typeface **5** : style, model ⟨un vestido tipo 60's : a 60's-style dress⟩
tipo², -pa *n fam* : guy *m*, gal *f*, character
tipografía *nf* : typography, printing
tipográfico, -ca *adj* : typographic, typographical
tipógrafo, -fa *n* : printer, typographer
tique *or* **tiquet** *nm* **1** : ticket **2** : receipt
tira *nf* **1** : strip, strap **2 tira cómica** : comic, comic strip
tirabuzón *nf, pl* **-zones** : corkscrew
tirada *nf* **1** : throw **2** : distance, stretch **3** IMPRESIÓN : printing, issue
tiradero *nm Mex* **1** : dump **2** : mess, clutter
tirador¹ *nm* : handle, knob
tirador², -dora *n* : marksman *m*, markswoman *f*
tiragomas *nms & pl* : slingshot
tiranía *nf* : tyranny
tiránico, -ca *adj* : tyrannical
tiranizar {21} *vt* : to tyrannize
tirano¹, -na *adj* : tyrannical, despotic
tirano², -na *n* : tyrant
tirante¹ *adj* **1** : tense, strained **2** : taut
tirante² *nm* **1** : shoulder strap **2 tirantes** *nmpl* : suspenders
tirantez *nf* **1** : tautness **2** : tension, friction, strain
tirar *vt* **1** : to throw, to hurl, to toss **2** BOTAR : to throw away, to throw out, to waste **3** DERRIBAR : to knock down **4** : to shoot, to fire, to launch **5** : to take (a photo) **6** : to print, to run off — *vi* **1** : to pull, to draw **2** : to shoot **3** : to attract **4** : to get by, to manage ⟨va tirando : he's getting along, he's managing⟩ **5** ∼ **a** : to tend towards, to be rather ⟨tira a picante : it's a bit spicy⟩ — **tirarse** *vr* **1** : to throw oneself **2** *fam* : to spend (time)
tiritar *vi* : to shiver, to tremble
tiro *nm* **1** BALAZO, DISPARO : shot, gunshot **2** : shot, kick (in sports) **3** : flue **4** : team (of horses, etc.) **5 a** ∼ : within range **6 al tiro** : right away **7 tiro de gracia** : coup de grace, death blow
tiroideo, -dea *adj* : thyroid
tiroides *nmf* : thyroid, thyroid gland — **tiroides** *adj*

tirolés, -lesa *adj* : Tyrolean
tirón *nm, pl* **tirones 1** : pull, tug, yank
2 de un tirón : all at once, in one go
tiroteo *nm* **1** : shooting **2** : gunfight,
shoot-out
tirria *nf* **tener tirria a** *fam* : to have a
grudge against
titánico, -ca *adj* : titanic, huge
titanio *nm* : titanium
títere *nm* : puppet
tití *nm* : marmoset
titilar *vi* : to twinkle, to flicker
titileo *nm* : twinkle, flickering
titiritero, -ra *n* **1** : puppeteer **2** : acrobat
titubear *vi* **1** : to hesitate **2** : to stutter,
to stammer — **titubeante** *adj*
titubeo *nm* **1** : hesitation **2** : stammering
titulado, -da *adj* **1** : titled, entitled **2**
: qualified
titular¹ *vt* : to title, to entitle — **titularse**
vr **1** : to be called, to be entitled **2** : to
receive a degree
titular² *adj* : titular, official
titular³ *nm* : headline
titular⁴ *nmf* **1** : owner, holder **2** : officeholder, incumbent
titularidad *nf* **1** : ownership, title **2** : position, office (with a title) **3** : starting
position (in sports)
título *nm* **1** : title **2** : degree, qualification **3** : security, bond **4 a título de**
: by way of, in the capacity of
tiza *nf* : chalk
tiznar *vt* : to blacken (with soot, etc.)
tizne *nm* HOLLÍN : soot
tiznón *nm, pl* **tiznones** : stain, smudge
tlapalería *nf Mex* : hardware store
TNT *nm* (trinitrotolueno) : TNT
toalla *nf* : towel
toallita *nf* : washcloth
tobillo *nm* : ankle
tobogán *nm, pl* **-ganes 1** : toboggan,
sled **2** : slide, chute
tocadiscos *nms & pl* : record player,
phonograph
tocado¹, -da *adj* **1** : bad, bruised (of
fruit) **2** *fam* : touched, not all there
tocado² *nm* : headdress
tocador¹ *nm* **1** : dressing table, vanity
table **2 artículos de tocador** : toiletries
tocador², -dora *n* : player (of music)
tocante *adj* ~ **a** : with regard to, regarding
tocar {72} *vt* **1** : to touch, to feel, to handle **2** : to touch on, to refer to **3** : to
concern, to affect **4** : to play (a musical instrument) — *vi* **1** : to knock, to
ring ⟨tocar a la puerta : to rap on the
door⟩ **2 ~ en** : to touch on, to border
on ⟨eso toca en lo ridículo : that's almost ludicrous⟩ **3 tocarle a** : to fall to,
to be up to, to be one's turn ⟨¿a quién
le toca manejar? : whose turn is it to
drive?⟩
tocayo, -ya *n* : namesake
tocineta *nf Col, Ven* : bacon
tocino *nm* **1** : bacon **2** : salt pork

tocología *nf* OBSTETRICIA : obstetrics
tocólogo, -ga *n* OBSTETRA : obstetrician
tocón *nm, pl* **tocones** CEPA : stump (of
a tree)
todavía *adv* **1** AÚN : still, yet ⟨todavía
puedes verlo : you can still see it⟩ **2**
: even ⟨todavía más rápido : even
faster⟩ **3 todavía no** : not yet
todo¹, -da *adj* **1** : all, whole, entire ⟨con
toda sinceridad : with all sincerity⟩
⟨toda la comunidad : the whole com-
munity⟩ **2** : every, each ⟨a todo nivel
: at every level⟩ **3** : maximum ⟨a toda
velocidad : at top speed⟩ **4 todo el
mundo** : everyone, everybody
todo² *nm* : whole
todo³, -da *pron* **1** : everything, all, every
bit ⟨lo sabe todo : he knows it all⟩ ⟨es
todo un soldado : he's every inch a sol-
dier⟩ **2 todos, -das** *pl* : everybody,
everyone, all
todopoderoso, -sa *adj* OMNIPOTENTE
: almighty, all-powerful
toga *nf* **1** : toga **2** : gown, robe (for mag-
istrates, etc.)
toldo *nm* : awning, canopy
tolerable *adj* : tolerable — **tolerable-
mente** *adv*
tolerancia *nf* : tolerance, toleration
tolerante *adj* : tolerant — **tolerante-
mente** *adv*
tolerar *vt* : to tolerate
tolete *nm* : oarlock
tolva *nf* : hopper (container)
toma *nf* **1** : taking, seizure, capture **2**
DOSIS : dose **3** : take, shot **4 toma de
corriente** : wall socket, outlet **5 toma
y daca** : give-and-take
tomar *vt* **1** : to take ⟨tomé el libro : I
took the book⟩ ⟨tomar un taxi : to take
a taxi⟩ ⟨tomar una foto : to take a pho-
to⟩ ⟨toma dos años : it takes two years⟩
⟨tomaron medidas drásticas : they
took drastic measures⟩ **2** BEBER : to
drink **3** CAPTURAR : to capture, to
seize **4 tomar el sol** : to sunbathe **5
tomar tierra** : to land — *vi* : to drink
(alcohol) — **tomarse** *vr* **1** : to take
⟨tomarse la molestia : to take the
trouble to⟩ **2** : to drink, to eat, to have
tomate *nm* : tomato
tomillo *nm* : thyme
tomo *nm* : volume, tome
ton *nm* **sin ton ni son** : without rhyme
or reason
tonada *nf* **1** : tune, song **2** : accent
tonalidad *nf* : tonality
tonel *nm* BARRICA : barrel, cask
tonelada *nf* : ton
tonelaje *nm* : tonnage
tónica *nf* **1** : tonic (water) **2** : tonic (in
music) **3** : trend, tone ⟨dar la tónica
: to set the tone⟩
tónico¹, -ca *adj* : tonic
tónico² *nm* : tonic ⟨tónico capilar : hair
tonic⟩
tono *nm* **1** : tone ⟨tono muscular : muscle tone⟩ **2** : shade (of colors) **3** : key
(in music)

tontamente *adv* : foolishly, stupidly
tontear *vi* **1** : to fool around, to play the fool **2** : to flirt
tontería *nf* **1** : foolishness **2** : stupid remark or action **3 decir tonterías** : to talk nonsense
tonto[1], **-ta** *adj* **1** : dumb, stupid **2** : silly **3 a tontas y a locas** : without thinking, haphazardly
tonto[2], **-ta** *n* : fool, idiot
topacio *nm* : topaz
toparse *vr* ~ **con** : to bump into, to run into, to come across ⟨me topé con algunas dificultades : I ran into some problems⟩
tope *nm* **1** : limit, end ⟨hasta el tope : to the limit, to the brim⟩ **2** : stop, check, buffer ⟨tope de puerta : doorstop⟩ **3** : bump, collision **4** *Mex* : speed bump
tópico[1], **-ca** *adj* **1** : topical, external **2** : trite, commonplace
tópico[2] *nm* **1** : topic, subject **2** : cliché, trite expression
topo *nm* **1** : mole (animal) **2** *fam* : clumsy person, blunderer
topografía *nf* : topography
topográfico, -ca *adj* : topographic, topographical
topógrafo, -fa *n* : topographer
toque[1], **etc.** → **tocar**
toque[2] *nm* **1** : touch ⟨el último toque : the finishing touch⟩ ⟨un toque de color : a touch of color⟩ **2** : ringing, peal, chime **3** *Mex* : shock, jolt **4 toque de queda** : curfew **5 toque de diana** : reveille
toquetear *vt* : to touch, to handle, to finger
tórax *nm* : thorax
torbellino *nm* : whirlwind
torcedura *nf* **1** : twisting, buckling **2** : sprain
torcer {14} *vt* **1** : to bend, to twist **2** : to sprain **3** : to turn (a corner) **4** : to wring, to wring out **5** : to distort — *vi* : to turn — **torcerse** *vr*
torcido, -da *adj* **1** : twisted, crooked **2** : devious
tordo *nm* ZORZAL : thrush
torear *vt* **1** : to fight (bulls) **2** : to dodge, to sidestep
toreo *nm* : bullfighting
torero, -ra *n* MATADOR : bullfighter, matador
tormenta *nf* **1** : storm ⟨tormenta de nieve : snowstorm⟩ **2** : turmoil, frenzy
tormento *nm* **1** : torment, anguish **2** : torture
tormentoso, -sa *adj* : stormy, turbulent
tornado *nm* : tornado
tornamesa *nmf* : turntable
tornar *vt* **1** : to return, to give back **2** : to make, to render — *vi* : to go back — **tornarse** *vr* : to become, to turn into
tornasol *nm* **1** : reflected light **2** : sunflower **3** : litmus
tornear *vt* : to turn (in carpentry)
torneo *nm* : tournament

tornillo *nm* **1** : screw **2 tornillo de banco** : vise
torniquete *nm* **1** : tourniquet **2** : turnstile
torno *nm* **1** : lathe **2** : winch **3 torno de banco** : vise **4 en torno a** : around, about ⟨en torno a este asunto : about this issue⟩ ⟨en torno suyo : around him⟩
toro *nm* : bull
toronja *nf* : grapefruit
toronjil *nm* : balm, lemon balm
torpe *adj* **1** DESMAÑADO : clumsy, awkward **2** : stupid, dull — **torpemente** *adv*
torpedear *vt* : to torpedo
torpedo *nm* : torpedo
torpeza *nf* **1** : clumsiness, awkwardness **2** : stupidity **3** : blunder
torre *nf* **1** : tower ⟨torre de perforación : oil rig⟩ **2** : turret **3** : rook, castle (in chess)
torrencial *adj* : torrential — **torrencialmente** *adv*
torrente *nm* **1** : torrent **2 torrente sanguíneo** : bloodstream
torreón *nm, pl* **-rreones** : tower (of a castle)
torreta *nf* : turret (of a tank, ship, etc.)
tórrido, -da *adj* : torrid
torsión *nf, pl* **torsiones** : torsion — **torsional** *adj*
torso *nm* : torso, trunk
torta *nf* **1** : torte, cake **2** *Mex* : sandwich
tortazo *nm fam* : blow, wallop
tortilla *nf* **1** : tortilla **2** *or* **tortilla de huevo** : omelet
tórtola *nf* : turtledove
tortuga *nf* **1** : turtle, tortoise **2 tortuga de agua dulce** : terrapin **3 tortuga boba** : loggerhead
tortuoso, -sa *adj* : tortuous, winding
tortura *nf* : torture
torturador, -dora *n* : torturer
torturar *vt* : to torture, to torment
torvo, -va *adj* : grim, stern, baleful
torzamos, etc. → **torcer**
tos *nf* **1** : cough **2 tos ferina** : whooping cough
tosco, -ca *adj* : rough, coarse
toser *vi* : to cough
tosquedad *nf* : crudeness, coarseness, roughness
tostada *nf* **1** : piece of toast **2** : tostada
tostador *nm* **1** : toaster **2** : roaster (for coffee)
tostar {19} *vt* **1** : to toast **2** : to roast (coffee) **3** : to tan — **tostarse** *vr* : to get a tan
tostón *nm, pl* **tostones** *Car* : fried plantain chip
total[1] *adv* : in the end, so ⟨total, que no fui : in short, I didn't go⟩
total[2] *adj & nm* : total — **totalmente** *adv*
totalidad *nf* : totality, whole
totalitario, -ria *adj & n* : totalitarian
totalitarismo *nm* : totalitarianism

totalizar {21} *vt* : total, to add up to
tótem *nm, pl* **tótems** : totem
totopo *nm CA, Mex* : tortilla chip
totuma *nf* : calabash
tour [ˈtur] *nm, pl* **tours** : tour, excursion
toxicidad *nf* : toxicity
tóxico[1], **-ca** *adj* : toxic, poisonous
tóxico[2] *nm* : poison
toxicomanía *nf* : drug addiction
toxicómano, -na *n* : drug addict
toxina *nf* : toxin
tozudez *nf* : stubbornness, obstinacy
tozudo, -da *adj* : stubborn, obstinate —
 tozudamente *adv*
traba *nf* **1** : tie, bond **2** : obstacle, hindrance
trabajador[1], **-dora** *adj* : hardworking
trabajador[2], **-dora** *n* : worker
trabajar *vi* **1** : to work ⟨trabaja mucho
 : he works hard⟩ ⟨trabajo de secretaria
 : I work as a secretary⟩ **2** : to strive
 ⟨trabajan por mejores oportunidades
 : they're striving for better opportuni-
 ties⟩ **3** : to act, to perform ⟨trabajar
 en una película : to be in a movie⟩ —
 vt **1** : to work (metal) **2** : to knead **3**
 : to till **4** : to work on ⟨tienes que trabajar el español : you need to work on
 your Spanish⟩
trabajo *nm* **1** : work, job **2** LABOR
 : labor, work ⟨tengo mucho trabajo : I
 have a lot of work to do⟩ **3** TAREA : task
 4 ESFUERZA : effort **5** costar trabajo
 : to be difficult **6** tomarse el trabajo
 : to take the trouble **7** trabajo en
 equipo : teamwork **8** trabajos *nmpl*
 : hardships, difficulties
trabajoso, -sa *adj* LABORIOSO : laborious — **trabajosamente** *adv*
trabalenguas *nms & pl* : tongue twister
trabar *vt* **1** : to join, to connect **2** : to
 impede, to hold back **3** : to strike up
 (a conversation), to form (a friendship)
 4 : to thicken (sauces) — **trabarse** *vr*
 1 : to jam **2** : to become entangled **3**
 : to be tongue-tied, to stammer
trabucar {72} *vt* : to confuse, to mix up
trabuco *nm* : blunderbuss
tracalero, -ra *adj Mex* : dishonest, tricky
tracción *nf* : traction
trace, etc. → trazar
tracto *nm* : tract
tractor *nm* : tractor
tradición *nf, pl* **-ciones** : tradition
tradicional *adj* : traditional — **tradi-
 cionalmente** *adv*
traducción *nf, pl* **-ciones** : translation
traducible *adj* : translatable
traducir {61} *vt* **1** : to translate **2** : to
 convey, to express — **traducirse** *vr* ~
 en : to result in
traductor, -tora *n* : translator
traer {81} *vt* **1** : to bring ⟨trae una ensalada : bring a salad⟩ **2** CAUSAR : to
 cause, to bring about ⟨el problema
 puede traer graves consecuencias : the
 problem could have serious conse-
 quences⟩ **3** : to carry, to have ⟨todos
 los periódicos traían las mismas noti-

cias : all of the newspapers carried the
 same news⟩ **4** LLEVAR : to wear —
 traerse *vr* **1** : to bring along **2 traérse-
 las** : to be difficult
traficante *nmf* : dealer, trafficker
traficar {72} *vi* **1** : to trade, to deal **2** ~
 con : to traffic in
tráfico *nm* **1** : trade **2** : traffic
tragaluz *nf, pl* **-luces** : skylight, fanlight
tragar {52} *v* : to swallow — **tragarse** *vr*
tragedia *nf* : tragedy
trágico, -ca *adj* : tragic — **trágicamente**
 adv
trago *nm* **1** : swallow, swig **2** : drink,
 liquor **3 trago amargo** : hard time
trague, etc. → tragar
traición *nf, pl* **traiciones** **1** : treason **2**
 : betrayal, treachery
traicionar *vt* : to betray
traicionero, -ra → traidor
traidor[1], **-dora** *adj* : traitorous, treason-
 ous
traidor[2], **-dora** *n* : traitor
traiga, etc. → traer
tráiler *or* **trailer** *nm* : trailer
traílla *nf* **1** : leash **2** : harrow
traje *nm* **1** : suit **2** : dress **3** : costume
 4 traje de baño : bathing suit
trajín *nm, pl* **trajines** **1** : transport **2** *fam*
 : hustle and bustle
trajinar *vt* : to transport, to carry — *vi*
 : to rush around
trajo, etc. → traer
trama *nf* **1** : plot **2** : weave, weft (fabric)
tramar *vt* **1** : to plot, to plan **2** : to weave
tramitar *vt* : to transact, to negotiate, to
 handle
trámite *nm* : procedure, step
tramo *nm* **1** : stretch, section **2** : flight
 (of stairs)
trampa *nf* **1** : trap **2 hacer trampas** : to
 cheat
trampear *vt* : to cheat
trampero, -ra *n* : trapper
trampilla *nf* : trapdoor
trampolín *nm, pl* **-lines** **1** : diving board
 2 : trampoline **3** : springboard ⟨un
 trampolín al éxito : a springboard to
 success⟩
tramposo[1], **-sa** *adj* : crooked, cheating
tramposo[2], **-sa** *n* : cheat, swindler
tranca *nf* **1** : stick, club **2** : bar, crossbar
trancar {72} *vt* : to bar (a door or window)
trancazo *nm* GOLPE : blow, hit
trance *nm* **1** : critical juncture, tough
 time **2** : trance **3 en trance de** : in the
 process of ⟨en trance de extinción : on
 the verge of extinction⟩
tranco *nm* **1** : stride **2** UMBRAL : threshold
tranque, etc. → trancar
tranquilidad *nf* : tranquility, peace
tranquilizador, -dora *adj* **1** : soothing **2**
 : reassuring
tranquilizante[1] *adj* **1** : reassuring **2**
 : tranquilizing

tranquilizante[2] *nm* : tranquilizer
tranquilizar {21} *vt* CALMAR : to calm down, to soothe ⟨tranquilizar la conciencia : to ease the conscience⟩ — **tranquilizarse** *vr*
tranquilo, -la *adj* CALMO : calm, tranquil ⟨una vida tranquila : a quiet life⟩ — **tranquilamente** *adv*
transacción *nf, pl* **-ciones** : transaction
transar *vi* TRANSIGIR : to give way, to compromise — *vt* : to buy and sell
transatlántico[1], **-ca** *adj* : transatlantic
transatlántico[2] *nm* : ocean liner
transbordador *nm* **1** : ferry **2 transbordador espacial** : space shuttle
transbordar *v* : to transfer
transbordo *nm* : transfer
transcendencia → **trascendencia**
transcender → **trascender**
transcribir {33} *vt* : to transcribe
transcrito *pp* → **transcribir**
transcripción *nf, pl* **-ciones** : transcription
transcurrir *vi* : to elapse, to pass
transcurso *nm* : course, progression ⟨en el transcurso de cien años : over the course of a hundred years⟩
transeúnte *nmf* **1** : passerby **2** : transient
transferencia *nf* : transfer, transference
transferir {76} *vt* TRASLADAR : to transfer — **transferible** *adj*
transfigurar *vt* : to transfigure, to transform — **transfiguración** *nf*
transformación *nf, pl* **-ciones** : transformation, conversion
transformador *nm* : transformer
transformar *vt* **1** CONVERTIR : to convert **2** : to transform, to change, to alter — **transformarse** *vr*
transfusión *nf, pl* **-siones** : transfusion
transgredir {1} *vt* : to transgress — **transgresión** *nf*
transgresor, -sora *n* : transgressor
transición *nf, pl* **-ciones** : transition ⟨período de transición : transition period⟩
transido, -da *adj* : overcome, beset ⟨transido de dolor : racked with pain⟩
transigir {35} *vi* **1** : to give in, to compromise **2 ~ con** : to tolerate, to put up with
transistor *nm* : transistor
transitable *adj* : passable
transitar *vi* : to go, to pass, to travel ⟨transitar por la ciudad : to travel through the city⟩
transitivo, -va *adj* : transitive
tránsito *nm* **1** TRÁFICO : traffic ⟨hora de máximo tránsito : rush hour⟩ **2** : transit, passage, movement **3** : death, passing
transitorio, -ria *adj* **1** : transitory **2** : provisional, temporary — **transitoriamente** *adv*
translúcido, -da *adj* : translucent
translucir → **traslucir**
transmisible *adj* : transmissible

transmisión *nf, pl* **-siones** **1** : transmission, broadcast **2** : transfer **3** : transmission (of an automobile)
transmisor *nm* : transmitter
transmitir *vt* **1** : to transmit, to broadcast **2** : to pass on, to transfer — *vi* : to transmit, to broadcast
transparencia *nf* : transparency
transparentar *vt* : to reveal, to betray — **transparentarse** *vr* **1** : to be transparent **2** : to show through
transparente[1] *adj* : transparent — **transparentemente** *adv*
transparente[2] *nm* : shade, blind
transpiración *nf, pl* **-ciones** SUDOR : perspiration, sweat
transpirado, -da *adj* : sweaty
transpirar *vi* **1** SUDAR : to perspire, to sweat **2** : to transpire
transplantar, transplante → **trasplantar, trasplante**
transponer {60} *vt* **1** : to transpose, to move about **2** TRASPLANTAR : to transplant — **transponerse** *vr* **1** OCULTARSE : to hide **2** PONERSE : to set, to go down (of the sun or moon) **3** DORMITAR : to doze off
transportación *nf, pl* **-ciones** : transportation
transportador *nm* **1** : protractor **2** : conveyor
transportar *vt* **1** : to transport, to carry **2** : to transmit **3** : to transpose (music) — **transportarse** *vr* : to get carried away
transporte *nm* : transport, transportation
transportista *nmf* : hauler, carrier, trucker
transpuso, etc. → **transponer**
transversal *adj* : transverse, cross ⟨corte transversal : cross section⟩
transversalmente *adv* : obliquely
transverso, -sa *adj* : transverse
tranvía *nm* : streetcar, trolley
trapeador *nm* : mop
trapear *vt* : to mop
trapecio *nm* **1** : trapezoid **2** : trapeze
trapezoide *nm* : trapezoid
trapo *nm* **1** : cloth, rag ⟨trapo de polvo : dust cloth⟩ **2 soltar el trapo** : to burst into tears **3 trapos** *nmpl fam* : clothes
tráquea *nf* : trachea, windpipe
traquetear *vi* : to clatter, to jolt
traqueteo *nm* **1** : jolting **2** : clattering, clatter
tras *prep* **1** : after ⟨día tras día : day after day⟩ ⟨uno tras otro : one after another⟩ **2** : behind ⟨tras la puerta : behind the door⟩
trasbordar, trasbordo → **transbordar, transbordo**
trascendencia *nf* **1** : importance, significance **2** : transcendence
trascendental *adj* **1** : transcendental **2** : important, momentous
trascendente *adj* **1** : important, significant **2** : transcendent

trascender {56} *vi* **1** : to leak out, to become known **2** : to spread, to have a wide effect **3** ~ **a** : to smell of ⟨la casa trascendía a flores : the house smelled of flowers⟩ **4** ~ **de** : to transcend, to go beyond — *vt* : to transcend

trasero[1], **-ra** *adj* POSTERIOR : rear, back

trasero[2] *nm* : buttocks

trasfondo *nm* **1** : background, backdrop **2** : undertone, undercurrent

trasformación → **transformación**

trasgo *nm* : goblin, imp

trasgredir → **transgredir**

trasladar *vt* **1** TRANSFERIR : to transfer, to move **2** POSPONER : to postpone **3** TRADUCIR : to translate **4** COPIAR : to copy, to transcribe — **trasladarse** *vr* MUDARSE : to move, to relocate

traslado *nm* **1** : transfer, move **2** : copy

traslapar *vt* : to overlap — **traslaparse** *vr*

traslapo *nm* : overlap

traslúcido, -da → **translúcido**

traslucir {45} *vi* : to reveal, to show — **traslucirse** *vr* : to show through

trasmano *nm* **a** ~ : out of the way, out of reach

trasmisión, trasmitir → **transmisión, transmitir**

trasnochar *vi* : to stay up all night

trasparencia *nf* **trasparente** → **transparencia, transparente**

traspasar *vt* **1** PERFORAR : to pierce, to go through **2** : to go beyond ⟨traspasar los límites : to overstep the limits⟩ **3** ATRAVESAR : to cross, to go across **4** : to sell, to transfer

traspaso *nm* : transfer, sale

traspié *nm* **1** : stumble **2** : blunder

traspiración → **transpiración**

trasplantar *vt* : to transplant

trasplante *nm* : transplant

trasponer → **transponer**

trasportar → **transportar**

trasquilar *vt* ESQUILAR : to shear

traste *nm* **1** : fret (on a guitar) **2** *CA, Mex, PRi* : kitchen utensil ⟨lavar los trastes : to do the dishes⟩ **3 dar al traste con** : to ruin, to destroy **4 irse al traste** : to fall through

trastornar *vt* : to disturb, to upset, to disrupt — **trastornarse** *vr*

trastorno *nm* **1** : disorder ⟨trastorno mental : mental disorder⟩ **2** : disturbance, upset

trastos *nmpl* **1** : implements, utensils **2** *fam* : pieces of junk, stuff

trasunto *nm* : image, likeness

tratable *adj* **1** : friendly, sociable **2** : treatable

tratado *nm* **1** : treatise **2** : treaty

tratamiento *nm* : treatment

tratante *nmf* : dealer, trader

tratar *vi* **1** ~ **con** : to deal with, to have contact with ⟨no trato mucho con los clientes : I don't have much contact with customers⟩ **2** ~ **de** : to try to ⟨estoy tratando de comer : I am trying to

eat⟩ **3** ~ **de** *or* ~ **sobre** : to be about, to concern ⟨el libro trata de las plantas : the book is about plants⟩ **4** ~ **en** : to deal in ⟨trata en herramientas : he deals in tools⟩ — *vt* **1** : to treat ⟨tratan bien a sus empleados : they treat their employees well⟩ **2** : to handle ⟨trató el tema con delicadeza : he handled the subject tactfully⟩ — **tratarse** *vr* ~ **de** : to be about, to concern

trato *nm* **1** : deal, agreement **2** : relationship, dealings *pl* **3** : treatment ⟨malos tratos : ill-treatment⟩

trauma *nm* : trauma

traumático, -ca *adj* : traumatic — **traumáticamente** *adv*

traumatismo *nm* : injury ⟨traumatismo cervical : whiplash⟩

través *nm* **1 a través de** : across, through **2 al través** : crosswise, across **3 de través** : sideways

travesaño *nm* **1** : crossbar **2** : crossbeam, crosspiece, transom (of a window)

travesía *nf* : voyage, crossing (of the sea)

travesura *nf* **1** : prank, mischievous act **2 travesuras** *nfpl* : mischief

travieso, -sa *adj* : mischievous, naughty — **traviesamente** *adv*

trayecto *nm* **1** : journey **2** : route **3** : trajectory, path

trayectoria *nf* : course, path, trajectory

trayendo → **traer**

traza *nf* **1** DISEÑO : design, plan **2** : appearance

trazado *nm* **1** BOSQUEJO : outline, sketch **2** PLAN : plan, layout

trazar {21} *vt* **1** : to trace **2** : to draw up, to devise **3** : to outline, to sketch

trazo *nm* **1** : stroke, line **2** : sketch, outline

trébol *nm* **1** : clover, shamrock **2** : club (playing card)

trece *adj* & *nm* : thirteen

treceavo[1], **-va** *adj* : thirteenth

treceavo[2] *nm* : thirteenth (fraction)

trecho *nm* **1** : stretch, period ⟨de trecho en trecho : at intervals⟩ **2** : distance, space

tregua *nf* **1** : truce **2** : lull, respite **3 sin** ~ : relentless, unrelenting

treinta *adj* & *nm* : thirty

treintavo[1], **-va** *adj* : thirtieth

treintavo[2] *nm* : thirtieth (fraction)

tremendo, -da *adj* **1** : tremendous, enormous **2** : terrible, dreadful **3** *fam* : great, super

trementina *nf* AGUARRÁS : turpentine

trémulo, -la *adj* **1** : trembling, shaky **2** : flickering

tren *nm* **1** : train **2** : set, assembly ⟨tren de aterrizaje : landing gear⟩ **3** : speed, pace ⟨a todo tren : at top speed⟩

trence, etc. → **trenzar**

trenza *nf* : braid, pigtail

trenzar {21} *vt* : to braid — **trenzarse** *vr* : to get involved

trepador, -dora *adj* : climbing ⟨rosal trepador : rambling rose⟩

trepadora *nf* **1** : climbing plant, climber **2** : nuthatch

trepar *vi* **1** : to climb ⟨trepar a un árbol : to climb up a tree⟩ **2** : to creep, to spread (of a plant)

trepidación *nf, pl* **-ciones** : vibration

trepidante *adj* **1** : vibrating **2** : fast, frantic

trepidar *vi* **1** : to shake, to vibrate **2** : to hesitate, to waver

tres *adj & nm* : three

trescientos[1], **-tas** *adj* : three hundred

trescientos[2] *nms & pl* : three hundred

treta *nf* : trick, ruse

tríada *nf* : triad

triángulo *nm* : triangle — **triangular** *adj*

tribal *adj* : tribal

tribu *nf* : tribe

tribulación *nf, pl* **-ciones** : tribulation

tribuna *nf* **1** : dais, platform **2** : stands *pl*, bleachers *pl,* grandstand

tribunal *nm* : court, tribunal

tributar *vt* : to pay, to render — *vi* : to pay taxes

tributario[1], **-ria** *adj* : tax ⟨evasión tributaria : tax evasion⟩

tributario[2] *nm* : tributary

tributo *nm* **1** : tax **2** : tribute

triciclo *nm* : tricycle

tricolor *adj* : tricolor, tricolored

tridente *nm* : trident

tridimensional *adj* : three-dimensional, 3-D

trienal *adj* : triennial

trifulca *nf fam* : row, ruckus

trigésimo[1], **-ma** *adj* : thirtieth, thirty-

trigésimo[2], **-ma** *n* : thirtieth, thirty- (in a series)

trigo *nm* **1** : wheat **2 trigo rubión** : buckwheat

trigonometría *nf* : trigonometry

trigueño, -ña *adj* **1** : light brown (of hair) **2** MORENO : dark, olive-skinned

trillado, -da *adj* : trite, hackneyed

trilladora *nf* : thresher, threshing machine

trillar *vt* : to thresh

trillizo, -za *n* : triplet

trilogía *nf* : trilogy

trimestral *adj* : quarterly — **trimestralmente** *adv*

trinar *vi* **1** : to thrill **2** : to warble

trinchar *vt* : to carve, to cut up

trinchera *nf* **1** : trench, ditch **2** : trench coat

trineo *nm* : sled, sleigh

trinidad *nf* **la Trinidad** : the Trinity

trino *nm* : trill, warble

trinquete *nm* : ratchet

trío *nm* : trio

tripa *nf* **1** INTESTINO : gut, intestine **2 tripas** *nfpl fam* : belly, tummy, insides *pl* ⟨dolerle a uno las tripas : to have a stomach ache⟩

tripartito, -ta *adj* : tripartite

triple *adj & nm* : triple

triplicado *nm* : triplicate

triplicar {72} *vt* : to triple, to treble

trípode *nm* : tripod

tripulación *nf, pl* **-ciones** : crew

tripulante *nmf* : crew member

tripular *vt* : to man

tris *nm* **estar en un tris de** : to be within an inch of, to be very close to

triste *adj* **1** : sad, gloomy ⟨ponerse triste : to become sad⟩ **2** : desolate, dismal ⟨una perspectiva triste : a dismal outlook⟩ **3** : sorry, sorry-looking ⟨la triste verdad : the sorry truth⟩

tristeza *nf* DOLOR : sadness, grief

tristón, -tona *adj, mpl* **-tones** : melancholy, downhearted

tritón *nm, pl* **tritones** : newt

triturar *vt* : to crush, to grind

triunfal *adj* : triumphal, triumphant — **triunfalmente** *adv*

triunfante *adj* : triumphant, victorious

triunfar *vi* : to triumph, to win

triunfo *nm* **1** : triumph, victory **2** ÉXITO : success **3** : trump (in card games)

triunvirato *nm* : triumvirate

trivial *adj* **1** : trivial **2** : trite, commonplace

trivialidad *nf* : triviality

triza *nf* **1** : shred, bit **2 hacer trizas** : to tear into shreds, to smash to pieces

trocar {82} *vt* **1** CAMBIAR : to exchange, to trade **2** CAMBIAR : to change, to alter, to transform **3** CONFUNDIR : to confuse, to mix up

trocha *nf* : path, trail

troce, etc. → **trozar**

trofeo *nm* : trophy

tromba *nf* **1** : whirlwind **2 tromba de agua** : downpour, cloudburst

trombón *nm, pl* **trombones** **1** : trombone **2** : trombonist — **trombonista** *nmf*

trombosis *nf* : thrombosis

trompa *nf* **1** : trunk (of an elephant), proboscis (of an insect) **2** : horn ⟨trompa de caza : hunting horn⟩ **3** : tube, duct (in the body)

trompada *nf fam* **1** : punch, blow **2** : bump, collision (of persons)

trompeta *nf* : trumpet

trompetista *nmf* : trumpet player, trumpeter

trompo *nm* : spinning top

tronada *nf* : thunderstorm

tronar {19} *vi* **1** : to thunder, to roar **2** : to be furious, to rage **3** *CA, Mex fam* : to shoot — *v impers* : to thunder ⟨está tronando : it's thundering⟩

tronchar *vt* **1** : to snap, to break off **2** : to cut off (relations)

tronco *nm* **1** : trunk (of a tree) **2** : log **3** : torso

trono *nm* **1** : throne **2** *fam* : toilet

tropa *nf* **1** : troop, soldiers *pl* **2** : crowd, mob **3** : herd (of livestock)

tropel *nm* : mob, swarm

tropezar {29} *vi* **1** : to trip, to stumble **2** : to slip up, to blunder **3 ~ con** : to run into, to bump into **4 ~ con** : to come up against (a problem)

tropezón *nm, pl* **-zones 1** : stumble **2** : mistake, slip

tropical *adj* : tropical

trópico *nm* **1** : tropic ⟨trópico de Cáncer : tropic of Cancer⟩ **2 el trópico** : the tropics

tropiezo *nm* **1** CONTRATIEMPO : snag, setback **2** EQUIVOCACIÓN : mistake, slip

troqué, etc. → **trocar**

troquel *nm* : die (for stamping)

trotamundos *nmf* : globe-trotter

trotar *vi* **1** : to trot **2** : to jog **3** *fam* : to rush about

trote *nm* **1** : trot **2** *fam* : rush, bustle **3 de** ～ : durable, for everyday use

trovador, -dora *n* : troubadour

trozar {21} *vt* : to cut up, to dice

trozo *nm* **1** PEDAZO : piece, bit, chunk **2** : passage, extract

trucha *nf* : trout

truco *nm* **1** : trick **2** : knack

truculento, -ta *adj* : horrifying, gruesome

trueca, trueque etc. → **trocar**

truena, etc. → **tronar**

trueno *nm* : thunder

trueque *nm* : barter, exchange

trufa *nf* : truffle

truncar {72} *vt* **1** : to truncate, to cut short **2** : to thwart, to frustrate ⟨truncó sus esperanzas : she shattered their hopes⟩

trunco, -ca *adj* **1** : truncated **2** : unfinished, incomplete

trunque, etc. → **truncar**

tu *adj* **1** : your ⟨tu vestido : your dress⟩ ⟨toma tus vitaminas : take your vitamins⟩ **2** : thy

tú *pron* **1** : you ⟨tú eres mi hijo : you are my son⟩ **2** : thou

tuba *nf* : tuba

tubérculo *nm* : tuber

tuberculosis *nf* : tuberculosis

tuberculoso, -sa *adj* : tuberculous, tubercular

tubería *nf* : pipes *pl*, tubing

tuberoso, -sa *adj* : tuberous

tubo *nm* **1** : tube ⟨tubo de ensayo : test tube⟩ **2** : pipe ⟨tubo de desagüe : drainpipe⟩ **3 tubo digestivo** : alimentary canal

tubular *adj* : tubular

tuerca *nf* : nut ⟨tuercas y tornillos : nuts and bolts⟩

tuerce, etc. → **torcer**

tuerto, -ta *adj* : one-eyed, blind in one eye

tuerza, etc. → **torcer**

tuesta, etc. → **tostar**

tuétano *nm* : marrow

tufo *nm* **1** : fume, vapor **2** *fam* : stench, stink

tugurio *nm* : hovel

tulipán *nm, pl* **-panes** : tulip

tumba *nf* **1** SEPULCRO : tomb **2** FOSA : grave **3** : felling of trees

tumbar *vt* **1** : to knock down **2** : to fell, to cut down — *vi* : to fall down

tumbarse *vr* ACOSTARSE : to lie down

tumbo *nm* **1** : tumble, fall **2 dar tumbos** : to jolt, to bump around

tumor *nm* : tumor

túmulo *nm* : burial mound

tumulto *nm* **1** ALBOROTO : commotion, tumult **2** MOTÍN : riot **3** MULTITUD : crowd

tumultuoso, -sa *adj* : tumultuous

tuna *nf* : prickly pear (fruit)

tundra *nf* : tundra

tunecino, -na *adj & n* : Tunisian

túnel *nm* : tunnel

tungsteno *nm* : tungsten

túnica *nf* : tunic

tupé *nm* PELUQUÍN : toupee

tupido, -da *adj* **1** DENSO : dense, thick **2** OBSTRUIDO : obstructed, blocked up

turba *nf* **1** : peat **2** : mob, throng

turbación *nf, pl* **-ciones 1** : disturbance **2** : alarm, concern **3** : confusion

turbante *nm* : turban

turbar *vt* **1** : to disturb, to disrupt **2** : to worry, to upset **3** : to confuse

turbina *nf* : turbine

turbio, -bia *adj* **1** : cloudy, murky, turbid **2** : dim, blurred **3** : shady, crooked

turbopropulsor *nm* : turboprop

turborreactor *nm* : turbojet

turbulencia *nf* : turbulence

turbulento, -ta *adj* : turbulent

turco¹, -ca *adj* : Turkish

turco², -ca *n* : Turk

turco³ *nm* : Turkish (language)

turgente *adj* : turgid, swollen

turismo *nm* : tourism, tourist industry

turista *nmf* : tourist, vacationer

turístico, -ca *adj* : tourist, travel

turnar *vi* : to take turns, to alternate

turno *nm* **1** : turn ⟨ya te tocará tu turno : you'll get your turn⟩ **2** : shift, duty ⟨turno de noche : night shift⟩ **3 por turno** : alternately

turón *nm, pl* **turones** : polecat

turquesa *nf* : turquoise

turrón *nm, pl* **turrones** : nougat

tusa *nf* : corn husk

tutear *vt* : to address as *tú*

tutela *nf* **1** : guardianship **2** : tutelage, protection

tuteo *nm* : addressing as *tú*

tutor, -tora *n* **1** : tutor **2** : guardian

tuvo, etc. → **tener**

tuyo¹, -ya *adj* : yours, of yours ⟨un amigo tuyo : a friend of yours⟩ ⟨¿es tuya esta casa? : is this house yours?⟩

tuyo², -ya *pron* **1** : yours ⟨ése es el tuyo : that one is yours⟩ ⟨trae la tuya : bring your own⟩ **2 los tuyos** : your relations, your friends ⟨¿vendrán los tuyos? : are your folks coming?⟩

tweed [ˈtwið] *nm* : tweed

U

u[1] *nf* : twenty-second letter of the Spanish alphabet

u[2] *conj* (*used instead of* **o** *before words beginning with o- or ho-*) : or

ualabí *nm* : wallaby

uapití *nm* : American elk, wapiti

ubicación *nf, pl* **-ciones** : location, position

ubicar {72} *vt* **1** SITUAR : to place, to put, to position **2** LOCALIZAR : to locate, to find — **ubicarse** *vr* **1** LOCALIZARSE : to be placed, to be located **2** SITUARSE : to position oneself

ubicuidad *nf* OMNIPRESENCIA : ubiquity

ubicuo, -cua *adj* OMNIPRESENTE : ubiquitous

ubre *nf* : udder

ucraniano[1], **-na** *adj & n* : Ukranian

ucraniano[2] *nm* : Ukranian (language)

Ud., Uds. → **usted**

ufanarse *vr* ~ **de** : to boast about, to pride oneself on

ufano, -na *adj* **1** ORGULLOSO : proud **2** : self-satisfied, smug

ugandés, -desa *adj & n, mpl* **-deses** : Ugandan

ukelele *nm* : ukulele

úlcera *nf* : ulcer — **ulceroso, -sa** *adj*

ulcerar *vt* : to ulcerate — **ulcerarse** *vr* — **ulceración** *nf*

ulceroso, -sa *adj* : ulcerous

ulterior *adj* : later, subsequent — **ulteriormente** *adv*

últimamente *adv* : lately, recently

ultimar *vt* **1** CONCLUIR : to complete, to finish, to finalize **2** MATAR : to kill

ultimátum *nm, pl* **-tums** : ultimatum

último, -ma *adj* **1** : last, final ⟨la última galleta : the last cookie⟩ ⟨en último caso : as a last resort⟩ **2** : last, latest, most recent ⟨su último viaje a España : her last trip to Spain⟩ ⟨en los últimos años : in recent years⟩ **3 por** ~ : finally

ultrajar *vt* INSULTAR : to offend, to outrage, to insult

ultraje *nm* INSULTO : outrage, insult

ultramar *nm* **de** ~ *or* **en** ~ : overseas, abroad

ultranza *nf* **1 a** ~ : to the extreme ⟨lo defendió a ultranza : she defended him fiercely⟩ **2 a** ~ : extreme, out-and-out ⟨perfeccionismo a ultranza : rabid perfectionism⟩

ultrarrojo, -ja *adj* : infrared

ultravioleta *adj* : ultraviolet

ulular *vi* **1** : to hoot **2** : to howl, to wail

ululato *nm* : hoot (of an owl), wail (of a person)

umbilical *adj* : umbilical ⟨cordón umbilical : umbilical cord⟩

umbral *nm* : threshold, doorstep

un[1] *adj* → **uno**[1]

un[2], **una** *art, mpl* **unos 1** : a, an **2 unos** *or* **unas** *pl* : some, a few ⟨hace unas se-manas : a few weeks ago⟩ **3 unos** *or* **unas** *pl* : about, approximately ⟨unos veinte años antes : about twenty years before⟩

unánime *adj* : unanimous — **unánimemente** *adv*

unanimidad *nf* **1** : unanimity **2 por** ~ : unanimously

unción *nf, pl* **-ciones** : unction

uncir {83} *vt* : to yoke

undécimo[1], **-ma** *adj* : eleventh

undécimo[2], **-ma** *n* : eleventh (in a series)

ungir {35} *vt* : to anoint

ungüento *nm* : ointment, salve

únicamente *adv* : only, solely

unicelular *adj* : unicellular

único[1], **-ca** *adj* **1** : only, sole **2** : unique, extraordinary

único[2], **-ca** *n* : only one ⟨los únicos que vinieron : the only ones who showed up⟩

unicornio *nm* : unicorn

unidad *nf* **1** : unity **2** : unit

unidireccional *adj* : unidirectional

unido, -da *adj* **1** : joined, united **2** : close ⟨unos amigos muy unidos : very close friends⟩

unificar {72} *vt* : to unify — **unificación** *nf*

uniformado, -da *adj* : uniformed

uniformar *vt* ESTANDARIZAR : to standardize, to make uniform

uniforme[1] *adj* : uniform — **uniformemente** *adv*

uniforme[2] *nm* : uniform

uniformidad *nf* : uniformity

unilateral *adj* : unilateral — **unilateralmente** *adv*

unión *nf, pl* **uniones 1** : union **2** JUNTURA : joint, coupling

unir *vt* **1** JUNTAR : to unite, to join, to link **2** COMBINAR : to combine, to blend — **unirse** *vr* **1** : to join together **2** : to combine, to mix together **3** ~ **a** : to join ⟨se unieron al grupo : they joined the group⟩

unísono *nm* : unison ⟨al unísono : in unison⟩

unitario, -ria *adj* : unitary, unit ⟨precio unitario : unit price⟩

universal *adj* : universal — **universalmente** *adv*

universidad *nf* : university

universitario[1], **-ria** *adj* : university, college

universitario[2], **-ria** *n* : university student, college student

universo *nm* : universe

unja, etc. → **ungir**

uno[1], **una** *adj* (**un** *before masculine singular nouns*) : one ⟨una silla : one chair⟩ ⟨tiene treinta y un años : he's thirty-one years old⟩ ⟨el tomo uno : volume one⟩

uno[2] *nm* : one, number one

uno³, una *pron* **1** : one (number) ⟨uno por uno : one by one⟩ ⟨es la una : it's one o'clock⟩ **2** : one (person or thing) ⟨una es mejor que las otras : one (of them) is better than the others⟩ ⟨hacerlo uno mismo : to do it oneself⟩ **3 unos, unas** *pl* : some (ones), some people **4 uno y otro** : both **5 unos y otros** : all of them **6 el uno al otro** : one another, each other ⟨se enseñaron los unos a los otros : they taught each other⟩

untar *vt* **1** : to anoint **2** : to smear, to grease **3** : to bribe

unza, etc. → **uncir**

uña *nf* **1** : fingernail, toenail **2** : claw, hoof, stinger

uranio *nm* : uranium

Urano *nm* : Uranus

urbanidad *nf* : urbanity, courtesy

urbanización *nf, pl* **-ciones** : housing development, residential area

urbanizar {21} *vt* : to develop (an area)

urbano, -na *adj* **1** : urban **2** CORTÉS : urbane, polite

urbe *nf* : large city, metropolis

urdimbre *nf* : warp (in a loom)

urdu *nm* : Urdu

uretra *nf* : urethra

urgencia *nf* **1** : urgency **2** EMERGENCIA : emergency

urgente *adj* : urgent — **urgentemente** *adv*

urgir {35} *v impers* : to be urgent, to be pressing ⟨me urge localizarlo : I urgently need to find him⟩ ⟨el tiempo urge : time is running out⟩

urinario¹, -ria *adj* : urinary

urinario² *nm* : urinal (place)

urja, etc. → **urgir**

urna *nf* **1** : urn **2** : ballot box ⟨acudir a las urnas : to go to the polls⟩

urogallo *nm* : grouse (bird)

urraca *nf* **1** : magpie **2 urraca de América** : blue jay

urticaria *nf* : hives

uruguayo, -ya *adj & n* : Uruguayan

usado, -da *adj* **1** : used, secondhand **2** : worn, worn-out

usanza *nf* : custom, usage

usar *vt* **1** EMPLEAR, UTILIZAR : to use, to make use of **2** CONSUMIR : to consume, to use (up) **3** LLEVAR : to wear **4 de usar y tirar** : disposable — **usarse** *vr* **1** : to be used **2** : to be in fashion

uso *nm* **1** EMPLEO, UTILIZACIÓN : use ⟨de uso personal : for personal use⟩ ⟨hacer uso de : to make use of⟩ **2** : wear ⟨uso y desgaste : wear and tear⟩ **3** USANZA : custom, usage, habit ⟨al uso de : in the manner of, in the style of⟩

usted *pron* **1** (*formal form of address in most countries; often written as* **Ud.** *or* **Vd.**) : you **2 ustedes** *pl* (*often written as* **Uds.** *or* **Vds.**) : you, all of you

usual *adj* : usual, common, normal ⟨poco usual : not very common⟩ — **usualmente** *adv*

usuario, -ria *n* : user

usura *nf* : usury — **usurario, -ria** *adj*

usurero, -ra *n* : usurer

usurpador, -dora *n* : usurper

usurpar *vt* : to usurp — **usurpación** *nf*

utensilio *nm* : utensil, tool

uterino, -na *adj* : uterine

útero *nm* : uterus, womb

útil *adj* : useful, handy, helpful

útiles *nmpl* : implements, tools

utilidad *nf* **1** : utility, usefulness **2 utilidades** *nfpl* : profits

utilitario, -ria *adj* : utilitarian

utilizable *adj* : usable, fit for use

utilización *nf, pl* **-ciones** : utilization, use

utilizar {21} *vt* : to use, to utilize

útilmente *adv* : usefully

utopía *nf* : utopia

utópico, -ca *adj* : utopian

uva *nf* : grape

uvular *adj* : uvular

V

v *nf* : twenty-third letter of the Spanish alphabet

va → **ir**

vaca *nf* : cow

vacación *nf, pl* **-ciones** **1** : vacation ⟨dos semanas de vacaciones : two weeks of vacation⟩ **2 estar de vacaciones** : to be on vacation **3 irse de vacaciones** : to go on vacation

vacacionar *vi Mex* : to vacation

vacacionista *nmf CA, Mex* : vacationer

vacante¹ *adj* : vacant, empty

vacante² *nf* : vacancy (for a job)

vaciado *nm* : cast, casting ⟨vaciado de yeso : plaster cast⟩

vaciar {85} *vt* **1** : to empty, to empty out, to drain **2** AHUECAR : to hollow out **3** : to cast (in a mold) — *vi* ~ **en** : to flow into, to empty into

vacilación *nf, pl* **-ciones** : hesitation, vacillation

vacilante *adj* **1** : hesitant, unsure **2** : shaky, unsteady **3** : flickering

vacilar *vi* **1** : to hesitate, to vacillate, to waver **2** : to be unsteady, to wobble **3** : to flicker **4** *fam* : to joke, to fool around

vacío¹, -cía *adj* **1** : vacant **2** : empty **3** : meaningless

vacío² *nm* **1** : emptiness, void **2** : space, gap **3** : vacuum **4 hacerle el vacío a alguien** : to ostracize someone, to give someone the cold shoulder

vacuidad *nf* : vacuity, vacuousness

vacuna *nf* : vaccine
vacunación *nf, pl* **-ciones** INOCULACIÓN : vaccination, inoculation
vacunar *vt* INOCULAR : to vaccinate, to inoculate
vacuno[1], **-na** *adj* : bovine ⟨ganado vacuno : beef cattle⟩
vacuno[2] *nm* : bovine
vacuo, -cua *adj* : empty, shallow, inane
vadear *vt* : to ford, to wade across
vado *nm* : ford
vagabundear *vi* : to wander, to roam about
vagabundo[1], **-da** *adj* **1** ERRANTE : wandering **2** : stray
vagabundo[2], **-da** *n* : vagrant, bum, vagabond
vagamente *adv* : vaguely
vagancia *nf* **1** : vagrancy **2** PEREZA : laziness, idleness
vagar {52} *vi* ERRAR : to roam, to wander
vagina *nf* : vagina — **vaginal** *adj*
vago[1], **-ga** *adj* **1** : vague **2** PEREZOSO : lazy, idle
vago[2], **-ga** *n* **1** : idler, loafer **2** VAGABUNDO : vagrant, bum
vagón *nm, pl* **vagones** : car (of a train)
vague, etc. → **vagar**
vaguear *vi* **1** : to loaf, to lounge around **2** VAGAR : to wander
vaguedad *nf* : vagueness
vahído *nm* : dizzy spell
vaho *nm* **1** : breath **2** : vapor, steam (on glass, etc.)
vaina *nf* **1** : sheath, scabbard **2** : pod (of a pea or bean) **3** *fam* : nuisance, bother
vainilla *nf* : vanilla
vaivén *nm, pl* **vaivenes 1** : swinging, swaying, rocking **2** : change, fluctuation ⟨los vaivenes de la vida : life's ups and downs⟩
vajilla *nf* : dishes *pl*, set of dishes
valdrá, etc. → **valer**
vale *nm* **1** : voucher **2** PAGARÉ : promissory note, IOU
valedero, -ra *adj* : valid
valentía *nf* : courage, valor
valer {84} *vt* **1** : to be worth ⟨valen una fortuna : they're worth a fortune⟩ ⟨no vale protestar : there's no point in protesting⟩ ⟨valer la pena : to be worth the trouble⟩ **2** : to cost ⟨¿cuánto vale? : how much does it cost?⟩ **3** : to earn, to gain ⟨le valió una reprimenda : it earned him a reprimand⟩ **4** : to protect, to aid ⟨¡válgame Dios! : God help me!⟩ **5** : to be equal to — *vi* **1** : to have value ⟨sus consejos no valen para nada : his advice is worthless⟩ **2** : to be valid, to count ⟨¡eso no vale! : that doesn't count!⟩ **3 hacerse valer** : to assert oneself **4 más vale** : it's better ⟨más vale que te vayas : you'd better go⟩ — **valerse** *vr* **1 ~ de** : to take advantage of **2 valerse solo** *or* **valerse por sí mismo** : to look after oneself **3** *Mex* : to be fair ⟨no se vale : it's not fair⟩

valeroso, -sa *adj* : brave, valiant
valet ['balɛt, -'le] *nm* : jack (in playing cards)
valga, etc. → **valer**
valía *nf* : value, worth
validar *vt* : to validate — **validación** *nf*
validez *nf* : validity
válido, -da *adj* : valid
valiente *adj* **1** : brave, valiant **2** (*used ironically*) : fine, great ⟨¡valiente amiga! : what a fine friend!⟩ — **valientemente** *adv*
valija *nf* : suitcase, valise
valioso, -sa *adj* PRECIOSO : valuable, precious
valla *nf* **1** : fence, barricade **2** : hurdle (in sports) **3** : obstacle, hindrance
vallar *vt* : to fence, to put a fence around
valle *nm* : valley, vale
valor *nm* **1** : value, worth, importance **2** CORAJE : courage, valor **3 valores** *nmpl* : values, principles **4 valores** *nmpl* : securities, bonds **5 sin ~** : worthless
valoración *nf, pl* **-ciones 1** EVALUACIÓN : valuation, appraisal, assessment **2** APRECIACIÓN : appreciation
valorar *vt* **1** EVALUAR : to evaluate, to appraise, to assess **2** APRECIAR : to value, to appreciate
valorizarse {21} *vr* : to appreciate, to increase in value — **valorización** *nf*
vals *nm* : waltz
valsar *vi* : to waltz
valuación *nf, pl* **-ciones** : valuation, appraisal
valuar {3} *vt* : to value, to appraise, to assess
válvula *nf* **1** : valve **2 válvula reguladora** : throttle
vamos → **ir**
vampiro *nm* : vampire
van → **ir**
vanadio *nm* : vanadium
vanagloriarse *vr* : to boast, to brag
vanamente *adv* : vainly, in vain
vandalismo *nm* : vandalism
vándalo *nm* : vandal — **vandalismo** *nm*
vanguardia *nf* **1** : vanguard **2** : avante-garde **3 a la vanguardia** : at the forefront
vanidad *nf* : vanity
vanidoso, -sa *adj* PRESUMIDO : vain, conceited
vano, -na *adj* **1** INÚTIL : vain, useless **2** : vain, worthless ⟨vanas promesas : empty promises⟩ **3 en ~** : in vain, of no avail
vapor *nm* **1** : vapor, steam **2** : steamer, steamship **3 al vapor** : steamed
vaporizador *nm* : vaporizer
vaporizar {21} *vt* : to vaporize — **vaporizarse** *vr* — **vaporización** *nf*
vaporoso, -sa *adj* **1** : vaporous **2** : sheer, airy
vapulear *vt* : to beat, to thrash
vaquero[1], **-ra** *adj* : cowboy ⟨pantalón vaquero : jeans⟩

vaquero², -ra n : cowboy m, cowgirl f
vaqueros nmpl JEANS : jeans
vaquilla nf : heifer
vara nf 1 : pole, stick, rod 2 : staff (of office) 3 : lance, pike (in bullfighting) 4 : yardstick 5 **vara de oro** : goldenrod
varado, -da adj 1 : beached, aground 2 : stranded
varar vt : to beach (a ship), to strand — vi : to run aground
variable adj & nf : variable — **variabilidad** nf
variación nf, pl **-ciones** : variation
variado, -da adj : varied, diverse
variante adj & nf : variant
varianza nf : variance
variar {85} vt 1 : to change, to alter 2 : to diversify — vi 1 : to vary, to change 2 **variar de opinión** : to change one's mind
varicela nf : chicken pox
varices or **várices** nfpl : varicose veins
varicoso, -sa adj : varicose
variedad nf DIVERSIDAD : variety, diversity
varilla nf 1 : rod, bar 2 : spoke (of a wheel) 3 : rib (of an umbrella)
vario, -ria adj 1 : varied, diverse 2 : variegated, motley 3 : changeable 4 **varios, varias** pl : various, several
variopinto, -ta adj : diverse, assorted, motley
varita nf : wand ⟨varita mágica : magic wand⟩
varón nm, pl **varones** 1 HOMBRE : man, male 2 NIÑO : boy
varonil adj 1 : masculine, manly 2 : mannish
vas → ir
vasallo nm : vassal — **vasallaje** nm
vasco¹, -ca adj & n : Basque
vasco² nm : Basque (language)
vascular adj : vascular
vasija nf : container, vessel
vaso nm 1 : glass, tumbler 2 : glassful 3 : vessel ⟨vaso sanguíneo : blood vessel⟩
vástago nm 1 : offspring, descendant 2 : shoot (of a plant)
vastedad nf : vastness, immensity
vasto, -ta adj : vast, immense
vataje nm : wattage
vaticinar vt : to predict, to foretell
vaticinio nm : prediction, prophecy
vatio nm : watt
vaya, etc. → ir
Vd., Vds. → usted
ve, etc. → ir, ver
vea, etc. → ver
vecinal adj : local
vecindad nf 1 : neighborhood, vicinity 2 **casa de vecindad** : tenement
vecindario nm 1 : neighborhood, area 2 : residents pl
vecino, -na n 1 : neighbor 2 : resident, inhabitant
veda nf 1 PROHIBICIÓN : prohibition 2 : closed season (for hunting or fishing)

vedar vt 1 : to prohibit, to ban 2 IMPEDIR : to impede, to prevent
vega nf : fertile lowland
vegetación nf, pl **-ciones** 1 : vegetation 2 **vegetaciones** nfpl : adenoids
vegetal adj & nm : vegetable, plant
vegetar vi : to vegetate
vegetarianismo nm : vegetarianism
vegetariano, -na adj & n : vegetarian
vegetativo, -va adj : vegetative
vehemente adj : vehement — **vehemencia** nf
vehículo nm : vehicle — **vehicular** adj
veía, etc. → ver
veinte adj & nm : twenty
veinteavo¹, -va adj : twentieth
veinteavo² nm : twentieth (fraction)
veintena nf : group of twenty, score ⟨una veintena de participantes : about twenty participants⟩
vejación nf, pl **-ciones** : ill-treatment, humiliation
vejar vt : to mistreat, to ridicule, to harass
vejete nm : old fellow, codger
vejez nf : old age
vejiga nf 1 : bladder 2 AMPOLLA : blister
vela nf 1 VIGILIA : wakefulness ⟨pasé la noche en vela : I stayed awake all night⟩ 2 : watch, vigil, wake 3 : candle 4 : sail
velada nf : evening party, soirée
velado, -da adj 1 : veiled, hidden 2 : blurred 3 : muffled
velador¹, -dora n : guard, night watchman
velador² nm 1 : candlestick 2 : night table
velar vt 1 : to hold a wake over 2 : to watch over, to sit up with 3 : to blur, to expose (a photo) 4 : to veil, to conceal — vi 1 : to stay awake 2 ~ **por** : to watch over, to look after
velatorio nm VELORIO : wake (for the dead)
veleidad nf 1 : fickleness 2 : whim, caprice
veleidoso, -sa : fickle, capricious
velero nm 1 : sailing ship 2 : sailboat
veleta nf : weather vane
vello nm 1 : body hair 2 : down, fuzz
vellocino nm : fleece
vellón nm, pl **vellones** 1 : fleece, sheepskin 2 PRi : nickel (coin)
vellosidad nf : downiness, hairiness
velloso, -sa adj : downy, fluffy, hairy
velo nm : veil
velocidad nf 1 : speed, velocity ⟨velocidad máxima : speed limit⟩ 2 MARCHA : gear (of an automobile)
velocímetro nm : speedometer
velocista nmf : sprinter
velorio nm VELATORIO : wake (for the dead)
velour nm : velour, velours
veloz adj, pl **veloces** : fast, quick, swift — **velozmente** adv
ven → venir

vena *nf* **1** : vein ⟨vena yugular : jugular vein⟩ **2** : vein, seam, lode **3** : grain (of wood) **4** : style ⟨en vena lírica : in a lyrical vein⟩ **5** : strain, touch ⟨una vena de humor : a touch of humor⟩ **6** : mood

venado *nm* **1** : deer **2** : venison

venal *adj* : venal — **venalidad** *nf*

vencedor, -dora *n* : winner, victor

vencejo *nm* : swift (bird)

vencer {86} *vt* **1** DERROTAR : to vanquish, to defeat **2** SUPERAR : to overcome, to surmount — *vi* **1** GANAR : to win, to triumph **2** CADUCAR : to expire ⟨el plazo vence el jueves : the deadline is Thursday⟩ **3** : to fall due, to mature — **vencerse** *vr* **1** DOMINARSE : to control oneself **2** : to break, to collapse

vencido, -da *adj* **1** : defeated **2** : expired **3** : due, payable **4 darse por vencido** : to give up

vencimiento *nm* **1** : defeat **2** : expiration **3** : maturity (of a loan)

venda *nf* : bandage

vendaje *nm* : bandage, dressing

vendar *vt* **1** : to bandage **2 vendar los ojos** : to blindfold

vendaval *nm* : gale, strong wind

vendedor, -dora *n* : salesperson, salesman *m*, saleswoman *f*

vender *vt* **1** : to sell **2** : to sell out, to betray — **venderse** *vr* **1** : to be sold ⟨se vende : for sale⟩ **2** : to sell out

vendetta *nf* : vendetta

vendible *adj* : salable, marketable

vendimia *nf* : grape harvest

vendrá, etc. → **venir**

veneno *nm* **1** : poison **2** : venom

venenoso, -sa *adj* : poisonous, venomous

venerable *adj* : venerable

veneración *nf, pl* **-ciones** : veneration, reverence

venerar *vt* : to venerate, to revere

venéreo, -rea *adj* : venereal

venero *nm* **1** VENA : seam, lode, vein **2** MANANTIAL : spring **3** FUENTE : origin, source

venezolano, -na *adj & n* : Venezuelan

venga, etc. → **venir**

vengador, -dora *n* : avenger

venganza *nf* : vengeance, revenge

vengar {52} *vt* : to avenge — **vengarse** *vr* : to get even, to revenge oneself

vengativo, -va *adj* : vindictive, vengeful

vengue, etc. → **vengar**

venia *nf* **1** PERMISO : permission, leave **2** PERDÓN : pardon **3** : bow (of the head)

venial *adj* : venial

venida *nf* **1** LLEGADA : arrival, coming **2** REGRESO : return **3 idas y venidas** : comings and goings

venidero, -ra *adj* : coming, future

venir {87} *vi* **1** : to come ⟨lo vi venir : I saw him coming⟩ ⟨¡venga! : come on!⟩ **2** : to arrive ⟨vinieron en coche : they came by car⟩ **3** : to come, to originate ⟨sus zapatos vienen de Italia : her shoes are from Italy⟩ **4** : to come, to be available ⟨viene envuelto en plástico : it comes wrapped in plastic⟩ **5** : to come back, to return **6** : to affect, to overcome ⟨me vino un vahído : a dizzy spell came over me⟩ **7** : to fit ⟨te viene un poco grande : it's a little big for you⟩ **8** (*with the present participle*) : to have been ⟨viene entrenando diariamente : he's been training daily⟩ **9 ~ a** (*with the infinitive*) : to end up, to turn out ⟨viene a ser lo mismo : it comes out the same⟩ **10 que viene** : coming, next ⟨el año que viene : next year⟩ **11 venir bien** : to be suitable, to be just right — **venirse** *vr* **1** : to come, to arrive **2** : to come back **3 venirse abajo** : to fall apart, to collapse

venta *nf* **1** : sale **2 venta al por menor** *or* **venta al detalle** : retail sales

ventaja *nf* **1** : advantage **2** : lead, head start **3 ventajas** *nfpl* : perks, extras

ventajoso, -sa *adj* **1** : advantageous **2** : profitable — **ventajosamente** *adv*

ventana *nf* **1** : window (of a building) **2 ventana de la nariz** : nostril

ventanal *nm* : large window

ventanilla *nf* **1** : window (of a vehicle or airplane) **2** : ticket window, box office

ventero, -ra *n* : innkeeper

ventilación *nf, pl* **-ciones** : ventilation

ventilador *nm* **1** : ventilator **2** : fan

ventilar *vt* **1** : to ventilate, to air out **2** : to air, to discuss **3** : to make public, to reveal — **ventilarse** *vr* : to get some air

ventisca *nf* : snowstorm, blizzard

ventisquero *nm* : snowdrift

ventosear *vi* : to break wind

ventosidad *nf* : wind, flatulence

ventoso, -sa *adj* : windy

ventrículo *nm* : ventricle

ventrílocuo, -cua *n* : ventriloquist

ventriloquia *nf* : ventriloquism

ventura *nf* **1** : fortune, luck, chance **2** : happiness **3 a la ventura** : at random, as it comes

venturoso, -sa *adj* **1** AFORTUNADO : fortunate, lucky **2** : successful

Venus *nm* : Venus

venza, etc. → **vencer**

ver[1] {88} *vt* **1** : to see ⟨vimos la película : we saw the movie⟩ **2** ENTENDER : to understand ⟨ya lo veo : now I get it⟩ **3** EXAMINAR : to examine, to look into ⟨lo veré : I'll take a look at it⟩ **4** JUZGAR : to see, to judge ⟨a mi manera de ver : to my way of thinking⟩ **5** VISITAR : to meet with, to visit **6** AVERIGUAR : to find out **7 a ver** *or* **vamos a ver** : let's see — *vi* **1** : to see **2** ENTERARSE : to learn, to find out **3** ENTENDER : to understand — **verse** *vr* **1** HALLARSE : to find oneself **2** PARECER : to look, to appear **3** ENCONTRARSE : to see each other, to meet

ver[2] *nm* **1** : looks *pl*, appearance **2** : opinion ⟨a mi ver : in my view⟩

vera *nf* : side ⟨a la vera del camino : alongside the road⟩
veracidad *nf* : truthfulness, veracity
veranda *nf* : veranda
veraneante *nmf* : summer vacationer
veranear *vi* : to spend the summer
veraniego, -ga *adj* **1** ESTIVAL : summer ⟨el sol veraniego : the summer sun⟩ **2** : summery
verano *nm* : summer
veras *nfpl* **de ~** : really, truly
veraz *adj, pl* **veraces** : truthful, veracious
verbal *adj* : verbal — **verbalmente** *adv*
verbalizar {21} *vt* : to verbalize, to express
verbena *nf* **1** FIESTA : festival, fair **2** : verbena, vervain
verbigracia *adv* : for example
verbo *nm* : verb
verborrea *nf* : verbiage
verbosidad *nf* : verbosity, wordiness
verboso, -sa *adj* : verbose, wordy
verdad *nf* **1** : truth **2 de ~** : really, truly **3 ¿verdad?** : right?, isn't that so?
verdaderamente *adv* : really, truly
verdadero, -dera *adj* **1** REAL, VERÍDICO : true, real **2** AUTÉNTICO : genuine
verde[1] *adj* **1** : green (in color) **2** : green, unripe **3** : inexperienced, green **4** : dirty, risqué
verde[2] *nm* : green
verdear *vi* : to turn green, to become verdant
verdín *nm, pl* **verdines** : slime, scum
verdor *nm* **1** : greenness **2** : verdure
verdoso, -sa *adj* : greenish
verdugo *nm* **1** : executioner, hangman **2** : tyrant
verdugón *nm, pl* **-gones** : welt, wheal
verdura *nf* : vegetable(s), green(s)
vereda *nf* **1** SENDA : path, trail **2** : sidewalk, pavement
veredicto *nm* : verdict
verga *nf* : spar, yard (of a ship)
vergonzoso, -sa *adj* **1** : disgraceful, shameful **2** : bashful, shy — **vergonzosamente** *adv*
vergüenza *nf* **1** : disgrace, shame **2** : embarrassment **3** : bashfulness, shyness
vericueto *nm* : rough terrain
verídico, -ca *adj* **1** REAL, VERDADERO : true, real **2** VERAZ : truthful
verificación *nf, pl* **-ciones 1** : verification **2** : testing, checking
verificador, -dora *n* : inspector, tester
verificar {72} *vt* **1** : to verify, to confirm **2** : to test, to check **3** : to carry out, to conduct — **verificarse** *vr* **1** : to take place, to occur **2** : to come true
verja *nf* **1** : rails *pl* (of a fence) **2** : grating, grille **3** : gate
vermut *nm, pl* **vermuts** : vermouth
vernáculo, -la *adj* : vernacular
vernal *adj* : vernal, spring
verosímil *adj* **1** : probable, likely **2** : credible, realistic

verosimilitud *nf* **1** : probability, likeliness **2** : verisimilitude
verraco *nm* : boar
verruga *nf* : wart
versado, -da *adj* **~ en** : versed in, knowledgeable about
versar *vi* **~ sobre** : to deal with, to be about
versátil *adj* **1** : versatile **2** : fickle
versatilidad *nf* **1** : versatility **2** : fickleness
versículo *nm* : verse (in the Bible)
versión *nf, pl* **versiones 1** : version **2** : translation
verso *nm* : verse
versus *prep* : versus, against
vértebra *nf* : vertebra — **vertebral** *adj*
vertebrado[1], **-da** *adj* : vertebrate
vertebrado[2] *nm* : vertebrate
vertedero *nm* **1** : garbage dump **2** DESAGÜE : drain, outlet
verter {56} *vt* **1** : to pour **2** : to spill, to shed **3** : to empty out **4** : to express, to voice **5** : to translate, to render — *vi* : to flow
vertical *adj* & *nf* : vertical — **verticalmente** *adv*
vértice *nm* : vertex, apex
vertido *nm* : spilling, spill
vertiente *nf* **1** : slope **2** : aspect, side, element
vertiginoso, -sa *adj* : vertiginous — **vertiginosamente** *adv*
vértigo *nm* : vertigo, dizziness
vesícula *nf* **1** : vesicle **2 vesícula biliar** : gallbladder
vesicular *adj* : vesicular
vestíbulo *nm* : vestibule, hall, lobby, foyer
vestido *nm* **1** : dress, costume, clothes *pl* **2** : dress (garment)
vestidor *nm* : dressing room
vestiduras *nfpl* **1** : clothing, raiment, regalia **2** *or* **vestiduras sacerdotales** : vestments
vestigio *nm* : vestige, sign, trace
vestimenta *nf* ROPA : clothing, clothes *pl*
vestir {54} *vt* **1** : to dress, to clothe **2** LLEVAR : to wear **3** ADORNAR : to decorate, to dress up — *vi* **1** : to dress ⟨vestir bien : to dress well⟩ **2** : to look good, to suit the occasion — **vestirse** *vr* **1** : to get dressed **2 ~ de** : to dress up as ⟨se vistieron de soldados : they dressed up as soldiers⟩ **3 ~ de** : to wear, to dress in
vestuario *nm* **1** : wardrobe **2** : dressing room, locker room
veta *nf* **1** : grain (in wood) **2** : vein, seam, lode **3** : trace, streak ⟨una veta de terco : a stubborn streak⟩
vetar *vt* : to veto
veteado, -da *adj* : streaked, veined
veterano, -na *adj* & *n* : veteran
veterinaria *nf* : veterinary medicine
veterinario[1], **-ria** *adj* : veterinary
veterinario[2], **-ria** *n* : veterinarian

veto *nm* : veto

vetusto, -ta *adj* ANTIGUO : ancient, very old

vez *nf, pl* **veces 1** : time, occasion ⟨a la vez : at the same time⟩ ⟨a veces : at times, occasionally⟩ ⟨de vez en cuando : from time to time⟩ **2** (*with numbers*) : time ⟨una vez : once⟩ ⟨de una vez : all at once⟩ ⟨de una vez para siempre : once and for all⟩ ⟨dos veces : twice⟩ **3** : turn ⟨a su vez : in turn⟩ ⟨en vez de : instead of⟩ ⟨hacer las veces de : to act as, to stand in for⟩

vía¹ *nf* **1** RUTA, CAMINO : road, route, way ⟨Vía Láctea : Milky Way⟩ **2** MEDIO : means, way ⟨por vía oficial : through official channels⟩ **3** : track, line (of a railroad) **4** : tract, passage ⟨por vía oral : orally⟩ **5 en vías de** : in the process of ⟨en vías de solución : on the road to a solution⟩ **6 por ~** : by (in transportation) ⟨por vía aérea : by air, airmail⟩

vía² *prep* : via

viable *adj* : viable, feasible — **viabilidad** *nf*

viaducto *nm* : viaduct

viajante *mf* : traveling salesman, traveling saleswoman

viajar *vi* : to travel, to journey

viaje *nm* : trip, journey ⟨viaje de negocios : business trip⟩

viajero¹, **-ra** *adj* : traveling

viajero², **-ra** *n* **1** : traveler **2** PASAJERO : passenger

vial *adj* : road, traffic

viático *nm* : travel allowance, travel expenses *pl*

víbora *nf* : viper

vibración *nf, pl* **-ciones** : vibration

vibrador *nm* : vibrator

vibrante *adj* **1** : vibrant **2** : vibrating

vibrar *vi* : to vibrate

vibratorio, -ria *adj* : vibratory

vicario, -ria *n* : vicar

vicealmirante *nmf* : vice admiral

vicepresidente, -ta *n* : vice president — **vicepresidencia** *nf*

viceversa *adv* : vice versa, conversely

viciado, -da *adj* : stuffy, close

viciar *vt* **1** : to corrupt **2** : to invalidate **3** FALSEAR : to distort **4** : to pollute, to adulterate

vicio *nm* **1** : vice, depravity **2** : bad habit **3** : defect, blemish

vicioso, -sa *adj* : depraved, corrupt

vicisitud *nf* : vicissitude

víctima *nf* : victim

victimario, -ria *n* ASESINO : killer, murderer

victimizar {21} *vt Arg, Mex* : to victimize

victoria *nf* : victory — **victorioso, -sa** *adj* — **victoriosamente** *adv*

victoriano, -na *adj* : Victorian

vid *nf* : vine, grapevine

vida *nf* **1** : life ⟨la vida cotidiana : everyday life⟩ **2** : life span, lifetime **3** BI-

OGRAFÍA : biography, life **4** : way of life, lifestyle **5** : livelihood ⟨ganarse la vida : to earn one's living⟩ **6** VIVEZA : liveliness **7 media vida** : half-life

vidente *nmf* **1** : psychic, clairvoyant **2** : sighted person

video *or* **vídeo** *nm* : video

videocasete *or* **videocassette** *nm* : videocassette

videocasetera *or* **videocassettera** *nf* : videocassette recorder, VCR

videocinta *nf* : videotape

videograbar *vt* : to videotape

vidriado *nm* : glaze

vidriar *vt* : to glaze (pottery, tile, etc.)

vidriera *nf* **1** : stained-glass window **2** : glass door or window **3** : store window

vidriero, -ra *n* : glazier

vidrio *nm* **1** : glass, piece of glass **2** : windowpane

vidrioso, -sa *adj* **1** : brittle, fragile **2** : slippery **3** : glassy, glazed (of eyes) **4** : touchy, delicate

vieira *nf* **1** : scallop **2** : scallop shell

viejo¹, **-ja** *adj* **1** ANCIANO : old, elderly **2** ANTIGUO : former, longstanding ⟨viejas tradiciones : old traditions⟩ ⟨viejos amigos : old friends⟩ **3** GASTADO : old, worn, worn-out

viejo², **-ja** *n* ANCIANO : old man *m*, old woman *f*

viene, etc. → **venir**

viento *nm* **1** : wind **2 hacer viento** : to be windy **3 contra viento y marea** : against all odds **4 viento alisio** : trade wind **5 viento en popa** : splendidly, successfully

vientre *nm* **1** : abdomen, belly **2** : womb **3** : bowels *pl*

viernes *nms & pl* : Friday

vierte, etc. → **verter**

vietnamita¹ *adj & nmf* : Vietnamese

vietnamita² *nm* : Vietnamese (language)

viga *nf* **1** : beam, rafter, girder **2 viga voladiza** : cantilever

vigencia *nf* **1** : validity **2** : force, effect ⟨entrar en vigencia : to go into effect⟩

vigente *adj* : valid, in force

vigésimo¹, **-ma** *adj* : twentieth, twenty- ⟨la vigésima segunda edición : the twenty-second edition⟩

vigésimo², **-ma** *n* : twentieth, twenty- (in a series)

vigía *nmf* : lookout

vigilancia *nf* : vigilance, watchfulness ⟨bajo vigilancia : under surveillance⟩

vigilante¹ *adj* : vigilant, watchful

vigilante² *nmf* : watchman, guard

vigilar *vt* **1** CUIDAR : to look after, to keep an eye on **2** GUARDAR : to watch over, to guard — *vi* **1** : to be watchful **2** : to keep watch

vigilia *nf* **1** VELA : wakefulness **2** : night work **3** : vigil (in religion)

vigor *nm* **1** : vigor, energy, strength **2** VIGENCIA : force, effect

vigorizante *adj* : invigorating

vigorizar {21} *vt* : to strengthen, to invigorate

vigoroso, -sa *adj* : vigorous — **vigorosamente** *adv*

VIH *nm* (virus de *i*nmunodeficiencia humana) : HIV

vikingo, -ga *adj & n* : Viking

vil *adj* : vile, despicable

vileza *nf* **1** : vileness **2** : despicable action, villainy

vilipendiar *vt* : to vilify, to revile

villa *nf* **1** : town, village **2** : villa

villancico *nm* : carol, Christmas carol

villano, -na *n* **1** : villain **2** : peasant

vilo *nm* **1 en** ∼ : in the air **2 en** ∼ : uncertain, in suspense

vinagre *nm* : vinegar

vinagrera *nf* : cruet (for vinegar)

vinatería *nf* : wine shop

vinculación *nf, pl* **-ciones 1** : linking **2** RELACIÓN : bond, link, connection

vincular *vt* CONECTAR, RELACIONAR : to tie, to link, to connect

vínculo *nm* LAZO : tie, link, bond

vindicación *nf, pl* **-ciones** : vindication

vindicar *vt* **1** : to vindicate **2** : to avenge

vinilo *nm* : vinyl

vino¹, etc. → **venir**

vino² *nm* : wine

viña *nf* : vineyard

viñedo *nm* : vineyard

vio, etc. → **ver**

viola *nf* : viola

violación *nf, pl* **-ciones 1** : violation, offense **2** : rape

violador¹, -dora *n* : violator, offender

violador² *nm* : rapist

violar *vt* **1** : to rape **2** : to violate (a law or right) **3** PROFANAR : to desecrate

violencia *nf* : violence

violentamente *adv* : by force, violently

violentar *vt* **1** FORZAR : to break open, to force **2** : to distort (words or ideas) — **violentarse** *vr* : to force oneself

violento, -ta *adj* **1** : violent **2** EMBARAZOSO, INCÓMODO : awkward, embarassing

violeta¹ *adj & nm* : violet (color)

violeta² *nf* : violet (flower)

violín *nm, pl* **-lines** : violin

violinista *nmf* : violinist

violonchelista *nmf* : cellist

violonchelo *nm* : cello, violoncello

VIP *nmf, pl* **VIPs** : VIP

vira *nf* : welt (of a shoe)

virago *nf* : virago, shrew

viraje *nm* **1** : turn, swerve **2** : change

viral *adj* : viral

virar *vi* : to tack, to turn, to veer

virgen¹ *adj* : virgin ⟨lana virgen : virgin wool⟩

virgen² *nmf, pl* **vírgenes** : virgin ⟨la Santísima Virgen : the Blessed Virgin⟩

virginal *adj* : virginal, chaste

virginidad *nf* : virginity

Virgo *nmf* : Virgo

vírico, -ca *adj* : viral

viril *adj* : virile — **virilidad** *nf*

virrey, -rreina *n* : viceroy *m*, vicereine *f*

virtual *adj* : virtual — **virtualmente** *adv*

virtud *nf* **1** : virtue **2 en virtud de** : by virtue of

virtuosismo *nm* : virtuosity

virtuoso¹, -sa *adj* : virtuous — **virtuosamente** *adv*

virtuoso², -sa *n* : virtuoso

viruela *nf* **1** : smallpox **2** : pockmark

virulencia *nf* : virulence

virulento, -ta *adj* : virulent

virus *nm* : virus

viruta *nf* : shaving

visa *nf* : visa

visado *nm Spain* : visa

visaje *nm* : face, grimace ⟨hacer visajes : to make faces⟩

visceral *adj* : visceral

vísceras *nfpl* : viscera, entrails

visconde, -desa *n* : viscount *m*, viscountess *f*

viscosidad *nf* : viscosity

viscoso, -sa *adj* : viscous

visera *nf* : visor

visibilidad *nf* : visibility

visible *adj* : visible — **visiblemente** *adv*

visión *nf, pl* **visiones 1** : vision, eyesight **2** : view, perspective **3** : vision, illusion ⟨ver visiones : to be seeing things⟩

visionario, -ria *adj & n* : visionary

visita *nf* **1** : visit, call **2** : visitor **3 ir de visita** : to go visiting

visitador, -dora *n* : visitor, frequent caller

visitante¹ *adj* : visiting

visitante² *nmf* : visitor

visitar *vt* : to visit

vislumbrar *vt* **1** : to discern, to make out **2** : to begin to see, to have an inkling of

vislumbre *nf* : glimmer, gleam

viso *nm* **1** APARIENCIA : appearance ⟨tener visos de : to seem, to show signs of⟩ **2** DESTELLO : glint, gleam **3** : sheen, iridescence

visón *nm, pl* **visones** : mink

víspera *nf* **1** : eve, day before **2** **vísperas** *nfpl* : vespers

vista *nf* **1** VISIÓN : vision, eyesight **2** MIRADA : look, gaze, glance **3** PANORAMA : view, vista, panorama **4** : hearing (in court) **5 a primera vista** : at first sight **6 en vista de** : in view of **7 hacer la vista gorda** : to turn a blind eye **8 ¡hasta la vista!** : so long!, see you! **9 perder de vista** : to lose sight of **10 punto de vista** : point of view

vistazo *nm* : glance, look

viste, etc. → **ver¹, vestir**

visto¹ *pp* → **ver**

visto², -ta *adj* **1** : obvious, clear **2** : in view of, considering **3 estar bien visto** : to be approved of **4 estar mal visto** : to be frowned upon **5 por lo visto** : apparently **6 nunca visto** : unheard-of **7 visto que** : since, given that

visto³ *nm* **visto bueno** : approval

vistoso, -sa *adj* : colorful, bright
visual *adj* : visual — **visualmente** *adv*
visualización *nf, pl* **-ciones** : visualization
visualizar {21} *vt* **1** : to visualize **2** : to display (on a screen)
vital *adj* **1** : vital **2** : lively, dynamic
vitalicio, -cia *adj* : life, lifetime
vitalidad *nf* : vitality
vitamina *nf* : vitamin
vitamínico, -ca *adj* : vitamin ⟨complejos vitamínicos : vitamin compounds⟩
vitorear *vt* : to cheer, to acclaim
vitral *nm* : stained-glass window
vítreo, -rea *adj* : vitreous, glassy
vitrina *nf* **1** : showcase, display case **2** : store window
vitriolo *nm* : vitriol
vituperar *vt* : to condemn, to vituperate against
vituperio *nm* : vituperation, censure
viudez *nf* : widowerhood, widowhood
viudo, -da *n* : widower *m*, widow *f*
vivacidad *nf* VIVEZA : vivacity, liveliness
vivamente *adv* **1** : in a lively manner **2** : vividly **3** : strongly, acutely ⟨lo recomendamos vivamente : we strongly recommend it⟩
vivaque *nm* : bivouac
vivaquear *vi* : to bivouac
vivar *vi* : to cheer
vivaz *adj, pl* **vivaces** **1** : lively, vivacious **2** : clever, sharp **3** : perennial
víveres *nmpl* : provisions, supplies, food
vivero *nm* **1** : nursery (for plants) **2** : hatchery, fish farm
viveza *nf* **1** VIVACIDAD : liveliness **2** BRILLO : vividness, brightness **3** ASTUCIA : cleverness, sharpness
vívido, -da *adj* : vivid, lively
vividor, -dora *n* : sponger, parasite
vivienda *nf* **1** : housing **2** MORADA : dwelling, home
viviente *adj* : living
vivificar {72} *vt* : to vivify, to give life to
vivir[1] *vi* **1** : to live, to be alive **2** SUBSISTIR : to subsist, to make a living **3** RESIDIR : to reside **4** : to spend one's life ⟨vive para trabajar : she lives to work⟩ **5** ~ **de** : to live on — *vt* **1** : to live ⟨vivir su vida : to live one's life⟩ **2** EXPERIMENTAR : to go through, to experience
vivir[2] *nm* **1** : life, lifestyle **2 de mal vivir** : disreputable
vivisección *nf, pl* **-ciones** : vivisection
vivo, -va *adj* **1** : alive **2** INTENSO : vivid, bright, intense **3** ANIMADO : lively, vivacious **4** ASTUTO : sharp, clever **5 en** ~ : live ⟨transmisión en vivo : live broadcast⟩ **6 al rojo vivo** : red-hot
vizconde, -desa *n* : viscount *m*, viscountess *f*
vocablo *nm* PALABRA : word
vocabulario *nm* : vocabulary
vocación *nf, pl* **-ciones** : vocation
vocacional *adj* : vocational
vocal[1] *adj* : vocal

vocal[2] *nmf* : member (of a committee, board, etc.)
vocal[3] *nf* : vowel
vocalista *nmf* CANTANTE : singer, vocalist
vocalizar {21} *vi* : to vocalize
vocear *v* : to shout
vocerío *nm* : clamor, shouting
vocero, -ra *n* PORTAVOZ : spokesperson, spokesman *m*, spokeswoman *f*
vociferante *adj* : vociferous
vociferar *vi* GRITAR : to shout, to yell
vodevil *nm* : vaudeville
vodka *nm* : vodka
voladizo[1]**, -za** *adj* : projecting
voladizo[2] *nm* : projection
volador, -dora *adj* : flying
volando *adv* : quickly, in a hurry
volante[1] *adj* : flying
volante[2] *nm* **1** : steering wheel **2** FOLLETO : flier, circular **3** : shuttlecock **4** : flywheel **5** : balance wheel (of a watch) **6** : ruffle, flounce
volar {19} *vi* **1** : to fly **2** CORRER : to hurry, to rush ⟨el tiempo vuela : time flies⟩ ⟨pasar volando : to fly past⟩ **3** DIVULGARSE : to spread ⟨unos rumores volaban : rumors were spreading around⟩ **4** DESAPARECER : to disappear ⟨el dinero ya voló : the money's already gone⟩ — *vt* **1** : to blow up, to demolish **2** : to irritate
volátil *adj* : volatile — **volatilidad** *nf*
volatilizar {21} *vt* : to volatize — **volatilizarse** *vr*
volcán *nm, pl* **volcanes** : volcano
volcánico, -ca *adj* : volcanic
volcar {82} *vt* **1** : to upset, to knock over, to turn over **2** : to empty out **3** : to make dizzy **4** : to cause a change of mind in **5** : to irritate — *vi* **1** : to overturn, to tip over **2** : to capsize — **volcarse** *vr* **1** : to overturn **2** : to do one's utmost
volea *nf* : volley (in sports)
volear *vi* : to volley (in sports)
voleibol *nm* : volleyball
voleo *nm* **al voleo** : haphazardly, at random
volframio *nm* : wolfram, tungsten
volición *nf, pl* **-ciones** : volition
volqué, etc. → **volcar**
voltaje *nm* : voltage
voltear *vt* **1** : to turn over, to turn upside down **2** : to reverse, to turn inside out **3** : to turn ⟨voltear la cara : to turn one's head⟩ **4** : to knock down — *vi* **1** : to roll over, to do somersaults **2** : to turn ⟨volteó a la izquierda : he turned left⟩ — **voltearse** *vr* **1** : to turn around **2** : to change one's allegiance
voltereta *nf* : somersault, tumble
voltio *nm* : volt
volubilidad *nf* : fickleness, changeableness
voluble *adj* : fickle, changeable
volumen *nm, pl* **-lúmenes** **1** TOMO : volume, book **2** : capacity, size, bulk **3** CANTIDAD : amount ⟨el volumen de

ventas : the volume of sales〉 **4** : volume, loudness

voluminoso, -sa *adj* : voluminous, massive, bulky

voluntad *nf* **1** : will, volition **2** DESEO : desire, wish **3** INTENCIÓN : intention **4 a voluntad** : at will **5 buena voluntad** : good will **6 mala voluntad** : ill will **7 fuerza de voluntad** : willpower

voluntario¹, -ria *adj* : voluntary — **voluntariamente** *adv*

voluntario², -ria *n* : volunteer

voluntarioso, -sa *adj* **1** : stubborn **2** : willing, eager

voluptuosidad *nf* : voluptuousness

voluptuoso, -sa *adj* : voluptuous — **voluptuosamente** *adv*

voluta *nf* : spiral, column (of smoke)

volver {89} *vi* **1** : to return, to come or go back 〈volver a casa : to return home〉 **2** : to revert 〈volver al tema : to get back to the subject〉 **3 ~ a** : to do again 〈volvieron a llamar : they called again〉 **4 volver en sí** : to come to, to regain consciousness — *vt* **1** : to turn, to turn over, to turn inside out **2** : to return, to repay, to restore **3** : to cause, to make 〈la volvía loca : it was driving her crazy〉 — **volverse** *vr* **1** : to become 〈se volvió deprimido : he became depressed〉 **2** : to turn around

vomitar *vi* : to vomit — *vt* **1** : to vomit **2** : to spew out (lava, etc.)

vómito *nm* **1** : vomiting **2** : vomit

voracidad *nf* : voracity

vorágine *nf* : whirlpool, maelstrom

voraz *adj, pl* **voraces** : voracious — **vorazmente** *adv*

vórtice *nm* **1** : whirlpool, vortex **2** TORBELLINO : whirlwind

vos *pron* (*in some regions of Latin America*) : you

vosear *vt* : to address as *vos*

vosotros, -tras *pron pl Spain* **1** : you, yourselves **2** : ye

votación *nf, pl* **-ciones** : vote, voting

votante *nmf* : voter

votar *vi* : to vote — *vt* : to vote for

votivo, -va *adj* : votive

voto *nm* **1** : vote **2** : vow (in religion) **3 votos** *nmpl* : good wishes

voy → **ir**

voz *nf, pl* **voces** **1** : voice **2** : opinion, say **3** GRITO : shout, yell **4** : sound **5** VOCABLO : word, term **6** : rumor **7 a**

voz en cuello : at the top of one's lungs **8 dar voces** : to shout **9 en voz alta** : aloud, in a loud voice **10 en voz baja** : softly, in a low voice

vudú *nm* : voodoo

vuelco *nm* : upset, overturning 〈me dio un vuelco el corazón : my heart skipped a beat〉

vuela, etc. → **volar**

vuelca, vuelque etc. → **volcar**

vuelo *nm* **1** : flight, flying 〈alzar el vuelo : to take flight〉 **2** : flight (of an aircraft) 〈vuelo espacial : space flight〉 **3** : flare, fullness (of clothing) **4 al vuelo** : on the wing

vuelta *nf* **1** GIRO : turn 〈se dio la vuelta : he turned around〉 **2** REVOLUCIÓN : circle, revolution 〈dio la vuelta al mundo : she went around the world〉 〈las ruedas daban vueltas : the wheels were spinning〉 **3** : flip, turn 〈le dio la vuelta : she flipped it over〉 **4** : bend, curve 〈a la vuelta de la esquina : around the corner〉 **5** REGRESO : return 〈de ida y vuelta : round trip〉 〈a vuelta de correo : return mail〉 **6** : round, lap (in sports or games) **7** PASEO : walk, drive, ride 〈dio una vuelta : he went for a walk〉 **8** DORSO, REVÉS : back, other side 〈a la vuelta : on the back〉 **9** : cuff (of pants) **10 darle vueltas** : to think over **11 estar de vuelta** : to be back

vuelto *pp* → **volver**

vuelve, etc. → **volver**

vuestro¹, -stra *adj Spain* : your, of yours 〈vuestros coches : your cars〉 〈una amiga vuestra : a friend of yours〉

vuestro², -stra *pron Spain,* (*with definite article*) : yours 〈la vuestra es más grande : yours is bigger〉 〈esos son los vuestros : those are yours〉

vulcanizar {21} *vt* : to vulcanize

vulgar *adj* **1** : common **2** : vulgar

vulgaridad *nf* : vulgarity

vulgarismo *nm* : vulgarism

vulgarizar {21} *vt* : to vulgarize, to popularize

vulgarmente *adv* : vulgarly, popularly

vulgo *nm* **el vulgo** : the masses, common people

vulnerable *adj* : vulnerable — **vulnerabilidad** *nf*

vulnerar *vt* **1** : to injure, to damage (one's reputation or honor) **2** : to violate, to break (a law or contract)

W

w *nf* : twenty-fourth letter of the Spanish alphabet

wafle *nm* : waffle

waflera *nf* : waffle iron

wapití *nm* : wapiti, elk

whisky *nm, pl* **whiskys** *or* **whiskies** : whiskey

wigwam *nm* : wigwam

X

x *nf* : twenty-fifth letter of the Spanish alphabet
xenofobia *nf* : xenophobia
xenófobo¹, -ba *adj* : xenophobic

xenófobo², -ba *n* : xenophobe
xenón *nm* : xenon
xerocopiar *vt* : to photocopy, to xerox
xilófono *nm* : xylophone

Y

y¹ *nf* : twenty-sixth letter of the Spanish alphabet
y² *conj* (**e** *before words beginning with i- or hi-*) **1** : and ⟨mi hermano y yo : my brother and I⟩ ⟨¿y los demás? : and (what about) the others?⟩ **2** (*used in numbers*) ⟨cincuenta y cinco : fifty-five⟩ **3** *fam* : well ⟨y por supuesto : well, of course⟩
ya¹ *adv* **1** : already ⟨ya terminó : she's finished already⟩ **2** : now, right now ⟨¡hazlo ya! : do it now!⟩ ⟨ya mismo : right away⟩ **3** : later, soon ⟨ya iremos : we'll go later on⟩ **4** : no longer, anymore ⟨ya no fuma : he no longer smokes⟩ **5** (*used for emphasis*) ⟨¡ya lo sé! : I know!⟩ ⟨ya lo creo : of course⟩ **6 no ya** : not only ⟨no ya lloran sino gritan : they're not only crying but screaming⟩ **7 ya que** : now that, since ⟨ya que sabe la verdad : now that she knows the truth⟩
ya² *conj* **ya ... ya** : whether ... or, first ... then ⟨ya le gusta, ya no : first he likes it, then he doesn't⟩
yac *nm* : yak
yacer {90} *vi* : to lie ⟨en esta tumba yacen sus abuelos : his grandparents lie in this grave⟩
yacimiento *nm* : bed, deposit ⟨yacimiento petrolífero : oil field⟩
yaga, etc. → **yacer**
yanqui *adj & nmf* : Yankee
yarda *nf* : yard
yate *nm* : yacht
yaz, yazca, yazga etc. → **yacer**
yedra *nf* : ivy
yegua *nf* : mare
yelmo *nm* : helmet
yema *nf* **1** : bud, shoot **2** : yolk (of an egg) **3 yema del dedo** : fingertip
yemenita *adj & nmf* : Yemenite
yen *nm* : yen (currency)
yendo → **ir**

yerba *nf* **1** *or* **yerba mate** : maté **2** → **hierba**
yerga, yergue etc. → **erguir**
yermo¹, -ma *adj* : barren, deserted
yermo² *nm* : wasteland
yerno *nm* : son-in-law
yerra, etc. → **errar**
yerro *nm* : blunder, mistake
yerto, -ta *adj* : rigid, stiff
yesca *nf* : tinder
yeso *nm* **1** : plaster **2** : gypsum
yo¹ *nm* : ego, self
yo² *pron* **1** : I **2** : me ⟨todos menos yo : everyone except me⟩ ⟨tan bajo como yo : as short as me⟩ **3 soy yo** : it is I, it's me
yodado, -da *adj* : iodized
yodo *nm* : iodine
yoduro *nm* : iodide
yoga *nm* : yoga
yogui *nm* : yogi
yogurt *or* **yogur** *nm* : yogurt
yola *nf* : yawl
yoyo *or* **yoyó** *nm* : yo-yo
yuca *nf* **1** : yucca (plant) **2** : cassava, manioc
yucateco¹, -ca *adj* : of or from the Yucatán
yucateco², -ca *n* : person from the Yucatán
yudo → **judo**
yugo *nm* : yoke
yugoslavo, -va *adj & n* : Yugoslavian
yugular *adj* : jugular ⟨vena yugular : jugular vein⟩
yungas *nfpl Bol, Chile, Peru* : warm tropical valleys
yunque *nm* : anvil
yunta *nf* : yoke, team (of oxen)
yuppy *nmf, pl* **yuppies** : yuppie
yute *nm* : jute
yuxtaponer {60} *vt* : to juxtapose — **yuxtaposición** *nf*

Z

z *nf* : twenty-seventh letter of the Spanish alphabet
zacate *nm CA, Mex* **1** : grass, forage **2** : hay
zafacón *nm, pl* **-cones** *Car* : wastebasket
zafar *vt* : to loosen, to untie — **zafarse**

vr **1** : to loosen up, to come undone **2** : to get free of
zafio, -fia *adj* : coarse, crude
zafiro *nm* : sapphire
zaga *nf* **1** : defense (in sports) **2 a la zaga** *or* **en ~** : behind, in the rear
zagual *nm* : paddle (of a canoe)

zaguán *nm, pl* **zaguanes** : front hall, vestibule
zaherir {76} *vt* **1** : to criticize sharply **2** : to wound, to mortify
zahones *nmpl* : chaps
zaino, -na *adj* : chestnut (color)
zalamería *nf* : flattery, sweet talk
zalamero¹, -ra *adj* : flattering, fawning
zalamero², -ra *n* : flatterer
zambiano, -na *adj & nmf* : Zambian
zambullida *nf* : dive, plunge
zambullirse {38} *vr* : to dive, to plunge
zanahoria *nf* : carrot
zancada *nf* : stride, step
zancadilla *nf* **1** : trip, stumble **2** *fam* : trick, ruse
zancos *nmpl* : stilts
zancuda *nf* : wading bird
zancudo *nm* MOSQUITO : mosquito
zángano *nm* : drone, male bee
zanja *nf* : ditch, trench
zanjar *vt* ACLARAR : to settle, to clear up, to resolve
zapallo *nm Arg, Chile, Peru, Uru* : pumpkin
zapapico *nm* : pickax
zapata *nf* : brake shoe
zapatería *nf* **1** : shoemaker's, shoe factory **2** : shoe store
zapatero¹, -ra *adj* : dry, tough, poorly cooked
zapatero², -ra *n* : shoemaker, cobbler
zapatilla *nf* **1** PANTUFLA : slipper **2** *or* **zapatilla de deporte** : sneaker
zapato *nm* : shoe
zar, zarina *n* : czar *m*, czarina *f*
zarandear *vt* **1** : to sift, to sieve **2** : to shake, to jostle, to jiggle
zarapito *nm* : curlew
zarcillo *nm* **1** : earring **2** : tendril (of a plant)
zarigüeya *nf* : opossum
zarista *adj & nmf* : czarist
zarpa *nf* : paw
zarpar *vi* : to set sail, to raise anchor
zarza *nf* : bramble, blackberry bush
zarzamora *nf* **1** : blackberry **2** : bramble, blackberry bush

zarzaparrilla *nf* : sarsaparilla
zepelín *nm, pl* **-lines** : zeppelin
zigoto *nm* : zygote
zigzag *nm, pl* **zigzags** *or* **zigzagues** : zigzag
zigzaguear *vi* : to zigzag
zimbabuense *adj & nmf* : Zimbabwean
zinc *nm* : zinc
zinnia *nf* : zinnia
zíper *nm CA, Mex* : zipper
zircón *nm, pl* **zircones** : zircon
zócalo *nm Mex* : main square
zodíaco *or* **zodiaco** *nm* : zodiac — **zodíacal** *adj*
zombi *or* **zombie** *nmf* : zombie
zona *nf* : zone, district, area
zonzo¹, -za *adj* : stupid, silly
zonzo², -za *n* : idiot, nitwit
zoo *nm* : zoo
zoología *nf* : zoology
zoológico¹, -ca *adj* : zoological
zoológico² *nm* : zoo
zoólogo, -ga *n* : zoologist
zoom *nm* : zoom lens
zopilote *nm CA, Mex* : buzzard
zoquete *nmf fam* : oaf, blockhead
zorrillo *nm* MOFETA : skunk
zorro¹, -rra *adj* : sly, crafty
zorro², -rra *n* **1** : fox, vixen **2** : sly crafty person
zorzal *nm* : thrush
zozobra *nf* : anxiety, worry
zozobrar *vi* : to capsize
zueco *nm* : clog (shoe)
zulú¹ *adj & nmf* : Zulu
zulú² *nm* : Zulu (language)
zumaque *nm* : sumac
zumbar *vi* : to buzz, to hum — *vt fam* **1** : to hit, to thrash **2** : to make fun of
zumbido *nm* : buzzing, humming
zumo *nf* JUGO : juice
zurcir {83} *vt* : to darn, to mend
zurdo¹, -da *adj* : left-handed
zurdo², -da *n* : left-handed person
zurza, etc. → **zurcir**
zutano, -na → **fulano**

English–Spanish Dictionary

A

a¹ ['eɪ] *n, pl* **a's** *or* **as** ['eɪz] : primera letra del alfabeto inglés

a² [ə, 'eɪ] *art* (**an** /ən, 'æn] before vowel or silent h) **1** : un *m*, una *f* ⟨a house : una casa⟩ ⟨half an hour : media hora⟩ ⟨what a surprise! : ¡qué sorpresa!⟩ **2** PER : por, a la, al ⟨30 kilometers an hour : 30 kilómetros por hora⟩ ⟨twice a month : dos veces al mes⟩

aardvark ['ɑrd,vɑrk] *n* : oso *m* hormiguero

aback [ə'bæk] *adv* **1** : por sorpresa **2 to be taken aback** : quedarse desconcertado

abacus ['æbəkəs] *n, pl* **abaci** ['æbə,saɪ, -,ki:] *or* **abacuses** : ábaco *m*

abaft [ə'bæft] *adv* : a popa

abalone [,æbə'lo:ni] *n* : abulón *m*, oreja *f* marina

abandon¹ [ə'bændən] *vt* **1** DESERT, FORSAKE : abandonar, desamparar (a alguien), desertar de (algo) **2** GIVE UP, SUSPEND : renunciar a, suspender ⟨he abandoned the search : suspendió la búsqueda⟩ **3** EVACUATE, LEAVE : abandonar, evacuar, dejar ⟨to abandon ship : abandonar el buque⟩ **4 to abandon oneself** : entregarse, abandonarse

abandon² *n* : desenfreno *m* ⟨with wild abandon : desenfrenadamente⟩

abandoned [ə'bændənd] *adj* **1** DESERTED : abandonado **2** UNRESTRAINED : desenfrenado, desinhibido

abandonment [ə'bændənmənt] *n* : abandono *m*, desamparo *m*

abase [ə'beɪs] *vt* **abased; abasing** : degradar, humillar, rebajar

abash [ə'bæʃ] *vt* : avergonzar, abochornar

abashed [ə'bæʃt] *adj* : avergonzado

abate [ə'beɪt] *vi* **abated; abating** : amainar, menguar, disminuir

abattoir ['æbə,twɑr] *n* : matadero *m*

abbess ['æbɪs, -,bɛs, -bəs] *n* : abadesa *f*

abbey ['æbi] *n, pl* **-beys** : abadía *f*

abbot ['æbət] *n* : abad *m*

abbreviate [ə'bri:vi,eɪt] *vt* **-ated; -ating** : abreviar

abbreviation [ə,bri:vi'eɪʃən] *n* : abreviación *f*, abreviatura *f*

ABC's [,eɪ,bi:'si:z] *npl* : abecé *m*

abdicate ['æbdɪ,keɪt] *v* **-cated; -cating** : abdicar

abdication [,æbdɪ'keɪʃən] *n* : abdicación *f*

abdomen ['æbdəmən, æb'do:mən] *n* : abdomen *m*, vientre *m*

abdominal [æb'dɑmənəl] *adj* : abdominal — **abdominally** *adv*

abduct [æb'dʌkt] *vt* : raptar, secuestrar

abduction [æb'dʌkʃən] *n* : rapto *m*, secuestro *m*

abductor [æb'dʌktər] *n* : raptor *m*, -tora *f*; secuestrador *m*, -dora *f*

abed [ə'bɛd] *adv & adj* : en cama

aberrant [æ'bɛrənt, 'æbərənt] *adj* **1** ABNORMAL : anormal, aberrante **2** ATYPICAL : anómalo, atípico

aberration [,æbə'reɪʃən] *n* **1** : aberración *f* **2** DERANGEMENT : perturbación *f* mental

abet [ə'bɛt] *vt* **abetted; abetting** ASSIST : ayudar ⟨to aid and abet : ser cómplice de⟩

abeyance [ə'beɪənts] *n* : desuso *m*, suspensión *f*

abhor [əb'hɔr, æb-] *vt* **-horred; -horring** : abominar, aborrecer

abhorrence [əb'hɔrənts, æb-] *n* : aborrecimiento *m*, odio *m*

abhorrent [əb'hɔrənt, æb-] *adj* : abominable, aborrecible, odioso

abide [ə'baɪd] *v* **abode** [ə'bo:d] *or* **abided; abiding** *vt* STAND : soportar, tolerar ⟨I can't abide them : no los puedo ver⟩ — *vi* **1** ENDURE : quedar, permanecer **2** DWELL : morar, residir **3 to abide by** : atenerse a

ability [ə'bɪləti] *n, pl* **-ties 1** CAPABILITY : aptitud *f*, capacidad *f*, facultad *f* **2** COMPETENCE : competencia *f* **3** TALENT : talento *m*, don *m*, habilidad *f*

abject ['æb,dʒɛkt, æb'-] *adj* **1** WRETCHED : miserable, desdichado **2** HOPELESS : abatido, desesperado **3** SERVILE : servil ⟨abject flattery : halagos serviles⟩ — **abjectly** *adv*

abjure [æb'dʒʊr] *vt* **-jured; -juring** : abjurar de

ablaze [ə'bleɪz] *adj* **1** BURNING : ardiendo, en llamas **2** RADIANT : resplandeciente, radiante

able ['eɪbəl] *adj* **abler; ablest 1** CAPABLE : capaz, hábil **2** COMPETENT : competente

ablution [ə'blu:ʃən] *n* : ablución *f* ⟨to perform one's ablutions : lavarse⟩

ably ['eɪbəli] *adv* : hábilmente, eficientemente

abnormal [æb'nɔrməl] *adj* : anormal — **abnormally** *adv*

abnormality [,æbnər'mæləti, -nɔr-] *n, pl* **-ties** : anormalidad *f*

aboard¹ [ə'bord] *adv* : a bordo

aboard² *prep* : a bordo de

abode¹ → **abide**

abode² [ə'bo:d] *n* : morada *f*, residencia *f*, vivienda *f*

abolish [ə'bɑlɪʃ] *vt* : abolir, suprimir

abolition [,æbə'lɪʃən] *n* : abolición *f*, supresión *f*

abominable [ə'bɑmənəbəl] *adj* DETESTABLE : abominable, aborrecible, espantoso

abominate [ə'bɑmə,neɪt] *vt* **-nated; -nating** : abominar, aborrecer

abomination [ə,bɑmə'neɪʃən] *n* : abominación *f*

aboriginal [,æbə'rɪdʒənəl] *adj* : aborigen, indígena

aborigine [,æbə'rɪdʒəni] *n* NATIVE : aborigen *mf*, indígena *mf*

abort [ə'bɔrt] *vt* **1** : abortar (en medicina) **2** CALL OFF : suspender, abandonar — *vi* : abortar, hacerse un aborto

abortion [ə'bɔrʃən] *n* : aborto *m*

abortive [ə'bɔrtɪv] *adj* UNSUCCESSFUL : fracasado, frustrado, malogrado

abound [ə'baʊnd] *vi* **to abound in** : abundar en, estar lleno de

about¹ [ə'baʊt] *adv* **1** APPROXIMATELY : aproximadamente, casi, más o menos **2** AROUND : por todas partes, alrededor ⟨the children are running about : los niños están corriendo por todas partes⟩ **3 to be about to** : estar a punto de **4 to be up and about** : estar levantado

about² *prep* **1** AROUND : alrededor de **2** CONCERNING : de, acerca de, sobre ⟨he always talks about politics : siempre habla de política⟩

above¹ [ə'bʌv] *adv* **1** OVERHEAD : por encima, arriba **2** : más arriba ⟨as stated above : como se indica más arriba⟩

above² *adj* : anterior, antedicho ⟨for the above reasons : por las razones antedichas⟩

above³ *prep* **1** OVER : encima de, arriba de, sobre **2** : superior a, por encima de ⟨he's above those things : él está por encima de esas cosas⟩ **3** : más de, superior a ⟨he earns above $50,000 : gana más de $50,000⟩ ⟨a number above 10 : un número superior a 10⟩ **4 above all** : sobre todo

aboveboard¹ [ə'bʌv'bord, -ˌbord] *adv* **open and aboveboard** : sin tapujos

aboveboard² *adj* : legítimo, sincero

abrade [ə'breɪd] *vt* **abraded; abrading 1** ERODE : erosionar, corroer **2** SCRAPE : escoriar, raspar

abrasion [ə'breɪʒən] *n* **1** SCRAPE, SCRATCH : raspadura *f*, rasguño *m* **2** EROSION : erosión *f*

abrasive¹ [ə'breɪsɪv] *adj* **1** ROUGH : abrasivo, áspero **2** BRUSQUE, IRRITATING : brusco, irritante

abrasive² *n* : abrasivo *m*

abreast [ə'brɛst] *adv* **1** : en fondo, al lado ⟨to march three abreast : marchar de tres en fondo⟩ **2 to keep abreast** : mantenerse al día

abridge [ə'brɪdʒ] *vt* **abridged; abridging** : compendiar, resumir

abridgment *or* **abridgement** [ə'brɪdʒmənt] *n* : compendio *m*, resumen *m*

abroad [ə'brɔd] *adv* **1** ABOUT, WIDELY : por todas partes, en todas direcciones ⟨the news spread abroad : la noticia corrió por todas partes⟩ **2** OVERSEAS : en el extranjero, en el exterior

abrogate ['æbrəˌgeɪt] *vt* **-gated; -gating** : abrogar

abrupt [ə'brʌpt] *adj* **1** SUDDEN : abrupto, repentino, súbito **2** BRUSQUE, CURT : brusco, cortante — **abruptly** *adv*

abscess ['æbˌsɛs] *n* : absceso *m*

abscond [æb'skɑnd] *vi* : huir, fugarse

absence ['æbsənts] *n* **1** : ausencia *f* (de una persona) **2** LACK : falta *f*, carencia *f*

absent¹ [æb'sɛnt] *vt* **to absent oneself** : ausentarse

absent² ['æbsənt] *adj* : ausente

absentee [ˌæbsən'ti:] *n* : ausente *mf*

absentminded [ˌæbsənt'maɪndəd] *adj* : distraído, despistado

absentmindedly [ˌæbsənt'maɪndədli] *adv* : distraídamente

absentmindedness [ˌæbsənt'maɪndədnəs] *n* : distracción *f*, despiste *m*

absolute ['æbsəˌlu:t, ˌæbsə'lu:t] *adj* **1** COMPLETE, PERFECT : completo, pleno, perfecto **2** UNCONDITIONAL : absoluto, incondicional **3** DEFINITE : categórico, definitivo

absolutely ['æbsəˌlu:tli, ˌæbsə'lu:tli] *adv* **1** COMPLETELY : completamente, solutamente **2** CERTAINLY : desde luego ⟨do you agree? absolutely! : ¿estás de acuerdo? ¡desde luego!⟩

absolution [ˌæbsə'lu:ʃən] *n* : absolución *f*

absolutism ['æbsəˌlu:ˌtɪzəm] *n* : absolutismo *m*

absolve [əb'zɑlv, æb-, -'sɑlv] *vt* **-solved; -solving** : absolver, perdonar

absorb [əb'zɔrb, æb-, -'sɔrb] *vt* **1** : absorber, embeber (un líquido), amortiguar (un golpe, la luz) **2** ENGROSS : absorber **3** ASSIMILATE : asimilar

absorbed [əb'zɔrbd, æb-, -'sɔrbd] *adj* ENGROSSED : absorto, ensimismado

absorbency [əb'zɔrbəntsi, æb-, -'sɔr-] *n* : absorbencia *f*

absorbent [əb'zɔrbənt, æb-, -'sɔr-] *adj* : absorbente

absorbing [əb'zɔrbɪŋ, æb-, -'sɔr-] *adj* : absorbente, fascinante

absorption [əb'zɔrpʃən, æb-, -'sɔrp-] *n* **1** : absorción *f* **2** CONCENTRATION : concentración *f*

abstain [əb'steɪn, æb-] *vi* : abstenerse

abstainer [əb'steɪnər, æb-] *n* : abstemio *m*, -mia *f*

abstemious [æb'sti:miəs] *adj* : abstemio, sobrio — **abstemiously** *adv*

abstention [əb'stɛntʃən, æb-] *n* : abstención *f*

abstinence ['æbstənənts] *n* : abstinencia *f*

abstract¹ [æb'strækt, 'æbˌ-] *vt* **1** EXTRACT : abstraer, extraer **2** SUMMARIZE : compendiar, resumir

abstract² *adj* : abstracto — **abstractly** [æb'stræktli, 'æbˌ-] *adv*

abstract³ ['æbˌstrækt] *n* : resumen *m*, compendio *m*, sumario *m*

abstraction [æb'strækʃən] *n* **1** : abstracción *f*, idea *f* abstracta **2** ABSENTMINDEDNESS : distracción *f*

abstruse [əb'stru:s, æb-] *adj* : abstruso, recóndito — **abstrusely** *adv*

absurd [əb'sərd, -'zərd] *adj* : absurdo, ridículo, disparatado — **absurdly** *adv*

absurdity [əb'sərdəti, -'zər-] *n, pl* **-ties** **1**
: absurdo *m* **2** NONSENSE : disparate
m, despropósito *m*
abundance [ə'bʌndənts] *n* : abundancia
f
abundant [ə'bʌndənt] *adj* : abundante,
cuantioso, copioso
abundantly [ə'bʌndəntli] *adv* : abundantemente, en abundancia
abuse¹ [ə'bju:z] *vt* **abused; abusing 1**
MISUSE : abusar de **2** MISTREAT : maltratar **3** REVILE : insultar, injuriar,
denostar
abuse² [ə'bju:s] *n* **1** MISUSE : abuso *m*
2 MISTREATMENT : abuso *m*, maltrato
m **3** INSULTS : insultos *mpl*, impro-
perios *mpl* ⟨a string of abuse : una serie
de improperios⟩
abuser [ə'bju:zər] *n* : abusador *m*, -dora
f
abusive [ə'bju:sɪv] *adj* **1** ABUSING : abusivo **2** INSULTING : ofensivo, injurioso,
insultante — **abusively** *adv*
abut [ə'bʌt] *v* **abutted; abutting** *vt* : bordear — *vi* **to abut on** : colindar con
abutment [ə'bʌtmənt] *n* **1** BUTTRESS
: contrafuerte *m*, estribo *m* **2** CLOSE-
NESS : contigüidad *f*
abysmal [ə'bɪzməl] *adj* **1** DEEP : abismal, insondable **2** TERRIBLE : atroz,
desastroso
abysmally [ə'bɪzməli] *adv* : desastrosa-
mente, terriblemente
abyss [ə'bɪs, 'æbɪs] *n* : abismo *m*, sima
f
acacia [ə'keɪʃə] *n* : acacia *f*
academic¹ [,ækə'dɛmɪk] *adj* **1** : académico **2** THEORETICAL : teórico —
academically [-mɪkli] *adv*
academic² *n* : académico *m*, -ca *f*
academician [,ækədə'mɪʃən] *n* → **academic**
academy [ə'kædəmi] *n, pl* **-mies** : academia *f*
acanthus [ə'kæntθəs] *n* : acanto *m*
accede [æk'si:d] *vi* **-ceded; -ceding 1**
AGREE : acceder, consentir **2** ASCEND
: subir, acceder ⟨he acceded to the
throne : subió al trono⟩
accelerate [ɪk'sɛlə,reɪt, æk-] *v* **-ated;
-ating** *vt* : acelerar, apresurar — *vi*
: acelerar (dícese de un carro)
acceleration [ɪk,sɛlə'reɪʃən, æk-] *n*
: aceleración *f*
accelerator [ɪk'sɛlə,reɪtər, æk-] *n* : acelerador *m*
accent¹ ['æk,sɛnt, æk'sɛnt] *vt* : acentuar
accent² ['æk,sɛnt, -sənt] *n* **1** : acento *m*
2 EMPHASIS, STRESS : énfasis *m*, acento *m*
accentuate [ɪk'sɛntʃu,eɪt, æk-] *vt* **-ated;
-ating** : acentuar, poner énfasis en
accept [ɪk'sɛpt, æk-] *vt* **1** : aceptar **2** AC-
KNOWLEDGE : admitir, reconocer
acceptability [ɪk,sɛptə'bɪləti, æk-] *n*
: aceptabilidad *f*

acceptable [ɪk'sɛptəbəl, æk-] *adj*
: aceptable, admisible — **acceptably**
[-bli] *adv*
acceptance [ɪk'sɛptənts, æk-] *n* : aceptación *f*, aprobación *f*
access¹ ['æk,sɛs] *vt* : obtener acceso a,
entrar a
access² *n* : acceso *m*
accessibility [ɪk,sɛsə'bɪləti] *n, pl* **-ties**
: accesibilidad *f*
accessible [ɪk'sɛsəbəl, æk-] *adj* : accesible, asequible
accession [ɪk'sɛʃən, æk-] *n* **1** : ascenso
f, subida *f* (al trono, etc.) **2** ACQUISI-
TION : adquisición *f*
accessory¹ [ɪk'sɛsəri, æk-] *adj* : auxiliar
accessory² *n, pl* **-ries** **1** : accesorio *m*,
complemento *m* **2** ACCOMPLICE : cóm-
plice *mf*
accident ['æksədənt] *n* **1** MISHAP : accidente *m* **2** CHANCE : casualidad *f*
accidental [,æksə'dɛntəl] *adj* : accidental, casual, imprevisto, fortuito
accidentally [,æksə'dɛntəli, -'dɛntli] *adv*
1 BY CHANCE : por casualidad **2** UN-
INTENTIONALLY : sin querer, involuntariamente
acclaim¹ [ə'kleɪm] *vt* : aclamar, elogiar
acclaim² *n* : aclamación *f*, elogio *m*
acclamation [,æklə'meɪʃən] *n* : aclamación *f*
acclimate ['æklə,meɪt, ə'klaɪmət] → **acclimatize**
acclimatize [ə'klaɪmə,taɪz] *v* **-tized;
-tizing** *vt* **1** : aclimatar **2 to acclimatize oneself** : aclimatarse
accolade ['ækə,leɪd, -,lɑd] *n* **1** PRAISE
: elogio *m* **2** AWARD : galardón *m*
accommodate [ə'kɑmə,deɪt] *vt* **-dated;
-dating 1** ADAPT : acomodar, adaptar
2 SATISFY : tener en cuenta, satisfacer
3 HOLD : dar cabida a, tener cabida
para
accommodation [ə,kɑmə'deɪʃən] *n* **1**
: adaptación *f*, adecuación *f* **2 accommodations** *npl* LODGING : alojamiento *m*, hospedaje *m*
accompaniment [ə'kʌmpənəmənt,
-'kɑm-] *n* : acompañamiento *m*
accompanist [ə'kʌmpənɪst, -'kɑm-] *n*
: acompañante *mf*
accompany [ə'kʌmpəni, -'kɑm-] *vt*
-nied; -nying : acompañar
accomplice [ə'kɑmpləs, -'kʌm-] *n* : cómplice *mf*
accomplish [ə'kʌmplɪʃ, -'kʌm-] *vt* : efectuar, realizar, lograr, llevar a cabo
accomplished [ə'kʌmplɪʃt, -'kʌm-] *adj*
: consumado, logrado
accomplishment [ə'kʌmplɪʃmənt,
-'kʌm-] *n* **1** ACHIEVEMENT : logro *m*,
éxito *m* **2** SKILL : destreza *f*, habilidad
f
accord¹ [ə'kɔrd] *vt* GRANT : conceder,
otorgar — *vi* **to accord with** : concordar con, conformarse con
accord² *n* **1** AGREEMENT : acuerdo *m*,
convenio *m* **2** VOLITION : voluntad *f*

⟨on one's own accord : voluntariamente, de motu proprio⟩
accordance [əˈkɔrdənts] *n* **1** ACCORD : acuerdo *m*, conformidad *f* **2 in accordance with** : conforme a, según, de acuerdo con
accordingly [əˈkɔrdɪŋli] *adv* **1** CORRESPONDINGLY : en consecuencia **2** CONSEQUENTLY : por consiguiente, por lo tanto
according to [əˈkɔrdɪŋ] *prep* : según, de acuerdo con, conforme a
accordion [əˈkɔrdiən] *n* : acordeón *m*
accordionist [əˈkɔrdiənɪst] *n* : acordeonista *mf*
accost [əˈkɔst] *vt* : abordar, dirigirse a
account[1] [əˈkaʊnt] *vt* : considerar, estimar ⟨he accounts himself lucky : se considera afortunado⟩ — *vi* **to account for** : dar cuenta de, explicar
account[2] *n* **1** : cuenta *f* ⟨savings account : cuenta de ahorros⟩ **2** EXPLANATION : versión *f*, explicación *f* **3** REPORT : relato *m*, informe *m* **4** IMPORTANCE : importancia *f* ⟨to be of no account : no tener importancia⟩ **5 on account of** BECAUSE OF : a causa de, debido a, por **6 on no account** : de ninguna manera
accountability [əˌkaʊntəˈbɪləti] *n* : responsabilidad *f*
accountable [əˈkaʊntəbəl] *adj* : responsable
accountant [əˈkaʊntənt] *n* : contador *m*, -dora *f*; contable *mf Spain*
accounting [əˈkaʊntɪŋ] *n* : contabilidad *f*
accoutrements *or* **accouterments** [əˈkuːtrəmənts, -ˈkuːtər-] *npl* **1** EQUIPMENT : equipo *m*, avíos *mpl* **2** ACCESSORIES : accesorios *mpl* **3** TRAPPINGS : símbolos *mpl* ⟨the accoutrements of power : los símbolos del poder⟩
accredit [əˈkrɛdət] *vt* : acreditar, autorizar
accreditation [əˌkrɛdəˈteɪʃən] *n* : acreditación *f*, homologación *f*
accretion [əˈkriːʃən] *n* **1** : acrecentamiento *m* (proceso) **2** : acreción *f*, acrecencia *f* (producto)
accrual [əˈkruːəl] *n* : incremento *m*, acumulación *f*
accrue [əˈkruː] *vi* **-crued; -cruing** : acumularse, aumentarse
accumulate [əˈkjuːmjəˌleɪt] *v* **-lated; -lating** *vt* : acumular, amontonar — *vi* : acumularse, amontonarse
accumulation [əˌkjuːmjəˈleɪʃən] *n* : acumulación *f*, amontonamiento *m*
accuracy [ˈækjərəsi] *n* : exactitud *f*, precisión *f*
accurate [ˈækjərət] *adj* : exacto, correcto, fiel, preciso — **accurately** *adv*
accusation [ˌækjəˈzeɪʃən] *n* : acusación *f*
accusatory [əˈkjuːzəˌtori] *adj* : acusatorio
accuse [əˈkjuːz] *vt* **-cused; -cusing** : acusar, delatar, denunciar

accused [əˈkjuːzd] *ns & pl* DEFENDANT : acusado *m*, -da *f*
accuser [əˈkjuːzər] *n* : acusador *m*, -dora *f*
accustom [əˈkʌstəm] *vt* : acostumbrar, habituar
ace [ˈeɪs] *n* : as *m*
acerbic [əˈsərbɪk, æ-] *adj* : acerbo, mordaz
acetate [ˈæsəˌteɪt] *n* : acetato *m*
acetic [əˈsiːtɪk] *adj* : acético
acetone [ˈæsəˌtoːn] *n* : acetona *f*
acetylene [əˈsɛtələn, -ˌtəˌliːn] *n* : acetileno *m*
ache[1] [ˈeɪk] *vi* **ached; aching 1** : doler **2 to ache for** : anhelar, ansiar
ache[2] *n* : dolor *m*
achieve [əˈtʃiːv] *vt* **achieved; achieving** : lograr, alcanzar, conseguir, realizar
achievement [əˈtʃiːvmənt] *n* : logro *m*, éxito *m*, realización *f*
acid[1] [ˈæsəd] *adj* **1** SOUR : ácido, agrio **2** CAUSTIC, SHARP : acerbo, mordaz — **acidly** *adv*
acid[2] *n* : ácido *m*
acidic [əˈsɪdɪk, æ-] *adj* : ácido
acidity [əˈsɪdəti, æ-] *n*, *pl* **-ties** : acidez *f*
acknowledge [ɪkˈnɑlɪdʒ, æk-] *vt* **-edged; -edging 1** ADMIT : reconocer, admitir **2** RECOGNIZE : reconocer **3 to acknowledge receipt of** : acusar recibo de
acknowledgment [ɪkˈnɑlɪdʒmənt, æk-] *n* **1** RECOGNITION : reconocimiento *m* **2** THANKS : agradecimiento *m*
acme [ˈækmi] *n* : colmo *m*, apogeo *m*, cúspide *f*
acne [ˈækni] *n* : acné *m*
acolyte [ˈækəˌlaɪt] *n* : acólito *m*
acorn [ˈeɪˌkɔrn, -kərn] *n* : bellota *f*
acoustic [əˈkuːstɪk] *or* **acoustical** [-stɪkəl] *adj* : acústico — **acoustically** *adv*
acoustics [əˈkuːstɪks] *ns & pl* : acústica *f*
acquaint [əˈkweɪnt] *vt* **1** INFORM : enterar, informar **2** FAMILIARIZE : familiarizar **3 to be acquainted with** : conocer a (una persona), estar al tanto de (un hecho)
acquaintance [əˈkweɪntənts] *n* **1** KNOWLEDGE : conocimiento *m* **2** : conocido *m*, -da *f* ⟨friends and acquaintances : amigos y conocidos⟩
acquiesce [ˌækwiˈɛs] *vi* **-esced; -escing** : consentir, conformarse
acquiescence [ˌækwiˈɛsənts] *n* : consentimiento *m*, aquiescencia *f*
acquire [əˈkwaɪr] *vt* **-quired; -quiring** : adquirir, obtener
acquisition [ˌækwəˈzɪʃən] *n* : adquisición *f*
acquisitive [əˈkwɪzətɪv] *adj* : adquisitivo, codicioso
acquit [əˈkwɪt] *vt* **-quitted; -quitting 1** : absolver, exculpar **2 to acquit oneself** : comportarse, defenderse
acquittal [əˈkwɪtəl] *n* : absolución *f*, exculpación *f*

acre ['eɪkər] *n* : acre *m*

acreage ['eɪkərɪʤ] *n* : superficie *f* en acres

acrid ['ækrəd] *adj* **1** BITTER : acre **2** CAUSTIC : acre, mordaz — **acridly** *adv*

acrimonious [ˌækrə'moːniəs] *adj* : áspero, cáustico, sarcástico

acrimony ['ækrəˌmoːni] *n, pl* **-nies** : acrimonia *f*

acrobat ['ækrəˌbæt] *n* : acróbata *mf*, saltimbanqui *mf*

acrobatic [ˌækrə'bæṭɪk] *adj* : acrobático

acrobatics [ˌækrə'bæṭɪks] *ns & pl* : acrobacia *f*

acronym ['ækrəˌnɪm] *n* : acrónimo *m*

across[1] [ə'krɔs] *adv* **1** CROSSWISE : al través **2** : a través, del otro lado ⟨he's already across : ya está del otro lado⟩ **3** : de ancho ⟨40 feet across : 40 pies de ancho⟩

across[2] *prep* **1** : al otro lado de ⟨across the street : al otro lado de la calle⟩ **2** : a través de ⟨a log across the road : un tronco a través del camino⟩

acrylic [ə'krɪlɪk] *n* : acrílico *m*

act[1] ['ækt] *vi* **1** PERFORM : actuar, interpretar **2** FEIGN, PRETEND : fingir, simular **3** BEHAVE : comportarse **4** FUNCTION : actuar, servir, funcionar **5** : tomar medidas ⟨he acted to save the business : tomó medidas para salvar el negocio⟩ **6 to act as** : servir de, hacer de

act[2] *n* **1** DEED : acto *m*, hecho *m*, acción *f* **2** DECREE : ley *f*, decreto *m* **3** : acto *m* (en una obra de teatro), número *m* (en un espectáculo) **4** PRETENSE : fingimiento *m*

action ['ækʃən] *n* **1** DEED : acción *f*, acto *m*, hecho *m* **2** BEHAVIOR : actuación *f*, comportamiento *m* **3** LAWSUIT : demanda *f* **4** MOVEMENT : movimiento *m* **5** COMBAT : combate *m* **6** PLOT : acción *f*, trama *f* **7** MECHANISM : mecanismo *m*

activate ['æktəˌveɪt] *vt* **-vated; -vating** : activar

activation [ˌæktə'veɪʃən] *n* : activación *f*

active ['æktɪv] *adj* **1** MOVING : activo, en movimiento **2** LIVELY : vigoroso, enérgico **3** : en actividad ⟨an active volcano : un volcán en actividad⟩ **4** OPERATIVE : vigente

actively ['æktɪvli] *adv* : activamente, enérgicamente

activist ['æktɪvɪst] *n* : activista *mf* — **activist** *adj*

activity [æk'tɪvəṭi] *n, pl* **-ties** **1** MOVEMENT : actividad *f*, movimiento *m* **2** VIGOR : vigor *m*, energía *f* **3** OCCUPATION : actividad *f*, ocupación *f*

actor ['æktər] *n* : actor *m*, artista *mf*

actress ['æktrəs] *n* : actriz *f*

actual ['æktʃuəl] *adj* : real, verdadero

actuality [ˌæktʃu'æləṭi] *n, pl* **-ties** : realidad *f*

actually ['æktʃuəli, -ʃəli] *adv* : realmente, en realidad

actuary ['æktʃuˌeri] *n, pl* **-aries** : actuario *m*, -ria *f* de seguros

acumen [ə'kjuːmən] *n* : perspicacia *f*

acupuncture ['ækjuˌpʌŋktʃər] *n* : acupuntura *f*

acute [ə'kjuːt] *adj* **acuter; acutest** **1** SHARP : agudo **2** PERCEPTIVE : perspicaz, sagaz **3** KEEN : fino, muy desarrollado, agudo ⟨an acute sense of smell : un fino olfato⟩ **4** SEVERE : grave **5 acute angle** : ángulo *m* agudo

acutely [ə'kjuːtli] *adv* : intensamente ⟨to be acutely aware : estar perfectamente consciente⟩

acuteness [ə'kjuːtnəs] *n* : agudeza *f*

ad ['æd] → **advertisement**

adage ['ædɪʤ] *n* : adagio *m*, refrán *m*, dicho *m*

adamant ['ædəmənt, -ˌmænt] *adj* : firme, categórico, inflexible — **adamantly** *adv*

Adam's apple ['ædəmz] *n* : nuez *f* de Adán

adapt [ə'dæpt] *vt* : adaptar, ajustar — *vi* : adaptarse

adaptability [əˌdæptə'bɪləṭi] *n* : adaptabilidad *f*, flexibilidad *f*

adaptable [ə'dæptəbəl] *adj* : adaptable, amoldable

adaptation [ˌæˌdæp'teɪʃən, -dəp-] *n* **1** : adaptación *f*, modificación *f* **2** VERSION : versión *f*

adapter [ə'dæptər] *n* : adaptador *m*

add ['æd] *vt* **1** : añadir, agregar ⟨to add a comment : añadir una observación⟩ **2** : sumar ⟨add these numbers : suma estos números⟩ — *vi* : sumar (en total)

adder ['ædər] *n* : víbora *f*

addict[1] [ə'dɪkt] *vt* : causar adicción en

addict[2] ['ædɪkt] *n* **1** : adicto *m*, -ta *f* **2 drug addict** : drogadicto *m*, -ta *f*; toxicómano *m*, -na *f*

addiction [ə'dɪkʃən] *n* **1** : adicción *f*, dependencia *f* **2 drug addiction** : drogadicción *f*

addictive [ə'dɪktɪv] *adj* : adictivo

addition [ə'dɪʃən] *n* **1** : adición *f*, añadidura *f* **2 in ~** : además, también

additional [ə'dɪʃənəl] *adj* : extra, adicional, de más

additionally [ə'dɪʃənəli] *adv* : además, adicionalmente

additive ['ædəṭɪv] *n* : aditivo *m*

addle ['ædəl] *vt* **-dled; -dling** : confundir, enturbiar

address[1] [ə'drɛs] *vt* **1** : dirigirse a, pronunciar un discurso ante ⟨to address a jury : dirigirse a un jurado⟩ **2** : dirigir, ponerle la dirección a ⟨to address a letter : dirigir una carta⟩

address[2] [ə'drɛs, 'æˌdrɛs] *n* **1** SPEECH : discurso *m*, alocución *f* **2** : dirección *f* (de una residencia, etc.)

addressee [ˌæˌdrɛ'siː, ə-] *n* : destinatario *m*, -ria *f*

adduce [ə-'du:s, 'dju:s] *vt* **-duced; -ducing** : aducir

adenoids ['æd,nɔɪd, -dən,ɔɪd] *npl* : adenoides *fpl*

adept [ə'dɛpt] *adj* : experto, hábil — **adeptly** *adv*

adequacy ['ædɪkwəsi] *n, pl* **-cies** : cantidad *f* suficiente

adequate ['ædɪkwət] *adj* **1** SUFFICIENT : adecuado, suficiente **2** ACCEPTABLE, PASSABLE : adecuado, aceptable

adequately ['ædɪkwətli] *adv* : suficientemente, apropiadamente

adhere [æd'hɪr, əd-] *vi* **-hered; -hering 1** STICK : pegarse, adherirse **2 to adhere to** : adherirse a (una política, etc.), cumplir con (una promesa)

adherence [æd'hɪrənts, əd-] *n* : adhesión *f*, adherencia *f*, observancia *f* (de una ley, etc.)

adherent¹ [æd'hɪrənt, əd-] *adj* : adherente, adhesivo, pegajoso

adherent² *n* : adepto *m*, -ta *f*; partidario *m*, -ria *f*

adhesion [æd'hi:ʒən, əd-] *n* : adhesión *f*

adhesive¹ [æd'hi:sɪv, əd-, -zɪv] *adj* : adhesivo

adhesive² *n* : adhesivo *m*, pegamento *m*

adjacent [ə'dʒeɪsənt] *adj* : adyacente, colindante, contiguo

adjective ['ædʒɪktɪv] *n* : adjetivo *m* — **adjectival** [,ædʒɪk'taɪvəl] *adj*

adjoin [ə'dʒɔɪn] *vt* : lindar con, colindar con

adjoining [ə'dʒɔɪnɪŋ] *adj* : contiguo, colindante

adjourn [ə'dʒərn] *vt* : levantar, suspender ⟨the meeting is adjourned : se levanta la sesión⟩ — *vi* : aplazarse

adjournment [ə'dʒərnmənt] *n* : suspensión *f*, aplazamiento *m*

adjudicate [ə'dʒu:dɪ,keɪt] *vt* **-cated; -cating** : juzgar, arbitrar

adjudication [ə,dʒu:dɪ'keɪʃən] *n* **1** JUDGING : arbitrio *m* (judicial) **2** JUDGMENT : fallo *m*

adjunct ['æ,dʒʌŋkt] *n* : adjunto *m*, complemento *m*

adjust [ə'dʒʌst] *vt* : ajustar, arreglar, regular — *vi* **to adjust to** : adaptarse a

adjustable [ə'dʒʌstəbəl] *adj* : ajustable, regulable, graduable

adjustment [ə'dʒʌstmənt] *n* : ajuste *m*, modificación *f*

ad–lib¹ ['æd'lɪb] *v* **-libbed; -libbing** : improvisar

ad–lib² *adj* : improvisado

administer [æd'mɪnəstər, əd-] *vt* : administrar

administration [æd,mɪnə'streɪʃən, əd-] *n* **1** MANAGING : administración *f*, dirección *f* **2** GOVERNMENT, MANAGEMENT : administración *f*, gobierno *m*

administrative [æd'mɪnə,streɪtɪv, əd-] *adj* : administrativo — **administratively** *adv*

administrator [æd'mɪnə,streɪtər, əd-] *n* : administrador *m*, -dora *f*

admirable ['ædmərəbəl] *adj* : admirable, loable — **admirably** *adv*

admiral ['ædmərəl] *n* : almirante *mf*

admiration [,ædmə'reɪʃən] *n* : admiración *f*

admire [æd'maɪr] *vt* **-mired; -miring** : admirar

admirer [æd'maɪrər] *n* : admirador *m*, -dora *f*

admiring [æd'maɪrɪŋ] *adj* : admirativo, de admiración

admiringly [æd'maɪrɪŋli] *adv* : con admiración

admissible [æd'mɪsəbəl] *adj* : admisible, aceptable

admission [æd'mɪʃən] *n* **1** ADMITTANCE : entrada *f*, admisión *f* **2** ACKNOWLEDGMENT : reconocimiento *m*, admisión *f*

admit [æd'mɪt, əd-] *vt* **-mitted; -mitting 1** : admitir, dejar entrar ⟨the museum admits children : el museo deja entrar a los niños⟩ **2** ACKNOWLEDGE : reconocer, admitir

admittance [æd'mɪtənts, əd-] *n* : admisión *f*, entrada *f*, acceso *m*

admittedly [æd'mɪtədli, əd-] *adv* : la verdad es que, lo cierto es que ⟨admittedly we went too fast : la verdad es que fuimos demasiado de prisa⟩

admonish [æd'manɪʃ, əd-] *vt* : amonestar, reprender

admonition [,ædmə'nɪʃən] *n* : admonición *f*

ado [ə'du:] *n* **1** FUSS : ruido *m*, alboroto *m* **2** TROUBLE : dificultad *f*, lío *m* **3 without further ado** : sin más preámbulos

adobe [ə'do:bi] *n* : adobe *m*

adolescence [,ædəl'ɛsənts] *n* : adolescencia *f*

adolescent¹ [,ædəl'ɛsənt] *adj* : adolescente, de adolescencia

adolescent² *n* : adolescente *mf*

adopt [ə'dapt] *vt* : adoptar

adoption [ə'dapʃən] *n* : adopción *f*

adoptive [ə'daptɪv] *adj* : adoptivo

adorable [ə'dorəbəl] *adj* : adorable, encantador

adorably [ə'dorəbli] *adv* : de manera adorable

adoration [,ædə'reɪʃən] *n* : adoración *f*

adore [ə'dor] *vt* **adored; adoring 1** WORSHIP : adorar **2** LOVE : querer, adorar **3** LIKE : encantarle (algo a uno), gustarle mucho (algo a uno) ⟨I adore your new dress : me encanta tu vestido nuevo⟩

adorn [ə'dɔrn] *vt* : adornar, ornar, engalanar

adornment [ə'dɔrnmənt] *n* : adorno *m*, decoración *f*

adrenaline [ə'drɛnələn] *n* : adrenalina *f*

adrift [ə'drɪft] *adj & adv* : a la deriva

adroit [ə'drɔɪt] *adj* : diestro, hábil — **adroitly** *adv*

adroitness [ə'drɔɪtnəs] *n* : destreza *f*, habilidad *f*

adult¹ [ə'dʌlt, 'æˌdʌlt] *adj* : adulto
adult² *n* : adulto *m*, -ta *f*
adulterate [ə'dʌltəˌreɪt] *vt* **-ated; -ating**
: adulterar
adulterous [ə'dʌltərəs] *adj* : adúltero
adultery [ə'dʌltəri] *n, pl* **-teries** : adulterio *m*
adulthood [ə'dʌltˌhʊd] *n* : adultez *f*, edad *f* adulta
advance¹ [æd'væn*t*s, əd-] *v* **-vanced; -vancing** *vt* **1** : avanzar, adelantar ⟨to advance troops : avanzar las tropas⟩ **2** PROMOTE : ascender, promover **3** PROPOSE : proponer, presentar **4** : adelantar, anticipar ⟨they advanced me next month's salary : me adelantaron el sueldo del próximo mes⟩ — *vi* **1** PROCEED : avanzar, adelantarse **2** PROGRESS : progresar
advance² *adj* : anticipado ⟨advance notice : previo aviso⟩
advance³ *n* **1** PROGRESSION : avance *m* **2** PROGRESS : adelanto *m*, mejora *f*, progreso *m* **3** RISE : aumento *m*, alza *f* **4** LOAN : anticipo *m*, préstamo *m* **5** in ∼ : por adelantado
advanced [æd'væn*t*st, əd-] *adj* **1** DEVELOPED : avanzado, desarrollado **2** PRECOCIOUS : adelantado, precoz **3** HIGHER : superior
advancement [æd'væn*t*smənt, əd-] *n* **1** FURTHERANCE : fomento *m*, adelantamiento *m*, progreso *m* **2** PROMOTION : ascenso *m*
advantage [əd'væntɪʤ, æd-] *n* **1** SUPERIORITY : ventaja *f*, superioridad *f* **2** GAIN : provecho *m*, partido *m* **3 to take advantage of** : aprovecharse de
advantageous [ˌædˌvæn'teɪʤəs, -vən-] *adj* : ventajoso, provechoso — **advantageously** *adv*
advent ['ædˌvɛnt] *n* **1 Advent** : Adviento *m* **2** ARRIVAL : advenimiento *m*, venida *f*
adventure [æd'vɛntʃər, əd-] *n* : aventura *f*
adventurer [æd'vɛntʃərər, əd-] *n* : aventurero *m*, -ra *f*
adventurous [æd'vɛntʃərəs, əd-] *adj* **1** : intrépido, aventurero ⟨an adventurous traveler : un viajero intrépido⟩ **2** RISKY : arriesgado, aventurado
adverb ['ædˌvərb] *n* : adverbio *m* — **adverbial** [æd'vərbiəl] *adj*
adversary ['ædvərˌsɛri] *n, pl* **-saries** : adversario *m*, -ria *f*
adverse [æd'vərs, 'ædˌ] *adj* **1** OPPOSING : opuesto, contrario **2** UNFAVORABLE : adverso, desfavorable — **adversely** *adv*
adversity [æd'vərsəti, əd-] *n, pl* **-ties** : adversidad *f*
advertise ['ædvərˌtaɪz] *v* **-tised; -tising** *vt* : anunciar, hacerle publicidad a — *vi* : hacer publicidad, hacer propaganda
advertisement ['ædvərˌtaɪzmənt; æd'vərtəzmənt] *n* : anuncio *m*

advertiser ['ædvərˌtaɪzər] *n* : anunciante *mf*
advertising ['ædvərˌtaɪzɪŋ] *n* : publicidad *f*, propaganda *f*
advice [æd'vaɪs] *n* : consejo *m*, recomendación *f* ⟨take my advice : sigue mis consejos⟩
advisability [ædˌvaɪzə'bɪləti, əd-] *n* : conveniencia *f*
advisable [æd'vaɪzəbəl, əd-] *adj* : aconsejable, recomendable, conveniente
advise [æd'vaɪz, əd-] *v* **-vised; -vising** *vt* **1** COUNSEL : aconsejar, asesorar **2** RECOMMEND : recomendar **3** INFORM : informar, notificar — *vi* : dar consejo
adviser *or* **advisor** [æd'vaɪzər, əd-] *n* : consejero *m*, -ra *f*; asesor *m*, -sora *f*
advisory [æd'vaɪzəri, əd-] *adj* **1** : consultivo **2 in an advisory capacity** : como asesor
advocacy ['ædvəkəsi] *n* : promoción *f*, apoyo *m*
advocate¹ ['ædvəˌkeɪt] *vt* **-cated; -cating** : recomendar, abogar por, ser partidario de
advocate² ['ædvəkət] *n* : defensor *m*, -sora *f*; partidario *m*, -ria *f*
adze ['ædz] *n* : azuela *f*
aeon ['i:ən, 'i:ˌɑn] *n* : eón *m*, siglo *m*, eternidad *f*
aerate ['ærˌeɪt] *vt* **-ated; -ating** : gasear (un líquido), oxigenar (la sangre)
aerial¹ ['æriəl] *adj* : aéreo
aerial² *n* : antena *f*
aerie ['æri, 'ɪri, 'eɪəri] *n* : aguilera *f*
aerobic [ˌær'o:bɪk] *adj* : aerobio, aeróbico ⟨aerobic exercises : ejercicios aeróbicos⟩
aerobics [ˌær'o:bɪks] *ns & pl* : aeróbic *m*
aerodynamic [ˌæro:daɪ'næmɪk] *adj* : aerodinámico — **aerodynamically** [-mɪkli] *adv*
aerodynamics [ˌæro:daɪ'næmɪks] *n* : aerodinámica *f*
aeronautical [ˌærə'nɔtɪkəl] *adj* : aeronáutico
aeronautics [ˌærə'nɔtɪks] *n* : aeronáutica *f*
aerosol ['ærəˌsɔl] *n* : aerosol *m*
aerospace¹ ['æroˌspeɪs] *adj* : aeroespacial
aerospace² *n* : espacio *m*
aesthetic [ɛs'θɛtɪk] *adj* : estético — **aesthetically** [-tɪkli] *adv*
aesthetics [ɛs'θɛtɪks] *n* : estética *f*
afar [ə'far] *adv* : lejos, a lo lejos
affability [ˌæfə'bɪləti] *n* : afabilidad *f*
affable ['æfəbəl] *adj* : afable — **affably** *adv*
affair [ə'fær] *n* **1** MATTER : asunto *m*, cuestión *f*, caso *m* **2** EVENT : ocasión *f*, acontecimiento *m* **3** LIAISON : amorío *m*, aventura *f* **4 business affairs** : negocios *mpl* **5 current affairs** : actualidades *fpl*
affect [ə'fɛkt, æ-] *vt* **1** INFLUENCE, TOUCH : afectar, tocar **2** FEIGN : fingir

affectation [ˌæˌfɛkˈteɪʃən] *n* : afectación *f*

affected [əˈfɛktəd, æ-] *adj* **1** FEIGNED : afectado, fingido **2** MOVED : conmovido

affecting [əˈfɛktɪŋ, æ-] *adj* : conmovedor

affection [əˈfɛkʃən] *n* : afecto *m*, cariño *m*

affectionate [əˈfɛkʃənət] *adj* : afectuoso, cariñoso — **affectionately** *adv*

affidavit [ˌæfəˈdeɪvət, ˈæfəˌ-] *n* : declaración *f* jurada, affidávit *m*

affiliate¹ [əˈfɪliˌeɪt] *v* **-ated; -ating** *vt* : afiliar, asociar ⟨to be affiliated with : estar afiliado a⟩

affiliate² [əˈfɪliət] *n* : afiliado *m*, -da *f* (persona), filial *f* (organización)

affiliation [əˌfɪliˈeɪʃən] *n* : afiliación *f*, filiación *f*

affinity [əˈfɪnəti] *n, pl* **-ties** : afinidad *f*

affirm [əˈfərm] *vt* : afirmar, aseverar, declarar

affirmation [ˌæfərˈmeɪʃən] *n* : afirmación *f*, aserto *m*, declaración *f*

affirmative¹ [əˈfərmətɪv] *adj* : afirmativo ⟨affirmative action : acción afirmativa⟩

affirmative² *n* **1** : afirmativa *f* **2 to answer in the affirmative** : responder afirmativamente, dar una respuesta afirmativa

affix [əˈfɪks] *vt* : fijar, poner, pegar

afflict [əˈflɪkt] *vt* **1** : afligir, aquejar **2 to be afflicted with** : padecer de, sufrir de

affliction [əˈflɪkʃən] *n* **1** TRIBULATION : aflicción *f*, tribulación *f* **2** AILMENT : enfermedad *f*, padecimiento *m*

affluence [ˈæˌfluːənts; æˈfluː-, ə-] *n* : afluencia *f*, abundancia *f*, prosperidad *f*

affluent [ˈæˌfluːənt; æˈfluː-, ə-] *adj* : próspero, adinerado

afford [əˈford] *vt* **1** : tener los recursos para, permitirse el lujo de ⟨I can afford it : puedo permitírmelo, tengo con que comprarlo⟩ **2** PROVIDE : ofrecer, proporcionar, dar

affront¹ [əˈfrʌnt] *vt* : afrentar, insultar, ofender

affront² *n* : afrenta *f*, insulto *m*, ofensa *f*

Afghan [ˈæfˌgæn, -gən] *n* : afgano *m*, -na *f* — **Afghan** *adj*

afire [əˈfaɪr] *adj* : ardiendo, en llamas

aflame [əˈfleɪm] *adj* : llameante, en llamas

afloat [əˈfloːt] *adv & adj* : a flote

afoot [əˈfʊt] *adv* **1** WALKING : a pie, andando **2** UNDER WAY : en marcha ⟨something suspicious is afoot : algo sospechoso se está tramando⟩

aforementioned [əˈforˈmɛntʃ ənd] *adj* : antedicho, susodicho

aforesaid [əˈforˌsɛd] *adj* : antes mencionado, antedicho

afraid [əˈfreɪd] *adj* **1 to be afraid** : tener miedo **2 to be afraid that** : temerse que ⟨I'm afraid not : me temo que no⟩

afresh [əˈfrɛʃ] *adv* **1** : de nuevo, otra vez **2 to start afresh** : volver a empezar

African [ˈæfrɪkən] *n* : africano *m*, -na *f* — **African** *adj*

Afro–American¹ [ˌæfroəˈmɛrɪkən] *adj* : afroamericano *m*, -na *f*

Afro–American² *n* : afroamericano

aft [ˈæft] *adv* : a popa

after¹ [ˈæftər] *adv* **1** AFTERWARD : después **2** BEHIND : detrás, atrás

after² *adj* : posterior, siguiente ⟨in after years : en los años posteriores⟩

after³ *conj* : después de, después de que ⟨after we ate : después de que comimos, después de comer⟩

after⁴ *prep* **1** FOLLOWING : después de, tras ⟨after Saturday : después del sábado⟩ ⟨day after day : día tras día⟩ **2** BEHIND : tras de, después de ⟨I ran after the dog : corrí tras del perro⟩ **3** CONCERNING : por ⟨they asked after you : preguntaron por ti⟩ **4 after all** : después de todo

aftereffect [ˈæftərɪˌfɛkt] *n* : efecto *m* secundario

afterlife [ˈæftərˌlaɪf] *n* : vida *f* venidera, vida *f* después de la muerte

aftermath [ˈæftərˌmæθ] *n* : consecuencias *fpl*, resultados *mpl*

afternoon [ˌæftərˈnuːn] *n* : tarde *f*

aftertaste [ˈæftərˌteɪst] *n* : resabio *m*, regusto *m*

afterthought [ˈæftərˌθɔt] *n* : ocurrencia *f* tardía, idea *f* tardía

afterward [ˈæftərwərd] *or* **afterwards** [-wərdz] *adv* : después, luego ⟨soon afterward : poco después⟩

again [əˈgɛn, -ˈgɪn] *adv* **1** ANEW, OVER : de nuevo, otra vez **2** BESIDES : además **3 then again** : por otra parte ⟨I may stay, then again I may not : puede ser que me quede, por otra parte, puede que no⟩

against [əˈgɛntst, -ˈgɪntst] *prep* **1** TOUCHING : contra ⟨against the wall : contra la pared⟩ **2** OPPOSING : contra, en contra de ⟨I will vote against the proposal : votaré en contra de la propuesta⟩ ⟨against the grain : a contrapelo⟩

agape [əˈgeɪp] *adj* : boquiabierto

agate [ˈæɡət] *n* : ágata *f*

age¹ [ˈeɪʤ] *vi* **aged; aging** : envejecer, madurar

age² *n* **1** : edad *f* ⟨ten years of age : diez años de edad⟩ ⟨to be of age : ser mayor de edad⟩ **2** PERIOD : era *f*, siglo *m*, época *f* **3 old age** : vejez *f* **4 ages** *npl* : siglos *mpl*, eternidad *f*

aged *adj* **1** [ˈeɪʤəd, ˈeɪʤd] OLD : anciano, viejo, vetusto **2** [ˈeɪʤd] (*indicating a specified age*) ⟨a girl aged 10 : una niña de 10 años de edad⟩

ageless [ˈeɪʤləs] *adj* **1** YOUTHFUL : eternamente joven **2** TIMELESS : eterno, perenne

agency [ˈeɪʤəntsi] *n, pl* **-cies 1** : agencia *f*, oficina *f* ⟨travel agency : agencia

de viajes⟩ **2 through the agency of** : a
través de, por medio de
agenda [ə'dʒndə] *n* : agenda *f*, orden *m*
del día
agent ['eɪdʒənt] *n* **1** MEANS : agente *m*,
medio *m*, instrumento *m* **2** REPRE-
SENTATIVE : agente *mf*, representante
mf
aggravate ['ægrə,veɪt] *vt* **-vated; -vating**
1 WORSEN : agravar, empeorar **2** AN-
NOY : irritar, exasperar
aggravation [,ægrə'veɪʃən] *n* **1** WORS-
ENING : empeoramiento *m* **2** ANNOY-
ANCE : molestia *f*, irritación *f*, exasperación *f*
aggregate[1] ['ægrɪ,geɪt] *vt* **-gated; -gat-
ing** : juntar, sumar
aggregate[2] ['ægrɪgət] *adj* : total, global,
conjunto
aggregate[3] ['ægrɪgət] *n* **1** CONGLOM-
ERATE : agregado *m*, conglomerado *m*
2 WHOLE : total *m*, conjunto *m*
aggression [ə'grɛʃən] *n* **1** ATTACK
: agresión *f* **2** AGGRESSIVENESS : agresividad *f*
aggressive [ə'grɛsɪv] *adj* : agresivo —
aggressively *adv*
aggressiveness [ə'grɛsɪvnəs] *n* : agresividad *f*
aggressor [ə'grɛsər] *n* : agresor *m*, -sora
f
aggrieved [ə'gri:vd] *adj* : ofendido, herido
aghast [ə'gæst] *adj* : espantado, aterrado, horrorizado
agile ['ædʒəl] *adj* : ágil
agility [ə'dʒɪləti] *n, pl* **-ties** : agilidad *f*
agitate ['ædʒə,teɪt] *v* **-tated; -tating** *vt* **1**
SHAKE : agitar **2** UPSET : inquietar,
perturbar — *vi* **to agitate against** : hacer campaña en contra de
agitation [,ædʒə'teɪʃən] *n* : agitación *f*,
inquietud *f*
agitator ['ædʒə,teɪtər] *n* : agitador *m*,
-dora *f*
agnostic [æg'nɑstɪk] *n* : agnóstico *m*, -ca
f
ago [ə'go:] *adv* : hace ⟨two years ago
: hace dos años⟩ ⟨long ago : hace tiempo, hace mucho tiempo⟩
agog [ə'gɑg] *adj* : ansioso, curioso
agonize ['ægə,naɪz] *vi* **-nized; -nizing**
: tormentarse, angustiarse
agonizing ['ægə,naɪzɪŋ] *adj* : angustioso, terrible — **agonizingly** [-zɪŋli]
adv
agony ['ægəni] *n, pl* **-nies 1** PAIN : dolor *m* **2** ANGUISH : angustia *f*
agrarian [ə'grɛriən] *adj* : agrario
agree [ə'gri:] *v* **agreed; agreeing** *vt* AC-
KNOWLEDGE : estar de acuerdo ⟨he
agreed that I was right : estuvo de
acuerdo en que tenía razón⟩ — *vi* **1**
CONCUR : estar de acuerdo **2** CONSENT
: ponerse de acuerdo **3** TALLY : concordar **4 to agree with** : sentarle bien
(a alguien) ⟨this climate agrees with me
: este clima me sienta bien⟩

agreeable [ə'gri:əbəl] *adj* **1** PLEASING
: agradable, simpático **2** WILLING : dispuesto **3** AGREEING : de acuerdo, conforme
agreeably [ə'gri:əbli] *adv* : agradablemente
agreement [ə'gri:mənt] *n* **1** : acuerdo
m, conformidad *f* ⟨in agreement with
: de acuerdo con⟩ **2** CONTRACT, PACT
: acuerdo *m*, pacto *m*, convenio *m* **3**
CONCORD, HARMONY : concordia *f*
agriculture ['ægrɪ,kʌltʃər] *n* : agricultura
f — **agricultural** [,ægrɪ'kʌltʃərəl] *adj*
aground [ə'graʊnd] *adj* : encallado,
varado
ahead [ə'hɛd] *adv* **1** : al frente, delante,
adelante ⟨he walked ahead : caminó
delante⟩ **2** BEFOREHAND : por adelantado, con antelación **3** LEADING : a
la delantera **4 to get ahead** : adelantar, progresar
ahead of *prep* **1** : al frente de, delante
de, antes de **2 to get ahead of** : adelantarse a
ahoy [ə'hɔɪ] *interj* **ship ahoy!** : ¡barco a
la vista!
aid[1] ['eɪd] *vt* : ayudar, auxiliar
aid[2] *n* **1** HELP : ayuda *f*, asistencia *f* **2**
ASSISTANT : asistente *mf*
aide ['eɪd] *n* : ayudante *mf*
AIDS ['eɪdz] *n* : SIDA *m*, sida *m*
ail ['eɪl] *vt* : molestar, afligir — *vi* : sufrir,
estar enfermo
aileron ['eɪlə,rɑn] *n* : alerón *m*
ailment ['eɪlmənt] *n* : enfermedad *f*, dolencia *f*, achaque *m*
aim[1] ['eɪm] *vt* **1** : apuntar (un arma), dirigir (una observación) **2** INTEND
: proponerse, querer ⟨he aims to do it
tonight : se propone hacerlo esta
noche⟩ — *vi* **1** POINT : apuntar **2 to
aim at** : aspirar a
aim[2] *n* **1** MARKSMANSHIP : puntería *f* **2**
GOAL : propósito *m*, objetivo *m*, fin *m*
aimless ['eɪmləs] *adj* : sin rumbo, sin objeto
aimlessly ['eɪmləsli] *adv* : sin rumbo, sin
objeto
air[1] ['ær] *vt* **1** : airear, ventilar ⟨to air
out a mattress : airear un colchón⟩ **2**
EXPRESS : airear, manifestar, comunicar **3** BROADCAST : transmitir, emitir
air[2] *n* **1** : aire *m* **2** MELODY : aire *m* **3**
APPEARANCE : aire *m*, aspecto *m* **4 airs**
npl : aires *mpl*, afectación *f* **5 by ∼**
: por avión (dícese de una carta), en
avión (dícese de una persona) **6 to be
on the air** : estar en el aire, estar emi-
tiendo
airborne ['ær,bɔrn] *adj* **1** : aerotransportado ⟨airborne troops : tropas aero-
transportadas⟩ **2** FLYING : volando, en
el aire
air–condition [,ærkən'dɪʃən] *vt* : climatizar, condicionar con el aire
air conditioner [,ærkən'dɪʃənər] *n*
: acondicionador *m* de aire

air–conditioning [ˌærkən'dɪʃənɪŋ] *n* : aire *m* acondicionado

aircraft ['ærˌkræft] *ns & pl* **1** : avión *m*, aeronave *f* **2 aircraft carrier** : portaaviones *m*

airfield ['ærˌfiːld] *n* : aeródromo *m*, campo *m* de aviación

air force *n* : fuerza *f* aérea

airlift ['ærˌlɪft] *n* : puente *m* aéreo, transporte *m* aéreo

airline ['ærˌlaɪn] *n* : aerolínea *f*, línea *f* aérea

airliner ['ærˌlaɪnər] *n* : avión *m* de pasajeros

airmail¹ ['ærˌmeɪl] *vt* : enviar por vía aérea

airmail² *n* : correo *m* aéreo

airman ['ærmən] *n, pl* **-men** [-mən, -ˌmɛn] **1** AVIATOR : aviador *m*, -dora *f* **2** : soldado *m* de la fuerza aérea

airplane ['ærˌpleɪn] *n* : avión *m*

airport ['ærˌpɔrt] *n* : aeropuerto *m*

airship ['ærˌʃɪp] *n* : dirigible *m*, zepelín *m*

airstrip ['ærˌstrɪp] *n* : pista *f* de aterrizaje

airtight ['ær'taɪt] *adj* : hermético, herméticamente cerrado

airwaves ['ærˌweɪvz] *npl* : radio *m*, televisión *f*

airy ['æri] *adj* **airier** [-iər]; **-est 1** DELICATE, LIGHT : delicado, ligero **2** BREEZY : aireado, bien ventilado

aisle ['aɪl] *n* : pasillo *m*, nave *f* lateral (de una iglesia)

ajar [ə'dʒɑr] *adj* : entreabierto, entornado

akimbo [ə'kɪmbo] *adj & adv* : en jarras

akin [ə'kɪn] *adj* **1** RELATED : emparentado **2** SIMILAR : semejante, parecido

alabaster ['æləˌbæstər] *n* : alabastro *m*

alacrity [ə'lækrəti] *n* : presteza *f*, prontitud *f*

alarm¹ [ə'lɑrm] *vt* **1** WARN : alarmar, alertar **2** FRIGHTEN : asustar

alarm² *n* **1** WARNING : alarma *f*, alerta *f* **2** APPREHENSION, FEAR : aprensión *f*, inquietud *f*, temor *m* **3 alarm clock** : despertador *m*

alarming [ə'lɑrmɪŋ] *adj* : alarmante

alas [ə'læs] *interj* : ¡ay!

Albanian [æl'beɪniən] *n* : albanés *m*, -nesa *f* — **Albanian** *adj*

albatross ['ælbəˌtrɔs] *n, pl* **-tross** or **-trosses** : albatros *m*

albeit [ɔl'biːət, æl-] *conj* : aunque

albino [æl'baɪno] *n, pl* **-nos** : albino *m*, -na *f*

album ['ælbəm] *n* : álbum *m*

albumen [æl'bjuːmən] *n* **1** : clara *f* de huevo **2** → **albumin**

albumin [æl'bjuːmən] *n* : albúmina *f*

alchemist ['ælkəmɪst] *n* : alquimista *mf*

alchemy ['ælkəmi] *n, pl* **-mies** : alquimia *f*

alcohol ['ælkəˌhɔl] *n* **1** ETHANOL : alcohol *m*, etanol *m* **2** LIQUOR : alcohol *m*, bebidas *fpl* alcohólicas

alcoholic¹ [ˌælkə'hɔlɪk] *adj* : alcohólico

alcoholic² *n* : alcohólico *m*, -ca *f*

alcoholism ['ælkəhɔˌlɪzəm] *n* : alcoholismo *m*

alcove ['ælˌkoːv] *n* : nicho *m*, hueco *m*

alderman ['ɔldərmən] *n, pl* **-men** [-mən, -ˌmɛn] : concejal *mf*

ale ['eɪl] *n* : cerveza *f*

alert¹ [ə'lərt] *vt* : alertar, poner sobre aviso

alert² *adj* **1** WATCHFUL : alerta, vigilante **2** QUICK : listo, vivo

alert³ *n* : alerta *f*, alarma *f*

alertly [ə'lərtli] *adv* : con listeza

alertness [ə'lərtnəs] *n* **1** WATCHFULNESS : vigilancia *f* **2** ASTUTENESS : listeza *f*, viveza *f*

alfalfa [æl'fælfə] *n* : alfalfa *f*

alga ['ælgə] *n, pl* **-gae** ['ælˌdʒiː] : alga *f*

algebra ['ældʒəbrə] *n* : álgebra *m*

algebraic [ˌældʒə'breɪɪk] *adj* : algebraico — **algebraically** [-ɪkli] *adv*

Algerian [æl'dʒɪriən] *n* : argelino *m*, -na *f* — **Algerian** *adj*

algorithm ['ælgəˌrɪðəm] *n* : algoritmo *m*

alias¹ ['eɪliəs] *adv* : alias

alias² *n* : alias *m*

alibi¹ ['æləˌbaɪ] *vi* : ofrecer una coartada

alibi² *n* **1** : coartada *f* **2** EXCUSE : pretexto *m*, excusa *f*

alien¹ ['eɪliən] *adj* **1** STRANGE : ajeno, extraño **2** FOREIGN : extranjero, foráneo **3** EXTRATERRESTRIAL : extraterrestre

alien² *n* **1** FOREIGNER : extranjero *m*, -ra *f*; forastero *m*, -ra *f* **2** EXTRATERRESTRIAL : extraterrestre *mf*

alienate ['eɪliəˌneɪt] *vt* **-ated; -ating 1** ESTRANGE : alienar, enajenar **2 to alienate oneself** : alejarse, distanciarse

alienation [ˌeɪliə'neɪʃən] *n* : alienación *f*, enajenación *f*

alight [ə'laɪt] *vi* **1** DISMOUNT : bajarse, apearse **2** LAND : posarse, aterrizar

align [ə'laɪn] *vt* : alinear

alignment [ə'laɪnmənt] *n* : alineación *f*, alineamiento *m*

alike¹ [ə'laɪk] *adv* : igual, del mismo modo

alike² *adj* : igual, semejante, parecido

alimentary [ˌælə'mɛntəri] *adj* **1** : alimenticio **2 alimentary canal** : tubo *m* digestivo

alimony ['æləˌmoːni] *n, pl* **-nies** : pensión *f* alimenticia

alive [ə'laɪv] *adj* **1** LIVING : vivo, viviente **2** LIVELY : animado, activo **3** ACTIVE : vigente, en uso **4** AWARE : consciente ⟨alive to the danger : consciente del peligro⟩

alkali ['ælkəˌlaɪ] *n, pl* **-lies** [-ˌlaɪz] or **-lis** [-ˌlaɪz] : álcali *m*

alkaline ['ælkələn, -ˌlaɪn] *adj* : alcalino

all¹ ['ɔl] *adv* **1** COMPLETELY : todo, completamente **2** : igual ⟨the score is 14 all : es 14 iguales, están empatados a 14⟩

3 all the better : tanto mejor **4 all the more** : aún más, todavía más

all² *adj* : todo ⟨all the children : todos los niños⟩ ⟨in all likelihood : con toda probabilidad, con la mayor probabilidad⟩

all³ *pron* **1** : todo, -da ⟨they ate it all : lo comieron todo⟩ ⟨that's all : eso es todo⟩ ⟨enough for all : suficiente para todos⟩ **2 all in all** : en general **3 not at all** (*in negative constructions*) : en absoluto, para nada

Allah ['ɑlɑ, ɑ'lɑ] *n* : Alá *m*

all–around [ˌɔlə'raʊnd] *adj* : completo, amplio

allay [ə'leɪ] *vt* **1** ALLEVIATE : aliviar, mitigar **2** CALM : aquietar, calmar

allegation [ˌælɪ'geɪʃən] *n* : alegato *m*, acusación *f*

allege [ə'lɛdʒ] *vt* **-leged; -leging 1** : alegar, afirmar **2 to be alleged** : decirse, pretenderse ⟨she is alleged to be wealthy : se dice que es adinerada⟩

alleged [ə'lɛdʒd, ə'lɛdʒəd] *adj* : presunto, supuesto

allegedly [ə'lɛdʒədli] *adv* : supuestamente, según se alega

allegiance [ə'liːdʒənts] *n* : lealtad *f*, fidelidad *f*

allegorical [ˌælə'gɔrɪkəl] *adj* : alegórico

allegory ['æləˌgɔri] *n, pl* **-ries** : alegoría *f*

alleluia [ˌɑlə'luːjə, ˌæ-] → **hallelujah**

allergen ['ælərdʒən] *n* : alérgeno *m*

allergic [ə'lərdʒɪk] *adj* : alérgico

allergy ['ælərdʒi] *n, pl* **-gies** : alergia *f*

alleviate [ə'liːviˌeɪt] *vt* **-ated; -ating** : aliviar, mitigar, paliar

alleviation [əˌliːvi'eɪʃən] *n* : alivio *m*

alley ['æli] *n, pl* **-leys 1** : callejón *m* **2 bowling alley** : bolera *f*

alliance [ə'laɪənts] *n* : alianza *f*, coalición *f*

alligator ['æləˌgeɪtər] *n* : caimán *m*

alliteration [əˌlɪtə'reɪʃən] *n* : aliteración *f*

allocate ['æləˌkeɪt] *vt* **-cated; -cating** : asignar, adjudicar

allocation [ˌælə'keɪʃən] *n* : asignación *f*, reparto *m*, distribución *f*

allot [ə'lɑt] *vt* **-lotted; -lotting** : repartir, distribuir, asignar

allotment [ə'lɑtmənt] *n* : reparto *m*, asignación *f*, distribución *f*

allow [ə'laʊ] *vt* **1** PERMIT : permitir, dejar **2** ALLOT : conceder, dar **3** ADMIT, CONCEDE : admitir, conceder — *vi* **to allow for** : tener en cuenta

allowable [ə'laʊəbəl] *adj* **1** PERMISSIBLE : permisible, lícito **2** : deducible ⟨allowable expenditure : gasto deducible⟩

allowance [ə'laʊənts] *n* **1** : complemento *m* (para gastos, etc.), mesada *f* (para niños) **2 to make allowance(s)** : tener en cuenta, disculpar

alloy ['æˌlɔɪ] *n* : aleación *f*

all–purpose ['ɔl'pərpəs] *adj* : multiuso ⟨all-purpose flour : harina común⟩

all right¹ *adv* **1** YES : sí, por supuesto **2** WELL : bien ⟨I did all right : me fue bien⟩ **3** DEFINITELY : bien, ciertamente, sin duda ⟨he's sick all right : está bien enfermo⟩

all right² *adj* **1** OK : bien ⟨are you all right? : ¿estás bien?⟩ **2** SATISFACTORY : bien, bueno ⟨your work is all right : tu trabajo es bueno⟩

all–round [ˌɔl'raʊnd] → **all–around**

allspice ['ɔlspaɪs] *n* : pimienta *f* de Jamaica

allude [ə'luːd] *vi* **-luded; -luding** : aludir, referirse

allure¹ [ə'lʊr] *vt* **-lured; -luring** : cautivar, atraer

allure² *n* : atractivo *m*, encanto *m*

allusion [ə'luːʒən] *n* : alusión *f*

ally¹ [ə'laɪ, 'æˌlaɪ] *vi* **-lied; -lying** : aliarse

ally² ['æˌlaɪ, ə'laɪ] *n* : aliado *m*, -da *f*

almanac ['ɔlməˌnæk, 'æl-] *n* : almanaque *m*

almighty [ɔl'maɪti] *adj* : omnipotente, todopoderoso

almond ['ɑmənd, 'ɑl-, 'æ-, 'æl-] *n* : almendra *f*

almost ['ɔlˌmoːst, ɔl'moːst] *adv* : casi, prácticamente

alms ['ɑmz, 'ɑlmz, 'ælmz] *ns & pl* : limosna *f*, caridad *f*

aloe ['æloː] *n* : áloe *m*

aloft [ə'lɔft] *adv* : en alto, en el aire

alone¹ [ə'loːn] *adv* : sólo, solamente, únicamente

alone² *adj* : solo ⟨they're alone in the house : están solos en la casa⟩

along¹ [ə'lɔŋ] *adv* **1** FORWARD : adelante ⟨farther along : más adelante⟩ ⟨move along! : ¡circulen, por favor!⟩ **2 to bring along** : traer **3 ~ with** : con, junto con **4 all along** : desde el principio

along² *prep* **1** : por, a lo largo de ⟨along the coast : a lo largo de la costa⟩ **2** : en, en el curso de, por ⟨along the way : en el curso del viaje⟩

alongside¹ [əˌlɔŋ'saɪd] *adv* : al costado, al lado

alongside² *or* **alongside of** *prep* : junto a, al lado de

aloof [ə'luːf] *adj* : distante, reservado

aloofness [ə'luːfnəs] *n* : reserva *f*, actitud *f* distante

aloud [ə'laʊd] *adv* : en voz alta

alpaca [æl'pækə] *n* : alpaca *f*

alphabet ['ælfəˌbɛt] *n* : alfabeto *m*

alphabetical [ˌælfə'bɛtɪkəl] *or* **alphabetic** [-'bɛtɪk] *adj* : alfabético — **alphabetically** [-tɪkli] *adv*

alphabetize ['ælfəbəˌtaɪz] *vt* **-ized; -izing** : alfabetizar, poner en orden alfabético

alpine ['ælˌpaɪn] *adj* : alpino

already [ɔl'rɛdi] *adv* : ya

also ['ɔlˌsoː] *adv* : también, además

altar ['ɔltər] *n* : altar *m*

alter ['ɔltər] *vt* : alterar, cambiar, modificar

alteration [ˌɔltə'reɪʃən] *n* : alteración *f*, cambio *m*, modificación *f*

altercation [ˌɔltər'keɪʃən] *n* : altercado *m*, disputa *f*

alternate[1] ['ɔltərˌneɪt] *v* **-nated; -nating** : alternar

alternate[2] ['ɔltərnət] *adj* **1** : alterno ⟨alternate cycles of inflation and depression : ciclos alternos de inflación y depresión⟩ **2** : uno sí y otro no ⟨he cooks on alternate days : cocina un día sí y otro no⟩

alternate[3] ['ɔltərnət] *n* : suplente *mf*; sustituto *m*, -ta *f*

alternately ['ɔltərnətli] *adv* : alternativemente, por turno

alternating current ['ɔltərˌneɪtɪŋ] *n* : corriente *f* alterna

alternation [ˌɔltər'neɪʃən] *n* : alternancia *f*, rotación *f*

alternative[1] [ɔl'tərnətɪv] *adj* : alternativo

alternative[2] *n* : alternativa *f*

alternator ['ɔltərˌneɪtər] *n* : alternador *m*

although [ɔl'ðoː] *conj* : aunque, a pesar de que

altitude ['æltəˌtuːd, -ˌtjuːd] *n* : altitud *f*, altura *f*

alto ['ælˌtoː] *n*, *pl* **-tos** : alto *mf*, contralto *mf*

altogether [ˌɔltə'gɛðər] *adv* **1** COMPLETELY : completamente, totalmente, del todo **2** ON THE WHOLE : en suma, en general

altruism ['æltruˌɪzəm] *n* : altruismo *m*

altruistic [ˌæltru'ɪstɪk] *adj* : altruista — **altruistically** [-tɪkli] *adv*

alum ['æləm] *n* : alumbre *m*

aluminum [ə'luːmənəm] *n* : aluminio *m*

alumna [ə'lʌmnə] *n*, *pl* **-nae** [-ˌniː] : exalumna *f*

alumnus [ə'lʌmnəs] *n*, *pl* **-ni** [-ˌnaɪ] : exalumno *m*

always ['ɔlwiz, -ˌweɪz] *adv* **1** INVARIABLY : siempre, invariablemente **2** FOREVER : para siempre

am → **be**

amalgam [ə'mælgəm] *n* : amalgama *f*

amalgamate [ə'mælgəˌmeɪt] *vt* **-ated; -ating** : amalgamar, unir, fusionar

amalgamation [əˌmælgə'meɪʃən] *n* : fusión *f*, unión *f*

amaryllis [ˌæmə'rɪləs] *n* : amarilis *f*

amass [ə'mæs] *vt* : amasar, acumular

amateur ['æməˌtʃər, -tər, -ˌtur, -ˌtjur] *n* **1** : amateur *mf* **2** BEGINNER : principiante *mf*; aficionado *m*, -da *f*

amateurish ['æməˌtʃərɪʃ, -ˌtər-, -ˌtur-, -ˌtjur-] *adj* : amateur, inexperto

amaze [ə'meɪz] *vt* **amazed; amazing** : asombrar, maravillar, pasmar

amazement [ə'meɪzmənt] *n* : asombro *m*, sorpresa *f*

amazing [ə'meɪzɪŋ] *adj* : asombroso, sorprendente — **amazingly** [-zɪŋli] *adv*

Amazon ['æməˌzɑn] *n* : amazona *f* (en mitología)

Amazonian [ˌæmə'zoːniən] *adj* : amazónico

ambassador [æm'bæsədər] *n* : embajador *m*, -dora *f*

amber ['æmbər] *n* : ámbar *m*

ambergris ['æmbərˌgrɪs, -ˌgriːs] *n* : ámbar *m* gris

ambidextrous [ˌæmbɪ'dɛkstrəs] *adj* : ambidextro — **ambidextrously** *adv*

ambience *or* **ambiance** ['æmbiənts, 'ambiˌants] *n* : ambiente *m*, atmósfera *f*

ambiguity [ˌæmbə'gjuːəti] *n*, *pl* **-ties** : ambigüedad *f*

ambiguous [æm'bɪgjuəs] *adj* : ambiguo

ambition [æm'bɪʃən] *n* : ambición *f*

ambitious [æm'bɪʃəs] *adj* : ambicioso — **ambitiously** *adv*

ambivalence [æm'bɪvələnts] *n* : ambivalencia *f*

ambivalent [æm'bɪvələnt] *adj* : ambivalente

amble[1] ['æmbəl] *vi* **-bled; -bling** : ir tranquilamente, pasearse despreocupadamente

amble[2] *n* : paseo *m* tranquilo

ambulance ['æmbjələnts] *n* : ambulancia *f*

ambush[1] ['æmˌbuʃ] *vt* : emboscar

ambush[2] *n* : emboscada *f*, celada *f*

ameliorate [ə'miːljəˌreɪt] *v* **-rated; -rating** IMPROVE : mejorar

amelioration [əˌmiːljə'reɪʃən] *n* : mejora *f*

amen ['eɪ'mɛn, 'ɑ-] *interj* : amén

amenable [ə'miːnəbəl, -'mɛ-] *adj* RESPONSIVE : susceptible, receptivo, sensible

amend [ə'mɛnd] *vt* **1** IMPROVE : mejorar, enmendar **2** CORRECT : enmendar, corregir

amendment [ə'mɛndmənt] *n* : enmienda *f*

amends [ə'mɛndz] *ns & pl* : compensación *f*, reparación *f*, desagravio *m*

amenity [ə'mɛnəti, -'miː-] *n*, *pl* **-ties 1** PLEASANTNESS : lo agradable, amenidad *f* **2 amenities** *npl* : servicios *mpl*, comodidades *fpl*

American [ə'mɛrɪkən] *n* : americano *m*, -na *f* — **American** *adj*

American Indian *n* : indio *m* (americano), india *f* (americana)

amethyst ['æməθəst] *n* : amatista *f*

amiability [ˌeɪmiə'bɪləti] *n* : amabilidad *f*, afabilidad *f*

amiable ['eɪmiːəbəl] *adj* : amable, afable — **amiably** [-bli] *adv*

amicable ['æmɪkəbəl] *adj* : amigable, amistoso, cordial — **amicably** [-bli] *adv*

amid [ə'mɪd] *or* **amidst** [ə'mɪdst] *prep* : en medio de, entre

amino acid [ə'miːno] *n* : aminoácido *m*

amiss[1] [ə'mɪs] *adv* : mal, fuera de lugar ⟨to take amiss : tomar a mal, llevar a mal⟩

amiss[2] *adj* **1** WRONG : malo, inoportuno **2 there's something amiss** : pasa algo, algo anda mal

ammeter ['æˌmiːtər] *n* : amperímetro *m*

ammonia [ə'mo:njə] *n* : amoníaco *m*
ammunition [ˌæmjə'nɪʃən] *n* **1** : municiones *fpl* **2** ARGUMENTS : argumentos *mpl*
amnesia [æm'ni:ʒə] *n* : amnesia *f*
amnesty ['æmnəsti] *n, pl* **-ties** : amnistía *f*
amoeba [ə'mi:bə] *n, pl* **-bas** *or* **-bae** [-ˌbi:] : ameba *f*
amoebic [ə'mi:bɪk] *adj* : amébico
amok [ə'mʌk, -'mɑk] *adv* **to run amok** : correr a ciegas, enloquecerse, desbocarse (dícese de la economía, etc.)
among [ə'mʌŋ] *prep* : entre
amoral [eɪ'mɔrəl] *adj* : amoral
amorous ['æmərəs] *adj* **1** PASSIONATE : enamoradizo, apasionado **2** ENAMORED : enamorado **3** LOVING : amoroso, cariñoso
amorously ['æmərəsli] *adv* : con cariño
amorphous [ə'mɔrfəs] *adj* : amorfo, informe
amortize ['æmərˌtaɪz, ə'mɔr-] *vt* **-tized; -tizing** : amortizar
amount[1] [ə'maʊnt] *vi* **to amount to 1** : equivaler a, significar ⟨that amounts to treason : eso equivale a la traición⟩ **2** : ascender (a) ⟨my debts amount to $2000 : mis deudas ascienden a $2000⟩
amount[2] *n* : cantidad *f*, suma *f*
ampere ['æmˌpɪr] *n* : amperio *m*
ampersand ['æmpərˌsænd] *n* : el signo &
amphetamine [æm'fɛtəˌmi:n] *n* : anfetamina *f*
amphibian [æm'fɪbiən] *n* : anfibio *m*
amphibious [æm'fɪbiəs] *adj* : anfibio
amphitheater ['æmfəˌθi:ətər] *n* : anfiteatro *m*
ample ['æmpəl] *adj* **-pler; -plest 1** LARGE, SPACIOUS : amplio, extenso, grande **2** ABUNDANT : abundante, generoso
amplifier ['æmpləˌfaɪər] *n* : amplificador *m*
amplify ['æmpləˌfaɪ] *vt* **-fied; -fying** : amplificar
amply ['æmpli] *adv* : ampliamente, abundantemente, suficientemente
amputate ['æmpjəˌteɪt] *vt* **-tated; -tating** : amputar
amputation [ˌæmpjə'teɪʃən] *n* : amputación *f*
amuck [ə'mʌk] → **amok**
amulet ['æmjələt] *n* : amuleto *m*, talismán *m*
amuse [ə'mju:z] *vt* **amused; amusing 1** ENTERTAIN : entretener, distraer **2** : hacer reír, divertir ⟨the joke amused us : la broma nos hizo reír⟩
amusement [ə'mju:zmənt] *n* **1** ENTERTAINMENT : diversión *f*, entretenimiento *m*, pasatiempo *m* **2** LAUGHTER : risa *f*
an *art* → **a**[2]
anachronism [ə'nækrəˌnɪzəm] *n* : anacronismo *m*
anachronistic [əˌnækrə'nɪstɪk] *adj* : anacrónico

anaconda [ˌænə'kɑndə] *n* : anaconda *f*
anagram ['ænəˌgræm] *n* : anagrama *m*
anal ['eɪnəl] *adj* : anal
analgesic [ˌænəl'dʒi:zɪk, -sɪk] *n* : analgésico *m*
analog ['ænəˌlɔg] *adj* : analógico
analogical [ˌænə'lɑdʒɪkəl] *adj* : analógico — **analogically** [-kli] *adv*
analogous [ə'næləgəs] *adj* : análogo
analogy [ə'nælədʒi] *n, pl* **-gies** : analogía *f*
analysis [ə'næləsəs] *n, pl* **-yses** [-ˌsi:z] **1** : análisis *m* **2** PSYCHOANALYSIS : psicoanálisis *m*
analyst ['ænəlɪst] *n* **1** : analista *mf* **2** PSYCHOANALYST : psicoanalista *mf*
analytic [ˌænə'lɪtɪk] *or* **analytical** [-tɪkəl] *adj* : analítico — **analytically** [-tɪkli] *adv*
analyze ['ænəˌlaɪz] *vt* **-lyzed; -lyzing** : analizar
anarchic [æ'nɑrkɪk] *adj* : anárquico — **anarchically** [-kɪkli] *adv*
anarchism ['ænərˌkɪzəm, -nɑr-] *n* : anarquismo *m*
anarchist ['ænərkɪst, -nɑr-] *n* : anarquista *mf*
anarchy ['ænərki, -nɑr-] *n* : anarquía *f*
anathema [ə'næθəmə] *n* : anatema *m*
anatomic [ˌænə'tɑmɪk] *or* **anatomical** [-mɪkəl] *adj* : anatómico — **anatomically** [-mɪkli] *adv*
anatomy [ə'nætəmi] *n, pl* **-mies** : anatomía *f*
ancestor ['ænˌsɛstər] *n* : antepasado *m*, -da *f*; antecesor *m*, -sora *f*
ancestral [æn'sɛstrəl] *adj* : ancestral, de los antepasados
ancestry ['ænˌsɛstri] *n* **1** DESCENT : ascendencia *f*, linaje *m*, abolengo *m* **2** ANCESTORS : antepasados *mpl*, -das *fpl*
anchor[1] ['æŋkər] *vt* **1** MOOR : anclar, fondear **2** FASTEN : sujetar, asegurar, fijar
anchor[2] *n* **1** : ancla *f* **2** : presentador *m*, -dora *f* (en televisión)
anchorage ['æŋkərɪdʒ] *n* : anclaje *m*
anchovy ['ænˌtʃo:vi, æn'tʃo:-] *n, pl* **-vies** *or* **-vy** : anchoa *f*
ancient ['eɪntʃənt] *adj* **1** : antiguo ⟨ancient history : historia antigua⟩ **2** OLD : viejo
ancients ['eɪntʃənts] *npl* : los antiguos *mpl*
and ['ænd] *conj* **1** : y (**e** *before words beginning with i- or hi-*) **2** : con ⟨ham and eggs : huevos con jamón⟩ **3** : a ⟨go and see : ve a ver⟩ **4** : de ⟨try and finish it soon : trata de terminarlo pronto⟩
Andalusian [ˌændə'lu:ʒən] *n* : andaluz *m*, -luza *f* — **Andalusian** *adj*
Andean ['ændiən] *adj* : andino
andiron ['ænˌdaɪərn] *n* : morillo *m*
Andorran [æn'dɔrən] *n* : andorrano *m*, -na *f* — **Andorran** *adj*
androgynous [æn'drɑdʒənəs] *adj* : andrógino
anecdotal [ˌænɪk'do:t̬əl] *adj* : anecdótico

anecdote ['ænɪk,do:t] *n* : anécdota *f*
anemia [ə'ni:miə] *n* : anemia *f*
anemic [ə'ni:mɪk] *adj* : anémico
anemone [ə'nɛmənɪ] *n* : anémona *f*
anesthesia [,ænəs'θi:ʒə] *n* : anestesia *f*
anesthetic[1] [,ænəs'θɪk] *adj* : anestésico
anesthetic[2] *n* : anestésico *m*
anesthetist [ə'nɛsθətɪst] *n* : anestesista *mf*
anesthetize [ə'nɛsθə,taɪz] *vt* **-tize; -tized** : anestesiar
aneurysm ['ænjə,rɪzəm] *n* : aneurisma *mf*
anew [ə'nu:, -'nju:] *adv* : de nuevo, otra vez, nuevamente
angel ['eɪndʒəl] *n* : ángel *m*
angelic [æn'dʒɛlɪk] *or* **angelical** [-lɪkəl] *adj* : angélico, angelical — **angelically** [-lɪkli] *adv*
anger[1] ['æŋgər] *vt* : enojar, enfadar
anger[2] *n* : enojo *m*, enfado *m*, ira *f*, cólera *f*, rabia *f*
angina [æn'dʒaɪnə] *n* : angina *f*
angle[1] ['æŋgəl] *v* **angled; angling** *vt* DIRECT, SLANT : orientar, dirigir — *vi* FISH : pescar (con caña)
angle[2] *n* **1** : ángulo *m* **2** POINT OF VIEW : perspectiva *f*, punto *m* de vista
angler ['æŋglər] *n* : pescador *m*, -dora *f*
Anglican ['æŋglɪkən] *n* : anglicano *m*, -na *f* — **Anglican** *adj*
Anglo–Saxon[1] [,æŋglo'sæksən] *adj* : anglosajón
Anglo–Saxon[2] *n* : anglosajón *m*, -jona *f*
Angolan [æŋ'go:lən, æn-] *n* : angoleño *m*, -ña *f* — **Angolan** *adj*
angora [æŋ'gorə, æn-] *n* : angora *f*
angrily ['æŋgrəli] *adv* : furiosamente, con ira
angry ['æŋgri] *adj* **-grier; -est** : enojado, enfadado, furioso
anguish ['æŋgwɪʃ] *n* : angustia *f*, congoja *f*
anguished ['æŋgwɪʃt] *adj* : angustiado, acongojado
angular ['æŋgjələr] *adj* : angular (dícese de las formas), anguloso (dícese de las caras)
animal ['ænəməl] *n* **1** : animal *m* **2** BRUTE : bruto *m*, -ta *f*
animate[1] ['ænə,meɪt] *vt* **-mated; -mating** : animar
animate[2] ['ænəmət] *adj* : animado
animated ['ænə,meɪtəd] *adj* **1** LIVELY : animado, vivo, vivaz **2 animated cartoon** : dibujos *mpl* animados
animation [,ænə'meɪʃən] *n* : animación *f*
animosity [,ænə'masəti] *n*, *pl* **-ties** : animosidad *f*, animadversión *f*
anise ['ænəs] *n* : anís *m*
aniseed ['ænəs,si:d] *n* : anís *m*, semilla *f* de anís
ankle ['æŋkəl] *n* : tobillo *m*
anklebone ['æŋkəl,bo:n] *n* : taba *f*
annals ['ænəlz] *npl* : anales *mpl*, crónica *f*
anneal [ə'ni:l] *vt* **1** TEMPER : templar **2** STRENGTHEN : fortalecer

annex[1] [ə'nɛks, 'æ,nɛks] *vt* : anexar
annex[2] ['æ,nɛks, -nɪks] *n* : anexo *m*, anejo *m*
annexation [,æ,nɛk'seɪʃən] *n* : anexión *f*
annihilate [ə'naɪə,leɪt] *vt* **-lated; -lating** : aniquilar
annihilation [ə,naɪə'leɪʃən] *n* : aniquilación *f*, aniquilamiento *m*
anniversary [,ænə'vərsəri] *n*, *pl* **-ries** : aniversario *m*
annotate ['ænə,teɪt] *vt* **-tated; -tating** : anotar
annotation [,ænə'teɪʃən] *n* : anotación *f*
announce [ə'naʊnts] *vt* **-nounced; -nouncing** : anunciar
announcement [ə'naʊntsmənt] *n* : anuncio *m*
announcer [ə'naʊntsər] *n* : anunciador *m*, -dora *f*; comentarista *mf*; locutor *m*, -tora *f*
annoy [ə'nɔɪ] *vt* : molestar, fastidiar, irritar
annoyance [ə'nɔɪənts] *n* **1** IRRITATION : irritación *f*, fastidio *m* **2** NUISANCE : molestia *f*, fastidio *m*
annoying [ə'nɔɪɪŋ] *adj* : molesto, fastidioso, engorroso — **annoyingly** [-ɪŋli] *adv*
annual[1] ['ænjʊəl] *adj* : anual — **annually** *adv*
annual[2] *n* **1** : planta *f* anual **2** YEARBOOK : anuario *m*
annuity [ə'nu:əti] *n*, *pl* **-ties** : anualidad *f*
annul [ə'nʌl] *vt* **anulled; anulling** : anular, invalidar
annulment [ə'nʌlmənt] *n* : anulación *f*
anode ['æ,no:d] *n* : ánodo *m*
anoint [ə'nɔɪnt] *vt* : ungir
anomalous [ə'namələs] *adj* : anómalo
anomaly [ə'naməli] *n*, *pl* **-lies** : anomalía *f*
anonymity [,ænə'nɪməti] *n* : anonimato *m*
anonymous [ə'nanəməs] *adj* : anónimo — **anonymously** *adv*
anorexia [,ænə'rɛksiə] *n* : anorexia *f*
anorexic [,ænə'rɛksɪk] *adj* : anoréxico
another[1] [ə'nʌðər] *adj* : otro
another[2] *pron* : otro, otra
answer[1] ['æntsər] *vt* **1** : contestar (a), responder (a) ⟨to answer the telephone : contestar el teléfono⟩ **2** FULFILL : satisfacer **3 to answer for** : ser responsable de, pagar por ⟨she'll answer for that mistake : pagará por ese error⟩ — *vi* : contestar, responder
answer[2] *n* **1** REPLY : respuesta *f*, contestación *f* **2** SOLUTION : solución *f*
answerable ['æntsərəbəl] *adj* : responsable
ant ['ænt] *n* : hormiga *f*
antacid [ænt'æsəd, 'æn,tæ-] *n* : antiácido *m*
antagonism [æn'tægə,nɪzəm] *n* : antagonismo *m*, hostilidad *f*
antagonist [æn'tægənɪst] *n* : antagonista *mf*

antagonistic [æn,tægə'nıstık] *adj* : antagonista, hostil
antagonize [æn'tægə,naız] *vt* **-nized; -nizing** : antagonizar
antarctic [ænt'arktık, -'artık] *adj* : antártico
antarctic circle *n* : círculo *m* antártico
anteater ['ænt,i:ʈər] *n* : oso *m* hormiguero
antebellum [,æntı'bɛləm] *adj* : prebélico
antecedent[1] [,æntə'si:dənt] *adj* : antecedente, precedente
antecedent[2] *n* : antecedente *mf*; precursor *m*, -sora *f*
antelope ['æntəl,o:p] *n, pl* **-lope** *or* **-lopes** : antílope *m*
antenna [æn'tɛnə] *n, pl* **-nae** [-,ni:, -,naı] *or* **-nas** : antena *f*
anterior [æn'tıriər] *adj* : anterior
anthem ['ænθəm] *n* : himno *m* ⟨national anthem : himno nacional⟩
anther ['ænθər] *n* : antera *f*
anthill ['ænt,hıl] *n* : hormiguero *m*
anthology [æn'θalədʒi] *n, pl* **-gies** : antología *f*
anthracite ['ænθrə,saıt] *n* : antracita *f*
anthropoid[1] ['ænθrə,pɔıd] *adj* : antropoide
anthropoid[2] *n* : antropoide *mf*
anthropological [,ænθrəpə'ladʒıkəl] *adj* : antropológico
anthropologist [,ænθrə'palədʒıst] *n* : antropólogo *m*, -ga *f*
anthropology [,ænθrə'palədʒi] *n* : antropología *f*
antiabortion [,æntiə'borʃən, ,æntaı-] *adj* : antiaborto
antiaircraft [,ænti'ær,kræft, ,æntaı-] *adj* : antiaéreo
anti–American [,æntiə'mɛrıkən, ,æntaı-] *adj* : antiamericano
antibiotic[1] [,æntibaı'aʈık, ,æntaı-, -bi-] *adj* : antibiótico
antibiotic[2] *n* : antibiótico *m*
antibody ['ænti,badi] *n, pl* **-bodies** : anticuerpo *m*
antic[1] ['æntık] *adj* : extravagante, juguetón
antic[2] *n* : payasada *f*, travesura *f*
anticipate [æn'tısə,peıt] *vt* **-pated; -pating 1** FORESEE : anticipar, prever **2** EXPECT : esperar, contar con
anticipation [æn,tısə'peıʃən] *n* **1** FORESIGHT : previsión *f* **2** EXPECTATION : anticipación *f*, expectación *f*, esperanza *f*
anticipatory [æn'tısəpə,tori] *adj* : en anticipación, en previsión
anticlimactic [,æntiklaı'mæktık] *adj* : anticlimático, decepcionante
anticlimax [,ænti'klaı,mæks] *n* : anticlímax *m*
anticommunism [,ænti'kamjə,nızəm, ,æntaı-] *n* : anticomunismo *m*
anticommunist[1] [,ænti'kamjənıst, ,æntaı-] *adj* : anticomunista
anticommunist[2] *n* : anticomunista *mf*

antidemocratic [,ænti,dɛmə'krætık, ,æntaı-] *adj* : antidemocrático
antidepressant [,æntidi'prɛsənt] *n* : antidepresivo *m* — **antidepressant** *adj*
antidote ['ænti,do:t] *n* : antídoto *m*
antidrug [,ænti'drʌg, ,æntaı-; 'ænti,drʌg, 'æntaı-] *adj* : antidrogas
antifascist [,ænti'fæʃıst, ,æntaı-] *adj* : antifascista
antifeminist [,ænti'fɛmənıst, ,æntaı-] *adj* : antifeminista
antifreeze ['ænti,fri:z] *n* : anticongelante *m*
antigen ['æntıdʒən, -,dʒɛn] *n* : antígeno *m*
antihistamine [,ænti'hıstə,mi:n, -mən] *n* : antihistamínico *m*
anti–imperialism [,æntiım'pıriə,lızəm, ,æntaı-] *n* : antiimperialismo *m*
anti–imperialist [,æntiım'pırialıst, ,æntaı-] *adj* : antiimperialista
anti–inflammatory [,ætiın'flæmətori] *adj* : antiinflamatorio
anti–inflationary [,æntiın'fleıʃə,nɛri, ,æntaı-] *adj* : antiinflacionario
antimony ['æntə,mo:ni] *n* : antimonio *m*
antipathy [æn'tıpəθi] *n, pl* **-thies** : antipatía *f*, aversión *f*
antiperspirant [,ænti'pərspərənt, ,æntaı-] *n* : antitranspirante *m*
antiquarian[1] [,æntə'kwɛriən] *adj* : antiguo, anticuario ⟨an antiquarian book : un libro antiguo⟩
antiquarian[2] *n* : anticuario *m*, -ria *f*
antiquary ['æntə,kwɛri] *n* → **antiquarian**[2]
antiquated ['æntə,kweıʈəd] *adj* : anticuado, pasado de moda
antique[1] [æn'ti:k] *adj* **1** OLD : antiguo, de época ⟨an antique mirror : un espejo antiguo⟩ **2** OLD-FASHIONED : anticuado, pasado de moda
antique[2] *n* : antigüedad *f*
antiquity [æn'tıkwəti] *n, pl* **-ties** : antigüedad
antirevolutionary [,ænti,rɛvə'lu:ʃə,nɛri, ,æntaı-] *adj* : antirrevolucionario
anti–Semitic [,æntisə'mıʈık, ,æntaı-] *adj* : antisemita
anti–Semitism [,ænti'sɛmə,tızəm, ,æntaı-] *n* : antisemitismo *m*
antiseptic[1] [,æntə'sɛptık] *adj* : antiséptico — **antiseptically** [-tıkli] *adv*
antiseptic[2] *n* : antiséptico *m*
antismoking [,ænti'smo:kıŋ, ,æntaı-] *adj* : antitabaco
antisocial [,ænti'so:ʃəl, ,æntaı-] *adj* **1** : antisocial **2** UNSOCIABLE : poco sociable
antitheft [,ænti'θɛft, ,æntaı-] *adj* : antirrobo
antithesis [æn'tıθəsıs] *n, pl* **-eses** [-,si:z] : antítesis *f*
antitoxin [,ænti'taksən, ,æntaı-] *n* : antitoxina *f*
antitrust [,ænti'trʌst, ,æntaı-] *adj* : antimonopolista
antler ['æntlər] *n* : asta *f*, cuerno *m*

antonym ['æntə,nɪm] *n* : antónimo *m*
anus ['eɪnəs] *n* : ano *m*
anvil ['ænvəl, -vɪl] *n* : yunque *m*
anxiety [æŋk'zaɪəti] *n, pl* **-eties 1** UN-EASINESS : inquietud *f*, preocupación *f*, ansiedad *f* **2** APPREHENSION : ansiedad *f*, angustia *f*
anxious ['æŋkʃəs] *adj* **1** WORRIED : inquieto, preocupado, ansioso **2** WORRISOME : preocupante, inquietante **3** EAGER : ansioso, deseoso
anxiously ['æŋkʃəsli] *adv* : con inquietud, con ansiedad
any¹ ['ɛni] *adv* **1** : algo ⟨is it any better? : ¿está (algo) mejor?⟩ **2** : para nada ⟨it is not any good : no sirve para nada⟩
any² *adj* **1** : alguno ⟨is there any doubt? : ¿hay alguna duda?⟩ ⟨call me if you have any questions : llámeme si tiene alguna pregunta⟩ **2** : cualquier ⟨I can answer any question : puedo responder a cualquier pregunta⟩ **3** : todo ⟨in any case : en todo caso⟩ **4** : ningún ⟨he would not accept it under any circumstances : no lo aceptaría bajo ninguna circunstancia⟩
any³ *pron* **1** : alguno *m*, -na *f* ⟨are there any left? : ¿queda alguno?⟩ **2** : ninguno *m*, -na *f* ⟨I don't want any : no quiero ninguno⟩
anybody ['ɛni,bʌdi, -,bɑ-] → **anyone**
anyhow ['ɛni,haʊ] *adv* **1** HAPHAZARDLY : de cualquier manera **2** IN ANY CASE : de todos modos, en todo caso
anymore [,ɛni'mor] *adv* **1** : ya, ya más ⟨he doesn't dance anymore : ya no baila más⟩ **2** : todavía ⟨do they sing anymore? : ¿cantan todavía?⟩
anyone ['ɛni,wʌn] *pron* **1** : alguien ⟨is anyone here? : ¿hay alguien aquí?⟩ ⟨if anyone wants to come : si alguno quiere venir⟩ **2** : cualquiera ⟨anyone can play : cualquiera puede jugar⟩ **3** : nadie ⟨I don't want anyone here : no quiero a nadie aquí⟩
anyplace ['ɛni,pleɪs] → **anywhere**
anything ['ɛni,θɪŋ] *pron* **1** : algo, alguna cosa ⟨do you want anything? : ¿quieres algo?, ¿quieres alguna cosa?⟩ **2** : nada ⟨hardly anything : casi nada⟩ **3** : cualquier cosa ⟨I eat anything : como de todo⟩
anytime ['ɛni,taɪm] *adv* : en cualquier momento, a cualquier hora, cuando sea
anyway ['ɛni,weɪ] → **anyhow**
anywhere ['ɛni,hwɛr] *adv* **1** : en algún sitio, en alguna parte ⟨do you see it anywhere? : ¿lo ves en alguna parte?⟩ **2** : en ningún sitio, por ninguna parte ⟨I can't find it anywhere : no puedo encontrarlo por ninguna parte⟩ **3** : en cualquier parte, dondequiera ⟨put it anywhere : ponlo dondequiera⟩
aorta [eɪ'ɔrtə] *n, pl* **-tas** *or* **-tae** [-ti, -taɪ] : aorta *f*

Apache [ə'pætʃi] *n, pl* **Apache** *or* **Apaches** : apache *mf*
apart [ə'pɑrt] *adv* **1** SEPARATELY : aparte, separadamente **2** ASIDE : aparte, a un lado **3 to fall apart** : deshacerse, hacerse pedazos **4 to take apart** : desmontar, desmantelar
apartheid [ə'pɑr,teɪt, -,taɪt] *n* : apartheid *m*
apartment [ə'pɑrtmənt] *n* : apartamento *m*, departamento *m*, piso *m* *Spain*
apathetic [,æpə'θɛtɪk] *adj* : apático, indiferente — **apathetically** [-tɪkli] *adv*
apathy ['æpəθi] *n* : apatía *f*, indiferencia *f*
ape¹ ['eɪp] *vt* **aped; aping** : imitar, remedar
ape² *n* : simio *m*; mono *m*, -na *f*
aperitif [ə,pɛrə'ti:f] *n* : aperitivo *m*
aperture ['æpərtʃər, -,tʃʊr] *n* : abertura *f*, rendija *f*, apertura *f* (en fotografía)
apex ['eɪ,pɛks] *n, pl* **apexes** *or* **apices** ['eɪpə,si:z, 'æ-] : ápice *m*, cúspide *f*, cima *f*
aphid ['eɪfɪd, 'æ-] *n* : áfido *m*
aphorism ['æfə,rɪzəm] *n* : aforismo *m*
aphrodisiac [,æfrə'di:zi,æk, -'dɪ-] *n* : afrodisíaco *m*
apiary ['eɪpi,ɛri] *n, pl* **-aries** : apiario *m*, colmenar *m*
apiece [ə'pi:s] *adv* : cada uno
aplenty [ə'plɛnti] *adj* : en abundancia
aplomb [ə'plɑm, -'plʌm] *n* : aplomo *m*
apocalypse [ə'pɑkə,lɪps] *n* : apocalipsis *m*
apocalyptic [ə,pɑkə'lɪptɪk] *adj* : apocalíptico
apocrypha [ə'pɑkrəfə] *n* : textos *mpl* apócrifos
apocryphal [ə'pɑkrəfəl] *adj* : apócrifo
apologetic [ə,pɑlə'dʒɛtɪk] *adj* : lleno de disculpas
apologetically [ə,pɑlə'dʒɛtɪkli] *adv* : disculpándose, con aire de disculpas
apologize [ə'pɑlə,dʒaɪz] *vi* **-gized; -gizing** : disculparse, pedir perdón
apology [ə'pɑlədʒi] *n, pl* **-gies** : disculpa *f*, excusa *f*
apoplectic [,æpə'plɛktɪk] *adj* : apopléti-co
apoplexy ['æpə,plɛksi] *n* : apoplejía *f*
apostasy [ə'pɑstəsi] *n, pl* **-sies** : apostasía *f*
apostate [ə'pɑs,teɪt] *n* : apóstata *mf*
apostle [ə'pɑsəl] *n* : apóstol *m*
apostolic [,æpə'stɑlɪk] *adj* : apostólico
apostrophe [ə'pɑstrə,fi:] *n* : apóstrofo *m* (ortográfico)
apothecary [ə'pɑθə,kɛri] *n, pl* **-caries** : boticario *m*, -ria *f*
appall [ə'pɔl] *vt* : consternar, horrorizar
apparatus [,æpə'rætəs, -'reɪ-] *n, pl* **-tuses** *or* **-tus** : aparato *m*, equipo *m*
apparel [ə'pærəl] *n* : atavío *m*, ropa *f*
apparent [ə'pærənt] *adj* **1** VISIBLE : visible **2** OBVIOUS : claro, evidente, manifiesto **3** SEEMING : aparente, ostensible

apparently [ə'pærəntli] *adv* : aparentemente, al parecer

apparition [ˌæpə'rɪʃən] *n* : aparición *f*, visión *f*

appeal[1] [ə'piːl] *vt* : apelar ⟨to appeal a decision : apelar contra una decisión⟩ — *vi* **1 to appeal for** : pedir, solicitar **2 to appeal to** : atraer a ⟨that doesn't appeal to me : eso no me atrae⟩

appeal[2] *n* **1** : apelación *f* (en derecho) **2** PLEA : ruego *m*, súplica *f* **3** ATTRACTION : atracción *f*, atractivo *m*, interés *m*

appear [ə'pɪr] *vi* **1** : aparecer, aparecerse, presentarse ⟨he suddenly appeared : apareció de repente⟩ **2** COME OUT : aparecer, salir, publicarse **3** : comparecer (ante el tribunal), actuar (en el teatro) **4** SEEM : parecer

appearance [ə'pɪrənʦ] *n* **1** APPEARING : aparición *f*, presentación *f*, comparecencia *f* (ante un tribunal), publicación *f* (de un libro) **2** LOOK : apariencia *f*, aspecto *m*

appease [ə'piːz] *vt* **-peased; -peasing 1** CALM, PACIFY : aplacar, apaciguar, sosegar **2** SATISFY : satisfacer, mitigar

appeasement [ə'piːzmənt] *n* : aplacamiento *m*, apaciguamiento *m*

append [ə'pɛnd] *vt* : agregar, añadir, adjuntar

appendage [ə'pɛndɪʤ] *n* **1** ADDITION : apéndice *m*, añadidura *f* **2** LIMB : miembro *m*, extremidad *f*

appendectomy [ˌæpən'dɛktəmi] *n, pl* **-mies** : apendicectomía *f*

appendicitis [ə,pɛndə'saɪtəs] *n* : apendicitis *f*

appendix [ə'pɛndɪks] *n, pl* **-dixes** *or* **-dices** [-də,siːz] : apéndice *m*

appetite ['æpə,taɪt] *n* **1** CRAVING : apetito *m*, deseo *m*, ganas *fpl* **2** PREFERENCE : gusto *m*, preferencia *f* ⟨the cultural appetites of today : los gustos culturales de hoy⟩

appetizer ['æpə,taɪzər] *n* : aperitivo *m*, entremés *m*, botana *f Mex*, tapa *f Spain*

appetizing ['æpə,taɪzɪŋ] *adj* : apetecible, apetitoso — **appetizingly** [-zɪŋli] *adv*

applaud [ə'plɔd] *v* : aplaudir

applause [ə'plɔz] *n* : aplauso *m*

apple ['æpəl] *n* : manzana *f*

appliance [ə'plaɪənʦ] *n* **1** : aparato *m* **2 household appliance** : electrodoméstico *m*, aparato *m* electrodoméstico

applicability [ˌæplɪkə'bɪləti, ə,plɪkə-] *n* : aplicabilidad *f*

applicable ['æplɪkəbəl, ə'plɪkə-] *adj* : aplicable, pertinente

applicant ['æplɪkənt] *n* : solicitante *mf*, aspirante *mf*, postulante *mf*; candidato *m*, -ta *f*

application [ˌæplə'keɪʃən] *n* **1** USE : aplicación *f*, empleo *m*, uso *m* **2** DILIGENCE : aplicación *f*, diligencia *f*, dedicación *f* **3** REQUEST : solicitud *f*, petición *f*, demanda *f*

applicator ['æplə,keɪtər] *n* : aplicador *m*

appliqué[1] [ˌæplə'keɪ] *vt* : decorar con apliques

appliqué[2] *n* : aplique *m*

apply [ə'plaɪ] *v* **-plied; -plying** *vt* **1** : aplicar (una sustancia, los frenos, el conocimiento) **2 to apply oneself** : dedicarse, aplicarse — *vi* **1** : aplicarse, referirse ⟨the rules apply to everyone : las reglas se aplican a todos⟩ **2 to apply for** : solicitar, pedir

appoint [ə'pɔɪnt] *vt* **1** NAME : nombrar, designar **2** FIX, SET : fijar, señalar, designar ⟨to appoint a date : fijar una fecha⟩ **3** EQUIP : equipar ⟨a well-appointed office : una oficina bien equipada⟩

appointee [ə,pɔɪn'tiː, ,æ-] *n* : persona *f* designada

appointment [ə'pɔɪntmənt] *n* **1** APPOINTING : nombramiento *m*, designación *f* **2** ENGAGEMENT : cita *f*, hora *f* **3** POST : puesto *m*

apportion [ə'pɔrʃən] *vt* : distribuir, repartir

apportionment [ə'pɔrʃənmənt] *n* : distribución *f*, repartición *f*, reparto *m*

apposite ['æpəzət] *adj* : apropiado, oportuno, pertinente — **appositely** *adv*

appraisal [ə'preɪzəl] *n* : evaluación *f*, valoración *f*, tasación *f*, apreciación *f*

appraise [ə'preɪz] *vt* **-praised; -praising** : evaluar, valorar, tasar, apreciar

appraiser [ə'preɪzər] *n* : tasador *m*, -dora *f*

appreciable [ə'priːʃəbəl, -'prɪʃiə-] *adj* : apreciable, sensible, considerable — **appreciably** [-bli] *adv*

appreciate [ə'priːʃi,eɪt, -'prɪ-] *v* **-ated; -ating** *vt* **1** VALUE : apreciar, valorar **2** : agradecer ⟨we appreciate his frankness : agradecemos su franqueza⟩ **3** UNDERSTAND : darse cuenta de, entender — *vi* : apreciarse, valorizarse

appreciation [ə,priːʃi'eɪʃən, -,prɪ-] *n* **1** GRATITUDE : agradecimiento *m*, reconocimiento *m* **2** VALUING : apreciación *f*, valoración *f*, estimación *f* ⟨art appreciation : apreciación artística⟩ **3** UNDERSTANDING : comprensión *f*, entendimiento *m*

appreciative [ə'priːʃətɪv, -'prɪ-; ə'priːʃi,eɪ-] *adj* **1** : apreciativo ⟨an appreciative audience : un público apreciativo⟩ **2** GRATEFUL : agradecido **3** ADMIRING : de admiración

apprehend [ˌæprɪ'hɛnd] *vt* **1** ARREST : aprehender, detener, arrestar **2** DREAD : temer **3** COMPREHEND : comprender, entender

apprehension [ˌæprɪ'hɛnʧən] *n* **1** ARREST : arresto *m*, detención *f*, aprehensión *f* **2** ANXIETY : aprensión *f*, ansiedad *f*, temor *m* **3** UNDERSTANDING : comprensión *f*, percepción *f*

apprehensive [ˌæprɪ'hɛnʦɪv] *adj* : aprensivo, inquieto — **apprehensively** *adv*

apprentice[1] [ə'prɛntɪs] *vt* **-ticed; -ticing** : colocar de aprendiz
apprentice[2] *n* : aprendiz *m*, -diza *f*
apprenticeship [ə'prɛntɪsˌʃɪp] *n* : aprendizaje *f*
apprise [ə'praɪz] *vt* **-prised; -prising** : informar, avisar
approach[1] [ə'proːtʃ] *vt* **1** NEAR : acercarse a **2** APPROXIMATE : aproximarse a **3** : abordar, dirigirse a ⟨I approached my boss with the proposal : me dirigí a mi jefe con la propuesta⟩ **4** TACKLE : abordar, enfocar, considerar — *vi* : acercarse, aproximarse
approach[2] *n* **1** NEARING : acercamiento *m*, aproximación *f* **2** POSITION : enfoque *m*, planteamiento *m* **3** OFFER : propuesta *f*, oferta *f* **4** ACCESS : acceso *m*, vía *f* de acceso
approachable [ə'proːtʃəbəl] *adj* : accesible, asequible
approbation [ˌæprə'beɪʃən] *n* : aprobación *f*
appropriate[1] [ə'proːpriˌeɪt] *vt* **-ated; -ating 1** SEIZE : apropiarse de **2** ALLOCATE : destinar, asignar
appropriate[2] [ə'proːpriət] *adj* : apropiado, adecuado, idóneo — **appropriately** *adv*
appropriateness [ə'proːpriətnəs] *n* : idoneidad *f*, propiedad *f*
appropriation [əˌproːpri'eɪʃən] *n* **1** SEIZURE : apropiación *f* **2** ALLOCATION : asignación *f*
approval [ə'pruːvəl] *n* **1** : aprobación *f*, visto *m* bueno **2 on approval** : a prueba
approve [ə'pruːv] *vt* **-proved; -proving 1** : aprobar, sancionar, darle el visto bueno a **2 to approve of** : consentir en, aprobar ⟨he doesn't approve of smoking : está en contra del tabaco⟩
approximate[1] [ə'prɑksəˌmeɪt] *vt* **-mated; -mating** : aproximarse a, acercarse a
approximate[2] [ə'prɑksəmət] *adj* : aproximado
approximately [ə'prɑksəmətli] *adv* : aproximadamente, más o menos
approximation [əˌprɑksə'meɪʃən] *n* : aproximación *f*
appurtenance [ə'pərtənənts] *n* : accesorio *m*
apricot ['æprəˌkɑt, 'eɪ-] *n* : albaricoque *m*, chabacano *m Mex*
April ['eɪprəl] *n* : abril *m*
apron ['eɪprən] *n* : delantal *m*, mandil *m*
apropos[1] [ˌæprə'poː, 'æprəˌpoː] *adv* : a propósito
apropos[2] *adj* : pertinente, oportuno, acertado
apropos of *prep* : a propósito de
apt ['æpt] *adj* **1** FITTING : apto, apropiado, acertado, oportuno **2** LIABLE : propenso, inclinado **3** CLEVER, QUICK : listo, despierto
aptitude ['æptəˌtuːd, -ˌtjuːd] *n* **1** : aptitud *f*, capacidad *f* ⟨aptitude test : prueba de aptitud⟩ **2** TALENT : talento *m*, facilidad *f*

aptly ['æptli] *adv* : acertadamente
aqua ['ækwə, 'ɑ-] *n* : color *m* aguamarina
aquarium [ə'kwæriəm] *n*, *pl* **-iums** *or* **-ia** [-iə] : acuario *m*
Aquarius [ə'kwæriəs] *n* : Acuario *mf*
aquatic [ə'kwɑtɪk, -'kwæ-] *adj* : acuático
aqueduct ['ækwəˌdʌkt] *n* : acueducto *m*
aqueous ['eɪkwiəs, 'æ-] *adj* : acuoso
aquiline ['ækwəˌlaɪn, -lən] *adj* : aguileño
Arab[1] ['ærəb] *adj* : árabe
Arab[2] *n* : árabe *mf*
arabesque [ˌærə'bɛsk] *n* : arabesco *m*
Arabian[1] [ə'reɪbiən] *adj* : árabe
Arabian[2] *n* → **Arab**[2]
Arabic[1] ['ærəbɪk] *adj* : árabe
Arabic[2] *n* : árabe *m* (idioma)
arable ['ærəbəl] *adj* : arable, cultivable
arbiter ['ɑrbətər] *n* : árbitro *m*, -tra *f*
arbitrary ['ɑrbəˌtreri] *adj* : arbitrario — **arbitrarily** [ˌɑrbə'trerəli] *adv*
arbitrate ['ɑrbəˌtreɪt] *v* **-trated; -trating** : arbitrar
arbitration [ˌɑrbə'treɪʃən] *n* : arbitraje *m*
arbitrator ['ɑrbəˌtreɪtər] *n* : árbitro *m*, -tra *f*
arbor ['ɑrbər] *n* : cenador *m*, pérgola *f*
arboreal [ɑr'boriəl] *adj* : arbóreo
arc[1] ['ɑrk] *vi* **arced; arcing** : formar un arco
arc[2] *n* : arco *m*
arcade [ɑr'keɪd] *n* **1** ARCHES : arcada *f* **2** MALL : galería *f* comercial
arcane [ɑr'keɪn] *adj* : arcano, secreto, misterioso
arch[1] ['ɑrtʃ] *vt* : arquear, enarcar — *vi* : formar un arco, arquearse
arch[2] *adj* **1** CHIEF : principal **2** MISCHIEVOUS : malicioso, pícaro
arch[3] *n* : arco *m*
archaeological [ˌɑrkiə'lɑdʒɪkəl] *adj* : arqueológico
archaeologist [ˌɑrki'ɑlədʒɪst] *n* : arqueólogo *m*, -ga *f*
archaeology *or* **archeology** [ˌɑrki-'ɑlədʒi] *n* : arqueología *f*
archaic [ɑr'keɪɪk] *adj* : arcaico — **archaically** [-ɪkli] *adv*
archangel ['ɑrkˌeɪndʒəl] *n* : arcángel *m*
archbishop [ɑrtʃ'bɪʃəp] *n* : arzobispo *m*
archdiocese [ɑrtʃ'daɪəsəs, -ˌsiːz, -ˌsiːs] *n* : archidiócesis *f*
archer ['ɑrtʃər] *n* : arquero *m*, -ra *f*
archery ['ɑrtʃəri] *n* : tiro *m* al arco
archetypal [ˌɑrkɪ'taɪpəl] *adj* : arquetípico
archetype ['ɑrkɪˌtaɪp] *n* : arquetipo *m*
archipelago [ˌɑrkə'pɛləˌgoː, ˌɑrtʃə-] *n*, *pl* **-goes** *or* **-gos** [-goːz] : archipiélago *m*
architect ['ɑrkəˌtɛkt] *n* : arquitecto *m*, -ta *f*
architectural [ˌɑrkə'tɛktʃərəl] *adj* : arquitectónico — **architecturally** *adv*
architecture ['ɑrkəˌtɛktʃər] *n* : arquitectura *f*
archive ['ɑrˌkaɪv] *n* *or* **archives** ['ɑrˌkaɪvz] *npl* : archivo *m*

archivist ['ɑrkəvɪst, -ˌkaɪ-] *n* : archivero
m, -ra *f*; archivista *mf*
archway ['ɑrtʃˌweɪ] *n* : arco *m*, pasadizo
m abovedado
arctic ['ɑrktɪk, 'ɑrt-] *adj* **1** : ártico ⟨arc-
tic regions : zonas árticas⟩ **2** FRIGID
: glacial
arctic circle *n* : círculo *m* ártico
ardent ['ɑrdənt] *adj* **1** PASSIONATE : ardiente, fogoso, apasionado **2** FERVENT
: ferviente, fervoroso — **ardently** *adv*
ardor ['ɑrdər] *n* : ardor *m*, pasión *f*, fervor *m*
arduous ['ɑrdʒuəs] *adj* : arduo, duro, riguroso — **arduously** *adv*
arduousness ['ɑrdʒuəsnəs] *n* : dureza *f*,
rigor *m*
are → **be**
area ['æriə] *n* **1** SURFACE : área *f*, superficie *f* **2** REGION : área *f*, región *f*,
zona *f* **3** FIELD : área *f*, terreno *m*, campo *m* (de conocimiento)
area code *n* : código *m* de la zona, prefijo *m Spain*
arena [ə'ri:nə] *n* **1** : arena *f*, estadio *m*
⟨sports arena : estadio deportivo⟩ **2**
: arena *f*, ruedo *m* ⟨the political arena
: el ruedo político⟩
Argentine ['ɑrdʒənˌtaɪn, -ˌti:n] *or* **Argentinean** *or* **Argentinian** [ˌɑrdʒən-
'tɪniən] *n* : argentino *m*, -na *f* —
Argentine *or* **Argentinean** *or* **Argentinian** *adj*
argon ['ɑrˌgɑn] *n* : argón *m*
argot ['ɑrgət, -ˌgo:] *n* : argot *m*
arguable ['ɑrgjuəbəl] *adj* : discutible
argue ['ɑrˌgju:] *v* **-gued; -guing** *vi* **1**
REASON : argüir, argumentar, razonar
2 DISPUTE : discutir, pelear(se), alegar
— *vt* **1** SUGGEST : sugerir **2** MAINTAIN
: alegar, argüir, sostener **3** DISCUSS
: discutir, debatir
argument ['ɑrgjəmənt] *n* **1** REASONING
: argumento *m*, razonamiento *m* **2**
DISCUSSION : discusión *f*, debate *m* **3**
QUARREL : pelea *f*, riña *f*, disputa *f*
argumentative [ˌɑrgjə'mɛntətɪv] *adj*
: discutidor
argyle ['ɑrˌgaɪl] *n* : diseño *m* de rombos
aria ['ɑriə] *n* : aria *f*
arid ['ærəd] *adj* : árido
aridity [ə'rɪdəṭi, æ-] *n* : aridez *f*
Aries ['ɛri:z, -iˌi:z] *n* : Aries *mf*
arise [ə'raɪz] *vi* **arose** [ə'ro:z]; **arisen**
[ə'rɪzən]; **arising 1** ASCEND : ascender,
subir, elevarse **2** ORIGINATE : originarse, surgir, presentarse **3** GET UP
: levantarse
aristocracy [ˌærə'stɑkrəsi] *n, pl* **-cies**
: aristocracia *f*
aristocrat [ə'rɪstəˌkræt] *n* : aristócrata
mf
aristocratic [əˌrɪstə'krætɪk] *adj* : aristocrático, noble
arithmetic¹ [ˌærɪθ'mɛtɪk] *or* **arithmetical** [-tɪkəl] *adj* : aritmético
arithmetic² [ə'rɪθməˌtɪk] *n* : aritmética
ark ['ɑrk] *n* : arca *f*

arm¹ ['ɑrm] *vt* : armar — *vi* : armarse
arm² *n* **1** : brazo *m* (del cuerpo o de un
sillón), manga *f* (de una prenda) **2**
BRANCH : rama *f*, sección *f* **3** WEAPON
: arma *f* ⟨to take up arms : tomar las
armas⟩ **4** → **coat of arms**
armada [ɑr'mɑdə, -'meɪ-] *n* : armada *f*,
flota *f*
armadillo [ˌɑrmə'dɪlo] *n, pl* **-los** : armadillo *m*
armament ['ɑrməmənt] *n* : armamento
m
armchair ['ɑrmˌtʃɛr] *n* : butaca *f*, sillón
m
armed ['ɑrmd] *adj* **1** : armado ⟨armed
robbery : robo a mano armada⟩ **2**
armed forces : fuerzas *fpl* armadas
Armenian [ɑr'mi:niən] *n* : armenio *m*,
-nia *f* — **Armenian** *adj*
armistice ['ɑrməstɪs] *n* : armisticio *m*
armor ['ɑrmər] *n* : armadura *f*, coraza *f*
armored ['ɑrmərd] *adj* : blindado, acorazado
armory ['ɑrməri] *n, pl* **-mories** : arsenal
m (almacén), armería *f* (museo), fábrica *f* de armas
armpit ['ɑrmˌpɪt] *n* : axila *f*, sobaco *m*
army ['ɑrmi] *n, pl* **-mies 1** : ejército *m*
(militar) **2** MULTITUDE : legión *f*, multitud *f*, ejército *m*
aroma [ə'ro:mə] *n* : aroma *f*
aromatic [ˌærə'mætɪk] *adj* : aromático
around¹ [ə'raund] *adv* **1** : de circunferencia ⟨a tree three feet around : un árbol de tres pies de circunferencia⟩ **2**
: alrededor, a la redonda ⟨for miles
around : por millas a la redonda⟩ ⟨all
around : por todos lados, todo alrede-
dor⟩ **3** : por ahí ⟨they're somewhere
around : deben estar por ahí⟩ **4** AP-
PROXIMATELY : más o menos, aproximadamente ⟨around 5 o'clock : a eso
de las 5⟩ **5 to turn around** : darse la
vuelta, voltearse
around² *prep* **1** SURROUNDING : alrededor de, en torno a **2** THROUGH : por,
en ⟨he traveled around Mexico : viajó
por México⟩ ⟨around the house : en
casa⟩ **3** : a la vuelta de ⟨around the
corner : a la vuelta de la esquina⟩ **4**
NEAR : alrededor de, cerca de
arousal [ə'rauzəl] *n* : excitación *f*
arouse [ə'rauz] *vt* **aroused; arousing 1**
AWAKE : despertar **2** EXCITE : despertar, suscitar, excitar
arraign [ə'reɪn] *vt* : hacer comparecer
(ante un tribunal)
arraignment [ə'reɪnmənt] *n* : orden *m* de
comparecencia, acusación *f*
arrange [ə'reɪndʒ] *vt* **-ranged; -ranging
1** ORDER : arreglar, poner en orden,
disponer **2** SETTLE : arreglar, fijar,
concertar **3** ADAPT : arreglar, adaptar
arrangement [ə'reɪndʒmənt] *n* **1** ORDER
: arreglo *m*, orden *m* **2** ARRANGING
: disposición *f* ⟨floral arrangement : arreglo floral⟩ **3** AGREEMENT : arreglo
m, acuerdo *m*, convenio *m* **4 arrange-**

ments *npl* : preparativos *mpl*, planes *mpl*

array¹ [ə'reɪ] *vt* **1** ORDER : poner en orden, presentar, formar **2** GARB : vestir, ataviar, engalanar

array² *n* **1** ORDER : orden *m*, formación *f* **2** ATTIRE : atavío *m*, galas *mpl* **3** RANGE, SELECTION : selección *f*, serie *f*, gama *f* ⟨an array of problems : una serie de problemas⟩

arrears [ə'rɪrz] *npl* : atrasos *mpl* ⟨to be in arrears : estar atrasado en los pagos⟩

arrest¹ [ə'rɛst] *vt* **1** APPREHEND : arrestar, detener **2** CHECK, STOP : detener, parar

arrest² *n* **1** APPREHENSION : arresto *m*, detención *f* ⟨under arrest : detenido⟩ **2** STOPPING : paro *m*

arrival [ə'raɪvəl] *n* : llegada *f*, venida *f*, arribo *m*

arrive [ə'raɪv] *vi* **-rived; -riving 1** COME : llegar, arribar **2** SUCCEED : triunfar, tener éxito

arrogance ['ærəgənts] *n* : arrogancia *f*, soberbia *f*, altanería *f*, altivez *f*

arrogant ['ærəgənt] *adj* : arrogante, soberbio, altanero, altivo — **arrogantly** *adv*

arrogate ['ærə,geɪt] *vt* **-gated; -gating to arrogate to oneself** : arrogarse

arrow ['æro] *n* : flecha *f*

arrowhead ['æro,hɛd] *n* : punta *f* de flecha

arroyo [ə'rɔɪo] *n* : arroyo *m*

arsenal ['arsənəl] *n* : arsenal *m*

arsenic ['arsənɪk] *n* : arsénico *m*

arson ['arsən] *n* : incendio *m* premeditado

arsonist ['arsənɪst] *n* : incendiario *m*, -ria *f*; pirómano *m*, -na *f*

art ['art] *n* **1** : arte *m* **2** SKILL : destreza *f*, habilidad *f*, maña *f* **3 arts** *npl* : letras *fpl* (en la educación) **4 fine arts** : bellas artes *fpl*

arterial [ar'tɪriəl] *adj* : arterial

arteriosclerosis [ar,tɪrioskla'ro:sɪs] *n* : arteriosclerosis *f*

artery ['artəri] *n, pl* **-teries 1** : arteria *f* **2** THOROUGHFARE : carretera *f* principal, arteria *f*

artesian well [ar'ti:ʒən] *n* : pozo *m* artesiano

artful ['artfəl] *adj* **1** INGENIOUS : ingenioso, diestro **2** CRAFTY : astuto, taimado, ladino, artero — **artfully** *adv*

arthritic [ar'θrɪtɪk] *adj* : artrítico

arthritis [ar'θraɪtəs] *n, pl* **-tides** [ar-'θrɪtə,di:z] : artritis *f*

arthropod ['arθrə,pad] *n* : artrópodo *m*

artichoke ['artə,ʧo:k] *n* : alcachofa *f*

article ['artɪkəl] *n* **1** ITEM : artículo *m*, objeto *m* **2** ESSAY : artículo *m* **3** CLAUSE : artículo *m*, cláusula *f* **4** : artículo *m* ⟨definite article : artículo determinado⟩

articulate¹ [ar'tɪkjə,leɪt] *vt* **-lated; -lating 1** UTTER : articular, enunciar, expresar **2** CONNECT : articular (en anatomía)

articulate² [ar'tɪkjələt] *adj* **to be articulate** : poder articular palabras, expresarse bien

articulately [ar'tɪkjələtli] *adv* : elocuentemente, con fluidez

articulateness [ar'tɪkjələtnəs] *n* : elocuencia *f*, fluidez *f*

articulation [ar,tɪkjə'leɪʃən] *n* **1** JOINT : articulación *f* **2** UTTERANCE : articulación *f*, declaración *f* **3** ENUNCIATION : articulación *f*, pronunciación *f*

artifact ['artə,fækt] *n* : artefacto *m*

artifice ['artəfəs] *n* : artificio *m*

artificial [,artə'fɪʃəl] *adj* **1** SYNTHETIC : artificial, sintético **2** FEIGNED : artificial, falso, afectado

artificially [,artə'fɪʃəli] *adv* : artificialmente, con afectación

artillery [ar'tɪləri] *n, pl* **-leries** : artillería *f*

artisan ['artəzən, -sən] *n* : artesano *m*, -na *f*

artist ['artɪst] *n* : artista *mf*

artistic [ar'tɪstɪk] *adj* : artístico — **artistically** [-tɪkli] *adv*

artistry ['artəstri] *n* : maestría *f*, arte *m*

artless ['artləs] *adj* : sencillo, natural, ingenuo, cándido — **artlessly** *adv*

artlessness ['artləsnəs] *n* : ingenuidad *f*, candidez *f*

arty ['arti] *adj* **artier; -est** : pretenciosamente artístico

as¹ ['æz] *adv* **1** : tan, tanto ⟨this one's not as difficult : éste no es tan difícil⟩ **2** : como ⟨some trees, as oak and pine : algunos árboles, como el roble y el pino⟩

as² *conj* **1** LIKE : como, igual que **2** WHEN, WHILE : cuando, mientras, a la vez que **3** BECAUSE : porque **4** THOUGH : aunque, por más que ⟨strange as it may appear : por extraño que parezca⟩ **5 as is** : tal como está

as³ *prep* **1** : de ⟨I met her as a child : la conocí de pequeña⟩ **2** LIKE : como ⟨behave as a man : compórtate como un hombre⟩

as⁴ *pron* : que ⟨in the same building as my brother : en el mismo edificio que mi hermano⟩

asbestos [æz'bɛstəs, æs-] *n* : asbesto *m*, amianto *m*

ascend [ə'sɛnd] *vi* : ascender, subir — *vt* : subir, subir a, escalar

ascendancy [ə'sɛndəntsi] *n* : ascendiente *m*, predominio *m*

ascendant¹ [ə'sɛndənt] *adj* **1** RISING : ascendente **2** DOMINANT : superior, dominante

ascendant² *n* **to be in the ascendant** : estar en alza, ir ganando predominio

ascension [ə'sɛnʧən] *n* : ascensión *f*

ascent [ə'sɛnt] *n* **1** RISE : ascensión *f*, subida *f*, ascenso *m* **2** SLOPE : cuesta *f*, pendiente *f*

ascertain [,æsər'teɪn] *vt* : determinar, establecer, averiguar

ascertainable [,æsər'teɪnəbəl] *adj* : determinable, averiguable

ascetic[1] [ə'sɛtɪk] *adj* : ascético
ascetic[2] *n* : asceta *mf*
asceticism [ə'sɛtə,sɪzəm] *n* : ascetismo *m*
ascribable [ə'skraɪbəbəl] *adj* : atribuible, imputable
ascribe [ə'skraɪb] *vt* **-cribed; -cribing** : atribuir, imputar
aseptic [eɪ'sɛptɪk] *adj* : aséptico
asexual [,eɪ'sɛkʃʊəl] *adj* : asexual
as for *prep* CONCERNING : en cuanto a, respecto a, para
ash ['æʃ] *n* **1** : ceniza *f* ⟨to reduce to ashes : reducir a cenizas⟩ **2** : fresno *m* (árbol)
ashamed [ə'ʃeɪmd] *adj* : avergonzado, abochornado, apenado — **ashamedly** [ə'ʃeɪmədli] *adv*
ashen ['æʃən] *adj* : lívido, ceniciento, pálido
ashore [ə'ʃor] *adv* **1** : en tierra **2 to go ashore** : desembarcar
ashtray ['æʃ,treɪ] *n* : cenicero *m*
Asian[1] ['eɪʒən, -ʃən] *adj* : asiático
Asian[2] *n* : asiático *m*, -ca *f*
aside [ə'saɪd] *adv* **1** : a un lado ⟨to step aside : hacerse a un lado⟩ **2** : de lado, aparte ⟨jesting aside : bromas aparte⟩ **3 to set aside** : guardar, apartar, reservar
aside from *prep* **1** BESIDES : además de **2** EXCEPT : aparte de, menos
as if *conj* : como si
asinine ['æsən,aɪn] *adj* : necio, estúpido
ask ['æsk] *vt* **1** : preguntar ⟨ask him if he's coming : pregúntale si viene⟩ **2** REQUEST : pedir, solicitar ⟨to ask a favor : pedir un favor⟩ **3** INVITE : invitar — *vi* **1** INQUIRE : preguntar ⟨I asked about her children : pregunté por sus niños⟩ **2** REQUEST : pedir ⟨we asked for help : pedimos ayuda⟩
askance [ə'skænts] *adv* **1** SIDELONG : de reojo, de soslayo **2** SUSPICIOUSLY : con recelo, con desconfianza
askew [ə'skju:] *adj* : torcido, ladeado
asleep [ə'sli:p] *adj* **1** : dormido, durmiendo **2 to fall asleep** : quedarse dormido
as of *prep* : desde, a partir de
asparagus [ə'spærəgəs] *n* : espárrago *m*
aspect ['æ,spɛkt] *n* : aspecto *m*
aspen ['æspən] *n* : álamo *m* temblón
asperity [æ'spɛrəti, ə-] *n*, *pl* **-ties** : aspereza *f*
aspersion [ə'spərʒən] *n* : difamación *f*, calumnia *f*
asphalt ['æs,fɔlt] *n* : asfalto *m*
asphyxia [æ'sfɪksiə, ə-] *n* : asfixia *f*
asphyxiate [æ'sfɪksi,eɪt] *v* **-ated; -ating** *vt* : asfixiar — *vi* : asfixiarse
asphyxiation [æ,sfɪksi'eɪʃən] *n* : asfixia *f*
aspirant ['æspərənt, ə'spaɪrənt] *n* : aspirante *mf*, pretendiente *mf*
aspiration [,æspə'reɪʃən] *n* **1** DESIRE : aspiración *f*, anhelo *m*, ambición *f* **2** BREATHING : aspiración *f*

aspire [ə'spaɪr] *vi* **-pired; -piring** : aspirar
aspirin ['æsprən, 'æspə-] *n*, *pl* **aspirin** *or* **aspirins** : aspirina *f*
ass ['æs] *n* **1** : asno *m* **2** IDIOT : imbécil *mf*, idiota *mf*
assail [ə'seɪl] *vt* : atacar, asaltar
assailant [ə'seɪlənt] *n* : asaltante *mf*, atacante *mf*
assassin [ə'sæsən] *n* : asesino *m*, -na *f*
assassinate [ə'sæsən,eɪt] *vt* **-nated; -nating** : asesinar
assassination [ə,sæsən'eɪʃən] *n* : asesinato *m*
assault[1] [ə'sɔlt] *vt* : atacar, asaltar, agredir
assault[2] *n* : ataque *m*, asalto *m*, agresión *f*
assay[1] [æ'seɪ, 'æ,seɪ] *vt* : ensayar
assay[2] ['æ,seɪ, æ'seɪ] *n* : ensayo *m*
assemble [ə'sɛmbəl] *v* **-bled; -bling** *vt* **1** GATHER : reunir, recoger, juntar **2** CONSTRUCT : ensamblar, montar, construir — *vi* : reunirse, congregarse
assembly [ə'sɛmbli] *n*, *pl* **-blies 1** MEETING : reunión *f* **2** CONSTRUCTING : ensamblaje *m*, montaje *m*
assemblyman [ə'sɛmblimən] *n*, *pl* **-men** [-mən, -,mɛn] : asambleísta *m*
assemblywoman [ə'sɛmbli,wʊmən] *n*, *pl* **-women** [-,wɪmən] : asambleísta *f*
assent[1] [ə'sɛnt] *vi* : asentir, consentir
assent[2] *n* : asentimiento *m*, aprobación *f*
assert [ə'sərt] *vt* **1** AFFIRM : afirmar, aseverar, mantener **2 to assert oneself** : imponerse, hacerse valer
assertion [ə'sərʃən] *n* : afirmación *f*, aseveración *f*, aserto *m*
assertive [ə'sərtɪv] *adj* : firme, enérgico
assertiveness [ə'sərtɪvnəs] *n* : seguridad *f* en sí mismo
assess [ə'sɛs] *vt* **1** IMPOSE : gravar (un impuesto), imponer **2** EVALUATE : evaluar, valorar, aquilatar
assessment [ə'sɛsmənt] *n* : evaluación *f*, valoración *f*
assessor [ə'sɛsər] *n* : evaluador *m*, -dora *f*; tasador *m*, -dora *f*
asset ['æ,sɛt] *n* **1** : ventaja *f*, recurso *m* **2 assets** *npl* : bienes *mpl*, activo *m* ⟨assets and liabilities : activo y pasivo⟩
assiduous [ə'sɪdʒʊəs] *adj* : diligente, aplicado, asiduo — **assiduously** *adv*
assign [ə'saɪn] *vt* **1** APPOINT : designar, nombrar **2** ALLOT : asignar, señalar **3** ATTRIBUTE : atribuir, dar, conceder
assignment [ə'saɪnmənt] *n* **1** TASK : función *f*, tarea *f*, misión *f* **2** HOMEWORK : tarea *f*, asignación *f* PRi, deberes *mpl* Spain **3** APPOINTMENT : nombramiento *m* **4** ALLOCATION : asignación *f*
assimilate [ə'sɪmə,leɪt] *v* **-lated; -lating** *vt* : asimilar — *vi* : adaptarse, integrarse
assimilation [ə,sɪmə'leɪʃən] *n* : asimilación *f*
assist[1] [ə'sɪst] *vt* : asistir, ayudar
assist[2] *n* : asistencia *f*, contribución *f*

assistance [ə'sɪstənts] *n* : asistencia *f*, ayuda *f*, auxilio *m*

assistant [ə'sɪstənt] *n* : ayudante *mf*, asistente *mf*

associate[1] [ə'so:ʃi,eɪt, -si-] *v* **-ated; -ating** *vt* **1** CONNECT, RELATE : asociar, relacionar **2 to be associated with** : estar relacionado con, estar vinculado a — *vi* **to associate with** : relacionarse con, frecuentar

associate[2] [ə'so:ʃiət, -siət] *n* : asociado *m*, -da *f*; colega *mf*; socio *m*, -cia *f*

association [ə,so:ʃi'eɪʃən, -si-] *n* **1** ORGANIZATION : asociación *f*, sociedad *f* **2** RELATIONSHIP : asociación *f*, relación *f*

as soon as *conj* : en cuanto, tan pronto como

assorted [ə'sɔrtəd] *adj* : surtido

assortment [ə'sɔrtmənt] *n* : surtido *m*, variedad *f*, colección *f*

assuage [ə'sweɪdʒ] *vt* **-suaged; -suaging 1** EASE : aliviar, mitigar **2** CALM : calmar, aplacar **3** SATISFY : saciar, satisfacer

assume [ə'su:m] *vt* **-sumed; -suming 1** SUPPOSE : suponer, asumir **2** UNDERTAKE : asumir, encargarse de **3** TAKE ON : adquirir, adoptar, tomar ⟨to assume importance : tomar importancia⟩ **4** FEIGN : adoptar, afectar, simular

assumption [ə'sʌmpʃən] *n* : asunción *f*, presunción *f*

assurance [ə'ʃurənts] *n* **1** CERTAINTY : certidumbre *f*, certeza *f* **2** CONFIDENCE : confianza *f*, aplomo *m*, seguridad *f*

assure [ə'ʃur] *vt* **-sured; -suring** : asegurar, garantizar ⟨I assure you that I'll do it : te aseguro que lo haré⟩

assured [ə'ʃurd] *adj* **1** CERTAIN : seguro, asegurado **2** CONFIDENT : confiado, seguro de sí mismo

aster ['æstər] *n* : aster *m*

asterisk ['æstə,rɪsk] *n* : asterisco *m*

astern [ə'stərn] *adv* **1** BEHIND : detrás, a popa **2** BACKWARDS : hacia atrás

asteroid ['æstə,rɔɪd] *n* : asteroide *m*

asthma ['æzmə] *n* : asma *m*

asthmatic [æz'mætɪk] *adj* : asmático

as though → **as if**

astigmatism [ə'stɪgmə,tɪzəm] *n* : astigmatismo *m*

as to *prep* **1** ABOUT : sobre, acerca de **2** → **according to**

astonish [ə'stɑnɪʃ] *vt* : asombrar, sorprender, pasmar

astonishing [ə'stɑnɪʃɪŋ] *adj* : asombroso, sorprendente, increíble — **astonishingly** *adv*

astonishment [ə'stɑnɪʃmənt] *n* : asombro *m*, estupefacción *f*, sorpresa *f*

astound [ə'staund] *vt* : asombrar, pasmar, dejar estupefacto

astounding [ə'staundɪŋ] *adj* : asombroso, pasmoso — **astoundingly** *adv*

astraddle [ə'strædəl] *adv* : a horcajadas

astral ['æstrəl] *adj* : astral

astray [ə'streɪ] *adv & adj* : perdido, extraviado, descarriado

astride [ə'straɪd] *adv* : a horcajadas

astringency [ə'strɪndʒəntsi] *n* : astringencia *f*

astringent[1] [ə'strɪndʒənt] *adj* : astringente

astringent[2] *n* : astringente *m*

astrologer [ə'strɑlədʒər] *n* : astrólogo *m*, -ga *f*

astrological [,æstrə'lɑdʒɪkəl] *adj* : astrológico

astrology [ə'strɑlədʒi] *n* : astrología *f*

astronaut ['æstrə,nɔt] *n* : astronauta *mf*

astronautic [,æstrə'nɔtɪk] *or* **astronautical** [-tɪkəl] *adj* : astronáutico

astronautics [,æstrə'nɔtɪks] *ns & pl* : astronáutica *f*

astronomer [ə'strɑnəmər] *n* : astrónomo *m*, -ma *f*

astronomical [,æstrə'nɑmɪkəl] *adj* **1** : astronómico **2** ENORMOUS : astronómico, enorme, gigantesco

astronomy [ə'strɑnəmi] *n, pl* **-mies** : astronomía *f*

astute [ə'stu:t, -'stju:t] *adj* : astuto, sagaz, perspicaz — **astutely** *adv*

astuteness [ə'stu:tnəs, -'stju:t-] *n* : astucia *f*, sagacidad *f*, perspicacia *f*

asunder [ə'sʌndər] *adv* : en dos, en pedazos ⟨to tear asunder : hacer pedazos⟩

as well as[1] *conj* : tanto como

as well as[2] *prep* BESIDES : además de, aparte de

as yet *adv* : aún, todavía

asylum [ə'saɪləm] *n* **1** REFUGE : refugio *m*, santuario *m*, asilo *m* **2 insane asylum** : manicomio *m*

asymmetrical [,eɪsə'mɛtrɪkəl] *or* **asymmetric** [-'mɛtrɪk] *adj* : asimétrico

asymmetry [,eɪ'sɪmətri] *n* : asimetría *f*

at ['æt] *prep* **1** : en ⟨at the top : en lo alto⟩ ⟨at peace : en paz⟩ ⟨at Ann's house : en casa de Ana⟩ **2** : a ⟨at the rear : al fondo⟩ ⟨at 10 o'clock : a las diez⟩ **3** : por ⟨at last : por fin⟩ ⟨to be surprised at something : sorprenderse por algo⟩ **4** : de ⟨he's laughing at you : está riéndose de ti⟩ **5** : para ⟨you're good at this : eres bueno para esto⟩

at all *adv* : en absoluto, para nada

ate → **eat**

atheism ['eɪθi,ɪzəm] *n* : ateísmo *m*

atheist ['eɪθiɪst] *n* : ateo *m*, atea *f*

atheistic [,eɪθi'ɪstɪk] *adj* : ateo

athlete ['æθ,li:t] *n* : atleta *mf*

athletic [æθ'lɛtɪk] *adj* : atlético

athletics [æθ'lɛtɪks] *ns & pl* : atletismo *m*

Atlantic [ət'læntɪk, æt-] *adj* : atlántico

atlas ['ætləs] *n* : atlas *m*

ATM [,eɪ,ti:'ɛm] *n* : cajero *m* automático

atmosphere ['ætmə,sfɪr] *n* **1** AIR : atmósfera *f*, aire *m* **2** AMBIENCE : ambiente *m*, atmósfera *f*, clima *m*

atmospheric [,ætmə'sfɪrɪk, -'sfɛr-] *adj* : atmosférico — **atmospherically** [-ɪkli] *adv*

atoll ['æˌtɔl, 'eɪ-, -ˌtɑl] *n* : atolón *m*
atom ['æt̬əm] *n* **1** : átomo *m* **2** SPECK : ápice *m*, pizca *f*
atomic [ə'tɑmɪk] *adj* : atómico
atomic bomb *n* : bomba *f* atómica
atomizer ['æt̬əˌmaɪzər] *n* : atomizador *m*, pulverizador *m*
atone [ə'toːn] *vt* **atoned; atoning to atone for** : expiar
atonement [ə'toːnmənt] *n* : expiación *f*, desagravio *m*
atop¹ [ə'tɑp] *adj* : encima
atop² *prep* : encima de, sobre
atrium ['eɪtriəm] *n, pl* **atria** [-triə] *or* **atriums 1** : atrio *m* **2** : aurícula *f* (del corazón)
atrocious [ə'troːʃəs] *adj* : atroz — **atrociously** *adv*
atrocity [ə'trɑsət̬i] *n, pl* **-ties** : atrocidad *f*
atrophy¹ ['ætrəfi] *vt* **-phied; -phying** : atrofiar
atrophy² *n, pl* **-phies** : atrofia *f*
attach [ə'tætʃ] *vt* **1** FASTEN : sujetar, atar, amarrar, pegar **2** JOIN : juntar, adjuntar **3** ATTRIBUTE : dar, atribuir ⟨I attached little importance to it : le di poca importancia⟩ **4** SEIZE : embargar **5 to become attached to someone** : encariñarse con alguien
attaché [ˌæt̬ə'ʃeɪ, ˌæˌtæ-, ə̩tæ-] *n* : agregado *m*, -da *f*
attachment [ə'tætʃmənt] *n* **1** ACCESSORY : accesorio *m* **2** CONNECTION : conexión *f*, acoplamiento *m* **3** FONDNESS : apego *m*, cariño *m*, afición *f*
attack¹ [ə'tæk] *vt* **1** ASSAULT : atacar, asaltar, agredir **2** TACKLE : acometer, combatir, enfrentarse con
attack² *n* **1** : ataque *m*, asalto *m*, acometida *f* ⟨to launch an attack : lanzar un ataque⟩ **2** : ataque *m*, crisis *f* ⟨heart attack : ataque cardíaco, infarto⟩ ⟨attack of nerves : crisis nerviosa⟩
attacker [ə'tækər] *n* : asaltante *mf*
attain [ə'teɪn] *vt* **1** ACHIEVE : lograr, conseguir, alcanzar, realizar **2** REACH : alcanzar, llegar a
attainable [ə'teɪnəbəl] *adj* : alcanzable, realizable, asequible
attainment [ə'teɪnmənt] *n* : logro *m*, consecución *f*, realización *f*
attempt¹ [ə'tempt] *vt* : intentar, tratar de
attempt² *n* : intento *m*, tentativa *f*
attend [ə'tend] *vt* **1** : asistir a ⟨to attend a meeting : asistir a una reunión⟩ **2** : atender, ocuparse de, cuidar ⟨to attend a patient : atender a un paciente⟩ **3** HEED : atender a, hacer caso de **4** ACCOMPANY : acompañar
attendance [ə'tendənts] *n* **1** ATTENDING : asistencia *f* **2** TURNOUT : concurrencia *f*
attendant¹ [ə'tendənt] *adj* : concomitante, inherente
attendant² *n* : asistente *mf*, acompañante *mf*, guarda *mf*

attention [ə'tentʃən] *n* **1** : atención *f* **2 to pay attention** : prestar atención, hacer caso **3 to stand at attention** : estar firme
attentive [ə'tentɪv] *adj* : atento — **attentively** *adv*
attentiveness [ə'tentɪvnəs] *n* **1** THOUGHTFULNESS : cortesía *f*, consideración *f* **2** CONCENTRATION : atención *f*, concentración *f*
attest [ə'test] *vt* : atestiguar, dar fe de
attestation [ˌæˌts'teɪʃən] *n* : testimonio *m*
attic ['ætɪk] *n* : ático *m*, desván *m*, buhardilla *f*
attire¹ [ə'taɪr] *vt* **-tired; -tiring** : ataviar
attire² *n* : atuendo *m*, atavío *m*
attitude ['æt̬əˌtuːd, -ˌtjuːd] *n* **1** FEELING : actitud *f* **2** POSTURE : postura *f*
attorney [ə'tərni] *n, pl* **-neys** : abogado *m*, -da *f*
attract [ə'trækt] *vt* **1** : atraer **2 to attract attention** : llamar la atención
attraction [ə'trækʃən] *n* : atracción *f*, atractivo *m*
attractive [ə'træktɪv] *adj* : atractivo, atrayente
attractively [ə'træktɪvli] *adv* : de manera atractiva, de buen gusto, hermosamente
attractiveness [ə'træktɪvnəs] *n* : atractivo *m*
attributable [ə'trɪbjʊt̬əbəl] *adj* : atribuible, imputable
attribute¹ [ə'trɪˌbjuːt] *vt* **-tributed; -tributing** : atribuir
attribute² ['ætrəˌbjuːt] *n* : atributo *m*, cualidad *f*
attribution [ˌætrə'bjuːʃən] *n* : atribución *f*
attune [ə'tuːn, -'tjuːn] *vt* **-tuned; -tuning 1** ADAPT : adaptar, adecuar **2 to be attuned to** : estar en armonía con
atypical [ˌeɪ'tɪpɪkəl] *adj* : atípico
auburn ['ɔbərn] *adj* : castaño rojizo
auction¹ ['ɔkʃən] *vt* : subastar, rematar
auction² *n* : subasta *f*, remate *m*
auctioneer [ˌɔkʃə'nɪr] *n* : subastador *m*, -dora *f*; rematador *m*, -dora *f*
audacious [ɔ'deɪʃəs] *adj* : audaz, atrevido
audacity [ɔ'dæsət̬i] *n, pl* **-ties** : audacia *f*, atrevimiento *m*, descaro *m*
audible ['ɔdəbəl] *adj* : audible — **audibly** [-bli] *adv*
audience ['ɔdiənts] *n* **1** INTERVIEW : audiencia *f* **2** PUBLIC : audiencia *f*, público *m*, auditorio *m*, espectadores *mpl*
audio¹ ['ɔdiˌoː] *adj* : de sonido, de audio
audio² *n* : audio *m*
audiovisual [ˌɔdio'vɪʒʊəl] *adj* : audiovisual
audit¹ ['ɔdət] *vt* **1** : auditar (finanzas) **2** : asistir como oyente a (una clase o un curso)
audit² *n* : auditoría *f*
audition¹ [ɔ'dɪʃən] *vi* : hacer una audición

audition² *n* : audición *f*
auditor ['ɔdətər] *n* **1** : auditor *m*, -tora *f* (de finanzas) **2** STUDENT : oyente *mf*
auditorium [,ɔdə'toriəm] *n*, *pl* **-riums** *or* **-ria** [-riə] : auditorio *m*, sala *f*
auditory ['ɔdə,tori] *adj* : auditivo
auger ['ɔgər] *n* : taladro *m*, barrena *f*
augment [ɔg'mɛnt] *vt* : aumentar, incrementar
augmentation [,ɔgmən'teɪʃən] *n* : aumento *m*, incremento *m*
augur¹ ['ɔgər] *vt* : augurar, presagiar — *vi* **to augur well** : ser de buen agüero
augur² *n* : augur *m*
augury ['ɔgjuri, -gər-] *n*, *pl* **-ries** : augurio *m*, presagio *m*, agüero *m*
august [ɔ'gʌst] *adj* : augusto
August ['ɔgəst] *n* : agosto *m*
auk ['ɔk] *n* : alca *f*
aunt ['ænt, 'ɑnt] *n* : tía *f*
aura ['ɔrə] *n* : aura *f*
aural ['ɔrəl] *adj* : auditivo
auricle ['ɔrɪkəl] *n* : aurícula *f*
aurora borealis [ə'rorə,bori'æləs] *n* : aurora *f* boreal
auspices ['ɔspəsəz, -,si:z] *npl* : auspicios *mpl*
auspicious [ɔ'spɪʃəs] *adj* : prometedor, propicio, de buen augurio
austere [ɔ'stɪr] *adj* : austero, severo, adusto — **austerely** *adv*
austerity [ɔ'stɛrəti] *n*, *pl* **-ties** : austeridad *f*
Australian [ɔ'streɪljən] *n* : australiano *m*, -na *f* — **Australian** *adj*
Austrian ['ɔstriən] *n* : austriaco *m*, -ca *f* — **Austrian** *adj*
authentic [ə'θɛntɪk, ɔ-] *adj* : auténtico, genuino — **authentically** [-tɪkli] *adv*
authenticate [ə'θɛntɪ,keɪt, ɔ-] *vt* **-cated; -cating** : autenticar, autentificar
authenticity [,ɔ,θɛn'tɪsəti] *n* : autenticidad *f*
author ['ɔθər] *n* **1** WRITER : escritor *m*, -tora *f*; autor *m*, -tora *f* **2** CREATOR : autor *m*, -tora *f*; creador *m*, -dora *f*; artífice *mf*
authoritarian [ɔ,θɔrə'tɛriən, ə-] *adj* : autoritario
authoritative [ə'θɔrə,teɪtɪv, ɔ-] *adj* **1** RELIABLE : fidedigno, autorizado **2** DICTATORIAL : autoritario, dictatorial, imperioso
authoritatively [ə'θɔrə,teɪtɪvli, ɔ-] *adv* **1** RELIABLY : con autoridad **2** DICTATORIALLY : de manera autoritaria
authority [ə'θɔrəti, ɔ-] *n*, *pl* **-ties** **1** EXPERT : autoridad *f*; experto *m*, -ta *f* **2** POWER : autoridad *f*, poder *m* **3** AUTHORIZATION : autorización *f*, licencia *f* **4 the authorities** : las autoridades **5 on good authority** : de buena fuente
authorization [,ɔθərə'zeɪʃən] *n* : autorización *f*
authorize ['ɔθə,raɪz] *vt* **-rized; -rizing** : autorizar, facultar
authorship ['ɔθər,ʃɪp] *n* : autoría *f*
autism ['ɔ,tɪzəm] *n* : autismo *m*

autistic [ɔ'tɪstɪk] *adj* : autista
auto ['ɔto] → **automobile**
autobiographical [,ɔto,baɪə'græfɪkəl] *adj* : autobiográfico
autobiography [,ɔtobaɪ'ɑgrəfi] *n*, *pl* **-phies** : autobiografía *f*
autocracy [ɔ'tɑkrəsi] *n*, *pl* **-cies** : autocracia *f*
autocrat ['ɔtə,kræt] *n* : autócrata *mf*
autocratic [,ɔtə'krætɪk] *adj* : autocrático — **autocratically** [-tɪkli] *adv*
autograph¹ ['ɔtə,græf] *vt* : autografiar
autograph² *n* : autógrafo *m*
automaker ['ɔto:meɪkər] *n* : fabricante *mf* de autos, automotriz *f*
automate ['ɔtə,meɪt] *vt* **-mated; -mating** : automatizar
automatic [,ɔtə'mætɪk] *adj* : automático — **automatically** [-tɪkli] *adv*
automation [,ɔtə'meɪʃən] *n* : automatización *f*
automaton [ɔ'tɑmə,tɑn] *n*, *pl* **-atons** *or* **-ata** [-tə, -,tɑ] : autómata *m*
automobile [,ɔtəmo'bi:l, -'mo:,bi:l] *n* : automóvil *m*, auto *m*, carro *m*, coche *m*
automotive [,ɔtə'mo:tɪv] *adj* : automotor
autonomous [ɔ'tɑnəməs] *adj* : autónomo — **autonomously** *adv*
autonomy [ɔ'tɑnəmi] *n*, *pl* **-mies** : autonomía *f*
autopsy ['ɔ,tɑpsi, -təp-] *n*, *pl* **-sies** : autopsia *f*
autumn ['ɔtəm] *n* : otoño *m*
autumnal [ɔ'tʌmnəl] *adj* : otoñal
auxiliary¹ [ɔg'zɪljəri, -'zɪləri] *adj* : auxiliar
auxiliary² *n*, *pl* **-ries** : auxiliar *mf*, ayudante *mf*
avail¹ [ə'veɪl] *vt* **to avail oneself** : aprovecharse, valerse
avail² *n* **1** : provecho *m*, utilidad *f* **2 to no avail** : en vano **3 to be of no avail** : no servir de nada, ser inútil
availability [ə,veɪlə'bɪləti] *n*, *pl* **-ties** : disponibilidad *f*
available [ə'veɪləbəl] *adj* : disponible
avalanche ['ævə,læntʃ] *n* : avalancha *f*, alud *m*
avarice ['ævərəs] *n* : avaricia *f*, codicia *f*
avaricious [,ævə'rɪʃəs] *adj* : avaricioso, codicioso
avenge [ə'vɛndʒ] *vt* **avenged; avenging** : vengar
avenger [ə'vɛndʒər] *n* : vengador *m*, -dora *f*
avenue ['ævə,nu:, -,nju:] *n* **1** : avenida *f* **2** MEANS : vía *f*, camino *m*
average¹ ['ævrɪdʒ, 'ævə-] *vt* **-aged; -aging** **1** : hacer un promedio de ⟨he averages 8 hours a day : hace un promedio de 8 horas diarias⟩ **2** : calcular el promedio de, promediar (en matemáticas)
average² *adj* **1** MEAN : medio ⟨the average temperature : la temperatura media⟩ **2** ORDINARY : común, ordinario ⟨the average man : el hombre común⟩

average³ *n* : promedio *m*
averse [ə'vərs] *adj* : reacio, opuesto
aversion [ə'vərʒən] *n* : aversión *f*
avert [ə'vərt] *vt* 1 : apartar, desviar ⟨he averted his eyes from the scene : apartó los ojos de la escena⟩ 2 AVOID, PREVENT : evitar, prevenir
aviary ['eɪvi,eri] *n*, *pl* -aries : pajarera *f*
aviation [,eɪvi'eɪʃən] *n* : aviación *f*
aviator ['eɪvi,eɪtər] *n* : aviador *m*, -dora *f*
avid ['ævɪd] *adj* 1 GREEDY : ávido, codicioso 2 ENTHUSIASTIC : ávido, entusiasta, ferviente — **avidly** *adv*
avocado [,ævə'kɑdo, ,ɑvə-] *n*, *pl* -dos : aguacate *m*, palta *f*
avocation [,ævə'keɪʃən] *n* : pasatiempo *m*, afición *f*
avoid [ə'vɔɪd] *vt* 1 SHUN : evitar, eludir 2 FORGO : evitar, abstenerse de ⟨I always avoided gossip : siempre evitaba los chismes⟩ 3 EVADE : evitar ⟨if I can avoid it : si puedo evitarlo⟩
avoidable [ə'vɔɪdəbəl] *adj* : evitable
avoidance [ə'vɔɪdənts] *n* : el evitar
avoirdupois [,ævərdə'pɔɪz] *n* : sistema *m* inglés de pesos y medidas
avow [ə'vaʊ] *vt* : reconocer, confesar
avowal [ə'vaʊəl] *n* : reconocimiento *m*, confesión *f*
await [ə'weɪt] *vt* : esperar
awake¹ [ə'weɪk] *v* **awoke** [ə'wo:k]; **awoken** [ə'wo:kən] *or* **awaked**; **awaking** : despertar
awake² *adj* : despierto
awaken [ə'weɪkən] → **awake¹**
award¹ [ə'wɔrd] *vt* : otorgar, conceder, conferir
award² *n* 1 PRIZE : premio *m*, galardón *m* 2 MEDAL : condecoración *f*
aware [ə'wær] *adj* : consciente ⟨to be aware of : darse cuenta de, estar consciente de⟩
awareness [ə'wærnəs] *n* : conciencia *f*, conocimiento *m*
awash [ə'wɔʃ] *adj* : inundado
away¹ [ə'weɪ] *adv* 1 : de aquí ⟨go away! : ¡fuera de aquí!, ¡vete!⟩ 2 : de distancia ⟨10 miles away : 10 millas de distancia, queda a 10 millas⟩ 3 far away : lejos, a lo lejos 4 right away : en segui-

da, ahora mismo 5 to be away : estar ausente, estar de viaje 6 to give away : regalar (una posesión), revelar (un secreto) 7 to go away : irse, largarse 8 to put away : guardar 9 to turn away : volver la cara
away² *adj* 1 ABSENT : ausente ⟨away for the week : ausente por la semana⟩ 2
away game : partido *m* que se juega fuera
awe¹ ['ɔ] *vt* **awed; awing** : abrumar, asombrar, impresionar
awe² *n* : asombro *m*
awesome ['ɔsəm] *adj* 1 IMPOSING : imponente, formidable 2 AMAZING : asombroso
awestruck ['ɔ,strʌk] *adj* : asombrado
awful ['ɔfəl] *adj* 1 AWESOME : asombroso 2 DREADFUL : horrible, terrible, atroz 3 ENORMOUS : enorme, tremendo ⟨an awful lot of people : muchísima gente, la mar de gente⟩
awfully ['ɔfəli] *adv* 1 EXTREMELY : terriblemente, extremadamente 2 BADLY : muy mal, espantosamente
awhile [ə'hwaɪl] *adv* : un rato, algún tiempo
awkward ['ɔkwərd] *adj* 1 CLUMSY : torpe, desmañado 2 EMBARRASSING : embarazoso, delicado — **awkwardly** *adv*
awkwardness ['ɔkwərdnəs] *n* 1 CLUMSINESS : torpeza *f* 2 INCONVENIENCE : incomodidad *f*
awl ['ɔl] *n* : punzón *m*
awning ['ɔnɪŋ] *n* : toldo *m*
awry [ə'raɪ] *adj* 1 ASKEW : torcido 2 to go awry : salir mal, fracasar
ax *or* **axe** ['æks] *n* : hacha *m*
axiom ['æksiəm] *n* : axioma *m*
axiomatic [,æksiə'mætɪk] *adj* : axiomático
axis ['æksɪs] *n*, *pl* **axes** [-,si:z] : eje *m*
axle ['æksəl] *n* : eje *m*
aye¹ ['aɪ] *adv* : sí
aye² *n* : sí *m*
azalea [ə'zeɪljə] *n* : azalea *f*
azimuth ['æzəməθ] *n* : azimut *m*, acimut *m*
Aztec ['æz,tɛk] *n* : azteca *mf*
azure¹ ['æʒər] *adj* : azur, celeste
azure² *n* : azur *m*

B

b ['bi:] *n*, *pl* **b's** *or* **bs** ['bi:z] : segunda letra del alfabeto inglés
babble¹ ['bæbəl] *vi* -bled; -bling 1 PRATTLE : balbucear 2 CHATTER : charlatanear, parlotear *fam* 3 MURMUR : murmurar
babble² *n* : balbuceo *m* (de bebé), parloteo *m* (de adultos), murmullo *m* (de voces, de un arroyo)
babe ['beɪb] *n* → **baby³**
babel ['beɪbəl, 'bæ-] *n* : babel *f*, caos *m*

baboon [bæ'bu:n] *n* : babuino *m*
baby¹ ['beɪbi] *vt* -bied; -bying : mimar, consentir
baby² *adj* 1 : de niño ⟨a baby carriage : un cochecito⟩ ⟨baby talk : habla infantil⟩ 2 TINY : pequeño, minúsculo
baby³ *n*, *pl* -bies : bebé *m*; niño *m*, -ña *f*
babyhood ['beɪbi,hʊd] *n* : niñez *f*, primera infancia *f*
babyish ['beɪbiɪʃ] *adj* : infantil, pueril

baby–sit ['beɪbiˌsɪt] *vi* **-sat** [-ˌsæt]; **-sitting** : cuidar niños, hacer de canguro *Spain*

baby–sitter ['beɪbiˌsɪtər] *n* : niñero *m*, -ra *f*; canguro *mf Spain*

baccalaureate [ˌbækəˈlɔriət] *n* : licenciatura *f*

bachelor ['bætʃələr] *n* **1** : soltero *m* **2** : licenciado *m*, -da *f* ⟨bachelor of arts degree : licenciatura en filosofía y letras⟩

bacillus [bəˈsɪləs] *n*, *pl* **-li** [-ˌlaɪ] : bacilo *m*

back¹ ['bæk] *vt* **1** *or* **to back up** SUPPORT : apoyar, respaldar **2** *or* **to back up** REVERSE : darle marcha atrás a (un vehículo) **3** : estar detrás de, formar el fondo de ⟨trees back the garden : unos árboles están detrás del jardín⟩ — *vi* **1** *or* **to back up** : retroceder **2 to back away** : echarse atrás **3 to back down** *or* **to back out** : volverse atrás, echarse para atrás

back² *adv* **1** : atrás, hacia atrás, detrás ⟨to move back : moverse atrás⟩ ⟨back and forth : de acá para allá⟩ **2** AGO : atrás, antes, ya ⟨some years back : unos años atrás, ya unos años⟩ ⟨10 months back : hace diez meses⟩ **3** : de vuelta, de regreso ⟨we're back : estamos de vuelta⟩ ⟨she ran back : volvió corriendo⟩ ⟨to call back : llamar de nuevo⟩

back³ *adj* **1** REAR : de atrás, posterior, trasero **2** OVERDUE : atrasado **3 back pay** : atrasos *mpl*

back⁴ *n* **1** : espalda *f* (de un ser humano), lomo *m* (de un animal) **2** : respaldo *m* (de una silla), espalda *f* (de ropa) **3** REVERSE : reverso *m*, dorso *m*, revés *m* **4** REAR : fondo *m*, parte *f* de atrás **5** : defensa *mf* (en deportes)

backache ['bækˌeɪk] *n* : dolor *m* de espalda

backbite ['bækˌbaɪt] *v* **-bit** [-ˌbɪt]; **-bitten** [-ˌbɪtən]; **-biting** *vt* : calumniar, hablar mal de — *vi* : murmurar

backbiter ['bækˌbaɪtər] *n* : calumniador *m*, -dora *f*

backbone ['bækˌboːn] *n* **1** : columna *f* vertebral **2** FIRMNESS : firmeza *f*, carácter *m*

backdrop ['bækˌdrɑp] *n* : telón *m* de fondo

backer ['bækər] *n* **1** SUPPORTER : partidario *m*, -ria *f* **2** SPONSOR : patrocinador *m*, -dora *f*

backfire¹ ['bækˌfaɪr] *vi* **-fired**; **-firing 1** : petardear (dícese de un automóvil) **2** FAIL : fallar, salir el tiro por la culata

backfire² *n* : petardeo *m*, explosión *f*

background ['bækˌɡraʊnd] *n* **1** : fondo *m* (de un cuadro, etc.), antecedentes *mpl* (de una situación) **2** EXPERIENCE, TRAINING : experiencia *f* profesional, formación *f*

backhand¹ ['bækˌhænd] *adv* : de revés, con el revés

backhand² *n* : revés *m*

backhanded ['bækˌhændəd] *adj* **1** : dado con el revés, de revés **2** INDIRECT : indirecto, ambiguo

backing ['bækɪŋ] *n* **1** SUPPORT : apoyo *m*, respaldo *m* **2** REINFORCEMENT : refuerzo *m* **3** SUPPORTERS : partidarios *mpl*, -rias *fpl*

backlash ['bækˌlæʃ] *n* : reacción *f* violenta

backlog ['bækˌlɔɡ] *n* : atraso *m*, trabajo *m* acumulado

backpack¹ ['bækˌpæk] *vi* : viajar con mochila

backpack² *n* : mochila *f*

backrest ['bækˌrɛst] *n* : respaldo *m*

backside ['bækˌsaɪd] *n* : trasero *m*

backslide ['bækˌslaɪd] *vi* **-slid** [-ˌslɪd]; **-slid** *or* **-slidden** [-ˌslɪdən]; **-sliding** : recaer, reincidir

backstage [ˌbækˈsteɪdʒ, 'bækˌ-] *adv* & *adj* : entre bastidores

backtrack ['bækˌtræk] *vi* : dar marcha atrás, volverse atrás

backup ['bækˌʌp] *n* **1** SUPPORT : respaldo *m*, apoyo *m* **2** : copia *f* de seguridad (para computadoras)

backward¹ ['bækwərd] *or* **backwards** [-wərdz] *adv* **1** : hacia atrás **2** : de espaldas ⟨he fell backwards : se cayó de espaldas⟩ **3** : al revés ⟨you're doing it backwards : lo estás haciendo al revés⟩ **4 to bend over backwards** : hacer todo lo posible

backward² *adj* **1** : hacia atrás ⟨a backward glance : una mirada hacia atrás⟩ **2** RETARDED : retrasado **3** SHY : tímido **4** UNDERDEVELOPED : atrasado

backwardness ['bækwərdnəs] *n* : atraso *m* (dícese de una región), retraso *m* (dícese de una persona)

backwoods [ˌbækˈwʊdz] *npl* : monte *m*, región *f* alejada

bacon ['beɪkən] *n* : tocino *m*, tocineta *f Col, Ven*, bacon *m Spain*

bacterial [bækˈtɪriəl] *adj* : bacteriano

bacteriologist [bækˌtɪriˈɑlədʒɪst] *n* : bacteriólogo *m*, -ga *f*

bacteriology [bækˌtɪriˈɑlədʒi] *n* : bacteriología *f*

bacterium [bækˈtɪriəm] *n*, *pl* **-ria** [-iə] : bacteria *f*

bad¹ ['bæd] *adv* → **badly**

bad² *adj* **1** : malo **2** ROTTEN : podrido **3** SERIOUS, SEVERE : grave **4** DEFECTIVE : defectuoso ⟨a bad check : un cheque sin fondos⟩ **5** HARMFUL : perjudicial **6** CORRUPT, EVIL : malo, corrompido **7** NAUGHTY : travieso **8 from bad to worse** : de mal en peor **9 too bad!** : ¡qué lástima!

bad³ *n* : lo malo ⟨the good and the bad : lo bueno y lo malo⟩

bade → **bid**

badge ['bædʒ] *n* : insignia *f*, botón *m*, chapa *f*

badger¹ ['bædʒər] *vt* : fastidiar, acosar, importunar

badger² *n* : tejón *m*
badly ['bædli] *adv* **1** : mal **2** URGENTLY : mucho, con urgencia **3** SEVERELY : gravemente
badminton ['bæd,mɪntən, -,mɪt-] *n* : bádminton *m*
badness ['bædnəs] *n* : maldad *f*
baffle¹ ['bæfəl] *vi* **-fled; -fling 1** PERPLEX : desconcertar, confundir **2** FRUSTRATE : frustrar
baffle² *n* : deflector *m*, bafle *m* (acústico)
bafflement ['bæfəlmənt] *n* : desconcierto *m*, confusión *f*
bag¹ ['bæg] *v* **bagged; bagging** *vi* SAG : formar bolsas — *vt* **1** : ensacar, poner en una bolsa **2** : cobrar (en la caza), cazar
bag² *n* **1** : bolsa *f*, saco *m* **2** HANDBAG : cartera *f*, bolso *m*, bolsa *f Mex* **3** SUITCASE : maleta *f*, valija *f*
bagatelle [,bægə'tɛl] *n* : bagatela *f*
bagel ['beɪgəl] *n* : rosquilla *f* de pan
baggage ['bægɪʤ] *n* : equipaje *m*
baggy ['bægi] *adj* **-gier; -est** : holgado, ancho
bagpipe ['bæg,paɪp] *n or* **bagpipes** ['bæg,paɪps] *npl* : gaita *f*
bail¹ ['beɪl] *vt* **1** : achicar (agua de un bote) **2 to bail out** : poner en libertad (de una cárcel) bajo fianza **3 to bail out** EXTRICATE : sacar de apuros
bail² *n* : fianza *f*, caución *f*
bailiff ['beɪləf] *n* : alguacil *mf*
bailiwick ['beɪli,wɪk] *n* : dominio *m*
bailout ['beɪl,aʊt] *n* : rescate *m* (financiero)
bait¹ ['beɪt] *vt* **1** : cebar (un anzuelo o cepo) **2** HARASS : acosar
bait² *n* : cebo *m*, carnada *f*
bake¹ ['beɪk] *vt* **baked; baking** : hornear, hacer al horno
bake² *n* : fiesta con platos hechos al horno
baker ['beɪkər] *n* : panadero *m*, -ra *f*
baker's dozen *n* : docena *f* de fraile
bakery ['beɪkəri] *n, pl* **-ries** : panadería *f*
bakeshop ['beɪk,ʃɑp] *n* : pastelería *f*, panadería *f*
baking powder *n* : levadura *f* en polvo
baking soda → **sodium bicarbonate**
balance¹ ['bælənts] *v* **-anced; -ancing** *vt* **1** : hacer el balance de (una cuenta) ⟨to balance the books : cuadrar las cuentas⟩ **2** EQUALIZE : balancear, equilibrar **3** HARMONIZE : armonizar — *vi* : balancearse
balance² *n* **1** SCALES : balanza *f*, báscula *f* **2** COUNTERBALANCE : contrapeso *m* **3** EQUILIBRIUM : equilibrio *m* **4** REMAINDER : balance *m*, resto *m*
balanced ['bæləntst] *adj* : equilibrado, balanceado
balcony ['bælkəni] *n, pl* **-nies 1** : balcón *m*, terraza *f* (de un edificio) **2** : galería *f* (de un teatro)

bald ['bɔld] *adj* **1** : calvo, pelado, pelón **2** PLAIN : simple, puro ⟨the bald truth : la pura verdad⟩
balding ['bɔldɪŋ] *adj* : quedándose calvo
baldly ['bɔldli] *adv* : sin reparos, sin rodeos, francamente
baldness ['bɔldnəs] *n* : calvicie *f*
bale¹ ['beɪl] *vt* **baled; baling** : empacar, hacer balas de
bale² *n* : bala *f*, fardo *m*, paca *f*
baleful ['beɪlfəl] *adj* **1** DEADLY : mortífero **2** SINISTER : siniestro, funesto, torvo ⟨a baleful glance : una mirada torva⟩
balk¹ ['bɔk] *vt* : obstaculizar, impedir — *vi* **1** : plantarse (dícese de un caballo, etc.) **2 to balk at** : resistarse a, mostrarse reacio a
balk² *n* : obstáculo *m*
Balkan ['bɔlkən] *adj* : balcánico
balky ['bɔki] *adj* **balkier; -est** : reacio, obstinado, terco
ball¹ ['bɔl] *vt* : apelotonar, ovillar
ball² *n* **1** : pelota *f*, bola *f*, balón *m*, ovillo *m* (de lana) **2** : juego *m* con pelota o bola **3** DANCE : baile *m*, baile *m* de etiqueta
ballad ['bæləd] *n* : romance *m*, balada *f*
balladeer [,bælə'dɪr] *n* : cantante *mf* de baladas
ballast¹ ['bæləst] *vt* : lastrar
ballast² *n* : lastre *m*
ball bearing *n* : cojinete *m* de bola
ballerina [,bælə'ri:nə] *n* : bailarina *f*
ballet [bæ'leɪ, 'bæ,leɪ] *n* : ballet *m*
ballistic [bə'lɪstɪk] *adj* : balístico
ballistics [bə'lɪstɪks] *ns & pl* : balística *f*
balloon¹ [bə'lu:n] *vi* **1** : viajar en globo **2** SWELL : hincharse, inflarse
balloon² *n* : globo *m*
balloonist [bə'lu:nɪst] *n* : aeróstata *mf*
ballot¹ ['bælət] *vi* : votar
ballot² *n* **1** : papeleta *f* (de voto) **2** BALLOTING : votación *f* **3** VOTE : voto *m*
ballpoint pen ['bɔl,pɔɪnt] *n* : bolígrafo *m*
ballroom ['bɔl,ru:m, -,rʊm] *n* : sala *f* de baile
ballyhoo ['bæli,hu:] *n* : propaganda *f*, publicidad *f*, bombo *m fam*
balm ['bɑm, 'bɑlm] *n* : bálsamo *m*, ungüento *m*
balmy ['bɑmi, 'bɑl-] *adj* **balmier; -est 1** MILD : templado, agradable **2** SOOTHING : balsámico **3** CRAZY : chiflado *fam*, chalado *fam*
baloney [bə'lo:ni] *n* NONSENSE : tonterías *fpl*, estupideces *fpl*
balsa ['bɔlsə] *n* : balsa *f*
balsam ['bɔlsəm] *n* **1** : bálsamo *m* **2 or balsam fir** : abeto *m* balsámico
Baltic ['bɔltɪk] *adj* : báltico
baluster ['bæləstər] *n* : balaustre *m*
balustrade ['bælə,streɪd] *n* : balaustrada *f*
bamboo [bæm'bu:] *n* : bambú *m*
bamboozle [bæm'bu:zəl] *vt* **-zled; -zling** : engañar, embaucar

ban¹ ['bæn] *vt* **banned; banning** : prohibir, proscribir

ban² *n* : prohibición *f*, proscripción *f*

banal [bə'nɑl, bə'næl, 'beɪnəl] *adj* : banal, trivial

banality [bə'næləti] *n*, *pl* **-ties** : banalidad *f*, trivialidad *f*

banana [bə'nænə] *n* : banano *m*, plátano *m*, banana *f*, cambur *m Ven*, guineo *m Car*

band¹ ['bænd] *vt* **1** BIND : fajar, atar **2 to band together** : unirse, juntarse

band² *n* **1** STRIP : banda *f*, cinta *f* (de un sombrero, etc.) **2** STRIPE : franja *f* **3** : banda *f* (de radiofrecuencia) **4** RING : anillo *m* **5** GROUP : banda *f*, grupo *m*, conjunto *m* ⟨jazz band : conjunto de jazz⟩

bandage¹ ['bændɪdʒ] *vt* **-daged; -daging** : vendar

bandage² *n* : vendaje *m*, venda *f*

bandanna *or* **bandana** [bæn'dænə] *n* : pañuelo *m* (de colores)

bandit ['bændət] *n* : bandido *m*, -da *f*; bandolero *m*, -ra *f*

banditry ['bændətri] *n* : bandolerismo *m*, bandidaje *m*

bandstand ['bænd,stænd] *n* : quiosco *m* de música

bandwagon ['bænd,wægən] *n* **1** : carroza *f* de músicos **2 to jump on the bandwagon** : subirse al carro, seguir la moda

bandy¹ ['bændi] *vt* **-died; -dying 1** EXCHANGE : intercambiar **2 to bandy about** : circular, propagar

bandy² *adj* : arqueado, torcido ⟨bandy-legged : de piernas arqueadas⟩

bane ['beɪn] *n* **1** POISON : veneno *m* **2** RUIN : ruina *f*, pesadilla *f*

baneful ['beɪnfəl] *adj* : nefasto, funesto

bang¹ ['bæŋ] *vt* **1** STRIKE : golpear, darse ⟨he banged his elbow against the door : se dio con el codo en la puerta⟩ **2** SLAM : cerrar (la puerta) con un portazo — *vi* **1** SLAM : cerrarse de un golpe **2 to bang on** : aporrear, golpear ⟨she was banging on the table : aporreaba la mesa⟩

bang² *adv* : directamente, exactamente

bang³ *n* **1** BLOW : golpe *m*, porrazo *m*, trancazo *m* **2** EXPLOSION : explosión *f*, estallido *m* **3** SLAM : portazo *m* **4 bangs** *npl* : flequillo *m*, fleco *m*

Bangladeshi [,bɑŋglə'dɛʃi, ,bæŋ-, ,bʌŋ-, -'deɪ-] *n* : bangladesí *mf* — **Bangladeshi** *adj*

bangle ['bæŋgəl] *n* : brazalete *m*, pulsera *f*

banish ['bænɪʃ] *vt* **1** EXILE : desterrar, exiliar **2** EXPEL : expulsar

banishment ['bænɪʃmənt] *n* **1** EXILE : destierro *m*, exilio *m* **2** EXPULSION : expulsión *f*

banister ['bænəstər] *n* **1** BALUSTER : balaustre *m* **2** HANDRAIL : pasamanos *m*, barandilla *f*, barandal *m*

banjo ['bæn,dʒoː] *n*, *pl* **-jos** : banjo *m*

bank¹ ['bæŋk] *vt* **1** TILT : peraltar (una carretera), ladear (un avión) **2** HEAP : amontonar **3** : cubrir (un fuego) **4** : depositar (dinero en un banco) — *vi* **1** : ladearse (dícese de un avión) **2** : tener una cuenta (en un banco) **3 to bank on** : contar con

bank² *n* **1** MASS : montón *m*, montículo *m*, masa *f* **2** : orilla *f*, ribera *f* (de un río) **3** : peralte *m* (de una carretera) **4** : banco *m* ⟨World Bank : Banco Mundial⟩ ⟨banco de sangre : blood bank⟩

bankbook ['bæŋk,bʊk] *n* : libreta *f* bancaria, libreta *f* de ahorros

banker ['bæŋkər] *n* : banquero *m*, -ra *f*

banking ['bæŋkɪŋ] *n* : banca *f*

bankrupt¹ ['bæŋ,krʌpt] *vt* : hacer quebrar, llevar a la quiebra, arruinar

bankrupt² *adj* **1** : en bancarrota, en quiebra **2 ~ of** LACKING : carente de, falto de

bankrupt³ *n* : fallido *m*, -da *f*; quebrado *m*, -da *f*

bankruptcy ['bæŋ,krʌptsi] *n*, *pl* **-cies** : ruina *f*, quiebra *f*, bancarrota *f*

banner¹ ['bænər] *adj* : excelente

banner² *n* : estandarte *m*, bandera *f*

banns ['bænz] *npl* : amonestaciones *fpl*

banquet¹ ['bæŋkwət] *vi* : celebrar un banquete

banquet² *n* : banquete *m*

banter¹ ['bæntər] *vi* : bromear, hacer bromas

banter² *n* : bromas *fpl*

baptism ['bæp,tɪzəm] *n* : bautismo *m*

baptismal [bæp'tɪzməl] *adj* : bautismal

Baptist ['bæptɪst] *n* : bautista *mf* — **Baptist** *adj*

baptize [bæp'taɪz, 'bæp,taɪz] *vt* **-tized; -tizing** : bautizar

bar¹ ['bɑr] *vt* **barred; barring 1** OBSTRUCT : obstruir, bloquear **2** EXCLUDE : excluir **3** PROHIBIT : prohibir **4** SECURE : atrancar, asegurar ⟨bar the door! : ¡atranca la puerta!⟩

bar² *n* **1** : barra *f*, barrote *m* (de una ventana), tranca *f* (de una puerta) **2** BARRIER : barrera *f*, obstáculo *m* **3** LAW : abogacía *f* **4** STRIPE : franja *f* **5** COUNTER : mostrador *m*, barra *f* **6** TAVERN : bar *m*, taberna *f*

bar³ *prep* **1** : excepto, con excepción de **2 bar none** : sin excepción

barb ['bɑrb] *n* **1** POINT : púa *f*, lengüeta *f* **2** GIBE : pulla *f*

barbarian¹ [bɑr'bæriən] *adj* **1** : bárbaro **2** CRUDE : tosco, bruto

barbarian² *n* : bárbaro *m*, -ra *f*

barbaric [bɑr'bærɪk] *adj* **1** PRIMITIVE : primitivo **2** CRUEL : brutal, cruel

barbarity [bɑr'bærəti] *n*, *pl* **-ties** : barbaridad *f*

barbarous ['bɑrbərəs] *adj* **1** UNCIVILIZED : bárbaro **2** MERCILESS : despiadado, cruel

barbarously ['bɑrbərəsli] *adv* : bárbaramente

barbecue¹ ['bɑrbɪˌkju:] *vt* **-cued; -cuing**
: asar a la parrilla
barbecue² *n* : barbacoa *f*, parrillada *f*
barbed ['bɑrbd] *adj* **1** : con púas
⟨barbed wire : alambre de púas⟩ **2** BIT-
ING : mordaz
barber ['bɑrbər] *n* : barbero *m*, -ra *f*
barbiturate [bɑr'bɪtʃərət] *n* : barbitúrico
m
bard ['bɑrd] *n* : bardo *m*
bare¹ ['bær] *vt* **bared; baring** : desnudar
bare² *adj* **1** NAKED : desnudo **2** EX-
POSED : descubierto, sin protección **3**
EMPTY : desprovisto, vacío **4** MINI-
MUM : mero, mínimo ⟨the bare neces-
sities : las necesidades mínimas⟩ **5**
PLAIN : puro, sencillo
bareback ['bærˌbæk] *or* **barebacked**
[-ˌbækt] *adv & adj* : a pelo
barefaced ['bærˌfeɪst] *adj* : descarado
barefoot ['bærˌfʊt] *or* **barefooted**
[-ˌfʊtəd] *adv & adj* : descalzo
bareheaded ['bærˌhɛdəd] *adv & adj* : sin
sombrero, con la cabeza descubierta
barely ['bærli] *adv* : apenas, por poco
bareness ['bærnəs] *n* : desnudez *f*
bargain¹ ['bɑrgən] *vi* HAGGLE : regatear,
negociar — *vt* BARTER : trocar, cambiar
bargain² *n* **1** AGREEMENT : acuerdo *m*,
convenio *m* ⟨to strike a bargain : cerrar un trato⟩ **2** : ganga*f*⟨bargain price
: precio de ganga⟩
barge¹ ['bɑrdʒ] *vi* **barged; barging 1**
: mover con torpeza **2 to barge in** : entrometerse, interrumpir
barge² *n* : barcaza *f*, gabarra *f*
bar graph *n* : gráfico *m* de barras
baritone ['bærəˌtoːn] *n* : barítono *m*
barium ['bæriəm] *n* : bario *m*
bark¹ ['bɑrk] *vi* : ladrar — *vt or* **to bark
out** : gritar ⟨to bark out an order : dar
una orden a gritos⟩
bark² *n* **1** : ladrido *m* (de un perro) **2**
: corteza *f* (de un árbol) **3** *or* **barque**
: tipo de embarcación con velas de proa
y popa
barley ['bɑrli] *n* : cebada *f*
barn ['bɑrn] *n* : granero *m* (para cosechas), establo *m* (para ganado)
barnacle ['bɑrnɪkəl] *n* : percebe *m*
barnyard ['bɑrnˌjɑrd] *n* : corral *m*
barometer [bə'rɑmətər] *n* : barómetro
m
barometric [ˌbærə'mɛtrɪk] *adj* : barométrico
baron ['bærən] *n* **1** : barón *m* **2** TYCOON
: magnate *mf*
baroness ['bærənɪs, -nəs, -ˌnɛs] *n*
: baronesa *f*
baronet [ˌbærə'nɛt, 'bærənət] *n*
: baronet *m*
baronial [bə'roːniəl] *adj* **1** : de barón **2**
STATELY : señorial, majestuoso
baroque [bə'roːk, -'rɑk] *adj* : barroco
barracks ['bærəks] *ns & pl* : cuartel *m*
barracuda [ˌbærə'kuːdə] *n, pl* **-da** *or* **-das**
: barracuda *f*

barrage [bə'rɑʒ, -'rɑdʒ] *n* **1** : descarga *f*
(de artillería) **2** DELUGE : aluvión *m*
⟨a barrage of questions : un aluvión de
preguntas⟩
barred ['bɑrd] *adj* : excluido, prohibido
barrel¹ ['bærəl] *v* **-reled** *or* **-relled;
-reling** *or* **-relling** *vt* : embarrilar — *vi*
: ir disparado
barrel² *n* **1** : barril *m*, tonel *m* **2** : cañón
m (de un arma de fuego), cilindro *m*
(de una cerradura)
barren ['bærən] *adj* **1** STERILE : estéril
(dícese de las plantas o la mujer), árido (dícese del suelo) **2** DESERTED
: yermo, desierto
barrette [bɑ'rɛt, bə-] *n* : pasador *m*,
broche *m* para el cabello
barricade¹ ['bærəˌkeɪd, ˌbærə'-] *vt*
-caded; -cading : cerrar con barri-
cadas
barricade² *n* : barricada *f*
barrier ['bæriər] *n* **1** : barrera *f* **2** OB-
STACLE : obstáculo *m*, impedimento *m*
barring ['bɑrɪŋ] *prep* : excepto, salvo, a
excepción de
barrio ['bɑrio, 'bær-] *n* : barrio *m*
barroom ['bɑrˌruːm, -ˌrʊm] *n* : bar *m*
barrow ['bærˌoː] → **wheelbarrow**
bartender ['bɑrˌtɛndər] *n* : camarero *m*,
-ra *f*; barman *m*
barter¹ ['bɑrtər] *vt* : cambiar, trocar
barter² *n* : trueque *m*, permuta *f*
basalt [bə'sɔlt, 'beɪˌ-] *n* : basalto *m*
base¹ ['beɪs] *vt* **based; basing** : basar,
fundamentar, establecer
base² *adj* **baser; basest 1** : de baja ley
(dícese de un metal) **2** CONTEMPTIBLE
: vil, despreciable
base³ *n, pl* **bases** : base *f*
baseball ['beɪsˌbɔl] *n* : beisbol *m*, béisbol *m*
baseless ['beɪsləs] *adj* : infundado
basely ['beɪsli] *adv* : vilmente
basement ['beɪsmənt] *n* : sótano *m*
baseness ['beɪsnəs] *n* : vileza *f*, bajeza *f*
bash¹ ['bæʃ] *vt* : golpear violentamente
bash² *n* **1** BLOW : golpe *m*, porrazo *m*,
madrazo *m Mex fam* **2** PARTY : fiesta
f, juerga *f fam*
bashful ['bæʃfəl] *adj* : tímido, vergonzoso, penoso
bashfulness ['bæʃfəlnəs] *n* : timidez *f*
basic¹ ['beɪsɪk] *adj* **1** FUNDAMENTAL
: básico, fundamental **2** RUDIMENTA-
RY : básico, elemental **3** : básico (en
química)
basic² *n* : fundamento *m*, rudimento *m*
basically ['beɪsɪkli] *adv* : fundamentalmente
basil ['beɪzəl, 'bæzəl] *n* : albahaca *f*
basilica [bə'sɪlɪkə] *n* : basílica *f*
basin ['beɪsən] *n* **1** WASHBOWL : palangana *f*, lavamanos *m*, lavabo *m* **2**
: cuenca *f* (de un río)
basis ['beɪsəs] *n, pl* **bases** [-ˌsiːz] **1** BASE
: base *f*, pilar *m* **2** FOUNDATION : fundamento *m*, base *f* **3 on a weekly basis** : semanalmente

bask ['bæsk] *vi* : disfrutar, deleitarse ⟨to bask in the sun : disfrutar del sol⟩

basket ['bæskət] *n* : cesta *f*, cesto *m*, canasta *f*

basketball ['bæskət,bɔl] *n* : baloncesto *m*, basquetbol *m*

bas–relief [,bɑrɪ'li:f] *n* : bajorrelieve *m*

bass¹ ['bæs] *n*, *pl* **bass** *or* **basses** : róbalo *m* (pesca)

bass² ['beɪs] *n* : bajo *m* (tono, voz, cantante)

bass drum *n* : bombo *m*

basset hound ['bæsət,haʊnd] *n* : basset *m*

bassinet [,bæsə'nɛt] *n* : moisés *m*, cuna *f*

bassist ['beɪsɪst] *n* : bajista *mf*

bassoon [bə'su:n, bæ-] *n* : fagot *m*

bass viol ['beɪs'vaɪəl, -,o:l] → **double bass**

bastard¹ ['bæstərd] *adj* : bastardo

bastard² *n* : bastardo *m*, -da *f*

bastardize ['bæstər,daɪz] *vt* -**ized**; -**izing** DEBASE : degradar, envilecer

baste ['beɪst] *vt* **basted**; **basting** 1 STITCH : hilvanar 2 : bañar (con su jugo durante la cocción)

bastion ['bæstʃən] *n* : bastión *m*, baluarte *m*

bat¹ ['bæt] *vt* **batted**; **batting** 1 HIT : batear 2 **without batting an eye** : sin pestañear

bat² *n* 1 : murciélago *m* (animal) 2 : bate *m* ⟨baseball bat : bate de beisbol⟩

batch ['bætʃ] *n* : hornada *f*, tanda *f*, grupo *m*, cantidad *f*

bate ['beɪt] *vt* **bated**; **bating** 1 : aminorar, reducir 2 **with bated breath** : con ansiedad, aguantando la respiración

bath ['bæθ, 'baθ] *n*, *pl* **baths** ['bæðz, 'bæθs, 'baðz, 'baθs] 1 BATHING : baño *m* ⟨to take a bath : bañarse⟩ 2 : baño *m* (en fotografía, etc.) 3 BATHROOM : baño *m*, cuarto *m* de baño 4 SPA : balneario *m* 5 LOSS : pérdida *f*

bathe ['beɪð] *v* **bathed**; **bathing** *vt* 1 WASH : bañar, lavar 2 SOAK : poner en remojo 3 FLOOD : inundar ⟨to bathe with light : inundar de luz⟩ — *vi* : bañarse, ducharse

bather ['beɪðər] *n* : bañista *mf*

bathrobe ['bæθ,ro:b] *n* : bata *f* (de baño)

bathroom ['bæθ,ru:m, -,rʊm] *n* : baño *m*, cuarto *m* de baño

bathtub ['bæθ,tʌb] *n* : bañera *f*, tina *f* (de baño)

batiste [bə'ti:st] *n* : batista *f*

baton [bə'tɑn] *n* : batuta *f*, bastón *m*

battalion [bə'tæljən] *n* : batallón *m*

batten ['bætən] *vt* **to batten down the hatches** : cerrar las escotillas

batter¹ ['bætər] *vt* 1 BEAT : aporrear, golpear 2 MISTREAT : maltratar

batter² *n* 1 : masa *f* para rebozar 2 HITTER : bateador *m*, -dora *f*

battering ram *n* : ariete *m*

battery ['bætəri] *n*, *pl* -**teries** 1 : lesiones *fpl* ⟨assault and battery : agresión con lesiones⟩ 2 ARTILLERY : batería *f* 3 : batería *f*, pila *f* (de electricidad) 4 SERIES : serie *f*

batting ['bætɪŋ] *n* 1 *or* **cotton batting** : algodón *m* en láminas 2 : bateo *m* (en beisbol)

battle¹ ['bætəl] *vi* -**tled**; -**tling** : luchar, pelear

battle² *n* : batalla *f*, lucha *f*, pelea *f*

battle–ax ['bætəl,æks] *n* : hacha *f* de guerra

battlefield ['bætəl,fi:ld] *n* : campo *m* de batalla

battlements ['bætəlmənts] *npl* : almenas *fpl*

battleship ['bætəl,ʃɪp] *n* : acorazado *m*

batty ['bæti] *adj* -**tier**; -**est** : chiflado *fam*, chalado *fam*

bauble ['bɔbəl] *n* : chuchería *f*, baratija *f*

Bavarian [bə'vɛriən] *n* : bávaro *m*, -ra *f* — **Bavarian** *adj*

bawdiness ['bɔdinəs] *n* : picardía *f*

bawdy ['bɔdi] *adj* **bawdier**; -**est** : subido de tono, verde, colorado *Mex*

bawl¹ ['bɔl] *vi* : llorar a gritos

bawl² *n* : grito *m*, alarido *m*

bawl out *vt* SCOLD : regañar

bay¹ ['beɪ] *vi* HOWL : aullar

bay² *adj* : castaño, zaino (dícese de los caballos)

bay³ *n* 1 : bahía *f* ⟨Bay of Campeche : Bahía de Campeche⟩ 2 *or* **bay horse** : caballo *m* castaño 3 LAUREL : laurel *m* 4 HOWL : aullido *m* 5 : saliente *m* ⟨bay window : ventana en saliente⟩ 6 COMPARTMENT : área *f*, compartimento *m* 7 **at** ~ : acorralado

bayberry ['beɪ,bɛri] *n*, *pl* -**ries** : arrayán *m* brabántico

bayonet¹ [,beɪə'nɛt, 'beɪə,nɛt] *vt* -**neted**; -**neting** : herir (o matar) con bayoneta

bayonet² *n* : bayoneta *f*

bayou ['baɪ,u:, -,o:] *n* : pantano *m*

bazaar [bə'zɑr] *n* 1 : bazar *m* 2 SALE : venta *f* benéfica

bazooka [bə'zu:kə] *n* : bazuca *f*

BB ['bi:bi] *n* : balín *m*

be ['bi:] *v* **was** ['wəz, 'wɑz]; **were** ['wər]; **been** ['bɪn]; **being**; **am** ['æm]; **is** ['ɪz]; **are** ['ɑr] *vi* 1 (*expressing equality*) : ser ⟨José is a doctor : José es doctor⟩ ⟨I'm Ann's sister : soy la hermana de Ana⟩ 2 (*expressing quality*) : ser ⟨the tree is tall : el árbol es alto⟩ ⟨you're silly! : ¡eres tonto!⟩ 3 (*expressing origin or possession*) : ser ⟨she's from Managua : es de Managua⟩ ⟨it's mine : es mío⟩ 4 (*expressing location*) : estar ⟨my mother is at home : mi madre está en casa⟩ ⟨the cups are on the table : las tazas están en la mesa⟩ 5 (*expressing existence*) : ser, existir ⟨to be or not to be : ser, o no ser⟩ ⟨I think, therefore I am : pienso, luego existo⟩ 6 (*expressing a state of being*) : estar, tener ⟨how are you? : ¿cómo estás?⟩ ⟨I'm cold : tengo frío⟩ ⟨she's 10 years old : tiene 10 años⟩ ⟨they're both sick : están enfermos los dos⟩ — *v impers* **1** (*indicating time*) : ser ⟨it's eight o'clock : son las ocho⟩ ⟨it's Friday : hoy es viernes⟩ **2** (*indicating a condition*) : hacer, estar ⟨it's sunny : hace sol⟩ ⟨it's very dark outside : está bien oscuro afuera⟩ — *v aux* **1** (*expressing progression*) : estar ⟨what are you doing?—I'm working : ¿qué haces?—estoy trabajando⟩ **2** (*expressing occurrence*) : ser ⟨it was finished yesterday : fue acabado ayer, se acabó ayer⟩ ⟨it was cooked in the oven : se cocinó en el horno⟩ **3** (*expressing possibility*) : poderse ⟨can she be trusted? : ¿se puede confiar en ella?⟩ **4** (*expressing obligation*) : deber ⟨you are to stay here : debes quedarte aquí⟩ ⟨he was to come yesterday : se esperaba que viniese ayer⟩

beach¹ [ˈbiːtʃ] *vt* : hacer embarrancar, hacer varar, hacer encallar

beach² *n* : playa *f*

beachcomber [ˈbiːtʃˌkoːmər] *n* : raquero *m*, -ra *f*

beachhead [ˈbiːtʃˌhɛd] *n* : cabeza *f* de playa

beacon [ˈbiːkən] *n* : faro *m*

bead¹ [ˈbiːd] *vi* : formarse en gotas

bead² *n* **1** : cuenta *f* **2** DROP : gota *f* **3 beads** *npl* NECKLACE : collar *m*

beady [ˈbiːdi] *adj* **beadier, -est 1** : de forma de cuenta **2 beady eyes** : ojos *mpl* pequeños y brillantes

beagle [ˈbiːgəl] *n* : beagle *m*

beak [ˈbiːk] *n* : pico *m*

beaker [ˈbiːkər] *n* **1** CUP : taza *f* alta **2** : vaso *m* de precipitados (en un laboratorio)

beam¹ [ˈbiːm] *vi* **1** SHINE : brillar **2** SMILE : sonreír radiantemente — *vt* BROADCAST : transmitir, emitir

beam² *n* **1** : viga *f*, barra *f* **2** RAY : rayo *m*, haz *m* de luz **3** : haz *m* de radiofaro (para guiar pilotos, etc.)

bean [ˈbiːn] *n* **1** : habichuela *f*, frijol *m* **2 broad bean** : haba *f* **3 string bean** : judía *f*

bear¹ [ˈbær] *v* **bore** [ˈbor]; **borne** [ˈborn]; **bearing** *vt* **1** CARRY : llevar, portar **2** : dar a luz a (un niño) **3** PRODUCE : dar (frutas, cosechas) **4** ENDURE, SUPPORT : soportar, resistir, aguantar — *vi* **1** TURN : doblar, dar la vuelta ⟨bear right : doble a la derecha⟩ **2 to bear up** : resistir

bear² *n, pl* **bears** *or* **bear** : oso *m*, osa *f*

bearable [ˈbærəbəl] *adj* : soportable

beard [ˈbɪrd] *n* **1** : barba *f* **2** : arista *f* (de plantas)

bearded [ˈbɪrdəd] *adj* : barbudo, de barba

bearer [ˈbærər] *n* : portador *m*, -dora *f*

bearing [ˈbærɪŋ] *n* **1** CONDUCT, MANNERS : comportamiento *m*, modales *mpl* **2** SUPPORT : soporte *f* **3** SIGNIFICANCE : relación *f*, importancia *f* ⟨to have no bearing on : no tener nada que ver con⟩ **4** : cojinete *m*, rodamiento *m*

(de una máquina) **5** COURSE, DIRECTION : dirección *f*, rumbo *m* ⟨to get one's bearings : orientarse⟩

beast [ˈbiːst] *n* **1** : bestia *f*, fiera *f* ⟨beast of burden : animal de carga⟩ **2** BRUTE : bruto *m*, -ta *f*; bestia *mf*

beastly [ˈbiːstli] *adj* : detestable, repugnante

beat¹ [ˈbiːt] *v* **beat; beaten** [ˈbiːtən] *or* **beat; beating** *vt* **1** STRIKE : golpear, pegar, darle una paliza (a alguien) **2** DEFEAT : vencer, derrotar **3** AVOID : anticiparse a, evitar ⟨to beat the crowd : evitar el gentío⟩ **4** MASH, WHIP : batir — *vi* THROB : palpitar, latir

beat² *adj* EXHAUSTED : derrengado, muy cansado ⟨I'm beat! : ¡estoy molido!⟩

beat³ *n* **1** : golpe *m*, redoble *m* (de un tambor), latido *m* (del corazón) **2** RHYTHM : ritmo *m*, tiempo *m*

beater [ˈbiːtər] *n* **1** : batidor *m*, -dora *f* **2** EGGBEATER : batidor *m*

beatific [ˌbiːəˈtɪfɪk] *adj* : beatífico

beatitude [biˈætəˌtuːd] *n* **1** : beatitud *f* **2 the Beatitudes** : las bienaventuranzas

beau [ˈboː] *n, pl* **beaux** *or* **beaus** : pretendiente *m*, galán *m*

beautification [ˌbjuːtəfəˈkeɪʃən] *n* : embellecimiento *m*

beautiful [ˈbjuːtɪfəl] *adj* : hermoso, bello, lindo, precioso

beautifully [ˈbjuːtɪfəli] *adv* **1** ATTRACTIVELY : hermosamente **2** EXCELLENTLY : maravillosamente, excelentemente

beauty [ˈbjuːti] *n, pl* **-ties** : belleza *f*, hermosura *f*, beldad *f*

beauty shop *or* **beauty salon** *n* : salón *m* de belleza

beaver [ˈbiːvər] *n* : castor *m*

because [bɪˈkʌz, -ˈkɔz] *conj* : porque

because of *prep* : por, a causa de, debido a

beck [ˈbɛk] *n* **to be at the beck and call of** : estar a la entera disposición de, estar sometido a la voluntad de

beckon [ˈbɛkən] *vi* **to beckon to someone** : hacerle señas a alguien

become [bɪˈkʌm] *v* **-came** [-ˈkeɪm]; **-come; -coming** *vi* : hacerse, volverse, ponerse ⟨he became famous : se hizo famoso⟩ ⟨to become sad : ponerse triste⟩ ⟨to become accustomed to : acostumbrarse a⟩ — *vt* **1** BEFIT : ser apropiado para **2** SUIT : favorecer, quedarle bien (a alguien) ⟨that dress becomes you : ese vestido te favorece⟩

becoming [bɪˈkʌmɪŋ] *adj* **1** SUITABLE : apropiado **2** FLATTERING : favorecedor

bed¹ [ˈbɛd] *v* **bedded; bedding** *vt* : acostar — *vi* : acostarse

bed² *n* **1** : cama *f*, lecho *m* **2** : cauce *m* (de un río), fondo *m* (del mar) **3** : arriate *m* (para plantas) **4** LAYER, STRATUM : estrato *m*, capa *f*

bedbug ['bɛd,bʌg] *n* : chinche *f*
bedclothes ['bɛd,klo:ðz, -,klo:z] *npl*
: ropa *f* de cama, sábanas *fpl*
bedding ['bɛdɪŋ] *n* 1 → **bedclothes** 2
: cama *f* (para animales)
bedeck [bɪ'dɛk] *vt* : adornar, engalanar
bedevil [bɪ'dɛvəl] *vt* **-iled** *or* **-illed; -iling**
or **-illing** : acosar, plagar
bedlam ['bɛdləm] *n* : locura *f*, caos *m*,
alboroto *m*
bedraggled [bɪ'drægəld] *adj* : desaliñado, despeinado
bedridden ['bɛd,rɪdən] *adj* : postrado en
cama
bedrock ['bɛd,rɑk] *n* : lecho *m* de roca
bedroom ['bɛd,ru:m, -,rʊm] *n* : dormitorio *m*, habitación *f*, pieza *f*, recámara
f Col, Mex, Pan
bedspread ['bɛd,sprd] *n* : cubrecama *m*,
colcha *f*, cobertor *m*
bee ['bi:] *n* 1 : abeja *f* (insecto) 2 GATH-
ERING : círculo *m*, reunión *f*
beech ['bi:tʃ] *n, pl* **beeches** *or* **beech**
: haya *f*
beechnut ['bi:tʃ,nʌt] *n* : hayuco *m*
beef[1] ['bi:f] *vt* **to beef up** : fortalecer, reforzar — *vi* COMPLAIN : quejarse
beef[2] *n, pl* **beefs** ['bi:fs] *or* **beeves**
['bi:vz] : carne *f* de vaca, carne *f* de res
CA, Mex
beefsteak ['bi:f,steɪk] *n* : filete *m*, bistec
m
beehive ['bi:,haɪv] *n* : colmena *f*
beekeeper ['bi:,ki:pər] *n* : apicultor *m*,
-tora *f*
beeline ['bi:,laɪn] *n* **to make a beeline**
for : ir derecho a, ir directo hacia
been → **be**
beep[1] ['bi:p] *v* : pitar
beep[2] *n* : pitido *m*
beeper ['bi:pər] *n* : busca *m*, buscapersonas *m*
beer ['bɪr] *n* : cerveza *f*
beeswax ['bi:z,wæks] *n* : cera *f* de abejas
beet ['bi:t] *n* : remolacha *f*, betabel *m*
Mex
beetle ['bi:təl] *n* : escarabajo *m*
befall [bɪ'fɔl] *v* **-fell** [-'fɛl]; **-fallen** [-'fɔlən]
vt : sucederle a, acontecerle a — *vi*
: acontecer
befit [bɪ'frt] *vt* **-fitted; -fitting** : convenir
a, ser apropiado para
before[1] [bɪ'for] *adv* 1 : antes ⟨before and
after : antes y después⟩ 2 : anterior
⟨the month before : el mes anterior⟩
before[2] *conj* : antes que ⟨he would die
before surrendering : moriría antes que
rendirse⟩
before[3] *prep* 1 : antes de ⟨before eating
: antes de comer⟩ 2 : delante de, ante
⟨I stood before the house : estaba parada delante de la casa⟩ ⟨before the judge
: ante el juez⟩
beforehand [bɪ'for,hænd] *adv* : antes,
por adelantado, de antemano, con anticipación
befriend [bɪ'frɛnd] *vt* : hacerse amigo de

befuddle [bɪ'fʌdəl] *vt* **-dled; -dling** : aturdir, ofuscar, confundir
beg ['bɛg] *v* **begged; begging** *vt* : pedir,
mendigar, suplicar ⟨I begged him to go
: le supliqué que fuera⟩ — *vi* : mendigar, pedir limosna
beget [bɪ'gɛt] *vt* **-got** [-'gɑt]; **-gotten**
[-'gɑtən] *or* **-got; -getting** : engendrar
beggar ['bɛgər] *n* : mendigo *m*, -ga *f*;
pordiosero *m*, -ra *f*
begin [bɪ'gɪn] *v* **-gan** [-'gæn]; **-gun**
[-'gʌn]; **-ginning** *vi* 1 : empezar, comenzar, iniciar — *vi* 1 START : empezar,
comenzar, iniciarse 2 ORIGINATE
: nacer, originarse 3 **to begin with** : en
primer lugar, para empezar
beginner [bɪ'gɪnər] *n* : principiante *mf*
beginning [bɪ'gɪnɪŋ] *n* : principio *m*,
comienzo *m*
begone [bɪ'gɔn] *interj* : ¡fuera de aquí!
begonia [bɪ'go:njə] *n* : begonia *f*
begrudge [bɪ'grʌʤ] *vt* **-grudged;**
-grudging 1 : dar de mala gana 2 ENVY
: envidiar, resentir
beguile [bɪ'gaɪl] *vt* **-guiled; -guiling** 1
DECEIVE : engañar 2 AMUSE : divertir,
entretener
behalf [bɪ'hæf, -'haf] *n* 1 : favor *m*, beneficio *m*, parte *f* 2 **on behalf of** *or* **in**
behalf of : de parte de, en nombre de
behave [bɪ'heɪv] *vi* **-haved; -having**
: comportarse, portarse
behavior [bɪ'heɪvjər] *n* : comportamiento *m*, conducta *f*
behead [bɪ'hd] *vt* : decapitar
behest [bɪ'hɛst] *n* 1 : mandato *m*, orden
f 2 **at the behest of** : a instancia de
behind[1] [bɪ'haɪnd] *adv* : atrás, detrás ⟨to
fall behind : quedarse atrás⟩
behind[2] *prep* 1 : atrás de, detrás de, tras
⟨behind the house : detrás de la casa⟩
⟨one behind another : uno tras otro⟩
2 : atrasado con, después de ⟨behind
schedule : atrasado con el trabajo⟩ ⟨I
arrived behind the others : llegué después de los otros⟩ 3 SUPPORTING : en
apoyo de, detrás
behind[3] [bɪ'haɪnd, 'bi:,haɪnd] *n* : trasero
m
behold [bɪ'ho:ld] *vt* **-held; -holding**
: contemplar
beholder [bɪ'ho:ldər] *n* : observador *m*,
-dora *f*
behoove [bɪ'hu:v] *vt* **-hooved; -hooving**
: convenirle a, corresponderle a ⟨it be-
hooves us to help him : nos conviene
ayudarlo⟩
beige[1] ['beɪʒ] *adj* : beige
beige[2] *n* : beige *m*
being ['bi:ɪŋ] *n* 1 EXISTENCE : ser *m*, existencia *f* 2 CREATURE : ser *m*, ente *m*
belabor [bɪ'leɪbər] *vt* **to belabor the**
point : extenderse sobre el tema
belated [bɪ'leɪtəd] *adj* : tardío, retrasado
belch[1] ['bɛltʃ] *vi* 1 BURP : eructar 2 EX-
PEL : expulsar, arrojar
belch[2] *n* : eructo *m*

beleaguer [bɪ'li:gər] *vt* **1** BESIEGE : asediar, sitiar **2** HARASS : fastidiar, molestar

belfry ['bɛlfri] *n, pl* **-fries** : campanario *m*

Belgian ['bɛldʒən] *n* : belga *mf* — **Belgian** *adj*

belie [bɪ'laɪ] *vt* **-lied; -lying 1** MISREPRESENT : falsear, ocultar **2** CONTRADICT : contradecir, desmentir

belief [bə'li:f] *n* **1** TRUST : confianza *f* **2** CONVICTION : creencia *f*, convicción *f* **3** FAITH : fe *f*

believable [bə'li:vəbəl] *adj* : verosímil, creíble

believe [bə'li:v] *v* **-lieved; -lieving** : creer

believer [bə'li:vər] *n* **1** : creyente *mf* **2** : partidario *m*, -ria *f*; entusiasta *mf* ⟨she's a great believer in vitamins : ella es una gran partidaria de las vitaminas⟩

belittle [bɪ'lɪtəl] *vt* **-littled; -littling 1** DISPARAGE : menospreciar, denigrar, rebajar **2** MINIMIZE : minimizar, quitar importancia a

Belizean [bə'li:ziən] *n* : beliceño *m*, -ña *f* — **Belizean** *adj*

bell¹ ['bɛl] *vt* : ponerle un cascabel a

bell² *n* : campana *f*, cencerro *m* (para una vaca o cabra), cascabel *m* (para un gato), timbre *m* (de teléfono, de la puerta)

belle ['bɛl] *n* : belleza *f*, beldad *f*

bellhop ['bɛl,hɑp] *n* : botones *m*

bellicose ['bɛlɪ,ko:s] *adj* : belicoso *m* — **bellicosity** [,bɛlɪ'kɑsəti] *n*

belligerence [bə'lɪdʒərənts] *n* : agresividad *f*, beligerancia *f*

belligerent¹ [bə'lɪdʒərənt] *adj* : agresivo, beligerante

belligerent² *n* : beligerante *mf*

bellow¹ ['bɛ,lo:] *vi* : bramar, mugir — *vt* : gritar

bellow² *n* : bramido *m*, grito *m*

bellows ['bɛ,lo:z] *ns & pl* : fuelle *m*

bellwether ['bɛl,wɛðər] *n* : líder *mf*

belly¹ ['bɛli] *vi* **-lied; -lying** SWELL : hincharse, inflarse

belly² *n, pl* **-lies** : abdomen *m*, vientre *m*, barriga *f*, panza *f*

belong [bɪ'lɔŋ] *vi* **1** : pertenecer (a), ser propiedad (de) ⟨it belongs to her : pertenece a ella, es suyo, es de ella⟩ **2** : ser parte (de), ser miembro (de) ⟨he belongs to the club : es miembro del club⟩ **3** : deber estar, ir ⟨your coat belongs in the closet : tu abrigo va en el ropero⟩

belongings [bɪ'lɔŋɪŋz] *npl* : pertenencias *fpl*, efectos *mpl* personales

beloved¹ [bɪ'lʌvəd, -'lʌvd] *adj* : querido, amado

beloved² *n* : amado *m*, -da *f*; enamorado *m*, -da *f*; amor *m*

below¹ [bɪ'lo:] *adv* : abajo

below² *prep* **1** : abajo de, debajo de ⟨below the window : debajo de la ventana⟩ **2** : por debajo de, bajo ⟨below average : por debajo del promedio⟩ ⟨5 degrees below zero : 5 grados bajo cero⟩

belt¹ ['bɛlt] *vt* **1** : ceñir con un cinturón, ponerle un cinturón a **2** THRASH : darle una paliza a, darle un trancazo a

belt² *n* **1** : cinturón *m*, cinto *m* (para el talle) **2** BAND, STRAP : cinta *f*, correa *f*, banda *f Mex* **3** AREA : frente *m*, zona *f*

beltway ['bɛlt,weɪ] *n* : carretera *f* de circunvalación; periférico *m CA, Mex*; libramiento *m Mex*

bemoan [bɪ'mo:n] *vt* : lamentarse de

bemuse [bɪ'mju:z] *vt* **-mused; -musing 1** BEWILDER : confundir, desconcertar **2** ENGROSS : absorber

bench ['bɛntʃ] *n* **1** SEAT : banco *m*, escaño *m*, banca *f* **2** : estrado *m* (de un juez) **3** COURT : tribunal *m*

bend¹ ['bɛnd] *v* **bent** ['bɛnt]; **bending** *vt* : torcer, doblar, curvar, flexionar — *vi* **1** : torcerse, agacharse ⟨to bend over : inclinarse⟩ **2** TURN : torcer, hacer una curva

bend² *n* **1** TURN : vuelta *f*, recodo *m* **2** CURVE : curva *f*, ángulo *m*, codo *m*

beneath¹ [bɪ'ni:θ] *adv* : bajo, abajo, debajo

beneath² *prep* : bajo de, abajo de, por debajo de

benediction [,bɛnə'dɪkʃən] *n* : bendición *f*

benefactor ['bɛnə,fæktər] *n* : benefactor *m*, -tora *f*

beneficence [bə'nɛfəsənts] *n* : beneficencia *f*

beneficent [bə'nɛfəsənt] *adj* : benéfico, caritativo

beneficial [,bɛnə'fɪʃəl] *adj* : beneficioso, provechoso — **beneficially** *adv*

beneficiary [,bɛnə'fɪʃi,ɛri, -'fɪʃəri] *n, pl* **-ries** : beneficiario *m*, -ria *f*

benefit¹ ['bɛnəfɪt] *vt* : beneficiar — *vi* : beneficiarse

benefit² *n* **1** ADVANTAGE : beneficio *m*, ventaja *f*, provecho *m* **2** AID : asistencia *f*, beneficio *m* **3** : función *f* benéfica (para recaudar fondos)

benevolence [bə'nɛvələnts] *n* : bondad *f*, benevolencia *f*

benevolent [bə'nɛvələnt] *adj* : benévolo, bondadoso — **benevolently** *adv*

Bengali [bɛn'gɑli, bɛŋ-] *n* **1** : bengalí *mf* **2** : bengalí *m* (idioma) — **Bengali** *adj*

benign [bɪ'naɪn] *adj* **1** GENTLE, KIND : benévolo, amable **2** FAVORABLE : propicio, favorable **3** MILD : benigno ⟨a benign tumor : un tumor benigno⟩

Beninese [bə,nɪ'ni:z, -,ni:-, -'ni:s; ,bɪni'-] *n* : beninés *m*, -nesa *f* — **Beninese** *adj*

bent ['bɛnt] *n* : aptitud *f*, inclinación *f*

benumb [bɪ'nʌm] *vt* : entumecer

benzene ['bɛn,zi:n] *n* : benceno *m*

bequeath [bɪ'kwi:θ, -'kwi:ð] *vt* : legar, dejar en testamento

bequest [bɪ'kwɛst] *n* : legado *m*

berate [bɪ'reɪt] *vt* **-rated; -rating** : reprender, regañar

bereaved¹ [bɪ'ri:vd] *adj* : que está de luto, afligido (por la muerte de alguien)

bereaved² *n* **the bereaved** : los deudos del difunto (o de la difunta)

bereavement [bɪ'riːvmənt] *n* **1** SORROW : dolor *m*, pesar *m* **2** LOSS : pérdida *f*

bereft [bɪ'rɛft] *adj* : privado, desprovisto

beret [bə'reɪ] *n* : boina *f*

beriberi [ˌbɛri'bɛri] *n* : beriberi *m*

berm ['bərm] *n* : arcén *m*

berry ['bɛri] *n, pl* **-ries** : baya *f*

berserk [bər'sərk, -'zərk] *adj* **1** : enloquecido **2 to go beserk** : volverse loco

berth¹ ['bərθ] *vi* : atracar

berth² *n* **1** DOCK : atracadero *m* **2** ACCOMMODATION : litera *f*, camarote *m* **3** POSITION : trabajo *m*, puesto *m*

beryl ['bɛrəl] *n* : berilo *m*

beseech [bɪ'siːtʃ] *vt* **-seeched** *or* **-sought** [-'sɔt]; **-seeching** : suplicar, implorar, rogar

beset [bɪ'sɛt] *vt* **-set**; **-setting 1** HARASS : acosar **2** SURROUND : rodear

beside [bɪ'saɪd] *prep* : al lado de, junto a

besides¹ [bɪ'saɪdz] *adv* **1** ALSO : además, también, aparte **2** MOREOVER : además, por otra parte

besides² *prep* **1** : además de, aparte de ⟨six others besides you : seis otros además de ti⟩ **2** EXCEPT : excepto, fuera de, aparte de

besiege [bɪ'siːdʒ] *vt* **-sieged**; **-sieging** : asediar, sitiar, cercar

besmirch [bɪ'smərtʃ] *vt* : ensuciar, mancillar

best¹ ['bɛst] *vt* : superar, ganar a

best² *adv* (*superlative* of **well**) : mejor ⟨as best I can : lo mejor que puedo⟩

best³ *adj* (*superlative* of **good**) : mejor ⟨my best friend : mi mejor amigo⟩

best⁴ *n* **1 the best** : lo mejor, el mejor, la mejor, los mejores, las mejores **2 at ~** : a lo más **3 to do one's best** : hacer todo lo posible

bestial ['bɛstʃəl, 'biːs-] *adj* **1** : bestial **2** BRUTISH : brutal, salvaje

best man *n* : padrino *m*

bestow [bɪ'stoː] *vt* : conferir, otorgar, conceder

bestowal [bɪ'stoːəl] *n* : concesión *f*, otorgamiento *m*

bet¹ ['bɛt] *v* **bet**; **betting** *vt* : apostar — *vi* **to bet on** : apostarle a

bet² *n* : apuesta *f*

betoken [bɪ'toːkən] *vt* : denotar, ser indicio de

betray [bɪ'treɪ] *vt* **1** : traicionar ⟨to betray one's country : traicionar uno a su patria⟩ **2** DIVULGE, REVEAL : delatar, revelar ⟨to betray a secret : revelar un secreto⟩

betrayal [bɪ'treɪəl] *n* : traición *f*, delación *f*, revelación *f* ⟨betrayal of trust : abuso de confianza⟩

betrothal [bɪ'troːðəl, -'troː-] *n* : esponsales *mpl*, compromiso *m*

betrothed [bɪ'troːðd, -'trɔθt] *n* FIANCÉ : prometido *m*, -da *f*

better¹ ['bɛtər] *vt* **1** IMPROVE : mejorar **2** SURPASS : superar

better² *adv* (*comparative* of **well**) **1** : mejor **2** MORE : más ⟨better than 50 miles : más de 50 millas⟩

better³ *adj* (*comparative* of **good**) **1** : mejor ⟨the weather is better today : hace mejor tiempo hoy⟩ ⟨I was sick, but now I'm better : estuve enfermo, pero ahora estoy mejor⟩ **2** : mayor ⟨the better part of a month : la mayor parte de un mes⟩

better⁴ *n* **1** : el mejor, la mejor ⟨the better of the two : el mejor de los dos⟩ **2 to get the better of** : vencer a, quedar por encima de, superar

betterment ['bɛtərmənt] *n* : mejoramiento *m*, mejora *f*

bettor *or* **better** ['bɛtər] *n* : apostador *m*, -dora *f*

between¹ [bɪ'twiːn] *adv* **1** : en medio, por lo medio **2 in ~** : intermedio

between² *prep* : entre

bevel¹ ['bɛvəl] *v* **-eled** *or* **-elled**; **-eling** *or* **-elling** *vt* : biselar — *vi* INCLINE : inclinarse

bevel² *n* : bisel *m*

beverage ['bɛvrɪdʒ, 'bɛvə-] *n* : bebida *f*

bevy ['bɛvi] *n, pl* **bevies** : grupo *m* (de personas), bandada *f* (de pájaros)

bewail [bɪ'weɪl] *vt* : lamentarse de, llorar

beware [bɪ'wær] *vi* **to beware of** : tener cuidado con ⟨beware of the dog! : ¡cuidado con el perro!⟩ — *vt* : guardarse de, cuidarse de

bewilder [bɪ'wɪldər] *vt* : desconcertar, dejar perplejo

bewilderment [bɪ'wɪldərmənt] *n* : desconcierto *m*, perplejidad *f*

bewitch [bɪ'wɪtʃ] *vt* **1** : hechizar, embrujar **2** CHARM : cautivar, encantar

bewitchment [bɪ'wɪtʃmənt] *n* : hechizo *m*

beyond¹ [bi'jɑnd] *adv* **1** FARTHER, LATER : más allá, más lejos (en el espacio), más adelante (en el tiempo) **2** MORE : más ⟨$50 and beyond : $50 o más⟩

beyond² *n* **the beyond** : el más allá, lo desconocido

beyond³ *prep* **1** : más allá de ⟨beyond the frontier : más allá de la frontera⟩ **2** : fuera de ⟨beyond one's reach : fuera de su alcance⟩ **3** BESIDES : además de

biannual [ˌbaɪ'ænjuəl] *adj* : bianual — **biannually** *adv*

bias¹ ['baɪəs] *vt* **-ased** *or* **-assed**; **-asing** *or* **-assing 1** : predisponer, sesgar, influir en, afectar **2 to be biased against** : tener prejuicio contra

bias² *n* **1** : sesgo *m*, bies *m* (en la costura) **2** PREJUDICE : prejuicio *m* **3** TENDENCY : inclinación *f*, tendencia *f*

biased ['baɪəst] *adj* : tendencioso, parcial

bib ['bɪb] *n* **1** : peto *m* **2** : babero *m* (para niños)

Bible ['baɪbəl] *n* : Biblia *f*

biblical ['bɪblɪkəl] *adj* : bíblico

bibliographer [ˌbɪbliˈɑgrəfər] *n* : bibliógrafo *m*, -fa *f*
bibliographic [ˌbɪbliəˈgræfɪk] *adj* : bibliográfico
bibliography [ˌbɪbliˈɑgrəfi] *n, pl* **-phies** : bibliografía *f*
bicameral [ˌbaɪˈkæmərəl] *adj* : bicameral
bicarbonate [ˌbaɪˈkɑrbənət, -ˌneɪt] *n* : bicarbonato *m*
bicentennial [ˌbaɪsɛnˈtɛniəl] *n* : bicentenario *m*
biceps [ˈbaɪˌsɛps] *ns & pl* : bíceps *m*
bicker[1] [ˈbɪkər] *vi* : pelear, discutir, reñir
bicker[2] *n* : pelea *f*, riña *f*, discusión *f*
bicuspid [baɪˈkʌspɪd] *n* : premolar *m*, diente *m* bicúspide
bicycle[1] [ˈbaɪsɪkəl, -ˌsɪ-] *vi* **-cled; -cling** : ir en bicicleta
bicycle[2] *n* : bicicleta *f*
bicycling [ˈbaɪsɪkəlɪŋ] *n* : ciclismo *m*
bicyclist [ˈbaɪsɪkəlɪst] *n* : ciclista *mf*
bid[1] [ˈbɪd] *vt* **bade** [ˈbæd, ˈbeɪd] *or* **bid; bidden** [ˈbɪdən] *or* **bid; bidding 1** ORDER : pedir, mandar **2** INVITE : invitar **3** SAY : dar, decir ⟨to bid good evening : dar las buenas noches⟩ ⟨to bid farewell to : decir adiós a⟩ **4** : ofrecer (en una subasta), declarar (en juegos de cartas)
bid[2] *n* **1** OFFER : oferta *f* (en una subasta), declaración *f* (en juegos de cartas) **2** INVITATION : invitación *f* **3** ATTEMPT : intento *m*, tentativa *f*
bidder [ˈbɪdər] *n* : postor *m*, -tora *f*
bide [ˈbaɪd] *v* **bode** [ˈboːd] *or* **bided; bided; biding** *vt* : esperar, aguardar ⟨to bide one's time : esperar el momento oportuno⟩ — *vi* DWELL : morar, vivir
biennial [baɪˈɛniəl] *adj* : bienal — **biennially** *adv*
bier [ˈbɪr] *n* **1** STAND : andas *fpl* **2** COFFIN : ataúd *m*, féretro *m*
bifocals [ˈbaɪˌfoːkəlz] *npl* : lentes *mpl* bifocales, bifocales *mpl*
big [ˈbɪg] *adj* **bigger; biggest 1** LARGE : grande **2** PREGNANT : embarazada **3** IMPORTANT, MAJOR : importante, grande ⟨a big decision : una gran decisión⟩ **4** POPULAR : popular, famoso, conocido
bigamist [ˈbɪgəmɪst] *n* : bígamo *m*, -ma *f*
bigamous [ˈbɪgəməs] *adj* : bígamo
bigamy [ˈbɪgəmi] *n* : bigamia *f*
Big Dipper → **dipper**
bighorn [ˈbɪgˌhɔrn] *n, pl* **-horn** *or* **-horns** *or* **bighorn sheep** : oveja *f* salvaje de las montañas
bight [ˈbaɪt] *n* : bahía *f*, ensenada *f*, golfo *m*
bigot [ˈbɪgət] *n* : intolerante *mf*
bigoted [ˈbɪgətəd] *adj* : intolerante, prejuiciado, fanático
bigotry [ˈbɪgətri] *n, pl* **-tries** : intolerancia *f*
big shot *n* : pez *m* gordo *fam*, mandamás *mf*

bigwig [ˈbɪgˌwɪg] → **big shot**
bike [ˈbaɪk] *n* **1** : bicicleta *f*, bici *f fam* **2** : motocicleta *f*, moto *f*
bikini [bəˈkiːni] *n* : bikini *m*
bilateral [baɪˈlætərəl] *adj* : bilateral — **bilaterally** *adv*
bile [ˈbaɪl] *n* **1** : bilis *f* **2** IRRITABILITY : mal genio *m*
bilingual [baɪˈlɪŋgwəl] *adj* : bilingüe
bilious [ˈbɪliəs] *adj* **1** : bilioso **2** IRRITABLE : bilioso, colérico
bilk [ˈbɪlk] *vt* : burlar, estafar, defraudar
bill[1] [ˈbɪl] *vt* : pasarle la cuenta a — *vi* : acariciar ⟨to bill and coo : acariciarse⟩
bill[2] *n* **1** LAW : proyecto *m* de ley, ley *f* **2** INVOICE : cuenta *f*, factura *f* **3** POSTER : cartel *m* **4** PROGRAM : programa *m* (del teatro) **5** : billete *m* ⟨a five-dollar bill : un billete de cinco dólares⟩ **6** BEAK : pico *m*
billboard [ˈbɪlˌbɔrd] *n* : cartelera *f*
billet[1] [ˈbɪlət] *vt* : acuartelar, alojar
billet[2] *n* : alojamiento *m*
billfold [ˈbɪlˌfoːld] *n* : billetera *f*, cartera *f*
billiards [ˈbɪljərdz] *n* : billar *m*
billion [ˈbɪljən] *n, pl* **billions** *or* **billion** : mil millones *mpl*
billow[1] [ˈbɪlo] *vi* : hincharse, inflarse
billow[2] *n* **1** WAVE : ola *f* **2** CLOUD : nube *f* ⟨a billow of smoke : un nube de humo⟩
billowy [ˈbɪlowi] *adj* : ondulante
billy goat [ˈbɪliˌgoːt] *n* : macho *m* cabrío
bin [ˈbɪn] *n* : cubo *m*, cajón *m*
binary [ˈbaɪnəri, -ˌnɛri] *adj* : binario *m*
bind [ˈbaɪnd] *vt* **bound** [ˈbaʊnd]; **binding 1** TIE : atar, amarrar **2** OBLIGATE : obligar **3** UNITE : aglutinar, ligar, unir **4** BANDAGE : vendar **5** : encuadernar (un libro)
binder [ˈbaɪndər] *n* **1** FOLDER : carpeta *f* **2** : encuadernador *m*, -dora *f* (de libros)
binding [ˈbaɪndɪŋ] *n* **1** : encuadernación *f* (de libros) **2** COVER : cubierta *f*, forro *m*
binge [ˈbɪndʒ] *n* : juerga *f*, parranda *f fam*
bingo [ˈbɪŋˌgoː] *n, pl* **-gos** : bingo *m*
binocular [baɪˈnɑkjələr, bə-] *adj* : binocular
binoculars [bəˈnɑkjələrz, baɪ-] *npl* : binoculares *mpl*
biochemical[1] [ˌbaɪoˈkɛmɪkəl] *adj* : bioquímico
biochemical[2] *n* : bioquímico *m*
biochemist [ˌbaɪoˈkɛmɪst] *n* : bioquímico *m*, -ca *f*
biochemistry [ˌbaɪoˈkɛməstri] *n* : bioquímica *f*
biodegradable [ˌbaɪodɪˈgreɪdəbəl] *adj* : biodegradable
biodegradation [ˌbaɪodɛgrəˈdeɪʃən] *n* : biodegradación *f*
biodegrade [ˌbaɪodɪˈgreɪd] *vi* **-graded; -grading** : biodegradarse

biodiversity [ˌbaɪodəˈvərsəti, -daɪ-] *n, pl* **-ties** : bioversidad *f*
biographer [baɪˈɑgrəfər] *n* : biógrafo *m*, -fa *f*
biographical [ˌbaɪəˈgræfɪkəl] *adj* : biográfico
biography [baɪˈɑgrəfi, bi:-] *n, pl* **-phies** : biografía *f*
biologic [ˌbaɪəˈlɑʤɪk] *or* **biological** [-ʤɪkəl] *adj* : biológico
biologist [baɪˈɑləʤɪst] *n* : biólogo *m*, -ga *f*
biology [baɪˈɑləʤi] *n* : biología *f*
biophysical [ˌbaɪoˈfɪzɪkəl] *adj* : biofísico
biophysicist [ˌbaɪoˈfɪzəsɪst] *n* : biofísico *m*, -ca *f*
biophysics [ˌbaɪoˈfɪzɪks] *ns & pl* : biofísica *f*
biopsy [ˈbaɪˌɑpsi] *n, pl* **-sies** : biopsia *f*
biosphere [ˈbaɪəˌsfɪr] *n* : biosfera *f*, biósfera *f*
biotechnology [ˌbaɪotɛkˈnɑləʤi] *n* : biotecnología *f*
biotic [baɪˈɑtɪk] *adj* : biótico
bipartisan [baɪˈpɑrtəzən, -sən] *adj* : bipartidista, de dos partidas
biped [ˈbaɪˌpɛd] *n* : bípedo *m*
birch [ˈbərʧ] *n* : abedul *m*
bird [ˈbərd] *n* : pájaro *m* (pequeño), ave *f* (grande)
birdbath [ˈbərdˌbæθ, -ˌbɑθ] *n* : pila *f* para pájaros
bird dog *n* : perro *m*, -rra *f* de caza
bird of prey *n* : ave *f* rapaz, ave *f* de presa
birdseed [ˈbərdˌsi:d] *n* : alpiste *m*
bird's-eye [ˈbərdzˌaɪ] *adj* **1** : visto desde arriba ⟨bird's-eye view : vista aérea⟩ **2** CURSORY : rápido, somero
birth [ˈbərθ] *n* **1** : nacimiento *m*, parto *m* **2** ORIGIN : origen *m*, nacimiento *m*
birthday [ˈbərθˌdeɪ] *n* : cumpleaños *m*, aniversario *m*
birthmark [ˈbərθˌmɑrk] *n* : mancha *f* de nacimiento
birthplace [ˈbərθˌpleɪs] *n* : lugar *m* de nacimiento
birthrate [ˈbərθˌreɪt] *n* : índice *m* de natalidad
birthright [ˈbərθˌraɪt] *n* : derecho *m* de nacimiento
biscuit [ˈbɪskət] *n* : bizcocho *m*
bisect [ˈbaɪˌsɛkt, ˌbaɪˈ-] *vt* : bisecar
bisexual [ˌbaɪˈsɛkʃuəl] *adj* : bisexual
bishop [ˈbɪʃəp] *n* **1** : obispo *m* **2** : alfil *m* (en ajedrez)
bismuth [ˈbɪzməθ] *n* : bismuto *m*
bison [ˈbaɪzən, -sən] *ns & pl* : bisonte *m*
bistro [ˈbiːstro, ˈbɪs-] *n, pl* **-tros** : bar *m*, restaurante *m* pequeño
bit [ˈbɪt] *n* **1** FRAGMENT, PIECE : pedazo *m*, trozo *m* ⟨a bit of luck : un poco de suerte⟩ **2** : freno *m*, bocado *m* (de una brida) **3** : broca *f* (de un taladro) **4** : bit *m* (de información)
bitch¹ [ˈbɪʧ] *vi* COMPLAIN : quejarse, reclamar

bitch² *n* : perra *f*
bite¹ [ˈbaɪt] *v* **bit** [ˈbɪt]; **bitten** [ˈbɪtən]; **biting** *vt* **1** : morder **2** STING : picar **3** PUNCTURE : punzar, pinchar **4** GRIP : agarrar — *vi* **1** : morder ⟨that dog bites : ese perro muerde⟩ **2** STING : picar (dícese de un insecto), cortar (dícese del viento) **3** : picar ⟨the fish are biting now : ya están picando los peces⟩ **4** GRAB : agarrarse
bite² *n* **1** BITING : mordisco *m*, dentellada *f* **2** SNACK : bocado *m* ⟨a bite to eat : algo de comer⟩ **3** : picadura *f* (de un insecto), mordedura *f* (de un animal) **4** SHARPNESS : mordacidad *f*, penetración *f*
biting *adj* **1** PENETRATING : cortante, penetrante **2** CAUSTIC : mordaz, sarcástico
bitter [ˈbɪtər] *adj* **1** ACRID : amargo, acre **2** PENETRATING : cortante, penetrante ⟨bitter cold : frío glacial⟩ **3** HARSH : duro, amargo ⟨to the bitter end : hasta el final⟩ **4** INTENSE, RELENTLESS : intenso, extremo, implacable ⟨bitter hatred : odio implacable⟩
bitterly [ˈbɪtərli] *adv* : amargamente
bitterness [ˈbɪtərnəs] *n* : amargura *f*
bittersweet [ˈbɪtərˌswi:t] *adj* : agridulce
bivalve [ˈbaɪˌvælv] *n* : bivalvo *m* — **bivalve** *adj*
bivouac¹ [ˈbɪvəˌwæk, ˈbɪvˌwæk] *vi* **-ouacked; -ouacking** : acampar, vivaquear
bivouac² *n* : vivaque *m*
bizarre [bəˈzɑr] *adj* : extraño, singular, estrafalario, estrambótico — **bizarrely** *adv*
blab [ˈblæb] *vi* **blabbed; blabbing** : parlotear *fam*, cotorrear *fam*
black¹ [ˈblæk] *vt* : ennegrecer
black² *adj* **1** : negro (color, raza) **2** SOILED : sucio **3** DARK : oscuro, negro **4** WICKED : malvado, perverso, malo **5** GLOOMY : negro, sombrío, deprimente
black³ *n* **1** : negro *m* (color) **2** : negro *m*, -gra *f* (persona)
black-and-blue [ˌblækənˈblu:] *adj* : amoratado
blackball [ˈblækˌbɔl] *vt* **1** OSTRACIZE : hacerle el vacío a, aislar **2** BOYCOTT : boicotear
blackberry [ˈblækˌbɛri] *n, pl* **-ries** : mora *f*
blackbird [ˈblækˌbərd] *n* : mirlo *m*
blackboard [ˈblækˌbɔrd] *n* : pizarra *f*, pizarrón *m*
blacken [ˈblækən] *vt* **1** BLACK : ennegrecer **2** DEFAME : deshonrar, difamar, manchar
blackhead [ˈblækˌhɛd] *n* : espinilla *f*, punto *m* negro
black hole *n* : agujero *m* negro
blackjack [ˈblækˌʤæk] *n* **1** : cachiporra *f* (arma) **2** : veintiuna *f* (juego de cartas)
blacklist¹ [ˈblækˌlɪst] *vt* : poner en la lista negra

blacklist² *n* : lista *f* negra
blackmail¹ ['blæk,meɪl] *vt* : chantajear, hacer chantaje a
blackmail² *n* : chantaje *m*
blackmailer ['blæk,meɪlər] *n* : chantajista *mf*
blackout ['blæk,aʊt] *n* **1** : apagón *m* (de poder eléctrico) **2** FAINT : desmayo *m*, desvanecimiento *m*
black out *vt* : dejar sin luz — *vi* FAINT : perder el conocimiento, desmayarse
blacksmith ['blæk,smɪθ] *n* : herrero *m*
blacktop ['blæk,tɑp] *n* : asfalto *m*
bladder ['blædər] *n* : vejiga *f*
blade ['bleɪd] *n* : hoja *f* (de un cuchillo), cuchilla *f* (de un patín), pala *f* (de un remo o una hélice), brizna *f* (de hierba)
blamable ['bleɪməbəl] *adj* : culpable
blame¹ ['bleɪm] *vt* **blamed; blaming** : culpar, echar la culpa a
blame² *n* : culpa *f*
blameless ['bleɪmləs] *adj* : intachable, sin culpa, inocente — **blamelessly** *adv*
blameworthiness ['bleɪm,wərðinəs] *n* : culpa *f*, culpabilidad *f*
blameworthy ['bleɪm,wərði] *adj* : culpable, reprochable, censurable
blanch ['blæntʃ] *vt* WHITEN : blanquear — *vi* PALE : palidecer
bland ['blænd] *adj* : soso, insulso, desabrido ⟨a bland smile : una sonrisa insulsa⟩ ⟨a bland diet : una dieta fácil de digerir⟩
blandishments ['blændɪʃmənts] *npl* : lisonjas *fpl*, halagos *mpl*
blandly ['blændli] *adv* : de manera insulsa
blandness ['blændnəs] *n* : lo insulso, lo desabrido
blank¹ ['blæŋk] *vt* OBLITERATE : borrar
blank² *adj* **1** DAZED : perplejo, desconcertado **2** EXPRESSIONLESS : sin expresión, inexpresivo **3** : en blanco (dícese de un papel), liso (dícese de una pared) **4** EMPTY : vacío, en blanco ⟨a blank stare : una mirada vacía⟩ ⟨his mind went blank : se quedó en blanco⟩
blank³ *n* **1** SPACE : espacio *m* en blanco **2** FORM : formulario *m* **3** CARTRIDGE : cartucho *m* de fogueo **4** *or* **blank key** : llave *f* ciega
blanket¹ ['blæŋkət] *vt* : cubrir
blanket² *adj* : global
blanket³ *n* : manta *f*, cobija *f*, frazada *f*
blankly ['blæŋkli] *adv* : sin comprender
blankness ['blæŋknəs] *n* **1** PERPLEXITY : desconcierto *m*, perplejidad *f* **2** EMPTINESS : vacío *m*, vacuidad *f*
blare¹ ['blær] *vi* **blared; blaring** : resonar
blare² *n* : estruendo *m*
blarney ['blɑrni] *n* : labia *f fam*
blasé [blɑˈzeɪ] *adj* : displicente, indiferente
blaspheme [blæsˈfiːm, 'blæs,-] *vi* **-phemed; -pheming** : blasfemar
blasphemer [blæsˈfiːmər, 'blæs,-] *n* : blasfemo *m*, -ma *f*

blasphemous ['blæsfəməs] *adj* : blasfemo
blasphemy ['blæsfəmi] *n, pl* **-mies** : blasfemia *f*
blast¹ ['blæst] *vt* **1** BLOW UP : volar, hacer volar **2** ATTACK : atacar, arremeter contra
blast² *n* **1** GUST : ráfaga *f* **2** EXPLOSION : explosión *f*
blast–off ['blæst,ɔf] *n* : despegue *m*
blast off *vi* : despegar
blatant ['bleɪtənt] *adj* : descarado — **blatantly** ['bleɪtəntli] *adv*
blaze¹ ['bleɪz] *v* **blazed; blazing** *vi* SHINE : arder, brillar, resplandecer — *vt* MARK : marcar, señalar ⟨to blaze a trail : abrir un camino⟩
blaze² *n* **1** FIRE : fuego *m* **2** BRIGHTNESS : resplandor *m*, brillantez *f* **3** OUTBURST : arranque *m* ⟨a blaze of anger : un arranque de cólera⟩ **4** DISPLAY : alarde *m*, llamarada *f* ⟨a blaze of color : un derroche de color⟩
blazer ['bleɪzər] *n* : chaqueta *f* deportiva, blazer *m*
bleach¹ ['bliːtʃ] *vt* : blanquear, decolorar
bleach² *n* : lejía *f*, blanqueador *m*
bleachers ['bliːtʃərz] *ns & pl* : gradas *fpl*, tribuna *f* descubierta
bleak ['bliːk] *adj* **1** DESOLATE : inhóspito, sombrío, desolado **2** DEPRESSING : deprimente, triste, sombrío
bleakly ['bliːkli] *adv* : sombríamente
bleakness ['bliːknəs] *n* : lo inhóspito, lo sombrío
blear ['blɪr] *adj* : empañado, nublado
bleary ['blɪri] *adj* **1** : adormilado, fatigado **2 bleary–eyed** : con los ojos nublados
bleat¹ ['bliːt] *vi* : balar
bleat² *n* : balido *m*
bleed ['bliːd] *v* **bled** ['blɛd]; **bleeding** *vi* **1** : sangrar **2** GRIEVE : sufrir, afligirse **3** EXUDE : exudar (dícese de una planta), correrse (dícese de los colores) — *vt* **1** : sangrar (a una persona), purgar (frenos) **2 to bleed someone dry** : sacarle todo el dinero a alguien
blemish¹ ['blɛmɪʃ] *vt* : manchar, marcar
blemish² *n* : imperfección *f*, mancha *f*, marca *f*
blend¹ ['blɛnd] *vt* **1** MIX : mezclar **2** COMBINE : combinar, aunar
blend² *n* : mezcla *f*, combinación *f*
blender ['blɛndər] *n* : licuadora *f*
bless ['blɛs] *vt* **blessed** ['blɛst]; **blessing 1** CONSECRATE : bendecir, consagrar **2** : bendecir ⟨may God bless you! : ¡que Dios te bendiga!⟩ **3 to bless with** : dotar de **4 to bless oneself** : santiguarse
blessed ['blɛsəd] *or* **blest** ['blɛst] *adj* : bienaventurado, bendito, dichoso
blessedly ['blɛsədli] *adv* : felizmente, alegremente, afortunadamente
blessing ['blɛsɪŋ] *n* **1** : bendición *f* **2** APPROVAL : aprobación *f*, consentimiento *m*

blew → blow

blight[1] ['blaɪt] *vt* : arruinar, infestar

blight[2] *n* **1** : añublo *m* **2** PLAGUE : peste *f*, plaga *f* **3** DECAY : deterioro *m*, ruina *f*

blimp ['blɪmp] *n* : dirigible *m*

blind[1] ['blaɪnd] *vt* **1** : cegar, dejar ciego **2** DAZZLE : deslumbrar

blind[2] *adj* **1** SIGHTLESS : ciego **2** IN-SENSITIVE : ciego, insensible, sin razón **3** CLOSED : sin salida ⟨blind alley : callejón sin salida⟩

blind[3] *n* **1** : persiana *f* (para una ventana) **2** COVER : escondite *m*, escondrijo *m*

blinders ['blaɪndərz] *npl* : anteojeras *fpl*

blindfold[1] ['blaɪnd,fo:ld] *vt* : vendar los ojos

blindfold[2] *n* : venda *f* (para los ojos)

blinding ['blaɪndɪŋ] *adj* : enceguecedor, cegador ⟨with blinding speed : con una rapidez inusitada⟩

blindly ['blaɪndli] *adv* : a ciegas, ciegamente

blindness ['blaɪndnəs] *n* : ceguera *f*

blink[1] ['blɪŋk] *vi* **1** WINK : pestañear, parpadear **2** : brillar intermitentemente

blink[2] *n* : pestañeo *m*, parpadeo *m*

blinker ['blɪŋkər] *n* : intermitente *m*, direccional *f*

bliss ['blɪs] *n* **1** HAPPINESS : dicha *f*, felicidad *f* absoluta **2** PARADISE : paraíso *m*

blissful ['blɪsfəl] *adj* : dichoso, feliz — **blissfully** *adv*

blister[1] ['blɪstər] *vi* : ampollarse

blister[2] *n* : ampolla *f* (en la piel o una superficie), burbuja *f* (en una superficie)

blithe ['blaɪθ, 'blaɪð] *adj* **blither; blithest** **1** CAREFREE : despreocupado **2** CHEERFUL : alegre, risueño — **blithely** *adv*

blitz[1] ['blɪts] *vt* **1** BOMBARD : bombardear **2** : atacar con rapidez

blitz[2] *n* **1** : bombardeo *m* aéreo **2** CAMPAIGN : ataque *m*, acometida *f*

blizzard ['blɪzərd] *n* : tormenta *f* de nieve, ventisca *f*

bloat ['blo:t] *vi* : hincharse, inflarse

blob ['blɑb] *n* : gota *f*, mancha *f*, borrón *m*

bloc ['blɑk] *n* : bloque *m*

block[1] ['blɑk] *vt* **1** OBSTRUCT : obstruir, bloquear **2** CLOG : atascar, atorar

block[2] *n* **1** PIECE : bloque *m* ⟨building blocks : cubos de construcción⟩ ⟨auction block : plataforma de subastas⟩ ⟨starting block : taco de salida⟩ **2** OB-STRUCTION : obstrucción *f*, bloqueo *m* **3** : cuadra *f*, manzana *f* (de edificios) ⟨to go around the block : dar la vuelta a la cuadra⟩ **4** BUILDING : edificio *m* (de apartamentos, oficinas, etc.) **5** GROUP, SERIES : serie *f*, grupo *m* ⟨a block of tickets : una serie de entradas⟩ **6** block and tackle : aparejo *m* de poleas

blockade[1] [blɑ'keɪd] *vt* **-aded; -ading** : bloquear

blockade[2] *n* : bloqueo *m*

blockage ['blɑkɪʤ] *n* : bloqueo *m*, obstrucción *f*

blockhead ['blɑk,hɛd] *n* : bruto *m*, -ta *f*; estúpido *m*, -da *f*

blond[1] *or* **blonde** ['blɑnd] *adj* : rubio, güero *Mex*, claro (dícese de la madera)

blond[2] *or* **blonde** *n* : rubio *m*, -bia *f*; güero *m*, -ra *f* *Mex*

blood ['blʌd] *n* **1** : sangre *f* **2** LIFEBLOOD : vida *f*, alma *f* **3** LINEAGE : linaje *m*, sangre *f*

blood bank *n* : banco *m* de sangre

bloodcurdling ['blʌd,kərdəlɪŋ] *adj* : espeluznante, aterrador

blooded ['blʌdəd] *adj* : de sangre ⟨cold-blooded animal : animal de sangre fría⟩

bloodhound ['blʌd,haʊnd] *n* : sabueso *m*

bloodless ['blʌdləs] *adj* **1** : incruento, sin derramamiento de sangre **2** LIFE-LESS : desanimado, insípido, sin vida

bloodmobile ['blʌdmo,bi:l] *n* : unidad *f* móvil para donantes de sangre

blood pressure *n* : tensión *f*, presión *f* (arterial)

bloodshed ['blʌd,ʃɛd] *n* : derramamiento *m* de sangre

bloodshot ['blʌd,ʃɑt] *adj* : inyectado de sangre

bloodstain ['blʌd,steɪn] *n* : mancha *f* de sangre

bloodstained ['blʌd,steɪnd] *adj* : manchado de sangre

bloodstream ['blʌd,stri:m] *n* : torrente *m* sanguíneo, corriente *f* sanguínea

bloodsucker ['blʌd,sʌkər] *n* : sanguijuela *f*

bloodthirsty ['blʌd,θərsti] *adj* : sanguinario

blood vessel *n* : vaso *m* sanguíneo

bloody ['blʌdi] *adj* **bloodier; -est** : ensangrentado, sangriento

bloom[1] ['blu:m] *vi* **1** FLOWER : florecer **2** MATURE : madurar

bloom[2] *n* **1** FLOWER : flor *f* ⟨to be in bloom : estar en flor⟩ **2** FLOWERING : floración *f* ⟨in full bloom : en plena floración⟩ **3** : rubor *m* (de la tez) ⟨in the bloom of youth : en plena juventud, en la flor de la vida⟩

bloomers ['blu:mərz] *npl* : bombachos *mpl*

blooper ['blu:pər] *n* : metedura *f* de pata *fam*

blossom[1] ['blɑsəm] *vi* : florecer, dar flor

blossom[2] *n* : flor *f*

blot[1] ['blɑt] *vt* **blotted; blotting** **1** SPOT : emborronar, borronear **2** DRY : secar

blot[2] *n* **1** STAIN : mancha *f*, borrón *m* **2** BLEMISH : mancha *f*, tacha *f*

blotch[1] ['blɑʧ] *vt* : emborronar, borronear

blotch[2] *n* : mancha *f*, borrón *m*

blotchy ['blɑʧi] *adj* **blotchier; -est** : lleno de manchas

blotter [ˈblɑṭər] *n* : hoja *f* de papel secante, secante *m*

blouse [ˈblaʊs, ˈblaʊz] *n* : blusa *f*

blow¹ [ˈbloː] *v* **blew** [ˈbluː]; **blown** [ˈbloːn]; **blowing** *vi* **1** : soplar, volar ⟨the wind is blowing hard : el viento está soplando con fuerza⟩ ⟨it blew out the door : voló por la puerta⟩ ⟨the window blew shut : se cerró la ventana⟩ **2** SOUND : sonar ⟨the whistle blew : sonó el silbato⟩ **3 to blow out** : fundirse (dícese de un fusible eléctrico), reventarse (dícese de una llanta) **4 to blow off** : dejar plantado (a alguien), flatar a (una cita, etc.) — *vt* **1** : soplar, echar ⟨to blow smoke : echar humo⟩ **2** SOUND : tocar, sonar **3** SHAPE : soplar, dar forma a ⟨to blow glass : soplar vidrio⟩ **4** BUNGLE : echar a perder

blow² *n* **1** PUFF : soplo *m*, soplido *m* **2** GALE : vendaval *f* **3** HIT, STROKE : golpe *m* **4** CALAMITY : golpe *m*, desastre *m* **5 to come to blows** : llegar a las manos

blower [ˈbloːər] *n* FAN : ventilador *m*

blowout [ˈbloːˌaʊt] *n* : reventón *m*

blowtorch [ˈbloːˌtɔrtʃ] *n* : soplete *m*

blow up *vi* EXPLODE : estallar, hacer explosión — *vt* BLAST : volar, hacer volar

blubber¹ [ˈblʌbər] *vi* : lloriquear

blubber² *n* : esperma *f* de ballena

bludgeon [ˈblʌdʒən] *vt* : aporrear

blue¹ [ˈbluː] *adj* **bluer; bluest 1** : azul **2** MELANCHOLY : melancólico, triste

blue² *n* : azul *m*

blueberry [ˈbluːˌbɛri] *n*, *pl* **-ries** : arándano *m*

bluebird [ˈbluːˌbərd] *n* : azulejo *m*

blue cheese *n* : queso *m* azul

blueprint [ˈbluːˌprɪnt] *n* **1** : plano *m*, proyecto *m*, cianotipo *m* **2** PLAN : anteproyecto *m*, programa *m*

blues [ˈbluːz] *npl* **1** DEPRESSION : depresión *f*, melancolía *f* **2** : blues *m* ⟨to sing the blues : cantar blues⟩

bluff¹ [ˈblʌf] *vi* : hacer un farol, blofear *Col, Mex*

bluff² *adj* **1** STEEP : escarpado **2** FRANK : campechano, franco, directo

bluff³ *n* **1** : farol *m*, blof *m Col, Mex* **2** CLIFF : acantilado *m*, risco *m*

bluing *or* **blueing** [ˈbluːɪŋ] *n* : añil *m*, azulete *m*

bluish [ˈbluːɪʃ] *adj* : azulado

blunder¹ [ˈblʌndər] *vi* **1** STUMBLE : tropezar, dar traspiés **2** ERR : cometer un error, tropezar, meter la pata *fam*

blunder² *n* : error *m*, fallo *m* garrafal, metedura *f* de pata *fam*

blunderbuss [ˈblʌndərˌbʌs] *n* : trabuco *m*

blunt¹ [ˈblʌnt] *vt* : despuntar (aguja o lápiz), desafilar (cuchillo o tijeras), suavizar (crítica)

blunt² *adj* **1** DULL : desafilado, despuntado **2** DIRECT : directo, franco, categórico

bluntly [ˈblʌntli] *adv* : sin rodeos, francamente, bruscamente

bluntness [ˈblʌntnəs] *n* **1** DULLNESS : falta *f* de filo, embotadura *f* **2** FRANKNESS : franqueza *f*

blur¹ [ˈblər] *vt* **blurred; blurring** : desdibujar, hacer borroso

blur² *n* **1** SMEAR : mancha *f*, borrón *m* **2** : aspecto *m* borroso ⟨everything was just a blur : todo se volvió borroso⟩

blurb [ˈblərb] *n* : propaganda *f*, nota *f* publicitaria

blurry [ˈbləri] *adj* : borroso

blurt [ˈblərt] *vt* : espetar, decir impulsivamente

blush¹ [ˈblʌʃ] *vi* : ruborizarse, sonrojarse, hacerse colorado

blush² *n* : rubor *m*, sonrojo *m*

bluster¹ [ˈblʌstər] *vi* **1** BLOW : soplar con fuerza **2** BOAST : fanfarronear, echar bravatas

bluster² *n* : fanfarronada *f*, bravatas *fpl*

blustery [ˈblʌstəri] *adj* : borrascoso, tempestuoso

boa [ˈboːə] *n* : boa *f*

boar [ˈbor] *n* : cerdo *m* macho, verraco *m*

board¹ [ˈbord] *vt* **1** : embarcarse en, subir a bordo de (una nave o un avión), subir a (un tren o un carro) **2** LODGE : hospedar, dar hospedaje con comidas a **3 to board up** : cerrar con tablas

board² *n* **1** PLANK : tabla *f*, tablón *m* **2** : tablero *m* ⟨chessboard : tablero de ajedrez⟩ **3** MEALS : comida *f* ⟨board and lodging : comida y alojamiento⟩ **4** COMMITTEE, COUNCIL : junta *f*, consejo *m*

boarder [ˈbordər] *n* LODGER : huésped *m*, -peda *f*

boardinghouse [ˈbordɪŋˌhaʊs] *n* : casa *f* de huéspedes

boarding school *n* : internado *m*

boardwalk [ˈbordˌwɔk] *n* : paseo *m* marítimo

boast¹ [ˈboːst] *vi* : alardear, presumir, jactarse

boast² *n* : jactancia *f*, alarde *m*

boaster [ˈboːstər] *n* : presumido *m*, -da *f*; fanfarrón *m*, -rrona *f fam*

boastful [ˈboːstfəl] *adj* : jactancioso, fanfarrón *fam*

boastfully [ˈboːstfəli] *adv* : de manera jactanciosa

boat¹ [ˈboːt] *vt* : transportar en barco, poner a bordo

boat² *n* : barco *m*, embarcación *f*, bote *m*, barca *f*

boatman [ˈboːtmən] *n*, *pl* **-men** [-mən, -ˌmɛn] : barquero *m*

boatswain [ˈboːsən] *n* : contramaestre *m*

bob¹ [ˈbɑb] *v* **bobbed; bobbing** *vi* **1** : balancearse, mecerse ⟨to bob up and down : subir y bajar⟩ **2** *or* **to bob up** APPEAR : presentarse, surgir — *vt* **1** : inclinar (la cabeza o el cuerpo) **2** CUT : cortar, recortar ⟨she bobbed her hair : se cortó el pelo⟩

bob² *n* **1** : inclinación *f* (de la cabeza, del cuerpo), sacudida *f* **2** FLOAT : flotador *m*, corcho *m* (de pesca) **3** : pelo *m* corto

bobbin ['bɑbən] *n* : bobina *f*, carrete *m*

bobby pin ['bɑbi,pɪn] *n* : horquilla *f*

bobcat ['bɑb,kæt] *n* : lince *m* rojo

bobolink ['bɑbə,lɪŋk] *n* : tordo *m* arrocero

bobsled ['bɑb,slɛd] *n* : bobsleigh *m*

bobwhite ['bɑb'hwaɪt] *n* : codorniz *m* (del Nuevo Mundo)

bode¹ ['bo:d] *v* **boded; boding** *vt* : presagiar, augurar — *vi* **to bode well** : ser de buen agüero

bode² → **bide**

bodice ['bɑdəs] *n* : corpiño *m*

bodied ['bɑdid] *adj* : de cuerpo ⟨lean-bodied : de cuerpo delgado⟩ ⟨able-bodied : no discapacitado⟩

bodiless ['bɑdiləs, 'bɑdələs] *adj* : incorpóreo

bodily¹ ['bɑdəli] *adv* : en peso ⟨to lift someone bodily : levantar a alguien en peso⟩

bodily² *adj* : corporal, del cuerpo ⟨bodily harm : daños corporales⟩

body ['bɑdi] *n, pl* **bodies 1** : cuerpo *m*, organismo *m* **2** CORPSE : cadáver *m* **3** PERSON : persona *f*, ser *m* humano **4** : nave *f* (de una iglesia), carrocería (de un automóvil), fuselaje *m* (de un avión), casco *m* (de una nave) **5** COLLECTION, MASS : conjunto *m*, grupo *m*, masa *f* ⟨in a body : todos juntos, en masa⟩ **6** ORGANIZATION : organismo *m*, organización *f*

bodyguard ['bɑdi,gɑrd] *n* : guardaespaldas *mf*

bog¹ ['bɑg, 'bɔg] *vt* **bogged; bogging** : empantanar, inundar ⟨to get bogged down : empantanarse⟩

bog² *n* : lodazal *m*, ciénaga *f*, cenagal *m*

bogey ['bʊgi, 'bo:-] *n, pl* **-geys** : terror *m*, coco *m fam*

boggle ['bɑgəl] *vi* **-gled; -gling** : quedarse atónito, quedarse pasmado ⟨the mind boggles! : ¡es increíble!⟩

boggy ['bɑgi, 'bɔ-] *adj* **boggier; -est** : cenagoso

bogus ['bo:gəs] *adj* : falso, fingido, falaz

bohemian [bo:'hi:miən] *n* : bohemio *m*, -mia *f* — **bohemian** *adj*

boil¹ ['bɔɪl] *vi* **1** : hervir **2 to make one's blood boil** : hervirle la sangre a uno — *vt* **1** : hervir, hacer hervir ⟨to boil water : hervir agua⟩ **2** : cocer, hervir ⟨to boil potatoes : cocer papas⟩

boil² *n* **1** BOILING : hervor *m* **2** : furúnculo *m*, divieso *m* (en medicina)

boiler ['bɔɪlər] *n* : caldera *f*

boisterous ['bɔɪstərəs] *adj* : bullicioso, escandaloso — **boisterously** *adv*

bold ['bo:ld] *adj* **1** COURAGEOUS : valiente **2** INSOLENT : insolente, descarado **3** DARING : atrevido, audaz — **boldly** *adv*

boldface ['bo:ld,feɪs] *or* **boldface type** *n* : negrita *f*

boldness ['bo:ldnəs] *n* **1** COURAGE : valor *m*, coraje *m* **2** INSOLENCE : atrevimiento *m*, insolencia *f*, descaro *m* **3** DARING : audacia *f*

bolero [bə'lɛro] *n, pl* **-ros** : bolero *m*

Bolivian [bə'lɪviən] *n* : boliviano *m*, -na *f* — **Bolivian** *adj*

boll ['bo:l] *n* : cápsula *f* (del algodón)

boll weevil *n* : gorgojo *m* del algodón

bologna [bə'lo:ni] *n* : salchicha *f* ahumada

bolster¹ ['bo:lstər] *vt* **-stered; -stering** : reforzar, reafirmar ⟨to bolster morale : levantar la moral⟩

bolster² *n* : cabezal *m*, almohadón *m*

bolt¹ ['bo:lt] *vt* **1** : atornillar, sujetar con pernos ⟨bolted to the floor : sujetado con pernos al suelo⟩ **2** : cerrar con pestillo, echar el cerrojo a ⟨to bolt the door : echar el cerrojo a la puerta⟩ **3 to bolt down** : engullir ⟨she bolted down her dinner : engulló su comida⟩ — *vi* : echar a correr, salir corriendo ⟨he bolted from the room : salió corriendo de la sala⟩

bolt² *n* **1** LATCH : pestillo *m*, cerrojo *m* **2** : tornillo *m*, perno *m* ⟨nuts and bolts : tuercas y tornillos⟩ **3** : rollo *m* ⟨a bolt of cloth : un rollo de tela⟩ **4 lightning bolt** : relámpago *m*, rayo *m*

bomb¹ ['bɑm] *vt* : bombardear

bomb² *n* : bomba *f*

bombard [bɑm'bɑrd, bəm-] *vt* : bombardear

bombardier [,bɑmbə'dɪr] *n* : bombardero *m*, -ra *f*

bombardment [bɑm'bɑrdmənt] *n* : bombardeo *m*

bombast ['bɑm,bæst] *n* : grandilocuencia *f*, ampulosidad *f*

bombastic [bɑm'bæstɪk] *adj* : grandilocuente, ampuloso, bombástico

bomber ['bɑmər] *n* : bombardero *m*

bombproof ['bɑm,pru:f] *adj* : a prueba de bombas

bombshell ['bɑm,ʃɛl] *n* : bomba *f* ⟨a political bombshell : una bomba política⟩

bona fide ['bo:nə,faɪd, 'bɑ-; ,bo:nə'faɪdi] *adj* **1** : de buena fe ⟨a bona fide offer : una oferta de buena fe⟩ **2** GENUINE : genuino, auténtico

bonanza [bə'nænzə] *n* : bonanza *f*

bonbon ['bɑn,bɑn] *n* : bombón *m*

bond¹ ['bɑnd] *vt* **1** INSURE : dar fianza a, asegurar **2** STICK : adherir, pegar — *vi* : adherirse, pegarse

bond² *n* **1** LINK, TIE : vínculo *m*, lazo *m* **2** BAIL : fianza *f*, caución *f* **3** : bono *m* ⟨stocks and bonds : acciones y bonos⟩ **4 bonds** *npl* FETTERS : cadenas *fpl*

bondage ['bɑndɪdʒ] *n* : esclavitud *f*

bondholder ['bɑnd,ho:ldər] *n* : tenedor *m*, -dora *f* de bonos

bondsman ['bɑndzmən] *n, pl* **-men** [-mən, -,mɪn] **1** SLAVE : esclavo *m* **2** SURETY : fiador *m*, -dora *f*

bone¹ ['bo:n] *vt* **boned; boning** : deshuesar

bone² *n* : hueso *m*

boneless ['bo:nləs] *adj* : sin huesos, sin espinas

boner ['bo:nər] *n* : metedura *f* de pata, metida *f* de pata

bonfire ['ban,faɪr] *n* : hoguera *f*, fogata *f*, fogón *m*

bonito [bə'ni:ɵo] *n, pl* **-tos** *or* **-to** : bonito *m*

bonnet ['banət] *n* : sombrero *m* (de mujer), gorra *f* (de niño)

bonus ['bo:nəs] *n* **1** : prima *f*, bonificación *f* (pagado al empleado) **2** ADVANTAGE, BENEFIT : beneficio *m*, provecho *m*

bony ['bo:ni] *adj* **bonier; -est** : huesudo

boo¹ ['bu:] *vt* : abuchear

boo² *n, pl* **boos** : abucheo *m*

booby ['bu:bi] *n, pl* **-bies** : bobo *m*, -ba *f*; tonto *m*, -ta *f*

book¹ ['bʊk] *vt* : reservar ⟨to book a flight : reservar un vuelo⟩

book² *n* **1** : libro *m* **2 the Book** : la Biblia **3 by the book** : según las reglas

bookcase ['bʊk,keɪs] *n* : estantería *f*, librero *m Mex*

bookend ['bʊk,ɛnd] *n* : sujetalibros *m*

bookie ['bʊki] → **bookmaker**

bookish ['bʊkɪʃ] *adj* : libresco

bookkeeper ['bʊk,ki:pər] *n* : tenedor *m*, -dora *f* de libros; contable *mf Spain*

bookkeeping ['bʊk,ki:pɪŋ] *n* : contabilidad *f*, teneduría *f* de libros

booklet ['bʊklət] *n* : folleto *m*

bookmaker ['bʊk,meɪkər] *n* : corredor *m*, -dora *f* de apuestas

bookmark ['bʊk,mɑrk] *n* : señalador *m* de libros, marcador *m* de libros

bookseller ['bʊk,slər] *n* : librero *m*, -ra *f*

bookshelf ['bʊk,ʃɛlf] *n, pl* **-shelves 1** : estante *m* **2 bookshelves** *npl* : estantería *f*

bookstore ['bʊk,stor] *n* : librería *f*

bookworm ['bʊk,wərm] *n* : ratón *m* de biblioteca *fam*

boom¹ ['bu:m] *vi* **1** THUNDER : tronar, resonar **2** FLOURISH, PROSPER : estar en auge, prosperar

boom² *n* **1** BOOMING : bramido *m*, estruendo *m* **2** FLOURISHING : auge *m* ⟨population boom : auge de población⟩

boomerang ['bu:mə,ræŋ] *n* : bumerán *m*

boon¹ ['bu:n] *adj* **boon companion** : amigo *m*, -ga *f* del alma

boon² *n* : ayuda *f*, beneficio *m*, adelanto *m*

boondocks ['bu:n,dɑks] *npl* : área *f* rural remota, región *f* alejada

boor ['bʊr] *n* : grosero *m*, -ra *f*

boorish ['bʊrɪʃ] *adj* : grosero

boost¹ ['bu:st] *vt* **1** LIFT : levantar, alzar **2** INCREASE : aumentar, incrementar **3** PROMOTE : promover, fomentar, hacer publicidad por

boost² *n* **1** THRUST : impulso *m*, empujón *m* **2** ENCOURAGEMENT : estímulo *m*, aliento *m* **3** INCREASE : aumento *m*, incremento *m*

booster ['bu:stər] *n* **1** SUPPORTER : partidario *m*, -ria *f* **2 booster rocket** : cohete *m* propulsor **3 booster shot** : vacuna *f* de refuerzo

boot¹ ['bu:t] *vt* KICK : dar una patada a, patear

boot² *n* **1** : bota *f*, botín *m* **2** KICK : puntapié *m*, patada *f*

bootee *or* **bootie** ['bu:ʈi] *n* : botita *f*, botín *m*

booth ['bu:θ] *n, pl* **booths** ['bu:ðz, 'bu:θs] : cabina *f* (de teléfono, de votar), caseta *f* (de información), barraca *f* (a una feria)

bootlegger ['bu:t,lɛgər] *n* : contrabandista *mf* del alcohol

booty ['bu:ʈi] *n, pl* **-ties** : botín *m*

booze ['bu:z] *n fam* : alcohol *m*

borax ['bor,æks] *n* : bórax *m*

border¹ ['bordər] *vt* **1** EDGE : ribetear, bordear **2** BOUND : limitar con, lindar con — *vi* VERGE : rayar, lindar ⟨that borders on absurdity : eso raya en el absurdo⟩

border² *n* **1** EDGE : borde *m*, orilla *f* **2** TRIM : ribete *m* **3** FRONTIER : frontera *f*

bore¹ ['bor] *vt* **bored; boring 1** PIERCE : taladrar, perforar ⟨to bore metals : taladrar metales⟩ **2** OPEN : hacer, abrir ⟨to bore a tunnel : abrir un túnel⟩ **3** WEARY : aburrir

bore² → **bear¹**

bore³ *n* **1** : pesado *m*, -da *f* (persona aburrida) **2** TEDIOUSNESS : pesadez *f*, lo aburrido **3** DIAMETER : calibre *m*

boredom ['bordəm] *n* : aburrimiento *m*

boring ['borɪŋ] *adj* : aburrido, pesado

born ['born] *adj* **1** : nacido **2** : nato ⟨she's a born singer : es una cantante nata⟩ ⟨he's a born leader : nació para mandar⟩

borne *pp* → **bear¹**

boron ['bor,ɑn] *n* : boro *m*

borough ['bɔro] *n* : distrito *m* municipal

borrow ['bɑro] *vt* **1** : pedir prestado, tomar prestado **2** APPROPRIATE : apropiarse de, adoptar

borrower ['bɑrəwər] *n* : prestatario *m*, -ria *f*

Bosnian ['bɑzniən, 'bɔz-] *n* : bosnio *m*, -nia *f* — **Bosnian** *adj*

bosom¹ ['bʊzəm, 'bu:-] *adj* : íntimo

bosom² *n* **1** CHEST : pecho *m* **2** BREAST : pecho *m*, seno *m* **3** CLOSENESS : seno *m* ⟨in the bosom of her family : en el seno de su familia⟩

bosomed ['bʊzəmd, 'bu:-] *adj* : con busto ⟨big-bosomed : con mucho busto⟩

boss¹ ['bɔs] *vt* **1** SUPERVISE : dirigir, supervisar **2 to boss around** : mandonear *fam*, mangonear *fam*

boss² *n* : jefe *m*, -fa *f*; patrón *m*, -trona *f*

bossy ['bɔsi] *adj* **bossier; -est** : mandón *fam*, autoritario, dominante

botanist [ˈbɑtənɪst] *n* : botánico *m*, -ca *f*
botany [ˈbɑtəni] *n* : botánica *f* — **botanical** [bəˈtænɪkəl] *adj*
botch¹ [ˈbɑtʃ] *vt* : hacer una chapuza de, estropear
botch² *n* : chapuza *f*
both¹ [ˈboːθ] *adj* : ambos, los dos, las dos ⟨both books : ambos libros, los dos libros⟩
both² *conj* : tanto como ⟨both Ann and her mother are tall : tanto Ana como su madre son altas⟩
both³ *pron* : ambos *m*, -bas *f*; los dos, las dos
bother¹ [ˈbɑðər] *vt* **1** IRK : preocupar ⟨nothing's bothering me : nada me preocupa⟩ ⟨what's bothering him? : ¿qué le pasa?⟩ **2** PESTER : molestar, fastidiar — *vi* **to bother to** : molestarse en, tomar la molestia de
bother² *n* **1** TROUBLE : molestia *f*, problemas *mpl* **2** ANNOYANCE : molestia *f*, fastidio *m*
bothersome [ˈbɑðərsəm] *adj* : molesto, fastidioso
bottle¹ [ˈbɑtəl] *vt* **bottled; bottling** : embotellar, envasar
bottle² *n* : botella *f*, frasco *m*
bottleneck [ˈbɑtəlˌnɛk] *n* **1** : cuello *m* de botella (en un camino) **2** : embotellamiento *m*, atasco *m* (de tráfico) **3** OBSTACLE : obstáculo *m*
bottom¹ [ˈbɑtəm] *adj* : más bajo, inferior, de abajo
bottom² *n* **1** : fondo *m* (de una caja, de una taza, del mar), pie *m* (de una escalera, una página, una montaña), asiento *m* (de una silla), parte *f* de abajo (de una pila) **2** CAUSE : origen *m*, causa *f* ⟨to get to the bottom of : llegar al fondo de⟩ **3** BUTTOCKS : trasero *m*, nalgas *fpl*
bottomless [ˈbɑtəmləs] *adj* : sin fondo, sin límites
botulism [ˈbɑtʃəˌlɪzəm] *n* : botulismo *m*
boudoir [bəˈdwɑr, bʊ-; ˈbuːˌ-, ˈbʊ-] *n* : tocador *m*
bough [ˈbaʊ] *n* : rama *f*
bought → **buy¹**
bouillon [ˈbuːˌjɑn; ˈbʊlˌjɑn, -jən] *n* : caldo *m*
boulder [ˈboːldər] *n* : canto *m* rodado, roca *f* grande
boulevard [ˈbʊləˌvɑrd, ˈbuː-] *n* : bulevar *m*, boulevard *m*
bounce¹ [ˈbaʊnts] *v* **bounced; bouncing** *vt* : hacer rebotar — *vi* : rebotar
bounce² *n* : rebote *m*
bouncy [ˈbaʊntsi] *adj* **bouncier; -est 1** LIVELY : vivo, exuberante, animado **2** RESILIENT : elástico, flexible **3** : que rebota (dícese de una pelota)
bound¹ [ˈbaʊnd] *vt* : delimitar, rodear — *vi* LEAP : saltar, dar brincos
bound² *adj* **1** OBLIGED : obligado **2** : encuadernado, empastado ⟨a book bound in leather : un libro encuadernado en cuero⟩ **3** DETERMINED : decidido, empeñado **4 to be bound to** : ser seguro que, tener que, no caber duda que ⟨it was bound to happen : tenía que suceder⟩ **5 bound for** : con rumbo a ⟨bound for Chicago : con rumbo a Chicago⟩ ⟨to be homeward bound : ir camino a casa⟩
bound³ *n* **1** LIMIT : límite *m* **2** LEAP : salto *m*, brinco *m*
boundary [ˈbaʊndri, -dəri] *n, pl* **-aries** : límite *m*, línea *f* divisoria, linde *mf*
boundless [ˈbaʊndləs] *adj* : sin límites, infinito
bounteous [ˈbaʊntiəs] *adj* **1** GENEROUS : generoso **2** ABUNDANT : copioso, abundante — **bounteously** *adv*
bountiful [ˈbaʊntɪfəl] *adj* **1** GENEROUS, LIBERAL : munificente, pródigo, generoso **2** ABUNDANT : copioso, abundante
bounty [ˈbaʊnti] *n, pl* **-ties 1** GENEROSITY : generosidad *f*, munificencia *f* **2** REWARD : recompensa *f*
bouquet [boːˈkeɪ, buː-] *n* **1** : ramo *m*, ramillete *m* **2** FRAGRANCE : bouquet *m*, aroma *m*
bourbon [ˈbɑrbən, ˈbʊr-] *n* : bourbon *m*, whisky *m* americano
bourgeois¹ [ˈbʊrʒˌwɑ, bʊrʒˈwɑ] *adj* : burgués
bourgeois² *n* : burgués *m*, -guesa *f*
bourgeoisie [ˌbʊrʒˌwɑˈzi] *n* : burguesía *f*
bout [ˈbaʊt] *n* **1** : encuentro *m*, combate *m* (en deportes) **2** ATTACK : ataque *m* (de una enfermedad) **3** PERIOD, SPELL : período *m* (de actividad)
boutique [buːˈtiːk] *n* : boutique *f*
bovine¹ [ˈboːˌvaɪn, -ˌviːn] *adj* : bovino, vacuno
bovine² *n* : bovino *m*
bow¹ [ˈbaʊ] *vi* **1** : hacer una reverencia, inclinarse **2** SUBMIT : ceder, resignarse, someterse — *vt* **1** LOWER : inclinar, bajar **2** BEND : doblar
bow² [ˈbaʊ] *n* **1** BOWING : reverencia *f*, inclinación *f* **2** : proa *f* (de un barco)
bow³ [ˈboː] *vi* CURVE : arquearse, doblarse
bow⁴ [ˈboː] *n* **1** ARCH, CURVE : arco *m*, curva *f* **2** : arco *m* (arma o vara para tocar varios instrumentos de música) **3** : lazo *m*, moño *m* ⟨to tie a bow : hacer un moño⟩
bowels [ˈbaʊəls] *npl* **1** INTESTINES : intestinos *mpl* **2** : entrañas *fpl* ⟨in the bowels of the earth : en las entrañas de la tierra⟩
bower [ˈbaʊər] *n* : enramada *f*
bowl¹ [ˈboːl] *vi* : jugar a los bolos
bowl² *n* : tazón *m*, cuenco *m*
bowler [ˈboːlər] *n* : jugador *m*, -dora *f* de bolos
bowling [ˈboːlɪŋ] *n* : bolos *mpl*
box¹ [ˈbɑks] *vt* **1** PACK : empaquetar, embalar, encajonar **2** SLAP : bofetear, cachetear — *vi* : boxear

box² *n* **1** CONTAINER : caja *f*, cajón *m* **2** COMPARTMENT : compartimento *m*, palco *m* (en el teatro) **3** SLAP : bofetada *f*, cachetada *f* **4** : boj *m* (planta)

boxcar ['bɑks,kɑr] *n* : vagón *m* de carga, furgón *m*

boxer ['bɑksər] *n* : boxeador *m*, -dora *f*

boxing ['bɑksɪŋ] *n* : boxeo *m*

box office *n* : taquilla *f*, boletería *f*

boxwood ['bɑks,wʊd] *n* : boj *m*

boy ['bɔɪ] *n* **1** : chico *m*, muchacho *m* **2** *or* **little boy** : niño *m*, chico *m* **3** SON : hijo *m*

boycott¹ ['bɔɪ,kɑt] *vt* : boicotear

boycott² *n* : boicot *m*

boyfriend ['bɔɪ,frɛnd] *n* **1** FRIEND : amigo *m* **2** SWEETHEART : novio *m*

boyhood ['bɔɪ,hʊd] *n* : niñez *f*

boyish ['bɔɪɪʃ] *adj* : de niño, juvenil

bra ['brɑ] → **brassiere**

brace¹ ['breɪs] *v* **braced; bracing** *vt* **1** PROP UP, SUPPORT : apuntalar, apoyar, sostener **2** INVIGORATE : vigorizar **3** REINFORCE : reforzar — *vi* **to brace oneself** PREPARE : prepararse

brace² *n* **1** : berbiquí *m* ⟨brace and bit : berbiquí y barrena⟩ **2** CLAMP, REINFORCEMENT : abrazadera *f*, refuerzo *m* **3** : llave *f* (signo de puntuación) **4 braces** *npl* : aparatos *mpl* (de ortodoncia), frenos *mpl Mex*

bracelet ['breɪslət] *n* : brazalete *m*, pulsera *f*

bracken ['brækən] *n* : helecho *m*

bracket¹ ['brækət] *vt* **1** SUPPORT : asegurar, apuntalar **2** : poner entre corchetes **3** CATEGORIZE, GROUP : catalogar, agrupar

bracket² *n* **1** SUPPORT : soporte *m* **2** : corchete *m* (marca de puntuación) **3** CATEGORY, CLASS : clase *f*, categoría *f*

brackish ['brækɪʃ] *adj* : salobre

brad ['bræd] *n* : clavo *m* con cabeza pequeña, clavito *m*

brag¹ ['bræg] *vi* **bragged; bragging** : alardear, fanfarronear, jactarse

brag² *n* : alarde *m*, jactancia *f*, fanfarronada *f*

braggart ['brægərt] *n* : fanfarrón *m*, -rrona *f fam*; jactancioso *m*, -sa *f*

braid¹ ['breɪd] *vt* : trenzar

braid² *n* : trenza *f*

braille ['breɪl] *n* : braille *m*

brain¹ ['breɪn] *vt* : romper la crisma a, aplastar el cráneo a

brain² *n* **1** : cerebro *m* **2 brains** *npl* INTELLECT : inteligencia *f*, sesos *mpl*

brainless ['breɪnləs] *adj* : estúpido, tonto

brainstorm ['breɪn,stɔrm] *n* : idea *f* brillante, idea *f* genial

brainy ['breɪni] *adj* **brainier; -est** : inteligente, listo

braise ['breɪz] *vt* **braised; braising** : cocer a fuego lento, estofar

brake¹ ['breɪk] *v* **braked; braking** : frenar

brake² *n* : freno *m*

bramble ['bræmbəl] *n* : zarza *f*, zarzamora *f*

bran ['bræn] *n* : salvado *m*

branch¹ ['bræntʃ] *vi* **1** : echar ramas (dícese de una planta) **2** DIVERGE : ramificarse, separarse

branch² *n* **1** : rama *f* (de una planta) **2** EXTENSION : ramal *m* (de un camino, un ferrocarril, un río), rama *f* (de una familia o un campo de estudiar), sucursal *f* (de una empresa), agencia *f* (del gobierno)

brand¹ ['brænd] *vt* **1** : marcar (ganado) **2** LABEL : tachar, tildar ⟨they branded him as a liar : lo tacharon de mentiroso⟩

brand² *n* **1** : marca *f* (de ganado) **2** STIGMA : estigma *m* **3** MAKE : marca *f* ⟨brand name : marca de fábrica⟩

brandish ['brændɪʃ] *vt* : blandir

brand-new ['brænd'nu:, -'nju:] *adj* : nuevo, flamante

brandy ['brændi] *n, pl* **-dies** : brandy *m*

brash ['bræʃ] *adj* **1** IMPULSIVE : impulsivo, impetuoso **2** BRAZEN : excesivamente desenvuelto, descarado

brass ['bræs] *n* **1** : latón *m* **2** GALL, NERVE : descaro *m*, cara *f fam* **3** OFFICERS : mandamases *mpl fam*

brassiere [brə'zɪr, brɑ-] *n* : sostén *m*, brasier *m Col, Mex*

brassy ['bræsi] *adj* **brassier; -est** : dorado

brat ['bræt] *n* : mocoso *m*, -sa *f*; niño *m* mimado, niña *f* mimada

bravado [brə'vɑdo] *n, pl* **-does** *or* **-dos** : bravuconadas *fpl*, bravatas *fpl*

brave¹ ['breɪv] *vt* **braved; braving** : afrontar, hacer frente a

brave² *adj* **braver; bravest** : valiente, valeroso — **bravely** *adv*

brave³ *n* : guerrero *m* indio

bravery ['breɪvəri] *n* : valor *m*, valentía *f*

bravo ['brɑ,vo:] *n, pl* **-vos** : bravo *m*

brawl¹ ['brɔl] *vi* : pelearse, pegarse

brawl² *n* : pelea *f*, reyerta *f*

brawn ['brɔn] *n* : fuerza *f* muscular

brawny ['brɔni] *adj* **brawnier; -est** : musculoso

bray¹ ['breɪ] *vi* : rebuznar

bray² *n* : rebuzno *m*

brazen ['breɪzən] *adj* **1** : de latón **2** BOLD : descarado, directo

brazenly ['breɪzənli] *adv* : descaradamente, insolentemente

brazenness ['breɪzənnəs] *n* : descaro *m*, atrevimiento *m*

brazier ['breɪzər] *n* : brasero *m*

Brazilian [brə'zɪljən] *n* : brasileño *m*, -ña *f* — **Brazilian** *adj*

Brazil nut [brə'zɪl,nʌt] *n* : nuez *f* de Brasil

breach¹ ['bri:tʃ] *vt* **1** PENETRATE : abrir una brecha en, penetrar **2** VIOLATE : infringir, violar

breach² *n* **1** VIOLATION : infracción *f*, violación *f* ⟨breach of trust : abuso de confianza⟩ **2** GAP, OPENING : brecha *f*

bread[1] ['brɛd] *vt* : empanar
bread[2] *n* : pan *m*
breadth ['brɛtθ] *n* : ancho *m*, anchura *f*
breadwinner ['brɛd,wɪnər] *n* : sostén *m* de la familia
break[1] ['breɪk] *v* **broke** ['broːk]; **broken** ['broːkən]; **breaking** *vt* **1** SMASH : romper, quebrar **2** VIOLATE : infringir, violar, romper **3** SURPASS : batir, superar **4** CRUSH, RUIN : arruinar, deshacer, destrozar ⟨to break one's spirit : quebrantar su espíritu⟩ **5** : dar, comunicar ⟨to break the news : dar las noticias⟩ **6** INTERRUPT : cortar, interrumpir — *vi* **1** : romperse, quebrarse ⟨my calculator broke : se me rompió la calculadora⟩ **2** DISPERSE : dispersarse, despejarse **3** : estallar (dícese de una tormenta), romper (dícese del día) **4** CHANGE : cambiar (dícese del tiempo o de la voz) **5** DECREASE : bajar ⟨my fever broke : me bajó la fiebre⟩ **6** : divulgarse, revelarse ⟨the news broke : la noticia se divulgó⟩ **7 to break into** : forzar, abrir **8 to break out of** : escaparse de **9 to break through** : penetrar
break[2] *n* **1** : ruptura *f*, rotura *f*, fractura *f* (de un hueso), claro *m* (entre las nubes), cambio *m* (del tiempo) **2** CHANCE : oportunidad *f* ⟨a lucky break : un golpe de suerte⟩ **3** REST : descanso *m* ⟨to take a break : tomar(se) un descanso⟩
breakable ['breɪkəbəl] *adj* : quebradizo, frágil
breakage ['breɪkɪdʒ] *n* **1** BREAKING : rotura *f* **2** DAMAGE : destrozos *mpl*, daños *mpl*
breakdown ['breɪk,daʊn] *n* **1** : avería *f* (de máquinas), interrupción *f* (de comunicaciones), fracaso *m* (de negociaciones) **2** ANALYSIS : análisis *m*, desglose *m* **3** *or* **nervous breakdown** : crisis *f* nerviosa
break down *vi* **1** : estropearse, descomponerse ⟨the machine broke down : la máquina se descompuso⟩ **2** FAIL : fracasar **3** CRY : echarse a llorar — *vt* **1** DESTROY : derribar, echar abajo **2** OVERCOME : vencer (la resistencia), disipar (sospechas) **3** ANALYZE : analizar, descomponer
breaker ['breɪkər] *n* **1** WAVE : ola *f* grande **2** : interruptor *m* automático (de electricidad)
breakfast[1] ['brɛkfəst] *vi* : desayunar
breakfast[2] *n* : desayuno *m*
breakneck ['breɪk,nɛk] *adj* **at breakneck speed** : a una velocidad vertiginosa
break out *vi* **1** : salirse ⟨she broke out in spots : le salieron granos⟩ **2** ERUPT : estallar (dícese de una guerra, la violencia, etc.) **3** ESCAPE : fugarse, escaparse
breakup ['breɪk,əp] *n* **1** DIVISION : desintegración *f* **2** : ruptura *f*

break up *vt* **1** DIVIDE : dividir **2** : disolver (una muchedumbre, una pelea, etc.) — *vi* **1** BREAK : romperse **2** SEPARATE : deshacerse, separarse ⟨I broke up with him : terminé con él⟩
breast ['brɛst] *n* **1** : pecho *m*, seno *m* (de una mujer) **2** CHEST : pecho *m*
breastbone ['brɛst,boːn] *n* : esternón *m*
breast–feed ['brɛst,fiːd] *vt* **-fed** [-,fɛd]; **-feeding** : amamantar, darle de mamar (a un niño)
breath ['brɛθ] *n* **1** BREATHING : aliento *m* ⟨to hold one's breath : aguantar la respiración⟩ **2** BREEZE : soplo *m* ⟨a breath of fresh air : un soplo de aire fresco⟩
breathe ['briːð] *v* **breathed; breathing** *vi* **1** : respirar **2** LIVE : vivir, respirar — *vt* **1** : respirar, aspirar ⟨to breathe fresh air : respirar el aire fresco⟩ **2** UTTER : decir ⟨I won't breathe a word of this : no diré nada de esto⟩
breathless ['brɛθləs] *adj* : sin aliento, jadeante
breathlessly ['brɛθləsli] *adv* : entrecortadamente, jadeando
breathlessness ['brɛθləsnəs] *n* : dificultad *f* al respirar
breathtaking ['brɛθ,teɪkɪŋ] *adj* IMPRESSIVE : impresionante, imponente
breeches ['brɪtʃəz, 'briː-] *npl* : pantalones *mpl*, calzones *mpl*, bombachos *mpl*
breed[1] ['briːd] *v* **bred** ['brɛd]; **breeding** *vt* **1** : criar (animales) **2** ENGENDER : engendrar, producir ⟨familiarity breeds contempt : la confianza hace perder el respeto⟩ **3** RAISE, REAR : criar, educar — *vi* REPRODUCE : reproducirse
breed[2] *n* **1** : variedad *f* (de plantas), raza *f* (de animales) **2** CLASS : clase *f*, tipo *m*
breeder ['briːdər] *n* : criador *m*, -dora *f* (de animales); cultivador *m*, -dora *f* (de plantas)
breeze[1] ['briːz] *vi* **breezed; breezing** : pasar con ligereza ⟨to breeze in : entrar como si nada⟩
breeze[2] *n* : brisa *f*, soplo *m* (de aire)
breezy ['briːzi] *adj* **breezier; -est 1** AIRY, WINDY : aireado, ventoso **2** LIVELY : animado, alegre **3** NONCHALANT : despreocupado
brethren → **brother**
brevity ['brɛvəti] *n, pl* **-ties** : brevedad *f*, concisión *f*
brew[1] ['bruː] *vt* **1** : fabricar, elaborar (cerveza) **2** FOMENT : tramar, maquinar, fomentar — *vi* **1** : fabricar cerveza **2** : amenazar ⟨a storm is brewing : una tormenta amenaza⟩
brew[2] *n* **1** BEER : cerveza *f* **2** POTION : brebaje *m*
brewer ['bruːər] *n* : cervecero *m*, -ra *f*
brewery ['bruːəri, 'bruri] *n, pl* **-eries** : cervecería *f*
briar ['braɪər] → **brier**

bribe¹ ['braɪb] *vt* **bribed; bribing** : sobornar, cohechar, coimear *Arg, Chile, Peru*

bribe² *n* : soborno *m*, cohecho *m*, coima *f Arg, Chile, Peru*, mordida *f CA, Mex*

bribery ['braɪbəri] *n, pl* **-eries** : soborno *m*, cohecho *m*, coima *f*, mordida *f CA, Mex*

bric–a–brac ['brɪkə‚bræk] *npl* : baratijas *fpl*, chucherías *fpl*

brick¹ ['brɪk] *vt* **to brick up** : tabicar, tapiar

brick² *n* : ladrillo *m*

bricklayer ['brɪk‚leɪər] *n* : albañil *mf*

bricklaying ['brɪk‚leɪŋ] *n* : albañilería *f*

bridal ['braɪdəl] *adj* : nupcial, de novia

bride ['braɪd] *n* : novia *f*

bridegroom ['braɪd‚gru:m] *n* : novio *m*

bridesmaid ['braɪdz‚meɪd] *n* : dama *f* de honor

bridge¹ ['brɪdʒ] *vt* **bridged; bridging 1** : tender un puente sobre **2 to bridge the gap** : salvar las diferencias

bridge² *n* **1** : puente *m* **2** : caballete *m* (de la nariz) **3** : puente *m* de mando (de un barco) **4** DENTURE : puente *m* (dental) **5** : bridge *m* (juego de naipes)

bridle¹ ['braɪdəl] *v* **-dled; -dling** *vt* **1** : embridar (un caballo) **2** RESTRAIN : refrenar, dominar, contener — *vi* **to bridle at** : molestarse por, picarse por

bridle² *n* : brida *f*

brief¹ ['bri:f] *vt* : dar órdenes a, instruir

brief² *adj* : breve, sucinto, conciso

brief³ *n* **1** : resumen *m*, sumario *m* **2 briefs** *npl* : calzoncillos *mpl*

briefcase ['bri:f‚keɪs] *n* : portafolio *m*, maletín *m*

briefly ['bri:fli] *adv* : brevemente, por poco tiempo ⟨to speak briefly : discursar en pocas palabras⟩

brier ['braɪər] *n* **1** BRAMBLE : zarza *f*, rosal *m* silvestre **2** HEATH : brezo *m* veteado

brig ['brɪg] *n* **1** : bergantín *m* (barco) **2** : calabozo *m* (en un barco)

brigade [brɪ'geɪd] *n* : brigada *f*

brigadier general [‚brɪgə'dɪr] *n* : general *m* de brigada

brigand ['brɪgənd] *n* : bandolero *m*, -ra *f*; forajido *m*, -da *f*

bright ['braɪt] *adj* **1** : brillante (dícese del sol, de los ojos), vivo (dícese de un color), claro, fuerte **2** CHEERFUL : alegre, animado ⟨bright and early : muy temprano⟩ **3** INTELLIGENT : listo, inteligente ⟨a bright idea : una idea luminosa⟩

brighten ['braɪtən] *vt* **1** ILLUMINATE : iluminar **2** ENLIVEN : alegrar, animar — *vi* **1** : hacerse más brillante **2 to brighten up** : animarse, alegrarse, mejorar

brightly ['braɪtli] *adv* : vivamente, intensamente, alegremente

brightness ['braɪtnəs] *n* **1** LUMINOSITY : luminosidad *f*, brillantez *f*, resplandor *m*, brillo *m* **2** CHEERFULNESS : alegría *f*, ánimo *m*

brilliance ['brɪljənts] *n* **1** BRIGHTNESS : resplandor *m*, fulgor *m*, brillo *m*, brillantez *f* **2** INTELLIGENCE : inteligencia *f*, brillantez *f*

brilliancy ['brɪljəntsi] → **brilliance**

brilliant ['brɪljənt] *adj* : brillante

brilliantly ['brɪljəntli] *adv* : brillantemente, con brillantez

brim¹ ['brɪm] *vi* **brimmed; brimming 1** *or* **to brim over** : desbordarse, rebosar **2 to brim with tears** : llenarse de lágrimas

brim² *n* **1** : ala *f* (de un sombrero) **2** : borde *m* (de una taza o un vaso)

brimful ['brɪm'fʊl] *adj* : lleno hasta el borde, repleto, rebosante

brimless ['brɪmləs] *adj* : sin ala

brimstone ['brɪm‚sto:n] *n* : azufre *m*

brindled ['brɪndəld] *adj* : manchado, pinto

brine ['braɪn] *n* **1** : salmuera *f*, escabeche *m* (para encurtir) **2** OCEAN : océano *m*, mar *m*

bring ['brɪŋ] *vt* **brought** ['brɔt]; **bringing 1** CARRY : traer ⟨bring me some coffee : tráigame un café⟩ **2** PRODUCE : traer, producir, conseguir ⟨his efforts will bring him success : sus esfuerzos le conseguirán el éxito⟩ **3** PERSUADE : convencer, persuadir **4** YIELD : rendir, alcanzar, venderse por ⟨to bring a good price : alcanzar un precio alto⟩ **5 to bring to an end** : terminar (con) **6 to bring to light** : sacar a la luz

bring about *vt* : ocasionar, provocar, determinar

bring forth *vt* PRODUCE : producir

bring out *vt* : sacar, publicar (un libro, etc.)

bring to *vt* REVIVE : resucitar

bring up *vt* **1** REAR : criar **2** MENTION : sacar, mencionar

brininess ['braɪnɪnəs] *n* : salinidad *f*

brink ['brɪŋk] *n* : borde *m*

briny ['braɪni] *adj* **brinier; -est** : salobre

briquette *or* **briquet** [brɪ'kɛt] *n* : briqueta *f*

brisk ['brɪsk] *adj* **1** LIVELY : rápido, enérgico, brioso **2** INVIGORATING : fresco, estimulante

brisket ['brɪskət] *n* : falda *f*

briskly ['brɪskli] *adv* : rápidamente, enérgicamente, con brío

briskness ['brɪsknəs] *n* : brío *m*, rapidez *f*

bristle¹ ['brɪsəl] *vi* **-tled; -tling 1** : erizarse, ponerse de punta **2** : enfurecerse, enojarse ⟨she bristled at the suggestion : se enfureció ante tal sugerencia⟩ **3** : estar plagado, estar repleto ⟨a city bristling with tourists : una ciudad repleta de turistas⟩

bristle² *n* : cerda *f* (de un animal), pelo *m* (de una planta)

bristly ['brɪsəli] *adj* **bristlier; -est** : áspero y erizado

British¹ ['brɪtɪʃ] *adj* : británico

British² *n* **the British** *npl* : los británicos

brittle ['brɪtəl] *adj* **-tler; -tlest** : frágil, quebradizo

brittleness ['brɪtəlnəs] *n* : fragilidad *f*

broach ['broːtʃ] *vt* BRING UP : mencionar, abordar, sacar

broad ['brɔd] *adj* **1** WIDE : ancho **2** SPACIOUS : amplio, extenso **3** FULL : pleno ⟨in broad daylight : en pleno día⟩ **4** OBVIOUS : claro, evidente **5** TOLERANT : tolerante, liberal **6** GENERAL : general **7** ESSENTIAL : principal, esencial ⟨the broad outline : los rasgos esenciales⟩

broadcast¹ ['brɔd,kæst] *vt* **-cast; -casting 1** SCATTER : esparcir, diseminar **2** CIRCULATE, SPREAD : divulgar, difundir, propagar **3** TRANSMIT : transmitir, emitir

broadcast² *n* **1** TRANSMISSION : transmisión *f*, emisión *f* **2** PROGRAM : programa *m*, emisión *f*

broadcaster ['brɔd,kæstər] *n* : presentador *m*, -dora *f*; locutor *m*, -tora *f*

broadcloth ['brɔd,klɔθ] *n* : paño *m* fino

broaden ['brɔdən] *vt* : ampliar, ensanchar — *vi* : ampliarse, ensancharse

broadloom ['brɔd,luːm] *adj* : tejido en telar ancho

broadly ['brɔdli] *adv* **1** GENERALLY : en general, aproximadamente **2** WIDELY : extensivamente

broad–minded ['brɔd'maɪndəd] *adj* : tolerante, de amplias miras

broad-mindedness [brɔd'maɪndədnəs] *n* : tolerancia *f*

broadside ['brɔd,saɪd] *n* **1** VOLLEY : andanada *f* **2** ATTACK : ataque *m*, invectiva *f*, andanada *f*

brocade [bro'keɪd] *n* : brocado *m*

broccoli ['brɑkəli] *n* : brócoli *m*, brécol *m*

brochure [bro'ʃʊr] *n* : folleto *m*

brogue ['broːg] *n* : acento *m* irlandés

broil¹ ['brɔɪl] *vt* : asar a la parrilla

broil² *n* : asado *m*

broiler ['brɔɪlər] *n* **1** GRILL : parrilla *f* **2** : pollo *m* para asar

broke¹ ['broːk] → **break¹**

broke² *adj* : pelado, arruinado ⟨to go broke : arruinarse, quebrar⟩

broken ['broːkən] *adj* **1** DAMAGED, SHATTERED : roto, quebrado, fracturado **2** IRREGULAR, UNEVEN : accidentado, irregular, recortado **3** VIOLATED : roto, quebrantado **4** INTERRUPTED : interrumpido, descontinuo **5** CRUSHED : abatido, quebrantado ⟨a broken man : un hombre destrozado⟩ **6** IMPERFECT : mal ⟨to speak broken English : hablar el inglés con dificultad⟩

brokenhearted [,broːkən'hɑrtəd] *adj* : descorazonado, desconsolado

broker¹ ['broːkər] *vt* : hacer corretaje de

broker² *n* **1** : agente *mf*; corredor *m*, -dora *f* **2** → **stockbroker**

brokerage ['broːkərɪdʒ] *n* : corretaje *m*, agencia *f* de corredores

bromine ['bro:,miːn] *n* : bromo *m*

bronchitis [brɑn'kaɪtəs, brɑŋ-] *n* : bronquitis *f*

bronze¹ ['brɑnz] *vt* **bronzed; bronzing** : broncear

bronze² *n* : bronce *m*

brooch ['broːtʃ, 'bruːtʃ] *n* : broche *m*, prendedor *m*

brood¹ ['bruːd] *vt* **1** INCUBATE : empollar, incubar **2** PONDER : sopesar, considerar — *vi* **1** INCUBATE : empollar **2** REFLECT : rumiar, reflexionar **3** WORRY : ponerse melancólico, inquietarse

brood² *adj* : de cría

brood³ *n* : nidada *f* (de pájaros), camada *f* (de mamíferos)

brooder ['bruːdər] *n* **1** THINKER : pensador *m*, -dora *f* **2** INCUBATOR : incubadora *f*

brook¹ ['brʊk] *vt* TOLERATE : tolerar, admitir

brook² *n* : arroyo *m*

broom ['bruːm, 'brʊm] *n* **1** : retama *f*, hiniesta *f* **2** : escoba *f* (para barrer)

broomstick ['bruːm,stɪk, 'brʊm-] *n* : palo *m* de escoba

broth ['brɔθ] *n*, *pl* **broths** ['brɔθs, 'brɔðz] : caldo *m*

brothel ['brɑθəl, 'brɔ-] *n* : burdel *m*

brother ['brʌðər] *n*, *pl* **brothers** *also* **brethren** ['brɔðrən, -ðərn] **1** : hermano *m* **2** KINSMAN : pariente *m*, familiar *m*

brotherhood ['brʌðər,hʊd] *n* **1** FELLOWSHIP : fraternidad *f* **2** ASSOCIATION : hermandad *f*

brother–in–law ['brʌðərɪn,lɔ] *n*, *pl* **brothers–in–law** : cuñado *m*

brotherly ['brʌðərli] *adj* : fraternal

brought → **bring**

brow ['braʊ] *n* **1** EYEBROW : ceja *f* **2** FOREHEAD : frente *f* **3** : cima *f* ⟨the brow of a hill : la cima de una colina⟩

browbeat ['braʊ,biːt] *vt* **-beat; -beaten** [-,biːtən] *or* **-beat; -beating** : intimidar

brown¹ ['braʊn] *vt* **1** : dorar (en cocina) **2** TAN : broncear — *vi* **1** : dorarse (en cocina) **2** TAN : broncearse

brown² *adj* : marrón, café, castaño (dícese del pelo), moreno (dícese de la piel)

brown³ *n* : marrón *m*, café *m*

brownish ['braʊnɪʃ] *adj* : pardo

browse ['braʊz] *vi* **browsed; browsing 1** GRAZE : pacer **2** LOOK : mirar, echar un vistazo

bruin ['bruːɪn] *n* BEAR : oso *m*

bruise¹ ['bruːz] *vt* **bruised; bruising 1** : contusionar, machucar, magullar (a una persona) **2** DAMAGE : magullar, dañar (frutas) **3** CRUSH : majar **4** HURT : herir (los sentimientos)

bruise² *n* : moretón *m*, cardenal *m*, magulladura *f* (dícese de frutas)

brunch ['brʌntʃ] *n* : combinación *f* de desayuno y almuerzo

brunet¹ *or* **brunette** [bru'nɛt] *adj* : moreno

brunet² *or* **brunette** *n* : moreno *m*, -na *f*

brunt ['brʌnt] *n* **to bear the brunt of** : llevar el peso de, aguantar el mayor impacto de
brush¹ ['brʌʃ] *vt* **1** : cepillar ⟨to brush one's teeth : cepillarse uno los dientes⟩ **2** SWEEP : barrer, quitar con un cepillo **3** GRAZE : rozar **4 to brush off** DISREGARD : hacer caso omiso de, ignorar — *vi* **to brush up on** : repasar, refrescar, dar un repaso a
brush² *n* **1** *or* **brushwood** ['brʌʃ,wʊd] : broza *f* **2** SCRUB, UNDERBRUSH : maleza *f* **3** : cepillo *m*, pincel *m* (de artista), brocha *f* (de pintor) **4** TOUCH : roce *m* **5** SKIRMISH : escaramuza *f*
brush–off ['brʌʃ,ɒf] *n* **to give the brush–off to** : dar calabazas a
brusque ['brʌsk] *adj* : brusco — **brusquely** *adv*
brussels sprout ['brʌsəlz,spraʊt] *n* : col *f* de Bruselas
brutal ['bruːt̬əl] *adj* : brutal, cruel, salvaje — **brutally** *adv*
brutality [bruːˈtælət̬i] *n, pl* **-ties** : brutalidad *f*
brutalize ['bruːt̬əl,aɪz] *vt* **-ized; -izing** : brutalizar, maltratar
brute¹ ['bruːt] *adj* : bruto ⟨brute force : fuerza bruta⟩
brute² *n* **1** BEAST : bestia *f*, animal *m* **2** : bruto *m*, -ta *f*; bestia *mf* (persona)
brutish ['bruːt̬ɪʃ] *adj* **1** : de animal **2** CRUEL : brutal, salvaje **3** STUPID : bruto, estúpido
bubble¹ ['bʌbəl] *vi* **-bled; -bling** : burbujear ⟨to bubble over with joy : rebosar de alegría⟩
bubble² *n* : burbuja *f*
bubbly ['bʌbəli] *adj* **bubblier; -est 1** BUBBLING : burbujeante **2** LIVELY : vivaz, lleno de vida
bubonic plague [buːˈbɑnɪk, bjuː-] *n* : peste *f* bubónica
buccaneer [,bʌkəˈnɪr] *n* : bucanero *m*
buck¹ ['bʌk] *vi* **1** : corcovear (dícese de un caballo o un burro) **2** JOLT : dar sacudidas **3 to buck against** : resistirse a, rebelarse contra **4 to buck up** : animarse, levantar el ánimo — *vt* OPPOSE : oponerse a, ir en contra de
buck² *n, pl* **buck** *or* **bucks 1** : animal *m* macho, ciervo *m* (macho) **2** DOLLAR : dólar *m* **3 to pass the buck** *fam* : pasar la pelota *fam*
bucket ['bʌkət] *n* : balde *m*, cubo *m*, cubeta *f Mex*
bucketful ['bʌkət,fʊl] *n* : balde *m* lleno
buckle¹ ['bʌkəl] *v* **-led; -ling** *vt* **1** FASTEN : abrochar **2** BEND, TWIST : combar, torcer — *vi* **1** BEND, TWIST : combarse, torcerse, doblarse (dícese de las rodillas) **2 to buckle down** : ponerse a trabajar con esmero **3 to buckle up** : abrocharse
buckle² *n* **1** : hebilla *f* **2** TWISTING : torcedura *f*
buckshot ['bʌk,ʃɑt] *n* : perdigón *m*
buckskin ['bʌk,skɪn] *n* : gamuza *f*

bucktooth ['bʌk,tuːθ] *n* : diente *m* saliente, diente *m* salido
buckwheat ['bʌk,ʍiːt] *n* : trigo *m* rubión, alforfón *m*
bucolic [bjuːˈkɑlɪk] *adj* : bucólico
bud¹ ['bʌd] *v* **budded; budding** *vt* GRAFT : injertar — *vi* : brotar, hacer brotes
bud² *n* : brote *m*, yema *f*, capullo *m* (de una flor)
Buddhism ['buː,dɪzəm, 'bʊ-] *n* : budismo *m*
Buddhist ['buː,dɪst, 'bʊ-] *n* : budista *mf* — **Buddhist** *adj*
buddy ['bʌdi] *n, pl* **-dies** : amigo *m*, -ga *f*; compinche *mf fam*; cuate *m*, -ta *f Mex fam*
budge ['bʌdʒ] *vi* **budged; budging 1** MOVE : moverse, desplazarse **2** YIELD : ceder
budget¹ ['bʌdʒət] *vt* : presupuestar (gastos), asignar (dinero) — *vi* : presupuestar, planear el presupuesto
budget² *n* : presupuesto
budgetary ['bʌdʒə,tɛri] *adj* : presupuestario
buff¹ ['bʌf] *vt* POLISH : pulir, sacar brillo a, lustrar
buff² *adj* : beige, amarillento
buff³ *n* **1** : beige *m*, amarillento *m* **2** ENTHUSIAST : aficionado *m*, -da *f*; entusiasta *mf*
buffalo ['bʌfə,loː] *n, pl* **-lo** *or* **-loes 1** : búfalo *m* **2** BISON : bisonte *m*
buffer ['bʌfər] *n* **1** BARRIER : barrera *f* ⟨buffer state : estado tapón⟩ **2** SHOCK ABSORBER : amortiguador *m*
buffet¹ ['bʌfət] *vt* : golpear, zarandear, sacudir
buffet² *n* BLOW : golpe *m*
buffet³ [,bʌˈfeɪ, ,buː-] *n* **1** : bufete *m*, bufé *m* (comida) **2** SIDEBOARD : aparador *m*
buffoon [,bʌˈfuːn] *n* : bufón *m*, -fona *f*; payaso *m*, -sa *f*
buffoonery [,bʌˈfuːnəri] *n, pl* **-eries** : bufonada *f*, payasada *f*
bug¹ ['bʌg] *vt* **bugged; bugging 1** PESTER : fastidiar, molestar **2** : ocultar micrófonos en
bug² *n* **1** INSECT : bicho *m*, insecto *m* **2** DEFECT : defecto *m*, falla *f*, problema *m* **3** GERM : microbio *m*, virus *m* **4** MICROPHONE : micrófono *m*
bugaboo ['bʌgə,buː] → **bogey**
bugbear ['bʌg,bær] *n* : pesadilla *f*, coco *m*
buggy ['bʌgi] *n, pl* **-gies** : calesa *f* (tirada por caballos), cochecito *m* (para niños)
bugle ['bjuːgəl] *n* : clarín *m*, corneta *f*
bugler ['bjuːgələr] *n* : corneta *mf*
build¹ ['bɪld] *v* **built** ['bɪlt]; **building** *vt* **1** CONSTRUCT : construir, edificar, ensamblar, levantar **2** DEVELOP : desarrollar, elaborar, forjar **3** INCREASE : incrementar, aumentar — *vi* **to build up** : aumentar, intensificar
build² *n* PHYSIQUE : físico *m*, complexión *f*

builder ['bɪldər] *n* : constructor *m*, -tora *f*; contratista *mf*

building ['bɪldɪŋ] *n* 1 EDIFICE : edificio *m* 2 CONSTRUCTION : construcción *f*

built–in ['bɪlt'ɪn] *adj* 1 : empotrado ⟨built-in cabinets : armarios empotrados⟩ 2 INHERENT : incorporado, intrínseco

bulb ['bʌlb] *n* 1 : bulbo *m* (de una planta), cabeza *f* (de ajo), cubeta *f* (de un termómetro) 2 LIGHTBULB : bombilla *f*, foco *m*, bombillo *m* CA, Col, Ven

bulbous ['bʌlbəs] *adj* : bulboso

Bulgarian [bʌl'gæriən, bʊl-] *n* 1 : búlgaro *m*, -ra *f* 2 : búlgaro *m* (idioma) — **Bulgarian** *adj*

bulge[1] ['bʌldʒ] *vi* **bulged; bulging** : abultar, sobresalir

bulge[2] *n* : bulto *m*, protuberancia *f*

bulk[1] ['bʌlk] *vt* : hinchar — *vi* EXPAND, SWELL : ampliarse, hincharse

bulk[2] *n* 1 SIZE, VOLUME : volumen *m*, tamaño *m* 2 FIBER : fibra *f* 3 MASS : mole *f* 4 **the bulk of** : la mayor parte de 5 **in ~** : en grandes cantidades

bulkhead ['bʌlk,hɛd] *n* : mamparo *m*

bulky ['bʌlki] *adj* **bulkier; -est** : voluminoso, grande

bull[1] ['bʊl] *adj* : macho

bull[2] *n* 1 : toro *m*, macho *m* (de ciertas especies) 2 : bula *f* (papal) 3 DECREE : decreto *m*, edicto *m*

bulldog ['bʊl,dɔg] *n* : bulldog *m*

bulldoze ['bʊl,do:z] *vt* **-dozed; -dozing** 1 LEVEL : nivelar (el terreno), derribar (un edificio) 2 FORCE : forzar ⟨he bulldozed his way through : se abrió paso a codazos⟩

bulldozer ['bʊl,do:zər] *n* : bulldozer *m*

bullet ['bʊlət] *n* : bala *f*

bulletin ['bʊlətən, -lətən] *n* 1 NOTICE : comunicado *m*, anuncio *m*, boletín *m* 2 NEWSLETTER : boletín *m* (informativo)

bulletin board *n* : tablón *m* de anuncios

bulletproof ['bʊlət,pru:f] *adj* : antibalas, a prueba de balas

bullfight ['bʊl,faɪt] *n* : corrida *f* (de toros)

bullfighter ['bʊl,faɪtər] *n* : torero *m*, -ra *f*; matador *m*

bullfrog ['bʊl,frɔg] *n* : rana *f* toro

bullheaded ['bʊl'hɛdəd] *adj* : testarudo

bullion ['bʊljən] *n* : oro *m* en lingotes, plata *f* en lingotes

bullock ['bʊlək] *n* 1 STEER : buey *m*, toro *m* castrado 2 : toro *m* joven, novillo *m*

bull's–eye ['bʊlz,aɪ] *n*, *pl* **bull's–eyes** : diana *f*, blanco *m*

bully[1] ['bʊli] *vt* **-lied; -lying** : intimidar, amedrentar, mangonear

bully[2] *n*, *pl* **-lies** : matón *m*; bravucón *m*, -cona *f*

bulrush ['bʊl,rʌʃ] *n* : especie *f* de junco

bulwark ['bʊl,wərk, -,wɔrk; 'bʌl,wərk] *n* : baluarte *m*, bastión *f*

bum[1] ['bʌm] *v* **bummed; bumming** *vi* **to bum around** : vagabundear, vagar — *vt* : gorronear *fam*, sablear *fam*

bum[2] *adj* : inútil, malo ⟨a bum rap : una acusación falsa⟩

bum[3] *n* 1 LOAFER : vago *m*, -ga *f* 2 HOBO, TRAMP : vagabundo *m*, -da *f*

bumblebee ['bʌmbəl,bi:] *n* : abejorro *m*

bump[1] ['bʌmp] *vt* : chocar contra, golpear contra, dar ⟨to bump one's head : darse (un golpe) en la cabeza⟩ — *vi* **to bump into** MEET : encontrarse con, tropezarse con

bump[2] *n* 1 BULGE : bulto *m*, protuberancia *f* 2 IMPACT : golpe *m*, choque *m* 3 JOLT : sacudida *f*

bumper[1] ['bʌmpər] *adj* : extraordinario, récord ⟨a bumper crop : una cosecha abundante⟩

bumper[2] *n* : parachoques *mpl*

bumpkin ['bʌmpkən] *n* : palurdo *m*, -da *f*

bumpy ['bʌmpi] *adj* **bumpier; -est** : desigual, lleno de baches (dícese de un camino), agitado (dícese de un vuelo en avión)

bun ['bʌn] *n* : bollo *m*

bunch[1] ['bʌntʃ] *vt* : agrupar, amontonar — *vi* **to bunch up** : amontonarse, agruparse, fruncirse (dícese de una tela)

bunch[2] *n* : grupo *m*, montón *m*, ramo *m* (de flores)

bundle[1] ['bʌndəl] *vt* **-dled; -dling** : liar, atar

bundle[2] *n* 1 : fardo *m*, atado *m*, bulto *m*, haz *m* (de palos) 2 PARCEL : paquete *m* 3 LOAD : montón *m* ⟨a bundle of money : un montón de dinero⟩

bungalow ['bʌŋgə,lo:] *n* : tipo de casa de un solo piso

bungle[1] ['bʌŋgəl] *vt* **-gled; -gling** : echar a perder, malograr

bungle[2] *n* : chapuza *f*, desatino *m*

bungler ['bʌŋgələr] *n* : chapucero *m*, -ra *f*; inepto *m*, -ta *f*

bunion ['bʌnjən] *n* : juanete *m*

bunk[1] ['bʌŋk] *vi* : dormir (en una litera)

bunk[2] *n* 1 *or* **bunk bed** : litera *f* 2 NONSENSE : tonterías *fpl*, bobadas *fpl*

bunker ['bʌŋkər] *n* 1 : carbonera *f* (en un barco) 2 SHELTER : búnker *m*

bunny ['bʌni] *n*, *pl* **-nies** : conejo *m*, -ja *f*

buoy[1] ['bu:i, 'bɔɪ] *vt* **to buoy up** 1 : mantener a flote 2 CHEER, HEARTEN : animar, levantar el ánimo a

buoy[2] *n* : boya *f*

buoyancy ['bɔɪəntsi, 'bu:jən-] *n* 1 : flotabilidad *f* 2 OPTIMISM : confianza *f*, optimismo *m*

buoyant ['bɔɪənt, 'bu:jənt] *adj* : boyante, flotante

bur *or* **burr** ['bər] *n* : abrojo *m* (de una planta)

burden[1] ['bərdən] *vt* : cargar, oprimir

burden[2] *n* : carga *f*, peso *m*

burdensome ['bərdənsəm] *adj* : oneroso

burdock ['bər,dɑk] *n* : bardana *f*

bureau ['bjʊro] *n* 1 CHEST OF DRAWERS : cómoda *f* 2 DEPARTMENT : departamento *m* (del gobierno) 3 AGENCY

: agencia *f* ⟨travel bureau : agencia de viajes⟩

bureaucracy [bjʊ'rɑkrəsi] *n, pl* **-cies** : burocracia *f*

bureaucrat ['bjʊrə,kræt] *n* : burócrata *mf*

bureaucratic [,bjʊrə'krætɪk] *adj* : burocrático

burgeon ['bərdʒən] *vi* : florecer, retoñar, crecer

burglar ['bərglər] *n* : ladrón *m*, -drona *f*

burglarize ['bərglə,raɪz] *vt* **-ized; -izing** : robar

burglary ['bərgləri] *n, pl* **-glaries** : robo *m*

burgle ['bərgəl] *vt* **-gled; -gling** : robar

burgundy ['bərgəndi] *n, pl* **-dies** : borgoña *m*, vino *m* de Borgoña

burial ['beriəl] *n* : entierro *m*, sepelio *m*

burlap ['bər,læp] *n* : arpillera *f*

burlesque¹ [bər'lesk] *vt* **-lesqued; -lesquing** : parodiar

burlesque² *n* **1** PARODY : parodia *f* **2** REVUE : revista *f* (musical)

burly ['bərli] *adj* **-lier; -liest** : fornido, corpulento, musculoso

Burmese [,bər'miːz, -'miːs] *n* : birmano *m*, -na *f* — **Burmese** *adj*

burn¹ ['bərn] *v* **burned** ['bərnd, 'bərnt] *or* **burnt** ['bərnt]; **burning** *vt* **1** : quemar, incendiar ⟨to burn a building : incendiar un edificio⟩ ⟨I burned my hand : me quemé la mano⟩ **2** CONSUME : usar, gastar, consumir — *vi* **1** : arder (dícese de un fuego o un edificio), quemarse (dícese de la comida, etc.) **2** : estar prendido, estar encendido ⟨we left the lights burning : dejamos las luces encendidas⟩ **3 to burn out** : consumirse, apagarse **4 to burn with** : arder de ⟨he was burning with jealousy : ardía de celos⟩

burn² *n* : quemadura *f*

burner ['bərnər] *n* : quemador *m*

burnish ['bərnɪʃ] *vt* : bruñir

burp¹ ['bərp] *vi* : eructar — *vt* : hacer eructar

burp² *n* : eructo *m*

burr → **bur**

burro ['bəro, 'bʊr-] *n, pl* **-os** : burro *m*

burrow¹ ['bəro] *vi* **1** : cavar, hacer una madriguera ⟨to burrow into : hurgar en — *vt* : cavar, excavar

burrow² *n* : madriguera *f*, conejera *f* (de un conejo)

bursar ['bərsər] *n* : administrador *m*, -dora *f*

bursitis [bər'saɪtəs] *n* : bursitis *f*

burst¹ ['bərst] *v* **burst; bursting** *vi* **1** : reventarse (dícese de una llanta o un globo), estallar (dícese de obuses o fuegos artificiales), romperse (dícese de un dique) **2 to burst in** : irrumpir en **3 to burst into** : empezar a, echar a ⟨to burst into tears : echarse a llorar⟩ — *vt* : reventar

burst² *n* **1** EXPLOSION : estallido *m*, explosión *f*, reventón *m* (de una llanta) **2** OUTBURST : arranque *m* (de actividad,

de velocidad), arrebato *m* (de ira), salva *f* (de aplausos)

Burundian [bʊ'ruːndiən, -'rʊn-] *n* : burundés *m*, -desa *f* — **Burundian** *adj*

bury ['beri] *vt* **buried; burying 1** INTER : enterrar, sepultar **2** HIDE : esconder, ocultar **3 to bury oneself in** : enfrascarse en

bus¹ ['bʌs] *v* **bused** *or* **bussed** ['bʌst]; **busing** *or* **bussing** ['bʌsɪŋ] *vt* : transportar en autobús — *vi* : viajar en autobús

bus² *n* : autobús *m*, bus *m*, camión *m* *Mex*, colectivo *m* *Arg, Bol, Peru*

busboy ['bʌs,bɔɪ] *n* : ayudante *mf* de camarero

bush ['bʊʃ] *n* **1** SHRUB : arbusto *m*, mata *f* **2** THICKET : maleza *f*, matorral *m*

bushel ['bʊʃəl] *n* : medida de áridos igual a 35.24 litros

bushing ['bʊʃɪŋ] *n* : cojinete *m*

bushy ['bʊʃi] *adj* **bushier; -est** : espeso, poblado ⟨bushy eyebrows : cejas pobladas⟩

busily ['bɪzəli] *adv* : afanosamente, diligentemente

business ['bɪznəs, -nəz] *n* **1** OCCUPATION : ocupación *f*, oficio *m* **2** DUTY, MISSION : misión *f*, deber *m*, responsabilidad *f* **3** ESTABLISHMENT, FIRM : empresa *f*, firma *f*, negocio *m*, comercio *m* **4** COMMERCE : negocios *mpl*, comercio *m* **5** AFFAIR, MATTER : asunto *m*, cuestión *f*, cosa *f* ⟨it's none of your business : no es asunto tuyo⟩

businessman ['bɪznəs,mæn, -nəz-] *n, pl* **-men** [-mən, -,mɛn] : empresario *m*, hombre *m* de negocios

businesswoman ['bɪznəs,wʊmən, -nəz-] *n, pl* **-women** [-,wɪmən] : empresaria *f*, mujer *f* de negocios

bust¹ ['bʌst] *vt* **1** BREAK, SMASH : romper, estropear, destrozar **2** TAME : domar, amansar (un caballo) — *vi* : romperse, estropearse

bust² *n* **1** : busto *m* (en la escultura) **2** BREASTS : pecho *m*, senos *mpl*, busto *m*

bustle¹ ['bʌsəl] *vi* **-tled; -tling to bustle about** : ir y venir, trajinar, ajetrearse

bustle² *n* **1** *or* **hustle and bustle** : bullicio *m*, ajetreo *m* **2** : polisón *m* (en la ropa femenina)

busy¹ ['bɪzi] *vt* **busied; busying to busy oneself with** : ocuparse con, ponerse a, entretenerse con

busy² *adj* **busier; -est 1** OCCUPIED : ocupado, atareado ⟨he's busy working : está ocupado en su trabajo⟩ ⟨the telephone was busy : el teléfono estaba ocupado⟩ **2** BUSTLING : concurrido, animado ⟨a busy street : una calle concurrida, una calle con mucho tránsito⟩

busybody ['bɪzi,bɑdi] *n, pl* **-bodies** : entrometido *m*, -da *f*; metiche *mf* *fam*; metomentodo *mf*

but¹ ['bʌt] *conj* **1** THAT : que ⟨there is no doubt but he is lazy : no cabe duda que sea perezoso⟩ **2** WITHOUT : sin que **3** NEVERTHELESS : pero, no obstante, sin embargo ⟨I called her but she didn't answer : la llamé pero no contestó⟩ **4** YET : pero ⟨he was poor but proud : era pobre pero orgulloso⟩

but² *prep* EXCEPT : excepto, menos ⟨everyone but Carlos : todos menos Carlos⟩ ⟨the last but one : el penúltimo⟩

butcher¹ [ˈbʊtʃər] *vt* **1** SLAUGHTER : matar (animales) **2** KILL : matar, asesinar, masacrar **3** BOTCH : estropear, hacer una chapuza

butcher² *n* **1** : carnicero *m*, -ra *f* **2** KILLER : asesino *m*, -na *f* **3** BUNGLER : chapucero *m*, -ra *f*

butler [ˈbʌtlər] *n* : mayordomo *m*

butt¹ [ˈbʌt] *vt* **1** : embestir (con los cuernos), darle un cabezazo a **2** ABUT : colindar con, bordear — *vi* **to butt in 1** INTERRUPT : interrumpir **2** MEDDLE : entrometerse, meterse

butt² *n* **1** BUTTING : embestida *f* (de cuernos), cabezazo *m* **2** TARGET : blanco *m* ⟨the butt of their jokes : el blanco de sus bromas⟩ **3** BOTTOM, END : extremo *m*, culata *f* (de un rifle), colilla *f* (de un cigarrillo)

butte [ˈbjuːt] *n* : colina *f* empinada y aislada

butter¹ [ˈbʌtər] *vt* **1** : untar con mantequilla **2 to butter up** : halagar

butter² *n* : mantequilla *f*

buttercup [ˈbʌtərˌkʌp] *n* : ranúnculo *m*

butterfat [ˈbʌtərˌfæt] *n* : grasa *f* de la leche

butterfly [ˈbʌtərˌflaɪ] *n, pl* **-flies** : mariposa *f*

buttermilk [ˈbʌtərˌmɪlk] *n* : suero *m* de la leche

butternut [ˈbʌtərˌnʌt] *n* : nogal *m* ceniciento (árbol)

butterscotch [ˈbʌtərˌskɑtʃ] *n* : caramelo *m* duro hecho con mantequilla

buttery [ˈbʌtəri] *adj* : mantecoso

buttocks [ˈbʌtəks, -ˌtaks] *npl* : nalgas *fpl*, trasero *m*

button¹ [ˈbʌtən] *vt* : abrochar, abotonar — *vi* : abrocharse, abotonarse

button² *n* : botón *m*

buttonhole¹ [ˈbʌtənˌhoːl] *vt* **-holed; -holing** : acorralar

buttonhole² *n* : ojal *m*

buttress¹ [ˈbʌtrəs] *vt* : apoyar, reforzar

buttress² *n* **1** : contrafuerte *m* (en la arquitectura) **2** SUPPORT : apoyo *m*, sostén *m*

buxom [ˈbʌksəm] *adj* : con mucho busto, con mucho pecho

buy¹ [ˈbaɪ] *vt* **bought** [ˈbɔt]; **buying** : comprar

buy² *n* BARGAIN : compra *f*, ganga *f*

buyer [ˈbaɪər] *n* : comprador *m*, -dora *f*

buzz¹ [ˈbʌz] *vi* : zumbar (dícese de un insecto), sonar (dícese de un teléfono o un despertador)

buzz² *n* **1** : zumbido *m* (de insectos) **2** : murmullo *m*, rumor *m* (de voces)

buzzard [ˈbʌzərd] *n* VULTURE : buitre *m*, zopilote *m* CA, Mex

buzzer [ˈbʌzər] *n* : timbre *m*, chicharra *f*

buzzword [ˈbʌzˌwərd] *n* : palabra *f* de moda

by¹ [ˈbaɪ] *adv* **1** NEAR : cerca ⟨he lives close by : vive muy cerca⟩ **2 to stop by** : pasar por casa, hacer una visita **3 to go by** : pasar ⟨they rushed by : pasaron corriendo⟩ **4 to put by** : reservar, poner a un lado **5 by and by** : poco después, dentro de poco **6 by and large** : en general

by² *prep* **1** NEAR : cerca de, al lado de, junto a **2** VIA : por ⟨she left by the door : salió por la puerta⟩ **3** PAST : por, por delante de ⟨they walked by him : pasaron por delante de él⟩ **4** DURING : de, durante ⟨by night : de noche⟩ **5** (*in expressions of time*) : para ⟨we'll be there by ten : estaremos allí para las diez⟩ ⟨by then : para entonces⟩ **6** (*indicating cause or agent*) : por, de, a ⟨built by the Romans : construido por los romanos⟩ ⟨a book by Borges : un libro de Borges⟩ ⟨made by hand : hecho a mano⟩

by and by *adv* : dentro de poco

bygone¹ [ˈbaɪˌgɔn] *adj* : pasado

bygone² *n* **let bygones be bygones** : lo pasado, pasado está

bylaw *or* **byelaw** [ˈbaɪˌlɔ] *n* : norma *f*, reglamento *m*

by–line [ˈbaɪˌlaɪn] *n* : data *f*

bypass¹ [ˈbaɪˌpæs] *vt* : evitar

bypass² *n* **1** BELTWAY : carretera *f* de circunvalación **2** DETOUR : desvío *m*

by–product [ˈbaɪˌprɑdəkt] *n* : subproducto *m*, producto *m* derivado

bystander [ˈbaɪˌstændər] *n* : espectador *m*, -dora *f*

byte [ˈbaɪt] *n* : byte *m*

byway [ˈbaɪˌweɪ] *n* : camino *m* (apartado), carretera *f* secundaria

byword [ˈbaɪˌwərd] *n* **1** PROVERB : proverbio *m*, refrán *m* **2 to be a byword for** : estar sinónimo de

C

c ['si:] *n, pl* **c's** *or* **cs** : tercera letra del alfabeto inglés
cab ['kæb] *n* **1** TAXI : taxi *m* **2** : cabina *f* (de un camión o una locomotora) **3** CARRIAGE : coche *m* de caballos
cabal [kə'bɑl, -'bæl] *n* **1** INTRIGUE, PLOT : conspiración *f*, complot *m*, intriga *f* **2** : grupo *m* de conspiradores
cabaret [ˌkæbə'reɪ] *n* : cabaret *m*
cabbage ['kæbɪʤ] *n* : col *f*, repollo *m*
cabbie *or* **cabby** ['kæbi] *n* : taxista *mf*
cabin ['kæbən] *n* **1** HUT : cabaña *f*, choza *f*, barraca *f* **2** STATEROOM : camarote *m* **3** : cabina *f* (de un automóvil o avión)
cabinet ['kæbnət] *n* **1** CUPBOARD : armario *m* **2** : gabinete *m*, consejo *m* de ministros **3** medicine cabinet : botiquín *m*
cabinetmaker ['kæbnətˌmeɪkər] *n* : ebanista *mf*
cabinetmaking ['kæbnətˌmeɪkɪŋ] *n* : ebanistería *f*
cable¹ ['keɪbəl] *vt* **-bled; -bling** : enviar un cable, telegrafiar
cable² *n* **1** : cable *m* (para colgar o sostener algo) **2** : cable *m* eléctrico **3** → **cablegram**
cablegram ['keɪbəlˌgræm] *n* : telegrama *m*, cable *m*
caboose [kə'bu:s] *n* : furgón *m* de cola, cabús *m Mex*
cabstand ['kæbˌstænd] *n* : parada *f* de taxis
cacao [kə'kaʊ, -'keɪo] *n, pl* **cacaos** : cacao *m*
cache¹ ['kæʃ] *vt* **cached; caching** : esconder, guardar en un escondrijo
cache² *n* **1** : escondite *m*, escondrijo *m* ⟨cache of weapons : escondite de armas⟩ **2** : cache *m* ⟨cache memory : memoria cache⟩
cachet [kæ'ʃeɪ] *n* : caché *m*, prestigio *m*
cackle¹ ['kækəl] *vi* **-led; -ling 1** CLUCK : cacarear **2** : reírse o carcajearse estridentemente ⟨he was cackling with delight : estaba carcajeándose de gusto⟩
cackle² *n* **1** : cacareo *m* (de una polla) **2** LAUGH : risa *f* estridente
cacophony [kæ'kɑfəni, -'kɔ-] *n, pl* **-nies** : cacofonía *f*
cactus ['kæktəs] *n, pl* **cacti** [-ˌtaɪ] *or* **-tuses** : cacto *m*, cactus *m*
cadaver [kə'dævər] *n* : cadáver *m*
cadaverous [kə'dævərəs] *adj* : cadavérico
caddie¹ *or* **caddy** ['kædi] *vi* **caddied; caddying** : trabajar de caddie, hacer de caddie
caddie² *or* **caddy** *n, pl* **-dies** : caddie *mf*
caddy ['kædi] *n, pl* **-dies** : cajita *f* para té
cadence ['keɪdənts] *n* : cadencia *f*, ritmo *m*
cadenced ['keɪdəntst] *adj* : cadencioso, rítmico

cadet [kə'dɛt] *n* : cadete *mf*
cadmium ['kædmiəm] *n* : cadmio *m*
cadre ['kæˌdreɪ, 'kɑ-, -ˌdri:] *n* : cuadro *m* (de expertos)
café [kæ'feɪ, kə-] *n* : café *m*, cafetería *f*
cafeteria [ˌkæfə'tɪriə] *n* : cafetería *f*, restaurante *m* de autoservicio
caffeine [kæ'fi:n] *n* : cafeína *f*
cage¹ ['keɪʤ] *vt* **caged; caging** : enjaular
cage² *n* : jaula *f*
cagey ['keɪʤi] *adj* **-gier; -est 1** CAUTIOUS : cauteloso, reservado **2** SHREWD : astuto, vivo — **cagily** [-ʤəli] *adv*
caisson ['keɪˌsan, -sən] *n* **1** : cajón *m* de municiones **2** : cajón *m* hidráulico
cajole [kə'ʤo:l] *vt* **-joled; -joling** : engatusar
cajolery [kə'ʤo:ləri] *n* : engatusamiento *m*
cake¹ ['keɪk] *v* **caked; caking** *vt* : cubrir ⟨caked with mud : cubierto de barro⟩ — *vi* : endurecerse
cake² *n* **1** : torta *f*, bizcocho *m*, pastel *m* **2** : pastilla *f* (de jabón) **3 to take the cake** : llevarse la palma, ser el colmo
calabash ['kælə,bæʃ] *n* : calabaza *f*
calamari [ˌkalə'mari] *ns & pl* : calamares *mpl*
calamine ['kælə,maɪn] *n* : calamina *f* ⟨calamine lotion : loción de calamina⟩
calamitous [kə'læmətəs] *adj* : desastroso, catastrófico, calamitoso — **calamitously** *adv*
calamity [kə'læməti] *n, pl* **-ties** : desastre *m*, desgracia *f*, calamidad *f*
calcium ['kælsiəm] *n* : calcio *m*
calcium carbonate ['kɑrbə,neɪt, -nət] *n* : carbonato *m* de calcio
calculable ['kælkjələbəl] *adj* : calculable, computable
calculate ['kælkjə,leɪt] *v* **-lated; -lating** *vt* **1** COMPUTE : calcular, computar **2** ESTIMATE : calcular, creer **3** INTEND : planear, tener la intención de ⟨I calculated on spending $100 : planeaba gastar $100⟩ — *vi* : calcular, hacer cálculos
calculated ['kælkjə,leɪtəd] *adj* **1** ESTIMATED : calculado **2** DELIBERATE : intencional, premeditado, deliberado
calculating ['kælkjə,leɪtɪŋ] *adj* SHREWD : calculador, astuto
calculation [ˌkælkjə'leɪʃən] *n* : cálculo *m*
calculator ['kælkjə,leɪtər] *n* : calculadora *f*
calculus ['kælkjələs] *n, pl* **-li** [-ˌlaɪ] **1** : cálculo *m* ⟨differential calculus : cálculo diferencial⟩ **2** TARTAR : sarro *m* (dental)
caldron ['kɔldrən] → **cauldron**
calendar ['kæləndər] *n* **1** : calendario *m* **2** SCHEDULE : calendario *m*, programa *m*, agenda *f*

calf ['kæf, 'kɑf] *n, pl* **calves** ['kævz, 'kavz] **1** : becerro *m*, -rra *f*; ternero *m*, -ra *f* (de vacunos) **2** : cría *f* (de otros mamíferos) **3** : pantorrilla *f* (de la pierna)
calfskin ['kæf,skɪn] *n* : piel *f* de becerro
caliber *or* **calibre** ['kæləbər] *n* **1** : calibre *m* ⟨a .38 caliber gun : una pistola de calibre .38⟩ **2** ABILITY : calibre *m*, valor *m*, capacidad *f*
calibrate ['kælə,breɪt] *vt* **-brated; -brating** : calibrar (armas), graduar (termómetros)
calibration [,kælə'breɪʃən] *n* : calibrado *m*, calibración *f*
calico ['kælɪ,koː] *n, pl* **-coes** *or* **-cos 1** : calicó *m*, percal *m* **2** *or* **calico cat** : gato *m* manchado
calipers ['kæləpərz] *npl* : calibrador *m*
caliph *or* **calif** ['keɪləf, 'kæ-] *n* : califa *m*
calisthenics [,kæləs'θɛnɪks] *ns & pl* : calistenia *f*
calk ['kɔk] → **caulk**
call[1] ['kɔl] *vi* **1** CRY, SHOUT : gritar, vociferar **2** VISIT : hacer (una) visita, visitar **3 to call for** : exigir, requerir, necesitar ⟨it calls for patience : requiere mucha paciencia⟩ — *vt* **1** SUMMON : llamar, convocar **2** TELEPHONE : llamar por teléfono, telefonear **3** NAME : llamar, apodar
call[2] *n* **1** SHOUT : grito *m*, llamada *f* **2** : grito *m* (de un animal), reclamo *m* (de un pájaro) **3** SUMMONS : llamada *f* **4** DEMAND : llamado *m*, petición *f* **5** VISIT : visita *f* **6** DECISION : decisión *f* (en deportes) **7** *or* **telephone call** : llamada *f* (telefónica)
call down *vt* REPRIMAND : reprender, reñir
caller ['kɔlər] *n* **1** VISITOR : visita *f* **2** : persona *f* que llama (por teléfono)
calligraphy [kə'lɪgrəfi] *n, pl* **-phies** : caligrafía *f*
calling ['kɔlɪŋ] *n* : vocación *f*, profesión *f*
calliope [kə'laɪə,piː, 'kæli,oːp] *n* : órgano *m* de vapor
call off *vt* CANCEL : cancelar, suspender
callous[1] ['kæləs] *vt* : encallecer
callous[2] *adj* **1** CALLUSED : calloso, encallecido **2** UNFEELING : insensible, desalmado, cruel
callously ['kæləsli] *adv* : cruelmente, insensiblemente
callousness ['kæləsnəs] *n* : insensibilidad *f*, crueldad *f*
callow ['kælo] *adj* : inexperto, inmaduro
callus ['kæləs] *n* : callo *m*
callused ['kæləst] *adj* : encallecido, calloso
calm[1] ['kɑm, 'kɑlm] *vt* : tranquilizar, calmar, sosegar — *vi* : tranquilizarse, calmarse ⟨calm down! : ¡tranquilízate!⟩
calm[2] *adj* **1** TRANQUIL : calmo, tranquilo, sereno, ecuánime **2** STILL : en calma (dícese del mar), sin viento (dícese del aire)

calm[3] *n* : tranquilidad *f*, calma *f*
calmly ['kɑmli, 'kɑlm-] *adv* : con calma, tranquilamente
calmness ['kɑmnəs, 'kɑlm-] *n* : calma *f*, tranquilidad *f*
caloric [kə'lɔrɪk] *adj* : calórico (dícese de los alimentos), calorífico (dícese de la energía)
calorie ['kæləri] *n* : caloría *f*
calumniate [kə'lʌmni,eɪt] *vt* **-ated; -ating** : calumniar, difamar
calumny ['kæləmni] *n, pl* **-nies** : calumnia *f*, difamación *f*
calve ['kæv, 'kav] *vi* **calved; calving** : parir (dícese de los mamíferos)
calves → **calf**
calypso [kə'lɪp,soː] *n, pl* **-sos** : calipso *m*
calyx ['keɪlɪks, 'kæ-] *n, pl* **-lyxes** *or* **-lyces** [-lə,siːz] : cáliz *m*
cam ['kæm] *n* : leva *f*
camaraderie [,kam'radəri, ,kæm-; ,kamə'ra-] *n* : compañerismo *m*, camaradería *f*
Cambodian [kæm'boːdiən] *n* : camboyano *m*, -na *f* — **Cambodian** *adj*
came → **come**
camel ['kæməl] *n* : camello *m*
camellia [kə'miːljə] *n* : camelia *f*
cameo ['kæmi,oː] *n, pl* **-eos 1** : camafeo *m* **2** *or* **cameo performance** : actuación *f* especial
camera ['kæmrə, 'kæmərə] *n* : cámara *f*, máquina *f* fotográfica
Cameroonian [,kæmə'ruːniən] *n* : camerunés *m*, -nesa *f*
camouflage[1] ['kæmə,flaʒ, -,flaʤ] *vt* **-flaged; -flaging** : camuflajear, camuflar
camouflage[2] *n* : camuflaje *m*
camp[1] ['kæmp] *vi* : acampar, ir de camping
camp[2] *n* **1** : campamento *m* **2** FACTION : campo *m*, bando *m* ⟨in the same camp : del mismo bando⟩ **3 to pitch camp** : acampar, poner el campamento **4 to break camp** : levantar el campamento
campaign[1] [kæm'peɪn] *vi* : hacer (una) campaña
campaign[2] *n* : campaña *f*
campanile [,kæmpə'niː,li:, -'ni:l] *n, pl* **-niles** *or* **-nili** [-'ni:,li:] : campanario *m*
camper ['kæmpər] *n* **1** : campista *mf* (persona) **2** : cámper *m* (vehículo)
campground ['kæmp,graund] *n* : campamento *m*, camping *m*
camphor ['kæmpfər] *n* : alcanfor *m*
campsite ['kæmp,saɪt] *n* : campamento *m*, camping *m*
campus ['kæmpəs] *n* : campus *m*, recinto *m* universitario
can[1] ['kæn] *v aux, past* **could** ['kʊd]; *present s & pl* **can 1** : poder ⟨could you help me? : ¿podría ayudarme?⟩ **2** : saber ⟨she can't drive yet : todavía no sabe manejar⟩ **3** MAY : poder, tener permiso para ⟨can I sit down? : ¿puedo sentarme?⟩ **4** : poder ⟨it can't be! : ¡no

puede ser!⟩ ⟨where can they be? : ¿dónde estarán?⟩

can² ['kæn] *vt* **canned; canning 1** : enlatar, envasar ⟨to can tomatoes : enlatar tomates⟩ **2** DISMISS, FIRE : despedir, echar

can³ *n* : lata *f*, envase *m*, cubo *m* ⟨a can of beer : una lata de cerveza⟩ ⟨garbage can : cubo de basura⟩

Canadian [kə'neɪdiən] *n* : canadiense *mf* — **Canadian** *adj*

canal [kə'næl] *n* **1** : canal *m*, tubo *m* ⟨alimentary canal : tubo digestivo⟩ **2** : canal *m* ⟨Panama Canal : Canal de Panamá⟩

canapé ['kænəpi, -ˌpeɪ] *n* : canapé *m*

canary [kə'nɛri] *n, pl* **-naries** : canario *m*

cancel ['kæntsəl] *vt* **-celed** *or* **-celled; -celing** *or* **-celling** : cancelar

cancellation [ˌkæntsə'leɪʃən] *n* : cancelación *f*

cancer ['kæntsər] *n* : cáncer *m*

Cancer *n* : Cáncer *mf*

cancerous ['kæntsərəs] *adj* : canceroso

candelabrum [ˌkændə'labrəm, -'læ-] *or* **candelabra** [-brə] *n, pl* **-bra** *or* **-bras** : candelabro *m*

candid ['kændɪd] *adj* **1** FRANK : franco, sincero, abierto **2** : natural, espontáneo (en la fotografía)

candidacy ['kændədəsi] *n, pl* **-cies** : candidatura *f*

candidate ['kændəˌdeɪt, -dət] *n* : candidato *m*, -ta *f*

candidly ['kændɪdli] *adv* : con franqueza

candied ['kændid] *adj* : confitado

candle ['kændəl] *n* : vela *f*, candela *f*, cirio *m* (ceremonial)

candlestick ['kændəlˌstɪk] *n* : candelero *m*

candor ['kændər] *n* : franqueza *f*

candy ['kændi] *n, pl* **-dies** : dulce *m*, caramelo *m*

cane¹ ['keɪn] *vt* **caned; caning 1** : tapizar (muebles) con mimbre **2** FLOG : azotar con una vara

cane² *n* **1** : bastón *m* (para andar), vara *f* (para castigar) **2** REED : caña *f*, mimbre *m* (para muebles)

canine¹ ['keɪˌnaɪn] *adj* : canino

canine² *n* **1** DOG : canino *m*; perro *m*, -rra *f* **2** *or* **canine tooth** : colmillo *m*, diente *m* canino

canister ['kænəstər] *n* : lata *f*, bote *m*

canker ['kæŋkər] *n* : úlcera *f* bucal

cannery ['kænəri] *n, pl* **-ries** : fábrica *f* de conservas

cannibal ['kænəbəl] *n* : caníbal *mf*; antropófago *m*, -ga *f*

cannibalism ['kænəbəˌlɪzəm] *n* : canibalismo *m*, antropofagia *f*

cannibalize ['kænəbəˌlaɪz] *vt* **-ized; -izing** : canibalizar

cannily ['kænəli] *adv* : astutamente, sagazmente

cannon ['kænən] *n, pl* **-nons** *or* **-non** : cañón *m*

cannot (can not) ['kænˌɑt, kə'nɑt] → **can¹**

canny ['kæni] *adj* **-nier; -est** SHREWD : astuto, sagaz

canoe¹ [kə'nu:] *vt* **-noed; -noeing** : ir en canoa

canoe² *n* : canoa *f*, piragua *f*

canon ['kænən] *n* **1** : canon *m* ⟨canon law : derecho canónico⟩ **2** WORKS : canon *m* ⟨the canon of American literature : el canon de la literatura americana⟩ **3** : canónigo *m* (de una catedral) **4** STANDARD : canon *m*, norma *f*

canonical [kə'nɑnɪkəl] *adj* : canónico

canonize ['kænəˌnaɪz] *vt* **-ized; -izing** : canonizar

canopy ['kænəpi] *n, pl* **-pies** : dosel *m*, toldo *m*

cant¹ ['kænt] *vt* TILT : ladear, inclinar — *vi* **1** SLANT : ladearse, inclinarse, escorar (dícese de un barco) **2** : hablar insinceramente

cant² *n* **1** SLANT : plano *m* inclinado **2** JARGON : jerga *f* **3** : palabras *fpl* insinceras

can't ['kænt, 'kant] (*contraction of* **can not**) → **can¹**

cantaloupe ['kæntəlˌo:p] *n* : melón *m*, cantalupo *m*

cantankerous [kæn'tæŋkərəs] *adj* : irritable, irascible — **cantankerously** *adv*

cantankerousness [kæn'tæŋkərəsnəs] *n* : irritabilidad *f*, irascibilidad *f*

cantata [kən'tɑtə] *n* : cantata *f*

canteen [kæn'ti:n] *n* **1** FLASK : cantimplora *f* **2** CAFETERIA : cantina *f*, comedor *m* **3** : club *m* para actividades sociales y recreativas

canter¹ ['kæntər] *vi* : ir a medio galope

canter² *n* : medio galope *m*

cantilever ['kæntəˌliːvər, -ˌlevər] *n* **1** : viga *f* voladiza **2 cantilever bridge** : puente *m* voladizo

canto ['kænˌto:] *n, pl* **-tos** : canto *m*

canton ['kæntən, -ˌtɑn] *n* : cantón *m*

Cantonese [ˌkæntən'i:z, -'i:s] *n* **1** : cantonés *m*, -nesa *f* **2** : cantonés *m* (idioma) — **Cantonese** *adj*

cantor ['kæntər] *n* : solista *mf*

canvas ['kænvəs] *n* **1** : lona *f* **2** SAILS : velas *fpl* (de un barco) **3** : lienzo *m*, tela *f* (de pintar) **4** PAINTING : pintura *f*, óleo *m*, cuadro *m*

canvass¹ ['kænvəs] *vt* **1** SOLICIT : solicitar votos o pedidos de, hacer campaña entre **2** SOUND OUT : sondear (opiniones, etc.)

canvass² *n* SURVEY : sondeo *m*, encuesta *f*

canyon ['kænjən] *n* : cañón *m*

cap¹ ['kæp] *vt* **capped; capping 1** COVER : tapar (un recipiente), enfundar (un diente), cubrir (una montaña) **2** CLIMAX : coronar, ser el punto culminante de ⟨to cap it all off : para colmo⟩ **3** LIMIT : limitar, poner un tope a

cap² *n* **1** : gorra *f*, gorro *m*, cachucha *f* Mex ⟨baseball cap : gorra de béisbol⟩

2 COVER, TOP : tapa *f*, tapón *m* (de botellas), corcholata *f* *Mex* 3 LIMIT : tope *m*, límite *m*

capability [ˌkeɪpə'bɪləti] *n, pl* **-ties** : capacidad *f*, habilidad *f*, competencia *f*

capable ['keɪpəbəl] *adj* : competente, capaz, hábil — **capably** [-bli] *adv*

capacious [kə'peɪʃəs] *adj* : amplio, espacioso, de gran capacidad

capacity[1] [kə'pæsəti] *adj* : completo, total ⟨a capacity crowd : un lleno completo⟩

capacity[2] *n, pl* **-ties** 1 ROOM, SPACE : capacidad *f*, cabida *f*, espacio *m* 2 CAPABILITY : habilidad *f*, competencia *f* 3 FUNCTION, ROLE : calidad *f*, función *f* ⟨in his capacity as ambassador : en su calidad de embajador⟩

cape ['keɪp] *n* 1 : capa *f* 2 : cabo *m* ⟨Cape Horn : el Cabo de Hornos⟩

caper[1] ['keɪpər] *vi* : dar saltos, correr y brincar

caper[2] *n* 1 : alcaparra *f* ⟨olives and capers : aceitunas y alcaparras⟩ 2 ANTIC, PRANK : broma *f*, travesura *f* 3 LEAP : brinco *m*, salto *m*

Cape Verdean ['keɪp'vərdiən] *n* : caboverdiano *m*, -na *f* — **Cape Verdean** *adj*

capful ['kæp,fʊl] *n* : tapa *f*, tapita *f*

capillary[1] ['kæpə,leri] *adj* : capilar

capillary[2] *n, pl* **-ries** : capilar *m*

capital[1] ['kæpətəl] *adj* 1 : capital ⟨capital punishment : pena capital⟩ 2 : mayúsculo (dícese de las letras) 3 : de capital ⟨capital assets : activo fijo⟩ ⟨capital gain : ganancia de capital, plusvalía⟩ 4 EXCELLENT : excelente, estupendo

capital[2] *n* 1 *or* **capital city** : capital *f*, sede *f* del gobierno 2 WEALTH : capital *m* 3 *or* **capital letter** : mayúscula *f* 4 : capitel *m* (de una columna)

capitalism ['kæpətəl,ɪzəm] *n* : capitalismo *m*

capitalist[1] ['kæpətəlɪst] *or* **capitalistic** [ˌkæpətəl'ɪstɪk] *adj* : capitalista

capitalist[2] *n* : capitalista *mf*

capitalization [ˌkæpətələ'zeɪʃən] *n* : capitalización *f*

capitalize ['kæpətəl,aɪz] *v* **-ized; -izing** *vt* 1 FINANCE : capitalizar, financiar 2 : escribir con mayúscula — *vi* to **capitalize on** : sacar partido de, aprovechar

capitol ['kæpətəl] *n* : capitolio *m*

capitulate [kə'pɪtʃə,leɪt] *vi* **-lated; -lating** : capitular

capitulation [kə,pɪtʃə'leɪʃən] *n* : capitulación *f*

capon ['keɪ,pɑn, -pən] *n* : capón *m*

cappuccino [ˌkɑpə'tʃi:no:] *n* : capuchino *m* (café)

caprice [kə'pri:s] *n* : capricho *m*, antojo *m*

capricious [kə'prɪʃəs, -'pri:-] *adj* : caprichoso — **capriciously** *adv*

Capricorn ['kæprɪ,kɔrn] *n* : Capricornio *mf*

capsize ['kæp,saɪz, kæp'saɪz] *v* **-sized; -sizing** *vi* : volcar, volcarse — *vt* : hacer volcar

capstan ['kæpstən, -,stæn] *n* : cabrestante *m*

capsule ['kæpsəl, -,su:l] *n* 1 : cápsula *f* (en la farmacéutica y botánica) 2 **space capsule** : cápsula *f* espacial

captain[1] ['kæptən] *vt* : capitanear

captain[2] *n* 1 : capitán *m*, -tana *f* 2 HEADWAITER : jefe *m*, -fa *f* de comedor 3 **captain of industry** : magnate *mf*

caption[1] ['kæpʃən] *vt* : ponerle una leyenda a (una ilustración), titular (un artículo), subtitular (una película)

caption[2] *n* 1 HEADING : titular *m*, encabezamiento *m* 2 : leyenda *f* (al pie de una ilustración) 3 SUBTITLE : subtítulo *m*

captivate ['kæptə,veɪt] *vt* **-vated; -vating** CHARM : cautivar, hechizar, encantar

captivating ['kæptə,veɪtɪŋ] *adj* : cautivador, hechicero, encantador

captive[1] ['kæptɪv] *adj* : cautivo

captive[2] *n* : cautivo *m*, -va *f*

captivity [kæp'tɪvəti] *n* : cautiverio *m*

captor ['kæptər] *n* : captor *m*, -tora *f*

capture[1] ['kæpʃər] *vt* **-tured; -turing** 1 SEIZE : capturar, apresar 2 CATCH : captar ⟨to capture one's interest : captar el interés de uno⟩

capture[2] *n* : captura *f*, apresamiento *m*

car ['kɑr] *n* 1 AUTOMOBILE : automóvil *m*, coche *m*, carro *m* 2 : vagón *m*, coche *m* (de un tren) 3 : cabina *f* (de un ascensor)

carafe [kə'ræf, -'rɑf] *n* : garrafa *f*

caramel ['kɑrməl; 'kærəməl, -,mɛl] *n* 1 : caramelo *m*, azúcar *f* quemada 2 *or* **caramel candy** : caramelo *m*, dulce *m* de leche

carat ['kærət] *n* : quilate *m*

caravan ['kærə,væn] *n* : caravana *f*

caraway ['kærə,weɪ] *n* : alcaravea *f*

carbine ['kɑr,baɪn, -,bi:n] *n* : carabina *f*

carbohydrate [ˌkɑrbo'haɪ,dreɪt, -drət] *n* : carbohidrato *m*, hidrato *m* de carbono

carbon ['kɑrbən] *n* 1 : carbono *m* 2 → carbon paper 3 → carbon copy

carbonated ['kɑrbə,neɪtəd] *adj* : carbonatado (dícese del agua), gaseoso (dícese de las bebidas)

carbon copy *n* 1 : copia *f* al carbón 2 DUPLICATE : duplicado *m*, copia *f* exacta

carbon paper *n* : papel *m* carbón

carbuncle ['kɑr,bʌŋkəl] *n* : carbunco *m*

carburetor ['kɑrbə,reɪtər, -bjə-] *n* : carburador *m*

carcass ['kɑrkəs] *n* : cuerpo *m* (de un animal muerto)

carcinogen [kɑr'sɪnədʒən, 'kɑrsənə-,dʒɛn] *n* : carcinógeno *m*, cancerígeno *m*

carcinogenic [ˌkɑrsəno'dʒɛnɪk] *adj* : carcinogénico

carcinoma [ˌkɑrsə'no:mə] *n* : carcinoma *m*

card¹ ['kɑrd] *vt* : cardar (fibras)
card² *n* 1 : carta *f*, naipe *m* ⟨to play cards
: jugar a las cartas⟩ ⟨a deck of cards
: una baraja⟩ 2 : tarjeta *f* ⟨birthday
card : tarjeta de cumpleaños⟩ ⟨busi-
ness card : tarjeta (de visita)⟩
cardboard ['kɑrd,bord] *n* : cartón *m*,
cartulina *f*
cardiac ['kɑrdi,æk] *adj* : cardíaco, cardiaco
cardigan ['kɑrdɪgən] *n* : cárdigan *m*,
chaqueta *f* de punto
cardinal¹ ['kɑrdənəl] *adj* FUNDAMEN-
TAL : cardinal, fundamental
cardinal² *n* : cardenal *m*
cardinal number *n* : número *m* cardinal
cardinal point *n* : punto *m* cardinal
cardiologist [,kɑrdi'ɑlədʒɪst] *n* : cardiólogo *m*, -ga *f*
cardiology [,kɑrdi'ɑlədʒi] *n* : cardiología
f
cardiovascular [,kɑrdio'væskjələr] *adj*
: cardiovascular
care¹ ['kær] *v* cared; caring *vi* 1 : importarle a uno ⟨they don't care : no les
importa⟩ 2 : preocuparse, inquietarse
⟨she cares about the poor : se preocupa por los pobres⟩ 3 to care for TEND
: cuidar (de), atender, encargarse de 4
to care for CHERISH : querer, sentir
cariño por 5 to care for LIKE : gustarle (algo a uno) ⟨I don't care for your
attitude : tu actitud no me agrada⟩ —
vt WISH : desear, querer ⟨if you care to
go : si deseas ir⟩
care² *n* 1 ANXIETY : inquietud *f*, preocupación *f* 2 CAREFULNESS : cuidado *m*, atención *f* ⟨handle with care
: manejar con cuidado⟩ 3 CHARGE
: cargo *m*, cuidado *m* 4 to take care of
: cuidar (de), atender, encargarse de
careen [kə'ri:n] *vi* 1 SWAY : oscilar, balancearse 2 CAREER : ir a toda velocidad
career¹ [kə'rɪr] *vi* : ir a toda velocidad
career² *n* VOCATION : vocación *f*, profesión *f*, carrera *f*
carefree ['kær,fri:, 'kær'-] *adj* : despreocupado
careful ['kærfəl] *adj* 1 CAUTIOUS
: cuidadoso, cauteloso 2 PAINSTAKING
: cuidadoso, esmerado, meticuloso
carefully ['kærfəli] *adv* : con cuidado,
cuidadosamente
carefulness ['kærfəlnəs] *n* 1 CAUTION
: cuidado *m*, cautela *f* 2 METICULOUS-
NESS : esmero *m*, meticulosidad *f*
caregiver ['kær,gɪvər] *n* : persona *f* que
cuida a niños o enfermos
careless ['kærləs] *adj* : descuidado, negligente — carelessly *adv*
carelessness ['kærləsnəs] *n* : descuido
m, negligencia *f*
caress¹ [kə'rɛs] *vt* : acariciar
caress² *n* : caricia *f*
caret ['kærət] *n* : signo *m* de intercalación
caretaker ['kɛr,teɪkər] *n* : conserje *mf*;
velador *m*, -dora *f*

cargo ['kɑr,go:] *n*, *pl* -goes *or* -gos
: cargamento *m*, carga *f*
Caribbean [kærə'bi:ən, kə'rɪbiən] *adj*
: caribeño ⟨the Caribbean Sea : el mar
Caribe⟩
caribou ['kærə,bu:] *n*, *pl* -bou *or* -bous
: caribú *m*
caricature¹ ['kærɪkə,tʃʊr] *vt* -tured; -tur-
ing : caricaturizar
caricature² *n* : caricatura *f*
caricaturist ['kærɪkə,tʃʊrɪst] *n* : caricaturista *mf*
caries ['kær,i:z] *ns & pl* : caries *f*
carillon ['kærə,lɑn] *n* : carillón *m*
carmine ['kɑrmən, -,maɪn] *n* : carmín *m*
carnage ['kɑrnɪdʒ] *n* : matanza *f*, carnicería *f*
carnal ['kɑrnəl] *adj* : carnal
carnation [kɑr'neɪʃən] *n* : clavel *m*
carnival ['kɑrnəvəl] *n* : carnaval *m*,
feria *f*
carnivore ['kɑrnə,vor] *n* : carnívoro *m*
carnivorous [kɑr'nɪvərəs] *adj* : carnívoro
carol¹ ['kærəl] *vi* -oled *or* -olled; -oling
or -olling : cantar villancicos
carol² *n* : villancico *m*
caroler *or* caroller ['kærələr] *n* : persona
f que canta villancicos
carom¹ ['kærəm] *vi* 1 REBOUND : rebotar ⟨the bullet caromed off the wall : la
bala rebotó contra el muro⟩ 2 : hacer
carambola (en billar)
carom² *n* : carambola *f*
carouse [kə'rauz] *vt* -roused; -rousing
: irse de parranda, irse de juerga
carousel *or* carrousel [,kærə'sɛl, 'kær-
ə,-] *n* : carrusel *m*, tiovivo *m*
carouser [kə'rauzər] *n* : juerguista *mf*
carp¹ ['kɑrp] *vi* 1 COMPLAIN : quejarse
2 to carp at : criticar
carp² *n*, *pl* carp *or* carps : carpa *f*
carpel ['kɑrpəl] *n* : carpelo *m*
carpenter ['kɑrpəntər] *n* : carpintero *m*,
-ra *f*
carpentry ['kɑrpəntri] *n* : carpintería *f*
carpet¹ ['kɑrpət] *vt* : alfombrar
carpet² *n* : alfombra *f*
carpeting ['kɑrpətɪŋ] *n* : alfombrado *m*
carport ['kɑr,port] *n* : cochera *f*, garaje
m abierto
carriage ['kærɪdʒ] *n* 1 TRANSPORT
: transporte *m* 2 POSTURE : porte *m*,
postura *f* 3 horse-drawn carriage
: carruaje *m*, coche *m* 4 baby carriage
: cochecito *m*
carrier ['kæriər] *n* 1 : transportista *mf*,
empresa *f* de transportes 2 : portador
m, -dora *f* (de una enfermedad) 3 aircraft carrier : portaaviones *m*
carrier pigeon : paloma *f* mensajera
carrion ['kæriən] *n* : carroña *f*
carrot ['kærət] *n* : zanahoria *f*
carry ['kæri] *v* -ried; -rying *vt* 1 TRANS-
PORT : llevar, cargar, transportar
(cargamento), conducir (electricidad),
portar (un virus) ⟨to carry a bag : cargar una bolsa⟩ ⟨to carry money : llevar dinero encima, traer dinero consi-

go⟩ **2** BEAR : soportar, aguantar, resistir (peso) **3** STOCK : vender, tener en abasto **4** ENTAIL : llevar, implicar, acarrear **5** WIN : ganar (una elección o competición), aprobar (una moción) **6 to carry oneself** : portarse, comportarse ⟨he carried himself honorably : se comportó dignamente⟩ — *vi* : oírse, proyectarse ⟨her voice carries well : su voz se puede oír desde lejos⟩

carryall ['kæri,ɔl] *n* : bolsa *f* de viaje

carry away *vt* **to get carried away** : exaltarse, entusiasmarse

carry on *vt* CONDUCT : realizar, ejercer, mantener ⟨to carry on research : realizar investigaciones⟩ ⟨to carry on a correspondence : mantener una correspondencia⟩ — *vi* **1** : portarse de manera escandalosa o inapropiada ⟨it's embarrassing how he carries on : su manera de comportarse da vergüenza⟩ **2** CONTINUE : seguir, continuar

carry out *vt* **1** PERFORM : llevar a cabo, realizar **2** FULFILL : cumplir

cart¹ ['kɑrt] *vt* : acarrear, llevar

cart² *n* : carreta *f*, carro *m*

cartel [kɑr'tɛl] *n* : cártel *m*

cartilage ['kɑrt̬əlɪdʒ] *n* : cartílago *m*

cartilaginous [,kɑrt̬əl'ædʒənəs] *adj* : cartilaginoso

cartographer [kɑr'tɑgrəfər] *n* : cartógrafo *m*, -fa *f*

cartography [kɑr'tɑgrəfi] *n* : cartografía *f*

carton ['kɑrtən] *n* : caja *f* de cartón

cartoon [kɑr'tu:n] *n* **1** : chiste *m* (gráfico), caricatura *f* ⟨a political cartoon : un chiste político⟩ **2** COMIC STRIP : tira *f* cómica, historieta *f* **3** *or* **animated cartoon** : dibujo *m* animado

cartoonist [kɑr'tu:nɪst] *n* : caricaturista *mf*, dibujante *mf* (de chistes)

cartridge ['kɑrtrɪdʒ] *n* : cartucho *m*

carve ['kɑrv] *vt* **carved; carving 1** : tallar (madera), esculpir (piedra), grabar ⟨he carved his name in the bark : grabó su nombre en la corteza⟩ **2** SLICE : cortar, trinchar (carne)

cascade¹ [kæs'keɪd] *vi* **-caded; -cading** : caer en cascada

cascade² *n* : cascada *f*, salto *m* de agua

case¹ ['keɪs] *vt* **cased; casing 1** BOX, PACK : embalar, encajonar **2** INSPECT : observar, inspeccionar (antes de cometer un delito)

case² *n* **1** : caso *m* ⟨an unusual case : un caso insólito⟩ ⟨ablative case : caso ablativo⟩ ⟨a case of the flu : un caso de gripe⟩ **2** BOX : caja *f* **3** CONTAINER : funda *f*, estuche *m* **4 in any case** : de todos modos, en cualquier caso **5 in case** : como precaución ⟨just in case : por si acaso⟩ **6 in case of** : en caso de

casement ['keɪsmənt] *n* : ventana *f* con bisagras

cash¹ ['kæʃ] *vt* : convertir en efectivo, cobrar, cambiar (un cheque)

cash² *n* : efectivo *m*, dinero *m* en efectivo

cashew ['kæ,ʃu:, kə'ʃu:] *n* : anacardo *m*

cashier¹ [kæ'ʃɪr] *vt* : destituir, despedir

cashier² *n* : cajero *m*, -ra *f*

cashmere ['kæʒ,mɪr, 'kæʃ-] *n* : cachemir *m*

casino [kə'si:,no:] *n, pl* **-nos** : casino *m*

cask ['kæsk] *n* : tonel *m*, barrica *f*, barril *m*

casket ['kæskət] *n* COFFIN : ataúd *m*, féretro *m*

cassava [kə'sɑvə] *n* : mandioca *f*, yuca *f*

casserole ['kæsə,ro:l] *n* **1** : cazuela *f* **2** : guiso *m*, guisado *m* ⟨tuna casserole : guiso de atún⟩

cassette [kə'sɛt, kæ-] *n* : cassette *mf*

cassock ['kæsək] *n* : sotana *f*

cast¹ ['kæst] *vt* **cast; casting 1** THROW : tirar, echar, arrojar ⟨the die is cast : la suerte está echada⟩ **2** : depositar (un voto) **3** : asignar (papeles en una obra de teatro) **4** MOLD : moldear, fundir, vaciar **5 to cast off** ABANDON : desamparar, abandonar

cast² *n* **1** THROW : lance *m*, lanzamiento *m* **2** APPEARANCE : aspecto *m*, forma *f* **3** : elenco *m*, reparto *m* (de una obra de teatro) **4 plaster cast** : molde *m* de yeso, escayola *f*

castanets [,kæstə'nɛts] *npl* : castañuelas *fpl*

castaway¹ ['kæstə,weɪ] *adj* : náufrago

castaway² *n* : náufrago *m*, -ga *f*

caste ['kæst] *n* : casta *f*

caster ['kæstər] *n* : ruedita *f* (de un mueble)

castigate ['kæstə,geɪt] *vt* **-gated; -gating** : castigar severamente, censurar, reprobar

Castilian [kæ'stɪljən] *n* **1** : castellano *m*, -na *f* **2** : castellano *m* (idioma) — **Castilian** *adj*

cast iron *n* : hierro *m* fundido

castle ['kæsəl] *n* **1** : castillo *m* **2** : torre *f* (en ajedrez)

cast–off ['kæst,ɔf] *adj* : desechado

castoff ['kæst,ɔf] *n* : desecho *m*

castrate ['kæs,treɪt] *vt* **-trated; -trating** : castrar

castration [kæ'streɪʃən] *n* : castración *f*

casual ['kæʒuəl] *adj* **1** FORTUITOUS : casual, fortuito **2** INDIFFERENT : indiferente, despreocupado **3** INFORMAL : informal — **casually** ['kæʒuəli, 'kæʒəli] *adv*

casualness ['kæʒuəlnəs] *n* **1** FORTUITOUSNESS : casualidad *f* **2** INDIFFERENCE : indiferencia *f*, despreocupación *f* **3** INFORMALITY : informalidad *f*

casualty ['kæʒuəlti, 'kæʒəl-] *n, pl* **-ties 1** ACCIDENT : accidente *m* serio, desastre *m* **2** VICTIM : víctima *f*; baja *f*; herido *m*, -da *f*

cat ['kæt] *n* : gato *m*, -ta *f*

cataclysm ['kæt̬ə,klɪzəm] *n* : cataclismo *m*

cataclysmal [ˌkæt̬ə'klızməl] *or* **cataclysmic** [ˌkæt̬ə'klızmık] *adj* : catastrófico

catacombs ['kæt̬ə,ko:mz] *npl* : catacumbas *fpl*

Catalan ['kæt̬ələn, -,læn] *n* **1** : catalán *m*, catalana *f* **2** : catalán *m* (idioma) — **Catalan** *adj*

catalog[1] *or* **catalogue** ['kæt̬ə,lɔg] *vt* **-loged** *or* **-logued; -loging** *or* **-loguing** : catalogar

catalog[2] *n* : catálogo *m*

catalyst ['kæt̬ələst] *n* : catalizador *m*

catalytic [ˌkæt̬əl'ıt̬ık] *adj* : catalítico

catamaran [ˌkæt̬əmə'ræn, 'kæt̬əmə-,ræn] *n* : catamarán *m*

catapult[1] ['kæt̬ə,pʌlt, -,pʊlt] *vt* : catapultar

catapult[2] *n* : catapulta *f*

cataract ['kæt̬ə,rækt] *n* : catarata *f*

catarrh [kə'tɑr] *n* : catarro *m*

catastrophe [kə'tæstrə,fi:] *n* : catástrofe *f*

catastrophic [ˌkæt̬ə'strɑfık] *adj* : catastrófico — **catastrophically** [-fıkli] *adv*

catcall ['kæt,kɔl] *n* : rechifla *f*, abucheo *m*

catch[1] ['kæʧ, 'kɛʧ] *v* **caught** ['kɔt]; **catching** *vt* **1** CAPTURE, TRAP : capturar, agarrar, atrapar, coger **2** : agarrar, pillar *fam*, tomar de sorpresa ⟨they caught him red-handed : lo pillaron con las manos en la masa⟩ **3** GRASP : agarrar, captar **4** ENTANGLE : enganchar, enredar **5** : tomar (un tren, etc.) **6** : contagiarse de ⟨to catch a cold : contagiarse de un resfriado, resfriarse⟩ — *vi* **1** GRASP : agarrar **2** HOOK : engancharse **3** IGNITE : prender, agarrar

catch[2] *n* **1** CATCHING : captura *f*, atrapada *f*, parada *f* (de una pelota) **2** : redada *f* (de pescado), presa *f* (de caza) ⟨he's a good catch : es un buen partido⟩ **3** LATCH : pestillo *m*, pasador *m* **4** DIFFICULTY, TRICK : problema *m*, trampa *f*, truco *m*

catcher ['kæʧər, 'kɛ-] *n* : catcher *mf*; receptor *m*, -tora *f* (en béisbol)

catching ['kæʧıŋ, 'kɛ-] *adj* : contagioso

catchup ['kæʧəp, 'kɛ-] → **ketchup**

catchword ['kæʧ,wərd, 'kɛʧ-] *n* : eslogan *m*, lema *m*

catchy ['kæʧi, 'kɛ-] *adj* **catchier; -est** : pegajoso ⟨a catchy song : una canción pegajosa⟩

catechism ['kæt̬ə,kızəm] *n* : catecismo *m*

categorical [ˌkæt̬ə'gɔrıkəl] *adj* : categórico, absoluto, rotundo — **categorically** [-kli] *adv*

categorize ['kæt̬ıgə,raız] *vt* **-rized; -rizing** : clasificar, catalogar

category ['kæt̬ə,gori] *n, pl* **-ries** : categoría *f*, género *m*, clase *f*

cater ['keıt̬ər] *vi* **1** : proveer alimentos (para fiestas, bodas, etc.) **2 to cater to** : atender a ⟨to cater to all tastes : atender a todos los gustos⟩

catercorner[1] ['kæt̬i,kɔrnər, 'kæt̬ə-, 'kıt̬i-] *or* **cater–cornered** [-,kɔrnərd] *adv* : diagonalmente, en diagonal

catercorner[2] *or* **cater–cornered** *adj* : diagonal

caterer ['keıt̬ərər] *n* : proveedor *m*, -dora *f* de comida

caterpillar ['kæt̬ər,pılər] *n* : oruga *f*

catfish ['kæt,fıʃ] *n* : bagre *m*

catgut ['kæt,gʌt] *n* : cuerda *f* de tripa

catharsis [kə'θɑrsıs] *n, pl* **catharses** [-,si:z] : catarsis *f*

cathartic[1] [kə'θɑrt̬ık] *adj* : catártico

cathartic[2] *n* : purgante *m*

cathedral [kə'θi:drəl] *n* : catedral *f*

catheter ['kæθət̬ər] *n* : catéter *m*, sonda *f*

cathode ['kæ,θo:d] *n* : cátodo *m*

catholic ['kæθəlık] *adj* **1** BROAD, UNIVERSAL : liberal, universal **2 Catholic** : católico

Catholic *n* : católico *m*, -ca *f*

Catholicism [kə'θɑlə,sızəm] *n* : catolicismo *m*

catlike ['kæt,laık] *adj* : gatuno, felino

catnap[1] ['kæt,næp] *vi* **-napped; -napping** : tomarse una siestecita

catnap[2] *n* : siesta *f* breve, siestecita *f*

catnip ['kæt,nıp] *n* : nébeda *f*

catsup ['kɛʧəp, 'kæt̬səp] → **ketchup**

cattail ['kæt,teıl] *n* : espadaña *f*, anea *f*

cattiness ['kæt̬inəs] *n* : malicia *f*

cattle ['kæt̬əl] *npl* : ganado *m*, reses *fpl*

cattleman ['kæt̬əlmən, -,mæn] *n, pl* **-men** [-mən, -,mɛn] : ganadero *m*

catty ['kæt̬i] *adj* **-tier; -est** : malicioso, malintencionado

catwalk ['kæt,wɔk] *n* : pasarela *f*

Caucasian[1] [kɔ'keıʒən] *adj* : caucásico

Caucasian[2] *n* : caucásico *m*, -ca *f*

caucus ['kɔkəs] *n* : junta *f* de políticos

caught → **catch**

cauldron ['kɔldrən] *n* : caldera *f*

cauliflower ['kɑlı,flaʊər, 'kɔ-] *n* : coliflor *f*

caulk[1] ['kɔk] *vt* : calafatear (un barco), enmasillar (una grieta)

caulk[2] *n* : masilla *f*

causal ['kɔzəl] *adj* : causal

causality [kɔ'zæləti] *n* : causalidad *f*

cause[1] ['kɔz] *vt* **caused; causing** : causar, provocar, ocasionar

cause[2] *n* **1** ORIGIN : causa *f*, origen *m* **2** REASON : causa *f*, razón *f*, motivo *m* **3** LAWSUIT : litigio *m*, pleito *m* **4** MOVEMENT : causa *f*, movimiento *m*

causeless ['kɔzləs] *adj* : sin causa

causeway ['kɔz,weı] *n* : camino *m* elevado

caustic ['kɔstık] *adj* **1** CORROSIVE : cáustico, corrosivo **2** BITING : mordaz, sarcástico

cauterize ['kɔt̬ə,raız] *vt* **-ized; -izing** : cauterizar

caution[1] ['kɔʃən] *vt* : advertir

caution[2] *n* **1** WARNING : advertencia *f*, aviso *m* **2** CARE, PRUDENCE : precaución *f*, cuidado *m*, cautela *f*

cautionary ['kɔʃə,nɛri] *adv* : admonitorio ⟨cautionary tale : cuento moral⟩

cautious ['kɔʃəs] *adj* : cauteloso, cuidadoso, precavido

cautiously ['kɔʃəsli] *adv* : cautelosamente, con precaución

cautiousness ['kɔʃəsnəs] *n* : cautela *f*, precaución *f*

cavalcade [,kævəl'keɪd, 'kævəl,-] *n* **1** : cabalgata *f* **2** SERIES : serie *f*

cavalier[1] [,kævə'lɪr] *adj* : altivo, desdeñoso — **cavalierly** *adv*

cavalier[2] *n* : caballero *m*

cavalry ['kævəlri] *n, pl* **-ries** : caballería *f*

cave[1] ['keɪv] *vi* **caved; caving** *or* **to cave in** : derrumbarse

cave[2] *n* : cueva *f*

cavern ['kævərn] *n* : caverna *f*

cavernous ['kævərnəs] *adj* : cavernoso — **cavernously** *adv*

caviar *or* **caviare** ['kævi,ɑr, 'kɑ-] *n* : caviar *m*

cavity ['kævəti] *n, pl* **-ties 1** HOLE : cavidad *f*, hueco *m* **2** CARIES : caries *f*

cavort [kə'vɔrt] *vi* : brincar, hacer cabriolas

caw[1] ['kɔ] *vi* : graznar

caw[2] *n* : graznido *m*

cayenne pepper [,kaɪ'ɛn, ,keɪ-] *n* : pimienta *f* cayena, pimentón *m*

CD [,si:'di:] *n* : CD *m*, disco *m* compacto

CD–ROM [,si:,di:'rɑm] *n* : CD-ROM *m*

cease ['si:s] *v* **ceased; ceasing** *vt* : dejar de ⟨they ceased bickering : dejaron de discutir⟩ — *vi* : cesar, pararse

ceaseless ['si:sləs] *adj* : incesante, continuo

cedar ['si:dər] *n* : cedro *m*

cede ['si:d] *vt* **ceded; ceding** : ceder, conceder

ceiling ['si:lɪŋ] *n* **1** : techo *m*, cielo *m* raso **2** LIMIT : límite *m*, tope *m*

celebrant ['sɛləbrənt] *n* : celebrante *mf*, oficiante *m*

celebrate ['sɛlə,breɪt] *v* **-brated; -brating** *vt* **1** : celebrar, oficiar ⟨to celebrate Mass : celebrar la misa⟩ **2** : celebrar, festejar ⟨we're celebrating our anniversary : estamos celebrando nuestro aniversario⟩ **3** EXTOL : alabar, ensalzar, exaltar — *vi* : estar de fiesta, divertirse

celebrated ['sɛlə,breɪtəd] *adj* : célebre, famoso, renombrado

celebration [,sɛlə'breɪʃən] *n* : celebración *f*, festejos *mpl*

celebrity [sə'lɛbrəti] *n, pl* **-ties 1** RENOWN : fama *f*, renombre *m*, celebridad *f* **2** PERSONALITY : celebridad *f*, personaje *m*

celery ['sɛləri] *n, pl* **-eries** : apio *m*

celestial [sə'lɛstʃəl, -'lɪstɪəl] *adj* **1** : celeste **2** HEAVENLY : celestial, paradisiaco

celibacy ['sɛləbəsi] *n* : celibato *m*

celibate[1] ['sɛləbət] *adj* : célibe

celibate[2] *n* : célibe *mf*

cell ['sɛl] *n* **1** : célula *f* (de un organismo) **2** : celda *f* (en una cárcel, etc.) **3** : elemento *m* (de una pila)

cellar ['sɛlər] *n* **1** BASEMENT : sótano *m* **2** : bodega *f* (de vinos)

cellist ['tʃɛlɪst] *n* : violonchelista *mf*

cello ['tʃɛ,lo:] *n, pl* **-los** : violonchelo *m*

cellophane ['sɛlə,feɪn] *n* : celofán *m*

cell phone *n* : teléfono *m* celular

cellular ['sɛljələr] *adj* : celular

celluloid ['sɛljə,lɔɪd] *n* : celuloide

cellulose ['sɛljə,lo:s] *n* : celulosa *f*

Celsius ['sɛlsiəs] *adj* : centígrado ⟨100 degrees Celsius : 100 grados centígrados⟩

Celt ['kɛlt, 'sɛlt] *n* : celta *mf*

Celtic[1] ['kɛltɪk, 'sɛl-] *adj* : celta

Celtic[2] *n* : celta *m*

cement[1] [sɪ'mɛnt] *vi* : unir o cubrir algo con cemento, cementar

cement[2] *n* **1** : cemento *m* **2** GLUE : pegamento *m*

cemetery ['sɛmə,teri] *n, pl* **-teries** : cementerio *m*, panteón *m*

censer ['sɛntsər] *n* : incensario *m*

censor[1] ['sɛntsər] *vt* : censurar

censor[2] *n* : censor *m*, -sora *f*

censorious [sɛn'soriəs] *adj* : de censura, crítico

censorship ['sɛntsər,ʃɪp] *n* : censura *f*

censure[1] ['sɛntʃər] *vt* **-sured; -suring** : censurar, criticar, reprobar — **censurable** [-tʃərəbəl] *adj*

censure[2] *n* : censura *f*, reproche *m* oficial

census ['sɛntsəs] *n* : censo *m*

cent ['sɛnt] *n* : centavo *m*

centaur ['sɛn,tɔr] *n* : centauro *m*

centennial[1] [sɛn'tɛniəl] *adj* : del centenario

centennial[2] *n* : centenario *m*

center[1] ['sɛntər] *vt* **1** : centrar **2** CONCENTRATE : concentrar, fijar, enfocar — *vi* : centrarse, enfocarse

center[2] *n* **1** : centro *m* ⟨center of gravity : centro de gravedad⟩ **2** : centro *mf* (en futbol americano), pívot *mf* (en basquetbol)

centerpiece ['sɛntər,pi:s] *n* : centro *m* de mesa

centigrade ['sɛntə,greɪd, 'sɑn-] *adj* : centígrado

centigram ['sɛntə,græm, 'sɑn-] *n* : centigramo *m*

centimeter ['sɛntə,mi:tər, 'sɑn-] *n* : centímetro *m*

centipede ['sɛntə,pi:d] *n* : ciempiés *m*

central ['sɛntrəl] *adj* **1** : céntrico, central ⟨in a central location : en un lugar céntrico⟩ **2** MAIN, PRINCIPAL : central, fundamental, principal

Central American[1] *adj* : centroamericano

Central American[2] *n* : centroamericano *m*, -na *f*

centralization [,sɛntrələ'zeɪʃən] *n* : centralización *f*

centralize ['sɛntrə,laɪz] *vt* **-ized; -izing** : centralizar

centrally ['sɛntrəli] *adv* **1 centrally heated** : con calefacción central **2 centrally located** : céntrico, en un lugar céntrico

centre ['sɛntər] → **center**

centrifugal [sɛn'trɪfjəgəl, -'trɪfɪ-] *adj* : centrífugo

centrifugal force *n* : fuerza *f* centrífuga

century ['sɛntʃəri] *n, pl* **-ries** : siglo *m*

ceramic[1] [sə'ræmɪk] *adj* : de cerámica

ceramic[2] *n* **1** : objeto *m* de cerámica, cerámica *f* **2 ceramics** *npl* : cerámica *f*

cereal[1] ['sɪriəl] *adj* : cereal

cereal[2] *n* : cereal *m*

cerebellum [ˌsɛrə'bɛləm] *n, pl* **-bellums** *or* **-bella** [-'bɛlə] : cerebelo *m*

cerebral [sə'ri:brəl, 'sɛrə-] *adj* : cerebral

cerebral palsy *n* : parálisis *f* cerebral

cerebrum [sə'ri:brəm, 'sɛrə-] *n, pl* **-brums** *or* **-bra** [-brə] : cerebro *m*

ceremonial[1] [ˌsɛrə'mo:niəl] *adj* : ceremonial

ceremonial[2] *n* : ceremonial *m*

ceremonious [ˌsɛrə'mo:niəs] *adj* **1** FORMAL : ceremonioso, formal **2** CEREMONIAL : ceremonial

ceremony ['sɛrəˌmo:ni] *n, pl* **-nies** : ceremonia *f*

cerise [sə'ri:s] *n* : rojo *m* cereza

certain[1] ['sərtən] *adj* **1** DEFINITE : cierto, determinado ⟨a certain percentage : un porcentaje determinado⟩ **2** TRUE : cierto, con certeza ⟨I don't know for certain : no sé exactamente⟩ **3** : cierto, alguno ⟨it has a certain charm : tiene cierta gracia⟩ **4** INEVITABLE : seguro, inevitable **5** ASSURED : seguro, asegurado ⟨she's certain to do well : seguro que le irá bien⟩

certain[2] *pron* : ciertos *pl*, algunos *pl* ⟨certain of my friends : algunos de mis amigos⟩

certainly ['sərtənli] *adv* **1** DEFINITELY : ciertamente, seguramente **2** OF COURSE : por supuesto

certainty ['sərtənti] *n, pl* **-ties** : certeza *f*, certidumbre *f*, seguridad *f*

certifiable [ˌsərtə'faɪəbəl] *adj* : certificable

certificate [sər'tɪfɪkət] *n* : certificado *m*, acta *f* ⟨birth certificate : acta de nacimiento⟩

certification [ˌsərtəfə'keɪʃən] *n* : certificación *f*

certify ['sərtəˌfaɪ] *vt* **-fied; -fying 1** VERIFY : certificar, verificar, confirmar **2** ENDORSE : endosar, aprobar oficialmente

certitude ['sərtəˌtu:d, -ˌtju:d] *n* : certeza *f*, certidumbre *f*

cervical ['sərvɪkəl] *adj* **1** : cervical (dícese del cuello) **2** : del cuello del útero

cervix ['sərvɪks] *n, pl* **-vices** [-və-ˌsi:z] *or* **-vixes 1** NECK : cerviz *f* **2** *or* **uterine cervix** : cuello *m* del útero

cesarean[1] [sɪ'zæriən] *adj* : cesáreo

cesarean[2] *n* : cesárea *f*

cesium ['si:ziəm] *n* : cesio *m*

cessation [s'seɪʃən] *n* : cesación *f*, cese *m*

cesspool ['sɛsˌpu:l] *n* : pozo *m* séptico

Chadian ['tʃædiən] *n* : chadiano *m*, -na *f* — **Chadian** *adj*

chafe ['tʃeɪf] *v* **chafed; chafing** *vi* : enojarse, irritarse — *vt* : rozar

chaff ['tʃæf] *n* **1** : barcia *f*, granzas *fpl* **2 to separate the wheat from the chaff** : separar el grano de la paja

chafing dish ['tʃeɪfɪŋˌdɪʃ] *n* : escalfador *m*

chagrin[1] [ʃə'grɪn] *vt* : desilusionar, avergonzar

chagrin[2] *n* : desilusión *f*, disgusto *m*

chain[1] ['tʃeɪn] *vt* : encadenar

chain[2] *n* **1** : cadena *f* ⟨steel chain : cadena de acero⟩ ⟨restaurant chain : cadena de restaurantes⟩ **2** SERIES : serie *f* ⟨chain of events : serie de eventos⟩ **3 chains** *npl* FETTERS : grillos *mpl*

chair[1] ['tʃɛr] *vt* : presidir, moderar

chair[2] *n* **1** : silla *f* **2** CHAIRMANSHIP : presidencia *f* **3** → **chairman, chairwoman**

chairman ['tʃɛrmən] *n, pl* **-men** [-mən, -ˌmɛn] : presidente *m*

chairmanship ['tʃɛrmənˌʃɪp] *n* : presidencia *f*

chairwoman ['tʃɛrˌwʊmən] *n, pl* **-women** [-ˌwɪmən] : presidenta *f*

chaise longue ['ʃeɪz'lɔŋ] *n, pl* **chaise longues** [-lɔŋ, -'lɔŋz] : chaise longue *f*

chalet [ʃæ'leɪ] *n* : chalet *m*, chalé *m*

chalice ['tʃælɪs] *n* : cáliz *m*

chalk[1] ['tʃɔk] *vt* : escribir con tiza

chalk[2] *n* **1** LIMESTONE : creta *f*, caliza *f* **2** : tiza *f*, gis *m Mex* (para escribir)

chalkboard ['tʃɔkˌbord] → **blackboard**

chalk up *vt* **1** ASCRIBE : atribuir, adscribir **2** SCORE : apuntarse, anotarse (una victoria, etc.)

chalky ['tʃɔki] *adj* **chalkier; -est 1** : calcáreo **2** PALE : pálido **3** POWDERY : polvoriento

challenge[1] ['tʃælɪndʒ] *vt* **-lenged; -lenging 1** DISPUTE : disputar, cuestionar, poner en duda **2** DARE : desafiar, retar **3** STIMULATE : estimular, incentivar

challenge[2] *n* : reto *m*, desafío *m*

challenger ['tʃælɪndʒər] *n* : retador *m*, -dora *f*; contendiente *mf*

chamber ['tʃeɪmbər] *n* **1** ROOM : cámara *f*, sala *f* ⟨the senate chamber : la cámara del senado⟩ **2** : recámara *f* (de un arma de fuego), cámara *f* (de combustión) **3** : cámara *f* ⟨chamber of commerce : cámara de comercio⟩ **4 chambers** *npl* *or* **judge's chambers** : despacho *m* del juez

chambermaid ['tʃeɪmbərˌmeɪd] *n* : camarera *f*

chamber music *n* : música *f* de cámara

chameleon [kə'mi:ljən, -liən] *n* : camaleón *m*

chamois [ˈʃæmi] *n, pl* **chamois** [-mi, -miz] : gamuza *f*

champ¹ [ˈʧæmp, ˈʧɑmp] *vi* **1** : masticar ruidosamente **2 to champ at the bit** : impacientarse, comerle a uno la impaciencia

champ² [ˈʧæmp] *n* : campeón *m*, -peona *f*

champagne [ʃæmˈpeɪn] *n* : champaña *m*, champán *m*

champion¹ [ˈʧæmpiən] *vt* : defender, luchar por (una causa)

champion² *n* **1** ADVOCATE, DEFENDER : paladín *m*; campeón *m*, -peona *f*; defensor *m*, -sora *f* **2** WINNER : campeón *m*, -peona *f* ⟨world champion : campeón mundial⟩

championship [ˈʧæmpiənˌʃɪp] *n* : campeonato *m*

chance¹ [ˈʧænʦ] *v* **chanced; chancing** *vi* **1** HAPPEN : ocurrir por casualidad **2 to chance upon** : encontrar por casualidad — *vt* RISK : arriesgar

chance² *adj* : fortuito, casual ⟨a chance encounter : un encuentro casual⟩

chance³ *n* **1** FATE, LUCK : azar *m*, suerte *f*, fortuna *f* **2** OPPORTUNITY : oportunidad *f*, ocasión *f* **3** PROBABILITY : probabilidad *f*, posibilidad *f* **4** RISK : riesgo *m* **5** : boleto *m* (de una rifa o lotería) **6 by chance** : por casualidad

chancellor [ˈʧænʦələr] *n* **1** : canciller *m* **2** : rector *m*, -tora *f* (de una universidad)

chancre [ˈʃæŋkər] *n* : chancro *m*

chancy [ˈʧænʦi] *adj* **chancier; -est** : riesgoso, arriesgado

chandelier [ˌʃændəˈlɪr] *n* : araña *f* de luces

change¹ [ˈʧeɪnʤ] *v* **changed; changing** *vt* **1** ALTER : cambiar, alterar, modificar **2** EXCHANGE : cambiar de, intercambiar ⟨to change places : cambiar de sitio⟩ — *vi* **1** VARY : cambiar, variar, transformarse ⟨you haven't changed : no has cambiado⟩ **2** *or* **to change clothes** : cambiarse (de ropa)

change² *n* **1** ALTERATION : cambio *m* **2** : cambio *m*, vuelto *m* ⟨two dollars change : dos dólares de vuelto⟩ **3** COINS : cambio *m*, monedas *fpl*

changeable [ˈʧeɪnʤəbəl] *adj* : cambiante, variable

changeless [ˈʧeɪnʤləs] *adj* : invariable, constante

changer [ˈʧeɪnʤər] *n* **1** : cambiador *m* ⟨record changer : cambiador de discos⟩ **2** *or* **money changer** : cambista *mf* (de dinero)

channel¹ [ˈʧænəl] *vt* **-neled** *or* **-nelled; -neling** *or* **-nelling** : encauzar, canalizar

channel² *n* **1** RIVERBED : cauce *m* **2** STRAIT : canal *m*, estrecho *m* ⟨English Channel : Canal de la Mancha⟩ **3** COURSE, MEANS : vía *f*, conducto *m* ⟨the usual channels : las vías normales⟩ **4** : canal *m* (de televisión)

chant¹ [ˈʧænt] *v* : salmodiar, cantar

chant² *n* **1** : salmodia *f* **2 Gregorian chant** : canto *m* gregoriano

Chanukah [ˈxɑnəkə, ˈhɑ-] → **Hanukkah**

chaos [ˈkeɪˌɑs] *n* : caos *m*

chaotic [keɪˈɑtɪk] *adj* : caótico — **chaotically** [-tɪkli] *adv*

chap¹ [ˈʧæp] *vi* **chapped; chapping** : partirse, agrietarse

chap² *n* FELLOW : tipo *m*, hombre *m*

chapel [ˈʧæpəl] *n* : capilla *f*

chaperon¹ *or* **chaperone** [ˈʃæpəˌroːn] *vt* **-oned; -oning** : ir de chaperón, acompañar

chaperon² *or* **chaperone** *n* : chaperón *m*, -rona *f*; acompañante *mf*

chaplain [ˈʧæplɪn] *n* : capellán *m*

chapter [ˈʧæptər] *n* **1** : capítulo *m* (de un libro) **2** BRANCH : sección *f*, división *f* (de una organización)

char [ˈʧɑr] *vt* **charred; charring 1** BURN : carbonizar **2** SCORCH : chamuscar

character [ˈkærɪktər] *n* **1** LETTER, SYMBOL : carácter *m* ⟨Chinese characters : caracteres chinos⟩ **2** DISPOSITION : carácter *m*, personalidad *f* ⟨of good character : de buena reputación⟩ **3** : tipo *m*, personaje *m* peculiar ⟨he's quite a character! : ¡él es algo serio!⟩ **4** : personaje *m* (ficticio)

characteristic¹ [ˌkærɪktəˈrɪstɪk] *adj* : característico, típico — **characteristically** [-tɪkli] *adv*

characteristic² *n* : característica *f*

characterization [ˌkærɪktərəˈzeɪʃən] *n* : caracterización *f*

characterize [ˈkærɪktəˌraɪz] *vt* **-ized; -izing** : caracterizar

charades [ʃəˈreɪdz] *ns & pl* : charada *f*

charcoal [ˈʧɑrˌkoːl] *n* : carbón *m*

chard [ˈʧɑrd] → **Swiss chard**

charge¹ [ˈʧɑrʤ] *v* **charged; charging** *vt* **1** : cargar ⟨to charge the batteries : cargar las pilas⟩ **2** ENTRUST : encomendar, encargar **3** COMMAND : ordenar, mandar **4** ACCUSE : acusar ⟨charged with robbery : acusado de robo⟩ **5** : cargar a una cuenta, comprar a crédito — *vi* **1** : cargar (contra el enemigo) ⟨charge! : ¡a la carga!⟩ **2** : cobrar ⟨they charge too much : cobran demasiado⟩

charge² *n* **1** : carga *f* (eléctrica) **2** BURDEN : carga *f*, peso *m* **3** RESPONSIBILITY : cargo *m*, responsabilidad *f* ⟨to take charge of : hacerse cargo de⟩ **4** ACCUSATION : cargo *m*, acusación *f* **5** COST : costo *m*, cargo *m*, precio *m* **6** ATTACK : carga *f*, ataque *m*

charge card → **credit card**

chargeable [ˈʧɑrʤəbəl] *adj* **1** : acusable, perseguible (dícese de un delito) **2 ~ to** : a cargo de (una cuenta)

charger [ˈʧɑrʤər] *n* : corcel *m*, caballo *m* (de guerra)

chariot [ˈʧæriət] *n* : carro *m* (de guerra)

charisma [kəˈrɪzmə] *n* : carisma *m*

charismatic [ˌkærəzˈmætɪk] *adj* : carismático

charitable [ˈʧærət̬əbəl] *adj* **1** GENER-OUS : caritativo ⟨a charitable organization : una organización benéfica⟩ **2** KIND, UNDERSTANDING : generoso, benévolo, comprensivo — **charitably** [-bli] *adv*

charitableness [ˈʧærət̬əbəlnəs] *n* : caridad *f*

charity [ˈʧærət̬i] *n, pl* **-ties 1** GENEROSITY : caridad *f* **2** ALMS : caridad *f*, limosna *f* **3** : organización *f* benéfica, obra *f* de beneficencia

charlatan [ˈʃɑrlətən] *n* : charlatán *m*, -tana *f*; farsante *mf*

charley horse [ˈʧɑrliˌhɔrs] *n* : calambre *m*

charm¹ [ˈʧɑrm] *vt* : encantar, cautivar, fascinar

charm² *n* **1** AMULET : amuleto *m*, talismán *m* **2** ATTRACTION : encanto *m*, atractivo *m* ⟨it has a certain charm : tiene cierto atractivo⟩ **3** : dije *m*, colgante *m* ⟨charm bracelet : pulsera de dijes⟩

charmer [ˈʧɑrmər] *n* : persona *f* encantadora

charming [ˈʧɑrmɪŋ] *adj* : encantador, fascinante

chart¹ [ˈʧɑrt] *vt* **1** : trazar un mapa de, hacer un gráfico de **2** PLAN : trazar, planear ⟨to chart a course : trazar un derrotero⟩

chart² *n* **1** MAP : carta *f*, mapa *m* **2** DIAGRAM : gráfico *m*, cuadro *m*, tabla *f*

charter¹ [ˈʧɑrtər] *vt* **1** : establecer los estatutos de (una organización) **2** RENT : alquilar, fletar

charter² *n* **1** STATUTES : estatutos *mpl* **2** CONSTITUTION : carta *f*, constitución *f*

chartreuse [ʃɑrˈtruːz, -ˈtruːs] *n* : color *m* verde-amarillo intenso

chary [ˈʧæri] *adj* **charier; -est 1** WARY : cauteloso, precavido **2** SPARING : parco

chase¹ [ˈʧeɪs] *vt* **chased; chasing 1** PURSUE : perseguir, ir a la caza de **2** DRIVE : ahuyentar, echar ⟨he chased the dog from the garden : ahuyentó al perro del jardín⟩ **3** : grabar (metales)

chase² *n* **1** PURSUIT : persecución *f*, caza *f* **2 the chase** HUNTING : caza *f*

chaser [ˈʧeɪsər] *n* **1** PURSUER : perseguidor *m*, -dora *f* **2** : bebida *f* que se toma después de un trago de licor

chasm [ˈkæzəm] *n* : abismo *m*, sima *f*

chassis [ˈʧæsi, ˈʃæsi] *n, pl* **chassis** [-siz] : chasis *m*, armazón *m*

chaste [ˈʧeɪst] *adj* **chaster; -est 1** : casto **2** MODEST : modesto, puro **3** AUSTERE : austero, sobrio

chastely [ˈʧeɪstli] *adv* : castamente

chasten [ˈʧeɪsən] *vt* : castigar, sancionar

chasteness [ˈʧeɪstnəs] *n* **1** MODESTY : modestia *f*, castidad *f* **2** AUSTERITY : sobriedad *f*, austeridad *f*

chastise [ˈʧæsˌtaɪz, ʧæsˈ-] *vt* **-tised; -tising 1** REPRIMAND : reprender, corregir, reprobar **2** PUNISH : castigar

chastisement [ˈʧæsˌtaɪzmənt, ʧæsˈtaɪz-, -ˈʧæstəz-] *n* : castigo *m*, corrección *f*

chastity [ˈʧæstət̬i] *n* : castidad *f*, decencia *f*, modestia *f*

chat¹ [ˈʧæt] *vi* **chatted; chatting** : charlar, platicar

chat² *n* : charla *f*, plática *f*

château [ʃæˈtoː] *n, pl* **-teaus** [-ˈtoːz] *or* **-teaux** [-ˈtoː, -ˈtoːz] : mansión *f* campestre

chattel [ˈʧæt̬əl] *n* : bienes *fpl* muebles, enseres *mpl*

chatter¹ [ˈʧæt̬ər] *vi* **1** : castañetear (dícese de los dientes) **2** GAB : parlotear *fam*, cotorrear *fam*

chatter² *n* **1** CHATTERING : castañeteo *m* (de dientes) **2** GABBING : parloteo *m fam*, cotorreo *m fam*, cháchara *f fam*

chatterbox [ˈʧæt̬ərˌbɑks] *n* : parlanchín *m*, -china *f*; charlatán *m*, -tana *f*; hablador *m*, -dora *f*

chatty [ˈʧæt̬i] *adj* **chattier; chattiest 1** TALKATIVE : parlanchín, charlatán **2** CONVERSATIONAL : familiar, conversador ⟨a chatty letter : una carta llena de noticias⟩

chauffeur¹ [ˈʃoːfər, ʃoˈfər] *vi* : trabajar de chofer privado — *vt* : hacer de chofer para

chauffeur² *n* : chofer *m* privado

chauvinism [ˈʃoːvəˌnɪzəm] *n* : chauvinismo *m*, patriotería *f*

chauvinist [ˈʃoːvənɪst] *n* : chauvinista *mf*; patriotero *m*, -ra *f*

chauvinistic [ˌʃoːvəˈnɪstɪk] *adj* : chauvinista, patriotero

cheap¹ [ˈʧiːp] *adv* : barato ⟨to sell cheap : vender barato⟩

cheap² *adj* **1** INEXPENSIVE : barato, económico **2** SHODDY : barato, mal hecho **3** STINGY : tacaño, agarrado *fam*, codo *Mex*

cheapen [ˈʧiːpən] *vt* : degradar, rebajar

cheaply [ˈʧiːpli] *adv* : barato, a precio bajo

cheapness [ˈʧiːpnəs] *n* **1** : baratura *f*, precio *m* bajo **2** STINGINESS : tacañería *f*

cheapskate [ˈʧiːpˌskeɪt] *n* : tacaño *m*, -ña *f*; codo *m*, -da *f Mex*

cheat¹ [ˈʧiːt] *vt* : defraudar, estafar, engañar — *vi* : hacer trampa

cheat² *n* **1** CHEATING : engaño *m*, fraude *m*, trampa *f* **2** → **cheater**

cheater [ˈʧiːt̬ər] *n* : estafador *m*, -dora *f*; tramposo *m*, -sa *f*

check¹ [ˈʧɛk] *vt* **1** HALT : frenar, parar, detener **2** RESTRAIN : refrenar, contener, reprimir **3** VERIFY : verificar, comprobar **4** INSPECT : revisar, chequear, inspeccionar **5** MARK : marcar, señalar **6** : chequear, facturar (maletas, equipaje) **7** CHECKER : marcar con cuadros **8 to check in** : registrarse en un hotel **9 to check out** : irse de un hotel

check² *n* **1** HALT : detención *f* súbita, parada *f* **2** RESTRAINT : control *m*, freno *m* **3** INSPECTION : inspección *f*, verificación *f*, chequeo *m* **4** : cheque *m* ⟨to pay by check : pagar con cheque⟩ **5** VOUCHER : resguardo *m*, comprobante *m* **6** BILL : cuenta *f* (en un restaurante) **7** SQUARE : cuadro *m* **8** MARK : marca *f* **9** : jaque *m* (en ajedrez)

checkbook ['tʃɛk,bʊk] *n* : chequera *f*

checker¹ ['tʃɛkər] *vt* : marcar con cuadros

checker² *n* **1** : pieza *f* (en el juego de damas) **2** : verificador *m*, -dora *f* **3** CASHIER : cajero *m*, -ra *f*

checkerboard ['tʃɛkər,bord] *n* : tablero *m* de damas

checkers ['tʃɛkərz] *n* : damas *fpl*

checkmate¹ ['tʃɛk,meɪt] *vt* **-mated; -mating 1** : dar jaque mate a (en ajedrez) **2** THWART : frustrar, arruinar

checkmate² *n* : jaque mate *m*

checkout ['tʃɛk,aʊt] *n or* **checkout counter** : caja *f*

checkpoint ['tʃɛk,pɔɪnt] *n* : puesto *m* de control

checkup ['tʃɛk,ʌp] *n* : examen *m* médico, chequeo *m*

cheddar ['tʃɛdər] *n* : queso *m* Cheddar

cheek ['tʃiːk] *n* **1** : mejilla *f*, cachete *m* **2** IMPUDENCE : insolencia *f*, descaro *m*

cheekbone ['tʃiːk,boːn] *n* : pómulo *m*

cheeky ['tʃiːki] *adj* **cheekier; -est** : descarado, insolente, atrevido

cheep¹ ['tʃiːp] *vi* : piar

cheep² *n* : pío *m*

cheer¹ ['tʃɪr] *vt* **1** ENCOURAGE : alentar, animar **2** GLADDEN : alegrar, levantar el ánimo a **3** ACCLAIM : aclamar, vitorear, echar porras a

cheer² *n* **1** CHEERFULNESS : alegría *f*, buen humor *m*, jovialidad *f* **2** APPLAUSE : aclamación *f*, ovación *f*, aplausos *mpl* ⟨three cheers for the chief! : ¡viva el jefe!⟩ **3 cheers!** : ¡salud!

cheerful ['tʃɪrfəl] *adj* : alegre, de buen humor

cheerfully ['tʃɪrfəli] *adv* : alegremente, jovialmente

cheerfulness ['tʃɪrfəlnəs] *n* : buen humor *m*, alegría *f*

cheerily ['tʃɪrəli] *adv* : alegremente

cheeriness ['tʃɪrinəs] *n* : buen humor *m*, alegría *f*

cheerleader ['tʃɪr,liːdər] *n* : porrista *mf*

cheerless ['tʃɪrləs] *adj* BLEAK : triste, sombrío

cheerlessly ['tʃɪrləsli] *adv* : desanimadamente

cheery ['tʃɪri] *adj* **cheerier; -est** : alegre, de buen humor

cheese ['tʃiːz] *n* : queso *m*

cheesecloth ['tʃiːz,klɔθ] *n* : estopilla *f*

cheesy ['tʃiːzi] *adj* **cheesier; -est 1** : a queso **2** : que contiene queso **3** CHEAP : barato, de mala calidad

cheetah ['tʃiːtə] *n* : guepardo *m*

chef ['ʃɛf] *n* : chef *m*

chemical¹ ['kɛmɪkəl] *adj* : químico — **chemically** [-mɪkli] *adv*

chemical² *n* : sustancia *f* química

chemise [ʃə'miːz] *n* **1** : camiseta *f*, prenda *f* interior de una pieza **2** : vestido *m* holgado

chemist ['kɛmɪst] *n* : químico *m*, -ca *f*

chemistry ['kɛmɪstri] *n, pl* **-tries** : química *f*

chemotherapy [,kiːmo'θɛrəpi, ,kɛmo-] *n, pl* **-pies** : quimioterapia *f*

chenille [ʃə'niːl] *n* : felpilla *f*

cherish ['tʃɛrɪʃ] *vt* **1** VALUE : apreciar, valorar **2** HARBOR : abrigar, albergar

cherry ['tʃɛri] *n, pl* **-ries 1** : cereza *f* (fruta) **2** : cerezo *m* (árbol)

cherub ['tʃɛrəb] *n* **1** *pl* **-ubim** ['tʃɛrə,bɪm, 'tʃɛrjə-] ANGEL : ángel *m*, querubín *m* **2** *pl* **-ubs** : niño *m* regordete, niña *f* regordeta

cherubic [tʃə'ruːbɪk] *adj* : querúbico, angelical

chess ['tʃɛs] *n* : ajedrez *m*

chessboard ['tʃɛs,bord] *n* : tablero *m* de ajedrez

chessman ['tʃɛsmən, -,mæn] *n, pl* **-men** [-mən, -,mɛn] : pieza *f* de ajedrez

chest ['tʃɛst] *n* **1** : cofre *m*, baúl *m* **2** : pecho *m* ⟨chest pains : dolores de pecho⟩

chestnut ['tʃɛst,nʌt] *n* **1** : castaña *f* (fruto) **2** : castaño *m* (árbol)

chest of drawers *n* : cómoda *f*

chevron ['ʃɛvrən] *n* : galón *m* (de un oficial militar)

chew¹ ['tʃuː] *vt* : masticar, mascar

chew² *n* : algo que se masca (como tabaco)

chewable ['tʃuːəbəl] *adj* : masticable

chewing gum *n* : goma *f* de mascar, chicle *m*

chewy ['tʃuːi] *adj* **chewier; -est 1** : fibroso (dícese de las carnes o los vegetales) **2** : pegajoso, chicloso (dícese de los dulces)

chic¹ ['ʃiːk] *adj* : chic, elegante, de moda

chic² *n* : chic *m*, elegancia *f*

Chicano [tʃɪ'kano] *n* : chicano *m*, -na *f* — **Chicano** *adj*

chick ['tʃɪk] *n* : pollito *m*, -ta *f*; polluelo *m*, -la *f*

chicken ['tʃɪkən] *n* **1** FOWL : pollo *m* **2** COWARD : cobarde *mf*

chickenhearted ['tʃɪkən,hɑrtəd] *n* : miedoso, cobarde

chicken pox *n* : varicela *f*

chickpea ['tʃɪk,piː] *n* : garbanzo *m*

chicle ['tʃɪkəl] *n* : chicle *m* (resina)

chicory ['tʃɪkəri] *n, pl* **-ries 1** : endibia *f* (para ensaladas) **2** : achicoria *f* (aditivo de café)

chide ['tʃaɪd] *vt* **chid** ['tʃɪd] *or* **chided; chid** *or* **chidden** ['tʃɪdən] *or* **chided; chiding** ['tʃaɪdɪŋ] : regañar, reprender

chief¹ ['tʃiːf] *adj* : principal, capital ⟨chief negotiator : negociador en jefe⟩ — **chiefly** *adv*

chief² *n* : jefe *m*, -fa *f*

chieftain [ˈʧiːftən] *n* : jefe *m*, -fa *f* (de una tribu)
chiffon [ʃɪˈfɑn, ˈʃɪ̱-] *n* : chifón *m*
chigger [ˈʧɪɡər] *n* : nigua *f*
chignon [ˈʃiːnˌjɑn, -ˌjɔn] *n* : moño *m*, chongo *m Mex*
chilblain [ˈʧɪlˌbleɪn] *n* : sabañón *m*
child [ˈʧaɪld] *n, pl* **children** [ˈʧɪldrən] **1** BABY, YOUNGSTER : niño *m*, -ña *f*; criatura *f* **2** OFFSPRING : hijo *m*, -ja *f*; progenie *f*
childbearing¹ [ˈʧaɪlˌberɪŋ] *adj* : relativo al parto ⟨of childbearing age : en edad fértil⟩
childbearing² → **childbirth**
childbirth [ˈʧaɪldˌbərθ] *n* : parto *m*
childhood [ˈʧaɪldˌhʊd] *n* : infancia *f*, niñez *f*
childish [ˈʧaɪldɪʃ] *adj* : infantil, inmaduro — **childishly** *adv*
childishness [ˈʧaɪldɪʃnəs] *n* : infantilismo *m*, inmadurez *f*
childless [ˈʧaɪldləs] *adj* : sin hijos
childlike [ˈʧaɪldˌlaɪk] *adj* : infantil, inocente ⟨a childlike imagination : una imaginación infantil⟩
childproof [ˈʧaɪldˌpruːf] *adj* : a prueba de niños
Chilean [ˈʧɪliən, ʧɪˈleɪən] *n* : chileno *m*, -na *f* — **Chilean** *adj*
chili *or* **chile** *or* **chilli** [ˈʧɪli] *n, pl* **chilies** *or* **chiles** *or* **chillies 1** *or* **chili pepper** : chile *m*, ají *m* **2** : chile *m* con carne
chill¹ [ˈʧɪl] *v* : enfriar
chill² *adj* : frío, gélido ⟨a chill wind : un viento frío⟩
chill³ *n* **1** CHILLINESS : fresco *m*, frío *m* **2** SHIVER : escalofrío *m* **3** DAMPER : enfriamiento *m*, frío *m* ⟨to cast a chill over : enfriar⟩
chilliness [ˈʧɪlinəs] *n* : frío *m*, fresco *m*
chilly [ˈʧɪli] *adj* **chillier; -est** : frío ⟨it's chilly tonight : hace frío esta noche⟩
chime¹ [ˈʧaɪm] *v* **chimed; chiming** *vt* : hacer sonar (una campana) — *vi* : sonar una campana, dar campanadas
chime² *n* **1** BELLS : juego *m* de campanitas sintonizadas, carillón *m* **2** PEAL : tañido *m*, campanada *f*
chime in *vi* : meterse en una conversación
chimera *or* **chimaera** [kaɪˈmɪrə, kə-] *n* : quimera *f*
chimney [ˈʧɪmni] *n, pl* **-neys** : chimenea *f*
chimney sweep *n* : deshollinador *m*, -dora *f*
chimp [ˈʧɪmp, ˈʃɪmp] → **chimpanzee**
chimpanzee [ˌʧɪmˌpænˈziː, ˌʃɪm-; ʧɪm ˈpænzi, ʃɪm-] *n* : chimpancé *m*
chin [ˈʧɪn] *n* : barbilla *f*, mentón *m*, barba *f*
china [ˈʧaɪnə] *n* **1** PORCELAIN : porcelana *f*, loza *f* **2** CROCKERY, TABLEWARE : loza *f*, vajilla *f*
chinchilla [ʧɪnˈʧɪlə] *n* : chinchilla *f*
Chinese [ˈʧaɪˈniːz, -ˈniːs] *n* **1** : chino *m*, -na *f* **2** : chino *m* (idioma) — **Chinese** *adj*

chink [ˈʧɪŋk] *n* : grieta *f*, abertura *f*
chintz [ˈʧɪnts] *n* : chintz *m*, chinz *m*
chip¹ [ˈʧɪp] *v* **chipped; chipping** *vt* : desportillar, desconchar, astillar (madera) — *vi* : desportillarse, desconcharse, descascararse (dícese de la pintura, etc.)
chip² *n* **1** : astilla *f* (de madera o vidrio), lasca *f* (de piedra) ⟨he's a chip off the old block : de tal palo, tal astilla⟩ **2** : bocado *m* pequeño (en rodajas o rebanadas) ⟨tortilla chips : totopos, tortillitas tostadas⟩ **3** : ficha *f* (de póker, etc.) **4** NICK : desportilladura *f*, mella *f* **5** : chip *m* ⟨memory chip : chip de memoria⟩
chip in *v* CONTRIBUTE : contribuir
chipmunk [ˈʧɪpˌmʌŋk] *n* : ardilla *f* listada
chipper [ˈʧɪpər] *adj* : alegre y vivaz
chiropodist [kəˈrɑpədɪst, ʃə-] *n* : podólogo *m*, -ga *f*
chiropody [kəˈrɑpədi, ʃə-] *n* : podología *f*
chiropractic [ˈkaɪrəˌpræktɪk] *n* : quiropráctica *f*
chiropractor [ˈkaɪrəˌpræktər] *n* : quiropráctico *m*, -ca *f*
chirp¹ [ˈʧərp] *vi* : gorjear (dícese de los pájaros), chirriar (dícese de los grillos)
chirp² *n* : gorjeo *m* (de un pájaro), chirrido *m* (de un grillo)
chisel¹ [ˈʧɪzəl] *vt* **-eled** *or* **-elled; -eling** *or* **-elling 1** : cincelar, tallar, labrar **2** CHEAT : estafar, defraudar
chisel² *n* : cincel *m* (para piedras y metales), escoplo *m* (para madera), formón *m*
chiseler [ˈʧɪzələr] *n* SWINDLER : estafador *m*, -dora *f*; fraude *mf*
chit [ˈʧɪt] *n* : resguardo *m*, recibo *m*
chitchat [ˈʧɪtˌʧæt] *n* : cotorreo *m*, charla *f*
chivalric [ʃəˈvælrɪk] → **chivalrous**
chivalrous [ˈʃɪvəlrəs] *adj* **1** KNIGHTLY : caballeresco, relativo a la caballería **2** GENTLEMANLY : caballeroso, honesto, cortés
chivalrousness [ˈʃɪvəlrəsnəs] *n* : caballerosidad *f*, cortesía *f*
chivalry [ˈʃɪvəlri] *n, pl* **-ries 1** KNIGHTHOOD : caballería *f* **2** CHIVALROUSNESS : caballerosidad *f*, nobleza *f*, cortesía *f*
chive [ˈʧaɪv] *n* : cebollino *m*
chloride [ˈklorˌaɪd] *n* : cloruro *m*
chlorinate [ˈklorəˌneɪt] *vt* **-nated; -nating** : clorar
chlorination [ˌklorəˈneɪʃən] *n* : cloración *f*
chlorine [ˈklorˌiːn] *n* : cloro *m*
chloroform [ˈklorəˌfɔrm] *n* : cloroformo *m*
chlorophyll [ˈklorəˌfɪl] *n* : clorofila *f*
chock–full [ˈʧɑkˈfʊl, ˈʧʌk-] *adj* : colmado, repleto
chocolate [ˈʧɑkələt, ˈʧɔk-] *n* **1** : chocolate *m* **2** BONBON : bombón *m* **3** : color *m* chocolate, marrón *m*

choice¹ [ˈʧɔɪs] *adj* **choicer; -est** : selecto, escogido, de primera calidad

choice² *n* **1** CHOOSING : elección *f*, selección *f* **2** OPTION : elección *f*, opción *f* ⟨I have no choice : no tengo alternativa⟩ **3** PREFERENCE : preferencia *f*, elección *f* **4** VARIETY : surtido *m*, selección *f* ⟨a wide choice : un gran surtido⟩

choir [ˈkwaɪr] *n* : coro *m*

choirboy [ˈkwaɪrˌbɔɪ] *n* : niño *m* de coro

choke¹ [ˈʧoːk] *v* **choked; choking** *vt* **1** ASPHYXIATE, STRANGLE : sofocar, asfixiar, ahogar, estrangular **2** BLOCK : tapar, obstruir — *vi* **1** SUFFOCATE : asfixiarse, sofocarse, ahogarse, atragantarse (con comida) **2** CLOG : taparse, obstruirse

choke² *n* **1** CHOKING : estrangulación *f* **2** : choke *m* (de un motor)

choker [ˈʧoːkər] *n* : gargantilla *f*

cholera [ˈkɑlərə] *n* : cólera *m*

cholesterol [kəˈlɛstəˌrɔl] *n* : colesterol *m*

choose [ˈʧuːz] *v* **chose** [ˈʧoːz]; **chosen** [ˈʧoːzən]; **choosing** *vt* **1** SELECT : escoger, elegir ⟨choose only one : escoja sólo uno⟩ **2** DECIDE : decidir ⟨he chose to leave : decidió irse⟩ **3** PREFER : preferir ⟨which one do you choose? : ¿cuál prefiere?⟩ — *vi* : escoger ⟨much to choose from : mucho de donde escoger⟩

choosy *or* **choosey** [ˈʧuːzi] *adj* **choosier; -est** : exigente, remilgado

chop¹ [ˈʧɑp] *vt* **chopped; chopping 1** MINCE : picar, cortar, moler (carne) **2 to chop down** : cortar, talar (un árbol)

chop² *n* **1** CUT : hachazo *m* (con una hacha), tajo *m* (con una cuchilla) **2** BLOW : golpe *m* (penetrante) ⟨karate chop : golpe de karate⟩ **3** : chuleta *f* ⟨pork chops : chuletas de cerdo⟩

chopper [ˈʧɑpər] → **helicopter**

choppy [ˈʧɑpi] *adj* **choppier; -est 1** : agitado, picado (dícese del mar) **2** DISCONNECTED : incoherente, inconexo

chops [ˈʧɑps] *npl* **1** : quijada *f*, mandíbula *f*, boca *f* (de una persona) **2 to lick one's chops** : relamerse

chopsticks [ˈʧɑpˌstɪks] *npl* : palillos *mpl*

choral [ˈkorəl] *adj* : coral

chorale [kəˈræl, -ˈrɑl] *n* **1** : coral *f* (composición musical vocal) **2** CHOIR, CHORUS : coral *f*, coro *m*

chord [ˈkɔrd] *n* **1** : acorde *m* (en música) **2** : cuerda *f* (en anatomía o geometría)

chore [ˈʧor] *n* **1** TASK : tarea *f* rutinaria **2** BOTHER, NUISANCE : lata *f fam*, fastidio *m* **3 chores** *npl* WORK : quehaceres *mpl*, faenas *fpl*

choreograph [ˈkoriəˌgræf] *vt* : coreografiar

choreographer [ˌkoriˈɑgrəfər] *n* : coreógrafo *m*, -fa *f*

choreographic [ˌkoriəˈgræfɪk] *adj* : coreográfico

choreography [ˌkoriˈɑgrəfi] *n, pl* **-phies** : coreografía *f*

chorister [ˈkorəstər] *n* : corista *mf*

chortle¹ [ˈʧɔrtəl] *vi* **-tled; -tling** : reírse (con satisfacción o júbilo)

chortle² *n* : risa *f* (de satisfacción o júbilo)

chorus¹ [ˈkorəs] *vt* : corear

chorus² *n* **1** : coro *m* (grupo o composición musical) **2** REFRAIN : coro *m*, estribillo *m*

chose → **choose**

chosen [ˈʧoːzən] *adj* : elegido, selecto

chow [ˈʧaʊ] *n* **1** FOOD : comida *f* **2** : chow-chow *m* (perro)

chowder [ˈʧaʊdər] *n* : sopa *f* de pescado

Christ [ˈkraɪst] *n* **1** : Cristo *m* **2 for Christ's sake** : ¡por Dios!

christen [ˈkrɪsən] *vt* **1** BAPTIZE : bautizar **2** NAME : bautizar con el nombre de

Christendom [ˈkrɪsəndəm] *n* : cristiandad *f*

christening [ˈkrɪsənɪŋ] *n* : bautismo *m*, bautizo *m*

Christian¹ [ˈkrɪsʧən] *adj* : cristiano

Christian² *n* : cristiano *m*, -na *f*

Christianity [ˌkrɪsʧiˈænəti, ˌkrɪsˈʧæ-] *n* : cristianismo *m*

Christian name *n* : nombre *m* de pila

Christmas [ˈkrɪsməs] *n* : Navidad *f* ⟨Christmas season : las Navidades⟩

chromatic [kroˈmætɪk] *adj* : cromático ⟨chromatic scale : escala cromática⟩

chrome [ˈkroːm] *n* : cromo *m* (metal)

chromium [ˈkroːmiəm] *n* : cromo *m* (elemento)

chromosome [ˈkroːməˌsoːm, -ˌzoːm] *n* : cromosoma *m*

chronic [ˈkrɑnɪk] *adj* : crónico — **chronically** [-nɪkli] *adv*

chronicle¹ [ˈkrɑnɪkəl] *vt* **-cled; -cling** : escribir (una crónica o historia)

chronicle² *n* : crónica *f*, historia *f*

chronicler [ˈkrɑnɪklər] *n* : historiador *m*, -dora *f*; cronista *mf*

chronological [ˌkrɑnəlˈɑʤɪkəl] *adj* : cronológico — **chronologically** [-kli] *adv*

chronology [krəˈnɑləʤi] *n, pl* **-gies** : cronología *f*

chronometer [krəˈnɑmətər] *n* : cronómetro *m*

chrysalis [ˈkrɪsələs] *n, pl* **chrysalides** [krɪˈsæləˌdiːz] *or* **chrysalises** : crisálida *f*

chrysanthemum [krɪˈsænθəməm] *n* : crisantemo *m*

chubbiness [ˈʧʌbinəs] *n* : gordura *f*

chubby [ˈʧʌbi] *adj* **-bier; -est** : gordito, regordete, rechoncho

chuck [ˈʧʌk] *vt* **1** TOSS : tirar, lanzar, aventar *Col, Mex* **2 to chuck under the chin** : hacer la mamola

chuck² *n* **1** PAT : mamola *f*, palmada *f* **2** TOSS : lanzamiento *m* **3** *or* **chuck steak** : corte *m* de carne de res

chuckle¹ [ˈʧʌkəl] *vi* **-led; -ling** : reírse entre dientes

chuckle² *n* : risita *f*, risa *f* ahogada

chug¹ ['tʃʌg] *vi* **chugged; chugging** : resoplar, traquetear

chug² *n* : resoplido *m*, traqueteo *m*

chum¹ ['tʃʌm] *vi* **chummed; chumming** : ser camaradas, ser cuates *Mex fam*

chum² *n* : amigo *m*, -ga *f*; camarada *mf*; compinche *mf fam*

chummy ['tʃʌmi] *adj* **-mier; -est** : amistoso ⟨they're very chummy : son muy amigos⟩

chump ['tʃʌmp] *n* : tonto *m*, -ta *f*; idiota *mf*

chunk ['tʃʌnk] *n* **1** PIECE : cacho *m*, pedazo *m*, trozo *m* **2** : cantidad *f* grande ⟨a chunk of money : mucho dinero⟩

chunky ['tʃʌnki] *adj* **chunkier; -est 1** STOCKY : fornido, robusto **2** : que contiene pedazos

church ['tʃərtʃ] *n* **1** : iglesia *f* ⟨to go to church : ir a la iglesia⟩ **2** CHRISTIANS : iglesia *f*, conjunto *m* de fieles cristianos **3** DENOMINATION : confesión *f*, secta *f* **4** CONGREGATION : feligreses *mpl*, fieles *mpl*

churchgoer ['tʃərtʃ,go:ər] *n* : practicante *mf*

churchyard ['tʃərtʃ,jard] *n* : cementerio *m* (junto a una iglesia)

churn¹ ['tʃərn] *vt* **1** : batir (crema), hacer (mantequilla) **2** : agitar con fuerza, revolver — *vi* : agitarse, arremolinarse

churn² *n* : mantequera *f*

chute ['ʃu:t] *n* : conducto *m* inclinado, vertedero *m* (para basuras)

chutney ['tʃʌtni] *n*, *pl* **-neys** : chutney *m*

chutzpah ['hʊtspə, 'xʊt-, -,spɑ] *n* : descaro *m*, frescura *f*, cara *f fam*

cicada [sə'keɪdə, -'kɑ-] *n* : cigarra *f*, chicharra *f*

cider ['saɪdər] *n* **1** : jugo *m* (de manzana, etc.) **2 hard cider** : sidra *f*

cigar [sɪ'gɑr] *n* : puro *m*, cigarro *m*

cigarette [,sɪgə'rɛt, 'sɪgə,rɛt] *n* : cigarrillo *m*, cigarro *m*

cilantro [sɪ'lɑntro:, -'læn-] *n* : cilantro *m*

cinch¹ ['sɪntʃ] *vt* **1** : cinchar (un caballo) **2** ASSURE : asegurar

cinch² *n* **1** : cincha *f* (para caballos) **2** : algo fácil o seguro ⟨it's a cinch : es bien fácil, es pan comido⟩

cinchona [sɪŋ'ko:nə] *n* : quino *m*

cinder ['sɪndər] *n* **1** EMBER : brasa *f*, ascua *f* **2 cinders** *npl* ASHES : cenizas *fpl*

cinema ['sɪnəmə] *n* : cine *m*

cinematic [,sɪnə'mætɪk] *adj* : cinematográfico

cinnamon ['sɪnəmən] *n* : canela *f*

cipher ['saɪfər] *n* **1** ZERO : cero *m* **2** CODE : cifra *f*, clave *f*

circa ['sərkə] *prep* : alrededor de, hacia ⟨circa 1800 : hacia el año 1800⟩

circle¹ ['sərkəl] *v* **-cled; -cling** *vt* **1** : encerrar en un círculo, poner un círculo alrededor de **2** : girar alrededor de, dar vueltas a ⟨we circled the building twice : le dimos vueltas al edificio dos veces⟩ — *vi* : dar vueltas

circle² *n* **1** : círculo *m* **2** CYCLE : ciclo *m* ⟨to come full circle : volver al punto de partida⟩ **3** GROUP : círculo *m*, grupo *m* (social)

circuit ['sərkət] *n* **1** BOUNDARY : circuito *m*, perímetro *m* (de una zona o un territorio) **2** TOUR : circuito *m*, recorrido *m*, tour *m* **3** : circuito *m* (eléctrico) ⟨a short circuit : un cortocircuito⟩

circuitous [,sər'kju:ətəs] *adj* : sinuoso, tortuoso

circuitry ['sərkətri] *n*, *pl* **-ries** : sistema *m* de circuitos

circular¹ ['sərkjələr] *adj* ROUND : circular, redondo

circular² *n* : circular *f*

circulate ['sərkjə,leɪt] *v* **-lated; -lating** *vi* : circular — *vt* **1** : circular (noticias, etc.) **2** DISSEMINATE : hacer circular, divulgar

circulation [,sərkjə'leɪʃən] *n* : circulación *f*

circulatory ['sərkjələ,tori] *adj* : circulatorio

circumcise ['sərkəm,saɪz] *vt* **-cised; -cising** : circuncidar

circumcision [,sərkəm'sɪʒən, 'sərkəm,-] *n* : circuncisión *f*

circumference [sər'kʌmpfrənts] *n* : circunferencia *f*

circumflex ['sərkəm,flɛks] *n* : acento *m* circunflejo

circumlocution [,sərkəmlo'kju:ʃən] *n* : circunlocución *f*

circumnavigate [,sərkəm'nævə,geɪt] *vt* **-gated; -gating** : circunnavegar

circumscribe ['sərkəm,skraɪb] *vt* **-scribed; -scribing 1** : circunscribir, trazar una figura alrededor de **2** LIMIT : circunscribir, limitar

circumspect ['sərkəm,spɛkt] *adj* : circunspecto, prudente, cauto

circumspection [,sərkəm'spɛkʃən] *n* : circunspección *f*, cautela *f*

circumstance ['sərkəm,stænts] *n* **1** EVENT : circunstancia *f*, acontecimiento *m* **2 circumstances** *npl* SITUATION : circunstancias *fpl*, situación *f* ⟨under the circumstances : dadas las circunstancias⟩ ⟨under no circumstances : de ninguna manera, bajo ningún concepto⟩ **3 circumstances** *npl* : situación *f* económica

circumstantial [,sərkəm'stæntʃəl] *adj* : circunstancial

circumvent [,sərkəm'vɛnt] *vt* : evadir, burlar (una ley o regla), sortear (una responsabilidad o dificultad)

circumvention [,sərkəm'vɛntʃən] *n* : evasión *f*

circus ['sərkəs] *n* : circo *m*

cirrhosis [sə'ro:sɪs] *n*, *pl* **-rhoses** [-'ro:,si:z] : cirrosis *f*

cirrus ['sɪrəs] *n*, *pl* **-ri** ['sɪr,aɪ] : cirro *m*

cistern ['sɪstərn] *n* : cisterna *f*, aljibe *m*

citadel ['sɪtədəl, -,dɛl] *n* FORTRESS : ciudadela *f*, fortaleza *f*

citation [saɪ'teɪʃən] *n* **1** SUMMONS : emplazamiento *m*, citación *f*, convocatoria *f* (judicial) **2** QUOTATION : cita *f* **3** COMMENDATION : elogio *m*, mención *f* (de honor)

cite ['saɪt] *vt* **cited; citing 1** ARRAIGN, SUBPOENA : emplazar, citar, hacer comparecer (ante un tribunal) **2** QUOTE : citar **3** COMMEND : elogiar, honrar (oficialmente)

citizen ['sɪt̬əzən] *n* : ciudadano *m*, -na *f*

citizenry ['sɪt̬əzənri] *n, pl* **-ries** : ciudadanía *f*, conjunto *m* de ciudadanos

citizenship ['sɪt̬əzən,ʃɪp] *n* : ciudadanía *f* ⟨Nicaraguan citizenship : ciudadanía nicaragüense⟩

citron ['sɪtrən] *n* : cidra *f*

citrus ['sɪtrəs] *n, pl* **-rus** *or* **-ruses** : cítrico *m*

city ['sɪt̬i] *n, pl* **cities** : ciudad *f*

civic ['sɪvɪk] *adj* : cívico

civics ['sɪvɪks] *ns & pl* : civismo *m*

civil ['sɪvəl] *adj* **1** : civil ⟨civil law : derecho civil⟩ **2** POLITE : civil, cortés

civilian [sə'vɪljən] *n* : civil *mf* ⟨soldiers and civilians : soldados y civiles⟩

civility [sə'vɪlət̬i] *n, pl* **-ties** : cortesía *f*, educación *f*

civilization [ˌsɪvələ'zeɪʃən] *n* : civilización *f*

civilize ['sɪvə,laɪz] *vt* **-lized; -lizing** : civilizar — **civilized** *adj*

civil liberties *npl* : derechos *mpl* civiles

civilly ['sɪvəli] *adv* : cortésmente

civil rights *npl* : derechos *mpl* civiles

civil service *n* : administración *f* pública

civil war *n* : guerra *f* civil

clack¹ ['klæk] *vi* : tabletear

clack² *n* : tableteo *m*

clad ['klæd] *adj* **1** CLOTHED : vestido **2** COVERED : cubierto

claim¹ ['kleɪm] *vt* **1** DEMAND : reclamar, reivindicar ⟨she claimed her rights : reclamó sus derechos⟩ **2** MAINTAIN : afirmar, sostener ⟨they claim it's theirs : sostienen que es suyo⟩

claim² *n* **1** DEMAND : demanda *f*, reclamación *f* **2** DECLARATION : declaración *f*, afirmación *f* **3 to stake a claim** : reclamar, reivindicar

claimant ['kleɪmənt] *n* : demandante *mf* (ante un juez), pretendiente *mf* (al trono, etc.)

clairvoyance [klær'vɔɪənts] *n* : clarividencia *f*

clairvoyant¹ [klær'vɔɪənt] *adj* : clarividente

clairvoyant² *n* : clarividente *mf*

clam ['klæm] *n* : almeja *f*

clamber ['klæmbər] *vi* : treparse o subirse torpemente

clammy ['klæmi] *adj* **-mier; -est** : húmedo y algo frío

clamor¹ ['klæmər] *vi* : gritar, clamar

clamor² *n* : clamor *m*

clamorous ['klæmərəs] *adj* : clamoroso, ruidoso, estrepitoso

clamp¹ ['klæmp] *vt* : sujetar con abrazaderas

clamp² *n* : abrazadera *f*

clan ['klæn] *n* : clan *m*

clandestine [klæn'dɛstɪn] *adj* : clandestino, secreto

clang¹ ['klæŋ] *vi* : hacer resonar (dícese de un objeto metálico)

clang² *n* : ruido *m* metálico fuerte

clangor ['klæŋər, -gər] *n* : estruendo *m* metálico

clank¹ ['klæŋk] *vi* : producir un ruido metálico seco

clank² *n* : ruido *m* metálico seco

clannish ['klænɪʃ] *adj* : exclusivista

clap¹ ['klæp] *v* **clapped; clapping** *vt* **1** SLAP, STRIKE : golpear ruidosamente, dar una palmada ⟨to clap one's hands : batir palmas, dar palmadas⟩ **2** APPLAUD : aplaudir — *vi* APPLAUD : aplaudir

clap² *n* **1** SLAP : palmada *f*, golpecito *m* **2** NOISE : ruido *m* seco ⟨a clap of thunder : un trueno⟩

clapboard ['klæbərd, 'klæp,bord] *n* : tabla *f* de madera (para revestir muros)

clapper ['klæpər] *n* : badajo *m* (de una campana)

clarification [ˌklærəfə'keɪʃən] *n* : clarificación *f*

clarify ['klærə,faɪ] *vt* **-fied; -fying 1** EXPLAIN : aclarar **2** : clarificar (un líquido)

clarinet [ˌklærə'nɛt] *n* : clarinete *m*

clarion ['klæriən] *adj* : claro y sonoro

clarity ['klærət̬i] *n* : claridad *f*, nitidez *f*

clash¹ ['klæʃ] *vi* **1** : sonar, chocarse ⟨the cymbals clashed : los platillos sonaron⟩ **2** : chocar, enfrentarse ⟨the students clashed with the police : los estudiantes se enfrentaron con la policía⟩ **3** CONFLICT : estar en conflicto, oponerse **4** : desentonar (dícese de los colores), coincidir (dícese de los datos)

clash² *n* **1** : ruido *m* (producido por un choque) **2** CONFLICT, CONFRONTATION : enfrentamiento *m*, conflicto *m*, choque *m* **3** : desentono *m* (de colores), coincidencia *f* (de datos)

clasp¹ ['klæsp] *vt* **1** FASTEN : sujetar, abrochar **2** EMBRACE, GRASP : agarrar, sujetar, abrazar

clasp² *n* **1** FASTENING : broche *m*, cierre *m* **2** EMBRACE, SQUEEZE : apretón *m*, abrazo *m*

class¹ ['klæs] *vt* : clasificar, catalogar

class² *n* **1** KIND, TYPE : clase *f*, tipo *m*, especie *f* **2** : clase *f*, rango *m* social ⟨the working class : la clase obrera⟩ **3** LESSON : clase *f*, curso *m* ⟨English class : clase de inglés⟩ **4** : conjunto *m* de estudiantes, clase *f* ⟨the class of '97 : la promoción del 97⟩

classic¹ ['klæsɪk] *adj* : clásico

classic² *n* : clásico *m*, obra *f* clásica

classical ['klæsɪkəl] *adj* : clásico — **classically** [-kli] *adv*

classicism ['klæsə,sɪzəm] *n* : clasicismo *m*

classification [,klæsəfə'keɪʃən] *n* : clasificación *f*

classified ['klæsə,faɪd] *adj* 1 : clasificado ⟨classified ads : avisos clasificados⟩ 2 RESTRICTED : confidencial, secreto ⟨classified documents : documentos secretos⟩

classify ['klæsə,faɪ] *vt* -**fied**; -**fying** : clasificar, catalogar

classless ['klæsləs] *adj* : sin clases

classmate ['klæs,meɪt] *n* : compañero *m*, -ra *f* de clase

classroom ['klæs,ru:m] *n* : aula *f*, salón *m* de clase

clatter¹ ['klæṭər] *vi* : traquetear, hacer ruido

clatter² *n* : traqueteo *m*, ruido *m*, estrépito *m*

clause ['klɔz] *n* : cláusula *f*

claustrophobia [,klɔstrə'fo:biə] *n* : claustrofobia *f*

claustrophobic [,klɔstrə'fo:bɪk] *adj* : claustrofóbico

clavicle ['klævɪkəl] *n* : clavícula *f*

claw¹ ['klɔ] *v* : arañar

claw² *n* : garra *f*, uña *f* (de un gato), pinza *f* (de un crustáceo)

clay ['kleɪ] *n* : arcilla *f*, barro *m*

clayey ['kleɪi] *adj* : arcilloso

clean¹ ['kli:n] *vt* : limpiar, lavar, asear

clean² *adv* : limpio, limpiamente ⟨to play clean : jugar limpio⟩

clean³ *adj* 1 : limpio 2 UNADULTERATED : puro 3 IRREPROACHABLE : intachable, sin mancha ⟨to have a clean record : no tener antecedentes penales⟩ 4 DECENT : decente 5 COMPLETE : completo, absoluto ⟨a clean break with the past : un corte radical con el pasado⟩

cleaner ['kli:nər] *n* 1 : limpiador *m*, -dora *f* 2 : producto *m* de limpieza 3 DRY CLEANER : tintorería *f* (servicio)

cleanliness ['klɛnlinəs] *n* : limpieza *f*, aseo *m*

cleanly¹ ['kli:nli] *adv* : limpiamente, con limpieza

cleanly² ['klɛnli] *adj* -**lier**; -**est** : limpio, pulcro

cleanness ['kli:nnəs] *n* : limpieza *f*

cleanse ['klɛnz] *vt* **cleansed**; **cleansing** : limpiar, purificar

cleanser ['klɛnzər] *n* : limpiador *m*, purificador *m*

clear¹ ['klɪr] *vt* 1 CLARIFY : aclarar, clarificar (un líquido) 2 : despejar (una superficie), desatascar (un tubo), desmontar (una selva) ⟨to clear the table : levantar la mesa⟩ ⟨to clear one's throat : carraspear, aclararse la voz⟩ 3 EXONERATE : absolver, limpiar el nombre de 4 EARN : ganar, sacar (una ganancia de) 5 : pasar sin tocar ⟨he cleared the hurdle : saltó por encima de la valla⟩ 6 **to clear up** RESOLVE : aclarar, resolver, esclarecer — *vi* 1

DISPERSE : irse, despejarse, disiparse 2 : ser compensado (dícese de un cheque) 3 **to clear up** : despejar (dícese del tiempo), mejorarse (dícese de una enfermedad)

clear² *adv* : claro, claramente

clear³ *adj* 1 BRIGHT : claro, lúcido 2 FAIR : claro, despejado 3 TRANSPARENT : transparente, translúcido 4 EVIDENT, UNMISTAKABLE : evidente, claro, obvio 5 CERTAIN : seguro 6 UNOBSTRUCTED : despejado, libre

clear⁴ *n* 1 **in the clear** : inocente, libre de toda sospecha 2 **in the clear** SAFE : fuera de peligro

clearance ['klɪrənts] *n* 1 CLEARING : despeje *m* 2 SPACE : espacio *m* (libre), margen *m* 3 AUTHORIZATION : autorización *f*, despacho *m* (de la aduana)

clearing ['klɪrɪŋ] *n* : claro *m* (de un bosque)

clearly ['klɪrli] *adv* 1 DISTINCTLY : claramente, directamente 2 OBVIOUSLY : obviamente, evidentemente

cleat ['kli:t] *n* 1 : taco *m* 2 **cleats** *npl* : zapatos *mpl* deportivos (con tacos)

cleavage ['kli:vɪdʒ] *n* 1 CLEFT : hendidura *f*, raja *f* 2 : escote *m* (del busto)

cleave¹ ['kli:v] *vi* **cleaved** ['kli:vd] *or* **clove** ['klo:v]; **cleaving** ADHERE : adherirse, unirse

cleave² *vt* **cleaved**; **cleaving** SPLIT : hender, dividir, partir

cleaver ['kli:vər] *n* : cuchilla *f* de carnicero

clef ['klɛf] *n* : clave *f*

cleft ['klɛft] *n* : hendidura *f*, raja *f*, grieta *f*

clemency ['klɛməntsi] *n* : clemencia *f*

clement ['klɛmənt] *adj* 1 MERCIFUL : clemente, piadoso 2 MILD : clemente, apacible

clench ['klɛntʃ] *vt* 1 CLUTCH : agarrar 2 TIGHTEN : apretar (el puño, los dientes)

clergy ['klərdʒi] *n, pl* -**gies** : clero *m*

clergyman ['klərdʒimən] *n, pl* -**men** [-mən, -,mɛn] : clérigo *m*

cleric ['klɛrɪk] *n* : clérigo *m*, -ga *f*

clerical ['klɛrɪkəl] *adj* 1 : clerical ⟨a clerical collar : un alzacuello⟩ 2 : de oficina ⟨clerical staff : personal de oficina⟩

clerk¹ ['klərk, *Brit* 'klɑrk] *vi* : trabajar de oficinista, trabajar de dependiente

clerk² *n* 1 : funcionario *m*, -ria *f* (de una oficina gubernamental) 2 : oficinista *mf*, empleado *m*, -da *f* de oficina 3 SALESPERSON : dependiente *m*, -ta *f*

clever ['klɛvər] *adj* 1 SKILLFUL : ingenioso, hábil 2 SMART : listo, inteligente, astuto

cleverly ['klɛvərli] *adv* 1 SKILLFULLY : ingeniosamente, hábilmente 2 INTELLIGENTLY : inteligentemente

cleverness ['klɛvərnəs] *n* 1 SKILL : ingenio *m*, habilidad *f* 2 INTELLIGENCE : inteligencia *f*

clew ['klu:] → **clue**

cliché [kli'ʃeɪ] *n* : cliché *m*, tópico *m*

click¹ ['klɪk] *vt* 1 : chasquear (los dedos, etc.) ⟨to click one's heels : dar un taconazo⟩ 2 : hacer clic en (un botón, etc.) — *vi* 1 : hacer clic 2 SNAP : chasquear 3 SUCCEED : tener éxito 4 GET ALONG : congeniar, llevarse bien

click² *n* : chasquido *m* (de los dedos, etc.), clic *m* (de un botón, etc.)

client ['klaɪənt] *n* : cliente *m*, -ta *f*

clientele [ˌklaɪən'tɛl, ˌkli:-] *n* : clientela *f*

cliff ['klɪf] *n* : acantilado *m*, precipicio *m*, risco *m*

climate ['klaɪmət] *n* : clima *m*

climatic [klaɪ'mætɪk, klə-] *adj* : climático

climax¹ ['klaɪˌmæks] *vi* : llegar al punto culminante, culminar — *vt* : ser el punto culminante de

climax² *n* : clímax *m*, punto *m* culminante

climb¹ ['klaɪm] *vt* : escalar, trepar a, subir a ⟨to climb a mountain : escalar una montaña⟩ — *vi* 1 RISE : subir, ascender ⟨prices are climbing : los precios están subiendo⟩ 2 : subirse, treparse ⟨to climb up a tree : treparse a un árbol⟩

climb² *n* : ascenso *m*, subida *f*

climber ['klaɪmər] *n* 1 : escalador *m*, -dora *f* ⟨a mountain climber : un alpinista⟩ 2 : trepadora *f* (planta)

clinch¹ ['klɪntʃ] *vt* 1 FASTEN, SECURE : remachar (un clavo), afianzar, abrochar 2 SETTLE : decidir, cerrar ⟨to clinch the title : ganar el título⟩

clinch² *n* : abrazo *m*, clinch *m* (en el boxeo)

clincher ['klɪntʃər] *n* : argumento *m* decisivo

cling ['klɪŋ] *vi* **clung** ['klʌŋ]; **clinging** 1 STICK : adherirse, pegarse 2 : aferrarse, agarrarse ⟨he clung to the railing : se aferró a la barandilla⟩

clinic ['klɪnɪk] *n* : clínica *f*

clinical ['klɪnɪkəl] *adj* : clínico — **clinically** [-kli] *adv*

clink¹ ['klɪŋk] *vi* : tintinear

clink² *n* : tintineo *m*

clip¹ ['klɪp] *vt* **clipped**; **clipping** 1 CUT : cortar, recortar 2 HIT : golpear, dar un puñetazo a 3 FASTEN : sujetar (con un clip)

clip² *n* 1 → **clippers** 2 BLOW : golpe *m*, puñetazo *m* 3 PACE : paso *m* rápido 4 FASTENER : clip *m* ⟨a paper clip : un sujetapapeles⟩

clipper ['klɪpər] *n* 1 : clíper *m* (buque de vela) 2 **clippers** *npl* : tijeras *fpl* ⟨nail clippers : cortauñas⟩

clique ['kli:k, 'klɪk] *n* : grupo *m* exclusivo, camarilla *f* (de políticos)

clitoris ['klɪtərəs, klɪ'tɔrəs] *n*, *pl* **clitorides** [-'tɔrəˌdi:z] : clítoris *m*

cloak¹ ['klo:k] *vt* : encubrir, envolver (en un manto de)

cloak² *n* : capa *f*, capote *m*, manto *m* ⟨under the cloak of darkness : al amparo de la oscuridad⟩

clobber ['klɑbər] *vt* : dar una paliza a

clock¹ ['klɑk] *vt* : cronometrar

clock² *n* 1 : reloj *m* (de pared), cronómetro *m* (en deportes o competencias) 2 **around the clock** : las veinticuatro horas

clockwise ['klɑkˌwaɪz] *adv* & *adj* : en la dirección de las manecillas del reloj

clockwork ['klɑkˌwərk] *n* : mecanismo *m* de relojería

clod ['klɑd] *n* 1 : terrón *m* 2 OAF : zoquete *mf*

clog¹ ['klɑg] *v* **clogged**; **clogging** *vt* 1 HINDER : estorbar, impedir 2 BLOCK : atascar, tapar — *vi* : atascarse, taparse

clog² *n* 1 OBSTACLE : traba *f*, impedimento *m*, estorbo *m* 2 : zueco *m* (zapato)

cloister¹ ['klɔɪstər] *vt* : enclaustrar

cloister² *n* : claustro *m*

clone ['klo:n] *n* 1 : clon *m* (de un organismo) 2 COPY : copia *f*, reproducción *f*

close¹ ['klo:z] *v* **closed**; **closing** *vt* : cerrar — *vi* 1 : cerrarse, cerrar 2 TERMINATE : concluirse, terminar 3 **to close in** APPROACH : acercarse, aproximarse

close² ['klo:s] *adv* : cerca, de cerca

close³ *adj* **closer**; **closest** 1 CONFINING : restrictivo, estrecho 2 SECRETIVE : reservado 3 STRICT : estricto, detallado 4 STUFFY : cargado, bochornoso (dícese del tiempo) 5 TIGHT : apretado, entallado, ceñido ⟨it's a close fit : es muy apretado⟩ 6 NEAR : cercano, próximo 7 INTIMATE : íntimo ⟨close friends : amigos íntimos⟩ 8 ACCURATE : fiel, exacto 9 : reñido ⟨a close election : una elección muy reñida⟩

close⁴ ['klo:z] *n* : fin *m*, final *m*, conclusión *f*

closely ['klo:sli] *adv* : cerca, de cerca

closeness ['klo:snəs] *n* 1 NEARNESS : cercanía *f*, proximidad *f* 2 INTIMACY : intimidad *f*

closet¹ ['klɑzət] *vt* **to be closeted with** : estar encerrado con

closet² *n* : armario *m*, guardarropa *f*, clóset *m*

closure ['klo:ʒər] *n* 1 CLOSING, END : cierre *m*, clausura *f*, fin *m* 2 FASTENER : cierre *m*

clot¹ ['klɑt] *v* **clotted**; **clotting** *vt* : coagular, cuajar — *vi* : cuajarse, coagularse

clot² *n* : coágulo *m*

cloth ['klɔθ] *n*, *pl* **cloths** ['klɔðz, 'klɔθs] 1 FABRIC : tela *f* 2 RAG : trapo *m* 3 TABLECLOTH : mantel *m*

clothe ['klo:ð] *vt* **clothed** *or* **clad** ['klæd]; **clothing** DRESS : vestir, arropar, ataviar

clothes ['klo:z, 'klo:ðz] *npl* 1 CLOTHING : ropa *f* 2 BEDCLOTHES : ropa *f* de cama

clothespin ['klo:zˌpɪn] *n* : pinza *f* (para la ropa)

clothing [ˈkloːðɪŋ] *n* : ropa *f*, indumentaria *f*

cloud[1] [ˈklaʊd] *vt* : nublar, oscurecer — *vi* **to cloud over** : nublarse

cloud[2] *n* : nube *f*

cloudburst [ˈklaʊdˌbərst] *n* : chaparrón *m*, aguacero *m*

cloudless [ˈklaʊdləs] *adj* : despejado, claro

cloudy [ˈklaʊdi] *adj* **cloudier; -est** : nublado, nuboso

clout[1] [ˈklaʊt] *vt* : bofetear, dar un tortazo a

clout[2] *n* **1** BLOW : golpe *m*, tortazo *m* *fam* **2** INFLUENCE : influencia *f*, palanca *f fam*

clove[1] [ˈkloːv] *n* **1** : diente *m* (de ajo) **2** : clavo *m* (especia)

clove[2] → **cleave**

cloven hoof [ˈkloːvən] *n* : pezuña *f* hendida

clover [ˈkloːvər] *n* : trébol *m*

cloverleaf [ˈkloːvərˌliːf] *n*, *pl* **-leafs** *or* **-leaves** [-ˌliːvz] : intersección *f* en trébol

clown[1] [ˈklaʊn] *vi* : payasear, bromear ⟨stop clowning around : déjate de payasadas⟩

clown[2] *n* : payaso *m*, -sa *f*

clownish [ˈklaʊnɪʃ] *adj* **1** : de payaso **2** BOORISH : grosero — **clownishly** *adv*

cloying [ˈklɔɪɪŋ] *adj* : empalagoso, meloso

club[1] [ˈklʌb] *vt* **clubbed; clubbing** : aporrear, dar garrotazos a

club[2] *n* **1** CUDGEL : garrote *m*, porra *f* **2** : palo *m* ⟨golf club : palo de golf⟩ **3** : trébol *m* (naipe) **4** ASSOCIATION : club *m*

clubfoot [ˈklʌbˌfʊt] *n*, *pl* **-feet** : pie *m* deforme

clubhouse [ˈklʌbˌhaʊs] *n* : sede *f* de un club

cluck[1] [ˈklʌk] *vi* : cloquear, cacarear

cluck[2] *n* : cloqueo *m*, cacareo *m*

clue[1] [ˈkluː] *vt* **clued; clueing** *or* **cluing** *or* **to clue in** : dar una pista a, informar

clue[2] *n* : pista *f*, indicio *m*

clump[1] [ˈklʌmp] *vi* **1** : caminar con pisadas fuertes **2** LUMP : agruparse, aglutinarse — *vt* : amontonar

clump[2] *n* **1** : grupo *m* (de arbustos o árboles), terrón *m* (de tierra) **2** : pisada *f* fuerte

clumsily [ˈklʌmzəli] *adv* : torpemente, sin gracia

clumsiness [ˈklʌmzinəs] *n* : torpeza *f*

clumsy [ˈklʌmzi] *adj* **-sier; -est 1** AWKWARD : torpe, desmañado **2** TACTLESS : carente de tacto, poco delicado

clung → **cling**

clunky [ˈklʌŋki] *adj* : torpe, poco elegante

cluster[1] [ˈklʌstər] *vt* : agrupar, juntar — *vi* : agruparse, apiñarse, arracimarse

cluster[2] *n* : grupo *m*, conjunto *m*, racimo *m* (de uvas)

clutch[1] [ˈklʌtʃ] *vt* : agarrar, asir — *vi* **to clutch at** : tratar de agarrar

clutch[2] *n* **1** GRASP, GRIP : agarre *m*, apretón *m* **2** : embrague *m*, clutch *m* (de una máquina) **3** **clutches** *npl* : garras *fpl* ⟨he fell into their clutches : cayó en sus garras⟩

clutter[1] [ˈklʌtər] *vt* : atiborrar o atestar de cosas, llenar desordenadamente

clutter[2] *n* : desorden *m*, revoltijo *m*

coach[1] [ˈkoːtʃ] *vt* : entrenar (atletas, artistas), preparar (alumnos)

coach[2] *n* **1** CARRIAGE : coche *m*, carruaje *m*, carroza *f* **2** : vagón *m* de pasajeros (de un tren) **3** BUS : autobús *m*, ómnibus *m* **4** : pasaje *m* aéreo de segunda clase **5** TRAINER : entrenador *m*, -dora *f*

coagulate [koˈægjəˌleɪt] *v* **-lated; -lating** *vt* : coagular, cuajar — *vi* : coagularse, cuajarse

coal [ˈkoːl] *n* **1** EMBER : ascua *f*, brasa *f* **2** : carbón *m* ⟨a coal mine : una mina de carbón⟩

coalesce [ˌkoːəˈlɛs] *vi* **-alesced; -alescing** : unirse

coalition [ˌkoːəˈlɪʃən] *n* : coalición *f*

coarse [ˈkors] *adj* **coarser; -est 1** : grueso (dícese de la arena o la sal), basto (dícese de las telas), áspero (dícese de la piel) **2** CRUDE, ROUGH : basto, tosco, ordinario **3** VULGAR : grosero — **coarsely** *adv*

coarsen [ˈkorsən] *vt* : hacer áspero o basto — *vi* : volverse áspero o basto

coarseness [ˈkorsnəs] *n* : aspereza *f*, tosquedad *f*

coast[1] [ˈkoːst] *vi* : deslizarse, rodar sin impulso

coast[2] *n* : costa *f*, litoral *m*

coastal [ˈkoːstəl] *adj* : costero

coaster [ˈkoːstər] *n* : posavasos *m*

coast guard *n* : guardia *f* costera, guardacostas *mpl*

coastline [ˈkoːstˌlaɪn] *n* : costa *f*

coat[1] [ˈkoːt] *vt* : cubrir, revestir, bañar (en un líquido)

coat[2] *n* **1** : abrigo *m* ⟨a sport coat : una chaqueta, un saco⟩ **2** : pelaje *m* (de animales) **3** LAYER : capa *f*, mano *f* (de pintura)

coating [ˈkoːtɪŋ] *n* : capa *f*

coat of arms *n* : escudo *m* de armas

coax [ˈkoːks] *vt* : engatusar, persuadir

cob [ˈkɑb] → **corncob**

cobalt [ˈkoːˌbɔlt] *n* : cobalto *m*

cobble [ˈkɑbəl] *vt* **cobbled; cobbling 1** : fabricar o remendar (zapatos) **2** **to cobble together** : improvisar, hacer apresuradamente

cobbler [ˈkɑblər] *n* **1** SHOEMAKER : zapatero *m*, -ra *f* **2 fruit cobbler** : tarta *f* de fruta

cobblestone [ˈkɑbəlˌstoːn] *n* : adoquín *m*

cobra [ˈkoːbrə] *n* : cobra *f*

cobweb [ˈkɑbˌwɛb] *n* : telaraña *f*

coca [ˈkoːkə] *n* : coca *f*

cocaine [ko:'keɪn, 'ko:ˌkeɪn] n : cocaína f

cock¹ ['kak] vt 1 : ladear ⟨to cock one's head : ladear la cabeza⟩ 2 : montar, amartillar (un arma de fuego)

cock² n 1 ROOSTER : gallo m 2 FAUCET : grifo m, llave f 3 : martillo m (de un arma de fuego)

cockatoo ['kakəˌtu:] n, pl -toos : cacatúa f

cockeyed ['kakˌaɪd] adj 1 ASKEW : ladeado, torcido, chueco 2 ABSURD : disparatado, absurdo

cockfight ['kakˌfaɪt] n : pelea f de gallos

cockiness ['kakinəs] n : arrogancia f

cockle ['kakəl] n : berberecho m

cockpit ['kakˌpɪt] n : cabina f

cockroach ['kakˌro:ʧ] n : cucaracha f

cocktail ['kakˌteɪl] n 1 : coctel m, cóctel m 2 APPETIZER : aperitivo m

cocky ['kaki] adj cockier; -est : creído, engreído

cocoa ['ko:ˌko:] n 1 CACAO : cacao m 2 : cocoa f, chocolate m (bebida)

coconut ['ko:kəˌnʌt] n : coco m

cocoon [kə'ku:n] n : capullo m

cod ['kad] n, pl cod : bacalao m

coddle ['kadəl] vt -dled; -dling : mimar, consentir

code ['ko:d] n 1 : código m ⟨civil code : código civil⟩ 2 : código m, clave f ⟨secret code : clave secreta⟩

codeine ['ko:ˌdi:n] n : codeína f

codex ['ko:ˌdɛks] n, pl -dexes [-ˌdɛksəz] or -dices [-dəˌsi:z] : códice m

codger ['kaʤər] n : viejo m, vejete m

codify ['kadəˌfaɪ, 'ko:-] vt -fied; -fying : codificar

coeducation [ˌko:ˌɛʤə'keɪʃən] n : coeducación f, enseñanza f mixta

coeducational [ˌko:ˌɛʤə'keɪʃənəl] adj : mixto

coefficient [ˌko:ə'fɪʃənt] n : coeficiente m

coerce [ko'ərs] vt -erced; -ercing : coaccionar, forzar, obligar

coercion [ko'ərʒən, -ʃən] n : coacción f

coercive [ko'ərsɪv] adj : coactivo

coexist [ˌko:ɪg'zɪst] vi : coexistir

coexistence [ˌko:ɪg'zɪstənts] n : coexistencia f

coffee ['kɔfi] n : café m

coffeepot ['kɔfiˌpat] n : cafetera f

coffee table n : mesa f de centro

coffer ['kɔfər] n : cofre m

coffin ['kɔfən] n : ataúd m, féretro m

cog ['kag] n : diente m (de una rueda dentada)

cogent ['ko:ʤənt] adj : convincente, persuasivo

cogitate ['kaʤəˌteɪt] vi -tated; -tating : reflexionar, meditar, discurrir

cogitation [ˌkaʤə'teɪʃən] n : reflexión f, meditación f

cognac ['ko:nˌjæk] n : coñac m

cognate ['kagˌneɪt] adj : relacionado, afín

cognition [kag'nɪʃən] n : cognición f

cognitive ['kagnətɪv] adj : cognitivo

cogwheel ['kagˌʍi:l] n : rueda f dentada

cohabit [ˌko:'hæbət] vi : cohabitar

cohere [ko'hɪr] vi -hered; -hering 1 ADHERE : adherirse, pegarse 2 : ser coherente o congruente

coherence [ko'hɪrənts] n : coherencia f, congruencia f

coherent [ko'hɪrənt] adj : coherente, congruente — coherently adv

cohesion [ko'hi:ʒən] n : cohesión f

cohesive [ko:'hi:sɪv, -zɪv] adj : cohesivo

cohort ['ko:ˌhɔrt] n 1 : cohorte f (de soldados) 2 COMPANION : compañero m, -ra f; colega mf

coiffure [kwa'fjʊr] n : peinado m

coil¹ ['kɔɪl] vt : enrollar — vi : enrollarse, enroscarse

coil² n : rollo m (de cuerda, etc.), espiral f (de humo)

coin¹ ['kɔɪn] vt 1 MINT : acuñar (moneda) 2 INVENT : acuñar, crear, inventar ⟨to coin a phrase : como se suele decir⟩

coin² n : moneda f

coincide [ˌko:ɪn'saɪd, 'ko:ɪnˌsaɪd] vi -cided; -ciding : coincidir

coincidence [ko'ɪntsədənts] n : coincidencia f, casualidad f ⟨what a coincidence! : ¡qué casualidad!⟩

coincident [ko'ɪntsədənt] adj : coincidente, concurrente

coincidental [koˌɪntsə'dɛntəl] adj : casual, accidental, fortuito

coitus ['ko:ətəs] n : coito m

coke ['ko:k] n : coque m

colander ['kaləndər, 'kʌ-] n : colador m

cold¹ ['ko:ld] adj : frío ⟨it's cold out : hace frío⟩ ⟨a cold reception : una fría recepción⟩ ⟨in cold blood : a sangre fría⟩

cold² n 1 : frío m ⟨to feel the cold : sentir frío⟩ 2 : resfriado m, catarro m ⟨to catch a cold : resfriarse⟩

cold-blooded ['ko:ld'blʌdəd] adj 1 CRUEL : cruel, despiadado 2 : de sangre fría (dícese de los reptiles, etc.)

coldly ['ko:ldli] adv : fríamente, con frialdad

coldness ['ko:ldnəs] n : frialdad f (de una persona o una actitud), frío m (de la temperatura)

coleslaw ['ko:lˌslɔ] n : ensalada f de col

colic ['kalɪk] n : cólico m

coliseum [ˌkalə'si:əm] n : coliseo m, arena f

collaborate [kə'læbəˌreɪt] vi -rated; -rating : colaborar

collaboration [kəˌlæbə'reɪʃən] n : colaboración f

collaborator [kə'læbəˌreɪtər] n 1 COLLEAGUE : colaborador m, -dora f 2 TRAITOR : colaboracionista mf

collage [kə'laʒ] n : collage m

collapse¹ [kə'læps] vi -lapsed; -lapsing 1 : derrumbarse, desplomarse, hundirse ⟨the building collapsed : el edificio se derrumbó⟩ **2** FALL : desplomarse, caerse ⟨he collapsed on the bed : se desplomó en la cama⟩ ⟨to collapse with laughter : morirse de risa⟩ **3** FAIL : fracasar, quebrar, arruinarse **4** FOLD : plegarse

collapse² *n* **1** FALL : derrumbe *m*, desplome *m* **2** BREAKDOWN, FAILURE : fracaso *m*, colapso *m* (físico), quiebra *f* (económica)

collapsible [kə'læpsəbəl] *adj* : plegable

collar¹ ['kɑlər] *vt* : agarrar, atrapar

collar² *n* : cuello *m*

collarbone ['kɑlər₁bo:n] *n* : clavícula *f*

collate [kə'leɪt; 'kɑ₁leɪt, 'ko:-] *vt* **-lated; -lating 1** COMPARE : cotejar, comparar **2** : ordenar, recopilar (páginas)

collateral¹ [kə'lætərəl] *adj* : colateral

collateral² *n* : garantía *f*, fianza *f*, prenda *f*

colleague ['kɑ₁li:g] *n* : colega *mf*; compañero *m*, -ra *f*

collect¹ [kə'lɛkt] *vt* **1** GATHER : recopilar, reunir, recoger ⟨she collected her thoughts : puso en orden sus ideas⟩ **2** : coleccionar, juntar ⟨to collect stamps : coleccionar timbres⟩ **3** : cobrar (una deuda), recaudar (un impuesto) **4** DRAW : cobrar, percibir (un sueldo, etc.) — *vi* **1** ACCUMULATE : acumularse, juntarse **2** CONGREGATE : congregarse, reunirse

collect² *adv & adj* : por cobrar, a cobro revertido

collectible *or* **collectable** [kə'lɛktəbəl] *adj* : coleccionable

collection [kə'lɛkʃən] *n* **1** COLLECTING : colecta *f* (de contribuciones), cobro *m* (de deudas), recaudación *f* (de impuestos) **2** GROUP : colección *f* (de objetos), grupo *m* (de personas)

collective¹ [kə'lɛktɪv] *adj* : colectivo — **collectively** *adv*

collective² *n* : colectivo *m*

collector [kə'lɛktər] *n* **1** : coleccionista *mf* (de objetos) **2** : cobrador *m*, -dora *f* (de deudas)

college ['kɑlɪʤ] *n* **1** : universidad *f* **2** : colegio *m* (de electores o profesionales)

collegiate [kə'li:ʤət] *adj* : universitario

collide [kə'laɪd] *vi* **-lided; -liding** : chocar, colisionar, estrellarse

collie ['kɑli] *n* : collie *mf*

collision [kə'lɪʒən] *n* : choque *m*, colisión *f*

colloquial [kə'lo:kwiəl] *adj* : coloquial

colloquialism [kə'lo:kwiə₁lɪzəm] *n* : expresión *f* coloquial

collusion [kə'lu:ʒən] *n* : colusión *f*

cologne [kə'lo:n] *n* : colonia *f*

Colombian [kə'lʌmbiən] *n* : colombiano *m*, -na *f* — **Colombian** *adj*

colon¹ ['ko:lən] *n*, *pl* **colons** *or* **cola** [-lə] : colon *m* (de los intestinos)

colon² *n*, *pl* **colons** : dos puntos *mpl* (signo ortográfico)

colonel ['kərnəl] *n* : coronel *m*

colonial¹ [kə'lo:niəl] *adj* : colonial

colonial² *n* : colono *m*, -na *f*

colonist ['kɑlənɪst] *n* : colono *m*, -na *f*; colonizador *m*, -dora *f*

colonization [₁kɑlənə'zeɪʃən] *n* : colonización *f*

colonize ['kɑlə₁naɪz] *vt* **-nized; -nizing 1** : establecer una colonia en **2** SETTLE : colonizar

colonnade [₁kɑlə'neɪd] *n* : columnata *f*

colony ['kɑləni] *n*, *pl* **-nies** : colonia *f*

color¹ ['kʌlər] *vt* **1** : colorear, pintar **2** INFLUENCE : influir en, influenciar — *vi* BLUSH : sonrojarse, ruborizarse

color² *n* **1** : color *m* ⟨primary colors : colores primarios⟩ **2** INTEREST, VIVIDNESS : color *m*, colorido *m* ⟨local color : color local⟩

coloration [kələ'reɪʃən] *n* : coloración *f*

color-blind ['kʌlər₁blaɪnd] *adj* : daltónico

color blindness *n* : daltonismo *m*

colored ['kʌlərd] *adj* **1** : de color (dícese de los objetos) **2** : de color, negro (dícese de las personas)

colorfast ['kʌlər₁fæst] *adj* : que no se destiñe

colorful ['kʌlərfəl] *adj* **1** : lleno de colorido, de colores vivos **2** PICTURESQUE, STRIKING : pintoresco, llamativo

coloring ['kələrɪŋ] *n* **1** : color *m*, colorido *m* **2 food coloring** : colorante *m*

colorless ['kʌlərləs] *adj* **1** : incoloro, sin color **2** DULL : soso, aburrido

colossal [kə'lɑsəl] *adj* : colosal

colossus [kə'lɑsəs] *n*, *pl* **-si** [-₁saɪ] : coloso *m*

colt ['ko:lt] *n* : potro *m*, potranco *m*

column ['kɑləm] *n* : columna *f*

columnist ['kɑləmnɪst, -ləmɪst] *n* : columnista *mf*

coma ['ko:mə] *n* : coma *m*, estado *m* de coma

Comanche [kə'mænʧi] *n* : comanche *mf* — **Comanche** *adj*

comatose ['ko:mə₁to:s, 'kɑ-] *adj* : comatoso, en estado de coma

comb¹ ['ko:m] *vt* **1** : peinar (el pelo) **2** SEARCH : peinar, rastrear, registrar a fondo

comb² *n* **1** : peine *m* **2** : cresta *f* (de un gallo)

combat¹ [kəm'bæt, 'kɑm₁bæt] *vt* **-bated** *or* **-batted; -bating** *or* **-batting** : combatir, luchar contra

combat² ['kɑm₁bæt] *n* : combate *m*, lucha *f*

combatant [kəm'bætənt] *n* : combatiente *mf*

combative [kəm'bætɪv] *adj* : combativo

combination [₁kɑmbə'neɪʃən] *n* : combinación *f*

combine¹ [kəm'baɪn] *v* **-bined; -bining** *vt* : combinar, aunar — *vi* : combinarse, mezclarse

combine² ['kɑm₁baɪn] *n* **1** ALLIANCE : alianza *f* comercial o política **2** HARVESTER : cosechadora *f*

combustible [kəm'bʌstəbəl] *adj* : inflamable, combustible

combustion [kəm'bʌstʃən] *n* : combustión *f*

come ['kʌm] *vi* **came** ['keɪm]; **come**; **coming** 1 APPROACH : venir, aproximarse ⟨here they come : acá vienen⟩ 2 ARRIVE : venir, llegar, alcanzar ⟨they came yesterday : vinieron ayer⟩ 3 ORIGINATE : venir, provenir ⟨this wine comes from France : este vino viene de Francia⟩ 4 AMOUNT : llegar, ascender ⟨the investment came to two million : la inversión llegó a dos millones⟩ 5 **to come clean** : confesar, desahogar la conciencia 6 **to come into** ACQUIRE : adquirir ⟨to come into a fortune : heredar una fortuna⟩ 7 **to come off** SUCCEED : tener éxito, ser un éxito 8 **to come out** : salir, aparecer, publicarse 9 **to come to** REVIVE : recobrar el conocimiento, volver en sí 10 **to come to pass** HAPPEN : acontecer 11 **to come to terms** : llegar a un acuerdo

comeback ['kʌm,bæk] *n* 1 RETORT : réplica *f*, respuesta *f* 2 RETURN : retorno *m*, regreso *m* ⟨the champion announced his comeback : el campeón anunció su regreso⟩

come back *vi* 1 RETORT : replicar, contestar 2 RETURN : volver ⟨come back here! : ¡vuelve acá!⟩ ⟨that style's coming back : ese estilo está volviendo⟩

comedian [kə'mi:diən] *n* : cómico *m*, -ca *f*; humorista *mf*

comedienne [kə,mi:di'ɛn] *n* : cómica *f*, humorista *f*

comedy ['kamədi] *n, pl* **-dies** : comedia *f*

comely ['kʌmli] *adj* **-lier; -est** : bello, bonito

comet ['kamət] *n* : cometa *m*

comfort[1] ['kʌmpfərt] *vt* 1 CHEER : confortar, alentar 2 CONSOLE : consolar

comfort[2] *n* 1 CONSOLATION : consuelo *m* 2 WELL-BEING : confort *m*, bienestar *m* 3 CONVENIENCE : comodidad *f* ⟨the comforts of home : las comodidades del hogar⟩

comfortable ['kʌmpfərtəbəl, 'kʌmpftə-] *adj* : cómodo, confortable — **comfortably** ['kʌmpfərtəbli, 'kʌmpftə-] *adv*

comforter ['kʌmpfərtər] *n* QUILT : edredón *m*, cobertor *m*

comic[1] ['kamɪk] *adj* : cómico, humorístico

comic[2] *n* 1 COMEDIAN : cómico *m*, -ca *f*; humorista *mf* 2 *or* **comic book** : historieta *f*, cómic *m*

comical ['kamɪkəl] *adj* : cómico, gracioso, chistoso

comic strip *n* : tira *f* cómica, historieta *f*

coming ['kʌmɪŋ] *adj* : siguiente, próximo, que viene

comma ['kamə] *n* : coma *f*

command[1] [kə'mænd] *vt* 1 ORDER : ordenar, mandar 2 CONTROL, DIRECT : comandar, tener el mando de — *vi* 1 : dar órdenes 2 GOVERN : estar al mando *m*, gobernar

command[2] *n* 1 CONTROL, LEADERSHIP : mando *m*, control *m*, dirección *f* 2 ORDER : orden *f*, mandato *m* 3 MASTERY : maestría *f*, destreza *f*, dominio *m* 4 : tropa *f* asignada a un comandante

commandant ['kamən,dant, -,dænt] *n* : comandante *mf*

commandeer [,kamən'dɪr] *vt* : piratear, secuestrar (un vehículo, etc.)

commander [kə'mændər] *n* : comandante *mf*

commandment [kə'mændmənt] *n* : mandamiento *m*, orden *f* ⟨the Ten Commandments : los diez mandamientos⟩

commando [kə'mændo:] *n* : comando *m*

commemorate [kə'mɛmə,reɪt] *vt* **-rated; -rating** : conmemorar

commemoration [kə,mɛmə'reɪʃən] *n* : conmemoración *f*

commemorative [kə'mɛmrətɪv, -'mɛmə,reɪtɪv] *adj* : conmemorativo

commence [kə'mɛnts] *v* **-menced; -mencing** *vt* : iniciar, comenzar — *vi* : iniciarse, comenzar

commencement [kə'mɛntsmənt] *n* 1 BEGINNING : inicio *m*, comienzo *m* 2 : ceremonia *f* de graduación

commend [kə'mɛnd] *vt* 1 ENTRUST : encomendar 2 RECOMMEND : recomendar 3 PRAISE : elogiar, alabar

commendable [kə'mɛndəbəl] *adj* : loable, meritorio, encomiable

commendation [,kamən'deɪʃən, -,mɛn-] *n* : elogio *m*, encomio *m*

commensurate [kə'mɛntsərət, -'mɛntʃurət] *adj* : proporcionado ⟨commensurate with : en proporción a⟩

comment[1] ['ka,mɛnt] *vi* 1 : hacer comentarios 2 **to comment on** : comentar, hacer observaciones sobre

comment[2] *n* : comentario *m*, observación *f*

commentary ['kamən,tɛri] *n, pl* **-taries** : comentario *m*, crónica *f* (deportiva)

commentator ['kamən,teɪtər] *n* : comentarista *mf*, cronista *mf* (de deportes)

commerce ['kamərs] *n* : comercio *m*

commercial[1] [kə'mərʃəl] *adj* : comercial — **commercially** *adv*

commercial[2] *n* : comercial *m*

commercialize [kə'mərʃə,laɪz] *vt* **-ized; -izing** : comercializar

commiserate [kə'mɪzə,reɪt] *vi* **-ated; -ating** : compadecerse, consolarse

commiseration [kə,mɪzə'reɪʃən] *n* : conmiseración *f*

commission[1] [kə'mɪʃən] *vt* 1 : nombrar (un oficial) 2 : comisionar, encargar ⟨to commission a painting : encargar una pintura⟩

commission² *n* **1** : nombramiento *m* (al grado de oficial) **2** COMMITTEE : comisión *f*, comité *m* **3** COMMITTING : comisión *f*, realización *f* (de un acto) **4** PERCENTAGE : comisión *f* ⟨sales commissions : comisiones de venta⟩

commissioned officer *n* : oficial *mf*

commissioner [kə'mɪʃənər] *n* **1** : comisionado *m*, -da *f*; miembro *m* de una comisión **2** : comisario *m*, -ria *f* (de policía, etc.)

commit [kə'mɪt] *vt* -mitted; -mitting **1** ENTRUST : encomendar, confiar **2** CONFINE : internar (en un hospital), encarcelar (en una prisión) **3** PERPETRATE : cometer ⟨to commit a crime : cometer un crimen⟩ **4 to commit oneself** : comprometerse

commitment [kə'mɪtmənt] *n* **1** RESPONSIBILITY : compromiso *m*, responsabilidad *f* **2** DEDICATION : dedicación *f*, devoción *f* ⟨commitment to the cause : devoción a la causa⟩

committee [kə'mɪṭi] *n* : comité *m*

commodious [kə'mo:diəs] *adj* SPACIOUS : amplio, espacioso

commodity [kə'mɑdəṭi] *n*, *pl* -ties : artículo *m* de comercio, mercancía *f*, mercadería *f*

commodore ['kɑmə,dor] *n* : comodoro *m*

common¹ ['kɑmən] *adj* **1** PUBLIC : común, público ⟨the common good : el bien común⟩ **2** SHARED : común ⟨a common interest : un interés común⟩ **3** GENERAL : común, general ⟨it's common knowledge : todo el mundo lo sabe⟩ **4** ORDINARY : ordinario, común y corriente ⟨the common man : el hombre medio, el hombre de la calle⟩

common² *n* **1** : tierra *f* comunal **2 in ~** : en común

common cold *n* : resfriado *m* común

common denominator *n* : denominador *m* común

commoner ['kɑmənər] *n* : plebeyo *m*, -ya *f*

commonly ['kɑmənli] *adv* **1** FREQUENTLY : comúnmente, frecuentemente **2** USUALLY : normalmente

common noun *n* : nombre *m* común

commonplace¹ ['kɑmən,pleɪs] *adj* : común, ordinario

commonplace² *n* : cliché *m*, tópico *m*

common sense *n* : sentido *m* común

commonwealth ['kɑmən,wɛlθ] *n* : entidad *f* política ⟨the British Commonwealth : la Mancomunidad Británica⟩

commotion [kə'mo:ʃən] *n* **1** RUCKUS : alboroto *m*, jaleo *m*, escándalo *m* **2** STIR, UPSET : revuelo *m*, conmoción *f*

communal [kə'mju:nəl] *adj* : comunal

commune¹ [kə'mju:n] *vi* -muned; -muning : estar en comunión

commune² ['kɑ,mju:n, kə'mju:n] *n* : comuna *f*

communicable [kə'mju:nɪkəbəl] *adj* CONTAGIOUS : transmisible, contagioso

communicate [kə'mju:nə,keɪt] *v* -cated; -cating *vt* **1** CONVEY : comunicar, expresar, hacer saber **2** TRANSMIT : transmitir (una enfermedad), contagiar — *vi* : comunicarse, expresarse

communication [kə,mju:nə'keɪʃən] *n* : comunicación *f*

communicative [kə'mju:nɪ,keɪṭɪv, -kəṭɪv] *adj* : comunicativo

communion [kə'mju:njən] *n* **1** SHARING : comunión *f* **2 Communion** : comunión *f*, eucaristía *f*

communiqué [kə'mju:nə,keɪ, -,mju:nə'keɪ] *n* : comunicado *m*

communism *or* **Communism** ['kɑmjə,nɪzəm] *n* : comunismo *m*

communist¹ *or* **Communist** ['kɑmjə,nɪst] *adj* : comunista ⟨the Communist Party : el Partido Comunista⟩

communist² *or* **Communist** *n* : comunista *mf*

communistic *or* **Communistic** [,kɑmjə'nɪstɪk] *adj* : comunista

community [kə'mju:nəṭi] *n*, *pl* -ties : comunidad *f*

commute [kə'mju:t] *v* -muted; -muting *vt* REDUCE : conmutar, reducir (una sentencia) — *vi* : viajar de la residencia al trabajo

commuter [kə'mju:ṭər] *n* : persona *f* que viaja diariamente al trabajo

compact¹ [kəm'pækt, 'kɑm,pækt] *vt* : compactar, consolidar, comprimir

compact² [kəm'pækt, 'kɑm,pækt] *adj* **1** DENSE, SOLID : compacto, macizo, denso **2** CONCISE : breve, conciso

compact³ ['kɑm,pækt] *n* **1** AGREEMENT : acuerdo *m*, pacto *m* **2** : polvera *f*, estuche *m* de maquillaje **3** *or* **compact car** : auto *m* compacto

compact disc ['kɑm,pækt'dɪsk] *n* : disco *m* compacto, compact disc *m*

compactly [kəm'pæktli, 'kɑm,pækt-] *adv* **1** DENSELY : densamente, macizamente **2** CONCISELY : concisamente, brevemente

companion [kəm'pænjən] *n* **1** COMRADE : compañero *m*, -ra *f*; acompañante *mf* **2** MATE : pareja *f* (de un zapato, etc.)

companionable [kəm'pænjənəbəl] *adj* : sociable, amigable

companionship [kəm'pænjən,ʃɪp] *n* : compañerismo *m*, camaradería *f*

company ['kʌmpəni] *n*, *pl* -nies **1** FIRM : compañía *f*, empresa *f* **2** GROUP : compañía *f* (de actores o soldados) **3** GUESTS : visita *f* ⟨we have company : tenemos visita⟩

comparable ['kɑmpərəbəl] *adj* : comparable, parecido

comparative¹ [kəm'pærəṭɪv] *adj* RELATIVE : comparativo, relativo — **comparatively** *adv*

comparative² *n* : comparativo *m*

compare¹ [kəm'pær] v -pared; -paring vt : comparar — vi **to compare with** : poder comparar con, tener comparación con

compare² n : comparación f ⟨beyond compare : sin igual, sin par⟩

comparison [kəm'pærəsən] n : comparación f

compartment [kəm'pɑrtmənt] n : compartimento m, compartimiento m

compass ['kʌmpəs, 'kɑm-] n 1 RANGE, SCOPE : alcance m, extensión f, límites mpl 2 : compás m (para trazar circunferencias) 3 : compás m, brújula f ⟨the points of the compass : los puntos cardinales⟩

compassion [kəm'pæʃən] n : compasión f, piedad f, misericordia f

compassionate [kəm'pæʃənət] adj : compasivo

compatibility [kəm,pætə'bɪləti] n : compatibilidad f

compatible [kəm'pætəbəl] adj : compatible, afín

compatriot [kəm'peɪtriət, -'pæ-] n : compatriota mf; paisano m, -na f

compel [kəm'pɛl] vt -pelled; -pelling : obligar, compeler

compelling [kəm'pɛlɪŋ] adj 1 FORCEFUL : fuerte 2 ENGAGING : absorbente 3 PERSUASIVE : persuasivo, convincente

compendium [kəm'pɛndiəm] n, pl -diums or -dia [-diə] : compendio m

compensate ['kɑmpən,seɪt] v -sated; -sating vi **to compensate for** : compensar — vt : indemnizar, compensar

compensation [,kɑmpən'seɪʃən] n : compensación f, indemnización f

compensatory [kəm'pɛnsə,tori] adj : compensatorio

compete [kəm'piːt] vi -peted; -peting : competir, contender, rivalizar

competence ['kɑmpətənts] n : competencia f, aptitud f

competency ['kɑmpətəntsi] → **competence**

competent ['kɑmpətənt] adj : competente, capaz

competition [,kɑmpə'tɪʃən] n : competencia f, concurso m

competitive [kəm'pɛtətɪv] adj : competitivo

competitor [kəm'pɛtətər] n : competidor m, -dora f

compilation [,kɑmpə'leɪʃən] n : recopilación f, compilación f

compile [kəm'paɪl] vt -piled; -piling : compilar, recopilar

complacency [kəm'pleɪsəntsi] n : satisfacción f consigo mismo, suficiencia f

complacent [kəm'pleɪsənt] adj : satisfecho de sí mismo, suficiente

complain [kəm'pleɪn] vi 1 GRIPE : quejarse, regañar, rezongar 2 PROTEST : reclamar, protestar

complaint [kəm'pleɪnt] n 1 GRIPE : queja f 2 AILMENT : afección f, dolencia f

3 ACCUSATION : reclamo m, acusación f

complement¹ ['kɑmplə,mɛnt] vt : complementar

complement² ['kɑmpləmənt] n : complemento m

complementary [,kɑmplə'mɛntəri] adj : complementario

complete¹ [kəm'pliːt] vt -pleted; -pleting 1 : completar, hacer entero ⟨this piece completes the collection : esta pieza completa la colección⟩ 2 FINISH : completar, acabar, terminar ⟨she completed her studies : completó sus estudios⟩

complete² adj -pleter; -est 1 WHOLE : completo, entero, íntegro 2 FINISHED : terminado, acabado 3 TOTAL : completo, total, absoluto

completely [kəm'pliːtli] adv : completamente, totalmente

completion [kəm'pliːʃən] n : finalización f, cumplimiento m

complex¹ [kɑm'plɛks, kəm-; 'kɑm,plɛks] adj : complejo, complicado

complex² ['kɑm,plɛks] n : complejo m

complexion [kəm'plɛkʃən] n : cutis m, tez f ⟨of dark complexion : de tez morena⟩

complexity [kəm'plɛksəti, kɑm-] n, pl -ties : complejidad f

compliance [kəm'plaɪənts] n : conformidad f ⟨in compliance with the law : conforme a la ley⟩

compliant [kəm'plaɪənt] adj : dócil, sumiso

complicate ['kɑmplə,keɪt] vt -cated; -cating : complicar

complicated ['kɑmplə,keɪt̬əd] adj : complicado

complication [,kɑmplə'keɪʃən] n : complicación f

complicity [kəm'plɪsəti] n, pl -ties : complicidad f

compliment¹ ['kɑmplə,mɛnt] vt : halagar, florear Mex

compliment² ['kɑmpləmənt] n 1 : halago m, cumplido m 2 **compliments** npl : saludos mpl ⟨give them my compliments : déles saludos de mi parte⟩

complimentary [,kɑmplə'mɛntəri] adj 1 FLATTERING : halagador, halagüeño 2 FREE : de cortesía, gratis

comply [kəm'plaɪ] vi -plied; -plying : cumplir, acceder, obedecer

component¹ [kəm'poːnənt, 'kɑm-,poː-] adj : componente

component² n : componente m, elemento m, pieza f

compose [kəm'poːz] vt -posed; -posing 1 : componer, crear ⟨to compose a melody : componer una melodía⟩ 2 CALM : calmar, serenar ⟨to compose oneself : serenarse⟩ 3 CONSTITUTE : constar, componer ⟨to be composed of : constar de⟩ 4 : componer (un texto a imprimirse)

composer [kəm'poːzər] n : compositor m, -tora f

composite¹ [kɑmˈpɑzət, kəm-; ˈkɑm-pəzət] *adj* : compuesto (de varias partes)

composite² *n* : compuesto *m*, mezcla *f*

composition [ˌkɑmpəˈzɪʃən] *n* **1** MAKE-UP : composición *f* **2** ESSAY : ensayo *m*, trabajo *m*

compost [ˈkɑmˌpoːst] *n* : abono *m* vegetal

composure [kəmˈpoːʒər] *n* : compostura *f*, serenidad *f*

compound¹ [kɑmˈpaʊnd, kəm-; ˈkɑm-ˌpaʊnd] *vt* **1** COMBINE, COMPOSE : combinar, componer **2** AUGMENT : agravar, aumentar ⟨to compound a problem : agravar un problema⟩

compound² [ˈkɑmˌpaʊnd; kɑmˈpaʊnd, kəm-] *adj* : compuesto ⟨compound interest : interés compuesto⟩

compound³ [ˈkɑmˌpaʊnd] *n* **1** MIXTURE : compuesto *m*, mezcla *f* **2** ENCLOSURE : recinto *m* (de residencias, etc.)

compound fracture *n* : fractura *f* complicada

comprehend [ˌkɑmprɪˈhɛnd] *vt* **1** UNDERSTAND : comprender, entender **2** INCLUDE : comprender, incluir, abarcar

comprehensible [ˌkɑmprɪˈhɛntsəbəl] *adj* : comprensible

comprehension [ˌkɑmprɪˈhɛntʃən] *n* : comprensión *f*

comprehensive [ˌkɑmprɪˈhɛntsɪv] *adj* **1** INCLUSIVE : inclusivo, exhaustivo **2** BROAD : extenso, amplio

compress¹ [kəmˈprɛs] *vt* : comprimir

compress² [ˈkɑmˌprɛs] *n* : compresa *f*

compression [kəmˈprɛʃən] *n* : compresión *f*

compressor [kəmˈprɛsər] *n* : compresor *m*

comprise [kəmˈpraɪz] *vt* -prised; -prising **1** INCLUDE : comprender, incluir **2** : componerse de, constar de ⟨the installation comprises several buildings : la instalación está compuesta de varios edificios⟩

compromise¹ [ˈkɑmprəˌmaɪz] *v* -mised; -mising *vi* : transigir, avenirse — *vt* JEOPARDIZE : comprometer, poner en peligro

compromise² *n* : acuerdo *m* mutuo, compromiso *m*

comptroller [kənˈtroːlər, ˈkɑmp-ˌtroː-] *n* : contralor *m*, -lora *f*; interventor *m*, -tora *f*

compulsion [kəmˈpʌlʃən] *n* **1** COERCION : coacción *f* **2** URGE : compulsión *f*, impulso *m*

compulsive [kəmˈpʌlsɪv] *adj* : compulsivo

compulsory [kəmˈpʌlsəri] *adj* : obligatorio

compunction [kəmˈpʌŋkʃən] *n* **1** QUALM : reparo *m*, escrúpulo *m* **2** REMORSE : remordimiento *m*

computation [ˌkɑmpjuˈteɪʃən] *n* : cálculo *m*, cómputo *m*

compute [kəmˈpjuːt] *vt* -puted; -puting : computar, calcular

computer [kəmˈpjuːt̬ər] *n* : computadora *f*, computador *m*, ordenador *m* *Spain*

computerize [kəmˈpjuːt̬əˌraɪz] *vt* -ized; -izing : computarizar, informatizar

comrade [ˈkɑmˌræd] *n* : camarada *mf*; compañero *m*, -ra *f*

con¹ [ˈkɑn] *vt* conned; conning SWINDLE : estafar, timar

con² *adv* : contra

con³ *n* : contra *m* ⟨the pros and cons : los pros y los contras⟩

concave [kɑnˈkeɪv, ˈkɑnˌkeɪv] *adj* : cóncavo

conceal [kənˈsiːl] *vt* : esconder, ocultar, disimular

concealment [kənˈsiːlmənt] *n* : escondimiento *m*, ocultación *f*

concede [kənˈsiːd] *vt* -ceded; -ceding **1** ALLOW, GRANT : conceder **2** ADMIT : conceder, reconocer ⟨to concede defeat : reconocer la derrota⟩

conceit [kənˈsiːt] *n* : engreimiento *m*, presunción *f*

conceited [kənˈsiːt̬əd] *adj* : presumido, engreído, presuntuoso

conceivable [kənˈsiːvəbəl] *adj* : concebible, imaginable

conceivably [kənˈsiːvəbli] *adv* : posiblemente, de manera concebible

conceive [kənˈsiːv] *v* -ceived; -ceiving *vi* : concebir, embarazarse — *vt* IMAGINE : concebir, imaginar

concentrate¹ [ˈkɑntsənˌtreɪt] *v* -trated; -trating *vt* : concentrar — *vi* : concentrarse

concentrate² *n* : concentrado *m*

concentration [ˌkɑntsənˈtreɪʃən] *n* : concentración *f*

concentric [kənˈsɛntrɪk] *adj* : concéntrico

concept [ˈkɑnˌspt] *n* : concepto *m*, idea *f*

conception [kənˈsɛpʃən] *n* **1** : concepción *f* (de un bebé) **2** IDEA : concepto *m*, idea *f*

concern¹ [kənˈsərn] *vt* **1** : tratarse de, tener que ver con ⟨the novel concerns a sailor : la novela se trata de un marinero⟩ **2** INVOLVE : concernir, incumbir a, afectar ⟨that does not concern me : eso no me incumbe⟩

concern² *n* **1** AFFAIR : asunto *m* **2** WORRY : inquietud *f*, preocupación *f* **3** BUSINESS : negocio *m*

concerned [kənˈsərnd] *adj* **1** ANXIOUS : preocupado, ansioso **2** INTERESTED, INVOLVED : interesado, afectado

concerning [kənˈsərnɪŋ] *prep* REGARDING : con respecto a, acerca de, sobre

concert [ˈkɑnˌsərt] *n* **1** AGREEMENT : concierto *m*, acuerdo *m* **2** : concierto *m* (musical)

concerted [kənˈsərt̬əd] *adj* : concertado, coordinado ⟨to make a concerted effort : coordinar los esfuerzos⟩

concertina [ˌkɑntsərˈtiːnə] *n* : concertina *f*

concerto [kən'tʃɛrtoː] *n, pl* **-ti** [-ṭi, -,tiː] *or* **-tos** : concierto *m* ⟨violin concerto : concierto para violín⟩

concession [kən'sɛʃən] *n* : concesión *f*

conch ['kaŋk, 'kantʃ] *n, pl* **conchs** ['kaŋks] *or* **conches** ['kantʃəz] : caracol *m* (animal), caracola *f* (concha)

conciliatory [kən'sɪliə,tori] *adj* : conciliador, conciliatorio

concise [kən'saɪs] *adj* : conciso, breve — **concisely** *adv*

conclave ['kan,kleɪv] *n* : cónclave *m*

conclude [kən'kluːd] *v* **-cluded; -cluding** *vt* **1** END : concluir, finalizar ⟨to conclude a meeting : concluir una reunión⟩ **2** DECIDE : concluir, llegar a la conclusión de — *vi* END : concluir, terminar

conclusion [kən'kluːʒən] *n* **1** INFERENCE : conclusión *f* **2** END : fin *m*, final *m*

conclusive [kən'kluːsɪv] *adj* : concluyente, decisivo — **conclusively** *adv*

concoct [kən'kakt, kan-] *vt* **1** PREPARE : preparar, confeccionar **2** DEVISE : inventar, tramar

concoction [kən'kakʃən] *n* : invención *f*, mejunje *m*, brebaje *m*

concomitant [kən'kamətənt] *adj* : concomitante

concord ['kan,kord, 'kaŋ-] *n* **1** HARMONY : concordia *f*, armonía *f* **2** AGREEMENT : acuerdo *m*

concordance [kən'kordənts] *n* : concordancia *f*

concourse ['kan,kors] *n* : explanada *f*, salón *m* (para pasajeros)

concrete¹ [kan'kriːt, 'kan,kriːt] *adj* **1** REAL : concreto ⟨concrete objects : objetos concretos⟩ **2** SPECIFIC : determinado, específico **3** : de concreto, de hormigón ⟨concrete walls : paredes de concreto⟩

concrete² ['kan,kriːt, kan'kriːt] *n* : concreto *m*, hormigón *m*

concur [kən'kər] *vi* **concurred; concurring 1** COINCIDE : concurrir, coincidir **2** AGREE : concurrir, estar de acuerdo

concurrent [kən'kərənt] *adj* : concurrente, simultáneo

concussion [kən'kʌʃən] *n* : conmoción *f* cerebral

condemn [kən'dɛm] *vt* **1** CENSURE : condenar, reprobar, censurar **2** : declarar insalubre (alimentos), declarar ruinoso (un edificio) **3** SENTENCE : condenar ⟨condemned to death : condenado a muerte⟩

condemnation [,kan,dɛm'neɪʃən] *n* : condena *f*, reprobación *f*

condensation [,kan,dɛn'seɪʃən, -dən-] *n* : condensación *f*

condense [kən'dɛns] *v* **-densed; -densing** *vt* **1** ABRIDGE : condensar, resumir **2** : condensar (vapor, etc.) — *vi* : condensarse

condescend [,kandɪ'sɛnd] *vi* **1** DEIGN : condescender, dignarse **2** **to condescend to someone** : tratar a alguien con condescendencia

condescension [,kandɪ'sɛntʃən] *n* : condescendencia *f*

condiment ['kandəmənt] *n* : condimento *m*

condition¹ [kən'dɪʃən] *vt* **1** DETERMINE : condicionar, determinar **2** : acondicionar (el pelo o el aire), poner en forma (el cuerpo)

condition² *n* **1** STIPULATION : condición *f*, estipulación *f* ⟨on the condition that : a condición de que⟩ **2** STATE : condición *f*, estado *m* ⟨in poor condition : en malas condiciones⟩ **3 conditions** *npl* : condiciones *fpl*, situación *f* ⟨working conditions : condiciones del trabajo⟩

conditional [kən'dɪʃənəl] *adj* : condicional — **conditionally** *adv*

conditioner [kən'dɪʃənər] *n* : acondicionador *m*

condo ['kando:] → **condominium**

condolence [kən'doːlənts] *n* **1** SYMPATHY : condolencia *f* **2 condolences** *npl* : pésame *m*

condom ['kandəm] *n* : condón *m*

condominium [,kandə'mɪniəm] *n, pl* **-ums** : condominio *m*

condone [kən'doːn] *vt* **-doned; -doning** : aprobar, perdonar, tolerar

condor ['kandər, -,dor] *n* : cóndor *m*

conducive [kən'duːsɪv, -'djuː-] *adj* : propicio, favorable

conduct¹ [kən'dʌkt] *vt* **1** GUIDE : guiar, conducir ⟨to conduct a tour : guiar una visita⟩ **2** DIRECT : conducir, dirigir ⟨to conduct an orchestra : dirigir una orquesta⟩ **3** CARRY OUT : realizar, llevar a cabo ⟨to conduct an investigation : llevar a cabo una investigación⟩ **4** TRANSMIT : conducir, transmitir (calor, electricidad, etc.) **5 to conduct oneself** BEHAVE : conducirse, comportarse

conduct² ['kan,dʌkt] *n* **1** MANAGEMENT : conducción *f*, dirección *f*, manejo *m* ⟨the conduct of foreign affairs : la conducción de asuntos exteriores⟩ **2** BEHAVIOR : conducta *f*, comportamiento *m*

conduction [kən'dʌkʃən] *n* : conducción *f*

conductivity [,kan,dʌk'tɪvəṭi] *n, pl* **-ties** : conductividad *f*

conductor [kən'dʌktər] *n* **1** : conductor *m*, -tora *f*; revisor *m*, -sora *f* (en un tren); cobrador *m*, -dora *f* (en un bus); director *m*, -tora *f* (de una orquesta) **2** : conductor *m* (de electricidad, etc.)

conduit ['kan,duː.ət, -,djuː-] *n* : conducto *m*, canal *m*, vía *f*

cone ['koːn] *n* **1** : piña *f* (fruto de las coníferas) **2** : cono *m* (en geometría) **3 ice–cream cone** : cono *m*, barquillo *m*, cucurucho *m*

confection [kən'fɛkʃən] *n* : dulce *m*

confectioner [kən'fɛkʃənər] *n* : confitero *m*, -ra *f*

confederacy [kən'fɛdərəsi] *n, pl* **-cies** : confederación *f*

confederate[1] [kən'fɛdə,reɪt] *v* **-ated; -ating** *vt* : unir, confederar — *vi* : confederarse, aliarse

confederate[2] [kən'fɛdərət] *adj* : confederado

confederate[3] *n* : cómplice *mf*; aliado *m*, -da *f*

confederation [kən,fɛdə'reɪʃən] *n* : confederación *f*, alianza *f*

confer [kən'fər] *v* **-ferred; -ferring** *vt* : conferir, otorgar — *vi* **to confer with** : consultar

conference ['kɑnfrənts, -fərənts] *n* : conferencia *f* ⟨press conference : conferencia de prensa⟩

confess [kən'fɛs] *vt* : confesar — *vi* 1 : confesar ⟨the prisoner confessed : el detenido confesó⟩ 2 : confesarse (en religión)

confession [kən'fɛʃən] *n* : confesión *f*

confessional [kən'fɛʃənəl] *n* : confesionario *m*

confessor [kən'fɛsər] *n* : confesor *m*

confetti [kən'fɛti] *n* : confeti *m*

confidant ['kɑnfə,dɑnt, -,dænt] *n* : confidente *mf*

confide [kən'faɪd] *v* **-fided; -fiding** : confiar

confidence ['kɑnfədənts] *n* 1 TRUST : confianza *f* 2 SELF-ASSURANCE : confianza *f* en sí mismo, seguridad *f* en sí mismo 3 SECRET : confidencia *f*, secreto *m*

confident ['kɑnfədənt] *adj* 1 SURE : seguro 2 SELF-ASSURED : confiado, seguro de sí mismo

confidential [,kɑnfə'dɛntʃəl] *adj* : confidencial — **confidentially** [,kɑnfə-'dɛntʃəli] *adv*

confidently ['kɑnfədəntli] *adv* : con seguridad, con confianza

configuration [kən,fɪgjə'reɪʃən] *n* : configuración *f*

confine [kən'faɪn] *vt* **-fined; -fining** 1 LIMIT : confinar, restringir, limitar 2 IMPRISON : recluir, encarcelar, encerrar

confinement [kən'faɪnmənt] *n* : confinamiento *m*, reclusión *f*, encierro *m*

confines ['kɑn,faɪnz] *npl* : límites *mpl*, confines *mpl*

confirm [kən'fərm] *vt* 1 RATIFY : ratificar 2 VERIFY : confirmar, verificar 3 : confirmar (en religión)

confirmation [,kɑnfər'meɪʃən] *n* : confirmación *f*

confiscate ['kɑnfə,skeɪt] *vt* **-cated; -cating** : confiscar, incautar, decomisar

confiscation [,kɑnfə'skeɪʃən] *n* : confiscación *f*, incautación *f*, decomiso *m*

conflagration [,kɑnflə'greɪʃən] *n* : conflagración *f*

conflict[1] [kən'flɪkt] *vi* : estar en conflicto, oponerse

conflict[2] ['kɑn,flɪkt] *n* : conflicto *m* ⟨to be in conflict : estar en desacuerdo⟩

confluence ['kɑn,flu:ənts, kən'flu:ənts] *n* : confluencia *f*

conform [kən'fɔrm] *vi* 1 ACCORD, COMPLY : ajustarse, adaptarse, conformarse ⟨it conforms with our standards : se ajusta a nuestras normas⟩ 2 CORRESPOND : corresponder, encajar ⟨to conform to the truth : corresponder a la verdad⟩

conformity [kən'fɔrməti] *n, pl* **-ties** : conformidad *f*

confound [kən'faʊnd, kɑn-] *vt* : confundir, desconcertar

confront [kən'frʌnt] *vt* : afrontar, enfrentarse a, encarar

confrontation [,kɑnfrən'teɪʃən] *n* : enfrentamiento *m*, confrontación *f*

confuse [kən'fju:z] *vt* **-fused; -fusing** 1 PUZZLE : confundir, enturbiar 2 COMPLICATE : confundir, enredar, complicar ⟨to confuse the issue : complicar las cosas⟩

confusing [kən'fju:zɪŋ] *adj* : complicado, que confunde

confusion [kən'fju:ʒən] *n* 1 PERPLEXITY : confusión *f* 2 MESS, TURMOIL : confusión *f*, embrollo *m*, lío *m fam*

congeal [kən'dʒi:l] *vi* 1 FREEZE : congelarse 2 COAGULATE, CURDLE : coagularse, cuajarse

congenial [kən'dʒi:niəl] *adj* : agradable, simpático

congenital [kən'dʒɛnət̬əl] *adj* : congénito

congest [kən'dʒɛst] *vt* 1 : congestionar (en la medicina) 2 OVERCROWD : abarrotar, atestar, congestionar (el tráfico) — *vi* : congestionarse

congestion [kən'dʒɛstʃən] *n* : congestión *f*

conglomerate[1] [kən'glɑmərət] *adj* : conglomerado

conglomerate[2] [kən'glɑmərət] *n* : conglomerado *m*

conglomeration [kən,glɑmə'reɪʃən] *n* : conglomerado *m*, acumulación *f*

Congolese [,kɑŋgə'li:z, -'li:s] *n* : congoleño *m*, -ña *f* — **Congolese** *adj*

congratulate [kən'grædʒə,leɪt, -'grætʃə-] *vt* **-lated; -lating** : felicitar

congratulation [kən,grædʒə'leɪʃən, -,grætʃə-] *n* : felicitación *f* ⟨congratulations! : ¡felicidades!, ¡enhorabuena!⟩

congregate ['kɑŋgrɪ,geɪt] *v* **-gated; -gating** *vt* : congregar, reunir — *vi* : congregarse, reunirse

congregation [,kɑŋgrɪ'geɪʃən] *n* 1 GATHERING : congregación *f*, fieles *mpl* (a un servicio religioso) 2 PARISHIONERS : feligreses *mpl*

congress ['kɑŋgrəs] *n* : congreso *m*

congressional [kən'grɛʃənəl, kɑn-] *adj* : del congreso

congressman ['kɑŋgrəsmən] *n, pl* **-men** [-mən, -,mɛn] : congresista *m*, diputado *m*

congresswoman ['kɑŋgrəs,wʊmən] *n*, *pl* **-women** [-,wɪmən] : congresista *f*, diputada *f*

congruence [kən'gruːənts, 'kɑŋgruənts] *n* : congruencia *f*

congruent [kən'gruːənt, 'kɑŋgruənt] *adj* : congruente

conic ['kɑnɪk] → **conical**

conical ['kɑnɪkəl] *adj* : cónico

conifer ['kɑnəfər, 'koː-] *n* : conífera *f*

coniferous [koˈnɪfərəs, kə-] *adj* : conífero

conjecture¹ [kən'ʤɛktʃər] *v* **-tured; -turing** : conjeturar

conjecture² *n* : conjetura *f*, presunción *f*

conjugal ['kɑnʤɪgəl, kən'ʤuː-] *adj* : conyugal

conjugate ['kɑnʤə,geɪt] *vt* **-gated; -gating** : conjugar

conjugation [,kɑnʤə'geɪʃən] *n* : conjugación *f*

conjunction [kən'ʤʌŋkʃən] *n* : conjunción *f* ⟨in conjunction with : en combinación con⟩

conjure ['kɑnʤər, 'kʌn-] *v* **-jured; -juring** *vt* **1** ENTREAT : rogar, suplicar **2 to conjure up** : hacer aparecer (apariciones), evocar (memorias, etc.) — *vi* : practicar la magia

conjurer *or* **conjuror** ['kɑnʤərər, 'kʌn-] *n* : mago *m*, -ga *f*; prestidigitador *m*, -dora *f*

connect [kə'nɛkt] *vi* : conectar, enlazar, empalmar, comunicarse — *vt* **1** JOIN, LINK : conectar, unir, juntar, vincular **2** RELATE : relacionar, asociar (ideas)

connection [kə'nɛkʃən] *n* : conexión *f*, enlace *m* ⟨professional connections : relaciones profesionales⟩

connective [kə'nɛktɪv] *adj* : conectivo, conjuntivo ⟨connective tissue : tejido conjuntivo⟩

connector [kə'nɛktər] *n* : conector *m*

connivance [kə'naɪvənts] *n* : connivencia *f*, complicidad *f*

connive [kə'naɪv] *vi* **-nived; -niving** CONSPIRE, PLOT : actuar en connivencia, confabularse, conspirar

connoisseur [,kɑnə'sər, -'sʊr] *n* : conocedor *m*, -dora *f*; entendido *m*, -da *f*

connotation [,kɑnə'teɪʃən] *n* : connotación *f*

connote [kə'noːt] *vt* **-noted; -noting** : connotar

conquer ['kɑŋkər] *vt* : conquistar, vencer

conqueror ['kɑŋkərər] *n* : conquistador *m*, -dora *f*

conquest ['kɑn,kwɛst, 'kɑŋ-] *n* : conquista *f*

conscience ['kɑntʃənts] *n* : conciencia *f*, consciencia *f* ⟨to have a clear conscience : tener la conciencia limpia⟩

conscientious [,kɑntʃi'ɛntʃəs] *adj* : concienzudo — **conscientiously** *adv*

conscious ['kɑntʃəs] *adj* **1** AWARE : consciente ⟨to become conscious of : darse

cuenta de⟩ **2** ALERT, AWAKE : consciente **3** INTENTIONAL : intencional, deliberado

consciously ['kɑntʃəsli] *adv* INTENTIONALLY : intencionalmente, deliberadamente, a propósito

consciousness ['kɑntʃəsnəs] *n* **1** AWARENESS : conciencia *f*, consciencia *f* **2** : conocimiento *m* ⟨to lose consciousness : perder el conocimiento⟩

conscript¹ [kən'skrɪpt] *vt* : reclutar, alistar, enrolar

conscript² ['kɑn,skrɪpt] *n* : conscripto *m*, -ta *f*; recluta *mf*

consecrate ['kɑntsə,kreɪt] *vt* **-crated; -crating** : consagrar

consecration [,kɑntsə'kreɪʃən] *n* : consagración *f*, dedicación *f*

consecutive [kən'sɛkjətɪv] *adj* : consecutivo, seguido ⟨on five consecutive days : cinco días seguidos⟩

consecutively [kən'sɛkjətɪvli] *adv* : consecutivamente

consensus [kən'sɛntsəs] *n* : consenso *m*

consent¹ [kən'sɛnt] *vi* **1** AGREE : acceder, ponerse de acuerdo **2 to consent to do something** : consentir en hacer algo

consent² *n* : consentimiento *m*, permiso *m* ⟨by common consent : de común acuerdo⟩

consequence ['kɑntsə,kwɛnts, -kwənts] *n* **1** RESULT : consecuencia *f*, secuela *f* **2** IMPORTANCE : importancia *f*, trascendencia *f*

consequent ['kɑntsəkwənt, -,kwɛnt] *adj* : consiguiente

consequential [,kɑntsə'kwɛntʃəl] *adj* **1** CONSEQUENT : consiguiente **2** IMPORTANT : importante, trascendente, trascendental

consequently ['kɑntsəkwəntli, -,kwɛnt-] *adv* : por consiguiente, por ende, por lo tanto

conservation [,kɑntsər'veɪʃən] *n* : conservación *f*, protección *f*

conservationist [,kɑntsər'veɪʃənɪst] *n* : conservacionista *mf*

conservatism [kən'sərvə,tɪzəm] *n* : conservadurismo *m*

conservative¹ [kən'sərvətɪv] *adj* **1** : conservador **2** CAUTIOUS : moderado, cauteloso ⟨a conservative estimate : un cálculo moderado⟩

conservative² *n* : conservador *m*, -dora *f*

conservatory [kən'sərvə,tori] *n*, *pl* **-ries** : conservatorio *m*

conserve¹ [kən'sərv] *vt* **-served; -serving** : conservar, preservar

conserve² ['kɑn,sərv] *n* PRESERVES : confitura *f*

consider [kən'sɪdər] *vt* **1** CONTEMPLATE : considerar, pensar en ⟨we'd considered attending : habíamos pensado en asistir⟩ **2** : considerar, tener en cuenta ⟨consider the consequences : considera las consecuencias⟩ **3** JUDGE, REGARD : considerar, estimar

considerable [kən'sɪdərəbəl] *adj* : considerable — **considerably** [-bli] *adv*

considerate [kən'sɪdərət] *adj* : considerado, atento

consideration [kən‚sɪdə'reɪʃən] *n* : consideración *f* ⟨to take into consideration : tener en cuenta⟩

considering [kən'sɪdərɪŋ] *prep* : teniendo en cuenta, visto

consign [kən'saɪn] *vt* **1** COMMIT, ENTRUST : confiar, encomendar **2** TRANSFER : consignar, transferir **3** SEND : consignar, enviar (mercancía)

consignment [kən'saɪnmənt] *n* **1** : envío *m*, remesa *f* **2 on** ~ : en consignación

consist [kən'sɪst] *vi* **1** LIE : consistir ⟨success consists in hard work : el éxito consiste en trabajar duro⟩ **2** : constar, componerse ⟨the set consists of 5 pieces : el juego se compone de 5 piezas⟩

consistency [kən'sɪstəntsi] *n, pl* **-cies 1** : consistencia *f* (de una mezcla o sustancia) **2** COHERENCE : coherencia *f* **3** UNIFORMITY : regularidad *f*, uniformidad *f*

consistent [kən'sɪstənt] *adj* **1** COMPATIBLE : compatible, coincidente ⟨consistent with policy : coincidente con la política⟩ **2** UNIFORM : uniforme, constante, regular — **consistently** [kən'sɪstəntli] *adv*

consolation [‚kɑntsə'leɪʃən] *n* **1** : consuelo *m* **2 consolation prize** : premio *m* de consolación

console[1] [kən'so:l] *vt* **-soled; -soling** : consolar

console[2] ['kɑn‚so:l] *n* : consola *f*

consolidate [kən'sɑlə‚deɪt] *vt* **-dated; -dating** : consolidar, unir

consolidation [kən‚sɑlə'deɪʃən] *n* : consolidación *f*

consommé [‚kɑntsə'meɪ] *n* : consomé *m*

consonant ['kɑntsənənt] *n* : consonante *m*

consort[1] [kən'sɔrt] *vi* : asociarse, relacionarse, tener trato ⟨to consort with criminals : tener trato con criminales⟩

consort[2] ['kɑn‚sɔrt] *n* : consorte *mf*

consortium [kən'sɔrʃəm] *n, pl* **-tia** [-ʃə] *or* **-tiums** [-ʃəmz] : consorcio *m*

conspicuous [kən'spɪkjʊəs] *adj* **1** OBVIOUS : visible, evidente **2** STRIKING : llamativo

conspicuously [kən'spɪkjʊəsli] *adv* : de manera llamativa

conspiracy [kən'spɪrəsi] *n, pl* **-cies** : conspiración *f*, complot *m*, confabulación *f*

conspirator [kən'spɪrətər] *n* : conspirador *m*, -dora *f*

conspire [kən'spaɪr] *vi* **-spired; -spiring** : conspirar, confabularse

constable ['kɑntstəbəl, 'kʌntstə-] *n* : agente *mf* de policía (en un pueblo)

constancy ['kɑntstəntsi] *n, pl* **-cies** : constancia *f*

constant[1] ['kɑntstənt] *adj* **1** FAITHFUL : leal, fiel **2** INVARIABLE : constante, invariable **3** CONTINUAL : constante, continuo

constant[2] *n* : constante *f*

constantly ['kɑntstəntli] *adv* : constantemente, continuamente

constellation [‚kɑntstə'leɪʃən] *n* : constelación *f*

consternation [‚kɑntstər'neɪʃən] *n* : consternación *f*

constipate ['kɑntstə‚peɪt] *vt* **-pated; -pating** : estreñir

constipation ['kɑntstə'peɪʃən] *n* : estreñimiento *m*, constipación *f* (de vientre)

constituency [kən'stɪtʃʊəntsi] *n, pl* **-cies 1** : distrito *m* electoral **2** : residentes *mpl* de un distrito electoral

constituent[1] [kən'stɪtʃʊənt] *adj* **1** COMPONENT : constituyente, componente **2** : constituyente, constitutivo ⟨a constituent assembly : una asamblea constituyente⟩

constituent[2] *n* **1** COMPONENT : componente *m* **2** ELECTOR, VOTER : elector *m*, -tora *f*; votante *mf*

constitute ['kɑntstə‚tu:t, -‚tju:t] *vt* **-tuted; -tuting 1** ESTABLISH : constituir, establecer **2** COMPOSE, FORM : constituir, componer

constitution [‚kɑntstə'tu:ʃən, -'tju:-] *n* : constitución *f*

constitutional [‚kɑntstə'tu:ʃənəl, -'tju:-] *adj* : constitucional

constitutionality [‚kɑntstə‚tu:ʃə'næləti, -‚tju:-] *n* : constitucionalidad *f*

constrain [kən'streɪn] *vt* **1** COMPEL : constreñir, obligar **2** CONFINE : constreñir, limitar, restringir **3** RESTRAIN : contener, refrenar

constraint [kən'streɪnt] *n* : restricción *f*, limitación *f*

constrict [kən'strɪkt] *vt* : estrechar, apretar, comprimir

constriction [kən'strɪkʃən] *n* : estrechamiento *m*, compresión *f*

construct [kən'strʌkt] *vt* : construir

construction [kən'strʌkʃən] *n* : construcción *f*

constructive [kən'strʌktɪv] *adj* : constructivo

construe [kən'stru:] *vt* **-strued; -struing** : interpretar

consul ['kɑntsəl] *n* : cónsul *mf*

consular ['kɑntsələr] *adj* : consular

consulate ['kɑntsələt] *n* : consulado *m*

consult [kən'sʌlt] *vt* : consultar — *vi* **to consult with** : consultar con, solicitar la opinión de

consultant [kən'sʌltənt] *n* : consultor *m*, -tora *f*; asesor *m*, -sora *f*

consultation [‚kɑntsəl'teɪʃən] *n* : consulta *f*

consumable [kən'su:məbəl] *adj* : consumible

consume [kən'su:m] *vt* **-sumed; -suming** : consumir, usar, gastar

consumer [kən'su:mər] *n* : consumidor *m*, -dora *f*

consummate¹ ['kαntsə,meit] *vt* **-mated; -mating** : consumar

consummate² [kən'sʌmət, 'kαntsə-mət] *adj* : consumado, perfecto

consummation [,kαntsə'meiʃən] : consumación *f*

consumption [kən'sʌmpʃən] *n* **1** USE : consumo *m*, uso *m* ⟨consumption of electricity : consumo de electricidad⟩ **2** TUBERCULOSIS : tisis *f*, consunción *f*

contact¹ ['kαn,tækt, kən'-] *vt* : ponerse en contacto con, contactar (con)

contact² ['kαn,tækt] *n* **1** TOUCHING : contacto *m* ⟨to come into contact with : entrar en contacto con⟩ **2** TOUCH : contacto *m*, comunicación *f* ⟨to lose contact with : perder contacto con⟩ **3** CONNECTION : contacto *m* (en negocios) **4** → **contact lens**

contact lens ['kαn,tækt'lɛnz] *n* : lente *mf* de contacto, pupilente *m* Mex

contagion [kən'teidʒən] *n* : contagio *m*

contagious [kən'teidʒəs] *adj* : contagioso

contain [kən'tein] *vt* **1** : contener **2 to contain oneself** : contenerse

container [kən'teinər] *n* : recipiente *m*, envase *m*

containment [kən'teinmənt] *n* : contención *f*

contaminant [kən'tæmənənt] *n* : contaminante *m*

contaminate [kən'tæmə,neit] *vt* **-nated; -nating** : contaminar

contamination [kən,tæmə'neiʃən] *n* : contaminación *f*

contemplate ['kαntəm,pleit] *v* **-plated; -plating** *vt* **1** VIEW : contemplar **2** PONDER : contemplar, considerar **3** CONSIDER, PROPOSE : proponerse, proyectar, pensar en ⟨to contemplate a trip : pensar en viajar⟩ — *vi* MEDITATE : meditar

contemplation [,kαntəm'pleiʃən] *n* : contemplación *f*

contemplative [kən'templətiv, 'kαntəm,pleitiv] *adj* : contemplativo

contemporaneous [kən,tempə'reiniəs] *adj* → **contemporary¹**

contemporary¹ [kən'tempə,reri] *adj* : contemporáneo

contemporary² *n, pl* **-raries** : contemporáneo *m*, -nea *f*

contempt [kən'tempt] *n* **1** DISDAIN : desprecio *m*, desdén *m* ⟨to hold in contempt : despreciar⟩ **2** : desacato *m* (ante un tribunal)

contemptible [kən'temptəbəl] *adj* : despreciable, vil

contemptuous [kən'temptʃuəs] *adj* : despectivo, despreciativo, desdeñoso

contemptuously [kən'temptʃuəsli] *adv* : despectivamente, con desprecio

contend [kən'tend] *vi* **1** STRUGGLE : luchar, lidiar, contender ⟨to contend with a problem : lidiar con un proble-

ma⟩ **2** COMPETE : competir ⟨to contend for a position : competir por un puesto⟩ — *vt* **1** ARGUE, MAINTAIN : argüir, sostener, afirmar ⟨he contended that he was right : afirmó que tenía razón⟩ **2** CONTEST : protestar contra (una decisión, etc.), disputar

contender [kən'tendər] *n* : contendiente *mf*; aspirante *mf*; competidor *m*, -dora *f*

content¹ [kən'tent] *vt* SATISFY : contentar, satisfacer

content² *adj* : conforme, contento, satisfecho

content³ *n* CONTENTMENT : contento *m*, satisfacción *f* ⟨to one's heart's content : hasta quedar satisfecho, a más no poder⟩

content⁴ ['kαn,tent] *n* **1** MEANING : contenido *m*, significado *m* **2** PROPORTION : contenido *m*, proporción *f* ⟨fat content : contenido de grasa⟩ **3 contents** *npl* : contenido *m*, sumario *m* (de un libro) ⟨table of contents : índice de materias⟩

contented [kən'tentəd] *adj* : conforme, satisfecho ⟨a contented smile : una sonrisa de satisfacción⟩

contentedly [kən'tentədli] *adv* : con satisfacción

contention [kən'tentʃən] *n* **1** DISPUTE : disputa *f*, discusión *f* **2** COMPETITION : competencia *f*, contienda *f* **3** OPINION : argumento *m*, opinión *f*

contentious [kən'tentʃəs] *adj* : disputador, pugnaz, combativo

contentment [kən'tentmənt] *n* : satisfacción *f*, contento *m*

contest¹ [kən'test] *vt* : disputar, cuestionar, impugnar ⟨to contest a will : impugnar un testamento⟩

contest² ['kαn,test] *n* **1** STRUGGLE : lucha *f*, contienda *f* **2** GAME : concurso *m*, competencia *f*

contestable [kən'testəbəl] *adj* : discutible, cuestionable

contestant [kən'testənt] *n* : concursante *mf*; competidor *m*, -dora *f*

context ['kαn,tekst] *n* : contexto *m*

contiguous [kən'tigjuəs] *adj* : contiguo

continence ['kαntənənts] *n* : continencia *f*

continent¹ ['kαntənənt] *adj* : continente

continent² *n* : continente *m* — **continental** [,kαntən'entəl] *adj*

contingency [kən'tindʒəntsi] *n, pl* **-cies** : contingencia *f*, eventualidad *f*

contingent¹ [kən'tindʒənt] *adj* **1** POSSIBLE : contingente, eventual **2** ACCIDENTAL : fortuito, accidental **3 to be contingent on** : depender de, estar sujeto a

contingent² *n* : contingente *m*

continual [kən'tinjuəl] *adj* : continuo, constante — **continually** [kən-'tinjuəli, -'tinjəli] *adv*

continuance [kən'tinjuənts] *n* **1** CONTINUATION : continuación *f* **2** DURA-

TION : duración *f* **3** : aplazamiento *m* (de un proceso)

continuation [kən͵tɪnjuˈeɪʃən] *n* : continuación *f*, prolongación *f*

continue [kənˈtɪnju:] *v* **-tinued; -tinuing** *vi* **1** CARRY ON : continuar, seguir, proseguir ⟨please continue : continúe, por favor⟩ **2** ENDURE, LAST : continuar, prolongarse, durar **3** RESUME : continuar, reanudarse — *vt* **1** : continuar, seguir ⟨she continued writing : continuó escribiendo⟩ **2** RESUME : continuar, reanudar **3** EXTEND, PROLONG : continuar, prolongar

continuity [͵kɑntəˈnu:əṭi, -ˈnju:-] *n, pl* **-ties** : continuidad *f*

continuous [kənˈtɪnjuəs] *adj* : continuo — **continuously** *adv*

contort [kənˈtɔrt] *vt* : torcer, retorcer, contraer (el rostro) — *vi* : contraerse, demudarse

contortion [kənˈtɔrʃən] *n* : contorsión *f*

contour [ˈkɑn͵tʊr] *n* **1** OUTLINE : contorno *m* **2** **contours** *npl* SHAPE : forma *f*, curvas *fpl* **3** **contour map** : mapa *m* topográfico

contraband [ˈkɑntrə͵bænd] *n* : contrabando *m*

contraception [͵kɑntrəˈsɛpʃən] *n* : anticoncepción *f*, contracepción *f*

contraceptive[1] [͵kɑntrəˈsɛptɪv] *adj* : anticonceptivo, contraceptivo

contraceptive[2] *n* : anticonceptivo *m*, contraceptivo *m*

contract[1] [kənˈtrækt, 1 *usu* ˈkɑn-͵trækt] *vt* **1** : contratar (servicios profesionales) **2** : contraer (una enfermedad, una deuda) **3** TIGHTEN : contraer (un músculo) **4** SHORTEN : contraer (una palabra) — *vi* : contraerse, reducirse

contract[2] [ˈkɑn͵trækt] *n* : contrato *m*

contraction [kənˈtrækʃən] *n* : contracción *f*

contractor [ˈkɑn͵træktər, kənˈtræk-] *n* : contratista *mf*

contractual [kənˈtræktʃuəl] *adj* : contractual — **contractually** *adv*

contradict [͵kɑntrəˈdɪkt] *vt* : contradecir, desmentir

contradiction [͵kɑntrəˈdɪkʃən] *n* : contradicción *f*

contradictory [͵kɑntrəˈdɪktəri] *adj* : contradictorio

contralto [kənˈtræl͵to:] *n, pl* **-tos** : contralto *m* (voz), contralto *mf* (vocalista)

contraption [kənˈtræpʃən] *n* DEVICE : aparato *m*, artefacto *m*

contrary[1] [ˈkɑn͵trɛri, 2 *often* kənˈtrɛri] *adj* **1** OPPOSITE : contrario, opuesto **2** BALKY, STUBBORN : terco, testarudo **3** **contrary to** : al contrario de, en contra de ⟨contrary to the facts : en contra de los hechos⟩

contrary[2] [ˈkɑn͵trɛri] *n, pl* **-traries 1** OPPOSITE : lo contrario, lo opuesto **2 on the contrary** : al contrario, todo lo contrario

contrast[1] [kənˈtræst] *vi* DIFFER : contrastar, diferir — *vt* COMPARE : contrastar, comparar

contrast[2] [ˈkɑn͵træst] *n* : contraste *m*

contravene [͵kɑntrəˈvi:n] *vt* **-vened; -vening** : contravenir, infringir

contribute [kənˈtrɪbjət] *v* **-uted; -uting** *vt* : contribuir, aportar (dinero, bienes, etc.) — *vi* : contribuir

contribution [͵kɑntrəˈbju:ʃən] *n* : contribución *f*

contributor [kənˈtrɪbjəṭər] *n* : contribuidor *m*, -dora *f*; colaborador *m*, -dora *f* (en periodismo)

contrite [ˈkɑn͵traɪt, kənˈtraɪt] *adj* REPENTANT : contrito, arrepentido

contrition [kənˈtrɪʃən] *n* : contrición *f*, arrepentimiento *m*

contrivance [kənˈtraɪvənts] *n* **1** DEVICE : aparato *m*, artefacto *m* **2** SCHEME : artimaña *f*, treta *f*, ardid *m*

contrive [kənˈtraɪv] *vt* **-trived; -triving 1** DEVISE : idear, ingeniar, maquinar **2** MANAGE : lograr, ingeniárselas para ⟨she contrived a way out of the mess : se las ingenió para salir del enredo⟩

control[1] [kənˈtro:l] *vt* **-trolled; -trolling** : controlar, dominar

control[2] *n* **1** : control *m*, dominio *m*, mando *m* ⟨to be under control : estar bajo control⟩ **2** RESTRAINT : control *m*, limitación *f* ⟨birth control : control natal⟩ **3** : control *m*, dispositivo *m* de mando ⟨remote control : control remoto⟩

controllable [kənˈtro:ləbəl] *adj* : controlable

controller [kənˈtro:lər, ˈkɑn͵-] *n* **1** → **comptroller 2** : controlador *m*, -dora *f* ⟨air traffic controller : controlador aéreo⟩

controversial [͵kɑntrəˈvərʃəl, -siəl] *adj* : controvertido ⟨a controversial decision : una decisión controvertida⟩

controversy [ˈkɑntrə͵vərsi] *n, pl* **-sies** : controversia *f*

controvert [ˈkɑntrə͵vərt, ͵kɑntrəˈ-] *vt* : controvertir, contradecir

contusion [kənˈtu:ʒən, -tju:-] *n* BRUISE : contusión *f*, moretón *m*

conundrum [kəˈnʌndrəm] *n* RIDDLE : acertijo *m*, adivinanza *f*

convalesce [͵kɑnvəˈlɛs] *vi* **-lesced; -lescing** : convalecer

convalescence [͵kɑnvəˈlɛsənts] *n* : convalecencia *f*

convalescent[1] [͵kɑnvəˈlɛsənt] *adj* : convaleciente

convalescent[2] *n* : convaleciente *mf*

convection [kənˈvɛkʃən] *n* : convección *f*

convene [kənˈvi:n] *v* **-vened; -vening** *vt* : convocar — *vi* : reunirse

convenience [kənˈvi:njənts] *n* **1** : conveniencia *f* ⟨at your convenience : cuando le resulte conveniente⟩ **2** AMENITY : comodidad *f* ⟨modern conveniences : comodidades modernas⟩

convenience store *n* : tienda *f* de conveniencia

convenient [kən'vi:njənt] *adj* : conveniente, cómodo — **conveniently** *adv*

convent ['kɑnvənt, -ˌvɛnt] *n* : convento *m*

convention [kən'vɛntʃən] *n* **1** PACT : convención *f*, convenio *m*, pacto *m* ⟨the Geneva Convention : la Convención de Ginebra⟩ **2** MEETING : convención *f*, congreso *m* **3** CUSTOM : convención *f*, convencionalismo *m*

conventional [kən'vɛntʃənəl] *adj* : convencional — **conventionally** *adv*

converge [kən'vərdʒ] *vi* **-verged; -verging** : converger, convergir

convergence [kən'vərdʒənts] *n* : convergencia *f*

convergent [kən'vərdʒənt] *adj* : convergente

conversant [kən'vərsənt] *adj* **conversant with** : versado con, experto en

conversation [ˌkɑnvər'seɪʃən] *n* : conversación *f*

conversational [ˌkɑnvər'seɪʃənəl] *adj* : familiar ⟨a conversational style : un estilo familiar⟩

converse[1] [kən'vərs] *vi* **-versed; -versing** : conversar

converse[2] [kən'vərs, 'kɑnˌvərs] *adj* : contrario, opuesto, inverso

conversely [kən'vərsli, 'kɑnˌvərs-] *adv* : a la inversa

conversion [kən'vərʒən] *n* **1** CHANGE : conversión *f*, transformación *f*, cambio *m* **2** : conversión *f* (a una religión)

convert[1] [kən'vərt] *vt* **1** : convertir (a una religión o un partido) **2** CHANGE : convertir, cambiar — *vi* : convertirse

convert[2] ['kɑnˌvərt] *n* : converso *m*, -sa *f*

converter *or* **convertor** [kən'vərtər] *n* : convertidor *m*

convertible[1] [kən'vərtəbəl] *adj* : convertible

convertible[2] *n* : convertible *m*, descapotable *m*

convex [kɑn'vɛks, 'kɑnˌ-, kən'-] *adj* : convexo

convey [kən'veɪ] *vt* **1** TRANSPORT : transportar, conducir **2** TRANSMIT : transmitir, comunicar, expresar (noticias, ideas, etc.)

conveyance [kən'veɪənts] *n* **1** TRANSPORT : transporte *m*, transportación *f* **2** COMMUNICATION : transmisión *f*, comunicación *f* **3** TRANSFER : transferencia *f*, traspaso *m* (de una propiedad)

conveyor [kən'veɪər] *n* : transportador *m*, -dora *f* ⟨conveyor belt : cinta transportadora⟩

convict[1] [kən'vɪkt] *vt* : declarar culpable

convict[2] ['kɑnˌvɪkt] *n* : preso *m*, -sa *f*; presidiario *m*, -ria *f*; recluso *m*, -sa *f*

conviction [kən'vɪkʃən] *n* **1** : condena *f* (de un acusado) **2** BELIEF : convicción *f*, creencia *f*

convince [kən'vɪnts] *vt* **-vinced; -vincing** : convencer

convincing [kən'vɪntsɪŋ] *adj* : convincente, persuasivo

convincingly [kən'vɪntsɪŋli] *adv* : de forma convincente

convivial [kən'vɪvjəl, -'vɪviəl] *adj* : jovial, festivo, alegre

conviviality [kənˌvɪvi'æləti] *n, pl* **-ties** : jovialidad *f*

convoke [kən'vo:k] *vt* **-voked; -voking** : convocar

convoluted ['kɑnvəˌlu:tǝd] *adj* : intrincado, complicado

convoy ['kɑnˌvɔɪ] *n* : convoy *m*

convulse [kən'vʌls] *v* **-vulsed; -vulsing** *vt* : convulsionar ⟨convulsed with laughter : muerto de risa⟩ — *vi* : sufrir convulsiones

convulsion [kən'vʌlʃən] *n* : convulsión *f*

convulsive [kən'vʌlsɪv] *adj* : convulsivo — **convulsively** *adv*

coo[1] ['ku:] *vi* : arrullar

coo[2] *n* : arrullo *m* (de una paloma)

cook[1] ['kʊk] *vi* : cocinar — *vt* **1** : preparar (comida) **2 to cook up** CONCOCT : inventar, tramar

cook[2] *n* : cocinero *m*, -ra *f*

cookbook ['kʊkˌbʊk] *n* : libro *m* de cocina

cookery ['kʊkəri] *n, pl* **-eries** : cocina *f*

cookie *or* **cooky** ['kʊki] *n, pl* **-ies** : galleta *f* (dulce)

cooking ['kʊkɪŋ] *n* **1** COOKERY : cocina *f* **2** : cocción *f*, cocimiento *m* ⟨cooking time : tiempo de cocción⟩

cookout ['kʊkˌaʊt] *n* : comida *f* al aire libre

cool[1] ['ku:l] *vt* : refrescar, enfriar — *vi* **1** : refrescarse, enfriarse ⟨the pie is cooling : el pastel se está enfriando⟩ **2** : calmarse, tranquilizarse ⟨his anger cooled : su ira se calmó⟩

cool[2] *adj* **1** : fresco, frío ⟨cool weather : tiempo fresco⟩ **2** CALM : tranquilo, sereno **3** ALOOF : frío, distante

cool[3] *n* **1** : fresco *m* ⟨the cool of the evening : el fresco de la tarde⟩ **2** COMPOSURE : calma *f*, serenidad *f*

coolant ['ku:lənt] *n* : refrigerante *m*

cooler ['ku:lər] *n* : nevera *f* portátil

coolie ['ku:li] *n* : culi *m*

coolly ['ku:lli] *adv* **1** CALMLY : con calma, tranquilamente **2** COLDLY : fríamente, con frialdad

coolness ['ku:lnəs] *n* **1** : frescura *f*, frescor *m* ⟨the coolness of the evening : el frescor de la noche⟩ **2** CALMNESS : tranquilidad *f*, serenidad *f* **3** COLDNESS, INDIFFERENCE : frialdad *f*, indiferencia *f*

coop[1] ['ku:p, 'kʊp] *vt or* **to coop up** : encerrar ⟨cooped up in the house : encerrado en la casa⟩

coop[2] *n* : gallinero *m*

co-op ['ko:ˌɑp] *n* → **cooperative**[2]

cooperate [ko'ɑpəˌreɪt] *vi* **-ated; -ating** : cooperar, colaborar

cooperation [ko͵ɑpə'reɪʃən] *n* : cooperación *f*, colaboración *f*

cooperative¹ [ko'ɑpərət͵ɪv, -'ɑpə͵reɪt͵ɪv] *adj* : cooperativo

cooperative² [ko'ɑpərət͵ɪv] *n* : cooperativa *f*

co–opt [ko'ɑpt] *vt* **1** : nombrar como miembro, cooptar **2** APPROPRIATE : apropiarse de

coordinate¹ [ko'ɔrdən͵eɪt] *v* **-nated; -nating** *vt* : coordinar — *vi* : coordinarse, combinar, acordar

coordinate² [ko'ɔrdənət] *adj* **1** COORDINATED : coordinado **2** EQUAL : igual, semejante

coordinate³ [ko'ɔrdənət] *n* : coordenada *f*

coordination [ko͵ɔrdən'eɪʃən] *n* : coordinación *f*

coordinator [ko'ɔrdən͵eɪtər] *n* : coordinador *m*, -dora *f*

cop ['kɑp] → **police officer**

cope ['ko:p] *vi* **coped; coping 1** : arreglárselas **2 to cope with** : hacer frente a, poder con ⟨I can't cope with all this! : ¡no puedo con todo esto!⟩

copier ['kɑpiər] *n* : copiadora *f*, fotocopiadora *f*

copilot ['ko:͵paɪlət] *n* : copiloto *m*

copious ['ko:piəs] *adj* : copioso, abundante — **copiously** *adv*

copiousness ['ko:piəsnəs] *n* : abundancia *f*

copper ['kɑpər] *n* : cobre *m*

coppery ['kɑpəri] *adj* : cobrizo

copra ['ko:prə, 'kɑ-] *n* : copra *f*

copse ['kɑps] *n* THICKET : soto *m*, matorral *m*

copulate ['kɑpjə͵leɪt] *vi* **-lated; -lating** : copular

copulation [͵kɑpjə'leɪʃən] *n* : cópula *f*, relaciones *fpl* sexuales

copy¹ ['kɑpi] *vt* **copied; copying 1** DUPLICATE : hacer una copia de, duplicar, reproducir **2** IMITATE : copiar, imitar

copy² *n, pl* **copies 1** : copia *f*, duplicado *m* (de un documento), reproducción *f* (de una obra de arte) **2** : ejemplar *m* (de un libro), número *m* (de una revista) **3** TEXT : manuscrito *m*, texto *m*

copyright¹ ['kɑpi͵raɪt] *vt* : registrar los derechos de

copyright² *n* : derechos *mpl* de autor

coral¹ ['kɔrəl] *adj* : de coral ⟨a coral reef : un arrecife de coral⟩

coral² *n* : coral *m*

coral snake *n* : serpiente *f* de coral

cord ['kɔrd] *n* **1** ROPE, STRING : cuerda *f*, cordón *m*, cordel *m* **2** : cuerda *f*, cordón *m*, médula *f* (en la anatomía) ⟨vocal cords : cuerdas vocales⟩ **3** : cuerda *f* ⟨a cord of firewood : una cuerda de leña⟩ **4** *or* **electric cord** : cable *m* eléctrico

cordial¹ ['kɔrdʒəl] *adj* : cordial — **cordially** *adv*

cordial² *n* : cordial *m*

cordiality [͵kɔrdʒi'ælət̬i] *n* : cordialidad *f*

cordless ['kɔrdləs] *adj* : inalámbrico

cordon¹ ['kɔrdən] *vt* **to cordon off** : acordonar

cordon² *n* : cordón *m*

corduroy ['kɔrdə͵rɔɪ] *n* **1** : pana *f* **2 corduroys** *npl* : pantalones *mpl* de pana

core¹ ['kor] *vt* **cored; coring** : quitar el corazón a (una fruta)

core² *n* **1** : corazón *m*, centro *m* (de algunas frutas) **2** CENTER : núcleo *m*, centro *m* **3** ESSENCE : núcleo *m*, meollo *m* ⟨to the core : hasta la médula⟩

coriander ['kori͵ændər] *n* : cilantro *m*

cork¹ ['kɔrk] *vt* : ponerle un corcho a

cork² *n* : corcho *m*

corkscrew ['kɔrk͵skru:] *n* : tirabuzón *m*, sacacorchos *m*

cormorant ['kɔrmərənt, -͵rænt] *n* : cormorán *m*

corn¹ ['kɔrn] *vt* : conservar en salmuera ⟨corned beef : carne en conserva⟩

corn² *n* **1** GRAIN : grano *m* **2** : maíz *m*, elote *m* *Mex* ⟨corn tortillas : tortillas de maíz⟩ **3** : callo *m* ⟨corn plaster : emplasto para callos⟩

corncob ['kɔrn͵kɑb] *n* : mazorca *f* (de maíz), choclo *m*, elote *m* *CA, Mex*

cornea ['kɔrniə] *n* : córnea *f*

corner¹ ['kɔrnər] *vt* **1** TRAP : acorralar, arrinconar **2** MONOPOLIZE : monopolizar, acaparar (un mercado) — *vi* : tomar una curva, doblar una esquina (en un automóvil)

corner² *n* **1** ANGLE : rincón *m*, esquina *f*, ángulo *m* ⟨the corner of a room : el rincón de una sala⟩ ⟨all corners of the world : todos los rincones del mundo⟩ ⟨to cut corners : atajar, economizar esfuerzos⟩ **2** INTERSECTION : esquina *f* **3** IMPASSE, PREDICAMENT : aprieto *m*, impasse *m* ⟨to be backed into a corner : estar acorralado⟩

cornerstone ['kɔrnər͵sto:n] *n* : piedra *f* angular

cornet [kɔr'nɛt] *n* : corneta *f*

cornfield ['kɔrn͵fi:ld] *n* : maizal *m*; milpa *f* *CA, Mex*

cornice ['kɔrnɪs] *n* : cornisa *f*

cornmeal ['kɔrn͵mi:l] *n* : harina *f* de maíz

cornstalk ['kɔrn͵stɔk] *n* : tallo *m* del maíz

cornstarch ['kɔrn͵stɑrtʃ] *n* : maicena *f*, almidón *m* de maíz

cornucopia [͵kɔrnə'ko:piə, -njə-] *n* : cornucopia *f*

corolla [kə'rɑlə] *n* : corola *f*

corollary ['kɔrə͵lɛri] *n, pl* **-laries** : corolario *m*

corona [kə'ro:nə] *n* : corona *f* (del sol)

coronary¹ ['kɔrə͵nɛri] *adj* : coronario

coronary² *n, pl* **-naries 1** : trombosis *f* coronaria **2** HEART ATTACK : infarto *m*, ataque *m* al corazón

coronation [͵kɔrə'neɪʃən] *n* : coronación *f*

coroner ['kɔrənər] n : médico m forense

corporal¹ ['kɔrpərəl] adj : corporal ⟨corporal punishment : castigos corporales⟩

corporal² n : cabo m

corporate ['kɔrpərət] adj : corporativo, empresarial

corporation [,kɔrpə'reɪʃən] n : sociedad f anónima, corporación f, empresa f

corporeal [kɔr'poriəl] adj 1 PHYSICAL : corpóreo 2 MATERIAL : material, tangible — corporeally adv

corps ['kor] n, pl corps ['korz] : cuerpo m ⟨medical corps : cuerpo médico⟩ ⟨diplomatic corps : cuerpo diplomático⟩

corpse ['kɔrps] n : cadáver m

corpulence ['kɔrpjələnts] n : obesidad f, gordura f

corpulent ['kɔrpjələnt] adj : obeso, gordo

corpuscle ['kɔr,pʌsəl] n : corpúsculo m, glóbulo m (sanguíneo)

corral¹ [kə'ræl] vt -ralled; -ralling : acorralar, encorralar (ganado)

corral² n : corral m

correct¹ [kə'rɛkt] vt 1 RECTIFY : corregir, rectificar 2 REPRIMAND : corregir, reprender

correct² adj 1 ACCURATE, RIGHT : correcto, exacto ⟨to be correct : estar en lo cierto⟩ 2 PROPER : correcto, apropiado

correction [kə'rɛkʃən] n : corrección f

corrective [kə'rɛktɪv] adj : correctivo

correctly [kə'rɛktli] adv : correctamente

correctness [kə'rɛk(t)nəs] n 1 ACCURACY : exactitud f 2 PROPRIETY : corrección f

correlate ['kɔrə,leɪt] vt -lated; -lating : relacionar, poner en correlación

correlation [,kɔrə'leɪʃən] n : correlación f

correspond [,kɔrə'spand] vi 1 MATCH : corresponder, concordar, coincidir 2 WRITE : corresponderse, escribirse

correspondence [,kɔrə'spandənts] n : correspondencia f

correspondent [,kɔrə'spandənt] n : corresponsal mf

corresponding [kɔrə'spandɪŋ, kar-] adj : correspondiente

correspondingly [,kɔrə'spandɪŋli] adv : en consecuencia, de la misma manera

corridor ['kɔrədər, -,dor] n : corredor m, pasillo m

corroborate [kə'rabə,reɪt] vt -rated; -rating : corroborar

corroboration [kə,rabə'reɪʃən] n : corroboración f

corrode [kə'ro:d] v -roded; -roding vt : corroer — vi : corroerse

corrosion [kə'ro:ʒən] n : corrosión f

corrosive [kə'ro:sɪv] adj : corrosivo

corrugate ['kɔrə,geɪt] vt -gated; -gating : ondular, acanalar, corrugar

corrugated ['kɔrə,geɪtəd] adj : ondulado, acanalado ⟨corrugated cardboard : cartón ondulado⟩

corrupt¹ [kə'rʌpt] vt 1 PERVERT : corromper, pervertir, degradar (información) 2 BRIBE : sobornar

corrupt² adj : corrupto, corrompido

corruptible [kə'rʌptəbəl] adj : corruptible

corruption [kə'rʌpʃən] n : corrupción f

corsage [kɔr'saʒ, -'saʤ] n : ramillete m que se lleva como adorno

corset ['kɔrsət] n : corsé m

cortex ['kɔr,tɛks] n, pl -tices ['kɔrtə,si:z] or -texes : corteza f ⟨cerebral cortex : corteza cerebral⟩

cortisone ['kɔrtə,so:n, -zo:n] n : cortisona f

cosmetic¹ [kaz'mɛtɪk] adj : cosmético

cosmetic² n : cosmético m

cosmic ['kazmɪk] adj 1 : cósmico ⟨cosmic ray : rayo cósmico⟩ 2 VAST : grandioso, inmenso, vasto

cosmonaut ['kazmə,nɔt] n : cosmonauta mf

cosmopolitan¹ [,kazmə'palətən] adj : cosmopolita

cosmopolitan² n : cosmopolita mf

cosmos ['kazməs, -,mo:s, -,mas] n : cosmos m, universo m

cost¹ ['kɔst] v cost; costing vt : costar ⟨how much does it cost? : ¿cuánto cuesta?, ¿cuánto vale?⟩ — vi : costar ⟨these cost more : éstos cuestan más⟩

cost² n : costo m, precio m, coste m ⟨cost of living : costo de vida⟩ ⟨victory at all costs : victoria a toda costa⟩

Costa Rican¹ [,kɔstə'ri:kən] adj : costarricense

Costa Rican² n : costarricense mf

costly ['kɔstli] adj : costoso, caro

costume ['kas,tu:m, -,tju:m] n 1 : traje m ⟨national costume : traje típico⟩ 2 : disfraz m ⟨costume party : fiesta de disfraces⟩ 3 OUTFIT : vestimenta f, traje m, conjunto m

cosy ['ko:zi] → cozy

cot ['kat] n : catre m

coterie ['ko:ṭə,ri, ,ko:ṭə'-] n : tertulia f, círculo m (social)

cottage ['kaṭɪʤ] n : casita f (de campo)

cottage cheese n : requesón m

cotton ['katən] n : algodón m

cottonmouth ['katən,mauθ] → moccasin

cottonseed ['katən,si:d] n : semilla f de algodón

cotton swab → swab

cottontail ['katən,teɪl] n : conejo m de cola blanca

couch¹ ['kauʧ] vt : expresar, formular ⟨couched in strong language : expresado en lenguaje enérgico⟩

couch² n SOFA : sofá m

couch potato n : haragán m, -gana f; vago m, -ga f

cougar ['ku:gər] n : puma m

cough¹ ['kɔf] vi : toser

cough[2] *n* : tos *f*

could ['kʊd] → **can**

council ['kaʊntsəl] *n* **1** : concejo *m* ⟨city council : concejo municipal, ayuntamiento⟩ **2** MEETING : concejo *m*, junta *f* **3** BOARD : consejo *m* **4** : concilio *m* (eclesiástico)

councillor *or* **councilor** ['kaʊntsələr] *n* : concejal *m*, -jala *f*

councilman ['kaʊntsəlmən] *n, pl* **-men** [-mən, -ˌmɛn] : concejal *m*

councilwoman ['kaʊntsəlˌwʊmən] *n, pl* **-women** [-ˌwɪmən] : concejala *f*

counsel[1] ['kaʊntsəl] *v* **-seled** *or* **-selled**; **-seling** *or* **-selling** *vt* ADVISE : aconsejar, asesorar, recomendar — *vi* CONSULT : consultar

counsel[2] *n* **1** ADVICE : consejo *m*, recomendación *f* **2** CONSULTATION : consulta *f* **3** **counsel** *ns & pl* LAWYER : abogado *m*, -da *f*

counselor *or* **counsellor** ['kaʊntsələr] *n* : consejero *m*, -ra *f*; consultor *m*, -tora *f*; asesor *m*, -sora *f*

count[1] ['kaʊnt] *vt* : contar, enumerar — *vi* **1** : contar ⟨to count out loud : contar en voz alta⟩ **2** MATTER : contar, valer, importar ⟨that's what counts : eso es lo que cuenta⟩ **3** **to count on** : contar con

count[2] *n* **1** COMPUTATION : cómputo *m*, recuento *m*, cuenta *f* ⟨to lose count : perder la cuenta⟩ **2** CHARGE : cargo *m* ⟨two counts of robbery : dos cargos de robo⟩ **3** : conde *m* (noble)

countable ['kaʊntəbəl] *adj* : numerable

countdown ['kaʊntˌdaʊn] *n* : cuenta *f* atrás

countenance[1] ['kaʊntənənts] *vt* **-nanced; -nancing** : permitir, tolerar

countenance[2] *n* FACE : semblante *m*, rostro *m*

counter[1] ['kaʊntər] *vt* **1** → **counteract** **2** OPPOSE : oponerse a, resistir — *vi* RETALIATE : responder, contraatacar

counter[2] *adv* **counter to** : contrario a, en contra de

counter[3] *adj* : contrario, opuesto

counter[4] *n* **1** PIECE : ficha *f* (de un juego) **2** : mostrador *m* (de un negocio), ventanilla *f* (en un banco) **3** : contador *m* (aparato) **4** COUNTERBALANCE : fuerza *f* opuesta, contrapeso *m*

counteract [ˌkaʊntər'ækt] *vt* : contrarrestar

counterattack ['kaʊntərəˌtæk] *n* : contraataque *m*

counterbalance[1] [ˌkaʊntər'bælənts] *vt* **-anced; -ancing** : contrapesar

counterbalance[2] ['kaʊntərˌbælənts] *n* : contrapeso *m*

counterclockwise [ˌkaʊntər'klɑkˌwaɪz] *adv & adj* : en el sentido opuesto al de las manecillas del reloj

counterfeit[1] ['kaʊntərˌfɪt] *vt* **1** : falsificar (dinero) **2** PRETEND : fingir, aparentar

counterfeit[2] *adj* : falso, inauténtico

counterfeit[3] *n* : falsificación *f*

counterfeiter ['kaʊntərˌfɪtər] *n* : falsificador *m*, -dora *f*

countermand ['kaʊntərˌmænd, ˌkaʊntər'-] *vt* : contramandar

countermeasure ['kaʊntərˌmɛʒər] *n* : contramedida *f*

counterpart ['kaʊntərˌpɑrt] *n* : homólogo *m*, contraparte *f Mex*

counterpoint ['kaʊntərˌpɔɪnt] *n* : contrapunto *m*

counterproductive [ˌkaʊntərprə'dʌktɪv] *adj* : contraproducente

counterrevolution [ˌkaʊntərˌrɛvə-'luːʃən] *n* : contrarrevolución *f*

counterrevolutionary[1] [ˌkaʊntərˌrɛvə-'luːʃənˌɛri] *adj* : contrarrevolucionario

counterrevolutionary[2] *n, pl* **-ries** : contrarrevolucionario *m*, -ria *f*

countersign ['kaʊntərˌsaɪn] *n* : contraseña *f*

countess ['kaʊntɪs] *n* : condesa *f*

countless ['kaʊntləs] *adj* : incontable, innumerable

country[1] ['kʌntri] *adj* : campestre, rural

country[2] *n, pl* **-tries** **1** NATION : país *m*, nación *f*, patria *f* ⟨country of origin : país de origen⟩ ⟨love of one's country : amor a la patria⟩ **2** : campo *m* ⟨they left the city for the country : se fueron de la ciudad al campo⟩

countryman ['kʌntrimən] *n, pl* **-men** [-mən, -ˌmɛn] : compatriota *mf*; paisano *m*, -na *f*

countryside ['kʌntriˌsaɪd] *n* : campo *m*, campiña *f*

county ['kaʊnti] *n, pl* **-ties** : condado *m*

coup ['kuː] *n, pl* **coups** ['kuːz] **1** : golpe *m* maestro **2** *or* **coup d'etat** : golpe *m* (de estado), cuartelazo *m*

coupe ['kuːp] *n* : cupé *m*

couple[1] ['kʌpəl] *vt* **-pled; -pling** : acoplar, enganchar, conectar

couple[2] *n* **1** PAIR : par *m* ⟨a couple of hours : un par de horas, unas dos horas⟩ **2** : pareja *f* ⟨a young couple : una pareja joven⟩

coupling ['kʌplɪŋ] *n* : acoplamiento *m*

coupon ['kuːˌpɑn, 'kjuː-] *n* : cupón *m*

courage ['kərɪdʒ] *n* : valor *m*, valentía *f*, coraje *m*

courageous [kə'reɪdʒəs] *adj* : valiente, valeroso

courier ['kʊriər, 'kəriər] *n* : mensajero *m*, -ra *f*

course[1] ['kors] *vi* **coursed; coursing** : correr (a toda velocidad)

course[2] *n* **1** PROGRESS : curso *m*, transcurso *m* ⟨to run its course : seguir su curso⟩ **2** DIRECTION : rumbo *m* (de un avión), derrota *f*, derrotero *m* (de un barco) **3** PATH, WAY : camino *m*, vía *f* ⟨course of action : línea de conducta⟩ **4** : plato *m* (de una cena) ⟨the main course : el plato principal⟩ **5** : curso *m* (académico) **6** **of course** : desde luego, por supuesto ⟨yes, of course! : ¡claro que sí!⟩

court¹ ['kort] *vt* WOO : cortejar, galantear

court² *n* **1** PALACE : palacio *m* **2** RETINUE : corte *f*, séquito *m* **3** COURTYARD : patio *m* **4** : cancha *f* (de tenis, baloncesto, etc.) **5** TRIBUNAL : corte *f*, tribunal *m* ⟨the Supreme Court : la Corte Suprema⟩

courteous ['kərṭiəs] *adj* : cortés, atento, educado — **courteously** *adv*

courtesan ['kortəzən, 'kər-] *n* : cortesana *f*

courtesy ['kərṭəsi] *n, pl* **-sies** : cortesía *f*

courthouse ['kort,haʊs] *n* : palacio *m* de justicia, juzgado *m*

courtier ['korṭiər, 'kortjər] *n* : cortesano *m*, -na *f*

courtly ['kortli] *adj* **-lier; -est** : distinguido, elegante, cortés

court–martial¹ ['kort,marʃəl] *vt* : someter a consejo de guerra

court–martial² *n, pl* **courts–martial** ['korts,marʃəl] : consejo *m* de guerra

court order *n* : mandamiento *m* judicial

courtroom ['kort,ru:m] *n* : tribunal *m*, corte *f*

courtship ['kort,ʃɪp] *n* : cortejo *m*, noviazgo *m*

courtyard ['kort,jard] *n* : patio *m*

cousin ['kʌzən] *n* : primo *m*, -ma *f*

couture [ku:'tʊr] *n* : industria *f* de la moda ⟨haute couture : alta costura⟩

cove ['ko:v] *n* : ensenada *f*, cala *f*

covenant ['kʌvənənt] *n* : pacto *m*, contrato *m*

cover¹ ['kʌvər] *vt* **1** : cubrir, tapar ⟨cover your head : tápate la cabeza⟩ ⟨covered with mud : cubierto de lodo⟩ **2** HIDE, PROTECT : encubrir, proteger **3** TREAT : tratar **4** INSURE : asegurar, cubrir

cover² *n* **1** SHELTER : cubierta *f*, abrigo *m*, refugio *m* ⟨to take cover : ponerse a cubierto⟩ ⟨under cover of darkness : al amparo de la oscuridad⟩ **2** LID, TOP : cubierta *f*, tapa *f* **3** : cubierta *f* (de un libro), portada *f* (de una revista) **4 covers** *npl* BEDCLOTHES : ropa *f* de cama, cobijas *fpl*, mantas *fpl*

coverage ['kʌvərɪdʒ] *n* : cobertura *f*

coverlet ['kʌvərlət] *n* : cobertor *m*

covert¹ ['ko:,vərt, 'kʌvərt] *adj* : encubierto, secreto ⟨covert operations : operaciones encubiertas⟩

covert² ['kʌvərt, 'ko:-] *n* THICKET : espesura *f*, maleza *f*

cover-up ['kʌvər,ʌp] *n* : encubrimiento *m* (de algo ilícito)

covet ['kʌvət] *vt* : codiciar

covetous ['kʌvəṭəs] *adj* : codicioso

covey ['kʌvi] *n, pl* **-eys 1** : bandada *f* pequeña (de codornices, etc.) **2** GROUP : grupo *m*

cow¹ ['kaʊ] *vt* : intimidar, acobardar

cow² *n* : vaca *f*, hembra *f* (de ciertas especies)

coward ['kaʊərd] *n* : cobarde *mf*

cowardice ['kaʊərdɪs] *n* : cobardía *f*

cowardly ['kaʊərdli] *adj* : cobarde

cowboy ['kaʊ,bɔɪ] *n* : vaquero *m*, cowboy *m*

cower ['kaʊər] *vi* : encogerse (de miedo), acobardarse

cowgirl ['kaʊ,gərl] *n* : vaquera *f*

cowherd ['kaʊ,hərd] *n* : vaquero *m*, -ra *f*

cowhide ['kaʊ,haɪd] *n* : cuero *m*, piel *f* de vaca

cowl ['kaʊl] *n* : capucha *f* (de un monje)

cowlick ['kaʊ,lɪk] *n* : remolino *m*

cowpuncher ['kaʊ,pʌntʃər] → **cowboy**

cowslip ['kaʊ,slɪp] *n* : prímula *f*, primavera *f*

coxswain ['kaksən, -,sweɪn] *n* : timonel *m*

coy ['kɔɪ] *adj* **1** SHY : tímido, cohibido **2** COQUETTISH : coqueto

coyote [kaɪ'o:ṭi, 'kaɪ,o:t] *n, pl* **coyotes** *or* **coyote** : coyote *m*

cozy ['ko:zi] *adj* **-zier; -est** : acogedor, cómodo

CPU [,si:,pi:'ju:] *n* (central processing unit) : CPU *f*

crab ['kræb] *n* : cangrejo *m*, jaiba *f*

crabby ['kræbi] *adj* **-bier; -est** : gruñón, malhumorado

crabgrass ['kræb,græs] *n* : garranchuelo *m*

crack¹ ['kræk] *vi* **1** : chasquear, restallar ⟨the whip cracked : el látigo restalló⟩ **2** SPLIT : rajarse, resquebrajarse, agrietarse **3** : quebrarse (dícese de la voz) — *vt* **1** : restallar, chasquear (un látigo, etc.) **2** SPLIT : rajar, agrietar, resquebrajar **3** BREAK : romper (un huevo), cascar (nueces), forzar (una caja fuerte) **4** SOLVE : resolver, descifrar (un código)

crack² *adj* FIRST-RATE : buenísimo, de primera

crack³ *n* **1** : chasquido *m*, restallido *m*, estallido *m* (de un arma de fuego), crujido *m* (de huesos) ⟨a crack of thunder : un trueno⟩ **2** WISECRACK : chiste *m*, ocurrencia *f*, salida *f* **3** CREVICE : raja *f*, grieta *f*, fisura *f* **4** BLOW : golpe *m* **5** ATTEMPT : intento *m*

crackdown ['kræk,daʊn] *n* : medidas *fpl* enérgicas

crack down *vt* : tomar medidas enérgicas

cracker ['krækər] *n* : galleta *f* (de soda, etc.)

crackle¹ ['krækəl] *vi* **-led; -ling** : crepitar, chisporrotear

crackle² *n* : crujido *m*, chisporroteo *m*

crackpot ['kræk,pat] *n* : excéntrico *m*, -ca *f*; chiflado *m*, -da *f*

crack-up ['kræk,ʌp] *n* **1** CRASH : choque *m*, estrellamiento *m* **2** BREAKDOWN : crisis *f* nerviosa

crack up *vt* **1** : estrellar (un vehículo) **2** : hacer reír **3** : elogiar ⟨it isn't all that it's cracked up to be : no es tan bueno como se dice⟩ — *vi* **1** : estrellarse **2** LAUGH : echarse a reír

cradle[1] ['kreɪdəl] *vt* **-dled; -dling** : acunar, mecer (a un niño)

cradle[2] *n* : cuna *f*

craft ['kræft] *n* **1** TRADE : oficio *m* ⟨the craft of carpentry : el oficio de carpintero⟩ **2** CRAFTSMANSHIP, SKILL : arte *m*, artesanía *f*, destreza *f* **3** CRAFTINESS : astucia *f*, maña *f* **4** *pl usually* **craft** BOAT : barco *m*, embarcación *f* **5** *pl usually* **craft** AIRCRAFT : avión *m*, aeronave *f*

craftiness ['kræftinəs] *n* : astucia *f*, maña *f*

craftsman ['kræftsmən] *n, pl* **-men** [-mən, -ˌmen] : artesano *m*, -na *f*

craftsmanship ['kræftsmənˌʃip] *n* : artesanía *f*, destreza *f*

crafty ['kræfti] *adj* **craftier; -est** : astuto, taimado

crag ['kræg] *n* : peñasco *m*

craggy ['krægi] *adj* **-gier; -est** : peñascoso

cram ['kræm] *v* **crammed; cramming** *vt* **1** JAM : embutir, meter **2** STUFF : atiborrar, abarrotar ⟨crammed with people : atiborrado de gente⟩ — *vi* : estudiar a última hora, memorizar (para un examen)

cramp[1] ['kræmp] *vt* **1** : dar calambre en **2** RESTRICT : limitar, restringir, entorpecer ⟨to cramp someone's style : cortarle el vuelo a alguien⟩ — *vi or* **to cramp up** : acalambrarse

cramp[2] *n* **1** SPASM : calambre *m*, espasmo *m* (de los músculos) **2 cramps** *npl* : retorcijones *mpl* ⟨stomach cramps : retorcijones de estómago⟩

cranberry ['krænˌberi] *n, pl* **-berries** : arándano *m* (rojo y agrio)

crane[1] ['kreɪn] *vt* **craned; craning** : estirar ⟨to crane one's neck : estirar el cuello⟩

crane[2] *n* **1** : grulla *f* (ave) **2** : grúa *f* (máquina)

cranial ['kreɪniəl] *adj* : craneal, craneano

cranium ['kreɪniəm] *n, pl* **-niums** *or* **-nia** [-niə] : cráneo *m*

crank[1] ['kræŋk] *vt or* **to crank up** : arrancar (con una manivela)

crank[2] *n* **1** : manivela *f*, manubrio *m* **2** ECCENTRIC : excéntrico *m*, -ca *f*

cranky ['kræŋki] *adj* **crankier; -est** : irritable, malhumorado, enojadizo

cranny ['kræni] *n, pl* **-nies** : grieta *f* ⟨every nook and cranny : todos los rincones⟩

crash[1] ['kræʃ] *vi* **1** SMASH : caerse con estrépito, estrellarse **2** COLLIDE : estrellarse, chocar **3** BOOM, RESOUND : retumbar, resonar — *vt* **1** SMASH : estrellar **2 to crash a party** : colarse en una fiesta **3 to crash one's car** : tener un accidente

crash[2] *n* **1** DIN : estrépito *m* **2** COLLISION : choque *m*, colisión *f* ⟨car crash : accidente automovilístico⟩ **3** FAILURE : quiebra *f* (de un negocio), crac *m* (de la bolsa)

crass ['kræs] *adj* : grosero, de mal gusto

crate[1] ['kreɪt] *vt* **crated; crating** : empacar en un cajón

crate[2] *n* : cajón *m* (de madera)

crater ['kreɪtər] *n* : cráter *m*

cravat [krə'væt] *n* : corbata *f*

crave ['kreɪv] *vt* **craved; craving** : ansiar, apetecer, tener muchas ganas de

craven ['kreɪvən] *adj* : cobarde, pusilánime

craving ['kreɪviŋ] *n* : ansia *f*, antojo *m*, deseo *m*

crawfish ['krɔˌfiʃ] → **crayfish**

crawl[1] ['krɔl] *vi* **1** CREEP : arrastrarse, gatear (dícese de un bebé) **2** TEEM : estar plagado

crawl[2] *n* : paso *m* lento

crayfish ['kreɪˌfiʃ] *n* **1** : ástaco *m* (de agua dulce) **2** : langostino *m* (de mar)

crayon ['kreɪˌɑn, -ən] *n* : crayón *m*

craze ['kreɪz] *n* : moda *f* pasajera, manía *f*

crazed ['kreɪzd] *adj* : enloquecido

crazily ['kreɪzəli] *adv* : locamente, erráticamente, insensatamente

craziness ['kreɪzinəs] *n* : locura *f*, demencia *f*

crazy ['kreɪzi] *adj* **-zier; -est** **1** INSANE : loco, demente ⟨to go crazy : volverse loco⟩ **2** ABSURD, FOOLISH : loco, insensato, absurdo **3 like crazy** : como loco **4 to be crazy about** : estar loco por

creak[1] ['kri:k] *vi* : chirriar, rechinar, crujir

creak[2] *n* : chirrido *m*, crujido *m*

creaky ['kri:ki] *adj* **creakier; -est** : chirriante, que cruje

cream[1] ['kri:m] *vt* **1** BEAT, MIX : batir, mezclar (azúcar y mantequilla, etc.) **2** : preparar (alimentos) con crema

cream[2] *n* **1** : crema *f* (de leche) **2** LOTION : crema *f*, loción *f* **3** ELITE : crema *f*, elite *f* ⟨the cream of the crop : la crema y nata, lo mejor⟩

creamery ['kri:məri] *n, pl* **-eries** : fábrica *f* de productos lácteos

creamy ['kri:mi] *adj* **creamier; -est** : cremoso

crease[1] ['kri:s] *vt* **creased; creasing** **1** : plegar, poner una raya en (pantalones) **2** WRINKLE : arrugar

crease[2] *n* **1** : pliegue *m*, doblez *m*, raya *f* (de pantalones)

create [kri'eɪt] *vt* **-ated; -ating** : crear, hacer

creation [kri'eɪʃən] *n* : creación *f*

creative [kri'eɪtɪv] *adj* : creativo, original ⟨creative people : personas creativas⟩ ⟨a creative work : un obra original⟩

creatively [kri'eɪtɪvli] *adv* : creativamente, con originalidad

creativity [ˌkri:eɪ'tɪvəti] *n* : creatividad *f*

creator [kri'eɪtər] *n* : creador *m*, -dora *f*

creature ['kri:tʃər] *n* : ser *m* viviente, criatura *f*, animal *m*

credence ['kri:dənts] *n* : crédito *m*
credentials [krɪ'dɛntʃəlz] *npl* : referencias *fpl* oficiales, cartas *fpl* credenciales
credibility [ˌkrɛdə'bɪləti] *n* : credibilidad *f*
credible ['krɛdəbəl] *adj* : creíble
credit[1] ['krɛdɪt] *vt* **1** BELIEVE : creer, dar crédito a **2** : ingresar, abonar ⟨to credit $100 to an account : ingresar $100 en (una) cuenta⟩ **3** ATTRIBUTE : atribuir ⟨they credit the invention to him : a él se le atribuye el invento⟩
credit[2] *n* **1** : saldo *m* positivo, saldo *m* a favor (de una cuenta) **2** : crédito *m* ⟨to buy on credit : comprar a crédito⟩ ⟨credit card : tarjeta de crédito⟩ **3** CREDENCE : crédito *m* ⟨I gave credit to everything he said : di crédito a todo lo que dijo⟩ **4** RECOGNITION : reconocimiento *m* **5** : orgullo *m*, honor *m* ⟨she's a credit to the school : ella es el orgullo de la escuela⟩
creditable ['krɛdɪtəbəl] *adj* : encomiable, loable — **creditably** [-bli] *adv*
credit card *n* : tarjeta de crédito
creditor ['krɛdɪtər] *n* : acreedor *m*, -dora *f*
credo ['kri:do:, 'krei-] *n* : credo *m*
credulity [krɪ'du:ləti, -'dju:-] *n* : credulidad *f*
credulous ['krɛdʒələs] *adj* : crédulo
creed ['kri:d] *n* : credo *m*
creek ['kri:k, 'krɪk] *n* : arroyo *m*, riachuelo *m*
creel ['kri:l] *n* : nasa *f*, cesta *f* (de pescador)
creep[1] ['kri:p] *vi* **crept** ['krɛpt]; **creeping 1** CRAWL : arrastrarse, gatear **2** : moverse lentamente o sigilosamente ⟨he crept out of the house : salió sigilosamente de la casa⟩ **3** SPREAD : trepar (dícese de una planta)
creep[2] *n* **1** CRAWL : paso *m* lento **2** : asqueroso *m*, -sa *f* **3** **creeps** *npl* : escalofríos *mpl* ⟨that gives me the creeps : eso me da escalofríos⟩
creeper ['kri:pər] *n* : planta *f* trepadora, trepadora *f*
creepy ['kri:pi] *adj* **1** SPOOKY : espeluznante **2** UNPLEASANT : asqueroso
cremate ['kri:ˌmeɪt] *vt* **-mated; -mating** : cremar
cremation [krɪ'meɪʃən] *n* : cremación *f*
Creole ['kri:ˌo:l] *n* **1** : criollo *m*, criolla *f* **2** : criollo *m* (idioma) — **Creole** *adj*
creosote ['kri:əˌso:t] *n* : creosota *f*
crepe *or* **crêpe** ['kreɪp] *n* **1** : crespón *m* (tela) **2** PANCAKE : crepe *mf*, crepa *f* *Mex*
crescendo [krɪ'ʃɛnˌdo:] *n, pl* **-dos** *or* **-does** : crescendo *m*
crescent ['krɛsənt] *n* : creciente *m*
crest ['krɛst] *n* **1** : cresta *f*, penacho *m* (de un ave) **2** PEAK, TOP : cresta *f* (de una ola), cima *f* (de una colina) **3** : emblema *m* (sobre un escudo de armas)
crestfallen ['krɛstˌfɔlən] *adj* : alicaído, abatido

cretin ['kri:tən] *n* : cretino *m*, -na *f*
crevasse [krɪ'væs] *n* : grieta *f*, fisura *f*
crevice ['krɛvɪs] *n* : grieta *f*, hendidura *f*
crew ['kru:] *n* **1** : tripulación *f* (de una nave) **2** TEAM : equipo *m* (de trabajadores o atletas)
crib ['krɪb] *n* **1** MANGER : pesebre *m* **2** GRANARY : granero *m* **3** : cuna *f* (de un bebé)
crick ['krɪk] *n* : calambre *m*, espasmo *m* muscular
cricket ['krɪkət] *n* **1** : grillo *m* (insecto) **2** : críquet *m* (juego)
crime ['kraɪm] *n* **1** : crimen *m*, delito *m* ⟨to commit a crime : cometer un delito⟩ **2** : crimen *m*, delincuencia *f* ⟨organized crime : crimen organizado⟩
criminal[1] ['krɪmənəl] *adj* : criminal
criminal[2] *n* : criminal *mf*, delincuente *mf*
crimp ['krɪmp] *vt* : ondular, rizar (el pelo), arrugar (una tela, etc.)
crimson ['krɪmzən] *n* : carmesí *m*
cringe ['krɪndʒ] *vi* **cringed; cringing** : encogerse
crinkle[1] ['krɪŋkəl] *v* **-kled; -kling** *vt* : arrugar — *vi* : arrugarse
crinkle[2] *n* : arruga *f*
crinkly ['krɪŋkəli] *adj* : arrugado
cripple[1] ['krɪpəl] *vt* **-pled; -pling 1** DISABLE : lisiar, dejar inválido **2** INCAPACITATE : inutilizar, incapacitar
cripple[2] *n* : lisiado *m*, -da *f*
crisis ['kraɪsɪs] *n, pl* **crises** [-ˌsi:z] : crisis *f*
crisp[1] ['krɪsp] *vt* : tostar, hacer crujiente
crisp[2] *adj* **1** CRUNCHY : crujiente, crocante **2** FIRM, FRESH : firme, fresco ⟨crisp lettuce : lechuga fresca⟩ **3** LIVELY : vivaz, alegre ⟨a crisp tempo : un ritmo alegre⟩ **4** INVIGORATING : fresco, vigorizante ⟨the crisp autumn air : el fresco aire otoñal⟩ — **crisply** *adv*
crisp[3] *n* : postre *m* de fruta (con pedacitos de masa dulce por encima)
crispy ['krɪspi] *adj* **crispier; -est** : crujiente ⟨crispy potato chips : papitas crujientes⟩
crisscross ['krɪsˌkrɔs] *vt* : entrecruzar
criterion [kraɪ'tɪriən] *n, pl* **-ria** [-iə] : criterio *m*
critic ['krɪtɪk] *n* **1** : crítico *m*, -ca *f* (de las artes) **2** FAULTFINDER : detractor *m*, -tora *f*; criticón *m*, -cona *f*
critical ['krɪtɪkəl] *adj* : crítico
critically ['krɪtɪkli] *adv* : críticamente ⟨critically ill : gravemente enfermo⟩
criticism ['krɪtəˌsɪzəm] *n* : crítica *f*
criticize ['krɪtəˌsaɪz] *vt* **-cized; -cizing 1** EVALUATE, JUDGE : criticar, analizar, evaluar **2** CENSURE : criticar, reprobar
critique [krɪ'ti:k] *n* : crítica *f*, evaluación *f*
croak[1] ['kro:k] *vi* : croar
croak[2] *n* : croar *m*, canto *m* (de la rana)
Croatian [kro'eɪʃən] *n* : croata *mf* — **Croatian** *adj*

crochet[1] [kro:'ʃeɪ] *v* : tejer al croché

crochet[2] *n* : croché *m*, crochet *m*

crock ['krak] *n* : vasija *f* de barro

crockery ['krakəri] *n* : vajilla *f* (de barro)

crocodile ['krakə,daɪl] *n* : cocodrilo *m*

crocus ['kro:kəs] *n, pl* **-cuses** : azafrán *m*

croissant [krə'sant] *n* : croissant *m*

crone ['kro:n] *n* : vieja *f* arpía, vieja *f* bruja

crony ['kro:ni] *n, pl* **-nies** : amigote *m* *fam*; compinche *mf fam*

crook[1] ['krʊk] *vt* : doblar (el brazo o el dedo)

crook[2] *n* **1** STAFF : cayado *m* (de pastor), báculo *m* (de obispo) **2** THIEF : ratero *m*, -ra *f*; ladrón *m*, -drona *f*

crooked ['krʊkəd] *adj* **1** BENT : chueco, torcido **2** DISHONEST : deshonesto

crookedness ['krʊkədnəs] *n* **1** : lo torcido, lo chueco **2** DISHONESTY : falta *f* de honradez

croon ['kru:n] *v* : cantar suavemente

crop[1] ['krap] *v* **cropped; cropping** *vt* TRIM : recortar, cortar — *vi* **to crop up** : aparecer, surgir ⟨these problems keep cropping up : estos problemas no cesan de surgir⟩

crop[2] *n* **1** : buche *m* (de un ave o insecto) **2** WHIP : fusta *f* (de jinete) **3** HARVEST : cosecha *f*, cultivo *m*

croquet [,kro:'keɪ] *n* : croquet *m*

croquette [,kro:'kɛt] *n* : croqueta *f*

cross[1] ['krɔs] *vt* **1** : cruzar, atravesar ⟨to cross the street : cruzar la calle⟩ ⟨several canals cross the city : varios canales atraviesan la ciudad⟩ **2** CANCEL : tachar, cancelar ⟨he crossed his name off the list : tachó su nombre de la planilla⟩ **3** INTERBREED : cruzar (en genética)

cross[2] *adj* **1** : que atraviesa ⟨cross ventilation : ventilación que atraviesa un cuarto⟩ **2** CONTRARY : contrario, opuesto ⟨cross purposes : objetivos opuestos⟩ **3** ANGRY : enojado, de mal humor

cross[3] *n* **1** : cruz *f* ⟨the sign of the cross : la señal de la cruz⟩ **2** : cruza *f* (en biología)

crossbones ['krɔs,bo:nz] *npl* **1** : huesos *mpl* cruzados **2** → skull

crossbow ['krɔs,bo:] *n* : ballesta *f*

crossbreed ['krɔs,bri:d] *vt* **-bred** [-,brɛd]; **-breeding** : cruzar

crosscurrent ['krɔs,kərənt] *n* : contracorriente *f*

cross–examination [,krɔsɪg,zæmə'neɪʃən] *n* : repreguntas *fpl*, interrogatorio *m*

cross–examine [,krɔsɪg'zæmən] *vt* **-ined; -ining** : repreguntar

cross–eyed ['krɔs,aɪd] *adj* : bizco

crossing ['krɔsɪŋ] *n* **1** INTERSECTION : cruce *m*, paso *m* ⟨pedestrian crossing : paso de peatones⟩ **2** VOYAGE : travesía *f* (del mar)

crossly ['krɔsli] *adv* : con enojo, con enfado

cross–reference [,krɔs'rɛfrənts, -'rɛfərənts] *n* : referencia *f*, remisión *f*

crossroads ['krɔs,ro:dz] *n* : cruce *m*, encrucijada *f*, crucero *m Mex*

cross section *n* **1** SECTION : corte *m* transversal **2** SAMPLE : muestra *f* representativa ⟨a cross section of the population : una muestra representativa de la población⟩

crosswalk ['krɔs,wɔk] *n* : cruce *m* peatonal, paso *m* de peatones

crossways ['krɔs,weɪz] → **crosswise**

crosswise[1] ['krɔs,waɪz] *adv* : transversalmente, diagonalmente

crosswise[2] *adj* : transversal, diagonal

crossword puzzle ['krɔs,wərd] *n* : crucigrama *m*

crotch ['kratʃ] *n* : entrepierna *f*

crotchety ['kratʃəti] *adj* CRANKY : malhumorado, irritable, enojadizo

crouch ['krautʃ] *vi* : agacharse, ponerse de cuclillas

croup ['kru:p] *n* : crup *m*

crouton ['kru:,tan] *n* : crutón *m*

crow[1] ['kro:] *vi* **1** : cacarear, cantar (como un cuervo) **2** BRAG : alardear, presumir

crow[2] *n* **1** : cuervo *m* (ave) **2** : cantar *m* (del gallo)

crowbar ['kro:,bar] *n* : palanca *f*

crowd[1] ['kraud] *vi* : aglomerarse, amontonarse — *vt* : atestar, atiborrar, llenar

crowd[2] *n* : multitud *f*, muchedumbre *f*, gentío *m*

crown[1] ['kraun] *vt* : coronar

crown[2] *n* : corona *f*

crow's nest *n* : cofa *f*

crucial ['kru:ʃəl] *adj* : crucial, decisivo

crucible ['kru:səbəl] *n* : crisol *m*

crucifix ['kru:sə,fɪks] *n* : crucifijo *m*

crucifixion [,kru:sə'fɪkʃən] *n* : crucifixión *f*

crucify ['kru:sə,faɪ] *vt* **-fied; -fying** : crucificar

crude ['kru:d] *adj* **cruder; -est** **1** RAW, UNREFINED : crudo, sin refinar ⟨crude oil : petróleo crudo⟩ **2** VULGAR : grosero, de mal gusto **3** ROUGH : tosco, burdo, rudo

crudely ['kru:dli] *adv* **1** VULGARLY : groseramente **2** ROUGHLY : burdamente, de manera rudimentaria

crudity ['kru:dəti] *n, pl* **-ties** **1** VULGARITY : grosería *f* **2** COARSENESS, ROUGHNESS : tosquedad *f*, rudeza *f*

cruel ['kru:əl] *adj* **-eler** *or* **-eller; -elest** *or* **-ellest** : cruel

cruelly ['kru:əli] *adv* : cruelmente

cruelty ['kru:əlti] *n, pl* **-ties** : crueldad *f*

cruet ['kru:ɪt] *n* : vinagrera *f*, aceitera *f*

cruise[1] ['kru:z] *vi* **cruised; cruising** **1** : hacer un crucero **2** : navegar o conducir a una velocidad constante ⟨cruising speed : velocidad de crucero⟩

cruise[2] *n* : crucero *m*

cruiser ['kru:zər] *n* **1** WARSHIP : crucero *m*, buque *m* de guerra **2** : patrulla *f* (de policía)

crumb ['krʌm] *n* : miga *f*, migaja *f*

crumble ['krʌmbəl] *v* **-bled; -bling** *vt* : desmigajar, desmenuzar — *vi* : desmigajarse, desmoronarse, desmenuzarse

crumbly ['krʌmbli] *adj* : que se desmenuza fácilmente, friable

crumple ['krʌmpəl] *v* **-pled; -pling** *vt* RUMPLE : arrugar — *vi* **1** WRINKLE : arrugarse **2** COLLAPSE : desplomarse

crunch[1] ['krʌntʃ] *vt* **1** : ronzar (con los dientes) **2** : hacer crujir (con los pies, etc.) — *vi* : crujir

crunch[2] *n* : crujido *m*

crunchy ['krʌntʃi] *adj* **crunchier; -est** : crujiente

crusade[1] [kru:'seɪd] *vi* **-saded; -sading** : hacer una campaña (a favor de o contra algo)

crusade[2] *n* **1** : campaña *f* (de reforma, etc.) **2 Crusade** : cruzada *f*

crusader [kru:'seɪdər] *n* **1** : cruzado *m* (en la Edad Media) **2** : campeón *m*, -peona *f* (de una causa)

crush[1] ['krʌʃ] *vt* **1** SQUASH : aplastar, apachurrar **2** GRIND, PULVERIZE : triturar, machacar **3** SUPPRESS : aplastar, suprimir

crush[2] *n* **1** CROWD, MOB : gentío *m*, multitud *f*, aglomeración *f* **2** INFATUATION : enamoramiento *m*

crushing ['krʌʃɪŋ] *adj* : aplastante, abrumador

crust ['krʌst] *n* **1** : corteza *f*, costra *f* (de pan) **2** : tapa *f* de masa, pasta *f* (de un pastel) **3** LAYER : capa *f*, corteza *f* ⟨the earth's crust : la corteza terrestre⟩

crustacean [ˌkrʌs'teɪʃən] *n* : crustáceo *m*

crusty ['krʌsti] *adj* **crustier; -est 1** : de corteza dura **2** CROSS, GRUMPY : enojado, malhumorado

crutch ['krʌtʃ] *n* : muleta *f*

crux ['krʌks, 'krʊks] *n, pl* **cruxes** : quid *m*, esencia *f*, meollo *m* ⟨the crux of the problem : el quid del problema⟩

cry[1] ['kraɪ] *vi* **cried; crying 1** SHOUT : gritar ⟨they cried for more : a gritos pidieron más⟩ **2** WEEP : llorar

cry[2] *n, pl* **cries 1** SHOUT : grito *m* **2** WEEPING : llanto *m* **3** : chillido *m* (de un animal)

crybaby ['kraɪˌbeɪbi] *n, pl* **-bies** : llorón *m*, -rona *f*

crypt ['krɪpt] *n* : cripta *f*

cryptic ['krɪptɪk] *adj* : enigmático, críptico

crystal ['krɪstəl] *n* : cristal *m*

crystalline ['krɪstəlɪn] *adj* : cristalino

crystallize ['krɪstəˌlaɪz] *v* **-lized; -lizing** *vt* : cristalizar, materializar ⟨to crystallize one's thoughts : cristalizar uno sus pensamientos⟩ — *vi* : cristalizarse

cub ['kʌb] *n* : cachorro *m*

Cuban ['kju:bən] *n* : cubano *m*, -na *f* — **Cuban** *adj*

cubbyhole ['kʌbiˌho:l] *n* : chiribitil *m*

cube[1] ['kju:b] *vt* **cubed; cubing 1** : elevar (un número) al cubo **2** : cortar en cubos

cube[2] *n* **1** : cubo *m* **2 ice cube** : cubito *m* de hielo **3 sugar cube** : terrón *m* de azúcar

cubic ['kju:bɪk] *adj* : cúbico

cubicle ['kju:bɪkəl] *n* : cubículo *m*

cuckoo[1] ['ku:ˌku:, 'kʊ-] *adj* : loco, chiflado

cuckoo[2] *n, pl* **-oos** : cuco *m*, cuclillo *m*

cucumber ['kju:ˌkʌmbər] *n* : pepino *m*

cud ['kʌd] *n* **to chew the cud** : rumiar

cuddle ['kʌdəl] *v* **-dled; -dling** *vi* : abrazarse tiernamente, acurrucarse — *vt* : abrazar

cudgel[1] ['kʌdʒəl] *vt* **-geled** *or* **-gelled; -geling** *or* **-gelling** : apalear, aporrear

cudgel[2] *n* : garrote *m*, porra *f*

cue[1] ['kju:] *vt* **cued; cuing** *or* **cueing** : darle el pie a, darle la señal a

cue[2] *n* **1** SIGNAL : señal *f*, pie *m* (en teatro), entrada *f* (en música) **2** : taco *m* (de billar)

cuff[1] ['kʌf] *vt* : bofetear, cachetear

cuff[2] *n* **1** : puño *m* (de una camisa), vuelta *f* (de pantalones) **2** SLAP : bofetada *f*, cachetada *f* **3 cuffs** *npl* HANDCUFFS : esposas *fpl*

cuisine [kwɪ'zi:n] *n* : cocina *f* ⟨Mexican cuisine : la cocina mexicana⟩

culinary ['kʌləˌnɛri, 'kju:lə-] *adj* : culinario

cull ['kʌl] *vt* : seleccionar, entresacar

culminate ['kʌlməˌneɪt] *vi* **-nated; -nating** : culminar

culmination [ˌkʌlmə'neɪʃən] *n* : culminación *f*, punto *m* culminante

culpable ['kʌlpəbəl] *adj* : culpable

culprit ['kʌlprɪt] *n* : culpable *mf*

cult ['kʌlt] *n* : culto *m*

cultivate ['kʌltəˌveɪt] *vt* **-vated; -vating 1** TILL : cultivar, labrar **2** FOSTER : cultivar, fomentar **3** REFINE : cultivar, refinar ⟨to cultivate the mind : cultivar la mente⟩

cultivation [ˌkʌltə'veɪʃən] *n* **1** : cultivo *m* ⟨under cultivation : en cultivo⟩ **2** CULTURE, REFINEMENT : cultura *f*, refinamiento *m*

cultural ['kʌltʃərəl] *adj* : cultural — **culturally** *adv*

culture ['kʌltʃər] *n* **1** CULTIVATION : cultivo *m* **2** REFINEMENT : cultura *f*, educación *f*, refinamiento *m* **3** CIVILIZATION : cultura *f*, civilización *f* ⟨the Incan culture : la cultura inca⟩

cultured ['kʌltʃərd] *adj* **1** EDUCATED, REFINED : culto, educado, refinado **2** : de cultivo, cultivado ⟨cultured pearls : perlas de cultivo⟩

culvert ['kʌlvərt] *n* : alcantarilla *f*

cumbersome ['kʌmbərsəm] *adj* : torpe y pesado, difícil de manejar

cumin ['kʌmən] *n* : comino *m*

cumulative ['kju:mjələtɪv, -ˌleɪtɪv] *adj* : acumulativo

cumulus ['kju:mjələs] *n, pl* -**li** [-ˌlaɪ, -ˌli:] : cúmulo *m*

cunning[1] ['kʌnɪŋ] *adj* **1** CRAFTY : astuto, taimado **2** CLEVER : ingenioso, hábil **3** CUTE : mono, gracioso, lindo

cunning[2] *n* **1** SKILL : habilidad *f* **2** CRAFTINESS : astucia *f*, maña *f*

cup[1] ['kʌp] *vt* **cupped; cupping** : ahuecar (las manos)

cup[2] *n* **1** : taza *f* ⟨a cup of coffee : una taza de café⟩ **2** CUPFUL : taza *f* **3** : media pinta *f* (unidad de medida) **4** GOBLET : copa *f* **5** TROPHY : copa *f*, trofeo *m*

cupboard ['kʌbərd] *n* : alacena *f*, armario *m*

cupcake ['kʌpˌkeɪk] *n* : pastelito *m*

cupful ['kʌpˌfʊl] *n* : taza *f*

cupola ['kju:pələ, -ˌlo:] *n* : cúpula *f*

cur ['kər] *n* : perro *m* callejero, perro *m* corriente *Mex*

curate ['kjurət] *n* : cura *m*, párroco *m*

curator ['kjurˌeɪtər, kjuˈreɪtər] *n* : conservador *m*, -dora *f* (de un museo); director *m*, -tora *f* (de un zoológico)

curb[1] ['kərb] *vt* : refrenar, restringir, controlar

curb[2] *n* **1** RESTRAINT : freno *m*, control *m* **2** : borde *m* de la acera

curd ['kərd] *n* : cuajada *f*

curdle ['kərdəl] *v* -**dled; -dling** *vi* : cuajarse — *vt* : cuajar ⟨to curdle one's blood : helarle la sangre a uno⟩

cure[1] ['kjur] *vt* **cured; curing** **1** HEAL : curar, sanar **2** REMEDY : remediar **3** PROCESS : curar (alimentos, etc.)

cure[2] *n* **1** RECOVERY : curación *f*, recuperación *f* **2** REMEDY : cura *f*, remedio *m*

curfew ['kərˌfju:] *n* : toque *m* de queda

curio ['kjuriˌo:] *n, pl* -**rios** : curiosidad *f*, objeto *m* curioso

curiosity [ˌkjuriˈɑsəti] *n, pl* -**ties** : curiosidad *f*

curious ['kjuriəs] *adj* **1** INQUISITIVE : curioso **2** STRANGE : curioso, raro

curl[1] ['kərl] *vt* **1** : rizar, ondular (el pelo) **2** COIL : enrollar **3** TWIST : torcer ⟨to curl one's lip : hacer una mueca⟩ — *vi* **1** : rizarse, ondularse **2 to curl up** : acurrucarse (con un libro, etc.)

curl[2] *n* **1** RINGLET : rizo *m* **2** COIL : espiral *f*, rosca *f*

curler ['kərlər] *n* : rulo *m*

curlew ['kərˌlu:, 'kərlˌju:] *n, pl* -**lews** *or* -**lew** : zarapito *m*

curly ['kərli] *adj* **curlier; -est** : rizado, crespo

currant ['kərənt] *n* **1** : grosella *f* (fruta) **2** RAISIN : pasa *f* de Corinto

currency ['kərənsi] *n, pl* -**cies** **1** PREVALENCE, USE : uso *m*, aceptación *f*, difusión *f* ⟨to be in currency : estar en uso⟩ **2** MONEY : moneda *f*, dinero *m*

current[1] ['kərənt] *adj* **1** PRESENT : actual ⟨current events : actualidades⟩ **2** PREVALENT : corriente, común — **currently** *adv*

current[2] *n* : corriente *f*

curriculum [kəˈrɪkjələm] *n, pl* -**la** [-lə] : currículum *m*, currículo *m*, programa *m* de estudio

curriculum vitae ['vi:ˌtaɪ, 'vaɪt̬i] *n, pl* **curricula vitae** : currículum *m*, currículo *m*

curry[1] ['kəri] *vt* -**ried; -rying** **1** GROOM : almohazar (un caballo) **2** : condimentar con curry **3 to curry favor** : congraciarse (con alguien)

curry[2] *n, pl* -**ries** : curry *m*

curse[1] ['kərs] *v* **cursed; cursing** *vt* **1** DAMN : maldecir **2** INSULT : injuriar, insultar, decir malas palabras a **3** AFFLICT : afligir — *vi* : maldecir, decir malas palabras

curse[2] *n* **1** : maldición *f* ⟨to put a curse on someone : echarle una maldición a alguien⟩ **2** AFFLICTION : maldición *f*, aflicción *f*, cruz *f*

cursor ['kərsər] *n* : cursor *m*

cursory ['kərsəri] *adj* : rápido, superficial, somero

curt ['kərt] *adj* : cortante, brusco, seco — **curtly** *adv*

curtail [kərˈteɪl] *vt* : acortar, limitar, restringir

curtailment [kərˈteɪlmənt] *n* : restricción *f*, limitación *f*

curtain ['kərtən] *n* : cortina *f* (de una ventana), telón *m* (en un teatro)

curtness ['kərtnəs] *n* : brusquedad *f*, sequedad *f*

curtsy[1] *or* **curtsey** ['kərtsi] *vt* -**sied** *or* -**seyed; -sying** *or* -**seying** : hacer una reverencia

curtsy[2] *or* **curtsey** *n, pl* -**sies** *or* -**seys** : reverencia *f*

curvature ['kərvəˌtʃur] *n* : curvatura *f*

curve[1] ['kərv] *v* **curved; curving** *vi* : torcerse, describir una curva — *vt* : encorvar

curve[2] *n* : curva *f*

cushion[1] ['kuʃən] *vt* **1** : poner cojines o almohadones a **2** SOFTEN : amortiguar, mitigar, suavizar ⟨to cushion a blow : amortiguar un golpe⟩

cushion[2] *n* **1** : cojín *m*, almohadón *m* **2** PROTECTION : colchón *m*, protección *f*

cusp ['kʌsp] *n* : cúspide *f* (de un diente), cuerno *m* (de la luna)

cuspid ['kʌspɪd] *n* : diente *m* canino, colmillo *m*

custard ['kʌstərd] *n* : natillas *fpl*

custodian [ˌkʌˈsto:diən] *n* : custodio *m*, -dia *f*; guardián, -diana *f*

custody ['kʌstədi] *n, pl* -**dies** : custodia *f*, cuidado *m* ⟨to be in custody : estar detenido⟩

custom[1] ['kʌstəm] *adj* : a la medida, a la orden

custom[2] *n* **1** : costumbre *f*, tradición *f* **2 customs** *npl* : aduana *f*

customarily [ˌkʌstəˈmɛrəli] *adv* : habitualmente, normalmente, de costumbre

customary ['kʌstə,mɛri] *adj* **1** TRADITIONAL : tradicional **2** USUAL : habitual, de costumbre

customer ['kʌstəmər] *n* : cliente *m*, -ta *f*

custom–made ['kʌstəm'meɪd] *adj* : hecho a la medida

cut¹ ['kʌt] *v* cut; cutting *vt* **1** : cortar ⟨cut paper : cortar papel⟩ **2** : cortarse ⟨to cut one's finger : cortarse uno el dedo⟩ **3** TRIM : cortar, recortar ⟨to have one's hair cut : cortarse el pelo⟩ **4** INTERSECT : cruzar, atravesar **5** SHORTEN : acortar, abreviar **6** REDUCE : reducir, rebajar ⟨to cut prices : rebajar los precios⟩ **7 to cut one's teeth** : salirle los dientes a uno — *vi* **1** : cortar, cortarse **2 to cut in** : entrometerse

cut² *n* **1** : corte *m* ⟨a cut of meat : un corte de carne⟩ **2** SLASH : tajo *m*, corte *m*, cortadura *f* **3** REDUCTION : rebaja *f*, reducción *f* ⟨a cut in the rates : una rebaja en las tarifas⟩

cute ['kju:t] *adj* cuter; -est : mono *fam*, lindo

cuticle ['kju:tɪkəl] *n* : cutícula *f*

cutlass ['kʌtləs] *n* : alfanje *m*

cutlery ['kʌtləri] *n* : cubiertos *mpl*

cutlet ['kʌtlət] *n* : chuleta *f*

cutter ['kʌtər] *n* **1** : cortadora *f* (implemento) **2** : cortador *m*, -dora *f* (persona) **3** : cúter *m* (embarcación)

cutthroat ['kʌt,θro:t] *adj* : despiadado, desalmado ⟨cutthroat competition : competencia feroz⟩

cutting¹ ['kʌtɪŋ] *adj* **1** : cortante ⟨a cutting wind : un viento cortante⟩ **2** CAUSTIC : mordaz

cutting² *n* : esqueje *m* (de una planta)

cuttlefish ['kʌtəl,fɪʃ] *n, pl* **-fish** *or* **-fishes** : jibia *f*, sepia *f*

cyanide ['saɪə,naɪd, -nɪd] *n* : cianuro *m*

cycle¹ ['saɪkəl] *vi* **-cled; -cling** : andar en bicicleta, ir en bicicleta

cycle² *n* **1** : ciclo *m* ⟨life cycle : ciclo de vida, ciclo vital⟩ **2** BICYCLE : bicicleta *f* **3** MOTORCYCLE : motocicleta *f*

cyclic ['saɪklɪk, 'sɪ-] *or* **cyclical** [-klɪkəl] *adj* : cíclico

cyclist ['saɪklɪst] *n* : ciclista *mf*

cyclone ['saɪ,klo:n] *n* **1** : ciclón *m* **2** TORNADO : tornado *m*

cyclopedia *or* **cyclopaedia** [,saɪklə'pi:diə] → **encyclopedia**

cylinder ['sɪləndər] *n* : cilindro *m*

cylindrical [sə'lɪndrɪkəl] *adj* : cilíndrico

cymbal ['sɪmbəl] *n* : platillo *m*, címbalo *m*

cynic ['sɪnɪk] *n* : cínico *m*, -ca *f*

cynical ['sɪnɪkəl] *adj* : cínico

cynicism ['sɪnə,sɪzəm] *n* : cinismo *m*

cypress ['saɪprəs] *n* : ciprés *m*

Cypriot ['sɪpriət, -,at] *n* : chipriota *mf* — **Cypriot** *adj*

cyst ['sɪst] *n* : quiste *m*

cytoplasm ['saɪto,plæzəm] *n* : citoplasma *m*

czar ['zar, 'sar] *n* : zar *m*

czarina [za'ri:nə, sa-] *n* : zarina *f*

Czech ['tʃɛk] *n* **1** : checo *m*, -ca *f* **2** : checo *m* (idioma) — **Czech** *adj*

Czechoslovak [,tʃɛko'slo:,vak, -,væk] *or* **Czechoslovakian** [-slo'vakiən, -'væ-] *n* : checoslovaco *m*, -ca *f* — **Czechoslovak** *or* **Czechoslovakian** *adj*

D

d ['di:] *n, pl* **d's** *or* **ds** ['di:z] : cuarta letra del alfabeto inglés

dab¹ ['dæb] *vt* dabbed; dabbing : darle toques ligeros a, aplicar suavemente

dab² *n* **1** BIT : toque *m*, pizca *f*, poco *m* ⟨a dab of ointment : un toque de ungüento⟩ **2** PAT : toque *m* ligero, golpecito *m*

dabble ['dæbəl] *v* **-bled; -bling** *vt* SPATTER : salpicar — *vi* **1** SPLASH : chapotear **2** TRIFLE : jugar, interesarse superficialmente

dabbler ['dæbələr] *n* : diletante *mf*

dachshund ['daks,hʊnt, -,hʊnd; 'daksənt, -sənd] *n* : perro *m* salchicha

dad ['dæd] *n* : papá *m fam*

daddy ['dædi] *n, pl* **-dies** : papi *m fam*

daffodil ['dæfə,dɪl] *n* : narciso *m*

daft ['dæft] *adj* : tonto, bobo

dagger ['dægər] *n* : daga *f*, puñal *m*

dahlia ['dæljə, 'dal-, 'deɪl-] *n* : dalia *f*

daily¹ ['deɪli] *adv* : a diario, diariamente

daily² *adj* : diario, cotidiano

daily³ *n, pl* **-lies** : diario *m*, periódico *m*

daintily ['deɪntəli] *adv* : delicadamente, con delicadeza

daintiness ['deɪntinəs] *n* : delicadeza *f*, finura *f*

dainty¹ ['deɪnti] *adj* **-tier; -est** **1** DELICATE : delicado **2** FASTIDIOUS : remilgado, melindroso **3** DELICIOUS : exquisito, sabroso

dainty² *n, pl* **-ties** DELICACY : exquisitez *f*, manjar *m*

dairy ['dæri] *n, pl* **-ies** **1** *or* **dairy store** : lechería *f* **2** *or* **dairy farm** : granja *f* lechera

dairymaid ['dæri,meɪd] *n* : lechera *f*

dairyman ['dærimən, -,mæn] *n, pl* **-men** [-mən, -,mɛn] : lechero *m*

dais ['deɪəs] *n* : tarima *f*, estrado *m*

daisy ['deɪzi] *n, pl* **-sies** : margarita *f*

dale ['deɪl] *n* : valle *m*

dally ['dæli] *vi* **-lied; -lying** **1** TRIFLE : juguetear **2** DAWDLE : entretenerse, perder tiempo

dalmatian [dæl'meɪʃən, dɔl-] *n* : dálmata *m*

dam¹ ['dæm] *vt* dammed; damming : represar, embalsar

dam² *n* **1** : represa *f*, dique *m* **2** : madre *f* (de animales domésticos)

damage¹ ['dæmɪʤ] *vt* **-aged; -aging** : dañar (un objeto o una máquina), perjudicar (la salud o una reputación)

damage² *n* **1** : daño *m*, perjuicio *m* **2 damages** *npl* : daños y perjuicios *mpl*

damaging ['dæməʤɪŋ] *adj* : perjudicial

damask ['dæməsk] *n* : damasco *m*

dame ['deɪm] *n* LADY : dama *f*, señora *f*

damn¹ ['dæm] *vt* **1** CONDEMN : condenar **2** CURSE : maldecir

damn² *or* **damned** ['dæmd] *adj* : condenado *fam*, maldito *fam*

damn³ *n* : pito *m*, bledo *m*, comino *m* ⟨it's not worth a damn : no vale un pito⟩ ⟨I don't give a damn : me importa un comino⟩

damnable ['dæmnəbəl] *adj* : condenable, detestable

damnation [dæm'neɪʃən] *n* : condenación *f*

damned¹ ['dæmd] *adv* VERY : muy

damned² *adj* **1** → **damnable 2** REMARKABLE : extraordinario

damp¹ ['dæmp] *vt* → **dampen**

damp² *adj* : húmedo

damp³ *n* MOISTURE : humedad *f*

dampen ['dæmpən] *vt* **1** MOISTEN : humedecer **2** DISCOURAGE : desalentar, desanimar

damper ['dæmpər] *n* **1** : regulador *m* de tiro (de una chimenea) **2** : sordina *f* (de un piano) **3 to put a damper on** : desanimar, apagar (el entusiasmo), enfriar

dampness ['dæmpnəs] *n* : humedad *f*

damsel ['dæmzəl] *n* : damisela *f*

dance¹ ['dænts] *v* **danced; dancing** : bailar

dance² *n* : baile *m*

dancer ['dæntsər] *n* : bailarín *m*, -rina *f*

dandelion ['dændə,aɪən] *n* : diente *m* de león

dandruff ['dændrəf] *n* : caspa *f*

dandy¹ ['dændi] *adj* **-dier; -est** : excelente, magnífico, macanudo *fam*

dandy² *n, pl* **-dies 1** FOP : dandi *m* **2** : algo *m* excelente ⟨this new program is a dandy : este programa nuevo es algo excelente⟩

Dane ['deɪn] *n* : danés *m*, -nesa *f*

danger ['deɪnʤər] *n* : peligro *m*

dangerous ['deɪnʤərəs] *adj* : peligroso

dangle ['dæŋgəl] *v* **-gled; -gling** *vi* HANG : colgar, pender — *vt* **1** SWING : hacer oscilar **2** PROFFER : ofrecer (como incentivo) **3 to keep someone dangling** : dejar a alguien en suspenso

Danish¹ ['deɪnɪʃ] *adj* : danés

Danish² *n* : danés *m* (idioma)

dank ['dæŋk] *adj* : frío y húmedo

dapper ['dæpər] *adj* : pulcro, atildado

dappled ['dæpəld] *adj* : moteado ⟨a dappled horse : un caballo rodado⟩

dare¹ ['dær] *v* **dared; daring** *vi* : osar, atreverse ⟨how dare you! : ¡cómo te atreves!⟩ — *vt* **1** CHALLENGE : desafiar, retar **2 to dare to do something** : atreverse a hacer algo, osar hacer algo

dare² *n* : desafío *m*, reto *m*

daredevil ['dær,dɛvəl] *n* : persona *f* temeraria

daring¹ ['dærɪŋ] *adj* : osado, atrevido, audaz

daring² *n* : arrojo *m*, coraje *m*, audacia *f*

dark ['dɑrk] *adj* **1** : oscuro (dícese del ambiente o de los colores), moreno (dícese del pelo o de la piel) **2** SOMBER : sombrío, triste

darken ['dɑrkən] *vt* **1** DIM : oscurecer **2** SADDEN : entristecer — *vi* : ensombrecerse, nublarse

darkly ['dɑrkli] *adv* **1** DIMLY : oscuramente **2** GLOOMILY : tristemente **3** MYSTERIOUSLY : misteriosamente, enigmáticamente

darkness ['dɑrknəs] *n* : oscuridad *f*, tinieblas *f*

darling¹ ['dɑrlɪŋ] *adj* **1** BELOVED : querido, amado **2** CHARMING : encantador, mono *fam*

darling² *n* **1** BELOVED : querido *m*, -da *f*; amado *m*, -da *f*; cariño *m*, -ña *f* **2** FAVORITE : preferido *m*, -da *f*; favorito *m*, -ta *f*

darn¹ ['dɑrn] *vt* : zurcir

darn² *n* **1** : zurcido *m* **2** → **damn³**

dart¹ ['dɑrt] *vt* THROW : lanzar, tirar — *vi* DASH : lanzarse, precipitarse

dart² *n* **1** : dardo *m* **2 darts** *npl* : juego *m* de dardos

dash¹ ['dæʃ] *vt* **1** SMASH : romper, estrellar **2** HURL : arrojar, lanzar **3** SPLASH : salpicar **4** FRUSTRATE : frustrar **5 to dash off** : hacer (algo) rápidamente — *vi* **1** SMASH : romperse, estrellarse **2** DART : lanzarse, irse apresuradamente

dash² *n* **1** BURST, SPLASH : arranque *m*, salpicadura *f* (de aguas) **2** : guión *m* largo (signo de puntuación) **3** DROP : gota *f*, pizca *f* **4** VERVE : brío *m* **5** RACE : carrera *f* ⟨a 100-meter dash : una carrera de 100 metros⟩ **6 to make a dash for it** : precipitarse (hacia), echarse a correr **7** → **dashboard**

dashboard ['dæʃ,bord] *n* : tablero *m* de instrumentos

dashing ['dæʃɪŋ] *adj* : gallardo, apuesto

data ['deɪtə, 'dæ-, 'dɑ-] *ns & pl* : datos *mpl*, información *f*

database ['deɪtə,beɪs, 'dæ-, 'dɑ-] *n* : base *f* de datos

date¹ ['deɪt] *v* **dated; dating** *vt* **1** : fechar (una carta, etc.), datar (un objeto) ⟨it was dated June 9 : estaba fechada el 9 de junio⟩ **2** : salir con ⟨she's dating my brother : sale con mi hermano⟩ — *vi* : datar

date² *n* **1** : fecha *f* ⟨to date : hasta la fecha⟩ **2** EPOCH, PERIOD : época *f*, período *m* **3** APPOINTMENT : cita *f* **4** COMPANION : acompañante *mf* **5** : dátil *m* (fruta)

dated ['deɪtəd] *adj* OUT-OF-DATE : anticuado, pasado de moda

datum ['deɪt̬əm, 'dæ-, 'dɑ-] *n, pl* **-ta** [-t̬ə] *or* **-tums** : dato *m*

daub¹ ['dɔb] *vt* : embadurnar

daub² *n* : mancha *f*

daughter ['dɔt̬ər] *n* : hija *f*

daughter–in–law ['dɔt̬ərɪn,lɔ] *n, pl* **daughters–in–law** : nuera *f*, hija *f* política

daunt ['dɔnt] *vt* : amilanar, acobardar, intimidar

dauntless ['dɔntləs] *adj* : intrépido, impávido

davenport ['dævən,port] *n* : sofá *m*

dawdle ['dɔdəl] *vi* **-dled; -dling** **1** DALLY : demorarse, entretenerse, perder tiempo **2** LOITER : vagar, holgazanear, haraganear

dawn¹ ['dɔn] *vi* **1** : amanecer, alborear, despuntar ⟨Saturday dawned clear and bright : el sábado amaneció claro y luminoso⟩ **2 to dawn on** : hacerse obvio ⟨it dawned on me that she was right : me di cuenta de que tenía razón⟩

dawn² *n* **1** DAYBREAK : amanecer *m*, alba *f* **2** BEGINNING : albor *m*, comienzo *m* ⟨the dawn of history : los albores de la historia⟩ **3 from dawn to dusk** : de sol a sol

day ['deɪ] *n* **1** : día *m* **2** DATE : fecha *f* **3** TIME : día *m*, tiempo *m* ⟨in olden days : intaño⟩ **4** WORKDAY : jornada *f* laboral

daybreak ['deɪ,breɪk] *n* : alba *f*, amanecer *m*

day care *n* : servicio *m* de guardería infantil

daydream¹ ['deɪ,dri:m] *vi* : soñar despierto, fantasear

daydream² *n* : ensueño *m*, ensoñación *f*, fantasía *f*

daylight ['deɪ,laɪt] *n* **1** : luz *f* del día ⟨in broad daylight : a plena luz del día⟩ → **daybreak 3** → **daytime**

daylight saving time *n* : hora *f* de verano

daytime ['deɪ,taɪm] *n* : horas *fpl* diurnas, día *m*

daze¹ ['deɪz] *vt* **dazed; dazing 1** STUN : aturdir **2** DAZZLE : deslumbrar, ofuscar

daze² *n* **1** : aturdimiento *m* **2 in a daze** : aturdido, atontado

dazzle¹ ['dæzəl] *vt* **-zled; -zling** : deslumbrar, ofuscar

dazzle² *n* : resplandor *m*, brillo *m*

DDT [,di:,di:'ti:] *n* : DDT *m*

deacon ['di:kən] *n* : diácono *m*

dead¹ ['dɛd] *adv* **1** ABRUPTLY : repentinamente, súbitamente ⟨to stop dead : parar en seco⟩ **2** ABSOLUTELY : absolutamente ⟨I'm dead certain : estoy absolutamente seguro⟩ **3** DIRECTLY : justo ⟨dead ahead : justo adelante⟩

dead² *adj* **1** LIFELESS : muerto **2** NUMB : entumecido **3** INDIFFERENT : indiferente, frío **4** INACTIVE : inactivo ⟨a dead volcano : un volcán inactivo⟩ **5** : desconectado (dícese del teléfono),

descargado (dícese de una batería) **6** EXHAUSTED : agotado, derrengado, muerto **7** OBSOLETE : obsoleto, muerto ⟨a dead language : una lengua muerta⟩ **8** EXACT : exacto ⟨in the dead center : justo en el blanco⟩

dead³ *n* **1 the dead** : los muertos **2 in the dead of night** : a las altas horas de la noche **3 in the dead of winter** : en pleno invierno

deadbeat ['dɛd,bi:t] *n* **1** LOAFER : vago *m*, -ga *f*; holgazán *m*, -zana *f* **2** FREELOADER : gorrón *m*, -rrona *f fam*; gorrero *m*, -ra *f fam*

deaden ['dɛdən] *vt* **1** : atenuar (un dolor), entorpecer (sensaciones) **2** DULL : deslustrar **3** DISPIRIT : desanimar **4** MUFFLE : amortiguar, reducir (sonidos)

dead–end ['dɛd'ɛnd] *adj* **1** : sin salida ⟨dead-end street : calle sin salida⟩ **2** : sin futuro ⟨a dead-end job : un trabajo sin porvenir⟩

dead end *n* : callejón *m* sin salida

dead heat *n* : empate *m*

deadline ['dɛd,laɪn] *n* : fecha *f* límite, fecha *f* tope, plazo *m* (determinado)

deadlock¹ ['dɛd,lɑk] *vt* : estancar — *vi* : estancarse, llegar a punto muerto

deadlock² *n* : punto *m* muerto, impasse *m*

deadly¹ ['dɛdli] *adv* : extremadamente, sumamente ⟨deadly serious : muy en serio⟩

deadly² *adj* **-lier; -est 1** LETHAL : mortal, letal, mortífero **2** ACCURATE : certero, preciso ⟨a deadly aim : una puntería infalible⟩ **3** CAPITAL : capital ⟨the seven deadly sins : los siete pecados capitales⟩ **4** DULL : funesto, aburrido **5** EXTREME : extremo, absoluto ⟨a deadly calm : una calma absoluta⟩

deadpan¹ ['dɛd,pæn] *adv* : de manera inexpresiva, sin expresión

deadpan² *adj* : inexpresivo, impasible

deaf ['dɛf] *adj* : sordo

deafen ['dɛfən] *vt* **-ened; -ening** : ensordecer

deafening ['dɛfənɪŋ] *adj* : ensordecedor

deaf–mute ['dɛf'mju:t] *n* : sordomudo *m*, -da *f*

deafness ['dɛfnəs] *n* : sordera *f*

deal¹ ['di:l] *v* **dealt; dealing** *vt* **1** APPORTION : repartir ⟨to deal justice : repartir la justicia⟩ **2** DISTRIBUTE : repartir, dar (naipes) **3** DELIVER : asestar, propinar ⟨to deal a blow : asestar un golpe⟩ — *vi* **1** : dar, repartir (en juegos de naipes) **2 to deal in** : comerciar en, traficar con (drogas) **3 to deal with** CONCERN : tratar de, tener que ver con ⟨the book deals with poverty : el libro trata de la pobreza⟩ **4 to deal with** HANDLE : tratar (con), encargarse de **5 to deal with** TREAT : tratar ⟨the judge dealt with him severely : el juez lo trató con severidad⟩ **6 to deal with** ACCEPT : aceptar (una situación o desgracia)

deal² *n* **1** : reparto *m* (de naipes) **2** AGREEMENT, TRANSACTION : trato *m*, acuerdo *m*, transacción *f* **3** TREATMENT : trato *m* ⟨he got a raw deal : le hicieron una injusticia⟩ **4** BARGAIN : ganga *f*, oferta *f* **5 a good deal** *or* **a great deal** : mucho, una gran cantidad

dealer ['di:lər] *n* : comerciante *mf*, traficante *mf*

dealership ['di:lər‚ʃɪp] *n* : concesión *f*

dealings ['di:lɪŋz] *npl* **1** : relaciones *fpl* (personales) **2** TRANSACTIONS : negocios *mpl*, transacciones *fpl*

dean ['di:n] *n* **1** : deán *m* (del clero) **2** : decano *m*, -na *f* (de una facultad o profesión)

dear¹ ['dɪr] *adj* **1** ESTEEMED, LOVED : querido, estimado ⟨a dear friend : un amigo querido⟩ ⟨Dear Sir : Estimado Señor⟩ **2** COSTLY : caro, costoso

dear² *n* : querido *m*, -da *f*; amado *m*, -da *f*

dearly ['dɪrli] *adv* **1** : mucho ⟨I love them dearly : los quiero mucho⟩ **2** : caro ⟨to pay dearly : pagar caro⟩

dearth ['dərθ] *n* : escasez *f*, carestía *f*

death ['dɛθ] *n* **1** : muerte *f*, fallecimiento *m* ⟨to be the death of : matar⟩ **2** FATALITY : víctima *f* (mortal); muerto *m*, -ta *f* **3** END : fin *m* ⟨the death of civilization : el fin de la civilización⟩

deathbed ['dɛθ‚bɛd] *n* : lecho *m* de muerte

deathblow ['dɛθ‚blo:] *n* : golpe *m* mortal

deathless ['dɛθləs] *adj* : eterno, inmortal

deathly ['dɛθli] *adj* : de muerte, sepulcral (dícese del silencio), cadavérico (dícese de la palidez)

debacle [dɪ'bɑkəl, -'bæ-] *n* : desastre *m*, debacle *m*, fiasco *m*

debar [di'bɑr] *vt* **-barred; -barring** : excluir, prohibir

debase [di'beɪs] *vt* **-based; -basing** : degradar, envilecer

debasement [di'beɪsmənt] *n* : degradación *f*, envilecimiento *m*

debatable [di'beɪtəbəl] *adj* : discutible

debate¹ [di'beɪt] *vt* **-bated; -bating** : debatir, discutir

debate² *n* : debate *m*, discusión *f*

debauch [di'bɔtʃ] *vt* : pervertir, corromper

debauchery [di'bɔtʃəri] *n, pl* **-eries** : libertinaje *m*, disipación *f*, intemperancia *f*

debilitate [di'bɪlə‚teɪt] *vt* **-tated; -tating** : debilitar

debility [di'bɪləti] *n, pl* **-ties** : debilidad *f*

debit¹ ['dɛbɪt] *vt* : adeudar, cargar, debitar

debit² *n* : débito *m*, cargo *m*, debe *m*

debonair [‚dɛbə'nær] *adj* : elegante y desenvuelto, apuesto

debris [də'bri:, deɪ-; 'deɪ‚bri:] *n, pl* **-bris** [-'bri:z, -‚bri:z] **1** RUBBLE, RUINS : escombros *mpl*, ruinas *fpl*, restos *mpl* **2** RUBBISH : basura *f*, deshechos *mpl*

debt ['dɛt] *n* **1** : deuda *f* ⟨to pay a debt : saldar una deuda⟩ **2** INDEBTEDNESS : endeudamiento *m*

debtor ['dɛtər] *n* : deudor *m*, -dora *f*

debunk [di'bʌŋk] *vt* DISCREDIT : desacreditar, desprestigiar

debut¹ [deɪ'bju:, 'deɪ‚bju:] *vi* : debutar

debut² *n* **1** : debut *m* (de un actor), estreno *m* (de una obra) **2** : debut *m*, presentación *f* (en sociedad)

debutante ['dɛbju‚tɑnt] *n* : debutante *f*

decade ['dɛ‚keɪd, dɛ'keɪd] *n* : década *f*

decadence ['dɛkədənts] *n* : decadencia *f*

decadent ['dɛkədənt] *adj* : decadente

decaf¹ ['di:‚kæf] → **decaffeinated**

decaf² *n* : café *m* descafeinado

decaffeinated [di'kæfə‚neɪtəd] *adj* : descafeinado

decal ['di:‚kæl, di'kæl] *n* : calcomanía *f*

decamp [di'kæmp] *vi* : irse, largarse *fam*

decant [di'kænt] *vt* : decantar

decanter [di'kæntər] *n* : licorera *f*, garrafa *f*

decapitate [di'kæpə‚teɪt] *vt* **-tated; -tating** : decapitar

decay¹ [di'keɪ] *vi* **1** DECOMPOSE : descomponerse, pudrirse **2** DETERIORATE : deteriorarse **3** : cariarse (dícese de los dientes)

decay² *n* **1** DECOMPOSITION : descomposición *f* **2** DECLINE, DETERIORATION : decadencia *f*, deterioro *m* **3** : caries *f* (de los dientes)

decease¹ [di'si:s] *vi* **-ceased; -ceasing** : morir, fallecer

decease² *n* : fallecimiento *m*, defunción *f*, deceso *m*

deceit [di'si:t] *n* **1** DECEPTION : engaño *m* **2** DISHONESTY : deshonestidad *f*

deceitful [di'si:tfəl] *adj* : falso, embustero, engañoso, mentiroso

deceitfully [di'si:tfəli] *adv* : con engaño, con falsedad

deceitfulness [di'si:tfəlnəs] *n* : falsedad *f*, engaño *m*

deceive [di'si:v] *vt* **-ceived; -ceiving** : engañar, burlar

deceiver [di'si:vər] *n* : impostor *m*, -tora *f*

decelerate [di'sɛlə‚reɪt] *vi* **-ated; -ating** : reducir la velocidad, desacelerar

December [di'sɛmbər] *n* : diciembre *m*

decency ['disəntsi] *n, pl* **-cies** : decencia *f*, decoro *m*

decent ['di:sənt] *adj* **1** CORRECT, PROPER : decente, decoroso, correcto **2** CLOTHED : vestido, presentable **3** MODEST : púdico, modesto **4** ADEQUATE : decente, adecuado ⟨decent wages : paga adecuada⟩

decently ['di:səntli] *adv* : decentemente

decentralize [di'sɛntrə‚laɪz] *v* **-lized** [-‚laɪzd]; **-lizing** [-‚laɪzɪŋ] *vt* : descentralizar — *vi* : descentralizarse

deception [di'sɛpʃən] *n* : engaño *m*

deceptive [dɪ'sɛptɪv] *adj* : engañoso, falaz — **deceptively** *adv*

decibel ['dɛsəbəl, -ˌbɛl] *n* : decibelio *m*

decide [dɪ'saɪd] *v* -**cided; -ciding** *vt* **1** CONCLUDE : decidir, llegar a la conclusión de ⟨he decided what to do : decidió qué iba a hacer⟩ **2** DETERMINE : decidir, determinar ⟨one blow decided the fight : un solo golpe determinó la pelea⟩ **3** CONVINCE : decidir ⟨her pleas decided me to help : sus súplicas me decidieron a ayudarla⟩ **4** RESOLVE : resolver — *vi* : decidirse

decided [dɪ'saɪdəd] *adj* **1** UNQUESTIONABLE : indudable **2** RESOLUTE : decidido, resuelto — **decidedly** *adv*

deciduous [dɪ'sɪdʒuəs] *adj* : caduco, de hoja caduca

decimal[1] ['dɛsəməl] *adj* : decimal

decimal[2] *n* : número *m* decimal

decipher [dɪ'saɪfər] *vt* : descifrar — **decipherable** [-əbəl] *adj*

decision [dɪ'sɪʒən] *n* : decisión *f*, determinación *f* ⟨to make a decision : tomar una decisión⟩

decisive [dɪ'saɪsɪv] *adj* **1** DECIDING : decisivo ⟨the decisive vote : el voto decisivo⟩ **2** CONCLUSIVE : decisivo, concluyente, contundente ⟨a decisive victory : una victoria contundente⟩ **3** RESOLUTE : decidido, resuelto, firme

decisively [dɪ'saɪsɪvli] *adv* : con decisión, de manera decisiva

decisiveness [dɪ'saɪsɪvnəs] *n* **1** FORCEFULNESS : contundencia *f* **2** RESOLUTION : firmeza *f*, decisión *f*, determinación *f*

deck[1] ['dɛk] *vt* **1** FLOOR : tumbar, derribar ⟨she decked him with one blow : lo tumbó de un solo golpe⟩ **2 to deck out** : adornar, engalanar

deck[2] *n* **1** : cubierta *f* (de un barco) **2** *or* **deck of cards** : baraja *f* (de naipes)

declaim [dɪ'kleɪm] *v* : declamar

declaration [ˌdɛklə'reɪʃən] *n* : declaración *f*, pronunciamiento *m* (oficial)

declare [dɪ'klær] *vt* -**clared; -claring** : declarar, manifestar ⟨to declare war : declarar la guerra⟩ ⟨they declared their support : manifestaron su apoyo⟩

decline[1] [dɪ'klaɪn] *v* -**clined; -clining** *vi* **1** DESCEND : descender **2** DETERIORATE : deteriorarse, decaer ⟨her health is declining : su salud se está deteriorando⟩ **3** DECREASE : disminuir, decrecer, decaer **4** REFUSE : rehusar — *vt* **1** INFLECT : declinar **2** REFUSE, TURN DOWN : declinar, rehusar

decline[2] *n* **1** DETERIORATION : decadencia *f*, deterioro *m* **2** DECREASE : disminución *f*, descenso *m* **3** SLOPE : declive *m*, pendiente *f*

decode [dɪ'koːd] *vt* -**coded; -coding** : descifrar (un mensaje), descodificar (una señal)

decoder [dɪ'koːdər] *n* : descodificador *m*

decompose [ˌdiːkəm'poːz] *v* -**posed; -posing** *vt* **1** BREAK DOWN : descomponer **2** ROT : descomponer, pudrir — *vi* : descomponerse, pudrirse

decomposition [ˌdiːˌkɑmpə'zɪʃən] *n* : descomposición *f*

decongestant [ˌdiːkən'dʒɛstənt] *n* : descongestionante *m*

decor *or* **décor** [deɪ'kɔr, 'deɪˌkɔr] *n* : decoración *f*

decorate ['dɛkəˌreɪt] *vt* -**rated; -rating 1** ADORN : decorar, adornar **2** : condecorar ⟨he was decorated for bravery : lo condecoraron por valor⟩

decoration [ˌdɛkə'reɪʃən] *n* **1** ADORNMENT : decoración *f*, adorno *m* **2** : condecoración *f* (de honor)

decorative ['dɛkərətɪv, -ˌreɪ-] *adj* : decorativo, ornamental, de adorno

decorator ['dɛkəˌreɪtər] *n* : decorador *m*, -dora *f*

decorum [dɪ'korəm] *n* : decoro *m*

decoy[1] ['diːˌkɔɪ, dɪ'-] *vt* : atraer (con señuelo)

decoy[2] *n* : señuelo *m*, reclamo *m*, cimbel *m*

decrease[1] [dɪ'kriːs] *v* -**creased; -creasing** *vi* : decrecer, disminuir, bajar — *vt* : reducir, disminuir

decrease[2] ['diːˌkriːs] *n* : disminución *f*, descenso *m*, bajada *f*

decree[1] [dɪ'kriː] *vt* -**creed; -creeing** : decretar

decree[2] *n* : decreto *m*

decrepit [dɪ'krɛpɪt] *adj* **1** FEEBLE : decrépito, débil **2** DILAPIDATED : deteriorado, ruinoso

decry [dɪ'kraɪ] *vt* -**cried; -crying** : censurar, criticar

dedicate ['dɛdɪˌkeɪt] *vt* -**cated; -cating 1** : dedicar ⟨she dedicated the book to Carlos : le dedicó el libro a Carlos⟩ **2** : consagrar, dedicar ⟨to dedicate one's life : consagrar uno su vida⟩

dedication [ˌdɛdɪ'keɪʃən] *n* **1** DEVOTION : dedicación *f*, devoción *f* **2** : dedicatoria *f* (de un libro, una canción, etc.) **3** CONSECRATION : dedicación *f*

deduce [dɪ'duːs, -'djuːs] *vt* -**duced; -ducing** : deducir, inferir

deduct [dɪ'dʌkt] *vt* : deducir, descontar, restar

deductible [dɪ'dʌktəbəl] *adj* : deducible

deduction [dɪ'dʌkʃən] *n* : deducción *f*

deed[1] ['diːd] *vt* : ceder, transferir

deed[2] *n* **1** ACT : acto *m*, acción *f*, hecho *m* ⟨a good deed : una buena acción⟩ **2** FEAT : hazaña *f*, proeza *f* **3** TITLE : escritura *f*, título *m*

deem ['diːm] *vt* : considerar, juzgar

deep[1] ['diːp] *adv* : hondo, profundamente ⟨to dig deep : cavar hondo⟩

deep[2] *adj* **1** : hondo, profundo ⟨the deep end : la parte honda⟩ ⟨a deep wound : una herida profunda⟩ **2** WIDE : ancho **3** INTENSE : profundo, intenso **4** DARK : intenso, subido ⟨deep red : rojo subido⟩ **5** LOW : profundo ⟨a deep tone

: un tono profundo〉 **6** ABSORBED : absorto 〈deep in thought : absorto en la meditación〉

deep³ *n* **1 the deep** : lo profundo, el piélago **2 the deep of night** : lo más profundo de la noche

deepen ['di:pən] *vt* **1** : ahondar, profundizar **2** INTENSIFY : intensificar — *vi* **1** : hacerse más profundo **2** INTENSIFY : intensificarse

deeply ['di:pli] *adv* : hondo, profundamente 〈I'm deeply sorry : lo siento sinceramente〉

deep-seated ['di:p'si:t̬əd] *adj* : profundamente arraigado, enraizado

deer ['dɪr] *ns & pl* : ciervo *m*, venado *m*

deerskin ['dɪr,skɪn] *n* : piel *f* de venado

deface [di'feɪs] *vt* **-faced; -facing** MAR : desfigurar

defacement [di'feɪsmənt] *n* : desfiguración *f*

defamation [,dɛfə'meɪʃən] *n* : difamación *f*

defamatory [di'fæmə,tori] *adj* : difamatorio

defame [di'feɪm] *vt* **-famed; -faming** : difamar, calumniar

default¹ [di'fɔlt, 'di:,fɔlt] *vi* **1** : no cumplir (con una obligación), no pagar **2** : no presentarse (en un tribunal)

default² *n* **1** NEGLECT : omisión *f*, negligencia *f* **2** NONPAYMENT : impago *m*, falta *f* de pago **3 to win by default** : ganar por abandono

defaulter [di'fɔltər] *n* : moroso *m*, -sa *f*; rebelde *mf* (en un tribunal)

defeat¹ [di'fi:t] *vt* **1** FRUSTRATE : frustrar **2** BEAT : vencer, derrotar

defeat² *n* : derrota *f*, rechazo *m* (de legislación), fracaso *m* (de planes, etc.)

defecate ['dɛfɪ,keɪt] *vi* **-cated; -cating** : defecar

defect¹ [di'fɛkt] *vi* : desertar

defect² ['di:,fɛkt, di'fɛkt] *n* : defecto *m*

defection [di'fɛkʃən] *n* : deserción *f*, defección *f*

defective [di'fɛktɪv] *adj* **1** FAULTY : defectuoso **2** DEFICIENT : deficiente

defector [di'fɛktər] *n* : desertor *m*, -tora *f*

defend [di'fɛnd] *vt* : defender

defendant [di'fɛndənt] *n* : acusado *m*, -da *f*; demandado *m*, -da *f*

defender [di'fɛndər] *n* **1** ADVOCATE : defensor *m*, -sora *f* **2** : defensa *mf* (en deportes)

defense [di'fɛnts, 'di:,fɛnts] *n* : defensa *f*

defenseless [di'fɛntsləs] *adj* : indefenso

defensive¹ [di'fɛntsɪv] *adj* : defensivo

defensive² *n* **on the defensive** : a la defensiva

defer [di'fər] *v* **-ferred; -ferring** *vt* POSTPONE : diferir, aplazar, posponer — *vi* **to defer to** : deferir a

deference ['dɛfərənts] *n* : deferencia *f*

deferential [,dɛfə'rɛntʃəl] *adj* : respetuoso

deferment [di'fərmənt] *n* : aplazamiento *m*

defiance [di'faɪənts] *n* : desafío *m*

defiant [di'faɪənt] *adj* : desafiante, insolente

deficiency [di'fɪʃəntsi] *n, pl* **-cies** : deficiencia *f*, carencia *f*

deficient [di'fɪʃənt] *adj* : deficiente, carente

deficit ['dɛfəsɪt] *n* : déficit *m*

defile [di'faɪl] *vt* **-filed; -filing 1** DIRTY : ensuciar, manchar **2** CORRUPT : corromper **3** DESECRATE, PROFANE : profanar **4** DISHONOR : deshonrar

defilement [di'faɪlmənt] *n* **1** DESECRATION : profanación *f* **2** CORRUPTION : corrupción *f* **3** CONTAMINATION : contaminación *f*

define [di'faɪn] *vt* **-fined; -fining 1** BOUND : delimitar, demarcar **2** CLARIFY : aclarar, definir **3** : definir 〈to define a word : definir una palabra〉

definite ['dɛfənɪt] *adj* **1** CERTAIN : definido, determinado **2** CLEAR : claro, explícito **3** UNQUESTIONABLE : seguro, incuestionable

definite article *n* : artículo *m* definido

definitely ['dɛfənɪtli] *adv* **1** DOUBTLESSLY : indudablemente, sin duda **2** DEFINITIVELY : definitivamente, seguramente

definition [,dɛfə'nɪʃən] *n* : definición *f*

definitive [di'fɪnət̬ɪv] *adj* **1** CONCLUSIVE : definitivo, decisivo **2** AUTHORITATIVE : de autoridad, autorizado

deflate [di'fleɪt] *v* **-flated; -flating** *vt* **1** : desinflar (una llanta, etc.) **2** REDUCE : rebajar 〈to deflate one's ego : bajarle los humos a uno〉 — *vi* : desinflarse

deflation [di'fleɪʃən] *n* **1** : desinflación *f* (de una llanta, etc.) **2** : deflación *f* (económica)

deflect [di'flɛkt] *vt* : desviar — *vi* : desviarse

defoliant [di'foːliənt] *n* : defoliante *m*

deforestation [di,fɔrə'steɪʃən] *n* : deforestación *f*, desforestación *f*

deform [di'fɔrm] *vt* : deformar

deformation [,di:,fɔr'meɪʃən] *n* : deformación *f*

deformed [di'fɔrmd] *adj* : deforme

deformity [di'fɔrmət̬i] *n, pl* **-ties** : deformidad *f*

defraud [di'frɔd] *vt* : estafar, defraudar

defray [di'freɪ] *vt* : sufragar, costear

defrost [di'frɔst] *vt* : descongelar, deshelar — *vi* : descongelarse, deshelarse

deft ['dɛft] *adj* : hábil, diestro — **deftly** *adv*

defunct [di'fʌŋkt] *adj* **1** DECEASED : difunto, fallecido **2** EXTINCT : extinto, fenecido

defuse [di'fju:z] *vt* : desactivar 〈to defuse the situation : reducir las tensiones〉

defy [di'faɪ] *vt* **-fied; -fying 1** CHALLENGE : desafiar, retar **2** DISOBEY : desobedecer **3** RESIST : resistir, hacer imposible, hacer inútil

degenerate[1] [di'dʒenə,reɪt] *vi* -ated; -ating : degenerar

degenerate[2] [di'dʒenərət] *adj* : degenerado

degeneration [di,dʒenə'reɪʃən] *n* : degeneración *f*

degenerative [di'dʒenərətɪv] *adj* : degenerative

degradation [,dɛgrə'deɪʃən] *n* : degradación *f*

degrade [di'greɪd] *vt* -graded; -grading 1 : degradar, envilecer 2 to degrade oneself : rebajarse

degrading [di'greɪdɪŋ] *adj* : degradante

degree [di'gri:] *n* 1 EXTENT : grado *m* ⟨a third degree burn : una quemadura de tercer grado⟩ 2 : título *m* (de enseñanza superior) 3 : grado *m* (de un círculo, de la temperatura) 4 by degrees : gradualmente, poco a poco

dehydrate [di'haɪ,dreɪt] *v* -drated; -drating *vt* : deshidratar — *vi* : deshidratarse

dehydration [,di:haɪ'dreɪʃən] *n* : deshidratación *f*

deice [,di:'aɪs] *vt* -iced; -icing : deshelar, descongelar

deify ['di:ə,faɪ, 'deɪ-] *vt* -fied; -fying : deificar

deign ['deɪn] *vi* : dignarse, condescender

deity ['di:əṭi, 'deɪ-] *n, pl* -ties 1 the Deity : Dios *m* 2 GOD, GODDESS : deidad *f*; dios *m*, diosa *f*

dejected [di'dʒektəd] *adj* : abatido, desalentado, desanimado

dejection [di'dʒekʃən] *n* : abatimiento *m*, desaliento *m*, desánimo *m*

delay[1] [di'leɪ] *vt* 1 POSTPONE : posponer, postergar 2 HOLD UP : retrasar, demorar — *vi* : tardar, demorar

delay[2] *n* 1 LATENESS : tardanza *f* 2 HOLDUP : demora *f*, retraso *m*

delectable [di'lektəbəl] *adj* 1 DELICIOUS : delicioso, exquisito 2 DELIGHTFUL : encantador

delegate[1] ['dɛlɪ,geɪt] *v* -gated; -gating : delegar

delegate[2] ['dɛlɪgət, -,geɪt] *n* : delegado *m*, -da *f*

delegation [,dɛlɪ'geɪʃən] *n* : delegación *f*

delete [di'li:t] *vt* -leted; -leting : suprimir, tachar, eliminar

deletion [di'li:ʃən] *n* : supresión *f*, tachadura *f*, eliminación *f*

deli ['dɛli] → delicatessen

deliberate[1] [di'lɪbə,reɪt] *v* -ated; -ating *vt* : deliberar sobre, reflexionar sobre, considerar — *vi* : deliberar

deliberate[2] [di'lɪbərət] *adj* 1 CONSIDERED : reflexionado, premeditado 2 INTENTIONAL : deliberado, intencional 3 SLOW : lento, pausado

deliberately [di'lɪbərətli] *adv* 1 INTENTIONALLY : adrede, a propósito 2 SLOWLY : pausadamente, lentamente

deliberation [di,lɪbə'reɪʃən] *n* 1 CONSIDERATION : deliberación *f*, consideración *f* 2 SLOWNESS : lentitud *f*

delicacy ['dɛlɪkəsi] *n, pl* -cies 1 : manjar *m*, exquisitez *f* ⟨caviar is a real delicacy : el caviar es un verdadero manjar⟩ 2 FINENESS : delicadeza *f* 3 FRAGILITY : fragilidad *f*

delicate ['dɛlɪkət] *adj* 1 SUBTLE : delicado ⟨a delicate fragrance : una fragancia delicada⟩ 2 DAINTY : delicado, primoroso, fino 3 FRAGILE : frágil 4 SENSITIVE : delicado ⟨a delicate matter : un asunto delicado⟩

delicately ['dɛlɪkətli] *adv* : delicadamente, con delicadeza

delicatessen [,dɛlɪkə'tɛsən] *n* : charcutería *f*, fiambrería *f*, salchichonería *f* Mex

delicious [di'lɪʃəs] *adj* : delicioso, exquisito, rico — **deliciously** *adv*

delight[1] [di'laɪt] *vt* : deleitar, encantar — *vi* to delight in : deleitarse con, complacerse en

delight[2] *n* 1 JOY : placer *m*, deleite *m*, gozo *m* 2 : encanto *m* ⟨your garden is a delight : su jardín es un encanto⟩

delightful [di'laɪtfəl] *adj* : delicioso, encantador

delightfully [di'laɪtfəli] *adv* : de manera encantadora, de maravilla

delineate [di'lɪni,eɪt] *vt* -eated; -eating : delinear, trazar, bosquejar

delinquency [di'lɪŋkwəntsi] *n, pl* -cies : delincuencia *f*

delinquent[1] [di'lɪŋkwənt] *adj* 1 : delincuente 2 OVERDUE : vencido y sin pagar, moroso

delinquent[2] *n* : delincuente *mf* ⟨juvenile delinquent : delincuente juvenil⟩

delirious [di'lɪriəs] *adj* : delirante ⟨delirious with joy : loco de alegría⟩

delirium [di'lɪriəm] *n* : delirio *m*, desvarío *m*

deliver [di'lɪvər] *vt* 1 FREE : liberar, librar 2 DISTRIBUTE, HAND : entregar, repartir 3 : asistir en el parto de (un niño) 4 : pronunciar ⟨to deliver a speech : pronunciar un discurso⟩ 5 PROJECT : despachar, lanzar ⟨he delivered a fast ball : lanzó un pelota rápida⟩ 6 DEAL : propinar, asestar ⟨to deliver a blow : asestar un golpe⟩

deliverance [di'lɪvərənts] *n* : liberación *f*, rescate *m*, salvación *f*

deliverer [di'lɪvərər] *n* RESCUER : libertador *m*, -dora *f*; salvador *m*, -dora *f*

delivery [di'lɪvəri] *n, pl* -eries 1 LIBERATION : liberación *f* 2 : entrega *f*, reparto *m* ⟨cash on delivery : entrega contra reembolso⟩ ⟨home delivery : servicio a domicilio⟩ 3 CHILDBIRTH : parto *m*, alumbramiento *m* 4 SPEECH : expresión *f* oral, modo *m* de hablar 5 THROW : lanzamiento *m*

dell ['dɛl] *n* : hondonada *f*, valle *m* pequeño

delta ['dɛltə] *n* : delta *m*

delude [di'lu:d] *vt* -luded; -luding 1 : engañar 2 to delude oneself : engañarse

deluge[1] ['dɛl,juːʤ, -,juːʒ] *vt* **-uged;**
-uging 1 FLOOD : inundar **2** OVER-
WHELM : abrumar ⟨deluged with re-
quests : abrumado de pedidos⟩
deluge[2] *n* **1** FLOOD : inundación *f* **2**
DOWNPOUR : aguacero *m* **3** BARRAGE
: aluvión *m*
delusion [di'luːʒən] *n* **1** : ilusión *f*
(falsa) **2 delusions of grandeur**
: delirios *mpl* de grandeza
deluxe [di'lʌks, -'luks] *adj* : de lujo
delve ['dɛlv] *vi* **delved; delving 1** DIG
: escarbar **2 to delve into** PROBE
: cavar en, ahondar en
demagogue ['dɛmə,gɑg] *n* : demagogo
m, demagoga *f*
demand[1] [di'mænd] *vt* : demandar, exigir, reclamar
demand[2] *n* **1** REQUEST : petición *f*, pedido *m*, demanda *f* ⟨by popular de-
mand : a petición del público⟩ **2** CLAIM
: reclamación *f*, exigencia *f* **3** MARKET
: demanda *f* ⟨supply and demand : la
oferta y la demanda⟩
demanding [di'mændɪŋ] *adj* : exigente
demarcation [,diː,mɑr'keɪʃən] *n* : demarcación *f*, deslinde *m*
demean [di'miːn] *vt* : degradar, rebajar
demeanor [di'miːnər] *n* : comportamiento *m*, conducta *f*
demented [di'mɛntəd] *adj* : demente,
loco
dementia [di'mɛntʃə] *n* : demencia *f*
demerit [di'mɛrət] *n* : demérito *m*
demigod ['dɛmi,gɑd, -,gɔd] *n* : semidiós
m
demise [di'maɪz] *n* **1** DEATH : fallecimiento *m*, deceso *m* **2** END : hundimiento *m*, desaparición *f* (de una institución, etc.)
demitasse ['dɛmi,tæs, -,tɑs] *n* : taza *f* pequeña (de café)
demobilization [di,moːbələ'zeɪʃən] *n*
: desmovilización *f*
demobilize [di'moːbə,laɪz] *vt* **-lized;**
-lizing : desmovilizar
democracy [di'mɑkrəsi] *n, pl* **-cies**
: democracia *f*
democrat ['dɛmə,kræt] *n* : demócrata
mf
democratic [,dɛmə'kræt̬ɪk] *adj* : democrático — **democratically** [-t̬ɪkli] *adv*
demographic [dɛmə'græfɪk] *adj* : demográfico
demolish [di'mɑlɪʃ] *vt* **1** RAZE : demoler, derribar, arrasar **2** DESTROY : destruir, destrozar
demolition [,dɛmə'lɪʃən, ,diː-] *n* : demolición *f*, derribo *m*
demon ['diːmən] *n* : demonio *m*, diablo *m*
demonstrably [di'mɑnstrəbli] *adv* : manifiestamente, claramente
demonstrate ['dɛmən,streɪt] *vt* **-strated;**
-strating 1 SHOW : demostrar **2** PROVE
: probar, demostrar **3** EXPLAIN : explicar, ilustrar

demonstration [,dɛmən'streɪʃən] *n* **1**
SHOW : muestra *f*, demostración *f* **2**
RALLY : manifestación *f*
demonstrative [di'mɑnstrət̬ɪv] *adj* **1**
EFFUSIVE : efusivo, expresivo,
demostrativo **2** : demostrativo (en
lingüística) ⟨demonstrative pronoun
: pronombre demostrativo⟩
demonstrator ['dɛmən,streɪt̬ər] *n* **1**
: demostrador *m*, -dora *f* (de productos) **2** PROTESTER : manifestante *mf*
demoralize [di'mɔrə,laɪz] *vt* **-ized; -izing**
: desmoralizar
demote [di'moːt] *vt* **-moted; -moting**
: degradar, bajar de categoría
demotion [di'moːʃən] *n* : degradación *f*,
descenso *m* de categoría
demur [di'mər] *vi* **-murred; -murring 1**
OBJECT : oponerse **2 to demur at** : ponerle objeciones a (algo)
demure [di'mjur] *adj* : recatado, modesto — **demurely** *adv*
den ['dɛn] *n* **1** LAIR : cubil *m*, madriguera *f* **2** HIDEOUT : guarida *f* **3**
STUDY : estudio *m*, gabinete *m*
denature [di'neɪtʃər] *vt* **-tured; -turing**
: desnaturalizar
denial [di'naɪəl] *n* **1** REFUSAL : rechazo
m, denegación *f*, negativa *f* **2** REPUDI-
ATION : negación *f* (de una creencia,
etc.), rechazo *m*
denigrate ['dɛni,greɪt] *vt* **-grated; -grat-**
ing : denigrar
denim ['dɛnəm] *n* **1** : tela *f* vaquera,
mezclilla *f* *Chile, Mex* **2 denims** *npl* →
jeans
denizen ['dɛnəzən] *n* : habitante *mf*;
morador *m*, -dora *f*
denomination [di,nɑmə'neɪʃən] *n* **1**
FAITH : confesión *f*, fe *f* **2** VALUE : denominación *f*, valor *m* (de una moneda)
denominator [di'nɑmə,neɪt̬ər] *n* : denominador *m*
denote [di'noːt] *vt* **-noted; -noting 1** IN-
DICATE, MARK : indicar, denotar, se-
ñalar **2** MEAN : significar
denouement [,deɪ,nuː'mɑ] *n* : desenlace
m
denounce [di'naʊnts] *vt* **-nounced;**
-nouncing 1 CENSURE : denunciar,
censurar **2** ACCUSE : denunciar,
acusar, delatar
dense ['dɛnts] *adj* **denser; -est 1** THICK
: espeso, denso ⟨dense vegetation : vegetación densa⟩ ⟨a dense fog : una
niebla espesa⟩ **2** STUPID : estúpido,
burro *fam*
densely ['dɛntsli] *adv* **1** THICKLY : densamente **2** STUPIDLY : torpemente
denseness ['dɛntsnəs] *n* **1** → **density 2**
STUPIDITY : estupidez *f*
density ['dɛntsət̬i] *n, pl* **-ties** : densidad
f
dent[1] ['dɛnt] *vt* : abollar, mellar
dent[2] *n* : abolladura *f*, mella *f*
dental ['dɛntəl] *adj* : dental
dental floss *n* : hilo *m* dental

dentifrice ['dɛntəfrɪs] n : dentífrico m, pasta f de dientes
dentist ['dɛntɪst] n : dentista mf
dentistry ['dɛntɪstri] n : odontología f
dentures ['dɛntʃərz] npl : dentadura f postiza
denude [di'nu:d, -'nju:d] vt **-nuded; -nuding** STRIP : desnudar, despojar
denunciation [di,nʌnsi'eɪʃən] n : denuncia f, acusación f
deny [di'naɪ] vt **-nied; -nying 1** REFUTE : desmentir, negar **2** DISOWN, REPUDIATE : negar, renegar de **3** REFUSE : denegar **4 to deny oneself** : privarse, sacrificarse
deodorant [di'o:dərənt] n : desodorante m
deodorize [di'o:də,raɪz] vt **-ized; -izing** : desodorizar
depart [di'part] vt : salirse de — vi **1** LEAVE : salir, partir, irse **2** DIE : morir
department [di'partmənt] n **1** DIVISION : sección f (de una tienda, una organización, etc.), departamento m (de una empresa, una universidad, etc.), ministerio m (del gobierno) **2** PROVINCE, SPHERE : esfera f, campo m, competencia f
departmental [di,part'mɛntəl, ,di:-] adj : departamental
department store n : grandes almacenes mpl
departure [di'partʃər] n **1** LEAVING : salida f, partida f **2** DEVIATION : desviación f
depend [di'pɛnd] vi **1** RELY : contar (con), confiar (en) ⟨depend on me! : ¡cuenta conmigo!⟩ **2 to depend on** : depender de ⟨success depends on hard work : el éxito depende de trabajar duro⟩ **3 that depends** : según, eso depende
dependable [di'pɛndəbəl] adj : responsable, digno de confianza, fiable
dependence [di'pɛndənts] n : dependencia f
dependency [di'pɛndəntsi] n, pl **-cies** → dependence **2** : posesión f (de una unidad política)
dependent¹ [di'pɛndənt] adj : dependiente
dependent² n : persona f a cargo de alguien
depict [di'pɪkt] vt **1** PORTRAY : representar **2** DESCRIBE : describir
depiction [di'pɪkʃən] n : representación f, descripción f
deplete [di'pli:t] vt **-pleted; -pleting 1** EXHAUST : agotar **2** REDUCE : reducir
depletion [di'pli:ʃən] n **1** EXHAUSTION : agotamiento m **2** REDUCTION : reducción f, disminución f
deplorable [di'plorəbəl] adj **1** CONTEMPTIBLE : deplorable, despreciable **2** LAMENTABLE : lamentable
deplore [di'plor] vt **-plored; -ploring 1** REGRET : deplorar, lamentar **2** CONDEMN : condenar, deplorar

deploy [di'plɔɪ] vt : desplegar
deployment [di'plɔɪmənt] n : despliegue m
deport [di'port] vt **1** EXPEL : deportar, expulsar (de un país) **2 to deport oneself** BEHAVE : comportarse
deportation [,di:,por'teɪʃən] n : deportación f
depose [di'po:z] vt **-posed; -posing** : deponer
deposit¹ [di'pazət] vt **-ited; -iting** : depositar
deposit² n **1** : depósito m (en el banco) **2** DOWN PAYMENT : entrega f inicial **3** : depósito m, yacimiento m (en geología)
deposition [,dɛpə'zɪʃən] n TESTIMONY : deposición f
depositor [di'pazətər] n : depositante mf
depository [di'pazə,tori] n, pl **-ries** : almacén m, depósito m
depot [in sense 1 usu 'dɛ,po:, 2 usu 'di:-] n **1** STOREHOUSE : almacén m, depósito m **2** STATION, TERMINAL : terminal mf, estación f (de autobuses, ferrocarriles, etc.)
deprave [di'preɪv] vt **-praved; -praving** : depravar, pervertir
depraved [di'preɪvd] adj : depravado, degenerado
depravity [di'prævəti] n, pl **-ties** : depravación f
depreciate [di'pri:ʃi,eɪt] v **-ated; -ating** vt **1** DEVALUE : depreciar, devaluar **2** DISPARAGE : menospreciar, despreciar — vi : depreciarse, devaluarse
depreciation [di,pri:ʃi'eɪʃən] n : depreciación f, devaluación f
depress [di'prɛs] vt **1** PRESS, PUSH : apretar, presionar, pulsar **2** REDUCE : reducir, hacer bajar (precios, ventas, etc.) **3** SADDEN : deprimir, abatir, entristecer **4** DEVALUE : depreciar
depressant¹ [di'prɛsənt] adj : depresivo
depressant² n : depresivo m
depressed [di'prɛst] adj **1** DEJECTED : deprimido, abatido **2** : deprimido, en crisis (dícese de la economía)
depressing [di'prɛsɪŋ] adj : deprimente, triste
depression [di'prɛʃən] n **1** DESPONDENCY : depresión f, abatimiento m **2** : depresión (en una superficie) **3** RECESSION : depresión f económica, crisis f
deprivation [,dɛprə'veɪʃən] n : privación f
deprive [di'praɪv] vt **-prived; -priving** : privar
depth ['dɛpθ] n, pl **depths** ['dɛpθs, 'dɛps] : profundidad f, fondo m ⟨to study in depth : estudiar a fondo⟩ ⟨in the depths of winter : en pleno invierno⟩
deputize ['dɛpju,taɪz] vt **-tized; -tizing** : nombrar como segundo
deputy ['dɛpjuti] n, pl **-ties** : suplente mf; sustituto m, -ta f
derail [di'reɪl] v : descarrilar

derailment [di'reɪlmənt] *n* : descarril-
amiento *m*
derange [di'reɪndʒ] *vt* **-ranged; -ranging**
1 DISARRANGE : desarreglar, desordenar **2** DISTURB, UPSET : trastornar,
perturbar **3** MADDEN : enloquecer,
volver loco
derangement [di'reɪndʒmənt] *n* **1** DIS-
TURBANCE, UPSET : trastorno *m* **2** IN-
SANITY : locura *f*, perturbación *f* mental
derby ['dərbi] *n*, *pl* **-bies 1** : derby *m*
⟨the Kentucky Derby : el Derby de
Kentucky⟩ **2** : sombrero *m* hongo
deregulate [di'rɛgjʊˌleɪt] *vt* **-lated;**
-lating : desregular
deregulation [diˌrɛgjʊˈleɪʃən] *n* : desregulación *f*
derelict[1] ['dɛrəˌlɪkt] *adj* **1** ABANDONED
: abandonado, en ruinas **2** REMISS
: negligente, remiso
derelict[2] *n* **1** : propiedad *f* abandonada
2 VAGRANT : vagabundo *m*, -da *f*
deride [di'raɪd] *vt* **-rided; -riding** : ridiculizar, burlarse de
derision [di'rɪʒən] *n* : escarnio *m*, irrisión *f*, mofa *f*
derisive [di'raɪsɪv] *adj* : burlón
derivation [ˌdɛrəˈveɪʃən] *n* : derivación
f
derivative[1] [di'rɪvəṭɪv] *adj* **1** DERIVED
: derivado **2** BANAL : carente de originalidad, banal
derivative[2] *n* : derivado *m*
derive [di'raɪv] *v* **-rived; -riving** *vt* **1** OB-
TAIN : obtener, sacar **2** DEDUCE : de-
ducir, inferir — *vi* : provenir, derivar,
proceder
dermatologist [ˌdərməˈtɑləʤɪst] *n* : dermatólogo *m*, -ga *f*
dermatology [ˌdərməˈtɑləʤi] *n* : dermatología *f*
derogatory [di'rɑgəˌtori] *adj* : despectivo, despreciativo
derrick ['dɛrɪk] *n* **1** CRANE : grúa *f* **2**
: torre *f* de perforación (sobre un pozo
de petróleo)
descend [di'sɛnd] *vt* : descender, bajar
— *vi* **1** : descender, bajar ⟨he de-
scended from the platform : descendió
del estrado⟩ **2** DERIVE : descender,
provenir **3** STOOP : rebajarse ⟨I de-
scended to his level : me rebajé a su
nivel⟩ **4 to descend upon** : caer sobre, invadir
descendant[1] [di'sɛndənt] *adj* : descendente
descendant[2] *n* : descendiente *mf*
descent [di'sɛnt] *n* **1** : bajada *f*, descenso *m* ⟨the descent from the mountain
: el descenso de la montaña⟩ **2** AN-
CESTRY : ascendencia *f*, linaje *f* **3**
SLOPE : pendiente *f*, cuesta *f* **4** FALL
: caída *f* **5** ATTACK : incursión *f*, ataque
m
describe [di'skraɪb] *vt* **-scribed; -scrib-**
ing : describir
description [di'skrɪpʃən] *n* : descripción
f

descriptive [di'skrɪptɪv] *adj* : descriptivo ⟨descriptive adjective : adjetivo cal-
ificativo⟩
desecrate ['dɛsɪˌkreɪt] *vt* **-crated; -crat-**
ing : profanar
desecration [ˌdɛsɪˈkreɪʃən] *n* : profanación *f*
desegregate [di'sɛgrəˌgeɪt] *vt* **-gated;**
-gating : eliminar la segregación racial
de
desegregation [diˌsɛgrəˈgeɪʃən] *n*
: eliminación *f* de la segregación racial
desert[1] [di'zərt] *vt* : abandonar (una persona o un lugar), desertar de (una
causa, etc.) — *vi* : desertar
desert[2] ['dɛzərt] *adj* : desierto ⟨a desert
island : una isla desierta⟩
desert[3] *n* **1** ['dɛzərt] : desierto *m* (en geografía) **2** [di'zərt] → **deserts**
deserter [di'zərtər] *n* : desertor *m*, -tora
f
desertion [di'zərʃən] *n* : abandono *m*,
deserción *f* (militar)
deserts [di'zərts] *npl* : merecido *m* ⟨to
get one's just deserts : llevarse uno su
merecido⟩
deserve [di'zərv] *vt* **-served; -serving**
: merecer, ser digno de
deserving [di'zərvɪŋ] *adj* : meritorio
⟨deserving of : digno de⟩
desiccate ['dɛsɪˌkeɪt] *vt* **-cated; -cating**
: desecar, deshidratar
design[1] [di'zaɪn] *vt* **1** DEVISE : diseñar,
concebir, idear **2** PLAN : proyectar **3**
SKETCH : trazar, bosquejar
design[2] *n* **1** PLAN, SCHEME : plan *m*,
proyecto *m* ⟨by design : a propósito,
intencionalmente⟩ **2** SKETCH : diseño
m, bosquejo *m* **3** PATTERN, STYLE : diseño *m*, estilo *m* **4 designs** *npl* INTEN-
TIONS : propósitos *mpl*, designios *mpl*
designate ['dɛzɪgˌneɪt] *vt* **-nated; -nat-**
ing 1 INDICATE, SPECIFY : indicar, especificar **2** APPOINT : nombrar, designar
designation [ˌdɛzɪgˈneɪʃən] *n* **1** NAM-
ING : designación *f* **2** NAME : denominación *f*, nombre *m* **3** APPOINTMENT
: designación *f*, nombramiento *m*
designer [di'zaɪnər] *n* : diseñador *m*,
-dora *f*
desirability [diˌzaɪrəˈbɪləṭi] *n*, *pl* **-ties 1**
ADVISABILITY : conveniencia *f* **2** AT-
TRACTIVENESS : atractivo *m*
desirable [di'zaɪrəbəl] *adj* **1** ADVISABLE
: conveniente, aconsejable **2** ATTRAC-
TIVE : deseable, atractivo
desire[1] [di'zaɪr] *vt* **-sired; -siring 1**
WANT : desear **2** REQUEST : rogar, solicitar
desire[2] *n* : deseo *m*, anhelo *m*, ansia *m*
desist [di'sɪst, -'zɪst] *vi* **to desist from**
: desistir de, abstenerse de
desk [di'dɛsk] *n* : escritorio *m*, pupitre *m*
(en la escuela)
desktop ['dɛskˌtɑp] *adj* : de escritorio
desolate[1] ['dɛsəˌleɪt, -zə-] *vt* **-lated;**
-lating : devastar, desolar

desolate² ['dɛsələt, -zə-] *adj* **1** BARREN : desolado, desierto, yermo **2** DISCONSOLATE : desconsolado, desolado

desolation [ˌdɛsə'leɪʃən, -zə-] *n* : desolación *f*

despair¹ [di'spær] *vi* : desesperar, perder las esperanzas

despair² *n* : desesperación *f*, desesperanza *f*

desperate ['dɛspərət] *adj* **1** HOPELESS : desesperado, sin esperanzas **2** RASH : desesperado, precipitado **3** SERIOUS, URGENT : grave, urgente, apremiante ⟨a desperate need : una necesidad apremiante⟩

desperately ['dɛspərətli] *adv* : desesperadamente, urgentemente

desperation [ˌdɛspə'reɪʃən] *n* : desesperación *f*

despicable [di'spɪkəbəl, 'dɛspɪ-] *adj* : vil, despreciable, infame

despise [di'spaɪz] *vt* **-spised; -spising** : despreciar

despite [də'spaɪt] *prep* : a pesar de, aún con

despoil [di'spɔɪl] *vt* : saquear

despondency [di'spandən(t)si] *n* : desaliento *m*, desánimo *m*, depresión *f*

despondent [di'spandənt] *adj* : desalentado, desanimado

despot ['dɛspət, -ˌpat] *n* : déspota *mf*; tirano *m*, -na *f*

despotic [dɛs'patɪk] *adj* : despótico

despotism ['dɛspəˌtɪzəm] *n* : despotismo *m*

dessert [di'zərt] *n* : postre *m*

destination [ˌdɛstə'neɪʃən] *n* : destino *m*, destinación *f*

destined ['dɛstənd] *adj* **1** FATED : predestinado **2** BOUND : destinado, con destino (a), con rumbo (a)

destiny ['dɛstəni] *n, pl* **-nies** : destino *m*

destitute ['dɛstəˌtuːt, -ˌtjuːt] *adj* **1** LACKING : carente, desprovisto **2** POOR : indigente, en miseria

destitution [ˌdɛstə'tuːʃən, -'tjuː-] *n* : indigencia *f*, miseria *f*

destroy [di'strɔɪ] *vt* **1** KILL : matar **2** DEMOLISH : destruir, destrozar

destroyer [di'strɔɪər] *n* : destructor *m* (buque)

destructible [di'strʌktəbəl] *adj* : destructible

destruction [di'strʌkʃən] *n* : destrucción *f*, ruina *f*

destructive [di'strʌktɪv] *adj* : destructor, destructivo

desultory ['dɛsəlˌtori] *adj* **1** AIMLESS : sin rumbo, sin objeto **2** DISCONNECTED : inconexo

detach [di'tætʃ] *vt* : separar, quitar, desprender

detached [di'tætʃt] *adj* **1** SEPARATE : separado, suelto **2** ALOOF : distante, indiferente **3** IMPARTIAL : imparcial, objetivo

detachment [di'tætʃmənt] *n* **1** SEPARATION : separación *f* **2** DETAIL : destacamento *m* (de tropas) **3** ALOOFNESS : reserva *f*, indiferencia *f* **4** IMPARTIALITY : imparcialidad *f*

detail¹ [di'teɪl, 'diːˌteɪl] *vt* : detallar, exponer en detalle

detail² *n* **1** : detalle *m*, pormenor *m* **2** : destacamento *m* (de tropas)

detailed [di'teɪld, 'diːˌteɪld] *adj* : detallado, minucioso

detain [di'teɪn] *vt* **1** HOLD : detener **2** DELAY : entretener, demorar, retrasar

detect [di'tɛkt] *vt* : detectar, descubrir

detection [di'tɛkʃən] *n* : descubrimiento *m*

detective [di'tɛktɪv] *n* : detective *mf* ⟨private detective : detective privado⟩

detector [di'tɛktər] *n* : detector *m*

detention [di'tɛnʃən] *n* : detención *m*

deter [di'tər] *vt* **-terred; -terring** : disuadir, impedir

detergent [di'tərdʒənt] *n* : detergente *m*

deteriorate [di'tɪriəˌreɪt] *vi* **-rated; -rating** : deteriorarse, empeorar

deterioration [diˌtɪriə'reɪʃən] *n* : deterioro *m*, empeoramiento *m*

determinant¹ [di'tərmənənt] *adj* : determinante

determinant² *n* **1** : factor *m* determinante **2** : determinante *m* (en matemáticas)

determination [diˌtərmə'neɪʃən] *n* **1** DECISION : determinación *f*, decisión *f* **2** RESOLUTION : resolución *f*, determinación *f* ⟨with grim determination : con una firme resolución⟩

determine [di'tərmən] *vt* **-mined; -mining** **1** ESTABLISH : determinar, establecer **2** SETTLE : decidir **3** FIND OUT : averiguar **4** BRING ABOUT : determinar

determined [di'tərmənd] *adj* RESOLUTE : decidido, resuelto

deterrent [di'tərənt] *n* : medida *f* disuasiva

detest [di'tɛst] *vt* : detestar, odiar, aborrecer

detestable [di'tɛstəbəl] *adj* : detestable, odioso, aborrecible

dethrone [di'θroːn] *vt* **-throned; -throning** : destronar

detonate ['dɛtənˌeɪt] *v* **-nated; -nating** *vt* : hacer detonar — *vi* : detonar, estallar

detonation [ˌdɛtə'neɪʃən] *n* : detonación *f*

detour¹ ['diːˌtʊr, di'tʊr] *vi* : desviarse

detour² *n* : desvío *m*, rodeo *m*

detract [di'trækt] *vi* **to detract from** : restarle valor a, quitarle méritos a

detractor [di'træktər] *n* : detractor *m*, -tora *f*

detriment ['dɛtrəmənt] *n* : detrimento *m*, perjuicio *m*

detrimental [ˌdɛtrə'mɛntəl] *adj* : perjudicial — **detrimentally** *adv*

devaluation [diˌvæljuˈeɪʃən] *n* : devaluación *f*

devalue [di'vælˌjuː] *vt* **-ued; -uing** : devaluar, depreciar

devastate [ˈdɛvəˌsteɪt] *vt* **-tated; -tating** : devastar, arrasar, asolar

devastation [ˌdɛvəˈsteɪʃən] *n* : devastación *f*, estragos *mpl*

develop [dɪˈvɛləp] *vt* **1** FORM, MAKE : desarrollar, elaborar, formar **2** : revelar (en fotografía) **3** FOSTER : desarrollar, fomentar **4** EXPLOIT : explotar (recursos), urbanizar (un área) **5** ACQUIRE : adquirir ⟨to develop an interest : adquirir un interés⟩ **6** CONTRACT : contraer (una enfermedad) — *vi* **1** GROW : desarrollarse **2** ARISE : aparecer, surgir

developed [dɪˈvɛləpt] *adj* : avanzado, desarrollado

developer [dɪˈvɛləpər] *n* **1** : inmobiliaria *f*, urbanizadora *f* **2** : revelador *m* (en fotografía)

development [dɪˈvɛləpmənt] *n* **1** : desarrollo *m* ⟨physical development : desarrollo físico⟩ **2** : urbanización *f* (de un área), explotación *f* (de recursos), creación *f* (de inventos) **3** EVENT : acontecimiento *m*, suceso *m* ⟨to await developments : esperar acontecimientos⟩

deviant [ˈdiːviənt] *adj* : desviado, anormal

deviate [ˈdiːviˌeɪt] *v* **-ated; -ating** *vi* : desviarse, apartarse — *vt* : desviar

deviation [ˌdiːviˈeɪʃən] *n* : desviación *f*

device [dɪˈvaɪs] *n* **1** MECHANISM : dispositivo *m*, aparato *m*, mecanismo *m* **2** EMBLEM : emblema *m*

devil[1] [ˈdɛvəl] *vt* **-iled** *or* **-illed; -iling** *or* **-illing 1** : sazonar con picante y especias **2** PESTER : molestar

devil[2] *n* **1** SATAN : el diablo, Satanás *m* **2** DEMON : diablo *m*, demonio *m* **3** FIEND : persona *f* diabólica; malvado *m*, -da *f*

devilish [ˈdɛvəlɪʃ] *adj* : diabólico

devilry [ˈdɛvəlri] *n*, *pl* **-ries** : diabluras *fpl*, travesuras *fpl*

devious [ˈdiːviəs] *adj* **1** CRAFTY : taimado, artero **2** WINDING : tortuoso, sinuoso

devise [dɪˈvaɪz] *vt* **-vised; -vising 1** INVENT : idear, concebir, inventar **2** PLOT : tramar

devoid [dɪˈvɔɪd] *adj* ∼ **of** : carente de, desprovisto de

devote [dɪˈvoːt] *vt* **-voted; -voting 1** DEDICATE : consagrar, dedicar ⟨to devote one's life : dedicar uno su vida⟩ **2 to devote oneself** : dedicarse

devoted [dɪˈvoːtəd] *adj* **1** FAITHFUL : leal, fiel **2 to be devoted to someone** : tenerle mucho cariño a alguien

devotee [ˌdɛvəˈtiː, -ˈteɪ] *n* : devoto *m*, -ta *f*

devotion [dɪˈvoːʃən] *n* **1** DEDICATION : dedicación *f*, devoción *f* **2 devotions** PRAYERS : oraciones *fpl*, devociones *fpl*

devour [dɪˈvaʊər] *vt* : devorar

devout [dɪˈvaʊt] *adj* **1** PIOUS : devoto, piadoso **2** EARNEST, SINCERE : sincero, ferviente — **devoutly** *adv*

devoutness [dɪˈvaʊtnəs] *n* : devoción *f*, piedad *f*

dew [ˈduː, ˈdjuː] *n* : rocío *m*

dewlap [ˈduːˌlæp, ˈdjuː-] *n* : papada *f*

dew point *n* : punto *m* de condensación

dewy [ˈduːi, ˈdjuːi] *adj* **dewier; -est** : cubierto de rocío

dexterity [dɛkˈstɛrəti] *n*, *pl* **-ties** : destreza *f*, habilidad *f*

dexterous [ˈdɛkstrəs] *adj* : diestro, hábil

dexterously [ˈdɛkstrəsli] *adv* : con destreza, con habilidad, hábilmente

dextrose [ˈdɛkˌstroːs] *n* : dextrosa *f*

diabetes [ˌdaɪəˈbiːtiz] *n* : diabetes *f*

diabetic[1] [ˌdaɪəˈbɛtɪk] *adj* : diabético

diabetic[2] *n* : diabético *m*, -ca *f*

diabolic [ˌdaɪəˈbɑlɪk] *or* **diabolical** [-lɪkəl] *adj* : diabólico, satánico

diacritical mark [ˌdaɪəˈkrɪtɪkəl] *n* : signo *m* diacrítico

diadem [ˈdaɪəˌdɛm, -dəm] *n* : diadema *f*

diagnose [ˈdaɪɪɡˌnoːs, ˌdaɪɡˈnoːs] *vt* **-nosed; -nosing** : diagnosticar

diagnosis [ˌdaɪɡˈnoːsɪs] *n*, *pl* **-noses** [-ˈnoːˌsiːz] : diagnóstico *m*

diagnostic [ˌdaɪɡˈnɑstɪk] *adj* : diagnóstico

diagonal[1] [daɪˈæɡənəl] *adj* : diagonal, en diagonal

diagonal[2] *n* : diagonal *f*

diagonally [daɪˈæɡənəli] *adv* : diagonalmente, en diagonal

diagram[1] [ˈdaɪəˌɡræm] *vt* **-gramed** *or* **-grammed; -graming** *or* **-gramming** : hacer un diagrama de

diagram[2] *n* : diagrama *m*, gráfico *m*, esquema *m*

dial[1] [ˈdaɪl] *v* **dialed** *or* **dialled; dialing** *or* **dialling** : marcar, discar

dial[2] *n* : esfera *f* (de un reloj), dial *m* (de un radio), disco *m* (de un teléfono)

dialect [ˈdaɪəˌlɛkt] *n* : dialecto *m*

dialogue [ˈdaɪəˌlɔɡ] *n* : diálogo *m*

diameter [daɪˈæmətər] *n* : diámetro *m*

diamond [ˈdaɪmənd, ˈdaɪə-] *n* **1** : diamante *m*, brillante *m* ⟨a diamond necklace : un collar de brillantes⟩ **2** : rombo *m*, forma *f* de rombo **3** : diamante *m* (en naipes) **4** INFIELD : cuadro *m*, diamante *m* (en béisbol)

diaper [ˈdaɪpər, ˈdaɪə-] *n* : pañal *m*

diaphragm [ˈdaɪəˌfræm] *n* : diafragma *m*

diarrhea [ˌdaɪəˈriːə] *n* : diarrea *f*

diary [ˈdaɪəri] *n*, *pl* **-ries** : diario *m*

diatribe [ˈdaɪəˌtraɪb] *n* : diatriba *f*

dice[1] [ˈdaɪs] *vt* **diced; dicing** : cortar en cubos

dice[2] *ns & pl* **1** → **die**[2] **2** : dados *mpl* (juego)

dicker [ˈdɪkər] *vt* : regatear

dictate[1] [ˈdɪkˌteɪt, dɪkˈteɪt] *v* **-tated; -tating** *vt* **1** : dictar ⟨to dictate a letter : dictar una carta⟩ **2** ORDER : mandar, ordenar — *vi* : dar órdenes

dictate² ['dɪk,teɪt] *n* **1** : mandato *m*, orden *f* **2 dictates** *npl* : dictados *mpl* ⟨the dictates of conscience : los dictados de la conciencia⟩

dictation [dɪk'teɪʃən] *n* : dictado *m*

dictator ['dɪk,teɪtər] *n* : dictador *m*, -dora *f*

dictatorial [,dɪktə'toriəl] *adj* : dictatorial — **dictatorially** *adv*

dictatorship [dɪk'teɪtər,ʃɪp, 'dɪk,-] *n* : dictadura *f*

diction ['dɪkʃən] *n* **1** : lenguaje *m*, estilo *m* **2** ENUNCIATION : dicción *f*, articulación *f*

dictionary ['dɪkʃə,neri] *n, pl* **-naries** : diccionario *m*

did → **do**

didactic [daɪ'dæktɪk] *adj* : didáctico

die¹ ['daɪ] *vi* **died** ['daɪd]; **dying** ['daɪɪŋ] **1** : morir **2** CEASE : morir, morirse ⟨a dying civilization : una civilización moribunda⟩ **3** STOP : apagarse, dejar de funcionar ⟨the motor died : el motor se apagó⟩ **4 to die down** SUBSIDE : amainar, disminuir **5 to die out** : extinguirse **6 to be dying for** *or* **to be dying to** : morirse por ⟨I'm dying to leave : me muero por irme⟩

die² ['daɪ] *n, pl* **dice** ['daɪs] : dado *m*

die³ *n, pl* **dies** ['daɪz] **1** STAMP : troquel *m*, cuño *m* **2** MOLD : matriz *f*, molde *m*

diesel ['di:zəl, -səl] *n* : diesel *m*

diet¹ ['daɪət] *vi* : ponerse a régimen, hacer dieta

diet² *n* : régimen *m*, dieta *f*

dietary ['daɪə,teri] *adj* : alimenticio, dietético

dietitian *or* **dietician** [,daɪə'tɪʃən] *n* : dietista *mf*

differ ['dɪfər] *vi* **-ferred; -ferring 1** : diferir, diferenciarse **2** VARY : variar **3** DISAGREE : discrepar, diferir, no estar de acuerdo

difference ['dɪfrənts, 'dɪfərənts] *n* : diferencia *f*

different ['dɪfrənt, 'dɪfərənt] *adj* : distinto, diferente

differentiate [,dɪfə'rentʃi,eɪt] *v* **-ated; -ating** *vt* **1** : hacer diferente **2** DISTINGUISH : distinguir, diferenciar — *vi* : distinguir

differentiation [,dɪfə,rentʃi'eɪʃən] *n* : diferenciación *f*

differently ['dɪfrəntli, 'dɪfərənt-] *adv* : de otra manera, de otro modo, distintamente

difficult ['dɪfɪ,kʌlt] *adj* : difícil

difficulty ['dɪfɪ,kʌlti] *n, pl* **-ties 1** : dificultad *f* **2** PROBLEM : problema *f*, dificultad *f*

diffidence ['dɪfədənts] *n* **1** SHYNESS : retraimiento *m*, timidez *f*, apocamiento *m* **2** RETICENCE : reticencia *f*

diffident ['dɪfədənt] *adj* **1** SHY : tímido, apocado, inseguro **2** RESERVED : reservado

diffuse¹ [dɪ'fju:z] *v* **-fused; -fusing** *vt* : difundir, esparcir — *vi* : difundirse, esparcirse

diffuse² [dɪ'fju:s] *adj* **1** WORDY : prolijo, verboso **2** WIDESPREAD : difuso

diffusion [dɪ'fju:ʒən] *n* : difusión *f*

dig¹ ['dɪg] *v* **dug** ['dʌg]; **digging** *vt* **1** : cavar, excavar ⟨to dig a hole : cavar un hoyo⟩ **2** EXTRACT : sacar ⟨to dig up potatoes : sacar papas del suelo⟩ **3** POKE, THRUST : clavar, hincar ⟨he dug me in the ribs : me dio un codazo en las costillas⟩ **4 to dig up** DISCOVER : descubrir, sacar a luz — *vi* : cavar, excavar

dig² *n* **1** POKE : codazo *m* **2** GIBE : pulla *f* **3** EXCAVATION : excavación *f*

digest¹ ['daɪ,ʤest, dɪ-] *vt* **1** ASSIMILATE : digerir, asimilar **2** : digerir (comida) **3** SUMMARIZE : compendiar, resumir

digest² ['daɪ,ʤest] *n* : compendio *m*, resumen *m*

digestible [daɪ'ʤestəbəl, dɪ-] *adj* : digerible

digestion [daɪ'ʤestʃən, dɪ-] *n* : digestión *f*

digestive [daɪ'ʤestɪv, dɪ-] *adj* : digestivo ⟨the digestive system : el sistema digestivo⟩

digit ['dɪʤət] *n* **1** NUMERAL : dígito *m*, número *m* **2** FINGER, TOE : dedo *m*

digital ['dɪʤətəl] *adj* : digital — **digitally** *adv*

dignified ['dɪgnə,faɪd] *adj* : digno, decoroso

dignify ['dɪgnə,faɪ] *vt* **-fied; -fying** : dignificar, honrar

dignitary ['dɪgnə,teri] *n, pl* **-taries** : dignatario *m*, -ria *f*

dignity ['dɪgnəti] *n, pl* **-ties** : dignidad *f*

digress [daɪ'gres, də-] *vi* : desviarse del tema, divagar

digression [daɪ'greʃən, də-] *n* : digresión *f*

dike *or* **dyke** ['daɪk] *n* : dique *m*

dilapidated [də'læpə,deɪtəd] *adj* : ruinoso, desvencijado, destartalado

dilapidation [də,læpə'deɪʃən] *n* : deterioro *m*, estado *m* ruinoso

dilate [daɪ'leɪt, 'daɪ,leɪt] *v* **-lated; -lating** *vt* : dilatar — *vi* : dilatarse

dilemma [dɪ'lɛmə] *n* : dilema *m*

dilettante ['dɪlə,tɑnt, -,tænt] *n, pl* **-tantes** [-,tɑnts, -,tænts] *or* **-tanti** [,dɪlə'tɑnti, -'tæn-] : diletante *mf*

diligence ['dɪləʤənts] *n* : diligencia *f*, aplicación *f*

diligent¹ ['dɪləʤənt] *adj* : diligente ⟨a diligent search : una búsqueda minuciosa⟩ — **diligently** *adv*

dill ['dɪl] *n* : eneldo *m*

dillydally ['dɪli,dæli] *vi* **-lied; lying** : demorarse, perder tiempo

dilute [daɪ'lu:t, də-] *vt* **-luted; -luting** : diluir, aguar

dilution [daɪ'lu:ʃən, də-] *n* : dilución *f*

dim¹ ['dɪm] *v* **dimmed; dimming** *vt* : atenuar (la luz), nublar (la vista), borrar (la memoria), opacar (una superficie) — *vi* : oscurecerse, apagarse

dim² *adj* **dimmer; dimmest 1** FAINT : oscuro, tenue (dícese de la luz), nublado (dícese de la vista), borrado (dícese de la memoria) **2** DULL : deslustrado **3** STUPID : tonto, torpe

dime [ˈdaɪm] *n* : moneda *f* de diez centavos

dimension [dəˈmɛntʃən, daɪ-] *n* **1** : dimensión *f* **2 dimensions** *npl* EXTENT, SCOPE : dimensiones *fpl*, extensión *f*, medida *f*

diminish [dəˈmɪnɪʃ] *vt* LESSEN : disminuir, reducir, amainar — *vi* DWINDLE, WANE : menguar, reducirse

diminutive [dəˈmɪnjuṭɪv] *adj* : diminutivo, minúsculo

dimly [ˈdɪmli] *adv* : indistintamente, débilmente

dimmer [ˈdɪmər] *n* : potenciómetro *m*, conmutador *m* de luces (en automóviles)

dimness [ˈdɪmnəs] *n* : oscuridad *f*, debilidad *f* (de la vista), imprecisión *f* (de la memoria)

dimple [ˈdɪmpəl] *n* : hoyuelo *m*

din [ˈdɪn] *n* : estrépito *m*, estruendo *m*

dine [ˈdaɪn] *vi* **dined; dining** : cenar

diner [ˈdaɪnər] *n* **1** : comensal *mf* (persona) **2** : vagón *m* restaurante (en un tren) **3** : cafetería *f*, restaurante *m* barato

dinghy [ˈdɪŋi, ˈdɪŋgi, ˈdɪŋki] *n, pl* **-ghies** : bote *m*

dinginess [ˈdɪndʒinəs] *n* **1** DIRTINESS : suciedad *f* **2** SHABBINESS : lo gastado, lo deslucido

dingy [ˈdɪndʒi] *adj* **-gier; -est 1** DIRTY : sucio **2** SHABBY : gastado, deslucido

dinner [ˈdɪnər] *n* : cena *f*, comida *f*

dinosaur [ˈdaɪnəˌsɔr] *n* : dinosaurio *m*

dint [ˈdɪnt] *n* **by dint of** : a fuerza de

diocese [ˈdaɪəsəs, -ˌsiːz, -ˌsiːs] *n, pl* **-ceses** [ˈdaɪəsəsəz] : diócesis *f*

dip¹ [ˈdɪp] *v* **dipped; dipping** *vt* **1** DUNK, PLUNGE : sumergir, mojar, meter **2** LADLE : servir con cucharón **3** LOWER : bajar, arriar (una bandera) — *vi* **1** DESCEND, DROP : bajar en picada, descender **2** SLOPE : bajar, inclinarse

dip² *n* **1** SWIM : chapuzón *m* **2** DROP : descenso *m*, caída *f* **3** SLOPE : cuesta *f*, declive *m* **4** SAUCE : salsa *f*

diphtheria [dɪfˈθɪriə] *n* : difteria *f*

diphthong [ˈdɪfˌθɔŋ] *n* : diptongo *m*

diploma [dəˈploːmə] *n, pl* **-mas** : diploma *m*

diplomacy [dəˈploːməsi] *n* **1** : diplomacia *f* **2** TACT : tacto *m*, discreción *f*

diplomat [ˈdɪpləˌmæt] *n* **1** : diplomático *m*, -ca *f* (en relaciones internacionales) **2** : persona *f* diplomática

diplomatic [ˌdɪpləˈmæṭɪk] *adj* : diplomático ⟨diplomatic immunity : inmunidad diplomática⟩

dipper [ˈdɪpər] *n* **1** LADLE : cucharón *m*, cazo *m* **2 Big Dipper** : Osa *f* Mayor **3 Little Dipper** : Osa *f* Menor

dire [ˈdaɪr] *adj* **direr; direst 1** HORRIBLE : espantoso, terrible, horrendo **2** EXTREME : extremo ⟨dire poverty : pobreza extrema⟩

direct¹ [dəˈrɛkt, daɪ-] *vt* **1** ADDRESS : dirigir, mandar **2** AIM, POINT : dirigir **3** GUIDE : indicarle el camino (a alguien), orientar **4** MANAGE : dirigir ⟨to direct a film : dirigir una película⟩ **5** COMMAND : ordenar, mandar

direct² *adv* : directamente

direct³ *adj* **1** STRAIGHT : directo **2** FRANK : franco

direct current *n* : corriente *f* continua

direction [dəˈrɛkʃən, daɪ-] *n* **1** SUPERVISION : dirección *f* **2** INSTRUCTION, ORDER : instrucción *f*, orden *f* **3** COURSE : dirección *f*, rumbo *m* ⟨to change direction : cambiar de dirección⟩ **4 to ask directions** : pedir indicaciones

directional [dəˈrɛkʃənəl, daɪ-] *adj* : direccional

directive [dəˈrɛktɪv, daɪ-] *n* : directiva *f*

directly [dəˈrɛktli, daɪ-] *adv* **1** STRAIGHT : directamente ⟨directly north : directamente al norte⟩ **2** FRANKLY : francamente **3** EXACTLY : exactamente, justo ⟨directly opposite : justo enfrente⟩ **4** IMMEDIATELY : en seguida, inmediatamente

directness [dəˈrɛktnəs, daɪ-] *n* : franqueza *f*

director [dəˈrɛktər, daɪ-] *n* **1** : director *m*, -tora *f* **2 board of directors** : junta *f* directiva, directorio *m*

directory [dəˈrɛktəri, daɪ-] *n, pl* **-ries** : guía *f*, directorio *m* ⟨telephone directory : directorio telefónico⟩

dirge [ˈdərdʒ] *n* : canto *m* fúnebre

dirigible [ˈdɪrədʒəbəl, dəˈrɪdʒə-] *n* : dirigible *m*, zepelín *m*

dirt [ˈdərt] *n* **1** FILTH : suciedad *f*, mugre *f*, porquería *f* **2** SOIL : tierra *f*

dirtiness [ˈdərṭinəs] *n* : suciedad *f*

dirty¹ [ˈdərṭi] *vt* **dirtied; dirtying** : ensuciar, manchar

dirty² *adj* **dirtier; -est 1** SOILED, STAINED : sucio, manchado **2** DISHONEST : sucio, deshonesto ⟨a dirty player : un jugador tramposo⟩ ⟨a dirty trick : una mala pasada⟩ **3** INDECENT : indecente, cochino ⟨a dirty joke : un chiste verde⟩

disability [ˌdɪsəˈbɪləṭi] *n, pl* **-ties** : minusvalía *f*, discapacidad *f*, invalidez *f*

disable [dɪsˈeɪbəl] *vt* **-abled; -abling** : dejar inválido, inutilizar, incapacitar

disabled [dɪsˈeɪbəld] *adj* : minusválido, discapacitado

disabuse [ˌdɪsəˈbjuːz] *vt* **-bused; -busing** : desengañar, sacar del error

disadvantage [ˌdɪsədˈvæntɪdʒ] *n* : desventaja *f*

disadvantageous [ˌdɪsˌædˌvænˈteɪ-dʒəs] *adj* : desventajoso, desfavorable

disagree [ˌdɪsə'gri:] *vi* **1** DIFFER : discrepar, no coincidir **2** DISSENT : disentir, discrepar, no estar de acuerdo

disagreeable [ˌdɪsə'gri:əbəl] *adj* : desagradable

disagreement [ˌdɪsə'gri:mənt] *n* **1** : desacuerdo *m* **2** DISCREPANCY : discrepancia *f* **3** ARGUMENT : discusión *f*, altercado *m*, disputa *f*

disappear [ˌdɪsə'pɪr] *vi* : desaparecer, desvanecerse ⟨to disappear from view : perderse de vista⟩

disappearance [ˌdɪsə'pɪrənts] *n* : desaparición *f*

disappoint [ˌdɪsə'pɔɪnt] *vt* : decepcionar, defraudar, fallar

disappointing [ˌdɪsə'pɔɪntɪŋ] *adj* : decepcionante

disappointment [ˌdɪsə'pɔɪntmənt] *n* : decepción *f*, desilusión *f*, chasco *m*

disapproval [ˌdɪsə'pru:vəl] *n* : desaprobación *f*

disapprove [ˌdɪsə'pru:v] *vi* **-proved; -proving** : desaprobar, estar en contra

disapprovingly [ˌdɪsə'pru:vɪŋli] *adv* : con desaprobación

disarm [dɪs'ɑrm] *vt* : desarmar

disarmament [dɪs'ɑrməmənt] *n* : desarme *m* ⟨nuclear disarmament : desarme nuclear⟩

disarrange [ˌdɪsə'reɪndʒ] *vt* **-ranged; -ranging** : desarreglar, desordenar

disarray [ˌdɪsə'reɪ] *n* : desorden *m*, confusión *f*, desorganización *f*

disaster [dɪ'zæstər] *n* : desastre *m*, catástrofe *f*

disastrous [dɪ'zæstrəs] *adj* : desastroso

disband [dɪs'bænd] *vt* : disolver — *vi* : disolverse, dispersarse

disbar [dɪs'bɑr] *vt* **-barred; -barring** : prohibir de ejercer la abogacía

disbelief [ˌdɪsbɪ'li:f] *n* : incredulidad *f*

disbelieve [ˌdɪsbɪ'li:v] *v* **-lieved; -lieving** : no creer, dudar

disburse [dɪs'bərs] *vt* **-bursed; -bursing** : desembolsar

disbursement [dɪs'bərsmənt] *n* : desembolso *m*

disc → **disk**

discard [dɪs'kɑrd, 'dɪsˌkɑrd] *vt* : desechar, deshacerse de, botar — *vi* : descartarse (en juegos de naipes)

discern [dɪ'sərn, -'zərn] *vt* : discernir, distinguir, percibir

discernible [dɪ'sərnəbəl, -'zər-] *adj* : perceptible, visible

discernment [dɪ'sərnmənt, -'zərn-] *n* : discernimiento *m*, criterio *m*

discharge¹ [dɪs'tʃɑrdʒ, 'dɪsˌ-] *v* **-charged; -charging** **1** UNLOAD : descargar (carga), desembarcar (pasajeros) **2** SHOOT : descargar, disparar **3** FREE : liberar, poner en libertad **4** DISMISS : despedir **5** EMIT : despedir (humo, etc.), descargar (electricidad) **6** : cumplir con (una obligación), saldar (una deuda) — *vi* **1** : descargarse (dícese de una batería) **2** OOZE : supurar

discharge² ['dɪsˌtʃɑrdʒ, dɪs'-] *n* **1** EMISSION : descarga *f* (de electricidad), emisión *f* (de gases) **2** DISMISSAL : despido *m* (del empleo), baja *f* (del ejército) **3** SECRETION : secreción *f*

disciple [dɪ'saɪpəl] *n* : discípulo *m*, -la *f*

discipline¹ ['dɪsəplən] *vt* **-plined; -plining** **1** PUNISH : castigar, sancionar (a los empleados) **2** CONTROL : disciplinar **3 to discipline oneself** : disciplinarse

discipline² *n* **1** FIELD : disciplina *f*, campo *m* **2** TRAINING : disciplina *f* **3** PUNISHMENT : castigo *m* **4** SELF-CONTROL : dominio *m* de sí mismo

disc jockey *n* : disc jockey *mf*

disclaim [dɪs'kleɪm] *vt* DENY : negar

disclose [dɪs'klo:z] *vt* **-closed; -closing** : revelar, poner en evidencia

disclosure [dɪs'klo:ʒər] *n* : revelación *f*

disco ['dɪsko:] *n* **1** → **discotheque** **2** *or* **disco music** : disco *f*, música *f* disco

discolor [dɪs'kʌlər] *vt* **1** BLEACH : decolorar **2** FADE : desteñir **3** STAIN : manchar — *vi* : decolorarse, desteñirse

discoloration [dɪsˌkʌlə'reɪʃən] *n* **1** FADING : decoloración *f* **2** STAIN : mancha *f*

discomfort [dɪs'kʌmfərt] *n* **1** PAIN : molestia *f*, malestar *m* **2** UNEASINESS : inquietud *f*

disconcert [ˌdɪskən'sərt] *vt* : desconcertar

disconcerting [ˌdɪskən'sərtɪŋ] *adj* : desconcertante

disconnect [ˌdɪskə'nɛkt] *vt* : desconectar

disconnected [ˌdɪskə'nɛktəd] *adj* : inconexo

disconsolate [dɪs'kɑntsələt] *adj* : desconsolado

discontent [ˌdɪskən'tɛnt] *n* : descontento *m*

discontented [ˌdɪskən'tɛntəd] *adj* : descontento

discontinue [ˌdɪskən'tɪnˌju:] *vt* **-ued; -uing** : suspender, descontinuar

discontinuity [dɪsˌkɑntə'nu:əti, -'nju:-] *n, pl* **-ties** : discontinuidad *f*

discontinuous [ˌdɪskən'tɪnjəwəs] *adj* : discontinuo

discord ['dɪsˌkɔrd] *n* **1** STRIFE : discordia *f*, discordancia *f* **2** : disonancia *f* (en música)

discordant [dɪs'kɔrdənt] *adj* : discordante, discorde — **discordantly** *adv*

discotheque ['dɪskəˌtɛk, ˌdɪskə'tɛk] *n* : discoteca *f*

discount¹ ['dɪsˌkaʊnt, dɪs'-] *vt* **1** REDUCE : descontar, rebajar (precios) **2** DISREGARD : descartar, ignorar

discount² ['dɪsˌkaʊnt] *n* : descuento *m*, rebaja *f*

discourage [dɪs'kərɪdʒ] *vt* **-aged; -aging** **1** DISHEARTEN : desalentar, desanimar **2** DISSUADE : disuadir

discouragement [dɪs'kərɪdʒmənt] *n* : desánimo *m*, desaliento *m*

discouraging [dɪs'kərədʒɪŋ] *adj* : desalentador

discourse[1] [dɪs'kors] *vi* **-coursed; -coursing** : disertar, conversar

discourse[2] ['dɪs,kors] *n* **1** TALK : conversación *f* **2** SPEECH, TREATISE : discurso *m*, tratado *m*

discourteous [dɪs'kərt̬iəs] *adj* : descortés — **discourteously** *adv*

discourtesy [dɪs'kərt̬əsi] *n, pl* **-sies** : descortesía *f*

discover [dɪs'kʌvər] *vt* : descubrir

discoverer [dɪs'kʌvərər] *n* : descubridor *m*, -dora *f*

discovery [dɪs'kʌvəri] *n, pl* **-ries** : descubrimiento *m*

discredit[1] [dɪs'krɛdət] *vt* **1** DISBELIEVE : no creer, dudar **2** : desacreditar, desprestigiar, poner en duda ⟨they discredited his research : desacreditaron sus investigaciones⟩

discredit[2] *n* **1** DISREPUTE : descrédito *m*, desprestigio *m* **2** DOUBT : duda *f*

discreet [dɪs'kriːt] *adj* : discreto — **discreetly** *adv*

discrepancy [dɪs'krɛpəntsi] *n, pl* **-cies** : discrepancia *f*

discretion [dɪs'krɛʃən] *n* **1** CIRCUMSPECTION : discreción *f*, circunspección *f* **2** JUDGMENT : discernimiento *m*, criterio *m*

discretionary [dɪs'krɛʃə,nɛri] *adj* : discrecional

discriminate [dɪs'krɪmə,neɪt] *v* **-nated; -nating** *vt* DISTINGUISH : distinguir, discriminar, diferenciar — *vi* : discriminar ⟨to discriminate against women : discriminar a las mujeres⟩

discrimination [dɪs,krɪmə'neɪʃən] *n* **1** PREJUDICE : discriminación *f* **2** DISCERNMENT : discernimiento *m*

discriminatory [dɪs'krɪmənə,tori] *adj* : discriminatorio

discus ['dɪskəs] *n, pl* **-cuses** [-kəsəz] : disco *m*

discuss [dɪs'kʌs] *vt* : hablar de, discutir, tratar (de)

discussion [dɪs'kʌʃən] *n* : discusión *f*, debate *m*, conversación *f*

disdain[1] [dɪs'deɪn] *vt* : desdeñar, despreciar ⟨they disdained to reply : no se dignaron a responder⟩

disdain[2] *n* : desdén *m*

disdainful [dɪs'deɪnfəl] *adj* : desdeñoso — **disdainfully** *adv*

disease [dɪ'ziːz] *n* : enfermedad *f*, mal *m*, dolencia *f*

diseased [dɪ'ziːzd] *adj* : enfermo

disembark [,dɪsɪm'bark] *v* : desembarcar

disembarkation [dɪs,ɛm,bar'keɪʃən] *n* : desembarco *m*, desembarque *m*

disembodied [,dɪsɪm'badɪd] *adj* : incorpóreo

disenchant [,dɪsɪn'tʃænt] *vt* : desilusionar, desencantar, desengañar

disenchantment [,dɪsɪn'tʃæntmənt] *n* : desencanto *m*, desilusión *f*

disengage [,dɪsɪn'geɪdʒ] *vt* **-gaged; -gaging 1** : soltar, desconectar (un mecanismo) **2 to disengage the clutch** : desembragar

disentangle [,dɪsɪn'tæŋgəl] *vt* **-gled; -gling** UNTANGLE : desenredar, desenmarañar

disfavor [dɪs'feɪvər] *n* : desaprobación *f*

disfigure [dɪs'fɪgjər] *vt* **-ured; -uring** : desfigurar (a una persona), afear (un edificio, un área)

disfigurement [dɪs'fɪgjərmənt] *n* : desfiguración *f*, afeamiento *m*

disfranchise [dɪs'fræn,tʃaɪz] *vt* **-chised; -chising** : privar del derecho a votar

disgrace[1] [dɪs'kreɪs] *vt* **-graced; -gracing** : deshonrar

disgrace[2] *n* **1** DISHONOR : desgracia *f*, deshonra *f* **2** SHAME : vergüenza *f* ⟨he's a disgrace to his family : es una vergüenza para su familia⟩

disgraceful [dɪ'skreɪsfəl] *adj* : vergonzoso, deshonroso, ignominioso

disgracefully [dɪ'skreɪsfəli] *adv* : vergonzosamente

disgruntle [dɪs'grʌntəl] *vt* **-tled; -tling** : enfadar, contrariar

disguise[1] [dɪ'skaɪz] *vt* **-guised; -guising 1** : disfrazar, enmascarar (el aspecto) **2** CONCEAL : encubrir, disimular

disguise[2] *n* : disfraz *m*

disgust[1] [dɪ'skʌst] *vt* : darle asco (a alguien), asquear, repugnar ⟨that disgusts me : eso me da asco⟩

disgust[2] *n* : asco *m*, repugnancia *f*

disgusting [dɪ'skʌstɪŋ] *adj* : asqueroso, repugnante — **disgustingly** *adv*

dish[1] ['dɪʃ] *vt* SERVE : servir

dish[2] *n* **1** : plato *m* ⟨the national dish : el plato nacional⟩ **2** PLATE : plato *m* ⟨to wash the dishes : lavar los platos⟩ **3 serving dish** : fuente *f*

dishcloth ['dɪʃ,klɔθ] *n* : paño *m* de cocina (para secar), trapo *m* de fregar (para lavar)

dishearten [dɪs'hart̬ən] *vt* : desanimar, desalentar

dishevel [dɪ'ʃɛvəl] *vt* **-eled** *or* **-elled; -eling** *or* **-elling** : desarreglar, despeinar (el pelo)

disheveled *or* **dishevelled** [dɪ'ʃɛvəld] *adj* : despeinado (dícese del pelo), desarreglado, desaliñado

dishonest [dɪ'sanəst] *adj* : deshonesto, fraudulento — **dishonestly** *adv*

dishonesty [dɪ'sanəsti] *n, pl* **-ties** : deshonestidad *f*, falta *f* de honradez

dishonor[1] [dɪ'sanər] *vt* : deshonrar

dishonor[2] *n* : deshonra *f*

dishonorable [dɪ'sanərəbəl] *adj* : deshonroso — **dishonorably** [-bli] *adv*

dishrag ['dɪʃ,ræg] → **dishcloth**

dishwasher ['dɪʃ,wɔʃər] *n* : lavaplatos *m*, lavavajillas *m*

disillusion [,dɪsə'luːʒən] *vt* : desilusionar, desencantar, desengañar

disillusionment [,dɪsə'luːʒənmənt] *n* : desilusión *f*, desencanto *m*

disinclination [dɪs,ɪnklə'neɪʃən, -,ɪŋ-] *n* : aversión *f*

disinclined [,dɪsɪn'klaɪnd] *adv* : poco dispuesto

disinfect [,dɪsɪn'fɛkt] *vt* : desinfectar

disinfectant¹ [,dɪsɪn'fɛktənt] *adj* : desinfectante

disinfectant² *n* : desinfectante *m*

disinherit [,dɪsɪn'hɛrət] *vt* : desheredar

disintegrate [dɪs'ɪntə,ɡreɪt] *v* **-grated; -grating** *vt* : desintegrar, deshacer — *vi* : desintegrarse, deshacerse

disintegration [dɪs,ɪntə'ɡreɪʃən] *n* : desintegración *f*

disinterested [dɪs'ɪntərəstəd, -,rɛs-] *adj* **1** INDIFFERENT : indiferente **2** IMPARTIAL : imparcial, desinteresado

disinterestedness [dɪs'ɪntərəstədnəs, -,rɛs-] *n* : desinterés *m*

disjointed [dɪs'dʒɔɪntəd] *adj* : inconexo, incoherente

disk *or* **disc** ['dɪsk] *n* : disco *m*

disk drive *n* : unidad *f* de disco

diskette [,dɪs'kɛt] *n* : diskette *m*, disquete *m*

dislike¹ [dɪs'laɪk] *vt* **-liked; -liking** : tenerle aversión a (algo), tenerle antipatía (a alguien), no gustarle (algo a uno)

dislike² *n* : aversión *f*, antipatía *f*

dislocate ['dɪslo,keɪt, dɪs'lo:-] *vt* **-cated; -cating** : dislocar

dislocation [,dɪslo'keɪʃən] *n* : dislocación *f*

dislodge [dɪs'lɑdʒ] *vt* **-lodged; -lodging** : sacar, desalojar, desplazar

disloyal [dɪs'lɔɪəl] *adj* : desleal

disloyalty [dɪs'lɔɪəlti] *n, pl* **-ties** : deslealtad *f*

dismal ['dɪzməl] *adj* **1** GLOOMY : sombrío, lúgubre, tétrico **2** DEPRESSING : deprimente, triste

dismantle [dɪs'mæntəl] *vt* **-tled; -tling** : desmantelar, desmontar, desarmar

dismay¹ [dɪs'meɪ] *vt* : consternar

dismay² *n* : consternación *f*

dismember [dɪs'mɛmbər] *vt* : desmembrar

dismiss [dɪs'mɪs] *vt* **1** : dejar salir, darle permiso (a alguien) para retirarse **2** DISCHARGE : despedir, destituir **3** REJECT : descartar, desechar, rechazar

dismissal [dɪs'mɪsəl] *n* **1** : permiso *m* para retirarse **2** DISCHARGE : despido *m* (de un empleado), destitución *f* (de un funcionario) **3** REJECTION : rechazo *m*

dismount [dɪs'maʊnt] *vi* : desmontar, bajarse, apearse

disobedience [,dɪsə'bi:diənts] *n* : desobediencia *f* — **disobedient** [-ənt] *adj*

disobey [,dɪsə'beɪ] *v* : desobedecer

disorder¹ [dɪs'ɔrdər] *vt* : desordenar, desarreglar

disorder² *n* **1** DISARRAY : desorden *m* **2** UNREST : disturbios *mpl*, desórdenes *mpl* **3** AILMENT : afección *f*, indisposición *f*, dolencia *f*

disorderly [dɪs'ɔrdərli] *adj* **1** UNTIDY : desordenado, desarreglado **2** UNRULY : indisciplinado, alborotado **3 disorderly conduct** : conducta *f* escandalosa

disorganization [dɪs,ɔrgənə'zeɪʃən] *n* : desorganización *f*

disorganize [dɪs'ɔrgə,naɪz] *vt* **-nized; -nizing** : desorganizar

disorient [dɪs'ori,ɛnt] *vt* : desorientar

disown [dɪs'o:n] *vt* : renegar de, repudiar

disparage [dɪs'pærɪdʒ] *vt* **-aged; -aging** : menospreciar, denigrar

disparagement [dɪs'pærɪdʒmənt] *n* : menosprecio *m*

disparate ['dɪspərət, dɪs'pærət] *adj* : dispar, diferente

disparity [dɪs'pærəti] *n, pl* **-ties** : disparidad *f*

dispassionate [dɪs'pæʃənət] *adj* : desapasionado, imparcial — **dispassionately** *adv*

dispatch¹ [dɪs'pætʃ] *vt* **1** SEND : despachar, enviar **2** KILL : despachar, matar **3** HANDLE : despachar

dispatch² *n* **1** SENDING : envío *m*, despacho *m* **2** MESSAGE : despacho *m*, reportaje *m* (de un periodista), parte *m* (en el ejército) **3** PROMPTNESS : prontitud *f*, rapidez *f*

dispel [dɪs'pɛl] *vt* **-pelled; -pelling** : disipar, desvanecer

dispensable [dɪ'spɛntsəbəl] *adj* : prescindible

dispensation [,dɪspɛn'seɪʃən] *n* EXEMPTION : exención *m*, dispensa *f*

dispense [dɪs'pɛnts] *v* **-pensed; -pensing** *vt* **1** DISTRIBUTE : repartir, distribuir, dar **2** ADMINISTER, BESTOW : administrar (justicia), conceder (favores, etc.) **3** : preparar y despachar (medicamentos) — *vi* **to dispense with** : prescindir de

dispenser [dɪs'pɛntsər] *n* : dispensador *m*, distribuidor *m* automático

dispersal [dɪs'pərsəl] *n* : dispersión *f*

disperse [dɪs'pərs] *v* **-persed; -persing** *vt* : dispersar, diseminar — *vi* : dispersarse

dispersion [dɪ'spərʒən] *n* : dispersión *f*

dispirit [dɪ'spɪrət] *vt* : desalentar, desanimar

displace [dɪs'pleɪs] *vt* **-placed; -placing** **1** : desplazar (un líquido, etc.) **2** REPLACE : reemplazar

displacement [dɪs'pleɪsmənt] *n* **1** : desplazamiento *m* (de personas) **2** REPLACEMENT : sustitución *f*, reemplazo *m*

display¹ [dɪs'pleɪ] *vt* : exponer, exhibir, mostrar

display² *n* **1** : muestra *f*, exposición *f*, alarde *m* **2** : visualizador *m* (de una computadora)

displease [dɪs'pli:z] *vt* **-pleased; -pleasing** : desagradar a, disgustar, contrariar

displeasure [dɪs'plɛʒər] *n* : desagrado *m*

disposable [dɪs'po:zəbəl] *adj* **1** : desechable ⟨disposable diapers : pañales desechables⟩ **2** AVAILABLE : disponible

disposal [dɪs'po:zəl] *n* **1** PLACEMENT : disposición *f*, colocación *f* **2** REMOVAL : eliminación *f* **3 to have at one's disposal** : disponer de, tener a su disposición

dispose [dɪs'po:z] *v* **-posed; -posing** *vt* **1** ARRANGE : disponer, colocar **2** INCLINE : predisponer — *vi* **1 to dispose of** DISCARD : desechar, deshacerse de **2 to dispose of** HANDLE : despachar

disposition [ˌdɪspə'zɪʃən] *n* **1** ARRANGEMENT : disposición *f* **2** TENDENCY : predisposición *f*, inclinación *f* **3** TEMPERAMENT : temperamento *m*, carácter *m*

dispossess [ˌdɪspə'zɛs] *vt* : deposeer

disproportion [ˌdɪsprə'porʃən] *n* : desproporción *f*

disproportionate [ˌdɪsprə'porʃənət] *adj* : desproporcionado — **disproportionately** *adv*

disprove [dɪs'pru:v] *vt* **-proved; -proving** : rebatir, refutar

disputable [dɪs'pju:təbəl, 'dɪspjʊtəbəl] *adj* : disputable, discutible

dispute¹ [dɪs'pju:t] *v* **-puted; -puting** *vt* **1** QUESTION : discutir, cuestionar **2** OPPOSE : combatir, resistir — *vi* ARGUE, DEBATE : discutir

dispute² *n* **1** DEBATE : debate *m*, discusión *f* **2** QUARREL : disputa *f*, discusión *f*

disqualification [dɪsˌkwaləfə'keɪʃən] *n* : descalificación *f*

disqualify [dɪs'kwalə,faɪ] *vt* **-fied; -fying** : descalificar, inhabilitar

disquiet¹ [dɪs'kwaɪət] *vt* : inquietar

disquiet² *n* : ansiedad *f*, inquietud *f*

disregard¹ [ˌdɪsrɪ'gard] *vt* : ignorar, no prestar atención a

disregard² *n* : indiferencia *f*

disrepair [ˌdɪsrɪ'pær] *n* : mal estado *m*

disreputable [dɪs'rɛpjʊtəbəl] *adj* : de mala fama (dícese de una persona o un lugar), vergonzoso (dícese de la conducta)

disreputably [dɪs'rɛpjʊtəbli] *adv* : vergonzosamente

disrepute [ˌdɪsrɪ'pju:t] *n* : descrédito *m*, mala fama *f*, deshonra *f*

disrespect [ˌdɪsrɪ'spɛkt] *n* : falta *f* de respeto

disrespectful [ˌdɪsrɪ'spɛktfəl] *adj* : irrespetuoso — **disrespectfully** *adv*

disrobe [dɪs'ro:b] *v* **-robed; -robing** *vt* : desvestir, desnudar — *vi* : desvestirse, desnudarse

disrupt [dɪs'rʌpt] *vt* : trastornar, perturbar

disruption [dɪs'rʌpʃən] *n* : trastorno *m*

disruptive [dɪs'rʌptɪv] *adj* : perjudicial, perturbador — **disruptively** *adv*

dissatisfaction [dɪsˌsætəs'fækʃən] *n* : descontento *m*, insatisfacción *f*

dissatisfied [dɪs'sætəs,faɪd] *adj* : descontento, insatisfecho

dissatisfy [dɪs'sætəs,faɪ] *vt* **-fied; -fying** : no contentar, no satisfacer

dissect [dɪ'sɛkt] *vt* : disecar

dissection [dɪ'sɛkʃən] *n* : disección *f*

dissemble [dɪ'sɛmbəl] *v* **-bled; -bling** *vt* HIDE : ocultar, disimular — *vi* PRETEND : fingir, disimular

disseminate [dɪ'sɛmə,neɪt] *vt* **-nated; -nating** : diseminar, difundir, divulgar

dissemination [dɪ,sɛmə'neɪʃən] *n* : diseminación *f*, difusión *f*

dissension [dɪ'sɛntʃən] *n* : disensión *f*, desacuerdo *m*

dissent¹ [dɪ'sɛnt] *vi* : disentir

dissent² *n* : disentimiento *m*, disensión *f*

dissertation [ˌdɪsər'teɪʃən] *n* **1** DISCOURSE : disertación *f*, discurso *m* **2** THESIS : tesis *f*

disservice [dɪs'sərvɪs] *n* : perjuicio *m*

dissident¹ ['dɪsədənt] *adj* : disidente

dissident² *n* : disidente *mf*

dissimilar [dɪ'sɪmələr] *adj* : distinto, diferente, disímil

dissipate ['dɪsə,peɪt] *vt* **-pated; -pating** **1** DISPERSE : disipar, dispersar **2** SQUANDER : malgastar, desperdiciar, derrochar, disipar

dissipation [ˌdɪsə'peɪʃən] *n* : disipación *f*, libertinaje *m*

dissociate [dɪ'so:ʃi,eɪt, -si-] *v* **-ated** [-,eɪtəd]; **-ating** [-,eɪtɪŋ] *vt* : disociar ⟨to disassociate oneself : disociarse⟩ — *vi* : disociarse

dissociation [dɪ,so:ʃi'eɪʃən, -si-] *n* : disociación *f*

dissolute ['dɪsə,lu:t] *adj* : disoluto

dissolution [ˌdɪsə'lu:ʃən] *n* : disolución *f*

dissolve [dɪ'zalv] *v* **-solved; -solving** *vt* : disolver — *vi* : disolverse

dissonance ['dɪsənənts] *n* : disonancia *f*

dissuade [dɪ'sweɪd] *vt* **-suaded; -suading** : disuadir

distance¹ ['dɪstənts] *vt* **-tanced** [-təntst]; **-tancing** [-təntsɪŋ] **to distance oneself** : distanciarse

distance² *n* **1** : distancia *f* ⟨the distance between two points : la distancia entre dos puntos⟩ ⟨in the distance : a lo lejos⟩ **2** RESERVE : actitud *f* distante, reserva *f* ⟨to keep one's distance : guardar las distancias⟩

distant ['dɪstənt] *adj* **1** FAR : distante, lejano **2** REMOTE : distante, lejano, remoto **3** ALOOF : distante, frío

distantly ['dɪstəntli] *adv* **1** LOOSELY : aproximadamente, vagamente **2** COLDLY : fríamente, con frialdad

distaste [dɪs'teɪst] *n* : desagrado *m*, aversión *f*

distasteful [dɪs'teɪstfəl] *adj* : desagradable, de mal gusto

distemper [dɪs'tɛmpər] *n* : moquillo *m*

distend [dɪs'tɛnd] *vt* : dilatar, hinchar — *vi* : dilatarse, hincharse

distill [dɪ'stɪl] *vt* : destilar
distillation [ˌdɪstə'leɪʃən] *n* : destilación *f*
distiller [dɪ'stɪlər] *n* : destilador *m*, -dora *f*
distillery [dɪ'stɪləri] *n, pl* **-ries** [-riz] : destilería *f*
distinct [dɪ'stɪŋkt] *adj* **1** DIFFERENT : distinto, diferente **2** CLEAR, UNMISTAKABLE : marcado, claro, evidente ⟨a distinct possibility : una clara posibilidad⟩
distinction [dɪ'stɪŋkʃən] *n* **1** DIFFERENTIATION : distinción *f* **2** DIFFERENCE : diferencia *f* **3** EXCELLENCE : distinción *f*, excelencia *f* ⟨a writer of distinction : un escritor destacado⟩
distinctive [dɪ'stɪŋktɪv] *adj* : distintivo, característico — **distinctively** *adv*
distinctiveness [dɪ'stɪŋktɪvnəs] *n* : peculiaridad *f*
distinctly [dɪ'stɪŋktli] *adv* : claramente, con claridad
distinguish [dɪs'tɪŋgwɪʃ] *vt* **1** DIFFERENTIATE : distinguir, diferenciar **2** DISCERN : distinguir ⟨he distinguished the sound of the piano : distinguió el sonido del piano⟩ **3 to distinguish oneself** : señalarse, distinguirse — *vi* DISCRIMINATE : distinguir
distinguishable [dɪs'tɪŋgwɪʃəbəl] *adj* : distinguible
distinguished [dɪs'tɪŋgwɪʃt] *adj* : distinguido
distort [dɪ'stɔrt] *vt* **1** MISREPRESENT : distorsionar, tergiversar **2** DEFORM : distorsionar, deformar
distortion [dɪ'stɔrʃən] *n* : distorsión *f*, deformación *f*, tergiversación *f*
distract [dɪ'strækt] *vt* : distraer, entretener
distracted [dɪ'stræktəd] *adj* : distraído
distraction [dɪ'strækʃən] *n* **1** INTERRUPTION : distracción *f*, interrupción *f* **2** CONFUSION : confusión *f* **3** AMUSEMENT : diversión *f*, entretenimiento *m*, distracción *f*
distraught [dɪ'strɔt] *adj* : afligido, turbado
distress[1] [dɪ'strɛs] *vt* : afligir, darle pena (a alguien), hacer sufrir
distress[2] *n* **1** SORROW : dolor *m*, angustia *f*, aflicción *f* **2** PAIN : dolor *m* **3 in ～** : en peligro
distressful [dɪ'strɛsfəl] *adj* : doloroso, penoso
distribute [dɪ'strɪˌbjuːt, -bjʊt] *vt* **-uted; -uting** : distribuir, repartir
distribution [ˌdɪstrə'bjuːʃən] *n* : distribución *f*, reparto *m*
distributive [dɪ'strɪbjʊtɪv] *adj* : distributivo
distributor [dɪ'strɪbjʊtər] *n* : distribuidor *m*, -dora *f*
district ['dɪsˌtrɪkt] *n* **1** REGION : región *f*, zona *f*, barrio *m* (de una ciudad) **2** : distrito *m* (zona política)
distrust[1] [dɪs'trʌst] *vt* : desconfiar de

distrust[2] *n* : desconfianza *f*, recelo *m*
distrustful [dɪs'trʌstfəl] *adj* : desconfiado, receloso, suspicaz
disturb [dɪ'stɜrb] *vt* **1** BOTHER : molestar, perturbar ⟨sorry to disturb you : perdone la molestia⟩ **2** DISARRANGE : desordenar **3** WORRY : inquietar, preocupar **4 to disturb the peace** : alterar el orden público
disturbance [dɪ'stɜrbənɹs] *n* **1** COMMOTION : alboroto *m*, disturbio *m* **2** INTERRUPTION : interrupción *f*
disuse [dɪs'juːs] *n* : desuso *m*
ditch[1] ['dɪtʃ] *vt* **1** : cavar zanjas en **2** DISCARD : deshacerse de, botar
ditch[2] *n* : zanja *f*, fosa *f*, cuneta *f* (en una carretera)
dither ['dɪðər] *n* **to be in a dither** : estar nervioso, ponerse como loco
ditto ['dɪtoː] *n, pl* **-tos 1** : lo mismo, ídem *m* **2 ditto marks** : comillas *fpl*
ditty ['dɪti] *n, pl* **-ties** : canción *f* corta y simple
diurnal [daɪ'ɜrnəl] *adj* **1** DAILY : diario, cotidiano **2** : diurno ⟨a diurnal animal : un animal diurno⟩
divan ['daɪˌvæn, dɪ'-] *n* : diván *m*
dive[1] ['daɪv] *vi* **dived** *or* **dove** ['doːv]; **dived; diving 1** PLUNGE : tirarse al agua, zambullirse, dar un clavado **2** SUBMERGE : sumergirse **3** DROP : bajar en picada (dícese de un avión), caer en picada
dive[2] *n* **1** PLUNGE : zambullida *f*, clavado *m* (en el agua) **2** DESCENT : descenso *m* en picada **3** BAR, JOINT : antro *m*
diver ['daɪvər] *n* : saltador *m*, -dora *f*; clavadista *mf*
diverge [də'vɜrdʒ, daɪ-] *vi* **-verged; -verging 1** SEPARATE : divergir, separarse **2** DIFFER : divergir, discrepar
divergence [də'vɜrdʒənɹs, daɪ-] *n* : divergencia *f* — **divergent** [-ənt] *adj*
diverse [daɪ'vɜrs, də-, 'daɪ,vɜrs] *adj* : diverso, variado
diversification [daɪ,vɜrsəfə'keɪʃən, də-] *n* : diversificación *f*
diversify [daɪ'vɜrsə,faɪ, də-] *vt* **-fied; -fying** : diversificar, variar
diversion [daɪ'vɜrʒən, də-] *n* **1** DEVIATION : desviación *f* **2** AMUSEMENT, DISTRACTION : diversión *f*, distracción *f*, entretenimiento *m*
diversity [daɪ'vɜrsəti, də-] *n, pl* **-ties** : diversidad *f*
divert [də'vɜrt, daɪ-] *vt* **1** DEFLECT : desviar **2** DISTRACT : distraer **3** AMUSE : divertir, entretener
divest [daɪ'vɛst, də-] *vt* **1** UNDRESS : desnudar, desvestir **2 to divest of** : despojar *m*
divide [də'vaɪd] *v* **-vided; -viding** *vt* **1** HALVE : dividir, partir por la mitad **2** SHARE : repartir, dividir **3** : dividir (números) — *vi* : dividirse, dividir (en matemáticas)

dividend ['dɪvə,dɛnd, -dənd] *n* **1** : dividendo *m* (en finanzas) **2** BONUS : beneficio *m*, provecho *m* **3** : dividendo *m* (en matemáticas)

divider [dɪ'vaɪdər] *n* **1** : separador *m* (para ficheros, etc.) **2** *or* **room divider** : mampara *f*, biombo *m*

divination [,dɪvə'neɪʃən] *n* : adivinación *f*

divine¹ [də'vaɪn] *adj* **-viner; -est 1** : divino **2** SUPERB : divino, espléndido — **divinely** *adv*

divine² *n* : clérigo *m*, eclesiástico *m*

divinity [də'vɪnəti] *n, pl* **-ties** : divinidad *f*

divisible [dɪ'vɪzəbəl] *adj* : divisible

division [dɪ'vɪʒən] *n* **1** DISTRIBUTION : división *f*, reparto *m* ⟨division of labor : distribución del trabajo⟩ **2** PART : división *f*, sección *f* **3** : división *f* (en matemáticas)

divisive [də'vaɪsɪv] *adj* : divisivo

divisor [dɪ'vaɪzər] *n* : divisor *m*

divorce¹ [də'vors] *v* **-vorced; -vorcing** *vt* : divorciar — *vi* : divorciarse

divorce² *n* : divorcio *m*

divorcé [dɪ,vor'seɪ, -'si:; -'vor,-] *n* : divorciado *m*

divorcée [dɪ,vor'seɪ, -'si:; -'vor,-] *n* : divorciada *f*

divulge [də'vʌldʒ, daɪ-] *vt* **-vulged; -vulging** : revelar, divulgar

dizzily ['dɪzəli] *adv* : vertiginosamente

dizziness ['dɪzinəs] *n* : mareo *m*, vahído *m*, vértigo *m*

dizzy ['dɪzi] *adj* **dizzier; -est 1** : mareado ⟨I feel dizzy : estoy mareado⟩ **2** : vertiginoso ⟨a dizzy speed : una velocidad vertiginosa⟩

DNA [,di:,ɛn'eɪ] *n* : ADN *m*

do ['du:] *v* **did** ['dɪd]; **done** ['dʌn]; **doing; does** ['dʌz] *vt* **1** CARRY OUT, PERFORM : hacer, realizar, llevar a cabo ⟨she did her best : hizo todo lo posible⟩ **2** PREPARE : preparar, hacer ⟨do your homework : haz tu tarea⟩ **3** ARRANGE : arreglar, peinar (el pelo) **4 to do in** RUIN : estropear, arruinar **5 to do in** KILL : matar, liquidar *fam* — *vi* **1** : hacer ⟨you did well : hiciste bien⟩ **2** FARE : estar, ir, andar ⟨how are you doing? : ¿cómo estás?, ¿cómo te va?⟩ **3** FINISH : terminar ⟨now I'm done : ya terminé⟩ **4** SERVE : servir, ser suficiente, alcanzar ⟨this will do for now : esto servirá por el momento⟩ **5 to do away with** ABOLISH : abolir, suprimir **6 to do away with** KILL : eliminar, matar **7 to do by** TREAT : tratar ⟨he does well by her : él la trata bien⟩ — *v aux* **1** (*used in interrogative sentences and negative statements*) ⟨do you know her? : ¿la conoces?⟩ ⟨I don't like that : a mí no me gusta eso⟩ **2** (*used for emphasis*) ⟨I do hope you'll come : espero que vengas⟩ **3** (*used as a substitute verb to avoid repetition*) ⟨do you speak English? yes, I do : ¿habla inglés? sí⟩

docile ['dɑsəl] *adj* : dócil, sumiso

dock¹ ['dɑk] *vt* **1** CUT : cortar **2** : descontar dinero de (un sueldo) — *vi* ANCHOR, LAND : fondear, atracar

dock² *n* **1** PIER : atracadero *m* **2** WHARF : muelle *m* **3** : banquillo *m* de los acusados (en un tribunal)

doctor¹ ['dɑktər] *vt* **1** TREAT : tratar, curar **2** ALTER : adulterar, alterar, falsificar (un documento)

doctor² *n* **1** : doctor *m*, -tora *f* ⟨Doctor of Philosophy : doctor en filosofía⟩ **2** PHYSICIAN : médico *m*, -ca *f*; doctor *m*, -tora *f*

doctorate ['dɑktərət] *n* : doctorado *m*

doctrine ['dɑktrɪn] *n* : doctrina *f*

document¹ ['dɑkju,mɛnt] *vt* : documentar

document² ['dɑkjumənt] *n* : documento *m*

documentary¹ [,dɑkju'mɛntəri] *adj* : documental

documentary² *n, pl* **-ries** : documental *m*

documentation [,dɑkjumən'teɪʃən] *n* : documentación *f*

dodge¹ ['dɑdʒ] *v* **dodged; dodging** *vt* : esquivar, eludir, evadir (impuestos) — *vi* : echarse a un lado

dodge² *n* **1** RUSE : truco *m*, treta *f*, artimaña *f* **2** EVASION : regate *m*, evasión *f*

dodo ['do:,do:] *n, pl* **-does** *or* **-dos** : dodo *m*

doe ['do:] *n, pl* **does** *or* **doe** : gama *f*, cierva *f*

doer ['du:ər] *n* : hacedor *m*, -dora *f*

does → **do**

doff ['dɑf, 'dɔf] *vt* : quitarse ⟨to doff one's hat : quitarse el sombrero⟩

dog¹ ['dɔg, 'dɑg] *vt* **dogged; dogging** : seguir de cerca, perseguir, acosar ⟨to dog someone's footsteps : seguir los pasos de alguien⟩ ⟨dogged by bad luck : perseguido por la mala suerte⟩

dog² *n* : perro *m*, -rra *f*

dogcatcher ['dɔg,kætʃər] *n* : perrero *m*, -ra *f*

dog-eared ['dɔg,ɪrd] *adj* : con las esquinas dobladas

dogged ['dɔgəd] *adj* : tenaz, terco, obstinado

doggy ['dɔgi] *n, pl* **doggies** : perrito *m*, -ta *f*

doghouse ['dɔg,haʊs] *n* : casita *f* de perro

dogma ['dɔgmə] *n* : dogma *m*

dogmatic [dɔg'mætɪk] *adj* : dogmático

dogmatism ['dɔgmə,tɪzəm] *n* : dogmatismo *m*

dogwood ['dɔg,wʊd] *n* : cornejo *m*

doily ['dɔɪli] *n, pl* **-lies** : pañito *m*

doings ['du:ɪŋz] *npl* : eventos *mpl*, actividades *fpl*

doldrums ['do:ldrəmz, 'dɑl-] *npl* **1** : zona *f* de las calmas ecuatoriales **2 to be in the doldrums** : estar abatido (dícese de una persona), estar estancado (dícese de una empresa)

dole ['do:l] *n* 1 ALMS : distribución *f* a los necesitados, limosna *f* 2 : subsidios *mpl* de desempleo

doleful ['do:lfəl] *adj* : triste, lúgubre

dolefully ['do:lfəli] *adv* : con pesar, de manera triste

dole out *vt* **doled out; doling out** : repartir

doll ['dal, 'dɔl] *n* : muñeco *m*, -ca *f*

dollar ['dalər] *n* : dólar *m*

dolly ['dali] *n, pl* **-lies** 1 → **doll** 2 : plataforma *f* rodante

dolphin ['dalfən, 'dɔl-] *n* : delfín *m*

dolt ['do:lt] *n* : imbécil *mf*; tonto *m*, -ta *f*

domain [do'meın, də-] *n* 1 TERRITORY : dominio *m*, territorio *m* 2 FIELD : campo *m*, esfera *f*, ámbito *m* ⟨the domain of art : el ámbito de las artes⟩

dome ['do:m] *n* : cúpula *f*, bóveda *f*

domestic[1] [də'mɛstık] *adj* 1 HOUSEHOLD : doméstico, casero 2 : nacional, interno ⟨domestic policy : política interna⟩ 3 TAME : domesticado

domestic[2] *n* : empleado *m* doméstico, empleada *f* doméstica

domestically [də'mɛstıkli] *adv* : domésticamente

domesticate [də'mɛstı,keıt] *vt* **-cated; -cating** : domesticar

domicile ['damə,saıl, 'do:-; 'daməsıl] *n* : domicilio *m*

dominance ['damənənts] *n* : dominio *m*, dominación *f*

dominant ['damənənt] *adj* : dominante

dominate ['damə,neıt] *v* **-nated; -nating** : dominar

domination [,damə'neıʃən] *n* : dominación *f*

domineer [,damə'nır] *vt* : dominar sobre, avasallar, tiranizar

Dominican [də'mınıkən] *n* : dominicano *m*, -na *f* — **Dominican** *adj*

dominion [də'mınjən] *n* 1 POWER : dominio *m* 2 DOMAIN, TERRITORY : dominio *m*, territorio *m*

domino ['damə,no:] *n, pl* **-noes** *or* **-nos** 1 : dominó *m* 2 **dominoes** *npl* : dominó *m* (juego)

don ['dan] *vt* **donned; donning** : ponerse

donate ['do:,neıt, do:'-] *vt* **-nated; -nating** : donar, hacer un donativo de

donation [do:'neıʃən] *n* : donación *f*, donativo *m*

done[1] ['dʌn] → **do**

done[2] *adj* 1 FINISHED : terminado, acabado, concluido 2 COOKED : cocinado

donkey ['daŋki, 'dʌŋ-] *n, pl* **-keys** : burro *m*, asno *m*

donor ['do:nər] *n* : donante *mf*; donador *m*, -dora *f*

don't ['do:nt] (*contraction* of **do not**) → **do**

doodle[1] ['du:dəl] *v* **-dled; -dling** : garabatear

doodle[2] *n* : garabato *m*

doom[1] ['du:m] *vt* : condenar

doom[2] *n* 1 JUDGMENT : sentencia *f*, condena *f* 2 DEATH : muerte *f* 3 FATE : destino *m* 4 RUIN : perdición *f*, ruina *f*

door ['dor] *n* : puerta *f*

doorbell ['dor,bɛl] *n* : timbre *m*

doorknob ['dor,nab] *n* : pomo *m*, perilla *f*

doorman ['dormən] *n, pl* **-men** [-mən, -,mɛn] : portero *m*

doormat ['dor,mæt] : felpudo *m*

doorstep ['dor,stɛp] *n* : umbral *m*

doorway ['dor,weı] *n* : entrada *f*, portal *m*

dope[1] ['do:p] *vt* **doped; doping** : drogar, narcotizar

dope[2] *n* 1 DRUG : droga *f*, estupefaciente *m*, narcótico *m* 2 IDIOT : idiota *mf*; tonto *m*, -ta *f* 3 INFORMATION : información *f*

dormant ['dɔrmənt] *adj* : inactivo, latente

dormer ['dɔrmər] *n* : buhardilla *f*

dormitory ['dɔrmə,tori] *n, pl* **-ries** : dormitorio *m*, residencia *f* de estudiantes

dormouse ['dɔr,maus] *n* : lirón *m*

dorsal ['dɔrsəl] *adj* : dorsal — **dorsally** *adv*

dory ['dori] *n, pl* **-ries** : bote *m* de fondo plano

dosage ['do:sıʤ] *n* : dosis *f*

dose[1] ['do:s] *vt* **dosed; dosing** : medicinar

dose[2] *n* : dosis *f*

dossier ['dɔs,jeı, 'das-] *n* : dossier *m*

dot[1] ['dat] *vt* **dotted; dotting** 1 : poner el punto sobre (una letra) 2 SCATTER : esparcir, salpicar

dot[2] *n* : punto *m* ⟨at six on the dot : a las seis en punto⟩ ⟨dots and dashes : puntos y rayas⟩

dote ['do:t] *vi* **doted; doting** : chochear

double[1] ['dʌbəl] *v* **-bled; -bling** *vt* 1 : doblar, duplicar (una cantidad), redoblar (esfuerzos) 2 FOLD : doblar, plegar 3 to double one's fist : apretar el puño — *vi* 1 : doblarse, duplicarse 2 to double over : retorcerse

double[2] *adj* : doble — **doubly** *adv*

double[3] *n* : doble *mf*

double bass *n* : contrabajo *m*

double–cross [,dʌbəl'krɔs] *vt* : traicionar

double–crosser [,dʌbəl'krɔsər] *n* : traidor *m*, -dora *f*

double–jointed [,dʌbəl'ʤɔıntəd] *adj* : con articulaciones dobles

double–talk ['dʌbəl,tɔk] *n* : ambigüedades *fpl*, lenguaje *m* con doble sentido

doubt[1] ['daut] *vt* 1 QUESTION : dudar de, cuestionar 2 DISTRUST : desconfiar de 3 : dudar, creer poco probable ⟨I doubt it very much : lo dudo mucho⟩

doubt[2] *n* 1 UNCERTAINTY : duda *f*, incertidumbre *f* 2 DISTRUST : desconfianza *f* 3 SKEPTICISM : duda *f*, escepticismo *m*

doubtful ['daʊtfəl] *adj* **1** QUESTIONABLE : dudoso **2** UNCERTAIN : dudoso, incierto

doubtfully ['daʊtfəli] *adv* : dudosamente, sin estar convencido

doubtless ['daʊtləs] *or* **doubtlessly** *adv* : sin duda

douche[1] ['du:ʃ] *vt* **douched; douching** : irrigar

douche[2] *n* : ducha *f*, irrigación *f*

dough ['do:] *n* : masa *f*

doughnut *or* **donut** ['do:,nʌt] *n* : rosquilla *f*, dona *f Mex*

doughty ['daʊti] *adj* **-tier; -est** : fuerte, valiente

dour ['daʊər, 'dʊr] *adj* **1** STERN : severo, adusto **2** SULLEN : hosco, taciturno — **dourly** *adv*

douse ['daʊs, 'daʊz] *vt* **doused; dousing 1** DRENCH : empapar, mojar **2** EXTINGUISH : extinguir, apagar

dove[1] ['do:v] → **dive**

dove[2] ['dʌv] *n* : paloma *f*

dovetail ['dʌv,teɪl] *vi* : encajar, enlazar

dowdy ['daʊdi] *adj* **dowdier; -est** : sin gracia, poco elegante

dowel ['daʊəl] *n* : clavija *f*

down[1] ['daʊn] *vt* **1** FELL : tumbar, derribar, abatir **2** DEFEAT : derrotar

down[2] *adv* **1** DOWNWARD : hacia abajo **2 to lie down** : acostarse, echarse **3 to put down (money)** : pagar un depósito (de dinero) **4 to sit down** : sentarse **5 to take down, to write down** : apuntar, anotar

down[3] *adj* **1** DESCENDING : de bajada ⟨the down elevator : el ascensor de bajada⟩ **2** REDUCED : reducido, rebajado ⟨attendance is down : la concurrencia ha disminuido⟩ **3** DOWNCAST : abatido, deprimido

down[4] *n* **1** : plumón *m* **2** : down *m* (en deportes) **3 ups and downs** : altibajos *mpl*

down[5] *prep* **1** : (hacia) abajo ⟨down the mountain : montaña abajo⟩ ⟨I walked down the stairs : bajé por la escalera⟩ **2** ALONG : por, a lo largo de ⟨we ran down the beach : corrimos por la playa⟩ **3** : a través de ⟨down the years : a través de los años⟩

downcast ['daʊn,kæst] *adj* **1** SAD : triste, abatido **2 with downcast eyes** : con los ojos bajos, con los ojos mirando al suelo

downfall ['daʊn,fɔl] *n* : ruina *f*, perdición *f*

downgrade[1] ['daʊn,greɪd] *vt* **-graded; -grading** : bajar de categoría

downgrade[2] *n* : bajada *f*

downhearted ['daʊn,hɑrtəd] *adj* : desanimado, descorazonado

downhill ['daʊn'hɪl] *adv & adj* : cuesta abajo

download[1] ['daʊn,lo:d] *vt* : descargar (un archivo)

download[2] *n* : descarga *f* (de archivos, etc.)

down payment *n* : entrega *f* inicial

downplay ['daʊn,pleɪ] *vt* : minimizar

downpour ['daʊn,por] *n* : aguacero *m*, chaparrón *m*

downright[1] ['daʊn,raɪt] *adv* THOROUGHLY : absolutamente, completamente

downright[2] *adj* : patente, manifiesto, absoluto ⟨a downright refusal : un rechazo categórico⟩

downside ['daʊn,saɪd] *n* : desventaja *f*

downstairs[1] ['daʊn'stærz] *adv* : abajo

downstairs[2] ['daʊn,stærz] *adj* : del piso de abajo

downstairs[3] ['daʊn'stærz, -,stærz] *n* : planta *f* baja

downstream ['daʊn'stri:m] *adv* : río abajo

down-to-earth [,daʊntu'ərθ] *adj* : práctico, realista

downtown[1] [,daʊn'taʊn] *adv* : hacia el centro, al centro, en el centro (de la ciudad)

downtown[2] *adj* : del centro (de la ciudad) ⟨downtown Chicago : el centro de Chicago⟩

downtown[3] [,daʊn'taʊn, 'daʊn,taʊn] *n* : centro *m* (de la ciudad)

downtrodden ['daʊn,trɑdən] *adj* : oprimido

downward ['daʊnwərd] *or* **downwards** [-wərdz] *adv & adj* : hacia abajo

downwind ['daʊn'wɪnd] *adv & adj* : en la dirección del viento

downy ['daʊni] *adj* **downier; -est 1** : cubierto de plumón, plumoso **2** VELVETY : aterciopelado, velloso

dowry ['daʊri] *n, pl* **-ries** : dote *f*

doze[1] ['do:z] *vi* **dozed; dozing** : dormitar

doze[2] *n* : sueño *m* ligero, cabezada *f*

dozen ['dʌzən] *n, pl* **dozens** *or* **dozen** : docena *f*

drab ['dræb] *adj* **drabber; drabbest 1** BROWNISH : pardo **2** DULL, LACKLUSTER : monótono, gris, deslustrado

draft[1] ['dræft, 'draft] *vt* **1** CONSCRIPT : reclutar **2** COMPOSE, SKETCH : hacer el borrador de, redactar

draft[2] *adj* **1** : de barril ⟨draft beer : cerveza de barril⟩ **2** : de tiro ⟨draft horses : caballos de tiro⟩

draft[3] *n* **1** HAULAGE : tiro *m* **2** DRINK, GULP : trago *m* **3** OUTLINE, SKETCH : bosquejo *m*, borrador *m*, versión *f* **4** : corriente *f* de aire, chiflón *m*, tiro *m* (de una chimenea) **5** CONSCRIPTION : conscripción *f* **6 bank draft** : giro *m* bancario, letra *f* de cambio

draftee [dræf'ti:] *n* : recluta *mf*

draftsman ['dræftsmən] *n, pl* **-men** [-mən, -,mɛn] : dibujante *mf*

drafty ['dræfti] *adj* **draftier; -est** : con corrientes de aire

drag[1] ['dræg] *v* **dragged; dragging** *vt* **1** HAUL : arrastrar, jalar **2** DREDGE : dragar — *vi* **1** TRAIL : arrastrarse **2** LAG : rezagarse **3** : hacerse pesado, hacerse largo ⟨the day dragged on : el día se hizo largo⟩

drag² *n* **1** RESISTANCE : resistencia *f* (aerodinámica) **2** HINDRANCE : traba *f*, estorbo *m* **3** BORE : pesadez *f*, plomo *m fam*

dragnet ['dræg,nɛt] *n* **1** : red *f* barredera (en pesca) **2** : operativo *m* policial de captura

dragon ['drægən] *n* : dragón *m*

dragonfly ['drægən,flaɪ] *n, pl* **-flies** : libélula *f*

drain¹ ['dreɪn] *vt* **1** EMPTY : vaciar, drenar **2** EXHAUST : agotar, consumir — *vi* **1** : escurrir, escurrirse ⟨the dishes are draining : los platos están escurriéndose⟩ **2** EMPTY : desaguar **3 to drain away** : irse agotando

drain² *n* **1** : desagüe *m* **2** SEWER : alcantarilla *f* **3** GRATING : sumidero *m*, resumidero *m*, rejilla *f* **4** EXHAUSTION : agotamiento *m*, disminución *f* (de energía, etc.) ⟨to be a drain on : agotar, consumir⟩ **5 to throw down the drain** : tirar por la ventana

drainage ['dreɪnɪʤ] *n* : desagüe *m*, drenaje *m*

drainpipe ['dreɪn,paɪp] *n* : tubo *m* de desagüe, caño *m*

drake ['dreɪk] *n* : pato *m* (macho)

drama ['drɑmə, 'dræ-] *n* **1** THEATER : drama *m*, teatro *m* **2** PLAY : obra *f* de teatro, drama *m*

dramatic [drə'mætɪk] *adj* : dramático — **dramatically** [-tɪkli] *adv*

dramatist ['dræmətɪst, 'drɑ-] *n* : dramaturgo *m*, -ga *f*

dramatization [,dræmətə'zeɪʃən, ,drɑ-] *n* : dramatización *f*

dramatize ['dræmə,taɪz, 'drɑ-] *vt* **-tized; -tizing** : dramatizar

drank → **drink**

drape¹ ['dreɪp] *vt* **draped; draping 1** COVER : cubrir (con tela) **2** HANG : drapear, disponer los pliegues de

drape² *n* **1** HANG : caída *f* **2 drapes** *npl* : cortinas *fpl*

drapery ['dreɪpəri] *n, pl* **-eries 1** CLOTH : pañería *f*, tela *f* para cortinas **2 draperies** *npl* : cortinas *fpl*

drastic ['dræstɪk] *adj* **1** HARSH, SEVERE : drástico, severo **2** EXTREME : radical, excepcional — **drastically** [-tɪkli] *adv*

draught ['dræft, 'draft] *n* → **draft³**

draughty ['drafti] → **drafty**

draw¹ ['drɔ] *v* **drew** ['dru:]; **drawn** ['drɔn]; **drawing** *vt* **1** PULL : tirar de, jalar, correr (cortinas) **2** ATTRACT : atraer **3** PROVOKE : provocar, suscitar **4** INHALE : aspirar ⟨to draw breath : respirar⟩ **5** EXTRACT : sacar, extraer **6** TAKE : sacar ⟨to draw a number : sacar un número⟩ **7** COLLECT : cobrar, percibir (un sueldo, etc.) **8** BEND : tensar (un arco) **9** TIE : empatar (en deportes) **10** SKETCH : dibujar, trazar **11** FORMULATE : sacar, formular, llegar a ⟨to draw a conclusion : llegar a

una conclusión⟩ **12 to draw out** : hacer hablar (sobre algo), hacer salir de sí mismo **13 to draw up** DRAFT : redactar — *vi* **1** SKETCH : dibujar **2** TUG : tirar, jalar **3 to draw near** : acercarse **4 to draw to a close** : terminar, finalizar **5 to draw up** STOP : parar

draw² *n* **1** DRAWING, RAFFLE : sorteo *m* **2** TIE : empate *m* **3** ATTRACTION : atracción *f* **4** PUFF : chupada *f* (de un cigarrillo, etc.)

drawback ['drɔ,bæk] *n* : desventaja *f*, inconveniente *m*

drawbridge ['drɔ,brɪʤ] *n* : puente *m* levadizo

drawer ['drɔr, 'drɔər] *n* **1** ILLUSTRATOR : dibujante *mf* **2** : gaveta *f*, cajón *m* (en un mueble) **3 drawers** *npl* UNDERPANTS : calzones *mpl*

drawing ['drɔɪŋ] *n* **1** LOTTERY : sorteo *m*, lotería *f* **2** SKETCH : dibujo *m*, bosquejo *m*

drawl¹ ['drɔl] *vi* : hablar arrastrando las palabras

drawl² *n* : habla *f* lenta y con vocales prolongadas

dread¹ ['drɛd] *vt* : tenerle pavor a, temer

dread² *adj* : pavoroso, aterrado

dread³ *n* : pavor *m*, temor *m*

dreadful ['drɛdfəl] *adj* **1** DREAD : pavoroso **2** TERRIBLE : espantoso, atroz, terrible — **dreadfully** *adv*

dream¹ ['dri:m] *v* **dreamed** ['drɛmpt, 'dri:md] *or* **dreamt** ['drɛmpt]; **dreaming** *vi* : soñar ⟨to dream about : soñar con⟩ **2** FANTASIZE : fantasear — *vt* **1** : soñar **2** IMAGINE : imaginarse **3 to dream up** : inventar, idear

dream² *n* **1** : sueño *m*, ensueño *m* **2 bad dream** NIGHTMARE : pesadilla *f*

dreamer ['dri:mər] *n* : soñador *m*, -dora *f*

dreamlike ['dri:m,laɪk] *adj* : de ensueño

dreamy ['dri:mi] *adj* **dreamier; -est 1** DISTRACTED : soñador, distraído **2** DREAMLIKE : de ensueño **3** MARVELOUS : maravilloso

drearily ['drɪrəli] *adv* : sombríamente

dreary ['drɪri] *adj* **-rier; -est** : deprimente, lóbrego, sombrío

dredge¹ ['drɛʤ] *vt* **dredged; dredging 1** DIG : dragar **2** COAT : espolvorear, enharinar

dredge² *n* : draga *f*

dredger ['drɛʤər] *n* : draga *f*

dregs ['drɛgz] *npl* **1** LEES : posos *mpl*, heces *fpl* (de un líquido) **2** : heces *fpl*, escoria *f* ⟨the dregs of society : la escoria de la sociedad⟩

drench ['drɛnʧ] *vt* : empapar, mojar, calar

dress¹ ['drɛs] *vt* **1** CLOTHE : vestir **2** DECORATE : decorar, adornar **3** : preparar (pollo o pescado), aliñar (ensalada) **4** : curar, vendar (una herida) **5** FERTILIZE : abonar (la tierra) — *vi* **1** : vestirse **2 to dress up** : ataviarse, engalanarse, ponerse de etiqueta

dress² *n* **1** APPAREL : indumentaria *f*, ropa *f* **2** : vestido *m*, traje *m* (de mujer)

dresser ['drɛsər] *n* : cómoda *f* con espejo

dressing ['drɛsɪŋ] *n* **1** : vestirse *m* **2** : aderezo *m*, aliño *m* (de ensalada), relleno *m* (de pollo) **3** BANDAGE : vendaje *m*, gasa *f*

dressmaker ['drɛs,meɪkər] *n* : modista *mf*

dressmaking ['drɛs,meɪkɪŋ] *n* : costura *f*

dressy ['drɛsi] *adj* **dressier; -est** : de mucho vestir, elegante

drew → **draw**

dribble¹ ['drɪbəl] *vi* **-bled; -bling 1** DRIP : gotear **2** DROOL : babear **3** : driblar (en basquetbol)

dribble² *n* **1** TRICKLE : goteo *m*, hilo *m* **2** DROOL : baba *f* **3** : drible *m* (en basquetbol)

drier → **dry², dryer**

driest *adj* → **dry²**

drift¹ ['drɪft] *vi* **1** : dejarse llevar por la corriente, ir a la deriva (dícese de un bote), ir sin rumbo (dícese de una persona) **2** ACCUMULATE : amontonarse, acumularse, apilarse

drift² *n* **1** DRIFTING : deriva *f* **2** HEAP, MASS : montón *m* (de arena, etc.), ventisquero *m* (de nieve) **3** MEANING : sentido *m*

drifter ['drɪftər] *n* : vagabundo *m*, -da *f*

driftwood ['drɪft,wʊd] *n* : madera *f* flotante

drill¹ ['drɪl] *vt* **1** BORE : perforar, taladrar **2** INSTRUCT : instruir por repetición — *vi* **1** TRAIN : entrenarse **2 to drill for oil** : perforar en busca de petróleo

drill² *n* **1** : taladro *m*, barrena *f* **2** EXERCISE, PRACTICE : ejercicio *m*, instrucción *f*

drily → **dryly**

drink¹ ['drɪŋk] *v* **drank** ['dræŋk]; **drunk** ['drʌŋk] *or* **drank; drinking** *vt* **1** IMBIBE : beber, tomar **2 to drink up** ABSORB : absorber — *vi* **1** : beber **2** : beber alcohol, tomar

drink² *n* **1** : bebida *f* **2** : bebida *f* alcohólica

drinkable ['drɪŋkəbəl] *adj* : potable

drinker ['drɪŋkər] *n* : bebedor *m*, -dora *f*

drip¹ ['drɪp] *vi* **dripped; dripping** : gotear, chorrear

drip² *n* **1** DROP : gota *f* **2** DRIPPING : goteo *m*

drive¹ ['draɪv] *v* **drove** ['droːv]; **driven** ['drɪvən]; **driving** *vt* **1** IMPEL : impeler, impulsar **2** OPERATE : guiar, conducir, manejar (un vehículo) **3** COMPEL : obligar, forzar **4** : clavar, hincar ⟨to drive a stake : clavar una estaca⟩ **5** *or* **to drive away** : ahuyentar, echar **6 to drive crazy** : volver loco — *vi* : manejar, conducir ⟨do you know how to drive? : ¿sabes manejar?⟩

drive² *n* **1** RIDE : paseo *m* en coche **2** CAMPAIGN : campaña *f* ⟨fund-raising drive : campaña para recaudar fondos⟩ **3** DRIVEWAY : camino *m* de entrada, entrada *f* **4** TRANSMISSION : transmisión *f* ⟨front-wheel drive : tracción delantera⟩ **5** ENERGY : dinamismo *m*, energía *f* **6** INSTINCT, NEED : instinto *m*, necesidad *f* básica **7** → **disk drive**

drivel ['drɪvəl] *n* : tontería *f*, estupidez *f*

driver ['draɪvər] *n* : conductor *m*, -tora *f*; chofer *m*

driveway ['draɪv,weɪ] *n* : camino *m* de entrada, entrada *f* (para coches)

drizzle¹ ['drɪzəl] *vi* **-zled; -zling** : lloviznar, garuar

drizzle² *n* : llovizna *f*, garúa *f*

droll ['droːl] *adj* : cómico, gracioso, chistoso — **drolly** *adv*

dromedary ['drɑmə,dɛri] *n*, *pl* **-daries** : dromedario *m*

drone¹ ['droːn] *vi* **droned; droning 1** BUZZ : zumbar **2** MURMUR : hablar con monotonía, murmurar

drone² *n* **1** : zángano *m* (abeja) **2** FREELOADER : gorrón *m*, -rrona *f fam*; parásito *m*, -ta *f* **3** BUZZ, HUM : zumbido *m*, murmullo *m*

drool¹ ['druːl] *vi* : babear

drool² *n* : baba *f*

droop¹ ['druːp] *vi* **1** HANG : inclinarse (dícese de la cabeza), encorvarse (dícese de los escombros), marchitarse (dícese de las flores) **2** FLAG : decaer, flaquear ⟨his spirits drooped : se desanimó⟩

droop² *n* : inclinación *f*, caída *f*

drop¹ ['drɑp] *v* **dropped; dropping** *vt* **1** : dejar caer, soltar ⟨she dropped the glass : se le cayó el vaso⟩ ⟨to drop a hint : dejar caer una indirecta⟩ **2** SEND : mandar ⟨drop me a line : mándame unas líneas⟩ **3** ABANDON : abandonar, dejar ⟨to drop the subject : cambiar de tema⟩ **4** LOWER : bajar ⟨he dropped his voice : bajó la voz⟩ **5** OMIT : omitir **6 to drop off** : dejar — *vi* **1** DRIP : gotear **2** FALL : caer(se) **3** DECREASE, DESCEND : bajar, descender ⟨the wind dropped : amainó el viento⟩ **4 to drop back** *or* **to drop behind** : rezagarse, quedarse atrás **5 to drop by** *or* **to drop in** : pasar

drop² *n* **1** : gota *f* (de líquido) **2** DECLINE : caída *f*, bajada *f*, descenso *m* **3** INCLINE : caída *f*, pendiente *f* ⟨a 20-foot drop : una caída de 20 pies⟩ **4** SWEET : pastilla *f*, dulce *m* **5 drops** *npl* : gotas *fpl* (de medicina)

droplet ['drɑplət] *n* : gotita *f*

dropper ['drɑpər] *n* : gotero *m*, cuentagotas *m*

dross ['drɑs, 'drɔs] *n* : escoria *f*

drought ['draʊt] *n* : sequía *f*

drove¹ → **drive**

drove² ['droːv] *n* : multitud *f*, gentío *m*, manada *f* (de ganado) ⟨in droves : en manada⟩

drown ['draʊn] *vt* **1** : ahogar **2** INUN-DATE : anegar, inundar **3 to drown out** : ahogar — *vi* : ahogarse
drowse[1] ['draʊz] *vi* **drowsed; drowsing** DOZE : dormitar
drowse[2] *n* : sueño *m* ligero, cabezada *f*
drowsiness ['draʊzinəs] *n* : somnolencia *f*, adormecimiento *m*
drowsy ['draʊzi] *adj* **drowsier; -est** : somnoliento, soñoliento
drub ['drʌb] *vt* **drubbed; drubbing 1** BEAT, THRASH : golpear, apalear **2** DEFEAT : derrotar por completo
drudge[1] ['drʌdʒ] *vi* **drudged; drudging** : trabajar como esclavo, trabajar duro
drudge[2] *n* : esclavo *m*, -va *f* del trabajo
drudgery ['drʌdʒəri] *n, pl* **-eries** : trabajo *m* pesado
drug[1] ['drʌg] *vt* **drugged; drugging** : drogar, narcotizar
drug[2] *n* **1** MEDICATION : droga *f*, medicina *f*, medicamento *m* **2** NARCOTIC : narcótico *m*, estupefaciente *m*, droga *f*
druggist ['drʌgɪst] *n* : farmacéutico *m*, -ca *f*
drugstore ['drʌg,stor] *n* : farmacia *f*, botica *f*, droguería *f*
drum[1] ['drʌm] *v* **drummed; drumming** *vt* : meter a fuerza ⟨he drummed it into my head : me lo metió en la cabeza a fuerza⟩ — *vi* : tocar el tambor
drum[2] *n* **1** : tambor *m* **2** : bidón *m* ⟨oil drum : bidón de petróleo⟩
drummer ['drʌmər] *n* : baterista *mf*
drumstick ['drʌm,stɪk] *n* **1** : palillo *m* (de tambor), baqueta *f* **2** : muslo *m* de pollo
drunk[1] *pp* → **drink**[1]
drunk[2] ['drʌŋk] *adj* : borracho, embriagado, ebrio
drunk[3] *n* : borracho *m*, -cha *f*
drunkard ['drʌŋkərd] *n* : borracho *m*, -cha *f*
drunken ['drʌŋkən] *adj* : borracho, ebrio ⟨drunken driver : conductor ebrio⟩ ⟨drunken brawl : pleito de borrachos⟩
drunkenly ['drʌŋkənli] *adv* : como un borracho
drunkenness ['drʌŋkənnəs] *n* : borrachera *f*, embriaguez *f*, ebriedad *f*
dry[1] ['draɪ] *v* **dried; drying** *vt* : secar — *vi* : secarse
dry[2] *adj* **drier; driest 1** : seco **2** THIRSTY : sediento **3** : donde la venta de bebidas alcohólicas está prohibida ⟨a dry county : un condado seco⟩ **4** DULL : aburrido, árido **5** : seco (dícese del vino), brut (dícese de la champaña)
dry–clean ['draɪ,kliːn] *v* : limpiar en seco
dry cleaner *n* : tintorería *f* (servicio)
dry cleaning *n* : limpieza *f* en seco
dryer ['draɪər] *n* **1 hair dryer** : secador *m* **2 clothes dryer** : secadora *f*
dry goods *npl* : artículos *mpl* de confección
dry ice *n* : hielo *m* seco

dryly ['draɪli] *adv* : secamente
dryness ['draɪnəs] *n* : sequedad *f*, aridez *f*
dual ['duːəl, 'djuː-] *adj* : doble
dualism ['duːə,lɪzəm] *n* : dualismo *m*
dub ['dʌb] *vt* **dubbed; dubbing 1** CALL : apodar **2** : doblar (una película), mezclar (una grabación)
dubious ['duːbiəs, 'djuː-] *adj* **1** UNCERTAIN : dudoso, indeciso **2** QUESTIONABLE : sospechoso, dudoso, discutible
dubiously ['duːbiəsli, 'djuː-] *adv* **1** UNCERTAINLY : dudosamente, con desconfianza **2** SUSPICIOUSLY : de modo sospechoso, con recelo
duchess ['dʌtʃəs] *n* : duquesa *f*
duck[1] ['dʌk] *vt* **1** LOWER : agachar, bajar (la cabeza) **2** PLUNGE : zambullir **3** EVADE : eludir, evadir — *vi* **to duck down** : agacharse
duck[2] *n, pl* **duck** *or* **ducks** : pato *m*, -ta *f*
duckling ['dʌklɪŋ] *n* : patito *m*, -ta *f*
duct ['dʌkt] *n* : conducto *m*
ductile ['dʌktəl] *adj* : dúctil
dude ['duːd, 'djuːd] *n* **1** DANDY : dandi *m*, dandy *m* **2** GUY : tipo *m*
due[1] ['duː, 'djuː] *adv* : justo a, derecho hacia ⟨due north : derecho hacia el norte⟩
due[2] *adj* **1** PAYABLE : pagadero, sin pagar **2** APPROPRIATE : debido, apropiado ⟨after due consideration : con las debidas consideraciones⟩ **3** EXPECTED : esperado ⟨the train is due soon : esperamos el tren muy pronto, el tren debe llegar pronto⟩ **4 due to** : debido a, por
due[3] *n* **1 to give someone his (her) due** : darle a alguien su merecido **2 dues** *npl* : cuota *f*
duel[1] ['duːəl, 'djuː-] *vi* : batirse en duelo
duel[2] *n* : duelo *m*
duet [duˈɛt, djuː-] *n* : dúo *m*
due to *prep* : debido a
dug → **dig**
dugout ['dʌg,aʊt] *n* **1** CANOE : piragua *f* **2** SHELTER : refugio *m* subterráneo
duke ['duːk, 'djuːk] *n* : duque *m*
dull[1] ['dʌl] *vt* **1** DIM : opacar, quitar el brillo a, deslustrar **2** BLUNT : embotar (un filo), entorpecer (los sentidos), aliviar (el dolor), amortiguar (sonidos)
dull[2] *adj* **1** STUPID : torpe, lerdo, lento **2** BLUNT : desafilado, despuntado **3** LACKLUSTER : sin brillo, deslustrado **4** BORING : aburrido, soso, pesado — **dully** *adv*
dullness ['dʌlnəs] *n* **1** STUPIDITY : estupidez *f* **2** : embotamiento *m* (de los sentidos) **3** MONOTONY : monotonía *f*, insipidez *f* **4** : falta *f* de brillo **5** BLUNTNESS : falta *f* de filo, embotadura *f*
duly ['duːli, 'djuː-] *adv* PROPERLY : debidamente, a su debido tiempo
dumb ['dʌm] *adj* **1** MUTE : mudo **2** STUPID : estúpido, tonto, bobo — **dumbly** *adv*

dumbbell ['dʌm,bɛl] *n* **1** WEIGHT : pesa *f* **2** : estúpido *m*, -da *f*
dumbfound *or* **dumfound** [,dʌm-'faʊnd] *vt* : dejar atónito, dejar sin habla
dummy ['dʌmi] *n, pl* **-mies 1** SHAM : imitación *f*, sustituto *m* **2** PUPPET : muñeco *m* **3** MANNEQUIN : maniquí *m* **4** IDIOT : tonto *m*, -ta *f*; idiota *mf*
dump¹ ['dʌmp] *vt* : descargar, verter
dump² *n* **1** : vertedero *m*, tiradero *m* *Mex* **2 down in the dumps** : triste, deprimido
dumpling ['dʌmplɪŋ] *n* : bola *f* de masa hervida
dumpy ['dʌmpi] *adj* **dumpier; -est** : rechoncho, regordete
dun¹ ['dʌn] *vt* **dunned; dunning** : apremiar (a un deudor)
dun² *adj* : pardo (color)
dunce ['dʌnts] *n* : estúpido *m*, -da *f*; burro *m*, -rra *f fam*
dune ['du:n, 'dju:n] *n* : duna *f*
dung ['dʌŋ] *n* **1** FECES : excrementos *mpl* **2** MANURE : estiércol *m*
dungaree [,dʌŋɡə'ri:] *n* **1** DENIM : tela *f* vaquera, mezclilla *f Chile, Mex* **2 dungarees** *npl* : pantalones *mpl* de trabajo hechos de tela vaquera
dungeon ['dʌndʒən] *n* : mazmorra *f*, calabozo *m*
dunk ['dʌŋk] *vt* : mojar, ensopar
duo ['du:o:, 'dju:-] *n, pl* **duos** : dúo *m*, par *m*
dupe¹ ['du:p, dju:p] *vt* **duped; duping** : engañar, embaucar
dupe² *n* : inocentón *m*, -tona *f*; simple *mf*
duplex¹ ['du:,plɛks, 'dju:-] *adj* : doble
duplex² *n* : casa *f* de dos viviendas, dúplex *m*
duplicate¹ ['du:plɪ,keɪt, 'dju:-] *vt* **-cated; -cating 1** COPY : duplicar, hacer copias de **2** REPEAT : repetir, reproducir
duplicate² ['du:plɪkət, 'dju:-] *adj* : duplicado ⟨a duplicate invoice : una factura por duplicado⟩
duplicate³ ['du:plɪkət, 'dju:-] *n* : duplicado *m*, copia *f*
duplication [,du:plɪ'keɪʃən, ,dju:-] *n* **1** DUPLICATING : duplicación *f*, repetición *f* (de esfuerzos) **2** DUPLICATE : copia *f*, duplicado *m*
duplicity [du'plɪsəti, ,dju:-] *n, pl* **-ties** : duplicidad *f*
durability [,dʊrə'bɪləti, ,djʊr-] *n* : durabilidad *f* (de un producto) permanencia *f*
durable ['dʊrəbəl, 'djʊr] *adj* : duradero
duration [dʊ'reɪʃən, djʊ-] *n* : duración *f*
duress [dʊ'rɛs, dju-] *n* : coacción *f*

during ['dʊrɪŋ, 'djʊr-] *prep* : durante
dusk ['dʌsk] *n* : anochecer *m*, crepúsculo *m*
dusky ['dʌski] *adj* **duskier; -est** : oscuro (dícese de los colores)
dust¹ ['dʌst] *vt* **1** : quitar el polvo de **2** SPRINKLE : espolvorear
dust² *n* : polvo *m*
duster ['dʌstər] *n* **1** *or* **dust cloth** : trapo *m* de polvo **2** HOUSECOAT : guardapolvo *m* **3 feather duster** : plumero *m*
dustpan ['dʌst,pæn] *n* : recogedor *m*
dusty ['dʌsti] *adj* **dustier; -est** : cubierto de polvo, polvoriento
Dutch¹ ['dʌtʃ] *adj* : holandés
Dutch² *n* **1** : holandés *m* (idioma) **2 the Dutch** *npl* : los holandeses
Dutch treat *n* : invitación o pago a escote
dutiful ['du:tɪfəl, 'dju:-] *adj* : motivado por sus deberes, responsable
duty ['du:ti, 'dju:-] *n, pl* **-ties 1** OBLIGATION : deber *m*, obligación *f*, responsabilidad *f* **2** TAX : impuesto *m*, arancel *m*
DVD [,di:,vi:'di:] *n* : DVD *m*
dwarf¹ ['dwɔrf] *vt* **1** STUNT : arrestar el crecimiento de **2** : hacer parecer pequeño
dwarf² *n, pl* **dwarfs** ['dwɔrfs] *or* **dwarves** ['dwɔrvz] : enano *m*, -na *f*
dwell ['dwɛl] *vi* **dwelled** *or* **dwelt** ['dwɛlt]; **dwelling 1** RESIDE : residir, morar, vivir **2 to dwell on** : pensar demasiado en, insistir en
dweller ['dwɛlər] *n* : habitante *mf*
dwelling ['dwɛlɪŋ] *n* : morada *f*, vivienda *f*, residencia *f*
dwindle ['dwɪndəl] *vi* **-dled; -dling** : menguar, reducirse, disminuir
dye¹ ['daɪ] *vt* **dyed; dyeing** : teñir
dye² *n* : tintura *f*, tinte *m*
dying → **die**
dyke → **dike**
dynamic [daɪ'næmɪk] *adj* : dinámico
dynamics [daɪ'næmɪks] *npl* : dinámica *f*
dynamite¹ ['daɪnə,maɪt] *vt* **-mited; -miting** : dinamitar
dynamite² *n* : dinamita *f*
dynamo ['daɪnə,mo:] *n, pl* **-mos** : dínamo *m*, generador *m* de electricidad
dynasty ['daɪnəsti, -,næs-] *n, pl* **-ties** : dinastía *f*
dysentery ['dɪsən,tɛri] *n, pl* **-teries** : disentería *f*
dysfunction [dɪs'fʌŋkʃən] *n* : disfunción *f*
dystrophy ['dɪstrəfi] *n, pl* **-phies 1** : distrofia *f* **2** → **muscular dystrophy**

E

e [ˈiː] *n, pl* **e's** *or* **es** [ˈiːz] : quinta letra del alfabeto inglés

each¹ [ˈiːtʃ] *adv* : cada uno, por persona ⟨they cost $10 each : costaron $10 cada uno⟩

each² *adj* : cada ⟨each student : cada estudiante⟩ ⟨each and every one : todos sin excepción⟩

each³ *pron* **1** : cada uno *m*, cada una *f* ⟨each of us : cada uno de nosotros⟩ **2 each other** : el uno al otro, mutuamente ⟨we are helping each other : nos ayudamos el uno al otro⟩ ⟨they love each other : se aman⟩

eager [ˈiːgər] *adj* **1** ENTHUSIASTIC : entusiasta, ávido, deseoso **2** ANXIOUS : ansioso, impaciente

eagerly [ˈiːgərli] *adv* : con entusiasmo, ansiosamente

eagerness [ˈiːgərnəs] *n* : entusiasmo *m*, deseo *m*, impaciencia *f*

eagle [ˈiːgəl] *n* : águila *f*

ear [ˈɪr] *n* **1** : oído *m*, oreja *f* ⟨inner ear : oído interno⟩ ⟨big ears : orejas grandes⟩ **2 ear of corn** : mazorca *f*, choclo *m*

earache [ˈɪr,eɪk] *n* : dolor *m* de oído

eardrum [ˈɪr,drʌm] *n* : tímpano *m*

earl [ˈərl] *n* : conde *m*

earlobe [ˈɪr,loːb] *n* : lóbulo *m* de la oreja, perilla *f* de la oreja

early¹ [ˈərli] *adv* **earlier; -est** : temprano, pronto ⟨he arrived early : llegó temprano⟩ ⟨as early as possible : lo más pronto posible, cuanto antes⟩ ⟨ten minutes early : diez minutos de adelanto⟩

early² *adj* **earlier; -est 1** (*referring to a beginning*) : primero ⟨the early stages : las primeras etapas⟩ ⟨in early May : a principios de mayo⟩ **2** (*referring to antiquity*) : primitivo, antiguo ⟨early man : el hombre primitivo⟩ ⟨early painting : la pintura antigua⟩ **3** (*referring to a designated time*) : temprano, antes de la hora, prematuro ⟨he was early : llegó temprano⟩ ⟨early fruit : frutas tempraneras⟩ ⟨an early death : una muerte prematura⟩

earmark [ˈɪr,mɑrk] *vt* : destinar ⟨earmarked funds : fondos destinados⟩

earn [ˈərn] *vt* **1** : ganar ⟨to earn money : ganar dinero⟩ **2** DESERVE : ganarse, merecer

earnest¹ [ˈərnəst] *adj* : serio, sincero

earnest² *n* **in ~** : en serio, de verdad ⟨we began in earnest : empezamos en verdad⟩

earnestly [ˈərnəstli] *adv* **1** SERIOUSLY : con seriedad, en serio **2** FERVENTLY : de todo corazón

earnestness [ˈərnəstnəs] *n* : seriedad *f*, sinceridad *f*

earnings [ˈərnɪŋz] *npl* : ingresos *mpl*, ganancias *fpl*, utilidades *fpl*

earphone [ˈɪr,foːn] *n* : audífono *m*

earring [ˈɪr,rɪŋ] *n* : zarcillo *m*, arete *m*, aro *m* *Arg, Chile, Uru*, pendiente *m* *Spain*

earshot [ˈɪr,ʃɑt] *n* : alcance *m* del oído

earth [ˈərθ] *n* **1** LAND, SOIL : tierra *f*, suelo *m* **2 the Earth** : la Tierra

earthen [ˈərθən, -ðən] *adj* : de tierra, de barro

earthenware [ˈərθən,wær, -ðən-] *n* : loza *f*, vajillas *fpl* de barro

earthly [ˈərθli] *adj* : terrenal, mundano

earthquake [ˈərθ,kweɪk] *n* : terremoto *m*, temblor *m*

earthworm [ˈərθ,wərm] *n* : lombriz *f* (de tierra)

earthy [ˈərθi] *adj* **earthier; -est 1** : terroso ⟨earthy colors : colores terrosos⟩ **2** DOWN-TO-EARTH : realista, práctico, llano **3** COARSE, CRUDE : basto, grosero, tosco ⟨earthy jokes : chistes groseros⟩

earwax [ˈɪr,wæks] *n* → **wax²**

earwig [ˈɪr,wɪg] *n* : tijereta *f*

ease¹ [ˈiːz] *v* **eased; easing** *vt* **1** ALLEVIATE : aliviar, calmar, hacer disminuir **2** LOOSEN, RELAX : aflojar (una cuerda), relajar (restricciones), descargar (tensiones) **3** FACILITATE : facilitar — *vi* : calmarse, relajarse

ease² *n* **1** CALM, RELIEF : tranquilidad *f*, comodidad *f*, desahogo *m* **2** FACILITY : facilidad *f* **3 at ~** : relajado, cómodo ⟨to put someone at ease : tranquilizar a alguien⟩

easel [ˈiːzəl] *n* : caballete *m*

easily [ˈiːzəli] *adv* **1** : fácilmente, con facilidad **2** UNQUESTIONABLY : con mucho, de lejos

easiness [ˈiːzinəs] *n* : facilidad *f*, soltura *f*

east¹ [ˈiːst] *adv* : al este

east² *adj* : este, del este, oriental ⟨east winds : vientos del este⟩

east³ *n* **1** : este *m* **2 the East** : el Oriente

Easter [ˈiːstər] *n* : Pascua *f* (de Resurrección)

easterly [ˈiːstərli] *adv & adj* : del este

eastern [ˈiːstərn] *adj* **1** : Oriental, del Este ⟨Eastern Europe : Europa del Este⟩ **2** : oriental, este

Easterner [ˈiːstərnər] *n* : habitante *mf* del este

eastward [ˈiːstwərd] *adv & adj* : hacia el este

easy [ˈiːzi] *adj* **easier; -est 1** : fácil **2** LENIENT : indulgente

easygoing [ˌiːziˈgoːɪŋ] *adj* : acomodaticio, tolerante, poco exigente

eat [ˈiːt] *v* **ate** [ˈeɪt]; **eaten** [ˈiːtən]; **eating** *vt* **1** : comer **2** CONSUME : consumir, gastar, devorar ⟨expenses ate up profits : los gastos devoraron las ganancias⟩ **3** CORRODE : corroer — *vi* **1** : comer **2 to eat away at** *or* **to eat into** : comerse **3 to eat out** : comer fuera

eatable[1] ['i:t̬əbəl] *adj* : comestible, comible *fam*
eatable[2] *n* **1** : algo para comer **2 eatables** *npl* : comestibles *mpl*, alimentos *mpl*
eater ['i:t̬ər] *n* : comedor *m*, -dora *f*
eaves ['i:vz] *npl* : alero *m*
eavesdrop ['i:vz̩drɑp] *vi* **-dropped; -dropping** : escuchar a escondidas
eavesdropper ['i:vz̩drɑpər] *n* : persona *f* que escucha a escondidas
ebb[1] ['ɛb] *vi* **1** : bajar, menguar (dícese de la marea) **2 DECLINE** : decaer, disminuir
ebb[2] *n* **1** : reflujo *m* (de una marea) **2 DECLINE** : decadencia *f*, declive *m*, disminución *f*
ebony[1] ['ɛbəni] *adj* **1** : de ébano **2 BLACK** : de color ébano, negro
ebony[2] *n*, *pl* **-nies** : ébano *m*
ebullience [ɪ'bʊljənts, -'bʌl-] *n* : efervescencia *f*, vivacidad *f*
ebullient [ɪ'bʊljənt, -'bʌl-] *adj* : efervescente, vivaz
eccentric[1] [ɪk'sɛntrɪk] *adj* **1** : excéntrico ⟨an eccentric wheel : una rueda excéntrica⟩ **2 ODD, SINGULAR** : excéntrico, extraño, raro — **eccentrically** [-trɪkli] *adv*
eccentric[2] *n* : excéntrico *m*, -ca *f*
eccentricity [ˌkˌsen'trɪsət̬i] *n*, *pl* **-ties** : excentricidad *f*
ecclesiastic [ɪˌkli:zi'æstɪk] *n* : eclesiástico *m*, clérigo *m*
ecclesiastical [ɪˌkli:zi'æstɪkəl] *or* **ecclesiastic** *adj* : eclesiástico — **ecclesiastically** *adv*
echelon ['ɛʃəˌlɑn] *n* **1** : escalón *m* (de tropas o aviones) **2 LEVEL** : nivel *m*, esfera *f*, estrato *m*
echo[1] ['ɛˌko:] *v* **echoed; echoing** *vi* : hacer eco, resonar — *vt* : repetir
echo[2] *n*, *pl* **echoes** : eco *m*
éclair [eɪ'klær, i-] *n* : pastel *m* relleno de crema
eclectic [ɛ'klɛktɪk, ɪ-] *adj* : ecléctico
eclipse[1] [ɪ'klɪps] *vt* **eclipsed; eclipsing** : eclipsar
eclipse[2] *n* : eclipse *m*
ecological [ˌi:kə'lɑdʒɪkəl, ˌɛkə-] *adj* : ecológico — **ecologically** *adv*
ecologist [i'kɑlədʒɪst, ɛ-] *n* : ecólogo *m*, -ga *f*
ecology [i'kɑlədʒi, ɛ-] *n*, *pl* **-gies** : ecología *f*
economic [ˌi:kə'nɑmɪk, ˌɛkə-] *adj* : económico
economical [ˌi:kə'nɑmɪkəl, ˌɛkə-] *adj* : económico — **economically** *adv*
economics [ˌi:kə'nɑmɪks, ˌɛkə-] *n* : economía *f*
economist [i'kɑnəmɪst] *n* : economista *mf*
economize [i'kɑnəˌmaɪz] *v* **-mized; -mizing** : economizar, ahorrar
economy [i'kɑnəmi] *n*, *pl* **-mies** **1** : economía *f*, sistema *m* económico **2 THRIFT** : economía *f*, ahorro *m*

ecosystem ['i:koˌsɪstəm] *n* : ecosistema *m*
ecru ['ɛˌkru:, 'eɪ-] *n* : color *m* crudo
ecstasy ['ɛkstəsi] *n*, *pl* **-sies** : éxtasis *m*
ecstatic [ɛk'stæt̬ɪk, ɪk-] *adj* : extático
ecstatically [ɛk'stæt̬ɪkli, ɪk-] *adv* : con éxtasis, con gran entusiasmo
Ecuadoran [ˌɛkwə'dorən] *or* **Ecuadorean** *or* **Ecuadorian** [-'dorian] *n* : ecuatoriano *m*, -na *f* — **Ecuadorean** *or* **Ecuadorian** *adj*
ecumenical [ˌɛkju'mnɪkəl] *adj* : ecuménico
eczema [ɪg'zi:mə, 'ɛgzəmə, 'ɛksə-] *n* : eczema *m*
eddy[1] ['ɛdi] *vi* **eddied; eddying** : arremolinarse, hacer remolinos
eddy[2] *n*, *pl* **-dies** : remolino *m*
edema [ɪ'di:mə] *n* : edema *m*
Eden ['i:dən] *n* : Edén *m*
edge[1] ['ɛdʒ] *v* **edged; edging** *vt* **1 BORDER** : bordear, ribetear, orlar **2 SHARPEN** : afilar, aguzar **3** *or* **to edge one's way** : avanzar poco a poco **4 to edge out** : derrotar por muy poco — *vi* **ADVANCE** : ir avanzando (poco a poco)
edge[2] *n* **1** : filo *m* (de un cuchillo) **2 BORDER** : borde *m*, orilla *f*, margen *m* **3 ADVANTAGE** : ventaja *f*
edger ['ɛdʒər] *n* : cortabordes *m*
edgewise ['ɛdʒˌwaɪz] *adv* **SIDEWAYS** : de lado, de canto
edginess ['ɛdʒinəs] *n* : tensión *f*, nerviosismo *m*
edgy ['ɛdʒi] *adj* **edgier; -est** : tenso, nervioso
edible ['ɛdəbəl] *adj* : comestible
edict ['i:ˌdɪkt] *n* : edicto *m*, mandato *m*, orden *f*
edification [ˌɛdəfə'keɪʃən] *n* : edificación *f*, instrucción *f*
edifice ['ɛdəfɪs] *n* : edificio *m*
edify ['ɛdəˌfaɪ] *vt* **-fied; -fying** : edificar
edit ['ɛdɪt] *vt* **1** : editar, redactar, corregir **2** *or* **to edit out DELETE** : recortar, cortar
edition [ɪ'dɪʃən] *n* : edición *f*
editor ['ɛdɪt̬ər] *n* : editor *m*, -tora *f*; redactor *m*, -tora *f*
editorial[1] [ˌɛdɪ'toriəl] *adj* **1** : de redacción **2** : editorial ⟨an editorial comment : un comentario editorial⟩
editorial[2] *n* : editorial *m*
editorship ['ɛdət̬ərˌʃɪp] *n* : dirección *f*
educable ['ɛdʒəkəbəl] *adj* : educable
educate ['ɛdʒəˌkeɪt] *vt* **-cated; -cating** **1 TEACH** : educar, enseñar **2 INSTRUCT** : formar, educar, instruir **3 INFORM** : informar, concientizar
education [ˌɛdʒə'keɪʃən] *n* : educación *f*
educational [ˌɛdʒə'keɪʃənəl] *adj* **1** : docente, de enseñanza ⟨an educational institution : una institución docente⟩ **2 PEDAGOGICAL** : pedagógico **3 INSTRUCTIONAL** : educativo, instructivo
educator ['ɛdʒəˌkeɪt̬ər] *n* : educador *m*, -dora *f*
eel ['i:l] *n* : anguila *f*

eerie ['ɪri] *adj* **-rier; -est 1** SPOOKY : que da miedo, espeluznante **2** GHOSTLY : fantasmagórico

eerily ['ɪrəli] *adv* : de manera extraña y misteriosa

efface [ɪ'feɪs, -] *vt* **-faced; -facing** : borrar

effect[1] [ɪ'fɛkt] *vt* **1** CARRY OUT : efectuar, llevar a cabo **2** ACHIEVE : lograr, realizar

effect[2] *n* **1** RESULT : efecto *m*, resultado *m*, consecuencia *f* ⟨to no effect : sin resultado⟩ **2** MEANING : sentido *m* ⟨something to that effect : algo por el estilo⟩ **3** INFLUENCE : efecto *m*, influencia *f* **4 effects** *npl* BELONGINGS : efectos *mpl*, pertenencias *fpl* **5 to go into effect** : entrar en vigor **6 in ~** REALLY : en realidad, efectivamente

effective [ɪ'fɛktɪv] *adj* **1** EFFECTUAL : efectivo, eficaz **2** OPERATIVE : vigente — **effectively** *adv*

effectiveness [ɪ'fɛktɪvnəs] *n* : eficacia *f*, efectividad *f*

effectual [ɪ'fɛktʃʊəl] *adj* : eficaz, efectivo — **effectually** *adv*

effeminate [ə'fɛmənət] *adj* : afeminado

effervesce [ˌɛfər'vɛs] *vi* **-vesced; -vescing 1** : estar en efervescencia, burbujear (dícese de líquidos) **2** : estar eufórico, estar muy animado (dícese de las personas)

effervescence [ˌɛfər'vɛsənts] *n* **1** : efervescencia *f* **2** LIVELINESS : vivacidad *f*

effervescent [ˌɛfər'vɛsənt] *adj* **1** : efervescente **2** LIVELY, VIVACIOUS : vivaz, animado

effete ['ɛfiːt, ɪ-] *adj* **1** WORN-OUT : desgastado, agotado **2** DECADENT : decadente **3** EFFEMINATE : afeminado

efficacious [ˌɛfə'keɪʃəs] *adj* : eficaz, efectivo

efficacy ['ɛfɪkəsi] *n, pl* **-cies** : eficacia *f*

efficiency [ɪ'fɪʃəntsi] *n, pl* **-cies** : eficiencia *f*

efficient [ɪ'fɪʃənt] *adj* : eficiente — **efficiently** *adv*

effigy ['ɛfədʒi] *n, pl* **-gies** : efigie *f*

effluent ['ɛˌfluːənt, ɛ'fluː-] *n* : efluente *m* — **effluent** *adj*

effort ['ɛfərt] *n* **1** EXERTION : esfuerzo *m* **2** ATTEMPT : tentativa *f*, intento *m* ⟨it's not worth the effort : no vale la pena⟩

effortless ['ɛfərtləs] *adj* : fácil, sin esfuerzo

effortlessly ['ɛfərtləsli] *adv* : sin esfuerzo, fácilmente

effrontery [ɪ'frʌntəri] *n, pl* **-teries** : insolencia *f*, desfachatez *f*, descaro *m*

effusion [ɪ'fjuːʒən, ɛ-] *n* : efusión *f*

effusive [ɪ'fjuːsɪv, ɛ-] *adj* : efusivo — **effusively** *adv*

egg[1] ['ɛg] *vt* **to egg on** : incitar, azuzar, provocar

egg[2] *n* **1** : huevo *m* **2** OVUM : óvulo *m*

eggbeater ['ɛgˌbiːtər] *n* : batidor *m* (de huevos)

eggnog ['ɛgˌnɑg] *n* : ponche *m* de huevo, rompope *m* CA, Mex

eggplant ['ɛgˌplænt] *n* : berenjena *f*

eggshell ['ɛgˌʃl] *n* : cascarón *m*

ego ['iːˌgoː] *n, pl* **egos 1** SELF-ESTEEM : amor *m* propio **2** SELF : ego *m*, yo *m*

egocentric [ˌiːgoː'sɛntrɪk] *adj* : egocéntrico

egoism ['iːgoːˌwɪzəm] *n* : egoísmo *m*

egoist ['iːgoːwɪst] *n* : egoísta *mf*

egoistic [ˌiːgoː'wɪstɪk] *adj* : egoísta

egotism ['iːgəˌtɪzəm] *n* : egotismo *m*

egotist ['iːgətɪst] *n* : egotista *mf*

egotistic [ˌiːgə'tɪstɪk] *or* **egotistical** [-'tɪstɪkəl] *adj* : egotista — **egotistically** *adv*

egregious [ɪ'griːdʒəs] *adj* : atroz, flagrante, mayúsculo — **egregiously** *adv*

egress ['iːˌgrɛs] *n* : salida *f*

egret ['iːgrət, -ˌgrɛt] *n* : garceta *f*

Egyptian [ɪ'dʒɪpʃən] *n* **1** : egipcio *m*, -cia *f* **2** : egipcio *m* (idioma) — **Egyptian** *adj*

eiderdown ['aɪdərˌdaʊn] *n* **1** : plumón *m* **2** COMFORTER : edredón *m*

eight[1] ['eɪt] *adj* : ocho

eight[2] *n* : ocho *m*

eight hundred[1] *adj* : ochocientos

eight hundred[2] *n* : ochocientos *m*

eighteen[1] [eɪt'tiːn] *adj* : dieciocho

eighteen[2] *n* : dieciocho *m*

eighteenth[1] [eɪt'tiːnθ] *adj* : decimoctavo

eighteenth[2] *n* **1** : decimoctavo *m*, -va *f* (en una serie) **2** : dieciochoavo *m*, dieciochoava parte *f*

eighth[1] ['eɪtθ] *adj* : octavo

eighth[2] *n* **1** : octavo *m*, -va *f* (en una serie) **2** : octavo *m*, octava parte *f*

eightieth[1] ['eɪtiəθ] *adj* : octogésimo

eightieth[2] *n* **1** : octogésimo *m*, -ma *f* (en una serie) **2** : ochentavo *m*, ochentava parte *f*

eighty[1] ['eɪti] *adj* : ochenta

eighty[2] *n, pl* **eighties 1** : ochenta *m* **2 the eighties** : los ochenta *mpl*

either[1] ['iːðər, 'aɪ-] *adj* **1** : cualquiera (de los dos) ⟨we can watch either movie : podemos ver cualquiera de las dos películas⟩ **2** : ninguno de los dos ⟨she wasn't in either room : no estaba en ninguna de las dos salas⟩ **3** EACH : cada ⟨on either side of the street : a cada lado de la calle⟩

either[2] *pron* **1** : cualquiera *mf* (de los dos) ⟨either is fine : cualquiera de los dos está bien⟩ **2** : ninguno *m*, -na *f* (de los dos) ⟨I don't like either : no me gusta ninguno⟩ **3** : algún *m*, alguna *f* ⟨is either of you interested? : ¿está alguno de ustedes (dos) interesado?⟩

either[3] *conj* **1** : o, u ⟨either David or Daniel could go : puede ir (o) David o Daniel⟩ **2** : ni ⟨we won't watch either this movie or the other : no veremos ni esta película ni la otra⟩

ejaculate [i'dʒækjəˌleɪt] *v* **-lated; -lating** *vt* **1** : eyacular **2** EXCLAIM : exclamar — *vi* : eyacular

ejaculation [i,dʒækjə'leɪʃən] *n* **1** : eyaculación *f* (en fisiología) **2** EXCLAMATION : exclamación *f*

eject [i'dʒɛkt] *vt* : expulsar, expeler

ejection [i'dʒɛkʃən] *n* : expulsión *f*

eke ['i:k] *vt* **eked; eking** *or* **to eke out** : ganar a duras penas

elaborate[1] [i'læbə,reɪt] *v* **-rated; -rating** *vt* : elaborar, idear, desarrollar — *vi* **to elaborate on** : ampliar, entrar en detalles

elaborate[2] [i'læbərət] *adj* **1** DETAILED : detallado, minucioso, elaborado **2** COMPLICATED : complicado, intrincado, elaborado — **elaborately** *adv*

elaboration [i,læbə'reɪʃən] *n* : elaboración *f*

elapse [i'læps] *vi* **elapsed; elapsing** : transcurrir, pasar

elastic[1] [i'læstɪk] *adj* : elástico

elastic[2] *n* **1** : elástico *m* **2** RUBBER BAND : goma *f*, gomita *f*, elástico *m*, liga *f*

elasticity [i,læs'tɪsəti, ,i:,læs-] *n, pl* **-ties** : elasticidad *f*

elate [i'leɪt] *vt* **elated; elating** : alborozar, regocijar

elation [i'leɪʃən] *n* : euforia *f*, júbilo *m*, alborozo *m*

elbow[1] ['ɛl,bo:] *vt* : darle un codazo a

elbow[2] *n* : codo *m*

elder[1] ['ɛldər] *adj* : mayor

elder[2] *n* **1 to be someone's elder** : ser mayor que alguien **2** : anciano *m*, -na *f* (de un pueblo o una tribu) **3** : miembro *m* del consejo (en varias religiones)

elderberry ['ɛldər,bɛri] *n, pl* **-berries** : baya *f* de saúco (fruta), saúco *m* (árbol)

elderly ['ɛldərli] *adj* : mayor, de edad, anciano

eldest ['ɛldəst] *adj* : mayor, de más edad

elect[1] [i'lɛkt] *vt* : elegir

elect[2] *adj* : electo ⟨the president-elect : el presidente electo⟩

elect[3] *npl* **the elect** : los elegidos *mpl*

election [i'lɛkʃən] *n* : elección *f*

elective[1] [i'lɛktɪv] *adj* **1** : electivo **2** OPTIONAL : facultativo, optativo

elective[2] *n* : asignatura *f* electiva

elector [i'lɛktər] *n* : elector *m*, -tora *f*

electoral [i'lɛktərəl] *adj* : electoral

electorate [i'lɛktərət] *n* : electorado *m*

electric [i'lɛktrɪk] *adj* **1** *or* **electrical** [-trɪkəl] : eléctrico **2** THRILLING : electrizante, emocionante

electrician [i,lɛk'trɪʃən] *n* : electricista *mf*

electricity [i,lɛk'trɪsəti] *n, pl* **-ties 1** : electricidad *f* **2** CURRENT : corriente *m* eléctrica

electrification [i,lɛktrəfə'keɪʃən] *n* : electrificación *f*

electrify [i'lɛktrə,faɪ] *vt* **-fied; -fying 1** : electrificar **2** THRILL : electrizar, emocionar

electrocardiogram [i,lɛktro'kardiə,græm] *n* : electrocardiograma *m*

electrocardiograph [i,lɛktro'kardiə,græf] *n* : electrocardiógrafo *m*

electrocute [i'lɛktrə,kju:t] *vt* **-cuted; -cuting** : electrocutar

electrocution [i,lɛktrə'kju:ʃən] *n* : electrocución *f*

electrode [i'lɛk,tro:d] *n* : electrodo *m*

electrolysis [i,lɛk'traləsɪs] *n* : electrólisis *f*

electrolyte [i'lɛktrə,laɪt] *n* : electrolito *m*

electromagnet [i,lɛktro'mægnət] *n* : electroimán *m*

electromagnetic [i,lɛktromæg'nɪtɪk] *adj* : electromagnético — **electromagnetically** [-ţikli] *adv*

electromagnetism [i,lɛktro'mægnə,tɪzəm] *n* : electromagnetismo *m*

electron [i'lɛk,tran] *n* : electrón *m*

electronic [i,lɛk'tranɪk] *adj* : electrónico — **electronically** [-nɪkli] *adv*

electronic mail *n* : correo *m* electrónico

electronics [i,lɛk'tranɪks] *n* : electrónica *f*

electroplate [i'lɛktrə,pleɪt] *vt* **-plated; plating** : galvanizar mediante electrólisis

elegance ['ɛlɪgənts] *n* : elegancia *f*

elegant ['ɛlɪgənt] *adj* : elegante — **elegantly** *adv*

elegy ['ɛlədʒi] *n, pl* **-gies** : elegía *f*

element ['ɛləmənt] *n* **1** COMPONENT : elemento *m*, factor *m* **2** : elemento *m* (en la química) **3** MILIEU : elemento *m*, medio *m* ⟨to be in one's element : estar en su elemento⟩ **4 elements** *npl* RUDIMENTS : elementos *mpl*, rudimentos *mpl*, bases *fpl* **5 the elements** WEATHER : los elementos *mpl*

elemental [,ɛlə'mɛntəl] *adj* **1** BASIC : elemental, primario **2** : elemental (dícese de los elementos químicos)

elementary [,ɛlə'mɛntri] *adj* **1** SIMPLE : elemental, simple, fundamental **2** : de enseñanza primaria

elementary school *n* : escuela *f* primaria

elephant ['ɛləfənt] *n* : elefante *m*, -ta *f*

elevate ['ɛlə,veɪt] *vt* **-vated; -vating 1** RAISE : elevar, levantar, alzar **2** EXALT, PROMOTE : elevar, exaltar, ascender **3** ELATE : alborozar, regocijar

elevation [,ɛlə'veɪʃən] *n* **1** : elevación *f* **2** ALTITUDE : altura *f*, altitud *f* **3** PROMOTION : ascenso *m*

elevator ['ɛlə,veɪţər] *n* : ascensor *m*, elevador *m*

eleven[1] [i'lɛvən] *adj* : once

eleven[2] *n* : once *m*

eleventh[1] [ɪlɛvəntθ] *adj* : undécimo

eleventh[2] *n* **1** : undécimo *m*, -ma *f* (en una serie) **2** : onceavo *m*, onceava *f* (parte)

elf ['ɛlf] *n, pl* **elves** ['ɛlvz] : elfo *m*, geniecillo *m*, duende *m*

elfin ['ɛlfən] *adj* **1** : de elfo, menudo **2** ENCHANTING, MAGIC : mágico, encantador

elfish ['ɛlfɪʃ] *adj* **1** : de elfo **2** MISCHIEVOUS : travieso

elicit [ɪ'lɪsət] *vt* : provocar

eligibility [ˌɛlədʒəˈbɪləti] *n, pl* **-ties** : elegibilidad *f*

eligible [ˈɛlədʒəbəl] *adj* **1** QUALIFIED : elegible **2** SUITABLE : idóneo

eliminate [ɪˈlɪməˌneɪt] *vt* **-nated; -nating** : eliminar

elimination [ɪˌlɪməˈneɪʃən] *n* : eliminación *f*

elite [eɪˈliːt, i-] *n* : elite *f*

elixir [ɪˈlɪksər] *n* : elixir *m*

elk [ˈɛlk] *n* : alce *m* (de Europa), uapití *m* (de América)

ellipse [ɪˈlɪps, -] *n* : elipse *f*

ellipsis [ɪˈlɪpsəs, -] *n, pl* **-lipses** [-ˌsiːz] **1** : elipsis *f* **2** : puntos *mpl* suspensivos (en la puntuación)

elliptical [ɪˈlɪptɪkəl, -] *or* **elliptic** [-tɪk] *adj* : elíptico

elm [ˈɛlm] *n* : olmo *m*

elocution [ˌɛləˈkjuːʃən] *n* : elocución *f*

elongate [iˈlɔŋˌgeɪt] *vt* **-gated; -gating** : alargar

elongation [ˌiːˌlɔŋˈgeɪʃən] *n* : alargamiento *m*

elope [iˈloːp] *vi* **eloped; eloping** : fugarse

elopement [iˈloːpmənt] *n* : fuga *f*

eloquence [ˈɛləkwənts] *n* : elocuencia *f*

eloquent [ˈɛləkwənt] *adj* : elocuente — **eloquently** *adv*

El Salvadoran [ˌɛlˌsælvəˈdorən] *n* : salvadoreño *m*, -ña *f* — **El Salvadoran** *adj*

else¹ [ˈɛls] *adv* **1** DIFFERENTLY : de otro modo, de otra manera ⟨how else? : ¿de qué otro modo?⟩ **2** ELSEWHERE : de otro sitio, de otro lugar ⟨where else? : ¿en qué otro sitio?⟩ **3 or else** OTHERWISE : si no, de lo contrario

else² *adj* **1** OTHER : otro ⟨anyone else : cualquier otro⟩ ⟨everyone else : todos los demás⟩ ⟨nobody else : ningún otro, nadie más⟩ ⟨somebody else : otra persona⟩ **2** MORE : más ⟨nothing else : nada más⟩ ⟨what else? : ¿qué más?⟩

elsewhere [ˈɛlsˌʍɛr] *adv* : en otra parte, en otro sitio, en otro lugar

elucidate [iˈluːsəˌdeɪt] *vt* **-dated; -dating** : dilucidar, elucidar, esclarecer

elucidation [iˌluːsəˈdeɪʃən] *n* : elucidación *f*, esclarecimiento *m*

elude [iˈluːd] *vt* **eluded; eluding** : eludir, evadir

elusive [iˈluːsɪv] *adj* **1** EVASIVE : evasivo, esquivo **2** SLIPPERY : huidizo, escurridizo **3** FLEETING, INTANGIBLE : impalpable, fugaz

elusively [iˈluːsɪvli] *adv* : de manera esquiva

elves → **elf**

emaciate [iˈmeɪʃiˌeɪt] *vt* **-ated; -ating** : enflaquecer

emaciation [iˌmeɪsiˈeɪʃən, -ʃi-] *n* : enflaquecimiento *m*, escualidez *f*, delgadez *f* extrema

e-mail [ˈiːˌmeɪl] *n* : e-mail *m*

emanate [ˈɛməˌneɪt] *v* **-nated; -nating** *vi* : emanar, provenir, proceder — *vt* : emanar

emanation [ˌɛməˈneɪʃən] *n* : emanación *f*

emancipate [iˈmæntsəˌpeɪt] *vt* **-pated; -pating** : emancipar

emancipation [iˌmæntsəˈpeɪʃən] *n* : emancipación *f*

emasculate [iˈmæskjəˌleɪt] *vt* **-lated; -lating** **1** CASTRATE : castrar, emascular **2** WEAKEN : debilitar

embalm [ɪmˈbam, ɛm-, -ˈbalm] *vt* : embalsamar

embankment [ɪmˈbæŋkmənt, ɛm-] *n* : terraplén *m*, muro *m* de contención

embargo¹ [ɪmˈbargo, ɛm-] *vt* **-goed; -going** : imponer un embargo sobre

embargo² *n, pl* **-goes** : embargo *m*

embark [ɪmˈbark, ɛm-] *vt* : embarcar — *vi* **1** : embarcarse **2 to embark on** START : emprender, embarcarse en

embarkation [ˌɛmˌbarˈkeɪʃən] *n* : embarque *m*, embarco *m*

embarrass [ɪmˈbærəs, ɛm-] *vt* : avergonzar, abochornar

embarrassing [ɪmˈbærəsɪŋ, ɛm-] *adj* : embarazoso, violento

embarrassment [ɪmˈbærəsmənt, ɛm-] *n* : vergüenza *f*, pena *f*

embassy [ˈɛmbəsi] *n, pl* **-sies** : embajada *f*

embed [ɪmˈbɛd, ɛm-] *vt* **-bedded; -bedding** : incrustar, empotrar, grabar (en la memoria)

embellish [ɪmˈbɛlɪʃ, ɛm-] *vt* : adornar, embellecer

embellishment [ɪmˈbɛlɪʃmənt, ɛm-] *n* : adorno *m*

ember [ˈɛmbər] *n* : ascua *f*, brasa *f*

embezzle [ɪmˈbɛzəl, ɛm-] *vt* **-zled; -zling** : desfalcar, malversar

embezzlement [ɪmˈbɛzəlmənt, ɛm-] *n* : desfalco *m*, malversación *f*

embezzler [ɪmˈbɛzələr, ɛm-] *n* : desfalcador *m*, -dora *f*; malversador *m*, -dora *f*

embitter [ɪmˈbɪtər, ɛm-] *vt* : amargar

emblem [ˈɛmbləm] *n* : emblema *m*, símbolo *m*

emblematic [ˌɛmbləˈmætɪk] *adj* : emblemático, simbólico

embodiment [ɪmˈbadimənt, ɛm-] *n* : encarnación *f*, personificación *f*

embody [ɪmˈbadi, ɛm-] *vt* **-bodied; -bodying** : encarnar, personificar

emboss [ɪmˈbas, ɛm-, -ˈbɔs] *vt* : repujar, grabar en relieve

embrace¹ [ɪmˈbreɪs, ɛm-] *vt* **-braced; -bracing** **1** HUG : abrazar **2** ADOPT, TAKE ON : adoptar, aceptar **3** INCLUDE : abarcar, incluir

embrace² *n* : abrazo *m*

embroider [ɪmˈbrɔɪdər, ɛm-] *vt* : bordar (una tela), adornar (una historia)

embroidery [ɪmˈbrɔɪdəri, ɛm-] *n, pl* **-deries** : bordado *m*

embroil [ɪmˈbrɔɪl, ɛm-] *vt* : embrollar, enredar

embryo [ˈɛmbriˌoː] *n, pl* **embryos** : embrión *m*

embryonic [ˌɛmbri'ɑnɪk] *adj* : embrionario

emend [i'mɛnd] *vt* : enmendar, corregir

emendation [ˌiːˌmɛn'deɪʃən] *n* : enmienda *f*

emerald¹ ['ɛmrəld, 'ɛmə-] *adj* : verde esmeralda

emerald² *n* : esmeralda *f*

emerge [i'mərdʒ] *vi* **emerged; emerging** : emerger, salir, aparecer, surgir

emergence [i'mərdʒənts] *n* : aparición *f*, surgimiento *m*

emergency [i'mərdʒəntsi] *n, pl* **-cies** : emergencia *f*

emergent [i'mərdʒənt] *adj* : emergente

emery ['ɛməri] *n, pl* **-eries** : esmeril *m*

emetic¹ [i'mɛtɪk] *adj* : vomitivo, emético

emetic² *n* : vomitivo *m*, emético *m*

emigrant ['ɛmɪgrənt] *n* : emigrante *mf*

emigrate ['ɛməˌgreɪt] *vi* **-grated; -grating** : emigrar

emigration [ˌɛmə'greɪʃən] *n* : emigración *f*

eminence ['ɛmənənts] *n* **1** PROMINENCE : eminencia *f*, prestigio *m*, renombre *m* **2** DIGNITARY : eminencia *f*; dignatario *m*, -ria *f* ⟨Your Eminence : Su Eminencia⟩

eminent ['ɛmənənt] *adj* : eminente, ilustre

eminently ['ɛmənəntli] *adv* : sumamente

emissary ['ɛməˌsɛri] *n, pl* **-saries** : emisario *m*, -ria *f*

emission [i'mɪʃən] *n* : emisión *f*

emit [i'mɪt] *vt* **emitted; emitting** : emitir, despedir, producir

emote [i'moːt] *vi* **emoted; emoting** : exteriorizar las emociones

emotion [i'moːʃən] *n* : emoción *f*, sentimiento *m*

emotional [i'moːʃənəl] *adj* **1** : emocional, afectivo ⟨an emotional reaction : una reacción emocional⟩ **2** MOVING : emocionante, emotivo, conmovedor

emotionally [i'moːʃənəli] *adv* : emocionalmente

empathy ['ɛmpəθi] *n* : empatía *f*

emperor ['ɛmpərər] *n* : emperador *m*

emphasis ['ɛmfəsɪs] *n, pl* **-phases** [-ˌsiːz] : énfasis *m*, hincapié *m*

emphasize ['ɛmfəˌsaɪz] *vt* **-sized; -sizing** : enfatizar, destacar, subrayar, hacer hincapié en

emphatic [ɪm'fætɪk, ɛm-] *adj* : enfático, enérgico, categórico — **emphatically** [-ɪkli] *adv*

empire ['ɛmˌpaɪr] *n* : imperio *m*

empirical [ɪm'pɪrɪkəl, ɛm-] *adj* : empírico — **empirically** [-ɪkli] *adv*

employ¹ [ɪm'plɔɪ, ɛm-] *vt* **1** USE : usar, utilizar **2** HIRE : contratar, emplear **3** OCCUPY : ocupar, dedicar, emplear

employ² [ɪm'plɔɪ, ɛm-; 'ɪmˌ-, 'ɛmˌ-] *n* **1** : puesto *m*, cargo *m*, ocupación *f* **2 to be in the employ of** : estar al servicio de, trabajar para

employee [ɪmˌplɔɪ'iː, ɛm-, -'plɔɪˌiː] *n* : empleado *m*, -da *f*

employer [ɪm'plɔɪər, ɛm-] *n* : patrón *m*, -trona *f*; empleador *m*, -dora *f*

employment [ɪm'plɔɪmənt, ɛm-] *n* : trabajo *m*, empleo *m*

empower [ɪm'paʊər, ɛm-] *vt* : facultar, autorizar, conferirle poder a

empowerment [ɪm'paʊərmənt, ɛm-] *n* : autorización *f*

empress ['ɛmprəs] *n* : emperatriz *f*

emptiness ['ɛmptinəs] *n* : vacío *m*, vacuidad *f*

empty¹ ['ɛmpti] *v* **-tied; -tying** *vt* : vaciar — *vi* : desaguar (dícese de un río)

empty² *adj* **emptier; -est 1** : vacío **2** VACANT : desocupado, libre **3** MEANINGLESS : vacío, hueco, vano

empty–handed [ˌɛmpti'hændəd] *adj* : con las manos vacías

empty–headed [ˌɛmpti'hɛdəd] *adj* : cabeza hueca, tonto

emu ['iːˌmjuː] *n* : emú *m*

emulate ['ɛmjəˌleɪt] *vt* **-lated; -lating** : emular

emulation [ˌɛmjə'leɪʃən] *n* : emulación *f*

emulsifier [ɪ'mʌlsəˌfaɪər] *n* : emulsionante *m*

emulsify [ɪ'mʌlsəˌfaɪ] *vt* **-fied; -fying** : emulsionar

emulsion [ɪ'mʌlʃən] *n* : emulsión *f*

enable [ɪ'neɪbəl, ɛ-] *vt* **-abled; -abling 1** EMPOWER : habilitar, autorizar, facultar **2** PERMIT : hacer posible, posibilitar, permitir

enact [ɪ'nækt, ɛ-] *vt* **1** : promulgar (un ley o decreto) **2** : representar (un papel en el teatro)

enactment [ɪ'næktmənt, ɛ-] *n* : promulgación *f*

enamel¹ [ɪ'næməl] *vt* **-eled** *or* **-elled; -eling** *or* **-elling** : esmaltar

enamel² *n* : esmalte *m*

enamor [ɪ'næmər] *vt* **1** : enamorar **2 to be enamored of** : estar enamorado de (una persona), estar entusiasmado con (algo)

encamp [ɪn'kæmp, ɛn-] *vi* : acampar

encampment [ɪn'kæmpmənt, ɛn-] *n* : campamento *m*

encase [ɪn'keɪs, ɛn-] *vt* **-cased; -casing** : encerrar, revestir

encephalitis [ɪnˌsfə'laɪtəs, ɛn-] *n, pl* **-litides** ['lɪʃəˌdiːz] : encefalitis *f*

enchant [ɪn'tʃænt, ɛn-] *vt* **1** BEWITCH : hechizar, encantar, embrujar **2** CHARM, FASCINATE : cautivar, fascinar, encantar

enchanting [ɪn'tʃæntɪŋ, ɛn-] *adj* : encantador

enchanter [ɪn'tʃæntər, ɛn-] *n* SORCERER : mago *m*, encantador *m*

enchantment [ɪn'tʃæntmənt, ɛn-] *n* **1** SPELL : encanto *m*, hechizo *m* **2** CHARM : encanto *m*

enchantress [ɪn'tʃæntrəs, ɛn-] *n* **1** SORCERESS : maga *f*, hechicera *f* **2** CHARMER : mujer *f* cautivadora

encircle [ɪn'sərkəl, ɛn-] *vt* **-cled; -cling** : rodear, ceñir, cercar

enclose [ɪn'kloːz, ɛn-] *vt* **-closed; -closing 1** SURROUND : encerrar, cercar, rodear **2** INCLUDE : incluir, adjuntar, acompañar ⟨please find enclosed : le enviamos adjunto⟩

enclosure [ɪn'kloːʒər, ɛn-] *n* **1** ENCLOSING : encierro *m* **2** : cercado *m* (de terreno), recinto *m* ⟨an enclosure for the press : un recinto para la prensa⟩ **3** ADJUNCT : anexo *m* (con una carta), documento *m* adjunto

encode [ɪn'koːd, ɛn-] *vt* : cifrar (mensajes, etc.), codificar (en informática)

encompass [ɪn'kʌmpəs, ɛn-, -'kɑm-] *vt* **1** SURROUND : circundar, rodear **2** INCLUDE : abarcar, comprender

encore ['ɑn,kor] *n* : bis *m*, repetición *f*

encounter[1] [ɪn'kaʊntər, ɛn-] *vt* **1** MEET : encontrar, encontrarse con, toparse con, tropezar con **2** FIGHT : combatir, luchar contra

encounter[2] *n* : encuentro *m*

encourage [ɪn'kərɪʤ, ɛn-] *vt* **-aged; -aging 1** HEARTEN, INSPIRE : animar, alentar **2** FOSTER : fomentar, promover

encouragement [ɪn'kərɪʤmənt, ɛn-] *n* : ánimo *m*, aliento *m*

encouraging [ɪn'kərədʒɪŋ, ɛn-] *adj* : alentador, esperanzador

encroach [ɪn'kroːʧ, ɛn-] *vi* to encroach on : invadir, abusar (derechos), quitar (tiempo)

encroachment [ɪn'kroːʧmənt, ɛn-] *n* : invasión *f*, usurpación *f*

encrust [ɪn'krʌst, ɛn-] *vt* **1** : recubrir con una costra **2** INLAY : incrustar ⟨encrusted with gems : incrustado de gemas⟩

encumber [ɪn'kʌmbər, ɛn-] *vt* **1** BLOCK : obstruir, estorbar **2** BURDEN : cargar, gravar

encumbrance [ɪn'kʌmbrənts, ɛn-] *n* : estorbo *m*, carga *f*, gravamen *m*

encyclopedia [ɪn,saɪklə'piːdiə, ɛn-] *n* : enciclopedia *f*

encyclopedic [ɪn,saɪklə'piːdɪk, ɛn-] *adj* : enciclopédico

end[1] ['ɛnd] *vt* **1** STOP : terminar, poner fin a **2** CONCLUDE : concluir, terminar — *vi* : terminar(se), acabar, concluir(se)

end[2] *n* **1** EXTREMITY : extremo *m*, final *m*, punta *f* **2** CONCLUSION : fin *m*, final *m* **3** AIM : fin *m*

endanger [ɪn'deɪnʤər, ɛn-] *vt* : poner en peligro

endear [ɪn'dɪr, ɛn-] *vt* to endear oneself to : ganarse la simpatía de, granjearse el cariño de

endearment [ɪn'dɪrmənt, ɛn-] *n* : expresión *f* de cariño

endeavor[1] [ɪn'dɛvər, ɛn-] *vt* : intentar, esforzarse por ⟨he endeavored to improve his work : intentó por mejorar su trabajo⟩

endeavor[2] *n* : intento *m*, esfuerzo *m*

endemic [ɛn'dɛmɪk, ɪn-] *adj* : endémico

ending ['ɛndɪŋ] *n* **1** CONCLUSION : final *m*, desenlace *m* **2** SUFFIX : sufijo *m*, terminación *f*

endive ['ɛn,daɪv, ,ɑn'diːv] *n* : endibia *f*, endivia *f*

endless ['ɛndləs] *adj* **1** INTERMINABLE : interminable, inacabable, sin fin **2** INNUMERABLE : innumerable, incontable

endlessly ['ɛndləsli] *adv* : interminablemente, eternamente, sin parar

endocrine ['ɛndəkrən, -,kraɪn, -,kriːn] *adj* : endocrino

endorse [ɪn'dors, ɛn-] *vt* **-dorsed; -dorsing 1** SIGN : endosar, firmar **2** APPROVE : aprobar, sancionar

endorsement [ɪn'dorsmənt, ɛn-] *n* **1** SIGNATURE : endoso *m*, firma *f* **2** APPROVAL : aprobación *f*, aval *m*

endow [ɪn'daʊ, ɛn-] *vt* : dotar

endowment [ɪn'daʊmənt, ɛn-] *n* **1** FUNDING : dotación *f* **2** DONATION : donación *f*, legado *m* **3** ATTRIBUTE, GIFT : atributo *m*, dotes *fpl*

endurable [ɪn'dʊrəbəl, ɛn-, -'djʊr-] *adj* : tolerable, soportable

endurance [ɪn'dʊrənts, ɛn-, -'djʊr-] *n* : resistencia *f*, aguante *m*

endure [ɪn'dʊr, ɛn-, -'djʊr] *v* **-dured; -during** *vt* **1** BEAR : resistir, soportar, aguantar **2** TOLERATE : tolerar, soportar — *vi* LAST : durar, perdurar

enema ['ɛnəmə] *n* : enema *m*, lavativa *f*

enemy ['ɛnəmi] *n, pl* **-mies** : enemigo *m*, -ga *f*

energetic [,ɛnər'ʤɛtɪk] *adj* : enérgico, vigoroso — **energetically** [-ʈɪkli] *adv*

energize ['ɛnər,ʤaɪz] *vt* **-gized; -gizing 1** ACTIVATE : activar **2** INVIGORATE : vigorizar

energy ['ɛnərʤi] *n, pl* **-gies 1** VITALITY : energía *f*, vitalidad *f* **2** EFFORT : esfuerzo *m*, energías *fpl* **3** POWER : energía *f* ⟨atomic energy : energía atómica⟩

enervate ['ɛnər,veɪt] *vt* **-vated; -vating** : enervar, debilitar

enfold [ɪn'foːld, ɛn-] *vt* : envolver

enforce [ɪn'fors, ɛn-] *vt* **-forced; -forcing 1** : hacer respetar, hacer cumplir (una ley, etc.) **2** IMPOSE : imponer ⟨to enforce obedience : imponer la obediencia⟩

enforcement [ɪn'forsmənt, ɛn-] *n* : imposición *f*

enfranchise [ɪn'fræn,ʧaɪz, ɛn-] *vt* **-chised; -chising** : conceder el voto a

enfranchisement [ɪn'fræn,ʧaɪzmənt, ɛn-] *n* : concesión *f* del voto

engage [ɪn'geɪʤ, ɛn-] *v* **-gaged; -gaging** *vt* **1** ATTRACT : captar, atraer, llamar ⟨to engage one's attention : captar la atención⟩ **2** MESH : engranar (engage the clutch : embragar⟩ **3** COMMIT : comprometer ⟨to get engaged : comprometerse⟩ **4** HIRE : contratar **5** : entablar combate con (un enemigo)

— *vi* **1** PARTICIPATE : participar **2 to engage in combat** : entrar en combate

engagement [ɪnˈgeɪdʒmənt, ɛn-] *n* **1** APPOINTMENT : cita *f*, hora *f* **2** BETROTHAL : compromiso *m*

engaging [ɪnˈgeɪdʒɪŋ, ɛn-] *adj* : atractivo, encantador, interesante

engender [ɪnˈdʒɛndər, ɛn-] *vt* **-dered; -dering** : engendrar

engine [ˈɛndʒən] *n* **1** MOTOR : motor *m* **2** LOCOMOTIVE : locomotora *f*, máquina *f*

engineer¹ [ˌɛndʒəˈnɪr] *vt* **1** : diseñar, construir (un sistema, un mecanismo, etc.) **2** CONTRIVE : maquinar, tramar, fraguar

engineer² *n* **1** : ingeniero *m*, -ra *f* **2** : maquinista *mf* (de locomotoras)

engineering [ˌɛndʒəˈnɪrɪŋ] *n* : ingeniería *f*

English¹ [ˈɪŋglɪʃ, ˈɪŋlɪʃ] *adj* : inglés

English² *n* **1** : inglés *m* (idioma) **2 the English** : los ingleses

Englishman [ˈɪŋglɪʃmən, ˈɪŋlɪʃ-] *n, pl* **-men** [-mən, -ˌmɛn] : inglés *m*

Englishwoman [ˈɪŋglɪʃˌwʊmən, ˈɪŋlɪʃ-] *n, pl* **-women** [-ˌwɪmən] : inglesa *f*

engrave [ɪnˈgreɪv, ɛn-] *vt* **-graved; -graving** : grabar

engraver [ɪnˈgreɪvər, ɛn-] *n* : grabador *m*, -dora *f*

engraving [ɪnˈgreɪvɪŋ, ɛn-] *n* : grabado *m*

engross [ɪnˈgroːs, ɛn-] *vt* : absorber

engrossed [ɪnˈgroːst, ɛn-] *adj* : absorto

engrossing [ɪnˈgroːsɪŋ, ɛn-] *adj* : fascinante, absorbente

engulf [ɪnˈgʌlf, ɛn-] *vt* : envolver, sepultar

enhance [ɪnˈhænts, ɛn-] *vt* **-hanced; -hancing** : realzar, aumentar, mejorar

enhancement [ɪnˈhæntsmənt, ɛn-] *n* : mejora *f*, realce *m*, aumento *m*

enigma [ɪˈnɪgmə] *n* : enigma *m*

enigmatic [ˌɛnɪgˈmætɪk, ˌiːnɪg-] *adj* : enigmático — **enigmatically** [-tɪkli] *adv*

enjoin [ɪnˈdʒɔɪn, ɛn-] *vt* **1** COMMAND : ordenar, imponer **2** FORBID : prohibir, vedar

enjoy [ɪnˈdʒɔɪ, ɛn-] *vt* **1** : disfrutar, gozar de ⟨did you enjoy the book? : ¿te gustó el libro?⟩ ⟨to enjoy good health : gozar de buena salud⟩ **2 to enjoy oneself** : divertirse, pasarlo bien

enjoyable [ɪnˈdʒɔɪəbəl, ɛn-] *adj* : agradable, placentero, divertido

enjoyment [ɪnˈdʒɔɪmənt, ɛn-] *n* : placer *m*, goce *m*, disfrute *m*, deleite *m*

enlarge [ɪnˈlɑrdʒ, ɛn-] *v* **-larged; -larging** *vt* : extender, agrandar, ampliar — *vi* **1** : ampliarse **2 to enlarge upon** : extenderse sobre, entrar en detalles sobre

enlargement [ɪnˈlɑrdʒmənt, ɛn-] *n* : expansión *f*, ampliación *f* (dícese de fotografías)

enlarger [ɪnˈlɑrdʒər, ɛn-] *n* : ampliadora *f*

enlighten [ɪnˈlaɪtən, ɛn-] *vt* : iluminar, aclarar

enlightenment [ɪnˈlaɪtənmənt, ɛn-] *n* **1** : ilustración *f* ⟨the Enlightenment : la Ilustración⟩ **2** CLARIFICATION : aclaración *f*

enlist [ɪnˈlɪst, ɛn-] *vt* **1** ENROLL : alistar, reclutar **2** SECURE : conseguir ⟨to enlist the support of : conseguir el apoyo de⟩ — *vi* : alistarse

enlisted man [ɪnˈlɪstəd, ɛn-] *n* : soldado *m* raso

enlistment [ɪnˈlɪstmənt, ɛn-] *n* : alistamiento *m*, reclutamiento *m*

enliven [ɪnˈlaɪvən, ɛn-] *vt* : animar, alegrar, darle vida a

enmity [ˈɛnməti] *n, pl* **-ties** : enemistad *f*, animadversión *f*

ennoble [ɪˈnoːbəl, ɛ-] *vt* **-bled; -bling** : ennoblecer

ennui [ˌɑnˈwiː] *n* : hastío *m*, tedio *m*, fastidio *m*, aburrimiento *m*

enormity [ɪˈnɔrməti] *n, pl* **-ties** **1** ATROCITY : atrocidad *f*, barbaridad *f* **2** IMMENSITY : enormidad *f*, inmensidad *f*

enormous [ɪˈnɔrməs] *adj* : enorme, inmenso, tremendo — **enormously** *adv*

enough¹ [ɪˈnʌf] *adv* **1** : bastante, suficientemente **2 fair enough!** : ¡está bien!, ¡de acuerdo! **3 strangely enough** : por extraño que parezca **4 sure enough** : en efecto, sin duda alguna **5 well enough** : muy bien, bastante bien

enough² *adj* : bastante, suficiente ⟨do we have enough chairs? : ¿tenemos suficientes sillas?⟩

enough³ *pron* : (lo) suficiente, (lo) bastante ⟨enough to eat : lo suficiente para comer⟩ ⟨it's not enough : no basta⟩ ⟨I've had enough! : ¡estoy harto!, ¡está bueno ya!⟩

enquire [ɪnˈkwaɪr, ɛn-] **enquiry** [ˈɪnˌkwaɪri, ˈɛn-, -kwəri; ɪnˈkwaɪri, ɛn-] → **inquire, inquiry**

enrage [ɪnˈreɪdʒ, ɛn-] *vt* **-raged; -raging** : enfurecer, encolerizar

enraged [ɪnˈreɪdʒd, ɛn-] *adj* : enfurecido, furioso

enrich [ɪnˈrɪtʃ, ɛn-] *vt* : enriquecer

enrichment [ɪnˈrɪtʃmənt, ɛn-] *n* : enriquecimiento *m*

enroll *or* **enrol** [ɪnˈroːl, ɛn-] *v* **-rolled; -rolling** *vt* : matricular, inscribir — *vi* : matricularse, inscribirse

enrollment [ɪnˈroːlmənt, ɛn-] *n* : matrícula *f*, inscripción *f*

en route [ɑˈruːt, ɛnˈraʊt] *adv* : de camino, por el camino

ensconce [ɪnˈskɑnts, ɛn-] *vt* **-sconced; -sconcing** : acomodar, instalar, establecer cómodamente

ensemble [ɑnˈsɑmbəl] *n* : conjunto *m*

enshrine [ɪnˈʃraɪn, ɛn-] *vt* **-shrined; -shrining** : conservar religiosamente, preservar

ensign [ˈɛntsən, ˈɛnˌsaɪn] *n* **1** FLAG : enseña *f*, pabellón *m* **2** : alférez *mf* (de fragata)

enslave [ɪn'sleɪv, ɛn-] vt **-slaved; -slav-**
ing : esclavizar
enslavement [ɪn'sleɪvmənt, ɛn-] n : esclavización f
ensnare [ɪn'snær, ɛn-] vt **-snared;**
-snaring : atrapar
ensue [ɪn'suː, ɛn-] vi **-sued; -suing**
: seguir, resultar
ensure [ɪn'ʃʊr, ɛn-] vt **-sured; -suring**
: asegurar, garantizar
entail [ɪn'teɪl, ɛn-] vt : implicar, suponer, conllevar
entangle [ɪn'tæŋgəl, ɛn-] vt **-gled; -gling**
: enredar
entanglement [ɪn'tæŋgəlmənt, ɛn-] n
: enredo m
enter ['ɛntər] vt **1** : entrar en, entrar a
2 BEGIN : entrar en, comenzar, iniciar
3 RECORD : anotar, inscribir, dar entrada a ⟨to enter data : introducir
datos⟩ **4** JOIN : entrar en, alistarse en,
hacerse socio de — vi **1** : entrar **2 to**
enter into : entrar en, firmar (un acuerdo), entablar (negociaciones, etc.)
enterprise ['ɛntər,praɪz] n **1** UNDER-
TAKING : empresa f **2** BUSINESS : empresa f, firma f **3** INITIATIVE : iniciativa f, empuje m
enterprising ['ɛntər,praɪzɪŋ] adj : emprendedor
entertain [,ɛntər'teɪn] vt **1** : recibir,
agasajar ⟨to entertain guests : tener in-
vitados⟩ **2** CONSIDER : considerar,
contemplar **3** AMUSE : entretener, divertir
entertainer [,ɛntər'teɪnər] n : artista mf
entertaining [,ɛntər'teɪnɪŋ] adj : entretenido, divertido
entertainment [,ɛntər'teɪnmənt] n : entretenimiento m, diversión f
enthrall or **enthral** [ɪn'θrɔl, ɛn-] vt
-thralled; -thralling : cautivar, embelesar
enthuse [ɪn'θuɪz, ɛn-] v **-thused; -thus-**
ing vt **1** EXCITE : entusiasmar **2** : decir con entusiasmo — vi **to enthuse**
over : hablar con entusiasmo sobre
enthusiasm [ɪn'θuːzi,æzəm, ɛn-, -'θjuː-]
n : entusiasmo m
enthusiast [ɪn'θuːzi,æst, ɛn-, -'θjuː-, -əst]
n : entusiasta mf; aficionado m, -da f
enthusiastic [ɪn,θuːzi'æstɪk, ɛn-, -,θjuː-]
adj : entusiasta, aficionado
enthusiastically [ɪn,θuːzi'æstɪkli, ɛn-,
-,θjuː-] adv : con entusiasmo
entice [ɪn'taɪs, ɛn-] vt **-ticed; -ticing**
: atraer, tentar
enticement [ɪn'taɪsmənt, ɛn-] n
: tentación f, atracción f, señuelo m
entire [ɪn'taɪr, ɛn-] adj : entero, completo
entirely [ɪn'taɪrli, ɛn-] adv : completamente, totalmente
entirety [ɪn'taɪrți, ɛn-, -'taɪrəți] n, pl **-ties**
: totalidad f
entitle [ɪn'taɪțəl, ɛn-] vt **-tled; -tling 1**
NAME : titular, intitular **2** : dar derecho a ⟨it entitles you to enter free : le

da derecho a entrar gratis⟩ **3 to be en-**
titled to : tener derecho a
entitlement [ɪn'taɪțəlmənt, ɛn-] n RIGHT
: derecho m
entity ['ɛntəți] n, pl **-ties** : entidad f, ente
m
entomologist [,ɛntə'mɑlədʒɪst] n : entomólogo m, -ga f
entomology [,ɛntə'mɑlədʒi] n : entomología f
entourage [,ɑntu'rɑʒ] n : séquito m
entrails ['ɛn,treɪlz, -trəlz] npl : entrañas
fpl, vísceras fpl
entrance[1] [ɪn'træns, ɛn-] vt **-tranced;**
-trancing : encantar, embelesar, fascinar
entrance[2] ['ɛntrənts] n **1** ENTERING : entrada f ⟨to make an entrance : entrar
en escena⟩ **2** ENTRY : entrada f, puerta f **3** ADMISSION : entrada f, ingreso
m ⟨entrance examination : examen de
ingreso⟩
entrant ['ɛntrənt] n : candidato m, -ta f
(en un examen); participante mf (en un
concurso)
entrap [ɪn'træp, ɛn-] vt **-trapped; -trap-**
ping : atrapar, entrampar, hacer caer
en una trampa
entrapment [ɪn'træpmənt, ɛn-] n : captura f
entreat [ɪn'triːt, ɛn-] vt : suplicar, rogar
entreaty [ɪn'triːți, ɛn-] n, pl **-treaties**
: ruego m, súplica f
entrée or **entree** ['ɑn,treɪ, 'ɑn'-] n : plato m principal
entrench [ɪn'trɛntʃ, ɛn-] vt **1** FORTIFY
: atrincherar (una posición militar) **2**
: consolidar, afianzar ⟨firmly en-
trenched in his job : afianzado en su
puesto⟩
entrepreneur [,ɑntrəprə'nər, -'njʊr] n
: empresario m, -ria f
entrust [ɪn'trʌst, ɛn-] vt : confiar, encomendar
entry ['ɛntri] n, pl **-tries 1** ENTRANCE
: entrada f **2** NOTATION : entrada f, anotación f
entwine [ɪn'twaɪn, ɛn-] vt **-twined; -twin-**
ing : entrelazar, entretejer, entrecruzar
enumerate [ɪ'nuːmə,reɪt, ɛ-, -'njuː-] vt
-ated; -ating 1 LIST : enumerar **2**
COUNT : contar, enumerar
enumeration [ɪ,nuːmə'reɪʃən, ɛ-, -,njuː-]
n : enumeración f, lista f
enunciate [i'nʌnʦi,eɪt, ɛ-] vt **-ated;**
-ating 1 STATE : enunciar, decir **2** PRO-
NOUNCE : articular, pronunciar
enunciation [i,nʌnʦi'eɪʃən, ɛ-] n **1**
STATEMENT : enunciación f, declaración f **2** ARTICULATION : articulación f, pronunciación f, dicción f
envelop [ɪn'vləp, ɛn-] vt : envolver,
cubrir
envelope ['ɛnvə,loːp, 'ɑn-] n : sobre m
enviable ['ɛnviəbəl] adj : envidiable
envious ['ɛnviəs] adj : envidioso — **en-**
viously adv

environment [ɪn'vaɪrənmənt, ɛn-, -'vaɪərn-] *n* : medio *m* (ambiente), ambiente *m*, entorno *m*

environmental [ɪn,vaɪrən'mɛntəl, ɛn-, -,vaɪərn-] *adj* : ambiental

environmentalist [ɪn,vaɪrən'mɛntəlɪst, ɛn-, -,vaɪərn-] *n* : ecologista *mf*

environs [ɪn'vaɪrənz, ɛn-, -'vaɪərnz] *npl* : alrededores *mpl*, entorno *m*, inmediaciones *fpl*

envisage [ɪn'vɪzɪʤ, ɛn-] *vt* **-aged; -aging** **1** IMAGINE : imaginarse, concebir **2** FORESEE : prever

envision [ɪn'vɪʒən, ɛn-] *vt* : imaginar

envoy ['ɛn,vɔɪ, 'ɑn-] *n* : enviado *m*, -da *f*

envy¹ ['ɛnvi] *vt* **-vied; -vying** : envidiar

envy² *n, pl* **envies** : envidia *f*

enzyme ['ɛn,zaɪm] *n* : enzima *f*

eon ['iːən, iː,ɑn] → **aeon**

epaulet [,pə'lɛt] *n* : charretera *f*

ephemeral [ɪ'fɛmərəl, -'fiː-] *adj* : efímero, fugaz

epic¹ ['ɛpɪk] *adj* : épico

epic² *n* : poema *m* épico, epopeya *f*

epicure ['ɛpɪ,kjʊr] *n* : epicúreo *m*, -rea *f*; gastrónomo *m*, -ma *f*

epicurean [,ɛpɪkjʊ'riːən, -'kjʊriən] *adj* : epicúreo

epidemic¹ [,ɛpə'dɛmɪk] *adj* : epidémico

epidemic² *n* : epidemia *f*

epidermis [,ɛpə'dərməs] *n* : epidermis *f*

epigram ['ɛpə,græm] *n* : epigrama *m*

epilepsy ['ɛpə,lɛpsi] *n, pl* **-sies** : epilepsia *f*

epileptic¹ [,ɛpə'lɛptɪk] *adj* : epiléptico

epileptic² *n* : epiléptico *m*, -ca *f*

epilogue ['ɛpə,lɔg, -,lɑg] *n* : epílogo *m*

epiphany [ɪ'pɪfəni] *n, pl* **-nies** **1** **Epiphany** : Epifanía *f* **2** **to have an epiphany** : tener una revelación

episcopal [ɪ'pɪskəpəl] *adj* : episcopal

Episcopalian [ɪ,pɪskə'peɪljən] *n* : episcopalista *mf*; episcopaliano *m*, -na *f*

episode ['ɛpə,soːd] *n* : episodio *m*

episodic [,ɛpə'sɑdɪk] *adj* : episódico

epistle [ɪ'pɪsəl] *n* : epístola *f*, carta *f*

epitaph ['ɛpə,tæf] *n* : epitafio *m*

epithet ['ɛpə,θɛt, -θət] *n* : epíteto *m*

epitome [ɪ'pɪtəmi] *n* **1** SUMMARY : epítome *m*, resumen *m* **2** EMBODIMENT : personificación *f*

epitomize [ɪ'pɪtə,maɪz] *vt* **-mized; -mizing** **1** SUMMARIZE : resumir **2** EMBODY : ser la personificación de, personificar

epoch ['ɛpək, 'ɛ,pɑk, 'iː,pɑk] *n* : época *f*, era *f*

epoxy [ɪ'pɑksi] *n, pl* **epoxies** : resina *f* epoxídica

equable ['ɛkwəbəl, 'iː-] *adj* **1** CALM, STEADY : ecuánime **2** UNIFORM : estable (dícese de la temperatura), constante (dícese del clima), uniforme

equably ['ɛkwəbli, 'iː-] *adv* : con ecuanimidad

equal¹ ['iːkwəl] *vt* **equaled** *or* **equalled; equaling** *or* **equalling** **1** : ser igual a

⟨two plus three equals five : dos más tres es igual a cinco⟩ **2** MATCH : igualar

equal² *adj* **1** SAME : igual **2** ADEQUATE : adecuado, capaz

equal³ *n* : igual *mf*

equality [ɪ'kwɑləṭi] *n, pl* **-ties** : igualdad *f*

equalize ['iːkwə,laɪz] *vt* **-ized; -izing** : igualar, equiparar

equally ['iːkwəli] *adv* : igualmente, por igual

equanimity [,iːkwə'nɪməṭi, ,ɛ-] *n, pl* **-ties** : ecuanimidad *f*

equate [ɪ'kweɪt] *vt* **equated; equating** : equiparar, identificar

equation [ɪ'kweɪʒən] *n* : ecuación *f*

equator [ɪ'kweɪṭər] *n* : ecuador *m*

equatorial [,iːkwə'toriəl, ,ɛ-] *adj* : ecuatorial

equestrian¹ [ɪ'kwɛstriən, ɛ-] *adj* : ecuestre

equestrian² *n* : jinete *mf*, caballista *mf*

equilateral [,iːkwə'læṭərəl, ,ɛ-] *adj* : equilátero

equilibrium [,iːkwə'lɪbriəm, ,ɛ-] *n, pl* **-riums** *or* **-ria** [-briə] : equilibrio *m*

equine ['iː,kwaɪn, 'ɛ-] *adj* : equino, hípico

equinox ['iːkwə,nɑks, 'ɛ-] *n* : equinoccio *m*

equip [ɪ'kwɪp] *vt* **equipped; equipping** **1** FURNISH : equipar **2** PREPARE : preparar

equipment [ɪ'kwɪpmənt] *n* : equipo *m*

equitable ['ɛkwəṭəbəl] *adj* : equitativo, justo, imparcial

equity ['ɛkwəṭi] *n, pl* **-ties** **1** FAIRNESS : equidad *f*, imparcialidad *f* **2** VALUE : valor *m* líquido

equivalence [ɪ'kwɪvələn*t*s] *n* : equivalencia *f*

equivalent¹ [ɪ'kwɪvələnt] *adj* : equivalente

equivalent² *n* : equivalente *m*

equivocal [ɪ'kwɪvəkəl] *adj* **1** AMBIGUOUS : equívoco, ambiguo **2** QUESTIONABLE : incierto, dudoso, sospechoso

equivocate [ɪ'kwɪvə,keɪt] *vi* **-cated; -cating** : usar lenguaje equívoco, andarse con evasivas

equivocation [ɪ,kwɪvə'keɪʃən] *n* : evasiva *f*, subterfugio *m*

era ['ɪrə, 'ɛrə, 'iːrə] *n* : era *f*, época *f*

eradicate [ɪ'rædə,keɪt] *vt* **-cated; -cating** : erradicar

erase [ɪ'reɪs] *vt* **erased; erasing** : borrar

eraser [ɪ'reɪsər] *n* : goma *f* de borrar, borrador *m*

erasure [ɪ'reɪʃər] *n* : tachadura *f*

ere¹ ['ɛr] *conj* : antes de que

ere² *prep* **1** : antes de **2 ere long** : dentro de poco

erect¹ [ɪ'rɛkt] *vt* **1** CONSTRUCT : erigir, construir **2** RAISE : levantar **3** ESTABLISH : establecer

erect² *adj* : erguido, derecho, erecto

erection [ɪ'rɛkʃən] *n* **1** : erección *f* (en fisiología) **2** BUILDING : construcción *f*

ergonomics [,ərgə'namɪks] *npl* : ergonomía *f*

ermine ['ərmən] *n* : armiño *m*

erode [ɪ'ro:d] *vt* **eroded; eroding** : erosionar (el suelo), corroer (metales)

erosion [ɪ'ro:ʒən] *n* : erosión *f*, corrosión *f*

erotic [ɪ'ratɪk] *adj* : erótico — **erotically** [-tɪkli] *adv*

eroticism [ɪ'ratə,sɪzəm] *n* : erotismo *m*

err ['ɛr, 'ər] *vi* : cometer un error, equivocarse, errar

errand ['ɛrənd] *n* : mandado *m*, encargo *m*, recado *m Spain* ⟨an errand of mercy : una misión de caridad⟩

errant ['ɛrənt] *adj* **1** WANDERING : errante **2** ASTRAY : descarriado

erratic [ɪ'rætɪk] *adj* **1** INCONSISTENT : errático, irregular, inconsistente **2** ECCENTRIC : excéntrico, raro

erratically [ɪ'rætɪkli] *adv* : erráticamente, de manera irregular

erroneous [ɪ'ro:niəs, ɛ-] *adj* : erróneo — **erroneously** *adv*

error ['ɛrər] *n* : error *m*, equivocación *f* ⟨to be in error : estar equivocado⟩

ersatz ['ɛr,sats, 'ər,sæts] *adj* : artificial, sustituto

erstwhile ['ərst,hwaɪl] *adj* : antiguo

erudite ['ɛrə,daɪt, 'ɛrjʊ-] *adj* : erudito, letrado

erudition [,ɛrə'dɪʃən, ,ɛrjʊ-] *n* : erudición *f*

erupt [ɪ'rʌpt] *vi* **1** : hacer erupción (dícese de un volcán o un sarpullido) **2** : estallar (dícese de la cólera o la violencia)

eruption [ɪ'rʌpʃən] *n* : erupción *f*, estallido *m*

eruptive [ɪ'rʌptɪv] *adj* : eruptivo

escalate ['ɛskə,leɪt] *v* **-lated; -lating** *vt* : intensificar (un conflicto), aumentar (precios) — *vi* : intensificarse, aumentarse

escalation [,ɛskə'leɪʃən] *n* : intensificación *f*, escalada *f*, aumento *m*, subida *f*

escalator ['ɛskə,leɪtər] *n* : escalera *f* mecánica

escapade ['ɛskə,peɪd] *n* : aventura *f*

escape¹ [ɪ'skeɪp, ɛ-] *v* **-caped; -caping** *vt* : escaparse de, librarse de, evitar — *vi* : escaparse, fugarse, huir

escape² *n* **1** FLIGHT : fuga *f*, huida *f*, escapada *f* **2** LEAKAGE : escape *m*, fuga *f* **3** : escapatoria *f*, evasión *f* ⟨to have no escape : no tener escapatoria⟩ ⟨escape from reality : evasión de la realidad⟩

escapee [ɪ,skeɪ'pi:, ,ɛ-] *n* : fugitivo *m*, -va *f*

escarole ['ɛskə,ro:l] *n* : escarola *f*

escarpment [ɪs'karpmənt, ɛs-] *n* : escarpa *f*, escarpadura *f*

eschew [ɛ'ʃu:, ɪs'tʃu:] *vt* : evitar, rehuir, abstenerse de

escort¹ [ɪ'skɔrt, ɛ-] *vt* **1** : escoltar ⟨to escort a ship : escoltar un barco⟩ **2** ACCOMPANY : acompañar

escort² ['ɛs,kɔrt] *n* **1** : escolta *f* ⟨armed escort : escolta armada⟩ **2** COMPANION : acompañante *mf*; compañero *m*, -ra *f*

escrow ['ɛs,kro:] *n* **in escrow** : en depósito, en custodia de un tercero

Eskimo ['ɛskə,mo:] *n* **1** : esquimal *mf* **2** : esquimal *m* (idioma) — **Eskimo** *adj*

esophagus [ɪ'safəgəs, i:-] *n, pl* **-gi** [-,gaɪ, -,dʒaɪ] : esófago *m*

esoteric [,ɛsə'tɛrɪk] *adj* : esotérico, hermético

especially [ɪ'spɛʃəli] *adv* : especialmente, particularmente

espionage ['ɛspiə,naʒ, -,nadʒ] *n* : espionaje *m*

espouse [ɪ'spauz, ɛ-] *vt* **espoused; espousing** **1** MARRY : casarse con **2** ADOPT, ADVOCATE : apoyar, adherirse a, adoptar

espresso ['ɛspre,so:] *n, pl* **-sos** : café *m* exprés

essay¹ ['ɛseɪ, 'ɛ,seɪ] *vt* : intentar, tratar

essay² ['ɛ,seɪ] *n* **1** COMPOSITION : ensayo *m*, trabajo *m* **2** ATTEMPT : intento *m*

essayist ['ɛ,seɪɪst] *n* : ensayista *mf*

essence ['ɛsənts] *n* **1** CORE : esencia *f*, núcleo *m*, meollo *m* ⟨in essence : esencialmente⟩ **2** EXTRACT : esencia *f*, extracto *m* **3** PERFUME : esencia *f*, perfume *m*

essential¹ [ɪ'sɛntʃəl] *adj* : esencial, imprescindible, fundamental — **essentially** *adv*

essential² *n* : elemento *m* esencial, lo imprescindible

establish [ɪ'stæblɪʃ, ɛ-] *vt* **1** FOUND : establecer, fundar **2** SET UP : establecer, instaurar, instituir **3** PROVE : demostrar, probar

establishment [ɪ'stæblɪʃmənt, ɛ-] *n* **1** ESTABLISHING : establecimiento *m*, fundación *f*, instauración *f* **2** BUSINESS : negocio *m*, establecimiento *m* **3 the Establishment** : la clase dirigente

estate [ɪ'steɪt, ɛ-] *n* **1** POSSESSIONS : bienes *mpl*, propiedad *f*, patrimonio *m* **2** PROPERTY : hacienda *f*, finca *f*, propiedad *f*

esteem¹ [ɪ'sti:m, ɛ-] *vt* : estimar, apreciar

esteem² *n* : estima *f*, aprecio *m*

ester ['ɛstər] *n* : éster *m*

esthetic [ɛs'θɛtɪk] → **aesthetic**

estimable ['ɛstəməbəl] *adj* : estimable

estimate¹ ['ɛstə,meɪt] *vt* **-mated; -mating** : calcular, estimar

estimate² ['ɛstəmət] *n* **1** : cálculo *m* aproximado ⟨to make an estimate : hacer un cálculo⟩ **2** ASSESSMENT : valoración *f*, estimación *f*

estimation [,ɛstə'meɪʃən] *n* **1** JUDGMENT : juicio *m*, opinión *f* ⟨in my estimation : en mi opinión, según mis cálculos⟩ **2** ESTEEM : estima *f*, aprecio *m*

estimator [ˈɛstəˌmeɪt̬ər] n : tasador m, -dora f

Estonian [ɛˈstoːniən] n : estonio m, -nia f — **Estonian** adj

estrange [ɪˈstreɪndʒ, ɛ-] vt **-tranged; -tranging** : enajenar, apartar, alejar

estrangement [ɪˈstreɪndʒmənt, ɛ-] n : alejamiento m, distanciamiento m

estrogen [ˈɛstrədʒən] n : estrógeno m

estrus [ˈɛstrəs] n : celo m

estuary [ˈɛstʃuˌwɛri] n, pl **-aries** : estuario m, -ría f

et cetera [ɛtˈsɛtərə, -ˈsɛtrə] : etcétera

etch [ˈɛtʃ] v : grabar al aguafuerte

etching [ˈɛtʃɪŋ] n : aguafuerte m, grabado m al aguafuerte

eternal [ɪˈtərnəl, iː-] adj 1 EVERLASTING : eterno 2 INTERMINABLE : constante, incesante

eternally [ɪˈtərnəli, iː-] adv : eternamente, para siempre

eternity [ɪˈtərnət̬i, iː-] n, pl **-ties** : eternidad f

ethane [ˈɛˌθeɪn] n : etano m

ethanol [ˈɛθəˌnɔl, -ˌnoːl] n : etanol m

ether [ˈiːθər] n : éter m

ethereal [ɪˈθɪriəl, iː-] adj 1 CELESTIAL : etéreo, celeste 2 DELICATE : delicado

ethical [ˈɛθɪkəl] adj : ético — **ethically** adv

ethics [ˈɛθɪks] ns & pl 1 : ética f 2 MORALITY : ética f, moral f, moralidad f

Ethiopian [ˌiːθiˈoːpiən] n : etíope mf — **Ethiopian** adj

ethnic [ˈɛθnɪk] adj : étnico

ethnologist [ɛθˈnɑlədʒɪst] n : etnólogo m, -ga f

ethnology [ɛθˈnɑlədʒi] n : etnología f

etiquette [ˈɛtɪkət, -ˌkɛt] n : etiqueta f, protocolo m

etymological [ˌɛtəməˈlɑdʒɪkəl] adj : etimológico

etymology [ˌɛtəˈmɑlədʒi] n, pl **-gies** : etimología f

eucalyptus [ˌjuːkəˈlɪptəs] n, pl **-ti** [-ˌtaɪ] or **-tuses** [-təsəz] : eucalipto m

Eucharist [ˈjuːkərɪst] n : Eucaristía f

eulogize [ˈjuːləˌdʒaɪz] vt **-gized; -gizing** : elogiar, encomiar

eulogy [ˈjuːlədʒi] n, pl **-gies** : elogio m, encomio m, panegírico m

eunuch [ˈjuːnək] n : eunuco m

euphemism [ˈjuːfəˌmɪzəm] n : eufemismo m

euphemistic [ˌjuːfəˈmɪstɪk] adj : eufemístico

euphony [ˈjuːfəni] n, pl **-nies** : eufonía f

euphoria [juˈforiə] n : euforia f

euphoric [juˈforɪk] adj : eufórico

European [ˌjʊrəˈpiːən] n : europeo m, europea f — **European** adj

euthanasia [ˌjuːθəˈneɪʒə, -ʒiə] n : eutanasia f

evacuate [ɪˈvækjuˌeɪt] v **-ated; -ating** vt VACATE : evacuar, desalojar — vi WITHDRAW : retirarse

evacuation [ɪˌvækjuˈeɪʃən] n : evacuación f, desalojo m

evade [ɪˈveɪd] vt **evaded; evading** : evadir, eludir, esquivar

evaluate [ɪˈvæljuˌeɪt] vt **-ated; -ating** : evaluar, valorar, tasar

evaluation [ɪˌvæljuˈeɪʃən] n : evaluación f, valoración f, tasación f

evangelical [ˌiː-ˌvænˈdʒɛlɪkəl, ˌɛvən-] adj : evangélico

evangelist [ɪˈvændʒəlɪst] n 1 : evangelista m 2 PREACHER : predicador m, -dora f

evaporate [ɪˈvæpəˌreɪt] vi **-rated; -rating** 1 VAPORIZE : evaporarse 2 VANISH : evaporarse, desvanecerse, esfumarse

evaporation [ɪˌvæpəˈreɪʃən] n : evaporación f

evasion [ɪˈveɪʒən] n : evasión f

evasive [ɪˈveɪsɪv] adj : evasivo

evasiveness [ɪˈveɪsɪvnəs] n : carácter m evasivo

eve [ˈiːv] n 1 : víspera f ⟨on the eve of the festivities : en vísperas de las festividades⟩ 2 → evening

even¹ [ˈiːvən] vt 1 LEVEL : allanar, nivelar, emparejar 2 EQUALIZE : igualar, equilibrar — vi **to even out** : nivelarse, emparejarse

even² adv 1 : hasta, incluso ⟨even a child can do it : hasta un niño puede hacerlo⟩ ⟨he looked content, even happy : se le veía satisfecho, incluso feliz⟩ 2 (in negative constructions) : ni siquiera ⟨he didn't even try : ni siquiera lo intentó⟩ 3 (in comparisons) : aún, todavía ⟨even better : aún mejor, todavía mejor⟩ 4 **even if** : aunque 5 **even so** : aun así 6 **even though** : aun cuando, a pesar de que

even³ adj 1 SMOOTH : uniforme, liso, parejo 2 FLAT : plano, llano 3 EQUAL : igual, igualado ⟨an even score : un marcador igualado⟩ 4 REGULAR : regular, constante ⟨an even pace : un ritmo constante⟩ 5 EXACT : exacto, justo ⟨even number : número par⟩ 7 **to be even** : estar en paz, estar a mano 8 **to get even** : desquitarse, vengarse

evening [ˈiːvnɪŋ] n : tarde f, noche f ⟨in the evening : por la noche⟩

evenly [ˈiːvənli] adv 1 UNIFORMLY : de modo uniforme, de manera constante 2 FAIRLY : igualmente, equitativamente

evenness [ˈiːvənnəs] n : uniformidad f, igualdad f, regularidad f

event [ɪˈvɛnt] n 1 : acontecimiento m, suceso m, prueba f (en deportes) 2 **in the event that** : en caso de que

eventful [ɪˈvɛntfəl] adj : lleno de incidentes, memorable

eventual [ɪˈvɛntʃuəl] adj : final, consiguiente

eventuality [ɪˌvɛntʃuˈæləti] n, pl **-ties** : eventualidad f

eventually [ɪˈvɛntʃuəli] adv : al fin, con el tiempo, algún día

ever ['ɛvər] *adv* **1** ALWAYS : siempre ⟨as ever : como siempre⟩ ⟨ever since : desde entonces⟩ **2** (*in questions*) : alguna vez, algún día ⟨have you ever been to Mexico? : ¿has estado en México alguna vez?⟩ **3** (*in negative constructions*) : nunca ⟨doesn't he ever work? : ¿es que nunca trabaja?⟩ ⟨nobody ever helps me : nadie nunca me ayuda⟩ **4** (*in comparisons*) : nunca ⟨better than ever : mejor que nunca⟩ **5** (*as intensifier*) ⟨I'm ever so happy! : ¡estoy tan y tan feliz!⟩ ⟨he looks ever so angry : parece estar muy enojado⟩

evergreen¹ ['ɛvər,gri:n] *adj* : de hoja perenne

evergreen² *n* : planta *f* de hoja perenne

everlasting [,ɛvər'læstɪŋ] *adj* : eterno, perpetuo, imperecedero

evermore [,ɛvər'mor] *adv* : eternamente

every ['ɛvri] *adj* **1** EACH : cada ⟨every time : cada vez⟩ ⟨every other house : cada dos casas⟩ **2** ALL : todo ⟨every month : todos los meses⟩ ⟨every woman : toda mujer, todas las mujeres⟩ **3** COMPLETE : pleno, entero ⟨to have every confidence : tener plena confianza⟩

everybody ['ɛvri,bʌdi, -,bɑ-] *pron* : todos *mpl*, -das *fpl*; todo el mundo

everyday [,ɛvri'deɪ, 'ɛvri,-] *adj* : cotidiano, diario, corriente ⟨everyday clothes : ropa de todos los días⟩

everyone ['ɛvri,wʌn] → **everybody**

everything ['ɛvri,θɪŋ] *pron* : todo

everywhere ['ɛvri,hwɛr] *adv* : en todas partes, por todas partes, dondequiera ⟨I looked everywhere : busqué en todas partes⟩ ⟨everywhere we go : dondequiera que vayamos⟩

evict [ɪ'vɪkt] *vt* : desalojar, desahuciar

eviction [ɪ'vɪkʃən] *n* : desalojo *m*, desahucio *m*

evidence ['ɛvədənts] *n* **1** INDICATION : indicio *m*, señal *m* ⟨to be in evidence : estar a la vista⟩ **2** PROOF : evidencia *f*, prueba *f* **3** TESTIMONY : testimonio *m*, declaración *f* ⟨to give evidence : declarar como testigo, prestar declaración⟩

evident ['ɛvɪdənt] *adj* : evidente, patente, manifiesto

evidently ['ɛvɪdəntli, ,ɛvi'dɛntli] *adv* **1** CLEARLY : claramente, obviamente **2** APPARENTLY : aparentemente, evidentemente, al parecer

evil¹ ['i:vəl, -vɪl] *adj* **eviler** *or* **eviller**; **evilest** *or* **evillest** **1** WICKED : malvado, malo, maligno **2** HARMFUL : nocivo, dañino, pernicioso **3** UNPLEASANT : desagradable ⟨an evil odor : un olor horrible⟩

evil² *n* **1** WICKEDNESS : mal *m*, maldad *f* **2** MISFORTUNE : desgracia *f*, mal *m*

evildoer [,i:vəl'du:ər, ,i:vɪl-] *n* : malvado *m*, -da *f*

evince [ɪ'vɪnts] *vt* **evinced**; **evincing** : mostrar, manifestar, revelar

eviscerate [ɪ'vɪsə,reɪt] *vt* **-ated**; **-ating** : eviscerar, destripar (un pollo, etc.)

evocation [,i:vo'keɪʃən, ,ɛ-] *n* : evocación *f*

evocative [i'vɑkətɪv] *adj* : evocador

evoke [i'vo:k] *vt* **evoked**; **evoking** : evocar, provocar

evolution [,ɛvə'lu:ʃən, ,i:-] *n* : evolución *f*, desarrollo *m*

evolutionary [,ɛvə'lu:ʃə,nɛri, ,i:-] *adj* : evolutivo

evolve [i'vɑlv] *vi* **evolved**; **evolving** : evolucionar, desarrollarse

ewe ['ju:] *n* : oveja *f*

exacerbate [ɪg'zæsər,beɪt] *vt* **-bated**; **-bating** : exacerbar

exact¹ [ɪg'zækt, ɛ-] *vt* : exigir, imponer, arrancar

exact² *adj* : exacto, preciso — **exactly** *adv*

exacting [ɪ'zæktɪŋ, ɛg-] *adj* : exigente, riguroso

exactitude [ɪg'zæktə,tu:d, ɛg-, -,tju:d] : exactitud *f*, precisión *f*

exaggerate [ɪg'zædʒə,reɪt, ɛg-] *v* **-ated**; **-ating** : exagerar

exaggerated [ɪg'zædʒə,reɪtəd, ɛg-] *adj* : exagerado — **exaggeratedly** *adv*

exaggeration [ɪg,zædʒə'reɪʃən, ɛg-] *n* : exageración *f*

exalt [ɪg'zɔlt, ɛg-] *vt* : exaltar, ensalzar, glorificar

exaltation [,ɛg,zɔl'teɪʃən, ,ɛk,sɔl-] *n* : exaltación *f*

exam [ɪg'zæm, ɛg-] → **examination**

examination [ɪg,zæmə'neɪʃən, ɛg-] *n* **1** TEST : examen *m* **2** INSPECTION : inspección *f*, revisión *f* **3** INVESTIGATION : examen *m*, estudio *m*

examine [ɪg'zæmən, ɛg-] *vt* **-ined**; **-ining** **1** TEST : examinar **2** INSPECT : inspeccionar, revisar **3** STUDY : examinar

example [ɪg'zæmpəl, ɛg-] *n* : ejemplo *m* ⟨for example : por ejemplo⟩ ⟨to set an example : dar ejemplo⟩

exasperate [ɪg'zæspə,reɪt, ɛg-] *vt* **-ated**; **-ating** : exasperar, sacar de quicio

exasperation [ɪg,zæspə'reɪʃən, ɛg-] *n* : exasperación *f*

excavate ['ɛkskə,veɪt] *vt* **-vated**; **-vating** : excavar

excavation [,ɛkskə'veɪʃən] *n* : excavación *f*

exceed [ɪk'si:d, ɛk-] *vt* **1** SURPASS : exceder, rebasar, sobrepasar **2** : exceder de, sobrepasar ⟨not exceeding two months : que no exceda de dos meses⟩

exceedingly [ɪk'si:dɪŋli, ɛk-] *adv* : extremadamente, sumamente

excel [ɪk'sɛl, ɛk-] *v* **-celled**; **-celling** *vi* : sobresalir, descollar, lucirse — *vt* : superar

excellence ['ɛksələnts] *n* : excelencia *f*

excellency ['ɛksələntsi] *n*, *pl* **-cies** : excelencia *f* ⟨His Excellency : Su Excelencia⟩

excellent ['ɛksələnt] *adj* : excelente, sobresaliente — **excellently** *adv*

except[1] [ɪk'sɛpt] *vt* : exceptuar, excluir
except[2] *conj* : pero, si no fuera por
except[3] *prep* : excepto, menos, salvo ⟨everyone except Carlos : todos menos Carlos⟩
exception [ɪk'sɛpʃən] *n* 1 : excepción *f* 2 **to take exception to** : ofenderse por, objetar a
exceptional [ɪk'sɛpʃənəl] *adj* : excepcional, extraordinario — **exceptionally** *adv*
excerpt[1] [ɛk'sərpt, ɛg'zərpt, 'ɛk,-, 'g,-] *vt* : escoger, seleccionar
excerpt[2] ['ɛk,sərpt, 'ɛg,zərpt] *n* : pasaje *m*, selección *f*
excess[1] ['ɛk,sɛs, ɪk'sɛs] *adj* 1 : excesivo, de sobra 2 **excess baggage** : exceso *m* de equipaje
excess[2] [ɪk'sɛs, 'ɛk,sɛs] *n* 1 SUPERFLUITY : exceso *m*, superfluidad *f* ⟨an excess of energy : un exceso de energía⟩ 2 SURPLUS : excedente *m*, sobrante *m* ⟨in excess of : superior a⟩
excessive [ɪk'sɛsɪv, ɛk-] *adj* : excesivo, exagerado, desmesurado — **excessively** *adv*
exchange[1] [ɪks'tʃeɪndʒ, ɛks-; 'ɛks,tʃeɪndʒ] *vt* **-changed; -changing** : cambiar, intercambiar, canjear
exchange[2] *n* 1 : cambio *m*, intercambio *m*, canje *m* 2 **stock exchange** : bolsa *f* (de valores)
exchangeable [ɪks'tʃeɪndʒəbəl, ɛks-] *adj* : canjeable
excise[1] [ɪk'saɪz, ɛk-] *vt* **-cised; -cising** : extirpar
excise[2] ['ɛk,saɪz] *n* **excise tax** : impuesto *m* interno, impuesto *m* sobre el consumo
excision [ɪk'sɪʒən, ɛk-] *n* : extirpación *f*, excisión *f*
excitability [ɪk,saɪtə'bɪləti, ɛk-] *n* : excitabilidad *f*
excitable [ɪk'saɪtəbəl, ɛk-] *adj* : excitable
excitation [,ɛk,saɪ'teɪʃən] *n* : excitación *f*
excite [ɪk'saɪt, ɛk-] *vt* **-cited; -citing** 1 AROUSE, STIMULATE : excitar, mover, estimular 2 ANIMATE : entusiasmar, animar 3 EVOKE, PROVOKE : provocar, despertar, suscitar ⟨to excite curiosity : despertar la curiosidad⟩
excited [ɪk'saɪtəd, ɛk-] *adj* 1 STIMULATED : excitado, estimulado 2 ENTHUSIASTIC : entusiasmado, emocionado
excitedly [ɪk'saɪtədli, ɛk-] *adv* : con excitación, con entusiasmo
excitement [ɪk'saɪtmənt, ɛk-] *n* 1 ENTHUSIASM : entusiasmo *m*, emoción *f* 2 AGITATION : agitación *f*, alboroto *m*, conmoción *f* 3 AROUSAL : excitación *f*
exciting [ɪk'saɪtɪŋ, ɛk-] *adj* 1 : emocionante 2 AROUSING : excitante
exclaim [ɪks'kleɪm, ɛk-] *v* : exclamar
exclamation [,ɛksklə'meɪʃən] *n* : exclamación *f*
exclamation point *n* : signo *m* de admiración

exclamatory [ɪks'klæmə,tori, ɛks-] *adj* : exclamativo
exclude [ɪks'klu:d, ɛks-] *vt* **-cluded; -cluding** 1 BAR : excluir, descartar, no admitir 2 EXPEL : expeler, expulsar
exclusion [ɪks'klu:ʒən, ɛks-] *n* : exclusión *f*
exclusive[1] [ɪks'klu:sɪv, ɛks-] *adj* 1 SOLE : exclusivo, único 2 SELECT : exclusivo, selecto
exclusive[2] *n* : exclusiva *f*
exclusively [ɪks'klu:sɪvli, ɛks-] *adv* : exclusivamente, únicamente
exclusiveness [ɪks'klu:sɪvnəs, ɛks-] *n* : exclusividad *f*
excommunicate [,ɛkskə'mju:nə,keɪt] *vt* **-cated; -cating** : excomulgar
excommunication [,ɛkskə,mju:nə'keɪʃən] *n* : excomunión *f*
excrement ['ɛkskrəmənt] *n* : excremento *m*
excrete [ɪk'skri:t, ɛk-] *vt* **-creted; -creting** : excretar
excretion [ɪk'skri:ʃən, ɛk-] *n* : excreción *f*
excruciating [ɪk'skru:ʃi,eɪtɪŋ, ɛk-] *adj* : insoportable, atroz, terrible — **excruciatingly** *adv*
exculpate ['ɛkskəl,peɪt] *vt* **-pated; -pating** : exculpar
excursion [ɪk'skərʒən, ɛk-] *n* 1 OUTING : excursión *f*, paseo *m* 2 DIGRESSION : digresión *f*
excuse[1] [ɪk'skju:z, ɛk-] *vt* **-cused; -cusing** 1 PARDON : disculpar, perdonar ⟨excuse me : con permiso, perdóneme, perdón⟩ 2 EXEMPT : eximir, disculpar 3 JUSTIFY : excusar, justificar
excuse[2] [ɪk'skju:s, ɛk-] *n* 1 JUSTIFICATION : excusa *f*, justificación *f* 2 PRETEXT : pretexto *m* 3 **to make one's excuses to someone** : pedirle disculpas a alguien
execute ['ɛksɪ,kju:t] *vt* **-cuted; -cuting** 1 CARRY OUT : ejecutar, llevar a cabo, desempeñar 2 ENFORCE : ejecutar, cumplir (un testamento, etc.) 3 KILL : ejecutar, ajusticiar
execution [,ɛksɪ'kju:ʃən] *n* 1 PERFORMANCE : ejecución *f*, desempeño *m* 2 IMPLEMENTATION : cumplimiento *m* 3 : ejecución *f* (por un delito)
executioner [,ɛksɪ'kju:ʃənər] *n* : verdugo *m*
executive[1] [ɪg'zɛkjətɪv, ɛg-] *adj* : ejecutivo
executive[2] *n* : ejecutivo *m*, -va *f*
executor [ɪg'zɛkjətər, ɛg-] *n* : albacea *m*, testamentario *m*
executrix [ɪg'zɛkjə,trɪks, ɛg-] *n, pl* **executrices** [-,zɛkjə'traɪ,si:z] *or* **executrixes** [-'zɛkjə,trɪksəz] : albacea *f*, testamentaria *f*
exemplary [ɪg'zɛmpləri, ɛg-] *adj* : ejemplar
exemplify [ɪg'zɛmplə,faɪ, ɛg-] *vt* **-fied; -fying** : ejemplificar, ilustrar, demostrar

exempt[1] [ɪg'zɛmpt, ɛg-] *vt* : eximir, dispensar, exonerar

exempt[2] *adj* : exento, eximido

exemption [ɪg'zɛmpʃən, ɛg-] *n* : exención *f*

exercise[1] ['ɛksər,saɪz] *v* -cised; -cising *vt* 1 : ejercitar (el cuerpo) 2 USE : ejercer, hacer uso de — *vi* : hacer ejercicio

exercise[2] *n* 1 : ejercicio *m* 2 **exercises** *npl* WORKOUT : ejercicios *mpl* físicos 3 **exercises** *npl* CEREMONY : ceremonia *f*

exert [ɪg'zərt, ɛg-] *vt* 1 : ejercer, emplear 2 **to exert oneself** : esforzarse

exertion [ɪg'zərʃən, ɛg-] *n* 1 USE : ejercicio *m* (de autoridad, etc.), uso *m* (de fuerza, etc.) 2 EFFORT : esfuerzo *m*, empeño *m*

exhalation [,ɛksə'leɪʃən, ,ɛkshə-] *n* : exhalación *f*, espiración *f*

exhale [ɛks'heɪl] *v* -haled; -haling *vt* 1 : exhalar, espirar 2 EMIT : exhalar, despedir, emitir — *vi* : espirar

exhaust[1] [ɪg'zɔst, ɛg-] *vt* 1 DEPLETE : agotar 2 TIRE : cansar, fatigar, agotar 3 EMPTY : vaciar

exhaust[2] *n* 1 **exhaust fumes** : gases *mpl* de escape 2 **exhaust pipe** : tubo *m* de escape 3 **exhaust system** : sistema *m* de escape

exhausted [ɪg'zɔstəd, ɛg-] *adj* : agotado, derrengado

exhausting [ɪg'zɔstɪŋ, ɛg-] *adj* : extenuante, agotador

exhaustion [ɪg'zɔstʃən, ɛg-] *n* : agotamiento *m*

exhaustive [ɪg'zɔstɪv, ɛg-] *adj* : exhaustivo

exhibit[1] [ɪg'zɪbət, ɛg-] *vt* 1 DISPLAY : exhibir, exponer 2 PRODUCE, SHOW : mostrar, presentar

exhibit[2] *n* 1 OBJECT : objeto *m* expuesto 2 EXHIBITION : exposición *f*, exhibición *f* 3 EVIDENCE : prueba *f* instrumental

exhibition [,ɛksə'bɪʃən] *n* 1 : exposición *f*, exhibición *f* 2 **to make an exhibition of oneself** : dar el espectáculo, hacer el ridículo

exhibitor [ɪg'zɪbətər] *n* : expositor *m*, -tora *f*

exhilarate [ɪg'zɪlə,reɪt, ɛg-] *vt* -rated; -rating : alegrar, levantar el ánimo de

exhilaration [ɪg,zɪlə'reɪʃən, ɛg-] *n* : alegría *f*, regocijo *m*, júbilo *m*

exhort [ɪg'zɔrt, ɛg-] *vt* : exhortar

exhortation [,ɛk,sɔr'teɪʃən, -sər-; ,ɛg-,zɔr-] *n* : exhortación *f*

exhumation [,ɛksju'meɪʃən, -hju-; ,ɛgzu-, -zju-] *n* : exhumación *f*

exhume [ɪg'zu:m, -'zju:m; ɪks'ju:m, -'hju:m] *vt* -humed; -huming : exhumar, desenterrar

exigencies ['ɛksɪʤəntsiz, ɪg'zɪʤən,si:z] *npl* : exigencias *fpl*

exile[1] ['ɛg,zaɪl, 'ɛk,saɪl] *vt* exiled; exiling : exiliar, desterrar

exile[2] *n* 1 BANISHMENT : exilio *m*, destierro *m* 2 OUTCAST : exiliado *m*, -da *f*; desterrado *m*, -da *f*

exist [ɪg'zɪst, ɛg-] *vi* 1 BE : existir 2 LIVE : subsistir, vivir

existence [ɪg'zɪstənts, ɛg-] *n* : existencia *f*

existent [ɪg'zɪstənt, ɛg-] *adj* : existente

existing [ɪg'zɪstɪŋ] *adj* : existente

exit[1] ['ɛgzət, 'ɛksət] *vi* : salir, hacer mutis (en el teatro) — *vt* : salir de

exit[2] *n* 1 DEPARTURE : salida *f*, partida *f* 2 EGRESS : salida *f* ⟨emergency exit : salida de emergencia⟩

exodus ['ɛksədəs] *n* : éxodo *m*

exonerate [ɪg'zɑnə,reɪt, ɛg-] *vt* -ated; -ating : exonerar, disculpar, absolver

exoneration [ɪg,zɑnə'reɪʃən, ɛg-] *n* : exoneración *f*

exorbitant [ɪg'zɔrbətənt, ɛg-] *adj* : exorbitante, excesivo

exorcise ['ɛk,sɔr,saɪz, -sər-] *vt* -cised; -cising : exorcizar

exorcism ['ɛksər,sɪzəm] *n* : exorcismo *m*

exotic[1] [ɪg'zɑtɪk, ɛg-] *adj* : exótico — **exotically** [-ɪkli] *adv*

exotic[2] *n* : planta *f* exótica

expand [ɪk'spænd, ɛk-] *vt* 1 ENLARGE : expandir, dilatar, aumentar, ampliar 2 EXTEND : extender — *vi* 1 ENLARGE : ampliarse, extenderse 2 : expandirse, dilatarse (dícese de los metales, gases, etc.)

expanse [ɪk'spænts, ɛk-] *n* : extensión *f*

expansion [ɪk'spænʃən, ɛk-] *n* 1 ENLARGEMENT : expansión *f*, ampliación *f* 2 EXPANSE : extensión *f*

expansive [ɪk'spæntsɪv, ɛk-] *adj* 1 : expansivo 2 OUTGOING : expansivo, comunicativo 3 AMPLE : ancho, amplio — **expansively** *adv*

expansiveness [ɪk'spæntsɪvnəs, ɛk-] *n* : expansibilidad *f*

expatriate[1] [ɛks'peɪtri,eɪt] *vt* -ated; -ating : expatriar

expatriate[2] [ɛks'peɪtriət, -,eɪt] *adj* : expatriado

expatriate[3] [ɛks'peɪtriət, -,eɪt] *n* : expatriado *m*, -da *f*

expect [ɪk'spkt, ɛk-] *vt* 1 SUPPOSE : suponer, imaginarse 2 ANTICIPATE : esperar 3 COUNT ON, REQUIRE : contar con, esperar — *vi* **to be expecting** : estar embarazada

expectancy [ɪk'spɛktəntsi, ɛk-] *n, pl* -cies : expectativa *f*, esperanza *f*

expectant [ɪk'spɛktənt, ɛk-] *adj* 1 ANTICIPATING : expectante 2 EXPECTING : futuro ⟨expectant mother : futura madre⟩

expectantly [ɪk'spɛktəntli, ɛk-] *adv* : con expectación

expectation [,ɛk,spɛk'teɪʃən] *n* 1 ANTICIPATION : expectación *f* 2 EXPECTANCY : expectativa *f*

expedient[1] [ɪk'spi:diənt, ɛk-] *adj* : conveniente, oportuno

expedient[2] *n* : expediente *m*, recurso *m*

expedite ['ɛkspə,daɪt] *vt* **-dited; -diting**
1 FACILITATE : facilitar, dar curso a **2**
HASTEN : acelerar
expedition [,ɛkspə'dɪʃən] *n* : expedición
f
expeditious [,ɛkspə'dɪʃəs] *adj* : pronto,
rápido
expel [ɪk'spɛl, ɛk-] *vt* **-pelled; -pelling**
: expulsar, expeler
expend [ɪk'spɛnd, ɛk-] *vt* **1** DISBURSE
: gastar, desembolsar **2** CONSUME
: consumir, agotar
expendable [ɪk'spɛndəbəl, ɛk-] *adj* : prescindible
expenditure [ɪk'spɛndɪtʃər, ɛk-, -,tʃʊr] *n*
: gasto *m*
expense [ɪk'spɛnts, ɛk-] *n* **1** COST : gasto *m* **2 expenses** *npl* : gastos *mpl*, expensas *fpl* **3 at the expense of** : a expensas de
expensive [ɪk'spɛntsɪv, ɛk-] *adj* : costoso, caro — **expensively** *adv*
experience[1] [ɪk'spɪriənts, ɛk-] *vt* **-enced;**
-encing : experimentar (sentimientos),
tener (dificultades), sufrir (una pérdida)
experience[2] *n* : experiencia *f*
experienced [ɪk'spɪriəntst, ɛk-] *adj* : con
experiencia, experimentado
experiment[1] [ɪk'spɛrəmənt, ɛk-, -'spɪr-]
vi : experimentar, hacer experimentos
experiment[2] *n* : experimento *m*
experimental [ɪk,spɛrə'mntəl, ɛk-,
-,spɪr-] *adj* : experimental — **experi-**
mentally *adv*
experimentation [ɪk,spɛrəmən'teɪʃən,
ɛk-, -,spɪr-] *n* : experimentación *f*
expert[1] ['ɛk,spərt, ɪk'spərt] *adj* : experto, de experto, pericial (dícese de un
testigo) — **expertly** *adv*
expert[2] ['ɛk,spərt] *n* : experto *m*, -ta *f*;
perito *m*, -ta *f*; especialista *mf*
expertise [,ɛkspər'ti:z] *n* : pericia *f*, competencia *f*
expiate ['ɛkspi,eɪt] *vt* **-ated; -ating** : expiar
expiation [,ɛkspi'eɪʃən] *n* : expiación *f*
expiration [,ɛkspə'reɪʃən] *n* **1** EXHALA-
TION : exhalación *f*, espiración *f* **2**
DEATH : muerte *f* **3** TERMINATION
: vencimiento *m*, caducidad *f*
expire [ɪk'spaɪr, ɛk-] *vi* **-pired; -piring 1**
EXHALE : espirar **2** DIE : expirar, morir
3 TERMINATE : caducar, vencer
explain [ɪk'spleɪn, ɛk-] *vt* : explicar
explanation [,ɛksplə'neɪʃən] *n* : explicación *f*
explanatory [ɪk'splænə,tori, ɛk-] *adj*
: explicativo, aclaratorio
expletive ['ɛksplətɪv] *n* : improperio *m*,
palabrota *f fam*, grosería *f*
explicable [ɛk'splɪkəbəl, 'ɛksplɪ-] *adj*
: explicable
explicit [ɪk'splɪsət, ɛk-] *adj* : explícito,
claro, categórico, rotundo — **explicit-**
ly *adv*
explicitness [ɪk'splɪsətnəs, ɛk-] *n* : claridad *f*, carácter *m* explícito

explode [ɪk'splo:d, ɛk-] *v* **-ploded;**
-ploding *vt* **1** BURST : hacer explosionar, hacer explotar **2** REFUTE : rebatir, refutar, desmentir — *vi* **1** BURST
: explotar, estallar, reventar **2** SKY-
ROCKET : dispararse
exploit[1] [ɪk'splɔɪt, ɛk-] *vt* : explotar,
aprovecharse de
exploit[2] ['ɛk,splɔɪt] *n* : hazaña *f*, proeza
f
exploitation [,ɛk,splɔɪ'teɪʃən] *n* : explotación *f*
exploration [,ɛksplə'reɪʃən] *n* : exploración *f*
exploratory [ɪk'splorə,tori, ɛk-] *adj* : exploratorio
explore [ɪk'splor, ɛk-] *vt* **-plored;**
-ploring : explorar, investigar, examinar
explorer [ɪk'splorər, ɛk-] *n* : explorador
m, -dora *f*
explosion [ɪk'splo:ʒən, ɛk-] *n* : explosión
f, estallido *m*
explosive[1] [ɪk'splo:sɪv, ɛk-] *adj* : explosivo, fulminante — **explosively** *adv*
explosive[2] *n* : explosivo *m*
exponent [ɪk'spo:nənt, 'ɛk,spo:-] *n* **1**
: exponente *m* **2** ADVOCATE : defensor
m, -sora *f*; partidario *m*, -ria *f*
exponential [,ɛkspə'nɛntʃəl] *adj* : exponencial — **exponentially** *adv*
export[1] [ɛk'sport, 'ɛk,sport] *vt* : exportar
export[2] ['ɛk,sport] *n* **1** : artículo *m* de
exportación **2** → **exportation**
exportation [,ɛk,spor'teɪʃən] *n* : exportación *f*
exporter [ɛk'sportər, 'ɛk,spor-] *n* : exportador *m*, -dora *f*
expose [ɪk'spo:z, ɛk-] *vt* **-posed;**
-posing 1 : exponer (al peligro, a los
elementos, a una enfermedad) **2** : exponer (una película a la luz) **3** DIS-
CLOSE : descubrir, revelar, poner en evidencia **4** UNMASK : desenmascarar
exposé *or* **expose** [,ɛkspo'zeɪ] *n* : exposición *f* (de hechos), revelación *f* (de
un escándalo)
exposed [ɪk'spo:zd, ɛk-] *adj* : descubierto, sin protección
exposition [,ɛkspə'zɪʃən] *n* : exposición
f
exposure [ɪk'spo:ʒər, ɛk-] *n* **1** : exposición *f* **2** CONTACT : exposición *f*, experiencia *f*, contacto *m* **3** UNMASKING
: desenmascaramiento *m* **4** ORIENTA-
TION : orientación *f* ⟨a room with a
northern exposure : una sala orienta-
da al norte⟩
expound [ɪk'spaund, ɛk-] *vt* : exponer,
explicar — *vi* : hacer comentarios de-
tallados
express[1] [ɪk'sprɛs, ɛk-] *vt* **1** SAY : expresar, comunicar **2** SHOW : expresar,
manifestar, externar *Mex* **3** SQUEEZE
: exprimir ⟨to express the juice from a
lemon : exprimir el jugo de un limón⟩
express[2] *adv* : por correo exprés, por
correo urgente

express[3] *adj* **1** EXPLICIT : expreso, manifiesto **2** SPECIFIC : específico ⟨for that express purpose : con ese fin específico⟩ **3** RAPID : expreso, rápido

express[4] *n* **1** : correo *m* exprés, correo *m* urgente **2** : expreso *m* (tren)

expression [ɪk'sprɛʃən, ɛk-] *n* **1** UTTERANCE : expresión *f* ⟨freedom of expression : libertad de expresión⟩ **2** : expresión *f* (en la matemática) **3** PHRASE : frase *f*, expresión *f* **4** LOOK : expresión *f*, cara *f*, gesto *m* ⟨with a sad expression : con un gesto de tristeza⟩

expressionless [ɪk'sprɛʃənləs, ɛk-] *adj* : inexpresivo

expressive [ɪk'sprɛsɪv, ɛk-] *adj* : expresivo

expressway [ɪk'sprɛs‚weɪ, ɛk-] *n* : autopista *f*

expulsion [ɪk'spʌlʃən, ɛk-] *n* : expulsión *f*

expurgate ['ɛkspər‚ɡeɪt] *vt* **-gated; -gating** : expurgar

exquisite [ɛk'skwɪzət, 'ɛk‚skwɪ-] *adj* **1** FINE : exquisito, delicado, primoroso **2** INTENSE : intenso, extremo

extant ['ɛkstənt, ɛk'stænt] *adj* : existente

extemporaneous [ɛk‚stɛmpə'reɪniəs] *adj* : improvisado — **extemporaneously** *adv*

extend [ɪk'stɛnd, ɛk-] *vt* **1** STRETCH : extender, tender **2** PROLONG : prolongar, prorrogar **3** ENLARGE : agrandar, ampliar, aumentar **4** PROFFER : extender, dar, ofrecer — *vi* : extenderse

extended [ɪk'stɛndəd, ɛk-] *adj* LENGTHY : prolongado, largo

extension [ɪk'stɛnʧən, ɛk-] *n* **1** EXTENDING : extensión *f*, ampliación *f*, prórroga *f*, prolongación *f* **2** ANNEX : ampliación *f*, anexo *m* **3** : extensión *f* (de teléfono)

extensive [ɪk'stɛnsɪv, ɛk-] *adj* : extenso, vasto, amplio — **extensively** *adv*

extent [ɪk'stɛnt, ɛk-] *n* **1** SIZE : extensión *f*, magnitud *f* **2** DEGREE, SCOPE : alcance *m*, grado *m* ⟨to a certain extent : hasta cierto punto⟩

extenuate [ɪk'stɛnjə‚weɪt, ɛk-] *vt* **-ated; -ating** : atenuar, aminorar, mitigar ⟨extenuating circumstances : circunstancias atenuantes⟩

extenuation [ɪk‚stɛnjə'weɪʃən, ɛk-] *n* : atenuación *f*, aminoración *f*

exterior[1] [ɛk'stɪriər] *adj* : exterior

exterior[2] *n* : exterior *m*

exterminate [ɪk'stərmə‚neɪt, ɛk-] *vt* **-nated; -nating** : exterminar

extermination [ɪk‚stərmə'neɪʃən, ɛk-] *n* : exterminación *f*, exterminio *m*

exterminator [ɪk'stərmə‚neɪtər, ɛk-] *n* : exterminador *m*, -dora *f*

external [ɪk'stərnəl, ɛk-] *adj* : externo, exterior — **externally** *adv*

extinct [ɪk'stɪŋkt, ɛk-] *adj* : extinto

extinction [ɪk'stɪŋkʃən, ɛk-] *n* : extinción *f*

extinguish [ɪk'stɪŋgwɪʃ, ɛk-] *vt* : extinguir, apagar

extinguisher [ɪk'stɪŋgwɪʃər, ɛk-] *n* : extinguidor *m*, extintor *m*

extirpate ['ɛkstər‚peɪt] *vt* **-pated; -pating** : extirpar, exterminar

extol [ɪk'stoːl, ɛk-] *vt* **-tolled; -tolling** : exaltar, ensalzar, alabar

extort [ɪk'stɔrt, ɛk-] *vt* : extorsionar

extortion [ɪk'stɔrʃən, ɛk-] *n* : extorsión *f*

extra[1] ['ɛkstrə] *adv* : extra, más, extremadamente, super ⟨extra special : super especial⟩

extra[2] *adj* **1** ADDITIONAL : adicional, suplementario, de más **2** SUPERIOR : superior

extra[3] *n* : extra *m*

extract[1] [ɪk'strækt, ɛk-] *vt* : extraer, sacar

extract[2] ['ɛk‚strækt] *n* **1** EXCERPT : pasaje *m*, selección *f*, trozo *m* **2** : extracto *m* ⟨vanilla extract : extracto de vainilla⟩

extraction [ɪk'strækʃən, ɛk-] *n* : extracción *f*

extractor [ɪk'stræktər, ɛk-] *n* : extractor *m*

extracurricular [‚ɛkstrəkə'rɪkjələr] *adj* : extracurricular

extradite ['ɛkstrə‚daɪt] *vt* **-dited; -diting** : extraditar

extradition [‚ɛkstrə'dɪʃən] *n* : extradición *f*

extramarital [‚ɛkstrə'mærətəl] *adj* : extramatrimonial

extraneous [ɛk'streɪniəs] *adj* **1** OUTSIDE : extrínseco, externo **2** SUPERFLUOUS : superfluo, ajeno — **extraneously** *adv*

extraordinary [ɪk'strɔrdən‚ɛri, ‚ɛkstrə'ɔrd-] *adj* : extraordinario, excepcional — **extraordinarily** [ɪk‚strɔrdən'ɛrəli, ‚kstrə‚ɔrd-] *adv*

extrasensory [‚ɛkstrə'sɛntsəri] *adj* : extrasensorial

extraterrestrial[1] [‚ɛkstrətə'rɛstriəl] *adj* : extraterrestre

extraterrestrial[2] *n* : extraterrestre *mf*

extravagance [ɪk'strævɪgənts, ɛk-] *n* **1** EXCESS : exceso *m*, extravagancia *f* **2** WASTEFULNESS : derroche *m*, despilfarro *m* **3** LUXURY : lujo *m*

extravagant [ɪk'strævɪgənt, ɛk-] *adj* **1** EXCESSIVE : excesivo, extravagante **2** WASTEFUL : despilfarrador, derrochador, gastador **3** EXORBITANT : costoso, exorbitante

extravagantly [ɪk'strævɪgəntli, ɛk-] *adv* **1** LAVISHLY : a lo grande **2** EXCESSIVELY : exageradamente, desmesuradamente

extravaganza [ɪk‚strævə'gænzə, ɛk-] *n* : gran espectáculo *m*

extreme[1] [ɪk'striːm, ɛk-] *adj* **1** UTMOST : extremo, sumo ⟨of extreme importance : de suma importancia⟩ **2** INTENSE : intenso, extremado ⟨extreme cold : frío extremado⟩ **3** EXCESSIVE : excesivo, extremo ⟨extreme views : opiniones extremas⟩ ⟨extreme measures : medidas excepcionales, medi-

das drásticas⟩ **4** OUTERMOST : extremo ⟨the extreme north : el norte extremo⟩
extreme² *n* **1** : extremo *m* **2 in the extreme** : en extremo, en sumo grado
extremely [ɪk'striːmli, ɛk-] *adv* : sumamente, extremadamente, terriblemente
extremist [ɪk'striːmɪst, ɛk-] *n* : extremista *mf* — **extremist** *adj*
extremity [ɪk'strɛməti, ɛk-] *n, pl* **-ties 1** EXTREME : extremo *m* **2 extremities** *npl* LIMBS : extremidades *fpl*
extricate ['ɛkstrə,keɪt] *vt* **-cated; -cating** : librar, sacar
extrinsic [ɪk'strɪnzɪk, -'strɪntsɪk] *adj* : extrínseco
extrovert ['ɛkstrə,vərt] *n* : extrovertido *m*, **-da** *f*
extroverted ['ɛkstrə,vərtəd] *adj* : extrovertido
extrude [ɪk'struːd, ɛk-] *vt* **-truded; -truding** : extrudir, expulsar
exuberance [ɪg'zuːbərənts, ɛg-] *n* **1** JOYOUSNESS : euforia *f*, exaltación *f* **2** VIGOR : exuberancia *f*, vigor *m*
exuberant [ɪg'zuːbərənt, ɛg-] *adj* **1** JOYOUS : eufórico **2** LUSH : exuberante — **exuberantly** *adv*
exude [ɪg'zuːd, ɛg-] *vt* **-uded; -uding 1** OOZE : rezumar, exudar **2** EMANATE : emanar, irradiar
exult [ɪg'zʌlt, ɛg-] *vi* : exultar, regocijarse
exultant [ɪg'zʌltənt, ɛg-] *adj* : exultante, jubiloso — **exultantly** *adv*
exultation [,ɛksəl'teɪʃən, ,ɛgzəl-] *n* : exultación *f*, júbilo *m*, alborozo *m*

eye¹ ['aɪ] *vt* **eyed; eyeing** *or* **eying** : mirar, observar
eye² *n* **1** : ojo *m* **2** VISION : visión *f*, vista *f*, ojo *m* ⟨a good eye for bargains : un buen ojo para las gangas⟩ **3** GLANCE : mirada *f*, ojeada *f* **4** ATTENTION : atención *f* ⟨to catch one's eye : llamar la atención⟩ **5** POINT OF VIEW : punto *m* de vista ⟨in the eyes of the law : según la ley⟩ **6** : ojo *m* (de una aguja, una papa, una tormenta)
eyeball ['aɪ,bɔl] *n* : globo *m* ocular
eyebrow ['aɪ,braʊ] *n* : ceja *f*
eyedropper ['aɪ,drɑpər] *n* : cuentagotas *f*
eyeglasses ['aɪ,glæsəz] *npl* : anteojos *mpl*, lentes *mpl*, espejuelos *mpl*, gafas *fpl*
eyelash ['aɪ,læʃ] *n* : pestaña *f*
eyelet ['aɪlət] *n* : ojete *m*
eyelid ['aɪ,lɪd] *n* : párpado *m*
eye–opener ['aɪ,oːpənər] *n* : revelación *f*, sorpresa *f*
eye–opening ['aɪ,oːpənɪŋ] *adj* : revelador
eyepiece ['aɪ,piːs] *n* : ocular *m*
eyesight ['aɪ,saɪt] *n* : vista *f*, visión *f*
eyesore ['aɪ,sor] *n* : monstruosidad *f*, adefesio *m*
eyestrain ['aɪ,streɪn] *n* : fatiga *f* visual, vista *f* cansada
eyetooth ['aɪ,tuːθ] *n* : colmillo *m*
eyewitness ['aɪ'wɪtnəs] *n* : testigo *mf* ocular, testigo *mf* presencial
eyrie ['aɪri] → **aerie**

F

f ['ɛf] *n, pl* **f's** *or* **fs** ['ɛfs] : sexta letra del alfabeto inglés
fable ['feɪbəl] *n* : fábula *f*
fabled ['feɪbəld] *adj* : legendario, fabuloso
fabric ['fæbrɪk] *n* **1** MATERIAL : tela *f*, tejido *m* **2** STRUCTURE : estructura *f* ⟨the fabric of society : la estructura de la sociedad⟩
fabricate ['fæbrɪ,keɪt] *vt* **-cated; -cating 1** CONSTRUCT, MANUFACTURE : construir, fabricar **2** INVENT : inventar (excusas o mentiras)
fabrication [,fæbrɪ'keɪʃən] *n* **1** LIE : mentira *f*, invención *f* **2** MANUFACTURE : fabricación *f*
fabulous ['fæbjələs] *adj* **1** LEGENDARY : fabuloso, legendario **2** INCREDIBLE : increíble, fabuloso ⟨fabulous wealth : riqueza fabulosa⟩ **3** WONDERFUL : magnífico, estupendo, fabuloso — **fabulously** *adv*
facade [fə'sɑd] *n* : fachada *f*
face¹ ['feɪs] *v* **faced; facing** *vt* **1** LINE : recubrir (una superficie), forrar (ropa) **2** CONFRONT : enfrentarse a, afrontar, hacer frente a ⟨to face the

music : afrontar las consecuencias⟩ ⟨to face the facts : aceptar la realidad⟩ **3** : estar de cara a, estar enfrente de ⟨she's facing her brother : está de cara a su hermano⟩ **4** OVERLOOK : dar a — *vi* : mirar (hacia), estar orientado (a)
face² *n* **1** : cara *f*, rostro *m* ⟨he told me to my face : me lo dijo a la cara⟩ **2** EXPRESSION : cara *f*, expresión *f* ⟨to pull a long face : poner mala cara⟩ **3** GRIMACE : mueca *f* ⟨to make faces : hacer muecas⟩ **4** APPEARANCE : fisonomía *f*, aspecto *m* ⟨the face of society : la fisonomía de la sociedad⟩ **5** EFFRONTERY : desfachatez *f* **6** PRESTIGE : prestigio *m* ⟨to lose face : desprestigiarse⟩ **7** FRONT, SIDE : cara *f* (de una moneda), esfera *f* (de un reloj), fachada *f* (de un edificio), pared *f* (de una montaña) **8** SURFACE : superficie *f*, faz *f* (de la tierra), cara *f* (de la luna) **9 in the face of** DESPITE : en medio de, en visto de, ante
facedown ['feɪs,daʊn] *adv* : boca abajo
faceless ['feɪsləs] *adj* ANONYMOUS : anónimo
face–lift ['feɪs,lɪft] *n* **1** : estiramiento *m*

facial **2** RENOVATION : renovación *f*, remozamiento *m*

facet ['fæsət] *n* **1** : faceta *f* (de una piedra) **2** ASPECT : faceta *f*, aspecto *m*

facetious [fə'si:ʃəs] *adj* : gracioso, burlón, bromista

facetiously [fə'si:ʃəsli] *adv* : en tono de burla

facetiousness [fə'si:ʃəsnəs] *n* : jocosidad *f*

face–to–face *adv & adj* : cara a cara

faceup ['feɪs'ʌp] *adv* : boca arriba

face value *n* : valor *m* nominal

facial[1] ['feɪʃəl] *adj* : de la cara, facial

facial[2] *n* : tratamiento *m* facial, limpieza *f* de cutis

facile ['fæsəl] *adj* SUPERFICIAL : superficial, simplista

facilitate [fə'sɪləˌteɪt] *vt* **-tated; -tating** : facilitar

facility [fə'sɪləṭi] *n, pl* **-ties** **1** EASE : facilidad *f* **2** CENTER, COMPLEX : centro *m*, complejo *m* **3 facilities** *npl* AMENITIES : comodidades *fpl*, servicios *mpl*

facing ['feɪsɪŋ] *n* **1** LINING : entretela *f* (de una prenda) **2** : revestimiento *m* (de un edificio)

facsimile [fæk'sɪməli] *n* : facsímile *m*, facsímil *m*

fact ['fækt] *n* **1** : hecho *m* ⟨as a matter of fact : de hecho⟩ **2** INFORMATION : información *f*, datos *mpl* ⟨facts and figures : datos y cifras⟩ **3** REALITY : realidad *f* ⟨in fact : en realidad⟩

faction ['fækʃən] *n* : facción *m*, bando *m*

factional ['fækʃənəl] *adj* : entre facciones

factious ['fækʃəs] *adj* : faccioso, contencioso

factitious [fæk'tɪʃəs] *adj* : artificial, facticio

factor ['fæktər] *n* : factor *m*

factory ['fæktəri] *n, pl* **-ries** : fábrica *f*

factual ['fæktʃuəl] *adj* : basado en hechos, objetivo

factually ['fæktʃuəli] *adv* : en cuanto a los hechos

faculty ['fækəlti] *n, pl* **-ties** **1** : facultad *f* ⟨the faculty of sight : las facultades visuales, el sentido de la vista⟩ **2** APTITUDE : aptitud *f*, facilidad *f* **3** TEACHERS : cuerpo *m* docente

fad ['fæd] *n* : moda *f* pasajera, manía *f*

fade ['feɪd] *v* **faded; fading** *vi* **1** WITHER : debilitarse (dícese de las personas), marchitarse (dícese de las flores y las plantas) **2** DISCOLOR : desteñirse, decolorarse **3** DIM : apagarse (dícese de la luz), perderse (dícese de los sonidos), fundirse (dícese de las imágenes) **4** VANISH : desvanecerse, decaer — *vt* DISCOLOR : desteñir

fag ['fæg] *vt* **fagged; fagging** EXHAUST : cansar, fatigar

fagot *or* **faggot** ['fægət] *n* : haz *m* de leña

Fahrenheit ['færənˌhaɪt] *adj* : Fahrenheit

fail[1] ['feɪl] *vi* **1** WEAKEN : fallar, deteriorarse **2** STOP : fallar, detenerse ⟨his heart failed : le falló el corazón⟩ **3** : fracasar, fallar ⟨her plan failed : su plan fracasó⟩ ⟨the crops failed : se perdió la cosecha⟩ **4** : quebrar ⟨a business about to fail : una empresa a punto de quebrar⟩ **5 to fail in** : faltar a, no cumplir con ⟨to fail in one's duties : faltar a sus deberes⟩ — *vt* **1** FLUNK : reprobar (un examen) **2** : fallar ⟨words fail me : las palabras me fallan, no encuentro palabras⟩ **3** DISAPPOINT : fallar, decepcionar ⟨don't fail me! : ¡no me falles!⟩

fail[2] *n* : fracaso *m*

failing ['feɪlɪŋ] *n* : defecto *m*

failure ['feɪljər] *n* **1** : fracaso *m*, malogro *m* ⟨crop failure : pérdida de la cosecha⟩ ⟨heart failure : insuficiencia cardíaca⟩ ⟨engine failure : falla mecánica⟩ **2** BANKRUPTCY : bancarrota *f*, quiebra *f* **3** : fracaso *m* (persona) ⟨he was a failure as a manager : como gerente, fue un fracaso⟩

faint[1] ['feɪnt] *vi* : desmayarse

faint[2] *adj* **1** COWARDLY, TIMID : cobarde, tímido **2** DIZZY : mareado ⟨faint with hunger : desfallecido de hambre⟩ **3** SLIGHT : leve, ligero, vago ⟨I haven't the faintest idea : no tengo la más mínima idea⟩ **4** INDISTINCT : tenue, indistinto, apenas perceptible

faint[3] *n* : desmayo *m*

fainthearted ['feɪnt'hɑrṭəd] *adj* : cobarde, pusilánime

faintly ['feɪntli] *adv* : débilmente, ligeramente, levemente

faintness ['feɪntnəs] *n* **1** INDISTINCTNESS : lo débil, falta *f* de claridad **2** FAINTING : desmayo *m*, desfallecimiento *m*

fair[1] ['fær] *adj* **1** ATTRACTIVE, BEAUTIFUL : bello, hermoso, atractivo **2** (*relating to weather*) : bueno, despejado ⟨fair weather : tiempo despejado⟩ **3** JUST : justo, imparcial **4** ALLOWABLE : permisible **5** BLOND, LIGHT : rubio (dícese del pelo), blanco (dícese de la tez) **6** ADEQUATE : bastante, adecuado ⟨fair to middling : mediano, regular⟩ **7 fair game** : presa *f* fácil **8 to play fair** : jugar limpio

fair[2] *n* : feria *f*

fairground ['fær,graʊnd] *n* : parque *m* de diversiones

fairly ['færli] *adv* **1** IMPARTIALLY : imparcialmente, limpiamente, equitativamente **2** QUITE : bastante **3** MODERATELY : medianamente

fairness ['færnəs] *n* **1** IMPARTIALITY : imparcialidad *f*, justicia *f* **2** LIGHTNESS : blancura *f* (de la piel), lo rubio (del pelo)

fairy ['færi] *n, pl* **fairies** **1** : hada *f* **2 fairy tale** : cuento *m* de hadas

fairyland ['færi,lænd] *n* **1** : país *m* de las hadas **2** : lugar *m* encantador

faith ['feɪθ] *n, pl* **faiths** ['feɪθs, 'feɪðz] **1**
BELIEF : fe *f* **2** ALLEGIANCE : lealtad *f*
3 CONFIDENCE, TRUST : confianza *f*, fe
f **4** RELIGION : religión *f*

faithful ['feɪθfəl] *adj* : fiel — **faithfully**
adv

faithfulness ['feɪθfəlnəs] *n* : fidelidad *f*

faithless ['feɪθləs] *adj* **1** DISLOYAL
: desleal **2** : infiel (en la religión) —
faithlessly *adv*

faithlessness ['feɪθləsnəs] *n* : deslealtad
f

fake¹ ['feɪk] *v* **faked; faking** *vt* **1** FALSI-
FY : falsificar, falsear **2** FEIGN : fingir
— *vi* **1** PRETEND : fingir **2** : hacer un
engaño, hacer una finta (en deportes)

fake² *adj* : falso, fingido, postizo

fake³ *n* **1** IMITATION : imitación *f*, falsificación *f* **2** IMPOSTOR : impostor *m*,
-tora *f*; charlatán *m*, -tana *f*; farsante *mf*
3 FEINT : engaño *m*, finta *f* (en deportes)

faker ['feɪkər] *n* : impostor *m*, -tora *f*;
charlatán *m*, -tana *f*; farsante *mf*

fakir [fə'kɪr, 'feɪkər] *n* : faquir *m*

falcon ['fælkən, 'fɔl-] *n* : halcón *m*

falconry ['fælkənri, 'fɔl-] *n* : cetrería *f*

fall¹ ['fɔl] *vi* **fell** ['fɛl]; **fallen** [fɔlən]; **falling**
1 : caer, caerse ⟨to fall out of bed : caer
de la cama⟩ ⟨to fall down : caerse⟩ **2**
HANG : caer **3** DESCEND : caer (dícese
de la lluvia o de la noche), bajar (dícese
de los precios), descender (dícese de la
temperatura) **4** : caer (a un enemigo),
rendirse ⟨the city fell : la ciudad se
rindió⟩ **5** OCCUR : caer ⟨Christmas
falls on a Friday : la Navidad cae en
viernes⟩ **6 to fall asleep** : dormirse,
quedarse dormido **7 to fall from grace**
SIN : perder la gracia **8 to fall sick** : caer
enfermo, enfermarse **9 to fall through**
: fracasar, caer en la nada **10 to fall to**
: tocar a, corresponder a ⟨the task fell
to him : le tocó hacerlo⟩

fall² *n* **1** TUMBLE : caída *f* ⟨to break one's
fall : frenar uno su caída⟩ ⟨a fall of
three feet : una caída de tres pies⟩ **2**
FALLING : derrumbe *m* (de rocas),
aguacero *m* (de lluvia), nevada *f* (de
nieve), bajada *f* (de precios), disminución *f* (de cantidades) **3** AUTUMN
: otoño *m* **4** DOWNFALL : caída *f*, ruina *f* **5 falls** *npl* WATERFALL : cascada
f, catarata *f*

fallacious [fə'leɪʃəs] *adj* : erróneo, engañoso, falaz

fallacy ['fæləsi] *n, pl* **-cies** : falacia *f*

fall back *vi* RETREAT : retirarse, replegarse **2 to fall back on** : recurrir a

fall guy *n* SCAPEGOAT : chivo *m* expiatorio

fallible ['fæləbəl] *adj* : falible

fallout ['fɔl,aʊt] *n* **1** : lluvia *f* radioacti-
va **2** CONSEQUENCES : secuelas *fpl*,
consecuencias *fpl*

fallow¹ ['fælo] *vt* : barbechar

fallow² *adj* **to lie fallow** : estar en barbecho

fallow³ *n* : barbecho *m*

false ['fɔls] *adj* **falser; falsest 1** UNTRUE
: falso **2** ERRONEOUS : erróneo, equivocado **3** FAKE : falso, postizo **4** UN-
FAITHFUL : infiel **5** FRAUDULENT
: fraudulento ⟨under false pretenses
: por fraude⟩

falsehood ['fɔls,hʊd] *n* : mentira *f*, falsedad *f*

falsely ['fɔlsli] *adv* : falsamente, con
falsedad

falseness ['fɔlsnəs] *n* : falsedad *f*

falsetto [fɔl'sɛtoː] *n, pl* **-tos** : falsete *m*

falsification [,fɔlsəfə'keɪʃən] *n* : falsificación *f*, falseamiento *m*

falsify ['fɔlsə,faɪ] *vt* **-fied; fying** : falsificar, falsear

falsity ['fɔlsəti] *n, pl* **-ties** : falsedad *f*

falter ['fɔltər] *vi* **-tered; -tering 1** TOT-
TER : tambalearse **2** STAMMER
: titubear, tartamudear **3** WAVER : vacilar

faltering ['fɔltərɪŋ] *adj* : titubeante, vacilante

fame ['feɪm] *n* : fama *f*

famed ['feɪmd] *adj* : famoso, célebre,
afamado

familial [fə'mɪljəl, -liəl] *adj* : familiar

familiar¹ [fə'mɪljər] *adj* **1** KNOWN : familiar, conocido ⟨to be familiar with
: estar familiarizado con⟩ **2** INFORMAL
: familiar, informal **3** INTIMATE : íntimo, de confianza **4** FORWARD : confianzudo, atrevido — **familiarly** *adv*

familiar² *n* : espíritu *m* guardián

familiarity [fə,mɪli'ærəti, -,mɪl'jær-] *n, pl*
-ties 1 KNOWLEDGE : conocimiento
m, familiaridad *f* **2** INFORMALITY, IN-
TIMACY : confianza *f*, familiaridad *f* **3**
FORWARDNESS : exceso *m* de confianza, descaro *m*

familiarize [fə'mɪljə,raɪz] *vt* **-ized; -izing**
1 : familiarizar **2 to familiarize oneself** : familiarizarse

family ['fæmli, 'fæmə-] *n, pl* **-lies** : familia *f*

family room *n* : living *m*, sala *f* (informal)

family tree *n* : árbol *m* genealógico

famine ['fæmən] *n* : hambre *f*, hambruna
f

famish ['fæmɪʃ] *vi* **to be famished** : estar famélico, estar hambriento, morir
de hambre *fam*

famous ['feɪməs] *adj* : famoso

famously ['feɪməsli] *adv* **to get on famously** : llevarse de maravilla

fan¹ ['fæn] *vt* **fanned; fanning 1**
: abanicar (a una persona), avivar (un
fuego) **2** STIMULATE : avivar, estimular

fan² *n* **1** : ventilador *m*, abanico *m* **2**
ADMIRER, ENTHUSIAST : aficionado
m, -da *f*; entusiasta *mf*; admirador *m*,
-dora *f*

fanatic¹ [fə'nætɪk] *or* **fanatical** [-ṭɪ-kəl]
adj : fanático

fanatic² *n* : fanático *m*, -ca *f*

fanaticism [fə'nætə,sızəm] *n* : fanatismo *m*

fanciful ['fænʧıfəl] *adj* **1** CAPRICIOUS : caprichoso, fantástico, extravagante **2** IMAGINATIVE : imaginativo — **fancifully** *adv*

fancy¹ ['fænʧsi] *vt* **-cied; -cying 1** IMAGINE : imaginarse, figurarse ⟨fancy that! : ¡figúrate!, ¡imagínate!⟩ **2** CRAVE : apetecer, tener ganas de

fancy² *adj* **-cier; -est 1** ELABORATE : elaborado **2** LUXURIOUS : lujoso, elegante — **fancily** ['fænʧsəli] *adv*

fancy³ *n, pl* **-cies 1** LIKING : gusto *m*, afición *f* **2** WHIM : antojo *m*, capricho *m* **3** IMAGINATION : fantasía *f*, imaginación *f*

fandango [fæn'dæŋgo] *n, pl* **-gos** : fandango *m*

fanfare ['fæn,fær] *n* : fanfarria *f*

fang ['fæŋ] *n* : colmillo *m* (de un animal), diente *m* (de una serpiente)

fanlight ['fæn,laıt] *n* : tragaluz *m*

fantasia [fæn'teıʒə, -ziə; ,fæntə-'zi:ə] *n* : fantasía *f*

fantasize ['fæntə,saız] *vi* **-sized; -sizing** : fantasear

fantastic [fæn'tæstık] *adj* **1** UNBELIEVABLE : fantástico, increíble, extraño **2** ENORMOUS : fabuloso, inmenso ⟨fantastic sums : sumas fabulosas⟩ **3** WONDERFUL : estupendo, fantástico, bárbaro *fam*, macanudo *fam* — **fantastically** [-tıkli] *adv*

fantasy ['fæntəsi] *n, pl* **-sies** : fantasía *f*

far¹ ['fɑr] *adv* **farther** ['fɑrðər] *or* **further** ['fər-]; **farthest** *or* **furthest** [-ðəst] **1** : lejos ⟨far from here : lejos de aquí⟩ ⟨to go far : llegar lejos⟩ ⟨as far as Chicago : hasta Chicago⟩ ⟨far away : a lo lejos⟩ **2** MUCH : muy, mucho ⟨far bigger : mucho más grande⟩ ⟨far superior : muy superior⟩ ⟨it's by far the best : es con mucho el mejor⟩ **3** (*expressing degree or extent*) ⟨the results are far off : salieron muy inexactos los resultados⟩ ⟨to go so far as : decir tanto como⟩ ⟨to go far enough : tener el alcance necesario⟩ **4** (*expressing progress*) ⟨the work is far advanced : el trabajo está muy avanzado⟩ ⟨to take (something) too far : llevar (algo) demasiado lejos⟩ **5 far and wide** : por todas partes **6 far from it!** : ¡todo lo contrario! **7 so far** : hasta ahora, todavía

far² *adj* **farther** *or* **further; farthest** *or* **furthest 1** REMOTE : lejano, remoto ⟨the Far East : el Lejano Oriente, el Extremo Oriente⟩ ⟨a far country : un país lejano⟩ **2** LONG : largo ⟨a far journey : un viaje largo⟩ **3** EXTREME : extremo ⟨the far right : la extrema derecha⟩ ⟨at the far end of the room : en el otro extremo de la sala⟩

faraway ['fɑrə,weı] *adj* : remoto, lejano

farce ['fɑrs] *n* : farsa *f*

farcical ['fɑrsıkəl] *adj* : absurdo, ridículo

fare¹ ['fær] *vi* **fared; faring** : ir, salir ⟨how did you fare? : ¿cómo te fue?⟩

fare² *n* **1** : pasaje *m*, billete *m*, boleto *m* ⟨half fare : medio pasaje⟩ **2** FOOD : comida *f*

farewell¹ [fær'wɛl] *adj* : de despedida

farewell² *n* : despedida *f*

far–fetched ['fɑr'fɛʧt] *adj* : improbable, exagerado

farina [fə'ri:nə] *n* : harina *f*

farm¹ ['fɑrm] *vt* **1** : cultivar, labrar **2** : criar (animales) — *vi* : ser agricultor

farm² *n* : granja *f*, hacienda *f*, finca *f*, estancia *f*

farmer ['fɑrmər] *n* : agricultor *m*, granjero *m*

farmhand ['fɑrm,hænd] *n* : peón *m*

farmhouse ['fɑrm,haʊs] *n* : granja *f*, vivienda *f* del granjero, casa *f* de hacienda

farming ['fɑrmıŋ] *n* : labranza *f*, cultivo *m*, crianza *f* (de animales)

farmland ['fɑrm,lænd] *n* : tierras *fpl* de labranza

farmyard ['fɑrm,jɑrd] *n* : corral *m*

far–off ['fɑr,ɔf, -'ɔf] *adj* : remoto, distante, lejano

far–reaching ['fɑr'ri:ʧıŋ] *adj* : de gran alcance

farsighted ['fɑr,saıtəd] *adj* **1** : hipermétrope **2** JUDICIOUS : con visión de futuro, previsor, precavido

farsightedness ['fɑr,saıtədnəs] *n* **1** : hipermetropía *f* **2** PRUDENCE : previsión *f*

farther¹ ['fɑrðər] *adv* **1** AHEAD : más lejos (en el espacio), más adelante (en el tiempo) **2** MORE : más

farther² *adj* : más lejano, más remoto

farthermost ['fɑrðər,mo:st] *adj* : (el) más lejano

farthest¹ ['fɑrðəst] *adv* **1** : lo más lejos ⟨I jumped farthest : salté lo más lejos⟩ **2** : lo más avanzado ⟨he progressed farthest : progresó al punto más avanzado⟩ **3** : más ⟨the farthest developed plan : el plan más desarrollado⟩

farthest² *adj* : más lejano

fascicle ['fæsıkəl] *n* : fascículo *m*

fascinate ['fæsən,eıt] *vt* **-nated; -nating** : fascinar, cautivar

fascinating ['fæsən,eıtıŋ] *adj* : fascinante

fascination [,fæsən'eıʃən] *n* : fascinación *f*

fascism ['fæʃ,ızəm] *n* : fascismo *m*

fascist¹ ['fæʃıst] *adj* : fascista

fascist² *n* : fascista *mf*

fashion¹ ['fæʃən] *vt* : formar, moldear

fashion² *n* **1** MANNER : manera *f*, modo *m* **2** CUSTOM : costumbre *f* **3** STYLE : moda *f*

fashionable ['fæʃənəbəl] *adj* : de moda, chic

fashionably ['fæʃənəbli] *adv* : a la moda

fast¹ ['fæst] *vi* : ayunar

fast² *adv* **1** SECURELY : firmemente, seguramente ⟨to hold fast : agarrarse

bien⟩ 2 RAPIDLY : rápidamente, rápido, de prisa 3 **to run fast** : ir adelantado (dícese de un reloj) 4 SOUNDLY
: profundamente ⟨fast asleep : profundamente dormido⟩
fast³ *adj* 1 SECURE : firme, seguro ⟨to
make fast : amarrar (un barco)⟩ 2
FAITHFUL : leal ⟨fast friends : amigos
leales⟩ 3 RAPID : rápido, veloz 4 : adelantado ⟨my watch is fast : tengo el
reloj adelantado⟩ 5 DEEP : profundo
⟨a fast sleep : un sueño profundo⟩ 6
COLORFAST : inalterable, que no destiñe 7 DISSOLUTE : extravagante, disi-
pado, disoluto
fast⁴ *n* : ayuno *m*
fasten ['fæsən] *vt* 1 ATTACH : sujetar,
atar 2 FIX : fijar ⟨to fasten one's eyes
on : fijar los ojos en⟩ 3 SECURE
: abrochar (ropa o cinturones), atar
(cordones), cerrar (una maleta) — *vi*
: abrocharse, cerrar
fastener ['fæsənər] *n* : cierre *m*, sujetador *m*
fastening ['fæsənɪŋ] *n* : cierre *m*, sujetador *m*
fast food *n* : comida *f* rápida
fastidious [fæs'tɪdiəs] *adj* : quisquilloso,
exigente — **fastidiously** *adv*
fat¹ ['fæt] *adj* **fatter; fattest** 1 OBESE
: gordo, obeso 2 THICK : grueso
fat² *n* : grasa *f*
fatal ['feɪtəl] *adj* 1 DEADLY : mortal 2
ILL-FATED : malhadado, fatal 3 MO-
MENTOUS : fatídico
fatalism ['feɪtəl,ɪzəm] *n* : fatalismo *m*
fatalist ['feɪtəlɪst] *n* : fatalista *mf*
fatalistic [,feɪtəl'ɪstɪk] *adj* : fatalista
fatality [feɪ'tæləti, fə-] *n, pl* **-ties** : víctima *f* mortal
fatally ['feɪtəli] *adv* : mortalmente
fate ['feɪt] *n* 1 DESTINY : destino *m* 2
END, LOT : final *m*, suerte *f*
fated ['feɪtəd] *adj* : predestinado
fateful ['feɪtfəl] *adj* 1 MOMENTOUS
: fatídico, aciago 2 PROPHETIC
: profético — **fatefully** *adv*
father¹ ['fɑðər] *vt* : engendrar
father² *n* 1 : padre *m* ⟨my father and
my mother : mi padre y mi madre⟩ ⟨Fa-
ther Smith : el padre Smith⟩ 2 **the Father** GOD : el Padre, Dios *m*
fatherhood ['fɑðər,hʊd] *n* : paternidad *f*
father-in-law ['fɑðərɪn,lɔ] *n, pl* **fa-
thers-in-law** : suegro *m*
fatherland ['fɑðər,lænd] *n* : patria *f*
fatherless ['fɑðərləs] *adj* : huérfano de
padre, sin padre
fatherly ['fɑðərli] *adj* : paternal
fathom¹ ['fæðəm] *vt* UNDERSTAND : entender, comprender
fathom² *n* : braza *f*
fatigue¹ [fə'tiːg] *vt* **-tigued; -tiguing**
: fatigar, cansar
fatigue² *n* : fatiga *f*
fatness ['fætnəs] *n* : gordura *f* (de una
persona o un animal), grosor *m* (de un
objeto)

fatten ['fætən] *vt* : engordar, cebar
fatty ['fæti] *adj* **fattier; -est** : graso, grasoso, adiposo (dícese de los tejidos)
fatuous ['fætʃuəs] *adj* : necio, fatuo —
fatuously *adv*
faucet ['fɔsət] *n* : llave *f*, canilla *f Arg,
Uru*, grifo *m*
fault¹ ['fɔlt] *vt* : encontrar defectos a
fault² *n* 1 SHORTCOMING : defecto *m*,
falta *f* 2 DEFECT : falta *f*, defecto *m*,
falla *f* 3 BLAME : culpa *f* 4 FRACTURE
: falla *f* (geológica)
faultfinder ['fɔlt,faɪndər] *n* : criticón *m*,
-cona *f*
faultfinding ['fɔlt,faɪndɪŋ] *n* : crítica *f*
faultless ['fɔltləs] *adj* : sin culpa, sin im-
perfecciones, impecable
faultlessly ['fɔltləsli] *adv* : impecablemente, perfectamente
faulty ['fɔlti] *adj* **faultier; -est** : defectuoso, imperfecto — **faultily** ['fɔltəli] *adv*
fauna ['fɔnə] *n* : fauna *f*
faux ['fo:] *adj* : de imitación
faux pas [,fo:'pɑ] *n, pl* **faux pas** [*same
or* -'pɑz] : metedura *f* de pata *fam*
favor¹ ['feɪvər] *vt* 1 SUPPORT : estar a favor de, ser partidario de, apoyar 2
OBLIGE : hacerle un favor a 3 PREFER
: preferir 4 RESEMBLE : parecerse a,
salir a
favor² *n* : favor *m* ⟨in favor of : a favor
de⟩ ⟨an error in his favor : un error a
su favor⟩
favorable ['feɪvərəbəl] *adj* : favorable,
propicio
favorably ['feɪvərəbli] *adv* : favorablemente, bien
favorite¹ ['feɪvərət] *adj* : favorito,
preferido
favorite² *n* : favorito *m*, -ta *f*; preferido
m, -da *f*
favoritism ['feɪvərə,tɪzəm] *n* : favoritismo *m*
fawn¹ ['fɔn] *vi* : adular, lisonjear
fawn² *n* : cervato *m*
fax ['fæks] *n* : facsímil *m*, facsímile *m*
faze ['feɪz] *vt* **fazed; fazing** : desconcertar, perturbar
fear¹ ['fɪr] *vt* : temer, tener miedo de —
vi : temer
fear² *n* : miedo *m*, temor *m* ⟨for fear of
: por temor a⟩
fearful ['fɪrfəl] *adj* 1 FRIGHTENING : espantoso, aterrador, horrible 2 FRIGHT-
ENED : temeroso, miedoso
fearfully ['fɪrfəli] *adv* 1 EXTREMELY : extremadamente, terriblemente 2 TIMID-
LY : con temor
fearless ['fɪrləs] *adj* : intrépido, impávido
fearlessly ['fɪrləsli] *adv* : sin temor
fearlessness ['fɪrləsnəs] *n* : intrepidez *f*,
impavidez *f*
fearsome ['fɪrsəm] *adj* : aterrador
feasibility [,fiːzə'bɪləti] *n* : viabilidad *f*,
factibilidad *f*
feasible ['fiːzəbəl] *adj* : viable, factible,
realizable

feast¹ ['fiːst] *vi* : banquetear — *vt* **1** : agasajar, festejar **2 to feast one's eyes on** : regalarse la vista con

feast² *n* **1** BANQUET : banquete *m*, festín *m* **2** FESTIVAL : fiesta *f*

feat ['fiːt] *n* : proeza *f*, hazaña *f*

feather¹ ['fɛðər] *vt* **1** : emplumar **2 to feather one's nest** : hacer su agosto

feather² *n* **1** : pluma *f* **2 a feather in one's cap** : un triunfo personal

feathered ['fɛðərd] *adj* : con plumas

feathery ['fɛðəri] *adj* **1** DOWNY : plumoso **2** LIGHT : liviano

feature¹ ['fiːtʃər] *v* **-tured; -turing** *vt* **1** IMAGINE : imaginarse **2** PRESENT : presentar — *vi* : figurar

feature² *n* **1** CHARACTERISTIC : característica *f*, rasgo *m* **2** : largometraje *m* (en el cine), artículo *m* (en un periódico), documental *m* (en la televisión) **3 features** *npl* : rasgos *mpl*, facciones *fpl* ⟨delicate features : facciones delicadas⟩

February ['fɛbjuˌri, 'fɛbu-, 'fbru-] *n* : febrero *m*

fecal ['fiːkəl] *adj* : fecal

feces ['fiːˌsiːz] *npl* : heces *fpl*, excrementos *mpl*

feckless ['fɛkləs] *adj* : irresponsable

fecund ['fɛkənd, 'fiː-] *adj* : fecundo

fecundity [fɪˈkʌndəti, fɛ-] *n* : fecundidad *f*

federal ['fɛdrəl, -dərəl] *adj* : federal

federalism ['fɛdrəˌlɪzəm, -dərə-] *n* : federalismo *m*

federalist¹ ['fɛdrəlɪst, -dərə-] *adj* : federalista

federalist² *n* : federalista *mf*

federate ['fɛdəˌreɪt] *vt* **-ated; -ating** : federar

federation [ˌfɛdəˈreɪʃən] *n* : federación *f*

fedora [fɪˈdorə] *n* : sombrero *m* flexible de fieltro

fed up *adj* : harto

fee ['fiː] *n* **1** : honorarios *mpl* (a un médico, un abogado, etc.) **2 entrance fee** : entrada *f*

feeble ['fiːbəl] *adj* **-bler; -blest** **1** WEAK : débil, endeble **2** INEFFECTIVE : flojo, pobre, poco convincente

feebleminded [ˌfiːbəlˈmaɪndəd] *adj* **1** : débil mental **2** FOOLISH, STUPID : imbécil, tonto

feebleness ['fiːbəlnəs] *n* : debilidad *f*

feebly ['fiːbli] *adv* : débilmente

feed¹ ['fiːd] *v* **fed** ['fɛd]; **feeding** *vt* **1** : dar de comer a, nutrir, alimentar (a una persona) **2** : alimentar (un fuego o una máquina), proveer (información), introducir (datos) — *vi* : comer, alimentarse

feed² *n* **1** NOURISHMENT : alimento *m* **2** FODDER : pienso *m*

feedback ['fiːdˌbæk] *n* **1** : realimentación *f* (electrónica) **2** RESPONSE : reacción *f*

feeder ['fiːdər] *n* : comedero *m* (para animales)

feel¹ ['fiːl] *v* **felt** ['fɛlt]; **feeling** *vi* **1** : sentirse, encontrarse ⟨I feel tired : me siento cansada⟩ ⟨he feels hungry : tiene hambre⟩ ⟨she feels like a fool : se siente como una idiota⟩ ⟨to feel like doing something : tener ganas de hacer algo⟩ **2** SEEM : parecer ⟨it feels like spring : parece primavera⟩ **3** THINK : parecerse, opinar, pensar ⟨how does he feel about that? : ¿qué opina él de eso?⟩ — *vt* **1** TOUCH : tocar, palpar **2** SENSE : sentir ⟨to feel the cold : sentir el frío⟩ **3** CONSIDER : sentir, creer, considerar ⟨to feel (it) necessary : creer necesario⟩

feel² *n* **1** SENSATION, TOUCH : sensación *f*, tacto *m* **2** ATMOSPHERE : ambiente *m*, atmósfera *f* **3 to have a feel for** : tener un talento especial para

feeler ['fiːlər] *n* : antena *f*, tentáculo *m*

feeling ['fiːlɪŋ] *n* **1** SENSATION : sensación *f*, sensibilidad *f* **2** EMOTION : sentimiento *m* **3** OPINION : opinión *f* **4 feelings** *npl* SENSIBILITIES : sentimientos *mpl* ⟨to hurt someone's feelings : herir los sentimientos de alguien⟩

feet → foot

feign ['feɪn] *vt* : simular, aparentar, fingir

feint¹ ['feɪnt] *vi* : fintar, fintear

feint² *n* : finta *f*

feldspar ['fɛldˌspar] *n* : feldespato *m*

felicitate [fɪˈlɪsəˌteɪt] *vt* **-tated; -tating** : felicitar, congratular

felicitation [fɪˌlɪsəˈteɪʃən] *n* : felicitación *f*

felicitous [fɪˈlɪsətəs] *adj* : acertado, oportuno

feline¹ ['fiːˌlaɪn] *adj* : felino

feline² *n* : felino *m*, -na *f*

fell¹ ['fɛl] *vt* : talar (un árbol), derribar (a una persona)

fell² → fall

fellow ['fɛˌloː] *n* **1** COMPANION : compañero *m*, -ra *f*; camarada *mf* **2** ASSOCIATE : socio *m*, -cia *f* **3** MAN : tipo *m*, hombre *m*

fellowman [ˌfɛloˈmæn] *n*, *pl* **-men** : prójimo *m*, semejante *m*

fellowship ['fɛloˌʃɪp] *n* **1** COMPANIONSHIP : camaradería *f*, compañerismo *m* **2** ASSOCIATION : fraternidad *f* **3** GRANT : beca *f* (de investigación)

felon ['fɛlən] *n* : malhechor *m*, -chora *f*; criminal *mf*

felonious [fəˈloniəs] *adj* : criminal

felony ['fɛləni] *n*, *pl* **-nies** : delito *m* grave

felt¹ ['fɛlt] *n* : fieltro *m*

felt² → feel

female¹ ['fiːˌmeɪl] *adj* : femenino

female² *n* **1** : hembra *f* (de animal) **2** WOMAN : mujer *f*

feminine ['fɛmənən] *adj* : femenino

femininity [ˌfɛməˈnɪnəti] *n* : feminidad *f*, femineidad *f*

feminism ['fɛməˌnɪzəm] *n* : feminismo *m*

feminist¹ ['fɛmənɪst] *adj* : feminista

feminist² *n* : feminista *mf*

femoral ['fɛmərəl] *adj* : femoral
femur ['fi:mər] *n, pl* **femurs** *or* **femora** ['fɛmərə] : fémur *m*
fence[1] ['fɛnts] *v* **fenced; fencing** *vt* : vallar, cercar — *vi* : hacer esgrima
fence[2] *n* : cerca *f*, valla *f*, cerco *m*
fencer ['fɛntsər] *n* : esgrimista *mf*; esgrimidor *m*, -dora *f*
fencing ['fɛntsɪŋ] *n* **1** : esgrima *m* (deporte) **2** : materiales *mpl* para cercas **3** ENCLOSURE : cercado *m*
fend ['fɛnd] *vt* **to fend off** : rechazar (un enemigo), parar (un golpe), eludir (una pregunta) — *vi* **to fend for oneself** : arreglárselas sólo, valerse por sí mismo
fender ['fɛndər] *n* : guardabarros *mpl*, salpicadera *f Mex*
fennel ['fɛnəl] *n* : hinojo *m*
ferment[1] [fər'mɛnt] *v* : fermentar
ferment[2] ['fər,mɛnt] *n* **1** : fermento *m* (en la química) **2** TURMOIL : agitación *f*, conmoción *f*
fermentation [,fərmən'teɪʃən, -,mɛn-] *n* : fermentación *f*
fern ['fərn] *n* : helecho *m*
ferocious [fə'roːʃəs] *adj* : feroz — **ferociously** *adv*
ferociousness [fə'roːʃəsnəs] *n* : ferocidad *f*
ferocity [fə'rɑsəti] *n* : ferocidad *f*
ferret[1] ['fɛrət] *vi* SNOOP : hurgar, husmear — *vt* **to ferret out** : descubrir
ferret[2] *n* : hurón *m*
ferric ['fɛrɪk] *or* **ferrous** ['fɛrəs] *adj* : férrico
Ferris wheel ['fɛrɪs] *n* : noria *f*
ferry[1] ['fɛri] *vt* **-ried; -rying** : llevar, transportar
ferry[2] *n, pl* **-ries** : transbordador *m*, ferry *m*
ferryboat ['fɛri,boːt] *n* : transbordador *m*, ferry *m*
fertile ['fərtəl] *adj* : fértil, fecundo
fertility [fər'tɪləti] *n* : fertilidad *f*
fertilization [,fərtələ'zeɪʃən] *n* : fertilización *f* (del suelo), fecundación (de un huevo)
fertilize ['fərtəl,aɪz] *vt* **-ized; -izing** **1** : fecundar (un huevo) **2** : fertilizar, abonar (el suelo)
fertilizer ['fərtəl,aɪzər] *n* : fertilizante *m*, abono *m*
fervent ['fərvənt] *adj* : ferviente, fervoroso, ardiente — **fervently** *adv*
fervid ['fərvɪd] *adj* : ardiente, apasionado — **fervidly** *adv*
fervor ['fərvər] *n* : fervor *m*, ardor *m*
fester ['fɛstər] *vi* : enconarse, supurar
festival ['fɛstəvəl] *n* : fiesta *f*, festividad *f*, festival *m*
festive ['fɛstɪv] *adj* : festivo — **festively** *adv*
festivity [fɛs'tɪvəti] *n, pl* **-ties** : festividad *f*, celebración *f*
festoon[1] [fɛs'tuːn] *vt* : adornar, engalanar
festoon[2] *n* GARLAND : guirnalda *f*
fetal ['fiːtəl] *adj* : fetal

fetch ['fɛtʃ] *vt* **1** BRING : traer, recoger, ir a buscar **2** REALIZE : realizar, venderse por ⟨the jewelry fetched $10,000 : las joyas se vendieron por $10,000⟩
fetching ['fɛtʃɪŋ] *adj* : atractivo, encantador
fête[1] ['feɪt, 'fɛt] *vt* **fêted; fêting** : festejar, agasajar
fête[2] *n* : fiesta *f*
fetid ['fɛtəd] *adj* : fétido
fetish ['fɛtɪʃ] *n* : fetiche *m*
fetlock ['fɛt,lɑk] *n* : espolón *m*
fetter ['fɛtər] *vt* : encadenar, poner grillos a
fetters ['fɛtərz] *npl* : grillos *mpl*, grilletes *mpl*, cadenas *fpl*
fettle ['fɛtəl] *n* **in fine fettle** : en buena forma, en plena forma
fetus ['fiːtəs] *n* : feto *m*
feud[1] ['fjuːd] *vi* : pelear, contender
feud[2] *n* : contienda *f*, enemistad *f* (heredada)
feudal ['fjuːdəl] *adj* : feudal
feudalism ['fjuːdəl,ɪzəm] *n* : feudalismo *m*
fever ['fiːvər] *n* : fiebre *f*, calentura *f*
feverish ['fiːvərɪʃ] *adj* **1** : afiebrado, con fiebre, febril **2** FRANTIC : febril, frenético
few[1] ['fjuː] *adj* : pocos ⟨with few exceptions : con pocas excepciones⟩ ⟨a few times : varias veces⟩
few[2] *pron* **1** : pocos ⟨few (of them) were ready : pocos estaban listos⟩ **2 a few** : algunos, unos cuantos **3 few and far between** : contados
fewer ['fjuːər] *pron* : menos ⟨the fewer the better : cuantos menos mejor⟩
fez ['fɛz] *n, pl* **fezzes** : fez *m*
fiancé [,fiː,ɑnˈseɪ, fiːˈɑn,seɪ] *n* : prometido *m*, novio *m*
fiancée [,fiː,ɑnˈseɪ, ,fiːˈɑn,seɪ] *n* : prometida *f*, novia *f*
fiasco [fiˈæs,koː] *n, pl* **-coes** : fiasco *m*, fracaso *m*
fiat ['fiː,ɑt, -,æt, -ət; 'faɪət, -,æt] *n* : decreto *m*, orden *m*
fib[1] ['fɪb] *vi* **fibbed; fibbing** : decir mentirillas
fib[2] *n* : mentirilla *f*, bola *f fam*
fibber ['fɪbər] *n* : mentirosillo *m*, -lla *f*; cuentista *mf fam*
fiber *or* **fibre** ['faɪbər] *n* : fibra *f*
fiberboard ['faɪbər,bord] *n* : cartón *m* madera
fiberglass ['faɪbər,glæs] *n* : fibra *f* de vidrio
fibrillate ['fɪbrə,leɪt, 'faɪ-] *vi* **-lated; -lating** : fibrilar
fibrillation [,fɪbrə'leɪʃən, ,faɪ-] *n* : fibrilación *f*
fibrous ['faɪbrəs] *adj* : fibroso
fibula ['fɪbjələ] *n, pl* **-lae** [-,liː, -,laɪ] *or* **-las** : peroné *m*
fickle ['fɪkəl] *adj* : inconstante, voluble, veleidoso
fickleness ['fɪkəlnəs] *n* : volubilidad *f*, inconstancia *f*, veleidad *f*

fiction ['fɪkʃən] *n* : ficción *f*
fictional ['fɪkʃənəl] *adj* : ficticio
fictitious [fɪk'tɪʃəs] *adj* **1** IMAGINARY : ficticio, imaginario **2** FALSE : falso, ficticio
fiddle[1] ['fɪdəl] *vi* **-dled; -dling 1** : tocar el violín **2 to fiddle with** : juguetear con, toquetear
fiddle[2] *n* : violín *m*
fiddler ['fɪdlər, 'fɪdələr] *n* : violinista *mf*
fiddlesticks ['fɪdəl,stɪks] *interj* : ¡tonterías!
fidelity [fə'dɛləti, faɪ-] *n, pl* **-ties** : fidelidad *f*
fidget[1] ['fɪʤət] *vi* **1** : moverse, estarse inquieto **2 to fidget with** : juguetear con
fidget[2] *n* **1** : persona *f* inquieta **2 fidgets** *npl* RESTLESSNESS : inquietud *f*
fidgety ['fɪʤəti] *adj* : inquieto
fiduciary[1] [fə'du:ʃi,ɛri, -'dju:-, -ʃəri] *adj* : fiduciario
fiduciary[2] *n, pl* **-ries** : fiduciario *m*, -ria *f*
field[1] ['fi:ld] *vt* : interceptar y devolver (una pelota), presentar (un candidato), sortear (una pregunta)
field[2] *adj* : de campaña, de campo ⟨field hospital : hospital de campaña⟩ ⟨field goal : gol de campo⟩ ⟨field trip : viaje de estudio⟩
field[3] *n* **1** : campo *m* (de cosechas, de batalla, de magnetismo) **2** : campo *m*, cancha *f* (en deportes) **3** : campo *m* (de trabajo), esfera *f* (de actividades)
fielder ['fi:ldər] *n* : jugador *m*, -dora *f* de campo; fildeador *m*, -dora *f*
field glasses *n* : binoculares *mpl*, gemelos *mpl*
fiend ['fi:nd] *n* **1** DEMON : demonio *m* **2** EVILDOER : persona *f* maligna; malvado *m*, -da *f* **3** FANATIC : fanático *m*, -ca *f*
fiendish ['fi:ndɪʃ] *adj* : diabólico — **fiendishly** *adv*
fierce ['fɪrs] *adj* **fiercer; -est 1** FEROCIOUS : fiero, feroz **2** HEATED : acalorado **3** INTENSE : intenso, violento, fuerte — **fiercely** *adv*
fierceness ['fɪrsnəs] *n* **1** FEROCITY : ferocidad *f*, fiereza *f* **2** INTENSITY : intensidad *f*, violencia *f*
fieriness ['faɪərinəs] *n* : pasión *f*, ardor *m*
fiery ['faɪəri] *adj* **fierier; -est 1** BURNING : ardiente, llameante **2** GLOWING : encendido **3** PASSIONATE : acalorado, ardiente, fogoso
fiesta [fi'ɛstə] *n* : fiesta *f*
fife ['faɪf] *n* : pífano *m*
fifteen[1] [fɪf'ti:n] *adj* : quince
fifteen[2] *n* : quince *m*
fifteenth[1] [fɪf'ti:nθ] *adj* : decimoquinto
fifteenth[2] *n* **1** : decimoquinto *m*, -ta *f* (en una serie) **2** : quinceavo *m*, quinceava parte *f*
fifth[1] ['fɪfθ] *adj* : quinto

fifth[2] *n* **1** : quinto *m*, -ta *f* (en una serie) **2** : quinto *m*, quinta parte *f* **3** : quinta *f* (en la música)
fiftieth[1] ['fɪftiəθ] *adj* : quincuagésimo
fiftieth[2] *n* **1** : quincuagésimo *m*, -ma *f* (en una serie) **2** : cincuentavo *m*, cincuentava parte *f*
fifty[1] ['fɪfti] *adj* : cincuenta
fifty[2] *n, pl* **-ties** : cincuenta *m*
fifty-fifty[1] [,fɪfti'fɪfti] *adv* : a medias, mitad y mitad
fifty-fifty[2] *adj* **to have a fifty-fifty chance** : tener un cincuenta por ciento de posibilidades
fig ['fɪg] *n* : higo *m*
fight[1] ['faɪt] *v* **fought** ['fɔt]; **fighting** *vi* : luchar, combatir, pelear — *vt* : luchar contra, combatir contra
fight[2] *n* **1** COMBAT : lucha *f*, pelea *f*, combate *m* **2** MATCH : pelea *f*, combate *m* (en boxeo) **3** QUARREL : disputa *f*, pelea *f*, pleito *m*
fighter ['faɪtər] *n* **1** COMBATANT : luchador *m*, -dora *f*; combatiente *mf* **2** BOXER : boxeador *m*, -dora *f*
figment ['fɪgmənt] *n* **figment of the imagination** : producto *m* de la imaginación
figurative ['fɪgjərətɪv, -gə-] *adj* : figurado, metafórico
figuratively ['fɪgjərətɪvli, -gə-] *adv* : en sentido figurado, de manera metafórica
figure[1] ['fɪgjər, -gər] *v* **-ured; -uring** *vt* **1** CALCULATE : calcular **2** ESTIMATE : figurarse, calcular ⟨he figured it was possible : se figuró que era posible⟩ — *vi* **1** FEATURE, STAND OUT : figurar, destacar **2 that figures!** : ¡obvio!, ¡no me extraña nada!
figure[2] *n* **1** DIGIT : número *m*, cifra *f* **2** PRICE : precio *m*, cifra *f* **3** PERSONAGE : figura *f*, personaje *m* **4** : figura *f*, tipo *m*, físico *m* ⟨to have a good figure : tener buen tipo, tener un buen físico⟩ **5** DESIGN, OUTLINE : figura *f* **6 figures** *npl* : aritmética *f*
figurehead ['fɪgjər,hɛd, -gər-] *n* : testaferro *m*, líder *mf* sin poder
figure of speech *n* : figura *f* retórica, figura *f* de hablar
figure out *vt* **1** UNDERSTAND : entender **2** RESOLVE : resolver (un problema, etc.)
figurine [,fɪgjə'ri:n] *n* : estatuilla *f*
Fijian ['fi:ʤiən, fɪ'ji:ən] *n* : fijiano *m*, -na *f* — **Fijian** *adj*
filament ['fɪləmənt] *n* : filamento *m*
filbert ['fɪlbərt] *n* : avellana *f*
filch ['fɪltʃ] *vt* : hurtar, birlar *fam*
file[1] ['faɪl] *v* **filed; filing** *vt* **1** CLASSIFY : clasificar **2** : archivar (documentos) **3** SUBMIT : presentar ⟨to file charges : presentar cargos⟩ **4** SMOOTH : limar — *vi* : desfilar, entrar (o salir) en fila
file[2] *n* **1** : lima *f* ⟨nail file : lima de uñas⟩ **2** DOCUMENTS : archivo *m* **3** LINE : fila *f*

filial ['fɪliəl, 'fɪljəl] *adj* : filial
filibuster[1] ['fɪlə,bʌstər] *vi* : practicar el obstruccionismo
filibuster[2] *n* : obstruccionismo *m*
filibusterer ['fɪlə,bʌstərər] *n* : obstruccionista *mf*
filigree ['fɪlə,gri:] *n* : filigrana *f*
Filipino [,fɪlə'pi:no:] *n* : filipino *m*, -na *f* — **Filipino** *adj*
fill[1] ['fɪl] *vt* **1** : llenar, ocupar ⟨to fill a cup : llenar una taza⟩ ⟨to fill a room : ocupar una sala⟩ **2** STUFF : rellenar **3** PLUG : tapar, rellenar, empastar (un diente) **4** SATISFY : cumplir con, satisfacer **5** *or* **to fill out** : llenar, re- llenar ⟨to fill out a form : rellenar un formulario⟩
fill[2] *n* **1** FILLING, STUFFING : relleno *m* **2 to eat one's fill** : comer lo suficiente **3 to have one's fill of** : estar harto de
filler ['fɪlər] *n* : relleno *m*
fillet[1] ['fɪlət, fɪ'leɪ, 'fɪ,leɪ] *vt* : cortar en filetes
fillet[2] *n* : filete *m*
fill in *vt* INFORM : informar, poner al corriente — *vi* **to fill in for** : reemplazar a
filling ['fɪlɪŋ] *n* **1** : relleno *m* **2** : empaste *m* (de un diente)
filling station → **gas station**
filly ['fɪli] *n, pl* **-lies** : potra *f*, potranca *f*
film[1] ['fɪlm] *vt* : filmar — *vi* : rodar
film[2] *n* **1** COATING : capa *f*, película *f* **2** : película *f* (fotográfica) **3** MOVIE : película *f*, filme *m*
filmmaker ['fɪlm,meɪkər] *n* : cineasta *mf*
filmy ['fɪlmi] *adj* **filmier; -est 1** GAUZY : diáfano, vaporoso **2** : cubierto de una película
filter[1] ['fɪltər] *vt* : filtrar
filter[2] *n* : filtro *m*
filth ['fɪlθ] *n* : mugre *f*, porquería *f*, roña *f*
filthiness ['fɪlθinəs] *n* : suciedad *f*
filthy ['fɪlθi] *adj* **filthier; -est 1** DIRTY : mugriento, sucio **2** OBSCENE : obsceno, indecente
filtration [fɪl'treɪʃən] *n* : filtración *f*
fin ['fɪn] *n* **1** : aleta *f* **2** : alerón *m* (de un automóvil o un avión)
finagle [fə'neɪgəl] *vt* **-gled; -gling** : arreglárselas para conseguir
final[1] ['faɪnəl] *adj* **1** DEFINITIVE : definitivo, final, inapelable **2** ULTIMATE : final **3** LAST : último, final
final[2] *n* **1** : final *f* (en deportes) **2 finals** *npl* : exámenes *mpl* finales
finale [fɪ'næli, -'nɑ-] *n* : final *m* ⟨grand finale : final triunfal⟩
finalist ['faɪnəlɪst] *n* : finalista *mf*
finality [faɪ'næləti, fə-] *n, pl* **-ties** : finalidad *f*
finalize ['faɪnəl,aɪz] *vt* **-ized; -izing** : finalizar
finally ['faɪnəli] *adv* **1** LASTLY : por último, finalmente **2** EVENTUALLY : por fin, al final **3** DEFINITIVELY : definitivamente

finance[1] [fə'nænts, 'faɪ,nænts] *vt* **-nanced; -nancing** : financiar
finance[2] *n* **1** : finanzas *fpl* **2 finances** *npl* RESOURCES : recursos *mpl* financieros
financial [fə'næntʃəl, faɪ-] *adj* : financiero, económico
financially [fə'næntʃəli, faɪ-] *adv* : económicamente
financier [,fɪnən'sɪr, ,faɪ,næn-] *n* : financiero *m*, -ra *f*; financista *mf*
financing [fə'næntsɪŋ, 'fæɪ,næntsɪŋ] *n* : financiación *f*, financiamiento *m*
finch ['fɪntʃ] *n* : pinzón *m*
find[1] ['faɪnd] *vt* **found** ['faʊnd]; **finding 1** LOCATE : encontrar, hallar ⟨I can't find it : no lo encuentro⟩ ⟨to find one's way : encontrar el camino, orientarse⟩ **2** DISCOVER, REALIZE : descubrir, darse cuenta de ⟨he found it difficult : descubrió que era difícil⟩ **3** DECLARE : declarar, hallar ⟨they found him guilty : lo declararon culpable⟩
find[2] *n* : hallazgo *m*
finder ['faɪndər] *n* : descubridor *m*, -dora *f*
finding ['faɪndɪŋ] *n* **1** FIND : hallazgo *m* **2 findings** *npl* : conclusiones *fpl*
find out *vt* DISCOVER : descubrir, averiguar — *vi* LEARN : enterarse
fine[1] ['faɪn] *vt* **fined; fining** : multar
fine[2] *adj* **finer; -est 1** PURE : puro (dícese del oro y de la plata) **2** THIN : fino, delgado **3** : fino ⟨fine sand : arena fina⟩ **4** SMALL : pequeño, minúsculo ⟨fine print : letras minúsculas⟩ **5** SUBTLE : sutil, delicado **6** EXCELLENT : excelente, magnífico, selecto **7** FAIR : bueno ⟨it's a fine day : hace buen tiempo⟩ **8** EXQUISITE : exquisito, delicado, fino **9 fine arts** : bellas artes *fpl*
fine[3] *n* : multa *f*
finely ['faɪnli] *adv* **1** EXCELLENTLY : con arte **2** ELEGANTLY : elegantemente **3** PRECISELY : con precisión **4 to chop finely** : picar muy fino, picar en trozos pequeños
fineness ['faɪnnəs] *n* **1** EXCELLENCE : excelencia *f* **2** ELEGANCE : elegancia *f*, refinamiento *m* **3** DELICACY : delicadeza *f*, lo fino **4** PRECISION : precisión *f* **5** SUBTLETY : sutileza *f* **6** PURITY : ley *f* (de oro y plata)
finery ['faɪnəri] *n* : galas *fpl*, adornos *mpl*
finesse[1] [fə'nɛs] *vt* **-nessed; -nessing** : ingeniar
finesse[2] *n* **1** REFINEMENT : refinamiento *m*, finura *f* **2** TACT : delicadeza *f*, tacto *m*, diplomacia *f* **3** CRAFTINESS : astucia *f*
finger[1] ['fɪŋgər] *vt* **1** HANDLE : tocar, toquetear **2** ACCUSE : acusar, delatar
finger[2] *n* : dedo *m*
fingerling ['fɪŋgərlɪŋ] *n* : pez *m* pequeño y joven
fingernail ['fɪŋgər,neɪl] *n* : uña *f*
fingerprint[1] ['fɪŋgər,prɪnt] *vt* : tomar las huellas digitales a

fingerprint² *n* : huella *f* digital
fingertip ['fɪŋɡər₁tɪp] *n* : punta *f* del dedo, yema *f* del dedo
finicky ['fɪnɪki] *adj* : maniático, melindroso, mañoso
finish¹ ['fɪnɪʃ] *vt* **1** COMPLETE : acabar, terminar **2** : aplicar un acabado a (muebles, etc.)
finish² *n* **1** END : fin *m*, final *m* **2** REFINEMENT : refinamiento *m* **3** : acabado *m* ⟨a glossy finish : un acabado brillante⟩
finite ['faɪˌnaɪt] *adj* : finito
fink ['fɪŋk] *n* : mequetrefe *mf fam*
Finn ['fɪn] *n* : finlandés *m*, -desa *f*
Finnish¹ ['fɪnɪʃ] *adj* : finlandés
Finnish² *n* : finlandés *m* (idioma)
fiord [fi'ɔrd] → **fjord**
fir ['fər] *n* : abeto *m*
fire¹ ['faɪr] *vt* **fired; firing 1** IGNITE, KINDLE : encender **2** ENLIVEN : animar, avivar **3** DISMISS : despedir **4** SHOOT : disparar **5** BAKE : cocer (cerámica)
fire² *n* **1** : fuego *m* **2** BURNING : incendio *m* ⟨fire alarm : alarma contra incendios⟩ ⟨to be on fire : estar en llamas⟩ **3** ENTHUSIASM : ardor *m*, entusiasmo *m* **4** SHOOTING : disparos *mpl*, fuego *m*
firearm ['faɪr₁ɑrm] *n* : arma *f* de fuego
fireball ['faɪr₁bɔl] *n* **1** : bola *f* de fuego **2** METEOR : bólido *m*
firebreak ['faɪr₁breɪk] *n* : cortafuegos *m*
firebug ['faɪr₁bʌɡ] *n* : pirómano *m*, -na *f*; incendiario *m*, -ria *f*
firecracker ['faɪr₁krækər] *n* : petardo *m*
fire escape *n* : escalera *f* de incendios
firefighter ['faɪr₁faɪtər] *n* : bombero *m*, -ra *f*
firefly ['faɪr₁flaɪ] *n, pl* **-flies** : luciérnaga *f*
fireman ['faɪrmən] *n, pl* **-men** [-mən, -₁mɛn] **1** FIREFIGHTER : bombero *m*, -ra *f* **2** STOKER : fogonero *m*, -ra *f*
fireplace ['faɪr₁pleɪs] *n* : hogar *m*, chimenea *f*
fireproof¹ ['faɪr₁pru:f] *vt* : hacer incombustible
fireproof² *adj* : incombustible, ignífugo
fireside¹ ['faɪr₁saɪd] *adj* : informal ⟨fireside chat : charla informal⟩
fireside² *n* **1** HEARTH : chimenea *f*, hogar *m* **2** HOME : hogar *m*, casa *f*
firewall ['faɪr₁wɔl] *n* : cortafuegos *m*
firewood ['faɪr₁wʊd] *n* : leña *f*
fireworks ['faɪr₁wərks] *npl* : fuegos *mpl* artificiales, pirotecnia *f*
firm¹ ['fərm] *vt or* **to firm up** : endurecer
firm² *adj* **1** VIGOROUS : fuerte, vigoroso **2** SOLID, UNYIELDING : firme, duro, sólido **3** UNCHANGING : firme, inalterable **4** RESOLUTE : firme, resuelto
firm³ *n* : empresa *f*, firma *f*, compañía *f*
firmament ['fərməmənt] *n* : firmamento *m*
firmly ['fərmli] *adv* : firmemente
firmness ['fərmnəs] *n* : firmeza *f*
first¹ ['fərst] *adv* **1** : primero ⟨finish your homework first : primero termina tu tarea⟩ ⟨first and foremost : ante todo⟩ ⟨first of all : en primer lugar⟩ **2** : por primera vez ⟨I saw it first in Boston : lo vi por primera vez en Boston⟩
first² *adj* **1** : primero ⟨the first time : la primera vez⟩ ⟨at first sight : a primera vista⟩ ⟨in the first place : en primer lugar⟩ ⟨the first ten applicants : los diez primeros candidatos⟩ **2** FOREMOST : principal, primero ⟨first tenor : tenor principal⟩
first³ *n* **1** : primero *m*, -ra *f* **2** *or* **first gear** : primera *f* **3** at ~ : al principio
first aid *n* : primeros auxilios *mpl*
first-class¹ ['fərst'klæs] *adv* : en primera ⟨to travel first-class : viajar en primera⟩
first-class² *adj* : de primera
first class *n* : primera clase *f*
firsthand¹ ['fərst'hænd] *adv* : directamente
firsthand² *adj* : de primera mano
first lieutenant *n* : teniente *mf*; teniente primero *m*, teniente primera *f*
firstly ['fərstli] *adv* : primeramente, principalmente, en primer lugar
first-rate¹ ['fərst'reɪt] *adv* : muy bien
first-rate² *adj* : de primera, de primera clase
first sergeant *n* : sargento *mf*
firth ['fərθ] *n* : estuario *m*
fiscal ['fɪskəl] *adj* : fiscal — **fiscally** *adv*
fish¹ ['fɪʃ] *vi* **1** *or* **to fish for** SEEK : buscar, rebuscar ⟨to fish for compliments : andar a la caza de cumplidos⟩ — *vt* : pescar
fish² *n, pl* **fish** *or* **fishes** : pez *m* (vivo), pescado *m* (para comer)
fisherman ['fɪʃərmən] *n, pl* **-men** [-mən, -₁mɛn] : pescador *m*, -dora *f*
fishery ['fɪʃəri] *n, pl* **-eries 1** → **fishing 2** : zona *f* pesquera, pesquería *f*
fishhook ['fɪʃ₁hʊk] *n* : anzuelo *m*
fishing ['fɪʃɪŋ] *n* : pesca *f*, industria *f* pesquera
fishing pole *n* : caña *f* de pescar
fish market *n* : pescadería *f*
fishy ['fɪʃi] *adj* **fishier; -est 1** : a pescado ⟨a fishy taste : un sabor a pescado⟩ **2** QUESTIONABLE : dudoso, sospechoso ⟨there's something fishy going on : aquí hay gato encerrado⟩
fission ['fɪʃən, -ʒən] *n* : fisión *f*
fissure ['fɪʃər] *n* : fisura *f*, hendidura *f*
fist ['fɪst] *n* : puño *m*
fistful ['fɪst₁fʊl] *n* : puñado *m*
fisticuffs ['fɪstɪ₁kʌfs] *npl* : lucha *f* a puñetazos
fit¹ ['fɪt] *v* **fitted; fitting** *vt* **1** MATCH : corresponder a, coincidir con ⟨the punishment fits the crime : el castigo corresponde al crimen⟩ **2** : quedar ⟨the dress doesn't fit me : el vestido no me queda⟩ **3** GO : caber, encajar en ⟨her key fits the lock : su llave encaja en la cerradura⟩ **4** INSERT, INSTALL : poner, colocar **5** ADAPT : adecuar, ajustar, adaptar **6** *or* **to fit out** EQUIP : equipar

— *vi* **1** : quedar, entallar ⟨these pants don't fit : estos pantalones no me quedan⟩ **2** CONFORM : encajar, cuadrar **3 to fit in** : encajar, estar integrado

fit² *adj* **fitter; fittest 1** SUITABLE : adecuado, apropiado, conveniente **2** QUALIFIED : calificado, competente **3** HEALTHY : sano, en forma

fit³ *n* **1** ATTACK : ataque *m*, acceso *m*, arranque *m* **2 to be a good fit** : quedar bien **3 to be a tight fit** : ser muy entallado (de ropa), estar apretado (de espacios)

fitful ['fɪtfəl] *adj* : irregular, intermitente — **fitfully** *adv*

fitness ['fɪtnəs] *n* **1** HEALTH : salud *f*, buena forma *f* (física) **2** SUITABILITY : idoneidad *f*

fitting¹ ['fɪtɪŋ] *adj* : adecuado, apropiado

fitting² *n* : accesorio *m*

five¹ ['faɪv] *adj* : cinco

five² *n* : cinco *m*

five hundred¹ *adj* : quinientos

five hundred² *n* : quinientos *m*

fix¹ ['fɪks] *vt* **1** ATTACH, SECURE : sujetar, asegurar, fijar **2** ESTABLISH : fijar, concretar, establecer **3** REPAIR : arreglar, reparar **4** PREPARE : preparar ⟨to fix dinner : preparar la cena⟩ **5** : arreglar, amañar ⟨to fix a race : arreglar una carrera⟩ **6** RIVET : fijar (los ojos, la mirada, etc.)

fix² *n* **1** PREDICAMENT : aprieto *m*, apuro *m* **2** : posición *f* ⟨to get a fix on : establecer la posición de⟩

fixate ['fɪkˌseɪt] *vi* **-ated; -ating** : obsesionarse

fixation [fɪk'seɪʃən] *n* : fijación *f*, obsesión *f*

fixed ['fɪkst] *adj* **1** STATIONARY : estacionario, inmóvil **2** UNCHANGING : fijo, inalterable **3** INTENT : fijo ⟨a fixed stare : una mirada fija⟩ **4 to be comfortably fixed** : estar en posición acomodada

fixedly ['fɪksədli] *adv* : fijamente

fixedness ['fɪksədnəs, 'fɪkst-] *n* : rigidez *f*

fixture ['fɪkstʃər] *n* **1** : parte *f* integrante, elemento *m* fijo **2 fixtures** *npl* : instalaciones *fpl* (de una casa)

fizz¹ ['fɪz] *vi* : burbujear

fizz² *n* : efervescencia *f*, burbujeo *m*

fizzle¹ ['fɪzəl] *vi* **-zled; -zling 1** FIZZ : burbujear **2** FAIL : fracasar

fizzle² *n* : fracaso *m*, fiasco *m*

fjord [fi'ɔrd] *n* : fiordo *m*

flab ['flæb] *n* : gordura *f*

flabbergast ['flæbərˌgæst] *vt* : asombrar, pasmar, dejar atónito

flabby ['flæbi] *adj* **-bier; -est** : blando, fofo, aguado *CA, Col, Mex*

flaccid ['flæksəd, 'flæsəd] *adj* : fláccido

flag¹ ['flæg] *vi* **flagged; flagging 1** : hacer señales con banderas **2** WEAKEN : flaquear, desfallecer

flag² *n* : bandera *f*, pabellón *m*, estandarte *m*

flagon ['flægən] *n* : jarra *f* grande

flagpole ['flægˌpoːl] *n* : asta *f*, mástil *m*

flagrant ['fleɪgrənt] *adj* : flagrante — **flagrantly** *adv*

flagship ['flægˌʃɪp] *n* : buque *m* insignia

flagstaff ['flægˌstæf] → **flagpole**

flagstone ['flægˌstoːn] *n* : losa *f*, piedra *f*

flail¹ ['fleɪl] *vt* **1** : trillar (grano) **2** : sacudir, agitar (los brazos)

flail² *n* : mayal *m*

flair ['flær] *n* : don *m*, facilidad *f*

flak ['flæk] *ns & pl* **1** : fuego *m* antiaéreo **2** CRITICISM : críticas *fpl*

flake¹ ['fleɪk] *vi* **flaked; flaking** : desmenuzarse, pelarse (dícese de la piel)

flake² *n* : copo *m* (de nieve), escama *f* (de la piel), astilla *f* (de madera)

flamboyance [flæm'bɔɪənts] *n* : extravagancia *f*, rimbombancia *f*

flamboyant [flæm'bɔɪənt] *adj* : exuberante, extravagante, rimbombante

flame¹ ['fleɪm] *vi* **flamed; flaming 1** BLAZE : arder, llamear **2** GLOW : brillar, encenderse

flame² *n* BLAZE : llama *f* ⟨to burst into flames : estallar en llamas⟩ ⟨to go up in flame : incendiarse⟩

flamethrower ['fleɪmˌθroːər] *n* : lanzallamas *m*

flamingo [flə'mɪŋgo] *n, pl* **-gos** : flamenco *m*

flammable ['flæməbəl] *adj* : inflamable, flamable

flange ['flændʒ] *n* : reborde *m*, pestaña *f*

flank¹ ['flæŋk] *vt* **1** : flanquear (para defender o atacar) **2** BORDER, LINE : bordear

flank² *n* : ijada *f* (de un animal), costado *m* (de una persona), falda *f* (de una colina), flanco *m* (de un cuerpo de soldados)

flannel ['flænəl] *n* : franela *f*

flap¹ ['flæp] *v* **flapped; flapping** *vi* **1** : aletear ⟨the bird was flapping (its wings) : el pájaro aleteaba⟩ **2** FLUTTER : ondear, agitarse — *vt* : batir, agitar

flap² *n* **1** FLAPPING : aleteo *m*, aletazo *m* (de alas) **2** : soplada *f* (de un sobre), hoja *f* (de una mesa), faldón *m* (de una chaqueta)

flapjack ['flæpˌdʒæk] → **pancake**

flare¹ ['flær] *vi* **flared; flaring 1** FLAME, SHINE : llamear, brillar **2 to flare up** : estallar, explotar (de cólera)

flare² *n* **1** FLASH : destello *m* **2** SIGNAL : (luz *f* de) bengala *f* **3 solar flare** : erupción *f* solar

flash¹ ['flæʃ] *vi* **1** SHINE, SPARKLE : destellar, brillar **2** : pasar como un relámpago ⟨an idea flashed through my mind : una idea me cruzó la mente como un relámpago⟩ — *vt* : despedir, lanzar (una luz), transmitir (un mensaje)

flash² *adj* SUDDEN : repentino
flash³ *n* **1** : destello *m* (de luz), fogonazo *m* (de una explosión) **2 flash of lightning** : relámpago *m* **3 in a flash** : de repente, de un abrir y cerrar los ojos
flashback ['flæʃ,bæk] *n* : flashback *m*
flashiness ['flæʃinəs] *n* : ostentación *f*
flashlight ['flæʃ,laɪt] *n* : linterna *f*
flashy ['flæʃi] *adj* **flashier; -est** : llamativo, ostentoso
flask ['flæsk] *n* : frasco *m*
flat¹ ['flæt] *vt* **flatted; flatting 1** FLATTEN : aplanar, achatar **2** : bajar de tono (en música)
flat² *adv* **1** EXACTLY : exactamente ⟨in ten minutes flat : en diez minutos exactos⟩ **2** : desafinado, demasiado bajo (en la música)
flat³ *adj* **flatter; flattest 1** EVEN, LEVEL : plano, llano **2** SMOOTH : liso **3** DEFINITE : categórico, rotundo, explícito ⟨a flat refusal : una negativa categórica⟩ **4** DULL : aburrido, soso, monótono (dícese la voz) **5** DEFLATED : desinflado, pinchado, ponchado *Mex* **6** : bemol (en música) ⟨to sing flat : cantar desafinado⟩
flat⁴ *n* **1** PLAIN : llano *m*, terreno *m* llano **2** : bemol *m* (en la música) **3** APARTMENT : apartamento *m*, departamento *m* **4 or flat tire** : pinchazo *m*, ponchadura *f Mex*
flatbed ['flæt,bɛd] *n* : camión *m* de plataforma
flatcar ['flæt,kar] *n* : vagón *m* abierto
flatfish ['flæt,fɪʃ] *n* : platija *f*
flat-footed ['flæt,fʊtəd, ,flæt'-] *adj* : de pies planos
flatly ['flætli] *adv* DEFINITELY : categóricamente, rotundamente
flatness ['flætnəs] *n* **1** EVENNESS : lo llano, lisura *f*, uniformidad *f* **2** DULLNESS : monotonía *f*
flat-out ['flæt'aʊt] *adj* **1** : frenético, a toda máquina ⟨a flat-out effort : un esfuerzo frenético⟩ **2** CATEGORICAL : descarado, rotundo, categórico
flatten ['flætən] *vt* : aplanar, achatar
flatter ['flætər] *vt* **1** OVERPRAISE : adular **2** COMPLIMENT : halagar **3** : favorecer ⟨the photo flatters you : la foto te favorece⟩
flatterer ['flætərər] *n* : adulador *m*, -dora *f*
flattering ['flætərɪŋ] *adj* **1** COMPLIMENTARY : halagador **2** BECOMING : favorecedor
flattery ['flætəri] *n, pl* **-ries** : halagos *mpl*
flatulence ['flætʃələnts] *n* : flatulencia *f*, ventosidad *f*
flatulent ['flætʃələnt] *adj* : flatulento
flatware ['flæt,wær] *n* : cubertería *f*, cubiertos *mpl*
flaunt¹ ['flɔnt] *vt* : alardear, hacer alarde de
flaunt² *n* : alarde *m*, ostentación *f*
flavor¹ ['fleɪvər] *vt* : dar sabor a, sazonar

flavor² *n* **1** : gusto *m*, sabor *m* **2** FLAVORING : sazón *f*, condimento *m*
flavorful ['fleɪvərfəl] *adj* : sabroso
flavoring ['fleɪvərɪŋ] *n* : condimento *m*, sazón *f*
flavorless ['fleɪvərləs] *adj* : sin sabor
flaw ['flɔ] *n* : falla *f*, defecto *m*, imperfección *f*
flawed ['flɔd] *adj* : imperfecto, con defectos
flawless ['flɔləs] *adj* : impecable, perfecto — **flawlessly** *adv*
flax ['flæks] *n* : lino *m*
flaxen ['flæksən] *adj* : rubio, blondo (dícese del pelo)
flay ['fleɪ] *vt* **1** SKIN : desollar, despellejar **2** VILIFY : criticar con dureza, vilipendiar
flea ['fli:] *n* : pulga *f*
fleck¹ ['flɛk] *vt* : salpicar
fleck² *n* : mota *f*, pinta *f*
fledgling ['flɛdʒlɪŋ] *n* : polluelo *m*, pollito *m*
flee ['fli:] *v* **fled** ['flɛd]; **fleeing** *vi* : huir, escapar(se) — *vt* : huir de
fleece¹ ['fli:s] *vt* **fleeced; fleecing 1** SHEAR : esquilar, trasquilar **2** SWINDLE : estafar, defraudar
fleece² *n* : lana *f*, vellón *m*
fleet¹ ['fli:t] *vi* : moverse con rapidez
fleet² *adj* SWIFT : rápido, veloz
fleet³ *n* : flota *f*
fleet admiral *n* : almirante *mf*
fleeting ['fli:tɪŋ] *adj* : fugaz, breve
flesh ['flɛʃ] *n* **1** : carne *f* (de seres humanos y animales) **2** : pulpa *f* (de frutas)
flesh out *vt* : desarrollar, darle cuerpo a
fleshy ['flɛʃi] *adj* **fleshier; -est** : gordo (dícese de las personas), carnoso (dícese de la fruta)
flew → **fly**
flex ['flɛks] *vt* : doblar, flexionar
flexibility [,flɛksə'bɪləti] *n, pl* **-ties** : flexibilidad *f*, elasticidad *f*
flexible ['flɛksəbəl] *adj* : flexible — **flexibly** [-bli] *adv*
flick¹ ['flɪk] *vt* : dar un capirotazo a (con el dedo) ⟨to flick a switch : darle al interruptor⟩ — *vi* **1** FLIT : revolotear **2 to flick through** : hojear (un libro)
flick² *n* : coletazo *m* (de una cola), capirotazo *m* (de un dedo)
flicker¹ ['flɪkər] *vi* **1** FLUTTER : revolotear, aletear **2** BLINK, TWINKLE : parpadear, titilar
flicker² *n* **1** : parpadeo *m*, titileo *m* **2** HINT, TRACE : indicio *m*, rastro *m* ⟨a flicker of hope : un rayo de esperanza⟩
flier ['flaɪər] *n* **1** AVIATOR : aviador *m*, -dora *f* **2** CIRCULAR : folleto *m* publicitario, circular *f*
flight ['flaɪt] *n* **1** : vuelo *m* (de aves o aviones), trayectoria *f* (de proyectiles) **2** TRIP : vuelo *m* **3** FLOCK, SQUADRON : bandada *f* (de pájaros), escuadrilla *f* (de aviones) **4** ESCAPE : huida *f*, fuga

f **5 flight of fancy** : ilusiones *fpl*, fantasía *f* **6 flight of stairs** : tramo *m*

flight attendant *n* : auxiliar *mf* de vuelo

flightless ['flaɪtləs] *adj* : no volador

flighty ['flaɪti] *adj* **flightier; -est** : caprichoso, frívolo

flimsy [flɪmzi] *adj* **flimsier; -est** **1** LIGHT, THIN : ligero, fino **2** WEAK : endeble, poco sólido **3** IMPLAUSIBLE : pobre, flojo, poco convincente ⟨a flimsy excuse : una excusa floja⟩

flinch ['flɪntʃ] *vi* **1** WINCE : estremecerse **2** RECOIL : recular, retroceder

fling¹ ['flɪŋ] *vt* **flung** ['flʌŋ] **flinging 1** THROW : lanzar, tirar, arrojar **2 to fling oneself** : lanzarse, tirarse, precipitarse

fling² *n* **1** THROW : lanzamiento *m* **2** ATTEMPT : intento *m* **3** AFFAIR : aventura *f* **4** BINGE : juerga *f*

flint ['flɪnt] *n* : pedernal *m*

flinty ['flɪnti] *adj* **flintier; -est 1** : de pedernal **2** STERN, UNYIELDING : severo, inflexible

flip¹ ['flɪp] *v* **flipped; flipping** *vt* **1** TOSS : tirar ⟨to flip a coin : echar a cara o cruz⟩ **2** OVERTURN : dar la vuelta a, voltear — *vi* **1** : moverse bruscamente **2 to flip through** : hojear (un libro)

flip² *adj* : insolente, descarado

flip³ *n* **1** FLICK : capirotazo *m*, golpe *m* ligero **2** SOMERSAULT : voltereta *f*

flip–flop ['flɪp,flɑp] *n* **1** REVERSAL : giro *m* radical **2** THONG : chancla *f*, chancleta *f*

flippancy ['flɪpəntsi] *n*, *pl* **-cies** : ligereza *f*, falta *f* de seriedad

flippant ['flɪpənt] *adj* : ligero, frívolo, poco serio

flipper ['flɪpər] *n* : aleta *f*

flirt¹ ['flərt] *vi* **1** : coquetear, flirtear **2** TRIFLE : jugar ⟨to flirt with death : jugar con la muerte⟩

flirt² *n* : coqueto *m*, -ta *f*

flirtation [,flər'teɪʃən] *n* : devaneo *m*, coqueteo *m*

flirtatious [,flər'teɪʃəs] *adj* : insinuante, coqueto

flit ['flɪt] *vi* **flitted; flitting 1** : revolotear **2 to flit about** : ir y venir rápidamente

float¹ ['flo:t] *vi* **1** : flotar **2** WANDER : vagar, errar — *vt* **1** : poner a flote, hacer flotar (un barco) **2** LAUNCH : hacer flotar (una empresa) **3** ISSUE : emitir (acciones en la bolsa)

float² *n* **1** : flotador *m*, corcho *m* (para pescar) **2** BUOY : boya *f* **3** : carroza *f* (en un desfile)

floating ['flo:ţɪŋ] *adj* : flotante

flock¹ ['flɑk] *vi* **1** : moverse en rebaño **2** CONGREGATE : congregarse, reunirse

flock² *n* : rebaño *m* (de ovejas), bandada *f* (de pájaros)

floe ['flo:] *n* : témpano *m* de hielo

flog ['flɑg] *vt* **flogged; flogging** : azotar, fustigar

flood¹ ['flʌd] *vt* : inundar, anegar

flood² *n* **1** INUNDATION : inundación *f* **2** TORRENT : avalancha *f*, diluvio *m*, torrente *m* ⟨a flood of tears : un mar de lágrimas⟩

floodlight ['flʌd,laɪt] *n* : foco *m*

floodwater ['flʌd,wɔtər] *n* : crecida *f*, creciente *f*

floor¹ ['flor] *vt* **1** : solar, poner suelo a (una casa o una sala) **2** KNOCK DOWN : derribar, echar al suelo **3** NONPLUS : desconcertar, confundir, dejar perplejo

floor² *n* **1** : suelo *m*, piso *m* ⟨dance floor : pista de baile⟩ **2** STORY : piso *m*, planta *f* ⟨ground floor : planta baja⟩ ⟨second floor : primer piso⟩ **3** : mínimo *m* (de sueldos, precios, etc.)

floorboard ['flor,bord] *n* : tabla *f* del suelo, suelo *m*, piso *m*

flooring ['florɪŋ] *n* : entarimado *m*

flop¹ ['flɑp] *vi* **flopped; flopping 1** FLAP : golpearse, agitarse **2** COLLAPSE : dejarse caer, desplomarse **3** FAIL : fracasar

flop² *n* **1** FAILURE : fracaso *m* **2 to take a flop** : caerse

floppy ['flɑpi] *adj* **-pier; -est 1** : blando, flexible **2 floppy disk** : diskette *m*, disquete *m*

flora ['florə] *n* : flora *f*

floral ['florəl] *adj* : floral, floreado

florid ['florɪd] *adj* **1** FLOWERY : florido **2** REDDISH : rojizo

florist ['florɪst] *n* : florista *mf*

floss¹ ['flɔs] *vi* : limpiarse los dientes con hilo dental

floss² *n* **1** : hilo *m* de seda (de bordar) **2 → dental floss**

flotation [flo'teɪʃən] *n* : flotación *f*

flotilla [flo'tɪlə] *n* : flotilla *f*

flotsam ['flɑtsəm] *n* **1** : restos *mpl* flotantes (en el mar) **2 flotsam and jetsam** : desechos *mpl*, restos *mpl*

flounce¹ ['flaunts] *vi* **flounced; flouncing** : moverse haciendo aspavientos ⟨she flounced into the room : entró en la sala haciendo aspavientos⟩

flounce² *n* **1** RUFFLE : volante *m* **2** FLOURISH : aspaviento *m*

flounder¹ ['flaundər] *vi* **1** STRUGGLE : forcejear **2** STUMBLE : no saber qué hacer o decir, perder el hilo (en un discurso)

flounder² *n*, *pl* **flounder** *or* **flounders** : platija *f*

flour¹ ['flauər] *vt* : enharinar

flour² *n* : harina *f*

flourish¹ ['flərɪʃ] *vi* THRIVE : florecer, prosperar, crecer (dícese de las plantas) — *vt* BRANDISH : blandir

flourish² *n* : floritura *f*, floreo *m*

flourishing ['flərɪʃɪŋ] *adj* : floreciente, próspero

flout ['flaut] *vt* : desacatar, burlarse de

flow¹ ['flo:] *vi* **1** COURSE : fluir, manar, correr **2** CIRCULATE : circular, correr ⟨traffic is flowing smoothly : el tránsito está circulando con fluidez⟩

flow² *n* **1** FLOWING : flujo *m*, circulación *f* **2** STREAM : corriente *f*, chorro *m*
flower¹ ['flaʊər] *vi* : florecer, florear
flower² *n* : flor *f*
flowered ['flaʊərd] *adj* : florido, floreado
floweriness ['flaʊərinəs] *n* : floritura *f*
flowering¹ ['flaʊərɪŋ] *adj* : floreciente
flowering² *n* : floración *f*, florecimiento *m*
flowerpot ['flaʊər,pɑt] *n* : maceta *f*, tiesto *m*, macetero *m*
flowery ['flaʊəri] *adj* **1** : florido, FLOWERED : floreado, de flores
flowing ['flo:ɪŋ] *adj* : fluido, corriente
flown → fly
flu ['flu:] *n* : gripe *f*, gripa *f Col, Mex*
fluctuate ['flʌktʃʊ,eɪt] *vi* -ated; -ating : fluctuar
fluctuation [,flʌktʃʊ'eɪʃən] *n* : fluctuación *f*
flue ['flu:] *n* : tiro *m*, salida *f* de humos
fluency ['flu:əntsi] *n* : fluidez *f*, soltura *f*
fluent ['flu:ənt] *adj* : fluido
fluently ['flu:əntli] *adv* : con soltura, con fluidez
fluff¹ ['flʌf] *vt* **1** : mullir ⟨to fluff up the pillows : mullir las almohadas⟩ **2** BUNGLE : echar a perder, equivocarse
fluff² *n* **1** FUZZ : pelusa *f* **2** DOWN : plumón *m*
fluffy ['flʌfi] *adj* **fluffier; -est 1** DOWNY : lleno de pelusa, velloso **2** SPONGY : esponjoso
fluid¹ ['flu:ɪd] *adj* : fluido
fluid² *n* : fluido *m*, líquido *m*
fluidity [flu'ɪdəti] *n* : fluidez *f*
fluid ounce *n* : onza *f* líquida (29.57 mililitros)
fluke ['flu:k] *n* : golpe *m* de suerte, chiripa *f*, casualidad *f*
flung → fling
flunk ['flʌŋk] *vt* FAIL : reprobar — *vi* : salir reprobando
fluorescence [,flʊr'ɛsənts, ,flɔr-] *n* : fluorescencia *f*
fluorescent [,flʊr'ɛsənt, ,flɔr-] *adj* : fluorescente
fluoridate ['flɔrə,deɪt, 'flʊr-] *vt* -dated; -dating : fluorizar
fluoridation [,flɔrə'deɪʃən, ,flʊr-] *n* : fluorización *f*, fluoración *f*
fluoride ['flɔr,aɪd, 'flʊr-] *n* : fluoruro *m*
fluorine ['flʊr,i:n] *n* : flúor *m*
fluorocarbon [,flɔro'karbən, ,flʊr-] *n* : fluorocarbono *m*
flurry ['flɔri] *n, pl* -ries **1** GUST : ráfaga *f* **2** SNOWFALL : nevisca *f* **3** BUSTLE : frenesí *m*, bullicio *m* **4** BARRAGE : aluvión *m*, oleada *f* ⟨a flurry of questions : un aluvión de preguntas⟩
flush¹ ['flʌʃ] *vt* **1** : limpiar con agua ⟨to flush the toilet : jalar la cadena⟩ **2** RAISE : hacer salir, levantar (en la caza) — *vi* BLUSH : ruborizarse, sonrojarse
flush² *adv* : al mismo nivel, a ras
flush³ *adj* **1** *or* **flushed** ['flʌʃt] : colorado, rojo, encendido (dícese de la

cara) **2** FILLED : lleno a rebosar **3** ABUNDANT : copioso, abundante **4** AFFLUENT : adinerado **5** ALIGNED, SMOOTH : alineado, liso **6** **flush against** : pegado a, contra
flush⁴ *n* **1** FLOW, JET : chorro *m*, flujo *m* rápido **2** SURGE : arrebato *m*, arranque *m* ⟨a flush of anger : un arrebato de cólera⟩ **3** BLUSH : rubor *m*, sonrojo *m* **4** GLOW : resplandor *m*, flor *f* ⟨the flush of youth : la flor de la juventud⟩ ⟨in the flush of victory : en la euforia del triunfo⟩
fluster¹ ['flʌstər] *vt* : poner nervioso, aturdir
fluster² *n* : agitación *f*, confusión *f*
flute ['flu:t] *n* : flauta *f*
fluted ['flu:təd] *adj* **1** GROOVED : estriado, acanalado **2** WAVY : ondulado
fluting ['flu:tɪŋ] *n* : estrías *fpl*
flutist ['flu:tɪst] *n* : flautista *mf*
flutter¹ ['flʌtər] *vi* **1** : revolotear (dícese de un pájaro), ondear (dícese de una bandera), palpitar con fuerza (dícese del corazón) **2** **to flutter about** : ir y venir, revolotear — *vt* : sacudir, batir
flutter² *n* **1** FLUTTERING : revoloteo *m*, aleteo *m* **2** COMMOTION, STIR : revuelo *m*, agitación *f*
flux ['flʌks] *n* **1** : flujo *m* (en física y medicina) **2** CHANGE : cambio *m* ⟨to be in a state of flux : estar cambiando continuamente⟩
fly¹ ['flaɪ] *v* **flew** ['flu:]; **flown** ['flo:n]; **flying** *vi* **1** : volar (dícese de los pájaros, etc.) **2** TRAVEL : volar (dícese de los aviones), ir en avión (dícese de los pasajeros) **3** FLOAT : flotar, ondear **4** FLEE : huir, escapar **5** RUSH : correr, irse volando **6** PASS : pasar (volando) ⟨how time flies! : ¡cómo pasa el tiempo!⟩ **7** **to fly open** : abrir de golpe — *vt* : pilotar (un avión), hacer volar (una cometa)
fly² *n, pl* **flies 1** : mosca *f* ⟨to drop like flies : caer como moscas⟩ **2** : bragueta *f* (de pantalones, etc.)
flyer → flier
flying saucer *n* : platillo *m* volador
flypaper ['flaɪ,peɪpər] *n* : papel *m* matamoscas
flyspeck ['flaɪ,spɛk] *n* **1** : excremento *m* de mosca **2** SPECK : motita *f*, puntito *m*
flyswatter ['flaɪ,swɑtər] *n* : matamoscas *m*
flywheel ['flaɪ,ʍi:l] *n* : volante *m*
foal¹ ['fo:l] *vi* : parir
foal² *n* : potro *m*, -tra *f*
foam¹ ['fo:m] *vi* : hacer espuma
foam² *n* : espuma *f*
foamy ['fo:mi] *adj* **foamier; -est** : espumoso
focal ['fo:kəl] *adj* **1** : focal, central **2** **focal point** : foco *m*, punto *m* de referencia
fo'c'sle ['fo:ksəl] → **forecastle**

focus[1] ['fo:kəs] *v* **-cused** *or* **-cussed;**
-cusing *or* **-cussing** *vt* **1** : enfocar (un
instrumento) **2** CONCENTRATE : con-
centrar, centrar — *vi* : enfocar, fijar la
vista

focus[2] *n, pl* **-ci** ['fo:ˌsaɪ, -ˌkaɪ] **1** : foco *m*
⟨to be in focus : estar enfocado⟩ **2** FO-
CUSING : enfoque *m* **3** CENTER : centro *m*, foco *m*

fodder ['fadər] *n* : pienso *m*, forraje *m*

foe ['fo:] *n* : enemigo *m*, -ga *f*

fog[1] ['fɔg, 'fag] *v* **fogged; fogging** *vt*
: empañar — *vi* **to fog up** : empañarse

fog[2] *n* : niebla *f*, neblina *f*

foggy ['fɔgi, 'fa-] *adj* **foggier; -est** : nebuloso, brumoso

foghorn ['fɔgˌhɔrn, 'fag-] *n* : sirena *f* de
niebla

fogy ['fo:gi] *n, pl* **-gies** : carca *mf fam*,
persona *f* chapada a la antigua

foible ['fɔɪbəl] *n* : flaqueza *f*, debilidad *f*

foil[1] ['fɔɪl] *vt* : frustrar, hacer fracasar

foil[2] *n* **1** : lámina *f* de metal, papel *m* de
aluminio **2** CONTRAST : contraste *m*,
complemento *m* **3** SWORD : florete *m*
(en esgrima)

foist ['fɔɪst] *vt* : encajar, endilgar *fam*,
colocar

fold[1] ['fo:ld] *vt* **1** BEND : doblar, plegar
2 CLASP : cruzar (brazos), enlazar
(manos), plegar (alas) **3** EMBRACE : estrechar, abrazar **4 to fold in** : incorporar ⟨fold in the cream : incorpore la
crema⟩ — *vi* **1** FAIL : fracasar **2 to fold
up** : doblarse, plegarse

fold[2] *n* **1** SHEEPFOLD : redil *m* (para ovejas) **2** FLOCK : rebaño *m* ⟨to return to
the fold : volver al redil⟩ **3** CREASE
: pliegue *m*, doblez *m*

folder ['fo:ldər] *n* **1** CIRCULAR : circular *f*, folleto *m* **2** BINDER : carpeta *f*

foliage ['fo:liidʒ, -lidʒ] *n* : follaje *m*

folio ['fo:liˌo:] *n, pl* **-lios** : folio *m*

folk[1] ['fo:k] *adj* : popular, folklórico
⟨folk customs : costumbres populares⟩
⟨folk dance : danza folklórica⟩

folk[2] *n, pl* **folk** *or* **folks 1** PEOPLE : gente
f **2 folks** *npl* : familia *f*, padres *mpl*

folklore ['fo:kˌlor] *n* : folklore *m*

folklorist ['fo:kˌlorɪst] *n* : folklorista *mf*

folksy ['fo:ksi] *adj* **folksier; -est**
: campechano

follicle ['falɪkəl] *n* : folículo *m*

follow ['falo] *vt* **1** : seguir ⟨follow the
guide : siga al guía⟩ ⟨she followed the
road : siguió el camino, continuó por
el camino⟩ **2** PURSUE : perseguir,
seguir **3** OBEY : seguir, cumplir, observar **4** UNDERSTAND : entender —
vi **1** : seguir **2** UNDERSTAND : entender **3 it follows that ...** : se deduce
que ...

follower ['faloər] *n* : seguidor *m*, -dora *f*

following[1] ['faloɪŋ] *adj* NEXT : siguiente

following[2] *n* FOLLOWERS : seguidores
mpl

following[3] *prep* AFTER : después de

follow through *vi* **to follow through with**
: continuar con, realizar

follow up *vt* : seguir (una sugerencia,
etc.), investigar (una huella)

folly ['fali] *n, pl* **-lies** : locura *f*, desatino
m

foment [fo'mɛnt] *vt* : fomentar

fond ['fand] *adj* **1** LOVING : cariñoso,
tierno **2** PARTIAL : aficionado **3** FER-
VENT : ferviente, fervoroso

fondle ['fandəl] *vt* **-dled; -dling** : acariciar

fondly ['fandli] *adv* : cariñosamente,
afectuosamente

fondness ['fandnəs] *n* **1** LOVE : cariño
m **2** LIKING : afición *f*

fondue [fan'du:, -'dju:] *n* : fondue *f*

font ['fant] *n* **1** *or* **baptismal font** : pila
f bautismal **2** FOUNTAIN : fuente *f*

food ['fu:d] *n* : comida *f*, alimento *m*

food chain *n* : cadena *f* alimenticia

foodstuffs ['fu:dˌstʌfs] *npl* : comestibles
mpl

fool[1] ['fu:l] *vi* **1** JOKE : bromear, hacer
el tonto **2** TOY : jugar, juguetear ⟨don't
fool with the computer : no juegues con
la computadora⟩ **3 to fool around**
: perder el tiempo ⟨he fools around instead of working : pierde el tiempo en
vez de trabajar⟩ — *vt* DECEIVE : engañar, burlar

fool[2] *n* **1** IDIOT : idiota *mf*; tonto *m*, -ta
f; bobo *m*, -ba *f* **2** JESTER : bufón *m*,
-fona *f*

foolhardiness ['fu:lˌhardinəs] *n* : imprudencia *f*

foolhardy ['fu:lˌhardi] *adj* RASH : imprudente, temerario, precipitado

foolish ['fu:lɪʃ] *adj* **1** STUPID : insensato,
estúpido **2** SILLY : idiota, tonto

foolishly ['fu:lɪʃli] *adv* : tontamente

foolishness ['fu:lɪʃnəs] *n* : insensatez *f*,
estupidez *f*, tontería *f*

foolproof ['fu:lˌpru:f] *adj* : infalible

foot ['fʊt] *n, pl* **feet** ['fi:t] : pie *m*

footage ['fʊtɪdʒ] *n* : medida *f* en pies, metraje *m* (en el cine)

football ['fʊtˌbɔl] *n* : futbol *m* americano, fútbol *m* americano

footbridge ['fʊtˌbrɪdʒ] *n* : pasarela *f*,
puente *m* peatonal

foothills ['fʊtˌhɪlz] *npl* : estribaciones *fpl*

foothold ['fʊtˌho:ld] *n* **1** : punto *m* de
apoyo **2 to gain a foothold** : afianzarse
en una posición

footing ['fʊtɪŋ] *n* **1** BALANCE : equilibrio *m* **2** FOOTHOLD : punto *m* de apoyo
3 BASIS : base *f* ⟨on an equal footing
: en igualdad⟩

footlights ['fʊtˌlaɪts] *npl* : candilejas *fpl*

footlocker ['fʊtˌlakər] *n* : baúl *m* pequeño, cofre *m*

footloose ['fʊtˌlu:s] *adj* : libre y sin compromiso

footman ['fʊtmən] *n, pl* **-men** [-mən,
-ˌmɛn] : lacayo *m*

footnote ['fʊtˌno:t] *n* : nota *f* al pie de la
página

footpath ['fʊtˌpæθ] *n* : sendero *m*, senda *f*, vereda *f*

footprint ['fʊt,prɪnt] *n* : huella *f*
footrace ['fʊt,reɪs] *n* : carrera *f* pedestre
footrest ['fʊt,rɛst] *n* : apoyapiés *m*, reposapiés *m*
footstep ['fʊt,stɛp] *n* **1** STEP : paso *m* **2** FOOTPRINT : huella *f*
footstool ['fʊt,stu:l] *n* : taburete *m*, escabel *m*
footwear ['fʊt,wær] *n* : calzado *m*
footwork ['fʊt,wərk] *n* : juego *m* de piernas, juego *m* de pies
fop ['fɑp] *n* : petimetre *m*, dandi *m*
for¹ ['fɔr] *conj* : puesto que, porque
for² *prep* **1** (*indicating purpose*) : para, de ⟨clothes for children : ropa para niños⟩ ⟨it's time for dinner : es la hora de comer⟩ **2** BECAUSE OF : por ⟨for fear of : por miedo de⟩ **3** (*indicating a recipient*) : para, por ⟨a gift for you : un regalo para ti⟩ **4** (*indicating support*) : por ⟨he fought for his country : luchó por su patria⟩ **5** (*indicating a goal*) : por, para ⟨a cure for cancer : una cura para el cáncer⟩ ⟨for your own good : por tu propio bien⟩ **6** (*indicating correspondence or exchange*) : por, para ⟨I bought it for $5 : lo compré por $5⟩ ⟨a lot of trouble for nothing : mucha molestia para nada⟩ **7** AS FOR : para, con respecto a **8** (*indicating duration*) : durante, por ⟨he's going for two years : se va por dos años⟩ ⟨I spoke for ten minutes : hablé (durante) diez minutos⟩ ⟨she has known it for three months : lo sabe desde hace tres meses⟩
forage¹ ['fɔrɪdʒ] *v* **-aged; -aging** *vi* : hurgar (en busca de alimento) — *vt* : buscar (provisiones)
forage² *n* : forraje *m*
foray ['fɔr,eɪ] *n* : incursión *f*
forbear¹ [fɔr'bær] *vi* **-bore** [-'bor]; **-borne** [-'born]; **-bearing 1** ABSTAIN : abstenerse **2** : tener paciencia
forbear² → forbear
forbearance [fɔr'bærənts] *n* **1** ABSTAINING : abstención *f* **2** PATIENCE : paciencia *f*
forbid [fər'bɪd] *vt* **-bade** [-'bæd, -'beɪd]; **-bidden** [-'bɪdən]; **-bidding 1** PROHIBIT : prohibir **2** PREVENT : impedir
forbidding [fər'bɪdɪŋ] *adj* **1** IMPOSING : imponente **2** DISAGREEABLE : desagradable, ingrato **3** GRIM : severo
force¹ ['fors] *vt* **forced; forcing 1** COMPEL : obligar, forzar **2** : forzar ⟨to force open the window : forzar la ventana⟩ ⟨to force a lock : forzar una cerradura⟩ **3** IMPOSE : imponer, obligar
force² *n* **1** : fuerza *f* **2 by force** : por la fuerza **3 in force** : en vigor, en vigencia
forced ['forst] *adj* : forzado, forzoso
forceful ['forsfəl] *adj* : fuerte, energético, contundente
forcefully ['forsfəli] *adv* : con energía, con fuerza
forcefulness ['forsfəlnəs] *n* : contundencia *f*, fuerza *f*

forceps ['fɔrsəps, -,sɛps] *ns & pl* : fórceps *m*
forcible ['forsəbəl] *adj* **1** FORCED : forzoso **2** CONVINCING : contundente, convincente — **forcibly** [-bli] *adv*
ford¹ ['ford] *vt* : vadear
ford² *n* : vado *m*
fore¹ ['for] *adv* **1** FORWARD : hacia adelante **2 fore and aft** : de popa a proa
fore² *adj* **1** FORWARD : delantero, de adelante **2** FORMER : anterior
fore³ *n* **1** : frente *m*, delantera *f* **2 to come to the fore** : empezar a destacar, saltar a primera plana
fore-and-aft ['forən'æft, -ənd-] *adj* : longitudinal
forearm ['for,ɑrm] *n* : antebrazo *m*
forebear ['for,bær] *n* : antepasado *m*, -da *f*
foreboding [for'bo:dɪŋ] *n* : premonición *f*, presentimiento *m*
forecast¹ ['for,kæst] *vt* **-cast; -casting** : pronosticar, predecir
forecast² *n* : predicción *f*, pronóstico *m*
forecastle ['fo:ksəl] *n* : castillo *m* de proa
foreclose [for'klo:z] *vt* **-closed; -closing** : ejecutar (una hipoteca)
forefather ['for,fɑðər] *n* : antepasado *m*, ancestro *m*
forefinger ['for,fɪŋgər] *n* : índice *m*, dedo *m* índice
forefoot ['for,fʊt] *n* : pata *f* delantera
forefront ['for,frʌnt] *n* : frente *m*, vanguardia *f* ⟨in the forefront : a la vanguardia⟩
forego [for'go:] *vt* **-went; -gone; -going 1** PRECEDE : preceder **2** → forgo
foregoing [for'go:ɪŋ] *adj* : precedente, anterior
foregone [for'gɔn] *adj* : previsto ⟨a foregone conclusion : un resultado inevitable⟩
foreground ['for,graʊnd] *n* : primer plano *m*
forehand¹ ['for,hænd] *adj* : directo, derecho
forehand² *n* : golpe *m* del derecho
forehead ['forəd, 'for,hɛd] *n* : frente *f*
foreign ['forən] *adj* **1** : extranjero, exterior ⟨foreign countries : países extranjeros⟩ ⟨foreign trade : comercio exterior⟩ **2** ALIEN : ajeno, extraño ⟨foreign to their nature : ajeno a su carácter⟩ ⟨a foreign body : un cuerpo extraño⟩
foreigner ['forənər] *n* : extranjero *m*, -ra *f*
foreknowledge [for'nɑlɪdʒ] *n* : conocimiento *m* previo
foreleg ['for,lɛg] *n* : pata *f* delantera
foreman ['formən] *n, pl* **-men** [-mən, -,mɛn] : capataz *mf* ⟨foreman of the jury : presidente del jurado⟩
foremost¹ ['for,mo:st] *adv* : en primer lugar
foremost² *adj* : más importante, principal, grande
forenoon ['for,nu:n] *n* : mañana *m*

forensic [fə'rɛntsɪk] *adj* **1** RHETORICAL : retórico, de argumentación **2** : forense ⟨forensic medicine : medicina forense⟩

foreordain [ˌforɔr'deɪn] *vt* : predestinar, predeterminar

forequarter ['for,kwɔrt̬ər] *n* : cuarto *m* delantero

forerunner ['for,rʌnər] *n* : precursor *m*, -sora *f*

foresee [for'si:] *vt* **-saw; -seen; -seeing** : prever

foreseeable [for'si:əbəl] *adj* : previsible ⟨in the foreseeable future : en el futuro inmediato⟩

foreshadow [for'ʃædo:] *vt* : anunciar, prefigurar

foresight ['for,saɪt] *n* : previsión *f*

foresighted ['for,saɪt̬əd] *adj* : previsto

forest ['fɔrəst] *n* : bosque *m* (en zonas templadas), selva *f* (en zonas tropicales)

forestall [for'stɔl] *vt* **1** PREVENT : prevenir, impedir **2** PREEMPT : adelantarse a

forested ['fɔrəstəd] *adj* : arbolado

forester ['fɔrəstər] *n* : silvicultor *m*, -tora *f*

forestland ['fɔrəst,lænd] *n* : zona *f* boscosa

forest ranger → **ranger**

forestry ['fɔrəstri] *n* : silvicultura *f*, ingeniería *f* forestal

foreswear → **forswear**

foretaste[1] ['for,teɪst] *vt* **-tasted; -tasting** : anticipar

foretaste[2] *n* : anticipo *m*

foretell [for'tɛl] *vt* **-told; -telling** : predecir, pronosticar, profetizar

forethought ['for,θɔt] *n* : previsión *f*, reflexión *f* previa

forever [fɔr'ɛvər] *adv* **1** PERPETUALLY : para siempre, eternamente **2** CONTINUALLY : siempre, constantemente

forevermore [fɔr,ɛvər'mor] *adv* : por siempre jamás

forewarn [for'wɔrn] *vt* : prevenir, advertir

foreword ['forword] *n* : prólogo *m*

forfeit[1] ['fɔrfət] *vt* : perder el derecho a

forfeit[2] *n* **1** FINE, PENALTY : multa *f* **2** : prenda *f* (en un juego)

forge[1] ['fɔrʤ] *v* **forged; forging** *vt* **1** : forjar (metal o un plan) **2** COUNTERFEIT : falsificar — *vi* **to forge ahead** : avanzar, seguir adelante

forge[2] *n* : forja *f*

forger ['forʤər] *n* : falsificador *m*, -dora *f*

forgery ['forʤəri] *n, pl* **-eries** : falsificación *f*

forget [fər'gɛt] *v* **-got** [-'gɑt]; **-gotten** [-'gɑt̬ən] *or* **-got; -getting** *vt* : olvidar — *vi* **to forget about** : olvidarse de, no acordarse de

forgetful [fər'gɛtfəl] *adj* : olvidadizo

forget–me–not [fər'gɛtmi,nɑt] *n* : nomeolvides *mf*

forgettable [fər'gɛt̬əbəl] *adj* : poco memorable

forgivable [fər'gɪvəbəl] *adj* : perdonable

forgive [fər'gɪv] *vt* **-gave** [-'geɪv]; **-given** [-'gɪvən]; **-giving** : perdonar

forgiveness [fər'gɪvnəs] *n* : perdón *m*

forgiving [fər'gɪvɪŋ] *adj* : indulgente, comprensivo, clemente

forgo *or* **forego** [for'go:] *vt* **-went; -gone; -going** : privarse de, renunciar a

fork[1] ['fɔrk] *vi* : ramificarse, bifurcarse — *vt* **1** : levantar (con un tenedor, una horca, etc.) **2 to fork over** : desembolsar

fork[2] *n* **1** : tenedor *m* (utensilio de cocina) **2** PITCHFORK : horca *f*, horquilla *f* **3** : bifurcación *f* (de un río o camino), horqueta *f* (de un árbol)

forked ['fɔrkt, 'fɔrkəd] *adj* : bífido, ahorquillado

forklift ['fɔrk,lɪft] *n* : carretilla *f* elevadora

forlorn [fɔr'lɔrn] *adj* **1** DESOLATE : abandonado, desolado, desamparado **2** SAD : triste **3** DESPERATE : desesperado

forlornly [fɔr'lɔrnli] *adv* **1** SADLY : con tristeza **2** HALFHEARTEDLY : sin ánimo

form[1] ['fɔrm] *vt* **1** FASHION, MAKE : formar **2** DEVELOP : moldear, desarrollar **3** CONSTITUTE : constituir, formar **4** ACQUIRE : adquirir (un hábito), formar (una idea) — *vi* : tomar forma, formarse

form[2] *n* **1** SHAPE : forma *f*, figura *f* **2** MANNER : manera *f*, forma *f* **3** DOCUMENT : formulario *m* **4** : forma *f* ⟨in good form : en buena forma⟩ ⟨true to form : en forma consecuente⟩ **5** MOLD : molde *m* **6** KIND, VARIETY : clase *f*, tipo *m* **7** : forma *f* (en gramática) ⟨plural forms : formas plurales⟩

formal[1] ['fɔrməl] *adj* **1** CEREMONIOUS : formal, de etiqueta, ceremonioso **2** OFFICIAL : formal, oficial, de forma

formal[2] *n* **1** BALL : baile *m* formal, baile *m* de etiqueta **2** *or* **formal dress** : traje *m* de etiqueta

formaldehyde [fɔr'mældə,haɪd] *n* : formaldehído *m*

formality [fɔr'mælət̬i] *n, pl* **-ties** : formalidad *f*

formalize ['fɔrmə,laɪz] *vt* **-ized; -izing** : formalizar

formally ['fɔrməli] *adv* : formalmente

format[1] ['fɔr,mæt] *vt* **-matted; -matting** : formatear

format[2] *n* : formato *m*

formation [fɔr'meɪʃən] *n* **1** FORMING : formación *f* **2** SHAPE : forma *f* **3 in formation** : en formación

formative ['fɔrmət̬ɪv] *adj* : formativo

former ['fɔrmər] *adj* **1** PREVIOUS : antiguo, anterior ⟨the former president : el antiguo presidente⟩ **2** : primero (de dos)

formerly ['fɔrmərli] *adv* : anteriormente, antes

formidable ['fɔrmədəbəl, fɔr'mɪdə-] *adj*
: formidable — **formidably** *adv*
formless ['fɔrmləs] *adj* : informe, amorfo
formula ['fɔrmjələ] *n, pl* **-las** *or* **-lae** [-ˌli:,
-ˌlaɪ] **1** : fórmula *f* **2 baby formula**
: preparado *m* para biberón
formulate ['fɔrmjəˌleɪt] *vt* **-lated; -lating**
: formular, hacer
formulation [ˌfɔrmjə'leɪʃən] *n* : formulación *f*
fornicate ['fɔrnəˌkeɪt] *vi* **-cated; -cating**
: fornicar
fornication [ˌfɔrnə'keɪʃən] *n* : fornicación *f*
forsake [fər'seɪk] *vt* **-sook** [-'sʊk];
-saken [-'seɪkən]; **-saking 1** ABANDON
: abandonar, desamparar **2** RELIN-
QUISH : renunciar a
forswear [fɔr'swær] *v* **-swore; -sworn;**
-swearing *vt* RENOUNCE : renunciar a
— *vi* : perjurar
forsythia [fər'sɪθiə] *n* : forsitia *f*
fort ['fɔrt] *n* **1** STRONGHOLD : fuerte *m*,
fortaleza *f*, fortín *m* **2** BASE : base *f* militar
forte ['fɔrt, 'fɔrˌteɪ] *n* : fuerte *m*
forth ['fɔrθ] *adv* **1** : adelante ⟨from this
day forth : de hoy en adelante⟩ **2 and
so forth** : etcétera
forthcoming [forθ'kʌmɪŋ, 'forθˌ-] *adj* **1**
COMING : próximo **2** DIRECT, OPEN
: directo, franco, comunicativo
forthright ['forθˌraɪt] *adj* : directo, franco — **forthrightly** *adv*
forthrightness ['forθˌraɪtnəs] *n* : franqueza *f*
forthwith [forθ'wɪθ, -'wɪð] *adv* : inmediatamente, en el acto, enseguida
fortieth¹ ['fɔrtiəθ] *adj* : cuadragésimo
fortieth² *n* **1** : cuadragésimo *m*, -ma *f*
(en una serie) **2** : cuarentavo *m*,
cuarentava parte *f*
fortification [ˌfɔrtəfə'keɪʃən] *n* : fortificación *f*
fortify ['fɔrtəˌfaɪ] *vt* **-fied; -fying** : fortificar
fortitude ['fɔrtəˌtu:d, -ˌtju:d] *n* : fortaleza
f, valor *m*
fortnight ['fɔrtˌnaɪt] *n* : quince días *mpl*,
dos semanas *fpl*
fortnightly¹ ['fɔrtˌnaɪtli] *adv* : cada
quince días
fortnightly² *adj* : quincenal
fortress ['fɔrtrəs] *n* : fortaleza *f*
fortuitous [fɔr'tu:ətəs, -'tju:-] *adj* : fortuito, accidental
fortunate ['fɔrtʃənət] *adj* : afortunado
fortunately ['fɔrtʃənətli] *adv* : afortunadamente, con suerte
fortune ['fɔrtʃən] *n* **1** : fortuna *f* ⟨to seek
one's fortune : buscar uno su fortuna⟩
2 LUCK : suerte *f*, fortuna *f* **3** DESTINY,
FUTURE : destino *m*, buenaventura *f* **4**
: dineral *m*, platal *m* ⟨she spent a fortune : se gastó un dineral⟩
fortune–teller ['fɔrtʃənˌtɛlər] *n* : adivino
m, -na *f*

fortune–telling ['fɔrtʃənˌtɛlɪŋ] *n* : adivinación *f*
forty¹ ['fɔrti] *adj* : cuarenta
forty² *n, pl* **forties** : cuarenta *m*
forum ['forəm] *n, pl* **-rums** : foro *m*
forward¹ ['forwərd] *vt* **1** PROMOTE : promover, adelantar, fomentar **2** SEND
: remitir, enviar
forward² *adv* **1** : adelante, hacia adelante ⟨to go forward : irse adelante⟩ **2**
from this day forward : de aquí en adelante
forward³ *adj* **1** : hacia adelante, delantero **2** BRASH : atrevido, descarado
forward⁴ *n* : delantero *m*, -ra *f* (en deportes)
forwarder ['forwərdər] *n* : agencia *f* de
transportes, agente *mf* expedidor
forwardness ['forwərdnəs] *n* : atrevimiento *m*, descaro *m*
forwards ['forwərdz] *adv* → **forward²**
fossil¹ ['fɑsəl] *adj* : fósil
fossil² *n* : fósil *m*
fossilize ['fɑsəˌlaɪz] *vt* **-ized; -izing** : fos-
ilizar — *vi* : fosilizarse
foster¹ ['fɔstər] *vt* : promover, fomentar
foster² *adj* : adoptivo ⟨foster child : niño
adoptivo⟩
fought → fight
foul¹ ['faʊl] *vi* : cometer faltas (en deportes) — *vt* **1** DIRTY, POLLUTE : contaminar, ensuciar **2** TANGLE : enredar
foul² *adv* **1** → **foully 2** : contra las reglas
foul³ *adj* **1** REPULSIVE : asqueroso, repugnante **2** CLOGGED : atascado, obstruido **3** TANGLED : enredado **4** OB-
SCENE : obsceno **5** BAD : malo ⟨foul
weather : mal tiempo⟩ **6** : antirreglamentario (en deportes)
foul⁴ *n* : falta *f*, faul *m*
foully ['faʊli] *adv* : asquerosamente
foulmouthed ['faʊlˌmæʊːðd, -ˌmaʊθt]
adj : malhablado
foulness ['faʊlnəs] *n* **1** DIRTINESS : suciedad *f* **2** INCLEMENCY : inclemencia
f **3** OBSCENITY : obscenidad *f*, grosería
f
foul play *n* : actos *mpl* criminales
foul–up ['faʊlˌʌp] *n* : lío *m*, confusión *f*,
desastre *m*
foul up *vt* SPOIL : estropear, arruinar —
vi BUNGLE : echar todo a perder
found¹ → find
found² ['faʊnd] *vt* : fundar, establecer
foundation [faʊn'deɪʃən] *n* **1** FOUND-
ING : fundación *f* **2** BASIS : fundamento
m, base *f* **3** INSTITUTION : fundación *f*
4 : cimientos *mpl* (de un edificio)
founder¹ ['faʊndər] *vi* SINK : hundirse,
irse a pique
founder² *n* : fundador *m*, -dora *f*
founding ['faʊndɪŋ] *adj* : fundador ⟨the
founding fathers : los fundadores⟩
foundling ['faʊndlɪŋ] *n* : expósito *m*, -ta
f
foundry ['faʊndri] *n, pl* **-dries** : fundición *f*

fount ['faʊnt] *n* SOURCE : fuente *f*, origen *m*

fountain ['faʊntən] *n* **1** SPRING : fuente *f*, manantial *m* **2** SOURCE : fuente *f*, origen *m* **3** JET : chorro *m* (de agua), surtidor *m*

fountain pen *n* : pluma *f* fuente

four[1] ['for] *adj* : cuatro

four[2] *n* **1** : cuatro *m* **2 on all fours** : a gatas

fourfold ['for,fo:ld, -'fo:ld] *adj* : cuadruple

four hundred[1] *adj* : cuatrocientos

four hundred[2] *n* : cuatrocientos *m*

fourscore ['for'skor] *adj* EIGHTY : ochenta

fourteen[1] [for'ti:n] *adj* : catorce

fourteen[2] *n* : catorce *m*

fourteenth[1] [for'ti:nθ] *adj* : decimocuarto

fourteenth[2] *n* **1** : decimocuarto *m*, -ta *f* (en una serie) **2** : catorceavo *m*, catorceava parte *f*

fourth[1] ['forθ] *adj* : cuarto

fourth[2] *n* **1** : cuarto *m*, -ta *f* (en una serie) **2** : cuarto *m*, cuarta parte *f*

fowl ['faʊl] *n*, *pl* **fowl** *or* **fowls** **1** BIRD : ave *f* **2** CHICKEN : pollo *m*

fox[1] ['faks] *vt* **1** TRICK : engañar **2** BAFFLE : confundir

fox[2] *n*, *pl* **foxes** : zorro *m*, -ra *f*

foxglove ['faks,glʌv] *n* : dedalera *f*, digital *f*

foxhole ['faks,ho:l] *n* : hoyo *m* para atrincherarse, trinchera *f* individual

foxy ['faksi] *adj* **foxier; -est** SHREWD : astuto

foyer ['fɔɪər, 'fɔɪ,jeɪ] *n* : vestíbulo *m*

fracas ['freɪkəs, 'fræ-] *n*, *pl* **-cases** [-kəsəz] : altercado *m*, pelea *f*, reyerta *f*

fraction ['frækʃən] *n* **1** : fracción *f*, quebrado *m* **2** PORTION : porción *f*, parte *f*

fractional ['frækʃənəl] *adj* **1** : fraccionario **2** TINY : minúsculo, mínimo, insignificante

fractious ['frækʃəs] *adj* **1** UNRULY : rebelde **2** IRRITABLE : malhumorado, irritable

fracture[1] ['fræktʃər] *vt* **-tured; -turing** : fracturar

fracture[2] *n* **1** : fractura *f* (de un hueso) **2** CRACK : fisura *f*, grieta *f*, falla *f* (geológica)

fragile ['frædʒəl, -,dʒaɪl] *adj* : frágil

fragility [frə'dʒɪləti] *n*, *pl* **-ties** : fragilidad *f*

fragment[1] ['fræg,mɛnt] *vt* : fragmentar — *vi* : fragmentarse, hacerse añicos

fragment[2] ['frægmənt] *n* : fragmento *m*, trozo *m*, pedazo *m*

fragmentary ['frægmən,tɛri] *adj* : fragmentario, incompleto

fragmentation [,frægmən'teɪʃən, -,mn-] *n* : fragmentación *f*

fragrance ['freɪgrənts] *n* : fragancia *f*, aroma *m*

fragrant ['freɪgrənt] *adj* : fragante, aromático — **fragrantly** *adv*

frail ['freɪl] *adj* : débil, delicado

frailty ['freɪlti] *n*, *pl* **-ties** : debilidad *f*, flaqueza *f*

frame[1] ['freɪm] *vt* **framed; framing** **1** FORMULATE : formular, elaborar **2** BORDER : enmarcar, encuadrar **3** INCRIMINATE : incriminar

frame[2] *n* **1** BODY : cuerpo *m* **2** : armazón *f* (de un edificio, un barco, o un avión), bastidor *m* (de un automóvil), cuadro *m* (de una bicicleta), marco *m* (de un cuadro, una ventana, una puerta, etc.) **3 frames** *npl* : armazón *mf*, montura *f* (para anteojos) **4 frame of mind** : estado *m* de ánimo

framework ['freɪm,wərk] *n* **1** SKELETON, STRUCTURE : armazón *f*, estructura *f* **2** BASIS : marco *m*

franc ['fræŋk] *n* : franco *m*

franchise ['fræn,tʃaɪz] *n* **1** LICENSE : licencia *f* exclusiva, concesión *f* (en comercio) **2** SUFFRAGE : sufragio *m*

franchisee [,fræn,tʃaɪ'zi:, -'tʃə-] *n* : concesionario *m*, -ria *f*

Franciscan [fræn'sɪskən] *n* : franciscano *m*, -na *f* — **Franciscan** *adj*

frank[1] ['fræŋk] *vt* : franquear

frank[2] *adj* : franco, sincero, cándido — **frankly** *adv*

frank[3] *n* : franqueo *m* (de correo)

frankfurter ['fræŋkfərtər, -,fər-] *or* **frankfurt** [-fərt] *n* : salchicha *f* (de Frankfurt, de Viena), perro *m* caliente

frankincense ['fræŋkən,sɛnts] *n* : incienso *m*

frankness ['fræŋknəs] *n* : franqueza *f*, sinceridad *f*, candidez *f*

frantic ['fræntɪk] *adj* : frenético, desesperado — **frantically** *adv*

fraternal [frə'tərnəl] *adj* : fraterno, fraternal

fraternity [frə'tərnəti] *n*, *pl* **-ties** : fraternidad *f*

fraternization [,frætərnə'zeɪʃən] *n* : fraternización *f*, confraternización *f*

fraternize ['frætər,naɪz] *vi* **-nized; -nizing** : fraternizar, confraternizar

fratricidal [,frætrə'saɪdəl] *adj* : fratricida

fratricide ['frætrə,saɪd] *n* : fratricidio *m*

fraud ['frɔd] *n* **1** DECEPTION, SWINDLE : fraude *m*, estafa *f*, engaño *m* **2** IMPOSTOR : impostor *m*, -tora *f*; farsante *mf*

fraudulent ['frɔdʒələnt] *adj* : fraudulento — **fraudulently** *adv*

fraught ['frɔt] *adj* **fraught with** : lleno de, cargado de

fray[1] ['freɪ] *vt* **1** WEAR : desgastar, deshilachar **2** IRRITATE : crispar, irritar (los nervios) — *vi* : desgastarse, deshilacharse

fray[2] *n* : pelea *f* ⟨to join the fray : salir a la palestra⟩ ⟨to return to the fray : volver a la carga⟩

frazzle[1] ['fræzəl] *vt* **-zled; -zling 1** FRAY : desgastar, deshilachar **2** EXHAUST : agotar, fatigar

frazzle[2] *n* EXHAUSTION : agotamiento *m*

freak ['fri:k] *n* **1** ODDITY : ejemplar *m* anormal, fenómeno *m*, rareza *f* **2** ENTHUSIAST : entusiasta *mf*

freakish ['fri:kɪʃ] *adj* : extraño, estrafalario, raro

freak out *vi* : ponerse como loco — *vt* : darle un ataque (a alguien)

freckle[1] ['frɛkəl] *vi* **-led; -ling** : cubrirse de pecas

freckle[2] *n* : peca *f*

free[1] ['fri:] *vt* **freed; freeing 1** LIBERATE : libertar, liberar, poner en libertad **2** RELIEVE, RID : librar, eximir **3** RELEASE, UNTIE : desatar, soltar **4** UNCLOG : desatascar, destapar

free[2] *adv* **1** FREELY : libremente **2** GRATIS : gratuitamente, gratis

free[3] *adj* **freer; freest 1** : libre ⟨free as a bird : libre como un pájaro⟩ **2** EXEMPT : libre ⟨tax-free : libre de impuestos⟩ **3** GRATIS : gratuito, gratis **4** VOLUNTARY : espontáneo, voluntario, libre **5** UNOCCUPIED : desocupado, libre **6** LOOSE : suelto

freebooter ['fri:,bu:ʈər] *n* : pirata *mf*

freeborn ['fri:'bɔrn] *adj* : nacido libre

freedom ['fri:dəm] *n* : libertad *f*

free-for-all ['fri:fər,ɔl] *n* : pelea *f*, batalla *f* campal

freelance[1] ['fri:,lænʦ] *vi* **-lanced; -lancing** : trabajar por cuenta propia

freelance[2] *adj* : por cuenta propia, independiente

freeload ['fri:,lo:d] *vi* : gorronear *fam*, gorrear *fam*

freeloader ['fri:,lo:dər] *n* : gorrón *m*, -rrona *f*; gorrero *m*, -ra *f*; vividor *m*, -dora *f*

freely ['fri:li] *adv* **1** FREE : libremente **2** GRATIS : gratis, gratuitamente

freestanding ['fri:'stændɪŋ] *adj* : de pie, no empotrado, independiente

freeway ['fri:,weɪ] *n* : autopista *f*

freewill ['fri:,wɪl] *adj* : de propia voluntad

free will *n* : libre albedrío *m*, propia voluntad *f*

freeze[1] ['fri:z] *v* **froze** ['fro:z]; **frozen** ['fro:zən]; **freezing** *vi* **1** : congelarse, helarse ⟨the water froze in the lake : el agua se congeló en el lago⟩ ⟨my blood froze : se me heló la sangre⟩ ⟨I'm freezing : me estoy helando⟩ **2** STOP : quedarse inmóvil — *vt* : helar, congelar (líquidos), congelar (alimentos, precios, activos)

freeze[2] *n* **1** FROST : helada *f* **2** FREEZING : congelación *f*, congelamiento *m*

freeze-dried ['fri:z'draɪd] *adj* : liofilizado

freeze-dry ['fri:z'draɪ] *vt* **-dried; -drying** : liofilizar

freezer ['fri:zər] *n* : congelador *m*

freezing ['fri:zɪŋ] *adj* : helando ⟨it's freezing! : ¡hace un frío espantoso!⟩

freezing point *n* : punto *m* de congelación

freight[1] ['freɪt] *vt* : enviar como carga

freight[2] *n* **1** SHIPPING, TRANSPORT : transporte *m*, porte *m*, flete *m* **2** GOODS : mercancías *fpl*, carga *f*

freighter ['freɪtər] *n* : carguero *m*, buque *m* de carga

French[1] ['frɛnʧ] *adj* : francés

French[2] *n* **1** : francés *m* (idioma) **2 the French** *npl* : los franceses

french fries ['frɛnʧ,fraɪz] *npl* : papas *fpl* fritas

Frenchman ['frɛnʧmən] *n, pl* **-men** [-mən, -ˌmɛn] : francés *m*

Frenchwoman ['frɛnʧ,wumən] *n, pl* **-women** [-ˌwɪmən] : francesa *f*

frenetic [frɪ'nɛtɪk] *adj* : frenético — **frenetically** [-tɪkli] *adv*

frenzied ['frɛnzid] *adj* : frenético

frenzy ['frɛnzi] *n, pl* **-zies** : frenesí *m*

frequency ['fri:kwəntsi] *n, pl* **-cies** : frecuencia *f*

frequent[1] [fri'kwɛnt] *vt* : frecuentar

frequent[2] ['fri:kwənt] *adj* : frecuente — **frequently** *adv*

fresco ['frɛs,ko:] *n, pl* **-coes** : fresco *m*

fresh ['frɛʃ] *adj* **1** : dulce ⟨freshwater : agua dulce⟩ **2** PURE : puro **3** : fresco ⟨fresh fruits : frutas frescas⟩ **4** CLEAN, NEW : limpio, nuevo ⟨fresh clothes : ropa limpia⟩ ⟨fresh evidence : evidencia nueva⟩ **5** REFRESHED : fresco, descansado **6** IMPERTINENT : descarado, impertinente

freshen ['frɛʃən] *vt* : refrescar, arreglar — *vi* **to freshen up** : arreglarse, lavarse

freshet ['frɛʃət] *n* : arroyo *m* desbordado

freshly ['frɛʃli] *adv* : recientemente, recién

freshman ['frɛʃmən] *n, pl* **-men** [-mən, -ˌmɛn] : estudiante *mf* de primer año universitario

freshness ['frɛʃnəs] *n* : frescura *f*

freshwater ['frɛʃ,wɔtər] *n* : agua *f* dulce

fret[1] ['frɛt] *vi* **fretted; fretting** : preocuparse, inquietarse

fret[2] *n* **1** VEXATION : irritación *f*, molestia *f* **2** WORRY : preocupación *f* **3** : traste *m* (de un instrumento musical)

fretful ['frɛtfəl] *adj* : fastidioso, quejoso, neurótico

fretfully ['frɛtfəli] *adv* : ansiosamente, fastidiosamente, inquieto

fretfulness ['frɛtfəlnəs] *n* : inquietud *f*, irritabilidad *f*

friable ['fraɪəbəl] *adj* : friable, pulverizable

friar ['fraɪər] *n* : fraile *m*

fricassee[1] ['frɪkə,si:, ˌfrɪkə'si:] *vt* **-seed; -seeing** : cocinar al fricasé

fricassee[2] *n* : fricasé *m*

friction ['frɪkʃən] *n* **1** RUBBING : fricción *f* **2** CONFLICT : fricción *f*, roce *m*

Friday ['fraɪ,deɪ, -di] *n* : viernes *m*

fridge ['frɪʤ] → **refrigerator**

friend ['frɛnd] *n* : amigo *m*, -ga *f*
friendless ['frɛndləs] *adj* : sin amigos
friendliness ['frɛndlinəs] *n* : simpatía *f*, amabilidad *f*
friendly ['frɛndli] *adj* **-lier; -est 1** : simpático, amable, de amigo ⟨a friendly child : un niño simpático⟩ ⟨friendly advice : consejo de amigo⟩ **2** : agradable, acogedor ⟨a friendly atmosphere : un ambiente agradable⟩ **3** GOOD-NATURED : amigable, amistoso ⟨friendly competition : competencia amistosa⟩
friendship [frɛnd,ʃɪp] *n* : amistad *f*
frieze ['fri:z] *n* : friso *m*
frigate ['frɪgət] *n* : fragata *f*
fright ['fraɪt] *n* : miedo *m*, susto *m*
frighten ['fraɪtən] *vt* : asustar, espantar
frightened ['fraɪtənd] *adj* : asustado, temeroso
frightening ['fraɪtənɪŋ] *adj* : espantoso, aterrador
frightful ['fraɪtfəl] *adj* **1** → **frightening 2** TREMENDOUS : espantoso, tremendo
frightfully ['fraɪtfəli] *adv* : terriblemente, tremendamente
frigid ['frɪdʒɪd] *adj* : glacial, extremadamente frío
frigidity [frɪ'dʒɪdəti] *n* **1** COLDNESS : frialdad *f* **2** : frigidez *f* (sexual)
frill ['frɪl] *n* **1** RUFFLE : volante *m* **2** EMBELLISHMENT : floritura *f*, adorno *m*
frilly ['frɪli] *adj* **frillier; -est 1** RUFFLY : con volantes **2** OVERDONE : recargado
fringe[1] ['frɪndʒ] *vt* **fringed; fringing** : orlar, bordear
fringe[2] *n* **1** BORDER : fleco *m*, orla *f* **2** EDGE : periferia *f*, margen *m* **3 fringe benefits** : incentivos *mpl*, extras *mpl*
frisk ['frɪsk] *vi* FROLIC : retozar, juguetear — *vt* SEARCH : cachear, registrar
friskiness ['frɪskinəs] *n* : vivacidad *f*
frisky ['frɪski] *adj* **friskier; -est** : retozón, juguetón
fritter[1] ['frɪtər] *vt* : desperdiciar, malgastar ⟨I frittered away the money : malgasté el dinero⟩
fritter[2] *n* : buñuelo *m*
frivolity [frɪ'valəti] *n, pl* **-ties** : frivolidad *f*
frivolous ['frɪvələs] *adj* : frívolo, de poca importancia
frivolously ['frɪvələsli] *adv* : frívolamente, a la ligera
frizz[1] ['frɪz] *vi* : rizarse, encresparse, ponerse chino *Mex*
frizz[2] *n* : rizos *mpl* muy apretados
frizzy ['frɪzi] *adj* **frizzier; -est** : rizado, crespo, chino *Mex*
fro ['fro:] *adv* **to and fro** : de aquí para allá, de un lado para otro
frock ['frak] *n* DRESS : vestido *m*
frog ['frɔg, 'frag] *n* **1** : rana *f* **2** FASTENER : alamar *m* **3 to have a frog in one's throat** : tener carraspera
frogman ['frɔg,mæn, 'frag-, -mən] *n, pl* **-men** [-mən, -,mɛn] : hombre *m* rana, submarinista *mf*

frolic[1] ['fralɪk] *vi* **-icked; -icking** : retozar, juguetear
frolic[2] *n* FUN : diversión *f*
frolicsome ['fralɪksəm] *adj* : juguetón
from ['frʌm, 'fram] *prep* **1** (*indicating a starting point*) : desde, de, a partir de ⟨from Cali to Bogota : de Cali a Bogotá⟩ ⟨where are you from? : ¿de dónde eres?⟩ ⟨from that time onward : desde entonces⟩ ⟨from tomorrow : a partir de mañana⟩ **2** (*indicating a source or sender*) : de ⟨a letter from my friend : una carta de mi amiga⟩ ⟨a quote from Shakespeare : una cita de Shakespeare⟩ **3** (*indicating distance*) : de ⟨10 feet from the entrance : a 10 pies de la entrada⟩ **4** (*indicating a cause*) : de ⟨red from crying : rojos de llorar⟩ ⟨he died from the cold : murió del frío⟩ **5** OFF, OUT OF : de ⟨she took it from the drawer : lo sacó del cajón⟩ **6** (*with adverbs or adverbial phrases*) : de, desde ⟨from above : desde arriba⟩ ⟨from among : de entre⟩
frond ['frand] *n* : fronda *f*, hoja *f*
front[1] ['frʌnt] *vi* **1** FACE : dar, estar orientado ⟨the house fronts north : la casa da al norte⟩ **2** : servir de pantalla ⟨he fronts for his boss : sirve de pantalla para su jefe⟩
front[2] *adj* : delantero, de adelante, primero ⟨the front row : la primera fila⟩
front[3] *n* **1** : frente *m*, parte *f* de adelante, delantera *f* ⟨the front of the class : el frente de la clase⟩ ⟨at the front of the train : en la parte delantera del tren⟩ **2** AREA, ZONE : frente *m*, zona *f* ⟨the Eastern front : el frente oriental⟩ ⟨on the educational front : en el frente de la enseñanza⟩ **3** FACADE : fachada *f* (de un edificio o una persona) **4** : frente *m* (en meteorología)
frontage ['frʌntɪdʒ] *n* : fachada *f*, frente *m*
frontal ['frʌntəl] *adj* : frontal, de frente
frontier [,frʌn'tɪr] *n* : frontera *f*
frontiersman [,frʌn'tɪrzmən] *n, pl* **-men** [-mən, -,mɛn] : hombre *m* de la frontera
frontispiece ['frʌntəs,pi:s] *n* : frontispicio *m*
frost[1] ['frɔst] *vt* **1** FREEZE : helar **2** ICE : escarchar (pasteles)
frost[2] *n* **1** : helada *f* (en meteorología) **2** : escarcha *f* ⟨frost on the window : escarcha en la ventana⟩
frostbite ['frɔst,baɪt] *n* : congelación *f*
frostbitten ['frɔst,bɪtən] *adj* : congelado (dícese de una persona), quemado (dícese de una planta)
frosting ['frɔstɪŋ] *n* ICING : glaseado *m*, betún *m Mex*
frosty ['frɔsti] *adj* **frostier; -est 1** CHILLY : helado, frío **2** COOL, UNFRIENDLY : frío, glacial
froth ['frɔθ] *n, pl* **froths** ['frɔθs, 'frɔðz] : espuma *f*

frothy ['froθi] *adj* **frothier; -est** : espumoso

frown[1] ['fraʊn] *vi* **1** : fruncir el ceño, fruncir el entrecejo **2 to frown at** : mirar (algo) con ceño, mirar (a alguien) con ceño

frown[2] *n* : ceño *m* (fruncido)

frowsy *or* **frowzy** ['fraʊzi] *adj* **frowsier** *or* **frowzier; -est** : desaliñado, desaseado

froze → **freeze**

frozen → **freeze**

frugal ['fru:gəl] *adj* : frugal, ahorrativo, parco — **frugally** *adv*

frugality [fru'gæləti] *n* : frugalidad *f*

fruit[1] ['fru:t] *vi* : dar fruto

fruit[2] *n* **1** : fruta *f* (término genérico), fruto *m* (término particular) **2 fruits** *npl* REWARDS : frutos *mpl* ⟨the fruits of his labor : los frutos de su trabajo⟩

fruitcake ['fru:t,keɪk] *n* : pastel *m* de frutas

fruitful ['fru:tfəl] *adj* : fructífero, provechoso

fruition [fru'ɪʃən] *n* **1** : cumplimiento *m*, realización *f* **2 to bring to fruition** : realizar

fruitless ['fru:tləs] *adj* : infructuoso, inútil — **fruitlessly** *adv*

fruity ['fru:ti] *adj* **fruitier; -est** : (con sabor) a fruta

frumpy ['frʌmpi] *adj* **frumpier; -est** : anticuado y sin atractivo

frustrate ['frʌs,treɪt] *vt* **-trated; -trating** : frustrar

frustrating ['frʌs,treɪtɪŋ] *adj* : frustrante — **frustratingly** *adv*

frustration [,frʌs'treɪʃən] *n* : frustración *f*

fry[1] ['fraɪ] *vt* **fried; frying** : freír

fry[2] *n, pl* **fries 1** : fritura *f*, plato *m* frito **2** : fiesta *f* en que se sirven frituras **3** *pl* **fry** : alevín *m* (pez)

frying pan *n* : sartén *mf*

fuchsia ['fju:ʃə] *n* **1** : fucsia *f* (planta) **2** : fucsia *m* (color)

fuddle ['fʌdəl] *vt* **-dled; -dling** : confundir, atontar

fuddy-duddy ['fʌdi,dʌdi] *n, pl* **-dies** : persona *f* chapada a la antigua, carca *mf*

fudge[1] ['fʌdʒ] *vt* **fudged; fudging 1** FALSIFY : amañar, falsificar **2** DODGE : esquivar

fudge[2] *n* : dulce *m* blando de chocolate y leche

fuel[1] ['fju:əl] *vt* **-eled** *or* **-elled; -eling** *or* **-elling 1** : abastecer de combustible **2** STIMULATE : estimular

fuel[2] *n* : combustible *m*, carburante *m* (para motores)

fugitive[1] ['fju:dʒətɪv] *adj* **1** RUNAWAY : fugitivo **2** FLEETING : efímero, pasajero, fugaz

fugitive[2] *n* : fugitivo *m*, -va *f*

fugue ['fju:g] *n* : fuga *f*

fulcrum ['fʊlkrəm, 'fʌl-] *n, pl* **-crums** *or* **-cra** [-krə] : fulcro *m*

fulfill *or* **fulfil** [fʊl'fɪl] *vt* **-filled; -filling 1** PERFORM : cumplir con, realizar, llevar a cabo **2** SATISFY : satisfacer

fulfillment [fʊl'fɪlmənt] *n* **1** PERFORMANCE : cumplimiento *m*, ejecución *f* **2** SATISFACTION : satisfacción *f*, realización *f*

full[1] ['fʊl, 'fʌl] *adv* **1** VERY : muy ⟨full well : muy bien, perfectamente⟩ **2** ENTIRELY : completamente ⟨she swung full around : giró completamente⟩ **3** DIRECTLY : de lleno, directamente ⟨he looked me full in the face : me miró directamente a la cara⟩

full[2] *adj* **1** FILLED : lleno **2** COMPLETE : completo, detallado **3** MAXIMUM : todo, pleno ⟨at full speed : a toda velocidad⟩ ⟨in full bloom : en plena flor⟩ **4** PLUMP : redondo, llenito *fam*, regordete *fam* ⟨a full face : una cara redonda⟩ ⟨a full figure : un cuerpo llenito⟩ **5** AMPLE : amplio ⟨a full skirt : una falda amplia⟩

full[3] *n* **1 to pay in full** : pagar en su totalidad **2 to the full** : al máximo

full-fledged ['fʊl'flɛdʒd] *adj* : hecho y derecho

fullness ['fʊlnəs] *n* **1** ABUNDANCE : plenitud *f*, abundancia *f* **2** : amplitud *f* (de una falda)

fully ['fʊli] *adv* **1** COMPLETELY : completamente, totalmente **2** : al menos, por lo menos ⟨fully half of them : al menos la mitad de ellos⟩

fulsome ['fʊlsəm] *adj* : excesivo, exagerado, efusivo

fumble[1] ['fʌmbəl] *v* **-bled; -bling** *vt* **1** : dejar caer, fumblear **2 to fumble one's way** : ir a tientas — *vi* **1** GROPE : hurgar, tantear **2 to fumble with** : manejar con torpeza

fumble[2] *n* : fumble *m* (en futbol americano)

fume[1] ['fju:m] *vi* **fumed; fuming 1** SMOKE : echar humo, humear **2** : estar furioso

fume[2] *n* : gas *m*, humo *m*, vapor *m*

fumigate ['fju:mə,geɪt] *vt* **-gated; -gating** : fumigar

fumigation [,fju:mə'geɪʃən] *n* : fumigación *f*

fun[1] ['fʌn] *adj* : divertido, entretenido

fun[2] *n* **1** AMUSEMENT : diversión *f*, entretenimiento *m* **2** ENJOYMENT : disfrute *m* **3 to have fun** : divertirse **4 to make fun of** : reírse de, burlarse de

function[1] ['fʌŋkʃən] *vi* : funcionar, desempeñarse, servir

function[2] *n* **1** PURPOSE : función *f* **2** GATHERING : reunión *f* social, recepción *f* **3** CEREMONY : ceremonia *f*, acto *m*

functional ['fʌŋkʃənəl] *adj* : funcional — **functionally** *adv*

functionary ['fʌŋkʃə,nɛri] *n, pl* **-aries** : funcionario *m*, -ria *f*

fund[1] ['fʌnd] *vt* : financiar

fund² *n* **1** SUPPLY : reserva *f*, cúmulo *m* **2** : fondo *m* ⟨investment fund : fondo de inversiones⟩ **3 funds** *npl* RESOURCES : fondos *mpl*

fundamental¹ [ˌfʌndəˈmɛntəl] *adj* **1** BASIC : fundamental, básico **2** PRINCIPAL : esencial, principal **3** INNATE : innato, intrínseco

fundamental² *n* : fundamento *m*

fundamentalism [ˌfʌndəˈmɛntəlˌɪzəm] *n* : integrismo *m*, fundamentalismo *m*

fundamentalist [ˌfʌndəˈmɛntəlɪst] *n* : integrista *mf*, fundamentalista *mf* — **fundamentalist** *adj*

fundamentally [ˌfʌndəˈmɛntəli] *adv* : fundamentalmente, básicamente

funding [ˈfʌndɪŋ] *n* : financiación *f*

fund–raiser [ˈfʌndˌreɪzər] *n* : función *f* para recaudar fondos

funeral¹ [ˈfjuːnərəl] *adj* **1** : funeral, funerario, fúnebre ⟨funeral procession : cortejo fúnebre⟩ **2 funeral home** : funeraria *f*

funeral² *n* : funeral *m*, funerales *mpl*

funereal [fjuˈnɪriəl] *adj* : fúnebre

fungal [ˈfʌŋɡəl] *adj* : de hongos, micótico

fungicidal [ˌfʌndʒəˈsaɪdəl, ˌfʌŋɡə-] *adj* : fungicida

fungicide [ˈfʌndʒəˌsaɪd, ˈfʌŋɡə-] *n* : fungicida *m*

fungous [ˈfʌŋɡəs] *adj* : fungoso

fungus [ˈfʌŋɡəs] *n, pl* **fungi** [ˈfʌnˌdʒaɪ, ˈfʌŋˌɡaɪ] : hongo *m*

funk [ˈfʌŋk] *n* **1** FEAR : miedo *m* **2** DEPRESSION : depresión *f*

funky [ˈfʌŋki] *adj* **funkier; -est** ODD, QUAINT : raro, extraño, original

funnel¹ [ˈfʌnəl] *vt* **-neled; -neling** CHANNEL : canalizar, encauzar

funnel² *n* **1** : embudo *m* **2** SMOKESTACK : chimenea *f* (de un barco o vapor)

funnies [ˈfʌniz] *npl* : tiras *fpl* cómicas

funny [ˈfʌni] *adj* **funnier; -est** **1** AMUSING : divertido, cómico **2** STRANGE : extraño, raro

fur¹ [ˈfər] *adj* : de piel

fur² *n* **1** : pelaje *m*, piel *f* **2** : prenda *f* de piel

furbish [ˈfərbɪʃ] *vt* : pulir, limpiar

furious [ˈfjuriəs] *adj* **1** ANGRY : furioso **2** FRANTIC : violento, frenético, vertiginoso (dícese de la velocidad)

furiously [ˈfjuriəsli] *adv* **1** ANGRILY : furiosamente **2** FRANTICALLY : frenéticamente

furlong [ˈfərˌlɔŋ] *n* : estadio *m* (201.2 m)

furlough¹ [ˈfərˌloː] *vt* : dar permiso a, dar licencia a

furlough² *n* LEAVE : permiso *m*, licencia *f*

furnace [ˈfərnəs] *n* : horno *m*

furnish [ˈfərnɪʃ] *vt* **1** SUPPLY : proveer, suministrar **2** : amueblar ⟨furnished apartment : departamento amueblado⟩

furnishings [ˈfərnɪʃɪŋz] *npl* **1** ACCESSORIES : accesorios *mpl* **2** FURNITURE : muebles *mpl*, mobiliario *m*

furniture [ˈfərnɪtʃər] *n* : muebles *mpl*, mobiliario *m*

furor [ˈfjurˌor, -ər] *n* **1** RAGE : furia *f*, rabia *f* **2** UPROAR : escándalo *m*, jaleo *m*, alboroto *m*

furrier [ˈfəriər] *n* : peletero *m*, -ra *f*

furrow¹ [ˈfəroː] *vt* **1** : surcar **2 to furrow one's brow** : fruncir el ceño

furrow² *n* **1** GROOVE : surco *m* **2** WRINKLE : arruga *f*, surco *m*

furry [ˈfəri] *adj* **furrier; -est** : peludo (dícese de un animal), peluche (dícese de un objeto)

further¹ [ˈfərðər] *vt* : promover, fomentar

further² *adv* **1** FARTHER : más lejos, más adelante **2** MOREOVER : además **3** MORE : más ⟨I'll consider it further in the morning : lo consideraré más en la mañana⟩

further³ *adj* **1** FARTHER : más lejano **2** ADDITIONAL : adicional, más

furtherance [ˈfərðərənts] *n* : promoción *f*, fomento *m*, adelantamiento *m*

furthermore [ˈfərðərˌmor] *adv* : además

furthermost [ˈfərðərˌmoːst] *adj* : más lejano, más distante

furthest [ˈfərðəst] → **farthest¹, farthest²**

furtive [ˈfərtɪv] *adj* : furtivo, sigiloso — **furtively** *adv*

furtiveness [ˈfərtɪvnəs] *n* STEALTH : sigilo *m*

fury [ˈfjuri] *n, pl* **-ries** **1** RAGE : furia *f*, ira *f* **2** VIOLENCE : furia *f*, furor *m*

fuse¹ [ˈfjuːz] *or* **fuze** *vt* **fused** *or* **fuzed; fusing** *or* **fuzing** : equipar con un fusible

fuse² *v* **fused; fusing** *vt* **1** SMELT : fundir **2** MERGE : fusionar, fundir — *vi* : fundirse, fusionarse

fuse³ *n* : fusible *m*

fuselage [ˈfjuːsəˌlɑʒ, -zə-] *n* : fuselaje *m*

fusillade [ˈfjuːsəˌlɑd, -ˌleɪd, ˌfjuːsəˈ-, -zə-] *n* : descarga *f* de fusilería

fusion [ˈfjuːʒən] *n* : fusión *f*

fuss¹ [ˈfʌs] *vi* **1** WORRY : preocuparse **2 to fuss with** : juguetear con, toquetear **3 to fuss over** : mimar

fuss² *n* **1** COMMOTION : alboroto *m*, escándalo *m* **2** ATTENTION : atenciones *fpl* **3** COMPLAINT : quejas *fpl*

fussbudget [ˈfʌsˌbʌdʒət] *n* : quisquilloso *m*, -sa *f*; melindroso *m*, -sa *f*

fussiness [ˈfʌsinəs] *n* **1** IRRITABILITY : irritabilidad *f* **2** ORNATENESS : lo recargado **3** METICULOUSNESS : meticulosidad *f*

fussy [ˈfʌsi] *adj* **fussier; -est** **1** IRRITABLE : irritable, nervioso **2** OVERELABORATE : recargado **3** METICULOUS : meticuloso **4** FASTIDIOUS : quisquilloso, exigente

futile [ˈfjuːtəl, ˈfjuːˌtaɪl] *adj* : inútil, vano

futility [fjuˈtɪləti] *n, pl* **-ties** : inutilidad *f*

future¹ [ˈfjuːtʃər] *adj* : futuro

future² *n* : futuro *m*

futuristic [ˌfjuːtʃəˈrɪstɪk] *adj* : futurista

fuze → **fuse¹**

fuzz ['fʌz] *n* : pelusa *f*
fuzziness ['fʌzinəs] *n* **1** DOWNINESS : vellosidad *f* **2** INDISTINCTNESS : falta *f* de claridad

fuzzy ['fʌzi] *adj* **fuzzier; -est** **1** FLUFFY, FURRY : con pelusa, peludo **2** INDISTINCT : indistinto ⟨a fuzzy image : una imagen borrosa⟩

G

g ['ʤiː] *n, pl* **g's** *or* **gs** ['ʤiːz] : séptima letra del alfabeto inglés
gab[1] ['gæb] *vi* **gabbed; gabbing** : charlar, cotorrear *fam*, parlotear *fam*
gab[2] *n* CHATTER : cotorreo *m fam*, parloteo *m fam*
gabardine ['gæbər,diːn] *n* : gabardina *f*
gabby ['gæbi] *adj* **gabbier; -est** : hablador, parlanchín
gable ['geɪbəl] *n* : hastial *m*, aguilón *m*
Gabonese [,gæbəˈniːz, -ˈniːs] *n* : gabonés *m*, -nesa *f* — **Gabonese** *adj*
gad ['gæd] *vi* **gadded; gadding** WANDER : deambular, vagar, callejear
gadfly ['gæd,flaɪ] *n, pl* **-flies 1** : tábano *m* (insecto) **2** FAULTFINDER : criticón *m*, -cona *f fam*
gadget ['gæʤət] *n* : artilugio *m*, aparato *m*
gadgetry ['gæʤətri] *n* : artilugios *mpl*, aparatos *mpl*
Gaelic ['geɪlɪk, 'gæ] *n* : gaélico *m* (idioma) — **Gaelic** *adj*
gaff ['gæf] *n* **1** : garfio *m* **2** → **gaffe**
gaffe ['gæf] *n* : metedura *f* de pata *fam*
gag[1] ['gæg] *v* **gagged; gagging** *vt* : amordazar ⟨to tie up and gag : atar y amordazar⟩ — *vi* **1** CHOKE : atragantarse **2** RETCH : hacer arcadas
gag[2] *n* **1** : mordaza *f* (para la boca) **2** JOKE : chiste *m*
gage → **gauge**
gaggle ['gægəl] *n* : bandada *f*, manada *f* (de gansos)
gaiety ['geɪəti] *n, pl* **-eties 1** MERRYMAKING : juerga *f* **2** MERRIMENT : alegría *f*, regocijo *m*
gaily ['geɪli] *adv* : alegremente
gain[1] ['geɪn] *vt* **1** ACQUIRE, OBTAIN : ganar, obtener, adquirir, conseguir ⟨to gain knowledge : adquirir conocimientos⟩ ⟨to gain a victory : obtener una victoria⟩ **2** REACH : alcanzar, llegar a **3** INCREASE : ganar, aumentar ⟨to gain weight : aumentar de peso⟩ **4** : adelantarse, ganar ⟨the watch gains two minutes a day : el reloj se adelanta dos minutos por día⟩ — *vi* **1** PROFIT : beneficiarse **2** INCREASE : aumentar
gain[2] *n* **1** PROFIT : beneficio *m*, ganancia *f*, lucro *m*, provecho *m* **2** INCREASE : aumento *m*
gainful ['geɪnfəl] *adj* : lucrativo, beneficioso, provechoso ⟨gainful employment : trabajo remunerado⟩
gait ['geɪt] *n* : paso *m*, andar *m*, manera *f* de caminar
gal ['gæl] *n* : muchacha *f*
gala[1] ['geɪlə, 'gæ-, 'gɑ-] *adj* : de gala

gala[2] *n* : gala *f*, fiesta *f*
galactic [gəˈlæktɪk] *adj* : galáctico
galaxy ['gæləksi] *n, pl* **-axies** : galaxia *f*
gale ['geɪl] *n* **1** WIND : vendaval *f*, viento *m* fuerte **2** gales of laughter : carcajadas *fpl*
gall[1] ['gɔl] *vt* **1** CHAFE : rozar **2** IRRITATE, VEX : irritar, molestar
gall[2] *n* **1** BILE : bilis *f*, hiel *f* **2** INSOLENCE : audacia *f*, insolencia *f*, descaro *m* **3** SORE : rozadura *f* (de un caballo) **4** : agalla *f* (de una planta)
gallant ['gælənt] *adj* **1** BRAVE : valiente, gallardo **2** CHIVALROUS, POLITE : galante, cortés
gallantry ['gæləntri] *n, pl* **-ries** : galantería *f*, caballerosidad *f*
gallbladder ['gɔl,blædər] *n* : vesícula *f* biliar
galleon ['gæljən] *n* : galeón *m*
gallery ['gæləri] *n, pl* **-leries 1** BALCONY : galería *f* (para espectadores) **2** CORRIDOR : pasillo *m*, galería *f*, corredor *m* **3** : galería *f* (para exposiciones)
galley ['gæli] *n, pl* **-leys** : galera *f*
gallium ['gæliəm] *n* : galio *m*
gallivant ['gælə,vænt] *vi* : callejear
gallon ['gælən] *n* : galón *m*
gallop[1] ['gæləp] *vi* : galopar
gallop[2] *n* : galope *m*
gallows ['gæ,loːz] *n, pl* **-lows** *or* **-lowses** [-,loːzəz] : horca *f*
gallstone ['gɔl,stoːn] *n* : cálculo *m* biliar
galore [gəˈlor] *adj* : en abundancia ⟨bargains galore : muchísimas gangas⟩
galoshes [gəˈlɑʃəz] *npl* : galochas *fpl*, chanclos *mpl*
galvanize ['gælvən,aɪz] *vt* **-nized; -nizing 1** STIMULATE : estimular, excitar, impulsar **2** : galvanizar (metales)
Gambian ['gæmbiən] *n* : gambiano *m*, -na *f* — **Gambian** *adj*
gambit ['gæmbɪt] *n* **1** : gambito *m* (en ajedrez) **2** STRATAGEM : estratagema *f*, táctica *f*
gamble[1] ['gæmbəl] *v* **-bled; -bling** *vi* : jugar, arriesgarse — *vt* **1** BET, WAGER : apostar, jugarse **2** RISK : arriesgar
gamble[2] *n* **1** BET : apuesta *f* **2** RISK : riesgo *m*
gambler ['gæmbələr] *n* : jugador *m*, -dora *f*
gambling ['gæmbəlɪŋ] *n* : juego *m*
gambol ['gæmbəl] *vi* **-boled** *or* **-bolled; -boling** *or* **-bolling** FROLIC : retozar, juguetear
game[1] ['geɪm] *adj* **1** READY : listo, dispuesto ⟨we're game for anything : es-

tamos listos para lo que sea⟩ **2** LAME
: cojo
game² *n* **1** AMUSEMENT : juego *m*, diversión *f* **2** CONTEST : juego *m*, partido
m, concurso *m* **3** : caza *f* ⟨big game
: caza mayor⟩
gamecock ['geɪm,kɑk] *n* : gallo *m* de pelea
gamekeeper ['geɪm,ki:pər] *n* : guardabosque *mf*
gamely ['geɪmli] *adv* : animosamente
gamma ray ['gæmə] *n* : rayo *m* gamma
gamut ['gæmət] *n* : gama *f*, espectro *m*
⟨to run the gamut : pasar por toda la
gama⟩
gamy *or* **gamey** ['geɪmi] *adj* **gamier; -est**
: con sabor de animal de caza, fuerte
gander ['gændər] *n* **1** : ganso *m* (animal) **2** GLANCE : mirada *f*, vistazo *m*,
ojeada *f*
gang¹ ['gæŋ] *vi* **to gang up** : agruparse,
unirse
gang² *n* : banda *f*, pandilla *f*
gangling ['gæŋglɪŋ] *adj* LANKY : larguirucho *fam*
ganglion ['gæŋgliən] *n, pl* **-glia** [-gliə]
: ganglio *m*
gangplank ['gæŋ,plæŋk] *n* : pasarela *f*
gangrene ['gæŋ,gri:n, 'gæn-; gæŋ'-,
gæn'-] *n* : gangrena *f*
gangrenous ['gæŋgrənəs] *adj* : gangrenoso
gangster ['gæŋstər] *n* : gángster *mf*
gangway ['gæŋ,weɪ] *n* **1** : pasarela *f* **2**
gangway! : ¡abran paso!
gap ['gæp] *n* **1** BREACH, OPENING : espacio *m*, brecha *f*, abertura *f* **2** GORGE
: desfiladero *m*, barranco *m* **3** : laguna *f* ⟨a gap in my education : una laguna en mi educación⟩ **4** INTERVAL
: pausa *f*, intervalo *m* **5** DISPARITY
: brecha *f*, disparidad *f*
gape¹ ['geɪp] *vi* **gaped; gaping 1** OPEN
: abrirse, estar abierto **2** STARE : mirar fijamente con la boca abierta, mirar boquiabierto
gape² *n* **1** OPENING : abertura *f*, brecha
f **2** STARE : mirada *f* boquiabierta
garage¹ [gə'rɑʒ, -'rɑʤ] *vt* **-raged;
-raging** : dejar en un garaje
garage² *n* : garaje *m*, cochera *f*
garb¹ ['gɑrb] *vt* : vestir, ataviar
garb² *n* : vestimenta *f*, atuendo *f*
garbage ['gɑrbɪʤ] *n* : basura *f*, desechos
mpl
garbageman ['gɑrbɪʤmən] *n, pl* **-men**
[-mən, -,mɛn] : basurero *m*
garble ['gɑrbəl] *vt* **-bled; -bling** : tergiversar, distorsionar
garbled ['gɑrbəld] *adj* : incoherente, incomprensible
garden¹ ['gɑrdən] *vi* : trabajar en el
jardín
garden² *n* : jardín *m*
gardener ['gɑrdənər] *n* : jardinero *m*, -ra
f
gardenia [gɑr'di:njə] *n* : gardenia *f*
gardening ['gɑrdənɪŋ] *n* : jardinería *f*

gargantuan [gɑr'gænʧʊən] *adj* : gigantesco, colosal
gargle¹ ['gɑrgəl] *vi* **-gled; -gling** : hacer
gárgaras, gargarizar
gargle² *n* : gárgara *f*
gargoyle ['gɑr,gɔɪl] *n* : gárgola *f*
garish ['gærɪʃ] *adj* GAUDY : llamativo,
chillón, charro — **garishly** *adv*
garland¹ ['gɑrlənd] *vt* : adornar con
guirnaldas
garland² *n* : guirnalda *f*
garlic ['gɑrlɪk] *n* : ajo *m*
garment ['gɑrmənt] *n* : prenda *f*
garner ['gɑrnər] *vt* : recoger, cosechar
garnet ['gɑrnət] *n* : granate *m*
garnish¹ ['gɑrnɪʃ] *vt* : aderezar, guarnecer
garnish² *n* : aderezo *m*, guarnición *f*
garret ['gærət] *n* : buhardilla *f*, desván
m
garrison¹ ['gærəsən] *vt* **1** QUARTER
: acuartelar (tropas) **2** OCCUPY : guarnecer, ocupar (con tropas)
garrison² *n* **1** : guarnición *f* (ciudad) **2**
FORT : fortaleza *f*, poste *m* militar
garrulous ['gærələs] *adj* : charlatán, parlanchín, garlero *Col fam*
garter ['gɑrtər] *n* : liga *f*
gas¹ ['gæs] *v* **gassed; gassing** *vt* : gasear
— *vi* **to gas up** : llenar el tanque con
gasolina
gas² *n, pl* **gases** ['gæsəz] **1** : gas *m* ⟨tear
gas : gas lacrimógeno⟩ **2** GASOLINE
: gasolina *f*
gaseous ['gæʃəs, 'gæsiəs] *adj* : gaseoso
gash¹ ['gæʃ] *vt* : hacer un tajo en, cortar
gash² *n* : cuchillada *f*, tajo *m*
gasket ['gæskət] *n* : junta *f*
gas mask *n* : máscara *f* antigás
gasoline ['gæsə,li:n, ,gæsə'-] *n* : gasolina *f*, nafta *f*
gasp¹ ['gæsp] *vi* **1** : boquear ⟨to gasp
with surprise : gritar de asombro⟩ **2**
PANT : jadear, respirar con dificultad
gasp² *n* **1** : boqueada *f* ⟨a gasp of surprise : un grito sofocado⟩ **2** PANTING
: jadeo *m*
gas station *n* : estación *f* de servicio,
gasolinera *f*
gastric ['gæstrɪk] *adj* : gástrico ⟨gastric
juice : jugo gástrico⟩
gastronomic [,gæstrə'nɑmɪk] *adj* : gastronómico
gastronomy [gæs'trɑnəmi] *n* : gastronomía *f*
gate ['geɪt] *n* : portón *m*, verja *f*, puerta
f
gatekeeper ['geɪt,ki:pər] *n* : guarda *mf*;
guardián *m*, -diana *f*
gateway ['geɪt,weɪ] *n* : puerta *f* (de acceso), entrada *f*
gather ['gæðər] *vt* **1** ASSEMBLE : juntar,
recoger, reunir **2** HARVEST : recoger,
cosechar **3** : fruncir (una tela) **4** IN-
FER : deducir, suponer
gathering ['gæðərɪŋ] *n* : reunión *f*
gauche ['goʃ] *adj* : torpe, falto de tacto

gaudy ['gɔdi] *adj* **gaudier; -est** : chillón, llamativo

gauge[1] ['geɪʤ] *vt* **gauged; gauging 1** MEASURE : medir **2** ESTIMATE, JUDGE : estimar, evaluar, juzgar

gauge[2] *n* **1** : indicador *m* ⟨pressure gauge : indicador de presión⟩ **2** CALIBER : calibre *m* **3** INDICATION : indicio *m*, muestra *f*

gaunt ['gɔnt] *adj* : demacrado, enjuto, descarnado

gauntlet ['gɔntlət] *n* : guante *m* ⟨to run the gauntlet of : exponerse a⟩

gauze ['gɔz] *n* : gasa *f*

gauzy ['gɔzi] *adj* **gauzier; -est** : diáfano, vaporoso

gave → **give**

gavel ['gævəl] *n* : martillo *m* (de un juez, un subastador, etc.)

gawk ['gɔk] *vi* GAPE : mirar boquiabierto

gawky ['gɔki] *adj* **gawkier; -est** : desmañado, torpe, desgarbado

gay ['geɪ] *adj* **1** MERRY : alegre **2** BRIGHT, COLORFUL : vistoso, vivo **3** HOMOSEXUAL : homosexual

gaze[1] ['geɪz] *vi* **gazed; gazing** : mirar (fijamente)

gaze[2] *n* : mirada *f* (fija)

gazelle [gə'zɛl] *n* : gacela *f*

gazette [gə'zɛt] *n* : gaceta *f*

gazetteer [,gæzə'tɪr] *n* : diccionario *m* geográfico

gear[1] ['gɪr] *vt* ADAPT, ORIENT : adaptar, ajustar, orientar ⟨a book geared to children : un libro adaptado a los niños⟩ — *vi* **to gear up** : prepararse

gear[2] *n* **1** CLOTHING : ropa *f* **2** BELONGINGS : efectos *mpl* personales **3** EQUIPMENT, TOOLS : equipo *m*, aparejo *m*, herramientas *fpl* ⟨fishing gear : aparejo de pescar⟩ ⟨landing gear : tren de aterrizaje⟩ **4** COGWHEEL : rueda *f* dentada **5** : marcha *f*, velocidad *f* (de un vehículo) ⟨to put in gear : poner en marcha⟩ ⟨to change gear(s) : cambiar de velocidad⟩

gearshift ['gɪr,ʃɪft] *n* : palanca *f* de cambio, palanca *f* de velocidad

geek ['gi:k] *n fam* : intelectual *mf*

geese → **goose**

Geiger counter ['gaɪgər,kaʊntər] *n* : contador *m* Geiger

gel ['ʤɛl] *n* : gel *m*

gelatin ['ʤɛlətən] *n* : gelatina *f*

gem ['ʤɛm] *n* : joya *f*, gema *f*, alhaja *f*

Gemini ['ʤɛmə,naɪ] *n* : Géminis *mf*

gemstone ['ʤɛm,sto:n] *n* : piedra *f* (semipreciosa o preciosa), gema *f*

gender ['ʤɛndər] *n* **1** SEX : sexo *m* **2** : género *m* (en la gramática)

gene ['ʤi:n] *n* : gen *m*, gene *m*

genealogical [,ʤi:niə'lɑʤɪkəl] *adj* : genealógico

genealogy [,ʤi:ni'ɑləʤi, ,ʤɛ-, -'æ-] *n, pl* **-gies** : genealogía *f*

genera → **genus**

general[1] ['ʤɛnrəl, 'ʤɛnə-] *adj* : general ⟨in general : en general, por lo general⟩

general[2] *n* : general *mf*

generality [,ʤɛnə'ræləti] *n, pl* **-ties** : generalidad *f*

generalization [,ʤɛnrələ'zeɪʃən, ,ʤɛnərə-] *n* : generalización *f*

generalize ['ʤɛnrə,laɪz, 'ʤɛnərə-] *v* **-ized; -izing** : generalizar

generally ['ʤɛnrəli, 'ʤɛnərə-] *adv* : generalmente, por lo general, en general

generate ['ʤɛnə,reɪt] *vt* **-ated; -ating** : generar, producir

generation [,ʤɛnə'reɪʃən] *n* : generación *f*

generator ['ʤɛnə,reɪtər] *n* : generador *m*

generic [ʤə'nɛrɪk] *adj* : genérico

generosity [,ʤɛnə'rɑsəti] *n, pl* **-ties** : generosidad *f*

generous ['ʤɛnərəs] *adj* **1** OPENHANDED : generoso, dadivoso, desprendido **2** ABUNDANT, AMPLE : abundante, amplio, generoso — **generously** *adv*

genetic [ʤə'nɛtɪk] *adj* : genético — **genetically** [-tɪkli] *adv*

geneticist [ʤə'nɛtəsɪst] *n* : genetista *mf*

genetics [ʤə'nɛtɪks] *n* : genética *f*

genial ['ʤi:niəl] *adj* GRACIOUS : simpático, cordial, afable — **genially** *adv*

geniality [,ʤi:ni'æləti] *n* : simpatía *f*, afabilidad *f*

genie ['ʤi:ni] *n* : genio *m*

genital ['ʤɛnətəl] *adj* : genital

genitals ['ʤɛnətəlz] *npl* : genitales *mpl*

genius ['ʤi:njəs] *n* : genio *m*

genocide ['ʤɛnə,saɪd] *n* : genocidio *m*

genre ['ʒɑnrə, 'ʒɑr] *n* : género *m*

genteel [ʤɛn'ti:l] *adj* : cortés, fino, refinado

gentile[1] ['ʤɛn,taɪl] *adj* : gentil

gentile[2] *n* : gentil *mf*

gentility [ʤɛn'tɪləti] *n, pl* **-ties 1** : nobleza *f* (de nacimiento) **2** POLITENESS, REFINEMENT : cortesía *f*, refinamiento *m*

gentle ['ʤɛntəl] *adj* **-tler; -tlest 1** NOBLE : bien nacido, noble **2** DOCILE : dócil, manso **3** KINDLY : bondadoso, amable **4** MILD : suave, apacible ⟨a gentle breeze : una brisa suave⟩ **5** SOFT : suave (dícese de un sonido), ligero (dícese del tacto) **6** MODERATE : moderado, gradual ⟨a gentle slope : una cuesta gradual⟩

gentleman ['ʤɛntəlmən] *n, pl* **-men** [-mən, -,mɛn] : caballero *m*, señor *m*

gentlemanly ['ʤɛntəlmənli] *adj* : caballeroso

gentleness ['ʤɛntəlnəs] *n* : delicadeza *f*, suavidad *f*, ternura *f*

gentlewoman ['ʤɛntəl,wʊmən] *n, pl* **-women** [-,wɪmən] : dama *f*, señora *f*

gently ['ʤɛntli] *adv* **1** CAREFULLY, SOFTLY : con cuidado, suavemente, ligeramente **2** KINDLY : amablemente, con delicadeza

gentry ['ʤɛntri] *n, pl* **-tries** : aristocracia *f*
genuflect ['ʤɛnjʊˌflɛkt] *vi* : doblar la rodilla, hacer una genuflexión
genuflection [ˌʤɛnjʊ'flɛkʃən] *n* : genuflexión *f*
genuine ['ʤɛnjʊwən] *adj* **1** AUTHENTIC, REAL : genuino, verdadero, auténtico **2** SINCERE : sincero — **genuinely** *adv*
genus ['ʤiːnəs] *n, pl* **genera** ['ʤɛnərə] : género *m*
geographer [ʤi'ɑgrəfər] *n* : geógrafo *m*, -fa *f*
geographical [ˌʤiːə'græfɪkəl] *or* **geographic** [-fɪk] *adj* : geográfico — **geographically** [-fɪkli] *adv*
geography [ʤi'ɑgrəfi] *n, pl* **-phies** : geografía *f*
geologic [ˌʤiːə'lɑʤɪk] *or* **geological** [-ʤɪkəl] *adj* : geológico — **geologically** [-ʤɪkli] *adv*
geologist [ʤi'ɑləʤɪst] *n* : geólogo *m*, -ga *f*
geology [ʤi'ɑləʤi] *n* : geología *f*
geometric [ˌʤiːə'mɛtrɪk] *or* **geometrical** [-trɪkəl] *adj* : geométrico
geometry [ʤi'ɑmətri] *n, pl* **-tries** : geometría *f*
geopolitical [ˌʤiːopə'lɪtɪkəl] *adj* : geopolítico
Georgian ['ʤɔrʤən] *n* **1** : georgiano *m* (idioma) **2** : georgiano *m*, -na *f* — **Georgian** *adj*
geranium [ʤə'reɪniəm] *n* : geranio *m*
gerbil ['ʤərbəl] *n* : jerbo *m*, gerbo *m*
geriatric [ˌʤɛri'ætrɪk] *adj* : geriátrico
geriatrics [ˌʤɛri'ætrɪks] *n* : geriatría *f*
germ ['ʤərm] *n* **1** MICROORGANISM : microbio *m*, germen *m* **2** BEGINNING : germen *m*, principio *m* ⟨the germ of a plan : el germen de un plan⟩
German ['ʤərmən] *n* **1** : alemán *m*, -mana *f* **2** : alemán *m* (idioma) — **German** *adj*
germane [ʤər'meɪn] *adj* : relevante, pertinente
Germanic[1] [ʤər'mænɪk] *adj* : germánico, germano
Germanic[2] *n* : germánico *m* (idioma)
germanium [ʤər'meɪniəm] *n* : germanio *m*
germ cell *n* : célula *f* germen
germicide ['ʤərməˌsaɪd] *n* : germicida *m*
germinate ['ʤərməˌneɪt] *v* **-nated; -nating** *vi* : germinar — *vt* : hacer germinar
germination [ˌʤərmə'neɪʃən] *n* : germinación *f*
gerund ['ʤɛrənd] *n* : gerundio *m*
gestation [ʤɛ'steɪʃən] *n* : gestación *f*
gesture[1] ['ʤɛsʧər] *vi* **-tured; -turing** : gesticular, hacer gestos
gesture[2] *n* **1** : gesto *m*, ademán *m* **2** SIGN, TOKEN : gesto *m*, señal *f* ⟨a gesture of friendship : una señal de amistad⟩

get ['gɛt] *v* **got** ['gɑt]; **got** *or* **gotten** ['gɑtən]; **getting** *vt* **1** OBTAIN : conseguir, obtener, adquirir **2** RECEIVE : recibir ⟨to get a letter : recibir una carta⟩ **3** EARN : ganar ⟨he gets $10 an hour : gana $10 por hora⟩ **4** FETCH : traer ⟨get me my book : tráigame el libro⟩ **5** CATCH : tomar (un tren, etc.), agarrar (una pelota, una persona, etc.) **6** CONTRACT : contagiarse de, contraer ⟨she got the measles : le dio el sarampión⟩ **7** PREPARE : preparar (una comida) **8** PERSUADE : persuadir, mandar a hacer ⟨I got him to agree : logré convencerlo⟩ **9** (*to cause to be*) ⟨to get one's hair cut : cortarse el pelo⟩ **10** UNDERSTAND : entender ⟨now I get it! : ¡ya entiendo!⟩ **11 to have got** : tener ⟨I've got a headache : tengo un dolor de cabeza⟩ **12 to have got to** : tener que ⟨you've got to come : tienes que venir⟩ — *vi* **1** BECOME : ponerse, volverse, hacerse ⟨to get angry : ponerse furioso, enojarse⟩ **2** GO, MOVE : ir, avanzar ⟨he didn't get far : no avanzó mucho⟩ **3** ARRIVE : llegar ⟨to get home : llegar a casa⟩ **4 to get to be** : llegar a ser ⟨she got to be the director : llegó a ser directora⟩ **5 to get ahead** : adelantarse, progresar **6 to get along** : llevarse bien (con alguien), congeniar **7 to get by** MANAGE : arreglárselas **8 to get over** OVERCOME : superar, consolarse de **9 to get together** MEET : reunirse **10 to get up** : levantarse
getaway ['gɛtəˌweɪ] *n* ESCAPE : fuga *f*, huida *f*, escapada *f*
geyser ['gaɪzər] *n* : géiser *m*
Ghanaian ['gɑnɪən, 'gæ-] *n* : ghanés *m*, -nesa *f* — **Ghanaian** *adj*
ghastly ['gæstli] *adj* **-lier; -est 1** HORRIBLE : horrible, espantoso **2** PALE : pálido, cadavérico
gherkin ['gərkən] *n* : pepinillo *m*
ghetto ['gɛtoː] *n, pl* **-tos** *or* **-toes** : gueto *m*
ghost ['goːst] *n* **1** : fantasma *f*, espectro *m* **2 the Holy Ghost** : el Espíritu Santo
ghostly ['goːstli] *adv* : fantasmal
ghoul ['guːl] *n* **1** : demonio *m* necrófago **2** : persona *f* de gustos macabros
GI [ˌʤiː'aɪ] *n, pl* **GI's** *or* **GIs** : soldado *m* estadounidense
giant[1] ['ʤaɪənt] *adj* : gigante, gigantesco, enorme
giant[2] *n* : gigante *m*, -ta *f*
gibberish ['ʤɪbərɪʃ] *n* : galimatías *m*, jerigonza *f*
gibbon ['gɪbən] *n* : gibón *m*
gibe[1] ['ʤaɪb] *vi* **gibed; gibing** : mofarse, burlarse
gibe[2] *n* : pulla *f*, burla *f*, mofa *f*
giblets ['ʤɪbləts] *npl* : menudos *mpl*, menudencias *fpl*
giddiness ['gɪdinəs] *n* **1** DIZZINESS : vértigo *m*, mareo *m* **2** SILLINESS : frivolidad *f*, estupidez *f*

giddy ['gɪdi] *adj* **-dier; -est 1** DIZZY : mareado, vertiginoso **2** FRIVOLOUS, SILLY : frívolo, tonto

gift ['gɪft] *n* **1** TALENT : don *m*, talento *m*, dotes *fpl* **2** PRESENT : regalo *m*, obsequio *m*

gifted ['gɪftəd] *adj* TALENTED : talentoso

gig ['gɪg] *vi* : trabajo *m* (de duración limitada) ⟨to play a gig : tocar en un concierto⟩

gigabyte ['dʒɪgə,baɪt, 'gɪ-] *n* : gigabyte *m*

gigantic [dʒaɪ'gæntɪk] *adj* : gigantesco, enorme, colosal

giggle¹ ['gɪgəl] *vi* **-gled; -gling** : reírse tontamente

giggle² *n* : risita *f*, risa *f* tonta

gild ['gɪld] *vt* **gilded** *or* **gilt** ['gɪlt]; **gilding** : dorar

gill ['gɪl] *n* : agalla *f*, branquia *f*

gilt¹ ['gɪlt] *adj* : dorado

gilt² *n* : dorado *m*

gimlet ['gɪmlət] *n* **1** : barrena *f* (herramienta) **2** : bebida *f* de vodka o ginebra y limón

gimmick ['gɪmɪk] *n* **1** GADGET : artilugio *m* **2** CATCH : engaño *m*, trampa *f* **3** SCHEME, TRICK : ardid *m*, truco *m*

gin ['dʒɪn] *n* **1** : desmotadora *f* (de algodón) **2** : ginebra *f* (bebida alcohólica)

ginger ['dʒɪndʒər] *n* : jengibre *m*

ginger ale *n* : ginger ale *m*, gaseosa *f* de jengibre

gingerbread ['dʒɪndʒər,brɛd] *n* : pan *m* de jengibre

gingerly ['dʒɪndʒərli] *adv* : con cuidado, cautelosamente

gingham ['gɪŋəm] *n* : guinga *f*

ginseng ['dʒɪn,sɪŋ, -,sɛŋ] *n* : ginseng *m*

giraffe [dʒə'ræf] *n* : jirafa *f*

gird ['gərd] *vt* **girded** *or* **girt** ['gərt]; **girding 1** BIND : ceñir, atar **2** ENCIRCLE : rodear **3 to gird oneself** : prepararse

girder ['gərdər] *n* : viga *f*

girdle¹ ['gərdəl] *vt* **-dled; -dling 1** GIRD : ceñir, atar **2** SURROUND : rodear, circundar

girdle² *n* : faja *f*

girl ['gərl] *n* **1** : chica *f*, muchacha *f* *or* **little girl** : niña *f*, chica *f* **3** SWEETHEART : novia *f* **4** DAUGHTER : hija *f*

girlfriend ['gərl,frɛnd] *n* : novia *f*, amiga *f*

girlhood ['gərl,hʊd] *n* : niñez *f*, juventud *f* (de una muchacha)

girlish ['gərlɪʃ] *adj* : de niña

girth ['gərθ] *n* **1** : circunferencia *f* (de un árbol, etc.), cintura *f* (de una persona) **2** CINCH : cincha *f* (para caballos, etc.)

gist ['dʒɪst] *n* : quid *m*, meollo *m*

give¹ ['gɪv] *v* **gave** ['geɪv]; **given** ['gɪvən]; **giving** *vt* **1** HAND, PRESENT : dar, regalar, obsequiar ⟨give it to me : dámelo⟩ ⟨they gave him a gold watch : le regalaron un reloj de oro⟩ **2** PAY : dar, pagar ⟨I'll give you $10 for this one : te daré $10 por éste⟩ **3** UTTER : dar, pronunciar ⟨to give a shout : dar un grito⟩ ⟨to give a speech : pronunciar un discurso⟩ ⟨to give a verdict : dictar sentencia⟩ **4** PROVIDE : dar ⟨to give one's word : dar uno su palabra⟩ ⟨to give a party : dar una fiesta⟩ **5** CAUSE : dar, causar, ocasionar ⟨to give trouble : causar problemas⟩ ⟨to give someone to understand : darle a entender a alguien⟩ **6** GRANT : dar, otorgar ⟨to give permission : dar permiso⟩ — *vi* **1** : hacer regalos **2** YIELD : ceder, romperse ⟨it gave under the weight of the crowd : cedió bajo el peso de la muchedumbre⟩ **3 to give in** *or* **to give up** SURRENDER : rendirse, entregarse **4 to give out** : agotarse, acabarse ⟨the supplies gave out : las provisiones se agotaron⟩

give² *n* FLEXIBILITY : flexibilidad *f*, elasticidad *f*

giveaway ['gɪvə,weɪ] *n* **1** : revelación *f* involuntaria **2** GIFT : regalo *m*, obsequio *m*

given ['gɪvən] *adj* **1** INCLINED : dado, inclinado ⟨he's given to quarreling : es muy dado a discutir⟩ **2** SPECIFIC : dado, determinado ⟨at a given time : en un momento dado⟩

given name *n* : nombre *m* de pila

give up *vt* **1** : dejar, renunciar a, abandonar ⟨to give up smoking : dejar de fumar⟩

gizzard ['gɪzərd] *n* : molleja *f*

glacial ['gleɪʃəl] *adj* : glacial — **glacially** *adv*

glacier ['gleɪʃər] *n* : glaciar *m*

glad ['glæd] *adj* **gladder; gladdest 1** PLEASED : alegre, contento ⟨she was glad I came : se alegró de que haya venido⟩ ⟨glad to meet you! : ¡mucho gusto!⟩ **2** HAPPY, PLEASING : feliz, agradable ⟨glad tidings : buenas nuevas⟩ **3** WILLING : dispuesto, gustoso ⟨I'll be glad to do it : lo haré con mucho gusto⟩

gladden ['glædən] *vt* : alegrar

glade ['gleɪd] *n* : claro *m*

gladiator ['glædi,eɪtər] *n* : gladiador *m*

gladiolus [,glædi'o:ləs] *n, pl* **-li** [-li, -,laɪ] : gladiolo *m*, gladíolo *m*

gladly ['glædli] *adv* : con mucho gusto

gladness ['glædnəs] *n* : alegría *f*, gozo *m*

glamor *or* **glamour** ['glæmər] *n* : atractivo *m*, hechizo *m*, encanto *m*

glamorous ['glæmərəs] *adj* : atractivo, encantador

glance¹ ['glænts] *vi* **glanced; glancing 1** RICOCHET : rebotar ⟨it glanced off the wall : rebotó en la pared⟩ **2 to glance at** : mirar, echar un vistazo a **3 to glance away** : apartar los ojos

glance² *n* : mirada *f*, vistazo *m*, ojeada *f*

gland ['glænd] *n* : glándula *f*

glandular ['glændʒʊlər] *adj* : glandular

glare¹ ['glær] *vi* **glared; glaring 1** SHINE : brillar, relumbrar **2** STARE : mirar con ira, lanzar una mirada feroz

glare² *n* **1** BRIGHTNESS : resplandor *m*, luz *f* deslumbrante **2** : mirada *f* feroz

glaring ['glærɪŋ] *adj* **1** BRIGHT : deslumbrante, brillante **2** FLAGRANT, OBVIOUS : flagrante, manifiesto ⟨a glaring error : un error que salta a la vista⟩

glass ['glæs] *n* **1** : vidrio *m*, cristal *m* ⟨stained glass : vidrio de color⟩ **2** : vaso *m* ⟨a glass of milk : un vaso de leche⟩ **3 glasses** *npl* SPECTACLES : gafas *fpl*, anteojos *mpl*, lentes *mpl*, espejuelos *mpl*

glassblowing ['glæs,blo:ɪŋ] *n* : soplado *m* del vidrio

glassful ['glæs,fʊl] *n* : vaso *m*, copa *f*

glassware ['glæs,wær] *n* : cristalería *f*

glassy ['glæsi] *adj* **glassier; -est 1** VITREOUS : vítreo **2** : vidrioso ⟨glassy eyes : ojos vidriosos⟩

glaucoma [glaʊ'ko:mə, glɔ-] *n* : glaucoma *m*

glaze¹ ['gleɪz] *vt* **glazed; glazing 1** : ponerle vidrios a (una ventana, etc.) **2** : vidriar (cerámica) **3** : glasear (papel, verduras, etc.)

glaze² *n* : vidriado *m*, glaseado *m*, barniz *m*

glazier ['gleɪʒər] *n* : vidriero *m*, -ra *f*

gleam¹ ['gli:m] *vi* : brillar, destellar, relucir

gleam² *n* **1** LIGHT : luz *f* (oscura) **2** GLINT : destello *m* **3** GLIMMER : rayo *m*, vislumbre *f* ⟨a gleam of hope : un rayo de esperanza⟩

glean ['gli:n] *vt* : recoger, espigar

glee ['gli:] *n* : alegría *f*, júbilo *m*, regocijo *m*

gleeful ['gli:fəl] *adj* : lleno de alegría

glen ['glɛn] *n* : cañada *f*

glib ['glɪb] *adj* **glibber; glibbest 1** : simplista ⟨a glib reply : una respuesta simplista⟩ **2** : con mucha labia (dícese de una persona)

glibly ['glɪbli] *adv* : con mucha labia

glide¹ ['glaɪd] *vi* **glided; gliding** : deslizarse (en una superficie), planear (en el aire)

glide² *n* : planeo *m*

glider ['glaɪdər] *n* **1** : planeador *m* (aeronave) **2** : mecedor *m* (tipo de columpio)

glimmer¹ ['glɪmər] *vi* : brillar con luz trémula

glimmer² *n* **1** : luz *f* trémula, luz *f* tenue **2** GLEAM : rayo *m*, vislumbre *f* ⟨a glimmer of understanding : un rayo de entendimiento⟩

glimpse¹ ['glɪmps] *vt* **glimpsed; glimpsing** : vislumbrar, entrever

glimpse² *n* : mirada *f* breve ⟨to catch a glimpse of : alcanzar a ver, vislumbrar⟩

glint¹ ['glɪnt] *vi* GLEAM, SPARKLE : destellar, fulgurar

glint² *n* **1** SPARKLE : destello *m*, centelleo *m* **2 to have a glint in one's eye** : chispearle los ojos a uno

glisten¹ ['glɪsən] *vi* : brillar, centellear

glisten² *n* : brillo *m*, centelleo *m*

glitch ['glɪtʃ] *n* **1** MALFUNCTION : mal funcionamiento *m* **2** SNAG : problema *m*, complicación *f*

glitter¹ ['glɪtər] *vi* **1** SPARKLE : destellar, relucir, brillar **2** FLASH : relampaguear ⟨his eyes glittered in anger : le relampagueaban los ojos de ira⟩

glitter² *n* **1** BRIGHTNESS : brillo *m* **2** : purpurina *f* (para decoración)

glitz ['glɪts] *n* : oropel *m*

gloat ['glo:t] *vi* **to gloat over** : regodearse en

glob ['glɑb] *n* : plasta *f*, masa *f*, grumo *m*

global ['glo:bəl] *adj* **1** SPHERICAL : esférico **2** WORLDWIDE : global, mundial — **globally** *adv*

globe ['glo:b] *n* **1** SPHERE : esfera *f*, globo *m* **2** EARTH : globo *m*, Tierra *f* **3** : globo *m* terráqueo (modelo de la Tierra)

globe–trotter ['glo:b,trɑtər] *n* : trotamundos *mf*

globular ['glɑbjʊlər] *adj* : globular

globule ['glɑ,bju:l] *n* : glóbulo *m*

gloom ['glu:m] *n* **1** DARKNESS : penumbra *f*, oscuridad *f* **2** MELANCHOLY : melancolía *f*, tristeza *f*

gloomily ['glu:məli] *adv* : tristemente

gloomy ['glu:mi] *adj* **gloomier; -est 1** DARK : oscuro, tenebroso ⟨gloomy weather : tiempo gris⟩ **2** MELANCHOLY : melancólico **3** PESSIMISTIC : pesimista **4** DEPRESSING : deprimente, lúgubre

glorification [,glorəfə'keɪʃən] *n* : glorificación *f*

glorify ['glorə,faɪ] *vt* **-fied; -fying** : glorificar

glorious ['gloriəs] *adj* **1** ILLUSTRIOUS : glorioso, ilustre **2** MAGNIFICENT : magnífico, espléndido, maravilloso — **gloriously** *adv*

glory¹ ['glori] *vi* **-ried; -rying** EXULT : exultar, regocijarse

glory² *n, pl* **-ries 1** RENOWN : gloria *f*, fama *f*, honor *m* **2** PRAISE : gloria *f* ⟨glory to God : gloria a Dios⟩ **3** MAGNIFICENCE : magnificencia *f*, esplendor *m*, gloria *f* **4 to be in one's glory** : estar uno en su gloria

gloss¹ ['glɔs, 'glɑs] *vt* **1** EXPLAIN : glosar, explicar **2** POLISH : lustrar, pulir **3 to gloss over** : quitarle importancia a, minimizar

gloss² *n* **1** SHINE : lustre *m*, brillo *m* **2** EXPLANATION : glosa *f*, explicación *f* breve **3** → **glossary**

glossary ['glɔsəri, 'glɑ-] *n, pl* **-ries** : glosario *m*

glossy ['glɔsi, 'glɑ-] *adj* **glossier; -est** : brillante, lustroso, satinado (dícese del papel)

glove ['glʌv] *n* : guante *m*

glow¹ ['glo:] *vi* **1** SHINE : brillar, resplandecer **2** BRIM : rebosar ⟨to glow with health : rebosar de salud⟩

glow² *n* **1** BRIGHTNESS : resplandor *m*, brillo *m*, luminosidad *f* **2** FEELING : sensación *f* (de bienestar), oleada *f* (de sentimiento) **3** INCANDESCENCE : incandescencia *f*

glower ['glaʊər] *vi* : fruncir el ceño

glowworm ['gloˌwərm] *n* : luciérnaga *f*

glucose ['gluˌkoːs] *n* : glucosa *f*

glue¹ ['gluː] *vt* **glued; gluing** *or* **glueing** : pegar, encolar

glue² *n* : pegamento *m*, cola *f*

gluey ['gluːi] *adj* **gluier; -est** : pegajoso

glum ['glʌm] *adj* **glummer; glummest** **1** SULLEN : hosco, sombrío **2** DREARY, GLOOMY : sombrío, triste, melancólico

glut¹ ['glʌt] *vt* **glutted; glutting** **1** SATIATE : saciar, hartar **2** : inundar (el mercado)

glut² *n* : exceso *m*, superabundancia *f*

glutinous ['gluːtənəs] *adj* STICKY : pegajoso, glutinoso

glutton ['glʌtən] *n* : glotón *m*, -tona *f*

gluttonous ['glʌtənəs] *adj* : glotón

gluttony ['glʌtəni] *n, pl* **-tonies** : glotonería *f*, gula *f*

gnarled ['nɑrld] *adj* **1** KNOTTY : nudoso **2** TWISTED : retorcido

gnash ['næʃ] *vt* : hacer rechinar (los dientes)

gnat ['næt] *n* : jején *m*

gnaw ['nɔ] *vt* : roer

gnome ['noːm] *n* : gnomo *m*

gnu ['nuː, 'njuː] *n, pl* **gnu** *or* **gnus** : ñu *m*

go¹ ['goː] *v* **went** ['wɛnt]; **gone** ['gɔn, 'gɑn]; **going; goes** ['goːz] *vi* **1** PROCEED : ir ⟨to go slow : ir despacio⟩ ⟨to go shopping : ir de compras⟩ **2** LEAVE : irse, marcharse, salir ⟨let's go! : ¡vámonos!⟩ ⟨the train went on time : el tren salió a tiempo⟩ **3** DISAPPEAR : desaparecer, pasarse, irse ⟨her fear is gone : se le ha pasado el miedo⟩ ⟨my pen is gone! : ¡mi pluma desapareció!⟩ **4** EXTEND : ir, extenderse, llegar ⟨this road goes to the river : este camino se extiende hasta el río⟩ ⟨to go from top to bottom : ir de arriba abajo⟩ **5** FUNCTION : funcionar, marchar ⟨the car won't go : el coche no funciona⟩ ⟨to get something going : poner algo en marcha⟩ **6** SELL : venderse ⟨it goes for $15 : se vende por $15⟩ **7** PROGRESS : ir, andar, seguir ⟨my exam went well : me fue bien en el examen⟩ ⟨how did the meeting go? : ¿qué tal la reunión?⟩ **8** BECOME : volverse, quedarse ⟨he's going crazy : está volviéndose loco⟩ ⟨the tire went flat : la llanta se desinfló⟩ **9** FIT : caber ⟨it will go through the door : cabe por la puerta⟩ **10** anything goes! : ¡todo vale! **11** to go : faltar ⟨only 10 days to go : faltan sólo 10 días⟩ **12** to go back on : faltar uno a (su promesa) **13** to go bad SPOIL : estropearse, echarse a perder **14** to go for : interesarse uno en, gustarle a uno (algo, alguien) ⟨I don't go for that : eso

no me interesa⟩ **15** to go off EXPLODE : estallar **16** to go with MATCH : armonizar con, hacer juego con — *v aux* to be going to : ir a ⟨I'm going to write a letter : voy a escribir una carta⟩ ⟨it's not going to last : no va a durar⟩

go² *n, pl* **goes 1** ATTEMPT : intento *m* ⟨to have a go at : intentar, probar⟩ **2** SUCCESS : éxito *m* **3** ENERGY : energía *f*, empuje *m* ⟨to be on the go : no parar, no descansar⟩

goad¹ ['goːd] *vt* : aguijonear (un animal), incitar (a una persona)

goad² *n* : aguijón *m*

goal ['goːl] *n* **1** : gol *m* (en deportes) ⟨to score a goal : anotar un gol⟩ **2** *or* **goalposts** : portería *f* **3** AIM, OBJECTIVE : meta *m*, objetivo *m*

goalie ['goːli] → **goalkeeper**

goalkeeper ['goːlˌkiːpər] *n* : portero *m*, -ra *f*; guardameta *mf*; arquero *m*, -ra *f*

goaltender ['goːlˌtɛndər] → **goalkeeper**

goat ['goːt] *n* **1** : cabra *f* (hembra) **2** billy goat : macho *m* cabrío, chivo *m*

goatee [goːˈtiː] *n* : barbita *f* de chivo, piocha *f* Mex

goatskin ['goːtˌskɪn] *n* : piel *f* de cabra

gob ['gɑb] *n* : masa *f*, grumo *m*

gobble ['gɑbəl] *v* **-bled; -bling** *vt* to gobble up : tragar, engullir — *vi* : hacer ruidos de pavo

gobbledygook ['gɑbəldiˌgʊk, -ˌguːk] *n* GIBBERISH : jerigonza *f*

go-between ['goːbɪˌtwiːn] *n* : intermediario *m*, -ria *f*; mediador *m*, -dora *f*

goblet ['gɑblət] *n* : copa *f*

goblin ['gɑblən] *n* : duende *m*, trasgo *m*

god ['gɑd, 'gɔd] *n* **1** : dios *m* **2** God : Dios *m*

godchild ['gɑdˌtʃaɪld, 'gɔd-] *n, pl* **-children** : ahijado *m*, -da *f*

goddess ['gɑdəs, 'gɔ-] *n* : diosa *f*

godfather ['gɑdˌfɑðər, 'gɔd-] *n* : padrino *m*

godless ['gɑdləs, 'gɔd-] *adj* : ateo

godlike ['gɑdˌlaɪk, 'gɔd-] *adj* : divino

godly ['gɑdli, 'gɔd-] *adj* **-lier; -est 1** DIVINE : divino **2** DEVOUT, PIOUS : piadoso, devoto, beato

godmother ['gɑdˌmʌðər, 'gɔd-] *n* : madrina *f*

godparents ['gɑdˌpærənts, 'gɔd-] *npl* : padrinos *mpl*

godsend ['gɑdˌsɛnd, 'gɔd-] *n* : bendición *f*, regalo *m* divino

goes → **go**

go-getter ['goːˌgɛtər] *n* : persona *f* ambiciosa, buscavidas *mf fam*

goggle ['gɑgəl] *vi* **-gled; -gling** : mirar con ojos desorbitados

goggles ['gɑgəlz] *npl* : gafas *fpl* (protectoras), anteojos *mpl*

goings-on [ˌgoːɪŋzˈɑn, -ˈɔn] *npl* : sucesos *mpl*, ocurrencias *fpl*

goiter ['gɔɪtər] *n* : bocio *m*

gold ['goːld] *n* : oro *m*

golden ['goːldən] *adj* **1** : (hecho) de oro **2** : dorado, de color oro ⟨golden hair

: pelo rubio⟩ **3** FLOURISHING, PROS-
PEROUS : dorado, próspero ⟨golden
years : años dorados⟩ **4** FAVORABLE
: favorable, excelente ⟨a golden opportunity : una excelente oportu-
nidad⟩
goldenrod ['goːldən,rɑd] *n* : vara *f* de
oro
golden rule *n* : regla *f* de oro
goldfinch ['goːld,fɪntʃ] *n* : jilguero *m*
goldfish ['goːld,fɪʃ] *n* : pez *m* de colores
goldsmith ['goːld,smɪθ] *n* : orífice *mf*,
orfebre *mf*
golf¹ ['gɑlf, 'gɔlf] *vi* : jugar (al) golf
golf² *n* : golf *m*
golfer ['gɑlfər, 'gɔl-] *n* : golfista *mf*
gondola ['gɑndələ, gɑn'doːlə] *n* : góndola *f*
gone ['gɔn] *adj* **1** DEAD : muerto **2** PAST
: pasado, ido **3** LOST : perdido, desaparecido **4 to be far gone** : estar muy
avanzado **5 to be gone on** : estar loco
por
goner ['gɔnər] *n* **to be a goner** : estar en
las últimas
gong ['gɔŋ, 'gɑŋ] *n* : gong *m*
gonorrhea [,gɑnə'riːə] *n* : gonorrea *f*
good¹ ['gʊd] *adv* **1** (*used as an intensifier*) : bien ⟨a good strong rope : una
cuerda bien fuerte⟩ **2** WELL : bien
good² *adj* **better** ['bɛţər]; **best** ['bɛst] **1**
PLEASANT : bueno, agradable ⟨good
news : buenas noticias⟩ ⟨to have a good
time : divertirse⟩ **2** BENEFICIAL
: bueno, beneficioso ⟨good for a cold
: beneficioso para los resfriados⟩ ⟨it's
good for you : es bueno para uno⟩ **3**
FULL : completo, entero ⟨a good hour
: una hora entera⟩ **4** CONSIDERABLE
: bueno, bastante ⟨a good many people : muchísima gente, un buen
número de gente⟩ **5** ATTRACTIVE, DE-
SIRABLE : bueno, bien ⟨a good salary
: un buen sueldo⟩ ⟨to look good
: quedar bien⟩ **6** KIND, VIRTUOUS
: bueno, amable ⟨she's a good person
: es buena gente⟩ ⟨that's good of you!
: ¡qué amable!⟩ ⟨good deeds : buenas
obras⟩ **7** SKILLED : bueno, hábil ⟨to
be good at : tener facilidad para⟩ **8**
SOUND : bueno, sensato ⟨good advice
: buenos consejos⟩ **9** (*in greetings*)
: bueno ⟨good morning : buenos días⟩
⟨good afternoon (evening) : buenas
tardes⟩ ⟨good night : buenas noches⟩
good³ *n* **1** RIGHT : bien *m* ⟨to do good
: hacer el bien⟩ **2** GOODNESS : bondad
f **3** BENEFIT : bien *m*, provecho *m* ⟨it's
for your own good : es por tu propio
bien⟩ **4 goods** *npl* PROPERTY : efectos
mpl personales, posesiones *fpl* **5 goods**
npl WARES : mercancía *f*, mercadería *f*,
artículos *mpl* **6 for ~** : para siempre
good–bye *or* **good–by** [gʊd'baɪ] *n*
: adiós *m*
good–for–nothing ['gʊdfər,nʌθɪŋ] *n*
: inútil *mf*; haragán *m*, -gana *f*; holgazán
m, -zana *f*

Good Friday *n* : Viernes *m* Santo
good–hearted ['gʊd'hɑrţəd] *adj* : bondadoso, benévolo, de buen corazón
good–looking ['gʊd'lʊkɪŋ] *adj* : bello,
bonito, guapo
goodly ['gʊdli] *adj* **-lier; -est** : considerable, importante ⟨a goodly number
: un número considerable⟩
good–natured ['gʊd'neɪtʃərd] *adj* : amigable, amistoso, bonachón *fam*
goodness ['gʊdnəs] *n* **1** : bondad *f* **2
thank goodness!** : ¡gracias a Dios!,
¡menos mal!
good–tempered ['gʊd'tɛmpərd] *adj* : de
buen genio
goodwill [,gʊd'wɪl] *n* **1** BENEVOLENCE
: benevolencia *f*, buena voluntad *f* **2**
: buen nombre *m* (de comercios),
renombre *m* comercial
goody ['gʊdi] *n, pl* **goodies** : cosa *f* rica
para comer, golosina *f*
gooey ['guːi] *adj* **gooier; gooiest** : pegajoso
goof¹ ['guːf] *vi* **1 to goof off** : holgazanear **2 to goof around** : hacer tonterías **3 to goof up** BLUNDER : cometer un error
goof² *n* **1** : bobo *m*, -ba *f*; tonto *m*, -ta *f*
2 BLUNDER : error *m*, planchazo *m* *fam*
goofy ['guːfi] *adj* **goofier; -est** SILLY
: tonto, bobo
goose ['guːs] *n, pl* **geese** ['giːs] : ganso
m, -sa *f*; ánsar *m*; oca *f*
gooseberry ['guːs,bɛriː, 'guːz-] *n, pl*
-berries : grosella *f* espinosa
goose bumps *npl* : carne *f* de gallina
gooseflesh ['guːs,flɛʃ] → **goose bumps**
goose pimples → **goose bumps**
gopher ['goːfər] *n* : taltuza *f*
gore¹ ['gor] *vt* **gored; goring** : cornear
gore² *n* BLOOD : sangre *f*
gorge¹ ['gɔrdʒ] *vt* **gorged; gorging 1** SA-
TIATE : saciar, hartar **2 to gorge oneself** : hartarse, atiborrarse, atracarse
fam
gorge² *n* RAVINE : desfiladero *m*
gorgeous ['gɔrdʒəs] *adj* : hermoso, espléndido, magnífico
gorilla [gə'rɪlə] *n* : gorila *m*
gory ['gori] *adj* **gorier; -est** BLOODY
: sangriento
gosling ['gɑzlɪŋ, 'gɔz-] *n* : ansarino *m*
gospel ['gɑspəl] *n* **1** *or* **Gospel** : evangelio *m* ⟨the four Gospels : los cuatro
evangelios⟩ **2 the gospel truth** : el
evangelio, la pura verdad
gossamer ['gɑsəmər, 'gɑzə-] *adj* : tenue,
sutil ⟨gossamer wings : alas tenues⟩
gossip¹ ['gɑsɪp] *vi* : chismear, contar
chismes
gossip² *n* **1** : chismoso *m*, -sa *f* (persona) **2** RUMOR : chisme *m*, rumor *m*
gossipy ['gɑsɪpi] *adj* : chismoso
got → get
Gothic ['gɑθɪk] *adj* : gótico
gotten → get
gouge¹ ['gaʊdʒ] *vt* **gouged; gouging 1**
: excavar, escoplear (con una gubia) **2**
SWINDLE : estafar, extorsionar

gouge² *n* **1** CHISEL : gubia *f*, formón *m* **2** GROOVE : ranura *f*, hoyo *m* (hecho por un formón)

goulash ['guːˌlɑʃ, -ˌlæʃ] *n* : estofado *m*, guiso *m* al estilo húngaro

gourd ['gord, 'gʊrd] *n* : calabaza *f*

gourmand ['gʊrˌmɑnd] *n* **1** GLUTTON : glotón *m*, -tona *f* **2** → **gourmet**

gourmet ['gʊrˌmeɪ, gʊrˈmeɪ] *n* : gourmet *mf*; gastrónomo *m*, -ma *f*

gout ['gaʊt] *n* : gota *f*

govern ['gʌvərn] *vt* **1** RULE : gobernar **2** CONTROL, DETERMINE : determinar, controlar, guiar **3** RESTRAIN : dominar (las emociones, etc.) — *vi* : gobernar

governess ['gʌvərnəs] *n* : institutriz *f*

government ['gʌvərmənt] *n* : gobierno *m*

governmental [ˌgʌvərˈmɛntəl] *adj* : gubernamental, gubernativo

governor ['gʌvənər, 'gʌvərnər] *n* **1** : gobernador *m*, - dora *f* (de un estado, etc.) **2** : regulador *m* (de una máquina)

governorship ['gʌvənərˌʃɪp, 'gʌvərnər-] *n* : cargo *m* de gobernador

gown ['gaʊn] *n* **1** : vestido *m* ⟨evening gown : traje de fiesta⟩ **2** : toga *f* (de magistrados, clérigos, etc.)

grab¹ ['græb] *v* **grabbed; grabbing** *vt* SNATCH : agarrar, arrebatar — *vi* : agarrarse

grab² *n* **1** to make a grab for : tratar de agarrar **2** up for grabs : disponible, libre

grace¹ ['greɪs] *vt* **graced; gracing** **1** HONOR : honrar **2** ADORN : adornar, embellecer

grace² *n* **1** : gracia *f* ⟨by the grace of God : por la gracia de Dios⟩ **2** BLESSING : bendición *f* (de la mesa) **3** RESPITE : plazo *m*, gracia *f* ⟨a five days' grace (period) : un plazo de cinco días⟩ **4** GRACIOUSNESS : gentileza *f*, cortesía *f* **5** ELEGANCE : elegancia *f*, gracia *f* **6** to be in the good graces of : estar en buenas relaciones con **7** with good grace : de buena gana

graceful ['greɪsfəl] *adj* : lleno de gracia, garboso, grácil

gracefully ['greɪsfəli] *adv* : con gracia, con garbo

gracefulness ['greɪsfəlnəs] *n* : gracilidad *f*, apostura *f*, gallardía *f*

graceless ['greɪsləs] *adj* **1** DISCOURTEOUS : descortés **2** CLUMSY, INELEGANT : torpe, desgarbado, poco elegante

gracious ['greɪʃəs] *adj* : cortés, gentil, cordial

graciously ['greɪʃəsli] *adv* : gentilmente

graciousness ['greɪʃəsnəs] *n* : gentileza *f*

gradation [greɪˈdeɪʃən, grə-] *n* : gradación *f*

grade¹ ['greɪd] *vt* **graded; grading** **1** SORT : clasificar **2** LEVEL : nivelar **3** : calificar (exámenes, alumnos)

grade² *n* **1** QUALITY : categoría *f*, calidad *f* **2** RANK : grado *m*, rango *m* (mil-

itar) **3** YEAR : grado *m*, curso *m*, año *m* ⟨sixth grade : el sexto grado⟩ **4** MARK : nota *f*, calificación *f* (en educación) **5** SLOPE : cuesta *f*, pendiente *f*, gradiente *f*

grade school → **elementary school**

gradient ['greɪdiənt] *n* : gradiente *f*

gradual ['grædʒʊəl] *adj* : gradual, paulatino

gradually ['grædʒʊəli, 'grædʒəli] *adv* : gradualmente, poco a poco

graduate¹ ['grædʒʊˌeɪt] *v* **-ated; -ating** *vi* : graduarse, licenciarse — *vt* : graduar ⟨a graduated thermometer : un termómetro graduado⟩

graduate² ['grædʒʊət] *adj* : de postgrado ⟨graduate course : curso de postgrado⟩

graduate³ *n* **1** : licenciado *m*, -da *f*; graduado *m*, -da *f* (de la universidad) **2** : bachiller *mf* (de la escuela secundaria)

graduate student *n* : postgraduado *m*, -da *f*

graduation [ˌgrædʒʊˈeɪʃən] *n* : graduación *f*

graffiti [grəˈfiːˌti, græ-] *npl* : pintadas *fpl*, graffiti *mpl*

graft¹ ['græft] *vt* : injertar

graft² *n* **1** : injerto *m* ⟨skin graft : injerto cutáneo⟩ **2** CORRUPTION : soborno *m* (político), ganancia *f* ilegal

grain ['greɪn] *n* **1** : grano *m* ⟨a grain of corn : un grano de maíz⟩ ⟨like a grain of sand : como grano de arena⟩ **2** CEREALS : cereales *mpl* **3** : veta *f*, vena *f*, grano *m* (de madera) **4** SPECK, TRACE : pizca *f*, ápice *m* ⟨a grain of truth : una pizca de verdad⟩ **5** grano *m* (unidad de peso)

gram ['græm] *n* : gramo *m*

grammar ['græmər] *n* : gramática *f*

grammar school → **elementary school**

grammatical [grəˈmætɪkəl] *adj* : gramatical — **grammatically** [-kli] *adv*

granary ['greɪnəri, 'græ-] *n, pl* **-ries** : granero *m*

grand ['grænd] *adj* **1** FOREMOST : grande **2** IMPRESSIVE : impresionante, magnífica ⟨a grand view : una vista magnífica⟩ **3** LAVISH : grandioso, suntuoso, lujoso ⟨to live in a grand manner : vivir a lo grande⟩ **4** FABULOUS : fabuloso, magnífico ⟨to have a grand time : pasarlo estupendamente, pasarlo en grande⟩ **5** grand total : total *m*, suma *f* total

grandchild ['grændˌtʃaɪld] *n, pl* **-children** : nieto *m*, -ta *f*

granddaughter ['grændˌdɔtər] *n* : nieta *f*

grandeur ['grændʒər] *n* : grandiosidad *f*, esplendor *m*

grandfather ['grændˌfɑðər] *n* : abuelo *m*

grandiose ['grændiˌoːs, ˌgrændiˈ-] *adj* **1** IMPOSING : imponente, grandioso **2** POMPOUS : pomposo, presuntuoso

grandma ['grænˌmɑ, -ˌmɔ] *n* : abuelita *f*, nana *f*

grandmother ['grænd,mʌðər] *n* : abuela *f*

grandpa ['græm,pɑ, -,pɔ] *n* : abuelito *m*

grandparents ['grænd,pærənts] *npl* : abuelos *mpl*

grandson ['grænd,sʌn] *n* : nieto *m*

grandstand ['grænd,stænd] *n* : tribuna *f*

granite ['grænɪt] *n* : granito *m*

grant[1] ['grænt] *vt* **1** ALLOW : conceder ⟨to grant a request : conceder una petición⟩ **2** BESTOW : conceder, dar, otorgar ⟨to grant a favor : otorgar un favor⟩ **3** ADMIT : reconocer, admitir ⟨I'll grant that he's clever : reconozco que es listo⟩ **4 to take for granted** : dar (algo) por sentado

grant[2] *n* **1** GRANTING : concesión *f*, otorgamiento *m* **2** SCHOLARSHIP : beca *f* **3** SUBSIDY : subvención *f*

granular ['grænjʊlər] *adj* : granular

granulated ['grænjʊ,leɪt̬əd] *adj* : granulado

grape ['greɪp] *n* : uva *f*

grapefruit ['greɪp,fru:t] *n* : toronja *f*, pomelo *m*

grapevine ['greɪp,vaɪn] *n* **1** : vid *f*, parra *f* **2 through the grapevine** : por vías secretas ⟨I heard it through the grapevine : me lo contaron⟩

graph ['græf] *n* : gráfica *f*, gráfico *m*

graphic ['græfɪk] *adj* **1** VIVID : vívido, gráfico **2 graphic arts** : artes gráficas

graphically ['græfɪkli] *adv* : gráficamente

graphite ['græ,faɪt] *n* : grafito *m*

grapnel ['græpnəl] *n* : rezón *m*

grapple ['græpəl] *v* **-pled; -pling** *vt* GRIP : agarrar (con un garfio) — *vi* STRUGGLE : forcejear, luchar (con un problema, etc.)

grasp[1] ['græsp] *vt* **1** GRIP, SEIZE : agarrar, asir **2** COMPREHEND : entender, comprender — *vi* **to grasp at** : aprovechar

grasp[2] *n* **1** GRIP : agarre *m* **2** CONTROL : control *m*, garras *fpl* **3** REACH : alcance *m* ⟨within your grasp : a su alcance⟩ **4** UNDERSTANDING : comprensión *f*, entendimiento *m*

grass ['græs] *n* **1** : hierba *f* (planta) **2** PASTURE : pasto *m*, zacate *m CA, Mex* **3** LAWN : césped *m*, pasto *m*

grasshopper ['græs,hɑpər] *n* : saltamontes *m*

grassland ['græs,lænd] *n* : pradera *f*

grassy ['græsi] *adj* **grassier; -est** : cubierto de hierba

grate[1] ['greɪt] *v* **grated; -ing** *vt* **1** : rallar (en cocina) **2** SCRAPE : rascar **3 to grate one's teeth** : hacer rechinar los dientes — *vi* **1** RASP, SQUEAK : chirriar **2** IRRITATE : irritar ⟨to grate on one's nerves : crisparle los nervios a uno⟩

grate[2] *n* **1** : parrilla *f* (para cocinar) **2** GRATING : reja *f*, rejilla *f*, verja *f* (en una ventana)

grateful ['greɪtfəl] *adj* : agradecido

gratefully ['greɪtfəli] *adv* : con agradecimiento

gratefulness ['greɪtfəlnəs] *n* : gratitud *f*, agradecimiento *m*

grater ['greɪt̬ər] *n* : rallador *m*

gratification [,græt̬əfə'keɪʃən] *n* : gratificación *f*

gratify ['græt̬ə,faɪ] *vt* **-fied; -fying 1** PLEASE : complacer **2** SATISFY : satisfacer, gratificar

grating ['greɪt̬ɪŋ] *n* : reja *f*, rejilla *f*

gratis[1] ['græt̬əs, 'greɪ-] *adv* : gratis, gratuitamente

gratis[2] *adj* : gratis, gratuito

gratitude ['græt̬ə,tu:d, -,tju:d] *n* : gratitud *f*, agradecimiento *m*

gratuitous [grə'tu:ət̬əs] *adj* : gratuito

gratuity [grə'tu:ət̬i] *n*, *pl* **-ities** TIP : propina *f*

grave[1] ['greɪv] *adj* **graver; -est 1** IMPORTANT : grave, de mucha gravedad **2** SERIOUS, SOLEMN : grave, serio

grave[2] *n* : tumba *f*, sepultura *f*

gravel ['grævəl] *n* : grava *f*, gravilla *f*

gravelly ['grævəli] *adj* **1** : de grava **2** HARSH : áspero (dícese de la voz)

gravely ['greɪvli] *adv* : gravemente

gravestone ['greɪv,sto:n] *n* : lápida *f*

graveyard ['greɪv,jɑrd] *n* CEMETERY : cementerio *m*, panteón *m*, camposanto *m*

gravitate ['grævə,teɪt] *vi* **-tated; -tating** : gravitar

gravitation [,grævə'teɪʃən] *n* : gravitación *f*

gravitational [,grævə'teɪʃənəl] *adj* : gravitacional

gravity ['grævət̬i] *n*, *pl* **-ties 1** SERIOUSNESS : gravedad *f*, seriedad *f* **2** : gravedad *f* ⟨the law of gravity : la ley de la gravedad⟩

gravy ['greɪvi] *n*, *pl* **-vies** : salsa *f* (preparada con el jugo de la carne asada)

gray[1] ['greɪ] *vt* : hacer gris — *vi* : encanecer, ponerse gris

gray[2] *adj* **1** : gris (dícese del color) **2** : cano, canoso ⟨gray hair : pelo canoso⟩ ⟨to go gray : volverse cano⟩ **3** DISMAL, GLOOMY : gris, triste

gray[3] *n* : gris *m*

grayish ['greɪɪʃ] *adj* : grisáceo

graze ['greɪz] *v* **grazed; grazing** *vi* : pastar, pacer — *vt* **1** : pastorear (ganado) **2** BRUSH : rozar **3** SCRATCH : raspar

grease[1] ['gri:s, 'gri:z] *vt* **greased; greasing** : engrasar, lubricar

grease[2] ['gri:s] *n* : grasa *f*

greasy ['gri:si, -zi] *adj* **greasier; -est 1** : grasiento **2** OILY : graso, grasoso

great ['greɪt] *adj* **1** LARGE : grande ⟨a great mountain : una montaña grande⟩ ⟨a great crowd : una gran muchedumbre⟩ **2** INTENSE : intenso, fuerte, grande ⟨great pain : gran dolor⟩ **3** EMINENT : grande, eminente, distinguido ⟨a great poet : un gran poeta⟩ **4** EXCELLENT, TERRIFIC : excelente, estupendo, fabuloso ⟨to have a great time : pasarlo en grande⟩ **5 a great while** : mucho tiempo

great–aunt [ˌɡreɪtˈænt, -ˈant] *n* : tía *f* abuela

greater [ˈɡreɪt̬ər] (*comparative* of **great**) : mayor

greatest [ˈɡreɪt̬əst] (*superlative* of **great**) : el mayor, la mayor

great–grandchild [ˌɡreɪtˈɡrænd-ˌtʃaɪld] *n, pl* **-children** [-ˌtʃɪldrən] : bisnieto *m*, -ta *f*

great–grandfather [ˌɡreɪtˈɡrænd-ˌfɑðər] *n* : bisabuelo *m*

great–grandmother [ˌɡreɪtˈɡrænd-ˌmʌðər] *n* : bisabuela *f*

greatly [ˈɡreɪtli] *adv* **1** MUCH : mucho, sumamente ⟨to be greatly improved : haber mejorado mucho⟩ **2** VERY : muy ⟨greatly superior : muy superior⟩

greatness [ˈɡreɪtnəs] *n* : grandeza *f*

great–uncle [ˌɡreɪtˈʌŋkəl] *n* : tío *m* abuelo

grebe [ˈɡriːb] *n* : somorgujo *m*

greed [ˈɡriːd] *n* **1** AVARICE : avaricia *f*, codicia *f* **2** GLUTTONY : glotonería *f*, gula *f*

greedily [ˈɡriːdəli] *adv* : con avaricia, con gula

greediness [ˈɡriːdinəs] → **greed**

greedy [ˈɡriːdi] *adj* **greedier; -est 1** AVARICIOUS : codicioso, avaricioso **2** GLUTTONOUS : glotón

Greek [ˈɡriːk] *n* **1** : griego *m*, -ga *f* **2** : griego *m* (idioma) — **Greek** *adj*

green¹ [ˈɡriːn] *adj* **1** : verde (dícese del color) **2** UNRIPE : verde, inmaduro **3** INEXPERIENCED : verde, novato

green² *n* **1** : verde *m* **2 greens** *npl* VEGETABLES : verduras *fpl*

greenery [ˈɡriːnəri] *n, pl* **-eries** : plantas *fpl* verdes, vegetación *f*

greenhorn [ˈɡriːnˌhɔrn] *n* : novato *m*, -ta *f*

greenhouse [ˈɡriːnˌhaʊs] *n* : invernadero *m*

greenhouse effect : efecto *m* invernadero

greenish [ˈɡriːnɪʃ] *adj* : verdoso

Greenlander [ˈɡriːnləndər, -ˌlæn-] *n* : groenlandés *m*, -desa *f*

greenness [ˈɡriːnnəs] *n* **1** : verdor *m* **2** INEXPERIENCE : inexperiencia *f*

green thumb *n* **to have a green thumb** : tener buena mano para las plantas

greet [ˈɡriːt] *vt* **1** : saludar ⟨to greet a friend : saludar a un amigo⟩ **2** : acoger, recibir ⟨they greeted him with boos : lo recibieron con abucheos⟩

greeting [ˈɡriːt̬ɪŋ] *n* **1** : saludo *m* **2 greetings** *npl* REGARDS : saludos *mpl*, recuerdos *mpl*

gregarious [ɡrɪˈɡæriəs] *adj* : gregario (dícese de los animales), sociable (dícese de las personas) — **gregariously** *adv*

gregariousness [ɡrɪˈɡæriəsnəs] *n* : sociabilidad *f*

gremlin [ˈɡrɛmlən] *n* : duende *m*

grenade [ɡrəˈneɪd] *n* : granada *f*

Grenadian [ɡrəˈneɪdiən] *n* : granadino *m*, -na *f* — **Grenadian** *adj*

grew → **grow**

grey → **gray**

greyhound [ˈɡreɪˌhaʊnd] *n* : galgo *m*

grid [ˈɡrɪd] *n* **1** GRATING : rejilla *f* **2** NETWORK : red *f* (de electricidad, etc.) **3** : cuadriculado *m* (de un mapa)

griddle [ˈɡrɪdəl] *n* : plancha *f*

griddle cake → **pancake**

gridiron [ˈɡrɪdˌaɪərn] *n* **1** GRILL : parrilla *f* **2** : campo *m* de futbol americano

gridlock [ˈɡrɪdˌlɑk] *n* : atasco *m* completo (de una red de calles)

grief [ˈɡriːf] *n* **1** SORROW : dolor *m*, pena *f* **2** ANNOYANCE, TROUBLE : problemas *mpl*, molestia *f*

grievance [ˈɡriːvənts] *n* COMPLAINT : queja *f*

grieve [ˈɡriːv] *v* **grieved; grieving** *vt* DISTRESS : afligir, entristecer, apenar — *vi* **1** : sufrir, afligirse **2 to grieve for** *or* **to grieve over** : llorar, lamentar

grievous [ˈɡriːvəs] *adj* **1** OPPRESSIVE : gravoso, opresivo, severo **2** GRAVE, SERIOUS : grave, severo, doloroso

grievously [ˈɡriːvəsli] *adv* : gravemente, de gravedad

grill¹ [ˈɡrɪl] *vt* **1** : asar (a la parrilla) **2** INTERROGATE : interrogar

grill² *n* **1** : parrilla *f* (para cocinar) **2** : parrillada *f* (comida) **3** RESTAURANT : grill *m*

grille *or* **grill** [ˈɡrɪl] *n* : reja *f*, enrejado *m*

grim [ˈɡrɪm] *adj* **grimmer; grimmest 1** CRUEL : cruel, feroz **2** STERN : adusto, severo ⟨a grim expression : un gesto severo⟩ **3** GLOOMY : sombrío, deprimente **4** SINISTER : macabro, siniestro **5** UNYIELDING : inflexible, persistente ⟨with grim determination : con una voluntad de hierro⟩

grimace¹ [ˈɡrɪməs, ɡrɪˈmeɪs] *vi* **-maced; -macing** : hacer muecas

grimace² *n* : mueca *f*

grime [ˈɡraɪm] *n* : mugre *f*, suciedad *f*

grimly [ˈɡrɪmli] *adv* **1** STERNLY : severamente **2** RESOLUTELY : inexorablemente

grimy [ˈɡraɪmi] *adj* **grimier; -est** : mugriento, sucio

grin¹ [ˈɡrɪn] *vi* **grinned; grinning** : sonreír abiertamente

grin² *n* : sonrisa *f* abierta

grind¹ [ˈɡraɪnd] *v* **ground** [ˈɡraʊnd]; **grinding** *vt* **1** CRUSH : moler, machacar, triturar **2** SHARPEN : afilar **3** POLISH : pulir, esmerilar (lentes, espejos) **4 to grind one's teeth** : rechinarle los dientes a uno **5 to grind down** OPPRESS : oprimir, agobiar — *vi* **1** : funcionar con dificultad, rechinar ⟨to grind to a halt : pararse poco a poco, llegar a un punto muerto⟩ **2** STUDY : estudiar mucho

grind² *n* : trabajo *m* pesado ⟨the daily grind : la rutina diaria⟩

grinder ['graɪndər] *n* : molinillo *m* ⟨coffee grinder : molinillo de café⟩

grindstone ['graɪnd,sto:n] *n* : piedra *m* de afilar

grip¹ ['grɪp] *vt* **gripped; gripping 1** GRASP : agarrar, asir **2** HOLD, INTEREST : captar el interés de

grip² *n* **1** GRASP : agarre *m*, asidero *m* ⟨to have a firm grip on something : agarrarse bien de algo⟩ **2** CONTROL, HOLD : control *m*, dominio *m* ⟨to lose one's grip on : perder el control de⟩ ⟨inflation tightened its grip on the economy : la inflación se afianzó en su dominio de la economía⟩ **3** UNDERSTANDING : comprensión *f*, entendimiento *m* ⟨to come to grips with : llegar a entender⟩ **4** HANDLE : asidero *m*, empuñadura *f* (de un arma)

gripe¹ ['graɪp] *v* **griped; griping** *vt* IRRITATE, VEX : irritar, fastidiar, molestar — *vi* COMPLAIN : quejarse, rezongar

gripe² *n* : queja *f*

grippe ['grɪp] *n* : influenza *f*, gripe *f*, gripa *f Col, Mex*

grisly ['grɪzli] *adj* **-lier; -est** : horripilante, horroroso, truculento

grist ['grɪst] *n* : molienda *f* ⟨it's all grist for the mill : todo ayuda, todo es provechoso⟩

gristle ['grɪsəl] *n* : cartílago *m*

gristly ['grɪsli] *adj* **-tlier; -est** : cartilaginoso

grit¹ ['grɪt] *vt* **gritted; gritting** : hacer rechinar (los dientes, etc.)

grit² *n* **1** SAND : arena *f* **2** GRAVEL : grava *f* **3** COURAGE : valor *m*, coraje *m* **4 grits** *npl* : sémola *f* de maíz

gritty ['grɪt̬i] *adj* **-tier; -est 1** : arenoso ⟨a gritty surface : una superficie arenosa⟩ **2** PLUCKY : valiente

grizzled ['grɪzəld] *adj* : entrecano

grizzly bear ['grɪzli] *n* : oso *m* pardo

groan¹ ['gro:n] *vi* **1** MOAN : gemir, quejarse **2** CREAK : crujir

groan² *n* **1** MOAN : gemido *m*, quejido *m* **2** CREAK : crujido *m*

grocer ['gro:sər] *n* : tendero *m*, -ra *f*

grocery ['gro:səri, -ʃəri] *n, pl* **-ceries 1** *or* **grocery store** : tienda *f* de comestibles, tienda *f* de abarrotes **2 groceries** *npl* : comestibles *mpl*, abarrotes *mpl*

groggy ['grɑgi] *adj* **-gier; -est** : atontado, grogui, tambaleante

groin ['grɔɪn] *n* : ingle *f*

grommet ['grɑmət, 'grʌ-] *n* : arandela *f*

groom¹ ['gru:m, 'grʊm] *vt* **1** : cepillar, almohazar (un animal) **2** : arreglar, cuidar ⟨well-groomed : bien arreglado⟩ **3** PREPARE : preparar

groom² *n* **1** : mozo *m*, -za *f* de cuadra **2** BRIDEGROOM : novio *m*

groove¹ ['gru:v] *vt* **grooved; grooving** : acanalar, hacer ranuras en, surcar

groove² *n* **1** FURROW, SLOT : ranura *f*, surco *m* **2** RUT : rutina *f*

grope ['gro:p] *v* **groped; groping** *vi* : andar a tientas, tantear ⟨he groped for the switch : buscó el interruptor a tientas⟩ — *vt* **to grope one's way** : avanzar a tientas

gross¹ ['gro:s] *vt* : tener entrada bruta de, recaudar en bruto

gross² *adj* **1** FLAGRANT : flagrante, grave ⟨a gross error : un error flagrante⟩ ⟨a gross injustice : una injusticia grave⟩ **2** FAT : muy gordo, obeso **3** : bruto ⟨gross national product : producto nacional bruto⟩ **4** COARSE, VULGAR : grosero, basto

gross³ *n* **1** *pl* **gross** : gruesa *f* (12 docenas) **2** *or* **gross income** : ingresos *mpl* brutos

grossly ['gro:sli] *adv* **1** EXTREMELY : extremadamente ⟨grossly unfair : totalmente injusto⟩ **2** CRUDELY : groseramente

grotesque [gro:'tɛsk] *adj* : grotesco

grotesquely [gro:'tɛskli] *adv* : de forma grotesca

grotto ['grɑto:] *n, pl* **-toes** : gruta *f*

grouch¹ ['graʊtʃ] *vi* : refunfuñar, rezongar

grouch² *n* **1** COMPLAINT : queja *f* **2** GRUMBLER : gruñón *m*, -ñona *f*; cascarrabias *mf fam*

grouchy ['graʊtʃi] *adj* **grouchier; -est** : malhumorado, gruñón

ground¹ ['graʊnd] *vt* **1** BASE : fundar, basar **2** INSTRUCT : enseñar los conocimientos básicos a ⟨to be well grounded in : ser muy entendido en⟩ **3** : conectar a tierra (un aparato eléctrico) **4** : varar, hacer encallar (un barco) **5** : restringir (un avión o un piloto) a la tierra

ground² *n* **1** EARTH, SOIL : suelo *m*, tierra *f* ⟨to dig (in) the ground : cavar la tierra⟩ ⟨to fall to the ground : caerse al suelo⟩ **2** LAND, TERRAIN : terreno *m* ⟨hilly ground : terreno alto⟩ ⟨to lose ground : perder terreno⟩ **3** BASIS, REASON : razón *f*, motivo *m* ⟨grounds for complaint : motivos de queja⟩ **4** BACKGROUND : fondo *m* **5** FIELD : campo *m*, plaza *f* ⟨parade ground : plaza de armas⟩ **6** : tierra *f* (para electricidad) **7 grounds** *npl* PREMISES : recinto *m*, terreno *m* **8 grounds** *npl* DREGS : posos *mpl* (de café)

ground³ → **grind**

groundhog ['graʊnd,hɔg] *n* : marmota *f* (de América)

groundless ['graʊndləs] *adj* : infundado

groundwork ['graʊnd,wərk] *n* **1** FOUNDATION : fundamento *m*, base *f* **2** PREPARATION : trabajo *m* preparatorio

group¹ ['gru:p] *vt* : agrupar

group² *n* : grupo *m*, agrupación *f*, conjunto *m*, compañía *f*

grouper ['gru:pər] *n* : mero *m*

grouse[1] ['graʊs] *vi* **groused; grousing** : quejarse, rezongar, refunfuñar

grouse[2] *n, pl* **grouse** *or* **grouses** : urogallo *m* (ave)

grout ['graʊt] *n* : lechada *f*

grove ['groːv] *n* : bosquecillo *m*, arboleda *f*, soto *m*

grovel ['grɑvəl, 'grʌ-] *vi* **-eled** *or* **-elled; -eling** *or* **-elling** **1** CRAWL : arrastrarse **2** : humillarse, postrarse ⟨to grovel before someone : postrarse ante alguien⟩

grow ['groː] *v* **grew** ['gruː]; **grown** ['groːn]; **growing** *vi* **1** : crecer ⟨palm trees grow on the islands : las palmas crecen en las islas⟩ ⟨my hair grows very fast : mi pelo crece muy rápido⟩ **2** DEVELOP, MATURE : desarrollarse, madurar **3** INCREASE : crecer, aumentar **4** BECOME : hacerse, volverse, ponerse ⟨she was growing angry : se estaba poniendo furiosa⟩ ⟨to grow dark : oscurecerse⟩ **5 to grow up** : hacerse mayor ⟨grow up! : ¡no seas niño!⟩ — *vt* **1** CULTIVATE, RAISE : cultivar **2** : dejar crecer ⟨to grow one's hair : dejarse crecer el pelo⟩

grower ['groːər] *n* : cultivador *m*, -dora *f*

growl[1] ['graʊl] *vi* : gruñir (dícese de un animal), refunfuñar (dícese de una persona)

growl[2] *n* : gruñido *m*

grown-up[1] ['groːn,əp] *adj* : adulto, mayor

grown-up[2] *n* : adulto *m*, -ta *f*; persona *f* mayor

growth ['groːθ] *n* **1** : crecimiento *m* ⟨to stunt one's growth : detener el crecimiento⟩ **2** INCREASE : aumento *m*, crecimiento *m*, expansión *f* **3** DEVELOPMENT : desarrollo *m* ⟨economic growth : desarrollo económico⟩ ⟨a five days' growth of beard : una barba de cinco días⟩ **4** LUMP, TUMOR : bulto *m*, tumor *m*

grub[1] ['grʌb] *vi* **grubbed; grubbing** **1** DIG : escarbar **2** RUMMAGE : hurgar, buscar **3** DRUDGE : trabajar duro

grub[2] *n* **1** : larva *f* ⟨beetle grub : larva del escarabajo⟩ **2** DRUDGE : esclavo *m*, -va *f* del trabajo **3** FOOD : comida *f*

grubby ['grʌbi] *adj* **grubbier; -est** : mugriento, sucio

grudge[1] ['grʌdʒ] *vt* **grudged; grudging** : resentir, envidiar

grudge[2] *n* : rencor *m*, resentimiento *m* ⟨to hold a grudge : guardar rencor⟩

grueling *or* **gruelling** ['gruːlɪŋ, 'gruːə-] *adj* : extenuante, agotador, duro

gruesome ['gruːsəm] *adj* : horripilante, truculento, horroroso

gruff ['grʌf] *adj* **1** BRUSQUE : brusco ⟨a gruff reply : una respuesta brusca⟩ **2** HOARSE : ronco — **gruffly** *adv*

grumble[1] ['grʌmbəl] *vi* **-bled; -bling** **1** COMPLAIN : refunfuñar, rezongar, quejarse **2** RUMBLE : hacer un ruido sordo, retumbar (dícese del trueno)

grumble[2] *n* **1** COMPLAINT : queja *f* **2** RUMBLE : ruido *m* sordo, estruendo *m*

grumbler ['grʌmbələr] *n* : gruñón *m*, -ñona *f*

grumpy ['grʌmpi] *adj* **grumpier; -est** : malhumorado, gruñón

grungy ['grʌndʒi] *adj* : sucio

grunt[1] ['grʌnt] *vi* : gruñir

grunt[2] *n* : gruñido *m*

guacamole [ˌgwɑkəˈmoːli] *n* : guacamole *m*, guacamol *m*

guarantee[1] [ˌgærənˈtiː] *vt* **-teed; -teeing** **1** PROMISE : asegurar, prometer **2** : poner bajo garantía, garantizar (un producto o servicio)

guarantee[2] *n* **1** PROMISE : garantía *f*, promesa *f* ⟨lifetime guarantee : garantía de por vida⟩ **2** → **guarantor**

guarantor [ˌgærənˈtɔr] *n* : garante *mf*; fiador *m*, -dora *f*

guaranty [ˌgærənˈtiː] → **guarantee**

guard[1] ['gɑrd] *vt* **1** DEFEND, PROTECT : defender, proteger **2** : guardar, vigilar, custodiar ⟨to guard the frontier : vigilar la frontera⟩ ⟨she guarded my secret well : guardó bien mi secreto⟩ — *vi* **to guard against** : protegerse contra, evitar

guard[2] *n* **1** WATCHMAN : guarda *mf* ⟨security guard : guarda de seguridad⟩ **2** VIGILANCE : guardia *f*, vigilancia *f* ⟨to be on guard : estar en guardia⟩ ⟨to let one's guard down : bajar la guardia⟩ **3** SAFEGUARD : salvaguardia *f*, dispositivo *m* de seguridad (en una máquina) **4** PRECAUTION : precaución *f*, protección *f*

guardhouse ['gɑrd,haʊs] *n* : cuartel *m* de la guardia

guardian ['gɑrdiən] *n* **1** PROTECTOR : guardián *m*, -diana *f*; custodio *m*, -dia *f* **2** : tutor *m*, -tora *f* (de un niño)

guardianship ['gɑrdiənˌʃɪp] *n* : custodia *f*, tutela *f*

Guatemalan [ˌgwɑtəˈmɑlən] *n* : guatemalteco *m*, -ca *f* — **Guatemalan** *adj*

guava ['gwɑvə] *n* : guayaba *f*

gubernatorial [ˌguːbənəˈtoːriəl, ˌgjuː-] *adj* : del gobernador

guerrilla *or* **guerilla** [gəˈrɪlə] *n* : guerrillero *m*, -ra *f*

guess[1] ['gɛs] *vt* **1** CONJECTURE : adivinar, conjeturar ⟨guess what happened! : ¡adivina lo que pasó!⟩ **2** SUPPOSE : pensar, creer, suponer ⟨I guess so : supongo que sí⟩ **3** : adivinar correctamente, acertar ⟨to guess the answer : acertar la respuesta⟩ — *vi* : adivinar

guess[2] *n* : conjetura *f*, suposición *f*

guesswork ['gɛs,wərk] *n* : suposiciones *fpl*, conjeturas *fpl*

guest ['gɛst] *n* : huésped *mf*; invitado *m*, -da *f*

guffaw[1] [gəˈfɔ] *vi* : reírse a carcajadas, carcajearse *fam*

guffaw[2] [gəˈfɔ, ˈgʌˌfɔ] *n* : carcajada *f*, risotada *f*

guidance ['gaɪdənts] *n* : orientación *f*, consejos *mpl*

guide[1] ['gaɪd] *vt* **guided; guiding 1** DI-RECT, LEAD : guiar, dirigir, conducir **2** ADVISE, COUNSEL : aconsejar, orientar

guide[2] *n* : guía *f*

guidebook ['gaɪd,bʊk] *n* : guía *f* (para viajeros)

guideline ['gaɪd,laɪn] *n* : pauta *f*, directriz *f*

guild ['gɪld] *n* : gremio *m*, sindicato *m*, asociación *f*

guile ['gaɪl] *n* : astucia *f*, engaño *m*

guileless ['gaɪlləs] *adj* : inocente, cándido, sin malicia

guillotine[1] ['gɪlə,ti:n, 'gi:jə,-] *vt* **-tined; -tining** : guillotinar

guillotine[2] *n* : guillotina *f*

guilt ['gɪlt] *n* : culpa *f*, culpabilidad *f*

guilty ['gɪlti] *adj* **guiltier; -est** : culpable

guinea fowl ['gɪni] *n* : gallina *f* de Guinea

guinea pig *n* : conejillo *m* de Indias, cobaya *f*

guise ['gaɪz] *n* : apariencia *f*, aspecto *m*, forma *f*

guitar [gə'tɑr, gɪ-] *n* : guitarra *f*

guitarist [gə'tɑrɪst, gɪ-] *n* : guitarrista *mf*

gulch ['gʌltʃ] *n* : barranco *m*, quebrada *f*

gulf ['gʌlf] *n* **1** : golfo *m* ⟨the Gulf of Mexico : el Golfo de México⟩ **2** GAP : brecha *f* ⟨the gulf between generations : la brecha entre las generaciones⟩ **3** CHASM : abismo *m*

gull ['gʌl] *n* : gaviota *f*

gullet ['gʌlət] *n* : garganta *f*

gullible ['gʌlɪbəl] *adj* : crédulo

gully ['gʌli] *n, pl* **-lies** : barranco *m*, hondonada *f*

gulp[1] ['gʌlp] *vt* **1** : engullir, tragar ⟨he gulped down the whiskey : engulló el whisky⟩ **2** SUPPRESS : suprimir, reprimir, tragar ⟨to gulp down a sob : reprimir un sollozo⟩ — *vi* : tragar saliva, tener un nudo en la garganta

gulp[2] *n* : trago *m*

gum[1] ['gʌm] *n* **1** CHEWING GUM : goma *f* de mascar, chicle *m* **2 gums** *npl* : encías *fpl*

gumbo ['gʌm,bo:] *n* : sopa *f* de quingombó

gumdrop ['gʌm,drɑp] *n* : pastilla *f* de goma

gummy ['gʌmi] *adj* **gummier; -est** : gomoso

gumption ['gʌmpʃən] *n* : iniciativa *f*, agallas *fpl fam*

gun[1] ['gʌn] *vt* **gunned; gunning 1** *or* **to gun down** : matar a tiros, asesinar **2** : acelerar (rápidamente) ⟨to gun the engine : acelerar el motor⟩

gun[2] *n* **1** CANNON : cañón *m* **2** FIREARM : arma *f* de fuego **3** SPRAY GUN : pistola *f* **4 to jump the gun** : adelantarse, salir antes de tiempo

gunboat ['gʌn,bo:t] *n* : cañonero *m*

gunfight ['gʌn,faɪt] *n* : tiroteo *m*, balacera *f*

gunfire ['gʌn,faɪr] *n* : disparos *mpl*

gunman ['gʌnmən] *n, pl* **-men** [-mən, -,mɛn] : pistolero *m*, gatillero *m* *Mex*

gunner ['gʌnər] *n* : artillero *m*, -ra *f*

gunnysack ['gʌni,sæk] *n* : saco *m* de yute

gunpowder ['gʌn,paʊdər] *n* : pólvora *f*

gunshot ['gʌn,ʃat] *n* : disparo *m*, tiro *m*, balazo *m*

gunwale ['gʌnəl] *n* : borda *f*

guppy ['gʌpi] *n, pl* **-pies** : lebistes *m*

gurgle[1] ['gərgəl] *vi* **-gled; -gling 1** : borbotar, gorgotear (dícese de un líquido) **2** : gorjear (dícese de un niño)

gurgle[2] *n* **1** : borboteo *m*, gorgoteo *m* (de un líquido) **2** : gorjeo *m* (de un niño)

gush ['gʌʃ] *vi* **1** SPOUT : surgir, salir a chorros, chorrear **2** : hablar con entusiasmo efusivo ⟨she gushed with praise : se deshizo en elogios⟩

gust ['gʌst] *n* : ráfaga *f*, racha *f*

gusto ['gʌs,to:] *n, pl* **gustoes** : entusiasmo *m* ⟨with gusto : con deleite, con ganas⟩

gusty ['gʌsti] *adj* **gustier; -est** : racheado

gut[1] ['gʌt] *vt* **gutted; gutting 1** EVISCERATE : destripar (un pollo, etc.), limpiar (un pescado) **2** : destruir el interior de (un edificio)

gut[2] *n* **1** INTESTINE : intestino *m* **2 guts** *npl* INNARDS : tripas *fpl fam*, entrañas *fpl* **3 guts** *npl* COURAGE : valentía *f*, agallas *fpl*

gutter ['gʌtər] *n* **1** : canal *mf*, canaleta *f* (de un techo) **2** : cuneta *f*, arroyo *m* (de una calle)

guttural ['gʌtərəl] *adj* : gutural

guy ['gaɪ] *n* **1** *or* **guyline** : cuerda *f* tensora, cable *m* **2** FELLOW : tipo *m*, hombre *m*

guzzle ['gʌzəl] *vt* **-zled; -zling** : chupar, tragarse

gym ['dʒɪm] → **gymnasium**

gymnasium [dʒɪm'neɪziəm, -ʒəm] *n, pl* **-siums** *or* **-sia** [-zi:ə, -ʒə] : gimnasio *m*

gymnast ['dʒɪmnəst, -,næst] *n* : gimnasta *mf*

gymnastic [dʒɪm'næstɪk] *adj* : gimnástico

gymnastics [dʒɪm'næstɪks] *ns & pl* : gimnasia *f*

gynecologist [,gaɪnə'kɑlədʒɪst, ,dʒɪnə-] *n* : ginecólogo *m*, -ga *f*

gynecology [,gaɪnə'kɑlədʒi, ,dʒɪnə-] *n* : ginecología *f*

gyp[1] ['dʒɪp] *vt* **gypped; gypping** : estafar, timar

gyp[2] *n* **1** SWINDLER : estafador *m*, -dora *f* **2** FRAUD, SWINDLE : estafa *f*, timo *m* *fam*

gypsum ['dʒɪpsəm] *n* : yeso *m*

Gypsy ['dʒɪpsi] *n, pl* **-sies** : gitano *m*, -na *f*

gyrate ['dʒaɪ,reɪt] *vi* **-rated; -rating** : girar, rotar

gyration [dʒaɪ'reɪʃən] *n* : giro *m*, rotación *f*

gyroscope ['dʒaɪrə,sko:p] *n* : giroscopio *m*, giróscopo *m*

H

h ['eɪtʃ] *n, pl* **h's** *or* **hs** ['eɪtʃəz] : octava letra del alfabeto inglés

ha ['hɑ] *interj* : ¡ja!

haberdashery ['hæbər,dæʃəri] *n, pl* **-eries** : tienda *f* de ropa para caballeros

habit ['hæbɪt] *n* **1** CUSTOM : hábito *m*, costumbre *f* **2** : hábito *m* (de un monje o una religiosa) **3** ADDICTION : dependencia *f*, adicción *f*

habitable ['hæbɪtəbəl] *adj* : habitable

habitat ['hæbɪ,tæt] *n* : hábitat *m*

habitation [,hæbɪ'teɪʃən] *n* **1** OCCUPANCY : habitación *f* **2** RESIDENCE : residencia *f*, morada *f*

habit–forming ['hæbɪt,fɔrmɪŋ] *adj* : que crea dependencia

habitual [hə'bɪtʃuəl] *adj* **1** CUSTOMARY : habitual, acostumbrado **2** INVETERATE : incorregible, empedernido — **habitually** *adv*

habituate [hə'bɪtʃu,eɪt] *vt* **-ated; -ating** : habituar, acostumbrar

hack¹ ['hæk] *vt* : cortar, tajear (a hachazos, etc.) ⟨to hack one's way : abrirse paso⟩ — *vi* **1** : hacer tajos **2** COUGH : toser

hack² *n* **1** CHOP : hachazo *m*, tajo *m* **2** HORSE : caballo *m* de alquiler **3** WRITER : escritor *m*, -tora *f* a sueldo; escritorzuelo *m*, -la *f* **4** COUGH : tos *f* seca

hackles ['hækəlz] *npl* **1** : pluma *f* erizada (de un ave), pelo *m* erizado (de un perro, etc.) **2 to get one's hackles up** : ponerse furioso

hackney ['hækni] *n, pl* **-neys** : caballo *m* de silla, caballo *m* de tiro

hackneyed ['hæknid] *adj* TRITE : trillado, gastado

hacksaw ['hæk,sɔ] *n* : sierra *f* para metales

had → **have**

haddock ['hædək] *ns & pl* : eglefino *m*

hadn't ['hædənt] (*contraction of* **had not**) → **have**

haft ['hæft] *n* : mango *m*, empuñadura *f*

hag ['hæg] *n* **1** WITCH : bruja *f*, hechicera *f* **2** CRONE : vieja *f* fea

haggard ['hægərd] *adj* : demacrado, macilento — **haggardly** *adv*

haggle ['hægəl] *vi* **-gled; -gling** : regatear

ha–ha [,hɑ'hɑ, 'hɑ'hɑ] *interj* : ¡ja, ja!

hail¹ ['heɪl] *vt* **1** GREET : saludar **2** SUMMON : llamar ⟨to hail a taxi : llamar un taxi⟩ — *vi* : granizar (en meteorología)

hail² *n* **1** : granizo *m* **2** BARRAGE : aluvión *m*, lluvia *f*

hail³ *interj* : ¡salve!

hailstone ['heɪl,stoːn] *n* : granizo *m*, piedra *f* de granizo

hailstorm ['heɪl,stɔrm] *n* : granizada *f*

hair ['hær] *n* **1** : pelo *m*, cabello *m* ⟨to get one's hair cut : cortarse el pelo⟩ **2** : vello *m* (en las piernas, etc.)

hairbreadth ['hær,brɛdθ] *or* **hairsbreadth** ['hærz-] *n* **by a hairbreadth** : por un pelo

hairbrush ['hær,brʌʃ] *n* : cepillo *m* (para el pelo)

haircut ['hær,kʌt] *n* : corte *m* de pelo

hairdo ['hær,duː] *n, pl* **-dos** : peinado *m*

hairdresser ['hær,drɛsər] *n* : peluquero *m*, -ra *f*

hairiness ['hærinəs] *n* : vellosidad *f*

hairless ['hærləs] *adj* : sin pelo, calvo, pelón

hairline ['hær,laɪn] *n* **1** : línea *f* delgada **2** : nacimiento *m* del pelo ⟨to have a receding hairline : tener entradas⟩

hairpin ['hær,pɪn] *n* : horquilla *f*

hair–raising ['hær,reɪzɪŋ] *adj* : espeluznante

hair spray *n* : laca *f*, fijador *m* (para el pelo)

hairstyle ['hær,staɪl] *n* : peinado *m*

hairy ['hæri] *adj* **hairier; -est** : peludo, velludo

Haitian ['heɪʃən, 'heɪtiən] *n* : haitiano *m*, -na *f* — **Haitian** *adj*

hake ['heɪk] *n* : merluza *f*

hale¹ ['heɪl] *vt* **haled; haling** : arrastrar, halar ⟨to hale to court : arrastrar al tribunal⟩

hale² *adj* : saludable, robusto

half¹ ['hæf, 'hɑf] *adv* : medio, a medias ⟨half cooked : medio cocido⟩

half² *adj* : medio, a medias ⟨a half hour : una media hora⟩ ⟨a half truth : una verdad a medias⟩

half³ *n, pl* **halves** ['hævz, 'hɑvz] **1** : mitad *f* ⟨half of my friends : la mitad de mis amigos⟩ ⟨in half : por la mitad⟩ **2** : tiempo *m* (en deportes)

half brother *n* : medio hermano *m*, hermanastro *m*

halfhearted ['hæf'hɑrtəd] *adj* : sin ánimo, poco entusiasta

halfheartedly ['hæf'hɑrtədli] *adv* : con poco entusiasmo, sin ánimo

half–life ['hæf,laɪf] *n, pl* **half–lives** : media vida *f*

half sister *n* : media hermana *f*, hermanastra *f*

halfway¹ ['hæf'weɪ] *adv* : a medio camino, a mitad de camino

halfway² *adj* : medio, intermedio ⟨a halfway point : un punto intermedio⟩

half–wit ['hæf,wɪt] *n* : tonto *m*, -ta *f*; imbécil *mf*

half–witted ['hæf'wɪtəd] *adj* : estúpido

halibut ['hælɪbət] *ns & pl* : halibut *m*

hall ['hɔl] *n* **1** BUILDING : residencia *f* estudiantil, facultad *f* (de una universidad) **2** VESTIBULE : entrada *f*, vestíbulo *m*, zaguán *m* **3** CORRIDOR : corredor *m*, pasillo *m* **4** AUDITORIUM : sala *f*, salón *m* ⟨concert hall : sala de conciertos⟩ **5 city hall** : ayuntamiento *m*

hallelujah [,hælə'luːjə, ,hɑ-] *interj* : ¡aleluya!

hallmark ['hɔl,mɑrk] *n* : sello *m* (distintivo)

hallow ['hæ,lo:] *vt* : santificar, consagrar

hallowed ['hæ,lo:d, 'hæ,lo:əd, 'hɑ,lo:d] *adj* : sagrado

Halloween [,hælə'wi:n, ,hɑ-] *n* : víspera *f* de Todos los Santos

hallucinate [hæ'lu:sən,eɪt] *vi* -nated; -nating : alucinar

hallucination [hə,lu:sən'eɪʃən] *n* : alucinación *f*

hallucinatory [hə'lu:sənə,tori] *adj* : alucinante

hallucinogen [hə'lu:sənədʒən] *n* : alucinógeno *m*

hallucinogenic [hə,lu:sənə'dʒɛnɪk] *adj* : alucinógeno

hallway ['hɔl,weɪ] *n* **1** ENTRANCE : entrada *f* **2** CORRIDOR : corredor *m*, pasillo *m*

halo ['heɪ,lo:] *n, pl* **-los** *or* **-loes** : aureola *f*, halo *m*

halt[1] ['hɔlt] *vi* : detenerse, pararse — *vt* **1** STOP : detener, parar (a una persona) **2** INTERRUPT : interrumpir (una actividad)

halt[2] *n* **1** : alto *m*, parada *f* **2 to come to a halt** : pararse, detenerse

halter ['hɔltər] *n* **1** : cabestro *m*, ronzal *m* (para un animal) **2** : blusa *f* sin espalda

halting ['hɔltɪŋ] *adj* HESITANT : vacilante, titubeante — **haltingly** *adv*

halve ['hæv, 'hav] *vt* **halved; halving 1** DIVIDE : partir por la mitad **2** REDUCE : reducir a la mitad

halves → **half**

ham ['hæm] *n* **1** : jamón *m* **2** *or* **ham actor** : comicastro *m*, -tra *f* **3** *or* **ham radio operator** : radioaficionado *m*, -da *f* **4 hams** *npl* HAUNCHES : ancas *fpl*

hamburger ['hæm,bərgər] *or* **hamburg** [-,bərg] *n* **1** : carne *f* molida **2** : hamburguesa *f* (emparedado)

hamlet ['hæmlət] *n* VILLAGE : aldea *f*, poblado *m*

hammer[1] ['hæmər] *vt* **1** STRIKE : clavar, golpear **2** NAIL : clavar, martillar **3 to hammer out** NEGOTIATE : elaborar, negociar, llegar a — *vi* : martillar, golpear

hammer[2] *n* **1** : martillo *m* **2** : percusor *m*, percutor *m* (de un arma de fuego)

hammock ['hæmək] *n* : hamaca *f*

hamper[1] ['hæmpər] *vt* : obstaculizar, dificultar

hamper[2] *n* : cesto *m*, canasta *f*

hamster ['hæmpstər] *n* : hámster *m*

hamstring ['hæm,strɪŋ] *vt* -strung [-,strʌŋ]; -stringing **1** : cortarle el tendón del corvejón a (un animal) **2** INCAPACITATE : incapacitar, inutilizar

hand[1] ['hænd] *vt* : pasar, dar, entregar

hand[2] *n* **1** : mano *f* ⟨made by hand : hecho a mano⟩ **2** POINTER : manecilla *f*, aguja *f* (de un reloj o instrumento) **3** SIDE : lado *m* ⟨on the other hand : por otro lado⟩ **4** HANDWRITING : letra *f*, escritura *f* **5** APPLAUSE : aplauso *m* **6** : mano *f*, cartas *fpl* (en juegos de naipes)

7 WORKER : obrero *m*, -ra *f*; trabajador *m*, -dora *f* **8 to ask for someone's hand (in marriage)** : pedir la mano de alguien **9 to lend a hand** : echar una mano

handbag ['hænd,bæg] *n* : cartera *f*, bolso *m*, bolsa *f Mex*

handball ['hænd,bɔl] *n* : frontón *m*, pelota *f*

handbill ['hænd,bɪl] *n* : folleto *m*, volante *m*

handbook ['hænd,bʊk] *n* : manual *m*

handcuff ['hænd,kʌf] *vt* : esposar, ponerle esposas (a alguien)

handcuffs ['hænd,kʌfs] *npl* : esposas *fpl*

handful ['hænd,fʊl] *n* : puñado *m*

handgun ['hænd,gʌn] *n* : pistola *f*, revólver *m*

handheld ['hænd,hɛld] *adj* : de mano

handicap[1] ['hændi,kæp] *vt* -capped; -capping **1** : asignar un handicap a (en deportes) **2** HAMPER : obstaculizar, poner en desventaja

handicap[2] *n* **1** DISABILITY : minusvalía *f*, discapacidad *f* **2** DISADVANTAGE : desventaja *f*, handicap *m* (en deportes)

handicapped ['hændi,kæpt] *adj* DISABLED : minusválido, discapacitado

handicraft ['hændi,kræft] *n* : artesanía *f*

handily ['hændəli] *adv* EASILY : fácilmente, con facilidad

handiwork ['hændi,wɔrk] *n* **1** WORK : trabajo *m* **2** CRAFTS : artesanías *fpl*

handkerchief ['hæŋkərtʃəf, -,tʃi:f] *n, pl* **-chiefs** : pañuelo *m*

handle[1] ['hændəl] *v* -dled; -dling *vt* **1** TOUCH : tocar **2** MANAGE : tratar, manejar, despachar **3** SELL : comerciar con, vender — *vi* : responder, conducirse (dícese de un vehículo)

handle[2] *n* : asa *m*, asidero *m*, mango *m* (de un cuchillo, etc.), pomo *m* (de una puerta), tirador *m* (de un cajón)

handlebars ['hændəl,bɑrz] *npl* : manubrio *m*, manillar *m*

handler ['hændələr] *n* : cuidador *m*, -dora *f*

handling ['hændəlɪŋ] *n* **1** MANAGEMENT : manejo *m* **2** TOUCHING : manoseo *m* **3 shipping and handling** : porte *m*, transporte *m*

handmade ['hænd,meɪd] *adj* : hecho a mano

hand–me–downs ['hændmi,daʊnz] *npl* : ropa *f* usada

handout ['hænd,aʊt] *n* **1** AID : dádiva *f*, limosna *f* **2** LEAFLET : folleto *m*

handpick ['hænd'pɪk] *vt* : seleccionar con cuidado

handrail ['hænd,reɪl] *n* : pasamanos *m*, barandilla *f*, barandal *m*

handsaw ['hænd,sɔ] *n* : serrucho *m*

hands down *adv* **1** EASILY : con facilidad **2** UNQUESTIONABLY : con mucho, de lejos

handshake ['hænd,ʃeɪk] *n* : apretón *m* de manos

handsome ['hæn*t*səm] *adj* **-somer; -est**
1 ATTRACTIVE : apuesto, guapo, atractivo **2** GENEROUS : generoso **3** SIZ-
ABLE : considerable
handsomely ['hæn*t*səmli] *adv* **1** ELE-
GANTLY : elegantemente **2** GENER-
OUSLY : con generosidad
handspring ['hænd,sprɪŋ] *n* : voltereta *f*
handstand ['hænd,stænd] *n* **to do a
handstand** : pararse de manos
hand–to–hand ['hæn*d*tə'hænd] *adj*
: cuerpo a cuerpo
handwriting ['hænd,raɪtɪŋ] *n* : letra *f*, escritura *f*
handwritten ['hænd,rɪtən] *adj* : escrito a
mano
handy ['hændi] *adj* **handier; -est 1**
NEARBY : a mano, cercano **2** USEFUL
: útil, práctico **3** DEXTEROUS : hábil
hang¹ ['hæŋ] *v* **hung** ['hʌŋ]; **hanging** *vt*
1 SUSPEND : colgar, tender, suspender
2 *past tense often* **hanged** EXECUTE
: colgar, ahorcar **3 to hang one's head**
: bajar la cabeza — *vi* **1** FALL : caer
(dícese de las telas y la ropa) **2** DAN-
GLE : colgar **3** HOVER : flotar, sostenerse en el aire **4** : ser ahorcado **5**
DROOP : inclinarse **6 to hang up** : colgar ⟨he hung up on me : me colgó⟩
hang² *n* **1** DRAPE : caída *f* **2 to get the
hang of something** : agarrarle la onda
a algo
hangar ['hæŋər, 'hæŋgər] *n* : hangar *m*
hanger ['hæŋər] *n* : percha *f*, gancho *m*
(para ropa)
hangman ['hæŋmən] *n*, *pl* **-men** [-mən,
-,mɛn] : verdugo *m*
hangnail ['hæŋ,neɪl] *n* : padrastro *m*
hangout ['hæŋ,aʊt] *n* : lugar *m* popular,
sitio *m* muy frecuentado
hangover ['hæŋ,o:vər] *n* : resaca *f*
hank ['hæŋk] *n* : madeja *f*
hanker ['hæŋkər] *vi* **to hanker for** : tener ansias de, tener ganas de
hankering ['hæŋkərɪŋ] *n* : ansia *f*, anhelo *m*
hansom ['hæn*t*səm] *n* : coche *m* de caballos
Hanukkah ['xɑnəkə, 'hɑ-] *n* : Januká,
Hanukkah
haphazard [hæp'hæzərd] *adj* : casual,
fortuito, al azar — **haphazardly** *adv*
hapless ['hæpləs] *adj* UNFORTUNATE
: desafortunado, desventurado — **hap-
lessly** *adv*
happen ['hæpən] *vi* **1** OCCUR : pasar,
ocurrir, suceder, tener lugar **2** BEFALL
: pasar, acontecer ⟨what happened to
her? : ¿qué le ha pasado?⟩ **3** CHANCE
: resultar, ocurrir por casualidad ⟨it
happened that I wasn't home : resulta
que estaba fuera de casa⟩ ⟨he happens
to be right : da la casualidad de que
tiene razón⟩
happening ['hæpənɪŋ] *n* : suceso *m*,
acontecimiento *m*
happiness ['hæpinəs] *n* : felicidad *f*,
dicha *f*

happy ['hæpi] *adj* **-pier; -est 1** JOYFUL
: feliz, contento, alegre **2** FORTUNATE
: afortunado, feliz — **happily** [-pəli] *adv*
happy–go–lucky ['hæpigo:'lʌki] *adj*
: despreocupado
harangue¹ [hə'ræŋ] *vt* **-rangued; -ran-
guing** : arengar
harangue² *n* : arenga *f*
harass [hə'ræs, 'hærəs] *vt* **1** BESIEGE,
HOUND : acosar, asediar, hostigar **2**
ANNOY : molestar
harassment [hə'ræsmənt, 'hærəsmənt]
n : acoso *m*, hostigamiento *m* ⟨sexual
harrassment : acoso sexual⟩
harbinger ['hɑrbɪndʒər] *n* **1** HERALD
: heraldo *m*, precursor *m* **2** OMEN : presagio *m*
harbor¹ ['hɑrbər] *vt* **1** SHELTER : dar
refugio a, albergar **2** CHERISH, KEEP
: abrigar, guardar, albergar ⟨to harbor
doubts : guardar dudas⟩
harbor² *n* **1** REFUGE : refugio *m* **2** PORT
: puerto *m*
hard¹ ['hɑrd] *adv* **1** FORCEFULLY
: fuerte, con fuerza ⟨the wind blew
hard : el viento sopló fuerte⟩ **2** STREN-
UOUSLY : duro, mucho ⟨to work hard
: trabajar duro⟩ **3 to take something
hard** : tomarse algo muy mal, estar muy
afectado por algo
hard² *adj* **1** FIRM, SOLID : duro, firme,
sólido **2** DIFFICULT : difícil, arduo **3**
SEVERE : severo, duro ⟨a hard winter
: un invierno severo⟩ **4** UNFEELING
: insensible, duro **5** DILIGENT : diligente ⟨to be a hard worker : ser muy
trabajador⟩ **6 hard liquor** : bebidas *fpl*
fuertes **7 hard water** : agua *f* dura
hardcover ['hɑrd,kʌvər] *adj* : de pasta
dura, de tapa dura
hard disk *n* : disco *m* duro
hard drive → **hard disk**
harden ['hɑrdən] *vt* : endurecer
hardheaded [,hɑrd'hɛdəd] *adj* **1** STUB-
BORN : testarudo, terco **2** REALISTIC
: realista, práctico — **hardheadedly**
adv
hard–hearted [,hɑrd'hɑrtəd] *adj* : despiadado, insensible — **hard–hearted-
ly** *adv*
hard–heartedness [,hɑrd'hɑrtədnəs] *n*
: dureza *f* de corazón
hardly ['hɑrdli] *adv* **1** SCARCELY : apenas, casi ⟨I hardly knew her : apenas
la conocía⟩ ⟨hardly ever : casi nunca⟩
2 NOT : difícilmente, poco, no ⟨they
can hardly blame me! : ¡difícilmente
pueden echarme la culpa!⟩ ⟨it's hardly likely : es poco probable⟩
hardness ['hɑrdnəs] *n* **1** FIRMNESS
: dureza *f* **2** DIFFICULTY : dificultad *f*
3 SEVERITY : severidad *f*
hardship ['hɑrd,ʃɪp] *n* : dificultad *f*, privación *f*
hardware ['hɑrd,wær] *n* **1** TOOLS : ferretería *f* **2** : hardware *m* (de una computadora)
hardwood ['hɑrd,wʊd] *n* : madera *f* dura,
madera *f* noble

hardworking ['hɑrd'wərkɪŋ] *adj* : trabajador

hardy ['hɑrdi] *adj* **-dier; -est** : fuerte, robusto, resistente (dícese de las plantas) — **hardily** [-dəli] *adv*

hare ['hær] *n, pl* **hare** *or* **hares** : liebre *f*

harebrained ['hær‚breɪnd] *adj* : estúpido, absurdo, disparatado

harelip ['hær‚lɪp] *n* : labio *m* leporino

harem ['hærəm] *n* : harén *m*

hark ['hɑrk] *vi* **1** (*used only in the imperative*) LISTEN : escuchar **2 hark back** RETURN : volver **3 hark back** RECALL : recordar

harlequin ['hɑrlɪkən, -kwən] *n* : arlequín *m*

harm[1] ['hɑrm] *vt* : hacerle daño a, perjudicar

harm[2] *n* : daño *m*, perjuicio *m*

harmful ['hɑrmfəl] *adj* : dañino, perjudicial — **harmfully** *adv*

harmless ['hɑrmləs] *adj* : inofensivo, inocuo — **harmlessly** *adv*

harmlessness ['hɑrmləsnəs] *n* : inocuidad *f*

harmonic [hɑr'mɑnɪk] *adj* : armónico — **harmonically** [-nɪkli] *adv*

harmonica [hɑr'mɑnɪkə] *n* : armónica *f*

harmonious [hɑr'mo:niəs] *adj* : armonioso — **harmoniously** *adv*

harmonize ['hɑrmə‚naɪz] *v* **-nized; -nizing** : armonizar

harmony ['hɑrməni] *n, pl* **-nies** : armonía *f*

harness[1] ['hɑrnəs] *vt* **1** : enjaezar (un animal) **2** UTILIZE : utilizar, aprovechar

harness[2] *n* : arreos *mpl*, guarniciones *fpl*, arnés *m*

harp[1] ['hɑrp] *vi* **to harp on** : insistir sobre, machacar sobre

harp[2] *n* : arpa *m*

harpist ['hɑrpɪst] *n* : arpista *mf*

harpoon[1] [hɑr'pu:n] *vt* : arponear

harpoon[2] *n* : arpón *m*

harpsichord ['hɑrpsɪ‚kɔrd] *n* : clavicémbalo *m*

harrow[1] ['hær‚o:] *vt* **1** CULTIVATE : gradar, labrar (la tierra) **2** TORMENT : atormentar

harrow[2] *n* : grada *f*, rastra *f*

harry ['hæri] *vt* **-ried; -rying** HARASS : acosar, hostigar

harsh ['hɑrʃ] *adj* **1** ROUGH : áspero **2** SEVERE : duro, severo **3** : discordante (dícese de los sonidos) — **harshly** *adv*

harshness ['hɑrʃnəs] *n* **1** ROUGHNESS : aspereza *f* **2** SEVERITY : dureza *f*, severidad *f*

harvest[1] ['hɑrvəst] *v* : cosechar

harvest[2] *n* **1** HARVESTING : siega *f*, recolección *f* **2** CROP : cosecha *f*

harvester ['hɑrvəstər] *n* : segador *m*, -dora *f*; cosechadora *f* (máquina)

has → have

hash[1] ['hæʃ] *vt* **1** MINCE : picar **2 to hash over** DISCUSS : discutir, repasar

hash[2] *n* **1** : picadillo *m* (comida) **2** JUMBLE : revoltijo *m*, fárrago *m*

hasn't ['hæzənt] (*contraction* of **has not**) → **has**

hasp ['hæsp] *n* : picaporte *m*, pestillo *m*

hassle[1] ['hæsəl] *vt* **-sled; -sling** : fastidiar, molestar

hassle[2] *n* **1** ARGUMENT : discusión *f*, disputa *f*, bronca *f* **2** FIGHT : pelea *f*, riña *f* **3** BOTHER, TROUBLE : problemas *mpl*, lío *m*

hassock ['hæsək] *n* **1** CUSHION : almohadón *m*, cojín *m* **2** FOOTSTOOL : escabel *m*

haste ['heɪst] *n* **1** : prisa *f*, apuro *m* **2 to make haste** : darse prisa, apurarse

hasten ['heɪsən] *vt* : acelerar, precipitar — *vi* : apresurarse, apurarse

hasty ['heɪsti] *adj* **hastier; -est** **1** HURRIED, QUICK : rápido, apresurado, apurado **2** RASH : precipitado — **hastily** [-təli] *adv*

hat ['hæt] *n* : sombrero *m*

hatch[1] ['hætʃ] *vt* **1** : incubar, empollar (huevos) **2** DEVISE : idear, tramar — *vi* : salir del cascarón

hatch[2] *n* : escotilla *f*

hatchery ['hætʃəri] *n, pl* **-ries** : criadero *m*

hatchet ['hætʃət] *n* : hacha *f*

hatchway ['hætʃ‚weɪ] *n* : escotilla *f*

hate[1] ['heɪt] *vt* **hated; hating** : odiar, aborrecer, detestar

hate[2] *n* : odio *m*

hateful ['heɪtfəl] *adj* : odioso, aborrecible, detestable — **hatefully** *adv*

hatred ['heɪtrəd] *n* : odio *m*

hatter ['hætər] *n* : sombrerero *m*, -ra *f*

haughtiness ['hɔtinəs] *n* : altanería *f*, altivez *f*

haughty ['hɔti] *adj* **-tier; -est** : altanero, altivo — **haughtily** [-təli] *adv*

haul[1] ['hɔl] *vt* **1** DRAG, PULL : arrastrar, jalar **2** TRANSPORT : transportar

haul[2] *n* **1** PULL : tirón *m*, jalón *m* **2** CATCH : redada *f* **3** JOURNEY : viaje *m*, trayecto *m* ⟨it's a long haul : es un trayecto largo⟩

haulage ['hɔlɪdʒ] *n* : transporte *m*, tiro *m*

hauler ['hɔlər] *n* : transportista *mf*

haunch ['hɔntʃ] *n* **1** HIP : cadera *f* **2 haunches** *npl* HINDQUARTERS : ancas *fpl*, cuartos *mpl* traseros

haunt[1] ['hɔnt] *vt* **1** : aparecer en (dícese de un fantasma) **2** FREQUENT : frecuentar, rondar **3** PREOCCUPY : perseguir, obsesionar

haunt[2] *n* : guarida *f* (de animales o ladrones), lugar *m* predilecto

haunting ['hɔntɪŋ] *adj* : obsesionante, evocador — **hauntingly** *adv*

haute ['o:t] *adj* **1** : de moda, de categoría **2 haute couture** [‚o:tku'tur] : alta costura *f* **3 haute cuisine** [‚o:tkwɪ'zi:n] : alta cocina *f*

have ['hæv, *in sense 3 as an auxiliary verb usu* 'hæf] *v* **had** ['hæd]; **having; has** ['hæz, *in sense 3 as an auxiliary verb usu* 'hæs] *vt* **1** POSSESS : tener ⟨do you have change? : ¿tienes cambio?⟩ **2** EXPERI-ENCE, UNDERGO : tener, experimen-tar, sufrir ⟨I have a toothache : tengo un dolor de muelas⟩ **3** INCLUDE : ten-er, incluir ⟨April has 30 days : abril tiene 30 días⟩ **4** CONSUME : comer, tomar **5** RECEIVE : tener, recibir ⟨he had my permission : tenía mi permiso⟩ **6** ALLOW : permitir, dejar ⟨I won't have it! : ¡no lo permitiré!⟩ **7** HOLD : hacer ⟨to have a party : dar una fiesta⟩ ⟨to have a meeting : convocar una re-unión⟩ **8** HOLD : tener ⟨he had me in his power : me tenía en su poder⟩ **9** BEAR : tener (niños) **10** (*indicating causation*) ⟨she had a dress made : mandó hacer un vestido⟩ ⟨to have one's hair cut : cortarse el pelo⟩ — *v aux* **1** : haber ⟨she has been very busy : ha estado muy ocupada⟩ ⟨I've lived here three years : hace tres años que vivo aquí⟩ **2** (*used in tags*) ⟨you've fin-ished, haven't you? : ha terminado, ¿no?⟩ **3 to have to** : deber, tener que ⟨we have to leave : tenemos que salir⟩

haven ['heɪvən] *n* : refugio *m*
havoc ['hævək] *n* **1** DESTRUCTION : es-tragos *mpl*, destrucción *f* **2** CHAOS, DISORDER : desorden *m*, caos *m*
Hawaiian[1] [hə'waɪən] *adj* : hawaiano
Hawaiian[2] *n* : hawaiano *m*, -na *f*
hawk[1] ['hɔk] *vt* : pregonar, vender (mer-cancías) en la calle
hawk[2] *n* : halcón *m*
hawker ['hɔkər] *n* : vendedor *m*, -dora *f* ambulante
hawthorn ['hɔ,θɔrn] *n* : espino *m*
hay ['heɪ] *n* : heno *m*
hay fever *n* : fiebre *f* del heno
hayloft ['heɪ,lɔft] *n* : pajar *m*
hayseed ['heɪ,siːd] *n* : palurdo *m*, -da *f*
haystack ['heɪ,stæk] *n* : almiar *m*
haywire ['heɪ,waɪr] *adj* : descompuesto, desbaratado ⟨to go haywire : estro-pearse⟩
hazard[1] ['hæzərd] *vt* : arriesgar, aventu-rar
hazard[2] *n* **1** DANGER : peligro *m*, ries-go *m* **2** CHANCE : azar *m*
hazardous ['hæzərdəs] *adj* : arriesgado, peligroso
haze[1] ['heɪz] *vt* **hazed; hazing** : abru-mar, acosar
haze[2] *n* : bruma *f*, neblina *f*
hazel ['heɪzəl] *n* **1** : avellano *m* (árbol) **2** : color *m* avellana
hazelnut ['heɪzəl,nʌt] *n* : avellana *f*
haziness ['heɪzinəs] *n* **1** MISTINESS : nebulosidad *f* **2** VAGUENESS : vaguedad *f*
hazy ['heɪzi] *adj* **hazier; -est 1** MISTY : brumoso, neblinoso, nebuloso **2** VAGUE : vago, confuso
he ['hiː] *pron* : él
head[1] ['hɛd] *vt* **1** LEAD : encabezar **2** DIRECT : dirigir — *vi* : dirigirse
head[2] *adj* MAIN : principal ⟨the head of-fice : la oficina central, la sede⟩

head[3] *n* **1** : cabeza *f* ⟨from head to foot : de pies a cabeza⟩ **2** MIND : mente *f*, cabeza *f* **3** TIP, TOP : cabeza *f* (de un clavo, un martillo, etc.), cabecera *f* (de una mesa o un río), punta *f* (de una flecha), flor *m* (de un repollo, etc.), en-cabezamiento *m* (de una carta, etc.), espuma *f* (de cerveza) **4** DIRECTOR, LEADER : director *m*, -tora *f*; jefe *m*, -fa *f*; cabeza *f* (de una familia) **5** : cara *f* (de una moneda) ⟨heads or tails : cara o cruz⟩ **6** : cabeza *f* ⟨500 head of cat-tle : 500 cabezas de ganado⟩ ⟨$10 a head : $10 por cabeza⟩ **7 to come to a head** : llegar a un punto crítico
headache ['hɛd,eɪk] *n* : dolor *m* de cabeza, jaqueca *f*
headband ['hɛd,bænd] *n* : cinta *f* del pelo
headdress ['hɛd,drɛs] *n* : tocado *m*
headfirst ['hɛd'fərst] *adv* : de cabeza
headgear ['hɛd,gɪr] *n* : gorro *m*, casco *m*, sombrero *m*
heading ['hɛdɪŋ] *n* **1** DIRECTION : di-rección *f* **2** TITLE : encabezamiento *m*, título *m* **3** : membrete *m* (de una car-ta)
headland ['hɛdlənd, -,lænd] *n* : cabo *m*
headlight ['hɛd,laɪt] *n* : faro *m*, foco *m*, farol *m Mex*
headline ['hɛd,laɪn] *n* : titular *m*
headlong[1] ['hɛd'lɔŋ] *adv* **1** HEADFIRST : de cabeza **2** HASTILY : precipitada-mente
headlong[2] ['hɛd,lɔŋ] *adj* : precipitado
headmaster ['hɛd,mæstər] *n* : director *m*
headmistress ['hɛd,mɪstrəs, -'mɪs-] *n* : directora *f*
head-on ['hɛd'ɑn, -'ɔn] *adv & adj* : de frente
headphones ['hɛd,foːnz] *npl* : audífonos *mpl*, cascos *mpl*
headquarters ['hɛd,kwɔrtərz] *ns & pl* **1** SEAT : oficina *f* central, sede *f* **2** : cuar-tel *m* general (de los militares)
headrest ['hɛd,rɛst] *n* : apoyacabezas *m*
headship ['hɛd,ʃɪp] *n* : dirección *f*
head start *n* : ventaja *f*
headstone ['hɛd,stoːn] *n* : lápida *f*
headstrong ['hɛd'strɔŋ] *adj* : testarudo, obstinado, empecinado
headwaiter ['hɛd'weɪtər] *n* : jefe *m*, -fa *f* de comedor
headwaters ['hɛd,wɔtərz, -,wɑ-] *npl* : cabecera *f*
headway ['hɛd,weɪ] *n* : progreso *m* ⟨to make headway against : avanzar con-tra⟩
heady ['hɛdi] *adj* **headier; -est 1** IN-TOXICATING : embriagador, excitante **2** SHREWD : astuto, sagaz
heal ['hiːl] *vt* : curar, sanar — *vi* **1** : sa-nar, curarse **2 to heal up** : cicatrizarse
healer ['hiːlər] *n* **1** : curandero *m*, -dera *f* **2** : curador *m*, -dora *f* (cosa)
health ['hɛlθ] *n* : salud *f*

healthful ['hɛlθfəl] *adj* : saludable, salubre — **healthfully** *adv*

healthy ['hɛlθi] *adj* **healthier; -est** : sano, bien — **healthily** [-θəli] *adv*

heap¹ ['hi:p] *vt* **1** PILE : amontonar, apilar **2** SHOWER : colmar

heap² *n* : montón *m*, pila *f*

hear ['hɪr] *v* **heard** ['hərd]; **hearing** *vt* **1** : oír ⟨do you hear me? : ¿me oyes?⟩ **2** HEED : oír, prestar atención a **3** LEARN : oír, enterarse de — *vi* **1** : oír ⟨to hear about : oír hablar de⟩ **2 to hear from** : tener noticias de

hearing ['hɪrɪŋ] *n* **1** : oído *m* ⟨hard of hearing : duro de oído⟩ **2** : vista *f* (en un tribunal) **3** ATTENTION : consideración *f*, oportunidad *f* de expresarse **4** EARSHOT : alcance *m* del oído

hearing aid *n* : audífono *m*

hearken ['harkən] *vt* : escuchar

hearsay ['hɪr,seɪ] *n* : rumores *mpl*

hearse ['hərs] *n* : coche *m* fúnebre

heart ['hart] *n* **1** : corazón *m* **2** CENTER, CORE : corazón *m*, centro *m* ⟨the heart of the matter : el meollo del asunto⟩ **3** FEELINGS : corazón *m*, sentimientos *mpl* ⟨a broken heart : un corazón destrozado⟩ ⟨to have a good heart : tener buen corazón⟩ ⟨to take something to heart : tomarse algo a pecho⟩ **4** COURAGE : valor *m*, corazón *m* ⟨to take heart : animarse, cobrar ánimos⟩ **5** hearts *npl* : corazones *mpl* (en juegos de naipes) **6 by heart** : de memoria

heartache ['hart,eɪk] *n* : pena *f*, angustia *f*

heart attack *n* : infarto *m*, ataque *m* al corazón

heartbeat ['hart,bi:t] *n* : latido *m* (del corazón)

heartbreak ['hart,breɪk] *n* : congoja *f*, angustia *f*

heartbreaking ['hart,breɪkɪŋ] *adj* : desgarrador, que parte el corazón

heartbroken ['hart,bro:kən] *adj* : desconsolado, destrozado

heartburn ['hart,bərn] *n* : acidez *f* estomacal

hearten ['hartən] *vt* : alentar, animar

heartfelt ['hart,fɛlt] *adj* : sentido

hearth ['harθ] *n* : hogar *m*, chimenea *f*

heartily ['hartəli] *adv* **1** ENTHUSIASTICALLY : de buena gana, con entusiasmo **2** TOTALLY : totalmente, completamente

heartless ['hartləs] *adj* : desalmado, despiadado, cruel

heartsick ['hart,sɪk] *adj* : abatido, desconsolado

heartstrings ['hart,strɪŋz] *npl* : fibras *fpl* del corazón

heartwarming ['hart,wɔrmɪŋ] *adj* : conmovedor, emocionante

hearty ['harti] *adj* **heartier; -est 1** CORDIAL, WARM : cordial, caluroso **2** STRONG : fuerte ⟨to have a hearty appetite : ser de buen comer⟩ **3** SUBSTANTIAL : abundante, sustancioso ⟨a

hearty breakfast : un desayuno abundante⟩

heat¹ ['hi:t] *vt* : calentar

heat² *n* **1** WARMTH : calor *m* **2** HEATING : calefacción *f* **3** EXCITEMENT : calor *m*, entusiasmo *m* ⟨in the heat of the moment : en el calor del momento⟩ **4** ESTRUS : celo *m*

heated ['hi:ţəd] *adj* **1** WARMED : calentado **2** IMPASSIONED : acalorado, apasionado

heater ['hi:ţər] *n* : calentador *m*, estufa *f*, calefactor *m*

heath ['hi:θ] *n* **1** MOOR : brezal *m*, páramo *m* **2** HEATHER : brezo *m*

heathen¹ ['hi:ðən] *adj* : pagano

heathen² *n, pl* **-thens** *or* **-then** : pagano *m*, -na *f*; infiel *mf*

heather ['hɛðər] *n* : brezo *m*

heave¹ ['hi:v] *v* **heaved** *or* **hove** ['ho:v]; **heaving** *vt* **1** LIFT, RAISE : levantar con esfuerzo **2** HURL : lanzar, tirar **3 to heave a sigh** : echar un suspiro, suspirar — *vi* **1** : subir y bajar, palpitar (dícese del pecho) **2 to heave up** RISE : levantarse

heave² *n* **1** EFFORT : gran esfuerzo *m* (para levantar algo) **2** THROW : lanzamiento *m*

heaven ['hɛvən] *n* **1** : cielo *m* ⟨for heaven's sake : por Dios⟩ **2 heavens** *npl* SKY : cielo *m* ⟨the heavens opened up : empezó a llover a cántaros⟩

heavenly ['hɛvənli] *adj* **1** : celestial, celeste **2** DELIGHTFUL : divino, encantador

heavily ['hɛvəli] *adv* **1** : pesadamente, con mucho peso **2** LABORIOUSLY : trabajosamente, penosamente **3** : mucho

heaviness ['hɛvinəs] *n* : peso *m*, pesadez *f*

heavy ['hɛvi] *adj* **heavier; -est 1** WEIGHTY : pesado **2** DENSE, THICK : denso, espeso, grueso **3** BURDENSOME : oneroso, gravoso **4** PROFOUND : profundo **5** SLUGGISH : lento, tardo **6** STOUT : corpulento **7** SEVERE : severo, duro, fuerte

heavy–duty ['hɛvi'du:ţi, -'dju:-] *adj* : muy resistente, fuerte

heavyweight ['hɛvi,weɪt] *n* : peso *m* pesado (en deportes)

Hebrew¹ ['hi:,bru:] *adj* : hebreo

Hebrew² *n* **1** : hebreo *m*, -brea *f* **2** : hebreo *m* (idioma)

heck ['hɛk] *n* : ¡caramba!, ¡caray! ⟨a heck of a lot : un montón⟩ ⟨what the heck is . . . ? : ¿que diablos es . . . ?⟩

heckle ['hɛkəl] *vt* **-led; -ling** : interrumpir (a un orador)

hectare ['hɛk,tær] *n* : hectárea *f*

hectic ['hɛktɪk] *adj* : agitado, ajetreado — **hectically** [-tɪkli] *adv*

he'd ['hi:d] (*contraction* of **he had** *or* **he would**) → **have, would**

hedge¹ ['hɛʤ] *v* **hedged; hedging** *vt* **1** : cercar con un seto **2 to hedge one's bet** : cubrirse — *vi* **1** : dar rodeos, con testar con evasivas **2 to hedge against** : cubrirse contra, protegerse contra

hedge² *n* **1** : seto *m* vivo **2** SAFEGUARD : salvaguardia *f*, protección *f*

hedgehog [ˈhɛʤˌhɔg, -hɑg] *n* : erizo *m*

heed¹ [ˈhiːd] *vt* : prestar atención a, hacer caso de

heed² *n* : atención *f*

heedless [ˈhiːdləs] *adj* : descuidado, despreocupado, inconsciente ⟨to be heedless of : hacer caso omiso de⟩ — **heedlessly** *adv*

heel¹ [ˈhiːl] *vi* : inclinarse

heel² *n* : talón *m* (del pie), tacón *m* (de calzado)

heft [ˈhɛft] *vt* : sopesar

hefty [ˈhɛfti] *adj* **heftier; -est** : robusto, fornido, pesado

hegemony [hɪˈʤɛməni] *n, pl* **-nies** : hegemonía *f*

heifer [ˈhɛfər] *n* : novilla *f*

height [ˈhaɪt] *n* **1** PEAK : cumbre *f*, cima *f*, punto *m* alto ⟨at the height of her career : en la cumbre de su carrera⟩ ⟨the height of stupidity : el colmo de la estupidez⟩ **2** TALLNESS : estatura *f* (de una persona), altura *f* (de un objeto) **3** ALTITUDE : altura *f*

heighten [ˈhaɪtən] *vt* **1** : hacer más alto **2** INTENSIFY : aumentar, intensificar — *vi* : aumentarse, intensificarse

heinous [ˈheɪnəs] *adj* : atroz, abominable, nefando

heir [ˈær] *n* : heredero *m*, -ra *f*

heiress [ˈærəs] *n* : heredera *f*

heirloom [ˈærˌluːm] *n* : reliquia *f* de familia

held → **hold**

helicopter [ˈhɛləˌkɑptər] *n* : helicóptero *m*

helium [ˈhiːliəm] *n* : helio *m*

helix [ˈhiːlɪks] *n, pl* **helices** [ˈhɛləˌsiːz, ˈhiː-] *or* **helixes** [ˈhiːlɪksəz] : hélice *f*

hell [ˈhɛl] *n* : infierno *m*

he'll [ˈhiːl, ˈhɪl] (*contraction of* **he shall** *or* **he will**) → **shall, will**

hellish [ˈhɛlɪʃ] *adj* : horroroso, infernal

hello [həˈloː, hɛ-] *interj* : ¡hola!

helm [ˈhɛlm] *n* **1** : timón *m* **2 to take the helm** : tomar el mando

helmet [ˈhɛlmət] *n* : casco *m*

help¹ [ˈhɛlp] *vt* **1** AID, ASSIST : ayudar, auxiliar, socorrer, asistir **2** ALLEVIATE : aliviar **3** SERVE : servir ⟨help yourself! : ¡sírvete!⟩ **4** AVOID : evitar ⟨it can't be helped : no lo podemos evitar, no hay más remedio⟩ ⟨I couldn't help smiling : no pude menos que sonreír⟩

help² *n* **1** ASSISTANCE : ayuda *f* ⟨help! : ¡socorro!, ¡auxilio!⟩ **2** STAFF : personal *m* (en una oficina), servicio *m* doméstico

helper [ˈhɛlpər] *n* : ayudante *mf*

helpful [ˈhɛlpfəl] *adj* **1** OBLIGING : servicial, amable, atento **2** USEFUL : útil, práctico — **helpfully** *adv*

helpfulness [ˈhɛlpfəlnəs] *n* **1** KINDNESS : bondad *f*, amabilidad *f* **2** USEFULNESS : utilidad *f*

helping [ˈhɛlpɪŋ] *n* : porción *f*

helpless [ˈhɛlpləs] *adj* **1** POWERLESS : incapaz, impotente **2** DEFENSELESS : indefenso

helplessly [ˈhɛlpləsli] *adv* : en vano, inútilmente

helplessness [ˈhɛlpləsnəs] *n* POWERLESSNESS : incapacidad *f*, impotencia *f*

helter–skelter [ˌhɛltərˈskɛltər] *adv* : atropelladamente, precipitadamente

hem¹ [ˈhɛm] *vt* **hemmed; hemming 1** : dobladillar **2 to hem in** : encerrar

hem² *n* : dobladillo *m*, bastilla *f*

hemisphere [ˈhɛməˌsfɪr] *n* : hemisferio *m*

hemispheric [ˌhɛməˈsfɪrɪk, -ˈsfr-] *or* **hemispherical** [-ɪkəl] *adj* : hemisférico

hemlock [ˈhɛmˌlɑk] *n* : cicuta *f*

hemoglobin [ˈhiːməˌgloːbən] *n* : hemoglobina *f*

hemophilia [ˌhiːməˈfɪliə] *n* : hemofilia *f*

hemorrhage¹ [ˈhɛmərɪʤ] *vi* **-rhaged; -rhaging** : sufrir una hemorragia

hemorrhage² *n* : hemorragia *f*

hemorrhoids [ˈhɛməˌrɔɪdz, ˈhɛm-ˌrɔɪdz] *npl* : hemorroides *fpl*, almorranas *fpl*

hemp [ˈhɛmp] *n* : cáñamo *m*

hen [ˈhɛn] *n* : gallina *f*

hence [ˈhɛnts] *adv* **1** : de aquí, de ahí ⟨10 years hence : de aquí a 10 años⟩ ⟨a dog bit me, hence my dislike of animals : un perro me mordió, de ahí mi aversión a los animales⟩ **2** THEREFORE : por lo tanto, por consiguiente

henceforth [ˈhɛntsˌforθ, ˌhɛnts-] *adv* : de ahora en adelante

henchman [ˈhɛntʃmən] *n, pl* **-men** [-mən, -ˌmɛn] : secuaz *mf*, esbirro *m*

henpeck [ˈhɛnˌpɛk] *vt* : dominar (al marido)

hepatitis [ˌhɛpəˈtaɪtəs] *n, pl* **-titides** [-ˈtɪtəˌdiːz] : hepatitis *f*

her¹ [ˈhər] *adj* : su, sus, de ella ⟨her house : su casa, la casa de ella⟩

her² [ˈhər, ər] *pron* **1** (*used as direct object*) : la ⟨I saw her yesterday : la vi ayer⟩ **2** (*used as indirect object*) : le, se ⟨he gave her the book : le dio el libro⟩ ⟨he sent it to her : se lo mandó⟩ **3** (*used as object of a preposition*) : ella ⟨we did it for her : lo hicimos por ella⟩ ⟨taller than her : más alto que ella⟩

herald¹ [ˈhɛrəld] *vt* ANNOUNCE : anunciar, proclamar

herald² *n* **1** MESSENGER : heraldo *m* **2** HARBINGER : precursor *m*

heraldic [hɛˈrældɪk, hə-] *adj* : heráldico

heraldry [ˈhɛrəldri] *n, pl* **-ries** : heráldica *f*

herb [ˈərb, ˈhərb] *n* : hierba *f*

herbal [ˈərbəl, ˈhər-] *adj* : herbario

herbicide [ˈərbəˌsaɪd, ˈhər-] *n* : herbicida *m*

herbivore [ˈərbəˌvor, ˈhər-] *n* : herbívoro *m*

herbivorous [ˌərˈbɪvərəs, ˌhər-] *adj* : herbívoro

herculean [ˌhərkjəˈliːən, ˌhərˈkjuː-liən] *adj* : hercúleo, sobrehumano

herd¹ ['hərd] *vt* : reunir en manada, conducir en manada — *vi* : ir en manada (dícese de los animales), apiñarse (dícese de la gente)

herd² *n* : manada *f*

herder ['hərdər] → **herdsman**

herdsman ['hərdzmən] *n, pl* **-men** [-mən, -ˌmɛn] : vaquero *m* (de ganado), pastor *m* (de ovejas)

here ['hɪr] *adv* **1** : aquí, acá ⟨come here! : ¡ven acá!⟩ ⟨right here : aquí mismo⟩ **2** NOW : en este momento, ahora, ya ⟨here he comes : ya viene⟩ ⟨here it's three o'clock (already) : ahora son las tres⟩ **3** : en este punto ⟨here we agree : estamos de acuerdo en este punto⟩ **4** **here you are! : ¡toma!**

hereabouts ['hɪrəˌbaʊts] *or* **hereabout** [-ˌbaʊt] *adv* : por aquí (cerca)

hereafter¹ [hɪr'æftər] *adv* **1** : de aquí en adelante, a continuación **2** : en el futuro

hereafter² *n* **the hereafter** : el más allá

hereby [hɪr'baɪ] *adv* : por este medio

hereditary [hə'rɛdəˌtɛri] *adj* : hereditario

heredity [hə'rɛdəti] *n* : herencia *f*

herein [hɪr'ɪn] *adv* : aquí

hereof [hɪr'ʌv] *adv* : de aquí

hereon [hɪr'ɑn, -'ɔn] *adv* : sobre esto

heresy ['hɛrəsi] *n, pl* **-sies** : herejía *f*

heretic ['hɛrəˌtɪk] *n* : hereje *mf*

heretical [hə'rɛtɪkəl] *adj* : herético

hereto [hɪr'tu:] *adv* : a esto

heretofore ['hɪrtəˌfor] *adv* HITHERTO : hasta ahora

hereunder [hɪr'ʌndər] *adv* : a continuación, abajo

hereupon [hɪrə'pɑn, -'pɔn] *adv* : con esto, en ese momento

herewith [hɪr'wɪθ] *adv* : adjunto

heritage ['hɛrətɪdʒ] *n* : patrimonio *m* (nacional)

hermaphrodite [hər'mæfrəˌdaɪt] *n* : hermafrodita *mf*

hermetic [hər'mɛtɪk] *adj* : hermético — **hermetically** [-tɪkli] *adv*

hermit ['hərmət] *n* : ermitaño *m*, -ña *f*; eremita *mf*

hernia ['hərniə] *n, pl* **-nias** *or* **-niae** [-niˌiː, -niˌaɪ] : hernia *f*

hero ['hɪˌroː, 'hɪrˌoː] *n, pl* **-roes** **1** : héroe *m* **2** PROTAGONIST : protagonista *mf*

heroic [hɪ'roːɪk] *adj* : heroico — **heroically** [-ɪkli] *adv*

heroics [hɪ'roːɪks] *npl* : actos *mpl* heroicos

heroin ['hɛroən] *n* : heroína *f*

heroine ['hɛroən] *n* **1** : heroína *f* **2** PROTAGONIST : protagonista *f*

heroism ['hɛroˌɪzəm] *n* : heroísmo *m*

heron ['hɛrən] *n* : garza *f*

herpes ['hərˌpiːz] *n* : herpes *m*

herring ['hɛrɪŋ] *n, pl* **-ring** *or* **-rings** : arenque *m*

hers ['hərz] *pron* : suyo, -ya; suyos, -yas; de ella ⟨these shoes are hers : estos zapatos son suyos⟩ ⟨hers are bigger : los de ella son más grandes⟩

herself [hər'sɪlf] *pron* **1** (*used reflexively*) : se ⟨she dressed herself : se vistió⟩ **2** (*used emphatically*) : ella misma ⟨she fixed it herself : lo arregló ella misma, lo arregló por sí sola⟩

hertz ['hərts, 'hrts] *ns & pl* : hercio *m*

he's ['hiːz] (*contraction of* **he is** *or* **he has**) → **be, have**

hesitancy ['hɛzətəntsi] *n, pl* **-cies** : vacilación *f*, titubeo *m*, indecisión *f*

hesitant ['hɛzətənt] *adj* : titubeante, vacilante — **hesitantly** *adv*

hesitate ['hɛzəˌteɪt] *vi* **-tated; -tating** : vacilar, titubear

hesitation [ˌhɛzə'teɪʃən] *n* : vacilación *f*, indecisión *f*, titubeo *m*

heterogeneous [ˌhɛtərə'dʒiːniəs, -njəs] *adj* : heterogéneo

heterosexual¹ [ˌhɛtəro'skʃʊəl] *adj* : heterosexual

heterosexual² *n* : heterosexual *mf*

heterosexuality [ˌhɛtəroˌskʃʊ'ælətɪ] *n* : heterosexualidad *f*

hew ['hjuː] *v* **hewed; hewed** *or* **hewn** ['hjuːn]; **hewing** *vt* **1** CUT : cortar, talar (árboles) **2** SHAPE : labrar, tallar — *vi* CONFORM : conformarse, ceñirse

hex¹ ['hɛks] *vt* : hacerle un maleficio (a alguien)

hex² *n* : maleficio *m*

hexagon ['hɛksəˌgɑn] *n* : hexágono *m*

hexagonal [hɛk'sægənəl] *adj* : hexagonal

hey ['heɪ] *interj* : ¡eh!, ¡oye!

heyday ['heɪˌdeɪ] *n* : auge *m*, apogeo *m*

hi ['haɪ] *interj* : ¡hola!

hiatus [haɪ'eɪtəs] *n* **1** : hiato *m* **2** PAUSE : pausa *f*

hibernate ['haɪbərˌneɪt] *vi* **-nated; -nating** : hibernar, invernar

hibernation [ˌhaɪbər'neɪʃən] *n* : hibernación *f*

hiccup¹ ['hɪkəp] *vi* **-cuped; -cuping** : hipar, tener hipo

hiccup² *n* : hipo *m* ⟨to have the hiccups : tener hipo⟩

hick ['hɪk] *n* BUMPKIN : palurdo *m*, -da *f*

hickory ['hɪkəri] *n, pl* **-ries** : nogal *m* americano

hidden ['hɪdən] *adj* : oculto

hide¹ ['haɪd] *v* **hid** ['hɪd]; **hidden** ['hɪdən] *or* **hid; hiding** *vt* **1** CONCEAL : esconder **2** : ocultar ⟨to hide one's motives : ocultar unos sus motivos⟩ **3** SCREEN : tapar, no dejar ver — *vi* : esconderse

hide² *n* : piel *f*, cuero *m* ⟨to save one's hide : salvar el pellejo⟩

hide-and-seek ['haɪdənd'siːk] *n* **to play hide-and-seek** : jugar a las escondidas

hidebound ['haɪdˌbaʊnd] *adj* : rígido, conservador

hideous ['hɪdiəs] *adj* : horrible, horroroso, espantoso — **hideously** *adv*

hideout ['haɪdˌaʊt] *n* : guarida *f*, escondrijo *m*

hierarchical [ˌhaɪə'rɑrkɪkəl] *adj* : jerárquico

hierarchy ['haɪə,rɑrki] *n, pl* **-chies** : jerarquía *f*

hieroglyphic [,haɪərə'glɪfɪk] *n* : jeroglífico *m*

hi–fi ['haɪ'faɪ] *n* **1** → **high fidelity 2** : equipo *m* de alta fidelidad

high¹ ['haɪ] *adv* : alto

high² *adj* **1** TALL : alto ⟨a high wall : una pared alta⟩ **2** ELEVATED : alto, elevado ⟨high prices : precios elevados⟩ ⟨high blood pressure : presión alta⟩ **3** GREAT, IMPORTANT : grande, importante, alto ⟨a high number : un número grande⟩ ⟨high society : alta sociedad⟩ ⟨high hopes : grandes esperanzas⟩ **4** : alto (en música) **5** INTOXICATED : borracho, drogado

high³ *n* **1** : récord *m*, punto *m* máximo ⟨to reach an all-time high : batir el récord⟩ **2** : zona *f* de alta presión (en meteorología) **3** *or* **high gear** : directa *f* **4 on high** : en las alturas

highbrow ['haɪ,braʊ] *n* : intelectual *mf*

higher ['haɪər] *adj* : superior

high fidelity *n* : alta fidelidad *f*

high–flown ['haɪ'floːn] *adj* : altisonante

high–handed ['haɪ'hændəd] *adj* : arbitrario

highlands ['haɪləndz] *npl* : tierras *fpl* altas, altiplano *m*

highlight¹ ['haɪ,laɪt] *vt* **1** EMPHASIZE : destacar, poner en relieve, subrayar **2** : ser el punto culminante de

highlight² *n* : punto *m* culminante

highly ['haɪli] *adv* **1** VERY : muy, sumamente **2** FAVORABLY : muy bien ⟨to speak highly of : hablar muy bien de⟩ ⟨to think highly of : tener en mucho a⟩

highness ['haɪnəs] *n* **1** HEIGHT : altura *f* **2 Highness** : Alteza *f* ⟨Your Royal Highness : Su Alteza Real⟩

high–pitched ['haɪ'pɪtʃt] *adj* : agudo

high–rise ['haɪ,raɪz] *adj* : alto, de muchas plantas

high school *n* : escuela *f* superior, escuela *f* secundaria

high seas *npl* : alta mar *f*

high–spirited ['haɪ'spɪrətəd] *adj* : vivaz, muy animado, brioso

high–strung [,haɪ'strʌŋ] *adj* : nervioso, excitable

highway ['haɪ,weɪ] *n* : carretera *f*

highwayman ['haɪ,weɪmən] *n, pl* **-men** [-mən, -,mɛn] : salteador *m* (de caminos), bandido *m*

hijack¹ ['haɪ,dʒæk] *vt* : secuestrar

hijack² *n* : secuestro *m*

hijacker ['haɪ,dʒækər] *n* : secuestrador *m*, -dora *f*

hike¹ ['haɪk] *v* **hiked; hiking** *vi* : hacer una caminata — *vt* RAISE : subir

hike² *n* **1** : caminata *f*, excursión *f* **2** INCREASE : subida *f* (de precios)

hiker ['haɪkər] *n* : excursionista *mf*

hilarious [hɪ'læriəs, haɪ-] *adj* : muy divertido, hilarante

hilarity [hɪ'lærəti, haɪ-] *n* : hilaridad *f*

hill ['hɪl] *n* **1** : colina *f*, cerro *m* **2** SLOPE : cuesta *f*, pendiente *f*

hillbilly ['hɪl,bɪli] *n, pl* **-lies** : palurdo *m*, -da *f* (de las montañas)

hillock ['hɪlək] *n* : loma *f*, altozano *m*, otero *m*

hillside ['hɪl,saɪd] *n* : ladera *f*, cuesta *f*

hilltop ['hɪl,tɑp] *n* : cima *f*, cumbre *f*

hilly ['hɪli] *adj* **hillier; -est** : montañoso, accidentado

hilt ['hɪlt] *n* : puño *m*, empuñadura *f*

him ['hɪm, əm] *pron* **1** (*used as direct object*) : lo ⟨I found him : lo encontré⟩ **2** (*used as indirect object*) : le, se ⟨we gave him a present : le dimos un regalo⟩ ⟨I sent it to him : se lo mandé⟩ **3** (*used as object of a preposition*) : él ⟨she was thinking of him : pensaba en él⟩ ⟨younger than him : más joven que él⟩

himself [hɪm'sɛlf] *pron* **1** (*used reflexively*) : se ⟨he washed himself : se lavó⟩ **2** (*used emphatically*) : él mismo ⟨he did it himself : lo hizo él mismo, lo hizo por sí solo⟩

hind¹ ['haɪnd] *adj* : trasero, posterior ⟨hind legs : patas traseras⟩

hind² *n* : cierva *f*

hinder ['hɪndər] *vt* : dificultar, impedir, estorbar

Hindi ['hɪndi:] *n* : hindi *m*

hindquarters ['haɪnd,kwɔrtərz] *npl* : cuartos *mpl* traseros

hindrance ['hɪndrənts] *n* : estorbo *m*, obstáculo *m*, impedimento *m*

hindsight ['haɪnd,saɪt] *n* : retrospectiva *f* ⟨with the benefit of hindsight : en retrospectiva, con la perspectiva que da la experiencia⟩

Hindu¹ ['hɪn,du:] *adj* : hindú

Hindu² *n* : hindú *mf*

Hinduism ['hɪndu,ɪzəm] *n* : hinduismo *m*

hinge¹ ['hɪndʒ] *v* **hinged; hinging** *vt* : unir con bisagras — *vi* **to hinge on** : depender de

hinge² *n* : bisagra *f*, gozne *m*

hint¹ ['hɪnt] *vt* : insinuar, dar a entender — *vi* : soltar indirectas

hint² *n* **1** INSINUATION : insinuación *f*, indirecta *f* **2** TIP : consejo *m*, sugerencia *f* **3** TRACE : pizca *f*, indicio *m*

hinterland ['hɪntər,lænd, -lənd] *n* : interior *m* (de un país)

hip ['hɪp] *n* : cadera *f*

hip-hop ['hɪp,hɑp] *n* : hip-hop *m*

hippie ['hɪpi] *n* : hippie *mf*, hippy *mf*

hippopotamus [,hɪpə'pɑtəməs] *n, pl* **-muses** *or* **-mi** [-,maɪ] : hipopótamo *m*

hippo ['hɪpo:] *n, pl* **hippos** → **hippopotamus**

hire¹ ['haɪr] *vt* **hired; hiring 1** EMPLOY : contratar, emplear **2** RENT : alquilar, arrendar

hire² *n* **1** RENT : alquiler *m* ⟨for hire : se alquila⟩ **2** WAGES : paga *f*, sueldo *m* **3** EMPLOYEE : empleado *m*, -da *f*

his¹ ['hɪz, ɪz] *adj* : su, sus, de él ⟨his hat : su sombrero, el sombrero de él⟩

his² *pron* : suyo, -ya; suyos, suyas; de él ⟨the decision is his : la decisión es suya⟩ ⟨it's his, not hers : es de él, no de ella⟩

Hispanic¹ [hɪ'spænɪk] *adj* : hispano, hispánico
Hispanic² *n* : hispano *m*, -na *f*; hispánico *m*, -ca *f*
hiss¹ ['hɪs] *vi* : sisear, silbar — *vt* : decir entre dientes
hiss² *n* : siseo *m*, silbido *m*
historian [hɪ'stɔriən] *n* : historiador *m*, -dora *f*
historic [hɪ'stɔrɪk] *or* **historical** [-ɪkəl] *adj* : histórico — **historically** [-ɪkli] *adv*
history ['hɪstəri] *n*, *pl* **-ries** 1 : historia *f* 2 RECORD : historial *m*
histrionics [ˌhɪstri'ɑnɪks] *ns & pl* : histrionismo *m*
hit¹ ['hɪt] *v* **hit; hitting** *vt* 1 STRIKE : golpear, pegar, batear (una pelota) ⟨he hit the dog : le pegó al perro⟩ 2 : chocar contra, dar con, dar en (el blanco) ⟨the car hit a tree : el coche chocó contra un árbol⟩ 3 AFFECT : afectar ⟨the news hit us hard : la noticia nos afectó mucho⟩ 4 ENCOUNTER : tropezar con, toparse con ⟨to hit a snag : tropezar con un obstáculo⟩ 5 REACH : llegar a, alcanzar ⟨the price hit $10 a pound : el precio alcanzó los $10 dólares por libra⟩ ⟨to hit town : llegar a la ciudad⟩ ⟨to hit the headlines : ser noticia⟩ **6 to hit on** *or* **to hit upon** : dar con — *vi* : golpear
hit² *n* 1 BLOW : golpe *m* 2 : impacto *m* (de un arma) 3 SUCCESS : éxito *m*
hitch¹ ['hɪtʃ] *vt* 1 : mover con sacudidas 2 ATTACH : enganchar, atar, amarrar 3 → **hitchhike** **4 to hitch up** : subirse (los pantalones, etc.)
hitch² *n* 1 JERK : tirón *m*, jalón *m* 2 OBSTACLE : obstáculo *m*, impedimento *m*, tropiezo *m*
hitchhike ['hɪtʃˌhaɪk] *vi* **-hiked; -hiking** : hacer autostop, ir de aventón *Col, Mex fam*
hitchhiker ['hɪtʃˌhaɪkər] *n* : autostopista *mf*
hither ['hɪðər] *adv* : acá, por aquí
hitherto ['hɪðərˌtuː, ˌhɪðər'-] *adv* : hasta ahora
hitter ['hɪtər] *n* BATTER : bateador *m*, -dora *f*
HIV [ˌeɪtʃˌaɪ'viː] *n* (*human immunodeficiency virus*) : VIH *m*, virus *m* del sida
hive ['haɪv] *n* 1 : colmena *f* 2 SWARM : enjambre *m* 3 : lugar *m* muy activo ⟨a hive of activity : un hervidero de actividad⟩
hives ['haɪvz] *ns & pl* : urticaria *f*
hoard¹ ['hɔrd] *vt* : acumular, atesorar
hoard² *n* : tesoro *m*, reserva *f*, provisión *f*
hoarfrost ['hɔrˌfrɔst] *n* : escarcha *f*
hoarse ['hɔrs] *adj* **hoarser; -est** : ronco — **hoarsely** *adv*
hoarseness ['hɔrsnəs] *n* : ronquera *f*
hoary ['hɔri] *adj* **hoarier; -est** 1 : cano, canoso 2 OLD : vetusto, antiguo
hoax¹ ['hoːks] *vt* : engañar, embaucar, bromear

hoax² *n* : engaño *m*, broma *f*
hobble¹ ['hɑbəl] *v* **-bled; -bling** *vi* LIMP : cojear, renguear — *vt* : manear (un animal)
hobble² *n* 1 LIMP : cojera *f*, rengo *m* 2 : maniota *f* (para un animal)
hobby ['hɑbi] *n*, *pl* **-bies** : pasatiempo *m*, afición *f*
hobgoblin ['hɑbˌgɑblən] *n* : duende *m*
hobnail ['hɑbˌneɪl] *n* : tachuela *f*
hobnob ['hɑbˌnɑb] *vi* **-nobbed; -nobbing** : codearse
hobo ['hoːˌboː] *n*, *pl* **-boes** : vagabundo *m*, -da *f*
hock¹ ['hɑk] *vt* PAWN : empeñar
hock² *n* in hock : empeñado
hockey ['hɑki] *n* : hockey *m*
hodgepodge ['hɑdʒˌpɑdʒ] *n* : mezcolanza *f*
hoe¹ ['hoː] *vt* **hoed; hoeing** : azadonar
hoe² *n* : azada *f*, azadón *m*
hog¹ ['hɔg, 'hɑg] *vt* **hogged; hogging** : acaparar, monopolizar
hog² *n* 1 PIG : cerdo *m*, -da *f* 2 GLUTTON : glotón *m*, -tona *f*
hogshead ['hɔgzˌhɛd, 'hɑgz-] *n* : tonel *m*
hoist¹ ['hɔɪst] *vt* : levantar, alzar, izar (una bandera, una vela)
hoist² *n* : grúa *f*
hold¹ ['hoːld] *v* **held** ['hɛld]; **holding** *vt* 1 POSSESS : tener ⟨to hold office : ocupar un puesto⟩ 2 RESTRAIN : detener, controlar ⟨to hold one's temper : controlar su mal genio⟩ 3 CLASP, GRASP : agarrar, coger ⟨to hold hands : agarrarse de la mano⟩ 4 : sujetar, mantener fijo ⟨hold this nail for me : sujétame este clavo⟩ 5 CONTAIN : contener, dar cabida a 6 SUPPORT : aguantar, sostener 7 REGARD : considerar, tener ⟨he held me responsible : me consideró responsable⟩ 8 CONDUCT : celebrar (una reunión), realizar (un evento), mantener (una conversación) — *vi* 1 : aguantar, resistir ⟨the rope will hold : la cuerda resistirá⟩ 2 : ser válido, valer ⟨my offer still holds : mi oferta todavía es válida⟩ **3 to hold forth** : perorar, arengar **4 to hold to** : mantenerse firme en **5 to hold with** : estar de acuerdo con
hold² *n* 1 GRIP : agarre *m*, llave *f* (en deportes) 2 CONTROL : control *m*, dominio *m* ⟨to get hold of oneself : controlarse⟩ 3 DELAY : demora *f* ⟨to put on hold : suspender temporalmente⟩ 4 : bodega *f* (en un barco o un avión) 5 **to get hold of** : conseguir, localizar
holder ['hoːldər] *n* : poseedor *m*, -dora *f*; titular *mf*
holdings ['hoːldɪŋz] *npl* : propiedades *fpl*
hold out *vi* 1 LAST : aguantar, durar 2 RESIST : resistir
holdup ['hoːldˌʌp] *n* 1 ROBBERY : atraco *m* 2 DELAY : retraso *m*, demora *f*
hold up *vt* 1 ROB : robarle (a alguien), atracar, asaltar 2 DELAY : retrasar
hole ['hoːl] *n* : agujero *m*, hoyo *m*

holiday [ˈhɑləˌdeɪ] *n* **1** : día *m* feriado, fiesta *f* **2** VACATION : vacaciones *fpl*

holiness [ˈhoːlinəs] *n* **1** : santidad *f* **2** **His Holiness** : Su Santidad

holistic [hoːˈlɪstɪk] *adj* : holístico

holler¹ [ˈhɑlər] *vi* : gritar, chillar

holler² *n* : grito *m*, chillido *m*

hollow¹ [ˈhɑˌloː] *vt or* **to hollow out** : ahuecar

hollow² *adj* **-lower; -est 1** : hueco, hundido (dícese de las mejillas, etc.), cavernoso (dícese de un sonido) **2** EMPTY, FALSE : vacío, falso

hollow³ *n* **1** CAVITY : hueco *m*, depresión *f*, cavidad *f* **2** VALLEY : hondonada *f*, valle *m*

hollowness [ˈhɑˌloːnəs] *n* **1** HOLLOW : hueco *m*, cavidad *f* **2** FALSENESS : falsedad *f* **3** EMPTINESS : vacuidad *f*

holly [ˈhɑli] *n, pl* **-lies** : acebo *m*

hollyhock [ˈhɑliˌhɑk] *n* : malvarrosa *f*

holocaust [ˈhɑləˌkɔst, ˈhoː-, ˈhɔ-] *n* : holocausto *m*

hologram [ˈhoːləˌgræm, ˈhɑ-] *n* : holograma *m*

holster [ˈhoːlstər] *n* : pistolera *f*

holy [ˈhoːli] *adj* **-lier; -est** : santo, sagrado

Holy Ghost → Holy Spirit

Holy Spirit *n* **the Holy Spirit** : el Espíritu Santo

homage [ˈɑmɪdʒ, ˈhɑ-] *n* : homenaje *m*

home [ˈhoːm] *n* **1** : casa *f*, hogar *m*, domicilio *m* ⟨to feel at home : sentirse en casa⟩ **2** INSTITUTION : residencia *f*, asilo *m*

homecoming [ˈhoːmˌkʌmɪŋ] *n* : regreso *m* (a casa)

homegrown [ˈhoːmˈgroːn] *adj* **1** : de cosecha propia **2** LOCAL : local

homeland [ˈhoːmˌlænd] *n* : patria *f*, tierra *f* natal, terruño *m*

homeless [ˈhoːmləs] *adj* : sin hogar, sin techo

homely [ˈhoːmli] *adj* **-lier; -est 1** DOMESTIC : casero, hogareño **2** UGLY : feo, poco atractivo

homemade [ˈhoːmˈmeɪd] *adj* : casero, hecho en casa

homemaker [ˈhoːmˌmeɪkər] *n* : ama *f* de casa, persona *f* que se ocupa de la casa

home plate *n* : base *f* del bateador

home run *n* : jonrón *m*

homesick [ˈhoːmˌsɪk] *adj* : nostálgico ⟨to be homesick : echar de menos a la familia⟩

homesickness [ˈhoːmˌsɪknəs] *n* : nostalgia *f*, morriña *f*

homespun [ˈhoːmˌspʌn] *adj* : simple, sencillo

homestead [ˈhoːmˌstɛd] *n* : estancia *f*, hacienda *f*

homeward¹ [ˈhoːmwərd] *or* **homewards** [-wərdz] *adv* : de vuelta a casa, hacia casa

homeward² *adj* : de vuelta, de regreso

homework [ˈhoːmˌwərk] *n* : tarea *f*, deberes *mpl Spain*, asignación *f PRi*

homey [ˈhoːmi] *adj* **homier; -est** : hogareño

homicidal [ˌhɑməˈsaɪdəl, ˌhoː-] *adj* : homicida

homicide [ˈhɑməˌsaɪd, ˈhoː-] *n* : homicidio *m*

hominy [ˈhɑməni] *n* : maíz *m* descascarillado

homogeneity [ˌhoːmədʒəˈniːəti, -ˈneɪ-] *n, pl* **-ties** : homogeneidad *f*

homogeneous [ˌhoːməˈdʒiːniəs, -njəs] *adj* : homogéneo — **homogeneously** *adv*

homogenize [hoːˈmɑdʒəˌnaɪz, hə-] *vt* **-nized; -nizing** : homogeneizar

homograph [ˈhɑməˌgræf, ˈhoː-] *n* : homógrafo *m*

homologous [hoːˈmɑləgəs, hə-] *adj* : homólogo

homonym [ˈhɑməˌnɪm, ˈhoː-] *n* : homónimo *m*

homophone [ˈhɑməˌfoːn, ˈhoː-] *n* : homófono *m*

homosexual¹ [ˌhoːməˈsɛkʃuəl] *adj* : homosexual

homosexual² *n* : homosexual *mf*

homosexuality [ˌhoːməˌsɛkʃuˈæləti] *n* : homosexualidad *f*

honcho [ˈhɑnˌtʃoː] *n* : pez *m* gordo ⟨the head honcho : el jefe⟩

Honduran [hɑnˈdʊrən, -ˈdjʊr-] *n* : hondureño *m*, -ña *f* — **Honduran** *adj*

hone [ˈhoːn] *vt* **honed; honing** : afilar

honest [ˈɑnəst] *adj* : honesto, honrado — **honestly** *adv*

honesty [ˈɑnəsti] *n, pl* **-ties** : honestidad *f*, honradez *f*

honey [ˈhʌni] *n, pl* **-eys** : miel *f*

honeybee [ˈhʌniˌbiː] *n* : abeja *f*

honeycomb [ˈhʌniˌkoːm] *n* : panal *m*

honeymoon¹ [ˈhʌniˌmuːn] *vi* : pasar la luna de miel

honeymoon² *n* : luna *f* de miel

honeysuckle [ˈhʌniˌsʌkəl] *n* : madreselva *f*

honk¹ [ˈhɑŋk, ˈhɔŋk] *vi* **1** : graznar (dícese del ganso) **2** : tocar la bocina (dícese de un vehículo), pitar

honk² *n* : graznido *m* (del ganso), bocinazo *m* (de un vehículo)

honor¹ [ˈɑnər] *vt* **1** RESPECT : honrar **2** : cumplir con ⟨to honor one's word : cumplir con su palabra⟩ **3** : aceptar (un cheque, etc.)

honor² *n* **1** : honor *m* ⟨in honor of : en honor de⟩ **2 honors** *npl* AWARDS : honores *mpl*, condecoraciones *fpl* **3 Your Honor** : Su Señoría

honorable [ˈɑnərəbəl] *adj* : honorable, honroso — **honorably** [-bli] *adv*

honorary [ˈɑnəˌrɛri] *adj* : honorario

hood [ˈhʊd] *n* **1** : capucha *f* **2** : capó *m*, bonete *m Car* (de un automóvil)

hooded [ˈhʊdəd] *adj* : encapuchado

hoodlum [ˈhʊdləm, ˈhuː-] *n* THUG : maleante *mf*, matón *m*

hoodwink [ˈhʊdˌwɪŋk] *vt* : engañar

hoof ['hʊf, 'hu:f] *n, pl* **hooves** ['hʊvz, 'hu:vz] *or* **hoofs** : pezuña *f*, casco *m*
hoofed ['hʊft, 'hu:ft] *adj* : ungulado
hook¹ ['hʊk] *vt* : enganchar — *vi* : abrocharse, engancharse
hook² *n* : gancho *m*, percha *f*
hooked ['hʊkt] *adj* **1** : en forma de gancho **2 to be hooked on** : estar enganchado a
hooker ['hʊkər] *n* : prostituta *f*, fulana *f* fam
hookworm ['hʊk,wərm] *n* : anquilostoma *m*
hooligan ['hu:lɪgən] *n* : gamberro *m*, -rra *f*
hoop ['hu:p] *n* : aro *m*
hooray [hʊ'reɪ] → **hurrah**
hoot¹ ['hu:t] *vi* **1** SHOUT : gritar ⟨to hoot with laughter : morirse de risa, reírse a carcajadas⟩ **2** : ulular (dícese de un búho), tocar la bocina (dícese de un vehículo), silbar (dícese de un tren o un barco)
hoot² *n* **1** : ululato *m* (de un búho), silbido *m* (de un tren), bocinazo *m* (de un vehículo) **2** GUFFAW : carcajada *f*, risotada *f* **3 I don't give a hoot** : me vale un comino, me importa un pito
hop¹ ['hɑp] *vi* **hopped; hopping** : brincar, saltar
hop² *n* **1** LEAP : salto *m*, brinco *m* **2** FLIGHT : vuelo *m* corto **3** : lúpulo *m* (planta)
hope¹ ['ho:p] *v* **hoped; hoping** *vi* : esperar — *vt* : esperar que ⟨we hope she comes : esperamos que venga⟩ ⟨I hope not : espero que no⟩
hope² *n* : esperanza *f*
hopeful ['ho:pfəl] *adj* : esperanzado — **hopefully** *adv*
hopeless ['ho:pləs] *adj* **1** DESPAIRING : desesperado **2** IMPOSSIBLE : imposible ⟨a hopeless case : un caso perdido⟩
hopelessly ['ho:pləsli] *adv* **1** : sin esperanzas, desesperadamente **2** COMPLETELY : totalmente, completamente **3** IMPOSSIBLY : imposiblemente
hopelessness ['ho:pləsnəs] *n* : desesperanza *f*
hopper ['hɑpər] *n* : tolva *f*
hopscotch ['hɑp,skɑtʃ] *n* : tejo *m*
horde ['hord] *n* : horda *f*, multitud *f*
horizon [hə'raɪzən] *n* : horizonte *m*
horizontal [,hɔrə'zɑntəl] *adj* : horizontal — **horizontally** *adv*
hormone ['hɔr,mo:n] *n* : hormona *f* — **hormonal** [hɔr'mo:nəl] *adj*
horn ['hɔrn] *n* **1** : cuerno *m* (de un toro, una vaca, etc.) **2** : cuerno *m*, trompa *f* (instrumento musical) **3** : bocina *f*, claxon *m* (de un vehículo)
horned ['hɔrnd, 'hɔrnəd] *adj* : cornudo, astado, con cuernos
hornet ['hɔrnət] *n* : avispón *m*
horny ['hɔrni] *adj* **hornier; -est 1** CALLOUS : calloso **2** LUSTFUL *fam* : caliente *fam*
horoscope ['hɔrə,sko:p] *n* : horóscopo *m*

horrendous [hɔ'rɛndəs] *adj* : horrendo, horroroso, atroz
horrible ['hɔrəbəl] *adj* : horrible, espantoso, horroroso — **horribly** [-bli] *adv*
horrid ['hɔrɪd] *adj* : horroroso, horrible — **horridly** *adv*
horrific [hɔ'rɪfɪk] *adj* : terrorífico, horroroso
horrify ['hɔrə,faɪ] *vt* **-fied; -fying** : horrorizar
horrifying ['hɔrə,faɪɪŋ] *adj* : horripilante, horroroso
horror ['hɔrər] *n* : horror *m*
hors d'oeuvre [ɔr'dərv] *n, pl* **hors d'oeuvres** [-'dərvz] : entremés *m*
horse ['hɔrs] *n* : caballo *m*
horseback ['hɔrs,bæk] *n* **on ~** : a caballo
horse chestnut *n* : castaña *f* de Indias
horsefly ['hɔrs,flaɪ] *n, pl* **-flies** : tábano *m*
horsehair ['hɔrs,hær] *n* : crin *f*
horseman ['hɔrsmən] *n, pl* **-men** [-mən, -,mɛn] : jinete *m*, caballista *m*
horsemanship ['hɔrsmən,ʃɪp] *n* : equitación *f*
horseplay ['hɔrs,pleɪ] *n* : payasadas *fpl*
horsepower ['hɔrs,paʊər] *n* : caballo *m* de fuerza
horseradish ['hɔrs,rædɪʃ] *n* : rábano *m* picante
horseshoe ['hɔrs,ʃu:] *n* : herradura *f*
horsewhip ['hɔrs,ʰwɪp] *vt* **-whipped; -whipping** : azotar, darle fuetazos (a alguien)
horsewoman ['hɔrs,wʊmən] *n, pl* **-women** [-,wɪmən] : amazona *f*, jinete *f*, caballista *f*
horsey *or* **horsy** ['hɔrsi] *adj* **horsier; -est** : relacionado a los caballos, caballar
horticultural [,hɔrtə'kʌltʃərəl] *adj* : hortícola
horticulture ['hɔrtə,kʌltʃər] *n* : horticultura *f*
hose¹ ['ho:z] *vt* **hosed; hosing** : regar o lavar con manguera
hose² *n* **1** *pl* **hose** SOCKS : calcetines *mpl*, medias *fpl* **2** *pl* **hose** STOCKINGS : medias *fpl* **3** *pl* **hoses** : manguera *f*, manga *f*
hosiery ['ho:ʒəri, 'ho:zə-] *n* : calcetería *f*, medias *fpl*
hospice ['hɑspəs] *n* : hospicio *m*
hospitable [hɑ'spɪtəbəl, 'hɑs,pɪ-] *adj* : hospitalario — **hospitably** [-bli] *adv*
hospital ['hɑs,pɪtəl] *n* : hospital *m*
hospitality [,hɑspə'tæləti] *n, pl* **-ties** : hospitalidad *f*
hospitalization [,hɑs,pɪtələ'zeɪʃən] *n* : hospitalización *f*
hospitalize ['hɑs,pɪtəl,aɪz] *vt* **-ized; -izing** : hospitalizar
host¹ ['ho:st] *vt* : presentar (un programa de televisión, etc.)
host² *n* **1** : anfitrión *m*, -triona *f* (en la casa, a un evento); presentador *m*, -dora *f* (de un programa de televisión, etc.) **2** *or* **host organism** : huésped *m*

3 TROOPS : huestes *fpl* 4 MULTITUDE : multitud *f* ⟨for a host of reasons : por muchas razones⟩ 5 EUCHARIST : hostia *f*, Eucaristía *f*

hostage ['hɑstɪdʒ] *n* : rehén *m*

hostel ['hɑstəl] *n* : albergue *m* juvenil

hostess ['ho:stɪs] *n* : anfitriona *f* (en la casa), presentadora *f* (de un programa)

hostile ['hɑstəl, -ˌtaɪl] *adj* : hostil — **hostilely** *adv*

hostility [hɑs'tɪləti] *n, pl* -**ties** : hostilidad *f*

hot ['hɑt] *adj* **hotter; hottest** 1 : caliente, cálido, caluroso ⟨hot water : agua caliente⟩ ⟨a hot climate : un clima cálido⟩ ⟨a hot day : un día caluroso⟩ 2 ARDENT, FIERY : ardiente, acalorado ⟨to have a hot temper : tener mal genio⟩ 3 SPICY : picante 4 FRESH : reciente, nuevo ⟨hot news : noticias de última hora⟩ 5 EAGER : ávido 6 STOLEN : robado

hot air *n* : palabrería *f*

hotbed ['hɑt,bɛd] *n* 1 : semillero *m* (de plantas) 2 : hervidero *m*, semillero *m* (de crimen, etc.)

hot dog *n* : perro *m* caliente

hotel [ho:'tɛl] *n* : hotel *m*

hothead ['hɑt,hɛd] *n* : exaltado *m*, -da *f*

hotheaded ['hɑt,hɛdəd] *adj* : exaltado

hothouse ['hɑt,haʊs] *n* : invernadero *m*

hot plate *n* : placa *f* (de cocina)

hot rod *n* : coche *m* con motor modificado

hot water *n* **to get into hot water** : meterse en un lío

hound[1] ['haʊnd] *vt* : acosar, perseguir

hound[2] *n* : perro *m* (de caza)

hour ['aʊər] *n* : hora *f*

hourglass ['aʊər,glæs] *n* : reloj *m* de arena

hourly ['aʊərli] *adv & adj* : cada hora, por hora

house[1] ['haʊz] *vt* **housed; housing** : albergar, alojar, hospedar

house[2] ['haʊs] *n, pl* **houses** ['haʊzəz, -səz] 1 HOME : casa *f* 2 : cámara *f* (del gobierno) 3 BUSINESS : casa *f*, empresa *f*

houseboat ['haʊs,bo:t] *n* : casa *f* flotante

housebroken ['haʊs,bro:kən] *adj* : enseñado

housefly ['haʊs,flaɪ] *n, pl* -**flies** : mosca *f* común

household[1] ['haʊs,ho:ld] *adj* 1 DOMESTIC : doméstico, de la casa 2 FAMILIAR : conocido por todos

household[2] *n* : casa *f*, familia *f*

householder ['haʊs,ho:ldər] *n* : dueño *m*, -ña *f* de casa

housekeeper ['haʊs,ki:pər] *n* : ama *f* de llaves

housekeeping ['haʊs,ki:pɪŋ] *n* : gobierno *m* de la casa, quehaceres *mpl* domésticos

housemaid ['haʊs,meɪd] *n* : criada *f*, mucama *f*, muchacha *f*, sirvienta *f*

housewarming ['haʊs,wɔrmɪŋ] *n* : fiesta *f* de estreno de una casa

housewife ['haʊs,waɪf] *n, pl* -**wives** : ama *f* de casa

housework ['haʊs,wərk] *n* : faenas *fpl* domésticas, quehaceres *mpl* domésticos

housing ['haʊzɪŋ] *n* 1 HOUSES : vivienda *f* 2 COVERING : caja *f* protectora

hove → **heave**

hovel ['hʌvəl, 'hɑ-] *n* : casucha *f*, tugurio *m*

hover ['hʌvər, 'hɑ-] *vi* 1 : cernerse, sostenerse en el aire 2 **to hover about** : rondar

how ['haʊ] *adv* 1 : cómo ⟨how are you? : ¿cómo estás?⟩ ⟨I don't know how to fix it : no se cómo arreglarlo⟩ 2 : qué ⟨how beautiful! : ¡qué bonito!⟩ 3 : cuánto ⟨how old are you? : ¿cuántos años tienes?⟩ 4 **how about...?** : ¿qué te parece...?

however[1] [haʊ'ɛvər] *adv* 1 : por mucho que, por más que ⟨however hot it is : por mucho calor que haga⟩ 2 NEVERTHELESS : sin embargo, no obstante

however[2] *conj* : comoquiera que, de cualquier manera que

howl[1] ['haʊl] *vi* : aullar

howl[2] *n* : aullido *m*, alarido *m*

hub ['hʌb] *n* 1 CENTER : centro *m* 2 : cubo *m* (de una rueda)

hubbub ['hʌ,bʌb] *n* : algarabía *f*, alboroto *m*, jaleo *m*

hubcap ['hʌb,kæp] *n* : tapacubos *m*

huckster ['hʌkstər] *n* : buhonero *m*, -ra *f*; vendedor *m*, -dora *f* ambulante

huddle[1] ['hʌdəl] *vi* -**dled; -dling** 1 : apiñarse, amontonarse 2 **to huddle together** : acurrucarse

huddle[2] *n* : grupo *m* (cerrado) ⟨to go into a huddle : conferenciar en secreto⟩

hue ['hju:] *n* : color *m*, tono *m*

huff ['hʌf] *n* : enojo *m*, enfado *m* ⟨to be in a huff : estar enojado⟩

huffy ['hʌfi] *adj* **huffier; -est** : enojado, enfadado

hug[1] ['hʌg] *vt* **hugged; hugging** 1 EMBRACE : abrazar 2 : ir pegado a ⟨the road hugs the river : el camino está pegado al río⟩

hug[2] *n* : abrazo *m*

huge ['hju:dʒ] *adj* **huger; hugest** : inmenso, enorme — **hugely** *adv*

hulk ['hʌlk] *n* 1 : persona *f* fornida 2 : casco *m* (barco), armatoste *m* (edificio, etc.)

hulking ['hʌlkɪŋ] *adj* : grandote *fam*, pesado

hull[1] ['hʌl] *vt* : pelar

hull[2] *n* 1 HUSK : cáscara *f* 2 : casco *m* (de un barco, un avión, etc.)

hullabaloo ['hʌləbə,lu:] *n, pl* -**loos** : alboroto *m*, jaleo *m*

hum[1] ['hʌm] *v* **hummed; humming** *vi* 1 BUZZ : zumbar 2 : estar muy activo, moverse ⟨to hum with activity : bullir de actividad⟩ — *vt* : tararear (una melodía)

hum² *n* : zumbido *m*, murmullo *m*

human¹ ['hju:mən, 'ju:-] *adj* : humano — **humanly** *adv*

human² *n* : ser *m* humano

humane [hju:'meɪn, ju:-] *adj* : humano, humanitario — **humanely** *adv*

humanism ['hju:mə,nɪzəm, 'ju:-] *n* : humanismo *m*

humanist¹ ['hju:mənɪst, 'ju:-] *n* : humanista *mf*

humanist² *or* **humanistic** [,hju:mə-'nɪstɪk, ,ju:-] *adj* : humanístico

humanitarian¹ [hju:,mænə'triən, ju:-] *adj* : humanitario

humanitarian² *n* : humanitario *m*, -ria *f*

humanity [hju:'mænəṭi, ju:-] *n*, *pl* **-ties** : humanidad *f*

humankind ['hju:mən'kaɪnd, 'ju:-] *n* : género *m* humano

humble¹ ['hʌmbəl] *vt* **-bled; -bling** **1** : humillar **2 to humble oneself** : humillarse

humble² *adj* **-bler; -blest** : humilde, modesto — **humbly** ['hʌmbli] *adv*

humbug ['hʌm,bʌg] *n* **1** FRAUD : charlatán *m*, -tana *f*; farsante *mf* **2** NONSENSE : patrañas *fpl*, tonterías *fpl*

humdrum ['hʌm,drʌm] *adj* : monótono, rutinario

humid ['hju:məd, 'ju:-] *adj* : húmedo

humidifier [hju:'mɪdə,faɪər, ju:-] *n* : humidificador *m*

humidify [hju:'mɪdə,faɪ, ju:-] *vt* **-fied; -fying** : humidificar

humidity [hju:'mɪdəṭi, ju:-] *n*, *pl* **-ties** : humedad *f*

humiliate [hju:'mɪli,eɪt, ju:-] *vt* **-ated; -ating** : humillar

humiliating [hju:'mɪli,eɪṭɪŋ, ju:-] *adj* : humillante

humiliation [hju:,mɪli'eɪʃən, ju:-] *n* : humillación *f*

humility [hju:'mɪləṭi, ju:-] *n* : humildad *f*

hummingbird ['hʌmɪŋ,bərd] *n* : colibrí *m*, picaflor *m*

hummock ['hʌmək] *n* : montículo *m*

humor¹ ['hju:mər, 'ju:-] *vt* : seguir el humor a, complacer

humor² *n* : humor *m*

humorist ['hju:mərɪst, 'ju:-] *n* : humorista *mf*

humorless ['hju:mərləs, 'ju:-] *adj* : sin sentido del humor ⟨a humorless smile : una sonrisa forzada⟩

humorous ['hju:mərəs, 'ju:-] *adj* : humorístico, cómico — **humorously** *adv*

hump ['hʌmp] *n* : joroba *f*, giba *f*

humpback ['hʌmp,bæk] *n* **1** HUMP : joroba *f*, giba *f* **2** HUNCHBACK : jorobado *m*, -da *f*; giboso *m*, -sa *f*

humpbacked ['hʌmp,bækt] *adj* : jorobado, giboso

humus ['hju:məs, 'ju:-] *n* : humus *m*

hunch¹ ['hʌntʃ] *vt* : encorvar — *vi or* **to hunch up** : encorvarse

hunch² *n* PREMONITION : presentimiento *m*

hunchback ['hʌntʃ,bæk] *n* **1** HUMP : joroba *f*, giba *f* **2** HUMPBACK : jorobado *m*, -da *f*; giboso *m*, -sa *f*

hunchbacked ['hʌntʃ,bækt] *adj* : jorobado, giboso

hundred¹ ['hʌndrəd] *adj* : cien, ciento

hundred² *n*, *pl* **-dreds** *or* **-dred** : ciento *m*

hundredth¹ ['hʌndrədθ] *adj* : centésimo

hundredth² *n* **1** : centésimo *m*, -ma *f* (en una serie) **2** : centésimo *m*, centésima parte *f*

hung → **hang**

Hungarian [hʌŋ'gæriən] *n* **1** : húngaro *m*, -ra *f* **2** : húngaro *m* (idioma) — **Hungarian** *adj*

hunger¹ ['hʌŋgər] *vi* **1** : tener hambre **2 to hunger for** : ansiar, anhelar

hunger² *n* : hambre *m*

hungrily ['hʌŋgrəli] *adv* : ávidamente

hungry ['hʌŋgri] *adj* **-grier; -est** **1** : hambriento **2 to be hungry** : tener hambre

hunk ['hʌŋk] *n* : trozo *m*, pedazo *m*

hunt¹ ['hʌnt] *vt* **1** PURSUE : cazar **2 to hunt for** : buscar

hunt² *n* **1** PURSUIT : caza *f*, cacería *f* **2** SEARCH : búsqueda *f*, busca *f*

hunter ['hʌntər] *n* : cazador *m*, -dora *f*

hunting ['hʌntɪŋ] *n* : caza *f* ⟨to go hunting : ir de caza⟩

hurdle¹ ['hərdəl] *vt* **-dled; -dling** : saltar, salvar (un obstáculo)

hurdle² *n* : valla *f* (en deportes), obstáculo *m*

hurl ['hərl] *vt* : arrojar, tirar, lanzar

hurrah [hʊ'rɑ, -'rɔ] *interj* : ¡hurra!

hurricane ['hərə,keɪn] *n* : huracán *m*

hurried ['hərid] *adj* : apresurado, precipitado

hurriedly ['hərədli] *adv* : apresuradamente, de prisa

hurry¹ ['həri] *v* **-ried; -rying** *vi* : apurarse, darse prisa, apresurarse — *vt* : apurar, darle prisa (a alguien)

hurry² *n* : prisa *f*, apuro *f*

hurt¹ ['hərt] *v* **hurt; hurting** *vt* **1** INJURE : hacer daño a, herir, lastimar ⟨to hurt oneself : hacerse daño⟩ **2** DISTRESS, OFFEND : hacer sufrir, ofender, herir — *vi* : doler ⟨my foot hurts : me duele el pie⟩

hurt² *n* **1** INJURY : herida *f* **2** DISTRESS, PAIN : dolor *m*, pena *f*

hurtful ['hərtfəl] *adj* : hiriente, doloroso

hurtle ['hərtəl] *vi* **-tled; -tling** : lanzarse, precipitarse

husband¹ ['hʌzbənd] *vt* : economizar, bien administrar

husband² *n* : esposo *m*, marido *m*

husbandry ['hʌzbəndri] *n* **1** MANAGEMENT, THRIFT : economía *f*, buena administración *f* **2** AGRICULTURE : agricultura *f* ⟨animal husbandry : cría de animales⟩

hush¹ ['hʌʃ] *vt* **1** SILENCE : hacer callar, acallar **2** CALM : calmar, apaciguar

hush² *n* : silencio *m*

hush–hush ['hʌʃ,hʌʃ, ,hʌʃ'hʌʃ] *adj*
: muy secreto, confidencial
husk[1] ['hʌsk] *vt* : descascarar
husk[2] *n* : cáscara *f*
huskily ['hʌskəli] *adv* : con voz ronca
husky[1] ['hʌski] *adj* **-kier; -est 1** HOARSE
: ronco **2** BURLY : fornido
husky[2] *n, pl* **-kies** : perro *m*, -rra *f* esquimal
hustle[1] ['həsəl] *v* **-tled; -tling** *vt* : darle
prisa (a alguien), apurar ⟨they hustled
me in : me hicieron entrar a empu-
jones⟩ — *vi* : apurarse, ajetrearse
hustle[2] *n* BUSTLE : ajetreo *m*
hut ['hʌt] *n* : cabaña *f*, choza *f*, barraca
f
hutch ['hʌtʃ] *n* **1** CUPBOARD : alacena *f*
2 rabbit hutch : conejera *f*
hyacinth ['haɪə,sɪnθ] *n* : jacinto *m*
hybrid[1] ['haɪbrɪd] *adj* : híbrido
hybrid[2] *n* : híbrido *m*
hydrant ['haɪdrənt] *n* : boca *f* de riego,
hidrante *m CA, Col* ⟨fire hydrant : boca
de incendios⟩
hydraulic [haɪ'drɔlɪk] *adj* : hidráulico —
hydraulically *adv*
hydrocarbon [,haɪdro'karbən] *n* : hidrocarburo *m*
hydrochloric acid [,haɪdro'klorɪk] *n*
: ácido *m* clorhídrico
hydroelectric [,haɪdroɪ'lɛktrɪk] *adj*
: hidroeléctrico
hydrogen ['haɪdrədʒən] *n* : hidrógeno *m*
hydrogen bomb *n* : bomba *f* de
hidrógeno
hydrogen peroxide *n* : agua *f* oxigenada, peróxido *m* de hidrógeno
hydrophobia [,haɪdrə'fobiə] *n* : hidrofobia *f*, rabia *f*
hydroplane ['haɪdrə,pleɪn] *n* : hidroplano *m*
hyena [haɪ'inə] *n* : hiena *f*
hygiene ['haɪ,dʒin] *n* : higiene *f*
hygienic [haɪ'dʒɛnɪk, -'dʒi-; ,haɪ-dʒi'nɪk]
adj : higiénico — **hygienically** [-nɪkli]
adv
hygienist [haɪ'dʒi:nɪst, -'dʒɛ-; 'haɪ-,dʒi:-]
n : higienista *mf*
hygrometer [haɪ'gramətər] *n* : higrómetro *m*
hymn ['hɪm] *n* : himno *m*

hymnal ['hɪmnəl] *n* : himnario *m*
hype ['haɪp] *n* : bombo *m* publicitario
hyperactive [,haɪpər'æktɪv] *adj* : hiperactivo
hyperactivity [,haɪpər,æk'tɪvəti] *n, pl*
-ties : hiperactividad *f*
hyperbole [haɪ'pərbəli] *n* : hipérbole *f*
hyperbolic [,haɪpər'balɪk] *adj* : hiperbólico
hypercritical [,haɪpər'krɪtəkəl] *adj*
: hipercrítico
hypersensitivity [,haɪpər,sɛntsə'tɪ-vəti]
n : hipersensibilidad *f*
hypertension ['haɪpər,tɛntʃən] *n* : hipertensión *f*
hyphen ['haɪfən] *n* : guión *m*
hyphenate ['haɪfən,eɪt] *vt* **-ated; -ating**
: escribir con guión
hypnosis [hɪp'no:sɪs] *n, pl* **-noses** [-,si:z]
: hipnosis *f*
hypnotic [hɪp'natɪk] *adj* : hipnótico,
hipnotizador
hypnotism ['hɪpnə,tɪzəm] *n* : hipnotismo
m
hypnotize ['hɪpnə,taɪz] *vt* **-tized; -tizing**
: hipnotizar
hypochondria [,haɪpə'kandriə] *n*
: hipocondría *f*
hypochondriac [,haɪpə'kandri,æk] *n*
: hipocondríaco *m*, -ca *f*
hypocrisy [hɪp'akrəsi] *n, pl* **-sies** : hipocresía *f*
hypocrite ['hɪpə,krɪt] *n* : hipócrita *mf*
hypocritical [,hɪpə'krɪtɪkəl] *adj* : hipócrita
hypodermic[1] [,haɪpə'dərmɪk] *adj* : hipodérmico
hypodermic[2] *n* : aguja *f* hipodérmica
hypotenuse [haɪ'patən,u:s, -,u:z, -,ju:s,
-,ju:z] *n* : hipotenusa *f*
hypothesis [haɪ'paθəsɪs] *n, pl* **-eses**
[-,si:z] : hipótesis *f*
hypothetical [,haɪpə'θɛtɪkəl] *adj*
: hipotético — **hypothetically** [-tɪkli]
adv
hysteria [hɪs'tɛriə, -tɪr-] *n* : histeria *f*, histerismo *m*
hysterical [hɪs'tɛrɪkəl] *adj* : histérico —
hysterically [-ɪkli] *adv*
hysterics [hɪs'tɛrɪks] *n* : histeria *f*, histerismo *m*

I

i ['aɪ] *n, pl* **i's** *or* **is** ['aɪz] : novena letra
del alfabeto inglés
I ['aɪ] *pron* : yo
Iberian [aɪ'bɪriən] *adj* : ibérico
ibis ['aɪbəs] *n, pl* **ibis** *or* **ibises** : ibis *f*
ice[1] ['aɪs] *v* **iced; icing** *vt* **1** FREEZE : congelar, helar **2** CHILL : enfriar **3 to ice
a cake** : escarchar un pastel — *vi*
: helarse, congelarse
ice[2] *n* **1** : hielo *m* **2** SHERBET : sorbete
m, nieve *f Cuba, Mex, PRi*

iceberg ['aɪs,bərg] *n* : iceberg *m*
icebox ['aɪs,baks] → **refrigerator**
icebreaker ['aɪs,breɪkər] *n* : rompehielos *m*
ice cap *n* : casquete *m* glaciar
ice-cold ['aɪs'ko:ld] *adj* : helado
ice cream *n* : helado *m*, mantecado *m*
PRi
Icelander ['aɪs,lændər, -lən-] *n* : islandés
m, -desa *f*
Icelandic[1] [aɪs'lændɪk] *adj* : islandés

Icelandic² *n* : islandés *m* (idioma)
ice–skate ['aɪsˌskeɪt] *vi* **-skated; -skating** : patinar
ice skater *n* : patinador *m*, -dora *f*
ichthyology [ˌɪkthiˈɑlədʒi] *n* : ictiología *f*
icicle ['aɪˌsɪkəl] *n* : carámbano *m*
icily ['aɪsəli] *adv* : fríamente, con frialdad ⟨he stared at me icily : me fijó la mirada con mucha frialdad⟩
icing ['aɪsɪŋ] *n* : glaseado *m*, betún *m Mex*
icon ['aɪˌkɑn, -kən] *n* : icono *m*
iconoclasm [aɪˈkɑnəˌklæzəm] *n* : iconoclasia *f*
iconoclast [aɪˈkɑnəˌklæst] *n* : iconoclasta *mf*
icy ['aɪsi] *adj* **icier; -est 1** : cubierto de hielo ⟨an icy road : una carretera cubierta de hielo⟩ **2** FREEZING : helado, gélido, glacial **3** ALOOF : frío, distante
id ['ɪd] *n* : id *m*
I'd ['aɪd] (*contraction of* **I should** *or* **I would**) → **should, would**
idea [aɪˈdiːə] *n* : idea *f*
ideal¹ [aɪˈdiːəl] *adj* : ideal
ideal² *n* : ideal *m*
idealism [aɪˈdiːəˌlɪzəm] *n* : idealismo *m*
idealist [aɪˈdiːəlɪst] *n* : idealista *mf*
idealistic [aɪˌdiːəˈlɪstɪk] *adj* : idealista
idealistically [aɪˌdiːəˈlɪstɪkli] *adv* : con idealismo
idealization [aɪˌdiːəlɪˈzeɪʃən] *n* : idealización *f*
idealize [aɪˈdiːəˌlaɪz] *vt* **-ized; -izing** : idealizar
ideally [aɪˈdiːəli] *adv* : perfectamente
identical [aɪˈdɛntɪkəl] *adj* : idéntico — **identically** [-tɪkli] *adv*
identifiable [aɪˌdɛntəˈfaɪəbəl] *adj* : identificable
identification [aɪˌdɛntəfəˈkeɪʃən] *n* **1** : identificación *f* **2 identification card** : carnet *m*, cédula *f* de identidad, identificación *f*
identify [aɪˈdɛntəˌfaɪ] *v* **-fied; -fying** *vt* : identificar — *vi* **to identify with** : identificarse con
identity [aɪˈdɛntəti] *n, pl* **-ties** : identidad *f*
ideological [ˌaɪdiəˈlɑdʒɪkəl, ˌɪ-] *adj* : ideológico — **ideologically** [-dʒɪkli] *adv*
ideology [ˌaɪdiˈɑlədʒi, ˌɪ-] *n, pl* **-gies** : ideología *f*
idiocy ['ɪdiəsi] *n, pl* **-cies 1** : idiotez *f* **2** NONSENSE : estupidez *f*, tontería *f*
idiom ['ɪdiəm] *n* **1** LANGUAGE : lenguaje *m* **2** EXPRESSION : modismo *m*, expresión *f* idiomática
idiomatic [ˌɪdiəˈmætɪk] *adj* : idiomático
idiosyncrasy [ˌɪdioˈsɪŋkrəsi] *n, pl* **-sies** : idiosincrasia *f*
idiosyncratic [ˌɪdiosɪnˈkrætɪk] *adj* : idiosincrásico — **idiosyncratically** [-tɪkli] *adv*
idiot ['ɪdiət] *n* **1** : idiota *mf* (en medicina) **2** FOOL : idiota *mf*; tonto *m*, -ta *f*; imbécil *mf fam*

idiotic [ˌɪdiˈɑtɪk] *adj* : estúpido, idiota
idiotically [ˌɪdiˈɑtɪkli] *adv* : estúpidamente
idle¹ ['aɪdəl] *v* **idled; idling** *vi* **1** LOAF : holgazanear, flojear, haraganear **2** : andar al ralentí (dícese de un automóvil), marchar en vacío (dícese de una máquina) — *vt* : dejar sin trabajo
idle² *adj* **idler; idlest 1** VAIN : frívolo, vano, infundado ⟨idle curiosity : pura curiosidad⟩ **2** INACTIVE : inactivo, parado, desocupado **3** LAZY : holgazán, haragán, perezoso
idleness ['aɪdəlnəs] *n* **1** INACTIVITY : inactividad *f*, ociosidad *f* **2** LAZINESS : holgazanería *f*, flojera *f*, pereza *f*
idler ['aɪdələr] *n* : haragán *m*, -gana *f*; holgazán *m*, -zana *f*
idly ['aɪdəli] *adv* : ociosamente
idol ['aɪdəl] *n* : ídolo *m*
idolater *or* **idolator** [aɪˈdɑlətər] *n* : idólatra *mf*
idolatrous [aɪˈdɑlətrəs] *adj* : idólatra
idolatry [aɪˈdɑlətri] *n, pl* **-tries** : idolatría *f*
idolize ['aɪdəlaɪz] *vt* **-ized; -izing** : idolatrar
idyll ['aɪdəl] *n* : idilio *m*
idyllic [aɪˈdɪlɪk] *adj* : idílico
if ['ɪf] *conj* **1** : si ⟨I would do it if I could : lo haría si pudiera⟩ ⟨if so : si es así⟩ ⟨as if : como si⟩ ⟨if I were you : yo que tú⟩ **2** WHETHER : si ⟨I don't know if they're ready : no sé si están listos⟩ **3** THOUGH : aunque, si bien ⟨it's pretty, if somewhat old-fashioned : es lindo aunque algo anticuado⟩
igloo ['ɪˌgluː] *n, pl* **-loos** : iglú *m*
ignite [ɪgˈnaɪt] *v* **-nited; -niting** *vt* : prenderle fuego a, encender — *vi* : prender, encenderse
ignition [ɪgˈnɪʃən] *n* **1** IGNITING : ignición *f*, encendido *m* **2** *or* **ignition switch** : encendido *m*, arranque *m* ⟨to turn on the ignition : arrancar el motor⟩
ignoble [ɪgˈnoːbəl] *adj* : innoble — **ignobly** *adv*
ignominious [ˌɪgnəˈmɪniəs] *adj* : ignominioso, deshonroso — **ignominiously** *adv*
ignominy ['ɪgnəˌmini] *n, pl* **-nies** : ignominia *f*
ignoramus [ˌɪgnəˈreɪməs] *n* : ignorante *mf*; bestia *mf*; bruto *m*, -ta *f*
ignorance ['ɪgnərənts] *n* : ignorancia *f*
ignorant ['ɪgnərənt] *adj* **1** : ignorante **2 to be ignorant of** : no ser consciente de, desconocer, ignorar
ignorantly ['ɪgnərəntli] *adv* : ignorantemente, con ignorancia
ignore [ɪgˈnor] *vt* **-nored; -noring** : ignorar, hacer caso omiso de, no hacer caso de
iguana [ɪˈgwɑnə] *n* : iguana *f*, garrobo *f CA*
ilk ['ɪlk] *n* : tipo *m*, clase *f*, índole *f*
ill¹ ['ɪl] *adv* **worse** ['wərs]; **worst** ['wərst] : mal ⟨to speak ill of : hablar mal de⟩

⟨he can ill afford to fail : mal puede permitirse el lujo de fracasar⟩

ill² *adj* **worse; worst 1** SICK : enfermo **2** BAD : malo ⟨ill luck : mala suerte⟩

ill³ *n* **1** EVIL : mal *m* **2** MISFORTUNE : mal *m*, desgracia *f* **3** AILMENT : enfermedad *f*

I'll ['aɪl] (*contraction of* **I shall** *or* **I will**) → **shall, will**

illegal [ɪl'li:gəl] *adj* : ilegal — **illegally** *adv*

illegality [ˌɪli'gæləti] *n* : ilegalidad *f*

illegibility [ɪlˌlɛdʒə'bɪləti] *n, pl* **-ties** : ilegibilidad *f*

illegible [ɪl'lɛdʒəbəl] *adj* : ilegible — **illegibly** [-bli] *adv*

illegitimacy [ˌɪli'dʒɪtəməsi] *n* : ilegitimidad *f*

illegitimate [ˌɪli'dʒɪtəmət] *adj* **1** BASTARD : ilegítimo, bastardo **2** UNLAWFUL : ilegítimo, ilegal — **illegitimately** *adv*

ill–fated ['ɪl'feɪtəd] *adj* : malhadado, infortunado, desventurado

illicit [ɪl'lɪsət] *adj* : ilícito — **illicitly** *adv*

illiteracy [ɪl'lɪtərəsi] *n, pl* **-cies** : analfabetismo *m*

illiterate¹ [ɪl'lɪtərət] *adj* : analfabeto

illiterate² *n* : analfabeto *m*, -ta *f*

ill–mannered [ˌɪl'mænərd] *adj* : descortés, maleducado

ill–natured [ˌɪl'neɪtʃərd] *adj* : desagradable, de mal genio

ill–naturedly [ˌɪl'neɪtʃərdli] *adv* : desagradablemente

illness ['ɪlnəs] *n* : enfermedad *f*

illogical [ɪl'lɑdʒɪkəl] *adj* : ilógico — **illogically** [-kli] *adv*

ill–tempered [ˌɪl'tempərd] → **ill–natured**

ill–treat [ˌɪl'tri:t] *vt* : maltratar

ill–treatment [ˌɪl'tri:tmənt] *n* : maltrato *m*

illuminate [ɪ'lu:mə,neɪt] *vt* **-nated; -nating 1** : iluminar, alumbrar **2** ELUCIDATE : esclarecer, elucidar

illumination [ɪˌlu:mə'neɪʃən] *n* **1** LIGHTING : iluminación *f*, luz *f* **2** ELUCIDATION : esclarecimiento *m*, elucidación *f*

ill–use ['ɪl'ju:z] → **ill–treat**

illusion [ɪ'lu:ʒən] *n* : ilusión *f*

illusory [ɪ'lu:səri, -zəri] *adj* : engañoso, ilusorio

illustrate ['ɪləs,treɪt] *v* **-trated; -trating** : ilustrar

illustration [ˌɪlə'streɪʃən] *n* **1** PICTURE : ilustración *f* **2** EXAMPLE : ejemplo *m*, ilustración *f*

illustrative [ɪ'lʌstrətɪv, 'ɪlə,streɪtɪv] *adj* : ilustrativo — **illustratively** *adv*

illustrator ['ɪlə,streɪtər] *n* : ilustrador *m*, -dora *f*; dibujante *mf*

illustrious [ɪ'lʌstriəs] *adj* : ilustre, eminente, glorioso

illustriousness [ɪ'lʌstriəsnəs] *n* : eminencia *f*, prestigio *m*

ill will *n* : animosidad *f*, malquerencia *f*, mala voluntad *f*

I'm ['aɪm] (*contraction of* **I am**) → **be**

image¹ ['ɪmɪdʒ] *vt* **-aged; -aging** : imaginar, crear una imagen de

image² *n* : imagen *f*

imagery ['ɪmɪdʒri] *n, pl* **-eries 1** IMAGES : imágenes *fpl* **2** : imaginería *f* (en el arte)

imaginable [ɪ'mædʒənəbəl] *adj* : imaginable — **imaginably** [-bli] *adv*

imaginary [ɪ'mædʒə,neri] *adj* : imaginario

imagination [ɪˌmædʒə'neɪʃən] *n* : imaginación *f*

imaginative [ɪ'mædʒənətɪv, -ə,neɪtɪv] *adj* : imaginativo — **imaginatively** *adv*

imagine [ɪ'mædʒən] *vt* **-ined; -ining** : imaginar(se)

imbalance [ɪm'bælənts] *n* : desajuste *m*, desbalance *m*, desequilibrio *m*

imbecile¹ ['ɪmbəsəl, -,sɪl] *or* **imbecilic** [ˌɪmbə'sɪlɪk] *adj* : imbécil, estúpido

imbecile² *n* **1** : imbécil *mf* (en medicina) **2** FOOL : idiota *mf*; imbécil *mf fam*; estúpido *m*, -da *f*

imbecility [ˌɪmbə'sɪləti] *n, pl* **-ties** : imbecilidad *f*

imbibe [ɪm'baɪb] *v* **-bibed; -bibing** *vt* **1** DRINK : beber **2** ABSORB : absorber, embeber — *vi* : beber

imbue [ɪm'bju:] *vt* **-bued; -buing** : imbuir

imitate ['ɪmə,teɪt] *vt* **-tated; -tating** : imitar, remedar

imitation¹ [ˌɪmə'teɪʃən] *adj* : de imitación, artificial

imitation² *n* : imitación *f*

imitative ['ɪmə,teɪtɪv] *adj* : imitativo, imitador, poco original

imitator ['ɪmə,teɪtər] *n* : imitador *m*, -dora *f*

immaculate [ɪ'mækjələt] *adj* **1** PURE : inmaculado, puro **2** FLAWLESS : impecable, intachable — **immaculately** *adv*

immaterial [ˌɪmə'tɪriəl] *adj* **1** INCORPOREAL : incorpóreo **2** UNIMPORTANT : irrelevante, sin importancia

immature [ˌɪmə'tʃur, -'tjur, -'tur] *adj* : inmaduro, verde (dícese de la fruta)

immaturity [ˌɪmə'tʃurəti, -'tjur-, -'tur-] *n, pl* **-ties** : inmadurez *f*, falta *f* de madurez

immeasurable [ɪ'mɛʒərəbəl] *adj* : inconmensurable, incalculable — **immeasurably** [-bli] *adv*

immediacy [ɪ'mi:diəsi] *n* : inmediatez *f*

immediate [ɪ'mi:diət] *adj* **1** INSTANT : inmediato, instantáneo ⟨immediate relief : alivio instantáneo⟩ **2** DIRECT : inmediato, directo ⟨the immediate cause of death : la causa directa de la muerte⟩ **3** URGENT : urgente, apremiante **4** CLOSE : cercano, próximo, inmediato ⟨her immediate family : sus familiares más cercanos⟩ ⟨in the immediate vicinity : en los alrededores, en las inmediaciones⟩

immediately [ɪ'mi:diətli] *adv* : inmediatamente, enseguida

immemorial [ˌɪmə'moriəl] *adj* : inmemorial

immense [ɪ'mɛnts] *adj* : inmenso, enorme — **immensely** *adv*

immensity [ɪ'mɛntsəti] *n, pl* **-ties** : inmensidad *f*

immerse [ɪ'mərs] *vt* **-mersed; -mersing** 1 SUBMERGE : sumergir **2 to immerse oneself in** : enfrascarse en

immersion [ɪ'mərʒən] *n* 1 : inmersión *f* (en un líquido) 2 : enfrascamiento *m* (en una actividad)

immigrant ['ɪmɪgrənt] *n* : inmigrante *mf*

immigrate ['ɪmə,greɪt] *vi* **-grated; -grating** : inmigrar

immigration [ˌɪmə'greɪʃən] *n* : inmigración *f*

imminence ['ɪmənənts] *n* : inminencia *f*

imminent ['ɪmənənt] *adj* : inminente — **imminently** *adv*

immobile [ɪm'o:bəl] *adj* 1 FIXED, IMMOVABLE : inmovible, fijo 2 MOTIONLESS : inmóvil

immobility [ˌɪmo'bɪləti] *n, pl* **-ties** : inmovilidad *f*

immobilize [ɪ'mo:bə,laɪz] *vt* **-lized; -lizing** : inmovilizar, paralizar

immoderate [ɪ'mɑdərət] *adj* : inmoderado, desmesurado, desmedido, excesivo — **immoderately** *adv*

immodest [ɪ'mɑdəst] *adj* 1 INDECENT : inmodesto, indecente, impúdico 2 CONCEITED : inmodesto, presuntuoso, engreído — **immodestly** *adv*

immodesty [ɪ'mɑdəsti] *n* : inmodestia *f*

immoral [ɪ'mɔrəl] *adj* : inmoral

immorality [ˌɪmo'ræləti, ˌɪmə-] *n, pl* **-ties** : inmoralidad *f*

immorally [ɪ'mɔrəli] *adv* : de manera inmoral

immortal¹ [ɪ'mɔrtəl] *adj* : inmortal

immortal² *n* : inmortal *mf*

immortality [ˌɪˌmɔr'tæləti] *n* : inmortalidad *f*

immortalize [ɪ'mɔrtəl,aɪz] *vt* **-ized; -izing** : inmortalizar

immovable [ɪ'mu:vəbəl] *adj* 1 FIXED : fijo, inmovible 2 UNYIELDING : inflexible

immune [ɪ'mju:n] *adj* 1 : inmune ⟨immune to smallpox : inmune a la viruela⟩ 2 EXEMPT : exento, inmune

immune system *n* : sistema *m* inmunológico

immunity [ɪ'mju:nəti] *n, pl* **-ties** 1 : inmunidad *f* 2 EXEMPTION : exención *f*

immunization [ˌɪmjʊnə'zeɪʃən] *n* : inmunización *f*

immunize ['ɪmjʊ,naɪz] *vt* **-nized; -nizing** : inmunizar

immunology [ˌɪmjʊ'nɑlədʒi] *n* : inmunología *f*

immutable [ɪ'mju:təbəl] *adj* : inmutable

imp ['ɪmp] *n* RASCAL : diablillo *m*; pillo *m*, -lla *f*

impact¹ [ɪm'pækt] *vt* 1 STRIKE : chocar con, impactar 2 AFFECT : afectar, impactar, impresionar — *vi* 1 STRIKE

: hacer impacto, golpear **2 to impact on** : tener un impacto sobre

impact² ['ɪm,pækt] *n* 1 COLLISION : impacto *m*, choque *m*, colisión *f* 2 EFFECT : efecto *m*, impacto *m*, consecuencias *fpl*

impacted [ɪm'pæktəd] *adj* : impactado, incrustado (dícese de los dientes)

impair [ɪm'pær] *vt* : perjudicar, dañar, afectar

impairment [ɪm'pærmənt] *n* : perjuicio *m*, daño *m*

impala [ɪm'pɑlə, -'pæ-] *n, pl* **impalas** *or* **impala** : impala *m*

impale [ɪm'peɪl] *vt* **-paled; -paling** : empalar

impanel [ɪm'pænəl] *vt* **-eled** *or* **-elled; -eling** *or* **-elling** : elegir (un jurado)

impart [ɪm'pɑrt] *vt* 1 CONVEY : impartir, dar, conferir 2 DISCLOSE : revelar, divulgar

impartial [ɪm'pɑrʃəl] *adj* : imparcial — **impartially** *adv*

impartiality [ɪm,pɑrʃi'æləti] *n, pl* **-ties** : imparcialidad *f*

impassable [ɪm'pæsəbəl] *adj* : infranqueable, intransitable — **impassably** [-bli] *adv*

impasse ['ɪm,pæs] *n* 1 DEADLOCK : impasse *m*, punto *m* muerto 2 DEAD END : callejón *m* sin salida

impassioned [ɪm'pæʃənd] *adj* : apasionado, vehemente

impassive [ɪm'pæsɪv] *adj* : impasible, indiferente

impassively [ɪm'pæsɪvli] *adv* : impasiblemente, sin emoción

impatience [ɪm'peɪʃənts] *n* : impaciencia *f*

impatient [ɪm'peɪʃənt] *adj* : impaciente — **impatiently** *adv*

impeach [ɪm'pi:tʃ] *vt* : destituir (a un funcionario) de su cargo

impeachment [ɪm'pi:tʃmənt] *n* 1 ACCUSATION : acusación *f* 2 DISMISSAL : destitución *f*

impeccable [ɪm'pɛkəbəl] *adj* : impecable — **impeccably** [-bli] *adv*

impecunious [ˌɪmpɪ'kju:niəs] *adj* : falto de dinero

impede [ɪm'pi:d] *vt* **-peded; -peding** : impedir, dificultar, obstaculizar

impediment [ɪm'pɛdəmənt] *n* 1 HINDRANCE : impedimento *m*, obstáculo *m* 2 **speech impediment** : defecto *m* del habla

impel [ɪm'pɛl] *vt* **-pelled; -pelling** : impeler

impend [ɪm'pɛnd] *vi* : ser inminente

impenetrable [ɪm'pɛnətrəbəl] *adj* 1 : impenetrable ⟨an impenetrable forest : una selva impenetrable⟩ 2 INSCRUTABLE : incomprensible, inescrutable, impenetrable — **impenetrably** [-bli] *adv*

impenitent [ɪm'pɛnətənt] *adj* : impenitente

imperative¹ [ɪm'pɛrəṭɪv] *adj* **1** AUTHOR-
ITATIVE : imperativo, imperioso **2**
NECESSARY : imprescindible — **im-
peratively** *adv*
imperative² *n* : imperativo *m*
imperceptible [,ɪmpər'sɛptəbəl] *adj* : imperceptible — **imperceptibly** [-bli] *adv*
imperfect [ɪm'pərfɪkt] *adj* : imperfecto,
defectuoso — **imperfectly** *adv*
imperfection [ɪm,pər'fɪkʃən] *n* : imperfección *f*, defecto *m*
imperial [ɪm'pɪriəl] *adj* **1** : imperial **2**
SOVEREIGN : soberano **3** IMPERIOUS
: imperioso, señorial
imperialism [ɪm'pɪriə,lɪzəm] *n* : imperialismo *m*
imperialist¹ [ɪm'pɪriəlɪst] *adj* : imperialista
imperialist² *n* : imperialista *mf*
imperialistic [ɪm,pɪri:ə'lɪstɪk] *adj* : imperialista
imperil [ɪm'pɛrəl] *vt* **-iled** *or* **-illed; -iling**
or **-illing** : poner en peligro
imperious [ɪm'pɪriəs] *adj* : imperioso —
imperiously *adv*
imperishable [ɪm'pɛrɪʃəbəl] *adj* : imperecedero
impermanent [ɪm'pərmənənt] *adj*
: pasajero, inestable, efímero — **im-
permanently** *adv*
impermeable [ɪm'pərmiəbəl] *adj* : impermeable
impersonal [ɪm'pərsənəl] *adj* : impersonal — **impersonally** *adv*
impersonate [ɪm'pərsən,eɪt] *vt* **-ated;
-ating** : hacerse pasar por, imitar
impersonation [ɪm,pərsən'eɪʃən] *n* : imitación *f*
impersonator [ɪm'pərsən,eɪṭər] *n* : imitador *m*, -dora *f*
impertinence [ɪm'pərtənənts] *n* : impertinencia *f*
impertinent [ɪm'pərtənənt] *adj* **1** IR-
RELEVANT : impertinente, irrelevante
2 INSOLENT : impertinente, insolente
impertinently [ɪm'pərtənəntli] *adv* : con
impertinencia, impertinentemente
imperturbable [,ɪmpər'tərbəbəl] *adj*
: imperturbable
impervious [ɪm'pərviəs] *adj* **1** IMPENE-
TRABLE : impermeable **2** INSENSITIVE
: insensible ⟨impervious to criticism
: insensible a la crítica⟩
impetuosity [ɪm,pɛtʃu'asəṭi] *n, pl* **-ties**
: impetuosidad *f*
impetuous [ɪm'pɛtʃuəs] *adj* : impetuoso,
impulsivo
impetuously [ɪm'pɛtʃuəsli] *adv* : de manera impulsiva, impetuosamente
impetus ['ɪmpəṭəs] *n* : ímpetu *m*, impulso *m*
impiety [ɪm'paɪəṭi] *n, pl* **-ties** : impiedad
f
impinge [ɪm'pɪndʒ] *vi* **-pinged; -pinging
1 to impinge on** AFFECT : afectar a, incidir en **2 to impinge on** VIOLATE : violar, vulnerar
impious ['ɪmpiəs, ɪm'paɪəs] *adj* : impío,
irreverente

impish ['ɪmpɪʃ] *adj* MISCHIEVOUS : pícaro, travieso
impishly ['ɪmpɪʃli] *adv* : con picardía
implacable [ɪm'plækəbəl] *adj* : implacable — **implacably** [-bli] *adv*
implant¹ [ɪm'plænt] *vt* **1** INCULCATE, IN-
STILL : inculcar, implantar **2** INSERT
: implantar, insertar
implant² ['ɪm,plænt] *n* : implante *m* (de
pelo), injerto *m* (de piel)
implantation [,ɪm,plæn'teɪʃən] *n* : implantación *f*
implausibility [ɪm,plɔzə'bɪləṭi] *n, pl* **-ties**
: inverosimilitud *f*
implausible [ɪm'plɔzəbəl] *adj* : inverosímil, poco convincente
implement¹ ['ɪmplə,mnt] *vt* : poner en
práctica, implementar
implement² ['ɪmpləmənt] *n* : utensilio *m*,
instrumento *m*, implemento *m*
implementation [,ɪmpləmən'teɪʃən] *n*
: implementación *f*, ejecución *f*, cumplimiento *m*
implicate ['ɪmplə,keɪt] *vt* **-cated; -cating**
: implicar, involucrar
implication [,ɪmplə'keɪʃən] *n* **1** CONSE-
QUENCE : implicación *f*, consecuencia
f **2** INFERENCE : insinuación *f*, inferencia *f*
implicit [ɪm'plɪsət] *adj* **1** IMPLIED : implícito, tácito **2** ABSOLUTE : absoluto,
completo ⟨implicit faith : fe ciega⟩ —
implicitly *adv*
implied [ɪm'plaɪd] *adj* : implícito, tácito
implode [ɪm'plo:d] *vi* **-ploded; -ploding**
: implosionar
implore [ɪm'plor] *vt* **-plored; -ploring**
: implorar, suplicar
implosion [ɪm'plo:ʒən] *n* : implosión *f*
imply [ɪm'plaɪ] *vt* **-plied; -plying 1** SUG-
GEST : insinuar, dar a entender **2** IN-
VOLVE : implicar, suponer ⟨rights imply obligations : los derechos implican
unas obligaciones⟩
impolite [,ɪmpə'laɪt] *adj* : descortés,
maleducado
impoliteness [,ɪmpə'laɪtnəs] *n* : descortesía *f*, falta *f* de educación
impolitic [ɪm'pɑlə,tɪk] *adj* : imprudente,
poco político
imponderable¹ [ɪm'pɑndərəbəl] *adj*
: imponderable
imponderable² *n* : imponderable *m*
import¹ [ɪm'port] *vt* **1** SIGNIFY : significar **2** : importar ⟨to import foreign
cars : importar autos extranjeros⟩
import² ['ɪm,port] *n* **1** SIGNIFICANCE
: importancia *f*, significación *f* **2** → **importation**
importance [ɪm'portənts] *n* : importancia *f*
important [ɪm'portənt] *adj* : importante
importantly [ɪm'portəntli] *adv* **1** : con
importancia **2 more importantly** : lo
que es más importante
importation [,ɪm,por'teɪʃən] *n* : importación *f*
importer [ɪm'portər] *n* : importador *m*,
-dora *f*

importunate [ɪm'pɔrt͡ʃənət] *adj* : importuno, insistente

importune [ˌɪmpər'tuːn, -'tjuːn; ɪm'pɔrt͡ʃən] *vt* **-tuned; -tuning** : importunar, implorar

impose [ɪm'poːz] *v* **-posed; -posing** *vt* : imponer ⟨to impose a tax : imponer un impuesto⟩ — *vi* **to impose on** : abusar de, molestar ⟨to impose on her kindness : abusar de su bondad⟩

imposing [ɪm'poːzɪŋ] *adj* : imponente, impresionante

imposition [ˌɪmpə'zɪʃən] *n* : imposición *f*

impossibility [ɪmˌpasə'bɪləti] *n, pl* **-ties** : imposibilidad *f*

impossible [ɪm'pasəbəl] *adj* **1** : imposible ⟨an impossible task : una tarea imposible⟩ ⟨to make life impossible for : hacerle la vida imposible a⟩ **2** UN-ACCEPTABLE : inaceptable

impossibly [ɪm'pasəbli] *adv* : imposiblemente, increíblemente

impostor *or* **imposter** [ɪm'pastər] *n* : impostor *m*, -tora *f*

impotence ['ɪmpətənt͡s] *n* : impotencia *f*

impotency ['ɪmpətənt͡si] → **impotence**

impotent ['ɪmpətənt] *adj* : impotente

impound [ɪm'paʊnd] *vt* : incautar, embargar, confiscar

impoverish [ɪm'pavərɪʃ] *vt* : empobrecer

impoverishment [ɪm'pavərɪʃmənt] *n* : empobrecimiento *m*

impracticable [ɪm'præktɪkəbəl] *adj* : impracticable

impractical [ɪm'præktɪkəl] *adj* : poco práctico

imprecise [ˌɪmprɪ'saɪs] *adj* : impreciso

imprecisely [ˌɪmprɪ'saɪsli] *adv* : con imprecisión

impreciseness [ˌɪmprɪ'saɪsnəs] → **imprecision**

imprecision [ˌɪmprɪ'sɪʒən] *n* : imprecisión *f*, falta de precisión *f*

impregnable [ɪm'prɛgnəbəl] *adj* : inexpugnable, impenetrable, inconquistable

impregnate [ɪm'prɛgˌneɪt] *vt* **-nated; -nating 1** FERTILIZE : fecundar **2** PERMEATE, SATURATE : impregnar, empapar, saturar

impresario [ˌɪmprə'sari͜o, -'sær-] *n, pl* **-rios** : empresario *m*, -ria *f*

impress [ɪm'prɛs] *vt* **1** IMPRINT : imprimir, estampar **2** : impresionar, causar impresión a ⟨I was not impressed : no me hizo buena impresión⟩ **3 to impress (something) on someone** : recalcarle (algo) a alguien — *vi* : impresionar, hacer una impresión

impression [ɪm'prɛʃən] *n* **1** IMPRINT : marca *f*, huella *f*, molde *m* (de los dientes) **2** EFFECT : impresión *f*, efecto *m*, impacto *m* **3** PRINTING : impresión *f* **4** NOTION : impresión *f*, noción *f*

impressionable [ɪm'prɛʃənəbəl] *adj* : impresionable

impressionism [ɪm'prɛʃəˌnɪzəm] *n* : impresionismo *m*

impressionist [ɪm'prɛʃənɪst] *n* : impresionista *mf* — **impressionist** *adj*

impressive [ɪm'prɛsɪv] *adj* : impresionante — **impressively** *adv*

impressiveness [ɪm'prɛsɪvnəs] *n* : calidad de ser impresionante

imprint[1] [ɪm'prɪnt, 'ɪm-] *vt* : imprimir, estampar

imprint[2] ['ɪmˌprɪnt] *n* : marca *f*, huella *f*

imprison [ɪm'prɪzən] *vt* **1** JAIL : encarcelar, aprisionar **2** CONFINE : recluir, encerrar

imprisonment [ɪm'prɪzənmənt] *n* : encarcelamiento *m*

improbability [ɪmˌprabə'bɪləti] *n, pl* **-ties** : improbabilidad *f*, inverosimilitud *f*

improbable [ɪm'prabəbəl] *adj* : improbable, inverosímil

impromptu[1] [ɪm'pramp͜tuː, -ˌtjuː] *adv* : sin preparación, espontáneamente

impromptu[2] *adj* : espontáneo, improvisado

impromptu[3] *n* : improvisación *f*

improper [ɪm'prapər] *adj* **1** INCORRECT : incorrecto, impropio **2** INDECOROUS : indecoroso

improperly [ɪm'prapərli] *adv* : incorrectamente, indebidamente

impropriety [ˌɪmprə'praɪəti] *n, pl* **-eties 1** INDECOROUSNESS : indecoro *m*, falta *f* de decoro **2** ERROR : impropiedad *f*, incorrección *f*

improve [ɪm'pruːv] *v* **-proved; -proving** : mejorar

improvement [ɪm'pruːvmənt] *n* : mejoramiento *m*, mejora *f*

improvidence [ɪm'pravədənt͡s] *n* : imprevisión *f*

improvisation [ɪmˌpravə'zeɪʃən, ˌɪmprəvə-] *n* : improvisación *f*

improvise ['ɪmprəˌvaɪz] *v* **-vised; -vising** : improvisar

imprudence [ɪm'pruːdənt͡s] *n* : imprudencia *f*, indiscreción *f*

imprudent [ɪm'pruːdənt] *adj* : imprudente, indiscreto

impudence ['ɪmpjədənt͡s] *n* : insolencia *f*, descaro *m*

impudent ['ɪmpjədənt] *adj* : insolente, descarado — **impudently** *adv*

impugn [ɪm'pjuːn] *vt* : impugnar

impulse ['ɪmˌpʌls] *n* **1** : impulso *m* **2 on impulse** : sin reflexionar

impulsive [ɪm'pʌlsɪv] *adj* : impulsivo — **impulsively** *adv*

impulsiveness [ɪm'pʌlsɪvnəs] *n* : impulsividad *f*

impunity [ɪm'pjuːnəti] *n* **1** : impunidad *f* **2 with impunity** : impunemente

impure [ɪm'pjʊr] *adj* **1** : impuro ⟨impure thoughts : pensamientos impuros⟩ **2** CONTAMINATED : con impurezas, impuro

impurity [ɪm'pjʊrəti] *n, pl* **-ties** : impureza *f*

impute [ɪm'pju:t] *vt* **-puted; -puting** AT-TRIBUTE : imputar, atribuir

in¹ ['ɪn] *adv* **1** INSIDE : dentro, adentro ⟨let's go in : vamos adentro⟩ **2** HAR-VESTED : recogido ⟨the crops are in : las cosechas ya están recogidas⟩ **3 to be in** : estar ⟨is Linda in? : ¿está Linda?⟩ **4 to be in** : estar en poder ⟨the De-mocrats are in : los demócratas están en el poder⟩ **5 to be in for** : ser obje-to de, estar a punto de ⟨they're in for a treat : los van a agasajar⟩ ⟨he's in for a surprise : se va a llevar una sorpre-sa⟩ **6 to be in on** : participar en, tomar parte en

in² *adj* **1** INSIDE : interior ⟨the in part : la parte interior⟩ **2** FASHIONABLE : de moda

in³ *prep* **1** (*indicating location or posi-tion*) ⟨in the lake : en el lago⟩ ⟨a pain in the leg : un dolor en la pierna⟩ ⟨in the sun : al sol⟩ ⟨in the rain : bajo la lluvia⟩ ⟨the best restaurant in Buenos Aires : el mejor restaurante de Buenos Aires⟩ **2** INTO : en, a ⟨he broke it in pieces : lo rompió en pedazos⟩ ⟨she went in the house : se metió a la casa⟩ **3** DURING : por, durante ⟨in the after-noon : por la tarde⟩ **4** WITHIN : den-tro de ⟨I'll be back in a week : vuelvo dentro de una semana⟩ **5** (*indicating manner*) : en, con, de ⟨in Spanish : en español⟩ ⟨written in pencil : escrito con lápiz⟩ ⟨in this way : de esta mane-ra⟩ **6** (*indicating states or circum-stances*) ⟨to be in luck : tener suerte⟩ ⟨to be in love : estar enamorado⟩ ⟨to be in a hurry : tener prisa⟩ **7** (*indicat-ing purpose*) : en ⟨in reply : en re-spuesta, como réplica⟩

in⁴ *n* **ins and outs** : pormenores *mpl*

inability [ˌɪnə'bɪləti] *n, pl* **-ties** : inca-pacidad *f*

inaccessibility [ˌɪnɪkˌsɛsə'bɪləti] *n, pl* **-ties** : inaccesibilidad *f*

inaccessible [ˌɪnɪk'sɛsəbəl] *adj* : inac-cesible

inaccuracy [ɪn'ækjərəsi] *n, pl* **-cies 1** : inexactitud *f* **2** MISTAKE : error *m*

inaccurate [ɪn'ækjərət] *n* : inexacto, erróneo, incorrecto

inaccurately [ɪn'ækjərətli] *adv* : inco-rrectamente, con inexactitud

inaction [ɪn'ækʃən] *n* : inactividad *f*, in-acción *f*

inactive [ɪn'æktɪv] *adj* : inactivo

inactivity [ˌɪnˌæk'tɪvəti] *n, pl* **-ties** : in-actividad *f*, ociosidad *f*

inadequacy [ɪn'ædɪkwəsi] *n, pl* **-cies 1** INSUFFICIENCY : insuficiencia *f* **2** IN-COMPETENCE : ineptitud *f*, incompe-tencia *f*

inadequate [ɪn'ædɪkwət] *adj* **1** INSUF-FICIENT : insuficiente, inadecuado **2** INCOMPETENT : inepto, incompetente

inadmissible [ˌɪnæd'mɪsəbəl] *adj* : inad-misible

inadvertent [ˌɪnəd'vərtənt] *adj* : inad-vertido, involuntario — **inadvertently** *adv*

inadvisable [ˌɪnæd'vaɪzəbəl] *adj* : de-saconsejable

inalienable [ɪn'eɪljənəbəl, -'eɪliənə-] *adj* : inalienable

inane [ɪ'neɪn] *adj* **inaner; -est** : estúpi-do, idiota, necio

inanimate [ɪn'ænəmət] *adj* : inanimado, exánime

inanity [ɪ'nænəti] *n, pl* **-ties 1** STUPIDI-TY : estupidez *f* **2** NONSENSE : idiotez *f*, disparate *m*

inapplicable [ɪn'æplɪkəbəl, ˌɪnə-'plɪkə-bəl] *adj* IRRELEVANT : inaplicable, ir-relevante

inappreciable [ˌɪnə'pri:ʃəbəl] *adj* : ina-preciable, imperceptible

inappropriate [ˌɪnə'pro:priət] *adj* : in-apropiado, inadecuado, impropio

inappropriateness [ˌɪnə'pro:priətnəs] *n* : lo inapropiado, impropiedad *f*

inapt [ɪn'æpt] *adj* **1** UNSUITABLE : in-adecuado, inapropiado **2** INEPT : in-epto

inarticulate [ˌɪnɑr'tɪkjələt] *adj* : inartic-ulado, incapaz de expresarse

inarticulately [ˌɪnɑr'tɪkjələtli] *adv* : inar-ticuladamente

inasmuch as [ˌɪnæz'mʌtʃæz] *conj* : ya que, dado que, puesto que

inattention [ˌɪnə'tɛntʃən] *n* : falta *f* de atención, distracción *f*

inattentive [ˌɪnə'tɛntɪv] *adj* : distraído, despistado

inattentively [ˌɪnə'tɛntɪvli] *adv* : distraí-damente, sin prestar atención

inaudible [ɪn'ɔdəbəl] *adj* : inaudible

inaudibly [ɪn'ɔdəbli] *adv* : de forma in-audible

inaugural¹ [ɪ'nɔgjərəl, -gərəl] *adj* : inau-gural, de investidura

inaugural² *n* **1** *or* **inaugural address** : discurso *m* de investidura **2** INAU-GURATION : investidura *f* (de una per-sona)

inaugurate [ɪ'nɔgjəˌreɪt, -gə-] *vt* **-rated; -rating 1** BEGIN : inaugurar **2** INDUCT : investir ⟨to inaugurate the president : investir al presidente⟩

inauguration [ɪˌnɔgjə'reɪʃən, -gə-] *n* **1** : inauguración *f* (de un edificio, un sis-tema, etc.) **2** : investidura *f* (de una per-sona)

inauspicious [ˌɪnə'spɪʃəs] *adj* : desfa-vorable, poco propicio

inborn ['ɪnˌbɔrn] *adj* **1** CONGENITAL, IN-NATE : innato, congénito **2** HEREDI-TARY : hereditario

inbred ['ɪnˌbred] *adj* **1** : engendrado por endogamia **2** INNATE : innato

inbreed ['ɪnˌbri:d] *vt* **-bred; -breeding** : engendrar por endogamia

inbreeding ['ɪnˌbri:dɪŋ] *n* : endogamia *f*

Inca ['ɪŋkə] *n* : inca *mf*

incalculable [ɪn'kælkjələbəl] *adj* : incal-culable — **incalculably** [-bli] *adv*

incandescence [ˌɪnkənˈdɛsənts] *n* : incandescencia *f*

incandescent [ˌɪnkənˈdɛsənt] *adj* **1** : incandescente **2** BRILLIANT : brillante

incantation [ˌɪnˌkænˈteɪʃən] *n* : conjuro *m*, ensalmo *m*

incapable [ɪnˈkeɪpəbəl] *adj* : incapaz

incapacitate [ˌɪnkəˈpæsəˌteɪt] *vt* **-tated; -tating** : incapacitar

incapacity [ˌɪnkəˈpæsəti] *n, pl* **-ties** : incapacidad *f*

incarcerate [ɪnˈkɑrsəˌreɪt] *vt* **-ated; -ating** : encarcelar

incarceration [ɪnˌkɑrsəˈreɪʃən] *n* : encarcelamiento *m*, encarcelación *f*

incarnate[1] [ɪnˈkɑrˌneɪt] *vt* **-nated; -nating** : encarnar

incarnate[2] [ɪnˈkɑrnət, -ˌneɪt] *adj* : encarnado

incarnation [ˌɪnˌkɑrˈneɪʃən] *n* : encarnación *f*

incendiary[1] [ɪnˈsɛndiˌri] *adj* : incendiario

incendiary[2] *n, pl* **-aries** : incendiario *m*, -ria *f*; pirómano *m*, -na *f*

incense[1] [ɪnˈsɛnts] *vt* **-censed; -censing** : indignar, enfadar, enfurecer

incense[2] [ˈɪnˌsɛnts] *n* : incienso *m*

incentive [ɪnˈsɛntɪv] *n* : incentivo *m*, aliciente *m*, motivación *f*, acicate *m*

inception [ɪnˈsɛpʃən] *n* : comienzo *m*, principio *m*

incessant [ɪnˈsɛsənt] *adj* : incesante, continuo — **incessantly** *adv*

incest [ˈɪnˌsɛst] *n* : incesto *m*

incestuous [ɪnˈsɛstʃʊəs] *adj* : incestuoso

inch[1] [ˈɪntʃ] *v* : avanzar poco a poco

inch[2] *n* **1** : pulgada *f* **2 every inch** : absoluto, seguro ⟨every inch a winner : un seguro ganador⟩ **3 within an inch of** : a punto de

incidence [ˈɪntsədənts] *n* **1** FREQUENCY : frecuencia *f*, índice *m* ⟨a high incidence of crime : un alto índice de crímenes⟩ **2 angle of incidence** : ángulo *m* de incidencia

incident[1] [ˈɪntsədənt] *adj* : incidente

incident[2] *n* : incidente *m*, incidencia *f*, episodio *m* (en una obra de ficción)

incidental[1] [ˌɪntsəˈdɛntəl] *adj* **1** SECONDARY : incidental, secundario **2** ACCIDENTAL : casual, fortuito

incidental[2] *n* **1** : algo incidental **2 incidentals** *npl* : imprevistos *mpl*

incidentally [ˌɪntsəˈdɛntəli, -ˈdɛntli] *adv* **1** BY CHANCE : incidentalmente, casualmente **2** BY THE WAY : a propósito, por cierto

incinerate [ɪnˈsɪnəˌreɪt] *vt* **-ated; -ating** : incinerar

incinerator [ɪnˈsɪnəˌreɪt̬ər] *n* : incinerador *m*

incipient [ɪnˈsɪpiənt] *adj* : incipiente, naciente

incise [ɪnˈsaɪz] *vt* **-cised; -cising** **1** ENGRAVE : grabar, cincelar, inscribir **2** : hacer una incisión en

incision [ɪnˈsɪʒən] *n* : incisión *f*

incisive [ɪnˈsaɪsɪv] *adj* : incisivo, penetrante

incisively [ɪnˈsaɪsɪvli] *adv* : con agudeza

incisor [ɪnˈsaɪzər] *n* : incisivo *m*

incite [ɪnˈsaɪt] *vt* **-cited; -citing** : incitar, instigar

incitement [ɪnˈsaɪtmənt] *n* : incitación *f*

inclemency [ɪnˈklɛməntsi] *n, pl* **-cies** : inclemencia *f*

inclement [ɪnˈklɛmənt] *adj* : inclemente, tormentoso

inclination [ˌɪnkləˈneɪʃən] *n* **1** PROPENSITY : inclinación *f*, tendencia *f* **2** DESIRE : deseo *m*, ganas *fpl* **3** BOW : inclinación *f*

incline[1] [ɪnˈklaɪn] *v* **-clined; -clining** *vi* **1** SLOPE : inclinarse **2** TEND : inclinarse, tender ⟨he is inclined to be late : tiende a llegar tarde⟩ — *vt* **1** LOWER : inclinar, bajar ⟨to incline one's head : bajar la cabeza⟩ **2** SLANT : inclinar **3** PREDISPOSE : predisponer

incline[2] [ˈɪnˌklaɪn] *n* : inclinación *f*, pendiente *f*

inclined [ɪnˈklaɪnd] *adj* **1** SLOPING : inclinado **2** PRONE : prono, dispuesto, dado

inclose, inclosure → **enclose, enclosure**

include [ɪnˈkluːd] *vt* **-cluded; -cluding** : incluir, comprender

inclusion [ɪnˈkluːʒən] *n* : inclusión *f*

inclusive [ɪnˈkluːsɪv] *adj* : inclusivo

incognito [ˌɪnˌkɑgˈniːt̬o, ɪnˈkɑgnəˌto:] *adv & adj* : de incógnito

incoherence [ˌɪnkoˈhɪrənts, -ˈhɛr-] *n* : incoherencia *f*

incoherent [ˌɪnkoˈhɪrənt, -ˈhɛr-] *adj* : incoherente — **incoherently** *adv*

incombustible [ˌɪnkəmˈbʌstəbəl] *adj* : incombustible

income [ˈɪnˌkʌm] *n* : ingresos *mpl*, entradas *fpl*

income tax *n* : impuesto *m* sobre la renta

incoming [ˈɪnˌkʌmɪŋ] *adj* **1** ARRIVING : que se recibe (dícese del correo), que llega (dícese de las personas), ascendente (dícese de la marea) **2** NEW : nuevo, entrante ⟨the incoming president : el nuevo presidente⟩ ⟨the incoming year : el año entrante⟩

incommunicado [ˌɪnkəˌmjuːnəˈkɑdo] *adj* : incomunicado

incomparable [ɪnˈkɑmpərəbəl] *adj* : incomparable, sin igual

incompatible [ˌɪnkəmˈpæt̬əbəl] *adj* : incompatible

incompetence [ɪnˈkɑmpətənts] *n* : incompetencia *f*, impericia *f*, ineptitud *f*

incompetent [ɪnˈkɑmpətənt] *adj* : incompetente, inepto, incapaz

incomplete [ˌɪnkəmˈpliːt] *adj* : incompleto — **incompletely** *adv*

incomprehensible [ˌɪnˌkɑmprɪˈhɛntsəbəl] *adj* : incomprensible

inconceivable [ˌɪnkənˈsiːvəbəl] *adj* **1** INCOMPREHENSIBLE : incomprensible **2** UNBELIEVABLE : inconcebible, increíble

inconceivably [,ınkən'si:vəbli] *adv* : inconcebiblemente, increíblemente
inconclusive [,ınkən'klu:sıv] *adj* : inconcluyente, no decisivo
incongruity [,ınkən'gru:əti, -,kan-] *n, pl* -ties : incongruencia *f*
incongruous [ın'kaŋgruəs] *adj* : incongruente, inapropiado, fuera de lugar
incongruously [ın'kaŋgruəsli] *adv* : de manera incongruente, inapropiadamente
inconsequential [,ın,kansə'kwentʃəl] *adj* : intrascendente, de poco importancia
inconsiderable [,ınkən'sıdərəbəl] *adj* : insignificante
inconsiderate [,ınkən'sıdərət] *adj* : desconsiderado, sin consideración — **inconsiderately** *adv*
inconsistency [,ınkən'sıstəntsi] *n, pl* -cies : inconsecuencia *f*, inconsistencia *f*
inconsistent [,ınkən'sıstənt] *adj* : inconsecuente, inconsistente
inconsolable [,ınkən'so:ləbəl] *adj* : inconsolable — **inconsolably** [-bli] *adv*
inconspicuous [,ınkən'spıkjuəs] *adj* : discreto, no conspicuo, que no llama la atención
inconspicuously [,ınkən'spıkjuəsli] *adv* : discretamente, sin llamar la atención
incontestable [,ınkən'testəbəl] *adj* : incontestable, indiscutible — **incontestably** [-bli] *adv*
incontinence [ın'kantənənts] *n* : incontinencia *f*
incontinent [ın'kantənənt] *adj* : incontinente
inconvenience¹ [,ınkən'vi:njənts] *vt* -nienced; -niencing : importunar, incomodar, molestar
inconvenience² *n* : incomodidad *f*, molestia *f*
inconvenient [,ınkən'vi:njənt] *adj* : inconveniente, importuno, incómodo — **inconveniently** *adv*
incorporate [ın'kɔrpə,reıt] *vt* -rated; -rating 1 INCLUDE : incorporar, incluir 2 : incorporar, constituir en sociedad (dícese de un negocio)
incorporation [ın,kɔrpə'reıʃən] *n* : incorporación *f*
incorporeal [,ın,kɔr'poriəl] *adj* : incorpóreo
incorrect [,ınkə'rekt] *adj* 1 INACCURATE : incorrecto 2 WRONG : equivocado, erróneo 3 IMPROPER : impropio — **incorrectly** *adv*
incorrigible [ın'kɔrədʒəbəl] *adj* : incorregible
incorruptible [,ınkə'rʌptəbəl] *adj* : incorruptible
increase¹ [ın'kri:s, 'ın,kri:s] *v* -creased; -creasing *vi* GROW : aumentar, crecer, subir (dícese de los precios) — *vt* AUGMENT : aumentar, acrecentar
increase² ['ın,kri:s, ın'kri:s] *n* : aumento *m*, incremento *m*, subida *f* (de precios)

increasing [ın'kri:sıŋ, 'ın,kri:sıŋ] *adj* : creciente
increasingly [ın'kri:sıŋli] *adv* : cada vez más
incredible [ın'kredəbəl] *adj* : increíble — **incredibly** [-bli] *adv*
incredulity [,ınkrı'du:ləti, -'dju:-] *n* : incredulidad *f*
incredulous [ın'kredʒələs] *adj* : incrédulo, escéptico
incredulously [ın'kredʒələsli] *adv* : con incredulidad
increment ['ıŋkrəmənt, 'ın-] *n* : incremento *m*, aumento *m*
incremental [,ıŋkrə'mentəl, ,ın-] *adj* : de incremento
incriminate [ın'krımə,neıt] *vt* -nated; -nating : incriminar
incrimination [ın,krımə'neıʃən] *n* : incriminación *f*
incriminatory [ın'krımənə,tori] *adj* : incriminatorio
incubate ['ıŋkju,beıt, 'ın-] *v* -bated; -bating *vt* : incubar, empollar — *vi* : incubar(se), empollar
incubation [,ıŋkju'beıʃən, ,ın-] *n* : incubación *f*
incubator ['ıŋkju,beıtər, 'ın-] *n* : incubadora *f*
inculcate [ın'kʌl,keıt, 'ın,kʌl-] *vt* -cated; -cating : inculcar
incumbency [ın'kʌmbəntsi] *n, pl* -cies 1 OBLIGATION : incumbencia *f* 2 : mandato *m* (en la política)
incumbent¹ [ın'kʌmbənt] *adj* : obligatorio
incumbent² *n* : titular *mf*
incur [ın'kər] *vt* **incurred; incurring** : provocar (al enojo), incurrir en (gastos, obligaciones)
incurable [ın'kjurəbəl] *adj* : incurable, sin remedio
incursion [ın'kərʒən] *n* : incursión *f*
indebted [ın'detəd] *adj* 1 : endeudado 2 to be indebted to : estar en deuda con, estarle agradecido a
indebtedness [ın'detədnəs] *n* : endeudamiento *m*
indecency [ın'di:səntsi] *n, pl* -cies : indecencia *f*
indecent [ın'di:sənt] *adj* : indecente — **indecently** *adv*
indecipherable [,ındı'saıfərəbəl] *adj* : indescifrable
indecision [,ındı'sıʒən] *n* : indecisión *f*, irresolución *f*
indecisive [,ındı'saısıv] *adj* 1 INCONCLUSIVE : indeciso, que no es decisivo 2 IRRESOLUTE : indeciso, irresoluto, vacilante 3 INDEFINITE : indefinido — **indecisively** *adv*
indecorous [ın'dekərəs, ,ındı'korəs] *adj* : indecoroso — **indecorously** *adv*
indecorousness [ın'dkərəsnəs, ,ındı'korəs-] *n* : indecoro *m*
indeed [ın'di:d] *adv* 1 TRULY : verdaderamente, de veras 2 (*used as intensifier*) ⟨thank you very much indeed

: muchísimas gracias〉 **3** OF COURSE : claro, por supuesto

indefatigable [ˌɪndɪˈfætɪɡəbəl] *adj* : incansable, infatigable — **indefatigably** [-bli] *adv*

indefensible [ˌɪndɪˈfɛntsəbəl] *adj* **1** VULNERABLE : indefendible, vulnerable **2** INEXCUSABLE : inexcusable

indefinable [ˌɪndɪˈfaɪnəbəl] *adj* : indefinible

indefinite [ɪnˈdɛfənət] *adj* **1** : indefinido, indeterminado 〈indefinite pronouns : pronombres indefinidos〉 **2** VAGUE : vago, impreciso

indefinitely [ɪnˈdɛfənətli] *adv* : indefinidamente, por un tiempo indefinido

indelible [ɪnˈdɛləbəl] *adj* : indeleble, imborrable — **indelibly** [-bli] *adv*

indelicacy [ɪnˈdɛləkəsi] *n* : falta *f* de delicadeza

indelicate [ɪnˈdɛlɪkət] *adj* **1** IMPROPER : indelicado, indecoroso **2** TACTLESS : indiscreto, falto de tacto

indemnify [ɪnˈdɛmnəˌfaɪ] *vt* **-fied; -fying 1** INSURE : asegurar **2** COMPENSATE : indemnizar, compensar

indemnity [ɪnˈdɛmnəti] *n, pl* **-ties 1** INSURANCE : indemnidad *f* **2** COMPENSATION : indemnización *f*

indent [ɪnˈdɛnt] *vt* : sangrar (un párrafo)

indentation [ˌɪnˌdɛnˈteɪʃən] *n* **1** NOTCH : muesca *f*, mella *f* **2** INDENTING : sangría *f* (de un párrafo)

indenture[1] [ɪnˈdɛntʃər] *vt* **-tured; -turing** : ligar por contrato

indenture[2] *n* : contrato de aprendizaje

independence [ˌɪndəˈpɛndənts] *n* : independencia *f*

Independence Day *n* : día *m* de la Independencia (4 de julio en los EE.UU.)

independent[1] [ˌɪndəˈpɛndənt] *adj* : independiente — **independently** *adv*

independent[2] *n* : independiente *mf*

indescribable [ˌɪndɪˈskraɪbəbəl] *adj* : indescriptible, incalificable — **indescribably** [-bli] *adv*

indestructibility [ˌɪndɪˌstrʌktəˈbɪləti] *n* : indestructibilidad *f*

indestructible [ˌɪndɪˈstrʌktəbəl] *adj* : indestructible

indeterminate [ˌɪndɪˈtərmənət] *adj* **1** VAGUE : vago, impreciso, indeterminado **2** INDEFINITE : indeterminado, indefinido

index[1] [ˈɪnˌdɛks] *vt* **1** : ponerle un índice a (un libro o una revista) **2** : incluir en un índice 〈all proper names are indexed : todos los nombres propios están incluidos en el índice〉 **3** INDICATE : indicar, señalar **4** REGULATE : indexar, indiciar 〈to index prices : indiciar los precios〉

index[2] *n, pl* **-dexes** *or* **-dices** [ˈɪndəˌsiz] **1** : índice *m* (de un libro, de precios) **2** INDICATION : indicio *m*, índice *m*, señal *f* 〈an index of her character : una señal de su carácter〉

index finger *n* FOREFINGER : dedo *m* índice

Indian [ˈɪndiən] *n* **1** : indio *m*, -dia *f* **2** → **American Indian** — **Indian** *adj*

indicate [ˈɪndəˌkeɪt] *vt* **-cated; -cating 1** POINT OUT : indicar, señalar **2** SHOW, SUGGEST : ser indicio de, ser señal de **3** EXPRESS : expresar, señalar **4** REGISTER : marcar, poner (una medida, etc.)

indication [ˌɪndəˈkeɪʃən] *n* : indicio *m*, señal *f*

indicative [ɪnˈdɪkətɪv] *adj* : indicativo

indicator [ˈɪndəˌkeɪtər] *n* : indicador *m*

indict [ɪnˈdaɪt] *vt* : acusar, procesar (por un crimen)

indictment [ɪnˈdaɪtmənt] *n* : acusación *f*

indifference [ɪnˈdɪfrənts, -ˈdɪfə-] *n* : indiferencia *f*

indifferent [ɪnˈdɪfrənt, -ˈdɪfə-] *adj* **1** UNCONCERNED : indiferente **2** MEDIOCRE : mediocre

indifferently [ɪnˈdɪfrəntli, -ˈdɪfə-] *adv* **1** : con indiferencia, indiferentemente **2** SO-SO : de modo regular, más o menos

indigence [ˈɪndɪdʒənts] *n* : indigencia *f*

indigenous [ɪnˈdɪdʒənəs] *adj* : indígena, nativo

indigent [ˈɪndɪdʒənt] *adj* : indigente, pobre

indigestible [ˌɪndaɪˈdʒɛstəbəl, -dɪ-] *adj* : difícil de digerir

indigestion [ˌɪndaɪˈdʒɛstʃən, -dɪ-] *n* : indigestión *f*, empacho *m*

indignant [ɪnˈdɪɡnənt] *adj* : indignado

indignantly [ɪnˈdɪɡnəntli] *adv* : con indignación

indignation [ˌɪndɪɡˈneɪʃən] *n* : indignación *f*

indignity [ɪnˈdɪɡnəti] *n, pl* **-ties** : indignidad *f*

indigo [ˈɪndɪˌɡoː] *n, pl* **-gos** *or* **-goes** : añil *m*, índigo *m*

indirect [ˌɪndəˈrɛkt, -daɪ-] *adj* : indirecto — **indirectly** *adv*

indiscernible [ˌɪndɪˈsərnəbəl, -ˈzər-] *adj* : imperceptible

indiscreet [ˌɪndɪˈskriːt] *adj* : indiscreto, imprudente — **indiscreetly** *adv*

indiscretion [ˌɪndɪˈskrɛʃən] *n* : indiscreción *f*, imprudencia *f*

indiscriminate [ˌɪndɪˈskrɪmənət] *adj* : indiscriminado

indiscriminately [ˌɪndɪˈskrɪmənətli] *adv* : sin discriminación, sin discernimiento

indispensable [ˌɪndɪˈspɛntsəbəl] *adj* : indispensable, necesario, imprescindible — **indispensably** [-bli] *adv*

indisposed [ˌɪndɪˈspoːzd] *adj* **1** ILL : indispuesto, enfermo **2** AVERSE, DISINCLINED : opuesto, reacio 〈to be indisposed toward working : no tener ganas de trabajar〉

indisputable [ˌɪndɪˈspjuːtəbəl, ɪnˈdɪspjutə-] *adj* : indiscutible, incuestionable, incontestable — **indisputably** [-bli] *adv*

indistinct [ˌɪndɪ'stɪŋkt] *adj* : indistinto — **indistinctly** *adv*

indistinctness [ˌɪndɪ'stɪŋktnəs] *n* : falta *f* de claridad

indistinguishable [ˌɪndɪ'stɪŋgwɪʃəbəl] *adj* : indistinguible

individual¹ [ˌɪndə'vɪdʒʊəl] *adj* **1** PERSONAL : individual, personal ⟨individual traits : características personales⟩ **2** SEPARATE : individual, separado **3** PARTICULAR : particular, propio

individual² *n* : individuo *m*

individualism [ˌɪndə'vɪdʒəwə,lɪzəm] *n* : individualismo *m*

individualist [ˌɪndə'vɪdʒʊəlɪst] *n* : individualista *mf*

individuality [ˌɪndə,vɪdʒu'æləti] *n*, *pl* **-ties** : individualidad *f*

individually [ˌɪndə'vɪdʒʊəli, -dʒəli] *adv* : individualmente

indivisible [ˌɪndɪ'vɪzəbəl] *adj* : indivisible

indoctrinate [ɪn'dɑktrə,neɪt] *vt* **-nated; -nating 1** TEACH : enseñar, instruir **2** PROPAGANDIZE : adoctrinar

indoctrination [ɪn,dɑktrə'neɪʃən] *n* : adoctrinamiento *m*

indolence ['ɪndələnts] *n* : indolencia *f*

indolent ['ɪndələnt] *adj* : indolente

indomitable [ɪn'dɑmətəbəl] *adj* : invencible, indomable, indómito — **indomitably** [-bli] *adv*

Indonesian [ˌɪndo'niːʒən, -ʃən] *n* : indonesio *m*, -sia *f* — **Indonesian** *adj*

indoor ['ɪn,dor] *adj* : interior (dícese de las plantas), para estar en casa (dícese de la ropa), cubierto (dícese de las piscinas, etc.), bajo techo (dícese de los deportes)

indoors ['ɪn'dorz] *adv* : adentro, dentro

indubitable [ɪn'duːbəţəbəl, -'dju:-] *adj* : indudable, incuestionable, indiscutible

indubitably [ɪn'duːbəţəbli, -'dju:-] *adv* : indudablemente

induce [ɪn'duːs, -'djuːs] *vt* **-duced; -ducing 1** PERSUADE : persuadir, inducir **2** CAUSE : inducir, provocar ⟨to induce labor : provocar un parto⟩

inducement [ɪn'duːsmənt, -'djuːs-] *n* **1** INCENTIVE : incentivo *m*, aliciente *m* **2** : inducción *f*, provocación *f* (de un parto)

induct [ɪn'dʌkt] *vt* **1** INSTALL : instalar, investir **2** ADMIT : admitir (como miembro) **3** CONSCRIPT : reclutar (al servicio militar)

inductee [ˌɪn,dʌk'tiː] *n* : recluta *mf*, conscripto *m*, -ta *f*

induction [ɪn'dʌkʃən] *n* **1** INTRODUCTION : iniciación *f*, introducción *f* **2** : inducción *f* (en la lógica o la electricidad)

inductive [ɪn'dʌktɪv] *adj* : inductivo

indulge [ɪn'dʌldʒ] *v* **-dulged; -dulging** *vt* **1** GRATIFY : gratificar, satisfacer **2** SPOIL : consentir, mimar — *vi* **to indulge in** : permitirse

indulgence [ɪn'dʌldʒənts] *n* **1** SATISFYING : satisfacción *f*, gratificación *f* **2** HUMORING : complacencia *f*, indulgencia *f* **3** SPOILING : consentimiento *m* **4** : indulgencia *f* (en la religión)

indulgent [ɪn'dʌldʒənt] *adj* : indulgente, consentido — **indulgently** *adv*

industrial [ɪn'dʌstriəl] *adj* : industrial — **industrially** *adv*

industrialist [ɪn'dʌstriəlɪst] *n* : industrial *mf*

industrialization [ɪn,dʌstriələ'zeɪʃən] *n* : industrialización *f*

industrialize [ɪn'dʌstriə,laɪz] *vt* **-ized; -izing** : industrializar

industrious [ɪn'dʌstriəs] *adj* : diligente, industrioso, trabajador

industriously [ɪn'dʌstriəsli] *adv* : con diligencia, con aplicación

industriousness [ɪn'dʌstriəsnəs] *n* : diligencia *f*, aplicación *f*

industry ['ɪndəstri] *n*, *pl* **-tries 1** DILIGENCE : diligencia *f*, aplicación *f* **2** : industria *f* ⟨the steel industry : la industria siderúrgica⟩

inebriated [ɪ'niːbri,eɪţəd] *adj* : ebrio, embriagado

inebriation [ɪ,niːbri'eɪʃən] *n* : ebriedad *f*, embriaguez *f*

ineffable [ɪn'ɛfəbəl] *adj* : inefable — **ineffably** [-bli] *adv*

ineffective [ˌɪnɪ'fɛktɪv] *adj* **1** INEFFECTUAL : ineficaz, inútil **2** INCAPABLE : incompetente, ineficiente, incapaz

ineffectively [ˌɪnɪ'fɛktɪvli] *adv* : ineficazmente, infructuosamente

ineffectual [ˌɪnɪ'fɛktʃʊəl] *adj* : inútil, ineficaz — **ineffectually** *adv*

inefficiency [ˌɪnɪ'fɪʃəntsi] *n*, *pl* **-cies** : ineficiencia *f*, ineficacia *f*

inefficient [ˌɪnɪ'fɪʃənt] *adj* **1** : ineficiente, ineficaz **2** INCAPABLE, INCOMPETENT : incompetente, incapaz — **inefficiently** *adv*

inelegance [ɪn'ɛləgənts] *n* : inelegancia *f*

inelegant [ɪn'ɛləgənt] *adj* : inelegante, poco elegante

ineligibility [ɪn,ɛlədʒə'bɪləţi] *n* : inelegibilidad *f*

ineligible [ɪn'ɛlədʒəbəl] *adj* : inelegible

inept [ɪ'nɛpt] *adj* : inepto ⟨inept at : incapaz para⟩

ineptitude [ɪ'nɛptə,tuːd, -,tjuːd] *n* : ineptitud *f*, incompetencia *f*, incapacidad *f*

inequality [ˌɪnɪ'kwɑləţi] *n*, *pl* **-ties** : desigualdad *f*

inert [ɪ'nərt] *adj* **1** INACTIVE : inerte, inactivo **2** SLUGGISH : lento

inertia [ɪ'nərʃə] *n* : inercia *f*

inescapable [ˌɪnɪ'skeɪpəbəl] *adj* : inevitable, ineludible — **inescapably** [-bli] *adv*

inessential [ˌɪnɪ'sɛntʃəl] *adj* : que no es esencial, innecesario

inestimable [ɪn'ɛstəməbəl] *adj* : inestimable, inapreciable

inevitability [ɪn,ɛvətə'bɪləti] *n, pl* **-ties**
: inevitabilidad *f*
inevitable [ɪn'ɛvətəbəl] *adj* : inevitable
— **inevitably** [-bli] *adv*
inexact [,ɪnɪg'zækt] *adj* : inexacto
inexactly [,ɪnɪg'zæktli] *adv* : sin exactitud
inexcusable [,ɪnɪk'skju:zəbəl] *adj* : inexcusable, imperdonable — **inexcus-
ably** [-bli] *adv*
inexhaustible [,ɪnɪg'zɔstəbəl] *adj* 1 IN-
DEFATIGABLE : infatigable, incansable
2 ENDLESS : inagotable — **inex-
haustibly** [-bli] *adv*
inexorable [ɪn'ɛksərəbəl] *adj* : inexorable — **inexorably** [-bli] *adv*
inexpensive [,ɪnɪk'spɛntsɪv] *adj* : barato, económico
inexperience [,ɪnɪk'spɪriənts] *n* : inexperiencia *f*
inexperienced [,ɪnɪk'spɪriəntst] *adj* : inexperto, novato
inexplicable [,ɪnɪk'splɪkəbəl] *adj* : inexplicable — **inexplicably** [-bli] *adv*
inexpressible [,ɪnɪk'sprɛsəbəl] *adj* : inexpresable, inefable
inextricable [,ɪnɪk'strɪkəbəl, ɪ'nɛk-,strɪ-]
adj : inextricable — **inextricably** [-bli]
adv
infallibility [ɪn,fælə'bɪləti] *n* : infalibilidad *f*
infallible [ɪn'fæləbəl] *adj* : infalible — **in-
fallibly** [-bli] *adv*
infamous ['ɪnfəməs] *adj* : infame — **in-
famously** *adv*
infamy ['ɪnfəmi] *n, pl* **-mies** : infamia *f*
infancy ['ɪnfəntsi] *n, pl* **-cies** : infancia *f*
infant ['ɪnfənt] *n* : bebé *m*; niño *m*, -ña *f*
infantile ['ɪnfən,taɪl, -təl, -,ti:l] *adj* : infantil, pueril
infantile paralysis → **poliomyelitis**
infantry ['ɪnfəntri] *n, pl* **-tries** : infantería
f
infatuated [ɪn'fætʃu,eɪtəd] *adj* **to be infatuated with** : estar encaprichado con
infatuation [ɪn,fætʃu'eɪʃən] *n* : encaprichamiento *m*, enamoramiento *m*
infect [ɪn'fɛkt] *vt* : infectar, contagiar
infection [ɪn'fɛkʃən] *n* : infección *f*, contagio *m*
infectious [ɪn'fɛkʃəs] *adj* : infeccioso,
contagioso
infer [ɪn'fər] *vt* **inferred; inferring** 1 DE-
DUCE : deducir, inferir 2 SURMISE
: concluir, suponer, tener entendido 3
IMPLY : sugerir, insinuar
inference ['ɪnfərənts] *n* : deducción *f*, inferencia *f*, conclusión *f*
inferior[1] [ɪn'fɪriər] *adj* : inferior, malo
inferior[2] *n* : inferior *mf*
inferiority [ɪn,fɪri'orəti] *n, pl* **-ties** : inferioridad *f* ⟨inferiority complex : com-
plejo de inferioridad⟩
infernal [ɪn'fərnəl] *adj* 1 : infernal ⟨in-
fernal fires : fuegos infernales⟩ 2 DIA-
BOLICAL : infernal, diabólico 3
DAMNABLE : maldito, condenado
inferno [ɪn'fər,no:] *n, pl* **-nos** : infierno
m

infertile [ɪn'fərtəl, -,taɪl] *adj* : estéril, infecundo
infertility [,ɪnfər'tɪləti] *n* : esterilidad *f*,
infecundidad *f*
infest [ɪn'fɛst] *vt* : infestar, plagar
infestation [,ɪn,fɛs'teɪʃən] *n* : infestación
f, plaga *f*
infidel ['ɪnfədəl, -,dɛl] *n* : infiel *mf*
infidelity [,ɪnfə'dɛləti, -faɪ-] *n, pl* **-ties** 1
UNFAITHFULNESS : infidelidad *f* 2 DIS-
LOYALTY : deslealtad *f*
infield ['ɪn,fi:ld] *n* : cuadro *m*, diamante
m
infiltrate [ɪn'fɪl,treɪt, 'ɪnfɪl-] *v* **-trated;
-trating** *vt* : infiltrar — *vi* : infiltrarse
infiltration [,ɪnfɪl'treɪʃən] *n* : infiltración
f
infinite ['ɪnfənət] *adj* 1 LIMITLESS : infinito, sin límites 2 VAST : infinito, vasto, extenso
infinitely ['ɪnfənətli] *adv* : infinitamente
infinitesimal [,ɪn,fɪnə'tɛsəməl] *adj* : in-
finitésimo, infinitesimal — **infinitesi-
mally** *adv*
infinitive [ɪn'fɪnətɪv] *n* : infinitivo *m*
infinity [ɪn'fɪnəti] *n, pl* **-ties** 1 : infinito
m (en matemáticas, etc.) 2 : infinidad
f ⟨an infinity of stars : una infinidad de
estrellas⟩
infirm [ɪn'fərm] *adj* 1 FEEBLE : enfermizo, endeble 2 INSECURE : inseguro
infirmary [ɪn'fərməri] *n, pl* **-ries** : enfermería *f*, hospital *m*
infirmity [ɪn'fərməti] *n, pl* **-ties** 1
FRAILTY : debilidad *f*, endeblez *f* 2 AIL-
MENT : enfermedad *f*, dolencia *f* ⟨the
infirmities of age : los achaques de la
vejez⟩
inflame [ɪn'fleɪm] *v* **-flamed; -flaming** *vt*
1 KINDLE : inflamar, encender 2 : in-
flamar (una herida) 3 STIR UP : encender, provocar, inflamar — *vi* : in-
flamarse
inflammable [ɪn'flæməbəl] *adj* 1 FLAM-
MABLE : inflamable 2 IRASCIBLE : irascible, explosivo
inflammation [,ɪnflə'meɪʃən] *n* : inflamación *f*
inflammatory [ɪn'flæmə,tori] *adj* : inflamatorio, incendiario
inflatable [ɪn'fleɪtəbəl] *adj* : inflable
inflate [ɪn'fleɪt] *vt* **-flated; -flating** : inflar, hinchar
inflation [ɪn'fleɪʃən] *n* : inflación *f*
inflationary [ɪn'fleɪʃə,nɛri] *adj* : inflacionario, inflacionista
inflect [ɪn'flɛkt] *vt* 1 CONJUGATE, DE-
CLINE : conjugar, declinar 2 MODU-
LATE : modular (la voz)
inflection [ɪn'flɛkʃən] *n* : inflexión *f*
inflexibility [ɪn,flɛksə'bɪləti] *n, pl* **-ties**
: inflexibilidad *f*
inflexible [ɪn'flɛksɪbəl] *adj* : inflexible
inflict [ɪn'flɪkt] *vt* 1 : infligir, causar, imponer 2 **to inflict oneself on** : imponer uno su presencia (a alguien)
infliction [ɪn'flɪkʃən] *n* : imposición *f*

influence¹ [ˈɪnˌfluːənts, ɪnˈfluːənts] *vt* **-enced; -encing** : influenciar, influir en

influence² *n* **1** : influencia *f*, influjo *m* ⟨to exert influence over : ejercer influencia sobre⟩ ⟨the influence of gravity : el influjo de la gravedad⟩ **2 under the influence** : bajo la influencia del alcohol, embriagado

influential [ˌɪnfluˈɛntʃəl] *adj* : influyente

influenza [ˌɪnfluˈɛnzə] *n* : gripe *f*, influenza *f*, gripa *f Col, Mex*

influx [ˈɪnˌflʌks] *n* : afluencia *f* (de gente), entrada *f* (de mercancías), llegada *f* (de ideas)

inform [ɪnˈfɔrm] *vt* : informar, notificar, avisar — *vi* **to inform on** : delatar, denunciar

informal [ɪnˈfɔrməl] *adj* **1** UNCEREMONIOUS : sin ceremonia, sin etiqueta **2** CASUAL : informal, familiar (dícese del lenguaje) **3** UNOFFICIAL : extraoficial

informality [ˌɪnfɔrˈmæləti, -fər-] *n, pl* **-ties** : informalidad *f*, familiaridad *f*, falta *f* de ceremonia

informally [ɪnˈfɔrməli] *adv* : sin ceremonias, de manera informal, informalmente

informant [ɪnˈfɔrmənt] *n* : informante *mf*; informador *m*, -dora *f*

information [ˌɪnfərˈmeɪʃən] *n* : información *f*

informative [ɪnˈfɔrmətɪv] *adj* : informativo, instructivo

informer [ɪnˈfɔrmər] *n* : informante *mf*; informador *m*, -dora *f*

infraction [ɪnˈfrækʃən] *n* : infracción *f*, violación *f*, transgresión *f*

infrared [ˌɪnfrəˈrɛd] *adj* : infrarrojo

infrastructure [ˈɪnfrəˌstrʌktʃər] *n* : infraestructura *f*

infrequent [ɪnˈfriːkwənt] *adj* : infrecuente, raro

infrequently [ɪnˈfriːkwəntli] *adv* : raramente, con poca frecuencia

infringe [ɪnˈfrɪndʒ] *v* **-fringed; -fringing** *vt* : infringir, violar — *vi* **to infringe on** : abusar de, violar

infringement [ɪnˈfrɪndʒmənt] *n* **1** VIOLATION : violación *f* (de la ley), incumplimiento *m* (de un contrato) **2** ENCROACHMENT : usurpación *f* (de derechos, etc.)

infuriate [ɪnˈfjʊriˌeɪt] *vt* **-ated; -ating** : enfurecer, poner furioso

infuriating [ɪnˈfjʊriˌeɪtɪŋ] *adj* : indignante, exasperante

infuse [ɪnˈfjuːz] *vt* **-fused; -fusing 1** INSTILL : infundir **2** STEEP : hacer una infusión de

infusion [ɪnˈfjuːʒən] *n* : infusión *f*

ingenious [ɪnˈdʒiːnjəs] *adj* : ingenioso — **ingeniously** *adv*

ingenue *or* **ingénue** [ˈɑndʒəˌnuː, ˈæn-; ˈæʒə-, ˈɑ-] *n* : ingenua *f*

ingenuity [ˌɪndʒəˈnuːəti, -ˈnjuː-] *n, pl* **-ities** : ingenio

ingenuous [ɪnˈdʒɛnjʊəs] *adj* **1** FRANK : cándido, franco **2** NAIVE : ingenuo — **ingenuously** *adv*

ingenuousness [ɪnˈdʒɛnjʊəsnəs] *n* **1** FRANKNESS : candidez *f*, candor *m* **2** NAÏVETÉ : ingenuidad *f*

ingest [ɪnˈdʒɛst] *vt* : ingerir

ingestion [ɪnˈdʒɛstʃən] *n* : ingestión *f*

inglorious [ɪnˈgloriəs] *adj* : deshonroso, ignominioso

ingot [ˈɪŋgət] *n* : lingote *m*

ingrained [ɪnˈgreɪnd] *adj* : arraigado

ingrate [ˈɪnˌgreɪt] *n* : ingrato *m*, -ta *f*

ingratiate [ɪnˈgreɪʃiˌeɪt] *vt* **-ated; -ating** : conseguir la benevolencia de ⟨to ingratiate oneself with someone : congraciarse con alguien⟩

ingratiating [ɪnˈgreɪʃiˌeɪtɪŋ] *adj* : halagador, zalamero, obsequioso

ingratitude [ɪnˈgrætəˌtuːd, -ˌtjuːd] *n* : ingratitud *f*

ingredient [ɪnˈgriːdiənt] *n* : ingrediente *m*, componente *m*

ingrown [ˈɪnˌgroːn] *adj* **1** : crecido hacia adentro **2 ingrown toenail** : uña *f* encarnada

inhabit [ɪnˈhæbət] *vt* : vivir en, habitar, ocupar

inhabitable [ɪnˈhæbətəbəl] *adj* : habitable

inhabitant [ɪnˈhæbətənt] *n* : habitante *mf*

inhalant [ɪnˈheɪlənt] *n* : inhalante *m*

inhalation [ˌɪnhəˈleɪʃən, ˌɪnə-] *n* : inhalación *f*

inhale [ɪnˈheɪl] *v* **-haled; -haling** *vt* : inhalar, aspirar — *vi* : inspirar

inhaler [ɪnˈheɪlər] *n* : inhalador *m*

inhere [ɪnˈhɪr] *vi* **-hered; -hering** : ser inherente

inherent [ɪnˈhɪrənt, -ˈhɛr-] *adj* : inherente, intrínseco — **inherently** *adv*

inherit [ɪnˈhɛrət] *vt* : heredar

inheritance [ɪnˈhɛrətənts] *n* : herencia *f*

inheritor [ɪnˈhɛrətər] *n* : heredero *m*, -da *f*

inhibit [ɪnˈhɪbət] *vt* IMPEDE : inhibir, impedir

inhibition [ˌɪnhəˈbɪʃən, ˌɪnə-] *n* : inhibición *f*, cohibición *f*

inhuman [ɪnˈhjuːmən, -ˈjuː-] *adj* : inhumano, cruel — **inhumanly** *adv*

inhumane [ˌɪnhjuˈmeɪn, -ju-] *adj* INHUMAN : inhumano, cruel

inhumanity [ˌɪnhjuˈmænəti, -ju-] *n, pl* **-ties** : inhumanidad *f*, crueldad *f*

inimical [ɪˈnɪmɪkəl] *adj* **1** UNFAVORABLE : adverso, desfavorable **2** HOSTILE : hostil — **inimically** *adv*

inimitable [ɪˈnɪmətəbəl] *adj* : inimitable

iniquitous [ɪˈnɪkwətəs] *adj* : inicuo, malvado

iniquity [ɪˈnɪkwəti] *n, pl* **-ties** : iniquidad *f*

initial¹ [ɪˈnɪʃəl] *vt* **-tialed** *or* **-tialled; -tialing** *or* **-tialling** : poner las iniciales a, firmar con las iniciales

initial² *adj* : inicial, primero — **initially** *adv*

initial³ *n* : inicial *f*

initiate¹ [ɪˈnɪʃiˌeɪt] *vt* **-ated; -ating 1** BE-GIN : comenzar, iniciar **2** INDUCT : instruir **3** INTRODUCE : introducir, instruir

initiate² [ɪˈnɪʃiət] *n* : iniciado *m*, -da *f*

initiation [ɪˌnɪʃiˈeɪʃən] *n* : iniciación *f*

initiative [ɪˈnɪʃətɪv] *n* : iniciativa *f*

initiatory [ɪˈnɪʃiəˌtori] *adj* **1** INTRODUCTORY : introductorio **2** : de iniciación ⟨initiatory rites : ritos de iniciación⟩

inject [ɪnˈdʒɛkt] *vt* : inyectar

injection [ɪnˈdʒɛkʃən] *n* : inyección *f*

injudicious [ˌɪndʒʊˈdɪʃəs] *adj* : imprudente, indiscreto, poco juicioso

injunction [ɪnˈdʒʌŋkʃən] *n* **1** ORDER : orden *f*, mandato *m* **2** COURT ORDER : mandamiento *m* judicial

injure [ˈɪndʒər] *vt* **-jured; -juring 1** WOUND : herir, lesionar **2** HURT : lastimar, dañar, herir **3 to injure oneself** : hacerse daño

injurious [ɪnˈdʒʊriəs] *adj* : perjudicial ⟨injurious to one's health : perjudicial a la salud⟩

injury [ˈɪndʒəri] *n, pl* **-ries 1** WRONG : mal *m*, injusticia *f* **2** DAMAGE, HARM : herida *f*, daño *m*, perjuicio *m*

injustice [ɪnˈdʒʌstəs] *n* : injusticia *f*

ink¹ [ˈɪŋk] *vt* : entintar

ink² *n* : tinta *f*

inkling [ˈɪŋklɪŋ] *n* : presentimiento *m*, indicio *m*, sospecha *f*

inkwell [ˈɪŋkˌwɛl] *n* : tintero *m*

inky [ˈɪŋki] *adj* **1** : manchado de tinta **2** BLACK : negro, impenetrable ⟨inky darkness : negra oscuridad⟩

inland¹ [ˈɪnˌlænd, -lənd] *adv* : hacia el interior, tierra adentro

inland² *adj* : interior

inland³ *n* : interior *m*

in—law [ˈɪnˌlɔ] *n* **1** : pariente *m* político **2 in—laws** *npl* : suegros *mpl*

inlay¹ [ɪnˈleɪ, ˈɪnˌleɪ] *vt* **-laid** [-ˈleɪd, -ˌleɪd]; **-laying** : incrustar, taracear

inlay² [ˈɪnˌleɪ] *n* **1** : incrustación *f* **2** : empaste *m* (de un diente)

inlet [ˈɪnˌlɛt, -lət] *n* : cala *f*, ensenada *f*

inmate [ˈɪnˌmeɪt] *n* : paciente *mf* (en un hospital); preso *m*, -sa *f* (en una prisión); interno *m*, -na *f* (en un asilo)

in memoriam [ˌɪnməˈmoriəm] *prep* : en memoria de

inmost [ˈɪnˌmoːst] → **innermost**

inn [ˈɪn] *n* **1** : posada *f*, hostería *f*, fonda *f* **2** TAVERN : taberna *f*

innards [ˈɪnərdz] *npl* : entrañas *fpl*, tripas *fpl fam*

innate [ɪˈneɪt] *adj* **1** INBORN : innato **2** INHERENT : inherente

inner [ˈɪnər] *adj* : interior, interno

innermost [ˈɪnərˌmoːst] *adj* : más íntimo, más profundo

innersole [ˈɪnərˈsoːl] → **insole**

inning [ˈɪnɪŋ] *n* : entrada *f*

innkeeper [ˈɪnˌkiːpər] *n* : posadero *m*, -ra *f*

innocence [ˈɪnəsənts] *n* : inocencia *f*

innocent¹ [ˈɪnəsənt] *adj* : inocente — **innocently** *adv*

innocent² *n* : inocente *mf*

innocuous [ɪˈnɑkjəwəs] *adj* **1** HARMLESS : inocuo **2** INOFFENSIVE : inofensivo

innovate [ˈɪnəˌveɪt] *vi* **-vated; -vating** : innovar

innovation [ˌɪnəˈveɪʃən] *n* : innovación *f*, novedad *f*

innovative [ˈɪnəˌveɪtɪv] *adj* : innovador

innovator [ˈɪnəˌveɪtər] *n* : innovador *m*, -dora *f*

innuendo [ˌɪnjʊˈɛndo] *n, pl* **-dos** *or* **-does** : insinuación *f*, indirecta *f*

innumerable [ɪˈnuːmərəbəl, -ˈnjuː-] *adj* : innumerable

inoculate [ɪˈnɑkjəˌleɪt] *vt* **-lated; -lating** : inocular

inoculation [ɪˌnɑkjəˈleɪʃən] *n* : inoculación *f*

inoffensive [ˌɪnəˈfɛntsɪv] *adj* : inofensivo

inoperable [ɪnˈɑpərəbəl] *adj* : inoperable

inoperative [ɪnˈɑpərətɪv, -ˌreɪ-] *adj* : inoperante

inopportune [ɪnˌɑpərˈtuːn, -ˈtjuːn] *adj* : inoportuno — **inopportunely** *adv*

inordinate [ɪnˈɔrdənət] *adj* : excesivo, inmoderado, desmesurado — **inordinately** *adv*

inorganic [ˌɪnˌɔrˈgænɪk] *adj* : inorgánico

inpatient [ˈɪnˌpeɪʃənt] *n* : paciente *mf* hospitalizado

input¹ [ˈɪnˌpʊt] *vt* **inputted** *or* **input; inputting** : entrar (datos, información)

input² *n* **1** CONTRIBUTION : aportación *f*, contribución *f* **2** ENTRY : entrada *f* (de datos) **3** ADVICE, OPINION : consejos *mpl*, opinión *f*

inquest [ˈɪnˌkwɛst] *n* INQUIRY, INVESTIGATION : investigación *f*, averiguación *f*, pesquisa *f* (judicial)

inquire [ɪnˈkwaɪr] *v* **-quired; -quiring** *vt* : preguntar, informarse de, inquirir ⟨he inquired how to get in : preguntó como entrar⟩ — *vi* **1** ASK : preguntar, informarse ⟨to inquire about : informarse sobre⟩ ⟨to inquire after (someone) : preguntar por (alguien)⟩ **2 to inquire into** INVESTIGATE : investigar, inquirir sobre

inquiringly [ɪnˈkwaɪrɪŋli] *adv* : inquisitivamente

inquiry [ˈɪnˌkwaɪri, ɪnˈkwaɪri; ˈɪnkwəri, ˈɪŋ-] *n, pl* **-ries 1** QUESTION : pregunta *f* ⟨to make inquiries about : pedir información sobre⟩ **2** INVESTIGATION : investigación *f*, inquisición *f*, pesquisa *f*

inquisition [ˌɪnkwəˈzɪʃən, ˌɪŋ-] *n* **1** : inquisición *f*, interrogatorio *m*, investigación *f* **2 the Inquisition** : la Inquisición *f*

inquisitive [ɪnˈkwɪzətɪv] *adj* : inquisidor, inquisitivo, curioso — **inquisitively** *adv*

inquisitiveness [ɪn'kwɪzətɪvnəs] *n* : curiosidad *f*

inquisitor [ɪn'kwɪzətər] *n* : inquisidor *m*, -dora *f*; interrogador *m*, -dora *f*

inroad ['ɪn,ro:d] *n* **1** ENCROACHMENT, INVASION : invasión *f*, incursión *f* **2 to make inroads into** : ocupar parte de (un tiempo), agotar parte de (ahorros, recursos), invadir (un territorio)

insane [ɪn'seɪn] *adj* **1** MAD : loco, demente ⟨to go insane : volverse loco⟩ **2** ABSURD : absurdo, insensato ⟨an insane scheme : un proyecto insensato⟩

insanely [ɪn'seɪnli] *adv* : como un loco ⟨insanely suspicious : loco de recelo⟩

insanity [ɪn'sænəti] *n*, *pl* **-ties 1** MADNESS : locura *f* **2** FOLLY : locura *f*, insensatez *f*

insatiable [ɪn'seɪʃəbəl] *adj* : insaciable — **insatiably** [-bli] *adv*

inscribe [ɪn'skraɪb] *vt* **-scribed; -scribing 1** ENGRAVE : inscribir, grabar **2** ENROLL : inscribir **3** DEDICATE : dedicar (un libro)

inscription [ɪn'skrɪpʃən] *n* : inscripción *f* (en un monumento), dedicación *f* (en un libro), leyenda *f* (de una ilustración, etc.)

inscrutable [ɪn'skru:təbəl] *adj* : inescrutable, misterioso — **inscrutably** [-bli] *adv*

inseam ['ɪn,si:m] *n* : entrepierna *f*

insect ['ɪn,sɛkt] *n* : insecto *m*

insecticidal [ɪn,sɛktə'saɪdəl] *adj* : insecticida

insecticide [ɪn'sɛktə,saɪd] *n* : insecticida *m*

insecure [,ɪnsɪ'kjʊr] *adj* : inseguro, poco seguro — **insecurely** *adv*

insecurely [,ɪnsɪ'kjʊrli] *adv* : inseguramente

insecurity [,ɪnsɪ'kjʊrəti] *n*, *pl* **-ties** : inseguridad *f*

inseminate [ɪn'sɛmə,neɪt] *vt* **-nated; -nating** : inseminar

insemination [ɪn,sɛmə'neɪʃən] *n* : inseminación *f*

insensibility [ɪn,sɛntsə'bɪləti] *n*, *pl* **-ties** : insensibilidad *f*

insensible [ɪn'sɛntsəbəl] *adj* **1** UNCONSCIOUS : inconsciente, sin conocimiento **2** NUMB : insensible, entumecido **3** UNAWARE : inconsciente

insensitive [ɪn'sɛntsətɪv] *adj* : insensible

insensitivity [ɪn,sɛntsə'tɪvəti] *n*, *pl* **-ties** : insensibilidad *f*

inseparable [ɪn'sɛpərəbəl] *adj* : inseparable

insert[1] [ɪn'sərt] *vt* **1** : insertar, introducir, poner, meter ⟨insert your key in the lock : mete tu llave en la cerradura⟩ **2** INTERPOLATE : interpolar, intercalar

insert[2] ['ɪn,sərt] *n* : inserción *f*, hoja *f* insertada (en una revista, etc.)

insertion [ɪn'sərʃən] *n* : inserción *f*

inset ['ɪn,sɛt] *n* : página *f* intercalada (en un libro), entredós *m* (de encaje en la ropa)

inshore[1] ['ɪn'ʃor] *adv* : hacia la costa

inshore[2] *adj* : cercano a la costa, costero ⟨inshore fishing : pesca costera⟩

inside[1] [ɪn'saɪd, 'ɪn,saɪd] *adv* : adentro, dentro ⟨to run inside : correr para adentro⟩ ⟨inside and out : por dentro y por fuera⟩

inside[2] *adj* **1** : interior, de adentro, de dentro ⟨the inside lane : el carril interior⟩ **2** : confidencial ⟨inside information : información confidencial⟩

inside[3] *n* **1** : interior *m*, parte *f* de adentro **2 insides** *npl* BELLY, GUTS : tripas *fpl fam* **3 inside out** : al revés

inside[4] *prep* **1** INTO : al interior de **2** WITHIN : dentro de **3** (*referring to time*) : en menos de ⟨inside an hour : en menos de una hora⟩

inside of *prep* INSIDE : dentro de

insider [ɪn'saɪdər] *n* : persona *f* enterada

insidious [ɪn'sɪdiəs] *adj* : insidioso — **insidiously** *adv*

insidiousness [ɪn'sɪdiəsnəs] *n* : insidia *f*

insight ['ɪn,saɪt] *n* : perspicacia *f*, penetración *f*

insightful [ɪn'saɪtfəl] *adj* : perspicaz

insignia [ɪn'sɪgniə] *or* **insigne** [-,ni:] *n*, *pl* **-nia** *or* **-nias** : insignia *f*, enseña *f*

insignificance [,ɪnsɪg'nɪfɪkənts] *n* : insignificancia *f*

insignificant [,ɪnsɪg'nɪfɪkənt] *adj* : insignificante

insincere [,ɪnsɪn'sɪr] *adj* : insincero, poco sincero

insincerely [,ɪnsɪn'sɪrli] *adv* : con poca sinceridad

insincerity [,ɪnsɪn'sɛrəti, -'sɪr-] *n*, *pl* **-ties** : insinceridad *f*

insinuate [ɪn'sɪnjʊ,eɪt] *vt* **-ated; -ating** : insinuar

insinuation [ɪn,sɪnjʊ'eɪʃən] *n* : insinuación *f*

insipid [ɪn'sɪpəd] *adj* : insípido

insist [ɪn'sɪst] *v* : insistir

insistence [ɪn'sɪstənts] *n* : insistencia *f*

insistent [ɪn'sɪstənt] *adj* : insistente — **insistently** *adv*

insofar as [,ɪnso'faræz] *conj* : en la medida en que, en tanto que, en cuanto a

insole ['ɪn,so:l] *n* : plantilla *f*

insolence ['ɪntsələnts] *n* : insolencia *f*

insolent ['ɪntsələnt] *adj* : insolente

insolubility [ɪn,saljʊ'bɪləti] *n* : insolubilidad *f*

insoluble [ɪn'saljʊbəl] *adj* : insoluble

insolvency [ɪn'salvəntsi] *n*, *pl* **-cies** : insolvencia *f*

insolvent [ɪn'salvənt] *adj* : insolvente

insomnia [ɪn'samniə] *n* : insomnio *m*

insomuch as [,ɪnso'mʌtʃæz] → **inasmuch as**

insomuch that *conj* SO : así que, de manera que

inspect [ɪn'spɛkt] *vt* : inspeccionar, examinar, revisar

inspection [ɪn'spɛkʃən] *n* : inspección *f*, examen *m*, revisión *f*, revista *f* (de tropas)

inspector [ɪn'spɛktər] *n* : inspector *m*, -tora *f*

inspiration [ˌɪntspə'reɪʃən] *n* : inspiración *f*

inspirational [ˌɪntspə'reɪʃənəl] *adj* : inspirador

inspire [ɪn'spaɪr] *v* -spired; -spiring *vt* 1 INHALE : inhalar, aspirar 2 STIMULATE : estimular, animar, inspirar 3 INSTILL : inspirar, infundir — *vi* : inspirar

instability [ˌɪntstə'bɪləti] *n, pl* -ties : inestabilidad *f*

install [ɪn'stɔl] *vt* -stalled; -stalling 1 : instalar ⟨to install the new president : instalar el presidente nuevo⟩ ⟨to install a fan : montar un abanico⟩ 2 to install oneself : instalarse

installation [ˌɪntstə'leɪʃən] *n* : instalación *f*

installment [ɪn'stɔlmənt] *n* 1 : plazo *m*, cuota *f* ⟨to pay in four installments : pagar a cuatro plazos⟩ 2 : entrega *f* (de una publicación o telenovela) 3 INSTALLATION : instalación *f*

instance ['ɪntstənts] *n* 1 INSTIGATION : instancia *f* 2 EXAMPLE : ejemplo *m* ⟨for instance : por ejemplo⟩ 3 OCCASION : instancia *f*, caso *m*, ocasión *f* ⟨he prefers, in this instance, to remain anonymous : en este caso prefiere quedarse anónimo⟩

instant¹ ['ɪntstənt] *adj* 1 IMMEDIATE : inmediato, instantáneo ⟨an instant reply : una respuesta inmediata⟩ 2 : instantáneo ⟨instant coffee : café instantáneo⟩

instant² *n* : momento *m*, instante *m*

instantaneous [ˌɪntstən'teɪniəs] *adj* : instantáneo

instantaneously [ˌɪntstən'teɪniəsli] *adv* : instantáneamente, al instante

instantly ['ɪntstəntli] *adv* : al instante, instantáneamente

instead [ɪn'stɛd] *adv* 1 : en cambio, en lugar de eso, en su lugar ⟨Dad was going, but Mom went instead : papá iba a ir, pero mamá fue en su lugar⟩ 2 RATHER : al contrario

instead of *prep* : en vez de, en lugar de

instep ['ɪnˌstɛp] *n* : empeine *m*

instigate ['ɪntstəˌgeɪt] *vt* -gated; -gating INCITE, PROVOKE : instigar, incitar, provocar, fomentar

instigation [ˌɪntstə'geɪʃən] *n* : instancia *f*, incitación *f*

instigator ['ɪntstəˌgeɪtər] *n* : instigador *m*, -dora *f*; incitador *m*, -dora *f*

instill [ɪn'stɪl] *vt* -stilled; -stilling : inculcar, infundir

instinct ['ɪnˌstɪŋkt] *n* 1 TALENT : instinto *m*, don *m* ⟨an instinct for the right word : un don para escoger la palabra apropiada⟩ 2 : instinto *m* ⟨maternal instincts : instintos maternales⟩

instinctive [ɪn'stɪŋktɪv] *adj* : instintivo

instinctively [ɪn'stɪŋktɪvli] *adv* : instintivamente, por instinto

instinctual [ɪn'stɪŋktʃuəl] *adj* : instintivo

institute¹ ['ɪntstəˌtuːt, -ˌtjuːt] *vt* -tuted; -tuting 1 ESTABLISH : establecer, instituir, fundar 2 INITIATE : iniciar, empezar, entablar

institute² *n* : instituto *m*

institution [ˌɪntstə'tuːʃən, -'tjuː-] *n* 1 ESTABLISHING : institución *f*, establecimiento *m* 2 CUSTOM : institución *f*, tradición *f* ⟨the institution of marriage : la institución del matrimonio⟩ 3 ORGANIZATION : institución *f*, organismo *m* 4 ASYLUM : asilo *m*

institutional [ˌɪntstə'tuːʃənəl, -'tjuː-] *adj* : institucional

institutionalize [ˌɪntstə'tuːʃənəˌlaɪz, -'tjuː-] *vt* -ized; -izing 1 : institucionalizar ⟨institutionalized values : valores institucionalizados⟩ 2 : internar ⟨institutionalized orphans : huérfanos internados⟩

instruct [ɪn'strʌkt] *vt* 1 TEACH, TRAIN : instruir, adiestrar, enseñar 2 COMMAND : mandar, ordenar, dar instrucciones a

instruction [ɪn'strʌkʃən] *n* 1 TEACHING : instrucción *f*, enseñanza *f* 2 COMMAND : orden *f*, instrucción *f* 3 **instructions** *npl* DIRECTIONS : instrucciones *fpl*, modo *m* de empleo

instructional [ɪn'strʌkʃənəl] *adj* : instructivo, educativo

instructive [ɪn'strʌktɪv] *adj* : instructivo

instructor [ɪn'strʌktər] *n* : instructor *m*, -tora *f*

instrument ['ɪntstrəmənt] *n* : instrumento *m*

instrumental [ˌɪntstrə'mɛntəl] *adj* : instrumental

instrumentalist [ˌɪntstrə'mɛntəlɪst] *n* : instrumentista *mf*

insubordinate [ˌɪnsə'bɔrdənət] *adj* : insubordinado

insubordination [ˌɪnsəˌbɔrdən'eɪʃən] *n* : insubordinación *f*

insubstantial [ˌɪnsəb'stæntʃəl] *adj* : insustancial, poco nutritivo (dícese de una comida), poco sólido (dícese de una estructura o un argumento)

insufferable [ɪn'sʌfərəbəl] *adj* UNBEARABLE : insufrible, intolerable, inaguantable, insoportable — **insufferably** [-bli] *adv*

insufficiency [ˌɪnsə'fɪʃəntsi] *n, pl* -cies : insuficiencia *f*

insufficient [ˌɪnsə'fɪʃənt] *adj* : insuficiente — **insufficiently** *adv*

insular ['ɪntsulər, -sju-] *adj* 1 : isleño (dícese de la gente), insular (dícese del clima) ⟨insular residents : residentes de la isla⟩ 2 NARROW-MINDED : de miras estrechas

insularity [ˌɪntsʊ'lærəti, -sjʊ-] *n* : insularidad *f*

insulate ['ɪntsəˌleɪt] *vt* -lated; -lating : aislar

insulation [ˌɪntsə'leɪʃən] *n* : aislamiento *m*

insulator ['ɪntsəˌleɪtər] *n* : aislador *m* (pieza), aislante *m* (material)

insulin [ˈɪntsələn] *n* : insulina *f*
insult¹ [ɪnˈsʌlt] *vt* : insultar, ofender, injuriar
insult² [ˈɪnˌsʌlt] *n* : insulto *m*, injuria *f*, agravio *m*
insulting [ɪnˈsʌltɪŋ] *adj* : ofensivo, injurioso, insultante
insultingly [ɪnˈsʌltɪŋli] *adv* : ofensivamente, de manera insultante
insuperable [ɪnˈsuːpərəbəl] *adj* : insuperable — **insuperably** [-bli] *adv*
insurable [ɪnˈʃʊrəbəl] *adj* : asegurable
insurance [ɪnˈʃʊrənts, ˈɪnˌʃʊr-] *n* : seguro *m* ⟨life insurance : seguro de vida⟩ ⟨insurance company : compañía de seguros⟩
insure [ɪnˈʃʊr] *vt* **-sured; -suring 1** UNDERWRITE : asegurar **2** ENSURE : asegurar, garantizar
insured [ɪnˈʃʊrd] *n* : asegurado *m*, -da *f*
insurer [ɪnˈʃʊrər] *n* : asegurador *m*, -dora *f*
insurgent¹ [ɪnˈsərdʒənt] *adj* : insurgente
insurgent² *n* : insurgente *mf*
insurmountable [ˌɪnsərˈmaʊntəbəl] *adj* : insuperable, insalvable — **insurmountably** [-bli] *adv*
insurrection [ˌɪnsəˈrɛkʃən] *n* : insurrección *f*, levantamiento *m*, alzamiento *m*
intact [ɪnˈtækt] *adj* : intacto
intake [ˈɪnˌteɪk] *n* **1** OPENING : entrada *f*, toma *f* ⟨fuel intake : toma de combustible⟩ **2** : entrada *f* (de agua o aire), consumo *m* (de sustancias nutritivas) **3 intake of breath** : inhalación *f*
intangible [ɪnˈtændʒəbəl] *adj* : intangible, impalpable — **intangibly** [-bli] *adv*
integer [ˈɪntɪdʒər] *n* : entero *m*
integral [ˈɪntɪgrəl] *adj* : integral, esencial
integrate [ˈɪntəˌgreɪt] *v* **-grated; -grating** *vt* **1** UNITE : integrar, unir **2** DESEGREGATE : eliminar la segregación de — *vi* : integrarse
integration [ˌɪntəˈgreɪʃən] *n* : integración *f*
integrity [ɪnˈtɛgrəti] *n* : integridad *f*
intellect [ˈɪntəlˌɛkt] *n* : intelecto *m*, inteligencia *f*, capacidad *f* intelectual
intellectual¹ [ˌɪntəˈlɛktʃuəl] *adj* : intelectual — **intellectually** *adv*
intellectual² *n* : intelectual *mf*
intellectualism [ˌɪntəˈlɛktʃuəˌlɪzəm] *n* : intelectualismo *m*
intelligence [ɪnˈtɛlədʒənts] *n* **1** : inteligencia *f* **2** INFORMATION, NEWS : inteligencia *f*, información *f*, noticias *fpl*
intelligent [ɪnˈtɛlədʒənt] *adj* : inteligente — **intelligently** *adv*
intelligentsia [ɪnˌtɛləˈdʒɛntsiə, -ˈgɛn-] *ns & pl* : intelectualidad *f*
intelligibility [ɪnˌtɛlədʒəˈbɪləti] *n* : inteligibilidad *f*
intelligible [ɪnˈtɛlədʒəbəl] *adj* : inteligible, comprensible — **intelligibly** [-bli] *adv*
intemperance [ɪnˈtɛmpərənts] *n* : inmoderación *f*, intemperancia *f*

intemperate [ɪnˈtɛmpərət] *adj* : excesivo, inmoderado, desmedido
intend [ɪnˈtɛnd] *vt* **1** MEAN : querer decir ⟨that's not what I intended : eso no es lo que quería decir⟩ **2** PLAN : tener planeado, proyectar, proponerse ⟨I intend to finish by Thursday : me propongo acabar para el jueves⟩
intended [ɪnˈtɛndəd] *adj* **1** PLANNED : previsto, proyectado **2** INTENTIONAL : intencional, deliberado
intense [ɪnˈtɛnts] *adj* **1** EXTREME : intenso, extremo ⟨intense pain : dolor intenso⟩ **2** : profundo, intenso ⟨to my intense relief : para mi alivio profundo⟩ ⟨intense enthusiasm : entusiasmo ardiente⟩
intensely [ɪnˈtɛntsli] *adv* : sumamente, profundamente, intensamente
intensification [ɪnˌtɛntsəfəˈkeɪʃən] *n* : intensificación *f*
intensify [ɪnˈtɛntsəˌfaɪ] *v* **-fied; -fying** *vt* **1** STRENGTHEN : intensificar, redoblar ⟨to intensify one's efforts : redoblar uno sus esfuerzos⟩ **2** SHARPEN : intensificar, agudizar (dolor, ansiedad) — *vi* : intensificarse, hacerse más intenso
intensity [ɪnˈtɛntsəti] *n, pl* **-ties** : intensidad *f*
intensive [ɪnˈtɛntsɪv] *adj* : intensivo — **intensively** *adv*
intent¹ [ɪnˈtɛnt] *adj* **1** FIXED : concentrado, fijo ⟨an intent stare : una mirada fija⟩ **2 intent on** *or* **intent upon** : resuelto a, atento a
intent² *n* **1** PURPOSE : intención *f*, propósito *m* **2 for all intents and purposes** : a todos los efectos, prácticamente
intention [ɪnˈtɛntʃən] *n* : intención *f*, propósito *m*
intentional [ɪnˈtɛntʃənəl] *adj* : intencional, deliberado
intentionally [ɪnˈtɛntʃənəli] *adv* : a propósito, adrede
intently [ɪnˈtɛntli] *adv* : atentamente, fijamente
inter [ɪnˈtər] *vt* **-terred; -terring** : enterrar, inhumar
interact [ˌɪntərˈækt] *vi* : interactuar, actuar recíprocamente, relacionarse
interaction [ˌɪntərˈækʃən] *n* : interacción *f*, interrelación *f*
interactive [ˌɪntərˈæktɪv] *adj* : interactivo
interbreed [ˌɪntərˈbriːd] *v* **-bred** [-ˈbrɛd]; **-breeding** *vt* : cruzar — *vi* : cruzarse
intercalate [ɪnˈtərkəˌleɪt] *vt* **-lated; -lating** : intercalar
intercede [ˌɪntərˈsiːd] *vi* **-ceded; -ceding** : interceder
intercept [ˌɪntərˈsɛpt] *vt* : interceptar
interception [ˌɪntərˈsɛpʃən] *n* : intercepción *f*
intercession [ˌɪntərˈsɛʃən] *n* : intercesión *f*

interchange¹ [ˌɪntərˈtʃeɪndʒ] *vt* -changed; -changing : intercambiar
interchange² [ˈɪntərˌtʃeɪndʒ] *n* 1 EXCHANGE : intercambio *m*, cambio *m* 2 JUNCTION : empalme *m*, enlace *m* de carreteras
interchangeable [ˌɪntərˈtʃeɪndʒəbəl] *adj* : intercambiable
intercity [ˈɪntərˈsɪti] *adj* : interurbano
intercollegiate [ˌɪntərkəˈliːdʒət, -dʒiət] *adj* : interuniversitario
interconnect [ˌɪntərkəˈnɛkt] *vt* 1 : conectar, interconectar (en tecnología) 2 RELATE : interrelacionar — *vi* 1 : conectar 2 : interrelacionarse
intercontinental [ˌɪntərˌkɑntənˈnɛtəl] *adj* : intercontinental
intercourse [ˈɪntərˌkors] *n* 1 RELATIONS : relaciones *fpl*, trato *m* 2 COPULATION : acto *m* sexual, relaciones *fpl* sexuales, coito *m*
interdenominational [ˌɪntərdɪˌnɑməˈneɪʃənəl] *adj* : interconfesional
interdepartmental [ˌɪntərdɪˌpartˈmɛntəl, -ˌdiː-] *adj* : interdepartamental
interdependence [ˌɪntərdɪˈpɛndənts] *n* : interdependencia *f*
interdependent [ˌɪntərdɪˈpɛndənt] *adj* : interdependiente
interdict [ˌɪntərˈdɪkt] *vt* 1 PROHIBIT : prohibir 2 : cortar (las líneas de comunicación o provisión del enemigo)
interest¹ [ˈɪntrəst, -təˌrest] *vt* : interesar
interest² *n* 1 SHARE, STAKE : interés *m*, participación *f* 2 BENEFIT : provecho *m*, beneficio *m*, interés *m* ⟨in the public interest : en el interés público⟩ 3 CHARGE : interés *m*, cargo *m* ⟨compound interest : interés compuesto⟩ 4 CURIOSITY : interés *m*, curiosidad *f* 5 COLOR : color *m*, interés *m* ⟨places of local interest : lugares de color local⟩ 6 HOBBY : afición *f*
interesting [ˈɪntrəstɪŋ, -təˌrestɪŋ] *adj* : interesante — **interestingly** *adv*
interface [ˈɪntərˌfeɪs] *n* 1 : punto *m* de contacto ⟨oil-water interface : punto de contacto entre el agua y el aceite⟩ 2 : interfaz *f* (de una computadora), interfase *f*
interfere [ˌɪntərˈfɪr] *vi* -fered; -fering 1 INTERPOSE : interponerse, hacer interferencia ⟨to interfere with a play : obstruir una jugada⟩ 2 MEDDLE : entrometerse, interferir, intervenir 3 **to interfere with** DISRUPT : afectar (una actividad), interferir (la radiotransmisión) 4 **to interfere with** TOUCH : tocar ⟨someone interfered with my papers : alguien tocó mis papeles⟩
interference [ˌɪntərˈfɪrənts] *n* : interferencia *f*, intromisión *f*
intergalactic [ˌɪntərgəˈlæktɪk] *adj* : intergaláctico
intergovernmental [ˌɪntərˌgʌvərˈmɛntəl, -vərn-] *adj* : intergubernamental
interim¹ [ˈɪntərəm] *adj* : interino, provisional

interim² *n* 1 : interín *m*, intervalo *m* 2 **in the interim** : en el interín, mientras tanto
interior¹ [ɪnˈtɪriər] *adj* : interior
interior² *n* : interior *m*
interject [ˌɪntərˈdʒɛkt] *vt* : interponer, agregar
interjection [ˌɪntərˈdʒɛkʃən] *n* 1 : interjección *f* (en lingüística) 2 EXCLAMATION : exclamación *f* 3 INTERPOSITION, INTERRUPTION : interposición *f*, interrupción *f*
interlace [ˌɪntərˈleɪs] *vt* -laced; -lacing 1 INTERWEAVE : entrelazar 2 INTERSPERSE : intercalar
interlock [ˌɪntərˈlɑk] *vt* 1 UNITE : trabar, unir 2 ENGAGE, MESH : engranar — *vi* : entrelazarse, trabarse
interloper [ˌɪntərˈloːpər] *n* 1 INTRUDER : intruso *m*, -sa *f* 2 MEDDLER : entrometido *m*, -da *f*
interlude [ˈɪntərˌluːd] *n* 1 INTERVAL : intervalo *m*, intermedio *m* (en el teatro) 2 : interludio *m* (en música)
intermarriage [ˌɪntərˈmærɪdʒ] *n* 1 : matrimonio *m* mixto (entre miembros de distintas razas o religiones) 2 : matrimonio *m* entre miembros del mismo grupo
intermarry [ˌɪntərˈmæri] *vi* -married; -marrying 1 : casarse (con miembros de otros grupos) 2 : casarse entre sí (con miembros del mismo grupo)
intermediary¹ [ˌɪntərˈmiːdiˌɛri] *adj* : intermediario
intermediary² *n, pl* -aries : intermediario *m*, -ria *f*
intermediate¹ [ˌɪntərˈmiːdiət] *adj* : intermedio
intermediate² *n* GO-BETWEEN : intermediario *m*, -ria *f*; mediador *m*, -dora *f*
interment [ɪnˈtərmənt] *n* : entierro *m*
interminable [ɪnˈtərmənəbəl] *adj* : interminable, constante — **interminably** [-bli] *adv*
intermingle [ˌɪntərˈmɪŋgəl] *vt* -mingled; -mingling : entremezclar, mezclar — *vi* : entremezclarse
intermission [ˌɪntərˈmɪʃən] *n* : intermisión *f*, intervalo *m*, intermedio *m*
intermittent [ˌɪntərˈmɪtənt] *adj* : intermitente — **intermittently** *adv*
intermix [ˌɪntərˈmɪks] *vt* : entremezclar
intern¹ [ˈɪn̩tərn, ɪnˈtərn] *vt* : confinar (durante la guerra) — *vi* : servir de interno, hacer las prácticas
intern² [ˈɪn̩tərn] *n* : interno *m*, -na *f*
internal [ɪnˈtərnəl] *adj* : interno, interior ⟨internal bleeding : hemorragia interna⟩ ⟨internal affairs : asuntos interiores, asuntos domésticos⟩ — **internally** *adv*
international [ˌɪntərˈnæʃənəl] *adj* : internacional — **internationally** *adv*
internationalize [ˌɪntərˈnæʃənəˌlaɪz] *vt* -ized; -izing : internacionalizar
internee [ˌɪn̩tərˈniː] *n* : interno *m*, -na *f*
Internet [ˈɪntərˌnɛt] *n* : Internet *mf*

internist ['ɪn,tərnɪst] *n* : internista *mf*
interpersonal [,ɪntər'pərsənəl] *adj* : interpersonal
interplay ['ɪntər,pleɪ] *n* : interacción *f*, juego *m*
interpolate [ɪn'tərpə,leɪt] *vt* **-lated;** **-lating** : interpolar
interpose [,ɪntər'po:z] *v* **-posed; -posing** *vt* : interponer, interrumpir con — *vi* : interponerse
interposition [,ɪntərpə'zɪʃən] *n* : interposición *f*
interpret [ɪn'tərprət] *vt* : interpretar
interpretation [ɪn,tərprə'teɪʃən] *n* : interpretación *f*
interpretative [ɪn'tərprə,teɪtɪv] *adj* : interpretativo
interpreter [ɪn'tərprətər] *n* : intérprete *mf*
interpretive [ɪn'tərprətɪv] *adj* : interpretativo
interracial [,ɪntər'reɪʃəl] *adj* : interracial
interrelate [,ɪntərɪ'leɪt] *v* **-related; -relating** : interrelacionar
interrelationship [,ɪntərɪ'leɪʃən,ʃɪp] *n* : interrelación *f*
interrogate [ɪn'tɛrə,geɪt] *vt* **-gated; -gating** : interrogar, someter a un interrogatorio
interrogation [ɪn,tɛrə'geɪʃən] *n* : interrogación *f*
interrogative¹ [,ɪntə'rɑgətɪv] *adj* : interrogativo
interrogative² *n* : interrogativo *m*
interrogator [ɪn'tɛrə,geɪtər] *n* : interrogador *m*, -dora *f*
interrogatory [,ɪntə'rɑgə,tori] *adj* → **interrogative¹**
interrupt [,ɪntə'rʌpt] *v* : interrumpir
interruption [,ɪntə'rʌpʃən] *n* : interrupción *f*
intersect [,ɪntər'sɛkt] *vt* : cruzar, cortar — *vi* : cruzarse (dícese de los caminos), intersectarse (dícese de las líneas o figuras), cortarse
intersection [,ɪntər'sɛkʃən] *n* : intersección *f*, cruce *m*
intersperse [,ɪntər'spərs] *vt* **-spersed; -spersing** : intercalar, entremezclar
interstate [,ɪntər'steɪt] *adj* : interestatal
interstellar [,ɪntər'stɛlər] *adj* : interestelar
interstice [ɪn'tərstəs] *n, pl* **-stices** [-stə,si:z, -stəsəz] : intersticio *m*
intertwine [,ɪntər'twaɪn] *vi* **-twined; -twining** : entrelazarse
interval ['ɪntərvəl] *n* : intervalo *m*
intervene [,ɪntər'vi:n] *vi* **-vened; -vening** 1 ELAPSE : transcurrir, pasar ⟨the intervening years : los años intermediarios⟩ 2 INTERCEDE : intervenir, interceder, mediar
intervention [,ɪntər'vɛnʧən] *n* : intervención *f*
interview¹ ['ɪntər,vju:] *vt* : entrevistar — *vi* : hacer entrevistas
interview² *n* : entrevista *f*
interviewer ['ɪntər,vju:ər] *n* : entrevistador *m*, -dora *f*

interweave [,ɪntər'wi:v] *v* **-wove** [-'wo:v]; **-woven** [-'wo:vən]; **-weaving** *vt* : entretejer, entrelazar — *vi* INTERTWINE : entrelazarse, entretejerse
interwoven [,ɪntər'wo:vən] *adj* : entretejido
intestate [ɪn'tɛs,teɪt, -tət] *adj* : intestado
intestinal [ɪn'tɛstənəl] *adj* : intestinal
intestine [ɪn'tɛstən] *n* **1** : intestino *m* **2 small intestine** : intestino *m* delgado **3 large intestine** : intestino *m* grueso
intimacy ['ɪntəməsi] *n, pl* **-cies** **1** CLOSENESS : intimidad *f* **2** FAMILIARITY : familiaridad *f*
intimate¹ ['ɪntə,meɪt] *vt* **-mated; -mating** : insinuar, dar a entender
intimate² ['ɪntəmət] *adj* **1** CLOSE : íntimo, de confianza ⟨intimate friends : amigos íntimos⟩ **2** PRIVATE : íntimo, privado ⟨intimate clubs : clubes íntimos⟩ **3** INNERMOST, SECRET : íntimo, secreto ⟨intimate fantasies : fantasías secretas⟩
intimate³ *n* : amigo *m* íntimo, amiga *f* íntima
intimidate [ɪn'tɪmə,deɪt] *vt* **-dated; -dating** : intimidar
intimidation [ɪn,tɪmə'deɪʃən] *n* : intimidación *f*
into ['ɪn,tu:] *prep* **1** (*indicating motion*) : en, a, contra, dentro de ⟨she got into bed : se metió en la cama⟩ ⟨to get into a plane : subir a un avión⟩ ⟨he crashed into the wall : chocó contra la pared⟩ ⟨looking into the sun : mirando al sol⟩ **2** (*indicating state or condition*) : a, en ⟨to burst into tears : echarse a llorar⟩ ⟨the water turned into ice : el agua se convirtió en hielo⟩ ⟨to translate into English : traducir al inglés⟩ **3** (*indicating time*) ⟨far into the night : hasta bien entrada la noche⟩ ⟨he's well into his eighties : tiene los ochenta bien cumplidos⟩ **4** (*in mathematics*) ⟨3 into 12 is 4 : 12 dividido por 3 es 4⟩
intolerable [ɪn'tɑlərəbəl] *adj* : intolerable — **intolerably** [-bli] *adv*
intolerance [ɪn'tɑlərənts] *n* : intolerancia *f*
intolerant [ɪn'tɑlərənt] *adj* : intolerante
intonation [,ɪnto'neɪʃən] *n* : entonación *f*
intone [ɪn'to:n] *vt* **-toned; -toning** : entonar
intoxicant [ɪn'tɑksɪkənt] *n* : bebida *f* alcohólica
intoxicate [ɪn'tɑksə,keɪt] *vt* **-cated; -cating** : emborrachar, embriagar
intoxicated [ɪn'tɑksə,keɪtəd] *adj* : borracho, embriagado
intoxicating [ɪn'tɑksə,keɪtɪŋ] *adj* : embriagador
intoxication [ɪn,tɑksə'keɪʃən] *n* : embriaguez *f*
intractable [ɪn'træktəbəl] *adj* : obstinado, intratable
intramural [,ɪntrə'mjʊrəl] *adj* : interno, dentro de la universidad

intransigence [ɪn'træntsədʒənts, -'trænzə-] *n* : intransigencia *f*

intransigent [ɪn'træntsədʒənt, -'trænzə-] *adj* : intransigente

intransitive [ɪn'træntsətɪv, -'trænzə-] *adj* : intransitivo

intravenous [ˌɪntrə'viːnəs] *adj* : intravenoso — **intravenously** *adv*

intrepid [ɪn'trɛpəd] *adj* : intrépido

intricacy ['ɪntrɪkəsi] *n, pl* **-cies** : complejidad *f*, lo intrincado

intricate ['ɪntrɪkət] *adj* : intrincado, complicado — **intricately** *adv*

intrigue¹ [ɪn'triːg] *v* **-trigued; -triguing** : intrigar

intrigue² ['ɪn,triːg, ɪn'triːg] *n* : intriga *f*

intriguing [ɪn'triːgɪŋ] *adj* : intrigante, fascinante

intrinsic [ɪn'trɪnzɪk, -'trɪntsɪk] *adj* : intrínseco, esencial — **intrinsically** [-zɪkli, -sɪ-] *adv*

introduce [ˌɪntrə'duːs, -'djuːs] *vt* **-duced; -ducing 1** : presentar ⟨let me introduce my father : permítame presentar a mi padre⟩ **2** : introducir (algo nuevo), lanzar (un producto), presentar (una ley), proponer (una idea o un tema)

introduction [ˌɪntrə'dʌkʃən] *n* : introducción *f*, presentación *f*

introductory [ˌɪntrə'dʌktəri] *adj* : introductorio, preliminar, de introducción

introspection [ˌɪntrə'spɛkʃən] *n* : introspección *f*

introspective [ˌɪntrə'spɛktɪv] *adj* : introspectivo — **introspectively** *adv*

introvert ['ɪntrə,vərt] *n* : introvertido *m*, -da *f*

introverted ['ɪntrə,vərtəd] *adj* : introvertido

intrude [ɪn'truːd] *v* **-truded; -truding** *vi* **1** INTERFERE : inmiscuirse, entrometerse **2** DISTURB, INTERRUPT : molestar, estorbar, interrumpir — *vt* : introducir por fuerza

intruder [ɪn'truːdər] *n* : intruso *m*, -sa *f*

intrusion [ɪn'truːʒən] *n* : intrusión *f*

intrusive [ɪn'truːsɪv] *adj* : intruso

intuit [ɪn'tuːɪt, -'tjuː-] *vt* : intuir

intuition [ˌɪntu'ɪʃən, -tju-] *n* : intuición *f*

intuitive [ɪn'tuːətɪv, -'tjuː-] *adj* : intuitivo — **intuitively** *adv*

inundate ['ɪnən,deɪt] *vt* **-dated; -dating** : inundar

inundation [ˌɪnən'deɪʃən] *n* : inundación *f*

inure [ɪ'nʊr, -'njʊr] *vt* **-ured; -uring** : acostumbrar, habituar

invade [ɪn'veɪd] *vt* **-vaded; -vading** : invadir

invader [ɪn'veɪdər] *n* : invasor *m*, -sora *f*

invalid¹ [ɪn'væləd] *adj* : inválido, nulo

invalid² ['ɪnvələd] *adj* : inválido, discapacitado

invalid³ ['ɪnvələd] *n* : inválido *m*, -da *f*

invalidate [ɪn'vælə,deɪt] *vt* **-dated; -dating** : invalidar

invalidity [ˌɪnvə'lɪdəti] *n, pl* **-ties** : invalidez *f*, falta de validez *f*

invaluable [ɪn'væljəbəl, -'væljuə-] *adj* : invalorable, inestimable, inapreciable

invariable [ɪn'væriəbəl] *adj* : invariable, constante — **invariably** [-bli] *adv*

invasion [ɪn'veɪʒən] *n* : invasión *f*

invasive [ɪn'veɪsɪv] *adj* : invasivo

invective [ɪn'vɛktɪv] *n* : invectiva *f*, improperio *m*, vituperio *m*

inveigh [ɪn'veɪ] *vi* to inveigh against : arremeter contra, lanzar invectivas contra

inveigle [ɪn'veɪgəl, -'viː-] *vt* **-gled; -gling** : engatusar, embaucar, persuadir con engaños

invent [ɪn'vɛnt] *vt* : inventar

invention [ɪn'vɛntʃən] *n* : invención *f*, invento *m*

inventive [ɪn'vɛntɪv] *adj* : inventivo

inventiveness [ɪn'vɛntɪvnəs] *n* : ingenio *m*, inventiva *f*

inventor [ɪn'vɛntər] *n* : inventor *m*, -tora *f*

inventory¹ ['ɪnvən,tɔri] *vt* **-ried; -rying** : inventariar

inventory² *n, pl* **-ries 1** LIST : inventario *m* **2** STOCK : existencias *fpl*

inverse¹ [ɪn'vərs, 'ɪn,vərs] *adj* : inverso — **inversely** *adv*

inverse² *n* : inverso *m*

inversion [ɪn'vərʒən] *n* : inversión *f*

invert [ɪn'vərt] *vt* : invertir

invertebrate¹ [ɪn'vərtəbrət, -,breɪt] *adj* : invertebrado

invertebrate² *n* : invertebrado *m*

invest [ɪn'vɛst] *vt* **1** AUTHORIZE : investir, autorizar **2** CONFER : conferir **3** : invertir, dedicar ⟨he invested his savings in stocks : invirtió sus ahorros en acciones⟩ ⟨to invest one's time : dedicar uno su tiempo⟩

investigate [ɪn'vɛstə,geɪt] *v* **-gated; -gating** : investigar

investigation [ɪn,vɛstə'geɪʃən] *n* : investigación *f*, estudio *m*

investigative [ɪn'vɛstə,geɪtɪv] *adj* : investigador

investigator [ɪn'vɛstə,geɪtər] *n* : investigador *m*, -dora *f*

investiture [ɪn'vɛstə,tʃʊr, -tʃər] *n* : investidura *f*

investment [ɪn'vɛstmənt] *n* : inversión *f*

investor [ɪn'vɛstər] *n* : inversor *m*, -sora *f*; inversionista *mf*

inveterate [ɪn'vɛtərət] *adj* **1** DEEP-SEATED : inveterado, enraizado **2** HABITUAL : empedernido, incorregible

invidious [ɪn'vɪdiəs] *adj* **1** OBNOXIOUS : repugnante, odioso **2** UNJUST : injusto — **invidiously** *adv*

invigorate [ɪn'vɪgə,reɪt] *vt* **-rated; -rating** : vigorizar, animar

invigorating [ɪn'vɪgə,reɪtɪŋ] *adj* : vigorizante, estimulante

invigoration [ɪn,vɪgə'reɪʃən] *n* : animación *f*

invincibility [ɪn,vɪntsə'bɪləti] *n* : invencibilidad *f*

invincible [ɪn'vɪntsəbəl] *adj* : invencible — **invincibly** [-bli] *adv*

inviolable [ɪn'vaɪələbəl] *adj* : inviolable

inviolate [ɪn'vaɪələt] *adj* : inviolado, puro

invisibility [ɪn,vɪzə'bɪləti] *n* : invisibilidad *f*

invisible [ɪn'vɪzəbəl] *adj* : invisible — **invisibly** [-bli] *adv*

invitation [,ɪnvə'teɪʃən] *n* : invitación *f*

invite [ɪn'vaɪt] *vt* **-vited; -viting 1** ATTRACT : atraer, tentar ⟨a book that invites interest : un libro que atrae el interés⟩ **2** PROVOKE : provocar, buscar ⟨to invite trouble : buscarse problemas⟩ **3** ASK : invitar ⟨we invited them for dinner : los invitamos a cenar⟩ **4** SOLICIT : solicitar, buscar (preguntas, comentarios, etc.)

inviting [ɪn'vaɪtɪŋ] *adj* : atractivo, atrayente

invocation [,ɪnvə'keɪʃən] *n* : invocación *f*

invoice¹ ['ɪn,vɔɪs] *vt* **-voiced; -voicing** : facturar

invoice² *n* : factura *f*

invoke [ɪn'vo:k] *vt* **-voked; -voking 1** : invocar, apelar a ⟨she invoked our aid : apeló a nuestra ayuda⟩ **2** CITE : invocar, citar ⟨to invoke a precedent : invocar un precedente⟩ **3** CONJURE UP : hacer aparecer, invocar

involuntary [ɪn'valən,teri] *adj* : involuntario — **involuntarily** [ɪn-,valən'trəli] *adv*

involve [ɪn'valv] *vt* **-volved; -volving 1** ENGAGE : ocupar (con una tarea, etc.) **2** IMPLICATE : involucrar, enredar, implicar ⟨to be involved in a crime : estar involucrado en un crimen⟩ **3** CONCERN : concernir, afectar **4** CONNECT : conectar, relacionar **5** ENTAIL, INCLUDE : suponer, incluir, consistir en ⟨what does the job involve? : ¿en qué consiste el trabajo?⟩ **6 to be involved with someone** : tener una relación (amorosa) con alguien

involved [ɪn'valvd] *adj* **1** COMPLEX, INTRICATE : complicado, complejo **2** CONCERNED : interesado, afectado

involvement [ɪn'valvmənt] *n* **1** PARTICIPATION : participación *f*, complicidad *f* **2** RELATIONSHIP : relación *f*

invulnerable [ɪn'vʌlnərəbəl] *adj* : invulnerable

inward¹ ['ɪnwərd] *or* **inwards** [-wərdz] *adv* : hacia adentro, hacia el interior

inward² *adj* INSIDE : interior, interno

inwardly ['ɪnwərdli] *adv* **1** MENTALLY, SPIRITUALLY : por dentro **2** INTERNALLY : internamente, interiormente **3** PRIVATELY : para sus adentros, para sí

iodide ['aɪə,daɪd] *n* : yoduro *m*

iodine ['aɪə,daɪn, -dən] *n* : yodo *m*, tintura *f* de yodo

iodize ['aɪə,daɪz] *vt* **-dized; -dizing** : yodar

ion ['aɪən, 'aɪ,ɑn] *n* : ion *m*

ionic [aɪ'ɑnɪk] *adj* : iónico

ionize ['aɪə,naɪz] *v* **ionized; ionizing** : ionizar

ionosphere [aɪ'ɑnə,sfɪr] *n* : ionosfera *f*

iota [aɪ'o:tə] *n* : pizca *f*, ápice *m*

IOU [,aɪ,o:'ju:] *n* : pagaré *m*, vale *m*

IPA [,aɪ,pi:'eɪ] *n* International Phonetic Alphabet : AFI *m*

IQ [,aɪ'kju:] *n* (intelligence quotient) : CI *m*, coeficiente *m* intelectual

Iranian [ɪ'reɪniən, -'ræ-, -'rɑ-; aɪ'-] *n* : iraní *mf* — **Iranian** *adj*

Iraqi [ɪ'rɑki:] *n* : iraquí *mf* — **Iraqi** *adj*

irascibility [ɪ,ræsə'bɪləti] *n* : irascibilidad *f*

irascible [ɪ'ræsəbəl] *adj* : irascible

irate [aɪ'reɪt] *adj* : furioso, airado, iracundo — **irately** *adv*

ire ['aɪr] *n* : ira *f*, cólera *f*

iridescence [,ɪrə'dɛsənts] *n* : iridiscencia *f*

iridescent [,ɪrə'dɛsənt] *adj* : iridiscente

iridium [ɪ'rɪdiəm] *n* : iridio *m*

iris ['aɪrəs] *n, pl* **irises** *or* **irides** ['aɪrə,di:z, 'ɪr-] **1** : iris *m* (del ojo) **2** : lirio *m* (planta)

Irish¹ ['aɪrɪʃ] *adj* : irlandés

Irish² **1** : irlandés *m* (idioma) **2 the Irish** *npl* : los irlandeses

Irishman ['aɪrɪʃmən] *n, pl* **-men** : irlandés *m*

Irishwoman ['aɪrɪʃ,wʊmən] *n, pl* **-women** : irlandesa *f*

irk ['ərk] *vt* : fastidiar, irritar, preocupar

irksome ['ərksəm] *adj* : irritante, fastidioso — **irksomely** *adv*

iron¹ ['aɪərn] *v* : planchar

iron² *n* **1** : hierro *m*, fierro *m* ⟨a will of iron : una voluntad de hierro, una voluntad férrea⟩ **2** : plancha *f* (para planchar la ropa)

ironclad ['aɪərn'klæd] *adj* **1** : acorazado, blindado **2** STRICT : riguroso, estricto

ironic [aɪ'rɑnɪk] *or* **ironical** [-nɪkəl] *adj* : irónico — **ironically** [-kli] *adv*

ironing ['aɪərnɪŋ] *n* **1** PRESSING : planchada *f* **2** : ropa *f* para planchar

ironing board *n* : tabla *f* (de planchar)

ironwork ['aɪərn,wərk] *n* **1** : obra *f* de hierro **2 ironworks** *npl* : fundición *f*

ironworker ['aɪərn,wərkər] *n* : fundidor *m*, -dora *f*

irony ['aɪrəni] *n, pl* **-nies** : ironía *f*

irradiate [ɪ'reɪdi,eɪt] *vt* **-ated; -ating** : irradiar, radiar

irradiation [ɪ,reɪdi'eɪʃən] *n* : irradiación *f*, radiación *f*

irrational [ɪ'ræʃənəl] *adj* : irracional — **irrationally** *adv*

irrationality [ɪ,ræʃə'næləti] *n, pl* **-ties** : irracionalidad *f*

irreconcilable [ɪ,rɛkən'saɪləbəl] *adj* : irreconciliable

irrecoverable [,ɪrɪ'kʌvərəbəl] *adj* : irrecuperable — **irrecoverably** [-bli] *adv*

irredeemable [ˌɪrɪˈdiːməbəl] *adj* **1** : irredimible (dícese de un bono) **2** HOPELESS : irremediable, irreparable

irreducible [ˌɪrɪˈduːsəbəl, -ˈdjuː-] *adj* : irreducible — **irreducibly** [-bli] *adv*

irrefutable [ˌɪrɪˈfjuːtəbəl, ɪrˈrɛfjə-] *adj* : irrefutable

irregular¹ [ɪˈrɛgjələr] *adj* : irregular — **irregularly** *adv*

irregular² *n* **1** : soldado *m* irregular **2 irregulars** *npl* : artículos *mpl* defectuosos

irregularity [ɪˌrɛgjəˈlærəti] *n, pl* **-ties** : irregularidad *f*

irrelevance [ɪˈrɛləvənts] *n* : irrelevancia *f*

irrelevant [ɪˈrɛləvənt] *adj* : irrelevante

irreligious [ˌɪrɪˈlɪdʒəs] *adj* : irreligioso

irreparable [ɪˈrɛpərəbəl] *adj* : irreparable

irreplaceable [ˌɪrɪˈpleɪsəbəl] *adj* : irreemplazable, insustituible

irrepressible [ˌɪrɪˈprɛsəbəl] *adj* : incontenible, incontrolable

irreproachable [ɪrɪˈproːtʃəbəl] *adj* : irreprochable, intachable

irresistible [ˌɪrɪˈzɪstəbəl] *adj* : irresistible — **irresistibly** [-bli] *adv*

irresolute [ɪˈrɛzəˌluːt] *adj* : irresoluto, indeciso

irresolutely [ɪˈrɛzəˌluːtli, -ˌrzəˈluːt-] *adv* : de manera indecisa

irresolution [ɪˌrɛzəˈluːʃən] *n* : irresolución *f*

irrespective of [ˌɪrɪˈspɛktɪvəv] *prep* : sin tomar en consideración, sin tener en cuenta

irresponsibility [ˌɪrɪˌspɑntsəˈbɪləti] *n, pl* **-ties** : irresponsabilidad *f*, falta *f* de responsabilidad

irresponsible [ˌɪrɪˈspɑntsəbəl] *adj* : irresponsable — **irresponsibly** [-bli] *adv*

irretrievable [ˌɪrɪˈtriːvəbəl] *adj* IRRECOVERABLE : irrecuperable

irreverence [ɪˈrɛvərənts] *n* : irreverencia *f*, falta *f* de respeto

irreverent [ɪˈrɛvərənt] *adj* : irreverente, irrespetuoso

irreversible [ˌɪrɪˈvərsəbəl] *adj* : irreversible

irrevocable [ɪˈrɛvəkəbəl] *adj* : irrevocable — **irrevocably** [-bli] *adv*

irrigate [ˈɪrəˌgeɪt] *vt* **-gated; -gating** : irrigar, regar

irrigation [ˌɪrəˈgeɪʃən] *n* : irrigación *f*, riego *m*

irritability [ˌɪrətəˈbɪləti] *n, pl* **-ties** : irritabilidad *f*

irritable [ˈɪrətəbəl] *adj* : irritable, colérico

irritably [ˈɪrətəbli] *adv* : con irritación

irritant¹ [ˈɪrətənt] *adj* : irritante

irritant² *n* : agente *m* irritante

irritate [ˈɪrəˌteɪt] *vt* **-tated; -tating 1** ANNOY : irritar, molestar **2** : irritar (en medicina)

irritating [ˈɪrəˌteɪtɪŋ] *adj* : irritante

irritatingly [ˈɪrəˌteɪtɪŋli] *adv* : de modo irritante, fastidiosamente

irritation [ˌɪrəˈteɪʃən] *n* : irritación *f*

is → be

Islam [ɪsˈlɑm, ɪz-, -ˈlæm; ˈɪsˌlɑm, ˈɪz-, -ˌlæm] *n* : el Islam

Islamic [ɪsˈlɑmɪk, ɪz-, -ˈlæ-] *adj* : islámico

island [ˈaɪlənd] *n* : isla *f*

islander [ˈaɪləndər] *n* : isleño *m*, -ña *f*

isle [ˈaɪl] *n* : isla *f*, islote *m*

islet [ˈaɪlət] *n* : islote *m*

isolate [ˈaɪsəˌleɪt] *vt* **-lated; -lating** : aislar

isolated [ˈaɪsəˌleɪtəd] *adj* : aislado, solo

isolation [ˌaɪsəˈleɪʃən] *n* : aislamiento *m*

isometric [ˌaɪsəˈmɛtrɪk] *adj* : isométrico

isometrics [ˌaɪsəˈmɛtrɪks] *ns & pl* : isometría *f*

isosceles [aɪˈsɑsəˌliːz] *adj* : isósceles

isotope [ˈaɪsəˌtoːp] *n* : isótopo *m*

Israeli [ɪzˈreɪli] *n* : israelí *mf* — **Israeli** *adj*

issue¹ [ˈɪˌʃuː] *v* **-sued; -suing** *vi* **1** EMERGE : emerger, salir, fluir **2** DESCEND : descender (dícese de los padres o antepasados específicos) **3** EMANATE, RESULT : emanar, surgir, resultar — *vt* **1** EMIT : emitir **2** DISTRIBUTE : emitir, distribuir ⟨to issue a new stamp : emitir un sello nuevo⟩ **3** PUBLISH : publicar

issue² *n* **1** EMERGENCE, FLOW : emergencia *f*, flujo *m* **2** PROGENY : descendencia *f*, progenie *f* **3** OUTCOME, RESULT : desenlace *m*, resultado *m*, consecuencia *f* **4** MATTER, QUESTION : asunto *m*, cuestión *f* **5** PUBLICATION : publicación *f*, distribución *f*, emisión *f* **6** : número *m* (de un periódico o una revista)

isthmus [ˈɪsməs] *n* : istmo *m*

it [ˈɪt] *pron* **1** (*as subject; generally omitted*) : él, ella, ello ⟨it's a big building : es un edificio grande⟩ ⟨who was it? : ¿quién era?⟩ **2** (*as indirect object*) : le ⟨I'll give it some water : voy a darle agua⟩ **3** (*as direct object*) : lo, la ⟨give it to me : dámelo⟩ **4** (*as object of a preposition; generally omitted*) : él, ella, ello ⟨behind it : detrás, detrás de él⟩ **5** (*in impersonal constructions*) ⟨it's raining : está lloviendo⟩ ⟨it's 8 o'clock : son las ocho⟩ **6** (*as the implied subject or object of a verb*) ⟨it is necessary to study : es necesario estudiar⟩ ⟨to give it all one's got : dar lo mejor de sí⟩

Italian [ɪˈtæliən, aɪ-] *n* **1** : italiano *m*, -na *f* **2** : italiano *m* (idioma) — **Italian** *adj*

italic¹ [ɪˈtælɪk, aɪ-] *adj* : en cursiva, en bastardilla

italic² *n* : cursiva *f*, bastardilla *f*

italicize [ɪˈtæləˌsaɪz, aɪ-] *vt* **-cized; -cizing** : poner en cursiva

itch¹ [ˈɪtʃ] *vi* **1** : picar ⟨her arm itched : le pica el brazo⟩ **2** : morirse ⟨they were itching to go outside : se morían por salir⟩ — *vt* : dar picazón, hacer picar

itch² *n* **1** ITCHING : picazón *f*, picor *m*, comezón *f* **2** RASH : sarpullido *m*, erupción *f* **3** DESIRE : ansia *f*, deseo *m*

itchy [ˈɪtʃi] *adj* **itchier; -est** : que pica, que da comezón

it'd [ˈɪtəd] (*contraction of* **it had** *or* **it would**) → **have, would**

item [ˈaɪtəm] *n* **1** OBJECT : artículo *m*, pieza *f* ⟨item of clothing : prenda de vestir⟩ **2** : punto *m* (en una agenda), número *m* (en el teatro), ítem *m* (en un documento) **3** news item : noticia *f*

itemize [ˈaɪtəˌmaɪz] *vt* **-ized; -izing** : detallar, enumerar, listar

itinerant [aɪˈtɪnərənt] *adj* : itinerante, ambulante

itinerary [aɪˈtɪnəˌrɛri] *n, pl* **-aries** : itinerario *m*

it'll [ˈɪtəl] (*contraction of* **it shall** *or* **it will**) → **shall, will**

its [ˈɪts] *adj* : su, sus ⟨its kennel : su perrera⟩ ⟨a city and its inhabitants : una ciudad y sus habitantes⟩

it's [ˈɪts] (*contraction of* **it is** *or* **it has**) → **be, have**

itself [ɪtˈsɛlf] *pron* **1** (*used reflexively*) : se ⟨the cat gave itself a bath : el gato se bañó⟩ **2** (*used for emphasis*) : (él) mismo, (ella) misma, sí (mismo), solo ⟨he is courtesy itself : es la misma cortesía⟩ ⟨in and of itself : por sí mismo⟩ ⟨it opened by itself : se abrió solo⟩

IUD [ˌaɪˌjuːˈdiː] *n* : intrauterine *d*evice : DIU *m*, dispositivo *m* intrauterino

I've [ˈaɪv] (*contraction of* **I have**) → **have**

ivory [ˈaɪvəri] *n, pl* **-ries** **1** : marfil *m* **2** : color *m* de marfil

ivy [ˈaɪvi] *n, pl* **ivies** **1** : hiedra *f*, yedra *f* **2** → **poison ivy**

J

j [ˈdʒeɪ] *n, pl* **j's** *or* **js** [ˈdʒeɪz] : décima letra del alfabeto inglés

jab¹ [ˈdʒæb] *v* **jabbed; jabbing** *vt* **1** PUNCTURE : clavar, pinchar **2** POKE : dar, golpear (con la punta de algo) ⟨he jabbed me in the ribs : me dio un codazo en las costillas⟩ — *vi* **to jab at** : dar, golpear

jab² *n* **1** PRICK : pinchazo *m* **2** POKE : golpe *m* abrupto

jabber¹ [ˈdʒæbər] *v* : farfullar

jabber² *n* : galimatías *m*, farfulla *f*

jack¹ [ˈdʒæk] *vt* **to jack up 1** : levantar (con un gato) **2** INCREASE : subir, aumentar

jack² *n* **1** : gato *m*, cric *m* ⟨hydraulic jack : gato hidráulico⟩ **2** FLAG : pabellón *m* **3** SOCKET : enchufe *m* hembra **4** : jota *f*, valet *m* ⟨jack of hearts : jota de corazones⟩ **5 jacks** *npl* : cantillos *mpl*

jackal [ˈdʒækəl] *n* : chacal *m*

jackass [ˈdʒækˌæs] *n* : asno *m*, burro *m*

jacket [ˈdʒækət] *n* **1** : chaqueta *f* **2** COVER : sobrecubierta *f* (de un libro), carátula *f* (de un disco)

jackhammer [ˈdʒækˌhæmər] *n* : martillo *m* neumático

jack–in–the–box [ˈdʒækɪnðəˌbɑks] *n* : caja *f* de sorpresa

jackknife¹ [ˈdʒækˌnaɪf] *vi* **-knifed; -knifing** : doblarse como una navaja, plegarse

jackknife² *n* : navaja *f*

jack–of–all–trades *n* : persona *f* que sabe un poco de todo, persona *f* de muchos oficios

jack–o'–lantern [ˈdʒækəˌlæntərn] *n* : linterna *f* hecha de una calabaza

jackpot [ˈdʒækˌpɑt] *n* **1** : primer premio *m*, gordo *m* **2 to hit the jackpot** : sacarse la lotería, sacarse el gordo

jackrabbit [ˈdʒækˌræbət] *n* : liebre *f* grande de Norteamérica

jade [ˈdʒeɪd] *n* : jade *m*

jaded [ˈdʒeɪdəd] *adj* **1** TIRED : agotado **2** BORED : hastiado

jagged [ˈdʒægəd] *adj* : dentado, mellado

jaguar [ˈdʒæɡˌwɑr, ˈdʒæɡjʊˌwɑr] *n* : jaguar *m*

jai alai [ˈhaɪˌlaɪ] *n* : jai alai *m*, pelota *f* vasca

jail¹ [ˈdʒeɪl] *vt* : encarcelar

jail² *n* : cárcel *f*

jailbreak [ˈdʒeɪlˌbreɪk] *n* : fuga *f*, huida *f* (de la cárcel)

jailer *or* **jailor** [ˈdʒeɪlər] *n* : carcelero *m*, -ra *f*

jalapeño [ˌhɑləˈpeɪnjo, ˌhæ-, -ˈpiːno] *n* : jalapeño *m*

jalopy [dʒəˈlɑpi] *n, pl* **-lopies** : cacharro *m fam*, carro *m* destartalado

jalousie [ˈdʒæləsi] *n* : celosía *f*

jam¹ [ˈdʒæm] *v* **jammed; jamming** *vt* **1** CRAM : apiñar, embutir **2** BLOCK : atascar, atorar **3 to jam on the brakes** : frenar en seco — *vi* STICK : atascarse, atrancarse

jam² *n* **1** *or* **traffic jam** : atasco *m*, embotellamiento *m* (de tráfico) **2** PREDICAMENT : lío *m*, aprieto *m*, apuro *m* **3** : mermelada *f* ⟨strawberry jam : mermelada de fresa⟩

Jamaican [dʒəˈmeɪkən] *n* : jamaiquino *m*, -na *f*; jamaicano *m*, -na *f* — **Jamaican** *adj*

jamb [ˈdʒæm] *n* : jamba *f*

jamboree [ˌdʒæmbəˈriː] *n* : fiesta *f* grande

jangle¹ [ˈdʒæŋɡəl] *v* **-gled; -gling** *vi* : hacer un ruido metálico — *vt* **1** : hacer sonar **2 to jangle one's nerves** : irritar, crispar

jangle² *n* : ruido *m* metálico

janitor [ˈdʒænətər] *n* : portero *m*, -ra *f*; conserje *mf*

January [ˈdʒænjʊˌɛri] *n* : enero *m*

Japanese [ˌdʒæpəˈniːz, -ˈniːs] *n* **1**

: japonés *m*, -nesa *f* **2** : japonés *m* (idioma) — **Japanese** *adj*

jar¹ ['dʒɑr] *v* **jarred; jarring** *vi* **1** GRATE : chirriar **2** CLASH : desentonar **3** SHAKE : sacudirse **4 to jar on** : crispar, enervar — *vt* JOLT : sacudir

jar² *n* **1** GRATING : chirrido *m* **2** JOLT : vibración *f*, sacudida *f* **3** : tarro *m*, bote *m*, pote *m* ⟨a jar of honey : un tarro de miel⟩

jargon ['dʒɑrgən] *n* : jerga *f*

jasmine ['dʒæzmən] *n* : jazmín *m*

jasper ['dʒæspər] *n* : jaspe *m*

jaundice ['dʒɔndɪs] *n* : ictericia *f*

jaundiced ['dʒɔndɪst] *adj* **1** : ictérico **2** EMBITTERED, RESENTFUL : amargado, resentido, negativo ⟨with a jaundiced eye : con una actitud de cinismo⟩

jaunt ['dʒɔnt] *n* : excursión *f*, paseo *m*

jauntily ['dʒɔntəli] *adv* : animadamente

jauntiness ['dʒɔntinəs] *n* : animación *f*, vivacidad *f*

jaunty ['dʒɔnti] *adj* **-tier; -est** **1** SPRIGHTLY : animado, alegre **2** RAKISH : desenvuelto, desenfadado

Javanese [ˌdʒævə'niːz, ˌdʒɑ-, -'niːs] *n* **1** : javanés *m* (idioma) **2** : javanés *m*, -nesa *f* — **Javanese** *adj*

javelin ['dʒævələn] *n* : jabalina *f*

jaw¹ ['dʒɔ] *vi* GAB : cotorrear *fam*, parlotear *fam*

jaw² *n* **1** : mandíbula *f*, quijada *f* **2** : mordaza *f* (de una herramienta) **3 the jaws of death** : las garras *f* de la muerte

jawbone ['dʒɔˌboːn] *n* : mandíbula *f*

jay ['dʒeɪ] *n* : arrendajo *m*, chara *f Mex*, azulejo *m Mex*

jaybird ['dʒeɪˌbərd] → **jay**

jaywalk ['dʒeɪˌwɔk] *vi* : cruzar la calle sin prudencia

jaywalker ['dʒeɪˌwɔkər] *n* : peatón *m* imprudente

jazz¹ ['dʒæz] *vt* **to jazz up** : animar, alegrar

jazz² *n* : jazz *m*

jazzy ['dʒæzi] *adj* **jazzier; -est** **1** : con ritmo de jazz **2** FLASHY, SHOWY : llamativo, ostentoso

jealous ['dʒɛləs] *adj* : celoso, envidioso — **jealously** *adv*

jealousy ['dʒɛləsi] *n* : celos *mpl*, envidia *f*

jeans ['dʒiːnz] *npl* : jeans *mpl*, vaqueros *mpl*

jeep ['dʒiːp] *n* : jeep *m*

jeer¹ ['dʒɪr] *vi* **1** BOO : abuchear **2** SCOFF : mofarse, burlarse — *vt* RIDICULE : mofarse de, burlarse de

jeer² *n* **1** : abucheo *m* **2** TAUNT : mofa *f*, burla *f*

Jehovah [dʒɪ'hoːvə] *n* : Jehová *m*

jell ['dʒɛl] *vi* **1** SET : gelificarse, cuajar **2** FORM : cuajar, formarse (una idea, etc.)

jelly¹ ['dʒɛli] *v* **jellied; jellying** *vi* **1** JELL : gelificarse, cuajar **2** : hacer jalea — *vt* : gelificar

jelly² *n*, *pl* **-lies** **1** : jalea *f* **2** GELATIN : gelatina *f*

jellyfish ['dʒɛliˌfɪʃ] *n* : medusa *f*

jeopardize ['dʒɛpərˌdaɪz] *vt* **-dized; -dizing** : arriesgar, poner en peligro

jeopardy ['dʒɛpərdi] *n* : peligro *m*, riesgo *m*

jerk¹ ['dʒərk] *vt* **1** JOLT : sacudir **2** TUG, YANK : darle un tirón a — *vi* JOLT : dar sacudidas ⟨the train jerked along : el tren iba moviéndose a sacudidas⟩

jerk² *n* **1** TUG : tirón *m*, jalón *m* **2** JOLT : sacudida *f* brusca **3** FOOL : estúpido *m*, -da *f*; idiota *mf*

jerkin ['dʒərkən] *n* : chaqueta *f* sin mangas, chaleco *m*

jerky ['dʒərki] *adj* **jerkier; -est** **1** : espasmódico (dícese de los movimientos) **2** CHOPPY : inconexo (dícese de la prosa) — **jerkily** [-kəli] *adv*

jerry–built ['dʒɛriˌbɪlt] *adj* : mal construido, chapucero

jersey ['dʒərzi] *n*, *pl* **-seys** : jersey *m*

jest¹ ['dʒɛst] *vi* : bromear

jest² *n* : broma *f*, chiste *m*

jester ['dʒɛstər] *n* : bufón *m*, -fona *f*

Jesuit ['dʒɛzuət] *n* : jesuita *m* — **Jesuit** *adj*

Jesus ['dʒiːzəs, -zəz] *n* **1** : Jesús *m* **2 Jesus Christ** : Jesucristo *m* **3 Jesus (Christ)!** *fam* : ¡por Dios!

jet¹ ['dʒɛt] *v* **jetted; jetting** *vt* SPOUT : arrojar a chorros — *vi* **1** GUSH : salir a chorros, chorrear **2** FLY : viajar en avión, volar

jet² *n* **1** STREAM : chorro *m* **2** *or* **jet airplane** : avión *m* a reacción, reactor *m* **3** : azabache *m* (mineral) **4 jet engine** : reactor *m*, motor *m* a reacción **5 jet lag** : desajuste *m* de horario (debido a un vuelo largo)

jet–propelled *adj* : a reacción

jetsam ['dʒɛtsəm] *n* **flotsam and jetsam** : restos *mpl*, desechos *mpl*

jettison ['dʒɛtəsən] *vt* **1** : echar al mar **2** DISCARD : desechar, deshacerse de

jetty ['dʒɛti] *n*, *pl* **-ties** **1** PIER, WHARF : desembarcadero *m*, muelle *m* **2** BREAKWATER : malecón *m*, rompeolas *m*

Jew ['dʒuː] *n* : judío *m*, -día *f*

jewel ['dʒuːəl] *n* **1** : joya *f*, alhaja *f* **2** GEM : piedra *f* preciosa, gema *f* **3** : rubí *m* (de un reloj) **4** TREASURE : joya *f*, tesoro *m*

jeweler *or* **jeweller** ['dʒuːələr] *n* : joyero *m*, -ra *f*

jewelry ['dʒuːəlri] *n* : joyas *fpl*, alhajas *fpl*

Jewish ['dʒuːɪʃ] *adj* : judío

jib ['dʒɪb] *n* : foque *m* (de un barco)

jibe ['dʒaɪb] *vi* **jibed; jibing** AGREE : concordar

jiffy ['dʒɪfi] *n*, *pl* **-fies** : santiamén *m*, segundo *m*, momento *m*

jig¹ ['dʒɪg] *vi* **jigged; jigging** : bailar la giga

jig² *n* **1** : giga *f* **2 the jig is up** : se acabó la fiesta

jigger ['dʒɪgər] *n* : medida de 1 a 2 onzas (para licores)

jiggle¹ ['dʒɪgəl] v **-gled; -gling** vt : agitar o sacudir ligeramente — vi : agitarse, vibrar

jiggle² n : sacudida f, vibración f

jigsaw ['dʒɪg,sɔ] n **1** : sierra f de vaivén **2 jigsaw puzzle** : rompecabezas m

jilt ['dʒɪlt] vt : dejar plantado, dar calabazas a

jimmy¹ ['dʒɪmi] vt **-mied; -mying** : forzar con una palanqueta

jimmy² n, pl **-mies** : palanqueta f

jingle¹ ['dʒɪŋgəl] v **-gled; -gling** vi : tintinear — vt : hacer sonar

jingle² n **1** TINKLE : tintineo m, retintín m **2** : canción f rimada

jingoism ['dʒɪŋgo,ɪzəm] n : jingoísmo m, patriotería f

jingoistic [,dʒɪŋgo'ɪstɪk] or **jingoist** ['dʒɪŋgoɪst] adj : jingoísta, patriotero

jinx¹ ['dʒɪŋks] vt : traer mala suerte a, salar CoRi, Mex

jinx² n **1** : cenizo m, -za f **2 to put a jinx on** : echarle el mal de ojo a

jitters ['dʒɪtərz] npl : nervios mpl ⟨he got the jitters : se puso nervioso⟩

jittery ['dʒɪtəri] adj : nervioso

job ['dʒab] n **1** : trabajo m ⟨he did odd jobs for her : le hizo algunos trabajos⟩ **2** CHORE, TASK : tarea f, quehacer m **3** EMPLOYMENT : trabajo m, empleo m, puesto m

jobber ['dʒabər] n MIDDLEMAN : intermediario m, -ria f

jock ['dʒak] n : deportista mf, atleta mf

jockey¹ ['dʒaki] v **-eyed; -eying** vt **1** MANIPULATE : manipular **2** MANEUVER : maniobrar — vi **to jockey for position** : maniobrar para conseguir algo

jockey² n, pl **-eys** : jockey mf

jocose [dʒo'ko:s] adj : jocoso

jocular ['dʒakjulər] adj : jocoso — **jocularly** adv

jocularity [,dʒakju'lærəti] n : jocosidad f

jodhpurs ['dʒadpərz] npl : pantalones mpl de montar

jog¹ ['dʒag] v **jogged; jogging** vt **1** NUDGE : dar, empujar, codear **2 to jog one's memory** : refrescar la memoria — vi **1** RUN : correr despacio, trotar, hacer footing (como ejercicio) **2** TRUDGE : andar a trote corto

jog² n **1** PUSH, SHAKE : empujoncito m, sacudida f leve **2** TROT : trote m corto, footing m (en deportes) **3** TWIST : recodo m, vuelta f, curva f

jogger ['dʒagər] n : persona f que hace footing

join ['dʒɔɪn] vt **1** CONNECT, LINK : unir, juntar ⟨to join in marriage : unir en matrimonio⟩ **2** ADJOIN : lindar con, colindar con **3** MEET : reunirse con, encontrarse con ⟨we joined them for lunch : nos reunimos con ellos para almorzar⟩ **4** : hacerse socio de (una organización), afiliarse a (un partido), entrar en (una empresa) — vi **1** UNITE : unirse **2** MERGE : empalmar (dícese de las carreteras), confluir (dícese de los ríos) **3 to join up** : hacerse socio, enrolarse

joiner ['dʒɔɪnər] n **1** CARPENTER : carpintero m, -ra f **2** : persona f que se une a varios grupos

joint¹ ['dʒɔɪnt] adj : conjunto, colectivo, mutuo ⟨a joint effort : un esfuerzo conjunto⟩ — **jointly** adv

joint² n **1** : articulación f, coyuntura f ⟨out of joint : dislocado⟩ **2** ROAST : asado m **3** JUNCTURE : juntura f, unión f **4** DIVE : antro m, tasca f

joist ['dʒɔɪst] n : viga f

joke¹ ['dʒo:k] vi **joked; joking** : bromear

joke² n **1** STORY : chiste m **2** PRANK : broma f

joker ['dʒo:kər] n **1** PRANKSTER : bromista mf **2** : comodín m (en los naipes)

jokingly ['dʒo:kɪŋli] adv : en broma

jollity ['dʒaləti] n, pl **-ties** MERRIMENT : alegría f, regocijo m

jolly ['dʒali] adj **-lier; -est** : alegre, jovial

jolt¹ ['dʒo:lt] vi JERK : dar tumbos, dar sacudidas — vt : sacudir

jolt² n **1** JERK : sacudida f brusca **2** SHOCK : golpe m (emocional)

jonquil ['dʒankwɪl] n : junquillo m

Jordanian [dʒor'deɪniən] n : jordano m, -na f — **Jordanian** adj

josh ['dʒaʃ] vt TEASE : tomarle el pelo (a alguien) — vi JOKE : bromear

jostle ['dʒasəl] v **-tled; -tling** vi **1** SHOVE : empujar, dar empellones **2** CONTEND : competir — vt **1** SHOVE : empujar **2 to jostle one's way** : abrirse paso a empellones

jot¹ ['dʒat] vt **jotted; jotting** : anotar, apuntar ⟨jot it down : apúntalo⟩

jot² n BIT : ápice m, jota f, pizca f

jounce¹ ['dʒæunts] v **jounced; jouncing** vt JOLT : sacudir — vi : dar tumbos, dar sacudidas

jounce² n JOLT : sacudida f, tumbo m

journal ['dʒərnəl] n **1** DIARY : diario m **2** PERIODICAL : revista f, publicación f periódica **3** NEWSPAPER : periódico m, diario m

journalism ['dʒərnəl,ɪzəm] n : periodismo m

journalist ['dʒərnəlɪst] n : periodista mf

journalistic [,dʒərnəl'ɪstɪk] adj : periodístico

journey¹ ['dʒərni] vi **-neyed; -neying** : viajar

journey² n, pl **-neys** : viaje m

journeyman ['dʒərnimən] n, pl **-men** [-mən, -,mɛn] : oficial m

joust¹ ['dʒæust] vi : justar

joust² n : justa f

jovial ['dʒo:viəl] adj : jovial — **jovially** adv

joviality [,dʒo:vi'æləti] n : jovialidad f

jowl ['dʒæul] n **1** JAW : mandíbula f **2** CHEEK : mejilla f, cachete m

joy ['dʒɔɪ] n **1** HAPPINESS : gozo m, alegría f, felicidad f **2** DELIGHT : placer m, deleite m ⟨the child is a real joy : el niño es un verdadero placer⟩

joyful ['dʒɔɪfəl] *adj* : gozoso, alegre, feliz — **joyfully** *adv*
joyless ['dʒɔɪləs] *adj* : sin alegría, triste
joyous ['dʒɔɪəs] *adj* : alegre, feliz, eufórico — **joyously** *adv*
joyousness ['dʒɔɪəsnəs] *n* : alegría *f*, felicidad *f*, euforia *f*
joyride ['dʒɔɪ,raɪd] *n* : paseo *m* temerario e irresponsable (en coche)
joystick ['dʒɔɪ,stɪk] *n* : joystick *m*
jubilant ['dʒuːbələnt] *adj* : jubiloso, alborozado — **jubilantly** *adv*
jubilation [,dʒuːbə'leɪʃən] *n* : júbilo *m*
jubilee ['dʒuːbə,liː] *n* 1 : quincuagésimo aniversario *m* 2 CELEBRATION : celebración *f*, festejos *mpl*
Judaic [dʒu'deɪɪk] *adj* : judaico
Judaism ['dʒuːdə,ɪzəm, 'dʒuːdi-, 'dʒuː-,deɪ-] *n* : judaísmo *m*
judge[1] ['dʒʌdʒ] *vt* **judged; judging** 1 ASSESS : evaluar, juzgar 2 DEEM : juzgar, considerar 3 TRY : juzgar (ante el tribunal) 4 **judging by** : a juzgar por
judge[2] *n* 1 : juez *mf*, jueza *f* 2 **to be a good judge of** : saber juzgar a, entender mucho de
judgment *or* **judgement** ['dʒʌdʒmənt] *n* 1 RULING : fallo *m*, sentencia *f* 2 OPINION : opinión *f* 3 DISCERNMENT : juicio *m*, discernimiento *m*
judgmental [,dʒʌdʒ'mntəl] *adj* : crítico — **judgmentally** *adv*
judicature ['dʒuːdɪkə,tʃʊr] *n* : judicatura *f*
judicial [dʒu'dɪʃəl] *adj* : judicial — **judicially** *adv*
judiciary[1] [dʒu'dɪʃi,ri, -'dɪʃəri] *adj* : judicial
judiciary[2] *n* 1 JUDICATURE : judicatura *f* 2 : poder *m* judicial
judicious [dʒu'dɪʃəs] *adj* SOUND, WISE : juicioso, sensato — **judiciously** *adv*
judo ['dʒuː,doː] *n* : judo *m*
jug ['dʒʌg] *n* 1 : jarra *f*, jarro *m*, cántaro *m* 2 JAIL : cárcel *f*, chirona *f fam*
juggernaut ['dʒʌgər,nɔt] *n* : gigante *m*, fuerza *f* irresistible ⟨a political juggernaut : un gigante político⟩
juggle ['dʒʌgəl] *v* **-gled; -gling** *vt* 1 : hacer juegos malabares con 2 MANIPULATE : manipular, jugar con — *vi* : hacer juegos malabares
juggler ['dʒʌgələr] *n* : malabarista *mf*
jugular ['dʒʌgjʊlər] *adj* : yugular ⟨jugular vein : vena yugular⟩
juice ['dʒuːs] *n* 1 : jugo *m* (de carne, de frutas) *m*, zumo *m* (de frutas) 2 ELECTRICITY : electricidad *f*, luz *f*
juicer ['dʒuːsər] *n* : exprimidor *m*
juiciness ['dʒuːsinəs] *n* : jugosidad *f*
juicy ['dʒuːsi] *adj* **juicier; -est** 1 SUCCULENT : jugoso, suculento 2 PROFITABLE : jugoso, lucrativo 3 RACY : picante
jukebox ['dʒuːk,baks] *n* : rocola *f*, máquina *f* de discos
julep ['dʒuːləp] *n* : bebida *f* hecha con whisky americano y menta

July [dʒu'laɪ] *n* : julio *m*
jumble[1] ['dʒʌmbəl] *vt* **-bled; -bling** : mezclar, revolver
jumble[2] *n* : revoltijo *m*, fárrago *m*, embrollo *m*
jumbo[1] ['dʒʌm,boː] *adj* : gigante, enorme, de tamaño extra grande
jumbo[2] *n, pl* **-bos** : coloso *m*, cosa *f* de tamaño extra grande
jump[1] ['dʒʌmp] *vi* 1 LEAP : saltar, brincar 2 START : levantarse de un salto, sobresaltarse 3 MOVE, SHIFT : moverse, pasar ⟨to jump from job to job : pasar de un empleo a otro⟩ 4 INCREASE, RISE : dar un salto, aumentarse de golpe, subir bruscamente 5 BUSTLE : animarse, ajetrearse 6 **to jump to conclusions** : sacar conclusiones precipitadas — *vt* 1 : saltar ⟨to jump a fence : saltar una valla⟩ 2 SKIP : saltarse 3 ATTACK : atacar, asaltar 4 **to jump the gun** : precipitarse
jump[2] *n* 1 LEAP : salto *m* 2 START : sobresalto *m*, respingo *m* 3 INCREASE : subida *f* brusca, aumento *m* 4 ADVANTAGE : ventaja *f* ⟨we got the jump on them : les llevamos la ventaja⟩
jumper ['dʒʌmpər] *n* 1 : saltador *m*, -dora *f* (en deportes) 2 : jumper *m*, vestido *m* sin mangas
jumpy ['dʒʌmpi] *adj* **jumpier; -est** : asustadizo, nervioso
junction ['dʒʌŋkʃən] *n* 1 JOINING : unión *f* 2 : cruce *m* (de calles), empalme *m* (de un ferrocarril), confluencia *f* (de ríos)
juncture ['dʒʌŋktʃər] *n* 1 UNION : juntura *f*, unión *f* 2 MOMENT, POINT : coyuntura *f* ⟨at this juncture : en esta coyuntura, en este momento⟩
June ['dʒuːn] *n* : junio *m*
jungle ['dʒʌŋgəl] *n* : jungla *f*, selva *f*
junior[1] ['dʒuːnjər] *adj* 1 YOUNGER : más joven ⟨John Smith, Junior : John Smith, hijo⟩ 2 SUBORDINATE : subordinado, subalterno
junior[2] *n* 1 : persona *f* de menor edad ⟨she's my junior : es menor que yo⟩ 2 SUBORDINATE : subalterno *m*, -na *f*; subordinado *m*, -da *f* 3 : estudiante *mf* de penúltimo año
juniper ['dʒuːnəpər] *n* : enebro *m*
junk[1] ['dʒʌŋk] *vt* : echar a la basura
junk[2] *n* 1 RUBBISH : desechos *mpl*, desperdicios *mpl* 2 STUFF : trastos *mpl fam*, cachivaches *mpl fam* 3 **piece of junk** : cacharro *m*, porquería *f*
junket ['dʒʌŋkət] *n* : viaje *m* (pagado con dinero público)
junta ['hʊntə, 'dʒʌn-, 'hʌn-] *n* : junta *f* militar
Jupiter ['dʒuːpətər] *n* : Júpiter *m*
jurisdiction [,dʒʊrəs'dɪkʃən] *n* : jurisdicción *f*
jurisprudence [,dʒʊrəs'pruːdənts] *n* : jurisprudencia *f*
jurist ['dʒʊrɪst] *n* : jurista *mf*; magistrado *m*, -da *f*

juror ['dʒʊrər] *n* : jurado *m*, -da *f*
jury ['dʒʊri] *n, pl* **-ries** : jurado *m*
just¹ ['dʒʌst] *adv* **1** EXACTLY : justo, precisamente, exactamente **2** POSSIBLY : posiblemente ⟨it just might work : tal vez resulte⟩ **3** BARELY : justo, apenas ⟨just in time : justo a tiempo⟩ **4** ONLY : sólo, solamente, nada más ⟨just us : sólo nosotros⟩ **5** QUITE : muy, simplemente ⟨it's just horrible! : ¡qué horrible!⟩ **6 to have just (done something)** : acabar de (hacer algo) ⟨he just called : acaba de llamar⟩
just² *adj* : justo — **justly** *adv*
justice ['dʒʌstɪs] *n* **1** : justicia *f* **2** JUDGE : juez *mf*, jueza *f*

justification [,dʒʌstəfə'keɪʃən] *n* : justificación *f*
justify ['dʒʌstə,faɪ] *vt* **-fied; -fying** : justificar — **justifiable** [,dʒʌstə-'faɪəbəl] *adj*
jut ['dʒʌt] *vi* **jutted; jutting** : sobresalir
jute ['dʒuːt] *n* : yute *m*
juvenile¹ ['dʒuːvə,naɪl, -vənəl] *adj* **1** : juvenil ⟨juvenile delinquent : delincuente juvenil⟩ ⟨juvenile court : tribunal de menores⟩ **2** CHILDISH : infantil
juvenile² *n* : menor *mf*
juxtapose ['dʒʌkstə,poːz] *vt* **-posed; -posing** : yuxtaponer
juxtaposition [,dʒʌkstəpə'zɪʃən] *n* : yuxtaposición *f*

K

k ['keɪ] *n, pl* **k's** *or* **ks** ['keɪz] : undécima letra del alfabeto inglés
kaiser ['kaɪzər] *n* : káiser *m*
kale ['keɪl] *n* : col *f* rizada
kaleidoscope [kə'laɪdə,skoːp] *n* : calidoscopio *m*
kamikaze [,kɑmɪ'kɑzi] *n* : kamikaze *m* — **kamikaze** *adj*
kangaroo [,kæŋgə'ruː] *n, pl* **-roos** : canguro *m*
kaolin ['keɪələn] *n* : caolín *m*
karaoke [,kæri'oːki] *n* : karaoke *m*
karat ['kærət] *n* : quilate *m*
karate [kə'rɑti] *n* : karate *m*
katydid ['keɪti,dɪd] *n* : saltamontes *m*
kayak ['kaɪ,æk] *n* : kayac *m*, kayak *m*
keel¹ ['kiːl] *vi* **to keel over** : volcar (dícese de un barco), desplomarse (dícese de una persona)
keel² *n* : quilla *f*
keen ['kiːn] *adj* **1** SHARP : afilado, filoso ⟨a keen blade : una hoja afilada⟩ **2** PENETRATING : cortante, penetrante ⟨a keen wind : un viento cortante⟩ **3** ENTHUSIASTIC : entusiasta **4** ACUTE : agudo, fino ⟨keen hearing : oído fino⟩ ⟨keen intelligence : inteligencia aguda⟩
keenly ['kiːnli] *adv* **1** ENTHUSIASTICALLY : con entusiasmo **2** INTENSELY : vivamente, profundamente ⟨keenly aware of : muy consciente de⟩
keenness ['kiːnnəs] *n* **1** SHARPNESS : lo afilado, lo filoso **2** ENTHUSIASM : entusiasmo *m* **3** ACUTENESS : agudeza *f*
keep¹ ['kiːp] *v* **kept** ['kɛpt]; **keeping** *vt* **1** : cumplir (la palabra a uno), acudir a (una cita) **2** OBSERVE : observar (una fiesta) **3** GUARD : guardar, cuidar **4** CONTINUE : mantener ⟨to keep silence : mantener silencio⟩ **5** SUPPORT : mantener (una familia) **6** RAISE : criar (animales) **7** : llevar, escribir (un diario, etc.) **8** RETAIN : guardar, conservar, quedarse con **9** STORE : guardar **10** DETAIN : hacer quedar, detener **11** PRESERVE : guardar ⟨to keep a secret : guardar un secreto⟩ — *vi* **1** : conser-

varse (dícese de los alimentos) **2** CONTINUE : seguir, no dejar ⟨he keeps on pestering us : no deja de molestarnos⟩ **3 to keep from** : abstenerse de ⟨I couldn't keep from laughing : no podía contener la risa⟩
keep² *n* **1** TOWER : torreón *m* (de un castillo), torre *f* del homenaje **2** SUSTENANCE : manutención *f*, sustento *m* **3 for keeps** : para siempre
keeper ['kiːpər] *n* **1** : guarda *mf* (en un zoológico); conservador *m*, -dora *f* (en un museo) **2** GAMEKEEPER : guardabosque *mf*
keeping ['kiːpɪŋ] *n* **1** CONFORMITY : conformidad *f*, acuerdo *m* ⟨in keeping with : de acuerdo con⟩ **2** CARE : cuidado *m* ⟨in the keeping of : al cuidado de⟩
keepsake ['kiːp,seɪk] *n* : recuerdo *m*
keep up *vt* CONTINUE, MAINTAIN : mantener, seguir con — *vi* **1** : mantenerse al corriente ⟨he kept up with the news : se mantenía al tanto de las noticias⟩ **2** CONTINUE : continuar **3 to keep up with someone** : mantener contacto con alguien
keg ['kɛg] *n* : barril *m*
kelp ['kɛlp] *n* : alga *f* marina
ken ['kɛn] *n* **1** SIGHT : vista *f*, alcance *m* de la vista **2** UNDERSTANDING : comprensión *f*, alcance *m* del conocimiento ⟨it's beyond his ken : no lo puede entender⟩
kennel ['kɛnəl] *n* : caseta *f* para perros, perrera *f*
Kenyan ['kɛnjən, 'kiːn-] *n* : keniano *m*, -na *f* — **Kenyan** *adj*
kept → **keep**
kerchief ['kərtʃəf, -,tʃiːf] *n* : pañuelo *m*
kernel ['kərnəl] *n* **1** : almendra *f* (de semillas y nueces) **2** : grano *m* (de cereales) **3** CORE : meollo *m* ⟨a kernel of truth : un fondo de verdad⟩
kerosene *or* **kerosine** ['kɛrə,siːn, ,kɛrə'-] *n* : queroseno *m*, kerosén *m*, kerosene *m*

ketchup ['kɛtʃəp, 'kæ-] *n* : salsa *f* catsup
kettle ['kɛtəl] *n* **1** : hervidor *m*, pava *f*
Arg, Bol, Chile **2** → **teakettle**
kettledrum ['kɛtəl,drʌm] *n* : timbal *m*
key¹ ['ki:] *vt* **1** ATTUNE : adaptar, adecuar **2 to key up** : poner nervioso, inquietar
key² *adj* : clave, fundamental
key³ *n* **1** : llave *f* **2** SOLUTION : clave *f*,
soluciones *fpl* **3** : tecla *f* (de un piano
o una máquina) **4** : tono *m*, tonalidad
f (en la música) **5** ISLET, REEF : cayo
m, islote *m*
keyboard ['ki:,bord] *n* : teclado *m*
keyhole ['ki:,ho:l] *n* : bocallave *f*, ojo *m*
(de una cerradura)
keynote¹ ['ki:,no:t] *vt* **-noted; -noting 1**
: establecer la tónica de (en música) **2**
: pronunciar el discurso principal de
keynote² *n* **1** : tónica *f* (en música) **2**
: idea *f* fundamental
keystone ['ki:,sto:n] *n* : clave *f*, dovela *f*
keystroke ['ki:,stro:k] *n* : pulsación *f* (de
tecla)
khaki ['kæki, 'kɑ-] *n* : caqui *m*
khan ['kɑn, 'kæn] *n* : kan *m*
kibbutz [kə'bʊts, -'bu:ts] *n, pl* **-butzim**
[-,bʊt'si:m, -,bu:t-] : kibutz *m*
kibitz ['kɪbɪts] *vi* : dar consejos molestos
kibitzer ['kɪbɪtsər, kɪ'bɪt-] *n* : persona *f*
que da consejos molestos
kick¹ ['kɪk] *vi* **1** : dar patadas (dícese de
una persona), cocear (dícese de un an-
imal) **2** PROTEST : patalear, protestar
3 RECOIL : dar un culatazo (dícese de
un arma de fuego) — *vt* : patear, darle una patada (a alguien)
kick² *n* **1** : patada *f*, puntapié *m*, coz *f*
(de un animal) **2** RECOIL : culatazo *m*
(de un arma de fuego) **3** : fuerza *f* ⟨a
drink with a kick : una bebida fuerte⟩
kicker ['kɪkər] *n* : pateador *m*, -dora *f*
(en deportes)
kickoff ['kɪk,ɔf] *n* : saque *m* (inicial)
kick off *vi* **1** : hacer el saque inicial (en
deportes) **2** BEGIN : empezar — *vt* : empezar
kid¹ ['kɪd] *v* **kidded; kidding** *vt* **1** FOOL
: engañar **2** TEASE : tomarle el pelo (a
alguien) — *vi* JOKE : bromear ⟨I'm only
kidding : lo digo en broma⟩
kid² *n* **1** : chivo *m*, -va *f*; cabrito *m*, -ta
f **2** CHILD : chico *m*, -ca *f*; niño *m*, -ña
f
kidder ['kɪdər] *n* : bromista *mf*
kiddingly ['kɪdɪŋli] *adv* : en broma
kidnap ['kɪd,næp] *vt* **-napped** *or* **-naped**
[-,næpt]; **-napping** *or* **-naping** [-,næpɪŋ]
: secuestrar, raptar
kidnapper *or* **kidnaper** ['kɪd,næpər] *n*
: secuestrador *m*, -dora *f*; raptor *m*,
-tora *f*
kidnapping ['kɪd,næpɪŋ] *n* : secuestro *m*
kidney ['kɪdni] *n, pl* **-neys** : riñón *m*
kidney bean *n* : frijol *m*
kill¹ ['kɪl] *vt* **1** : matar **2** END : acabar
con, poner fin a **3 to kill time** : matar
el tiempo

kill² *n* **1** KILLING : matanza *f* **2** PREY
: presa *f*
killer ['kɪlər] *n* : asesino *m*, -na *f*
killjoy ['kɪl,dʒɔɪ] *n* : aguafiestas *mf*
kiln ['kɪl, 'kɪln] *n* : horno *m*
kilo ['ki:,lo:] *n, pl* **-los** : kilo *m*
kilobyte ['kɪlə,baɪt] *n* : kilobyte *m*
kilocycle ['kɪlə,saɪkəl] *n* : kilociclo *m*
kilogram ['kɪlə,græm, 'ki:-] *n* : kilogramo *m*
kilohertz ['kɪlə,hərts] *n* : kilohertzio *m*
kilometer [kɪ'lɑmətər, 'kɪlə,mi:-] *n*
: kilómetro *m*
kilowatt ['kɪlə,wɑt] *n* : kilovatio *m*
kilt ['kɪlt] *n* : falda *f* escocesa
kilter ['kɪltər] *n* **1** ORDER : buen estado
m **2 out of kilter** : descompuesto, es-
tropeado
kimono [kə'mo:no, -nə] *n, pl* **-nos** : kimono *m*, quimono *m*
kin ['kɪn] *n* : familiares *mpl*, parientes
mpl
kind¹ ['kaɪnd] *adj* : amable, bondadoso,
benévolo
kind² *n* **1** ESSENCE : esencia *f* ⟨a difference in degree, not in kind : una diferencia cuantitativa y no cualitativa⟩ **2**
CATEGORY : especie *f*, género *m* **3** TYPE
: clase *f*, tipo *m*, índole *f*
kindergarten ['kɪndər,gɑrtən, -dən] *n*
: kinder *m*, kindergarten *m*, jardín *m*
de infantes, jardín *m* de niños *Mex*
kindhearted [,kaɪnd'hɑrtəd] *adj* : bondadoso, de buen corazón
kindle ['kɪndəl] *v* **-dled; -dling** *vt* **1** IG-
NITE : encender **2** AROUSE : despertar,
suscitar — *vi* : encenderse
kindliness ['kaɪndlinəs] *n* : bondad *f*
kindling ['kɪndlɪŋ, 'kɪndlən] *n* : astillas
fpl, leña *f*
kindly¹ ['kaɪndli] *adv* **1** AMIABLY : amablemente, bondadosamente **2** COUR-
TEOUSLY : cortésmente, con cortesía
⟨we kindly ask you not smoke : les rog-
amos que no fumen⟩ **3** PLEASE : por
favor **4 to take kindly to** : aceptar de
buena gana
kindly² *adj* **-lier; -est** : bondadoso, amable
kindness ['kaɪndnəs] *n* : bondad *f*
kind of *adv* SOMEWHAT : un tanto, algo
kindred¹ ['kɪndrəd] *adj* SIMILAR : similar, afín ⟨kindred spirits : almas geme-
las⟩
kindred² *n* **1** FAMILY : familia *f*, parentela *f* **2** → **kin**
kinfolk ['kɪn,fo:k] *or* **kinfolks** [-,fo:ks]
npl → **kin**
king ['kɪŋ] *n* : rey *m*
kingdom ['kɪŋdəm] *n* : reino *m*
kingfisher ['kɪŋ,fɪʃər] *n* : martín *m*
pescador
kingly ['kɪŋli] *adj* **-lier; -est** : regio, real
king-size ['kɪŋ,saɪz] *or* **king-sized**
[-,saɪzd] *adj* : de tamaño muy grande,
extra largo (dícese de cigarrillos)
kink ['kɪŋk] *n* **1** : rizo *m* (en el pelo),
vuelta *f* (en una cuerda) **2** CRAMP

: calambre *m* ⟨to have a kink in the neck : tener tortícolis⟩

kinky ['kıŋki] *adj* **-kier; -est** : rizado (dícese del pelo), enroscado (dícese de una cuerda)

kinship ['kın,ʃıp] *n* : parentesco *m*

kinsman ['kınzmən] *n, pl* **-men** [-mən, -,mɛn] : familiar *m*, pariente *m*

kinswoman ['kınz,wumən] *n, pl* **-women** [-,wımən] : familiar *f*, pariente *f*

kiosk ['ki:,ask] *n* : quiosco *m*

kipper ['kıpər] *n* : arenque *m* ahumado

kiss¹ ['kıs] *vt* : besar — *vi* : besarse

kiss² *n* : beso *m*

kit ['kıt] *n* **1** SET : juego *m*, kit *m* **2** CASE : estuche *m*, caja *f* **3 first–aid kit** : botiquín *m* **4 tool kit** : caja *f* de herramientas **5 travel kit** : neceser *m*

kitchen ['kıtʃən] *n* : cocina *f*

kite ['kaıt] *n* **1** : milano *m* (ave) **2** : cometa *f*, papalote *m Mex* ⟨to fly a kite : hacer volar una cometa⟩

kith ['kıθ] *n* : amigos *mpl* ⟨kith and kin : amigos y parientes⟩

kitten ['kıtən] *n* : gatito *m*, -ta *f*

kitty ['kıti] *n, pl* **-ties 1** FUND, POOL : bote *m*, fondo *m* común **2** CAT : gato *m*, gatito *m*

kitty–corner ['kıti,kɔrnər] *or* **kitty–cornered** [-nərd] → **catercorner**

kiwi ['ki:,wi:] *n* : kiwi *m*

kleptomania [,klɛptə'meınıə] *n* : cleptomanía *f*

kleptomaniac [,klɛptə'meını,æk] *n* : cleptómano *m*, -na *f*

knack ['næk] *n* : maña *f*, facilidad *f*

knapsack ['næp,sæk] *n* : mochila *f*, morral *m*

knave ['neıv] *n* : bellaco *m*, pícaro *m*

knead ['ni:d] *vt* **1** : amasar, sobar **2** MASSAGE : masajear

knee ['ni:] *n* : rodilla *f*

kneecap ['ni:,kæp] *n* : rótula *f*

kneel ['ni:l] *vi* **knelt** ['nɛlt] *or* **kneeled** ['ni:ld]; **kneeling** : arrodillarse, ponerse de rodillas

knell ['nɛl] *n* : doble *m*, toque *m* ⟨death knell : toque de difuntos⟩

knew → **know**

knickers ['nıkərz] *npl* : pantalones *mpl* bombachos de media pierna

knickknack ['nık,næk] *n* : chuchería *f*, baratija *f*

knife¹ ['naıf] *vt* **knifed** ['naıft]; **knifing** : acuchillar, apuñalar

knife² *n, pl* **knives** ['naıvz] : cuchillo *m*

knight¹ ['naıt] *vt* : conceder el título de *Sir* a

knight² *n* **1** : caballero *m* ⟨knight errant : caballero andante⟩ **2** : caballo *m* (en ajedrez) **3** : uno que tiene el título de *Sir*

knighthood ['naıt,hud] *n* **1** : caballería *f* **2** : título *m* de *Sir*

knightly ['naıtli] *adj* : caballeresco

knit¹ ['nıt] *v* **knit** *or* **knitted** ['nıtəd]; **knitting** *vt* **1** UNITE : unir, enlazar **2** : tejer ⟨to knit a sweater : tejer un suéter⟩ **3**

to knit one's brows : fruncir el ceño — *vi* **1** : tejer **2** : soldarse (dícese de los huesos)

knit² *n* : prenda *f* tejida

knitter ['nıtər] *n* : tejedor *m*, -dora *f*

knob ['nab] *n* **1** LUMP : bulto *m*, protuberancia *f* **2** HANDLE : perilla *f*, tirador *m*, botón *m*

knobbed ['nabd] *adj* **1** KNOTTY : nudoso **2** : que tiene perilla o botón

knobby ['nabi] *adj* **knobbier; -est 1** KNOTTY : nudoso **2 knobby knees** : rodillas *fpl* huesudas

knock¹ ['nak] *vt* **1** HIT, RAP : golpear, golpetear **2** : hacer chocar ⟨they knocked heads : se dieron en la cabeza⟩ **3** CRITICIZE : criticar — *vi* **1** RAP : dar un golpe, llamar (a la puerta) **2** COLLIDE : darse, chocar

knock² *n* : golpe *m*, llamada *f* (a la puerta), golpeteo *m* (de un motor)

knock down *vt* : derribar, echar al suelo

knocker ['nakər] *n* : aldaba *f*, llamador *m*

knock–kneed ['nak'ni:d] *adj* : patizambo

knockout ['nak,aut] *n* : nocaut *m*, knockout *m* (en deportes)

knock out *vt* : dejar sin sentido, poner fuera de combate (en el boxeo)

knoll ['no:l] *n* : loma *f*, otero *m*, montículo *m*

knot¹ ['nat] *v* **knotted; knotting** *vt* : anudar — *vi* : anudarse

knot² *n* **1** : nudo *m* (en cordel o madera), nódulo *m* (en los músculos) **2** CLUSTER : grupo *m* **3** : nudo *m* (unidad de velocidad)

knotty ['nati] *adj* **-tier; -est 1** GNARLED : nudoso **2** COMPLEX : espinoso, enredado, complejo

know ['no:] *v* **knew** ['nu:, 'nju:]; **known** ['no:n]; **knowing** *vt* **1** : saber ⟨he knows the answer : sabe la respuesta⟩ **2** : conocer (a una persona, un lugar) ⟨do you know Julia? : ¿conoces a Julia?⟩ **3** RECOGNIZE : reconocer **4** DISCERN, DISTINGUISH : distinguir, discernir **5 to know how to** : saber ⟨I don't know how to dance : no sé bailar⟩ — *vi* : saber

knowable ['no:əbəl] *adj* : conocible

knowing ['no:ıŋ] *adj* **1** KNOWLEDGEABLE : informado ⟨a knowing look : una mirada de complicidad⟩ **2** ASTUTE : astuto **3** DELIBERATE : deliberado, intencional

knowingly ['no:ıŋli] *adv* **1** : con complicidad ⟨she smiled knowingly : sonrió con una mirada de complicidad⟩ **2** DELIBERATELY : a sabiendas, adrede, a propósito

know–it–all ['no:ıt,ɔl] *n* : sabelotodo *mf fam*

knowledge ['nalıʤ] *n* **1** AWARENESS : conocimiento *m* **2** LEARNING : conocimientos *mpl*, saber *m*

knowledgeable ['nalıʤəbəl] *adj* : informado, entendido, enterado

known ['noːn] *adj* : conocido, familiar
knuckle ['nʌkəl] *n* : nudillo *m*
koala [ko'wɑlə] *n* : koala *m*
kohlrabi [ˌkoːl'rɑbi, -'ræ-] *n, pl* **-bies** : colinabo *m*
Koran [kə'rɑn, -'ræn] *n* **the Koran** : el Corán
Korean [kə'riːən] *n* **1** : coreano *m*, -na *f* **2** : coreano *m* (idioma) — **Korean** *adj*
kosher ['koːʃər] *adj* : aprobado por la ley judía

kowtow [ˌkau'tau, 'kauˌtau] *vi* **to kowtow to** : humillarse ante, doblegarse ante
krypton ['krɪpˌtɑn] *n* : criptón *m*
kudos ['kjuːˌdɑs, 'kuː-, -ˌdoːz] *n* : fama *f*, renombre *m*
kumquat ['kʌmˌkwɑt] *n* : naranjita *f* china
Kurd ['kurd, 'kərd] *n* : kurdo *m*, -da *f*
Kurdish ['kurdɪʃ, 'kər-] *adj* : kurdo
Kuwaiti [ku'weiti] *n* : kuwaití *mf* — **Kuwaiti** *adj*

L

l ['ɛl] *n, pl* **l's** *or* **ls** ['lz] : duodécima letra del alfabeto inglés
lab ['læb] → **laboratory**
label[1] ['leɪbəl] *vt* **-beled** *or* **-belled; -beling** *or* **-belling** **1** : etiquetar, poner etiqueta a **2** BRAND, CATEGORIZE : calificar, tildar, tachar ⟨they labeled him as a fraud : lo calificaron de farsante⟩
label[2] *n* **1** : etiqueta *f*, rótulo *m* **2** DESCRIPTION : calificación *f*, descripción *f* **3** BRAND : marca *f*
labial ['leɪbiəl] *adj* : labial
labor[1] ['leɪbər] *vi* **1** WORK : trabajar **2** STRUGGLE : avanzar penosamente (dícese de una persona), funcionar con dificultad (dícese de un motor) **3 to labor under a delusion** : hacerse ilusiones, tener una falsa impresión — *vt* BELABOR : insistir en, extenderse sobre
labor[2] *n* **1** EFFORT, WORK : trabajo *m*, esfuerzos *mpl* **2** : parto *m* ⟨to be in labor : estar de parto⟩ **3** TASK : tarea *f*, labor *m* **4** WORKERS : mano *f* de obra
laboratory ['læbrəˌtori, lə'bɔrə-] *n, pl* **-ries** : laboratorio *m*
Labor Day *n* : Día *m* del Trabajo
laborer ['leɪbərər] *n* : peón *m*; trabajador *m*, -dora *f*
laborious [lə'boriəs] *adj* : laborioso, difícil
laboriously [lə'boriəsli] *adv* : laboriosamente, trabajosamente
labor union → **union**
labyrinth ['læbəˌrɪnθ] *n* : laberinto *m*
lace[1] ['leɪs] *vt* **laced; lacing** **1** TIE : acordonar, atar los cordones de **2** : adornar de encaje ⟨I laced the dress in white : adorné el vestido de encaje blanco⟩ **3** SPIKE : echar licor a
lace[2] *n* **1** : encaje *m* **2** SHOELACE : cordón *m* (de zapatos), agujeta *f Mex*
lacerate ['læsəˌreɪt] *vt* **-ated; -ating** : lacerar
laceration [ˌlæsə'reɪʃən] *n* : laceración *f*
lack[1] ['læk] *vt* : carecer de, no tener ⟨she lacks patience : carece de paciencia⟩ — *vi* : faltar ⟨they lack for nothing : no les falta nada⟩
lack[2] *n* : falta *f*, carencia *f*
lackadaisical [ˌlækə'deɪzɪkəl] *adj*

: apático, indiferente, lánguido — **lackadaisically** [-kli] *adv*
lackey ['læki] *n, pl* **-eys** **1** FOOTMAN : lacayo *m* **2** TOADY : adulador *m*, -dora *f*
lackluster ['lækˌlʌstər] *adj* **1** DULL : sin brillo, apagado, deslustrado **2** MEDIOCRE : deslucido, mediocre
laconic [lə'kɑnɪk] *adj* : lacónico — **laconically** [-nɪkli] *adv*
lacquer[1] ['lækər] *vt* : laquear, pintar con laca
lacquer[2] *n* : laca *f*
lacrosse [lə'krɔs] *n* : lacrosse *f*
lactic acid ['læktɪk] *n* : ácido *m* láctico
lacuna [lə'kuːnə, -'kjuː-] *n, pl* **-nae** [-ˌniː, -ˌnai] *or* **-nas** : laguna *f*
lacy ['leɪsi] *adj* **lacier; -est** : de encaje, como de encaje
lad ['læd] *n* : muchacho *m*, niño *m*
ladder ['lædər] *n* : escalera *f*
laden ['leɪdən] *adj* : cargado
ladle[1] ['leɪdəl] *vt* **-dled; -dling** : servir con cucharón
ladle[2] *n* : cucharón *m*, cazo *m*
lady ['leɪdi] *n, pl* **-dies** **1** : señora *f*, dama *f* **2** WOMAN : mujer *f*
ladybird ['leɪdiˌbərd] → **ladybug**
ladybug ['leɪdiˌbʌg] *n* : mariquita *f*
lag[1] ['læg] *vi* **lagged; lagging** : quedarse atrás, retrasarse, rezagarse
lag[2] *n* **1** DELAY : retraso *m*, demora *f* **2** INTERVAL : lapso *m*, intervalo *m*
lager ['lɑgər] *n* : cerveza *f* rubia
laggard[1] ['lægərd] *adj* : retardado, retrasado
laggard[2] *n* : rezagado *m*, -da *f*
lagoon [lə'guːn] *n* : laguna *f*
laid → **lay**[1]
laid–back ['leɪd'bæk] *adj* : tranquilo, relajado
lain *pp* → **lie**[1]
lair ['lær] *n* : guarida *f*, madriguera *f*
laissez–faire [ˌlɛˌseɪ'fær, ˌleɪˌzeɪ-] *n* : liberalismo *m* económico
laity ['leɪəti] *n* **the laity** : los laicos, el laicado
lake ['leɪk] *n* : lago *m*
lama ['lɑmə] *n* : lama *m*
lamb ['læm] *n* **1** : cordero *m*, borrego *m* (animal) **2** : carne *f* de cordero

lambaste [læm'beɪst] *or* **lambast** [-'bæst] *vt* **-basted; -basting 1** BEAT, THRASH : golpear, azotar, darle una paliza (a alguien) **2** CENSURE : arremeter contra, censurar

lame[1] ['leɪm] *vt* **lamed; laming** : lisiar, hacer cojo

lame[2] *adj* **lamer; lamest 1** : cojo, renco, rengo **2** WEAK : pobre, débil, poco convincente ⟨a lame excuse : una excusa débil⟩

lamé [lɑ'meɪ, læ-] *n* : lamé *m*

lame duck *n* : persona *f* sin poder ⟨a lame-duck President : un presidente saliente⟩

lamely ['leɪmli] *adv* : sin convicción

lameness ['leɪmnəs] *n* **1** : cojera *f*, renquera *f* **2** : falta *f* de convicción, debilidad *f*, pobreza *f* ⟨the lameness of her response : la pobreza de su respuesta⟩

lament[1] [lə'mɛnt] *vt* **1** MOURN : llorar, llorar por **2** DEPLORE : lamentar, deplorar — *vi* : llorar

lament[2] *n* : lamento *m*

lamentable ['læməntəbəl, lə'mɛntə-] *adj* : lamentable, deplorable — **lamentably** [-bli] *adv*

lamentation [,læmən'teɪʃən] *n* : lamentación *f*, lamento *m*

laminate[1] ['læmə,neɪt] *vt* **-nated; -nating** : laminar

laminate[2] ['læmənət] *n* : laminado *m*

laminated ['læmə,neɪtəd] *adj* : laminado

lamp ['læmp] *n* : lámpara *f*

lampoon[1] [læm'pu:n] *vt* : satirizar

lampoon[2] *n* : sátira *f*

lamprey ['læmpri] *n, pl* **-preys** : lamprea *f*

lance[1] ['lænts] *vt* **lanced; lancing** : abrir con lanceta, sajar

lance[2] *n* : lanza *f*

lance corporal *n* : cabo *m* interino, soldado *m* de primera clase

lancet ['læntsət] *n* : lanceta *f*

land[1] ['lænd] *vt* **1** : desembarcar (pasajeros de un barco), hacer aterrizar (un avión) **2** CATCH : pescar, sacar (un pez) del agua **3** GAIN, SECURE : conseguir, ganar ⟨to land a job : conseguir empleo⟩ **4** DELIVER : dar, asestar ⟨he landed a punch : asestó un puñetazo⟩ — *vi* **1** : aterrizar, tomar tierra, atracar ⟨the plane just landed : el avión acaba de aterrizar⟩ ⟨the ship landed an hour ago : el barco atracó hace una hora⟩ **2** ALIGHT : posarse, aterrizar ⟨to land on one's feet : caer de pie⟩

land[2] *n* **1** GROUND : tierra *f* ⟨dry land : tierra firme⟩ **2** TERRAIN : terreno *m* **3** NATION : país *m*, nación *f* **4** DOMAIN : mundo *m*, dominio *m* ⟨the land of dreams : el mundo de los sueños⟩

landfill ['lænd,fɪl] *n* : vertedero *m* (de basuras)

landing ['lændɪŋ] *n* **1** : aterrizaje *m* (de aviones), desembarco *m* (de barcos) **2** : descansillo *m* (de una escalera)

landing field *n* : campo *m* de aterrizaje

landing strip → **airstrip**

landlady ['lænd,leɪdi] *n, pl* **-dies** : casera *f*, dueña *f*, arrendadora *f*

landless ['lændləs] *adj* : sin tierra

landlocked ['lænd,lɑkt] *adj* : sin salida al mar

landlord ['lænd,lɔrd] *n* : dueño *m*, casero *m*, arrendador *m*

landlubber ['lænd,lʌbər] *n* : marinero *m* de agua dulce

landmark ['lænd,mɑrk] *n* **1** : señal *f* (geográfica), punto *m* de referencia **2** MILESTONE : hito *m* ⟨a landmark in our history : un hito en nuestra historia⟩ **3** MONUMENT : monumento *m* histórico

landowner ['lænd,o:nər] *n* : hacendado *m*, -da *f*; terrateniente *mf*

landscape[1] ['lænd,skeɪp] *vt* **-scaped; -scaping** : ajardinar

landscape[2] *n* : paisaje *m*

landslide ['lænd,slaɪd] *n* **1** : desprendimiento *m* de tierras, derrumbe *m* **2** **landslide victory** : victoria *f* arrolladora

landward ['lændwərd] *adv* : en dirección de la tierra, hacia tierra

lane ['leɪn] *n* **1** PATH, WAY : camino *m*, sendero *m* **2** : carril *m* (de una carretera)

language ['læŋgwɪʤ] *n* **1** : idioma *m*, lengua *f* ⟨the English language : el idioma inglés⟩ **2** : lenguaje *m* ⟨body language : lenguaje corporal⟩

languid ['læŋgwɪd] *adj* : lánguido — **languidly** *adv*

languish ['læŋgwɪʃ] *vi* **1** WEAKEN : languidecer, debilitarse **2** PINE : consumirse, suspirar (por) ⟨to languish for love : suspirar por el amor⟩ ⟨he languished in prison : estuvo pudriéndose en la cárcel⟩

languor ['læŋgər] *n* : languidez *f*

languorous ['læŋgərəs] *adj* : lánguido — **languorously** *adv*

lank ['læŋk] *adj* **1** THIN : delgado, larguirucho *fam* **2** LIMP : lacio

lanky ['læŋki] *adj* **lankier; -est** : delgado, larguirucho *fam*

lanolin ['lænəlɪn] *n* : lanolina *f*

lantern ['læntərn] *n* : linterna *f*, farol *m*

Laotian [leɪ'o:ʃən, 'lauʃən] *n* : laosiano *m*, -na *f* — **Laotian** *adj*

lap[1] ['læp] *v* **lapped; lapping** *vt* **1** FOLD : plegar, doblar **2** WRAP : envolver **3** : lamer, besar ⟨waves were lapping the shore : las olas lamían la orilla⟩ **4 lap up** : beber a lengüetadas (como un gato) — *vi* OVERLAP : traslaparse

lap[2] *n* **1** : falda *f*, regazo *m* (del cuerpo) **2** OVERLAP : traslapo *m* **3** : vuelta *f* (en deportes) **4** STAGE : etapa *f* (de un viaje)

lapdog ['læp,dɔg] *n* : perro *m* faldero

lapel [lə'pɛl] *n* : solapa *f*

lapp ['læp] *n* : lapón *m*, -pona *f* — **Lapp** *adj*

lapse[1] ['læps] *vi* **lapsed; lapsing 1** FALL, SLIP : caer ⟨to lapse into bad habits : caer en malos hábitos⟩ ⟨to lapse into unconsciousness : perder el conocimiento⟩ ⟨to lapse into silence : quedarse callado⟩ 2 FADE : decaer, desvanecerse ⟨her dedication lapsed : su dedicación se desvaneció⟩ 3 CEASE : cancelarse, perderse 4 ELAPSE : transcurrir, pasar 5 EXPIRE : caducar

lapse² *n* 1 SLIP : lapsus *m*, desliz *m*, falla *f* ⟨a lapse of memory : una falla de memoria⟩ 2 INTERVAL : lapso *m*, intervalo *m*, período *m* 3 EXPIRATION : caducidad *f*

laptop¹ ['læp,tɑp] *adj* : portátil, laptop

laptop² *n* : laptop *m*

larboard ['lɑrbərd] *n* : babor *m*

larcenous ['lɑrsənəs] *adj* : de robo

larceny ['lɑrsəni] *n, pl* **-nies** : robo *m*, hurto *m*

larch ['lɑrtʃ] *n* : alerce *f*

lard ['lɑrd] *n* : manteca *f* de cerdo

larder ['lɑrdər] *n* : despensa *f*, alacena *f*

large ['lɑrdʒ] *adj* **larger; largest** 1 BIG : grande 2 COMPREHENSIVE : amplio, extenso 3 **by and large** : por lo general

largely ['lɑrdʒli] *adv* : en gran parte, en su mayoría

largeness ['lɑrdʒnəs] *n* : lo grande

largesse *or* **largess** [lɑr'ʒɛs, -'dʒɛs] *n* : generosidad *f*, largueza *f*

lariat ['læriət] *n* : lazo *m*

lark ['lɑrk] *n* 1 FUN : diversión *f* ⟨what a lark! : ¡qué divertido!⟩ 2 : alondra *f* (pájaro)

larva ['lɑrvə] *n, pl* **-vae** [-,vi:, -,vaɪ] : larva *f* — **larval** [-vəl] *adj*

laryngitis [,lærən'dʒaɪtəs] *n* : laringitis *f*

larynx ['lærɪŋks] *n, pl* **-rynges** [lə'rɪndʒi:z] *or* **-ynxes** ['lærɪŋksəz] : laringe *f*

lasagna [lə'zɑnjə] *n* : lasaña *f*

lascivious [lə'sɪviəs] *adj* : lascivo

lasciviousness [lə'sɪviəsnəs] *n* : lascivia *f*, lujuria *f*

laser ['leɪzər] *n* : láser *m*

laser disc *n* : disco *m* láser

lash¹ ['læʃ] *vt* 1 WHIP : azotar 2 BIND : atar, amarrar

lash² *n* 1 WHIP : látigo *m* 2 STROKE : latigazo *m* 3 EYELASH : pestaña *f*

lass ['læs] *or* **lassie** ['læsi] *n* : muchacha *f*, chica *f*

lassitude ['læsə,tu:d, -,tju:d] *n* : lasitud *f*

lasso¹ ['læ,so:, læ'su:] *vt* : lazar

lasso² *n, pl* **-sos** *or* **-soes** : lazo *m*, reata *f Mex*

last¹ ['læst] *vi* 1 CONTINUE : durar ⟨how long will it last? : ¿cuánto durará?⟩ 2 ENDURE : aguantar, durar 3 SURVIVE : durar, sobrevivir 4 SUFFICE : durar, bastar — *vt* 1 : durar ⟨it will last a lifetime : durará toda la vida⟩ 2 **to last out** : aguantar

last² *adv* 1 : en último lugar, al último ⟨we came in last : llegamos en último lugar⟩ 2 : por última vez, la última vez ⟨I saw him last in Bogota : lo vi por última vez en Bogotá⟩ 3 FINALLY : por último, en conclusión

last³ *adj* 1 FINAL : último, final 2 PREVIOUS : pasado ⟨last year : el año pasado⟩

last⁴ *n* 1 : el último, la última, lo último ⟨at last : por fin, al fin, finalmente⟩ 2 : horma *f* (de zapatero)

lasting ['læstɪŋ] *adj* : perdurable, duradero, estable

lastly ['læstli] *adv* : por último, finalmente

latch¹ ['lætʃ] *vt* : cerrar con picaporte

latch² *n* : picaporte *m*, pestillo *m*, pasador *m*

late¹ ['leɪt] *adv* **later; latest** 1 : tarde ⟨to arrive late : llegar tarde⟩ ⟨to sleep late : dormir hasta tarde⟩ 2 : a última hora, a finales ⟨late in the month : a finales del mes⟩ 3 RECENTLY : recién, últimamente ⟨as late as last year : todavía en el año pasado⟩

late² *adj* **later; latest** 1 TARDY : tardío, de retraso ⟨to be late : llegar tarde⟩ 2 : avanzado ⟨because of the late hour : a causa de la hora avanzada⟩ 3 DECEASED : difunto, fallecido 4 RECENT : reciente, último ⟨our late quarrel : nuestra última pelea⟩

latecomer ['leɪt,kʌmər] *n* : rezagado *m*, -da *f*

lately ['leɪtli] *adv* : recientemente, últimamente

lateness ['leɪtnəs] *n* 1 DELAY : retraso *m*, atraso *m*, tardanza *f* 2 : lo avanzado (de la hora)

latent ['leɪtənt] *adj* : latente — **latently** *adv*

lateral ['lætərəl] *adj* : lateral — **laterally** *adv*

latex ['leɪ,tɛks] *n, pl* **-tices** ['leɪtə,si:z, 'lætə-] *or* **-texes** : látex *m*

lath ['læθ, 'læð] *n, pl* **laths** *or* **lath** : listón *m*

lathe ['leɪð] *n* : torno *m*

lather¹ ['læðər] *vt* : enjabonar — *vi* : espumar, hacer espuma

lather² *n* 1 : espuma *f* (de jabón) 2 : sudor *m* (de caballo) 3 **to get into a lather** : ponerse histérico

Latin¹ *adj* : latino

Latin² *n* 1 : latín *m* (idioma) 2 → **Latin American**

Latin–American ['lætənə'mrikən] *adj* : latinoamericano

Latin American *n* : latinoamericano *m*, -na *f*

latitude ['lætə,tu:d, -,tju:d] *n* : latitud *f*

latrine [lə'tri:n] *n* : letrina *f*

latte ['lɑ,teɪ] *n* : café *m* con leche

latter¹ ['lætər] *adj* 1 SECOND : segundo 2 LAST : último

latter² *pron* **the latter** : éste, ésta, éstos *pl*, éstas *pl*

lattice ['lætəs] *n* : enrejado *m*, celosía *f*

Latvian ['lætviən] *n* : letón *m*, -tona *f* — **Latvian** *adj*

laud¹ ['lɔd] *vt* : alabar, loar

laud² *n* : alabanza *f*, loa *f*

laudable ['lɔdəbəl] *adj* : loable — **laudably** [-bli] *adv*
laugh¹ ['læf] *vi* : reír, reírse
laugh² *n* **1** LAUGHTER : risa *f* **2** JOKE : chiste *m*, broma *f* ⟨he did it for a laugh : lo hizo en broma, lo hizo para divertirse⟩
laughable ['læfəbəl] *adj* : risible, de risa
laughingstock ['læfɪŋ,stɑk] *n* : hazmerreír *m*
laughter ['læftər] *n* : risa *f*, risas *fpl*
launch¹ ['lɔntʃ] *vt* **1** HURL : lanzar **2** : botar (un barco) **3** START : iniciar, empezar
launch² *n* **1** : lancha *f* (bote) **2** LAUNCHING : lanzamiento *m*
launder ['lɔndər] *vt* **1** : lavar y planchar (ropa) **2** : blanquear, lavar (dinero)
launderer ['lɔndərər] *n* : lavandero *m*, -ra *f*
laundress ['lɔndrəs] *n* : lavandera *f*
laundry ['lɔndri] *n, pl* **laundries 1** : ropa *f* sucia, ropa *f* para lavar ⟨to do the laundry : lavar la ropa⟩ **2** : lavandería *f* (servicio de lavar)
laureate ['lɔriət] *n* : laureado *m*, -da *f* ⟨poet laureate : poeta laureado⟩
laurel ['lɔrəl] *n* **1** : laurel *m* (planta) **2** **laurels** *npl* : laureles *mpl* ⟨to rest on one's laurels : dormirse uno en sus laureles⟩
lava ['lɑvə, 'læ-] *n* : lava *f*
lavatory ['lævə,tori] *n, pl* **-ries** : baño *m*, cuarto *m* de baño
lavender ['lævəndər] *n* : lavanda *f*, espliego *m*
lavish¹ ['lævɪʃ] *vt* : prodigar (a), colmar (de)
lavish² *adj* **1** EXTRAVAGANT : pródigo, generoso, derrochador **2** ABUNDANT : abundante **3** LUXURIOUS : lujoso, espléndido
lavishly ['lævɪʃli] *adv* : con generosidad, espléndidamente ⟨to live lavishly : vivir a lo grande⟩
lavishness ['lævɪʃnəs] *n* : generosidad *f*, esplendidez *f*
law ['lɔ] *n* **1** : ley *f* ⟨to break the law : violar la ley⟩ **2** : derecho *m* ⟨criminal law : derecho criminal⟩ **3** : abogacía *f* ⟨to practice law : ejercer la abogacía⟩
law–abiding ['lɔə,baɪdɪŋ] *adj* : observante de la ley
lawbreaker ['lɔ,breɪkər] *n* : infractor *m*, -tora *f* de la ley
lawful ['lɔfəl] *adj* : legal, legítimo, lícito — **lawfully** *adv*
lawgiver ['lɔ,gɪvər] *n* : legislador *m*, -dora *f*
lawless ['lɔləs] *adj* : anárquico, ingobernable — **lawlessly** *adv*
lawlessness ['lɔləsnəs] *n* : anarquía *f*, desorden *m*
lawmaker ['lɔ,meɪkər] *n* : legislador *m*, -dora *f*
lawman ['lɔmən] *n, pl* **-men** [-mən, -,mɛn] : agente *m* del orden
lawn ['lɔn] *n* : césped *m*, pasto *m*

lawn mower *n* : cortadora *f* de césped
lawsuit ['lɔ,su:t] *n* : pleito *m*, litigio *m*, demanda *f*
lawyer ['lɔiər, 'lɔjər] *n* : abogado *m*, -da *f*
lax ['læks] *adj* : laxo, relajado — **laxly** *adv*
laxative ['læksətɪv] *n* : laxante *m*
laxity ['læksəti] *n* : relajación *f*, descuido *m*, falta *f* de rigor
lay¹ ['leɪ] *vt* **laid** ['leɪd]; **laying 1** PLACE, PUT : poner, colocar ⟨she laid it on the table : lo puso en la mesa⟩ ⟨to lay eggs : poner huevos⟩ **2** : hacer ⟨to lay a bet : hacer una apuesta⟩ **3** IMPOSE : imponer ⟨to lay a tax : imponer un impuesto⟩ ⟨to lay the blame on : echarle la culpa a⟩ **4 to lay out** PRESENT : presentar, exponer ⟨he laid out his plan : presentó su proyecto⟩ **5 to lay out** DESIGN : diseñar (el trazado de)
lay² → **lie¹**
lay³ *adj* SECULAR : laico, lego
lay⁴ *n* **1** : disposición *f*, configuración *f* ⟨the lay of the land : la configuración del terreno⟩ **2** BALLAD : romance *m*, balada *f*
layer ['leɪər] *n* **1** : capa *f* (de pintura, etc.), estrato *m* (de roca) **2** : gallina *f* ponedora
layman ['leɪmən] *n, pl* **-men** [-mən, -,mɛn] : laico *m*, lego *m*
layoff ['leɪ,ɔf] *n* : despido *m*
lay off *vt* : despedir
layout ['leɪ,aʊt] *n* : disposición *f*, distribución *f* (de una casa, etc.), trazado *m* (de una ciudad)
lay up *vt* **1** STORE : guardar, almacenar **2 to be laid up** : estar enfermo, tener que guardar cama
laywoman ['leɪ,wʊmən] *n, pl* **-women** [-,wɪmən] : laica *f*, lega *f*
laziness ['leɪzinəs] *n* : pereza *f*, flojera *f*
lazy ['leɪzi] *adj* **-zier; -est** : perezoso, holgazán — **lazily** ['leɪzəli] *adv*
leach ['li:tʃ] *vt* : filtrar
lead¹ ['li:d] *vt* **led** ['lɛd]; **leading 1** GUIDE : conducir, llevar, guiar **2** DIRECT : dirigir **3** HEAD : encabezar, ir al frente de **4 to lead to** : resultar en, llevar a ⟨it only leads to trouble : sólo resulta en problemas⟩
lead² *n* : delantera *f*, primer lugar *m* ⟨to take the lead : tomar la delantera⟩
lead³ ['lɛd] *n* **1** : plomo *m* (metal) **2** : mina *f* (de lápiz) **3 lead poisoning** : saturnismo *m*
leaden ['lɛdən] *adj* **1** : plomizo ⟨a leaden sky : un ciel plomizo⟩ **2** HEAVY : pesado
leader ['li:dər] *n* : jefe *m*, -fa *f*; líder *mf*; dirigente *mf*; gobernante *mf*
leadership ['li:dər,ʃɪp] *n* : mando *m*, dirección *f*
leaf¹ ['li:f] *vi* **1** : echar hojas (dícese de un árbol) **2 to leaf through** : hojear (un libro)

leaf² *n, pl* **leaves** ['liːvz] **1 :** hoja *f* (de plantas o libros) **2 to turn over a new leaf :** hacer borrón y cuenta nueva
leafless ['liːfləs] *adj* : sin hojas, pelado
leaflet ['liːflət] *n* : folleto *m*
leafy ['liːfi] *adj* **leafier; -est** : frondoso
league¹ ['liːg] *v* **leagued; leaguing** *vt* : aliar, unir — *vi* : aliarse, unirse
league² *n* **1** : legua *f* (medida de distancia) **2** ASSOCIATION : alianza *f*, sociedad *f*, liga *f*
leak¹ ['liːk] *vt* **1** : perder, dejar escapar (un líquido o un gas) **2** : filtrar (información) — *vi* **1** : gotear, escaparse, fugarse (dícese de un líquido o un gas) **2** : hacer agua (dícese de un bote) **3** : filtrarse, divulgarse (dícese de información)
leak² *n* **1** HOLE : agujero *m* (en recipientes), gotera *f* (en un tejado) **2** ESCAPE : fuga *f*, escape *m* **3** : filtración *f* (de información)
leakage ['liːkɪdʒ] *n* : escape *m*, fuga *f*
leaky ['liːki] *adj* **leakier; -est** : agujereado (dícese de un recipiente), que hace agua (dícese de un bote), con goteras (dícese de un tejado)
lean¹ ['liːn] *vi* **1** BEND : inclinarse, ladearse **2** RECLINE : reclinarse **3** RELY : apoyarse (en), depender (de) **4** INCLINE, TEND : inclinarse, tender — *vt* : apoyar
lean² *adj* **1** THIN : delgado, flaco **2** : sin grasa, magro (dícese de la carne)
leanness ['liːnnəs] *n* : delgadez *f*
lean-to ['liːnˌtuː] *n* : cobertizo *m*
leap¹ ['liːp] *vi* **leaped** ['liːpt, 'lɛpt] *or* **leapt; leaping** : saltar, brincar
leap² *n* : salto *m*, brinco *m*
leap year *n* : año *m* bisiesto
learn ['lərn] *vt* **1** : aprender ⟨to learn to sing : aprender a cantar⟩ **2** MEMORIZE : aprender de memoria **3** DISCOVER : saber, enterarse de — *vi* **1** : aprender ⟨to learn from experience : aprender por experiencia⟩ **2** FIND OUT : enterarse, saber
learned ['lərnəd] *adj* : erudito
learner ['lərnər] *n* : principiante *mf*, estudiante *mf*
learning ['lərnɪŋ] *n* : erudición *f*, saber *m*
lease¹ ['liːs] *vt* **leased; leasing** : arrendar
lease² *n* : contrato *m* de arrendamiento
leash¹ ['liːʃ] *vt* : atraillar (un animal)
leash² *n* : traílla *f*
least¹ ['liːst] *adv* : menos ⟨when least expected : cuando menos se espera⟩
least² *adj* (*superlative of* **little**) : menor, más mínimo
least³ *n* **1** : lo menos ⟨at least : por lo menos⟩ **2 to say the least** : por no decir más
leather ['lɛðər] *n* : cuero *m*
leathery ['lɛðəri] *adj* : curtido (dícese de la piel), correoso (dícese de la carne)

leave¹ ['liːv] *v* **left** ['lɛft]; **leaving** *vt* **1** BEQUEATH : dejar, legar **2** DEPART : dejar, salir(se) de **3** ABANDON : abandonar, dejar **4** FORGET : dejar, olvidarse de ⟨I left the books at the library : dejé los libros en la biblioteca⟩ **5 to be left** : quedar ⟨it's all I have left : es todo lo que me queda⟩ **6 to be left over** : sobrar **7 to leave out** : omitir, excluir — *vi* : irse, salir, partir, marcharse ⟨she left yesterday morning : se fue ayer por la mañana⟩
leave² *n* **1** PERMISSION : permiso *m* ⟨by your leave : con su permiso⟩ **2 or leave of absence** : permiso *m*, licencia *f* ⟨maternity leave : licencia por maternidad⟩ **3 to take one's leave** : despedirse
leaven ['lɛvən] *n* : levadura *f*
leaves → **leaf²**
leaving ['liːvɪŋ] *n* **1** : salida *f*, partida *f* **2 leavings** *npl* : restos *mpl*, sobras *fpl*
Lebanese [ˌlɛbəˈniːz, -ˈniːs] *n* : libanés *m*, -nesa *f* — **Lebanese** *adj*
lecherous ['lɛtʃərəs] *adj* : lascivo, libidinoso — **lecherously** *adv*
lechery ['lɛtʃəri] *n* : lascivia *f*, lujuria *f*
lecture¹ ['lɛktʃər] *v* **-tured; -turing** *vi* : dar clase, dictar clase, dar una conferencia — *vt* SCOLD : sermonear, echar una reprimenda a, regañar
lecture² *n* **1** : conferencia *f* **2** REPRIMAND : reprimenda *f*
lecturer ['lɛktʃərər] *n* **1** SPEAKER : conferenciante *mf* **2** TEACHER : profesor *m*, -sora *f*
led → **lead¹**
ledge ['lɛdʒ] *n* : repisa *f* (de una pared), antepecho *m* (de una ventana), saliente *m* (de una montaña)
ledger ['lɛdʒər] *n* : libro *m* mayor, libro *m* de contabilidad
lee¹ ['liː] *adj* : de sotavento
lee² *n* : sotavento *m*
leech ['liːtʃ] *n* : sanguijuela *f*
leek ['liːk] *n* : puerro *m*
leer¹ ['lɪr] *vi* : mirar con lascivia
leer² *n* : mirada *f* lasciva
leery ['lɪri] *adj* : receloso
lees ['liːz] *npl* : posos *mpl*, heces *fpl*
leeward¹ ['liːwərd, 'luːərd] *adj* : de sotavento
leeward² *n* : sotavento *m*
leeway ['liːˌweɪ] *n* : libertad *f*, margen *m*
left¹ ['lɛft] *adv* : hacia la izquierda
left² → **leave¹**
left³ *adj* : izquierdo
left⁴ *n* : izquierda *f* ⟨on the left : a la izquierda⟩
left-hand ['lɛftˈhand] *adj* **1** : de la izquierda **2** → **left-handed**
left-handed ['lɛftˈhandəd] *adj* **1** : zurdo (dícese de una persona) **2** : con doble sentido ⟨a left-handed compliment : un cumplido a medias⟩
leftist ['lɛftɪst] *n* : izquierdista *mf* — **leftist** *adj*
leftover ['lɛftˌoːvər] *adj* : sobrante, que sobra

leftovers ['lɛft,o:vərz] *npl* : restos *mpl*, sobras *fpl*

left wing *n* **the left wing** : la izquierda

left–winger ['lɛft'wɪŋər] *n* : izquierdista *mf*

leg ['lɛg] *n* **1** : pierna *f* (de una persona, de carne, de ropa), pata *f* (de un animal, de muebles) **2** STAGE : etapa *f* (de un viaje), vuelta *f* (de una carrera)

legacy ['lɛgəsi] *n, pl* **-cies** : legado *m*, herencia *f*

legal ['li:gəl] *adj* **1** : legal, jurídico ⟨legal advisor : asesor jurídico⟩ ⟨the legal profession : la abogacía⟩ **2** LAWFUL : legítimo, legal

legalistic [,li:gə'lɪstɪk] *adj* : legalista

legality [li'gæləti] *n, pl* **-ties** : legalidad *f*

legalize ['li:gə,laɪz] *vt* **-ized; -izing** : legalizar

legally ['li:gəli] *adv* : legalmente

legate ['lɛgət] *n* : legado *m*

legation [lɪ'geɪʃən] *n* : legación *f*

legend ['lɛʤənd] *n* **1** STORY : leyenda *f* **2** INSCRIPTION : leyenda *f*, inscripción *f* **3** : signos *mpl* convencionales (en un mapa)

legendary ['lɛʤən,dɛri] *adj* : legendario

legerdemain [,lɛʤərdə'meɪn] → **sleight of hand**

leggings ['lɛgɪnz, 'lɛgənz] *npl* : mallas *fpl*

legibility [,lɛʤə'bɪləti] *n* : legibilidad *f*

legible ['lɛʤəbəl] *adj* : legible

legibly ['lɛʤəbli] *adv* : de manera legible

legion ['li:ʤən] *n* : legión *f*

legionnaire [,li:ʤə'nær] *n* : legionario *m*, -ria *f*

legislate ['lɛʤəs,leɪt] *vi* **-lated; -lating** : legislar

legislation [,lɛʤəs'leɪʃən] *n* : legislación *f*

legislative ['lɛʤəs,leɪtɪv] *adj* : legislativo, legislador

legislator ['lɛʤəs,leɪtər] *n* : legislador *m*, -dora *f*

legislature ['lɛʤəs,leɪtʃər] *n* : asamblea *f* legislativa

legitimacy [lɪ'ʤɪtəməsi] *n* : legitimidad *f*

legitimate [lɪ'ʤɪtəmət] *adj* **1** VALID : legítimo, válido, justificado **2** LAWFUL : legítimo, legal

legitimately [lɪ'ʤɪtəmətli] *adv* : legítimamente

legitimize [lɪ'ʤɪtə,maɪz] *vt* **-mized; -mizing** : legitimar, hacer legítimo

legume ['lɛ,gju:m, lɪ'gju:m] *n* : legumbre *f*

leisure ['li:ʒər, 'lɛ-] *n* **1** : ocio *m*, tiempo *m* libre ⟨a life of leisure : una vida de ocio⟩ **2** **to take one's leisure** : reposar **3 at your leisure** : cuando te venga bien, cuando tengas tiempo

leisurely ['li:ʒərli, 'lɛ-] *adj & adv* : lento, sin prisas

lemming ['lɛmɪŋ] *n* : lemming *m*

lemon ['lɛmən] *n* : limón *m*

lemonade [,lɛmə'neɪd] *n* : limonada *f*

lemony ['lɛməni] *adj* : a limón

lend ['lɛnd] *vt* **lent** ['lɛnt]; **lending 1** : prestar ⟨to lend money : prestar dinero⟩ **2** GIVE : dar ⟨it lends force to his criticism : da fuerza a su crítica⟩ **3 to lend oneself to** : prestarse a

length ['lɛŋkθ] *n* **1** : longitud *f*, largo *m* ⟨10 feet in length : 10 pies de largo⟩ **2** DURATION : duración *f* **3** : trozo *m* (de madera), corte *m* (de tela) **4 to go to any lengths** : hacer todo lo posible **5 at ~** : extensamente ⟨to speak at length : hablar largo y tendido⟩

lengthen ['lɛŋkθən] *vt* **1** : alargar ⟨can they lengthen the dress? : ¿se puede alargar el vestido?⟩ **2** EXTEND, PROLONG : prolongar, extender — *vi* : alargarse, crecer ⟨the days are lengthening : los días están creciendo⟩

lengthways ['lɛŋkθ,weɪz] → **lengthwise**

lengthwise ['lɛŋkθ,waɪz] *adv* : a lo largo, longitudinalmente

lengthy ['lɛŋkθi] *adj* **lengthier; -est 1** OVERLONG : largo y pesado **2** EXTENDED : prolongado, largo

leniency ['li:niəntsi] *n, pl* **-cies** : lenidad *f*, indulgencia *f*

lenient ['li:niənt] *adj* : indulgente, poco severo

leniently ['li:niəntli] *adv* : con lenidad, con indulgencia

lens ['lɛnz] *n* **1** : cristalino *m* (del ojo) **2** : lente *mf* (de un instrumento o una cámara) **3** → **contact lens**

lent → **lend**

Lent ['lɛnt] *n* : Cuaresma *f*

lentil ['lɛntəl] *n* : lenteja *f*

Leo ['li:o:] *n* : Leo *mf*

leopard ['lɛpərd] *n* : leopardo *m*

leotard ['li:ə,tard] *n* : leotardo *m*, malla *f*

leper ['lɛpər] *n* : leproso *m*, -sa *f*

leprechaun ['lɛprə,kan] *n* : duende *m* (irlandés)

leprosy ['lɛprəsi] *n* : lepra *f* — **leprous** ['lɛprəs] *adj*

lesbian¹ ['lɛzbiən] *adj* : lesbiano

lesbian² *n* : lesbiana *f*

lesbianism ['lɛzbiə,nɪzəm] *n* : lesbianismo *m*

lesion ['li:ʒən] *n* : lesión *f*

less¹ ['lɛs] *adv* (*comparative of* **little¹**) : menos ⟨the less you know, the better : cuanto menos sepas, mejor⟩ ⟨less and less : cada vez menos⟩

less² *adj* (*comparative of* **little²**) : menos ⟨less than three : menos de tres⟩ ⟨less money : menos dinero⟩ ⟨nothing less than perfection : nada menos que la perfección⟩

less³ *pron* : menos ⟨I'm earning less : estoy ganando menos⟩

less⁴ *prep* : menos ⟨one month less two days : un mes menos dos días⟩

lessee [lɛ'si:] *n* : arrendatario *m*, -ria *f*

lessen ['lɛsən] *vt* : disminuir, reducir — *vi* : disminuir, reducirse

lesser ['lɛsər] *adj* : menor ⟨to a lesser degree : en menor grado⟩

lesson ['lɛsən] *n* **1** CLASS : clase *f*, curso *m* **2** : lección *f* ⟨the lessons of history : las lecciones de la historia⟩

lessor ['lɛˌsɔr, l'sɔr] *n* : arrendador *m*, -dora *f*

lest ['lɛst] *conj* : para (que) no ⟨lest we forget : para que no olvidemos⟩

let ['lɛt] *vt* **let; letting 1** ALLOW : dejar, permitir ⟨let me see it : déjame verlo⟩ **2** MAKE : hacer ⟨let me know : házmelo saber, avísame⟩ ⟨let them wait : que esperen, haz que esperen⟩ **3** RENT : alquilar **4** (*used in the first person plural imperative*) ⟨let's go! : ¡vamos!, ¡vámonos!⟩ ⟨let us pray : oremos⟩ **5 to let down** DISAPPOINT : fallar **6 to let off** FORGIVE : perdonar **7 to let out** REVEAL : revelar **8 to let up** ABATE : amainar, disminuir ⟨the pace never lets up : el ritmo nunca disminuye⟩

letdown *n* : chasco *m*, decepción *f*

lethal ['li:θəl] *adj* : letal — **lethally** *adv*

lethargic [lɪ'θɑrdʒɪk] *adj* : letárgico

lethargy ['lɛθərdʒi] *n* : letargo *m*

let on *vi* **1** ADMIT : reconocer ⟨don't let on! : ¡no digas nada!⟩ **2** PRETEND : fingir

let's ['lɛts] (*contraction of* **let us**) → **let**

letter[1] ['lɛtər] *vt* : marcar con letras, inscribir letras en

letter[2] *n* **1** : letra *f* (del alfabeto) **2** : carta *f* ⟨a letter to my mother : una carta a mi madre⟩ **3 letters** *npl* ARTS : letras *fpl* **4 to the letter** : al pie de la letra

lettering ['lɛtərɪŋ] *n* : letra *f*

lettuce ['lɛtəs] *n* : lechuga *f*

leukemia [lu:'ki:miə] *n* : leucemia *f*

levee ['lɛvi] *n* : dique *m*

level[1] ['lɛvəl] *vt* **-eled** *or* **-elled; -eling** *or* **-elling 1** FLATTEN : nivelar, aplanar **2** AIM : apuntar (una pistola), dirigir (una acusación) **3** RAZE : rasar, arrasar

level[2] *adj* **1** EVEN : llano, plano, parejo **2** CALM : tranquilo ⟨to keep a level head : no perder la cabeza⟩

level[3] *n* : nivel *m*

leveler ['lɛvələr] *n* : nivelador *m*, -dora *f*

levelheaded ['lɛvəl'hɛdəd] *adj* : sensato, equilibrado

levelly ['lɛvəli] *adv* CALMLY : con ecuanimidad *f*, con calma

levelness ['lɛvəlnəs] *n* : uniformidad *f*

lever ['lɛvər, 'li:-] *n* : palanca *f*

leverage ['lɛvərɪdʒ, 'li:-] *n* **1** : apalancamiento *m* (en física) **2** INFLUENCE : influencia *f* fam

leviathan [lɪ'vaɪəθən] *n* : leviatán *m*, gigante *m*

levity ['lɛvəti] *n* : ligereza *f*, frivolidad *f*

levy[1] ['lɛvi] *vt* **levied; levying 1** IMPOSE : imponer, exigir, gravar (un impuesto) **2** COLLECT : recaudar (un impuesto)

levy[2] *n, pl* **levies** : impuesto *m*, gravamen *m*

lewd ['lu:d] *adj* : lascivo — **lewdly** *adv*

lewdness ['lu:dnəs] *n* : lascivia *f*

lexical ['lɛksikəl] *adj* : léxico

lexicographer [ˌlɛksə'kɑgrəfər] *n* : lexicógrafo *m*, -fa *f*

lexicographical [ˌlɛksəko'græfɪkəl] *or* **lexicographic** [-'græfɪk] *adj* : lexicográfico

lexicography [ˌlɛksə'kɑgrəfi] *n* : lexicografía *f*

lexicon ['lɛksɪˌkɑn] *n, pl* **-ica** [-kə] *or* **-icons** : léxico *m*, lexicón *m*

liability [ˌlaɪə'bɪləti] *n, pl* **-ties 1** RESPONSIBILITY : responsabilidad *f* **2** SUSCEPTIBILITY : propensión *f* **3** DRAWBACK : desventaja *f* **4 liabilities** *npl* DEBTS : deudas *fpl*, pasivo *m*

liable ['laɪəbəl] *adj* **1** RESPONSIBLE : responsable **2** SUSCEPTIBLE : propenso **3** PROBABLE : probable ⟨it's liable to happen : es probable que suceda⟩

liaison ['li:əˌzɑn, li'eɪ-] *n* **1** CONNECTION : enlace *m*, relación *f* **2** AFFAIR : amorío *m*, aventura *f*

liar ['laɪər] *n* : mentiroso *m*, -sa *f*; embustero *m*, -ra *f*

libel[1] ['laɪbəl] *vt* **-beled** *or* **-belled; -beling** *or* **-belling** : difamar, calumniar

libel[2] *n* : difamación *f*, calumnia *f*

libeler ['laɪbələr] *n* : difamador *m*, -dora *f*; calumniador *m*, -dora *f*; libelista *mf*

libelous *or* **libellous** ['laɪbələs] *adj* : difamatorio, calumnioso, injurioso

liberal[1] ['lɪbrəl, 'lɪbərəl] *adj* **1** TOLERANT : liberal, tolerante **2** GENEROUS : generoso **3** ABUNDANT : abundante **4 liberal arts** : humanidades *fpl*, artes *fpl* liberales

liberal[2] *n* : liberal *mf*

liberalism ['lɪbrəˌlɪzəm, 'lɪbərə-] *n* : liberalismo *m*

liberality [ˌlɪbə'ræləti] *n, pl* **-ties** : liberalidad *f*, generosidad *f*

liberalize ['lɪbrəˌlaɪz, 'lɪbərə-] *vt* **-ized; -izing** : liberalizar

liberally ['lɪbrəli, 'lɪbərə-] *adv* **1** GENEROUSLY : generosamente **2** ABUNDANTLY : abundantemente **3** FREELY : libremente

liberate ['lɪbəˌreɪt] *vt* **-ated; -ating** : liberar, libertar

liberation [ˌlɪbə'reɪʃən] *n* : liberación *f*

liberator ['lɪbəˌreɪtər] *n* : libertador *m*, -dora *f*

Liberian [laɪ'bɪriən] *n* : liberiano *m*, -na *f* — **Liberian** *adj*

libertine ['lɪbərˌti:n] *n* : libertino *m*, -na *f*

liberty ['lɪbərti] *n, pl* **-ties 1** : libertad *f* **2 to take the liberty of** : tomarse la libertad de **3 to take liberties with** : tomarse confianzas con, tomarse libertades con

libido [lə'bi:do:, -'baɪ-] *n, pl* **-dos** : libido *f* — **libidinous** [lə'bɪdənəs] *adj*

Libra ['li:brə] *n* : Libra *mf*

librarian [laɪ'brɛriən] *n* : bibliotecario *m*, -ria *f*

library ['laɪˌbrɛri] *n, pl* **-braries** : biblioteca *f*

librettist [lɪ'brɛṭɪst] *n* : libretista *mf*
libretto [lɪ'brɛṭo] *n, pl* **-tos** *or* **-ti** [-ṭiː] : libreto *m*
Libyan ['lɪbiən] *n* : libio *m*, -bia *f* — **Libyan** *adj*
lice → **louse**
license[1] ['laɪsənts] *vt* **licensed; licensing** : licenciar, autorizar, dar permiso a
license[2] *or* **licence** *n* **1** PERMISSION : licencia *f*, permiso *m* **2** PERMIT : licencia *f*, carnet *m Spain* ⟨driver's license : licencia de conducir⟩ **3** FREEDOM : libertad *f* **4** LICENTIOUSNESS : libertinaje *m*
licentious [laɪ'sɛntʃəs] *adj* : licencioso, disoluto — **licentiously** *adv*
licentiousness [laɪ'sɛntʃəsnəs] *n* : libertinaje *m*
lichen ['laɪkən] *n* : liquen *m*
licit ['lɪsət] *adj* : lícito
lick[1] ['lɪk] *vt* **1** : lamer **2** BEAT : darle una paliza (a alguien)
lick[2] *n* **1** : lamida *f*, lengüetada *f* ⟨a lick of paint : una mano de pintura⟩ **2** BIT : pizca *f*, ápice *m* **3 a lick and a promise** : una lavada a la carrera
licorice ['lɪkərɪʃ, -rəs] *n* : regaliz *m*, dulce *m* de regaliz
lid ['lɪd] *n* **1** COVER : tapa *f* **2** EYELID : párpado *m*
lie[1] ['laɪ] *vi* **lay** ['leɪ]; **lain** ['leɪn]; **lying** ['laɪŋ] **1** : acostarse, echarse ⟨I lay down : me acosté⟩ **2** : estar, estar situado, encontrarse ⟨the book lay on the table : el libro estaba en la mesa⟩ ⟨the city lies to the south : la ciudad se encuentra al sur⟩ **3** CONSIST : consistir **4 to lie in** : residir en ⟨the power lies in the people : el poder reside en el pueblo⟩
lie[2] *vi* **lied; lying** ['laɪŋ] : mentir
lie[3] *n* **1** UNTRUTH : mentira *f* ⟨to tell lies : decir mentiras⟩ **2** POSITION : posición *f*
liege ['liːdʒ] *n* : señor *m* feudal
lien ['liːn, 'liːən] *n* : derecho *m* de retención
lieutenant [luː'tɛnənt] *n* : teniente *mf*
lieutenant colonel *n* : teniente *mf* coronel
lieutenant commander *n* : capitán *m*, -tana *f* de corbeta
lieutenant general *n* : teniente *mf* general
life ['laɪf] *n, pl* **lives** ['laɪvz] **1** : vida *f* ⟨plant life : la vida vegetal⟩ **2** EXISTENCE : vida *f*, existencia *f* **3** BIOGRAPHY : biografía *f*, vida *f* **4** DURATION : duración *f*, vida *f* **5** LIVELINESS : vivacidad *f*, animación *f*
lifeblood ['laɪf,blʌd] *n* : parte *f* vital, sustento *m*
lifeboat ['laɪf,boːt] *n* : bote *m* salvavidas
lifeguard ['laɪf,gard] *n* : socorrista *mf*, salvavidas *mf*
lifeless ['laɪfləs] *adj* : sin vida, muerto
lifelike ['laɪf,laɪk] *adj* : que parece vivo, natural, verosímil

lifelong ['laɪf'lɔŋ] *adj* : de toda la vida ⟨a lifelong friend : un amigo de toda la vida⟩
life preserver *n* : salvavidas *m*
lifesaver ['laɪf,seɪvər] *n* **1** : salvación *f* **2** → **lifeguard**
lifesaving ['laɪf,seɪvɪŋ] *n* : socorrismo *m*
lifestyle ['laɪf,staɪl] *n* : estilo *m* de vida
lifetime ['laɪf,taɪm] *n* : vida *f*, curso *m* de la vida
lift[1] ['lɪft] *vt* **1** RAISE : levantar, alzar, subir **2** END : levantar ⟨to lift a ban : levantar una prohibición⟩ — *vi* **1** RISE : levantarse, alzarse **2** CLEAR UP : despejar ⟨the fog lifted : se disipó la niebla⟩
lift[2] *n* **1** LIFTING : levantamiento *m*, alzamiento *m* **2** BOOST : impulso *m*, estímulo *m* **3 to give someone a lift** : llevar en coche a alguien
liftoff ['lɪft,ɔf] *n* : despegue *m*
ligament ['lɪgəmənt] *n* : ligamento *m*
ligature ['lɪgə,tʃʊr, -tʃər] *n* : ligadura *f*
light[1] ['laɪt] *v* **lit** ['lɪt] *or* **lighted; lighting** *vt* **1** ILLUMINATE : iluminar, alumbrar **2** IGNITE : encender, prenderle fuego a — *vi* : encenderse, prender
light[2] *vi* **lighted** *or* **lit** ['lɪt]; **lighting** **1** LAND, SETTLE : posarse **2** DISMOUNT : bajarse, apearse
light[3] ['laɪt] *adv* **1** LIGHTLY : suavemente, ligeramente **2 to travel light** : viajar con poco equipaje
light[4] *adj* **1** LIGHTWEIGHT : ligero, liviano, poco pesado **2** EASY : fácil, ligero, liviano ⟨light reading : lectura fácil⟩ ⟨light work : trabajo liviano⟩ **3** GENTLE, MILD : fino, suave, leve ⟨a light breeze : una brisa suave⟩ ⟨a light rain : una lluvia fina⟩ **4** FRIVOLOUS : de poca importancia, superficial **5** BRIGHT : bien iluminado, claro **6** PALE : claro (dícese de los colores), rubio (dícese del pelo)
light[5] *n* **1** ILLUMINATION : luz *f* **2** DAYLIGHT : luz *f* del día **3** DAWN : amanecer *m*, madrugada *f* **4** LAMP : lámpara *f* ⟨to turn on off the light : apagar la luz⟩ **5** ASPECT : aspecto *m* ⟨in a new light : con otros ojos⟩ ⟨in the light of : en vista de, a la luz de⟩ **6** MATCH : fósforo *m*, cerillo *m* **7 to bring to light** : sacar a (la) luz
lightbulb ['laɪt,bʌlb] *n* : bombilla *f*, foco *m*, bombillo *m CA, Col, Ven*
lighten ['laɪtən] *vt* **1** ILLUMINATE : iluminar, dar más luz a **2** : aclararse (el pelo) **3** : aligerar (una carga, etc.) **4** RELIEVE : aliviar **5** GLADDEN : alegrar ⟨it lightened his heart : alegró su corazón⟩
lighter ['laɪtər] *n* : encendedor *m*
lighthearted ['laɪt'hɑrṭəd] *adj* : alegre, despreocupado, desenfadado — **lightheartedly** *adv*
lightheartedness ['laɪt'hɑrṭədnəs] *n* : desenfado *m*, alegría *f*
lighthouse ['laɪt,haʊs] *n* : faro *m*

lighting [ˈlaɪtɪŋ] n : iluminación f
lightly [ˈlaɪtli] adv 1 GENTLY : suavemente 2 SLIGHTLY : ligeramente 3 FRIVOLOUSLY : a la ligera 4 **to let off lightly** : tratar con indulgencia
lightness [ˈlaɪtnəs] n 1 BRIGHTNESS : luminosidad f, claridad f 2 GENTLENESS : ligereza f, suavidad f, delicadeza f 3 : ligereza f, liviandad f (de peso)
lightning [ˈlaɪtnɪŋ] n : relámpago m, rayo m
lightning bug → firefly
lightproof [ˈlaɪtˌpruːf] adj : impenetrable por la luz, opaco
lightweight [ˈlaɪtˌweɪt] adj : ligero, liviano, de poco peso
light-year [ˈlaɪtˌjɪr] n : año m luz
lignite [ˈlɪgˌnaɪt] n : lignito m
likable or **likeable** [ˈlaɪkəbəl] adj : simpático, agradable
like[1] [ˈlaɪk] v **liked; liking** vt 1 : agradar, gustarle (algo a uno) ⟨he likes rice : le gusta el arroz⟩ ⟨she doesn't like flowers : a ella no le gustan las flores⟩ ⟨I like you : me caes bien⟩ 2 WANT : querer, desear ⟨I'd like a hamburger : quiero una hamburguesa⟩ ⟨he would like more help : le gustaría tener más ayuda⟩ — vi : querer ⟨do as you like : haz lo que quieras⟩
like[2] adj : parecido, semejante, similar
like[3] n 1 PREFERENCE : preferencia f, gusto m 2 **the like** : cosa f parecida, cosas fpl por el estilo ⟨I've never seen the like : nunca he visto cosa parecida⟩
like[4] conj 1 AS IF : como si ⟨they looked at me like I was crazy : se me quedaron mirando como si estuviera loca⟩ 2 AS : como, igual que ⟨she doesn't love you like I do : ella no te quiere como yo⟩
like[5] prep 1 : como, parecido a ⟨she acts like my mother : se comporta como mi madre⟩ ⟨he looks like me : se parece a mí⟩ 2 : propio de, típico de ⟨that's just like her : eso es muy típico de ella⟩ 3 : como ⟨animals like cows : animales como vacas⟩ 4 **like this, like that** : así ⟨do it like that : hazlo así⟩
likelihood [ˈlaɪkliˌhʊd] n : probabilidad f ⟨in all likelihood : con toda probabilidad⟩
likely[1] [ˈlaɪkli] adv : probablemente ⟨most likely he's sick : lo más probable es que esté enfermo⟩ ⟨they're likely to come : es probable que vengan⟩
likely[2] adj **-lier; -est** 1 PROBABLE : probable ⟨to be likely to : ser muy probable que⟩ 2 SUITABLE : apropiado, adecuado 3 BELIEVABLE : verosímil, creíble 4 PROMISING : prometedor
liken [ˈlaɪkən] vt : comparar
likeness [ˈlaɪknəs] n 1 SIMILARITY : semejanza f, parecido m 2 PORTRAIT : retrato m
likewise [ˈlaɪkˌwaɪz] adv 1 SIMILARLY : de la misma manera, asimismo 2 ALSO : también, además, asimismo

liking [ˈlaɪkɪŋ] n 1 FONDNESS : afición f (por una cosa), simpatía f (por una persona) 2 TASTE : gusto m ⟨is it to your liking? : ¿te gusta?⟩
lilac [ˈlaɪlək, -ˌlæk, -ˌlɑk] n : lila f
lilt [ˈlɪlt] n : cadencia f, ritmo m alegre
lily [ˈlɪli] n, pl **lilies** 1 : lirio m, azucena f 2 **lily of the valley** : lirio m de los valles, muguete m
lima bean [ˈlaɪmə] n : frijol m de media luna
limb [ˈlɪm] n 1 APPENDAGE : miembro m, extremidad f 2 BRANCH : rama f
limber[1] [ˈlɪmbər] vi or **to limber up** : calentarse, prepararse
limber[2] adj : ágil (dícese de las personas), flexible (dícese de los objetos)
limbo [ˈlɪmˌboː] n, pl **-bos** 1 : limbo m (en la religión) 2 OBLIVION : olvido m ⟨the project is in limbo : el proyecto ha caído en el olvido⟩
lime [ˈlaɪm] n 1 : cal f (óxido) 2 : lima f (fruta), limón m verde Mex
limelight [ˈlaɪmˌlaɪt] n **to be in the limelight** : ser el centro de atención, estar en el candelero
limerick [ˈlɪmərɪk] n : poema m jocoso de cinco versos
limestone [ˈlaɪmˌstoːn] n : piedra f caliza, caliza f
limit[1] [ˈlɪmət] vt : limitar, restringir
limit[2] n 1 MAXIMUM : límite m, máximo m ⟨speed limit : límite de velocidad⟩ 2 **limits** npl : límites mpl, confines mpl ⟨city limits : límites de la ciudad⟩ 3 **that's the limit!** : ¡eso es el colmo!
limitation [ˌlɪməˈteɪʃən] n : limitación f, restricción f
limited [ˈlɪmətəd] adj : limitado, restringido
limitless [ˈlɪmətləs] adj : ilimitado, sin límites
limousine [ˈlɪməˌziːn, ˌlɪməˈ-] n : limusina f
limp[1] [ˈlɪmp] vi : cojear
limp[2] adj 1 FLACCID : fláccido 2 LANK : lacio (dícese del pelo) 3 WEAK : débil ⟨to feel limp : sentirse desfallecer, sentirse sin fuerzas⟩
limp[3] n : cojera f
limpid [ˈlɪmpəd] adj : límpido, claro
limply [ˈlɪmpli] adv : sin fuerzas
limpness [ˈlɪmpnəs] n : flaccidez f, debilidad f
linden [ˈlɪndən] n : tilo m
line[1] [ˈlaɪn] v **lined; lining** vt 1 : forrar, cubrir ⟨to line a dress : forrar un vestido⟩ ⟨to line the walls : cubrir las paredes⟩ 2 MARK : rayar, trazar líneas en 3 BORDER : bordear 4 ALIGN : alinear — vi **to line up** : ponerse in fila, hacer cola
line[2] n 1 CORD, ROPE : cuerda f 2 WIRE : cable m ⟨power line : cable eléctrico⟩ 3 : línea f (de teléfono) 4 ROW : fila f, hilera f 5 NOTE : nota f, líneas fpl ⟨drop me a line : mándame unas líneas⟩ 6 COURSE : línea f ⟨line of inquiry : línea

de investigación⟩ **7** AGREEMENT : conformidad *f* ⟨to be in line with : ser conforme a⟩ ⟨to fall into line : estar de acuerdo⟩ **8** OCCUPATION : ocupación *f*, rama *f*, especialidad *f* **9** LIMIT : línea *f*, límite *m* ⟨dividing line : línea divisoria⟩ ⟨to draw the line : fijar límites⟩ **10** SERVICE : línea *f* ⟨bus line : línea de autobuses⟩ **11** MARK : línea *f*, arruga *f* (de la cara)

lineage ['lɪniɪʤ] *n* : linaje *m*, abolengo *m*

lineal ['lɪniəl] *adj* : en línea directa

lineaments ['lɪniəmənts] *npl* : facciones *fpl* (de la cara), rasgos *mpl*

linear ['lɪniər] *adj* : lineal

linen ['lɪnən] *n* : lino *m*

liner ['laɪnər] *n* **1** LINING : forro *m* **2** SHIP : buque *m*, transatlántico *m*

lineup ['laɪn‚ʌp] *n* **1** : fila *f* de sospechosos **2** : formación *f* (en deportes) **3** ALIGNMENT : alineación *f*

linger ['lɪŋgər] *vi* **1** TARRY : quedarse, entretenerse, rezagarse **2** PERSIST : persistir, sobrevivir

lingerie [‚lɑnʤə'reɪ, ‚lænʒə'riː] *n* : ropa *f* íntima femenina, lencería *f*

lingo ['lɪŋgo] *n, pl* **-goes 1** LANGUAGE : idioma *m* **2** JARGON : jerga *f*

linguist ['lɪŋgwɪst] *n* : lingüista *mf*

linguistic [lɪŋ'gwɪstɪk] *adj* : lingüístico

linguistics [lɪŋ'gwɪstɪks] *n* : lingüística *f*

liniment ['lɪnəmənt] *n* : linimento *m*

lining ['laɪnɪŋ] *n* : forro *m*

link[1] ['lɪŋk] *vt* : unir, enlazar, conectar — *vi* **to link up** : unirse, conectar

link[2] *n* **1** : eslabón *m* (de una cadena) **2** BOND : conexión *f*, lazo *m*, vínculo *m*

linkage ['lɪŋkɪʤ] *n* : conexión *f*, unión *f*, enlace *m*

linoleum [lə'noːliəm] *n* : linóleo *m*

linseed oil ['lɪn‚siːd] *n* : aceite *m* de linaza

lint ['lɪnt] *n* : pelusa *f*

lintel ['lɪntəl] *n* : dintel *m*

lion ['laɪən] *n* : león *m*

lioness ['laɪənɪs] *n* : leona *f*

lionize ['laɪə‚naɪz] *vt* **-ized; -izing** : tratar a una persona como muy importante

lip ['lɪp] *n* **1** : labio *m* **2** EDGE, RIM : pico *m* (de una jarra), borde *m* (de una taza)

lipreading ['lɪp‚riːdɪŋ] *n* : lectura *f* de los labios

lipstick ['lɪp‚stɪk] *n* : lápiz *m* de labios, barra *f* de labios

liquefy ['lɪkwə‚faɪ] *v* **-fied; -fying** *vt* : licuar — *vi* : licuarse

liqueur [lɪ'kʊr, -'kər, -'kjʊr] *n* : licor *m*

liquid[1] ['lɪkwəd] *adj* : líquido

liquid[2] *n* : líquido *m*

liquidate ['lɪkwə‚deɪt] *vt* **-dated; -dating** : liquidar

liquidation [‚lɪkwə'deɪʃən] *n* : liquidación *f*

liquidity [lɪk'wɪdəti] *n* : liquidez *f*

liquor ['lɪkər] *n* : alcohol *m*, bebidas *fpl* alcohólicas, licor *m*

lisp[1] ['lɪsp] *vi* : cecear

lisp[2] *n* : ceceo *m*

lissome ['lɪsəm] *adj* **1** FLEXIBLE : flexible **2** LITHE : ágil y grácil

list[1] ['lɪst] *vt* **1** ENUMERATE : hacer una lista de, enumerar **2** INCLUDE : poner en una lista, incluir — *vi* : escorar (dícese de un barco)

list[2] *n* **1** ENUMERATION : lista *f* **2** SLANT : escora *f*, inclinación *f*

listen ['lɪsən] *vi* **1** : escuchar, oír **2 to listen to** HEED : prestar atención a, hacer caso de, escuchar **3 to listen to reason** : atender a razones

listener ['lɪsənər] *n* : oyente *mf*, persona *f* que sabe escuchar

listless ['lɪstləs] *adj* : lánguido, apático — **listlessly** *adv*

listlessness ['lɪstləsnəs] *n* : apatía *f*, languidez *f*, desgana *f*

lit ['lɪt] → **light**

litany ['lɪtəni] *n, pl* **-nies** : letanía *f*

liter ['liːtər] *n* : litro *m*

literacy ['lɪtərəsi] *n* : alfabetismo *m*

literal ['lɪtərəl] *adj* : literal — **literally** *adv*

literary ['lɪtə‚rri] *adj* : literario

literate ['lɪtərət] *adj* : alfabetizado

literature ['lɪtərə‚tʃur, -tʃər] *n* : literatura *f*

lithe ['laɪð, 'laɪθ] *adj* : ágil y grácil

lithesome ['laɪðsəm, 'laɪθ-] → **lissome**

lithium ['lɪθiəm] *n* : litio *m*

lithograph ['lɪθə‚græf] *n* : litografía *f*

lithographer [lɪ'θɑgrəfər, 'lɪθə-‚græfər] *n* : litógrafo *m*, -fa *f*

lithography [lɪ'θɑgrəfi] *n* : litografía *f*

lithosphere ['lɪθə‚sfɪr] *n* : litosfera *f*

Lithuanian [‚lɪθə'weɪniən] *n* **1** : lituano *m* (idioma) **2** : lituano *m*, -na *f* — **Lithuanian** *adj*

litigant ['lɪtɪgənt] *n* : litigante *mf*

litigate ['lɪtə‚geɪt] *vi* **-gated; -gating** : litigar

litigation [‚lɪtə'geɪʃən] *n* : litigio *m*

litmus paper ['lɪtməs] *n* : papel *m* de tornasol

litter[1] ['lɪtər] *vt* : tirar basura en, ensuciar — *vi* : tirar basura

litter[2] *n* **1** : camada *f*, cría *f* ⟨a litter of kittens : una cría de gatitos⟩ **2** STRETCHER : camilla *f* **3** RUBBISH : basura *f* **4** : arena *f* higiénica (para gatos)

little[1] ['lɪtəl] *adv* **less** ['lɛs]; **least** ['liːst] **1** : poco ⟨she sings very little : canta muy poco⟩ **2 little did I know that . . .** : no tenía la menor idea de que . . . **3 as little as possible** : lo menos posible

little[2] *adj* **littler** *or* **less** ['lɛs] *or* **lesser** ['lɛsər]; **littlest** *or* **least** ['liːst] **1** SMALL : pequeño **2** : poco ⟨they speak little Spanish : hablan poco español⟩ ⟨little by little : poco a poco⟩ **3** TRIVIAL : sin importancia, trivial

little[3] *n* **1** : poco *m* ⟨little has changed : poco ha cambiado⟩ **2 a little** : un poco, algo ⟨it's a little surprising : es algo sorprendente⟩

Little Dipper → **dipper**

liturgical [lə'tərʤɪkəl] *adj* : litúrgico — **liturgically** [-kli] *adv*

liturgy ['lɪtərdʒi] *n, pl* **-gies** : liturgia *f*
livable ['lɪvəbəl] *adj* : habitable
live¹ ['lɪv] *vi* **lived; living 1** EXIST : vivir ⟨as long as I live : mientras viva⟩ ⟨to live from day to day : vivir al día⟩ **2** : llevar una vida, vivir ⟨he lived simply : llevó una vida sencilla⟩ **3** SUBSIST : mantenerse, vivir **4** RESIDE : vivir, residir
live² ['laɪv] *adj* **1** LIVING : vivo **2** BURNING : encendido ⟨a live coal : una brasa⟩ **3** : con corriente ⟨live wires : cables con corriente⟩ **4** : cargado, sin estallar ⟨a live bomb : una bomba sin estallar⟩ **5** CURRENT : de actualidad ⟨a live issue : un asunto de actualidad⟩ **6** : en vivo, en directo ⟨a live interview : una entrevista en vivo⟩
livelihood ['laɪvli,hʊd] *n* : sustento *m*, vida *f*, medio *m* de vida
liveliness ['laɪvlinəs] *n* : animación *f*, vivacidad *f*
livelong ['lɪv'lɔŋ] *adj* : entero, completo
lively ['laɪvli] *adj* **-lier; -est** : animado, vivaz, vivo, enérgico
liven ['laɪvən] *vt* : animar — *vi* : animarse
liver ['lɪvər] *n* : hígado *m*
livery ['lɪvəri] *n, pl* **-eries** : librea *f*
lives → **life**
livestock ['laɪv,stɑk] *n* : ganado *m*
live wire *n* : persona *f* vivaz y muy activa
livid ['lɪvəd] *adj* **1** BLACK-AND-BLUE : amoratado **2** PALE : lívido **3** ENRAGED : furioso
living¹ ['lɪvɪŋ] *adj* : vivo
living² *n* **to make a living** : ganarse la vida
living room *n* : living *m*, sala *f* de estar
lizard ['lɪzərd] *n* : lagarto *m*
llama ['lɑmə, 'jɑ-] *n* : llama *f*
load¹ ['lo:d] *vt* : cargar, embarcar
load² *n* **1** CARGO : carga *f* **2** WEIGHT : peso *m* **3** BURDEN : carga *f*, peso *m* **4 loads** *npl* : montón *m*, pila *f*, cantidad *f* ⟨loads of work : un montón de trabajo⟩
loaf¹ ['lo:f] *vi* : holgazanear, flojear, haraganear
loaf² *n, pl* **loaves** ['lo:vz] **1** : pan *m*, pan *m* de molde, barra *f* de pan **2 meat loaf** : pan *m* de carne
loafer ['lo:fər] *n* : holgazán *m*, -zana *f*; haragán *m*, -gana *f*; vago *m*, -ga *f*
loam ['lo:m] *n* : marga *f*, suelo *m*
loan¹ ['lo:n] *vt* : prestar
loan² *n* : préstamo *m*, empréstito *m* (del banco)
loath ['lo:θ, 'lo:ð] *adj* : poco dispuesto ⟨I am loath to say it : me resisto a decirlo⟩
loathe ['lo:ð] *vt* **loathed; loathing** : odiar, aborrecer
loathing ['lo:ðɪŋ] *n* : aversión *f*, odio *m*, aborrecimiento *m*
loathsome ['lo:θsəm, 'lo:ð-] *adj* : odioso, repugnante
lob¹ ['lɑb] *vt* **lobbed; lobbing** : hacerle un globo (a otro jugador)

lob² *n* : globo *m* (en deportes)
lobby¹ ['lɑbi] *v* **-bied; -bying** *vt* : presionar, ejercer presión sobre — *vi* **to lobby for** : presionar para (lograr algo)
lobby² *n, pl* **-bies 1** FOYER : vestíbulo *m* **2** LOBBYISTS : grupo *m* de presión, lobby *m*
lobbyist ['lɑbiɪst] *n* : miembro *m* de un lobby
lobe ['lo:b] *n* : lóbulo *m*
lobed ['lo:bd] *adj* : lobulado
lobotomy [lə'bɑtəmi, lo-] *n, pl* **-mies** : lobotomía *f*
lobster ['lɑbstər] *n* : langosta *f*
local¹ ['lo:kəl] *adj* : local
local² *n* **1** : anestesia *f* local **2 the locals** : los vecinos del lugar, los habitantes
locale [lo'kæl] *n* : lugar *m*, escenario *m*
locality [lo'kæləti] *n, pl* **-ties** : localidad *f*
localize ['lo:kə,laɪz] *vt* **-ized; -izing** : localizar
locally ['lo:kəli] *adv* : en la localidad, en la zona
locate ['lo:,keɪt, lo'keɪt] *v* **-cated; -cating** *vt* **1** POSITION : situar, ubicar **2** FIND : localizar, ubicar — *vi* SETTLE : establecerse
location [lo'keɪʃən] *n* **1** POSITION : posición *f*, emplazamiento *m*, ubicación *f* **2** PLACE : lugar *m*, sitio *m*
lock¹ ['lɑk] *vt* **1** FASTEN : cerrar **2** CONFINE : encerrar ⟨they locked me in the room : me encerraron en la sala⟩ **3** IMMOBILIZE : bloquear (una rueda) — *vi* **1** : cerrarse (dícese de una puerta) **2** : trabarse, bloquearse (dícese de una rueda)
lock² *n* **1** : mechón *m* (de pelo) **2** FASTENER : cerradura *f*, cerrojo *m*, chapa *f* **3** : esclusa *f* (de un canal)
locker ['lɑkər] *n* : armario *m*, cajón *m* con llave, lócker *m*
locket ['lɑkət] *n* : medallón *m*, guardapelo *m*, relicario *m*
lockjaw ['lɑk,jɔ] *n* : tétano *m*
lockout ['lɑk,aʊt] *n* : cierre *m* patronal, lockout *m*
locksmith ['lɑk,smɪθ] *n* : cerrajero *m*, -ra *f*
lockup ['lɑk,ʌp] *n* JAIL : cárcel *f*
locomotion [,lo:kə'mo:ʃən] *n* : locomoción *f*
locomotive¹ [,lo:kə'mo:tɪv] *adj* : locomotor
locomotive² *n* : locomotora *f*
locust ['lo:kəst] *n* **1** : langosta *f*, chapulín *m* CA, Mex **2** CICADA : cigarra *f*, chicharra *f* **3** : acacia *f* blanca (árbol)
locution [lo'kju:ʃən] *n* : locución *f*
lode ['lo:d] *n* : veta *f*, vena *f*, filón *m*
lodestar ['lo:d,stɑr] *n* : estrella *f* polar
lodestone ['lo:d,sto:n] *n* : piedra *f* imán
lodge¹ ['lɑdʒ] *v* **lodged; lodging** *vt* **1** HOUSE : hospedar, alojar **2** FILE : presentar ⟨to lodge a complaint : presentar una demanda⟩ — *vi* **1** : posarse, meterse ⟨the bullet lodged in the door

: la bala se incrustó en la puerta⟩ **2**
STAY : hospedarse, alojarse

lodge² *n* **1** : pabellón *m*, casa *f* de campo ⟨hunting lodge : refugio de caza⟩ **2** : madriguera *f* (de un castor) **3** : logia *f* ⟨Masonic lodge : logia masónica⟩

lodger ['lɑdʒər] *n* : inquilino *m*, -na *f*; huésped *m*, -peda *f*

lodging ['lɑdʒɪŋ] *n* **1** : alojamiento *m* **2 lodgings** *npl* ROOMS : habitaciones *fpl*

loft ['lɔft] *n* **1** ATTIC : desván *m*, ático *m*, buhardilla *f* **2** : loft *m* (en un depósito comercial) **3** HAYLOFT : pajar *m* **4** : galería *f* ⟨choir loft : galería del coro⟩

loftily ['lɔftəli] *adv* : altaneramente, con altivez

loftiness ['lɔftinəs] *n* **1** NOBILITY : nobleza *f* **2** ARROGANCE : altanería *f*, arrogancia *f* **3** HEIGHT : altura *f*, elevación *f*

lofty ['lɔfti] *adj* **loftier; -est 1** NOBLE : noble, elevado **2** HAUGHTY : altivo, arrogante, altanero **3** HIGH : majestuoso, elevado

log¹ ['lɔg, 'lɑg] *vi* **logged; logging 1** : talar (árboles) **2** RECORD : registrar, anotar **3 to log on** : entrar (al sistema) **4 to log off** : salir (del sistema)

log² *n* **1** : tronco *m*, leño *m* **2** RECORD : diario *m*

logarithm ['lɔgə,rɪðəm, 'lɑ-] *n* : logaritmo *m*

logger ['lɔgər, 'lɑ-] *n* : leñador *m*, -dora *f*

loggerhead ['lɔgər,hd, 'lɑ-] *n* **1** : tortuga *f* boba **2 to be at loggerheads** : estar en pugna, estar en desacuerdo

logic ['lɑdʒɪk] *n* : lógica *f* — **logical** ['lɑdʒɪkəl] *adj* — **logically** [-kli] *adv*

logistic [lə'dʒɪstɪk] *adj* : logístico

logistics [lə'dʒɪstɪks, lo-] *ns & pl* : logística *f*

logo ['lo:,go:] *n, pl* **logos** [-,go:z] : logotipo *m*

loin ['lɔɪn] *n* **1** : lomo *m* ⟨pork loin : lomo de cerdo⟩ **2 loins** *npl* : lomos *mpl* ⟨to gird one's loins : prepararse para la lucha⟩

loiter ['lɔɪtər] *vi* : vagar, perder el tiempo

loll ['lɑl] *vi* **1** SLOUCH : repantigarse **2** IDLE : holgazanear, hacer el vago

lollipop *or* **lollypop** ['lɑli,pɑp] *n* : dulce *m* en palito, chupete *m* Chile, Peru, paleta *f* CA, Mex

lone ['lo:n] *adj* **1** SOLITARY : solitario **2** ONLY : único

loneliness ['lo:nlinəs] *n* : soledad *f*

lonely ['lo:nli] *adj* **-lier; -est 1** SOLITARY : solitario, aislado **2** LONESOME : solo ⟨to feel lonely : sentirse muy solo⟩

loner ['lo:nər] *n* : solitario *m*, -ria *f*; recluso *m*, -sa *f*

lonesome ['lo:nsəm] *adj* : solo, solitario

long¹ ['lɔŋ] *vi* **1 to long for** : añorar, desear, anhelar **2 to long to** : anhelar, estar deseando ⟨they longed to see her : estaban deseando verla, tenían muchas ganas de verla⟩

long² *adv* **1** : mucho, mucho tiempo ⟨it didn't take long : no llevó mucho tiempo⟩ ⟨will it last long? : ¿va a durar mucho?⟩ **2 all day long** : todo el día **3 as long as** *or* **so long as** : mientras, con tal que **4 long before** : mucho antes **5 so long!** : ¡hasta luego!, ¡adiós!

long³ *adj* **longer** ['lɔŋgər]; **longest** ['lɔŋgəst] **1** (*indicating length*)) : largo ⟨the dress is too long : el vestido es demasiado largo⟩ ⟨a long way from : bastante lejos de⟩ ⟨in the long run : a la larga⟩ **2** (*indicating time*)) : largo, prolongado ⟨a long illness : una enfermedad prolongada⟩ ⟨a long walk : un paseo largo⟩ ⟨at long last : por fin⟩ **3 to be long on** : estar cargado de

long⁴ *n* **1 before long** : dentro de poco **2 the long and the short** : lo esencial, lo fundamental

longevity [lɑn'dʒvəti] *n* : longevidad *f*

longhand ['lɔŋ,hænd] *n* : escritura *f* a mano, escritura *f* cursiva

longhorn ['lɔŋ,hɔrn] *n* : longhorn *mf*

longing [lɔŋɪŋ] *n* : vivo deseo *m*, ansia *f*, anhelo *m*

longingly [lɔŋɪŋli] *adv* : ansiosamente, con ansia

longitude ['lɑndʒə,tu:d, -,tju:d] *n* : longitud *f*

longitudinal [,lɑndʒə'tu:dənəl, -'tju:-] *adj* : longitudinal — **longitudinally** *adv*

long–lived ['lɔŋ'lɪvd, -'laɪvd] *adj* : longevo

longshoreman ['lɔŋ'ʃɔrmən] *n, pl* **-men** [-mən, -,mɛn] : estibador *m*, -dora *f*

long–standing ['lɔŋ'stændɪŋ] *adj* : de larga data

long–suffering ['lɔŋ'sʌfərɪŋ] *adj* : paciente, sufrido

look¹ ['lʊk] *vi* **1** GLANCE : mirar ⟨to look out the window : mirar por la ventana⟩ **2** INVESTIGATE : buscar, mirar ⟨look in the closet : busca en el closet⟩ ⟨look before you leap : mira lo que haces⟩ **3** SEEM : parecer ⟨he looks happy : parece estar contento⟩ ⟨I look like my mother : me parezco a mi madre⟩ **4 to look after** : cuidar, cuidar de **5 to look for** EXPECT : esperar **6 to look for** SEEK : buscar — *vt* : mirar

look² *n* **1** GLANCE : mirada *f* **2** EXPRESSION : cara *f* ⟨a look of disapproval : una cara de desaprobación⟩ **3** ASPECT : aspecto *m*, apariencia *f*, aire *m* **4** looks *npl* : belleza *f*

lookout ['lʊk,aʊt] *n* **1** : centinela *mf*, vigía *mf* **2 to be on the lookout for** : estar al acecho de, andar a la caza de

loom¹ ['lu:m] *vi* **1** : aparecer, surgir ⟨the city loomed up in the distance : la ciudad surgió en la distancia⟩ **2** IMPEND : amenazar, ser inminente **3 to loom large** : cobrar mucha importancia

loom² *n* : telar *m*

loon ['lu:n] *n* : somorgujo *m*, somormujo *m*

loony *or* **looney** ['lu:ni] *adj* **-nier; -est** : loco, chiflado *fam*

loop¹ ['lu:p] *vt* **1** : hacer lazadas con **2 to loop around** : pasar alrededor de — *vi* **1** : rizar el rizo (dícese de un avión) **2** : serpentear (dícese de una carretera)

loop² *n* **1** : lazada *f* (en hilo o cuerda) **2** BEND : curva *f* **3** CIRCUIT : circuito *m* cerrado **4** : rizo *m* (en la aviación) ⟨to loop the loop : rizar el rizo⟩

loophole ['lu:p,ho:l] *n* : escapatoria *f*, pretexto *m*

loose¹ ['lu:s] *vt* **loosed; loosing 1** RELEASE : poner en libertad, soltar **2** UNTIE : deshacer, desatar **3** DISCHARGE, UNLEASH : descargar, desatar

loose² → **loosely**

loose³ *adj* **looser; -est 1** INSECURE : flojo, suelto, poco seguro ⟨a loose tooth : un diente flojo⟩ **2** ROOMY : suelto, holgado ⟨loose clothing : ropa holgada⟩ **3** OPEN : suelto, abierto ⟨loose soil : suelo suelto⟩ ⟨a loose weave : una tejida abierta⟩ **4** FREE : suelto ⟨to break loose : soltarse⟩ **5** SLACK : flojo, flexible **6** APPROXIMATE : libre, aproximado ⟨a loose translation : una traducción aproximada⟩

loosely ['lu:sli] *adv* **1** : sin apretar **2** ROUGHLY : aproximadamente, más o menos

loosen ['lu:sən] *vt* : aflojar

loose-leaf ['lu:s'li:f] *adj* : de hojas sueltas

looseness ['lu:snəs] *n* **1** : aflojamiento *m*, holgura *f* (de ropa) **2** IMPRECISION : imprecisión *f*

loot¹ ['lu:t] *vt* : saquear, robar

loot² *n* : botín *m*

looter ['lu:t̬ər] *n* : saqueador *m*, -dora *f*

lop ['lɑp] *vt* **lopped; lopping** : cortar, podar

lope¹ ['lo:p] *vi* **loped; loping** : correr a paso largo

lope² *n* : paso *m* largo

lopsided ['lɑp,saɪdəd] *adj* **1** CROOKED : torcido, chueco, ladeado **2** ASYMETRICAL : asimétrico

loquacious [lo'kweɪʃəs] *adj* : locuaz

lord ['lɔrd] *n* **1** : señor *m*, noble *m* **2** : lord *m* (en la Gran Bretaña) **3 the Lord** : el Señor **4 good Lord!** : ¡Dios mío!

lordly ['lɔrdli] *adj* **-lier; -est** HAUGHTY : arrogante, altanero

lordship ['lɔrd,ʃɪp] *n* : señoría *f*

Lord's Supper *n* : Eucaristía *f*

lore ['lor] *n* : saber *m* popular, tradición *f*

lose ['lu:z] *v* **lost** ['lɔst]; **losing** ['lu:-zɪŋ] *vt* **1** : perder ⟨I lost my umbrella : perdí mi paraguas⟩ ⟨to lose blood : perder sangre⟩ ⟨to lose one's voice : quedarse fónico⟩ ⟨to have nothing to lose : no tener nada que perder⟩ ⟨to lose no time : no perder tiempo⟩ ⟨to lose weight : perder peso, adelgazar⟩ ⟨to lose one's temper : perder los estribos, enojarse, enfadarse⟩ ⟨to lose sight of : perder de vista⟩ **2** : costar, hacer perder ⟨the errors lost him his job : los errores le

costaron su empleo⟩ **3** : atrasar ⟨my watch loses 5 minutes a day : mi reloj atrasa 5 minutos por día⟩ **4 to lose oneself** : perderse, ensimismarse — *vi* **1** : perder ⟨we lost to the other team : perdimos contra el otro equipo⟩ **2** : atrasarse ⟨the clock loses time : el reloj se atrasa⟩

loser ['lu:zər] *n* : perdedor *m*, -dora *f*

loss ['lɔs] *n* **1** LOSING : pérdida *f* ⟨loss of memory : pérdida de memoria⟩ ⟨to sell at a loss : vender con pérdida⟩ ⟨to be at a loss to : no saber como⟩ **2** DEFEAT : derrota *f*, juego *m* perdido **3**

losses *npl* DEATHS : muertos *mpl*

lost ['lɔst] *adj* **1** : perdido ⟨a lost cause : una causa perdida⟩ ⟨lost in thought : absorto⟩ **2 to get lost** : perderse **3 to make up for lost time** : recuperar el tiempo perdido

lot ['lɑt] *n* **1** DRAWING : sorteo *m* ⟨by lot : por sorteo⟩ **2** SHARE : parte *f*, porción *f* **3** FATE : suerte *f* **4** LAND, PLOT : terreno *m*, solar *m*, lote *m*, parcela *f* ⟨parking lot : estacionamiento⟩ **5 a lot of** *or* **lots of** : mucho, un montón de, bastante ⟨lots of books : un montón de libros, muchos libros⟩ ⟨a lot of people : mucha gente⟩

loth ['lo:θ, 'lo:ð] → **loath**

lotion ['lo:ʃən] *n* : loción *f*

lottery ['lɑt̬əri] *n, pl* **-teries** : lotería *f*

lotus ['lo:t̬əs] *n* : loto *m*

loud¹ ['laʊd] *adv* : alto, fuerte ⟨out loud : en voz alta⟩

loud² *adj* **1** : alto, fuerte ⟨a loud voice : una voz alta⟩ **2** NOISY : ruidoso ⟨a loud party : una fiesta ruidosa⟩ **3** FLASHY : llamativo, chillón

loudly ['laʊdli] *adv* : alto, fuerte, en voz alta

loudness ['laʊdnəs] *n* : volumen *m*, fuerza *f* (del ruido)

loudspeaker ['laʊd,spi:kər] *n* : altavoz *m*, altoparlante *m*

lounge¹ ['laʊndʒ] *vi* **lounged; lounging** : holgazanear, gandulear

lounge² *n* : salón *m*, sala *f* de estar

louse ['laʊs] *n, pl* **lice** ['laɪs] : piojo *m*

lousy ['laʊzi] *adj* **lousier; -est 1** : piojoso, lleno de piojos **2** BAD : pésimo, muy malo

lout ['laʊt] *n* : bruto *m*, patán *m*

louver *or* **louvre** ['lu:vər] *n* : persiana *f*, listón *m* de persiana

lovable ['lʌvəbəl] *adj* : adorable, amoroso, encantador

love¹ ['lʌv] *v* **loved; loving** *vt* **1** : querer, amar ⟨I love you : te quiero⟩ **2** ENJOY : encantarle a alguien, ser (muy) aficionado a, gustarle mucho a uno (algo) ⟨she loves flowers : le encantan las flores⟩ ⟨he loves golf : es muy aficionado al golf⟩ ⟨I'd love to go with you : me gustaría mucho acompañarte⟩ — *vi* : querer, amar

love² *n* **1** : amor *m*, cariño *m* ⟨to be in love with : estar enamorado de⟩ ⟨to fall

in love with : enamorarse de⟩ **2** EN-
THUSIASM, INTEREST : amor *m*, afición
m, gusto *m* ⟨love of music : afición a
la música⟩ **3** BELOVED : amor *m*; amado *m*, -da *f*; enamorado *m*, -da *f*
loveless ['lʌvləs] *adj* : sin amor
loveliness ['lʌvlinəs] *n* : belleza *f*, hermosura *f*
lovelorn ['lʌv,lɔrn] *adj* : herido de amor,
perdidamente enamorado
lovely ['lʌvli] *adj* **-lier; -est** : hermoso,
bello, lindo, precioso
lover ['lʌvər] *n* : amante *mf* (de personas); aficionado *m*, -da *f* (a alguna actividad)
loving ['lʌvɪŋ] *adj* : amoroso, cariñoso
lovingly ['lʌvɪŋli] *adv* : cariñosamente
low¹ ['lo:] *vi* : mugir
low² *adv* : bajo, profundo ⟨to aim low
: apuntar bajo⟩ ⟨to lie low : mantenerse escondido⟩ ⟨to turn the lights
down low : bajar las luces⟩
low³ *adj* **lower; -est** **1** : bajo ⟨a
low building : un edificio bajo⟩ ⟨a low
bow : una profunda reverencia⟩ **2**
SOFT : bajo, suave ⟨in a low voice : en
voz baja⟩ **3** SHALLOW : bajo, poco profundo **4** HUMBLE : humilde, modesto
5 DEPRESSED : deprimido, bajo de
moral **6** INFERIOR : bajo, inferior **7**
UNFAVORABLE : mal ⟨to have a low
opinion of him : tener un mal concepto de él⟩ **8 to be low on** : tener poco
de, estar escaso de
low⁴ *n* **1** : punto *m* bajo ⟨to reach an all-
time low : estar más bajo que nunca⟩
2 *or* **low gear** : primera velocidad *f* **3**
: mugido *m* (de una vaca)
lowbrow ['lo:,braʊ] *n* : persona *f* inculta
lower¹ ['lo:ər] *vt* **1** DROP : bajar ⟨to lower one's voice : bajar la voz⟩ **2** : arriar, bajar ⟨to lower the flag : arriar la
bandera⟩ **3** REDUCE : reducir, bajar **4**
to lower oneself : rebajarse
lower² ['lo:ər] *adj* : inferior, más bajo, de
abajo
lowland ['lo:lənd, -,lænd] *n* : tierras *fpl*
bajas
lowly ['lo:li] *adj* **-lier; -est** : humilde,
modesto
loyal ['lɔɪəl] *adj* : leal, fiel — **loyally** *adv*
loyalist ['lɔɪəlɪst] *n* : partidario *m*, -ria *f*
del régimen
loyalty ['lɔɪəlti] *n*, *pl* **-ties** : lealtad *f*, fidelidad *f*
lozenge ['lazəndʒ] *n* : pastilla *f*
LSD [,ɛl,ɛs'di:] *n* : LSD *m*
lubricant ['lu:brɪkənt] *n* : lubricante *m*
lubricate ['lu:brɪ,keɪt] *vt* **-cated; -cating**
: lubricar — **lubrication** [,lu:brɪ
'keɪʃən] *n*
lucid ['lu:səd] *adj* : lúcido, claro — **lu-
cidly** *adv*
lucidity [lu:'sɪdəti] *n* : lucidez *f*
luck ['lʌk] *n* **1** : suerte *f* **2 to have bad
luck** : tener mala suerte **3 good luck!**
: ¡(buena) suerte!
luckily ['lʌkəli] *adv* : afortunadamente,
por suerte

luckless ['lʌkləs] *adj* : desafortunado
lucky ['lʌki] *adj* **luckier; -est** **1** : afortunado, que tiene suerte ⟨a lucky
woman : una mujer afortunada⟩ **2**
FORTUITOUS : fortuito, de suerte **3** OP-
PORTUNE : oportuno **4** : de (la) suerte
⟨lucky number : número de la suerte⟩
lucrative ['lu:krətɪv] *adj* : lucrativo,
provechoso — **lucratively** *adv*
ludicrous ['lu:dəkrəs] *adj* : ridículo, absurdo — **ludicrously** *adv*
ludicrousness ['lu:dəkrəsnəs] *n* : ridiculez *f*, absurdo *m*
lug ['lʌg] *vt* **lugged; lugging** : arrastrar,
transportar con dificultad
luggage ['lʌgɪdʒ] *n* : equipaje *m*
lugubrious [lʊ'gu:briəs] *adj* : lúgubre —
lugubriously *adv*
lukewarm ['lu:k'wɔrm] *adj* **1** TEPID
: tibio **2** HALFHEARTED : poco entusiasta
lull¹ ['lʌl] *vt* **1** CALM, SOOTHE : calmar,
sosegar **2 to lull to sleep** : arrullar,
adormecer
lull² *n* : calma *f*, pausa *f*
lullaby ['lʌlə,baɪ] *n*, *pl* **-bies** : canción *f*
de cuna, arrullo *m*, nana *f*
lumber¹ ['lʌmbər] *vt* : aserrar (madera)
— *vi* : moverse pesadamente
lumber² *n* : madera *f*
lumberjack ['lʌmbər,dʒæk] *n* : leñador
m, -dora *f*
lumberyard ['lʌmbər,jard] *n* : almacén
m de maderas
luminary ['lu:mə,nɛri] *n*, *pl* **-naries**
: lumbrera *f*, luminaria *f*
luminescence [,lu:mə'nɛsənts] *n* : luminiscencia *f* — **luminescent** [-'nɛs-
ənt] *adj*
luminosity [,lu:mə'nasəti] *n*, *pl* **-ties**
: luminosidad *f*
luminous ['lu:mənəs] *adj* : luminoso —
luminously *adv*
lump¹ ['lʌmp] *vt* *or* **to lump together**
: juntar, agrupar, amontonar — *vi*
CLUMP : agruparse, aglutinarse
lump² *n* **1** GLOB : grumo *m* **2** PIECE
: pedazo *m*, trozo *m*, terrón *m* ⟨a lump
of coal : un trozo de carbón⟩ ⟨a lump
of sugar : un terrón de azúcar⟩ **3**
SWELLING : bulto *m*, hinchazón *f*,
protuberancia *f* **4 to have a lump in
one's throat** : tener un nudo en la garganta
lumpy ['lʌmpi] *adj* **lumpier; -est** **1**
: lleno de grumos (dícese de una salsa)
2 UNEVEN : desigual, disparejo
lunacy ['lu:nəsi] *n*, *pl* **-cies** : locura *f*
lunar ['lu:nər] *adj* : lunar
lunatic¹ ['lu:nə,tɪk] *adj* : lunático, loco
lunatic² *n* : loco *m*, -ca *f*
lunch¹ ['lʌntʃ] *vi* : almorzar, comer
lunch² *n* : almuerzo *m*, comida *f*, lonche
m
luncheon ['lʌntʃən] *n* **1** : comida *f*, almuerzo *m* **2 luncheon meat** : fiambres
fpl

lung ['lʌŋ] *n* : pulmón *m*
lunge¹ ['lʌndʒ] *vi* **lunged; lunging 1**
THRUST : atacar (en la esgrima) **2 to
lunge forward** : arremeter, lanzarse
lunge² *n* **1** : arremetida *f*, embestida *f* **2**
: estocada *f* (en la esgrima)
lurch¹ ['lərtʃ] *vi* **1** PITCH : cabecear, dar
bandazos, dar sacudidas **2** STAGGER
: tambalearse
lurch² *n* **1** : sacudida *f*, bandazo *m* (de
un vehículo) **2** : tambaleo *m* (de una
persona)
lure¹ ['lʊr] *vt* **lured; luring** : atraer
lure² *n* **1** ATTRACTION : atractivo *m* **2**
ENTICEMENT : señuelo *m*, aliciente
m **3** BAIT : cebo *m* artificial (en la
pesca)
lurid ['lʊrəd] *adj* **1** GRUESOME : espeluznante, horripilante **2** SENSA-
TIONAL : sensacionalista, chocante **3**
GAUDY : chillón
lurk ['lərk] *vi* : estar al acecho
luscious ['lʌʃəs] *adj* **1** DELICIOUS : delicioso, exquisito **2** SEDUCTIVE : seductor, cautivador
lush ['lʌʃ] *adj* **1** LUXURIANT : exuberante, lozano **2** LUXURIOUS : suntuoso,
lujoso
lust¹ ['lʌst] *vi* **to lust after** : desear (a una
persona), codiciar (riquezas, etc.)
lust² *n* **1** LASCIVIOUSNESS : lujuria *f*, lascivia *f* **2** CRAVING : deseo *m*, ansia *f*,
anhelo *m*
luster *or* **lustre** ['lʌstər] *n* **1** GLOSS,

SHEEN : lustre *m*, brillo *m* **2** SPLEN-
DOR : lustre *m*, esplendor *m*
lusterless ['lʌstərləs] *adj* : deslustrado,
sin brillo
lustful ['lʌstfəl] *adj* : lujurioso, lascivo,
lleno de deseo
lustrous ['lʌstrəs] *adj* : brillante, brilloso, lustroso
lusty ['lʌsti] *adj* **lustier; -est** : fuerte, robusto, vigoroso — **lustily** ['lʌstəli] *adv*
lute ['luːt] *n* : laúd *m*
luxuriant [ˌlʌɡ'ʒʊriənt, ˌlʌk'ʃʊr-] *adj* **1**
: exuberante, lozano (dícese de las
plantas) **2** : abundante y hermoso
(dícese del pelo) — **luxuriantly** *adv*
luxuriate [ˌlʌɡ'ʒʊriˌeɪt, ˌlʌk'ʃʊr-] *vi*
-ated; -ating 1 : disfrutar **2 to luxuriate in** : deleitarse con
luxurious [ˌlʌɡ'ʒʊriəs, ˌlʌk'ʃʊr-] *adj* : lujoso, suntuoso — **luxuriously** *adv*
luxury ['lʌkʃəri, 'lʌɡʒə-] *n*, *pl* **-ries** : lujo
m
lye ['laɪ] *n* : lejía *f*
lying → **lie¹, lie²**
lymph ['lɪmpf] *n* : linfa *f*
lymphatic [lɪm'fætɪk] *adj* : linfático
lynch ['lɪntʃ] *vt* : linchar
lynx ['lɪŋks] *n*, *pl* **lynx** *or* **lynxes** : lince
m
lyre ['laɪr] *n* : lira *f*
lyric¹ ['lɪrɪk] *adj* : lírico
lyric² *n* **1** : poema *m* lírico **2 lyrics** *npl*
: letra *f* (de una canción)
lyrical ['lɪrɪkəl] *adj* : lírico, elocuente

M

m ['ɛm] *n*, *pl* **m's** *or* **ms** ['ɛmz] : deci-
motercera letra del alfabeto inglés
ma'am ['mæm] → **madam**
macabre [mə'kɑb, -'kɑbər, -'kɑbrə] *adj*
: macabro
macadam [mə'kædəm] *n* : macadán *m*
macaroni [ˌmækə'roːni] *n* : macarrones
mpl
macaroon [ˌmækə'ruːn] *n* : macarrón *m*,
mostachón *m*
macaw [mə'kɔ] *n* : guacamayo *m*
mace ['meɪs] *n* **1** : maza *f* (arma o símbolo) **2** : macis *f* (especia)
machete [mə'ʃɛti] *n* : machete *m*
machination [ˌmækə'neɪʃən, ˌmæʃə-] *n*
: maquinación *f*, intriga *f*
machine¹ [mə'ʃiːn] *vt* **-chined; -chining**
: trabajar a máquina
machine² *n* **1** : máquina *f* ⟨machine
shop : taller de máquinas⟩ ⟨machine
language : lenguaje de la máquina⟩ **2**
: aparato *m*, maquinaria *f* (en política)
machine gun *n* : ametralladora *f*
machinery [mə'ʃiːnəri] *n*, *pl* **-eries 1**
: maquinaria *f* **2** WORKS : mecanismo
m
machinist [mə'ʃiːnɪst] *n* : maquinista *mf*
machismo [mɑ'tʃizmoː] *n* : machismo
m, masculinidad *f*

macho ['mɑtʃoː] *adj* : machote, macho
mackerel ['mækərəl] *n*, *pl* **-el** *or* **-els** : caballa *f*
mackinaw ['mækəˌnɔ] *n* : chaqueta *f* escocesa de lana
mad ['mæd] *adj* **madder; maddest 1** IN-
SANE : loco, demente **2** RABID : rabioso **3** FOOLISH : tonto, insensato **4**
ANGRY : enojado, furioso **5** CRAZY
: loco ⟨I'm mad about you : estoy loco
por ti⟩
Madagascan [ˌmædə'ɡæskən] *n* : malgache *mf* — **Madagascan** *adj*
madam ['mædəm] *n*, *pl* **mesdames**
[meɪ'dɑm, -'dæm] : señora *f*
madcap¹ ['mædˌkæp] *adj* ZANY : alocado, disparatado
madcap² *n* : alocado *m*, -da *f*
madden ['mædən] *vt* : enloquecer, enfurecer
maddening ['mædənɪŋ] *adj* : enloquecedor, exasperante ⟨I find it maddening : me saca de quicio⟩
made → **make¹**
madhouse ['mædˌhaʊs] *n* : manicomio
m ⟨the office was a madhouse : la oficina parecía una casa de locos⟩
madly ['mædli] *adv* : como un loco, locamente

madman ['mæd₁mæn, -mən] *n, pl* **-men** [-mən, -₁mɛn] : loco *m*, demente *m*

madness ['mædnəs] *n* : locura *f*, demencia *f*

madwoman ['mæd₁wʊmən] *n, pl* **-women** [-₁wɪmən] : loca *f*, demente *f*

maelstrom ['meɪlstrəm] *n* : remolino *m*, vorágine *f*

maestro ['maɪ₁stro:] *n, pl* **-stros** *or* **-stri** [-₁stri:] : maestro *m*

Mafia ['mɑfiə] *n* : Mafia *f*

magazine ['mægə₁zi:n] *n* **1** STOREHOUSE : almacén *m*, polvorín *m* (de explosivos) **2** PERIODICAL : revista *f* **3** : cargador *m* (de un arma de fuego)

magenta [mə'ʤɛntə] *n* : magenta *f*, color *m* magenta

maggot ['mægət] *n* : gusano *m*

magic¹ ['mæʤɪk] *or* **magical** ['mæʤɪkəl] *adj* : mágico

magic² *n* : magia *f*

magically ['mæʤɪkli] *adv* : mágicamente ⟨they magically appeared : aparecieron como por arte de magia⟩

magician [mə'ʤɪʃən] *n* **1** SORCERER : mago *m*, -ga *f* **2** CONJURER : prestidigitador *m*, -dora *f*; mago *m*, -ga *f*

magistrate ['mæʤə₁streɪt] *n* : magistrado *m*, -da *f*

magma ['mægmə] *n* : magma *m*

magnanimity [₁mægnə'nɪməti] *n, pl* **-ties** : magnanimidad *f*

magnanimous [mæg'nænəməs] *adj* : magnánimo, generoso — **magnanimously** *adv*

magnate ['mæg₁neɪt, -nət] *n* : magnate *mf*

magnesium [mæg'ni:ziəm, -ʒəm] *n* : magnesio *m*

magnet ['mægnət] *n* : imán *m*

magnetic [mæg'nɛtɪk] *adj* : magnético — **magnetically** [-tɪkli] *adv*

magnetic field *n* : campo *m* magnético

magnetism ['mægnə₁tɪzəm] *n* : magnetismo *m*

magnetize ['mægnə₁taɪz] *vt* **-tized; -tizing 1** : magnetizar, imantar **2** ATTRACT : magnetizar, atraer

magnification [₁mægnəfə'keɪʃən] *n* : aumento *m*, ampliación *f*

magnificence [mæg'nɪfəsənts] *n* : magnificencia *f*

magnificent [mæg'nɪfəsənt] *adj* : magnífico — **magnificently** *adv*

magnify ['mægnə₁faɪ] *vt* **-fied; -fying 1** ENLARGE : ampliar **2** EXAGGERATE : magnificar, exagerar

magnifying glass *n* : lupa *f*

magnitude ['mægnə₁tu:d, -₁tju:d] *n* **1** GREATNESS : magnitud *f*, grandeza *f* **2** QUANTITY : cantidad *f* **3** IMPORTANCE : magnitud *f*, envergadura *f*

magnolia [mæg'no:ljə] *n* : magnolia *f* (flor), magnolio *m* (árbol)

magpie ['mæg₁paɪ] *n* : urraca *f*

mahogany [mə'hɑgəni] *n, pl* **-nies** : caoba *f*

maid ['meɪd] *n* **1** MAIDEN : doncella *f* **2** *or* **maidservant** ['meɪd₁sərvənt] : sirvienta *f*, muchacha *f*, mucama *f*, criada *f*

maiden¹ ['meɪdən] *adj* **1** UNMARRIED : soltera **2** FIRST : primero ⟨maiden voyage : primera travesía⟩

maiden² *n* : doncella *f*

maidenhood ['meɪdən₁hʊd] *n* : doncellez *f*

maiden name *n* : nombre *m* de soltera

mail¹ ['meɪl] *vt* : enviar por correo, echar al correo

mail² *n* **1** : correo *m* ⟨airmail : correo aéreo⟩ **2** : malla *f* ⟨coat of mail : cota de malla⟩

mailbox ['meɪl₁bɑks] *n* : buzón *m*

mailman ['meɪl₁mæn, -mən] *n, pl* **-men** [-mən, -₁mɛn] : cartero *m*

maim ['meɪm] *vt* : mutilar, desfigurar, lisiar

main¹ ['meɪn] *adj* : principal, central ⟨the main office : la oficina central⟩

main² *n* **1** HIGH SEAS : alta mar *f* **2** : tubería *f* principal (de agua o gas), cable *m* principal (de un circuito) **3 with might and main** : con todas sus fuerzas

mainframe ['meɪn₁freɪm] *n* : mainframe *m*, computadora *f* central

mainland ['meɪn₁lænd, -lənd] *n* : continente *m*

mainly ['meɪnli] *adv* **1** PRINCIPALLY : principalmente, en primer lugar **2** MOSTLY : principalmente, en la mayor parte

mainstay ['meɪn₁steɪ] *n* : pilar *m*, sostén *m* principal

mainstream¹ ['meɪn₁stri:m] *adj* : dominante, corriente, convencional

mainstream² *n* : corriente *f* principal

maintain [meɪn'teɪn] *vt* **1** SERVICE : dar mantenimiento a (una máquina) **2** PRESERVE : mantener, conservar ⟨to maintain silence : guardar silencio⟩ **3** SUPPORT : mantener, sostener **4** ASSERT : mantener, sostener, afirmar

maintenance ['meɪntənənts] *n* : mantenimiento *m*

maize ['meɪz] *n* : maíz *m*

majestic [mə'ʤɛstɪk] *adj* : majestuoso — **majestically** [-tɪkli] *adv*

majesty ['mæʤəsti] *n, pl* **-ties 1** : majestad *f* ⟨Your Majesty : su Majestad⟩ **2** SPLENDOR : majestuosidad *f*, esplendor *m*

major¹ ['meɪʤər] *vi* **-jored; -joring** : especializarse

major² *adj* **1** GREATER : mayor **2** NOTEWORTHY : mayor, notable **3** SERIOUS : grave **4** : mayor (en la música)

major³ *n* **1** : mayor *mf*, comandante *mf* (en las fuerzas armadas) **2** : especialidad *f* (universitaria)

Majorcan [mɑ'ʤɔrkən, mə-, -'jɔr-] *n* : mallorquín *m*, -quina *f* — **Majorcan** *adj*

major general *n* : general *mf* de división

majority [mə'dʒɔrəʈi] *n, pl* **-ties 1**
ADULTHOOD : mayoría *f* de edad **2**
: mayoría *f*, mayor parte *f* ⟨the vast majority : la inmensa mayoría⟩
make¹ ['meɪk] *v* **made** ['meɪd;]; **making**
vt **1** CREATE : hacer ⟨to make noise
: hacer ruido⟩ **2** FASHION, MANUFAC-
TURE : hacer, fabricar ⟨she made a
dress : hizo un vestido⟩ **3** DEVISE,
FORM : desarrollar, elaborar, formar **4**
CONSTITUTE : hacer, constituir ⟨made
of stone : hecho de piedra⟩ **5** PREPARE
: hacer, preparar **6** RENDER : hacer,
poner ⟨it makes him nervous : lo pone
nervioso⟩ ⟨to make someone happy
: hacer feliz a alguien⟩ ⟨it made me sad
: me dio pena⟩ **7** PERFORM : hacer ⟨to
make a gesture : hacer un gesto⟩ **8**
COMPEL : hacer, forzar, obligar **9**
EARN : ganar ⟨to make a living : ganarse la vida⟩ — *vi* **1** HEAD : ir, dirigirse ⟨we made for home : nos fuimos
a casa⟩ **2 to make do** : arreglárselas **3
to make good** REPAY : pagar **4 to make
good** SUCCEED : tener éxito
make² *n* BRAND : marca *f*
make–believe¹ [ˌmeɪkbə'liːv] *adj* : imaginario
make–believe² *n* : fantasía *f*, invención
f ⟨a world of make-believe : un mundo de ensueño⟩
make out *vt* **1** WRITE : hacer (un cheque)
2 DISCERN : distinguir, divisar **3** UN-
DERSTAND : comprender, entender —
vi : arreglárselas ⟨how did you make
out? : ¿qué tal te fue?⟩
maker ['meɪkər] *n* : fabricante *mf*
makeshift ['meɪkˌʃɪft] *adj* : provisional,
improvisado
makeup ['meɪkˌʌp] *n* **1** COMPOSITION
: composición *f* **2** CHARACTER : carácter *m*, temperamento *m* **3** COSMETICS
: maquillaje *m*
make up *vt* **1** INVENT : inventar **2** : recuperar ⟨she made up the time : recu-
peró las horas perdidas⟩ — *vi* RECON-
CILE : hacer las paces, reconciliarse
making ['meɪkɪŋ] *n* **1** : creación *f*, producción *f* ⟨in the making : en ciernes⟩
2 to have the makings of : tener
madera de (dícese de personas), tener
los ingredientes para
maladjusted [ˌmælə'dʒʌstəd] *adj* : inadaptado
malady ['mælədi] *n, pl* **-dies** : dolencia
f, enfermedad *f*, mal *m*
malaise [mæ'leɪz, mæ-] *n* : malestar *m*
malapropism ['mælə,prɑ,pɪzəm] *n* : uso
m incorrecto y cómico de una palabra
malaria [mə'lɛriə] *n* : malaria *f*, paludismo *m*
malarkey [mə'lɑrki] *n* : tonterías *fpl*, estupideces *fpl*
Malawian [mə'lɑwiən] *n* : malauiano *m*,
-na *f* — **Malawian** *adj*
Malay [mə'leɪ, 'meɪˌleɪ] *n* **1** *or* **Malayan**
[mə'leɪən, meɪ-; 'meɪˌleɪən] : malayo *m*,

-ya *f* **2** : malayo *m* (idioma) — **Malay**
or **Malayan** *adj*
Malaysian [mə'leɪʒən, -ʃən] *n* : malasio
m, -sia *f*; malaisio *m*, -sia *f* — **Malaysian**
adj
male¹ ['meɪl] *adj* **1** : macho **2** MASCU-
LINE : masculino
male² *n* : macho *m* (de animales o plantas), varón *m* (de personas)
malefactor ['mælə,fæktər] *n* : malhechor *m*, -chora *f*
maleness ['meɪlnəs] *n* : masculinidad *f*
malevolence [mə'lɛvələn/s] *n* : malevolencia *f*
malevolent [mə'lɛvələnt] *adj* : malévolo
malformation [ˌmælfɔr'meɪʃən] *n* : malformación *f*
malformed [mæl'fɔrmd] *adj* : mal formado, deforme
malfunction¹ [mæl'fʌŋkʃən] *vi* : funcionar mal
malfunction² *n* : mal funcionamiento *m*
malice ['mæləs] *n* **1** : malicia *f*, malevolencia *f* **2 with malice aforethought**
: con premeditación
malicious [mə'lɪʃəs] *adj* : malicioso,
malévolo — **maliciously** *adv*
malign¹ [mə'laɪn] *vt* : calumniar, difamar
malign² *adj* : maligno
malignancy [mə'lɪgnən/si] *n, pl* **-cies**
: malignidad *f*
malignant [mə'lɪgnənt] *adj* : maligno
malinger [mə'lɪŋgər] *vi* : fingirse enfermo
malingerer [mə'lɪŋgərər] *n* : uno que se
finge enfermo
mall ['mɔl] *n* **1** PROMENADE : alameda
f, paseo *m* (arbolado) **2** : centro *m* comercial ⟨shopping mall : galería comer-
cial⟩
mallard ['mælərd] *n, pl* **-lard** *or* **-lards**
: pato *m* real, ánade *mf* real
malleable ['mæliəbəl] *adj* : maleable
mallet ['mælət] *n* : mazo *m*
malnourished [mæl'nərɪʃt] *adj* : desnutrido, malnutrido
malnutrition [ˌmælnʊ'trɪʃən, -njʊ-] *n*
: desnutrición *f*, malnutrición *f*
malodorous [mæl'oːdərəs] *adj* : maloliente
malpractice [ˌmæl'præktəs] *n* : mala
práctica *f*, negligencia *f*
malt ['mɔlt] *n* : malta *f*
maltreat [mæl'triːt] *vt* : maltratar
mama *or* **mamma** ['mɑmə] *n* : mamá *f*
mammal ['mæməl] *n* : mamífero *m*
mammalian [mə'meɪliən, mæ-] *adj*
: mamífero
mammary ['mæməri] *adj* **1** : mamario
2 mammary gland : glándula mamaria
mammogram ['mæmə,græm] *n* : mamografía *f*
mammoth¹ ['mæməθ] *adj* : colosal, gigantesco
mammoth² *n* : mamut *m*
man¹ ['mæn] *vt* **manned; manning** : tripular (un barco o avión), encargarse de
(un servicio)

man² *n, pl* **men** ['mɛn] **1** PERSON : hombre *m*, persona *f* **2** MALE : hombre *m* **3** MANKIND : humanidad *f*

manacles ['mænɪkəlz] *npl* HANDCUFFS : esposas *fpl*

manage ['mænɪʤ] *v* **-aged; -aging** *vt* **1** HANDLE : controlar, manejar **2** DIRECT : administrar, dirigir **3** CONTRIVE : lograr, ingeniárselas para — *vi* COPE : arreglárselas

manageable ['mænɪʤəbəl] *adj* : manejable

management ['mænɪʤmənt] *n* **1** DIRECTION : administración *f*, gestión *f*, dirección *f* **2** HANDLING : manejo *m* **3** MANAGERS : dirección *f*, gerencia *f*

manager ['mænɪʤər] *n* : director *m*, -tora *f*; gerente *mf*; administrador *m*, -dora *f*

managerial [ˌmænə'ʤɪriəl] *adj* : directivo, gerencial

mandarin ['mændərən] *n* **1** : mandarín *m* **2** *or* **mandarin orange** : mandarina *f*

mandate ['mæn‚deɪt] *n* : mandato *m*

mandatory ['mændə‚tori] *adj* : obligatorio

mandible ['mændəbəl] *n* : mandíbula *f*

mandolin [ˌmændə'lɪn, 'mændələn] *n* : mandolina *f*

mane ['meɪn] *n* : crin *f* (de un caballo), melena *f* (de un león o una persona)

maneuver¹ [mə'nu:vər, -'nju:-] *vt* **1** PLACE, POSITION : maniobrar, posicionar, colocar **2** MANIPULATE : manipular, maniobrar — *vi* : maniobrar

maneuver² *n* : maniobra *f*

manfully ['mænfəli] *adj* : valientemente

manganese ['mæŋɡə‚ni:z, -‚ni:s] *n* : manganeso *m*

mange ['meɪnʤ] *n* : sarna *f*

manger ['meɪnʤər] *n* : pesebre *m*

mangle ['mæŋɡəl] *vt* **-gled; -gling 1** CRUSH, DESTROY : aplastar, despedazar, destrozar **2** MUTILATE : mutilar ⟨to mangle a text : mutilar un texto⟩

mango ['mæŋ‚go:] *n, pl* **-goes** : mango *m*

mangrove ['mæn‚gro:v, 'mæŋ-] *n* : mangle *m*

mangy ['meɪnʤi] *adj* **mangier; -est 1** : sarnoso **2** SHABBY : gastado

manhandle ['mæn‚hændəl] *vt* **-dled; -dling** : maltratar, tratar con poco cuidado

manhole ['mæn‚ho:l] *n* : boca *f* de alcantarilla

manhood ['mæn‚hʊd] *n* **1** : madurez *f* (de un hombre) **2** COURAGE, MANLINESS : hombría *f*, valor *m* **3** MEN : hombres *mpl*

manhunt ['mæn‚hʌnt] *n* : búsqueda *f* (de un criminal)

mania ['meɪniə, -njə] *n* : manía *f*

maniac ['meɪni‚æk] *n* : maníaco *m*, -ca *f*; maniático *m*, -ca *f*

maniacal [mə'naɪəkəl] *adj* : maníaco, maniaco

manicure¹ ['mænə‚kjʊr] *vt* **-cured; -curing 1** : hacer la manicura a **2** TRIM : recortar

manicure² *n* : manicura *f*

manicurist ['mænə‚kjʊrɪst] *n* : manicuro *m*, -ra *f*

manifest¹ ['mænə‚fɛst] *vt* : manifestar

manifest² *adj* : manifiesto, patente — **manifestly** *adv*

manifestation [ˌmænəfə'steɪʃən] *n* : manifestación *f*

manifesto [ˌmænə'fɛs‚to:] *n, pl* **-tos** *or* **-toes** : manifiesto *m*

manifold¹ ['mænə‚fo:ld] *adj* : diverso, variado

manifold² *n* : colector *m* (de escape)

manipulate [mə'nɪpjə‚leɪt] *vt* **-lated; -lating** : manipular

manipulation [mə‚nɪpjə'leɪʃən] *n* : manipulación *f*

manipulative [mə'nɪpjə‚leɪtɪv, -lətɪv] *adj* : manipulador

mankind ['mæn'kaɪnd, ‚kaɪnd] *n* : género *m* humano, humanidad *f*

manliness ['mænlinəs] *n* : hombría *f*, masculinidad *f*

manly ['mænli] *adj* **-lier; -est** : varonil, viril

man–made ['mæn'meɪd] *adj* : artificial ⟨man-made fabrics : telas sintéticas⟩

manna ['mænə] *n* : maná *m*

mannequin ['mænɪkən] *n* **1** DUMMY : maniquí *m* **2** MODEL : modelo *mf*

manner ['mænər] *n* **1** KIND, SORT : tipo *m*, clase *f* **2** WAY : manera *f*, modo *m* **3** STYLE : estilo *m* (artístico) **4** **manners** *npl* CUSTOMS : costumbres *fpl* ⟨Victorian manners : costumbres victorianas⟩ **5** **manners** *npl* ETIQUETTE : modales *mpl*, educación *f*, etiqueta *f* ⟨good manners : buenos modales⟩

mannered ['mænərd] *adj* **1** AFFECTED, ARTIFICIAL : amanerado, afectado **2** **well–mannered** : educado, cortés **3** → **ill–mannered**

mannerism ['mænə‚rɪzəm] *n* : peculiaridad *f*, gesto *m* particular

mannerly ['mænərli] *adj* : cortés, bien educado

mannish ['mænɪʃ] *adj* : masculino, hombruno

man–of–war [ˌmænə'wɔr, -əv'wɔr] *n, pl* **men–of–war** [ˌmɛn-] WARSHIP : buque *m* de guerra

manor ['mænər] *n* **1** : casa *f* solariega, casa *f* señorial **2** ESTATE : señorío *m*

manpower ['mæn‚paʊər] *n* : personal *m*, mano *f* de obra

mansion ['mænʧən] *n* : mansión *f*

manslaughter ['mæn‚slɔtər] *n* : homicidio *m* sin premeditación

mantel ['mæntəl] *n* : repisa *f* de chimenea

mantelpiece ['mæntəl‚pi:s] → **mantel**

mantis ['mæntəs] *n, pl* **-tises** *or* **-tes** ['mæn‚ti:z] : mantis *f* religiosa

mantle ['mæntəl] *n* : manto *m*

manual[1] ['mænjʊəl] *adj* : manual — **manually** *adv*

manual[2] *n* : manual *m*

manufacture[1] [ˌmænjə'fækʧər] *vt* **-tured; -turing** : fabricar, manufacturar, confeccionar (ropa), elaborar (comestibles)

manufacture[2] *n* : manufactura *f*, fabricación *f*, confección *f* (de ropa), elaboración *f* (de comestibles)

manufacturer [ˌmænjə'fækʧərər] *n* : fabricante *m*; manufacturero *m*, -ra *f*

manure [mə'nʊr, -'njʊr] *n* : estiércol *m*

manuscript ['mænjəˌskrɪpt] *n* : manuscrito *m*

many[1] ['mɛni] *adj* **more** ['mor]; **most** ['moːst] : muchos

many[2] *pron* : muchos *pl*, -chas *pl*

map[1] ['mæp] *vt* **mapped; mapping** 1 : trazar el mapa de 2 PLAN : planear, proyectar ⟨to map out a program : planear un programa⟩

map[2] *n* : mapa *m*

maple ['meɪpəl] *n* : arce *m*

mar[1] ['mar] *vt* **marred; marring** 1 SPOIL : estropear, echar a perder 2 DEFACE : desfigurar

maraschino [ˌmærə'skiːnoː, -'ʃiː-] *n*, *pl* **-nos** : cereza *f* al marrasquino

marathon ['mærəˌθɑn] *n* 1 RACE : maratón *m* 2 CONTEST : competencia *f* de resistencia

maraud [mə'rɑd] *vi* : merodear

marauder [mə'rɑdər] *n* : merodeador *m*, -dora *f*

marble ['marbəl] *n* 1 : mármol *m* 2 : canica *f* ⟨to play marbles : jugar a las canicas⟩

march[1] ['marʧ] *vi* 1 : marchar, desfilar ⟨they marched past the grandstand : desfilaron ante la tribuna⟩ 2 : caminar con resolución ⟨she marched right up to him : se le acercó sin vacilación⟩

march[2] *n* 1 MARCHING : marcha *f* 2 PASSAGE : paso *m* (del tiempo) 3 PROGRESS : avance *m*, progreso *m* 4 : marcha *f* (en música)

March ['marʧ] *n* : marzo *m*

marchioness ['marʃənɪs] *n* : marquesa *f*

Mardi Gras ['mardiˌgra] *n* : martes *m* de Carnaval

mare ['mær] *n* : yegua *f*

margarine ['marʤərən] *n* : margarina *f*

margin ['marʤən] *n* : margen *m*

marginal ['marʤənəl] *adj* 1 : marginal 2 MINIMAL : mínimo — **marginally** *adv*

marigold ['mærəˌgoːld] *n* : maravilla *f*, caléndula *f*

marijuana [ˌmærə'hwanə] *n* : marihuana *f*

marina [mə'riːnə] *n* : puerto *m* deportivo

marinade [ˌmærə'nɑd] *n* : adobo *m*, marinada *f*

marinate ['mærəˌneɪt] *vt* **-nated; -nating** : marinar

marine[1] [mə'riːn] *adj* 1 : marino ⟨marine life : vida marina⟩ 2 NAUTICAL : náutico, marítimo 3 : de la infantería de marina

marine[2] *n* : soldado *m* de marina

mariner ['mærɪnər] *n* : marinero *m*, marino *m*

marionette [ˌmæriə'nɛt] *n* : marioneta *f*, títere *m*

marital ['mærətəl] *adj* 1 : matrimonial 2 **marital status** : estado *m* civil

maritime ['mærəˌtaɪm] *adj* : marítimo

marjoram ['marʤərəm] *n* : mejorana *f*

mark[1] ['mark] *vt* 1 : marcar 2 CHARACTERIZE : caracterizar 3 SIGNAL : señalar 4 NOTICE : prestar atención a, hacer caso de 5 **to mark off** : demarcar, delimitar

mark[2] *n* 1 TARGET : blanco *m* 2 : marca *f*, señal *f* ⟨put a mark where you left off : pon una señal donde terminaste⟩ 3 INDICATION : señal *f*, indicio *m* 4 GRADE : nota *f* 5 IMPRINT : huella *f*, marca *f* 6 BLEMISH : marca *f*, imperfección *f*

marked ['markt] *adj* : marcado, notable — **markedly** ['markədli] *adv*

marker ['markər] *n* : marcador *m*

market[1] ['markət] *vt* : poner en venta, comercializar

market[2] *n* 1 MARKETPLACE : mercado *m* ⟨the open market : el mercado libre⟩ 2 DEMAND : demanda *f*, mercado *m* 3 STORE : tienda *f* 4 → **stock market**

marketable ['markətəbəl] *adj* : vendible

marketing ['markətɪŋ] *n* : mercadotecnia *f*, mercadeo *m*

marketplace ['markətˌpleɪs] *n* : mercado *m*

marksman ['marksmən] *n*, *pl* **-men** [-mən, -ˌmɛn] : tirador *m*

marksmanship ['marksmənˌʃɪp] *n* : puntería *f*

marlin ['marlɪn] *n* : marlín *m*

marmalade ['marməˌleɪd] *n* : mermelada *f*

marmoset ['marməˌsɛt] *n* : tití *m*

marmot ['marmət] *n* : marmota *f*

maroon[1] [mə'ruːn] *vt* : abandonar, aislar

maroon[2] *n* : rojo *m* oscuro, granate *m*

marquee [mar'kiː] *n* : marquesina *f*

marquess ['markwɪs] *or* **marquis** ['markwɪs, mar'kiː] *n*, *pl* **-quesses** *or* **-quises** [-'kiːz, -'kiːzəz] *or* **-quis** [-'kiː, -'kiːz] : marqués *m*

marquise [mar'kiːz] → **marchioness**

marriage ['mærɪʤ] *n* 1 : matrimonio *m* 2 WEDDING : casamiento *m*, boda *f*

marriageable ['mærɪʤəbəl] *adj* **of marriageable age** : de edad de casarse

married ['mærid] *adj* 1 : casado 2 **to get married** : casarse

marrow ['mæroː] *n* : médula *f*, tuétano *m*

marry ['mæri] *vt* **-ried; -rying** 1 : casar ⟨the priest married them : el cura los casó⟩ 2 : casarse con ⟨she married John : se casó con John⟩

Mars · match 522

Mars ['marz] *n* : Marte *m*

marsh ['marʃ] *n* 1 : pantano *m* 2 salt marsh : marisma *f*

marshal¹ ['marʃəl] *vt* -shaled *or* -shalled; -shaling *or* -shalling 1 : poner en orden, reunir 2 USHER : conducir

marshal² *n* 1 : maestro *m* de ceremonias 2 : mariscal *m* (en el ejército); jefe *m*, -fa *f* (de la policía, de los bomberos, etc.)

marshmallow ['marʃ,mɛlo:, -,mælo:] *n* : malvavisco *m*

marshy ['marʃi] *adj* marshier; -est : pantanoso

marsupial [mar'su:piəl] *n* : marsupial *m*

mart ['mart] *n* MARKET : mercado *m*

marten ['martən] *n, pl* -ten *or* -tens : marta *f*

martial ['marʃəl] *adj* : marcial

martin ['martən] *n* 1 SWALLOW : golondrina *f* 2 SWIFT : vencejo *m*

martyr¹ ['martər] *vt* : martirizar

martyr² *n* : mártir *mf*

martyrdom ['martərdəm] *n* : martirio *m*

marvel¹ ['marvəl] *vi* -veled *or* -velled; -veling *or* -velling : maravillarse

marvel² *n* : maravilla *f*

marvelous ['marvələs] *or* marvellous *adj* : maravilloso — marvelously *adv*

Marxism ['mark,sizəm] *n* : marxismo *m*

Marxist¹ ['marksist] *adj* : marxista

Marxist² *n* : marxista *mf*

mascara [mæs'kærə] *n* : rímel *m*, rimel *m*

mascot ['mæs,kat, -kət] *n* : mascota *f*

masculine ['mæskjələn] *adj* : masculino

masculinity [,mæskjə'linəti] *n* : masculinidad *f*

mash¹ ['mæʃ] *vt* 1 : hacer puré de (papas, etc.) 2 CRUSH : aplastar, majar

mash² *n* 1 FEED : afrecho *m* 2 : malta *f* (para hacer bebidas alcohólicas) 3 PASTE, PULP : papilla *f*, pasta *f*

mask¹ ['mæsk] *vt* 1 CONCEAL, DISGUISE : enmascarar, ocultar 2 COVER : cubrir, tapar

mask² *n* : máscara *f*, careta *f*, mascarilla *f* (de un cirujano o dentista)

masochism ['mæsə,kizəm, 'mæzə-] *n* : masoquismo *m*

masochist ['mæsə,kist, 'mæzə-] *n* : masoquista *mf*

masochistic [,mæsə'kistik, ,mæzə-] *adj* : masoquista

mason ['meisən] *n* 1 BRICKLAYER : albañil *mf* 2 *or* stonemason ['sto:n,-] : mampostero *m*, cantero *m*

masonry ['meisənri] *n, pl* -ries 1 BRICKLAYING : albañería *f* 2 *or* stonemasonry ['sto:n,-] : mampostería *f*

masquerade¹ [,mæskə'reid] *vi* -aded; -ading 1 : disfrazarse (de), hacerse pasar (por) 2 : asistir a una mascarada

masquerade² *n* 1 : mascarada *f*, baile *m* de disfraces 2 FACADE : farsa *f*, fachada *f*

mass¹ ['mæs] *vi* : concentrarse, juntarse en masa — *vt* : concentrar

mass² *n* 1 : masa *f* ⟨atomic mass : masa atómica⟩ 2 BULK : mole *f*, volumen *m* 3 MULTITUDE : cantidad *f*, montón *m* (de cosas), multitud *f* (de gente) 4 the masses : las masas, el pueblo, el populacho

Mass ['mæs] *n* : misa *f*

massacre¹ ['mæsikər] *vt* -cred; -cring : masacrar

massacre² *n* : masacre *f*

massage¹ [mə'saʒ, -'sadʒ] *vt* -saged; -saging : masajear

massage² *n* : masaje *m*

masseur [mæ'sər] *n* : masajista *m*

masseuse [mæ'søz, -'su:z] *n* : masajista *f*

massive ['mæsiv] *adj* 1 BULKY : voluminoso, macizo 2 HUGE : masivo, enorme — massively *adv*

mast ['mæst] *n* : mástil *m*, palo *m*

master¹ ['mæstər] *vt* 1 SUBDUE : dominar 2 : llegar a dominar ⟨she mastered French : llegó a dominar el francés⟩

master² *n* 1 TEACHER : maestro *m*, profesor *m* 2 EXPERT : experto *m*, -ta *f*; maestro *m*, -tra *f* 3 : amo *m* (de animales o esclavos), señor *m* (de la casa) 4 master's degree : maestría *f*

masterful ['mæstərfəl] *adj* 1 IMPERIOUS : autoritario, imperioso, dominante 2 SKILLFUL : magistral — masterfully *adv*

masterly ['mæstərli] *adj* : magistral

mastermind ['mæstər,maind] *n* : cerebro *m*, artífice *mf*

masterpiece ['mæstər,pi:s] *n* : obra *f* maestra

masterwork ['mæstər,wərk] → masterpiece

mastery ['mæstəri] *n* 1 DOMINION : dominio *m*, autoridad *f* 2 SUPERIORITY : superioridad *f* 3 EXPERTISE : maestría *f*

masticate ['mæstə,keit] *v* -cated; -cating : masticar

mastiff ['mæstif] *n* : mastín *m*

mastodon ['mæstə,dan] *n* : mastodonte *m*

masturbate ['mæstər,beit] *v* -bated; bating *vi* : masturbarse — *vt* : masturbar

masturbation [,mæstər'beiʃən] *n* : masturbación *f*

mat¹ ['mæt] *v* matted; matting *vt* TANGLE : enmarañar — *vi* : enmarañarse

mat² *n* 1 : estera *f* 2 TANGLE : maraña *f* 3 PAD : colchoneta *f* (de gimnasia) 4 *or* matt *or* matte ['mæt] FRAME : marco *m* (de cartón)

mat³ → matte

matador ['mætə,dor] *n* : matador *m*

match¹ ['mætʃ] *vt* 1 PIT : enfrentar, oponer 2 EQUAL, FIT : igualar, corresponder a, coincidir con 3 : combinar con, hacer juego con ⟨her shoes match her dress : sus zapatos hacen juego con su vestido⟩ — *vi* 1 CORRESPOND : concordar, coincidir 2 : hacer juego ⟨with a tie to match : con una corbata que hace juego⟩

match² *n* **1** EQUAL : igual *mf* ⟨he's no match for her : no puede competir con ella⟩ **2** FIGHT, GAME : partido *m*, combate *m* (en boxeo) **3** MARRIAGE : matrimonio *m*, casamiento *m* **4** : fósforo *m*, cerilla *f*, cerillo *m in various countries*) ⟨he lit a match : encendió un fósforo⟩ **5 to be a good match** : hacer buena pareja (dícese de las personas), hacer juego (dícese de la ropa)

matchless ['mætʃləs] *adj* : sin igual, sin par

matchmaker ['mætʃ,meɪkər] *n* : casamentero *m*, -ra *f*

mate¹ ['meɪt] *v* **mated; mating** *vi* **1** FIT : encajar **2** PAIR : emparejarse **3** (*relating to animals*) : aparearse, copular — *vt* : aparear, acoplar (animales)

mate² *n* **1** COMPANION : compañero *m*, -ra *f*; camarada *mf* **2** : macho *m*, hembra *f* (de animales) **3** : oficial *mf* (de un barco) ⟨first mate : primer oficial⟩ **4** : compañero *m*, -ra *f*; pareja *f* (de un zapato, etc.)

material¹ [mə'tɪriəl] *adj* **1** PHYSICAL : material, físico ⟨the material world : el mundo material⟩ ⟨material needs : necesidades materiales⟩ **2** IMPORTANT : importante, esencial **3** material evidence : prueba *f* sustancial

material² *n* **1** : material *m* **2** CLOTH : tejido *m*, tela *f*

materialism [mə'tɪriə,lɪzəm] *n* : materialismo *m*

materialist [mə'tɪriəlɪst] *n* : materialista *mf*

materialistic [mə,tɪriə'lɪstɪk] *adj* : materialista

materialize [mə'tɪriə,laɪz] *v* **-ized; -izing** *vt* : materializar, hacer aparecer — *vi* : materializarse, aparecer

maternal [mə'tərnəl] *adj* MOTHERLY : maternal — **maternally** *adv*

maternity¹ [mə'tərnəti] *adj* : de maternidad ⟨maternity clothes : ropa de futura mamá⟩ ⟨maternity leave : licencia por maternidad⟩

maternity² *n, pl* **-ties** : maternidad *f*

math ['mæθ] → **mathematics**

mathematical [,mæθə'mætɪkəl] *adj* : matemático — **mathematically** *adv*

mathematician [,mæθəmə'tɪʃən] *n* : matemático *m*, -ca *f*

mathematics [,mæθə'mætɪks] *ns & pl* : matemáticas *fpl*, matemática *f*

matinee *or* **matinée** [,mætən'eɪ] *n* : matiné *f*

matriarch ['meɪtri,ɑrk] *n* : matriarca *f*

matriarchy ['meɪtri,ɑrki] *n, pl* **-chies** : matriarcado *m*

matriculate [mə'trɪkjə,leɪt] *v* **-lated; -lating** *vt* : matricular — *vi* : matricularse

matriculation [mə,trɪkjə'leɪʃən] *n* : matrícula *f*, matriculación *f*

matrimony ['mætrə,moːni] *n* : matrimonio *m* — **matrimonial** [,mætrə'moːniəl] *adj*

matrix ['meɪtrɪks] *n, pl* **-trices** ['meɪtrə,siːz, 'mæ-] *or* **-trixes** ['meɪtrɪksəz] : matriz *f*

matron ['meɪtrən] *n* : matrona *f*

matronly ['meɪtrənli] *adj* : de matrona, matronal

matte ['mæt] *adj* : mate, de acabado mate

matter¹ ['mætər] *vi* : importar ⟨it doesn't matter : no importa⟩

matter² *n* **1** QUESTION : asunto *m*, cuestión *f* ⟨a matter of taste : una cuestión de gusto⟩ **2** SUBSTANCE : materia *f*, sustancia *f* **3 matters** *npl* CIRCUMSTANCES : situación *f*, cosas *fpl* ⟨to make matters worse : para colmo de males⟩ **4 to be the matter** : pasar ⟨what's the matter? : ¿qué pasa?⟩ **5 as a matter of fact** : en efecto, en realidad **6 for that matter** : de hecho **7 no matter how much** : por mucho que

matter–of–fact [,mætərəv'fækt] *adj* : práctico, realista

mattress ['mætrəs] *n* : colchón *m*

mature¹ [mə'tʊr, -'tjʊr, -'tʃʊr] *vi* **-tured; -turing 1** : madurar **2** : vencer ⟨when does the loan mature? : ¿cuándo vence el préstamo?⟩

mature² *adj* **-turer; -est 1** : maduro **2** DUE : vencido

maturity [mə'tʊrəti, -'tjʊr-, -'tʃʊr-] *n* : madurez *f*

maudlin ['mɔdlɪn] *adj* : sensiblero

maul¹ ['mɔl] *vt* **1** BEAT : golpear, pegar **2** MANGLE : mutilar **3** MANHANDLE : maltratar

maul² *n* MALLET : mazo *m*

Mauritanian [,mɔrə'teɪniən] *n* : mauritano *m*, -na *f* — **Mauritanian** *adj*

mausoleum [,mɔsə'liːəm, ,mɔzə-] *n, pl* **-leums** *or* **-lea** [-'liːə] : mausoleo *m*

mauve ['moːv, 'mɔv] *n* : malva *m*

maven *or* **mavin** ['meɪvən] *n* EXPERT : experto *m*, -ta *f*

maverick ['mævrɪk, 'mævə-] *n* **1** : ternero *m* sin marcar **2** NONCONFORMIST : inconformista *mf*, disidente *mf*

mawkish ['mɔkɪʃ] *adj* : sensiblero

maxim ['mæksəm] *n* : máxima *f*

maximize ['mæksə,maɪz] *vt* **-mized; -mizing** : maximizar, llevar al máximo

maximum¹ ['mæksəməm] *adj* : máximo

maximum² *n, pl* **-ma** ['mæksəmə] *or* **-mums** : máximo *m*

may ['meɪ] *v aux, past* **might** ['maɪt] *present s & pl* **may 1** (*expressing permission*) : poder ⟨you may go : puedes ir⟩ **2** (*expressing possibility or probability*) : poder ⟨you may be right : puede que tengas razón⟩ ⟨it may happen occasionally : puede pasar de vez en cuando⟩ **3** (*expressing desires, intentions, or contingencies*) ⟨may the best man win : que gane el mejor⟩ ⟨I laugh that I may not weep : me río para no llorar⟩ ⟨come what may : pase lo que pase⟩

May ['meɪ] *n* : mayo *m*

Maya ['maɪə] *or* **Mayan** ['maɪən] *n* : maya *mf* — **Maya** *or* **Mayan** *adj*

maybe ['meɪbi] *adv* PERHAPS : quizás, tal vez

mayfly ['meɪˌflaɪ] *n, pl* **-flies** : efímera *f*

mayhem ['meɪˌhɛm, 'meɪəm] *n* **1** MUTILATION : mutilación *f* **2** DEVASTATION : estragos *mpl*

mayonnaise ['meɪəˌneɪz] *n* : mayonesa *f*

mayor ['meɪər, 'mɛr] *n* : alcalde *m*, -desa *f*

mayoral ['meɪərəl, 'mɛrəl] *adj* : de alcalde

maze ['meɪz] *n* : laberinto *m*

me ['mi:] *pron* **1** : me ⟨she called me : me llamó⟩ ⟨give it to me : dámelo⟩ **2** (*after a preposition*) : mí ⟨for me : para mí⟩ ⟨with me : conmigo⟩ **3** (*after conjunctions and verbs*) : yo ⟨it's me : soy yo⟩ ⟨as big as me : tan grande como yo⟩ **4** (*emphatic use*) : yo ⟨me, too! : ¡yo también!⟩ ⟨who, me? : ¿quién, yo?⟩

meadow ['mɛdo:] *n* : prado *m*, pradera *f*

meadowland ['mɛdoˌlænd] *n* : pradera *f*

meadowlark ['mɛdoˌlɑrk] *n* : pájaro *m* cantor con el pecho amarillo

meager *or* **meagre** ['mi:gər] *adj* **1** THIN : magro, flaco **2** POOR, SCANTY : exiguo, escaso, pobre

meagerly ['mi:gərli] *adv* : pobremente

meagerness ['mi:gərnəs] *n* : escasez *f*, pobreza *f*

meal ['mi:l] *n* **1** : comida *f* ⟨a hearty meal : una comida sustanciosa⟩ **2** : harina *f* (de maíz, etc.)

mealtime ['mi:lˌtaɪm] *n* : hora *f* de comer

mean¹ ['mi:n] *vt* **meant** ['mɛnt]; **meaning 1** INTEND : querer, pensar, tener la intención de ⟨I didn't mean to do it : lo hice sin querer⟩ ⟨what do you mean to do? : ¿qué piensas hacer?⟩ **2** SIGNIFY : querer decir, significar ⟨what does that mean? : ¿qué quiere decir eso?⟩ **3** : importar ⟨health means everything : lo que más importa es la salud⟩

mean² *adj* **1** HUMBLE : humilde **2** NEGLIGIBLE : despreciable ⟨it's no mean feat : no es poca cosa⟩ **3** STINGY : mezquino, tacaño **4** CRUEL : malo, cruel ⟨to be mean to someone : tratar mal a alguien⟩ **5** AVERAGE, MEDIAN : medio

mean³ *n* **1** MIDPOINT : término *m* medio **2** AVERAGE : promedio *m*, media *f* aritmética **3 means** *npl* WAY : medio *m*, manera *f*, vía *f* **4 means** *npl* RESOURCES : medios *mpl*, recursos *mpl* **5 by all means** : por supuesto, cómo no **6 by means of** : por medio de **7 by no means** : de ninguna manera, de ningún modo

meander [mi'ændər] *vi* **-dered; -dering 1** WIND : serpentear **2** WANDER : vagar, andar sin rumbo fijo

meaning ['mi:nɪŋ] *n* **1** : significado *m*, sentido *m* ⟨double meaning : doble sentido⟩ **2** INTENT : intención *f*, propósito *m*

meaningful ['mi:nɪŋfəl] *adj* : significativo — **meaningfully** *adv*

meaningless ['mi:nɪŋləs] *adj* : sin sentido

meanness ['mi:nnəs] *n* **1** CRUELTY : crueldad *f*, mezquindad *f* **2** STINGINESS : tacañería *f*

meantime¹ ['mi:nˌtaɪm] *adv* → **meanwhile¹**

meantime² *n* **1** : interín *m* **2 in the meantime** : entretanto, mientras tanto

meanwhile¹ ['mi:nˌhwaɪl] *adv* : entretanto, mientras tanto

meanwhile² *n* → **meantime²**

measles ['mi:zəlz] *ns & pl* : sarampión *m*

measly ['mi:zli] *adj* **-slier; -est** : miserable, mezquino

measurable ['mɛʒərəbəl, 'meɪ-] *adj* : mensurable — **measurably** [-bli] *adv*

measure¹ ['mɛʒər, 'meɪ-] *v* **-sured; -suring** : medir ⟨he measured the table : midió la mesa⟩ ⟨it measures 15 feet tall : mide 15 pies de altura⟩

measure² *n* **1** AMOUNT : medida *f*, cantidad *f* ⟨in large measure : en gran medida⟩ ⟨a full measure : una cantidad exacta⟩ ⟨a measure of proficiency : una cierta competencia⟩ ⟨for good measure : de ñapa, por añadidura⟩ **2** DIMENSIONS, SIZE : medida *f*, tamaño *m* **3** RULER : regla *f* ⟨tape measure : cinta métrica⟩ **4** MEASUREMENT : medida *f* ⟨cubic measure : medida de capacidad⟩ **5** MEASURING : medición *f* **6 measures** *npl* : medidas *fpl* ⟨security measures : medidas de seguridad⟩

measureless ['mɛʒərləs, 'meɪ-] *adj* : inmensurable

measurement ['mɛʒərmənt, 'meɪ-] *n* **1** MEASURING : medición *f* **2** DIMENSION : medida *f*

measure up *vi* **to measure up to** : estar a la altura de

meat ['mi:t] *n* **1** FOOD : comida *f* **2** : carne *f* ⟨meat and fish : carne y pescado⟩ **3** SUBSTANCE : sustancia *f*, esencia *f* ⟨the meat of the story : la sustancia del cuento⟩

meatball ['mi:tˌbɔl] *n* : albóndiga *f*

meaty ['mi:ti] *adj* **meatier; -est** : con mucha carne, carnoso

mechanic [mɪ'kænɪk] *n* : mecánico *m*, -ca *f*

mechanical [mɪ'kænɪkəl] *adj* : mecánico — **mechanically** *adv*

mechanics [mɪ'kænɪks] *ns & pl* **1** : mecánica *f* ⟨fluid mechanics : la mecánica de fluidos⟩ **2** MECHANISMS : mecanismos *mpl*, aspectos *mpl* prácticos

mechanism ['mɛkəˌnɪzəm] *n* : mecanismo *m*

mechanization [ˌmɛkənə'zeɪʃən] *n* : mecanización *f*

mechanize ['mɛkə,naɪz] *vt* **-nized; -nizing** : mecanizar

medal ['mɛdəl] *n* : medalla *f*, condecoración *f*

medalist ['mɛdəlɪst] *or* **medallist** *n* : medallista *mf*

medallion [mə'dæljən] *n* : medallón *m*

meddle ['mɛdəl] *vi* **-dled; -dling** : meterse, entrometerse

meddler ['mɛdələr] *n* : entrometido *m*, -da *f*

meddlesome ['mɛdəlsəm] *adj* : entrometido

media[1] ['mi:diə] *npl* : medios *mpl* de comunicación

median[1] ['mi:diən] *adj* : medio

median[2] *n* : valor *m* medio

mediate ['mi:di,eɪt] *vi* **-ated; -ating** : mediar

mediation [,mi:di'eɪʃən] *n* : mediación *f*

mediator ['mi:di,eɪtər] *n* : mediador *m*, -dora *f*

medical ['mɛdɪkəl] *adj* : médico

medicate ['mɛdə,keɪt] *vt* **-cated; -cating** : medicar ⟨medicated powder : polvos medicinales⟩

medication [,mɛdə'keɪʃən] *n* **1** TREATMENT : tratamiento *m*, medicación *f* **2** MEDICINE : medicamento *m* ⟨to be on medication : estar medicado⟩

medicinal [mə'dɪsənəl] *adj* : medicinal

medicine ['mɛdəsən] *n* **1** MEDICATION : medicina *f*, medicamento *m* **2** : medicina *f* ⟨he's studying medicine : estudia medicina⟩

medicine man *n* : hechicero *m*

medieval *or* **mediaeval** [mɪ'di:vəl, ,mi:-, ,m-, -di'i:vəl] *adj* : medieval

mediocre [,mi:di'o:kər] *adj* : mediocre

mediocrity [,mi:di'ɑkrəti] *n, pl* **-ties** : mediocridad *f*

meditate ['mɛdə,teɪt] *vi* **-tated; -tating** : meditar

meditation [,mɛdə'teɪʃən] *n* : meditación *f*

meditative ['mɛdə,teɪtɪv] *adj* : meditabundo

medium[1] ['mi:diəm] *adj* : mediano ⟨of medium height : de estatura mediana, de estatura regular⟩

medium[2] *n, pl* **-diums** *or* **-dia** ['mi:-diə] **1** MEAN : punto *m* medio, término *m* medio ⟨happy medium : justo medio⟩ **2** MEANS : medio *m* **3** SUBSTANCE : medio *m*, sustancia *f* ⟨a viscous medium : un medio viscoso⟩ **4** : medio *m* de comunicación **5** : medio *m* (artístico)

medley ['mɛdli] *n, pl* **-leys** : popurrí *m* (de canciones)

meek ['mi:k] *adj* **1** LONG-SUFFERING : paciente, sufrido **2** SUBMISSIVE : sumiso, dócil, manso

meekly ['mi:kli] *adv* : dócilmente

meekness ['mi:knəs] *n* : mansedumbre *f*, docilidad *f*

meet[1] ['mi:t] *v* **met** ['mɛt]; **meeting** *vt* **1** ENCOUNTER : encontrarse con **2** JOIN : unirse con **3** CONFRONT : enfrentarse a **4** SATISFY : satisfacer, cumplir con ⟨to meet costs : pagar los gastos⟩ **5** : conocer ⟨I met his sister : conocí a su hermana⟩ — *vi* ASSEMBLE : reunirse, congregarse

meet[2] *n* : encuentro *m*

meeting ['mi:tɪŋ] *n* **1** : reunión *f* ⟨to open the meeting : abrir la sesión⟩ **2** ENCOUNTER : encuentro *m* **3** : entrevista *f* (formal)

meetinghouse ['mi:tɪŋ,haʊs] *n* : iglesia *f* (de ciertas confesiones protestantes)

megabyte ['mɛgə,baɪt] *n* : megabyte *m*

megahertz ['mɛgə,hərts, -,hrts] *n* : megahercio *m*

megaphone ['mɛgə,fo:n] *n* : megáfono *m*

melancholy[1] ['mɛlən,kɑli] *adj* : melancólico, triste, sombrío

melancholy[2] *n, pl* **-cholies** : melancolía *f*

melanoma [,mɛlə'no:mə] *n, pl* **-mas** : melanoma *m*

meld ['mɛld] *vt* : fusionar, unir — *vi* : fusionarse, unirse

melee ['meɪ,leɪ, meɪ'leɪ] *n* BRAWL : reyerta *f*, riña *f*, pelea *f*

meliorate ['mi:ljə,reɪt, 'mi:liə-] → **ameliorate**

mellow[1] ['mɛlo:] *vt* : suavizar, endulzar — *vi* : suavizarse, endulzarse

mellow[2] *adj* **1** RIPE : maduro **2** MILD : apacible ⟨a mellow character : un carácter apacible⟩ ⟨mellow wines : vinos añejos⟩ **3** : suave, dulce ⟨mellow colors : colores suaves⟩ ⟨mellow tones : tonos dulces⟩

mellowness ['mɛlonəs] *n* : suavidad *f*, dulzura *f*

melodic [mə'lɑdɪk] *adj* : melódico — **melodically** [-dɪkli] *adv*

melodious [mə'lo:diəs] *adj* : melodioso — **melodiously** *adv*

melodiousness [mə'lo:diəsnəs] *n* : calidad *f* de melódico

melodrama ['mɛlə,drɑmə, -,dræ-] *n* : melodrama *m*

melodramatic [,mɛlədrə'mætɪk] *adj* : melodramático — **melodramatically** [-tɪkli] *adv*

melody ['mɛlədi] *n, pl* **-dies** : melodía *f*, tonada *f*

melon ['mɛlən] *n* : melón *m*

melt ['mɛlt] *vt* **1** : derretir, disolver **2** SOFTEN : ablandar ⟨it melted his heart : ablandó su corazón⟩ — *vi* **1** : derretirse, disolverse **2** SOFTEN : ablandarse **3** DISAPPEAR : desvanecerse, esfumarse ⟨the clouds melted away : las nubes se desvanecieron⟩

melting point *n* : punto *m* de fusión

member ['mɛmbər] *n* **1** LIMB : miembro *m* **2** : miembro *m* (de un grupo); socio *m*, -cia *f* (de un club) **3** PART : miembro *m*, parte *f*

membership ['mɛmbər,ʃɪp] *n* **1** : membresía *f* ⟨application for membership

: solicitud de entrada⟩ **2** MEMBERS
: membresía *f*, miembros *mpl*, socios
mpl

membrane ['mɛm,breɪn] *n* : membrana
f — **membranous** ['mɛmbrə-nəs] *adj*

memento [mɪ'mɛn,to:] *n*, *pl* **-tos** *or* **-toes**
: recuerdo *m*

memo ['mɛmo:] *n*, *pl* **memos** : memorándum *m*

memoirs ['mɛm,wɑrz] *npl* : memorias
fpl, autobiografía *f*

memorabilia [,mɛmərə'bɪliə, -'bɪljə] *npl*
1 : objetos *mpl* de interés histórico **2**
MEMENTOS : recuerdos *mpl*

memorable ['mɛmərəbəl] *adj* : memorable, notable — **memorably** [-bli] *adv*

memorandum [,mɛmə'rændəm] *n*, *pl*
-dums *or* **-da** [-də] : memorándum *m*

memorial[1] [mə'moriəl] *adj* : conmemorativo

memorial[2] *n* : monumento *m* conmemorativo

Memorial Day *n* : el último lunes de
mayo (observado en Estados Unidos
como día feriado para conmemorar a
los caídos en guerra)

memorialize [mə'moriə,laɪz] *vt* **-ized**;
-izing COMMEMORATE : conmemorar

memorization [,mɛmərə'zeɪʃən] *n*
: memorización *f*

memorize ['mɛmə,raɪz] *vt* **-rized**; **-rizing**
: memorizar, aprender de memoria

memory ['mɛmri, 'mɛmə-] *n*, *pl* **-ries 1**
: memoria *f* ⟨he has a good memory
: tiene buena memoria⟩ **2** RECOLLEC-
TION : recuerdo *m* **3** COMMEMORA-
TION : memoria *f*, conmemoración *f*

men → **man**[2]

menace[1] ['mɛnəs] *vt* **-aced**; **-acing 1**
THREATEN : amenazar **2** ENDANGER
: poner en peligro

menace[2] *n* : amenaza *f*

menacing ['mɛnəsɪŋ] *adj* : amenazador,
amenazante

menagerie [mə'nædʒəri, -'næʒəri] *n*
: colección *f* de animales salvajes

mend[1] ['mɛnd] *vt* **1** CORRECT : enmendar, corregir ⟨to mend one's ways
: enmendarse⟩ **2** REPAIR : remendar,
arreglar, reparar — *vi* HEAL : curarse

mend[2] *n* : remiendo *m*

mendicant ['mɛndɪkənt] *n* BEGGAR
: mendigo *m*, -ga *f*

menhaden [mɛn'heɪdən, mən-] *ns & pl*
: pez *m* de la misma familia que los
arenques

menial[1] ['mi:niəl] *adj* : servil, bajo

menial[2] *n* : sirviente *m*, -ta *f*

meningitis [,mɛnən'dʒaɪtəs] *n*, *pl*
-gitides [-'dʒɪtə,di:z] : meningitis *f*

menopause ['mɛnə,pɔz] *n* : menopausia
f

menorah [mə'norə] *n* : candelabro *m*
(usado en los oficios religiosos judíos)

menstrual ['mɛnstruəl] *adj* : menstrual

menstruate ['mɛnstru,eɪt] *vi* **-ated**; **-at-
ing** : menstruar

menstruation [,mɛnstru'eɪʃən] *n* : menstruación *f*

mental ['mɛntəl] *adj* : mental ⟨mental
hospital : hospital psiquiátrico⟩ —
mentally *adv*

mentality [mɛn'tæləti] *n*, *pl* **-ties** : mentalidad *f*

menthol ['mɛn,θɔl, -,θo:l] *n* : mentol *m*

mentholated [,mɛnθə,leɪtəd] *adj* : men-
tolado

mention[1] ['mɛntʃən] *vt* : mencionar,
mentar, referirse a ⟨don't mention it!
: ¡de nada!, ¡no hay de qué!⟩

mention[2] *n* : mención *f*

mentor ['mɛn,tɔr, 'mɛntər] *n* : mentor *m*

menu ['mɛn,ju:] *n* **1** : menú *m*, carta *f*
(en un restaurante) **2** : menú *m* (de
computadoras)

meow[1] [mi:'aʊ] *vi* : maullar

meow[2] *n* : maullido *m*, miau *m*

mercantile ['mərkən,ti:l, -,taɪl] *adj* : mercantil

mercenary[1] ['mərsəˌnɛ,ri] *adj* : mercenario

mercenary[2] *n*, *pl* **-naries** : mercenario
m, -ria *f*

merchandise ['mərtʃən,daɪz, -,daɪs] *n*
: mercancía *f*, mercadería *f*

merchandiser ['mərtʃən,daɪzər] *n* : comerciante *mf*; vendedor *m*, -dora *f*

merchant ['mərtʃənt] *n* : comerciante *mf*

merchant marine *n* : marina *f* mercante

merciful ['mərsɪfəl] *adj* : misericordioso,
clemente

mercifully ['mərsɪfli] *adv* **1** : con misericordia, con compasión **2** FORTU-
NATELY : afortunadamente

merciless ['mərsɪləs] *adj* : despiadado —
mercilessly *adv*

mercurial [,mər'kjʊriəl] *adj* TEMPERA-
MENTAL : temperamental, volátil

mercury ['mərkjəri] *n*, *pl* **-ries** : mercurio *m*

Mercury *n* : Mercurio *m*

mercy ['mərsi] *n*, *pl* **-cies 1** CLEMENCY
: misericordia *f*, clemencia *f* **2** BLESS-
ING : bendición *f*

mere ['mɪr] *adj*, *superlative* **merest**
: mero, simple

merely ['mɪrli] *adv* : solamente, simplemente

merge ['mərdʒ] *v* **merged**; **merging** *vi*
: unirse, fusionarse (dícese de las com-
pañías), confluir (dícese de los ríos, las
calles, etc.) — *vt* : unir, fusionar, combinar

merger ['mərdʒər] *n* : unión *f*, fusión *f*

meridian [mə'rɪdiən] *n* : meridiano *m*

meringue [mə'ræŋ] *n* : merengue *m*

merino [mə'ri:no] *n*, *pl* **-nos 1** : merino
m, -na *f* **2** *or* **merino wool** : lana *f* merino

merit[1] ['mɛrət] *vt* : merecer, ser digno de

merit[2] *n* : mérito *m*, valor *m*

meritorious [,mɛrə'toriəs] *adj* : meritorio

mermaid ['mər,meɪd] *n* : sirena *f*

merriment ['mɛrimənt] *n* : alegría *f*, júbilo *m*, regocijo *m*

merry ['mɛri] *adj* **-rier; -est** : alegre —
merrily ['mɛrəli] *adv*
merry–go–round ['mɛrigo,raʊnd] *n*
: carrusel *m*, tiovivo *m*
merrymaker ['mɛri,meɪkər] *n* : juerguista *mf*
merrymaking ['mɛri,meɪkɪŋ] *n* : juerga
f
mesa ['meɪsə] *n* : mesa *f*
mesdames → **madam, Mrs.**
mesh[1] ['mɛʃ] *vi* **1** ENGAGE : engranar
(dícese de las piezas mecánicas) **2** TAN-
GLE : enredarse **3** COORDINATE : coordinarse, combinar
mesh[2] *n* **1** : malla *f* ⟨wire mesh : malla
metálica⟩ **2** NETWORK : red *f* **3** MESH-
ING : engranaje *m* ⟨in mesh : engrana-
do⟩
mesmerize ['mɛzmə,raɪz] *vt* **-ized;**
-izing 1 HYPNOTIZE : hipnotizar **2**
FASCINATE : cautivar, embelesar, fascinar
mess[1] ['mɛs] *vt* **1** SOIL : ensuciar **2 to**
mess up DISARRANGE : desordenar,
desarreglar **3 to mess up** BUNGLE
: echar a perder — *vi* **1** PUTTER : entretenerse **2** INTERFERE : meterse, entrometerse ⟨don't mess with me : no te
metas conmigo⟩
mess[2] *n* **1** : rancho *m* (para soldados,
etc.) **2** DISORDER : desorden *m* ⟨your
room is a mess : tienes el cuarto hecho
un desastre⟩ **3** CONFUSION, TURMOIL
: confusión *f*, embrollo *m*, lío *m fam*
message ['mɛsɪʤ] *n* : mensaje *m*, recado *m*
messenger ['mɛsənʤər] *n* : mensajero
m, -ra *f*
Messiah [mə'saɪə] *n* : Mesías *m*
Messrs. → **Mr.**
messy ['mɛsi] *adj* **messier; -est** UNTIDY
: desordenado, sucio
met → **meet**
metabolic [,mɛtə'balɪk] *adj* : metabólico
metabolism [mə'tæbə,lɪzəm] *n* : metabolismo *m*
metabolize [mə'tæbə,laɪz] *vt* **-lized;**
-lizing : metabolizar
metal ['mɛtəl] *n* : metal *m*
metallic [mə'tælɪk] *adj* : metálico
metallurgical [,mɛtəl'ərʤɪkəl] *adj* : me-
talúrgico
metallurgy ['mɛtəl,ərʤi] *n* : metalurgia
f
metalwork ['mɛtəl,wərk] *n* : objeto *m* de
metal
metalworking ['mɛtəl,wərkɪŋ] *n* : metalistería *f*
metamorphosis [,mɛtə'mɔrfəsɪs] *n, pl*
-phoses [-,siːz] : metamorfosis *f*
metaphor ['mɛtə,fɔr, -fər] *n* : metáfora
f
metaphoric [,mɛtə'fɔrɪk] *or* **metaphori-**
cal [-ɪkəl] *adj* : metafórico
metaphysical [,mɛtə'fɪzəkəl] *adj*
: metafísico
metaphysics [,mɛtə'fɪzɪks] *n* : metafísica *f*

mete ['miːt] *vt* **meted; meting** ALLOT
: repartir, distribuir ⟨to mete out punishment : imponer castigos⟩
meteor ['miːtiər, -ti:,ɔr] *n* : meteoro *m*
meteoric [,miːti'ɔrɪk] *adj* : meteórico
meteorite ['miːtiə,raɪt] *n* : meteorito *m*
meteorologic [,miːti,ɔrə'laʤɪk] *or* **me-**
teorological [-'laʤɪkəl] *adj* : meteorológico
meteorologist [,miːti'ɑrələʤɪst] *n* : meteorólogo *m*, -ga *f*
meteorology [,miːti'ɑrələʤi] *n* : meteorología *f*
meter ['miːtər] *n* **1** : metro *m* ⟨it measures 2 meters : mide 2 metros⟩ **2** : contador *m*, medidor *m* (de electricidad,
etc.) ⟨parking meter : parquímetro⟩ **3**
: metro *m* (en literatura o música)
methane ['mɛ,θeɪn] *n* : metano *m*
method ['mɛθəd] *n* : método *m*
methodical [mə'θɑdɪkəl] *adj* : metódico
— **methodically** *adv*
Methodist ['mɛθədɪst] *n* : metodista *mf*
— **Methodist** *adj*
methodology [,mɛθə'dɑləʤi] *n, pl* **-gies**
: metodología *f*
meticulous [mə'tɪkjələs] *adj* : meticuloso — **meticulously** *adv*
meticulousness [mə'tɪkjələsnəs] *n*
: meticulosidad *f*
metric ['mɛtrɪk] *or* **metrical** [-trɪkəl] *adj*
: métrico
metric system *n* : sistema *m* métrico
metronome ['mɛtrə,no:m] *n*
: metrónomo *m*
metropolis [mə'trɑpələs] *n* : metrópoli
f, metrópolis *f*
metropolitan [,mɛtrə'pɑlətən] *adj* : metropolitano
mettle ['mɛtəl] *n* : temple *m*, valor *m* ⟨on
one's mettle : dispuesto a mostrar su
valía⟩
Mexican ['mɛksɪkən] *n* : mexicano *m*,
-na *f* — **Mexican** *adj*
mezzanine ['mɛzə,ni:n, ,mɛzə'ni:n] *n* **1**
: entrepiso *m*, entresuelo *m* **2** : primer
piso *m* (de un teatro)
miasma [maɪ'æzmə] *n* : miasma *m*
mica ['maɪkə] *n* : mica *f*
mice → **mouse**
micro ['maɪkro] *adj* : muy pequeño, microscópico
microbe ['maɪ,kro:b] *n* : microbio *m*
microbiology [,maɪkrobaɪ'ɑləʤi] *n* : microbiología *f*
microchip ['maɪkro,ʧɪp] *n* : microchip
m
microcomputer ['maɪkrokəm,pju:tər] *n*
: microcomputadora *f*
microcosm ['maɪkro,kazəm] *n* : micro-
cosmo *m*
microfilm ['maɪkro,fɪlm] *n* : microfilm
m
micrometer [maɪ'krɑmətər] *n* : micrómetro *m*
micron ['maɪ,krɑn] *n* : micrón *m*
microorganism [,maɪkro'ɔrgə,nɪzəm] *n*
: microorganismo *m*, microbio *m*

microphone ['maɪkrə,foːn] *n* : micrófono *m*

microprocessor ['maɪkro,prɑ,ssər] *n* : microprocesador *m*

microscope ['maɪkrə,skoːp] *n* : microscopio *m*

microscopic [,maɪkrə'skɑpɪk] *adj* : microscópico

microscopy [maɪ'krɑskəpi] *n* : microscopía *f*

microwave ['maɪkrə,weɪv] *n* **1** : microonda *f* **2** *or* **microwave oven** : microondas *m*

mid ['mɪd] *adj* : medio ⟨mid morning : a media mañana⟩ ⟨in mid-August : a mediados de agosto⟩ ⟨in mid ocean : en alta mar⟩

midair ['mɪd'ær] *n* **in ~** : en el aire ⟨to catch in midair : agarrar al vuelo⟩

midday ['mɪd'deɪ] *n* NOON : mediodía *m*

middle¹ ['mɪdəl] *adj* **1** CENTRAL : medio, del medio, de en medio **2** INTERMEDIATE : intermedio, mediano ⟨middle age : la mediana edad⟩

middle² *n* **1** CENTER : medio *m*, centro *m* ⟨fold it down the middle : dóblalo por la mitad⟩ **2 in the middle of** : en medio de (un espacio), a mitad de (una actividad) ⟨in the middle of the month : a mediados del mes⟩

Middle Ages *npl* : Edad *f* Media

middle class *n* : clase *f* media

middleman ['mɪdəl,mæn] *n*, *pl* **-men** [-mən, -,mɛn] : intermediario *m*, -ria *f*

middling ['mɪdlɪŋ, -lən] *adj* **1** MEDIUM, MIDDLE : mediano **2** MEDIOCRE : mediocre, regular

midfielder ['mɪd,fiːldər] *n* : mediocampista *mf*

midge ['mɪdʒ] *n* : mosca *f* pequeña

midget ['mɪdʒət] *n* **1** : enano *m*, -na *f* (persona) **2** : cosa *f* diminuta

midland ['mɪdlənd, -,lænd] *n* : región *f* central (de un país)

midnight ['mɪd,naɪt] *n* : medianoche *f*

midpoint ['mɪd,pɔɪnt] *n* : punto *m* medio, término *m* medio

midriff ['mɪd,rɪf] *n* : diafragma *m*

midshipman ['mɪd,ʃɪpmən, ,mɪd'ʃɪp-] *n*, *pl* **-men** [-mən, -,mɛn] : guardiamarina *m*

midst¹ ['mɪdst] *n* : medio *m* ⟨in our midst : entre nosotros⟩ ⟨in the midst of : en medio de⟩

midst² *prep* : entre

midstream ['mɪd'striːm, -,striːm] *n* : medio *m* de la corriente ⟨in the midstream of his career : en medio de su carrera⟩

midsummer ['mɪd'sʌmər, -,sʌ-] *n* : pleno verano *m*

midtown ['mɪd,taʊn] *n* : centro *m* (de una ciudad)

midway ['mɪd,weɪ] *adv* HALFWAY : a mitad de camino

midweek ['mɪd,wiːk] *n* : medio *m* de la semana ⟨in midweek : a media semana⟩

midwife ['mɪd,waɪf] *n*, *pl* **-wives** [-,waɪvz] : partera *f*, comadrona *f*

midwinter ['mɪd'wɪntər, -,win-] *n* : pleno invierno *m*

midyear ['mɪd,jɪr] *n* : medio *m* del año ⟨at midyear : a mediados del año⟩

mien ['miːn] *n* : aspecto *m*, porte *m*, semblante *m*

miff ['mɪf] *vt* : ofender

might¹ ['maɪt] (*used to express permission or possibility or as a polite alternative to* **may**) → **may** ⟨it might be true : podría ser verdad⟩ ⟨might I speak with Sarah? : ¿se puede hablar con Sarah?⟩

might² *n* : fuerza *f*, poder *m*

mightily ['maɪtəli] *adv* : con mucha fuerza, poderosamente

mighty¹ ['maɪti] *adv* VERY : muy ⟨mighty good : muy bueno, buenísimo⟩

mighty² *adj* **mightier; -est 1** POWERFUL : poderoso, potente **2** GREAT : grande, imponente

migraine ['maɪ,greɪn] *n* : jaqueca *f*, migraña *f*

migrant ['maɪgrənt] *n* : trabajador *m*, -dora *f* ambulante

migrate ['maɪ,greɪt] *vi* **-grated; -grating** : emigrar

migration [maɪ'greɪʃən] *n* : migración *f*

migratory ['maɪgrə,tori] *adj* : migratorio

mild ['maɪld] *adj* **1** GENTLE : apacible, suave ⟨a mild disposition : un temperamento suave⟩ **2** LIGHT : leve, ligero ⟨a mild punishment : un castigo leve, un castigo poco severo⟩ **3** TEMPERATE : templado (dícese del clima) — **mildly** *adv*

mildew¹ ['mɪl,duː, -,djuː] *vi* : enmohecerse

mildew² *n* : moho *m*

mildness ['maɪldnəs] *n* : apacibilidad *f*, suavidad *f*

mile ['maɪl] *n* : milla *f*

mileage ['maɪlɪdʒ] *n* **1** ALLOWANCE : viáticos *mpl* (pagados por milla recorrida) **2** : distancia *f* recorrida (en millas), kilometraje *m*

milestone ['maɪl,stoːn] *n* LANDMARK : hito *m*, jalón *m* ⟨a milestone in his life : un hito en su vida⟩

milieu [miːˈljuː, -ˈjø] *n*, *pl* **-lieus** *or* **-lieux** [-ˈjuːz, -ˈjø] SURROUNDINGS : entorno *m*, medio *m*, ambiente *m*

militant¹ ['mɪlətənt] *adj* : militante, combativo

militant² *n* : militante *mf*

militarism ['mɪlətə,rɪzəm] *n* : militarismo *m*

militaristic [,mɪlətə'rɪstɪk] *adj* : militarista

military¹ ['mɪlə,teri] *adj* : militar

military² *n* **the military** : las fuerzas armadas

militia [mə'lɪʃə] *n* : milicia *f*

milk¹ ['mɪlk] *vt* **1** : ordeñar (una vaca, etc.) **2** EXPLOIT : explotar

milk² *n* : leche *f*

milkman ['mɪlk,mæn, -mən] *n*, *pl* **-men** [-mən, -,mɛn] : lechero *m*

milk shake *n* : batido *m*, licuado *m*

milkweed ['mɪlk,wi:d] *n* : algodoncillo *m*

milky ['mɪlki] *adj* **milkier; -est** : lechoso

Milky Way *n* : Vía *f* Láctea

mill¹ ['mɪl] *vt* : moler (granos), fresar (metales), acordonar (monedas) — *vi* **to mill about** : arremolinarse

mill² *n* **1** : molino *m* (para moler granos) **2** FACTORY : fábrica *f* ⟨textile mill : fábrica textil⟩ **3** GRINDER : molinillo *m*

millennium [mə'lɛniəm] *n*, *pl* **-nia** [-niə] *or* **-niums** : milenio *m*

miller ['mɪlər] *n* : molinero *m*, -ra *f*

millet ['mɪlət] *n* : mijo *m*

milligram ['mɪlə,græm] *n* : miligramo *m*

milliliter ['mɪlə,li:tər] *n* : mililitro *m*

millimeter ['mɪlə,mi:tər] *n* : milímetro *m*

milliner ['mɪlənər] *n* : sombrerero *m*, -ra *f* (de señoras)

millinery ['mɪlə,nɛri] *n* : sombreros *mpl* de señora

million¹ ['mɪljən] *adj* **a million** : un millón *p*

million² *n*, *pl* **millions** *or* **million** : millón *m*

millionaire [,mɪljə'nær, 'mɪljə,nær] *n* : millonario *m*, -ria *f*

millionth¹ ['mɪljənθ] *adj* : millonésimo

millionth² *n* : millonésimo *m*

millipede ['mɪlə,pi:d] *n* : milpiés *m*

millstone ['mɪl,sto:n] *n* : rueda *f* de molino, muela *f*

mime¹ ['maɪm] *v* **mimed; miming** *vt* MIMIC : imitar, remedar — *vi* PANTOMIME : hacer la mímica

mime² *n* **1** : mimo *mf* **2** PANTOMIME : pantomima *f*

mimeograph ['mɪmiə,græf] *n* : mimeógrafo *m*

mimic¹ ['mɪmɪk] *vt* **-icked; -icking** : imitar, remedar

mimic² *n* : imitador *m*, -dora *f*

mimicry ['mɪmɪkri] *n*, *pl* **-ries** : mímica *f*, imitación *f*

minaret [,mɪnə'rɛt] *n* : alminar *m*, minarete *m*

mince ['mɪnts] *v* **minced; mincing** *vt* **1** CHOP : picar, moler (carne) **2 not to mince one's words** : no tener uno pelos en la lengua — *vi* : caminar de manera afectada

mincemeat ['mɪnts,mi:t] *n* : mezcla *f* de fruta picada, sebo, y especias

mind¹ ['maɪnd] *vt* **1** TEND : cuidar, atender ⟨mind the children : cuida a los niños⟩ **2** OBEY : obedecer **3** : preocuparse por, sentirse molestado por ⟨I don't mind his jokes : sus bromas no me molestan⟩ **4** : tener cuidado con ⟨mind the ladder! : ¡cuidado con la escalera!⟩ — *vi* **1** OBEY : obedecer **2** CARE : importarle a uno ⟨I don't mind : no me importa, me es igual⟩

mind² *n* **1** MEMORY : memoria *f*, recuerdo *m* ⟨keep it in mind : téngalo en

cuenta⟩ **2** : mente *f* ⟨the mind and the body : la mente y el cuerpo⟩ **3** INTENTION : intención *f*, propósito *m* ⟨to have a mind to do something : tener intención de hacer algo⟩ **4** : razón *f* ⟨he's out of his mind : está loco⟩ **5** OPINION : opinión *f* ⟨to change one's mind : cambiar de opinión⟩ **6** INTELLECT : capacidad *f* intelectual

minded ['maɪndəd] *adj* **1** (*used in combination*) ⟨narrow-minded : de mentalidad cerrada⟩ ⟨health-minded : preocupado por la salud⟩ **2** INCLINED : inclinado

mindful ['maɪndfəl] *adj* AWARE : consciente — **mindfully** *adv*

mindless ['maɪndləs] *adj* **1** SENSELESS : estúpido, sin sentido ⟨mindless violence : violencia sin sentido⟩ **2** HEEDLESS : inconsciente

mindlessly ['maɪndləsli] *adv* **1** SENSELESSLY : sin sentido **2** HEEDLESSLY : inconscientemente

mine¹ ['maɪn] *vt* **mined; mining 1** : extraer (oro, etc.) **2** : minar (con artefactos explosivos)

mine² *n* : mina *f* ⟨gold mine : mina de oro⟩

mine³ *pron* : mío, mía ⟨that one's mine : ése es el mío⟩ ⟨some friends of mine : unos amigos míos⟩

minefield ['maɪn,fi:ld] *n* : campo *m* de minas

miner ['maɪnər] *n* : minero *m*, -ra *f*

mineral ['mɪnərəl] *n* : mineral *m* — **mineral** *adj*

mineralogy [,mɪnə'rɑlədʒi, -'ræ-] *n* : mineralogía *f*

mingle ['mɪŋgəl] *v* **-gled; -gling** *vt* MIX : mezclar — *vi* **1** MIX : mezclarse **2** CIRCULATE : circular

miniature¹ ['mɪniə,tʃʊr, 'mɪni,tʃʊr, -tʃər] *adj* : en miniatura, diminuto

miniature² *n* : miniatura *f*

minibus ['mɪni,bʌs] *n* : microbús *m*, pesera *f Mex*

minicomputer ['mɪnikəm,pju:tər] *n* : minicomputadora *f*

minimal ['mɪnəməl] *adj* : mínimo

minimally ['mɪnəməli] *adv* : en grado mínimo

minimize ['mɪnə,maɪz] *vt* **-mized; -mizing** : minimizar

minimum¹ ['mɪnəməm] *adj* : mínimo

minimum² *n*, *pl* **-ma** ['mɪnəmə] *or* **-mums** : mínimo *m*

miniseries ['mɪni,sɪri:z] *n* : miniserie *f*

miniskirt ['mɪni,skərt] *n* : minifalda *f*

minister¹ ['mɪnəstər] *vi* **to minister to** : cuidar (de), atender a

minister² *n* **1** : pastor *m*, -tora *f* (de una iglesia) **2** : ministro *m*, -tra *f* (en política)

ministerial [,mɪnə'stɪriəl] *adj* : ministerial

ministry ['mɪnəstri] *n*, *pl* **-tries 1** : ministerio *m* (en política) **2** : sacerdocio *m* (en el catolicismo), clerecía *f* (en el protestantismo)

minivan ['mɪni,væn] *n* : minivan *f*

mink ['mɪŋk] *n, pl* **mink** *or* **minks** : visón *m*

minnow ['mɪno:] *n, pl* **-nows** : pececillo *m* de agua dulce

minor¹ ['maɪnər] *adj* : menor

minor² *n* **1** : menor *mf* (de edad) **2** : asignatura *f* secundaria (de estudios)

minority [mə'nɔrəṭi, maɪ-] *n, pl* **-ties** : minoría *f*

minstrel ['mɪntstrəl] *n* : juglar *m*, trovador *m* (en el medioevo)

mint¹ ['mɪnt] *vt* : acuñar

mint² *adj* : sin usar ⟨in mint condition : como nuevo⟩

mint³ *n* **1** : menta *f* ⟨mint tea : té de menta⟩ **2** : pastilla *f* de menta **3** : casa *f* de la moneda ⟨the U.S. Mint : la casa de la moneda de los EE.UU.⟩ **4** FORTUNE : dineral *m*, fortuna *f*

minuet [,mɪnju'ɛt] *n* : minué *m*

minus¹ ['maɪnəs] *n* **1** : cantidad *f* negativa **2 minus sign** : signo *m* de menos

minus² *prep* **1** : menos ⟨four minus two : cuatro menos dos⟩ **2** WITHOUT : sin ⟨minus his hat : sin su sombrero⟩

minuscule *or* **miniscule** ['mɪnəs,kju:l, mɪ'nʌs-] *adj* : minúsculo

minute¹ [maɪ'nu:t, mɪ-, -'nju:t] *adj* **-nuter; -est 1** TINY : diminuto, minúsculo **2** DETAILED : minucioso

minute² ['mɪnət] *n* **1** : minuto *m* ⟨ten minutes late : diez minutos de retraso⟩ **2** MOMENT : momento *m* **3 minutes** *npl* : actas *fpl* (de una reunión)

minutely [maɪ'nu:tli, mɪ-, -'nju:t-] *adv* : minuciosamente

miracle ['mɪrɪkəl] *n* : milagro *m*

miraculous [mə'rækjələs] *adj* : milagroso — **miraculously** *adv*

mirage [mɪ'rɑ:ʒ, *chiefly Brit* 'mɪr,ɑʒ] *n* : espejismo *m*

mire¹ ['maɪr] *vi* **mired; miring** : atascarse

mire² *n* **1** MUD : barro *m*, lodo *m* **2** : atolladero *m* ⟨stuck in a mire of debt : agobiado por la deuda⟩

mirror¹ ['mɪrər] *vt* : reflejar

mirror² *n* : espejo *m*

mirth ['mərθ] *n* : alegría *f*, regocijo *m*

mirthful ['mərθfəl] *adj* : alegre, regocijado

misadventure [,mɪsəd'vɛntʃər] *n* : malaventura *f*, desventura *f*

misanthrope ['mɪsən,θro:p] *n* : misántropo *m*, -pa *f*

misanthropic [,mɪsən'θrɑpɪk] *adj* : misantrópico

misanthropy [mɪ'sænθrəpi] *n* : misantropía *f*

misapprehend [,mɪs,æprə'hɛnd] *vt* : entender mal

misapprehension [,mɪs,æprə'hɛntʃən] *n* : malentendido *m*

misappropriate [,mɪsə'pro:pri,eɪt] *vt* **-ated; -ating** : malversar

misbegotten [,mɪsbi'gɑtən] *adj* **1** ILLEGITIMATE : ilegítimo **2** : mal concebido ⟨misbegotten laws : leyes mal concebidas⟩

misbehave [,mɪsbi'heɪv] *vi* **-haved; -having** : portarse mal

misbehavior [,mɪsbi'heɪvjər] *n* : mala conducta *f*

miscalculate [mɪs'kælkjə,leɪt] *v* **-lated; -lating** : calcular mal

miscalculation [mɪs,kælkjə'leɪʃən] *n* : error *m* de cálculo, mal cálculo *m*

miscarriage [mɪs'kærɪdʒ, 'mɪs,kærɪdʒ] *n* **1** : aborto *m* **2** FAILURE : fracaso *m*, malogro *m* ⟨a miscarriage of justice : una injusticia, un error judicial⟩

miscarry [,mɪs'kæri, 'mɪs,kæri] *vi* **-ried; -rying 1** ABORT : abortar **2** FAIL : malograrse, fracasar

miscellaneous [,mɪsə'leɪniəs] *adj* : misceláneo

miscellany ['mɪsə,leɪni] *n, pl* **-nies** : miscelánea *f*

mischance [mɪs'tʃænts] *n* : desgracia *f*, infortunio *m*, mala suerte *f*

mischief ['mɪstʃəf] *n* : diabluras *fpl*, travesuras *fpl*

mischievous ['mɪstʃəvəs] *adj* : travieso, pícaro

mischievously ['mɪstʃəvəsli] *adv* : de manera traviesa

misconception [,mɪskən'sɛpʃən] *n* : concepto *m* erróneo, idea *f* falsa

misconduct [mɪs'kɑndəkt] *n* : mala conducta *f*

misconstrue [,mɪskən'stru:] *vt* **-strued; -struing** : malinterpretar

misdeed [mɪs'di:d] *n* : fechoría *f*

misdemeanor [,mɪsdɪ'mi:nər] *n* : delito *m* menor

miser ['maɪzər] *n* : avaro *m*, -ra *f*; tacaño *m*, -ña *f*

miserable ['mɪzərəbəl] *adj* **1** UNHAPPY : triste, desdichado **2** WRETCHED : miserable, desgraciado ⟨a miserable hut : una choza miserable⟩ **3** UNPLEASANT : desagradable, malo ⟨miserable weather : tiempo malísimo⟩ **4** CONTEMPTIBLE : despreciable, mísero ⟨for a miserable $10 : por unos míseros diez dólares⟩

miserably ['mɪzərəbli] *adv* **1** SADLY : tristemente **2** WRETCHEDLY : miserablemente, lamentablemente **3** UNFORTUNATELY : desgraciadamente

miserly ['maɪzərli] *adj* : avaro, tacaño

misery ['mɪzəri] *n, pl* **-eries** : miseria *f*, sufrimiento *m*

misfire [mɪs'faɪr] *vi* **-fired; -firing** : fallar

misfit ['mɪs,fɪt] *n* : inadaptado *m*, -da *f*

misfortune [mɪs'fɔrtʃən] *n* : desgracia *f*, desventura *f*, infortunio *m*

misgiving [mɪs'gɪvɪŋ] *n* : duda *f*, recelo *m*

misguided [mɪs'gaɪdəd] *adj* : desacertado, equivocado, mal informado

mishap ['mɪs,hæp] *n* : contratiempo *m*, percance *m*, accidente *m*

misinform [,mɪsɪn'fɔrm] *vt* : informar mal

misinterpret [,mɪsɪn'tərprət] *vt* : malinterpretar

misinterpretation [ˌmɪsɪnˌtərprə'teɪ-ʃən] n : mala interpretación f, malentendido m

misjudge [mɪs'dʒʌdʒ] vt **-judged; -judging** : juzgar mal

mislay [mɪs'leɪ] vt **-laid** [-leɪd]; **-laying** : extraviar, perder

mislead [mɪs'li:d] vt **-led** [-'lɛd]; **-leading** : engañar

misleading [mɪs'li:dɪŋ] adj : engañoso

mismanage [mɪs'mænɪdʒ] vt **-aged; -aging** : administrar mal

mismanagement [mɪs'mænɪdʒmənt] n : mala administración f

misnomer [mɪs'no:mər] n : nombre m inapropiado

misogynist [mɪ'sɑdʒənɪst] n : misógino m

misogyny [mə'sɑdʒəni] n : misoginia f

misplace [mɪs'pleɪs] vt **-placed; -placing** : extraviar, perder

misprint ['mɪsˌprɪnt, mɪs'-] n : errata f, error m de imprenta

mispronounce [ˌmɪsprə'naʊnts] vt **-nounced; -nouncing** : pronunciar mal

mispronunciation [ˌmɪsprəˌnʌntsi'eɪʃən] n : pronunciación f incorrecta

misquote [mɪs'kwo:t] vt **-quoted; -quoting** : citar incorrectamente

misread [mɪs'ri:d] vt **-read; -reading 1** : leer mal ⟨she misread the sentence : leyó mal la frase⟩ **2** MISUNDERSTAND : malinterpretar ⟨they misread his intention : malinterpretaron su intención⟩

misrepresent [ˌmɪsˌrprɪ'zɛnt] vt : distorsionar, falsear, tergiversar

misrule[1] [mɪs'ru:l] vt **-ruled; -ruling** : gobernar mal

misrule[2] n : mal gobierno m

miss[1] ['mɪs] vt **1** : errar, faltar ⟨to miss the target : no dar en el blanco⟩ **2** : no encontrar, perder ⟨they missed each other : no se encontraron⟩ ⟨I missed the plane : perdí el avión⟩ **3** : echar de menos, extrañar ⟨we miss him a lot : lo echamos mucho de menos⟩ **4** OVERLOOK : pasar por alto, perder (una oportunidad, etc.) **5** AVOID : evitar ⟨they just missed hitting the tree : por muy poco chocan contra el árbol⟩ **6** OMIT : saltarse ⟨he missed breakfast : se saltó el desayuno⟩

miss[2] n **1** : fallo m (de un tiro, etc.) **2** FAILURE : fracaso m **3** : señorita f ⟨Miss Jones called us : nos llamó la señorita Jones⟩ ⟨excuse me, miss : perdone, señorita⟩

missal ['mɪsəl] n : misal m

misshapen [mɪ'ʃeɪpən] adj : deforme

missile ['mɪsəl] n **1** : misil m ⟨guided missile : misil guiado⟩ **2** PROJECTILE : proyectil m

missing ['mɪsɪŋ] adj **1** ABSENT : ausente ⟨who's missing? : ¿quién falta?⟩ **2** LOST : perdido, desaparecido ⟨missing persons : los desaparecidos⟩

mission ['mɪʃən] n **1** : misión f (mandada por una iglesia) **2** DELEGATION : misión f, delegación f, embajada f **3** TASK : misión f

missionary[1] ['mɪʃəˌnɛri] adj : misionero

missionary[2] n, pl **-aries** : misionero m, -ra f

missive ['mɪsɪv] n : misiva f

misspell [mɪs'spɛl] vt : escribir mal

misspelling [mɪs'spɛlɪŋ] n : falta f de ortografía

misstep ['mɪsˌstɛp] n : traspié m, tropezón m

mist ['mɪst] n **1** HAZE : neblina f, niebla f **2** SPRAY : rocío m

mistake[1] [mɪ'steɪk] vt **-took** [-'stʊk]; **-taken** [-'steɪkən]; **-taking 1** MISINTERPRET : malinterpretar **2** CONFUSE : confundir ⟨he mistook her for Clara : la confundió con Clara⟩

mistake[2] n **1** MISUNDERSTANDING : malentendido m, confusión f **2** ERROR : error m ⟨I made a mistake : me equivoqué, cometí un error⟩

mistaken [mɪ'steɪkən] adj WRONG : equivocado — **mistakenly** adv

mister ['mɪstər] n : señor m ⟨watch out, mister : cuidado, señor⟩

mistiness ['mɪstinəs] n : nebulosidad f

mistletoe ['mɪsəlˌto:] n : muérdago m

mistreat [mɪs'tri:t] vt : maltratar

mistreatment [mɪs'tri:tmənt] n : maltrato m, abuso m

mistress ['mɪstrəs] n **1** : dueña f, señora f (de una casa) **2** LOVER : amante f

mistrust[1] [mɪs'trʌst] vt : desconfiar de

mistrust[2] n : desconfianza f

mistrustful [mɪs'trʌstfəl] adj : desconfiado

misty ['mɪsti] adj **mistier; -est 1** : nebuloso, nebuloso **2** TEARFUL : lloroso

misunderstand [ˌmɪsˌʌndər'stænd] vt **-stood** [-'stʊd]; **-standing 1** : entender mal **2** MISINTERPRET : malinterpretar ⟨don't misunderstand me : no me malinterpretes⟩

misunderstanding [ˌmɪsˌʌndər'stændɪŋ] n **1** MISINTERPRETATION : malentendido m **2** DISAGREEMENT, QUARREL : disputa f, discusión f

misuse[1] [mɪs'ju:z] vt **-used; -using 1** : emplear mal **2** ABUSE, MISTREAT : abusar de, maltratar

misuse[2] [mɪs'ju:s] n **1** : mal empleo m, mal uso m **2** WASTE : derroche m, despilfarro m **3** ABUSE : abuso m

mite ['maɪt] n **1** : ácaro m **2** BIT : poco m ⟨a mite tired : un poquito cansado⟩

miter or **mitre** ['maɪtər] n **1** : mitra f (de un obispo) **2** or **miter joint** : inglete m

mitigate ['mɪtəˌgeɪt] vt **-gated; -gating** : mitigar, aliviar

mitigation [ˌmɪtə'geɪʃən] n : mitigación f, alivio m

mitosis [maɪ'to:sɪs] n, pl **-toses** [-ˌsi:z] : mitosis f

mitt ['mɪt] n : manopla f, guante m (de béisbol)

mitten ['mɪtən] *n* : manopla *f*, mitón *m*

mix¹ ['mɪks] *vt* **1** COMBINE : mezclar **2** STIR : remover, revolver **3 to mix up** CONFUSE : confundir — *vi* : mezclarse

mix² *n* : mezcla *f*

mixer ['mɪksər] *n* **1** : batidora *f* (de la cocina) **2 cement mixer** : hormigonera *f*

mixture ['mɪkstʃər] *n* : mezcla *f*

mix–up ['mɪks,ʌp] *n* CONFUSION : confusión *f*, lío *m fam*

mnemonic [nɪ'manɪk] *adj* : mnemónico

moan¹ ['mo:n] *vi* : gemir

moan² *n* : gemido *m*

moat ['mo:t] *n* : foso *m*

mob¹ ['mab] *vt* **mobbed; mobbing 1** ATTACK : atacar en masa **2** HOUND : acosar, rodear

mob² *n* **1** THRONG : multitud *f*, turba *f*, muchedumbre *f* **2** GANG : pandilla *f*

mobile¹ ['mo:bəl, -ˌbi:l, -ˌbaɪl] *adj* : móvil ⟨mobile home : caravana, casa rodante⟩

mobile² ['mo,bi:l] *n* : móvil *m*

mobility [mo'bɪləti] *n* : movilidad *f*

mobilize ['mo:bə,laɪz] *vt* **-lized; -lizing** : movilizar

moccasin ['makəsən] *n* **1** : mocasín *m* **2** *or* **water moccasin** : serpiente *f* venenosa de Norteamérica

mocha ['mo:kə] *n* **1** : mezcla *f* de café y chocolate **2** : color *m* chocolate

mock¹ ['mak, 'mɔk] *vt* **1** RIDICULE : burlarse de, mofarse de **2** MIMIC : imitar, remedar (de manera burlona)

mock² *adj* **1** SIMULATED : simulado **2** PHONY : falso

mockery ['makəri, 'mɔ-] *n, pl* **-eries 1** JEER, TAUNT : burla *f*, mofa *f* ⟨to make a mockery of : burlarse de⟩ **2** FAKE : imitación *f* (burlona)

mockingbird ['makɪŋ,bərd, 'mɔ-] *n* : sinsonte *m*

mode ['mo:d] *n* **1** FORM : modo *m*, forma *f* **2** MANNER : modo *m*, manera *f*, estilo *m* **3** FASHION : moda *f*

model¹ ['madəl] *v* **-eled** *or* **-elled; -eling** *or* **-elling** *vt* SHAPE : modelar — *vi* : trabajar de modelo

model² *adj* **1** EXEMPLARY : modelo, ejemplar ⟨a model student : un estudiante modelo⟩ **2** MINIATURE : en miniatura

model³ *n* **1** PATTERN : modelo *m* **2** MINIATURE : modelo *m*, miniatura *f* **3** EXAMPLE : modelo *m*, ejemplo *m* **4** MANNEQUIN : modelo *mf* **5** DESIGN : modelo *m* ⟨the '97 model : el modelo '97⟩

modem ['mo:dəm, -ˌdɛm] *n* : módem *m*

moderate¹ ['madə,reɪt] *v* **-ated; -ating** *vt* : moderar, temperar — *vi* **1** CALM : moderarse, calmarse **2** : fungir como moderador (en un debate, etc.)

moderate² ['madərət] *adj* : moderado

moderate³ ['madərət] *n* : moderado *m*, -da *f*

moderately ['madərətli] *adv* **1** : con moderación **2** FAIRLY : medianamente

moderation [ˌmadə'reɪʃən] *n* : moderación *f*

moderator ['madəˌreɪtər] *n* : moderador *m*, -dora *f*

modern ['madərn] *adj* : moderno

modernism ['madərˌnɪzəm] *n* : modernismo *m*

modernist ['madərnɪst] *n* : modernista *mf* — **modernist** *adj*

modernity [mə'dərnəti] *n* : modernidad *f*

modernization [ˌmadərnə'zeɪʃən] *n* : modernización *f*

modernize ['madərˌnaɪz] *v* **-ized; -izing** *vt* : modernizar — *vi* : modernizarse

modest ['madəst] *adj* **1** HUMBLE : modesto **2** DEMURE : recatado, pudoroso **3** MODERATE : modesto, moderado — **modestly** *adv*

modesty ['madəsti] *n* : modestia *f*

modicum ['madɪkəm] *n* : mínimo *m*, pizca *f*

modification [ˌmadəfə'keɪʃən] *n* : modificación *f*

modifier ['madəˌfaɪər] *n* : modificante *m*, modificador *m*

modify ['madəˌfaɪ] *vt* **-fied; -fying** : modificar, calificar (en gramática)

modish ['mo:dɪʃ] *adj* STYLISH : a la moda, de moda

modular ['madʒələr] *adj* : modular

modulate ['madʒəˌleɪt] *vt* **-lated; -lating** : modular

modulation [ˌmadʒə'leɪʃən] *n* : modulación *f*

module ['maˌdʒu:l] *n* : módulo *m*

mogul ['mo:gəl] *n* : magnate *mf*; potentado *m*, -da *f*

mohair ['mo:ˌhær] *n* : mohair *m*

moist ['mɔɪst] *adj* : húmedo

moisten ['mɔɪsən] *vt* : humedecer

moistness ['mɔɪstnəs] *n* : humedad *f*

moisture ['mɔɪstʃər] *n* : humedad *f*

moisturize ['mɔɪstʃəˌraɪz] *vt* **-ized; -izing** : humedecer (el aire), humectar (la piel)

moisturizer ['mɔɪstʃəˌraɪzər] *n* : crema *f* hidratante, crema *f* humectante

molar ['mo:lər] *n* : muela *f*, molar *m*

molasses [mə'læsəz] *n* : melaza *f*

mold¹ ['mo:ld] *vt* : moldear, formar (carácter, etc.) — *vi* : enmohecerse ⟨the bread will mold : el pan se enmohecerá⟩

mold² *n* **1** *or* **leaf mold** : mantillo *m* **2** FORM : molde *m* ⟨to break the mold : romper el molde⟩ **3** FUNGUS : moho *m*

molder ['mo:ldər] *vi* CRUMBLE : desmoronarse

molding ['mo:ldɪŋ] *n* : moldura *f* (en arquitectura)

moldy ['mo:ldi] *adj* **moldier; -est** : mohoso

mole ['mo:l] *n* **1** : lunar *m* (en la piel) **2** : topo *m* (animal)

molecule ['mɑlɪˌkjuːl] *n* : molécula *f* —
  molecular [mə'lɛkjələr] *adj*
molehill ['moːlˌhɪl] *n* : topera *f*
molest [mə'lɛst] *vt* **1** ANNOY, DISTURB
  : molestar **2** : abusar (sexualmente)
mollify ['mɑləˌfaɪ] *vt* **-fied; -fying**
  : apaciguar, aplacar
mollusk *or* **mollusc** ['mɑləsk] *n* : molusco *m*
mollycoddle ['mɑliˌkɑdəl] *vt* **-dled;
-dling** PAMPER : consentir, mimar
molt ['moːlt] *vi* : mudar, hacer la muda
molten ['moːltən] *adj* : fundido
mom ['mɑm, 'mʌm] *n* : mamá *f*
moment ['moːmənt] *n* **1** INSTANT : momento *m* ⟨one moment, please : un momento, por favor⟩ **2** TIME : momento
  m ⟨at the moment : de momento, ac-
  tualmente⟩ ⟨from that moment : desde entonces⟩ **3** IMPORTANCE : importancia *f* ⟨of great moment : de gran
  importancia⟩
momentarily [ˌmoːmən'tɛrəli] *adv* **1**
  : momentáneamente **2** SOON : dentro
  de poco, pronto
momentary ['moːmənˌtɛri] *adj* : momentáneo
momentous [moˈmɛntəs] *adj* : de suma
  importancia, fatídico
momentum [moˈmɛntəm] *n, pl* **-ta** [-tə]
  or **-tums 1** : momento *m* (en física) **2**
  IMPETUS : ímpetu *m*, impulso *m*
mommy ['mɑmi, 'mʌ-] *n* : mami *f*
monarch ['mɑˌnɑrk, -nərk] *n* : monarca
  mf
monarchism ['mɑˌnɑrˌkɪzəm, -nər-] *n*
  : monarquismo *m*
monarchist ['mɑˌnɑrkɪst, -nər-] *n*
  : monárquico *m*, -ca *f*
monarchy ['mɑˌnɑrki, -nər-] *n, pl* **-chies**
  : monarquía *f*
monastery ['mɑnəˌstɛri] *n, pl* **-teries**
  : monasterio *m*
monastic [mə'næstɪk] *adj* : monástico
  — **monastically** [-tɪkli] *adv*
Monday ['mʌnˌdeɪ, -di] *n* : lunes *m*
monetary ['mɑnəˌtɛri, 'mʌnə-] *adj*
  : monetario
money ['mʌni] *n, pl* **-eys** *or* **-ies** ['mʌniz]
  : dinero *m*, plata *f*
moneyed ['mʌnid] *adj* : adinerado
moneylender ['mʌniˌlɛndər] *n* : prestamista *mf*
money order *n* : giro *m* postal
Mongol ['mɑŋgəl, -ˌgoːl] → **Mongolian**
Mongolian [mɑnˈgoːliən, mɑŋ-] *n* : mongol *m*, -gola *f* — **Mongolian** *adj*
mongoose ['mɑŋˌguːs, 'mɑn-] *n, pl*
  -gooses : mangosta *f*
mongrel ['mɑŋgrəl, 'mʌŋ-] *n* **1** : perro
  m mestizo, perro *m* corriente *Mex* **2**
  HYBRID : híbrido *m*
monitor[1] ['mɑnətər] *vt* : controlar, monitorear
monitor[2] *n* **1** : ayudante *mf* (en una escuela) **2** : monitor *m* (de una computadora, etc.)
monk ['mʌŋk] *n* : monje *m*

monkey[1] ['mʌŋki] *vi* **-keyed; -keying 1**
  to monkey around : hacer payasadas,
  payasear **2 to monkey with** : juguetear
  con
monkey[2] *n, pl* **-keys** : mono *m*, -na *f*
monkeyshines ['mʌŋkiˌʃaɪnz] *npl*
  PRANKS : picardías *fpl*, travesuras *fpl*
monkey wrench *n* : llave *f* inglesa
monocle ['mɑnɪkəl] *n* : monóculo *m*
monogamous [mə'nɑgəməs] *adj*
  : monógamo
monogamy [mə'nɑgəmi] *n* : monogamia *f*
monogram[1] ['mɑnəˌgræm] *vt*
  -grammed; -gramming : marcar con
  monograma ⟨monogrammed towels
  : toallas con monograma⟩
monogram[2] *n* : monograma *m*
monograph ['mɑnəˌgræf] *n* : monografía *f*
monolingual [ˌmɑnəˈlɪŋgwəl] *adj* : monolingüe
monolith ['mɑnəˌlɪθ] *n* : monolito *m*
monolithic [ˌmɑnəˈlɪθɪk] *adj* : monolítico
monologue ['mɑnəˌlɔg] *n* : monólogo *m*
monoplane ['mɑnəˌpleɪn] *n* : mono-
  plano *m*
monopolize [mə'nɑpəˌlaɪz] *vt* **-lized;
-lizing** : monopolizar
monopoly [mə'nɑpəli] *n, pl* **-lies** : monopolio *m*
monosyllabic [ˌmɑnosəˈlæbɪk] *adj*
  : monosilábico
monosyllable ['mɑnoˌsɪləbəl] *n* : monosílabo *m*
monotheism ['mɑnoθiːˌɪzəm] *n* : monoteísmo *m*
monotheistic [ˌmɑnoθiːˈɪstɪk] *adj* : mo-
  noteísta
monotone ['mɑnəˌtoːn] *n* : voz *f* monó-
  tona
monotonous [mə'nɑtənəs] *adj* : monótono — **monotonously** *adv*
monotony [mə'nɑtəni] *n* : monotonía *f*,
  uniformidad *f*
monoxide [mə'nɑkˌsaɪd] *n* : monóxido
  m
monsoon [mɑn'suːn] *n* : monzón *m*
monster ['mɑntstər] *n* : monstruo *m*
monstrosity [mɑn'strɑsəti] *n, pl* **-ties**
  : monstruosidad *f*
monstrous ['mɑntstrəs] *adj* : monstruoso — **monstrously** *adv*
montage [mɑn'tɑʒ] *n* : montaje *m*
month ['mʌnθ] *n* : mes *m*
monthly[1] ['mʌnθli] *adv* : mensualmente
monthly[2] *adj* : mensual
monthly[3] *n, pl* **-lies** : publicación *f* mensual
monument ['mɑnjəmənt] *n* : monumento *m*
monumental [ˌmɑnjəˈmɛntəl] *adj* : monumental — **monumentally** *adv*
moo[1] ['muː] *vi* : mugir
moo[2] *n* : mugido *m*
mood ['muːd] *n* : humor *m* ⟨to be in a
  good mood : estar de buen humor⟩ ⟨to

be in the mood for : tener ganas de⟩
⟨to be in no mood for : no estar para⟩
moodiness ['mu:dinəs] *n* **1** SADNESS
: melancolía *f*, tristeza *f* **2** : cambios
mpl de humor, carácter *m* temperamental
moody ['mu:di] *adj* **moodier; -est 1**
GLOOMY : melancólico, deprimido **2**
TEMPERAMENTAL : temperamental, de
humor variable
moon ['mu:n] *n* : luna *f*
moonbeam ['mu:n,bi:m] *n* : rayo *m* de
luna
moonlight¹ ['mu:n,laɪt] *vi* : estar pluriempleado
moonlight² *n* : claro *m* de luna, luz *f* de
la luna
moonlit ['mu:n,lɪt] *adj* : iluminado por
la luna ⟨a moonlit night : una noche
de luna⟩
moonshine ['mu:n,ʃaɪn] *n* **1** MOON-
LIGHT : luz *f* de la luna **2** NONSENSE
: disparates *mpl*, tonterías *fpl* **3**
: whisky *m* destilado ilegalmente
moor¹ ['mʊr, 'mɔr] *vt* : amarrar
moor² *n* : brezal *m*, páramo *m*
Moor ['mʊr] *n* : moro *m*, -ra *f*
mooring ['mʊrɪŋ, 'mɔr-] *n* DOCK : atracadero *m*
Moorish ['mʊrɪʃ] *adj* : moro
moose ['mu:s] *ns & pl* : alce *m* (norteamericano)
moot ['mu:t] *adj* DEBATABLE : discutible
mop¹ ['map] *vt* **mopped; mopping** : trapear
mop² *n* : trapeador *m*
mope ['mo:p] *vi* **moped; moping** : andar deprimido, quedar abatido
moped ['mo:,pɛd] *n* : ciclomotor *m*
moraine [mə'reɪn] *n* : morena *f*
moral¹ ['mɔrəl] *adj* : moral ⟨moral judgment : juicio moral⟩ ⟨moral support
: apoyo moral⟩ — **morally** *adv*
moral² *n* **1** : moraleja *f* (de un cuento,
etc.) **2 morals** *npl* : moral *f*, moralidad
f
morale [mə'ræl] *n* : moral *f*
moralist ['mɔrəlɪst] *n* : moralista *mf*
moralistic [,mɔrə'lɪstɪk] *adj* : moralista
morality [mə'ræləti] *n, pl* **-ties** : moralidad *f*
morass [mə'ræs] *n* **1** SWAMP : ciénaga
f, pantano *m* **2** CONFUSION, MESS : lío
m fam, embrollo *m*
moratorium [,mɔrə'toriəm] *n, pl* **-riums**
or **-ria** [-iə] : moratoria *f*
moray ['mɔr,eɪ, mə'reɪ] *n* : morena *f*
morbid ['mɔrbɪd] *adj* **1** : mórbido, morboso (en medicina) **2** GRUESOME
: morboso, horripilante
morbidity [mɔr'bɪdəti] *n, pl* **-ties** : morbosidad *f*
more¹ ['mor] *adv* : más ⟨what more can
I say? : ¿qué más puedo decir?⟩ ⟨more
important : más importante⟩ ⟨once
more : una vez más⟩
more² *adj* : más ⟨nothing more than that
: nada más que eso⟩ ⟨more work : más
trabajo⟩

more³ *n* : más *m* ⟨the more you eat, the
more you want : cuanto más comes,
tanto más quieres⟩
more⁴ *pron* : más ⟨more were found : se
encontraron más⟩
moreover [mor'o:vər] *adv* : además
mores ['mɔr,eɪz, -i:z] *npl* CUSTOMS : costumbres *fpl*, tradiciones *fpl*
morgue ['mɔrg] *n* : morgue *f*
moribund ['mɔrə,bʌnd] *adj* : moribun-
do
Mormon ['mɔrmən] *n* : mormón *m*,
-mona *f* — **Mormon** *adj*
morn ['mɔrn] → **morning**
morning ['mɔrnɪŋ] *n* : mañana *f* ⟨good
morning! : ¡buenos días!⟩
Moroccan [mə'rakən] *n* : marroquí *mf*
— **Moroccan** *adj*
moron ['mɔr,ɑn] *n* **1** : retrasado *m*, -da
f mental **2** DUNCE : estúpido *m*, -da *f*;
tonto *m*, -ta *f*
morose [mə'ro:s] *adj* : hosco, sombrío
— **morosely** *adv*
moroseness [mə'ro:snəs] *n* : malhumor
m
morphine ['mɔr,fi:n] *n* : morfina *f*
morphology [mɔr'falədʒi] *n, pl* **-gies**
: morfología *f*
morrow ['mɑro:] *n* : día *m* siguiente
Morse code ['mɔrs] *n* : código *m* morse
morsel ['mɔrsəl] *n* **1** BITE : bocado *m* **2**
FRAGMENT : pedazo *m*
mortal¹ ['mɔrtəl] *adj* : mortal ⟨mortal
blow : golpe mortal⟩ ⟨mortal fear
: miedo mortal⟩ — **mortally** *adv*
mortal² *n* : mortal *mf*
mortality [mɔr'tæləti] *n* : mortalidad *f*
mortar ['mɔrtər] *n* **1** : mortero *m*, molcajete *m Mex* ⟨mortar and pestle
: mortero y maja⟩ **2** : mortero *m* ⟨mor-
tar shell : granada de mortero⟩ **3** CE-
MENT : mortero *m*, argamasa *f*
mortgage¹ ['mɔrgɪdʒ] *vt* **-gaged;**
-gaging : hipotecar
mortgage² *n* : hipoteca *f*
mortification [,mɔrtəfə'keɪʃən] *n* **1**
: mortificación *f* **2** HUMILIATION : humillación *f*, vergüenza *f*
mortify ['mɔrtə,faɪ] *vt* **-fied; -fying 1**
: mortificar (en religión) **2** HUMILIATE
: humillar, avergonzar
mortuary ['mɔrtʃə,wɛri] *n, pl* **-aries** FU-
NERAL HOME : funeraria *f*
mosaic [mo'zeɪɪk] *n* : mosaico *m*
Moslem ['mazləm] → **Muslim**
mosque ['mask] *n* : mezquita *f*
mosquito [mə'ski:ʈo] *n, pl* **-toes** : mosquito *m*, zancudo *m*
moss ['mɔs] *n* : musgo *m*
mossy ['mɔsi] *adj* **-ier; -est** : musgoso
most¹ ['mo:st] *adv* : más ⟨the most interesting book : el libro más intere-
sante⟩
most² *adj* **1** : la mayoría de, la mayor
parte de ⟨most people : la mayoría de
la gente⟩ **2** GREATEST : más (dícese de
los números), mayor (dícese de las cantidades) ⟨the most ability : la mayor ca-
pacidad⟩

most³ *n* : más *m*, máximo *m* ⟨the most I can do : lo más que puedo hacer⟩ ⟨three weeks at the most : tres semanas como máximo⟩

most⁴ *pron* : la mayoría, la mayor parte ⟨most will go : la mayoría irá⟩

mostly ['mo:stli] *adv* MAINLY : en su mayor parte, principalmente

mote ['mo:t] *n* SPECK : mota *f*

motel [mo'tel] *n* : motel *m*

moth ['mɔθ] *n* : palomilla *f*, polilla *f*

mother¹ ['mʌðər] *vt* **1** BEAR : dar a luz a **2** PROTECT : cuidar de, proteger

mother² *n* : madre *f*

motherhood ['mʌðər,hʊd] *n* : maternidad *f*

mother–in–law ['mʌðərɪn,lɔ] *n, pl* **mothers–in–law** : suegra *f*

motherland ['mʌðər,lænd] *n* : patria *f*

motherly ['mʌðərli] *adj* : maternal

mother–of–pearl [,mʌðərəv'pərl] *n* : nácar *m*, madreperla *f*

motif [mo'ti:f] *n* : motivo *m*

motion¹ ['mo:ʃən] *vt* : hacerle señas a alguien ⟨she motioned us to come in : nos hizo señas para que entráramos⟩

motion² *n* **1** MOVEMENT : movimiento *m* ⟨to set in motion : poner en marcha⟩ **2** PROPOSAL : moción *f* ⟨to second a motion : apoyar una moción⟩

motionless ['mo:ʃənləs] *adj* : inmóvil, quieto

motion picture *n* MOVIE : película *f*

motivate ['mo:tə,veɪt] *vt* **-vated; -vating** : motivar, mover, inducir

motivation [,mo:tə'veɪʃən] *n* : motivación *f*

motive¹ ['mo:tɪv] *adj* : motor ⟨motive power : fuerza motriz⟩

motive² *n* : motivo *m*, móvil *m*

motley ['mɑtli] *adj* : abigarrado, variopinto

motor¹ ['mo:tər] *vi* : viajar en coche

motor² *n* : motor *m*

motorbike ['mo:tər,baɪk] *n* : motocicleta *f* (pequeña), moto *f*

motorboat ['mo:tər,bo:t] *n* : bote *m* a motor, lancha *f* motora

motorcar ['mo:tər,kɑr] *n* : automóvil *m*

motorcycle ['mo:tər,saɪkəl] *n* : motocicleta *f*

motorcyclist ['mo:tər,saɪkəlɪst] *n* : motociclista *mf*

motorist ['mo:tərɪst] *n* : automovilista *mf*, motorista *mf*

mottle ['mɑtəl] *vt* **-tled; -tling** : manchar, motear ⟨mottled skin : piel manchada⟩ ⟨a mottled surface : una superficie moteada⟩

motto ['mɑto] *n, pl* **-toes** : lema *m*

mould ['mo:ld] → **mold**

mound ['maʊnd] *n* **1** PILE : montón *m* **2** KNOLL : montículo *m* **3** burial mound : túmulo *m*

mount¹ ['maʊnt] *vt* **1** : montar a (un caballo), montar en (una bicicleta), subir a **2** : montar (artillería, etc.) — *vi* INCREASE : aumentar

mount² *n* **1** SUPPORT : soporte *m* **2** HORSE : caballería *f*, montura *f* **3** MOUNTAIN : monte *m*, montaña *f*

mountain ['maʊntən] *n* : montaña *f*

mountaineer [,maʊntən'ɪr] *n* : alpinista *mf*; montañero *m*, -ra *f*

mountaineering [,maʊntən'ɪrɪŋ] *n* : alpinismo *m*

mountainous ['maʊntənəs] *adj* : montañoso

mountaintop ['maʊntən,tɑp] *n* : cima *f*, cumbre *f*

mourn ['morn] *vt* : llorar (por), lamentar ⟨to mourn the death of : llorar la muerte de⟩ — *vi* : llorar, estar de luto

mourner ['mornər] *n* : doliente *mf*

mournful ['mornfəl] *adj* **1** SORROWFUL : lloroso, plañidero, triste **2** GLOOMY : deprimente, entristecedor — **mournfully** *adv*

mourning ['mornɪŋ] *n* : duelo *m*, luto *m*

mouse ['maʊs] *n, pl* **mice** ['maɪs] **1** : ratón *m*, -tona *f* **2** : ratón *m* (de una computadora)

mousetrap ['maʊs,træp] *n* : ratonera *f*

mousse ['mu:s] *n* : mousse *mf*

moustache ['mʌ,stæʃ, mə'stæʃ] → **mustache**

mouth¹ ['maʊð] *vt* **1** : decir con poca sinceridad, repetir sin comprensión **2** : articular en silencio ⟨she mouthed the words : formó las palabras con los labios⟩

mouth² ['maʊθ] *n* : boca *f* (de una persona o un animal), entrada *f* (de un túnel), desembocadura *f* (de un río)

mouthful ['maʊθ,fʊl] *n* : bocado *m* (de comida), bocanada *f* (de líquido o humo)

mouthpiece ['maʊθ,pi:s] *n* : boquilla *f* (de un instrumento musical)

mouthwash ['maʊθ,wɔʃ, -,wɑʃ] *n* : enjuague *m* bucal

movable ['mu:vəbəl] *or* **moveable** *adj* : movible, móvil

move¹ ['mu:v] *v* **moved; moving** *vi* **1** GO : ir **2** RELOCATE : mudarse, trasladarse **3** STIR : moverse ⟨don't move! : ¡no te muevas!⟩ **4** ACT : actuar — *vt* **1** : mover ⟨move it over there : ponlo allí⟩ ⟨he kept moving his feet : no dejaba de mover los pies⟩ **2** INDUCE, PERSUADE : inducir, persuadir, mover **3** TOUCH : conmover ⟨it moved him to tears : lo hizo llorar⟩ **4** PROPOSE : proponer

move² *n* **1** MOVEMENT : movimiento *m* **2** RELOCATION : mudanza *f* (de casa), traslado *m* **3** STEP : paso *m* ⟨a good move : un paso acertado⟩

movement ['mu:vmənt] *n* : movimiento *m*

mover ['mu:vər] *n* : persona *f* que hace mudanzas

movie ['mu:vi] *n* **1** : película *f* **2 movies** *npl* : cine *m*

moving ['mu:vɪŋ] *adj* **1** : en movimiento ⟨a moving target : un blanco móvil⟩

2 TOUCHING : conmovedor, emocionante

mow[1] ['mo:] *vt* **mowed; mowed** *or* **mown** ['mo:n]; **mowing** : cortar (la hierba)

mow[2] ['mau] *n* : pajar *m*

mower ['mo:ər] → **lawn mower**

Mr. ['mɪstər] *n, pl* **Messrs.** ['mɛsərz] : señor *m*

Mrs. ['mɪsəz, -səs, *esp South* 'mɪzəz, -zəs] *n, pl* **Mesdames** [meɪ'dɑm, -'dæm] : señora *f*

Ms. ['mɪz] *n* : señora *f*, señorita *f*

much[1] ['mʌtʃ] *adv* **more** ['mor]; **most** ['mo:st] : mucho ⟨I'm much happier : estoy mucho más contenta⟩ ⟨she talks as much as I do : habla tanto como yo⟩

much[2] *adj* **more; most** : mucho ⟨it has much validity : tiene mucha validez⟩ ⟨too much time : demasiado tiempo⟩

much[3] *pron* : mucho, -cha ⟨I don't need much : no necesito mucho⟩

mucilage ['mju:səlɪdʒ] *n* : mucílago *m*

muck ['mʌk] *n* **1** MANURE : estiércol *m* **2** DIRT, FILTH : mugre *f*, suciedad *f* **3** MIRE, MUD : barro *m*, fango *m*, lodo *m*

mucous ['mju:kəs] *adj* : mucoso ⟨mucous membrane : membrana mucosa⟩

mucus ['mju:kəs] *n* : mucosidad *f*

mud ['mʌd] *n* : barro *m*, fango *m*, lodo *m*

muddle[1] ['mʌdəl] *v* **-dled; -dling** *vt* **1** CONFUSE : confundir **2** BUNGLE : echar a perder, malograr — *vi* : andar confundido ⟨to muddle through : arreglárselas⟩

muddle[2] *n* : confusión *f*, embrollo *m*, lío *m*

muddleheaded [,mʌdəl'hɛdəd, 'mʌdəl,-] *adj* CONFUSED : confuso, despistado

muddy[1] ['mʌdi] *vt* **-died; -dying** : llenar de barro

muddy[2] *adj* **-dier; -est** : barroso, fangoso, lodoso, enlodado ⟨you're all muddy : estás cubierto de barro⟩

muff[1] ['mʌf] *vt* BUNGLE : echar a perder, fallar (un tiro, etc.)

muff[2] *n* : manguito *m*

muffin ['mʌfən] *n* : magdalena *f*, mantecada *f Mex*

muffle ['mʌfəl] *vt* **-fled; -fling 1** ENVELOP : cubrir, tapar **2** DEADEN : amortiguar (un sonido)

muffler ['mʌflər] *n* **1** SCARF : bufanda *f* **2** : silenciador *m*, mofle *m CA, Mex* (de un automóvil)

mug[1] ['mʌg] *v* **mugged; mugging** *vi* : posar (con afectación), hacer muecas ⟨mugging for the camera : haciendo muecas para la cámara⟩ — *vt* ASSAULT : asaltar, atracar

mug[2] *n* CUP : tazón *m*

mugger ['mʌgər] *n* : atracador *m*, -dora *f*

mugginess ['mʌginəs] *n* : bochorno *m*

muggy ['mʌgi] *adj* **-gier; -est** : bochornoso

mulatto [mu'lɑto, -'læ-] *n, pl* **-toes** *or* **-tos** : mulato *m*, -ta *f*

mulberry ['mʌl,bɛri] *n, pl* **-ries** : morera *f* (árbol), mora *f* (fruta)

mulch[1] ['mʌltʃ] *vt* : cubrir con pajote

mulch[2] *n* : pajote *m*

mule ['mju:l] *n* **1** : mula *f* **2** : obstinado *m*, -da *f*; terco *m*, -ca *f*

mulish ['mju:lɪʃ] *adj* : obstinado, terco

mull ['mʌl] *vt* **to mull over** : reflexionar sobre

mullet ['mʌlət] *n, pl* **-let** *or* **-lets** : mújol *m*, múgil *m*

multicolored [,mʌlti'kʌlərd, ,mʌltaɪ-] *adj* : multicolor, abigarrado

multicultural [,mʌlti'kʌltʃərəl] *adj* : multicultural

multifaceted [,mʌlti'fæsətəd, ,mʌltaɪ-] *adj* : multifacético

multifamily [,mʌlti'fæmli, ,mʌltaɪ-] *adj* : multifamiliar

multifarious [,mʌltə'færiəs] *adj* DIVERSE : diverso, variado

multilateral [,mʌlti'lætərəl, ,mʌltaɪ-] *adj* : multilateral

multimedia [,mʌlti'mi:diə, ,mʌltaɪ-] *adj* : multimedia

multimillionaire [,mʌlti,mɪljə'nær, ,mʌltaɪ-, -'mɪljə,nær] *adj* : multimillonario

multinational [,mʌlti'næʃənəl, ,mʌltaɪ-] *adj* : multinacional

multiple[1] ['mʌltəpəl] *adj* : múltiple

multiple[2] *n* : múltiplo *m*

multiple sclerosis [sklə'ro:sɪs] *n* : esclerosis *f* múltiple

multiplication [,mʌltəplə'keɪʃən] *n* : multiplicación *f*

multiplicity [,mʌltə'plɪsəti] *n, pl* **-ties** : multiplicidad *f*

multiplier ['mʌltə,plaɪər] *n* : multiplicador *m* (en matemáticas)

multiply ['mʌltə,plaɪ] *v* **-plied; -plying** *vt* : multiplicar — *vi* : multiplicarse

multipurpose [,mʌlti'pərpəs, ,mʌltaɪ-] *adj* : multiuso

multitude ['mʌltə,tu:d, -,tju:d] *n* **1** CROWD : multitud *f*, muchedumbre *f* **2** HOST : multitud *f*, gran cantidad *f* ⟨a multitude of ideas : numerosas ideas⟩

multivitamin [,mʌlti'vaɪtəmən, ,mʌltaɪ-] *adj* : multivitamínico

mum[1] ['mʌm] *adj* SILENT : callado

mum[2] *n* → **chrysanthemum**

mumble[1] ['mʌmbəl] *v* **-bled; -bling** *vt* : mascullar, musitar — *vi* : mascullar, hablar entre dientes, murmurar

mumble[2] *n* **to speak in a mumble** : hablar entre dientes

mummy ['mʌmi] *n, pl* **-mies** : momia *f*

mumps ['mʌmps] *ns & pl* : paperas *fpl*

munch ['mʌntʃ] *v* : mascar, masticar

mundane [,mʌn'deɪn, 'mʌn,-] *adj* **1** EARTHLY, WORLDLY : mundano, terrenal **2** COMMONPLACE : rutinario, ordinario

municipal [mju'nɪsəpəl] *adj* : municipal

municipality [mju,nɪsə'pælət̮i] *n, pl* **-ties** : municipio *m*

munitions [mju'nɪʃənz] *npl* : municiones *fpl*

mural¹ ['mjʊrəl] *adj* : mural
mural² ['mjʊrəlıst] *n* : mural *m*
murder¹ ['mərdər] *vt* : asesinar, matar —
vi : matar
murder² *n* : asesinato *m*, homicidio *m*
murderer ['mərdərər] *n* : asesino *m*, -na
f; homicida *mf*
murderess ['mərdərıs, -də̩rɛs, -dərəs] *n*
: asesina *f*, homicida *f*
murderous ['mərdərəs] *adj* : asesino,
homicida
murk ['mərk] *n* DARKNESS : oscuridad *f*,
tinieblas *fpl*
murkiness ['mərkinəs] *n* : oscuridad *f*,
tenebrosidad *f*
murky ['mərki] *adj* -kier; -est : oscuro,
tenebroso
murmur¹ ['mərmər] *vi* 1 DRONE : murmurar 2 GRUMBLE : refunfuñar, regañar, rezongar — *vt* MUMBLE : murmurar
murmur² *n* 1 COMPLAINT : queja *f* 2
DRONE : murmullo *m*, rumor *m*
muscle¹ ['mʌsəl] *vi* -cled; -cling : meterse ⟨to muscle in on : meterse por la
fuerza en, entrometerse en⟩
muscle² *n* 1 : músculo *m* 2 STRENGTH
: fuerza *f*
muscular ['mʌskjələr] *adj* 1 : muscular
⟨muscular tissue : tejido muscular⟩ 2
BRAWNY : musculoso
muscular dystrophy *n* : distrofia *f* muscular
musculature ['mʌskjələ̩tʃʊr, -tʃər] *n*
: musculatura *f*
muse¹ ['mjuːz] *vi* mused; musing PON-
DER, REFLECT : cavilar, meditar, reflexionar
muse² *n* : musa *f*
museum [mjʊ'ziːəm] *n* : museo *m*
mush ['mʌʃ] *n* 1 : gachas *fpl* (de maíz)
2 SENTIMENTALITY : sensiblería *f*
mushroom¹ ['mʌʃ̩ruːm, -̩rʊm] *vi* GROW,
MULTIPLY : crecer rápidamente, multiplicarse
mushroom² *n* : hongo *m*, champiñón *m*,
seta *f*
mushy ['mʌʃi] *adj* mushier; -est 1 SOFT
: blando 2 MAWKISH : sensiblero
music ['mjuːzık] *n* : música *f*
musical¹ ['mjuːzıkəl] *adj* : musical, de
música — **musically** *adv*
musical² *n* : comedia *f* musical
music box *n* : cajita *f* de música
musician [mjʊ'zıʃən] *n* : músico *m*, -ca
f
musk ['mʌsk] *n* : almizcle *m*
musket ['mʌskət] *n* : mosquete *m*
musketeer [̩mʌskə'tır] *n* : mosquetero
m
muskrat ['mʌsk̩ræt] *n*, *pl* -rat *or* -rats
: rata *f* almizclera
Muslim¹ ['mʌzləm, 'mʊs-, 'mʊz-] *adj*
: musulmán
Muslim² *n* : musulmán *m*, -mana *f*
muslin ['mʌzlın] *n* : muselina *f*
muss¹ ['mʌs] *vt* : desordenar, despeinar
(el pelo)

muss² *n* : desorden *m*
mussel ['mʌsəl] *n* : mejillón *m*
must¹ ['mʌst] *v aux* 1 (*expressing obligation or necessity*) : deber, tener que
⟨you must stop : debes parar⟩ ⟨we
must obey : tenemos que obedecer⟩ 2
(*expressing probability*) : deber (de),
haber de ⟨you must be tired : debes de
estar cansado⟩ ⟨it must be late : ha de
ser tarde⟩
must² *n* : necesidad *f* ⟨exercise is a must
: el ejercicio es imprescindible⟩
mustache ['mʌ̩stæʃ, mʌ'stæʃ] *n* : bigote
m, bigotes *mpl*
mustang ['mʌ̩stæŋ] *n* : mustang *m*
mustard ['mʌstərd] *n* : mostaza *f*
muster¹ ['mʌstər] *vt* 1 ASSEMBLE : reunir 2 **to muster up** : armarse de, cobrar (valor, fuerzas, etc.)
muster² *n* 1 INSPECTION : revista *f* (de
tropas) ⟨it didn't pass muster : no re-
sistió un examen minucioso⟩ 2 COL-
LECTION : colección *f*
mustiness ['mʌstinəs] *n* : lo mohoso
musty ['mʌsti] *adj* mustier; -est : mohoso, que huele a moho, que huele a
encerrado
mutant¹ ['mjuːtənt] *adj* : mutante
mutant² *n* : mutante *m*
mutate ['mjuː̩teɪt] *vi* -tated; -tating 1
: mutar (genéticamente) 2 CHANGE
: transformarse
mutation [mjuː'teɪʃən] *n* : mutación *f*
(genética)
mute¹ ['mjuːt] *vt* muted; muting MUF-
FLE : amortiguar, ponerle sordina a (un
instrumento musical)
mute² *adj* muter; mutest : mudo —
mutely *adv*
mute³ *n* 1 : mudo *m*, -da *f* (persona) 2
: sordina *f* (para un instrumento musical)
mutilate ['mjuːtə̩leɪt] *vt* -lated; -lating
: mutilar
mutilation [̩mjuːtə'leɪʃən] *n* : mutilación
f
mutineer [̩mjuːtən'ır] *n* : amotinado *m*,
-da *f*
mutinous ['mjuːtənəs] *adj* : amotinado
mutiny¹ ['mjuːtəni] *vi* -nied; -nying
: amotinarse
mutiny² *n*, *pl* -nies : amotinamiento *m*,
motín *m*
mutt ['mʌt] *n* MONGREL : perro *m* mestizo, perro *m* corriente *Mex*
mutter ['mʌtər] *vi* 1 MUMBLE : mascullar, hablar entre dientes, murmurar
2 GRUMBLE : refunfuñar, regañar, rezongar
mutton ['mʌtən] *n* : carne *f* de carnero
mutual ['mjuːtʃʊəl] *adj* 1 : mutuo ⟨mu-
tual respect : respeto mutuo⟩ 2 COM-
MON : común ⟨a mutual friend : un
amigo común⟩
mutually ['mjuːtʃʊəli, -tʃəli] *adv* 1 : mutuamente ⟨mutually beneficial : mutuamente beneficioso⟩ 2 JOINTLY
: conjuntamente

muzzle¹ ['mʌzəl] *vt* **-zled; -zling** : ponerle un bozal a (un animal), amordazar

muzzle² *n* **1** SNOUT : hocico *m* **2** : bozal *m* (para un perro, etc.) **3** : boca *f* (de un arma de fuego)

my¹ ['maɪ] *adj* : mi ⟨my parents : mis padres⟩

my² *interj* : ¡caramba!, ¡Dios mío!

myopia [maɪ'o:piə] *n* : miopía *f*

myopic [maɪ'o:pɪk, -'ɑ-] *adj* : miope

myriad¹ ['mɪriəd] *adj* INNUMERABLE : innumerable

myriad² *n* : miríada *f*

myrrh ['mər] *n* : mirra *f*

myrtle ['mərtəl] *n* : mirto *m*, arrayán *m*

myself [maɪ'sɛlf] *pron* **1** (*used reflexively*) : me ⟨I washed myself : me lavé⟩ **2** (*used for emphasis*) : yo mismo, yo misma ⟨I did it myself : lo hice yo mismo⟩

mysterious [mɪ'stɪriəs] *adj* : misterioso — **mysteriously** *adv*

mysteriousness [mɪ'stɪriəsnəs] *n* : lo misterioso

mystery ['mɪstəri] *n, pl* **-teries** : misterio *m*

mystic¹ ['mɪstɪk] *adj* : místico

mystic² *n* : místico *m*, -ca *f*

mystical ['mɪstɪkəl] *adj* : místico — **mystically** *adv*

mysticism ['mɪstə,sɪzəm] *n* : misticismo *m*

mystify ['mɪstə,faɪ] *vt* **-fied; -fying** : dejar perplejo, confundir

mystique [mɪ'sti:k] *n* : aura *f* de misterio *m*

myth ['mɪθ] *n* : mito *m*

mythic ['mɪθɪk] *adj* : mítico

mythical ['mɪθɪkəl] *adj* : mítico

mythological [,mɪθə'lɑdʒɪkəl] *adj* : mitológico

mythology [mɪ'θɑlədʒi] *n, pl* **-gies** : mitología *f*

N

n ['ɛn] *n, pl* **n's** *or* **ns** ['ɛnz] : decimocuarta letra del alfabeto inglés

nab ['næb] *vt* **nabbed; nabbing** : prender, pillar *fam*, pescar *fam*

nadir ['neɪdər, 'neɪ,dɪr] *n* : nadir *m*, punto *m* más bajo

nag¹ ['næg] *v* **nagged; nagging** *vi* **1** COMPLAIN : quejarse, rezongar **2 to nag at** HASSLE : molestar, darle (la) lata (a alguien) — *vt* **1** PESTER : molestar, fastidiar **2** SCOLD : regañar, estarle encima a *fam*

nag² *n* **1** GRUMBLER : gruñón *m*, -ñona *f* **2** HORSE : jamelgo *m*

naiad ['neɪəd, 'naɪ-, -,æd] *n, pl* **-iads** *or* **-iades** [-ə,di:z] : náyade *f*

nail¹ ['neɪl] *vt* : clavar, sujetar con clavos

nail² *n* **1** FINGERNAIL : uña *f* ⟨nail file : lima (de uñas)⟩ ⟨nail polish : laca de uñas⟩ **2** : clavo *m* ⟨to hit the nail on the head : dar en el clavo⟩

naive *or* **naïve** [nɑ'i:v] *adj* **-iver; -est 1** INGENUOUS : ingenuo, cándido **2** GULLIBLE : crédulo

naively [nɑ'i:vli] *adv* : ingenuamente

naïveté [,nɑ,i:və'teɪ, nɑ'i:və,-] *n* : ingenuidad *f*

naked ['neɪkəd] *adj* **1** UNCLOTHED : desnudo **2** UNCOVERED : desenvainado (dícese de una espada), pelado (dícese de los árboles), expuesto al aire (dícese de una llama) **3** OBVIOUS, PLAIN : manifiesto, puro, desnudo ⟨the naked truth : la pura verdad⟩ **4 to the naked eye** : a simple vista

nakedly ['neɪkədli] *adv* : manifiestamente

nakedness ['neɪkədnəs] *n* : desnudez *f*

name¹ ['neɪm] *vt* **named; naming 1** CALL : llamar, bautizar, ponerle nombre a **2** MENTION : mentar, mencionar, dar el nombre de ⟨they have named a suspect : han dado el nombre de un sospechoso⟩ **3** APPOINT : nombrar **4 to name a price** : fijar un precio

name² *adj* **1** KNOWN : de nombre ⟨name brand : marca conocida⟩ **2** PROMINENT : de renombre, de prestigio

name³ *n* **1** : nombre *m* ⟨what is your name? : ¿cómo se llama?⟩ **2** SURNAME : apellido *m* **3** EPITHET : epíteto *m* ⟨to call somebody names : llamar a alguien de todo⟩ **4** REPUTATION : fama *f*, reputación *f* ⟨to make a name for oneself : darse a conocer, hacerse famoso⟩

nameless ['neɪmləs] *adj* **1** ANONYMOUS : anónimo **2** INDESCRIBABLE : indecible, indescriptible

namelessly ['neɪmləsli] *adv* : anónimamente

namely ['neɪmli] *adv* : a saber

namesake ['neɪm,seɪk] *n* : tocayo *m*, -ya *f*; homónimo *m*, -ma *f*

Namibian [nə'mɪbiən] *n* : namibio *m*, -bia *f* — **Namibian** *adj*

nanny ['næni] *n, pl* **nannies** : niñera *f*; nana *f* *CA, Col, Mex, Ven*

nap¹ ['næp] *vi* **napped; napping 1** : dormir, dormir la siesta **2 to be caught napping** : estar desprevenido

nap² *n* **1** SLEEP : siesta *f* ⟨to take a nap : echarse una siesta⟩ **2** FUZZ, PILE : pelo *m*, pelusa *f* (de telas)

nape ['neɪp, 'næp] *n* : nuca *f*, cerviz *f*, cogote *m*

naphtha ['næfθə] *n* : nafta *f*

napkin ['næpkən] *n* : servilleta *f*

narcissism ['nɑrsə,sɪzəm] *n* : narcisismo *m*

narcissist ['nɑrsəsɪst] *n* : narcisista *mf*

narcissistic [,nɑrsə'sɪstɪk] *adj* : narcisista

narcissus [nɑr'sɪsəs] *n, pl* **-cissus** *or*

-cissuses *or* **-cissi** [-'sɪˌsaɪ, -ˌsiː] : narciso *m*
narcotic¹ [nɑr'kɑṭɪk] *adj* : narcótico
narcotic² *n* : narcótico *m*, estupefaciente *m*
narrate ['nærˌeɪt] *vt* **-rated; -rating** : narrar, relatar
narration [næ'reɪʃən] *n* : narración *f*
narrative¹ ['nærəṭɪv] *adj* : narrativo
narrative² *n* : narración *f*, narrativa *f*, relato *m*
narrator ['nærˌeɪṭər] *n* : narrador *m*, -dora *f*
narrow¹ ['nærˌoː] *vi* : estrecharse, angostarse ⟨the river narrowed : el río se estrechó⟩ — *vt* **1** : estrechar, angostar **2** LIMIT : restringir, limitar ⟨to narrow the search : limitar la búsqueda⟩
narrow² *adj* **1** : estrecho, angosto **2** LIMITED : estricto, limitado ⟨in the narrowest sense of the word : en el sentido más estricto de la palabra⟩ **3 to have a narrow escape** : escapar por un pelo
narrowly ['næroli] *adv* **1** BARELY : por poco **2** CLOSELY : de cerca
narrow–minded [ˌnæro'maɪndəd] *adj* : de miras estrechas
narrowness ['næronəs] *n* : estrechez *f*
narrows ['næroːz] *npl* STRAIT : estrecho *m*
narwhal ['nɑrˌhwɑl, 'nɑrwəl] *n* : narval *m*
nasal ['neɪzəl] *adj* : nasal, gangoso ⟨a nasal voice : una voz gangosa⟩
nasally ['neɪzəli] *adv* **1** : por la nariz **2** : con voz gangosa
nastily ['næstəli] *adv* : con maldad, cruelmente
nastiness ['næstinəs] *n* : porquería *f*
nasturtium [nə'stərʃəm, næ-] *n* : capuchina *f*
nasty ['næsti] *adj* **-tier; -est 1** FILTHY : sucio, mugriento **2** OBSCENE : obsceno **3** MEAN, SPITEFUL : malo, malicioso **4** UNPLEASANT : desagradable, feo **5** REPUGNANT : asqueroso, repugnante ⟨a nasty smell : un olor asqueroso⟩
natal ['neɪṭəl] *adj* : natal
nation ['neɪʃən] *n* : nación *f*
national¹ ['næʃənəl] *adj* : nacional
national² *n* : ciudadano *m*, -na *f*; nacional *mf*
nationalism ['næʃənəˌlɪzəm] *n* : nacionalismo *m*
nationalist¹ ['næʃənəlɪst] *adj* : nacionalista
nationalist² *n* : nacionalista *mf*
nationalistic [ˌnæʃənə'lɪstɪk] *adj* : nacionalista
nationality [ˌnæʃə'næləṭi] *n, pl* **-ties** : nacionalidad *f*
nationalization [ˌnæʃənələ'zeɪʃən] *n* : nacionalización *f*
nationalize ['næʃənəˌlaɪz] *vt* **-ized; -izing** : nacionalizar
nationally ['næʃənəli] *adv* : a escala nacional, a nivel nacional

nationwide ['neɪʃən'waɪd] *adj* : en toda la nación, por todo el país
native¹ ['neɪṭɪv] *adj* **1** INNATE : innato **2** : natal ⟨her native city : su ciudad natal⟩ **3** INDIGENOUS : indígena, autóctono
native² *n* **1** ABORIGINE : nativo *m*, -va *f*; indígena *mf* **2** : natural *m* ⟨he's a native of Mexico : es natural de México⟩
Native American → **American Indian**
nativity [nə'tɪvəṭi, neɪ-] *n, pl* **-ties 1** BIRTH : navidad *f* **2 the Nativity** : la Natividad, la Navidad
natty ['næṭi] *adj* **-tier; -est** : elegante, garboso
natural¹ ['nætʃərəl] *adj* **1** : natural, de la naturaleza ⟨natural woodlands : bosques naturales⟩ ⟨natural childbirth : parto natural⟩ **2** INNATE : innato, natural **3** UNAFFECTED : natural, sin afectación **4** LIFELIKE : natural, vivo
natural² *n* **to be a natural** : tener un talento innato (para algo)
natural gas *n* : gas *m* natural
natural history *n* : historia *f* natural
naturalism ['nætʃərəˌlɪzəm] *n* : naturalismo *m*
naturalist ['nætʃərəlɪst] *n* : naturalista *mf* — **naturalist** *adj*
naturalistic [ˌnætʃərə'lɪstɪk] *adj* : naturalista
naturalization [ˌnætʃərələ'zeɪʃən] *n* : naturalización *f*
naturalize ['nætʃərəˌlaɪz] *vt* **-ized; -izing** : naturalizar
naturally ['nætʃərəli] *adv* **1** INHERENTLY : naturalmente, intrínsecamente **2** UNAFFECTEDLY : de manera natural **3** OF COURSE : por supuesto, naturalmente
naturalness ['nætʃərəlnəs] *n* : naturalidad *f*
natural science *n* : ciencias *fpl* naturales
nature ['neɪtʃər] *n* **1** : naturaleza *f* ⟨the laws of nature : las leyes de la naturaleza⟩ **2** KIND, SORT : índole *f*, clase *f* ⟨things of this nature : cosas de esta índole⟩ **3** DISPOSITION : carácter *m*, natural *m*, naturaleza *f* ⟨it is his nature to be friendly : es de natural simpático⟩ ⟨human nature : la naturaleza humana⟩
naught ['nɔt] *n* **1** : nada *f* ⟨to come to naught : reducirse a nada, fracasar⟩ **2** ZERO : cero *m*
naughtily ['nɔṭəli] *adv* : traviesamente, con malicia
naughtiness ['nɔṭinəs] *n* : mala conducta *f*, travesuras *fpl*, malicia *f*
naughty ['nɔṭi] *adj* **-tier; -est 1** MISCHIEVOUS : travieso, pícaro **2** RISQUÉ : picante, subido de tono
nausea ['nɔziə, 'nɔʃə] *n* **1** SICKNESS : náuseas *fpl* **2** DISGUST : asco *m*
nauseate ['nɔziˌeɪt, -ʒɪ-, -si-, -ʃi-] *vt* **-ated; -ating 1** SICKEN : darle náuseas (a alguien) **2** DISGUST : asquear, darle asco (a alguien)

nauseating *adj* : nauseabundo, repugnante

nauseatingly [ˈnɔziˌeɪtɪŋli, -ʒi-, -si-, -ʃi-] *adv* : hasta el punto de dar asco ⟨nauseatingly sweet : tan dulce que da asco⟩

nauseous [ˈnɔʃəs, -ziəs] *adj* **1** SICK : mareado, con náuseas **2** SICKENING : nauseabundo

nautical [ˈnɔtɪkəl] *adj* : náutico

nautilus [ˈnɔtələs] *n, pl* **-luses** *or* **-li** [-ˌlaɪ, -ˌliː] : nautilo *m*

Navajo [ˈnævəˌhoː, ˈnɑ-] *n* : navajo *m*, -ja *f* — **Navajo** *adj*

naval [ˈneɪvəl] *adj* : naval

nave [ˈneɪv] *n* : nave *f*

navel [ˈneɪvəl] *n* : ombligo *m*

navigability [ˌnævɪgəˈbɪləti] *n* : navegabilidad *f*

navigable [ˈnævɪgəbəl] *adj* : navegable

navigate [ˈnævəˌgeɪt] *v* **-gated; -gating** *vi* : navegar — *vt* **1** STEER : gobernar (un barco), pilotar (un avión) **2** : navegar por (un río, etc.)

navigation [ˌnævəˈgeɪʃən] *n* : navegación *f*

navigator [ˈnævəˌgeɪtər] *n* : navegante *mf*

navy [ˈneɪvi] *n, pl* **-vies 1** FLEET : flota *f* **2** : marina *f* de guerra, armada *f* ⟨the United States Navy : la armada de los Estados Unidos⟩ **3** *or* **navy blue** : azul *m* marino

nay[1] [ˈneɪ] *adv* : no

nay[2] *n* : no *m*, voto *m* en contra

Nazi [ˈnɑtsi, ˈnæt-] *n* : nazi *mf*

Nazism [ˈnɑtˌsɪzəm, ˈnæt-] *or* **Naziism** [ˈnɑtsiˌɪzəm, ˈnæt-] *n* : nazismo *m*

Neanderthal man [niˈændərˌθɑl, -ˌtɑl] *n* : hombre *m* de Neanderthal

near[1] [ˈnɪr] *vt* **1** : acercarse a ⟨the ship is nearing port : el barco se está acercando al puerto⟩ **2** : estar a punto de ⟨she is nearing graduation : está a punto de graduarse⟩

near[2] *adv* **1** CLOSE : cerca ⟨my family lives quite near : mi familia vive muy cerca⟩ **2** NEARLY : casi ⟨I came near to finishing : casi terminé⟩

near[3] *adj* **1** CLOSE : cercano, próximo **2** SIMILAR : parecido, semejante

near[4] *prep* : cerca de

nearby[1] [ˈnɪrˈbaɪ, ˈnɪrˌbaɪ] *adv* : cerca

nearby[2] *adj* : cercano

nearly [ˈnɪrli] *adv* **1** ALMOST : casi ⟨nearly asleep : casi dormido⟩ **2** not nearly : ni con mucho, ni mucho menos ⟨it was not nearly so bad as I had expected : no fue ni con mucho tan malo como esperaba⟩

nearness [ˈnɪrnəs] *n* : proximidad *f*

nearsighted [ˈnɪrˌsaɪtəd] *adj* : miope, corto de vista

nearsightedly [ˈnɪrˌsaɪtədli] *adv* : con miopía

nearsightedness [ˈnɪrˌsaɪtədnəs] *n* : miopía *f*

neat [ˈniːt] *adj* **1** CLEAN, ORDERLY : ordenado, pulcro, limpio **2** UNDILUTED : solo, sin diluir **3** SIMPLE, TASTEFUL : sencillo y de buen gusto **4** CLEVER : hábil, ingenioso ⟨a neat trick : un truco ingenioso⟩

neatly [ˈniːtli] *adv* **1** TIDILY : ordenadamente **2** CLEVERLY : ingeniosamente

neatness [ˈniːtnəs] *n* : pulcritud *f*, limpieza *f*, orden *m*

nebula [ˈnɛbjʊlə] *n, pl* **-lae** [-ˌliː, -ˌlaɪ] : nebulosa *f*

nebulous [ˈnɛbjʊləs] *adj* : nebuloso, vago

necessarily [ˌnɛsəˈsɛrəli] *adv* : necesariamente, forzosamente

necessary[1] [ˈnɛsəˌsɛri] *adj* **1** INEVITABLE : inevitable **2** COMPULSORY : necesario, obligatorio **3** ESSENTIAL : imprescindible, preciso, necesario

necessary[2] *n, pl* **-saries** : lo esencial, lo necesario

necessitate [nɪˈsɛsəˌteɪt] *vt* **-tated; -tating** : necesitar, requerir

necessity [nɪˈsɛsəti] *n, pl* **-ties 1** NEED : necesidad *f* **2** REQUIREMENT : requisito *m* indispensable **3** POVERTY : indigencia *f*, necesidad *f* **4** INEVITABILITY : inevitabilidad *f*

neck[1] [ˈnɛk] *vi* : besuquearse

neck[2] *n* **1** : cuello *m* (de una persona), pescuezo *m* (de un animal) **2** COLLAR : cuello *m* **3** : cuello *m* (de una botella), mástil *m* (de una guitarra)

neckerchief [ˈnɛkərtʃəf, -ˌtʃiːf] *n, pl* **-chiefs** [-tʃəfs, -ˌtʃiːfs] : pañuelo *m* (para el cuello), mascada *f Mex*

necklace [ˈnɛkləs] *n* : collar *m*

neckline [ˈnɛkˌlaɪn] *n* : escote *m*

necktie [ˈnɛkˌtaɪ] *n* : corbata *f*

nectar [ˈnɛktər] *n* : néctar *m*

nectarine [ˌnɛktəˈriːn] *n* : nectarina *f*

née *or* **nee** [ˈneɪ] *adj* : de soltera ⟨Mrs. Smith, née Whitman : la señora Smith, de soltera Whitman⟩

need[1] [ˈniːd] *vt* **1** : necesitar ⟨I need your help : necesito su ayuda⟩ ⟨I need money : me falta dinero⟩ **2** REQUIRE : requerir, exigir ⟨that job needs patience : ese trabajo exige paciencia⟩ **3** to need to** : tener que ⟨he needs to study : tiene que estudiar⟩ ⟨they need to be scolded : hay que reprenderlos⟩ — *v aux* **1** MUST : tener que, deber ⟨need you shout? : ¿tienes que gritar?⟩ **2** to be needed** : hacer falta ⟨you needn't worry : no hace falta que te preocupes, no hay por qué preocuparse⟩

need[2] *n* **1** NECESSITY : necesidad *f* ⟨in case of need : en caso de necesidad⟩ **2** LACK : falta *f* ⟨the need for better training : la falta de mejor capacitación⟩ ⟨to be in need : necesitar⟩ **3** POVERTY : necesidad *f*, indigencia *f* **4** needs *npl* : requisitos *mpl*, carencias *fpl*

needful [ˈniːdfəl] *adj* : necesario

needle[1] [ˈniːdəl] *vt* **-dled; -dling** : pinchar

needle[2] *n* **1** : aguja *f* ⟨to thread a needle : enhebrar una aguja⟩ ⟨knitting

needle : aguja de tejer〉 **2** POINTER : aguja *f*, indicador *m*

needlepoint ['ni:dəl,pɔint] *n* **1** LACE : encaje *m* de mano **2** EMBROIDERY : bordado *m* en cañamazo

needless ['ni:dləs] *adj* : innecesario

needlessly ['ni:dləsli] *adv* : sin ninguna necesidad, innecesariamente

needlework ['ni:dəl,wərk] *n* : bordado *m*

needn't ['ni:dənt] (*contraction of* **need not**) → **need**

needy¹ ['ni:di] *adj* **needier; -est** : necesitado

needy² *n* **the needy** : los necesitados *mpl*

nefarious [nɪ'færiəs] *adj* : nefario, nefando, infame

negate [nɪ'geɪt] *vt* **-gated; -gating 1** DENY : negar **2** NULLIFY : invalidar, anular

negation [nɪ'geɪʃən] *n* : negación *f*

negative¹ ['nɛgətɪv] *adj* : negativo

negative² *n* **1** : negación *f* (en lingüística) **2** : negativa *f* 〈to answer in the negative : contestar con una negativa〉 **3** : término *m* negativo (en matemáticas) **4** : negativo *m*, imagen *f* en negativo (en fotografía)

negatively ['nɛgətɪvli] *adv* : negativamente

neglect¹ [nɪ'glɛkt] *vt* **1** : desatender, descuidar 〈to neglect one's health : descuidar la salud〉 **2** : no cumplir con, faltar a 〈to neglect one's obligations : faltar uno a sus obligaciones〉 〈he neglected to tell me : omitió decírmelo〉

neglect² *n* **1** : negligencia *f*, descuido *m*, incumplimiento *m* 〈through neglect : por negligencia〉 〈neglect of duty : incumplimiento del deber〉 **2 in a state of neglect** : abandonado, descuidado

neglectful [nɪ'glɛktfəl] *adj* : descuidado *m*

negligee [,nɛglə'ʒeɪ] *n* : negligé *m*

negligence ['nɛglɪdʒənts] *n* : descuido *m*, negligencia *f*

negligent ['nɛglɪdʒənt] *adj* : negligente, descuidado — **negligently** *adv*

negligible ['nɛglɪdʒəbəl] *adj* : insignificante, despreciable

negotiable [nɪ'goːʃəbəl, -ʃiə-] *adj* : negociable

negotiate [nɪ'goːʃi,eɪt] *v* **-ated; -ating** *vi* : negociar — *vt* **1** : negociar, gestionar 〈to negotiate a treaty : negociar un trato〉 **2** : salvar, franquear 〈they negotiated the obstacles : salvaron los obstáculos〉 〈to negotiate a turn : tomar una curva〉

negotiation [nɪ,goːʃi'eɪʃən, -si'eɪ-] *n* : negociación *f*

negotiator [nɪ'goːʃi,eɪtər, -si,eɪ-] *n* : negociador *m*, -dora *f*

Negro ['niː,groː] *n, pl* **-groes** : negro *m*, -gra *f*

neigh¹ ['neɪ] *vi* : relinchar

neigh² *n* : relincho *m*

neighbor¹ ['neɪbər] *vt* : ser vecino de, estar junto a 〈her house neighbors mine : su casa está junto a la mía〉 — *vi* : estar cercano, lindar, colindar 〈her land neighbors on mine : sus tierras lindan con las mías〉

neighbor² *n* **1** : vecino *m*, -na *f* **2 love thy neighbor** : ama a tu prójimo

neighborhood ['neɪbər,hʊd] *n* **1** : barrio *m*, vecindad *f*, vecindario *m* **2 in the neighborhood of** : alrededor de, cerca de

neighborly ['neɪbərli] *adv* : amable, de buena vecindad

neither¹ ['niːðər, 'naɪ-] *adj* : ninguno (de los dos)

neither² *conj* **1** : ni 〈neither asleep nor awake : ni dormido ni despierto〉 **2** NOR : ni (tampoco) 〈I'm not asleep—neither am I : no estoy dormido—ni yo tampoco〉

neither³ *pron* : ninguno

nemesis ['nɛməsɪs] *n, pl* **-eses** [-,siːz] **1** RIVAL : rival *mf* **2** RETRIBUTION : justo castigo *m*

Neoclassical [,niːoʊ'klæsɪkəl] *adj* : neoclásico

neologism [ni'alə,dʒɪzəm] *n* : neologismo *m*

neon¹ ['niː,an] *adj* : de neón 〈neon sign : letrero de neón〉

neon² *n* : neón *m*

neophyte ['niːə,faɪt] *n* : neófito *m*, -ta *f*

Nepali [nə'pɔli, -'pɑ-, -'pæ-] *n* : nepalés *m*, -lesa *f* — **Nepali** *adj*

nephew ['nɛ,fjuː, *chiefly British* 'nɛ,vjuː] *n* : sobrino *m*

nepotism ['nɛpə,tɪzəm] *n* : nepotismo *m*

Neptune ['nɛp,tuːn, -,tjuːn] *n* : Neptuno *m*

nerd ['nərd] *n* : ganso *m*, -sa *f*

nerve ['nərv] *n* **1** : nervio *m* **2** COURAGE : coraje *m*, valor *m*, fuerza *f* de la voluntad 〈to lose one's nerve : perder el valor〉 **3** AUDACITY, GALL : atrevimiento *m*, descaro *m* 〈of all the nerve! : ¡qué descaro!〉 **4 nerves** *npl* : nervios *mpl* 〈a fit of nerves : un ataque de nervios〉

nervous ['nərvəs] *adj* **1** : nervioso 〈the nervous system : el sistema nervioso〉 **2** EXCITABLE : nervioso, excitable 〈to get nervous : excitarse, ponerse nervioso〉 **3** FEARFUL : miedoso, temeroso

nervously ['nərvəsli] *adv* : nerviosamente

nervousness ['nərvəsnəs] *n* : nerviosismo *m*, nerviosidad *f*, ansiedad *f*

nervy ['nərvi] *adj* **nervier; -est 1** COURAGEOUS : valiente **2** IMPUDENT : atrevido, descarado, fresco *fam* **3** NERVOUS : nervioso

nest¹ ['nɛst] *vi* : anidar

nest² *n* **1** : nido *m* (de un ave), avispero *m* (de una avispa), madriguera *f* (de un animal) **2** REFUGE : nido *m*, refugio *m* **3** SET : juego *m* 〈a nest of tables : un juego de mesitas〉

nestle ['nɛsəl] *vi* **-tled; -tling** : acurrucarse, arrimarse cómodamente

net¹ ['nɛt] *vt* **netted; netting 1** CATCH : pescar, atrapar con una red **2** CLEAR : ganar neto ⟨they netted $5000 : ganaron $5000 netos⟩ **3** YIELD : producir neto

net² *adj* : neto ⟨net weight : peso neto⟩ ⟨net gain : ganancia neta⟩

net³ *n* : red *f*, malla *f*

nether ['nɛðər] *adj* **1** : inferior, más bajo **2 the nether regions** : el infierno

nettle¹ ['nɛtəl] *vt* **-tled; -tling** : irritar, provocar, molestar

nettle² *n* : ortiga *f*

network ['nɛt,wərk] *n* **1** SYSTEM : red *f* **2** CHAIN : cadena *f* ⟨a network of supermarkets : una cadena de supermercados⟩

neural ['nʊrəl, 'njʊr-] *adj* : neural

neuralgia [nʊ'rældʒə, njʊ-] *n* : neuralgia *f*

neuritis [nʊ'raɪtəs, njʊ-] *n, pl* **-ritides** [-'rɪtə,diːz] *or* **-ritises** : neuritis *f*

neurological [,nʊrə'lɑdʒɪkəl, ,njʊr-] *or* **neurologic** [,nʊrə'lɑdʒɪk, ,njʊr-] *adj* : neurológico

neurologist [nʊ'rɑlədʒɪst, njʊ-] *n* : neurólogo *m*, -ga *f*

neurology [nʊ'rɑlədʒi, njʊ-] *n* : neurología *f*

neurosis [nʊ'roːsɪs, njʊ-] *n, pl* **-roses** [-,siːz] : neurosis *f*

neurotic¹ [nʊ'rɑtɪk, njʊ-] *adj* : neurótico

neurotic² *n* : neurótico *m*, -ca *f*

neuter¹ ['nuːtər, 'njuː-] *vt* : castrar

neuter² *adj* : neutro

neutral¹ ['nuːtrəl, 'njuː-] *adj* **1** IMPARTIAL : neutral, imparcial ⟨to remain neutral : permanecer neutral⟩ **2** : neutro ⟨a neutral color : un color neutro⟩ **3** : neutro (en la química o la electricidad)

neutral² *n* : punto *m* muerto (de un automóvil)

neutrality [nuː'træləti:, njuː-] *n* : neutralidad *f*

neutralization [,nuːtrələ'zeɪʃən, ,njuː-] *n* : neutralización *f*

neutralize ['nuːtrə,laɪz, 'njuː-] *vt* **-ized; -izing** : neutralizar

neutron ['nuː,trɑn, 'njuː-] *n* : neutrón *m*

never ['nɛvər] *adv* **1** : nunca, jamás ⟨he never studies : nunca estudia⟩ **2 never again** : nunca más, nunca jamás **3 never mind** : no importa

nevermore [,nɛvər'mor] *adv* : nunca más

nevertheless [,nɛvərðə'lɛs] *adv* : sin embargo, no obstante

new ['nuː, 'njuː] *adj* **1** : nuevo ⟨a new dress : un vestido nuevo⟩ **2** RECENT : nuevo, reciente ⟨what's new? : ¿qué hay de nuevo?⟩ ⟨a new arrival : un recién llegado⟩ **3** DIFFERENT : nuevo, distinto ⟨this problem is new : este problema es distinto⟩ ⟨new ideas : ideas nuevas⟩ **4 like new** : como nuevo

newborn ['nuː,bɔrn, 'njuː-] *adj* : recién nacido

newcomer ['nuː,kʌmər, 'njuː-] *n* : recién llegado *m*, recién llegada *f*

newfangled ['nuː'fæŋgəld, 'njuː-] *adj* : novedoso

newfound ['nuː'faʊnd, 'njuː-] *adj* : recién descubierto

newly ['nuːli, 'njuː-] *adv* : recién, recientemente

newlywed ['nuːli,wɛd, 'njuː-] *n* : recién casado *m*, -da *f*

new moon *n* : luna *f* nueva

newness ['nuːnəs, 'njuː-] *n* : novedad *f*

news ['nuːz, 'njuːz] *n* : noticias *fpl*

newscast ['nuːz,kæst, 'njuːz-] *n* : noticiero *m*, informativo *m*

newscaster ['nuːz,kæstər, 'njuːz-] *n* : presentador *m*, -dora *f*; locutor *m*, -tora *f*

newsletter ['nuːz,lɛtər, 'njuːz-] *n* : boletín *m* informativo

newsman ['nuːzmən, 'njuːz-, -,mæn] *n, pl* **-men** [-mən, -,mɛn] : periodista *m*, reportero *m*

newspaper ['nuːz,peɪpər, 'njuːz-] *n* : periódico *m*, diario *m*

newspaperman ['nuːz,peɪpər,mæn, 'njuːz-] *n, pl* **-men** [-mən, -,mɛn] **1** REPORTER : periodista *m*, reportero *m* **2** : dueño *m* de un periódico

newsprint ['nuːz,prɪnt, 'njuːz-] *n* : papel *m* de prensa

newsstand ['nuːz,stænd, 'njuːz-] *n* : quiosco *m*, puesto *m* de periódicos

newswoman ['nuːz,wʊmən, 'njuːz-] *n, pl* **-women** [-,wɪmən] : periodista *f*, reportera *f*

newsworthy ['nuːz,wərði, 'njuːz-] *adj* : de interés periodístico

newsy ['nuːzi:, 'njuː-] *adj* **newsier; -est** : lleno de noticias

newt ['nuːt, 'njuːt] *n* : tritón *m*

New Testament *n* : Nuevo Testamento *m*

New Year *n* : Año *m* Nuevo

New Year's Day *n* : día *m* del Año Nuevo

New Yorker [nuː'jɔrkər, njuː-] *n* : neoyorquino *m*, -na *f*

New Zealander [nuː'ziːləndər, njuː-] *n* : neozelandés *m*, -desa *f*

next¹ ['nɛkst] *adv* **1** AFTERWARD : después, luego ⟨what will you do next? : ¿qué harás después?⟩ **2** NOW : después, ahora, entonces ⟨next I will sing a song : ahora voy a cantar una canción⟩ **3** : la próxima vez ⟨when next we meet : la próxima vez que nos encontremos⟩

next² *adj* **1** ADJACENT : contiguo, de al lado **2** COMING : que viene, próximo ⟨next Friday : el viernes que viene⟩ **3** FOLLOWING : siguiente ⟨the next year : el año siguiente⟩

next–door ['nɛkst'dor] *adj* : de al lado

next to¹ *adv* ALMOST : casi, prácticamente ⟨next to impossible : casi imposible⟩

next to² *prep* : junto a, al lado de
nexus ['nɛksəs] *n* : nexo *m*
nib ['nɪb] *n* : plumilla *f*
nibble¹ ['nɪbəl] *v* **-bled; -bling** *vt* : pellizcar, mordisquear, picar — *vi* : picar
nibble² *n* : mordisco *m*
Nicaraguan [ˌnɪkə'rɑgwən] *n* : nicaragüense *mf* — **Nicaraguan** *adj*
nice ['naɪs] *adj* **nicer; nicest 1** REFINED : pulido, refinado **2** SUBTLE : fino, sutil **3** PLEASING : agradable, bueno, lindo ⟨nice weather : buen tiempo⟩ **4** RESPECTABLE : bueno, decente **5 nice and** : bien, muy ⟨nice and hot : bien caliente⟩ ⟨nice and slow : despacito⟩
nicely ['naɪsli] *adv* **1** KINDLY : amablemente **2** POLITELY : con buenos modales **3** ATTRACTIVELY : de buen gusto
niceness ['naɪsnəs] *n* : simpatía *f*, amabilidad *f*
nicety ['naɪsəti] *n, pl* **-ties 1** DETAIL, SUBTLETY : sutileza *f*, detalle *m* **2**
niceties *npl* : lujos *mpl*, detalles *mpl*
niche ['nɪtʃ] *n* **1** RECESS : nicho *m*, hornacina *f* **2** : nicho *m*, hueco *m* ⟨to make a niche for oneself : hacerse un hueco, encontrarse una buena posición⟩
nick¹ ['nɪk] *vt* : cortar, hacer una muesca en
nick² *n* **1** CUT : corte *m*, muesca *f* **2 in the nick of time** : en el momento crítico, justo a tiempo
nickel ['nɪkəl] *n* **1** : níquel *m* **2** : moneda *f* de cinco centavos
nickname¹ ['nɪkˌneɪm] *vt* **-named; -naming** : apodar
nickname² *n* : apodo *m*, mote *m*, sobrenombre *m*
nicotine ['nɪkəˌtiːn] *n* : nicotina *f*
niece ['niːs] *n* : sobrina *f*
Nigerian [naɪ'dʒɪriən] *n* : nigeriano *m*, -na *f* — **Nigerian** *adj*
niggardly ['nɪgərdli] *adj* : mezquino, tacaño
niggling ['nɪgəlɪŋ] *adj* **1** PETTY : insignificante **2** PERSISTENT : constante, persistente ⟨a niggling doubt : una duda constante⟩
nigh¹ ['naɪ] *adv* **1** NEARLY : casi **2 to draw nigh** : acercarse, avecinarse
nigh² *adj* : cercano, próximo
night¹ ['naɪt] *adj* : nocturno, de la noche ⟨the night sky : el cielo nocturno⟩ ⟨night shift : turno de la noche⟩
night² *n* **1** EVENING : noche *f* ⟨at night : de noche⟩ ⟨last night : anoche⟩ ⟨tomorrow night : mañana por la noche⟩ **2** DARKNESS : noche *f*, oscuridad *f* ⟨night fell : cayó la noche⟩
nightclothes ['naɪtˌkloːðz, -ˌkloːz] *npl* : ropa *f* de dormir
nightclub ['naɪtˌklʌb] *n* : cabaret *m*, club *m* nocturno
night crawler ['naɪtˌkrɔlər] *n* EARTHWORM : lombriz *f* (de tierra)
nightfall ['naɪtˌfɔl] *n* : anochecer *m*
nightgown ['naɪtˌgaʊn] *n* : camisón *m* (de noche)

nightingale ['naɪtən̩ˌgeɪl, 'naɪtɪŋ-] *n* : ruiseñor *m*
nightly¹ ['naɪtli] *adv* : cada noche, todas las noches
nightly² *adj* : de todas las noches
nightmare ['naɪtˌmær] *n* : pesadilla *f*
nightmarish ['naɪtˌmærɪʃ] *adj* : de pesadilla
night owl *n* : noctámbulo *m*, -la *f*
nightshade ['naɪtˌʃeɪd] *n* : hierba *f* mora
nightshirt ['naɪtˌʃərt] *n* : camisa *f* de dormir
nightstick ['naɪtˌstɪk] *n* : porra *f*
nighttime ['naɪtˌtaɪm] *n* : noche *f*
nihilism ['naɪəˌlɪzəm] *n* : nihilismo *m*
nil ['nɪl] *n* : nada *f*, cero *m*
nimble ['nɪmbəl] *adj* **-bler; -blest 1** AGILE : ágil **2** CLEVER : hábil, ingenioso
nimbleness ['nɪmbəlnəs] *n* : agilidad *f*
nimbly ['nɪmbli] *adv* : con agilidad, ágilmente
nincompoop ['nɪnkəmˌpuːp, 'nɪŋ-] *n* FOOL : tonto *m*, -ta *f*; bobo *m*, -ba *f*
nine¹ ['naɪn] *adj* **1** : nueve **2 nine times out of ten** : casi siempre
nine² *n* : nueve *m*
nine hundred¹ *adj* : novecientos
nine hundred² *n* : novecientos *m*
ninepins ['naɪnˌpɪnz] *n* : bolos *mpl*
nineteen¹ [naɪn'tiːn] *adj* : diecinueve
nineteen² *n* : diecinueve *m*
nineteenth¹ [naɪn'tiːnθ] *adj* : decimonoveno, decimonono ⟨the nineteenth century : el siglo diecinueve⟩
nineteenth² *n* **1** : decimonoveno *m*, -na *f*; decimonono *m*, -na *f* (en una serie) **2** : diecinueveavo *m*, diecinueveava parte *f*
ninetieth¹ ['naɪntiəθ] *adj* : nonagésimo
ninetieth² *n* **1** : nonagésimo *m*, -ma *f* (en una serie) **2** : noventavo *m*, noventava parte *f*
ninety¹ ['naɪnti] *adj* : noventa
ninety² *n, pl* **-ties** : noventa *m*
ninth¹ ['naɪnθ] *adj* : noveno
ninth² *n* **1** : noveno *m*, -na *f* (en una serie) **2** : noveno *m*, novena parte *f*
ninny ['nɪni] *n, pl* **ninnies** FOOL : tonto *m*, -ta *f*; bobo *m*, -ba *f*
nip¹ ['nɪp] *vt* **nipped; nipping 1** PINCH : pellizcar **2** BITE : morder, mordisquear **3 to nip in the bud** : cortar de raíz
nip² *n* **1** TANG : sabor *m* fuerte **2** PINCH : pellizco *m* **3** NIBBLE : mordisco *m* **4** SWALLOW : trago *m*, traguito *m* **5 there's a nip in the air** : hace fresco
nipple ['nɪpəl] *n* : pezón *m* (de una mujer), tetilla *f* (de un hombre)
nippy ['nɪpi] *adj* **-pier; -est 1** SHARP : fuerte, picante **2** CHILLY : frío ⟨it's nippy today : hoy hace frío⟩
nit ['nɪt] *n* : liendre *f*
nitrate ['naɪˌtreɪt] *n* : nitrato *m*
nitric acid ['naɪtrɪk] *n* : ácido *m* nítrico
nitrite ['naɪˌtraɪt] *n* : nitrito *m*
nitrogen ['naɪtrədʒən] *n* : nitrógeno *m*
nitroglycerin *or* **nitroglycerine** [ˌnaɪtro-'glɪsərən] *n* : nitroglicerina *f*

nitwit ['nɪt,wɪt] *n* : zonzo *m*, -za *f*; bobo *m*, -ba *f*
no¹ ['no:] *adv* : no ⟨are you leaving?— no : ¿te vas?—no⟩ ⟨no less than : no menos de⟩ ⟨to say no : decir que no⟩ ⟨like it or no : quieras o no quieras⟩
no² *adj* **1** : ninguno ⟨it's no trouble : no es ningún problema⟩ ⟨she has no money : no tiene dinero⟩ **2** (*indicating a small amount*) ⟨we'll be there in no time : llegamos dentro de poco, no tardamos nada⟩ **3** (*expressing a negation*) ⟨he's no liar : no es mentiroso⟩
no³ *n, pl* **noes** *or* **nos** ['no:z] **1** DENIAL : no *m* ⟨I won't take no for an answer : no aceptaré un no por respuesta⟩ **2** : vota *f* en contra ⟨the noes have it : se ha rechazado la moción⟩
nobility [no'bɪləti] *n* : nobleza *f*
noble¹ ['no:bəl] *adj* **-bler; -blest 1** ILLUSTRIOUS : noble, glorioso **2** ARISTOCRATIC : noble **3** STATELY : majestuoso, magnífico **4** LOFTY : noble, elevado ⟨noble sentiments : sentimientos elevados⟩
noble² *n* : noble *mf*, aristócrata *mf*
nobleman ['no:bəlmən] *n, pl* **-men** [-mən, -,mɛn] : noble *m*, aristócrata *m*
nobleness ['no:bəlnəs] *n* : nobleza *f*
noblewoman ['no:bəl,wʊmən] *n, pl* **-women** [-,wɪmən] : noble *f*, aristócrata *f*
nobly ['no:bli] *adv* : noblemente
nobody¹ ['no:bədi, -,badi] *n, pl* **-bodies** : don nadie *m* ⟨he's a mere nobody : es un don nadie⟩
nobody² *pron* : nadie
nocturnal [nak'tərnəl] *adj* : nocturno
nocturne ['nak,tərn] *n* : nocturno *m*
nod¹ ['nad] *v* **nodded; nodding** *vi* **1** : saludar con la cabeza, asentir con la cabeza **2 to nod off** : dormirse, quedarse dormido — *vt* : inclinar (la cabeza) ⟨to nod one's head in agreement : asentir con la cabeza⟩
nod² *n* : saludo *m* con la cabeza, señal *m* con la cabeza, señal *m* de asentimiento
node ['no:d] *n* : nudo *m* (de una planta)
nodule ['na,dʒu:l] *n* : nódulo *m*
noel [no'ɛl] *n* **1** CAROL : villancico *m* de Navidad **2 Noel** CHRISTMAS : Navidad *f*
noes → **no³**
noise¹ ['nɔɪz] *vt* **noised; noising** : rumorear, publicar
noise² *n* : ruido *m*
noiseless ['nɔɪzləs] *adj* : silencioso, sin ruido
noiselessly ['nɔɪzləsli] *adv* : silenciosamente
noisemaker ['nɔɪz,meɪkər] *n* : matraca *f*
noisiness ['nɔɪzinəs] *n* : ruido *m*
noisome ['nɔɪsəm] *adj* : maloliente, fétido
noisy ['nɔɪzi] *adj* **noisier; -est** : ruidoso — **noisily** ['nɔɪzəli] *adv*
nomad¹ ['no:,mæd] → **nomadic**

nomad² *n* : nómada *mf*
nomadic [no'mædɪk] *adj* : nómada
nomenclature ['no:mən,kleɪtʃər] *n* : nomenclatura *f*
nominal ['namənəl] *adj* **1** : nominal ⟨the nominal head of his party : el jefe nominal de su partido⟩ **2** TRIFLING : insignificante
nominally ['namənəli] *adv* : sólo de nombre, nominalmente
nominate ['namə,neɪt] *vt* **-nated; -nating 1** PROPOSE : proponer (como candidato), nominar **2** APPOINT : nombrar
nomination [,namə'neɪʃən] *n* **1** PROPOSAL : propuesta *f*, postulación *f* **2** APPOINTMENT : nombramiento *m*
nominative¹ ['namənətɪv] *adj* : nominativo
nominative² *n or* **nominative case** : nominativo *m*
nominee [,namə'ni:] *n* : candidato *m*, -ta *f*
nonaddictive [,nanə'dɪktɪv] *adj* : que no crea dependencia
nonalcoholic [,nan,ælkə'hɔlɪk] *adj* : sin alcohol, no alcohólico
nonaligned [,nanə'laɪnd] *adj* : no alineado
nonbeliever [,nanbə'li:vər] *n* : no creyente *mf*
nonbreakable [,nan'breɪkəbəl] *adj* : irrompible
nonce ['nants] *n* **for the nonce** : por el momento
nonchalance [,nanʃə'lants] *n* : indiferencia *f*, despreocupación *f*
nonchalant [,nanʃə'lant] *adj* : indiferente, despreocupado, impasible
nonchalantly [,nanʃə'lantli] *adv* : con aire despreocupado, con indiferencia
noncombatant [,nankəm'bætənt, -'kam-bə-] *n* : no combatiente *mf*
noncommissioned officer [,nankə-'mɪʃənd] *n* : suboficial *mf*
noncommittal [,nankə'mɪtəl] *adj* : evasivo, que no se compromete
nonconductor [,nankən'dʌktər] *n* : aislante *m*
nonconformist [,nankən'fɔrmɪst] *n* : inconformista *mf*, inconforme *mf*
nonconformity [,nankən'fɔrməti] *n* : inconformidad *f*, no conformidad *f*
noncontagious [,nankən'teɪdʒəs] *adj* : no contagioso
nondenominational [,nandɪ,namə-'neɪʃənəl] *adj* : no sectario
nondescript [,nandɪ'skrɪpt] *adj* : anodino, soso
nondiscriminatory [,nandɪ'skrɪmənə-,tori] *adj* : no discriminatorio
nondrinker [,nan'drɪŋkər] *n* : abstemio *m*, -mia *f*
none¹ ['nʌn] *adv* : de ninguna manera, de ningún modo, nada ⟨he was none too happy : no se sintió nada contento⟩ ⟨I'm none the worse for it : no estoy peor por ello⟩ ⟨none too soon : a buena hora⟩

545 none · northwest

none² *pron* : ninguno, ninguna
nonentity [ˌnɑn'ɛntəti] *n, pl* **-ties** : persona *f* insignificante, nulidad *f*
nonessential [ˌnɑnɪ'sɛntʃəl] *adj* : secundario, no esencial
nonessentials [ˌnɑnɪ'sɛntʃəlz] *npl* : cosas *fpl* secundarias, cosas *fpl* accesorias
nonetheless [ˌnʌnðə'lɛs] *adv* : sin embargo, no obstante
nonexistence [ˌnɑnɪg'zɪstənts] *n* : inexistencia *f*
nonexistent [ˌnɑnɪg'zɪstənt] *adj* : inexistente
nonfat [ˌnɑn'fæt] *adj* : sin grasa
nonfattening [ˌnɑn'fætənɪŋ] *adj* : que no engorda
nonfiction [ˌnɑn'fɪkʃən] *n* : no ficción *f*
nonflammable [ˌnɑn'flæməbəl] *adj* : no inflamable
nonintervention [ˌnɑnˌɪntər'vɛntʃən] *n* : no intervención *f*
nonmalignant [ˌnɑnmə'lɪgnənt] *adj* : no maligno, benigno
nonnegotiable [ˌnɑnnɪ'goːʃəbəl, -ʃiə-] *adj* : no negociable
nonpareil¹ [ˌnɑnpə'rɛl] *adj* : sin parangón, sin par
nonpareil² *n* : persona *f* sin igual, cosa *f* sin par
nonpartisan [ˌnɑn'pɑrtəzən, -sən] *adj* : imparcial
nonpaying [ˌnɑn'peɪɪŋ] *adj* : que no paga
nonpayment [ˌnɑn'peɪmənt] *n* : impago *m*, falta *f* de pago
nonperson [ˌnɑn'pərsən] *n* : persona *f* sin derechos
nonplus [ˌnɑn'plʌs] *vt* **-plussed; -plussing** : confundir, desconcertar, dejar perplejo
nonprescription [ˌnɑnprɪ'skrɪpʃən] *adj* : disponible sin receta del médico
nonproductive [ˌnɑnprə'dʌktɪv] *adj* : improductivo
nonprofit [ˌnɑn'prɑfət] *adj* : sin fines lucrativos
nonproliferation [ˌnɑnprəˌlɪfə'reɪʃən] *adj* : no proliferación
nonresident [ˌnɑn'rɛzədənt, -ˌdɛnt] *n* : no residente *mf*
nonscheduled [ˌnɑn'skɛˌdʒuːld] *adj* : no programado, no regular
nonsectarian [ˌnɑnˌsɛk'tæriən] *adj* : no sectario
nonsense ['nɑnˌsɛnts, 'nɑntsənts] *n* : tonterías *fpl*, disparates *mpl*
nonsensical [nɑn'sɛntsɪkəl] *adj* ABSURD : absurdo, disparatado — **nonsensically** [-kli] *adv*
nonsmoker [ˌnɑn'smoːkər] *n* : no fumador *m*, -dora *f*; persona *f* que no fuma
nonstandard [ˌnɑn'stændərd] *adj* : no regular, no estándar
nonstick [ˌnɑn'stɪk] *adj* : antiadherente
nonstop¹ [ˌnɑn'stɑp] *adv* : sin parar ⟨he talked nonstop : habló sin parar⟩
nonstop² *adj* : directo, sin escalas ⟨nonstop flight : vuelo directo⟩

nonsupport [ˌnɑnsə'pɔrt] *n* : falta *f* de manutención
nontaxable [ˌnɑn'tæksəbəl] *adj* : exento de impuestos
nontoxic [ˌnɑn'tɑksɪk] *adj* : no tóxico
nonviolence [ˌnɑn'vaɪlənts, -'vaɪə-] *n* : no violencia *f*
nonviolent [ˌnɑn'vaɪlənt, -'vaɪə-] *adj* : pacífico, no violento
noodle ['nuːdəl] *n* : fideo *m*, tallarín *m*
nook ['nʊk] *n* : rincón *m*, recoveco *m*, escondrijo *m* ⟨in every nook and cranny : en todos los rincones⟩
noon ['nuːn] *n* : mediodía *m*
noonday ['nuːnˌdeɪ] *n* : mediodía *m* ⟨the noonday sun : el sol de mediodía⟩
no one *pron* NOBODY : nadie
noontime ['nuːnˌtaɪm] *n* : mediodía *m*
noose ['nuːs] *n* **1** LASSO : lazo *m* **2** hangman's noose : dogal *m*, soga *f*
nor ['nɔr] *conj* : ni ⟨neither good nor bad : ni bueno ni malo⟩ ⟨nor I! : ¡ni yo tampoco!⟩
Nordic ['nɔrdɪk] *adj* : nórdico
norm ['nɔrm] *n* **1** STANDARD : norma *f*, modelo *m* **2** CUSTOM, RULE : regla *f* general, lo normal
normal ['nɔrməl] *adj* : normal — **normally** *adv*
normalcy ['nɔrməlsi] *n* : normalidad *f*
normality [nɔr'mæləti] *n* : normalidad *f*
normalize ['nɔrməˌlaɪz] *vt* : normalizar
Norse ['nɔrs] *adj* : nórdico
north¹ ['nɔrθ] *adv* : al norte
north² *adj* : norte, del norte ⟨the north coast : la costa del norte⟩
north³ *n* **1** : norte *m* **2** the North : el Norte *m*
North American *n* : norteamericano *m*, -na *f* — **North American** *adj*
northbound ['nɔrθˌbaʊnd] *adv* : con rumbo al norte
northeast¹ [nɔrθ'iːst] *adv* : hacia el nordeste
northeast² *adj* : nordeste, del nordeste
northeast³ *n* : nordeste *m*, noreste *m*
northeasterly¹ [nɔrθ'iːstərli] *adv* : hacia el nordeste
northeasterly² *adj* : nordeste, del nordeste
northeastern [nɔrθ'iːstərn] *adj* : nordeste, del nordeste
northerly¹ ['nɔrðərli] *adv* : hacia el norte
northerly² *adj* : del norte ⟨a northerly wind : un viento del norte⟩
northern ['nɔrðərn] *adj* : norte, norteño, septentrional
Northerner ['nɔrðərnər] *n* : norteño *m*, -ña *f*
northern lights → aurora borealis
North Pole : Polo *m* Norte
North Star *n* : estrella *f* polar
northward ['nɔrθwərd] *adv & adj* : hacia el norte
northwest¹ [nɔrθ'wɛst] *adv* : hacia el noroeste
northwest² *adj* : del noroeste
northwest³ *n* : noroeste *m*

northwesterly[1] [nɔrθ'wɛstərli] *adv* : hacia el noroeste

northwesterly[2] *adj* : del noroeste

northwestern [nɔrθ'wɛstərn] *adj* : noroeste, del noroeste

Norwegian [nɔr'wi:ʤən] *n* **1** : noruego *m*, -ga *f* **2** : noruego *m* (idioma) — **Norwegian** *adj*

nose[1] ['no:z] *v* **nosed; nosing** *vt* **1** SMELL : olfatear **2** : empujar con el hocico ⟨the dog nosed open the bag : el perro abrió el saco con el hocico⟩ **3** EDGE, MOVE : mover poco a poco — *vi* **1** PRY : entrometerse, meter las narices **2** EDGE : avanzar poco a poco

nose[2] *n* **1** : nariz *f* (de una persona), hocico *m* (de un animal) ⟨to blow one's nose : sonarse las narices⟩ **2** SMELL : olfato *m*, sentido *m* del olfato **3** FRONT : parte *f* delantera, nariz *f* (de un avión), proa *f* (de un barco) **4 to follow one's nose** : dejarse guiar por el instinto

nosebleed ['no:z,bli:d] *n* : hemorragia *f* nasal

nosedive ['no:z,daɪv] *n* **1** : descenso *m* en picada (de un avión) **2** : caída *f* súbita (de precios, etc.)

nose–dive ['no:z,daɪv] *vi* : descender en picada, caer en picada

nostalgia [na'stælʤə, nə-] *n* : nostalgia *f*

nostalgic [na'stælʤɪk, nə-] *adj* : nostálgico

nostril ['nastrəl] *n* : ventana *f* de la nariz

nostrum ['nastrəm] *n* : panacea *f*

nosy *or* **nosey** ['no:zi] *adj* **nosier; -est** : entrometido

not ['nat] *adv* **1** (*used to form a negative*) : no ⟨she is not tired : no está cansada⟩ ⟨not to say something would be wrong : no decir nada sería injusto⟩ **2** (*used to replace a negative clause*) : no ⟨are we going or not? : ¿vamos a ir o no?⟩ ⟨of course not! : ¡claro que no!⟩

notable[1] ['no:təbəl] *adj* **1** NOTEWORTHY : notable, de notar **2** DISTINGUISHED, PROMINENT : distinguido, destacado

notable[2] *n* : persona *f* importante, personaje *m*

notably ['no:təbli] *adv* : notablemente, particularmente

notarize ['no:tə,raɪz] *vt* **-rized; -rizing** : autenticar, autorizar

notary public ['no:təri] *n, pl* **-ries public** *or* **-ry publics** : notario *m*, -ria *f*; escribano *m*, -na *f*

notation [no'teɪʃən] *n* **1** NOTE : anotación *f*, nota *f* **2** : notación *f* ⟨musical notation : notación musical⟩

notch[1] ['naʧ] *vt* : hacer una muesca en, cortar

notch[2] *n* : muesca *f*, corte *m*

note[1] ['no:t] *vt* **noted; noting** **1** NOTICE : notar, observar, tomar nota de **2** RECORD : anotar, apuntar

note[2] *n* **1** : nota *f* (musical) **2** COMMENT : nota *f*, comentario *m* **3** LETTER : nota *f*, cartita *f* **4** PROMINENCE : prestigio *m* ⟨a musician of note : un músico destacado⟩ **5** ATTENTION : atención *f* ⟨to take note of : prestar atención a⟩

notebook ['no:t,bʊk] *n* **1** : libreta *f*, cuaderno *m* **2** : notebook *m* (computadora)

noted ['no:təd] *adj* EMINENT : renombrado, eminente, celebrado

noteworthy ['no:t,wərði] *adj* : notable, de notar, de interés

nothing[1] ['nʌθɪŋ] *adv* **1** : de ninguna manera ⟨nothing daunted, we carried on : sin amilanarnos, seguimos adelante⟩ **2 nothing like** : no . . . en nada ⟨he's nothing like his brother : no se parece en nada a su hermano⟩

nothing[2] *n* **1** NOTHINGNESS : nada *f* **2** ZERO : cero *m* **3** : persona *f* de poca importancia, cero *m* **4** TRIFLE : nimiedad *f*

nothing[3] *pron* : nada ⟨there's nothing better : no hay nada mejor⟩ ⟨nothing else : nada más⟩ ⟨nothing but : solamente⟩ ⟨they mean nothing to me : ellos me son indiferentes⟩

nothingness ['nʌθɪŋnəs] *n* **1** VOID : vacío *m*, nada *f* **2** NONEXISTENCE : inexistencia *f* **3** TRIFLE : nimiedad *f*

notice[1] ['no:tɪs] *vt* **-ticed; -ticing** : notar, observar, advertir, darse cuenta de

notice[2] *n* **1** NOTIFICATION : aviso *m*, notificación *f* **2** ATTENTION : atención *f* ⟨to take notice of : prestar atención a⟩

noticeable ['no:tɪsəbəl] *adj* : evidente, perceptible — **noticeably** [-bli] *adv*

notification [,no:təfə'keɪʃən] *n* : notificación *f*, aviso *m*

notify ['no:tə,faɪ] *vt* **-fied; -fying** : notificar, avisar

notion ['no:ʃən] *n* **1** IDEA : idea *f*, noción *f* **2** WHIM : capricho *m*, antojo *m* **3 notions** *npl* : artículos *mpl* de mercería

notoriety [,no:tə'raɪəti] *n* : mala fama *f*, notoriedad *f*

notorious [no'to:riəs] *adj* : de mala fama, célebre, bien conocido

notwithstanding[1] [,natwɪθ'stændɪŋ, -wɪð-] *adv* NEVERTHELESS : no obstante, sin embargo

notwithstanding[2] *conj* : a pesar de que

notwithstanding[3] *prep* : a pesar de, no obstante

nougat ['nu:gət] *n* : turrón *m*

nought ['nɔt, 'nat] → **naught**

noun ['naʊn] *n* : nombre *m*, sustantivo *m*

nourish ['nərɪʃ] *vt* **1** FEED : alimentar, nutrir, sustentar **2** FOSTER : fomentar, alentar

nourishing ['nərɪʃɪŋ] *adj* : alimenticio, nutritivo

nourishment ['nərɪʃmənt] *n* : nutrición *f*, alimento *m*, sustento *m*

novel[1] ['navəl] *adj* : original, novedoso

novel² *n* : novela *f*

novelist ['nɑvəlɪst] *n* : novelista *mf*

novelty ['nɑvəlti] *n, pl* **-ties 1** : novedad *f* **2 novelties** *npl* TRINKETS : baratijas *fpl*, chucherías *fpl*

November [noˈvɛmbər] *n* : noviembre *m*

novice ['nɑvɪs] *n* : novato *m*, -ta *f*; principiante *mf*; novicio *m*, -cia *f*

now¹ ['nau] *adv* **1** PRESENTLY : ahora, ya, actualmente ⟨from now on : de ahora en adelante⟩ ⟨long before now : ya hace tiempo⟩ ⟨now and then : de vez en cuando⟩ **2** IMMEDIATELY : ahora (mismo), inmediatamente ⟨do it right now! : ¡hazlo ahora mismo!⟩ **3** THEN : ya, entonces ⟨now they were ready : ya estaban listos⟩ **4** (*used to introduce a statement, a question, a command, or a transition*) ⟨now hear this! : ¡presten atención!⟩ ⟨now what do you think of that? : ¿qué piensas de eso?⟩

now² *n* (*indicating the present time*) ⟨until now : hasta ahora⟩ ⟨by now : ya⟩ ⟨ten years from now : dentro de 10 años⟩

now³ *conj* **now that** : ahora que, ya que

nowadays ['nauəˌdeɪz] *adv* : hoy en día, actualmente, en la actualidad

nowhere¹ ['noːˌhwɛr] *adv* **1** : en ninguna parte, a ningún lado ⟨nowhere to be found : en ninguna parte, por ningún lado⟩ ⟨you're going nowhere : no estás yendo a ningún lado, no estás yendo a ninguna parte⟩ **2 nowhere near** : ni con mucho, nada cerca ⟨it's nowhere near here : no está nada cerca de aquí⟩

nowhere² *n* **1** : ninguna parte *f* **2 out of nowhere** : de la nada

noxious ['nɑkʃəs] *adj* : nocivo, dañino, tóxico

nozzle ['nɑzəl] *n* : boca *f*

nuance ['nuːˌɑns, 'njuː-] *n* : matiz *m*

nub ['nʌb] *n* **1** KNOB, LUMP : protuberancia *f*, nudo *m* **2** GIST : quid *m*, meollo *m*

nuclear ['nuːkliər, 'njuː-] *adj* : nuclear

nucleus ['nuːkliəs, 'njuː-] *n, pl* **-clei** [-kliˌaɪ] : núcleo *m*

nude¹ ['nuːd, 'njuːd] *adj* **nuder; nudest** : desnudo

nude² *n* : desnudo *m*

nudge¹ ['nʌdʒ] *vt* **nudged; nudging** : darle con el codo (a alguien)

nudge² *n* : toque *m* que se da con el codo

nudism ['nuːˌdɪzəm, 'njuː-] *n* : nudismo *m*

nudist ['nuːdɪst, 'njuː-] *n* : nudista *mf*

nudity ['nuːdəti, 'njuː-] *n* : desnudez *f*

nugget ['nʌgət] *n* : pepita *f*

nuisance ['nuːsənts, 'njuː-] *n* **1** BOTHER : fastidio *m*, molestia *f*, lata *f* **2** PEST : pesado *m*, -da *f fam*

null ['nʌl] *adj* : nulo ⟨null and void : nulo y sin efecto⟩

nullify ['nʌləˌfaɪ] *vt* **-fied; -fying** : invalidar, anular

nullity ['nʌləti] *n, pl* **-ties** : nulidad *f*

numb¹ ['nʌm] *vt* : entumecer, adormecer

numb² *adj* : entumecido, dormido ⟨numb with fear : paralizado de miedo⟩

number¹ ['nʌmbər] *vt* **1** COUNT, INCLUDE : contar, incluir **2** : numerar ⟨number the pages : numera las páginas⟩ **3** TOTAL : ascender a, sumar

number² *n* **1** : número *m* ⟨in round numbers : en números redondos⟩ ⟨telephone number : número de teléfono⟩ **2 a number of** : varios, unos pocos, unos cuantos

numberless ['nʌmbərləs] *adj* : innumerable, sin número

numbness ['nʌmnəs] *n* : entumecimiento *m*

numeral ['nuːmərəl, 'njuː-] *n* : número *m* ⟨Roman numeral : número romano⟩

numerator ['nuːməˌreɪtər, 'njuː-] *n* : numerador *m*

numeric [nuˈmɛrɪk, njʊ-] *adj* : numérico

numerical [nʊˈmɛrɪkəl, njʊ-] *adj* : numérico — **numerically** [-kli] *adv*

numerous ['nuːmərəs, 'njuː-] *adj* : numeroso

numismatics [ˌnuːməzˈmætɪks, ˌnjuː-] *n* : numismática *f*

numskull ['nʌmˌskʌl] *n* : tonto *m*, -ta *f*; mentecato *m*, -ta *f*; zoquete *m fam*

nun ['nʌn] *n* : monja *f*

nuptial ['nʌpʃəl] *adj* : nupcial

nuptials ['nʌpʃəlz] *npl* WEDDING : nupcias *fpl*, boda *f*

nurse¹ ['nərs] *vt* **nursed; nursing 1** SUCKLE : amamantar **2** : cuidar (de), atender ⟨to nurse the sick : cuidar a los enfermos⟩ ⟨to nurse a cold : curarse de un resfriado⟩

nurse² *n* **1** : enfermero *m*, -ra *f* **2** → **nursemaid**

nursemaid ['nərsˌmeɪd] *n* : niñera *f*

nursery ['nərsəri] *n, pl* **-eries 1** *or* **day nursery** : guardería *f* **2** : vivero *m* (de plantas)

nursing home *n* : hogar *m* de ancianos, clínica *f* de reposo

nurture¹ ['nərtʃər] *vt* **-tured; -turing 1** FEED, NOURISH : nutrir, alimentar **2** EDUCATE : criar, educar **3** FOSTER : alimentar, fomentar

nurture² *n* **1** UPBRINGING : crianza *f*, educación *f* **2** FOOD : alimento *m*

nut ['nʌt] *n* **1** : nuez *f* **2** : tuerca *f* ⟨nuts and bolts : tuercas y tornillos⟩ **3** LUNATIC : loco *m*, -ca *f*; chiflado *m*, -da *f fam* **4** ENTHUSIAST : fanático *m*, -ca *f*; entusiasta *mf*

nutcracker ['nʌtˌkrækər] *n* : cascanueces *m*

nuthatch ['nʌtˌhætʃ] *n* : trepador *m*

nutmeg ['nʌtˌmɛg] *n* : nuez *f* moscada

nutrient ['nuːtriənt, 'njuː-] *n* : nutriente *m*, alimento *m* nutritivo

nutriment ['nuːtrəmənt, 'njuː-] *n* : nutrimento *m*

nutrition [nʊˈtrɪʃən, njʊ-] *n* : nutrición *f*

nutritional [nʊˈtrɪʃənəl, njʊ-] *adj* : alimenticio

nutritious [nʊˈtrɪʃəs, njʊ-] *adj* : nutritivo, alimenticio

nuts ['nʌts] *adj* 1 FANATICAL : fanático
2 CRAZY : loco, chiflado *fam*
nutshell ['nʌt,ʃɛl] *n* 1 : cáscara *f* de nuez
2 **in a nutshell** : en pocas palabras
nutty ['nʌti] *adj* **-tier; -tiest** : loco, chiflado *fam*

nuzzle ['nʌzəl] *v* **-zled; -zling** *vi* NESTLE
: acurrucarse, arrimarse — *vt* : acariciar con el hocico
nylon ['naɪ,lɑn] *n* 1 : nilón *m* 2 **nylons**
npl : medias *fpl* de nilón
nymph ['nɪmpf] *n* : ninfa *f*

O

o ['o:] *n, pl* **o's** *or* **os** ['o:z] 1 : decimoquinta letra del alfabeto inglés 2 ZERO
: cero *m*
O ['o:] → **oh**
oaf ['o:f] *n* : zoquete *m*; bruto *m*, -ta *f*
oafish ['o:fɪʃ] *adj* : torpe, lerdo
oak ['o:k] *n, pl* **oaks** *or* **oak** : roble *m*
oaken ['o:kən] *adj* : de roble
oar ['or] *n* : remo *m*
oarlock ['or,lɑk] *n* : tolete *m*, escálamo *m*
oasis [o'eɪsɪs] *n, pl* **oases** [-,si:z] : oasis *m*
oat ['o:t] *n* : avena *f*
oath ['o:θ] *n, pl* **oaths** ['o:ðz, 'o:θs] 1 : juramento *m* ⟨to take an oath : prestar juramento⟩ 2 SWEARWORD : mala palabra *f*, palabrota *f*
oatmeal ['o:t,mi:l] *n* : avena *f* ⟨instant oatmeal : avena instantánea⟩
obdurate ['ɑbdʊrət, -djʊ-] *adj* : inflexible, firme, obstinado
obedience [o'bi:diənts] *n* : obediencia *f*
obedient [o'bi:diənt] *adj* : obediente — **obediently** *adv*
obelisk ['ɑbə,lɪsk] *n* : obelisco *m*
obese [o'bi:s] *adj* : obeso
obesity [o'bi:səti] *n* : obesidad *f*
obey [o'beɪ] *v* **obeyed; obeying** : obedecer ⟨to obey the law : cumplir la ley⟩
obfuscate ['ɑbfə,skeɪt] *vt* **-cated; -cating** : ofuscar, confundir
obituary [o'bɪtʃʊ,ɛri] *n, pl* **-aries** : obituario *m*, necrología *f*
object¹ [əb'dʒɛkt] *vt* : objetar — *vi* : oponerse, poner reparos, hacer objeciones
object² ['ɑbdʒɪkt] *n* 1 : objeto *m* 2 OBJECTIVE, PURPOSE : objetivo *m*, propósito *m* 3 : complemento *m* (en gramática)
objection [əb'dʒɛkʃən] *n* : objeción *f*
objectionable [əb'dʒɛkʃənəbəl] *adj* : ofensivo, indeseable — **objectionably** [-bli] *adv*
objective¹ [əb'dʒɛktɪv] *adj* 1 IMPARTIAL : objetivo, imparcial 2 : de complemento, directo (en gramática)
objective² *n* 1 : objetivo *m* 2 *or* **objective case** : acusativo *m*
objectively [əb'dʒɛktɪvli] *adv* : objetivamente
objectivity [,ɑb,dʒɛk'tɪvəti] *n, pl* **-ties** : objetividad *f*
obligate ['ɑblə,geɪt] *vt* **-gated; -gating** : obligar
obligation [,ɑblə'geɪʃən] *n* : obligación *f*

obligatory [ə'blɪgə,tori] *adj* : obligatorio
oblige [ə'blaɪdʒ] *vt* **obliged; obliging** 1 COMPEL : obligar 2 : hacerle un favor (a alguien), complacer ⟨to oblige a friend : hacerle un favor a un amigo⟩ 3 **to be much obliged** : estar muy agradecido
obliging [ə'blaɪdʒɪŋ] *adj* : servicial, complaciente — **obligingly** *adv*
oblique [o'bli:k] *adj* 1 SLANTING : oblicuo 2 INDIRECT : indirecto — **obliquely** *adv*
obliterate [ə'blɪtə,reɪt] *vt* **-ated; -ating** 1 ERASE : obliterar, borrar 2 DESTROY : destruir, eliminar
obliteration [ə,blɪtə'reɪʃən] *n* : obliteración *f*
oblivion [ə'blɪviən] *n* : olvido *m*
oblivious [ə'blɪviəs] *adj* : inconsciente — **obliviously** *adv*
oblong¹ ['ɑ,blɔŋ] *adj* : oblongo
oblong² *n* : figura *f* oblonga, rectángulo *m*
obnoxious [ɑb'nɑkʃəs, əb-] *adj* : repugnante, odioso — **obnoxiously** *adv*
oboe ['o:,bo:] *n* : oboe *m*
oboist ['o,boɪst] *n* : oboe *mf*
obscene [ɑb'si:n, əb-] *adj* : obsceno, indecente — **obscenely** *adv*
obscenity [ɑb'sɛnəti, əb-] *n, pl* **-ties** : obscenidad *f*
obscure¹ [ɑb'skjʊr, əb-] *vt* **-scured; -scuring** 1 CLOUD, DIM : oscurecer, nublar 2 HIDE : ocultar
obscure² *adj* 1 DIM : oscuro 2 REMOTE, SECLUDED : recóndito 3 VAGUE : oscuro, confuso, vago 4 UNKNOWN : desconocido ⟨an obscure poet : un poeta desconocido⟩ — **obscurely** *adv*
obscurity [ɑb'skjʊrəti, əb-] *n, pl* **-ties** : oscuridad *f*
obsequious [ɑb'si:kwiəs] *adj* : servil, excesivamente atento
observable [əb'zɜrvəbəl] *adj* : observable, perceptible
observance [əb'zɜrvənts] *n* 1 FULFILLMENT : observancia *f*, cumplimiento *m* 2 PRACTICE : práctica *f*
observant [əb'zɜrvənt] *adj* : observador
observation [,ɑbsər'veɪʃən, -zər-] *n* : observación *f*
observatory [əb'zɜrvə,tori] *n, pl* **-ries** : observatorio *m*
observe [əb'zɜrv] *v* **-served; -serving** *vt* 1 OBEY : observar, obedecer 2 CELEBRATE : celebrar, guardar (una práctica religiosa) 3 WATCH : observar, mi-

rar **4** REMARK : observar, comentar — *vi* LOOK : mirar

observer [ab'zərvər] *n* : observador *m*, -dora *f*

obsess [əb'sɛs] *vt* : obsesionar

obsession [ab'sɛʃən, əb-] *n* : obsesión *f*

obsessive [ab'sɛsɪv, əb-] *adj* : obsesivo — **obsessively** *adv*

obsolescence [ˌabsə'lɛsənts] *n* : obsolescencia *f*

obsolescent [ˌabsə'lɛsənt] *adj* : obsolescente ⟨to become obsolescent : caer en desuso⟩

obsolete [ˌabsə'li:t, 'absəˌ-] *adj* : obsoleto, anticuado

obstacle ['abstɪkəl] *n* : obstáculo *m*, impedimento *m*

obstetric [əb'stɛtrɪk] *or* **obstetrical** [-trɪkəl] *adj* : obstétrico

obstetrician [ˌabstə'trɪʃən] *n* : obstetra *mf*; tocólogo *m*, -ga *f*

obstetrics [əb'stɛtrɪks] *ns & pl* : obstetricia *f*, tocología *f*

obstinacy ['abstənəsi] *n, pl* **-cies** : obstinación *f*, terquedad *f*

obstinate ['abstənət] *adj* : obstinado, terco — **obstinately** *adv*

obstreperous [əb'strɛpərəs] *adj* **1** CLAMOROUS : ruidoso, clamoroso **2** UNRULY : rebelde, indisciplinado

obstruct [əb'strʌkt] *vt* : obstruir, bloquear

obstruction [əb'strʌkʃən] *n* : obstrucción *f*, bloqueo *m*

obstructive [əb'strʌktɪv] *adj* : obstructor

obtain [əb'teɪn] *vt* : obtener, conseguir — *vi* PREVAIL : imperar, prevalecer

obtainable [əb'teɪnəbəl] *adj* : obtenible, asequible

obtrude [əb'tru:d] *v* **-truded; -truding** *vt* **1** EXTRUDE : expulsar **2** IMPOSE : imponer — *vi* INTRUDE : inmiscuirse, entrometerse

obtrusive [əb'tru:sɪv] *adj* **1** IMPERTINENT, MEDDLESOME : impertinente, entrometido **2** PROTRUDING : prominente

obtuse [ab'tu:s, əb-, -'tju:s] *adj* : obtuso, torpe

obtuse angle *n* : ángulo obtuso

obviate ['abviˌeɪt] *vt* **-ated; -ating** : obviar, evitar

obvious ['abviəs] *adj* : obvio, evidente, manifiesto

obviously ['abviəsli] *adv* **1** CLEARLY : obviamente, evidentemente **2** OF COURSE : claro, por supuesto

occasion[1] [ə'keɪʒən] *vt* : ocasionar, causar

occasion[2] *n* **1** OPPORTUNITY : oportunidad *f*, ocasión *f* **2** CAUSE : motivo *m*, razón *f* **3** INSTANCE : ocasión *f* **4** EVENT : ocasión *f*, acontecimiento *m* **5** on ~ : de vez en cuando, ocasionalmente

occasional [ə'keɪʒənəl] *adj* : ocasional

occasionally [ə'keɪʒənəli] *adv* : de vez en cuando, ocasionalmente

occidental [ˌaksə'dɛntəl] *adj* : oeste, del oeste, occidental

occult[1] [ə'kʌlt, 'aˌkʌlt] *adj* **1** HIDDEN, SECRET : oculto, secreto **2** ARCANE : arcano, esotérico

occult[2] *n* **the occult** : las ciencias ocultas

occupancy ['akjəpəntsi] *n, pl* **-cies** : ocupación *f*, habitación *f*

occupant ['akjəpənt] *n* : ocupante *mf*

occupation [ˌakjə'peɪʃən] *n* : ocupación *f*, profesión *f*, oficio *m*

occupational [ˌakjə'peɪʃənəl] *adj* : ocupacional

occupy ['akjəˌpaɪ] *vt* **-pied; -pying** : ocupar

occur [ə'kər] *vi* **occurred; occurring 1** EXIST : encontrarse, existir **2** HAPPEN : ocurrir, acontecer, suceder, tener lugar **3** : ocurrirse ⟨it occurred to him that . . . : se le ocurrió que . . . ⟩

occurrence [ə'kərənts] *n* : acontecimiento *m*, suceso *m*, ocurrencia *f*

ocean ['oːʃən] *n* : océano *m*

oceanic [ˌoːʃi'ænɪk] *adj* : oceánico

oceanography [ˌoːʃə'nagrəfi] *n* : oceanografía *f*

ocelot ['asəˌlat, 'oː-] *n* : ocelote *m*

ocher *or* **ochre** ['oːkər] *n* : ocre *m*

o'clock [ə'klak] *adv* (*used in telling time*) ⟨it's ten o'clock : son las diez⟩ ⟨at six o'clock : a las seis⟩

octagon ['aktəˌgan] *n* : octágono *m*

octagonal [ak'tægənəl] *adj* : octagonal

octave ['aktɪv] *n* : octava *f*

October [ak'toːbər] *n* : octubre *m*

octopus ['aktəˌpus, -pəs] *n, pl* **-puses** *or* **-pi** [-ˌpaɪ] : pulpo *m*

ocular ['akjələr] *adj* : ocular

oculist ['akjəlɪst] *n* **1** OPHTHALMOLOGIST : oftalmólogo *m*, -ga *f*; oculista *mf* **2** OPTOMETRIST : optometrista *mf*

odd ['ad] *adj* **1** : sin pareja, suelto ⟨an odd sock : un calcetín sin pareja⟩ **2** UNEVEN : impar ⟨odd numbers : números impares⟩ **3** : y pico, y tantos ⟨forty odd years ago : hace cuarenta y pico años⟩ **4** : alguno, uno que otro ⟨odd jobs : algunos trabajos⟩ **5** STRANGE : extraño, raro

oddball ['adˌbɔl] *n* : excéntrico *m*, -ca *f*; persona *f* rara

oddity ['adəti] *n, pl* **-ties** : rareza *f*, cosa *f* rara

oddly ['adli] *adv* : de manera extraña

oddness ['adnəs] *n* : rareza *f*, excentricidad *f*

odds ['adz] *npl* **1** CHANCES : probabilidades *fpl* **2** : puntos *mpl* de ventaja (de una apuesta) **3 to be at odds** : estar en desacuerdo

odds and ends *npl* : costillas *fpl*, cosas *fpl* sueltas, cachivaches *mpl*

ode ['oːd] *n* : oda *f*

odious ['oːdiəs] *adj* : odioso — **odiously** *adv*

odor ['oːdər] *n* : olor *m*

odorless ['oːdərləs] *adj* : inodoro, sin olor

odorous ['o:dərəs] *adj* : oloroso

odyssey ['adəsi] *n, pl* **-seys** : odisea *f*

o'er ['or] → **over**

of ['ʌv, 'ɑv] *prep* **1** FROM : de ⟨a man of the city : un hombre de la ciudad⟩ **2** (*indicating character or background*) : de ⟨a woman of great ability : una mujer de gran capacidad⟩ **3** (*indicating cause*) : de ⟨he died of the flu : murió de la gripe⟩ **4** BY : de ⟨the works of Shakespeare : las obras de Shakespeare⟩ **5** (*indicating contents, material, or quantity*) : de ⟨a house of wood : una casa de madera⟩ ⟨a glass of water : un vaso de agua⟩ **6** (*indicating belonging or connection*) : de ⟨the front of the house : el frente de la casa⟩ **7** ABOUT : sobre, de ⟨tales of the West : los cuentos del Oeste⟩ **8** (*indicating a particular example*) : de ⟨the city of Caracas : la ciudad de Caracas⟩ **9** FOR : por, a ⟨love of country : amor por la patria⟩ **10** (*indicating time or date*) ⟨five minutes of ten : las diez menos cinco⟩ ⟨the eighth of April : el ocho de abril⟩

off¹ ['ɔf] *adv* **1** (*indicating change of position or state*) ⟨to march off : marcharse⟩ ⟨he dozed off : se puso a dormir⟩ **2** (*indicating distance in space or time*) ⟨some miles off : a varias millas⟩ ⟨the holiday is three weeks off : faltan tres semanas para la fiesta⟩ **3** (*indicating removal*) ⟨the knob came off : se le cayó el pomo⟩ **4** (*indicating termination*) ⟨shut the television off : apaga la televisión⟩ **5** (*indicating suspension of work*) ⟨to take a day off : tomarse un día de descanso⟩ **6 off and on** : de vez en cuando

off² *adj* **1** FARTHER : más remoto, distante ⟨the off side of the building : el lado distante del edificio⟩ **2** STARTED : empezado ⟨to be off on a spree : irse de juerga⟩ **3** OUT : apagado ⟨the light is off : la luz está apagada⟩ **4** CANCELED : cancelado, suspendido **5** INCORRECT : erróneo, incorrecto **6** REMOTE : remoto, lejano ⟨an off chance : una posibilidad remota⟩ **7** FREE : libre ⟨I'm off today : hoy estoy libre⟩ **8 to be well off** : vivir con desahogo, tener bastante dinero

off³ *prep* **1** (*indicating physical separation*) : de ⟨she took it off the table : lo tomó de la mesa⟩ ⟨a shop off the main street : una tienda al lado de la calle principal⟩ **2** : a la costa de, a expensas de ⟨he lives off his sister : vive a expensas de su hermana⟩ **3** (*indicating the suspension of an activity*) ⟨to be off duty : estar libre⟩ ⟨he's off liquor : ha dejado el alcohol⟩ **4** BELOW : por debajo de ⟨he's off his game : está por debajo de su juego normal⟩

offal ['ɔfəl] *n* **1** RUBBISH, WASTE : desechos *mpl*, desperdicios *mpl* **2** VISCERA : vísceras *fpl*, asaduras *fpl*

offend [ə'fɛnd] *vt* **1** VIOLATE : violar, atentar contra **2** HURT : ofender ⟨to be easily offended : ser muy susceptible⟩

offender [ə'fɛndər] *n* : delincuente *mf*; infractor *m*, -tora *f*

offense *or* **offence** [ə'fɛnts, 'ɔ,fɛnts] *n* **1** INSULT : ofensa *f*, injuria *f*, agravio *m* ⟨to take offense : ofenderse⟩ **2** ASSAULT : ataque *m* **3** : ofensiva *f* (en deportes) **4** CRIME, INFRACTION : infracción *f*, delito *m*

offensive¹ [ə'fɛntsɪv, 'ɔ,fɛnt-] *adj* : ofensivo — **offensively** *adv*

offensive² *n* : ofensiva *f*

offer¹ ['ɔfər] *vt* **1** : ofrecer ⟨they offered him the job : le ofrecieron el puesto⟩ **2** PROPOSE : proponer, sugerir **3** SHOW : ofrecer, mostrar ⟨to offer resistance : ofrecer resistencia⟩

offer² *n* : oferta *f*, ofrecimiento *m*, propuesta *f*

offering ['ɔfərɪŋ] *n* : ofrenda *f*

offhand¹ ['ɔf'hænd] *adv* : sin preparación, sin pensarlo

offhand² *adj* **1** IMPROMPTU : improvisado **2** ABRUPT : brusco

office ['ɔfəs] *n* **1** : cargo *m* ⟨to run for office : presentarse como candidato⟩ **2** : oficina *f*, despacho *m*, gabinete *m* (en la casa) ⟨office hours : horas de oficina⟩

officeholder ['ɔfəs,ho:ldər] *n* : titular *mf*

officer ['ɔfəsər] *n* **1** *or* **police officer** : policía *mf*, agente *mf* de policía **2** OFFICIAL : oficial *mf*; funcionario *m*, -ria *f*; director *m*, -tora *f* (en una empresa) **3** COMMISSIONED OFFICER : oficial *mf*

official¹ [ə'fɪʃəl] *adj* : oficial — **officially** *adv*

official² *n* : funcionario *m*, -ria *f*; oficial *mf*

officiate [ə'fɪʃi,eɪt] *v* **-ated; -ating** *vi* **1** : arbitrar (en deportes) **2 to officiate at** : oficiar, celebrar — *vt* : arbitrar

officious [ə'fɪʃəs] *adj* : oficioso

offing ['ɔfɪŋ] *n* **in the offing** : en perspectiva

offset ['ɔf,sɛt] *vt* **-set; -setting** : compensar

offshoot ['ɔf,ʃuːt] *n* **1** OUTGROWTH : producto *m*, resultado *m* **2** BRANCH, SHOOT : retoño *m*, rama *f*, vástago *m* (de una planta)

offshore¹ ['ɔf'ʃor] *adv* : a una distancia de la costa

offshore² *adj* **1** : de (la) tierra ⟨an offshore wind : un viento que sopla de tierra⟩ **2** : (de) costa afuera, cercano a la costa ⟨an offshore island : una isla costera⟩

offspring ['ɔf,sprɪŋ] *ns & pl* **1** YOUNG : crías *fpl* (de los animales) **2** PROGENY : prole *f*, progenie *f*

off-white ['ɔf'hwaɪt] *adj* : blancuzco

often ['ɔfən, 'ɔftən] *adv* : muchas veces, a menudo, seguido

oftentimes ['ɔfən,taımz, 'ɔftən-] *or* **oft-times** ['ɔft,taımz] → **often**
ogle ['o:gəl] *vt* **ogled; ogling** : comerse con los ojos, quedarse mirando a
ogre ['o:gər] *n* : ogro *m*
oh ['o:] *interj* : ¡oh!, ¡ah!, ¡ay! ⟨oh, of course : ah, por supuesto⟩ ⟨oh no! : ¡ay no!⟩ ⟨oh really? : ¿de veras?⟩
ohm ['o:m] *n* : ohm *m*, ohmio *m*
oil[1] ['ɔıl] *vt* : lubricar, engrasar, aceitar
oil[2] *n* **1** : aceite *m* **2** PETROLEUM : petróleo *m* **3** *or* **oil painting** : óleo *m*, pintura *f* al óleo **4** *or* **oil paint(s)** : óleo *m*
oilcloth ['ɔıl,klɔθ] *n* : hule *m*
oiliness ['ɔılinəs] *n* : lo aceitoso
oilskin ['ɔıl,skın] *n* **1** : hule *m* **2 oilskins** *npl* : impermeable *m*
oily ['ɔıli] *adj* **oilier; -est** : aceitoso, grasiento, grasoso ⟨oily fingers : dedos grasientos⟩
ointment ['ɔıntmənt] *n* : ungüento *m*, pomada *f*
OK[1] [,o:'keı] *vt* **OK'd** *or* **okayed** [,o:'keıd]; **OK'ing** *or* **okaying** APPROVE, AUTHORIZE : dar el visto bueno a, autorizar, aprobar
OK[2] *or* **okay** [,o:'keı] *adv* **1** WELL : bien **2** YES : sí, por supuesto
OK[3] *adj* : bien ⟨he's OK : está bien⟩ ⟨it's OK with me : estoy de acuerdo⟩
OK[4] *n* : autorización *f*, visto *m* bueno
okra ['o:krə, *South also* -kri] *n* : quingombó *m*
old[1] ['o:ld] *adj* **1** ANCIENT : antiguo ⟨old civilizations : civilizaciones antiguas⟩ **2** FAMILIAR : viejo ⟨old friends : viejos amigos⟩ ⟨the same old story : el mismo cuento⟩ **3** (*indicating a certain age*) ⟨he's ten years old : tiene diez años (de edad)⟩ **4** AGED : viejo, anciano ⟨an old woman : una anciana⟩ **5** FORMER : antiguo ⟨her old neighborhood : su antiguo barrio⟩ **6** WORN-OUT : viejo, gastado
old[2] *n* **1 the old** : los viejos, los ancianos **2 in the days of old** : antaño, en los tiempos antiguos
olden ['o:ldən] *adj* : de antaño, de antigüedad
old-fashioned ['o:ld'fæʃənd] *adj* : anticuado, pasado de moda
old maid *n* **1** SPINSTER : soltera *f* **2** FUSS-BUDGET : maniático *m*, -ca *f*; melindroso *m*, -sa *f*
Old Testament *n* : Antiguo Testamento *m*
old-time ['o:ld'taım] *adj* : antiguo
old-timer ['o:ld'taımər] *n* **1** VETERAN : veterano *m*, -na *f* **2** *or* **oldster** : anciano *m*, -na *f*
old-world ['o:ld'wərld] *adj* : pintoresco (de antaño)
oleander ['o:li,ændər] *n* : adelfa *f*
oleomargarine [,o:lio'mardʒərən] → **margarine**
olfactory [al'fæktəri, ol-] *adj* : olfativo
oligarchy ['alə,garki, 'o:lə-] *n*, *pl* **-chies** : oligarquía *f*

olive ['alıv, -ləv] *n* **1** : aceituna *f*, oliva *f* (fruta) **2** : olivo *m* (árbol) **3** *or* **olive green** : color *m* aceituna, verde *m* oliva
Olmec ['al,mɛk, 'o:l-] *n* : olmeca *mf* — **Olmec** *adj*
Olympic [ə'lımpık, o-] *adj* : olímpico
Olympic Games *npl* : Juegos *mpl* Olímpicos
Olympics [ə'lımpıks, o-] *npl* : olimpiadas *fpl*
Omani [o'mani, -'mæ-] *n* : omaní *mf* — **Omani** *adj*
ombudsman ['am,bʊdzmən, am-'bʊdz-] *n*, *pl* **-men** [-mən, -,mɛn] : ombudsman *m*
omelet *or* **omelette** ['amlət, 'amə-] *n* : omelette *mf*, tortilla *f* (de huevo)
omen ['o:mən] *n* : presagio *m*, augurio *m*, agüero *m*
ominous ['amənəs] *adj* : ominoso, agorero, de mal agüero
ominously ['amənəsli] *adv* : de manera amenazadora
omission [o'mıʃən] *n* : omisión *f*
omit [o'mıt] *vt* **omitted; omitting 1** LEAVE OUT : omitir, excluir **2** NEGLECT : omitir ⟨they omitted to tell us : omitieron decírnoslo⟩
omnipotence [am'nıpətənts] *n* : omnipotencia *f* — **omnipotent** [am-'nıpətənt] *adj*
omnipresent [,amnı'prɛzənt] *adj* : omnipresente
omniscient [am'nıʃənt] *adj* : omnisciente
omnivorous [am'nıvərəs] *adj* **1** : omnívoro **2** AVID : ávido, voraz
on[1] ['an, 'ɔn] *adv* **1** (*indicating contact with a surface*) ⟨put the top on : pon la tapa⟩ ⟨he has a hat on : lleva un sombrero puesto⟩ **2** (*indicating forward movement*) ⟨from that moment on : a partir de ese momento⟩ ⟨farther on : más adelante⟩ **3** (*indicating operation or an operating position*) ⟨turn the light on : prende la luz⟩
on[2] *adj* **1** (*being in operation*) ⟨the radio is on : el radio está prendido⟩ **2** (*taking place*) ⟨the game is on : el juego ha comenzado⟩ **3 to be on to** : estar enterado de
on[3] *prep* **1** (*indicating position*) : en, sobre, encima de ⟨on the table : en (sobre, encima de) la mesa⟩ ⟨shadows on the wall : sombras en la pared⟩ ⟨on horseback : a caballo⟩ **2** AT, TO : a ⟨on the right : a la derecha⟩ **3** ABOARD, IN : en, a ⟨on the plane : en el avión⟩ ⟨he got on the train : subió al tren⟩ **4** (*indicating time*) ⟨she worked on Saturdays : trabajaba los sábados⟩ ⟨every hour on the hour : a la hora en punto⟩ **5** (*indicating means or agency*) : por ⟨he cut himself on a tin can : se cortó con una lata⟩ ⟨to talk on the telephone : hablar por teléfono⟩ **6** (*indicating a state or process*) : en ⟨on fire : en llamas⟩ ⟨on the increase : en aumen-

to⟩ 7 (*indicating connection or membership*) : en ⟨on a committee : en una comisión⟩ 8 (*indicating an activity*) ⟨on vacation : de vacaciones⟩ ⟨on a diet : a dieta⟩ 9 ABOUT, CONCERNING : sobre ⟨a book on insects : un libro sobre insectos⟩ ⟨reflect on that : reflexiona sobre eso⟩

once¹ ['wʌnʦ] *adv* 1 : una vez ⟨once a month : una vez al mes⟩ ⟨once and for all : de una vez por todas⟩ 2 EVER : alguna vez 3 FORMERLY : antes, anteriormente

once² *adj* FORMER : antiguo

once³ *n* 1 : una vez 2 at ～ SIMULTANEOUSLY : al mismo tiempo, simultáneamente 3 at ～ IMMEDIATELY : inmediatamente, en seguida

once⁴ *conj* : una vez que, tan pronto como

once–over [ˌwʌnʦ'oːvər, 'wʌnʦˌ-] *n* to give someone the once–over : echarle un vistazo a alguien

oncoming ['ɑnˌkʌmɪŋ, 'ɔn-] *adj* : que viene

one¹ ['wʌn] *adj* 1 (*being a single unit*) : un, una ⟨he only wants one apple : sólo quiere una manzana⟩ 2 (*being a particular one*) : un, una ⟨he arrived early one morning : llegó temprano una mañana⟩ 3 (*being the same*) : mismo, misma ⟨they're all members of one team : todos son miembros del mismo equipo⟩ ⟨one and the same thing : la misma cosa⟩ 4 SOME : alguno, alguna, un, una ⟨I'll see you again one day : algún día te veré otra vez⟩ ⟨at one time or another : en una u otra ocasión⟩

one² *n* 1 : uno *m* (número) 2 (*indicating the first of a set or series*) ⟨from day one : desde el primer momento⟩ 3 (*indicating a single person or thing*) ⟨the one (girl) on the right : la de la derecha⟩ ⟨he has the one but needs the other : tiene uno pero necesita el otro⟩

one³ *pron* 1 : uno, una ⟨one of his friends : una de sus amigas⟩ ⟨one never knows : uno nunca sabe, nunca se sabe⟩ ⟨to cut one's finger : cortarse el dedo⟩ 2 one and all : todos, todo el mundo 3 one another : el uno al otro, se ⟨they loved one another : se amaban⟩ 4 that one : aquél, aquella 5 which one? : ¿cuál?

one–on–one [wʌnɑn'wʌn, -ɑn-] *adj* : uno a uno — **one–on–one** *adv*

onerous ['ɑnərəs, 'oːnə-] *adj* : oneroso, gravoso

oneself [ˌwʌn'sɛlf] *pron* 1 (*used reflexively or for emphasis*) : se, sí mismo, uno mismo ⟨to control oneself : controlarse⟩ ⟨to talk to oneself : hablarse a sí mismo⟩ ⟨to do it oneself : hacérselo uno mismo⟩ 2 by ～ : solo

one–sided ['wʌn'saɪdəd] *adj* 1 : de un solo lado 2 LOPSIDED : asimétrico 3 BIASED : parcial, tendencioso 4 UNILATERAL : unilateral

onetime ['wʌn'taɪm] *adj* FORMER : antiguo

one–way ['wʌn'weɪ] *adj* 1 : de sentido único, de una sola dirección ⟨a one-way street : una calle de sentido único⟩ 2 : de ida, sencillo ⟨a one-way ticket : un boleto de ida⟩

ongoing ['ɑnˌgoːɪŋ] *adj* 1 CONTINUING : en curso, corriente 2 DEVELOPING : en desarrollo

onion ['ʌnjən] *n* : cebolla *f*

online ['ɔn'laɪn, 'ɑn-] *adj* : en línea

onlooker ['ɔnˌlʊkər, 'ɑn-] *n* : espectador *m*, -dora *f*, circunstante *mf*

only¹ ['oːnli] *adv* 1 MERELY : sólo, solamente, nomás ⟨for only two dollars : por tan sólo dos dólares⟩ ⟨only once : sólo una vez, no más de una vez⟩ ⟨I only did it to help : lo hice por ayudar nomás⟩ 2 SOLELY : únicamente, sólo, solamente ⟨only he knows it : solamente él lo sabe⟩ 3 (*indicating a result*) ⟨it will only cause him problems : no hará más que crearle problemas⟩ 4 if only : ojalá, por lo menos ⟨if only it were true! : ¡ojalá sea cierto!⟩ ⟨if he could only dance : si por lo menos pudiera bailar⟩

only² *adj* : único ⟨an only child : un hijo único⟩ ⟨the only chance : la única oportunidad⟩

only³ *conj* BUT : pero ⟨I would go, only I'm sick : iría, pero estoy enfermo⟩

onset ['ɑnˌsɛt] *n* : comienzo *m*, llegada *f*

onslaught ['ɑnˌslɔt, 'ɔn-] *n* : arremetida *f*, embestida *f*, embate *m*

onto ['ɑnˌtuː, 'ɔn-] *prep* : sobre

onus ['oːnəs] *n* : responsabilidad *f*, carga *f*

onward¹ ['ɑnwərd, 'ɔn-] *or* **onwards** *adv* FORWARD : adelante, hacia adelante

onward² *adj* : hacia adelante

onyx ['ɑnɪks] *n* : ónix *m*

ooze¹ ['uːz] *v* **oozed; oozing** *vi* : rezumar — *vt* 1 : rezumar 2 EXUDE : irradiar, rebosar ⟨to ooze confidence : irradiar confianza⟩

ooze² *n* SLIME : cieno *m*, limo *m*

opacity [oˈpæsəti] *n*, *pl* **-ties** : opacidad *f*

opal ['oːpəl] *n* : ópalo *m*

opaque [oˈpeɪk] *adj* 1 : opaco 2 UNCLEAR : poco claro

open¹ ['oːpən] *vt* 1 : abrir ⟨open the door : abre la puerta⟩ 2 UNCOVER : destapar 3 UNFOLD : desplegar, abrir 4 CLEAR : abrir (un camino, etc.) 5 INAUGURATE : abrir (una tienda), inaugurar (una exposición, etc.) 6 INITIATE : iniciar, entablar, abrir ⟨to open the meeting : abrir la sesión⟩ ⟨to open a discussion : entablar un debate⟩ — *vi* 1 : abrirse 2 BEGIN : empezar, comenzar

open² *adj* 1 : abierto ⟨an open window : una ventana abierta⟩ 2 FRANK : abierto, franco, directo 3 UNCOV-

ERED : descubierto, abierto **4** EX-TENDED : extendido, abierto ⟨with open arms : con los brazos abiertos⟩ **5** UNRESTRICTED : libre, abierto **6** UN-DECIDED : pendiente, por decidir, sin resolver ⟨an open question : una cuestión pendiente⟩ **7** AVAILABLE : vacante, libre ⟨the job is open : el puesto está vacante⟩

open³ *n* **in the open 1** OUTDOORS : al aire libre **2** KNOWN : conocido, sacado a la luz

open–air ['o:pən'ær] *adj* OUTDOOR : al aire libre

open–and–shut ['o:pənənd'ʃʌt] *adj* : claro, evidente ⟨an open-and-shut case : un caso muy claro⟩

opener ['o:pənər] *n* : destapador *m*, abrelatas *m*, abridor *m*

openhanded [,o:pən'hændəd] *adj* : generoso, liberal

openhearted [,o:pən'hɑrtəd] *adj* **1** FRANK : franco, sincero **2** : generoso, de gran corazón

opening ['o:pənɪŋ] *n* **1** BEGINNING : comienzo *m*, principio *m*, apertura *f* **2** APERTURE : abertura *f*, brecha *f*, claro *m* (en el bosque) **3** OPPORTUNITY : oportunidad *f*

openly ['o:pənli] *adv* **1** FRANKLY : abiertamente, francamente **2** PUBLICLY : públicamente, declaradamente

openness ['o:pənnəs] *n* : franqueza *f*

opera ['ɑprə, 'ɑpərə] *n* **1** : ópera *f* **2** → **opus**

opera glasses *npl* : gemelos *mpl* de teatro

operate ['ɑpə,reɪt] *v* **-ated; -ating** *vi* **1** ACT, FUNCTION : operar, funcionar, actuar **2 to operate on (someone)** : operar a (alguien) — *vt* **1** WORK : operar, manejar, hacer funcionar (una máquina) **2** MANAGE : manejar, administrar (un negocio)

operatic [,ɑpə'rætɪk] *adj* : operístico

operation [,ɑpə'reɪʃən] *n* **1** FUNCTIONING : funcionamiento *m* **2** USE : uso *m*, manejo *m* (de máquinas) **3** SURGERY : operación *f*, intervención *f* quirúrgica

operational [,ɑpə'reɪʃənəl] *adj* : operacional, de operación

operative ['ɑpərətɪv, -,reɪ-] *adj* **1** OPERATING : vigente, en vigor **2** WORKING : operativo **3** SURGICAL : quirúrgico

operator ['ɑpə,reɪtər] *n* : operador *m*, -dora *f*

operetta [,ɑpə'rɛtə] *n* : opereta *f*

ophthalmologist [,ɑf,θæl'mɑlədʒɪst, -θə'mɑ-] *n* : oftalmólogo *m*, -ga *f*

ophthalmology [,ɑf,θæl'mɑlədʒi, -θə'mɑ-] *n* : oftalmología *f*

opiate ['o:piət, -pi,eɪt] *n* : opiato *m*

opinion [ə'pɪnjən] *n* : opinión *f*

opinionated [ə'pɪnjə,neɪtəd] *adj* : testarudo, dogmático

opium ['o:piəm] *n* : opio *m*

opossum [ə'pɑsəm] *n* : zarigüeya *f*, oposum *m*

opponent [ə'po:nənt] *n* : oponente *mf*; opositor *m*, -tora *f*; contrincante *mf* (en deportes)

opportune [,ɑpər'tu:n, -'tju:n] *adj* : oportuno — **opportunely** *adv*

opportunist [,ɑpər'tu:nɪst, -'tju:-] *n* : oportunista *mf*

opportunistic [,ɑpərtu'nɪstɪk, -tju-] *adj* : oportunista *mf*

opportunity [,ɑpər'tu:nəti, -'tju:-] *n, pl* **-ties** : oportunidad *f*, ocasión *f*, chance *m*, posibilidades *fpl*

oppose [ə'po:z] *vt* **-posed; -posing 1** : ir en contra de, oponerse a ⟨good opposes evil : el bien se opone al mal⟩ **2** COMBAT : luchar contra, combatir, resistir

opposite¹ ['ɑpəzət] *adv* : enfrente

opposite² *adj* **1** FACING : de enfrente ⟨the opposite side : el lado de enfrente⟩ **2** CONTRARY : opuesto, contrario ⟨in opposite directions : en direcciones contrarias⟩ ⟨the opposite sex : el sexo opuesto, el otro sexo⟩

opposite³ *n* : lo contrario, lo opuesto

opposite⁴ *prep* : enfrente de, frente a

opposition [,ɑpə'zɪʃən] *n* **1** : oposición *f*, resistencia *f* **2 in opposition to** AGAINST : en contra de

oppress [ə'prɛs] *vt* **1** PERSECUTE : oprimir, perseguir **2** BURDEN : oprimir, agobiar

oppression [ə'prɛʃən] *n* : opresión *f*

oppressive [ə'prɛsɪv] *adj* **1** HARSH : opresivo, severo **2** STIFLING : agobiante, sofocante ⟨oppressive heat : calor sofocante⟩

oppressor [ə'prɛsər] *n* : opresor *m*, -sora *f*

opprobrium [ə'pro:briəm] *n* : oprobio *m*

opt ['ɑpt] *vi* : optar

optic ['ɑptɪk] *or* **optical** [-tɪkəl] *adj* : óptico

optical disk *n* : disco *m* óptico

optician [ɑp'tɪʃən] *n* : óptico *m*, -ca *f*

optics ['ɑptɪks] *npl* : óptica *f*

optimal ['ɑptəməl] *adj* : óptimo

optimism ['ɑptə,mɪzəm] *n* : optimismo *m*

optimist ['ɑptəmɪst] *n* : optimista *mf*

optimistic [,ɑptə'mɪstɪk] *adj* : optimista

optimistically [,ɑptə'mɪstɪkli] *adv* : con optimismo, positivamente

optimum¹ ['ɑptəməm] *adj* → **optimal**

optimum² *n, pl* **-ma** ['ɑptəmə] : lo óptimo, lo ideal

option ['ɑpʃən] *n* : opción *f* ⟨she has no option : no tiene más remedio⟩

optional ['ɑpʃənəl] *adj* : facultativo, optativo

optometrist [ɑp'tɑmətrɪst] *n* : optometrista *mf*

optometry [ɑp'tɑmətri] *n* : optometría *f*

opulence ['ɑpjələnts] *n* : opulencia *f*

opulent ['ɑpjələnt] *adj* : opulento

opus ['o:pəs] *n, pl* **opera** ['o:pərə, 'ɑpə-] : opus *m*, obra *f* (de música)

or ['ɔr] *conj* **1** (*indicating an alternative*) : o (u *before words beginning with o or ho*) ⟨coffee or tea : café o té⟩ ⟨one day or another : un día u otro⟩ 2 (*following a negative*) : ni ⟨he didn't have his keys or his wallet : no llevaba ni sus llaves ni su billetera⟩

oracle ['ɔrəkəl] *n* : oráculo *m*

oral ['ɔrəl] *adj* : oral — **orally** *adv*

orange ['ɔrɪndʒ] *n* 1 : naranja *f*, china *f* *PRi* (fruto) 2 : naranja *m* (color), color *m* de china *PRi*

orangeade [ˌɔrɪndʒ'eɪd] *n* : naranjada *f*

orangutan [ə'ræŋə,tæŋ, -'ræŋɡə-, -,tæn] *n* : orangután *m*

oration [ə'reɪʃən] *n* : oración *f*, discurso *m*

orator ['ɔrətər] *n* : orador *m*, -dora *f*

oratorio [ˌɔrə'tori,o:] *n, pl* **-rios** : oratorio *m*

oratory ['ɔrə,tori] *n, pl* **-ries** : oratoria *f*

orb ['ɔrb] *n* : orbe *m*

orbit[1] ['ɔrbət] *vt* 1 CIRCLE : girar alrededor de, orbitar 2 : poner en órbita (un satélite, etc.) — *vi* : orbitar

orbit[2] *n* : órbita *f*

orbital ['ɔrbətəl] *adj* : orbital

orchard ['ɔrtʃərd] *n* : huerto *m*

orchestra ['ɔrkəstrə] *n* : orquesta *f*

orchestral [ɔr'kɛstrəl] *adj* : orquestal

orchestrate ['ɔrkə,streɪt] *vt* **-trated; -trating** 1 : orquestar, instrumentar (en música) 2 ORGANIZE : arreglar, organizar

orchestration [ˌɔrkə'streɪʃən] *n* : orquestación *f*

orchid ['ɔrkɪd] *n* : orquídea *f*

ordain [ɔr'deɪn] *vt* 1 : ordenar (en religión) 2 DECREE : decretar, ordenar

ordeal [ɔr'di:l, 'ɔr,di:l] *n* : prueba *f* dura, experiencia *f* terrible

order[1] ['ɔrdər] *vt* 1 ORGANIZE : arreglar, ordenar, poner en orden 2 COMMAND : ordenar, mandar 3 REQUEST : pedir, encargar ⟨to order a meal : pedir algo de comer⟩ — *vi* : hacer un pedido

order[2] *n* 1 : orden *f* ⟨a religious order : una orden religiosa⟩ 2 COMMAND : orden *f*, mandato *m* ⟨to give an order : dar una orden⟩ 3 REQUEST : orden *f*, pedido *m* ⟨purchase order : orden de compra⟩ 4 ARRANGEMENT : orden *m* ⟨in chronological order : por orden cronológico⟩ 5 DISCIPLINE : orden *m* ⟨law and order : el orden público⟩ 6 **in order to** : para 7 **out of order** : descompuesto, averiado 8 **orders** *npl* or **holy orders** : órdenes *fpl* sagradas

orderliness ['ɔrdərlinəs] *n* : orden *m*

orderly[1] ['ɔrdərli] *adj* 1 METHODICAL : ordenado, metódico 2 PEACEFUL : pacífico, disciplinado

orderly[2] *n, pl* **-lies** 1 : ordenanza *m* (en el ejército) 2 : camillero *m* (en un hospital)

ordinal ['ɔrdənəl] *n or* **ordinal number** : ordinal *m*, número *m* ordinal

ordinance ['ɔrdənənts] *n* : ordenanza *f*, reglamento *m*

ordinarily [ˌɔrdən'ɛrəli] *adv* : ordinariamente, por lo general

ordinary ['ɔrdən,ɛri] *adj* 1 NORMAL, USUAL : normal, usual 2 AVERAGE : común y corriente, normal 3 MEDIOCRE : mediocre, ordinario

ordination [ˌɔrdən'eɪʃən] *n* : ordenación *f*

ordnance ['ɔrdnənts] *n* : artillería *f*

ore ['or] *n* : mineral *m* (metalífero), mena *f*

oregano [ə'rɛgə,no:] *n* : orégano *m*

organ ['ɔrgən] *n* 1 : órgano *m* (instrumento) 2 : órgano *m* (del cuerpo) 3 PERIODICAL : publicación *f* periódica, órgano *m*

organic [ɔr'gænɪk] *adj* : orgánico — **organically** *adv*

organism ['ɔrgə,nɪzəm] *n* : organismo *m*

organist ['ɔrgənɪst] *n* : organista *mf*

organization [ˌɔrgənə'zeɪʃən] *n* 1 ORGANIZING : organización *f* 2 BODY : organización *f*, organismo *m*

organizational [ˌɔrgənə'zeɪʃənəl] *adj* : organizativo

organize ['ɔrgə,naɪz] *vt* **-nized; -nizing** : organizar, arreglar, poner en orden

organizer ['ɔrgə,naɪzər] *n* : organizador *m*, -dora *f*

orgasm ['ɔr,gæzəm] *n* : orgasmo *m*

orgy ['ɔrdʒi] *n, pl* **-gies** : orgía *f*

orient ['ori,ɛnt] *vt* : orientar

Orient *n* **the Orient** : el Oriente

oriental [ˌori'ɛntəl] *adj* : del Oriente, oriental

Oriental *n* : oriental *mf*

orientation [ˌorian'teɪʃən] *n* : orientación *f*

orifice ['ɔrəfəs] *n* : orificio *m*

origin ['ɔrədʒən] *n* 1 ANCESTRY : origen *m*, ascendencia *f* 2 SOURCE : origen *m*, raíz *f*, fuente *f*

original[1] [ə'rɪdʒənəl] *adj* : original

original[2] *n* : original *m*

originality [ə,rɪdʒə'næləti] *n* : originalidad *f*

originally [ə'rɪdʒənəli] *adv* 1 AT FIRST : al principio, originariamente 2 CREATIVELY : originalmente, con originalidad

originate [ə'rɪdʒə,neɪt] *v* **-nated; -nating** *vt* : originar, iniciar, crear — *vi* 1 BEGIN : originarse, empezar 2 COME : provenir, proceder, derivarse

originator [ə'rɪdʒə,neɪtər] *n* : creador *m*, -dora *f*; inventor *m*, -tora *f*

oriole ['ori,o:l, -iəl] *n* : oropéndola *f*

ornament[1] ['ɔrnəmənt] *vt* : adornar, decorar, ornamentar

ornament[2] *n* : ornamento *m*, adorno *m*, decoración *f*

ornamental [ˌɔrnə'mɛntəl] *adj* : ornamental, de adorno, decorativo

ornamentation [ˌɔrnəmən'teɪʃən, -mɛn-] *n* : ornamentación *f*

ornate [ɔr'neɪt] *adj* : elaborado, recargado

ornery ['ɔrnəri, 'arnəri] *adj* **ornerier; -est** : de mal genio, malhumorado

ornithologist [ˌɔrnə'θalədʒɪst] *n* : ornitólogo *m*, -ga *f*

ornithology [ˌɔrnəˈθɑlədʒi] *n, pl* **-gies** : ornitología *f*

orphan[1] [ˈɔrfən] *vt* : dejar huérfano

orphan[2] *n* : huérfano *m*, -na *f*

orphanage [ˈɔrfənɪdʒ] *n* : orfelinato *m*, orfanato *m*

orthodontics [ˌɔrθəˈdɑntɪks] *n* : ortodoncia *f*

orthodontist [ˌɔrθəˈdɑntɪst] *n* : ortodoncista *mf*

orthodox [ˈɔrθəˌdɑks] *adj* : ortodoxo

orthodoxy [ˈɔrθəˌdɑksi] *n, pl* **-doxies** : ortodoxia *f*

orthographic [ˌɔrθəˈgræfɪk] *adj* : ortográfico

orthography [ɔrˈθɑgrəfi] *n, pl* **-phies** SPELLING : ortografía *f*

orthopedic [ˌɔrθəˈpiːdɪk] *adj* : ortopédico

orthopedics [ˌɔrθəˈpiːdɪks] *ns & pl* : ortopedia *f*

orthopedist [ˌɔrθəˈpiːdɪst] *n* : ortopedista *mf*

oscillate [ˈɑsəˌleɪt] *vi* **-lated; -lating** : oscilar

oscillation [ˌɑsəˈleɪʃən] *n* : oscilación *f*

osmosis [ɑzˈmoːsɪs, ɑs-] *n* : ósmosis *f*, osmosis *f*

osprey [ˈɑspri, -ˌpreɪ] *n* : pigargo *m*

ostensible [ɑˈstɛnʦəbəl] *adj* APPARENT : aparente, ostensible — **ostensibly** [-bli] *adv*

ostentation [ˌɑstənˈteɪʃən] *n* : ostentación *f*, boato *m*

ostentatious [ˌɑstənˈteɪʃəs] *adj* : ostentoso — **ostentatiously** *adv*

osteopath [ˈɑstiəˌpæθ] *n* : osteópata *mf*

osteopathy [ˌɑstiˈɑpəθi] *n* : osteopatía *f*

osteoporosis [ˌɑstiopəˈroːsɪs] *n, pl* **-roses** [-ˌsiːz] : osteoporosis *f*

ostracism [ˈɑstrəˌsɪzəm] *n* : ostracismo *m*

ostracize [ˈɑstrəˌsaɪz] *vt* **-cized; -cizing** : condenar al ostracismo, marginar, aislar

ostrich [ˈɑstrɪʧ, ˈɔs-] *n* : avestruz *m*

other[1] [ˈʌðər] *adv* **other than** : aparte de, fuera de

other[2] *adj* : otro ⟨the other boys : los otros muchachos⟩ ⟨smarter than other people : más inteligente que los demás⟩ ⟨on the other hand : por otra parte, por otro lado⟩ ⟨every other day : cada dos días⟩

other[3] *pron* : otro, otra ⟨one in front of the other : uno tras otro⟩ ⟨myself and three others : yo y tres otros, yo y tres más⟩ ⟨somewhere or other : en alguna parte⟩

otherwise[1] [ˈʌðərˌwaɪz] *adv* **1** DIFFERENTLY : de otro modo, de manera distinta ⟨he could not act otherwise : no pudo actuar de manera distinta⟩ **2** : eso aparte, por lo demás ⟨I'm dizzy, but otherwise I'm fine : estoy mareado pero, por lo demás, estoy bien⟩ **3** OR ELSE : de lo contrario, si no ⟨do what I tell you, otherwise you'll be sorry : haz

lo que te digo, de lo contrario, te arrepentirás⟩

otherwise[2] *adj* : diferente, distinto ⟨the facts are otherwise : la realidad es diferente⟩

otter [ˈɑtər] *n* : nutria *f*

Ottoman [ˈɑtəmən] *n* **1** : otomano *m*, -na *f* **2** : otomana *f* (mueble) — **Ottoman** *adj*

ouch [ˈaʊʧ] *interj* : ¡ay!, ¡huy!

ought [ˈɔt] *v aux* : deber ⟨you ought to take care of yourself : deberías cuidarte⟩

oughtn't [ˈɔtənt] (*contraction of* **ought not**) → **ought**

ounce [ˈaʊnʦ] *n* : onza *f*

our [ˈɑr, ˈaʊr] *adj* : nuestro

ours [ˈaʊrz, ˈɑrz] *pron* : nuestro, nuestra ⟨a cousin of ours : un primo nuestro⟩

ourselves [ɑrˈsɛlvz, aʊr-] *pron* **1** (*used reflexively*) : nos, nosotros ⟨we amused ourselves : nos divertimos⟩ ⟨we were always thinking of ourselves : siempre pensábamos en nosotros⟩ **2** (*used for emphasis*) : nosotros mismos, nosotras mismas ⟨we did it ourselves : lo hicimos nosotros mismos⟩

oust [ˈaʊst] *vt* : desbancar, expulsar

ouster [ˈaʊstər] *n* : expulsión *f* (de un país, etc.), destitución *f* (de un puesto)

out[1] [ˈaʊt] *vi* : revelarse, hacerse conocido

out[2] *adv* **1** (*indicating direction or movement*) : para afuera ⟨she opened the door and looked out : abrió la puerta y miró para afuera⟩ **2** (*indicating a location away from home or work*) : fuera, afuera ⟨to eat out : comer afuera⟩ **3** (*indicating loss of control or possession*) ⟨they let the secret out : sacaron el secreto a la luz⟩ **4** (*indicating completion or discontinuance*) ⟨his money ran out : se le acabó el dinero⟩ ⟨to turn out the light : apagar la luz⟩ **5** OUTSIDE : fuera, afuera ⟨out in the garden : afuera en el jardín⟩ **6** ALOUD : en voz alta, en alto ⟨to cry out : gritar⟩

out[3] *adj* **1** EXTERNAL : externo, exterior **2** OUTLYING : alejado, distante ⟨the out islands : las islas distantes⟩ **3** ABSENT : ausente **4** UNFASHIONABLE : fuera de moda **5** EXTINGUISHED : apagado

out[4] *prep* **1** (*used to indicate an outward movement*) : por ⟨I looked out the window : miré por la ventana⟩ ⟨she ran out the door : corrió por la puerta⟩ **2** → **out of**

out–and–out [ˈaʊtənˈaʊt] *adj* UTTER : redomado, absoluto

outboard motor [ˈaʊtˌbord] *n* : motor *m* fuera de borde

outbound [ˈaʊtˌbaʊnd] *adj* : que sale, de salida

outbreak [ˈaʊtˌbreɪk] *n* : brote *m* (de una enfermedad), comienzo *m* (de guerra), ola *f* (de violencia), erupción *f* (de granos)

outbuilding ['aʊt,bɪldɪŋ] *n* : edificio *m* anexo

outburst ['aʊt,bərst] *n* : arranque *m*, arrebato *m*

outcast ['aʊt,kæst] *n* : marginado *m*, -da *f*; paria *mf*

outcome ['aʊt,kʌm] *n* : resultado *m*, desenlace *m*, consecuencia *f*

outcrop ['aʊt,krɑp] *n* : afloramiento *m*

outcry ['aʊt,kraɪ] *n, pl* -**cries** : clamor *m*, protesta *f*

outdated [,aʊt'deɪtəd] *adj* : anticuado, fuera de moda

outdistance [,aʊt'dɪstənts] *vt* -**tanced**; -**tancing** : aventajar, dejar atrás

outdo [,aʊt'du:] *vt* -**did** [-'dɪd]; -**done** [-'dʌn]; -**doing**; -**does** [-'dʌz] : superar

outdoor ['aʊt'dor] *adj* : al aire libre ⟨outdoor sports : deportes al aire libre⟩ ⟨outdoor clothing : ropa de calle⟩

outdoors¹ ['aʊt'dorz] *adv* : afuera, al aire libre

outdoors² *n* : aire *m* libre

outer ['aʊt̮ər] *adj* **1** : exterior, externo **2 outer space** : espacio *m* exterior

outermost ['aʊt̮ər,mo:st] *adj* : más remoto, más exterior, extremo

outfield ['aʊt,fi:ld] *n* **the outfield** : los jardines

outfielder ['aʊt,fi:ldər] *n* : jardinero *m*, -ra *f*

outfit¹ ['aʊt,fɪt] *vt* -**fitted**; -**fitting** EQUIP : equipar

outfit² *n* **1** EQUIPMENT : equipo *m* **2** COSTUME, ENSEMBLE : traje *m*, conjunto *m* **3** GROUP : conjunto *m*

outgo ['aʊt,go:] *n, pl* **outgoes** : gasto *m*

outgoing ['aʊt,go:ɪŋ] *adj* **1** OUTBOUND : que sale **2** DEPARTING : saliente ⟨an outgoing president : un presidente saliente⟩ **3** EXTROVERTED : extrovertido, expansivo

outgrow [,aʊt'gro:] *vt* -**grew** [-'gru:]; -**grown** [-'gro:n]; -**growing** **1** : crecer más que ⟨that tree outgrew all the others : ese árbol creció más que todos los otros⟩ **2 to outgrow one's clothes** : quedarle pequeña la ropa a uno

outgrowth ['aʊt,gro:θ] *n* **1** OFFSHOOT : brote *m*, vástago *m* (de una planta) **2** CONSEQUENCE : consecuencia *f*, producto *m*, resultado *m*

outing ['aʊtɪŋ] *n* : excursión *f*

outlandish [aʊt'lændɪʃ] *adj* : descabellado, muy extraño

outlast [,aʊt'læst] *vt* : durar más que

outlaw¹ ['aʊt,lɔ] *vt* : hacerse ilegal, declarar fuera de la ley, prohibir

outlaw² *n* : bandido *m*, -da *f*; bandolero *m*, -ra *f*; forajido *m*, -da *f*

outlay ['aʊt,leɪ] *n* : gasto *m*, desembolso *m*

outlet ['aʊt,lɛt, -lət] *n* **1** EXIT : salida *f*, escape *m* ⟨electrical outlet : toma de corriente⟩ **2** RELIEF : desahogo *m* **3** MARKET : mercado *m*, salida *f*

outline¹ ['aʊt,laɪn] *vt* -**lined**; -**lining** **1** SKETCH : diseñar, esbozar, bosquejar **2** DEFINE, EXPLAIN : perfilar, delinear, explicar ⟨she outlined our responsibilities : delineó nuestras responsabilidades⟩

outline² *n* **1** PROFILE : perfil *m*, silueta *f*, contorno *m* **2** SKETCH : bosquejo *m*, boceto *m* **3** SUMMARY : esquema *m*, resumen *m*, sinopsis *m* ⟨an outline of world history : un esquema de la historia mundial⟩

outlive [,aʊt'lɪv] *vt* -**lived**; -**living** : sobrevivir a

outlook ['aʊt,lʊk] *n* **1** VIEW : vista *f*, panorama *f* **2** POINT OF VIEW : punto *m* de vista **3** PROSPECTS : perspectivas *fpl*

outlying ['aʊt,laɪɪŋ] *adj* : alejado, distante, remoto ⟨the outlying areas : las afueras⟩

outmoded [,aʊt'mo:dəd] *adj* : pasado de moda, anticuado

outnumber [,aʊt'nʌmbər] *vt* : superar en número a, ser más numeroso de

out of *prep* **1** (*indicating direction or movement from within*) : de, por ⟨we ran out of the house : salimos corriendo de la casa⟩ ⟨to look out of the window : mirar por la ventana⟩ **2** (*being beyond the limits of*) ⟨out of control : fuera de control⟩ ⟨to be out of sight : desaparecer de vista⟩ **3** OF : de ⟨one out of four : uno de cada cuatro⟩ **4** (*indicating absence or loss*) : sin ⟨out of money : sin dinero⟩ ⟨we're out of matches : nos hemos quedado sin fósforos⟩ **5** BECAUSE OF : por ⟨out of curiosity : por curiosidad⟩ **6** FROM : de ⟨made out of plastic : hecho de plástico⟩

out-of-date [,aʊt̮əv'deɪt] *adj* : anticuado, obsoleto, pasado de moda

out-of-door [,aʊt̮əv'dor] *or* **out-of-doors** [-'dorz] → **outdoor**

out-of-doors *n* → **outdoors²**

outpatient ['aʊt,peɪʃənt] *n* : paciente *m* externo, paciente *f* externa

outpost ['aʊt,po:st] *n* : puesto *m* avanzado

output¹ ['aʊt,pʊt] *vt* -**putted** *or* -**put**; -**putting** : producir

output² *n* : producción *f* (de una fábrica), rendimiento *m* (de una máquina), productividad *f* (de una persona)

outrage¹ ['aʊt,reɪdʒ] *vt* -**raged**; -**raging** **1** INSULT : ultrajar, injuriar **2** INFURIATE : indignar, enfurecer

outrage² *n* **1** ATROCITY : atropello *m*, atrocidad *f*, atentado *m* **2** SCANDAL : escándalo *m* **3** ANGER : ira *f*, furia *f*

outrageous [,aʊt'reɪdʒəs] *adj* **1** SCANDALOUS : escandaloso, ofensivo, atroz **2** UNCONVENTIONAL : poco convencional, extravagante **3** EXORBITANT : exorbitante, excesivo (dícese de los precios, etc.)

outright¹ [,aʊt'raɪt] *adv* **1** COMPLETELY : por completo, totalmente ⟨to sell outright : vender por completo⟩ ⟨he refused it outright : lo rechazó rotundamente⟩ **2** DIRECTLY : directamente, sin reserva **3** INSTANTLY : al instante, en el acto

outright² [ˈaʊtˌraɪt] *adj* **1** COMPLETE : completo, absoluto, categórico ⟨an outright lie : una mentira absoluta⟩ **2** : sin reservas ⟨an outright gift : un regalo sin reservas⟩

outset [ˈaʊtˌsɛt] *n* : comienzo *m*, principio *m*

outshine [ˌaʊtˈʃaɪn] *vt* **-shone** [-ˈʃoːn, -ˈʃɑn] *or* **-shined; -shining** : eclipsar

outside¹ [ˌaʊtˈsaɪd, ˈaʊtˌ-] *adv* : fuera, afuera

outside² *adj* **1** : exterior, externo ⟨the outside edge : el borde exterior⟩ ⟨outside influences : influencias externas⟩ **2** REMOTE : remoto ⟨an outside chance : una posibilidad remota⟩

outside³ *n* **1** EXTERIOR : parte *f* de afuera, exterior *m* **2** MOST : máximo *m* ⟨three weeks at the outside : tres semanas como máximo⟩ **3 from the outside** : desde afuera, desde fuera

outside⁴ *prep* : fuera de, afuera de ⟨outside my window : fuera de mi ventana⟩ ⟨outside regular hours : fuera del horario normal⟩ ⟨outside the law : afuera de la ley⟩

outside of *prep* **1** → **outside⁴ 2** → **besides²**

outsider [ˌaʊtˈsaɪdər] *n* : forastero *m*, -ra *f*

outskirts [ˈaʊtˌskərts] *npl* : afueras *fpl*, alrededores *mpl*

outsmart [ˌaʊtˈsmɑrt] → **outwit**

outspoken [ˌaʊtˈspoːkən] *adj* : franco, directo

outstanding [ˌaʊtˈstændɪŋ] *adj* **1** UNPAID : pendiente **2** NOTABLE : destacado, notable, excepcional, sobresaliente

outstandingly [ˌaʊtˈstændɪŋli] *adv* : excepcionalmente

outstretched [ˌaʊtˈstrɛtʃt] *adj* : extendido

outstrip [ˌaʊtˈstrɪp] *vt* **-stripped** *or* **-stript** [-ˈstrɪpt]; **-stripping 1** : aventajar, dejar atrás ⟨he outstripped the other runners : aventajó a los otros corredores⟩ **2** SURPASS : aventajar, sobrepasar

outward¹ [ˈaʊtwərd] *or* **outwards** [-wərdz] *adv* : hacia afuera, hacia el exterior

outward² *adj* **1** : hacia afuera ⟨an outward flow : un flujo hacia afuera⟩ **2** : externo ⟨outward beauty : belleza externa⟩

outwardly [ˈaʊtwərdli] *adv* **1** EXTERNALLY : exteriormente **2** APPARENTLY : aparentemente ⟨outwardly friendly : aparentemente simpático⟩

outwit [ˌaʊtˈwɪt] *vt* **-witted; -witting** : ser más listo que

ova → **ovum**

oval¹ [ˈoːvəl] *adj* : ovalado, oval

oval² *n* : óvalo *m*

ovarian [oˈværiən] *adj* : ovárico

ovary [ˈoːvəri] *n, pl* **-ries** : ovario *m*

ovation [oˈveɪʃən] *n* : ovación *f*

oven [ˈʌvən] *n* : horno *m*

over¹ [ˈoːvər] *adv* **1** (*indicating movement across*) ⟨he flew over to London : voló a Londres⟩ ⟨come on over! : ¡ven acá!⟩ **2** (*indicating an additional amount*) ⟨the show ran 10 minutes over : el espectáculo terminó 10 minutos de tarde⟩ **3** ABOVE, OVERHEAD : por encima **4** AGAIN : otra vez, de nuevo ⟨over and over : una y otra vez⟩ ⟨to start over : volver a empezar⟩ **5 all over** EVERYWHERE : por todas partes **6 to fall over** : caerse **7 to turn over** : poner boca abajo, voltear

over² *adj* **1** HIGHER, UPPER : superior **2** REMAINING : sobrante, que sobra **3** ENDED : terminado, acabado ⟨the work is over : el trabajo está terminado⟩

over³ *prep* **1** ABOVE : encima de, arriba de, sobre ⟨over the fireplace : encima de la chimenea⟩ ⟨the hawk flew over the hills : el halcón voló sobre los cerros⟩ **2** : más de ⟨over $50 : más de $50⟩ **3** ALONG : por, sobre ⟨to glide over the ice : deslizarse sobre el hielo⟩ **4** (*indicating motion through a place or thing*) ⟨they showed me over the house : me mostraron la casa⟩ **5** ACROSS : por encima de, sobre ⟨he jumped over the ditch : saltó por encima de la zanja⟩ **6** UPON : sobre ⟨a cape over my shoulders : una capa sobre los hombros⟩ **7** ON : por ⟨to speak over the telephone : hablar por teléfono⟩ **8** DURING : en, durante ⟨over the past 25 years : durante los últimos 25 años⟩ **9** BECAUSE OF : por ⟨they fought over the money : se pelearon por el dinero⟩

overabundance [ˌoːvərəˈbʌndənts] *n* : superabundancia *f*

overabundant [ˌoːvərəˈbʌndənt] *adj* : superabundante

overactive [ˌoːvərˈæktɪv] *adj* : hiperactivo

overall [ˌoːvərˈɔl] *adj* : total, global, de conjunto

overalls [ˈoːvərˌɔlz] *npl* : overol *m*

overawe [ˌoːvərˈɔ] *vt* **-awed; -awing** : intimidar, impresionar

overbearing [ˌoːvərˈbærɪŋ] *adj* : dominante, imperioso, prepotente

overblown [ˌoːvərˈbloːn] *adj* **1** INFLATED : inflado, exagerado **2** BOMBASTIC : grandilocuente, rimbombante

overboard [ˈoːvərˌbord] *adv* : por la borda, al agua

overburden [ˌoːvərˈbərdən] *vt* : sobrecargar, agobiar

overcast [ˈoːvərˌkæst] *adj* CLOUDY : nublado

overcharge [ˌoːvərˈtʃɑrdʒ] *vt* **-charged; -charging** : cobrarle de más (a alguien)

overcoat [ˈoːvərˌkoːt] *n* : abrigo *m*

overcome [ˌoːvərˈkʌm] *v* **-came** [-ˈkeɪm]; **-come; -coming** *vt* **1** CON-

QUER : vencer, derrotar, superar **2**
OVERWHELM : abrumar, agobiar — *vi*
: vencer

overconfidence [ˌoːvərˈkɑnfədən*t*s] *n*
: exceso *m* de confianza

overconfident [ˌoːvərˈkɑnfədənt] *adj*
: demasiado confiado

overcook [ˌoːvərˈkʊk] *vt* : recocer, cocer
demasiado

overcrowded [ˌoːvərˈkraʊdəd] *adj* **1**
PACKED : abarrotado, atestado de
gente **2** OVERPOPULATED : superpoblado

overdo [ˌoːvərˈduː] *vt* **-did** [-ˈdɪd]; **-done**
[-ˈdʌn]; **-doing**; **-does** [-ˈdʌz] **1** : hacer demasiado **2** EXAGGERATE : ex-
agerar **3** OVERCOOK : recocer

overdose [ˈoːvərˌdoːs] *n* : sobredosis *f*

overdraft [ˈoːvərˌdræft] *n* : sobregiro *m*,
descubierto *m*

overdraw [ˌoːvərˈdrɔ] *vt* **-drew** [-ˈdruː];
-drawn [-ˈdrɔn]; **-drawing** **1** : sobregirar ⟨my account is overdrawn : tengo
la cuenta en descubierto⟩ **2** EXAG-
GERATE : exagerar

overdue [ˌoːvərˈduː] *adj* **1** UNPAID : vencido y sin pagar **2** TARDY : de retraso,
tardío

overeat [ˌoːvərˈiːt] *vi* **-ate** [-ˈeɪt]; **-eaten**
[-ˈiːtən]; **-eating** : comer demasiado

overelaborate [ˌoːvərɪˈlæbərət] *adj* : recargado

overestimate [ˌoːvərˈɛstəˌmeɪt] *vt*
-mated; **-mating** : sobreestimar

overexcited [ˌoːvərɪkˈsaɪtəd] *adj* : sobreexcitado

overexpose [ˌoːvərɪkˈspoːz] *vt* **-posed**;
-posing : sobreexponer

overfeed [ˌoːvərˈfiːd] *vt* **-fed** [-ˈfɛd];
-feeding : sobrealimentar

overflow[1] [ˌoːvərˈfloː] *vt* **1** : desbordar **2**
INUNDATE : inundar — *vi* : desbor-
darse, rebosar

overflow[2] [ˈoːvərˌfloː] *n* **1** : derrame *m*,
desbordamiento *m* (de un río) **2** SUR-
PLUS : exceso *m*, excedente *m*

overfly [ˌoːvərˈflaɪ] *vt* **-flew** [-ˈfluː];
-flown [-ˈfloːn]; **-flying** : sobrevolar

overgrown [ˌoːvərˈgroːn] *adj* **1** : cubierto ⟨overgrown with weeds : cubierto de malas hierbas⟩ **2** : demasiado grande

overhand[1] [ˈoːvərˌhænd] *adv* : por encima de la cabeza

overhand[2] *adj* : por lo alto (tirada)

overhang[1] [ˌoːvərˈhæŋ] *v* **-hung** [-ˈhʌŋ];
-hanging *vt* **1** : sobresalir por encima
de **2** THREATEN : amenazar — *vi* : sobresalir

overhang[2] [ˈoːvərˌhæŋ] *n* : saliente *mf*

overhaul [ˌoːvərˈhɔl] *vt* **1** : revisar ⟨to
overhaul an engine : revisar un motor⟩
2 OVERTAKE : adelantar

overhead[1] [ˌoːvərˈhɛd] *adv* : por encima,
arriba, por lo alto

overhead[2] [ˈoːvərˌhɛd] *adj* : de arriba

overhead[3] [ˈoːvərˌhɛd] *n* : gastos *mpl*
generales

overhear [ˌoːvərˈhɪr] *vt* **-heard**; **-hearing**
: oír por casualidad

overheat [ˌoːvərˈhiːt] *vt* : recalentar, sobrecalentar, calentar demasiado

overjoyed [ˌoːvərˈdʒɔɪd] *adj* : rebosante
de alegría

overkill [ˈoːvərˌkɪl] *n* : exceso *m*, excedente *m*

overland[1] [ˈoːvərˌlænd, -lənd] *adv* : por
tierra

overland[2] *adj* : terrestre, por tierra

overlap[1] [ˌoːvərˈlæp] *v* **-lapped**; **-lapping**
vt : traslapar — *vi* : traslaparse, solaparse

overlap[2] [ˈoːvərˌlæp] *n* : traslapo *m*

overlay[1] [ˌoːvərˈleɪ] *vt* **-laid** [-ˈleɪd];
-laying : recubrir, revestir

overlay[2] [ˈoːvərˌleɪ] *n* : revestimiento *m*

overload [ˌoːvərˈloːd] *vt* : sobrecargar

overlong [ˌoːvərˈlɔŋ] *adj* : excesivamente largo, largo y pesado

overlook [ˌoːvərˈlʊk] *vt* **1** INSPECT : inspeccionar, revisar **2** : tener vista a, dar
a ⟨a house overlooking the valley : una
casa que tiene vista al valle⟩ **3** MISS
: pasar por alto **4** EXCUSE : dejar pasar,
disculpar

overly [ˈoːvərli] *adv* : demasiado

overnight[1] [ˌoːvərˈnaɪt] *adv* **1** : por la
noche, durante la noche **2** : de la noche
a la mañana ⟨we can't do it overnight
: no podemos hacerlo de la noche a la
mañana⟩

overnight[2] [ˈoːvərˈnaɪt] *adj* **1** : de noche
⟨an overnight stay : una estancia de
una noche⟩ ⟨an overnight bag : una
bolsa de viaje⟩ **2** SUDDEN : repentino

overpass [ˈoːvərˌpæs] *n* : paso *m* elevado, paso *m* a desnivel *Mex*

overpopulated [ˌoːvərˈpɑpjəˌleɪtəd] *adj*
: sobrepoblado

overpower [ˌoːvərˈpaʊər] *vt* **1** CON-
QUER, SUBDUE : vencer, superar **2**
OVERWHELM : abrumar, agobiar
⟨overpowered by the heat : sofocado
por el calor⟩

overpraise [ˌoːvərˈpreɪz] *vt* **-praised**;
-praising : adular

overrate [ˌoːvərˈreɪt] *vt* **-rated**; **-rating**
: sobrevalorar, sobrevaluar

override [ˌoːvərˈraɪd] *vt* **-rode** [-ˈroːd];
-ridden [-ˈrɪdən]; **-riding** **1** : predominar sobre, contar más que ⟨hunger
overrode our manners : el hambre pre-
dominó sobre los modales⟩ **2** ANNUL
: anular, invalidar ⟨to override a veto
: anular un veto⟩

overrule [ˌoːvərˈruːl] *vt* **-ruled**; **-ruling**
: anular (una decisión), desautorizar
(una persona), denegar (un pedido)

overrun [ˌoːvərˈrʌn] *v* **-ran** [-ˈræn];
-running *vt* **1** INVADE : invadir **2** IN-
FEST : infestar, plagar **3** EXCEED : exceder, rebasar — *vi* : rebasar el tiempo previsto

overseas[1] [ˌoːvərˈsiːz] *adv* : en el extranjero ⟨to travel overseas : viajar al
extranjero⟩

overseas² ['o:vər,si:z] *adj* : extranjero, exterior

oversee [,o:vər'si:] *vt* **-saw** [-'sɔ]; **-seen** [-'si:n]; **-seeing** SUPERVISE : supervisar

overseer ['o:vər,si:ər] *n* : supervisor *m*, -sora *f*; capataz *mf*

overshadow [,o:vər'ʃæ,do:] *vt* **1** DARKEN : oscurecer, ensombrecer **2** ECLIPSE, OUTSHINE : eclipsar

overshoe ['o:vər,ʃu:] *n* : chanclo *m*

overshoot [,o:vər'ʃu:t] *vt* **-shot** [-'ʃɑt]; **-shooting** : pasarse de ⟨to overshoot the mark : pasarse de la raya⟩

oversight ['o:vər,saɪt] *n* : descuido *m*, inadvertencia *f*

oversleep [,o:vər'sli:p] *vi* **-slept** [-'slɛpt]; **-sleeping** : no despertarse a tiempo, quedarse dormido

overspread [,o:vər'sprɛd] *vt* **-spread**; **-spreading** : extenderse sobre

overstaffed [,o:vər'stæft] *adj* : con exceso de personal

overstate [,o:vər'steɪt] *vt* **-stated**; **-stating** EXAGGERATE : exagerar

overstatement [,o:vər'steɪtmənt] *n* : exageración *f*

overstep [,o:vər'stɛp] *vt* **-stepped**; **-stepping** EXCEED : sobrepasar, traspasar, exceder

overt [o'vərt, 'o:,vərt] *adj* : evidente, manifiesto, patente

overtake [,o:vər'teɪk] *vt* **-took** [-'tʊk]; **-taken** [-'teɪkən]; **-taking** : pasar, adelantar, rebasar *Mex*

overthrow¹ [,o:vər'θro:] *vt* **-threw** [-'θru:]; **-thrown** [-'θro:n]; **-throwing** **1** OVERTURN : dar la vuelta a, volcar **2** DEFEAT, TOPPLE : derrocar, derribar, deponer

overthrow² ['o:vər,θro:] *n* : derrocamiento *m*, caída *f*

overtime ['o:vər,taɪm] *n* **1** : horas *fpl* extras (de trabajo) **2** : prórroga *f* (en deportes)

overtly [o'vərtli, 'o:,vərt-] *adv* OPENLY : abiertamente

overtone ['o:vər,to:n] *n* **1** : armónico *m* (en música) **2** HINT, SUGGESTION : tinte *m*, insinuación *f*

overture ['o:vər,tʃur, -tʃər] *n* **1** PROPOSAL : propuesta *f* **2** : obertura *f* (en música)

overturn [,o:vər'tərn] *vt* **1** UPSET : dar la vuelta a, volcar **2** NULLIFY : anular, invalidar — *vi* TURN OVER : volcar, dar un vuelco

overuse [,o:vər'ju:z] *vt* **-used**; **-using** : abusar de

overview ['o:vər,vju:] *n* : resumen *m*, visión *f* general

overweening [,o:vər'wi:nɪŋ] *adj* **1** ARROGANT : arrogante, soberbio **2** IMMODERATE : desmesurado

overweight [,o:vər'weɪt] *adj* : demasiado gordo, demasiado pesado

overwhelm [,o:vər'hwɛlm] *vt* **1** CRUSH, DEFEAT : aplastar, arrollar **2** SUBMERGE : inundar, sumergir **3** OVERPOWER : abrumar, agobiar ⟨overwhelmed by remorse : abrumado de remordimiento⟩

overwhelming [,o:vər'hwɛlmɪŋ] *adj* **1** CRUSHING : abrumador, apabullante **2** SWEEPING : arrollador, aplastante ⟨an overwhelming majority : una mayoría aplastante⟩

overwork [,o:vər'wərk] *vt* **1** : hacer trabajar demasiado **2** OVERUSE : abusar de — *vi* : trabajar demasiado

overwrought [,o:vər'rɔt] *adj* : alterado, sobreexcitado

ovoid ['o:,vɔɪd] *or* **ovoidal** [o'vɔɪdəl] *adj* : ovoide

ovulate ['ɑvjə,leɪt, 'o:-] *vi* **-lated**; **-lating** : ovular

ovulation [,ɑvjə'leɪʃən, ,o:-] *n* : ovulación *f*

ovum ['o:vəm] *n*, *pl* **ova** [-və] : óvulo *m*

owe ['o:] *vt* **owed**; **owing** : deber ⟨you owe me $10 : me debes $10⟩ ⟨he owes his wealth to his father : le debe su riqueza a su padre⟩

owing to *prep* : debido a

owl ['aʊl] *n* : búho *m*, lechuza *f*, tecolote *m Mex*

own¹ ['o:n] *vt* **1** POSSESS : poseer, tener, ser dueño de **2** ADMIT : reconocer, admitir — *vi* **to own up** : reconocer (algo), admitir (algo)

own² *adj* : propio, personal, particular ⟨his own car : su propio coche⟩

own³ *pron* **my; (your, his/her, our, their)**; **own** : el mío, la mía; el tuyo, la tuya; el suyo, la suya; el nuestro, la nuestra ⟨to each his own : cada uno a lo suyo⟩ ⟨money of my own : mi propio dinero⟩ ⟨to be on one's own : estar solo⟩

owner ['o:nər] *n* : dueño *m*, -ña *f*; propietario *m*, -ria *f*

ownership ['o:nər,ʃɪp] *n* : propiedad *f*

ox ['ɑks] *n*, *pl* **oxen** ['ɑksən] : buey *m*

oxidation [,ɑksə'deɪʃən] *n* : oxidación *f*

oxide ['ɑk,saɪd] *n* : óxido *m*

oxidize ['ɑksə,daɪz] *vt* **-dized**; **-dizing** : oxidar

oxygen ['ɑksɪdʒən] *n* : oxígeno *m*

oyster ['ɔɪstər] *n* : ostra *f*, ostión *m Mex*

ozone ['o:,zo:n] *n* : ozono *m*

P

p ['pi:] *n, pl* **p's** *or* **ps** ['pi:z] : decimosexta letra del alfabeto inglés

pace¹ ['peɪs] *v* **paced; pacing** *vi* : caminar, ir y venir — *vt* **1** : caminar por ⟨she paced the floor : caminaba de un lado a otro del cuarto⟩ **2 to pace a runner** : marcarle el ritmo a un corredor

pace² *n* **1** STEP : paso *m* **2** RATE : paso *m*, ritmo *m* ⟨to set the pace : marcar el paso, marcar la pauta⟩

pacemaker ['peɪsˌmeɪkər] *n* : marcapasos *m*

pacific [pə'sɪfɪk] *adj* : pacífico

pacifier ['pæsəˌfaɪər] *n* : chupete *m*, chupón *m*, mamila *f Mex*

pacifism ['pæsəˌfɪzəm] *n* : pacifismo *m*

pacifist ['pæsəfɪst] *n* : pacifista *mf*

pacify ['pæsəˌfaɪ] *vt* **-fied; -fying 1** SOOTHE : apaciguar, pacificar **2** : pacificar (un país, una región, etc.)

pack¹ ['pæk] *vt* **1** PACKAGE : empaquetar, embalar, envasar **2** : empacar, meter (en una maleta) ⟨to pack one's bag : hacer la maleta⟩ **3** FILL : llenar, abarrotar ⟨a packed theater : un teatro abarrotado⟩ **4 to pack off** SEND : mandar — *vi* : empacar, hacer las maletas

pack² *n* **1** BUNDLE : bulto *m*, fardo *m* **2** BACKPACK : mochila *f* **3** PACKAGE : paquete *m*, cajetilla *f* (de cigarrillos, etc.) **4** : manada *f* (de lobos, etc.), jauría *f* (de perros) ⟨a pack of thieves : una pandilla de ladrones⟩

package¹ ['pækɪdʒ] *vt* **-aged; -aging** : empaquetar, embalar

package² *n* : paquete *m*, bulto *m*

packaging ['pækɪdʒɪŋ] *n* **1** : embalaje *m* **2** WRAPPING : envoltorio *m*

packer ['pækər] *n* : empacador *m*, -dora *f*

packet ['pækət] *n* : paquete *m*

packing ['pækɪŋ] *n* : embalaje *m*

pact ['pækt] *n* : pacto *m*, acuerdo *m*

pad¹ ['pæd] *vt* **padded; padding 1** FILL, STUFF : rellenar, acolchar (una silla, una pared) **2** : meter paja en, rellenar ⟨to pad a speech : rellenar un discurso⟩

pad² *n* **1** CUSHION : almohadilla *f* ⟨a shoulder pad : una hombrera⟩ **2** TABLET : bloc *m* (de papel) **3** *or* **lily pad** : hoja *f* grande (de un nenúfar) **4 ink pad** : tampón *m* **5 launching pad** : plataforma *f* (de lanzamiento)

padding ['pædɪŋ] *n* **1** FILLING : relleno *m* **2** : paja *f* (en un discurso, etc.)

paddle¹ ['pædəl] *v* **-dled; -dling** *vt* **1** : hacer avanzar (una canoa) con canalete **2** HIT : azotar, darle nalgadas a (con una pala o paleta) — *vi* **1** : remar (en una canoa) **2** SPLASH : chapotear, mojarse los pies

paddle² *n* **1** : canalete *m*, zagual *m* (de una canoa, etc.) **2** : pala *f*, paleta *f* (en deportes)

paddock ['pædək] *n* **1** PASTURE : potrero *m* **2** : paddock *m*, cercado *m* (en un hipódromo)

paddy ['pædi] *n, pl* **-dies** : arrozal *m*

padlock¹ ['pædˌlɑk] *vt* : cerrar con candado

padlock² *n* : candado *m*

pagan¹ ['peɪgən] *adj* : pagano

pagan² *n* : pagano *m*, -na *f*

paganism ['peɪgənˌɪzəm] *n* : paganismo *m*

page¹ ['peɪdʒ] *vt* **paged; paging** : llamar por altavoz

page² *n* **1** BELLHOP : botones *m* **2** : página *f* (de un libro, etc.)

pageant ['pædʒənt] *n* **1** SPECTACLE : espectáculo *m* **2** PROCESSION : desfile *m*

pageantry ['pædʒəntri] *n* : pompa *f*, fausto *m*

pager ['peɪdʒər] *n* BEEPER : buscapersonas *m*

pagoda [pə'goːdə] *n* : pagoda *f*

paid → **pay**

pail ['peɪl] *n* : balde *m*, cubo *m*, cubeta *f Mex*

pailful ['peɪlˌful] *n* : balde *m*, cubo *m*, cubeta *f Mex*

pain¹ ['peɪn] *vt* : doler

pain² *n* **1** PENALTY : pena *f* ⟨under pain of death : so pena de muerte⟩ **2** SUFFERING : dolor *m*, malestar *m*, pena *f* (mental) **3 pains** *npl* EFFORT : esmero *m*, esfuerzo *m* ⟨to take pains : esmerarse⟩

painful ['peɪnfəl] *adj* : doloroso — **painfully** *adv*

painkiller ['peɪnˌkɪlər] *n* : analgésico *m*

painless ['peɪnləs] *adj* : indoloro, sin dolor

painlessly ['peɪnləsli] *adv* : sin dolor

painstaking ['peɪnˌsteɪkɪŋ] *adj* : esmerado, cuidadoso, meticuloso — **painstakingly** *adv*

paint¹ ['peɪnt] *v* : pintar

paint² *n* : pintura *f*

paintbrush ['peɪntˌbrʌʃ] *n* : pincel *m* (de un artista), brocha *f* (para pintar casas, etc.)

painter ['peɪntər] *n* : pintor *m*, -tora *f*

painting ['peɪntɪŋ] *n* : pintura *f*

pair¹ ['pær] *vt* : emparejar, poner en parejas — *vi* : emparejarse

pair² *n* : par *m* (de objetos), pareja *f* (de personas o animales) ⟨a pair of scissors : unas tijeras⟩

pajamas [pə'dʒɑməz, -'dʒæ-] *npl* : pijama *m*, piyama *mf*

Pakistani [ˌpækɪ'stæni, ˌpɑkɪ'stɑni] *n* : paquistaní *mf* — **Pakistani** *adj*

pal ['pæl] *n* : amigo *m*, -ga *f*; compinche *mf fam*; chamo *m*, -ma *f Ven fam*; cuate *m*, -ta *f Mex*

palace ['pæləs] *n* : palacio *m*

palatable ['pælətəbəl] *adj* : sabroso

palate ['pælət] *n* **1** : paladar *m* (de la boca) **2** TASTE : paladar *m*, gusto *m*

palatial [pə'leɪʃəl] *adj* : suntuoso, espléndido

palaver [pə'læːvər, -'lɑ-] *n* : palabrería *f*

pale¹ ['peɪl] *v* **paled; paling** *vi* : palidecer — *vt* : hacer pálido

pale² *adj* **paler; palest 1** : pálido ⟨to turn pale : palidecer, ponerse pálido⟩ **2** : claro (dícese de los colores)

paleness ['peɪlnəs] *n* : palidez *f*

paleontologist [ˌpeɪliˌɑn'tɑlədʒɪst] *n* : paleontólogo *m*, -ga *f*

paleontology [ˌpeɪliˌɑn'tɑlədʒi] *n* : paleontología *f*

Palestinian [ˌpælə'stɪniən] *n* : palestino *m*, -na *f* — **Palestinian** *adj*

palette ['pælət] *n* : paleta *f* (para mezclar pigmentos)

palisade [ˌpælə'seɪd] *n* **1** FENCE : empalizada *f*, estacada *f* **2** CLIFFS : acantilado *m*

pall¹ ['pɔl] *vi* : perder su sabor, dejar de gustar

pall² *n* **1** : paño *m* mortuorio (sobre un ataúd) **2** COVER : cortina *f* (de humo, etc.) **3 to cast a pall over** : ensombrecer

pallbearer ['pɔlˌbɛrər] *n* : portador *m*, -dora *f* del féretro

pallet ['pælət] *n* **1** BED : camastro *m* **2** PLATFORM : plataforma *f* de carga

palliative ['pæliˌeɪtɪv, 'pæljətɪv] *adj* : paliativo

pallid ['pæləd] *adj* : pálido

pallor ['pælər] *n* : palidez *f*

palm¹ ['pɑm, 'pɑlm] *vt* **1** CONCEAL : escamotear (un naipe, etc.) **2 to palm off** : encajar, endilgar *fam* ⟨he palmed it off on me : me lo endilgó⟩

palm² *n* **1** *or* **palm tree** : palmera *f* **2** : palma *f* (de la mano)

Palm Sunday *n* : Domingo *m* de Ramos

palomino [ˌpælə'miːˌnoː] *n, pl* **-nos** : caballo *m* de color dorado

palpable ['pælpəbəl] *adj* : palpable — **palpably** [-bli] *adv*

palpitate ['pælpəˌteɪt] *vi* **-tated; -tating** : palpitar

palpitation [ˌpælpə'teɪʃən] *n* : palpitación *f*

palsy ['pɔlzi] *n, pl* **-sies 1** : parálisis *f* → **cerebral palsy**

paltry ['pɔltri] *adj* **-trier; -est** : mísero, mezquino, insignificante ⟨a paltry excuse : una mala excusa⟩

pampas ['pæmpəz, 'pɑmpəs] *npl* : pampa *f*

pamper ['pæmpər] *vt* : mimar, consentir, chiquear *Mex*

pamphlet ['pæmpflət] *n* : panfleto *m*, folleto *m*

pan¹ ['pæn] *vt* **panned; panning** CRITICIZE : poner por los suelos — *vi* **to pan for gold** : cribar el oro con batea, lavar oro

pan² *n* **1** : cacerola *f*, cazuela *f* **2 frying pan** : sartén *mf*, freidera *f* *Mex*

panacea [ˌpænə'siːə] *n* : panacea *f*

Panamanian [ˌpænə'meɪniən] *n* : panameño *m*, -ña *f* — **Panamanian** *adj*

pancake ['pænˌkeɪk] *n* : panqueque *m*

pancreas ['pæŋkriəs, 'pæn-] *n* : páncreas *m*

panda ['pændə] *n* : panda *mf*

pandemonium [ˌpændə'moːniəm] *n* : pandemonio *m*, pandemónium *m*

pander ['pændər] *vi* **to pander to** : satisfacer, complacer (a alguien) ⟨to pander to popular taste : satisfacer el gusto popular⟩

pane ['peɪn] *n* : cristal *m*, vidrio *m*

panel¹ ['pænəl] *vt* **-eled** *or* **-elled; -eling** *or* **-elling** : adornar con paneles

panel² *n* **1** : lista *f* de nombres (de un jurado, etc.) **2** GROUP : panel *m*, grupo *m* ⟨discussion panel : panel de discusión⟩ **3** : panel *m* (de una pared, etc.) **4 instrument panel** : tablero *m* de instrumentos

paneling ['pænəlɪŋ] *n* : paneles *mpl*

pang ['pæŋ] *n* : puntada *f*, punzada *f*

panic¹ ['pænɪk] *v* **-icked; -icking** *vt* : llenar de pánico — *vi* : ser presa de pánico

panic² *n* : pánico *m*

panicky ['pænɪki] *adj* : presa de pánico

panorama [ˌpænə'ræmə, -'rɑ-] *n* : panorama *m*

panoramic [ˌpænə'ræmɪk, -'rɑ-] *adj* : panorámico

pansy ['pænzi] *n, pl* **-sies** : pensamiento *m*

pant¹ ['pænt] *vi* : jadear, resoplar

pant² *n* : jadeo *m*, resoplo *m*

pantaloons [ˌpæntə'luːnz] → **pants**

pantheon ['pænθiˌɑn, -ən] *n* : panteón *m*

panther ['pænθər] *n* : pantera *f*

panties ['pæntiz] *npl* : calzones *mpl*; pantaletas *fpl* *Mex, Ven*; bragas *fpl* *Spain*

pantomime¹ ['pæntəˌmaɪm] *v* **-mimed; -miming** *vt* : representar mediante la pantomima — *vi* : hacer la mímica

pantomime² *n* : pantomima *f*

pantry ['pæntri] *n, pl* **-tries** : despensa *f*

pants ['pænts] *npl* **1** TROUSERS : pantalón *m*, pantalones *mpl* **2** → **panties**

panty hose ['pænti] *ns & pl* : medias *fpl*, panties *mfpl*, pantimedias *fpl* *Mex*

pap ['pæp] *n* : papilla *f* (para bebés, etc.)

papa ['pɑpə] *n* : papá *m*

papal ['peɪpəl] *adj* : papal

papaya [pə'paɪə] *n* : papaya *f* (fruta)

paper¹ ['peɪpər] *vt* WALLPAPER : empapelar

paper² *adj* : de papel

paper³ *n* **1** : papel *m* ⟨a piece of paper : un papel⟩ **2** DOCUMENT : papel *m*, documento *m* **3** NEWSPAPER : periódico *m*, diario *m*

paperback ['peɪpərˌbæk] *n* : libro *m* en rústica

paper clip *n* : clip *m*, sujetapapeles *m*

paperweight ['peɪpərˌweɪt] *n* : pisapapeles *m*

paperwork ['peɪpər,wərk] *n* : papeleo *m*
papery ['peɪpəri] *adj* : parecido al papel
papier–mâché [,peɪpərmə'ʃeɪ, ,pæ-,pjeɪmæ'ʃeɪ] *n* : papel *m* maché
papoose [pæ'pu:s, pə-] *n* : niño *m*, -ña *f* de los indios norteamericanos
paprika [pə'pri:kə, pæ-] *n* : pimentón *m*, paprika *f*
papyrus [pə'paɪrəs] *n, pl* **-ruses** *or* **-ri** [-,ri, -,raɪ] : papiro *m*
par ['pɑr] *n* **1** VALUE : valor *m* (nominal), par *f* ⟨below par : debajo de la par⟩ **2** EQUALITY : igualdad *f* ⟨to be on a par with : estar al mismo nivel que⟩ **3** : par *m* (en golf)
parable ['pærəbəl] *n* : parábola *f*
parabola [pə'ræbələ] *n* : parábola *f* (en matemáticas)
parachute[1] ['pærə,ʃu:t] *vi* **-chuted; -chuting** : lanzarse en paracaídas
parachute[2] *n* : paracaídas *m*
parachutist ['pærə,ʃu:tɪst] *n* : paracaidista *mf*
parade[1] [pə'reɪd] *vi* **-raded; -rading 1** MARCH : desfilar **2** SHOW OFF : pavonearse, lucirse
parade[2] *n* **1** PROCESSION : desfile *m* **2** DISPLAY : alarde *m*
paradigm ['pærə,daɪm] *n* : paradigma *m*
paradise ['pærə,daɪs, -,daɪz] *n* : paraíso *m*
paradox ['pærə,dɑks] *n* : paradoja *f*
paradoxical [,pærə'dɑksɪkəl] *adj* : paradójico — **paradoxically** *adv*
paraffin ['pærəfən] *n* : parafina *f*
paragon ['pærə,gɑn, -gən] *n* : dechado *m*
paragraph[1] ['pærə,græf] *vt* : dividir en párrafos
paragraph[2] *n* : párrafo *m*, acápite *m*
Paraguayan [,pærə'gwaɪən, -'gweɪ-] *n* : paraguayo *m*, -ya *f* — **Paraguayan** *adj*
parakeet ['pærə,ki:t] *n* : periquito *m*
paralegal [,pærə'li:gəl] *n* : asistente *mf* de abogado
parallel[1] ['pærə,lɛl, -ləl] *vt* **1** MATCH, RESEMBLE : ser paralelo a, ser análogo a, corresponder con **2** : extenderse en línea paralela con ⟨the road parallels the river : el camino se extiende a lo largo del río⟩
parallel[2] *adj* : paralelo
parallel[3] *n* **1** : línea *f* paralela, superficie *f* paralela **2** : paralelo *m* (en geografía) **3** SIMILARITY : paralelismo *m*, semejanza *f*
parallelogram [,pærə'lɛlə,græm] *n* : paralelogramo *m*
paralysis [pə'ræləsɪs] *n, pl* **-yses** [-,si:z] : parálisis *f*
paralyze ['pærə,laɪz] *vt* **-lyzed; -lyzing** : paralizar
parameter [pə'ræmətər] *n* : parámetro *m*
paramount ['pærə,maʊnt] *adj* : supremo ⟨of paramount importance : de suma importancia⟩
paranoia [,pærə'nɔɪə] *n* : paranoia *f*

paranoid ['pærə,nɔɪd] *adj* : paranoico
parapet ['pærəpət, -,pɛt] *n* : parapeto *m*
paraphernalia [,pærəfə'neɪljə, -fər-] *ns & pl* : parafernalia *f*
paraphrase[1] ['pærə,freɪz] *vt* **-phrased; -phrasing** : parafrasear
paraphrase[2] *n* : paráfrasis *f*
paraplegic[1] [,pærə'pli:dʒɪk] *adj* : parapléjico
paraplegic[2] *n* : parapléjico *m*, -ca *f*
parasite ['pærə,saɪt] *n* : parásito *m*
parasitic [,pærə'sɪtɪk] *adj* : parasitario
parasol ['pærə,sɔl] *n* : sombrilla *f*, quitasol *m*, parasol *m*
paratrooper ['pærə,tru:pər] *n* : paracaidista *mf* (militar)
parboil ['pɑr,bɔɪl] *vt* : sancochar, cocer a medias
parcel[1] ['pɑrsəl] *vt* **-celed** *or* **-celled; -celing** *or* **-celling** *or* **to parcel out** : repartir, parcelar (tierras)
parcel[2] *n* **1** LOT : parcela *f*, lote *m* **2** PACKAGE : paquete *m*, bulto *m*
parch ['pɑrtʃ] *vt* : resecar
parchment ['pɑrtʃmənt] *n* : pergamino *m*
pardon[1] ['pɑrdən] *vt* **1** FORGIVE : perdonar, disculpar ⟨pardon me! : ¡perdone!, ¡disculpe la molestia!⟩ **2** REPRIEVE : indultar (a un delincuente)
pardon[2] *n* **1** FORGIVENESS : perdón *m* **2** REPRIEVE : indulto *m*
pardonable ['pɑrdənəbəl] *adj* : perdonable, disculpable
pare ['pær] *vt* **pared; paring 1** PEEL : pelar **2** TRIM : recortar **3** REDUCE : reducir ⟨he pared it (down) to 50 pages : lo redujo a 50 páginas⟩
parent ['pærənt] *n* **1** : madre *f*, padre *m* **2 parents** *npl* : padres *mpl*
parentage ['pærəntɪdʒ] *n* : linaje *m*, abolengo *m*, origen *m*
parental [pə'rɛntəl] *adj* : de los padres
parenthesis [pə'rɛnθəsɪs] *n, pl* **-theses** [-,si:z] : paréntesis *m*
parenthetic [,pærən'θɛtɪk] *or* **parenthetical** [-ʈɪkəl] *adj* : parentético — **parenthetically** [-ʈɪkli] *adv*
parenthood ['pærənt,hʊd] *n* : paternidad *f*
parfait [pɑr'feɪ] *n* : postre *m* elaborado con frutas y helado
pariah [pə'raɪə] *n* : paria *mf*
parish ['pærɪʃ] *n* : parroquia *f*
parishioner [pə'rɪʃənər] *n* : feligrés *m*, -gresa *f*
parity ['pærəti] *n, pl* **-ties** : paridad *f*
park[1] ['pɑrk] *vt* : estacionar, parquear, aparcar *Spain* — *vi* : estacionarse, parquearse, aparcar *Spain*
park[2] *n* : parque *m*
parka ['pɑrkə] *n* : parka *f*
parking ['pɑrkɪŋ] *n* : estacionamiento *m*, aparcamiento *m* Spain
parkway ['pɑrk,weɪ] *n* : carretera *f* ajardinada, bulevar *m*
parley[1] ['pɑrli] *vi* : parlamentar, negociar

parley[2] *n, pl* **-leys** : negociación *f*, parlamento *m*

parliament ['pɑrləmənt, 'pɑrljə-] *n* : parlamento *m*

parliamentary [ˌpɑrlə'mɛntəri, ˌpɑrljə-] *adj* : parlamentario

parlor ['pɑrlər] *n* **1** : sala *f*, salón *m* (en una casa) **2** : salón *m* ⟨beauty parlor : salón de belleza⟩ **3 funeral parlor** : funeraria *f*

parochial [pə'ro:kiəl] *adj* **1** : parroquial **2** PROVINCIAL : pueblerino, de miras estrechas

parody[1] ['pærədi] *vt* **-died; -dying** : parodiar

parody[2] *n, pl* **-dies** : parodia *f*

parole [pə'ro:l] *n* : libertad *f* condicional

paroxysm ['pærək,sɪzəm, pə'rɑk-] *n* : paroxismo *m*

parquet ['pɑr,keɪ, pɑr'keɪ] *n* : parquet *m*, parqué *m*

parrakeet → parakeet

parrot ['pærət] *n* : loro *m*, papagayo *m*

parry[1] ['pæri] *v* **-ried; -rying** *vi* : parar un golpe — *vt* EVADE : esquivar (una pregunta, etc.)

parry[2] *n, pl* **-ries** : parada *f*

parsimonious [ˌpɑrsə'mo:niəs] *adj* : tacaño, mezquino

parsley ['pɑrsli] *n* : perejil *m*

parsnip ['pɑrsnɪp] *n* : chirivía *f*

parson ['pɑrsən] *n* : pastor *m*, -tora *f*; clérigo *m*

parsonage ['pɑrsənɪʤ] *n* : rectoría *f*, casa *f* del párroco

part[1] ['pɑrt] *vi* **1** SEPARATE : separarse, despedirse ⟨we should part as friends : debemos separarnos amistosamente⟩ **2** OPEN : abrirse ⟨the curtains parted : las cortinas se abrieron⟩ **3 to part with** : deshacerse de — *vt* **1** SEPARATE : separar **2 to part one's hair** : hacerse la raya, peinarse con raya

part[2] *n* **1** SECTION, SEGMENT : parte *f*, sección *f* **2** PIECE : pieza *f* (de una máquina, etc.) **3** ROLE : papel *m* **4** : raya *f* (del pelo)

partake [pɑr'teɪk, pər-] *vi* **-took** [-'tʊk]; **-taken** [-'teɪkən;]; **-taking 1 to partake of** CONSUME : comer, beber, tomar **2 to partake in** : participar en (una actividad, etc.)

partial ['pɑrʃəl] *adj* **1** BIASED : parcial, tendencioso **2** INCOMPLETE : parcial, incompleto **3 to be partial to** : ser aficionado a

partiality [ˌpɑrʃi'æləti] *n, pl* **-ties** : parcialidad *f*

partially ['pɑrʃəli] *adv* : parcialmente

participant [pər'tɪsəpənt, pɑr-] *n* : participante *mf*

participate [pər'tɪsə,peɪt, pɑr-] *vi* **-pated; -pating** : participar

participation [pər,tɪsə'peɪʃən, pɑr-] *n* : participación *f*

participle ['pɑrtə,sɪpəl] *n* : participio *m*

particle ['pɑrtɪkəl] *n* : partícula *f*

particular[1] [pər'tɪkjələr] *adj* **1** SPECIFIC : particular, en particular ⟨this particular person : esta persona en particular⟩ **2** SPECIAL : particular, especial ⟨with particular emphasis : con un énfasis especial⟩ **3** FUSSY : exigente, maniático ⟨to be very particular : ser muy especial⟩ ⟨I'm not particular : me da igual⟩

particular[2] *n* **1** DETAIL : detalle *m*, sentido *m* **2 in particular** : en particular, en especial

particularly [pər'tɪkjələrli] *adv* **1** ESPECIALLY : particularmente, especialmente **2** SPECIFICALLY : específicamente, en especial

partisan ['pɑrtəzən, -sən] *n* **1** ADHERENT : partidario *m*, -ria *f* **2** GUERRILLA : partisano *m*, -na *f*; guerrillero *m*, -ra *f*

partition[1] [pər'tɪʃən, pɑr-] *vt* : dividir ⟨to partition off (a room) : dividir (una habitación) con un tabique⟩

partition[2] *n* **1** DISTRIBUTION : partición *f*, división *f*, reparto *m* **2** DIVIDER : tabique *m*, mampara *f*, biombo *m*

partly ['pɑrtli] *adv* : en parte, parcialmente

partner ['pɑrtnər] *n* **1** COMPANION : compañero *m*, -ra *f* **2** : pareja *f* (en un juego, etc.) ⟨dancing partner : pareja de baile⟩ **3** SPOUSE : cónyuge *mf* **4** *or* **business partner** : socio *m*, -cia *f*; asociado *m*, -da *f*

partnership ['pɑrtnər,ʃɪp] *n* **1** ASSOCIATION : asociación *f*, compañerismo *m* **2** : sociedad *f* (de negociantes) ⟨to form a partnership : asociarse⟩

part of speech : categoría *f* gramatical

partridge ['pɑrtrɪʤ] *n, pl* **-tridge** *or* **-tridges** : perdiz *f*

party ['pɑrti] *n, pl* **-ties 1** : partido *m* (político) **2** PARTICIPANT : parte *f*, participante *mf* **3** GROUP : grupo *m* (de personas) **4** GATHERING : fiesta *f* ⟨to throw a party : dar una fiesta⟩

parvenu ['pɑrvə,nu:, -,nju:] *n* : advenedizo *m*, -za *f*

pass[1] ['pæs] *vi* **1** : pasar, cruzarse ⟨a car passed by : pasó un coche⟩ ⟨we passed in the hallway : nos cruzamos en el pasillo⟩ **2** CEASE : pasarse ⟨the pain passed : se pasó el dolor⟩ **3** ELAPSE : pasar, transcurrir **4** PROCEED : pasar ⟨let me pass : déjame pasar⟩ **5** HAPPEN : pasar, ocurrir **6** : pasar, aprobar (en un examen) **7** RULE : fallar ⟨the jury passed on the case : el jurado falló en el caso⟩ **8** *or* **to pass down** : pasar ⟨the throne passed to his son : el trono pasó a su hijo⟩ **9 to let pass** OVERLOOK : pasar por alto **10 to pass as** : pasar por **11 to pass away** *or* **to pass on** DIE : fallecer, morir — *vt* **1** : pasar por ⟨they passed the house : pasaron por la casa⟩ **2** OVERTAKE : pasar, adelantar **3** SPEND : pasar (tiempo) **4** HAND : pasar ⟨pass me the salt : pásame la sal⟩ **5** : aprobar (un examen, una ley)

pass² *n* **1** CROSSING, GAP : paso *m*, desfiladero *m*, puerto *m* ⟨mountain pass : puerto de montaña⟩ **2** PERMIT : pase *m*, permiso *m* **3** : pase *m* (en deportes) **4** SITUATION : situación *f* (difícil) ⟨things have come to a pretty pass! : ¡hasta dónde hemos llegado!⟩

passable ['pæsəbəl] *adj* **1** ADEQUATE : adecuado, pasable **2** : transitable (dícese de un camino, etc.)

passably ['pæsəbli] *adv* : pasablemente

passage ['pæsɪʤ] *n* **1** PASSING : paso *m* ⟨the passage of time : el paso del tiempo⟩ **2** PASSAGEWAY : pasillo *m* (dentro de un edificio), pasaje *m* (entre edificios) **3** VOYAGE : travesía *f* (por el mar), viaje *m* ⟨to grant safe passage : dar un salvoconducto⟩ **4** SECTION : pasaje *m* (en música o literatura)

passageway ['pæsɪʤ,weɪ] *n* : pasillo *m*, pasadizo *m*, corredor *m*

passbook ['pæs,bʊk] *n* BANKBOOK : libreta *f* de ahorros

passé [pæ'seɪ] *adj* : pasado de moda

passenger ['pæsənʤər] *n* : pasajero *m*, -ra *f*

passerby [,pæsər'baɪ, 'pæsər,-] *n, pl* **passersby** : transeúnte *mf*

passing ['pæsɪŋ] *n* DEATH : fallecimiento *m*

passion ['pæʃən] *n* : pasión *f*, ardor *m*

passionate ['pæʃənət] *adj* **1** IRASCIBLE : irascible, iracundo **2** ARDENT : apasionado, ardiente, ferviente, fogoso

passionately ['pæʃənətli] *adv* : apasionadamente, fervientemente, con pasión

passive¹ ['pæsɪv] *adj* : pasivo — **passively** *adv*

passive² *n* : voz *f* pasiva (en gramática)

passivity [pæ'sɪvəti] *n* : pasividad *f*

Passover ['pæs,o,vər] *n* : Pascua *f* (en el judaísmo)

passport ['pæs,pɔrt] *n* : pasaporte *m*

password ['pæs,wərd] *n* : contraseña *f*

past¹ ['pæst] *adv* : por delante ⟨he drove past : pasamos en coche⟩

past² *adj* **1** AGO : hace ⟨10 years past : hace 10 años⟩ **2** LAST : último ⟨the past few months : los últimos meses⟩ **3** BYGONE : pasado ⟨in past times : en tiempos pasados⟩ **4** : pasado (en gramática)

past³ *n* : pasado *m*

past⁴ *prep* **1** BY : por, por delante de ⟨he ran past the house : pasó por la casa corriendo⟩ **2** BEYOND : más allá de ⟨just past the corner : un poco más allá de la esquina⟩ ⟨we went past the exit : pasamos la salida⟩ **3** AFTER : después de ⟨past noon : después del mediodía⟩ ⟨half past two : las dos y media⟩

pasta ['pɑstə, 'pæs-] *n* : pasta *f*

paste¹ ['peɪst] *vt* **pasted; pasting** : pegar (con engrudo)

paste² *n* **1** : pasta *f* ⟨tomato paste : pasta de tomate⟩ **2** : engrudo *m* (para pegar)

pasteboard ['peɪst,bɔrd] *n* : cartón *m*, cartulina *f*

pastel [pæ'stɛl] *n* : pastel *m* — **pastel** *adj*

pasteurization [,pæsʧərə'zeɪʃən, ,pæstjə-] *n* : pasteurización *f*

pasteurize ['pæsʧə,raɪz, 'pæstjə-] *vt* **-ized; -izing** : pasteurizar

pastime ['pæs,taɪm] *n* : pasatiempo *m*

pastor ['pæstər] *n* : pastor *m*, -tora *f*

pastoral ['pæstərəl] *adj* : pastoral

past participle *n* : participio *m* pasado

pastry ['peɪstri] *n, pl* **-ries 1** DOUGH : pasta *f*, masa *f* **2** **pastries** *npl* : pasteles *mpl*

pasture¹ ['pæsʧər] *v* **-tured; -turing** *vi* GRAZE : pacer, pastar — *vt* : apacentar, pastar

pasture² *n* : pastizal *m*, potrero *m*, pasto *m*

pasty ['peɪsti] *adj* **pastier; -est 1** : pastoso (en consistencia) **2** PALLID : pálido

pat¹ ['pæt] *vt* **patted; patting** : dar palmaditas a, tocar

pat² *adv* : de memoria ⟨to have down pat : saberse de memoria⟩

pat³ *adj* **1** APT : apto, apropiado **2** GLIB : fácil **3** UNYIELDING : firme ⟨to stand pat : mantenerse firme⟩

pat⁴ *n* **1** TAP : golpecito *m*, palmadita *f* ⟨a pat on the back : una palmadita en la espalda⟩ **2** CARESS : caricia *f* **3** : porción *f* ⟨a pat of butter : una porción de mantequilla⟩

patch¹ ['pæʧ] *vt* **1** MEND, REPAIR : remendar, parchar, ponerle un parche a **2 to patch together** IMPROVISE : confeccionar, improvisar **3 to patch up** : arreglar ⟨they patched things up : hicieron las paces⟩

patch² *n* **1** : parche *m*, remiendo *m* (para la ropa) ⟨eye patch : parche para el ojo⟩ **2** PIECE : mancha *f*, trozo *m* ⟨a patch of sky : un trozo de cielo⟩ **3** PLOT : parcela *f*, terreno *m* ⟨cabbage patch : parcela de repollos⟩

patchwork ['pæʧ,wərk] *n* : labor *f* de retazos

patchy ['pæʧi] *adj* **patchier; -est 1** IRREGULAR : irregular, desigual **2** INCOMPLETE : parcial, incompleto

patent¹ ['pætənt] *vt* : patentar

patent² ['pætənt, 'peɪt-] *adj* **1** OBVIOUS : patente, evidente **2** ['pæt-] PATENTED : patentado

patent³ ['pætənt] *n* : patente *f*

patently ['pætəntli] *adv* : patentemente, evidentemente

paternal [pə'tərnəl] *adj* **1** FATHERLY : paternal **2** : paterno ⟨paternal grandfather : abuelo paterno⟩

paternity [pə'tərnəti] *n* : paternidad *f*

path ['pæθ, 'pɑθ] *n* **1** TRACK, TRAIL : camino *m*, sendero *m*, senda *f* **2** COURSE, ROUTE : recorrido *m*, trayecto *m*, trayectoria *f*

pathetic [pə'θɛtɪk] *adj* : patético — **pathetically** [-tɪkli] *adv*

pathological [,pæθə'lɑʤɪkəl] *adj* : patológico

pathologist [pə'θɑlədʒɪst] *n* : patólogo *m*, -ga *f*
pathology [pə'θɑlədʒi] *n, pl* **-gies** : patología *f*
pathos ['peɪˌθɑs, 'pæ-, -ˌθɔs] *n* : patetismo *m*
pathway ['pæθˌweɪ] *n* : camino *m*, sendero *m*, senda *f*, vereda *f*
patience ['peɪʃənts] *n* : paciencia *f*
patient[1] ['peɪʃənt] *adj* : paciente — **patiently** *adv*
patient[2] *n* : paciente *mf*
patio ['pætiˌoː] *n, pl* **-tios** : patio *m*
patriarch ['peɪtriˌɑrk] *n* : patriarca *m*
patriarchy ['peɪtriˌɑrki] *n, pl* **-chies** : patriarcado *m*
patrimony ['pætrəˌmoːni] *n, pl* **-nies** : patrimonio *m*
patriot ['peɪtriət] *n* : patriota *mf*
patriotic [ˌpeɪtri'ɑtɪk] *adj* : patriótico — **patriotically** *adv*
patriotism ['peɪtriəˌtɪzəm] *n* : patriotismo *m*
patrol[1] [pə'troːl] *v* **-trolled; -trolling** : patrullar
patrol[2] *n* : patrulla *f*
patrolman [pə'troːlmən] *n, pl* **-men** [-mən, -ˌmɛn] : policía *mf*, guardia *mf*
patron ['peɪtrən] *n* **1** SPONSOR : patrocinador *m*, -dora *f* **2** CUSTOMER : cliente *m*, -ta *f* **3** *or* **patron saint** : patrono *m*, -na *f*
patronage ['peɪtrənɪʤ, 'pæ-] *n* **1** SPONSORSHIP : patrocinio *m* **2** CLIENTELE : clientela *f* **3** : influencia *f* (política)
patronize ['peɪtrəˌnaɪz, 'pæ-] *vt* **-ized; -izing 1** SPONSOR : patrocinar **2** : ser cliente de (un negocio) **3** : tratar con condescendencia
patter[1] ['pætər] *v* **1** TAP : golpetear, tamborilear (dícese de la lluvia) **2 to patter about** : corretear (con pasos ligeros)
patter[2] *n* **1** TAPPING : golpeteo *m*, tamborileo *m* (de la lluvia), correteo *m* (de pies) **2** CHATTER : palabrería *f*, parloteo *m fam*
pattern[1] ['pætərn] *vt* **1** BASE : basar (en un modelo) **2 to pattern after** : hacer imitación de
pattern[2] *n* **1** MODEL : modelo *m*, patrón *m* (de costura) **2** DESIGN : diseño *m*, dibujo *m*, estampado *m* (de tela) **3** NORM, STANDARD : pauta *f*, norma *f*, patrón *m*
patty ['pæti] *n, pl* **-ties** : porción *f* de carne picada (u otro alimento) en forma de ruedita ⟨a hamburger patty : una hamburguesa⟩
paucity ['pɔsəti] *n* : escasez *f*
paunch ['pɔntʃ] *n* : panza *f*, barriga *f*
pauper ['pɔpər] *n* : pobre *mf*, indigente *mf*
pause[1] ['pɔz] *vi* **paused; pausing** : hacer una pausa, pararse (brevemente)
pause[2] *n* : pausa *f*
pave ['peɪv] *vt* **paved; paving** : pavimentar ⟨to pave with stones : empedrar⟩

pavement ['peɪvmənt] *n* : pavimento *m*, empedrado *m*
pavilion [pə'vɪljən] *n* : pabellón *m*
paving ['peɪvɪŋ] → **pavement**
paw[1] ['pɔ] *vt* : tocar, manosear, sobar
paw[2] *n* : pata *f*, garra *f*, zarpa *f*
pawn[1] ['pɔn] *vt* : empeñar, prendar
pawn[2] *n* **1** PLEDGE, SECURITY : prenda *f* **2** PAWNING : empeño *m* **3** : peón *m* (en ajedrez)
pawnbroker ['pɔnˌbroːkər] *n* : prestamista *mf*
pawnshop ['pɔnˌʃɑp] *n* : casa *f* de empeños, monte *m* de piedad
pay[1] *v* **paid** ['peɪd]; **paying** *vt* **1** : pagar (una cuenta, a un empleado, etc.) **2 to pay attention** : poner atención, prestar atención, hacer caso **3 to pay back** : pagar, devolver ⟨she paid them back : les devolvió el dinero⟩ ⟨I'll pay you back for what you did! : ¡me las pagarás!⟩ **4 to pay off** SETTLE : saldar, cancelar (una deuda, etc.) **5 to pay one's respects** : presentar uno sus respetos **6 to pay a visit** : hacer una visita — *vi* : valer la pena ⟨crime doesn't pay : no hay crimen sin castigo⟩
pay[2] *n* : paga *f*
payable ['peɪəbəl] *adj* DUE : pagadero
paycheck ['peɪˌtʃɛk] *n* : sueldo *m*, cheque *m* del sueldo
payee [peɪ'iː] *n* : beneficiario *m*, -ria *f* (de un cheque, etc.)
payment ['peɪmənt] *n* **1** : pago *m* **2** INSTALLMENT : plazo *m*, cuota *f* **3** REWARD : recompensa *f*
payoff ['peɪˌɔf] *n* **1** REWARD : recompensa *f* **2** PROFIT : ganancia *f* **3** BRIBE : soborno *m*
payroll ['peɪˌroːl] *n* : nómina *f*
PC [ˌpiː'siː] *n, pl* **PCs** *or* **PC's** : PC *mf*, computadora *f* personal
pea ['piː] *n* : chícharo *m*, guisante *m*, arveja *f*
peace ['piːs] *n* **1** : paz *f* ⟨peace treaty : tratado de paz⟩ ⟨peace and tranquillity : paz y tranquilidad⟩ **2** ORDER : orden *m* (público)
peaceable ['piːsəbəl] *adj* : pacífico — **peaceably** [-bli] *adv*
peaceful ['piːsfəl] *adj* **1** PEACEABLE : pacífico **2** CALM, QUIET : tranquilo, sosegado — **peacefully** *adv*
peacemaker ['piːsˌmeɪkər] *n* : conciliador *m*, -dora *f*; mediador *m*, -dora *f*
peach ['piːtʃ] *n* : durazno *m*, melocotón *m*
peacock ['piːˌkɑk] *n* : pavo *m* real
peak[1] ['piːk] *vi* : alcanzar su nivel máximo
peak[2] *adj* : máximo
peak[3] *n* **1** POINT : punta *f* **2** CREST, SUMMIT : cima *f*, cumbre *f* **3** APEX : cúspide *f*, apogeo *m*, nivel *m* máximo
peaked ['piːkəd] *adj* SICKLY : pálido
peal[1] ['piːl] *vi* : repicar
peal[2] *n* : repique *m*, tañido *m* (de campanada) ⟨peals of laughter : carcajadas⟩

peanut ['pi:ˌnʌt] *n* : maní *m*, cacahuate *m Mex*, cacahuete *m Spain*

pear ['pær] *n* : pera *f*

pearl ['pərl] *n* : perla *f*

pearly ['pərli] *adj* **pearlier; -est** : nacarado

peasant ['pɛzənt] *n* : campesino *m*, -na *f*

peat ['pi:t] *n* : turba *f*

pebble ['pɛbəl] *n* : guijarro *m*, piedrecita *f*, piedrita *f*

pecan [pɪ'kɑn, -'kæn, 'pi:ˌkæn] *n* : pacana *f*, nuez *f Mex*

peccadillo [ˌpɛkə'dɪlo] *n, pl* **-loes** *or* **-los** : pecadillo *m*

peccary ['pɛkəri] *n, pl* **-ries** : pécari *m*, pecarí *m*

peck[1] ['pɛk] *vt* : picar, picotear

peck[2] *n* **1** : medida *f* de áridos equivalente a 8.810 litros **2** : picotazo *m* (de un pájaro) ⟨a peck on the cheek : un besito en la mejilla⟩

pectoral ['pɛktərəl] *adj* : pectoral

peculiar [pɪ'kju:ljər] *adj* **1** DISTINCTIVE : propio, peculiar, característico (peculiar to this area : propio de esta zona) **2** STRANGE : extraño, raro — **peculiarly** *adv*

peculiarity [pɪˌkju:l'jærəti, -ˌkju:li'ær-] *n, pl* **-ties** **1** DISTINCTIVENESS : peculiaridad *f* **2** ODDITY, QUIRK : rareza *f*, idiosincrasia *f*, excentricidad *f*

pecuniary [pɪ'kju:niˌɛri] *adj* : pecuniario

pedagogical [ˌpɛdə'gɑʤɪkəl, -'go:-] *adj* : pedagógico

pedagogy ['pɛdəˌgo:ʤi, -ˌgɑ-] *n* : pedagogía *f*

pedal[1] ['pɛdəl] *v* **-aled** *or* **-alled; -aling** *or* **-alling** *vi* : pedalear — *vt* : darle a los pedales de

pedal[2] *n* : pedal *m*

pedant ['pɛdənt] *n* : pedante *mf*

pedantic [pɪ'dæntɪk] *adj* : pedante

pedantry ['pɛdəntri] *n, pl* **-ries** : pedantería *f*

peddle ['pɛdəl] *vt* **-dled; -dling** : vender (en las calles)

peddler ['pɛdlər] *n* : vendedor *m*, -dora *f* ambulante; mercachifle *m*

pedestal ['pɛdəstəl] *n* : pedestal *m*

pedestrian[1] [pə'dɛstriən] *adj* **1** COMMONPLACE : pedestre, ordinario **2** : de peatón, peatonal ⟨pedestrian crossing : paso de peatones⟩

pedestrian[2] *n* : peatón *m*, -tona *f*

pediatric [ˌpi:di'ætrɪk] *adj* : pediátrico

pediatrician [ˌpi:diə'trɪʃən] *n* : pediatra *mf*

pediatrics [ˌpi:di'ætrɪks] *ns & pl* : pediatría *f*

pedigree ['pɛdəˌgri:] *n* **1** FAMILY TREE : árbol *m* genealógico **2** LINEAGE : pedigrí *m* (de un animal), linaje *m* (de una persona)

peek[1] ['pi:k] *vi* **1** PEEP : espiar, mirar furtivamente **2** GLANCE : echar un vistazo

peek[2] *n* **1** : miradita *f* (furtiva) **2** GLANCE : vistazo *m*, ojeada *f*

peel[1] ['pi:l] *vt* **1** : pelar (fruta, etc.) **2** *or* **to peel away** : quitar — *vi* : pelarse (dícese de la piel), desconcharse (dícese de la pintura)

peel[2] *n* : cáscara *f*

peep[1] ['pi:p] *vi* **1** PEEK : espiar, mirar furtivamente **2** CHEEP : piar **3** **to peep out** SHOW : asomarse

peep[2] *n* **1** CHEEP : pío *m* (de un pajarito) **2** GLANCE : vistazo *m*, ojeada *f*

peer[1] ['pɪr] *vi* : mirar detenidamente, mirar con atención

peer[2] *n* **1** EQUAL : par *m*, igual *mf* **2** NOBLE : noble *mf*

peerage ['pɪrɪʤ] *n* : nobleza *f*

peerless ['pɪrləs] *adj* : sin par, incomparable

peeve[1] ['pi:v] *vt* **peeved; peeving** : fastidiar, irritar, molestar

peeve[2] *n* : queja *f*

peevish ['pi:vɪʃ] *adj* : quejoso, fastidioso — **peevishly** *adv*

peevishness ['pi:vɪʃnəs] *n* : irritabilidad *f*

peg[1] ['pɛg] *vt* **pegged; pegging** **1** PLUG : tapar (con una clavija) **2** FASTEN, FIX : sujetar (con estaquillas) **3** **to peg out** MARK : marcar (con estaquillas)

peg[2] *n* : estaquilla *f* (para clavar), clavija *f* (para tapar)

pejorative [pɪ'ʤorətɪv] *adj* : peyorativo — **pejoratively** *adv*

pelican ['pɛlɪkən] *n* : pelícano *m*

pellagra [pə'lægrə, -'leɪ-] *n* : pelagra *f*

pellet ['pɛlət] *n* **1** BALL : bolita *f* ⟨food pellet : bolita de comida⟩ **2** SHOT : perdigón *m*

pell-mell ['pɛl'mɛl] *adv* : desordenadamente, atropelladamente

pelt[1] ['pɛlt] *vt* **1** THROW : lanzar, tirar (algo a alguien) **2** **to pelt with stones** : apedrear — *vi* BEAT : golpear con fuerza ⟨the rain was pelting down : llovía a cántaros⟩

pelt[2] *n* : piel *f*, pellejo *m*

pelvic ['pɛlvɪk] *adj* : pélvico

pelvis ['pɛlvɪs] *n, pl* **-vises** *or* **-ves** ['pɛlˌvi:z] : pelvis *f*

pen[1] ['pɛn] *vt* **penned; penning** **1** *or* **pen in** : encerrar (animales) **2** WRITE : escribir

pen[2] *n* **1** CORRAL : corral *m*, redil *m* (para ovejas) **2** : pluma *f* ⟨fountain pen : pluma fuente⟩ ⟨ballpoint pen : bolígrafo⟩

penal ['pi:nəl] *adj* : penal

penalize ['pi:nəlˌaɪz, 'pɛn-] *vt* **-ized; -izing** : penalizar, sancionar, penar

penalty ['pɛnəlti] *n, pl* **-ties** **1** PUNISHMENT : pena *f*, castigo *m* **2** DISADVANTAGE : desventaja *f*, castigo *m*, penalty *m* (en deportes) **3** FINE : multa *f*

penance ['pɛnənts] *n* : penitencia *f*

pence → **penny**

penchant ['pɛntʃənt] *n* : inclinación *f*, afición *f*

pencil[1] ['pɛntsəl] vt -ciled or -cilled; -ciling or -cilling : escribir con lápiz, dibujar con lápiz

pencil[2] n : lápiz m

pendant ['pɛndənt] n : colgante m

pending[1] ['pɛndɪŋ] adj : pendiente

pending[2] prep **1** DURING : durante **2** AWAITING : en espera de

pendulum ['pɛndʒələm, -djʊləm] n : péndulo m

penetrate ['pɛnə,treɪt] vt -trated; -trating : penetrar

penetrating ['pɛnə,treɪtɪŋ] adj : penetrante, cortante

penetration [,pɛnə'treɪʃən] n : penetración f

penguin ['pɛŋgwɪn, 'pɛn-] n : pingüino m

penicillin [,pɛnə'sɪlən] n : penicilina f

peninsula [pə'nɪntsələ, -'nɪntʃʊlə] n : península f

penis ['pi:nəs] n, pl -nes [-,ni:z] or -nises : pene m

penitence ['pɛnətənts] n : arrepentimiento m, penitencia f

penitent[1] ['pɛnətənt] adj : arrepentido, penitente

penitent[2] n : penitente mf

penitentiary [,pɛnə'tɛntʃəri] n, pl -ries : penitenciaría f, prisión m, presidio m

penmanship ['pɛnmən,ʃɪp] n : escritura f, caligrafía f

pen name n : seudónimo m

pennant ['pɛnənt] n : gallardete m (de un barco), banderín m

penniless ['pɛniləs] adj : sin un centavo

penny ['pɛni] n, pl -nies or pence ['pɛnts] **1** : penique m (del Reino Unido) **2** pl -nies CENT : centavo m (de los Estados Unidos)

pension[1] ['pɛntʃən] vt or to pension off : jubilar

pension[2] n : pensión m, jubilación f

pensive ['pɛntsɪv] adj : pensativo, meditabundo — **pensively** adv

pent ['pɛnt] adj : encerrado ⟨pent-up feelings : emociones reprimidas⟩

pentagon ['pɛntə,gɑn] n : pentágono m

pentagonal [pɛn'tægənəl] adj : pentagonal

penthouse ['pɛnt,haʊs] n : ático m, penthouse m

penultimate [pɪ'nʌltəmət] adj : penúltimo

penury ['pɛnjəri] n : penuria f, miseria f

peon ['pi:,ɑn, -ən] n, pl -ons or -ones [peɪ'o:ni:z] : peón m

peony ['pi:əni] n, pl -nies : peonía f

people[1] ['pi:pəl] vt -pled; -pling : poblar

people[2] ns & pl **1** people npl : gente f, personas fpl ⟨people like him : él le cae bien a la gente⟩ ⟨many people : mucha gente, muchas personas⟩ **2** pl peoples : pueblo m ⟨the Cuban people : el pueblo cubano⟩

pep[1] ['pɛp] vt pepped; pepping or to pep up : animar

pep[2] n : energía f, vigor m

pepper[1] ['pɛpər] vt **1** : añadir pimienta a **2** RIDDLE : acribillar (a balazos) **3** SPRINKLE : salpicar ⟨peppered with quotations : salpicado de citas⟩

pepper[2] n **1** : pimienta f (condimento) **2** : pimiento m, pimentón m (fruta) **3** → **chili**

peppermint ['pɛpər,mɪnt] n : menta f

peppery ['pɛpəri] adj : picante

peppy ['pɛpi] adj peppier; -est : lleno de energía, vivaz

peptic ['pɛptɪk] adj peptic ulcer : úlcera f estomacal

per ['pər] prep **1** : por ⟨miles per hour : millas por hora⟩ **2** ACCORDING TO : según ⟨per his specifications : según sus especificaciones⟩

per annum [pər'ænəm] adv : al año, por año

percale [,pər'keɪl, 'pər-,; ,pər'kæl] n : percal m

per capita [pər'kæpɪtə] adv & adj : per cápita

perceive [pər'si:v] vt -ceived; -ceiving **1** REALIZE : percatarse de, concientizarse de, darse cuenta de **2** NOTE : percibir, notar

percent[1] [pər'sɛnt] adv : por ciento

percent[2] n, pl -cent or -cents **1** : por ciento ⟨10 percent of the population : el 10 por ciento de la población⟩ **2** → **percentage**

percentage [pər'sɛntɪdʒ] n : porcentaje m

perceptible [pər'sɛptəbəl] adj : perceptible — **perceptibly** [-bli] adv

perception [pər'sɛpʃən] n **1** : percepción f ⟨color perception : la percepción de los colores⟩ **2** INSIGHT : perspicacia f **3** IDEA : idea f, imagen f

perceptive [pər'sɛptɪv] adj : perspicaz

perceptively [pər'sɛptɪvli] adv : con perspicacia

perch[1] ['pərtʃ] vi **1** ROOST : posarse **2** SIT : sentarse (en un sitio elevado) — vt PLACE : posar, colocar

perch[2] n **1** ROOST : percha f (para los pájaros) **2** pl perch or perches : perca f (pez)

percolate ['pərkə,leɪt] vi -lated; -lating : colarse, filtrarse ⟨percolated coffee : café filtrado⟩

percolator ['pərkə,leɪtər] n : cafetera f de filtro

percussion [pər'kʌʃən] n **1** STRIKING : percusión f **2** or percussion instruments : instrumentos mpl de percusión

peremptory [pə'rɛmptəri] adj : perentorio

perennial[1] [pə'rɛniəl] adj **1** : perenne, vivaz ⟨perennial flowers : flores perennes⟩ **2** RECURRENT : perenne, continuo ⟨a perennial problem : un problema eterno⟩

perennial[2] n : planta f perenne, planta f vivaz

perfect[1] [pər'fɛkt] vt : perfeccionar

perfect² ['pərfɪkt] *adj* : perfecto — **perfectly** *adv*

perfection [pər'fɛkʃən] *n* : perfección *f*

perfectionist [pər'fɛkʃənɪst] *n* : perfeccionista *mf*

perfidious [pər'fɪdiəs] *adj* : pérfido

perforate ['pərfə,reɪt] *vt* **-rated; -rating** : perforar

perforation [,pərfə'reɪʃən] *n* : perforación *f*

perform [pər'fɔrm] *vt* **1** CARRY OUT : realizar, hacer, desempeñar **2** PRESENT : representar, dar (una obra teatral), etc.) — *vi* : actuar (en una obra teatral), cantar (en una ópera, etc.), tocar (en un concierto, etc.), bailar (en un ballet, etc.)

performance [pər'fɔrmənts] *n* **1** EXECUTION : ejecución *f*, realización *f*, desempeño *m*, rendimiento *m* **2** INTERPRETATION : interpretación *f* ⟨his performance of Hamlet : su interpretación de Hamlet⟩ **3** PRESENTATION : representación *f* (de una obra teatral), función *f*

performer [pər'fɔrmər] *n* : artista *mf*; actor *m*, -triz *f*; intérprete *mf* (de música)

perfume¹ [pər'fju:m, 'pər,-] *vt* **-fumed; -fuming** : perfumar

perfume² ['pər,fju:m, pər'-] *n* : perfume *m*

perfunctory [pər'fʌŋktəri] *adj* : mecánico, superficial, somero

perhaps [pər'hæps] *adv* : tal vez, quizá, quizás

peril ['pɛrəl] *n* : peligro *m*

perilous ['pɛrələs] *adj* : peligroso — **perilously** *adv*

perimeter [pə'rɪmətər] *n* : perímetro *m*

period ['pɪriəd] *n* **1** : punto *m* (en puntuación) **2** : período *m* ⟨a two-hour period : un período de dos horas⟩ **3** STAGE : época *f* (histórica), fase *f*, etapa *f*

periodic [,pɪri'ɑdɪk] *or* **periodical** [-dɪkəl] *adj* : periódico — **periodically** [-dɪkli] *adv*

periodical [,pɪri'ɑdɪkəl] *n* : publicación *f* periódica, revista *f*

peripheral [pə'rɪfərəl] *adj* : periférico

periphery [pə'rɪfəri] *n*, *pl* **-eries** : periferia *f*

periscope ['pɛrə,sko:p] *n* : periscopio *m*

perish ['pɛrɪʃ] *vi* DIE : perecer, morirse

perishable¹ ['pɛrɪʃəbəl] *adj* : perecedero

perishable² *n* : producto *m* perecedero

perjure ['pərdʒər] *vt* **-jured; -juring** (*used in law*) **to perjure oneself** : perjurar, perjurarse

perjury ['pərdʒəri] *n* : perjurio *m*

perk¹ ['pərk] *vt* **1** : levantar (las orejas, etc.) **2** *or* **to perk up** FRESHEN : arreglar — *vi* **to perk up** : animarse, reanimarse

perk² *n* : extra *m*

perky ['pərki] *adj* **perkier; -est** : animado, alegre, lleno de vida

permanence ['pərmənənts] *n* : permanencia *f*

permanent¹ ['pərmənənt] *adj* : permanente — **permanently** *adv*

permanent² *n* : permanente *f*

permeability [,pərmiə'bɪləti] *n* : permeabilidad *f*

permeable ['pərmiəbəl] *adj* : permeable

permeate ['pərmi,eɪt] *v* **-ated; -ating** *vt* **1** PENETRATE : penetrar, impregnar **2** PERVADE : penetrar, difundirse por — *vi* : penetrar

permissible [pər'mɪsəbəl] *adj* : permisible, lícito

permission [pər'mɪʃən] *n* : permiso *m*

permissive [pər'mɪsɪv] *adj* : permisivo

permit¹ [pər'mɪt] *vt* **-mitted; -mitting** : permitir, dejar ⟨weather permitting : si el tiempo lo permite⟩

permit² ['pər,mɪt, pər'-] *n* : permiso *m*, licencia *f*

pernicious [pər'nɪʃəs] *adj* : pernicioso

peroxide [pə'rɑk,saɪd] *n* **1** : peróxido *m* **2** → **hydrogen peroxide**

perpendicular¹ [,pərpən'dɪkjələr] *adj* **1** VERTICAL : vertical **2** : perpendicular ⟨perpendicular lines : líneas perpendiculares⟩ — **perpendicularly** *adv*

perpendicular² *n* : perpendicular *f*

perpetrate ['pərpə,treɪt] *vt* **-trated; -trating** : perpetrar, cometer (un delito)

perpetrator ['pərpə,treɪtər] *n* : autor *m*, -tora *f* (de un delito)

perpetual [pər'pɛtʃuəl] *adj* **1** EVERLASTING : perpetuo, eterno **2** CONTINUAL : perpetuo, continuo, constante

perpetually [pər'pɛtʃuəli, -tʃəli] *adv* : para siempre, eternamente

perpetuate [pər'pɛtʃu,eɪt] *vt* **-ated; -ating** : perpetuar

perpetuity [,pərpə'tu:əti, -'tju:-] *n*, *pl* **-ties** : perpetuidad *f*

perplex [pər'plɛks] *vt* : dejar perplejo, confundir

perplexed [pər'plɛkst] *adj* : perplejo

perplexity [pər'plɛksəti] *n*, *pl* **-ties** : perplejidad *f*, confusión *f*

persecute ['pərsɪ,kju:t] *vt* **-cuted; -cuting** : perseguir

persecution [,pərsɪ'kju:ʃən] *n* : persecución *f*

perseverance [,pərsə'vɪrənts] *n* : perseverancia *f*

persevere [,pərsə'vɪr] *vi* **-vered; -vering** : perseverar

Persian ['pərʒən] *n* **1** : persa *mf* **2** : persa *m* (idioma) — **Persian** *adj*

persist [pər'sɪst] *vi* : persistir

persistence [pər'sɪstənts] *n* **1** CONTINUATION : persistencia *f* **2** TENACITY : perseverancia *f*, tenacidad *f*

persistent [pər'sɪstənt] *adj* : persistente — **persistently** *adv*

person ['pərsən] *n* **1** HUMAN, INDIVIDUAL : persona *f*, individuo *m*, ser *m* humano **2** : persona *f* (en gramática) **3 in person** : en persona

personable ['pərsənəbəl] *adj* : agradable

personage ['pərsənɪdʒ] *n* : personaje *m*
personal ['pərsənəl] *adj* **1** OWN, PRIVATE : personal, particular, privado ⟨for personal reasons : por razones personales⟩ **2** : en persona ⟨to make a personal appearance : presentarse en persona, hacerse acto de presencia⟩ **3** : íntimo, personal ⟨personal hygiene : higiene personal⟩ **4** INDISCREET, PRYING : indiscreto, personal
personal computer *n* : computadora *f* personal, ordenador *m* personal *Spain*
personal digital assistant *n* : asistente *m* personal digital
personality [,pərsən'ælət̪i] *n, pl* **-ties 1** DISPOSITION : personalidad *f*, temperamento *m* **2** CELEBRITY : personalidad *f*, personaje *m*, celebridad *f*
personalize ['pərsənə,laɪz] *vt* **-ized; -izing** : personalizar
personally ['pərsənəli] *adv* **1** : personalmente, en persona ⟨I'll do it personally : lo haré personalmente⟩ **2** : como persona ⟨personally she's very amiable : como persona es muy amable⟩ **3** : personalmente ⟨personally, I don't believe it : yo, personalmente, no me lo creo⟩
personification [pər,sɑnəfə'keɪʃən] *n* : personificación *f*
personify [pər'sɑnə,faɪ] *vt* **-fied; -fying** : personificar
personnel [,pərsən'ɛl] *n* : personal *m*
perspective [pər'spɛktɪv] *n* : perspectiva *f*
perspicacious [,pərspə'keɪʃəs] *adj* : perspicaz
perspiration [,pərspə'reɪʃən] *n* : transpiración *f*, sudor *m*
perspire [pər'spaɪr] *vi* **-spired; -spiring** : transpirar, sudar
persuade [pər'sweɪd] *vt* **-suaded; -suading** : persuadir, convencer
persuasion [pər'sweɪʒən] *n* : persuasión *f*
persuasive [pər'sweɪsɪv, -zɪv] *adj* : persuasivo — **persuasively** *adv*
persuasiveness [pər'sweɪsɪvnəs, -zɪv-] *n* : persuasión *f*
pert ['pərt] *adj* **1** SAUCY : descarado, impertinente **2** JAUNTY : alegre, animado ⟨a pert little hat : un sombrero coqueto⟩
pertain [pər'teɪn] *vi* **1** BELONG : pertenecer (a) **2** RELATE : estar relacionado (con)
pertinence ['pərtənənts] *n* : pertinencia *f*
pertinent ['pərtənənt] *adj* : pertinente
perturb [pər'tərb] *vt* : perturbar
perusal [pə'ru:zəl] *n* : lectura *f* cuidadosa
peruse [pə'ru:z] *vt* **-rused; -rusing 1** READ : leer con cuidado **2** SCAN : recorrer con la vista ⟨he perused the newspaper : echó un vistazo al periódico⟩

Peruvian [pə'ru:viən] *n* : peruano *m*, -na *f* — **Peruvian** *adj*
pervade [pər'veɪd] *vt* **-vaded; -vading** : penetrar, difundirse por
pervasive [pər'veɪsɪv, -zɪv] *adj* : penetrante
perverse [pər'vərs] *adj* **1** CORRUPT : perverso, corrompido **2** STUBBORN : obstinado, porfiado, terco (sin razón) — **perversely** *adv*
perversion [pər'vərʒən] *n* : perversión *f*
perversity [pər'vərsət̪i] *n, pl* **-ties 1** CORRUPTION : corrupción *f* **2** STUBBORNNESS : obstinación *f*, terquedad *f*
pervert[1] [pər'vərt] *vt* **1** DISTORT : pervertir, distorsionar **2** CORRUPT : pervertir, corromper
pervert[2] ['pər,vərt] *n* : pervertido *m*, -da *f*
pesky ['pɛski] *adj* : molestoso, molesto
peso ['peɪ,so:] *n, pl* **-sos** : peso *m*
pessimism ['pɛsə,mɪzəm] *n* : pesimismo *m*
pessimist ['pɛsəmɪst] *n* : pesimista *mf*
pessimistic [,pɛsə'mɪstɪk] *adj* : pesimista
pest ['pɛst] *n* **1** NUISANCE : peste *f*; latoso *m*, -sa *f fam* ⟨to be a pest : dar (la) lata⟩ **2** : insecto *m* nocivo, animal *m* nocivo ⟨the squirrels were pests : las ardillas eran una plaga⟩
pester ['pɛstər] *vt* **-tered; -tering** : molestar, fastidiar
pesticide ['pɛstə,saɪd] *n* : pesticida *m*
pestilence ['pɛstələnts] *n* : pestilencia *f*, peste *f*
pestle ['pɛsəl, 'pɛstəl] *n* : mano *f* de mortero, mazo *m*, maja *f*
pet[1] ['pɛt] *vt* **petted; petting** : acariciar
pet[2] *n* **1** : animal *m* doméstico **2** FAVORITE : favorito *m*, -ta *f*
petal ['pɛt̪əl] *n* : pétalo *m*
petite [pə'ti:t] *adj* : pequeña, menuda, chiquita
petition[1] [pə'tɪʃən] *vt* : peticionar
petition[2] *n* : petición *f*
petitioner [pə'tɪʃənər] *n* : peticionario *m*, -ria *f*
petrify ['pɛtrə,faɪ] *vt* **-fied; -fying** : petrificar
petroleum [pə'tro:liəm] *n* : petróleo *m*
petticoat ['pɛt̪i,ko:t] *n* : enagua *f*, fondo *m Mex*
pettiness ['pɛt̪inəs] *n* **1** INSIGNIFICANCE : insignificancia *f* **2** MEANNESS : mezquindad *f*
petty ['pɛt̪i] *adj* **-tier; -est 1** MINOR : menor ⟨petty cash : dinero para gastos menores⟩ **2** INSIGNIFICANT : insignificante, trivial, nimio **3** MEAN : mezquino
petty officer *n* : suboficial *mf*
petulance ['pɛtʃələnts] *n* : irritabilidad *f*, mal genio *m*
petulant ['pɛtʃələnt] *adj* : irritable, de mal genio
petunia [pɪ'tu:njə, -'tju:-] *n* : petunia *f*
pew ['pju:] *n* : banco *m* (de iglesia)

pewter ['pju:tər] *n* : peltre *m*
pH [,pi:'eitʃ] *n* : pH *m*
phallic ['fælik] *adj* : fálico
phallus ['fæləs] *n, pl* -li ['fæ,lai] *or* -luses : falo *m*
phantasy ['fæntəsi] → fantasy
phantom ['fæntəm] *n* : fantasma *m*
pharaoh ['fɛr,o:, 'fei,ro:] *n* : faraón *m*
pharmaceutical [,farmə'su:tikəl] *adj* : farmacéutico
pharmacist ['farməsist] *n* : farmacéutico *m*, -ca *f*
pharmacology [,farmə'kalədʒi] *n* : farmacología *f*
pharmacy ['farməsi] *n, pl* -cies : farmacia *f*
pharynx ['færiŋks] *n, pl* pharynges [fə'rin,dʒi:z] : faringe *f*
phase[1] ['feiz] *vt* phased; phasing 1 SYNCHRONIZE : sincronizar, poner en fase 2 STAGGER : escalonar 3 to phase in : introducir progresivamente 4 to phase out : retirar progresivamente, dejar de producir
phase[2] *n* 1 : fase *f* (de la luna, etc.) 2 STAGE : fase *f*, etapa *f*
pheasant ['fɛzənt] *n, pl* -ant *or* -ants : faisán *m*
phenomenal [fi'namənəl] *adj* : extraordinario, excepcional
phenomenon [fi'namə,nan, -nən] *n, pl* -na [-nə] *or* -nons 1 : fenómeno *m* 2 *pl* -nons PRODIGY : fenómeno *m*, prodigio *m*
philanthropic [,filən'θrapik] *adj* : filantrópico
philanthropist [fə'lænθrəpist] *n* : filántropo *m*, -pa *f*
philanthropy [fə'lænθrəpi] *n, pl* -pies : filantropía *f*
philately [fə'lætəli] *n* : filatelia *f*
philodendron [,filə'dɛndrən] *n, pl* -drons *or* -dra [-drə] : arácea *f*
philosopher [fə'lasəfər] *n* : filósofo *m*, -fa *f*
philosophic [,filə'safik] *or* philosophical [-fikəl] *adj* : filosófico — philosophically [-kli] *adv*
philosophize [fə'lasə,faiz] *vi* -phized; -phizing : filosofar
philosophy [fə'lasəfi] *n, pl* -phies : filosofía *f*
phlebitis [fli'baitəs] *n* : flebitis *f*
phlegm ['flɛm] *n* : flema *f*
phlox ['flaks] *n, pl* phlox *or* phloxes : polemonio *m*
phobia ['fo:biə] *n* : fobia *f*
phoenix ['fi:niks] *n* : fénix *m*
phone[1] ['fo:n] *v* → telephone[1]
phone[2] *n* → telephone[2]
phoneme ['fo:,ni:m] *n* : fonema *m*
phonetic [fə'nɛtik] *adj* : fonético
phonetics [fə'nɛtiks] *n* : fonética *f*
phonics ['faniks] *n* : método *m* fonético de aprender a leer
phonograph ['fo:nə,græf] *n* : fonógrafo *m*, tocadiscos *m*
phony[1] *or* phoney ['fo:ni] *adj* -nier; -est : falso

phony[2] *or* phoney *n, pl* -nies : farsante *mf*; charlatán *m*, -tana *f*
phosphate ['fas,feit] *n* : fosfato *m*
phosphorescence [,fasfə'rɛsənts] *n* : fosforescencia *f*
phosphorescent [,fasfə'rɛsənt] *adj* : fosforescente — phosphorescently *adv*
phosphorus ['fasfərəs] *n* : fósforo *m*
photo ['fo:to:] *n, pl* -tos : foto *f*
photocopier ['fo:to,kapiər] *n* : fotocopiadora *f*
photocopy[1] ['fo:to,kapi] *vt* -copied; -copying : fotocopiar
photocopy[2] *n, pl* -copies : fotocopia *f*
photoelectric [,fo:toi'lɛktrik] *adj* : fotoeléctrico
photogenic [,fo:tə'dʒɛnik] *adj* : fotogénico
photograph[1] ['fo:tə,græf] *vt* : fotografiar
photograph[2] *n* : fotografía *f*, foto *f* ⟨to take a photograph of : tomarle una fotografía a, tomar una fotografía de⟩
photographer [fə'tagrəfər] *n* : fotógrafo *m*, -fa *f*
photographic [,fo:tə'græfik] *adj* : fotográfico — photographically [-fikli] *adv*
photography [fə'tagrəfi] *n* : fotografía *f*
photosynthesis [,fo:to'sinθəsis] *n* : fotosíntesis *f*
photosynthetic [,fo:tosin'θɛtik] *adj* : fotosintético, de fotosíntesis
phrase[1] ['freiz] *vt* phrased; phrasing : expresar
phrase[2] *n* : frase *f*, locución *f* ⟨to coin a phrase : para decirlo así⟩
phylum ['failəm] *n, pl* -la [-lə] : phylum *m*
physical[1] ['fizikəl] *adj* 1 : físico ⟨physical laws : leyes físicas⟩ 2 MATERIAL : material, físico 3 BODILY : físico, corpóreo — physically [-kli] *adv*
physical[2] *n* CHECKUP : chequeo *m*, reconocimiento *m* médico
physician [fə'ziʃən] *n* : médico *m*, -ca *f*
physicist ['fizəsist] *n* : físico *m*, -ca *f*
physics ['fiziks] *ns & pl* : física *f*
physiognomy [,fizi'agnəmi] *n, pl* -mies : fisonomía *f*
physiological ['fiziə'ladʒikəl] *or* physiologic [-dʒik] *adj* : fisiológico
physiologist [,fizi'alədʒist] *n* : fisiólogo *m*, -ga *f*
physiology [,fizi'alədʒi] *n* : fisiología *f*
physique [fə'zi:k] *n* : físico *m*
pi ['pai] *n, pl* pis ['paiz] : pi *f*
pianist [pi'ænist, 'pi:ənist] *n* : pianista *mf*
piano [pi'æno:] *n, pl* -anos : piano *m*
piazza [pi'æzə, -'atsə] *n, pl* -zas *or* -ze [-'at,sei] : plaza *f*
picaresque [,pikə'rɛsk, ,pi:-] *adj* : picaresco
picayune [,piki'ju:n] *adj* : trivial, nimio, insignificante
piccolo ['pikə,lo:] *n, pl* -los : flautín *m*
pick[1] ['pik] *vt* 1 : picar, labrar (con un pico) ⟨he picked the hard soil : picó la

tierra dura⟩ **2** : quitar, sacar (poco a
poco) ⟨to pick meat off the bones
: quitar pedazos de carne de los hue-
sos⟩ **3** : recoger, arrancar (frutas, flores, etc.) **4** SELECT : escoger, elegir **5**
PROVOKE : provocar ⟨to pick a quar-
rel : buscar pleito, buscar pelea⟩ **6 to
pick a lock** : forzar una cerradura **7 to
pick someone's pocket** : robarle algo
del bolsillo de alguien ⟨someone
picked my pocket! : ¡me robaron la
cartera del bolsillo!⟩ — *vi* **1** NIBBLE
: picar, picotear **2 to pick and choose**
: ser exigente **3 to pick at** : tocar, rascarse (una herida, etc.) **4 to pick on**
TEASE : mofarse de, atormentar
pick² *n* **1** CHOICE : selección *f* **2** BEST
: lo mejor ⟨the pick of the crop : la crema y nata⟩ **3** → **pickax**
pickax ['pɪkˌæks] *n* : pico *m*, zapapico
m, piqueta *f*
pickerel ['pɪkərəl] *n, pl* **-el** *or* **-els** : lucio
m pequeño
picket¹ ['pɪkət] *v* : piquetear
picket² *n* **1** STAKE : estaca *f* **2** STRIKER
: huelguista *mf*, integrante *mf* de un piquete
pickle¹ ['pɪkəl] *vt* **-led; -ling** : encurtir,
escabechar
pickle² *n* **1** BRINE : escabeche *m* **2**
GHERKIN : pepinillo *m* (encurtido) **3**
JAM, TROUBLE : lío *m*, apuro *m*
pickpocket ['pɪkˌpɑkət] *n* : carterista *mf*
pickup ['pɪkˌəp] *n* **1** IMPROVEMENT
: mejora *f* **2** *or* **pickup truck** : camioneta *f*
pick up *vt* **1** LIFT : levantar **2** TIDY : arreglar, ordenar — *vi* IMPROVE : mejo-
rar
picnic¹ ['pɪkˌnɪk] *vi* **-nicked; -nicking** : ir
de picnic
picnic² *n* : picnic *m*
pictorial [pɪk'toriəl] *adj* : pictórico
picture¹ ['pɪktʃər] *vt* **-tured; -turing 1**
DEPICT : representar **2** IMAGINE
: imaginarse ⟨can you picture it? : ¿te
lo puedes imaginar?⟩
picture² *n* **1** : cuadro *m* (pintado o dibu-
jado), ilustración *f*, fotografía *f* **2** DE-
SCRIPTION : descripción *f* **3** IMAGE
: imagen *f* ⟨he's the picture of his father : es la viva imagen de su padre⟩ **4**
MOVIE : película *f*
picturesque [ˌpɪktʃə'rɛsk] *adj* : pintoresco
pie ['paɪ] *n* : pastel *m* (con fruta o carne),
empanada *f* (con carne)
piebald ['paɪˌbɔld] *adj* : picazo, pío
piece¹ ['piːs] *vt* **pieced; piecing 1** PATCH
: parchar, arreglar **2 to piece together** : construir pieza por pieza
piece² *n* **1** FRAGMENT : trozo *m*, pedazo *m* **2** COMPONENT : pieza *f* ⟨a three-
piece suit : un traje de tres piezas⟩ **3**
UNIT : pieza *f* ⟨a piece of fruit : una
(pieza de) fruta⟩ **4** WORK : obra *f*, pieza
f (de música, etc.) **5** (*in board games*)
: ficha *f*, pieza *f*, figura *f* (en ajedrez)

piecemeal¹ ['piːsˌmiːl] *adv* : poco a poco,
por partes
piecemeal² *adj* : hecho poco a poco,
poco sistemático
pied ['paɪd] *adj* : pío
pier ['pɪr] *n* **1** : pila *f* (de un puente) **2**
WHARF : muelle *m*, atracadero *m*, embarcadero *m* **3** PILLAR : pilar *m*
pierce ['pɪrs] *vt* **pierced; piercing 1** PEN-
ETRATE : atravesar, traspasar, penetrar
(en) ⟨the bullet pierced his leg : la bala
le atravesó la pierna⟩ ⟨to pierce one's
heart : traspasarle el corazón a uno⟩ **2**
PERFORATE : perforar, agujerear (las
orejas, etc.) **3 to pierce the silence**
: desgarrar el silencio
piety ['paɪəti] *n, pl* **-eties** : piedad *f*
pig ['pɪg] *n* **1** HOG, SWINE : cerdo *m*, -da
f; puerco *m*, -ca *f* **2** SLOB : persona *f*
desaliñada; cerdo *m*, -da *f* **3** GLUTTON
: glotón *m*, -tona *f* **4** *or* **pig iron** : lingote *m* de hierro
pigeon ['pɪdʒən] *n* : paloma *f*
pigeonhole ['pɪdʒənˌhoːl] *n* : casilla *f*
pigeon–toed ['pɪdʒənˌtoːd] *adj* : pat-
ituerto
piggish ['pɪgɪʃ] *adj* **1** GREEDY : glotón
2 DIRTY : cochino, sucio
piggyback ['pɪgiˌbæk] *adv & adj* : a cuestas
pigheaded ['pɪgˌhɛdəd] *adj* : terco, obstinado
piglet ['pɪglət] *n* : cochinillo *m*; lechón
m, -chona *f*
pigment ['pɪgmənt] *n* : pigmento *m*
pigmentation [ˌpɪgmən'teɪʃən] *n* : pigmentación *f*
pigmy → **pygmy**
pigpen ['pɪgˌpɛn] *n* : chiquero *m*, pocilga *f*
pigsty ['pɪgˌstaɪ] → **pigpen**
pigtail ['pɪgˌteɪl] *n* : coleta *f*, trenza *f*
pike ['paɪk] *n, pl* **pike** *or* **pikes 1** : lucio
m (pez) **2** LANCE : pica *f* **3** → **turnpike**
pile¹ ['paɪl] *v* **piled; piling** *vt* : amontonar,
apilar — *vi* **to pile up** : amontonarse,
acumularse
pile² *n* **1** STAKE : pilote *m* **2** HEAP : montón *m*, pila *f* **3** NAP : pelo *m* (de telas)
piles ['paɪlz] *npl* HEMORRHOIDS : hemorroides *fpl*, almorranas *fpl*
pilfer ['pɪlfər] *vt* : robar (cosas pe-
queñas), ratear
pilgrim ['pɪlgrəm] *n* : peregrino *m*, -na *f*
pilgrimage ['pɪlgrəmɪdʒ] *n* : peregrinación *f*
pill ['pɪl] *n* : pastilla *f*, píldora *f*
pillage¹ ['pɪlɪdʒ] *vt* **-laged; -laging**
: saquear
pillage² *n* : saqueo *m*
pillar ['pɪlər] *n* : pilar *m*, columna *f*
pillory ['pɪləri] *n, pl* **-ries** : picota *f*
pillow ['pɪˌloː] *n* : almohada *f*
pillowcase ['pɪˌloːˌkeɪs] *n* : funda *f*
pilot¹ ['paɪlət] *vt* : pilotar, pilotear
pilot² *n* : piloto *mf*
pilot light *n* : piloto *m*
pimento [pə'mɛnˌtoː] → **pimiento**

pimiento [pə'mɛn,to:, -'mjɛn-] *n, pl* **-tos**
: pimiento *m* morrón
pimp ['pɪmp] *n* : proxeneta *m*
pimple ['pɪmpəl] *n* : grano *m*
pimply ['pɪmpəli] *adj* **-plier; -est** : cubierto de granos
pin¹ ['pɪn] *vt* **pinned; pinning 1** FASTEN
: prender, sujetar (con alfileres) **2**
HOLD, IMMOBILIZE : inmovilizar, sujetar **3 to pin one's hopes on** : poner
sus esperanzas en
pin² *n* **1** : alfiler *m* ⟨safety pin : alfiler
de gancho⟩ ⟨a bobby pin : una horquilla⟩ **2** BROOCH : alfiler *m*, broche *m*,
prendedor *m* **3** *or* **bowling pin** : bolo
m
pinafore ['pɪnə,for] *n* : delantal *m*
pincer ['pɪntsər] *n* **1** CLAW : pinza *f* (de
una langosta, etc.) **2 pincers** *npl* : pinzas *fpl*, tenazas *fpl*, tenaza *f*
pinch¹ ['pɪntʃ] *vt* **1** : pellizcar ⟨she
pinched my cheek : me pellizcó el cachete⟩ **2** STEAL : robar — *vi* : apretar
⟨my shoes pinch : me aprietan los zapatos⟩
pinch² *n* **1** EMERGENCY : emergencia *f*
⟨in a pinch : en caso necesario⟩ **2** PAIN
: dolor *m*, tormento *m* **3** SQUEEZE : pellizco *m* (con los dedos) **4** BIT : pizca
f, pellizco *m* ⟨a pinch of cinnamon : una
pizca de canela⟩
pinch hitter *n* **1** SUBSTITUTE : sustituto
m, -ta *f* **2** : bateador *m* emergente (en
beisbol)
pincushion ['pɪn,kuʃən] *n* : acerico *m*,
alfiletero *m*
pine¹ ['paɪn] *vi* **pined; pining 1 to pine
away** : languidecer, consumirse **2 to
pine for** : añorar, suspirar por
pine² *n* **1** : pino *m* (árbol) **2** : madera *f*
de pino
pineapple ['paɪn,æpəl] *n* : piña *f*, ananá
m, ananás *m*
ping-pong ['pɪŋ,paŋ, -,pɔŋ] *n* : ping-
pong *m*
pinion¹ ['pɪnjən] *vt* : sujetar los brazos
de, inmovilizar
pinion² *n* : piñón *m*
pink¹ ['pɪŋk] *adj* : rosa, rosado
pink² *n* **1** : clavelito *m* (flor) **2** : rosa *m*,
rosado *m* (color) **3 to be in the pink**
: estar en plena forma, rebosar de salud
pinkeye ['pɪŋk,aɪ] *n* : conjuntivitis *f* aguda
pinkish ['pɪŋkɪʃ] *adj* : rosáceo
pinnacle ['pɪnɪkəl] *n* **1** : pináculo *m* (de
un edificio) **2** PEAK : cima *f*, cumbre *f*
(de una montaña) **3** ACME : pináculo
m, cúspide *f*, apogeo *m*
pinpoint ['pɪn,pɔɪnt] *vt* : precisar, localizar con precisión
pint ['paɪnt] *n* : pinta *f*
pinto ['pɪn,to:] *n, pl* **pintos** : caballo *m*
pinto
pinworm ['pɪn,wərm] *n* : oxiuro *m*
pioneer¹ [,paɪə'nɪr] *vt* : promover, iniciar, introducir
pioneer² *n* : pionero *m*, -ra *f*

pious ['paɪəs] *adj* **1** DEVOUT : piadoso,
devoto **2** SANCTIMONIOUS : beato
piously ['paɪəsli] *adv* **1** DEVOUTLY : piadosamente **2** SANCTIMONIOUSLY
: santurronamente
pipe¹ ['paɪp] *v* **piped; piping** *vi* : hablar
en voz chillona — *vt* **1** PLAY : tocar (el
caramillo o la flauta) **2** : conducir por
tuberías ⟨to pipe water : transportar el
agua por tubería⟩
pipe² *n* **1** : caramillo *m* (instrumento
musical) **2** BAGPIPE : gaita *f* **3** : tubo
m, caño *m* ⟨gas pipes : tubería de gas⟩
4 : pipa *f* (para fumar)
pipeline ['paɪp,laɪn] *n* **1** : conducto *m*,
oleoducto *m* (para petróleo), gasoducto *m* (para gas) **2** CONDUIT : vía *f* (de
información, etc.)
piper ['paɪpər] *n* : músico *m*, -ca *f* que
toca el caramillo o la gaita
piping ['paɪpɪŋ] *n* **1** : música *f* del
caramillo o de la gaita **2** TRIM : cordoncillo *m*, ribete *m* con cordón
piquant ['pi:kənt, 'pɪkwənt] *adj* **1** SPICY
: picante **2** INTRIGUING : intrigante,
estimulante
pique¹ ['pi:k] *vt* **piqued; piquing 1** IRRITATE : picar, irritar **2** AROUSE : despertar (la curiosidad, etc.)
pique² *n* : pique *m*, resentimiento *m*
piracy ['paɪrəsi] *n, pl* **-cies** : piratería *f*
piranha [pə'ranə, -'ranjə, -'rænjə] *n* : piraña *f*
pirate¹ ['paɪrət] *n* : pirata *mf*
pirate² *vt* **-rated; -rating** : piratear (software, etc.)
pirouette [,pɪrə'wɛt] *n* : pirueta *f*
pis → **pi**
Pisces ['paɪ,si:z, 'pɪ-; 'pɪs,keɪs] *n* : Piscis
mf
pistachio [pə'stæʃi,o:, -'sta-] *n, pl* **-chios**
: pistacho *m*
pistil ['pɪstəl] *n* : pistilo *m*
pistol ['pɪstəl] *n* : pistola *f*
piston ['pɪstən] *n* : pistón *m*, émbolo *m*
pit¹ ['pɪt] *v* **pitted; pitting** *vt* **1** : marcar
de hoyos, picar (una superficie) **2**
: deshuesar (una fruta) **3 to pit against**
: enfrentar a, oponer a — *vi* : quedar
marcado
pit² *n* **1** HOLE : fosa *f*, hoyo *m* ⟨a bottomless pit : un pozo sin fondo⟩ **2** MINE
: mina *f* **3** : foso *m* ⟨orchestra pit : foso
orquestal⟩ **4** POCKMARK : marca *f* (en
la cara), cicatriz *f* de viruela **5** STONE
: hueso *m*, pepa *f* (de una fruta) **6 pit
of the stomach** : boca *f* del estómago
pitch¹ ['pɪtʃ] *vt* **1** SET UP : montar, armar
(una tienda) **2** THROW : lanzar, arrojar **3** ADJUST, SET : dar el tono de (un
discurso, un instrumento musical) —
vi **1** *or* **pitch forward** FALL : caerse **2**
LURCH : cabecear (dícese de un barco
o un avión), dar bandazos
pitch² *n* **1** LURCHING : cabezada *f*,
cabeceo *m* (de un barco o un avión) **2**
SLOPE : (grado de) inclinación *f*, pendiente *f* **3** : tono *m* (en música) ⟨per-

fect pitch : oído absoluto⟩ **4** THROW
: lanzamiento *m* **5** DEGREE : grado *m*,
nivel *m*, punto *m* ⟨the excitement
reached a high pitch : la excitación
llegó a un punto culminante⟩ **6** *or*
sales pitch : presentación *f* (de un
vendedor) **7** TAR : pez *f*, brea *f*
pitcher ['pɪtʃər] *n* **1** JUG : jarra *f*, jarro
m, cántaro *m*, pichel *m* **2** : lanzador *m*,
-dora *f* (en béisbol, etc.)
pitchfork ['pɪtʃ,fɔrk] *n* : horquilla *f*, horca *f*
piteous ['pɪtiəs] *adj* : lastimoso, lastimero — **piteously** *adv*
pitfall ['pɪt,fɔl] *n* : peligro *m* (poco obvio), dificultad *f*
pith ['pɪθ] *n* **1** : médula *f* (de una planta) **2** CORE : meollo *m*, entraña *f*
pithy ['pɪθi] *adj* **pithier; -est** : conciso y
sustancioso ⟨pithy comments : co-
mentarios sucintos⟩
pitiable ['pɪtiəbəl] → **pitiful**
pitiful ['pɪtɪfəl] *adj* **1** LAMENTABLE : lastimero, lastimoso, lamentable **2** CON-
TEMPTIBLE : despreciable, lamentable
— **pitifully** [-fli] *adv*
pitiless ['pɪtɪləs] *adj* : despiadado — **piti-
lessly** *adv*
pittance ['pɪtənts] *n* : miseria *f*
pituitary [pə'tu:ə,teri, -'tju:-] *adj* : pituitario
pity[1] ['pɪti] *vt* **pitied; pitying** : compadecer, compadecerse de
pity[2] *n, pl* **pities** **1** COMPASSION : compasión *f*, piedad *f* **2** SHAME : lástima *f*,
pena *f* ⟨what a pity! : ¡qué lástima!⟩
pivot[1] ['pɪvət] *vi* **1** : girar sobre un eje **2
to pivot on** : girar sobre, depender de
pivot[2] *n* : pivote *m*
pivotal ['pɪvətəl] *adj* : fundamental, central
pixie *or* **pixy** ['pɪksi] *n, pl* **pixies** : elfo
m, hada *f*
pizza ['pi:tsə] *n* : pizza *f*
pizzazz *or* **pizazz** [pə'zæz] *n* **1** GLAMOR
: encanto *m* **2** VITALITY : animación *f*,
vitalidad *f*
placard ['plækərd, -,kɑrd] *n* POSTER
: cartel *m*, póster *m*, afiche *m*
placate ['pleɪ,keɪt, 'plæ-] *vt* **-cated;
-cating** : aplacar, apaciguar
place[1] ['pleɪs] *vt* **placed; placing** **1** PUT,
SET : poner, colocar **2** SITUATE : situ-
ar, ubicar, emplazar ⟨to be well placed
: estar bien situado⟩ ⟨to place in a job
: colocar en un trabajo⟩ **3** IDENTIFY,
RECALL : identificar, ubicar, recordar
⟨I can't place him : no lo ubico⟩ **4 to
place an order** : hacer un pedido
place[2] *n* **1** SPACE : sitio *m*, lugar *m*
⟨there's no place to sit : no hay sitio
para sentarse⟩ **2** LOCATION, SPOT : lugar *m*, sitio *m*, parte *f* ⟨place of work
: lugar de trabajo⟩ ⟨our summer place
: nuestra casa de verano⟩ ⟨all over the
place : por todas partes⟩ **3** RANK : lugar *m*, puesto *m* ⟨he took first place
: ganó el primer lugar⟩ **4** POSITION : lugar *m* ⟨everything in its place : todo en

su debido lugar⟩ ⟨to feel out of place
: sentirse fuera de lugar⟩ **5** SEAT
: asiento *m*, cubierto *m* (a la mesa) **6**
JOB : puesto *m* **7** ROLE : papel *m*, lugar *m* ⟨to change places : cambiarse los
papeles⟩ **8 to take place** : tener lugar
9 to take the place of : sustituir a
placebo [plə'si:,bo:] *n, pl* **-bos** : placebo
m
placement ['pleɪsmənt] *n* : colocación *f*
placenta [plə'sɛntə] *n, pl* **-tas** *or* **-tae** [-ti,
-,taɪ] : placenta *f*
placid ['plæsəd] *adj* : plácido, tranquilo
— **placidly** *adv*
plagiarism ['pleɪdʒə,rɪzəm] *n* : plagio *m*
plagiarist ['pleɪdʒərɪst] *n* : plagiario *m*,
-ria *f*
plagiarize ['pleɪdʒə,raɪz] *vt* **-rized;
-rizing** : plagiar
plague[1] ['pleɪg] *vt* **plagued; plaguing** **1**
AFFLICT : plagar, afligir **2** HARASS
: acosar, atormentar
plague[2] *n* **1** : plaga *f* (de insectos, etc.)
2 : peste *f* (en medicina)
plaid[1] ['plæd] *adj* : escocés, de cuadros
⟨a plaid skirt : una falda escocesa⟩
plaid[2] *n* TARTAN : tela *f* escocesa, tartán
m
plain[1] ['pleɪn] *adj* **1** SIMPLE, UN-
ADORNED : liso, sencillo, sin adornos
2 CLEAR : claro ⟨in plain language : en
palabras claras⟩ **3** FRANK : franco,
puro ⟨the plain truth : la pura verdad⟩
4 HOMELY : ordinario, poco atractivo
5 in plain sight : a la vista de todos
plain[2] *n* : llanura *f*, llano *m*, planicie *f*
plainly ['pleɪnli] *adv* **1** CLEARLY : claramente **2** FRANKLY : francamente, con
franqueza **3** SIMPLY : sencillamente
plaintiff ['pleɪntɪf] *n* : demandante *mf*
plaintive ['pleɪntɪv] *adj* MOURNFUL : lastimero, plañidero
plait[1] ['pleɪt, 'plæt] *vt* **1** PLEAT : plisar **2**
BRAID : trenzar
plait[2] *n* **1** PLEAT : pliegue *m* **2** BRAID
: trenza *f*
plan[1] ['plæn] *v* **planned; planning** *vt* **1**
: planear, proyectar, planificar ⟨to plan
a trip : planear un viaje⟩ ⟨to plan a city
: planificar una ciudad⟩ **2** INTEND
: tener planeado, proyectar — *vi* : hacer planes
plan[2] *n* **1** DIAGRAM : plano *m*, esquema
m **2** SCHEME : plan *m*, proyecto *m*, programa *m* ⟨to draw up a plan : elaborar
un proyecto⟩
plane[1] ['pleɪn] *vt* **planed; planing** : cepillar (madera)
plane[2] *adj* : plano
plane[3] *n* **1** : plano *m* (en matemáticas,
etc.) **2** LEVEL : nivel *m* **3** : cepillo *m*
(de carpintero) **4** → **airplane**
planet ['plænət] *n* : planeta *f*
planetarium [,plænə'teriəm] *n, pl* **-iums**
or **-ia** [-iə] : planetario *m*
planetary ['plænə,teri] *adj* : planetario
plank ['plæŋk] *n* **1** BOARD : tablón *m*,
tabla *f* **2** : artículo *m*, punto *m* (de una
plataforma política)

plankton ['plæŋktən] *n* : plancton *m*

plant¹ ['plænt] *vt* **1** : plantar, sembrar (semillas) ⟨planted with flowers : plantado de flores⟩ **2** PLACE : plantar, colocar ⟨to plant an idea : inculcar una idea⟩

plant² *n* **1** : planta *f* ⟨leafy plants : plantas frondosas⟩ **2** FACTORY : planta *f*, fábrica *f* ⟨hydroelectric plant : planta hidroeléctrica⟩ **3** MACHINERY : maquinaria *f*, equipo *m*

plantain ['plæntən] *n* **1** : llantén *m* (mala hierba) **2** : plátano *m*, plátano *m* macho *Mex* (fruta)

plantation [plæn'teɪʃən] *n* : plantación *f*, hacienda *f* ⟨a coffee plantation : un cafetal⟩

planter ['plæntər] *n* **1** : hacendado *m*, -da *f* (de una hacienda) **2** FLOWERPOT : tiesto *m*, maceta *f*

plaque ['plæk] *n* **1** TABLET : placa *f* **2** : placa *f* (dental)

plasma ['plæzmə] *n* : plasma *m*

plaster¹ ['plæstər] *vt* **1** : enyesar, revocar (con yeso) **2** COVER : cubrir, llenar ⟨a wall plastered with notices : una pared cubierta de avisos⟩

plaster² *n* **1** : yeso *m*, revoque *m* (para paredes, etc.) **2** : escayola *f*, yeso *m* (en medicina) **3 plaster of Paris** ['pærɪs] : yeso *m* mate

plaster cast *n* : vaciado *m* de yeso

plasterer ['plæstərər] *n* : revocador *m*, -dora *f*

plastic¹ ['plæstɪk] *adj* **1** : de plástico **2** PLIABLE : plástico, flexible **3 plastic surgery** : cirugía *f* plástica

plastic² *n* : plástico *m*

plasticity [plæ'stɪsəti] *n*, *pl* **-ties** : plasticidad *f*

plate¹ ['pleɪt] *vt* **plated; plating** : chapar (en metal)

plate² *n* **1** PLAQUE, SHEET : placa *f* ⟨a steel plate : una placa de acero⟩ **2** UTENSILS : vajilla *f* (de metal) ⟨silver plate : vajilla de plata⟩ **3** DISH : plato *m* **4** DENTURES : dentadura *f* postiza **5** ILLUSTRATION : lámina *f* (en un libro) **6 license plate** : matrícula *f*, placa *f* de matrícula

plateau [plæ'toː] *n*, *pl* **-teaus** *or* **-teaux** [-'toːz] : meseta *f*

platform ['plætˌfɔrm] *n* **1** STAGE : plataforma *f*, estrado *m*, tribuna *f* **2** : andén *m* (de una estación de ferrocarril) **3 political platform** : plataforma *f* política, programa *m* electoral

plating ['pleɪtɪŋ] *n* **1** : enchapado *m* **2 silver plating** : plateado *m*

platinum ['plætᵊnəm] *n* : platino *m*

platitude ['plætəˌtuːd, -ˌtjuːd] *n* : lugar *m* común, perogrullada *f*

platonic [plə'tɑnɪk] *adj* : platónico

platoon [plə'tuːn] *n* : sección *f* (en el ejército)

platter ['plætər] *n* : fuente *f*

platypus ['plætɪpəs, -ˌpʊs] *n*, *pl* **platypuses** *or* **platypi** [-ˌpaɪ, -ˌpiː] : ornitorrinco *m*

plausibility [ˌplɔzə'bɪləti] *n*, *pl* **-ties** : credibilidad *f*, verosimilitud *f*

plausible ['plɔzəbəl] *adj* : creíble, convincente, verosímil — **plausibly** [-bli] *adv*

play¹ ['pleɪ] *vi* **1** : jugar ⟨to play with a doll : jugar con una muñeca⟩ ⟨to play with an idea : darle vueltas a una idea⟩ **2** FIDDLE, TOY : jugar, juguetear ⟨don't play with your food : no juegues con la comida⟩ **3** : tocar ⟨to play in a band : tocar en un grupo⟩ **4** : actuar (en una obra de teatro) — *vt* **1** : jugar (un deporte, etc.), jugar a (un juego), jugar contra (un contrincante) **2** : tocar (música o un instrumento) **3** PERFORM : interpretar, hacer el papel de (un carácter), representar (una obra de teatro) ⟨she plays the lead : hace el papel principal⟩ **4 to play back** : poner (una grabación) **5 to play down** : minimizar **6 to play up** : resaltar

play² *n* **1** GAME, RECREATION : juego *m* ⟨children at play : niños jugando⟩ ⟨a play on words : un juego de palabras⟩ **2** ACTION : juego *m* ⟨the ball is in play : la pelota está en juego⟩ ⟨to bring into play : poner en juego⟩ **3** DRAMA : obra *f* de teatro, pieza *f* (de teatro) **4** MOVEMENT : juego *m* (de la luz, una brisa, etc.) **5** SLACK : juego *m* ⟨there's not enough play in the wheel : la rueda no da lo suficiente⟩

playacting ['pleɪˌæktɪŋ] *n* : actuación *f*, teatro *m*

player ['pleɪər] *n* **1** : jugador *m*, -dora *f* (en un juego) **2** ACTOR : actor *m*, actriz *f* **3** MUSICIAN : músico *m*, -ca *f*

playful ['pleɪfəl] *adj* **1** FROLICSOME : juguetón **2** JOCULAR : jocoso — **playfully** *adv*

playfulness ['pleɪfəlnəs] *n* : lo juguetón, jocosidad *f*, alegría *f*

playground ['pleɪˌɡraʊnd] *n* : patio *m* de recreo, jardín *m* para jugar

playhouse ['pleɪˌhaʊs] *n* **1** THEATER : teatro *m* **2** : casita *f* de juguete

playing card *n* : naipe *m*, carta *f*

playmate ['pleɪˌmeɪt] *n* : compañero *m*, -ra *f* de juego

play-off ['pleɪˌɔf] *n* : desempate *m*

playpen ['pleɪˌpɛn] *n* : corral *m* (para niños)

plaything ['pleɪˌθɪŋ] *n* : juguete *m*

playwright ['pleɪˌraɪt] *n* : dramaturgo *m*, -ga *f*

plaza ['plæzə, 'plɑ-] *n* **1** SQUARE : plaza *f* **2 shopping plaza** MALL : centro *m* comercial

plea ['pliː] *n* **1** : acto *m* de declararse ⟨he entered a plea of guilty : se declaró culpable⟩ **2** APPEAL : ruego *m*, súplica *f*

plead ['pliːd] *v* **pleaded** *or* **pled** ['plɛd]; **pleading** *vi* **1** : declararse (culpable o inocente) **2 to plead for** : suplicar, implorar — *vt* **1** : alegar, pretextar ⟨he pleaded illness : pretextó la enfermedad⟩ **2 to plead a case** : defender un caso

pleasant ['plɛzənt] *adj* : agradable, grato, bueno — **pleasantly** *adv*

pleasantness ['plɛzəntnəs] *n* : lo agradable, amenidad *f*

pleasantries ['plɛzəntriz] *npl* : cumplidos *mpl*, cortesías *fpl* ⟨to exchange pleasantries : intercambiar cumplidos⟩

please¹ ['pli:z] *v* **pleased; pleasing** *vt* **1** GRATIFY : complacer ⟨please yourself! : ¡cómo quieras!⟩ **2** SATISFY : contentar, satisfacer — *vi* **1** SATISFY : complacer, agradar ⟨anxious to please : deseoso de complacer⟩ **2** LIKE : querer ⟨do as you please : haz lo que quieras, haz lo que te parezca⟩

please² *adv* : por favor

pleased ['pli:zd] *adj* : contento, satisfecho, alegre

pleasing ['pli:zɪŋ] *adj* : agradable — **pleasingly** *adv*

pleasurable ['plɛʒərəbəl] *adj* PLEASANT : agradable

pleasure ['plɛʒər] *n* **1** WISH : deseo *m*, voluntad *f* ⟨at your pleasure : cuando guste⟩ **2** ENJOYMENT : placer *m*, disfrute *m*, goce *m* ⟨with pleasure : con mucho gusto⟩ **3** : placer *m*, gusto *m* ⟨it's a pleasure to be here : me da gusto estar aquí⟩ ⟨the pleasures of reading : los placeres de leer⟩

pleat¹ ['pli:t] *vt* : plisar

pleat² *n* : pliegue *m*

plebeian [plɪ'biən] *adj* : ordinario, plebeyo

pledge¹ ['plɛdʒ] *vt* **pledged; pledging 1** PAWN : empeñar, prendar **2** PROMISE : prometer, jurar

pledge² *n* **1** SECURITY : garantía *f*, prenda *f* **2** PROMISE : promesa *f*

plenteous ['plɛntiəs] *adj* : copioso, abundante

plentiful ['plɛntɪfəl] *adj* : abundante — **plentifully** [-fli] *adv*

plenty ['plɛnti] *n* : abundancia *f* ⟨plenty of time : tiempo de sobra⟩ ⟨plenty of visitors : muchos visitantes⟩

plethora ['plɛθərə] *n* : plétora *f*

pleurisy ['plʊrəsi] *n* : pleuresía *f*

pliable ['plaɪəbəl] *adj* : flexible, maleable

pliant ['plaɪənt] → **pliable**

pliers ['plaɪərz] *npl* : alicates *mpl*, pinzas *fpl*

plight ['plaɪt] *n* : situación *f* difícil, apuro *m*

plod ['plɑd] *vi* **plodded; plodding 1** TRUDGE : caminar pesadamente y lentamente **2** DRUDGE : trabajar laboriosamente

plot¹ ['plɑt] *v* **plotted; plotting** *vt* **1** DEVISE : tramar **2 to plot out** : trazar, determinar (una posición, etc.) — *vi* CONSPIRE : conspirar

plot² *n* **1** LOT : terreno *m*, parcela *f*, lote *m* **2** STORY : argumento *m* (en el teatro), trama *f* (en un libro, etc.) **3** CONSPIRACY, INTRIGUE : complot *m*, intriga *f*

plotter ['plɑtər] *n* : conspirador *m*, -dora *f*; intrigante *mf*

plow¹ *or* **plough** ['plaʊ] *vt* **1** : arar (la tierra) **2 to plow the seas** : surcar los mares

plow² *or* **plough** *n* **1** : arado *m* **2** → **snowplow**

plowshare ['plaʊˌʃɛr] *n* : reja *f* del arado

ploy ['plɔɪ] *n* : estratagema *f*, maniobra *f*

pluck¹ ['plʌk] *vt* **1** PICK : arrancar **2** : desplumar (un pollo, etc.) — *vi* **to pluck at** : tirar de

pluck² *n* **1** TUG : tirón *m* **2** COURAGE, SPIRIT : valor *m*, ánimo *m*

plucky ['plʌki] *adj* **pluckier; -est** : valiente, animoso

plug¹ ['plʌg] *vt* **plugged; plugging 1** BLOCK : tapar **2** PROMOTE : hacerle publicidad a, promocionar **3 to plug in** : enchufar

plug² *n* **1** STOPPER : tapón *m* **2** : enchufe *m* (eléctrico) **3** ADVERTISEMENT : publicidad *f*, propaganda *f*

plum ['plʌm] *n* **1** : ciruela *f* (fruta) **2** : color *m* ciruela **3** PRIZE : premio *m*, algo muy atractivo

plumage ['plu:mɪdʒ] *n* : plumaje *m*

plumb¹ ['plʌm] *vt* **1** : aplomar ⟨to plumb a wall : aplomar una pared⟩ **2** SOUND : sondear, sondar

plumb² *adv* **1** VERTICALLY : a plomo, verticalmente **2** EXACTLY : justo, exactamente **3** COMPLETELY : completamente, absolutamente ⟨plumb crazy : loco de remate⟩

plumb³ *adj* : a plomo

plumb⁴ *n or* **plumb line** : plomada *f*

plumber ['plʌmər] *n* : plomero *m*, -ra *f*; fontanero *m*, -ra *f*

plumbing ['plʌmɪŋ] *n* **1** : plomería *f*, fontanería *f* (trabajo del plomero) **2** PIPES : cañería *f*, tubería *f*

plume ['plu:m] *n* **1** FEATHER : pluma *f* **2** TUFT : penacho *m* (en un sombrero, etc.)

plumed ['plu:md] *adj* : con plumas ⟨white-plumed birds : aves de plumaje blanco⟩

plummet ['plʌmət] *vi* : caer en picada, desplomarse

plump¹ ['plʌmp] *vi or* **to plump down** : dejarse caer (pesadamente)

plump² *adv* **1** STRAIGHT : a plomo **2** DIRECTLY : directamente, sin rodeos ⟨he ran plump into the door : dio de cara con la puerta⟩

plump³ *adj* : llenito *fam*, regordete *fam*, rechoncho *fam*

plumpness ['plʌmpnəs] *n* : gordura *f*

plunder¹ ['plʌndər] *vi* : saquear, robar

plunder² *n* : botín *m*

plunderer ['plʌndərər] *n* : saqueador *m*, -dora *f*

plunge¹ ['plʌndʒ] *v* **plunged; plunging** *vt* **1** IMMERSE : sumergir **2** THRUST : hundir, clavar — *vi* **1** DIVE : zambullirse (en el agua) **2** : meterse precipitadamente o violentamente ⟨they plunged into war : se enfrascaron en una guerra⟩ ⟨he plunged into depression : cayó en la depresión⟩ **3** DESCEND : descender en picada ⟨the road plunges dizzily : la calle desciende vertiginosamente⟩

plunge² *n* **1** DIVE : zambullida *f* **2** DROP : descenso *m* abrupto ⟨the plunge in prices : el desplome de los precios⟩

plural¹ ['plʊrəl] *adj* : plural

plural² *n* : plural *m*

plurality [plʊ'ræləti] *n, pl* -**ties** : pluralidad *f*

pluralize ['plʊrə,laɪz] *vt* -**ized; -izing** : pluralizar

plus¹ ['plʌs] *adj* **1** POSITIVE : positivo ⟨a plus factor : un factor positivo⟩ **2** (*indicating a quantity in addition*) ⟨a grade of C plus : una calificación entre C y B⟩ ⟨a salary of $30,000 plus : un sueldo de más de $30,000⟩

plus² *n* **1** *or* **plus sign** : más *m*, signo *m* de más **2** ADVANTAGE : ventaja *f*

plus³ *prep* : más (en matemáticas)

plus⁴ *conj* AND : y

plush¹ ['plʌʃ] *adj* **1** : afelpado **2** LUXURIOUS : lujoso

plush² *n* : felpa *f*, peluche *m*

plushy ['plʌʃi] *adj* **plushier; -est** : lujoso

Pluto ['plu:to:] *n* : Plutón *m*

plutocracy [plu:'tɑkrəsi] *n, pl* -**cies** : plutocracia *f*

plutonium [plu:'to:niəm] *n* : plutonio *m*

ply¹ ['plaɪ] *v* **plied; plying** *vt* **1** USE, WIELD : manejar ⟨to ply an ax : manejar un hacha⟩ **2** PRACTICE : ejercer ⟨to ply a trade : ejercer un oficio⟩ **3 to ply with questions** : acosar con preguntas

ply² *n, pl* **plies 1** LAYER : chapa *f* (de madera), capa *f* (de papel) **2** STRAND : cabo *m* (de hilo, etc.)

plywood ['plaɪ,wʊd] *n* : contrachapado *m*

pneumatic [nʊ'mætɪk, njʊ-] *adj* : neumático

pneumonia [nʊ'mo:njə, njʊ-] *n* : pulmonía *f*, neumonía *f*

poach ['po:tʃ] *vt* **1** : cocer a fuego lento ⟨to poach an egg : escalfar un huevo⟩ **2 to poach game** : cazar ilegalmente — *vi* : cazar ilegalmente

poacher ['po:tʃər] *n* : cazador *m* furtivo, cazadora *f* furtiva

pock ['pɑk] *n* **1** PUSTULE : pústula *f* **2** → **pockmark**

pocket¹ ['pɑkət] *vt* **1** : meterse en el bolsillo ⟨he pocketed the pen : se metió la pluma en el bolsillo⟩ **2** STEAL : embolsarse

pocket² *n* **1** : bolsillo *m*, bolsa *f Mex* ⟨a coat pocket : el bolsillo de un abrigo⟩ ⟨air pockets : bolsas de aire⟩ **2** CENTER : foco *m*, centro *m* ⟨a pocket of resistance : un foco de resistencia⟩

pocketbook ['pɑkət,bʊk] *n* **1** PURSE : cartera *f*, bolso *m*, bolsa *f Mex* **2** MEANS : recursos *mpl*

pocketknife ['pɑkət,naɪf] *n, pl* -**knives** : navaja *f*

pocket–size ['pɑkət'saɪz] *adj* : de bolsillo

pockmark ['pɑk,mɑrk] *n* : cicatriz *f* de viruela, viruela *f*

pod ['pɑd] *n* : vaina *f* ⟨pea pod : vaina de guisantes⟩

podiatrist [pə'daɪətrɪst, po-] *n* : podólogo *m*, -ga *f*

podiatry [pə'daɪətri, po-] *n* : podología *f*, podiatría *f*

podium ['po:diəm] *n, pl* -**diums** *or* -**dia** [-diə] : podio *m*, estrado *m*, tarima *f*

poem ['po:əm] *n* : poema *m*, poesía *f*

poet ['po:ət] *n* : poeta *mf*

poetic [po'ɛtɪk] *or* **poetical** [-tɪkəl] *adj* : poético

poetry ['po:ətri] *n* : poesía *f*

pogrom ['po:grəm, pə'grɑm, 'pɑgrəm] *n* : pogrom *m*

poignancy ['pɔɪnjəntsi] *n, pl* -**cies** : lo conmovedor

poignant ['pɔɪnjənt] *adj* **1** PAINFUL : penoso, doloroso ⟨poignant grief : profundo dolor⟩ **2** TOUCHING : conmovedor, emocionante

poinsettia [pɔɪn'sɛtiə, -'sɛtə] *n* : flor *f* de Nochebuena

point¹ ['pɔɪnt] *vt* **1** SHARPEN : afilar (la punta de) **2** INDICATE : señalar, indicar ⟨to point the way : señalar el camino⟩ **3** AIM : apuntar **4 to point out** : señalar, indicar — *vi* **1 to point at** : señalar (con el dedo) **2 to point to** INDICATE : señalar, indicar

point² *n* **1** ITEM : punto *m* ⟨the main points : los puntos principales⟩ **2** QUALITY : cualidad *f* ⟨her good points : sus buenas cualidades⟩ ⟨it's not his strong point : no es su (punto) fuerte⟩ **3** (*indicating a chief idea or meaning*) ⟨it's beside the point : no viene al caso⟩ ⟨to get to the point : ir al grano⟩ ⟨to stick to the point : no salirse del tema⟩ **4** PURPOSE : fin *m*, propósito *m* ⟨there's no point to it : no vale la pena, no sirve para nada⟩ **5** PLACE : punto *m*, lugar *m* ⟨points of interest : puntos interesantes⟩ **6** : punto *m* (en una escala) ⟨boiling point : punto de ebullición⟩ **7** MOMENT : momento *m*, coyuntura *f* ⟨at this point : en este momento⟩ **8** TIP : punta *f* **9** HEADLAND : punta *f*, cabo *m* **10** PERIOD : punto *m* (marca de puntuación) **11** UNIT : punto *m* ⟨he scored 15 points : ganó 15 puntos⟩ ⟨shares fell 10 points : las acciones bajaron 10 enteros⟩ **12 compass points** : puntos *mpl* cardinales **13 decimal point** : punto *m* decimal, coma *f*

point–blank¹ ['pɔɪnt'blæŋk] *adv* **1** : a quemarropa ⟨to shoot point-blank : disparar a quemarropa⟩ **2** BLUNTLY, DIRECTLY : a bocajarro, sin rodeos, francamente

point–blank² *adj* **1** : a quemarropa ⟨point-blank shots : disparos a quemarropa⟩ **2** BLUNT, DIRECT : directo, franco

pointed ['pɔɪntəd] *adj* **1** POINTY : puntiagudo **2** PERTINENT : atinado **3** CONSPICUOUS : marcado, manifiesto

pointedly ['pɔɪntədli] *adv* : intencionadamente, directamente

pointer ['pɔɪntər] *n* **1** STICK : puntero *m* (para maestros, etc.) **2** INDICATOR, NEEDLE : indicador *m*, aguja *f* **3** : perro *m* de muestra **4** HINT, TIP : consejo *m*

pointless ['pɔɪntləs] *adj* : inútil, ocioso, vano ⟨it's pointless to continue : no tiene sentido continuar⟩

point of view *n* : perspectiva *f*, punto *m* de vista

pointy ['pɔɪnti] *adj* : puntiagudo

poise[1] ['pɔɪz] *vt* **poised; poising** BALANCE : equilibrar, balancear

poise[2] *n* : aplomo *m*, compostura *f*

poison[1] ['pɔɪzən] *vt* **1** : envenenar, intoxicar **2** CORRUPT : corromper

poison[2] *n* : veneno *m*

poison ivy *n* : hiedra *f* venenosa

poisonous ['pɔɪzənəs] *adj* : venenoso, tóxico, ponzoñoso

poke[1] ['po:k] *v* **poked; poking** *vt* **1** JAB : golpear (con la punta de algo), dar ⟨he poked me with his finger : me dio con el dedo⟩ **2** THRUST : introducir, asomar ⟨I poked my head out the window : asomé la cabeza por la ventana⟩ — *vi* **1 to poke around** RUMMAGE : hurgar **2 to poke along** DAWDLE : demorarse, entretenerse

poke[2] *n* : golpe *m* abrupto (con la punta de algo)

poker ['po:kər] *n* **1** : atizador *m* (para el fuego) **2** : póker *m*, poker *m* (juego de naipes)

polar ['po:lər] *adj* : polar

polar bear *n* : oso *m* blanco

Polaris [po'læris, -'lɑr-] → **North Star**

polarize ['po:lə,raɪz] *vt* **-ized; -izing** : polarizar

pole ['po:l] *n* **1** : palo *m*, poste *m*, vara *f* ⟨telephone pole : poste de teléfonos⟩ **2** : polo *m* ⟨the South Pole : el Polo Sur⟩ **3** : polo *m* (eléctrico o magnético)

Pole ['po:l] *n* : polaco *m*, -ca *f*

polecat ['po:l,kæt] *n, pl* **polecats** *or* **polecat** **1** : turón *m* (de Europa) **2** SKUNK : mofeta *f*, zorrillo *m*

polemical [pə'lɛmɪkəl] *adj* : polémico

polemics [pə'lɛmɪks] *ns & pl* : polémica *f*

polestar ['po:l,stɑr] → **North Star**

police[1] [pə'li:s] *vt* **-liced; -licing** : mantener el orden en ⟨to police the streets : patrullar las calles⟩

police[2] *ns & pl* **1** : policía *f* (organización) **2** POLICE OFFICERS : policías *mfpl*

policeman [pə'li:smən] *n, pl* **-men** [-mən, -,mɛn] : policía *m*

police officer *n* : policía *mf*, agente *mf* de policía

policewoman [pə'li:s,wumən] *n, pl* **-women** [-,wɪmən] : policía *f*, mujer *f* policía

policy ['pɑləsi] *n, pl* **-cies** **1** : política *f* ⟨foreign policy : política exterior⟩ **2** *or* **insurance policy** : póliza *f* de seguros, seguro *m*

polio[1] ['po:li,o:] *adj* : de polio ⟨polio vaccine : vacuna contra la polio⟩

polio[2] *n* → **poliomyelitis**

poliomyelitis [,po:li,o:,maɪə'laɪtəs] *n* : poliomielitis *f*, polio *f*

polish[1] ['pɑlɪʃ] *vt* **1** : pulir, lustrar, sacar brillo a ⟨to polish one's nails : pintarse las uñas⟩ **2** REFINE : pulir, perfeccionar

polish[2] *n* **1** LUSTER : brillo *m*, lustre *m* **2** REFINEMENT : refinamiento *m* **3** : betún *m* (para zapatos), cera *f* (para suelos y muebles), esmalte *m* (para las uñas)

Polish[1] ['po:lɪʃ] *adj* : polaco

Polish[2] *n* : polaco *m* (idioma)

polite [pə'laɪt] *adj* **-liter; -est** : cortés, correcto, educado

politely [pə'laɪtli] *adv* : cortésmente, correctamente, con buenos modales

politeness [pə'laɪtnəs] *n* : cortesía *f*

politic ['pɑlə,tɪk] *adj* : diplomático, prudente

political [pə'lɪtɪkəl] *adj* : político — **politically** [-tɪkli] *adv*

politician [,pɑlə'tɪʃən] *n* : político *m*, -ca *f*

politics ['pɑlə,tɪks] *ns & pl* : política *f*

polka ['po:lkə, 'po:kə] *n* : polka *f*

polka dot ['po:kə,dɑt] *n* : lunar *m* (en un diseño)

poll[1] ['po:l] *vt* **1** : obtener (votos) ⟨she polled over 1000 votes : obtuvo más de 1000 votos⟩ **2** CANVASS : encuestar, sondear — *vi* : obtener votos

poll[2] *n* **1** SURVEY : encuesta *f*, sondeo *m* **2 polls** *npl* : urnas *fpl* ⟨to go to the polls : acudir a las urnas, ir a votar⟩

pollen ['pɑlən] *n* : polen *m*

pollinate ['pɑlə,neɪt] *vt* **-nated; -nating** : polinizar

pollination [,pɑlə'neɪʃən] *n* : polinización *f*

pollster ['po:lstər] *n* : encuestador *m*, -dora *f*

pollutant [pə'lu:tənt] *n* : contaminante *m*

pollute [pə'lu:t] *vt* **-luted; -luting** : contaminar

pollution [pə'lu:ʃən] *n* : contaminación *f*

pollywog *or* **polliwog** ['pɑli,wɔg] *n* TADPOLE : renacuajo *m*

polo ['po:,lo:] *n* : polo *m*

poltergeist ['po:ltər,gaɪst] *n* : poltergeist *m*, fantasma *m* travieso

polyester ['pɑli,ɛstər, ,pɑli'-] *n* : poliéster *m*

polygamous [pə'lɪgəməs] *adj* : polígamo

polygamy [pə'lɪgəmi] *n* : poligamia *f*

polygon ['pɑli,gɑn] *n* : polígono *m*

polymer ['pɑləmər] *n* : polímero *m*

Polynesian [ˌpɑlə'niːʒən, -ʃən] *n* : polinesio *m*, -sia *f* — **Polynesian** *adj*

polyunsaturated [ˌpɑliˌʌn'sæʧə-ˌreɪtəd] *adj* : poliinsaturado

pomegranate ['pɑməˌgrænət, 'pɑm-ˌgrænət] *n* : granada *f* (fruta)

pommel[1] ['pʌməl] *vt* → **pummel**

pommel[2] ['pʌməl, 'pɑ-] *n* **1** : pomo *m* (de una espada) **2** : perilla *f* (de una silla de montar)

pomp ['pɑmp] *n* **1** SPLENDOR : pompa *f*, esplendor *m* **2** OSTENTATION : boato *m*, ostentación *f*

pom–pom ['pɑmˌpɑm] *n* : borla *f*, pompón *m*

pomposity [pɑm'pɑsəti] *n, pl* **-ties** : pomposidad *f*

pompous ['pɑmpəs] *adj* : pomposo — **pompously** *adv*

poncho ['pɑnˌʧoː] *n, pl* **-chos** : poncho *m*

pond ['pɑnd] *n* : charca *f* (natural), estanque *m* (artificial)

ponder ['pɑndər] *vt* : reflexionar, considerar — *vi* **to ponder over** : reflexionar sobre, sopesar

ponderous ['pɑndərəs] *adj* : pesado

pontiff ['pɑntɪf] *n* POPE : pontífice *m*

pontificate [pɑn'tɪfəˌkeɪt] *vi* **-cated; -cating** : pontificar

pontoon [pɑn'tuːn] *n* : pontón *m*

pony ['poːni] *n, pl* **-nies** : poni *m*, poney *m*, jaca *f*

ponytail ['poːniˌteɪl] *n* : cola *f* de caballo, coleta *f*

poodle ['puːdəl] *n* : caniche *m*

pool[1] ['puːl] *vt* : mancomunar, hacer un fondo común de

pool[2] *n* **1** : charca *f* ⟨a swimming pool : una piscina⟩ **2** PUDDLE : charco *m* **3** RESERVE, SUPPLY : fondo *m* común (de recursos), reserva *f* **4** : billar *m* (juego)

poor ['pur, 'por] *adj* **1** : pobre ⟨poor people : los pobres⟩ **2** SCANTY : pobre, escaso ⟨poor attendance : baja asistencia⟩ **3** UNFORTUNATE : pobre ⟨poor thing! : ¡pobrecito!⟩ **4** BAD : malo ⟨to be in poor health : estar mal de salud⟩

poorly ['purli, 'por-] *adv* : mal

pop[1] ['pɑp] *v* **popped; popping** *vi* **1** BURST : reventarse, estallar **2** : ir, venir, o aparecer abruptamente ⟨he popped into the house : se metió en la casa⟩ ⟨a menu pops up : aparece un menú⟩ **3 to pop out** PROTRUDE : salirse, saltarse ⟨my eyes popped out of my head : se me saltaban los ojos⟩ — *vt* **1** BURST : reventar **2** : hacer o meter abruptamente ⟨he popped it into his mouth : se lo metió en la boca⟩

pop[2] *adj* : popular ⟨pop music : música popular⟩

pop[3] *n* **1** : estallido *m* pequeño (de un globo, etc.) **2** SODA : refresco *m*, gaseosa *f*

popcorn ['pɑpˌkɔrn] *n* : palomitas *fpl* (de maíz)

pope ['poːp] *n* : papa *m* ⟨Pope John : el Papa Juan⟩

poplar ['pɑplər] *n* : álamo *m*

poplin ['pɑplɪn] *n* : popelín *m*, popelina *f*

poppy ['pɑpi] *n, pl* **-pies** : amapola *f*

populace ['pɑpjələs] *n* **1** MASSES : pueblo *m* **2** POPULATION : población *f*

popular ['pɑpjələr] *adj* **1** : popular ⟨the popular vote : el voto popular⟩ **2** COMMON : generalizado, común ⟨popular beliefs : creencias generalizadas⟩ **3** : popular, de gran popularidad ⟨a popular singer : un cantante popular⟩

popularity [ˌpɑpjə'lærəti] *n* : popularidad *f*

popularize ['pɑpjələˌraɪz] *vt* **-ized; -izing** : popularizar

popularly ['pɑpjələrli] *adv* : popularmente, vulgarmente

populate ['pɑpjəˌleɪt] *vt* **-lated; -lating** : poblar

population [ˌpɑpjə'leɪʃən] *n* : población *f*

populist ['pɑpjəlɪst] *n* : populista *mf* — **populist** *adj*

populous ['pɑpjələs] *adj* : populoso

porcelain ['porsələn] *n* : porcelana *f*

porch ['porʧ] *n* : porche *m*

porcupine ['porkjəˌpaɪn] *n* : puerco *m* espín

pore[1] ['por] *vi* **pored; poring 1** GAZE : mirar (con atención) **2 to pore over** : leer detenidamente, estudiar

pore[2] *n* : poro *m*

pork ['pork] *n* : carne *f* de cerdo, carne *f* de puerco

pornographic [ˌpornə'græfɪk] *adj* : pornográfico

pornography [por'nɑgrəfi] *n* : pornografía *f*

porous ['porəs] *adj* : poroso

porpoise ['porpəs] *n* **1** : marsopa *f* **2** DOLPHIN : delfín *m*

porridge ['porɪʤ] *n* : sopa *f* espesa de harina, gachas *fpl*

port[1] ['port] *adj* : de babor ⟨on the port side : a babor⟩

port[2] *n* **1** HARBOR : puerto *m* **2** ORIFICE : orificio *m* (de una válvula, etc.) **3** : puerto *m* (de una computadora) **4** PORTHOLE : portilla *f* **5** *or* **port side** : babor *m* (de un barco) **6** : oporto *m* (vino)

portable ['portəbəl] *adj* : portátil

portal ['portəl] *n* : portal *m*

portend [por'tend] *vt* : presagiar, augurar

portent ['porˌtent] *n* : presagio *m*, augurio *m*

portentous [por'tentəs] *adj* : profético, que presagia

porter ['portər] *n* : maletero *m*, mozo *m* (de estación)

portfolio [port'foːliˌo] *n, pl* **-lios 1** FOLDER : cartera *f* (para llevar papeles), carpeta *f* **2** : cartera *f* (diplomática) **3 investment portfolio** : cartera de inversiones

porthole ['port,ho:l] *n* : portilla *f* (de un barco), ventanilla *f* (de un avión)

portico ['porti,ko] *n, pl* **-coes** *or* **-cos** : pórtico *m*

portion¹ ['porʃən] *vt* DISTRIBUTE : repartir

portion² *n* PART, SHARE : porción *f*, parte *f*

portly ['portli] *adj* **-lier; -est** : corpulento

portrait ['portrət, -,treɪt] *n* : retrato *m*

portray [por'treɪ] *vt* **1** DEPICT : representar, retratar **2** DESCRIBE : describir **3** PLAY : interpretar (un personaje)

portrayal [por'treɪəl] *n* **1** REPRESENTATION : representación *f* **2** PORTRAIT : retrato *m*

Portuguese [,portʃə'gi:z, -'gi:s] *n* **1** : portugués *m*, -guesa *f* (persona) **2** : portugués *m* (idioma) — **Portuguese** *adj*

pose¹ ['po:z] *v* **posed; posing** *vt* PRESENT : plantear (una pregunta, etc.), representar (una amenaza) — *vi* **1** : posar (para una foto, etc.) **2 to pose as** : hacerse pasar por

pose² *n* **1** : pose *f* ⟨to strike a pose : asumir una pose⟩ **2** PRETENSE : pose *f*, afectación *f*

posh ['paʃ] *adj* : elegante, de lujo

position¹ [pə'zɪʃən] *vt* : colocar, situar, ubicar

position² *n* **1** APPROACH, STANCE : posición *f*, postura *f*, planteamiento *m* **2** LOCATION : posición *f*, ubicación *f* **3** STATUS : posición *f* (en una jerarquía) **4** JOB : puesto *m*

positive ['pazətɪv] *adj* **1** DEFINITE : incuestionable, inequívoco ⟨positive evidence : pruebas irrefutables⟩ **2** CONFIDENT : seguro **3** : positivo (en gramática, matemáticas, y física) **4** AFFIRMATIVE : positivo, afirmativo ⟨a positive response : una respuesta positiva⟩

positively ['pazətɪvli] *adv* **1** FAVORABLY : favorablemente **2** OPTIMISTICALLY : positivamente **3** DEFINITELY : definitivamente, en forma concluyente **4** (*used for emphasis*) : realmente, verdaderamente ⟨it's positively awful! : ¡es verdaderamente malo!⟩

possess [pə'zɛs] *vt* **1** HAVE, OWN : poseer, tener **2** SEIZE : apoderarse de ⟨he was possessed by fear : el miedo se apoderó de él⟩

possession [pə'zɛʃən] *n* **1** POSSESSING : posesión *f* **2** : posesión *f* (por un demonio, etc.) **3 possessions** *npl* PROPERTY : bienes *mpl*, propiedad *f*

possessive¹ [pə'zɛsɪv] *adj* **1** : posesivo (en gramática) **2** JEALOUS : posesivo, celoso

possessive² *n* *or* **possessive case** : posesivo *m*

possessor [pə'zɛsər] *n* : poseedor *m*, -dora *f*

possibility [,pasə'bɪləti] *n, pl* **-ties** : posibilidad *f*

possible ['pasəbəl] *adj* : posible

possibly ['pasəbli] *adv* **1** CONCEIVABLY : posiblemente ⟨it can't possibly be true! : ¡no puede ser!⟩ **2** PERHAPS : quizás, posiblemente

possum ['pasəm] → **opossum**

post¹ ['po:st] *vt* **1** MAIL : echar al correo, mandar por correo **2** ANNOUNCE : anunciar ⟨they've posted the grades : han anunciado las notas⟩ **3** AFFIX : fijar, poner (noticias, etc.) **4** STATION : apostar **5 to keep (someone) posted** : tener al corriente (a alguien)

post² *n* **1** POLE : poste *m*, palo *m* **2** STATION : puesto *m* **3** CAMP : puesto *m* (militar) **4** JOB, POSITION : puesto *m*, empleo *m*, cargo *m*

postage ['po:stɪʤ] *n* : franqueo *m*

postal ['po:stəl] *adj* : postal

postcard ['po:st,kard] *n* : postal *f*, tarjeta *f* postal

poster ['po:stər] *n* : póster *m*, cartel *m*, afiche *m*

posterior¹ [pa'stɪriər, po-] *adj* : posterior

posterior² *n* BUTTOCKS : trasero *m*, nalgas *fpl*, asentaderas *fpl*

posterity [pa'stɛrəti] *n* : posteridad *f*

postgraduate¹ [,po:st'græʤuət] *adj* : de postgrado

postgraduate² *n* : postgraduado *m*, -da *f*

posthaste ['po:st'heɪst] *adv* : a toda prisa

posthumous ['pastʃəməs] *adj* : póstumo — **posthumously** *adv*

postman ['po:stmən, -,mæn] → **mailman**

postmark¹ ['po:st,mark] *vt* : matasellar

postmark² *n* : matasellos *m*

postmaster ['po:st,mæstər] *n* : administrador *m*, -dora *f* de correos

postmodern [,po:st'madərn] *adj* : posmoderno

postmortem [,po:st'mortəm] *n* : autopsia *f*

postnatal [,po:st'neɪtəl] *adj* : postnatal ⟨postnatal depression : depresión posparto⟩

post office *n* : correo *m*, oficina *f* de correos

postoperative [,po:st'apərətɪv, -,reɪ-] *adj* : posoperatorio

postpaid [,po:st'peɪd] *adv* : con franqueo pagado

postpone [,po:st'po:n] *vt* **-poned; -poning** : postergar, aplazar, posponer

postponement [,po:st'po:nmənt] *n* : postergación *f*, aplazamiento *m*

postscript ['po:st,skrɪpt] *n* : postdata *f*, posdata *f*

postulate ['pastʃə,leɪt] *vt* **-lated; -lating** : postular

posture¹ ['pastʃər] *vi* **-tured; -turing** : posar, asumir una pose

posture² *n* : postura *f*

postwar [,po:st'wor] *adj* : de (la) posguerra

posy ['po:zi] *n, pl* **-sies 1** FLOWER : flor *f* **2** BOUQUET : ramo *m*, ramillete *m*
pot¹ ['pɑt] *vt* **potted; potting** : plantar (en una maceta)
pot² *n* **1** : olla *f* (de cocina) **2 pots and pans** : cacharros *mpl*
potable ['po:təbəl] *adj* : potable
potash ['pɑt,æʃ] *n* : potasa *f*
potassium [pə'tæsiəm] *n* : potasio *m*
potato [pə'teɪto] *n, pl* **-toes** : papa *f*, patata *f Spain*
potato chips *npl* : papas *fpl* fritas (de bolsa)
potbellied ['pɑt,bɛlid] *adj* : panzón, barrigón *fam*
potbelly ['pɑt,bɛli] *n* : panza *f*, barriga *f*
potency ['po:təntsi] *n, pl* **-cies 1** POWER : fuerza *f*, potencia *f* **2** EFFECTIVENESS : eficacia *f*
potent ['po:tənt] *adj* **1** POWERFUL : potente, poderoso **2** EFFECTIVE : eficaz ⟨a potent medicine : una medicina bien fuerte⟩
potential¹ [pə'tɛntʃəl] *adj* : potencial, posible
potential² *n* **1** : potencial *m* ⟨growth potential : potencial de crecimiento⟩ ⟨a child with potential : un niño que promete⟩ **2** : potencial *m* (eléctrico) — **potentially** *adv*
potful ['pɑt,fʊl] *n* : contenido *m* de una olla ⟨a potful of water : una olla de agua⟩
pothole ['pɑt,ho:l] *n* : bache *m*
potion ['po:ʃən] *n* : brebaje *m*, poción *f*
potluck ['pɑt,lʌk] *n* **to take potluck** : tomar lo que haya
potpourri [,po:pʊ'ri:] *n* : popurrí *m*
potshot ['pɑt,ʃɑt] *n* **1** : tiro *m* al azar ⟨to take potshots at : disparar al azar a⟩ **2** CRITICISM : crítica *f* (hecha al azar)
potter ['pɑtər] *n* : alfarero *m*, -ra *f*
pottery ['pɑtəri] *n, pl* **-teries** : cerámica *f*
pouch ['paʊtʃ] *n* **1** BAG : bolsa *f* pequeña **2** : bolsa *f* (de un animal)
poultice ['po:ltəs] *n* : emplasto *m*, cataplasma *f*
poultry ['po:ltri] *n* : aves *fpl* de corral
pounce ['paʊnts] *vi* **pounced; pouncing** : abalanzarse
pound¹ ['paʊnd] *vt* **1** CRUSH : machacar, machucar, majar **2** BEAT : golpear, machacar ⟨she pounded the lessons into them : les machacaba las lecciones⟩ ⟨he pounded home his point : les hizo entender su razonamiento⟩ — *vi* **1** BEAT : palpitar (dícese del corazón) **2** RESOUND : retumbar, resonar **3** : andar con paso pesado ⟨we pounded through the mud : caminamos pesadamente por el barro⟩
pound² *n* **1** : libra *f* (unidad de peso) **2** : libra *f* (unidad monetaria) **3 dog pound** : perrera *f*
pour ['por] *vt* **1** : echar, verter, servir (bebidas) ⟨pour it into a pot : viértalo en una olla⟩ **2** : proveer con abundancia ⟨they poured money into it : le invirtieron mucho dinero⟩ **3 to pour out** : dar salida a ⟨he poured out his feelings to her : se desahogó con ella⟩ — *vi* **1** FLOW : manar, fluir, salir ⟨blood was pouring from the wound : la sangre le salía de la herida⟩ **2 it's pouring (outside)** : está lloviendo a cántaros
pout¹ ['paʊt] *vi* : hacer pucheros
pout² *n* : puchero *m*
poverty ['pavərti] *n* : pobreza *f*, indigencia *f*
powder¹ ['paʊdər] *vt* **1** : empolvar ⟨to powder one's face : empolvarse la cara⟩ **2** PULVERIZE : pulverizar
powder² *n* : polvo *m*, polvos *mpl*
powdery ['paʊdəri] *adj* : polvoriento, como polvo
power¹ ['paʊər] *vt* : impulsar, propulsar
power² *n* **1** AUTHORITY : poder *m*, autoridad *f* ⟨executive powers : poderes ejecutivos⟩ **2** ABILITY : capacidad *f*, poder *m* **3** : potencia *f* (política) ⟨foreign powers : potencias extranjeras⟩ **4** STRENGTH : fuerza *f* **5** : potencia *f* (en física y matemáticas)
powerful ['paʊərfəl] *adj* : poderoso, potente — **powerfully** *adv*
powerhouse ['paʊər,haʊs] *n* : persona *f* dinámica
powerless ['paʊərləs] *adj* : impotente
power plant *n* : central *f* eléctrica
powwow ['paʊ,waʊ] *n* : conferencia *f*
pox ['pɑks] *n, pl* **pox** *or* **poxes 1** CHICKEN POX : varicela *f* **2** SYPHILIS : sífilis *f*
practicable ['præktɪkəbəl] *adj* : practicable, viable, factible
practical ['præktɪkəl] *adj* : práctico
practicality [,præktɪ'kæləti] *n, pl* **-ties** : factibilidad *f*, viabilidad *f*
practical joke *n* : broma *f* (pesada)
practically ['præktɪkli] *adv* **1** : de manera práctica **2** ALMOST : casi, prácticamente
practice¹ *or* **practise** ['præktəs] *vt* **-ticed** *or* **-tised; -ticing** *or* **-tising 1** : practicar ⟨he practiced his German on us : practicó el alemán con nosotros⟩ ⟨to practice politeness : practicar la cortesía⟩ **2** : ejercer ⟨to practice medicine : ejercer la medicina⟩
practice² *n* **1** USE : práctica *f* ⟨to put into practice : poner en práctica⟩ **2** CUSTOM : costumbre *f* ⟨it's a common practice here : por aquí se acostumbra hacerlo⟩ **3** TRAINING : práctica *f* **4** : ejercicio *m* (de una profesión)
practitioner [præk'tɪʃənər] *n* **1** : profesional *mf* **2 general practitioner** : médico *m*, -ca *f*
pragmatic [præg'mætɪk] *adj* : pragmático — **pragmatically** *adv*
pragmatism ['prægmə,tɪzəm] *n* : pragmatismo
prairie ['prɛri] *n* : pradera *f*, llanura *f*

praise¹ ['preɪz] *vt* **praised; praising** : elogiar, alabar ⟨to praise God : alabar a Dios⟩

praise² *n* : elogio *m*, alabanza *f*

praiseworthy ['preɪz,wərði] *adj* : digno de alabanza, loable

prance¹ ['prænʦ] *vi* **pranced; prancing 1** : hacer cabriolas, cabriolar ⟨a prancing horse : un caballo haciendo cabriolas⟩ **2** SWAGGER : pavonearse

prance² *n* : cabriola *f*

prank ['præŋk] *n* : broma *f*, travesura *f*

prankster ['præŋkstər] *n* : bromista *mf*

prattle¹ ['prætəl] *vt* **-tled; -tling** : parlotear *fam*, cotorrear *fam*, balbucear (como un niño)

prattle² *n* : parloteo *m fam*, cotorreo *m fam*, cháchara *f fam*

prawn ['prɔn] *n* : langostino *m*, camarón *m*, gamba *f*

pray ['preɪ] *vt* ENTREAT : rogar, suplicar — *vi* : rezar

prayer ['prɛr] *n* **1** : plegaria *f*, oración *f* ⟨to say one's prayers : orar, rezar⟩ ⟨the Lord's Prayer : el Padrenuestro⟩ **2** PRAYING : rezo *m*, oración *f* ⟨to kneel in prayer : arrodillarse para rezar⟩

praying mantis → **mantis**

preach ['pri:ʧ] *vi* : predicar — *vt* ADVOCATE : abogar por ⟨to preach cooperation : promover la cooperación⟩

preacher ['pri:ʧər] *n* **1** : predicador *m*, -dora *f* **2** MINISTER : pastor *m*, -tora *f*

preamble ['pri:,æmbəl] *n* : preámbulo *m*

prearrange [,pri:ə'reɪnʤ] *vt* **-ranged; -ranging** : arreglar de antemano

precarious [prɪ'kæriəs] *adj* : precario — **precariously** *adv*

precariousness [prɪ'kæriəsnəs] *n* : precariedad *f*

precaution [prɪ'kɔʃən] *n* : precaución *f*

precautionary [prɪ'kɔʃə,nɛri] *adj* : preventivo, cautelar, precautorio

precede [prɪ'si:d] *v* **-ceded; -ceding** : preceder a

precedence ['prɛsədənʦ, prɪ'si:dənʦ] *n* : precedencia *f*

precedent ['prɛsədənt] *n* : precedente *m*

precept ['pri:,sɛpt] *n* : precepto *m*

precinct ['pri:,sɪŋkt] *n* **1** DISTRICT : distrito *m* (policial, electoral, etc.) **2 precincts** *npl* PREMISES : recinto *m*, predio *m*, límites *mpl* (de una ciudad)

precious ['prɛʃəs] *adj* **1** : precioso ⟨precious gems : piedras preciosas⟩ **2** DEAR : querido **3** AFFECTED : afectado

precipice ['prɛsəpəs] *n* : precipicio *m*

precipitate [prɪ'sɪpə,teɪt] *v* **-tated; -tating** *vt* **1** HASTEN, PROVOKE : precipitar, provocar **2** HURL : arrojar **3** : precipitar (en química) — *vi* : precipitarse (en química), condensarse (en meteorología)

precipitation [prɪ,sɪpə'teɪʃən] *n* **1** HASTE : precipitación *f*, prisa *f* **2** : precipitaciones *fpl* (en meteorología)

precipitous [prɪ'sɪpətəs] *adj* **1** HASTY, RASH : precipitado **2** STEEP : escarpado, empinado ⟨a precipitous drop : una caída vertiginosa⟩

précis [preɪ'si:] *n, pl* **précis** [-'si:z] : resumen *m*

precise [prɪ'saɪs] *adj* **1** DEFINITE : preciso, explícito **2** EXACT : exacto, preciso ⟨precise calculations : cálculos precisos⟩ — **precisely** *adv*

preciseness [prɪ'saɪsnəs] *n* : precisión *f*, exactitud *f*

precision [prɪ'sɪʒən] *n* : precisión *f*

preclude [prɪ'klu:d] *vt* **-cluded; -cluding** : evitar, impedir, excluir (una posibilidad, etc.)

precocious [prɪ'ko:ʃəs] *adj* : precoz — **precociously** *adv*

precocity [prɪ'kasəṭi] *n* : precocidad *f*

preconceive [,pri:kən'si:v] *vt* **-ceived; -ceiving** : preconcebir

preconception [,pri:kən'spʃən] *n* : idea *f* preconcebida

precondition [,pri:kən'dɪʃən] *n* : precondición *f*, condición *f* previa

precook [,pri:'kʊk] *vt* : precocinar

precursor [prɪ'kərsər] *n* : precursor *m*, -sora *f*

predator ['prɛdəṭər] *n* : depredador *m*, -dora *f*

predatory ['prɛdə,tori] *adj* : depredador

predecessor ['prɛdə,sɛsər, 'pri:-] *n* : antecesor *m*, -sora *f*; predecesor *m*, -sora *f*

predestination [prɪ,dɛstə'neɪʃən] *n* : predestinación *f*

predestine [prɪ'dɛstən] *vt* **-tined; -tining** : predestinar

predetermine [,pri:dɪ'tərmən] *vt* **-mined; -mining** : predeterminar

predicament [prɪ'dɪkəmənt] *n* : apuro *m*, aprieto *m*

predicate¹ ['prɛdə,keɪt] *vt* **-cated; -cating 1** AFFIRM : afirmar, aseverar **2 to be predicated on** : estar basado en

predicate² ['prɛdɪkət] *n* : predicado *m*

predict [prɪ'dɪkt] *vt* : pronosticar, predecir

predictable [prɪ'dɪktəbəl] *adj* : previsible — **predictably** [-bli] *adv*

prediction [prɪ'dɪkʃən] *n* : pronóstico *m*, predicción *f*

predilection [,prɛdəl'ɛkʃən, ,pri:-] *n* : predilección *f*

predispose [,pri:dɪ'spo:z] *vt* **-posed; -posing** : predisponer

predisposition [,pri:,dɪspə'zɪʃən] *n* : predisposición *f*

predominance [prɪ'damənənʦ] *n* : predominio *m*

predominant [prɪ'damənənt] *adj* : predominante — **predominantly** *adv*

predominate [prɪ'damə,neɪt] *vi* **-nated; -nating 1** : predominar (en cantidad) **2** PREVAIL : prevalecer

preeminence [prɪ'ɛmənənʦ] *n* : preeminencia *f*

preeminent [prɪ'ɛmənənt] *adj* : preeminente

preeminently [prɪ'ɛmənəntli] *adv* : especialmente

preempt [pri'ɛmpt] *vt* **1** APPROPRIATE : apoderarse de, apropiarse de **2** : reemplazar (un programa de televisión, etc.) **3** FORESTALL : adelantarse a (un ataque, etc.)

preen ['pri:n] *vt* : arreglarse (el pelo, las plumas, etc.)

prefabricated [ˌpri:'fæbrəˌkeɪṭəd] *adj* : prefabricado

preface ['prɛfəs] *n* : prefacio *m*, prólogo *m*

prefatory ['prɛfəˌtori] *adj* : preliminar

prefer [pri'fər] *vt* **-ferred; -ferring 1** : preferir ⟨I prefer coffee : prefiero café⟩ **2 to prefer charges against** : presentar cargos contra

preferable ['prɛfərəbəl] *adj* : preferible

preferably ['prɛfərəbli] *adv* : preferentemente, de preferencia

preference ['prɛfrənts, 'prɛfər-] *n* : preferencia *f*, gusto *m*

preferential [ˌprɛfə'rɛntʃəl] *adj* : preferencial, preferente

prefigure [pri'fɪgjər] *vt* **-ured; -uring** FORESHADOW : prefigurar, anunciar

prefix ['pri:ˌfɪks] *n* : prefijo *m*

pregnancy ['prɛgnənsi] *n, pl* **-cies** : embarazo *m*, preñez *f*

pregnant ['prɛgnənt] *adj* **1** : embarazada (dícese de una mujer), preñada (dícese de un animal) **2** MEANINGFUL : significativo

preheat [ˌpri:'hi:t] *vt* : precalentar

prehensile [pri'hɛntsəl, -'hɛnˌsaɪl] *adj* : prensil

prehistoric [ˌpri:hɪs'tɔrɪk] *or* **prehistorical** [-ɪkəl] *adj* : prehistórico

prejudge [ˌpri:'dʒʌdʒ] *vt* **-judged; -judging** : prejuzgar

prejudice[1] ['prɛdʒədəs] *vt* **-diced; -dicing 1** DAMAGE : perjudicar **2** BIAS : predisponer, influir en

prejudice[2] *n* **1** DAMAGE : perjuicio *m* (en derecho) **2** BIAS : prejuicio *m*

prelate ['prɛlət] *n* : prelado *m*

preliminary[1] [pri'lɪməˌnɛri] *adj* : preliminar

preliminary[2] *n, pl* **-naries 1** : preámbulo *m*, preludio *m* **2 preliminaries** *npl* : preliminares *mpl*

prelude ['preɪˌlu:d, 'prɛlˌju:d; 'preɪˌlu:d, 'pri:-] *n* : preludio *m*

premarital [ˌpri:'mærəṭəl] *adj* : prematrimonial

premature [ˌpri:mə'tʊr, -'tjʊr, -'tʃʊr] *adj* : prematuro — **prematurely** *adv*

premeditate [pri'mɛdəˌteɪt] *vt* **-tated; -tating** : premeditar

premeditation [pri,mɛdə'teɪʃən] *n* : premeditación *f*

premenstrual [pri'mɛntstruəl] *adj* : premenstrual

premier[1] [pri'mɪr, -'mjɪr; 'pri:miər] *adj* : principal

premier[2] *n* PRIME MINISTER : primer ministro *m*, primera ministra *f*

premiere[1] [pri'mjɛr, -'mɪr] *vt* **-miered; -miering** : estrenar

premiere[2] *n* : estreno *m*

premise ['prɛmɪs] *n* **1** : premisa *f* ⟨the premise of his arguments : la premisa de sus argumentos⟩ **2 premises** *npl* : recinto *m*, local *m*

premium ['pri:miəm] *n* **1** BONUS : prima *f* **2** SURCHARGE : recargo *m* ⟨to sell at a premium : vender (algo) muy caro⟩ **3 insurance premium** : prima *f* (de seguros) **4 to set a premium on** : darle un gran valor (a algo)

premonition [ˌpri:mə'nɪʃən, ˌprɛmə-] *n* : presentimiento *m*, premonición *f*

prenatal [ˌpri:'neɪṭəl] *adj* : prenatal

preoccupation [pri,akjə'peɪʃən] *n* : preocupación *f*

preoccupied [pri'akjəˌpaɪd] *adj* : abstraído, ensimismado, preocupado

preoccupy [pri'akjəˌpaɪ] *vt* **-pied; -pying** : preocupar

preparation [ˌprɛpə'reɪʃən] *n* **1** PREPARING : preparación *f* **2** MIXTURE : preparado *m* ⟨a preparation for burns : un preparado para quemaduras⟩ **3 preparations** *npl* ARRANGEMENTS : preparativos *mpl*

preparatory [pri'pærəˌtori] *adj* : preparatorio

prepare [pri'pær] *v* **-pared; -paring** *vt* : preparar — *vi* : prepararse

prepay [ˌpri:'peɪ] *vt* **-paid; -paying** : pagar por adelantado

preponderance [pri'pandərənts] *n* : preponderancia *f*

preponderant [pri'pandərənt] *adj* : preponderante — **preponderantly** *adv*

preposition [ˌprɛpə'zɪʃən] *n* : preposición *f*

prepositional [ˌprɛpə'zɪʃənəl] *adj* : preposicional

prepossessing [ˌpri:pə'zɛsɪŋ] *adj* : atractivo, agradable

preposterous [pri'pastərəs] *adj* : absurdo, ridículo

prerequisite[1] [pri'rɛkwəzət] *adj* : necesario, esencial

prerequisite[2] *n* : condición *f* necesario, requisito *m* previo

prerogative [pri'ragəṭɪv] *n* : prerrogativa *f*

presage ['prɛsɪdʒ, pri'seɪdʒ] *vt* **-saged; -saging** : presagiar

preschool ['pri:ˌsku:l] *adj* : preescolar ⟨preschool students : estudiantes de preescolar⟩

prescribe [pri'skraɪb] *vt* **-scribed; -scribing 1** ORDAIN : prescribir, ordenar **2** : recetar (medicinas, etc.)

prescription [pri'skrɪpʃən] *n* : receta *f*

presence ['prɛzənts] *n* : presencia *f*

present[1] [pri'zɛnt] *vt* **1** INTRODUCE : presentar ⟨to present oneself : presentarse⟩ **2** : presentar (una obra de teatro, etc.) **3** GIVE : entregar (un regalo, etc.), regalar, obsequiar **4** SHOW : presentar, ofrecer ⟨it presents a lovely view : ofrece una vista muy linda⟩

present[2] ['prɛzənt] *adj* **1** : actual ⟨present conditions : condiciones actuales⟩

2 : presente ⟨all the students were present : todos los estudiantes estaban presentes⟩

present³ [ˈprɛzənt] *n* **1** GIFT : regalo *m*, obsequio *m* **2** : presente *m* ⟨at present : en este momento⟩ **3** *or* **present tense** : presente *m*

presentable [prɪˈzɛntəbəl] *adj* : presentable

presentation [ˌpriːˌzɛnˈteɪʃən, ˌprɛzən-] *n* : presentación *f* ⟨presentation ceremony : ceremonia de entrega⟩

presentiment [prɪˈzɛntəmənt] *n* : presentimiento *m*, premonición *f*

presently [ˈprɛzəntli] *adv* **1** SOON : pronto, dentro de poco **2** NOW : actualmente, ahora

present participle *n* : participio *m* presente, participio *m* activo

preservation [ˌprɛzərˈveɪʃən] *n* : conservación *f*, preservación *f*

preservative [prɪˈzərvətɪv] *n* : conservante *m*

preserve¹ [prɪˈzərv] *vt* **-served; -serving 1** PROTECT : proteger, preservar **2** : conservar (los alimentos, etc.) **3** MAINTAIN : conservar, mantener

preserve² *n* **1** *or* **preserves** *npl* : conserva *f* ⟨peach preserves : duraznos en conserva⟩ **2** : coto *m* ⟨game preserve : coto de caza⟩

preside [prɪˈzaɪd] *vi* **-sided; -siding 1 to preside over** : presidir ⟨he presided over the meeting : presidió la reunión⟩ **2 to preside over** : supervisar ⟨she presides over the department : dirige el departamento⟩

presidency [ˈprɛzədəntsi] *n, pl* **-cies** : presidencia *f*

president [ˈprɛzədənt] *n* : presidente *m*, -ta *f*

presidential [ˌprɛzəˈdɛntʃəl] *adj* : presidencial

press¹ [ˈprɛs] *vt* **1** PUSH : apretar **2** SQUEEZE : apretar, prensar (frutas, flores, etc.) **3** IRON : planchar (ropa) **4** URGE : instar, apremiar ⟨he pressed me to come : insistió en que viniera⟩ — *vi* **1** PUSH : apretar ⟨press hard : aprieta con fuerza⟩ **2** CROWD : apiñarse **3** : abrirse paso ⟨I pressed through the crowd : me abrí paso entre el gentío⟩ **4** URGE : presionar

press² *n* **1** CROWD : multitud *f* **2** : imprenta *f*, prensa *f* ⟨to go to press : entrar en prensa⟩ **3** URGENCY : urgencia *f*, prisa *f* **4** PRINTER, PUBLISHER : imprenta *f*, editorial *f* **5 the press** : la prensa ⟨freedom of the press : libertad de prensa⟩

pressing [ˈprɛsɪŋ] *adj* URGENT : urgente

pressure¹ [ˈprɛʃər] *vt* **-sured; -suring** : presionar, apremiar

pressure² *n* **1** : presión *f* ⟨to be under pressure : estar bajo presión⟩ **2** → **blood pressure**

pressurize [ˈprɛʃəˌraɪz] *vt* **-ized; -izing** : presurizar

prestige [prɛˈstiːʒ, -ˈstiːdʒ] *n* : prestigio *m*

prestigious [prɛˈstɪdʒəs] *adj* : prestigioso

presto [ˈprɛsˌtoː] *adv* : de pronto

presumably [prɪˈzuːməbli] *adv* : es de suponer, supuestamente ⟨presumably, he's guilty : supone que es culpable⟩

presume [prɪˈzuːm] *vt* **-sumed; -suming 1** ASSUME, SUPPOSE : suponer, asumir, presumir **2 to presume to** : atreverse a, osar

presumption [prɪˈzʌmpʃən] *n* **1** AUDACITY : atrevimiento *m*, osadía *f* **2** ASSUMPTION : presunción *f*, suposición *f*

presumptuous [prɪˈzʌmptʃuəs] *adj* : descarado, atrevido

presuppose [ˌpriːsəˈpoːz] *vt* **-posed; -posing** : presuponer

pretend [prɪˈtɛnd] *vt* **1** CLAIM : pretender **2** FEIGN : fingir, simular — *vi* : fingir

pretender [prɪˈtɛndər] *n* : pretendiente *mf* (al trono, etc.)

pretense *or* **pretence** [ˈpriːˌtɛnts, prɪˈtɛnts] *n* **1** CLAIM : afirmación *f* (falsa), pretensión *f* **2** FEIGNING : fingimiento *m*, simulación *f* ⟨to make a pretense of doing something : fingir hacer algo⟩ ⟨a pretense of order : una apariencia de orden⟩ **3** PRETEXT : pretexto *m* ⟨under false pretenses : con pretextos falsos, de manera fraudulenta⟩

pretension [prɪˈtɛntʃən] *n* **1** CLAIM : pretensión *f*, afirmación *f* **2** ASPIRATION : aspiración *f*, ambición *f* **3** PRETENTIOUSNESS : pretensiones *fpl*, presunción *f*

pretentious [prɪˈtɛntʃəs] *adj* : pretencioso

pretentiousness [prɪˈtɛntʃəsnəs] *n* : presunción *f*, pretensiones *fpl*

pretext [ˈpriːˌtɛkst] *n* : pretexto *m*, excusa *f*

prettily [ˈprɪtəli] *adv* : atractivamente

prettiness [ˈprɪtinəs] *n* : lindeza *f*

pretty¹ [ˈprɪti] *adv* : bastante, bien ⟨it's pretty obvious : está bien claro⟩ ⟨it's pretty much the same : es más o menos igual⟩

pretty² *adj* **-tier; -est** : bonito, lindo, guapo ⟨a pretty girl : una muchacha guapa⟩ ⟨what a pretty dress! : ¡qué vestido más lindo!⟩

pretzel [ˈprɛtsəl] *n* : galleta *f* salada (en forma de nudo)

prevail [prɪˈveɪl] *vi* **1** TRIUMPH : prevalecer **2** PREDOMINATE : predominar **3 to prevail upon** : persuadir, convencer ⟨I prevailed upon her to sing : la convencí para que cantara⟩

prevailing [prɪˈveɪlɪŋ] *adj* : imperante, prevaleciente

prevalence [ˈprɛvələnts] *n* : preponderancia *f*, predominio *m*

prevalent [ˈprɛvələnt] *adj* **1** COMMON : común y corriente, general **2** WIDESPREAD : extendido

prevaricate [prɪ'værə,keɪt] *vi* **-cated;
-cating** LIE : mentir
prevarication [prɪ,værə'keɪʃən] *n* : mentira *f*
prevent [prɪ'vɛnt] *vt* **1** AVOID : prevenir,
evitar ⟨steps to prevent war : medidas
para evitar la guerra⟩ **2** HINDER : impedir
preventable [prɪ'vɛntəbəl] *adj* : evitable
preventative [prɪ'vɛntəɪv] → **preventive**
prevention [prɪ'vɛntʃən] *n* : prevención
f
preventive [prɪ'vɛntɪv] *adj* : preventivo
preview ['pri:,vju] *n* : preestreno *m*
previous ['pri:viəs] *adj* : previo, anteri-
or ⟨previous knowledge : conocimien-
tos previos⟩ ⟨the previous day : el día
anterior⟩ ⟨in the previous year : en el
año pasado⟩
previously ['pri:viəsli] *adv* : antes
prewar [,pri:'wɔr] *adj* : de antes de la
guerra
prey ['preɪ] *n, pl* **preys** : presa *f*
prey on *vt* **1** : cazar, alimentarse de ⟨it
preys on fish : se alimenta de peces⟩ **2
to prey on one's mind** : hacer presa en
alguien, atormentar a alguien
price¹ ['praɪs] *vt* **priced; pricing** : poner
un precio a
price² *n* : precio *m* ⟨peace at any price
: la paz a toda costa⟩
priceless ['praɪsləs] *adj* : inestimable, inapreciable
pricey ['praɪsi] *adj* : caro
prick¹ ['prɪk] *vt* **1** : pinchar **2 to prick
up one's ears** : levantar las orejas —
vi : pinchar
prick² *n* **1** STAB : pinchazo *m* ⟨a prick
of conscience : un remordimiento⟩ **2**
→ **pricker**
pricker ['prɪkər] *n* THORN : espina *f*
prickle¹ ['prɪkəl] *vi* **-led; -ling** : sentir un
cosquilleo, tener un hormigueo
prickle² *n* **1** : espina *f* (de una planta) **2**
TINGLE : cosquilleo *m*, hormigueo *m*
prickly ['prɪkəli] *adj* **1** THORNY : espinoso **2** : que pica ⟨a prickly sensation : un hormigueo⟩
prickly pear *n* : tuna *f*
pride¹ ['praɪd] *vt* **prided; priding** : estar
orgulloso de ⟨to pride oneself on : preciarse de, enorgullecerse de⟩
pride² *n* : orgullo *m*
priest ['pri:st] *n* : sacerdote *m*, cura *m*
priestess ['pri:stəs] *n* : sacerdotisa *f*
priesthood ['pri:st,hʊd] *n* : sacerdocio *m*
priestly ['pri:stli] *adj* : sacerdotal
prig ['prɪg] *n* : mojigato *m*, -ta *f*; gazmoño *m*, -ña *f*
prim ['prɪm] *adj* **primmer; primmest 1**
PRISSY : remilgado **2** PRUDISH : mojigato, gazmoño
primarily [praɪ'mɛrəli] *adv* : principalmente, fundamentalmente
primary¹ ['praɪ,mɛri, 'praɪmərɪ] *adj* **1**
FIRST : primario **2** PRINCIPAL : principal **3** BASIC : fundamental

primary² *n, pl* **-ries** : elección *f* primaria
primary color *n* : color *m* primario
primary school → **elementary school**
primate *n* **1** ['praɪ,meɪt, -mət] : primado *m* (obispo) **2** [-,meɪt] : primate *m*
(animal)
prime¹ ['praɪm] *vt* **primed; priming 1**
: cebar ⟨to prime a pump : cebar una
bomba⟩ **2** PREPARE : preparar (una
superficie para pintar) **3** COACH
: preparar (a un testigo, etc.)
prime² *adj* **1** CHIEF, MAIN : principal,
primero **2** EXCELLENT : de primera
(categoría), excelente
prime³ *n* **the prime of one's life** : la flor
de la vida
prime minister *n* : primer ministro *m*,
primera ministra *f*
primer¹ ['prɪmər] *n* **1** READER : cartilla
f **2** MANUAL : manual *m*
primer² ['praɪmər] *n* **1** : cebo *m* (para
explosivos) **2** : base *f* (de pintura)
prime time *n* : horas *fpl* de mayor audiencia
primeval [praɪ'mi:vəl] *adj* : primitivo,
primigenio
primitive ['prɪmətɪv] *adj* : primitivo
primly ['prɪmli] *adv* : mojigatamente
primness ['prɪmnəs] *n* : mojigatería *f*,
gazmoñería *f*
primordial [praɪ'mɔrdiəl] *adj* : primordial, fundamental
primp ['prɪmp] *vi* : arreglarse, acicalarse
primrose ['prɪm,ro:z] *n* : primavera *f*,
prímula *f*
prince ['prɪnts] *n* : príncipe *m*
princely ['prɪntsli] *adj* : principesco
princess ['prɪntsəs, 'prɪn,sɛs] *n* : princesa *f*
principal¹ ['prɪntsəpəl] *adj* : principal —
principally *adv*
principal² *n* **1** PROTAGONIST : protagonista *mf* **2** : director *m*, -tora *f* (de una
escuela) **3** CAPITAL : principal *m*, capital *m* (en finanzas)
principality [,prɪntsə'pæləti] *n, pl* **-ties**
: principado *m*
principle ['prɪntsəpəl] *n* : principio *m*
print¹ ['prɪnt] *vt* : imprimir (libros, etc.)
— *vi* : escribir con letra de molde
print² *n* **1** IMPRESSION : marca *f*, huella
f, impresión *f* **2** : texto *m* impreso ⟨to
be out of print : estar agotado⟩ **3** LET-
TERING : letra *f* **4** ENGRAVING : grabado *m* **5** : copia *f* (en fotografía) **6** : estampado *m* (de tela)
printer ['prɪntər] *n* **1** : impresor *m*, -sora
f (persona) **2** : impresora *f* (máquina)
printing ['prɪntɪŋ] *n* **1** : impresión *f*
(acto) ⟨the third printing : la tercera
tirada⟩ **2** : imprenta *f* (profesión) **3**
LETTERING : letras *fpl* de molde
printing press *n* : prensa *f*
print out *vt* : imprimir (de una computadora)
printout ['prɪnt,aʊt] *n* : copia *f* impresa
(de una computadora)
prior ['praɪər] *adj* **1** : previo **2 prior to**
: antes de

priority ['praɪ'ɔrəti] *n, pl* **-ties** : prioridad *f*

priory ['praɪəri] *n, pl* **-ries** : priorato *m*

prism ['prɪzəm] *n* : prisma *m*

prison ['prɪzən] *n* : prisión *f*, cárcel *f*

prisoner ['prɪzənər] *n* : preso *m*, -sa *f*; recluso *m*, -sa *f* ⟨prisoner of war : prisionero de guerra⟩

prissy ['prɪsi] *adj* **-sier; -est** : remilgado, melindroso

pristine ['prɪsˌtiːn, prɪs'-] *adj* : puro, prístino

privacy ['praɪvəsi] *n, pl* **-cies** : privacidad *f*

private¹ ['praɪvət] *adj* **1** PERSONAL : privado, particular ⟨private property : propiedad privada⟩ **2** INDEPENDENT : privado, independiente ⟨private studies : estudios privados⟩ **3** SECRET : secreto **4** SECLUDED : aislado, privado — **privately** *adv*

private² *n* : soldado *m* raso

privateer [ˌpraɪvə'tɪr] *n* : corsario *m*

privation [praɪ'veɪʃən] *n* : privación *f*

privilege ['prɪvlɪdʒ, 'prɪvə-] *n* : privilegio *m*

privileged ['prɪvlɪdʒd, 'prɪvə-] *adj* : privilegiado

privy¹ ['prɪvi] *adj* **to be privy to** : estar enterado de

privy² *n, pl* **privies** : excusado *m*, retrete *m* (exterior)

prize¹ ['praɪz] *vt* **prized; prizing** : valorar, apreciar

prize² *adj* **1** : premiado ⟨a prize stallion : un semental premiado⟩ **2** OUTSTANDING : de primera, excepcional

prize³ *n* **1** AWARD : premio *m* ⟨third prize : el tercer premio⟩ **2** : joya *f*, tesoro *m* ⟨he's a real prize : es un tesoro⟩

prizefighter ['praɪzˌfaɪtər] *n* : boxeador *m*, -dora *f* profesional

prizewinning ['praɪzˌwɪnɪŋ] *adj* : premiado

pro¹ ['pro:] *adv* : a favor

pro² *adj* → **professional¹**

pro³ *n* **1** : pro *m* ⟨the pros and cons : los pros y los contras⟩ **2** → **professional²**

probability [ˌprɑbə'bɪləti] *n, pl* **-ties** : probabilidad *f*

probable ['prɑbəbəl] *adj* : probable — **probably** [-bli] *adv*

probate¹ ['pro:ˌbeɪt] *vt* **-bated; -bating** : autenticar (un testamento)

probate² *n* : autenticación *f* (de un testamento)

probation [pro'beɪʃən] *n* **1** : período *m* de prueba (para un empleado, etc.) **2** : libertad *f* condicional (para un preso)

probationary [pro'beɪʃəˌnɛri] *adj* : de prueba

probe¹ ['pro:b] *vt* **probed; probing 1** : sondar (en medicina y tecnología) **2** INVESTIGATE : investigar, sondear

probe² *n* **1** : sonda *f* (en medicina, etc.) ⟨space probe : sonda espacial⟩ **2** INVESTIGATION : investigación *f*, sondeo *m*

probity ['pro:bəti] *n* : probidad *f*

problem¹ ['prɑbləm] *adj* : difícil

problem² *n* : problema *m*

problematic [ˌprɑblə'mætɪk] *or* **problematical** [-tɪkəl] *adj* : problemático

proboscis [prə'bɑsɪs] *n, pl* **-cises** *also* **-cides** [-səˌdiːz] : probóscide *f*

procedural [prə'siːdʒərəl] *adj* : de procedimiento

procedure [prə'siːdʒər] *n* : procedimiento *m* ⟨administrative procedures : trámites administrativos⟩

proceed [pro'siːd] *vi* **1** : proceder ⟨to proceed to do something : proceder a hacer algo⟩ **2** CONTINUE : continuar, proseguir, seguir ⟨he proceeded to the next phase : pasó a la segunda fase⟩ **3** ADVANCE : avanzar ⟨as the conference proceeded : mientras seguía avanzando la conferencia⟩ ⟨the road proceeds south : la calle sigue hacia el sur⟩

proceeding [pro'siːdɪŋ] *n* **1** PROCEDURE : procedimiento *m* **2 proceedings** *npl* EVENTS : acontecimientos *mpl* **3 proceedings** *npl* MINUTES : actas *fpl* (de una reunión, etc.)

proceeds ['pro:ˌsiːdz] *npl* : ganancias *fpl*

process¹ ['prɑˌsɛs, 'pro:-] *vt* : procesar, tratar

process² *n, pl* **-cesses** ['prɑˌsɛsəz, 'pro:-, -səsəz, -səˌsiːz] **1** : proceso *m* ⟨the process of elimination : el proceso de eliminación⟩ **2** METHOD : proceso *m*, método *m* ⟨manufacturing processes : procesos industriales⟩ **3** : acción *f* judicial ⟨due process of law : el debido proceso (de la ley)⟩ **4** SUMMONS : citación *f* **5** PROJECTION : protuberancia *f* (anatómica) **6 in the process of** : en vías de ⟨in the process of repair : en reparaciones⟩

procession [prə'sɛʃən] *n* : procesión *f*, desfile *m* ⟨a funeral procession : un cortejo fúnebre⟩

processional [prə'sɛʃənəl] *n* : himno *m* para una procesión

processor ['prɑˌsɛsər, 'pro:-, -səsər] *n* **1** : procesador *m* (de una computadora) **2 food processor** : procesador *m* de alimentos

proclaim [pro'kleɪm] *vt* : proclamar

proclamation [ˌprɑklə'meɪʃən] *n* : proclamación *f*

proclivity [pro'klɪvəti] *n, pl* **-ties** : proclividad *f*

procrastinate [prə'kræstəˌneɪt] *vi* **-nated; -nating** : demorar, aplazar las responsabilidades

procrastination [prəˌkræstə'neɪʃən] *n* : aplazamiento *m*, demora *f*, dilación *f*

procreate ['pro:kriˌeɪt] *vi* **-ated; -ating** : procrear

procreation [ˌpro:kri'eɪʃən] *n* : procreación *f*

proctor¹ ['prɑktər] *vt* : supervisar (un examen)

proctor² *n* : supervisor *m*, -sora *f* (de un examen)

procure [prə'kjʊr] *vt* **-cured; -curing 1**
OBTAIN : procurar, obtener **2** BRING
ABOUT : provocar, lograr, conseguir
procurement [prə'kjʊrmənt] *n* : obtención *f*
prod¹ ['prɑd] *vt* **prodded; prodding 1**
JAB, POKE : pinchar, golpear (con la
punta de algo) **2** GOAD : incitar, estimular
prod² *n* **1** JAB, POKE : golpe *m* (con la
punta de algo), pinchazo *m* **2** STIMU-
LUS : estímulo *m* **3 cattle prod** : picana
f, aguijón *m*
prodigal¹ ['prɑdɪgəl] *adj* SPENDTHRIFT
: pródigo, despilfarrador, derrochador
prodigal² *n* : pródigo *m*, -ga *f*; derrochador *m*, -dora *f*
prodigious [prə'dɪdʒəs] *adj* **1** MAR-
VELOUS : prodigioso, maravilloso **2**
HUGE : enorme, vasto ⟨prodigious
sums : muchísimo dinero⟩ — **prodi-
giously** *adv*
prodigy ['prɑdədʒi] *n, pl* **-gies** : prodigio
m ⟨child prodigy : niño prodigio⟩
produce¹ [prə'du:s, -'dju:s] *vt* **-duced;
-ducing 1** EXHIBIT : presentar,
mostrar **2** YIELD : producir **3** CAUSE
: producir, causar **4** CREATE : producir
⟨to produce a poem : escribir un poe-
ma⟩ **5** : poner en escena (una obra de
teatro), producir (una película)
produce² ['prɑ,du:s, 'pro:-, -,dju:s] *n*
: productos *mpl* agrícolas
producer [prə'du:sər, -'dju:-] *n* : productor *m*, -tora *f*
product ['prɑ,dʌkt] *n* : producto *m*
production [prə'dʌkʃən] *n* : producción
f
productive [prə'dʌktɪv] *adj* : productivo
productivity [,pro:,dʌk'tɪvəti, ,prɑ-] *n*
: productividad *f*
profane¹ [pro'feɪn] *vt* **-faned; -faning**
: profanar
profane² *adj* **1** SECULAR : profano **2** IR-
REVERENT : irreverente, impío
profanity [pro'fænəti] *n, pl* **-ties 1** IR-
REVERENCE : irreverencia *f*, impiedad
f **2** : blasfemias *fpl*, obscenidades *fpl*
⟨don't use profanity : no digas blas-
femias⟩
profess [prə'fɛs] *vt* **1** DECLARE : declarar, manifestar **2** CLAIM : pretender
3 : profesar (una religión, etc.)
professedly [prə'fɛsədli] *adv* **1** OPENLY
: declaradamente **2** ALLEGEDLY
: supuestamente
profession [prə'fɛʃən] *n* : profesión *f*
professional¹ [prə'fɛʃənəl] *adj* : profesional — **professionally** *adv*
professional² *n* : profesional *mf*
professionalism [prə'fɛʃənə,lɪzəm] *n*
: profesionalismo *m*
professor [prə'fɛsər] *n* : profesor *m* (universitario), profesora *f* (universitaria);
catedrático *m*, -ca *f*
proffer ['prɑfər] *vt* **-fered; -fering** : ofrecer, dar

proficiency [prə'fɪʃəntsi] *n* : competencia *f*, capacidad *f*
proficient [prə'fɪʃənt] *adj* : competente,
experto — **proficiently** *adv*
profile ['pro:,faɪl] *n* : perfil *m* ⟨a portrait
in profile : un retrato de perfil⟩ ⟨to
keep a low profile : no llamar la atención, hacerse pasar desapercibido⟩
profit¹ ['prɑfət] *vi* : sacar provecho (de),
beneficiarse (de)
profit² *n* **1** ADVANTAGE : provecho *m*,
partido *m*, beneficio *m* **2** GAIN : beneficio *m*, utilidad *f*, ganancia *f* ⟨to make
a profit : sacar beneficios⟩
profitable ['prɑfətəbəl] *adj* : rentable, lucrativo — **profitably** [-bli] *adv*
profitless ['prɑfətləs] *adj* : infructuoso,
inútil
profligate ['prɑflɪgət, -,geɪt] *adj* **1** DIS-
SOLUTE : disoluto, licencioso **2** SPEND-
THRIFT : despilfarrador, derrochador,
pródigo
profound [prə'faʊnd] *adj* : profundo
profoundly [prə'faʊndli] *adv* : profundamente, en profundidad
profundity [prə'fʌndəti] *n, pl* **-ties** : profundidad *f*
profuse [prə'fju:s] *adj* **1** COPIOUS : profuso, copioso **2** LAVISH : pródigo —
profusely *adv*
profusion [prə'fju:ʒən] *n* : abundancia *f*,
profusión *f*
progenitor [pro'dʒɛnətər] *n* : progenitor
m, -tora *f*
progeny ['prɑdʒəni] *n, pl* **-nies** : progenie *f*
progesterone [pro'dʒɛstə,ro:n] *n* : progesterona *f*
prognosis [prɑg'no:sɪs] *n, pl* **-noses**
[-,si:z] : pronóstico *m* (médico)
program¹ ['pro:,græm, -grəm] *vt*
-grammed *or* **-gramed; -gramming** *or*
-graming : programar
program² *n* : programa *m*
programmable ['pro:,græməbəl] *adj*
: programable
programmer ['pro:,græmər] *n* : programador *m*, -dora *f*
programming ['pro:,græmɪŋ] *n* : programación *f*
progress¹ [prə'grɛs] *vi* **1** PROCEED
: progresar, adelantar **2** IMPROVE
: mejorar
progress² ['prɑgrəs, -,grɛs] *n* **1** AD-
VANCE : progreso *m*, adelanto *m*,
avance *m* ⟨to make progress : hacer
progresos⟩ **2** BETTERMENT : mejora *f*,
mejoramiento *m*
progression [prə'grɛʃən] *n* **1** ADVANCE
: avance *m* **2** SEQUENCE : desarrollo
m (de eventos)
progressive [prə'grɛsɪv] *adj* **1** : progresista ⟨a progressive society : una sociedad progresista⟩ **2** : progresivo ⟨a
progressive disease : una enfermedad
progresiva⟩ **3** *or* **Progressive** : progresista (en política) **4** : progresivo (en
gramática)

progressively [prə'grɛsɪvli] *adv* : progresivamente, poco a poco

prohibit [pro'hɪbət] *vt* : prohibir

prohibition [ˌproː'bɪʃən, ˌproːhə-] *n* : prohibición *f*

prohibitive [pro'hɪbətɪv] *adj* : prohibitivo

project[1] [prə'dʒɛkt] *vt* **1** PLAN : proyectar, planear **2** : proyectar (imágenes, misiles, etc.) — *vi* PROTRUDE : sobresalir, salir

project[2] ['prɑˌdʒɛkt, -dʒɪkt] *n* : proyecto *m*, trabajo *m* (de un estudiante) ⟨research project : proyecto de investigación⟩

projectile [prə'dʒɛktəl, -ˌtaɪl] *n* : proyectil *m*

projection [prə'dʒɛkʃən] *n* **1** PLAN : plan *m*, proyección *f* **2** : proyección *f* (de imágenes, misiles, etc.) **3** PROTRUSION : saliente *m*

projector [prə'dʒɛktər] *n* : proyector *m*

proletarian[1] [ˌproːlə'tɛriən] *adj* : proletario

proletarian[2] *n* : proletario *m*, -ria *f*

proletariat [ˌproːlə'tɛriət] *n* : proletariado *m*

proliferate [prə'lɪfəˌreɪt] *vi* -ated; -ating : proliferar

proliferation [prəˌlɪfə'reɪʃən] *n* : proliferación *f*

prolific [prə'lɪfɪk] *adj* : prolífico

prologue ['proːˌlɔg] *n* : prólogo *m*

prolong [prə'lɔŋ] *vt* : prolongar

prolongation [ˌproːˌlɔŋ'geɪʃən] *n* : prolongación *f*

prom [ˈprɑm] *n* : baile *m* formal (de un colegio)

promenade[1] [ˌprɑmə'neɪd, -'nɑd] *vi* -naded; -nading : pasear, pasearse, dar un paseo

promenade[2] *n* : paseo *m*

prominence ['prɑmənənts] *n* **1** PROJECTION : prominencia *f* **2** EMINENCE : eminencia *f*, prestigio *m*

prominent ['prɑmənənt] *adj* **1** OUTSTANDING : prominente, destacado **2** PROJECTING : prominente, saliente

prominently ['prɑmənəntli] *adv* : destacadamente, prominentemente

promiscuity [ˌprɑmɪs'kjuːəti] *n*, *pl* -ties : promiscuidad *f*

promiscuous [prə'mɪskjuəs] *adj* : promiscuo — **promiscuously** *adv*

promise[1] ['prɑməs] *v* -ised; -ising : prometer

promise[2] *n* **1** : promesa *f* ⟨he kept his promise : cumplió su promesa⟩ **2 to show promise** : prometer

promising ['prɑməsɪŋ] *adj* : prometedor

promissory ['prɑməˌsori] *adj* : que promete ⟨a promissory note : un pagaré⟩

promontory ['prɑmənˌtori] *n*, *pl* -ries : promontorio *m*

promote [prə'moːt] *vt* -moted; -moting **1** : ascender (a un alumno o un empleado) **2** ADVERTISE : promocionar,

hacerle publicidad a **3** FURTHER : promover, fomentar

promoter [prə'moːtər] *n* : promotor *m*, -tora *f*; empresario *m*, -ria *f* (en deportes)

promotion [prə'moːʃən] *n* **1** : ascenso *m* (de un alumno o un empleado) **2** FURTHERING : promoción *f*, fomento *m* **3** ADVERTISING : publicidad *f*, propaganda *f*

promotional [prə'moːʃənəl] *adj* : promocional

prompt[1] ['prɑmpt] *vt* **1** INDUCE : provocar (una cosa), inducir (a una persona) ⟨curiosity prompted me to ask you : la curiosidad me indujo a preguntarle⟩ **2** : apuntar (a un actor, etc.)

prompt[2] *adj* : pronto, rápido ⟨prompt payment : pago puntual⟩

prompter ['prɑmptər] *n* : apuntador *m*, -dora *f* (en teatro)

promptly ['prɑmptli] *adv* : inmediatamente, rápidamente

promptness ['prɑmptnəs] *n* : prontitud *f*, rapidez *f*

promulgate ['prɑməlˌgeɪt] *vt* -gated; -gating : promulgar

prone ['proːn] *adj* **1** LIABLE : propenso, proclive ⟨accident-prone : propenso a los accidentes⟩ **2** : boca abajo, decúbito prono ⟨in a prone position : en decúbito prono⟩

prong ['prɔŋ] *n* : punta *f*, diente *m*

pronoun ['proːˌnaʊn] *n* : pronombre *m*

pronounce [prə'naʊnts] *vt* -nounced; -nouncing **1** : pronunciar ⟨how do you pronounce your name? : ¿cómo se pronuncia su nombre?⟩ **2** DECLARE : declarar **3 to pronounce sentence** : dictar sentencia, pronunciar un fallo

pronounced [prə'naʊntst] *adj* MARKED : pronunciado, marcado

pronouncement [prə'naʊntsmənt] *n* : declaración *f*

pronunciation [prəˌnʌntsi'eɪʃən] *n* : pronunciación *f*

proof[1] ['pruːf] *adj* : a prueba ⟨proof against tampering : a prueba de manipulación⟩

proof[2] *n* : prueba *f*

proofread ['pruːfˌriːd] *v* -read; -reading *vt* : corregir — *vi* : corregir pruebas

proofreader ['pruːfˌriːdər] *n* : corrector *m*, -tora *f* (de pruebas)

prop[1] ['prɑp] *vt* propped; propping **1 to prop against** : apoyar contra **2 to prop up** SUPPORT : apoyar, apuntalar, sostener **3 to prop up** SUSTAIN : alentar (a alguien), darle ánimo (a alguien)

prop[2] *n* **1** SUPPORT : puntal *m*, apoyo *m*, soporte *m* **2** : accesorio *m* (en teatro)

propaganda [ˌprɑpə'gændə, ˌproː-] *n* : propaganda *f*

propagandize [ˌprɑpə'gænˌdaɪz, ˌproː-] *v* -dized; -dizing *vt* : someter a propaganda — *vi* : hacer propaganda

propagate ['prɑpə,geɪt] v **-gated; -gat-ing** vi : propagarse — vt : propagar
propagation [,prɑpə'geɪʃən] n : propagación f
propane ['pro:,peɪn] n : propano m
propel [prə'pɛl] vt **-pelled; -pelling** : impulsar, propulsar, impeler
propellant or **propellent** [prə'pɛlənt] n : propulsor m
propeller [prə'pɛlər] n : hélice f
propensity [prə'pɛntsəti] n, pl **-ties** : propensión f, tendencia f, inclinación f
proper ['prɑpər] adj **1** RIGHT, SUITABLE : apropiado, adecuado **2** : propio, mismo ⟨the city proper : la propia ciudad⟩ **3** CORRECT : correcto **4** GENTEEL : fino, refinado, cortés **5** OWN, SPECIAL : propio ⟨proper name : nombre propio⟩ — **properly** adv
property ['prɑpərti] n, pl **-ties 1** CHARACTERISTIC : característica f, propiedad f **2** POSSESSIONS : propiedad f **3** BUILDING : inmueble m **4** LAND, LOT : terreno m, lote m, parcela f **5** PROP : accesorio m (en teatro)
prophecy ['prɑfəsi] n, pl **-cies** : profecía f, vaticinio m
prophesy ['prɑfə,saɪ] v **-sied; -sying** vt **1** FORETELL : profetizar (como profeta) **2** PREDICT : profetizar, predecir, vaticinar — vi : hacer profecías
prophet ['prɑfət] n : profeta m, profetisa f
prophetic [prə'fɛtɪk] or **prophetical** [-tɪkəl] adj : profético — **prophetically** [-tɪkli] adv
propitiate [pro'pɪʃi,eɪt] vt **-ated; -ating** : propiciar
propitious [prə'pɪʃəs] adj : propicio
proponent [prə'po:nənt] n : defensor m, -sora f; partidario m, -ria f
proportion[1] [prə'porʃən] vt : proporcionar ⟨well-proportioned : de buenas proporciones⟩
proportion[2] n **1** RATIO : proporción f **2** SYMMETRY : proporción f, simetría f ⟨out of proportion : desproporcionado⟩ **3** SHARE : parte f **4 proportions** npl SIZE : dimensiones fpl
proportional [prə'porʃənəl] adj : proporcional — **proportionally** adv
proportionate [prə'porʃənət] adj : proporcional — **proportionately** adv
proposal [prə'po:zəl] n **1** PROPOSITION : propuesta f, proposición f ⟨marriage proposal : propuesta de matrimonio⟩ **2** PLAN : proyecto m, propuesta f
propose [prə'po:z] v **-posed; -posing** vi : proponer matrimonio — vt **1** INTEND : pensar, proponerse **2** SUGGEST : proponer
proposition [,prɑpə'zɪʃən] n **1** PROPOSAL : proposición f, propuesta f **2** STATEMENT : proposición f
propound [prə'paʊnd] vt : proponer, exponer
proprietary [prə'praɪə,tɛri] adj : propietario, patentado

proprietor [prə'praɪətər] n : propietario m, -ria f
propriety [prə'praɪəti] n, pl **-eties 1** DECORUM : decencia f, decoro m **2 proprieties** npl CONVENTIONS : convenciones fpl, cánones mpl sociales
propulsion [prə'pʌlʃən] n : propulsión f
prosaic [pro'zeɪɪk] adj : prosaico
proscribe [pro'skraɪb] vt **-scribed; -scribing** : proscribir
prose ['pro:z] n : prosa f
prosecute ['prɑsɪ,kju:t] vt **-cuted; -cuting 1** CARRY OUT : llevar a cabo **2** : procesar, enjuiciar ⟨prosecuted for fraud : procesado por fraude⟩
prosecution [,prɑsɪ'kju:ʃən] n **1** : procesamiento m ⟨the prosecution of forgers : el procesamiento de falsificadores⟩ **2** PROSECUTORS : acusación f ⟨witness for the prosecution : testigo de cargo⟩
prosecutor ['prɑsɪ,kju:tər] n : acusador m, -dora f; fiscal mf
prospect[1] ['prɑ,spɛkt] vi : prospectar (el terreno) ⟨to prospect for gold : buscar oro⟩
prospect[2] n **1** VISTA : vista f, panorama m **2** POSSIBILITY : posibilidad f **3** OUTLOOK : perspectiva f **4** : posible cliente m, -ta f ⟨a salesman looking for prospects : un vendedor buscando nuevos clientes⟩
prospective [prə'spɛktɪv, 'prɑ,spɛk-] adj **1** EXPECTANT : futuro ⟨prospective mother : futura madre⟩ **2** POTENTIAL : potencial, posible ⟨prospective employee : posible empleado⟩
prospector ['prɑ,spɛktər, prɑ'spɛk-] n : prospector m, -tora f; explorador m, -dora f
prospectus [prə'spɛktəs] n : prospecto m
prosper ['prɑspər] vi : prosperar
prosperity [prɑ'spɛrəti] n : prosperidad f
prosperous ['prɑspərəs] adj : próspero
prostate ['prɑ,steɪt] n : próstata f
prosthesis [prɑs'θi:sɪs, 'prɑsθə-] n, pl **-theses** [-,si:z] : prótesis f
prostitute[1] ['prɑstə,tu:t, -,tju:t] vt **-tuted; -tuting 1** : prostituir **2 to prostitute oneself** : prostituirse
prostitute[2] n : prostituto m, -ta f
prostitution [,prɑstə'tu:ʃən, -'tju:-] n : prostitución f
prostrate[1] ['prɑ,streɪt] vt **-trated; -trating 1** : postrar **2 to prostrate oneself** : postrarse
prostrate[2] adj : postrado
prostration [prɑ'streɪʃən] n : postración f
protagonist [pro'tægənɪst] n : protagonista mf
protect [prə'tɛkt] vt : proteger
protection [prə'tɛkʃən] n : protección f
protective [prə'tɛktɪv] adj : protector
protector [prə'tɛktər] n **1** : protector m, -tora f (persona) **2** GUARD : protector m (aparato)

protectorate [prə'tɛktərət] *n* : protectorado *m*

protégé ['proːtəˌʒeɪ] *n* : protegido *m*, -da *f*

protein ['proːˌtiːn] *n* : proteína *f*

protest¹ [pro'tɛst] *vt* 1 ASSERT : afirmar, declarar 2 : protestar ⟨they protested the decision : protestaron (por) la decisión⟩ — *vi* **to protest against** : protestar contra

protest² ['proːˌtɛst] *n* 1 DEMONSTRATION : manifestación *f* (de protesta) ⟨a public protest : una manifestación pública⟩ 2 COMPLAINT : queja *f*, protesta *f*

Protestant ['prɑtəstənt] *n* : protestante *mf*

Protestantism ['prɑtəstənˌtɪzəm] *n* : protestantismo *m*

protocol ['proːtəˌkɔl] *n* : protocolo *m*

proton ['proːˌtɑn] *n* : protón *m*

protoplasm ['proːtəˌplæzəm] *n* : protoplasma *m*

prototype ['proːtəˌtaɪp] *n* : prototipo *m*

protozoan [ˌproːtə'zoːən] *n* : protozoario *m*, protozoo *m*

protract [pro'trækt] *vt* : prolongar

protractor [pro'træktər] *n* : transportador *m* (instrumento)

protrude [pro'truːd] *vi* **-truded; -truding** : salir, sobresalir

protrusion [pro'truːʒən] *n* : protuberancia *f*, saliente *m*

protuberance [pro'tuːbərən̪ts, -'tjuː-] *n* : protuberancia *f*

proud ['praʊd] *adj* 1 HAUGHTY : altanero, orgulloso, arrogante 2 : orgulloso ⟨she was proud of her work : estaba orgullosa de su trabajo⟩ ⟨too proud to beg : demasiado orgulloso para rogar⟩ 3 GLORIOUS : glorioso — **proudly** *adv*

prove ['pruːv] *v* **proved; proved** *or* **proven** ['pruːvən]; **proving** *vt* 1 TEST : probar 2 DEMONSTRATE : probar, demostrar — *vi* : resultar ⟨it proved effective : resultó efectivo⟩

Provençal [ˌproːvan'sal, ˌprɑvɑn-] *n* 1 : provenzal *mf* 2 : provenzal *m* (idioma) — **Provençal** *adj*

proverb ['prɑˌvərb] *n* : proverbio *m*, refrán *m*

proverbial [prə'vərbiəl] *adj* : proverbial

provide [prə'vaɪd] *v* **-vided; -viding** *vt* 1 STIPULATE : estipular 2 **to provide with** : proveer de, proporcionar — *vi* 1 : proveer ⟨the Lord will provide : el Señor proveerá⟩ 2 **to provide for** SUPPORT : mantener 3 **to provide for** ANTICIPATE : hacer previsiones para, prever

provided [prə'vaɪdəd] *or* **provided that** *conj* : con tal (de) que, siempre que

providence ['prɑvədən̪ts] *n* 1 PRUDENCE : previsión *f*, prudencia *f* 2 *or* **Providence** : providencia *f* ⟨divine providence : la Divina Providencia⟩ 3 **Providence** GOD : Providencia *f*

provident ['prɑvədənt] *adj* 1 PRUDENT : previsor, prudente 2 FRUGAL : frugal, ahorrativo

providential [ˌprɑvə'dɛntʃəl] *adj* : providencial

provider [prə'vaɪdər] *n* 1 PURVEYOR : proveedor *m*, -dora *f* 2 BREADWINNER : sostén *m* (económico)

providing that → provided

province ['prɑvɪn̪ts] *n* 1 : provincia *f* (de un país) ⟨to live in the provinces : vivir en las provincias⟩ 2 FIELD, SPHERE : campo *m*, competencia *f* ⟨it's not in my province : no es de mi competencia⟩

provincial [prə'vɪntʃəl] *adj* 1 : provincial ⟨provincial government : gobierno provincial⟩ 2 : provinciano, pueblerino ⟨a provincial mentality : una mentalidad provinciana⟩

provision¹ [prə'vɪʒən] *vt* : aprovisionar, abastecer

provision² *n* 1 PROVIDING : provisión *f*, suministro *m* 2 STIPULATION : condición *f*, salvedad *f*, estipulación *f* 3 **provisions** *npl* : despensa *f*, víveres *mpl*, provisiones *fpl*

provisional [prə'vɪʒənəl] *adj* : provisional, provisorio — **provisionally** *adv*

proviso [prə'vaɪˌzoː] *n, pl* **-sos** *or* **-soes** : condición *f*, salvedad *f*, estipulación *f*

provocation [ˌprɑvə'keɪʃən] *n* : provocación *f*

provocative [prə'vɑkətɪv] *adj* : provocador, provocativo ⟨a provocative article : un artículo que hace pensar⟩

provoke [prə'voːk] *vt* **-voked; -voking** : provocar

prow ['praʊ] *n* : proa *f*

prowess ['praʊəs] *n* 1 VALOR : valor *m*, valentía *f* 2 SKILL : habilidad *f*, destreza *f*

prowl ['praʊl] *vi* : merodear, rondar — *vt* : rondar por

prowler ['praʊlər] *n* : merodeador *m*, -dora *f*

proximity [prɑk'sɪməti] *n* : proximidad *f*

proxy ['prɑksi] *n, pl* **proxies** 1 : poder *m* (de actuar en nombre de alguien) ⟨by proxy : por poder⟩ 2 AGENT : apoderado *m*, -da *f*; representante *mf*

prude ['pruːd] *n* : mojigato *m*, -ta *f*; gazmoño *m*, -ña *f*

prudence ['pruːdən̪ts] *n* 1 SHREWDNESS : prudencia *f*, sagacidad *f* 2 CAUTION : prudencia *f*, cautela *f* 3 THRIFTINESS : frugalidad *f*

prudent ['pruːdənt] *adj* 1 SHREWD : prudente, sagaz 2 CAUTIOUS, FARSIGHTED : prudente, previsor, precavido 3 THRIFTY : frugal, ahorrativo — **prudently** *adv*

prudery ['pruːdəri] *n, pl* **-eries** : mojigatería *f*, gazmoñería *f*

prudish ['pruːdɪʃ] *adj* : mojigato, gazmoño

prune¹ ['pru:n] vt pruned; pruning : podar (arbustos, etc.), acortar (un texto),
recortar (gastos, etc.)
prune² n : ciruela f pasa
prurient ['prʊriənt] adj : lascivo
pry ['praɪ] v pried; prying vi : curiosear,
huronear ⟨to pry into other people's
business : meterse uno en lo que no le
importa⟩ — vt or to pry open : abrir
(con una palanca), apalancar
psalm ['sɑm, 'sɑlm] n : salmo m
pseudonym ['su:də,nɪm] n : seudónimo
m
psoriasis [sə'raɪəsɪs] n : soriasis f, psoriasis f
psyche ['saɪki] n : psique f, psiquis f
psychedelic¹ [,saɪkə'dɛlɪk] adj : psi-
codélico
psychedelic² n : droga f psicodélica
psychiatric [,saɪki'ætrɪk] adj : psiquiátrico, siquiátrico
psychiatrist [sə'kaɪətrɪst, saɪ-] n : psiquia-
atra mf, siquiatra mf
psychiatry [sə'kaɪətri, saɪ-] n : psiquiatría f, siquiatría f
psychic¹ ['saɪkɪk] adj 1 : psíquico,
síquico (en psicología) 2 CLAIRVOY-
ANT : clarividente
psychic² n : vidente mf, clarividente mf
psychoanalysis [,saɪkoə'næləsɪs] n, pl
-yses : psicoanálisis m, sicoanálisis m
psychoanalyst [,saɪko'ænəlɪst] n : psicoanalista mf, sicoanalista mf
psychoanalytic [,saɪko,ænəl'ɪtɪk] adj
: psicoanalítico, sicoanalítico
psychoanalyze [,saɪko'ænə,laɪz] vt
-lyzed; -lyzing : psicoanalizar, sico-
analizar
psychological [,saɪkə'lɑdʒɪkəl] adj : psicológico, sicológico — psychological-
ly adv
psychologist [saɪ'kɑlədʒɪst] n : psicólogo m, -ga f; sicólogo m, -ga f
psychology [saɪ'kɑlədʒi] n, pl -gies : psicología f, sicología f
psychopath ['saɪkə,pæθ] n : psicópata
mf, sicópata mf
psychopathic [,saɪkə'pæθɪk] adj : psicopático, sicopático
psychosis [saɪ'ko:sɪs] n, pl -choses
[-'ko:,si:z] : psicosis f, sicosis f
psychosomatic [,saɪkəsə'mætɪk] adj
: psicosomático, sicosomático
psychotherapist [,saɪko'θɛrəpɪst] n
: psicoterapeuta mf, sicoterapeuta mf
psychotherapy [,saɪko'θɛrəpi] n, pl
-pies : psicoterapia f, sicoterapia f
psychotic¹ [saɪ'kɑtɪk] adj : psicótico,
sicótico
psychotic² n : psicótico m, -ca f; sicótico m, -ca f
puberty ['pju:bərti] n : pubertad f
pubic ['pju:bɪk] adj : pubiano, púbico
public¹ ['pʌblɪk] adj : público — publicly adv
public² n : público m
publication [,pʌblə'keɪʃən] n : publicación f

publicist ['pʌbləsɪst] n : publicista mf
publicity [pə'blɪsəti] n : publicidad f
publicize ['pʌblə,saɪz] vt -cized; -cizing
: publicitar
public school n : escuela f pública
publish ['pʌblɪʃ] vt : publicar
publisher ['pʌblɪʃər] n : casa f editorial
(compañía); editor m, -tora f (persona)
publishing ['pʌblɪʃɪŋ] n : industria f editorial
pucker¹ ['pʌkər] vt : fruncir, arrugar —
vi : arrugarse
pucker² n : arruga f, frunce m, fruncido
m
pudding ['pʊdɪŋ] n : budín m, pudín m
puddle ['pʌdəl] n : charco m
pudgy ['pʌdʒi] adj pudgier; -est : regordete fam, rechoncho fam, gordinflón fam
puerile ['pjʊrəl] adj : pueril
Puerto Rican¹ [,pwɛrtə'ri:kən, ,portə-]
adj : puertorriqueño
Puerto Rican² n : puertorriqueño m, -ña
f
puff¹ ['pʌf] vi 1 BLOW : soplar 2 PANT
: resoplar, jadear 3 to puff up SWELL
: hincharse — vt 1 BLOW : soplar ⟨to
puff smoke : echar humo⟩ 2 INFLATE
: inflar, hinchar ⟨to puff out one's
cheeks : inflar las mejillas⟩
puff² n 1 GUST : soplo m, ráfaga f, bocanada f (de humo) 2 DRAW : chupada f (a un cigarrillo) 3 SWELLING : hinchazón f 4 cream puff : pastelito m de
crema 5 powder puff : borla f
puffy ['pʌfi] adj puffier; -est 1 SWOLLEN
: hinchado, inflado 2 SPONGY : esponjoso, suave
pug ['pʌg] n 1 : doguillo m (perro) 2 or
pug nose : nariz f achatada
pugnacious [,pʌg'neɪʃəs] adj : pugnaz,
agresivo
puke ['pju:k] vi puked; puking : vomitar, devolver
pull¹ ['pʊl, 'pʌl] vt 1 DRAW, TUG : tirar
de, jalar 2 EXTRACT : sacar, extraer ⟨to
pull teeth : sacar muelas⟩ ⟨to pull a gun
on : amenazar a (alguien) con pistola⟩
3 TEAR : desgarrarse (un músculo, etc.)
4 to pull down : bajar, echar abajo, derribar (un edificio) 5 to pull in AT-
TRACT : atraer (una muchedumbre,
etc.) ⟨to pull in votes : conseguir vo-
tos⟩ 6 to pull off REMOVE : sacar,
quitar 7 to pull oneself together : calmarse, tranquilizarse 8 to pull up
RAISE : levantar, subir — vi 1 DRAW,
TUG : tirar, jalar 2 (indicating movement in a specific direction) ⟨they
pulled in front of us : se nos metieron
delante⟩ ⟨to pull to a stop : pararse⟩ 3
to pull through RECOVER : recobrarse,
reponerse 4 to pull together COOPER-
ATE : trabajar juntos, cooperar
pull² n 1 TUG : tirón m, jalón m ⟨he gave
it a pull : le dio un tirón⟩ 2 ATTRAC-
TION : atracción f, fuerza f ⟨the pull of
gravity : la fuerza de la gravedad⟩ 3

INFLUENCE : influencia *f* 4 HANDLE : tirador *m* (de un cajón, etc.) 5 bell pull : cuerda *f*

pullet ['pʊlət] *n* : polla *f*, gallina *f* (joven)

pulley ['pʊli] *n*, *pl* -**leys** : polea *f*

pullover ['pʊl,o:vər] *n* : suéter *m*

pulmonary ['pʊlmə,nɛri, 'pʌl-] *adj* : pulmonar

pulp ['pʌlp] *n* 1 : pulpa *f* (de una fruta, etc.) 2 MASH : papilla *f*, pasta *f* ⟨wood pulp : pasta de papel, pulpa de papel⟩ ⟨to beat to a pulp : hacer papilla (a alguien)⟩ 3 : pulpa *f* (de los dientes)

pulpit ['pʊl,pɪt] *n* : púlpito *m*

pulsate ['pʌl,seɪt] *vi* -**sated**; -**sating** 1 BEAT : latir, palpitar 2 VIBRATE : vibrar

pulsation [,pʌl'seɪʃən] *n* : pulsación *f*

pulse ['pʌls] *n* : pulso *m*

pulverize ['pʌlvə,raɪz] *vt* -**ized**; -**izing** : pulverizar

puma ['pu:mə, 'pju:-] *n* : puma *m*; león *m*, leona *f* (in various countries)

pumice ['pʌməs] *n* : piedra *f* pómez

pummel ['pʌməl] *vt* -**meled**; -**meling** : aporrear, apalear

pump¹ ['pʌmp] *vt* 1 : bombear ⟨to pump water : bombear agua⟩ ⟨to pump (up) a tire : inflar una llanta⟩ 2 : mover (una manivela, un pedal, etc.) de arriba abajo ⟨to pump someone's hand : darle un fuerte apretón de manos (a alguien)⟩ 3 **to pump out** : sacar, vaciar (con una bomba)

pump² *n* 1 : bomba *f* ⟨water pump : bomba de agua⟩ 2 SHOE : zapato *m* de tacón

pumpernickel ['pʌmpər,nɪkəl] *n* : pan *m* negro de centeno

pumpkin ['pʌmpkɪn, 'pʌŋkən] *n* : calabaza *f*, zapallo *m Arg, Chile, Peru, Uru*

pun¹ ['pʌn] *vi* **punned**; **punning** : hacer juegos de palabras

pun² *n* : juego *m* de palabras, albur *m Mex*

punch¹ ['pʌntʃ] *vt* 1 HIT : darle un puñetazo (a alguien), golpear ⟨she punched him in the nose : le dio un puñetazo en la nariz⟩ 2 PERFORATE : perforar (papel, etc.), picar (un boleto)

punch² *n* 1 : perforadora *f* ⟨paper punch : perforadora de papel⟩ 2 BLOW : golpe *m*, puñetazo *m* 3 : ponche *m* ⟨fruit punch : ponche de frutas⟩

punctilious [pəŋk'tɪliəs] *adj* : puntilloso

punctual ['pʌŋktʃʊəl] *adj* : puntual

punctuality [,pʌŋktʃʊ'æləti] *n* : puntualidad *f*

punctually ['pʌŋktʃʊəli] *adv* : puntualmente, a tiempo

punctuate ['pʌŋktʃʊ,eɪt] *vt* -**ated**; -**ating** : puntuar

punctuation [,pʌŋktʃʊ'eɪʃən] *n* : puntuación *f*

puncture¹ ['pʌŋktʃər] *vt* -**tured**; -**turing** : pinchar, punzar, perforar, ponchar *Mex*

puncture² *n* : pinchazo *m*, ponchadura *f Mex*

pundit ['pʌndɪt] *n* : experto *m*, -ta *f*

pungency ['pʌndʒəntsi] *n* : acritud *f*, acrimonia *f*

pungent ['pʌndʒənt] *adj* : acre

punish ['pʌnɪʃ] *vt* : castigar

punishable ['pʌnɪʃəbəl] *adj* : punible

punishment ['pʌnɪʃmənt] *n* : castigo *m*

punitive ['pju:nətɪv] *adj* : punitivo

punt¹ ['pʌnt] *vt* : impulsar (un barco) con una pértiga — *vi* : despejar (en deportes)

punt² *n* 1 : batea *f* (barco) 2 : patada *f* de despeje (en deportes)

puny ['pju:ni] *adj* -**nier**; -**est** : enclenque, endeble

pup ['pʌp] *n* : cachorro *m*, -rra *f* (de un perro); cría *f* (de otros animales)

pupa ['pju:pə] *n*, *pl* -**pae** [-pi, -,paɪ] *or* -**pas** : crisálida *f*, pupa *f*

pupil ['pju:pəl] *n* 1 : alumno *m*, -na *f* (de colegio) 2 : pupila *f* (del ojo)

puppet ['pʌpət] *n* : títere *m*, marioneta *f*

puppy ['pʌpi] *n*, *pl* -**pies** : cachorro *m*, -rra *f*

purchase¹ ['pərtʃəs] *vt* -**chased**; -**chasing** : comprar

purchase² *n* 1 PURCHASING : compra *f*, adquisición *f* 2 : compra *f* ⟨last-minute purchases : compras de última hora⟩ 3 GRIP : agarre *m*, asidero *m* ⟨she got a firm purchase on the wheel : se agarró bien del volante⟩

purchase order *n* : orden *f* de compra

pure ['pjʊr] *adj* purer; purest : puro

puree¹ [pjʊ'reɪ, -'ri:] *vt* -**reed**; -**reeing** : hacer un puré con

puree² *n* : puré *m*

purely ['pjʊrli] *adv* 1 WHOLLY : puramente, completamente ⟨purely by chance : por pura casualidad⟩ 2 SIMPLY : sencillamente, meramente

purgative ['pərgətɪv] *n* : purgante *m*

purgatory ['pərgə,tori] *n*, *pl* -**ries** : purgatorio *m*

purge¹ ['pərdʒ] *vt* purged; purging : purgar

purge² *n* : purga *f*

purification [,pjʊrəfə'keɪʃən] *n* : purificación *f*

purify ['pjʊrə,faɪ] *vt* -**fied**; -**fying** : purificar

puritan ['pjʊrətən] *n* : puritano *m*, -na *f* — **puritan** *adj*

puritanical [,pju:rə'tænɪkəl] *adj* : puritano

purity ['pjʊrəti] *n* : pureza *f*

purl¹ ['pərl] *v* : tejer al revés, tejer del revés

purl² *n* : punto *m* del revés

purloin [pər'lɔɪn, 'pər,lɔɪn] *vt* : hurtar, robar

purple ['pərpəl] *n* : morado *m*, color *m* púrpura

purport [pər'port] *vt* : pretender ⟨to purport to be : pretender ser⟩

purpose ['pərpəs] *n* 1 INTENTION : propósito *m*, intención *f* ⟨on purpose

: a propósito, adrede⟩ **2** FUNCTION
: función *f* **3** RESOLUTION : resolución
f, determinación *f*
purposeful [ˈpərpəsfəl] *adj* : determinado, decidido, resuelto
purposefully [ˈpərpəsfəli] *adv* : decididamente, resueltamente
purposely [ˈpərpəsli] *adv* : intencionadamente, a propósito, adrede
purr[1] [ˈpər] *vi* : ronronear
purr[2] *n* : ronroneo *m*
purse[1] [ˈpərs] *vt* **pursed; pursing** : fruncir ⟨to purse one's lips : fruncir la boca⟩
purse[2] *n* **1** HANDBAG : cartera *f*, bolso
m, bolsa *f Mex* ⟨a change purse : un
monedero⟩ **2** FUNDS : fondos *mpl* **3**
PRIZE : premio *m*
pursue [pərˈsuː] *vt* **-sued; -suing 1**
CHASE : perseguir **2** SEEK : buscar,
tratar de encontrar ⟨to pursue pleasure
: buscar el placer⟩ **3** FOLLOW : seguir
⟨the road pursues a northerly course
: el camino sigue hacia el norte⟩ **4**
: dedicarse a ⟨to pursue a hobby : dedicarse a un pasatiempo⟩
pursuer [pərˈsuːər] *n* : perseguidor *m*,
-dora *f*
pursuit [pərˈsuːt] *n* **1** CHASE : persecución *f* **2** SEARCH : búsqueda *f*, busca
f **3** ACTIVITY : actividad *f*, pasatiempo
m
purveyor [pərˈveɪər] *n* : proveedor *m*,
-dora *f*
pus [ˈpʌs] *n* : pus *m*
push[1] [ˈpʊʃ] *vt* **1** SHOVE : empujar **2**
PRESS : apretar, pulsar ⟨push that button : aprieta ese botón⟩ **3** PRESSURE,
URGE : presionar **4 to push around**
BULLY : intimidar, mangonear — *vi* **1**
SHOVE : empujar **2** INSIST : insistir,
presionar **3 to push off** LEAVE : marcharse, irse, largarse *fam* **4 to push on**
PROCEED : seguir
push[2] *n* **1** SHOVE : empujón *m* **2** DRIVE
: empuje *m*, energía *f*, dinamismo *m* **3**
EFFORT : esfuerzo *m*
push–button [ˈpʊʃˈbʌtən] *adj* : de botones
pushcart [ˈpʊʃˌkɑrt] *n* : carretilla *f* de
mano
pushy [ˈpʊʃi] *adj* **pushier; -est** : mandón, prepotente
pussy [ˈpʊsi] *n, pl* **pussies** : gatito *m*, -ta
f; minino *m*, -na *f*
pussy willow *n* : sauce *m* blanco
pustule [ˈpʌsˌtʃuːl] *n* : pústula *f*
put [ˈpʊt] *v* **put; putting** *vt* **1** PLACE : poner, colocar ⟨put it on the table : ponlo
en la mesa⟩ **2** INSERT : meter **3** (*indicating causation of a state or feeling*)
: poner ⟨it put her in a good mood : la
puso de buen humor⟩ ⟨to put into effect : poner en práctica⟩ **4** IMPOSE : imponer ⟨they put a tax on it : lo gravaron
con un impuesto⟩ **5** SUBJECT : someter, poner ⟨to put to the test : poner a
prueba⟩ ⟨to put to death : ejecutar⟩ **6**
EXPRESS : expresar, decir ⟨he put it

simply : lo dijo sencillamente⟩ **7** AP-
PLY : aplicar ⟨to put one's mind to
something : proponerse hacer algo⟩ **8**
SET : poner ⟨I put him to work : lo puse
a trabajar⟩ **9** ATTACH : dar ⟨to put a
high value on : dar gran valor a⟩ **10**
PRESENT : presentar, exponer ⟨to put
a question to someone : hacer una pregunta a alguien⟩ — *vi* **1 to put to sea**
: hacerse a la mar **2 to put up with**
: aguantar, soportar
put away *vt* **1** KEEP : guardar **2** *or* **to
put aside** : dejar a un lado
put by *vt* SAVE : ahorrar
put down *vt* **1** SUPPRESS : aplastar,
suprimir **2** ATTRIBUTE : atribuir ⟨she
put it down to luck : lo atribuyó a la
suerte⟩
put in *vi* : presentarse ⟨I've put in for the
position : me presenté para el puesto⟩
— *vt* DEVOTE : dedicar (unas horas,
etc.)
put off *vt* DEFER : aplazar, posponer
put on *vt* **1** ASSUME : afectar, adoptar **2**
PRODUCE : presentar (una obra de
teatro, etc.) **3** WEAR : ponerse
put out *vt* INCONVENIENCE : importunar, incomodar
putrefy [ˈpjuːtrəˌfaɪ] *v* **-fied; -fying** *vt*
: pudrir — *vi* : pudrirse
putrid [ˈpjuːtrɪd] *adj* : putrefacto, pútrido
putter [ˈpʌtər] *vi or* **to putter around** : entretenerse
putty[1] [ˈpʌti] *vt* **-tied; -tying** : poner masilla en
putty[2] *n, pl* **-ties** : masilla *f*
put up *vt* **1** LODGE : alojar **2** CON-
TRIBUTE : contribuir, pagar
puzzle[1] [ˈpʌzəl] *vt* **-zled; -zling 1** CON-
FUSE : confundir, dejar perplejo **2 to
puzzle out** : dar vueltas a, tratar de resolver
puzzle[2] *n* **1** : rompecabezas *m* ⟨a crossword puzzle : un crucigrama⟩ **2** MYS-
TERY : misterio *m*, enigma *m*
puzzlement [ˈpʌzəlmənt] *n* : desconcierto *m*, perplejidad *f*
pygmy[1] [ˈpɪgmi] *adj* : enano, pigmeo
pygmy[2] *n, pl* **-mies 1** DWARF : enano *m*,
-na *f* **2 Pygmy** : pigmeo *m*, -mea *f*
pylon [ˈpaɪˌlɑn, -lən] *n* **1** : torre *f* de conducta eléctrica **2** : pilón *m* (de un
puente)
pyramid [ˈpɪrəˌmɪd] *n* : pirámide *f*
pyre [ˈpaɪr] *n* : pira *f*
pyromania [ˌpaɪroˈmeɪniə] *n* : piromanía
f
pyromaniac [ˌpaɪroˈmeɪniˌæk] *n* : pirómano *m*, -na *f*
pyrotechnics [ˌpaɪrəˈtɛknɪks] *npl* **1**
FIREWORKS : fuegos *mpl* artificiales **2**
DISPLAY, SHOW : espectáculo *m*, muestra *f* de virtuosismo ⟨computer pyrotechnics : efectos especiales hechos
por computadora⟩
python [ˈpaɪˌθɑn, -θən] *n* : pitón *f*, serpiente *f* pitón

Q

q [ˈkjuː] *n, pl* **q's** *or* **qs** [ˈkjuːz] : decimoséptima letra del alfabeto inglés

quack[1] [ˈkwæk] *vi* : graznar

quack[2] *n* **1** : graznido *m* (de pato) **2** CHARLATAN : curandero *m*, -ra *f*; matasanos *m fam*

quadrangle [ˈkwɑˌdræŋgəl] *n* **1** COURTYARD : patio *m* interior **2** → quadrilateral

quadrant [ˈkwɑdrənt] *n* : cuadrante *m*

quadrilateral [ˌkwɑdrəˈlæt̬ərəl] *n* : cuadrilátero *m*

quadruped [ˈkwɑdrəˌped] *n* : cuadrúpedo *m*

quadruple [kwɑˈdruːpəl, -ˈdrʌ-; ˈkwɑdrə-] *v* **-pled; -pling** *vt* : cuadruplicar — *vi* : cuadruplicarse

quadruplet [kwɑˈdruːplət, -ˈdrʌ-; ˈkwɑdrə-] *n* : cuatrillizo *m*, -za *f*

quagmire [ˈkwægˌmaɪr, ˈkwɑg-] *n* **1** : lodazal *m*, barrizal *m* **2** PREDICAMENT : atolladero *m*

quail[1] [ˈkweɪl] *vi* : encogerse, acobardarse

quail[2] *n, pl* **quail** *or* **quails** : codorniz *f*

quaint [ˈkweɪnt] *adj* **1** ODD : extraño, curioso **2** PICTURESQUE : pintoresco — **quaintly** *adv*

quaintness [ˈkweɪntnəs] *n* : rareza *f*, lo curioso

quake[1] [ˈkweɪk] *vi* **quaked; quaking** : temblar

quake[2] *n* : temblor *m*, terremoto *m*

qualification [ˌkwɑləfəˈkeɪʃən] *n* **1** LIMITATION, RESERVATION : reserva *f*, limitación *f* ⟨without qualification : sin reservas⟩ **2** REQUIREMENT : requisito *m* **3 qualifications** *npl* ABILITY : aptitud *f*, capacidad *f*

qualified [ˈkwɑləˌfaɪd] *adj* : competente, capacitado

qualifier [ˈkwɑləˌfaɪər] *n* **1** : clasificado *m*, -da *f* (en deportes) **2** : calificativo *m* (en gramática)

qualify [ˈkwɑləˌfaɪ] *v* **-fied; -fying** *vt* **1** : matizar ⟨to qualify a statement : matizar una declaración⟩ **2** MODIFY : calificar (en gramática) **3** : habilitar ⟨the certificate qualified her to teach : el certificado la habilitó para enseñar⟩ — *vi* **1** : obtener el título, recibirse ⟨to qualify as an engineer : recibirse de ingeniero⟩ **2** : clasificarse (en deportes)

quality [ˈkwɑlət̬i] *n, pl* **-ties 1** NATURE : carácter *m* **2** ATTRIBUTE : cualidad *f* **3** GRADE : calidad *f* ⟨of good quality : de buena calidad⟩

qualm [ˈkwɑm, ˈkwɑlm, ˈkwɔm] *n* **1** MISGIVING : duda *f*, aprensión *f* **2** RESERVATION, SCRUPLE : escrúpulo *m*, reparo *m*

quandary [ˈkwɑndri] *n, pl* **-ries** : dilema *m*

quantitative [ˈkwɑntəˌteɪt̬ɪv] *adj* : cuantitativo

quantity [ˈkwɑntət̬i] *n, pl* **-ties** : cantidad *f*

quantum[1] [ˈkwɑntəm] *n* : cuanto *m* (en física)

quantum[2] *adj* : cuántico

quantum theory [ˈkwɑntəm] *n* : teoría *f* cuántica

quarantine[1] [ˈkwɔrənˌtiːn] *vt* **-tined; -tining** : poner en cuarentena

quarantine[2] *n* : cuarentena *f*

quarrel[1] [ˈkwɔrəl] *vi* **-reled** *or* **-relled; -reling** *or* **-relling** : pelearse, reñir, discutir

quarrel[2] *n* : pelea *f*, riña *f*, disputa *f*

quarrelsome [ˈkwɔrəlsəm] *adj* : pendenciero, discutidor

quarry[1] [ˈkwɔri] *vt* **quarried; quarrying 1** EXTRACT : extraer, sacar ⟨to quarry marble : extraer mármol⟩ **2** EXCAVATE : excavar ⟨to quarry a hill : excavar un cerro⟩

quarry[2] *n, pl* **quarries 1** PREY : presa *f* **2** *or* **stone quarry** : cantera *f*

quart [ˈkwɔrt] *n* : cuarto *m* de galón

quarter[1] [ˈkwɔrt̬ər] *vt* **1** : dividir en cuatro partes **2** LODGE : alojar, acuartelar (tropas)

quarter[2] *n* **1** : cuarto *m*, cuarta parte *f* ⟨a foot and a quarter : un pie y cuarto⟩ ⟨a quarter after three : las tres y cuarto⟩ **2** : moneda *f* de 25 centavos, cuarto *m* de dólar **3** DISTRICT : barrio *m* ⟨business quarter : barrio comercial⟩ **4** PLACE : parte *f* ⟨from all quarters : de todas partes⟩ ⟨at close quarters : de muy cerca⟩ **5** MERCY : clemencia *f*, cuartel *m* ⟨to give no quarter : no dar cuartel⟩ **6 quarters** *npl* LODGING : alojamiento *m*, cuartel *m* (militar)

quarterback [ˈkwɔrt̬ərˌbæk] *n* : mariscal *m* de campo

quarterly[1] [ˈkwɔrt̬ərli] *adv* : cada tres meses, trimestralmente

quarterly[2] *adj* : trimestral

quarterly[3] *n, pl* **-lies** : publicación *f* trimestral

quartermaster [ˈkwɔrt̬ərˌmæstər] *n* : intendente *mf*

quartet [kwɔrˈtet] *n* : cuarteto *m*

quartz [ˈkwɔrts] *n* : cuarzo *m*

quash [ˈkwɑʃ, ˈkwɔʃ] *vt* **1** ANNUL : anular **2** QUELL : sofocar, aplastar

quaver [ˈkweɪvər] *vi* **1** SHAKE : temblar ⟨her voice was quavering : le temblaba la voz⟩ **2** TRILL : trinar

quaver[2] *n* : temblor *m* (de la voz)

quay [ˈkiː, ˈkeɪ, ˈkweɪ] *n* : muelle *m*

queasiness [ˈkwiːzinəs] *n* : mareo *m*, náusea *f*

queasy [ˈkwiːzi] *adj* **-sier; -est** : mareado

queen [ˈkwiːn] *n* : reina *f*

queenly [ˈkwiːnli] *adj* **-lier; -est** : de reina, regio

queer [ˈkwɪr] *adj* : extraño, raro, curioso — **queerly** *adv*

quell [ˈkwl] *vt* : aplastar, sofocar

quench [ˈkwɛntʃ] *vt* **1** EXTINGUISH : apagar, sofocar **2** SATISFY : saciar, satisfacer (la sed)

querulous [ˈkwɛrələs, ˈkwɛrjələs, ˈkwɪr-] *adj* : quejumbroso, quejoso — **querulously** *adv*

query¹ [ˈkwɪri, ˈkwɛr-] *vt* **-ried; -rying 1** ASK : preguntar, interrogar ⟨we queried the professor : preguntamos al profesor⟩ **2** QUESTION : cuestionar, poner en duda ⟨to query a matter : cuestionar un asunto⟩

query² *n, pl* **-ries 1** QUESTION : pregunta *f* **2** DOUBT : duda *f*

quest¹ [ˈkwɛst] *v* : buscar

quest² *n* : búsqueda *f*

question¹ [ˈkwɛstʃən] *vt* **1** ASK : preguntar **2** DOUBT : poner en duda, cuestionar **3** INTERROGATE : interrogar — *vi* INQUIRE : inquirir, preguntar

question² *n* **1** QUERY : pregunta *f* **2** ISSUE : asunto *m*, problema *f*, cuestión *f* **3** POSSIBILITY : posibilidad *f* ⟨it's out of the question : es indiscutible⟩ **4** DOUBT : duda *f* ⟨to call into question : poner en duda⟩

questionable [ˈkwɛstʃənəbəl] *adj* : dudoso, discutible, cuestionable ⟨questionable results : resultados discutibles⟩ ⟨questionable motives : motivos sospechosos⟩

questioner [ˈkwɛstʃənər] *n* : interrogador *m*, -dora *f*

question mark *n* : signo *m* de interrogación

questionnaire [ˌkwɛstʃəˈnær] *n* : cuestionario *m*

queue¹ [ˈkjuː] *vi* **queued; queuing** *or* **queueing** : hacer cola

queue² *n* **1** PIGTAIL : coleta *f*, trenza *f* **2** LINE : cola *f*, fila *f*

quibble¹ [ˈkwɪbəl] *vi* **-bled; -bling** : quejarse por nimiedades, andar con sutilezas

quibble² *n* : objeción *f* de poca monta, queja *f* insignificante

quick¹ [ˈkwɪk] *adv* : rápidamente

quick² *adj* **1** RAPID : rápido **2** ALERT, CLEVER : listo, vivo, agudo **3 a quick temper** : un genio vivo

quick³ *n* **1** FLESH : carne *f* viva **2 to cut someone to the quick** : herir a alguien en lo más vivo

quicken [ˈkwɪkən] *vt* **1** REVIVE : resucitar **2** AROUSE : estimular, despertar **3** HASTEN : acelerar ⟨she quickened her pace : aceleró el paso⟩

quickly [ˈkwɪkli] *adv* : rápidamente, rápido, de prisa

quickness [ˈkwɪknəs] *n* : rapidez *f*

quicksand [ˈkwɪkˌsænd] *n* : arena *f* movediza

quicksilver [ˈkwɪkˌsɪlvər] *n* : mercurio *m*, azogue *m*

quick–tempered [ˈkwɪkˈtɛmpərd] *adj* : irascible, de genio vivo

quick–witted [ˈkwɪkˈwɪtəd] *adj* : agudo

quiet¹ [ˈkwaɪət] *vt* **1** SILENCE : hacer callar, acallar **2** CALM : calmar, tranquilizar — *vi* **to quiet down** : calmarse, tranquilizarse

quiet² *adv* : silenciosamente ⟨a quiet-running engine : un motor silencioso⟩

quiet³ *adj* **1** CALM : tranquilo, calmoso **2** MILD : sosegado, suave ⟨a quiet disposition : un temperamento sosegado⟩ **3** SILENT : silencioso **4** UNOBTRUSIVE : discreto **5** SECLUDED : aislado ⟨a quiet nook : un rincón aislado⟩ — **quietly** *adv*

quiet⁴ *n* **1** CALM : calma *f*, tranquilidad *f* **2** SILENCE : silencio *m*

quietness [ˈkwaɪətnəs] *n* : suavidad *f*, tranquilidad *f*, quietud *f*

quietude [ˈkwaɪəˌtuːd, -ˌtjuːd] *n* : quietud *f*, reposo *m*

quill [ˈkwɪl] *n* **1** SPINE : púa *f* (de un puerco espín) **2** : pluma *f* (para escribir)

quilt¹ [ˈkwɪlt] *vt* : acolchar

quilt² *n* : colcha *f*, edredón *m*

quince [ˈkwɪnts] *n* : membrillo *m*

quinine [ˈkwaɪˌnaɪn] *n* : quinina *f*

quintessence [kwɪnˈtɛsənts] *n* : quintaesencia *f*

quintet [kwɪnˈtɛt] *n* : quinteto *m*

quintuple [kwɪnˈtuːpəl, -ˈtjuː-, -ˈtʌ-; ˈkwɪntə-] *adj* : quíntuplo

quintuplet [kwɪnˈtʌplət, -ˈtuː-, -ˈtjuː-; ˈkwɪntə-] *n* : quintillizo *m*, -za *f*

quip¹ [ˈkwɪp] *vi* **quipped; quipping** : bromear

quip² *n* : ocurrencia *f*, salida *f*

quirk [ˈkwərk] *n* : peculiaridad *f*, rareza *f* ⟨a quirk of fate : un capricho del destino⟩

quirky [ˈkwərki] *adj* **-kier; -est** : peculiar, raro

quit [ˈkwɪt] *v* **quit; quitting** *vt* : dejar, abandonar ⟨to quit smoking : dejar de fumar⟩ — *vi* **1** STOP : parar **2** RESIGN : dimitir, renunciar

quite [ˈkwaɪt] *adv* **1** COMPLETELY : completamente, totalmente **2** RATHER : bastante ⟨quite near : bastante cerca⟩

quits [ˈkwɪts] *adj* **to call it quits** : quedar en paz

quitter [ˈkwɪtər] *n* : derrotista *mf*

quiver¹ [ˈkwɪvər] *vi* : temblar, estremecerse, vibrar

quiver² *n* **1** : carcaj *m*, aljaba *f* (para flechas) **2** TREMBLING : temblor *m*, estremecimiento *m*

quixotic [kwɪkˈsɑtɪk] *adj* : quijotesco

quiz¹ [ˈkwɪz] *vt* **quizzed; quizzing** : interrogar, hacer una prueba a (en el colegio)

quiz² *n, pl* **quizzes** : examen *m* corto, prueba *f*

quizzical [ˈkwɪzɪkəl] *adj* **1** TEASING : burlón **2** CURIOUS : curioso, interrogativo

quorum [ˈkworəm] *n* : quórum *m*

quota ['kwo:tə] *n* : cuota *f*, cupo *m*
quotable ['kwo:təbəl] *adj* : citable
quotation [kwo'teɪʃən] *n* **1** CITATION
: cita *f* **2** ESTIMATE : presupuesto *m*,
estimación *f* **3** PRICE : cotización *f*
quotation marks *npl* : comillas *fpl*

quote¹ ['kwo:t] *vt* **quoted; quoting 1**
CITE : citar **2** VALUE : cotizar (en finanzas)
quote² *n* **1** → **quotation 2 quotes** *npl*
→ **quotation marks**
quotient ['kwo:ʃənt] *n* : cociente *m*

R

r ['ɑr] *n*, *pl* **r's** *or* **rs** ['ɑrz] : decimoctava
letra del alfabeto inglés
rabbi ['ræ,baɪ] *n* : rabino *m*, -na *f*
rabbit ['ræbət] *n*, *pl* **-bit** *or* **-bits** : conejo *m*, -ja *f*
rabble ['ræbəl] *n* **1** MASSES : populacho
m **2** RIFFRAFF : chusma *f*, gentuza *f*
rabid ['ræbɪd] *adj* **1** : rabioso, afectado
con la rabia **2** FURIOUS : furioso **3**
FANATIC : fanático
rabies ['reɪbi:z] *ns & pl* : rabia *f*
raccoon [ræ'ku:n] *n*, *pl* **-coon** *or* **-coons**
: mapache *m*
race¹ ['reɪs] *vi* **raced; racing 1** : correr,
competir (en una carrera) **2** RUSH : ir
a toda prisa, ir corriendo
race² *n* **1** CURRENT : corriente *f* (de
agua) **2** : carrera *f* ⟨dog race : carrera
de perros⟩ ⟨the presidential race : la
carrera presidential⟩ **3** : raza *f* ⟨the
black race : la raza negra⟩ ⟨the human
race : el género humano⟩
racecourse ['reɪs,kors] *n* : pista *f* (de carreras)
racehorse ['reɪs,hors] *n* : caballo *m* de
carreras
racer ['reɪsər] *n* : corredor *m*, -dora *f*
racetrack ['reɪs,træk] *n* : pista *f* (de carreras)
racial ['reɪʃəl] *adj* : racial — **racially** *adv*
racism ['reɪ,sɪzəm] *n* : racismo *m*
racist ['reɪsɪst] *n* : racista *mf*
rack¹ ['ræk] *vt* **1** : atormentar ⟨racked
with pain : atormentado por el dolor⟩
2 to rack one's brains : devanarse los
sesos
rack² *n* **1** SHELF, STAND : estante *m* ⟨a
luggage rack : un portaequipajes⟩ ⟨a
coatrack : un perchero, una percha⟩ **2**
: potro *m* (instrumento de la tortura)
racket ['rækət] *n* **1** : raqueta *f* (en deportes) **2** DIN : estruendo *m*, bulla *f*,
jaleo *m fam* **3** SWINDLE : estafa *f*, timo
m fam
racketeer [,rækə'tɪr] *n* : estafador *m*,
-dora *f*
raconteur [,ræ,kɑn'tər] *n* : anecdotista
mf
racy ['reɪsi] *adj* **racier; -est** : subido de
tono, picante
radar ['reɪ,dɑr] *n* : radar *m*
radial ['reɪdiəl] *adj* : radial
radiance ['reɪdiənʦ] *n* : resplandor *m*
radiant ['reɪdiənt] *adj* : radiante — **ra-
diantly** *adv*
radiate ['reɪdi,eɪt] *v* **-ated; -ating** *vt* : irradiar, emitir ⟨to radiate heat : irradi-

ar el calor⟩ ⟨to radiate happiness : rebosar de alegría⟩ — *vi* **1** : irradiar **2**
SPREAD : salir, extenderse ⟨to radiate
(out) from the center : salir del centro⟩
radiation [,reɪdi'eɪʃən] *n* : radiación *f*
radiator ['reɪdi,eɪtər] *n* : radiador *m*
radical¹ ['rædɪkəl] *adj* : radical — **radi-
cally** [-kli] *adv*
radical² *n* : radical *mf*
radicalism ['rædɪkə,lɪzəm] *n* : radicalismo *m*
radii → **radius**
radio¹ ['reɪdi,o:] *v* : llamar por radio,
transmitir por radio
radio² *n*, *pl* **-dios** : radio *m* (aparato), radio *f* (emisora, radiodifusión)
radioactive ['reɪdio'æktɪv] *adj* : radiactivo, radioactivo
radioactivity [,reɪdio,æk'tɪvəti] *n*, *pl*
-ties : radiactividad *f*, radioactividad *f*
radiologist [,reɪdi'ɑləʤɪst] *n* : radiólogo
m, -ga *f*
radiology [,reɪdi'ɑləʤi] *n* : radiología *f*
radish ['rædɪʃ] *n* : rábano *m*
radium ['reɪdiəm] *n* : radio *m*
radius ['reɪdiəs] *n*, *pl* **radii** [-di,aɪ] : radio
m
radon ['reɪ,dɑn] *n* : radón *m*
raffle¹ ['ræfəl] *vt* **-fled; -fling** : rifar,
sortear
raffle² *n* : rifa *f*, sorteo *m*
raft ['ræft] *n* **1** : balsa *f* ⟨rubber rafts
: balsas de goma⟩ **2** LOT, SLEW : montón *m* ⟨a raft of documents : un montón de documentos⟩
rafter ['ræftər] *n* : par *m*, viga *f*
rag ['ræg] *n* **1** CLOTH : trapo *m* **2 rags**
npl TATTERS : harapos *mpl*, andrajos
mpl
ragamuffin ['rægə,mʌfən] *n* : pilluelo *m*,
-la *f*
rage¹ ['reɪʤ] *vi* **raged; raging 1** : estar
furioso, rabiar ⟨to fly into a rage : en-
furecerse⟩ **2** : bramar, hacer estragos
⟨the wind was raging : el viento bram-
aba⟩ ⟨flu raged through the school : la
gripe hizo estragos por el colegio⟩
rage² *n* **1** ANGER : furia *f*, ira *f*, cólera *f*
2 FAD : moda *f*, furor *m*
ragged ['rægəd] *adj* **1** UNEVEN : irregular, desigual **2** TORN : hecho jirones
3 TATTERED : andrajoso, harapiento
ragout [ræ'gu:] *n* : ragú *m*, estofado *m*
ragtime ['ræg,taɪm] *n* : ragtime *m*
ragweed ['ræg,wi:d] *n* : ambrosía *f*
raid¹ ['reɪd] *vt* **1** : invadir, hacer una incursión en ⟨raided by enemy troops

: invadido por tropas enemigas⟩ **2**
: asaltar, atracar ⟨the gang raided the
warehouse : la pandilla asaltó el al-
macén⟩ **3** : allanar, hacer una redada
en ⟨police raided the house : la policía
allanó la vivienda⟩

raid² *n* **1** : invasión *f* (militar) **2** : asalto
m (por delincuentes) **3** : redada *f*, allanamiento *m* (por la policía)

raider ['reɪdər] *n* **1** ATTACKER : asaltante
mf; invasor *m*, -sora *f* **2 corporate
raider** : tiburón *m*

rail¹ ['reɪl] *vi* **1 to rail against** REVILE
: denostar contra **2 to rail at** SCOLD
: regañar, reprender

rail² *n* **1** BAR : barra *f*, barrera *f* **2**
HANDRAIL : pasamanos *m*, barandilla
f **3** TRACK : riel *m* (para ferrocarriles)
4 RAILROAD : ferrocarril *m*

railing ['reɪlɪŋ] *n* **1** : baranda *f* (de un
balcón, etc.) **2** RAILS : verja *f*

raillery ['reɪləri] *n*, *pl* **-leries** : bromas *fpl*

railroad ['reɪl,roːd] *n* : ferrocarril *m*

railway ['reɪl,weɪ] → **railroad**

raiment ['reɪmənt] *n* : vestiduras *fpl*

rain¹ ['reɪn] *vi* **1** : llover ⟨it's raining : está
lloviendo⟩ **2 to rain down** SHOWER
: llover ⟨insults rained down on him : le
llovieron los insultos⟩

rain² *n* : lluvia *f*

rainbow ['reɪn,boː] *n* : arco *m* iris

raincoat ['reɪn,koːt] *n* : impermeable *m*

raindrop ['reɪn,drɑp] *n* : gota *f* de lluvia

rainfall ['reɪn,fɔl] *n* : lluvia *f*, precipitación *f*

rainstorm ['reɪn,stɔrm] *n* : temporal *m*
(de lluvia)

rainwater ['reɪn,wɔtər] *n* : agua *f* de lluvia

rainy ['reɪni] *adj* **rainier; -est** : lluvioso

raise¹ ['reɪz] *vt* **raised; raising 1** LIFT
: levantar, subir, alzar ⟨to raise one's
spirits : levantarle el ánimo a alguien⟩
2 ERECT : levantar, erigir **3** COLLECT
: recaudar ⟨to raise money : recaudar
dinero⟩ **4** REAR : criar ⟨to raise one's
children : criar uno a sus niños⟩ **5**
GROW : cultivar **6** INCREASE : aumentar, subir **7** PROMOTE : ascender **8**
PROVOKE : provocar ⟨it raised a laugh
: provocó una risa⟩ **9** BRING UP : sacar
(temas, objeciones, etc.)

raise² *n* : aumento *m*

raisin ['reɪzən] *n* : pasa *f*

raja *or* **rajah** ['rɑdʒə, -,dʒɑ, -,ʒɑ] *n* : rajá
m

rake¹ ['reɪk] *v* **raked; raking** *vt* **1** : rastrillar ⟨to rake leaves : rastrillar las ho-
jas⟩ **2** SWEEP : barrer ⟨raked with gunfire : barrido con metralla⟩ — *vi* **to rake
through** : revolver, hurgar en

rake² *n* **1** : rastrillo *m* **2** LIBERTINE : libertino *m*, -na *f*; calavera *m*

rakish ['reɪkɪʃ] *adj* **1** JAUNTY : desenvuelto, desenfadado **2** DISSOLUTE
: libertino, disoluto

rally¹ ['ræli] *v* **-lied; -lying** *vi* **1** MEET,
UNITE : reunirse, congregarse **2** RE-

COVER : recuperarse — *vt* **1** ASSEMBLE
: reunir (tropas, etc.) **2** RECOVER : recobrar (la fuerza, el ánimo, etc.)

rally² *n*, *pl* **-lies** : reunión *f*, mitin *m*, manifestación *f*

ram¹ ['ræm] *v* **rammed; ramming** *vt* **1**
DRIVE : hincar, clavar ⟨he rammed it
into the ground : lo hincó en la tierra⟩
2 SMASH : estrellar, embestir — *vi* COL-
LIDE : chocar (contra), estrellarse

ram² *n* **1** : carnero *m* (animal) **2 battering ram** : ariete *m*

RAM ['ræm] *n* : RAM *f*

ramble¹ ['ræmbəl] *vi* **-bled; -bling 1**
WANDER : pasear, deambular **2 to ram-
ble on** : divagar, perder el hilo **3**
SPREAD : trepar (dícese de una planta)

ramble² *n* : paseo *m*, excursión *f*

rambler ['ræmblər] *n* **1** WALKER : excursionista *mf* **2** ROSE : rosa *f* trepadora

rambunctious [ræm'bʌŋkʃəs] *adj* UN-
RULY : alborotado

ramification [,ræməfə'keɪʃən] *n* : ramificación *f*

ramify ['ræmə,faɪ] *vi* **-fied; -fying** : ramificarse

ramp ['ræmp] *n* : rampa *f*

rampage¹ ['ræm,peɪdʒ, ræm'peɪdʒ] *vi*
-paged; -paging : andar arrasando
todo, correr destrozando

rampage² ['ræm,peɪdʒ] *n* : alboroto *m*,
frenesí *m* (de violencia)

rampant ['ræmpənt] *adj* : desenfrenado

rampart ['ræm,pɑrt] *n* : terraplén *m*, muralla *f*

ramrod ['ræm,rɑd] *n* : baqueta *f*

ramshackle ['ræm,ʃækəl] *adj* : destartalado

ran → **run**

ranch ['ræntʃ] *n* **1** : hacienda *f*, rancho
m, finca *f* ganadera **2** FARM : granja *f*
⟨fruit ranch : granja de frutas⟩

rancher ['ræntʃər] *n* : estanciero *m*, -ra
f; ranchero *m*, -ra *f*

rancid ['rænsɪd] *adj* : rancio

rancor ['ræŋkər] *n* : rencor *m*

random ['rændəm] *adj* **1** : fortuito,
aleatorio **2 at ∼** : al azar — **randomly** *adv*

rang → **ring**

range¹ ['reɪndʒ] *v* **ranged; ranging** *vt*
ARRANGE : alinear, ordenar, arreglar
— *vi* **1** ROAM : deambular ⟨to range
through the town : deambular por el
pueblo⟩ **2** EXTEND : extenderse ⟨the
results range widely : los resultados se
extienden mucho⟩ **3** VARY : variar
⟨discounts range from 20% to 40% : los
descuentos varían entre 20% y 40%⟩

range² *n* **1** ROW : fila *f*, hilera *f* ⟨a mountain range : una cordillera⟩ **2** GRASS-
LAND : pradera *f*, pampa *f* **3** STOVE
: cocina *f* **4** VARIETY : variedad *f*, gama
f **5** SPHERE : ámbito *m*, esfera *f*, campo *m* **6** REACH : registro *m* (de la voz),
alcance *m* (de un arma de fuego) **7**
shooting range : campo *m* de tiro

ranger ['reɪnʤər] *n or* **forest ranger**
: guardabosque *mf*
rangy ['reɪnʤi] *adj* **rangier; -est** : alto y
delgado
rank¹ ['ræŋk] *vt* **1** RANGE : alinear, ordenar, poner en fila **2** CLASSIFY : clasificar — *vi* **1 to rank above** : ser superior a **2 to rank among** : encontrarse
entre, figurar entre
rank² *adj* **1** LUXURIANT : lozano, exuberante (dícese de una planta) **2**
SMELLY : fétido, maloliente **3** OUT-
RIGHT : completo, absoluto ⟨a rank injustice : una injusticia manifiesta⟩
rank³ *n* **1** LINE, ROW : fila *f* ⟨to close
ranks : cerrar filas⟩ **2** GRADE, POSI-
TION : grado *m*, rango *m* (militar) ⟨to
pull rank : abusar de su autoridad⟩ **3**
CLASS : categoría *f*, clase *f* **4 ranks** *npl*
: soldados *mpl* rasos
rank and file *n* **1** RANKS : soldados *mpl*
rasos **2** : bases *fpl* (de un partido, etc.)
rankle ['ræŋkəl] *v* **-kled; -kling** *vi* : doler — *vt* : irritar, herir
ransack ['ræn,sæk] *vt* : revolver, desvalijar, registrar de arriba abajo
ransom¹ ['ræntsəm] *vt* : rescatar, pagar
un rescate por
ransom² *n* : rescate *m*
rant ['rænt] *vi or* **to rant and rave**
: despotricar, desvariar
rap¹ ['ræp] *v* **rapped; rapping** *vt* **1**
KNOCK : golpetear, dar un golpe en **2**
CRITICIZE : criticar — *vi* **1** CHAT : charlar, cotorrear *fam* **2** KNOCK : dar un
golpe
rap² *n* **1** BLOW, KNOCK : golpe *m*,
golpecito *m* **2** CHAT : charla *f* **3** *or* **rap
music** : rap *m* **4 to take the rap** : pagar el pato *fam*
rapacious [rə'peɪʃəs] *adj* **1** GREEDY
: avaricioso, codicioso **2** PREDATORY
: rapaz, de rapiña **3** RAVENOUS : voraz
rape¹ ['reɪp] *vt* **raped; raping** : violar
rape² *n* **1** : colza *f* (planta) **2** : violación
f (de una persona)
rapid ['ræpɪd] *adj* : rápido — **rapidly** *adv*
rapidity [rə'pɪdəti] *n* : rapidez *f*
rapids ['ræpɪdz] *npl* : rápidos *mpl*
rapier ['reɪpiər] *n* : estoque *m*
rapist ['reɪpɪst] *n* : violador *m*, -dora *f*
rapper ['ræpər] *n* : cantante *mf* de rap;
rapero *m*, -ra *f*
rapport [ræ'por] *n* : relación *f* armo-
niosa, entendimiento *m*
rapt ['ræpt] *adj* : absorto, embelesado
rapture ['ræptʃər] *n* : éxtasis *m*
rapturous ['ræptʃərəs] *adj* : extasiado,
embelesado
rare ['rær] *adj* **rarer; rarest 1** RAREFIED
: enrarecido **2** FINE : excelente, excepcional ⟨a rare talent : un talento ex-
cepcional⟩ **3** UNCOMMON : raro, poco
común **4** : poco cocido (dícese de la
carne)
rarefy ['rærə,faɪ] *vt* **-fied; -fying** : rari-
ficar, enrarecer

rarely ['rærli] *adv* SELDOM : pocas veces,
rara vez
raring ['rærən, -ɪŋ] *adj* : lleno de entusiasmo, con muchas ganas
rarity ['rærəti] *n, pl* **-ties** : rareza *f*
rascal ['ræskəl] *n* : pillo *m*, -lla *f*; pícaro
m, -ra *f*
rash¹ ['ræʃ] *adj* : imprudente, precipitado — **rashly** *adv*
rash² *n* : sarpullido *m*, erupción *f*
rashness ['ræʃnəs] *n* : precipitación *f*,
impetuosidad *f*
rasp¹ ['ræsp] *vt* **1** SCRAPE : raspar, es-
cofinar **2 to rasp out** : decir en voz
áspera
rasp² *n* : escofina *f*
raspberry ['ræz,bɛri] *n, pl* **-ries** : frambuesa *f*
rat ['ræt] *n* : rata *f*
ratchet ['rætʃət] *n* : trinquete *m*
rate¹ ['reɪt] *vt* **rated; rating 1** CONSID-
ER, REGARD : considerar, estimar **2**
DESERVE : merecer
rate² *n* **1** PACE, SPEED : velocidad *f*, ritmo *m* ⟨at this rate : a este paso⟩ **2**
: índice *m*, tasa *f* ⟨birth rate : índice de
natalidad⟩ ⟨interest rate : tasa de in-
terés⟩ **3** CHARGE, PRICE : precio *m*,
tarifa *f*
rather ['ræðər, 'rɑ-, 'rɑ-] *adv* **1** (*indicating preference*) ⟨she would rather stay
in the house : preferiría quedarse en
casa⟩ ⟨I'd rather not : mejor que no⟩
2 (*indicating preciseness*) ⟨my father, or
rather my stepfather : mi padre, o
mejor dicho mi padrastro⟩ **3** INSTEAD
: sino que, más que, al contrario ⟨I'm
not pleased; rather I'm disappointed
: no estoy satisfecho, sino desilusiona-
do⟩ **4** SOMEWHAT : algo, un tanto
⟨rather strange : un poco extraño⟩ **5**
QUITE : bastante ⟨rather difficult : bastante difícil⟩
ratification [,rætəfə'keɪʃən] *n* : ratificación *f*
ratify ['rætə,faɪ] *vt* **-fied; -fying** : ratificar
rating ['reɪtɪŋ] *n* **1** STANDING : clasificación *f*, posición *f* **2 ratings** *npl*
: índice *m* de audiencia
ratio ['reɪʃio] *n, pl* **-tios** : proporción *f*,
relación *f*
ration¹ ['ræʃən, 'reɪʃən] *vt* : racionar
ration² *n* **1** : ración *f* **2 rations** *npl* PRO-
VISIONS : víveres *mpl*
rational ['ræʃənəl] *adj* : racional, razonable, lógico — **rationally** *adv*
rationale [,ræʃə'næl] *n* **1** EXPLANATION
: explicación *f* **2** BASIS : base *f*, razones
fpl
rationality [,ræʃə'næləti] *n, pl* **-ties**
: racionalidad *f*
rationalization [,ræʃənələ'zeɪʃən] *n*
: racionalización *f*
rationalize ['ræʃənə,laɪz] *vt* **-ized; -izing**
: racionalizar
rattle¹ ['rætəl] *v* **-tled; -tling** *vi* **1** CLAT-
TER : traquetear, hacer ruido **2 to rat-
tle on** CHATTER : parlotear *fam* — *vt*

1 : hacer sonar, agitar ⟨the wind rattled the door : el viento sacudió la puerta⟩ **2** DISCONCERT, WORRY : desconcertar, poner nervioso **3 to rattle off** : despachar, recitar, decir de corrido

rattle² *n* **1** CLATTER : traqueteo *m*, ruido *m* **2** *or* **baby's rattle** : sonajero *m* **3** : cascabel *m* (de una culebra)

rattler ['rætələr] → **rattlesnake**

rattlesnake ['rætəl,sneɪk] *n* : serpiente *f* de cascabel

ratty ['ræti] *adj* **rattier; -est** : raído, andrajoso

raucous ['rɔkəs] *adj* **1** HOARSE : ronco **2** BOISTEROUS : escandaloso, bullicioso — **raucously** *adv*

ravage¹ ['rævɪdʒ] *vt* **-aged; -aging** : devastar, arrasar, hacer estragos

ravage² *n* : destrozo *m*, destrucción *f* ⟨the ravages of war : los estragos de la guerra⟩

rave ['reɪv] *vi* **raved; raving** **1** : delirar, desvariar ⟨to rave like a maniac : desvariar como un loco⟩ **2 to rave about** : hablar con entusiasmo sobre, entusiasmarse por

ravel ['rævəl] *v* **-eled** *or* **-elled; -eling** *or* **-elling** *vt* UNRAVEL : desenredar, desenmarañar — *vi* FRAY : deshilacharse

raven ['reɪvən] *n* : cuervo *m*

ravenous ['rævənəs] *adj* : hambriento, voraz — **ravenously** *adv*

ravine [rə'vi:n] *n* : barranco *m*, quebrada *f*

ravish ['rævɪʃ] *vt* **1** PLUNDER : saquear **2** ENCHANT : embelesar, cautivar, encantar

raw ['rɔ] *adj* **rawer; rawest** **1** UNCOOKED : crudo **2** UNTREATED : sin tratar, sin refinar, puro ⟨raw data : datos en bruto⟩ ⟨raw materials : materias primas⟩ **3** INEXPERIENCED : novato, inexperto **4** OPEN : abierto, en carne viva ⟨a raw sore : una llaga abierta⟩ **5** : frío y húmedo ⟨a raw day : un día crudo⟩ **6** UNFAIR : injusto ⟨a raw deal : un trato injusto, una injusticia⟩

rawhide ['rɔ,haɪd] *n* : cuero *m* sin curtir

ray ['reɪ] *n* **1** : rayo *m* (de la luz, etc.) ⟨a ray of hope : un resquicio de esperanza⟩ **2** : raya *f* (pez)

rayon ['reɪ,ɑn] *n* : rayón *m*

raze ['reɪz] *vt* **razed; razing** : arrasar, demoler

razor ['reɪzər] *n* **1** *or* **straight razor** : navaja *f* (de afeitar) **2** *or* **safety razor** : maquinilla *f* de afeitar, rastrillo *m Mex* **3** SHAVER : afeitadora *f*, rasuradora *f*

reach¹ ['ri:tʃ] *vt* **1** EXTEND : extender, alargar ⟨to reach out one's hand : extender la mano⟩ **2** : alcanzar ⟨I couldn't reach the apple : no pude alcanzar la manzana⟩ **3** : llegar a, llegar hasta ⟨the shadow reached the wall : la sombra llegó hasta la pared⟩ **4** CONTACT : contactar, ponerse en contacto con — *vi* **1** *or* **to reach out** : extender la mano **2** STRETCH : extenderse **3 to**

reach for : tratar de agarrar

reach² *n* : alcance *m*, extensión *f*

react [ri'ækt] *vi* : reaccionar

reaction [ri'ækʃən] *n* : reacción *f*

reactionary¹ [ri'ækʃə,nɛri] *adj* : reaccionario

reactionary² *n, pl* **-ries** : reaccionario *m*, -ria *f*

reactor [ri'æktər] *n* : reactor *m* ⟨nuclear reactor : reactor nuclear⟩

read¹ ['ri:d] *v* **read** ['rɛd]; **reading** *vt* **1** : leer ⟨to read a story : leer un cuento⟩ **2** INTERPRET : interpretar ⟨it can be read two ways : se puede interpretar de dos maneras⟩ **3** : decir, poner ⟨the sign read "No smoking" : el letrero decía "No Fumar"⟩ **4** : marcar ⟨the thermometer reads 70° : el termómetro marca 70°⟩ — *vi* **1** : leer ⟨he can read : sabe leer⟩ **2** SAY : decir ⟨the list reads as follows : la lista dice lo siguiente⟩

read² *n* **to be a good read** : ser una lectura amena

readable ['ri:dəbəl] *adj* : legible — **readably** [-bli] *adv*

reader ['ri:dər] *n* : lector *m*, -tora *f*

readily ['rɛdəli] *adv* **1** WILLINGLY : de buena gana, con gusto **2** EASILY : fácilmente, con facilidad

readiness ['rɛdinəs] *n* **1** WILLINGNESS : buena disposición *f* **2 to be in readiness** : estar preparado

reading ['ri:dɪŋ] *n* : lectura *f*

readjust [,ri:ə'dʒʌst] *vt* : reajustar — *vi* : volverse a adaptar

readjustment [,ri:ə'dʒʌstmənt] *n* : reajuste *m*

ready¹ ['rɛdi] *vt* **readied; readying** : preparar

ready² *adj* **readier; -est** **1** PREPARED : listo, preparado **2** WILLING : dispuesto **3** : a punto de ⟨ready to cry : a punto de llorar⟩ **4** AVAILABLE : disponible ⟨ready cash : efectivo⟩ **5** QUICK : vivo, agudo ⟨a ready wit : un ingenio agudo⟩

ready–made ['rɛdi'meɪd] *adj* : preparado, confeccionado

reaffirm [,ri:ə'fərm] *vt* : reafirmar

real¹ ['ri:l] *adv* VERY : muy ⟨we had a real good time : lo pasamos muy bien⟩

real² *adj* **1** : inmobiliario ⟨real property : bien inmueble, bien raíz⟩ **2** GENUINE : auténtico, genuino **3** ACTUAL, TRUE : real, verdadero ⟨a real friend : un verdadero amigo⟩ **4 for real** SERIOUSLY : de veras, de verdad

real estate *n* : propiedad *f* inmobiliaria, bienes *mpl* raíces

realign [,ri:ə'laɪn] *vt* : realinear

realignment [,ri:ə'laɪnmənt] *n* : realineamiento *m*

realism ['ri:ə,lɪzəm] *n* : realismo *m*

realist ['ri:əlɪst] *n* : realista *mf*

realistic [,ri:ə'lɪstɪk] *adj* : realista

realistically [,ri:ə'lɪstɪkli] *adv* : de manera realista

reality [ri'æləti] *n, pl* **-ties** : realidad *f*
realizable [ˌri:ə'laizəbəl] *adj* : realizable, alcanzable
realization [ˌri:ələ'zeiʃən] *n* : realización *f*
realize ['ri:əˌlaiz] *vt* **-ized; -izing 1** AC-COMPLISH : realizar, llevar a cabo **2** GAIN : obtener, realizar, sacar ⟨to realize a profit : realizar beneficios⟩ **3** UNDERSTAND : darse cuenta de, saber
really ['rɪli, 'ri:-] *adv* **1** ACTUALLY : de verdad, en realidad **2** TRULY : verdaderamente, realmente **3** FRANKLY : francamente, en serio
realm ['rɛlm] *n* **1** KINGDOM : reino *m* **2** SPHERE : esfera *f*, campo *m*
ream¹ ['ri:m] *vt* : escariar
ream² *n* **1** : resma *f* (de papel) **2 reams** *npl* LOADS : montones *mpl*
reap ['ri:p] *v* : cosechar
reaper ['ri:pər] *n* **1** : cosechador *m*, -dora *f* (persona) **2** : cosechadora *f* (máquina)
reappear [ˌri:ə'pɪr] *vi* : reaparecer
reappearance [ˌri:ə'pɪrənts] *n* : reaparición *f*
rear¹ ['rɪr] *vt* **1** LIFT, RAISE : levantar **2** BREED, BRING UP : criar — *vi or* **to rear up** : encabritarse
rear² *adj* : trasero, posterior, de atrás
rear³ *n* **1** BACK : parte *f* de atrás ⟨to bring up the rear : cerrar la marcha⟩ **2 or rear end** : trasero *m*
rear admiral *n* : contraalmirante *mf*
rearrange [ˌri:ə'reindʒ] *vt* **-ranged; -ranging** : colocar de otra manera, volver a arreglar, reorganizar
rearview mirror ['rɪrˌvju:-] *n* : retrovisor *m*
reason¹ ['ri:zən] *vt* THINK : pensar — *vi* : razonar ⟨I can't reason with her : no puedo razonar con ella⟩
reason² *n* **1** CAUSE, GROUND : razón *f*, motivo *m* ⟨the reason for his trip : el motivo de su viaje⟩ ⟨for this reason : por esta razón, por lo cual⟩ ⟨the reason why : la razón por la cual, el porqué⟩ **2** SENSE : razón *f* ⟨to lose one's reason : perder los sesos⟩ ⟨to listen to reason : avenirse a razones⟩
reasonable ['ri:zənəbəl] *adj* **1** SENSIBLE : razonable **2** INEXPENSIVE : barato, económico
reasonably ['ri:zənəbli] *adv* **1** SENSIBLY : razonablemente **2** FAIRLY : bastante
reasoning ['ri:zənɪŋ] *n* : razonamiento *m*, raciocinio *m*, argumentos *mpl*
reassess [ˌri:ə'sɛs] *vt* : revaluar, reconsiderar
reassurance [ˌri:ə'ʃurənts] *n* : consuelo *m*, palabras *fpl* alentadoras
reassure [ˌri:ə'ʃur] *vt* **-sured; -suring** : tranquilizar
reassuring [ˌri:ə'ʃurɪŋ] *adj* : tranquilizador
reawaken [ˌri:ə'weikən] *vt* : volver a despertar, reavivar
rebate ['ri:ˌbeit] *n* : reembolso *m*, devolución *f*

rebel¹ [rɪ'bɛl] *vi* **-belled; -belling** : rebelarse, sublevarse
rebel² ['rɛbəl] *adj* : rebelde
rebel³ ['rɛbəl] *n* : rebelde *mf*
rebellion [rɪ'bɛljən] *n* : rebelión *f*
rebellious [rɪ'bɛljəs] *adj* : rebelde
rebelliousness [rɪ'bɛljəsnəs] *n* : rebeldía *f*
rebirth [ˌri:'bərθ] *n* : renacimiento *m*
reboot [ri'bu:t] *vt* : reiniciar (una computadora)
reborn [ri:'born] *adj* **to be reborn** : renacer
rebound¹ ['ri:ˌbaund, ˌri:'baund] *vi* : rebotar
rebound² ['ri:ˌbaund] *n* : rebote *m*
rebuff¹ [rɪ'bʌf] *vt* : desairar, rechazar
rebuff² *n* : desaire *m*, rechazo *m*
rebuild [ˌri:'bɪld] *vt* **-built** [-'bɪlt]; **-building** : reconstruir
rebuke¹ [rɪ'bju:k] *vt* **-buked; -buking** : reprender, regañar
rebuke² *n* : reprimenda *f*, reproche *m*
rebut [rɪ'bʌt] *vt* **-butted; -butting** : rebatir, refutar
rebuttal [rɪ'bʌtəl] *n* : refutación *f*
recalcitrant [rɪ'kælsətrənt] *adj* : recalcitrante
recall¹ [rɪ'kɔl] *vt* **1** : llamar, retirar ⟨recalled to active duty : llamado al servicio activo⟩ **2** REMEMBER : recordar, acordarse de **3** REVOKE : revocar
recall² [rɪ'kɔl, 'ri:ˌkɔl] *n* **1** : retirada *f* (de personas o mercancías) **2** MEMORY : memoria *f* ⟨to have total recall : poder recordar todo⟩
recant [rɪ'kænt] *vt* : retractarse de — *vi* : retractarse, renegar
recapitulate [ˌri:kə'pɪtʃəˌleit] *v* **-lated; -lating** : resumir, recapitular
recapture [ˌri:'kæptʃər] *vt* **-tured; -turing 1** REGAIN : volver a tomar, reconquistar **2** RELIVE : revivir (la juventud, etc.)
recast [ri:'kæst] *vt* **-cast; -casting 1** : refundir (metales) **2** REWRITE : refundir, modificar
recede [rɪ'si:d] *vi* **-ceded; -ceding 1** WITHDRAW : retirarse, retroceder **2** FADE : desvanecerse, alejarse **3** SLANT : inclinarse **4 to have a receding hairline** : tener entradas
receipt [rɪ'si:t] *n* **1** : recibo *m* **2 receipts** *npl* : ingresos *mpl*, entradas *fpl*
receivable [rɪ'si:vəbəl] *adj* **accounts receivable** : cuentas por cobrar
receive [rɪ'si:v] *vt* **-ceived; -ceiving 1** GET : recibir ⟨to receive a letter : recibir una carta⟩ ⟨to receive a blow : recibir un golpe⟩ **2** WELCOME : acoger, recibir ⟨to receive guests : tener invitados⟩ **3** : recibir, captar (señales de radio)
receiver [rɪ'si:vər] *n* **1** : receptor *m*, -tora *f* (en futbol americano) **2** : receptor *m* (de radio o televisión) **3 telephone receiver** : auricular *m*
recent ['ri:sənt] *adj* : reciente — **recently** *adv*

receptacle [ri'sɛptɪkəl] *n* : receptáculo *m*, recipiente *m*

reception [ri'sɛpʃən] *n* : recepción *f*

receptionist [ri'sɛpʃənɪst] *n* : recepcionista *mf*

receptive [ri'sɛptɪv] *adj* : receptivo

receptivity [ˌri:ˌsɛp'tɪvəti] *n* : receptividad *f*

recess¹ ['ri:ˌsɛs, rɪ'sɛs] *vt* 1 : poner en un hueco ⟨recessed lighting : iluminación empotrada⟩ 2 ADJOURN : suspender, levantar

recess² *n* 1 ALCOVE : hueco *m*, nicho *m* 2 BREAK : receso *m*, descanso *m*, recreo *m* (en el colegio)

recession [ri'sɛʃən] *n* : recesión *f*, depresión *f* económica

recessive [ri'sɛsɪv] *adj* : recesivo

recharge [ˌri:'tʃɑrdʒ] *vt* **-charged; -charging** : recargar

rechargeable [ˌri:'tʃɑrdʒəbəl] *adj* : recargable

recipe ['rɛsəˌpi:] *n* : receta *f*

recipient [ri'sɪpiənt] *n* : recipiente *mf*

reciprocal [ri'sɪprəkəl] *adj* : recíproco

reciprocate [ri'sɪprəˌkeɪt] *vi* **-cated; -cating** : reciprocar

reciprocity [ˌrɛsə'prɑsəti] *n, pl* **-ties** : reciprocidad *f*

recital [ri'saɪtəl] *n* 1 PERFORMANCE : recital *m* 2 ENUMERATION : relato *m*, enumeración *f*

recitation [ˌrɛsə'teɪʃən] *n* : recitación *f*

recite [ri'saɪt] *vt* **-cited; -citing** 1 : recitar (un poema, etc.) 2 RECOUNT : narrar, relatar, enumerar

reckless ['rɛkləs] *adj* : imprudente, temerario — **recklessly** *adv*

recklessness ['rɛkləsnəs] *n* : imprudencia *f*, temeridad *f*

reckon ['rɛkən] *vt* 1 CALCULATE : calcular, contar 2 CONSIDER : considerar

reckoning ['rɛkənɪŋ] *n* 1 CALCULATION : cálculo *m* 2 SETTLEMENT : ajuste *m* de cuentas ⟨day of reckoning : día del juicio final⟩

reclaim [ri'kleɪm] *vt* 1 : ganar, sanear ⟨to reclaim marshy land : sanear las tierras pantanosas⟩ 2 RECOVER : recobrar, reciclar ⟨to reclaim old tires : reciclar llantas desechadas⟩ 3 REGAIN : reclamar, recuperar ⟨to reclaim one's rights : reclamar uno sus derechos⟩

recline [ri'klaɪn] *vi* **-clined; -clining** 1 LEAN : reclinarse 2 REPOSE : recostarse

recluse ['rɛˌklu:s, ri'klu:s] *n* : solitario *m*, -ria *f*

recognition [ˌrɛkɪg'nɪʃən] *n* : reconocimiento *m*

recognizable ['rɛkəgˌnaɪzəbəl] *adj* : reconocible

recognize ['rɛkɪgˌnaɪz] *vt* **-nized; -nizing** : reconocer

recoil¹ [ri'kɔɪl] *vi* : retroceder, dar un culatazo

recoil² ['ri:ˌkɔɪl, ri'-] *n* : retroceso *m*, culatazo *m*

recollect [ˌrɛkə'lɛkt] *v* : recordar

recollection [ˌrɛkə'lɛkʃən] *n* : recuerdo *m*

recommend [ˌrɛkə'mɛnd] *vt* 1 : recomendar ⟨she recommended the medicine : recomendó la medicina⟩ 2 ADVISE, COUNSEL : aconsejar, recomendar

recommendation [ˌrɛkəmən'deɪʃən] *n* : recomendación *f*

recompense¹ ['rɛkəmˌpɛns] *vt* **-pensed; -pensing** : indemnizar, recompensar

recompense² *n* : indemnización *f*, compensación *f*

reconcile ['rɛkənˌsaɪl] *v* **-ciled; -ciling** *vt* 1 : reconciliar (personas), conciliar (ideas, etc.) 2 to reconcile oneself to : resignarse a — *vi* MAKE UP : reconciliarse, hacer las paces

reconciliation [ˌrɛkənˌsili'eɪʃən] *n* : reconciliación *f* (con personas), conciliación *f* (con ideas, etc.)

recondite ['rɛkənˌdaɪt, ri'kən-] *adj* : recóndito, abstruso

recondition [ˌri:kən'dɪʃən] *vt* : reacondicionar

reconnaissance [ri'kɑnəzənts, -sənts] *n* : reconocimiento *m*

reconnoiter *or* **reconnoitre** [ˌri:kə'nɔɪtər, ˌrɛkə-] *v* **-tered** *or* **-tred; -tering** *or* **-tring** *vt* : reconocer — *vi* : hacer un reconocimiento

reconsider [ˌri:kən'sɪdər] *vt* : reconsiderar, repensar

reconsideration [ˌri:kənˌsɪdə'reɪʃən] *n* : reconsideración *f*

reconstruct [ˌri:kən'strʌkt] *vt* : reconstruir

reconstruction [ˌri:kən'strʌkʃən] *n* : reconstrucción *f*

record¹ [ri'kɔrd] *vt* 1 WRITE DOWN : anotar, apuntar 2 REGISTER : registrar, hacer constar 3 INDICATE : marcar (una temperatura, etc.) 4 TAPE : grabar

record² ['rɛkərd] *n* 1 DOCUMENT : registro *m*, documento *m* oficial 2 HISTORY : historial *m* ⟨a good academic record : un buen historial académico⟩ ⟨criminal record : antecedentes penales⟩ 3 : récord *m* ⟨the world record : el récord mundial⟩ 4 : disco *m* (de música, etc.) ⟨to make a record : grabar un disco⟩

recorder [ri'kɔrdər] *n* 1 : flauta *f* dulce (instrumento de viento) 2 **tape recorder** : grabadora *f*

recording [ri'kɔrdɪŋ] *n* : grabación *f*

recount¹ [ri'kaʊnt] *vt* 1 NARRATE : narrar, relatar 2 : volver a contar (votos, etc.)

recount² ['ri:ˌkaʊnt, ˌri'-] *n* : recuento *m*

recoup [ri'ku:p] *vt* : recuperar, recobrar

recourse ['ri:ˌkors, ri'-] *n* : recurso *m* ⟨to have recourse to : recurrir a⟩

recover [ri'kʌvər] *vt* REGAIN : recobrar — *vi* RECUPERATE : recuperarse

recovery [ri'kʌvəri] *n, pl* **-eries** : recuperación *f*

re–create [ˌriːkri'eɪt] *vt* **-ated; -ating** : recrear

recreation [ˌrɛkri'eɪʃən] *n* : recreo *m*, esparcimiento *m*, diversión *f*

recreational [ˌrɛkri'eɪʃənəl] *adj* : recreativo, de recreo

recrimination [riˌkrɪmə'neɪʃən] *n* : recriminación *f*

recruit[1] [ri'kruːt] *vt* : reclutar

recruit[2] *n* : recluta *mf*

recruitment [ri'kruːtmənt] *n* : reclutamiento *m*, alistamiento *m*

rectal ['rɛktəl] *adj* : rectal

rectangle ['rɛkˌtæŋgəl] *n* : rectángulo *m*

rectangular [rɛk'tæŋgjələr] *adj* : rectangular

rectify ['rɛktəˌfaɪ] *vt* **-fied; -fying** : rectificar

rectitude ['rɛktəˌtuːd, -ˌtjuːd] *n* : rectitud *f*

rector ['rɛktər] *n* : rector *m*, -tora *f*

rectory ['rɛktəri] *n, pl* **-ries** : rectoría *f*

rectum ['rɛktəm] *n, pl* **-tums** *or* **-ta** [-tə] : recto *m*

recuperate [ri'kuːpəˌreɪt, -'kjuː-] *v* **-ated; -ating** *vt* : recuperar — *vi* : recuperarse, restablecerse

recuperation [riˌkuːpə'reɪʃən, -ˌkjuː-] *n* : recuperación *f*

recur [ri'kər] *vi* **-curred; -curring** : volver a ocurrir, volver a producirse, repetirse

recurrence [ri'kərənts] *n* : repetición *f*, reaparición *f*

recurrent [ri'kərənt] *adj* : recurrente, que se repite

recyclable [ri'saɪkələbəl] *adj* : reciclable

recycle [ri'saɪkəl] *vt* **-cled; -cling** : reciclar

recycling [ri'saɪkəlɪŋ] *n* : reciclaje *m*

red[1] ['rɛd] *adj* **1** : rojo, colorado ⟨to be red in the face : ponerse colorado⟩ ⟨to have red hair : ser pelirrojo⟩ **2** COMMUNIST : rojo, comunista

red[2] *n* **1** : rojo *m*, colorado *m* **2 Red** COMMUNIST : comunista *mf*

red blood cell *n* : glóbulo *m* rojo

red–blooded ['rɛd'blʌdəd] *adj* : vigoroso

redcap ['rɛdˌkæp] → **porter**

redden ['rɛdən] *vt* : enrojecer — *vi* BLUSH : enrojecerse, ruborizarse

reddish ['rɛdɪʃ] *adj* : rojizo

redecorate [ˌriː'dɛkəˌreɪt] *vt* **-rated; -rating** : renovar, pintar de nuevo

redeem [ri'diːm] *vt* **1** RESCUE, SAVE : rescatar, salvar **2** : desempeñar ⟨she redeemed it from the pawnshop : lo desempeñó de la casa de empeños⟩ **3** : redimir (en religión) **4** : canjear, vender ⟨to redeem coupons : canjear cupones⟩

redeemer [ri'diːmər] *n* : redentor *m*, -tora *f*

redefine [ˌriːdɪ'faɪn] *vt* : redefinir

redemption [ri'dɛmpʃən] *n* : redención *f*

redesign [ˌriːdi'zaɪn] *vt* : rediseñar

red–handed ['rɛd'hændəd] *adj* : con las manos en la masa

redhead ['rɛdˌhɛd] *n* : pelirrojo *m*, -ja *f*

red–hot ['rɛd'hɑt] *adj* **1** : al rojo vivo, candente **2** CURRENT : de candente actualidad **3** POPULAR : de gran popularidad

rediscover [ˌriːdi'skʌvər] *vt* : redescubrir

redistribute [ˌriːdi'strɪˌbjuːt] *vt* **-uted; -uting** : redistribuir

red–letter ['rɛd'lɛtər] *adj* **red–letter day** : día *m* memorable

redness ['rɛdnəs] *n* : rojez *f*

redo [ˌriː'duː] *vt* **-did** [-dɪd]; **-done** [-'dʌn]; **-doing** **1** : hacer de nuevo **2** → **redecorate**

redolence ['rɛdələnts] *n* : fragancia *f*

redolent ['rɛdələnt] *adj* **1** FRAGRANT : fragante, oloroso **2** SUGGESTIVE : evocador

redouble [ri'dʌbəl] *vt* **-bled; -bling** : redoblar, intensificar (esfuerzos, etc.)

redoubtable [r'dauɾəbəl] *adj* : temible

redress [ri'drɛs] *vt* : reparar, remediar, enmendar

red snapper *n* : pargo *m*, huachinango *m Mex*

red tape *n* : papeleo *m*

reduce [ri'duːs, -'djuːs] *v* **-duced; -ducing** *vt* **1** LESSEN : reducir, disminuir, rebajar (precios) **2** DEMOTE : bajar de categoría, degradar **3 to be reduced to** : verse rebajado a, verse forzado a **4 to reduce someone to tears** : hacer llorar a alguien — *vi* SLIM : adelgazar

reduction [ri'dʌkʃən] *n* : reducción *f*, rebaja *f*

redundancy [ri'dʌndəntsi] *n, pl* **-cies** **1** : superfluidad *f* **2** REPETITION : redundancia *f*

redundant [ri'dʌndənt] *adj* : superfluo, redundante

redwood ['rɛdˌwʊd] *n* : secoya *f*

reed ['riːd] *n* **1** : caña *f*, carrizo *m*, junco *m* **2** : lengüeta *f* (para instrumentos de viento)

reef ['riːf] *n* : arrecife *m*, escollo *m*

reek[1] ['riːk] *vi* : apestar

reek[2] *n* : hedor *m*

reel[1] ['riːl] *vt* **1 to reel in** : enrollar, sacar (un pez) del agua **2 to reel off** : recitar de un tirón — *vi* **1** SPIN, WHIRL : girar, dar vueltas **2** STAGGER : tambalearse

reel[2] *n* **1** : carrete *m* (de pescar etc.), rollo *m* (de fotos) **2** : baile *m* escocés **3** STAGGER : tambaleo *m*

reelect [ˌriːɪ'lɛkt] *vt* : reelegir

reenact [ˌriːɪ'nækt] *vt* : representar de nuevo, reconstruir

reenter [ˌriː'ɛntər] *vt* : volver a entrar

reestablish [ˌriːɪ'stæblɪʃ] *vt* : restablecer

reevaluate [ˌriːɪ'væljuˌeɪt] *vt* **-ated; -ating** : revaluar

reevaluation [ˌriːɪˌvæljuˈeɪʃən] *n* : revaluación *f*

reexamine [ˌriːɪgˈzæmən, -g-] vt **-ined; -ining** : volver a examinar, reexaminar

refer [riˈfər] v **-ferred; -ferring** vt DIRECT, SEND : remitir, enviar ⟨to refer a patient to a specialist : enviar a un paciente a un especialista⟩ — vi **to refer to** MENTION : referirse a, aludir a

referee¹ [ˌrɛfəˈriː] v **-eed; -eeing** : arbitrar

referee² n : árbitro m, -tra f; réferi mf

reference [ˈrɛfrənts, ˈrɛfə-] n **1** ALLUSION : referencia f, alusión f ⟨to make reference to : hacer referencia a⟩ **2** CONSULTATION : consulta f ⟨for future reference : para futuras consultas⟩ **3** or **reference book** : libro m de consulta **4** TESTIMONIAL : informe m, referencia f, recomendación f

referendum [ˌrɛfəˈrɛndəm] n, pl **-da** [-də] or **-dums** : referéndum m

refill¹ [ˌriːˈfɪl] vt : rellenar

refill² [ˈriːˌfɪl] n : recambio m

refinance [ˌriːˈfaɪˌnænts] vt **-nanced; -nancing** : refinanciar

refine [riˈfaɪn] vt **-fined; -fining 1** : refinar (azúcar, petróleo, etc.) **2** PERFECT : perfeccionar, pulir

refined [riˈfaɪnd] adj **1** : refinado (dícese del azúcar, etc.) **2** CULTURED : culto, educado, refinado

refinement [riˈfaɪnmənt] n : refinamiento m, fineza f, finura f

refinery [riˈfaɪnəri] n, pl **-eries** : refinería f

reflect [riˈflɛkt] vt **1** : reflejar ⟨to reflect light : reflejar la luz⟩ ⟨happiness is reflected in her face : la felicidad se refleja en su cara⟩ **2 to reflect that** : pensar que, considerar que — vi **1 to reflect on** : reflexionar sobre **2 to reflect badly on** : desacreditar, perjudicar

reflection [riˈflɛkʃən] n **1** : reflexión f, reflejo m (de la luz, de imágenes, etc.) **2** THOUGHT : reflexión f, meditación f

reflective [riˈflɛktɪv] adj **1** THOUGHTFUL : reflexivo, pensativo **2** : reflectante (en física)

reflector [riˈflɛktər] n : reflector m

reflex [ˈriːˌflɛks] n : reflejo m

reflexive [riˈflɛksɪv] adj : reflexivo ⟨a reflexive verb : un verbo reflexivo⟩

reform¹ [riˈfɔrm] vt : reformar — vi : reformarse

reform² n : reforma f

reformation [ˌrɛfərˈmeɪʃən] n : reforma f ⟨the Reformation : la Reforma⟩

reformatory [riˈfɔrməˌtori] n, pl **-ries** : reformatorio m

reformer [riˈfɔrmər] n : reformador m, -dora f

refract [riˈfrækt] vt : refractar — vi : refractarse

refraction [riˈfrækʃən] n : refracción f

refractory [riˈfræktəri] adj OBSTINATE : refractario, obstinado

refrain¹ [riˈfreɪn] vi **to refrain from** : abstenerse de

refrain² n : estribillo m (en música)

refresh [riˈfrɛʃ] vt : refrescar ⟨to refresh one's memory : refrescarle la memoria a uno⟩

refreshing [riˈfrɛʃɪŋ] adj : refrescante ⟨a refreshing sleep : un sueño reparador⟩

refreshment [riˈfrɛʃmənt] n **1** : refresco m **2 refreshments** npl : refrigerio m

refrigerate [riˈfrɪdʒəˌreɪt] vt **-ated; -ating** : refrigerar

refrigeration [riˌfrɪdʒəˈreɪʃən] n : refrigeración f

refrigerator [riˈfrɪdʒəˌreɪtər] n : refrigerador m, -dora f, nevera f

refuel [riːˈfjuːəl] v **-eled** or **-elled; -eling** or **-elling** vi : repostar — vt : llenar de combustible

refuge [ˈrɛˌfjuːdʒ] n : refugio m

refugee [ˌrɛfjʊˈdʒiː] n : refugiado m, -da f

refund¹ [riˈfʌnd, ˈriˌfʌnd] vt : reembolsar, devolver

refund² [ˈriːˌfʌnd] n : reembolso m, devolución f

refundable [riˈfʌndəbəl] adj : reembolsable

refurbish [riˈfərbɪʃ] vt : renovar, restaurar

refusal [riˈfjuːzəl] n : negativa f, rechazo m, denegación f (de una petición)

refuse¹ [riˈfjuːz] vt **-fused; -fusing 1** REJECT : rechazar, rehusar **2** DENY : negar, rehusar, denegar ⟨to refuse permission : negar el permiso⟩ **3 to refuse to** : negarse a

refuse² [ˈrɛˌfjuːs, -ˌfjuːz] n : basura f, desechos mpl, desperdicios mpl

refutation [ˌrɛfjʊˈteɪʃən] n : refutación f

refute [riˈfjuːt] vt **-futed; -futing 1** DENY : desmentir, negar **2** DISPROVE : refutar, rebatir

regain [riˈgeɪn] vt **1** RECOVER : recuperar, recobrar **2** REACH : alcanzar ⟨to regain the shore : llegar a la tierra⟩

regal [ˈriːgəl] adj : real, regio

regale [riˈgeɪl] vt **-galed; -galing 1** ENTERTAIN : agasajar, entretener **2** AMUSE, DELIGHT : deleitar, divertir

regalia [riˈgeɪljə] npl : ropaje m, vestiduras fpl, adornos mpl

regard¹ [riˈgɑrd] vt **1** OBSERVE : observar, mirar **2** HEED : tener en cuenta, hacer caso de **3** CONSIDER : considerar **4** RESPECT : respetar ⟨highly regarded : muy estimado⟩ **5 as regards** : en cuanto a, en lo que se refiere a

regard² n **1** CONSIDERATION : consideración f **2** ESTEEM : respeto m, estima f **3** PARTICULAR : aspecto m, sentido m ⟨in this regard : en este sentido⟩ **4 regards** npl : saludos mpl, recuerdos mpl **5 with regard to** : con relación a, con respecto a

regarding [riˈgɑrdɪŋ] prep : con respecto a, en cuanto a

regardless [riˈgɑrdləs] adv : a pesar de todo

regardless of *prep* : a pesar de, sin tener en cuenta ⟨regardless of our mistakes : a pesar de nuestros errores⟩ ⟨regardless of age : sin tener en cuenta la edad⟩

regenerate [ri'ʤɛnə,reɪt] *v* **-ated; -ating** *vt* : regenerar — *vi* : regenerarse

regeneration [ri,ʤɛnə'reɪʃən] *n* : regeneración *f*

regent ['ri:ʤənt] *n* **1** RULER : regente *mf* **2** : miembro *m* de la junta directiva (de una universidad, etc.)

regime [reɪ'ʒi:m, rɪ-] *n* : régimen *m*

regimen ['rɛʤəmən] *n* : régimen *m*

regiment¹ ['rɛʤə,mɛnt] *vt* : reglamentar

regiment² ['rɛʤəmənt] *n* : regimiento *m*

region ['ri:ʤən] *n* **1** : región *f* **2 in the region of** : alrededor de

regional ['ri:ʤənəl] *adj* : regional — **regionally** *adv*

register¹ ['rɛʤəstər] *vt* **1** RECORD : registrar, inscribir **2** INDICATE : marcar (temperatura, medidas, etc.) **3** REVEAL : manifestar, acusar ⟨to register surprise : acusar sorpresa⟩ **4** : certificar (correo) — *vi* ENROLL : inscribirse, matricularse

register² *n* : registro *m*

registrar ['rɛʤə,strar] *n* : registrador *m*, -dora *f* oficial

registration [,rɛʤə'streɪʃən] *n* **1** REGISTERING : inscripción *f*, matriculación *f*, registro *m* **2 or registration number** : matrícula *f*, número *m* de matrícula

registry ['rɛʤəstri] *n, pl* **-tries** : registro *m*

regress [ri'grɛs] *vi* : retroceder

regression [ri'grɛʃən] *n* : retroceso *m*, regresión *f*

regressive [ri'grɛsɪv] *adj* : regresivo

regret¹ [ri'grɛt] *vt* **-gretted; -gretting** : arrepentirse de, lamentar ⟨he regrets nothing : no se arrepiente de nada⟩ ⟨I regret to tell you : lamento decirle⟩

regret² *n* **1** REMORSE : arrepentimiento *m*, remordimientos *mpl* **2** SADNESS : pesar *m*, dolor *m* **3 regrets** *npl* : excusas *fpl* ⟨to send one's regrets : excusarse⟩

regretful [ri'grɛtfəl] *adj* : arrepentido, pesaroso

regretfully [ri'grɛtfəli] *adv* : con pesar

regrettable [ri'grɛtəbəl] *adj* : lamentable — **regrettably** [-bli] *adv*

regular¹ ['rɛgjələr] *adj* **1** NORMAL : regular, normal, usual **2** STEADY : uniforme, regular ⟨a regular pace : un paso regular⟩ **3** CUSTOMARY, HABITUAL : habitual, de costumbre

regular² *n* : cliente *mf* habitual

regularity [,rɛgjə'lærəti] *n, pl* **-ties** : regularidad *f*

regularly ['rɛgjələrli] *adv* : regularmente, con regularidad

regulate ['rɛgjə,leɪt] *vt* **-lated; -lating** : regular

regulation [,rɛgjə'leɪʃən] *n* **1** REGULATING : regulación *f* **2** RULE : regla *f*,

reglamento *m*, norma *f* ⟨safety regulations : reglas de seguridad⟩

regulator ['rɛgjə,leɪtər] *n* **1** : regulador *m* (mecanismo) **2** : persona *f* que regula

regulatory ['rɛgjələ,tori] *adj* : regulador

regurgitate [ri'gərʤə,teɪt] *v* **-tated; -tating** : regurgitar, vomitar

rehabilitate [,ri:hə'bɪlə,teɪt, ,ri:ə-] *vt* **-tated; -tating** : rehabilitar

rehabilitation [,ri:hə,bɪlə'teɪʃən, ,ri:ə-] *n* : rehabilitación *f*

rehearsal [ri'hərsəl] *n* : ensayo *m*

rehearse [ri'hərs] *v* **-hearsed; -hearsing** : ensayar

reheat [,ri:'hi:t] *vt* : recalentar

reign¹ ['reɪn] *vi* **1** RULE : reinar **2** PREVAIL : reinar, predominar ⟨the reigning champion : el actual campeón⟩

reign² *n* : reinado *m*

reimburse [,ri:əm'bərs] *vt* **-bursed; -bursing** : reembolsar

reimbursement [,ri:əm'bərsmənt] *n* : reembolso *m*

rein¹ ['reɪn] *vt* : refrenar (un caballo)

rein² *n* **1** : rienda *f* ⟨to give free rein to : dar rienda suelta a⟩ **2** CHECK : control *m* ⟨to keep a tight rein on : llevar un estricto control de⟩

reincarnation [,ri:ɪn,kɑr'neɪʃən] *n* : reencarnación *f*

reindeer ['reɪn,dɪr] *n* : reno *m*

reinforce [,ri:ən'fors] *vt* **-forced; -forcing** : reforzar

reinforcement [,ri:ən'forsmənt] *n* : refuerzo *m*

reinstate [,ri:ən'steɪt] *vt* **-stated; -stating** **1** : reintegrar, restituir (una persona) **2** RESTORE : restablecer (un servicio, etc.)

reinstatement [,ri:ən'steɪtmənt] *n* : reintegración *f*, restitución *f*, restablecimiento *m*

reiterate [ri'ɪtə,reɪt] *vt* **-ated; -ating** : reiterar, repetir

reiteration [ri,ɪtə'reɪʃən] *n* : reiteración *f*, repetición *f*

reject¹ [ri'ʤɛkt] *vt* : rechazar

reject² ['ri:,ʤɛkt] *n* : desecho *m* (cosa), persona *f* rechazada

rejection [ri'ʤɛkʃən] *n* : rechazo *m*

rejoice [ri'ʤɔɪs] *vi* **-joiced; -joicing** : alegrarse, regocijarse

rejoin [,ri:'ʤɔɪn] *vt* **1** : reincorporarse a, reintegrarse a ⟨he rejoined the firm : se reincorporó a la firma⟩ **2** [ri'-] REPLY, RETORT : replicar

rejoinder [ri'ʤɔɪndər] *n* : réplica *f*

rejuvenate [ri'ʤu:və,neɪt] *vt* **-nated; -nating** : rejuvenecer

rejuvenation [ri,ʤu:və'neɪʃən] *n* : rejuvenecimiento *m*

rekindle [,ri:'kɪndəl] *vt* **-dled; -dling** : reavivar

relapse¹ [ri'læps] *vi* **-lapsed; -lapsing** : recaer, volver a caer

relapse² ['ri:,læps, ri'læps] *n* : recaída *f*

relate [ri'leɪt] v **-lated; -lating** vt **1** TELL : relatar, contar **2** ASSOCIATE : relacionar, asociar ⟨to relate crime to poverty : relacionar la delincuencia a la pobreza⟩ — vi **1** CONNECT : conectar, estar relacionado (con) **2** INTERACT : relacionarse (con), llevarse bien (con) **3 to relate to** UNDERSTAND : identificarse con, simpatizar con

related [ri'leɪtəd] adj : emparentado ⟨to be related to : ser pariente de⟩

relation [ri'leɪʃən] n **1** NARRATION : relato m, narración f **2** RELATIVE : pariente mf, familiar mf **3** RELATIONSHIP : relación f ⟨in relation to : en relación con, con relación a⟩ **4 relations** npl : relaciones fpl ⟨public relations : relaciones públicas⟩

relationship [ri'leɪʃən͜ʃɪp] n **1** CONNECTION : relación f **2** KINSHIP : parentesco m

relative[1] ['rɛlətɪv] adj : relativo — **relatively** adv

relative[2] n : pariente mf, familiar mf

relativism ['rɛlətɪˌvɪzəm] n : relativismo m

relativity [ˌrɛlə'tɪvəti] n, pl **-ties** : relatividad f

relax [ri'læks] vt : relajar, aflojar — vi : relajarse

relaxation [ˌriːˌlæk'seɪʃən] n **1** RELAXING : relajación f, aflojamiento m **2** DIVERSION : esparcimiento m, distracción f

relaxing [ri'læksɪŋ] adj : relajante

relay[1] ['riːˌleɪ, ri'leɪ] vt **-layed; -laying** : transmitir

relay[2] ['riːˌleɪ] n **1** : relevo m **2** or **relay race** : carrera de relevos

release[1] [ri'liːs] vt **-leased; -leasing 1** FREE : liberar, poner en libertad **2** LOOSEN : soltar, aflojar ⟨to release the brake : soltar el freno⟩ **3** RELINQUISH : renunciar a, ceder **4** ISSUE : publicar (un libro), estrenar (una película), sacar (un disco)

release[2] n **1** LIBERATION : liberación f, puesta f en libertad **2** RELINQUISHMENT : cesión f (de propiedad, etc.) **3** ISSUE : estreno m (de una película), puesta f en venta (de un disco), publicación f (de un libro) **4** ESCAPE : escape m, fuga f (de un gas)

relegate ['rɛləˌgeɪt] vt **-gated; -gating** : relegar

relent [ri'lɛnt] vi : ablandarse, ceder

relentless [ri'lɛntləs] adj : implacable, sin tregua

relentlessly [ri'lɛntləsli] adv : implacablemente

relevance ['rɛləvənts] n : pertinencia f, relación f

relevant ['rɛləvənt] adj : pertinente — **relevantly** adv

reliability [riˌlaɪə'bɪləti] n, pl **-ties 1** : fiabilidad f, seguridad f (de una cosa) **2** : formalidad f, seriedad f (de una persona)

reliable [ri'laɪəbəl] adj : confiable, fiable, fidedigno, seguro

reliably [ri'laɪəbli] adv : sin fallar ⟨to be reliably informed : saber (algo) de fuentes fidedignas⟩

reliance [ri'laɪənts] n **1** DEPENDENCE : dependencia f **2** CONFIDENCE : confianza f

reliant [ri'laɪənt] adj : dependiente

relic ['rɛlɪk] n **1** : reliquia f **2** VESTIGE : vestigio m

relief [ri'liːf] n **1** : alivio m, desahogo m ⟨relief from pain : alivio del dolor⟩ **2** AID, WELFARE : ayuda f (benéfica), asistencia f social **3** : relieve m (en la escultura) ⟨relief map : mapa en relieve⟩ **4** REPLACEMENT : relevo m

relieve [ri'liːv] vt **-lieved; -lieving 1** ALLEVIATE : aliviar, mitigar ⟨to feel relieved : sentirse aliviado⟩ **2** FREE : liberar, eximir ⟨to relieve someone of responsibility for : eximir a alguien de la responsabilidad de⟩ **3** REPLACE : relevar (a un centinela, etc.) **4** BREAK : romper ⟨to relieve the monotony : romper la monotonía⟩

religion [ri'lɪdʒən] n : religión f

religious [ri'lɪdʒəs] adj : religioso — **religiously** adv

relinquish [ri'lɪŋkwɪʃ, -'lɪn-] vt **1** GIVE UP : renunciar a, abandonar **2** RELEASE : soltar

relish[1] ['rɛlɪʃ] vt : saborear (comida), disfrutar con (una idea, una perspectiva, etc.)

relish[2] n **1** ENJOYMENT : gusto m, deleite m **2** : salsa f (condimento)

relive [ˌriː'lɪv] vt **-lived; -living** : revivir

relocate [ˌriːˈloʊˌkeɪt, ˌriːloʊˈkeɪt] v **-cated; -cating** vt : reubicar, trasladar — vi : trasladarse

relocation [ˌriːloʊ'keɪʃən] n : reubicación f, traslado m

reluctance [ri'lʌktənts] n : renuencia f, reticencia f, desgana f

reluctant [ri'lʌktənt] adj : renuente, reacio, reticente

reluctantly [ri'lʌktəntli] adv : a regañadientes

rely [ri'laɪ] vi **-lied; -lying 1** DEPEND : depender (de), contar (con) **2** TRUST : confiar (en)

remain [ri'meɪn] vi **1** : quedar ⟨very little remains : queda muy poco⟩ ⟨the remaining 10 minutes : los 10 minutos que quedan⟩ **2** STAY : quedarse, permanecer **3** CONTINUE : continuar, seguir ⟨to remain the same : continuar siendo igual⟩ **4 to remain to** : quedar por ⟨to remain to be done : quedar por hacer⟩ ⟨it remains to be seen : está por ver⟩

remainder [ri'meɪndər] n : resto m, remanente m

remains [ri'meɪnz] npl : restos mpl ⟨mortal remains : restos mortales⟩

remake[1] [riː'meɪk] vt **-made; -making 1** TRANSFORM : rehacer **2** : hacer una nueva versión de (una película, etc.)

remake² ['ri:ˌmeɪk] *n* : nueva versión *f*
remark¹ [ri'mɑrk] *vt* **1** NOTICE : observar **2** SAY : comentar, observar — *vi* **to remark on** : hacer observaciones sobre
remark² *n* : comentario *m*, observación *f*
remarkable [ri'mɑrkəbəl] *adj* : extraordinario, notable — **remarkably** [-bli] *adv*
rematch ['ri:ˌmætʃ] *n* : revancha *f*
remedial [ri'mi:diəl] *adj* : correctivo ⟨remedial classes : clases para alumnos atrasados⟩
remedy¹ ['rɛmədi] *vt* **-died; -dying** : remediar
remedy² *n, pl* **-dies** : remedio *m*, medicamento *m*
remember [ri'mɛmbər] *vt* **1** RECOLLECT : acordarse de, recordar **2** : no olvidar ⟨remember my words : no olvides mis palabras⟩ ⟨to remember to : acordarse de⟩ **3** : dar saludos, dar recuerdos ⟨remember me to her : dale saludos de mi parte⟩ **4** COMMEMORATE : recordar, conmemorar
remembrance [ri'mɛmbrən/s] *n* **1** RECOLLECTION : recuerdo *m* ⟨in remembrance of : en conmemoración de⟩ **2** MEMENTO : recuerdo *m*
remind [ri'maɪnd] *vt* : recordar ⟨remind me to do it : recuérdame que lo haga⟩ ⟨she reminds me of Clara : me recuerda de Clara⟩
reminder [ri'maɪndər] *n* : recuerdo *m*
reminisce [ˌrɛmə'nɪs] *vi* **-nisced; -niscing** : rememorar los viejos tiempos
reminiscence [ˌrɛmə'nɪsən/s] *n* : recuerdo *m*, reminiscencia *f*
reminiscent [ˌrɛmə'nɪsənt] *adj* **1** NOSTALGIC : reminiscente, nostálgico **2** SUGGESTIVE : evocador, que recuerda — **reminiscently** *adv*
remiss [ri'mɪs] *adj* : negligente, descuidado, remiso
remission [ri'mɪʃən] *n* : remisión *f*
remit [ri'mɪt] *vt* **-mitted; -mitting 1** PARDON : perdonar **2** SEND : remitir, enviar (dinero)
remittance [ri'mɪtən/s] *n* : remesa *f*
remnant ['rɛmnənt] *n* : restos *mpl*, vestigio *m*
remodel [ri'mɑdəl] *vt* **-eled** *or* **-elled; -eling** *or* **-elling** : remodelar, reformar
remonstrate [ri'mɑnˌstreɪt] *vi* **-strated; -strating** : protestar ⟨to remonstrate with someone : quejarse a alguien⟩
remorse [ri'mɔrs] *n* : remordimiento *m*
remorseful [ri'mɔrsfəl] *adj* : arrepentido, lleno de remordimiento
remorseless [ri'mɔrsləs] *adj* **1** PITILESS : despiadado **2** RELENTLESS : implacable
remote [ri'mo:t] *adj* **-moter; -est 1** FAR-OFF : lejano, remoto ⟨remote countries : países remotos⟩ ⟨in the remote past : en el pasado lejano⟩ **2** SECLUDED : recóndito **3** : a distancia, remoto ⟨remote control : control remoto⟩ **4** SLIGHT : remoto **5** ALOOF : distante
remotely [ri'mo:tli] *adv* **1** SLIGHTLY : remotamente **2** DISTANTLY : en un lugar remoto, muy lejos
remoteness [ri'mo:tnəs] *n* : lejanía *f*
removable [ri'mu:vəbəl] *adj* : removible
removal [ri'mu:vəl] *n* : separación *f*, extracción *f*, supresión *f* (en algo escrito), eliminación *f* (de problemas, etc.)
remove [ri'mu:v] *vt* **-moved; -moving 1** : quitar, quitarse ⟨remove the lid : quite la tapa⟩ ⟨to remove one's hat : quitarse el sombrero⟩ **2** EXTRACT : sacar, extraer ⟨to remove the contents of : sacar el contenido de⟩ **3** ELIMINATE : eliminar, disipar
remunerate [ri'mju:nəˌreɪt] *vt* **-ated; -ating** : remunerar
remuneration [ri,mju:nə'reɪʃən] *n* : remuneración *f*
remunerative [ri'mju:nərətɪv, -ˌreɪ-] *adj* : remunerativo
renaissance [ˌrɛnə'sɑn/s, -'zɑn/s; 'rɛnə-ˌ-] *n* : renacimiento *m* ⟨the Renaissance : el Renacimiento⟩
renal ['ri:nəl] *adj* : renal
rename [ˌri:'neɪm] *vt* **-named; -naming** : ponerle un nombre nuevo a
rend ['rɛnd] *vt* **rent** ['rɛnt]; **rending** : desgarrar
render ['rɛndər] *vt* **1** : derretir ⟨to render lard : derretir la manteca⟩ **2** GIVE : prestar, dar ⟨to render aid : prestar ayuda⟩ **3** MAKE : hacer, volver, dejar ⟨it rendered him helpless : lo dejó incapacitado⟩ **4** TRANSLATE : traducir, verter ⟨to render into English : traducir al inglés⟩
rendezvous ['rɑndɪˌvu:, -deɪ-] *ns & pl* : encuentro *m*, cita *f*
rendition [rɛn'dɪʃən] *n* : interpretación *f*
renegade ['rɛnɪˌgeɪd] *n* : renegado *m*, -da *f*
renege [ri'nɪg, -'nɛg] *vi* **-neged; -neging** : no cumplir con (una promesa, etc.)
renew [ri'nu:, -'nju:] *vt* **1** REVIVE : renovar, reavivar ⟨to renew the sentiments of youth : renovar los sentimientos de la juventud⟩ **2** RESUME : reanudar **3** EXTEND : renovar ⟨to renew a subscription : renovar una suscripción⟩
renewable [ri'nu:əbəl, -'nju:-] *adj* : renovable
renewal [ri'nu:əl, -'nju:-] *n* : renovación *f*
renounce [ri'naʊn/s] *vt* **-nounced; -nouncing** : renunciar a
renovate ['rɛnəˌveɪt] *vt* **-vated; -vating** : restaurar, renovar
renovation [ˌrɛnə'veɪʃən] *n* : restauración *f*, renovación *f*
renown [ri'naʊn] *n* : renombre *m*, fama *f*, celebridad *f*
renowned [ri'naʊnd] *adj* : renombrado, célebre, famoso
rent¹ ['rɛnt] *vt* : rentar, alquilar

rent² *n* **1** : renta *f*, alquiler *m* ⟨for rent : se alquila⟩ **2** RIP : rasgadura *f*

rental¹ ['rɛntəl] *adj* RENT : de alquiler

rental² *n* : alquiler *m*

renter ['rɛntər] *n* : arrendatario *m*, -ria *f*

renunciation [ri,nʌntsi'eɪʃən] *n* : renuncia *f*

reopen [,riː'oːpən] *vt* : volver a abrir

reorganization [,riːˌɔrgənə'zeɪʃən] *n* : reorganización *f*

reorganize [,riː'ɔrgən,aɪz] *vt* **-nized; -nizing** : reorganizar

repair¹ [ri'pær] *vt* : reparar, arreglar, refaccionar

repair² *n* **1** : reparación *f*, arreglo *m* **2** CONDITION : estado *m* ⟨in bad repair : en mal estado⟩

reparation [,rɛpə'reɪʃən] *n* **1** AMENDS : reparación *f* **2 reparations** *npl* COMPENSATION : indemnización *f*

repartee [,rɛpər'tiː, -,pɑr-, -'teɪ] *n* : intercambio *m* de réplicas ingeniosas

repast [ri'pæst, 'ri:,pæst] *n* : comida *f*

repatriate [ri'peɪtri,eɪt] *vt* **-ated; -ating** : repatriar

repay [ri'peɪ] *vt* **-paid; -paying** : pagar, devolver, reembolsar

repeal¹ [ri'pi:l] *vt* : abrogar, revocar

repeal² *n* : abrogación *f*, revocación *f*

repeat¹ [ri'pi:t] *vt* : repetir

repeat² *n* : repetición *f*

repeatedly [ri'pi:tədli] *adv* : repetidamente, repetidas veces

repel [ri'pɛl] *vt* **-pelled; -pelling 1** REPULSE : repeler (un enemigo, etc.) **2** RESIST : repeler **3** REJECT : rechazar, repeler **4** DISGUST : repugnar, darle asco (a alguien)

repellent *or* **repellant** [ri'pɛlənt] *n* : repelente *m*

repent [ri'pɛnt] *vi* : arrepentirse

repentance [ri'pɛntənts] *n* : arrepentimiento *m*

repentant [ri'pɛntənt] *adj* : arrepentido

repercussion [,riːpər'kʌʃən, ,rɛpər-] *n* : repercusión *f*

repertoire ['rɛpər,twɑr] *n* : repertorio *m*

repertory ['rɛpər,tori] *n, pl* **-ries** : repertorio *m*

repetition [,rɛpə'tɪʃən] *n* : repetición *f*

repetitious [,rɛpə'tɪʃəs] *adj* : repetitivo, reiterativo — **repetitiously** *adv*

repetitive [ri'pɛtətɪv] *adj* : repetitivo, reiterativo

replace [ri'pleɪs] *vt* **-placed; -placing 1** : volver a poner ⟨replace it in the drawer : vuelve a ponerlo en el cajón⟩ **2** SUBSTITUTE : reemplazar, sustituir **3** : reponer ⟨to replace the worn carpet : reponer la alfombra raída⟩

replaceable [ri'pleɪsəbəl] *adj* : reemplazable

replacement [ri'pleɪsmənt] *n* **1** SUBSTITUTION : reemplazo *m*, sustitución *f* **2** SUBSTITUTE : sustituto *m*, -ta *f*; suplente *mf* (persona) **3 replacement part** : repuesto *m*, pieza *f* de recambio

replenish [ri'plɛnɪʃ] *vt* : rellenar, llenar de nuevo

replenishment [ri'plɛnɪʃmənt] *n* : reabastecimiento *m*

replete [ri'pli:t] *adj* : repleto, lleno

replica ['rɛplɪkə] *n* : réplica *f*, reproducción *f*

replicate ['rɛplə,keɪt] *v* **-cated; -cating** *vt* : duplicar, repetir — *vi* : duplicarse

replication [,rɛplə'keɪʃən] *n* **1** REPRODUCTION : reproducción *f* **2** REPETITION : repetición *f* **3** : replicación *f* (celular)

reply¹ [ri'plaɪ] *vi* **-plied; -plying** : contestar, responder

reply² *n, pl* **-plies** : respuesta *f*, contestación *f*

report¹ [ri'port] *vt* **1** ANNOUNCE : relatar, anunciar **2** : dar parte de, informar de, reportar ⟨he reported an accident : dio parte de un accidente⟩ ⟨to report a crime : denunciar un delito⟩ **3** : informar acerca de (en un periódico, la televisión, etc.) — *vi* **1** : hacer un informe, informar **2 to report for duty** : presentarse, reportarse

report² *n* **1** RUMOR : rumor *m* **2** REPUTATION : reputación *f* ⟨people of evil report : personas de mala fama⟩ **3** ACCOUNT : informe *m*, reportaje *m* (en un periódico, etc.) **4** BANG : estallido *m* (de un arma de fuego)

report card *n* : boletín *m* de calificaciones, boletín *m* de notas

reportedly [ri'portədli] *adv* : según se dice, según se informa

reporter [ri'portər] *n* : periodista *mf*; reportero *m*, -ra *f*

repose¹ [ri'po:z] *vi* **-posed; -posing** : reposar, descansar

repose² *n* **1** : reposo *m*, descanso *m* **2** CALM : calma *f*, tranquilidad *f*

repository [ri'pazə,tori] *n, pl* **-ries** : depósito *m*

repossess [,riːpə'zɛs] *vt* : recuperar, recobrar la posesión de

reprehensible [,rɛpri'hɛntsəbəl] *adj* : reprensible — **reprehensibly** *adv*

represent [,rɛpri'zɛnt] *vt* **1** SYMBOLIZE : representar ⟨the flag represents our country : la bandera representa a nuestro país⟩ **2** : representar, ser un representante de ⟨an attorney who represents his client : un abogado que representa su cliente⟩ **3** PORTRAY : presentar ⟨he represents himself as a friend : se presenta como amigo⟩

representation [,rɛpriˌzɛn'teɪʃən, -zən-] *n* : representación *f*

representative¹ [,rɛpri'zɛntətɪv] *adj* : representativo

representative² *n* **1** : representante *mf* **2** : diputado *m*, -da *f* (en la política)

repress [ri'prɛs] *vt* : reprimir

repression [ri'prɛʃən] *n* : represión *f*

repressive [ri'prɛsɪv] *adj* : represivo

reprieve¹ [ri'pri:v] *vt* **-prieved; -prieving** : indultar

reprieve² *n* : indulto *m*

reprimand¹ ['rɛprə,mænd] *vt* : reprender

reprimand² *n* : reprimenda *f*
reprint¹ [ri'prɪnt] *vt* : reimprimir
reprint² ['ri:ˌprɪnt, ri'prɪnt] *n* : reedición *f*
reprisal [ri'praɪzəl] *n* : represalia *f*
reproach¹ [ri'proːʧ] *vt* : reprochar
reproach² *n* **1** DISGRACE : deshonra *f* **2** REBUKE : reproche *m*, recriminación *f*
reproachful [ri'proːʧfəl] *adj* : de reproche
reproduce [ˌri:prə'duːs, -'djuːs] *v* **-duced; -ducing** *vt* : reproducir — *vi* BREED : reproducirse
reproduction [ˌri:prə'dʌkʃən] *n* : reproducción *f*
reproductive [ˌri:prə'dʌktɪv] *adj* : reproductor
reproof [ri'pruːf] *n* : reprobación *f*, reprimenda *f*, reproche *m*
reprove [ri'pruːv] *vt* **-proved; -proving** : reprender, censurar
reptile ['rɛpˌtaɪl] *n* : reptil *m*
republic [ri'pʌblɪk] *n* : república *f*
republican¹ [ri'pʌblɪkən] *adj* : republicano
republican² *n* : republicano *m*, -na *f*
repudiate [ri'pjuːdiˌeɪt] *vt* **-ated; -ating** **1** REJECT : rechazar **2** DISOWN : repudiar, renegar de
repudiation [riˌpjuːdi'eɪʃən] *n* : rechazo *m*, repudio *m*
repugnance [ri'pʌgnənts] *n* : repugnancia *f*
repugnant [ri'pʌgnənt] *adj* : repugnante, asqueroso
repulse¹ [ri'pʌls] *vt* **-pulsed; -pulsing** **1** REPEL : repeler **2** REBUFF : desairar, rechazar
repulse² *n* : rechazo *m*
repulsive [ri'pʌlsɪv] *adj* : repulsivo, repugnante, asqueroso — **repulsively** *adv*
reputable ['rɛpjətəbəl] *adj* : acreditado, de buena reputación
reputation [ˌrɛpjə'teɪʃən] *n* : reputación *f*, fama *f*
repute [ri'pjuːt] *n* : reputación *f*, fama *f*
reputed [ri'pjuːtəd] *adj* : reputado, supuesto ⟨she's reputed to be the best : tiene fama de ser la mejor⟩
reputedly [ri'pjuːtədli] *adv* : supuestamente, según se dice
request¹ [ri'kwɛst] *vt* : pedir, solicitar, rogar ⟨to request assistance : solicitar asistencia, pedir ayuda⟩ ⟨I requested him to do it : le pedí que lo hiciera⟩
request² *n* : petición *f*, solicitud *f*, pedido *m*
requiem ['rɛkwiəm, 'reɪ-] *n* : réquiem *m*
require [ri'kwaɪr] *vt* **-quired; -quiring 1** CALL FOR, DEMAND : requerir, exigir ⟨if required : si se requiere⟩ ⟨to require that something be done : exigir que algo se haga⟩ **2** NEED : necesitar, requerir
requirement [ri'kwaɪrmənt] *n* **1** NECESSITY : necesidad *f* **2** DEMAND : requisito *m*, demanda *f*

requisite¹ ['rɛkwəzɪt] *adj* : esencial, necesario
requisite² *n* : requisito *m*, necesidad *f*
requisition¹ [ˌrɛkwə'zɪʃən] *vt* : requisar
requisition² *n* : requisición *f*, requisa *f*
reread [ˌri:'riːd] *vt* **-read; -reading** : releer
reroute [ˌri:'ruːt, -'raʊt] *vt* **-routed; -routing** : desviar
rerun¹ [ri:'rʌn] *vt* **-ran; -run; -running** : reponer (un programa televisivo)
rerun² ['ri:ˌrʌn] *n* **1** : reposición *f* (de un programa televisivo) **2** REPEAT : repetición *f*
resale [ri'seɪl, ˌri:'seɪl] *n* : reventa *f* ⟨resale price : precio de venta⟩
rescind [ri'sɪnd] *vt* **1** CANCEL : rescindir, cancelar **2** REPEAL : abrogar, revocar
rescue¹ ['rɛsˌkjuː] *vt* **-cued; -cuing** : rescatar, salvar
rescue² *n* : rescate *m*
rescuer ['rɛskjuər] *n* : salvador *m*, -dora *f*
research¹ [ri'sərʧ, 'ri:ˌsərʧ] *v* : investigar
research² *n* : investigación *f*
researcher [ri'sərʧər, 'ri:ˌ-] *n* : investigador *m*, -dora *f*
resemblance [ri'zɛmblənts] *n* : semejanza *f*, parecido *m*
resemble [ri'zɛmbəl] *vt* **-sembled; -sembling** : parecerse a, asemejarse a
resent [ri'zɛnt] *vt* : resentirse de, ofenderse por
resentful [ri'zɛntfəl] *adj* : resentido, rencoroso — **resentfully** *adv*
resentment [ri'zɛntmənt] *n* : resentimiento *m*
reservation [ˌrɛzər'veɪʃən] *n* **1** : reservación *f*, reserva *f* ⟨to make a reservation : hacer una reservación⟩ **2** DOUBT, MISGIVING : reserva *f*, duda *f* ⟨without reservations : sin reservas⟩ **3** : reserva *f* (de indios americanos)
reserve¹ [ri'zərv] *vt* **-served; -serving** : reservar
reserve² *n* **1** STOCK : reserva *f* ⟨to keep in reserve : guardar en reserva⟩ **2** RESTRAINT : reserva *f*, moderación *f* **3 reserves** *npl* : reservas *fpl* (militares)
reserved [ri'zərvd] *adj* : reservado
reservoir ['rɛzərˌvwɑr, -ˌvwɔr, -ˌvɔr] *n* : embalse *m*
reset [ˌri:'sɛt] *vt* **-set; -setting** : reajustar, poner en hora (un reloj), reiniciar (una computadora)
reside [ri'zaɪd] *vi* **-sided; -siding 1** DWELL : residir **2** LIE : radicar, residir ⟨the power resides in the presidency : el poder radica en la presidencia⟩
residence ['rɛzədənts] *n* : residencia *f*
resident¹ ['rɛzədənt] *adj* : residente
resident² *n* : residente *mf*
residential [ˌrɛzə'dɛnʧəl] *adj* : residencial
residual [ri'zɪʤuəl] *adj* : residual
residue ['rɛzəˌduː, -ˌdjuː] *n* : residuo *m*, resto *m*

resign [ri'zaɪn] vt 1 QUIT : dimitir, renunciar 2 **to resign oneself** : aguantarse, resignarse
resignation [ˌrɛzɪg'neɪʃən] n : resignación f
resignedly [ri'zaɪnədli] adv : con resignación
resilience [ri'zɪljənts] n 1 : capacidad f
de recuperación, adaptabilidad f 2
ELASTICITY : elasticidad f
resiliency [ri'zɪljəntsi] → **resilience**
resilient [ri'zɪljənt] adj 1 STRONG : resistente, fuerte 2 ELASTIC : elástico
resin ['rɛzən] n : resina f
resist [ri'zɪst] vt 1 WITHSTAND : resistir
⟨to resist heat : resistir el calor⟩ 2 OP-
POSE : oponerse a
resistance [ri'zɪstənts] n : resistencia f
resistant [ri'zɪstənt] adj : resistente
resolute ['rɛzə,lu:t] adj : firme, resuelto, decidido
resolutely ['rɛzə,lu:tli, ˌrɛzə'-] adv : resueltamente, firmemente
resolution [ˌrɛzə'lu:ʃən] n 1 SOLUTION
: solución f 2 RESOLVE : resolución f,
determinación f 3 DECISION : propósito m, decisión f ⟨New Year's resolu-
tions : propósitos para el Año Nuevo⟩
4 MOTION, PROPOSAL : moción f, resolución f (legislativa)
resolve¹ [ri'zalv] vt **-solved; -solving** 1
SOLVE : resolver, solucionar 2 DECIDE
: resolver ⟨she resolved to get more
sleep : resolvió dormir más⟩
resolve² n : resolución f, determinación
f
resonance ['rɛzənənts] n : resonancia f
resonant ['rɛzənənt] adj : resonante, retumbante
resort¹ [ri'zɔrt] vi **to resort to** : recurrir
⟨to resort to force : recurrir a la fuerza⟩
resort² n 1 RECOURSE : recurso m ⟨as
a last resort : como último recurso⟩ 2
HANGOUT : lugar m popular, lugar m
muy frecuentado 3 : lugar m de vacaciones ⟨tourist resort : centro turísti-
co⟩
resound [ri'zaʊnd] vi : retumbar, resonar
resounding [ri'zaʊndɪŋ] adj 1 RESO-
NANT : retumbante, resonante 2 AB-
SOLUTE, CATEGORICAL : rotundo,
tremendo ⟨a resounding success : un
éxito rotundo⟩
resource ['ri:ˌsors, ri'sors] n 1 RE-
SOURCEFULNESS : ingenio m, recursos
mpl 2 **resources** npl : recursos mpl
⟨natural resources : recursos natu-
rales⟩ 3 **resources** npl MEANS : recursos mpl, medios mpl, fondos mpl
resourceful [ri'sorsfəl, -'zors-] adj : ingenioso
resourcefulness [ri'sorsfəlnəs, -'zors-] n
: ingenio m, recursos mpl, inventiva f
respect¹ [ri'spɛkt] vt : respetar, estimar
respect² n 1 REFERENCE : relación f,
respeto m ⟨with respect to : en lo que
respecta a⟩ 2 ESTEEM : respeto m, es-

tima f 3 DETAIL, PARTICULAR : detalle
m, sentido m, respeto m ⟨in some respects : en algunos sentidos⟩ 4 **respects** npl : respetos mpl ⟨to pay one's
respects : presentar uno susrespetos⟩
respectability [riˌspɛktə'bɪləti] n : respetabilidad f
respectable [ri'spɛktəbəl] adj 1 PROP-
ER : respetable, decente 2 CONSIDER-
ABLE : considerable, respetable ⟨a respectable amount : una cantidad
respetable⟩ — **respectably** [-bli] adv
respectful [ri'spɛktfəl] adj : respetuoso
— **respectfully** adv
respectfulness [ri'spɛktfəlnəs] n : respetuosidad f
respective [ri'spɛktɪv] adj : respectivo
⟨their respective homes : sus casas re-
spectivas⟩ — **respectively** adv
respiration [ˌrɛspə'reɪʃən] n : respiración f
respirator ['rɛspəˌreɪtər] n : respirador
m
respiratory ['rɛspərəˌtori, ri'spaɪrə-] adj
: respiratorio
respite ['rɛspɪt, ri'spaɪt] n : respiro m,
tregua f
resplendent [ri'splɛndənt] adj : resplandeciente — **resplendently** adv
respond [ri'spand] vi 1 ANSWER : contestar, responder 2 REACT : responder,
reaccionar ⟨to respond to treatment
: responder al tratamiento⟩
response [ri'spants] n : respuesta f
responsibility [riˌspantsə'bɪləti] n, pl
-ties : responsabilidad f
responsible [ri'spantsəbəl] adj : responsable — **responsibly** [-bli] adv
responsive [ri'spantsɪv] adj 1 ANSWER-
ING : que responde 2 SENSITIVE : sensible, receptivo
responsiveness [ri'spantsɪvnəs] n : receptividad f, sensibilidad f
rest¹ ['rɛst] vi 1 REPOSE : reposar, descansar 2 RELAX : quedarse tranquilo
3 STOP : pararse, detenerse 4 DEPEND
: basarse (en), descansar (sobre), depender (de) ⟨the decision rests with her
: la decisión pesa sobre ella⟩ 5 **to rest
on** : apoyarse en, descansar sobre ⟨to
rest on one's arm : apoyarse en el bra-
zo⟩ — vt 1 RELAX : descansar 2 SUP-
PORT : apoyar 3 **to rest one's eyes on**
: fijar la mirada en
rest² n 1 RELAXATION, REPOSE : reposo
m, descanso m 2 SUPPORT : soporte m,
apoyo m 3 : silencio m (en música) 4
REMAINDER : resto m 5 **to come to
rest** : pararse
restart [ri'start] vt 1 : volver a empezar
2 RESUME : reanudar 3 : volver a arrancar (un motor), reiniciar (una computadora) — vi 1 : reanudarse 2
: volver a arrancar
restatement [ˌriːˈsteɪtmənt] n : repetición f
restaurant ['rɛstəˌrant, -rənt] n : restaurante m

restful ['rɛstfəl] *adj* **1** RELAXING : relajante **2** PEACEFUL : tranquilo, sosegado

restitution [ˌrɛstə'tuːʃən, -'tjuː-] *n* : restitución *f*

restive ['rɛstɪv] *adj* : inquieto, nervioso

restless ['rɛstləs] *adj* **1** FIDGETY : inquieto, agitado **2** IMPATIENT : impaciente **3** SLEEPLESS : desvelado ⟨a restless night : una noche en blanco⟩

restlessly ['rɛstləsli] *adv* : nerviosamente

restlessness ['rɛstləsnəs] *n* : inquietud *f*, agitación *f*

restoration [ˌrɛstə'reɪʃən] *n* : restauración *f*, restablecimiento *m*

restore [ri'stor] *vt* **-stored; -storing 1** RETURN : volver **2** REESTABLISH : restablecer **3** REPAIR : restaurar

restrain [ri'streɪn] *vt* **1** : refrenar, contener **2 to restrain oneself** : contenerse

restrained [ri'streɪnd] *adj* : comedido, templado, contenido

restraint [ri'streɪnt] *n* **1** RESTRICTION : restricción *f*, limitación *f*, control *m* **2** CONFINEMENT : encierro *m* **3** RESERVE : reserva *f*, control *m* de sí mismo

restrict [ri'strɪkt] *vt* : restringir, limitar, constreñir

restricted [ri'strɪktəd] *adj* **1** LIMITED : limitado, restringido **2** CLASSIFIED : secreto, confidencial

restriction [ri'strɪkʃən] *n* : restricción *f*

restrictive [ri'strɪktɪv] *adj* : restrictivo — **restrictively** *adv*

rest room *n* : servicios *mpl*, baño *m*

restructure [ri'strʌktʃər] *vt* **-tured; -turing** : reestructurar

result[1] [ri'zʌlt] *vi* : resultar ⟨to result in : resultar en, tener por resultado⟩

result[2] *n* : resultado *m*, consecuencia *f* ⟨as a result of : como consecuencia de⟩

resultant [ri'zʌltənt] *adj* : resultante

resume [ri'zuːm] *v* **-sumed; -suming** *vt* : reanudar — *vi* : reanudarse

résumé *or* **resume** *or* **resumé** ['rɛzəˌmeɪ, ˌrɛzə'-] *n* **1** SUMMARY : resumen *m* **2** CURRICULUM VITAE : currículum *m*, currículo *m*

resumption [ri'zʌmpʃən] *n* : reanudación *f*

resurface [ˌri'sərfəs] *v* **-faced; -facing** *vt* : pavimentar (una carretera) de nuevo — *vi* : volver a salir en la superficie

resurgence [ri'sərdʒənts] *n* : resurgimiento *m*

resurrect [ˌrɛzə'rɛkt] *vt* : resucitar, desempolvar

resurrection [ˌrɛzə'rɛkʃən] *n* : resurrección *f*

resuscitate [ri'sʌsəˌteɪt] *vt* **-tated; -tating** : resucitar, revivir

resuscitation [riˌsʌsə'teɪʃən] *n* : reanimación *f*, resucitación *f*

retail[1] ['riːˌteɪl] *vt* : vender al por menor, vender al detalle

retail[2] *adv* : al por menor, al detalle

retail[3] *adj* : detallista, minorista

retail[4] *n* : venta *f* al detalle, venta *f* al por menor

retailer ['riːˌteɪlər] *n* : detallista *mf*, minorista *mf*

retain [ri'teɪn] *vt* : retener, conservar, guardar

retainer [ri'teɪnər] *n* **1** SERVANT : criado *m*, -da *f* **2** ADVANCE : anticipo *m*

retaliate [ri'tæliˌeɪt] *vi* **-ated; -ating** : responder, contraatacar, tomar represalias

retaliation [riˌtæli'eɪʃən] *n* : represalia *f*, retaliación *f*

retard [ri'tard] *vt* : retardar, retrasar

retardation [ˌriːˌtar'deɪʃən] *n* **1** : retardación *f* **2** *or* **mental retardation** : retraso *m* mental

retarded [ri'tardəd] *adj* : retrasado

retch ['rɛtʃ] *vi* : hacer arcadas

retention [ri'tɛntʃən] *n* : retención *f*

retentive [ri'tɛntɪv] *adj* : retentivo

rethink [riː'θɪŋk] *vt* **-thought; -thinking** : reconsiderar, repensar

reticence ['rɛtəsənts] *n* : reticencia *f*

reticent ['rɛtəsənt] *adj* : reticente

retina ['rɛtənə] *n, pl* **-nas** *or* **-nae** [-əni, -ənˌaɪ] : retina *f*

retinue ['rɛtənˌuː, -ˌjuː] *n* : séquito *m*, comitiva *f*, cortejo *m*

retire [ri'taɪr] *vi* **-tired; -tiring 1** RETREAT, WITHDRAW : retirarse, retraerse **2** : retirarse, jubilarse (de su trabajo) **3** : acostarse, irse a dormir

retiree [riˌtaɪ'riː] *n* : jubilado *m*, -da *f*

retirement [ri'taɪrmənt] *n* : jubilación *f*

retiring [ri'taɪrɪŋ] *adj* SHY : retraído

retort[1] [ri'tort] *vt* : replicar

retort[2] *n* : réplica *f*

retrace [ˌriː'treɪs] *vt* **-traced; -tracing** : volver sobre, desandar ⟨to retrace one's steps : volver uno sobre sus pasos⟩

retract [ri'trækt] *vt* **1** TAKE BACK, WITHDRAW : retirar, retractarse de **2** : retraer (las garras) — *vi* : retractarse

retractable [ri'træktəbəl] *adj* : retractable

retrain [ˌriː'treɪn] *vt* : reciclar, reconvertir

retreat[1] [ri'triːt] *vi* : retirarse

retreat[2] *n* **1** WITHDRAWAL : retirada *f*, repliegue *m*, retiro *m* ⟨to beat a retreat : batirse en retirada⟩ **2** REFUGE : retiro *m*, refugio *m*

retrench [ri'trɛntʃ] *vt* : reducir (gastos) — *vi* : economizar

retribution [ˌrɛtrə'bjuːʃən] *n* PUNISHMENT : castigo *m*, pena *f* merecida

retrieval [ri'triːvəl] *n* : recuperación *f* ⟨beyond retrieval : irrecuperable⟩ ⟨data retrieval : recuperación de datos⟩

retrieve [ri'triːv] *vt* **-trieved; -trieving 1** : cobrar ⟨to retrieve game : cobrar la caza⟩ **2** RECOVER : recuperar

retriever [ri'triːvər] *n* : perro *m* cobrador

retroactive [ˌrɛtroˈæktɪv] *adj* : retroactivo — **retroactively** *adv*

retrograde [ˈrɛtrəˌgreɪd] *adj* : retrógrado

retrospect [ˈrɛtrəˌspɛkt] *n* **in retrospect** : mirando hacia atrás, retrospectivamente

retrospective [ˌrɛtrəˈspɛktɪv] *adj* : retrospectivo

return¹ [rɪˈtərn] *vi* **1** : volver, regresar ⟨to return home : regresar a casa⟩ **2** REAPPEAR : reaparecer, resurgir **3** ANSWER : responder — *vt* **1** REPLACE, RESTORE : devolver, volver (a poner), restituir ⟨to return something to its place : volver a poner algo en su lugar⟩ **2** YIELD : producir, redituar, rendir **3** REPAY : pagar, devolver ⟨to return a compliment : devolver un cumplido⟩

return² *adj* : de vuelta

return³ *n* **1** RETURNING : regreso *m*, vuelta *f*, retorno *m* **2** *or* **tax return** : declaración *f* de impuestos **3** YIELD : rédito *m*, rendimiento *m*, ganancia *f* **4** **returns** *npl* DATA, RESULTS : resultados *mpl*, datos *mpl*

reunion [rɪˈjuːnjən] *n* : reunión *f*, reencuentro *m*

reunite [ˌriːjuˈnaɪt] *v* **-nited; -niting** *vt* : (volver a) reunir — *vi* : (volver a) reunirse

reusable [riˈjuːzəbəl] *adj* : reutilizable

reuse [riˈjuːz] *vt* **-used; -using** : reutilizar, usar de nuevo

revamp [ˌriˈvæmp] *vt* : renovar

reveal [rɪˈviːl] *vt* **1** DIVULGE : revelar, divulgar ⟨to reveal a secret : revelar un secreto⟩ **2** SHOW : manifestar, mostrar, dejar ver

revealing [rɪˈviːlɪŋ] *adj* : revelador

reveille [ˈrɛvəli] *n* : toque *m* de diana

revel¹ [ˈrɛvəl] *vi* **-eled** *or* **-elled; -eling** *or* **-elling** **1** CAROUSE : ir de juerga **2 to revel in** : deleitarse

revel² *n* : juerga *f*, parranda *f fam*

revelation [ˌrɛvəˈleɪʃən] *n* : revelación *f*

reveler *or* **reveller** [ˈrɛvələr] *n* : juerguista *mf*

revelry [ˈrɛvəlri] *n*, *pl* **-ries** : juerga *f*, parranda *f fam*, jarana *f fam*

revenge¹ [rɪˈvɛndʒ] *vt* **-venged; -venging** : vengar ⟨to revenge oneself on : vengarse de⟩

revenge² *n* : venganza *f*

revenue [ˈrɛvəˌnuː, -ˌnjuː] *n* : ingresos *mpl*, rentas *fpl*

reverberate [rɪˈvərbəˌreɪt] *vi* **-ated; -ating** : reverberar

reverberation [rɪˌvərbəˈreɪʃən] *n* : reverberación *f*

revere [rɪˈvɪr] *vt* **-vered; -vering** : reverenciar, venerar

reverence [ˈrɛvərənts] *n* : reverencia *f*, veneración *f*

reverend [ˈrɛvərənd] *adj* : reverendo ⟨the Reverend John Chapin : el reverendo John Chapin⟩

reverent [ˈrɛvərənt] *adj* : reverente — **reverently** *adv*

reverie [ˈrɛvəri] *n*, *pl* **-eries** : ensueño *m*

reversal [rɪˈvərsəl] *n* **1** INVERSION : inversión *f* (del orden normal) **2** CHANGE : cambio *m* total **3** SETBACK : revés *m*, contratiempo *m*

reverse¹ [rɪˈvərs] *v* **-versed; -versing** *vt* **1** INVERT : invertir **2** CHANGE : cambiar totalmente **3** ANNUL : anular, revocar — *vi* : dar marcha atrás

reverse² *adj* **1** : inverso ⟨in reverse order : en orden inverso⟩ ⟨the reverse side : el reverso⟩ **2** OPPOSITE : contrario, opuesto

reverse³ *n* **1** OPPOSITE : lo contrario, lo opuesto **2** SETBACK : revés *m*, contratiempo *m* **3** BACK : reverso *m*, dorso *m*, revés *m* **4** *or* **reverse gear** : marcha *f* atrás, reversa *f Col, Mex*

reversible [rɪˈvərsəbəl] *adj* : reversible

reversion [rɪˈvərʒən] *n* : reversión *f*, vuelta *f*

revert [rɪˈvərt] *vi* : revertir

review¹ [rɪˈvjuː] *vt* **1** REEXAMINE : volver a examinar, repasar (una lección) **2** CRITICIZE : reseñar, hacer una crítica de **3** EXAMINE : examinar, analizar ⟨to review one's life : examinar su vida⟩ **4 to review the troops** : pasar revista a las tropas

review² *n* **1** INSPECTION : revista *f* (de tropas) **2** ANALYSIS, OVERVIEW : resumen *m*, análisis *m* ⟨a review of current affairs : un análisis de las actualidades⟩ **3** CRITICISM : reseña *f*, crítica *f* (de un libro, etc.) **4** : repaso *m* (para un examen) **5** REVUE : revista *f* (musical)

reviewer [rɪˈvjuːər] *n* : crítico *m*, -ca *f*

revile [rɪˈvaɪl] *vt* **-viled; -viling** : injuriar, denostar

revise [rɪˈvaɪz] *vt* **-vised; -vising** : revisar, corregir, refundir ⟨to revise a dictionary : corregir un diccionario⟩

revision [rɪˈvɪʒən] *n* : revisión *f*

revival [rɪˈvaɪvəl] *n* **1** : renacimiento *m* (de ideas, etc.), restablecimiento *m* (de costumbres, etc.), reactivación *f* (de la economía) **2** : reanimación *f*, resucitación *f* (en medicina) **3** *or* **revival meeting** : asamblea *f* evangelista

revive [rɪˈvaɪv] *v* **-vived; -viving** *vt* **1** REAWAKEN : reavivar, reanimar, reactivar (la economía), resucitar (a un paciente) **2** REESTABLISH : restablecer — *vi* **1** : renacer, reanimarse, reactivarse **2** COME TO : recobrar el sentido, volver en sí

revoke [rɪˈvoːk] *vt* **-voked; -voking** : revocar

revolt¹ [rɪˈvoːlt] *vi* **1** REBEL : rebelarse, sublevarse **2 to revolt at** : sentir repugnancia por — *vt* DISGUST : darle asco (a alguien), repugnar

revolt² *n* REBELLION : rebelión *f*, revuelta *f*, sublevación *f*

revolting [rɪˈvoːltɪŋ] *adj* : asqueroso, repugnante

revolution [ˌrɛvəˈluːʃən] *n* : revolución *f*
revolutionary[1] [ˌrɛvəˈluːʃənɛˌri] *adj* : revolucionario
revolutionary[2] *n, pl* **-aries** : revolucionario *m*, -ria *f*
revolutionize [ˌrɛvəˈluːʃənˌaɪz] *vt* **-ized; -izing** : cambiar radicalmente, revolucionar
revolve [riˈvɑlv] *v* **-volved; -volving** *vt* ROTATE : hacer girar — *vi* 1 ROTATE : girar ⟨to revolve around : girar alrededor de⟩ 2 **to revolve in one's mind** : darle vueltas en la cabeza a alguien
revolver [riˈvɑlvər] *n* : revólver *m*
revue [riˈvjuː] *n* : revista *f* (musical)
revulsion [riˈvʌlʃən] *n* : repugnancia *f*
reward[1] [riˈwɔrd] *vt* : recompensar, premiar
reward[2] *n* : recompensa *f*
rewrite [ˌriːˈraɪt] *vt* **-wrote; -written; -writing** : escribir de nuevo, volver a escribir
rhapsody [ˈræpsədi] *n, pl* **-dies** 1 : elogio *m* excesivo ⟨to go into rhapsodies over : extasiarse por⟩ 2 : rapsodia *f* (en música)
rhetoric [ˈrɛtərɪk] *n* : retórica *f*
rhetorical [rɪˈtɔrɪkəl] *adj* : retórico
rheumatic [rʊˈmætɪk] *adj* : reumático
rheumatism [ˈruːməˌtɪzəm, ˈrʊ-] *n* : reumatismo *m*
rhinestone [ˈraɪnˌstoːn] *n* : diamante *m* de imitación
rhino [ˈraɪˌnoː] *n, pl* **rhino** *or* **rhinos** → **rhinoceros**
rhinoceros [raɪˈnɑsərəs] *n, pl* **-eroses** *or* **-eros** *or* **-eri** [-ˌraɪ] : rinoceronte *m*
rhododendron [ˌroːdəˈdɛndrən] *n* : rododendro *m*
rhombus [ˈrɑmbəs] *n, pl* **-buses** *or* **-bi** [-ˌbaɪ, -bi] : rombo *m*
rhubarb [ˈruːˌbɑrb] *n* : ruibarbo *m*
rhyme[1] [ˈraɪm] *vi* **rhymed; rhyming** : rimar
rhyme[2] *n* 1 : rima *f* 2 VERSE : verso *m* (en rima)
rhythm [ˈrɪðəm] *n* : ritmo *m*
rhythmic [ˈrɪðmɪk] *or* **rhythmical** [-mɪkəl] *adj* : rítmico — **rhythmically** [-mɪkli] *adv*
rib[1] [ˈrɪb] *vt* **ribbed; ribbing** 1 : hacer en canalé ⟨a ribbed sweater : un suéter en canalé⟩ 2 TEASE : tomarle el pelo (a alguien)
rib[2] *n* 1 : costilla *f* (de una persona o un animal) 2 : nervio *m* (de una bóveda o una hoja), varilla *f* (de un paraguas), canalé *m* (de una prenda tejida)
ribald [ˈrɪbəld] *adj* : escabroso, procaz
ribbon [ˈrɪbən] *n* 1 : cinta *f* 2 **to tear to ribbons** : hacer jirones
rice [ˈraɪs] *n* : arroz *m*
rich [ˈrɪtʃ] *adj* 1 WEALTHY : rico 2 SUMPTUOUS : suntuoso, lujoso 3 : pesado ⟨rich foods : comida pesada⟩ 4 ABUNDANT : abundante 5 : vivo, intenso ⟨rich colors : colores vivos⟩ 6 FERTILE : fértil, rico

riches [ˈrɪtʃəz] *npl* : riquezas *fpl*
richly [ˈrɪtʃli] *adv* 1 SUMPTUOUSLY : suntuosamente, ricamente 2 ABUNDANTLY : abundantemente 3 **richly deserved** : bien merecido
richness [ˈrɪtʃnəs] *n* : riqueza *f*
rickets [ˈrɪkəts] *n* : raquitismo *m*
rickety [ˈrɪkəti] *adj* : desvencijado, destartalado
ricksha *or* **rickshaw** [ˈrɪkˌʃɔ] *n* : cochecillo *m* tirado por un hombre
ricochet[1] [ˈrɪkəˌʃeɪ] *vi* **-cheted** [-ˌʃeɪd]; **-chetted** [-ˌʃɛtəd]; **-cheting** [-ˌʃeɪɪŋ] *or* **-chetting** [-ˌʃɛtɪŋ] : rebotar
ricochet[2] *n* : rebote *m*
rid [ˈrɪd] *vt* **rid; ridding** 1 FREE : librar ⟨to rid the city of thieves : librar la ciudad de ladrones⟩ 2 **to rid oneself of** : desembarazarse de
riddance [ˈrɪdənts] *n* : libramiento *m* ⟨good riddance! : ¡adiós y buen viaje!, ¡vete con viento fresco!⟩
riddle[1] [ˈrɪdəl] *vt* **-dled; -dling** : acribillar ⟨riddled with bullets : acribillado a balazos⟩ ⟨riddled with errors : lleno de errores⟩
riddle[2] *n* : acertijo *m*, adivinanza *f*
ride[1] [ˈraɪd] *v* **rode** [ˈroːd]; **ridden** [ˈrɪdən]; **riding** *vt* 1 : montar, ir, andar ⟨to ride a horse : montar a caballo⟩ ⟨to ride a bicycle : montar en bicicleta, andar en bicicleta⟩ ⟨to ride the bus : ir en autobús⟩ 2 TRAVERSE : recorrer ⟨he rode 5 miles : recorrió 5 millas⟩ 3 TEASE : burlarse de, ridiculizar 4 CARRY : llevar 5 WEATHER : capear ⟨they rode out the storm : capearon el temporal⟩ 6 **to ride the waves** : surcar los mares — *vi* 1 : montar a caballo, cabalgar 2 TRAVEL : ir, viajar (en coche, en bicicleta, etc.) 3 RUN : andar, marchar ⟨the car rides well : el coche anda bien⟩ 4 **to ride at anchor** : estar fondeado 5 **to let things ride** : dejar pasar las cosas
ride[2] *n* 1 : paseo *m*, vuelta *f* (en coche, en bicicleta, a caballo) ⟨to go for a ride : dar una vuelta⟩ ⟨to give someone a ride : llevar en coche a alguien⟩ 2 : aparato *m* (en un parque de diversiones)
rider [ˈraɪdər] *n* 1 : jinete *mf* ⟨the rider fell off his horse : el jinete se cayó de su caballo⟩ 2 CYCLIST : ciclista *mf* 3 MOTORCYCLIST : motociclista *mf* 4 CLAUSE : cláusula *f* añadida
ridge [ˈrɪdʒ] *n* 1 CHAIN : cadena *f* (de montañas o cerros) 2 : caballete *m* (de un techo), cresta *f* (de una ola o una montaña), cordoncillo *m* (de telas)
ridicule[1] [ˈrɪdəˌkjuːl] *vt* **-culed; -culing** : burlarse de, mofarse de, ridiculizar
ridicule[2] *n* : burlas *fpl*
ridiculous [rəˈdɪkjələs] *adj* : ridículo, absurdo
ridiculously [rəˈdɪkjələsli] *adv* : de forma ridícula
rife [ˈraɪf] *adj* : abundante, común ⟨to be rife with : estar plagado de⟩

riffraff ['rɪf,ræf] *n* : chusma *f*, gentuza *f*
rifle[1] ['raɪfəl] *v* -**fled**; -**fling** *vt* RANSACK : desvalijar, saquear — *vi* **to rifle through** : revolver
rifle[2] *n* : rifle *m*, fusil *m*
rift ['rɪft] *n* 1 FISSURE : grieta *f*, fisura *f* 2 BREAK : ruptura *f* (entre personas), división *f* (dentro de un grupo)
rig[1] ['rɪg] *vt* **rigged**; **rigging** 1 : aparejar (un barco) 2 EQUIP : equipar 3 FIX : amañar (una elección, etc.) 4 **to rig up** CONSTRUCT : construir, erigir 5 **to rig oneself out as** : vestirse de
rig[2] *n* 1 : aparejo *m* (de un barco) 2 *or* **oil rig** : torre *f* de perforación, plataforma *f* petrolífera
rigging ['rɪgɪŋ, -gən] *n* : jarcia *f*, aparejo *m*
right[1] ['raɪt] *vt* 1 FIX, RESTORE : reparar ⟨to right the economy : reparar la economía⟩ 2 STRAIGHTEN : enderezar
right[2] *adv* 1 : bien ⟨to live right : vivir bien⟩ 2 PRECISELY : precisamente, justo ⟨right in the middle : justo en medio⟩ 3 DIRECTLY, STRAIGHT : derecho, directamente ⟨he went right home : fue derecho a casa⟩ 4 IMMEDIATELY : inmediatamente ⟨right after lunch : inmediatamente después del almuerzo⟩ 5 COMPLETELY : completamente ⟨he felt right at home : se sintió completamente cómodo⟩ 6 : a la derecha ⟨to look left and right : mirar a la izquierda y a la derecha⟩
right[3] *adj* 1 UPRIGHT : bueno, honrado ⟨right conduct : conducta honrada⟩ 2 CORRECT : correcto ⟨the right answer : la respuesta correcta⟩ 3 APPROPRIATE : apropiado, adecuado, debido ⟨the right man for the job : el hombre perfecto para el trabajo⟩ 4 STRAIGHT : recto ⟨a right line : una línea recta⟩ 5 : derecho ⟨the right hand : la mano derecha⟩ 6 SOUND : bien ⟨he's not in his right mind : no está bien de la cabeza⟩
right[4] *n* 1 GOOD : bien *m* ⟨to do right : hacer el bien⟩ 2 : derecha *f* ⟨on the right : a la derecha⟩ 3 *or* **right hand** : mano *f* derecha 4 ENTITLEMENT : derecho *m* ⟨the right to vote : el derecho a votar⟩ ⟨women's rights : los derechos de la mujer⟩ 5 **the Right** : la derecha (en la política)
right angle *n* : ángulo *m* recto
right–angled ['raɪt'æŋgəld] *or* **right–angle** [-gəl] *adj* 1 : en ángulo recto 2 **right–angled triangle** : triángulo *m* rectángulo
righteous ['raɪtʃəs] *adj* : recto, honrado — **righteously** *adv*
righteousness ['raɪtʃəsnəs] *n* : rectitud *f*, honradez *f*
rightful ['raɪtfəl] *adj* 1 JUST : justo 2 LAWFUL : legítimo — **rightfully** *adv*
right–hand ['raɪt'hænd] *adj* 1 : situado a la derecha 2 RIGHT-HANDED : para

la mano derecha, con la mano derecha 3 **right–hand man** : brazo *m* derecho
right–handed ['raɪt'hændəd] *adj* 1 : diestro ⟨a right-handed pitcher : un lanzador diestro⟩ 2 : para la mano derecha, con la mano derecha 3 CLOCKWISE : en la dirección de las manecillas del reloj
rightly ['raɪtli] *adv* 1 JUSTLY : justamente, con razón 2 PROPERLY : debidamente, apropiadamente 3 CORRECTLY : correctamente
right–of–way ['raɪtə'weɪ, -əv-] *n*, *pl* **rights–of–way** 1 : preferencia (del tráfico) 2 ACCESS : derecho *m* de paso
rightward ['raɪtwərd] *adj* : a la derecha, hacia la derecha
right–wing ['raɪt'wɪŋ] *adj* : derechista
right wing *n* **the right wing** : la derecha
right–winger ['raɪt'wɪŋər] *n* : derechista *mf*
rigid ['rɪdʒɪd] *adj* : rígido — **rigidly** *adv*
rigidity [rɪ'dʒɪdəti] *n*, *pl* -**ties** : rigidez *f*
rigmarole ['rɪgmə,roːl, 'rɪgə-] *n* 1 NONSENSE : galimatías *m*, disparates *mpl* 2 PROCEDURES : trámites *mpl*
rigor ['rɪgər] *n* : rigor *m*
rigor mortis [,rɪgər'mɔrtəs] *n* : rigidez *f* cadavérica
rigorous ['rɪgərəs] *adj* : riguroso — **rigorously** *adv*
rile ['raɪl] *vt* **riled**; **riling** : irritar
rill ['rɪl] *n* : riachuelo *m*
rim ['rɪm] *n* 1 EDGE : borde *m* 2 : llanta *f*, rin *m* Col, Mex (de una rueda) 3 FRAME : montura *f* (de anteojos)
rime ['raɪm] *n* : escarcha *f*
rind ['raɪnd] *n* : corteza *f*
ring[1] ['rɪŋ] *v* **rang** ['ræŋ]; **rung** ['rʌŋ]; **ringing** *vi* 1 : sonar ⟨the doorbell rang : el timbre sonó⟩ ⟨to ring for : llamar⟩ 2 RESOUND : resonar 3 SEEM : parecer ⟨to ring true : parecer cierto⟩ — *vt* 1 : tocar, hacer sonar (un timbre, una alarma, etc.) 2 SURROUND : cercar, rodear
ring[2] *n* 1 : anillo *m*, sortija *f* ⟨wedding ring : anillo de matrimonio⟩ 2 BAND : aro *m*, anillo *m* ⟨piston ring : aro de émbolo⟩ 3 CIRCLE : círculo *m* 4 ARENA : arena *f*, ruedo *m* ⟨a boxing ring : un cuadrilátero, un ring⟩ 5 GANG : banda *f* (de ladrones, etc.) 6 SOUND : timbre *m*, sonido *m* 7 CALL : llamada *f* (por teléfono)
ringer ['rɪŋər] *n* **to be a dead ringer for** : ser un vivo retrato de
ringleader ['rɪŋ,liːdər] *n* : cabecilla *mf*
ringlet ['rɪŋlət] *n* : sortija *f*, rizo *m*
ringworm ['rɪŋ,wərm] *n* : tiña *f*
rink ['rɪŋk] *n* : pista *f* ⟨skating rink : pista de patinaje⟩
rinse[1] ['rɪnts] *vt* **rinsed**; **rinsing** : enjuagar ⟨to rinse out one's mouth : enjuagarse la boca⟩
rinse[2] *n* : enjuague *m*
riot[1] ['raɪət] *vi* : amotinarse
riot[2] *n* : motín *m*, tumulto *m*, alboroto *m*

rioter ['raɪətər] *n* : alborotador *m*, -dora *f*

riotous ['raɪətəs] *adj* **1** UNRULY, WILD : desenfrenado, alborotado **2** ABUNDANT : abundante

rip¹ ['rɪp] *v* **ripped; ripping** *vt* : rasgar, arrancar, desgarrar — *vi* : rasgarse, desgarrarse

rip² *n* : rasgón *m*, desgarrón *m*

ripe ['raɪp] *adj* **riper; ripest 1** MATURE : maduro ⟨ripe fruit : fruta madura⟩ **2** READY : listo, preparado

ripen ['raɪpən] *v* : madurar

ripeness ['raɪpnəs] *n* : madurez *f*

rip–off ['rɪpˌɔf] *n* **1** THEFT : robo *m* **2** SWINDLE : estafa *f*, timo *m fam*

rip off *vt* **1** : rasgar, arrancar, desgarrar **2** SWINDLE : estafar, timar

ripple¹ ['rɪpəl] *v* **-pled; -pling** *vi* : rizarse, ondear, ondular — *vt* : rizar

ripple² *n* : onda *f*, ondulación *f*

rise¹ ['raɪz] *vi* **rose** ['roːz]; **risen** ['rɪz-ən]; **rising 1** GET UP : levantarse ⟨to rise to one's feet : ponerse de pie⟩ **2** : elevarse, alzarse ⟨the mountains rose to the west : las montañas se elevaron al oeste⟩ **3** : salir (dícese del sol y de la luna) **4** : subir (dícese de las aguas, del humo, etc.) ⟨the river rose : las aguas subieron de nivel⟩ **5** INCREASE : aumentar, subir **6** ORIGINATE : nacer, proceder **7 to rise in rank** : ascender **8 to rise up** REBEL : sublevarse, rebelarse

rise² *n* **1** ASCENT : ascensión *f*, subida *f* **2** ORIGIN : origen *m* **3** ELEVATION : elevación *f* **4** INCREASE : subida *f*, aumento *m*, alzamiento *m* **5** SLOPE : pendiente *f*, cuesta *f*

riser ['raɪzər] *n* **1** : contrahuella *f* (de una escalera) **2 early riser** : madrugador *m*, -dora *f* **3 late riser** : dormilón *m*, -lona *f*

risk¹ ['rɪsk] *vt* : arriesgar

risk² *n* : riesgo *m*, peligro *m* ⟨at risk : en peligro⟩ ⟨at your own risk : por su cuenta y riesgo⟩

risky ['rɪski] *adj* **riskier; -est** : arriesgado, peligroso, riesgoso

risqué [rɪˈskeɪ] *adj* : escabroso, picante, subido de tono

rite ['raɪt] *n* : rito *m*

ritual¹ ['rɪtʃuəl] *adj* : ritual — **ritually** *adv*

ritual² *n* : ritual *m*

rival¹ ['raɪvəl] *vt* **-valed** *or* **-valled; -valing** *or* **-valling** : rivalizar con, competir con

rival² *adj* : competidor, rival

rival³ *n* : rival *mf*; competidor *m*, -dora *f*

rivalry ['raɪvəlri] *n, pl* **-ries** : rivalidad *f*, competencia *f*

river ['rɪvər] *n* : río *m*

riverbank ['rɪvərˌbæŋk] *n* : ribera *f*, orilla *f*

riverbed ['rɪvərˌbɛd] *n* : cauce *m*, lecho *m*

riverside ['rɪvərˌsaɪd] *n* : ribera *f*, orilla *f*

rivet¹ ['rɪvət] *vt* **1** : remachar **2** FIX : fijar (los ojos, etc.) **3** FASCINATE : fascinar, cautivar

rivet² *n* : remache *m*

rivulet ['rɪvjələt] *n* : arroyo *m*, riachuelo *m* ⟨rivulets of sweat : gotas de sudor⟩

roach ['roːtʃ] → **cockroach**

road ['roːd] *n* **1** : carretera *f*, calle *f*, camino *m* **2** PATH : camino *m*, sendero *m*, vía *f* ⟨on the road to a solution : en vías de una solución⟩

roadblock ['roːdˌblɑk] *n* : control *m*

roadrunner ['roːdˌrʌnər] *n* : correcaminos *m*

roadside ['roːdˌsaɪd] *n* : borde *m* de la carretera

roadway ['roːdˌweɪ] *n* : carretera *f*, calzada *f*

roam ['roːm] *vi* : vagar, deambular, errar — *vt* : vagar por

roan¹ ['roːn] *adj* : ruano

roan² *n* : caballo *m* ruano

roar¹ ['ror] *vi* : rugir, bramar ⟨to roar with laughter : reírse a carcajadas⟩ — *vt* : decir a gritos

roar² *n* **1** : rugido *m*, bramido *m* (de un animal) **2** DIN : clamor *m* (de gente), fragor *m* (del trueno), estruendo *m* (del tráfico, etc.)

roast¹ ['roːst] *vt* : asar (carne, papas), tostar (café, nueces) — *vi* : asarse

roast² *adj* **1** : asado ⟨roast chicken : pollo asado⟩ **2 roast beef** : rosbif *m*

roast³ *n* : asado *m*

rob ['rɑb] *v* **robbed; robbing** *vt* **1** STEAL : robar **2** DEPRIVE : privar, quitar — *vi* : robar

robber ['rɑbər] *n* : ladrón *m*, -drona *f*

robbery ['rɑbəri] *n, pl* **-beries** : robo *m*

robe¹ ['roːb] *vt* **robed; robing** : vestirse

robe² *n* **1** : toga *f* (de magistrados, etc.), sotana *f* (de eclesiásticos) ⟨robe of office : traje de ceremonias⟩ **2** BATHROBE : bata *f*

robin ['rɑbən] *n* : petirrojo *m*

robot ['roːˌbɑt, -bət] *n* : robot *m*

robotic [roˈbɑtɪk] *adj* : robótico, robotizado

robotics [roˈbɑtɪks] *ns & pl* : robótica *f*

robust [roˈbʌst, 'roːˌbʌst] *adj* : robusto, fuerte — **robustly** *adv*

rock¹ ['rɑk] *vt* **1** : acunar (a un niño), mecer (una cuna) **2** SHAKE : sacudir — *vi* SWAY : mecerse, balancearse

rock² *adj* : de rock

rock³ *n* **1** ROCKING : balanceo *m* **2** *or* **rock music** : rock *m*, música *f* rock **3** : roca *f* (substancia) **4** STONE : piedra *f*

rock and roll *n* : rock and roll *m*

rocker ['rɑkər] *n* **1** : balancín *m* **2** *or* **rocking chair** : mecedora *f*, balancín *m* **3 to be off one's rocker** : estar chiflado, estar loco

rocket¹ ['rɑkət] *vi* : dispararse, subir rápidamente

rocket² *n* : cohete *m*

rocking horse *n* : caballito *m* (de balancín)
rock salt *n* : sal *f* gema
rocky ['rɑki] *adj* **rockier; -est 1** : rocoso, pedregoso **2** UNSTEADY : inestable
rod ['rɑd] *n* **1** BAR : barra *f*, varilla *f*, vara *f* (de madera) ⟨a fishing rod : una caña (de pescar)⟩ **2** : medida *f* de longitud equivalente a 5.03 metros (5 yardas)
rode → **ride**[1]
rodent ['ro:dənt] *n* : roedor *m*
rodeo ['ro:di,o:, ro'dei,o:] *n, pl* **-deos** : rodeo *m*
roe ['ro:] *n* : hueva *f*
rogue ['ro:g] *n* SCOUNDREL : pícaro *m*, -ra *f*; pillo *m*, -lla *f*
roguish ['ro:gɪʃ] *adj* : pícaro, travieso
role ['ro:l] *n* : papel *m*, función *f*, rol *m*
roll[1] ['ro:l] *vt* **1** : hacer rodar ⟨to roll the ball : hacer rodar la pelota⟩ ⟨to roll one's eyes : poner los ojos en blanco⟩ **2** : liar (un cigarrillo) **3** *or* **to roll up** : enrollar ⟨to roll (oneself) up into a ball : hacerse una bola⟩ **4** FLATTEN : estirar (masa), laminar (metales), pasar el rodillo por (el césped) **5 to roll up one's sleeves** : arremangarse — *vi* **1** : rodar ⟨the ball kept on rolling : la pelota siguió rodando⟩ **2** SWAY : balancearse ⟨the ship rolled in the waves : el barco se balanceó en las olas⟩ **3** REVERBERATE, SOUND : tronar (dícese del trueno), redoblar (dícese de un tambor) **4 to roll along** PROCEED : ponerse en marcha **5 to roll around** : revolcarse **6 to roll by** : pasar **7 to roll over** : dar una vuelta
roll[2] *n* **1** LIST : lista *f* ⟨to call the roll : pasar lista⟩ ⟨to have on the roll : tener inscrito⟩ **2** *or* **bread roll** : panecito *m*, bolillo *m Mex* **3** : rollo *m* (de papel, de tela, etc.) ⟨a roll of film : un carrete⟩ ⟨a roll of bills : un fajo⟩ **4** : redoble *m* (de tambores), retumbo *m* (del trueno, etc.) **5** ROLLING, SWAYING : balanceo *m*
roller ['ro:lər] *n* **1** : rodillo *m* **2** CURLER : rulo *m*
roller coaster ['ro:lər,ko:stər] *n* : montaña *f* rusa
roller–skate ['ro:lər,skeit] *vi* **-skated; -skating** : patinar (sobre ruedas)
roller skate *n* : patín *m* (de ruedas)
rollicking ['rɑlɪkɪŋ] *adj* : animado, alegre
rolling pin *n* : rodillo *m*
Roman[1] ['ro:mən] *adj* : romano
Roman[2] *n* : romano *m*, -na *f*
Roman Catholic *n* : católico *m*, -ca *f* — **Roman Catholic** *adj*
Roman Catholicism *n* : catolicismo *m*
romance[1] [ro'mænts, 'ro:,mænts] *vi* **-manced; -mancing** FANTASIZE : fantasear
romance[2] *n* **1** : romance *m*, novela *f* de caballerías **2** : novela *f* de amor, novela *f* romántica **3** AFFAIR : romance *m*, amorío *m*

Romanian [ro'meiniən, ro-] *n* **1** : rumano *m*, -na *f* **2** : rumano *m* (idioma) — **Romanian** *adj*
Roman numeral *n* : número *m* romano
romantic [ro'mæntɪk] *adj* : romántico — **romantically** [-tɪkli] *adv*
romp[1] ['rɑmp] *vi* FROLIC : retozar, juguetear
romp[2] *n* : retozo *m*
roof[1] ['ru:f, 'ruf] *vt* : techar
roof[2] *n, pl* **roofs** ['ru:fs, 'rufs; 'ru:vz, 'ruvz] **1** : techo *m*, tejado *m*, techado *m* **2 roof of the mouth** : paladar *m*
roofing ['ru:fɪŋ, 'rufɪŋ] *n* : techumbre *f*
rooftop ['ru:f,tɑp, 'ruf-] *n* ROOF : tejado *m*
rook[1] ['ruk] *vt* CHEAT : defraudar, estafar, timar
rook[2] *n* **1** : grajo *m* (ave) **2** : torre *f* (en ajedrez)
rookie ['ruki] *n* : novato *m*, -ta *f*
room[1] ['ru:m, 'rum] *vi* LODGE : alojarse, hospedarse
room[2] *n* **1** SPACE : espacio *m*, sitio *m*, lugar *m* ⟨to make room for : hacer lugar para⟩ **2** : cuarto *m*, habitación *f* (en una casa), sala *f* (para reuniones, etc.) **3** BEDROOM : dormitorio *m*, habitación *f*, pieza *f* **4** (*indicating possibility or opportunity*) ⟨room for improvement : posibilidad de mejorar⟩ ⟨there's no room for error : no hay lugar para errores⟩
roomer ['ru:mər, 'rumər] *n* : inquilino *m*, -na *f*
rooming house *n* : pensión *f*
roommate ['ru:m,meit, 'rum-] *n* : compañero *m*, -ra *f* de cuarto
roomy ['ru:mi, 'rumi] *adj* **roomier; -est 1** SPACIOUS : espacioso, amplio **2** LOOSE : suelto, holgado ⟨a roomy blouse : una blusa holgada⟩
roost[1] ['ru:st] *vi* : posarse, dormir (en una percha)
roost[2] *n* : percha *f*
rooster ['ru:stər, 'rus-] *n* : gallo *m*
root[1] ['ru:t, 'rut] *vi* **1** : arraigar ⟨the plant rooted easily : la planta arraigó con facilidad⟩ ⟨deeply rooted traditions : tradiciones profundamente arraigadas⟩ **2** : hozar (dícese de los cerdos) ⟨to root around in : hurgar en⟩ **3 to root for** : apoyar a, alentar — *vt* **to root out** *or* **to root up** : desarraigar (plantas), extirpar (problemas, etc.)
root[2] *n* **1** : raíz *f* (de una planta) **2** ORIGIN : origen *m*, raíz *f* **3** CORE : centro *m*, núcleo *m* ⟨to get to the root of the matter : ir al centro del asunto⟩
rootless ['ru:tləs, 'rut-] *adj* : desarraigado
rope[1] ['ro:p] *vt* **roped; roping 1** TIE : amarrar, atar **2** LASSO : lazar **3 to rope off** : acordonar
rope[2] *n* : soga *f*, cuerda *f*
rosary ['ro:zəri] *n, pl* **-ries** : rosario *m*
rose[1] → **rise**[1]
rose[2] ['ro:z] *adj* : rosa, color de rosa

rose[3] *n* **1** : rosal *m* (planta), rosa *f* (flor)
2 : rosa *m* (color)
rosebush ['ro:z,buʃ] *n* : rosal *m*
rosemary ['ro:z,mɛri] *n, pl* **-maries**
: romero *m*
rosette [ro'zɛt] *n* : escarapela *f* (hecho
de cintas), roseta *f* (en arquitectura)
Rosh Hashanah [,rɑʃhɑ'ʃɑnə, ,ro:ʃ-] *n*
: el Año Nuevo judío
rosin ['rɑzən] *n* : colofonia *f*
roster ['rɑstər] *n* : lista *f*
rostrum ['rɑstrəm] *n, pl* **-trums** *or* **-tra**
[-trə] : tribuna *f*, estrado *m*
rosy ['ro:zi] *adj* **rosier; -est 1** : sonrosado, de color rosa **2** PROMISING
: prometedor, halagüeño
rot[1] ['rɑt] *v* **rotted; rotting** *vi* : pudrirse,
descomponerse — *vt* : pudrir, descom-
poner
rot[2] *n* : putrefacción *f*, descomposición
f, podredumbre *f*
rotary ['ro:t̬əri] *adj* : rotativo, rotatorio
rotary[2] *n, pl* **-ries 1** : máquina *f* rotati-
va **2** TRAFFIC CIRCLE : rotonda *f*, glorieta *f*
rotate ['ro:,teɪt] *v* **-tated; -tating** *vi* RE-
VOLVE : girar, rotar — *vt* **1** TURN : hacer girar, darle vueltas a **2** ALTERNATE
: alternar
rotation [ro'teɪʃən] *n* : rotación *f*
rote ['ro:t] *n* **to learn by rote** : aprender
de memoria
rotor ['ro:t̬ər] *n* : rotor *m*
rotten ['rɑtən] *adj* **1** PUTRID : podrido,
putrefacto **2** CORRUPT : corrompido **3**
BAD : malo ⟨a rotten day : un día malísi-
mo⟩
rottenness ['rɑtənnəs] *n* : podredumbre
f
rotund [ro'tʌnd] *adj* **1** ROUNDED : re-
dondeado **2** PLUMP : regordete *fam*,
llenito *fam*
rouge ['ru:ʒ, 'ru:dʒ] *n* : colorete *m*
rough[1] ['rʌf] *vt* **1** ROUGHEN : poner
áspero **2 to rough out** SKETCH : esbozar, bosquejar **3 to rough up** BEAT
: darle una paliza (a alguien) **4 to
rough it** : vivir sin comodidades
rough[2] *adj* **1** COARSE : áspero, basto **2**
UNEVEN : desigual, escabroso, acci-
dentado (dícese del terreno) **3** : agitado (dícese del mar), tempestuoso
(dícese del tiempo), violento (dícese del
viento) **4** VIOLENT : violento, brutal ⟨a
rough neighborhood : un barrio peli-
groso⟩ **5** DIFFICULT : duro, difícil **6**
CRUDE : rudo, tosco, burdo ⟨a rough
cottage : una casita tosca⟩ ⟨a rough
draft : un borrador⟩ ⟨a rough sketch
: un bosquejo⟩ **7** APPROXIMATE
: aproximado ⟨a rough idea : una idea
aproximada⟩
rough[3] *n* **1 the rough** : el rough (en golf)
2 in the rough : en borrador
roughage ['rʌfɪdʒ] *n* : fibra *f*
roughen ['rʌfən] *vt* : poner áspero — *vi*
: ponerse áspero

roughly ['rʌfli] *adv* **1** : bruscamente ⟨to
treat roughly : maltratar⟩ **2** CRUDELY
: burdamente **3** APPROXIMATELY
: aproximadamente, más o menos
roughneck ['rʌf,nɛk] *n* : matón *m*
roughness ['rʌfnəs] *n* : rudeza *f*, aspereza *f*
roulette [ru:'lɛt] *n* : ruleta *f*
round[1] ['raʊnd] *vt* **1** : redondear ⟨she
rounded the edges : redondeó los bor-
des⟩ **2** TURN : doblar ⟨to round the
corner : dar la vuelta a la esquina⟩ **3
to round off** : redondear (un número)
4 to round off *or* **to round out** COM-
PLETE : rematar, terminar **5 to round
up** GATHER : reunir
round[2] *adv* → **around**[1]
round[3] *adj* **1** : redondo ⟨a round table
: una mesa redonda⟩ ⟨in round num-
bers : en números redondos⟩ ⟨round
shoulders : espaldas cargadas⟩ **2
round trip** : viaje *m* de ida y vuelta
round[4] *n* **1** CIRCLE : círculo *m* **2** SERIES
: serie *f*, sucesión *f* ⟨a round of talks
: una ronda de negociaciones⟩ ⟨the daily round : la rutina cotidiana⟩ **3** : asalto
m (en boxeo), recorrido *m* (en golf),
vuelta *f* (en varios juegos) **4** : salva *f*
(de aplausos) **5 round of drinks** : ronda *f* **6 round of ammunition** : disparo
m, cartucho *m* **7 rounds** *npl* : recorridos *mpl* (de un cartero), rondas *fpl* (de
un vigilante), visitas *fpl* (de un médico)
⟨to make the rounds : hacer visitas⟩
round[5] *prep* → **around**[2]
roundabout ['raʊndə,baʊt] *adj* : indirecto ⟨to speak in a roundabout way
: hablar con rodeos⟩
roundly ['raʊndli] *adv* **1** THOROUGHLY
: completamente **2** BLUNTLY : francamente, rotundamente **3** VIGOROUSLY
: con vigor
roundness ['raʊndnəs] *n* : redondez *f*
roundup ['raʊnd,ʌp] *n* **1** : rodeo *m* (de
animales), redada *f* (de delincuentes,
etc.) **2** SUMMARY : resumen *m*
round up *vt* **1** : rodear (ganado), reunir
(personas) **2** SUMMARIZE : hacer un resumen de
roundworm ['raʊnd,wərm] *n* : lombriz *f*
intestinal
rouse ['raʊz] *vt* **roused; rousing 1**
AWAKE : despertar **2** EXCITE : excitar
⟨it roused him to fury : lo enfureció⟩
rout[1] ['raʊt] *vt* **1** DEFEAT : derrotar,
aplastar **2 to rout out** : hacer salir
rout[2] *n* **1** DISPERSAL : desbandada *f*, dispersión *f* **2** DEFEAT : derrota *f* aplastante
route[1] ['ru:t, 'raʊt] *vt* **routed; routing**
: dirigir, enviar, encaminar
route[2] *n* : camino *m*, ruta *f*, recorrido *m*
routine[1] [ru:'ti:n] *adj* : rutinario — **rou-
tinely** *adv*
routine[2] *n* : rutina *f*
rove ['ro:v] *v* **roved; roving** *vi* : vagar, errar — *vt* : errar por
rover ['ro:vər] *n* : vagabundo *m*, -da *f*

row¹ ['ro:] *vt* **1** : avanzar a remo ⟨to row a boat : remar⟩ **2** : llevar a remo ⟨he rowed me to shore : me llevó hasta la orilla⟩ — *vi* : remar

row² ['raʊ] *n* **1** : paseo *m* en barca ⟨to go for a row : salir a remar⟩ **2** LINE, RANK : fila *f*, hilera *f* **3** SERIES : serie *f* ⟨three days in a row : tres días seguidos⟩ **4** RACKET : estruendo *m*, bulla *f* **5** QUARREL : pelea *f*, riña *f*

rowboat ['ro:,bo:t] *n* : bote *m* de remos

rowdiness ['raʊdinəs] *n* : bulla *f*

rowdy¹ ['raʊdi] *adj* **-dier; -est** : escandaloso, alborotador

rowdy² *n, pl* **-dies** : alborotador *m*, -dora *f*

rower ['ro:ər] *n* : remero *m*, -ra *f*

royal¹ ['rɔɪəl] *adj* : real — **royally** *adv*

royal² *n* : persona de linaje real, miembro de la familia real

royalty ['rɔɪəlti] *n, pl* **-ties 1** : realeza *f* (posición) **2** : miembros *mpl* de la familia real **3 royalties** *npl* : derechos *mpl* de autor

rub¹ ['rʌb] *v* **rubbed; rubbing** *vt* **1** : frotar, restregar ⟨to rub one's hands together : frotarse las manos⟩ **2** MASSAGE : friccionar, masajear **3** CHAFE : rozar **4** POLISH : frotar, pulir **5** SCRUB : fregar **6 to rub elbows with** : codearse con **7 to rub someone the wrong way** : sacar de quicio a alguien, caerle mal a alguien — *vi* **to rub against** : rozar

rub² *n* **1** RUBBING : frotamiento *m*, fricción *f* **2** DIFFICULTY : problema *m*

rubber ['rʌbər] *n* **1** : goma *f*, caucho *m*, hule *m Mex* **2 rubbers** *npl* OVERSHOES : chanclos *mpl*

rubber band *n* : goma *f* (elástica), gomita *f*

rubber–stamp ['rʌbər'stæmp] *vt* **1** APPROVE : aprobar, autorizar **2** STAMP : sellar

rubber stamp *n* : sello *m* (de goma)

rubbery ['rʌbəri] *adj* : gomoso

rubbish ['rʌbɪʃ] *n* : basura *f*, desechos *mpl*, desperdicios *mpl*

rubble ['rʌbəl] *n* : escombros *mpl*, ripio *m*

ruble ['ru:bəl] *n* : rublo *m*

ruby ['ru:bi] *n, pl* **-bies 1** : rubí *m* (gema) **2** : color *m* de rubí

rudder ['rʌdər] *n* : timón *m*

ruddy ['rʌdi] *adj* **-dier; -est** : rubicundo (dícese de la cara, etc.), rojizo (dícese del cielo)

rude ['ru:d] *adj* **ruder; rudest 1** CRUDE : tosco, rústico **2** IMPOLITE : grosero, descortés, maleducado **3** ABRUPT : brusco ⟨a rude awakening : una sorpresa desagradable⟩

rudely ['ru:dli] *adv* : groseramente

rudeness ['ru:dnəs] *n* **1** IMPOLITENESS : grosería *f*, descortesía *f*, falta *f* de educación **2** ROUGHNESS : tosquedad *f* **3** SUDDENNESS : brusquedad *f*

rudiment ['ru:dəmənt] *n* : rudimento *m*, noción *f* básica ⟨the rudiments of Spanish : los rudimentos del español⟩

rudimentary [,ru:də'mentəri] *adj* : rudimentario, básico

rue ['ru:] *vt* **rued; ruing** : lamentar, arrepentirse de

rueful ['ru:fəl] *adj* **1** PITIFUL : lastimoso **2** REGRETFUL : arrepentido, pesaroso

ruffian ['rʌfiən] *n* : matón *m*

ruffle¹ ['rʌfəl] *vt* **-fled; -fling 1** AGITATE : agitar, rizar (agua) **2** RUMPLE : arrugar (ropa), despeinar (pelo) **3** ERECT : erizar (plumas) **4** VEX : alterar, irritar, perturbar **5** : fruncir volantes en (tela)

ruffle² *n* FLOUNCE : volante *m*

ruffly ['rʌfəli] *adj* : con volantes

rug ['rʌg] *n* : alfombra *f*, tapete *m*

rugged ['rʌgəd] *adj* **1** ROUGH, UNEVEN : accidentado, escabroso ⟨rugged mountains : montañas accidentadas⟩ **2** HARSH : duro, severo **3** ROBUST, STURDY : robusto, fuerte

ruin¹ ['ru:ən] *vt* **1** DESTROY : destruir, arruinar **2** BANKRUPT : arruinar, hacer quebrar

ruin² *n* **1** : ruina *f* ⟨to fall into ruin : caer en ruinas⟩ **2** : ruina *f*, perdición *f* ⟨to be the ruin of : ser la perdición de⟩ **3 ruins** *npl* : ruinas *fpl*, restos *mpl* ⟨the ruins of the ancient temple : las ruinas del templo antiguo⟩

ruinous ['ru:ənəs] *adj* : ruinoso

rule¹ ['ru:l] *v* **ruled; ruling** *vt* **1** CONTROL, GOVERN : gobernar (un país), controlar (las emociones) **2** DECIDE : decidir, fallar ⟨the judge ruled that . . . : el juez falló que . . . ⟩ **3** DRAW : trazar con una regla — *vi* **1** GOVERN : gobernar, reinar **2** PREVAIL : prevalecer, imperar **3 to rule against** : fallar en contra de

rule² *n* **1** REGULATION : regla *f*, norma *f* **2** CUSTOM, HABIT : regla *f* general ⟨as a rule : por lo general⟩ **3** GOVERNMENT : gobierno *m*, dominio *m* **4** RULER : regla *f* (para medir)

ruler ['ru:lər] *n* **1** LEADER, SOVEREIGN : gobernante *mf*; soberano *m*, -na *f* **2** : regla *f* (para medir)

ruling ['ru:lɪŋ] *n* : resolución *f*, fallo *m*

rum ['rʌm] *n* : ron *m*

Rumanian [rʊ'meɪniən] → **Romanian**

rumble¹ ['rʌmbəl] *vi* **-bled; -bling** : retumbar, hacer ruidos (dícese del estómago)

rumble² *n* : estruendo *m*, ruido *m* sordo, retumbo *m*

ruminant¹ ['ru:mənənt] *adj* : rumiante

ruminant² *n* : rumiante *m*

ruminate ['ru:mə,neɪt] *vi* **-nated; -nating 1** : rumiar (en zoología) **2** REFLECT : reflexionar, rumiar

rummage ['rʌmɪdʒ] *v* **-maged; -maging** *vi* : hurgar — *vt* RANSACK : revolver ⟨they rummaged the attic : revolvieron el ático⟩

rummy ['rʌmi] *n* : rummy *m* (juego de naipes)

rumor[1] ['ruːmər] *vt* : rumorear ⟨it is rumored that . . . : se rumorea que . . ., se dice que . . .⟩

rumor[2] *n* : rumor *m*

rump ['rʌmp] *n* **1** : ancas *fpl*, grupa *f* (de un animal) **2** : cadera *f* ⟨rump steak : filete de cadera⟩

rumple ['rʌmpəl] *vt* **-pled; -pling** : arrugar (ropa, etc.), despeinar (pelo)

rumpus ['rʌmpəs] *n* : lío *m*, jaleo *m fam*

run[1] ['rʌn] *v* **ran** ['ræn]; **run; running** *vi* **1** : correr ⟨she ran to catch the bus : corrió para alcanzar el autobús⟩ ⟨run and fetch the doctor : corre a buscar al médico⟩ **2** : circular, correr ⟨the train runs between Detroit and Chicago : el tren circula entre Detroit y Chicago⟩ ⟨to run on time : ser puntual⟩ **3** FUNCTION : funcionar, ir ⟨the engine runs on gasoline : el motor funciona con gasolina⟩ ⟨to run smoothly : ir bien⟩ **4** FLOW : correr, ir **5** LAST : durar ⟨the movie runs for two hours : la película dura dos horas⟩ ⟨the contract runs for three years : el contrato es válido por tres años⟩ **6** : desteñir, despintar ⟨dícese de los colores⟩ **7** EXTEND : correr, extenderse **8 to run for office** : postularse, presentarse — *vt* **1** : correr ⟨to run 10 miles : correr 10 millas⟩ ⟨to run errands : hacer los mandados⟩ ⟨to run out of town : hacer salir del pueblo⟩ **2** PASS : pasar **3** DRIVE : llevar en coche ⟨to run water : echar agua⟩ **6** MANAGE : dirigir, llevar (un negocio, etc.) **7** EXTEND : tender (un cable, etc.) **8 to run a risk** : correr un riesgo

run[2] *n* **1** : carrera *f* ⟨at a run : a la carrera, corriendo⟩ ⟨to go for a run : ir a correr⟩ **2** TRIP : vuelta *f*, paseo *m* (en coche), viaje *m* (en avión) **3** SERIES : serie *f* ⟨a run of disappointments : una serie de desilusiones⟩ ⟨in the long run : a la larga⟩ ⟨in the short run : a corto plazo⟩ **4** DEMAND : gran demanda *f* ⟨a run on the banks : una corrida bancaria⟩ **5** (*used for theatrical productions and films*) ⟨to have a long run : mantenerse mucho tiempo en la cartelera⟩ **6** TYPE : tipo *m* ⟨the average run of students : el tipo más común de estudiante⟩ **7** : carrera *f* (en béisbol) **8** : carrera *f* (en una media) **9 to have the run of** : tener libre acceso de (una casa, etc.) **10 ski run** : pista *f* (de esquí)

runaway[1] ['rʌnəˌweɪ] *adj* **1** FUGITIVE : fugitivo **2** UNCONTROLLABLE : incontrolable, fuera de control ⟨runaway inflation : inflación desenfrenada⟩ ⟨a runaway success : un éxito aplastante⟩

runaway[2] *n* : fugitivo *m*, -va *f*

rundown ['rʌnˌdaʊn] *n* SUMMARY : resumen *m*

run–down ['rʌn'daʊn] *adj* **1** DILAPIDATED : ruinoso, destartalado **2** SICKLY, TIRED : cansado, débil

rung[1] *pp* → **ring**[1]

rung[2] ['rʌŋ] *n* : peldaño *m*, escalón *m*

run–in ['rʌnˌɪn] *n* : disputa *f*, altercado *m*

runner ['rʌnər] *n* **1** RACER : corredor *m*, -dora *f* **2** MESSENGER : mensajero *m*, -ra *f* **3** TRACK : riel *m* (de un cajón, etc.) **4** : patín *m* (de un trineo), cuchilla *f* (de un patín) **5** : estolón *m* (planta)

runner–up [ˌrʌnərˈʌp] *n, pl* **runners–up** : subcampeón *m*, -peona *f*

running ['rʌnɪŋ] *adj* **1** FLOWING : corriente ⟨running water : agua corriente⟩ **2** CONTINUOUS : continuo ⟨a running battle : una lucha continua⟩ **3** CONSECUTIVE : seguido ⟨six days running : por seis días seguidos⟩

runny ['rʌni] *adj* **-nier; -est 1** WATERY : caldoso **2 to have a runny nose** : moquear

run over *vt* : atropellar — *vi* OVERFLOW : rebosar

runt ['rʌnt] *n* : animal *m* pequeño ⟨the runt of the litter : el más pequeño de la camada⟩

runway ['rʌnˌweɪ] *n* : pista *f* de aterrizaje

rupee [ruːˈpiː, ˈruːˌ-] *n* : rupia *f*

rupture[1] ['rʌptʃər] *v* **-tured; -turing** *vt* **1** BREAK, BURST : romper, reventar **2** : causar una hernia en — *vi* : reventarse

rupture[2] *n* **1** BREAK : ruptura *f* **2** HERNIA : hernia *f*

rural ['rʊrəl] *adj* : rural, campestre

ruse ['ruːs, 'ruːz] *n* : treta *f*, ardid *m*, estratagema *f*

rush[1] ['rʌʃ] *vi* : correr, ir de prisa ⟨to rush around : correr de un lado a otro⟩ ⟨to rush off : irse corriendo⟩ — *vt* **1** HURRY : apresurar, apurar **2** ATTACK : abalanzarse sobre, asaltar

rush[2] *adj* : urgente

rush[3] *n* **1** HASTE : prisa *f*, apuro *m* **2** SURGE : ráfaga *f* (de aire), torrente *m* (de aguas), avalancha *f* (de gente) **3** DEMAND : demanda *f* ⟨a rush on sugar : una gran demanda para el azúcar⟩ **4** : carga *f* (en futbol americano) **5** : junco *m* (planta)

russet ['rʌsət] *n* : color *m* rojizo

Russian ['rʌʃən] *n* **1** : ruso *m*, -sa *f* **2** : ruso *m* (idioma) — **Russian** *adj*

rust[1] ['rʌst] *vi* : oxidarse — *vt* : oxidar

rust[2] *n* **1** : herrumbre *f*, orín *m*, óxido *m* (en los metales) **2** : roya *f* (en las plantas)

rustic[1] ['rʌstɪk] *adj* : rústico, campestre — **rustically** [-tɪkli] *adv*

rustic[2] *n* : rústico *m*, -ca *f*; campesino *m*, -na *f*

rustle[1] ['rʌsəl] *v* **-tled; -tling** *vt* **1** : hacer susurrar, hacer crujir ⟨to rustle a newspaper : hacer crujir un periódico⟩ **2** STEAL : robar (ganado) — *vi* : susurrar, crujir

rustle² *n* : murmullo *m*, susurro *m*, crujido *m*
rustler ['rʌsələr] *n* : ladrón *m*, -drona *f* de ganado
rusty ['rʌsti] *adj* **rustier; -est** : oxidado, herrumbroso
rut ['rʌt] *n* **1** GROOVE, TRACK : rodada *f*, surco *m* **2 to be in a rut** : ser esclavo de la rutina

ruthless ['ru:θləs] *adj* : despiadado, cruel — **ruthlessly** *adv*
ruthlessness ['ru:θləsnəs] *n* : crueldad *f*, falta *f* de piedad
Rwandan [ru'andən] *n* : ruandés *m*, -desa *f* — **Rwandan** *adj*
rye ['raɪ] *n* **1** : centeno *m* **2** *or* **rye whiskey** : whisky *m* de centeno

S

s ['ɛs] *n, pl* **s's** *or* **ss** ['ɛsəz] : decimonovena letra del alfabeto inglés
Sabbath ['sæbəθ] *n* **1** : sábado *m* (en el judaísmo) **2** : domingo *m* (en el cristianismo)
saber ['seɪbər] *n* : sable *m*
sable ['seɪbəl] *n* **1** BLACK : negro *m* **2** : marta *f* cebellina (animal)
sabotage¹ ['sæbə,taʒ] *vt* **-taged; -taging** : sabotear
sabotage² *n* : sabotaje *m*
sac ['sæk] *n* : saco *m* (anatómico)
saccharin ['sækərən] *n* : sacarina *f*
saccharine ['sækərən, -,ri:n, -,raɪn] *adj* : meloso, empalagoso
sachet [sæ'ʃeɪ] *n* : bolsita *f* (perfumada)
sack¹ ['sæk] *vt* **1** FIRE : echar (del trabajo), despedir **2** PLUNDER : saquear
sack² *n* BAG : saco *m*
sacrament ['sækrəmənt] *n* : sacramento *m*
sacramental [,sækrə'mɛntəl] *adj* : sacramental
sacred ['seɪkrəd] *adj* **1** RELIGIOUS : sagrado, sacro ⟨sacred texts : textos sagrados⟩ **2** HOLY : sagrado **3 sacred to** : consagrado a
sacrifice¹ ['sækrə,faɪs] *vt* **-ficed; -ficing** **1** : sacrificar **2 to sacrifice oneself** : sacrificarse
sacrifice² *n* : sacrificio *m*
sacrilege ['sækrəlɪdʒ] *n* : sacrilegio *m*
sacrilegious [,sækrə'lɪdʒəs, -'li:-] *adj* : sacrílego
sacrosanct ['sækro,sæŋkt] *adj* : sacrosanto
sad ['sæd] *adj* **sadder; saddest** : triste — **sadly** *adv*
sadden ['sædən] *vt* : entristecer
saddle¹ ['sædəl] *vt* **-dled; -dling** : ensillar
saddle² *n* : silla *f* (de montar)
sadism ['seɪ,dɪzəm, 'sæ-] *n* : sadismo *m*
sadist ['seɪdɪst, 'sæ-] *n* : sádico *m*, -ca *f*
sadistic [sə'dɪstɪk] *adj* : sádico — **sadistically** [-tɪkli] *adv*
sadness ['sædnəs] *n* : tristeza *f*
safari [sə'fɑri, -'fær-] *n* : safari *m*
safe¹ ['seɪf] *adj* **safer; safest** **1** UNHARMED : ileso ⟨safe and sound : sano y salvo⟩ **2** SECURE : seguro **3 to be on the safe side** : para mayor seguridad **4 to play it safe** : ir a la segura
safe² *n* : caja *f* fuerte

safeguard¹ ['seɪf,gɑrd] *vt* : salvaguardar, proteger
safeguard² *n* : salvaguarda *f*, protección *f*
safekeeping ['seɪf'ki:pɪŋ] *n* : custodia *f*, protección *f* ⟨to put into safekeeping : poner en buen recaudo⟩
safely ['seɪfli] *adv* **1** UNHARMED : sin incidentes, sin novedades ⟨they landed safely : aterrizaron sin novedades⟩ **2** SECURELY : con toda seguridad, sin peligro
safety ['seɪfti] *n, pl* **-ties** : seguridad *f*
safety belt *n* : cinturón *m* de seguridad
safety pin *n* : alfiler *m* de gancho, alfiler *m* de seguridad, imperdible *m Spain*
saffron ['sæfrən] *n* : azafrán *m*
sag¹ ['sæg] *vi* **sagged; sagging** **1** DROOP, SINK : combarse, hundirse, inclinarse **2** : colgar, caer ⟨his jowls sagged : le colgaban las mejillas⟩ **3** FLAG : flaquear, decaer ⟨his spirits sagged : se le flaqueó el ánimo⟩
sag² *n* : combadura *f*
saga ['sɑgə, 'sæ-] *n* : saga *f*
sagacious [sə'geɪʃəs] *adj* : sagaz
sage¹ ['seɪdʒ] *adj* **sager; -est** : sabio — **sagely** *adv*
sage² *n* **1** : sabio *m*, -bia *f* **2** : salvia *f* (planta)
sagebrush ['seɪdʒ,brʌʃ] *n* : artemisa *f*
Sagittarius [,sædʒə'tɛriəs] *n* : Sagitario *mf*
said → say
sail¹ ['seɪl] *vi* **1** : navegar (en un barco) **2** : ir fácilmente ⟨we sailed right in : entramos sin ningún problema⟩ — *vt* **1** : gobernar (un barco) **2 to sail the seas** : cruzar los mares
sail² *n* **1** : vela *f* (de un barco) **2** : viaje *m* en velero ⟨to go for a sail : salir a navegar⟩
sailboat ['seɪl,bo:t] *n* : velero *m*, barco *m* de vela
sailfish ['seɪl,fɪʃ] *n* : pez *m* vela
sailor ['seɪlər] *n* : marinero *m*
saint ['seɪnt, *before a name* ,seɪnt *or* sənt] *n* : santo *m*, -ta *f* ⟨Saint Francis : San Francisco⟩ ⟨Saint Rose : Santa Rosa⟩
saintliness ['seɪntlinəs] *n* : santidad *f*
saintly ['seɪntli] *adj* **saintlier; -est** : santo
sake ['seɪk] *n* **1** BENEFIT : bien *m* ⟨for the children's sake : por el bien de los

niños⟩ **2** (*indicating an end or a purpose*) ⟨art for art's sake : el arte por el arte⟩ ⟨let's say, for argument's sake, that he's wrong : pongamos que está equivocado⟩ **3 for goodness' sake!** : ¡por (el amor de) Dios!

salable *or* **saleable** ['seɪləbəl] *adj* : vendible

salacious [sə'leɪʃəs] *adj* : salaz — **salaciously** *adv*

salad ['sæləd] *n* : ensalada *f*

salamander ['sælə,mændər] *n* : salamandra *f*

salami [sə'lɑmi] *n* : salami *m*

salary ['sæləri] *n, pl* **-ries** : sueldo *m*

sale ['seɪl] *n* **1** SELLING : venta *f* **2** : liquidación *f*, rebajas *fpl* ⟨on sale : de rebaja⟩ **3 sales** *npl* : ventas *fpl* ⟨to work in sales : trabajar en ventas⟩

salesman ['seɪlzmən] *n, pl* **-men** [-mən, -,mɛn] **1** : vendedor *m*, dependiente *m* (en una tienda) **2 traveling salesman** : viajante *m*, representante *m*

salesperson ['seɪlz,pərsən] *n* : vendedor *m*, -dora *f*; dependiente *m*, -ta *f* (en una tienda)

saleswoman ['seɪlz,wʊmən] *n, pl* **-women** [-,wɪmən] **1** : vendedora *f*, dependienta *f* (en una tienda) **2 traveling saleswoman** : viajante *f*, representante *f*

salient ['seɪljənt] *adj* : saliente, sobresaliente

saline ['seɪ,li:n, -,laɪn] *adj* : salino

saliva [sə'laɪvə] *n* : saliva *f*

salivary ['sælə,veri] *adj* : salival ⟨salivary gland : glándula salival⟩

salivate ['sælə,veɪt] *vi* **-vated; -vating** : salivar

sallow ['sælo:] *adj* : amarillento, cetrino

sally¹ ['sæli] *vi* **-lied; -lying** SET OUT : salir, hacer una salida

sally² *n, pl* **-lies 1** : salida *f* (militar), misión *f* **2** QUIP : salida *f*, ocurrencia *f*

salmon ['sæmən] *ns & pl* **1** : salmón *m* (pez) **2** : color *m* salmón

salon [sə'lɑn, 'sæ,lɑn, sæ'lɔ̃] *n* : salón *m* ⟨beauty salon : salón de belleza⟩

saloon [sə'lu:n] *n* **1** HALL : salón *m* (en un barco) **2** BARROOM : bar *m*

salsa ['sɔlsə, 'sɑl-] *n* : salsa *f* mexicana, salsa *f* picante

salt¹ ['sɔlt] *vt* : salar, echarle sal a

salt² *adj* : salado

salt³ *n* : sal *f*

saltwater ['sɔlt,wɔt̬ər, -,wɑ-] *adj* : de agua salada

salty ['sɔlti] *adj* **saltier; -est** : salado

salubrious [sə'lu:briəs] *adj* : salubre

salutary ['sæljə,teri] *adj* : saludable, salubre

salutation [,sæljə'teɪʃən] *n* : saludo *m*, salutación *f*

salute¹ [sə'lu:t] *v* **-luted; -luting** *vt* **1** : saludar (con gestos o ceremonias) **2** ACCLAIM : reconocer, aclamar — *vi* : hacer un saludo

salute² *n* **1** : saludo *m* (gesto), salva *f* (de cañonazos) **2** TRIBUTE : reconocimiento *m*, homenaje *m*

Salvadoran [,sælvə'dorən] → **El Salvadoran**

salvage¹ ['sælvɪdʒ] *vt* **-vaged; -vaging** : salvar, rescatar

salvage² *n* **1** SALVAGING : salvamento *m*, rescate *m* **2** : objetos *mpl* salvados

salvation [sæl'veɪʃən] *n* : salvación *f*

salve¹ ['sæv, 'sav] *vt* **salved; salving** : calmar, apaciguar ⟨to salve one's conscience : aliviarse la conciencia⟩

salve² *n* : ungüento *m*

salvo ['sæl,vo:] *n, pl* **-vos** *or* **-voes** : salva *f*

same¹ ['seɪm] *adj* : mismo, igual ⟨the results are the same : los resultados son iguales⟩ ⟨he said the same thing as you : dijo lo mismo que tú⟩

same² *pron* : mismo ⟨it's all the same to me : me da lo mismo⟩ ⟨the same to you! : ¡igualmente!⟩

sameness ['seɪmnəs] *n* **1** SIMILARITY : identidad *f*, semejanza *f* **2** MONOTONY : monotonía *f*

sample¹ ['sæmpəl] *vt* **-pled; -pling** : probar

sample² *n* : muestra *f*, prueba *f*

sampler ['sæmplər] *n* **1** : dechado *m* (de bordado) **2** COLLECTION : colección *f* **3** ASSORTMENT : surtido *m*

sanatorium [,sænə'toriəm] *n, pl* **-riums** *or* **-ria** [-iə] : sanatorio *m*

sanctify ['sæŋktə,faɪ] *vt* **-fied; -fying** : santificar

sanctimonious [,sæŋktə'mo:niəs] *adj* : beato, santurrón

sanction¹ ['sæŋkʃən] *vt* : sancionar, aprobar

sanction² *n* **1** AUTHORIZATION : sanción *f*, autorización *f* **2 sanctions** *npl* : sanciones *fpl* ⟨to impose sanctions on : imponer sanciones a⟩

sanctity ['sæŋktəti] *n, pl* **-ties** : santidad *f*

sanctuary ['sæŋktʃu,eri] *n, pl* **-aries 1** : presbiterio *m* (en una iglesia) **2** REFUGE : refugio *m*, asilo *m*

sand¹ ['sænd] *vt* : lijar (madera)

sand² *n* : arena *f*

sandal ['sændəl] *n* : sandalia *f*

sandbank ['sænd,bæŋk] *n* : banco *m* de arena

sandpaper *n* : papel *m* de lija

sandpiper ['sænd,paɪpər] *n* : andarríos *m*

sandstone ['sænd,sto:n] *n* : arenisca *f*

sandstorm ['sænd,storm] *n* : tormenta *f* de arena

sandwich¹ ['sænd,wɪtʃ] *vt* : intercalar, encajonar, meter (entre dos cosas)

sandwich² *n* : sandwich *m*, emparedado *m*, bocadillo *m* Spain

sandy ['sændi] *adj* **sandier; -est** : arenoso

sane ['seɪn] *adj* **saner; sanest 1** : cuerdo **2** SENSIBLE : sensato, razonable

sang → sing
sanguine ['sæŋgwən] *adj* **1** RUDDY
: sanguíneo, rubicundo **2** HOPEFUL
: optimista
sanitarium [ˌsænə'tɛriəm] *n, pl* **-iums** *or*
-ia [-iə] → **sanatorium**
sanitary ['sænəteri] *adj* **1** : sanitario
⟨sanitary measures : medidas sani-
tarias⟩ **2** HYGIENIC : higiénico **3** **sanitary napkin** : compresa *f*, paño *m*
higiénico
sanitation [ˌsænə'teɪʃən] *n* : sanidad *f*
sanitize ['sænəˌtaɪz] *vt* **-tized; -tizing 1**
: desinfectar **2** EXPURGATE : expurgar
sanity ['sænəti] *n* : cordura *f*, razón *f* ⟨to
lose one's sanity : perder el juicio⟩
sank → sink
Santa Claus ['sæntəˌklɔz] *n* : Papá Noel,
San Nicolás
sap[1] ['sæp] *vt* **sapped; sapping 1** UN-
DERMINE : socavar **2** WEAKEN : mi-
nar, debilitar
sap[2] *n* **1** : savia *f* (de una planta) **2** SUCK-
ER : inocentón *m*, -tona *f*
sapling ['sæplɪŋ] *n* : árbol *m* joven
sapphire ['sæˌfaɪr] *n* : zafiro *m*
sarcasm ['sɑrˌkæzəm] *n* : sarcasmo *m*
sarcastic [sɑr'kæstɪk] *adj* : sarcástico —
sarcastically [-tɪkli] *adv*
sarcophagus [sɑr'kafəgəs] *n, pl* **-gi**
[-ˌgaɪ, -ˌdʒaɪ] : sarcófago *m*
sardine [sɑr'diːn] *n* : sardina *f*
sardonic [sɑr'dɑnɪk] *adj* : sardónico —
sardonically [-nɪkli] *adv*
sarsaparilla [ˌsæspə'rɪlə, ˌsɑrs-] *n*
: zarzaparrilla *f*
sash ['sæʃ] *n* **1** : faja *f* (de un vestido),
fajín *m* (de un uniforme) **2** *pl* **sash**
: marco *m* (de una ventana)
sassafras ['sæsəˌfræs] *n* : sasafrás *m*
sassy ['sæsi] *adj* **sassier; -est** → **saucy**
sat → sit
Satan ['seɪtən] *n* : Satanás *m*, Satán *m*
satanic [sə'tænɪk, seɪ-] *adj* : satánico —
satanically [-nɪkli] *adv*
satchel ['sætʃəl] *n* : cartera *f*, saco *m*
sate ['seɪt] *vt* **sated; sating** : saciar
satellite ['sætəˌlaɪt] *n* : satélite *m* ⟨spy
satellite : satélite espía⟩
satiate ['seɪʃiˌeɪt] *vt* **-ated; -ating** : saciar,
hartar
satin ['sætən] *n* : raso *m*, satín *m*, satén
m
satire ['sæˌtaɪr] *n* : sátira *f*
satiric [sə'tɪrɪk] *or* **satirical** [-ɪkəl] *adj*
: satírico
satirize ['sætəˌraɪz] *vt* **-rized; -rizing**
: satirizar
satisfaction [ˌsætəs'fækʃən] *n* : satisfacción *f*
satisfactory [ˌsætəs'fæktəri] *adj* : satisfactorio, bueno — **satisfactorily** [-rəli]
adv
satisfy ['sætəsˌfaɪ] *v* **-fied; -fying** *vt* **1**
PLEASE : satisfacer, contentar **2** CON-
VINCE : convencer **3** FULFILL : satisfacer, cumplir con, llenar **4** SETTLE
: pagar, saldar (una cuenta) — *vi* SUF-
FICE : bastar

saturate ['sætʃəˌreɪt] *vt* **-rated; -rating 1**
SOAK : empapar **2** FILL : saturar
saturation [ˌsætʃə'reɪʃən] *n* : saturación
f
Saturday ['sætərˌdeɪ, -di] *n* : sábado *m*
Saturn ['sætərn] *n* : Saturno *m*
satyr ['seɪtər, 'sæ-] *n* : sátiro *m*
sauce ['sɔs] *n* : salsa *f*
saucepan ['sɔsˌpæn] *n* : cacerola *f*, cazo
m, cazuela *f*
saucer ['sɔsər] *n* : platillo *m*
sauciness ['sɔsinəs] *n* : descaro *m*, frescura *f*
saucy ['sɔsi] *adj* **saucier; -est** IMPU-
DENT : descarado, fresco *fam* — **sauci-
ly** *adv*
Saudi ['saʊdi, 'sɔ-] → **Saudi Arabian**
Saudi Arabian *n* : saudita *mf*, saudí *mf*
— **Saudi Arabian** *adj*
sauna ['sɔnə, 'saʊnə] *n* : sauna *mf*
saunter ['sɔntər, 'sɑn-] *vi* : pasear,
pasearse
sausage ['sɔsɪdʒ] *n* : salchicha *f*, embutido *m*
sauté [sɔ'teɪ, soʊ-] *vt* **-téed** *or* **-téd; -téing**
: saltear, sofreír
savage[1] ['sævɪdʒ] *adj* : salvaje, feroz —
savagely *adv*
savage[2] *n* : salvaje *mf*
savagery ['sævɪdʒri, -dʒəri] *n, pl* **-ries 1**
FEROCITY : ferocidad *f* **2** WILDNESS
: salvajismo *m*
savanna [sə'vænə] *n* : sabana *f*
save[1] ['seɪv] *vt* **saved; saving 1** RESCUE
: salvar, rescatar **2** PRESERVE : preservar, conservar **3** KEEP : guardar, ahorrar (dinero), almacenar (alimentos) **4**
: guardar (en informática)
save[2] *prep* EXCEPT : salvo, excepto,
menos
savior ['seɪvjər] *n* **1** : salvador *m*, -dora
f **2 the Savior** : el Salvador *m*
savor[1] ['seɪvər] *vt* : saborear
savor[2] *n* : sabor *m*
savory ['seɪvəri] *adj* : sabroso
saw[1] → see
saw[2] [sɔ] *vt* **sawed; sawed** *or* **sawn**
['sɔn]; **sawing** : serrar, cortar (con sierra)
saw[3] *n* : sierra *f*
sawdust ['sɔˌdʌst] *n* : aserrín *m*, serrín
m
sawhorse ['sɔˌhɔrs] *n* : caballete *m*, burro *m* (en carpintería)
sawmill ['sɔˌmɪl] *n* : aserradero *m*
saxophone ['sæksəˌfoːn] *n* : saxofón *m*
say[1] ['seɪ] *v* **said** ['sɛd]; **saying; says**
['sɛz] *vt* **1** EXPRESS, UTTER : decir, expresar ⟨to say no : decir que no⟩ ⟨that
goes without saying : ni que decir
tiene⟩ ⟨no sooner said than done : dicho y hecho⟩ ⟨to say again : repetir⟩
⟨to say one's prayers : rezar⟩ **2** INDI-
CATE : marcar, poner ⟨my watch says
three o'clock : mi reloj marca las tres⟩
⟨what does the sign say? : ¿qué pone
el letrero?⟩ **3** ALLEGE : decir ⟨it's said
that she's pretty : se dice que es boni-
ta⟩ — *vi* : decir

say² *n, pl* **says** ['seiz] : voz *f*, opinión *f* ⟨to have no say : no tener ni voz ni voto⟩ ⟨to have one's say : dar uno su opinión⟩

saying ['seiiŋ] *n* : dicho *m*, refrán *m*

scab ['skæb] *n* **1** : costra *f*, postilla *f* (en una herida) **2** STRIKEBREAKER : rompehuelgas *mf*, esquirol *mf*

scabbard ['skæbərd] *n* : vaina *f* (de una espada), funda *f* (de un puñal, etc.)

scabby ['skæbi] *adj* **scabbier; -est** : lleno de costras

scaffold ['skæfəld, -ˌfoːld] *n* **1** *or* **scaffolding** : andamio *m* (para obreros, etc.) **2** : patíbulo *m*, cadalso *m* (para ejecuciones)

scald ['skɔld] *vt* **1** BURN : escaldar **2** HEAT : calentar (hasta el punto de ebullición)

scale¹ ['skeɪl] *v* **scaled; scaling** *vt* **1** : escamar (un pescado) **2** CLIMB : escalar (un muro, etc.) **3 to scale down** : reducir — *vi* WEIGH : pesar ⟨he scaled in at 200 pounds : pesó 200 libras⟩

scale² *n* **1** *or* **scales** : balanza *f*, báscula *f* (para pesar) **2** : escama *f* (de un pez, etc.) **3** EXTENT : escala *f*, proporción *f* ⟨wage scale : escala salarial⟩ **4** : escala *f* (en música, en cartografía, etc.) ⟨to draw to scale : dibujar a escala⟩

scallion ['skæljən] *n* : cebollino *m*, cebolleta *f*

scallop ['skɑləp, 'skæ-] *n* **1** : vieira *f* (molusco) **2** : festón *m* (decoración)

scalp¹ ['skælp] *vt* : arrancar la cabellera a

scalp² *n* : cuero *m* cabelludo

scalpel ['skælpəl] *n* : bisturí *m*, escalpelo *m*

scaly ['skeɪli] *adj* **scalier; -est** : escamoso

scam ['skæm] *n* : estafa *f*, timo *m fam*, chanchullo *m fam*

scamp ['skæmp] *n* : bribón *m*, -bona *f*; granuja *mf*; travieso *m*, -sa *f*

scamper ['skæmpər] *vi* : corretear

scan¹ ['skæn] *vt* **scanned; scanning 1** : escandir (versos) **2** SCRUTINIZE : escudriñar, escrutar ⟨to scan the horizon : escudriñar el horizonte⟩ **3** PERUSE : echarle un vistazo a (un periódico, etc.) **4** EXPLORE : explorar (con radar), hacer un escáner de (en ecografía) **5** : escanear (una imagen)

scan² *n* **1** : ecografía *f*, examen *m* ultrasónico (en medicina) **2** : imagen *f* escaneada (en una computadora)

scandal ['skændəl] *n* **1** DISGRACE, OUTRAGE : escándalo *m* **2** GOSSIP : habladurías *fpl*, chismes *mpl*

scandalize ['skændəˌaɪz] *vt* **-ized; -izing** : escandalizar

scandalous ['skændələs] *adj* : de escándalo

Scandinavian¹ [ˌskændəˈneɪviən] *adj* : escandinavo

Scandinavian² *n* : escandinavo *m*, -va *f*

scanner ['skænər] *n* : escáner *m*, scanner *m*

scant ['skænt] *adj* : escaso

scanty ['skænti] *adj* **scantier; -est** : exiguo, escaso ⟨a scanty meal : una comida insuficiente⟩ — **scantily** [-təli] *adv*

scapegoat ['skeɪpˌgoːt] *n* : chivo *m* expiatorio, cabeza *f* de turco

scapula ['skæpjələ] *n, pl* **-lae** [-ˌliː, -ˌlaɪ] *or* **-las → shoulder blade**

scar¹ ['skɑr] *v* **scarred; scarring** *vt* : dejar una cicatriz en — *vi* : cicatrizar

scar² *n* : cicatriz *f*, marca *f*

scarab ['skærəb] *n* : escarabajo *m*

scarce ['skers] *adj* **scarcer; -est** : escaso

scarcely ['skersli] *adv* **1** BARELY : apenas **2** : ni mucho menos, ni nada que se le parezca ⟨he's scarcely an expert : ciertamente no es experto⟩

scarcity ['skersəti] *n, pl* **-ties** : escasez *f*

scare¹ ['sker] *vt* **scared; scaring** : asustar, espantar

scare² *n* **1** FRIGHT : susto *m*, sobresalto *m* **2** ALARM : pánico *m*

scarecrow ['skerˌkroː] *n* : espantapájaros *m*, espantajo *m*

scarf ['skɑrf] *n, pl* **scarves** ['skɑrvz] *or* **scarfs 1** MUFFLER : bufanda *f* **2** KERCHIEF : pañuelo *m*

scarlet ['skɑrlət] *n* : escarlata *f* — **scarlet** *adj*

scarlet fever *n* : escarlatina *f*

scary ['skeri] *adj* **scarier; -est** : espantoso, pavoroso

scathing ['skeɪðɪŋ] *adj* : mordaz, cáustico

scatter ['skæt̬ər] *vt* : esparcir, desparramar — *vi* DISPERSE : dispersarse

scavenge ['skævəndʒ] *v* **-venged; -venging** *vt* : rescatar (de la basura), pepenar *CA, Mex* — *vi* : rebuscar, hurgar en la basura ⟨to scavenge for food : andar buscando comida⟩

scavenger ['skævəndʒər] *n* **1** : persona *f* que rebusca en las basuras; pepenador *m*, -dora *f CA, Mex* **2** : carroñero *m*, -ra *f* (animal)

scenario [səˈnæriˌoː, -ˈnɑr-] *n, pl* **-ios 1** PLOT : argumento *m* (en teatro), guión *m* (en cine) **2** SITUATION : situación *f* hipotética ⟨in the worst-case scenario : en el peor de los casos⟩

scene ['siːn] *n* **1** : escena *f* (en una obra de teatro) **2** SCENERY : decorado *m* (en el teatro) **3** VIEW : escena *f* **4** LOCALE : escenario *m* **5** COMMOTION, FUSS : escándalo *m*, escena *f* ⟨to make a scene : armar un escándalo⟩

scenery ['siːnəri] *n, pl* **-eries 1** : decorado *m* (en el teatro) **2** LANDSCAPE : paisaje *m*

scenic ['siːnɪk] *adj* : pintoresco

scent¹ ['sent] *vt* **1** SMELL : oler, olfatear **2** PERFUME : perfumar **3** SENSE : sentir, percibir

scent² *n* **1** ODOR : olor *m*, aroma *m* **2** : olfato *m* ⟨a dog with a keen scent : un

perro con un buen olfato⟩ **3** PERFUME
: perfume *m*
scented ['sɛntəd] *adj* : perfumado
scepter ['sɛptər] *n* : cetro *m*
sceptic ['skɛptɪk] → **skeptic**
schedule¹ ['skɛˌdʒuːl, -dʒəl, *esp Brit*
'ʃɛdˌjuːl] *vt* **-uled; -uling** : planear, programar
schedule² *n* **1** PLAN : programa *m*, plan
m ⟨on schedule : según lo previsto⟩
⟨behind schedule : atrasado, con re-
traso⟩ **2** TIMETABLE : horario *m*
scheme¹ ['skiːm] *vi* **schemed; schem-
ing** : intrigar, conspirar
scheme² *n* **1** PLAN : plan *m*, proyecto
m **2** PLOT, TRICK : intriga *f*, ardid *m* **3**
FRAMEWORK : esquema *f* ⟨a color
scheme : una combinación de colores⟩
schemer ['skiːmər] *n* : intrigante *mf*
schism ['sɪzəm, 'skɪ-] *n* : cisma *m*
schizophrenia [ˌskɪtsəˈfriːniə, ˌskɪzə-,
-ˈfrɛ-] *n* : esquizofrenia *f*
schizophrenic [ˌskɪtsəˈfrɛnɪk, ˌskɪzə-] *n*
: esquizofrénico *m*, -ca *f* — **schizophrenic** *adj*
scholar ['skɑlər] *n* **1** STUDENT : escolar
mf; alumno *m*, -na *f* **2** EXPERT : especialista *mf*
scholarly ['skɑlərli] *adj* : erudito
scholarship ['skɑlərˌʃɪp] *n* **1** LEARNING
: erudición *f* **2** GRANT : beca *f*
scholastic [skəˈlæstɪk] *adj* : académico
school¹ ['skuːl] *vt* : instruir, enseñar
school² *n* **1** : escuela *f*, colegio *m* (institución) **2** : estudiantes *mfpl* y pro-
fesores *mpl* (de una escuela) **3** : escuela
f (en pintura, etc.) ⟨the Flemish school
: la escuela flamenca⟩ **4 school of fish**
: banco *m*, cardumen *m*
schoolboy ['skuːlˌbɔɪ] *n* : escolar *m*,
colegial *m*
schoolgirl ['skuːlˌgərl] *n* : escolar *f*, cole-
giala *f*
schoolhouse ['skuːlˌhaʊs] *n* : escuela *f*
schoolmate ['skuːlˌmeɪt] *n* : compañero
m, -ra *f* de escuela
schoolroom ['skuːlˌruːm, -ˌrʊm] →
classroom
schoolteacher ['skuːlˌtiːtʃər] *n* : maestro
m, -tra *f*; profesor *m*, -sora *f*
schoolwork ['skuːlˌwərk] *n* : trabajo *m*
escolar
schooner ['skuːnər] *n* : goleta *f*
science ['saɪənts] *n* : ciencia *f*
science fiction *n* : ciencia ficción *f*
scientific [ˌsaɪənˈtɪfɪk] *adj* : científico —
scientifically [-fɪkli] *adv*
scientist ['saɪəntɪst] *n* : científico *m*, -ca
f
scintillating ['sɪntəˌleɪtɪŋ] *adj* : chispeante, brillante
scissors ['sɪzərz] *npl* : tijeras *fpl*
sclerosis [skləˈroːsəs] *n, pl* **-roses** : esclerosis *f*
scoff ['skɑf] *vi* **to scoff at** : burlarse de,
mofarse de
scold ['skoːld] *vt* : regañar, reprender,
reñir

scoop¹ ['skuːp] *vt* **1** : sacar (con pala o
cucharón) **2 to scoop out** HOLLOW
: vaciar, ahuecar
scoop² *n* : pala *f* (para harina, etc.),
cucharón *m* (para helado, etc.)
scoot ['skuːt] *vi* : ir rápidamente ⟨she
scooted around the corner : volvió la
esquina a toda prisa⟩
scooter ['skuːtər] *n* : patineta *f*,
monopatín *m*, patinete *m*
scope ['skoːp] *n* **1** RANGE : alcance *m*,
ámbito *m*, extensión *f* **2** OPPORTUNI-
TY : posibilidades *fpl*, libertad *f*
scorch ['skɔrtʃ] *vt* : chamuscar, quemar
score¹ ['skor] *v* **scored; scoring** *vt* **1**
RECORD : anotar **2** MARK, SCRATCH
: marcar, rayar **3** : marcar, meter (en
deportes) **4** GAIN : ganar, apuntarse **5**
GRADE : calificar (exámenes, etc.) **6**
: instrumentar, orquestar (música) —
vi **1** : marcar (en deportes) **2** : obtener una puntuación (en un examen)
score² *n, pl* **scores 1** *or pl* **score** TWEN-
TY : veintena *f* **2** LINE, SCRATCH : línea
f, marca *f* **3** : resultado *m* (en deportes)
⟨what's the score? : ¿cómo va el marcador?⟩ **4** GRADE, POINTS : calificación *f* (en un examen), puntuación *f*
(en un concurso) **5** ACCOUNT : cuenta *f* ⟨to settle a score : ajustar una cuen-
ta⟩ ⟨on that score : a ese respecto⟩ **6**
: partitura *f* (musical)
scorn¹ ['skɔrn] *vt* : despreciar, menospreciar, desdeñar
scorn² *n* : desprecio *m*, menosprecio *m*,
desdén *m*
scornful ['skɔrnfəl] *adj* : desdeñoso, despreciativo — **scornfully** *adv*
Scorpio ['skɔrpiˌoː] *n* : Escorpio *mf*, Escorpión *mf*
scorpion ['skɔrpiən] *n* : alacrán *m*, escorpión *m*
Scot ['skɑt] *n* : escocés *m*, -cesa *f*
Scotch¹ ['skɑtʃ] *adj* → **Scottish¹**
Scotch² *npl* **the Scotch** : los escoceses
scot–free ['skɑtˈfriː] *adj* **to get off
scot–free** : salir impune, quedar sin
castigo
Scots ['skɑts] *n* : escocés *m* (idioma)
Scottish¹ ['skɑtɪʃ] *adj* : escocés
Scottish² *n* → **Scots**
scoundrel ['skaʊndrəl] *n* : sinvergüenza
mf; bellaco *m*, -ca *f*
scour ['skaʊər] *vt* **1** EXAMINE, SEARCH
: registrar (un área), revisar (documentos, etc.) **2** SCRUB : fregar, restregar
scourge¹ ['skərdʒ] *vt* **scourged; scourg-
ing** : azotar
scourge² *n* : azote *m*
scout¹ ['skaʊt] *vi* **1** RECONNOITER : reconocer **2 to scout around for** : explorar en busca de
scout² *n* **1** : explorador *m*, -dora *f* **2** *or*
talent scout : cazatalentos *mf*
scow ['skaʊ] *n* : barcaza *f*, gabarra *f*
scowl¹ ['skaʊl] *vi* : fruncir el ceño
scowl² *n* : ceño *m* fruncido

scram ['skræm] *vi* **scrammed; scram-ming** : largarse

scramble¹ ['skræmbəl] *v* **-bled; -bling** *vi* **1** : trepar, gatear (con torpeza) ⟨he scrambled over the fence : se trepó a la cerca con dificultad⟩ **2** STRUGGLE : pelearse (por) ⟨they scrambled for seats : se pelearon por los asientos⟩ — *vt* **1** JUMBLE : mezclar **2 to scramble eggs** : hacer huevos revueltos

scramble² *n* : rebatiña *f*, pelea *f*

scrap¹ ['skræp] *v* **scrapped; scrapping** *vt* DISCARD : desechar — *vi* FIGHT : pe-learse

scrap² *n* **1** FRAGMENT : pedazo *m*, tro-zo *m* **2** FIGHT : pelea *f* **3** *or* **scrap met-al** : chatarra *f* **4 scraps** *npl* LEFTOVERS : restos *mpl*, sobras *fpl*

scrapbook ['skræp,bʊk] *n* : álbum *m* de recortes

scrape¹ ['skreɪp] *v* **scraped; scraping** *vt* **1** GRAZE, SCRATCH : rozar, rascar ⟨to scrape one's knee : rasparse la rodilla⟩ **2** CLEAN : raspar ⟨to scrape carrots : raspar zanahorias⟩ **3 to scrape off** : raspar (pintura, etc.) **4 to scrape up** *or* **to scrape together** : juntar, reunir poco a poco — *vi* **1** RUB : rozar **2 to scrape by** : arreglárselas, ir tirando

scrape² *n* **1** SCRAPING : raspadura *f* **2** SCRATCH : rasguño *m* **3** PREDICAMENT : apuro *m*, aprieto *m*

scratch¹ ['skrætʃ] *vt* **1** : arañar, rasguñar ⟨to scratch an itch : rascarse⟩ **2** MARK : rayar, marcar **3 to scratch out** : tachar

scratch² *n* **1** : rasguño *m*, arañazo *m* (en la piel), rayón *m* (en un mueble, etc.) **2** : sonido *m* rasposo ⟨I heard a scratch at the door : oí como que raspaban a la puerta⟩

scratchy ['skrætʃi] *adj* **scratchier; -est** : áspero, que pica ⟨a scratchy sweater : un suéter que pica⟩

scrawl¹ ['skrɔl] *v* : garabatear

scrawl² *n* : garabato *m*

scrawny ['skrɔni] *adj* **scrawnier; -est** : flaco, escuálido

scream¹ ['skri:m] *vi* : chillar, gritar

scream² *n* : chillido *m*, grito *m*

screech¹ ['skri:tʃ] *vi* : chillar (dícese de las personas o de los animales), chirri-ar (dícese de los frenos, etc.)

screech² *n* **1** : chillido *m*, grito *m* (de una persona o un animal) **2** : chirrido *m* (de frenos, etc.)

screen¹ ['skri:n] *vt* **1** SHIELD : proteger **2** CONCEAL : tapar, ocultar **3** EXAM-INE : someter a una revisión, hacerle un chequeo (a un paciente) **4** SIEVE : cribar

screen² *n* **1** PARTITION : biombo *m*, pan-talla *f* **2** SIEVE : criba *f* **3** : pantalla *f* (de un televisor, una computadora, etc.) **4** MOVIES : cine *m* **5** *or* **window screen** : ventana *f* de tela metálica

screenplay ['skri:n,pleɪ] *n* SCRIPT : guión *m*

screw¹ ['skru:] *vt* : atornillar — *vi* **1 to screw in** : atornillarse **2 to screw up** *fam* : meter la pata

screw² *n* **1** : tornillo *m* (para fijar algo) **2** TWIST : vuelta *f* **3** PROPELLER : hélice *f*

screwdriver ['skru:,draɪvər] *n* : des-tornillador *m*, desarmador *m Mex*

scribble¹ ['skrɪbəl] *v* **-bled; -bling** : gara-batear

scribble² *n* : garabato *m*

scribe ['skraɪb] *n* : escriba *m*

scrimmage ['skrɪmɪdʒ] *n* : escaramuza *f*

scrimp ['skrɪmp] *vi* **1 to scrimp on** : es-catimar **2 to scrimp and save** : hacer economías

script ['skrɪpt] *n* **1** HANDWRITING : le-tra *f*, escritura *f* **2** : guión *m* (de una película, etc.)

scriptural ['skrɪptʃərəl] *adj* : bíblico

scripture ['skrɪptʃər] *n* **1** : escritos *mpl* sagrados (de una religión) **2 the Scrip-tures** *npl* : las Sagradas Escrituras

scriptwriter ['skrɪpt,raɪtər] *n* : guionista *mf*, libretista *mf*

scroll ['skro:l] *n* **1** : rollo *m* (de pergamino, etc.) **2** : voluta *f* (adorno en arquitectura)

scrotum ['skro:təm] *n, pl* **scrota** [-tə] *or* **scrotums** : escroto *m*

scrounge ['skraʊndʒ] *v* **scrounged; scrounging** *vt* **1** BUM : gorrear *fam*, sablear *fam* (dinero) **2 to scrounge around for** : buscar, andar a la busca de — *vi* **to scrounge off someone** : vivir a costa de alguien

scrub¹ ['skrʌb] *vt* **scrubbed; scrubbing** : restregar, fregar

scrub² *n* **1** THICKET, UNDERBRUSH : maleza *f*, matorral *m*, matorrales *mpl* **2** SCRUBBING : fregado *m*, restregadu-ra *f*

scrubby ['skrʌbi] *adj* **-bier; -est 1** STUNTED : achaparrado **2** : cubierto de maleza

scruff ['skrʌf] *n* **by the scruff of the neck** : por el cogote, por el pescuezo

scrumptious ['skrʌmpʃəs] *adj* : deli-cioso, muy rico

scruple ['skru:pəl] *n* : escrúpulo *m*

scrupulous ['skru:pjələs] *adj* : escrupu-loso — **scrupulously** *adv*

scrutinize ['skru:tən,aɪz] *vt* **-nized; -nizing** : escrutar, escudriñar

scrutiny ['skru:təni] *n, pl* **-nies** : escru-tinio *m*, inspección *f*

scuba ['sku:bə] *n* **1** *or* **scuba gear** : equipo *m* de submarinismo **2 scuba diver** : submarinista *mf* **3 scuba div-ing** : submarinismo *m*

scuff ['skʌf] *vt* : rayar, raspar ⟨to scuff one's feet : arrastrar los pies⟩

scuffle¹ ['skʌfəl] *vi* **-fled; -fling 1** TUS-SLE : pelearse **2** SHUFFLE : caminar ar-rastrando los pies

scuffle² *n* **1** TUSSLE : refriega *f*, pelea *f* **2** SHUFFLE : arrastre *m* de los pies

scull¹ ['skʌl] *vi* : remar (con espadilla)

scull² *n* OAR : espadilla *f*

sculpt ['skʌlpt] *v* : esculpir

sculptor ['skʌlptər] *n* : escultor *m*, -tora *f*

scuptural ['skʌlptʃərəl] *adj* : escultórico

sculpture¹ ['skʌlptʃər] *vt* **-tured; -turing** : esculpir

sculpture² *n* : escultura *f*

scum ['skʌm] *n* **1** FROTH : espuma *f*, nata *f* **2** : verdín *m* (encima de un líquido)

scurrilous ['skərələs] *adj* : difamatorio, calumnioso, injurioso

scurry ['skəri] *vi* **-ried; -rying** : corretear

scurvy ['skərvi] *n* : escorbuto *m*

scuttle¹ ['skʌt̬əl] *v* **-tled; -tling** *vt* : hundir (un barco) — *vi* SCAMPER : corretear

scuttle² *n* : cubo *m* (para carbón)

scythe ['saɪð] *n* : guadaña *f*

sea¹ ['si:] *adj* : del mar

sea² *n* **1** : mar *mf* ⟨the Black Sea : el Mar Negro⟩ ⟨on the high seas : en alta mar⟩ ⟨heavy seas : mar gruesa, mar agitada⟩ **2** MASS : mar *m*, multitud *f* ⟨a sea of faces : un mar de rostros⟩

seabird ['si:ˌbərd] *n* : ave *f* marina

seaboard ['si:ˌbord] *n* : litoral *m*

seacoast ['si:ˌko:st] *n* : costa *f*, litoral *m*

seafarer ['si:ˌfærər] *n* : marinero *m*

seafaring¹ ['si:ˌfærɪŋ] *adj* : marinero

seafaring² *n* : navegación *f*

seafood ['si:ˌfu:d] *n* : mariscos *mpl*

seagull ['si:ˌgʌl] *n* : gaviota *f*

sea horse ['si:ˌhɔrs] *n* : hipocampo *m*, caballito *m* de mar

seal¹ ['si:l] *vt* **1** CLOSE : sellar, cerrar ⟨to seal a letter : cerrar una carta⟩ ⟨to seal an agreement : sellar un acuerdo⟩ **2 to seal up** : tapar, rellenar (una grieta, etc.)

seal² *n* **1** : foca *f* (animal) **2** : sello *m* ⟨seal of approval : sello de aprobación⟩ **3** CLOSURE : cierre *m*, precinto *m*

sea level *n* : nivel *m* del mar

sea lion *n* : león *m* marino

sealskin ['si:l̩ˌskɪn] *n* : piel *f* de foca

seam¹ ['si:m] *vt* **1** STITCH : unir con costuras **2** MARK : marcar

seam² *n* **1** STITCHING : costura *f* **2** LODE, VEIN : veta *f*, filón *m*

seaman ['si:mən] *n, pl* **-men** [-mən, -ˌmɛn] **1** SAILOR : marinero *m* **2** : marino *m* (en la armada)

seamless ['si:mləs] *adj* **1** : sin costuras, de una pieza **2** : perfecto ⟨a seamless transition : una transición fluida⟩

seamstress ['si:mpstrəs] *n* : costurera *f*

seamy ['si:mi] *adj* **seamier; -est** : sórdido

séance ['seɪˌɑnts] *n* : sesión *f* de espiritismo

seaplane ['si:ˌpleɪn] *n* : hidroavión *m*

seaport ['si:ˌport] *n* : puerto *m* marítimo

sear ['sɪr] *vt* **1** PARCH, WITHER : secar, resecar **2** SCORCH : chamuscar, quemar

search¹ ['sərtʃ] *vt* : registrar (un edificio, un área), cachear (a una persona), buscar en — *vi* **to search for** : buscar

search² *n* : búsqueda *f*, registro *m* (de un edificio, etc.), cacheo *m* (de una persona)

searchlight ['sərtʃˌlaɪt] *n* : reflector *m*

seashell ['si:ˌʃɛl] *n* : concha *f* (marina)

seashore ['si:ˌʃor] *n* : orilla *f* del mar

seasick ['si:ˌsɪk] *adj* : mareado ⟨to get seasick : marearse⟩

seasickness ['si:ˌsɪknəs] *n* : mareo *m*

seaside → **seacoast**

season¹ ['si:zən] *vt* **1** FLAVOR, SPICE : sazonar, condimentar **2** CURE : curar, secar ⟨seasoned wood : madera seca⟩ ⟨a seasoned veteran : un veterano avezado⟩

season² *n* **1** : estación *f* (del año) **2** : temporada *f* (en deportes, etc.) ⟨baseball season : temporada de beisbol⟩

seasonable ['si:zənəbəl] *adj* **1** : propio de la estación (dícese del tiempo, de las temperaturas, etc.) **2** TIMELY : oportuno

seasonal ['si:zənəl] *adj* : estacional — **seasonally** *adv*

seasoning ['si:zənɪŋ] *n* : condimento *m*, sazón *f*

seat¹ ['si:t] *vt* **1** SIT : sentar ⟨please be seated : siéntense, por favor⟩ **2** HOLD : tener cabida para ⟨the stadium seats 40,000 : el estadio tiene 40,000 asientos⟩

seat² *n* **1** : asiento *m*, plaza *f* (en un vehículo) ⟨take a seat : tome asiento⟩ **2** BOTTOM : fondillos *mpl* (de la ropa), trasero *m* (del cuerpo) **3** : sede *f* (de un gobierno, etc.)

seat belt *n* : cinturón *m* de seguridad

sea urchin *n* : erizo *m* de mar

seawall ['si:ˌwɑl] *n* : rompeolas *m*, dique *m* marítimo

seawater ['si:ˌwɔt̬ər, -ˌwɑ-] *n* : agua *f* de mar

seaweed ['si:ˌwi:d] *n* : alga *f* marina

seaworthy ['si:ˌwərði] *adj* : en condiciones de navegar

secede [sɪ'si:d] *vi* **-ceded; -ceding** : separarse (de una nación, etc.)

seclude [sɪ'klu:d] *vt* **-cluded; -cluding** : aislar

seclusion [sɪ'klu:ʒən] *n* : aislamiento *m*

second¹ ['sɛkənd] *vt* : secundar, apoyar (una moción)

second² *or* **secondly** ['sɛkəndli] *adv* : en segundo lugar

second³ *adj* : segundo

second⁴ *n* **1** : segundo *m*, -da *f* (en una serie) **2** : segundo *m*, ayudante *m* (en deportes) **3** MOMENT : segundo *m*, momento *m*

secondary ['sɛkənˌdri] *adj* : secundario

secondhand ['sɛkəndˈhænd] *adj* : de segunda mano

second lieutenant *n* : alférez *mf*, subteniente *mf*

second–rate ['sɛkəndˈreɪt] *adj* : mediocre, de segunda categoría

secrecy ['si:krəsi] *n, pl* **-cies** : secreto *m*
secret[1] ['si:krət] *adj* : secreto — **secretly** *adv*
secret[2] *n* : secreto *m*
secretarial [ˌsɛkrə'triəl] *adj* : de secretario, de oficina
secretariat [ˌsɛkrə'triət] *n* : secretaría *f*, secretariado *m*
secretary ['sɛkrəˌtri] *n, pl* **-taries** 1 : secretario *m*, -ria *f* (en una oficina, etc.) 2 : ministro *m*, -tra *f*; secretario *m*, -ria *f* ⟨Secretary of State : Secretario de Estado⟩
secrete [sɪ'kri:t] *vt* **-creted; -creting** 1 : secretar, segregar (en fisiología) 2 HIDE : ocultar
secretion [sɪ'kri:ʃən] *n* : secreción *f*
secretive ['si:krətɪv, sɪ'kri:tɪv] *adj* : reservado, callado, secreto
sect ['sɛkt] *n* : secta *f*
sectarian [sɛk'triən] *adj* : sectario
section ['sɛkʃən] *n* : sección *f*, parte *f* (de un mueble, etc.), sector *m* (de la población), barrio *m* (de una ciudad)
sectional ['sɛkʃənəl] *adj* 1 : en sección, en corte ⟨a sectional diagram : un gráfico en corte⟩ 2 FACTIONAL : de grupo, entre facciones 3 : modular ⟨sectional furniture : muebles modulares⟩
sector ['sɛktər] *n* : sector *m*
secular ['sɛkjələr] *adj* 1 : secular, laico ⟨secular life : la vida secular⟩ 2 : seglar (dícese de los sacerdotes, etc.)
secure[1] [sɪ'kjʊr] *vt* **-cured; -curing** 1 FASTEN : asegurar (una puerta, etc.), sujetar 2 GET : conseguir
secure[2] *adj* **-curer; -est** : seguro — **securely** *adv*
security [sɪ'kjʊrəti] *n, pl* **-ties** 1 SAFETY : seguridad *f* 2 GUARANTEE : garantía *f* 3 **securities** *npl* : valores *mpl*
sedan [sɪ'dæn] *n* 1 *or* **sedan chair** : silla *f* de manos 2 : sedán *m* (automóvil)
sedate[1] [sɪ'deɪt] *vt* **-dated; -dating** : sedar
sedate[2] *adj* : sosegado — **sedately** *adv*
sedation [sɪ'deɪʃən] *n* : sedación *f*
sedative[1] ['sɛdətɪv] *adj* : sedante
sedative[2] *n* : sedante *m*, calmante *m*
sedentary ['sɛdənˌtɛri] *adj* : sedentario
sedge ['sɛdʒ] *n* : juncia *f*
sediment ['sɛdəmənt] *n* : sedimento *m* (geológico), poso *m* (en un líquido)
sedimentary [ˌsɛdə'mɛntəri] *adj* : sedimentario
sedition [sɪ'dɪʃən] *n* : sedición *f*
seditious [sɪ'dɪʃəs] *adj* : sedicioso
seduce [sɪ'du:s, -'dju:s] *vt* **-duced; -ducing** : seducir
seduction [sɪ'dʌkʃən] *n* : seducción *f*
seductive [sɪ'dʌktɪv] *adj* : seductor, seductivo
see[1] ['si:] *v* **saw** ['sɔ]; **seen** ['si:n]; **seeing** *vt* 1 : ver ⟨I saw a dog : vi un perro⟩ ⟨see you later! : ¡hasta luego!⟩ 2 EXPERIENCE : ver, conocer 3 UNDERSTAND : ver, entender 4 ENSURE : asegurarse ⟨see that it's correct : asegúrese de que sea correcto⟩ 5 ACCOMPANY : acompañar 6 **to see off** : despedir, despedirse de — *vi* 1 : ver ⟨seeing is believing : ver para creer⟩ 2 UNDERSTAND : entender, ver ⟨now I see! : ¡ya entiendo!⟩ 3 CONSIDER : ver ⟨let's see : vamos a ver⟩ 4 **to see to** : ocuparse de
see[2] *n* : sede *f* ⟨the Holy See : la Santa Sede⟩
seed[1] ['si:d] *vt* 1 SOW : sembrar 2 : despepitar, quitarle las semillas a
seed[2] *n, pl* **seed** *or* **seeds** 1 : semilla *f*, pepita *f* (de una fruta) 2 SOURCE : germen *m*, semilla *f*
seedless ['si:dləs] *adj* : sin semillas
seedling ['si:dlɪŋ] *n* : plantón *m*
seedpod ['si:dˌpɑd] → **pod**
seedy ['si:di] *adj* **seedier; -est** 1 : lleno de semillas 2 SHABBY : raído (dícese de la ropa) 3 RUN-DOWN : ruinoso (dícese de los edificios, etc.), sórdido
seek ['si:k] *v* **sought** ['sɔt]; **seeking** *vt* 1 : buscar ⟨to seek an answer : buscar una solución⟩ 2 REQUEST : solicitar, pedir 3 **to seek to** : tratar de, intentar de — *vi* SEARCH : buscar
seem ['si:m] *vi* : parecer
seeming ['si:mɪŋ] *adj* : aparente, ostensible
seemingly ['si:mɪŋli] *adv* : aparentemente, según parece
seemly ['si:mli] *adj* **seemlier; -est** : apropiado, decoroso
seep ['si:p] *vi* : filtrarse
seer ['si:ər] *n* : vidente *mf*, clarividente *mf*
seesaw[1] ['si:ˌsɔ] *vi* 1 : jugar en un subibaja 2 VACILLATE : vacilar, oscilar
seesaw[2] *n* : balancín *m*, subibaja *m*
seethe ['si:ð] *vi* **seethed; seething** 1 : bullir, hervir 2 **to seethe with anger** : rabiar, estar furioso
segment ['sɛgmənt] *n* : segmento *m*
segmented ['sɛgˌmɛntəd, sɛg'mɛn-] *adj* : segmentado
segregate ['sɛgrɪˌgeɪt] *vt* **-gated; -gating** : segregar
segregation [ˌsɛgrɪ'geɪʃən] *n* : segregación *f*
seismic ['saɪzmɪk, 'saɪs-] *adj* : sísmico
seize ['si:z] *v* **seized; seizing** *vt* 1 CAPTURE : capturar, tomar, apoderarse de 2 ARREST : detener 3 CLUTCH, GRAB : agarrar, coger, aprovechar (una oportunidad) 4 **to be seized with** : estar sobrecogido por — *vi or* **to seize up** : agarrotarse
seizure ['si:ʒər] *n* 1 CAPTURE : toma *f*, captura *f* 2 ARREST : detención *f* 3 : ataque *m* ⟨an epileptic seizure : un ataque epiléptico⟩
seldom ['sɛldəm] *adv* : pocas veces, rara vez, casi nunca
select[1] [sə'lɛkt] *vt* : escoger, elegir, seleccionar (a un candidato, etc.)
select[2] *adj* : selecto
selection [sə'lɛkʃən] *n* : selección *f*, elección *f*

selective [sə'lɛktɪv] *adj* : selectivo
selenium [sə'liːnɪəm] *n* : selenio *m*
self ['sɛlf] *n, pl* **selves** ['sɛlvz] **1** : ser *m*, persona *f* ⟨the self : el yo⟩ ⟨with his whole self : con todo su ser⟩ ⟨her own self : su propia persona⟩ **2** SIDE : lado (de la personalidad) ⟨his better self : su lado bueno⟩
self–addressed [ˌsɛlfə'drst] *adj* : con la dirección del remitente ⟨include a self-addressed envelope : incluya un sobre con su nombre y dirección⟩
self–appointed [ˌsɛlfə'pɔɪntəd] *adj* : autoproclamado, autonombrado
self–assurance [ˌsɛlfə'ʃʊrənts] *n* : seguridad *f* en sí mismo
self–assured [ˌsɛlfə'ʃʊrd] *adj* : seguro de sí mismo
self–centered [ˌsɛlf'sɛntərd] *adj* : egocéntrico
self–confidence [ˌsɛlf'kɑnfədənts] *n* : confianza *f* en sí mismo
self–confident [ˌsɛlf'kɑnfədənt] *adj* : seguro de sí mismo
self–conscious [ˌsɛlf'kɑntʃəs] *adj* : cohibido, tímido
self–consciously [ˌsɛlf'kɑntʃəsli] *adv* : de manera cohibida
self–consciousness [ˌsɛlf'kɑntʃəsnəs] *n* : vergüenza *f*, timidez *f*
self–contained [ˌsɛlfkən'teɪnd] *adj* **1** INDEPENDENT : independiente **2** RESERVED : reservado
self–control [ˌsɛlfkən'troːl] *n* : autocontrol *m*, control *m* de sí mismo
self–defense [ˌsɛlfdɪ'fɛnts] *n* : defensa *f* propia, defensa *f* personal ⟨to act in self-defense : actuar en defensa propia⟩ ⟨self-defense class : clase de defensa personal⟩
self–denial [ˌsɛlfdɪ'naɪəl] *n* : abnegación *f*
self–destructive [ˌsɛlfdɪ'strʌktɪv] *adj* : autodestructivo
self–determination [ˌsɛlfdɪˌtərmə'neɪʃən] *n* : autodeterminación *f*
self–discipline [ˌsɛlf'dɪsəplən] *n* : autodisciplina *f*
self–employed [ˌsɛlfɪm'plɔɪd] *adj* : que trabaja por cuenta propia, autónomo
self–esteem [ˌsɛlfɪ'stiːm] *n* : autoestima *f*, amor *m* propio
self–evident [ˌsɛlf'ɛvədənt] *adj* : evidente, manifiesto
self–explanatory [ˌsɛlfɪk'splænəˌtori] *adj* : fácil de entender, evidente
self–expression [ˌsɛlfɪk'sprʃən] *n* : expresión *f* personal
self–government [ˌsɛlf'gʌvərmənt, -vərn-] *n* : autogobierno *m*
self–help [ˌsɛlf'hɛlp] *n* : autoayuda *f*
self–important [ˌsɛlfɪm'pɔrtənt] *adj* **1** VAIN : vanidoso, presumido **2** ARROGANT : arrogante
self–indulgent [ˌsɛlfɪn'dʌldʒənt] *adj* : que se permite excesos
self–inflicted [ˌsɛlfɪn'flɪktəd] *adj* : autoinfligido

self–interest [ˌsɛlf'ɪntrəst, -tɚˌrst] *n* : interés *m* personal
selfish ['sɛlfɪʃ] *adj* : egoísta
selfishly ['sɛlfɪʃli] *adv* : de manera egoísta
selfishness ['sɛlfɪʃnəs] *n* : egoísmo *m*
selfless ['sɛlfləs] *adj* UNSELFISH : desinteresado
self–made [ˌsɛlf'meɪd] *adj* : próspero gracias a sus propios esfuerzos
self–pity [ˌsɛlf'pɪti] *n, pl* **-ties** : autocompasión *f*
self–portrait [ˌsɛlf'pɔrtrət] *n* : autorretrato *m*
self–propelled [ˌsɛlfproˈpɛld] *adj* : autopropulsado
self–reliance [ˌsɛlfri'laɪənts] *n* : independencia *f*, autosuficiencia *f*
self–respect [ˌsɛlfri'spɛkt] *n* : autoestima *f*, amor *m* propio
self–restraint [ˌsɛlfri'streɪnt] *n* : autocontrol *m*, moderación *f*
self–righteous [ˌsɛlf'raɪtʃəs] *adj* : santurrón, moralista
self–sacrifice [ˌsɛlf'sækrəˌfaɪs] *n* : abnegación *f*
selfsame ['sɛlfˌseɪm] *adj* : mismo
self–service [ˌsɛlf'sərvɪs] *adj* **1** : de autoservicio **2 self-service restaurant** : autoservicio *m*
self–sufficiency [ˌsɛlfsə'fɪʃəntsi] *n* : autosuficiencia *f*
self–sufficient [ˌsɛlfsə'fɪʃənt] *adj* : autosuficiente
self–taught [ˌsɛlf'tɔt] *adj* : autodidacta
sell ['sɛl] *v* **sold** ['soːld]; **selling** *vt* : vender — *vi* : venderse
seller ['sɛlər] *n* : vendedor *m*, -dora *f*
selves → **self**
semantic [sɪ'mæntɪk] *adj* : semántico
semantics [sɪ'mæntɪks] *ns & pl* : semántica *f*
semaphore ['sɛməˌfor] *n* : semáforo *m*
semblance ['sɛmblənts] *n* : apariencia *f*
semen ['siːmən] *n* : semen *m*
semester [sə'mɛstər] *n* : semestre *m*
semicolon ['sɛmiˌkoːlən, 'sɛˌmaɪ-] *n* : punto y coma *m*
semiconductor ['sɛmikənˌdʌktər, 'sɛˌmaɪ-] *n* : semiconductor *m*
semifinal ['sɛmiˌfaɪnəl, 'sɛˌmaɪ-] *n* : semifinal *f*
seminar ['sɛməˌnɑr] *n* : seminario *m*
seminary ['sɛməˌnɛri] *n, pl* **-naries** : seminario *m*
Semitic [sə'mɪtɪk] *adj* : semita
senate ['sɛnət] *n* : senado *m*
senator ['sɛnətər] *n* : senador *m*, -dora *f*
send ['sɛnd] *vt* **sent** ['sɛnt]; **sending 1** : mandar, enviar ⟨to send a letter : mandar una carta⟩ ⟨to send word : avisar, mandar decir⟩ **2** PROPEL : mandar, lanzar ⟨he sent it into left field : lo mandó al jardín izquierdo⟩ ⟨to send up dust : alzar polvo⟩ **3 to send into a rage** : poner furioso
sender ['sɛndər] *n* : remitente *mf* (de una carta, etc.)

Senegalese [ˌsɛnəgəˈliːz, -ˈliːs] *n* : senegalés *m*, -lesa *f* — **Senegalese** *adj*
senile [ˈsiːˌnaɪl] *adj* : senil
senility [sɪˈnɪləti] *n* : senilidad *f*
senior[1] [ˈsiːnjər] *adj* **1** ELDER : mayor ⟨John Doe, Senior : John Doe, padre⟩ **2** : superior (en rango), más antiguo (en años de servicio) ⟨a senior official : un alto oficial⟩
senior[2] *n* **1** : superior *m* (en rango) **2 to be someone's senior** : ser mayor que alguien ⟨she's two years my senior : me lleva dos años⟩
senior citizen *n* : persona *f* de la tercera edad
seniority [ˌsiːˈnjɔrəti] *n* : antigüedad *f* (en años de servicio)
sensation [sɛnˈseɪʃən] *n* : sensación *f*
sensational [sɛnˈseɪʃənəl] *adj* : que causa sensación ⟨sensational stories : historias sensacionalistas⟩
sense[1] [ˈsɛnts] *vt* **sensed; sensing** : sentir ⟨he sensed danger : se dio cuenta del peligro⟩
sense[2] *n* **1** MEANING : sentido *m*, significado *m* **2** : sentido *m* ⟨the sense of smell : el sentido del olfato⟩ **3 to make sense** : tener sentido
senseless [ˈsɛntsləs] *adj* **1** MEANINGLESS : sin sentido, sin razón **2** UNCONSCIOUS : inconsciente
senselessly [ˈsɛntsləsli] *adv* : sin sentido
sensibility [ˌsɛntsəˈbɪləti] *n, pl* -**ties** : sensibilidad *f*
sensible [ˈsɛntsəbəl] *adj* **1** PERCEPTIBLE : sensible, perceptible **2** AWARE : consciente **3** REASONABLE : sensato ⟨a sensible man : un hombre sensato⟩ ⟨sensible shoes : zapatos prácticos⟩ — **sensibly** [-bli] *adv*
sensibleness [ˈsɛntsəbəlnəs] *n* : sensatez *f*, solidez *f*
sensitive [ˈsɛntsətɪv] *adj* **1** : sensible, delicado ⟨sensitive skin : piel sensible⟩ **2** IMPRESSIONABLE : sensible, impresionable **3** TOUCHY : susceptible
sensitiveness [ˈsɛntsətɪvnəs] → **sensitivity**
sensitivity [ˌsɛntsəˈtɪvəti] *n, pl* -**ties** : sensibilidad *f*
sensitize [ˈsɛntsəˌtaɪz] *vt* -**tized; -tizing** : sensibilizar
sensor [ˈsɛnˌsɔr, ˈsɛntsər] *n* : sensor *m*
sensory [ˈsɛntsəri] *adj* : sensorial
sensual [ˈsɛntʃuəl] *adj* : sensual — **sensually** *adv*
sensuality [ˌsɛntʃəˈwæləti] *n, pl* -**ties** : sensualidad *f*
sensuous [ˈsɛntʃuəs] *adj* : sensual
sent → **send**
sentence[1] [ˈsɛntənts, -ənz] *vt* -**tenced; -tencing** : sentenciar
sentence[2] *n* **1** JUDGMENT : sentencia *f* **2** : oración *f*, frase *f* (en gramática)
sentiment [ˈsɛntəmənt] *n* **1** BELIEF : opinión *f* **2** FEELING : sentimiento *m* **3** → **sentimentality**

sentimental [ˌsɛntəˈmɛntəl] *adj* : sentimental
sentimentality [ˌsɛntəˌmɛnˈtæləti] *n, pl* -**ties** : sentimentalismo *m*, sensiblería *f*
sentinel [ˈsɛntənəl] *n* : centinela *mf*, guardia *mf*
sentry [ˈsɛntri] *n, pl* -**tries** : centinela *mf*
sepal [ˈsiːpəl, ˈsɛ-] *n* : sépalo *m*
separable [ˈsɛpərəbəl] *adj* : separable
separate[1] [ˈsɛpəˌreɪt] *v* -**rated; -rating** *vt* **1** DETACH, SEVER : separar **2** DISTINGUISH : diferenciar, distinguir — *vi* PART : separarse
separate[2] [ˈsɛprət, ˈsɛpə-] *adj* **1** INDIVIDUAL : separado, aparte ⟨a separate state : un estado separado⟩ ⟨in a separate envelope : en un sobre aparte⟩ **2** DISTINCT : distinto
separately [ˈsɛprətli, ˈsɛpə-] *adv* : por separado, separadamente, aparte
separation [ˌsɛpəˈreɪʃən] *n* : separación *f*
sepia [ˈsiːpiə] *n* : color *m* sepia
September [sɛpˈtɛmbər] *n* : septiembre *m*, setiembre *m*
septic [ˈsɛptɪk] *adj* : séptico ⟨septic tank : fosa séptica⟩
sepulchre [ˈsɛpəlkər] *n* : sepulcro *m*
sequel [ˈsiːkwəl] *n* **1** CONSEQUENCE : secuela *f*, consecuencia *f* **2** : continuación *f* (de una película, etc.)
sequence [ˈsiːkwənts] *n* **1** SERIES : serie *f*, sucesión *f*, secuencia *f* (matemática o musical) **2** ORDER : orden *m*
sequester [sɪˈkwɛstər] *vt* : aislar
sequin [ˈsiːkwən] *n* : lentejuela *f*
sequoia [sɪˈkwɔɪə] *n* : secoya *f*, secuoya *f*
sera → **serum**
Serb [ˈsərb] *or* **Serbian** [ˈsərbiən] *n* **1** : serbio *m*, -bia *f* **2** : serbio *m* (idioma) — **Serb** *or* **Serbian** *adj*
Serbo-Croatian [ˌsərbokroˈeɪʃən] *n* : serbocroata *m* (idioma) — **Serbo-Croatian** *adj*
serenade[1] [ˌsɛrəˈneɪd] *vt* -**naded; -nading** : darle una serenata (a alguien)
serenade[2] *n* : serenata *f*
serene [səˈriːn] *adj* : sereno — **serenely** *adv*
serenity [səˈrɛnəti] *n* : serenidad *f*
serf [ˈsərf] *n* : siervo *m*, -va *f*
serge [ˈsərdʒ] *n* : sarga *f*
sergeant [ˈsɑrdʒənt] *n* : sargento *mf*
serial[1] [ˈsɪriəl] *adj* : seriado
serial[2] *n* : serie *f*, serial *m* (de radio o televisión), publicación *f* por entregas
serially [ˈsɪriəli] *adv* : en serie
series [ˈsɪrˌiːz] *n, pl* **series** : serie *f*, sucesión *f*
serious [ˈsɪriəs] *adj* **1** SOBER : serio **2** DEDICATED, EARNEST : serio, dedicado ⟨to be serious about something : tomar algo en serio⟩ **3** GRAVE : serio, grave ⟨serious problems : problemas graves⟩
seriously [ˈsɪriəsli] *adv* **1** EARNESTLY : seriamente, con seriedad, en serio **2** SEVERELY : gravemente

seriousness ['sɪriəsnəs] *n* : seriedad *f*, gravedad *f*

sermon ['sərmən] *n* : sermón *m*

serpent ['sərpənt] *n* : serpiente *f*

serrated [sə'reɪtəd, 'sɛr,eɪtəd] *adj* : dentado, serrado

serum ['sɪrəm] *n, pl* **serums** *or* **sera** ['sɪrə] : suero *m*

servant ['sərvənt] *n* : criado *m*, -da *f*; sirviente *m*, -ta *f*

serve ['sərv] *v* **served; serving** *vi* **1** : servir ⟨to serve in the navy : servir en la armada⟩ ⟨to serve on a jury : ser miembro de un jurado⟩ **2** DO, FUNCTION : servir ⟨to serve as : servir de, servir como⟩ **3** : sacar (en deportes) — *vt* **1** : servir ⟨to serve God : servir a Dios⟩ **2** HELP : servir ⟨it serves no purpose : no sirve para nada⟩ **3** : servir (comida o bebida) ⟨dinner is served : la cena está servida⟩ **4** SUPPLY : abastecer **5** CARRY OUT : cumplir, hacer ⟨to serve time : servir una pena⟩ **6 to serve a summons** : entregar una citación

server ['sərvər] *n* **1** : camarero *m*, -ra *f*; mesero *m*, -ra *f* (en un restaurante) **2** *or* **serving dish** : fuente *f* (para servir comida) **3** : servidor *m* (en informática)

service¹ ['sərvəs] *vt* **-viced; -vicing 1** MAINTAIN : darle mantenimiento a (una máquina), revisar **2** REPAIR : arreglar, reparar

service² *n* **1** HELP, USE : servicio *m* ⟨to do someone a service : hacerle un servicio a alguien⟩ ⟨at your service : a sus órdenes⟩ ⟨to be out of service : no funcionar⟩ **2** CEREMONY : oficio *m* (religioso) **3** DEPARTMENT, SYSTEM : servicio *m* ⟨social services : servicios sociales⟩ ⟨train service : servicio de trenes⟩ **4** SET : juego *m*, servicio *m* ⟨tea service : juego de té⟩ **5** MAINTENANCE : mantenimiento *m*, revisión *f*, servicio *m* **6** : saque *m* (en deportes) **7 armed services** : fuerzas *fpl* armadas

serviceable ['sərvəsəbəl] *adj* **1** USEFUL : útil **2** DURABLE : duradero

serviceman ['sərvəs,mæn, -mən] *n, pl* **-men** [-mən, -,mɛn] : militar *m*

service station → **gas station**

servicewoman ['sərvəs,wumən] *n, pl* **-women** [-,wɪmən] : militar *f*

servile ['sərvəl, -,vaɪl] *adj* : servil

serving ['sərvɪŋ] *n* HELPING : porción *f*, ración *f*

servitude ['sərvə,tu:d, -,tju:d] *n* : servidumbre *f*

sesame ['sɛsəmi] *n* : ajonjolí *m*, sésamo *m*

session ['sɛʃən] *n* : sesión *f*

set¹ ['sɛt] *v* **set; setting** *vt* **1** SEAT : sentar **2** *or* **set down** PLACE : poner, colocar **3** ARRANGE : fijar, establecer ⟨to set the date : poner la fecha⟩ ⟨he set the agenda : estableció la agenda⟩ **4** ADJUST : poner (un reloj, etc.) **5** (*indicating the causing of a certain condition*) ⟨to set fire to : prenderle fuego a⟩ ⟨she

set it free : lo soltó⟩ **6** MAKE, START : poner, hacer ⟨I set them working : los puse a trabajar⟩ — *vi* **1** SOLIDIFY : fraguar (dícese del cemento, etc.), cuajar (dícese de la gelatina, etc.) **2** : ponerse (dícese del sol o de la luna)

set² *adj* **1** ESTABLISHED, FIXED : fijo, establecido **2** RIGID : inflexible ⟨to be set in one's ways : tener costumbres muy arraigadas⟩ **3** READY : listo, preparado

set³ *n* **1** COLLECTION : juego *m* ⟨a set of dishes : un juego de platos, una vajilla⟩ ⟨a tool set : una caja de herramientas⟩ **2** *or* **stage set** : decorado *m* (en el teatro), plató *m* (en el cine) **3** APPARATUS : aparato *m* ⟨a television set : un televisor⟩ **4** : conjunto *m* (en matemáticas)

setback ['sɛt,bæk] *n* : revés *m*, contratiempo *m*

set in *vi* BEGIN : comenzar, empezar

set off *vt* **1** PROVOKE : provocar **2** EXPLODE : hacer estallar (una bomba, etc.) — *vi or* **to set forth** : salir

set out *vi* : salir (de viaje) — *vt* INTEND : proponerse

settee [sɛ'ti:] *n* : sofá *m*

setter ['sɛtər] *n* : setter *mf* ⟨Irish setter : setter irlandés⟩

setting ['sɛtɪŋ] *n* **1** : posición *f*, ajuste *m* (de un control) **2** : engaste *m*, montura *f* (de una gema) **3** SCENE : escenario *m* (de una novela, etc.) **4** SURROUNDINGS : ambiente *m*, entorno *m*, marco *m*

settle ['sɛtəl] *v* **settled; settling** *vi* **1** ALIGHT, LAND : posarse (dícese de las aves), depositarse (dícese del polvo) **2** SINK : asentarse (dícese de los edificios) ⟨he settled into the chair : se arrellanó en la silla⟩ **3** : instalarse (en una casa), establecerse (en una ciudad o región) **4 to settle down** : calmarse, tranquilizarse ⟨settle down! : ¡tranquilízate!, ¡cálmate!⟩ **5 to settle down** : sentar cabeza, hacerse sensato ⟨to marry and settle down : casarse y sentar cabeza⟩ — *vt* **1** ARRANGE, DECIDE : fijar, decidir, acordar (planes, etc.) **2** RESOLVE : resolver, solucionar ⟨to settle an argument : resolver una discusión⟩ **3** PAY : pagar ⟨to settle an account : saldar una cuenta⟩ **4** CALM : calmar (los nervios), asentar (el estómago) **5** COLONIZE : colonizar **6 to settle oneself** : acomodarse, hacerse cómodo

settlement ['sɛtəlmənt] *n* **1** PAYMENT : pago *m*, liquidación *f* **2** COLONY : asentamiento *m* **3** RESOLUTION : acuerdo *m*

settler ['sɛtələr] *n* : poblador *m*, -dora *f*; colono *m*, -na *f*

setup ['sɛt,ʌp] *n* **1** ASSEMBLY : montaje *m*, ensamblaje *m* **2** ARRANGEMENT : disposición *f* **3** PREPARATION : preparación *f* **4** TRAP, TRICK : encerrona *f*

set up *vt* **1** ASSEMBLE : montar, armar **2** ERECT : levantar, erigir **3** ESTABLISH : establecer, fundar, montar (un negocio) **4** CAUSE : armar ⟨they set up a clamor : armaron un alboroto⟩

seven[1] ['sɛvən] *adj* : siete

seven[2] *n* : siete *m*

seven hundred[1] *adj* : setecientos

seven hundred[2] *n* : setecientos *m*

seventeen[1] [,sɛvən'ti:n] *adj* : diecisiete

seventeen[2] *n* : diecisiete *m*

seventeenth[1] [,sɛvən'ti:nθ] *adj* : decimoséptimo

seventeenth[2] *n* **1** : decimoséptimo *m*, -ma *f* (en una serie) **2** : diecisieteavo *m*, diecisieteava parte *f*

seventh[1] ['sɛvənθ] *adj* : séptimo

seventh[2] *n* **1** : séptimo *m*, -ma *f* (en una serie) **2** : séptimo *m*, séptima parte *f*

seventieth[1] ['sɛvəntiəθ] *adj* : septuagésimo

seventieth[2] *n* **1** : septuagésimo *m*, -ma *f* (en una serie) **2** : setentavo *m*, setentava parte *f*, septuagésima parte *f*

seventy[1] ['sɛvənti] *adj* : setenta

seventy[2] *n*, *pl* **-ties** : setenta *m*

sever ['sɛvər] *vt* **-ered; -ering** : cortar, romper

several[1] ['sɛvrəl, 'sɛvə-] *adj* **1** DISTINCT : distinto **2** SOME : varios ⟨several weeks : varias semanas⟩

several[2] *pron* : varios, varias

severance ['sɛvrənts, sɛvə-] *n* **1** : ruptura *f* (de relaciones, etc.) **2 severance pay** : indemnización *f* (por despido)

severe [sə'vɪr] *adj* **severer; -est 1** STRICT : severo **2** AUSTERE : sobrio, austero **3** SERIOUS : grave ⟨a severe wound : una herida grave⟩ ⟨severe aches : dolores fuertes⟩ **4** DIFFICULT : duro, difícil — **severely** *adv*

severity [sə'vrəti] *n* **1** HARSHNESS : severidad *f* **2** AUSTERITY : sobriedad *f*, austeridad *f* **3** SERIOUSNESS : gravedad *f* (de una herida, etc.)

sew ['so:] *v* **sewed; sewn** ['so:n] *or* **sewed; sewing** : coser

sewage ['su:ɪdʒ] *n* : aguas *fpl* negras, aguas *fpl* residuales

sewer[1] ['so:ər] *n* : uno que cose

sewer[2] ['su:ər] *n* : alcantarilla *f*, cloaca *f*

sewing ['so:ɪŋ] *n* : costura *f*

sex ['sɛks] *n* **1** : sexo *m* ⟨the opposite sex : el sexo opuesto⟩ **2** COPULATION : relaciones *fpl* sexuales

sexism ['sɛk,sɪzəm] *n* : sexismo *m*

sexist[1] ['sɛksɪst] *adj* : sexista

sexist[2] *n* : sexista *mf*

sextant ['sɛkstənt] *n* : sextante *m*

sextet [sɛk'stɛt] *n* : sexteto *m*

sexton ['sɛkstən] *n* : sacristán *m*

sexual ['sɛkʃuəl] *adj* : sexual — **sexually** *adv*

sexuality [,sɛkʃu'æləti] *n* : sexualidad *f*

sexy ['sɛksi] *adj* **sexier; -est** : sexy

shabbily ['ʃæbəli] *adv* **1** : pobremente ⟨shabbily dressed : pobremente vestido⟩ **2** UNFAIRLY : mal, injustamente

shabbiness ['ʃæbinəs] *n* **1** : lo gastado (de ropa, etc.) **2** : lo mal vestido (de personas) **3** UNFAIRNESS : injusticia *f*

shabby ['ʃæbi] *adj* **shabbier; -est 1** : gastado (dícese de la ropa, etc.) **2** : mal vestido (dícese de las personas) **3** UNFAIR : malo, injusto ⟨shabby treatment : mal trato⟩

shack ['ʃæk] *n* : choza *f*, rancho *m*

shackle[1] ['ʃækəl] *vt* **-led; -ling** : ponerle grilletes (a alguien)

shackle[2] *n* : grillete *m*

shad ['ʃæd] *n* : sábalo *m*

shade[1] ['ʃeɪd] *v* **shaded; shading** *vt* **1** SHELTER : proteger (del sol o de la luz) **2** *or* **to shade in** : matizar los colores de — *vi* : convertirse gradualmente ⟨his irritation shaded into rage : su irritación iba convirtiéndose en furia⟩

shade[2] *n* **1** : sombra *f* ⟨to give shade : dar sombra⟩ **2** : tono *m* (de un color) **3** NUANCE : matiz *m* **4** : pantalla *f* (de una lámpara), persiana *f* (de una ventana)

shadow[1] ['ʃædo:] *vt* **1** DARKEN : ensombrecer **2** TRAIL : seguir de cerca, seguirle la pista (a alguien)

shadow[2] *n* **1** : sombra *f* **2** DARKNESS : oscuridad *f* **3** TRACE : sombra *f*, atisbo *m*, indicio *m* ⟨without a shadow of a doubt : sin sombra de duda, sin lugar a dudas⟩ **4 to cast a shadow over** : ensombrecer

shadowy ['ʃædowi] *adj* **1** INDISTINCT : vago, indistinto **2** DARK : oscuro

shady ['ʃeɪdi] *adj* **shadier; -est 1** : sombreado (dícese de un lugar), que da sombra (dícese de un árbol) **2** DISREPUTABLE : sospechoso (dícese de una persona), turbio (dícese de un negocio, etc.)

shaft ['ʃæft] *n* **1** : asta *f* (de una lanza), astil *m* (de una flecha), mango *m* (de una herramienta) **2** *or* **mine shaft** : pozo *m*

shaggy ['ʃægi] *adj* **shaggier; -est 1** HAIRY : peludo ⟨a shaggy dog : un perro peludo⟩ **2** UNKEMPT : enmarañado, despeinado (dícese del pelo, de las barbas, etc.)

shake[1] ['ʃeɪk] *v* **shook** ['ʃʊk]; **shaken** ['ʃeɪkən]; **shaking** *vt* **1** : sacudir, agitar, hacer temblar ⟨he shook his head : negó con la cabeza⟩ **2** WEAKEN : debilitar, hacer flaquear ⟨it shook her faith : debilitó su confianza⟩ **3** UPSET : afectar, alterar **4 to shake hands with someone** : darle la mano a alguien, estrecharle la mano a alguien — *vi* : temblar, sacudirse

shake[2] *n* : sacudida *f*, apretón *m* (de manos)

shaker ['ʃeɪkər] *n* **1 salt shaker** : salero *m* **2 pepper shaker** : pimentero *m* **3 cocktail shaker** : coctelera *f*

shake-up ['ʃeɪk,ʌp] *n* : reorganización *f*

shakily ['ʃeɪkəli] *adv* : temblorosamente

shaky [ˈʃeɪki] *adj* **shakier; -est 1** SHAK-
ING : tembloroso **2** UNSTABLE : poco
firme, inestable **3** PRECARIOUS : precario, incierto **4** QUESTIONABLE : dudoso, cuestionable ⟨shaky arguments
: argumentos discutibles⟩
shale [ˈʃeɪl] *n* : esquisto *m*
shall [ˈʃæl] *v aux, past* **should** [ˈʃʊd] *present s & pl* **shall 1** (*used to express a
command*) ⟨you shall do as I say : harás
lo que te digo⟩ **2** (*used to express futu-
rity*) ⟨we shall see : ya veremos⟩ ⟨when
shall we expect you? : ¿cuándo te
podemos esperar?⟩ **3** (*used to express
determination*) ⟨you shall have the
money : tendrás el dinero⟩ **4** (*used to
express a condition*) ⟨if he should die
: si muriera⟩ ⟨if they should call, tell
me : si llaman, dímelo⟩ **5** (*used to express obligation*) ⟨he should have said
it : debería haberlo dicho⟩ **6** (*used to
express probability*) ⟨they should arrive
soon : deben (de) llegar pronto⟩ ⟨why
should he lie? : ¿porqué ha de mentir?⟩
shallow [ˈʃælo:] *adj* **1** : poco profundo
(dícese del agua, etc.) **2** SUPERFICIAL
: superficial
shallows [ˈʃælo:z] *npl* : bajío *m*, bajos
mpl
sham¹ [ˈʃæm] *v* **shammed; shamming**
: fingir
sham² *adj* : falso, fingido
sham³ *n* **1** FAKE, PRETENSE : farsa *f*,
simulación *f*, imitación *f* **2** FAKER : impostor *m*, -tora *f*; farsante *mf*
shamble [ˈʃæmbəl] *vi* **-bled; -bling**
: caminar arrastrando los pies
shambles [ˈʃæmbəlz] *ns & pl* : caos *m*,
desorden *m*, confusión *f*
shame¹ [ˈʃeɪm] *vt* **shamed; shaming 1**
: avergonzar ⟨he was shamed by their
words : sus palabras le dieron vergüen-
za⟩ **2** DISGRACE : deshonrar
shame² *n* **1** : vergüenza *f* ⟨to have no
shame : no tener vergüenza⟩ **2** DIS-
GRACE : vergüenza *f*, deshonra *f* **3** PITY
: lástima *f*, pena *f* ⟨what a shame! : ¡qué
pena!⟩
shamefaced [ˈʃeɪmˌfeɪst] *adj* : avergonzado
shameful [ˈʃeɪmfəl] *adj* : vergonzoso —
shamefully *adv*
shameless [ˈʃeɪmləs] *adj* : descarado,
desvergonzado — **shamelessly** *adv*
shampoo¹ [ʃæmˈpuː] *vt* : lavar (el pelo)
shampoo² *n, pl* **-poos** : champú *m*
shamrock [ˈʃæmˌrak] *n* : trébol *m*
shank [ˈʃæŋk] *n* : parte *f* baja de la pierna
shan't [ˈʃænt] (*contraction of* **shall not**)
→ **shall**
shanty [ˈʃænti] *n, pl* **-ties** : choza *f*, rancho *m*
shape¹ [ˈʃeɪp] *v* **shaped; shaping** *vt* **1**
: dar forma a, modelar (arcilla, etc.),
tallar (madera, piedra), formar (carácter) ⟨to be shaped like : tener forma
de⟩ **2** DETERMINE : decidir, determi-

nar — *vi or* **to shape up** : tomar forma
shape² *n* **1** : forma *f*, figura *f* ⟨in the
shape of a circle : en forma de círcu-
lo⟩ **2** CONDITION : estado *m*, condiciones *fpl*, forma *f* (física) ⟨to get in
shape : ponerse en forma⟩
shapeless [ˈʃeɪpləs] *adj* : informe
shapely [ˈʃeɪpli] *adj* **shapelier; -est**
: curvilíneo, bien proporcionado
shard [ˈʃard] *n* : fragmento *m*, casco *m*
(de cerámica, etc.)
share¹ [ˈʃɛr] *v* **shared; sharing** *vt* **1** AP-
PORTION : dividir, repartir **2** : compartir ⟨they share a room : comparten
una habitación⟩ — *vi* : compartir
share² *n* **1** PORTION : parte *f*, porción *f*
⟨one's fair share : lo que le corresponde
a uno⟩ **2** : acción *f* (en una compañía)
⟨to hold shares : tener acciones⟩
sharecropper [ˈʃɛrˌkrapər] *n* : aparcero
m, -ra *f*
shareholder [ˈʃɛrˌhoːldər] *n* : accionista
mf
shark [ˈʃark] *n* : tiburón *m*
sharp¹ [ˈʃarp] *adv* : en punto ⟨at two
o'clock sharp : a las dos en punto⟩
sharp² *adj* **1** : afilado, filoso ⟨a sharp
knife : un cuchillo afilado⟩ **2** PENE-
TRATING : cortante, fuerte **3** CLEVER
: agudo, listo, perspicaz **4** ACUTE : agudo ⟨sharp eyesight : vista aguda⟩ **5**
HARSH, SEVERE : duro, severo, agudo
⟨a sharp rebuke : una reprimenda mor-
daz⟩ **6** STRONG : fuerte ⟨sharp cheese
: queso fuerte⟩ **7** ABRUPT : brusco, repentino **8** DISTINCT : nítido, definido
⟨a sharp image : una imagen bien
definida⟩ **9** ANGULAR : anguloso
(dícese de la cara) **10** : sostenido (en
música)
sharp³ *n* : sostenido *m* (en música)
sharpen [ˈʃarpən] *vt* : afilar, aguzar ⟨to
sharpen a pencil : sacarle punta a un
lápiz⟩ ⟨to sharpen one's wits : aguzar
el ingenio⟩
sharpener [ˈʃarpənər] *n* : afilador *m*
(para cuchillos, etc.), sacapuntas *m*
(para lápices)
sharply [ˈʃarpli] *adv* **1** ABRUPTLY : bruscamente **2** DISTINCTLY : claramente,
marcadamente
sharpness [ˈʃarpnəs] *n* **1** : lo afilado (de
un cuchillo, etc.) **2** ACUTENESS
: agudeza *f* (de los sentidos o de la
mente) **3** INTENSITY : intensidad *f*,
agudeza *f* (de dolores, etc.) **4** HARSH-
NESS : dureza *f*, severidad *f* **5** ABRUPT-
NESS : brusquedad *f* **6** CLARITY : nitidez *f*
sharpshooter [ˈʃarpˌʃuːtər] *n* : tirador
m, -dora *f* de primera
shatter [ˈʃætər] *vt* **1** : hacer añicos ⟨to
shatter the silence : romper el silencio⟩
2 to be shattered by : quedar destrozado por — *vi* : hacerse añicos,
romperse en pedazos

shave¹ ['ʃeɪv] v **shaved; shaved** or **shaven** ['ʃeɪvən]; **shaving** vt **1** : afeitar, rasurar ⟨she shaved her legs : se rasuró las piernas⟩ ⟨they shaved (off) his beard : le afeitaron la barba⟩ **2** SLICE : cortar (en pedazos finos) — vi : afeitarse, rasurarse

shave² n : afeitada f, rasurada f

shaver ['ʃeɪvər] n : afeitadora f, máquina f de afeitar, rasuradora f

shawl ['ʃɔl] n : chal m, mantón m, rebozo m

she ['ʃi:] pron : ella

sheaf ['ʃi:f] n, pl **sheaves** ['ʃi:vz] : gavilla f (de cereales), haz m (de flechas), fajo m (de papeles)

shear ['ʃɪr] vt **sheared; sheared** or **shorn** ['ʃɔrn]; **shearing 1** : esquilar, trasquilar ⟨to shear sheep : trasquilar ovejas⟩ **2** CUT : cortar (el pelo, etc.)

shears ['ʃɪrz] npl : tijeras fpl (grandes)

sheath ['ʃi:θ] n, pl **sheaths** ['ʃi:ðz, 'ʃi:θs] : funda f, vaina f

sheathe ['ʃi:ð] vt **sheathed; sheathing** : envainar, enfundar

shed¹ ['ʃd] vt **shed; shedding 1** : derramar (sangre o lágrimas) **2** EMIT : emitir (luz) ⟨to shed light on : aclarar⟩ **3** DISCARD : mudar (la piel, etc.) ⟨to shed one's clothes : quitarse uno la ropa⟩

shed² n : cobertizo m

she'd ['ʃi:d] (contraction of **she had** or **she would**) → **have, would**

sheen ['ʃi:n] n : brillo m, lustre m

sheep ['ʃi:p] ns & pl : oveja f

sheepfold ['ʃi:p,fo:ld] n : redil m

sheepish ['ʃi:pɪʃ] adj : avergonzado

sheepskin ['ʃi:p,skɪn] n : piel f de oveja, piel f de borrego

sheer¹ ['ʃɪr] adv **1** COMPLETELY : completamente, totalmente **2** VERTICALLY : verticalmente

sheer² adj **1** TRANSPARENT : vaporoso, transparente **2** ABSOLUTE, UTTER : puro ⟨by sheer luck : por pura suerte⟩ **3** STEEP : escarpado, vertical

sheet ['ʃi:t] n **1** or **bedsheet** ['bɛd-,ʃi:t] : sábana f **2** : hoja f (de papel) **3** : capa f (de hielo, etc.) **4** : lámina f, placa f (de vidrio, metal, etc.), plancha f (de metal, madera, etc.) ⟨baking sheet : placa de horno⟩

sheikh or **sheik** ['ʃi:k, 'ʃeɪk] n : jeque m

shelf ['ʃɛlf] n, pl **shelves** ['ʃɛlvz] **1** : estante m, anaquel m (en una pared) **2** : banco m, arrecife m (en geología) ⟨continental shelf : plataforma continental⟩

shell¹ ['ʃɛl] vt **1** : desvainar (chícharos), pelar (nueces, etc.) **2** BOMBARD : bombardear

shell² n **1** SEASHELL : concha f **2** : cáscara f (de huevos, nueces, etc.), vaina f (de chícharos, etc.), caparazón m (de crustáceos, tortugas, etc.) **3** : cartucho m, casquillo m ⟨a .45 caliber shell : un cartucho calibre .45⟩ **4** or **racing shell** : bote m (para hacer regatas de remos)

she'll ['ʃi:l, 'ʃɪl] (contraction of **she shall** or **she will**) → **shall, will**

shellac¹ [ʃə'læk] vt **-lacked; -lacking 1** : laquear (madera, etc.) **2** DEFEAT : darle una paliza (a alguien), derrotar

shellac² n : laca f

shellfish ['ʃɛl,fɪʃ] n : marisco m

shelter¹ ['ʃɛltər] vt **1** PROTECT : proteger, abrigar **2** HARBOR : dar refugio a, albergar

shelter² n : refugio m, abrigo m ⟨to take shelter : refugiarse⟩

shelve ['ʃɛlv] vt **shelved; shelving 1** : poner en estantes **2** DEFER : dar carpetazo a

shenanigans [ʃə'nænɪgənz] npl **1** TRICKERY : artimañas fpl **2** MISCHIEF : travesuras fpl

shepherd¹ ['ʃɛpərd] vt **1** : cuidar (ovejas, etc.) **2** GUIDE : conducir, guiar

shepherd² n : pastor m

shepherdess ['ʃɛpərdəs] n : pastora f

sherbet ['ʃərbət] or **sherbert** [-bərt] n : sorbete m, nieve f Cuba, Mex, PRi

sheriff ['ʃɛrɪf] n : sheriff mf

sherry ['ʃɛri] n, pl **-ries** : jerez m

she's ['ʃi:z] (contraction of **she is** or **she has**) → **be, have**

shield¹ ['ʃi:ld] vt **1** PROTECT : proteger **2** CONCEAL : ocultar ⟨to shield one's eyes : taparse los ojos⟩

shield² n **1** : escudo m (armadura) **2** PROTECTION : protección f, blindaje m (de un cable)

shier, shiest → **shy**

shift¹ ['ʃɪft] vt **1** CHANGE : cambiar ⟨to shift gears : cambiar de velocidad⟩ **2** MOVE : mover **3** TRANSFER : transferir ⟨to shift the blame : echarle la culpa (a otro)⟩ — vi **1** CHANGE : cambiar **2** MOVE : moverse **3 to shift for oneself** : arreglárselas solo

shift² n **1** CHANGE, TRANSFER : cambio m ⟨a shift in priorities : un cambio de prioridades⟩ **2** : turno m ⟨night shift : turno de noche⟩ **3** DRESS : vestido m (suelto) **4** → **gearshift**

shiftless ['ʃɪftləs] adj : perezoso, vago, holgazán

shifty ['ʃɪfti] adj **shiftier; -est** : taimado, artero ⟨a shifty look : una mirada huidiza⟩

shilling ['ʃɪlɪŋ] n : chelín m

shimmer ['ʃɪmər] vi GLIMMER : brillar con luz trémula

shin¹ ['ʃɪn] vi **shinned; shinning** : trepar, subir ⟨she shinned up the pole : subió al poste⟩

shin² n : espinilla f, canilla f

shine¹ ['ʃaɪn] v **shone** ['ʃo:n] or **shined; shining** vi **1** : brillar, relucir ⟨the stars were shining : las estrellas brillaban⟩ **2** EXCEL : brillar, lucirse — vt **1** : alumbrar ⟨he shined the flashlight at it : lo alumbró con la linterna⟩ **2** POLISH : sacarle brillo a, lustrar

shine² n : brillo m, lustre m

shingle¹ ['ʃɪŋgəl] vt **-gled; -gling** : techar

shingle² *n* : tablilla *f* (para techar)
shingles [ˈʃɪŋgəlz] *npl* : herpes *m*
shinny [ˈʃɪni] *vi* -nied; -nying → shin¹
shiny [ˈʃaɪni] *adj* shinier; -est : brillante
ship¹ [ˈʃɪp] *vt* shipped; shipping 1 LOAD : embarcar (en un barco) 2 SEND : transportar (en barco), enviar ⟨to ship by air : enviar por avión⟩
ship² *n* 1 : barco *m*, buque *m* 2 → spaceship
shipboard [ˈʃɪpˌbord] *n* on ~ : a bordo
shipbuilder [ˈʃɪpˌbɪldər] *n* : constructor *m*, -tora *f* naval
shipment [ˈʃɪpmənt] *n* 1 SHIPPING : transporte *m*, embarque *m* 2 : envío *m*, remesa *f* ⟨a shipment of medicine : un envío de medicina⟩
shipping [ˈʃɪpɪŋ] *n* 1 SHIPS : barcos *mpl*, embarcaciones *fpl* 2 TRANSPORTATION : transporte *m* (de mercancías)
shipshape [ˈʃɪpˈʃeɪp] *adj* : ordenado
shipwreck¹ [ˈʃɪpˌrɛk] *vt* to be shipwrecked : naufragar
shipwreck² *n* : naufragio *m*
shipyard [ˈʃɪpˌjard] *n* : astillero *m*
shirk [ˈʃərk] *vt* : eludir, rehuir ⟨to shirk one's responsibilities : esquivar uno sus responsabilidades⟩
shirt [ˈʃərt] *n* : camisa *f*
shiver¹ [ˈʃɪvər] *vi* 1 : tiritar (de frío) 2 TREMBLE : estremecerse, temblar
shiver² *n* : escalofrío *m*, estremecimiento *m*
shoal [ˈʃoːl] *n* : banco *m*, bajío *m*
shock¹ [ˈʃɑk] *vt* 1 UPSET : conmover, conmocionar 2 STARTLE : asustar, sobresaltar 3 SCANDALIZE : escandalizar 4 : darle una descarga eléctrica a
shock² *n* 1 COLLISION, JOLT : choque *m*, sacudida *f* 2 UPSET : conmoción *f*, golpe *m* emocional 3 : shock *m* (en medicina) 4 *or* electric shock : descarga *f* eléctrica 5 SHEAVES : gavillas *fpl* 6 shock of hair : mata *f* de pelo
shock absorber *n* : amortiguador *m*
shocking [ˈʃɑkɪŋ] *adj* 1 : chocante 2 shocking pink : rosa *m* estridente
shoddy [ˈʃɑdi] *adj* shoddier; -est : de mala calidad ⟨a shoddy piece of work : un trabajo chapucero⟩
shoe¹ [ˈʃuː] *vt* shod [ˈʃɑd]; shoeing : herrar (un caballo)
shoe² *n* 1 : zapato *m* ⟨the shoe industry : la industria del calzado⟩ 2 HORSESHOE : herradura *f* 3 brake shoe : zapata *f*
shoelace [ˈʃuːˌleɪs] *n* : cordón *m* (de zapatos)
shoemaker [ˈʃuːˌmeɪkər] *n* : zapatero *m*, -ra *f*
shone → shine
shook → shake
shoot¹ [ˈʃuːt] *v* shot [ˈʃɑt]; shooting *vt* 1 : disparar, tirar ⟨to shoot a bullet : tirar una bala⟩ 2 : pegarle un tiro a, darle un balazo a ⟨he shot her : le pegó un tiro⟩ ⟨they shot and killed him : lo mataron a balazos⟩ 3 THROW : lanzar

(una pelota, etc.), echar (una mirada) 4 PHOTOGRAPH : fotografiar 5 FILM : filmar — *vi* 1 : disparar (con un arma de fuego) 2 DART : ir rápidamente ⟨it shot past : pasó como una bala⟩
shoot² *n* : brote *m*, retoño *m*, vástago *m*
shooting star *n* : estrella *f* fugaz
shop¹ [ˈʃɑp] *vi* shopped; shopping : hacer compras ⟨to go shopping : ir de compras⟩
shop² *n* 1 WORKSHOP : taller *m* 2 STORE : tienda *f*
shopkeeper [ˈʃɑpˌkiːpər] *n* : tendero *m*, -ra *f*
shoplift [ˈʃɑpˌlɪft] *vi* : hurtar mercancía (de una tienda) — *vt* : hurtar (de una tienda)
shoplifter [ˈʃɑpˌlɪftər] *n* : ladrón *m*, -drona *f* (que roba en una tienda)
shopper [ˈʃɑpər] *n* : comprador *m*, -dora *f*
shore¹ [ˈʃor] *vt* shored; shoring : apuntalar ⟨they shored up the wall : apuntalaron la pared⟩
shore² *n* 1 : orilla *f* (del mar, etc.) 2 PROP : puntal *m*
shoreline [ˈʃorˌlaɪn] *n* : orilla *f*
shorn → shear
short¹ [ˈʃort] *adv* 1 ABRUPTLY : repentinamente, súbitamente ⟨the car stopped short : el carro se paró en seco⟩ 2 to fall short : no alcanzar, quedarse corto
short² *adj* 1 : corto (de medida), bajo (de estatura) 2 BRIEF : corto ⟨short and sweet : corto y bueno⟩ ⟨a short time ago : hace poco⟩ 3 CURT : brusco, cortante, seco 4 : corto (de tiempo, de dinero) ⟨I'm one dollar short : me falta un dólar⟩
short³ *n* 1 shorts *npl* : shorts *mpl*, pantalones *mpl* cortos 2 → short circuit
shortage [ˈʃortɪdʒ] *n* : falta *f*, escasez *f*, carencia *f*
shortcake [ˈʃortˌkeɪk] *n* : tarta *f* de fruta
shortchange [ˈʃortˈtʃeɪndʒ] *vt* -changed; -changing : darle mal el cambio (a alguien)
short circuit *n* : cortocircuito *m*, corto *m* (eléctrico)
shortcoming [ˈʃortˌkʌmɪŋ] *n* : defecto *m*
shortcut [ˈʃortˌkʌt] *n* 1 : atajo *m* ⟨to take a shortcut : cortar camino⟩ 2 : alternativa *f* fácil, método *m* rápido
shorten [ˈʃortən] *vt* : acortar — *vi* : acortarse
shorthand [ˈʃortˌhænd] *n* : taquigrafía *f*
short–lived [ˈʃortˈlɪvd, -ˈlaɪvd] *adj* : efímero
shortly [ˈʃortli] *adv* 1 BRIEFLY : brevemente ⟨to put it shortly : para decirlo en pocas palabras⟩ 2 SOON : dentro de poco
shortness [ˈʃortnəs] *n* 1 : lo corto ⟨shortness of stature : estatura baja⟩ 2 BREVITY : brevedad *f* 3 CURTNESS : brusquedad *f* 4 SHORTAGE : falta *f*, escasez *f*, carencia *f*

shortsighted ['ʃɔrt,saɪtəd] → **nearsighted**

shot ['ʃɑt] n 1 : disparo m, tiro m ⟨to fire a shot : disparar⟩ 2 PELLETS : perdigones mpl 3 : tiro m (en deportes) 4 ATTEMPT : intento m, tentativa f ⟨to have a shot at : hacer un intento por⟩ 5 RANGE : alcance m ⟨a long shot : una posibilidad remota⟩ 6 PHOTOGRAPH : foto f 7 INJECTION : inyección f 8 : trago m (de licor)

shotgun ['ʃɑt,gʌn] n : escopeta f

should → **shall**

shoulder[1] ['ʃoːldər] vt 1 JOSTLE : empujar (con el hombro) 2 : ponerse al hombro (una mochila, etc.) 3 : cargar con (la responsabilidad, etc.)

shoulder[2] n 1 : hombro m ⟨to shrug one's shoulders : encogerse los hombros⟩ 2 : arcén m (de una carretera)

shoulder blade n : omóplato m, omoplato m, escápula f

shouldn't ['ʃʊdənt] (contraction of should not) → **shall**

shout[1] ['ʃaʊt] v : gritar, vocear

shout[2] n : grito m

shove[1] ['ʃʌv] v shoved; shoving : empujar bruscamente

shove[2] n : empujón m, empellón m

shovel[1] ['ʃʌvəl] vt -veled or -velled; -veling or -velling 1 : mover con (una) pala ⟨they shoveled the dirt out : sacaron la tierra con palas⟩ 2 DIG : cavar (con una pala)

shovel[2] n : pala f

show[1] ['ʃoː] v showed; shown ['ʃoːn] or showed; showing vt 1 DISPLAY : mostrar, enseñar 2 REVEAL : demostrar, manifestar, revelar ⟨he showed himself to be a coward : se reveló como cobarde⟩ 3 TEACH : enseñar 4 PROVE : demostrar, probar 5 CONDUCT, DIRECT : llevar, acompañar ⟨to show someone the way : indicarle el camino a alguien⟩ 6 : proyectar (una película), dar (un programa de televisión) — vi 1 : notarse, verse ⟨the stain doesn't show : la mancha no se ve⟩ 2 APPEAR : aparecer, dejarse ver

show[2] n 1 : demostración f ⟨a show of force : una demostración de fuerza⟩ 2 EXHIBITION : exposición f, exhibición f ⟨flower show : exposición de flores⟩ ⟨to be on show : estar expuesto⟩ 3 : espectáculo m (teatral), programa m (de televisión, etc.) ⟨to go to a show : ir al teatro⟩

showcase ['ʃoː,keɪs] n : vitrina f

showdown ['ʃoː,daʊn] n : confrontación f (decisiva)

shower[1] ['ʃaʊər] vt 1 SPRAY : regar, mojar 2 HEAP : colmar ⟨they showered him with gifts : lo colmaron de regalos, le llovieron los regalos⟩ — vi 1 BATHE : ducharse, darse una ducha 2 RAIN : llover

shower[2] n 1 : chaparrón m, chubasco m ⟨a chance of showers : una posibil-

idad de chaparrones⟩ 2 : ducha f ⟨to take a shower : ducharse⟩ 3 PARTY : fiesta f ⟨a bridal shower : una despedida de soltera⟩

show off vt : hacer alarde de, ostentar — vi : lucirse

show up vi APPEAR : aparecer — vt EXPOSE : revelar

showy ['ʃoːi] adj showier; -est : llamativo, ostentoso — **showily** adv

shrank → **shrink**

shrapnel ['ʃræpnəl] ns & pl : metralla f

shred[1] ['ʃrɛd] vt shredded; shredding : hacer trizas, desmenuzar (con las manos), triturar (con una máquina) ⟨to shred vegetables : cortar verduras en tiras⟩

shred[2] n 1 STRIP : tira f, jirón m (de tela) 2 BIT : pizca f ⟨not a shred of evidence : ni la mínima prueba⟩

shrew ['ʃruː] n 1 : musaraña f (animal) 2 : mujer f regañona, arpía f

shrewd ['ʃruːd] adj : astuto, inteligente, sagaz — **shrewdly** adv

shrewdness ['ʃruːdnəs] n : astucia f

shriek[1] ['ʃriːk] vi : chillar, gritar

shriek[2] n : chillido m, alarido m, grito m

shrill ['ʃrɪl] adj : agudo, estridente

shrilly ['ʃrɪli] adv : agudamente

shrimp ['ʃrɪmp] n : camarón m, langostino m

shrine ['ʃraɪn] n 1 TOMB : sepulcro m (de un santo) 2 SANCTUARY : lugar m sagrado, santuario m

shrink ['ʃrɪŋk] vi shrank ['ʃræŋk] or shrunk ['ʃrʌŋk]; shrunk or shrunken ['ʃrʌŋkən]; shrinking 1 RECOIL : retroceder ⟨he shrank back : se echó para atrás⟩ 2 : encogerse (dícese de la ropa)

shrinkage ['ʃrɪŋkɪdʒ] n : encogimiento m (de ropa, etc.), contracción f, reducción f

shrivel ['ʃrɪvəl] vi -veled or -velled; -veling or -velling : arrugarse, marchitarse

shroud[1] ['ʃraʊd] vt : envolver

shroud[2] n 1 : sudario m, mortaja f 2 VEIL : velo m ⟨wrapped in a shroud of mystery : envuelto en un aura de misterio⟩

shrub ['ʃrʌb] n : arbusto m, mata f

shrubbery ['ʃrʌbəri] n, pl -beries : arbustos mpl, matas fpl

shrug ['ʃrʌg] vi shrugged; shrugging : encogerse de hombros

shrunk → **shrink**

shuck[1] ['ʃʌk] vt : pelar (mazorcas, etc.), abrir (almejas, etc.)

shuck[2] n 1 HUSK : cascarilla f, cáscara f (de una nuez, etc.), hojas fpl (de una mazorca) 2 SHELL : concha f (de una almeja, etc.)

shudder[1] ['ʃʌdər] vi : estremecerse

shudder[2] n : estremecimiento m, escalofrío m

shuffle[1] ['ʃʌfəl] v -fled; -fling vt MIX : mezclar, revolver, barajar (naipes) — vi : caminar arrastrando los pies

shuffle² *n* **1** : acto *m* de revolver ⟨each player gets a shuffle : a cada jugador le toca barajar⟩ **2** JUMBLE : revoltijo *m* **3** : arrastramiento *m* de los pies

shun [ˈʃʌn] *vi* **shunned; shunning** : evitar, esquivar, eludir

shunt [ˈʃʌnt] *vt* : desviar, cambiar de vía (un tren)

shut [ˈʃʌt] *v* **shut; shutting** *vt* **1** CLOSE : cerrar ⟨shut the lid : tápalo⟩ **2 to shut out** EXCLUDE : excluir, dejar fuera a (personas), no dejar que entre (luz, ruido, etc.) **3 to shut up** CONFINE : encerrar — *vi* : cerrarse ⟨the factory shut down : la fábrica cerró suspuertas⟩

shut–in [ˈʃʌtˌɪn] *n* : inválido *m*, -da *f* (que no puede salir de casa)

shutter [ˈʃʌtər] *n* **1** : contraventana *f*, postigo *m* (de una ventana o puerta) **2** : obturador *m* (de una cámara)

shuttle¹ [ˈʃʌtəl] *v* **-tled; -tling** *vt* : transportar ⟨she shuttled him back and forth : lo llevaba de acá para allá⟩ — *vi* : ir y venir

shuttle² *n* **1** : lanzadera *f* (para tejer) **2** : vehículo *m* que hace recorridos cortos **3** → **space shuttle**

shuttlecock [ˈʃʌtəlˌkɑk] *n* : volante *m*

shut up *vi* : callarse ⟨shut up! : ¡cállate (la boca)!⟩

shy¹ [ˈʃaɪ] *vi* **shied; shying** : retroceder, asustarse

shy² *adj* **shier** *or* **shyer** [ˈʃaɪər]; **shiest** *or* **shyest** [ˈʃaɪəst] **1** TIMID : tímido **2** WARY : cauteloso ⟨he's not shy about asking : no vacila en preguntar⟩ **3** SHORT : corto (de dinero, etc.) ⟨I'm two dollars shy : me faltan dos dólares⟩

shyly [ˈʃaɪli] *adv* : tímidamente

shyness [ˈʃaɪnəs] *n* : timidez *f*

Siamese¹ [ˌsaɪəˈmiːz, -ˈmiːs-] *adj* : siamés ⟨Siamese twins : hermanos siameses⟩

Siamese² *n* **1** : siamés *m*, -mesa *f* **2** : siamés *m* (idioma) **3** *or* **Siamese cat** : gato *m* siamés

sibling [ˈsɪblɪŋ] *n* : hermano *m*, hermana *f*

Sicilian [səˈsɪljən] *n* : siciliano *m*, -na *f* — **Sicilian** *adj*

sick [ˈsɪk] *adj* **1** : enfermo **2** NAUSEOUS : mareado, con náuseas ⟨to get sick : vomitar⟩ **3** : para uso de enfermos ⟨sick day : día de permiso (por enfermedad)⟩

sickbed [ˈsɪkˌbɛd] *n* : lecho *m* de enfermo

sicken [ˈsɪkən] *vt* **1** : poner enfermo **2** REVOLT : darle asco (a alguien) — *vi* : enfermar(se), caer enfermo

sickening [ˈsɪkənɪŋ] *adj* : asqueroso, repugnante, nauseabundo

sickle [ˈsɪkəl] *n* : hoz *f*

sickly [ˈsɪkli] *adj* **sicklier; -est 1** : enfermizo **2** → **sickening**

sickness [ˈsɪknəs] *n* **1** : enfermedad *f* **2** NAUSEA : náuseas *fpl*

side [ˈsaɪd] *n* **1** : lado *m*, costado *m* (de una persona), ijada *f* (de un animal) **2** : lado *m*, cara *f* (de una moneda, etc.) **3** : lado *m*, parte *f* ⟨he's on my side : está de mi parte⟩ ⟨to take sides : tomar partido⟩

sideboard [ˈsaɪdˌbord] *n* : aparador *m*

sideburns [ˈsaɪdˌbərnz] *npl* : patillas *fpl*

sided [ˈsaɪdəd] *adj* : que tiene lados ⟨one-sided : de un lado⟩

side effect *n* : efecto *m* secundario

sideline [ˈsaɪdˌlaɪn] *n* **1** : línea *f* de banda (en deportes) **2** : actividad *f* suplementaria (en negocios) **3 to be on the sidelines** : estar al margen

sidelong [ˈsaɪdˌlɔŋ] *adj* : de reojo, de soslayo

sideshow [ˈsaɪdˌʃoː] *n* : espectáculo *m* secundario, atracción *f* secundaria

sidestep [ˈsaɪdˌstɛp] *v* **-stepped; -stepping** *vi* : dar un paso hacia un lado — *vt* AVOID : esquivar, eludir

sidetrack [ˈsaɪdˌtræk] *vt* : desviar (una conversación, etc.), distraer (a una persona)

sidewalk [ˈsaɪdˌwɔk] *n* : acera *f*, vereda *f*, andén *m CA, Col*, banqueta *f Mex*

sideways¹ [ˈsaɪdˌweɪz] *adv* **1** : hacia un lado ⟨it leaned sideways : se inclinaba hacia un lado⟩ **2** : de lado, de costado ⟨lie sideways : acuéstese de costado⟩

sideways² *adj* : hacia un lado ⟨a sideways glance : una mirada de reojo⟩

siding [ˈsaɪdɪŋ] *n* **1** : apartadero *m* (para trenes) **2** : revestimiento *m* exterior (de un edificio)

sidle [ˈsaɪdəl] *vi* **-dled; -dling** : moverse furtivamente

siege [ˈsiːdʒ, ˈsiːʒ] *n* : sitio *m* ⟨to be under siege : estar sitiado⟩

siesta [siˈɛstə] *n* : siesta *f*

sieve [ˈsɪv] *n* : tamiz *m*, cedazo *m*, criba *f* (en mineralogía)

sift [ˈsɪft] *vt* **1** : tamizar, cerner ⟨sift the flour : tamice la harina⟩ **2** *or* **to sift through** : examinar cuidadosamente, pasar por el tamiz

sifter [ˈsɪftər] *n* : tamiz *m*, cedazo *m*

sigh¹ [ˈsaɪ] *vi* : suspirar

sigh² *n* : suspiro *m*

sight¹ [ˈsaɪt] *vt* : ver (a una persona), divisar (la tierra, un barco)

sight² *n* **1** : vista *f* (facultad) ⟨out of sight : fuera de vista⟩ **2** : algo visto ⟨it's a familiar sight : se ve con frecuencia⟩ ⟨she's a sight for sore eyes : da gusto verla⟩ **3** : lugar *m* de interés (para turistas, etc.) **4** : mira *f* (de un rifle, etc.) **5** GLIMPSE : mirada *f* breve ⟨I caught sight of her : la divisé, alcancé a verla⟩

sighting [ˈsaɪtɪŋ] *n* : avistamiento *m*

sightless [ˈsaɪtləs] *adj* : invidente, ciego

sightseer [ˈsaɪtˌsiːər] *n* : turista *mf*

sign¹ [ˈsaɪn] *vt* **1** : firmar ⟨to sign a check : firmar un cheque⟩ **2** *or* **to sign on** HIRE : contratar (a un empleado), fichar (a un jugador) — *vi* **1** : hacer una seña ⟨she signed for him to stop : le hizo una seña para que se parara⟩ **2** : comunicarse por señas

sign² *n* **1** SYMBOL : símbolo *m*, signo *m* 〈minus sign : signo de menos〉 **2** GESTURE : seña *f*, señal *f*, gesto *m* **3** : letrero *m*, cartel *m* 〈neon sign : letrero de neón〉 **4** TRACE : señal *f*, indicio *m*

signal¹ ['sɪgnəl] *vt* **-naled** *or* **-nalled; -naling** *or* **-nalling 1** : hacerle señas (a alguien) 〈she signaled me to leave : me hizo señas para que saliera〉 **2** INDICATE : señalar, indicar — *vi* : hacer señas, comunicar por señas

signal² *adj* NOTABLE : señalado, notable

signal³ *n* : señal *f*

signature ['sɪgnə,tʃur] *n* : firma *f*

signet ['sɪgnət] *n* : sello *m*

significance [sɪg'nɪfɪkənts] *n* **1** MEANING : significado *m* **2** IMPORTANCE : importancia *f*

significant [sɪg'nɪfɪkənt] *adj* **1** IMPORTANT : importante **2** MEANINGFUL : significativo — **significantly** *adv*

signify ['sɪgnə,faɪ] *vt* **-fied; -fying 1** : indicar 〈he signified his desire for more : haciendo señas indicó que quería más〉 **2** MEAN : significar

sign language *n* : lenguaje *m* por señas

signpost ['saɪn,po:st] *n* : poste *m* indicador

silence¹ ['saɪlənts] *vt* **-lenced; -lencing** : silenciar, acallar

silence² *n* : silencio *m*

silent ['saɪlənt] *adj* **1** : callado 〈to remain silent : quedarse callado, guardar silencio〉 **2** QUIET, STILL : silencioso **3** MUTE : mudo 〈a silent letter : una letra muda〉

silently ['saɪləntli] *adv* : silenciosamente, calladamente

silhouette¹ [,sɪlə'wet] *vt* **-etted; -etting** : destacar la silueta de 〈it was silhouetted against the sky : se perfilaba contra el cielo〉

silhouette² *n* : silueta *f*

silica ['sɪlɪkə] *n* : sílice *f*

silicon ['sɪlɪkən, -,kɑn] *n* : silicio *m*

silk ['sɪlk] *n* : seda *f*

silken ['sɪlkən] *adj* **1** : de seda 〈a silken veil : un velo de seda〉 **2** SILKY : sedoso 〈silken hair : cabellos sedosos〉

silkworm ['sɪlk,wərm] *n* : gusano *m* de seda

silky ['sɪlki] *adj* **silkier; -est** : sedoso

sill ['sɪl] *n* : alféizar *m* (de una ventana), umbral *m* (de una puerta)

silliness ['sɪlinəs] *n* : tontería *f*, estupidez *f*

silly ['sɪli] *adj* **sillier; -est** : tonto, estúpido, ridículo

silo ['saɪ,lo:] *n*, *pl* **silos** : silo *m*

silt ['sɪlt] *n* : cieno *m*

silver¹ ['sɪlvər] *adj* **1** : de plata 〈a silver spoon : una cuchara de plata〉 **2** → silvery

silver² *n* **1** : plata *f* **2** COINS : monedas *fpl* **3** → silverware **4** : color *m* plata

silverware ['sɪlvər,wær] *n* **1** : artículos *mpl* de plata, platería *f* **2** FLATWARE : cubertería *f*

silvery ['sɪlvəri] *adj* : plateado

similar ['sɪmələr] *adj* : similar, parecido, semejante

similarity [,sɪmə'lærəti] *n*, *pl* **-ties** : semejanza *f*, parecido *m*

similarly ['sɪmələrli] *adv* : de manera similar

simile ['sɪmə,li:] *n* : símil *m*

simmer ['sɪmər] *v* : hervir a fuego lento

simper¹ ['sɪmpər] *vi* : sonreír como un tonto

simper² *n* : sonrisa *f* tonta

simple ['sɪmpəl] *adj* **simpler; -plest 1** INNOCENT : inocente **2** PLAIN : sencillo, simple **3** EASY : simple, sencillo, fácil **4** STRAIGHTFORWARD : puro, simple 〈the simple truth : la pura verdad〉 **5** NAIVE : ingenuo, simple

simpleton ['sɪmpəltən] *n* : bobo *m*, -ba *f*; tonto *m*, -ta *f*

simplicity [sɪm'plɪsəti] *n* : simplicidad *f*, sencillez *f*

simplification [,sɪmpləfə'keɪʃən] *n* : simplificación *f*

simplify ['sɪmplə,faɪ] *vt* **-fied; -fying** : simplificar

simply ['sɪmpli] *adv* **1** PLAINLY : sencillamente **2** SOLELY : simplemente, sólo **3** REALLY : absolutamente

simulate ['sɪmjə,leɪt] *vt* **-lated; -lating** : simular

simulation [,sɪmjə'leɪʃən] *n* : simulación *f*

simultaneous [,saɪməl'teɪniəs] *adj* : simultáneo — **simultaneously** *adv*

sin¹ ['sɪn] *vi* **sinned; sinning** : pecar

sin² *n* : pecado *m*

since¹ ['sɪnts] *adv* **1** : desde entonces 〈they've been friends ever since : desde entonces han sido amigos〉 **2** AGO : hace 〈he's long since dead : murió hace mucho〉

since² *conj* **1** : desde que 〈since he was born : desde que nació〉 **2** INASMUCH AS : ya que, puesto que, dado que

since³ *prep* : desde

sincere [sɪn'sɪr] *adj* **-cerer; -est** : sincero — **sincerely** *adv*

sincerity [sɪn'sɛrəti] *n* : sinceridad *f*

sinew ['sɪn,ju:, 'sɪ,nu:] *n* **1** TENDON : tendón *m*, nervio *m* (en la carne) **2** POWER : fuerza *f*

sinewy ['sɪnjui, 'sɪnui] *adj* **1** STRINGY : fibroso **2** STRONG, WIRY : fuerte, nervudo

sinful ['sɪnfəl] *adj* : pecador (dícese de las personas), pecaminoso

sing ['sɪŋ] *v* **sang** ['sæŋ] *or* **sung** ['sʌŋ]; **sung; singing** : cantar

singe ['sɪndʒ] *vt* **singed; singeing** : chamuscar, quemar

singer ['sɪŋər] *n* : cantante *mf*

single¹ ['sɪŋgəl] *vt* **-gled; -gling** *or* **to single out 1** SELECT : escoger **2** DISTINGUISH : señalar

single² *adj* **1** UNMARRIED : soltero **2** SOLE : solo 〈a single survivor : un solo sobreviviente⟩ ⟨every single one : cada uno, todos⟩

single³ *n* **1** : soltero *m*, -ra *f* ⟨for married couples and singles : para los matrimonios y los solteros⟩ **2** *or* **single room** : habitación *f* individual **3** DOLLAR : billete *m* de un dólar

single–handed [ˈsɪŋɡəlˈhændəd] *adj* : sin ayuda, solo

singly [ˈsɪŋɡli] *adv* : individualmente, uno por uno

singular¹ [ˈsɪŋɡjələr] *adj* **1** : singular (en gramática) **2** OUTSTANDING : singular, sobresaliente **3** STRANGE : singular, extraño

singular² *n* : singular *m*

singularity [ˌsɪŋɡjəˈlærəti] *n, pl* **-ties** : singularidad *f*

singularly [ˈsɪŋɡjələrli] *adv* : singularmente

sinister [ˈsɪnəstər] *adj* : siniestro

sink¹ [ˈsɪŋk] *v* **sank** [ˈsæŋk] *or* **sunk** [ˈsʌŋk]; **sunk**; **sinking** *vi* **1** : hundirse (dícese de un barco) **2** DROP, FALL : descender, caer ⟨to sink into a chair : dejarse caer en una silla⟩ ⟨her heart sank : se le cayó el alma a los pies⟩ **3** DECREASE : bajar — *vt* **1** : hundir (un barco, etc.) **2** EXCAVATE : excavar (un pozo para minar), perforar (un pozo de agua) **3** PLUNGE, STICK : clavar, hincar **4** INVEST : invertir (fondos)

sink² *n* **1** kitchen sink : fregadero *m*, lavaplatos *m Chile, Col, Mex* **2** bathroom sink : lavabo *m*, lavamanos *m*

sinner [ˈsɪnər] *n* : pecador *m*, -dora *f*

sinuous [ˈsɪnjuəs] *adj* : sinuoso — **sinuously** *adv*

sinus [ˈsaɪnəs] *n* : seno *m*

sip¹ [ˈsɪp] *v* **sipped; sipping** *vt* : sorber — *vi* : beber a sorbos

sip² *n* : sorbo *m*

siphon¹ [ˈsaɪfən] *vt* : sacar con sifón

siphon² *n* : sifón *m*

sir [ˈsər] *n* **1** (*in titles*) : sir *m* **2** (*as a form of address*) : señor *m* ⟨Dear Sir : Muy señor mío⟩ ⟨yes sir! : ¡sí, señor!⟩

sire¹ [ˈsaɪr] *vt* **sired; siring** : engendrar, ser el padre de

sire² *n* : padre *m*

siren [ˈsaɪrən] *n* : sirena *f*

sirloin [ˈsərˌlɔɪn] *n* : solomillo *m*

sirup → **syrup**

sisal [ˈsaɪsəl, -zəl] *n* : sisal *m*

sissy [ˈsɪsi] *n, pl* **-sies** : mariquita *f fam*

sister [ˈsɪstər] *n* **1** : hermana *f* **2 Sister** : hermana *f*, Sor *f* ⟨Sister Mary : Sor María⟩

sisterhood [ˈsɪstərˌhʊd] *n* **1** : condición *f* de ser hermana **2** : sociedad *f* de mujeres

sister–in–law [ˈsɪstərɪnˌlɔ] *n, pl* **sisters–in–law** : cuñada *f*

sisterly [ˈsɪstərli] *adj* : de hermana

sit [ˈsɪt] *v* **sat** [ˈsæt]; **sitting** *vi* **1** : sentarse, estar sentado ⟨he sat down : se sentó⟩ **2** ROOST : posarse **3** : sesionar ⟨the legislature is sitting : la legislatu-

ra está en sesión⟩ **4** POSE : posar (para un retrato) **5** LIE, REST : estar (ubicado) ⟨the house sits on a hill : la casa está en una colina⟩ — *vt* SEAT : sentar, colocar ⟨I sat him on the sofa : lo senté en el sofá⟩

sitcom [ˈsɪtˌkɑm] → **situation comedy**

site [ˈsaɪt] *n* **1** PLACE : sitio *m*, lugar *m* **2** LOCATION : emplazamiento *m*, ubicación *f*

sitter [ˈsɪtər] → **baby–sitter**

sitting room → **living room**

situated [ˈsɪtʃuˌeɪtəd] *adj* LOCATED : ubicado, situado

situation [ˌsɪtʃuˈeɪʃən] *n* **1** LOCATION : situación *f*, ubicación *f*, emplazamiento *m* **2** CIRCUMSTANCES : situación *f* **3** JOB : empleo *m*

situation comedy *n* : comedia *f* de situación

six¹ [ˈsɪks] *adj* : seis

six² *n* : seis *m*

six–gun [ˈsɪksˌɡʌn] *n* : revólver *m* (con seis cámaras)

six hundred¹ *adj* : seiscientos

six hundred² *n* : seiscientos *m*

six–shooter [ˈsɪksˌʃuːtər] → **six–gun**

sixteen¹ [sɪksˈtiːn] *adj* : dieciséis

sixteen² *n* : dieciséis *m*

sixteenth¹ [sɪksˈtiːnθ] *adj* : decimosexto

sixteenth² *n* **1** : decimosexto *m*, -ta *f* (en una serie) **2** : dieciseisavo *m*, dieciseisava parte *f*

sixth¹ [ˈsɪksθ, ˈsɪkst] *adj* : sexto

sixth² *n* **1** : sexto *m*, -ta *f* (en una serie) **2** : sexto *m*, sexta parte *f*

sixtieth¹ [ˈsɪkstiəθ] *adj* : sexagésimo

sixtieth² *n* **1** : sexagésimo *m*, -ma *f* (en una serie) **2** : sesentavo *m*, sesentava parte *f*

sixty¹ [ˈsɪksti] *adj* : sesenta

sixty² *n, pl* **-ties** : sesenta *m*

sizable *or* **sizeable** [ˈsaɪzəbəl] *adj* : considerable

size¹ [ˈsaɪz] *vt* **sized; sizing** **1** : clasificar según el tamaño **2 to size up** : evaluar, apreciar

size² *n* **1** DIMENSIONS : tamaño *m*, talla *f* (de ropa), número *m* (de zapatos) **2** MAGNITUDE : magnitud *f*

sizzle [ˈsɪzəl] *vi* **-zled; -zling** : chisporrotear

skate¹ [ˈskeɪt] *vi* **skated; skating** : patinar

skate² *n* **1** : patín *m* ⟨roller skate : patín de ruedas⟩ **2** : raya *f* (pez)

skateboard [ˈskeɪtˌbord] *n* : monopatín *m*

skater [ˈskeɪtər] *n* : patinador *m*, -dora *f*

skein [ˈskeɪn] *n* : madeja *f*

skeletal [ˈskelətəl] *adj* **1** : óseo (en anatomía) **2** EMACIATED : esquelético

skeleton [ˈskelətən] *n* **1** : esqueleto *m* (anatómico) **2** FRAMEWORK : armazón *mf*

skeptic [ˈskɛptɪk] *n* : escéptico *m*, -ca *f*

skeptical [ˈskɛptɪkəl] *adj* : escéptico

skepticism [ˈskɛptəˌsɪzəm] *n* : escepticismo *m*

sketch[1] ['skɛtʃ] *vt* : bosquejar — *vi* : hacer bosquejos
sketch[2] *n* 1 DRAWING, OUTLINE : esbozo *m*, bosquejo *m* 2 ESSAY : ensayo *m*
sketchy ['skɛtʃi] *adj* **sketchier; -est** : incompleto, poco detallado
skewer[1] ['skju:ər] *vt* : ensartar (carne, etc.)
skewer[2] *n* : brocheta *f*, broqueta *f*
ski[1] ['ski:] *vi* **skied; skiing** : esquiar
ski[2] *n, pl* **skis** : esquí *m*
skid[1] ['skɪd] *vi* **skidded; skidding** : derrapar, patinar
skid[2] *n* : derrape *m*, patinazo *m*
skier ['ski:ər] *n* : esquiador *m*, -dora *f*
skiff ['skɪf] *n* : esquife *m*
skill ['skɪl] *n* 1 DEXTERITY : habilidad *f*, destreza *f* 2 CAPABILITY : capacidad *f*, arte *m*, técnica *f* ⟨organizational skills : la capacidad para organizar⟩
skilled ['skɪld] *adj* : hábil, experto
skillet ['skɪlət] *n* : sartén *mf*
skillful ['skɪlfəl] *adj* : hábil, diestro
skillfully ['skɪlfəli] *adv* : con habilidad, con destreza
skim[1] ['skɪm] *vt* **skimmed; skimming** 1 *or* **to skim off** : espumar, descremar (leche) 2 : echarle un vistazo a (un libro, etc.), pasar rozando (una superficie)
skim[2] *adj* : descremado ⟨skim milk : leche descremada⟩
skimp ['skɪmp] *vi* **to skimp on** : escatimar
skimpy ['skɪmpi] *adj* **skimpier; -est** : exiguo, escaso, raquítico
skin[1] ['skɪn] *vt* **skinned; skinning** : despellejar, desollar
skin[2] *n* 1 : piel *f*, cutis *m* (de la cara) ⟨dark skin : piel morena⟩ 2 RIND : piel *f*
skin diving *n* : buceo *m*, submarinismo *m*
skinflint ['skɪn,flɪnt] *n* : tacaño *m*, -ña *f*
skinned ['skɪnd] *adj* : de piel ⟨tough-skinned : de piel dura⟩
skinny ['skɪni] *adj* **skinnier; -est** : flaco
skip[1] ['skɪp] *v* **skipped; skipping** *vi* : ir dando brincos — *vt* : saltarse
skip[2] *n* : brinco *m*, salto *m*
skipper ['skɪpər] *n* : capitán *m*, -tana *f*
skirmish[1] ['skərmɪʃ] *vi* : escaramuzar
skirmish[2] *n* : escaramuza *f*, refriega *f*
skirt[1] ['skərt] *vt* 1 BORDER : bordear 2 EVADE : evadir, esquivar
skirt[2] *n* : falda *f*, pollera *f*
skit ['skɪt] *n* : sketch *m* (teatral)
skittish ['skɪtɪʃ] *adj* : asustadizo, nervioso
skulk ['skʌlk] *vi* : merodear
skull ['skʌl] *n* 1 : cráneo *m*, calavera *f* 2 **skull and crossbones** : calavera *f* (bandera pirata)
skunk ['skʌŋk] *n* : zorrillo *m*, mofeta *f*
sky ['skaɪ] *n, pl* **skies** : cielo *m*
skylark ['skaɪ,lɑrk] *n* : alondra *f*
skylight ['skaɪ,laɪt] *n* : claraboya *f*, tragaluz *m*

skyline ['skaɪ,laɪn] *n* : horizonte *m*
skyrocket ['skaɪ,rɑkət] *vi* : dispararse
skyscraper ['skaɪ,skreɪpər] *n* : rascacielos *m*
slab ['slæb] *n* : losa *f* (de piedra), tabla *f* (de madera), pedazo *m* grueso (de pan, etc.)
slack[1] ['slæk] *adj* 1 CARELESS : descuidado, negligente 2 LOOSE : flojo 3 SLOW : de poco movimiento
slack[2] *n* 1 : parte *f* floja ⟨to take up the slack : tensar (una cuerda, etc.)⟩ 2 **slacks** *npl* : pantalones *mpl*
slacken ['slækən] *vt* : aflojar — *vi* : aflojarse
slacker ['slækər] *n* : vago *m*, -ga *f*; holgazán *m*, -zana *f*
slag ['slæg] *n* : escoria *f*
slain → slay
slake ['sleɪk] *vt* **slaked; slaking** : saciar (la sed), satisfacer (la curiosidad)
slam[1] ['slæm] *v* **slammed; slamming** *vt* 1 : cerrar de golpe ⟨he slammed the door : dio un portazo⟩ 2 : tirar o dejar caer de golpe ⟨he slammed down the book : dejó caer el libro de un golpe⟩ — *vi* 1 : cerrarse de golpe 2 **to slam into** : chocar contra
slam[2] *n* : golpe *m*, portazo *m* (de una puerta)
slander[1] ['slændər] *vt* : calumniar, difamar
slander[2] *n* : calumnia *f*, difamación *f*
slanderous ['slændərəs] *adj* : difamatorio, calumnioso
slang ['slæŋ] *n* : argot *m*, jerga *f*
slant[1] ['slænt] *vi* : inclinarse, ladearse — *vt* 1 SLOPE : inclinar 2 ANGLE : sesgar, orientar, dirigir ⟨a story slanted towards youth : un artículo dirigido a los jóvenes⟩
slant[2] *n* 1 INCLINE : inclinación *f* 2 PERSPECTIVE : perspectiva *f*, enfoque *m*
slap[1] ['slæp] *vt* **slapped; slapping** : bofetear, cachetear, dar una palmada (en la espalda, etc.)
slap[2] *n* : bofetada *f*, cachetada *f*, palmada *f*
slash[1] ['slæʃ] *vt* 1 GASH : cortar, hacer un tajo en 2 REDUCE : reducir, rebajar (precios)
slash[2] *n* : tajo *m*, corte *m*
slat ['slæt] *n* : tablilla *f*, listón *m*
slate ['sleɪt] *n* 1 : pizarra *f* ⟨a slate roof : un techo de pizarra⟩ 2 : lista *f* de candidatos (políticos)
slaughter[1] ['slɔtər] *vt* 1 BUTCHER : matar (animales) 2 MASSACRE : masacrar (personas)
slaughter[2] *n* 1 : matanza *f* (de animales) 2 MASSACRE : masacre *f*, carnicería *f*
slaughterhouse ['slɔtər,haʊs] *n* : matadero *m*
Slav ['slɑv, 'slæv] *n* : eslavo *m*, -va *f*
slave[1] ['sleɪv] *vi* **slaved; slaving** : trabajar como un burro
slave[2] *n* : esclavo *m*, -va *f*
slaver ['slævər, 'sleɪ-] *vi* : babear

slavery ['sleɪvəri] *n* : esclavitud *f*
Slavic ['slɑvɪk, 'slæ-] *adj* : eslavo
slavish ['sleɪvɪʃ] *adj* **1** SERVILE : servil **2** IMITATIVE : poco original
slay ['sleɪ] *vt* **slew** ['slu:]; **slain** ['sleɪn]; **slaying** : asesinar, matar
slayer ['sleɪər] *n* : asesino *m*, -na *f*
sleazy ['sli:zi] *adj* **sleazier; -est 1** SHODDY : chapucero, de mala calidad **2** DILAPIDATED : ruinoso **3** DISREPUTABLE : de mala fama
sled¹ ['slɛd] *v* **sledded; sledding** *vi* : ir en trineo — *vt* : transportar en trineo
sled² *n* : trineo *m*
sledge ['slɛdʒ] *n* **1** : trineo *m* (grande) **2** → **sledgehammer**
sledgehammer ['slɛdʒ,hæmər] *n* : almádena *f*, combo *m Chile, Peru*
sleek¹ ['sli:k] *vt* SLICK : alisar
sleek² *adj* : liso y brillante
sleep¹ ['sli:p] *vi* **slept** ['slɛpt]; **sleeping** : dormir
sleep² *n* **1** : sueño *m* **2 to go to sleep** : dormirse
sleeper ['sli:pər] *n* **1** : durmiente *mf* ⟨to be a light sleeper : tener el sueño ligero⟩ **2** *or* **sleeping car** : coche *m* cama, coche *m* dormitorio
sleepily ['sli:pəli] *adv* : de manera somnolienta
sleepiness ['sli:pinəs] *n* : somnolencia *f*
sleepless ['sli:pləs] *adj* : sin dormir, desvelado ⟨to have a sleepless night : pasar la noche en blanco⟩
sleepwalker ['sli:p,wɔkər] *n* : sonámbulo *m*, -la *f*
sleepy ['sli:pi] *adj* **sleepier; -est 1** DROWSY : somnoliento, soñoliento ⟨to be sleepy : tener sueño⟩ **2** LETHARGIC : aletargado, letárgico
sleet¹ ['sli:t] *vi* **to be sleeting** : caer aguanieve
sleet² *n* : aguanieve *f*
sleeve ['sli:v] *n* : manga *f* (de una camisa, etc.)
sleeveless ['sli:vləs] *adj* : sin mangas
sleigh¹ ['sleɪ] *vi* : ir en trineo
sleigh² *n* : trineo *m* (tirado por caballos)
sleight of hand [,slaɪtəv'hænd] : prestidigitación *f*, juegos *mpl* de manos
slender ['slɛndər] *adj* **1** SLIM : esbelto, delgado **2** SCANTY : exiguo, escaso ⟨a slender hope : una esperanza lejana⟩
sleuth ['slu:θ] *n* : detective *mf*; sabueso *m*, -sa *f*
slew → **slay**
slice¹ ['slaɪs] *vt* **sliced; slicing** : cortar
slice² *n* : rebanada *f*, tajada *f*, lonja *f* (de carne, etc.), rodaja *f* (de una verdura, fruta, etc.), trozo *m* (de pastel, etc.)
slick¹ ['slɪk] *vt* : alisar
slick² *adj* **1** SLIPPERY : resbaladizo, resbaloso **2** CRAFTY : astuto, taimado
slicker ['slɪkər] *n* : impermeable *m*
slide¹ ['slaɪd] *v* **slid** ['slɪd]; **sliding** ['slaɪdɪŋ] *vi* **1** SLIP : resbalar **2** GLIDE : deslizarse **3** DECLINE : bajar ⟨to let

things slide : dejar pasar las cosas⟩ — *vt* : correr, deslizar
slide² *n* **1** SLIDING : deslizamiento *m* **2** SLIP : resbalón *m* **3** : tobogán *m* (para niños) **4** TRANSPARENCY : diapositiva *f* (fotográfica) **5** DECLINE : descenso *m*
slier, sliest → **sly**
slight¹ ['slaɪt] *vt* : desairar, despreciar
slight² *adj* **1** SLENDER : esbelto, delgado **2** FLIMSY : endeble **3** TRIFLING : leve, insignificante ⟨a slight pain : un leve dolor⟩ **4** SMALL : pequeño, ligero ⟨not in the slightest : en absoluto⟩
slight³ *n* SNUB : desaire *m*
slightly ['slaɪtli] *adv* : ligeramente, un poco
slim¹ ['slɪm] *v* **slimmed; slimming** : adelgazar
slim² *adj* **slimmer; slimmest 1** SLENDER : esbelto, delgado **2** SCANTY : exiguo, escaso
slime ['slaɪm] *n* **1** : baba *f* (secretada por un animal) **2** MUD, SILT : fango *m*, cieno *m*
slimy ['slaɪmi] *adj* **slimier; -est** : viscoso
sling¹ ['slɪŋ] *vt* **slung** ['slʌŋ]; **slinging 1** THROW : lanzar, tirar **2** HANG : colgar
sling² *n* **1** : honda *f* (arma) **2** : cabestrillo *m* ⟨my arm is in a sling : llevo el brazo en cabestrillo⟩
slingshot ['slɪŋ,ʃat] *n* : tiragomas *m*, resortera *f Mex*
slink ['slɪŋk] *vi* **slunk** ['slʌŋk]; **slinking** : caminar furtivamente
slip¹ ['slɪp] *v* **slipped; slipping** *vi* **1** STEAL : ir sigilosamente ⟨to slip away : escabullirse⟩ ⟨to slip out the door : escaparse por la puerta⟩ **2** SLIDE : resbalarse, deslizarse **3** LAPSE : caer ⟨to slip into error : equivocarse⟩ **4 to let slip** : dejar escapar **5 to slip into** PUT ON : ponerse — *vt* **1** PUT : meter, poner **2** PASS : pasar ⟨she slipped me a note : me pasó una nota⟩ **3 to slip one's mind** : olvidársele a uno
slip² *n* **1** PIER : atracadero *m* **2** MISHAP : percance *m*, contratiempo *m* **3** MISTAKE : error *m*, desliz *m* ⟨a slip of the tongue : un lapsus⟩ **4** PETTICOAT : enagua *f* **5** : injerto *m*, esqueje *m* (de una planta) **6 slip of paper** : papelito *m*
slipper ['slɪpər] *n* : zapatilla *f*, pantufla *f*
slipperiness ['slɪpərinəs] *n* **1** : lo resbaloso, lo resbaladizo **2** TRICKINESS : astucia *f*
slippery ['slɪpəri] *adj* **slipperier; -est 1** : resbaloso, resbaladizo ⟨a slippery road : un camino resbaloso⟩ **2** TRICKY : artero, astuto, taimado **3** ELUSIVE : huidizo, escurridizo
slipshod ['slɪp,ʃad] *adj* : descuidado, chapucero
slip up *vi* : equivocarse
slit¹ ['slɪt] *vt* **slit; slitting** : cortar, abrir por lo largo

slit[2] *n* **1** OPENING : abertura *f*, rendija *f* **2** CUT : corte *m*, raja *f*, tajo *m*

slither ['slɪðər] *vi* : deslizarse

sliver ['slɪvər] *n* : astilla *f*

slob ['slɑb] *n* : persona *f* desaliñada ⟨what a slob! : ¡qué cerdo!⟩

slobber[1] ['slɑbər] *vi* : babear

slobber[2] *n* : baba *f*

slogan ['slo:gən] *n* : lema *m*, eslogan *m*

sloop ['slu:p] *n* : balandra *f*

slop[1] ['slɑp] *v* **slopped; slopping** *vt* : derramar — *vi* : derramarse

slop[2] *n* : bazofia *f*

slope[1] ['slo:p] *vi* **sloped; sloping** : inclinarse ⟨the road slopes upward : el camino sube (en pendiente)⟩

slope[2] *n* : inclinación *f*, pendiente *f*, declive *m*

sloppy ['slɑpi] *adj* **sloppier; -est 1** MUDDY, SLUSHY : lodoso, fangoso **2** UNTIDY : descuidado (en el trabajo, etc.), desaliñado (de aspecto)

slot ['slɑt] *n* : ranura *f*

sloth ['slɔθ, 'slo:θ] *n* **1** LAZINESS : pereza *f* **2** : perezoso *m* (animal)

slouch[1] ['slaʊtʃ] *vi* : andar con los hombros caídos, repantigarse (en un sillón)

slouch[2] *n* **1** SLUMPING : mala postura *f* **2** BUNGLER, IDLER : haragán *m*, -gana *f*; inepto *m*, -ta *f* ⟨to be no slouch : no quedarse atrás⟩

slough[1] ['slʌf] *vt* : mudar de (piel)

slough[2] ['slu:, 'slaʊ] *n* SWAMP : ciénaga *f*

Slovak ['slo:ˌvɑk, -ˌvæk] *or* **Slovakian** [slo:'vɑkiən, -'væ-] *n* : eslovaco *m*, -ca *f* — **Slovak** *or* **Slovakian** *adj*

Slovene ['slo:ˌvi:n] *or* **Slovenian** [slo:'vi:niən] *n* : esloveno *m*, -na *f* — **Slovene** *or* **Slovenian** *adj*

slovenly ['slʌvənli, 'slʌv-] *adj* : descuidado (en el trabajo, etc.), desaliñado (de aspecto)

slow[1] [slo:] *vt* : retrasar, reducir la marcha de — *vi* : ir más despacio

slow[2] *adv* : despacio, lentamente

slow[3] *adj* **1** : lento ⟨a slow process : un proceso lento⟩ **2** : atrasado ⟨my watch is slow : mi reloj está atrasado, mi reloj se atrasa⟩ **3** SLUGGISH : lento, poco activo **4** STUPID : lento, torpe, corto de alcances

slowly [slo:li] *adv* : lentamente, despacio

slowness [slo:nəs] *n* : lentitud *f*, torpeza *f*

sludge ['slʌdʒ] *n* : aguas *fpl* negras, aguas *fpl* residuales

slug[1] ['slʌg] *vt* **slugged; slugging** : pegarle un porrazo (a alguien)

slug[2] *n* **1** : babosa *f* (molusco) **2** BULLET : bala *f* **3** TOKEN : ficha *f* **4** BLOW : porrazo *m*, puñetazo *m*

sluggish ['slʌgɪʃ] *adj* : aletargado, lento

sluice[1] ['slu:s] *vt* **sluiced; sluicing** : lavar en agua corriente

sluice[2] *n* : canal *m*

slum ['slʌm] *n* : barriada *f*, barrio *m* bajo

slumber[1] ['slʌmbər] *vi* : dormir

slumber[2] *n* : sueño *m*

slump[1] ['slʌmp] *vi* **1** DECLINE, DROP : disminuir, bajar **2** SLOUCH : encorvarse, dejarse caer (en una silla, etc.)

slump[2] *n* : bajón *m*, declive *m* (económico)

slung → **sling**

slunk → **slink**

slur[1] ['slər] *vt* **slurred; slurring** : ligar (notas musicales), tragarse (las palabras)

slur[2] *n* **1** : ligado *m* (en música), mala pronunciación *f* (de las palabras) **2** ASPERSION : calumnia *f*, difamación *f*

slurp[1] ['slərp] *vi* : beber o comer haciendo ruido — *vt* : sorber ruidosamente

slurp[2] *n* : sorbo *m* (ruidoso)

slush ['slʌʃ] *n* : nieve *f* medio derretida

slut ['slʌt] *n* PROSTITUTE : ramera *f*, fulana *f*

sly ['slaɪ] *adj* **slier** ['slaɪər]; **sliest** ['slaɪəst] **1** CUNNING : astuto, taimado **2** UNDERHANDED : soplado — **slyly** *adv*

slyness ['slaɪnəs] *n* : astucia *f*

smack[1] ['smæk] *vi* **to smack of** : oler a, saber a — *vt* **1** KISS : besar, plantarle un beso (a alguien) **2** SLAP : pegarle una bofetada (a alguien) **3 to smack one's lips** : relamerse

smack[2] *adv* : justo, exactamente ⟨smack in the face : en plena cara⟩

smack[3] *n* **1** TASTE, TRACE : sabor *m*, indicio *m* **2** : chasquido *m* (de los labios) **3** SLAP : bofetada *f* **4** KISS : beso *m*

small ['smɔl] *adj* **1** : pequeño, chico ⟨a small house : una casa pequeña⟩ ⟨small change : monedas de poco valor⟩ **2** TRIVIAL : pequeño, insignificante

smallness ['smɔlnəs] *n* : pequeñez *f*

smallpox ['smɔlˌpɑks] *n* : viruela *f*

smart[1] ['smɑrt] *vi* **1** STING : escocer, picar, arder **2** HURT : dolerse, resentirse ⟨to smart under a rejection : dolerse ante un rechazo⟩

smart[2] *adj* **1** BRIGHT : listo, vivo, inteligente **2** STYLISH : elegante — **smartly** *adv*

smart[3] *n* PAIN : escozor *m*, dolor *m* **2 smarts** *npl* : inteligencia *f*

smartness ['smɑrtnəs] *n* **1** INTELLIGENCE : inteligencia *f* **2** ELEGANCE : elegancia *f*

smash[1] ['smæʃ] *vt* **1** BREAK : romper, quebrar, hacer pedazos **2** WRECK : destrozar, arruinar **3** CRASH : estrellar, chocar — *vi* **1** SHATTER : hacerse pedazos, hacerse añicos **2** COLLIDE, CRASH : estrellarse, chocar

smash[2] *n* **1** BLOW : golpe *m* **2** COLLISION : choque *m* **3** BANG, CRASH : estrépito *m*

smattering ['smæt̬ərɪŋ] *n* **1** : nociones *fpl* ⟨she has a smattering of programming : tiene nociones de programación⟩ **2** : un poco, unos cuantos ⟨a smattering of spectators : unos cuantos espectadores⟩

smear¹ ['smɪr] *vt* **1** DAUB : embadurnar, untar (mantequilla, etc.) **2** SMUDGE : emborronar **3** SLANDER : calumniar, difamar

smear² *n* **1** SMUDGE : mancha *f* **2** SLANDER : calumnia *f*

smell¹ ['smɛl] *v* **smelled** *or* **smelt** ['smɛlt]; **smelling** *vt* : oler, olfatear ⟨to smell danger : olfatear el peligro⟩ — *vi* : oler ⟨to smell good : oler bien⟩

smell² *n* **1** : olfato *m*, sentido *m* del olfato **2** ODOR : olor *m*

smelly ['smɛli] *adj* **smellier; -est** : maloliente

smelt¹ ['smɛlt] *vt* : fundir

smelt² *n, pl* **smelts** *or* **smelt** : eperlano *m* (pez)

smile¹ ['smaɪl] *vi* **smiled; smiling** : sonreír

smile² *n* : sonrisa *f*

smirk¹ ['smərk] *vi* : sonreír con suficiencia

smirk² *n* : sonrisa *f* satisfecha

smite ['smaɪt] *vt* **smote** ['smo:t]; **smitten** ['smɪtən] *or* **smote; smiting 1** STRIKE : golpear **2** AFFLICT : afligir

smith ['smɪθ] *n* : herrero *m*, -ra *f*

smithy ['smɪθi] *n, pl* **smithies** : herrería *f*

smock ['smɑk] *n* : bata *f*, blusón *m*

smog ['smɑg, 'smɔg] *n* : smog *m*

smoke¹ ['smo:k] *v* **smoked; smoking** *vi* **1** : echar humo, humear ⟨a smoking chimney : una chimenea que echa humo⟩ **2** : fumar ⟨I don't smoke : no fumo⟩ — *vt* : ahumar (carne, etc.)

smoke² *n* : humo *m*

smoke detector [dɪ'tɛktər] *n* : detector *m* de humo

smoker ['smo:kər] *n* : fumador *m*, -dora *f*

smokestack ['smo:k,stæk] *n* : chimenea *f*

smoky ['smo:ki] *adj* **smokier; -est 1** SMOKING : humeante **2** : a humo ⟨a smoky flavor : un sabor a humo⟩ **3** : lleno de humo ⟨a smoky room : un cuarto lleno de humo⟩

smolder ['smo:ldər] *vi* **1** : arder sin llama **2** : arder (en el corazón) ⟨his anger smoldered : su rabia ardía⟩

smooth¹ ['smu:ð] *vt* : alisar

smooth² *adj* **1** : liso (dícese de una superficie) ⟨smooth skin : piel lisa⟩ **2** : suave (dícese de un movimiento) ⟨a smooth landing : un aterrizaje suave⟩ **3** : sin grumos ⟨a smooth sauce : una salsa sin grumos⟩ **4** : fluido ⟨smooth writing : escritura fluida⟩

smoothly ['smu:ðli] *adv* **1** GENTLY, SOFTLY : suavemente **2** EASILY : con facilidad, sin problemas

smoothness ['smu:ðnəs] *n* : suavidad *f*

smother ['smʌðər] *vt* **1** SUFFOCATE : ahogar, sofocar **2** COVER : cubrir **3** SUPPRESS : contener — *vi* : asfixiarse

smudge¹ ['smʌdʒ] *v* **smudged; smudging** *vt* : emborronar — *vi* : correrse

smudge² *n* : mancha *f*, borrón *m*

smug ['smʌg] *adj* **smugger; smuggest** : suficiente, pagado de sí mismo

smuggle ['smʌgəl] *vt* **-gled; -gling** : contrabandear, pasar de contrabando

smuggler ['smʌgələr] *n* : contrabandista *mf*

smugly ['smʌgli] *adv* : con suficiencia

smut ['smʌt] *n* **1** SOOT : tizne *m*, hollín *m* **2** FUNGUS : tizón *m* **3** OBSCENITY : obscenidad *f*, inmundicia *f*

smutty ['smʌti] *adj* **smuttier; -est 1** SOOTY : tiznado **2** OBSCENE : obsceno, indecente

snack ['snæk] *n* : refrigerio *m*, bocado *m*, tentempié *m fam* ⟨an afternoon snack : una merienda⟩

snag¹ ['snæg] *v* **snagged; snagging** *vt* : enganchar — *vi* : engancharse

snag² *n* : problema *m*, inconveniente *m*

snail ['sneɪl] *n* : caracol *m*

snake ['sneɪk] *n* : culebra *f*, serpiente *f*

snakebite ['sneɪk,baɪt] *n* : mordedura *f* de serpiente

snap¹ ['snæp] *v* **snapped; snapping** *vi* **1** : intentar morder (dícese de un perro, etc.), picar (dícese de un pez) **2** : hablar con severidad ⟨he snapped at me! : ¡me gritó!⟩ **3** BREAK : romperse, quebrarse (haciendo un chasquido) — *vt* **1** BREAK : partir (en dos), quebrar **2** : hacer (algo) de un golpe ⟨to snap open : abrir de golpe⟩ **3** RETORT : decir bruscamente **4** CLICK : chasquear ⟨to snap one's fingers : chasquear los dedos⟩

snap² *n* **1** CLICK, CRACK : chasquido *m* **2** FASTENER : broche *m* **3** CINCH : cosa *f* fácil ⟨it's a snap : es facilísimo⟩

snapdragon ['snæp,drægən] *n* : dragón *m* (flor)

snapper ['snæpər] → **red snapper**

snappy ['snæpi] *adj* **snappier; -est 1** FAST : rápido ⟨make it snappy! : ¡date prisa!⟩ **2** LIVELY : vivaz **3** CHILLY : frío **4** STYLISH : elegante

snapshot ['snæp,ʃɑt] *n* : instantánea *f*

snare¹ ['snær] *vt* **snared; snaring** : atrapar

snare² *n* : trampa *f*, red *f*

snare drum *n* : tambor *m* con bordón

snarl¹ ['snɑrl] *vi* **1** TANGLE : enmarañar, enredar **2** GROWL : gruñir

snarl² *n* **1** TANGLE : enredo *m*, maraña *f* **2** GROWL : gruñido *m*

snatch¹ ['snætʃ] *vt* : arrebatar

snatch² *n* : fragmento *m*

sneak¹ ['sni:k] *vi* : ir a hurtadillas — *vt* : hacer furtivamente ⟨to sneak a look : mirar con disimulo⟩ ⟨he sneaked a smoke : fumó un cigarrillo a escondidas⟩

sneak² *n* : soplón *m*, -plona *f*

sneakers ['sni:kərz] *npl* : tenis *mpl*, zapatillas *fpl*

sneaky ['sni:ki] *adj* **sneakier; -est** : solapado

sneer¹ ['snɪr] *vi* : sonreír con desprecio
sneer² *n* : sonrisa *f* de desprecio
sneeze¹ ['sni:z] *vi* **sneezed; sneezing** : estornudar
sneeze² *n* : estornudo *m*
snicker¹ ['snɪkər] *vi* : reírse disimuladamente
snicker² *n* : risita *f*
snide ['snaɪd] *adj* : sarcástico
sniff¹ ['snɪf] *vi* **1** SMELL : oler, husmear (dícese de los animales) **2 to sniff at** : despreciar, desdeñar — *vt* **1** SMELL : oler **2 to sniff out** : olerse, husmear
sniff² *n* **1** SNIFFING : aspiración *f* por la nariz **2** SMELL : olor *m*
sniffle ['snɪfəl] *vi* **-fled; -fling** : respirar con la nariz congestionada
sniffles ['snɪfəlz] *npl* : resfriado *m*
snip¹ ['snɪp] *vt* **snipped; snipping** : cortar (con tijeras)
snip² *n* : tijeretada *f*, recorte *m*
snipe¹ ['snaɪp] *vi* **sniped; sniping** : disparar
snipe² *n, pl* **snipes** *or* **snipe** : agachadiza *f*
sniper ['snaɪpər] *n* : francotirador *m*, -dora *f*
snippet ['snɪpət] *n* : fragmento *m* (de un texto, etc.)
snivel ['snɪvəl] *vi* **-veled** *or* **-velled; -veling** *or* **-velling 1** → **snuffle 2** WHINE : lloriquear
snob ['snɑb] *n* : esnob *mf*, snob *mf*
snobbery ['snɑbəri] *n, pl* **-beries** : esnobismo *m*
snobbish ['snɑbɪʃ] *adj* : esnob, snob
snobbishness ['snɑbɪʃnəs] *n* : esnobismo *m*
snoop¹ ['snu:p] *vi* : husmear, curiosear
snoop² *n* : fisgón *m*, -gona *f*
snooze¹ ['snu:z] *vi* **snoozed; snoozing** : dormitar
snooze² *n* : siestecita *f*, siestita *f*
snore¹ ['snor] *vi* **snored; snoring** : roncar
snore² *n* : ronquido *m*
snort¹ ['snort] *vi* : bufar, resoplar
snort² *n* : bufido *m*, resoplo *m*
snout ['snaʊt] *n* : hocico *m*, morro *m*
snow¹ ['sno:] *vi* **1** : nevar ⟨I'm snowed in : estoy aislado por la nieve⟩ **2 to be snowed under** : estar inundado
snow² *n* : nieve *f*
snowball ['sno:ˌbɔl] *n* : bola *f* de nieve
snowdrift ['sno:ˌdrɪft] *n* : ventisquero *m*
snowfall ['sno:ˌfɔl] *n* : nevada *f*
snowplow ['sno:ˌplaʊ] *n* : quitanieves *m*
snowshoe ['sno:ˌʃu:] *n* : raqueta *f* (para nieve)
snowstorm ['sno:ˌstorm] *n* : tormenta *f* de nieve, ventisca *f*
snowy ['sno:i] *adj* **snowier; -est** : nevoso ⟨a snowy road : un camino nevado⟩
snub¹ ['snʌb] *vt* **snubbed; snubbing** : desairar
snub² *n* : desaire *m*
snub–nosed ['snʌbˌno:zd] *adj* : de nariz respingada

snuff¹ ['snʌf] *vt* **1** : apagar (una vela) **2** : sorber (algo) por la nariz
snuff² *n* : rapé *m*
snuffle ['snʌfəl] *vi* **-fled; -fling** : respirar con la nariz congestionada
snug ['snʌg] *adj* **snugger; snuggest 1** COMFORTABLE : cómodo **2** TIGHT : ajustado, ceñido ⟨snug pants : pantalones ajustados⟩
snuggle ['snʌgəl] *vi* **-gled; -gling** : acurrucarse ⟨to snuggle up to someone : arrimársele a alguien⟩
snugly ['snʌgli] *adv* **1** COMFORTABLY : cómodamente **2** : de manera ajustada ⟨the shirt fits snugly : la camisa queda ajustada⟩
so¹ ['so:] *adv* **1** (*referring to something indicated or suggested*) ⟨do you think so? : ¿tú crees?⟩ ⟨so it would seem : eso parece⟩ ⟨I told her so : se lo dije⟩ ⟨he's ready, or so he says : según dice, está listo⟩ ⟨it so happened that . . . : resultó que . . .⟩ ⟨do it like so : hazlo así⟩ ⟨so be it : así sea⟩ **2** ALSO : también ⟨so do I : yo también⟩ **3** THUS : así, de esta manera **4** : tan ⟨he'd never been so happy : nunca había estado tan contento⟩ **5** CONSEQUENTLY : por lo tanto
so² *conj* **1** THEREFORE : así que **2** *or* **so that** : para que, así que, de manera que **3 so what?** : ¿y qué?
soak¹ ['so:k] *vi* : estar en remojo — *vt* **1** : poner en remojo **2 to soak up** ABSORB : absorber
soak² *n* : remojo *m*
soap¹ ['so:p] *vt* : enjabonar
soap² *n* : jabón *m*
soapsuds ['so:pˌsʌdz] → **suds**
soapy ['so:pi] *adj* **soapier; -est** : jabonoso ⟨a soapy taste : un gusto a jabón⟩ ⟨a soapy texture : una textura de jabón⟩
soar ['sor] *vi* **1** FLY : volar **2** RISE : remontar el vuelo (dícese de las aves) ⟨her hopes soared : su esperanza renació⟩ ⟨prices are soaring : los precios están subiendo vertiginosamente⟩
sob¹ ['sɑb] *vi* **sobbed; sobbing** : sollozar
sob² *n* : sollozo *m*
sober ['so:bər] *adj* **1** : sobrio ⟨he's not sober enough to drive : está demasiado borracho para manejar⟩ **2** SERIOUS : serio
soberly ['so:bərli] *adv* **1** : sobriamente **2** SERIOUSLY : seriamente
sobriety [sə'braɪəti, so-] *n* **1** : sobriedad *f* ⟨sobriety test : prueba de alcoholemia⟩ **2** SERIOUSNESS : seriedad *f*
so–called ['so:'kɔld] *adj* : supuesto, presunto ⟨the so-called experts : los expertos, así llamados⟩
soccer ['sɑkər] *n* : futbol *m*, fútbol *m*
sociable ['so:ʃəbəl] *adj* : sociable
social¹ ['so:ʃəl] *adj* : social — **socially** *adv*
social² *n* : reunión *f* social

socialism ['soːʃəˌlɪzəm] *n* : socialismo *m*
socialist¹ ['soːʃəlɪst] *adj* : socialista
socialist² *n* : socialista *mf*
socialize ['soːʃəˌlaɪz] *v* **-ized; -izing** *vt* **1** NATIONALIZE : nacionalizar **2** : socializar (en psicología) — *vi* : alternar, circular ⟨to socialize with friends : alternar con amigos⟩
social work *n* : asistencia *f* social
society [səˈsaɪəti] *n, pl* **-eties 1** COMPANIONSHIP : compañía *f* **2** : sociedad *f* ⟨a democratic society : una sociedad democrática⟩ ⟨high society : alta sociedad⟩ **3** ASSOCIATION : sociedad *f*, asociación *f*
socioeconomic [ˌsoːsioˌiːkəˈnɑmɪk, -ˌɛkə-] *adj* : socioeconómico
sociology [ˌsoːsiˈɑləʤi] *n* : sociología *f*
sociological [ˌsoːsiəˈlɑʤɪkəl] *adj* : sociológico
sociologist [ˌsoːsiˈɑləʤɪst] *n* : sociólogo *m, -ga f*
sock¹ ['sɑk] *vt* : pegar, golpear, darle un puñetazo a
sock² *n* **1** *pl* **socks** *or* **sox** ['sɑks] : calcetín *m*, media *f* ⟨shoes and socks : zapatos y calcetines⟩ **2** *pl* **socks** ['sɑks] PUNCH : puñetazo *m*
socket ['sɑkət] *n* **1** *or* **electric socket** : enchufe *m*, toma *f* de corriente **2** : glena *f* (de una articulación) ⟨shoulder socket : glena del hombro⟩ **3 eye socket** : órbita *f*, cuenca *f*
sod¹ ['sɑd] *vt* **sodded; sodding** : cubrir de césped
sod² *n* TURF : césped *m*, tepe *m*
soda ['soːdə] *n* **1** *or* **soda water** : soda *f* **2** *or* **soda pop** : gaseosa *f*, refresco *m* **3** *or* **ice–cream soda** : refresco *m* con helado
sodden ['sɑdən] *adj* SOGGY : empapado
sodium ['soːdiəm] *n* : sodio *m*
sodium bicarbonate *n* : bicarbonato *m* de soda
sodium chloride → **salt**
sofa ['soːfə] *n* : sofá *m*
soft ['sɔft] *adj* **1** : blando ⟨a soft pillow : una almohada blanda⟩ **2** SMOOTH : suave (dícese de las texturas, de los sonidos, etc.) **3** NONALCOHOLIC : no alcohólico ⟨a soft drink : un refresco⟩
softball ['sɔftˌbɔl] *n* : softbol *m*
soften ['sɔfən] *vt* : ablandar (algo sólido), suavizar (la piel, un golpe, etc.), amortiguar (un impacto) — *vi* : ablandarse, suavizarse
softly ['sɔftli] *adv* : suavemente ⟨she spoke softly : habló en voz baja⟩
softness ['sɔftnəs] *n* **1** : blandura *f*, lo blando (de una almohada, de la mantequilla, etc.) **2** SMOOTHNESS : suavidad *f*
software ['sɔftˌwær] *n* : software *m*
soggy ['sɑgi] *adj* **soggier; -est** : empapado
soil¹ ['sɔɪl] *vt* : ensuciar — *vi* : ensuciarse

soil² *n* **1** DIRTINESS : suciedad *f* **2** DIRT, EARTH : suelo *m*, tierra *f* **3** COUNTRY : patria *f* ⟨her native soil : su tierra natal⟩
sojourn¹ ['soːˌʤərn, soːˈʤərn] *vi* : pasar una temporada
sojourn² *n* : estadía *f*, estancia *f*, permanencia *f*
solace ['sɑləs] *n* : consuelo *m*
solar ['soːlər] *adj* : solar ⟨the solar system : el sistema solar⟩
sold → **sell**
solder¹ ['sɑdər, 'sɔ-] *vt* : soldar
solder² *n* : soldadura *f*
soldier¹ ['soːlʤər] *vi* : servir como soldado
soldier² *n* : soldado *mf*
sole¹ ['soːl] *adj* : único
sole² *n* **1** : suela *f* (de un zapato) **2** : lenguado *m* (pez)
solely ['soːli] *adv* : únicamente, sólo
solemn ['sɑləm] *adj* : solemne, serio — **solemnly** *adv*
solemnity [səˈlɛmnəti] *n, pl* **-ties** : solemnidad *f*
solicit [səˈlɪsət] *vt* : solicitar
solicitous [səˈlɪsətəs] *adj* : solícito
solicitude [səˈlɪsəˌtuːd, -ˌtjuːd] *n* : solicitud *f*
solid¹ ['sɑləd] *adj* **1** : macizo ⟨a solid rubber ball : una bola maciza de caucho⟩ **2** CUBIC : tridimensional **3** COMPACT : compacto, denso **4** STURDY : sólido **5** CONTINUOUS : seguido, continuo ⟨two solid hours : dos horas seguidas⟩ ⟨a solid line : una línea continua⟩ **6** UNANIMOUS : unánime **7** DEPENDABLE : serio, fiable **8** PURE : macizo, puro ⟨solid gold : oro macizo⟩
solid² *n* : sólido *m*
solidarity [ˌsɑləˈdærəti] *n* : solidaridad *f*
solidify [səˈlɪdəˌfaɪ] *v* **-fied; -fying** *vt* : solidificar — *vi* : solidificarse
solidity [səˈlɪdəti] *n, pl* **-ties** : solidez *f*
solidly ['sɑlədli] *adv* **1** : sólidamente **2** UNANIMOUSLY : unánimemente
soliloquy [səˈlɪləkwi] *n, pl* **-quies** : soliloquio *m*
solitaire ['sɑləˌtɛr] *n* : solitario *m*
solitary ['sɑləˌtɛri] *adj* **1** ALONE : solitario **2** SECLUDED : apartado, retirado **3** SINGLE : solo
solitude ['sɑləˌtuːd, -ˌtjuːd] *n* : soledad *f*
solo¹ ['soːˌloː] *vi* : volar en solitario (dícese de un piloto)
solo² *adv & adj* : en solitario, a solas
solo³ *n, pl* **solos** : solo *m*
soloist ['soːloɪst] *n* : solista *mf*
solstice ['sɑlstɪs] *n* : solsticio *m*
soluble ['sɑljəbəl] *adj* : soluble
solution [səˈluːʃən] *n* : solución *f*
solve ['sɑlv] *vt* **solved; solving** : resolver, solucionar
solvency ['sɑlvəntsi] *n* : solvencia *f*
solvent ['sɑlvənt] *n* : solvente *m*
Somali [soˈmɑli, sə-] *n* : somalí *mf* — **Somali** *adj*
somber ['sɑmbər] *adj* **1** DARK : sombrío, oscuro ⟨somber colors : colores

oscuros⟩ **2** GRAVE : sombrío, serio **3**
MELANCHOLY : sombrío, lúgubre
sombrero [səm'brɛr͵oː] *n, pl* **-ros** : sombrero *m* (mexicano)
some¹ ['sʌm] *adj* **1** : un, algún ⟨some
lady stopped me : una mujer me detuvo⟩ ⟨some distant galaxy : alguna
galaxia lejana⟩ **2** : algo de, un poco de
⟨he drank some water : tomó (un poco
de) agua⟩ **3** : unos ⟨do you want some
apples? : ¿quieres unas manzanas?⟩
⟨some years ago : hace varios años⟩
some² *pron* **1** : algunos ⟨some went,
others stayed : algunos se fueron, otros
se quedaron⟩ **2** : un poco, algo ⟨there's
some left : queda un poco⟩ ⟨I have
gum; do you want some? : tengo chicle, ¿quieres?⟩
somebody ['sʌmbədi, -͵bɑdi] *pron* : alguien
someday ['sʌm͵deɪ] *adv* : algún día
somehow ['sʌm͵haʊ] *adv* **1** : de alguna
manera, de alguna modo ⟨I'll do it somehow : lo haré de alguna manera⟩ **2** : por
alguna razón ⟨somehow I don't trust
her : por alguna razón no me fío de
ella⟩
someone ['sʌm͵wʌn] *pron* : alguien
someplace ['sʌm͵pleɪs] → **somewhere**
somersault¹ ['sʌmər͵sɔlt] *vi* : dar
volteretas, dar un salto mortal
somersault² *n* : voltereta *f*, salto *m* mortal
something ['sʌmθɪŋ] *pron* : algo ⟨I want
something else : quiero otra cosa⟩
⟨she's writing a novel or something
: está escribiendo una novela o no sé
qué⟩
sometime ['sʌm͵taɪm] *adv* : algún día,
en algún momento ⟨sometime next
month : durante el mes que viene⟩
sometimes ['sʌm͵taɪmz] *adv* : a veces,
algunas veces, de vez en cuando
somewhat ['sʌm͵hwʌt, -͵hwɑt] *adv*
: algo, un tanto
somewhere ['sʌm͵hwɛr] *adv* **1** (*indicating location*) : en algún lugar ⟨it must
be somewhere else : estará en otra
parte⟩ **2** (*indicating destination*) : a algún lugar
son ['sʌn] *n* : hijo *m*
sonar ['so:͵nɑr] *n* : sonar *m*
sonata [sə'nɑtə] *n* : sonata *f*
song ['sɔŋ] *n* : canción *f*, canto *m* (de un
pájaro)
songbird ['sɔŋ͵bərd] *n* : pájaro *m* cantor
songwriter ['sɔŋ͵raɪtər] *n* : compositor
m, -tora *f*
sonic ['sɑnɪk] *adj* **1** : sónico **2 sonic
boom** : estampido *m* sónico
son–in–law ['sʌnɪn͵lɔ] *n, pl* **sons–
in–law** : yerno *m*, hijo *m* político
sonnet ['sɑnət] *n* : soneto *m*
sonorous ['sɑnərəs, sə'norəs] *adj*
: sonoro
soon ['suːn] *adv* **1** : pronto, dentro de
poco ⟨he'll arrive soon : llegará pron-

to⟩ **2** QUICKLY : pronto ⟨as soon as
possible : lo más pronto posible⟩ ⟨the
sooner the better : cuanto antes mejor⟩
3 : de buena gana ⟨I'd sooner walk
: prefiero caminar⟩
soot ['sʊt, 'suːt, 'sʌt] *n* : hollín *m*, tizne
m
soothe ['suːð] *vt* **soothed; soothing 1**
CALM : calmar, tranquilizar **2** RELIEVE
: aliviar
soothsayer ['suːθ͵seɪər] *n* : adivino *m*,
-na *f*
sooty ['sʊti, 'suː-, 'sʌ-] *adj* **sootier; -est**
: cubierto de hollín, tiznado
sop¹ ['sɑp] *vt* **sopped; sopping 1** DIP
: mojar **2** SOAK : empapar **3 to sop up**
: rebañar, absorber
sop² *n* **1** CONCESSION : concesión *f* **2**
BRIBE : soborno *m*
sophisticated [sə'fɪstə͵keɪtəd] *adj* **1**
COMPLEX : complejo **2** WORLDLY-
WISE : sofisticado
sophistication [sə͵fɪstə'keɪʃən] *n* **1**
COMPLEXITY : complejidad *f* **2** UR-
BANITY : sofisticación *f*
sophomore ['sɑf͵mor, 'sɑfə͵mor] *n* : estudiante *mf* de segundo año
soporific [͵sɑpə'rɪfɪk, ͵so:-] *adj* : soporífero
soprano [sə'præ͵noː] *n, pl* **-nos** : soprano *mf*
sorcerer ['sɔrsərər] *n* : hechicero *m*, brujo *m*, mago *m*
sorceress ['sɔrsərəs] *n* : hechicera *f*, bruja *f*, maga *f*
sorcery ['sɔrsəri] *n* : hechicería *f*, brujería *f*
sordid ['sɔrdɪd] *adj* : sórdido
sore¹ ['sor] *adj* **sorer; sorest 1** PAINFUL
: dolorido, doloroso ⟨I have a sore
throat : me duele la garganta⟩ **2**
ACUTE, SEVERE : extremo, grande ⟨in
sore straits : en grandes apuros⟩ **3** AN-
GRY : enojado, enfadado
sore² *n* : llaga *f*
sorely ['sorli] *adv* : muchísimo ⟨it was
sorely needed : se necesitaba urgentemente⟩ ⟨she was sorely missed : la echaban mucho de menos⟩
soreness ['sornəs] *n* : dolor *m*
sorghum ['sɔrgəm] *n* : sorgo *m*
sorority [sə'rɔrəṭi] *n, pl* **-ties** : hermandad *f* (de estudiantes femeninas)
sorrel ['sɔrəl] *n* **1** : alazán *m* (color o animal) **2** : acedera *f* (hierba)
sorrow ['sɑr͵oː] *n* : pesar *m*, dolor *m*,
pena *f*
sorrowful ['sɑrofəl] *adj* : triste, afligido,
apenado
sorrowfully ['sɑrofəli] *adv* : con tristeza
sorry ['sɑri] *adj* **sorrier; -est 1** PITIFUL
: lastimero, lastimoso **2 to be sorry**
: sentir, lamentar ⟨I'm sorry : lo siento⟩ **3 to feel sorry for** : compadecer ⟨I
feel sorry for him : me da pena⟩
sort¹ ['sɔrt] *vt* **1** : dividir en grupos **2**
CLASSIFY : clasificar **3 to sort out** OR-
GANIZE : poner en orden **4 to sort out**
RESOLVE : resolver

sort[2] *n* **1** KIND : tipo *m*, clase *f* ⟨a sort of writer : una especie de escritor⟩ **2** NATURE : índole *f* **3 out of sorts** : de mal humor

sortie ['sɔrṭi, sɔr'tiː] *n* : salida *f*

SOS [ˌɛsˌoː'ɛs] *n* : SOS *m*

so–so ['soː'soː] *adj & adv* : así así, de modo regular

soufflé [suː'fleɪ] *n* : suflé *m*

sought → **seek**

soul ['soːl] *n* **1** SPIRIT : alma *f* **2** ESSENCE : esencia *f* **3** PERSON : persona *f*, alma *f*

soulful ['soːlfəl] *adj* : conmovedor, lleno de emoción

sound[1] ['saʊnd] *vt* **1** : sondar (en navegación) **2** *or* **to sound out** PROBE : sondear **3** : hacer sonar, tocar (una trompeta, etc.) — *vi* **1** : sonar ⟨the alarm sounded : la alarma sonó⟩ **2** SEEM : parecer

sound[2] *adj* **1** HEALTHY : sano ⟨safe and sound : sano y salvo⟩ ⟨of sound mind and body : en pleno uso de sus facultades⟩ **2** FIRM, SOLID : sólido **3** SENSIBLE : lógico, sensato **4** DEEP : profundo ⟨a sound sleep : un sueño profundo⟩

sound[3] *n* **1** : sonido *m* ⟨the speed of sound : la velocidad del sonido⟩ **2** NOISE : sonido *m*, ruido *m* ⟨I heard a sound : oí un sonido⟩ **3** CHANNEL : brazo *m* de mar, canal *m* (ancho)

soundless ['saʊndləs] *adj* : sordo

soundlessly ['saʊndləsli] *adv* : silenciosamente

soundly ['saʊndli] *adv* **1** SOLIDLY : sólidamente **2** SENSIBLY : lógicamente, sensatamente **3** DEEPLY : profundamente ⟨sleeping soundly : durmiendo profundamente⟩

soundness ['saʊndnəs] *n* **1** SOLIDITY : solidez *f* **2** SENSIBLENESS : sensatez *f*, solidez *f*

soundproof ['saʊndˌpruːf] *adj* : insonorizado

soundtrack ['saʊndˌtræk] *n* : banda *f* sonora

sound wave *n* : onda *f* sonora

soup ['suːp] *n* : sopa *f*

sour[1] ['saʊər] *vi* : agriarse, cortarse (dícese de la leche) — *vt* : agriar, cortar (leche)

sour[2] *adj* **1** ACID : agrio, ácido (dícese de la fruta, etc.), cortado (dícese de la leche) **2** DISAGREEABLE : desagradable, agrio

source ['sors] *n* : fuente *f*, origen *m*, nacimiento *m* (de un río)

sourness ['saʊərnəs] *n* : acidez *f*

south[1] ['saʊθ] *adv* : al sur, hacia el sur ⟨the window looks south : la ventana mira al sur⟩ ⟨she continued south : continuó hacia el sur⟩

south[2] *adj* : sur, del sur ⟨the south entrance : la entrada sur⟩ ⟨South America : Sudamérica, América del Sur⟩

south[3] *n* : sur *m*

South African *n* : sudafricano *m*, -na *f* — **South African** *adj*

South American[1] *adj* : sudamericano, suramericano

South American[2] *n* : sudamericano *m*, -na *f*; suramericano *m*, -na *f*

southbound ['saʊθˌbaʊnd] *adj* : con rumbo al sur

southeast[1] [saʊ'θiːst] *adj* : sureste, sudeste, del sureste

southeast[2] *n* : sureste *m*, sudeste *m*

southeasterly [saʊ'θiːstərli] *adv & adj* **1** : del sureste (dícese del viento) **2** : hacia el sureste

southeastern [saʊ'θiːstərn] *adj* → **southeast**[1]

southerly ['sʌðərli] *adv & adj* : del sur

southern ['sʌðərn] *adj* : sur, sureño, meridional, austral ⟨a southern city : una ciudad del sur del país, una ciudad meridional⟩ ⟨the southern side : el lado sur⟩

Southerner ['sʌðərnər] *n* : sureño *m*, -ña *f*

South Pole : Polo *m* Sur

southward ['saʊθwərd] *or* **southwards** [-wərdz] *adv & adj* : hacia el sur

southwest[1] [saʊθ'wɛst, *as a nautical term often* saʊ'wɛst] *adj* : suroeste, sudoeste, del suroeste

southwest[2] *n* : suroeste *m*, sudoeste *m*

southwesterly [saʊθ'wɛstərli] *adv & adj* **1** : del suroeste (dícese del viento) **2** : hacia el suroeste

southwestern [saʊθ'wɛstərn] *adj* → **southwest**[1]

souvenir [ˌsuːvə'nɪr, 'suːvəˌ-] *n* : recuerdo *m*, souvenir *m*

sovereign[1] ['sʌvərən] *adj* : soberano

sovereign[2] *n* **1** : soberano *m*, -na *f* (monarca) **2** : soberano *m* (moneda)

sovereignty ['sʌvərənti] *n, pl* **-ties** : soberanía *f*

Soviet ['soːviˌɛt, 'sɑ-, -viət] *adj* : soviético

sow[1] ['soː] *vt* **sowed; sown** ['soːn] *or* **sowed; sowing 1** PLANT : sembrar **2** SCATTER : esparcir

sow[2] ['saʊ] *n* : cerda *f*

sox → **sock**

soy ['sɔɪ] *n* : soya *f*, soja *f*

soybean ['sɔɪˌbiːn] *n* : soya *f*, soja *f*

spa ['spɑ] *n* : balneario *m*

space[1] ['speɪs] *vt* **spaced; spacing** : espaciar

space[2] *n* **1** PERIOD : espacio *m*, lapso *m*, período *m* **2** ROOM : espacio *m*, sitio *m*, lugar *m* ⟨is there space for me? : ¿hay sitio para mí?⟩ **3** : espacio *m* ⟨blank space : espacio en blanco⟩ **4** : espacio *m* (en física) **5** PLACE : plaza *f*, sitio *m* ⟨to reserve space : reservar plazas⟩ ⟨parking space : sitio para estacionarse⟩

spacecraft ['speɪsˌkræft] *n* : nave *f* espacial

spaceflight ['speɪsˌflaɪt] *n* : vuelo *m* espacial

spaceman ['speɪsmən, -ˌmæn] *n, pl* **-men** [-mən, -ˌmɛn] : astronauta *m*, cosmonauta *m*

spaceship ['speɪsˌʃɪp] *n* : nave *f* espacial

space shuttle *n* : transbordador *m* espacial

space suit *n* : traje *m* espacial

spacious ['speɪʃəs] *adj* : espacioso, amplio

spade¹ ['speɪd] *v* **spaded; spading** *vt* : palear — *vi* : usar una pala

spade² *n* **1** SHOVEL : pala *f* **2** : pica *f* (naipe)

spaghetti [spə'gɛti] *n* : espagueti *m*, espaguetis *mpl*, spaghetti *mpl*

spam ['spæm] *n* : spam *m*, correo *m* electrónico no solicitado

span¹ ['spæn] *vt* **spanned; spanning** : abarcar (un período de tiempo), extenderse sobre (un espacio)

span² *n* **1** : lapso *m*, espacio *m* (de tiempo) ⟨life span : duración de la vida⟩ **2** : luz *f* (entre dos soportes)

spangle ['spæŋgəl] *n* : lentejuela *f*

Spaniard ['spænjərd] *n* : español *m*, -ñola *f*

spaniel ['spænjəl] *n* : spaniel *m*

Spanish¹ ['spænɪʃ] *adj* : español

Spanish² *n* **1** : español *m* (idioma) **2 the Spanish** *npl* : los españoles

spank ['spæŋk] *vt* : darle nalgadas (a alguien)

spar¹ ['spɑr] *vi* **sparred; sparring** : entrenarse (en boxeo)

spar² *n* : palo *m*, verga *f* (de un barco)

spare¹ ['spær] *vt* **spared; sparing 1** : perdonar ⟨to spare someone's life : perdonarle la vida a alguien⟩ **2** SAVE : ahorrar, evitar ⟨I'll spare you the trouble : le evitaré la molestia⟩ **3** : prescindir de ⟨I can't spare her : no puedo prescindir de ella⟩ ⟨can you spare a dollar? : ¿me das un dólar?⟩ **4** STINT : escatimar ⟨they spared no expense : no repararon en gastos⟩ **5 to spare** : de sobra

spare² *adj* **1** : de repuesto, de recambio ⟨spare tire : llanta de repuesto⟩ **2** EXCESS : de más, de sobra ⟨spare time : tiempo libre⟩ **3** LEAN : delgado

spare³ *n or* **spare part** : repuesto *m*, recambio *m*

sparing ['spærɪŋ] *adj* : parco, económico — **sparingly** *adv*

spark¹ ['spɑrk] *vi* : chispear, echar chispas — *vt* PROVOKE : despertar, provocar ⟨to spark interest : despertar interés⟩

spark² *n* **1** : chispa *f* ⟨to throw off sparks : echar chispas⟩ **2** GLIMMER, TRACE : destello *m*, pizca *f*

sparkle¹ ['spɑrkəl] *vi* **-kled; -kling 1** FLASH, SHINE : destellar, centellear, brillar **2** : estar muy animado (dícese de una conversación, etc.)

sparkle² *n* : destello *m*, centelleo *m*

sparkler ['spɑrklər] *n* : luz *f* de bengala

spark plug *n* : bujía *f*

sparrow ['spæro:] *n* : gorrión *m*

sparse ['spɑrs] *adj* **sparser; -est** : escaso — **sparsely** *adv*

spasm ['spæzəm] *n* **1** : espasmo *m* (muscular) **2** BURST, FIT : arrebato *m*

spasmodic [spæz'mɑdɪk] *adj* **1** : espasmódico **2** SPORADIC : irregular, esporádico — **spasmodically** [-dɪkli] *adv*

spastic ['spæstɪk] *adj* : espástico

spat¹ → **spit¹**

spat² ['spæt] *n* : discusión *f*, disputa *f*, pelea *f*

spatial ['speɪʃəl] *adj* : espacial

spatter¹ ['spætər] *v* : salpicar

spatter² *n* : salpicadura *f*

spatula ['spætʃələ] *n* : espátula *f*, paleta *f* (para servir)

spawn¹ ['spɔn] *vi* : desovar, frezar — *vt* GENERATE : generar, producir

spawn² *n* : hueva *f*, freza *f*

spay ['speɪ] *vt* : esterilizar (una perra, etc.)

speak ['spi:k] *v* **spoke** ['spo:k]; **spoken** ['spo:kən]; **speaking** *vi* **1** TALK : hablar ⟨to speak to someone : hablar con alguien⟩ ⟨who's speaking? : ¿de parte de quien?⟩ ⟨so to speak : por así decirlo⟩ **2 to speak out** : hablar claramente **3 to speak out against** : denunciar **4 to speak up** : hablar en voz alta **5 to speak up for** : defender — *vt* **1** SAY : decir ⟨she spoke her mind : habló con franqueza⟩ **2** : hablar (un idioma)

speaker ['spi:kər] *n* **1** : hablante *mf* ⟨a native speaker : un hablante nativo⟩ **2** : orador *m*, -dora *f* ⟨the keynote speaker : el orador principal⟩ **3** LOUDSPEAKER : altavoz *m*, altoparlante *m*

spear¹ ['spɪr] *vt* : atravesar con una lanza

spear² *n* : lanza *f*

spearhead¹ ['spɪrˌhɛd] *vt* : encabezar

spearhead² *n* : punta *f* de lanza

spearmint ['spɪrmɪnt] *n* : menta *f* verde

special ['spɛʃəl] *adj* : especial ⟨nothing special : nada en especial, nada en particular⟩ — **specially** *adv*

specialist ['spɛʃəlɪst] *n* : especialista *mf*

specialization [ˌspɛʃələ'zeɪʃən] *n* : especialización *f*

specialize ['spɛʃəˌlaɪz] *vi* **-ized; -izing** : especializarse

specialty ['spɛʃəlti] *n, pl* **-ties** : especialidad *f*

species ['spi:ˌʃi:z, -ˌsi:z] *ns & pl* : especie *f*

specific [spɪ'sɪfɪk] *adj* : específico, determinado — **specifically** [-fɪkli] *adv*

specification [ˌspɛsəfə'keɪʃən] *n* : especificación *f*

specify ['spɛsəˌfaɪ] *vt* **-fied; -fying** : especificar

specimen ['spɛsəmən] *n* **1** SAMPLE : espécimen *m*, muestra *f* **2** EXAMPLE : espécimen *m*, ejemplar *m*

speck ['spɛk] *n* **1** SPOT : manchita *f* **2** BIT, TRACE : mota *f*, pizca *f*, ápice *m*

speckled ['spɛkəld] *adj* : moteado

spectacle · spiny

spectacle ['spɛktɪkəl] *n* 1 : espectáculo *m* 2 **spectacles** *npl* GLASSES : lentes *fpl*, gafas *fpl*, anteojos *mpl*, espejuelos *mpl*

spectacular [spɛk'tækjələr] *adj* : espectacular

spectator ['spɛk,teɪṭər] *n* : espectador *m*, -dora *f*

specter *or* **spectre** ['spɛktər] *n* : espectro *m*, fantasma *m*

spectrum ['spɛktrəm] *n*, *pl* **spectra** [-trə] *or* **spectrums** 1 : espectro *m* (de colores, etc.) 2 RANGE : gama *f*, abanico *m*

speculate ['spɛkjə,leɪt] *vi* -**lated**; -**lating** 1 : especular (en finanzas) 2 WONDER : preguntarse, hacer conjeturas

speculation [,spɛkjə'leɪʃən] *n* : especulación *f*

speculative ['spɛkjə,leɪṭɪv] *adj* : especulativo

speculator ['spɛkjə,leɪṭər] *n* : especulador *m*, -dora *f*

speech ['spiːtʃ] *n* 1 : habla *f*, modo *m* de hablar, expresión *f* 2 ADDRESS : discurso *m*

speechless ['spiːtʃləs] *adj* : enmudecido, estupefacto

speed¹ ['spiːd] *v* **sped** ['spɛd] *or* **speeded; speeding** *vi* 1 : ir a toda velocidad, correr a toda prisa ⟨he sped off : se fue a toda velocidad⟩ 2 : conducir a exceso de velocidad ⟨a ticket for speeding : una multa por exceso de velocidad⟩ — *vt* **to speed up** : acelerar

speed² *n* 1 SWIFTNESS : rapidez *f* 2 VELOCITY : velocidad *f*

speedboat ['spiːd,boːt] *n* : lancha *f* motora

speed bump *n* : badén *m*

speed limit *n* : velocidad *f* máxima, límite *m* de velocidad

speedometer [spɪ'dɑməṭər] *n* : velocímetro *m*

speedup ['spiːd,ʌp] *n* : aceleración *f*

speedy ['spiːdi] *adj* **speedier; -est** : rápido — **speedily** [-dəli] *adv*

spell¹ ['spɛl] *vt* 1 : escribir, deletrear (verbalmente) ⟨how do you spell it? : ¿cómo se escribe?, ¿cómo se deletrea?⟩ 2 MEAN : significar ⟨that could spell trouble : eso puede significar problemas⟩ 3 RELIEVE : relevar

spell² *n* 1 TURN : turno *m* 2 PERIOD, TIME : período *m* (de tiempo) 3 ENCHANTMENT : encanto *m*, hechizo *m*, maleficio *m*

spellbound ['spɛl,baʊnd] *adj* : embelesado

speller ['spɛlər] *n* : persona *f* que escribe ⟨she's a good speller : tiene buena ortografía⟩

spelling ['spɛlɪŋ] *n* : ortografía *f*

spend ['spɛnd] *vt* **spent** ['spɛnt]; **spending** 1 : gastar (dinero, etc.) 2 PASS : pasar (el tiempo) ⟨to spend time on : dedicar tiempo a⟩

spendthrift ['spɛnd,θrɪft] *n* : derrochador *m*, -dora *f*; despilfarrador *m*, -dora *f*

sperm ['spərm] *n*, *pl* **sperm** *or* **sperms** : esperma *mf*

spew ['spjuː] *vi* : salir a chorros — *vt* : vomitar, arrojar (lava, etc.)

sphere ['sfɪr] *n* : esfera *f*

spherical ['sfɪrɪkəl, 'sfɛr-] *adj* : esférico

spice¹ ['spaɪs] *vt* **spiced; spicing** 1 SEASON : condimentar, sazonar 2 *or* **to spice up** : salpimentar, hacer más interesante

spice² *n* 1 : especia *f* 2 FLAVOR, INTEREST : sabor *m* ⟨the spice of life : la sal de la vida⟩

spick–and–span ['spɪkənd'spæn] *adj* : limpio y ordenado

spicy ['spaɪsi] *adj* **spicier; -est** 1 SPICED : condimentado, sazonado 2 HOT : picante 3 RACY : picante

spider ['spaɪdər] *n* : araña *f*

spigot ['spɪɡət, -kət] *n* : llave *f*, grifo *m*, canilla *Arg, Uru*

spike¹ ['spaɪk] *vt* **spiked; spiking** 1 FASTEN : clavar (con clavos grandes) 2 PIERCE : atravesar 3 : añadir alcohol a ⟨he spiked her drink with rum : le puso ron a la bebida⟩

spike² *n* 1 : clavo *m* grande 2 CLEAT : clavo *m* 3 : remache *m* (en voleibol) 4 PEAK : pico *m*

spill¹ ['spɪl] *vt* 1 SHED : derramar, verter ⟨to spill blood : derrame sangre⟩ 2 DIVULGE : revelar, divulgar — *vi* : derramarse

spill² *n* 1 SPILLING : derrame *m*, vertido *m* ⟨oil spill : derrame de petróleo⟩ 2 FALL : caída *f*

spin¹ ['spɪn] *v* **spun** ['spʌn]; **spinning** *vi* 1 : hilar 2 TURN : girar 3 REEL : dar vueltas ⟨my head is spinning : la cabeza me está dando vueltas⟩ — *vt* 1 : hilar (hilo, etc.) 2 : tejer ⟨to spin a web : tejer una telaraña⟩ 3 TWIRL : hacer girar

spin² *n* : vuelta *f*, giro *m* ⟨to go for a spin : dar una vuelta (en coche)⟩

spinach ['spɪnɪtʃ] *n* : espinacas *fpl*, espinaca *f*

spinal column ['spaɪnəl] *n* BACKBONE : columna *f* vertebral

spinal cord *n* : médula *f* espinal

spindle ['spɪndəl] *n* 1 : huso *m* (para hilar) 2 : eje *m* (de un mecanismo)

spindly ['spɪndli] *adj* : larguirucho *fam*, largo y débil (dícese de una planta)

spine ['spaɪn] *n* 1 BACKBONE : columna *f* vertebral, espina *f* dorsal 2 QUILL : púa *f* (de un animal) 3 THORN : espina *f* 4 : lomo *m* (de un libro)

spineless ['spaɪnləs] *adj* 1 : sin púas, sin espinas 2 INVERTEBRATE : invertebrado 3 WEAK : débil (de carácter)

spinet ['spɪnət] *n* : espineta *f*

spinster ['spɪnstər] *n* : soltera *f*

spiny ['spaɪni] *adj* **spinier; -est** : con púas (dícese de los animales), espinoso (dícese de las plantas)

spiral[1] ['spaɪrəl] *vi* **-raled** *or* **-ralled; -raling** *or* **-ralling** : ir en espiral

spiral[2] *adj* : espiral, en espiral ⟨a spiral staircase : una escalera de caracol⟩

spiral[3] *n* : espiral *f*

spire ['spaɪr] *n* : aguja *f*

spirit[1] ['spɪrət] *vt* **to spirit away** : hacer desaparecer

spirit[2] *n* 1 : espíritu *m* ⟨body and spirit : cuerpo y espíritu⟩ 2 GHOST : espíritu *m*, fantasma *m* 3 MOOD : espíritu *m*, humor *m* ⟨in the spirit of friendship : en el espíritu de amistad⟩ ⟨to be in good spirits : estar de buen humor⟩ 4 ENTHUSIASM, VIVACITY : espíritu *m*, ánimo *m*, brío *m* 5 **spirits** *npl* : licores *mpl*

spirited ['spɪrətəd] *adj* : animado, energético

spiritless ['spɪrətləs] *adj* : desanimado

spiritual[1] ['spɪrɪtʃʊəl, -tʃəl] *adj* : espiritual — **spiritually** *adv*

spiritual[2] *n* : espiritual *m* (canción)

spiritualism ['spɪrɪtʃʊə,lɪzəm, -tʃə-] *n* : espiritismo *m*

spirituality [ˌspɪrɪtʃʊ'æləti] *n*, *pl* **-ties** : espiritualidad *f*

spit[1] ['spɪt] *v* **spit** *or* **spat** ['spæt]; **spitting** : escupir

spit[2] *n* 1 SALIVA : saliva *f* 2 ROTISSERIE : asador *m* 3 POINT : lengua *f* (de tierra)

spite[1] ['spaɪt] *vt* **spited; spiting** : fastidiar, molestar

spite[2] *n* 1 : despecho *m*, rencor *m* 2 **in spite of** : a pesar de (que), pese a (que)

spiteful ['spaɪtfəl] *adj* : malicioso, rencoroso

spitting image *n* **to be the spitting image of** : ser el vivo retrato de

spittle ['spɪtəl] *n* : saliva *f*

splash[1] ['splæʃ] *vt* : salpicar — *vi* 1 : salpicar 2 **to splash around** : chapotear

splash[2] *n* 1 SPLASHING : salpicadura *f* 2 SQUIRT : chorrito *m* 3 SPOT : mancha *f*

splatter ['splætər] → **spatter**

splay ['spleɪ] *vt* : extender (hacia afuera) ⟨to splay one's fingers : abrir los dedos⟩ — *vi* : extenderse (hacia afuera)

spleen ['spli:n] *n* 1 : bazo *m* (órgano) 2 ANGER, SPITE : ira *f*, rencor *m*

splendid ['splendəd] *adj* : espléndido — **splendidly** *adv*

splendor ['splendər] *n* : esplendor *m*

splice[1] ['splaɪs] *vt* **spliced; splicing** : empalmar, unir

splice[2] *n* : empalme *m*, unión *f*

splint ['splɪnt] *n* : tablilla *f*

splinter[1] ['splɪntər] *vt* : astillar — *vi* : astillarse

splinter[2] *n* : astilla *f*

split[1] ['splɪt] *v* **split; splitting** *vt* 1 CLEAVE : partir, hender ⟨to split wood : partir madera⟩ 2 BURST : romper, rajar ⟨to split open : abrir⟩ 3 DIVIDE, SHARE : dividir, repartir — *vi* 1 : partirse (dícese de la madera, etc.) 2 BURST, CRACK : romperse, rajarse 3 *or* **to split up** : dividirse

split[2] *n* 1 CRACK : rajadura *f* 2 TEAR : rotura *f* 3 DIVISION : división *f*, escisión *f*

splurge[1] ['splərdʒ] *v* **splurged; splurging** *vt* : derrochar — *vi* : derrochar dinero

splurge[2] *n* : derroche *m*

spoil[1] ['spɔɪl] *vt* 1 PILLAGE : saquear 2 RUIN : estropear, arruinar 3 PAMPER : consentir, mimar — *vi* : estropearse, echarse a perder

spoil[2] *n* PLUNDER : botín *m*

spoke[1] → **speak**

spoke[2] ['spo:k] *n* : rayo *m* (de una rueda)

spoken → **speak**

spokesman ['spo:ksmən] *n*, *pl* **-men** [-mən, -ˌmɛn] : portavoz *mf*; vocero *m*, -ra *f*

spokeswoman ['spo:ks,wʊmən] *n*, *pl* **-women** [-ˌwɪmən] : portavoz *f*, vocera *f*

sponge[1] ['spʌndʒ] *vt* **sponged; sponging** : limpiar con una esponja

sponge[2] *n* : esponja *f*

spongy ['spʌndʒi] *adj* **spongier; -est** : esponjoso

sponsor[1] ['spantsər] *vt* : patrocinar, auspiciar, apadrinar (a una persona)

sponsor[2] *n* : patrocinador *m*, -dora *f*; padrino *m*, madrina *f*

sponsorship ['spantsər,ʃɪp] *n* : patrocinio *m*, apadrinamiento *m*

spontaneity [ˌspantə'ni:əti, -'neɪ-] : espontaneidad *f*

spontaneous [span'teɪniəs] *adj* : espontáneo — **spontaneously** *adv*

spoof ['spu:f] *n* : burla *f*, parodia *f*

spook[1] ['spu:k] *vt* : asustar

spook[2] *n* : fantasma *m*, espíritu *m*, espectro *m*

spooky ['spu:ki] *adj* **spookier; -est** : que da miedo, espeluzante

spool ['spu:l] *n* : carrete *m*

spoon[1] ['spu:n] *vt* : comer, servir, o echar con cuchara

spoon[2] *n* : cuchara *f*

spoonful ['spu:n,fʊl] *n* : cucharada *f* ⟨by the spoonful : a cucharadas⟩

spoor ['spʊr, 'spɔr] *n* : rastro *m*, pista *f*

sporadic [spə'rædɪk] *adj* : esporádico — **sporadically** [-dɪkli] *adv*

spore ['spɔr] *n* : espora *f*

sport[1] ['sport] *vi* FROLIC : retozar, juguetear — *vt* SHOW OFF : lucir, ostentar

sport[2] *n* 1 : deporte *m* ⟨outdoor sports : deportes al aire libre⟩ 2 JEST : broma *f* 3 **to be a good sport** : tener espíritu deportivo

sporting ['sportɪŋ] *adj* : deportivo ⟨a sporting chance : buenas posibilidades⟩

sportsman ['sportsmən] *n*, *pl* **-men** [-mən, -ˌmɛn] : deportista *m*

sportsmanship ['sportsmən,ʃɪp] *n* : espíritu *m* deportivo, deportividad *f* *Spain*

sportswoman ['sports,wumən] *n, pl* **-women** [-,wimən] : deportista *f*

sporty ['sporti] *adj* **sportier; -est** : deportivo

spot¹ ['spat] *v* **spotted; spotting** *vt* **1** STAIN : manchar **2** RECOGNIZE, SEE : ver, reconocer ⟨to spot an error : descubrir un error⟩ — *vi* : mancharse

spot² *adj* : hecho al azar ⟨a spot check : un vistazo, un control aleatorio⟩

spot³ *n* **1** STAIN : mancha *f* **2** DOT : punto *m* **3** PIMPLE : grano *m* ⟨to break out in spots : salirle granos a alguien⟩ **4** PREDICAMENT : apuro *m*, aprieto *m*, lío *m* ⟨in a tight spot : en apuros⟩ **5** PLACE : lugar *m*, sitio *m* ⟨to be on the spot : estar en el lugar⟩

spotless ['spatləs] *adj* : impecable, inmaculado — **spotlessly** *adv*

spotlight¹ ['spat,laɪt] *vt* **-lighted** *or* **-lit** [-,lɪt]; **-lighting 1** LIGHT : iluminar (con un reflector) **2** HIGHLIGHT : destacar, poner en relieve

spotlight² *n* **1** : reflector *m*, foco *m* **2 to be in the spotlight** : ser el centro de atención

spotty ['spati] *adj* **spottier; -est** : irregular, desigual

spouse ['spaʊs] *n* : cónyuge *mf*

spout¹ ['spaʊt] *vt* **1** : lanzar chorros de **2** DECLAIM : declamar — *vi* : salir a chorros

spout² *n* **1** : pico *m* (de una jarra, etc.) **2** STREAM : chorro *m*

sprain¹ ['spreɪn] *vt* : sufrir un esguince en

sprain² *n* : esguince *m*, torcedura *f*

sprawl¹ ['sprɔl] *vi* **1** LIE : tumbarse, echarse, despatarrarse **2** EXTEND : extenderse

sprawl² *n* **1** : postura *f* despatarrada **2** SPREAD : extensión *f*, expansión *f*

spray¹ ['spreɪ] *vt* : rociar (una superficie), pulverizar (un líquido)

spray² *n* **1** BOUQUET : ramillete *m* **2** MIST : rocío *m* **3** ATOMIZER : atomizador *m*, pulverizador *m*

spray gun *n* : pistola *f*

spread¹ ['sprɛd] *v* **spread; spreading** *vt* **1** *or* **to spread out** : desplegar, extender **2** SCATTER, STREW : esparcir **3** SMEAR : untar (mantequilla, etc.) **4** DISSEMINATE : difundir, sembrar, propagar — *vi* **1** : difundirse, correr, propagarse **2** EXTEND : extenderse

spread² *n* **1** EXTENSION : extensión *f*, difusión *f* (de noticias, etc.), propagación *f* (de enfermedades, etc.) **2** : colcha *f* (para una cama), mantel *m* (para una mesa) **3** PASTE : pasta *f* ⟨cheese spread : pasta de queso⟩

spreadsheet ['sprɛd,ʃi:t] *n* : hoja *f* de cálculo

spree ['spri] *n* **1** : acción *f* desenfrenada ⟨to go on a shopping spree : com-

prar como loco⟩ **2** BINGE : parranda *f*, juerga *f* ⟨on a spree : de parranda, de juerga⟩

sprig ['sprɪg] *n* : ramita *f*, ramito *m*

sprightly ['spraɪtli] *adj* **sprightlier; -est** : vivo, animado ⟨with a sprightly step : con paso ligero⟩

spring¹ ['sprɪŋ] *v* **sprang** ['spræŋ] *or* **sprung** ['sprʌŋ]; **sprung; springing** *vi* **1** LEAP : saltar **2** : mover rápidamente ⟨the lid sprang shut : la tapa se cerró de un golpe⟩ ⟨he sprang to his feet : se paró de un salto⟩ **3 to spring up** : brotar (dícese de las plantas), surgir **4 to spring from** : surgir de — *vt* **1** RELEASE : soltar (de repente) ⟨to spring the news on someone : sorprender a alguien con las noticias⟩ ⟨to spring a trap : hacer saltar una trampa⟩ **2** ACTIVATE : accionar (un mecanismo) **3 to spring a leak** : hacer agua

spring² *n* **1** SOURCE : fuente *f*, origen *m* **2** : manantial *m*, fuente *f* ⟨hot spring : fuente termal⟩ **3** : primavera *f* ⟨spring and summer : la primavera y el verano⟩ **4** : resorte *m*, muelle *m* (de metal, etc.) **5** LEAP : salto *m*, brinco *m* **6** RESILIENCE : elasticidad *f*

springboard ['sprɪŋ,bord] *n* : trampolín *m*

springtime ['sprɪŋ,taɪm] *n* : primavera *f*

springy ['sprɪŋi] *adj* **springier; -est 1** RESILIENT : elástico **2** LIVELY : enérgico

sprinkle¹ ['sprɪŋkəl] *vt* **-kled; -kling** : rociar (con agua), espolvorear (con azúcar, etc.), salpicar

sprinkle² *n* : llovizna *f*

sprinkler ['sprɪŋkələr] *n* : rociador *m*, aspersor *m*

sprint¹ ['sprɪnt] *vi* : echar la carrera, esprintar (en deportes)

sprint² *n* : esprint *m* (en deportes)

sprinter ['sprɪntər] *n* : esprínter *mf*

sprite ['spraɪt] *n* : hada *f*, elfo *m*

sprocket ['sprakət] *n* : diente *m* (de una rueda dentada)

sprout¹ ['spraʊt] *vi* : brotar

sprout² *n* : brote *m*, retoño *m*, vástago *m*

spruce¹ ['spru:s] *v* **spruced; sprucing** *vt* : arreglar — *vi* *or* **to spruce up** : arreglarse, acicalarse

spruce² *adj* **sprucer; sprucest** : pulcro, arreglado

spruce³ *n* : picea *f* (árbol)

spry ['spraɪ] *adj* **sprier** *or* **spryer** ['spraɪər]; **spriest** *or* **spryest** ['spraɪəst] : ágil, activo

spun → **spin**

spunk ['spʌŋk] *n* : valor *m*, coraje *m*, agallas *fpl fam*

spunky ['spʌŋki] *adj* **spunkier; -est** : animoso, corajudo

spur¹ ['spər] *vt* **spurred; spurring** *or* **to spur on** : espolear (un caballo), motivar (a una persona, etc.)

spur[2] *n* **1** : espuela *f*, acicate *m* **2** STIM-ULUS : acicate *m* **3** : espolón *m* (de aves gallináceas)

spurious ['spjuriəs] *adj* : espurio

spurn ['spərn] *vt* : desdeñar, rechazar

spurt[1] ['spərt] *vt* SQUIRT : lanzar un cho-rro de — *vi* SPOUT : salir a chorros

spurt[2] *n* **1** : actividad *f* repentina ⟨a spurt of energy : una explosión de en-ergía⟩ ⟨to do in spurts : hacer por rachas⟩ **2** JET : chorro *m* (de agua, etc.)

sputter[1] ['spʌtər] *vi* **1** JABBER : farfullar **2** : chisporrotear (dícese de la grasa, etc.), petardear (dícese de un motor)

sputter[2] *n* **1** JABBER : farfulla *f* **2** : chis-porroteo *m* (de grasa, etc.), petardeo *m* (de un motor)

spy[1] ['spaɪ] *v* **spied; spying** *vt* SEE : ver, divisar — *vi* : espiar ⟨to spy on some-one : espiar a alguien⟩

spy[2] *n* : espía *mf*

squab ['skwɑb] *n, pl* **squabs** *or* **squab** : pichón *m*

squabble[1] ['skwɑbəl] *vi* **-bled; -bling** : reñir, pelearse, discutir

squabble[2] *n* : riña *f*, pelea *f*, discusión *f*

squad ['skwɑd] *n* : pelotón *m* (militar), brigada *f* (de policías), cuadrilla *f* (de obreros, etc.)

squadron ['skwɑdrən] *n* : escuadrón *m* (de militares), escuadrilla *f* (de aviones), escuadra *f* (de naves)

squalid ['skwɑlɪd] *adj* : miserable

squall ['skwɔl] *n* **1** : aguacero *m* tor-mentoso, chubasco *m* tormentoso **2** **snow squall** : tormenta *f* de nieve

squalor ['skwɑlər] *n* : miseria *f*

squander ['skwɑndər] *vt* : derrochar (dinero, etc.), desaprovechar (una oportunidad, etc.), desperdiciar (talen-tos, energías, etc.)

square[1] ['skwær] *vt* **squared; squaring** **1** : cuadrar **2** : elevar al cuadrado (en matemáticas) **3** CONFORM : conciliar (con), ajustar (con) **4** SETTLE : saldar (una cuenta) ⟨I squared it with him : lo arreglé con él⟩

square[2] *adj* **squarer; -est 1** : cuadrado ⟨a square house : una casa cuadrada⟩ **2** RIGHT-ANGLED : a escuadra, en án-gulo recto **3** : cuadrado (en matemáti-cas) ⟨a square mile : una milla cuadra-da⟩ **4** HONEST : justo ⟨a square deal : un buen acuerdo⟩ ⟨fair and square : en buena lid⟩

square[3] *n* **1** : escuadra *f* (instrumento) **2** : cuadrado *m*, cuadro *m* ⟨to fold into squares : plegar en cuadrados⟩ **3** : plaza *f* (de una ciudad) **4** : cuadrado *m* (en matemáticas)

squarely ['skwærli] *adv* **1** EXACTLY : ex-actamente, directamente, justo **2** HON-ESTLY : honradamente, justamente

square root *n* : raíz *f* cuadrada

squash[1] ['skwɑʃ, 'skwɔʃ] *vt* **1** CRUSH : aplastar **2** SUPPRESS : acallar (protes-tas), sofocar (una rebelión)

squash[2] *n* **1** *pl* **squashes** *or* **squash** : calabaza *f* (vegetal) **2** *or* **squash rac-quets** : squash *m* (deporte)

squat[1] ['skwɑt] *vi* **squatted; squatting** **1** CROUCH : agacharse, ponerse en cu-clillas **2** : ocupar un lugar sin derecho

squat[2] *adj* **squatter; squattest** : bajo y ancho, rechoncho *fam* (dícese de una persona)

squat[3] *n* **1** : posición *f* en cuclillas **2** : ocupación *f* ilegal (de un lugar)

squaw ['skwɔ] *n* : india *f* (norteameri-cana)

squawk[1] ['skwɔk] *vi* : graznar (dícese de las aves), chillar

squawk[2] *n* : graznido *m* (de un ave), chillido *m*

squeak[1] ['skwi:k] *vi* : chillar (dícese de un animal), chirriar (dícese de un ob-jeto)

squeak[2] *n* : chillido *m*, chirrido *m*

squeaky ['skwi:ki] *adj* **squeakier; -est** : chirriante ⟨a squeaky voice : una voz chillona⟩

squeal[1] ['skwi:l] *vi* **1** : chillar (dícese de las personas o los animales), chirriar (dícese de los frenos, etc.) **2** PROTEST : quejarse

squeal[2] *n* **1** : chillido *m* (de una persona o un animal) **2** SCREECH : chirrido *m* (de frenos, etc.)

squeamish ['skwi:mɪʃ] *adj* : impresion-able, sensible ⟨he's squeamish about cockroaches : las cucarachas le dan asco⟩

squeeze[1] ['skwi:z] *vt* **squeezed; squeezing 1** PRESS : apretar, exprim-ir (naranjas, etc.) **2** EXTRACT : extraer (jugo, etc.)

squeeze[2] *n* : apretón *m*

squelch ['skwɛltʃ] *vt* : aplastar (una re-belión, etc.)

squid ['skwɪd] *n, pl* **squid** *or* **squids** : calamar *m*

squint[1] ['skwɪnt] *vi* : mirar con los ojos entornados

squint[2] *adj or* **squint—eyed** ['skwɪnt,aɪd] : bizco

squint[3] *n* : ojos *mpl* bizcos, bizquera *f*

squire ['skwaɪr] *n* : hacendado *m*, -da *f*; terrateniente *mf*

squirm ['skwərm] *vi* : retorcerse

squirrel ['skwərəl] *n* : ardilla *f*

squirt[1] ['skwərt] *vt* : lanzar un chorro de — *vi* SPURT : salir a chorros

squirt[2] *n* : chorrito *m*

stab[1] ['stæb] *vt* **stabbed; stabbing 1** KNIFE : acuchillar, apuñalar **2** STICK : clavar (con una aguja, etc.), golpear (con el dedo, etc.)

stab[2] *n* **1** : puñalada *f*, cuchillada *f* **2** JAB : pinchazo *m* (con una aguja, etc.), golpe *m* (con un dedo, etc.) **3 to take a stab at** : intentar

stability [stə'bɪləti] *n, pl* **-ties** : estabili-dad *f*

stabilize ['steɪbə,laɪz] *v* **-lized; -lizing** *vt* : estabilizar — *vi* : estabilizarse

stable[1] ['steɪbəl] *vt* **-bled; -bling** : poner (ganado) en un establo, poner (caballos) en una caballeriza
stable[2] *adj* **-bler; -blest 1** FIXED, STEADY : fijo, sólido, estable **2** LASTING : estable, perdurable ⟨a stable government : un gobierno estable⟩ **3** : estacionario (en medicina), equilibrado (en psicología)
stable[3] *n* : establo *m* (para ganado), caballeriza *f* o cuadra *f* (para caballos)
staccato [stə'kɑːtoː] *adj* : staccato
stack[1] ['stæk] *vt* **1** PILE : amontonar, apilar **2** COVER : cubrir, llenar ⟨he stacked the table with books : cubrió la mesa de libros⟩
stack[2] *n* **1** PILE : montón *m*, pila *f* **2** SMOKESTACK : chimenea *f*
stadium ['steɪdiəm] *n, pl* **-dia** [-diə] *or* **-diums** : estadio *m*
staff[1] ['stæf] *vt* : proveer de personal
staff[2] *n, pl* **staffs** ['stæfs, stævz] *or* **staves** ['stævz, 'steɪvz] **1** : bastón *m* (de mando), báculo *m* (de obispo) **2** *pl* **staffs** PERSONNEL : personal *m* **3** *or* **stave** : pentagrama *m* (en música)
stag[1] ['stæg] *adv* : solo, sin pareja ⟨to go stag : ir solo⟩
stag[2] *adj* : sólo para hombres
stag[3] *n, pl* **stags** *or* **stag** : ciervo *m*, venado *m*
stage[1] ['steɪdʒ] *vt* **staged; staging** : poner en escena (una obra de teatro)
stage[2] *n* **1** PLATFORM : estrado *m*, tablado *m*, escenario *m* (de un teatro) **2** PHASE, STEP : fase *f*, etapa *f* ⟨stage of development : fase de desarrollo⟩ ⟨in stages : por etapas⟩ **3 the stage** : el teatro *m*
stagecoach ['steɪdʒ,koːtʃ] *n* : diligencia *f*
stagger[1] ['stægər] *vi* TOTTER : tambalearse — *vt* **1** ALTERNATE : alternar, escalonar (turnos de trabajo) **2** : hacer tambalear ⟨to be staggered by : quedarse estupefacto por⟩
stagger[2] *n* : tambaleo *m*
staggering ['stægərɪŋ] *adj* : asombroso
stagnant ['stægnənt] *adj* : estancado
stagnate ['stæg,neɪt] *vi* **-nated; -nating** : estancarse
staid ['steɪd] *adj* : serio, sobrio
stain[1] ['steɪn] *vt* **1** DISCOLOR : manchar **2** DYE : teñir (madera, etc.) **3** SULLY : manchar, empañar
stain[2] *n* **1** SPOT : mancha *f* **2** DYE : tinte *m*, tintura *f* **3** BLEMISH : mancha *f*, mácula *f*
stainless ['steɪnləs] *adj* : sin mancha ⟨stainless steel : acero inoxidable⟩
stair ['stær] *n* **1** STEP : escalón *m*, peldaño *m* **2 stairs** *npl* : escalera *f*, escaleras *fpl*
staircase ['stær,keɪs] *n* : escalera *f*, escaleras *fpl*
stairway ['stær,weɪ] *n* : escalera *f*, escaleras *fpl*
stake[1] ['steɪk] *vt* **staked; staking 1** : estacar, marcar con estacas (una

propiedad) **2** BET : jugarse, apostar **3 to stake a claim to** : reclamar, reivindicar
stake[2] *n* **1** POST : estaca *f* **2** BET : apuesta *f* ⟨to be at stake : estar en juego⟩ **3** INTEREST, SHARE : interés *m*, participación *f*
stalactite [stə'læk,taɪt] *n* : estalactita *f*
stalagmite [stə'læg,maɪt] *n* : estalagmita *f*
stale ['steɪl] *adj* **staler; stalest** : viejo ⟨stale bread : pan duro⟩ ⟨stale news : viejas noticias⟩
stalemate ['steɪl,meɪt] *n* : punto *m* muerto, impasse *m*
stalk[1] ['stɔk] *vt* : acechar — *vi* : caminar rígidamente (por orgullo, ira, etc.)
stalk[2] *n* : tallo *m* (de una planta)
stall[1] ['stɔl] *vt* **1** : parar (un motor) **2** DELAY : entretener (a una persona), demorar — *vi* **1** : pararse (dícese de un motor) **2** DELAY : demorar, andar con rodeos
stall[2] *n* **1** : compartimiento *m* (de un establo) **2** : puesto *m* (en un mercado, etc.)
stallion ['stæljən] *n* : caballo *m* semental
stalwart ['stɔlwərt] *adj* **1** STRONG : fuerte ⟨a stalwart supporter : un firme partidario⟩ **2** BRAVE : valiente, valeroso
stamen ['steɪmən] *n* : estambre *m*
stamina ['stæmənə] *n* : resistencia *f*
stammer[1] ['stæmər] *vi* : tartamudear, titubear
stammer[2] *n* : tartamudeo *m*, titubeo *m*
stamp[1] ['stæmp] *vt* **1** : pisotear (con los pies) ⟨to stamp one's feet : patear, dar una patada⟩ **2** IMPRESS, IMPRINT : sellar (una factura, etc.), acuñar (monedas) **3** : franquear, ponerle estampillas a (correo)
stamp[2] *n* **1** : sello *m* (para documentos, etc.) **2** DIE : cuño *m* (para monedas) **3** *or* **postage stamp** : sello *m*, estampilla *f*, timbre *m* CA, Mex
stampede[1] [stæm'piːd] *vi* **-peded; -peding** : salir en estampida
stampede[2] *n* : estampida *f*
stance ['stænts] *n* : postura *f*
stanch ['stɔntʃ, 'stæntʃ] *vt* : detener, estancar (un líquido)
stand[1] ['stænd] *v* **stood** ['stʊd]; **standing** *vi* **1** : estar de pie, estar parado ⟨I was standing on the corner : estaba parada en la esquina⟩ **2** *or* **to stand up** : levantarse, pararse, ponerse de pie **3** *(indicating a specified position or location)* ⟨they stand third in the country : ocupan el tercer lugar en el país⟩ ⟨the machines are standing idle : las máquinas están paradas⟩ **4** *(referring to an opinion)* ⟨how does he stand on the matter? : ¿cuál es su postura respecto al asunto?⟩ **5** BE : estar ⟨the house stands on a hill : la casa está en una colina⟩ **6** CONTINUE : seguir ⟨the order still stands : el mandato sigue vi-

gente⟩ — vt **1** PLACE, SET : poner, colocar ⟨he stood them in a row : los colocó en hilera⟩ **2** TOLERATE : aguantar, soportar ⟨he can't stand her : no la puede tragar⟩ **3 to stand firm** : mantenerse firme **4 to stand guard** : hacer la guardia

stand² *n* **1** RESISTANCE : resistencia *f* ⟨to make a stand against : resistir a⟩ **2** BOOTH, STALL : stand *m*, puesto *m*, kiosko *m* (para vender periódicos, etc) **3** BASE : pie *m*, base *f* **4** : grupo *m* (de árboles, etc.) **5** POSITION : posición *f*, postura *f* **6 stands** *npl* GRANDSTAND : tribuna *f*

standard¹ ['stændərd] *adj* **1** ESTABLISHED : estándar, oficial ⟨standard measures : medidas oficiales⟩ ⟨standard English : el inglés estándar⟩ **2** NORMAL : normal, estándar, común **3** CLASSIC : estándar, clásico ⟨a standard work : una obra clásica⟩

standard² *n* **1** BANNER : estandarte *m* **2** CRITERION : criterio *m* **3** RULE : estándar *m*, norma *f*, regla *f* **4** LEVEL : nivel *m* ⟨standard of living : nivel de vida⟩ **5** SUPPORT : poste *m*, soporte *m*

standardization [ˌstændərdəˈzeɪʃən] *n* : estandarización *f*

standardize ['stændərˌdaɪz] *vt* **-ized; -izing** : estandarizar

standard time *n* : hora *f* oficial

stand by *vt* : atenerse a, cumplir con (una promesa, etc.) — *vi* **1** : mantenerse aparte (to stand by and do nothing : mirar sin hacer nada⟩ **2** : estar preparado, estar listo (para un anuncio, un ataque, etc.)

stand for *vt* **1** REPRESENT : significar **2** PERMIT, TOLERATE : permitir, tolerar

standing ['stændɪŋ] *n* **1** POSITION, RANK : posición *f* **2** DURATION : duración *f*

stand out *vi* **1** : destacar(se) ⟨she stands out from the rest : se destaca entre los otros⟩ **2 to stand out against** RESIST : oponerse a

standpoint ['stændˌpoɪnt] *n* : punto *m* de vista

standstill ['stændˌstɪl] *n* **1** STOP : detención *f*, paro *m* ⟨to come to a standstill : pararse⟩ **2** DEADLOCK : punto *m* muerto, impasse *m*

stand up *vt* : dejar plantado ⟨he stood me up again : otra vez me dejó plantado⟩ — *vi* **1** ENDURE : durar, resistir **2 to stand up for** : defender **3 to stand up to** : hacerle frente (a alguien)

stank → **stink**

stanza ['stænzə] *n* : estrofa *f*

staple¹ ['steɪpəl] *vt* **-pled; -pling** : engrapar, grapar

staple² *adj* : principal, básico ⟨a staple food : un alimento básico⟩

staple³ *n* **1** : producto *m* principal **2** : grapa *f* (para engrapar papeles)

stapler ['steɪplər] *n* : engrapadora *f*, grapadora *f*

star¹ ['stɑr] *v* **starred; starring** *vt* **1** : marcar con una estrella o un aster-

isco **2** FEATURE : estar protagonizado por — *vi* : tener el papel principal ⟨to star in : protagonizar⟩

star² *n* : estrella *f*

starboard ['stɑrbərd] *n* : estribor *m*

starch¹ ['stɑrtʃ] *vt* : almidonar

starch² *n* : almidón *m*, fécula *f* (comida)

starchy ['stɑrtʃi] *adj* **starchier; -est** : lleno de almidón ⟨a starchy diet : una dieta feculenta⟩

stardom ['stɑrdəm] *n* : estrellato *m*

stare¹ ['stær] *vi* **stared; staring** : mirar fijamente

stare² *n* : mirada *f* fija

starfish ['stɑrˌfɪʃ] *n* : estrella *f* de mar

stark¹ ['stɑrk] *adv* : completamente ⟨stark raving mad : loco de remate⟩ ⟨stark naked : completamente desnudo⟩

stark² *adj* **1** ABSOLUTE : absoluto **2** BARREN, DESOLATE : desolado, desierto **3** BARE : desnudo **4** HARSH : severo, duro

starlight ['stɑrˌlaɪt] *n* : luz *f* de las estrellas

starling ['stɑrlɪŋ] *n* : estornino *m*

starry ['stɑri] *adj* **starrier; -est** : estrellado

start¹ ['stɑrt] *vi* **1** JUMP : levantarse de un salto, sobresaltarse, dar un respingo **2** BEGIN : empezar, comenzar **3** SET OUT : salir (de viaje, etc.) **4** : arrancar (dícese de un motor) — *vt* **1** BEGIN : empezar, comenzar, iniciar **2** CAUSE : provocar, causar **3** ESTABLISH : fundar, montar, establecer ⟨to start a business : montar un negocio⟩ **4** : arrancar, poner en marcha, encender ⟨to start the car : arrancar el motor⟩

start² *n* **1** JUMP : sobresalto *m*, respingo *m* **2** BEGINNING : principio *m*, comienzo *m* ⟨to get an early start : salir temprano⟩

starter ['stɑrtər] *n* **1** : participante *mf* (en una carrera, etc.); jugador *m* titular, jugadora *f* titular (en beisbol, etc.) **2** APPETIZER : entremés *m*, aperitivo *m* **3** *or* **starter motor** : motor *m* de arranque

startle ['stɑrtəl] *vt* **-tled; -tling** : asustar, sobresaltar

start–up ['stɑrtˈʌp] *adj* : de puesta en marcha

starvation [stɑrˈveɪʃən] *n* : inanición *f*, hambre *f*

starve ['stɑrv] *v* **starved; starving** *vi* : morirse de hambre — *vt* : privar de comida

stash ['stæʃ] *vt* : esconder, guardar (en un lugar secreto)

stat ['stæt] → **statistic**

state¹ ['steɪt] *vt* **stated; stating 1** REPORT : puntualizar, exponer (los hechos, etc.) ⟨state your name : diga su nombre⟩ **2** ESTABLISH, FIX : establecer, fijar

state² *n* **1** CONDITION : estado *m*, condición *f* ⟨a liquid state : un estado líquido⟩ ⟨state of mind : estado de ánimo⟩

⟨in a bad state : en malas condiciones⟩ **2** NATION : estado *m*, nación *f* **3** : estado *m* (dentro de un país) ⟨the States : los Estados Unidos⟩

stateliness ['steɪtlinəs] *n* : majestuosidad *f*

stately ['steɪtli] *adj* **statelier; -est** : majestuoso

statement ['steɪtmənt] *n* **1** DECLARATION : declaración *f*, afirmación *f* **2** or **bank statement** : estado *m* de cuenta

stateroom ['steɪt,ruːm, -,rʊm] *n* : camarote *m*

statesman ['steɪtsmən] *n*, *pl* **-men** [-mən, -,mɛn] : estadista *mf*

static¹ ['stætɪk] *adj* : estático

static² *n* : estática *f*, interferencia *f*

station¹ ['steɪʃən] *vt* : apostar, estacionar

station² *n* **1** : estación *f* (de trenes, etc.) **2** RANK, STANDING : condición *f* (social) **3** : canal *m* (de televisión), estación *f* o emisora *f* (de radio) **4 police station** : comisaría *f* **5 fire station** : estación *f* de bomberos, cuartel *m* de bomberos

stationary ['steɪʃə,nɛri] *adj* **1** IMMOBILE : estacionario, inmovible **2** UNCHANGING : inmutable, inalterable

stationery ['steɪʃə,nɛri] *n* : papel *m* y sobres *mpl* (para correspondencia)

station wagon *n* : camioneta *f* ranchera, camioneta *f* guayín *Mex*

statistic [stə'tɪstɪk] *n* : estadística *f* ⟨according to statistics : según las estadísticas⟩

statistical [stə'tɪstɪkəl] *adj* : estadístico

statistician [,stætə'stɪʃən] *n* : estadístico *m*, -ca *f*

statue ['stæ,tʃuː] *n* : estatua *f*

statuesque [,stætʃu'ɛsk] *adj* : escultural

statuette [,stætʃu'ɛt] *n* : estatuilla *f*

stature ['stætʃər] *n* **1** HEIGHT : estatura *f*, talla *f* **2** PRESTIGE : talla *f*, prestigio *m*

status ['steɪtəs, 'stæ-] *n* : condición *f*, situación *f*, estatus *m* (social) ⟨marital status : estado civil⟩

statute ['stæ,tʃuːt] *n* : ley *f*, estatuto *m*

staunch ['stɔntʃ] *adj* : acérrimo, incondicional, leal ⟨a staunch supporter : un partidario incondicional⟩ — **staunchly** *adv*

stave¹ ['steɪv] *vt* **staved** *or* **stove** ['stoːv]; **staving 1 to stave in** : romper **2 to stave off** : evitar (un ataque), prevenir (un problema)

stave² *n* : duela *f* (de un barril)

staves → staff

stay¹ ['steɪ] *vi* **1** REMAIN : quedarse, permanecer ⟨to stay in : quedarse en casa⟩ ⟨he stayed in the city : permaneció en la ciudad⟩ **2** CONTINUE : seguir, quedarse ⟨it stayed cloudy : siguió nublado⟩ ⟨to stay awake : mantenerse despierto⟩ **3** LODGE : hospedarse, alojarse (en un hotel, etc.) — *vt* **1** HALT : detener, suspender (una ejecución, etc.) **2 to stay the course** : aguantar hasta el final

stay² *n* **1** SOJOURN : estadía *f*, estancia *f*, permanencia *f* **2** SUSPENSION : suspensión *f* (de una sentencia) **3** SUPPORT : soporte *m*

stead ['stɛd] *n* **1** : lugar *m* ⟨she went in his stead : fue en su lugar⟩ **2 to stand (someone) in good stead** : ser muy útil a, servir de mucho a

steadfast ['stɛd,fæst] *adj* : firme, resuelto ⟨a steadfast friend : un fiel amigo⟩ ⟨a steadfast refusal : una negativa categórica⟩

steadily ['stɛdəli] *adv* **1** CONSTANTLY : continuamente, sin parar **2** FIRMLY : con firmeza **3** FIXEDLY : fijamente

steady¹ ['stɛdi] *v* **steadied; steadying** *vt* : sujetar ⟨she steadied herself : recobró el equilibrio⟩ — *vi* : estabilizarse

steady² *adj* **steadier; -est 1** FIRM, SURE : seguro, firme ⟨to have a steady hand : tener buen pulso⟩ **2** FIXED, REGULAR : fijo ⟨a steady income : ingresos fijos⟩ **3** CALM : tranquilo, ecuánime ⟨she has steady nerves : es imperturbable⟩ **4** DEPENDABLE : responsable, fiable **5** CONSTANT : constante

steak ['steɪk] *n* : bistec *m*, filete *m*, churrasco *m*, bife *m* *Arg, Chile, Uru*

steal ['stiːl] *v* **stole** ['stoːl]; **stolen** ['stoːlən]; **stealing** *vt* : robar, hurtar — *vi* **1** : robar, hurtar **2** : ir sigilosamente ⟨to steal away : escabullirse⟩

stealth ['stɛlθ] *n* : sigilo *m*

stealthily ['stɛlθəli] *adv* : furtivamente

stealthy ['stɛlθi] *adj* **stealthier; -est** : furtivo, sigiloso

steam¹ ['stiːm] *vi* : echar vapor ⟨to steam away : moverse echando vapor⟩ — *vt* **1** : cocer al vapor (en cocina) **2 to steam open** : abrir con vapor

steam² *n* **1** : vapor *m* **2 to let off steam** : desahogarse

steamboat ['stiːm,boːt] → **steamship**

steam engine *n* : motor *m* de vapor

steamroller ['stiːm,roːlər] *n* : apisonadora *f*

steamship ['stiːm,ʃɪp] *n* : vapor *m*, barco *m* de vapor

steamy ['stiːmi] *adj* **steamier; -est 1** : lleno de vapor **2** EROTIC : erótico ⟨a steamy romance : un tórrido romance⟩

steed ['stiːd] *n* : corcel *m*

steel¹ ['stiːl] *vt* **to steel oneself** : armarse de valor

steel² *adj* : de acero

steel³ *n* : acero *m*

steely ['stiːli] *adj* **steelier; -est** : como acero ⟨a steely gaze : una mirada fría⟩ ⟨steely determination : determinación férrea⟩

steep¹ ['stiːp] *vt* : remojar, dejar (té, etc.) en infusión

steep² *adj* **1** : empinado, escarpado ⟨a steep cliff : un precipicio escarpado⟩ **2** CONSIDERABLE : considerable, marcado **3** EXCESSIVE : excesivo ⟨steep prices : precios muy altos⟩

steeple ['stiːpəl] *n* : aguja *f*, campanario *m*

steeplechase ['sti:pəl,ʧeɪs] *n* : carrera *f* de obstáculos

steeply ['sti:pli] *adv* : abruptamente

steer[1] ['stɪr] *vt* **1** : conducir (un coche), gobernar (un barco) **2** GUIDE : dirigir, guiar

steer[2] *n* : buey *m*

steering wheel *n* : volante *m*

stein ['staɪn] *n* : jarra *f* (para cerveza)

stellar ['stɛlər] *adj* : estelar

stem[1] ['stɛm] *v* **stemmed; stemming** *vt* : detener, contener, parar ⟨to stem the tide : detener el curso⟩ — *vi* **to stem from** : provenir de, ser el resultado de

stem[2] *n* : tallo *m* (de una planta)

stench ['stɛnʧ] *n* : hedor *m*, mal olor *m*

stencil[1] ['stɛntsəl] *vt* **-ciled** *or* **-cilled; -ciling** *or* **-cilling** : marcar utilizando una plantilla

stencil[2] *n* : plantilla *f* (para marcar)

stenographer [stə'nɑgrəfər] *n* : taquígrafo *m*, -fa *f*

stenographic [,stɛnə'græfɪk] *adj* : taquigráfico

stenography [stə'nɑgrəfi] *n* : taquigrafía *f*

step[1] ['stɛp] *vi* **stepped; stepping** **1** : dar un paso ⟨step this way, please : pase por aquí, por favor⟩ ⟨he stepped outside : salió⟩ **2 to step on** : pisar

step[2] *n* **1** : paso *m* ⟨step by step : paso por paso⟩ **2** STAIR : escalón *m*, peldaño *m* **3** RUNG : escalón *m*, travesaño *m* **4** MEASURE, MOVE : medida *f*, paso *m* ⟨to take steps : tomar medidas⟩ **5** STRIDE : paso *m* ⟨with a quick step : con paso rápido⟩

stepbrother ['stɛp,brʌðər] *n* : hermanastro *m*

stepdaughter ['stɛp,dɔtər] *n* : hijastra *f*

stepfather ['stɛp,faðər, -,fa-] *n* : padrastro *m*

stepladder ['stɛp,lædər] *n* : escalera *f* de tijera

stepmother ['stɛp,mʌðər] *n* : madrastra *f*

steppe ['stɛp] *n* : estepa *f*

stepping–stone ['stɛpɪŋ,stoːn] *n* : pasadera *f* (en un río, etc.), trampolín *m* (al éxito)

stepsister ['stɛp,sɪstər] *n* : hermanastra *f*

stepson ['stɛp,sʌn] *n* : hijastro *m*

step up *vt* INCREASE : aumentar

stereo[1] ['stɛri,oː, 'stɪr-] *adj* : estéreo

stereo[2] *n, pl* **stereos** : estéreo *m*

stereophonic [,stɛrio'fɑnɪk, ,stɪr-] *adj* : estereofónico

stereotype[1] ['stɛrio,taɪp, 'stɪr-] *vt* **-typed; -typing** : estereotipar

stereotype[2] *n* : estereotipo *m*

sterile ['stɛrəl] *adj* : estéril

sterility [stə'rɪləti] *n* : esterilidad *f*

sterilization [,stɛrələ'zeɪʃən] *n* : esterilización *f*

sterilize ['stɛrə,laɪz] *vt* **-ized; -izing** : esterilizar

sterling ['stərlɪŋ] *adj* **1** : de ley ⟨sterling silver : plata de ley⟩ **2** EXCELLENT : excelente

stern[1] ['stərn] *adj* : severo, adusto — **sternly** *adv*

stern[2] *n* : popa *f*

sternness ['stərnnəs] *n* : severidad *f*

sternum ['stərnəm] *n, pl* **sternums** *or* **sterna** [-nə] : esternón *m*

stethoscope ['stɛθə,skoːp] *n* : estetoscopio *m*

stevedore ['sti:və,dor] *n* : estibador *m*, -dora *f*

stew[1] ['stu:, 'stju:] *vt* : estofar, guisar — *vi* **1** : cocer (dícese de la carne, etc.) **2** FRET : preocuparse

stew[2] *n* **1** : estofado *m*, guiso *m* **2 to be in a stew** : estar agitado

steward ['stu:ərd, 'stju:-] *n* **1** MANAGER : administrador *m* **2** : auxiliar *m* de vuelo (en un avión), camarero *m* (en un barco)

stewardess ['stu:ərdəs, 'stju:-] *n* **1** MANAGER : administradora *f* **2** : camarera *f* (en un barco) **3** : auxiliar *f* de vuelo, azafata *f*, aeromoza *f* (en un avión)

stick[1] ['stɪk] *v* **stuck** ['stʌk]; **sticking** *vt* **1** STAB : clavar **2** ATTACH : pegar **3** PUT : poner **4 to stick out** : sacar (la lengua, etc.), extender (la mano) — *vi* **1** ADHERE : pegarse, adherirse **2** JAM : atascarse **3 to stick around** : quedarse **4 to stick out** PROJECT : sobresalir (de una superficie), asomar (por detrás o debajo de algo) **5 to stick to** : no abandonar ⟨stick to your guns : manténgase firme⟩ **6 to stick up** : estar parado (dícese del pelo, etc.), sobresalir (de una superficie) **7 to stick with** : serle fiel a (una persona), seguir con (una cosa) ⟨I'll stick with what I know : prefiero lo conocido⟩

stick[2] *n* **1** BRANCH, TWIG : ramita *f* **2** : palo *m*, vara *f* ⟨a walking stick : un bastón⟩

sticker ['stɪkər] *n* : etiqueta *f* adhesiva

stickler ['stɪklər] *n* : persona *f* exigente ⟨to be a stickler for : insistir mucho en⟩

sticky ['stɪki] *adj* **stickier; -est** **1** ADHESIVE : pegajoso, adhesivo **2** MUGGY : bochornoso **3** DIFFICULT : difícil

stiff ['stɪf] *adj* **1** RIGID : rígido, tieso ⟨a stiff dough : una masa firme⟩ **2** : agarrotado, entumecido ⟨stiff muscles : músculos entumecidos⟩ **3** STILTED : acartonado, poco natural **4** STRONG : fuerte (dícese del viento, etc.) **5** DIFFICULT, SEVERE : severo, difícil, duro

stiffen ['stɪfən] *vt* **1** STRENGTHEN : fortalecer, reforzar (tela, etc.) **2** : hacer más duro (un castigo, etc.) — *vi* **1** HARDEN : endurecerse **2** : entumecerse (dícese de los músculos)

stiffly ['stɪfli] *adv* **1** RIGIDLY : rígidamente **2** COLDLY : con frialdad

stiffness ['stɪfnəs] *n* **1** RIGIDITY : rigidez *f* **2** COLDNESS : frialdad *f* **3** SEVERITY : severidad *f*

stifle ['staɪfəl] *vt* **-fled; -fling** SMOTHER, SUPPRESS : sofocar, reprimir, contener ⟨to stifle a yawn : reprimir un bostezo⟩

stigma ['stɪgmə] *n, pl* **stigmata** [stɪg-'mɑṭə, 'stɪgməṭə] *or* **stigmas** : estigma *m*

stigmatize ['stɪgmə,taɪz] *vt* **-tized; -tizing** : estigmatizar

stile ['staɪl] *n* : escalones *mpl* para cruzar un cerco

stiletto [stə'lɛ,to:] *n, pl* **-tos** *or* **-toes** : estilete *m*

still[1] ['stɪl] *vt* CALM : pacificar, apaciguar — *vi* : pacificarse, apaciguarse

still[2] *adv* **1** QUIETLY : quieto ⟨sit still! : ¡quédate quieto!⟩ **2** : de todos modos, aún, todavía ⟨she still lives there : aún vive allí⟩ ⟨it's still the same : sigue siendo lo mismo⟩ **3** IN ANY CASE : de todos modos, aún así ⟨he still has doubts : aún así le quedan dudas⟩ ⟨I still prefer that you stay : de todos modos prefiero que te quedes⟩

still[3] *adj* **1** MOTIONLESS : quieto, inmóvil **2** SILENT : callado

still[4] *n* **1** SILENCE : quietud *f*, calma *f* **2** : alambique *m* (para destilar alcohol)

stillborn ['stɪl,bɔrn] *adj* : nacido muerto

stillness ['stɪlnəs] *n* : calma *f*, silencio *m*

stilt ['stɪlt] *n* : zanco *m*

stilted ['stɪltəd] *adj* : afectado, poco natural

stimulant ['stɪmjələnt] *n* : estimulante *m* — **stimulant** *adj*

stimulate ['stɪmjə,leɪt] *vt* **-lated; -lating** : estimular

stimulation [,stɪmjə'leɪʃən] *n* **1** STIMULATING : estimulación *f* **2** STIMULUS : estímulo *m*

stimulus ['stɪmjələs] *n, pl* **-li** [-,laɪ] **1** : estímulo *m* **2** INCENTIVE : acicate *m*

sting[1] ['stɪŋ] *v* **stung** ['stʌŋ]; **stinging** *vt* **1** : picar ⟨a bee stung him : le picó una abeja⟩ **2** HURT : hacer escocer (físicamente), herir (emocionalmente) — *vi* **1** : picar (dícese de las abejas, etc.) **2** SMART : escocer, arder

sting[2] *n* : picadura *f* (herida), escozor *m* (sensación)

stinger ['stɪŋər] *n* : aguijón *m* (de una abeja, etc.)

stinginess ['stɪndʒinəs] *n* : tacañería *f*

stingy ['stɪndʒi] *adj* **stingier; -est 1** MISERLY : tacaño, avaro **2** PALTRY : mezquino, mísero

stink[1] ['stɪŋk] *vi* **stank** ['stæŋk] *or* **stunk** ['stʌŋk]; **stunk; stinking** : apestar, oler mal

stink[2] *n* : hedor *m*, mal olor *m*, peste *f*

stint[1] ['stɪnt] *vt* : escatimar ⟨to stint oneself of : privarse de⟩ — *vi* **to stint on** : escatimar

stint[2] *n* : período *m*

stipend ['staɪ,pɛnd, -pənd] *n* : estipendio *m*

stipulate ['stɪpjə,leɪt] *vt* **-lated; -lating** : estipular

stipulation [,stɪpjə'leɪʃən] *n* : estipulación *f*

stir[1] ['stər] *v* **stirred; stirring** *vt* **1** AGITATE : mover, agitar **2** MIX : revolver, remover **3** INCITE : incitar, impulsar, motivar **4** *or* **to stir up** AROUSE : despertar (memorias, etc.), provocar (ira, etc.) — *vi* : moverse, agitarse

stir[2] *n* **1** MOTION : movimiento *m* **2** COMMOTION : revuelo *m*

stirrup ['stərəp, 'stɪr-] *n* : estribo *m*

stitch[1] ['stɪtʃ] *vt* : coser, bordar (para decorar) — *vi* : coser

stitch[2] *n* **1** : puntada *f* **2** TWINGE : punzada *f*, puntada *f*

stock[1] ['stɑk] *vt* : surtir, abastecer, vender — *vi* **to stock up** : abastecerse

stock[2] *n* **1** SUPPLY : reserva *f*, existencias *fpl* (en comercio) ⟨to be out of stock : estar agotadas las existencias⟩ **2** SECURITIES : acciones *fpl*, valores *mpl* **3** LIVESTOCK : ganado *m* **4** ANCESTRY : linaje *m*, estirpe *f* **5** BROTH : caldo *m* **6 to take stock** : evaluar

stockade [stɑ'keɪd] *n* : estacada *f*

stockbroker ['stɑk,bro:kər] *n* : corredor *m*, -dora *f* de bolsa

stockholder ['stɑk,ho:ldər] *n* : accionista *mf*

stocking ['stɑkɪŋ] *n* : media *f* ⟨a pair of stockings : unas medias⟩

stock market *n* : bolsa *f*

stockpile[1] ['stɑk,paɪl] *vt* **-piled; -piling** : acumular, almacenar

stockpile[2] *n* : reservas *fpl*

stocky ['stɑki] *adj* **stockier; -est** : robusto, fornido

stockyard ['stɑk,jɑrd] *n* : corral *m*

stodgy ['stɑdʒi] *adj* **stodgier; -est 1** DULL : aburrido, pesado **2** OLD-FASHIONED : anticuado

stoic[1] ['sto:ɪk] *or* **stoical** [-ɪkəl] *adj* : estoico — **stoically** [-ɪkli] *adv*

stoic[2] *n* : estoico *m*, -ca *f*

stoicism ['sto:ə,sɪzəm] *n* : estoicismo *m*

stoke ['sto:k] *vt* **stoked; stoking** : atizar (un fuego), echarle carbón a (un horno)

stole[1] → **steal**

stole[2] ['sto:l] *n* : estola *f*

stolen → **steal**

stolid ['stɑlɪd] *adj* : impasible, imperturbable — **stolidly** *adv*

stomach[1] ['stʌmɪk] *vt* : aguantar, soportar

stomach[2] *n* **1** : estómago *m* **2** BELLY : vientre *m*, barriga *f*, panza *f* **3** DESIRE : ganas *fpl* ⟨he had no stomach for a fight : no quería pelea⟩

stomachache ['stʌmɪk,eɪk] *n* : dolor *m* de estómago

stomp ['stɑmp, 'stɔmp] *vt* : pisotear — *vi* : pisar fuerte

stone[1] ['sto:n] *vt* **stoned; stoning** : apedrear, lapidar

stone[2] *n* **1** : piedra *f* **2** PIT : hueso *m*, pepa *f* (de una fruta)

Stone Age *n* : Edad *f* de Piedra

stony ['sto:ni] *adj* **stonier; -est 1** ROCKY : pedregoso **2** UNFEELING : insensible, frío ⟨a stony stare : una mirada glacial⟩

stood → **stand**

stool ['stu:l] *n* **1** SEAT : taburete *m*, banco *m* **2** FOOTSTOOL : escabel *m* **3** FECES : deposición *f* de heces

stoop¹ ['stu:p] *vi* **1** CROUCH : agacharse **2 to stoop to** : rebajarse a

stoop² *n* **1** : espaldas *fpl* encorvadas ⟨to have a stoop : ser encorvado⟩ **2** : entrada *f* (de una casa)

stop¹ ['stɑp] *v* **stopped; stopping** *vt* **1** PLUG : tapar **2** PREVENT : impedir, evitar ⟨she stopped me from leaving : me impidió que saliera⟩ **3** HALT : parar, detener **4** CEASE : dejar de ⟨he stopped talking : dejó de hablar⟩ — *vi* **1** HALT : detenerse, parar **2** CEASE : cesar, terminar ⟨the rain won't stop : no deja de llover⟩ **3** STAY : quedarse ⟨she stopped with friends : se quedó en casa de unos amigos⟩ **4 to stop by** : visitar

stop² *n* **1** STOPPER : tapón *m* **2** HALT : parada *f*, alto *m* ⟨to come to a stop : pararse, detenerse⟩ ⟨to put a stop to : poner fin a⟩ **3** : parada *f* ⟨bus stop : parada de autobús⟩

stopgap ['stɑp,gæp] *n* : arreglo *m* provisorio

stoplight ['stɑp,laɪt] *n* : semáforo *m*

stoppage ['stɑpɪdʒ] *n* : acto *m* de parar ⟨a work stoppage : un paro⟩

stopper ['stɑpər] *n* : tapón *m*

storage ['storɪdʒ] *n* : almacenamiento *m*, almacenaje *m*

storage battery *n* : acumulador *m*

store¹ ['stor] *vt* **stored; storing** : guardar, almacenar

store² *n* **1** RESERVE, SUPPLY : reserva *f* **2** SHOP : tienda *f* ⟨grocery store : tienda de comestibles⟩

storehouse ['stor,haʊs] *n* : almacén *m*, depósito *m*

storekeeper ['stor,ki:pər] *n* : tendero *m*, -ra *f*

storeroom ['stor,ru:m, -,rʊm] *n* : almacén *m*, depósito *m*

stork ['stork] *n* : cigüeña *f*

storm¹ ['storm] *vi* **1** : llover o nevar tormentosamente **2** RAGE : ponerse furioso, vociferar **3 to storm out** : salir echando pestes — *vt* ATTACK : asaltar

storm² *n* **1** : tormenta *f*, tempestad *f* **2** UPROAR : alboroto *m*, revuelo *m*, escándalo *m* ⟨a storm of abuse : un torrente de abusos⟩

stormy ['stormi] *adj* **stormier; -est** : tormentoso

story ['stori] *n, pl* **stories 1** NARRATIVE : cuento *m*, relato *m* **2** ACCOUNT : historia *f*, relato *m* **3** : piso *m*, planta *f* (de un edificio) ⟨first story : planta baja⟩

stout ['staʊt] *adj* **1** FIRM, RESOLUTE : firme, resuelto **2** STURDY : fuerte, robusto, sólido **3** FAT : corpulento, gordo

stove¹ ['sto:v] *n* : cocina *f* (para cocinar), estufa *f* (para calentar)

stove² → **stave**¹

stow ['sto:] *vt* **1** STORE : poner, meter, guardar **2** LOAD : cargar — *vi* **to stow away** : viajar de polizón

stowaway ['sto:ə,weɪ] *n* : polizón *m*

straddle ['strædəl] *vt* **-dled; -dling** : sentarse a horcajadas sobre

straggle ['strægəl] *vi* **-gled; -gling** : rezagarse, quedarse atrás

straggler ['strægələr] *n* : rezagado *m*, -da *f*

straight¹ ['streɪt] *adv* **1** : derecho, directamente ⟨go straight, then turn right : sigue derecho, luego gira a la derecha⟩ **2** HONESTLY : honestamente ⟨to go straight : enmendarse⟩ **3** CLEARLY : con claridad **4** FRANKLY : francamente, con franqueza

straight² *adj* **1** : recto (dícese de las líneas, etc.), derecho (dícese de algo vertical), lacio (dícese del pelo) **2** HONEST, JUST : honesto, justo **3** NEAT, ORDERLY : arreglado, ordenado

straighten ['streɪtən] *vt* **1** : enderezar, poner derecho **2 to straighten up** : arreglar, ordenar ⟨he straightened up the house : arregló la casa⟩

straightforward [streɪt'forwərd] *adj* **1** FRANK : franco, sincero **2** CLEAR, PRECISE : puro, simple, claro

straightway ['streɪt'weɪ, -,weɪ] *adv* : inmediatamente

strain¹ ['streɪn] *vt* **1** EXERT : forzar (la vista, la voz) ⟨to strain oneself : hacer un gran esfuerzo⟩ **2** FILTER : colar, filtrar **3** INJURE : lastimarse, hacerse daño en ⟨to strain a muscle : sufrir un esguince⟩

strain² *n* **1** LINEAGE : linaje *m*, abolengo *m* **2** STREAK, TRACE : veta *f* **3** VARIETY : tipo *m*, variedad *f* **4** STRESS : tensión *f*, presión *f* **5** SPRAIN : esguince *m*, torcedura *f* (del tobillo, etc.) **6 strains** *npl* TUNE : melodía *f*, acordes *mpl*, compases *fpl*

strainer ['streɪnər] *n* : colador *m*

strait ['streɪt] *n* **1** : estrecho *m* **2 straits** *npl* DISTRESS : aprietos *mpl*, apuros *mpl* ⟨in dire straits : en serios aprietos⟩

straitened ['streɪtənd] *adj* **in straitened circumstances** : en apuros económicos

strand¹ ['strænd] *vt* **1** : varar **2 to be left stranded** : quedar(se) varado, quedar colgado ⟨they left me stranded : me dejaron abandonado⟩

strand² *n* **1** : hebra *f* (de hilo, etc.) ⟨a strand of hair : un pelo⟩ **2** BEACH : playa *f*

strange ['streɪndʒ] *adj* **stranger; -est 1** QUEER, UNUSUAL : extraño, raro **2** UNFAMILIAR : desconocido, nuevo

strangely ['streɪndʒli] *adv* ODDLY : de manera extraña ⟨to behave strangely : portarse de una manera rara⟩ ⟨strangely, he didn't call : curiosamente, no llamó⟩

strangeness ['streɪndʒnəs] *n* **1** ODD-
NESS : rareza *f* **2** UNFAMILIARITY : lo
desconocido

stranger ['streɪndʒər] *n* : desconocido *m*,
-da *f*; extraño *m*, -ña *f*

strangle ['stræŋgəl] *vt* **-gled; -gling** : estrangular

strangler ['stræŋglər] *n* : estrangulador
m, -dora *f*

strap[1] ['stræp] *vt* **strapped; strapping 1**
FASTEN : sujetar con una correa **2**
FLOG : azotar (con una correa)

strap[2] *n* **1** : correa *f* **2 shoulder strap**
: tirante *m*

strapless ['stræpləs] *n* : sin tirantes

strapping ['stræpɪŋ] *adj* : robusto,
fornido

stratagem ['stræt̬ədʒəm, -ˌdʒɛm] *n* : estratagema *f*, artimaña *f*

strategic [strə'ti:dʒɪk] *adj* : estratégico

strategist ['stræt̬ədʒɪst] *n* : estratega *mf*

strategy ['stræt̬ədʒi] *n, pl* **-gies** : estrategia *f*

stratified ['stræt̬əˌfaɪd] *adj* : estratificado

stratosphere ['stræt̬əˌsfɪr] *n* : estratosfera *f*

stratospheric [ˌstræt̬ə'sfɪrɪk, -'sfɛr-] *adj*
: estratosférico

stratum ['streɪt̬əm, 'stræ-] *n, pl* **strata**
[-t̬ə] : estrato *m*, capa *f*

straw *n* **1** : paja *f* ⟨the last straw : el col-
mo⟩ **2** *or* **drinking straw** : pajita *f*,
popote *m* Mex

strawberry ['strɔˌbɛri] *n, pl* **-ries** : fresa
f

stray[1] ['streɪ] *vi* **1** WANDER : alejarse, extraviarse ⟨the cattle strayed away : el
ganado se descarrió⟩ **2** DIGRESS
: desviarse, divagar

stray[2] *adj* : perdido, callejero (dícese de
un perro o un gato), descarriado
(dícese del ganado)

stray[3] *n* : animal *m* perdido, animal *m*
callejero

streak[1] ['stri:k] *vt* : hacer rayas en ⟨blue
streaked with grey : azul veteado con
gris⟩ — *vi* : ir como una flecha

streak[2] *n* **1** : raya *f*, veta *f* (en mármol,
queso, etc.), mechón *m* (en el pelo) **2**
: rayo *m* (de luz) **3** TRACE : veta *f* **4**
: racha *f* ⟨a streak of luck : una racha
de suerte⟩

stream[1] ['stri:m] *vi* : correr, salir a chorros ⟨tears streamed from his eyes : las
lágrimas brotaban de sus ojos⟩ — *vt*
: derramar, dejar correr ⟨to stream
blood : derramar sangre⟩

stream[2] *n* **1** BROOK : arroyo *m*, riachuelo *m* **2** RIVER : río *m* **3** FLOW
: corriente *f*, chorro *m*

streamer ['stri:mər] *n* **1** PENNANT : banderín *m* **2** RIBBON : serpentina *f* (de papel), cinta *f* (de tela)

streamlined ['stri:mˌlaɪnd] *adj* **1**
: aerodinámico (dícese de los automóviles, etc.) **2** EFFICIENT : eficiente, racionalizado

street ['stri:t] *n* : calle *f*

streetcar ['stri:tˌkɑr] *n* : tranvía *m*

strength ['strɛŋkθ] *n* **1** POWER : fuerza
f **2** SOLIDITY, TOUGHNESS : solidez *f*,
resistencia *f*, dureza *f* **3** INTENSITY : intensidad *f* (de emociones, etc.), lo
fuerte (de un sabor, etc.) **4** : punto *m*
fuerte ⟨strengths and weaknesses : vir-
tudes y defectos⟩ **5** NUMBER : número
m, complemento *m* ⟨in full strength
: en gran número⟩

strengthen ['strɛŋkθən] *vt* **1** : fortalecer
(los músculos, el espíritu, etc.) **2** RE-
INFORCE : reforzar **3** INTENSIFY : intensificar, redoblar (esfuerzos, etc.) —
vi **1** : fortalecerse, hacerse más fuerte
2 INTENSIFY : intensificarse

strenuous ['strɛnjuəs] *adj* **1** VIGOROUS
: vigoroso, enérgico **2** ARDUOUS
: duro, riguroso

strenuously ['strɛnjuəsli] *adv* : vigorosamente, duro

stress[1] ['strɛs] *vt* **1** : someter a tensión
(física) **2** EMPHASIZE : enfatizar, recalcar **3 to stress out** : estresar

stress[2] *n* **1** : tensión *f* (en un material)
2 EMPHASIS : énfasis *m*, acento *m* (en
lingüística) **3** TENSION : tensión *f*
(nerviosa), estrés *m*

stressful ['strɛsfəl] *adj* : estresante

stretch[1] ['strɛtʃ] *vt* **1** EXTEND : estirar,
extender, desplegar (alas) **2 to stretch
the truth** : forzar la verdad, exagerar
— *vi* : estirarse

stretch[2] *n* **1** STRETCHING : extensión *f*,
estiramiento *m* (de músculos) **2** ELAS-
TICITY : elasticidad *f* **3** EXPANSE
: tramo *m*, trecho *m* ⟨the home stretch
: la recta final⟩ **4** PERIOD : período *m*
(de tiempo)

stretcher ['strɛtʃər] *n* : camilla *f*

strew ['stru:] *vt* **strewed; strewed** *or*
strewn ['stru:n]; **strewing 1** SCATTER
: esparcir (semillas, etc.), desparramar
(papeles, etc.) **2 to strew with** : cubrir
de

stricken ['strɪkən] *adj* **stricken with**
: aquejado de (una enfermedad), afligido por (tristeza, etc.)

strict ['strɪkt] *adj* : estricto — **strictly**
adv

strictness ['strɪktnəs] *n* : severidad *f*, lo
estricto

stricture ['strɪktʃər] *n* : crítica *f*, censura
f

stride[1] ['straɪd] *vi* **strode** ['stro:d]; **strid-
den** ['strɪdən]; **striding** : ir dando tran-
cos, ir dando zancadas

stride[2] *n* : tranco *m*, zancada *f*

strident ['straɪdənt] *adj* : estridente

strife ['straɪf] *n* : conflictos *mpl*, disensión *f*

strike[1] ['straɪk] *v* **struck** ['strʌk]; **striking** *vt* **1** HIT : golpear (a una persona)
⟨to strike a blow : pegar un golpe⟩ **2**
DELETE : suprimir, tachar **3** COIN,
MINT : acuñar (monedas) **4** : dar (la
hora) **5** AFFLICT : sobrevenir ⟨he was
stricken with a fever : le sobrevino una

fiebre⟩ **6** IMPRESS : impresionar, parecer ⟨her voice struck me : su voz me impresionó⟩ ⟨it struck him as funny : le pareció chistoso⟩ **7** : encender (un fósforo) **8** FIND : descubrir (oro, petróleo) **9** ADOPT : adoptar (una pose, etc.) — *vi* **1** HIT : golpear ⟨to strike against : chocar contra⟩ **2** ATTACK : atacar **3** : declararse en huelga

strike² *n* **1** BLOW : golpe *m* **2** : huelga *f*, paro *m* ⟨to be on strike : estar en huelga⟩ **3** ATTACK : ataque *m*

strikebreaker ['straɪk,breɪkər] *n* : rompehuelgas *mf*, esquirol *mf*

strike out *vi* **1** HEAD : salir (para) **2** : ser ponchado (en béisbol) ⟨the batter struck out : poncharon al bateador⟩

striker ['straɪkər] *n* : huelguista *mf*

strike up *vt* START : entablar, empezar

striking ['straɪkɪŋ] *adj* : notable, sorprendente, llamativo ⟨a striking beauty : una belleza imponente⟩ — **strikingly** *adv*

string¹ ['strɪŋ] *vt* **strung** ['strʌŋ]; **stringing** **1** THREAD : ensartar ⟨to string beads : ensartar cuentas⟩ **2** HANG : colgar (con un cordel)

string² *n* **1** : cordel *m*, cuerda *f* **2** SERIES : serie *f*, sarta *f* (de insultos, etc.) **3 strings** *npl* : cuerdas *fpl* (en música)

string bean *n* : judía *f*, ejote *m Mex*

stringent ['strɪndʒənt] *adj* : estricto, severo

stringy ['strɪŋi] *adj* **stringier; -est** : fibroso

strip¹ ['strɪp] *v* **stripped; stripping** *vt* : quitar (ropa, pintura, etc.), desnudar, despojar — *vi* UNDRESS : desnudarse

strip² *n* : tira *f* ⟨a strip of land : una faja⟩

stripe¹ ['straɪp] *vt* **striped** ['straɪpt]; **striping** : marcar con rayas o listas

stripe² *n* **1** : raya *f*, lista *f* **2** BAND : franja *f*

striped ['straɪpt, 'straɪpəd] *adj* : a rayas, de rayas, rayado, listado

strive ['straɪv] *vi* **strove** ['stroːv]; **striven** ['strɪvən] *or* **strived; striving 1 strive for** : luchar por lograr **2 to strive to** : esforzarse por

strobe ['stroːb] *or* **strobe light** *n* : luz *f* estroboscópica

strode → **stride**

stroke¹ ['stroːk] *vt* **stroked; stroking** : acariciar

stroke² *n* : golpe *m* ⟨a stroke of luck : un golpe de suerte⟩

stroll¹ ['stroːl] *vi* : pasear, pasearse, dar un paseo

stroll² *n* : paseo *m*

stroller ['stroːlər] *n* : cochecito *m* (para niños)

strong ['strɔŋ] *adj* **1** : fuerte **2** HEALTHY : sano **3** ZEALOUS : ferviente

stronghold ['strɔŋ,hoːld] *n* : fortaleza *f*, fuerte *m*, bastión *m* ⟨a cultural stronghold : un baluarte de la cultura⟩

strongly ['strɔŋli] *adv* **1** POWERFULLY : fuerte, con fuerza **2** STURDILY

: fuertemente, sólidamente **3** INTENSELY : intensamente, profundamente **4** WHOLEHEARTEDLY : totalmente

struck → **strike¹**

structural ['strʌktʃərəl] *adj* : estructural

structure¹ ['strʌktʃər] *vt* **-tured; -turing** : estructurar

structure² *n* **1** BUILDING : construcción *f* **2** ARRANGEMENT, FRAMEWORK : estructura *f*

struggle¹ ['strʌgəl] *vi* **-gled; -gling 1** CONTEND : forcejear (físicamente), luchar, contender **2** : hacer con dificultad ⟨she struggled forward : avanzó con dificultad⟩

struggle² *n* : lucha *f*, pelea *f* (física)

strum ['strʌm] *vt* **strummed; strumming** : rasguear

strung → **string¹**

strut¹ ['strʌt] *vi* **strutted; strutting** : pavonearse

strut² *n* **1** : pavoneo *m* ⟨he walked with a strut : se pavoneaba⟩ **2** : puntal *m* (en construcción, etc.)

strychnine ['strɪk,naɪn, -nən, -,niːn] *n* : estricnina *f*

stub¹ ['stʌb] *vt* **stubbed; stubbing 1 to stub one's toe** : darse en el dedo (del pie) **2 to stub out** : apagarse

stub² *n* : colilla *f* (de un cigarrillo), cabo *m* (de un lápiz, etc.), talón *m* (de un cheque)

stubble ['stʌbəl] *n* **1** : rastrojo *m* (de plantas) **2** BEARD : barba *f*

stubborn ['stʌbərn] *adj* **1** OBSTINATE : terco, obstinado, empecinado **2** PERSISTENT : pertinaz, persistente — **stubbornly** *adv*

stubbornness ['stʌbərnnəs] *n* **1** OBSTINACY : terquedad *f*, obstinación *f* **2** PERSISTENCE : persistencia *f*

stubby ['stʌbi] *adj* **stubbier; -est** : corto y grueso ⟨stubby fingers : dedos regordetes⟩

stucco ['stʌkoː] *n, pl* **stuccos** *or* **stuccoes** : estuco *m*

stuck → **stick¹**

stuck–up ['stʌk'ʌp] *adj* : engreído, creído *fam*

stud¹ ['stʌd] *vt* **studded; studding** : tachonar, salpicar

stud² *n* **1** *or* **stud horse** : semental *m* **2** : montante *m* (en construcción) **3** HOBNAIL : tachuela *f*, tachón *m*

student ['stuːdənt, 'stjuː-] *n* : estudiante *mf*; alumno *m*, -na *f* (de un colegio)

studied ['stʌdid] *adj* : intencionado, premeditado

studio ['stuːdi,oː, 'stjuː-] *n, pl* **studios** : estudio *m*

studious ['stuːdiəs, 'stjuː-] *adj* : estudioso — **studiously** *adv*

study¹ ['stʌdi] *v* **studied; studying 1** : estudiar **2** EXAMINE : examinar, estudiar

study² *n, pl* **studies 1** STUDYING : estudio *m* **2** OFFICE : estudio *m*, gabinete *m* (en una casa) **3** RESEARCH : investigación *f*, estudio *m*

stuff¹ [ˈstʌf] *vt* : rellenar, llenar, atiborrar ⟨a stuffed toy : un juguete de peluche⟩

stuff² *n* **1** POSSESSIONS : cosas *fpl* **2** ESSENCE : esencia *f* **3** SUBSTANCE : cosa *f*, cosas *fpl* ⟨some sticky stuff : una cosa pegajosa⟩ ⟨she knows her stuff : es experta⟩

stuffing [ˈstʌfɪŋ] *n* : relleno *m*

stuffy [ˈstʌfi] *adj* **stuffier; -est 1** CLOSE : viciado, cargado ⟨a stuffy room : una sala mal ventilada⟩ ⟨stuffy weather : tiempo bochornoso⟩ **2** : tapado (dícese de la nariz) **3** STODGY : pesado, aburrido

stumble¹ [ˈstʌmbəl] *vi* **-bled; -bling 1** TRIP : tropezar, dar un traspié **2** FLOUNDER : quedarse sin saber qué hacer o decir **3 to stumble across** *or* **to stumble upon** : dar con, tropezar con

stumble² *n* : tropezón *m*, traspié *m*

stump¹ [ˈstʌmp] *vt* : dejar perplejo ⟨to be stumped : no tener respuesta⟩

stump² *n* **1** : muñón *m* (de un brazo o una pierna) **2** *or* **tree stump** : cepa *f*, tocón *m* **3** STUB : cabo *m*

stun [ˈstʌn] *vt* **stunned; stunning 1** : aturdir (con un golpe) **2** ASTONISH, SHOCK : dejar estupefacto, dejar atónito, aturdir

stung → **sting¹**

stunk → **stink¹**

stunning [ˈstʌnɪŋ] *adj* **1** ASTONISHING : asombroso, pasmoso, increíble **2** STRIKING : imponente, impresionante (dícese de la belleza)

stunt¹ [ˈstʌnt] *vt* : atrofiar

stunt² *n* : proeza *f* (acrobática)

stupefy [ˈstuːpəˌfaɪ, ˈstjuː-] *vt* **-fied; -fying 1** : aturdir, atontar (con drogas, etc.) **2** AMAZE : dejar estupefacto, dejar atónito

stupendous [stʊˈpɛndəs, stjʊ-] *adj* **1** MARVELOUS : estupendo, maravilloso **2** TREMENDOUS : tremendo — **stupendously** *adv*

stupid [ˈstuːpəd, ˈstjuː-] *adj* **1** IDIOTIC, SILLY : tonto, bobo, estúpido **2** DULL, OBTUSE : lento, torpe, lerdo

stupidity [stʊˈpɪdəti, stjʊ-] *n* : tontería *f*, estupidez *f*

stupidly [ˈstuːpədli, ˈstjuː-] *adv* **1** IDIOTICALLY : estúpidamente, tontamente **2** DENSELY : torpemente

stupor [ˈstuːpər, ˈstjuː-] *n* : estupor *m*

sturdily [ˈstərdəli] *adv* : sólidamente

sturdiness [ˈstərdinəs] *n* : solidez *f* (de muebles, etc.), robustez *f* (de una persona)

sturdy [ˈstərdi] *adj* **sturdier; -est** : fuerte, robusto, sólido

sturgeon [ˈstərdʒən] *n* : esturión *m*

stutter¹ [ˈstʌtər] *vi* : tartamudear

stutter² *n* STAMMER : tartamudeo *m*

sty [ˈstaɪ] *n* **1** *pl* **sties** PIGPEN : chiquero *m*, pocilga *f* **2** *pl* **sties** *or* **styes** : orzuelo *m* (en el ojo)

style¹ [ˈstaɪl] *vt* **styled; styling 1** NAME : llamar **2** : peinar (pelo), diseñar (vestidos, etc.) ⟨carefully styled prose : prosa escrita con gran esmero⟩

style² *n* **1** : estilo *m* ⟨that's just his style : él es así⟩ ⟨to live in style : vivir a lo grande⟩ **2** FASHION : moda *f*

stylish [ˈstaɪlɪʃ] *adj* : de moda, elegante, chic

stylishly [ˈstaɪlɪʃli] *adv* : con estilo

stylishness [ˈstaɪlɪʃnəs] *n* : estilo *m*

stylist [ˈstaɪlɪst] *n* : estilista *mf*

stylize [ˈstaɪˌlaɪz, ˈstaɪə-] *vt* : estilizar

stylus [ˈstaɪləs] *n, pl* **styli** [ˈstaɪˌlaɪ] **1** PEN : estilo *m* **2** NEEDLE : aguja *f* (de un tocadiscos)

stymie [ˈstaɪmi] *vt* **-mied; -mieing** : obstaculizar

suave [ˈswɑv] *adj* : fino, urbano

sub¹ [ˈsʌb] *vi* **subbed; subbing** → **substitute¹**

sub² *n* **1** → **substitute² 2** → **submarine**

subcommittee [ˈsʌbkəˌmɪti] *n* : subcomité *m*

subconscious¹ [səbˈkɑntʃəs] *adj* : subconsciente — **subconsciously** *adv*

subconscious² *n* : subconsciente *m*

subcontract [ˌsʌbˈkɑnˌtrækt] *vt* : subcontratar

subculture [ˈsʌbˌkʌltʃər] *n* : subcultura *f*

subdivide [ˌsʌbdəˈvaɪd, ˈsʌbdəˌvaɪd] *vt* **-vided; -viding** : subdividir

subdivision [ˈsʌbdəˌvɪʒən] *n* : subdivisión *f*

subdue [səbˈduː, -ˈdjuː] *vt* **-dued; -duing 1** OVERCOME : sojuzgar (a un enemigo), vencer, superar **2** CONTROL : dominar **3** SOFTEN : suavizar, atenuar (luz, etc.), moderar (lenguaje)

subgroup [ˈsʌbˌgruːp] *n* : subgrupo *m*

subhead [ˈsʌbˌhɛd] *or* **subheading** [-ˌhɛdɪŋ] *n* : subtítulo *m*

subject¹ [səbˈdʒɛkt] *vt* **1** CONTROL, DOMINATE : controlar, dominar **2** : someter ⟨they subjected him to pressure : lo sometieron a presiones⟩

subject² [ˈsʌbdʒɪkt] *adj* **1** : subyugado, sometido ⟨a subject nation : una nación subyugada⟩ **2** PRONE : sujeto, propenso ⟨subject to colds : sujeto a resfriarse⟩ **3 subject to** : sujeto a ⟨subject to congressional approval : sujeto a la aprobación del congreso⟩

subject³ [ˈsʌbdʒɪkt] *n* **1** : súbdito *m*, -ta *f* (de un gobierno) **2** TOPIC : tema *m* **3** : sujeto *m* (en gramática)

subjection [səbˈdʒɛkʃən] *n* : sometimiento *m*

subjective [səbˈdʒɛktɪv] *adj* : subjetivo — **subjectively** *adv*

subjectivity [ˌsʌbˌdʒɛkˈtɪvəti] *n* : subjetividad *f*

subjugate [ˈsʌbdʒɪˌgeɪt] *vt* **-gated; -gating** : subyugar, someter, sojuzgar

subjunctive [səb'dʒʌŋktɪv] *n* : subjuntivo *m* — **subjunctive** *adj*

sublet ['sʌb,lɛt] *vt* **-let; -letting** : subarrendar

sublime [sə'blaɪm] *adj* : sublime

sublimely [sə'blaɪmli] *adv* **1** : de manera sublime **2** UTTERLY : absolutamente, completamente

submarine[1] ['sʌbmə,riːn, ,sʌbmə'-] *adj* : submarino

submarine[2] *n* : submarino *m*

submerge [səb'mərdʒ] *v* **-merged; -merging** *vt* : sumergir — *vi* : sumergirse

submission [səb'mɪʃən] *n* **1** YIELDING : sumisión *f* **2** PRESENTATION : presentación *f*

submissive [səb'mɪsɪv] *adj* : sumiso, dócil

submit [səb'mɪt] *v* **-mitted; -mitting** *vi* YIELD : rendirse ⟨to submit to : someterse a⟩ — *vt* PRESENT : presentar

subnormal [,sʌb'nɔrməl] *adj* : por debajo de lo normal

subordinate[1] [sə'bɔrdən,eɪt] *vt* **-nated; -nating** : subordinar

subordinate[2] [sə'bɔrdənət] *adj* : subordinado ⟨a subordinate clause : una oración subordinada⟩

subordinate[3] *n* : subordinado *m*, -da *f*; subalterno *m*, -na *f*

subordination [sə,bɔrdən'eɪʃən] *n* : subordinación *f*

subpoena[1] [sə'piːnə] *vt* **-naed; -naing** : citar

subpoena[2] *n* : citación *f*, citatorio *m*

subscribe [səb'skraɪb] *vi* **-scribed; -scribing 1** : suscribirse (a una revista, etc.) **2 to subscribe to** : suscribir (una opinión, etc.), estar de acuerdo con

subscriber [səb'skraɪbər] *n* : suscriptor *m*, -tora *f* (de una revista, etc.); abonado *m*, -da *f* (de un servicio)

subscription [səb'skrɪpʃən] *n* : suscripción *f*

subsequent ['sʌbsɪkwənt, -sə,kwɛnt] *adj* : subsiguiente ⟨subsequent to : posterior a⟩

subsequently ['sʌb,sɪkwəntli, -kwənt-] *adv* : posteriormente

subservient [səb'sərviənt] *adj* : servil

subside [səb'saɪd] *vi* **-sided; -siding 1** SINK : hundirse, descender **2** ABATE : calmarse (dícese de las emociones), amainar (dícese del viento, etc.)

subsidiary[1] [səb'sɪdi,ɛri] *adj* : secundario

subsidiary[2] *n, pl* **-ries** : filial *f*, subsidiaria *f*

subsidize ['sʌbsə,daɪz] *vt* **-dized; -dizing** : subvencionar, subsidiar

subsidy ['sʌbsədi] *n, pl* **-dies** : subvención *f*, subsidio *m*

subsist [səb'sɪst] *vi* : subsistir, mantenerse, vivir

subsistence [səb'sɪstənts] *n* : subsistencia *f*

substance ['sʌbstənts] *n* **1** ESSENCE : sustancia *f*, esencia *f* **2** : sustancia *f* ⟨a toxic substance : una sustancia tóxica⟩ **3** WEALTH : riqueza *f* ⟨a woman of substance : una mujer acaudalada⟩

substandard [,sʌb'stændərd] *adj* : inferior, deficiente

substantial [səb'stæntʃəl] *adj* **1** ABUNDANT : sustancioso ⟨a substantial meal : una comida sustanciosa⟩ **2** CONSIDERABLE : considerable, apreciable **3** SOLID, STURDY : sólido

substantially [səb'stæntʃəli] *adv* : considerablemente

substantiate [səb'stæntʃi,eɪt] *vt* **-ated; -ating** : confirmar, probar, justificar

substitute[1] ['sʌbstə,tuːt, -,tjuːt] *v* **-tuted; -tuting** *vt* : sustituir — *vi* **to substitute for** : sustituir

substitute[2] *n* **1** : sustituto *m*, -ta *f*; suplente *mf* (persona) **2** : sucedáneo *m* ⟨sugar substitute : sucedáneo de azúcar⟩

substitute teacher *n* : profesor *m*, -sora *f* suplente

substitution [,sʌbstə'tuːʃən, -'tjuː-] *n* : sustitución *f*

subterfuge ['sʌbtər,fjuːdʒ] *n* : subterfugio *m*

subterranean [,sʌbtə'reɪniən] *adj* : subterráneo

subtitle ['sʌb,taɪtəl] *n* : subtítulo *m*

subtle ['sʌtəl] *adj* **-tler; -tlest 1** DELICATE, ELUSIVE : sutil, delicado **2** CLEVER : sutil, ingenioso

subtlety ['sʌtəlti] *n, pl* **-ties** : sutileza *f*

subtly ['sʌtəli] *adv* : sutilmente

subtotal ['sʌb,toːtəl] *n* : subtotal *m*

subtract [səb'trækt] *vt* : restar, sustraer

subtraction [səb'trækʃən] *n* : resta *f*, sustracción *f*

suburb ['sʌ,bərb] *n* : municipio *m* periférico, suburbio *m*

suburban [sə'bərbən] *adj* : de las afueras (de una ciudad), suburbano

subversion [səb'vərʒən] *n* : subversión *f*

subversive [səb'vərsɪv] *adj* : subversivo

subway ['sʌb,weɪ] *n* : metro *m*, subterráneo *m Arg, Uru*

succeed [sək'siːd] *vt* FOLLOW : suceder a — *vi* : tener éxito (dícese de las personas), dar resultado (dícese de los planes, etc.) ⟨she succeeded in finishing : logró terminar⟩

success [sək'sɛs] *n* : éxito *m*

successful [sək'sɛsfəl] *adj* : exitoso, logrado — **successfully** *adv*

succession [sək'sɛʃən] *n* : sucesión *f* ⟨in succesion : sucesivamente⟩

successive [sək'sɛsɪv] *adj* : sucesivo, consecutivo — **successively** *adv*

successor [sək'sɛsər] *n* : sucesor *m*, -sora *f*

succinct [sək'sɪŋkt, sə'sɪŋkt] *adj* : sucinto — **succinctly** *adv*

succor[1] ['sʌkər] *vt* : socorrer

succor[2] *n* : socorro *m*

succotash [ˈsʌkəˌtæʃ] *n* : guiso *m* de maíz y frijoles

succulent¹ [ˈsʌkjələnt] *adj* : suculento, jugoso

succulent² *n* : suculenta *f* (planta)

succumb [səˈkʌm] *vi* : sucumbir

such¹ [ˈsʌtʃ] *adv* **1** SO : tan ⟨such tall buildings : edificios tan grandes⟩ **2** VERY : muy ⟨he's not in such good shape : anda un poco mal⟩ **3 such that** : de tal manera que

such² *adj* : tal ⟨there's no such thing : no existe tal cosa⟩ ⟨in such cases : en tales casos⟩ ⟨animals such as cows and sheep : animales como vacas y ovejas⟩

such³ *pron* **1** : tal ⟨such was the result : tal fue el resultado⟩ ⟨he's a child, and acts as such : es un niño, y se porta como tal⟩ **2** : algo o alguien semejante ⟨books, papers and such : libros, papeles y cosas por el estilo⟩

suck [ˈsʌk] *vi* **1** : chupar (por la boca), aspirar (dícese de las máquinas) **2** SUCKLE : mamar — *vt* : sorber (bebidas), chupar (dulces, etc.)

sucker [ˈsʌkər] *n* **1** : ventosa *f* (de un insecto, etc.) **2** : chupón *m* (de una planta) **3** → **lollipop 4** FOOL : tonto *m*, -ta *f*; idiota *mf*

suckle [ˈsʌkəl] *v* **-led; -ling** *vt* : amamantar — *vi* : mamar

suckling [ˈsʌklɪŋ] *n* : lactante *mf*

sucrose [ˈsuːˌkroːs, -ˌkroːz] *n* : sacarosa *f*

suction [ˈsʌkʃən] *n* : succión *f*

Sudanese [ˌsuːdənˈiːz, -ˈiːs] *n* : sudanés *m*, -nesa *f* — **Sudanese** *adj*

sudden [ˈsʌdən] *adj* **1** : repentino, súbito ⟨all of a sudden : de pronto, de repente⟩ **2** UNEXPECTED : inesperado, improviso **3** ABRUPT, HASTY : precipitado, brusco

suddenly [ˈsʌdənli] *adv* **1** : de repente, de pronto **2** ABRUPTLY : bruscamente

suddenness [ˈsʌdənnəs] *n* **1** : lo repentino **2** ABRUPTNESS : brusquedad *f* **3** HASTINESS : lo precipitado

suds [ˈsʌdz] *npl* : espuma *f* (de jabón)

sue [ˈsuː] *v* **sued; suing** *vt* : demandar — *vi* **to sue for** : demandar por (daños, etc.)

suede [ˈsweɪd] *n* : ante *m*, gamuza *f*

suet [ˈsuːət] *n* : sebo *m*

suffer [ˈsʌfər] *vi* : sufrir — *vt* **1** : sufrir, padecer (dolores, etc.) **2** PERMIT : permitir, dejar

sufferer [ˈsʌfərər] *n* : persona que padece (una enfermedad, etc.)

suffering [ˈsʌfərɪŋ] *n* : sufrimiento *m*

suffice [səˈfaɪs] *vi* **-ficed; -ficing** : ser suficiente, bastar

sufficient [səˈfɪʃənt] *adj* : suficiente

sufficiently [səˈfɪʃəntli] *adv* : (lo) suficientemente, bastante

suffix [ˈsʌˌfɪks] *n* : sufijo *m*

suffocate [ˈsʌfəˌkeɪt] *v* **-cated; -cating** *vt* : asfixiar, ahogar — *vi* : asfixiarse, ahogarse

suffocation [ˌsʌfəˈkeɪʃən] *n* : asfixia *f*, ahogo *m*

suffrage [ˈsʌfrɪdʒ] *n* : sufragio *m*, derecho *m* al voto

suffuse [səˈfjuːz] *vt* **-fused; -fusing** : impregnar (de olores, etc.), bañar (de luz), teñir (de colores), llenar (de emociones)

sugar¹ [ˈʃʊgər] *vt* : azucarar

sugar² *n* : azúcar *mf*

sugarcane [ˈʃʊgərˌkeɪn] *n* : caña *f* de azúcar

sugary [ˈʃʊgəri] *adj* **1** : azucarado ⟨sugary desserts : postres azucarados⟩ **2** SACCHARINE : empalagoso

suggest [səgˈdʒest, sə-] *vt* **1** PROPOSE : sugerir **2** IMPLY : indicar, dar a entender

suggestible [səgˈdʒestəbəl, sə-] *adj* : influenciable

suggestion [səgˈdʒestʃən, sə-] *n* **1** PROPOSAL : sugerencia *f* **2** INDICATION : indicio *m* **3** INSINUATION : insinuación *f*

suggestive [səgˈdʒestɪv, sə-] *adj* : insinuante — **suggestively** *adv*

suicidal [ˌsuːəˈsaɪdəl] *adj* : suicida

suicide [ˈsuːəˌsaɪd] *n* **1** : suicidio *m* (acto) **2** : suicida *mf* (persona)

suit¹ [ˈsuːt] *vt* **1** ADAPT : adaptar **2** BEFIT : convenir a, ser apropiado a **3** BECOME : favorecer, quedarle bien (a alguien) ⟨the dress suits you : el vestido te queda bien⟩ **4** PLEASE : agradecer, satisfacer, convenirle bien (a alguien) ⟨does Friday suit you? : ¿le conviene el viernes?⟩ ⟨suit yourself! : ¡como quieras!⟩

suit² *n* **1** LAWSUIT : pleito *m*, litigio *m* **2** : traje *m* (ropa) **3** : palo *m* (de naipes)

suitability [ˌsuːtəˈbɪləti] *n* : idoneidad *f*, lo apropiado

suitable [ˈsuːtəbəl] *adj* : apropiado, idóneo — **suitably** [-bli] *adv*

suitcase [ˈsuːtˌkeɪs] *n* : maleta *f*, valija *f*, petaca *f* Mex

suite [ˈswiːt, *for 2 also* ˈsuːt] *n* **1** : suite *f* (de habitaciones) **2** SET : juego *m* (de muebles)

suitor [ˈsuːtər] *n* : pretendiente *m*

sulfur [ˈsʌlfər] *n* : azufre *m*

sulfuric acid [ˌsʌlˈfjʊrɪk] *adj* : ácido *m* sulfúrico

sulfurous [ˌsʌlˈfjʊrəs, ˈsʌlfərəs, ˈsʌlfjə-] *adj* : sulfuroso

sulk¹ [ˈsʌlk] *vi* : estar de mal humor, enfurruñarse *fam*

sulk² *n* : mal humor *m*

sulky [ˈsʌlki] *adj* **sulkier; -est** : malhumorado, taimado *Chile*

sullen [ˈsʌlən] *adj* **1** MOROSE : hosco, taciturno **2** DREARY : sombrío, deprimente

sullenly [ˈsʌlənli] *adv* **1** MOROSELY : hoscamente **2** GLOOMILY : sombríamente

sully [ˈsʌli] *vt* **sullied; sullying** : manchar, empañar

sultan ['sʌltən] *n* : sultán *m*

sultry ['sʌltri] *adj* **sultrier; -est 1** : bochornoso ⟨sultry weather : tiempo sofocante, tiempo bochornoso⟩ **2** SENSUAL : sensual, seductor

sum¹ ['sʌm] *vt* **summed; summing 1** : sumar (números) **2** → sum up

sum² *n* **1** AMOUNT : suma *f*, cantidad *f* **2** TOTAL : suma *f*, total *f* **3** : suma *f*, adición *f* (en matemáticas)

sumac ['ʃu:ˌmæk, 'su:-] *n* : zumaque *m*

summarize ['sʌməˌraɪz] *v* **-rized; -rizing** : resumir, compendiar

summary¹ ['sʌməri] *adj* **1** CONCISE : breve, conciso **2** IMMEDIATE : inmediato ⟨a summary dismissal : un despido inmediato⟩

summary² *n, pl* **-ries** : resumen *m*, compendio *m*

summer ['sʌmər] *n* : verano *m*

summery ['sʌməri] *adj* : veraniego

summit ['sʌmət] *n* **1** : cumbre *f*, cima *f* (de una montaña) **2** *or* **summit conference** : cumbre *f*

summon ['sʌmən] *vt* **1** CALL : convocar (una reunión, etc.), llamar (a una persona) **2** : citar (en derecho) **3 to summon up** : armarse de (valor, etc.) ⟨to summon up one's strength : reunir fuerzas⟩

summons ['sʌmənz] *n, pl* **summonses 1** SUBPOENA : citación *f*, citatorio *m* *Mex* **2** CALL : llamada *f*, llamamiento *m*

sumptuous ['sʌmptʃuəs] *adj* : suntuoso

sum up *vt* **1** SUMMARIZE : resumir **2** EVALUATE : evaluar — *vi* : recapitular

sun¹ ['sʌn] *vt* **sunned; sunning 1** : poner al sol **2 to sun oneself** : asolearse, tomar el sol

sun² *n* **1** : sol *m* **2** SUNSHINE : luz *f* del sol

sunbeam ['sʌnˌbi:m] *n* : rayo *m* de sol

sunblock ['sʌnˌblɑk] *n* : filtro *m* solar

sunburn¹ ['sʌnˌbərn] *vi* **-burned [-ˌbərnd]** *or* **-burnt [-ˌbərnt]; -burning** : quemarse por el sol

sunburn² ['sʌnˌbərn] *n* : quemadura *f* de sol

sundae ['sʌndi] *n* : sundae *m*

Sunday ['sʌnˌdeɪ, -di] *n* : domingo *m*

sundial ['sʌnˌdaɪl] *n* : reloj *m* de sol

sundown ['sʌnˌdaʊn] → sunset

sundries ['sʌndriz] *npl* : artículos *mpl* diversos

sundry ['sʌndri] *adj* : varios, diversos

sunflower ['sʌnˌflaʊər] *n* : girasol *m*, mirasol *m*

sung → sing

sunglasses ['sʌnˌglæsəz] *npl* : gafas *fpl* de sol, lentes *mpl* de sol

sunk → sink¹

sunken ['sʌŋkən] *adj* : hundido

sunlight ['sʌnˌlaɪt] *n* : sol *m*, luz *f* del sol

sunny ['sʌni] *adj* **sunnier; -est** : soleado

sunrise ['sʌnˌraɪz] *n* : salida *f* del sol

sunscreen ['sʌnˌskri:n] *n* : filtro *m* solar

sunset ['sʌnˌsɛt] *n* : puesta *f* del sol

sunshine ['sʌnˌʃaɪn] *n* : sol *m*, luz *f* del sol

sunspot ['sʌnˌspɑt] *n* : mancha *f* solar

sunstroke ['sʌnˌstro:k] *n* : insolación *f*

suntan ['sʌnˌtæn] *n* : bronceado *m*

sup ['sʌp] *vi* **supped; supping** : cenar

super ['su:pər] *adj* : súper ⟨super! : ¡fantástico!⟩

superabundance [ˌsu:pərə'bʌndənts] *n* : superabundancia *f*

superb [su'pərb] *adj* : magnífico, espléndido — **superbly** *adv*

supercilious [ˌsu:pər'sɪliəs] *adj* : altivo, altanero, desdeñoso

supercomputer ['su:pərkəmˌpju:tər] *n* : supercomputadora *f*

superficial [ˌsu:pər'fɪʃəl] *adj* : superficial — **superficially** *adv*

superfluous [su'pərfluəs] *adj* : superfluo

superhighway ['su:pərˌhaɪˌweɪ, ˌsu:pər'-] *n* : autopista *f*

superhuman [ˌsu:pər'hju:mən] *adj* **1** SUPERNATURAL : sobrenatural **2** HERCULEAN : sobrehumano

superimpose [ˌsu:pərɪm'po:z] *vt* **-posed; -posing** : superponer, sobreponer

superintend [ˌsu:pərɪn'tɛnd] *vt* : supervisar

superintendent [ˌsu:pərɪn'tɛndənt] *n* : portero *m*, -ra *f* (de un edificio); director *m*, -tora *f* (de una escuela, etc.); superintendente *mf* (de policía)

superior¹ [su'pɪriər] *adj* **1** BETTER : superior **2** HAUGHTY : altivo, altanero

superior² *n* : superior *m*

superiority [suˌpɪri'ɔrəti] *n, pl* **-ties** : superioridad *f*

superlative¹ [su'pərlətɪv] *adj* **1** : superlativo (en gramática) **2** SUPREME : supremo **3** EXCELLENT : excelente, excepcional

superlative² *n* : superlativo *m*

supermarket ['su:pərˌmɑrkət] *n* : supermercado *m*

supernatural [ˌsu:pər'næt͡ʃərəl] *adj* : sobrenatural

supernaturally [ˌsu:pər'næt͡ʃərəli] *adv* : de manera sobrenatural

superpower ['su:pərˌpaʊər] *n* : superpotencia *f*

supersede [ˌsu:pər'si:d] *vt* **-seded; -seding** : suplantar, reemplazar, sustituir

supersonic [ˌsu:pər'sɑnɪk] *adj* : supersónico

superstar ['su:pərˌstɑr] *n* : superestrella *f*

superstition [ˌsu:pər'stɪʃən] *n* : superstición *f*

superstitious [ˌsu:pər'stɪʃəs] *adj* : supersticioso

superstructure ['su:pərˌstrʌkt͡ʃər] *n* : superestructura *f*

supervise ['su:pərˌvaɪz] *vt* **-vised; -vising** : supervisar, dirigir

supervision [ˌsu:pər'vɪʒən] *n* : supervisión *f*, dirección *f*

supervisor ['su:pər,vaɪzər] *n* : supervi-sor *m*, -sora *f*

supervisory [,su:pər'vaɪzəri] *adj* : de su-pervisor

supine [su'paɪn] *adj* **1** : en decúbito supino, en decúbito dorsal **2** ABJECT, INDIFFERENT : indiferente, apático

supper ['sʌpər] *n* : cena *f*, comida *f*

supplant [sə'plænt] *vt* : suplantar

supple ['sʌpəl] *adj* **-pler; -plest** : flexi-ble

supplement[1] ['sʌplə,mɛnt] *vt* : comple-mentar, completar

supplement[2] ['sʌpləmənt] *n* **1** : com-plemento *m* ⟨dietary supplement : complemento alimenticio⟩ **2** : suple-mento *m* (de un libro o periódico)

supplementary [,sʌplə'mɛntəri] *adj* : suplementario

supplicate ['sʌplə,keɪt] *v* **-cated; -cating** *vi* : rezar — *vt* : suplicar

supplier [sə'plaɪər] *n* : proveedor *m*, -dora *f*; abastecedor *m*, -dora *f*

supply[1] [sə'plaɪ] *vt* **-plied; -plying** : sum-inistrar, proveer de, proporcionar

supply[2] *n, pl* **-plies 1** PROVISION : pro-visión *f*, suministro *m* ⟨supply and de-mand : la oferta y la demanda⟩ **2** STOCK : reserva *f*, existencias *fpl* (de un negocio) **3 supplies** *npl* PROVISIONS : provisiones *fpl*, víveres *mpl*, despensa *f*

support[1] [sə'port] *vt* **1** BACK : apoyar, respaldar **2** MAINTAIN : mantener, sostener, sustentar **3** PROP UP : sosten-er, apoyar, apuntalar, soportar

support[2] *n* **1** : apoyo *m* (moral), ayuda *f* (económica) **2** PROP : soporte *m*, apoyo *m*

supporter [sə'portər] *n* : partidario *m*, -ria *f*

supportive [sə'portɪv] *adj* : que apoya ⟨his family is very supportive : su fa-milia lo apoya mucho⟩

suppose [sə'po:z] *vt* **-posed; -posing 1** ASSUME : suponer, imaginarse **2** BE-LIEVE : suponer, creer **3 to be sup-posed to** : tener que, deber

supposed [sə'po:zd, -'po:zəd] *adj* : supuesto — **supposedly** [sə'po:zədli] *adv*

supposition [,sʌpə'zɪʃən] *n* : suposición *f*

suppository [sə'pɑzə,tori] *n, pl* **-ries** : supositorio *m*

suppress [sə'prɛs] *vt* **1** SUBDUE : sofo-car, suprimir, reprimir (una rebelión, etc.) **2** : suprimir, ocultar (informa-ción) **3** REPRESS : reprimir, contener ⟨to suppress a yawn : reprimir un bostezo⟩

suppression [sə'prɛʃən] *n* **1** SUBDUING : represión *f* **2** : supresión *f* (de infor-mación) **3** REPRESSION : represión *f*, inhibición *f*

supremacy [su'prɛməsi] *n, pl* **-cies** : su-premacía *f*

supreme [su'pri:m] *adj* : supremo

Supreme Being *n* : Ser *m* Supremo

supremely [su'pri:mli] *adv* **1** : totalmente, sumamente

surcharge ['sər,tʃɑrdʒ] *n* : recargo *m*

sure[1] ['ʃur] *adv* **1** ALL RIGHT : por supuesto, claro **2** (*used as an intensifi-er*) ⟨it sure is hot! : ¡hace tanto calor!⟩ ⟨she sure is pretty! : ¡qué linda es!⟩

sure[2] *adj* **surer; -est** : seguro ⟨to be sure about something : estar seguro de algo⟩ ⟨a sure sign : una clara señal⟩ ⟨for sure : seguro, con seguridad⟩

surely ['ʃurli] *adv* **1** CERTAINLY : segu-ramente **2** (*used as an intensifier*) ⟨you surely don't mean that! : ¡no me digas que estás hablando en serio!⟩

sureness ['ʃurnəs] *n* : certeza *f*, seguri-dad *f*

surety ['ʃurəti] *n, pl* **-ties** : fianza *f*, garantía *f*

surf ['sərf] *n* **1** WAVES : oleaje *m* **2** FOAM : espuma *f*

surface[1] ['sərfəs] *v* **-faced; -facing** *vi* : salir a la superficie — *vt* : revestir (una carretera)

surface[2] *n* **1** : superficie *f* **2 on the sur-face** : en apariencia

surfboard ['sərf,bord] *n* : tabla *f* de surf, tabla *f* de surfing

surfeit ['sərfət] *n* : exceso *m*

surfer ['sərfər] *n* : surfista *mf*

surfing ['sərfɪŋ] *n* : surf *m*, surfing *m*

surge[1] ['sərdʒ] *vi* **surged; surging 1** : hincharse (dícese del mar), levantarse (dícese de las olas) **2** SWARM : salir en tropel (dícese de la gente, etc.)

surge[2] *n* **1** : oleaje *m* (del mar), oleada *f* (de gente) **2** FLUSH : arranque *m*, arrebato *m* (de ira, etc.) **3** INCREASE : aumento *m* (súbito)

surgeon ['sərdʒən] *n* : cirujano *m*, -na *f*

surgery ['sərdʒəri] *n, pl* **-geries** : cirugía *f*

surgical ['sərdʒɪkəl] *adj* : quirúrgico — **surgically** [-kli] *adv*

surly ['sərli] *adj* **surlier; -est** : hosco, arisco

surmise[1] [sər'maɪz] *vt* **-mised; -mising** : conjeturar, suponer, concluir

surmise[2] *n* : conjetura *f*

surmount [sər'maunt] *vt* **1** OVERCOME : superar, vencer, salvar **2** CLIMB : es-calar **3** CAP, TOP : coronar

surname ['sər,neɪm] *n* : apellido *m*

surpass [sər'pæs] *vt* : superar, exceder, rebasar, sobrepasar

surplus ['sər,plʌs] *n* : excedente *m*, so-brante *m*, superávit *m* (de dinero)

surprise[1] [sə'praɪz, sər-] *vt* **-prised; -prising** : sorprender

surprise[2] *n* : sorpresa *f* ⟨to take by sur-prise : sorprender⟩

surprising [sə'praɪzɪŋ, sər-] *adj* : sor-prendente — **surprisingly** *adv*

surrender[1] [sə'rɛndər] *vt* **1** : entregar, rendir **2 to surrender oneself** : entre-garse — *vi* : rendirse

surrender[2] *n* : rendición *m* (de una ciu-dad, etc.), entrega *f* (de posesiones)

surreptitious [,sərəp'tɪʃəs] *adj* : subrepticio — **surreptitiously** *adv*

surrogate ['sərəgət, -,geɪt] *n* : sustituto *m*

surround [sə'raʊnd] *vt* : rodear

surroundings [sə'raʊndɪŋz] *npl* : ambiente *m*, entorno *m*

surveillance [sər'veɪlənts, -'veɪljənts, -'veɪənts] *n* : vigilancia *f*

survey[1] [sər'veɪ] *vt* **-veyed; -veying** **1** : medir (un terreno) **2** EXAMINE : inspeccionar, examinar, revisar **3** POLL : hacer una encuesta de, sondear

survey[2] ['sər,veɪ] *n, pl* **-veys** **1** INSPECTION : inspección *f*, revisión *f* **2** : medición *f* (de un terreno) **3** POLL : encuesta *f*, sondeo *m*

surveyor [sər'veɪər] *n* : agrimensor *m*, -sora *f*

survival [sər'vaɪvəl] *n* : supervivencia *f*, sobrevivencia *f*

survive [sər'vaɪv] *v* **-vived; -viving** *vi* : sobrevivir — *vt* OUTLIVE : sobrevivir a

survivor [sər'vaɪvər] *n* : superviviente *mf*, sobreviviente *mf*

susceptibility [sə,septə'bɪləti] *n, pl* **-ties** : vulnerabilidad *f*, propensión *f* (a enfermedades, etc.)

susceptible [sə'septəbəl] *adj* **1** VULNERABLE : vulnerable, sensible ⟨susceptible to flattery : sensible a halagos⟩ **2** PRONE : propenso ⟨susceptible to colds : propenso a resfriarse⟩

suspect[1] [sə'spekt] *vt* **1** DISTRUST : dudar de **2** : sospechar (algo), sospechar de (una persona) **3** IMAGINE, THINK : imaginarse, creer

suspect[2] ['sʌs,pekt, sə'spekt] *adj* : sospechoso, dudoso, cuestionable

suspect[3] ['sʌs,pekt] *n* : sospechoso *m*, -sa *f*

suspend [sə'spend] *vt* : suspender

suspenders [sə'spendərz] *npl* : tirantes *mpl*

suspense [sə'spents] *n* : incertidumbre *f*, suspenso *m* (en una película, etc.)

suspenseful [sə'spentsfəl] *adj* : de suspenso

suspension [sə'spentʃən] *n* : suspensión *f*

suspicion [sə'spɪʃən] *n* **1** : sospecha *f* **2** TRACE : pizca *f*, atisbo *m*

suspicious [sə'spɪʃəs] *adj* **1** QUESTIONABLE : sospechoso, dudoso **2** DISTRUSTFUL : suspicaz, desconfiado

suspiciously [sə'spɪʃəsli] *adv* : de modo sospechoso, con recelo

sustain [sə'steɪn] *vt* **1** NOURISH : sustentar **2** PROLONG : sostener **3** SUFFER : sufrir **4** SUPPORT, UPHOLD : apoyar, respaldar, sostener

sustainable [sə'steɪnəbəl] *adj* : sostenible

sustenance ['sʌstənənts] *n* **1** NOURISHMENT : sustento *m* **2** SUPPORT : sostén *m*

svelte ['sfɛlt] *adj* : esbelto

swab[1] ['swɑb] *vt* **swabbed; swabbing** **1** CLEAN : lavar, limpiar **2** : aplicar a (con hisopo)

swab[2] *n or* **cotton swab** : hisopo *m* (para aplicar medicinas, etc.)

swaddle ['swɑdəl] *vt* **-dled; -dling** ['swɑdəlɪŋ] : envolver (en pañales)

swagger[1] ['swægər] *vi* : pavonearse

swagger[2] *n* : pavoneo *m*

swallow[1] ['swɑlo:] *vt* **1** : tragar (comida, etc.) **2** ENGULF : tragarse, envolver **3** REPRESS : tragarse (insultos, etc.) — *vi* : tragar

swallow[2] *n* **1** : golondrina *f* (pájaro) **2** GULP : trago *m*

swam → **swim**[1]

swamp[1] ['swɑmp] *vt* : inundar

swamp[2] *n* : pantano *m*, ciénaga *f*

swampy ['swɑmpi] *adj* **swampier; -est** : pantanoso, cenagoso

swan ['swɑn] *n* : cisne *f*

swap[1] ['swɑp] *vt* **swapped; swapping** : cambiar, intercambiar ⟨to swap places : cambiarse de sitio⟩

swap[2] *n* : cambio *m*, intercambio *m*

swarm[1] ['swɔrm] *vi* : enjambrar

swarm[2] *n* : enjambre *m*

swarthy ['swɔrði, -θi] *adj* **swarthier; -est** : moreno

swashbuckling ['swɑʃ,bʌklɪŋ] *adj* : de aventurero

swat[1] ['swɑt] *vt* **swatted; swatting** : aplastar (un insecto), darle una palmada (a alguien)

swat[2] *n* : palmada *f* (con la mano), golpe *m* (con un objeto)

swatch ['swɑtʃ] *n* : muestra *f*

swath ['swɑθ, 'swɔθ] *or* **swathe** ['swɑð, 'swɔð, 'sweɪð] *n* : franja *f* (de grano segado)

swathe ['swɑð, 'swɔð, 'sweɪð] *vt* **swathed; swathing** : envolver

swatter ['swɑtər] → **flyswatter**

sway[1] ['sweɪ] *vi* : balancearse, mecerse — *vt* INFLUENCE : influir en, convencer

sway[2] *n* **1** SWINGING : balanceo *m* **2** INFLUENCE : influjo *m*

swear ['swær] *v* **swore** ['swor]; **sworn** ['sworn]; **swearing** *vi* **1** VOW : jurar **2** CURSE : decir palabrotas — *vt* : jurar

swearword ['swær,wərd] *n* : mala palabra *f*, palabrota *f*

sweat[1] ['swet] *vi* **sweat** *or* **sweated; sweating** **1** PERSPIRE : sudar, transpirar **2** OOZE : rezumar **3 to sweat over** : sudar la gota gorda por

sweat[2] *n* : sudor *m*, transpiración *f*

sweater ['swetər] *n* : suéter *m*

sweatshirt ['swet,ʃərt] *n* : sudadera *f*

sweaty ['sweti] *adj* **sweatier; -est** : sudoroso, sudado, transpirado

Swede ['swi:d] *n* : sueco *m*, -ca *f*

Swedish[1] ['swi:dɪʃ] *adj* : sueco

Swedish[2] *n* **1** : sueco *m* (idioma) **2 the Swedish** *npl* : los suecos

sweep[1] ['swi:p] *v* **swept** ['swept]; **sweeping** *vt* **1** : barrer (el suelo, etc.), limpiar (suciedad, etc.) ⟨he swept the books aside : apartó los libros de un manotazo⟩ **2** *or* **to sweep through** : extenderse por (dícese del fuego, etc.), azotar (dícese de una tormenta) — *vi* **1** : barrer, limpiar **2** : extenderse (en una curva), describir una curva ⟨the sun swept across the sky : el sol describía una curva en el cielo⟩

sweep² *n* **1** : barrido *m*, barrida *f* (con una escoba) **2** : movimiento *m* circular **3** SCOPE : alcance *m*

sweeper ['swi:pər] *n* : barrendero *m*, -ra *f*

sweeping ['swi:pɪŋ] *adj* **1** WIDE : amplio (dícese de un movimiento) **2** EXTENSIVE : extenso, radical **3** INDISCRIMINATE : indiscriminado, demasiado general **4** OVERWHELMING : arrollador, aplastante

sweepstakes ['swi:p,steɪks] *ns & pl* **1** : carrera *f* (en que el ganador se lleva el premio entero) **2** LOTTERY : lotería *f*

sweet¹ ['swi:t] *adj* **1** : dulce ⟨sweet desserts : postres dulces⟩ **2** FRESH : fresco **3** : sin sal (dícese de la mantequilla, etc.) **4** PLEASANT : dulce, agradable **5** DEAR : querido

sweet² *n* : dulce *m*

sweeten ['swi:tən] *vt* : endulzar

sweetener ['swi:tənər] *n* : endulzante *m*

sweetheart ['swi:t,hɑrt] *n* : novio *m*, -via *f* ⟨thanks, sweetheart : gracias, cariño⟩

sweetly ['swi:tli] *adv* : dulcemente

sweetness ['swi:tnəs] *n* : dulzura *f*

sweet potato *n* : batata *f*, boniato *m*

swell¹ ['swɛl] *vi* **swelled; swelled** *or* **swollen** ['swo:lən, 'swʌl-]; **swelling 1** *or* **to swell up** : hincharse ⟨her ankle swelled : se le hinchó el tobillo⟩ **2** *or* **to swell out** : inflarse, hincharse (dícese de las velas, etc.) **3** INCREASE : aumentar, crecer

swell² *n* **1** : oleaje *m* (del mar) **2** → **swelling**

swelling ['swɛlɪŋ] *n* : hinchazón *f*

swelter ['swɛltər] *vi* : sofocarse de calor

swept → **sweep¹**

swerve¹ ['swərv] *vi* **swerved; swerving** : virar bruscamente

swerve² *n* : viraje *m* brusco

swift¹ ['swɪft] *adj* **1** FAST : rápido, veloz **2** SUDDEN : repentino, súbito — **swiftly** *adv*

swift² *n* : vencejo *m* (pájaro)

swiftness ['swɪftnəs] *n* : rapidez *f*, velocidad *f*

swig¹ ['swɪg] *vi* **swigged; swigging** : tomar a tragos, beber a tragos

swig² *n* : trago *m*

swill¹ ['swɪl] *vt* : chupar, beber a tragos grandes

swill² *n* **1** SLOP : bazofia *f* **2** GARBAGE : basura *f*

swim¹ ['swɪm] *vi* **swam** ['swæm]; **swum** ['swʌm]; **swimming 1** : nadar **2** FLOAT : flotar **3** REEL : dar vueltas ⟨his head was swimming : la cabeza le daba vueltas⟩

swim² *n* : baño *m*, chapuzón *m* ⟨to go for a swim : ir a nadar⟩

swimmer ['swɪmər] *n* : nadador *m*, -dora *f*

swindle¹ ['swɪndəl] *vt* **-dled; -dling** : estafar, timar

swindle² *n* : estafa *f*, timo *m fam*

swindler ['swɪndələr] *n* : estafador *m*, -dora *f*; timador *m*, -dora *f*

swine ['swaɪn] *ns & pl* : cerdo *m*, -da *f*

swing¹ ['swɪŋ] *v* **swung** ['swʌŋ]; **swinging** *vt* **1** : describir una curva con ⟨he swung the ax at the tree : le dio al arbol con el hacha⟩ **2** : balancear (los brazos, etc.), hacer oscilar **3** SUSPEND : colgar — *vi* **1** SWAY : balancearse (dícese de los brazos, etc.), oscilar (dícese de un objeto), columpiarse, mecerse (en un columpio) **2** SWIVEL : girar (en un pivote) ⟨the door swung shut : la puerta se cerró⟩ **3** CHANGE : virar, cambiar (dícese de las opiniones, etc.)

swing² *n* **1** SWINGING : vaivén *m*, balanceo *m* **2** CHANGE, SHIFT : viraje *m*, movimiento *m* **3** : columpio *m* (para niños) **4 to take a swing at someone** : intentar pegarle a alguien

swipe¹ ['swaɪp] *vt* **swiped; swiping 1** STRIKE : dar, pegar (con un movimiento amplio) **2** WIPE : limpiar **3** STEAL : birlar *fam*, robar

swipe² *n* BLOW : golpe *m*

swirl¹ ['swərl] *vi* : arremolinarse

swirl² *n* **1** EDDY : remolino *m* **2** SPIRAL : espiral *f*

swish¹ ['swɪʃ] *vt* : mover (produciendo un sonido) ⟨she swished her skirt : movía la falda⟩ — *vi* : moverse (produciendo un sonido) ⟨the cars swished by : se oían pasar los coches⟩

swish² *n* : silbido *m* (de un látigo, etc.), susurro *m* (de agua), crujido *m* (de ropa, etc.)

Swiss ['swɪs] *n* : suizo *m*, -za *f* — **Swiss** *adj*

swiss chard *n* : acelga *f*

switch¹ ['swɪtʃ] *vt* **1** LASH, WHIP : azotar **2** CHANGE : cambiar de **3** EXCHANGE : intercambiar **4 to switch on** : encender, prender **5 to switch off** : apagar — *vi* **1** : moverse de un lado al otro **2** CHANGE : cambiar **3** SWAP : intercambiarse

switch² *n* **1** WHIP : vara *f* **2** CHANGE, SHIFT : cambio *m* **3** : interruptor *m*, llave *f* (de la luz, etc.)

switchboard ['swɪtʃ,bord] *n* : conmutador *m*, centralita *f*

swivel¹ ['swɪvəl] *vi* **-veled** *or* **-velled; -veling** *or* **-velling** : girar (sobre un pivote)

swivel² *n* : base *f* giratoria

swollen *pp* → **swell¹**

swoon¹ ['swu:n] *vi* : desvanecerse, desmayarse

swoon² *n* : desvanecimiento *m*, desmayo *m*

swoop¹ ['swu:p] *vi* : abatirse (dícese de las aves), descender en picada (dícese de un avión)

swoop² *n* : descenso *m* en picada

sword ['sɔrd] *n* : espada *f*

swordfish ['sɔrd,fɪʃ] *n* : pez *m* espada

swore, sworn → **swear**

swum *pp* → **swim¹**

swung → **swing¹**

sycamore ['sɪkə,mor] *n* : sicomoro *m*

sycophant ['sɪkəfənt, -,fænt] *n* : adulador *m*, -dora *f*

syllabic [sə'læbɪk] *adj* : silábico

syllable ['sɪləbəl] *n* : sílaba *f*

syllabus ['sɪləbəs] *n, pl* **-bi** [-,baɪ] *or* **-buses** : programa *m* (de estudios)

symbol ['sɪmbəl] *n* : símbolo *m*

symbolic [sɪm'bɑlɪk] *adj* : simbólico — **symbolically** [-kli] *adv*

symbolism ['sɪmbə,lɪzəm] *n* : simbolismo *m*

symbolize ['sɪmbə,laɪz] *vt* **-ized; -izing** : simbolizar

symmetrical [sə'mɛtrɪkəl] *or* **symmetric** [-trɪk] *adj* : simétrico — **symmetrically** [-trɪkli] *adv*

symmetry ['sɪmətri] *n, pl* **-tries** : simetría *f*

sympathetic [,sɪmpə'θɛtɪk] *adj* **1** PLEASING : agradable **2** RECEPTIVE : receptivo, favorable **3** COMPASSIONATE, UNDERSTANDING : comprensivo, compasivo

sympathetically [,sɪmpə'θɛtɪkli] *adv* : con compasión, con comprensión

sympathize ['sɪmpə,θaɪz] *vi* **-thized; -thizing** : compadecer ⟨I sympathize with you : te compadezco⟩

sympathy ['sɪmpəθi] *n, pl* **-thies 1** COMPASSION : compasión *f* **2** UNDERSTANDING : comprensión *f* **3** AGREEMENT : solidaridad *f* ⟨in sympathy with : de acuerdo con⟩ **4** CONDOLENCES : pésame *m*, condolencias *fpl*

symphonic [sɪm'fɑnɪk] *adj* : sinfónico

symphony ['sɪmfəni] *n, pl* **-nies** : sinfonía *f*

symposium [sɪm'po:ziəm] *n, pl* **-sia** [-ziə] *or* **-siums** : simposio *m*

symptom ['sɪmptəm] *n* : síntoma *m*

symptomatic [,sɪmptə'mætɪk] *adj* : sintomático

synagogue ['sɪnə,gɑg, -,gɔg] *n* : sinagoga *f*

sync ['sɪŋk] *n* : sincronización *f* ⟨in sync : sincronizado⟩

synchronize ['sɪŋkrə,naɪz, 'sɪn-] *v* **-nized; -nizing** *vi* : estar sincronizado — *vt* : sincronizar

syncopate ['sɪŋkə,peɪt, 'sɪn-] *vt* **-pated; -pating** : sincopar

syncopation [,sɪŋkə'peɪʃən, ,sɪn-] *n* : síncopa *f*

syndicate¹ ['sɪndə,keɪt] *vi* **-cated; -cating** : formar una asociación

syndicate² ['sɪndɪkət] *n* : asociación *f*, agrupación *f*

syndrome ['sɪn,dro:m] *n* : síndrome *m*

synonym ['sɪnə,nɪm] *n* : sinónimo *m*

synonymous [sə'nɑnəməs] *adj* : sinónimo

synopsis [sə'nɑpsɪs] *n, pl* **-opses** [-,si:z] : sinopsis *f*

syntactic [sɪn'tæktɪk] *adj* : sintáctico

syntax ['sɪn,tæks] *n* : sintaxis *f*

synthesis ['sɪnθəsɪs] *n, pl* **-theses** [-,si:z] : síntesis *f*

synthesize ['sɪnθə,saɪz] *vt* **-sized; -sizing** : sintetizar

synthetic¹ [sɪn'θɛtɪk] *adj* : sintético, artificial — **synthetically** [-ţɪkli] *adv*

synthetic² *n* : producto *m* sintético

syphilis ['sɪfələs] *n* : sífilis *f*

Syrian ['sɪriən] *n* : sirio *m*, -ria *f* — **Syrian** *adj*

syringe [sə'rɪndʒ, 'sɪrɪndʒ] *n* : jeringa *f*, jeringuilla *f*

syrup ['sərəp, 'sɪrəp] *n* : jarabe *m*, almíbar *m* (de azúcar y agua)

system ['sɪstəm] *n* **1** METHOD : sistema *m*, método *m* **2** APPARATUS : sistema *m*, instalación *f*, aparato *m* ⟨electrical system : instalación eléctrica⟩ ⟨digestive system : aparato digestivo⟩ **3** BODY : organismo *m*, cuerpo *m* ⟨diseases that affect the whole system : enfermedades que afectan el organismo entero⟩ **4** NETWORK : red *f*

systematic [,sɪstə'mætɪk] *adj* : sistemático — **systematically** [-ţɪkli] *adv*

systematize ['sɪstəmə,taɪz] *vt* **-tized; -tizing** : sistematizar

systemic [sɪs'tɛmɪk] *adj* : sistémico

T

t ['ti:] *n, pl* **t's** *or* **ts** ['ti:z] : vigésima letra del alfabeto inglés

tab ['tæb] *n* **1** FLAP, TAG : lengüeta *f* (de un sobre, una caja, etc.), etiqueta *f* (de ropa) **2** → **tabulator 3** BILL, CHECK : cuenta *f* **4** to keep tabs on : tener bajo vigilancia

tabby ['tæbi] *n, pl* **-bies 1** *or* **tabby cat** : gato *m* atigrado **2** : gata *f*

tabernacle ['tæbər,nækəl] *n* : tabernáculo *m*

table ['teɪbəl] *n* **1** : mesa *f* ⟨a table for two : una mesa para dos⟩ **2** LIST : tabla *f* ⟨multiplication table : tabla de multiplicar⟩ **3** table of contents : índice *m* de materias

tableau [tæ'blo:, 'tæ,-] *n, pl* **-leaux** [-'blo:z, -,blo:z] : retablo *m*, cuadro *m* vivo (en teatro)

tablecloth ['teɪbəl,klɔθ] *n* : mantel *m*

tablespoon ['teɪbəl,spu:n] *n* **1** : cuchara *f* (de mesa) **2** → **tablespoonful**

tablespoonful ['teɪbəlˌspuːnˌfʊl] *n* : cucharada *f*

tablet ['tæblət] *n* **1** PLAQUE : placa *f* **2** PAD : bloc *m* (de papel) **3** PILL : tableta *f*, pastilla *f*, píldora *f* ⟨an aspirin tablet : una tableta de aspirina⟩

table tennis *n* : tenis *m* de mesa

tableware ['teɪbəlˌwær] *n* : vajillas *fpl*, cubiertos *mpl* (de mesa)

tabloid ['tæˌblɔɪd] *n* : tabloide *m*

taboo¹ [təˈbuː, tæ-] *adj* : tabú

taboo² *n* : tabú *m*

tabular ['tæbjələr] *adj* : tabular

tabulate ['tæbjəˌleɪt] *vt* **-lated; -lating** : tabular

tabulator ['tæbjəˌleɪtər] *n* : tabulador *m*

tacit ['tæsɪt] *adj* : tácito, implícito — **tacitly** *adv*

taciturn ['tæsɪˌtərn] *adj* : taciturno

tack¹ ['tæk] *vt* **1** : sujetar con tachuelas **2 to tack on** ADD : añadir, agregar

tack² *n* **1** : tachuela *f* **2** COURSE : rumbo *m* ⟨to change tack : cambiar de rumbo⟩

tackle¹ ['tækəl] *vt* **-led; -ling 1** : taclear (en futbol americano) **2** CONFRONT : abordar, enfrentar, emprender (un problema, un trabajo, etc.)

tackle² *n* **1** EQUIPMENT, GEAR : equipo *m*, aparejo *m* **2** : aparejo *m* (de un buque) **3** : tacleada *f* (en futbol americano)

tacky ['tæki] *adj* **tackier; -est 1** STICKY : pegajoso **2** CHEAP, GAUDY : de mal gusto, naco *Mex*

tact ['tækt] *n* : tacto *m*, delicadeza *f*, discreción *f*

tactful ['tæktfəl] *adj* : discreto, diplomático, de mucho tacto

tactfully ['tæktfəli] *adv* : discretamente, con mucho tacto

tactic ['tæktɪk] *n* : táctica *f*

tactical ['tæktɪkəl] *adj* : táctico, estratégico

tactics ['tæktɪks] *ns & pl* : táctica *f*, estrategia *f*

tactile ['tæktəl, -ˌtaɪl] *adj* : táctil

tactless ['tæktləs] *adj* : indiscreto, poco delicado

tactlessly ['tæktləsli] *adv* : rudamente, sin tacto

tadpole ['tædˌpoːl] *n* : renacuajo *m*

taffeta ['tæfətə] *n* : tafetán *m*, tafeta *f* *Arg, Mex, Uru*

taffy ['tæfi] *n, pl* **-fies** : caramelo *m* de melaza, chicloso *m Mex*

tag¹ ['tæg] *v* **tagged; tagging** *vt* **1** LABEL : etiquetar **2** TAIL : seguir de cerca **3** TOUCH : tocar (en varios juegos) — *vi* **to tag along** : pegarse, acompañar

tag² *n* **1** LABEL : etiqueta *f* **2** SAYING : dicho *m*, refrán *m*

tail¹ ['teɪl] *vt* FOLLOW : seguir de cerca, pegarse

tail² *n* **1** : cola *f*, rabo *m* (de un animal) **2** : cola *f*, parte *f* posterior ⟨a comet's tail : la cola de un cometa⟩ **3 tails** *npl* : cruz *f* (de una moneda) ⟨heads or tails : cara o cruz⟩

tailed ['teɪld] *adj* : que tiene cola

tailgate¹ ['teɪlˌgeɪt] *vi* **-gated; -gating** : seguir a un vehículo demasiado de cerca

tailgate² *n* : puerta *f* trasera (de un vehículo)

taillight ['teɪlˌlaɪt] *n* : luz *f* trasera (de un vehículo), calavera *f Mex*

tailor¹ ['teɪlər] *vt* **1** : confeccionar o alterar (ropa) **2** ADAPT : adaptar, ajustar

tailor² *n* : sastre *m*, -tra *f*

tailpipe ['teɪlˌpaɪp] *n* : tubo *m* de escape

tailspin ['teɪlˌspɪn] *n* : barrena *f*

taint¹ ['teɪnt] *vt* : contaminar, corromper

taint² *n* : corrupción *f*, impureza *f*

take¹ ['teɪk] *v* **took** ['tʊk]; **taken** ['teɪkən]; **taking** *vt* **1** CAPTURE : capturar, apresar **2** GRASP : tomar, agarrar ⟨to take the bull by the horns : tomar al toro por los cuernos⟩ **3** CATCH : tomar, agarrar ⟨taken by surprise : tomado por sorpresa⟩ **4** CAPTIVATE : encantar, fascinar **5** INGEST : tomar, ingerir ⟨take two pills : tome dos píldoras⟩ **6** REMOVE : sacar, extraer ⟨take an orange : saca una naranja⟩ **7** : tomar, coger (un tren, un autobús, etc.) **8** NEED, REQUIRE : tomar, requerir ⟨these things take time : estas cosas toman tiempo⟩ **9** BRING, CARRY : llevar, sacar, cargar ⟨take them with you : llévalos contigo⟩ ⟨take the trash out : saca la basura⟩ **10** BEAR, ENDURE : soportar, aguantar (dolores, etc.) **11** ACCEPT : aceptar (un cheque, etc.), seguir (consejos), asumir (la responsabilidad) **12** SUPPOSE : suponer ⟨I take it that . . . : supongo que . . . ⟩ **13** (*indicating an action or an undertaking*) ⟨to take a walk : dar un paseo⟩ ⟨to take a class : tomar una clase⟩ **14 to take place** HAPPEN : tener lugar, suceder, ocurrir — *vi* : agarrar (dícese de un tinte), prender (dícese de una vacuna)

take² *n* **1** PROCEEDS : recaudación *f*, ingresos *mpl*, ganancias *fpl* **2** : toma *f* (de un rodaje o una grabación)

take back *vt* : retirar (palabras, etc.)

take in *vt* **1** : tomarle a, achicar (un vestido, etc.) **2** INCLUDE : incluir, abarcar **3** ATTEND : ir a ⟨to take in a movie : ir al cine⟩ **4** GRASP, UNDERSTAND : captar, entender **5** DECEIVE : engañar

takeoff ['teɪkˌɔf] *n* **1** PARODY : parodia *f* **2** : despegue *m* (de un avión o cohete)

take off *vt* REMOVE : quitar ⟨take off your hat : quítate el sombrero⟩ — *vi* **1** : despegar (dícese de un avión o un cohete) **2** LEAVE : irse, partir

take on *vt* **1** TACKLE : abordar, emprender (problemas, etc.) **2** ACCEPT : aceptar, encargarse de, asumir (una responsabilidad) **3** CONTRACT : contratar (trabajadores) **4** ASSUME : adoptar, asumir, adquirir ⟨the neighborhood took on a dingy look : el barrio asumió una apariencia deprimente⟩

takeover ['teɪk,o:vər] *n* : toma *f* (de poder o de control), adquisición *f* (de una empresa por otra)

take over *vt* : tomar el poder de, tomar las riendas de — *vi* : asumir el mando

taker ['teɪkər] *n* : persona *f* interesada ⟨available to all takers : disponible a cuantos estén interesados⟩

take up *vt* **1** LIFT : levantar **2** SHORTEN : acortar (una falda, etc.) **3** BEGIN : empezar, dedicarse a (un pasatiempo, etc.) **4** OCCUPY : ocupar, llevar (tiempo, espacio) **5** PURSUE : volver a (una cuestión, un asunto) **6** CONTINUE : seguir con

talc ['tælk] *n* : talco *m*

talcum powder ['tælkəm] *n* : talco *m*, polvos *mpl* de talco

tale ['teɪl] *n* **1** ANECDOTE, STORY : cuento *m*, relato *m*, anécdota *f* **2** FALSEHOOD : cuento *m*, mentira *f*

talent ['tælənt] *n* : talento *m*, don *m*

talented ['tæləntəd] *adj* : talentoso

talisman ['tælɪsmən, -lɪz-] *n, pl* **-mans** : talismán *m*

talk[1] ['tɔk] *vi* **1** : hablar ⟨he talks for hours : se pasa horas hablando⟩ **2** CHAT : charlar, platicar — *vt* **1** SPEAK : hablar ⟨to talk French : hablar francés⟩ ⟨to talk business : hablar de negocios⟩ **2** PERSUADE : influenciar, convencer ⟨she talked me out of it : me convenció que no lo hiciera⟩ **3 to talk over** DISCUSS : hablar de, discutir

talk[2] *n* **1** CONVERSATION : charla *f*, plática *f*, conversación *f* **2** GOSSIP, RUMOR : chisme *m*, rumores *mpl*

talkative ['tɔkəṭɪv] *adj* : locuaz, parlanchín, charlatán

talker ['tɔkər] *n* : conversador *m*, -dora *f*; hablador *m*, -dora *f*

talk show *n* : programa *m* de entrevistas

tall ['tɔl] *adj* : alto ⟨how tall is he? : ¿cuánto mide?⟩

tallness ['tɔlnəs] *n* HEIGHT : estatura *f* (de una persona), altura *f* (de un objeto)

tallow ['tælo:] *n* : sebo *m*

tally[1] ['tæli] *v* **-lied; -lying** *vt* RECKON : contar, hacer una cuenta de — *vi* MATCH : concordar, corresponder, cuadrar

tally[2] *n, pl* **-lies** : cuenta *f* ⟨to keep a tally : llevar la cuenta⟩

talon ['tælən] *n* : garra *f* (de un ave de rapiña)

tambourine [,tæmbə'ri:n] *n* : pandero *m*, pandereta *f*

tame[1] ['teɪm] *vt* **tamed; taming** : domar, amansar, domesticar

tame[2] *adj* **tamer; -est 1** DOMESTICATED : domesticado, manso **2** DOCILE : manso, dócil **3** DULL : aburrido, soso

tamely ['teɪmli] *adv* : mansamente, dócilmente

tamer ['teɪmər] *n* : domador *m*, -dora *f*

tamp ['tæmp] *vt* : apisonar

tamper ['tæmpər] *vi* **to tamper with** : adulterar (una sustancia), forzar (un sello, una cerradura), falsear (documentos), manipular (una máquina)

tampon ['tæm,pɑn] *n* : tampón *m*

tan[1] ['tæn] *v* **tanned; tanning** *vt* **1** : curtir (pieles) **2** : broncear — *vi* : broncearse

tan[2] *n* **1** SUNTAN : bronceado *m* ⟨to get a tan : broncearse⟩ **2** : color *m* canela, color *m* café con leche

tandem[1] ['tændəm] *adv or* **in tandem** : en tándem

tandem[2] *n* : tándem *m* (bicicleta)

tang ['tæŋ] *n* : sabor *m* fuerte

tangent ['tændʒənt] *n* : tangente *f* ⟨to go off on a tangent : irse por la tangente⟩

tangerine ['tændʒə,ri:n, ,tændʒə'-] *n* : mandarina *f*

tangible ['tændʒəbəl] *adj* : tangible, palpable — **tangibly** [-bli] *adv*

tangle[1] ['tæŋgəl] *v* **-gled; -gling** *vt* : enredar, enmarañar — *vi* : enredarse

tangle[2] *n* : enredo *m*, maraña *f*

tango[1] ['tæŋ,go:] *vi* : bailar el tango

tango[2] *n, pl* **-gos** : tango *m*

tangy ['tæŋi] *adj* **tangier; -est** : que tiene un sabor fuerte

tank ['tæŋk] *n* **1** : tanque *m*, depósito *m* ⟨fuel tank : depósito de combustibles⟩

tankard ['tæŋkərd] *n* : jarra *f*

tanker ['tæŋkər] *n* : buque *m* cisterna, camión *m* cisterna, avión *m* cisterna ⟨an oil tanker : un petrolero⟩

tanner ['tænər] *n* : curtidor *m*, -dora *f*

tannery ['tænəri] *n, pl* **-neries** : curtiduría *f*, tenería *f*

tannin ['tænən] *n* : tanino *m*

tantalize ['tæntə,laɪz] *vt* **-lized; -lizing** : tentar, atormentar (con algo inasequible)

tantalizing ['tæntə,laɪzɪŋ] *adj* : tentador, seductor

tantamount ['tæntə,maunt] *adj* : equivalente

tantrum ['tæntrəm] *n* : rabieta *f*, berrinche *m* ⟨to throw a tantrum : hacer un berrinche⟩

tap[1] ['tæp] *vt* **tapped; tapping 1** : ponerle una espita a, sacar líquido de (un barril, un tanque, etc.) **2** : intervenir (una línea telefónica) **3** PAT, TOUCH : tocar, golpear ligeramente ⟨he tapped me on the shoulder : me tocó en el hombro⟩

tap[2] *n* **1** FAUCET : llave *f*, grifo *m* ⟨beer on tap : cerveza de barril⟩ **2** : extracción *f* (de líquido) ⟨a spinal tap : una punción lumbar⟩ **3** PAT, TOUCH : golpecito *m*, toque *m*

tape[1] ['teɪp] *vt* **taped; taping 1** : sujetar o arreglar con cinta adhesiva **2** RECORD : grabar

tape[2] *n* **1** : cinta *f* (adhesiva, magnética, etc.) **2 → tape measure**

tape measure *n* : cinta *f* métrica

taper[1] ['teɪpər] *vi* **1** : estrecharse gradualmente ⟨its tail tapers towards the tip : su cola va estrechándose hacia la punta⟩ **2** *or* **to taper off** : disminuir gradualmente

taper² *n* **1** CANDLE : vela *f* larga y delgada **2** TAPERING : estrechamiento *m* gradual

tapestry ['tæpəstri] *n, pl* **-tries** : tapiz *m*

tapeworm ['teɪp,wərm] *n* : solitaria *f*, tenia *f*

tapioca [,tæpi'o:kə] *n* : tapioca *f*

tar¹ ['tɑr] *vt* **tarred; tarring** : alquitranar

tar² *n* : alquitrán *m*, brea *f*, chapopote *m Mex*

tarantula [tə'ræntʃələ, -'ræntələ] *n* : tarántula *f*

tardiness ['tɑrdinəs] *n* : tardanza *f*, retraso *m*

tardy ['tɑrdi] *adj* **-dier; -est** LATE : tardío, de retraso

target¹ ['tɑrgət] *vt* : fijar como objetivo, dirigir, destinar

target² *n* **1** : blanco *m* ⟨target practice : tiro al blanco⟩ **2** GOAL, OBJECTIVE : meta *f*, objetivo *m*

tariff ['tærɪf] *n* DUTY : tarifa *f*, arancel *m*

tarnish¹ ['tɑrnɪʃ] *vt* **1** DULL : deslustrar **2** SULLY : empañar, manchar (una reputación, etc.) — *vi* : deslustrarse

tarnish² *n* : deslustre *m*

tarpaulin [tɑr'pɔlən, 'tɑrpə-] *n* : lona *f* (impermeable)

tarragon ['tærə,gɑn, -gən] *n* : estragón *m*

tarry¹ ['tæri] *vi* **-ried; -rying** : demorarse, entretenerse

tarry² ['tɑri] *adj* **1** : parecido al alquitrán **2** : cubierto de alquitrán

tart¹ ['tɑrt] *adj* **1** SOUR : ácido, agrio **2** CAUSTIC : mordaz, acrimonioso — **tartly** *adv*

tart² *n* : tartaleta *f*

tartan ['tɑrtən] *n* : tartán *m*

tartar ['tɑrtər] *n* **1** : tártaro *m* ⟨tartar sauce : salsa tártara⟩ **2** : sarro *m* (dental)

tartness ['tɑrtnəs] *n* **1** SOURNESS : acidez *f* **2** ACRIMONY, SHARPNESS : mordacidad *f*, acrimonia *f*, acritud *f*

task ['tæsk] *n* : tarea *f*, trabajo *m*

taskmaster ['tæsk,mæstər] *n* **to be a hard taskmaster** : ser exigente, ser muy estricto

tassel ['tæsəl] *n* : borla *f*

taste¹ ['teɪst] *v* **tasted; tasting** *vt* : probar (alimentos), degustar, catar (vinos) ⟨taste this soup : prueba esta sopa⟩ — *vi* : saber ⟨this tastes good : esto sabe bueno⟩

taste² *n* **1** SAMPLE : prueba *f*, bocado *m* (de comida), trago *m* (de bebidas) **2** FLAVOR : gusto *m*, sabor *m* **3** : gusto *m* ⟨she has good taste : tiene buen gusto⟩ ⟨in bad taste : de mal gusto⟩

taste bud *n* : papila *f* gustativa

tasteful ['teɪstfəl] *adj* : de buen gusto

tastefully ['teɪstfəli] *adv* : con buen gusto

tasteless ['teɪstləs] *adj* **1** FLAVORLESS : sin sabor, soso, insípido **2** : de mal

gusto ⟨a tasteless joke : un chiste de mal gusto⟩

taster ['teɪstər] *n* : degustador *m*, -dora *f*; catador *m*, -dora *f* (de vinos)

tastiness ['teɪstinəs] *n* : lo sabroso

tasty ['teɪsti] *adj* **tastier; -est** : sabroso, gustoso

tatter ['tætər] *n* **1** SHRED : tira *f*, jirón *m* (de tela) **2** **tatters** *npl* : andrajos *mpl*, harapos *mpl* ⟨to be in tatters : estar por los suelos⟩

tattered ['tætərd] *adj* : andrajoso, en jirones

tattle ['tætəl] *vi* **-tled; -tling 1** CHATTER : parlotear *fam*, cotorrear *fam* **2** **to tattle on someone** : acusar a alguien

tattletale ['tætəl,teɪl] *n* : soplón *m*, -plona *f fam*

tattoo¹ [tæ'tu:] *vt* : tatuar

tattoo² *n* : tatuaje *m* ⟨to get a tattoo : tatuarse⟩

taught → **teach**

taunt¹ ['tɔnt] *vt* MOCK : mofarse de, burlarse de

taunt² *n* : mofa *f*, burla *f*

Taurus ['tɔrəs] *n* : Tauro *mf*

taut ['tɔt] *adj* : tirante, tenso — **tautly** *adv*

tautness ['tɔtnəs] *n* : tirantez *f*, tensión *f*

tavern ['tævərn] *n* : taberna *f*

tawdry ['tɔdri] *adj* **-drier; -est** : chabacano, vulgar

tawny ['tɔni] *adj* **-nier; -est** : leonado

tax¹ ['tæks] *vt* **1** : gravar, cobrar un impuesto sobre **2** CHARGE : acusar ⟨they taxed him with neglect : fue acusado de incumplimiento⟩ **3** **to tax someone's strength** : ponerle a prueba las fuerzas (a alguien)

tax² *n* **1** : impuesto *m*, tributo *m* **2** BURDEN : carga *f*

taxable ['tæksəbəl] *adj* : sujeto a un impuesto

taxation [tæk'seɪʃən] *n* : impuestos *mpl*

tax–exempt ['tæksɪg'zɛmpt, -ɛg-] *adj* : libre de impuestos

taxi¹ ['tæksi] *vi* **taxied; taxiing** *or* **taxying; taxis** *or* **taxies 1** : ir en taxi **2** : rodar sobre la pista de aterrizaje (dícese de un avión)

taxi² *n, pl* **taxis** : taxi *m*, libre *m Mex*

taxicab ['tæksi,kæb] *n* → **taxi²**

taxidermist ['tæksə,dərmɪst] *n* : taxidermista *mf*

taxidermy ['tæksə,dərmi] *n* : taxidermia *f*

taxpayer ['tæks,peɪər] *n* : contribuyente *mf*, causante *mf Mex*

TB [,ti:'bi:] → **tuberculosis**

tea ['ti:] *n* **1** : té *m* (planta y bebida) **2** : merienda *f*, té *m* (comida)

teach ['ti:tʃ] *v* **taught** ['tɔt]; **teaching** *vt* : enseñar, dar clases de ⟨she teaches math : da clases de matemáticas⟩ ⟨she taught me everything I know : me enseñó todo lo que sé⟩ — *vi* : enseñar, dar clases

teacher ['ti:tʃər] *n* : maestro *m*, -tra *f* (de enseñanza primaria); profesor *m*, -sora *f* (de enseñanza secundaria)

teaching ['ti:tʃɪŋ] *n* : enseñanza *f*

teacup ['ti:ˌkʌp] *n* : taza *f* para té

teak ['ti:k] *n* : teca *f*

teakettle ['ti:ˌkɛtəl] *n* : tetera *f*

teal ['ti:l] *n, pl* **teal** *or* **teals** : cerceta *f* (pato)

team¹ ['ti:m] *vi or* **to team up** **1** : formar un equipo (en deportes) **2** COLLABORATE : asociarse, juntarse, unirse

team² *adj* : de equipo

team³ *n* **1** : tiro *m* (de caballos), yunta *f* (de bueyes o mulas) **2** : equipo *m* (en deportes, etc.)

teammate ['ti:mˌmeɪt] *n* : compañero *m*, -ra *f* de equipo

teamster ['ti:mstər] *n* : camionero *m*, -ra *f*

teamwork ['ti:mˌwərk] *n* : trabajo *m* en equipo, cooperación *f*

teapot ['ti:ˌpɑt] *n* : tetera *f*

tear¹ ['tær] *v* **tore** ['tor]; **torn** ['torn]; **tearing** *vt* **1** RIP : desgarrar, romper, rasgar (tela) ⟨to tear to pieces : hacer pedazos⟩ **2** *or* **to tear apart** DIVIDE : dividir **3** REMOVE : arrancar ⟨torn from his family : arrancado de su familia⟩ **4** **to tear down** : derribar — *vi* **1** RIP : desgarrarse, romperse **2** RUSH : ir a gran velocidad ⟨she went tearing down the street : se fue como rayo por la calle⟩

tear² *n* : desgarradura *f*, rotura *f*, desgarro *m* (muscular)

tear³ ['tɪr] *n* : lágrima *f*

teardrop ['tɪrˌdrɑp] *n* → **tear³**

tearful ['tɪrfəl] *adj* : lloroso, triste — **tearfully** *adv*

tease¹ ['ti:z] *vt* **teased; teasing** **1** MOCK : burlarse de, mofarse de **2** ANNOY : irritar, fastidiar

tease² *n* **1** TEASING : burla *f*, mofa *f* **2** : bromista *mf*; guasón *m*, -sona *f*

teaspoon ['ti:ˌspu:n] *n* **1** : cucharita *f* **2** → **teaspoonful**

teaspoonful ['ti:ˌspu:nˌfʊl] *n, pl* **-spoonfuls** [-ˌfʊlz] *or* **-spoonsful** [-ˌspu:nzˌfʊl] : cucharadita *f*

teat ['ti:t] *n* : tetilla *f*

technical ['tɛknɪkəl] *adj* : técnico — **technically** [-kli] *adv*

technicality [ˌtɛknəˈkæləti] *n, pl* **-ties** : detalle *m* técnico

technician [tɛkˈnɪʃən] *n* : técnico *m*, -ca *f*

technique [tɛkˈni:k] *n* : técnica *f*

technological [ˌtɛknəˈlɑdʒɪkəl] *adj* : tecnológico

technology [tɛkˈnɑlədʒi] *n, pl* **-gies** : tecnología *f*

teddy bear ['tɛdi] *n* : oso *m* de peluche

tedious ['ti:diəs] *adj* : aburrido, pesado, monótono — **tediously** *adv*

tediousness ['ti:diəsnəs] *n* : lo aburrido, lo pesado

tedium ['ti:diəm] *n* : tedio *m*, pesadez *f*

tee ['ti:] *n* : tee *mf*

teem ['ti:m] *vi* **to teem with** : estar repleto de, estar lleno de

teenage ['ti:nˌeɪdʒ] *or* **teenaged** [-eɪdʒd] *adj* : adolescente, de adolescencia

teenager ['ti:nˌeɪdʒər] *n* : adolescente *mf*

teens ['ti:nz] *npl* : adolescencia *f*

teepee → **tepee**

teeter¹ ['ti:tər] *vi* : balancearse, tambalearse

teeter² *n or* **teeter–totter** ['ti:tər-ˌtɑtər] → **seesaw**

teeth → **tooth**

teethe ['ti:ð] *vi* **teethed; teething** : formársele a uno los dientes ⟨the baby's teething : le están saliendo los dientes al niño⟩

telecast¹ ['tɛləˌkæst] *vt* **-cast; -casting** : televisar, transmitir por televisión

telecast² *n* : transmisión *f* por televisión

telecommunication [ˌtɛləkəˌmju:nəˈkeɪʃən] *n* : telecomunicación *f*

telegram ['tɛləˌgræm] *n* : telegrama *m*

telegraph¹ ['tɛləˌgræf] *v* : telegrafiar

telegraph² *n* : telégrafo *m*

telepathic [ˌtɛləˈpæθɪk] *adj* : telepático — **telepathically** [-θɪkli] *adv*

telepathy [təˈlɛpəθi] *n* : telepatía *f*

telephone¹ ['tɛləˌfo:n] *v* **-phoned; -phoning** *vt* : llamar por teléfono a, telefonear — *vi* : telefonear

telephone² *n* : teléfono *m*

telescope¹ ['tɛləˌsko:p] *vi* **-scoped; -scoping** : plegarse (como un telescopio)

telescope² *n* : telescopio *m*

telescopic [ˌtɛləˈskɑpɪk] *adj* : telescópico

televise ['tɛləˌvaɪz] *vt* **-vised; -vising** : televisar

television ['tɛləˌvɪʒən] *n* : televisión *f*

tell ['tɛl] *v* **told** ['to:ld]; **telling** *vt* **1** COUNT : contar, enumerar ⟨all told : en total⟩ **2** INSTRUCT : decir ⟨he told me how to fix it : me dijo cómo arreglarlo⟩ ⟨they told her to wait : le dijeron que esperara⟩ **3** RELATE : contar, relatar, narrar ⟨to tell a story : contar una historia⟩ **4** DIVULGE, REVEAL : revelar, divulgar ⟨he told me everything about her : me contó todo acerca de ella⟩ **5** DISCERN : discernir, notar ⟨I can't tell the difference : no noto la diferencia⟩ — *vi* **1** SAY : decir ⟨I won't tell : no voy a decírselo a nadie⟩ **2** KNOW : saber ⟨you never can tell : nunca se sabe⟩ **3** SHOW : notarse, hacerse sentir ⟨the strain is beginning to tell : la tensión se empieza a notar⟩

teller ['tɛlər] *n* **1** NARRATOR : narrador *m*, -dora *f* **2** *or* **bank teller** : cajero *m*, -ra *f*

temerity [təˈmɛrəti] *n, pl* **-ties** : temeridad *f*

temp ['tɛmp] *n* : empleado *m*, -da *f* temporal

temper¹ ['tɛmpər] *vt* **1** MODERATE : moderar, temperar **2** ANNEAL : templar (acero, etc.)

temper² *n* **1** DISPOSITION : carácter *m*, genio *m* **2** HARDNESS : temple *m*, dureza *f* (de un metal) **3** COMPOSURE : calma *f*, serenidad *f* ⟨to lose one's temper : perder los estribos⟩ **4** RAGE : furia *f* ⟨to fly into a temper : ponerse furioso⟩

temperament ['tɛmpərmənt, -prə-, -pərə-] *n* : temperamento *m*

temperamental [ˌtɛmpər'mɛntəl, -prə-, -pərə-] *adj* : temperamental

temperance ['tɛmprənts] *n* : templanza *f*, temperancia *f*

temperate ['tɛmpərət] *adj* : templado (dícese del clima, etc.), moderado

temperature ['tɛmpərˌtʃur, -prə-, -pərə-, -tʃər] *n* **1** : temperatura *f* **2** FEVER : calentura *f*, fiebre *f*

tempest ['tɛmpəst] *n* : tempestad *f*

tempestuous [tɛm'pɛstʃuəs] *adj* : tempestuoso

temple ['tɛmpəl] *n* **1** : templo *m* (en religión) **2** : sien *f* (en anatomía)

tempo ['tɛmˌpo:] *n, pl* **-pi** [-ˌpi:] *or* **-pos** : ritmo *m*, tempo *m* (en música)

temporal ['tɛmpərəl] *adj* : temporal

temporarily [ˌtɛmpə'rɛrəli] *adv* : temporalmente, provisionalmente

temporary ['tɛmpəˌrɛri] *adj* : temporal, provisional, provisorio

tempt ['tɛmpt] *vt* : tentar

temptation [tɛmp'teɪʃən] *n* : tentación *f*

tempter ['tɛmptər] *n* : tentador *m*

temptress ['tɛmptrəs] *n* : tentadora *f*

ten¹ ['tɛn] *adj* : diez

ten² *n* **1** : diez *m* (número) **2** : decena *f* ⟨tens of thousands : decenas de millares⟩

tenable ['tɛnəbəl] *adj* : sostenible, defendible

tenacious [tə'neɪʃəs] *adj* : tenaz

tenacity [tə'næsəti] *n* : tenacidad *f*

tenancy ['tɛnəntsi] *n, pl* **-cies** : tenencia *f*, inquilinato *m* (de un inmueble)

tenant ['tɛnənt] *n* : inquilino *m*, -na *f*; arrendatario *m*, -ria *f*

tend ['tɛnd] *vt* : atender, cuidar (de), ocuparse de — *vi* : tender ⟨it tends to benefit the consumer : tiende a beneficiar al consumidor⟩

tendency ['tɛndəntsi] *n, pl* **-cies** : tendencia *f*, proclividad *f*, inclinación *f*

tender¹ ['tɛndər] *vt* : entregar, presentar ⟨I tendered my resignation : presenté mi renuncia⟩

tender² *adj* **1** : tierno, blando ⟨tender steak : bistec tierno⟩ **2** AFFECTIONATE, LOVING : tierno, cariñoso, afectuoso **3** DELICATE : tierno, sensible, delicado

tender³ *n* **1** OFFER : propuesta *f*, oferta *f* (en negocios) **2 legal tender** : moneda *f* de curso legal

tenderize ['tɛndəˌraɪz] *vt* **-ized; -izing** : ablandar (carnes)

tenderloin ['tɛndrˌlɔɪn] *n* : lomo *f* (de res o de puerco)

tenderly ['tɛndərli] *adv* : tiernamente, con ternura

tenderness ['tɛndərnəs] *n* : ternura *f*

tendon ['tɛndən] *n* : tendón *m*

tendril ['tɛndrɪl] *n* : zarcillo *m*

tenement ['tɛnəmənt] *n* : casa *f* de vecindad

tenet ['tɛnət] *n* : principio *m*

tennis ['tɛnəs] *n* : tenis *m*

tenor ['tɛnər] *n* **1** PURPORT : tenor *m*, significado *m* **2** : tenor *m* (en música)

tenpins ['tɛnˌpɪnz] *npl* : bolos *mpl*, boliche *m*

tense¹ ['tɛnts] *v* **tensed; tensing** *vt* : tensar — *vi* : tensarse, ponerse tenso

tense² *adj* **tenser; tensest 1** TAUT : tenso, tirante **2** NERVOUS : tenso, nervioso

tense³ *n* : tiempo *m* (de un verbo)

tensely ['tɛntsli] *adv* : tensamente

tenseness ['tɛntsnəs] → **tension**

tension ['tɛntʃən] *n* **1** TAUTNESS : tensión *f*, tirantez *f* **2** STRESS : tensión *f*, nerviosismo *m*, estrés *m*

tent ['tɛnt] *n* : tienda *f* de campaña

tentacle ['tɛntɪkəl] *n* : tentáculo *m*

tentative ['tɛntətɪv] *adj* **1** HESITANT : indeciso, vacilante **2** PROVISIONAL : sujeto a cambios, provisional

tentatively ['tɛntətɪvli] *adv* : provisionalmente

tenth¹ ['tɛnθ] *adj* : décimo

tenth² *n* **1** : décimo *m*, -ma *f* (en una serie) **2** : décimo *m*, décima parte *f*

tenuous ['tɛnjuəs] *adj* : tenue, débil ⟨tenuous reasons : razones poco convincentes⟩

tenuously ['tɛnjuəsli] *adv* : tenuemente, ligeramente

tenure ['tɛnjər] *n* : tenencia *f* (de un cargo o una propiedad), titularidad *f* (de un puesto académico)

tepee ['ti:ˌpi:] *n* : tipi *m*

tepid ['tɛpɪd] *adj* : tibio

tequila [tə'ki:lə] *n* : tequila *m*

term¹ ['tərm] *vt* : calificar de, llamar, nombrar

term² *n* **1** PERIOD : término *m*, plazo *m*, período *m* **2** : término *m* (en matemáticas) **3** WORD : término *m*, vocablo *m* ⟨legal terms : términos legales⟩ **4 terms** *npl* CONDITIONS : términos *mpl*, condiciones *fpl* **5 terms** *npl* RELATIONS : relaciones *fpl* ⟨to be on good terms with : tener buenas relaciones con⟩ **6 in terms of** : con respecto a, en cuanto a

terminal¹ ['tərmənəl] *adj* : terminal

terminal² *n* **1** : terminal *m*, polo *m* (en electricidad) **2** : terminal *m* (de una computadora) **3** STATION : terminal *f*, estación *f* (de transporte público)

terminate ['tərməˌneɪt] *v* **-nated; -nating** *vi* : terminar(se), concluirse — *vt* : terminar, poner fin a

termination [ˌtərmə'neɪʃən] *n* : cese *m*, terminación *f*

terminology [ˌtərmə'nalədʒi] *n, pl* **-gies** : terminología *f*

terminus ['tərmənəs] *n, pl* **-ni** [-ˌnaɪ] *or* **-nuses 1** END : término *m*, fin *m* **2** : terminal *f* (de transporte público)

termite ['tər,maɪt] *n* : termita *f*
tern ['tərn] *n* : golondrina *f* de mar
terrace¹ ['terəs] *vt* **-raced; -racing** : formar en terrazas, disponer en bancales
terrace² *n* **1** PATIO : terraza *f*, patio *m* **2** : terraplén *m*, terraza *f*, bancal *m* (en agricultura)
terra–cotta [ˌterə'kɑtə] *n* : terracota *f*
terrain [tə'reɪn] *n* : terreno *m*
terrapin ['terəpɪn] *n* : galápago *m* norteamericano
terrarium [tə'ræriəm] *n, pl* **-ia** [-iə] *or* **-iums** : terrario *m*
terrestrial [tə'restriəl] *adj* : terrestre
terrible ['terəbəl] *adj* : atroz, horrible, terrible
terribly ['terəbli] *adv* **1** BADLY : muy mal **2** EXTREMELY : terriblemente, extremadamente
terrier ['teriər] *n* : terrier *mf*
terrific [tə'rɪfɪk] *adj* **1** FRIGHTFUL : aterrador **2** EXTRAORDINARY : extraordinario, excepcional **3** EXCELLENT : excelente, estupendo
terrify ['terə,faɪ] *vt* **-fied; -fying** : aterrorizar, aterrar, espantar
terrifying ['terə,faɪɪŋ] *adj* : espantoso, aterrador
territory ['terə,tori] *n, pl* **-ries** : territorio *m* — **territorial** [ˌterə'toriəl] *adj*
terror ['terər] *n* : terror *m*
terrorism ['terər,ɪzəm] *n* : terrorismo *m*
terrorist¹ ['terərɪst] *adj* : terrorista
terrorist² *n* : terrorista *mf*
terrorize ['terər,aɪz] *vt* **-ized; -izing** : aterrorizar
terry ['teri] *n, pl* **-ries** *or* **terry cloth** : (tela de) toalla *f*
terse ['tərs] *adj* **terser; tersest** : lacónico, conciso, seco — **tersely** *adv*
tertiary ['tər,ʃi,eri] *adj* : terciario
test¹ ['test] *vt* : examinar, evaluar — *vi* : hacer pruebas
test² *n* : prueba *f*, examen *m*, test *m* ⟨to put to the test : poner a prueba⟩
testament ['testəmənt] *n* **1** WILL : testamento *m* **2** : Testamento *m* (en la Biblia) ⟨the Old Testament : el Antiguo Testamento⟩
testicle ['testɪkəl] *n* : testículo *m*
testify ['testə,faɪ] *v* **-fied; -fying** *vi* : testificar, atestar, testimoniar — *vt* : testificar
testimonial [ˌtestə'mo:niəl] *n* **1** REFERENCE : recomendación *f* **2** TRIBUTE : homenaje *m*, tributo *m*
testimony ['testə,mo:ni] *n, pl* **-nies** : testimonio *m*, declaración *f*
test tube *n* : probeta *f*, tubo *m* de ensayo
testy ['testi] *adj* **-tier; -est** : irritable
tetanus ['tetənəs] *n* : tétano *m*, tétanos *m*
tête–à–tête [ˌtetə'tet, ˌteɪtə'teɪt] *n* : conversación *f* en privado
tether¹ ['teðər] *vt* : atar (con una cuerda), amarrar
tether² *n* : atadura *f*, cadena *f*, correa *f*

text ['tekst] *n* **1** : texto *m* **2** TOPIC : tema *m* **3** → **textbook**
textbook ['tekst,bʊk] *n* : libro *m* de texto
textile ['tek,staɪl, 'tekstəl] *n* : textil *m*, tela *f* ⟨the textile industry : la industria textil⟩
textual ['tekstʃuəl] *adj* : textual
texture ['tekstʃər] *n* : textura *f*
Thai ['taɪ] *n* **1** : tailandés *m*, -desa *f* **2** : tailandés *m* (idioma) — **Thai** *adj*
than¹ ['ðæn] *conj* : que, de ⟨it's worth more than that : vale más que eso⟩ ⟨more than you think : más de lo que piensas⟩
than² *prep* : que, de ⟨you're better than he is : eres mejor que él⟩ ⟨more than once : más de una vez⟩
thank ['θæŋk] *vt* : agradecer, darle (las) gracias (a alguien) ⟨thank you! : ¡gracias!⟩ ⟨I thanked her for the present : le di las gracias por el regalo⟩ ⟨I thank you for your help : le agradezco su ayuda⟩
thankful ['θæŋkfəl] *adj* : agradecido
thankfully ['θæŋkfəli] *adv* **1** GRATEFULLY : con agradecimiento **2** FORTUNATELY : afortunadamente, por suerte ⟨thankfully, it's over : se acabó, gracias a Dios⟩
thankfulness ['θæŋkfəlnəs] *n* : agradecimiento *m*, gratitud *f*
thankless ['θæŋkləs] *adj* : ingrato ⟨a thankless task : un trabajo ingrato⟩
thanks ['θæŋks] *npl* **1** : agradecimiento *m* **2** thanks! : ¡gracias!
Thanksgiving [θæŋks'gɪvɪŋ, 'θæŋks,-] *n* : el día de Acción de Gracias (fiesta estadounidense)
that¹ ['ðæt] *adv* (*in negative constructions*) : tan ⟨it's not that expensive : no es tan caro⟩ ⟨not that much : no tanto⟩
that² *adj, pl* **those** : ese, esa, aquel, aquella ⟨do you see those children? : ¿ves a aquellos niños?⟩
that³ *conj & pron* : que ⟨he said that he was afraid : dijo que tenía miedo⟩ ⟨the book that he wrote : el libro que escribió⟩
that⁴ *pron, pl* **those** ['ðo:z] **1** : ése, ésa, eso ⟨that's my father : ése es mi padre⟩ ⟨those are the ones he likes : ésos son los que le gustan⟩ ⟨what's that? : ¿qué es eso?⟩ **2** (*referring to more distant objects or time*) : aquél, aquélla, aquello ⟨those are maples and these are elms : aquéllos son arces y éstos son olmos⟩ ⟨that came to an end : aquello se acabó⟩
thatch¹ ['θætʃ] *vt* : cubrir o techar con paja
thatch² *n* : paja *f* (usada para techos)
thaw¹ ['θɔ] *vt* : descongelar — *vi* : derretirse (dícese de la nieve), descongelarse (dícese de los alimentos)
thaw² *n* : deshielo *m*

the¹ [ðə, *before vowel sounds usu* ði:] *adv*
1 (*used to indicate comparison*) ⟨the
sooner the better : cuanto más pronto,
mejor⟩ ⟨she likes this one the best : éste
es el que más le gusta⟩ **2** (*used as a conjunction*) : cuanto ⟨the more I learn,
the less I understand : cuanto más
aprendo, menos entiendo⟩

the² *art* : el, la, los, las ⟨the gloves : los
guantes⟩ ⟨the suitcase : la maleta⟩
⟨forty cookies to the box : cuarenta
galletas por caja⟩

theater *or* **theatre** ['θi:ətər] *n* **1** : teatro
m (edificio) **2** DRAMA : teatro *m*, drama *m*

theatrical [θi'ætrıkəl] *adj* : teatral,
dramático

thee ['ði:] *pron* : te, ti

theft ['θεft] *n* : robo *m*, hurto *m*

their ['ðεr] *adj* : su ⟨their friends : sus
amigos⟩

theirs ['ðεrz] *pron* : (el) suyo, (la) suya,
(los) suyos, (las) suyas ⟨they came for
theirs : vinieron por el suyo⟩ ⟨theirs is
bigger : la suya es más grande, la de ellos es más grande⟩ ⟨a brother of theirs
: un hermano suyo, un hermano de
ellos⟩

them ['ðεm] *pron* **1** (*as a direct object*)
: los (*Spain sometimes* les), las ⟨I know
them : los conozco⟩ **2** (*as indirect object*) : les, se ⟨I sent them a letter : les
mandé una carta⟩ ⟨give it to them
: dáselo a ellos⟩ **3** (*as object of a preposition*) : ellos, ellas ⟨go with them : ve
con ellos⟩ **4** (*for emphasis*) : ellos,
ellas ⟨I wasn't expecting them : no los
esperaba a ellos⟩

thematic [θi'mætık] *adj* : temático

theme ['θi:m] *n* **1** SUBJECT, TOPIC : tema
m **2** COMPOSITION : composición *f*, trabajo *m* (escrito) **3** : tema *m* (en música)

themselves [ðəm'sεlvz, ðεm-] *pron* **1**
(*as a reflexive*) : se, sí ⟨they enjoyed
themselves : se divirtieron⟩ ⟨they divided it among themselves : lo
repartieron entre sí, se lo repartieron⟩
2 (*for emphasis*) : ellos mismos, ellas
mismas ⟨they built it themselves : ellas
mismas lo construyeron⟩

then¹ ['ðεn] *adv* **1** : entonces, en ese
tiempo ⟨I was sixteen then : tenía entonces dieciséis años⟩ ⟨since then : desde entonces⟩ **2** NEXT : después, luego
⟨we'll go to Toronto, then to Winnipeg
: iremos a Toronto, y luego a Winnipeg⟩
3 BESIDES : además, aparte ⟨then
there's the tax : y aparte está el impuesto⟩ **4** : entonces, en ese caso ⟨if
you like music, then you should attend
: si te gusta la música, entonces deberías asistir⟩

then² *adj* : entonces ⟨the then governor
of Georgia : el entonces gobernador de
Georgia⟩

thence ['ðεnts, 'θεnts] *adv* : de ahí, de ahí
en adelante

theologian [ˌθi:ə'lo:ʤən] *n* : teólogo *m*,
-ga *f*

theological [ˌθi:ə'lɑʤıkəl] *adj* : teológico

theology [θi'ɑləʤi] *n, pl* **-gies** : teología
f

theorem ['θi:ərəm, 'θırəm] *n* : teorema
m

theoretical [ˌθi:ə'rεtıkəl] *adj* : teórico —
theoretically *adv*

theorist ['θi:ərıst] *n* : teórico *m*, -ca *f*

theorize ['θi:əˌraız] *vi* **-rized; -rizing**
: teorizar

theory ['θi:əri, 'θıri] *n, pl* **-ries** : teoría *f*

therapeutic [ˌθεrə'pju:tık] *adj* : terapéutico — **therapeutically** *adv*

therapist ['θεrəpıst] *n* : terapeuta *mf*

therapy ['θεrəpi] *n, pl* **-pies** : terapia *f*

there¹ ['ðær] *adv* **1** : ahí, allí, allá ⟨stand
over there : párate ahí⟩ ⟨over there
: por allí, por allá⟩ ⟨who's there?
: ¿quién es?⟩ **2** : ahí, en esto, en eso
⟨there is where we disagree : en eso es
donde no estamos de acuerdo⟩

there² *pron* **1** (*introducing a sentence or
clause*) ⟨there comes a time to decide
: llega un momento en que tiene uno
que decidir⟩ **2 there is, there are** : hay
⟨there are many children here : aquí
hay muchos niños⟩ ⟨there's a good hotel downtown : hay un buen hotel en
el centro⟩

thereabouts [ˌðærə'bauts, 'ðærəˌ-] *or*
thereabout [-'baut, -ˌbaut] *adv* **or**
thereabouts : por ahí, más o menos ⟨at
five o'clock or thereabouts : por ahí de
las cinco⟩

thereafter [ðær'æftər] *adv* : después
⟨shortly thereafter : poco después⟩

thereby [ðær'baı, 'ðærˌbaı] *adv* : de tal
modo, de ese manera, así

therefore ['ðærˌfor] *adv* : por lo tanto,
por consiguiente

therein [ðær'ın] *adv* **1** : allí adentro, ahí
adentro ⟨the contents therein : lo que
allí se contiene⟩ **2** : allí, en ese aspecto ⟨therein lies the problem : allí está
el problema⟩

thereof [ðær'ʌv, -'ɑv] *adv* : de eso, de
esto

thereupon ['ðærəˌpɑn, -ˌpɔn; ˌðærə'pɑn,
-'pɔn] *adv* : acto seguido, inmediatamente (después)

therewith [ðær'wıð, -'wıθ] *adv* : con eso,
con ello

thermal ['θərməl] *adj* **1** : térmico (en física) **2** HOT : termal

thermodynamics [ˌθərmodaı'næmıks]
ns & pl : termodinámica *f*

thermometer [θər'mɑmətər] *n* : termómetro *m*

thermos ['θərməs] *n* : termo *m*

thermostat ['θərməˌstæt] *n* : termostato
m

thesaurus [θı'sɔrəs] *n, pl* **-sauri** [-'sɔrˌaı]
or **-sauruses** [-'sɔrəsəz] : diccionario *m*
de sinónimos

these → **this**

thesis ['θi:sɪs] *n, pl* **theses** ['θi:ˌsi:z] : tesis *f*

they ['ðeɪ] *pron* : ellos, ellas ⟨they are here : están aquí⟩ ⟨they don't know : ellos no saben⟩

they'd ['ðeɪd] (*contraction of* **they had** *or* **they would**) → **have, would**

they'll ['ðeɪl, 'ðɛl] (*contraction of* **they shall** *or* **they will**) → **shall, will**

they're ['ðɛr] (*contraction of* **they are**) → **be**

they've ['ðeɪv] (*contraction of* **they have**) → **have**

thiamine ['θaɪəmɪn, -ˌmi:n] *n* : tiamina *f*

thick¹ ['θɪk] *adj* **1** : grueso ⟨a thick plank : una tabla gruesa⟩ **2** : espeso, denso ⟨thick syrup : jarabe espeso⟩ — **thickly** *adv*

thick² *n* **1 in the thick of** : en medio de ⟨in the thick of the battle : en lo más reñido de la batalla⟩ **2 through thick and thin** : a las duras y a las maduras

thicken ['θɪkən] *vt* : espesar (un líquido) — *vi* : espesarse

thickener ['θɪkənər] *n* : espesante *m*

thicket ['θɪkət] *n* : matorral *m*, maleza *f*, espesura *f*

thickness ['θɪknəs] *n* : grosor *m*, grueso *m*, espesor *m*

thickset ['θɪk'sɛt] *adj* STOCKY : robusto, fornido

thick–skinned ['θɪk'skɪnd] *adj* : poco sensible, que no se ofende fácilmente

thief ['θi:f] *n, pl* **thieves** ['θi:vz] : ladrón *m*, -drona *f*

thieve ['θi:v] *v* **thieved; thieving** : hurtar, robar

thievery ['θi:vəri] *n* : hurto *m*, robo *m*, latrocinio *m*

thigh ['θaɪ] *n* : muslo *m*

thighbone ['θaɪˌbo:n] *n* : fémur *m*

thimble ['θɪmbəl] *n* : dedal *m*

thin¹ ['θɪn] *v* **thinned; thinning** *vt* : hacer menos denso, diluir, aguar (un líquido), enrarecer (un gas) — *vi* : diluirse, aguarse (dícese de un líquido), enrarecerse (dícese de un gas)

thin² *adj* **thinner; -est 1** LEAN, SLIM : delgado, esbelto, flaco **2** SPARSE : ralo, escaso ⟨a thin beard : una barba rala⟩ **3** WATERY : claro, aguado, diluido **4** FINE : delgado, fino ⟨thin slices : rebanadas finas⟩

thing ['θɪŋ] *n* **1** AFFAIR, MATTER : cosa *f*, asunto *m* ⟨don't talk about those things : no hables de esas cosas⟩ ⟨how are things? : ¿cómo van las cosas?⟩ **2** ACT, EVENT : cosa *f*, suceso *m*, evento *m* ⟨the flood was a terrible thing : la inundación fue una cosa terrible⟩ **3** OBJECT : cosa *f*, objeto *m* ⟨don't forget your things : no olvides tus cosas⟩

think ['θɪŋk] *v* **thought** ['θɔt]; **thinking** *vt* **1** : pensar ⟨I thought to return early : pensaba regresar temprano⟩ **2** BELIEVE : pensar, creer, opinar **3** PONDER : pensar, reflexionar **4** CONCEIVE : ocurrirse, concebir ⟨we've thought up a plan : se nos ha ocurrido un plan⟩ —

vi **1** REASON : pensar, razonar **2** CONSIDER : pensar, considerar ⟨think of your family first : primero piensa en tu familia⟩

thinker ['θɪŋkər] *n* : pensador *m*, -dora *f*

thinly ['θɪnli] *adv* **1** LIGHTLY : ligeramente **2** SPARSELY : escasamente ⟨thinly populated : poco populado⟩ **3** BARELY : apenas

thinness ['θɪnnəs] *n* : delgadez *f*

thin–skinned ['θɪn'skɪnd] *adj* : susceptible, muy sensible

third¹ ['θərd] *or* **thirdly** [-li] *adv* : en tercer lugar ⟨she came in third : llegó en tercer lugar⟩

third² *adj* : tercero ⟨the third day : el tercer día⟩

third³ *n* **1** : tercero *m*, -ra *f* (en una serie) **2** : tercero *m*, tercera parte *f*

third world *n* **the Third World** : el Tercer Mundo *m*

thirst¹ ['θərst] *vi* **1** : tener sed **2 to thirst for** DESIRE : tener sed de, estar sediento de

thirst² *n* : sed *f*

thirsty ['θərsti] *adj* **thirstier; -est** : sediento, que tiene sed ⟨I'm thirsty : tengo sed⟩

thirteen¹ [ˌθər'ti:n] *adj* : trece

thirteen² *n* : trece *m*

thirteenth¹ [ˌθər'ti:nθ] *adj* : décimo tercero

thirteenth² *n* **1** : decimotercero *m*, -ra *f* (en una serie) **2** : treceavo *m*, treceava parte *f*

thirtieth¹ ['θərtʃəθ] *adj* : trigésimo

thirtieth² *n* **1** : trigésimo *m*, -ma *f* (en una serie) **2** : treintavo *m*, treintava parte *f*

thirty¹ ['θərti] *adj* : treinta

thirty² *n, pl* **thirties** : treinta *m*

this¹ ['ðɪs] *adv* : así, a tal punto ⟨this big : así de grande⟩

this² *adj, pl* **these** ['ði:z] : este ⟨these things : estas cosas⟩ ⟨read this book : lee este libro⟩

this³ *pron, pl* **these** : esto ⟨what's this? : ¿qué es esto?⟩ ⟨this wasn't here yesterday : esto no estaba aquí ayer⟩

thistle ['θɪsəl] *n* : cardo *m*

thong ['θɔŋ] *n* **1** STRAP : correa *f*, tira *f* **2** FLIP-FLOP : chancla *f*, chancleta *f*

thorax ['θorˌæks] *n, pl* **-raxes** *or* **-races** ['θorəˌsi:z] : tórax *m*

thorn ['θorn] *n* : espina *f*

thorny ['θorni] *adj* **thornier; -est** : espinoso

thorough ['θəro:] *adj* **1** CONSCIENTIOUS : concienzudo, meticuloso **2** COMPLETE : absoluto, completo — **thoroughly** *adv*

thoroughbred ['θəroˌbrɛd] *adj* : de pura sangre (dícese de un caballo)

Thoroughbred *n* *or* **Thoroughbred horse** : pura sangre *mf*

thoroughfare ['θəroˌfær] *n* : vía *f* pública, carretera *f*

thoroughness ['θəronəs] *n* : esmero *m*, meticulosidad *f*

those → **that**

thou ['ðaʊ] *pron* : tú

though¹ ['ðo:] *adv* **1** HOWEVER, NEVERTHELESS : sin embargo, no obstante **2** as ～ : como si ⟨as though nothing had happened : como si nada hubiera pasado⟩

though² *conj* : aunque, a pesar de ⟨though it was raining, we went out : salimos a pesar de la lluvia⟩

thought¹ → **think**

thought² ['θɔt] *n* **1** THINKING : pensamiento *m*, ideas *fpl* ⟨Western thought : el pensamiento occidental⟩ **2** COGITATION : pensamiento *m*, reflexión *f*, raciocinio *m* **3** IDEA : idea *f*, ocurrencia *f* ⟨it was just a thought : fue sólo una idea⟩

thoughtful ['θɔtfəl] *adj* **1** PENSIVE : pensativo, meditabundo **2** CONSIDERATE : considerado, atento, cortés — **thoughtfully** *adv*

thoughtfulness ['θɔtfəlnəs] *n* : consideración *f*, atención *f*, cortesía *f*

thoughtless ['θɔtləs] *adj* **1** CARELESS : descuidado, negligente **2** INCONSIDERATE : desconsiderado — **thoughtlessly** *adv*

thousand¹ ['θaʊzənd] *adj* : mil

thousand² *n*, *pl* **-sands** *or* **-sand** : mil *m*

thousandth¹ ['θaʊzəntθ] *adj* : milésimo

thousandth² *n* **1** : milésimo *m*, -ma *f* (en una serie) **2** : milésimo *m*, milésima parte *f*

thrash ['θræʃ] *vt* **1** → **thresh 2** BEAT : golpear, azotar, darle una paliza (a alguien) **3** FLAIL : sacudir, agitar bruscamente

thread¹ ['θrɛd] *vt* **1** : enhilar, enhebrar (una aguja) **2** STRING : ensartar (cuentas en un hilo) **3 to thread one's way** : abrirse paso

thread² *n* **1** : hilo *m*, hebra *f* ⟨needle and thread : aguja e hilo⟩ ⟨the thread of an argument : el hilo de un debate⟩ **2** : rosca *f*, filete *m* (de un tornillo)

threadbare ['θrɛd'bær] *adj* **1** SHABBY, WORN : raído, gastado **2** TRITE : trillado, tópico, manido

threat ['θrɛt] *n* : amenaza *f*

threaten ['θrɛtən] *v* : amenazar

threatening ['θrɛtəniŋ] *adj* : amenazador — **threateningly** *adv*

three¹ ['θri:] *adj* : tres

three² *n* : tres *m*

3–D ['θri:'di:] *adj* → **three–dimensional**

three–dimensional ['θri:də'mɛntʃənəl] *adj* : tridimensional

threefold ['θri:,fo:ld] *adj* TRIPLE : triple

three hundred¹ *adj* : trescientos

three hundred² *n* : trescientos *m*

threescore ['θri:'skor] *adj* SIXTY : sesenta

thresh ['θrɛʃ] *vt* : trillar (grano)

thresher ['θrɛʃər] *n* : trilladora *f*

threshold ['θrɛʃ,ho:ld, -,o:ld] *n* : umbral *m*

threw → **throw¹**

thrice ['θraɪs] *adv* : tres veces

thrift ['θrɪft] *n* : economía *f*, frugalidad *f*

thriftless ['θrɪftləs] *adj* : despilfarrador, manirroto

thrifty ['θrɪfti] *adj* **thriftier; -est** : económico, frugal — **thriftily** ['θrɪftəli] *adv*

thrill¹ ['θrɪl] *vt* : emocionar — *vi* **to thrill to** : dejarse conmover por, estremecerse con

thrill² *n* : emoción *f*

thriller ['θrɪlər] *n* **1** : evento *m* emocionante **2** : obra *f* de suspenso

thrilling ['θrɪlɪŋ] *adj* : emocionante, excitante

thrive ['θraɪv] *vi* **throve** ['θro:v] *or* **thrived; thriven** ['θrɪvən] **1** FLOURISH : florecer, crecer abundantemente **2** PROSPER : prosperar

throat ['θro:t] *n* : garganta *f*

throaty ['θro:ti] *adj* **throatier; -est** : ronco (dícese de la voz)

throb¹ ['θrɑb] *vi* **throbbed; throbbing** : palpitar, latir (dícese del corazón), vibrar (dícese de un motor, etc.)

throb² *n* : palpitación *f*, latido *m*, vibración *f*

throe ['θro:] *n* **1** PAIN, SPASM : espasmo *m*, dolor *m* ⟨the throes of childbirth : los dolores de parto⟩ **2 throes** *npl* : lucha *f* larga y ardua ⟨in the throes of : en el medio de⟩

throne ['θro:n] *n* : trono *m*

throng¹ ['θrɔŋ] *vt* CROWD : atestar, atiborrar, llenar — *vi* : aglomerarse, amontonarse

throng² *n* : muchedumbre *f*, gentío *m*, multitud *f*

throttle¹ ['θrɑtəl] *vt* **-tled; -tling 1** STRANGLE : estrangular, ahogar **2 to throttle down** : desacelerar (un motor)

throttle² *n* **1** : válvula *f* reguladora **2 at full throttle** : a toda máquina

through¹ ['θru:] *adv* **1** : a través, de un lado a otro ⟨let them through : déjenlos pasar⟩ **2** : de principio a fin ⟨she read the book through : leyó el libro de principio a fin⟩ **3** COMPLETELY : completamente ⟨soaked through : completamente empapado⟩

through² *adj* **1** DIRECT : directo ⟨a through train : un tren directo⟩ **2** FINISHED : terminado, acabado ⟨we're through : hemos terminado⟩

through³ *prep* **1** : a través de, por ⟨through the door : por la puerta⟩ ⟨a road through the woods : un camino que atraviesa el bosque⟩ **2** BETWEEN : entre ⟨a path through the trees : un sendero entre los árboles⟩ **3** BECAUSE OF : a causa de, como consecuencia de **4** (*in expressions of time*) ⟨through the night : durante la noche⟩ ⟨to go through an experience : pasar por una experiencia⟩ **5** : a, hasta ⟨from Monday through Friday : de lunes a viernes⟩

throughout¹ [θru:'aʊt] *adv* **1** EVERY-WHERE : por todas partes **2** THROUGH : desde el principio hasta el fin de (algo)
throughout² *prep* **1** : en todas partes de, a través de ⟨throughout the United States : en todo Estados Unidos⟩ **2** : de principio a fin de, durante ⟨throughout the winter : durante todo el invierno⟩
throve → **thrive**
throw¹ ['θro:] *vt* **threw** ['θru:]; **thrown** ['θro:n]; **throwing 1** TOSS : tirar, lanzar, echar, arrojar, aventar *Col, Mex* ⟨to throw a ball : tirar una pelota⟩ **2** UNSEAT : desmontar (a un jinete) **3** CAST : proyectar ⟨it threw a long shadow : proyectó una sombra larga⟩ **4 to throw a party** : dar una fiesta **5 to throw into confusion** : desconcertar **6 to throw out** DISCARD : botar, tirar (en la basura)
throw² *n* TOSS : tiro *m*, tirada *f*, lanzamiento *m*, lance *m* (de dados)
thrower ['θro:ər] *n* : lanzador *m*, -dora *f*
throw up *v* VOMIT : vomitar, devolver
thrush ['θrʌʃ] *n* : tordo *m*, zorzal *m*
thrust¹ ['θrʌst] *vt* **thrust; thrusting 1** SHOVE : empujar bruscamente **2** PLUNGE, STAB : apuñalar, clavar ⟨he thrust a dagger into her heart : la apuñaló en el corazón⟩ **3 to thrust one's way** : abrirse paso **4 to thrust upon** : imponer a
thrust² *n* **1** PUSH, SHOVE : empujón *m*, empellón *m* **2** LUNGE : estocada *f* (en esgrima) **3** IMPETUS : ímpetu *m*, impulso *m*, propulsión *f* (de un motor)
thud¹ ['θʌd] *vi* **thudded; thudding** : producir un ruido sordo
thud² *n* : ruido *m* sordo (que produce un objeto al caer)
thug ['θʌg] *n* : matón *m*
thumb¹ ['θʌm] *vt* : hojear (con el pulgar)
thumb² *n* : pulgar *m*, dedo *m* pulgar
thumbnail ['θʌm,neɪl] *n* : uña *f* del pulgar
thumbtack ['θʌm,tæk] *n* : tachuela *f*, chinche *f*
thump¹ ['θʌmp] *vt* POUND : golpear, aporrear — *vi* : latir con vehemencia (dícese del corazón)
thump² *n* THUD : ruido *m* sordo
thunder¹ ['θʌndər] *vi* **1** : tronar ⟨it rained and thundered all night : llovió y tronó durante la noche⟩ **2** BOOM : retumbar, bramar, resonar — *vt* ROAR, SHOUT : decir a gritos, vociferar
thunder² *n* : truenos *mpl*
thunderbolt ['θʌndər,bo:lt] *n* : rayo *m*
thunderclap ['θʌndər,klæp] *n* : trueno *m*
thunderous ['θʌndərəs] *adj* : atronador, ensordecedor, estruendoso
thundershower ['θʌndər,ʃaʊər] *n* : lluvia *f* con truenos y relámpagos
thunderstorm ['θʌndər,stɔrm] *n* : tormenta *f* con truenos y relámpagos
thunderstruck ['θʌndər,strʌk] *adj* : atónito

Thursday ['θərz,deɪ, -di] *n* : jueves *m*
thus ['ðʌs] *adv* **1** : así, de esta manera **2** SO : hasta (cierto punto) ⟨the weather's been nice thus far : hasta ahora ha hecho buen tiempo⟩ **3** HENCE : por consiguiente, por lo tanto
thwart ['θwɔrt] *vt* : frustrar
thy ['ðaɪ] *adj* : tu
thyme ['taɪm, 'θaɪm] *n* : tomillo *m*
thyroid ['θaɪ,rɔɪd] *n or* **thyroid gland** : tiroides *mf*, glándula *f* tiroidea
thyself [ðaɪ'sɛlf] *pron* : ti, ti mismo
tiara [ti'ærə, -'ɑr-] *n* : diadema *f*
Tibetan [tə'bɛtən] *n* **1** : tibetano *m*, -na *f* **2** : tibetano *m* (idioma) — **Tibetan** *adj*
tibia ['tɪbiə] *n, pl* **-iae** [-bi,i:] : tibia *f*
tic ['tɪk] *n* : tic *m*
tick¹ ['tɪk] *vi* **1** : hacer tictac **2** OPERATE, RUN : operar, andar (dícese de un mecanismo) ⟨what makes him tick? : ¿qué es lo que lo mueve?⟩ — *vt or* **to tick off** CHECK : marcar
tick² *n* **1** : tictac *m* (de un reloj) **2** CHECK : marca *f* **3** : garrapata *f* (insecto)
ticket¹ ['tɪkət] *vt* LABEL : etiquetar
ticket² *n* **1** : boleto *m*, entrada *f* (de un espectáculo), pasaje *m* (de avión, tren, etc.) **2** SLATE : lista *f* de candidatos
tickle¹ ['tɪkəl] *v* **-led; -ling** *vt* **1** AMUSE : divertir, hacerle gracia (a alguien) **2** : hacerle cosquillas (a alguien) ⟨don't tickle me! : ¡no me hagas cosquillas!⟩ — *vi* : picar
tickle² *n* : cosquilleo *m*, cosquillas *fpl*, picor *m* (en la garganta)
ticklish ['tɪkəlɪʃ] *adj* **1** : cosquilloso (dícese de una persona) **2** DELICATE, TRICKY : delicado, peliagudo
tidal ['taɪdəl] *adj* : de marea, relativo a la marea
tidal wave *n* : maremoto *m*
tidbit ['tɪd,bɪt] *n* **1** BITE, SNACK : bocado *m*, golosina *f* **2** : dato *m* o noticia *f* interesante ⟨useful tidbits of information : informaciones útiles⟩
tide¹ ['taɪd] *vt* **tided; tiding** *or* **to tide over** : proveer lo necesario para aguantar una dificultad ⟨this money will tide you over until you find work : este dinero te mantendrá hasta que encuentres empleo⟩
tide² *n* **1** : marea *f* **2** CURRENT : corriente *f* (de eventos, opiniones, etc.)
tidily ['taɪdəli] *adv* : ordenadamente
tidiness ['taɪdinəs] *n* : aseo *m*, limpieza *f*, orden *m*
tidings ['taɪdɪŋz] *npl* : nuevas *fpl*
tidy¹ ['taɪdi] *vt* **-died; -dying** : asear, limpiar, poner en orden
tidy² *adj* **-dier; -est 1** CLEAN, NEAT : limpio, aseado, en orden **2** SUBSTANTIAL : grande, considerable ⟨a tidy sum : una suma considerable⟩
tie¹ ['taɪ] *v* **tied; tying** *or* **tieing** *vt* **1** : atar, amarrar ⟨to tie a knot : atar un nudo⟩ ⟨to tie one's shoelaces : atarse los cordones⟩ **2** BIND, UNITE : ligar, atar **3** : empatar ⟨they tied the score : em-

pataron el marcador⟩ — *vi* : empatar ⟨the two teams were tied : los dos equipos empataron⟩

tie² *n* **1** : ligadura *f*, cuerda *f*, cordón *m* (para atar algo) **2** BOND, LINK : atadura *f*, ligadura *f*, vínculo *m*, lazo *m* ⟨family ties : lazos familiares⟩ **3** *or* **railroad tie** : traviesa *f* **4** DRAW : empate *m* (en deportes) **5** NECKTIE : corbata *f*

tier [ˈtɪr] *n* : hilera *f*, escalón *m*

tiff [ˈtɪf] *n* : disgusto *m*, disputa *f*

tiger [ˈtaɪɡər] *n* : tigre *m*

tight¹ [ˈtaɪt] *adv* TIGHTLY : bien, fuerte ⟨shut it tight : ciérralo bien⟩

tight² *adj* **1** : bien cerrado, hermético ⟨a tight seal : un cierre hermético⟩ **2** STRICT : estricto, severo **3** TAUT : tirante, tenso **4** SNUG : apretado, ajustado, ceñido ⟨a tight dress : un vestido ceñido⟩ **5** DIFFICULT : difícil ⟨to be in a tight spot : estar en un aprieto⟩ **6** STINGY : apretado, avaro, agarrado *fam* **7** CLOSE : reñido ⟨a tight game : un juego reñido⟩ **8** SCARCE : escaso ⟨money is tight : escasea el dinero⟩

tighten [ˈtaɪtən] *vt* : tensar (una cuerda, etc.), apretar (un nudo, un tornillo, etc.), apretarse (el cinturón), reforzar (las reglas)

tightly [ˈtaɪtli] *adv* : bien, fuerte

tightness [ˈtaɪtnəs] *n* : lo apretado, lo tenso, tensión *f*

tightrope [ˈtaɪtˌroːp] *n* : cuerda *f* floja

tights [ˈtaɪts] *npl* : leotardo *m*, malla *f*

tightwad [ˈtaɪtˌwɑd] *n* : avaro *m*, -ra *f*; tacaño *m*, -ña *f*

tigress [ˈtaɪɡrəs] *n* : tigresa *f*

tile¹ [ˈtaɪl] *vt* **tiled; tiling** : embaldosar (un piso), revestir de azulejos (una pared), tejar (un techo)

tile² *n* **1** *or* **floor tile** : losa *f*, baldosa *f*, mosaico *m* Mex (de un piso) **2** : azulejo *m* (de una pared) **3** : teja *f* (de un techo)

till¹ [ˈtɪl] *vt* : cultivar, labrar

till² *n* : caja *f*, caja *f* registradora

till³ *prep & conj* → until

tiller [ˈtɪlər] *n* **1** : cultivador *m*, -dora *f* (de la tierra) **2** : caña *f* del timón (de un barco)

tilt¹ [ˈtɪlt] *vt* : ladear, inclinar — *vi* : ladearse, inclinarse

tilt² *n* **1** SLANT : inclinación *f* **2 at full tilt** : a toda velocidad

timber [ˈtɪmbər] *n* **1** : madera *f* (para construcción) **2** BEAM : viga *f*

timberland [ˈtɪmbərˌlænd] *n* : bosque *m* maderero

timbre [ˈtæmbər, ˈtɪm-] *n* : timbre *m*

time¹ [ˈtaɪm] *vt* **timed; timing 1** SCHEDULE : fijar la hora de, calcular el momento oportuno para **2** CLOCK : cronometrar, medir el tiempo de (una competencia, etc.)

time² *n* **1** : tiempo *m* ⟨the passing of time : el paso del tiempo⟩ ⟨she doesn't have time : no tiene tiempo⟩ **2** MOMENT : tiempo *m*, momento *m* ⟨this is not the time to bring it up : no es el momento de sacar el tema⟩ **3** : vez *f* ⟨she called you three times : te llamó tres veces⟩ ⟨three times greater : tres veces mayor⟩ **4** AGE : tiempo *m*, era *f* ⟨in your grandparents' time : en el tiempo de tus abuelos⟩ **5** TEMPO : tiempo *m*, ritmo *m* (en música) **6** : hora *f* ⟨what time is it? : ¿qué hora es?⟩ ⟨it's time for dinner : es hora de comer⟩ ⟨at the usual time : a la hora acostumbrada⟩ ⟨to keep time : ir a la hora⟩ ⟨to lose time : atrasar⟩ **7** EXPERIENCE : rato *m*, experiencia *f* ⟨we had a nice time together : pasamos juntos un rato agradable⟩ ⟨to have a rough time : pasarlo mal⟩ ⟨have a good time! : ¡que se diviertan!⟩ **8 at times** SOMETIMES : a veces **9 for the time being** : por el momento, de momento **10 from time to time** OCCASIONALLY : de vez en cuando **11 in time** PUNCTUALLY : a tiempo **12 in time** EVENTUALLY : con el tiempo **13 time after time** : una y otra vez

timekeeper [ˈtaɪmˌkiːpər] *n* : cronometrador *m*, -dora *f*

timeless [ˈtaɪmləs] *adj* : eterno

timely [ˈtaɪmli] *adj* **-lier; -est** : oportuno

timepiece [ˈtaɪmˌpiːs] *n* : reloj *m*

timer [ˈtaɪmər] *n* : temporizador *m*, cronómetro *m*

times [ˈtaɪmz] *prep* : por ⟨3 times 4 is 12 : 3 por 4 son 12⟩

timetable [ˈtaɪmˌteɪbəl] *n* : horario *m*

timid [ˈtɪmɪd] *adj* : tímido — **timidly** *adv*

timidity [təˈmɪdəṭi] *n* : timidez *f*

timorous [ˈtɪmərəs] *adj* : timorato, miedoso

timpani [ˈtɪmpəni] *npl* : timbales *mpl*

tin [ˈtɪn] *n* **1** : estaño *m*, hojalata *f* (metal) **2** CAN : lata *f*, bote *m*, envase *m*

tincture [ˈtɪŋktʃər] *n* : tintura *f*

tinder [ˈtɪndər] *n* : yesca *f*

tine [ˈtaɪn] *n* : diente *m* (de un tenedor, etc.)

tinfoil [ˈtɪnˌfɔɪl] *n* : papel *m* (de) aluminio

tinge¹ [ˈtɪndʒ] *vt* **tinged; tingeing** *or* **tinging** [ˈtɪndʒɪŋ] TINT : matizar, teñir ligeramente

tinge² *n* **1** TINT : matiz *m*, tinte *m* sutil **2** TOUCH : dejo *m*, sensación *f* ligera

tingle¹ [ˈtɪŋɡəl] *vi* **-gled; -gling** : sentir (un) hormigueo, sentir (un) cosquilleo

tingle² *n* : hormigueo *m*, cosquilleo *m*

tinker [ˈtɪŋkər] *vi* **to tinker with** : arreglar con pequeños ajustes, toquetear (con intento de arreglar)

tinkle¹ [ˈtɪŋkəl] *vi* **-kled; -kling** : tintinear

tinkle² *n* : tintineo *m*

tinsel [ˈtɪntsəl] *n* : oropel *m*

tint¹ [ˈtɪnt] *vt* : teñir, colorear

tint² *n* : tinte *m*

tiny [ˈtaɪni] *adj* **-nier; -est** : diminuto, minúsculo

tip¹ [ˈtɪp] *v* **tipped; tipping** *vt* **1** *or* **to tip over** : volcar, voltear, hacer caer **2** TILT : ladear, inclinar ⟨to tip one's hat : saludar con el sombrero⟩ **3** TAP : tocar, golpear ligeramente **4** : darle una propina (a un mesero, etc.) ⟨I tipped him $5 : le di $5 de propina⟩ **5** : adornar o cubrir la punta de ⟨wings tipped in red : alas que tienen las puntas rojas⟩ **6 to tip off** : dar información a — *vi* TILT : ladearse, inclinarse

tip² *n* **1** END, POINT : punta *f*, extremo *m* ⟨on the tip of one's tongue : en la punta de la lengua⟩ **2** GRATUITY : propina *f* **3** ADVICE, INFORMATION : consejo *m*, información *f* (confidencial)

tip–off ['tɪpˌɔf] *n* **1** SIGN : indicación *f*, señal *f* **2** TIP : información *f* (confidencial)

tipple ['tɪpəl] *vi* **-pled; -pling** : tomarse unas copas

tipsy ['tɪpsi] *adj* **-sier; -est** : achispado

tiptoe¹ ['tɪpˌto:] *vi* **-toed; -toeing** : caminar de puntillas

tiptoe² *adv* : de puntillas

tiptoe³ *n* : punta *f* del pie

tip–top¹ ['tɪp'tɑp, -ˌtɑp] *adj* EXCELLENT : excelente

tip–top² *n* SUMMIT : cumbre *f*, cima *f*

tirade ['taɪˌreɪd] *n* : diatriba *f*

tire¹ ['taɪr] *v* **tired; tiring** *vt* : cansar, agotar, fatigar — *vi* : cansarse

tire² *n* : llanta *f*, neumático *m*, goma *f*

tired ['taɪrd] *adj* : cansado, agotado, fatigado ⟨to get tired : cansarse⟩

tireless ['taɪrləs] *adj* : incansable, infatigable — **tirelessly** *adv*

tiresome ['taɪrsəm] *adj* : fastidioso, pesado, tedioso — **tiresomely** *adv*

tissue ['tɪˌʃu:] *n* **1** : pañuelo *m* de papel **2** : tejido *m* ⟨lung tissue : tejido pulmonar⟩

titanic [taɪ'tænɪk, tə-] *adj* GIGANTIC : titánico, gigantesco

titanium [taɪ'teɪniəm, tə-] *n* : titanio *m*

titillate ['tɪtəlˌeɪt] *vt* **-lated; -lating** : excitar, estimular placenteramente

title¹ ['taɪtəl] *vt* **-tled; -tling** : titular, intitular

title² *n* : título *m*

titter¹ ['tɪtər] *vi* GIGGLE : reírse tontamente

titter² *n* : risita *f*, risa *f* tonta

tizzy ['tɪzi] *n, pl* **tizzies** : estado *m* agitado o nervioso ⟨I'm all in a tizzy : estoy todo alterado⟩

TNT [ˌti:ˌɛn'ti:] *n* : TNT *m*

to¹ ['tu:] *adv* **1** : a un estado consciente ⟨to come to : volver en sí⟩ **2 to and fro** : de aquí para allá, de un lado para otro

to² *prep* **1** (*indicating a place*) : a ⟨to go to the doctor : ir al médico⟩ ⟨I'm going to John's : voy a la casa de John⟩ **2** TOWARD : a, hacia ⟨two miles to the south : dos millas hacia el sur⟩ **3** ON : en, sobre ⟨apply salve to the wound : póngale ungüento a la herida⟩ **4** UP TO : hasta, a ⟨to a degree : hasta cierto grado⟩ ⟨from head to toe : de pies a cabeza⟩ **5** (*in expressions of time*) ⟨it's quarter to seven : son las siete menos

cuarto⟩ **6** UNTIL : a, hasta ⟨from May to December : de mayo a diciembre⟩ **7** (*indicating belonging or possession*) : de, a ⟨the key to the lock : la llave del candado⟩ **8** (*indicating response*) : a ⟨dancing to the rhythm : bailando al compás⟩ **9** (*indicating comparison or proportion*) : a ⟨it's similar to mine : es parecido al mío⟩ ⟨they won 4 to 2 : ganaron 4 a 2⟩ **10** (*indicating agreement or conformity*) : a, de acuerdo con ⟨made to order : hecho a la orden⟩ ⟨to my knowledge : a mi saber⟩ **11** (*indicating inclusion*) : en cada, por ⟨twenty to the box : veinte por caja⟩ **12** (*used to form the infinitive*) ⟨to understand : entender⟩ ⟨to go away : irse⟩

toad ['to:d] *n* : sapo *m*

toadstool ['to:dˌstu:l] *n* : hongo *m* (no comestible)

toady ['to:di] *n, pl* **toadies** : adulador *m*, -dora *f*

toast¹ ['to:st] *vt* **1** : tostar (pan) **2** : brindar por ⟨to toast the victors : brindar por los vencedores⟩ **3** WARM : calentar ⟨to toast oneself : calentarse⟩

toast² *n* **1** : pan *m* tostado, tostadas *fpl* **2** : brindis *m* ⟨to propose a toast : proponer un brindis⟩

toaster ['to:stər] *n* : tostador *m*

tobacco [tə'bæko:] *n, pl* **-cos** : tabaco *m*

toboggan¹ [tə'bɑgən] *vi* : deslizarse en tobogán

toboggan² *n* : tobogán *m*

today¹ [tə'deɪ] *adv* **1** : hoy ⟨she arrives today : hoy llega⟩ **2** NOWADAYS : hoy en día

today² *n* : hoy *m* ⟨today is a holiday : hoy es día de fiesta⟩

toddle ['tɑdəl] *vi* **-dled; -dling** : hacer pininos, hacer pinitos

toddler ['tɑdələr] *n* : niño *m* pequeño, niña *f* pequeña (que comienza a caminar)

to–do [tə'du:] *n, pl* **to–dos** [-'du:z] FUSS : lío *m*, alboroto *m*

toe ['to:] *n* : dedo *m* del pie

toenail ['to:ˌneɪl] *n* : uña *f* del pie

toffee *or* **toffy** ['tɔfi, 'tɑ-] *n, pl* **toffees** *or* **toffies** : caramelo *m* elaborado con azúcar y mantequilla

toga ['to:gə] *n* : toga *f*

together [tə'gɛðər] *adv* **1** : juntamente, juntos (el uno con el otro) ⟨Susan and Sarah work together : Susan y Sarah trabajan juntas⟩ **2** ~ **with** : junto con

togetherness [tə'gɛðərnəs] *n* : unión *f*, compañerismo *m*

togs ['tɑgz, 'tɔgz] *npl* : ropa *f*

toil¹ ['tɔɪl] *vi* : trabajar arduamente

toil² *n* : trabajo *m* arduo

toilet ['tɔɪlət] *n* **1** : arreglo *m* personal **2** BATHROOM : (cuarto de) baño *m*, servicios *mpl* (públicos), sanitario *m* Col, Mex, Ven **3** : inodoro *m* ⟨to flush the toilet : jalar la cadena⟩

toilet paper *n* : papel *m* higiénico

toiletries ['tɔɪlətriz] *npl* : artículos *mpl* de tocador

token ['to:kən] *n* 1 PROOF, SIGN : prueba *f*, muestra *f*, señal *m* 2 SYMBOL : símbolo *m* 3 SOUVENIR : recuerdo *m* 4 : ficha *f* (para transporte público, etc.)

told → **tell**

tolerable ['talərəbəl] *adj* : tolerable — **tolerably** [-bli] *adv*

tolerance ['talərənts] *n* : tolerancia *f*

tolerant ['talərənt] *adj* : tolerante — **tolerantly** *adv*

tolerate ['talə,reɪt] *vt* -ated; -ating 1 ACCEPT : tolerar, aceptar 2 BEAR, ENDURE : tolerar, aguantar, soportar

toleration [,talə'reɪʃən] *n* : tolerancia *f*

toll¹ ['to:l] *vt* : tañer, sonar (una campana) — *vi* : sonar, doblar (dícese de las campanas)

toll² *n* 1 : peaje *m* (de una carretera, un puente, etc.) 2 CASUALTIES : pérdida *f*, número *m* de víctimas 3 TOLLING : tañido *m* (de campanas)

tollbooth ['to:l,bu:θ] *n* : caseta *f* de peaje

tollgate ['to:l,geɪt] *n* : barrera *f* de peaje

tomahawk ['tamə,hɔk] *n* : hacha *f* de guerra (de los indígenas norteamericanos)

tomato [tə'meɪ,to, -'ma-] *n, pl* -toes : tomate *m*

tomb ['tu:m] *n* : sepulcro *m*, tumba *f*

tomboy ['tam,bɔɪ] *n* : marimacho *mf*; niña *f* que se porta como muchacho

tombstone ['tu:m,sto:n] *n* : lápida *f*

tomcat ['tam,kæt] *n* : gato *m* (macho)

tome ['to:m] *n* : tomo *m*

tomorrow¹ [tə'mɑro] *adv* : mañana

tomorrow² *n* : mañana *m*

tom–tom ['tam,tam] *n* : tam-tam *m*

ton ['tən] *n* : tonelada *f*

tone¹ ['to:n] *vt* **toned; toning** 1 *or* **to tone down** : atenuar, suavizar, moderar 2 *or* **to tone up** STRENGTHEN : tonificar, vigorizar

tone² *n* : tono *m* ⟨in a friendly tone : en tono amistoso⟩ ⟨a greyish tone : un tono grisáceo⟩

tongs ['taŋz, 'tɔŋz] *npl* : tenazas *fpl*

tongue ['tʌŋ] *n* 1 : lengua *f* 2 LANGUAGE : lengua *f*, idioma *m*

tongue–tied ['tʌŋ,taɪd] *adj* **to get tongue–tied** : trabársele la lengua a uno

tonic¹ ['tanɪk] *adj* : tónico

tonic² *n* 1 : tónico *m* 2 *or* **tonic water** : tónica *f*

tonight¹ [tə'naɪt] *adv* : esta noche

tonight² *n* : esta noche *f*

tonsil ['tantsəl] *n* : amígdala *f*, angina *f* Mex

tonsillitis [,tantsə'laɪtəs] *n* : amigdalitis *f*, anginas *fpl* Mex

too ['tu:] *adv* 1 ALSO : también 2 EXCESSIVELY : demasiado ⟨it's too hot in here : aquí hace demasiado calor⟩

took → **take¹**

tool¹ ['tu:l] *vt* 1 : fabricar, confeccionar (con herramientas) 2 EQUIP : instalar maquinaria en (una fábrica)

tool² *n* : herramienta *f*

toolbox ['tu:l,baks] *n* : caja *f* de herramientas

toot¹ ['tu:t] *vt* : sonar (un claxon o un pito)

toot² *n* : pitido *m*, bocinazo *m* (de un claxon)

tooth ['tu:θ] *n, pl* **teeth** ['ti:θ] : diente *m*

toothache ['tu:θ,eɪk] *n* : dolor *m* de muelas

toothbrush ['tu:θ,brʌʃ] *n* : cepillo *m* de dientes

toothless ['tu:θləs] *adj* : desdentado

toothpaste ['tu:θ,peɪst] *n* : pasta *f* de dientes, crema *f* dental, dentífrico *m*

toothpick ['tu:θ,pɪk] *n* : palillo *m* (de dientes), mondadientes *m*

top¹ ['tap] *vt* **topped; topping** 1 COVER : cubrir, coronar 2 SURPASS : sobrepasar, superar 3 CLEAR : pasar por encima de

top² *adj* : superior ⟨the top shelf : la repisa superior⟩ ⟨one of the top lawyers : uno de los mejores abogados⟩

top³ *n* 1 : parte *f* superior, cumbre *f*, cima *f* (de un monte, etc.) ⟨to climb to the top : subir a la cumbre⟩ 2 COVER : tapa *f*, cubierta *f* 3 : trompo *m* (juguete) 4 **on top of** : encima de

topaz ['to:,pæz] *n* : topacio *m*

topcoat ['tap,ko:t] *n* : sobretodo *m*, abrigo *m*

topic ['tapɪk] *n* : tema *m*, tópico *m*

topical ['tapɪkəl] *adj* : de interés actual

topmost ['tap,mo:st] *adj* : más alto

top–notch ['tap'natʃ] *adj* : de lo mejor, de primera categoría

topographic [,tapə'græfɪk] *or* **topographical** [-fɪkəl] *adj* : topográfico

topography [tə'pagrəfi] *n, pl* **-phies** : topografía *f*

topple ['tapəl] *v* **-pled; -pling** *vi* : caerse, venirse abajo — *vt* : volcar, derrocar (un gobierno, etc.)

topsoil ['tap,sɔɪl] *n* : capa *f* superior del suelo

topsy–turvy [,tapsi'tərvi] *adv & adj* : patas arriba, al revés

torch ['tɔrtʃ] *n* : antorcha *f*

tore → **tear¹**

torment¹ [tɔr'mɛnt, 'tɔr,-] *vt* : atormentar, torturar, martirizar

torment² ['tɔr,mɛnt] *n* : tormento *m*, suplicio *m*, martirio *m*

tormentor [tɔr'mɛntər] *n* : atormentador *m*, -dora *f*

torn *pp* → **tear¹**

tornado [tɔr'neɪdo] *n, pl* **-does** *or* **-dos** : tornado *m*

torpedo¹ [tɔr'pi:do] *vt* : torpedear

torpedo² *n, pl* **-does** : torpedo *m*

torpid ['tɔrpɪd] *adj* 1 SLUGGISH : aletargado 2 APATHETIC : apático

torpor ['tɔrpər] *n* : letargo *m*, apatía *f*

torrent ['tɔrənt] *n* : torrente *m*

torrential [tɔ'rɛntʃəl, tə-] *adj* : torrencial

torrid ['tɔrɪd] *adj* : tórrido

torso ['tɔr,so:] *n, pl* **-sos** *or* **-si** [-,si:] : torso *m*

tortilla [tɔr'tiːjə] *n* : tortilla *f* (de maíz)
tortoise ['tɔrtəs] *n* : tortuga *f* (terrestre)
tortoiseshell ['tɔrtəsˌʃɛl] *n* : carey *m*, concha *f*
tortuous ['tɔrtʃʊəs] *adj* : tortuoso
torture¹ ['tɔrtʃər] *vt* **-tured; -turing** : torturar, atormentar
torture² *n* : tortura *f*, tormento *m* ⟨it was sheer torture! : ¡fue un verdadero suplicio!⟩
torturer ['tɔrtʃərər] *n* : torturador *m*, -dora *f*
toss¹ ['tɔs, 'tɑs] *vt* **1** AGITATE, SHAKE : sacudir, agitar, mezclar (una ensalada) **2** THROW : tirar, echar, lanzar — *vi* : sacudirse, moverse agitadamente ⟨to toss and turn : dar vueltas⟩
toss² *n* THROW : lanzamiento *m*, tiro *m*, tirada *f*, lance *m* (de dados, etc.)
toss–up ['tɔsˌʌp] *n* : posibilidad *f* igual ⟨it's a toss-up : quizá sí, quizá no⟩
tot ['tɑt] *n* : pequeño *m*, -ña *f*
total¹ ['toːtəl] *vt* **-taled** *or* **-talled; -taling** *or* **-talling** **1** *or* **to total up** ADD : sumar, totalizar **2** AMOUNT TO : ascender a, llegar a
total² *adj* : total, completo, absoluto — **totally** *adv*
total³ *n* : total *m*
totalitarian [toːˌtælə'tɛriən] *adj* : totalitario
totalitarianism [toːˌtælə'tɛriəˌnɪzəm] *n* : totalitarismo *m*
totality [toː'tæləti] *n, pl* **-ties** : totalidad *f*
tote ['toːt] *vt* **toted; toting** : cargar, llevar
totem ['toːtəm] *n* : tótem *m*
totter ['tɑtər] *vi* : tambalearse
touch¹ ['tʌtʃ] *vt* **1** FEEL, HANDLE : tocar, tentar **2** AFFECT, MOVE : conmover, afectar, tocar ⟨his gesture touched our hearts : su gesto nos tocó el corazón⟩ — *vi* : tocarse
touch² *n* **1** : tacto *m* (sentido) **2** DETAIL : toque *m*, detalle *m* ⟨a touch of color : un toque de color⟩ **3** BIT : pizca *f*, gota *f*, poco *m* **4** ABILITY : habilidad *f* ⟨to lose one's touch : perder la habilidad⟩ **5** CONTACT : contacto *m*, comunicación *f* ⟨to keep in touch : mantenerse en contacto⟩
touchdown ['tʌtʃˌdaʊn] *n* : touchdown *m* (en futbol americano)
touching ['tʌtʃɪŋ] *adj* MOVING : conmovedor
touchstone ['tʌtʃˌstoːn] *n* : piedra *f* de toque
touch up *vt* : retocar
touchy ['tʌtʃi] *adj* **touchier; -est** **1** : sensible, susceptible (dícese de una persona) **2** : delicado ⟨a touchy subject : un tema delicado⟩
tough¹ ['tʌf] *adj* **1** STRONG : fuerte, resistente (dícese de materiales) **2** LEATHERY : correoso ⟨a tough steak : un bistec duro⟩ **3** HARDY : fuerte, robusto (dícese de una persona) **4** STRICT

: severo, exigente **5** DIFFICULT : difícil **6** STUBBORN : terco, obstinado
tough² *n* : matón *m*, persona *f* ruda y brusca
toughen ['tʌfən] *vt* : fortalecer, endurecer — *vi* : endurecerse, hacerse más fuerte
toughness ['tʌfnəs] *n* : dureza *f*
toupee [tuː'peɪ] *n* : peluquín *m*, bisoñé *m*
tour¹ ['tʊr] *vi* : tomar una excursión, viajar — *vt* : recorrer, hacer una gira por
tour² *n* **1** : gira *f*, tour *m*, excursión *f* **2** **tour of duty** : período *m* de servicio
tourism ['tʊrˌɪzəm] *n* : turismo *m*
tourist ['tʊrɪst, 'tər-] *n* : turista *mf*
tournament ['tərnəmənt, 'tʊr-] *n* : torneo *m*
tourniquet ['tərnɪkət, 'tʊr-] *n* : torniquete *m*
tousle ['taʊzəl] *vt* **-sled; -sling** : desarreglar, despeinar (el cabello)
tout ['taʊt] *vt* : promocionar, elogiar (con exageración)
tow¹ ['toː] *vt* : remolcar
tow² *n* : remolque *m*
toward ['tord, tə'word] *or* **towards** ['tordz, tə'wordz] *prep* **1** (*indicating direction*) : hacia, rumbo a ⟨heading toward town : dirigiéndose rumbo al pueblo⟩ ⟨efforts towards peace : esfuerzos hacia la paz⟩ **2** (*indicating time*) : alrededor de ⟨toward midnight : alrededor de la medianoche⟩ **3** REGARDING : hacia, con respecto a ⟨his attitude toward life : su actitud hacia la vida⟩ **4** FOR : para, como pago parcial de (una compra o deuda)
towel ['taʊəl] *n* : toalla *f*
tower¹ ['taʊər] *vi* **to tower over** : descollar sobre, elevarse sobre, dominar
tower² *n* : torre *f*
towering ['taʊərɪŋ] *adj* : altísimo, imponente
town ['taʊn] *n* : pueblo *m*, ciudad *f* (pequeña)
township ['taʊnˌʃɪp] *n* : municipio *m*
tow truck ['toːˌtrʌk] *n* : grúa *f*
toxic ['tɑksɪk] *adj* : tóxico
toxicity [tɑk'sɪsəti] *n, pl* **-ties** : toxicidad *f*
toxin ['tɑksɪn] *n* : toxina *f*
toy¹ ['tɔɪ] *vi* : juguetear, jugar
toy² *adj* : de juguete ⟨a toy rifle : un rifle de juguete⟩
toy³ *n* : juguete *m*
trace¹ ['treɪs] *vt* **traced; tracing** **1** : calcar (un dibujo, etc.) **2** OUTLINE : delinear, trazar (planes, etc.) **3** TRACK : describir (un curso, una historia) **4** FIND : localizar, ubicar
trace² *n* **1** SIGN, TRACK : huella *f*, rastro *m*, indicio *m*, vestigio *m* ⟨he disappeared without a trace : desapareció sin dejar rastro⟩ **2** BIT, HINT : pizca *f*, ápice *m*, dejo *m*
trachea ['treɪkiə] *n, pl* **-cheae** [-kiˌiː] : tráquea *f*

tracing paper *n* : papel *m* de calcar

track[1] ['træk] *vt* **1** TRAIL : seguir la pista de, rastrear **2** : dejar huellas de ⟨he tracked mud all over : dejó huellas de lodo por todas partes⟩

track[2] *n* **1** : rastro *m*, huella *f* (de animales), pista *f* (de personas) **2** PATH : pista *f*, sendero *m*, camino *m* **3** *or* **railroad track** : vía *f* (férrea) **4** → **racetrack 5** : oruga *f* (de un tanque, etc.) **6** : pista *f* (deporte) **7 to keep track of** : llevar la cuenta de

track–and–field ['trækənd'fi:ld] *adj* : de pista y campo

tract ['trækt] *n* **1** AREA : terreno *m*, extensión *f*, área *f* **2** : tracto *m* ⟨digestive tract : tracto digestivo⟩ **3** PAMPHLET : panfleto *m*, folleto *m*

traction ['trækʃən] *n* : tracción *f*

tractor ['træktər] *n* **1** : tractor *m* (vehículo agrícola) **2** TRUCK : camión *m* (con remolque)

trade[1] ['treɪd] *v* **traded; trading** *vi* : comerciar, negociar — *vt* EXCHANGE : intercambiar, canjear

trade[2] *n* **1** OCCUPATION : oficio *m*, profesión *f*, ocupación *f* ⟨a carpenter by trade : carpintero de oficio⟩ **2** COMMERCE : comercio *m*, industria *f* ⟨free trade : libre comercio⟩ ⟨the book trade : la industria del libro⟩ **3** EXCHANGE : intercambio *m*, canje *m*

trade–in ['treɪd,ɪn] *n* : artículo *m* que se canjea por otro

trademark ['treɪd,mɑrk] *n* **1** : marca *f* registrada **2** CHARACTERISTIC : sello *m* característico (de un grupo, una persona, etc.)

trader ['treɪdər] *n* : negociante *mf*, tratante *mf*, comerciante *mf*

tradesman ['treɪdzmən] *n, pl* **-men** [-mən, -,mɛn] **1** CRAFTSMAN : artesano *m*, -na *f* **2** SHOPKEEPER : tendero *m*, -ra *f*; comerciante *mf*

trade wind *n* : viento *m* alisio

tradition [trə'dɪʃən] *n* : tradición *f*

traditional [trə'dɪʃənəl] *adj* : tradicional — **traditionally** *adv*

traffic[1] ['træfɪk] *vi* **trafficked; trafficking** : traficar (con)

traffic[2] *n* **1** COMMERCE : tráfico *m*, comercio *m* ⟨the drug traffic : el narcotráfico⟩ **2** : tráfico *m*, tránsito *m*, circulación *f* (de vehículos, etc.)

traffic circle *n* : rotonda *f*, glorieta *f*

trafficker ['træfɪkər] *n* : traficante *mf*

traffic light *n* : semáforo *m*, luz *f* (de tránsito)

tragedy ['trædʒədi] *n, pl* **-dies** : tragedia *f*

tragic ['trædʒɪk] *adj* : trágico — **tragically** *adv*

trail[1] ['treɪl] *vi* **1** DRAG : arrastrarse **2** LAG : quedarse atrás, retrasarse **3 to trail away** *or* **to trail off** : disminuir, menguar, desvanecerse — *vt* **1** DRAG : arrastrar **2** PURSUE : perseguir, seguir la pista de

trail[2] *n* **1** TRACK : rastro *m*, huella *f*, pista *f* ⟨a trail of blood : un rastro de sangre⟩ **2** : cola *f*, estela *f* (de un meteoro) **3** PATH : sendero *m*, camino *m*, vereda *f*

trailer ['treɪlər] *n* **1** : remolque *m*, tráiler *m* (de un camión) **2** : caravana *f* (vivienda ambulante)

train[1] ['treɪn] *vt* **1** : adiestrar, entrenar (atletas), capacitar (trabajadores), amaestrar (animales) **2** POINT : apuntar (un arma, etc.) — *vi* : entrenar(se) (físicamente), prepararse (profesionalmente) ⟨she's training at the gym : se está entrenando en el gimnasio⟩

train[2] *n* **1** : cola *f* (de un vestido) **2** RETINUE : cortejo *m*, séquito *m* **3** SERIES : serie *f* (de eventos) **4** : tren *m* ⟨passenger train : tren de pasajeros⟩

trainee [treɪ'ni:] *n* : aprendiz *m*, -diza *f*

trainer ['treɪnər] *n* : entrenador *m*, -dora *f*

training ['treɪnɪŋ] *n* : adiestramiento *m*, entrenamiento *m* (físico), capacitación *f* (de trabajadores)

traipse ['treɪps] *vi* **traipsed; traipsing** : andar de un lado para otro, vagar

trait ['treɪt] *n* : rasgo *m*, característica *f*

traitor ['treɪtər] *n* : traidor *m*, -dora *f*

traitorous ['treɪtərəs] *adj* : traidor

trajectory [trə'dʒɛktəri] *n, pl* **-ries** : trayectoria *f*

tramp[1] ['træmp] *vi* : caminar (a paso pesado) — *vt* : deambular por, vagar por ⟨to tramp the streets : vagar por las calles⟩

tramp[2] *n* **1** VAGRANT : vagabundo *m*, -da *f* **2** HIKE : caminata *f*

trample ['træmpəl] *vt* **-pled; -pling** : pisotear, hollar

trampoline [,træmpə'li:n, 'træmpə,-] *n* : trampolín *m*, cama *f* elástica

trance ['træn*t*s] *n* : trance *m*

tranquil ['træŋkwəl] *adj* : calmo, tranquilo, sereno — **tranquilly** *adv*

tranquilize ['træŋkwə,laɪz] *vt* **-ized; -izing** : tranquilizar

tranquilizer ['træŋkwə,laɪzər] *n* : tranquilizante *m*

tranquillity *or* **tranquility** [træŋ'kwɪləti] *n* : sosiego *m*, tranquilidad *f*

transact [træn'zækt] *vt* : negociar, gestionar, hacer (negocios)

transaction [træn'zækʃən] *n* **1** : transacción *f*, negocio *m*, operación *f* **2 transactions** *npl* RECORDS : actas *fpl*

transatlantic [,træn*t*sət'læntɪk, ,trænz-] *adj* : transatlántico

transcend [træn'sɛnd] *vt* : trascender, sobrepasar

transcendent [træn'sɛndənt] *adj* : trascendente — **transcendence** [træn'sɛndən*t*s] *n*

transcendental [,træn*t*,sɛn'dɛntəl, -sən-] *adj* : trascendental ⟨transcendental meditation : meditación trascendental⟩

transcribe [træn'skraɪb] vt -scribed; -scribing : transcribir

transcript ['træn,skrɪpt] n : copia f oficial

transcription [træn'skrɪpʃən] n : transcripción f

transfer[1] [træn*ts*'fər, 'træn*ts*,fər] v -ferred; -ferring vt 1 : trasladar (a una persona), transferir (fondos) 2 : transferir, traspasar, ceder (propiedad) 3 PRINT : imprimir (un diseño) — vi 1 MOVE : trasladarse, cambiarse 2 CHANGE : transbordar, cambiar (de un transporte a otro) ⟨he transfers at E Street : hace un transborde a la calle E⟩

transfer[2] ['træn*ts*,fər] n 1 TRANSFERRING : transferencia f (de fondos, de propiedad, etc.), traslado m (de una persona) 2 DECAL : calcomanía f 3 : boleto m (para cambiar de un avión, etc., a otro)

transferable [træn*ts*'fərəbəl] adj : transferible

transference [træn*ts*'fərən*ts*] n : transferencia f

transfigure [træn*ts*'fɪgjər] vt -ured; -uring : transfigurar, transformar

transfix [træn*ts*'fɪks] vt 1 PIERCE : traspasar, atravesar 2 IMMOBILIZE : paralizar

transform [træn*ts*'fɔrm] vt : transformar

transformation [,træn*ts*fər'meɪʃən] n : transformación f

transformer [træn*ts*'fɔrmər] n : transformador m

transfusion [træn*ts*'fju:ʒən] n : transfusión f

transgress [træn*ts*'grɛs, trænz-] vt : transgredir, infringir

transgression [træn*ts*'grɛʃən, trænz-] n : transgresión f

transient[1] ['træn*t*ʃənt, 'trænsiənt] adj : pasajero, transitorio — transiently adv

transient[2] n : transeúnte mf

transistor [træn'zɪstər, -'sɪs-] n : transistor m

transit ['træn*ts*ɪt, 'trænzɪt] n 1 PASSAGE : pasaje m, tránsito m ⟨in transit : en tránsito⟩ 2 TRANSPORTATION : transporte m (público) 3 : teodolito m (instrumento topográfico)

transition [træn'sɪʃən, -'zɪʃ-] n : transición f

transitional [træn'sɪʃənəl, -'zɪʃ-] adj : de transición

transitive ['træn*ts*ətɪv, 'trænzə-] adj : transitivo

transitory ['træn*ts*ə,tori, 'trænzə-] adj : transitorio

translate [træn*ts*'leɪt, trænz-; 'træn*ts*,-, 'træns,-] vt -lated; -lating : traducir

translation [træn*ts*'leɪʃən, trænz-] n : traducción f

translator [træn*ts*'leɪtər, trænz-; 'træn*ts*,-, 'træns,-] n : traductor m, -tora f

translucent [træn*ts*'lu:sənt, trænz-] adj : translúcido

transmission [træn*ts*'mɪʃən, trænz-] n : transmisión f

transmit [træn*ts*'mɪt, trænz-] vt -mitted; -mitting : transmitir

transmitter [træn*ts*'mɪtər, trænz-; 'træn*ts*,-, 'træns,-] n : transmisor m, emisor m

transom ['træn*ts*əm] n : montante m (de una puerta), travesaño m (de una ventana)

transparency [træn*ts*'pærən*ts*i] n, pl -cies : transparencia f

transparent [træn*ts*'pærənt] adj 1 : transparente, traslúcido ⟨a transparent fabric : una tela transparente⟩ 2 OBVIOUS : transparente, obvio, claro — transparently adv

transpiration [,træn*ts*pə'reɪʃən] n : transpiración f

transpire [træn*ts*'paɪr] vi -spired; -spiring 1 : transpirar (en biología y botánica) 2 TURN OUT : resultar 3 HAPPEN : suceder, ocurrir, tener lugar

transplant[1] [træn*ts*'plænt] vt : trasplantar

transplant[2] ['træn*ts*,plænt] n : trasplante m

transport[1] [træn*ts*'port, 'træn*ts*,-] vt 1 CARRY : transportar, acarrear 2 ENRAPTURE : transportar, extasiar

transport[2] ['træn*ts*,port] n 1 TRANSPORTATION : transporte m, transportación f 2 RAPTURE : éxtasis m 3 or transport ship : buque m de transporte (de personal militar)

transportation [,træn*ts*pər'teɪʃən] n : transporte m, transportación f

transpose [træn*ts*'po:z] vt -posed; -posing : trasponer, trasladar, transportar (una composición musical)

transverse [træn*ts*'vərs, trænz-] adj : transversal, transverso, oblicuo — transversely adv

trap[1] ['træp] vt trapped; trapping : atrapar, apresar (en una trampa)

trap[2] n : trampa f ⟨to set a trap : tender una trampa⟩

trapdoor ['træp'dor] n : trampilla f, escotillón m

trapeze [træ'pi:z] n : trapecio m

trapezoid ['træpə,zɔɪd] n : trapezoide m, trapecio m

trapper ['træpər] n : trampero m, -ra f; cazador m, -dora f (que usa trampas)

trappings ['træpɪŋz] npl 1 : arreos mpl, jaeces mpl (de un caballo) 2 ADORNMENTS : adornos mpl, pompa f

trash ['træʃ] n : basura f

trashy ['træʃi] adj : de pacotilla

trauma ['trɔmə, 'traʊ-] n : trauma m

traumatic [trə'mætɪk, trɔ-, traʊ-] adj : traumático

travel[1] ['trævəl] vi -eled or -elled; -eling or -elling 1 JOURNEY : viajar 2 GO, MOVE : desplazarse, moverse, ir ⟨the waves travel at uniform speed : las ondas se desplazan a una velocidad uniforme⟩

travel² *n or* **travels** *npl* : viajes *mpl*

traveler *or* **traveller** ['trævələr] *n* : viajero *m*, -ra *f*

traverse [trə'vərs, træ'vərs, 'trævərs] *vt* **-versed; -versing** CROSS : atravesar, extenderse a través de, cruzar

travesty ['trævəsti] *n, pl* **-ties** : parodia *f*

trawl¹ ['trɔl] *vi* : pescar con red de arrastre, rastrear

trawl² *n or* **trawl net** : red *f* de arrastre

trawler ['trɔlər] *n* : barco *m* de pesca (utilizado para rastrear)

tray ['treɪ] *n* : bandeja *f*, charola *f Bol, Mex, Peru*

treacherous ['trɛtʃərəs] *adj* **1** TRAITOROUS : traicionero, traidor **2** DANGEROUS : peligroso

treacherously ['trɛtʃərəsli] *adv* : a traición

treachery ['trɛtʃəri] *n, pl* **-eries** : traición *f*

tread¹ ['trɛd] *v* **trod** ['trɑd]; **trodden** ['trɑdən] *or* **trod; treading** *vt* TRAMPLE : pisotear, hollar — *vi* **1** WALK : caminar, andar **2 to tread on** : pisar

tread² *n* **1** STEP : paso *m*, andar *m* **2** : banda *f* de rodadura (de un neumático, etc.) **3** : escalón *m* (de una escalera)

treadle ['trɛdəl] *n* : pedal *m* (de una máquina)

treadmill ['trɛd,mɪl] *n* **1** : rueda *f* de andar **2** ROUTINE : rutina *f*

treason ['tri:zən] *n* : traición *f* (a la patria, etc.)

treasure¹ ['trɛʒər, 'treɪ-] *vt* **-sured; -suring** : apreciar, valorar

treasure² *n* : tesoro *m*

treasurer ['trɛʒərər, 'treɪ-] *n* : tesorero *m*, -ra *f*

treasury ['trɛʒəri, 'treɪ-] *n, pl* **-suries** : tesorería *f*, tesoro *m*

treat¹ ['tri:t] *vt* **1** DEAL WITH : tratar (un asunto) ⟨the article treats of poverty : el artículo trata de la pobreza⟩ **2** HANDLE : tratar (a una persona), manejar (un objeto) ⟨to treat something as a joke : tomar(se) algo a broma⟩ **3** INVITE : invitar, convidar ⟨he treated me to a meal : me invitó a comer⟩ **4** : tratar, atender (en medicina) **5** PROCESS : tratar ⟨to treat sewage : tratar las aguas negras⟩

treat² *n* : gusto *m*, placer *m* ⟨it was a treat to see you : fue un placer verte⟩ ⟨it's my treat : yo invito⟩

treatise ['tri:tɪs] *n* : tratado *m*, estudio *m*

treatment ['tri:tmənt] *n* : trato *m*, tratamiento *m* (médico)

treaty ['tri:ti] *n, pl* **-ties** : tratado *m*, convenio *m*

treble¹ ['trɛbəl] *vt* **-bled; -bling** : triplicar

treble² *adj* **1** → **triple 2** : de tiple, soprano (en música) **3 treble clef** : clave *f* de sol

treble³ *n* : tiple *m*, parte *f* de soprano

tree ['tri:] *n* : árbol *m*

treeless ['tri:ləs] *adj* : carente de árboles

trek¹ ['trɛk] *vi* **trekked; trekking** : hacer un viaje largo y difícil

trek² *n* : viaje *m* largo y difícil

trellis ['trɛlɪs] *n* : enrejado *m*, espaldera *f*, celosía *f*

tremble ['trɛmbəl] *vi* **-bled; -bling** : temblar

tremendous [trɪ'mɛndəs] *adj* : tremendo — **tremendously** *adv*

tremor ['trɛmər] *n* : temblor *m*

tremulous ['trɛmjələs] *adj* : trémulo, tembloroso

trench ['trɛntʃ] *n* **1** DITCH : zanja *f* **2** : trinchera *f* (militar)

trenchant ['trɛntʃənt] *adj* : cortante, mordaz

trend¹ ['trɛnd] *vi* : tender, inclinarse

trend² *n* **1** TENDENCY : tendencia *f* **2** FASHION : moda *f*

trendy ['trɛndi] *adj* **trendier; -est** : de moda

trepidation [ˌtrɛpə'deɪʃən] *n* : inquietud *f*, ansiedad *f*

trespass¹ ['trɛspəs, -ˌpæs] *vi* **1** SIN : pecar, transgredir **2** : entrar ilegalmente (en propiedad ajena)

trespass² *n* **1** SIN : pecado *m*, transgresión *f* ⟨forgive us our trespasses : perdónanos nuestras deudas⟩ **2** : entrada *f* ilegal (en propiedad ajena)

tress ['trɛs] *n* : mechón *m*

trestle ['trɛsəl] *n* **1** : caballete *m* (armazón) **2** *or* **trestle bridge** : puente *m* de caballete

triad ['traɪ,æd] *n* : tríada *f*

trial¹ ['traɪəl] *adj* : de prueba ⟨trial period : período de prueba⟩

trial² *n* **1** : juicio *m*, proceso *m* ⟨to stand trial : ser sometido a juicio⟩ **2** AFFLICTION : aflicción *f*, tribulación *f* **3** TEST : prueba *f*, ensayo *m*

triangle ['traɪ,æŋgəl] *n* : triángulo *m*

triangular [traɪ'æŋgjələr] *adj* : triangular

tribal ['traɪbəl] *adj* : tribal

tribe ['traɪb] *n* : tribu *f*

tribesman ['traɪbzmən] *n, pl* **-men** [-mən, -ˌmɛn] : miembro *m* de una tribu

tribulation [ˌtrɪbjə'leɪʃən] *n* : tribulación *f*

tribunal [traɪ'bju:nəl, trɪ-] *n* : tribunal *m*, corte *f*

tributary ['trɪbjəˌtɛri] *n, pl* **-taries** : afluente *m*

tribute ['trɪbˌju:t] *n* : tributo *m*

trick¹ ['trɪk] *vt* : engañar, embaucar

trick² *n* **1** RUSE : trampa *f*, treta *f*, artimaña *f* **2** PRANK : broma *f* ⟨we played a trick on her : le gastamos una broma⟩ **3** : truco *m* ⟨magic tricks : trucos de magia⟩ ⟨the trick is to wait five minutes : el truco está en esperar cinco minutos⟩ **4** MANNERISM : peculiaridad *f*, manía *f* **5** : baza *f* (en juegos de naipes)

trickery ['trɪkəri] *n* : engaños *mpl*, trampas *fpl*

trickle¹ ['trɪkəl] *vi* **-led; -ling** : gotear, chorrear

trickle² *n* : goteo *m*, hilo *m*
trickster ['trɪkstər] *n* : estafador *m*, -dora *f*; embaucador *m*, -dora *f*
tricky ['trɪki] *adj* **trickier; -est 1** SLY : astuto, taimado **2** DIFFICULT : delicado, peliagudo, difícil
tricycle ['traɪsəkəl, -ˌsɪkəl] *n* : triciclo *m*
trident ['traɪdənt] *n* : tridente *m*
triennial ['traɪˈɛniəl] *adj* : trienal
trifle¹ ['traɪfəl] *vi* **-fled; -fling** : jugar, juguetear
trifle² *n* : nimiedad *f*, insignificancia *f*
trifling ['traɪflɪŋ] *adj* : trivial, insignificante
trigger¹ ['trɪgər] *vt* : causar, provocar
trigger² *n* : gatillo *m*
trigonometry [ˌtrɪgəˈnɑmətri] *n* : trigonometría *f*
trill¹ ['trɪl] *vi* QUAVER : trinar, gorjear — *vt* : vibrar ⟨to trill the *r* : vibrar la *r*⟩
trill² *n* **1** QUAVER : trino *m*, gorjeo *m* **2** : vibración *f* (en fonética)
trillion ['trɪljən] *n* : billón *m*
trilogy ['trɪlədʒi] *n, pl* **-gies** : trilogía *f*
trim¹ ['trɪm] *vt* **trimmed; trimming 1** DECORATE : adornar, decorar **2** CUT : recortar **3** REDUCE : recortar, reducir ⟨to trim the excess : recortar el exceso⟩
trim² *adj* **trimmer; trimmest 1** SLIM : esbelto **2** NEAT : limpio y arreglado, bien cuidado
trim³ *n* **1** CONDITION : condición *f*, estado *m* ⟨to keep in trim : mantenerse en buena forma⟩ **2** CUT : recorte *m* **3** TRIMMING : adornos *mpl*
trimming ['trɪmɪŋ] *n* : adornos *mpl*, accesorios *mpl*
Trinity ['trɪnəti] *n* : Trinidad *f*
trinket ['trɪŋkət] *n* : chuchería *f*, baratija *f*
trio ['triːˌoː] *n, pl* **trios** : trío *m*
trip¹ ['trɪp] *v* **tripped; tripping** *vi* **1** : caminar (a paso ligero) **2** STUMBLE : tropezar **3 to trip up** ERR : equivocarse, cometer un error — *vt* **1** : hacerle una zancadilla (a alguien) ⟨you tripped me on purpose! : ¡me hiciste la zancadilla a propósito!⟩ **2** ACTIVATE : activar (un mecanismo) **3 to trip up** : hacer equivocar (a alguien)
trip² *n* **1** JOURNEY : viaje *m* ⟨to take a trip : hacer un viaje⟩ **2** STUMBLE : tropiezo *m*, traspié *m*
tripartite [traɪˈpɑrˌtaɪt] *adj* : tripartito
tripe ['traɪp] *n* **1** : mondongo *m*, callos *mpl*, pancita *f Mex* **2** TRASH : porquería *f*
triple¹ ['trɪpəl] *vt* **-pled; -pling** : triplicar
triple² *adj* : triple
triple³ *n* : triple *m*
triplet ['trɪplət] *n* **1** : terceto *m* (en poesía, música, etc.) **2** : trillizo *m*, -za *f* (persona)
triplicate ['trɪplɪkət] *n* : triplicado *m*
tripod ['traɪˌpɑd] *n* : trípode *m*
trite ['traɪt] *adj* **triter; tritest** : trillado, tópico, manido

triumph¹ ['traɪəmpf] *vi* : triunfar
triumph² *n* : triunfo *m*
triumphal [traɪˈʌmpfəl] *adj* : triunfal
triumphant [traɪˈʌmpfənt] *adj* : triunfante, triunfal — **triumphantly** *adv*
trivia ['trɪviə] *ns & pl* : trivialidades *fpl*, nimiedades *fpl*
trivial ['trɪviəl] *adj* : trivial, intrascendente, insignificante
triviality [ˌtrɪviˈæləti] *n, pl* **-ties** : trivialidad *f*
trod, trodden → **tread¹**
troll ['troːl] *n* : duende *m* o gigante *m* de cuentos folklóricos
trolley ['trɑli] *n, pl* **-leys** : tranvía *m*
trombone [trɑmˈboːn] *n* : trombón *m*
trombonist [trɑmˈboːnɪst] *n* : trombón *m*
troop¹ ['truːp] *vi* : desfilar, ir en tropel
troop² *n* **1** : escuadrón *m* (de caballería) **2** GROUP : grupo *m*, banda *f* (de personas) **3 troops** *npl* SOLDIERS : tropas *fpl*, soldados *mpl*
trooper ['truːpər] *n* **1** : soldado *m* (de caballería) **2** : policía *m* montado **3** : policía *m* (estatal)
trophy ['troːfi] *n, pl* **-phies** : trofeo *m*
tropic¹ ['trɑpɪk] *or* **tropical** [-pɪkəl] *adj* : tropical
tropic² *n* **1** : trópico *m* ⟨tropic of Cancer : trópico de Cáncer⟩ **2 the tropics** : el trópico
trot¹ ['trɑt] *vi* **trotted; trotting** : trotar
trot² *n* : trote *m*
trouble¹ ['trʌbəl] *v* **-bled; -bling** *vt* **1** DISTURB, WORRY : molestar, perturbar, inquietar **2** AFFLICT : afligir, afectar — *vi* : molestarse, hacer un esfuerzo ⟨they didn't trouble to come : no se molestaron en venir⟩
trouble² *n* **1** PROBLEMS : problemas *mpl*, dificultades *fpl* ⟨to be in trouble : estar en un aprieto⟩ ⟨heart trouble : problemas de corazón⟩ **2** EFFORT : molestia *f*, esfuerzo *m* ⟨to take the trouble : tomarse la molestia⟩ ⟨it's not worth the trouble : no vale la pena⟩
troublemaker ['trʌbəlˌmeɪkər] *n* : agitador *m*, -dora *f*; alborotador *m*, -dora *f*
troublesome ['trʌbəlsəm] *adj* : problemático, dificultoso — **troublesomely** *adv*
trough ['trɔf] *n, pl* **troughs** ['trɔfs, 'trɔvz] **1** : comedero *m*, bebedero *m* (de animales) **2** CHANNEL, HOLLOW : depresión *f* (en el suelo), seno *m* (de olas)
trounce ['traʊnts] *vt* **trounced; trouncing 1** THRASH : apalear, darle una paliza (a alguien) **2** DEFEAT : derrotar contundentemente
troupe ['truːp] *n* : troupe *f*
trousers ['traʊzərz] *npl* : pantalón *m*, pantalones *mpl*
trout ['traʊt] *n, pl* **trout** : trucha *f*
trowel ['traʊəl] *n* **1** : llana *f*, paleta *f* (de albañil) **2** : desplantador *m* (de jardinero)
truant ['truːənt] *n* : alumno *m*, -na *f* que falta a clase sin permiso

truce ['tru:s] *n* : tregua *f*, armisticio *m*

truck¹ ['trʌk] *vt* : transportar en camión

truck² *n* **1** : camión *m* (vehículo automóvil), carro *m* (manual) **2** DEALINGS : tratos *mpl* ⟨to have no truck with : no tener nada que ver con⟩

trucker ['trʌkər] *n* : camionero *m*, -ra *f*

truculent ['trʌkjələnt] *adj* : agresivo, beligerante

trudge ['trʌdʒ] *vi* **trudged; trudging** : caminar a paso pesado

true¹ ['tru:] *vt* **trued; trueing** : aplomar (algo vertical), nivelar (algo horizontal), centrar (una rueda)

true² *adv* **1** TRUTHFULLY : lealmente, sinceramente **2** ACCURATELY : exactamente, certeramente

true³ *adj* **truer; truest 1** LOYAL : fiel, leal **2** : cierto, verdadero, verídico ⟨it's true : es cierto, es la verdad⟩ ⟨a true story : una historia verídica⟩ **3** GENUINE : auténtico, genuino — **truly** *adv*

true–blue ['tru:'blu:] *adj* LOYAL : leal, fiel

truffle ['trʌfəl] *n* : trufa *f*

truism ['tru:ˌɪzəm] *n* : perogrullada *f*, verdad *f* obvia

trump¹ ['trʌmp] *vt* : matar (en juegos de naipes)

trump² *n* : triunfo *m* (en juegos de naipes)

trumped–up ['trʌmpt'ʌp] *adj* : inventado, fabricado ⟨trumped-up charges : falsas acusaciones⟩

trumpet¹ ['trʌmpət] *vi* **1** : sonar una trompeta **2** : berrear, bramar (dícese de un animal) — *vt* : proclamar a los cuatro vientos

trumpet² *n* : trompeta *f*

trumpeter ['trʌmpətər] *n* : trompetista *mf*

truncate ['trʌŋˌkeɪt, 'trʌn-] *vt* **-cated; -cating** : truncar

trundle ['trʌndəl] *v* **-dled; -dling** *vi* : rodar lentamente — *vt* : hacer rodar, empujar lentamente

trunk¹ ['trʌŋk] *n* **1** : tronco *m* (de un árbol o del cuerpo) **2** : trompa *f* (de un elefante) **3** CHEST : baúl *m* **4** : maletero *m*, cajuela *f Mex* (de un auto) **5 trunks** *npl* : traje *m* de baño (de caballero)

truss¹ ['trʌs] *vt* : atar (con fuerza)

truss² *n* **1** FRAMEWORK : armazón *m* (de una estructura) **2** : braguero *m* (en medicina)

trust¹ ['trʌst] *vi* : confiar, esperar ⟨to trust in God : confiar en Dios⟩ — *vt* **1** ENTRUST : confiar, encomendar **2** : confiar en, tenerle confianza a ⟨I trust you : te tengo confianza⟩

trust² *n* **1** CONFIDENCE : confianza *f* **2** HOPE : esperanza *f*, fe *f* **3** CREDIT : crédito *m* ⟨to sell on trust : fiar⟩ **4** : fideicomiso *m* ⟨to hold in trust : guardar en fideicomiso⟩ **5** : trust *m* (consorcio empresarial) **6** CUSTODY : responsabilidad *f*, custodia *f*

trustee [ˌtrʌs'ti:] *n* : fideicomisario *m*, -ria *f*; fiduciario *m*, -ria *f*

trustful ['trʌstfəl] *adj* : confiado — **trustfully** *adv*

trustworthiness ['trʌstˌwərðinəs] *n* : integridad *f*, honradez *f*

trustworthy ['trʌstˌwərði] *adj* : digno de confianza, confiable

trusty ['trʌsti] *adj* **trustier; -est** : fiel, confiable

truth ['tru:θ] *n, pl* **truths** ['tru:ðz, 'tru:θs] : verdad *f*

truthful ['tru:θfəl] *adj* : sincero, veraz — **truthfully** *adv*

truthfulness ['tru:θfəlnəs] *n* : sinceridad *f*, veracidad *f*

try¹ ['traɪ] *v* **tried; trying** *vt* **1** : enjuiciar, juzgar, procesar ⟨he was tried for murder : fue procesado por homicidio⟩ **2** : probar ⟨did you try the salad? : ¿probaste la ensalada?⟩ **3** TEST : tentar, poner a prueba ⟨to try one's patience : tentarle la paciencia a uno⟩ **4** ATTEMPT : tratar (de), intentar **5** *or* **to try on** : probarse (ropa) — *vi* : tratar, intentar

try² *n, pl* **tries** : intento *m*, tentativa *f*

tryout ['traɪˌaʊt] *n* : prueba *f*

tsar ['zɑr, 'tsɑr, 'sɑr] → **czar**

T–shirt ['ti:ˌʃərt] *n* : camiseta *f*

tub ['tʌb] *n* **1** CASK : cuba *f*, barril *m*, tonel *m* **2** CONTAINER : envase *m* (de plástico, etc.) ⟨a tub of margarine : un envase de margarina⟩ **3** BATHTUB : tina *f* (de baño), bañera *f*

tuba ['tu:bə, 'tju:-] *n* : tuba *f*

tube ['tu:b, 'tju:b] *n* **1** PIPE : tubo *m* **2** : tubo *m* (de dentífrico, etc.) **3** *or* **inner tube** : cámara *f* **4** : tubo *m* (de un aparato electrónico) **5** : trompa *f* (en anatomía)

tubeless ['tu:bləs, 'tju:b-] *adj* : sin cámara (dícese de una llanta)

tuber ['tu:bər, 'tju:-] *n* : tubérculo *m*

tubercular [tʊ'bərkjələr, tju-] → **tuberculous**

tuberculosis [tʊˌbərkjə'lo:sɪs, tju-] *n, pl* **-loses** [-ˌsi:z] : tuberculosis *f*

tuberculous [tʊ'bərkjələs, tju-] *adj* : tuberculoso

tuberous ['tu:bərəs, 'tju:-] *adj* : tuberoso

tubing ['tu:bɪŋ, 'tju:-] *n* : tubería *f*

tubular ['tu:bjələr, 'tju:-] *adj* : tubular

tuck¹ ['tʌk] *vt* **1** PLACE, PUT : meter, colocar ⟨tuck in your shirt : métete la camisa⟩ **2** : guardar, esconder ⟨to tuck away one's money : guardar uno bien su dinero⟩ **3** COVER : arropar (a un niño en la cama)

tuck² *n* : pliegue *m*, alforza *f*

Tuesday ['tu:zˌdeɪ, 'tju:z-, -di] *n* : martes *m*

tuft ['tʌft] *n* : penacho *m* (de plumas), copete *m* (de pelo)

tug¹ ['tʌg] *v* **tugged; tugging** *vi* : tirar, jalar, dar un tirón — *vt* : jalar, arrastrar, remolcar (con un barco)

tug² *n* **1** : tirón *m*, jalón *m* **2** → **tugboat**

tugboat ['tʌgˌbo:t] *n* : remolcador *m*

tug–of–war [ˌtʌgəˈwɔr] *n*, *pl* **tugs–of–war** : tira y afloja *m*

tuition [tuˈɪʃən] *n or* **tuition fees** : tasas *fpl* de matrícula, colegiatura *f Mex*

tulip [ˈtuːlɪp, ˈtjuː-] *n* : tulipán *m*

tumble¹ [ˈtʌmbəl] *v* **-bled; -bling** *vi* 1 : dar volteretas (en acrobacia) 2 FALL : caerse, venirse abajo — *vt* 1 TOPPLE : volcar 2 TOSS : hacer girar

tumble² *n* : voltereta *f*, caída *f*

tumbler [ˈtʌmblər] *n* 1 ACROBAT : acróbata *mf*, saltimbanqui *mf* 2 GLASS : vaso *m* (de mesa) 3 : clavija *f* (de una cerradura)

tummy [ˈtʌmi] *n*, *pl* **-mies** BELLY : panza *f*, vientre *m*

tumor [ˈtuːmər, ˈtjuː-] *n* : tumor *m*

tumult [ˈtuːˌmʌlt, ˈtjuː-] *n* : tumulto *m*, alboroto *m*

tumultuous [tʊˈmʌlʧuəs, tju-] *adj* : tumultuoso

tuna [ˈtuːnə, ˈtjuː-] *n*, *pl* **-na** *or* **-nas** : atún *m*

tundra [ˈtʌndrə] *n* : tundra *f*

tune¹ [ˈtuːn, ˈtjuːn] *v* **tuned; tuning** *vt* 1 ADJUST : ajustar, hacer más preciso, afinar (un motor) 2 : afinar (un instrumento musical) 3 : sintonizar (un radio o televisor) — *vi* **to tune in** : sintonizar (con una emisora)

tune² *n* 1 MELODY : tonada *f*, canción *f*, melodía *f* 2 **in tune** : afinado (dícese de un instrumento o de la voz), sintonizado, en sintonía

tuneful [ˈtuːnfəl, ˈtjuːn-] *adj* : armonioso, melódico

tuner [ˈtuːnər, ˈtjuː-] *n* : afinador *m*, -dora *f* (de instrumentos); sintonizador *m* (de un radio o un televisor)

tungsten [ˈtʌŋkstən] *n* : tungsteno *m*

tunic [ˈtuːnɪk, ˈtjuː-] *n* : túnica *f*

tuning fork *n* : diapasón *m*

Tunisian [tuːˈniːʒən, tjuːˈnɪziən] *n* : tunecino *m*, -na *f* — **Tunisian** *adj*

tunnel¹ [ˈtʌnəl] *vi* **-neled** *or* **-nelled; -neling** *or* **-nelling** : hacer un túnel

tunnel² *n* : túnel *m*

turban [ˈtərbən] *n* : turbante *m*

turbid [ˈtərbɪd] *adj* : turbio

turbine [ˈtərbən, -ˌbaɪn] *n* : turbina *f*

turboprop [ˈtərboˌprɑp] *n* : turbopropulsor *m* (motor), avión *m* turbopropulsado

turbulence [ˈtərbjələn*t*s] *n* : turbulencia *f*

turbulent [ˈtərbjələnt] *adj* : turbulento — **turbulently** *adv*

tureen [təˈriːn, tjʊ-] *n* : sopera *f*

turf [ˈtərf] *n* SOD : tepe *m*

turgid [ˈtərdʒɪd] *adj* 1 SWOLLEN : turgente 2 : ampuloso, hinchado ⟨turgid style : estilo ampuloso⟩

Turk [ˈtərk] *n* : turco *m*, -ca *f*

turkey [ˈtərki] *n*, *pl* **-keys** : pavo *m*

Turkish¹ [ˈtərkɪʃ] *adj* : turco

Turkish² *n* : turco *m* (idioma)

turmoil [ˈtərˌmɔɪl] *n* : agitación *f*, desorden *m*, confusión *f*

turn¹ [ˈtərn] *vt* 1 : girar, voltear, volver ⟨to turn one's head : voltear la cabeza⟩ ⟨she turned her chair toward the fire : giró su asiento hacia la hoguera⟩ 2 ROTATE : darle vuelta a, hacer girar ⟨turn the handle : dale vuelta a la manivela⟩ 3 SPRAIN, WRENCH : dislocar, torcer 4 UPSET : revolver (el estómago) 5 TRANSFORM : convertir ⟨to turn water into wine : convertir el agua en vino⟩ 6 SHAPE : tornear (en carpintería) — *vi* 1 ROTATE : girar, dar vueltas 2 : girar, doblar, dar una vuelta ⟨turn left : doble a la izquierda⟩ ⟨to turn around : dar la media vuelta⟩ 3 BECOME : hacerse, volverse, ponerse 4 SOUR : agriarse, cortarse (dícese de la leche) 5 **to turn to** : recurrir a ⟨they have no one to turn to : no tienen quien les ayude⟩

turn² *n* 1 : vuelta *f*, giro *m* ⟨a sudden turn : una vuelta repentina⟩ 2 CHANGE : cambio *m* 3 CURVE : curva *f* (en un camino) 4 : turno *m* ⟨they're awaiting their turn : están esperando su turno⟩ ⟨whose turn is it? : ¿a quién le toca?⟩

turnaround [ˈtərnəˌraʊnd] *n* PROCESSING : procesamiento *m*

turncoat [ˈtərnˌkoːt] *n* : traidor *m*, -dora *f*

turn down *vt* 1 REFUSE : rehusar, rechazar ⟨they turned down our invitation : rehusaron nuestra invitación⟩ 2 LOWER : bajar (el volumen)

turn in *vt* : entregar ⟨to turn in one's work : entregar uno su trabajo⟩ ⟨they turned in the suspect : entregaron al sospechoso⟩ — *vi* : acostarse, irse a la cama

turnip [ˈtərnəp] *n* : nabo *m*

turn off *vt* : apagar (la luz, la radio, etc.)

turn on *vt* : prender (la luz, etc.), encender (un motor, etc.)

turnout [ˈtərnˌaʊt] *n* : concurrencia *f*

turn out *vt* 1 EVICT, EXPEL : expulsar, echar, desalojar 2 PRODUCE : producir 3 → **turn off** — *vi* 1 : concurrir, presentarse ⟨many turned out to vote : muchos concurrieron a votar⟩ 2 PROVE, RESULT : resultar

turnover [ˈtərnˌoːvər] *n* 1 : empanada *f* (salada o dulce) 2 : volumen *m* (de ventas) 3 : rotación *f* (de personal) ⟨a high turnover : un alto nivel de rotación⟩

turn over *vt* 1 TRANSFER : entregar, transferir (un cargo o una responsabilidad) 2 : voltear, darle la vuelta a ⟨turn the cassette over : voltea el cassette⟩

turnpike [ˈtərnˌpaɪk] *n* : carretera *f* de peaje

turnstile [ˈtərnˌstaɪl] *n* : torniquete *m* (de acceso)

turntable [ˈtərnˌteɪbəl] *n* : tornamesa *mf*

turn up *vi* 1 APPEAR : aparecer, presentarse 2 HAPPEN : ocurrir, suceder (inesperadamente) — *vt* : subir (el volumen)

turpentine [ˈtərpənˌtaɪn] *n* : aguarrás *m*, trementina *f*

turquoise ['tər‚kɔɪz, -‚kwɔɪz] *n* : turquesa *f*
turret ['tərət] *n* **1** TOWER : torre *f* pequeña **2** : torreta *f* (de un tanque, un avión, etc.)
turtle ['tərtəl] *n* : tortuga *f* (marina)
turtledove ['tərtəl‚dʌv] *n* : tórtola *f*
turtleneck ['tərtəl‚nɛk] *n* : cuello *m* de tortuga, cuello *m* alto
tusk ['tʌsk] *n* : colmillo *m*
tussle¹ ['tʌsəl] *vi* **-sled; -sling** SCUFFLE : pelearse, reñir
tussle² *n* : riña *f*, pelea *f*
tutor¹ ['tu:tər, 'tju:-] *vt* : darle clases particulares (a alguien)
tutor² *n* : tutor *m*, -tora *f*; maestro *m*, -tra *f* (particular)
tuxedo [‚tək'si:‚do:] *n, pl* **-dos** *or* **-does** : esmoquin *m*, smoking *m*
TV [‚ti:'vi:, 'ti:‚vi:] → **television**
twain ['tweɪn] *n* : dos *m*
twang¹ ['twæŋ] *vt* : pulsar la cuerda de (una guitarra) — *vi* : hablar en tono nasal
twang² *n* **1** : tañido *m* (de una cuerda de guitarra) **2** : tono *m* nasal (de voz)
tweak¹ ['twi:k] *vt* : pellizcar
tweak² *n* : pellizco *m*
tweed ['twi:d] *n* : tweed *m*
tweet¹ ['twi:t] *vi* : piar
tweet² *n* : gorjeo *m*, pío *m*
tweezers ['twi:zərz] *npl* : pinzas *fpl*
twelfth¹ ['twɛlfθ] *adj* : duodécimo
twelfth² *n* **1** : duodécimo *m*, -ma *f* (en una serie) **2** : doceavo *m*, doceava parte *f*
twelve¹ ['twɛlv] *adj* : doce
twelve² *n* : doce *m*
twentieth¹ ['twʌntiəθ, 'twɛn-] *adj* : vigésimo
twentieth² *n* **1** : vigésimo *m*, -ma *f* (en una serie) **2** : veinteavo *m*, veinteava parte *f*
twenty¹ ['twʌnti, 'twɛn-] *adj* : veinte
twenty² *n, pl* **-ties** : veinte *m*
twice ['twaɪs] *adv* : dos veces ⟨twice a day : dos veces al día⟩ ⟨it costs twice as much : cuesta el doble⟩
twig ['twɪg] *n* : ramita *f*
twilight ['twaɪ‚laɪt] *n* : crepúsculo *m*
twill ['twɪl] *n* : sarga *f*, tela *f* cruzada
twin¹ ['twɪn] *adj* : gemelo, mellizo
twin² *n* : gemelo *m*, -la *f*; mellizo *m*, -za *f*
twine¹ ['twaɪn] *v* **twined; twining** *vt* : entrelazar, entrecruzar — *vi* : enroscarse (alrededor de algo)
twine² *n* : cordel *m*, cuerda *f*, mecate *m* CA, Mex, Ven
twinge¹ ['twɪndʒ] *vi* **twinged; twinging** *or* **twingeing** : sentir punzadas
twinge² *n* : punzada *f*, dolor *m* agudo
twinkle¹ ['twɪŋkəl] *vi* **-kled; -kling 1** : centellear, titilar (dícese de las estrellas o de la luz) **2** : chispear, brillar (dícese de los ojos)
twinkle² *n* : centelleo *m* (de las estrellas), brillo *m* (de los ojos)
twirl¹ ['twərl] *vt* : girar, darle vueltas a — *vi* : girar, dar vueltas (rápidamente)

twirl² *n* : giro *m*, vuelta *f*
twist¹ ['twɪst] *vt* : torcer, retorcer ⟨he twisted my arm : me torció el brazo⟩ — *vi* : retorcerse, enroscarse, serpentear (dícese de un río, un camino, etc.)
twist² *n* **1** BEND : vuelta *f*, recodo *m* (en el camino, el río, etc.) **2** TURN : giro *m* ⟨give it a twist : hazlo girar⟩ **3** SPIRAL : espiral *f* ⟨a twist of lemon : una rodajita de limón⟩ **4** : giro *m* inesperado (de eventos, etc.)
twisted ['twɪstəd] *adj* : retorcido ⟨a twisted mind : una mente retorcida⟩
twister ['twɪstər] **1** → **tornado 2** → **waterspout**
twitch¹ ['twɪtʃ] *vi* : moverse nerviosamente, contraerse espasmódicamente (dícese de un músculo)
twitch² *n* : espasmo *m*, sacudida *f* ⟨a nervous twitch : un tic nervioso⟩
twitter¹ ['twɪtər] *vi* CHIRP : gorjear, cantar (dícese de los pájaros)
twitter² *n* : gorjeo *m*
two¹ ['tu:] *adj* : dos
two² *n, pl* **twos** : dos *m*
twofold¹ ['tu:'fo:ld] *adv* : al doble
twofold² ['tu:‚fo:ld] *adj* : doble
two hundred¹ *adj* : doscientos
two hundred² *n* : doscientos *m*
twosome ['tu:səm] *n* COUPLE : pareja *f*
tycoon [taɪ'ku:n] *n* : magnate *mf*
tying → **tie¹**
type¹ ['taɪp] *v* **typed; typing** *vt* **1** TYPEWRITE : escribir a máquina, pasar (un texto) a máquina **2** CATEGORIZE : categorizar, identificar — *vi* : escribir a máquina
type² *n* **1** KIND : tipo *m*, clase *f*, categoría *f* **2** *or* **printing type** : tipo *m*
typeface ['taɪp‚feɪs] *n* : tipo *m* de imprenta
typewrite ['taɪp‚raɪt] *v* **-wrote; -written** : escribir a máquina
typewriter ['taɪp‚raɪtər] *n* : máquina *f* de escribir
typhoid¹ ['taɪ‚fɔɪd, taɪ'-] *adj* : relativo al tifus o a la tifoidea
typhoid² *n* *or* **typhoid fever** : tifoidea *f*
typhoon [taɪ'fu:n] *n* : tifón *m*
typhus ['taɪfəs] *n* : tifus *m*, tifo *m*
typical ['tɪpɪkəl] *adj* : típico, característico — **typically** *adv*
typify ['tɪpə‚faɪ] *vt* **-fied; -fying** : ser típico o representativo de (un grupo, una clase, etc.)
typist ['taɪpɪst] *n* : mecanógrafo *m*, -fa *f*
typographic [‚taɪpə'græfɪk] *or* **typographical** [-fɪkəl] *adj* : tipográfico — **typographically** [-fɪkli] *adv*
typography [taɪ'pɑgrəfi] *n* : tipografía *f*
tyrannical [tə'rænɪkəl, taɪ-] *adj* : tiránico — **tyrannically** [-nɪkli] *adv*
tyrannize ['tɪrə‚naɪz] *vt* **-nized; -nizing** : tiranizar
tyranny ['tɪrəni] *n, pl* **-nies** : tiranía *f*
tyrant ['taɪrənt] *n* : tirano *m*, -na *f*
tzar ['zɑr, 'tsɑr, 'sɑr] → **czar**

U

u [ˈjuː] *n, pl* **u's** *or* **us** [ˈjuːz] : vigésima primera letra del alfabeto inglés

ubiquitous [juːˈbɪkwətəs] *adj* : ubicuo, omnipresente

udder [ˈʌdər] *n* : ubre *f*

UFO [ˌjuːˌɛfˈoː, ˈjuːˌfoː] *n, pl* **UFO's** *or* **UFOs** (*u*nidentified *f*lying *o*bject) : ovni *m*, OVNI *m*

Ugandan [juːˈgændən, -ˈgɑn-; uːˈgɑn-] *n* : ugandés *m*, -desa *f* — **Ugandan** *adj*

ugliness [ˈʌglinəs] *n* : fealdad *f*

ugly [ˈʌgli] *adj* **uglier; -est 1** UNATTRACTIVE : feo **2** DISAGREEABLE : desagradable, feo ⟨ugly weather : tiempo feo⟩ ⟨to have an ugly temper : tener mal genio⟩

Ukrainian [juːˈkreɪniən, -ˈkraɪ-] *n* **1** : ucraniano *m*, -na *f* **2** : ucraniano *m* (idioma) — **Ukrainian** *adj*

ukulele [ˌjuːkəˈleɪli] *n* : ukelele *m*

ulcer [ˈʌlsər] *n* : úlcera *f* (interna), llaga *f* (externa)

ulcerate [ˈʌlsəˌreɪt] *vi* **-ated; -ating** : ulcerarse

ulceration [ˌʌlsəˈreɪʃən] *n* **1** : ulceración *f* **2** ULCER : úlcera *f*, llaga *f*

ulcerous [ˈʌlsərəs] *adj* : ulceroso

ulna [ˈʌlnə] *n* : cúbito *m*

ulterior [ˌʌlˈtɪriər] *adj* : oculto ⟨ulterior motive : motivo oculto, segunda intención⟩

ultimate [ˈʌltəmət] *adj* **1** FINAL : último, final **2** SUPREME : supremo, máximo **3** FUNDAMENTAL : fundamental, esencial

ultimately [ˈʌltəmətli] *adv* **1** FINALLY : por último, finalmente **2** EVENTUALLY : a la larga, con el tiempo

ultimatum [ˌʌltəˈmeɪtəm, -ˈmɑ-] *n, pl* **-tums** *or* **-ta** [-tə] : ultimátum *m*

ultrasound [ˈʌltrəˌsaʊnd] *n* **1** : ultrasonido *m* **2** : ecografía *f* (técnica o imagen)

ultraviolet [ˌʌltrəˈvaɪələt] *adj* : ultravioleta

umbilical cord [ˌʌmˈbɪlɪkəl] *n* : cordón *m* umbilical

umbrage [ˈʌmbrɪdʒ] *n* **to take umbrage at** : ofenderse por

umbrella [ˌʌmˈbrɛlə] *n* **1** : paraguas *m* **2 beach umbrella** : sombrilla *f*

umpire¹ [ˈʌmˌpaɪr] *v* **-pired; -piring** : arbitrar

umpire² *n* : árbitro *m*, -tra *f*

umpteenth [ˈʌmpˈtiːnθ] *adj* : enésimo

unable [ˌʌnˈeɪbəl] *adj* : incapaz ⟨to be unable to : no poder⟩

unabridged [ˌʌnəˈbrɪdʒd] *adj* : íntegro

unacceptable [ˌʌnɪkˈsɛptəbəl] *adj* : inaceptable

unaccompanied [ˌʌnəˈkʌmpənid] *adj* : solo, sin acompañamiento (en música)

unaccountable [ˌʌnəˈkaʊntəbəl] *adj* : inexplicable, incomprensible — **unaccountably** [-bli] *adv*

unaccustomed [ˌʌnəˈkʌstəmd] *adj* **1** UNUSUAL : desacostumbrado, inusual **2** UNUSED : inhabituado ⟨unaccustomed to noise : inhabituado al ruido⟩

unacquainted [ˌʌnəˈkweɪntəd] *adj* **to be unacquainted with** : desconocer, ignorar

unadorned [ˌʌnəˈdɔrnd] *adj* : sin adornos, puro y simple

unadulterated [ˌʌnəˈdʌltəˌreɪtəd] *adj* **1** PURE : puro ⟨unadulterated food : comida pura⟩ **2** ABSOLUTE : completo, absoluto

unaffected [ˌʌnəˈfɛktəd] *adj* **1** : no afectado, indiferente **2** NATURAL : sin afectación, natural

unaffectedly [ˌʌnəˈfɛktədli] *adv* : de manera natural

unafraid [ˌʌnəˈfreɪd] *adj* : sin miedo

unaided [ˌʌnˈeɪdəd] *adj* : sin ayuda, solo

unambiguous [ˌʌnæmˈbɪgjuəs] *adj* : inequívoco

unanimity [ˌjuːnəˈnɪməti] *n* : unanimidad *f*

unanimous [juˈnænəməs] *adj* : unánime — **unanimously** *adv*

unannounced [ˌʌnəˈnaʊnst] *adj* : sin dar aviso

unanswered [ˌʌnˈæntsərd] *adj* : sin contestar

unappealing [ˌʌnəˈpiːlɪŋ] *adj* : desagradable

unappetizing [ˌʌnˈæpəˌtaɪzɪŋ] *adj* : poco apetitoso, poco apetecible

unarmed [ˌʌnˈɑrmd] *adj* : sin armas, desarmado

unassisted [ˌʌnəˈsɪstəd] *adj* : sin ayuda

unassuming [ˌʌnəˈsuːmɪŋ] *adj* : modesto, sin pretensiones

unattached [ˌʌnəˈtæʧt] *adj* **1** LOOSE : suelto **2** INDEPENDENT : independiente **3** : solo (ni casado ni prometido)

unattractive [ˌʌnəˈtræktɪv] *adj* : poco atractivo

unauthorized [ˌʌnˈɔθəˌraɪzd] *adj* : sin autorización, no autorizado

unavailable [ˌʌnəˈveɪləbəl] *adj* : no disponible

unavoidable [ˌʌnəˈvɔɪdəbəl] *adj* : inevitable, ineludible

unaware¹ [ˌʌnəˈwær] *adv* → **unawares**

unaware² *adj* : inconsciente

unawares [ˌʌnəˈwærz] *adv* **1** : por sorpresa ⟨to catch someone unawares : agarrar a alguien desprevenido⟩ **2** UNINTENTIONALLY : inconscientemente, inadvertidamente

unbalanced [ˌʌnˈbæləntst] *adj* : desequilibrado

unbearable [ˌʌnˈbærəbəl] *adj* : insoportable, inaguantable — **unbearably** *adv*

unbecoming [ˌʌnbɪˈkʌmɪŋ] *adj* **1** UNSEEMLY : impropio, indecoroso **2** UNFLATTERING : poco favorecedor

unbelievable [ˌʌnbə'liːvəbəl] *adj* : increíble — **unbelievably** [-bli] *adv*
unbend [ˌʌn'bɛnd] *vi* -**bent** [-'bɛnt]; -**bending** RELAX : relajarse
unbending [ˌʌn'bɛndɪŋ] *adj* : inflexible
unbiased [ˌʌn'baɪəst] *adj* : imparcial, objetivo
unbind [ˌʌn'baɪnd] *vt* -**bound** [-'baʊnd]; -**binding 1** UNFASTEN, UNTIE : desatar, desamarrar **2** RELEASE : liberar
unbolt [ˌʌn'boːlt] *vt* : abrir el cerrojo de, descorrer el pestillo de
unborn [ˌʌn'bɔrn] *adj* : aún no nacido, que va a nacer
unbosom [ˌʌn'buzəm, -'buː-] *vt* : revelar, divulgar
unbreakable [ˌʌn'breɪkəbəl] *adj* : irrompible
unbridled [ˌʌn'braɪdəld] *adj* : desenfrenado
unbroken [ˌʌn'broːkən] *adj* **1** INTACT : intacto, sano **2** CONTINUOUS : continuo, ininterrumpido
unbuckle [ˌʌn'bʌkəl] *vt* -**led**; -**ling** : desabrochar
unburden [ˌʌn'bərdən] *vt* **1** UNLOAD : descargar **2 to unburden oneself** : desahogarse
unbutton [ˌʌn'bʌtən] *vt* : desabrochar, desabotonar
uncalled–for [ˌʌn'kɔldˌfɔr] *adj* : inapropiado, innecesario
uncanny [ən'kæni] *adj* -**nier**; -**est 1** STRANGE : extraño **2** EXTRAORDINARY : raro, extraordinario — **uncannily** [-'kænəli] *adv*
unceasing [ˌʌn'siːsɪŋ] *adj* : incesante, continuo — **unceasingly** *adv*
unceremonious [ˌʌnˌsɛrə'moːniəs] *adj* **1** INFORMAL : sin ceremonia, sin pompa **2** ABRUPT : abrupto, brusco — **unceremoniously** *adv*
uncertain [ˌʌn'sərtən] *adj* **1** INDEFINITE : indeterminado **2** UNSURE : incierto, dudoso **3** CHANGEABLE : inestable, variable ⟨uncertain weather : tiempo inestable⟩ **4** HESITANT : indeciso **5** VAGUE : poco claro
uncertainly [ˌʌn'sərtənli] *adv* : dudosamente, con desconfianza
uncertainty [ˌʌn'sərtənti] *n, pl* -**ties** : duda *f*, incertidumbre *f*
unchangeable [ˌʌn'tʃeɪndʒəbəl] *adj* : inalterable, inmutable
unchanged [ˌʌn'tʃeɪndʒd] *adj* : sin cambiar
unchanging [ˌʌn'tʃeɪndʒɪŋ] *adj* : inalterable, inmutable, firme
uncharacteristic [ˌʌnˌkærɪktə'rɪstɪk] *adj* : inusual, desacostumbrado
uncharged [ˌʌn'tʃɑrdʒd] *adj* : sin carga (eléctrica)
uncivilized [ˌʌn'sɪvəˌlaɪzd] *adj* **1** BARBAROUS : incivilizado, bárbaro **2** WILD : salvaje
uncle ['ʌŋkəl] *n* : tío *m*
unclean [ˌʌn'kliːn] *adj* **1** IMPURE : impuro **2** DIRTY : sucio

unclear [ˌʌn'klɪr] *adj* : confuso, borroso, poco claro
Uncle Sam ['sæm] *n* : el Tío Sam
unclog [ˌʌn'klɑg] *vt* -**clogged**; -**clogging** : desatascar, destapar
unclothed [ˌʌn'kloːðd] *adj* : desnudo
uncomfortable [ˌʌn'kʌmpfərtəbəl] *adj* **1** : incómodo (dícese de una silla, etc.) **2** UNEASY : inquieto, incómodo
uncommitted [ˌʌnkə'mɪtəd] *adj* : sin compromisos
uncommon [ˌʌn'kɑmən] *adj* **1** UNUSUAL : raro, poco común **2** REMARKABLE : excepcional, extraordinario
uncommonly [ˌʌn'kɑmənli] *adv* : extraordinariamente
uncompromising [ˌʌn'kɑmprəˌmaɪzɪŋ] *adj* : inflexible, intransigente
unconcerned [ˌʌnkən'sərnd] *adj* : indiferente — **unconcernedly** [-'sərnədli] *adv*
unconditional [ˌʌnkən'dɪʃənəl] *adj* : incondicional — **unconditionally** *adv*
unconscious[1] [ˌʌn'kɑntʃəs] *adj* : inconsciente — **unconsciously** *adv*
unconscious[2] *n* : inconsciente *m*
unconsciousness [ˌʌn'kɑntʃəsnəs] *n* : inconsciencia *f*
unconstitutional [ˌʌnˌkɑntstə'tuːʃənəl, -'tjuː-] *adj* : inconstitucional
uncontrollable [ˌʌnkən'troːləbəl] *adj* : incontrolable, incontenible — **uncontrollably** [-bli] *adv*
uncontrolled [ˌʌnkən'troːld] *adj* : incontrolado
unconventional [ˌʌnkən'vɛntʃənəl] *adj* : poco convencional
unconvincing [ˌʌnkən'vɪntsɪŋ] *adj* : poco convincente
uncouth [ˌʌn'kuːθ] *adj* CRUDE, ROUGH : grosero, rudo
uncover [ˌʌn'kʌvər] *vt* **1** : destapar (un objeto), dejar al descubierto **2** EXPOSE, REVEAL : descubrir, revelar, exponer
uncultivated [ˌʌn'kʌltəˌveɪtəd] *adj* : inculto
uncurl [ˌʌn'kərl] *vt* UNROLL : desenrollar — *vi* : desenrollarse, desrizarse (dícese del pelo)
uncut [ˌʌn'kʌt] *adj* **1** : sin cortar ⟨uncut grass : hierba sin cortar⟩ **2** : sin tallar, en bruto ⟨an uncut diamond : un diamante en bruto⟩ **3** UNABRIDGED : completo, íntegro
undaunted [ˌʌn'dɔntəd] *adj* : impávido
undecided [ˌʌndi'saɪdəd] *adj* **1** IRRESOLUTE : indeciso, irresoluto **2** UNRESOLVED : pendiente, no resuelto
undefeated [ˌʌndi'fiːtəd] *adj* : invicto
undeniable [ˌʌndi'naɪəbəl] *adj* : innegable — **undeniably** [-bli] *adv*
under[1] ['ʌndər] *adv* **1** LESS : menos ⟨$10 or under : $10 o menos⟩ **2** UNDERWATER : debajo del agua **3** : bajo los efectos de la anestesia
under[2] *adj* **1** LOWER : (más) bajo, inferior **2** SUBORDINATE : inferior **3** : insuficiente ⟨an under dose of medicine : una dosis insuficiente de medicina⟩

under³ *prep* **1** BELOW, BENEATH : debajo de, abajo de ⟨under the table : abajo de la mesa⟩ ⟨we walked under the arch : pasamos por debajo del arco⟩ ⟨under the sun : bajo el sol⟩ **2** : menos de ⟨in under 20 minutes : en menos de 20 minutos⟩ **3** (*indicating rank or authority*) : bajo ⟨under the command of : bajo las órdenes de⟩ **4** SUBJECT TO : bajo ⟨under suspicion : bajo sospecha⟩ ⟨under the circumstances : dadas las circunstancias⟩ **5** ACCORDING TO : según, de acuerdo con, conforme a ⟨under the present laws : según las leyes actuales⟩

underage [ˌʌndərˈeɪʤ] *adj* : menor de edad

underbrush [ˈʌndərˌbrəʃ] *n* : maleza *f*

underclothes [ˈʌndərˌkloːz, -ˌkloːðz] → **underwear**

underclothing [ˈʌndərˌkloːðɪŋ] → **underwear**

undercover [ˌʌndərˈkʌvər] *adj* : secreto, clandestino

undercurrent [ˈʌndərˌkərənt] *n* **1** : corriente *f* submarina **2** UNDERTONE : corriente *f* oculta, trasfondo *m*

undercut [ˌʌndərˈkʌt] *vt* **-cut; -cutting** : vender más barato que

underdeveloped [ˌʌndərdɪˈvɛləpt] *adj* : subdesarrollado, atrasado

underdog [ˈʌndərˌdɔg] *n* : persona *f* que tiene menos posibilidades

underdone [ˌʌndərˈdʌn] *adj* RARE : poco cocido

underestimate [ˌʌndərˈɛstəˌmeɪt] *vt* **-mated; -mating** : subestimar, menospreciar

underexposed [ˌʌndərɪkˈspoːzd] *adj* : subexpuesto (en fotografía)

underfoot [ˌʌndərˈfʊt] *adv* **1** : bajo los pies ⟨to trample underfoot : pisotear⟩ **2 to be underfoot** : estorbar ⟨they're always underfoot : están siempre estorbando⟩

undergarment [ˈʌndərˌgɑrmənt] *n* : prenda *f* íntima

undergo [ˌʌndərˈgoː] *vt* **-went** [-ˈwɛnt]; **-gone** [-ˈgɔn]; **-going** : sufrir, experimentar ⟨to undergo an operation : someterse a una intervención quirúrgica⟩

undergraduate [ˌʌndərˈgræʤuət] *n* : estudiante *m* universitario, estudiante *f* universitaria

underground¹ [ˌʌndərˈgraʊnd] *adv* **1** : bajo tierra **2** SECRETLY : clandestinamente, en secreto ⟨to go underground : pasar a la clandestinidad⟩

underground² [ˈʌndərˌgraʊnd] *adj* **1** SUBTERRANEAN : subterráneo **2** SECRET : secreto, clandestino

underground³ [ˈʌndərˌgraʊnd] *n* : movimiento *m* o grupo *m* clandestino

undergrowth [ˈʌndərˌgroːθ] *n* : maleza *f*, broza *f*

underhand¹ [ˈʌndərˌhænd] *adv* **1** SECRETLY : de manera clandestina **2** *or*

underhanded : sin levantar el brazo por encima del hombro (en deportes)

underhand² *adj* **1** SLY : solapado **2** : por debajo del hombro (en deportes)

underhanded [ˌʌndərˈhændəd] *adj* **1** SLY : solapado **2** SHADY : turbio, poco limpio

underline [ˈʌndərˌlaɪn] *vt* **-lined; -lining** **1** : subrayar **2** EMPHASIZE : subrayar, acentuar, hacer hincapié en

underlying [ˌʌndərˈlaɪɪŋ] *adj* **1** : subyacente ⟨the underlying rock : la roca subyacente⟩ **2** FUNDAMENTAL : fundamental, esencial

undermine [ˌʌndərˈmaɪn] *vt* **-mined; -mining** **1** : socavar (una estructura, etc.) **2** SAP, WEAKEN : minar, debilitar

underneath¹ [ˌʌndərˈniːθ] *adv* : debajo, abajo ⟨the part underneath : la parte de abajo⟩

underneath² *prep* : debajo de, abajo de

undernourished [ˌʌndərˈnərɪʃt] *adj* : desnutrido

underpants [ˈʌndərˌpænts] *npl* : calzoncillos *mpl*, calzones *mpl*

underpass [ˈʌndərˌpæs] *n* : paso *m* a desnivel

underprivileged [ˌʌndərˈprɪvlɪʤd] *adj* : desfavorecido

underrate [ˌʌndərˈreɪt] *vt* **-rated; -rating** : subestimar, menospreciar

underscore [ˈʌndərˌskor] *vt* **-scored; -scoring** → **underline**

undersea¹ [ˌʌndərˈsiː] *or* **underseas** [-ˈsiːz] *adv* : bajo la superficie del mar

undersea² *adj* : submarino

undersecretary [ˌʌndərˈsɛkrəˌtɛri] *n, pl* **-ries** : subsecretario *m*, -ria *f*

undersell [ˌʌndərˈsɛl] *vt* **-sold; -selling** : vender más barato que

undershirt [ˈʌndərˌʃərt] *n* : camiseta *f*

undershorts [ˈʌndərˌʃɔrts] *npl* : calzoncillos *mpl*

underside [ˈʌndərˌsaɪd, ˌʌndərˈsaɪd] *n* : parte *f* de abajo

undersized [ˌʌndərˈsaɪzd] *adj* : más pequeño de lo normal

understand [ˌʌndərˈstænd] *v* **-stood** [-ˈstʊd]; **-standing** *vt* **1** COMPREHEND : comprender, entender ⟨I don't understand it : no lo entiendo⟩ ⟨that's understood : eso se comprende⟩ ⟨to make oneself understood : hacerse entender⟩ **2** BELIEVE : entender ⟨to give someone to understand : dar a alguien a entender⟩ **3** INFER : tener entendido ⟨I understand that she's leaving : tengo entendido que se va⟩ — *vi* : comprender, entender

understandable [ˌʌndərˈstændəbəl] *adj* : comprensible

understanding¹ [ˌʌndərˈstændɪŋ] *adj* : comprensivo, compasivo

understanding² *n* **1** GRASP : comprensión *f*, entendimiento *m* **2** SYMPATHY : comprensión *f* (mutua) **3** INTERPRETATION : interpretación *f* ⟨it's my understanding that ... : tengo la impresión de que ..., tengo entendido que ... ⟩ **4** AGREEMENT : acuerdo *m*, arreglo *m*

understate [ˌʌndərˈsteɪt] *vt* **-stated; -stating** : minimizar, subestimar

understatement [ˌʌndərˈsteɪtmənt] *n* : atenuación *f* ⟨that's an understatement : decir sólo eso es quedarse corto⟩

understudy [ˈʌndərˌstʌdi] *n, pl* **-dies** : sobresaliente *mf*, suplente *mf* (en el teatro)

undertake [ˌʌndərˈteɪk] *vt* **-took** [-ˈtʊk]; **-taken** [-ˈteɪkən]; **-taking 1** : emprender (una tarea), asumir (una responsabilidad) **2** PROMISE : comprometerse (a hacer algo)

undertaker [ˈʌndərˌteɪkər] *n* : director *m*, -tora *f* de funeraria

undertaking [ˈʌndərˌteɪkɪŋ, ˌʌndərˈ-] *n* **1** ENTERPRISE, TASK : empresa *f*, tarea *f* **2** PLEDGE : promesa *f*, garantía *f*

undertone [ˈʌndərˌtoːn] *n* **1** : voz *f* baja ⟨to speak in an undertone : hablar en voz baja⟩ **2** HINT, UNDERCURRENT : trasfondo *m*, matiz *m*

undertow [ˈʌndərˌtoː] *n* : resaca *f*

undervalue [ˌʌndərˈvælˌjuː] *vt* **-ued; -uing** : menospreciar, subestimar

underwater[1] [ˌʌndərˈwɔtər, -ˈwɑ-] *adv* : debajo (del agua)

underwater[2] *adj* : submarino

under way [ˌʌndərˈweɪ] *adv* : en marcha, en camino ⟨to get under way : ponerse en marcha⟩

underwear [ˈʌndərˌwær] *n* : ropa *f* interior, ropa *f* íntima

underworld [ˈʌndərˌwərld] *n* **1** HELL : infierno *m* **2 the underworld** CRIMINALS : la hampa, los bajos fondos

underwrite [ˈʌndərˌraɪt, ˌʌndərˈ-] *vt* **-wrote** [-ˌroːt, -ˈroːt]; **-written** [-ˌrɪtən, -ˈrɪtən]; **-writing 1** INSURE : asegurar **2** FINANCE : financiar **3** BACK, ENDORSE : suscribir, respaldar

underwriter [ˈʌndərˌraɪtər, ˌʌndərˈ-] *n* INSURER : asegurador *m*, -dora *f*

undeserving [ˌʌndiˈzərvɪŋ] *adj* : indigno

undesirable[1] [ˌʌndiˈzaɪrəbəl] *adj* : indeseable

undesirable[2] *n* : indeseable *mf*

undeveloped [ˌʌndiˈvɛləpt] *adj* : sin desarrollar, sin revelar (dícese de una película)

undies [ˈʌndiz] → **underwear**

undignified [ˌʌnˈdɪgnəfaɪd] *adj* : indecoroso

undiluted [ˌʌndaɪˈluːtəd, -də-] *adj* : sin diluir, concentrado

undiscovered [ˌʌndɪˈskʌvərd] *adj* : no descubierto

undisputed [ˌʌndɪˈspjuːtəd] *adj* : indiscutible

undisturbed [ˌʌndɪˈstərbd] *adj* : tranquilo (dícese de una persona), sin tocar (dícese de un objeto)

undivided [ˌʌndɪˈvaɪdəd] *adj* : íntegro, completo

undo [ˌʌnˈduː] *vt* **-did** [-ˈdɪd]; **-done** [-ˈdʌn]; **-doing 1** UNFASTEN : desabrochar, desatar, abrir **2** ANNUL : anular **3** REVERSE : deshacer, reparar (daños, etc.) **4** RUIN : arruinar, destruir

undoing [ˌʌnˈduːɪŋ] *n* : ruina *f*, perdición *f*

undoubted [ˌʌnˈdaʊtəd] *adj* : cierto, indudable — **undoubtedly** *adv*

undress [ˌʌnˈdrɛs] *vt* : desvestir, desabrigar, desnudar — *vi* : desvestirse, desnudarse

undrinkable [ˌʌnˈdrɪŋkəbəl] *adj* : no potable

undue [ˌʌnˈduː, -ˈdjuː] *adj* : excesivo, indebido — **unduly** *adv*

undulate [ˈʌndʒəˌleɪt] *vi* **-lated; -lating** : ondular

undulation [ˌʌndʒəˈleɪʃən] *n* : ondulación *f*

undying [ˌʌnˈdaɪɪŋ] *adj* : perpetuo, imperecedero

unearth [ˌʌnˈərθ] *vt* **1** EXHUME : desenterrar, exhumar **2** DISCOVER : descubrir

unearthly [ˌʌnˈərθli] *adj* **-lier; -est** : sobrenatural, de otro mundo

uneasily [ˌʌnˈiːzəli] *adv* : inquietamente, con inquietud

uneasiness [ˌʌnˈiːzinəs] *n* : inquietud *f*

uneasy [ˌʌnˈiːzi] *adj* **-easier; -est 1** AWKWARD : incómodo **2** WORRIED : preocupado, inquieto **3** RESTLESS : inquieto, agitado

uneducated [ˌʌnˈɛdʒəˌkeɪtəd] *adj* : inculto, sin educación

unemployed [ˌʌnɪmˈplɔɪd] *adj* : desempleado

unemployment [ˌʌnɪmˈplɔɪmənt] *n* : desempleo *m*

unending [ˌʌnˈɛndɪŋ] *adj* : sin fin, interminable

unendurable [ˌʌnɪmˈdʊrəbəl, -ɛn-, -ˈdjʊr-] *adj* : insoportable, intolerable

unequal [ˌʌnˈiːkwəl] *adj* **1** : desigual **2** INADEQUATE : incapaz, incompetente ⟨to be unequal to a task : no estar a la altura de una tarea⟩

unequaled *or* **unequalled** [ˌʌnˈiːkwəld] *adj* : sin igual

unequivocal [ˌʌniˈkwɪvəkəl] *adj* : inequívoco, claro — **unequivocally** *adv*

unerring [ˌʌnˈɛrɪŋ, -ˈər-] *adj* : infalible

unethical [ˌʌnˈɛθɪkəl] *adj* : poco ético

uneven [ˌʌnˈiːvən] *adj* **1** ODD : impar (dícese de un número) **2** : desigual, desnivelado (dícese de una superficie) ⟨uneven terrain : terreno accidentado⟩ **3** IRREGULAR : irregular, poco uniforme **4** UNEQUAL : desigual

unevenly [ˌʌnˈiːvənli] *adv* : desigualmente, irregularmente

uneventful [ˌʌnɪˈvɛntfəl] *adj* : sin incidentes, tranquilo

unexpected [ˌʌnɪkˈspɛktəd] *adj* : imprevisto, inesperado — **unexpectedly** *adv*

unfailing [ˌʌnˈfeɪlɪŋ] *adj* **1** CONSTANT : constante **2** INEXHAUSTIBLE : inagotable **3** SURE : a toda prueba, indefectible

unfair [ˌʌn'fær] *adj* : injusto — **unfairly** *adv*

unfairness [ˌʌn'færnəs] *n* : injusticia *f*

unfaithful [ˌʌn'feɪθfəl] *adj* : desleal, infiel — **unfaithfully** *adv*

unfaithfulness [ˌʌn'feɪθfəlnəs] *n* : infidelidad *f*, deslealtad *f*

unfamiliar [ˌʌnfə'mɪljər] *adj* **1** STRANGE : desconocido, extraño ⟨an unfamiliar place : un lugar nuevo⟩ **2 to be unfamiliar with** : no estar familiarizado con, desconocer

unfamiliarity [ˌʌnfəˌmɪli'ærəti] *n* : falta *f* de familiaridad

unfashionable [ˌʌn'fæʃənəbəl] *adj* : fuera de moda

unfasten [ˌʌn'fæsən] *vt* : desabrochar, desatar (una cuerda, etc.), abrir (una puerta)

unfavorable [ˌʌn'feɪvərəbəl] *adj* : desfavorable, mal — **unfavorably** [-bli] *adv*

unfeeling [ˌʌn'fiːlɪŋ] *adj* : insensible — **unfeelingly** *adv*

unfinished [ˌʌn'fɪnɪʃd] *adj* : inacabado, incompleto

unfit [ˌʌn'fɪt] *adj* **1** UNSUITABLE : inadecuado, impropio **2** UNSUITED : no apto, incapaz **3** : incapacitado (físicamente) ⟨to be unfit : no estar en forma⟩

unflappable [ˌʌn'flæpəbəl] *adj* : imperturbable

unflattering [ˌʌn'flætərɪŋ] *adj* : poco favorecedor

unfold [ˌʌn'foːld] *vt* **1** EXPAND : desplegar, desdoblar, extender ⟨to unfold a map : desplegar un mapa⟩ **2** DISCLOSE, REVEAL : revelar, exponer (un plan, etc.) — *vi* **1** DEVELOP : desarrollarse, desenvolverse ⟨the story unfolded : el cuento se desarrollaba⟩ **2** EXPAND : extenderse, desplegarse

unforeseeable [ˌʌnfor'siːəbəl] *adj* : imprevisible

unforeseen [ˌʌnfor'siːn] *adj* : imprevisto

unforgettable [ˌʌnfər'ɡɛtəbəl] *adj* : inolvidable, memorable — **unforgettably** [-bli] *adv*

unforgivable [ˌʌnfər'ɡɪvəbəl] *adj* : imperdonable

unfortunate[1] [ˌʌn'fɔrtʃənət] *adj* **1** UNLUCKY : desgraciado, infortunado, desafortunado ⟨how unfortunate! : ¡qué mala suerte!⟩ **2** INAPPROPRIATE : inoportuno ⟨an unfortunate comment : un comentario poco feliz⟩

unfortunate[2] *n* : desgraciado *m*, -da *f*

unfortunately [ˌʌn'fɔrtʃənətli] *adv* : desafortunadamente

unfounded [ˌʌn'faʊndəd] *adj* : infundado

unfreeze [ˌʌn'friːz] *v* **-froze** [-'froːz]; **-frozen** [-'froːzən]; **-freezing** *vt* : descongelar — *vi* : descongelarse

unfriendliness [ˌʌn'frɛndlinəs] *n* : hostilidad *f*, antipatía *f*

unfriendly [ˌʌn'frɛndli] *adj* **-lier; -est** : poco amistoso, hostil

unfurl [ˌʌn'fərl] *vt* : desplegar, desdoblar — *vi* : desplegarse

unfurnished [ˌʌn'fərnɪʃt] *adj* : desamueblado

ungainly [ˌʌn'ɡeɪnli] *adj* : desgarbado

ungodly [ˌʌn'ɡɔdli, -'ɡɑd-] *adj* **1** IMPIOUS : impío **2** OUTRAGEOUS : atroz, terrible ⟨at an ungodly hour : a una hora intempestiva⟩

ungrateful [ˌʌn'ɡreɪtfəl] *adj* : desagradecido, ingrato — **ungratefully** *adv*

ungratefulness [ˌʌn'ɡreɪtfəlnəs] *n* : ingratitud *f*

unhappily [ˌʌn'hæpəli] *adv* **1** SADLY : tristemente **2** UNFORTUNATELY : desafortunadamente, lamentablemente

unhappiness [ˌʌn'hæpinəs] *n* : infelicidad *f*, tristeza *f*, desdicha *f*

unhappy [ˌʌn'hæpi] *adj* **-pier; -est 1** UNFORTUNATE : desafortunado, desventurado **2** MISERABLE, SAD : infeliz, triste, desdichado **3** INOPPORTUNE : inoportuno, poco feliz

unharmed [ˌʌn'hɑrmd] *adj* : salvo, ileso

unhealthy [ˌʌn'hɛlθi] *adj* **-thier; -est 1** UNWHOLESOME : insalubre, malsano, nocivo a la salud ⟨an unhealthy climate : un clima insalubre⟩ **2** SICKLY : de mala salud, enfermizo

unheard–of [ˌʌn'hərdəv] *adj* : sin precedente, inaudito, insólito

unhinge [ˌʌn'hɪndʒ] *vt* **-hinged; -hinging 1** : desquiciar (una puerta, etc.) **2** DISRUPT, UNSETTLE : trastornar, perturbar

unholy [ˌʌn'hoːli] *adj* **-lier; -est 1** : profano, impío **2** UNGODLY : atroz, terrible

unhook [ˌʌn'hʊk] *vt* **1** : desenganchar, descolgar (de algo) **2** UNDO : desabrochar

unhurt [ˌʌn'hərt] *adj* : ileso

unicorn ['juːnəˌkɔrn] *n* : unicornio *m*

unidentified [ˌʌnaɪ'dɛntəˌfaɪd] *adj* : no identificado ⟨unidentified flying object : objeto volador no identificado⟩

unification [ˌjuːnəfə'keɪʃən] *n* : unificación *f*

uniform[1] ['juːnəˌfɔrm] *adj* : uniforme, homogéneo, constante

uniform[2] *n* : uniforme *m*

uniformed ['juːnəˌfɔrmd] *adj* : uniformado

uniformity [ˌjuːnə'fɔrməti] *n, pl* **-ties** : uniformidad *f*

unify ['juːnəˌfaɪ] *vt* **-fied; -fying** : unificar, unir

unilateral [ˌjuːnə'lætərəl] *adj* : unilateral — **unilaterally** *adv*

unimaginable [ˌʌni'mædʒənəbəl] *adj* : inimaginable, inconcebible

unimportant [ˌʌnim'pɔrtənt] *adj* : intrascendente, insignificante, sin importancia

uninhabited [ˌʌnin'hæbətəd] *adj* : deshabitado, desierto, despoblado

uninhibited [ˌʌnɪnˈhɪbətəd] *adj* : desenfadado, desinhibido, sin reservas

uninjured [ˌʌnˈɪndʒərd] *adj* : ileso

unintelligent [ˌʌnɪnˈtɛlədʒənt] *adj* : poco inteligente

unintelligible [ˌʌnɪnˈtɛlədʒəbəl] *adj* : ininteligible, incomprensible

unintentional [ˌʌnɪnˈtɛntʃənəl] *adj* : no deliberado, involuntario

unintentionally [ˌʌnɪnˈtɛntʃənəli] *adv* : involuntariamente, sin querer

uninterested [ˌʌnˈɪntəˌrɛstəd, -trəstəd] *adj* : indiferente

uninteresting [ˌʌnˈɪntəˌrɛstɪŋ, -trəstɪŋ] *adj* : poco interesante, sin interés

uninterrupted [ˌʌnˌɪntəˈrʌptəd] *adj* : ininterrumpido, continuo

union [ˈjuːnjən] *n* **1** : unión *f* **2** *or* **labor union** : sindicato *m*, gremio *m*

unionize [ˈjuːnjəˌnaɪz] *v* **-ized; -izing** *vt* : sindicalizar, sindicar — *vi* : sindicalizarse

unique [juˈniːk] *adj* **1** SOLE : único, solo **2** UNUSUAL : extraordinario

uniquely [juˈniːkli] *adv* **1** EXCLUSIVELY : exclusivamente **2** EXCEPTIONALLY : excepcionalmente

unison [ˈjuːnəsən, -zən] *n* **1** : unísono *m* (en música) **2** CONCORD : acuerdo *m*, armonía *f*, concordia *f* **3 in ~** SIMULTANEOUSLY : simultáneamente, al unísono

unit [ˈjuːnɪt] *n* **1** : unidad *f* **2** : módulo *m* (de un mobiliario)

unitary [ˈjuːnəˌtɛri] *adj* : unitario

unite [juˈnaɪt] *v* **united; uniting** *vt* : unir, juntar, combinar — *vi* : unirse, juntarse

unity [ˈjuːnəti] *n, pl* **-ties 1** UNION : unidad *f*, unión *f* **2** HARMONY : armonía *f*, acuerdo *m*

universal [ˌjuːnəˈvərsəl] *adj* **1** GENERAL : general, universal ⟨a universal rule : una regla universal⟩ **2** WORLDWIDE : universal, mundial — **universally** *adv*

universe [ˈjuːnəˌvərs] *n* : universo *m*

university [ˌjuːnəˈvərsəti] *n, pl* **-ties** : universidad *f*

unjust [ˌʌnˈdʒʌst] *adj* : injusto — **unjustly** *adv*

unjustifiable [ˌʌnˌdʒʌstəˈfaɪəbəl] *adj* : injustificable

unjustified [ˌʌnˈdʒʌstəˌfaɪd] *adj* : injustificado

unkempt [ˌʌnˈkɛmpt] *adj* : descuidado, desaliñado, despeinado (dícese del pelo)

unkind [ˌʌnˈkaɪnd] *adj* : poco amable, cruel — **unkindly** *adv*

unkindness [ˌʌnˈkaɪndnəs] *n* : crueldad *f*, falta *f* de amabilidad

unknowing [ˌʌnˈnoːɪŋ] *adj* : inconsciente, ignorante — **unknowingly** *adv*

unknown [ˌʌnˈnoːn] *adj* : desconocido

unlawful [ˌʌnˈlɔːfəl] *adj* : ilícito, ilegal — **unlawfully** *adv*

unleash [ˌʌnˈliːʃ] *vt* : soltar, desatar

unless [ənˈlɛs] *conj* : a menos que, salvo que, a no ser que

unlike¹ [ˌʌnˈlaɪk] *adj* **1** DIFFERENT : diferente, distinto **2** UNEQUAL : desigual

unlike² *prep* **1** : diferente de, distinto de ⟨unlike the others : distinto a los demás⟩ **2** : a diferencia de ⟨unlike her sister, she is shy : a diferencia de su hermana, es tímida⟩

unlikelihood [ˌʌnˈlaɪkliˌhʊd] *n* : improbabilidad *f*

unlikely [ˌʌnˈlaɪkli] *adj* **-lier; -est 1** IMPROBABLE : improbable, poco probable **2** UNPROMISING : poco prometedor

unlimited [ˌʌnˈlɪmətəd] *adj* : ilimitado

unload [ˌʌnˈloːd] *vt* **1** REMOVE : descargar, desembarcar (mercancías o pasajeros) **2** : descargar (un avión, un camión, etc.) **3** DUMP : deshacerse de — *vi* : descargar (dícese de un avión, un camión, etc.)

unlock [ˌʌnˈlɑk] *vt* **1** : abrir (con llave) **2** DISCLOSE, REVEAL : revelar

unluckily [ˌʌnˈlʌkəli] *adv* : desgraciadamente

unlucky [ˌʌnˈlʌki] *adj* **-luckier; -est 1** : de mala suerte, desgraciado, desafortunado ⟨an unlucky year : un año de mala suerte⟩ **2** INAUSPICIOUS : desfavorable, poco propicio **3** REGRETTABLE : lamentable

unmanageable [ˌʌnˈmænɪdʒəbəl] *adj* : difícil de controlar, poco manejable, ingobernable

unmarried [ˌʌnˈmærid] *adj* : soltero

unmask [ˌʌnˈmæsk] *vt* EXPOSE : desenmascarar

unmerciful [ˌʌnˈmərsɪfəl] *adj* MERCILESS : despiadado — **unmercifully** *adv*

unmistakable [ˌʌnmɪˈsteɪkəbəl] *adj* : evidente, inconfundible, obvio — **unmistakably** [-bli] *adv*

unmoved [ˌʌnˈmuːvd] *adj* : impasible ⟨to be unmoved by : permanecer impasible ante⟩

unnatural [ˌʌnˈnætʃərəl] *adj* **1** ABNORMAL, UNUSUAL : anormal, poco natural, poco normal **2** AFFECTED : afectado, forzado ⟨an unnatural smile : una sonrisa forzada⟩ **3** PERVERSE : perverso, antinatural

unnecessary [ˌʌnˈnɛsəˌsɛri] *adj* : innecesario — **unnecessarily** [-ˌnɛsəˈsɛrəli] *adv*

unnerve [ˌʌnˈnərv] *vt* **-nerved; -nerving** : turbar, desconcertar, poner nervioso

unnoticed [ˌʌnˈnoːtəst] *adj* : inadvertido ⟨to go unnoticed : pasar inadvertido⟩

unobstructed [ˌʌnəbˈstrʌktəd] *adj* : libre, despejado

unobtainable [ˌʌnəbˈteɪnəbəl] *adj* : inasequible

unobtrusive [ˌʌnəbˈstruːsɪv] *adj* : discreto

unoccupied [ˌʌnˈɑkjəˌpaɪd] *adj* **1** IDLE : desempleado, desocupado **2** EMPTY : desocupado, libre, deshabitado

unofficial [ˌʌnəˈfɪʃəl] *adj* : extraoficial, oficioso, no oficial

unorganized [ˌʌn'ɔrgəˌnaɪzd] *adj* : desorganizado

unorthodox [ˌʌn'ɔrθəˌdɑks] *adj* : poco ortodoxo, poco convencional

unpack [ˌʌn'pæk] *vt* : desempacar — *vi* : desempacar, deshacer las maletas

unpaid [ˌʌn'peɪd] *adj* : no remunerado, no retribuido ⟨an unpaid bill : una cuenta pendiente⟩

unparalleled [ˌʌn'pærəˌlɛld] *adj* : sin igual

unpatriotic [ˌʌnˌpeɪtri'ɑṭɪk] *adj* : antipatriótico

unpleasant [ˌʌn'plɛzənt] *adj* : desagradable — **unpleasantly** *adv*

unplug [ˌʌn'plʌg] *vt* **-plugged; -plugging 1** UNCLOG : destapar, desatascar **2** DISCONNECT : desconectar, desenchufar

unpopular [ˌʌn'pɑpjələr] *adj* : impopular, poco popular

unpopularity [ˌʌnˌpɑpjə'lærəṭi] *n* : impopularidad *f*

unprecedented [ˌʌn'prɛsəˌdɛntəd] *adj* : sin precedentes, inaudito, nuevo

unpredictable [ˌʌnpri'dɪktəbəl] *adj* : impredecible

unprejudiced [ˌʌn'prɛdʒədəst] *adj* : imparcial, objetivo

unprepared [ˌʌnpri'pærd] *adj* : no preparado ⟨an unprepared speech : un discurso improvisado⟩

unpretentious [ˌʌnpri'tɛntʃəs] *adj* : modesto, sin pretensiones

unprincipled [ˌʌn'prɪnṭsəpəld] *adj* : sin principios, carente de escrúpulos

unproductive [ˌʌnprə'dʌktɪv] *adj* : improductivo

unprofitable [ˌʌn'prɑfəṭəbəl] *adj* : no rentable, poco provechoso

unpromising [ˌʌn'prɑməsɪŋ] *adj* : poco prometedor

unprotected [ˌʌnprə'tɛktəd] *adj* : sin protección, desprotegido

unprovoked [ˌʌnprə'vo:kt] *adj* : no provocado

unpublished [ˌʌn'pʌblɪʃt] *adj* : inédito

unpunished [ˌʌn'pʌnɪʃt] *adj* : impune ⟨to go unpunished : escapar sin castigo⟩

unqualified [ˌʌn'kwɑləˌfaɪd] *adj* **1** : no calificado, sin título **2** COMPLETE : completo, absoluto ⟨an unqualified denial : una negación incondicional⟩

unquestionable [ˌʌn'kwɛstʃənəbəl] *adj* : incuestionable, indudable, indiscutible — **unquestionably** [-bli] *adv*

unquestioning [ˌʌn'kwɛstʃənɪŋ] *adj* : incondicional, absoluto, ciego

unravel [ˌʌn'rævəl] *v* **-eled** *or* **-elled; -eling** *or* **-elling** *vt* **1** DISENTANGLE : desenmarañar, desenredar **2** SOLVE : aclarar, desenmarañar, desentrañar — *vi* : deshacerse

unreal [ˌʌn'ri:l] *adj* : irreal

unrealistic [ˌʌnˌri:ə'lɪstɪk] *adj* : poco realista

unreasonable [ˌʌn'ri:zənəbəl] *adj* **1** IRRATIONAL : poco razonable, irrazon-

able, irracional **2** EXCESSIVE : excesivo ⟨unreasonable prices : precios excesivos⟩

unreasonably [ˌʌn'ri:zənəbli] *adv* **1** IRRATIONALLY : irracionalmente, de manera irrazonable **2** EXCESSIVELY : excesivamente

unrefined [ˌʌnri'faɪnd] *adj* **1** : no refinado, sin refinar (dícese del azúcar, de la harina, etc.) **2** : poco refinado, inculto (dícese de una persona)

unrelated [ˌʌnri'leɪṭəd] *adj* : no relacionado, inconexo

unrelenting [ˌʌnri'lɛntɪŋ] *adj* **1** STERN : severo, inexorable **2** CONSTANT, RELENTLESS : constante, implacable

unreliable [ˌʌnri'laɪəbəl] *adj* : que no es de fiar, de poca confianza, inestable (dícese del tiempo)

unrepentant [ˌʌnri'pɛntənt] *adj* : impenitente

unresolved [ˌʌnri'zɑlvd] *adj* : pendiente, no resuelto

unrest [ˌʌn'rɛst] *n* : inquietud *f*, malestar *m* ⟨political unrest : disturbios políticos⟩

unrestrained [ˌʌnri'streɪnd] *adj* : desenfrenado, incontrolado

unrestricted [ˌʌnri'strɪktəd] *adj* : sin restricción ⟨unrestricted access : libre acceso⟩

unrewarding [ˌʌnri'wɔrdɪŋ] *adj* THANKLESS : ingrato

unripe [ˌʌn'raɪp] *adj* : inmaduro, verde

unrivaled *or* **unrivalled** [ˌʌn'raɪvəld] *adj* : incomparable

unroll [ˌʌn'ro:l] *vt* : desenrollar — *vi* : desenrollarse

unruffled [ˌʌn'rʌfəld] *adj* **1** SERENE : sereno, tranquilo **2** SMOOTH : tranquilo, liso ⟨unruffled waters : aguas tranquilas⟩

unruliness [ˌʌn'ru:linəs] *n* : indisciplina *f*

unruly [ˌʌn'ru:li] *adj* : indisciplinado, díscolo, rebelde

unsafe [ˌʌn'seɪf] *adj* : inseguro

unsaid [ˌʌn'sɛd] *adj* : sin decir ⟨to leave unsaid : quedar por decir⟩

unsanitary [ˌʌn'sænəˌtɛri] *adj* : antihigiénico

unsatisfactory [ˌʌnˌsæṭəs'fæktəri] *adj* : insatisfactorio

unsatisfied [ˌʌn'sæṭəsˌfaɪd] *adj* : insatisfecho

unscathed [ˌʌn'skeɪðd] *adj* UNHARMED : ileso

unscheduled [ˌʌn'skɛˌdʒu:ld] *adj* : no programado, imprevisto

unscientific [ˌʌnˌsaɪən'tɪfɪk] *adj* : poco científico

unscrupulous [ˌʌn'skru:pjələs] *adj* : inescrupuloso, sin escrúpulos — **unscrupulously** *adv*

unseal [ˌʌn'si:l] *vt* : abrir, quitarle el sello a

unseasonable [ˌʌn'si:zənəbəl] *adj* **1** : extemporáneo ⟨unseasonable rain

: lluvia extemporánea⟩ **2** UNTIMELY : extemporáneo, inoportuno

unseemly [ˌʌnˈsiːmli] *adj* **-lier; -est 1** INDECOROUS : indecoroso **2** INAPPROPRIATE : impropio, inapropiado

unseen [ˌʌnˈsiːn] *adj* **1** UNNOTICED : inadvertido **2** INVISIBLE : oculto, invisible

unselfish [ˌʌnˈsɛlfɪʃ] *adj* : generoso, desinteresado — **unselfishly** *adv*

unselfishness [ˌʌnˈsɛlfɪʃnəs] *n* : generosidad *f*, desinterés *m*

unsettle [ˌʌnˈsɛtəl] *vt* **-tled; -tling** DISTURB : trastornar, alterar, perturbar

unsettled [ˌʌnˈsɛtəld] *adj* **1** CHANGEABLE : inestable, variable ⟨unsettled weather : tiempo inestable⟩ **2** DISTURBED : agitado, inquieto ⟨unsettled waters : aguas agitadas⟩ **3** UNDECIDED : pendiente (dícese de un asunto), indeciso (dícese de una persona) **4** UNPAID : sin saldar, pendiente **5** UNINHABITED : despoblado, no colonizado

unshaped [ˌʌnˈʃeɪpt] *adj* : sin forma, informe

unsightly [ˌʌnˈsaɪtli] *adj* UGLY : feo, de aspecto malo

unskilled [ˌʌnˈskɪld] *adj* : no calificado

unskillful [ˌʌnˈskɪlfəl] *adj* : inexperto, poco hábil

unsnap [ˌʌnˈsnæp] *vt* **-snapped; -snapping** : desabrochar

unsociable *adj* : poco sociable

unsolved [ˌʌnˈsɑlvd] *adj* : no resuelto, sin resolver

unsophisticated [ˌʌnsəˈfɪstəˌkeɪtəd] *adj* **1** NAIVE, UNWORLDLY : ingenuo, de poco mundo **2** SIMPLE : simple, poco sofisticado, rudimentario

unsound [ˌʌnˈsaʊnd] *adj* **1** UNHEALTHY : enfermizo, de mala salud **2** : poco sólido, defectuoso (dícese de una estructura, etc.) **3** INVALID : inválido, erróneo **4 of unsound mind** : mentalmente incapacitado

unspeakable [ˌʌnˈspiːkəbəl] *adj* **1** INDESCRIBABLE : indecible, inexpresable, incalificable **2** HEINOUS : atroz, nefando, abominable — **unspeakably** [-bli] *adv*

unspecified [ˌʌnˈspɛsəˌfaɪd] *adj* : indeterminado, sin especificar

unspoiled [ˌʌnˈspɔɪld] *adj* **1** : conservado, sin estropear (dícese de un lugar) **2** : que no está mimado (dícese de un niño)

unstable [ˌʌnˈsteɪbəl] *adj* **1** CHANGEABLE : variable, inestable, cambiable ⟨an unstable pulse : un pulso irregular⟩ **2** UNSTEADY : inestable, poco sólido (dícese de una estructura)

unsteadily [ˌʌnˈstɛdəli] *adv* : de modo inestable

unsteadiness [ˌʌnˈstɛdinəs] *n* : inestabilidad *f*, inseguridad *f*

unsteady [ˌʌnˈstɛdi] *adj* **1** UNSTABLE : inestable, variable **2** SHAKY : tembloroso

unstoppable [ˌʌnˈstɑpəbəl] *adj* : irrefrenable, incontenible

unsubstantiated [ˌʌnsəbˈstænʧiˌeɪtəd] *adj* : no corroborado, no demostrado

unsuccessful [ˌʌnsəkˈsɛsfəl] *adj* : fracasado, infructuoso

unsuitable [ˌʌnˈsuːʈəbəl] *adj* : inadecuado, impropio, inapropiado ⟨an unsuitable time : una hora inconveniente⟩

unsuited [ˌʌnˈsuːʈəd] *adj* : inadecuado, inepto

unsung [ˌʌnˈsʌŋ] *adj* : olvidado

unsure [ˌʌnˈʃʊr] *adj* : incierto, dudoso

unsurpassed [ˌʌnsərˈpæst] *adj* : sin par, sin igual

unsuspecting [ˌʌnsəˈspɛktɪŋ] *adj* : desprevenido, desapercibido, confiado

unsympathetic [ˌʌnˌsɪmpəˈθɛtɪk] *adj* : poco comprensivo, indiferente

untangle [ˌʌnˈteɪŋgəl] *vt* **-gled; -gling** : desenmarañar, desenredar

unthinkable [ˌʌnˈθɪŋkəbəl] *adj* : inconcebible, impensable

unthinking [ˌʌnˈθɪŋkɪŋ] *adj* : irreflexivo, inconsciente — **unthinkingly** *adv*

untidy [ˌʌnˈtaɪdi] *adj* **1** SLOVENLY : desaliñado **2** DISORDERLY : desordenado, desarreglado

untie [ˌʌnˈtaɪ] *vt* **-tied; -tying** *or* **-tieing** : desatar, deshacer

until[1] [ˌʌnˈtɪl] *prep* : hasta ⟨until now : hasta ahora⟩

until[2] *conj* : hasta que ⟨until they left : hasta que salieron⟩ ⟨don't answer until you're sure : no contestes hasta que (no) estés seguro⟩

untimely [ˌʌnˈtaɪmli] *adj* **1** PREMATURE : prematuro ⟨an untimely death : una muerte prematura⟩ **2** INOPPORTUNE : inoportuno, intempestivo

untold [ˌʌnˈtoːld] *adj* **1** : nunca dicho ⟨the untold secret : el secreto sin contar⟩ **2** INCALCULABLE : incalculable, indecible

untouched [ˌʌnˈtʌʧt] *adj* **1** INTACT : intacto, sin tocar, sin probar (dícese de la comida) **2** UNAFFECTED : insensible, indiferente

untoward [ˌʌnˈtɔrd, -ˈtoːərd, -təˈwɔrd] *adj* **1** : indecoroso, impropio (dícese del comportamiento) **2** ADVERSE, UNFORTUNATE : desafortunado, adverso ⟨untoward effects : efectos perjudiciales⟩ **3** UNSEEMLY : indecoroso

untrained [ˌʌnˈtreɪnd] *adj* : inexperto, no capacitado

untreated [ˌʌnˈtriːʈəd] *adj* : no tratado (dícese de una enfermedad, etc.), sin tratar (dícese de un material)

untroubled [ˌʌnˈtrʌbəld] *adj* : tranquilo ⟨to be untroubled by : no estar afectado por⟩

untrue [ˌʌnˈtruː] *adj* **1** UNFAITHFUL : infiel **2** FALSE : falso

untrustworthy [ˌʌnˈtrʌstˌwərði] *adj* : de poca confianza (dícese de una persona), no fidedigno (dícese de la información)

untruth [ˌʌnˈtruːθ, ˈʌnˌ-] *n* : mentira *f*, falsedad *f*

untruthful [ˌʌnˈtruːθfəl] *adj* : mentiroso, falso

unusable [ˌʌnˈjuːzəbəl] *adj* : inútil, inservible

unused [ˌʌnˈjuːzd, *in sense 1 usually* -ˈjuːst] *adj* **1** UNACCUSTOMED : inhabituado **2** NEW : nuevo **3** IDLE : no utilizado (dícese de la tierra) **4** REMAINING : restante ⟨the unused portion : la porción restante⟩

unusual [ˌʌnˈjuːʒʊəl] *adj* : inusual, poco común, raro

unusually [ˌʌnˈjuːʒʊəli, -ˈjuːʒəli] *adv* : excepcionalmente, extraordinariamente, fuera de lo común

unwanted [ˌʌnˈwɑntəd] *adj* : superfluo, de sobre

unwarranted [ˌʌnˈwɔrəntəd] *adj* : injustificado

unwary [ˌʌnˈwæri] *adj* : incauto

unwavering [ˌʌnˈweɪvərɪŋ] *adj* : firme, inquebrantable ⟨an unwavering gaze : una mirada fija⟩

unwelcome [ˌʌnˈwɛlkəm] *adj* : importuno, molesto

unwell [ˌʌnˈwɛl] *adj* : enfermo, mal

unwholesome [ˌʌnˈhoːlsəm] *adj* **1** UNHEALTHY : malsano, insalubre **2** PERNICIOUS : pernicioso **3** LOATHSOME : repugnante, muy desagradable

unwieldy [ˌʌnˈwiːldi] *adj* CUMBERSOME : difícil de manejar, torpe y pesado

unwilling [ˌʌnˈwɪlɪŋ] *adj* : poco dispuesto ⟨to be unwilling to : no estar dispuesto a⟩

unwillingly [ˌʌnˈwɪlɪŋli] *adv* : a regañadientes, de mala gana

unwind [ˌʌnˈwaɪnd] *v* **-wound** [-ˈwaʊnd]; **-winding** *vt* UNROLL : desenrollar — *vi* **1** : desenrollarse **2** RELAX : relajar

unwise [ˌʌnˈwaɪz] *adj* : imprudente, desacertado, poco aconsejable

unwisely [ˌʌnˈwaɪzli] *adv* : imprudentemente

unwitting [ˌʌnˈwɪtɪŋ] *adj* **1** UNAWARE : inconsciente **2** INADVERTENT : involuntario, inadvertido ⟨an unwitting mistake : un error inadvertido⟩ — **unwittingly** *adv*

unworthiness [ˌʌnˈwərðinəs] *n* : falta *f* de valía

unworthy [ˌʌnˈwərði] *adj* **1** UNDESERVING : indigno ⟨to be unworthy of : no ser digno de⟩ **2** UNMERITED : inmerecido

unwrap [ˌʌnˈræp] *vt* **-wrapped**; **-wrapping** : desenvolver, deshacer

unwritten [ˌʌnˈrɪtən] *adj* : no escrito

unyielding [ˌʌnˈjiːldɪŋ] *adj* : firme, inflexible, rígido

unzip [ˌʌnˈzɪp] *vt* **-zipped**; **-zipping** : abrir el cierre de

up¹ [ˈʌp] *v* **upped** [ˈʌpt]; **upping**; **ups** *vt* INCREASE : aumentar, subir ⟨they upped the prices : aumentaron los precios⟩ — *vi* **to up and** : agarrar y *fam* ⟨she up and left : agarró y se fue⟩

up² *adv* **1** ABOVE : arriba, en lo alto ⟨up in the mountains : arriba en las montañas⟩ **2** UPWARDS : hacia arriba ⟨push it up : empújalo hacia arriba⟩ ⟨the sun came up : el sol salió⟩ ⟨prices went up : los precios subieron⟩ **3** (*indicating an upright position or waking state*) ⟨to sit up : ponerse derecho⟩ ⟨they got up late : se levantaron tarde⟩ ⟨I stayed up all night : pasé toda la noche sin dormir⟩ **4** (*indicating volume or intensity*) ⟨to speak up : hablar más fuerte⟩ **5** (*indicating a northerly direction*) ⟨the climate up north : el clima del norte⟩ ⟨I'm going up to Canada : voy para Canadá⟩ **6** (*indicating the appearance or existence of something*) ⟨the book turned up : el libro apareció⟩ **7** (*indicating consideration*) ⟨she brought the matter up : mencionó el asunto⟩ **8** COMPLETELY : completamente ⟨eat it up : cómetelo todo⟩ **9** : en pedazos ⟨he tore it up : lo rompió en pedazos⟩ **10** (*indicating a stopping*) ⟨the car pulled up to the curb : el carro paró al borde de la acera⟩ **11** (*indicating an even score*) ⟨the game was 10 up : empataron a 10⟩

up³ *adj* **1** (*risen above the horizon*) ⟨the sun is up : ha salido el sol⟩ **2** (*being above a normal or former level*) ⟨prices are up : los precios han aumentado⟩ ⟨the river is up : las aguas están altas⟩ **3** : despierto, levantado ⟨up all night : despierto toda la noche⟩ **4** BUILT : construido ⟨the house is up : la casa está construida⟩ **5** OPEN : abierto ⟨the windows are up : las ventanas están abiertas⟩ **6** (*moving or going upward*) ⟨the up staircase : la escalera para subir⟩ **7** ABREAST : enterado, al día, al corriente ⟨to be up on the news : estar al corriente de las noticias⟩ **8** PREPARED : preparado ⟨we were up for the test : estuvimos preparados para el examen⟩ **9** FINISHED : terminado, acabado ⟨time is up : se ha terminado el tiempo permitido⟩ **10 to be up** : pasar ⟨what's up? : ¿qué pasa?⟩

up⁴ *prep* **1** (*to, toward, or at a higher point of*) ⟨he went up the stairs : subió la escalera⟩ **2** (*to or toward the source of*) ⟨to go up the river : ir río arriba⟩ **3** ALONG : a lo largo, por ⟨up the coast : a lo largo de la costa⟩ ⟨just up the way : un poco más adelante⟩ ⟨up and down the city : por toda la ciudad⟩

upbraid [ˌʌpˈbreɪd] *vt* : reprender, regañar

upbringing [ˈʌpˌbrɪŋɪŋ] *n* : crianza *f*, educación *f*

upcoming [ˌʌpˈkʌmɪŋ] *adj* : próximo

update¹ [ˌʌpˈdeɪt] *vt* **-dated**; **-dating** : poner al día, poner al corriente, actualizar

update² [ˈʌpˌdeɪt] *n* : actualización *f*, puesta *f* al día

upend [ˌʌpˈɛnd] *vt* **1** : poner vertical **2** OVERTURN : volcar

upgrade¹ [ˈʌpˌgreɪd, ˌʌpˈ-] vt **-graded; -grading 1** PROMOTE : ascender **2** IMPROVE : mejorar

upgrade² [ˈʌpˌgreɪd] n **1** SLOPE : cuesta f, pendiente f **2** RISE : aumento m de categoría (de un puesto), ascenso m (de un empleado) **3** IMPROVEMENT : mejoramiento m

upheaval [ˌʌpˈhiːvəl] n **1** : levantamiento m (en geología) **2** DISTURBANCE, UPSET : trastorno m, agitación f, conmoción f

uphill¹ [ˌʌpˈhɪl] adv : cuesta arriba

uphill² [ˈʌpˌhɪl] adj **1** ASCENDING : en subida **2** DIFFICULT : difícil, arduo

uphold [ˌʌpˈhoːld] vt **-held; -holding 1** SUPPORT : sostener, apoyar, mantener **2** RAISE : levantar **3** CONFIRM : confirmar (una decisión judicial)

upholster [ˌʌpˈhoːlstər] vt : tapizar

upholsterer [ˌʌpˈhoːlstərər] n : tapicero m, -ra f

upholstery [ˌʌpˈhoːlstəri] n, pl **-steries** : tapicería f

upkeep [ˈʌpˌkiːp] n : mantenimiento m

upland [ˈʌplənd, -ˌlænd] n : altiplanicie f, altiplano m

uplift¹ [ˌʌpˈlɪft] vt **1** RAISE : elevar, levantar **2** ELEVATE : elevar, animar (el espíritu, la mente, etc.)

uplift² [ˈʌpˌlɪft] n : elevación f

upon [əˈpɑn, əˈpʌn] prep : en, sobre ⟨upon the desk : sobre el escritorio⟩ ⟨upon leaving : al salir⟩ ⟨questions upon questions : pregunta tras pregunta⟩

upper¹ [ˈʌpər] adj **1** HIGHER : superior ⟨the upper classes : las clases altas⟩ **2** : alto (en geografía) ⟨the upper Mississippi : el alto Mississippi⟩

upper² n : parte f superior (del calzado, etc.)

uppercase [ˌʌpərˈkeɪs] adj : mayúsculo

upper hand n : ventaja f, dominio m

uppermost [ˈʌpərˌmoːst] adj : más alto ⟨it was uppermost in his mind : era lo que más le preocupaba⟩

upright¹ [ˈʌpˌraɪt] adj **1** VERTICAL : vertical **2** ERECT : erguido, derecho **3** JUST : recto, honesto, justo

upright² n : montante m, poste m, soporte m

uprising [ˈʌpˌraɪzɪŋ] n : insurrección f, revuelta f, alzamiento m

uproar [ˈʌpˌror] n COMMOTION : alboroto m, jaleo m, escándalo m

uproarious [ˌʌpˈroriəs] adj **1** CLAMOROUS : estrepitoso, clamoroso **2** HILARIOUS : muy divertido, hilarante — **uproariously** adv

uproot [ˌʌpˈruːt, -ˈrʊt] vt : desarraigar

upset¹ [ˌʌpˈsɛt] vt **-set; -setting 1** OVERTURN : volcar **2** SPILL : derramar **3** DISTURB : perturbar, disgustar, inquietar, alterar **4** SICKEN : sentar mal a ⟨it upsets my stomach : me sienta mal al estómago⟩ **5** DISRUPT : trastornar, desbaratar (planes, etc.) **6** DEFEAT : derrotar (en deportes)

upset² adj **1** DISPLEASED, DISTRESSED : disgustado, alterado **2 to have an upset stomach** : estar mal del estómago, estar descompuesto (de estómago)

upset³ [ˈʌpˌsɛt] n **1** OVERTURNING : vuelco m **2** DISRUPTION : trastorno m (de planes, etc.) **3** DEFEAT : derrota f (en deportes)

upshot [ˈʌpˌʃɑt] n : resultado m final

upside–down [ˌʌpˌsaɪdˈdaʊn] adj : al revés

upside down [ˌʌpˌsaɪdˈdaʊn] adv **1** : al revés **2** : en confusión, en desorden

upstairs¹ [ˌʌpˈstærz] adv : arriba, en el piso superior

upstairs² [ˈʌpˌstærz, ˌʌpˈ-] adj : de arriba

upstairs³ [ˈʌpˌstærz, ˌʌpˈ-] ns & pl : piso m de arriba, planta f de arriba

upstanding [ˌʌpˈstændɪŋ, ˈʌpˌ-] adj HONEST, UPRIGHT : honesto, íntegro, recto

upstart [ˈʌpˌstɑrt] n : advenedizo m, -za f

upswing [ˈʌpˌswɪŋ] n : alza f, mejora f notable ⟨to be on the upswing : estar mejorándose⟩

uptight [ˌʌpˈtaɪt] adj : tenso, nervioso

up to prep **1** : hasta ⟨up to a year : hasta un año⟩ ⟨in mud up to my ankles : en barro hasta los tobillos⟩ **2 to be up to** : estar a la altura de ⟨I'm not up to going : no estoy en condiciones de ir⟩ **3 to be up to** : depender de ⟨it's up to the director : depende del director⟩

up–to–date [ˌʌptəˈdeɪt] adj **1** CURRENT : corriente, al día ⟨to keep up-to-date : mantenerse al corriente⟩ **2** MODERN : moderno

uptown [ˈʌpˈtaʊn] adv : hacia la parte alta de la ciudad, hacia el distrito residencial

upturn [ˈʌpˌtərn] n : mejora f, auge m (económico)

upward¹ [ˈʌpwərd] or **upwards** [-wərdz] adv **1** : hacia arriba **2 ~ of** : más de

upward² adj : ascendente, hacia arriba

upwind [ˌʌpˈwɪnd] adv & adj : contra el viento

uranium [jʊˈreɪniəm] n : uranio m

Uranus [jʊˈreɪnəs, ˈjʊrənəs] n : Urano m

urban [ˈərbən] adj : urbano

urbane [ˌərˈbeɪn] adj : urbano, cortés

urchin [ˈərtʃən] n **1** SCAMP : granuja mf; pillo m, -lla f **2 sea urchin** : erizo m de mar

Urdu [ˈʊrduː, ˈər-] n : urdu m

urethra [jʊˈriːθrə] n, pl **-thras** or **-thrae** [-ˌθriː] : uretra f

urge¹ [ˈərdʒ] vt **urged; urging 1** PRESS : instar, apremiar, insistir ⟨we urged him to come : insistimos en que viniera⟩ **2** ADVOCATE : recomendar, abogar por **3 to urge on** : animar, alentar

urge² n : impulso m, ganas fpl, compulsión f

urgency [ˈərdʒəntsi] n, pl **-cies** : urgencia f

urgent ['ərʤənt] *adj* **1** PRESSING : urgente, apremiante **2** INSISTENT : insistente **3 to be urgent** : urgir

urgently ['ərʤəntli] *adv* : urgentemente

urinal ['jurənəl, *esp Brit* ju'rainəl] *n* : orinal *m* (recipiente), urinario *m* (lugar)

urinary ['jurə,nɛri] *adj* : urinario

urinate ['jurə,neit] *vi* **-nated; -nating** : orinar

urination [,jurə'neiʃən] *n* : orinación *f*

urine ['jurən] *n* : orina *f*

urn ['ərn] *n* **1** VASE : urna *f* **2** : recipiente *m* (para servir café, etc.)

Uruguayan [,urə'gwaiən, ,jur-, -'gwei-] *n* : uruguayo *m*, -ya *f* — **Uruguayan** *adj*

us ['ʌs] *pron* **1** (*as direct object*) : nos ⟨they were visiting us : nos visitaban⟩ **2** (*as indirect object*) : nos ⟨he gave us a present : nos dio un regalo⟩ **3** (*as object of preposition*) : nosotros, nosotras ⟨stay with us : quédese con nosotros⟩ ⟨both of us : nosotros dos⟩ **4** (*for emphasis*) : nosotros ⟨it's us! : ¡somos nosotros!⟩

usable ['ju:zəbəl] *adj* : utilizable

usage ['ju:sɪʤ, -zɪʤ] *n* **1** HABIT : costumbre *f*, hábito *m* **2** USE : uso *m*

use¹ ['ju:z] *v* **used** ['ju:zd, *in phrase "used to" usually* 'ju:stu:]; **using** *vt* **1** EMPLOY : emplear, usar **2** CONSUME : consumir, tomar (drogas, etc.) **3** UTILIZE : usar, utilizar ⟨to use tact : usar tacto⟩ ⟨he used his friends to get ahead : usó a sus amigos para mejorar su posición⟩ **4** TREAT : tratar ⟨they used the horse cruelly : maltrataron al caballo⟩ **5 to use up** : agotar, consumir, gastar — *vi* (*used in the past with* **to** *to indicate a former fact or state*) : soler, acostumbrar ⟨winters used to be colder : los inviernos solían ser más fríos, los inviernos eran más fríos⟩ ⟨she used to dance : acostumbraba bailar⟩

use² ['ju:s] *n* **1** APPLICATION, EMPLOYMENT : uso *m*, empleo *m*, utilización *f* ⟨out of use : en desuso⟩ ⟨ready for use : listo para usar⟩ ⟨to be in use : usarse, estar funcionando⟩ ⟨to make use of : servirse de, aprovechar⟩ **2** USEFULNESS : utilidad *f* ⟨to be of no use : no servir (para nada)⟩ ⟨it's no use! : ¡es inútil!⟩ **3 to have the use of** : poder usar, tener acceso a **4 to have no use for** : no necesitar ⟨she has no use for po-

etry : a ella no le gusta la poesía⟩

used ['ju:zd] *adj* **1** SECONDHAND : usado, de segunda mano ⟨used cars : coches usados⟩ **2** ACCUSTOMED : acostumbrado ⟨used to the heat : acostumbrado al calor⟩

useful ['ju:sfəl] *adj* : útil, práctico — **usefully** *adv*

usefulness ['ju:sfəlnəs] *n* : utilidad *f*

useless ['ju:sləs] *adj* : inútil — **uselessly** *adv*

uselessness ['ju:sləsnəs] *n* : inutilidad *f*

user ['ju:zər] *n* : usuario *m*, -ria *f*

usher¹ ['ʌʃər] *vt* **1** ESCORT : acompañar, conducir **2 to usher in** : hacer pasar (a alguien) ⟨to usher in a new era : anunciar una nueva época⟩

usher² *n* : acomodador *m*, -dora *f*

usherette [,ʌʃə'rɛt] *n* : acomodadora *f*

usual ['ju:ʒuəl] *adj* **1** NORMAL : usual, normal **2** CUSTOMARY : acostumbrado, habitual, de costumbre **3** ORDINARY : ordinario, típico

usually ['ju:ʒuəli, 'ju:ʒəli] *adv* : usualmente, normalmente

usurp [ju'sərp, -'zərp] *vt* : usurpar

usurper [ju'sərpər, -'zər-] *n* : usurpador *m*, -dora *f*

utensil [ju'tɛntsəl] *n* **1** : utensilio *m* (de cocina) **2** IMPLEMENT : implemento *m*, útil *m* (de labranza, etc.)

uterine ['ju:tə,rain, -rən] *adj* : uterino

uterus ['ju:tərəs] *n, pl* **uteri** [-,rai] : útero *m*, matriz *f*

utilitarian [ju,tɪlə'tɛriən] *adj* : utilitario

utility [ju'tɪləti] *n, pl* **-ties 1** USEFULNESS : utilidad *f* **2 public utility** : empresa *f* de servicio público

utilization [,ju:tələ'zeiʃən] *n* : utilización *f*

utilize ['ju:təl,aiz] *vt* **-lized; -lizing** : utilizar, hacer uso de

utmost¹ ['ʌt,mo:st] *adj* **1** FARTHEST : extremo, más lejano **2** GREATEST : sumo, mayor ⟨of the utmost importance : de suma importancia⟩

utmost² *n* : lo más posible ⟨to the utmost : al máximo⟩

utopia [ju'to:piə] *n* : utopía *f*

utopian [ju'to:piən] *adj* : utópico

utter¹ ['ʌtər] *vt* : decir, articular, pronunciar (palabras)

utter² *adj* : absoluto — **utterly** *adv*

utterance ['ʌtərənts] *n* : declaración *f*, articulación *f*

V

v ['vi:] *n, pl* **v's** *or* **vs** ['vi:z] : vigésima segunda letra del alfabeto inglés

vacancy ['veikəntsi] *n, pl* **-cies 1** EMPTINESS : vacío *m*, vacuidad *f* **2** : vacante *f*, puesto *m* vacante ⟨to fill a vacancy

: ocupar un puesto⟩ **3** : habitación *f* libre (en un hotel) ⟨no vacancies : completo⟩

vacant ['veikənt] *adj* **1** EMPTY : libre, desocupado (dícese de los edificios, etc.) **2** : vacante (dícese de los puestos) **3** BLANK : vacío, ausente ⟨a vacant stare : una mirada ausente⟩

vacate ['veɪˌkeɪt] *vt* **-cated; -cating** : desalojar, desocupar

vacation¹ [veɪˈkeɪʃən, və-] *vi* : pasar las vacaciones, vacacionar *Mex*

vacation² *n* : vacaciones *fpl* ⟨to be on vacation : estar de vacaciones⟩

vacationer [veɪˈkeɪʃənər, və-] *n* : turista *mf*, veraneante *mf*, vacacionista *mf CA, Mex*

vaccinate ['væksəˌneɪt] *vt* **-nated; -nating** : vacunar

vaccination [ˌvæksəˈneɪʃən] *n* : vacunación *f*

vaccine [vækˈsiːn, 'vækˌ-] *n* : vacuna *f*

vacillate ['væsəˌleɪt] *vi* **-lated; -lating 1** HESITATE : vacilar **2** SWAY : oscilar

vacillation [ˌvæsəˈleɪʃən] *n* : indecisión *f*, vacilación *f*

vacuous ['vækjuəs] *adj* **1** EMPTY : vacío **2** INANE : vacuo, necio, estúpido

vacuum¹ ['væˌkjuːm, -kjəm] *vt* : limpiar con aspiradora, pasar la aspiradora por

vacuum² *n, pl* **vacuums** *or* **vacua** ['vækjuə] : vacío *m*

vacuum cleaner *n* : aspiradora *f*

vagabond¹ ['vægəˌband] *adj* : vagabundo

vagabond² *n* : vagabundo *m*, -da *f*

vagary ['veɪgəri, vəˈgɛri] *n, pl* **-ries** : capricho *m*

vagina [vəˈdʒaɪnə] *n, pl* **-nae** [-ˌniː, -ˌnaɪ] *or* **-nas** : vagina *f*

vagrancy ['veɪgrəntsi] *n, pl* **-cies** : vagancia *f*

vagrant¹ ['veɪgrənt] *adj* : vagabundo

vagrant² *n* : vagabundo *m*, -da *f*

vague ['veɪg] *adj* **vaguer; -est 1** IMPRECISE : vago, impreciso ⟨a vague feeling : una sensación indefinida⟩ ⟨I haven't the vaguest idea : no tengo la más remota idea⟩ **2** UNCLEAR : borroso, poco claro ⟨a vague outline : un perfil indistinto⟩ **3** ABSENTMINDED : distraído

vaguely ['veɪgli] *adv* : vagamente, de manera imprecisa

vagueness ['veɪgnəs] *n* : vaguedad *f*, imprecisión *f*

vain ['veɪn] *adj* **1** WORTHLESS : vano **2** FUTILE : vano, inútil ⟨in vain : en vano⟩ **3** CONCEITED : vanidoso, presumido

vainly ['veɪnli] *adv* : en vano, vanamente, inútilmente

valance ['vælənts, 'veɪ-] *n* **1** FLOUNCE : volante *m* (de una cama, etc.) **2** : galería *f* de cortina (sobre una ventana)

vale ['veɪl] *n* : valle *m*

valedictorian [ˌvæləˌdɪkˈtoriən] *n* : estudiante *mf* que pronuncia el discurso de despedida en ceremonia de graduación

valedictory [ˌvæləˈdɪktəri] *adj* : de despedida

valentine ['væ|ənˌtaɪn] *n* : tarjeta *f* que se manda el Día de los Enamorados (el 14 de febrero)

Valentine's Day *n* : Día *m* de los Enamorados

valet ['væˌleɪ, væˈleɪ, 'vælət] *n* : ayuda *m* de cámara

valiant ['væljənt] *adj* : valiente, valeroso

valiantly ['væljəntli] *adv* : con valor, valientemente

valid ['væləd] *adj* : válido

validate ['væləˌdeɪt] *vt* **-dated; -dating** : validar, dar validez a

validity [vəˈlɪdəti, væ-] *n* : validez *f*

valise [vəˈliːs] *n* : maleta *f* (de mano)

valley ['væli] *n, pl* **-leys** : valle *m*

valor ['vælər] *n* : valor *m*, valentía *f*

valorous ['vælərəs] *adj* : valeroso, valiente

valuable¹ ['væljuəbəl, 'væljəbəl] *adj* **1** EXPENSIVE : valioso, de valor **2** WORTHWHILE : valioso, apreciable

valuable² *n* : objeto *m* de valor

valuation [ˌvæljuˈeɪʃən] *n* **1** APPRAISAL : valoración *f*, tasación *f* **2** VALUE : valuación *f*

value¹ ['væljuː] *vt* **-ued; -uing 1** APPRAISE : valorar, avaluar, tasar **2** APPRECIATE : valorar, apreciar

value² *n* **1** : valor *m* ⟨of little value : de poco valor⟩ ⟨to be a good value : estar bien de precio, tener buen precio⟩ ⟨at face value : en su sentido literal⟩ **2 values** *npl* : valores *mpl* (morales), principios *mpl*

valueless ['væljuːləs] *adj* : sin valor

valve ['vælv] *n* : válvula *f*

vampire ['væmˌpaɪr] *n* **1** : vampiro *m* **2** *or* **vampire bat** : vampiro *m*

van¹ ['væn] → **vanguard**

van² *n* : furgoneta *f*, camioneta *f*

vanadium [vəˈneɪdiəm] *n* : vanadio *m*

vandal ['vændəl] *n* : vándalo *m*

vandalism ['vændəlˌɪzəm] *n* : vandalismo *m*

vandalize ['vændəlˌaɪz] *vt* : destrozar, destruir, estropear

vane ['veɪn] *n or* **weather vane** : veleta *f*

vanguard ['vænˌgard] *n* : vanguardia *f*

vanilla [vəˈnɪlə, -ˈnɛ-] *n* : vainilla *f*

vanish ['vænɪʃ] *vi* : desaparecer, disiparse, desvanecerse

vanity ['vænəti] *n, pl* **-ties 1** : vanidad *f* **2** *or* **vanity table** : tocador *m*

vanquish ['væŋkwɪʃ, 'væn-] *vt* : vencer, conquistar

vantage point ['væntɪdʒ] *n* : posición *f* ventajosa

vapid ['væpəd, 'veɪ-] *adj* : insípido, insulso

vapor ['veɪpər] *n* : vapor *m*

vaporize ['veɪpəˌraɪz] *v* **-rized; -rizing** *vt* : vaporizar — *vi* : vaporizarse, evaporarse

vaporizer ['veɪpəˌraɪzər] *n* : vaporizador *m*

variability [ˌvɛriəˈbɪləti] *n, pl* **-ties** : variabilidad *f*

variable¹ ['vɛriəbəl] *adj* : variable ⟨variable cloudiness : nubosidad variable⟩

variable² *n* : variable *f*, factor *m*
variance [ˈvɛriənts] *n* **1** DISCREPANCY : varianza *f*, discrepancia *f* **2** DISAGREEMENT : desacuerdo *m* ⟨at variance with : en desacuerdo con⟩
variant¹ [ˈvɛriənt] *adj* : variante, divergente
variant² *n* : variante *f*
variation [ˌvɛriˈeɪʃən] *n* : variación *f*, diferencias *fpl*
varicose [ˈværəˌkoːs] *adj* : varicoso
varicose veins *npl* : varices *fpl*, várices *fpl*
varied [ˈvɛrid] *adj* : variado, dispar, diferente
variegated [ˈvɛriəˌgeɪtd] *adj* : abigarrado, multicolor
variety [vəˈraɪəti] *n, pl* **-ties 1** DIVERSITY : diversidad *f*, variedad *f* **2** ASSORTMENT : surtido *m* ⟨for a variety of reasons : por diversas razones⟩ **3** SORT : clase *f* **4** BREED : variedad *f* (de plantas)
various [ˈvɛriəs] *adj* : varios, diversos
varnish¹ [ˈvɑrnɪʃ] *vt* : barnizar
varnish² *n* : barniz *f*
varsity [ˈvɑrsəti] *n, pl* **-ties** : equipo *m* universitario
vary [ˈvɛri] *v* **varied; varying** *vt* : variar, diversificar — *vi* **1** CHANGE : variar, cambiar **2** DEVIATE : desviarse
vascular [ˈvæskjələr] *adj* : vascular
vase [ˈveɪs, ˈveɪz, ˈvɑz] *n* : jarrón *m*, florero *m*
vassal [ˈvæsəl] *n* : vasallo *m*, -lla *f*
vast [ˈvæst] *adj* : inmenso, enorme, vasto
vastly [ˈvæstli] *adv* : enormemente
vastness [ˈvæstnəs] *n* : vastedad *f*, inmensidad *f*
vat [ˈvæt] *n* : cuba *f*, tina *f*
vaudeville [ˈvɒdvəl, -ˌviːl; ˈvɒdəˌvɪl] *n* : vodevil *m*
vault¹ [ˈvɔlt] *vi* LEAP : saltar
vault² *n* **1** JUMP : salto *m* ⟨pole vault : salto de pértiga, salto con garrocha⟩ **2** DOME : bóveda *f* **3** : bodega *f* (para vino), bóveda *f* de seguridad (de un banco) **4** CRYPT : cripta *f*
vaulted [ˈvɔltəd] *adj* : abovedado
vaunted [ˈvɔntəd] *adj* : cacareado, alardeado ⟨a much vaunted wine : un vino muy alardeado⟩
VCR [ˌviːˌsiːˈɑr] *n* : video *m*, videocasetera *f*
veal [ˈviːl] *n* : ternera *f*, carne *f* de ternera
veer [ˈvɪr] *vi* : virar (dícese de un barco), girar (dícese de un coche), torcer (dícese de un camino)
vegetable¹ [ˈvɛdʒtəbəl, ˈvɛdʒətə-] *adj* : vegetal
vegetable² *n* **1** : vegetal *m* ⟨the vegetable kingdom : el reino vegetal⟩ **2** : verdura *f*, hortaliza *f* (para comer)
vegetarian [ˌvɛdʒəˈtɛriən] *n* : vegetariano *mf*
vegetarianism [ˌvɛdʒəˈtɛriəˌnɪzəm] *n* : vegetarianismo *m*

vegetate [ˈvɛdʒəˌteɪt] *vi* **-tated; -tating** : vegetar
vegetation [ˌvɛdʒəˈteɪʃən] *n* : vegetación *f*
vegetative [ˈvɛdʒəˌteɪtɪv] *adj* : vegetativo
vehemence [ˈviːəmənts] *n* : intensidad *f*, vehemencia *f*
vehement [ˈviːəmənt] *adj* : intenso, vehemente
vehemently [ˈviːəməntli] *adv* : vehementemente, con vehemencia
vehicle [ˈviːəkəl, ˈviːˌhɪkəl] *n* **1** *or* **motor vehicle** : vehículo *m* **2** MEDIUM : vehículo *m*, medio *m*
vehicular [viˈhɪkjələr, və-] *adj* : vehicular ⟨vehicular homicide : muerte por atropello⟩
veil¹ [ˈveɪl] *vt* **1** CONCEAL : velar, disimular **2** : cubrir con un velo ⟨to veil one's face : cubrirse con un velo⟩
veil² *n* : velo *m* ⟨bridal veil : velo de novia⟩
vein [ˈveɪn] *n* **1** : vena *f* (en anatomía, botánica, etc.) **2** LODE : veta *f*, vena *f*, filón *m* **3** STYLE : vena *f* ⟨in a humorous vein : en vena humorística⟩
veined [ˈveɪnd] *adj* : veteado (dícese del queso, de los minerales, etc.)
velocity [vəˈlɑsəti] *n, pl* **-ties** : velocidad *f*
velour [vəˈlʊr] *or* **velours** [-ˈlʊrz] *n* : velour *m*
velvet¹ [ˈvɛlvət] *adj* **1** : de terciopelo **2** → **velvety**
velvet² *n* : terciopelo *m*
velvety [ˈvɛlvəti] *adj* : aterciopelado
venal [ˈviːnəl] *adj* : venal, sobornable
vend [ˈvɛnd] *vt* : vender
vendetta [vɛnˈdɛtə] *n* : vendetta *f*
vendor [ˈvɛndər] *n* : vendedor *m*, -dora *f*; puestero *m*, -ra *f*
veneer¹ [vəˈnɪr] *vt* : enchapar, chapar
veneer² *n* **1** : enchapado *m*, chapa *f* **2** APPEARANCE : apariencia *f*, barniz *m* ⟨a veneer of culture : un barniz de cultura⟩
venerable [ˈvɛnərəbəl] *adj* : venerable
venerate [ˈvɛnəˌreɪt] *vt* **-ated; -ating** : venerar
veneration [ˌvɛnəˈreɪʃən] *n* : veneración *f*
venereal disease [vəˈnɪriəl] *n* : enfermedad *f* venérea
venetian blind [vəˈniːʃən] *n* : persiana *f* veneciana
Venezuelan [ˌvɛnəˈzweɪlən, -zuˈeɪ-] *n* : venezolano *m*, -na *f* — **Venezuelan** *adj*
vengeance [ˈvɛndʒənts] *n* : venganza *f* ⟨to take vengeance on : vengarse de⟩
vengeful [ˈvɛndʒfəl] *adj* : vengativo
venial [ˈviːniəl] *adj* : venial ⟨a venial sin : un pecado venial⟩
venison [ˈvɛnəsən, -zən] *n* : venado *m*, carne *f* de venado
venom [ˈvɛnəm] *n* **1** : veneno *m* **2** MALICE : veneno *m*, malevolencia *f*

venomous ['vɛnəməs] *adj* : venenoso

vent[1] ['vɛnt] *vt* : desahogar, dar salida a ⟨to vent one's feelings : desahogarse⟩

vent[2] *n* **1** OPENING : abertura *f* (de escape), orificio *m* **2** *or* **air vent** : respiradero *m*, rejilla *f* de ventilación **3** OUTLET : desahogo *m* ⟨to give vent to one's anger : desahogar la ira⟩

ventilate ['vɛntəl,eɪt] *vt* **-lated; -lating** : ventilar

ventilation [,vɛntəl'eɪʃən] *n* : ventilación *f*

ventilator ['vɛntəl,eɪtər] *n* : ventilador *m*

ventricle ['vɛntrɪkəl] *n* : ventrículo *m*

ventriloquism [vɛn'trɪlə,kwɪzəm] *n* : ventriloquia *f*

ventriloquist [vɛn'trɪlə,kwɪst] *n* : ventrílocuo *m*, -cua *f*

venture[1] ['vɛntʃər] *v* **-tured; -turing** *vt* **1** RISK : arriesgar **2** OFFER : aventurar ⟨to venture an opinion : aventurar una opinión⟩ — *vi* : arriesgarse, atreverse, aventurarse

venture[2] *n* **1** UNDERTAKING : empresa *f* **2** GAMBLE, RISK : aventura *f*, riesgo *m*

venturesome ['vɛntʃərsəm] *adj* **1** ADVENTUROUS : audaz, atrevido **2** RISKY : arriesgado

venue ['vɛn,ju:] *n* **1** PLACE : lugar *m* **2** : jurisdicción *f* (en derecho)

Venus ['vi:nəs] *n* : Venus *m*

veracity [və'ræsəti] *n, pl* **-ties** : veracidad *f*

veranda *or* **verandah** [və'rændə] *n* : terraza *f*, veranda *f*

verb ['vərb] *n* : verbo *m*

verbal ['vərbəl] *adj* : verbal

verbalize ['vərbə,laɪz] *vt* **-ized; -izing** : expresar con palabras, verbalizar

verbally ['vərbəli] *adv* : verbalmente, de palabra

verbatim[1] [vər'beɪtəm] *adv* : palabra por palabra, textualmente

verbatim[2] *adj* : literal, textual

verbose [vər'bo:s] *adj* : verboso, prolijo

verdant ['vərdənt] *adj* : verde, verdeante

verdict ['vərdɪkt] *n* **1** : veredicto *m* (de un jurado) **2** JUDGMENT, OPINION : juicio *m*, opinión *f*

verge[1] ['vərdʒ] *vi* **verged; verging** : estar al borde, rayar ⟨it verges on madness : raya en la locura⟩

verge[2] *n* **1** EDGE : borde *m* **2 to be on the verge of** : estar a pique de, estar al borde de, estar a punto de

verification [,vɛrəfə'keɪʃən] *n* : verificación *f*

verify ['vɛrə,faɪ] *vt* **-fied; -fying** : verificar, comprobar, confirmar

veritable ['vɛrətəbəl] *adj* : verdadero — **veritably** *adv*

vermicelli [,vərmə'tʃɛli, -'sɛli] *n* : fideos *mpl* finos

vermin ['vərmən] *ns & pl* : alimañas *fpl*, bichos *mpl*, sabandijas *fpl*

vermouth [vər'mu:th] *n* : vermut *m*

vernacular[1] [vər'nækjələr] *adj* : vernáculo

vernacular[2] *n* : lengua *f* vernácula

versatile ['vərsətəl] *adj* : versátil

versatility [,vərsə'tɪləti] *n* : versatilidad *f*

verse ['vərs] *n* **1** LINE, STANZA : verso *m*, estrofa *f* **2** POETRY : poesía *f* **3** : versículo *m* (en la Biblia)

versed ['vərst] *adj* : versado ⟨to be well versed in : ser muy versado en⟩

version ['vərʒən] *n* : versión *f*

versus ['vərsəs] *prep* : versus

vertebra ['vərtəbrə] *n, pl* **-brae** [-,breɪ, -,bri:] *or* **-bras** : vértebra *f*

vertebrate[1] ['vərtəbrət, -,breɪt] *adj* : vertebrado

vertebrate[2] *n* : vertebrado *m*

vertex ['vər,tɛks] *n, pl* **vertices** ['vərtə,si:z] **1** : vértice *m* (en matemáticas y anatomía) **2** SUMMIT, TOP : ápice *m*, cumbre *f*, cima *f*

vertical[1] ['vərtɪkəl] *adj* : vertical — **vertically** *adv*

vertical[2] *n* : vertical *f*

vertigo ['vərtɪ,go:] *n, pl* **-goes** *or* **-gos** : vértigo *m*

verve ['vərv] *n* : brío *m*

very[1] ['vɛri] *adv* **1** EXTREMELY : muy, sumamente ⟨very few : muy pocos⟩ ⟨I am very sorry : lo siento mucho⟩ **2** (*used for emphasis*) ⟨at the very least : por lo menos, como mínimo⟩ ⟨the very same dress : el mismo vestido⟩

very[2] *adj* **verier; -est 1** EXACT, PRECISE : mismo, exacto ⟨at that very moment : en ese mismo momento⟩ ⟨it's the very thing : es justo lo que hacía falta⟩ **2** BARE, MERE : solo, mero ⟨the very thought of it : sólo pensarlo⟩ **3** EXTREME : extremo, de todo ⟨at the very top : arriba de todo⟩

vesicle ['vɛsɪkəl] *n* : vesícula *f*

vespers ['vɛspərz] *npl* : vísperas *fpl*

vessel ['vɛsəl] *n* **1** CONTAINER : vasija *f*, recipiente *m* **2** BOAT, CRAFT : nave *f*, barco *m*, buque *m* **3** : vaso *m* ⟨blood vessel : vaso sanguíneo⟩

vest[1] ['vɛst] *vt* **1** CONFER : conferir ⟨to vest authority in : conferirle la autoridad a⟩ **2** CLOTHE : vestir

vest[2] *n* **1** : chaleco *m* **2** UNDERSHIRT : camiseta *f*

vestibule ['vɛstə,bju:l] *n* : vestíbulo *m*

vestige ['vɛstɪdʒ] *n* : vestigio *m*, rastro *m*

vestment ['vɛstmənt] *n* : vestidura *f*

vestry ['vɛstri] *n, pl* **-tries** : sacristía *f*

vet ['vɛt] *n* **1** → **veterinarian 2** → **veteran**[2]

veteran[1] ['vɛtərən, 'vɛtrən] *adj* : veterano

veteran[2] *n* : veterano *m*, -na *f*

Veterans Day *n* : día *m* del Armisticio (celebrado el 11 de noviembre en los Estados Unidos)

veterinarian [,vɛtərə'nɛriən, ,vɛtə'nɛr-] *n* : veterinario *m*, -ria *f*

veterinary ['vɛtərə,nɛri] *adj* : veterinario

veto[1] ['vi:to] *vt* **1** FORBID : prohibir **2** : vetar ⟨to veto a bill : vetar un proyecto de ley⟩

veto² *n, pl* **-toes 1** : veto *m* ⟨the power of veto : el derecho de veto⟩ **2** BAN : veto *m*, prohibición *f*

vex [ˈvɛks] *vt* : contrariar, molestar, irritar

vexation [vɛkˈseɪʃən] *n* : contrariedad *f*, irritación *f*

via [ˈvaɪə, ˈviːə] *prep* : por, vía

viability [ˌvaɪəˈbɪləti] *n* : viabilidad *f*

viable [ˈvaɪəbəl] *adj* : viable

viaduct [ˈvaɪəˌdʌkt] *n* : viaducto *m*

vial [ˈvaɪəl] *n* : frasco *m*

vibrant [ˈvaɪbrənt] *adj* **1** LIVELY : vibrante, animado, dinámico **2** BRIGHT : fuerte, vivo (dícese de los colores)

vibrate [ˈvaɪˌbreɪt] *vi* **-brated; -brating 1** OSCILLATE : vibrar, oscilar **2** THRILL : bullir ⟨to vibrate with excitement : bullir de emoción⟩

vibration [vaɪˈbreɪʃən] *n* : vibración *f*

vicar [ˈvɪkər] *n* : vicario *m*, -ria *f*

vicarious [vaɪˈkæriːəs, vɪ-] *adj* : indirecto — **vicariously** *adv*

vice [ˈvaɪs] *n* : vicio *m*

vice admiral *n* : vicealmirante *mf*

vice president *n* : vicepresidente *m*, -ta *f*

viceroy [ˈvaɪsˌrɔɪ] *n* : virrey *m*, -rreina *f*

vice versa [ˌvaɪsɪˈvərsə, ˌvaɪsˈvər-] *adv* : viceversa

vicinity [vəˈsɪnəti] *n, pl* **-ties 1** NEIGHBORHOOD : vecindad *f*, inmediaciones *fpl* **2** NEARNESS : proximidad *f*

vicious [ˈvɪʃəs] *adj* **1** DEPRAVED : depravado, malo **2** SAVAGE : malo, fiero, salvaje ⟨a vicious dog : un perro feroz⟩ **3** MALICIOUS : malicioso

viciously [ˈvɪʃəsli] *adv* : con saña, brutalmente

viciousness [ˈvɪʃəsnəs] *n* : brutalidad *f*, ferocidad *f* (de un animal), malevolencia *f* (de un comentario, etc.)

vicissitudes [vəˈsɪsəˌtuːdz, vaɪ-, -ˌtjuːdz] *npl* : vicisitudes *fpl*

victim [ˈvɪktəm] *n* : víctima *f*

victimize [ˈvɪktəˌmaɪz] *vt* **-mized; -mizing** : tomar como víctima, perseguir, victimizar *Arg, Mex*

victor [ˈvɪktər] *n* : vencedor *m*, -dora *f*

Victorian [vɪkˈtoːriən] *adj* : victoriano

victorious [vɪkˈtoːriəs] *adj* : victorioso — **victoriously** *adv*

victory [ˈvɪktəri] *n, pl* **-ries** : victoria *f*, triunfo *m*

victuals [ˈvɪtəlz] *npl* : víveres *mpl*, provisiones *fpl*

video [ˈvɪdiˌoː] *adj* : de video ⟨video recording : grabación de video⟩

video² *n* **1** : video *m* (medio o grabación) **2** → **videotape²**

video camera *n* : videocámara *f*

videocassette [ˌvɪdioʊkəˈsɛt] *n* : videocasete *m*, videocassette *m*

videocassette recorder → **VCR**

video game *n* : videojuego *m*, juego *m* de video

videotape¹ [ˈvɪdioˌteɪp] *vt* **-taped; -taping** : grabar en video, videograbar

videotape² *n* : videocinta *f*

vie [ˈvaɪ] *vi* **vied; vying** [ˈvaɪɪŋ] : competir, rivalizar

Vietnamese [viˌɛtnəˈmiːz, -ˈmiːs] *n* **1** : vietnamita *mf* **2** : vietnamita *m* (idioma) — **Vietnamese** *adj*

view¹ [ˈvjuː] *vt* **1** OBSERVE : mirar, ver, observar **2** CONSIDER : considerar, contemplar

view² *n* **1** SIGHT : vista *f* ⟨to come into view : aparecer⟩ **2** ATTITUDE, OPINION : opinión *f*, parecer *m*, actitud *f* ⟨in my view : en mi opinión⟩ **3** SCENE : vista *f*, panorama *f* **4** INTENTION : idea *f*, vista *f* ⟨with a view to : con vistas a, con la idea de⟩ **5 in view of** : dado que, en vista de (que)

viewer [ˈvjuːər] *n or* **television viewer** : telespectador *m*, -dora *f*; televidente *mf*

viewpoint [ˈvjuːˌpɔɪnt] *n* : punto *m* de vista

vigil [ˈvɪdʒəl] *n* **1** : vigilia *f*, vela *f* **2 to keep vigil** : velar

vigilance [ˈvɪdʒələnts] *n* : vigilancia *f*

vigilant [ˈvɪdʒələnt] *adj* : vigilante

vigilante [ˌvɪdʒəˈlænˌtiː] *n* : integrante *mf* de un comité de vigilancia (que actúa como policía)

vigilantly [ˈvɪdʒələntli] *adv* : con vigilancia

vigor [ˈvɪgər] *n* : vigor *m*, energía *f*, fuerza *f*

vigorous [ˈvɪgərəs] *adj* : vigoroso, enérgico — **vigorously** *adv*

Viking [ˈvaɪkɪŋ] *n* : vikingo *m*, -ga *f*

vile [ˈvaɪl] *adj* **viler; vilest 1** WICKED : vil, infame **2** REVOLTING : asqueroso, repugnante **3** TERRIBLE : horrible, atroz ⟨vile weather : tiempo horrible⟩ ⟨to be in a vile mood : estar de un humor de perros⟩

vilify [ˈvɪləˌfaɪ] *vt* **-fied; -fying** : vilipendiar, denigrar, difamar

villa [ˈvɪlə] *n* : casa *f* de campo, quinta *f*

village [ˈvɪlɪdʒ] *n* : pueblo *m* (grande), aldea *f* (pequeña)

villager [ˈvɪlɪdʒər] *n* : vecino *m*, -na *f* (de un pueblo); aldeano *m*, -na *f* (de una aldea)

villain [ˈvɪlən] *n* : villano *m*, -na *f*; malo *m*, -la *f* (en ficción, películas, etc.)

villainess [ˈvɪlənɪs, -nəs] *n* : villana *f*

villainous [ˈvɪlənəs] *adj* : infame, malvado

villainy [ˈvɪləni] *n, pl* **-lainies** : vileza *f*, maldad *f*

vim [ˈvɪm] *n* : brío *m*, vigor *m*, energía *f*

vindicate [ˈvɪndəˌkeɪt] *vt* **-cated; -cating 1** EXONERATE : vindicar, disculpar **2** JUSTIFY : justificar

vindication [ˌvɪndəˈkeɪʃən] *n* : vindicación *f*, justificación *f*

vindictive [vɪnˈdɪktɪv] *adj* : vengativo

vine [ˈvaɪn] *n* **1** GRAPEVINE : vid *f*, parra *f* **2** : planta *f* trepadora, enredadera *f*

vinegar [ˈvɪnɪgər] *n* : vinagre *m*

vinegary ['vɪnɪgəri] *adj* : avinagrado
vineyard ['vɪnjərd] *n* : viña *f*, viñedo *m*
vintage¹ ['vɪntɪʤ] *adj* 1 : añejo (dícese de un vino) 2 CLASSIC : clásico, de época
vintage² *n* 1 : cosecha *f* ⟨the 1947 vintage : la cosecha de 1947⟩ 2 ERA : época *f*, era *f* ⟨slang of recent vintage : argot de la época reciente⟩
vinyl ['vaɪnəl] *n* : vinilo
viola [vi:'o:lə] *n* : viola *f*
violate ['vaɪə,leɪt] *vt* -lated; -lating 1 BREAK : infringir, violar, quebrantar ⟨to violate the rules : violar las reglas⟩ 2 RAPE : violar 3 DESECRATE : profanar
violation [,vaɪə'leɪʃən] *n* 1 : violación *f*, infracción *f* (de una ley) 2 DESECRATION : profanación *f*
violence ['vaɪlənts, 'vaɪə-] *n* : violencia *f*
violent ['vaɪlənt, 'vaɪə-] *adj* : violento
violently ['vaɪləntli, 'vaɪə-] *adv* : violentamente, con violencia
violet ['vaɪlət, 'vaɪə-] *n* : violeta *f*
violin [,vaɪə'lɪn] *n* : violín *m*
violinist [,vaɪə'lɪnɪst] *n* : violinista *mf*
violoncello [,vaɪələn'ʧɛlo:, ,vi:-] → **cello**
VIP [,vi:,aɪ'pi:] *n, pl* **VIPs** [-'pi:z] : VIP *mf*, persona *f* de categoría
viper ['vaɪpər] *n* : víbora *f*
viral ['vaɪrəl] *adj* : viral, vírico ⟨viral pneumonia : pulmonía viral⟩
virgin¹ ['vərʤən] *adj* 1 CHASTE : virginal ⟨the virgin birth : el alumbramiento virginal⟩ 2 : virgen, intacto ⟨a virgin forest : una selva virgen⟩ ⟨virgin wool : lana virgen⟩
virgin² *n* : virgen *mf*
virginity [vər'ʤɪnəti] *n* : virginidad *f*
Virgo ['vər,go:, 'vɪr-] *n* : Virgo *mf*
virile ['vɪrəl, -,aɪl] *adj* : viril, varonil
virility [və'rɪləti] *n* : virilidad *f*
virtual ['vərʧuəl] *adj* : virtual ⟨a virtual dictator : un virtual dictador⟩ ⟨virtual reality : realidad virtual⟩
virtually ['vərʧuəli, 'vərʧəli] *adv* : en realidad, de hecho, casi
virtue ['vər,ʧu:] *n* 1 : virtud *f* 2 **by virtue of** : en virtud de, debido a
virtuosity [,vərʧu'asəti] *n, pl* -ties : virtuosismo *m*
virtuoso [,vərʧu'o:so:, -zo:] *n, pl* -sos *or* -si [-,si:, -,zi:] : virtuoso *m*, -sa *f*
virtuous ['vərʧuəs] *adj* : virtuoso, bueno — **virtuously** *adv*
virulence ['vɪrələnts, 'vɪrjə-] *n* : virulencia *f*
virulent ['vɪrələnt, 'vɪrjə-] *adj* : virulento
virus ['vaɪrəs] *n* : virus *m*
visa ['vi:zə, -sə] *n* : visa *f*
vis-à-vis [,vi:zə'vi:, -sə-] *prep* : con relación a, con respecto a
viscera ['vɪsərə] *npl* : vísceras *fpl*
visceral ['vɪsərəl] *adj* : visceral
viscosity [vɪs'kasəti] *n, pl* -ties : viscosidad *f*
viscount ['vaɪ,kæunt] *n* : vizconde *m*

viscountess ['vaɪ,kæuntɪs] *n* : vizcondesa *f*
viscous ['vɪskəs] *adj* : viscoso
vise ['vaɪs] *n* : torno *m* de banco, tornillo *m* de banco
visibility [,vɪzə'bɪləti] *n, pl* -ties : visibilidad *f*
visible ['vɪzəbəl] *adj* 1 : visible ⟨the visible stars : las estrellas visibles⟩ 2 OBVIOUS : evidente, patente
visibly ['vɪzəbli] *adv* : visiblemente
vision ['vɪʒən] *n* 1 EYESIGHT : vista *f*, visión *f* 2 APPARITION : visión *f*, aparición *f* 3 FORESIGHT : visión *f* (del futuro), previsión *f* 4 IMAGE : imagen *f* ⟨she had visions of a disaster : se imaginaba un desastre⟩
visionary¹ ['vɪʒə,nɛri] *adj* 1 FARSIGHTED : visionario, con visión de futuro 2 UTOPIAN : utópico, poco realista
visionary² *n, pl* -ries : visionario *m*, -ria *f*
visit¹ ['vɪzət] *vt* 1 : visitar, ir a ver 2 AFFLICT : azotar, afligir ⟨visited by troubles : afligido con problemas⟩ — *vi* : hacer (una) visita
visit² *n* : visita *f*
visitor ['vɪzətər] *n* : visitante *mf* (a una ciudad, etc.), visita *f* (a una casa)
visor ['vaɪzər] *n* : visera *f*
vista ['vɪstə] *n* : vista *f*
visual ['vɪʒuəl] *adj* : visual ⟨the visual arts : las artes visuales⟩ — **visually** *adv*
visualize ['vɪʒuə,laɪz] *vt* -ized; -izing : visualizar, imaginarse, hacerse una idea de — **visualization** [,vɪʒuwələ'zeɪʃən] *n*
vital ['vaɪtəl] *adj* 1 : vital ⟨vital organs : órganos vitales⟩ 2 CRUCIAL : esencial, crucial, decisivo ⟨of vital importance : de suma importancia⟩ 3 LIVELY : enérgico, lleno de vida, vital
vitality [vaɪ'tæləti] *n, pl* -ties : vitalidad *f*, energía *f*
vitally ['vaɪtəli] *adv* : sumamente
vital statistics *npl* : estadísticas *fpl* demográficas
vitamin ['vaɪtəmən] *n* : vitamina *f* ⟨vitamin deficiency : carencia vitamínica⟩
vitreous ['vɪtriəs] *adj* : vítreo
vitriolic [,vɪtri'alɪk] *adj* : mordaz, virulento
vituperation [vaɪ,tu:pə'reɪʃən, -,tju:-] *n* : vituperio *m*
vivacious [və'veɪʃəs, vaɪ-] *adj* : vivaz, animado, lleno de vida
vivaciously [və'veɪʃəsli, vaɪ-] *adv* : con vivacidad, animadamente
vivacity [və'væsəti, vaɪ-] *n* : vivacidad *f*
vivid ['vɪvəd] *adj* 1 LIVELY : lleno de vitalidad 2 BRILLIANT : vivo, intenso ⟨vivid colors : colores vivos⟩ 3 INTENSE, SHARP : vívido, gráfico ⟨a vivid dream : un sueño vívido⟩
vividly ['vɪvədli] *adv* 1 BRIGHTLY : con colores vivos 2 SHARPLY : vívidamente
vividness ['vɪvədnəs] *n* 1 BRIGHTNESS : intensidad *f*, viveza *f* 2 SHARPNESS : lo gráfico, nitidez *f*

vivisection [ˌvɪvə'sɛkʃən, 'vɪvəˌ-] *n* : vivisección *f*

vixen ['vɪksən] *n* : zorra *f*, raposa *f*

vocabulary [vo:'kæbjəˌlɛri] *n, pl* **-laries 1** : vocabulario *m* **2** LEXICON : léxico *m*

vocal ['vo:kəl] *adj* **1** : vocal **2** LOUD, OUTSPOKEN : ruidoso, muy franco

vocal cords *npl* : cuerdas *fpl* vocales

vocalist ['vo:kəlɪst] *n* : cantante *mf*, vocalista *mf*

vocalize ['vo:kəlˌaɪz] *vt* **-ized; -izing** : vocalizar

vocation [vo'keɪʃən] *n* : vocación *f* ⟨to have a vocation for : tener vocación de⟩

vocational [vo'keɪʃənəl] *adj* : profesional ⟨vocational guidance : orientación profesional⟩

vociferous [vo'sɪfərəs] *adj* : ruidoso, vociferante

vodka ['vɑdkə] *n* : vodka *m*

vogue ['vo:g] *n* : moda *f*, boga *f* ⟨to be in vogue : estar de moda, estar en boga⟩

voice[1] ['vɔɪs] *vt* **voiced; voicing** : expresar

voice[2] *n* **1** : voz *f* ⟨in a low voice : en voz baja⟩ ⟨to lose one's voice : quedarse sin voz⟩ ⟨the voice of the people : la voz del pueblo⟩ **2 to make one's voice heard** : hacerse oír

voice box → **larynx**

voiced ['vɔɪst] *adj* : sonoro

voice mail *n* : correo *m* de voz

void[1] ['vɔɪd] *vt* : anular, invalidar ⟨to void a contract : anular un contrato⟩

void[2] *adj* **1** EMPTY : vacío, desprovisto ⟨void of content : desprovisto de contenido⟩ **2** INVALID : inválido, nulo

void[3] *n* : vacío *m*

volatile ['vɑlətəl] *adj* : volátil, inestable

volatility [ˌvɑlə'tɪləti] *n* : volatilidad *f*, inestabilidad *f*

volcanic [vɑl'kænɪk] *adj* : volcánico

volcano [vɑl'keɪˌno:] *n, pl* **-noes** *or* **-nos** : volcán *m*

vole ['vo:l] *n* : campañol *m*

volition [vo'lɪʃən] *n* : volición *f*, voluntad *f* ⟨of one's own volition : por voluntad propia⟩

volley ['vɑli] *n, pl* **-leys 1** : descarga *f* (de tiros) **2** : torrente *m*, lluvia *f* (de insultos, etc.) **3** : salva *f* (de aplausos) **4** : volea *f* (en deportes)

volleyball ['vɑliˌbɔl] *n* : voleibol *m*

volt ['vo:lt] *n* : voltio *m*

voltage ['vo:ltɪʤ] *n* : voltaje *m*

volubility [ˌvɑljə'bɪləti] *n* : locuacidad *f*

voluble ['vɑljəbəl] *adj* : locuaz

volume ['vɑljəm, -ˌju:m] *n* **1** BOOK : volumen *m*, tomo *m* **2** SPACE : capacidad *f*, volumen *m* (en física) **3** AMOUNT : cantidad *f*, volumen *m* **4** LOUDNESS : volumen *m*

voluminous [və'lu:mənəs] *adj* : voluminoso

voluntary ['vɑlənˌteri] *adj* : voluntario — **voluntarily** [ˌvɑlən'terəli] *adv*

volunteer[1] [ˌvɑlən'tɪr] *vt* : ofrecer, dar ⟨to volunteer one's assistance : ofrecer la ayuda⟩ — *vi* : ofrecerse, alistarse como voluntario

volunteer[2] *n* : voluntario *m*, -ria *f*

voluptuous [və'lʌptʃuəs] *adj* : voluptuoso

vomit[1] ['vɑmət] *v* : vomitar

vomit[2] *n* : vómito *m*

voodoo ['vu:ˌdu:] *n, pl* **voodoos** : vudú *m*

voracious [vɔ'reɪʃəs, və-] *adj* : voraz

voraciously [vɔ'reɪʃəsli, və-] *adv* : vorazmente, con voracidad

vortex ['vɔrˌtɛks] *n, pl* **vortices** ['vɔrtəˌsi:z] : vórtice *m*

vote[1] ['vo:t] *vi* **voted; voting** : votar ⟨to vote Democratic : votar por los demócratas⟩

vote[2] *n* **1** : voto *m* **2** SUFFRAGE : sufragio *m*, derecho *m* al voto

voter ['vo:tər] *n* : votante *mf*

voting ['vo:ṭɪŋ] *n* : votación *f*

vouch ['væʊtʃ] *vi* **to vouch for** : garantizar (algo), responder de (algo), responder por (alguien)

voucher ['væʊtʃər] *n* **1** RECEIPT : comprobante *m* **2** : vale *m* ⟨travel voucher : vale de viajar⟩

vow[1] ['væʊ] *vt* : jurar, prometer, hacer voto de

vow[2] *n* : promesa *f*, voto *m* (en la religión) ⟨a vow of poverty : un voto de pobreza⟩

vowel ['væʊəl] *n* : vocal *m*

voyage[1] ['vɔɪɪʤ] *vi* **-aged; -aging** : viajar

voyage[2] *n* : viaje *m*

voyager ['vɔɪɪʤər] *n* : viajero *m*, -ra *f*

vulcanize ['vʌlkəˌnaɪz] *vt* **-nized; -nizing** : vulcanizar

vulgar ['vʌlgər] *adj* **1** COMMON, PLEBIAN : ordinario, populachero, del vulgo **2** COARSE, CRUDE : grosero, de mal gusto, majadero *Mex* **3** INDECENT : indecente, colorado (dícese de un chiste, etc.)

vulgarity [ˌvʌl'gærəti] *n, pl* **-ties** : grosería *f*, vulgaridad *f*

vulgarly ['vʌlgərli] *adv* : vulgarmente, groseramente

vulnerability [ˌvʌlnərə'bɪləti] *n, pl* **-ties** : vulnerabilidad *f*

vulnerable ['vʌlnərəbəl] *adj* : vulnerable

vulture ['vʌltʃər] *n* : buitre *m*, zopilote *m* *CA, Mex*

vying → **vie**

W

w ['dʌbəlˌjuː] *n, pl* **w's** *or* **ws** [-ˌjuːz] : vigésima tercera letra del alfabeto inglés

wad¹ ['wɑd] *vt* **wadded; wadding 1** : hacer un taco con, formar en una masa **2** STUFF : rellenar

wad² *n* : taco *m* (de papel), bola *f* (de algodón, etc.), fajo *m* (de billetes)

waddle¹ ['wɑdəl] *vi* **-dled; -dling** : andar como un pato

waddle² *n* : andar *m* de pato

wade ['weɪd] *v* **waded; wading** *vi* **1** : caminar por el agua **2 to wade through** : leer (algo) con dificultad — *vt or* **to wade across** : vadear

wading bird *n* : zancuda *f*, ave *f* zancuda

wafer ['weɪfər] *n* : barquillo *m*, galleta *f* de barquillo

waffle¹ ['wɑfəl] *n* **1** : wafle *m* **2 waffle iron** : waflera *f*

waft ['wɑft, 'wæft] *vt* : llevar por el aire — *vi* : flotar

wag¹ ['wæg] *v* **wagged; wagging** *vt* : menear — *vi* : menearse, moverse

wag² *n* **1** : meneo *m* (de la cola) **2** JOKER, WIT : bromista *mf*

wage¹ ['weɪdʒ] *vt* **waged; waging** : hacer, librar ⟨to wage war : hacer la guerra⟩

wage² *n or* **wages** *npl* : sueldo *m*, salario *m* ⟨minimum wage : salario mínimo⟩

wager¹ ['weɪdʒər] *v* : apostar

wager² *n* : apuesta *f*

waggish ['wægɪʃ] *adj* : burlón, bromista (dícese de una persona), chistoso (dícese de un comentario)

waggle ['wægəl] *vt* **-gled; -gling** : menear, mover (de un lado a otro)

wagon ['wægən] *n* **1** : carro *m* (tirado por caballos) **2** CART : carrito *m* **3** → **station wagon**

waif ['weɪf] *n* : niño *m* abandonado, animal *m* sin hogar

wail¹ ['weɪl] *vi* : gemir, lamentarse

wail² *n* : gemido *m*, lamento *m*

wainscot ['weɪnskət, -ˌskɑt, -ˌskoːt] *or* **wainscoting** [-skətɪŋ, -ˌskɑ-, -ˌskoː-] *n* : boiserie *f*, revestimiento *m* de paneles de madera

waist ['weɪst] *n* : cintura *f* (del cuerpo humano), talle *m* (de ropa)

waistline ['weɪstˌlaɪn] → **waist**

wait¹ ['weɪt] *vi* : esperar ⟨to wait for something : esperar algo⟩ ⟨wait and see! : ¡espera y verás!⟩ ⟨I can't wait : me muero de ganas⟩ — *vt* **1** AWAIT : esperar **2** DELAY : retrasar ⟨don't wait lunch : no retrase el almuerzo⟩ **3** SERVE : servir, atender ⟨to wait tables : servir (a la mesa)⟩

wait² *n* : espera *f* **2 to lie in wait** : estar al acecho

waiter ['weɪtər] *n* : mesero *m*, camarero *m*, mozo *m* Arg, Chile, Col, Peru

waiting room *n* : sala *f* de espera

waitress ['weɪtrəs] *n* : mesera *f*, camarera *f*, moza *f* Arg, Chile, Col, Peru

waive ['weɪv] *vt* **waived; waiving** : renunciar a ⟨to waive one's rights : renunciar a sus derechos⟩ ⟨to waive the rules : no aplicar las reglas⟩

waiver ['weɪvər] *n* : renuncia *f*

wake¹ ['weɪk] *v* **woke** ['woːk]; **woken** ['woːkən] *or* **waked; waking** *vi or* **to wake up** : despertar(se) ⟨he woke at noon : se despertó al mediodía⟩ ⟨wake up! : ¡despiértate!⟩ — *vt* : despertar

wake² *n* **1** VIGIL : velatorio *m*, velorio *m* (de un difunto) **2** TRAIL : estela *f* (de un barco, un huracán, etc.) **3** AFTERMATH : consecuencias *fpl* ⟨in the wake of : tras, como consecuencia de⟩

wakeful ['weɪkfəl] *adj* **1** SLEEPLESS : desvelado **2** VIGILANT : alerta, vigilante

waken ['weɪkən] → **awake**

walk¹ ['wɔk] *vi* **1** : caminar, andar, pasear ⟨you're walking too fast : estás caminando demasiado rápido⟩ ⟨to walk around the city : pasearse por la ciudad⟩ **2** : ir andando, ir a pie ⟨we had to walk home : tuvimos que ir a casa a pie⟩ **3** : darle base por bolas (a un bateador) — *vt* **1** : recorrer, caminar ⟨she walked two miles : caminó dos millas⟩ **2** ACCOMPANY : acompañar **3** : sacar a pasear (a un perro)

walk² *n* **1** : paseo *m*, caminata *f* ⟨to go for a walk : ir a caminar, dar un paseo⟩ **2** PATH : camino *m* **3** GAIT : andar *m* **4** : marcha *f* (en beisbol) **5 walk of life** : esfera *f*, condición *f*

walker ['wɔkər] *n* **1** : paseante *mf* **2** HIKER : excursionista *mf* **3** : andador *m* (aparato)

walking stick *n* : bastón *m*

walkout ['wɔkˌaʊt] *n* STRIKE : huelga *f*

walk out *vi* **1** STRIKE : declararse en huelga **2** LEAVE : salir, irse **3 to walk out on** : abandonar, dejar

walkway ['wɔkˌweɪ] *n* **1** SIDEWALK : acera *f* **2** PATH : sendero *m* **3** PASSAGEWAY : pasadizo *m*

wall¹ ['wɔl] *vt* **1 to wall in** : cercar con una pared o un muro, tapiar, amurallar **2 to wall off** : separar con una pared o un muro **3 to wall up** : tapiar, condenar (una ventana, etc.)

wall² *n* **1** : muro *m* (exterior) ⟨the walls of the city : las murallas de la ciudad⟩ **2** : pared *f* (interior) **3** BARRIER : barrera *f* ⟨a wall of mountains : una barrera de montañas⟩ **4** : pared *f* (en anatomía)

wallaby ['wɑləbi] *n, pl* **-bies** : ualabí *m*

walled ['wɔld] *adj* : amurallado

wallet ['wɑlət] *n* : billetera *f*, cartera *f*

wallflower ['wɔlˌflaʊər] *n* **1** : alhelí *m* (flor) **2 to be a wallflower** : comer pavo

wallop¹ ['wɑləp] *vt* **1** TROUNCE : darle una paliza (a alguien) **2** SOCK : pegar fuerte

wallop² *n* : golpe *m* fuerte, golpazo *m*

wallow¹ ['wɑ,lo:] *vi* **1** : revolcarse ⟨to wallow in the mud : revolcarse en el lodo⟩ **2** DELIGHT : deleitarse ⟨to wallow in luxury : nadar en lujos⟩

wallow² *n* : revolcadero *m* (para animales)

wallpaper¹ ['wɔl,peɪpər] *vt* : empapelar

wallpaper² *n* : papel *m* pintado

walnut ['wɔl,nʌt] *n* **1** : nuez *f* (fruta) **2** : nogal *m* (árbol y madera)

walrus ['wɔlrəs, 'wɑl-] *n, pl* **-rus** *or* **-ruses** : morsa *f*

waltz¹ ['wɔlts] *vi* **1** : valsar, bailar el vals **2** BREEZE : pasar con ligereza ⟨to waltz in : entrar tan campante⟩

waltz² *n* : vals *m*

wan ['wɑn] *adj* **wanner; -est 1** PALLID : pálido **2** DIM : tenue ⟨wan light : luz tenue⟩ **3** LANGUID : lánguido ⟨a wan smile : una sonrisa lánguida⟩ — **wanly** *adv*

wand ['wɑnd] *n* : varita *f* (mágica)

wander ['wɑndər] *vi* **1** RAMBLE : deambular, vagar, vagabundear **2** STRAY : alejarse, desviarse, divagar ⟨she let her mind wander : dejó vagar la imaginación⟩ — *vt* : recorrer ⟨to wander the streets : vagar por las calles⟩

wanderer ['wɑndərər] *n* : vagabundo *m*, -da *f*; viajero *m*, -ra *f*

wanderlust ['wɑndər,lʌst] *n* : pasión *f* por viajar

wane¹ ['weɪn] *vi* **waned; waning 1** : menguar (dícese de la luna) **2** DECLINE : disminuir, decaer, menguar

wane² *n* **on the wane** : decayendo, en decadencia

wangle ['wæŋgəl] *vt* **-gled; -gling** FINAGLE : arreglárselas para conseguir

wannabe ['wɑnə,bi:] *n* : aspirante *mf* (a algo); imitador *m*, -dora *f* (de alguien)

want¹ ['wɑnt, 'wɔnt] *vt* **1** LACK : faltar **2** REQUIRE : requerir, necesitar **3** DESIRE : querer, desear

want² *n* **1** LACK : falta *f* **2** DESTITUTION : indigencia *f*, miseria *f* **3** DESIRE, NEED : deseo *m*, necesidad *f*

wanting ['wɑntɪŋ, 'wɔn-] *adj* **1** ABSENT : ausente **2** DEFICIENT : deficiente ⟨he's wanting in common sense : le falta sentido común⟩

wanton ['wɑntən, 'wɔn-] *adj* **1** LEWD, LUSTFUL : lascivo, lujurioso, licencioso **2** INHUMANE, MERCILESS : despiadado ⟨wanton cruelty : crueldad despiadada⟩

wapiti ['wɑpəti] *n, pl* **-ti** *or* **-tis** : uapití *m*

war¹ ['wɔr] *vi* **warred; warring** : combatir, batallar, hacer la guerra

war² *n* : guerra *f* ⟨to go to war : entrar en guerra⟩

warble¹ ['wɔrbəl] *vi* **-bled; -bling** : gorjear, trinar

warble² *n* : trino *m*, gorjeo *m*

warbler ['wɔrblər] *n* : pájaro *m* gorjeador, curruca *f*

ward¹ ['wɔrd] *vt* **to ward off** : desviar, protegerse contra

ward² *n* **1** : sala *f* (de un hospital, etc.) ⟨maternity ward : sala de maternidad⟩ **2** : distrito *m* electoral o administrativo (de una ciudad) **3** : pupilo *m*, -la *f* (de un tutor, etc.)

warden ['wɔrdən] *n* **1** KEEPER : guarda *mf*; guardián *m*, -diana *f* ⟨game warden : guardabosque⟩ **2** *or* **prison warden** : alcaide *m*

wardrobe ['wɔrd,ro:b] *n* **1** CLOSET : armario *m* **2** CLOTHES : vestuario *m*, guardarropa *f*

ware ['wær] *n* **1** POTTERY : cerámica *f* **2 wares** *npl* GOODS : mercancía *f*, mercadería *f*

warehouse ['wær,haʊs] *n* : depósito *m*, almacén *m*, bodega *f* *Chile, Col, Mex*

warfare ['wɔr,fær] *n* **1** WAR : guerra *f* **2** STRUGGLE : lucha *f* ⟨the warfare against drugs : la lucha contra las drogas⟩

warhead ['wɔr,hɛd] *n* : ojiva *f*, cabeza *f* (de un misil)

warily ['wærəli] *adv* : cautelosamente, con cautela

wariness ['wærinəs] *n* : cautela *f*

warlike ['wær,laɪk] *adj* : belicoso, guerrero

warm¹ ['wɔrm] *vt* **1** HEAT : calentar, recalentar **2 to warm one's heart** : reconfortar a uno, alegrar el corazón **3 to warm up** : calentar (los músculos, un automóvil, etc.) — *vi* **1** : calentarse **2 to warm to** : tomarle simpatía (a alguien), entusiasmarse con (algo)

warm² *adj* **1** LUKEWARM : tibio, templado **2** : caliente, cálido, caluroso ⟨a warm wind : un viento cálido⟩ ⟨a warm day : un día caluroso, un día de calor⟩ ⟨warm hands : manos calientes⟩ **3** : caliente, que abriga ⟨warm clothes : ropa de abrigo⟩ ⟨I feel warm : tengo calor⟩ **4** CARING, CORDIAL : cariñoso, cordial **5** : cálido (dícese de colores) **6** FRESH : fresco, reciente ⟨a warm trail : un rastro reciente⟩ **7** (*used for riddles*) : caliente

warm–blooded ['wɔrm'blʌdəd] *adj* : de sangre caliente

warmhearted ['wɔrm'hɑrtəd] *adj* : cariñoso

warmly ['wɔrmli] *adv* **1** AFFECTIONATELY : calurosamente, afectuosamente **2 to dress warmly** : abrigarse

warmonger ['wɔr,mɑŋgər, -,mʌŋ-] *n* : belicista *mf*

warmth ['wɔrmpθ] *n* **1** : calor *m* **2** AFFECTION : cariño *m*, afecto *m* **3** ENTHUSIASM : ardor *m*, entusiasmo *m*

warm–up ['wɔrm,ʌp] *n* : calentamiento *m*

warn ['wɔrn] *vt* **1** CAUTION : advertir, alertar **2** INFORM : avisar, informar

warning ['wɔrnɪŋ] *n* **1** ADVICE : advertencia *f*, aviso *m* **2** ALERT : alerta *f*, alarma *f*

warp¹ ['wɔrp] *vt* **1** : alabear, combar **2** PERVERT : pervertir, deformar — *vi* : pandearse, alabearse, combarse

warp² *n* **1** : urdimbre *f* ⟨the warp and the weft : la urdimbre y la trama⟩ **2** : alabeo *m* (en la madera, etc.)

warrant¹ ['wɔrənt] *vt* **1** ASSURE : asegurar, garantizar **2** GUARANTEE : garantizar **3** JUSTIFY, MERIT : justificar, merecer

warrant² *n* **1** AUTHORIZATION : autorización *f*, permiso *m* ⟨an arrest warrant : una orden de detención⟩ **2** JUSTIFICATION : justificación *f*

warranty ['wɔrənti, ˌwɔrən'ti:] *n, pl* **-ties** : garantía *f*

warren ['wɔrən] *n* : madriguera *f* (de conejos)

warrior ['wɔriər] *n* : guerrero *m*, -ra *f*

warship ['wɔrˌʃɪp] *n* : buque *m* de guerra

wart ['wɔrt] *n* : verruga *f*

wartime ['wɔrˌtaɪm] *n* : tiempo *m* de guerra

wary ['wæri] *adj* **warier; -est** : cauteloso, receloso ⟨to be wary of : desconfiar de⟩

was → **be**

wash¹ ['wɔʃ, 'wɑʃ] *vt* **1** CLEAN : lavar(se), limpiar, fregar ⟨to wash the dishes : lavar los platos⟩ ⟨to wash one's hands : lavarse las manos⟩ **2** DRENCH : mojar **3** LAP : bañar ⟨waves were washing the shore : las olas bañaban la orilla⟩ **4** CARRY, DRAG : arrastrar **5 to wash away** : llevarse (un puente, etc.) — *vi* **1** : lavarse (dícese de una persona o la ropa) ⟨the dress washes well : el vestido se lava bien⟩ **2 to wash against** *or* **to wash over** : bañar

wash² *n* **1** : lavado *m* ⟨to give something a wash : lavar algo⟩ **2** LAUNDRY : artículos *mpl* para lavar, ropa *f* sucia **3** : estela *f* (de un barco)

washable ['wɔʃəbəl, 'wɑ-] *adj* : lavable

washboard ['wɔʃˌbord, 'wɑʃ-] *n* : tabla *f* de lavar

washbowl ['wɔʃˌboːl, 'wɑʃ-] *n* : lavabo *m*, lavamanos *m*

washcloth ['wɔʃˌklɔθ, 'wɑʃ-] *n* : toallita *f* (para lavarse)

washed–out ['wɔʃt'aʊt, 'wɑʃt-] *adj* **1** : desvaído (dícese de colores) **2** EXHAUSTED : agotado, desanimado

washed–up ['wɔʃt'ʌp, 'wɑʃt-] *adj* : acabado (dícese de una persona), fracasado (dícese de un negocio, etc.)

washer ['wɔʃər, 'wɑ-] *n* **1** → **washing machine 2** : arandela *f* (de una llave, etc.)

washing ['wɔʃɪŋ, 'wɑ-] *n* WASH : ropa *f* para lavar

washing machine *n* : máquina *f* de lavar, lavadora *f*

washout ['wɔʃˌaʊt, 'wɑʃ-] *n* **1** : erosión *f* (de la tierra) **2** FAILURE : fracaso *m* ⟨she's a washout : es un desastre⟩

washroom ['wɔʃˌruːm, 'wɑʃ-, -ˌrʊm] *n* : servicios *mpl* (públicos), baño *m*, sanitario *m Col, Mex, Ven*

wasn't ['wʌzənt] (*contraction of* **was not**) → **be**

wasp ['wɑsp] *n* : avispa *f*

waspish ['wɑspɪʃ] *adj* **1** IRRITABLE : irritable, irascible **2** CAUSTIC : cáustico, mordaz

waste¹ ['weɪst] *v* **wasted; wasting** *vt* **1** DEVASTATE : arrasar, arruinar, devastar **2** SQUANDER : desperdiciar, despilfarrar, malgastar ⟨to waste time : perder tiempo⟩ — *vi or* **to waste away** : consumirse, chuparse

waste² *adj* **1** BARREN : yermo, baldío **2** DISCARDED : de desecho **3** EXCESS : sobrante

waste³ *n* **1** → **wasteland 2** MISUSE : derroche *m*, desperdicio *m*, despilfarro *m* ⟨a waste of time : una pérdida de tiempo⟩ **3** RUBBISH : basura *f*, desechos *mpl*, desperdicios *mpl* **4** EXCREMENT : excremento *m*

wastebasket ['weɪstˌbæskət] *n* : cesto *m* (de basura), papelera *f*, zafacón *m Car*

wasteful ['weɪstfəl] *adj* : despilfarrador, derrochador, pródigo

wastefulness ['weɪstfəlnəs] *n* : derroche *m*, despilfarro *m*

wasteland ['weɪstˌlænd, -lənd] *n* : baldío *m*, yermo *m*, desierto *m*

watch¹ ['wɑtʃ] *vi* **1** *or* **to keep watch** : velar **2** OBSERVE : mirar, ver, observar **3 to watch for** AWAIT : esperar, quedar a la espera de **4 to watch out** : tener cuidado ⟨watch out! : ¡ten cuidado!, ¡ojo!⟩ — *vt* **1** OBSERVE : mirar, observar **2** *or* **to watch over** : vigilar, cuidar **3** : tener cuidado de ⟨watch what you do : ten cuidado con lo que haces⟩

watch² *n* **1** : guardia *f* ⟨to be on watch : estar de guardia⟩ **2** SURVEILLANCE : vigilancia *f* **3** LOOKOUT : guardia *mf*, centinela *f*, vigía *mf* **4** TIMEPIECE : reloj *m*

watchdog ['wɑtʃˌdɔg] *n* : perro *m* guardián

watcher ['wɑtʃər] *n* : observador *m*, -dora *f*

watchful ['wɑtʃfəl] *adj* : alerta, vigilante, atento

watchfulness ['wɑtʃfəlnəs] *n* : vigilancia *f*

watchman ['wɑtʃmən] *n, pl* **-men** [-mən, -ˌmɛn] : vigilante *m*, guarda *m*

watchword ['wɑtʃˌwərd] *n* **1** PASSWORD : contraseña *f* **2** SLOGAN : lema *m*, eslogan *m*

water¹ ['wɔtər, 'wɑ-] *vt* **1** : regar (el jardín, etc.) **2 to water down** DILUTE : diluir, aguar — *vi* : lagrimear (dícese de los ojos), hacérsele agua la boca a uno ⟨my mouth is watering : se me hace agua la boca⟩

water² *n* : agua *f*

water buffalo *n* : búfalo *m* de agua

watercolor ['wɔtərˌkʌlər, 'wɑ-] *n* : acuarela *f*

watercourse ['wɔtərˌkors, 'wɑ-] *n* : curso *m* de agua

watercress ['wɔtərˌkrɛs, 'wɑ-] *n* : berro *m*

waterfall ['wɔtər₁fɔl, 'wɑ-] *n* : cascada *f*, salto *m* de agua, catarata *f*

waterfowl ['wɔtər₁faʊl, 'wɑ-] *n* : ave *f* acuática

waterfront ['wɔtər₁frʌnt, 'wɑ-] *n* **1** : tierra *f* que bordea un río, un lago, o un mar **2** WHARF : muelle *m*

water lily *n* : nenúfar *m*

waterlogged ['wɔtər₁lɔgd, 'wɑtər-₁lɑgd] *adj* : lleno de agua, empapado, inundado (dícese del suelo)

watermark ['wɔtər₁mɑrk, 'wɑ-] *n* **1** : marca *f* del nivel de agua **2** : filigrana *f* (en el papel)

watermelon ['wɔtər₁mɛlən, 'wɑ-] *n* : sandía *f*

water moccasin → moccasin

waterpower ['wɔtər₁paʊər, 'wɑ-] *n* : energía *f* hidráulica

waterproof[1] ['wɔtər₁pru:f, 'wɑ-] *vt* : hacer impermeable, impermeabilizar

waterproof[2] *adj* : impermeable, a prueba de agua

watershed ['wɔtər₁ʃɛd, 'wɑ-] *n* **1** : línea *f* divisoria de aguas **2** BASIN : cuenca *f* (de un río)

waterskiing ['wɔtər₁ski:ɪŋ, 'wɑ-] *n* : esquí *m* acuático

waterspout ['wɔtər₁spaʊt, 'wɑ-] *n* WHIRLWIND : tromba *f* marina

watertight ['wɔtər₁taɪt, 'wɑ-] *adj* **1** : hermético **2** IRREFUTABLE : irrebatible, irrefutable ⟨a watertight contract : un contrato sin lagunas⟩

waterway ['wɔtər₁weɪ, 'wɑ-] *n* : vía *f* navegable

waterworks ['wɔtər₁wərks, 'wɑ-] *npl* : central *f* de abastecimiento de agua

watery ['wɔtəri, 'wɑ-] *adj* **1** : acuoso, como agua **2** : aguado, diluido ⟨watery soup : sopa aguada⟩ **3** : lloroso ⟨watery eyes : ojos llorosos⟩ **4** WASHED-OUT : desvaído (dícese de colores)

watt ['wɑt] *n* : vatio *m*

wattage ['wɑtɪdʒ] *n* : vataje *m*

wattle ['wɑtəl] *n* : carúncula *f* (de un ave, etc.)

wave[1] ['weɪv] *v* **waved; waving** *vi* **1** : saludar con la mano, hacer señas con la mano ⟨she waved at him : lo saludó con la mano⟩ **2** FLUTTER, SHAKE : ondear, agitarse **3** UNDULATE : ondular — *vt* **1** SHAKE : agitar **2** BRANDISH : blandir **3** CURL : ondular, marcar (el pelo) **4** SIGNAL : hacerle señas a (con la mano) ⟨he waved farewell : se despidió con la mano⟩

wave[2] *n* **1** : ola *f* (de agua) **2** CURL : onda *f* (en el pelo) **3** : onda *f* (en física) **4** SURGE : oleada *f* ⟨a wave of enthusiasm : una oleada de entusiasmo⟩ **5** GESTURE : señal *f* con la mano, saludo *m* con la mano

wavelength ['weɪv₁lɛŋkθ] *n* : longitud *f* de onda

waver ['weɪvər] *vi* **1** VACILLATE : vacilar, fluctuar **2** FLICKER : parpadear, titilar, oscilar **3** FALTER : flaquear, tambalearse

wavy ['weɪvi] *adj* **wavier; -est** : ondulado

wax[1] ['wæks] *vi* **1** : crecer (dícese de la luna) **2** BECOME : volverse, ponerse ⟨to wax indignant : indignarse⟩ — *vt* : encerar

wax[2] *n* **1** BEESWAX : cera *f* de abejas **2** : cera *f* ⟨floor wax : cera para el piso⟩ **3** *or* **earwax** ['ɪr₁wæks] : cerilla *f*, cerumen *m*

waxen ['wæksən] *adj* : de cera

waxy ['wæksi] *adj* **waxier; -est** : ceroso

way ['weɪ] *n* **1** PATH, ROAD : camino *m*, vía *f* **2** ROUTE : camino *m*, ruta *f* ⟨to go the wrong way : equivocarse de camino⟩ ⟨I'm on my way : estoy de camino⟩ **3** : línea *f* de conducta, camino *m* ⟨he chose the easy way : optó por el camino fácil⟩ **4** MANNER, MEANS : manera *f*, modo *m*, forma *f* ⟨in the same way : del mismo modo, igualmente⟩ ⟨there are no two ways about it : no cabe la menor duda⟩ ⟨no way! : ¡de ninguna manera!⟩ **5** (*indicating a wish*) ⟨have it your way : como tú quieras⟩ ⟨to get one's own way : salirse uno con la suya⟩ **6** STATE : estado *m* ⟨things are in a bad way : las cosas marchan mal⟩ **7** RESPECT : aspecto *m*, sentido *m* **8** CUSTOM : costumbre *f* ⟨to mend one's ways : dejar las malas costumbres⟩ **9** PASSAGE : camino *m* ⟨to get in the way : meterse en el camino⟩ **10** DISTANCE : distancia *f* ⟨to come a long way : hacer grandes progresos⟩ **11** DIRECTION : dirección *f* ⟨come this way : venga por aquí⟩ ⟨which way did he go? : ¿por dónde fue?⟩ **12 by the way** : a propósito, por cierto **13 by way of** VIA : vía, pasando por **14 out of the way** REMOTE : remoto, recóndito **15** → **under way**

wayfarer ['weɪ₁færər] *n* : caminante *mf*

waylay ['weɪ₁leɪ] *vt* **-laid** [-₁leɪd]; **-laying** ACCOST : abordar

wayside ['weɪ₁saɪd] *n* : borde *m* del camino

wayward ['weɪwərd] *adj* **1** UNRULY : díscolo, rebelde **2** UNTOWARD : adverso

we ['wi:] *pron* : nosotros, nosotras

weak ['wi:k] *adj* **1** FEEBLE : débil, endeble **2** : flojo, pobre ⟨a weak excuse : una excusa poco convincente⟩ **3** DILUTED : aguado, diluido ⟨weak tea : té poco cargado⟩ **4** FAINT : tenue (dícese de los colores, las luces, los sonidos, etc.)

weaken ['wi:kən] *vt* : debilitar — *vi* : debilitarse, flaquear

weakling ['wi:klɪŋ] *n* : alfeñique *m fam*; debilucho *m*, -cha *f*

weakly[1] ['wi:kli] *adv* : débilmente

weakly[2] *adj* **weaklier; -est** : débil, enclenque

weakness ['wi:knəs] *n* **1** FEEBLENESS : debilidad *f* **2** FAULT, FLAW : flaqueza *f*, punto *m* débil

wealth ['wεlθ] *n* **1** RICHES : riqueza *f* **2** PROFUSION : abundancia *f*, profusión *f*

wealthy ['wεlθi] *adj* **wealthier; -est** : rico, acaudalado, adinerado

wean ['wi:n] *vt* **1** : destetar (a los niños o las crías) **2 to wean someone away from** : quitarle a alguien la costumbre de

weapon ['wεpən] *n* : arma *f*

weaponless ['wεpənləs] *adj* : desarmado

weaponry ['wεpənri] *n* : armamento *m*

wear[1] ['wær] *v* **wore** ['wor]; **worn** ['worn]; **wearing** *vt* **1** : llevar (ropa, un reloj, etc.), calzar (zapatos) ⟨to wear a happy smile : sonreír alegremente⟩ **2** *or* **to wear away** : desgastar, erosionar (rocas, etc.) **3 to wear out** : gastar ⟨he wore out his shoes : gastó sus zapatos⟩ **4 to wear out** EXHAUST : agotar, fatigar ⟨to wear oneself out : agotarse⟩ — *vi* **1** LAST : durar **2 to wear off** DIMINISH : disminuir **3 to wear out** : gastarse

wear[2] *n* **1** USE : uso *m* ⟨for everyday wear : para todos los días⟩ **2** CLOTHING : ropa *f* ⟨children's wear : ropa de niños⟩ **3** DETERIORATION : desgaste *m* ⟨to be the worse for wear : estar deteriorado⟩

wearable ['wærəbəl] *adj* : que puede ponerse (dícese de una prenda)

wear and tear *n* : desgaste *m*

weariness ['wɪrinəs] *n* : fatiga *f*, cansancio *m*

wearisome ['wɪrisəm] *adj* : aburrido, pesado, cansado

weary[1] ['wɪri] *v* **-ried; -rying** *vt* **1** TIRE : cansar, fatigar **2** BORE : hastiar, aburrir — *vi* : cansarse

weary[2] *adj* **-rier; -est 1** TIRED : cansado **2** FED UP : harto **3** BORED : aburrido

weasel ['wi:zəl] *n* : comadreja *f*

weather[1] ['wεðər] *vt* **1** WEAR : erosionar, desgastar **2** ENDURE : aguantar, sobrellevar, capear ⟨to weather the storm : capear el temporal⟩

weather[2] *n* : tiempo *m*

weather–beaten ['wεðər,bi:tən] *adj* : curtido

weatherman ['wεðər,mæn] *n, pl* **-men** [-mən, -,mεn] METEOROLOGIST : meteorólogo *m*, -ga *f*

weatherproof ['wεðər,pru:f] *adj* : que resiste a la intemperie, impermeable

weather vane → **vane**

weave[1] ['wi:v] *v* **wove** ['wo:v] *or* **weaved; woven** ['wo:vən] *or* **weaved; weaving** *vt* **1** : tejer (tela) **2** INTERLACE : entretejer, entrelazar **3 to weave one's way through** : abrirse camino por — *vi* **1** : tejer **2** WIND : serpentear, zigzaguear

weave[2] *n* : tejido *m*, trama *f*

weaver ['wi:vər] *n* : tejedor *m*, -dora *f*

web[1] ['wεb] *vt* **webbed; webbing** : cubrir o proveer con una red

web[2] *n* **1** COBWEB, SPIDERWEB : telaraña *f*, tela *f* de araña **2** ENTANGLEMENT, SNARE : red *f*, enredo *m* ⟨a web of intrigue : una red de intriga⟩ **3** : membrana *f* interdigital (de aves) **4** NETWORK : red *f* ⟨a web of highways : una red de carreteras⟩ **5 the Web** : la web

webbed ['wεbd] *adj* : palmeado ⟨webbed feet : patas palmeadas⟩

Web site *n* : sitio *m* web

wed ['wεd] *vt* **wedded; wedding 1** MARRY : casarse con **2** UNITE : ligar, unir

we'd ['wi:d] (*contraction of* **we had, we should**, *or* **we would**) → **have, should, would**

wedding ['wεdɪŋ] *n* : boda *f*, casamiento *m*

wedge[1] ['wεdʒ] *vt* **wedged; wedging 1** : apretar (con una cuña) ⟨to wedge open : mantener abierto con una cuña⟩ **2** CRAM : meter, embutir

wedge[2] *n* **1** : cuña *f* **2** PIECE : porción *f*, trozo *m*

wedlock ['wεd,lɑk] → **marriage**

Wednesday ['wεnz,deɪ, -di] *n* : miércoles *m*

wee ['wi:] *adj* : pequeño, minúsculo ⟨in the wee hours : a las altas horas⟩

weed[1] ['wi:d] *vt* **1** : desherbar, desyerbar **2 to weed out** : eliminar, quitar

weed[2] *n* : mala hierba *f*

weedy ['wi:di] *adj* **weedier; -est 1** : cubierto de malas hierbas **2** LANKY, SKINNY : flaco, larguirucho *fam*

week ['wi:k] *n* : semana *f*

weekday ['wi:k,deɪ] *n* : día *m* laborable

weekend ['wi:k,εnd] *n* : fin *m* de semana

weekly[1] ['wi:kli] *adv* : semanalmente

weekly[2] *adj* : semanal

weekly[3] *n, pl* **-lies** : semanario *m*

weep ['wi:p] *v* **wept** ['wεpt]; **weeping** : llorar

weeping willow *n* : sauce *m* llorón

weepy ['wi:pi] *adj* **weepier; -est** : lloroso, triste

weevil ['wi:vəl] *n* : gorgojo *m*

weft ['wεft] *n* : trama *f*

weigh ['weɪ] *vt* **1** : pesar **2** CONSIDER : considerar, sopesar **3 to weigh anchor** : levar anclas **4 to weigh down** : sobrecargar (con una carga), abrumar (con preocupaciones, etc.) — *vi* **1** : pesar ⟨it weighs 10 pounds : pesa 10 libras⟩ **2** COUNT : tener importancia, contar **3 to weigh on one's mind** : preocuparle a uno

weight[1] ['weɪt] *vt* **1** : poner peso en, sujetar con un peso **2** BURDEN : cargar, oprimir

weight[2] *n* **1** HEAVINESS : peso *m* ⟨to lose weight : bajar de peso, adelgazar⟩ **2** : peso *m* ⟨weights and measures : pesos y medidas⟩ **3** : pesa *f* ⟨to lift weights : levantar pesas⟩ **4** BURDEN : peso *m*, carga *f* ⟨to take a weight off one's mind : quitarle un peso de encima a uno⟩ **5**

IMPORTANCE : peso *m* **6** INFLUENCE
: influencia *f*, autoridad *f* ⟨to throw
one's weight around : hacer sentir su
influencia⟩
weighty ['weɪţi] *adj* **weightier; -est 1**
HEAVY : pesado **2** IMPORTANT : importante, de peso
weird ['wɪrd] *adj* **1** MYSTERIOUS : misterioso **2** STRANGE : extraño, raro —
weirdly *adv*
welcome¹ ['wɛlkəm] *vt* **-comed; -com-
ing** : darle la bienvenida a, recibir
welcome² *adj* : bienvenido ⟨to make
someone welcome : acoger bien a al-
guien⟩ ⟨you're welcome! : ¡de nada!,
¡no hay de qué!⟩
welcome³ *n* : bienvenida *f*, recibimiento *m*, acogida *f*
weld¹ ['wɛld] *v* : soldar
weld² *n* : soldadura *f*
welder ['wɛldər] *n* : soldador *m*, -dora *f*
welfare ['wɛl,fær] *n* **1** WELL-BEING : bienestar *m* **2** : asistencia *f* social
well¹ ['wɛl] *vi or* **to well up** : brotar, manar
well² *adv* **better** ['bɛţər]; **best** ['bɛst] **1**
RIGHTLY : bien, correctamente **2** SAT-
ISFACTORILY : bien ⟨to turn out well
: resultar bien, salir bien⟩ **3** COM-
PLETELY : completamente ⟨well-hid-
den : completamente escondido⟩ **4** IN-
TIMATELY : bien ⟨I knew him well : lo
conocía bien⟩ **5** CONSIDERABLY, FAR
: muy, bastante ⟨well ahead : muy ade-
lante⟩ ⟨well before the deadline : bastante antes de la fecha⟩ **6 as well** ALSO
: también **7** → **as well as**
well³ *adj* **1** SATISFACTORY : bien ⟨all is
well : todo está bien⟩ **2** DESIRABLE
: conveniente ⟨it would be well if you
left : sería conveniente que te fueras⟩
3 HEALTHY : bien, sano
well⁴ *n* **1** : pozo *m* (de agua, petróleo,
gas, etc.), aljibe *m* (de agua) **2** SOURCE
: fuente *f* ⟨a well of information : una
fuente de información⟩ **3 or stairwell**
: caja *f*, hueco *m* (de la escalera)
well⁵ *interj* **1** (*used to introduce a remark*) : bueno **2** (*used to express surprise*) : ¡vaya!
we'll ['wiːl, wɪl] (*contraction of* **we shall**
or **we will**) → **shall, will**
well–balanced ['wɛl'bælənst] *adj* : equilibrado
well–being ['wɛl'biːɪŋ] *n* : bienestar *m*
well–bred ['wɛl'brɛd] *adj* : fino, bien educado
well–defined [,wɛldi'faɪnd] *adj* : bien
definido
well–done ['wɛl'dʌn] *adj* **1** : bien hecho
⟨well-done! : ¡bravo!⟩ **2** : bien cocido
well–known ['wɛl'noːn] *adj* : famoso,
bien conocido
well–meaning ['wɛl'miːnɪŋ] *adj* : bienintencionado, que tiene buenas inten-
ciones
well–nigh ['wɛl'naɪ] *adv* : casi ⟨well-nigh
impossible : casi imposible⟩

well–off ['wɛl'ɔf] → **well–to–do**
well–rounded ['wɛl'raʊndəd] *adj* : completo, equilibrado
well–to–do [,wɛltə'duː] *adj* : próspero,
adinerado, rico
Welsh ['wɛlʃ] *n* **1** : galés *m*, galesa *f* **2**
: galés *m* (idioma) — **Welsh** *adj*
welt ['wɛlt] *n* **1** : vira *f* (de un zapato) **2**
WHEAL : verdugón *m*
welter ['wɛltər] *n* : fárrago *m*, revoltijo
m ⟨a welter of data : un fárrago de
datos⟩
wend ['wɛnd] *vi* **to wend one's way**
: ponerse en camino, encaminar sus pasos
went → **go¹**
wept → **weep**
were → **be**
we're ['wɪr, 'wər, 'wiːər] (*contraction of*
we are) → **be**
werewolf ['wɪr,wʊlf, 'wɛr-, 'wər-, -,wʌlf]
n, pl **-wolves** [-,wʊlvz, -,wʌlvz] : hombre *m* lobo
west¹ ['wɛst] *adv* : al oeste
west² *adj* : oeste, del oeste, occidental
⟨west winds : vientos del oeste⟩
west³ *n* **1** : oeste *m* **2 the West** : el Oeste,
el Occidente
westerly ['wɛstərli] *adv & adj* : del oeste
western ['wɛstərn] *adj* **1** : Occidental,
del Oeste **2** : occidental, oeste
Westerner ['wɛstərnər] *n* : habitante *mf*
del oeste
West Indian *n* : antillano *m*, -na *f* —
West Indian *adj*
westward ['wɛstwərd] *adv & adj* : hacia
el oeste
wet¹ ['wɛt] *vt* **wet** *or* **wetted; wetting**
: mojar, humedecer
wet² *adj* **wetter; wettest 1** : mojado,
húmedo ⟨wet clothes : ropa mojada⟩
2 RAINY : lluvioso **3 wet paint** : pintura *f* fresca
wet³ *n* **1** MOISTURE : humedad *f* **2** RAIN
: lluvia *f*
we've ['wiːv] (*contraction of* **we have**) →
have
whack¹ ['hwæk] *vt* : golpear (fuertemente), aporrear
whack² *n* **1** : golpe *m* fuerte, porrazo *m*
2 ATTEMPT : intento *m*, tentativa *f*
whale¹ ['hweɪl] *vi* **whaled; whaling**
: cazar ballenas
whale² *n, pl* **whales** *or* **whale** : ballena *f*
whaleboat ['hweɪl,boːt] *n* : ballenero *m*
whalebone ['hweɪl,boːn] *n* : barba *f* de
ballena
whaler ['hweɪlər] *n* **1** : ballenero *m*, -ra
f **2** → **whaleboat**
wharf ['hwɔrf] *n, pl* **wharves** ['hwɔrvz]
: muelle *m*, embarcadero *m*
what¹ ['hwɑt, 'hwʌt] *adv* **1** HOW : cómo,
cúanto ⟨what he suffered! : ¡cómo
sufría!⟩ **2 what with** : entre ⟨what with
one thing and another : entre una cosa
y otra⟩
what² *adj* **1** (*used in questions*) : qué
⟨what more do you want? : ¿qué más
quieres?⟩ ⟨what color is it? : ¿de qué

color es?⟩ **2** (*used in exclamations*)
: qué ⟨what an idea! : ¡qué idea!⟩ **3**
ANY, WHATEVER : cualquier ⟨give what
help you can : da cualquier contribución que puedas⟩

what³ *pron* **1** (*used in direct questions*)
: qué ⟨what happened? : ¿qué pasó?⟩
⟨what does it cost? : ¿cuánto cuesta?⟩
2 (*used in indirect statements*) : lo que,
que ⟨I don't know what to do : no sé
que hacer⟩ ⟨do what I tell you : haz lo
que te digo⟩ **3 what for** WHY : porqué
4 what if : y si ⟨what if he knows? : ¿y
si lo sabe?⟩

whatever¹ [*h*waţ'ɛvər, ,*h*wʌt-] *adj* **1** ANY
: cualquier, cualquier ... que ⟨what-
ever way you prefer : de cualquier
manera que prefiera, como prefiera⟩ **2**
(*in negative constructions*) ⟨there's no
chance whatever : no hay ninguna posi-
bilidad⟩ ⟨nothing whatever : nada en
absoluto⟩

whatever² *pron* **1** ANYTHING : (todo) lo
que ⟨I'll do whatever I want : haré lo
que quiera⟩ **2** (*no matter what*) ⟨what-
ever it may be : sea lo que sea⟩ **3** WHAT
: qué ⟨whatever do you mean? : ¿qué
quieres decir?⟩

whatsoever¹ [,*h*wɑtso'ɛvər, ,*h*wʌt-] *adj*
→ **whatever¹**

whatsoever² *pron* → **whatever²**

wheal [*h*wi:l] *n* : verdugón *m*

wheat [*h*wi:t] *n* : trigo *m*

wheaten ['*h*wi:tən] *adj* : de trigo

wheedle ['*h*wi:dəl] *vt* **-dled; -dling** CA-
JOLE : engatusar ⟨to wheedle some-
thing out of someone : sonsacarle algo
a alguien⟩

wheel¹ ['*h*wi:l] *vt* : empujar (una bicicleta, etc.), mover (algo sobre ruedas)
— *vi* **1** ROTATE : girar, rotar **2 to wheel
around** TURN : darse la vuelta

wheel² *n* **1** : rueda *f* **2** *or* **steering wheel**
: volante *m* (de automóviles, etc.),
timón *m* (de barcos o aviones) **3**
wheels *npl* : maquinaria *f*, fuerza *f* im-
pulsora ⟨the wheels of government : la
maquinaria del gobierno⟩

wheelbarrow ['*h*wi:l,bær,o:] *n* : carretilla *f*

wheelchair ['*h*wi:l,ʧær] *n* : silla *f* de
ruedas

wheeze¹ ['*h*wi:z] *vi* **wheezed; wheezing**
: resollar, respirar con dificultad

wheeze² *n* : resuello *m*

whelk ['*h*wɛlk] *n* : buccino *m*

whelp¹ ['*h*wɛlp] *vi* : parir

whelp² *n* : cachorro *m*, -rra *f*

when¹ ['*h*wɛn] *adv* : cuándo ⟨when will
you return? : ¿cuándo volverás?⟩ ⟨he
asked me when I would be home : me
preguntó cuándo estaría en casa⟩

when² *conj* **1** (*referring to a particular
time*) : cuando, en que ⟨when you are
ready : cuando estés listo⟩ ⟨the days
when I clean the house : los días en que
limpio la casa⟩ **2** IF : cuando, si ⟨how
can I go when I have no money?⟩

: ¿cómo voy a ir si no tengo dinero?⟩
3 ALTHOUGH : cuando ⟨you said it was
big when actually it's small : dijiste que
era grande cuando en realidad es pe-
queño⟩

when³ *pron* : cuándo ⟨since when are
you the boss? : ¿desde cuándo eres el
jefe?⟩

whence ['*h*wɛnts] *adv* : de donde

whenever¹ [*h*wɛn'vər] *adv* **1** : cuando
sea ⟨tomorrow or whenever : mañana
o cuando sea⟩ **2** (*in questions*) : cuándo

whenever² *conj* **1** : siempre que, cada
vez que ⟨whenever I go, I'm disappointed : siempre que voy, quedo de-
silusionado⟩ **2** WHEN : cuando ⟨when-
ever you like : cuando quieras⟩

where¹ ['*h*wɛr] *adv* : dónde, adónde
⟨where is he? : ¿dónde está?⟩ ⟨where
did they go? : ¿adónde fueron?⟩

where² *conj* : donde, adonde ⟨she knows
where the house is : sabe donde está la
casa⟩ ⟨she goes where she likes : va
adonde quiera⟩

where³ *pron* : donde ⟨Chicago is where
I live : Chicago es donde vivo⟩

whereabouts¹ ['*h*wɛrə,baʊts] *adv*
: dónde, por dónde ⟨whereabouts is the
house? : ¿dónde está la casa?⟩

whereabouts² *ns & pl* : paradero *m*

whereas [*h*wɛr'æz] *conj* **1** : consideran-
do que (usado en documentos legales)
2 : mientras que ⟨I like the white one
whereas she prefers the black : me gusta el blanco mientras que ella prefiere
el negro⟩

whereby [*h*wɛr'baɪ] *adv* : por lo cual

wherefore ['*h*wɛr,for] *adv* : por qué

wherein [*h*wɛr'ɪn] *adv* : en el cual, en el
que

whereof [*h*wɛr'ʌv, -ɑv] *conj* : de lo cual

whereupon ['*h*wɛrə,pɑn, -,pɔn] *conj*
: con lo cual, después de lo cual

wherever¹ [*h*wɛr'ɛvər] *adv* **1** WHERE
: dónde, adónde **2** : en cualquier parte
⟨or wherever : o donde sea⟩

wherever² *conj* : dondequiera que,
donde sea ⟨wherever you go : dondequiera que vayas⟩

wherewithal ['*h*wɛrwɪ,ðɔl, -,θɔl] *n*
: medios *mpl*, recursos *mpl*

whet ['*h*wɛt] *vt* **whetted; whetting 1**
SHARPEN : afilar **2** STIMULATE : estimular ⟨to whet the appetite : estimular el apetito⟩

whether ['*h*wɛðər] *conj* **1** : si ⟨I don't
know whether it is finished : no sé si
está acabado⟩ ⟨we doubt whether he'll
show up : dudamos que aparezca⟩ **2**
(*used in comparisons*) ⟨whether I like
it or not : tanto si quiero como si no⟩
⟨whether he comes or he doesn't : venga o no⟩

whetstone ['*h*wɛt,sto:n] *n* : piedra *f* de
afilar

whey ['*h*weɪ] *n* : suero *m* (de la leche)

which¹ ['*h*wɪʧ] *adj* : qué, cuál ⟨which tie
do you prefer? : ¿cuál corbata pre-

fieres?⟩ ⟨which ones? : ¿cuáles?⟩ ⟨tell me which house is yours : dime qué casa es la tuya⟩
which² *pron* **1** : cuál ⟨which is the right answer? : ¿cuál es la respuesta correcta?⟩ **2** : que, el (la) cual ⟨the cup which broke : la taza que se quebró⟩ ⟨the house, which is made of brick : la casa, la cual es de ladrillo⟩
whichever¹ [*hwɪtʃˈɛvər*] *adj* : el (la) que, cualquiera que ⟨whichever book you like : cualquier libro que te guste⟩
whichever² *pron* : el (la) que, cualquiera que ⟨take whichever you want : toma el que quieras⟩ ⟨whichever I choose : cualquiera que elija⟩
whiff¹ [*hwɪf*] *v* PUFF : soplar
whiff² *n* **1** PUFF : soplo *m*, ráfaga *f* **2** SNIFF : olor *m* **3** HINT : dejo *m*, pizca *f*
while¹ [*hwaɪl*] *vt* **whiled; whiling** : pasar ⟨to while away the time : matar el tiempo⟩
while² *n* **1** TIME : rato *m*, tiempo *m* ⟨after a while : después de un rato⟩ ⟨in a while : dentro de poco⟩ **2 to be worth one's while** : valer la pena
while³ *conj* **1** : mientras ⟨whistle while you work : silba mientras trabajas⟩ **2** WHEREAS : mientras que **3** ALTHOUGH : aunque ⟨while it's very good, it's not perfect : aunque es muy bueno, no es perfecto⟩
whim [*hwɪm*] *n* : capricho *m*, antojo *m*
whimper¹ [*hwɪmpər*] *vi* : lloriquear, gimotear
whimper² *n* : quejido *m*
whimsical [*hwɪmzɪkəl*] *adj* **1** CAPRICIOUS : caprichoso, fantasioso **2** ERRATIC : errático — **whimsically** *adv*
whine¹ [*hwaɪn*] *vi* **whined; whining 1** : lloriquear, gimotear, gemir **2** COMPLAIN : quejarse
whine² *n* : quejido *m*, gemido *m*
whinny¹ [*hwɪni*] *vi* **-nied; -nying** : relinchar
whinny² *n, pl* **-nies** : relincho *m*
whip¹ [*hwɪp*] *v* **whipped; whipping** *vt* **1** SNATCH : sacar (rápidamente), arrebatar ⟨she whipped the cloth off the table : arrebató el mantel de la mesa⟩ **2** LASH : azotar **3** DEFEAT : vencer, derrotar **4** INCITE : incitar, despertar ⟨to whip up enthusiasm : despertar el entusiasmo⟩ **5** BEAT : batir (huevos, crema, etc.) — *vi* FLAP : agitarse
whip² *n* **1** : látigo *m*, azote *m*, fusta *f* (de jinete) **2** : miembro *m* de un cuerpo legislativo encargado de disciplina
whiplash [*hwɪpˌlæʃ*] *n or* **whiplash injury** : traumatismo *m* cervical
whippet [*hwɪpət*] *n* : galgo *m* pequeño, galgo *m* inglés
whir¹ [*hwər*] *vi* **whirred; whirring** : zumbar
whir² *n* : zumbido *m*
whirl¹ [*hwərl*] *vi* **1** SPIN : dar vueltas, girar ⟨my head is whirling : la cabeza me

está dando vueltas⟩ **2 to whirl about** : arremolinarse, moverse rápidamente
whirl² *n* **1** SPIN : giro *m*, vuelta *f*, remolino *m* (dícese del polvo, etc.) **2** BUSTLE : bullicio *m*, torbellino *m* (de actividad, etc.) **3 to give it a whirl** : intentar hacer, probar
whirlpool [*hwərlˌpu:l*] *n* : vorágine *f*, remolino *m*
whirlwind [*hwərlˌwɪnd*] *n* : remolino *m*, torbellino *m*, tromba *f*
whisk¹ [*hwɪsk*] *vt* **1** : llevar ⟨she whisked the children off to bed : llevó a los niños a la cama⟩ **2** : batir ⟨to whisk eggs : batir huevos⟩ **3 to whisk away** *or* **to whisk off** : sacudir
whisk² *n* **1** WHISKING : sacudida *f* (movimiento) **2** : batidor *m* (para batir huevos, etc.)
whisk broom *n* : escobilla *f*
whisker [*hwɪskər*] *n* **1** : pelo *m* (de la barba o el bigote) **2 whiskers** *npl* : bigotes *mpl* (de animales)
whiskey *or* **whisky** [*hwɪski*] *n, pl* **-keys** *or* **-kies** : whisky *m*
whisper¹ [*hwɪspər*] *vi* : cuchichear, susurrar — *vt* : decir en voz baja, susurrar
whisper² *n* **1** WHISPERING : susurro *m*, cuchicheo *m* **2** RUMOR : rumor *m* **3** TRACE : dejo *m*, pizca *f*
whistle¹ [*hwɪsəl*] *v* **-tled; -tling** *vi* : silbar, chiflar, pitar (dícese de un tren, etc.) — *vt* : silbar ⟨to whistle a tune : silbar una melodía⟩
whistle² *n* **1** WHISTLING : chiflido *m*, silbido *m* **2** : silbato *m*, pito *m* (instrumento)
whit [*hwɪt*] *n* BIT : ápice *m*, pizca *f*
white¹ [*hwaɪt*] *adj* **whiter; -est** : blanco
white² *n* **1** : blanco *m* (color) **2** : clara *f* (de huevos) **3** *or* **white person** : blanco *m*, -ca *f*
white blood cell *n* : glóbulo *m* blanco
whitecaps [*hwaɪtˌkæps*] *npl* : cabrillas *fpl*
white–collar [*hwaɪtˈkɑlər*] *adj* **1** : de oficina **2 white–collar worker** : oficinista *mf*
whitefish [*hwaɪtˌfɪʃ*] *n* : pescado *m* blanco
whiten [*hwaɪtən*] *vt* : blanquear — *vi* : ponerse blanco
whiteness [*hwaɪtnəs*] *n* : blancura *f*
white–tailed deer [*hwaɪtˈteɪld*] *n* : ciervo *f* de Virginia
whitewash¹ [*hwaɪtˌwɔʃ*] *vt* **1** : enjalbegar, blanquear ⟨to whitewash a fence : enjalbegar una valla⟩ **2** CONCEAL : encubrir (un escándalo, etc.)
whitewash² *n* **1** : jalbegue *m*, lechada *f* **2** COVER-UP : encubrimiento *m*
whither [*hwɪðər*] *adv* : adónde
whiting [*hwaɪtɪŋ*] *n* : merluza *f*, pescadilla *f* (pez)
whitish [*hwaɪtɪʃ*] *adj* : blancuzco
whittle [*hwɪtəl*] *vt* **-tled; -tling 1** : tallar (madera) **2 to whittle down** : reducir,

recortar ⟨to whittle down expenses : reducir los gastos⟩

whiz[1] *or* **whizz** ['hwɪz] *vi* **whizzed; whizzing 1** BUZZ : zumbar **2 to whiz by** : pasar muy rápido, pasar volando

whiz[2] *or* **whizz** *n, pl* **whizzes 1** BUZZ : zumbido *m* **2 to be a whiz** : ser un prodigio, ser muy hábil

who ['hu:] *pron* **1** (*used in direct and indirect questions*) : quién ⟨who is that? : ¿quién es ése?⟩ ⟨who did it? : ¿quién lo hizo?⟩ ⟨we know who they are : sabemos quiénes son⟩ **2** (*used in relative clauses*) : que, quien ⟨the lady who lives there : la señora que vive allí⟩ ⟨for those who wait : para los que esperan, para quienes esperan⟩

whodunit [hu:'dʌnɪt] *n* : novela *f* policíaca

whoever [hu:'ɛvər] *pron* **1** : quienquiera que, quien ⟨whoever did it : quienquiera que lo hizo⟩ ⟨give it to whoever you want : dalo a quien quieras⟩ **2** (*used in questions*) : quién ⟨whoever could that be? : ¿quién podría ser?⟩

whole[1] ['ho:l] *adj* **1** UNHURT : ileso **2** INTACT : intacto, sano **3** ENTIRE : entero, íntegro ⟨the whole island : toda la isla⟩ ⟨whole milk : leche entera⟩ **4 a whole lot** : muchísimo

whole[2] *n* **1** : todo *m* **2 as a whole** : en conjunto **3 on the whole** : en general

wholehearted ['ho:l'hɑrtəd] *adj* : sin reservas, incondicional

whole number *n* : entero *m*

wholesale[1] ['ho:l,seɪl] *v* -**saled; -saling** *vt* : vender al por mayor — *vi* : venderse al por mayor

wholesale[2] *adv* : al por mayor

wholesale[3] *adj* **1** : al por mayor ⟨wholesale grocer : tendero al por mayor⟩ **2** TOTAL : total, absoluto ⟨wholesale slaughter : matanza sistemática⟩

wholesale[4] *n* : mayoreo *m*

wholesaler ['ho:l,seɪlər] *n* : mayorista *mf*

wholesome ['ho:lsəm] *adj* **1** : sano ⟨wholesome advice : consejo sano⟩ **2** HEALTHY : sano, saludable

whole wheat *adj* : de trigo integral

wholly ['ho:li] *adv* **1** COMPLETELY : completamente **2** SOLELY : exclusivamente, únicamente

whom ['hu:m] *pron* **1** (*used in direct questions*) : a quién ⟨whom did you choose? : ¿a quién elegiste?⟩ **2** (*used in indirect questions*) : de quién, con quién, en quién ⟨I don't know whom to consult : no sé con quién consultar⟩ **3** (*used in relative clauses*) : que, a quien ⟨the lawyer whom I recommended to you : el abogado que te recomendé⟩

whomever [hu:m'ɛvər] *pron* WHOEVER : quienquiera, quien ⟨marry whomever you please : cásate con quien quieras⟩

whoop[1] ['hwu:p, 'hwʊp] *vi* : gritar, chillar

whoop[2] *n* : grito *m*

whooping cough *n* : tos *f* ferina

whopper ['hwɑpər] *n* **1** : cosa *f* enorme **2** LIE : mentira *f* colosal

whopping ['hwɑpɪŋ] *adj* : enorme

whore ['hor] *n* : puta *f*, ramera *f*

whorl ['hwɔrl, 'hwərl] *n* : espiral *f*, espira *f* (de una concha), línea *f* (de una huella digital)

whose[1] ['hu:z] *adj* **1** (*used in questions*) : de quién ⟨whose truck is that? : ¿de quién es ese camión?⟩ **2** (*used in relative clauses*) : cuyo ⟨the person whose work is finished : la persona cuyo trabajo está terminado⟩

whose[2] *pron* : de quién ⟨tell me whose it was : dime de quién era⟩

why[1] ['hwaɪ] *adv* : por qué ⟨why did you do it? : ¿por qué lo hizo?⟩

why[2] *n, pl* **whys** REASON : porqué *m*, razón *f*

why[3] *conj* : por qué ⟨I know why he left : yo sé por qué salió⟩ ⟨there's no reason why it should exist : no hay razón para que exista⟩

why[4] *interj* (*used to express surprise*) : ¡vaya!, ¡mira!

wick ['wɪk] *n* : mecha *f*

wicked ['wɪkəd] *adj* **1** EVIL : malo, malvado **2** MISCHIEVOUS : travieso, pícaro ⟨a wicked grin : una sonrisa traviesa⟩ **3** TERRIBLE : terrible, horrible ⟨a wicked storm : una tormenta horrible⟩

wickedly ['wɪkədli] *adv* : con maldad

wickedness ['wɪkədnəs] *n* : maldad *f*

wicker[1] ['wɪkər] *adj* : de mimbre

wicker[2] *n* **1** : mimbre *m* **2** → **wickerwork**

wickerwork ['wɪkər,wərk] *n* : artículos *mpl* de mimbre

wicket ['wɪkət] *n* **1** WINDOW : ventanilla *f* **2** *or* **wicket gate** : postigo *m* **3** : aro *m* (en croquet), palos *mpl* (en críquet)

wide[1] ['waɪd] *adv* **wider; widest 1** WIDELY : por todas partes ⟨to travel far and wide : viajar por todas partes⟩ **2** COMPLETELY : completamente, totalmente ⟨wide open : abierto de par en par⟩ **3 wide apart** : muy separados

wide[2] *adj* **wider; widest 1** VAST : vasto, extensivo ⟨a wide area : una área extensiva⟩ **2** : ancho ⟨three meters wide : tres metros de ancho⟩ **3** BROAD : ancho, amplio **4** *or* **wide-open** : muy abierto **5 wide of the mark** : desviado, lejos del blanco

wide-awake ['waɪdə'weɪk] *adj* : (completamente) despierto

wide-eyed ['waɪd'aɪd] *adj* **1** : con los ojos muy abiertos **2** NAIVE : inocente, ingenuo

widely ['waɪdli] *adv* : extensivamente, por todas partes

widen ['waɪdən] *vt* : ampliar, ensanchar — *vi* : ampliarse, ensancharse

widespread ['waɪd'sprɛd] *adj* : extendido, extenso, difuso

widow[1] ['wɪ,do:] *vt* : dejar viuda ⟨to be widowed : enviudar⟩

widow[2] *n* : viuda *f*

widower ['wɪdowər] *n* : viudo *m*
width ['wɪdθ] *n* : ancho *m*, anchura *f*
wield ['wi:ld] *vt* **1** USE : usar, manejar ⟨to wield a broom : usar una escoba⟩ **2** EXERCISE : ejercer ⟨to wield influence : influir⟩
wiener ['wi:nər] → **frankfurter**
wife ['waɪf] *n, pl* **wives** ['waɪvz] : esposa *f*, mujer *f*
wifely ['waɪfli] *adj* : de esposa, conyugal
wig ['wɪg] *n* : peluca *f*
wiggle¹ ['wɪgəl] *v* **-gled; -gling** *vt* : menear, contonear ⟨to wiggle one's hips : contonearse⟩ — *vi* : menearse
wiggle² *n* : meneo *m*, contoneo *m*
wiggly ['wɪgəli] *adj* **-glier; -est** **1** : que se menea **2** WAVY : ondulado
wigwag ['wɪg,wæg] *vi* **-wagged; -wagging** : comunicar por señales
wigwam ['wɪg,wɑm] *n* : wigwam *m*
wild¹ ['waɪld] *adv* **1** → **wildly** **2 to run wild** : descontrolarse
wild² *adj* **1** : salvaje, silvestre, cimarrón ⟨wild horses : caballos salvajes⟩ ⟨wild rice : arroz silvestre⟩ **2** DESOLATE : yermo, agreste **3** UNRULY : desenfrenado **4** CRAZY : loco, fantástico ⟨wild ideas : ideas locas⟩ **5** BARBAROUS : salvaje, bárbaro **6** ERRATIC : errático ⟨a wild throw : un tiro errático⟩
wild³ *n* → **wilderness**
wild card *n* **1** : factor *m* desconocido **2** : comodín *m* (carta o símbolo)
wildcat ['waɪld,kæt] *n* **1** : gato *m* montés **2** BOBCAT : lince *m* rojo
wilderness ['wɪldərnəs] *n* : yermo *m*, desierto *m*
wildfire ['waɪld,faɪr] *n* **1** : fuego *m* descontrolado **2 to spread like wildfire** : propagarse como un reguero de pólvora
wildflower ['waɪld,flaʊər] *n* : flor *f* silvestre
wildfowl ['waɪld,faʊl] *n* : ave *f* de caza
wildlife ['waɪld,laɪf] *n* : fauna *f*
wildly ['waɪldli] *adv* **1** FRANTICALLY : frenéticamente, como un loco **2** EXTREMELY : extremadamente ⟨wildly happy : loco de felicidad⟩
wile¹ ['waɪl] *vt* **wiled; wiling** LURE : atraer
wile² *n* : ardid *m*, artimaña *f*
will¹ ['wɪl] *v, past* **would** ['wʊd]; *pres sing & pl* **will** *vt* WISH : querer ⟨do what you will : haz lo que quieras⟩ — *v aux* **1** (*expressing willingness*) ⟨no one would take the job : nadie aceptaría el trabajo⟩ ⟨I won't do it : no lo haré⟩ **2** (*expressing habitual action*) ⟨he will get angry over nothing : se pone furioso por cualquier cosa⟩ **3** (*forming the future tense*) ⟨tomorrow we will go shopping : mañana iremos de compras⟩ **4** (*expressing capacity*) ⟨the couch will hold three people : en el sofá cabrán tres personas⟩ **5** (*expressing determination*) ⟨I will go despite them : iré a pesar de

ellos⟩ **6** (*expressing probability*) ⟨that will be the mailman : eso ha de ser el cartero⟩ **7** (*expressing inevitability*) ⟨accidents will happen : los accidentes ocurrirán⟩ **8** (*expressing a command*) ⟨you will do as I say : harás lo que digo⟩
will² *vt* **1** ORDAIN : disponer, decretar ⟨if God wills it : si Dios lo dispone, si Dios quiere⟩ **2** : lograr a fuerza de voluntad ⟨they were willing him to succeed : estaban deseando que tuviera éxito⟩ **3** BEQUEATH : legar
will³ *n* **1** DESIRE : deseo *m*, voluntad *f* **2** VOLITION : voluntad *f* ⟨free will : libre albedrío⟩ **3** WILLPOWER : voluntad *f*, fuerza *f* de voluntad ⟨a will of iron : una voluntad férrea⟩ **4** : testamento *m* ⟨to make a will : hacer testamento⟩
willful *or* **wilful** ['wɪlfəl] *adj* **1** OBSTINATE : obstinado, terco **2** INTENTIONAL : intencionado, deliberado — **willfully** *adv*
willing ['wɪlɪŋ] *adj* **1** INCLINED, READY : listo, dispuesto **2** OBLIGING : servicial, complaciente
willingly ['wɪlɪŋli] *adv* : con gusto
willingness ['wɪlɪŋnəs] *n* : buena voluntad *f*
willow ['wɪ,lo:] *n* : sauce *m*
willowy ['wɪlowi] *adj* : esbelto
willpower ['wɪl,paʊər] *n* : voluntad *f*, fuerza *f* de voluntad
wilt ['wɪlt] *vi* **1** : marchitarse (dícese de las flores) **2** LANGUISH : debilitarse, languidecer
wily ['waɪli] *adj* **wilier; -est** : artero, astuto
wimp ['wɪmp] *n* **1** COWARD : gallina *f*, cobarde *mf* **2** WEAKLING : debilucho *m*, -cha *f*, alfeñique *m*
win¹ ['wɪn] *v* **won** ['wʌn]; **winning** *vi* : ganar — *vt* **1** : ganar, conseguir **2 to win over** : ganarse a **3 to win someone's heart** : conquistar a alguien
win² *n* : triunfo *m*, victoria *f*
wince¹ ['wɪnts] *vi* **winced; wincing** : estremecerse, hacer una mueca de dolor
wince² *n* : mueca *f* de dolor
winch ['wɪntʃ] *n* : torno *m*
wind¹ ['wɪnd] *vt* : dejar sin aliento ⟨to be winded : quedarse sin aliento⟩
wind² ['waɪnd] *v* **wound** ['waʊnd]; **winding** *vi* MEANDER : serpentear — *vt* **1** COIL, ROLL : envolver, enrollar **2** TURN : hacer girar ⟨to wind a clock : darle cuerda a un reloj⟩
wind³ ['wɪnd] *n* **1** : viento *m* ⟨against the wind : contra el viento⟩ **2** BREATH : aliento *m* **3** FLATULENCE : flatulencia *f*, ventosidad *f* **4 to get wind of** : enterarse de
wind⁴ ['waɪnd] *n* **1** TURN : vuelta *f* **2** BEND : recodo *m*, curva *f*
windbreak ['wɪnd,breɪk] *n* : barrera *f* contra el viento, abrigadero *m*
windfall ['wɪnd,fɔl] *n* **1** : fruta *f* caída **2** : beneficio *m* imprevisto
wind instrument *n* : instrumento *m* de viento

windlass ['wɪndləs] *n* : cabrestante *m*

windmill ['wɪnd,mɪl] *n* : molino *m* de viento

window ['wɪn,do:] *n* **1** : ventana *f* (de un edificio o una computadora), ventanilla *f* (de un vehículo o avión), vitrina *f* (de una tienda) **2** → **windowpane**

windowpane ['wɪn,do:,peɪn] *n* : vidrio *m*

window–shop ['wɪndo,ʃɑp] *vi* **-shopped; -shopping** : mirar las vitrinas

windpipe ['wɪnd,paɪp] *n* : tráquea *f*

windshield ['wɪnd,ʃi:ld] *n* **1** : parabrisas *m* **2 windshield wiper** : limpiaparabrisas *m*

windup ['waɪnd,ʌp] *n* : conclusión *f*

wind up *vt* END : terminar, concluir — *vi* : terminar, acabar

windward[1] ['wɪndwərd] *adj* : de barlovento

windward[2] *n* : barlovento *m*

windy ['wɪndi] *adj* **windier; -est 1** : ventoso ⟨it's windy : hace viento⟩ **2** VERBOSE : verboso, prolijo

wine[1] ['waɪn] *v* **wined; wining** *vi* : beber vino — *vt* **to wine and dine** : agasajar

wine[2] *n* : vino *m*

wing[1] ['wɪŋ] *vi* FLY : volar

wing[2] *n* **1** : ala *f* (de un ave, un avión, o un edificio) **2** FACTION : ala *f* ⟨the right wing of the party : el ala derecha del partido⟩ **3 wings** *npl* : bastidores *mpl* (de un teatro) **4 on the wing** : al vuelo, volando **5 under one's wing** : bajo el cargo de uno

winged ['wɪŋd, 'wɪŋəd] *adj* : alado

wink[1] ['wɪŋk] *vi* **1** : guiñar el ojo **2** BLINK : pestañear, parpadear **3** FLICKER : parpadear, titilar

wink[2] *n* **1** : guiño *m* (del ojo) **2** NAP : siesta *f* ⟨not to sleep a wink : no pegar el ojo⟩

winner ['wɪnər] *n* : ganador *m*, -dora *f*

winning ['wɪnɪŋ] *adj* **1** VICTORIOUS : ganador **2** CHARMING : encantador

winnings ['wɪnɪŋz] *npl* : ganancias *fpl*

winnow ['wɪ,no:] *vt* : aventar (el grano, etc.)

winsome ['wɪnsəm] *adj* CHARMING : encantador

winter[1] ['wɪntər] *adj* : invernal, de invierno

winter[2] *n* : invierno *m*

wintergreen ['wɪntər,gri:n] *n* : gaulteria *f*

wintertime ['wɪntər,taɪm] *n* : invierno *m*

wintry ['wɪntri] *adj* **wintrier; -est 1** WINTER : invernal, de invierno **2** COLD : frío ⟨she gave us a wintry greeting : nos saludó fríamente⟩

wipe[1] ['waɪp] *vt* **wiped; wiping 1** : limpiar, pasarle un trapo a ⟨to wipe one's feet : limpiarse los pies⟩ **2 to wipe away** : enjugar (lágrimas), borrar (una memoria) **3 to wipe out** ANNIHILATE : aniquilar, destruir

wipe[2] *n* : pasada *f* (con un trapo, etc.)

wire[1] ['waɪr] *vt* **wired; wiring 1** : instalar el cableado en (una casa, etc.) **2** BIND : atar con alambre **3** TELEGRAPH : telegrafiar, mandarle un telegrama (a alguien)

wire[2] *n* **1** : alambre *m* ⟨barbed wire : alambre de púas⟩ **2** : cable *m* (eléctrico o telefónico) **3** CABLEGRAM, TELEGRAM : telegrama *m*, cable *m*

wireless ['waɪrləs] *adj* : inalámbrico

wiretapping ['waɪr,tæpɪŋ] *n* : intervención *f* electrónica

wiring ['waɪrɪŋ] *n* : cableado *m*

wiry ['waɪri] *adj* **wirier; -est 1** : hirsuto, tieso (dícese del pelo) **2** : esbelto y musculoso (dícese del cuerpo)

wisdom ['wɪzdəm] *n* **1** KNOWLEDGE : sabiduría *f* **2** JUDGMENT, SENSE : sensatez *f*

wisdom tooth *n* : muela *f* de juicio

wise[1] ['waɪz] *adj* **wiser; wisest 1** LEARNED : sabio **2** SENSIBLE : sabio, sensato, prudente **3** KNOWLEDGEABLE : entendido, enterado ⟨they're wise to his tricks : conocen muy bien sus mañas⟩

wise[2] *n* : manera *f*, modo *m* ⟨in no wise : de ninguna manera⟩

wisecrack ['waɪz,kræk] *n* : broma *f*, chiste *m*

wisely ['waɪzli] *adv* : sabiamente, sensatamente

wish[1] ['wɪʃ] *vt* **1** WANT : desear, querer **2 to wish (something) for** : desear ⟨they wished me well : me desearon lo mejor⟩ — *vi* **1** : pedir (como deseo) **2** : querer ⟨as you wish : como quieras⟩

wish[2] *n* **1** : deseo *m* ⟨to grant a wish : conceder un deseo⟩ **2 wishes** *npl* : saludos *mpl*, recuerdos *mpl* ⟨to send best wishes : mandar muchos recuerdos⟩

wishbone ['wɪʃ,bo:n] *n* : espoleta *f*

wishful ['wɪʃfəl] *adj* **1** HOPEFUL : deseoso, lleno de esperanza **2 wishful thinking** : ilusiones *fpl*

wishy–washy ['wɪʃi,wɔʃi, -,wɑʃi] *adj* : insípido, soso

wisp ['wɪsp] *n* **1** BUNCH : manojo *m* (de paja) **2** STRAND : mechón *m* (de pelo) **3** : voluta *f* (de humo)

wispy ['wɪspi] *adj* **wispier; -est** : tenue, ralo (dícese del pelo)

wisteria [wɪs'tɪriə] *n* : glicinia *f*

wistful ['wɪstfəl] *adj* : añorante, anhelante, melancólico — **wistfully** *adv*

wistfulness ['wɪstfəlnəs] *n* : añoranza *f*, melancolía *f*

wit ['wɪt] *n* **1** INTELLIGENCE : inteligencia *f* **2** CLEVERNESS : ingenio *m*, gracia *f*, agudeza *f* **3** HUMOR : humorismo *m* **4** JOKER : chistoso *m*, -sa *f* **5 wits** *npl* : razón *f*, buen juicio *m* ⟨scared out of one's wits : muerto de miedo⟩ ⟨to be at one's wit's end : estar desesperado⟩

witch ['wɪtʃ] *n* : bruja *f*

witchcraft ['wɪtʃ,kræft] *n* : brujería *f*, hechicería *f*

witch doctor *n* : hechicero *m*, -ra *f*
witchery ['wɪtʃəri] *n, pl* **-eries** 1 → **witch-craft** 2 CHARM : encanto *m*
witch–hunt ['wɪtʃ,hʌnt] *n* : caza *f* de brujas
with ['wɪð, 'wɪθ] *prep* 1 : con ⟨I'm going with you : voy contigo⟩ ⟨coffee with milk : café con leche⟩ 2 AGAINST : con ⟨to argue with someone : discutir con alguien⟩ 3 (*used in descriptions*) : con, de ⟨the girl with red hair : la muchacha de pelo rojo⟩ 4 (*indicating manner, means, or cause*) : con ⟨to cut with a knife : cortar con un cuchillo⟩ ⟨fix it with tape : arréglalo con cinta⟩ ⟨with luck : consuerte⟩ 5 DESPITE : a pesar de, aún con ⟨with all his work, the business failed : a pesar de su trabajo, el negocio fracasó⟩ 6 REGARDING : con respecto a, con ⟨the trouble with your plan : el problema con su plan⟩ 7 ACCORDING TO : según ⟨it varies with the season : varía según la estación⟩ 8 (*indicating support or understanding*) : con ⟨I'm with you all the way : estoy contigo hasta el fin⟩
withdraw [wɪð'drɔ, wɪθ-] *v* **-drew** [-'dru:]; **-drawn** [-'drɔn]; **-drawing** *vt* 1 REMOVE : retirar, apartar, sacar (dinero) 2 RETRACT : retractarse de — *vi* : retirarse, recluirse (de la sociedad)
withdrawal [wɪð'drɔəl, wɪθ-] *n* 1 : retirada *f*, retiro *m* (de fondos, etc.), retraimiento *m* (social) 2 RETRACTION : retractación *f* 3 **withdrawal symptoms** : síndrome *m* de abstinencia
withdrawn [wɪð'drɔn, wɪθ-] *adj* : retraído, reservado, introvertido
wither ['wɪðər] *vt* : marchitar, agostar — *vi* 1 WILT : marchitarse 2 WEAKEN : decaer, debilitarse
withhold [wɪθ'ho:ld, wɪð-] *vt* **-held** [-'hld]; **-holding** : retener (fondos), aplazar (una decisión), negar (permiso, etc.)
within[1] [wɪð'ɪn, wɪθ-] *adv* : dentro
within[2] *prep* 1 : dentro de ⟨within the limits : dentro de los límites⟩ 2 (*in expressions of distance*) : a menos de ⟨within 10 miles of the ocean : a menos de 10 millas del mar⟩ 3 (*in expressions of time*) : dentro de ⟨within an hour : dentro de una hora⟩ ⟨within a month of her birthday : a poco menos de un mes de su cumpleaños⟩
without[1] [wɪð'aut, wɪθ-] *adv* 1 OUTSIDE : fuera 2 **to do without** : pasar sin algo
without[2] *prep* 1 OUTSIDE : fuera de 2 : sin ⟨without fear : sin temor⟩ ⟨he left without his briefcase : se fue sin su portafolios⟩
withstand [wɪθ'stænd, wɪð-] *vt* **-stood** [-'stud]; **-standing** 1 BEAR : aguantar, soportar 2 RESIST : resistir, resistirse a
witless ['wɪtləs] *adj* : estúpido, tonto
witness[1] ['wɪtnəs] *vt* 1 SEE : presenciar, ver, ser testigo de 2 : atestiguar (una firma, etc.) — *vi* TESTIFY : atestiguar, testimoniar

witness[2] *n* 1 TESTIMONY : testimonio *m* ⟨to bear witness : atestiguar, testimoniar⟩ 2 : testigo *mf* ⟨witness for the prosecution : testigo de cargo⟩
witticism ['wɪtə,sɪzəm] *n* : agudeza *f*, ocurrencia *f*
witty ['wɪti] *adj* **-tier; -est** : ingenioso, ocurrente, gracioso
wives → **wife**
wizard ['wɪzərd] *n* 1 SORCERER : mago *m*, brujo *m*, hechicero *m* 2 : genio *m* ⟨a math wizard : un genio en matemáticas⟩
wizened ['wɪzənd, 'wi:-] *adj* : arrugado, marchito
wobble[1] ['wabəl] *vi* **-bled; -bling** : bambolearse, tambalearse, temblar (dícese de la voz)
wobble[2] *n* : tambaleo *m*, bamboleo *m*
wobbly ['wabəli] *adj* : bamboleante, tambaleante, inestable
woe ['wo:] *n* 1 GRIEF, MISFORTUNE : desgracia *f*, infortunio *m*, aflicción *f* 2 **woes** *npl* TROUBLES : penas *fpl*, males *mpl*
woeful ['wo:fəl] *adj* 1 SORROWFUL : afligido, apenado, triste 2 UNFORTUNATE : desgraciado, infortunado 3 DEPLORABLE : lamentable
woke, woken → **wake**[1]
wolf[1] ['wulf] *vt or* **to wolf down** : engullir
wolf[2] *n, pl* **wolves** ['wulvz] : lobo *m*, -ba *f*
wolfram ['wulfrəm] → **tungsten**
wolverine [,wulvə'ri:n] *n* : glotón *m* (animal)
woman ['wumən] *n, pl* **women** ['wɪmən] : mujer *f*
womanhood ['wumən,hud] *n* 1 : condición *f* de mujer 2 WOMEN : mujeres *fpl*
womanly ['wumənli] *adj* : femenino
womb ['wu:m] *n* : útero *m*, matriz *f*
won → **win**
wonder[1] ['wʌndər] *vi* 1 SPECULATE : preguntarse, pensar ⟨to wonder about : preguntarse por⟩ 2 MARVEL : asombrarse, maravillarse — *vt* : preguntarse ⟨I wonder if they're coming : me pregunto si vendrán⟩
wonder[2] *n* 1 MARVEL : maravilla *f*, milagro *m* ⟨to work wonders : hacer maravillas⟩ 2 AMAZEMENT : asombro *m*
wonderful ['wʌndərfəl] *adj* : maravilloso, estupendo
wonderfully ['wʌndərfəli] *adv* : maravillosamente, de maravilla
wonderland ['wʌndər,lænd, -lənd] *n* : país *m* de las maravillas
wonderment ['wʌndərmənt] *n* : asombro *m*
wondrous ['wʌndrəs] → **wonderful**
wont[1] ['wɔnt, 'wo:nt, 'want] *adj* : acostumbrado, habituado
wont[2] *n* : hábito *m*, costumbre *f*
won't ['wo:nt] (*contraction of* **will not**) → **will**[1]
woo ['wu:] *vt* 1 COURT : cortejar 2 : buscar el apoyo de (clientes, votantes, etc.)

wood¹ [ˈwʊd] *adj* : de madera
wood² *n* **1** *or* **woods** *npl* FOREST : bosque *m* **2** : madera *f* (materia) **3** FIREWOOD : leña *f*
woodchuck [ˈwʊdˌtʃʌk] *n* : marmota *f* de América
woodcut [ˈwʊdˌkʌt] *n* **1** : plancha *f* de madera (para imprimir imágenes) **2** : grabado *m* en madera
woodcutter [ˈwʊdˌkʌtər] *n* : leñador *m*, -dora *f*
wooded [ˈwʊdəd] *adj* : arbolado, boscoso
wooden [ˈwʊdən] *adj* **1** : de madera ⟨a wooden cross : una cruz de madera⟩ **2** STIFF : rígido, inexpresivo (dícese del estilo, de la cara, etc.)
woodland [ˈwʊdlənd, -ˌlænd] *n* : bosque *m*
woodpecker [ˈwʊdˌpɛkər] *n* : pájaro *m* carpintero
woodshed [ˈwʊdˌʃɛd] *n* : leñera *f*
woodsman [ˈwʊdzmən] → **woodcutter**
woodwind [ˈwʊdˌwɪnd] *n* : instrumento *m* de viento de madera
woodworking [ˈwʊdˌwərkɪŋ] *n* : carpintería *f*
woody [ˈwʊdi] *adj* **woodier; -est 1** → **wooded 2** : leñoso ⟨woody plants : plantas leñosas⟩ **3** : leñoso (dícese de la textura), a madera (dícese del aroma, etc.)
woof [ˈwʊf] → **weft**
wool [ˈwʊl] *n* : lana *f*
woolen¹ *or* **woollen** [ˈwʊlən] *adj* : de lana
woolen² *or* **woollen** *n* **1** : lana *f* (tela) **2 woolens** *npl* : prendas *fpl* de lana
woolly [ˈwʊli] *adj* **-lier; -est 1** : lanudo **2** CONFUSED : confuso, vago
woozy [ˈwuːzi] *adj* **-zier; -est** : mareado
word¹ [ˈwərd] *vt* : expresar, formular, redactar
word² *n* **1** : palabra *f*, vocablo *m*, voz *f* ⟨word for word : palabra por palabra⟩ ⟨in one's own words : en sus propias palabras⟩ ⟨words fail me : me quedo sin habla⟩ **2** REMARK : palabra *f* ⟨by word of mouth : de palabra⟩ ⟨to have a word with : hablar (dos palabras) con⟩ **3** COMMAND : orden *f* ⟨to give the word : dar la orden⟩ ⟨just say the word : no tienes que decirlo⟩ **4** MESSAGE, NEWS : noticias *fpl* ⟨is there any word from her? : ¿hay noticias de ella?⟩ ⟨to send word : mandar un recado⟩ **5** PROMISE : palabra *f* ⟨to keep one's word : cumplir uno su palabra⟩ **6 words** *npl* QUARREL : palabra *f*, riña *f* ⟨to have words with : tener unas palabras con, reñir con⟩ **7 words** *npl* TEXT : letra *f* (de una canción, etc.)
wordiness [ˈwərdinəs] *n* : verbosidad *f*
wording [ˈwərdɪŋ] *n* : redacción *f*, lenguaje *m* (de un documento)
word processing *n* : procesamiento *m* de textos
word processor *n* : procesador *m* de textos

wordy [ˈwərdi] *adj* **wordier; -est** : verboso, prolijo
wore → **wear¹**
work¹ [ˈwərk] *v* **worked** [ˈwərkt] *or* **wrought** [ˈrɔt]; **working** *vt* **1** OPERATE : trabajar, operar ⟨to work a machine : operar una máquina⟩ **2** : lograr, conseguir (algo) con esfuerzo ⟨to work one's way up : lograr subir por sus propios esfuerzos⟩ **3** EFFECT : efectuar, llevar a cabo, obrar (milagros) **4** MAKE, SHAPE : elaborar, fabricar, formar ⟨a beautifully wrought vase : un florero bellamente elaborado⟩ **5 to work up** : estimular, excitar ⟨don't get worked up : no te agites⟩ — *vi* **1** LABOR : trabajar ⟨to work full-time : trabajar a tiempo completo⟩ **2** FUNCTION : funcionar, servir
work² *adj* : laboral
work³ *n* **1** LABOR : trabajo *m*, labor *f* **2** EMPLOYMENT : trabajo *m*, empleo *m* **3** TASK : tarea *f*, faena *f* **4** DEED : obra *f*, labor *f* ⟨works of charity : obras de caridad⟩ **5** : obra *f* (de arte o literatura) **6** → **workmanship 7 works** *npl* FACTORY : fábrica *f* **8 works** *npl* MECHANISM : mecanismo *m*
workable [ˈwərkəbəl] *adj* **1** : explotable (dícese de una mina, etc.) **2** FEASIBLE : factible, realizable
workaday [ˈwərkəˌdeɪ] *adj* : ordinario, banal
workbench [ˈwərkˌbɛntʃ] *n* : mesa *f* de trabajo
workday [ˈwərkˌdeɪ] *n* **1** : jornada *f* laboral **2** WEEKDAY : día *m* hábil, día *m* laborable
worker [ˈwərkər] *n* : trabajador *m*, -dora *f*; obrero *m*, -ra *f*
working [ˈwərkɪŋ] *adj* **1** : que trabaja ⟨working mothers : madres que trabajan⟩ ⟨the working class : la clase obrera⟩ **2** : de trabajo ⟨working hours : horas de trabajo⟩ **3** FUNCTIONING : que funciona, operativo **4** SUFFICIENT : suficiente ⟨a working majority : una mayoría suficiente⟩ ⟨working knowledge : conocimientos básicos⟩
workingman [ˈwərkɪŋˌmæn] *n*, *pl* **-men** [-mən, -ˌmɛn] : obrero *m*
workman [ˈwərkmən] *n*, *pl* **-men** [-mən, -ˌmɛn] **1** → **workingman 2** ARTISAN : artesano *m*
workmanlike [ˈwərkmənˌlaɪk] *adj* : bien hecho, competente
workmanship [ˈwərkmənˌʃɪp] *n* **1** WORK : ejecución *f*, trabajo *m* **2** CRAFTSMANSHIP : artesanía *f*, destreza *f*
workout [ˈwərkˌaʊt] *n* : ejercicios *mpl* físicos, entrenamiento *m*
work out *vt* **1** DEVELOP, PLAN : idear, planear, desarrollar **2** RESOLVE : solucionar, resolver ⟨to work out the answer : calcular la solución⟩ — *vi* **1** TURN OUT : resultar **2** SUCCEED : lograr, dar resultado, salir bien **3** EXERCISE : hacer ejercicio

workroom ['wɔrk,ru:m, -,rʊm] *n* : taller *m*

workshop ['wɔrk,ʃɑp] *n* : taller *m* ⟨ceramics workshop : taller de cerámica⟩

workstation ['wɔrk,steɪʃən] *n* : estación *f* de trabajo (en informática)

world[1] ['wɔrld] *adj* : mundial, del mundo ⟨world championship : campeonato mundial⟩

world[2] *n* : mundo *m* ⟨around the world : alrededor del mundo⟩ ⟨a world of possibilities : un mundo de posibilidades⟩ ⟨to think the world of someone : tener a alguien en alta estima⟩ ⟨to be worlds apart : no tener nada que ver (uno con otro)⟩

worldly ['wɔrldli] *adj* **1** : mundano ⟨wordly goods : bienes materiales⟩ **2** SOPHISTICATED : sofisticado, de mundo

worldwide[1] ['wɔrld'waɪd] *adv* : mundialmente, en todo el mundo

worldwide[2] *adj* : global, mundial

World Wide Web *n* : World Wide Web *f*

worm[1] ['wɔrm] *vi* CRAWL : arrastrarse, deslizarse (como gusano) — *vt* **1** : desparasitar (un animal) **2 to worm one's way into** : introducirse en ⟨he wormed his way into her confidence : se ganó su confianza⟩ **3 to worm something out of someone** : sonsacarle algo a alguien

worm[2] *n* **1** : gusano *m*, lombriz *f* **2 worms** *npl* : lombrices *fpl* (parásitos)

wormy ['wɔrmi] *adj* **wormier; -est** : infestado de gusanos

worn *pp* → **wear**[1]

worn–out ['worn'aʊt] *adj* **1** USED : gastado, desgastado **2** TIRED : agotado

worried ['wɔrid] *adj* : inquieto, preocupado

worrier ['wɔriər] *n* : persona *f* que se preocupa mucho

worrisome ['wɔrisəm] *adj* **1** DISTURBING : preocupante, inquietante **2** : que se preocupa mucho (dícese de una persona)

worry[1] ['wɔri] *v* **-ried; -rying** *vt* : preocupar, inquietar — *vi* : preocuparse, inquietarse, angustiarse

worry[2] *n, pl* **-ries** : preocupación *f*, inquietud *f*, angustia *f*

worse[1] ['wɔrs] *adv* (*comparative of* **bad** *or of* **ill**) : peor

worse[2] *adj* (*comparative of* **bad** *or of* **ill**) : peor ⟨from bad to worse : de mal en peor⟩ ⟨to get worse : empeorar⟩ ⟨to feel worse : sentirse peor⟩

worse[3] *n* : estado *m* peor ⟨to take a turn for the worse : ponerse peor⟩ ⟨so much the worse : tanto peor⟩

worsen ['wɔrsən] *vt* : empeorar — *vi* : empeorar(se)

worship[1] ['wɔrʃəp] *v* **-shiped** *or* **-shipped; -shiping** *or* **-shipping** *vt* : adorar, venerar ⟨to worship God : adorar a Dios⟩ — *vi* : practicar una religión

worship[2] *n* : adoración *f*, culto *m*

worshiper *or* **worshipper** ['wɔrʃəpər] *n* : devoto *m*, -ta *f*; adorador *m*, -dora *f*

worst[1] ['wɔrst] *vt* DEFEAT : derrotar

worst[2] *adv* (*superlative of* **ill** *or of* **bad** *or* **badly**) : peor ⟨the worst dressed of all : el peor vestido de todos⟩

worst[3] *adj* (*superlative of* **bad** *or of* **ill**) : peor ⟨the worst movie : la peor película⟩

worst[4] *n* **the worst** : lo peor, el (la) peor ⟨the worst is over : ya ha pasado lo peor⟩

worsted ['wʊstəd, 'wɔrstəd] *n* : estambre *m*

worth[1] ['wɔrθ] *n* **1** : valor *m* (monetario) ⟨ten dollars' worth of gas : diez dólares de gasolina⟩ **2** MERIT : valor *m*, mérito *m*, valía *f* ⟨an employee of great worth : un empleado de gran valía⟩

worth[2] *prep* **to be worth** : valer ⟨her holdings are worth a fortune : sus propiedades valen una fortuna⟩ ⟨it's not worth it : no vale la pena⟩

worthiness ['wɔrðinəs] *n* : mérito *m*

worthless ['wɔrθləs] *adj* **1** : sin valor ⟨worthless trinkets : chucherías sin valor⟩ **2** USELESS : inútil

worthwhile [wɔrθ'hwaɪl] *adj* : que vale la pena

worthy ['wɔrði] *adj* **-thier; -est 1** : digno ⟨worthy of promotion : digno de un ascenso⟩ **2** COMMENDABLE : meritorio, encomiable

would ['wʊd] *past of* **will 1** (*expressing preference*) ⟨I would rather go alone than with her : preferiría ir sola que con ella⟩ **2** (*expressing intent*) ⟨those who would ban certain books : aquellos que prohibirían ciertos libros⟩ **3** (*expressing habitual action*) ⟨he would often take his kids to the park : solía llevar a sus hijos al parque⟩ **4** (*expressing contingency*) ⟨I would go if I had the money : iría yo si tuviera el dinero⟩ **5** (*expressing probability*) ⟨she would have won if she hadn't tripped : habría ganado si no hubiera tropezado⟩ **6** (*expressing a request*) ⟨would you kindly help me with this? : ¿tendría la bondad de ayudarme con esto?⟩

would–be ['wʊd'bi:] *adj* : potencial ⟨a would-be celebrity : un aspirante a celebridad⟩

wouldn't ['wʊd'ənt] (*contraction of* **would not**) → **would**

wound[1] ['wu:nd] *vt* : herir

wound[2] *n* : herida *f*

wound[3] ['waʊnd] → **wind**[2]

wove, woven → **weave**[1]

wow ['waʊ] *interj* : ¡guau!, ¡híjole! *Mex*, ¡hala! *Spain*

wrangle[1] ['ræŋgəl] *vi* **-gled; -gling** : discutir, reñir ⟨to wrangle over : discutir por⟩

wrangle[2] *n* : riña *f*, disputa *f*

wrap[1] ['ræp] *v* **wrapped; wrapping** *vt* **1** COVER : envolver, cubrir ⟨to wrap a package : envolver un paquete⟩

⟨wrapped in mystery : envuelto en misterio⟩ **2** ENCIRCLE : rodear, ceñir ⟨to wrap one's arms around someone : estrechar a alguien⟩ **3 to wrap up** FINISH : darle fin a (algo) — vi **1** COIL : envolverse, enroscarse **2 to wrap up** DRESS : abrigarse ⟨wrap up warmly : abrígate bien⟩

wrap² n **1** WRAPPER : envoltura f **2** : prenda f que envuelve (como un chal, una bata, etc.)

wrapper ['ræpər] n : envoltura f, envoltorio m

wrapping ['ræpɪŋ] n : envoltura f, envoltorio m

wrath ['ræθ] n : ira f, cólera f

wrathful ['ræθfəl] adj : iracundo

wreak ['riːk] vt : infligir, causar ⟨to wreak havoc : crear caos, causar estragos⟩

wreath ['riːθ] n, pl **wreaths** ['riːðz, 'riːθs] : corona f (de flores, etc.)

wreathe ['riːð] vt **wreathed; wreathing** **1** ADORN : coronar (de flores, etc.) **2** ENVELOP : envolver ⟨wreathed in mist : envuelto en niebla⟩

wreck¹ ['rɛk] vt : destruir, arruinar, estrellar (un automóvil), naufragar (un barco)

wreck² n **1** WRECKAGE : restos mpl (de un buque naufragado, un avión siniestrado, etc.) **2** RUIN : ruina f, desastre m ⟨this place is a wreck! : ¡este lugar está hecho un desastre!⟩ ⟨to be a nervous wreck : tener los nervios destrozados⟩

wreckage ['rɛkɪdʒ] n : restos mpl (de un buque naufragado, un avión siniestrado, etc.), ruinas fpl (de un edificio)

wrecker ['rɛkər] n **1** TOW TRUCK : grúa f **2** : desguazador m (de autos, barcos, etc.), demoledor m (de edificios)

wren ['rɛn] n : chochín m

wrench¹ ['rɛntʃ] vt **1** PULL : arrancar (de un tirón) **2** SPRAIN, TWIST : torcerse (un tobillo, un músculo, etc.)

wrench² n **1** TUG : tirón m, jalón m **2** SPRAIN : torcedura f **3** or **monkey wrench** : llave f inglesa

wrest ['rɛst] vt : arrancar

wrestle¹ ['rɛsəl] v **-tled; -tling** vi **1** : luchar, practicar la lucha (en deportes) **2** STRUGGLE : luchar ⟨to wrestle with a dilemma : lidiar con un dilema⟩ — vt : luchar contra

wrestle² n STRUGGLE : lucha f

wrestler ['rɛsələr] n : luchador m, -dora f

wrestling ['rɛsəlɪŋ] n : lucha f

wretch ['rɛtʃ] n : infeliz mf; desgraciado m, -da f

wretched ['rɛtʃəd] adj **1** MISERABLE, UNHAPPY : desdichado, afligido ⟨I feel wretched : me siento muy mal⟩ **2** UNFORTUNATE : miserable, desgraciado, lastimoso ⟨wretched weather : tiempo

espantoso⟩ **3** INFERIOR : inferior, malo

wretchedly ['rɛtʃədli] adv : miserablemente, lamentablemente

wriggle ['rɪgəl] vi **-gled; -gling** : retorcerse, menearse

wring ['rɪŋ] vt **wrung** ['rʌŋ]; **wringing 1** or **to wring out** : escurrir, exprimir (el lavado) **2** EXTRACT : arrancar, sacar (por la fuerza) **3** TWIST : torcer, retorcer **4 to wring someone's heart** : partirle el corazón a alguien

wringer ['rɪŋər] n : escurridor m

wrinkle¹ ['rɪŋkəl] v **-kled; -kling** vt : arrugar — vi : arrugarse

wrinkle² n : arruga f

wrinkly ['rɪŋkəli] adj **wrinklier; -est** : arrugado

wrist ['rɪst] n **1** : muñeca f (en anatomía) **2** or **wristband** ['rɪst-ˌbænd] CUFF : puño m

writ ['rɪt] n : orden f (judicial)

write ['raɪt] v **wrote** ['roːt]; **written** ['rɪtən]; **writing** : escribir

write down vt : apuntar, anotar

write off vt CANCEL : cancelar

writer ['raɪtər] n : escritor m, -tora f

writhe ['raɪð] vi **writhed; writhing** : retorcerse

writing ['raɪtɪŋ] n **1** : escritura f **2** HANDWRITING : letra f **3 writings** npl WORKS : escritos mpl, obra f

wrong¹ ['rɔŋ] vt **wronged; wronging** : ofender, ser injusto con

wrong² adv : mal, incorrectamente

wrong³ adj **wronger** ['rɔŋər]; **wrongest** ['rɔŋəst] **1** EVIL, SINFUL : malo, injusto, inmoral **2** IMPROPER, UNSUITABLE : inadecuado, inapropiado, malo **3** INCORRECT : incorrecto, erróneo, malo ⟨a wrong answer : una mala respuesta⟩ **4 to be wrong** : equivocarse, estar equivocado

wrong⁴ n **1** INJUSTICE : injusticia f, mal m **2** OFFENSE : ofensa f, agravio m (en derecho) **3 to be in the wrong** : haber hecho mal, estar equivocado

wrongdoer ['rɔŋˌduːər] n : malhechor m, -chora f

wrongdoing ['rɔŋˌduːɪŋ] n : fechoría f, maldad f

wrongful ['rɔŋfəl] adj **1** UNJUST : injusto **2** UNLAWFUL : ilegal

wrongly ['rɔŋli] adv **1** : injustamente **2** INCORRECTLY : erróneamente, incorrectamente

wrote → write

wrought ['rɔt] adj **1** SHAPED : formado, forjado ⟨wrought iron : hierro forjado⟩ **2** or **wrought up** : agitado, excitado

wrung → wring

wry ['raɪ] adj **wrier** ['raɪər]; **wriest** ['raɪəst] **1** TWISTED : torcido ⟨a wry neck : un cuello torcido⟩ **2** : irónico, sardónico (dícese del humor)

X

x¹ *n, pl* **x's** *or* **xs** [ˈɛksəz] **1** : vigésima cuarta letra del alfabeto inglés **2** : incógnita *f* (en matemáticas)
x² [ˈks] *vt* **x–ed** [ˈɛkst]; **x–ing** *or* **x'ing** [ˈɛksiŋ] DELETE : tachar
xenon [ˈziːˌnɑn, ˈzɛ-] *n* : xenón *m*

xenophobia [ˌzɛnəˈfoːbiə, ˌziː-] *n* : xenofobia *f*
Xmas [ˈkrɪsməs] *n* : Navidad *f*
x–ray [ˈɛksˌreɪ] *vt* : radiografiar
X ray [ˈɛksˌreɪ] *n* **1** : rayo *m* X **2** *or* **X–ray photograph** : radiografía *f*
xylophone [ˈzaɪləˌfoːn] *n* : xilófono *m*

Y

y [ˈwaɪ] *n, pl* **y's** *or* **ys** [ˈwaɪz] : vigésima quinta letra del alfabeto inglés
yacht¹ [ˈjɑt] *vi* : navegar (a vela), ir en yate ⟨to go yachting : irse a navegar⟩
yacht² *n* : yate *m*
yak [ˈjæk] *n* : yac *m*
yam [ˈjæm] *n* **1** : ñame *m* **2** SWEET POTATO : batata *f*, boniato *m*
yank¹ [ˈjæŋk] *vt* : tirar de, jalar, darle un tirón a
yank² *n* : tirón *m*
Yankee [ˈjæŋki] *n* : yanqui *mf*
yap¹ [ˈjæp] *vi* **yapped; yapping 1** BARK, YELP : ladrar, gañir **2** CHATTER : cotorrear *fam*, parlotear *fam*
yap² *n* : ladrido *m*, gañido *m*
yard [ˈjɑrd] *n* **1** : yarda *f* (medida) **2** SPAR : verga *f* (de un barco) **3** COURTYARD : patio *m* **4** : jardín *m* (de una casa) **5** : depósito *m* (de mercancías, etc.)
yardage [ˈjɑrdɪdʒ] *n* : medida *f* en yardas
yardarm [ˈjɑrdˌɑrm] *n* : penol *m*
yardstick [ˈjɑrdˌstɪk] *n* **1** : vara *f* **2** CRITERION : criterio *m*, norma *f*
yarn [ˈjɑrn] *n* **1** : hilado *m* **2** TALE : historia *f*, cuento *m* ⟨to spin a yarn : inventar una historia⟩
yawl [ˈjɔl] *n* : yola *f*
yawn¹ [ˈjɔn] *vi* **1** : bostezar **2** OPEN : abrirse
yawn² *n* : bostezo *m*
ye [ˈjiː] *pron* : vosotros, vosotras
yea¹ [ˈjeɪ] *adv* YES : sí
yea² *n* : voto *m* a favor
year [ˈjɪr] *n* **1** : año *m* ⟨last year : el año pasado⟩ ⟨he's ten years old : tiene diez años⟩ **2** : curso *m*, año *m* (escolar) **3** **years** *npl* AGES : siglos *mpl*, años *mpl* ⟨I haven't seen them in years : hace siglos que no los veo⟩
yearbook [ˈjɪrˌbʊk] *n* : anuario *m*
yearling [ˈjɪrlɪŋ, ˈjərlən] *n* : animal *m* menor de dos año
yearly¹ [ˈjɪrli] *adv* : cada año, anualmente
yearly² *adj* : anual
yearn [ˈjərn] *vi* : anhelar, ansiar
yearning [ˈjərnɪŋ] *n* : anhelo *m*
yeast [ˈjiːst] *n* : levadura *f*
yell¹ [ˈjɛl] *vi* : gritar, chillar — *vt* : gritar
yell² *n* : grito *m*, alarido *m* ⟨to let out a yell : dar un grito⟩

yellow¹ [ˈjɛlo] *vi* : ponerse amarillo, volverse amarillo
yellow² *adj* **1** : amarillo **2** COWARDLY : cobarde
yellow³ *n* : amarillo *m*
yellow fever *n* : fiebre *f* amarilla
yellowish [ˈjɛloɪʃ] *adj* : amarillento
yellow jacket *n* : avispa *f* (con rayas amarillas)
yelp¹ [ˈjɛlp] *vi* : dar un gañido (dícese de un animal), dar un grito (dícese de una persona)
yelp² *n* : gañido *m* (de un animal), grito *m* (de una persona)
yen [ˈjɛn] *n* **1** DESIRE : deseo *m*, ganas *fpl* **2** : yen *m* (moneda japonesa)
yeoman [ˈjoːmən] *n, pl* **-men** [-mən, -mɛn] : suboficial *mf* de marina
yes¹ [ˈjɛs] *adv* : sí ⟨to say yes : decir que sí⟩
yes² *n* : sí *m*
yesterday¹ [ˈjɛstərˌdeɪ, -di] *adv* : ayer
yesterday² *n* **1** : ayer *m* **2** **the day before yesterday** : anteayer
yet¹ [ˈjɛt] *adv* **1** BESIDES, EVEN : aún ⟨yet more problems : más problemas aún⟩ ⟨yet again : otra vez⟩ **2** SO FAR : aún, todavía ⟨not yet : todavía no⟩ ⟨as yet : hasta ahora, todavía⟩ **3** : ya ⟨has he come yet? : ¿ya ha venido?⟩ **4** EVENTUALLY : todavía, algún día **5** NEVERTHELESS : sin embargo
yet² *conj* : pero
yew [ˈjuː] *n* : tejo *m*
yield¹ [ˈjiːld] *vt* **1** SURRENDER : ceder ⟨to yield the right of way : ceder el paso⟩ **2** PRODUCE : producir, dar, rendir (en finanzas) — *vi* **1** GIVE : ceder ⟨to yield under pressure : ceder por la presión⟩ **2** GIVE IN, SURRENDER : ceder, rendirse, entregarse
yield² *n* : rendimiento *m*, rédito *m* (en finanzas)
yin and yang [ˈjɪnændˈjæŋ, -ˈjɑŋ] *n* : yin *m* y yang *f*
yodel¹ [ˈjoːdəl] *vi* **-deled** *or* **-delled; -deling** *or* **-delling** : cantar al estilo tirolés
yodel² *n* : canción *f* al estilo tirolés
yoga [ˈjoːgə] *n* : yoga *m*
yogurt [ˈjoːgərt] *n* : yogur *m*, yogurt *m*
yoke¹ [ˈjoːk] *vt* **yoked; yoking** : uncir (animales)
yoke² *n* **1** : yugo *m* (para uncir animales)

⟨the yoke of oppression : el yugo de la opresión⟩ **2** TEAM : yunta *f* (de bueyes) **3** : canesú *m* (de ropa)
yokel [ˈjoːkəl] *n* : palurdo *m*, -da *f*
yolk [ˈjoːk] *n* : yema *f* (de un huevo)
Yom Kippur [ˌjoːmkɪˈpʊr, ˌjɑm-, -ˈkɪpər] *n* : el Día *m* del Perdón, Yom Kippur
yon [ˈjɑn] → **yonder**
yonder[1] [ˈjɑndər] *adv* : allá ⟨over yonder : allá lejos⟩
yonder[2] *adj* : aquel ⟨yonder hill : aquella colina⟩
yore [ˈjoːr] *n* **in days of yore** : antaño
you [ˈjuː] *pron* **1** (*used as subject — familiar*) : tú; vos (*in some Latin American countries*); ustedes *pl*; vosotros, vosotras *pl Spain* **2** (*used as subject — formal*) : usted, ustedes *pl* **3** (*used as indirect object — familiar*) : te, les *pl* (*se before lo, la, los, las*), os *pl Spain* ⟨he told it to you : te lo contó⟩ ⟨I gave them to (all of, both of) you : se los di⟩ **4** (*used as indirect object — formal*) : lo (*Spain sometimes* le), la; los (*Spain sometimes* les), las *pl* **5** (*used after a preposition — familiar*) : ti; vos (*in some Latin American countries*); ustedes *pl*; vosotros, vosotras *pl Spain* **6** (*used after a preposition — formal*) : usted, ustedes *pl* **7** (*used as an impersonal subject*) ⟨you never know : nunca se sabe⟩ ⟨you have to be aware : hay que ser consciente⟩ ⟨you mustn't do that : eso no se hace⟩ **8 with you** (*familiar*) : contigo; con ustedes *pl*; con vosotros, con vosotras *pl Spain* **9 with you** (*formal*) : con usted, con ustedes *pl*
you'd [ˈjuːd, ˈjʊd] (*contraction of* **you had** *or* **you would**) → **have, would**
you'll [ˈjuːl, ˈjʊl] (*contraction of* **you shall** *or* **you will**) → **shall, will**
young[1] [ˈjʌŋ] *adj* **younger** [ˈjʌŋgər]; **youngest** [-gəst] **1** : joven, pequeño, menor ⟨young people : los jóvenes⟩ ⟨my younger brother : mi hermano menor⟩ ⟨she is the youngest : es la más pequeña⟩ **2** FRESH, NEW : tierno (dícese de las verduras), joven (dícese del vino) **3** YOUTHFUL : joven, juvenil
young[2] *npl* : jóvenes *mfpl* (de los humanos), crías *fpl* (de los animales)
youngster [ˈjʌŋkstər] *n* **1** YOUTH : joven *mf* **2** CHILD : chico *m*, -ca *f*; niño *m*, -ña *f*
your [ˈjʊr, ˈjoːr, jər] *adj* **1** (*familiar singular*) : tu ⟨your cat : tu gato⟩ ⟨your

books : tus libros⟩ ⟨wash your hands : lávate las manos⟩ **2** (*familiar plural*) : su, vuestro *Spain* ⟨your car : su coche, el coche de ustedes⟩ **3** (*formal*) : su ⟨your houses : sus casas⟩ **4** (*impersonal*) : el, la, los, las ⟨on your left : a la izquierda⟩
you're [ˈjʊr, ˈjoːr, ˈjər, ˈjuːər] (*contraction of* **you are**) → **be**
yours [ˈjʊrz, ˈjoːrz] *pron* **1** (*belonging to one person — familiar*) : (el) tuyo, (la) tuya, (los) tuyos, (las) tuyas ⟨those are mine; yours are there : ésas son mías; las tuyas están allí⟩ ⟨is this one yours? : ¿éste es tuyo?⟩ **2** (*belonging to more than one person — familiar*) : (el) suyo, (la) suya, (los) suyos, (las) suyas; (el) vuestro, (la) vuestra, (los) vuestros, (las) vuestras *Spain* ⟨our house and yours : nuestra casa y la suya⟩ **3** (*formal*) : (el) suyo, (la) suya, (los) suyos, (las) suyas
yourself [jərˈsɛlf] *pron, pl* **yourselves** [-ˈslvz] **1** (*used reflexively — familiar*) : te, se *pl*, os *pl Spain* ⟨wash yourself : lávate⟩ ⟨you dressed yourselves : se vistieron, os vestisteis⟩ **2** (*used reflexively — formal*) : se ⟨did you hurt yourself? : ¿se hizo daño?⟩ ⟨you've gotten yourselves dirty : se ensuciaron⟩ **3** (*used for emphasis*) : tú mismo, tú misma; usted mismo, usted misma; ustedes mismos, ustedes mismas *pl*; vosotros mismos, vosotras mismas *pl Spain* ⟨you did it yourselves? : ¿lo hicieron ustedes mismos?, ¿lo hicieron por sí solos?⟩
youth [ˈjuːθ] *n, pl* **youths** [ˈjuːðz, ˈjuːθs] **1** : juventud *f* ⟨in her youth : en su juventud⟩ **2** BOY : joven *m* **3** : jóvenes *mfpl*, juventud *f* ⟨the youth of our city : los jóvenes de nuestra ciudad⟩
youthful [ˈjuːθfəl] *adj* **1** : de juventud **2** YOUNG : joven **3** JUVENILE : juvenil
youthfulness [ˈjuːθfəlnəs] *n* : juventud *f*
you've [ˈjuːv] (*contraction of* **you have**) → **have**
yowl[1] [ˈjæʊl] *vi* : aullar
yowl[2] *n* : aullido *m*
yo-yo [ˈjoːˌjoː] *n, pl* **-yos** : yoyo *m*, yoyó *m*
yucca [ˈjʌkə] *n* : yuca *f*
Yugoslavian [ˌjuːgoˈslɑviən] *n* : yugoslavo *m*, -va *f* — **Yugoslavian** *adj*
yule [ˈjuːl] *n* CHRISTMAS : Navidad *f*
yuletide [ˈjuːlˌtaɪd] *n* : Navidades *fpl*
yuppie [ˈjʌpi] *n* : yuppy *mf*

Z

z ['zi:] *n, pl* **z's** *or* **zs** : vigésima sexta letra del alfabeto inglés

Zambian ['zæmbiən] *n* : zambiano *m*, -na *f* — **Zambian** *adj*

zany¹ ['zeini] *adj* **-nier; -est** : alocado, disparatado

zany² *n, pl* **-nies** : bufón *m*, -fona *f*

zap¹ ['zæp] *vt* **zapped; zapping 1** ELIMINATE : eliminar **2** : enviar o transportar rápidamente — *vi* : ir rápidamente

zap² *n* **1** ZEST : sabor *m*, sazón *f* **2** BLAST : golpe *m* fuerte!

zap³ *interj* : ¡zas!

zeal ['zi:l] *n* : fervor *m*, celo *m*, entusiasmo *m*

zealot ['zɛlət] *n* : fanático *m*, -ca *f*

zealous ['zɛləs] *adj* : celoso — **zealously** *adv*

zebra ['zi:brə] *n* : cebra *f*

zenith ['zi:nəθ] *n* **1** : cenit *m* (en astronomía) **2** PEAK : apogeo *m*, cenit *m* ⟨at the zenith of his career : en el apogeo de su carrera⟩

zephyr ['zɛfər] *n* : céfiro *m*

zeppelin ['zɛplən, -pəlin] *n* : zepelín *m*

zero¹ ['zi:ro, 'ziro] *vi* **to zero in on** : apuntar hacia, centrarse en (un problema, etc.)

zero² *adj* : cero, nulo ⟨zero degrees : cero grados⟩ ⟨zero opportunities : oportunidades nulas⟩

zero³ *n, pl* **-ros** : cero *m* ⟨below zero : bajo cero⟩

zest ['zɛst] *n* **1** GUSTO : entusiasmo *m*, brío *m* **2** FLAVOR : sabor *m*, sazón *f*

zestful ['zɛstfəl] *adj* : brioso

zigzag¹ ['zɪg,zæg] *vi* **-zagged; -zagging** : zigzaguear

zigzag² *adv & adj* : en zigzag

zigzag³ *n* : zigzag *m*

Zimbabwean [zɪm'babwiən, -bwei-] *n* : zimbabuense *mf* — **Zimbabwean** *adj*

zinc ['zɪŋk] *n* : cinc *m*, zinc *m*

zing ['zɪŋ] *n* **1** HISS, HUM : zumbido *m*, silbido *m* **2** ENERGY : brío *m*

zinnia ['zɪniə, 'zi:-, -njə] *n* : zinnia *f*

Zionism ['zaiə,nizəm] *n* : sionismo *m*

Zionist ['zaiənist] *n* : sionista *mf*

zip¹ ['zɪp] *v* **zipped; zipping** *vt* *or* **to zip up** : cerrar el cierre de — *vi* **1** SPEED : pasarse volando ⟨the day zipped by : el día se pasó volando⟩ **2** HISS, HUM : silbar, zumbar

zip² *n* **1** ZING : zumbido *m*, silbido *m* **2** ENERGY : brío *m*

zip code *n* : código *m* postal

zipper ['zɪpər] *n* : cierre *m*, cremallera *f*, zíper *m CA, Mex*

zippy ['zɪpi] *adj* **-pier; -est** : brioso

zircon ['zər,kan] *n* : circón *m*, zircón *m*

zirconium [,zər'ko:niəm] *n* : circonio *m*

zither ['zɪðər, -θər] *n* : cítara *f*

zodiac ['zo:di,æk] *n* : zodíaco *m*

zombie ['zambi] *n* : zombi *mf*, zombie *mf*

zone¹ ['zo:n] *vt* **zoned; zoning 1** : dividir en zonas **2** DESIGNATE : declarar ⟨to zone for business : declarar como zona comercial⟩

zone² *n* : zona *f*

zoo ['zu:] *n, pl* **zoos** : zoológico *m*, zoo *m*

zoological [,zo:ə'ladʒikəl, ,zu:ə-] *adj* : zoológico

zoologist [zo'alədʒist, zu:-] *n* : zoólogo *m*, -ga *f*

zoology [zo'alədʒi, zu:-] *n* : zoología *f*

zoom¹ ['zu:m] *vi* **1** : zumbar, ir volando ⟨to zoom past : pasar volando⟩ **2** CLIMB : elevarse ⟨the plane zoomed up : el avión se elevó⟩

zoom² *n* **1** : zumbido *m* ⟨the zoom of an engine : el zumbido de un motor⟩ **2** : subida *f* vertical (de un avión, etc.) **3** *or* **zoom lens** : zoom *m*

zucchini [zu'ki:ni] *n, pl* **-ni** *or* **-nis** : calabacín *m*, calabacita *f Mex*

Zulu ['zu:lu:] *n* **1** : zulú *mf* **2** : zulú *m* (idioma) — **Zulu** *adj*

zygote ['zai,go:t] *n* : zigoto *m*, cigoto *m*

Common Spanish Abbreviations

SPANISH ABBREVIATION AND EXPANSION		ENGLISH EQUIVALENT	
abr.	abril	**Apr.**	April
A.C., a.C.	antes de Cristo	**BC**	before Christ
a. de J.C.	antes de Jesucristo	**BC**	before Christ
admon., admón.	administración	—	administration
a/f	a favor	—	in favor
ago.	agosto	**Aug.**	August
Apdo.	apartado (de correos)	—	P.O. box
aprox.	aproximadamente	**approx.**	approximately
Aptdo.	apartado (de correos)	—	P.O. box
Arq.	arquitecto	**arch.**	architect
A.T.	Antiguo Testamento	**O.T.**	Old Testament
atte.	atentamente	—	sincerely
atto., atta.	atento, atenta	—	kind, courteous
av., avda.	avenida	**ave.**	avenue
a/v.	a vista	—	on receipt
BID	Banco Interamericano de Desarrollo	**IDB**	Interamerican Development Bank
Bo	banco	—	bank
BM	Banco Mundial	—	World Bank
c/, C/	calle	**st.**	street
C	centígrado, Celsius	**C**	centigrade, Celsius
C.	compañía	**Co.**	company
CA	corriente alterna	**AC**	alternating current
cap.	capítulo	**ch., chap.**	chapter
c/c	cuenta corriente	—	current account, checking account
c.c.	centímetros cúbicos	**cu. cm**	cubic centimeters
CC	corriente continua	**DC**	direct current
c/d	con descuento	—	with discount
Cd.	ciudad	—	city
CE	Comunidad Europea	**EC**	European Community
CEE	Comunidad Económica Europea	**EEC**	European Economic Community
cf.	confróntese	**cf.**	compare
cg.	centígramo	**cg**	centigram
CGT	Confederación General de Trabajadores *or* del Trabajo	—	confederation of workers, workers' union
CI	coeficiente intelectual *or* de inteligencia	**IQ**	intelligence quotient
Cía.	compañía	**Co.**	company
cm.	centímetro	**cm**	centimeter
Cnel.	coronel	**Col.**	colonel
col.	columna	**col.**	column
Col. *Mex*	colonia	—	residential area
Com.	comandante	**Cmdr.**	commander
comp.	compárese	**comp.**	compare
Cor.	coronel	**Col.**	colonel

SPANISH ABBREVIATION AND EXPANSION		ENGLISH EQUIVALENT	
C.P.	código postal	—	zip code
CSF, c.s.f.	coste, seguro y flete	**c.i.f.**	cost, insurance, and freight
cta.	cuenta	**ac., acct.**	account
cte.	corriente	**cur.**	current
c/u	cada uno, cada una	**ea.**	each
CV	caballo de vapor	**hp**	horsepower
D.	Don	—	—
Da., D.ª	Doña	—	—
d.C.	después de Cristo	**AD**	anno Domini (in the year of Our Lord)
dcha.	derecha	—	right
d. de J.C.	después de Jesucristo	**AD**	anno Domini (in the year of Our Lord)
dep.	departamento	**dept.**	department
DF, D.F.	Distrito Federal	—	Federal District
dic.	diciembre	**Dec.**	December
dir.	director, directora	**dir.**	director
dir.	dirección	—	address
Dña.	Doña	—	—
do.	domingo	**Sun.**	Sunday
dpto.	departamento	**dept.**	department
Dr.	doctor	**Dr.**	doctor
Dra.	doctora	**Dr.**	doctor
dto.	descuento	—	discount
E, E.	Este, este	**E**	East, east
Ed.	editorial	—	publishing house
Ed., ed.	edición	**ed.**	edition
edif.	edificio	**bldg.**	building
edo.	estado	**st.**	state
EEUU, EE.UU.	Estados Unidos	**US, U.S.**	United States
ej.	por ejemplo	**e.g.**	for example
E.M.	esclerosis multiple	**MS**	multiple sclerosis
ene.	enero	**Jan.**	January
etc.	etcétera	**etc.**	et cetera
ext.	extensión	**ext.**	extension
F	Fahrenheit	**F**	Fahrenheit
f.a.b.	franco a bordo	**f.o.b.**	free on board
FC	ferrocarril	**RR**	railroad
feb.	febrero	**Feb.**	February
FF AA, FF.AA.	Fuerzas Armadas	—	armed forces
FMI	Fondo Monetario Internacional	**IMF**	International Monetary Fund
g.	gramo	**g., gm, gr.**	gram
G.P.	giro postal	**M.O.**	money order
gr.	gramo	**g., gm, gr.**	gram
Gral.	general	**Gen.**	general
h.	hora	**hr.**	hour
Hnos.	hermanos	**Bros.**	brothers
I + D, I & D, I y D	investigación y desarrollo	**R & D**	research and development
i.e.	esto es, es decir	**i.e.**	that is
incl.	inclusive	**incl.**	inclusive, inclusively
Ing.	ingeniero, ingeniera	**eng.**	engineer

SPANISH ABBREVIATION AND EXPANSION		ENGLISH EQUIVALENT	
IPC	índice de precios al consumo	**CPI**	consumer price index
IVA	impuesto al valor agregado	**VAT**	value-added tax
izq.	izquierda	**l.**	left
juev.	jueves	**Thurs.**	Thursday
jul.	julio	**Jul.**	July
jun.	junio	**Jun.**	June
kg.	kilogramo	**kg**	kilogram
km.	kilómetro	**km**	kilometer
km/h	kilómetros por hora	**kph**	kilometers per hour
kv, kV	kilovatio	**kw, kW**	kilowatt
l.	litro	**l, lit.**	liter
Lic.	licenciado, licenciada	—	—
Ltda.	limitada	**Ltd.**	limited
lun.	lunes	**Mon.**	Monday
m	masculino	**m**	masculine
m	metro	**m**	meter
m	minuto	**m**	minute
mar.	marzo	**Mar.**	March
mart.	martes	**Tues.**	Tuesday
mg.	miligramo	**mg**	milligram
miérc.	miércoles	**Wednes.**	Wednesday
min	minuto	**min.**	minute
mm.	milímetro	**mm**	millimeter
M-N, m/n	moneda nacional	—	national currency
Mons.	monseñor	**Msgr.**	monsignor
Mtra.	maestra	—	teacher
Mtro.	maestro	—	teacher
N, N.	Norte, norte	**N, no.**	North, north
n/o	nuestro	—	our
n.⁰	número	**no.**	number
N. de (la) R.	nota de (la) redacción	—	editor's note
NE	nordeste	**NE**	northeast
NN.UU.	Naciones Unidas	**UN**	United Nations
NO	noroeste	**NW**	northwest
nov.	noviembre	**Nov.**	November
N.T.	Nuevo Testamento	**N.T.**	New Testament
ntra., ntro.	nuestra, nuestro	—	our
NU	Naciones Unidas	**UN**	United Nations
núm.	número	**num.**	number
O, O.	Oeste, oeste	**W**	West, west
oct.	octubre	**Oct.**	October
OEA, O.E.A.	Organización de Estados Americanos	**OAS**	Organization of American States
OMS	Organización Mundial de la Salud	**WHO**	World Health Organization
ONG	organización no gubernamental	**NGO**	non-governmental organization
ONU	Organización de las Naciones Unidas	**UN**	United Nations
OTAN	Organización del Tratado del Atlántico Norte	**NATO**	North Atlantic Treaty Organization
p.	página	**p.**	page
P, P.	padre	**Fr.**	father

SPANISH ABBREVIATION AND EXPANSION		ENGLISH EQUIVALENT	
pág.	página	**pg.**	page
pat.	patente	**pat.**	patent
PCL	pantalla de cristal líquido	**LCD**	liquid crystal display
P.D.	post data	**P.S.**	postscript
p. ej.	por ejemplo	**e.g.**	for example
PNB	Producto Nacional Bruto	**GNP**	gross national product
p^o	paseo	**Ave.**	avenue
p.p.	porte pagado	**ppd.**	postpaid
PP, p.p.	por poder, por poderes	**p.p.**	by proxy
prom.	promedio	**av., avg.**	average
ptas., pts.	pesetas	**—**	
q.e.p.d.	que en paz descanse	**R.I.P.**	may he/she rest in peace
R, R/	remite	**—**	sender
RAE	Real Academia Española	**—**	—
ref., ref.[a]	referencia	**ref.**	reference
rep.	república	**rep.**	republic
r.p.m.	revoluciones por minuto	**rpm.**	revolutions per minute
rte.	remite, remitente	**—**	sender
s.	siglo	**c., cent.**	century
s/	su, sus	**—**	his, her, your, their
S, S.	Sur, sur	**S, so.**	South, south
S.	san, santo	**St.**	saint
S.A.	sociedad anónima	**Inc.**	incorporated (company)
sáb.	sábado	**Sat.**	Saturday
s/c	su cuenta	**—**	your account
SE	sudeste, sureste	**SE**	southeast
seg.	segundo, segundos	**sec.**	second, seconds
sep., sept.	septiembre	**Sept.**	September
s.e.u.o.	salvo error u omisión	**—**	errors and omissions excepted
Sgto.	sargento	**Sgt.**	sergeant
S.L.	sociedad limitada	**Ltd.**	limited (corporation)
S.M.	Su Majestad	**HM**	His Majesty, Her Majesty
s/n	sin número	**—**	no (street) number
s.n.m.	sobre el nivel de mar	**a.s.l.**	above sea level
SO	sudoeste/suroeste	**SW**	southwest
S.R.C.	se ruega contestación	**R.S.V.P.**	please reply
ss.	siguientes	**—**	the following ones
SS, S.S.	Su Santidad	**H.H.**	His Holiness
Sta.	santa	**St.**	Saint
Sto.	santo	**St.**	saint
t, t.	tonelada	**t., tn.**	ton
TAE	tasa anual efectiva	**APR**	annual percentage rate
tb.	también	**—**	also
tel., Tel.	teléfono	**tel.**	telephone
Tm.	tonelada métrica	**MT**	metric ton
Tn.	tonelada	**t., tn.**	ton
trad.	traducido	**tr., trans., transl.**	translated

SPANISH ABBREVIATION AND EXPANSION		ENGLISH EQUIVALENT	
UE	Unión Europea	**EU**	European Union
Univ.	universidad	**Univ., U.**	university
UPC	unidad procesadora central	**CPU**	central processing unit
Urb.	urbanización	—	residential area
v	versus	**v., vs.**	versus
v	verso	**v., ver., vs.**	verse
v.	véase	**vid.**	see
Vda.	viuda	—	widow
v.g., v.gr.	verbigracia	**e.g.**	for example
vier., viern.	viernes	**Fri.**	Friday
V.M.	Vuestra Majestad	—	Your Majesty
V^{o}B^o, V.^{o}B.^{o}	visto bueno	—	OK, approved
vol, vol.	volumen	**vol.**	volume
vra., vro.	vuestra, vuestro	—	your

Common English Abbreviations

	ENGLISH ABBREVIATION AND EXPANSION	SPANISH EQUIVALENT	
AAA	American Automobile Association	—	—
AD	anno Domini (in the year of Our Lord)	d.C., d. de J.C.	después de Cristo, después de Jesucristo
AK	Alaska	—	Alaska
AL, Ala.	Alabama	—	Alabama
Alas.	Alaska	—	Alaska
a.m., AM	ante meridiem	a.m.	ante meridiem (de la mañana)
Am., Amer.	America, American	—	América, americano
amt.	amount	—	cantidad
anon.	anonymous	—	anónimo
ans.	answer	—	respuesta
Apr.	April	abr.	abril
AR	Arkansas	—	Arkansas
Ariz.	Arizona	—	Arizona
Ark.	Arkansas	—	Arkansas
asst.	assistant	ayte.	ayudante
atty.	attorney	—	abogado, -da
Aug.	August	ago.	agosto
ave.	avenue	av., avda.	avenida
AZ	Arizona	—	Arizona
BA	Bachelor of Arts	Lic.	Licenciado, -da en Filosofía y Letras
BA	Bachelor of Arts (degree)	—	Licenciatura en Filosofía y Letras
BC	before Christ	a.C., A.C., a. de J.C.	antes de Cristo, antes de Jesucristo
BCE	before the Christian Era, before the Common Era	—	antes de la era cristiana, antes de la era común
bet.	between	—	entre
bldg.	building	edif.	edificio
blvd.	boulevard	blvar., br.	bulevar
Br., Brit.	Britain, British	—	Gran Bretaña, británico
Bro(s).	brother(s)	Hno(s).	hermano(s)
BS	Bachelor of Science	Lic.	Licenciado, -da en Ciencias
BS	Bachelor of Science (degree)	—	Licenciatura en Ciencias
c	carat	—	quilate
c	cent	—	centavo
c	centimeter	cm.	centímetro
c	century	s.	siglo
c	cup	—	taza
C	Celsius, centigrade	C	Celsius, centígrado
CA, Cal., Calif.	California	—	California
Can., Canad.	Canada, Canadian	—	Canadá, canadiense
cap.	capital	—	capital
cap.	capital	—	mayúscula
Capt.	captain	—	capitán

ENGLISH ABBREVIATION AND EXPANSION		SPANISH EQUIVALENT	
cent.	century	s.	siglo
CEO	chief executive officer	—	presidente, -ta (de una corporación)
ch., chap.	chapter	cap.	capítulo
CIA	Central Intelligence Agency	—	—
cm	centimeter	cm.	centímetro
Co.	company	C., Cía.	compañía
co.	county	—	condado
CO	Colorado	—	Colorado
c/o	care of	a/c	a cargo de
COD	cash on delivery, collect on delivery	—	(pago) contra reembolso
col.	column	col.	columna
Col., Colo.	Colorado	—	Colorado
Conn.	Connecticut	—	Connecticut
corp.	corporation	—	corporación
CPR	cardiopulmonary resuscitation	RCP	reanimación cardiopulmonar, resucitación cardiopulmonar
ct.	cent	—	centavo
CT	Connecticut	—	Connecticut
D.A.	district attorney	—	fiscal (del distrito)
DC	District of Columbia	—	—
DDS	Doctor of Dental Surgery	—	doctor de cirugía dental
DE	Delaware	—	Delaware
Dec.	December	dic.	diciembre
Del.	Delaware	—	Delaware
DJ	disc jockey	—	disc-jockey
dept.	department	dep., dpto.	departamento
DMD	Doctor of Dental Medicine	—	doctor de medicina dental
doz.	dozen	—	docena
Dr.	doctor	Dr., Dra.	doctor, doctora
DST	daylight saving time	—	—
DVM	Doctor of Veterinary Medicine	—	doctor de medicina veterinaria
E	East, east	E, E.	Este, este
ea.	each	c/u	cada uno, cada una
e.g.	for example (exempli gratia)	v.g., v.gr.	verbigracia
EMT	emergency medical technician	—	técnico, -ca en urgencias médicas
Eng.	England, English	—	Inglaterra, inglés
esp.	especially	—	especialmente
EST	eastern standard time	—	—
etc.	et cetera	etc.	etcétera
f	false	—	falso
f	female	f	femenino
F	Fahrenheit	F	Fahrenheit
FBI	Federal Bureau of Investigation	—	—
Feb.	February	feb.	febrero
fem.	feminine	—	femenino
FL, Fla.	Florida	—	Florida

ENGLISH ABBREVIATION AND EXPANSION		SPANISH EQUIVALENT	
Fri.	Friday	**vier., viern.**	viernes
ft.	feet, foot	—	pie(s)
g	gram	**g., gr.**	gramo
Ga., GA	Georgia	—	Georgia
gal.	gallon	—	galón
Gen.	general	**Gral.**	general
gm	gram	**g., gr.**	gramo
gov.	governor	—	gobernador, -dora
govt.	government	—	gobierno
gr.	gram	**g., gr.**	gramo
HI	Hawaii	—	Hawai, Hawaii
hr.	hour	**h.**	hora
HS	high school	—	colegio secundario
ht.	height	—	altura
Ia., IA	Iowa	—	Iowa
ID	Idaho	—	Idaho
i.e.	that is (id est)	**i.e.**	id est (esto es, es decir)
IL, Ill.	Illinois	—	Illinois
in.	inch	—	pulgada
IN	Indiana	—	Indiana
Inc.	incorporated	**S.A.**	sociedad anónima
Ind.	Indian, Indiana	—	Indiana
Jan.	January	**ene.**	enero
Jul.	July	**jul.**	julio
Jun.	June	**jun.**	junio
Jr., Jun.	Junior	**Jr.**	Júnior
Kan., Kans.	Kansas	—	Kansas
kg	kilogram	**kg.**	kilogramo
km	kilometer	**km.**	kilómetro
KS	Kansas	—	Kansas
Ky., KY	Kentucky	—	Kentucky
l	liter	**l.**	litro
l.	left	**izq.**	izquierda
L	large	**G**	(talla) grande
La., LA	Louisiana	—	Luisiana, Louisiana
lb.	pound	—	libra
Ltd.	limited	**S.L.**	sociedad limitada
m	male	**m**	masculino
m	meter	**m**	metro
m	mile	—	milla
M	medium	**M**	(talla) mediana
MA	Massachusetts	—	Massachusetts
Maj.	major	—	mayor
Mar.	March	**mar.**	marzo
masc.	masculine	—	masculino
Mass.	Massachusetts	—	Massachusetts
Md., MD	Maryland	—	Maryland
M.D.	Doctor of Medicine	—	doctor de medicina
Me., ME	Maine	—	Maine
Mex.	Mexican, Mexico	**Méx.**	mexicano, México
mg	milligram	**mg.**	miligramo
mi.	mile	—	milla
MI, Mich.	Michigan	—	Michigan
min.	minute	**min**	minuto
Minn.	Minnesota	—	Minnesota
Miss.	Mississippi	—	Mississippi, Misisipí
ml	mililiter	**ml.**	mililitro

ENGLISH ABBREVIATION AND EXPANSION		SPANISH EQUIVALENT	
mm	millimeter	**mm.**	milímetro
MN	Minnesota	—	Minnesota
mo.	month	—	mes
Mo., MO	Missouri	—	Missouri
Mon.	Monday	**lun.**	lunes
Mont.	Montana	—	Montana
mpg	miles per gallon	—	millas por galón
mph	miles per hour	—	millas por hora
MS	Mississippi	—	Mississippi, Misisipí
mt.	mount, mountain	—	monte, montaña
MT	Montana	—	Montana
mtn.	mountain	—	montaña
N	North, north	**N**	Norte, norte
NASA	National Aeronautics and Space Administration	—	—
NC	North Carolina	—	Carolina del Norte, North Carolina
ND, N. Dak.	North Dakota	—	Dakota del Norte, North Dakota
NE	northeast	**NE**	nordeste
NE, Neb., Nebr.	Nebraska	—	Nebraska
Nev.	Nevada	—	Nevada
NH	New Hampshire	—	New Hampshire
NJ	New Jersey	—	Nueva Jersey, New Jersey
NM, N. Mex.	New Mexico	—	Nuevo México, New Mexico
no.	north	**N**	norte
no.	number	**n.º**	número
Nov.	November	**nov.**	noviembre
N.T.	New Testament	**N.T.**	Nuevo Testamento
NV	Nevada	—	Nevada
NW	northwest	**NO**	noroeste
NY	New York	**NY**	Nueva York, New York
O	Ohio	—	Ohio
Oct.	October	**oct.**	octubre
OH	Ohio	—	Ohio
OK, Okla.	Oklahoma	—	Oklahoma
OR, Ore., Oreg.	Oregon	—	Oregon
O.T.	Old Testament	**A.T.**	Antiguo Testamento
oz.	ounce, ounces	—	onza, onzas
p.	page	**p.**	página
Pa., PA	Pennsylvania	—	Pennsylvania, Pensilvania
pat.	patent	**pat.**	patente
PD	police department	—	departamento de policía
PE	physical education	—	educación física
Penn., Penna.	Pennsylvania	—	Pennsylvania, Pensilvania
pg.	page	**pág.**	página
PhD	Doctor of Philosophy	—	doctor, -tora (en filosofía)

ENGLISH ABBREVIATION AND EXPANSION		SPANISH EQUIVALENT	
pkg.	package	—	paquete
p.m., PM	post meridiem	p.m.	post meridiem (de la tarde)
P.O.	post office	—	oficina de correos, correo
pp.	pages	págs.	páginas
PR	Puerto Rico	PR	Puerto Rico
pres.	present	—	presente
pres.	president	—	presidente, -ta
prof.	professor	—	profesor, -sora
P.S.	postscript	P.D.	postdata
P.S.	public school	—	escuela pública
pt.	pint	—	pinta
pt.	point	pto.	punto
PTA	Parent-Teacher Association	—	—
PTO	Parent-Teacher Organization	—	—
q, qt.	quart	—	cuarto de galón
r.	right	dcha.	derecha
rd.	road	c/, C/	calle
RDA	recommended daily allowance	—	consumo diario recomendado
recd.	received	—	recibido
Rev.	reverend	Rdo.	reverendo
RI	Rhode Island	—	Rhode Island
rpm	revolutions per minute	r.p.m.	revoluciones por minuto
RR	railroad	FC	ferrocarril
R.S.V.P.	please reply (répondez s'il vous plaît)	S.R.C.	se ruega contestación
rt.	right	dcha.	derecha
rte.	route	—	ruta
S	small	P	(talla) pequeña
S	South, south	S	Sur, sur
S.A.	South America	—	Sudamérica, América del Sur
Sat.	Saturday	sáb.	sábado
SC	South Carolina	—	Carolina del Sur, South Carolina
SD, S. Dak.	South Dakota	—	Dakota del Sur, South Dakota
SE	southeast	SE	sudeste, sureste
Sept.	September	sep., sept.	septiembre
so.	south	S	sur
sq.	square	—	cuadrado
Sr.	Senior	Sr.	Sénior
Sr.	sister	—	sor
st.	state	—	estado
st.	street	c/, C/	calle
St.	saint	S., Sto., Sta.	santo, santa
Sun.	Sunday	dom.	domingo
SW	southwest	SO	sudoeste, suroeste
t.	teaspoon	—	cucharadita
T, tb., tbsp.	tablespoon	—	cucharada (grande)
Tenn.	Tennessee	—	Tennessee

ENGLISH ABBREVIATION AND EXPANSION		SPANISH EQUIVALENT	
Tex.	Texas	—	Texas
Thu., Thur., Thurs.	Thursday	**juev.**	jueves
TM	trademark	—	marca (de un producto)
TN	Tennessee	—	Tennessee
tsp.	teaspoon	—	cucharadita
Tue., Tues.	Tuesday	**mart.**	martes
TX	Texas	—	Texas
UN	United Nations	**NU, NN.UU.**	Naciones Unidas
US	United States	**EEUU, EE.UU.**	Estados Unidos
USA	United States of America	**EEUU, EE.UU.**	Estados Unidos de América
usu.	usually	—	usualmente
UT	Utah	—	Utah
v.	versus	**v**	versus
Va., VA	Virginia	—	Virginia
vol.	volume	**vol.**	volumen
VP	vice president	—	vicepresidente, -ta
vs.	versus	**v**	versus
Vt., VT	Vermont	—	Vermont
W	West, west	**O**	Oeste, oeste
WA, Wash.	Washington (estado)	—	Washington
Wed.	Wednesday	**miérc.**	miércoles
WI, Wis., Wisc.	Wisconsin	—	Wisconsin
wt.	weight	—	peso
WV, W. Va.	West Virginia	—	Virginia del Oeste, West Virginia
WY, Wyo.	Wyoming	—	Wyoming
yd.	yard	—	yarda
yr.	year	—	año

Spanish Numbers

Cardinal Numbers

1	uno	28	veintiocho
2	dos	29	veintinueve
3	tres	30	treinta
4	cuatro	31	treinta y uno
5	cinco	40	cuarenta
6	seis	50	cincuenta
7	siete	60	sesenta
8	ocho	70	setenta
9	nueve	80	ochenta
10	diez	90	noventa
11	once	100	cien
12	doce	101	ciento uno
13	trece	200	doscientos
14	catorce	300	trescientos
15	quince	400	cuatrocientos
16	dieciséis	500	quinientos
17	diecisiete	600	seiscientos
18	dieciocho	700	setecientos
19	diecinueve	800	ochocientos
20	veinte	900	novecientos
21	veintiuno	1,000	mil
22	veintidós	1,001	mil uno
23	veintitrés	2,000	dos mil
24	veinticuatro	100,000	cien mil
25	veinticinco	1,000,000	un millón
26	veintiséis	1,000,000,000	mil millones
27	veintisiete	1,000,000,000,000	un billón

Ordinal Numbers

1st	primero, -ra	18th	decimoctavo, -va
2nd	segundo, -da	19th	decimonoveno, -na;
3rd	tercero, -ra		*or* decimonono, -na
4th	cuarto, -ta	20th	vigésimo, -ma
5th	quinto, -ta	21st	vigésimoprimero,
6th	sexto, -ta		vigésimaprimera
7th	séptimo, -ta	22nd	vigésimosegundo,
8th	octavo, -ta		vigésimasegunda
9th	noveno, -na	30th	trigésimo, -ma
10th	décimo, -ma	40th	cuadragésimo, -ma
11th	undécimo, -ca	50th	quincuagésimo, -ma
12th	duodécimo, -ma	60th	sexagésimo, -ma
13th	decimotercero, -ra	70th	septuagésimo, -ma
14th	decimocuarto, -ta	80th	octogésimo, -ma
15th	decimoquinto, -ta	90th	nonagésimo, -ma
16th	decimosexto, -ta	100th	centésimo, -ma
17th	decimoséptimo, -ma	1,000th	milésimo, -ma

English Numbers

Cardinal Numbers

1	one	50	fifty
2	two	60	sixty
3	three	70	seventy
4	four	80	eighty
5	five	90	ninety
6	six	100	one hundred
7	seven	101	one hundred and one
8	eight	200	two hundred
9	nine	300	three hundred
10	ten	400	four hundred
11	eleven	500	five hundred
12	twelve	600	six hundred
13	thirteen	700	seven hundred
14	fourteen	800	eight hundred
15	fifteen	900	nine hundred
16	sixteen	1,000	one thousand
17	seventeen	1,001	one thousand and one
18	eighteen	2,000	two thousand
19	nineteen	10,000	ten thousand
20	twenty	100,000	one hundred thousand
21	twenty-one	1,000,000	one million
30	thirty	1,000,000,000	one billion
40	forty	1,000,000,000,000	one trillion

Ordinal Numbers

1st	first	17th	seventeenth
2nd	second	18th	eighteenth
3rd	third	19th	nineteenth
4th	fourth	20th	twentieth
5th	fifth	21st	twenty-first
6th	sixth	30th	thirtieth
7th	seventh	40th	fortieth
8th	eighth	50th	fiftieth
9th	ninth	60th	sixtieth
10th	tenth	70th	seventieth
11th	eleventh	80th	eightieth
12th	twelfth	90th	ninetieth
13th	thirteenth	100th	hundredth
14th	fourteenth	1,000th	thousandth
15th	fifteenth	1,000,000th	millionth
16th	sixteenth	1,000,000,000th	billionth

Nations of the World

ENGLISH	SPANISH

Africa/África

ENGLISH	SPANISH
Algeria	Argelia
Angola	Angola
Benin	Benin
Botswana	Botswana, Botsuana
Burkina Faso	Burkina Faso
Burundi	Burundi
Cameroon	Camerún
Cape Verde	Cabo Verde
Central African Republic	República Centroafricana
Chad	Chad
Comoro Islands	Islas Comores, Comoras
Congo	Congo
Democratic Republic of Congo	Congo, República Democrática del
Djibouti	Djibouti, Djibuti
Egypt	Egipto
Equatorial Guinea	Guinea Ecuatorial
Eritrea	Eritrea
Ethiopia	Etiopía
Gabon	Gabón
Gambia	Gambia
Ghana	Ghana
Guinea	Guinea
Guinea-Bissau	Guinea-Bissau
Ivory Coast	Costa de Marfil
Kenya	Kenya, Kenia
Lesotho	Lesotho, Lesoto
Liberia	Liberia
Libya	Libia
Madagascar	Madagascar
Malawi	Malawi, Malaui
Mali	Malí
Mauritania	Mauritania
Mauritius	Mauricio
Morocco	Marruecos
Mozambique	Mozambique
Namibia	Namibia
Niger	Níger
Nigeria	Nigeria
Rwanda	Ruanda, Rwanda
São Tomé and Principe	Santo Tomé y Príncipe
Senegal	Senegal
Seychelles	Seychelles
Sierra Leone	Sierra Leona
Somalia	Somalia
South Africa, Republic of	Sudáfrica, República de
Sudan	Sudán
Swaziland	Suazilandia, Swazilandia
Tanzania	Tanzanía, Tanzania
Togo	Togo

ENGLISH	SPANISH
Tunisia	Túnez
Uganda	Uganda
Zambia	Zambia
Zimbabwe	Zimbabwe, Zimbábue

Antarctica/Antártida

No independent countries

Asia/Asia

Afghanistan	Afganistán
Armenia	Armenia
Azerbaijan	Azerbaiyán, Azerbaiján
Bahrain	Bahrein
Bangladesh	Bangladesh
Bhutan	Bhután, Bután
Brunei	Brunei
Cambodia	Camboya
China	China
Cyprus	Chipre
Georgia, Republic of	Georgia
India	India
Indonesia	Indonesia
Iran	Irán
Iraq	Iraq, Irak
Israel	Israel
Japan	Japón
Jordan	Jordania
Kazakhstan	Kazajstán
Korea, North	Corea del Norte
Korea, South	Corea del Sur
Kuwait	Kuwait
Kyrgyzstan	Kirguistán, Kirguizistán
Laos	Laos
Lebanon	Líbano
Malaysia	Malasia
Maldive Islands	Maldivas
Mongolia	Mongolia
Myanmar	Myanmar
Nepal	Nepal
Oman	Omán
Pakistan	Pakistán
Philippines	Filipinas
Qatar	Qatar
Saudi Arabia	Arabia Saudita, Arabia Saudí
Singapore	Singapur
Sri Lanka	Sri Lanka
Syria	Siria
Taiwan	Taiwán
Tajikistan	Tayikistán
Thailand	Tailandia
Turkey	Turquía
Turkmenistan	Turkmenistán

ENGLISH	SPANISH
United Arab Emirates	Emiratos Árabes Unidos
Uzbekistan	Uzbekistán
Vietnam	Vietnam
Yemen	Yemen

Europe/Europa

Albania	Albania
Andorra	Andorra
Austria	Austria
Belarus	Belarús
Belgium	Bélgica
Bosnia and Herzegovina	Bosnia y Hercegovina, Bosnia y Herzegovina
Bulgaria	Bulgaria
Croatia	Croacia
Czech Republic	República Checa
Denmark	Dinamarca
Estonia	Estonia
Finland	Finlandia
France	Francia
Germany	Alemania
Greece	Grecia
Hungary	Hungría
Iceland	Islandia
Ireland	Irlanda
Italy	Italia
Latvia	Letonia
Liechtenstein	Liechtenstein
Lithuania	Lituania
Luxembourg	Luxemburgo
Macedonia	Macedonia
Malta	Malta
Moldavia	Moldavia
Monaco	Mónaco
Netherlands	Países Bajos
Norway	Noruega
Poland	Polonia
Portugal	Portugal
Romania	Rumania, Rumanía
Russian Federation	Rusia, Federación de
San Marino	San Marino
Serbia and Montenegro	Serbia y Montenegro
Slovakia	Eslovaquia
Slovenia	Eslovenia
Spain	España
Sweden	Suecia
Switzerland	Suiza
Ukraine	Ucrania
United Kingdom	Reino Unido
Vatican City	Ciudad del Vaticano

ENGLISH   SPANISH

North America/Norteamérica

Antigua and Barbuda	Antigua y Barbuda
Bahamas	Bahamas
Barbados	Barbados
Belize	Belice
Bermuda	Bermudas
Canada	Canadá
Costa Rica	Costa Rica
Cuba	Cuba
Dominica	Dominica
Dominican Republic	República Dominicana
El Salvador	El Salvador
Grenada	Granada
Guatemala	Guatemala
Haiti	Haití
Honduras	Honduras
Jamaica	Jamaica
Mexico	México, Méjico
Nicaragua	Nicaragua
Panama	Panamá
Saint Kitts-Nevis	Saint Kitts y Nevis
Saint Lucia	Santa Lucía
Saint Vincent and the Grenadines	San Vicente y las Granadinas
Trinidad and Tobago	Trinidad y Tobago
United States of America	Estados Unidos de América

Oceania/Oceanía

Australia	Australia
Fiji	Fiji
Kiribati	Kiribati
Marshall Islands	Islas Marshall
Nauru	Nauru
New Zealand	Nueva Zelanda, Nueva Zelandia
Papua New Guinea	Papua Nueva Guinea
Solomon Islands	Islas Salomón
Tonga	Tonga
Tuvalu	Tuvalu
Vanuatu	Vanuatu
Western Samoa	Samoa del Oeste

South America/Sudamérica

Argentina	Argentina
Bolivia	Bolivia
Brazil	Brasil
Chile	Chile
Colombia	Colombia
Ecuador	Ecuador
Guyana	Guyana
Paraguay	Paraguay
Peru	Perú
Suriname	Surinam
Uruguay	Uruguay
Venezuela	Venezuela

Metric System: Conversions

Length

unit	number of meters	approximate U.S. equivalents	
millimeter	0.001	0.039	inch
centimeter	0.01	0.39	inch
meter	1	39.37	inches
kilometer	1,000	0.62	mile

Longitud

unidad	número de metros	equivalentes aproximados de los EE.UU.	
milímetro	0.001	0.039	pulgada
centímetro	0.01	0.39	pulgada
metro	1	39.37	pulgadas
kilómetro	1,000	0.62	milla

Area

unit	number of square meters	approximate U.S. equivalents	
square centimeter	0.0001	0.155	square inch
square meter	1	10.764	square feet
hectare	10,000	2.47	acres
square kilometer	1,000,000	0.3861	square mile

Superficie

unidad	número de metros cuadrados	equivalentes aproximados de los EE.UU.	
centímetro cuadrado	0.0001	0.155	pulgada cuadrada
metro cuadrado	1	10.764	pies cuadrados
hectárea	10,000	2.47	acres
kilómetro cuadrado	1,000,000	0.3861	milla cuadrada

Volume

unit	number of cubic meters	approximate U.S. equivalents	
cubic centimeter	0.000001	0.061	cubic inch
cubic meter	1	1.307	cubic yards

Volumen

unidad	número de metros cúbicos	equivalentes aproximados de los EE.UU	
centímetro cúbico	0.000001	0.061	pulgada cúbica
metro cúbico	1	1.307	yardas cúbicas

Capacity

unit	number of liters	approximate U.S. equivalents		
		CUBIC	DRY	LIQUID
liter	1	61.02 cubic inches	0.908 quart	1.057 quarts

Capacidad

unidad	número de litros	equivalentes aproximados de los EE.UU.		
		CÚBICO	SECO	LÍQUIDO
litro	1	61.02 pulgadas cúbicas	0.908 cuarto	1.057 cuartos

Mass and Weight

unit	number of grams	approximate U.S. equivalents	
milligram	0.001	0.015	grain
centigram	0.01	0.154	grain
gram	1	0.035	ounce
kilogram	1,000	2.2046	pounds
metric ton	1,000,000	1.102	short tons

Masa y peso

unidad	número de gramos	equivalentes aproximados de los EE.UU.	
miligramo	0.001	0.015	grano
centigramo	0.01	0.154	grano
gramo	1	0.035	onza
kilogramo	1.000	2.2046	libras
tonelada métrica	1,000,000	1.102	toneladas cortas